Wycliffe Bible

Wycliffite Translators

Wycliffe Bible

Wycliffite Translators

Published by
PRAOTES PUBLISHING
1670 Salem Road
Cranbrook, BC, v1c 6v3
Canada
http://www.Praotes.Net

First Edition: September 2009

Library of Congress Cataloging Card Number: To be issued.

ISBN: 1449535615
EAN-13: 9781449535612

Foreword

"The Scriptures," Wycliffe stated, "are the property of the people and one which no party should be allowed to wrest from them. Christ and his apostles converted much people by uncovering of Scripture, and this in the tongue which was most known to them. Why then may not the modern disciples of Christ gather up the fragments of the same bread? The faith of Christ ought therefore to be recounted to the people in both languages, Latin and English[1]." Such was the belief of John Wycliffe, and what he taught dictated what he did, and its effect on civilization has been profound.

The most used and famous of all English Bible translations in history is the King James Version. Ordered by King James I of England in January 1604, and completed in 1611, the influence of this enduring work reverberates unto this day. Western Society is increasingly becoming a Libertarian and Post-Christian Society. For today's minds it is often hard to even conceive the centrality of the Lord Jesus Christ and His Word in all of culture and society until recent times.

The King James Version text helped shape the style and maturity of the English Language[2]. But her influence was not limited to the realm of linguistics. Lawmakers of old used its text, and the concepts contained therein, to shape the constitution and laws of the English-speaking world[3]. It was this same King James text that inspired many of our celebrated artists, in all fields of art. The King James text formed the moral and inspirational source for many of our world's greatest men. Sir Winston Churchill, for example, spoke of it with these words: "The scholars who produced this masterpiece are mostly unknown and unremembered. But they forged an enduring link, literary and religious, between the English-speaking people of the world.[4]"

All appropriate honor aside, its very magnitude and reputation also produced a negative: It made it very difficult for subsequent translators to argue with its assumed accuracy. When one compares the leading English translations from 1611 to today, one will find that even the most literal of these stay generally faithful to the interpretations of the King James Version text, even when the underlying Hebrew or Greek calls for a deviation. The fame of the King James did yet another thing: It made it very difficult to look beyond, or past, its place in history. And this has led to the fact that one translation - the very first complete European translation in

nearly a thousand years, preceding the King James Version by 222 years - has been nearly forgotten.

The King James Version came about by direct orders from the highest authority in England: King James I. We do well to ask ourselves what caused God's Word to have gained such acceptance and authority in England that her highest power ordered a formal translation for use in church and state. What natural and verifiable sources did God use to cause this to come about? One of the most noteworthy of these, without a doubt, was the emergence of that very first European translation in nearly a thousand years, known to us as the Wycliffe Bible, or the Wycliffite Translations.

Authorship has never been conclusively defined, but its popularity in its day is undisputable, evidenced by the nearly 200 manuscripts extant, most of them copied between 1420 and 1450. Separate books surfaced between 1382 and 1395 and it is safe to conclude that several people have been working on these books, which culminated into what is now know as the Wycliffe Bible. Scholars hold John Wycliffe to have been the author of the Gospels. Wycliffe died on New Year's Eve of 1384 - over a decade prior to the surfacing or completion of the last books. Another contributor is believed

---

1. Margaret Deanesly. The Lollard Bible: And Other Medieval Biblical Versions. Cambridge, United Kingdom: Cambridge University Press, November 27, 2008. 246. ISBN 0521090733.

2. Based upon "Stanley Malless and Jeffrey McQuain. Coined by God. London and New York: W.W. Norton and Co., 2003.", the Dunham Bible Museum carries a treatise on the influence in History and Culture, listing English words and phrases from early translations. Source: English Language Words/Phrases. Houston Baptist University. 23 September 2009 <http://www.hbu.edu/hbu/DBM_Words_first_introduced_into_English.asp?SnID=2>.

3. Commandments VI, VIII and IX of the Ten Commandments contained in Exodus 20 - respectively: thou shalt not kill, thou shalt not steal and thou shalt not bear false witness against thy neighbour - form an integral part of law in our Western legal systems (with commandment nine being applied in the realm of court witnessing).
Further, the formal British coronation oath demonstrates the centrality of the Word of God. The oath contains the following: "I [monarch's name] do solemnly and sincerely in the presence of God profess, testify and declare that I am a faithful Protestant, and that I will, according to the true intent of the enactments which secure the Protestant succession to the Throne of my Realm, uphold and maintain the said enactments to the best of my powers according to law.... maintaine the Laws of God the true profession of the Gospell and the Protestant reformed religion established by law." (Source: Lucinda Maer and Oonagh Gay. The Coronation Oath. London: Library House of Commons, 27 August 2008, Standard Note SN/PC/00435. 2-3. 23 September 2009 <http://www.parliament.uk/commons/lib/research/briefings/snpc-00435.pdf>).
Further, when we look at legislation surrounding land leases, we discover the occurrence of 50 year terms to be common. This 50 year term can be traced back to the instructions contained in Leviticus 25:8-9. Examples are manifold. It goes beyond the scope of this foreword to elaborate on this any further. On a closing note, political forces today seek to mitigate or even deny the role which Biblical thought played in the shaping of British and allied civilization.

to have been Nicholas of Hereford. One of the early manuscripts contains a closing note in the book of Baruch (*Bodl. Douce MS.* 369), stating "Here ends the translation of Nicholas of Hereford.[5]" Hereford survived Wycliffe by several decades, and was an active member of Wycliffe's movement until the near-final years in which the last manuscripts appeared. A third scholar considered to have played a major role is John Purvey, who is believed to have been instrumental in improving the readability of the English, as this very first complete translation in its primal edition was too literal to be properly readable. All three men, Wycliffe, Hereford and Purvey, were graduates of Oxford University.

The intellectual culture at Oxford at the time was a most fascinating one and seems to have been conducive to the willingness of Wycliffe, Hereford and Purvey to take stand against the institution of the then dominant Roman Catholic Church. It is appropriate to attend briefly to some Oxford men that went immediately before them, and who were operative in the same fields of Theology and Philosophy, and who created Wycliffe's scholastic background at Oxford[6].

We name Robert Grosseteste (ca. 1175 - 1253), scholastic philosopher, lecturer in Theology at Oxford, and Bishop of Lincoln: Regarded by some as the key founder of scientific thought in medieval Oxford. Franciscan philosopher Roger Bacon (ca. 1214 - 1294), also a graduate of Oxford. A brilliant thinker, with an incredibly vast area of profound knowledge and interest. William of Ockham (ca. 1288 - c. 1348), Franciscan philosopher and political critic. Finally, Thomas Bradwardine (ca. 1290 - 1349), scholar in English, mathematician, logician, and theologian. Bradwardine functioned as Professor of Divinity at Oxford, and even served a brief term as Archbishop of Canterbury. All these men were men of faith, highly educated, and critical in their thinking. Their collective scientific achievements cover the fields of philosophy, theology, mathematics, physics, astronomy and language. With the Roman Catholic Church holding a tight grip on society, these men stood at the forefront of the tension between pseudo or biased theology versus science, and pseudo or biased science verses theology: A tension which has risen to great prominence again in our own Twenty-First Century, in which intellectual thought and truth is increasingly strangled to silence by the forces of required political correctness - especially libertarian correctness where it relates to pseudo science versus theology, and dogmatic evangelicalism where it relates to pseudo theology versus science.

Born in Ipreswell (modern Hipswell), in the Richmondshire district of North Yorkshire, England, Mr.

John Wycliffe (ca. 1320 - 1384) became a regent master in arts at Balliol College, Oxford. In 1360 he was appointed master. His later studies at Oxford resulted in a Doctorate of Divinity in 1372. Though he died of natural causes, his grave was desecrated, his remains dug up and burned to ashes in 1428 under direct orders of Pope Martin V.

Little is known or published of the early life of Nicholas of Hereford. He too received a Doctorate in Theology at Oxford, in 1382: Ten years after Wycliffe. Hereford joined Wycliffe's reform movement, nicknamed at Oxford and later publicly known as the Lollards. It is interesting to note - or rather: sad to note - that even today, in September 2009, the latest edition of the Catholic Encyclopedia labels Wycliffe's reform movement as "a heretical body." Nicholas of Hereford, together with John Wycliffe, was summoned to appear before the Court of the Archbishop of Canterbury in 1382. Both men refused to appear and were subsequently excommunicated. In the next seven years Hereford spend several years in prison for his beliefs and was supposedly treated quite harshly. In 1391, Hereford reportedly disavowed his former beliefs and became one of the persecutors of the Lollard movement. In the remaining two decades of his life, he held various top positions in the established church. Shortly before his death he resigned his ecclesiastical appointment and disappeared into a Carthusian monastery. It is of relevance to note that Carthusian monks were called to lives of hermits. They left their private cells for three prayer services with their brethren. Who knows? Perhaps Hereford could no longer hold fast to his betrayals and yielded back into the arms of Christ.

John Purvey (ca. 1354 - 1427) is believed to have been born in Buckinghamshire, and also to have been educated at Oxford. Purvey was Wycliffe's curate at Lutterworth. He took it upon himself to produce a thorough linguistic revision of the works rendered by Wycliffe, Hereford and perhaps other contributors. Purvey took the text of his brothers and improved the readability, removing its cramped and over-latinized style. This was no small achievement. Purvey left an account of his approach:

> "A simple creature hath translated the Bible out of Latin into English. First, this simple creature had much travail, with divers fellows and helpers, to gather many old Bibles and other doctors and common glosses, and to make one Latin Bible some deal true; and then to study it a new the text with the gloss and other doctors as he might get, and specially Nicolaus de Lyra on the Old Testament that helped full much in this work; the third time to counsel with old grammarians and old divines of hard words and hard sentences, how they might be best understood and translated; the fourth time to translate as he could to the sentence, and to have many good fellows and cunning at the correcting of the translation.[7]"

It thus appears that his contribution went beyond the technical improvement of style. Even as Hereford, Purvey too

4. Sir Winston Churchill. The Island Race. New York: Dodd Mead, 1964. 146.

5. Margaret Deanesly. The Lollard Bible and other medieval biblical versions. London, United Kingdom: Cambridge University Press, November 27, 2008. 253.

6. For a treatise on the subject: J.A. Robson. Wyclif and the Oxford Schools: The Relation of the 'Summa de Ente' to Scholastic Debates at Oxford in the Later Fourteenth Century. London, United Kingdom: Cambridge University Press, 1961. Chapter: Scholastic background at Oxford.

7. Henry Paterson Cameron. History of the English Bible. London, United Kingdom: Alexander Gardner, 1885. 57. In facsimile reprint by General Books LL, 2009. ISBN 1459082028.

- at a later date and due to vigorous persecution - recanted his supposedly heretical beliefs. After only a few years, however, he returned to his soul's conviction and suffered persecution until his final imprisonment in 1421. The last known of Purvey's fate is his appeal to Cardinal Beaufort in 1427.

There are strong parallels in the thoughts and opinions of Dr. Martin Luther (1483 - 1546) and Wycliffe, Hereford and Purvey. Luther's Ninety-Five Thesis were hammered on the doors of the church in Wittenberg in 1517. Wycliffe, Hereford and Purvey held the same strong conviction as Luther that God's Word, the Bible, was to be authoritative in life. They also shared that firm believe that our justification is by faith in Jesus Christ. Through these and other positions, these three men and their followers became early dissidents of the Roman Catholic Church, well over a Century prior to the Reformation.

The Wycliffe Bible, as it has come to us, contains 77 books: All the books present in the current canon of the Protestant Old and New Testament, plus ten belonging to what Jerome called the Apocrypha. Its contents follows closely that of the Latin Vulgate[8], which was its main source. The final book is not the Revelation (or the Apocalypse), but rather the short apocryphal Letter -authored by Paul or possibly his associate Epaphroditus[9]- to the Church in Laodicea, entitled Laodicensis. This book was not a part of Jerome's Apocrypha, however.

With Wycliffe, Hereford, Purvey and others working from the Latin Vulgate -to an extend to be determined by those more qualified- one must acknowledge the fact that the Wycliffe Bible is a translation of a translation. Further, I already indicated in the third paragraph of this foreword, that the translators had to create new English words to give expression to what they sought to relay from the Vulgate[10]. Interpretive choices, possibly even of theological and doctrinal concepts, made by Wycliffe, Hereford, Purvey and others must have had their influence on the formulation of subsequent translation texts, theology and doctrine. To

manage the risk of the effects of intrinsic deviations from God's revelation, caused by the sequential processes of translation, I encourage the study of God's Word in Hebrew and Greek. With high quality reference materials available these days, this avenue of study has become more and more feasible[11].

It struck me as odd that the monumental work of Wycliffe et al., whose influence was instrumental in the growth of the faith in England, and whose passages have in part been adopted into the King James Version, was not available in print. Sections of it were, but not the whole work. Permission was requested and granted by the Wesley Center Online[12] to use their digital text as the source file for a single volume print edition of the Wycliffe Bible. For the cover of this single volume print edition I considered a facsimile of an original leaf of a hand-written copy of the Wycliffe Bible the only appropriate cover illustration, and to my joy I received two scanned pages from the Dunham Bible Museum, Houston Baptist University[13].

It is my hope and prayer that you may be blessed in your personal studies of God's Word and that these revived pages in print may proof to be a refreshing inspiration in your obedient walk with our Lord and Savior.

Cranbrook, BC, 23 September 2009

Hans J.A. Dekkers
Publisher

---

8. The Vulgate (from the Latin *editio vulgata* meaning "common version") was commissioned by Pope Damasus to Jerome in ca. 382. The work was completed in ca. 405. Source: Vulgate. Encyclopaedia Britannica, 15th Edition, Micropedia X. 1973. It is generally believed that the Vulgate formed the basis for the translation work culminating in the Wycliffe Bible.

9. Charles P. Anderson, of the Faculty of Religious Studies, University of British Columbia, wrote a five page treatise, entitled "Who wrote the epistle from Laodicea", in which he concludes that Epaphroditus (mentioned in Philippians 2:25, 4:18) is left as the only one whom we know to have the occasion, the relationship, and the motive for writing that letter. Source: Charles P. Anderson. Who wrote "The Epistle from Laodicea"? The Society of Biblical Literature, Journal of Biblical Literature, Vol. 85, No. 4 (Dec. 1966). 436-440.

10. Cf. footnote 2 within that paragraph.

---

11. Software such as BibleWorks (available at www.BibleWorks.com) offers students access to the Hebrew and the Greek, including searches on both form and lemma. The monumental reference works by Botterweck (Old Testament) and Kittel (New Testament) provide deep and profound insight in the words used. There is great doctrinal protection to be enjoyed in the usage of these volumes as opposed to the usage of commentaries. For in these, many different authors were assigned the task to comment on individual words only, making it much more difficult to introduce one's individual positions on doctrine or theology.
Botterweck, Ringgren, Fabry. Theological Dictionary of the Old Testament. Grand Rapids, Michigan, USA / Cambridge, United Kingdom: William B. Eerdmans Publishing Company, 1974-2006.
Kittel. Theological Dictionary of the New Testament. Grand Rapids, Michigan, USA: William B. Eerdmans Publishing Company, 1964-1976.

12. http://wesley.nnu.edu

13. http://www.hbu.edu/biblemuseum

Acknowledgements

In the direct context of this publication I desire to express my sincere gratitude to Dr. George Lyons, Ph.D., Professor of New Testament, and Director of the Wesley Center Online. Dr. Lyons instantly encouraged and said "Yes" to my proposal to produce a print-edition of the digital text of the Wycliffe Bible. I love the "yes" attitude in people. It empowers. Dr. Lyons also gracefully reviewed all files and draft, and edited my foreword.

Another heart-warming "Yes" came from Dr. Diana L. Severance, Ph.D., Director of the Dunham Bible Museum, associated with Houston Baptist University. I had been in contact with several antiquarian book stores specialized in old Bibles and hand-written manuscripts but to no avail. Dr. Severance indicated that the Houston Bible Museum had recently acquired a hand-written manuscript dating back to around 1450. A few weeks later I was in possession of digital scans of two leafs of Romans 6. These images reveal to us the antiquity of this work, and decorate the front and back cover.

Leaving the direct context of this publication, I desire to demonstrate the profound effects of role-modelling a love for God and His Word, and want to encourage you to nurture this love in all those around you: Especially those of the next generation. My Grandmother Dekkers had entire sections of God's Word memorized. My Dad read from the Word after all family evening meals. My first mentor in Christ, Christian and Missionary Alliance missionary to Irian Jaya Mr. John Schultz role-modelled a passionate love for God's Word. He has written commentaries on over 40 books of the Bible, which writings are freely accessible to all on www.Bible-Commentaries.com. My first home group leader and mentor, Dr. Andrew Perriman, Ph.D., encouraged thorough study. My brother in The Gideons International, Charles Vos, endlessly stressed the centrality of God's Word, and as a lay man was fluent in Hebrew and had mastered Biblical Hebrew. These dear people, and many more, grew my deep respect for God's Word, and it is my honor to acknowledge their investment and love.

There were also organizations which were instrumental in the growth of my respect and love for God's Word. I think of The Gideons International, as well as several smaller organizations who allowed me access to God's Word long before I was saved. For me, back then, the text was inaccessible. I could not stop reading it, but I hardly understood anything of it. The language was not the issue. The issue was the fact that without re-birth one reads the scriptures in English, or Dutch, or French, or German, or whatever the language may be - even Hebrew or Greek. But the Holy Scriptures need to be read in the Holy Spirit.

And so it follows that, most of all, I am eternally grateful to our Lord and Savior Jesus Christ: For saving a wretch like me and calling me his own. It was his Holy Spirit who opened the Scriptures and guided me into His Love and His Truth.

Lastly, I want to acknowledge you. For holding this Wycliffe Bible in your hands, and even reading these few words of mine, tells me that you care about the Word of God. And that means a lot to me, for there is no healthier food for the soul than that supernatural book that is known to mankind as the Bible.

Thank you all!

Hans J.A. Dekkers

Table of Contents

Apocrypha in italic type.

GENESIS - - - - - - - - - - - - - - - 1
EXODUS - - - - - - - - - - - - - - 34
LEVITICUS - - - - - - - - - - - 61
NUMBERS - - - - - - - - - - - - - 80
DEUTERONOMY - - - - - - - - - 108
JOSHUA - - - - - - - - - - - - - - 131
JUDGES - - - - - - - - - - - - - - 147
RUTH - - - - - - - - - - - - - - - 163
1 KINGS   (1 Samuel) - - - - - - - - - 166
2 KINGS   (2 Samuel) - - - - - - - - - 187
3 KINGS   (1 Kings) - - - - - - - - - 206
4 KINGS   (2 Kings) - - - - - - - - - 227
1 PARALIPOMENON   (1 Chr.) - - - - - 247
2 PARALIPOMENON   (2 Chr.) - - - - - 267
1 ESDRAS (Ezra) - - - - - - - - - - 290
2 ESDRAS (Nehemiah) - - - - - - - 296
3 ESDRAS   (1 Esdras) - - - - - - - - 306
TOBIT - - - - - - - - - - - - - - - 316
JUDITH - - - - - - - - - - - - - - 323
ESTHER - - - - - - - - - - - - - - 331
JOB - - - - - - - - - - - - - - - - 339
PSALMS - - - - - - - - - - - - - - 357
PROVERBS - - - - - - - - - - - - 403
ECCLESIASTES - - - - - - - - - - 418
SONGES OF SONGES - - - - - - - 423
WISDOM - - - - - - - - - - - - - - 426
SYRACH - - - - - - - - - - - - - - 436
ISAIAH - - - - - - - - - - - - - - 465
JEREMIAH - - - - - - - - - - - - 497
LAMENTATIONS - - - - - - - - - 533
PREIER OF JEREMYE - - - - - - - 537
BARUK - - - - - - - - - - - - - - 538
EZECHIEL - - - - - - - - - - - - 541
DANIEL - - - - - - - - - - - - - - 575
OSEE   (Hosea) - - - - - - - - - - - 589
JOEL - - - - - - - - - - - - - - - 593
AMOS - - - - - - - - - - - - - - 595
ABDIAS   (Obadiah) - - - - - - - - - 599
JONAS (Jonah) - - - - - - - - - - 599
MYCHEE (Micah) - - - - - - - - - 601
NAUM (Nahum) - - - - - - - - - 603
ABACUK (Habakkuk) - - - - - - - 604
SOFONYE (Zephaniah) - - - - - - - 606
AGGEY (Haggai) - - - - - - - - - 607
SACARIE (Zechariah) - - - - - - - - 608
MALACHIE (Malachi) - - - - - - - 614
1 MACHABEIS (1 Maccabees) - - - - - 615
2 MACHABEIS (2 Maccabees) - - - - - 635
MATHEU (Matthew) - - - - - - - - - 650

MARK - - - - - - - - - - - - - - 671
LUKE - - - - - - - - - - - - - - 684
JOHN - - - - - - - - - - - - - - 707
DEDIS OF APOSTLIS (Acts) - - - - - 724
ROMAYNES (Romans) - - - - - - - 746
1 CORINTHIS (1 Corinthians) - - - - 755
2 CORINTHIS (2 Corinthians) - - - - 763
GALATHIES (Galatians) - - - - - - 768
EFFESIES (Ephesians) - - - - - - - 771
FILIPENSIS (Philippians) - - - - - - 774
COLOSENCIS (Colossians) - - - - - - 776
1 THESSALONYCENSIS (1 Thessalonians) 778
2 THESSALONYCENSIS (2 Thessalonians) 779
1 TYMOTHE (1 Timothy) - - - - - - 780
2 TYMOTHE (2 Timothy) - - - - - - 783
TITE (Titus) - - - - - - - - - - - 784
FILEMON (Philemon) - - - - - - - 785
EBREWS (Hebrews) - - - - - - - - 785
JAMES   792
1 PETRE (1 Peter) - - - - - - - - - 794
2 PETRE (2 Peter) - - - - - - - - - 796
1 JOON (1 John) - - - - - - - - - 797
2 JOON (2 John) - - - - - - - - - - 800
3 JOON (3 John) - - - - - - - - - - 800
JUDAS - - - - - - - - - - - - - - 800
APOCALIPS (Revelation) - - - - - - 801
LAODICENSIS - - - - - - - - - - - 811

GENESIS
CAP 1

1 In the bigynnyng God made of nouyt heuene and erthe.

2 Forsothe the erthe was idel and voide, and derknessis weren on the face of depthe; and the Spiryt of the Lord was borun on the watris.

3 And God seide, Liyt be maad, and liyt was maad.

4 And God seiy the liyt, that it was good, and he departide the liyt fro derknessis; and he clepide the liyt,

5 dai, and the derknessis, nyyt. And the euentid and morwetid was maad, o daie.

6 And God seide, The firmament be maad in the myddis of watris, and departe watris fro watris.

7 And God made the firmament, and departide the watris that weren vndur the firmament fro these watris that weren on the firmament; and it was don so.

8 And God clepide the firmament, heuene. And the euentid and morwetid was maad, the secounde dai.

9 Forsothe God seide, The watris, that ben vndur heuene, be gaderid in to o place, and a drie place appere; and it was doon so.

10 And God clepide the drie place, erthe; and he clepide the gadryngis togidere of watris, the sees. And God seiy that it was good;

11 and seide, The erthe brynge forth greene eerbe and makynge seed, and appil tre makynge fruyt bi his kynde, whos seed be in it silf on erthe; and it was doon so.

12 And the erthe brouyte forth greene erbe and makynge seed bi his kynde, and a tre makynge fruyt, and ech hauynge seed by his kynde. And God seiy that it was good.

13 And the euentid and morwetid was maad, the thridde dai.

14 Forsothe God seide, Liytis be maad in the firmament of heuene, and departe tho the dai and niyt; and be tho in to signes, and tymes, and daies, and yeeris;

15 and shyne tho in the firmament of heuene, and liytne tho the erthe; and it was doon so.

16 And God made twei grete liytis, the gretter liyt that it schulde be bifore to the dai, and the lesse liyt that it schulde be bifore to the niyt;

17 and God made sterris; and settide tho in the firmament of heuene, that tho schulden schyne on erthe,

18 and that tho schulden be bifore to the dai and nyyt, and schulden departe liyt and derknesse. And God seiy that it was good.

19 And the euentid and the morwetid was maad, the fourthe dai.

20 Also God seide, The watris brynge forth a 'crepynge beeste of lyuynge soule, and a brid fleynge aboue erthe vndur the firmament of heuene.

21 And God made of nouyt grete whallis, and ech lyuynge soule and mouable, whiche the watris han brouyt forth in to her kyndis; and God made of nouyt ech volatile bi his kynde. And God seiy that it was good;

22 and blesside hem, and seide, Wexe ye, and be ye multiplied, and fille ye the watris of the see, and briddis be multiplied on erthe.

23 And the euentid and the morwetid was maad, the fyuethe dai.

24 And God seide, The erthe brynge forth a lyuynge soul in his kynde, werk beestis, and 'crepynge beestis, and vnresonable beestis of erthe, bi her kyndis; and it was don so.

25 And God made vnresonable beestis of erthe bi her kyndes, and werk beestis, 'and ech crepynge beeste of erthe in his kynde. And God seiy that it was good; and seide,

26 Make we man to oure ymage and liknesse, and be he souereyn to the fischis of the see, and to the volatilis of heuene, and to vnresonable beestis of erthe, and to ech creature, and to ech 'crepynge beest, which is moued in erthe.

27 And God made of nouyt a man to his ymage and liknesse; God made of nouyt a man, to the ymage of God; God made of nouyt hem, male and female.

28 And God blesside hem, and seide, Encreesse ye, and be ye multiplied, and fille ye the erthe, and make ye it suget, and be ye lordis to fischis of the see, and to volatilis of heuene, and to alle lyuynge beestis that ben moued on erthe.

29 And God seide, Lo! Y haue youe to you ech eerbe berynge seed on erthe, and alle trees that han in hem silf the seed of her kynde, that tho be in to mete to you;

30 and to alle lyuynge beestis of erthe, and to ech brid of heuene, and to alle thingis that ben moued in erthe, and in whiche is a lyuynge soule, that tho haue to ete; and it was doon so.

31 And God seiy alle thingis whiche he made, and tho weren ful goode. And the euentid and morwetid was maad, the sixte day.

CAP 2

1 Therfor heuenes and erthe ben maad perfit, and al the ournement of tho.

2 And God fillide in the seuenthe dai his werk which he made; and he restide in the seuenthe dai fro al his werk which he hadde maad;

3 and he blesside the seuenthe dai, and halewide it; for in that dai God ceesside of al his werk which he made of nouyt, that he schulde make.

4 These ben the generaciouns of heuene and of erthe, in the day wherynne the Lord God made heuene and erthe,

5 and ech litil tre of erthe bifore that it sprong out in erthe; and he made ech erbe of the feeld bifore that it buriownede. For the Lord God had not reyned on erthe, and no man was that wrouyte erthe;

6 but a welle stiede out of the erthe, and moistide al the hiyere part of erthe.

7 Therfor the Lord God formede man of the sliym of erthe, and brethide in to his face the brething of lijf; and man was maad in to a lyuynge soule.

8 Forsothe the Lord God plauntide at the bigynnyng paradis of likyng, wherynne he settide man whom he hadde formed.

9 And the Lord God brouyte forth of the erthe ech tre fair in siyt, and swete to ete; also he brouyte forth the tre of lijf in the middis of paradis, and the tre of kunnyng of good and of yuel.

10 And a ryuer yede out fro the place of likyng to moyste paradis, which ryuer is departid fro thennus in to foure heedis.

11 The name of the o ryuer is Fyson, thilke it is that cumpassith al the lond of Euilath, where gold cometh forth,

12 and the gold of that lond is the beste, and there is foundun delium, that is, a tree of spicerie, and the stoon onychyn;

13 and the name to the secounde ryuer is Gyon, thilke it is that cumpassith al the loond of Ethiopie;

14 forsothe the name of the thridde ryuer is Tigris, thilke goith ayens Assiriens; sotheli the fourthe ryuer is thilke Eufrates.

15 Therfor the Lord God took man, and settide hym in paradis of likyng, that he schulde worche and kepe it.

16 And God comaundide to hym and seide, Ete thou of ech tre of paradis;

17 forsothe ete thou not of the tre of kunnyng of good and of yuel; for in what euere dai thou schalt ete therof, thou schalt die bi deeth.

18 And the Lord God seide, It is not good that a man be aloone, make we to hym an help lijk to hym silf.

19 Therfor whanne alle lyuynge beestis of erthe, and alle the volatils of heuene weren formed of erthe, the Lord God brouyte tho to Adam, that he schulde se what he schulde clepe tho; for al thing that Adam clepide of lyuynge soule, thilke is the name therof.

20 And Adam clepide bi her names alle lyuynge thingis, and alle volatils, and alle vnresonable beestis of erthe. Forsothe to Adam was not foundun an helpere lijk hym.

21 Therfore the Lord God sente sleep in to Adam, and whanne he slepte, God took oon of hise ribbis, and fillide fleisch for it.

22 And the Lord God bildide the rib which he hadde take fro Adam in to a womman, and brouyte hir to Adam.

23 And Adam seide, This is now a boon of my boonys, and fleisch of my fleisch; this schal be clepid virago, 'for she is takun of man.

24 Wherfor a man schal forsake fadir and modir, and schal cleue to his wijf, and thei schulen be tweyne in o fleisch.

25 Forsothe euer eithir was nakid, that is, Adam and his wijf, and thei weren not aschamed.

CAP 3

1 But and the serpent was feller than alle lyuynge beestis of erthe, whiche the Lord God hadde maad. Which serpent seide to the womman, Why comaundide God to you, that ye schulden not ete of ech tre of paradis?

2 To whom the womman answerde, We eten of the fruyt of trees that ben in paradis;

3 sothely God commaundide to vs, that we schulden not eate of the fruyt of the tre, which is in the myddis of paradijs, and that we schulden not touche it, lest perauenture we dien.

4 Forsothe the serpent seide to the womman, ye schulen not die bi deeth;

5 for whi God woot that in what euere dai ye schulen ete therof, youre iyen schulen be opened, and ye schulen be as Goddis, knowynge good and yuel.

6 Therfore the womman seiy that the tre was good, and swete to ete, and fair to the iyen, and delitable in bi holdyng; and sche took of the fruyt therof, and eet, and yaf to hir hosebande, and he eet.

7 And the iyen of bothe weren openid; and whanne thei knowen that thei weren nakid, thei sewden the leeues of a fige tre, and maden brechis to hem silf.

8 And whanne thei herden the vois of the Lord God goynge in paradijs at the wynd after myddai, Adam and his wijf hidden hem fro the face of the Lord God in the middis of the tre of paradijs.

9 And the Lord God clepide Adam, and seide to hym, Where art thou?

10 And Adam seide, Y herde thi vois in paradijs, and Y drede, for Y was nakid, and Y hidde me.

11 To whom the Lord seide, Who forsothe schewide to thee that thou were nakid, no but for thou hast ete of the tre of which Y comaundide to thee that thou schuldist ete?

12 And Adam seide, The womman which thou yauest felowe to me, yaf me of the tre, and Y eet.

13 And the Lord seide to the womman, Whi didist thou this thing? Which answerde, The serpent disseyued me, and Y eet.

14 And the Lord God seide to the serpent, For thou didist this, thou schalt be cursid among alle lyuynge thingis and vnresonable beestis of erthe; thou schalt go on thi brest, and thou schalt ete erthe in alle daies of thi liif;

15 Y schal sette enemytees bitwixe thee and the womman, and bitwixe thi seed and hir seed; sche schal breke thin heed, and thou schalt sette aspies to hir heele.

16 Also God seide to the womman, Y schal multiplie thi wretchidnessis and thi conseyuyngis; in sorewe thou schalt bere thi children; and thou schalt be vndur power of the hosebonde, and he schal be lord of thee.

17 Sothely God seyde to Adam, For thou herdist the voys of thi wijf, and hast ete of the tree, of which Y comaundide to thee that thou schuldist not ete, the erthe schal be cursid in thi werk; in traueylis thou schalt ete therof in alle daies of thi lijf;

18 it schal brynge forth thornes and breris to thee, and thou schalt ete eerbis of the erthe;

19 in swoot of thi cheer thou schalt ete thi breed, til thou turne ayen in to the erthe of which thou art takun; for thou art dust, and thou schalt turne ayen in to dust.

20 And Adam clepide the name of his wijf Eue, for sche was the moder of alle men lyuynge. And the Lord God made cootis of skynnys to Adam and Eue his wijf, and clothide hem; and seide, Lo!

22 Adam is maad as oon of vs, and knowith good and yuel; now therfore se ye, lest perauenture he putte his hond, and take of the tre of lijf, and ete, and lyue with outen ende.

23 And the Lord God sente hym out of paradijs of likyng, that he schulde worche the erthe, of which he was takun.

24 And God castide out Adam, and settide bifore paradis of lykyng cherubyn, and a swerd of flawme and turnynge aboute to kepe the weie of the tre of lijf.

CAP 4

1 Forsothe Adam knewe Eue his wijf, which conseyuede, and childide Cayn, and seide, Y haue gete a man bi God.

2 And efte sche childide his brother Abel. Forsothe Abel was a kepere of scheep, and Cayn was an erthe tilyere.

3 Sotheli it was don after many daies, that Cayn offride yiftis to the Lord of the fruytis of erthe;

4 and Abel offride of the first gendrid of his floc, and of the fatnesse of tho. And the Lord bihelde to Abel and to the yiftis of hym;

5 sotheli he bihelde not to Cayn and to hise yiftis. And Cayn was wrooth greetli, and his cheer felde doun.

6 And the Lord seide to hym, Whi art thou wrooth, and whi felde doun thi face?

7 Whether not if thou schalt do wel, thou schalt resseyue; but if thou doist yuele, thi synne schal be present anoon in the yatis? but the desir therof schal be vndur thee, and thou schalt be lord therof.

8 And Cayn seide to Abel his brother, Go we out. And whanne thei weren in the feeld, Cayn roos ayens his brother Abel, and killide him.

9 And the Lord seide to Cayn, Where is Abel thi brother? Which answerde, Y woot not; whether Y am the kepere of my brothir?

10 And God seide to Cayn, What hast thou do? the vois of the blood of thi brother crieth to me fro erthe.

11 Now therfor thou schalt be cursid on erthe, that openyde his mouth, and resseyuede of thin hond the blood of thi brothir.

12 Whanne thou schalt worche the erthe, it schal not yyue his fruytis to thee; thou schalt be vnstable of dwellyng and fleynge aboute on erthe in alle the daies of thi lijf.

13 And Cayn seide to the Lord, My wickidnesse is more than that Y disserue foryyuenesse; lo!

14 to dai thou castist me out fro the face of the erthe; and Y schal be hid fro thi face, and Y schal be vnstable of dwellyng and fleynge aboute in erthe; therfore ech man that schal fynde me schal slee me.

15 And the Lord seide to hym, It schal not be don so, but ech man that schal slee Cayn shal be punyschid seuenfold. And the Lord settide a signe in Cayn, that ech man that schulde fynde hym schulde not slee hym.

16 And Cayn yede out fro the face of the Lord, and dwellide fleynge aboute in erthe, at the eest coost of Eden.

17 Forsothe Cayn knewe his wiif, which conseyuede, and childide Enoth; and Cayn bildide a citee, and clepide the name therof of the name of hise sone Enoth.

18 Forsothe Enoth gendride Irad, and Irad gendride Manyael, and Manyael gendride Matusael, and Matusael gendride Lameth;

19 that took twei wyues, the name to o wijf was Ada, and the name to the tother was Sella.

20 And Ada gendride Jabel, that was the fadir of dwellers in tentis and of shepherdis;

21 and the name of his brother was Tubal, he was the fadir of syngeris in harpe and orgun.

22 And Sella gendride Tubalcayn, that was an hamerbetere, and smyyt on alle werkis of bras and of yrun; forsothe the sistir of Tubalcayn was Neoma.

23 And Lameth seide to his wyues Ada and Sella, Ye wyues of Lameth, here my vois, and herkne my word; for Y haue slayn a man bi my wounde, and a yong wexynge man bi my 'violent betyng;

24 veniaunce schal be youun seuenfold of Cayn, forsothe of Lameth seuentisithis seuensithis.

25 Also yit Adam knewe his wijf, and sche childide a sone, and clepide his name Seth, and seide, God hath put to me another seed for Abel, whom Cayn killide.

26 But also a sone was borun to Seth, which sone he clepide Enos; this Enos bigan to clepe inwardli the name of the Lord.

CAP 5

1 This is the book of generacioun of Adam, in the dai wher ynne God made man of nouyt. God made man to the ymage and licnesse of God;

2 God formede hem male and female, and blesside hem, and clepide the name of hem Adam, in the day in which thei weren formed.

3 Forsothe Adam lyuede an hundrid yeer and thretti, and gendride a sone to his ymage and liknesse, and clepide his name Seth.

4 And the daies of Adam after that he gendride Seth weren maad eiyte hundrid yeer, and he gendride sones and douytris.

5 And al the tyme in which Adam lyuede was maad nyne hundrid yeer and thretti, and he was deed.

6 Also Seth lyuede an hundrid and fyue yeer, and gendride Enos.

7 And Seth lyuede aftir that he gendride Enos eiyte hundrid and seuen yeer, and gendride sones and douytris.

8 And alle the daies of Seth weren maad nyne hundrid and twelue yeer, and he was deed.

9 Forsothe Enos lyuede nynti yeer, and gendride Caynan;

10 aftir whos birthe Enos lyuede eiyte hundrid and fiftene yeer, and gendride sones and douytris.

11 And alle the daies of Enos weren maad nyne hundrid and fyue yeer, and he was deed.

12 Also Caynan lyuyde seuenti yeer, and gendride Malalehel.

13 And Caynan lyuede after that he gendride Malalehel eiyte hundrid and fourti yeer, and gendride sones and douytris.

14 And alle the dayes of Caynan weren maad nyn hundrid and ten yeer, and he was deed.

15 Forsothe Malalehel lyuede sixti yeer and fyue, and gendride Jared.

16 And Malalehel lyuede aftir that he gendride Jared eiyte hundrid and thretti yeer, and gendride sones and douytris.

17 And alle the daies of Malalehel weren maad eiyte hundrid nynti and fyue yeer, and he was deed.

18 And Jared lyuede an hundrid and two and sixti yeer, and gendride Enoth.

19 And Jared lyuede aftir that he gendride Enoth eiyte hundrid yeer, and gendride sones and douytris.

20 And alle the dayes of Jared weren maad nyn hundrid and twei and sexti yeer, and he was deed.

21 Forsothe Enoth lyuede fyue and sixti yeer, and gendride Matusalem.

22 And Enoth yede with God; and Enoth lyuede after that he gendride Matusalem thre hundrid yeer, and gendride sones and douytris.

23 And alle the daies of Enoth weren maad thre hundride and fyue and sexti yeer.

24 And Enoth yeed with God, and apperide not afterward, for God took hym awei.

25 Also Matusalem lyuede an hundrid and 'fourscoor yeer and seuene, and gendride Lameth.

26 And Matusalem lyuede after that he gendride Lameth seuene hundrid and 'fourscoor yeer and twei, and gendride sones and douytris.

27 And alle the daies of Matusale weren maad nyn hundrid and nyn and sixti yeer, and he was deed.

28 Forsothe Lameth lyuede an hundrid and 'fourscoor yeer and two, and gendride a sone;

29 and clepide his name Noe, and seide, This man schal comforte vs of the werkis and traueilis of oure hondis, in the loond which the Lord curside.

30 And Lameth lyuede after that he gendride Noe fyue hundrid 'nynti and fyue yeer, and gendride sones and douytris.

31 And alle the daies of Lameth weren maad seuene hundrid 'thre scoor and seuentene yeer, and he was deed.

CAP 6

1 Forsothe Noe whanne he was of fyue hundrid yeer gendride Sem, Cham, and Jafeth. And whanne men bigunnen to be multiplied on erthe, and hadden gendrid douytris,

2 the sones of God seiyen the douytris of men that thei weren faire, and token wyues to hem of alle whiche thei hadden chose.

3 And God seide, My spirit schal not dwelle in man with outen ende, for he is fleisch; and the daies of hym schulen be an hundrid and twenti yeer.

4 Sotheli giauntis weren on erthe in tho daies, forsothe aftir that the sones of God entriden to the douytris of men, and tho

douytris gendriden; these weren myyti of the world and famouse men.

5 Sotheli God seiy that myche malice of men was in erthe, and that al the thouyt of herte was ententif to yuel in al tyme,

6 and repentide him that he hadde maad man in erthe; and God was war bifore ayens tyme to comyng, and was touchid with sorewe of herte with ynne;

7 and seide, Y schal do awei man, whom Y made of nouyt, fro the face of the erthe, fro man til to lyuynge thingis, fro crepynge beeste til to the briddis of heuene; for it repentith me that Y made hem.

8 Forsothe Noe foond grace bifore the Lord.

9 These ben the generaciouns of Noe. Noe was a iust man and perfit in hise generaciouns; Noe yede with God,

10 and gendride thre sones, Sem, Cam, and Jafeth.

11 Forsothe the erthe was corrupt bifore God, and was fillid with wickidnes.

12 And whanne God seiy, that the erthe was corrupt, for ech fleisch ether man hadde corrupt his weie on erthe,

13 he seide to Noe, The ende of al fleisch is comen bifore me; the erthe is fillid with wickidnesse of the face of hem, and Y schal distrye hem with the erthe.

14 Make thou to thee a schip of trees hewun and planed; thou schalt make dwellynge placis in the schip, and thou schalt anoynte it with pitche with ynne and with outforth.

15 And so thou schalt make it. The lengthe of the schip schal be of thre hundrid cubitis, the brede schal be of fifti cubitis, and the hiynesse therof schal be of thretti cubitis.

16 Thou schalt make a wyndow in the schip, and thou schalt ende the hiynesse therof in a cubite; sotheli thou schalt sette the dore of the schip in the side binethe; thou schalt make soleris and placis of thre chaumbris in the schip.

17 Lo! Y schal brynge 'watris of diluuye ether greet flood on erthe, and Y schal sle ech fleisch in which is the spirit of lijf vndir heuene, and alle thingis that ben in erthe, schulen be wastid.

18 And Y schal sette my couenaunt of pees with thee; and thou schalt entre in to the schip, and thy sones, and thi wijf, and the wiues of thi sones schulen entre with thee.

19 And of alle lyuynge beestis of al fleisch thou schalt brynge in to the schip tweyne and tweyne, of male kynde and female, that thei lyue with thee;

20 of briddis bi her kynde, and of werk beestis in her kynde, and of ech crepynge beeste of erthe, by her kynde; tweyne and tweyne of alle schulen entre with thee, that thei moun lyue.

21 Therfore thou schalt take with thee of alle metis that moun be etun, and thou schalt bere to gidre at thee, and tho schulen be as well to thee as to the beestis in to mete.

22 Therfor Noe dide alle thingis whiche God comaundide to hym.

CAP 7

1 Also the Lord seide to Noe, Entre thou and al thin hous in to the schip, for Y seiy thee iust bifore me in this generacioun.

2 Of alle clene lyuynge beestis thou schalt take bi seuene and bi seuene, male and female; forsothe of vnclene lyuynge beestis thou schalt take bi tweyne and bi tweyne, male and female;

3 but also of volatils of heuene thou schalt take, bi seuene and bi seuene, male and female, that her seed be saued on the face of al erthe.

4 For yit and aftir seuene daies Y schal reyne on erthe fourti daies and fourti nyytis, and Y schal do awey al substaunce which Y made, fro the face of erthe.

5 Therfor Noe dide alle thingis whiche the Lord comaundide to hym.

6 And he was of six hundrid yeer, whanne the watris of the greet flood flowiden on erthe.

7 And Noe entride in to the schip, and hise sones, and hise wijf, and the wyues of his sones, entriden with him for the watris of the greet flood.

8 And of lyuynge beestis clene and vnclene, and of briddis of heuene, and of ech beeste which is moued on erthe,

9 bi tweyne and bi tweyne, male and female entriden to Noe in to the schip, as the Lord comaundide to Noe.

10 And whanne seuene daies hadden passid, the watris of the greet flood flowiden on erthe.

11 In the six hundrid yeer of the lijf of Noe, in the secunde moneth, in the seuententhe dai of the moneth, alle the wellis of the greet see weren brokun, and the wyndowis of heuene weren opened,

12 and reyn was maad on erthe fourti daies and fourti nyytis.

13 In the ende of that dai Noe entride, and Sem, Cham, and Japheth, hise sones, his wijf, and the wyues of hise sones, entriden with hem into the schip.

14 Thei entriden, and ech beeste bi his kynde, and alle werk beestis in her kynde, and ech beeste which is moued on erthe in his kynde, and ech volatil bi his kynde; alle briddis and alle volatils entriden to Noe in to the schip,

15 bi tweyne and bi tweyne of ech fleisch in whiche the spirit of lijf was.

16 And tho that entriden, entriden male and female of ech fleisch, as God comaundide to hym. And the Lord encloside hym fro with out-forth.

17 And the greet flood was maad fourti daies and fourti niytis on erthe, and the watris weren multiplied, and reiseden the schip on hiy fro erthe.

18 The watris flowiden greetli, and filliden alle thingis in the face of erthe. Forsothe the schip was borun on the watris.

19 And the watris hadden maistrie greetli on erthe, and alle hiye hillis vndur alle heuene weren hilid;

20 the watyr was hiyere bi fiftene cubitis ouer the hilis whiche it hilide.

21 And ech fleisch was wastid that was moued on erthe, of briddis, of lyuynge beestis, of vnresonable beestis, and of alle 'reptilis that crepen on erthe.

22 Alle men, and alle thingis in whiche the brething of lijf was in erthe, weren deed.

23 And God dide awei al substaunce that was on erthe, fro man til to beeste, as wel a crepynge beeste as the briddis of heuene; and tho weren doon awei fro erthe. Forsothe Noe dwellide aloone, and thei that weren with hym in the schip.

24 And the watris of the greet flood ouereyeden the erthe an hundrid and fifti daies.

CAP 8

1 Forsothe the Lord hadde mynde of Noe, and of alle lyuynge beestis, and of alle werk beestis, that weren with hym in the schip; and brouyte a wynd on the erthe.

2 And watris weren decreessid, and the wellis of the see weren closid, and the wyndowis of heuene weren closid, and reynes of heuene weren ceessid.

3 And watrys turneden ayen fro erthe, and yeden ayen, and bigunnen to be decreessid aftir an hundrid and fifti daies.

4 And the schip restide in the seuenthe monthe, in the seuene and twentithe dai of the monthe, on the hillis of Armenye.

5 And sotheli the watrys yeden and decresiden til to the tenthe monethe, for in the tenthe monethe, in the firste dai of the monethe, the coppis of hillis apperiden.

6 And whanne fourti daies weren passid, Noe openyde the wyndow of the schip which he hadde maad, and sente out a crowe,

7 which yede out, and turnede not ayen til the watris weren dried on erthe. Also Noe sente out a culuer aftir hym, to se if the watris hadden ceessid thanne on the face of erthe;

9 and whanne the culuer foond not where hir foot schulde reste, sche turnede ayen to hym in to the schip, for the watris weren on al erthe; and Noe helde forth his hoond, and brouyte the culuer takun in to the schip.

10 Sotheli whanne othere seuene daies weren abedun aftirward, eft he leet out a culuer fro the schip;

11 and sche cam to hym at euentid, and bare in hir mouth a braunche of olyue tre with greene leeuys. Therfor Noe vndirstood that the watris hadden ceessid on erthe;

12 and neuerthelesse he abood seuene othere daies, and sente out a culuer, which turnede 'no more ayen to hym.

13 Therfor in the sixe hundrid and o yeer of the lijf of Noe, in the firste monethe, in the firste day of the monethe, watris weren decreessid on erthe; and Noe openede the roof of the schip, and bihelde and seiy that the face of the erthe was dried.

14 In the secunde monethe, in the seuene and twentithe dai of the monethe, the erthe was maad drie.

15 Sotheli the Lord spak to Noe;

16 and seide, Go out of the schip, thou, and thi wijf, thi sones, and the wyues of thi sones with thee;

17 and lede out with thee alle lyuynge beestis that ben at thee of ech fleisch, as wel in volatilis as in vnresonable beestis, and alle 'reptils that crepen on erthe; and entre ye on the erthe, encreesse ye, and be ye multiplied on erthe.

18 Therfor Noe yede out, and hise sones, and his wijf, and the wyues of hise sones with hym;

19 but also alle lyuynge beestis, and werk beestis, and 'reptils that crepen on erthe, bi her kynde, yeden out of the schip.

20 Forsothe Noe bildide an auter to the Lord, and he took of alle clene beestis and briddis, and offride brent sacrifices on the auter.

21 And the Lord sauerede the odour of swetnesse, and seide to hym, Y schal no more curse the erthe for men, for the wit and thouyt of mannus herte ben redi in to yuel fro yong wexynge age; therfor Y schal no more smyte ech lyuynge soule as Y dide;

22 in alle the daies of erthe, seed and ripe corn, coold and heete, somer and wyntir, nyyt and dai, shulen not reste.

CAP 9

1 And God blisside Noe and hise sones, and seide to hem, Encreesse ye, and be ye multiplied, and fille ye the erthe;

2 and youre drede and tremblyng be on alle vnresonable beestis of erthe, and on alle briddis of heuene, with alle thingis that ben moued in erthe; alle fischis of the see ben youun to youre hond.

3 And al thing which is moued and lyueth schal be to you in to mete; Y have youe to you alle thingis as greene wortis,

4 outakun that ye schulen not ete fleisch with blood,

5 for Y schal seke the blood of youre lyues of the hoond of alle vnresonable beestis and of the hoond of man, of the hoond of man and of hys brother Y schal seke the lijf of man.

6 Who euere schedith out mannus blood, his blood schal be sched; for man is maad to the ymage of God.

7 Forsothe encreesse ye, and be ye multiplied, and entre ye on erthe, and fille ye it, Also the Lord seide thes thingis to Noe,

8 and to his sones with him, Lo!

9 Y schal make my couenaunt with you, and with your seed after you,

10 and to ech lyuynge soule which is with you, as wel in briddis as in werk beestis and smale beestis of erthe, and to alle thingis that yeden out of the schip, and to alle vnresonable beestis of erthe.

11 Y schal make my couenaunt with you, and ech fleisch schal no more be slayn of the watris of the greet flood, nethir the greet flood distriynge al erthe schal be more.

12 And God seide, This is the signe of boond of pees, which Y yyue bitwixe me and you, and to ech lyuynge soule which is with you, in to euerlastynge generaciouns.

13 Y schal sette my bowe in the cloudis, and it schal be a signe of boond of pees bitwixe me and erthe;

14 and whanne Y schal hile heuene with cloudis, my bowe schal appere in the cloudis,

15 and Y schal haue mynde of my boond of pees which Y made with you, and with ech soule lyuynge, that nurschith fleisch; and the watris of the greet flood schulen no more be to do awey al fleish.

16 And my bowe schal be in the cloudis, and Y schal se it, and Y schal haue mynde of euerlastynge boond of pees, which is maad bitwixe God and man, and ech soul lyuynge of al fleisch which is on erthe.

17 And God seide to Noe, This schal be a signe of boond of pees, which Y made bitwixe me and ech fleisch on erthe.

18 Therfore thei that yeden out of the schip weren Noe, Sem, Cham, and Japheth; forsothe Cham, thilke is the fadir of Chanaan.

19 These thre weren the sones of Noe, and al the kynde of men was sowun of hem on al erthe.

20 And Noe, an erthe tiliere, bigan to tile the erthe, and he plauntide a viner,

21 and he drank wyn, and was drunkun; and he was nakid, and lay in his tabernacle.

22 And whanne Cham, the fadir of Chanaan, hadde seien this thing, that is, that the schameful membris of his fadir weren maad nakid, he telde to hise tweye britheren with out forth.

23 And sotheli Sem and Jafeth puttiden a mentil on her schuldris, and thei yeden bacward, and hileden the schameful membris of her fadir, and her faces weren turned awei, and thei sien not the priuy membris of her fadir.

24 And forsothe Noe wakide of the wyn, and whanne he hadde lerned what thingis his lesse sone hadde do to hym,

25 he seide, Cursid be the child Canaan, he schal be seruaunt of seruauntis to hise britheren.

26 And Noe seide, Blessid be the Lord God of Sem,

27 and Chanaan be the seruaunt to Sem; God alarge Jafeth, and dwelle in the tabernaclis of Sem, and Chanaan be seruaunt of hym.

28 Forsothe Noe lyuede aftir the greet flood thre hundrid and fifti yeer;

29 and alle the daies of hym weren fillid nyn hundrid and fifty yeer, and he was deed.

CAP 10

1 These ben the generaciouns of the sones of Noe, Sem, Cham, and Jafeth. And sones weren borun to hem aftir the greet flood.

2 The sones of Jafeth weren Gomer, and Magog, and Madai, and Jauan, and Tubal, and Mosoth, and Thiras.

3 Forsothe the sones of Gomer weren Asseneth, and Rifath, and Thogorma.

4 Forsothe the sones of Jauan weren Helisa, and Tharsis, Cethym, and Dodanym;

5 of these sones the ylis of hethen men weren departid in her cuntrees, ech bi his langage and meynees, in hise naciouns.

6 Sotheli the sones of Cham weren Thus, and Mesraym, and Futh, and Chanaan.

7 Forsothe the sones of Thus weren Saba, and Euila, and Sabatha, and Regma, and Sabatacha. The sones of Regma weren Saba, and Dadan.

8 Forsothe Thus gendride Nemroth; he bigan to be myyti in erthe,

9 and he was a strong huntere of men bifore the Lord; of hym a prouerbe yede out, as Nemroth, a strong huntere bifore the Lord.

10 Sotheli the bigynnyng of his rewme was Babiloyne, and Arach, and Archad, and Thalamye, in the lond of Sennaar.

11 Assur yede out of that lond, and bildide Nynyue, 'and stretis of the citee,

12 and Chale, and Resen bitwixe Nynyue and Chale; this is a greet citee.

13 And sotheli Mesraym gendride Ludym, and Anamym, and Laabym, Neptuym, and Ferrusym, and Cesluym;

14 of which the Filisteis and Capturym camen forth.

15 Forsothe Chanaan gendride Sidon, his firste gendride sone, Ethei, and Jebusei,

16 and Amorrei, Gergesei,

17 Euei, and Arathei,

18 Ceney, and Aradie, Samarites, and Amathei; and puplis of Chananeis weren sowun abrood bi these men.

19 And the termes of Chanaan weren maad to men comynge fro Sidon to Gerara, til to Gasa, til thou entre in to Sodom and Gomore, and Adama, and Seboyne, til to Lesa.

20 These weren the sones of Cham, in her kynredis, and langagis, and generaciouns, and londis, and folkis.

21 Also of Sem weren borun the fadris of alle the sones of Heber, and Japhet was the more brother.

22 The sones of Sem weren Elam, and Assur, and Arfaxath, and Lud, and Aram.

23 The sones of Aram weren Vs, and Hul, and Gether, and Mes.

24 And sotheli Arfaxath gendride Sale, of whom Heber was borun.

25 And twei sones weren borun to Heber, the name to o sone was Faleg, for the lond was departid in hise daies; and the name of his brothir was Jectan.

26 And thilke Jectan gendride Elmodad, and Salech,

27 and Asamoth, Jare, and Adhuram, and Vsal,

28 and Deda, and Ebal, and Abymahel, Saba, and Ofir, and Euila, and Jobab;

29 alle these weren the sones of Jectan.

30 And the habitacioun of hem was maad fro Messa, as 'me goith til to Sefar, an hil of the eest.

31 These ben the sones of Sem, bi kynredis, and langagis, and cuntrees, in her folkis.

32 These ben the meynees of Noe, bi her puplis and naciouns; folkis in erthe weren departid of these aftir the greet flood.

CAP 11

1 Forsothe the lond was of o langage, and of the same speche.

2 And whanne thei yeden forth fro the eest, thei fonden a feeld in the lond of Sennaar, and dwelliden ther ynne.

3 And oon seide to his neiybore, Come ye, and make we tiel stonys, and bake we tho with fier; and thei hadden tiel for stonus, and pitche for morter;

4 and seiden, Come ye, and make we to vs a citee and tour, whos hiynesse stretche 'til to heuene; and make we solempne oure name bifor that we be departid in to alle londis.

5 Forsothe the Lord cam down to se the citee and tour, which the sones of Adam bildiden.

6 And he seide, Lo! the puple is oon, and o langage is to alle, and thei han bigunne to make this, nethir thei schulen ceesse of her thouytis, til thei fillen tho in werk; therfor come ye, go we doun,

7 and scheende we there the tunge of hem, that ech man here not the voys of his neiybore.

8 And so the Lord departide hem fro that place in to alle londis; and thei cessiden to bielde a cytee.

9 And therfor the name therof was clepid Babel, for the langage of al erthe was confoundide there; and fro thennus the Lord scaterede hem on the face of alle cuntrees.

10 These ben the generaciouns of Sem. Sem was of an hundrid yeer whanne he gendride Arfaxath, twey yeer aftir the greet flood.

11 And Sem lyuede aftir that he gendride Arfaxath fyue hundrid yeer, and gendride sones and douytris.

12 Forsothe Arfaxath lyuede fyue and thretti yeer, and gendride Sale;

13 and Arfaxath lyuede aftir that he gendride Sale thre hundride and thre yeer, and gendride sones and douytris.

14 Also Sale lyuede thretti yeer, and gendride Heber;

15 and Sale lyuede after that he gendride Heber foure hundrid and thre yeer, and gendride sones and douytris.

16 Sotheli Heber lyuede foure and thretti yeer, and gendride Falech;

17 and Heber lyuede aftir that he gendride Falech foure hundrid and thretti yeer, and gendride sones and douytris.

18 Also Falech lyuede thretti yeer, and gendride Reu;

19 and Falech lyuede aftir that he gendride Reu two hundrid and nyne yeer, and gendride sones and douytris.

20 And Reu lyuede two and thretti yeer, and gendride Saruch;

21 and Reu lyuede aftir that he gendride Saruch two hundrid and seuene yeer, and gendride sones and douytris.

22 Sotheli Saruch lyuede thretti yeer, and gendride Nachor;

23 and Saruch lyuede aftir that he gendride Nacor two hundrid yeer, and gendride sones and douytris.

24 Forsothe Nachor lyuede nyne and twenti yeer, and gendride Thare;

25 and Nachor lyuede after that he gendride Thare an hundrid and nynetene yeer, and gendride sones and douytris.

26 And Thare lyuede seuenti yeer, and gendride Abram, and Nachor, and Aran.

27 Sotheli these ben the generaciouns of Thare. Thare gendride Abram, Nachor, and Aran. Forsothe Aran gendride Loth;

28 and Aran diede bifore Thare, his fadir, in the lond of his natiuite, in Vr of Caldeis.

29 Forsothe Abram and Nachor weddiden wyues; the name of the wijf of Abram was Saray, and the name of the wiif of

Nachor was Melcha, the douyter of Aran, fadir of Melcha and fadir of Jescha.

30 Sotheli Saray was bareyn, and hadde no children.

31 And so Thare took Abram, his sone, and Loth, the sone of Aran his sone, and Saray, his douyter in lawe, the wijf of Abram, his sone, and ledde hem out of Vr of Caldeis, that thei schulen go in to the lond of Chanaan; and thei camen 'til to Aran, and dwelliden there.

32 And the daies of Thare weren maad two hundrid yeer and fyue, and he was deed in Aran.

CAP 12

1 Forsothe the Lord seide to Abram, Go thou out of thi lond, and of thi kynrede, and of the hous of thi fadir, and come thou in to the lond which Y schal schewe to thee;

2 and Y schal make thee in to a greet folk, and Y schal blisse thee, and Y schal magnyfie thi name, and thou schalt be blessid;

3 Y schal blesse hem that blessen thee, and Y schal curse hem that cursen thee; and alle kynredis of erthe schulen be blessid in thee.

4 And so Abram yede out, as the Lord comaundide hym, and Loth yede with hym. Abram was of 'thre scoor yeer and fiftene whanne he yede out of Aran.

5 And he took Saray, his wijf, and Loth, the sone of his brother, and al the substaunce which thei hadden in possessioun, and the men whiche thei hadden bigete in Aran; and thei yeden out that thei 'schulen go in to the loond of Chanaan. And whanne they camen in to it,

6 Abram passide thorou the lond til to the place of Sichem, and til to the noble valey. Forsothe Chananei was thanne in the lond.

7 Sotheli the Lord apperide to Abram, and seide to hym, Y schal yyue this lond to thi seed. And Abram bildide there an auter to the Lord, that apperide to hym.

8 And fro thennus he passide forth to the hil Bethel, that was ayens the eest, and settide there his tabernacle, hauynge Bethel fro the west, and Hay fro the eest. And he bildide also there an auter to the Lord, and inwardli clepide his name.

9 And Abram yede goynge and goynge forth ouer to the south.

10 Sotheli hungur was maad in the lond; and Abram yede doun in to Egipt, to be a pilgrime ther, for hungur hadde maistrie in the lond.

11 And whanne he was nyy to entre in to Egipt, he seide to Saray, his wijf, Y knowe that thou art a fair womman,

12 and that whanne Egipcians schulen se thee, thei schulen seie, it is his wijf, and thei schulen sle me, and 'schulen reserue thee.

13 Therfor, Y biseche thee, seie thou, that thou art my sistir, that it be wel to me for thee, and that my lijf lyue for loue of thee.

14 And so whanne Abram hadde entrid in to Egipt, Egipcians sien the womman that sche was ful fair; and the prynces telden to Farao, and preiseden hir anentis him;

15 and the womman was takun vp in to the hous of Farao.

16 Forsothe thei vsiden wel Abram for hir; and scheep, and oxun, and assis, and seruauntis, and seruauntessis, and sche assis, and camels weren to hym.

17 Forsothe the Lord beet Farao and his hous with moste veniaunces, for Saray, the wijf of Abram.

18 And Farao clepide Abram, and seide to hym, What is it that thou hast do to me? whi schewidist thou not to me, that sche was thi wijf?

19 for what cause seidist thou, that sche was thi sister, that Y schulde take hir in to wife to me? Now therfor lo! thi wiif; take thou hir, and go.

20 And Farao comaundide to men on Abram, and thei ledden forth hym, and his wijf, and alle thingis that he hadde.

CAP 13

1 Therfore Abram stiede fro Egipt, he, and his wijf, and alle thingis that he hadde; and Loth stiede with hym, to the south coost.

2 Forsothe he was ful riche in possessyoun of siluer and of gold.

3 And he turnede ayen bi the weye in which he cam fro the south in to Bethel, 'til to the place, in which bifore he hadde sett tabernacle, bitwixe Bethel and Hay,

4 in the place of the auter which he made bifore, and inwardli clepide there the name of the Lord.

5 But also flockis of scheep, and droues of oxun, and tabernaclis weren to Loth, that was with Abram;

6 and the lond miyte not take hem, that thei schulden dwelle togidre, for the catel of hem was myche, and thei miyten not dwelle in comyn.

7 Wherfor also strijf was maad bitwixe the keperis of flockis of Abram and of Loth. Forsothe Chananei and Feresei dwelliden in that lond in that tyme.

8 Therfor Abram seide to Loth, Y biseche, that no strijf be bitwixe me and thee, and bitwixe my scheepherdis and thi scheepherdis; for we ben britheren.

9 Lo! al the lond is bifore thee, Y biseche, departe thou fro me; if thou go to the left side, Y schal holde the riyt side; if thou chese the riyt side, Y schal go to the left side.

10 And so Loth reiside hise iyen, and seiy aboute al the cuntrei of Jordan, which was al moistid, bifor that the Lord distriede Sodom and Gomorre, as paradis of the Lord, and as Egipt, as men comen in to Segor.

11 And Loth chees to him the cuntre aboute Jordan, and departide fro the eest; and thei weren departid ech fro his brother.

12 Abram dwellide in the lond of Chanaan; sotheli Loth dwellide in townes aboute Jordan, and wonide in Sodom.

13 Forsothe men of Sodom weren ful wickid, and synneris greetly bifore the Lord.

14 And the Lord seide to Abram, aftir that Loth was departid fro him, Reise thin iyen forth riyt, and se fro the place in which thou art now, to the north and south, to the eest and west;

15 Y schal yyue al the lond which thou seest to thee and to thi seed, til in to with outen ende.

16 And Y schal make thi seed as the dust of erthe; if ony man may noumbre the dust of erthe, also he schal mowe noumbre thi seed.

17 Therfor rise thou, and passe thorou the lond in his lengthe and breede, for Y schal yyue it to thee.

18 Therfor Abram, mouynge his tabernacle, cam and dwellide bisidis the valei of Mambre, which is in Ebron; and he bildide there an auter to the Lord.

CAP 14

1 Forsothe it was don in that tyme, that Amrafel, kyng of Sennaar, and Ariok, kyng of Ponte, and Chodorlaomor, kyng of Elemytis,

2 and Tadal, kyng of folkis, bigunnen batel ayens Bara, kyng of Sodom, and ayens Bersa, kyng of Gomorre, and ayens Sennaar, kyng of Adama, and ayens Semeber, kyng of Seboym, and ayens the kyng of Bale; thilke Bale is Segor.

3 Alle these camen togidre in to the valey of wode, which is now the see of salt.

4 For in twelue yeer thei seruyden Chodorlaomor, and in the thrittenthe yeer thei departiden fro hym.

5 Therfor Chodorlaomor cam in the fourtenthe yeer, and kyngis that weren with him, and thei 'han smyte Rafaym in Astaroth Carnaym, and Susym with hem, and Emym in Sabe Cariathaym,

6 and Choreis in the hillis of Seir, til to the feldi placis of Faran, which is in wildirnesse.

7 And thei turneden ayen, and camen til to the welle Mesphath; thilke is Cades. And thei 'han smyte al the cuntre of men of Amalec, and Amorrei, that dwellide in Asason Thamar.

8 And the kyng of Sodom, and the king of Gomorre, and the kyng of Adama, and the kyng of Seboym, also and the kyng of Bale, which is Segor, yeden out, and dressiden scheltrun ayens hem in the valei of wode,

9 that is, ayens Chodorlaomor, kyng of Elamytis, and Thadal, kyng of folkis, and Amrafel, kyng of Sennaar, and Ariok, kyng of Ponte; foure kyngis ayens fyue.

10 Forsothe the valey of the wode hadde many pittis of pitche; and so the kyng of Sodom and the kyng of Gomorre turneden the backis, and felden doun there; and thei that leften fledden to the hil.

11 Sotheli thei token awei al the catel of Sodom and Gomorre, and alle thingis that perteynen to mete, and yeden awei;

12 also and thei token awey Loth and his catel, the sone of the brother of Abram, which Loth dwellide in Sodom.

13 And, lo! oon that ascapide, telde to Abram Ebrew, that dwellide in the valei of Mambre of Amorrei, brother of Escol, and brother of Aner; for these maden couenaunt of pees with Abram.

14 And whanne Abram hadde herd this thing, that is, Loth his brothir takun, he noumbride his borun seruauntis maad redy thre hundrid and eiytene, and pursuede hem 'til to Dan.

15 And whanne his felowis weren departid, he felde on hem in the niyt, and he smoot hem, and pursuede hem 'til to Hoba, and Fenyce, which is at the left side of Damask.

16 And he brouyte ayen al the catel, and Loth his brother with his catel, also wymmen and the puple.

17 Sotheli the kyng of Sodom yede out in to the metyng of him, after that he turnede ayen fro sleyng of Chodorlaomor, and of kyngis that weren with him, in the valei of Sabe, which is the valey of the kyng.

18 And sotheli Melchisedech, kyng of Salem, brouyte forth breed and wyn, for he was the preest of hiyeste God;

19 and he blesside Abram, and seide, Blessid be Abram of hiy God, that made heuene and erthe of nouyt,

20 and blessid be hiy God, bi whom defendynge, enemyes ben bitakun in thin hondis. And Abram yaf tithis of alle thingis to hym.

21 Forsothe the kyng of Sodom seide to Abram, Yyue thou the men to me; take thou othir thingis to thee.

22 And Abram answerde to hym, Y reyse myn hondis to the hiy Lord God,

23 Lord of heuene and of erthe, that fro the threde of oof til to the layner of the hose I schal not take of alle thingis that ben thine, lest thou seie, I made Abram riche;

24 out takun these thingis whiche the yonge men eeten, and the partis of men that camen with me, Aner, Escol, and Mambre; these men schulen take her partis.

CAP 15

1 And so whanne these thingis weren don, the word of the Lord was maad to Abram bi a visioun, and seide, Abram, nyle thou drede, Y am thi defender, and thi meede is ful greet.

2 And Abram seide, Lord God, what schalt thou yyue to me? Y schal go with oute fre children, and this Damask, sone of Elieser, the procuratour of myn hous, schal be myn eir.

3 And Abram addide, Sotheli thou hast not youe seed to me, and, lo! my borun seruaunt schal be myn eir.

4 And anoon the word of the Lord was maad to hym, and seide, This schal not be thin eir, but thou schalt haue hym eir, that schal go out of thi wombe.

5 And the Lord ledde out Abram, and seide to hym, Biholde thou heuene, and noumbre thou sterris, if thou maist. And the Lord seide to Abram, So thi seed schal be.

6 Abram bileuede to God, and it was arettid to hym to riytfulnesse.

7 And God seide to hym, Y am the Lord, that ladde thee out of Vr of Caldeis, that Y schulde yyue this lond to thee, and thou schuldist haue it in possessioun.

8 And Abram seide, Lord God, wherbi may I wite that Y schal welde it?

9 And the Lord answerde, and seide, Take thou to me a cow of thre yeer, and a geet of thre yeer, and a ram of thre yeer, a turtle also, and a culuer.

10 Which took alle these thingis, and departide tho bi the myddis, and settide euer eithir partis ech ayens other; but he departide not the briddis.

11 And foulis camen doun on the careyns, and Abram drof hem awey.

12 And whanne the sunne was gon doun, drede felde on Abram, and a greet hidousenesse and derk asaylide him.

13 And it was seid to hym, Wite thou bifore knowinge, that thi seed schal be pilgrim foure hundrid yeer in a lond not his owne, and thei schulen make hem suget to seruage, and thei schulen turment hem;

14 netheles Y schal deme the folk to whom thei schulen serue; and aftir these thingis thei schulen go out with greet catel.

15 Forsothe thou schalt go to thi fadris in pees, and schalt be biried in good age.

16 Sotheli in the fourthe generacioun thei schulen turne ayen hidir, for the wickidnesse of Amoreis ben not yit fillid, 'til to present tyme.

17 Therfor whanne the sunne was gon doun, a derk myst was maad, and a furneis smokynge apperide, and a laumpe of fier, and passide thorou tho departingis.

18 In that dai the Lord made a couenaunt of pees with Abram, and seide, Y schal yyue to thi seed this lond, fro the ryuer of Egipt til to the greet ryuer Eufrates; Cyneis,

19 and Cyneseis, and Cethmoneis, and Etheis,

20 and Fereseis, and Raphaym, and Amorreis,

21 and Cananeis, and Gergeseis, and Jebuseis.

CAP 16

1 Therfor Sarai, wijf of Abram, hadde not gendrid fre children; but sche hadde a seruauntesse of Egipt, Agar bi name, and seide to hir hosebonde, Lo!

2 the Lord hath closid me, that Y schulde not bere child; entre thou to my seruauntesse, if in hap Y schal take children, nameli of hir. And whanne he assentide to hir preiynge, sche took Agar Egipcian,

3 hir seruauntesse, after ten yeer aftir that thei begunne to enhabite in the lond of Chanaan, and sche yaf Agar wiif to hir hosebonde.

4 And Abram entride to Agar; and Agar seiy that sche hadde conseyued, and sche dispiside hir ladi.

5 And Saray seide to Abram, Thou doist wickidli ayens me; I yaf my seruauntesse in to thi bosum, which seeth, that sche conseyuede, and dispisith me; the Lord deme betwixe me and thee.

6 And Abram answerde and seide to hir, Lo! thi seruauntesse is in thin hond; vse thou hir as 'it likith. Therfor for Sarai turmentide hir, sche fledde awei.

7 And whanne the aungel of the Lord hadde founde hir bisidis a welle of watir in wildernesse, which welle is in the weie of Sur in deseert,

8 he seide to hir, Fro whennus comest thou Agar, the seruauntesse of Sarai, and whidur goist thou? Which answerde, Y fle fro the face of Sarai my ladi.

9 And the aungel of the Lord seide to hir, Turne thou ayen to thi ladi, and be thou mekid vndur hir hondis.

10 And eft he seide, Y multipliynge schal multiplie thi seed, and it schal not be noumbrid for multitude.

11 And aftirward he seide, Lo! thou hast conseyued, and thou schalt bere a sone, and thou schalt clepe his name Ismael, for the Lord hath herd thi turment;

12 this schal be a wielde man; his hond schal be ayens alle men, and the hondis of alle men schulen be ayens him; and he schal sette tabernaclis euene ayens alle his britheren.

13 Forsothe Agar clepide the name of the Lord that spak to hir, Thou God that seiyest me; for sche seide, Forsothe here Y seiy the hynderere thingis of him that siy me.

14 Therfor sche clepide thilke pit, the pit of hym that lyueth and seeth me; thilk pit is bitwixe Cades and Barad.

15 And Agar childide a sone to Abram, which clepide his name Ismael.

16 Abram was of 'eiyti yeere and sixe, whanne Agar childide Ysmael to hym.

CAP 17

1 Forsothe aftir that Abram bigan to be of nynti yeer and nyne, the Lord apperide to hym, and seide to him, Y am Almyyti God; go thou bifore me, and be thou perfit;

2 and Y schal sette my couenaunt of pees bitwixe me and thee; and Y schal multiplie thee ful greetli.

3 And Abram felde doun lowe on his face.

4 And God seide to hym, Y am, and my couenaunt of pees is with thee, and thou schalt be the fadir of many folkis;

5 and thi name schal no more be clepid Abram, but thou schalt be clepid Abraham, for Y haue maad thee fadir of many folkis;

6 and Y schal make thee to wexe ful greetli, and Y schal sette thee in folkis, and kyngis schulen go out of thee;

7 and Y schal make my couenaunt bitwixe me and thee, and bitwixe thi seed after thee, in her generaciouns, bi euer-

lastynge bond of pees, that Y be thi God, and of thi seed after thee;

8 and Y schal yyue to thee and to thi seed after thee the lond of thi pilgrymage, al the lond of Chanaan, in to euerlastynge possessioun, and Y schal be the God of hem.

9 God seide eft to Abraham, And therfor thou schalt kepe my couenaunt, and thi seed after thee, in her generaciouns.

10 This is my couenaunt, which ye schulen kepe bitwixe me and you, and thi seed after thee; ech male kynde of you schal be circumcidid,

11 and ye schulen circumside the fleisch of youre mannes yeerd, that it be in to a signe of boond of pees bytwixe me and you.

12 A yong child of eiyte daies schal be circumsidid in you, al male kynde in youre generaciouns, as wel a borun seruaunt as a seruaunt bouyt schal be circumsidid, and who euere is of youre kynrede he schal be circumsidid;

13 and my couenaunt schal be in youre fleisch in to euerlastynge boond of pees.

14 A man whos fleisch of his yerde schal not be circumsidid, thilke man schal be doon a wei fro his puple; for he made voide my couenaunt.

15 Also God seide to Abraham, Thou schalt not clepe Saray, thi wijf, Sarai, but Sara;

16 and Y schal blesse hir, and of hir I schal yyue to thee a sone, whom I schal blesse, and he schal be in to naciouns, and kyngis of puplis schulen be borun of hym.

17 Abraham felde doun on his face, and leiyede in his hert, and seide, Gessist thou, whethir a sone schal be borun to a man of an hundrid yeer, and Sara of nynti yeer schal bere child?

18 And he seide to the Lord, Y wolde that Ismael lyue bifore thee.

19 And the Lord seide to Abraham, Sara, thi wijf, schal bere a sone to thee, and thou schalt clepe his name Ysaac, and Y schal make my couenaunt to hym in to euerlastynge boond of pees, and to his seed aftir hym;

20 also on Ysmael Y haue herd thee, lo! Y schal blesse him, and Y schal encreesse, and Y schal multiplie him greetli; he schal gendre twelue dukis, and Y schal make hym in to a greet folk.

21 Forsothe Y schal make my couenaunt to Ysaac, whom Sare schal childe to thee in this tyme in the tother yeer.

22 And whanne the word of the spekere with hym was endid, God stiede fro Abraham.

23 Forsothe Abraham took Ismael, his sone, and alle the borun seruauntis of his hous, and alle which he hadde bouyte, alle the malis of alle men of his hous, and circumsidide the fleisch of her yerde, anoon in that dai, as the Lord comaundide him.

24 Abraham was of nynti yeer and nyne whanne he circumsidide the fleisch of his yeerd,

25 and Ismael, his sone, hadde fillid threttene yeer in the tyme of his circumsicioun.

26 Abraham was circumsidid in the same day, and Ismael his sone,

27 and alle men of his hows, as wel borun seruauntis as bouyt and aliens, weren circumcidid togidre.

CAP 18

1 Forsothe in the valei of Mambre the Lord apperide to Abraham, sittynge in the dore of his tabernacle, in thilke heete of the dai.

2 And whanne he hadde reisid his iyen, thre men apperiden to hym, and stoden nyy hym. And whanne he hadde seyn hem, he ran fro the dore of his tabernacle in to the meting of hem, and he worschipide on erthe,

3 and seide, Lord, if Y haue founde grace in thin iyen, passe thou not thi seruaunt,

4 but I schal brynge a litil watir, and youre feet be waischid, and reste ye vndur the tre;

5 and Y schal sette a mussel of breed, and youre herte be coumfortid; aftirward ye schulen passe; for herfor ye bowiden to youre seruaunt. Whiche seiden, Do thou as thou hast spoke.

6 Abraham hastide in to the tabernacle, to Sare, and seide to hir, Hast thou, meddle thou thre half buschelis of clene flour; and make thou looues bakun vndur aischis.

7 Forsothe he ran to the droue of beestis, and took therof a calf moost tendre and best, and yaf to a child, which hastide, and sethede the calfe;

8 and he took botere, and mylk, and the calf which he hadde sode, and settide bifore hem; forsothe Abraham stood bisidis hem vndur the tre.

9 And whanne thei hadden ete, thei seiden to hym, Where is Sare thi wijf? He answerde, Lo! sche is in the tabernacle.

10 To whom the Lord seide, Y schal turne ayen, and Y schal come to thee in this tyme, if Y lyue; and Sare, thi wijf, schal haue a sone. Whanne this was herd, Sare leiyede bihynde the dore of the tabernacle.

11 Forsothe bothe weren olde, and of greet age, and wommans termes ceessiden to be maad to Sare.

12 And she leiyede, seiynge pryueli, after that Y wexede eld, and my lord is eld, schal Y yyue diligence to lust?

13 Forsothe the Lord seide to Abraham, Whi leiyeth Sare, thi wijf, seiynge, whether Y an eld womman schal bere child ver-ili?

14 whether ony thing is hard to God? Bi the biheeste Y schal turne ayen to thee in this same tyme, if Y lyue; and Sara schal haue a sone.

15 Sare was aferd for drede, and denyede, seiynge, Y leiyede not. Forsothe the Lord seide, It is not so, but thou leiyedist.

16 Therfor whanne the men hadden risen fro thennus, thei dressiden the iyen ayens Sodom; and Abraham yede to gidre, ledynge hem forth.

17 And the Lord seide, Wher Y mowe hele fro Abraham what thingis Y schal do,

18 sithen he schal be in to a greet folk and moost strong, and alle naciouns of erthe schulen be blessid in hym?

19 For Y woot that Abraham schal comaunde hise children, and his hows after hym, that thei kepe the weie of the Lord, and that thei do riytfulnesse and dom, that the Lord bringe for Abraham alle thingis whiche he spak to Abraham.

20 And so the Lord seide, The cry of men of Sodom and of men of Gomorre is multiplied, and her synne is agreggid greetli; Y schal come doun,

21 and schal se whether thei han fillid in werk the cry that cam to me, that Y wite whether it is not so.

22 And thei turneden han fro thennus, and yeden to Sodom. Abraham sotheli stood yit bifore the Lord,

23 and neiyede, and seide, Whether thou schalt leese a iust man with the wickid man?

24 if fifti iust men ben in the citee, schulen thei perische togidere, and schalt thou not spare that place for fifti iust men, if thei ben ther ynne?

25 Fer be it fro thee that thou do this thing, and sle a iust man with a wickid man, and that a iust man be maad as a wickid man; this is not thin that demest al erthe; thou schalt not make this doom.

26 And the Lord seide to him, If Y schal fynde in Sodom fifti iust men in the myddis of the citee, Y schal foryyue to al the place for hem.

27 Abraham answerde and seide, For Y bigan onys, Y schal speke to my Lord, sithen Y am dust and aische;

28 what if lesse than fifti iust men bi fyue ben, schalt thou do a wey al the cite for fyue and fourti? And the Lord seide, Y schal not do a wei, if I schal fynde fyue and fourti there.

29 And eft Abraham seide to hym, But if fourti ben there, what schalt thou do? The Lord seide, Y schal not smyte for fourti.

30 Abraham seide, Lord, Y biseche, take thou not to indignacioun, if Y speke; what if thretti be foundun there? The Lord answerde, Y schal not do, if Y schal fynde thretti there.

31 Abraham seide, For Y bigan onys, Y schal speke to my Lord; what if twenti be foundun there? The Lord seide, Y schal not sle for twenti.

32 Abraham seide, Lord, Y biseche, be thou not wrooth, if Y speke yit onys; what if ten be founden there? The Lord seide, Y schal not do a wey for ten.

33 The Lord yede forth, after that he ceesside to speke to Abraham, and Abraham turnede ayen in to his place.

CAP 19

1 And tweyne aungels camen to Sodom in the euentide, while Loth sat in the yatis of the citee. And whanne he hadde seyn hem, he roos, and yede ayens hem, and worschipide lowe to erthe,

2 and seide, My lordis, Y biseche, bowe ye in to the hous of youre child, and dwelle ye there; waische ye youre feet, and in the morewtid ye schulen go in to youre weie. Whiche seiden, Nay, but we schulen dwelle in the street.

3 He constreynede hem greetli, that thei schulden turne to hym. And whanne thei weren entrid in to his hous, he made a feeste, he bakide therf breed, and thei eten.

4 Forsothe bifore that thei yeden to sleepe, men of the citee compassiden his hows, fro a child 'til to an eld man, al the puple togidre;

5 and thei clepiden Loth, and seiden to him, Where ben the men that entriden to thee to nyyt? brynge hem out hidur, that we 'knowe hem.

6 And Loth yede out to hem 'bihynde the bak, and closide the dore,

7 and seide, Y biseche, nyle ye, my britheren, nyle ye do this yuel.

8 Y haue twey douytris, that knewen not yit man; Y schal lede out hem to you, and mys vse ye hem as it plesith you, so that ye doon noon yuel to these men, for thei entriden vndur the schadewe of my roof.

9 And thei seiden, Go thou fro hennus. And eft thei seiden, Thou entridist as a comelyng; wher that thou deme? therfor we schulen turment thee more than these. And thei diden violentli to Loth ful greetli. Thanne it was nyy that thei wolden breke the doris; and lo!

10 the men puttiden hoond, and ledden in Loth to hem, and thei closiden the dore.

11 And thei smyten with blyndenesse hem that weren withoutforth, fro the leest til to the moost; so that thei myyten not fynde the dore.

12 Forsothe thei seiden to Loth, Hast thou here ony man of thine, hosebonde of thi douyter, ethir sones, ethir douytris; lede thou out of this citee alle men that ben thine,

13 for we schulen do a wey this place, for the cry of hem encreesside bifor the Lord, which sente vs that we leese hem.

14 And so Loth yede out, and spak to the hosebondys of his douytris, that schulden take hise douytris, and seide, Rise ye, and go ye out of this place; for the Lord schal do awey this citee. And he was seyn to hem to speke as pleiynge.

15 And whanne the morewtid was, the aungels constreyneden hym, and seiden, Rise thou, and take thi wijf, and thi twey douytris whiche thou hast, lest also thou perische to gidere in the synne of the citee.

16 While he dissymelide, thei token his hond, and the hond of his wijf, and of his twey doutris; for the Lord sparide hym.

17 And thei ledden out hym, and settiden with out the citee. There thei spaken to him, and seiden, Saue thou thi lijf; nyle thou biholde bihynde thi bac, nether stond thou in al the cuntre aboute, but make thee saaf in the hil; lest also thou perische togidere.

18 And Loth seide to hem, My lord, Y biseche,

19 for thi seruaunt hath founde grace bifore thee, and thou hast magnyfied thi grace and mercy, which thou hast do with me, that thou schuldist saue my lijf; Y may not be saued in the hil, lest perauenture yuel take me, and Y die;

20 a litil citee is here bisidis, to which Y may fle, and Y schal be saued ther ynne; where it is not a litil citee? and my soule schal lyue ther ynne.

21 And he seide to Loth, Lo! also in this Y haue resseyued thi preieris, that Y distrye not the citee, for which thou hast spoke;

22 haste thou, and be thou saued there, for Y may not do ony thing til thou entre thidur. Therfor the name of that citee was clepid Segor.

23 The sunne roos on erthe, and Loth entride in to Segor.

24 Therfor the Lord reynede on Sodom and Gomorre brynston and fier, fro the Lord fro heuene,

25 and distriede these citees, and al the cuntrey aboute; he destriede alle enhabiters of citees, and all grene thingis of erthe.

26 And his wijf lokide abac, and was turned in to an ymage of salt.

27 Forsothe Abraham risynge eerly, where he stood bifore with the Lord, bihelde Sodom and Gomorre,

28 and al the lond of that cuntrey; and he seiy a deed sparcle stiynge fro erthe, as the smoke of a furneis.

29 For whanne God distriede the citees of that cuntrey, he hadde mynde of Abraham, and delyuerede Loth fro destriynge of the citees in whiche he dwellide.

30 And Loth stiede fro Segor, and dwellide in the hil, and hise twey douytris with him, for he dredde to dwelle in Segor; and he dwellide in a denne, he and his twey douytris with hym.

31 And the more douytre seide to the lasse, Oure fadre is eld, and no man is left in erthe, that may entre to vs, bi the custom of al erthe;

32 come thou, make we him drunkun of wyn, and slepe we with him, that we moun kepe seed of oure fadir.

33 And so thei yauen to her fadir to drynke wyn in that nyyt, and the more douyter entrede, and slepte with hir fadir; and he feelide not, nethir whanne the douytir lay doun, nether whanne sche roos.

34 And in the tothir dai the more douytir seide to the lasse, Lo! Y slepte yistirdai with my fadir, yyue we to hym to drynk

wyn also in this nyyt; and thou schalt slepe with hym, that we saue seed of oure fadir.

35 And thei yauen to her fadir also in that nyyt to drynke wyn, and the lesse douytir entride, and slepte with him; and sotheli he feelide not thanne whanne sche lay doun, nether whanne sche roos.

36 Therfor the twei douytris of Loth conseyuede of hir fadir.

37 And the more douytre childide a sone, and clepide his name Moab; he is the fadir of men of Moab 'til in to present dai.

38 And the lesse douyter childide a sone, and clepide his name Amon, that is, the sone of my puple; he is the fadir of men of Amon til to day.

CAP 20

1 Abraham yede forth fro thennus in to the lond of the south, and dwellide bitwixe Cades and Sur, and was a pilgrym in Geraris;

2 and he seide of Sare, his wijf, Sche is my sistir. Therfor Abymalec, kyng of Gerare, sente, and took hir.

3 Sotheli God cam to Abymalec bi a sweuene in the nyyt, and seide to hym, Lo! thou schalt die, for the wooman which thou hast take, for sche hath an hosebond.

4 Forsothe Abymalech touchide not hir; and he seide, Lord, whether thou schalt sle folc vnkunnynge and iust?

5 Whether he seide not to me, Sche is my sistir, and sche seide, He is my brother? In the symplenesse of myn herte, and in the clennesse of myn hondis Y dide this.

6 And the Lord seide to hym, And Y woot that thou didist bi symple herte, and therfor Y kepte thee, lest thou didist synne ayens me, and I suffride not that thou touchidist hir;

7 now therfor yelde thou the wijf to hir hosebonde, for he is a profete; and he schal preye for thee, and thou schalt lyue; sotheli if thou nylte yelde, wite thou that thou schalt die bi deeth, thou and alle thingis that ben thine.

8 And anoon Abynalech roos bi nyyt, and clepide alle his seruauntis, and spak alle these wordis in the eeris of hem; and alle men dredden greetli.

9 Sotheli Abymalec clepide also Abraham, and seide to hym, What hast thou do to vs? what synneden we ayens thee, for thou hast brouyt in on me and on my rewme a greuouse synne? thou hast do to vs whiche thingis thou ouytist not do.

10 And eft Abimalech axide, and seide, What thing seiyist thou, that thou woldist do this?

11 Abraham answerde, Y thouyte with me, and seide, in hap the drede of God is not in this place; and thei schulen sle me for my wijf;

12 in other maner forsothe and sche is my sister verili, the douyter of my fadir, and not the douyter of my moder; and Y weddide hir in to wijf;

13 sotheli aftir that God ladde me out of the hous of my fadir, Y seide to hir, Thou schalt do this mercy with me in ech place to which we schulen entre; thou schalt seie, that Y am thi brother.

14 Therfore Abymelech took scheep, and oxun, and seruauntis, and handmaydenes, and yaf to Abraham; and he yeldide to him Sare, 'his wijf, and seide, The lond is bifor you;

15 dwelle thou, where euere it plesith thee. Forsothe Abymelech seide to Sare, Lo!

16 Y yaf a thousand platis of siluer to thi brother; this schal be to thee in to hiling of iyen to al men that ben with thee; and whider euere thou goist, haue thou mynde that thou art takun.

17 Sotheli for Abraham preiede, God curide Abymelech, and his wijf, and handmaydens, and thei childiden;
18 for God hadde closid ech wombe of the hows of Abymelech, for Sare, the wijf of Abraham.

CAP 21

1 Forsothe God visitide Sare, as he bihiyte, and fillide tho thingis, that he spak.
2 And sche conseyuede, and childide a sone in hir eeld, in the tyme wherynne God biforseide to hir.
3 And Abraham clepide the name of his sone, whom Sare childide to him, Ysaac.
4 And Abraham circumcidide hym in the eiyte dai, as God comaundide to him,
5 whanne he was of an hundrid yeer; for Ysaac was borun in this age of the fadir.
6 And Sare seide, The Lord made leiyynge to me, and who euer schal here schal leiye with me.
7 And eft sche seide, Who schulde here, and bileue to Abraham, that Sare schulde yyue soukyng to a sone, whom sche childide to him now an eld man?
8 Therfor the child encreesside, and was wenyd; and Abraham made a greet feeste in the dai of his wenyng.
9 And whanne Sare seiy the sone of Agar Egipcian pleiynge with Ysaac hir sone, sche seide to Abraham,
10 Cast thou out the handmayde and hir sone; for the sone of the handmayde schal not be eir with my sone Ysaac.
11 Abraham took this heuyli for his sone;
12 and God seide to hym, Be it not seyn scharp to thee on the child, and on thin handmayde; alle thingis whiche Sare seith to thee, here thou hir vois, for in Isaac seed schal be clepid to thee;
13 but also I schal make the sone of the handmaid in to a greet folk, for he is thi seed.
14 And so Abraham roos eerli, and took breed, and a botel of watir, and puttide on hir schuldre, and bitook the child, and lefte hir; and whanne sche hadde go, sche yede out of the weie in the wildirnesse of Bersabee.
15 And whanne the watir in the botel was endid, sche castide awei the child vndur a tre that was there;
16 and sche yede awei, and sche sat euene ayens as fer as a bowe may caste; for sche seide, Y schal not se the child diynge; and sche sat ayens, and reiside hir vois, and wepte.
17 Forsothe the Lord herde the vois of the child, and the aungel of the Lord clepide Agar fro heuene, and seide, What doist thou, Agar? nyle thou drede, for God hath herd the vois of the child fro the place where ynne he is.
18 Rise thou, and take the child, and holde his hoond; for Y schal make hym in to a greet folc.
19 And God openyde hir iyen, and sche seiy a pit of watir, and sche yede, and fillide the botel, and sche yaf drynk to the child;
20 and was with him, and he encresside, and dwellide in wildernesse, and he was maad a yong man an archer,
21 and dwellide in the deseert of Faran; and his modir took to him a wijf of the lond of Egipt.
22 In the same tyme Abymelech, and Ficol, prince of his oost, seide to Abraham, God is with thee in alle thingis whiche thou doist;
23 therfore swere thou bi God that thou noye not me, and myn eiris, and my kynrede; but bi the mersi whych Y dide to thee, do thou to me, and to the lond in which thou lyuedist a comelyng.

24 And Abraham seide, Y schal swere.
25 And he blamyde Abymelech for the pit of watir, which hise seruauntis token awey bi violence.
26 And Abymelech answerde, I wiste not who dide this thing, but also thou schewidist not to me, and Y herde not outakun to dai.
27 And so Abraham took scheep and oxun, and yaf to Abymalech, and bothe smyten a boond of pees.
28 And Abraham settide seuene ewe lambren of the flok asidis half.
29 And Abymelech seide to hym, What wolen these seuene ewe lambren to hem silf, whiche thou madist stonde asidis half?
30 And he seide, Thou schalt take of myn hond seuene ewe lambren, that tho be in to witnessyng to me, for Y diggide this pit.
31 Therfor thilke place was clepid Bersabee, for euere eithir swore there;
32 and thei maden boond of pees for the pit of an ooth.
33 Forsothe Abymelech roos, and Ficol, prince of his chyualrie, and thei turneden ayen in to the lond of Palestyns. Sotheli Abraham plauntide a wode in Bersabee, and inwardli clepide there the name of euerlastinge God;
34 and he was an erthetiliere ether a comelynge of the lond of Palestynes in many dayes.

CAP 22

1 And aftir that these thingis weren don, God assaiede Abraham, and seide to hym, Abraham! Abraham! He answerde, Y am present.
2 God seide to him, Take thi 'sone oon gendrid, whom thou louest, Ysaac; and go into the lond of visioun, and offre thou hym there in to brent sacrifice, on oon of the hillis whiche Y schal schewe to thee.
3 Therfor Abraham roos bi niyt, and sadlide his asse, and ledde with hym twey yonge men, and Ysaac his sone; and whanne he hadde hewe trees in to brent sacrifice, he yede to the place which God hadde comaundid to him.
4 Forsothe in the thridde dai he reiside hise iyen, and seiy a place afer;
5 and he seide to hise children, Abide ye here with the asse, Y and the child schulen go thidur; and aftir that we han worschipid, we schulen turne ayen to you.
6 And he took the trees of brent sacrifice, and puttide on Ysaac his sone; forsothe he bar fier, and a swerd in hise hondis. And whanne thei tweyne yeden togidere, Isaac seide to his fadir, My fadir!
7 And he answerde, What wolt thou, sone? He seide, Lo! fier and trees, where is the beeste of brent sacrifice?
8 Abraham seide, My sone, God schal puruey to hym the beeste of brent sacrifice.
9 Therfor thei yeden to gidere, and camen to the place whiche God hadde schewid to hym, in which place Abraham bildide an auter, and dresside trees a boue; and whanne he hadde bounde to gidere Ysaac, his sone, he puttide Ysaac in the auter, on the heep of trees.
10 And he helde forth his hond, and took the swerd to sacrifice his sone.
11 And lo! an aungel of the Lord criede fro heuene, and seide, Abraham! Abraham!
12 Which answerde, I am present. And the aungel seide to hym, Holde thou not forth thin honde on the child, nether do

thou ony thing to him; now Y haue knowe that thou dredist God, and sparidist not thin oon gendrid sone for me.

13 Abraham reiside hise iyen, and he seiy 'bihynde his bak a ram cleuynge bi hornes among breris, which he took, and offride brent sacrifice for the sone.

14 And he clepide the name of that place, The Lord seeth; wherfor it is seyd, til to dai, The Lord schal see in the hil.

15 Forsothe the aungel of the Lord clepide Abraham the secounde tyme fro heuene,

16 and seide, The Lord seith, Y haue swore bi my silf, for thou hast do this thing, and hast not sparid thin oon gendrid for me,

17 Y schal blesse thee, and Y schal multiplie thi seed as the sterris of heuene, and as grauel which is in the brynk of the see; thi seed schal gete the yatis of hise enemyes;

18 and alle the folkis of erthe schulen be blessid in thi seed, for thou obeiedist to my vois.

19 Abraham turnede ayen to hise children, and thei yeden to Bersabee to gidere, and he dwellide there.

20 And so whanne these thingis weren don, it was teld to Abraham that also Melcha hadde bore sones to Nachor his brother;

21 Hus the firste gendrid, and Buz his brothir, and Chamuhel the fadir of Sireis,

22 and Cased, and Asan, and Feldas,

23 and Jedlaf, and Batuhel, of whom Rebecca was borun; Melcha childide these eiyte to Nachor brother of Abraham.

24 Forsothe his concubyn, Roma bi name, childide Thabee, and Gaon, and Thaas, and Maacha.

CAP 23

1 Forsothe Sare lyuede an hundrid and seuene and twenti yeer,

2 and diede in the citee of Arbee, which is Ebron, in the lond of Chanaan; and Abraham cam to biweyle and biwepe hir.

3 And whanne he hadde rise fro the office of the deed bodi, he spak to the sones of Heth, and seide,

4 Y am a comelyng and a pilgrym anentis you; yyue ye to me riyt of sepulcre with you, that Y birie my deed body.

5 And the sones of Heth answeriden, and seiden, Lord, here thou vs;

6 thou art the prince of God anentis vs; birie thou thi deed bodi in oure chosun sepulcris, and no man schal mow forbede thee, that ne thou birie thi deed bodi in the sepulcre of him.

7 And Abraham roos, and worschipide the puple of the lond, that is, the sones of Heth.

8 And he seide to hem, If it plesith youre soule that Y birie my deed bodi, here ye me, and preie ye for me to Efron, the sone of Seor,

9 that he yyue to me the double caue, whiche he hath in the vttirmoste part of his feeld; for sufficiaunt money yyue he it to me bifore you into possessioun of sepulcre.

10 Forsothe Efron dwellide in the myddis of the sones of Heth. And Efron answerde to Abraham, while alle men herden that entriden bi the yate of that citee,

11 and seide, My lord, it schal not be doon so, but more herkne thou that that Y seie; Y yyue to thee the feeld, and the denne which is therine, while the sones of my puple ben present; birie thou thi deed bodi.

12 Abraham worschipide bifor the Lord, and bifor the puple of the lond,

13 and he spak to Efron, while his puple stood aboute, Y biseche, that thou here me; Y schal yyue money for the feeld,

resseyue thou it, and so Y schal birie my deed bodi in the feeld.

14 And Efron answerde, My lord,

15 here thou me, the lond which thou axist is worth foure hundrid siclis of siluer, that is the prijs bitwixe me and thee, but hou myche is this? birie thou thi deed bodi.

16 And whanne Abraham hadde herd this, he noumbride the monei which Efron axide, while the sones of Heth herden, foure hundrid siclis of siluer, and of preuyd comyn monei.

17 And the feeld that was sumtyme of Efron, in which feeld was a double denne, biholdinge to Mambre, as wel thilke feeld as the denne and alle the trees therof, in alle termes therof bi cumpas, was confermed to Abraham in to possessioun,

18 while the sones of Heth seiyen and alle men that entriden bi the yate of that citee.

19 And so Abraham biriede Sare, his wijf, in the double denne of the feeld, that bihelde to Mambre; this is Ebron in the lond of Chanaan.

20 And the feeld, and the denne that was therynne, was confermyd of the sones of Heth to Abraham, in to possessioun of sepulcre.

CAP 24

1 Forsothe Abraham was eld, and of many daies, and the Lord hadde blessid hym in alle thingis.

2 And he seide to the eldere seruaunt of his hows, that was souereyn on alle thingis that he hadde, Put thou thin hond vndur myn hipe,

3 that Y coniure thee bi the Lord God of heuene and of erthe, that thou take not a wijf to my sone of the douytris of Chanaan, among whiche Y dwelle;

4 but that thou go to my lond and kynrede, and therof take a wijf to my sone Ysaac.

5 The seruaunt aunswerde, If the womman nyle come with me in to this lond, whether Y owe lede ayen thi sone to the place, fro which thou yedist out?

6 Abraham seide, Be war, lest ony tyme thou lede ayen thidur my sone;

7 the Lord of heuene that took me fro the hows of my fadir, and fro the lond of my birthe, which spak to me, and swoor, and seide, Y schal yyue this lond to thi seed, he schal sende his aungel bifore thee, and thou schalt take fro thennus a wijf to my sone; forsothe if the womman nyle sue thee,

8 thou schalt not be holdun bi the ooth; netheles lede not ayen my sone thidur.

9 Therfore the seruaunt puttide his hond vndur the hipe of Abraham, his lord, and swoor to him on this word.

10 And he took ten camels of the floc of his lord, and yede forth, and bar with him of alle the goodis of his lord; and he yede forth, and cam to Mesopotanye, to the citee of Nachor.

11 And whanne he hadde maad the camels to reste with out the citee, bisidis the pit of watir, in the euentid, in that tyme in which wymmen ben wont to go out to drawe watir,

12 he seide, Lord God of my lord Abraham, Y biseche, meete with me to dai, and do mersi with my lord Abraham.

13 Lo! Y stonde nyy the welle of watir, and the douytris of enhabiters of this citee schulen go out to drawe watir;

14 therfor the damysel to which Y schal seie, Bowe doun thi watir pot that Y drynke, and schal answere, Drynke thou, but also Y schal yyue drynke to thi camels, thilke it is which thou hast maad redi to thi seruaunt Ysaac; and bi this Y schal vndirstonde that thou hast do mersi with my lord Abraham.

15 And he hadde not yit fillid the wordis with ynne hym silf, and lo! Rebecca, the douytir of Batuel, sone of Melcha, wijf of Nachor, brothir of Abraham, yede out, hauynge a watir pot in hir schuldre;

16 a damysel ful comeli, and faireste virgyn, and vnknowun of man. Sotheli sche cam doun to the welle, and fillide the watir pot, and turnide ayen.

17 And the seruaunt mette hir, and seide, Yyue thou to me a litil of the watir of thi pot to drynke.

18 Which answerde, Drynke thou, my lord. And anoon sche dide doun the watir pot on hir schuldre, and yaf drynk to hym.

19 And whanne he hadde drunke, sche addide, But also Y schal drawe watir to thi camelis, til alle drynken.

20 And sche helde out the watir pot in trouyis, and ran ayen to the pit, to drawe watir, and sche yaf watir drawun to alle the camels.

21 Sotheli he bihelde hir priueli, and wolde wite whether the Lord hadde sped his wei, ethir nay.

22 Therfor after that the camels drunken, the man brouyte forth goldun eere ryngis, weiynge twei siclis, and as many bies of the arm, in the weiyte of ten siclis.

23 And he seide to hir, Whos douyter art thou? schewe thou to me, is ony place in the hows of thi fadir to dwelle?

24 Which answerde, Y am the douyter of Batuel, sone of Nachor, whom Melcha childide to him.

25 And sche addide, seiynge, Also ful myche of prouendre and of hey is at vs, and a large place to dwelle.

26 The man bowide hym silf,

27 and worschipide the Lord, and seide, Blessid be the Lord God of my lord Abraham, which God took not aweie his mersy and treuthe fro my lord, and ledde me bi riyt weie in to the hous of the brother of my lord.

28 And so the damesel ran, and telde in the hous of hir modir alle thingis whiche sche hadde herd.

29 Sotheli Rebecca hadde a brothir, Laban bi name, whiche yede out hastili to the man, where he was with out forth.

30 And whanne he hadde seyn the eere ryngis and byes of the arm in the hondis of his sister, and hadde herd alle the wordis of hir tellynge, the man spak to me these thingis, he cam to the man that stood bisidis the camels, and nyy the welle of watir,

31 and seide to him, Entre thou, the blessid of the Lord; whi stondist thou with outforth? I haue maad redi the hows, and a place to thi camels.

32 And he brouyte hym in to the ynne, and unsadlide the camels, and yaf prouendre, and hey, and watir to waische the feet of camels, and of men that camen with hym.

33 And breed was set forth in his siyt, which seide, Y schal not ete til Y speke my wordis. He answerde to the man, Speke thou.

34 And the man seide, Y am the seruaunt of Abraham,

35 and the Lord hath blessid my lord greetli, and he is maad greet; and God yaf to hym scheep, and oxun, siluer, and gold, seruauntis, and handmaides, camels, and assis.

36 And Sare, 'the wijf of my lord, childide a sone to my lord in his eelde, and he yaf alle thingis that he hadde to that sone.

37 And my lord chargide me greetli, and seide, Thou schalt not take to my sone a wijf of the douytris of Canaan, in whos lond Y dwelle,

38 but thou schalt go to the hous of my fadir, and of myn kynrede thou schalt take a wijf to my sone.

39 Forsothe Y answerde to my lord, What if the womman nyle come with me?

40 He seide, The Lord in whose siyt Y go, schal sende his aungel with thee, and he schal dresse thi weie; and thou schalt take a wijf to my sone of my kynrede, and of my fadris hows.

41 Thou schalt be innocent fro my curs, whanne thou comest to my kynesmen, and thei yyuen not 'the womman to thee.

42 Therfor Y cam to day to the welle of watir, and Y seide, Lord God of my lord Abraham, if thou hast dressid my weie in which Y go now, lo!

43 Y stonde bisidis the welle of watir, and the maide that schal go out to drawe watir herith me, yyue thou to me a litil of water to drynke of thi pot,

44 and seith to me, And thou drynke, and Y schal drawe watir to thi camels, thilke is the womman which the Lord hath maad redi to the sone of my lord.

45 While Y turnede in thouyte these thingis with me, Rebecca apperide, comynge with a pot which sche bare in the schuldre; and sche yede doun to the welle, and drowe watir. And Y seide to hir, Yyue thou a litil to me to drynke; and sche hastide,

46 and dide doun the pot of the schuldre, and seide to me, And thou drynke, and Y schal yyue drynke to thi camels; Y drank, and watride the camels.

47 And Y axide hir, and seide, Whos douytir art thou? Which answerde, Y am the douytir of Batuel, sone of Nachor, whom Melcha childide to him. And so Y hangide eere ryngis to ourne hir face, and Y puttide bies of the arm in hir hondis,

48 and lowliche Y worschipide the Lord, and Y blessid the Lord God of my lord Abraham, which God ledde me bi riyt weie, that Y schulde take the douytir of the brothir of my lord to his sone.

49 Wherfor if ye don mercy and treuthe with 'my lord, schewe ye to me; ellis if othir thing plesith, also seie ye this, that Y go to the riyt side ethir to the left side.

50 Laban and Batuel answeriden, The word is gon out of the Lord; we moun not speke ony other thing with thee without his plesaunce.

51 Lo! Rebecca is bifore thee; take thou hir, and go forth, and be sche wijf of the sone of thi lord, as the Lord spak.

52 And whanne the child of Abraham hadde herd this, he felde doun, and worschipide the Lord in erthe.

53 And whanne vessels of siluer, and of gold, and clothis weren brouyt forth, he yaf tho to Rebecca for yifte, and he yaf yiftis to hir britheren, and modir.

54 And whanne a feeste was maad, thei eeten and drunken to gider, and dwelliden there. Forsothe the child roos eerli, and spak, Delyuere ye me, that Y go to my lord.

55 Hir britheren and modir answerden, The damesele dwelle nameli ten daies at vs, and aftirward sche schal go forth.

56 The child seide, Nyle ye holde me, for the Lord hath dressid my weie; delyuere ye me, that I go to my lord.

57 And thei seiden, Clepe we the damysele, and axe we hir wille.

58 And whanne sche was clepid, and cam, thei axiden, Wolt thou go with this man?

59 And sche seide, Y schal go. Therfor they delyueriden hir, and hir nurse, and the seruaunt of Abraham, and hise felowis,
and wischiden prosperitees to her sister,

60 and seiden, Thou art oure sister, encreesse thou in to a thousand thousandis, and thi seed gete the yatis of hise enemyes.

61 Therfor Rebecca and hir damesels stieden on the camels, and sueden the man, which turnede ayen hasteli to his lord.

62 In that tyme Ysaac walkide bi the weie that ledith to the pit, whos name is of hym that lyueth and seeth; for he dwellide in the south lond.

63 And he yede out to thenke in the feeld, for the dai was 'bowid thanne; and whanne he hadde reisid the iyen, he seiy camels comynge afer.

64 And whanne Ysaac was seyn, Rebecca liyte doun of the camel,

65 and seide to the child, Who is that man that cometh bi the feeld in to the metyng of vs? And the child seide to hir, He is my lord. And sche took soone a mentil, and hilide hir.

66 Forsothe the seruaunt tolde to his lord Ysaac alle thingis whiche he hadde do;

67 which Ysaac ledde hir in to the tabernacle of Sare, his modir, and took hir to wijf; and so myche he louede hir, that he temperide the sorewe which bifelde of the deeth of the modir.

CAP 25

1 Forsothe Abraham weddide another wijf, Ceture bi name,

2 which childide to him Samram, and Jexan, and Madan, and Madian, and Jesboth, and Sue.

3 Also Jexan gendride Saba and Dadan. Forsothe the sones of Dadan weren Asurym, and Lathusym, and Laomym.

4 And sotheli of Madian was borun Efa, and Ofer, and Enoth, and Abida, and Heldaa; alle these weren the sones of Cethure.

5 And Abraham yaf alle thingis whiche he hadde in possessioun to Isaac;

6 sotheli he yaf yiftis to the sones of concubyns; and Abraham, while he lyuede yit, departide hem fro Ysaac, his sone, to the eest coost.

7 Forsothe the daies of lijf of Abraham weren an hundrid and 'fyue and seuenti yeer;

8 and he failide, and diede in good eelde, and of greet age, and ful of daies, and he was gaderid to his puple.

9 And Ysaac and Ismael, his sones, birieden him in the doble denne, which is set in the feeld of Efron, sone of Seor Ethei,

10 euene ayens Mambre, which denne he bouyte of the sones of Heth; and he was biried there, and Sare his wijf.

11 And aftir the deeth of Abraham God blesside Isaac his sone, which dwellide bisidis the pit bi name of hym that lyueth and seeth.

12 These ben the generaciouns of Ismael, sone of Abraham, whom Agar Egipcian, seruauntesse of Sare, childide to Abraham;

13 and these ben the names of the sones of Ismael, in her names and generaciouns. The firste gendride of Ismael was Nabaioth, aftirward Cedar, and Abdeel, and Mabsan,

14 and Masma, and Duma, and Massa,

15 and Adad, and Thema, and Ithur, and Nafir, and Cedma.

16 These weren the sones of Ismael, and these weren names by castels and townes of hem, twelue princes of her lynagis.

17 And the yeeris of lijf of Ismael weren maad an hundrid and seuene and thretti, and he failide, and diede, and was put to his puple.

18 Forsothe he enhabitide fro Euila til to Sur, that biholdith Egipt, as me entrith in to Assiriens; he diede bifore alle his britheren.

19 Also these ben the generaciouns of Ysaac sone of Abraham. Abraham gendride Isaac,

20 and whanne Isaac was of fourti yeer, he weddide a wijf, Rebecca, douyter of Batuel, of Sirie of Mesopotanye, the sistir of Laban.

21 And Isaac bisouyte the Lord for his wijf, for sche was bareyn; and the Lord herde him, and yaf conseiuyng to Rebecca.

22 But the litle children weren hurtlid togidre in hir wombe; and sche seide, If it was so to comynge to me, what nede was it to conseyue? And sche yede and axide counsel of the Lord,

23 which answerde, and seide, Twei folkis ben in thi wombe, and twei puplis schulen be departid fro thi wombe, and a puple schal ouercome a puple, and the more schal serue the lesse.

24 Thanne the tyme of childberyng cam, and lo! twei children weren foundun in hir wombe.

25 He that yede out first was reed, and al rouy in the manere of a skyn; and his name was clepid Esau.

26 Anoon the tothir yede out, and helde with the hond the heele of the brother; and therfore he clepide him Jacob. Isaac was sixti yeer eeld, whanne the litle children weren borun.

27 And whanne thei weren woxun, Esau was maad a man kunnynge of huntyng, and a man erthe tilier; forsothe Jacob was a symple man, and dwellide in tabernaclis.

28 Isaac louyde Esau, for he eet of the huntyng of Esau; and Rebecca louyde Jacob.

29 Sotheli Jacob sethide potage; and whanne Esau cam weri fro the feld,

30 he seide to Jacob, Yyue thou to me of this reed sething, for Y am ful weri; for which cause his name was clepid Edom.

31 And Jacob seide to him, Sille to me the riyt of the first gendrid childe.

32 He answerde, Lo! Y die, what schulen the firste gendrid thingis profite to me?

33 Jacob seide, therfor swere thou to me. Therfor Esau swoor, and selde the firste gendrid thingis.

34 And so whanne he hadde take breed and potage, Esau eet and drank, and yede forth, and chargide litil that he hadde seld the riyt of the firste gendrid child.

CAP 26

1 Forsothe for hungur roos on the lond, aftir thilke bareynesse that bifelde in the daies of Abraham, Isaac yede forth to Abymelech, kyng of Palestyns, in Gerara.

2 And the Lord apperide to hym, and seide, Go not doun in to Egipt, but reste thou in the lond which Y schal seie to thee,

3 and be thou a pilgrym ther ynne; and Y schal be with thee, and Y schal blesse thee; for Y schal yyue alle these cuntrees to thee and to thi seed, and Y schal fille the ooth which Y bihiyte to Abraham, thi fadir.

4 And Y schal multiplie thi seed as the sterris of heuene, and Y schal yyue alle these thingis to thin eyris, and alle folkis of erthe schulen be blessid in thi seed, for Abraham obeide to my vois,

5 and kepte 'my preceptis and comaundementis, and kepte cerymonyes and lawis.

6 And so Ysaac dwellide in Geraris.

7 And whanne he was axid of men of that place of his wijf, he answarde, Sche is my sistir; for he dredde to knowleche that sche was felouschipid to hym in matrymonye, and gesside lest peraduenture thei wolden sle him for the fairnesse of hir.

8 And whanne ful many daies weren passid, and he dwellide there, Abymelech, kyng of Palestyns, bihelde bi a wyndow, and seiy hym pleiynge with Rebecca, his wijf.

9 And whanne Isaac was clepid, the kyng seide, It is opyn, that sche is thi wijf; whi liedist thou, that sche was thi sistir? Isaac answerde, Y dredde, lest Y schulde die for hir.

10 And Abymelech seide, Whi hast thou disseyued vs? Sum man of the puple myyte do letcherie with thi wijf, and thou haddist brouyt in greuous synne on vs. And the kyng comaundide to al the puple,

11 and seide, He that touchith the wijf of this man schal die bi deeth.

12 Forsothe Isaac sowide in that lond, and he foond an hundrid fold in that yeer; and the Lord blesside hym.

13 And the man was maad riche, and he yede profitynge and encreessynge til he was maad ful greet.

14 Also he hadde possessioun of scheep and grete beestis, and ful myche of meyne. For this thing Palestyns hadden enuye to hym,

15 and thei stoppiden in that tyme and filliden with erthe alle the pittis whiche the seruauntis of Abraham his fadir hadden diggid,

16 in so myche that Abymelech him silf seide to Ysaac, Go thou awei fro vs, for thou art maad greetly myytier than we.

17 And he yede awei, that he schulde come to the stronde of Gerare, and dwelle there.

18 And he diggide eft other pittis, whiche the seruauntis of Abraham his fadir hadden diggid, and whiche the Filisteis hadden stoppid sumtyme, whanne Abraham was deed; and he clepide tho pittis bi the same names, bi whiche his fadir hadde clepid bifore.

19 Thei diggiden in the stronde, and thei founden wellynge watir.

20 But also strijf of scheepherdis of Gerare was there ayens the scheepherdis of Isaac, and thei seiden, The watir is oure; wherfor of that that bifelde he clepide the name of the pit fals chaleng.

21 And thei diggiden anothir, and thei stryueden also for that, and Ysaac clepide that pit enemytes.

22 And he yede forth fro thennus, and diggide another pit, for which thei stryueden not, therfor he clepid the name of that pit largenesse; and seide, Now God hath alargid vs, and hath maad to encreesse on erthe.

23 Forsothe he stiede fro that place in to Bersabee,

24 where the Lord God apperide to him in that nyyt; and seide, Y am God of Abraham, thi fadir; nyle thou drede, for Y am with thee, and Y schal blesse thee, and Y schal multiplie thi seed for my seruaunt Abraham.

25 And so Ysaac bildide ther an auter to the Lord; and whanne the name of the Lord was inwardli clepid, he stretchide forth a tabernacle; and he comaundide hise seruauntis that thei schulden digge pittis.

26 And whanne Abymelech, and Ochosat, hise frendis, and Ficol, duk of knyytis, hadden comen fro Geraris to that place,

27 Isaac spak to hem, What camen ye to me, a man whom ye hatiden, and puttiden awei fro you?

28 Whiche answeriden, We seiyen that God is with thee, and therfor we seiden now, An ooth be bitwixe vs, and make we a couenaunt of pees,

29 that thou do not ony yuel to vs, as we touchiden 'not ony thing of thine, nethir diden that that hirtide thee, but with pees we leften thee encressid bi the blessyng of the Lord.

30 Therfor Isaac made a feeste to hem; and after mete and drynk thei risen eerli,

31 and sworen ech to other; and Isaac lefte hem peisibli in to her place.

32 Lo! forsothe in that dai the seruauntis of Ysaac camen, tellynge to him of the pit which thei hadden diggid, and seiden, We han foundun watir.

33 Wherfor Ysaac clepide that pit abundaunce; and the name of the citee was set Bersabee til in to present dai.

34 Esau forsothe fourti yeer eld weddide twei wyues, Judith, the douytir of Beeri Ethei, and Bethsamath, the douyter of Elon, of the same place;

35 whiche bothe offendiden the soule of Isaac and of Rebecca.

CAP 27

1 Forsothe Isaac wexe eld, and hise iyen dasewiden, and he miyte not se. And he clepide Esau, his more sone, and seide to hym, My sone! Which answerde, Y am present.

2 To whom the fadir seide, Thou seest that Y haue woxun eld, and Y knowe not the dai of my deeth.

3 Take thin armeres, 'arewe caas, and a bowe, and go out; and whanne thou hast take ony thing bi huntyng,

4 make to me a seew therof, as thou knowist that Y wole, and brynge that Y ete, and my soule blesse thee bifore that Y die.

5 And whanne Rebecca hadde herd this thing, and he hadde go in to the feeld to fille the comaundment of the fadir,

6 sche seide to hir sone Jacob, Y herde thi fadir spekynge with Esau, thi brothir, and seiynge to him, Brynge thou me of thin huntyng,

7 and make thow metis, that Y ete, and that Y blesse thee bifor the Lord bifor that Y die.

8 Now therfor, my sone, assent to my counsels,

9 and go to the floc, and brynge to me tweyne the beste kidis, that Y make metis of tho to thi fadir, whiche he etith gladli;

10 and that whanne thow hast brouyt in tho metis, and he hath ete, he blesse thee bifore that he die.

11 To whom Jacob answerde, Thou knowist that Esau my brother is an heeri man, and Y am smethe; if my fadir 'touchith and feelith me,

12 Y drede lest he gesse that Y wolde scorne him, and lest he brynge in cursyng on me for blessyng.

13 To whom the modir seide, My sone, this cursyng be in me; oonly here thou my vois, and go, and brynge that that Y seide.

14 He yede, and brouyte, and yaf to his modir. Sche made redi metis, as sche knewe that his fadir wolde,

15 and sche clothide Jacob in ful goode clothis of Esau, whiche sche hadde at home anentis hir silf.

16 And sche 'compasside the hondis with litle skynnys of kiddis, and kyuerede the 'nakide thingis of the necke;

17 and sche yaf seew, and bitook the loouys whiche sche hadde bake.

18 And whanne these weren brouyt in, he seide, My fadir! And he answerde, Y here; who art thou, my sone?

19 And Jacob seide, Y am Esau, thi first gendrid sone. Y haue do to thee as thou comaundist to me; rise thou, sitte, and ete of myn huntyng, that thi soule blesse me.

20 Eft Ysaac seide to his sone, My sone, hou miytist thou fynde so soone? Which answerde, It was Goddis wille, that this that Y wolde schulde come soone to me.

21 And Isaac seide, My sone, come thou hidir, that Y touche thee, and that Y preue wher thou art my sone Esau, ethir nay.

22 He neiyede to the fadir; and whanne he hadde feelid hym, Isaac seide, Sotheli the vois is the vois of Jacob, but the hondis ben the hondis of Esau.

23 And Isaac knew not Jacob, for the heery hondis expressiden the licnesse of the more sone.

24 Therfor Isaac blesside him, and seide, Art thou my sone Esau? Jacob answerde, Y am.

25 And Isaac seide, My sone, brynge thou to me metis of thin huntyng, that my soule blesse thee. And whanne Isaac hadde ete these metis brouyt, Jacob brouyte also wyn to Isaac, and whanne this was drunkun,

26 Isaac seide to him, My sone, come thou hidir, and yyue to me a cos.

27 Jacob neiyede, and kisside hym; and anoon as Isaac feelide the odour of hise clothis, he blesside him, and seide, Lo! the odour of my sone as the odour of a 'feeld ful which the Lord hath blessid.

28 God yyue to thee of the dewe of heuene, and of the fatnesse of erthe, aboundaunce of whete, and of wyn, and of oile;

29 and puplis serue thee, and lynagis worschipe thee; be thou lord of thi britheren, and the sones of thi modir be bowid bifor thee; be he cursid that cursith thee, and he that blessith thee, be fillid with blessyngis.

30 Vnnethis Isaac hadde fillid the word, and whanne Jacob was gon out,

31 Esau cam, and brouyte in metis sodun of the huntyng to the fadir, and seide, My fadir, rise thou, and ete of the huntyng of thi sone, that thi soule blesse me.

32 And Isaac seide, Who forsothe art thou? Which answerde, Y am Esau, thi firste gendrid sone.

33 Isaac dredde bi a greet astonying; and he wondride more, than it mai be bileued, and seide, Who therfor is he which a while ago brouyte to me huntyng takun, and Y eet of alle thingis bifor that thou camest; and Y blesside him? and he schal be blessid.

34 Whanne the wordis of the fadir weren herd, Esau rorid with a greet cry, and was astonyed, and seide, My fadir, blesse thou also me.

35 Which seide, Thy brother cam prudentli, and took thi blessyng.

36 And Esau addide, Justli his name is clepid Jacob, for lo! he supplauntide me another tyme; bifor he took awei 'my firste gendride thingis, and now the secounde tyme he rauyschide priueli my blessyng. And eft he seide to the fadir, Wher thou hast not reserued a blessyng also to me?

37 Ysaac answeride, Y haue maad him thi lord, and Y haue maad suget alle hise britheren to his seruage; Y haue stablischid him in whete, and wyn, and oile; and, my sone, what schal Y do to thee aftir these thingis?

38 To whom Esau saide, Fadir, wher thou hast oneli o blessyng? Y biseche that also thou blesse me. And whanne Esau wepte with greet yellyng,

39 Isaac was stirid, and seide to hym, Thi blessyng schal be in the fatnesse of erthe, and in the dew of heuene fro aboue;

40 thou schalt lyue bi swerd, and thou schalt serue thi brothir, and tyme schal come whanne thou schalt shake awei, and vnbynde his yok fro thi nollis.

41 Therfor Esau hatide euer Jacob for the blessyng bi which the fadir hadde blessid hym; and Esau seide in his herte, The daies of morenyng of my fadir schulen come, and Y schal sle Jacob, my brothir.

42 These thingis weren teld to Rebecca, and sche sente, and clepide hir sone Jacob, and seide to hym, Lo ! Esau, thi brothir, manaasith to sle thee;

43 now therfor, my sone, here thou my vois, and rise thou, and fle to Laban, my brother, in Aran;

44 and thou schalt dwelle with hym a fewe daies, til the woodnesse of thi brother reste,

45 and his indignacioun ceesse, and til he foryite tho thingis whiche thou hast don ayens hym. Aftirward Y schal sende, and Y schal brynge thee fro thennus hidir. Whi schal Y be maad soneles of euer eithir sone in o dai?

46 And Rebecca seide to Isaac, It anoieth me of my lijf for the douytris of Heth; if Jacob takith a wijf of the kynrede of this lond, Y nyle lyue.

CAP 28

1 And so Isaac clepide Jacob, and blesside hym, and comaundide to hym, and seide, Nyle thou take a wijf of the kyn of Canaan; but go thou,

2 and walke forth in to Mesopotanye of Sirie, to the hows of Batuel, fadir of thi modir, and take to thee of thennus a wijf of the douytris of Laban, thin vncle.

3 Sotheli Almyyti God blesse thee, and make thee to encreesse, and multiplie thee, that thou be in to cumpanyes of puplis;

4 and God yyue to thee the blessyngis of Abraham, and to thi seed aftir thee, that thou welde the lond of thi pilgrymage, which he bihiyte to thi grauntsir.

5 And whanne Ysaac hadde left hym, he yede forth, and cam in to Mesopotanye of Sirie, to Laban, the sone of Batuel of Sirie, the brother of Rebecca, his modir.

6 Forsothe Esau seiy that his fadir hadde blessid Jacob, and hadde sent him in to Mesopotanye of Sirie, that he schulde wedde a wijf of thennus, and that aftir the blessyng he comaundide to Jacob, and seide, Thou schalt not take a wijf of the douytris of Canaan;

7 and that Jacob obeiede to his fadir 'and modir, and yede in to Sirie;

8 also Esau preuyde that his fadir bihelde not gladli the douytris of Canaan.

9 And he yede to Ismael, and weddide a wijf, with out these whiche he hadde bifore, Melech, the douyter of Ismael, sone of Abraham, the sistir of Nabaioth.

10 Therfor Jacob yede out of Bersabee, and yede to Aran.

11 And whanne he hadde come to sum place, and wolde reste ther inne aftir the goynge doun of the sunne, he took of the stoonus that laien ther, and he puttide vndur his heed, and slepte in the same place.

12 And he seiye in sleep a laddir stondynge on the erthe, and the cop ther of touchinge heuene; and he seiy Goddis aungels stiynge vp and goynge doun ther bi,

13 and the Lord fastned to the laddir, seiynge to hym, Y am the Lord God of Abraham, thi fadir, and God of Isaac; Y schal yyue to thee and to thi seed the lond in which thou slepist.

14 And thi seed schal be as the dust of erthe, thou schalt be alargid to the eest, and west, and north, and south; and alle lynagis of erthe schulen be blessid in thee and in thi seed.

15 And Y schal be thi kepere, whidur euer thou schalt go; and Y schal lede thee ayen in to this lond, and Y schal not leeue no but Y schal fil alle thingis whiche Y seide.

16 And whanne Jacob hadde wakyd of sleep, he seide, Verili the Lord is in this place, and Y wiste not.

17 And he seide dredynge, Hou worschipful is this place! Here is noon other thing no but the hows of God, and the yate of heuene.

18 Therfor Jacob roos eerli, and took the stoon which he hadde put vndur his heed, and reiside in to a title, and helde oile aboue.

19 And he clepide the name of that citee Bethel, which was clepid Lusa bifore.

20 Also he auowide a vow, and seide, If God is with me, and kepith me in the weie in which Y go, and yyueth to me looues to ete, and clothis to be clothid,

21 and Y turne ayen in prosperite to the hows of my fadir, the Lord schal be in to God to me.

22 And this stoon, which Y reiside in to a title, schal be clepid the hows of God, and Y schal offre tithis to thee of alle thingis whiche thou schalt yyue to me.

CAP 29

1 Therfor Jacob passide forth, and cam in to the eest lond;

2 and seiy a pit in the feeld, and thre flockis of scheep restynge bisidis it, for whi scheep weren watrid therof, and the mouth therof was closid with a greet stoon.

3 And the custom was that whanne alle scheep weren gaderid togidere, thei schulden turne awei the stoon, and whanne the flockis weren fillid thei schulden put it eft on the mouth of the pit.

4 And Jacob seide to the scheepherdis, Brithren, of whennus ben ye? Whiche answeriden, Of Aran.

5 And he axide hem and seide, Wher ye knowen Laban, the sone of Nachor? Thei seiden, We knowen.

6 Jacob seide, Is he hool? Thei seiden, He is in good staat; and lo! Rachel, his douytir, cometh with his flok.

7 And Jacob seide, Yit myche of the dai is to come, and it is not tyme that the flockis be led ayen to the fooldis; sotheli yyue ye drynk to the scheep, and so lede ye hem ayen to mete.

8 Whiche answeriden, We moun not til alle scheep be gederid to gidere, and til we remouen the stoon fro the mouth of the pit to watir the flockis.

9 Yit thei spaken, and lo! Rachel cam with the scheep of hir fadir.

10 And whanne Jacob seiy hir, and knewe the douytir of his modris brothir, and the scheep of Laban his vncle, he remeuyde the stoon with which the pit was closid;

11 and whanne the flok was watrid, he kisside hir, and he wepte with 'vois reisid.

12 And he schewide to hir that he was the brothir of hir fadir, and the sone of Rebecca; and sche hastide, and telde to hir fadir.

13 And whanne he hadde herd, that Jacob, the sone of his sistir, cam, he ran ayens hym, and he biclippide Jacob and kisside hym, and ledde in to his hows. Forsothe whanne the causis of the iurney weren herd,

14 Laban answeride, Thou art my boon and my fleisch. And aftir that the daies of o moneth weren fillid, Laban seide to him,

15 'Whethir for thou art my brothir, thou schalt serue me frely? seie thou what mede thou schalt take.

16 Forsothe Laban hadde twei douytris, the name of the more was Lya, sotheli the lesse was clepid Rachel;

17 but Lya was blere iyed, Rachel was of fair face, and semeli in siyt.

18 And Jacob louede Rachel, and seide, Y schal serue thee seuene yeer for Rachel thi lesse douytir.

19 Laban answeride, It is betere that Y yyue hir to thee than to anothir man; dwelle thou at me.

20 Therfor Jacob seruyde seuene yeer for Rachel; and the daies semyden fewe to hym for the greetnesse of loue.

21 And he seide to Laban, Yyue thou my wijf to me, for the tyme is fillid that Y entre to hir.

22 And whanne many cumpenyes of freendis weren clepid to the feeste, he made weddyngis,

23 and in the euentid Laban brouyte in to hym Lya his douytir,

24 and yaf an handmaide, Selfa bi name, to the douyter. And whanne Jacob hadde entrid to hir bi custom, whanne the morewtid was maad, he seiy Lya,

25 and seide to his wyues fadir, What is it that thou woldist do? wher Y seruede not thee for Rachel? whi hast thou disseyued me?

26 Laban answerde, It is not custom in oure place that we yyue first the 'lesse douytris to weddyngis;

27 fille thou the wouke of daies of this couplyng, and Y schal yyue to thee also this Rachel, for the werk in which thou schalt serue me bi othere seuene yeer.

28 Jacob assentide to the couenaunt, and whanne the wouke was passid,

29 he weddide Rachel, to whom the fadir hadde youe Bala seruauntesse.

30 And at the laste he vside the weddyngis desirid, and settide the loue of the 'wijf suynge bifore the former; and he seruede at Laban seuene othere yeer.

31 Forsothe the Lord seiy that he dispiside Lya, and openyde hir wombe while the sistir dwellide bareyn.

32 And Lia childide a sone conseyued, and clepide his name Ruben, and seide, The Lord seiy my mekenesse; now myn hosebonde schal loue me.

33 And eft sche conseyuede, 'and childide a sone, and seide, For the Lord seiy that Y was dispisid, he yaf also this sone to me; and sche clepide his name Symeon.

34 And sche conseyuede the thridde tyme, and childide anothir sone, and she seide also, Now myn hosebonde schal be couplid to me, for Y childide thre sones to him; and therfor sche clepide his name Leuy.

35 The fourthe tyme sche conseyuede, and childide a sone, and seide, Now I schal knouleche to the Lord; and herfor she clepide his name Judas; and ceesside to childe.

CAP 30

1 Forsothe Rachel seiy, that sche was vnfruytful, and hadde enuye to the sister, and seide to hir hosebonde, Yyue thou fre children to me, ellis Y schal die.

2 To whom Jacob was wrooth, and answerde, Wher Y am for God, which haue priued thee fro the fruyt of thi wombe?

3 And sche seide, Y haue 'a seruauntesse Bala, entre thou to hir that she childe on my knees, and that Y haue sones of hir.

4 And sche yaf to hym Bala in to matrimony;

5 and whanne the hosebonde hadde entrid to hir, sche conseyuede, and childide a sone.

6 And Rachel seide, the Lord demede to me, and herde my preier, and yaf a sone to me; and therfor sche clepide his name Dan.

7 And eft Bala conseyuede, and childide anothir sone,

8 for whom Rachel seide, The Lord hath maad me lijk to my sistir, and Y wexide strong; and sche clepide hym Neptalym.

9 Lya feelide that sche ceesside to bere child, and sche yaf Selfa, hir handmayde, to the hosebonde.

10 And whanne Selfa aftir conseyuyng childide a sone, Lya seide, Blessidly;

11 and therfor sche clepide his name Gad.

12 Also Selfa childide anothir sone,

13 and Lia seide, This is for my blis, for alle wymmen schulen seie me blessid; therfor sche clepide hym Aser.

14 Forsothe Ruben yede out in to the feeld in the tyme of wheete heruest, and foond mandragis, whiche he brouyte to Lya, his modir. And Rachel seide, Yyue thou to me a part of the mandragis of thi sone.

15 Lya answeride, Whether it semeth litil to thee, that thou hast rauyschid the hosebonde fro me, no but thou take also the mandragis of my sone? Rachel seide, The hosebonde sleepe with thee in this nyyt for the mandragis of thi sone.

16 And whanne Jacob cam ayen fro the feeld at euentid, Lya yede out in to his comyng, and seide, Thou shalt entre to me, for Y haue hired thee with hire for the mandragis of my sone. He slepte with hir in that nyyt;

17 and God herde hir preiers, and sche conseyuede, and childide the fyuethe sone;

18 and seide, God yaf meede to me, for Y yaf myn hand-mayde to myn hosebond; and sche clepide his name Isacar.

19 Eft Lia conseyuede, and childide the sixte sone,

20 and seide, The Lord hath maad me riche with a good dower, also in this tyme myn hosebonde schal be with me, for Y childide sixe sones to hym; and therfore sche clepide his name Sabulon.

21 Aftir whom sche childide a douyter, Dyna bi name.

22 Also the Lord hadde mynde on Rachel, and herde hir, and openyde hir wombe.

23 And sche conseyuede, and childide a sone, and seide, God hath take a wey my schenschipe; and sche clepid his name Joseph,

24 and seide, The Lord yyue to me another sone.

25 Sotheli whanne Joseph was borun, Jacob seide to his wyues fadir, Delyuere thou me, that Y turne ayen in to my cuntrey and to my lond.

26 Yyue thou to me my wyues and fre children for whiche Y seruede thee, that Y go; forsothe thou knowist the seruyce bi which Y seruede thee.

27 Laban seide to hym, Fynde Y grace in thi siyt, Y haue lerned bi experience that God blesside me for thee;

28 ordeyne thou the meede which Y schal yyue to thee.

29 And he answeride, Thou woost hou Y seruede thee, and hou greet thi possessioun was in myn hondis;

30 thou haddist litil bifore that Y cam to thee, and now thou art maad riche, and the Lord blesside thee at myn entryng; therfor it is iust that Y purueye sum tyme also to myn hows.

31 And Laban seide, What schal Y yyue to thee? And Jacob seide, Y wole no thing but if thou doist that that Y axe, eft Y schal fede and kepe thi scheep.

32 Cumpasse thou alle thi flockis, and departe thou alle diuerse scheep and of spottid flees, and what euer thing schal be dun, and spottid, and dyuerse, as wel in scheep as in geet, it schal be my mede.

33 And my riytfulnesse schal answere to me to morewe, whanne the tyme of couenaunt schal come bifor thee; and alle that ben not dyuerse and spottid and dunne, as well in sheep as in geet, schulen repreue me of thefte.

34 And Laban seide, Y haue acceptable that that thou axist.

35 And he departide in that dai the geet, and scheep, geet buckis, and rammes, dyuerse and spottid. Sothely he bitook al the flok of o coloure, that is, of white and of blak flees in the hond of hise sones;

36 and he settide the space of weie of thre daies bitwixe hise sones and the hosebonde of hise douytris, that fedde othere flockis' of hym.

37 Therfor Jacob took greene yerdis of popeleris, and of almoundis, and of planes, and in parti dide awei the rynde of tho, and whanne the ryndis weren 'drawun a wei, whitnesse apperide in these that weren maad bare; sothely tho that weren hoole dwelliden grene, and bi this maner the coloure was maad dyuerse.

38 And Jacob puttide tho yerdis in the trowis, where the watir was held out, that whanne the flockis schulden come to drynke, thei schulden haue the yerdis bifor the iyen, and schulden conseyue in the siyt of the yerdis.

39 And it was doon that in thilke heete of riding the sheep schulde biholde the yerdis, and that thei schulden brynge forth spotti beestis, and dyuerse, and bispreynt with dyuerse colour.

40 And Jacob departide the floc, and puttide the yerdis in the trowis bifor the iyen of the rammys. Sotheli alle the white and blake weren Labans; sotheli the othere weren Jacobis; for the flockis weren departid bytwixe hem silf.

41 Therfor whanne the scheep weren ridun in the firste tyme, Jacob puttide the yerdis in the 'trouyis of watir bifor the iyen of rammys and of scheep, that thei schulden conseyue in the siyt of tho yerdis.

42 Forsothe whanne the late medlyng and the laste con-seyuyng weren, Jacob puttide not tho yerdis; and tho that weren late, weren maad Labans, and tho that weren of the firste tyme weren Jacobis.

43 And he was maad ful riche, and hadde many flockis, hand-maydis, and seruauntis, camels, and assis.

CAP 31

1 Aftir that Jacob herde the wordis of the sones of Laban, that seiden, Jacob hath take awei alle thingis that weren oure fadris, and of his catel Jacob is maad riche, and noble.

2 Also Jacob perseyuede the face of Laban, that it was not ayens hym as yistirdai, and the thridde dai agoon,

3 moost for the Lord seide to hym, Turne ayen into the lond of thi fadris, and to thi generacioun, and Y shal be with thee.

4 He sente, and clepide Rachel, and Lya, in to the feeld, where he kepte flockis, and he seide to hem,

5 Y se the face of youre fadir, that it is not ayens me as 'yis-terdai and the thridde dai agoon; but God of my fadir was with me.

6 And ye witen that with alle my strengthis Y seruede youre fadir;

7 but and youre fadir disseyuyde me, and chaungide my meede ten sithis; and netheles God suffride not hym to anoye me.

8 If he seide ony tyme, Dyuerse colourid sheep schulen be thi medis, alle sheep brouyten forth dyuerse colourid lambren; forsothe whanne he seide ayenward, Thou shalte take alle white for mede, alle the flockis brouyten forth white beestis;

9 and God took a wey the substaunce of youre fadir, and yaf to me.

10 For aftir that the tyme of conseyuyng of sheep cam, Y rei-side myn iyen, and seiy in sleep malis dyuerse, and spotti, and of dyuerse colouris, stiynge on femalis;

11 And the aungel of the Lord seide to me in sleep, Jacob! and Y answeride, Y am redy.

12 Which seide, Reise thin iyen, and se alle malis dyuerse, byspreynt, and spotti, stiynge on femalis; for Y seiy alle thingis whiche Laban dide to thee;

13 Y am God of Bethel, where thou anoyntidist a stoon, and madist auow to me. Now therefor rise thou, and go out of this lond, and turne ayen in to the lond of thi birthe.

14 And Rachel and Lya answeriden, Wher we han ony thing residue in the catels, and eritage of oure fadir?

15 Wher he 'arettide not vs as aliens, and selde, and eet oure prijs?

16 But God took awei the richessis of oure fadir, and yaf tho to vs, and to oure sones; wherfor do thou alle thingis whiche God hath comaundide to thee.

17 Forsothe Jacob roos, and puttide hise fre children and wyues on camels, and yede forth;

18 and he took al his catel, flockis, and what euer thing he hadde gete in Mesopotanye, and yede to Isaac, his fadir, into the lond of Canaan.

19 In that tyme Laban yede to schere scheep, and Rachel stal the idols of hir fadir.

20 And Jacob nolde knouleche to the fadir of his wijf, that he wolde fle;

21 and whanne he hadde go, as wel he as alle thingis that weren of his riyt, and whanne he hadde passid the water, and he yede ayens the hil of Galaad,

22 it was teld to Laban, in the thridde dai, that Jacob fledde.

23 And Laban took his britheren, and pursuede hym seuene daies, and took hym in the hil of Galaad.

24 And Laban seiy in sleep the Lord seiynge to him, Be war that thou speke not ony thing sharpli ayens Jacob.

25 And thanne Jacob hadde stretchid forth the tabernacle in the hil; and whanne he hadde sued Jacob with his britheren, 'he settide tente in the same hil of Galaad; and he seide to Jacob,

26 Whi hast thou do so, that the while I wiste not thou woldist dryue awey my douytris as caitifs by swerd?

27 Whi woldist thou fle the while Y wiste not, nether woldist shewe to me, that Y shulde sue thee with ioie, and songis, and tympans, and harpis?

28 Thou suffridist not that Y schulde kisse my sones and douytris; thou hast wrouyt folili.

29 And now sotheli myn hond mai yelde yuel to thee, but the God of thi fadir seide to me yisterdai, Be war that thou speke not ony harder thing with Jacob.

30 Suppose, if thou coueitedist to go to thi kynesmen, and the hows of thi fadir was in desir to thee, whi hast thou stole my goddis?

31 Jacob answeride, That Y yede forth while thou wistist not, Y dredde lest thou woldist take awey thi douytris violentli;

32 sotheli that thou repreuest me of thefte, at whom euer thou fyndist thi goddis, be he slayn bifor oure britheren; seke thou, what euer thing of thine thou fyndist at me, and take awei. Jacob seide these thingis, and wiste not that Rachel stal the idols.

33 And so Laban entride into the tabernacle of Jacob, and of Lya, and of euer eithir meyne, and foond not; and whanne Laban hadde entrid in to the tente of Rachel,

34 sche hastide, and hidde the idols vndur the strewyngis of the camel, and sat aboue. And sche seide to Laban, sekynge al the tente and fyndynge no thing,

35 My lord, be not wrooth that Y may not rise bifore thee, for it bifelde now to me bi the custom of wymmen; so the bisynesse of the sekere was scorned.

36 And Jacob bolnyde, and seide with strijf, For what cause of me, and for what synne of me, hast thou come so fersly aftir me,

37 and hast souyt al 'the portenaunce of myn hous? What 'hast thou founde of al the catel of thin hows? Putte thou here bifore my britheren and thi britheren, and deme thei betwixe me and thee.

38 Was I with thee herfore twenti yeer? Thi sheep and geet weren not bareyn, Y eet not the rammes of thi flok,

39 nether Y schewide to thee ony thing takun of a beeste; Y yeldide al harm; what euer thing perischide bi thefte, thou axidist of me;

40 Y was angwischid in dai and nyyt with heete and frost, and sleep fledde fro myn iyen;

41 so Y seruede thee bi twenti yeer in thin hows, fourtene yeer for thi douytris, and sixe yeer for thi flockis; and thou chaungidist my mede ten sithis.

42 If God of my fadir Abraham, and the drede of Isaac hadde not helpid me, perauenture now thou haddist left me nakid; the Lord bihelde my turmentyng and the traueyl of myn hondis, and repreuyde thee yistirdai.

43 Laban answeride hym, The douytris, and thi sones, and flockis, and alle thingis whiche thou seest, ben myne, what mai Y do to my sones, and to the sones of sones?

44 Therfor come thou, and make we boond of pees, that it be witnessyng bitwixe me, and thee.

45 And so Jacob took a stoon, and reiside it in to a signe, and seide to hise britheren,

46 Brynge ye stoonus; whiche gadriden, and maden an heep, and eten on it.

47 And Laban clepide it the heep of wittnesse, and Jacob clepide it the heep of witnessyng; euer eithir clepide bi the proprete of his langage.

48 And Laban seide, This heep schal be witnesse bytwixe me and thee to day, and herfor the name therof was clepid Galaad, that is, the heep of witnesse.

49 And Laban addide, The Lord biholde, and deme bitwixe vs, whanne we schulen go awei fro yow;

50 if thou schalt turmente my douytris, and if thou schal brynge yn othere wyues on hem, noon is witnesse of oure word, outakun God, whiche is present, and biholdith.

51 And eft he seide to Jacob, Lo! this heep, and stoon, whiche Y reiside bitwixe me and thee, schal be witnesse;

52 sotheli this heep, and stoon be in to witnessyng, forsothe if Y schal passe it, and go to thee, ether thou shalt passe, and thenke yuel to me.

53 God of Abraham, and God of Nachor, God of the fadir of hem, deme bitwixe vs. Therfor Jacob swoor by the drede of his fadir Ysaac;

54 and whanne slayn sacrifices weren offrid in the hil, he clepyde his britheren to ete breed, and whanne thei hadden ete, thei dwelliden there.

55 Forsothe Laban roos bi nyyt, and kisside his sones, and douytris, and blesside hem, and turnede ayen in to his place.

CAP 32

1 Forsothe Jacob wente forth in the weie in which he began, and the aungels of the Lord metten him.

2 And whanne he hadde seyn hem, he seide, These ben the castels of God; and he clepide the name of that place Manaym, that is, castels.

3 Sotheli Jacob sente bifore him also messangeris to Esau, his brother, in to the lond of Seir, in the cuntrey of Edom;

4 and comaundide to hem, and seide, Thus speke ye to my lord Esau, Thi brothir Jacob seith these thingis, Y was a pilgrym at Laban, 'and Y was 'til in to present dai;

5 Y haue oxun, and assis, and scheep, and seruauntis, and hand maydis, and Y sende now a message to my lord, that Y fynde grace in thi siyt.

6 And the messageris turneden ayen to Jacob, and seiden, We camen to Esau, thi brother, and lo! he hastith in to thi comyng, with foure hundrid men.

7 Jacob dredde greetli, and he was aferd, and departide the puple that was with hym, and he departide the flockis, and scheep, and oxun, and camels, in to twei cumpenyes;

8 and seide, If Esau schal come to o cumpeny, and schal smyte it, the tothir cumpeny which is residue schal be sauued.

9 And Jacob seide, A! God of my fadir Abraham, and God of my fadir Isaac, A! Lord, that seidist to me, Turne thou ayen in to thi lond, and in to the place of thi birthe, and Y schal do wel to thee,

10 Y am lesse than alle thi merciful doyngis, and than thi treuthe which thou hast fillid to thi seruaunt; with my staf Y passide this Jordan, and now Y go ayen with twei cumpanyes;

11 delyuere thou me fro the hond of my brothir Esau, for Y drede him greetli, lest he come and sle the modris with the sones.

12 Thou spakist that thou schuldist do wel to me, and shuldist alarge my seed as the grauel of the see, that mai not be noumbrid for mychilnesse.

13 And whanne Jacob hadde slept there in that nyyt, he departide of tho thingis whiche he hadde yiftis to Esau, his brothir,

14 two hundrid geet, and twenti buckis of geet, two hundrid scheep, and twenti rammys,

15 camels fulle with her foolis thretti, fourti kyen, and twenti boolis, twenti sche assis, and ten foolis of hem.

16 And he sente bi the hondis of his seruauntis alle flockis bi hem silf; and he seide to hise children, Go ye bifore me, and a space be betwixe flok and flok.

17 And he comaundide to the formere, and seide, If thou schalt mete my brothir Esau, and he schal axe thee, whos man thou art, ether whidir thou goist, ether whos ben these thingis whiche thou suest,

18 thou schalt answere, Of thi seruaunt Jacob, he hath sent yiftis to his lord Esau, and he cometh aftir vs.

19 In lijk maner, he yaf comaundementis to the secounde, and to the thridde, and to alle that sueden flockis; and seide, Speke ye bi the same wordis to Esau,

20 whanne ye fynden hym, and ye schulen adde, Also Jacob hym silf thi seruaunt sueth oure weie. For Jacob seide, Y schal plese Esau with yiftis that goon bifore, and aftirward Y schal se hym; in hap he schal be mercyful to me.

21 And so the yiftis yeden bifore hym; sotheli he dwellide in that nyyt in the tentis.

22 And whanne Jacob hadde arise ayysseli, he took hise twei wyues, and so many seruauntessis with enleuen sones, and passide the forthe of Jaboth.

23 And whanne alle thingis that perteyneden to hym weren led ouer, he dwellide aloone, and, lo!

24 a man wrastlide with him til to the morwetid.

25 And whanne the man seiy that he miyte not ouercome Jacob, he touchide the senewe of Jacobis hipe, and it driede anoon.

26 And he seide to Jacob, Leeue thou me, for the morewtid stieth now. Jacob answeride, Y schal not leeue thee, no but thou blesse me.

27 Therfore he seide, What name is to thee? He answeride, Jacob.

28 And the man seide, Thi name schal no more be clepid Jacob, but Israel; for if thou were strong ayens God, hou miche more schalt thou haue power ayens men.

29 Jacob axide him, Seie thou to me bi what name thou art clepid? He answerde, Whi axist thou my name, whiche is wondirful? And he blesside Jacob in the same place.

30 And Jacob clepide the name of that place Fanuel, and seide, Y siy the Lord face to face, and my lijf is maad saaf.

31 And anoon the sunne roos to hym, aftir that he passide Fanuel; forsothe he haltide in the foot.

32 For which cause the sones of Israel eten not 'til in to present day the senewe, that driede in the hipe of Jacob; for the man touchide the senewe of Jacobs hipe, and it driede.

CAP 33

1 Forsothe Jacob reiside hise iyen, and seiy Esau comynge, and foure hundrid men with hym; and he departide the sones of Lia, and of Rachel, and of bothe seruauntessis.

2 And he puttide euer either handmaide, and the fre children of hem, in the bigynnyng; sotheli he puttide Lia, and her sones, in the secounde place; forsothe he puttide Rachel and Joseph the laste.

3 And Jacob yede bifore, and worschipide lowli to erthe seuensithis, til his brothir neiyede.

4 And so Esau ran ayens his brothir, and collide hym, and Esau helde his necke, and kisside, and wepte.

5 And whanne the iyen weren reisid, he seiy the wymmen, and the litle children of hem, and seide, What wolen these to hem silf? and wher thei pertenen to thee? Jacob answeride, Thei ben the litle children, whiche God hath youe to me, thi seruaunt.

6 And the handmaydis and her sones neiyeden, and weren bowid.

7 Also Lya neiyede with hir fre children; and whanne thei hadden worschipid in lijk maner, Joseph and Rachel the laste worschipeden.

8 And Esau seide, What ben these cumpanyes, whiche Y mette? Jacob answerde, That Y schulde fynde grace bifore my lord.

9 And he seide, My brother, Y haue ful many thingis, thi thingis be to thee.

10 And Jacob seide, Y biseche, nyle thou so, but if Y foond grace in thin iyen, take thou a litil yifte of myn hondis; for Y seiy so thi face as I seiy the cheer of God;

11 be thou merciful to me, and resseyue the blessyng which Y brouyte to thee, and which blessyng God yyuynge alle thingis yaf to me. Vnnethis, while the brothir compellide,

12 he resseyuede, and seide, Go we to gidere, and Y schal be felowe of thi weie.

13 And Jacob seide, My lord, thou knowist that Y haue litle children tendre, and scheep, and kien with calue with me, and if Y schal make hem for to trauele more in goynge, alle the flockis schulen die in o dai;

14 my lord go bifore his seruaunt, and Y schal sue litil and litil hise steppis, as I shal se that my litle children mown, til Y come to my lord, in to Seir.

15 Esau answeride, Y preie thee, that of the puple which is with me, nameli felowis of thi weie dwelle. Jacob seide, It is

no nede; Y haue nede to this o thing oneli, that Y fynde grace in thi siyt, my lord.

16 And so Esau turnede ayen in that dai in the weie bi which he cam, in to Seir.

17 And Jacob cam in to Sochot, where whanne he hadde bildid an hows, and hadde set tentis, he clepide the name of that place Sochot, that is, tabernaclis.

18 And Jacob passide in to Salem, a citee of Sichimis, whiche is in the lond of Canaan, aftir that he turnede ayen fro Mesopotanye of Sirie, and he dwellide besidis the citee.

19 And he bouyte for an hundrid lambren a part of the feeld, in which he settide tabernaclis, of the sones of Emor, fadir of Sichem.

20 And whanne he hadde reisid an auter there, he inwardly clepide on it the strongeste God of Israel.

CAP 34

1 Forsothe Dyna, the douytir of Lya, yede out to se the wymmen of that cuntrey.

2 And whanne Sichem, the sone of Emor Euey, the prince of that lond, hadde seyn hir, he louede hir, and rauyschide, and sclepte with hir, and oppresside the virgyn bi violence.

3 And his soule was boundun faste with hir, and he pleiside hir sory with flateringis.

4 And he yede to Emor,

5 his fadir, and seide, Take to me this damysel a wijf. And whanne Jacob hadde herd this thing, while the sones weren absent, and ocupied in the fedyng of scheep, he was stille, til thei camen ayen.

6 Sotheli whanne Emor, the fadir of Sichem, was gon out, 'that he schulde speke to Jacob, lo!

7 hise sones camen fro the feeld. And whanne this thing that bifelde was herd, thei weren wroothe greetli; for he wrouyte a foul thing in Israel, and he hadde do a thing vnleueful in the defoulyng of the douyter of Jacob.

8 And so Emor spak to hem, The soule of my sone Sichem cleuyde to youre douytir, yeue ye hir a wijf to hym,

9 and ioyne we weddyngis to gidere; yyue ye youre douytris to vs,

10 and take ye oure douytris, and dwelle ye with vs; the lond is in youre power, tile ye, make ye marchaundise, and welde ye it.

11 But also Sichem seide to the fadir and britheren of hir, Fynde Y grace bifor you, and what euer thingis ye ordeynen Y schal yyue;

12 encreesse ye the dower, and axe ye yiftis, Y schal yyue wilfull that that ye axen; oonli yyue ye this damysele a wijf to me.

13 The sones of Jacob answeriden in gile to Sichem and his fadir, and weren feerse for the defoulyng of maidenhod of the sistir,

14 We moun not do this that ye axen, nether we moun yyue oure sistir to a man vncircumcidid, which thing is vnleueful and abhomynable anentis vs.

15 But in this we schulen mowe be boundun in pees, if ye wole be lijk vs, and ech of male kynde be circumcidid in you,

16 thanne we schulen yyue and take togidre oure douytris and youre; and we schulen dwelle with you, and we schulen be o puple.

17 Forsothe if ye nylen be circumcidid, we schulen take oure douytir, and schulen go a wei.

18 The profryng of hem pleiside Emor and Sichem,

19 his sone, and the yong wexynge man dilaiede not, that ne he fillide anoon that that was axid, for he louede the damysele greetli, and he was noble in al 'the hous of his fadir.

20 And thei entriden in to the yate of the citee, and spaken to the puple,

21 These men ben pesible, and wolen dwelle with vs; make thei marchaundie in the loond, and tile thei it, which is large and brood, and hath nede to tileris; we schulen take her douytris to wyues, and we schulen yyue oure douytris to hem.

22 O thing is, for which so greet good is dilaied; if we circumciden oure malis, and suen the custom of the folc,

23 bothe her substaunce, and scheep, and alle thingis which thei welden, schulen be oure; oneli assente we in this, that we dwelle to gidere, and make o puple.

24 And alle men assentiden, and alle malis weren circumcidid.

25 And lo! in the thridde day, whanne the sorewe of woundis was moost greuous, twei sones of acob, Symeon and Leuy, britheren of Dyna, token swerdis, and entriden in to the citee booldeli; and whanne alle malis weren slayn,

26 thei killiden Emor and Sichem togidere, and token Dyna, her sistir, fro the hous of Sichem.

27 And whanne thei weren goon out, othere sones of Jacob felden in on the slayn men, and rifeliden the citee for the veniaunce of defoulyng of a virgyn.

28 And thei wastiden the scheep of tho men, and droues of oxun, and assis, and alle thingis that weren in howsis and feeldis,

29 and ledden prisoneris the litle children, and wyues of tho men.

30 And whanne these thingis weren don hardili, Jacob seide to Symeon and Leuy, Ye han troblid me, and han maad me hateful to Cananeis and Fereseis, dwellers of this lond; we ben fewe, thei schulen be gaderid to gidere and schulen sle me, and Y schal be don a wey and myn hous.

31 Symeon and Leuy answeriden, Whether thei ouyten mysuse oure sistir as an hoore?

CAP 35

1 Yn the mene tyme the Lord spak to Jacob, Ryse thou, and stie to Bethel, and dwelle thou there, and make thou an auter to the Lord, that apperide to thee whanne thou fleddist Esau, thi brother.

2 Forsothe Jacob seide, whanne al his hous was clepid to gidere, Caste ye a wei alien goddis, that ben 'in the myddis of you, and be ye clensid, and chaunge ye youre clothis;

3 rise ye, and stie we into Bethel, that we make there an auter to the Lord, which herde me in the dai of my tribulacioun, and was felowe of my weie.

4 Therfor thei yauen to hym alle alien goddis which thei hadden, and eeris ryngis, that weren in 'the eeris of hem; and he deluyde tho vndur a 'tre, clepid therubynte, which is bihynde the citee of Sichem.

5 And whanne thei yeden, drede assailide alle men by cumpas of the citee, and thei weren not hardi to pursue hem goynge a wei.

6 Therfor Jacob cam to Lusa, which is in the lond of Canaan, bi 'sire name Bethel, he and al his puple with hym.

7 And he bildide there an auter to the Lord, and clepide the name of that place The hows of God, for God apperide there to hym, whanne he fledde his brothir.

8 Delbora, the nurische of Rebecca, diede in the same tyme, and sche was biried at the roote of Bethel, vndir an ook, and the name of the place was clepid The ook of wepyng.

9 Forsothe God apperide eft to Jacob, aftir that he turnede ayen fro Mesopotanye of Sirie, and cam into Bethel, and blesside hym,

10 and seide, Thou schalt no more be clepid Jacob, but Israel schal be thi name. And God clepide hym Israel, and seide to hym,

11 Y am God Almyyti, encreesse thou, and be thou multiplied, folkis and puplis of naciouns schulen be of thee, kyngis schulen go out of thi leendis;

12 and Y shal yyue to thee, and to thi seed after thee, the lond which Y yaf to Abraham, and Ysaac.

13 And God departide fro hym.

14 Forsothe Jacob reiside a title ether memorial of stoonys, in the place where ynne God spak to hym, and he sacrifiede ther onne fletynge sacrifices, and schedde out oile,

15 and clepide the name of that place Bethel.

16 Forsothe Jacob yede out fro thennus, and cam in the bigynnynge of somer to the lond that ledith to Effrata; in which lond whanne Rachel trauelide in child beryng,

17 sche bigan to be in perel for the hardnesse of childberyng; and the medewijf seide to hir, Nyle thou drede, for thou schalt haue also this sone.

18 Forsothe while the soule yede out for sorew, and deeth neiyede thanne, she clepide the name of hir sone Bennony, that is, the sone of my sorewe; forsothe the fadir clepide hym Beniamyn, that is the sone of the riyt side.

19 Therfor Rachel diede, and was biriede in the weie that ledith to Effrata, this is Bethleem.

20 And Jacob bildide a title on the sepulcre of hir; this is the title of biriel of Rachel 'til into present dai.

21 Jacob yede fro thennus, and settide tabernacle ouer the tour of the flok.

22 And while he dwellide in that cuntrei, Ruben yede, and slepte with Bala, the secundarie wijf of his fadir, which thing was not hid fro hym. Forsothe the sones of Jacob weren twelue;

23 the sones of Lia weren, the firste gendrid Ruben, and Symeon, and Leuy, and Judas, and Isachar, and Zabulon;

24 the sones of Rachel weren, Joseph and Beniamyn;

25 the sones of Bala, handmayde of Rachel, weren Dan, and Neptalym;

26 the sones of Zelfa, handmayde of Lya, weren Gad, and Aser. These weren the sones of Jacob, that weren borun to hym in Mesopotanye of Sirie.

27 Also Jacob came to Isaac, his fadir, in to Manbre, a citee Arabee, this is Ebron, in which Manbre Abraham 'and Isaac was a pylgrym.

28 And the daies of Isaac weren fillid an hundrid and foure scoore of yeris;

29 and he was wastid in age, and diede, and he was put to his puple, and was eeld, and ful of daies; and Esau and Jacob his sones birieden hym.

CAP 36

1 Forsothe these ben the generaciouns of Esau; he is Edom.

2 Esau took wyues of the douytris of Canaan, Ada, the douytir of Elom Ethey, and Oolibama, the douyter of Ana, sone of Sebeon Euey; also Bathsemath,

3 the douytir of Ismael, the sistir of Nabioth.

4 Forsothe Ada childide Elifath; Batsemath childide Rahuel; Oolibama childide Hieus,

5 and Hielon, and Chore. These weren the sones of Esau, that weren borun to hym in the lond of Canaan.

6 Sotheli Esau took hise wyues, and sones, and douytris, and ech soule of his hows, and catel, and scheep, and alle thingis whiche he 'myyte haue in the lond of Canaan, and yede into anothir cuntrey, and departide fro his brother Jacob; for thei weren ful riche,

7 and thei miyten not dwelle to gidere, and the erthe of her pilgrymage susteynede not hem, for the multitude of flockis.

8 And Esau dwellide in the hil of Seir; he is Edom.

9 Forsothe these weren the generaciouns of Esau, fader of Edom,

10 in the hil of Seir, and these weren the names of hise sones. Elifath, sone of Ada, 'wijf of Esau; also Rahuel sone of Bathsemath, 'wijf of hym.

11 And the sones of Elifath weren, Theman, Emath, Sephu, and Gathan, and Ceneth, and Chore.

12 Forsothe Tanna was the secundarie wijf of Elifath, 'sone of Esau, whiche Tanna childide to hym Amalech. These weren the sones of Ada, 'wijf of Esau.

13 Forsothe the sones of Rahuel weren, Naath, and Zara, and Semna, and Meza. These weren the sones of Bathsemath, 'wijf of Esau.

14 And these weren the sones of Oolibama, douyter of Ana, sone of Sebeon, 'wijf of Esau, whiche sche childide to hym; Hieus, and Hielon, and Chore.

15 These weren the dukis of the sones of Esau; the sones of Elifath first gendrid of Esau, duk Theman, duyk Omar,

16 duk Sephua, duyk Ceneth, duyk Chore, duyk Dathan, duyk Amalech. These weren the sones of Eliphat, in the lond of Edom, and these weren the sones of Ada.

17 Also these weren the sones of Rahuel, 'sone of Esau, duyk Naath, duyk Zara, duyk Senna, duyk Meza; forsothe these duykis weren of Rahuel in the lond of Edom. These weren the sones of Bathsamath, 'wijf of Esau.

18 Forsothe these weren the sones of Oolibama, 'wijf of Esau; duyk Hieus, duyk Hielon, duyk Chore; these weren duykis of Oolibama, douytir of Ana, 'wijf of Esau.

19 These weren the sones of Esau, and thei weren duykis of hem; he is Edom.

20 These weren the sones of Seir Horrei, enhabiteris of the lond; Jothan, and Sobal, and Sebeon,

21 and Anam, and Dison, and Eser, and Disan; these duikis weren of Horrey, sone of Seir, in the lond of Edom.

22 Forsothe the sones of Jothan weren maad, Horrey, and Theman; sotheli the sistir of Jothan was Tanna.

23 And these weren the sones of Sobal; Aluan, and Maneeth, and Ebal, Sephi, and Onam.

24 And these weren the sones of Sebeon; Achaia, and Ana; this is Ana that foonde hoote watris in wildirnesse, whanne he kepte the assis of Sebeon, his fadir;

25 and he hadde a sone Disan, and a douytir Oolibama.

26 And these weren the sones of Disan; Amadan, and Jesban, and Jethran, and Charan.

27 Also these weren the sones of Heser; Baalan, and Zeuan, and Acham.

28 And Disan hadde sones, Hus, and Haran.

29 These weren the duykis of Horreis; duyk Jothan, duyk Sobal, duyk Sebeon, duyk Ana, duyk Dison, duyk Heser, duik Disan;

30 these weren the duykis of Horreis, that weren lordis in the lond of Seir.

31 Forsothe kyngis that regneden in the lond of Edom, bifore that the sones of Israel hadden a kyng, weren these;

32 Balach, the sone of Beor, and the name of his citee was Deneba.

33 Forsothe Balach diede, and Jobab, sone of Sara of Bosra, regnede for hym.

34 And whanne Jobab was deed, Husam of the lond of Themayns regnede for hym.

35 And whanne he was deed, Adad, the sone of Badadi, that smoot Madian in the lond of Moab, and the name of his citee was Abyuth, 'regnede for him.

36 And whanne Adad was deed, Semla of Maseracha regnede for hym.

37 And whanne he was deed, Saul of the flood Robooth ragnede for hym.

38 And whanne he was deed, Balanam, the sone of Achobor, was successour in to the rewme.

39 And whanne this was deed, Adad regnede for hym, and the name of the citee of Adad was Phau, and the name of his wijf was clepid Meezabel, the douyter of Mathrect, douyter of Mesaab.

40 Therfor these weren the names of duykis of Esau, in her kynredis, and places, and names; duyk Thanna, duyk Alua,

41 duyk Jetech, duyk Oolibama, duyk Ela,

42 duyk Phinon, duyk Ceneth, duik Theman,

43 duyk Mabsar, duyk Madiel, duyk Iram; these weren the duykis of Edom, dwelleris in the lond of hys lordschip; he was Esau, the fadir of Ydumeis.

CAP 37

1 Forsothe Jacob dwellide in the lond of Canaan, in which his fadir was a pilgrym; and these weren the generaciouns of hym.

2 Joseph whanne he was of sixtene yeer, yit a child, kepte a flok with hise britheren, and was with the sones of Bala and Zelfa, wyues of his fadir; and he accuside his britheren at the fadir of 'the worste synne.

3 Forsothe Israel louyde Joseph ouer alle hise sones, for he hadde gendrid hym in eelde; and he made to Joseph a cote of many colours.

4 Forsothe hise britheren sien that he was loued of the fader more than alle, and thei hatiden hym, and myyten not speke ony thing pesibli to hym.

5 And it bifelde that he telde to hise britheren a sweuene seyn, which cause was 'the seed of more hatrede.

6 And Joseph seide to his britheren, Here ye the sweuene which Y seiy,

7 Y gesside that we bounden to gidere handfuls, and that as myn handful roos, and stood, and that youre handfuls stoden aboute and worschipiden myn handful.

8 Hise britheren answerden, Whether thou shalt be oure kyng, ethir we shulen be maad suget to thi lordschip? Therfor this cause of sweuenys and wordis mynystride the nurschyng of enuye, and of hatrede.

9 Also Joseph seiy another sweuene, which he telde to the britheren, and seide, Y seiy bi a sweuene that as the sunne, and moone, and enleuen sterris worschipiden me.

10 And whanne he hadde teld this sweuene to his fadir, and britheren, his fadir blamyde him, and seide, What wole this sweuene to it silf which thou hast seyn? Whether Y and thi modir, and thi britheren, schulen worschipe thee on erthe?

11 Therfor hise britheren hadden enuye to hym. Forsothe the fadir bihelde pryuely the thing,

12 and whanne his britheren dwelliden in Sichem, aboute flockis of the fadir 'to be kept,

13 Israel seide to Joseph, Thi britheren kepen scheep in Sichymys; come thou, Y schal sende thee to hem.

14 And whanne Joseph answerde, Y am redi, Israel seide, Go thou, and se whether alle thingis ben esi anentis thi britheren, and scheep; and telle thou to me what is doon. He was sent fro the valey of Ebron, and cam into Sichem;

15 and a man foond hym errynge in the feeld, and 'the man axide, what he souyte.

16 And he answerde, Y seke my britheren, schewe thou to me where thei kepten flockis.

17 And the man seide to hym, Thei yeden awei fro this place; forsothe Y herde hem seiynge, Go we into Dothaym. And Joseph yede aftir his britheren, and foond hem in Dothaym.

18 And whanne thei hadden seyn hym afer, bifor that he neiyede to hem,

19 thei thouyten to sle hym, and spaken to gidere, Lo! the dremere cometh, come ye,

20 sle we hym, and sende we into an eld sisterne, and we schulen seie, A wielde beeste ful wickid hath deuourid hym; and thanne it schal appere what hise dremes profiten to hym.

21 Sotheli Ruben herde this, and enforside to delyuere hym fro her hondis,

22 and seide, Sle we not the lijf of hym, nether schede we out his blood, but caste ye hym into an eeld cisterne, which is in the wildirnesse, and kepe ye youre hondis gilteles. Forsothe he seide this, willynge to delyuere hym fro her hondis, and to yelde to his fadir.

23 Therfor anoon as Joseph cam to hise britheren, thei dispuyliden hym of the coote, doun to the heele, and of many colours, and senten into the eeld cisterne,

24 that hadde no water.

25 And thei saten 'to ete breed; and thei sien that Ismaelitis weigoers camen fro Galaad, and that her camels baren swete smellynge spiceries, and 'rosyn, and stacten, into Egipt.

26 Therfor Judas seide to hise britheren, What schal it profite to vs, if we schulen sle oure brother, and schulen hide his blood?

27 It is betere that he be seeld to Ismalitis, and oure hondis be not defoulid, for he is oure brother and fleisch. The britheren assentiden to these wordis;

28 and whanne marchauntis of Madian passiden forth, thei drowen hym out of the cisterne, and seelden hym to Ismaelitis, for thriytti platis of siluer; whiche ledden hym in to Egipt.

29 And Ruben turnede ayen to the cisterne, and foond not the child;

30 and he to-rente his closis, and he yede to hise britheren, and seide, The child apperith not, and whidir schal Y go?

31 Forsothe thei token his coote, and dippiden in the blood of a kide, which thei hadden slayn; and senten men that baren to the fadir,

32 and seiden, We han founde this coote, se, whether it is the coote of thi sone, ether nai.

33 And whanne the fader hadde knowe it, he seide, It is the coote of my sone, a wielde beeste ful wickid hath ete hym, a beeste hath deuourid Joseph.

34 And he to-rente his clothis, and he was clothid with an heire, and biweilide his sone in myche tyme.

35 Sothely whanne hise fre children weren gaderid to gidere, that thei schulden peese the sorewe of the fadir, he nolde take

counfort, but seide, Y schal go doun in to helle, and schal biweile my sone. And the while Jacob contynude in wepyng, 36 Madianytis seelden Joseph into Egipt to Putifar, chast 'and onest seruaunt of Farao, maistir of the chyualrie.

CAP 38

1 Yn the same tyme Judas yede doun fro his britheren, and turnede to a man of Odolla, Hiram bi name;

2 and he siy ther a douytir of a man of Canaan, Sue bi name. And whanne he hadde takun hir to wijf,

3 he entride to hir, and sche conseyuede, and childide a sone, and clepide his name Her.

4 And eft whanne a child was conseyued, sche nemyde the child borun Onam.

5 And sche childide the thridde sone, whom sche clepide Cela, and whanne he was borun, sche ceesside to bere child more.

6 Forsothe Judas yaf a wijf, 'Thamar bi name, to his firste gendrid sone Her.

7 And Her, the firste gendrid sone of Judas, was weiward in the siyt of the Lord, and therfor he was slayn of the Lord.

8 Therfor Judas seide to Onam, his sone, Entre thou to the wijf of thi brothir, and be thou felouschipid to hir, that thou reise seed to thi brothir.

9 And he wiste that sones schulden not be borun to him, 'and he entride to the wijf of his brother, and schedde seed in to the erthe, lest the fre children schulden be borun bi the name of the brother;

10 and therfor the Lord smoot hym, for he dide abhomynable thing.

11 Wherfor Judas seide to Thamar, 'wijf of his sone, Be thou widewe in the hous of thi fadir, til Sela my sone wexe, for he dredde lest also he schulde die as hise britheren. And sche yede, and dwellide in the hous of hir fadir.

12 Forsothe whanne many yeeris weren passid, the douyter of Sue, 'the wijf of Juda, diede, and whanne coumfort was takun aftir morenyng, he stiede to the schereris of hise scheep, he and Iras of Odolla, that was kepere of the floc, stieden in to Thampnas.

13 And it was teld to Thamar, that 'the fadir of hir hosebonde stiede to Thampnas, to schere scheep.

14 And sche dide awei the clothis of widewehod, and sche took a roket, and whanne the clothinge was chaungid, sche sat in the weilot that ledith to Tampna; for Sela hadde woxe, and sche hadde not take hym to hosebonde.

15 And whanne Judas hadde seyn hir, he supposide hir to be an hoore, for sche hadde hilid hir face, lest sche were knowun.

16 And Judas entride to hir, and seide, Suffre me that Y ligge with thee; for he wiste not that sche was the wijf of his sone. And whanne sche answeride, What schalt thou yyue to me, that thou ligge bi me?

17 he seide, Y schal sende to thee a kide of the flockis. And eft whanne sche seide, Y schal suffre that that thou wolt, if thou schalt yyue to me a wed, til thou sendist that that thou bihetist.

18 Judas seide, What wolt thou that be youun to thee for a wed? She answeride, Thi ryng, and thi bie of the arm, and the staaf which thou holdist in the hond. Therfor the womman conseyuide at o liggyng bi, and sche roos, and yede;

19 and whanne the clooth was 'put awei which sche hadde take, sche was clothid in the clothis of widewhod.

20 Forsothe Judas sente a kide bi his scheepherde of Odolla, that he schulde resseyue the wed which he hadde youe to the womman; and whanne he hadde not founde hir,

21 he axide men of that place, Where is the womman that sat in the weie lot? And whanne alle men answeriden, An hoore was not in this place; he turnede ayen to Judas,

22 and seide to hym, Y foond not hir, but also men of that place seiden to me, that an hoore sat neuere there.

23 Judas seide, Haue sche to hir silf, certis sche may not repreue vs of a leesyng; Y sente the kyde which Y bihiyte, and thou foundist not hir.

24 Lo! sotheli aftir thre monethis thei telden to Judas, and seiden, Thamar, 'wijf of thi sone, hath do fornycacioun, and hir womb semeth to wexe greet. Judas seide, Brynge ye hir forth, that sche be brent.

25 And whanne sche was led to peyne, sche sente to 'the fadir of hir hosebonde, and seide, Y haue conseyued of the man, whose these thingis ben; knowe thou whose is the ryng, and bie of the arm, and staf?

26 And whanne the yiftis weren knowun, he seide, Sche is more iust than Y, for Y yaf not hir to Sela, my sone; netheles Judas knewe hir no more fleischli.

27 Sotheli whanne the childberyng neiyede, twei chyldren apperiden in the wombe, and in that birthe of children, oon brouyte forth the hond, in which the mydwijf boond a reed threed,

28 and seide, This schal go out 'the formere.

29 Sotheli while he withdrowe the hond, the tother yede out, and the womman seide, Whi was the skyn in which the child lay in the wombe departid for thee? And for this cause sche clepide his name Fares.

30 Afterward his brothir yede out, in whos hond was the reed threed, whom sche clepide Zaram.

CAP 39

1 Therfor Joseph was led in to Egipt, and Putifar, 'chast and onest seruaunt of Farao, prince of the oost, a man of Egipt, bouyte hym of the hondis of Ismaelitis, of which he was brouyt.

2 And the Lord was with hym, and he was a man doynge with prosperite in alle thingis. And Joseph dwellide in 'the hows of his lord,

3 which knew best that the Lord was with Joseph, and that alle thingis whiche he dide, weren dressid of the Lord in 'the hond of hym.

4 And Joseph foond grace bifor his lord, and 'mynystride to hym, of whom Joseph was maad souereyn of alle thingis, and gouernede the hows bitaken to hym, and alle thingis that weren bitakun to hym.

5 And the Lord blesside the 'hows of Egipcian for Joseph, and multipliede al his catel, as wel in howsis as in feeldis;

6 nether he knew ony other thing no but 'breed which he eet. Forsothe Joseph was fair in face, and schapli in siyt.

7 And so aftir many daies the ladi castide hir iyen in to Joseph, and seide, Slepe thou with me;

8 which assentide not to the vnleueful werk, and seide to hir, Lo! while alle thingis ben bitakun to me, my lord woot not what he hath in his hows,

9 nether ony thing is, which is not in my power, ether which 'he hath not bitake to me, outakun thee, which art his wijf; how therfor may Y do this yuel, and do synne ayens my lord?

10 Thei spaken siche wordis 'bi alle daies, and the womman was diseseful to the yong waxynge man, and he forsook auoutrie.

11 Forsothe it bifelde in a dai, that Joseph entride in to the hows, and dide sum werk with out witnessis.

12 And sche took 'the hem of his clooth, and sche seide, Slepe thou with me; and he lefte the mentil in hir hoond, and he fledde, and yede out.

13 And whanne the womman hadde seyn the clooth in hir hondis, and that sche was dispisid,

14 sche clepide to hir the men of hir hows, and seide to hem, Lo! my lord hath brouyt in an Ebrew man, that he schulde scorn vs; he entride to me to do leccherie with me, and whanne Y criede, and he herde my vois,

15 he lefte the mentil which Y helde, and he fledde out.

16 Therfor in to the preuyng of trouthe, sche schewide the mantil, holdun to the hosebonde turnynge ayen hoom.

17 And she seide, The Ebrew seruaunt, whom thou brouytist, entride to me to scorne me; and whanne he siy me crye,

18 he lefte the mentil which Y helde, and he fledde out.

19 And whanne these thingis weren herd, the lord bileuyde ouer myche to the wordis of the wijf, and was ful wrooth;

20 and he bitook Joseph in to prisoun, where the bounden men of the kyng weren kept, and he was closid there.

21 Forsothe the Lord was with Joseph, and hadde mercy on hym, and yaf grace to hym in the siyt of the prince of the prisoun,

22 which bitook in the hond of Joseph alle prisoneris that weren holdun in kepyng, and what euer thing was doon, it was vndur Joseph, nethir the prince knewe ony thing,

23 for alle thingis weren bitakun to Joseph; for the Lord was with hym, and dresside alle his werkis.

CAP 40

1 Whanne these thingis weren doon so, it bifelde that twei geldyngis, the boteler and the baker 'of the kyng of Egipt, synneden to her lord.

2 And Farao was wrooth ayens hem, for the toon was 'souereyn to boteleris, the tother was 'souereyn to bakeris.

3 And he sente hem in to the prisoun of the prince of knyytis, in which also Joseph was boundun.

4 And the keper of the prisoun bitook hem to Joseph, which also 'mynystride to hem. Sumdel of tyme passide, and thei weren hooldun in kepyng, and bothe sien a dreem in o nyyt,

5 bi couenable expownyng to hem.

6 And whanne Joseph hadde entrid to hem eerli, and hadde seyn hem sori,

7 he axide hem, and seide, Whi is youre 'face soriere to dai than it ys wont?

8 Whiche answeriden, We seiyen a dreem, and 'noon is that expowneth to vs. And Joseph seide to hem, Whether expownyng is not of God? Telle ye to me what ye han seyn.

9 The 'souereyn of boteleris telde first his dreem; Y seiy that a vyne bifore me,

10 in which weren thre siouns, wexide litil and litil in to buri-ounnyngis, and that aftir flouris grapys wexiden ripe,

11 and the cuppe of Farao was in myn hond; therfor Y took the grapis, and presside out in to the cuppe which Y helde, and Y yaf drynk to Farao.

12 Joseph answerde, This is the expownyng of the dreem; thre siouns ben yit thre daies,

13 aftir whiche Farao schal haue mynde of thi seruyce, and he schal restore thee in to the firste degree, and thou schal yyue

to hym the cuppe, bi thin office, as thou were wont to do bifore.

14 Oneli haue thou mynde on me, whanne it is wel to thee, and thou schalt do merci with me, that thou make suggestioun to Farao, that he lede me out of this prisoun;

15 for theefli Y am takun awei fro the lond of Ebrews, and here Y am sent innocent in to prisoun.

16 The 'maister of bakeris seiye that Joseph hadde expowned prudentli the dreem, and he seide, And Y seiy a dreem, that Y hadde thre panyeris of mele on myn heed,

17 and Y gesside that Y bar in o panyere, that was heiyere, alle metis that ben maad bi craft of bakers, and that briddis eeten therof.

18 Joseph answerde, This is the expownyng of the dreem; thre panyeris ben yit thre daies,

19 aftir whiche Farao schal take awei thin heed, and he schal hange thee in a cros, and briddis schulen todrawe thi fleischis.

20 Fro thennus the thridde dai was the dai of birthe of Farao, which made a greet feeste to hise children, and hadde mynde among metis on the maistir 'of boteleris, and on the prince of bakeris;

21 and he restoride the oon in to his place, that he schulde dresse cuppe to 'the kyng,

22 and he hangide 'the tothir in a gebat, that the treuthe of 'the expownere schulde be preued.

23 And netheles whanne prosperitees bifelden, the 'souereyn of boteleris foryat 'his expownere.

CAP 41

1 Aftir twei yeer Farao seiy a dreem; he gesside that he stood on a flood,

2 fro which seuene faire kiyn and ful fatte stieden, and weren fed in the places of mareis;

3 and othere seuene, foule and leene, camen out of the flood, and weren fed in thilk brenke of the watir, in grene places;

4 and tho deuoureden thilke kien of whiche the fairnesse and comelynesse of bodies was wondurful.

5 Farao wakide, and slepte eft, and seiy another dreem; seuen eeris of corn ful and faire camen forth in o stalke,

6 and othere as many eeris of corn, thinne and smytun with corrupcioun of brennynge wynd,

7 camen forth, deuourynge al the fairenesse of the firste. Farao wakide aftir reste,

8 and whanne morewtid was maad, he was aferd bi inward drede, and he sente to alle the expowneris of Egipt, and to alle wise men; and whanne thei weren clepid, he telde the dreem, and noon was that expownede.

9 Thanne at the laste the maistir 'of boteleris bithouyte, and seide, Y knowleche my synne;

10 the kyng was wrooth to hise seruauntis, and comaundide me and the maister 'of bakeris to be cast doun in to the prisoun of the prince of knyytis,

11 where we bothe saien a dreem in o nyyt, biforeschewynge of thingis to comynge.

12 An Ebrew child, seruaunt of the same duk of knyytis was there, to whom we telden the dremes,

13 and herden what euer thing the bifallyng of thing preuede afterward; for Y am restorid to myn office, and he was hangid in a cros.

14 Anoon at the comaundement of the kyng thei polliden Joseph led out of prisoun, and whanne 'the clooth was chaungid, thei brouyten Joseph to the kyng.

15 To whom the kyng seide, Y seiye dremes, and noon is that expowneth tho thingis that Y seiy, I haue herd that thou expownest moost prudentli.

16 Joseph answerde, With out me, God schal answere prosperitees to Farao.

17 Therfor Farao telde that that he seiy; Y gesside that Y stood on the brenke of the flood,

18 and seuene kiyn, ful faire and with fleischis able to etyng, stieden fro the watir, whiche kiyn gaderiden grene seggis in the pasture of the marreis;

19 and lo! seuene othere kiyn, so foule and leene, sueden these, that Y seiy neuere siche in the lond of Egipt;

20 and whanne the formere kien weren deuourid and wastid, tho secounde yauen no steppe of fulnesse,

21 but weren slowe bi lijk leenesse and palenesse. I wakide, and eft Y was oppressid bi sleep, and Y seiy a dreem;

22 seuene eeris of corn, ful and faireste, camen forth in o stalke,

23 and othere seuene, thinne and smytun with 'corrupcioun of brennynge wynd, camen forth of the stobil,

24 whiche deuouriden the fairenesse of the formere;

25 Y telde the dreem to expowneris, and no man is that expowneth. Joseph answerde, The dreem of the king is oon; God schewide to Farao what thingis he schal do.

26 Seuene faire kiyn, and seuene ful eeris of corn, ben seuene yeeris of plentee, and tho comprehenden the same strengthe of dreem;

27 and seuene kiyn thinne and leene, that stieden aftir tho, and seuene thinne eeris of corn and smytun with brennynge wynd, ben seuene yeer of hungur to comynge,

28 whiche schulen be fillid bi this ordre.

29 Lo! seuene yeer of greet plentee in al the lond of Egipt schulen come,

30 and seuene othre yeer of so greet bareynesse schulen sue tho, that al the abundaunce bifore be youun to foryetyng; for the hungur schal waste al the lond,

31 and the greetnesse of pouert schal leese the greetnesse of plentee.

32 Forsothe this that thou siyest the secunde tyme a dreem, perteynynge to the same thing, is a 'schewyng of sadnesse, for the word of God schal be doon, and schal be fillid ful swiftli.

33 Now therfor puruey the kyng a wijs man and a redi, and make the kyng hym souereyn to the lond of Egipt,

34 which man ordeyne gouernouris bi alle cuntreis, and gadere he in to bernys the fyuethe part of fruytis bi seuene yeer of plentee,

35 that schulen come now; and al the wheete be kept vndur the power of Farao, and be it kept in citees,

36 and be it maad redi to the hungur to comynge of seuene yeer that schal oppresse Egipt, and the lond be not wastid bi pouert.

37 The counsel pleside Farao,

38 and alle his mynystris, and he spak to hem, Wher we moun fynde sich a man which is ful of Goddis spirit?

39 Therfor Farao seide to Joseph, For God hath schewid to thee alle thingis whiche thou hast spoke, wher Y mai fynde a wisere man and lijk thee?

40 Therfor thou schalt be ouer myn hous, and al the puple schal obeie to the comaundement of thi mouth; Y schal passe thee onely by o trone of the rewme.

41 And eft Farao seide to Joseph, Lo! Y haue ordeyned thee on al the lond of Egipt.

42 And Farao took the ryng fro his hond, and yaf it in the hond of Joseph, and he clothide Joseph with a stoole of bijs, and puttide a goldun wrethe aboute the necke;

43 and Farao made Joseph to 'stie on his secounde chare, while a bidele criede, that alle men schulden knele bifore hym, and schulden knowe that he was souereyn of al the lond of Egipt.

44 And the kyng seide to Joseph, Y am Farao, without thi comaundement no man shal stire hond ether foot in al the lond of Egipt.

45 And he turnede the name of Joseph, and clepide him bi Egipcian langage, the sauyour of the world; and he yaf to Joseph a wijf, Asenech, the douyter of Potifar, preest of Heliopoleos. And so Joseph yede out to the lond of Egipt.

46 Forsothe Joseph was of thretti yeer, whanne he stood in the siyt of kyng Farao, and cumpasside alle the cuntreis of Egipt.

47 And the plente of seuene yeer cam, and ripe corn weren bounden into handfuls, and weren gaderid into the bernys of Egipt,

48 also al the aboundaunce of cornes weren kept in alle citeis,

49 and so greet aboundaunce was of wheete, that it was maad euene to the grauel of the see, and the plente passide mesure.

50 Sotheli twei sones were born to Joseph bifor that the hungur came, whiche Asenech, douytir of Putifar, preest of Heliopoleos, childide to hym.

51 And he clepide the name of the firste gendrid sone, Manasses, and seide, God hath maad me to foryete alle my traueilis, and the hous of my fadir;

52 and he clepide the name of the secunde sone Effraym, and seide, God hath maad me to encreesse in the lond of my pouert.

53 Therfor whanne seuene yeer of plentee that weren in Egipt weren passid,

54 seuene yeer of pouert bigunnen to come, whiche Joseph bifore seide, and hungur hadde the maistri in al the world; also hungur was in al the lond of Egipt;

55 and whanne that lond hungride, the puple criede to Farao, and axide metis; to whiche he answeride, Go ye to Joseph, and do ye what euer thing he seith to you.

56 Forsothe hungur encreesside ech dai in al the lond, and Joseph openyde alle the bernys, and seelde to Egipcians, for also hungur oppresside hem;

57 and alle prouynces camen in to Egipt to bie metis, and to abate the yuel of nedynesse.

CAP 42

1 Forsothe Jacob herde that foodis weren seeld in Egipt, and he seide to hise sones, Whi ben ye necgligent?

2 Y herde that wheete is seeld in Egipt, go ye doun, and bie ye necessaries to vs, that we moun lyue, and be not wastid bi nedynesse.

3 Therfor ten britheren of Joseph yeden doun to bie wheete in Egipt,

4 and Beniamyn was withholdun of Jacob at hoome, that seide to hise britheren, Lest perauenture in the weie he suffre ony yuel.

5 Sotheli thei entriden in to the lond of Egipt, with othere men that yeden to bie; forsothe hungur was in the lond of Canaan.

6 And Joseph was prince of Egipt, and at his wille whetis weren seeld to puplis. And whanne hise britheren hadden worschipid hym,

7 and he hadde knowe hem, he spak hardere as to aliens, and axide hem, Fro whennus camen ye? Whiche answeriden, Fro the lond of Canaan, that we bie necessaries to lyiflode.

8 And netheles he knewe the britheren, and he was not knowun of hem,

9 and he bithouyte on the dremys whiche he seiy sumtyme. And he seide to hem, Ye ben aspieris, ye camen to se the feblere thingis of the lond.

10 Whiche seiden, Lord, it is not so, but thi seruauntis camen to bie metis;

11 alle we ben the sones of o man, we comen pesible, and thi seruauntis ymaginen not ony yuel.

12 To 'whiche he answeride, It is in other maner, ye camen to se the feble thingis of the lond.

13 And thei seiden, 'We twelue britheren, thi seruauntis, ben sones of o man in the lond of Canaan; the leeste is with oure fadir, an other is not 'on erthe.

14 This it is, he seide, that Y spak to you,

15 ye ben aspieris, riyt now Y schal take experience of you, bi the helthe of Farao ye schulen not go fro hennus, til youre leeste brother come; sende ye oon of you,

16 that he brynge hym, forsothe ye schulen be in boondis, til tho thingis that ye seiden ben preued, whether tho ben false ether trewe; ellis, bi the helthe of Farao, ye ben aspieris.

17 Therfor he bitook hem to kepyng thre daies; sotheli in the thridde dai,

18 whanne thei weren led out of prisoun, he seide, Do ye that that Y seide, and ye schulen lyue, for Y drede God;

19 if ye ben pesible, o brother of you be boundun in prisoun; forsothe go ye, and bere wheetis, whiche ye bouyten,

20 in to youre housis, and brynge ye youre leeste brother to me, that Y may preue youre wordis, and ye die not. Thei diden as he seide,

21 and thei spaken togidere, Skilfuli we suffren these thingis, for we synneden ayens oure brother, and we seiyen the anguysch of his soule, while he preiede vs, and we herden not; herfore this tribulacioun cometh on vs.

22 Of which oon, Ruben, seide, Whether Y seide not to yow, Nyle ye do synne ayens the child, and ye herden not me? lo! his blood is souyt.

23 Sotheli thei wisten not that Joseph vndirstood, for he spak to hem by interpretour.

24 And he turnede awei hym silf a litil and wepte; and he turnede ayen, and spak to hem.

25 And he took Symeon, and boond hym, while thei weren present; and he comaundide the mynystris, that thei schulden fille her sackis with wheete, and that thei schulden putte the money 'of alle in her baggis, and ouer this yyue metis in the weie; whiche diden so.

26 And thei 'baren wetis on her assis, and yeden forth,

27 and whanne the sak of oon was opened that he schulde yyue meete to the werk beeste in the yn, he bihelde the money in the mouth of the bagge,

28 and seide to his britheren, My monei is yoldun to me, lo! it is had in the bagge; and thei weren astonyed, and troblid, and seiden togidere, What thing is this that God hath doon to us.

29 And thei camen to Jacob, her fadir, in the loond of Canaan, and telden to hym alle thingis that bifelden to hem, and seiden,

30 The lord of the lond spak harde to vs, and gesside that we weren aspieris of the prouynce;

31 to whom we answeriden, We ben pesible, nether we pur-posen ony tresouns;

32 we ben twelue britheren, gendrid of o fadir, oon is not 'on erthe, the leeste dwellith with the fadir in the lond of Canaan.

33 And he seide to vs, Thus Y schal preue that ye ben pesible; leeffe ye o brother of you with me, and take ye metis nedeful to youre housis, and go ye, and brynge ye to me youre leeste brother,

34 that Y wite that ye ben not aspieris, and that ye moun res-seyue this brother which is holdun in boondis, and that fro thennus forth ye haue licence to bie what thingis ye wolen.

35 While these thingis weren seide, whanne alle schedden out wheetis, thei founden money boundun in 'the mouth of sackis. And whanne alle togidere weren aferd,

36 the fadir Jacob seide, Ye han maad me to be with out chil-dren; Joseph is not alyue, Symeon is holdun in bondis, ye schulen take a wey fro me Beniamyn; alle these yuels felden in me.

37 To whom Ruben answeride, Sle thou my twei sones, if Y shal not brynge hym ayen to thee; take thou hym in myn hond, and Y schal restore hym to thee.

38 And Jacob seide, My sone schal not go doun with you; his brother is deed, he aloone is left; if ony aduersite schal bifalle 'to hym in the lond to which ye schulen go, ye schulen lede forth myn hoore heeris with sorewe to hellis.

CAP 43

1 In the meene tyme hungur oppresside greetli al the lond;

2 and whanne the meetis weren wastid, whiche thei brouyten fro Egipt, Jacob seide to hise sones, Turne ye ayen, and bie ye a litil of meetis to vs.

3 Judas answeride, The ilke man denounside to vs vndir wit-nessyng of an ooth, and seide, Ye schulen not se my face, if ye schulen not brynge with you youre leeste brother;

4 therfor if thou wolt sende hym with vs, we schulen go to gidere, and we schulen bie necessaries to thee;

5 ellis if thou wolt not, we schulen not go; for as we seiden ofte, the man denounside to vs, and seide, Ye schulen not se my face with out youre leeste brother.

6 Forsothe Israel seide to hem, Ye diden this in to my wretch-idnesse, that ye schewiden to hym, that ye hadden also another brother.

7 And thei answeriden, The man axide vs bi ordre oure gen-eracioun, if the fadir lyuede, if we hadden a brother; and we answeriden suyngli to hym, bi that that he axide; whether we myyten wite that he wolde seie, Brynge ye youre brothir with you?

8 And Judas seide to his fadir, Sende the child with me, that we go, and moun lyue, lest we dien, and oure litle children;

9 Y take the child, require thou hym of myn hoond; if Y schal not brynge ayen, and bitake hym to thee, Y schal be gilti of synne ayens thee in al tyme;

10 if delai hadde not be, we hadden come now anothir tyme.

11 Therfor Israel, 'the fadir of hem, seide to hem, If it is nede so, do ye that that ye wolen; 'take ye of the beste fruytis of the lond in youre vesselis, and 'bere ye yiftis to the man, a litil of gumme, and of hony, and of storax, and of mirre, and of therebynte, and of alemaundis;

12 and 'bere ye with you double money, and 'bere ye ayen that money which ye founden in baggis, lest perauenture it be doon bi errour;

13 but also take ye youre brother, and go ye to the man;

14 forsothe my God Almyyti mak him pesible to you, and sende he ayen youre brother, whom he holdith in boondis,

and this Beniamyn; forsothe Y schal be as maad bare without sones.

15 Therfor the men token yiftis, and double monei, and Beniamyn; and thei yeden doun in to Egipt, and stoden bifore Joseph.

16 And whanne he hadde seyn 'hem and Beniamyn togidere, he comaundide the dispendere of his hows, and seide, Lede these men in to the hous, and sle beestis, and make a feeste; for thei schulen ete with me to dai.

17 He dide as it was comaundid, and ledde the men in to the hows;

18 and there thei weren aferd, and seiden to gidere, We ben brouyt in for the monei which we baren ayen bifore in oure sackis, that he putte chalenge 'in to vs, and make suget bi violence to seruage bothe vs and oure assis.

19 Wherfor thei neiyeden in the 'yatis, and spaken to the dispendere,

20 Lord, we preien that thou here vs; we camen doun now bifore that we schulden bie metis;

21 whanne tho weren bouyt, whanne we camen to the ynne, we openeden oure baggis, and we founden money in the mouth of sackis, which money we han brouyt ayen now in the same weiyte;

22 but also we han brouyt other siluer, that we bie tho thingis that ben nedeful to vs; it is not in oure conscience, who puttide the money in oure pursis.

23 And he answerde, Pees be to you, nyle ye drede; youre God and God of youre fadir yaf to you tresouris in youre baggis; for I haue the monei preued, which ye yauen to me. And he ledde out Symeon to hem;

24 and whanne thei weren brouyt in to the hows, he brouyte watir, and thei waischiden her feet, and he yaf 'meetis to her assis.

25 Sotheli thei maden redi yiftis til Joseph entride at myd day, for thei hadden herd that thei schulden ete breed there.

26 Therfor Joseph entride in to his hows, and thei offriden yiftis to hym, and helden in the hondis, and worschipiden lowe to erthe.

27 And he grette hem ayen mekeli; and he axide hem, and seide, Whether youre fadir, the elde man, is saaf, of whom ye seiden to me? lyueth he yit?

28 Whiche answeriden, He is hool, thi seruaunt oure fadir lyueth yit; and thei weren bowid, and worschipiden hym.

29 Forsothe Joseph reyside hise iyen, and siy Beniamyn his brother of the same wombe, and seide, Is this youre litil brother, of whom ye seiden to me? And eft Joseph seide, My sone, God haue merci of thee.

30 And Joseph hastide in to the hous, for his entrailis weren moued on his brother, and teeris brasten out, and he entride into a closet, and wepte.

31 And eft whanne the face was waischun, he yede out, and refreynede hym silf, and seide, Sette ye looues.

32 'And whanne tho weren set to Joseph by hym silf, and to the britheren bi hem silf, and to Egipcyans that eeten to gidre by hem silf; for it is vnleueful to Egipcians to ete with Ebrewis, and thei gessen sich a feeste vnhooli;

33 Therfor thei saten bifore hym, the firste gendrid bi the rite of his firste gendryng, and the leeste bi his age; and thei wondriden greetli,

34 whanne the partis weren takun whiche thei hadden resseyued of him, and the more part cam to Beniamyn, so that it passide in fyue partis; and thei drunken, and weren fillid with him.

CAP 44

1 Forsothe Joseph comaundid the dispendere of his hous, and seide, Fille thou her sackis with wheete, as myche as tho moun take, and putte thou the money of ech in the hiynesse of the sak;

2 forsothe put thou in the mouth of the sak of the yongere my silueren cuppe, and the prijs of wheete which he yaf; and it was doon so.

3 And whanne the morewtid roos, thei weren delyuered with her assis.

4 And now thei hadden go out of the citee, and hadden go forth a litil; thanne Joseph seide, whanne the dispendere of his hous was clepid, Rise thou, pursue the men, and seye thou whanne thei ben takun, Whi han ye yolde yuel for good?

5 The cuppe, which ye han stole, is thilk in which my lord drynkith, and in which he is wont to dyuyne; ye han do a ful wickid thing.

6 He dide as Joseph comaundid, and whanne thei weren takun, he spak bi ordre.

7 Whiche answeriden, Whi spekith oure lord so, that thi seruauntis han do so greet trespas?

8 We brouyten ayen to thee fro the lond of Chanaan the monei which we founden in the hiynesse of sackis, and hou is it suynge that we han stole fro 'the hows of thi lord gold ether siluer?

9 At whom euere of thi seruauntis this that thou sekist is foundun, die he, and we schulen be seruauntis of my lord.

10 Which seide to hem, Be it doon bi youre sentence; at whom it is foundun, be he my seruaunt; forsothe ye schulen be gilteles.

11 And so thei diden doun hastili the sackis on erthe, and alle openyden tho whiche he souyte;

12 and bigan at the more til to the leeste, and foond the cuppe in 'the sak of Beniamyn.

13 And whanne thei hadden 'to-rent her clothis, and hadden chargid eft the assis, thei turneden ayen in to the citee.

14 And Judas entride 'the firste with brithren to Joseph; for he hadde not go yit fro the place; and alle felden togidere on erthe bifore hym.

15 To whiche he seide, Whi wolden ye do so? whether ye witen not, that noon is lijk me in the kunnyng of dyuinyng?

16 To whom Judas seide, What schulen we answere to my lord, ether what schulen we speke, ether moun iustli ayenseie? God hath founde the wickidnesse of thi seruauntis; lo! alle we ben the seruauntis of my lord, bothe we and he at whom the cuppe is foundun.

17 Joseph answeride, Fer be it fro me, that Y do so; he be my seruaunt that stal the cuppe; forsothe go ye fre to youre fadir.

18 Sotheli Judas neiyede neer, and seide tristili, My lord, Y preye, thi seruaunt speke a word in thin eeris, and be thou not wrooth to thi seruaunt; for aftir Farao thou art my lord.

19 Thou axidist first thi seruauntis, Han ye a fadir, ether a brother?

20 And we answeriden to thee, my lord, An eld fadir is to vs, and a litil child that was borun in his eelde, whos brother of the same wombe is deed, and his modir hath hym aloone; forsothe his fadir loueth hym tendirli.

21 And thou seidist to thi seruauntis, Brynge ye hym to me, and Y schal sette myn iyen on hym.

22 We maden suggestioun to thee, my lord, the child may not forsake his fadir; for if he schal leeue the fadir, he schal die.

23 And thou seidist to thi seruauntis, If youre leeste brother schal not come with you, ye schulen no more se my face.

24 Therfor whanne we hadden stied to thi seruaunt, oure fadir, we telden to hym alle thingis whiche my lord spak; and oure fadir seide,

25 Turne ye ayen, and bie ye to you a litil of wheete;

26 to whom we seiden, We moun not go; if oure leeste brother schal go doun with vs, we schulen go forth togidere; ellis, if he is absent, we doren not se the 'face of the lord.

27 To whiche thingis the fadir answeride, Ye witen that my wiif childide twei sones to me;

28 oon yede out, and ye seiden, a beeste deuouride hym, and hidir to he apperith not;

29 if ye taken also this sone, and ony thing bifallith to hym in the weye, ye schulen lede forth myn hoor heeris with morenyng to hellis.

30 Therfor if Y entre to thi seruaunt, oure fadir, and the child faile, sithen his lijf hangith of the lijf of the child,

31 and he se that the child is not with vs, he schal die, and thi seruauntis schulen lede forth hise hoor heeris with sorewe to hellis.

32 Be Y propirli thi seruaunt, which resseyuede this child on my feith, and bihiyte, and seide, If Y schal not brynge ayen hym, Y schal be gilti of synne ayens my fadir in al tyme;

33 and so Y schal dwelle thi seruaunt for the child in to the seruyce of my lord, and the child stie with hise britheren;

34 for Y may not go ayen to my fadir, if the child is absent, lest Y stonde a witnesse of the wretchidnesse that schal oppresse my fadir.

CAP 45

1 Joseph myyte no lengere absteyne hym silf, while many men stoden bifore; wherfor he comaundide that alle men schulden go out, and that noon alien were present in the knowyng of Joseph and hise britheren.

2 And Joseph reiside the vois with wepyng, which Egipcians herden, and al the hows of Farao.

3 And he seide to hise britheren, Y am Joseph; lyueth my fadir yit? The brithren myyten not answere, and weren agast bi ful myche drede.

4 To whiche he seide mekeli, Neiye ye to me. And whanne thei hadden neiyed nyy, he seide, Y am Joseph youre brother, whom ye selden in to Egipt;

5 nyle ye drede, nether seme it to be hard to you, that ye seelden me in to these cuntreis; for God hath sent me bifore you in to Egipt for youre helthe.

6 For it is twei yeer that hungur bigan 'to be in the lond, yit fyue yeer suen, in whiche me schal not mow ere, nether repe;

7 and God bifor sente me, that ye be reserued on erthe, and moun haue metis to lyue.

8 Y was sent hidur not bi youre counsel, but bi Goddis wille, which made me as the fadir of Farao, and the lord of al his hows, and prince in al the lond of Egipt.

9 Haste ye, and 'stie ye to my fadir, and ye schulen seie to hym, Thi sone Joseph sendith these thingis; God hath maad me lord of al the lond of Egipt; come doun to me, and tarie not, and dwelle in the lond of Gessen;

10 and thou schalt be bisidis me, thou, and thi sones, and the sones of thi sones, thi scheep, and thi grete beestis, and alle thingis whiche thou weldist,

11 and there Y schal fede thee; for yit fyue yeer of hungur ben residue, lest bothe thou perische, and thin hows, and alle thingis whiche thou weldist.

12 Lo! youre iyen, and the iyen of my brother Beniamyn seen, that my mouth spekith to you;

13 telle ye to my fadir al my glorie, and alle thingis whiche ye sien in Egipt; haste ye, and brynge ye hym to me.

14 And whanne he hadde biclippid, and hadde feld in to the necke of Beniamyn, his brother, he wepte, the while also Benjamin wepte in lijk maner on the necke of Joseph.

15 And Joseph kisside alle hise britheren, and wepte on alle; aftir whiche thingis thei weren hardi to speke to hym.

16 And it was herd, and pupplischid bi famouse word in the halle of the kyng, The britheren of Joseph ben comun. And Farao ioiede, and al his meynee;

17 and Farao seide to Joseph, that he schulde comaunde hise britheren, and 'seie, Charge youre beestis, and go ye in to the lond of Canaan,

18 and take ye fro thennus youre fadir, and kynrede, and come ye to me; and Y schal yyue to you alle the goodis of Egipt, that ye ete the merow of the lond.

19 Comaunde thou also, that thei take waynes of the lond of Egipt to the cariage of her litle children, and wyues, and seie thou, 'Take ye youre fadir, and haste ye comynge soone,

20 nether leeue ye ony thing of the purtenaunce of youre hows, for alle the richessis of Egipt schulen be youre.

21 The sones of Israel diden, as it was comaundid to hem; to whiche Joseph yaf waynes, bi the comaundement of Farao, and metis in the weie;

22 and he comaundide twei stoolis to be brouyt forth to ech; forsothe he yaf to Beniamyn thre hundrid platis of siluer, with fyue the beste stoolis;

23 and sente to his fadir so myche of siluer, and of cloothis, and he addide to hem ten male assis, that schulden bere of alle richessis of Egipt, and so many femal assis, berynge wheete and looues in the weie.

24 Therfor he lefte hise britheren, and seide to hem goynge forth, Be ye not wrooth in the weie.

25 Whiche stieden fro Egipt, and camen in to the lond of Canaan, to her fadir Jacob;

26 and telden to hym, and seiden, Joseph, thi sone, lyueth, and he is lord in al the lond of Egipt. And whanne this was herd, Jacob wakide as of a greuouse sleep; netheles he bile-uyde not to hem.

27 Thei telden ayenward al the ordre of the thing; and whanne Jacob hadde seyn the waynes, and alle thingis whiche Joseph hadde sent, his spirit lyuede ayen,

28 and he seide, It suffisith to me, if Joseph my sone lyueth yit, Y schal go and 'Y schal se hym bifore that Y die.

CAP 46

1 And Israel yede forth with alle thingis that he hadde, and he cam to the pit of ooth; and whanne sacrifices weren slayn there to God of his fadir Isaac,

2 he herde God bi a visioun in that nyyt clepynge hym, 'and seiynge to hym, Jacob! Jacob! To whom he answeride, Lo! Y am present.

3 God seide to hym, Y am the strongeste God of thi fadir; nyle thou drede, go doun in to Egipt, for Y schal make thee there in to a greet folk;

4 Y schal go doun thidir with thee, and Y schal brynge thee turnynge ayen fro thennus, and Joseph schal sette his hond on thin iyen.

5 Jacob roos fro the pit of ooth, and the sones token him, with her litle children, and wyues, in the waynes whiche Farao hadde sent to bere the eld man,

6 and alle thingis whiche he weldide in the lond of Canaan; and he cam in to Egipt with his seed,

7 hise sones, and her sones, and douytris, and al the generacioun togidere.

8 Forsothe thes ben the names of the sones of Israel, that entriden in to Egipte; he with hise fre children. The firste gendrid Ruben;

9 the sones of Ruben, Enoch, and Fallu, and Esrom, and Carmi.

10 The sones of Symeon, Jemuhel, and Jamyn, and Ahoth, and Jachyn, and Sab, and Saber, and Saul, the sone of a womman of Canaan.

11 The sones of Leuy, Gerson, Caath, and Merarie.

12 The sones of Juda, Her and Onam, and Sela, and Fares, and Zara. Forsothe Her and Onam dieden in the lond of Canaan; and the sones of Fares weren borun, Esrom, and Amul.

13 The sones of Isacar, Thola, and Fua, and Jobab, and Semron.

14 The sones of Zabulon, Sared, and Thelom, and Jahel.

15 These ben the sones of Lia, whiche sche childide in Mesopotanye of Sirie, with Dyna, hir douyter; alle the soules of hise sones and douytris, thre and thretti.

16 The sones of Gad, Sefion, and Aggi, Suny, and Hesebon, Heri, and Arodi, and Areli.

17 The sones of Aser, Jamne, and Jesua, and Jesui, and Beria; and Sara, the sister of hem. The sones of Beria, Heber and Melchiel.

18 These weren the sones of Zelfa, whom Laban yaf to Lia, his douyter, and Jacob gendryde these sixtene persones.

19 The sones of Rachel, 'wijf of Jacob, weren Joseph and Beniamyn.

20 And sones weren borun to Joseph in the loond of Egipt, Manasses and Effraym, whiche Asenech, 'douytir of Putifar, preest of Helipoleos, childide to hym.

21 The sones of Beniamin weren Bela, and Becor, and Asbel, Gera, and Naaman, and Jechi, 'Ros, and Mofym, and Ofym, and Ared.

22 These weren the sones of Rachel, whiche Jacob gendride; alle the persones weren fouretene.

23 The sone of Dan, Vsym.

24 The sones of Neptalym, Jasiel, and Guny, and Jeser, and Salem.

25 These weren 'the sones of Bala, whom Laban yaf to Rachel his douytir.

26 And Jacob gendride these; alle the soules weren seuene. And alle the men that entriden with Jacob in to Egipt, and yeden out of his thiy, with out 'the wyues of his sones, weren sixti and sixe.

27 Forsothe the sones of Joseph, that weren borun to hym in 'the loond of Egipt, weren two men. Alle the soulis of 'the hows of Jacob, that entriden in to Egipt, weren seuenti.

28 Forsothe Jacob sente Judas bifore hym to Joseph, that he schulde telle to hym, and he schulde 'come in to Gessen.

29 And whanne Jacob hadde come thidir, Joseph stiede in his chare to mete his fadir at the same place. And he siy Jacob, and felde on 'his necke, and wepte bitwixe collyngis.

30 And the fadir seide to Joseph, Now Y schal die ioiful, for Y siy thi face, and Y leeue thee lyuynge.

31 And Joseph spak to hise brithren, and to al 'the hows of his fadir, I schal stie, and 'Y schal telle to Farao, and Y schal seie to hym, My britheren, and the hows of my fadir, that weren in the lond of Canaan, ben comun to me,

32 and thei ben men kepers of scheep, and han bisynesse of flockis to be fed; thei brouyten with hem her scheep and grete beestis, and alle thingis whiche thei miyten haue.

33 And whanne Farao schal clepe you, and schal seie, What is youre werk? ye schulen answere, We ben thi seruauntis, men scheepherdis, fro oure childhed til in to present tyme, bothe we and oure fadris. Sotheli ye schulen seye these thingis, that ye moun dwelle in the lond of Gessen, for Egipcians wlaten alle keperis of scheep.

CAP 47

1 Therfor Joseph entride, and telde to Farao, and seide, My fadir and brethren, the scheep and grete beestis of hem, and alle thingis whiche thei welden, camen fro the lond of Canaan; and lo! thei stonden in the lond of Gessen.

2 And he ordeynede fyue, the laste men of hise britheren, bifore the kyng,

3 whiche he axide, What werk han ye? Thei answeriden, We thi seruauntis ben kepers of scheep, bothe we and oure faderis;

4 we camen in to thi lond to be pilgrymys, for noo gras is to the flockis of thi seruauntis; hungur wexith greuouse in the lond of Canaan, and we axen that thou comaunde vs thi seruauntis to be in the lond of Gessen.

5 And so the kyng seide to Joseph, Thi fadir and thi britheren camen to thee;

6 the lond of Egipt is in thi siyt, make thou hem to dwelle in the beste place, and yyue thou to hem the lond of Gessen; that if thou woost that witti men ben in hem, ordeyne thou hem maystris of my beestis.

7 After these thingis Joseph brouyte in his fader to the king, and settide him bifor the king, which blesside the king;

8 and he was axid of the king, Hou many ben the daies of the yeeris of thi lijf?

9 And he answeride, The daies of pilgrymage of my lijf, ben feewe and yuele, of an hundrid and thretti yeer, and tho 'camen not til to the daies of my fadris, in whiche thei weren pilgryms.

10 And whanne he hadde blessid the kyng, he yede out.

11 Forsothe Joseph yaf to hise fadir and britheren possessioun in Egipt, in Ramasses, the beste soile of erthe, as Farao comaundide;

12 and he fedde hem, and al the hows of his fadir, and yaf metis to alle.

13 For breed failide in al the world, and hungur oppresside the lond, moost of Egipt and of Canaan;

14 of whiche londis he gaderide al the money for the sillyng of wheete, and brouyte it in to the 'tresorie of the kyng.

15 And whanne prijs failide to the bieris, al Egipt cam to Joseph, and seide, Yyue thou 'looues to vs; whi shulen we die bifore thee, while monei failith?

16 To whiche he answeride, Brynge ye youre beestis, and Y schal yyue to you metis for tho, if ye han not prijs.

17 And whanne thei hadden brouyt tho, he yaf to hem metis for horsis, and scheep, and oxun, and assis; and he susteynede hem in that yeer for the chaungyng of beestis.

18 And thei camen in the secunde yeer, and seiden to hym, We helen not fro oure lord, that the while monei failith, also beestis failiden togidere, nether it is hid fro thee, that with out bodies and lond we han no thing;

19 whi therfor schulen we die, while thou seest? bothe we and oure lond schulen be thine, bie thou vs in to the kyngis seru-

age, and yyue thou seedis, lest the while the tiliere perischith, the lond be turned in to wildirnesse.

20 Therfor Joseph bouyte al the lond of Egipt, while all men seelden her possessiouns, for the greetnesse of hungur;

21 and he made it and alle puplis therof suget to Farao, fro the laste termes of Egipt til to the laste endis therof,

22 outakun the lond of preestis, that was youun of the kyng to hem, to whiche preestis also metis weren youun of the comun bernys, and therfor thei weren not compellid to sille her possessiouns.

23 Therfor Joseph seide to the puplis, Lo! as ye seen, Farao weldith bothe you and youre lond; take ye seedis, and 'sowe ye feeldis,

24 that ye moun haue fruytis; ye schulen yyue the fifthe part to the kyng; Y suffre to you the foure residue partis in to seed and in to meetis, to you, and to youre fre children.

25 Whiche answeriden, Oure helthe is in thin hond; oneli oure God biholde vs, and we schulen ioifuli serue the kyng.

26 For that tyme til in to present dai, in al the lond of Egipt, the fyuethe part is paied to the kyngis, and it is maad as in to a lawe, with out the lond of preestis, that was fre fro this condicioun.

27 Therfor Israel dwellide in Egipt, that is, in the lond of Jessen, and weldide it; and he was encreessid and multiplied ful mych.

28 And he lyuede therynne sixtene yeer; and alle the daies of his lijf weren maad of an hundrid and seuene and fourti yeer.

29 And whanne he seiy the dai of deeth nyye, he clepide his sone Joseph, and seide to hym, If Y haue founde grace in thi siyt; putte thin hond vndur myn hipe, and thou schal do merci and treuthe to me, that thou birie not me in Egipt;

30 but 'Y schal slepe with my fadris, and take thou awey me fro this lond, and birie in the sepulcre of my grettere. To whom Joseph answeride, Y schal do that that thou comaundist.

31 And Israel seide, Therfor swere thou to me; and whanne Joseph swoor, Israel turnede to the heed of the bed, and worschipide God.

CAP 48

1 And so whanne these thingis weren don, it was teld to Joseph, that his fadir was sijk. And he took hise twei sones, Manasses and Effraym, and he disposide to go.

2 And it was seid to the elde man, Lo! thi sone Joseph cometh to thee; which was coumfortid, and sat in the bed.

3 And whanne Joseph entride to hym, he seide, Almyyti God apperide to me in Luza, which is in the lond of Canaan, and blesside me,

4 and seide, Y schal encreesse and multiplie thee, and Y schal make thee in to cumpanyes of puplis, and Y schal yyue to thee this lond, and to thi seed aftir thee, in to euerlastinge possessioun.

5 Therfor thi twei sones, that ben borun to thee in the lond of Egipt bifore that Y cam hidir to thee, schulen be myne, Effraym and Manasses as Ruben and Symeon schulen be arettid to me;

6 forsothe the othere whiche thou schalt gendre aftir hem schulen be thine; and thei schulen be clepid bi the name of her britheren in her possessiouns.

7 Forsothe whanne Y cam fro Mesopotamye, Rachel was deed to me in the lond of Canaan, in thilke weie; and it was the bigynnyng of somer; and Y entride in to Effrata, and beriede hir bisidis the weie of Effrata, which bi anothir name is clepid Bethleem.

8 Forsothe Jacob seiy the sones of Joseph, and seide to him, Who ben these?

9 He answeride, Thei ben my sones, whiche God yaf to me in this place. Jacob seide, Brynge hem to me that Y blesse hem.

10 For 'the iyen of Israel, dasewiden for greet eelde, and he myyte not se clereli; and he kisside and collide tho children ioyned to hym, and seide to his sone,

11 Y am not defraudid of thi siyt; ferthermore God schewide to me thi seed.

12 And whanne Joseph hadde take hem fro 'the fadris lappe, he worschipide lowe to erthe.

13 And he sette Effraym on his riyt side, that is, on the lift side of Israel; forsothe he settide Manasses in his lift side, that is, on the riyt side of the fadir; and he ioynede bothe to hym.

14 Which helde forth the riyt hond, and settide on 'the heed of Effraym, the lesse brothir; sotheli he settide the left hond on 'the heed of Manasses, that was the more thury birthe. Jacob chaungide 'the hondes,

15 and blesside his sone Joseph, and seide, God, in whos siyt my fadris Abraham and Isaac yeden; God, that fedith me fro my yong wexynge age til in to present day;

16 the aungel that delyuerede me fro alle yuelis, blesse thes children, and my name be clepid on hem, and the names of my fadris Abraham and Ysaac; and wexe thei in multitude on erthe.

17 Forsothe Joseph seiy that his fadir hadde set the riyt hond on the heed of Effraym, and took heuyli, and he enforside to reise the fadris hond takun fro the heed of Effraym, and to bere 'ouer on 'the heed of Manasses.

18 And he seide to the fadir, Fadir, it acordith not so; for this is the firste gendrid; sette thi riyt hond on the heed 'of hym.

19 Which forsook and seide, Y woot, my sone, Y woot; and sotheli this child schal be in to puplis, and he schal be multiplied; but his yonger brother schal be more than he, and 'his seed schal encreesse in to folkis.

20 And he blesside hem in that tyme, and seide, Israel schal be blessid in thee, Joseph, and it schal be seid, God do to thee as to Effraym and as to Manasses. And he settide Effraym bifore Manasses;

21 and seide to Joseph, his sone, Lo! Y die, and God schal be with you, and schal lede you ayen to the lond of youre fadris;

22 Y yyue to thee o part ouer thi britheren which Y took fro the hand of Amorei, in my swerd and bowe.

CAP 49

1 Forsothe Jacob clepide hise sones, and seide to hem, Be ye gaderid that Y telle what thingis schulen come to you in the laste daies;

2 be ye gaderid, 'and here, ye sones of Jacob, here ye Israel youre fadir.

3 Ruben, my firste gendrid sone, thou art my strengthe and the bigynnyng of my sorewe; thou ouytist to be the former in yiftis, the more in lordschip;

4 thou art sched out as watir; wexe thou not, for thou stiedist on the bed of thi fader, and defoulidist his bed.

5 Symeon and Leuy, britheren, fiytynge vessils of wickidnesse;

6 my soule come not in to the councel of hem, and my glorie be not in the congregacioun of hem; for in her woodnesse thei killiden a man, and in her wille thei myneden the wal;

7 curside be the woodnesse of hem, for it is obstynat, and the indignacioun of hem for it is hard; Y schal departe hem in Jacob, and I schal scatere hem in Israel.

8 Judas, thi britheren schulen preise thee, thin hondis schulen be in the nollis of thin enemyes; the sones of thi fadir schulen worschipe thee.

9 'A whelp of lioun 'is Judas; my sone thou stiedist to prey; thou restidist, and hast leyn as a lioun, and as a lionesse who schal reise hym?

10 The septre schal not be takun awey fro Juda, and a duyk of his hipe, til he come that schal be sent, and he schal be abiding of hethene men;

11 and he schal tye his colt at the vyner, and his femal asse at the vyne; A! my sone, he schal waische his stoole in wyn, and his mentil in the blood of grape;

12 hise iyen ben fairere than wyn, and hise teeth ben whittere than mylk.

13 Zabulon schal dwelle in the brenk of the see, and in the stondyng of schipis; and schal stretche til to Sydon.

14 Isachar, a strong asse,

15 liggynge bitwixe termes, seiy reste, that it was good and seiy the lond that it was best, and he vndirsettide his schuldre to bere, and he was maad seruynge to tributis.

16 Dan schal deme his puple, as also another lynage in Israel.

17 Dan be maad a serpent in the weie, and cerastes in the path, and bite the feet of an hors, that the 'stiere therof falle bacward; Lord,

18 Y schal abide thin helthe.

19 Gad schal be gird, and schal fiyte bifor hym, and he schal be gird bihynde.

20 Aser his breed schal be plenteuouse, and he schal yyue delicis to kyngis.

21 Neptalym schal be an hert sent out, and yyuynge spechis of fairenesse.

22 Joseph, a sone encreessynge, 'a sone encresinge, and fair in biholdyng; douytris runnen aboute on the wal,

23 but hise brithren wraththeden hym, and chidden, and thei hadden dartis, and hadden enuye to hym.

24 His bowe sat in the stronge, and the boondis of his armes, and hondis weren vnboundun bi the hond of the myyti of Jacob; of hym a scheepherd yede out, the stoon of Israel.

25 God of thi fadir schal be thin helpere, and Almyyti God schal blesse thee with blessyngis of heuene fro aboue, and with blessyngis of the see liggynge binethe, with blessyngis of tetis, and of wombe;

26 the blessyngis of thi fadir ben coumfortid, the blessyngis of his fadris, til the desire of euerlastynge hillis cam; blessyngis ben maad in the heed of Joseph, and in the nol of Nazarei among his britheren.

27 Beniamyn, a rauyschynge wolf, schal ete prey eerly, and in the euentid he schal departe spuylis.

28 Alle these weren in twelue kynredis of Israel; her fadir spak these thingys to hem, and blesside hem alle by propre blessyngis,

29 and comaundide hem, and seide, Y am gaderid to my puple, birie ye me with my fadris in the double denne, which is in the lond of Efron Ethei, ayens Manbre,

30 in the lond of Canaan, which denne Abraham bouyte with the feeld of Efron Ethei, in to possessioun of sepulcre.

31 There thei birieden hym, and Sare his wijf, also Ysaac was biried there with Rebecca his wijf; there also Lia liggith biried.

32 And whanne the comaundementis weren endid, bi whiche he tauyte the sones, he gaderide hise feet on the bed, and diede, and he was put to his puple.

CAP 50

1 Which thing Joseph seiy, and felde on 'the face of the fader, and wepte, and kiste hym;

2 and he comaundide hise seruauntis, lechis, that thei schulden anoynte the fadir with swete smellynge spiceries.

3 While thei 'filliden the comaundementis, fourti daies passiden, for this was the custom of deed bodies anoyntid; and Egipt biwepte hym seuenti daies.

4 And whanne the tyme of weiling was fillid, Joseph spak to the meyne of Farao, If Y haue founde grace in youre siyt, speke ye in the eeris of Farao; for my fadir chargide me,

5 and seide, Lo! Y die, thou schalt birie me in my sepulcre which Y diggide to me in the lond of Canaan; therfor Y schal stie that Y birie my fadir, and Y schal turne ayen.

6 And Farao seide to hym, Stie, and birie thi fader, as thou art chargid.

7 And whanne 'he stiede, alle the elde men of 'the hous of Farao yeden with him, and alle the grettere men in birthe of the lond of Egipt; the hous of Joseph with her britheren,

8 without litle children, and flockis, and grete beestis, whiche thei leften in the lond of Gessen, yeden with him.

9 And he hadde charis, and horsmen, and felouschip, and cumpany was maad not litil.

10 And thei camen to the cornfloor of Adad, which is set ouer Jordan, where thei maden the seruice of the deed bodi, with greet weilyng and strong, and fillide seuen daies.

11 And whanne the dwellers of the lond of Canaan hadden seyn this, thei seiden, This is a greet weiling to Egipcians; and therfor thei clepiden the name of that place the weilyng of Egipt.

12 Therfor the sones of Jacob diden, as he hadde comaundid to hem;

13 and thei baren hym in to the lond of Canaan, and thei birieden hym in the double denne, which denne with the feeld Abraham hadde bouyt of Effron Ethei, ayens the face of Mambre, into possessioun of sepulcre.

14 And Joseph turnede ayen in to Egipt with hise britheren and al the felouschipe, whanne the fadir was biried.

15 And whanne the fadir was deed, the britheren of Joseph dredden, and spaken togidere, lest perauenture he be myndeful of the wrong which he suffride, and yelde to vs al the yuel, that we diden.

16 And thei senten to hym, and seiden, Thi fadir comaundide to vs,

17 bifore that he diede, that we schulden seie to thee these thingis bi hise wordis; Y beseche, that thou foryete the wickidnesse of thi britheren, and the synne, and malice which thei hauntiden ayens thee; also we preien, that thou foryyue this wickidnesse to thi fadir, the seruaunt of God. Whanne these thingis weren herd, Joseph wepte.

18 And hise britheren camen to hym, and worschipiden lowe to erthe, and seiden, We ben thi seruauntis.

19 To whiche he answeride, Nyle ye drede; whether we moun ayenstonde Goddis wille?

20 Ye thouyten yuel of me, and God turnede it in to good, that he schulde enhaunse me, as ye seen in present tyme, and that he schulde make saaf many puplis;

21 nyle ye drede, Y schal fede you and youre litle children. And he coumfortide hem, and spak swetli, and liytly;

22 and he dwellide in Egipt, with al the hows of his fadir. And he lyuyde an hundrid yeer, and he seiy the sones of Effraym til to the thridde generacioun; also the sones of Machir, son of Manasses, weren borun in the knees of Joseph.
23 Whanne these thingis weren don, Joseph spak to hise brithren, Aftir my deeth God schal visite you, and he schal make to stie fro this lond to the loond which he swoor to Abraham, Ysaac, and Jacob.
24 And whanne he hadde chargid hem, and hadde seid, God schal visite you, bere ye out with you my boonus fro this place,
25 he diede, whanne an hundrid and ten yeeris of his lijf weren fillid; and he was anoyntid with swete smellynge spiceries, and was kept in a beere in Egipt.

EXODUS

CAP 1

1 These ben the names of the sones of Israel, that entriden into Egipt with Jacob; alle entriden with her housis;
2 Ruben, Symeon,
3 Leuy, Judas, Isachar, Zabulon, and Benjamin,
4 Dan, and Neptalim, Gad, and Aser.
5 Therfor alle the soules of hem that yeden out of 'the hipe of Jacob weren seuenti and fyue.
6 Forsothe Joseph was in Egipt; and whanne he was deed, and alle hise brithren, and al his kynrede,
7 the sones of Israel encreessiden, and weren multiplied as buriounnyng, and thei weren maad strong greetli, and filliden the lond.
8 A newe kyng, that knewe not Joseph, roos in the meene tyme on Egipt, and seide to his puple, Lo!
9 the puple of the sones of Israel is myche, and strongere than we;
10 come ye, wiseli oppresse we it, lest perauenture it be multiplied; and lest, if batel risith ayens vs, it be addid to oure enemyes, and go out of the lond, whanne we ben ouercomun.
11 And so he made maistris of werkis souereyns to hem, that thei schulden turmente hem with chargis. And thei maden citees of tabernaclis to Farao, Fiton, and Ramesses.
12 And bi hou myche thei oppressiden hem, bi so myche thei weren multiplied, and encreessiden more.
13 And Egipcians hatiden the sones of Israel, and turmentiden, and scorneden hem;
14 and brouyten her lijf to bitternesse bi hard werkis of cley and to tijl stoon, and bi al seruage, bi which thei weren oppressid in the werkis of erthe.
15 Forsothe the kyng of Egipt seide to the mydwyues of Ebrews, of whiche oon was clepid Sefora, the tother Fua;
16 and he commaundide to hem, Whanne ye schulen do the office of medewyues to Ebrew wymmen, and the tyme of childberyng schal come, if it is a knaue child, sle ye him; if it is a womman, kepe ye.
17 Forsothe the medewyues dredden God, and diden not bi the comaundement of the kyng of Egipt, but kepten knaue children.
18 To whiche clepid to hym the kyng seide, What is this thing which ye wolden do, that ye wolden kepe the children?
19 Whiche answeriden, Ebrew wymmen ben not as the wymmen of Egipt, for thei han kunnyng of the craft of medewijf, and childen bifore that we comen to hem.
20 Therfor God dide wel to medewyues; and the puple encreesside, and was coumfortid greetli.

21 And for the mydewyues dredden God, he bildide 'housis to hem.
22 Therfor Farao comaundide al his puple, and seide, What euer thing of male kynde is borun to Ebrewis, 'caste ye into the flood; what euer thing of wymmen kynde, kepe ye.

CAP 2

1 Aftir these thingis a man of 'the hows of Leuy yede out, and took a wijf of his kyn,
2 which conseyuede, and childide a sone. And sche seiy hym wel farynge, and hidde him bi thre monethis.
3 And whanne sche myyte not hele, thanne sche took a 'leep of segge, and bawmede it with tar and pitch, and puttide the yong child with ynne, and puttide hym forth in a 'place of spier of the brenke of the flood,
4 the while his sistir stood afer, and bihelde the bifalling of the thing.
5 Lo! forsothe the douytir of Farao cam doun to be waischun in the flood, and hir damysels walkiden bi the brenke of the flood. And whanne sche hadde seyn a leep in the 'place of spier, sche sente oon of hir seruauntessis,
6 and sche openyde the leep brouyt to hir, and seiy a litil child wepynge ther ynne. And sche hadde mercy on the child, and seide, It is of the yonge children of Ebrews.
7 To whom the 'sister of the child seide, Wolt thou that Y go, and clepe to thee an Ebrew womman, that may nurische the yong child?
8 She answeride, Go thou. The damysel yede, and clepide the 'modir of the child.
9 To whom 'the douytir of Farao spak, and seide, Take thou this child, and nurische to me; Y schal yyue to thee thi mede. The womman took, and nurischide the child, and bitook hym woxun to 'the douytir of Farao,
10 whom sche purchaside 'in to the place of sone; and sche clepide his name Moises, and seide, For Y took hym fro the watir.
11 In tho daies, aftir that Moises encreesside, he yede out to hise britheren, and seiy the turment of hem, and a man Egipcian smytynge 'oon of Ebrews, hise britheren.
12 And whanne he hadde biholdun hidur and thidir, and hadde seyn, that no man was present, he killide the Egipcian, and hidde in soond.
13 And he yede out in another dai, and seiy tweyne Ebrews chidynge, and he seide to hym that dide wrong, Whi smytist thou thi brother?
14 Which answeride, Who ordeynede thee prince, ether iuge on vs? Whether thou wolt sle me, as thou killidist yisterdai the Egipcian? Moises dredde, and seide, Hou is this word maad opun?
15 And Farao herde this word, and souyte to sle Moyses, which fledde fro his siyt, and dwellide in the lond of Madian, and sat bisidis a pit.
16 Forsothe seuene douytris weren to the preest of Madian, that camen to drawe watir; and whanne the trouyis weren fillid, thei coueitiden to watere 'the flockis of her fadir.
17 Scheepherdis camen aboue, and dreuen hem awei; and Moises roos, and defendide the dameselis; and he watride 'the scheep of hem.
18 And whanne thei hadden turned ayen to Jetro, her fadir, he seide to hem, Whi camen ye swiftliere than ye weren wont?
19 Thei answeriden, A man of Egipt delyuerede vs fro the hond of scheepherdis; ferthermore and he drow watir with vs, and yaf drynk to the scheep.

20 And he seide, Where is that man? whi leften ye the man? clepe ye hym, that he ete breed.

21 Therfor Moises swoor, that he wolde dwelle with Jetro; and he took a wijf, Sefora, 'the douyter of Jetro.

22 And sche childide a sone to hym, whom he clepide Gersan, and seide, Y was a comelyng in an alyen lond. Forsothe sche childide an othir sone, whom he clepide Eliezer, and seide, For God of my fadir is myn helpere, and delyuerede me fro the hond of Farao.

23 Forsothe aftir myche tyme the kyng of Egipt diede, and the sones of Israel inwardli weiliden for werkis, and crieden, and the cry of hem for werkis stiede to God.

24 And he herde the weilyng of hem, and he hadde mynde of the boond of pees, which he hadde maad with Abraham, Ysaac, and Jacob; and he bihelde the sones of Israel,

25 and knewe hem.

CAP 3

1 Forsothe Moises kepte the scheep of Jetro, 'his wyues fadir, preest of Madian; and whanne he hadde dryue the floc to the ynnere partis of deseert, he cam to Oreb, the hil of God.

2 Forsothe the Lord apperide to hym in the flawme of fier fro the myddis of the buysch, and he seiy that the buysch brente, and was not forbrent.

3 Therfor Moyses seide, Y schal go and schal se this greet siyt, whi the buysch is not forbrent.

4 Sotheli the Lord seiy that Moises yede to se, and he clepide Moises fro the myddis of the buysch, and seide, Moyses! Moises! Which answeride, Y am present.

5 And the Lord seide, Neiye thou not hidur, but vnbynde thou the scho of thi feet, for the place in which thou stondist is hooli lond.

6 And the Lord seide, Y am God of thi fadir, God of Abraham, and God of Isaac, and God of Jacob. Moises hidde his face, for he durste not biholde ayens God.

7 To whom the Lord seide, Y seiy the affliccion of my puple in Egipt, and Y herde the cry therof, for the hardnesse of hem that ben souereyns of werkis.

8 And Y knew the sorewe of the puple, and Y cam down to delyuere it fro the hondis of Egipcians, and lede out of that lond in to a good lond and brood, into a lond that flowith with milk and hony, to the places of Cananey, and of Ethei, of Amorrey, and of Feresei, of Euey, and of Jebusei.

9 Therfor the cry of the sones of Israel cam to me, and Y seiy the turment of hem, bi which thei ben oppressid of Egipcians.

10 But come thou, I schal sende thee to Farao, that thou lede out my puple, the sones of Israel, fro Egipt.

11 And Moises seide to hym, Who am Y, that Y go to Farao, and lede out the sones of Israel fro Egipt?

12 And the Lord seide to Moises, Y schal be with thee, and thou schalt haue this signe, that Y haue sent thee, whanne thou hast led out my puple fro Egipt, thou schalt offre to God on this hil.

13 Moises seide to God, Lo! Y schal go to the sones of Israel, and Y schal seie to hem, God of youre fadris sente me to you; if thei schulen seie to me, what is his name, what schal Y seie to hem?

14 The Lord seide to Moises, Y am that am. The Lord seide, Thus thou schalt seie to the sones of Israel, He that is sente me to you.

15 And eft God seide to Moises, Thou schalt seie these thingis to the sones of Israel, The Lord God of youre fadris, God of Abraham, and of Isaac, and God of Jacob, sente me to you; this name is to me with outen ende, and this is my memorial in generacioun and in to generacioun.

16 Go thou, gadere thou the eldere men, that is, iugis, of Israel, and thou schalt seie to hem, The Lord God of youre fadris apperide to me, God of Abraham, and God of Ysaac, and God of Jacob, and seide, Y visitynge haue visitid you, and Y seiy alle thingis that bifelden to you in Egipt;

17 and Y seide, that Y lede out you fro the afflicsioun of Egipt in to the lond of Cananey, and of Ethei, and of Amorrei, and of Ferezei and of Euei, and of Jebusei, to the lond flowynge with mylk and hony.

18 And thei schulen here thi vois; and thou schalt entre, and the eldere men of Israel to the kyng of Egipt, and thou schalt seie to hym, The Lord God of Ebrews clepide vs; we schulen go the weie of thre daies in to wildirnesse, that we offre to oure Lord God.

19 But Y woot, that the kyng of Egipt schal not delyuere you that ye go, but bi strong hond;

20 for Y schal holde forthe myn hond, and I schal smyte Egipt in alle my marueils, whiche Y schal do in the myddis of hem; aftir these thingis he schal delyuere you.

21 And Y schal yyue grace to this puple bifore Egipcians, and whanne ye schulen go out, ye schulen not go out voide;

22 but a womman schal axe of hir neiyboresse and of her hoosteesse siluerne vesselis, and goldun, and clothis, and ye schulen putte tho on youre sones and douytris, and ye schulen make nakid Egipt.

CAP 4

1 Moyses answeride, and seide, The comyns schulen not bileue to me, nether thei schulen here my vois; but thei schulen seie, The Lord apperide not to thee.

2 Therfor the Lord seide to hym, What is this that thou holdist in thin hond? Moises answeride, A yerde.

3 And the Lord seide, Caste it forth into erthe; and he castide forth, and it was turned in to a serpent, so that Moises fledde.

4 And the Lord seide, Holde forth thin hond, and take the tail therof; he stretchide forth, and helde, and it was turned in to a yerde.

5 And the Lord seide, That thei bileue, that the Lord God of thi fadris apperide to thee, God of Abraham, and God of Isaac, and God of Jacob.

6 And the Lord seide eft, Putte thin hond in to thi bosum; and whanne he hadde put it in to the bosum, he brouyte forth it leprouse, at the licnesse of snow.

7 The Lord seide, Withdrawe thin hond in to thi bosum; he withdrow, and brouyte forth eft, and it was lijc the tother fleisch.

8 The Lord seide, If thei schulen not bileue to thee, nether schulen here the word of the formere signe, thei schulen bileue to the word of the signe suynge;

9 that if thei bileuen not sotheli to these twei signes, nether heren thi vois, take thou watir of the flood, and schedde out it on the drie lond, and what euer thing thou schalt drawe vp of the flood, it schal be turned in to blood.

10 Moises seide, Lord, Y biseche, Y am 'not eloquent fro yistirdai and the thridde dai ago; and sithen thou hast spokun to thi seruaunt, Y am of more lettid and slowere tunge.

11 The Lord seide to hym, Who made the mouth of man, ether who made a doumb man and 'deef, seynge and blynd? whether not Y?

12 Therfor go thou, and Y schal be in thi mouth, and Y schal teche thee what thou schalt speke.

13 And he seide, Lord, Y biseche, sende thou whom thou schalt sende.

14 And the Lord was wrooth ayens Moises, and seide, Y woot, that Aaron, thi brother, of the lynage of Leuy, is eloquent; lo! he schal go out in to thi comyng, and he schal se thee, and schal be glad in herte.

15 Speke thou to hym, and putte thou my wordis in his mouth, and Y schal be in thi mouth, and in the mouth of hym; and Y schal schewe to you what ye owen to do.

16 He schal speke for thee to the puple, and he schal be thi mouth; forsothe thou schalt be to him in these thingis, that perteynen to God.

17 Also take thou this yerde in thin hond, in which thou schalt do myraclis.

18 Moises yede, and turnede ayen to Jetro, his wyues fadir, and seide to hym, Y schal go, and turne ayen to my britheren in to Egipt, that Y se, whether thei lyuen yit. To whom Jetro seide, Go thou in pees.

19 Therfor the Lord seide to Moyses in Madian, Go thou, and turne ayen into Egipt; for alle thei ben deed that souyten thi lijf.

20 Moises took his wijf, and hise sones, and puttide hem on an asse, and he turnede ayen in to Egipt, and bar the yerde of God in his hond.

21 And the Lord seide to hym turnynge ayen in to Egipt, Se, that thou do alle wondris, whiche Y haue put in thin hond, bifore Farao; Y schal make hard his herte, and he schal not delyuere the puple; and thou schalt seie to hym,

22 The Lord seith these thingis, My firste gendrid sone is Israel;

23 Y seide to thee, delyuere thou my sone, that he serue me, and thou noldist delyuere hym; lo! Y schal sle thi firste gendrid sone.

24 And whanne Moises was in the weie, in an yn, the Lord cam to him, and wolde sle hym.

25 Sefora took anoon a moost scharp stoon, and circumcidide the yerde of hir sone; and sche towchide 'the feet of Moises, and seide, Thou art an hosebonde of bloodis to me.

26 And he lefte hym, aftir that sche hadde seid, Thou art an hosebonde of bloodis to me for circumcisioun.

27 Forsothe the Lord seide to Aaron, Go thou in to the comyng of Moises in to deseert; which yede ayens Moises in to the hil of God, and kisside him.

28 And Moises telde to Aaron alle the wordis of the Lord, for whiche he hadde sent Moises; and 'he telde the myraclis, whiche the Lord hadde comaundid.

29 And thei camen togidere, and gaderiden alle the eldere men of the sones of Israel.

30 And Aaron spak alle the wordis, whiche the Lord hadde seid to Moises, and he dide the signes bifore the puple;

31 and the puple bileuede; and thei herden, that the Lord hadde visitid the sones of Israel, and that he hadde biholde the turment of hem; and thei worschipiden lowe.

CAP 5

1 Aftir these thingis Moises and Aaron entriden, and seiden to Farao, The Lord God of Israel seith these thingis, Delyuere thou my puple, that it make sacrifice to me in deseert.

2 And he answeride, Who is the Lord, that Y here his vois, and delyuere Israel? I knowe not the Lord, and Y schal not delyuere Israel.

3 Thei seiden, God of Ebrews clepide vs, that we go the weie of thre daies in to wildirnesse, and that we make sacrifice to

oure Lord God, lest perauenture pestilence, ether swerd, bifalle to vs.

4 The kyng of Egipt seide to hem, Moises and Aaron, whi stiren ye the puple fro her werkis? Go ye to youre chargis.

5 And Farao seide, The puple of the loond is myche; ye seen that the cumpany hath encreessid; hou myche more schal it encreesse, if ye schulen yyue to hem reste fro werkis.

6 Therfor Farao comaundide in that dai to the maistris of werkis, and to rente gadereris of the puple,

7 and seide, Ye schulen no more yyue stre to the puple, to make tijl stoonys as bifore; but go thei, and gedere stobil;

8 and ye schulen sette on hem the mesure of tijl stoonys, which thei maden bifore, nether ye schulen abate ony thing; for thei ben idil, and therfor thei crien, and seien, Go we, and make we sacrifice to oure God;

9 be thei oppressid bi werkis, and fille thei tho, that thei assente not to the false wordis.

10 Therfor the maistris of the workis and the rente gadereris yeden out to the puple, and seiden, Thus seith Farao, Y yyue not to you stre;

11 go ye, and gadere, if ye moun fynde ony where; nether ony thing schal be decreessid of youre werk.

12 And the puple was scaterid bi al the lond of Egipt to gadre stre.

13 And the maystris of werkis weren bisi, and seiden, Fille ye youre werk ech dai, as ye weren wont to do, whanne the stre was youun to you.

14 And thei, that weren maistris of the werkis of the sones of Israel, weren betun of the rent gadereris of Farao, that seiden, Whi filliden ye not the mesure of tijl stoonus, as bifore, nether yistirdai nethir to dai?

15 And the souereyns of the sonys of Israel camen, and crieden to Farao, and seiden, Whi doist thou so ayens thi seruauntis?

16 Stre is not youun to vs, and tijl stoonus ben comaundid in lijk manere. Lo! we thi seruauntis ben betun with scourgis, and it is doon vniustli ayens thi puple.

17 Farao seide, Ye yyuen tent to idilnesse, and therfor ye seien, Go we, and make we sacrifice to the Lord;

18 therfor go ye, and worche; stre schal not be youun to you, and ye schulen yelde the customable noumbre of tijl stoonus.

19 And the souereyns of the children of Israel sien hem silf in yuel, for it was seid to hem, No thing schal be decreessid of tijl stoonus bi alle daies.

20 And thei 'camen to Moises and Aaron, that stoden euene ayens, and thei 'yeden out fro Farao,

21 and seiden to 'Moises and Aaron, The Lord se, and deme, for ye han maad oure odour to stynke bifore Farao and hise seruauntis; and ye han youe to hym a swerd, that he schulde sle vs.

22 And Moises turnede ayen to the Lord, and seide, Lord, whi hast thou turmentid this puple? why sentist thou me?

23 For sithen Y entride to Farao, that Y schulde speke in thi name, thou hast turmentid thi puple, and hast not delyuered hem.

CAP 6

1 And the Lord seide to Moises, Now thou schalt se, what thingis Y schal do to Farao; for bi strong hond he schal delyuere hem, and in myyti hond he schal caste hem out of his lond.

2 And the Lord spak to Moises,

3 and seide, Y am the Lord, that apperide to Abraham, and to Isaac, and to Jacob in Almyyti God; and Y schewide not to hem my greet name Adonai;

4 and Y made couenaunt with hem, that Y schulde yyue to hem the lond of Canaan, the lond of her pilgrymage, in which thei weren comelyngis.

5 Y herde the weilyng of the sones of Israel, in which the Egipcians oppresseden hem, and Y hadde mynde of my couenaunt.

6 Therfor seie thou to the sones of Israel, Y am the Lord, that schal lede out you of the prisoun of Egipcians; and Y schal delyuere fro seruage; and Y schal ayen bie in 'an hiy arm, and in grete domes;

7 and Y schal take you to me in to a puple, and Y schal be youre God; and ye schulen wite, for Y am youre Lord God, 'which haue led you out of the prisoun of Egipcians,

8 and haue led you in to the lond, on which Y reiside myn hond, that Y schulde yyue it to Abraham, and to Ysaac, and to Jacob; and Y schal yyue to you that lond to be weldid; I the Lord.

9 Therfor Moises telde alle thingis to the sones of Irael, whiche assentide not to hym for the angwisch of spirit, and for the hardest werk.

10 And the Lord spak to Moises,

11 and seide, Entre thou, and speke to Farao, kyng of Egipt, that he delyuere the children of Israel fro his lond.

12 Moises answeride bifore the Lord, Lo! the children of Israel here not me, and hou schal Farao here, moost sithen Y am vncircumcidid in lippis?

13 And the Lord spak to Moises and to Aaron, and yaf comaundementis to the sones of Israel, and to Farao, kyng of Egipt, that thei schulden lede out the sones of Israel fro the lond of Egipt.

14 These ben the princis of housis bi her meynees. The sones of Ruben, the firste gendrid of Israel, Enoch, and Fallu, Esrom, and Charmy; these ben the kynredis of Ruben.

15 The sones of Symeon, Jamuel, and Jamyn, and Aod, and Jachym, and Soer, and Saul, the sone of a womman of Canaan; these ben the kynretis of Symeon.

16 And these ben the names of the sones of Leuy by her kynredis, Gerson, and Caath, and Merary. Forsothe the yeeris of lijf of Leuy weren an hundrid and seuene and thretti.

17 The sones of Gerson, Lobny and Semei, bi her kynredis.

18 The sones of Caath, Amram, and Isuar, and Hebron, and Oziel; and the yeeris of lijf of Caath weren an hundrid and thre and thretti.

19 The sones of Merari weren Mooli and Musi. These weren the kynredis of Leuy bi her meynees.

20 Forsothe Amram took a wijf, Jocabed, douytir of his fadris brother, and sche childide to hym Aaron, and Moises, and Marie; and the yeeris of lijf of Amram weren an hundred and seuene and thretti.

21 Also the sones of Isuar weren Chore, and Nafeg, and Zechry.

22 Also the sones of Oziel weren Misael, and Elisaphan, and Sechery.

23 Sotheli Aaron took a wijf, Elizabeth, the douytir of Amynadab, the sistir of Naason, and sche childide to hym Nadab, and Abyu, and Eleazar, and Ythamar.

24 Also the sones of Chore weren Aser, and Elcana, and Abiasab; thes weren the kinredis of Chore.

25 And sotheli Eleazar, sone of Aaron, took a wijf of the douytris of Phatiel, and sche childide Fynees to hym. These ben the princis of the meynees of Leuy bi her kynredis.

26 This is Aaron and Moises, to whiche the Lord comaundide, that thei schulden lede out of the lond of Egipt the sones of Israel by her cumpanyes;

27 these it ben, that speken to Pharao king of Egipt, that thei lede the sones of Israel out of Egipt;

28 this is Moises and Aaron, in the dai in which the Lord spak to Moises in the lond of Egipt.

29 And the Lord spak to Moises, and seide, Y am the Lord; spek thou to Farao, kyng of Egipt, alle thingis whiche Y speke to thee.

30 And Moises seide bifore the Lord, Lo! Y am vncircumcidid in lippis; hou schal Farao here me?

CAP 7

1 And the Lord seide to Moises, Lo! Y haue maad thee the god of Farao; and Aaron, thi brother, schal be thi prophete.

2 Thou schalt speke to Aaron alle thingis whiche Y comaunde to thee, and he schal speke to Farao, that he delyuere the sones of Israel fro his hond.

3 But Y schal make hard his herte, and Y schal multiplie my signes and merueils in the lond of Egipt, and he schal not here you;

4 and Y schal sende myn hond on Egipt, and Y schal lede out myn oost, and my puple, the sones of Israel, fro the lond of Egipt bi mooste domes;

5 and Egipcians schulen wite, that Y am the Lord, which haue holde forth myn hond on Egipt, and haue led out of the myddis of hem the sones of Israel.

6 And so Moises dide and Aaron; as the Lord comaundide, so thei diden.

7 Forsothe Moyses was of fourescoor yeer, and Aaron was of fourescoor yeer and thre, whanne thei spaken to Farao.

8 And the Lord seide to Moises and to Aaron,

9 Whanne Farao schal seie to you, Schewe ye signes to vs, thou schalt seie to Aaron, Take thi yerde, and caste forth it before Farao, and be it turned into a serpent.

10 And so Moises and Aaron entriden to Farao, and diden as the Lord comaundide; and Aaron took the yeerde, and castide forth bifore Farao and hise seruauntis, which yerde was turned in to a serpent.

11 Forsothe Farao clepide wise men, and witchis, and thei also diden bi enchauntementis of Egipt, and bi summe priuy thingis in lijk maner;

12 and alle castiden forth her yerdis, whiche weren turned in to dragouns; but the yerde of Aaron deuouride 'the yerdis of hem.

13 And the herte of Farao was maad hard, and he herde not hem, as the Lord comaundide.

14 Forsothe the Lord seide to Moyses, The herte of Farao is maad greuouse, he nyle delyuere the puple;

15 go thou to hym eerli; lo! he schal go out to the watris, and thou schalt stonde in the comyng of hym on the brynke of the flood; and thou schalt take in thin honde the yerde, that was turned into a dragoun,

16 and thou schalt seie to hym, The Lord God of Ebrews sente me to thee, and seide, Delyuere thou my puple, that it make sacrifice to me in desert; til to present time thou noldist here.

17 Therfor the Lord seith these thingis, In this thou schalt wite, that Y am the Lord; lo! Y schal smyte with the yerde,

which is in myn hond, the watir of the flood, and it schal be turned in to blood;

18 and the fischis that ben in the flood schulen die; and the watris schulen wexe rotun, and Egipcians drynkynge the watir of the flood schulen be turmentid.

19 Also the Lord seide to Moises, Seie thou to Aaron, Take thi yerde, and holde forth thin hond on the watris of Egipt, and on the flodis of hem, and on the stremys 'of hem, and on the mareis, and alle lakis of watris, that tho be turned in to blood; and blood be in al the lond of Egipt, as wel in vessils of tree as of stoon.

20 And Moises and Aaron diden so, as the Lord comaundide; and Aaron reiside the yerde, and smoot the watir of the flood bifore Farao and hise seruauntis, which watir was turned in to blood;

21 and fischis, that weren in the flood, dieden; and the flood was rotun, and Egipcians myyten not drynke the water of the flood; and blood was in al the lond of Egipt.

22 And the witchis of Egipcians diden in lijk maner by her enchauntementis; and the herte of Farao was maad hard, and he herde not hem, as the Lord comaundide.

23 And he turnede awei hym silf, and entride in to his hows, nethir he took it to herte, yhe, in this tyme.

24 Forsothe alle Egipcians diggiden watir 'bi the cumpas of the flood, to drinke; for thei myyten not drynke of the 'watir of the flood.

25 And seuene daies weren fillid, aftir that the Lord smoot the flood.

CAP 8

1 Also the Lord seide to Moises, Entre thou to Farao, and thou schalt seie to hym, The Lord seith these thingis, Delyuere thou my puple, that it make sacrifice to me; sotheli if thou nylt delyuere, lo!

2 Y schal smyte alle thi termys with paddoks;

3 and the flood schal buyle out paddokis, that schulen stie, and schulen entre in to thin hows, and in to the closet of thi bed, and on thi bed, and in to 'the hous of thi seruauntis, and in to thi puple, and in to thin ouenes, and in to the relyues of thi metis;

4 and the paddoks schulen entre to thee, and to thi puple, and to alle thi seruauntis.

5 And the Lord seide to Moises, Seie thou to Aaron, Hold forth thin hond on the floodis, and on the streemes, and mareis; and bryng out paddoks on the lond of Egipt.

6 And Aaron helde forth the hond on the watris of Egipt; and paddoks stieden, and hileden the lond of Egipt.

7 Forsothe and the witchis diden in lijk maner bi her enchauntementis; and thei brouyten forth paddoks on the lond of Egipt.

8 Forsothe Farao clepide Moises and Aaron, and seide to hem, Preie ye the Lord, that he do a wei the paddoks fro me, and fro my puple; and Y schal delyuere the puple, that it make sacrifice to the Lord.

9 And Moises seide to Farao, Ordeyne thou a tyme to me, whanne Y schal preie for thee, and for thi seruauntis, and for thi puple, that the paddokis be dryuun awei fro thee, and fro thin hows, and fro thi seruauntis, and fro thi puple; and dwelle oneli in the flood.

10 And he answeride, To morewe. And Moises seide, Y schal do bi thi word, that thou wite, that noon is as oure Lord God; and the paddoks schulen go awei fro thee,

11 and fro thin hous, and fro thi children, and fro thi seruauntis, and fro thi puple; and tho schulen dwelle oneli in the flood.

12 And Moises and Aaron yeden out fro Farao. And Moises criede to the Lord, for the biheest of paddoks, which he hadde seid to Farao.

13 And the Lord dide bi the word of Moises; and the paddoks weren deed fro housis, and fro townes, and fro feeldis;

14 and thei gaderiden tho in to grete heepis, and the lond was rotun.

15 Sotheli Farao seiy that reste was youun, and he made greuous his herte, and herde not hem, as the Lord comaundide.

16 And the Lord seide to Moises, Spek thou to Aaron, Holde forth thi yerde, and smyte the dust of erthe, and litle flies, ether gnattis, be in al the lond of Egipt.

17 And thei diden so; and Aaron helde forth the hond, and helde the yerde, and smoot the duste of erthe; and gnattis weren maad in men, and in werk beestis; al the dust of erthe was turned in to gnattis bi al the lond of Egipt.

18 And witchis diden in lijk maner bi her enchauntementis, that thei schulden brynge forth gnattis, and thei miyten not; and gnattis weren as wel in men as in werk beestis.

19 And the witchis seiden to Farao, This is the fyngur of God. And the herte of Farao was maad hard, and he herde not hem, as the Lord comaundide.

20 And the Lord seide to Moises, Rise thou eerli, and stonde bifore Farao, for he schal go out to the watris; and thou schalt seie to hym, The Lord seith these thingis, Delyuere thou my puple, that it make sacrifice to me;

21 that if thou schalt not delyuere the puple, lo! Y schal sende in to thee, and in to thi seruauntis, and in to thi puple, and in to thin housis, al the kynde of flies; and the housis of Egipcians schulen be fillid with flies of dyuerse kyndis, and al the lond in which thei schulen be.

22 And in that dai Y schal make wondurful the lond of Gessen, in which my puple is, that flies be not there; and that thou wite that Y am the Lord in the myddis of erthe;

23 and Y schal sette departyng bitwixe my puple and thi puple; this signe schal be to morewe.

24 And the Lord dide so. And a moost greuouse flie cam in to the hows of Farao, and of hise seruauntis, and in to al the lond of Egipt; and the lond was corrupt of siche flies.

25 And Farao clepide Moises and Aaron, and seide to hem, Go ye, make ye sacrifice to 'youre Lord God in this lond.

26 And Moises seide, It may not be so, for 'we schulen offre to oure God the abhomynacioums of Egipcians; that if we schulen sle bifore Egipcians tho thingis whiche thei worschipen, thei schulen 'ouerleie vs with stoonus.

27 We schulen go the weie of thre daies in to wildirnesse, and we schulen make sacrifice to oure Lord God, as he comaundide vs.

28 And Farao seide, Y schal delyuere you, that ye make sacrifice to 'youre Lord God in deseert; netheles go ye not ferthere; preie ye for me.

29 And Moises seide, Y schal go out fro thee, and Y schal preie the Lord; and the fli schal go awei fro Farao, and fro hise seruauntis, and puple to morewe; netheles nyle thou more disseyue me, that thou delyuere not the puple to make sacrifice to the Lord.

30 And Moises yede out fro Farao, and preiede the Lord, whiche dide bi the word of Moyses,

31 and took awei flies fro Farao, and fro hise seruauntis, and puple; noon lefte, 'sotheli nether oon.

32 And the herte of Farao was maad hard, so that he delyueride not the puple, sothli nethir in this tyme.

CAP 9

1 Forsothe the Lord seide to Moises, Entre thou to Farao, and speke thou to hym, The Lord God of Ebrews seith these thingis, Delyuere thou my puple, that it make sacrifice to me;

2 that if thou forsakist yit, and withholdist hem, lo!

3 myn hond schal be on thi feeldis, on horsis, and assis, and camels, and oxun, and scheep, a pestilence ful greuous;

4 and the Lord schal make a merueilous thing bitwixe the possessiouns of Israel and the possessiouns of Egipcians, that outirli no thing perische of these thingis that perteynen to the sones of Israel.

5 And the Lord ordeinede a tyme, and seide, To morewe the Lord schal do this word in the lond.

6 Therfor the Lord made this word in the tother dai, and alle the lyuynge beestis of Egipcians weren deed; forsothe outirli no thing perischide of the beestis of the sones of Israel.

7 And Farao sente to se, nether ony thing was deed of these thingis whiche Israel weldide; and the herte of Farao was maad greuouse, and he delyuerede not the puple.

8 And the Lord seide to Moises and Aaron, Take ye the hondis ful of askis of the chymeney, and Moises sprynge it in to heuene bifore Farao;

9 and be there dust on al the lond of Egipt; for whi botchis schulen be in men and in werk beestis, and bolnynge bladdris schulen be in al the lond of Egipt.

10 And thei token askis of the chymney, and stoden bifore Farao; and Moises spreynt it into heuene; and woundis of bolnynge bladdris weren maad in men, and in werk beestis;

11 and the witchis myyten not stonde bifor Moises, for woundis that weren in hem, and in al the lond of Egipt.

12 And the Lord made hard the herte of Farao, and he herde not hem, as the Lord spak to Moises.

13 Also the Lord seide to Moises, Rise thou eerli, and stonde bifore Farao, and thou schalt seie to hym, The Lord God of Ebrews seth these thingis, Delyuere thou my puple, that it make sacrifice to me;

14 for in this tyme Y schal sende alle my veniauncis on thin herte, and on thi seruauntis, and on thi puple, that thou wite, that noon is lijk me in al erthe.

15 For now Y schal holde forth the hond, and Y schal smyte thee and thi puple with pestilence, and thou schalt perische fro erthe;

16 forsothe herfor Y haue set thee, that Y schewe my strengthe in thee, and that my name be teld in ech lond.

17 Yit thou withholdist my puple, and nylt delyuere it?

18 Lo! to morewe in this same our Y schal reyne ful myche hail, which maner hail was not in Egipt, fro the dai in which it was foundid, til in to present tyme.

19 Therfor sende thou 'riyt now, and gadere thi werk beestis, and alle thingis whiche thou hast in the feeld; for men and werk beestis and alle thingis that ben in feeldis with outforth, and ben not gaderid fro the feeldis, and haile falle on tho, schulen die.

20 He that dredde 'the Lordis word, of the seruauntis of Farao, made his seruauntis and werk beestis fle in to housis;

21 sotheli he that dispiside the 'Lordis word, lefte his seruauntis and werk beestis in the feeldis.

22 And the Lord seide to Moises, Holde forth thin hond in to heuene, that hail be maad in al the lond of Egipt, on men, and on werk beestis, and on ech eerbe of the feeld in the lond of Egipt.

23 And Moises held forth the yerde in to heuene; and the Lord yaf thundris, and hail, and leitis rennynge aboute on the lond; and the Lord reynede hail on the lond of Egipt;

24 and hail and fier meddlid togidere weren borun forth; and it was of so myche greetnesse, how greet apperide neuere bifore in al the lond of Egipt, sithen thilke puple was maad.

25 And the hail smoot in the lond of Egipt alle thingis that weren in the feeldis, fro man til to werk beeste; and the hail smoot al the eerbe of the feeld, and brak al the flex of the cuntrey;

26 oonli the hail felde not in the lond of Gessen, where the sones of Israel weren.

27 And Farao sente, and clepide Moises and Aaron, and seide to hem, Y haue synned also now; the Lord is iust, Y and my puple ben wickid;

28 preye ye the Lord, that the thundris and hail of God ceesse, and Y schal delyuere you, and dwelle ye no more here.

29 Moyses seide, Whanne Y schal go out of the citee, Y schal holde forth myn hondis to the Lord, and leitis and thundris schulen ceesse, and hail schal not be, that thou wite, that the lond is the Lordis;

30 forsothe Y knowe, that thou and thi seruauntis dreden not yit the Lord.

31 Therfor the flex and barli was hirt, for the barli was greene, and the flex hadde buriounned thanne knoppis;

32 forsothe wheete and beenys weren not hirt, for tho weren late.

33 And Moyses yede out fro Farao, and fro the citee, and helde forth the hondis to the Lord, and thundris and hail ceessiden, and reyn droppide no more on the erthe.

34 Sotheli Farao siy that the reyn hadde ceessid, and the hail, and thundris, and he encreesside synne;

35 and the herte of hym and of hise seruauntis was maad greuouse, and his herte was maad hard greetli; nethir he lefte the sones of Israel, as the Lord comaundide bi 'the hond of Moises.

CAP 10

1 And the Lord seide to Moises, Entre thou to Farao, for Y haue maad hard the herte of hym, and of hise seruauntis, that Y do these signes 'of me in hym;

2 and that thou telle in the eeris of thi sone and of 'thi sones sones, how ofte Y al to-brak Egipcians, and dide signes in hem; and that ye wyte that Y am the Lord.

3 Therfore Moises and Aaron entriden to Farao, and seiden to hym, The Lord God of Ebrews seith these thingis, How long 'nylt thou be maad suget to me? Delyuere thou my puple, that it make sacrifice to me; ellis sotheli if thou ayenstondist,

4 and nylt delyuere it, lo! Y schal brynge in to morewe a locuste in to thi coostis,

5 which schal hile the hiyere part of erthe, nether ony thing therof schal appere, but that, that was 'residue to the hail schal be etun; for it schal gnawe alle the trees that buriounnen in feeldis;

6 and tho schulen fille thin howsis, and the howsis of thi seruauntis, and of alle Egipcians, hou greet thi fadris and grauntsiris sien not, sithen thei weren borun on erthe, til in to present dai. And Moises turnede awei hym silf, and yede out fro Farao.

7 Forsothe the seruauntis of Farao seiden to hym, Hou longe schulen we suffre this sclaundre? Delyuere the men, that thei make sacrifice to 'her Lord God; seest thou not that Egipt perischide?

8 And thei ayen clepiden Moises and Aaron to Farao, and he seide to hem, Go ye, and make ye sacrifice to 'youre Lord God; whiche ben thei, that schulen go?

9 Moises seide, We schulen go with oure litle children and eldre, and with sones, and douytris, with scheep, and grete beestis; for it is the solempnyte of 'oure Lord God.

10 And Farao answeride, So the Lord be with you; hou therfor schal Y delyuere you and youre litle children? to whom is it doute, that ye thenken worst?

11 It schal 'not be so; but go ye men oneli, and make ye sacrifice to the Lord; for also ye axiden this. And anoon thei weren cast out fro the siyt of Farao.

12 Forsothe the Lord seide to Moises, Holde forth thi hond on the lond of Egipt, to a locust, that it stie on the lond, and deuoure al the eerbe which is residue to the hail.

13 And Moises helde forthe the yerde on the lond of Egipt, and the Lord brouyte in a brennynge wynd al that dai and niyt; and whanne the morewtid was maad, the brennynge wynd reiside locustis, whiche stieden on al the lond of Egipt,

14 and saten in alle the coostis of Egipcians; 'and the locustis weren vnnoumbrable, and suche weren not bifore that tyme, nether schulen come aftirward.

15 And tho hiliden al the face of the erthe, and wastiden alle thingis; therfor the eerbe of the erthe was deuourid, and what euere of applis was in trees, whiche the hail hadde left, 'it was deuourid; and outirli no green thing was left in trees and in eerbis of erthe, in al Egipt.

16 Wherfor Farao hastide, and clepide Moises and Aaron, and seide to hem, Y haue synned ayens youre Lord God, and ayens yow;

17 but now foryyue ye the synne to me; also in this tyme preie ye youre Lord God, that he take awey fro me this deeth.

18 And Moises yede out of the siyt of Farao, and preiede the Lord;

19 which made a moost strong wynd to blowe fro the west, and took, and castide the locust in to the reed see; 'noon dwellide, sotheli nether oon, in alle the coostis of Egipt.

20 And the Lord made hard the herte of Farao, and he lefte not the sones of Israel.

21 Forsothe the Lord seide to Moises, Holde forth thin hond in to heuene, and derknessis be on the lond of Egipt, so thicke that tho moun be gropid.

22 And Moises helde forth the hond in to heuene, and orrible derknessis weren maad in al the lond of Egipt;

23 in thre daies no man seiy his brother, nether mouede him silf fro that place in which he was. Whereuer the sones of Israel dwelliden, liyt was.

24 And Farao clepide Moises and Aaron, and seide to hem, Go ye, make ye sacrifice to the Lord; oneli youre scheep and grete beestis dwelle stille; youre litle children go with you.

25 Moises seide, Also thou schalt yyue to vs offryngis and brent sacrifices, whiche we schulen offre to 'oure Lord God;

26 alle the flockis schulen go with vs, for 'a cle schal not dwelle of tho thingis, that ben nedeful in to the worschipyng of 'oure Lord God, moost sithen we witen not what owith to be offrid, til we comen to that place.

27 Forsothe the Lord made hard the herte of Farao, and he nolde delyuere hem.

28 And Farao seide to Moises, Go awei fro me, and be war that thou se no more my face; in whateuer dai thou schalt appere to me, thou schalt die.

29 Moyses answeride, Be it doon so, as thou hast spokun; I schal no more se thi face.

CAP 11

1 And the Lord seide to Moises, Yit Y schal touche Farao and Egipt with o veniaunce, and after these thingis he schal delyuere you, and schal constreyne you to go out.

2 Therfor thou schalt seie to al the puple, that a man axe of his freend, and a womman of hir neiyboresse, silueren vessels and goldun, and clothis;

3 forsothe the Lord schal yyue grace to his puple bifor Egipcians. And Moises was a ful greet man in the lond of Egipt, bifore the seruauntis of Farao and al the puple;

4 and he seide, The Lord seith these thingis, At mydnyyt Y schal entre in to Egipt;

5 and ech firste gendrid thing in the lond of Egipcians schal die, fro the firste gendrid of Farao, that sittith in the trone of hym, til to the firste gendrid of the handmayde, which is at the querne; and alle the firste gendrid of beestis schulen die;

6 and greet cry schal be in al the lond of Egipt, which maner cry was not bifore, nether schal be aftirward.

7 Forsothe at alle the children of Israel a dogge schal not make priuy noise, fro man til to beeste; that ye wite bi how greet myracle the Lord departith Egipcians and Israel.

8 And alle these thi seruauntis schulen come doun to me, and thei schulen preye me, and schulen seie, Go out thou, and al the puple which is suget to thee; aftir these thingis we schulen go out.

9 And Moyses was ful wrooth, and yede out fro Farao. Forsothe the Lord seide to Moises, Farao schal not here you, that many signes be maad in the lond of Egipt.

10 Sotheli Moises and Aaron maden alle signes and wondris, that ben writun, bifor Farao; and the Lord made hard the herte of Farao, nether he delyuerede the sones of Israel fro his lond.

CAP 12

1 Also the Lord seide to Moises and Aaron in the lond of Egipt,

2 This monethe, the bigynnyng of monethis to you, schal be the firste in the monethis of the yeer.

3 Speke ye to al the cumpanye of the sones of Israel, and seie ye to hem, In the tenthe dai of this monethe ech man take a lomb by hise meynees and housis;

4 but if the noumbre is lesse, that it may not suffice to ete the lomb, he schal take his neiybore, which is ioyned to his hows, bi the noumbre of soulis, that moun suffice to the etyng of the lomb.

5 Forsothe the lomb schal be a male of o yeer, without wem; bi which custom ye schulen take also a kide;

6 and ye schulen kepe hym til to the fouretenthe dai of this monethe; and al the multitude of the sones of Israel schal offre hym at euentid.

7 And thei schulen take of his blood, and schulen put on euer either post, and in lyntels, 'ether hiyer threschfoldis, of the housis, in whiche thei schulen ete hym;

8 and in that niyt thei schulen ete fleischis, roostid with fier, and therf looues, with letusis of the feeld.

9 Ye schulen not ete therof ony raw thing, nether sodun in watir, but roostid oneli by fier; ye schulen deuoure the heed with feet and entrailis therof;

10 nether ony thing therof schal abide til the morewtid; if ony thing is residue, ye schulen brenne in the fier.

11 Forsothe thus ye schulen ete hym; ye schulen girde youre reynes, and ye schulen haue schoon in the feet, and ye schulen holde stauys in hondis, and ye schulen ete hastili; for it is fase, that is, the passyng of the Lord.

12 And Y schal passe thorou the lond of Egipt in that niyt, and Y schal smyte al the firste gendrid thing in the lond of Egipt, fro man til to beeste; and Y the Lord schal make domes in alle the goddis of Egipt.

13 Forsothe blood schal be to you in to signe, in the housis in whiche ye schulen be; and Y schal se the blood, and Y schal passe you; nether a wounde distriynge schal be in you, whanne Y schal smyte the lond of Egipt.

14 Forsothe ye schulen haue this dai in to mynde, and 'ye schulen make it solempne to the Lord in youre generaciouns bi euerlastynge worschipyng.

15 In seuene daies ye schulen ete therf breed; in the firste dai no thing diyt with sour douy schal be in youre housis; who euer schal ete ony thing diyt with sour douy, fro the firste dai til the seuenthe dai, that soule schal perische fro Israel.

16 The firste day schal be hooli and solempne, and the seuenthe dai schal be worschipful bi the same halewyng; ye schulen not do ony werk in tho daies, outakun these thingis that perteynen to mete;

17 and ye schulen kepe therf breed. For in that same dai Y schal lede out of the lond of Egipt youre oost; and ye schulen kepe this dai in youre generaciouns bi euerlastynge custom.

18 In the first monethe, in the fouretenthe dai of the monethe, at euentid, ye schulen ete therf breed, til to the oon and twentithe dai of the same monethe at euentid.

19 In seuene dayes no thing 'diyt with sour douy schal be foundun in youre housis; if ony etith ony thing diyt with sour dow, his soule schal perische fro the cumpeny of Israel, as wel of comelyngis, as of hem that ben borun in the lond.

20 Ye schulen not ete ony thing diyt with sour dow, and ye schulen ete therf breed in alle youre dwellyng placis.

21 Forsothe Moises clepide alle the eldre men of the sones of Israel, and seide to hem, Go ye, and take a beeste by youre meynees, and offre ye fase; and dippe ye a bundel of isope,

22 in the blood which 'is in the threisfold, and sprynge ye therof the lyntel, and euer either post; noon of you schal go out at the dore of his hows til the morewtid.

23 For the Lord schal passe smytynge Egipcians; and whanne he schal se the blood in the lyntel, and in euer either post, he schal passe the dore of the hows; and he schal not suffre the smytere to entre in to youre housis, and to hirte.

24 Kepe thou this word; it schal be a lawful thing to thee and to thi sones til in to with outen ende.

25 And whanne ye schulen entre in to the lond which the Lord schal yyue to you, as he bihiyte, ye schulen kepe these cerymonyes;

26 and whanne youre sones schulen seie to you, What is this religioun? ye schulen seie to hem,

27 It is the sacrifice of the passyng of the Lord, whanne he passide ouer the housis of the sones of Israel in Egipt, and smoot Egipcians, and delyueride oure housis. And the puple was bowid, and worschipide.

28 And the sones of Israel yeden out, and diden as the Lord comaundide to Moises and to Aaron.

29 Forsothe it was doon in the myddis of the nyyt, the Lord smoot al the firste gendrid thing in the lond of Egipt, fro the firste gendrid of Farao, that sat in the trone of hym, til to the first gendrid of the caitif womman, that was in the prisoun, and alle the first gendrid of beestis.

30 And Farao roos in the nyyt, and alle hise seruauntis, and al Egipt; and a greet cry was maad in Egipt, for noon hows was, in which a deed man lay not.

31 And whanne Moises and Aaron weren clepid in the nyyt, Farao seide, Rise ye, go ye out fro my puple, bothe ye and the sones of Israel; go ye, offre ye to the Lord, as ye seien;

32 take ye youre scheep and greete beestis, as ye axiden; and go ye, and blesse ye me.

33 And Egipcians constreyneden the puple to go out of the lond swiftli, and seiden, All we schulen die!

34 Therfor the puple took meele spreynd togidere, bifor that it was diyt with sour douy; and boond in mentils, and puttide on her schuldris.

35 And the sones of Israel diden as the Lord comaundide to Moises; and thei axiden of Egipcians siluerne vesselis and goldun, and ful myche clooth.

36 Forsothe the Lord yaf grace to the puple bifor Egipcians, that the Egipcians lenten to hem; and thei maden bare Egipcians.

37 And the sones of Israel yeden forth fro Ramasses in to Socoth, almest six hundrid thousind of foot men, with out litle children and wymmen;

38 but also comyn puple of malis and femalis vnnoumbrable stieden with hem; scheep, and oxun, and ful many beestis of diuerse kynde, stieden with hem.

39 And thei bakiden meele, which spreynd to gidere 'a while ago thei token fro Egipt, and maden therf looues bakun vnder the aischis; for the looues miyten not be diyt with sour dow, for Egipcians compelliden to go out, and suffriden not to make ony tariyng, nether it was leiser to make ony seew.

40 Forsothe the dwellyng of the sones of Israel, bi which thei dwelliden in Egipt, was of foure hundrid and thretti yeer;

41 and whanne tho weren fillid, al the oost of the Lord yede out of the lond of Egipt in the same dai.

42 This nyyt is worthi to be kept in the worschipyng of the Lord, whanne he ladde hem out of the lond of Egipt; alle the sones of Israel owen to kepe this in her generaciouns.

43 Also the Lord seide to Moises and Aaron, This is the religioun of fase; ech alien schal not ete therof;

44 sotheli ech seruaunt bouyt schal be circumcidid, and so he schal ete;

45 a comelyng and hirid man schulen not ete therof;

46 it schal be etun in oon hows; nether ye schulen bere out of the fleischis therof; nether ye schulen breke a boon therof.

47 Ech company of the sones of Israel schal make that fase;

48 that if ony pilgrym wole passe into youre feith and worschipyng, and make fase of the Lord, ech male kynde of hym schal be circumcidid bifore, and thanne he schal make lawfuli, and he schal be to gidere as a man borun of the lond; forsothe if ony man is not circumcidid, he schal not ete therof.

49 The same lawe schal be to a man borun of the lond, and to a comelyng, that takith youre feith, which is a pilgrym anentis you.

50 And alle the sones of Israel diden as the Lord comaundide to Moises and Aaron.

51 And in the same dai the Lord ladde out of 'the lond of Egipt the sones of Israel, bi her cumpanies.

CAP 13

1 Also the Lord spak to Moises, and seide,

2 Halewe thou to me ech firste gendrid thing that openeth the wombe among the sones of Israel, as wel of men as of beestis, for whi alle ben myn.

3 And Moises seide to the puple, Haue ye mynde of this dai, in which ye yeden out of Egipt, and of the hows of seruage, for in strong hond the Lord ledde you out of this place, that ye ete not breed diyt with sour dow.

4 To dai ye gon out, in the monethe of new fruytis;

5 and whanne the Lord hath led thee in to the lond of Cananey, and of Ethei, and of Amorrei, and of Euei, and of Jebusei, which lond he swoor to thi fadris, that he schulde yyue to thee, a lond flowynge with mylk and hony, thou schalt halowe this custom of holy thingis in this monethe.

6 In seuene daies thou schalt ete therf looues, and the solempnete of the Lord schal be in the seuenthe dai;

7 ye schulen ete therf looues seuene daies, no thing diyt with sour dow schal appere at thee, nether in alle thi coostis.

8 And thou schalt telle to thi sone in that dai, and schalt seie, This it is that the Lord dide to me, whanne Y yede out of Egipt.

9 And it schal be as a signe in thin hond, and as a memorial before thin iyen, and that the lawe of the Lord be euere in thi mouth; for in a strong hond the Lord ledde thee out of Egipt, and of the hows of seruage.

10 Thou schalt kepe siche a worschipyng in tyme ordeined, 'fro daies in to daies.

11 And whanne the Lord hath brouyt thee in to the lond of Cananey, as he swoor to thee, and to thi fadris, and hath youe it to thee,

12 thou schalt departe to the Lord al the thing that openeth the wombe, and that that is the firste in thi beestis; what euer thing thou hast of male kynde, thou schalt halewe to the Lord.

13 Thou schalt chaunge the firste gendrid of an asse for a scheep, that if thou ayen biest not, thou schalt sle; forsothe thou schalt ayen bie with prijs al the firste gendrid of man of thi sones.

14 And whanne thi sone schal axe thee to morewe, and seie, What is this? thou schalt answere to hym, In a strong hond the Lord ladde vs out of the lond of Egipt, of the hows of seruage; for whanne Farao was maad hard,

15 and nolde delyuere vs, the Lord killide alle the firste gendrid thing in the lond of Egipt, fro the firste gendrid of man til to the firste gendrid of beestis; therfor Y offre to the Lord al thing of male kynde that openeth the wombe, and Y ayen bie alle the firste gendrid thingis of my sones.

16 Therfor it schal be as a signe in thin hond, and as a thing hangid for mynde bifore thin iyen, for in a strong hond the Lord ledde vs out of Egipt.

17 Therfor whanne Farao hadde sent out the puple, God ledde not hem out bi the weie of 'the lond of Filisteis, which is niy; and arettid lest perauenture it wolde repente the puple, if he had seyn batelis rise ayens hym, and 'the puple wolde turn ayen in to Egipt;

18 but God ledde aboute by the weie of deseert, which weie is bisidis the reed see. And the sones of Israel weren armed, and stieden fro the lond of Egipte.

19 And Moises took the boonus of Joseph with hym, for he hadde chargid the sones of Israel, and hadde seid, God schal visite you, and bere ye out 'fro hennus my boonus with you.

20 And thei yeden forth fro Socoth, and settiden tentis in Etham, in the laste endis of wildirnesse.

21 Forsothe the Lord yede bifore hem to schewe the weie, bi dai in a piler of clowde, and bi nyyt in a piler of fier, that he schulde be ledere of the weie in euer either time;

22 the piler of clowde failide neuere bi dai, nether the piler of fier bi niyt, bifor the puple.

CAP 14

1 Forsothe the Lord spak to Moises, and seide, Speke thou to the sones of Israel;

2 turne thei ayen, and sette thei tentis euene ayens Fiayroth, which is bitwixe Magdalum and the see, ayens Beelsefon; in the siyt therof ye schulen sette tentis ouer the see.

3 And Farao schal seie on the sones of Israel, Thei ben maad streit in the lond, the deseert hath closid hem to gidere.

4 And Y schal make hard his herte, and he schal pursue you, and Y schal be glorified in Farao, and in al his oost; and Egipcians schulen wite that Y am the Lord; and thei diden so.

5 And it was teld to the kyng of Egipcians, that the puple hadde fled; and the herte of Farao and of hise seruauntis was chaungid on the puple, and thei seiden, What wolden we do, that we leften Israel, that it schulde not serue us?

6 Therfor Farao ioynede the chare, and took with him al his puple;

7 and he took sixe hundrid chosyn charis, and what euer thing of charis was in Egipt, and duykis of al the oost.

8 And the Lord made hard 'the herte of Farao, kyng of Egipt, and he pursuede the sones of Israel; and thei weren go out in an hiy hond.

9 And whanne Egipcians pursueden the steppis of the sones of Israel bifor goynge, thei founden hem in tentis on the see; al the chyualrye and charis of Farao, and al the oost weren in Fiayroth, ayens Beelsefon.

10 And whanne Farao hadde neiyed the sones of Israel, reisiden her iyen, and thei sien Egipcians bihynde hem, and dredden greetli; and thei crieden to the Lord,

11 and seiden to Moises, In hap sepulcris weren not in Egipt, therfor thou hast take vs awei, that we schulen die in wildirnesse? what woldist thou do this, that thou leddist vs out of Egipt?

12 Whether this is not the word which we spaken to thee in Egipt, 'and seiden, Go awei fro vs, that we serue Egipcians? for it is myche betere to serue hem, than to die in wildirnesse.

13 And Moises seide to the puple, Nyle ye drede, stonde ye, and 'se ye the grete werkys of God, whiche he schal do to dai; for ye schulen no more se Egipcians, whiche ye seen now, til in to with outen ende;

14 the Lord schal fiyte for you, and ye schulen be stille.

15 And the Lord seide to Moises, What criest thou to me? Speke thou to the sones of Israel, that thei go forth; forsothe reise thou thi yerde,

16 and stretche forth thin hond on the see, and departe thou it, that the sones of Israel go in the myddis of the see, by drie place.

17 Forsothe Y schal make hard the herte of Egipcians, that thei pursue you, and Y schal be glorified in Farao, and in al the oost of hym, and in the charis, and in the knyytis of hym;

18 and Egipcians schulen wite that Y am the Lord God, whanne Y schal be glorified in Farao, and in the charis, and in the knyytis of hym.

19 And the aungel of the Lord, that yede bifore the castellis of Israel, took hym silf, and yede bihynde hem; and the piler of cloude yede to gidir with hym, and lefte the formere thingis aftir the bak,

20 and stood bitwixe the 'castels of Egipcians and castels of Israel; and the cloude was derk toward Egipcians, and liytnynge 'the nyyt toward 'the children of Israel, so that in al the tyme of the niyt thei miyten not neiy togidere to hem silf.

21 And whanne Moises hadde stretchid forth the hond on the see, the Lord took it awei, the while a greet wynde and brennynge blew in al the niyt, and turnede in to dryenesse; and the watir was departid.

22 And the sones of Israel entriden by the myddis of the drye see; for the watir was as a wal at the riyt side and left side of hem.

23 And Egipcians pursueden, and entriden aftir hem, al the ridyng of Farao, hise charis, and knyytis, bi the myddis of the see.

24 And the wakyng of the morewtid cam thanne, and lo! the Lord bihelde on the castels of Egipcians, bi a piler of fier, and of cloude, and killide the oost of hem; and he destriede the wheelis of charis,

25 and tho weren borun in to the depthe. Therfor Egipcians seiden, Fle we Israel; for the Lord fiytith for hem ayenus vs.

26 And the Lord seide to Moises, Holde forth thin hond on the see, that the watris turne ayen to Egipcians, on the charis, and knyytis of hem.

27 And whanne Moises hadde hold forth the hoond ayens the see, it turnede ayen first in the morewtid to the formere place; and whanne Egipcians fledden, the watris camen ayen, and the Lord wlappide hem in the myddis of the floodis.

28 And the watris turneden ayen, and hiliden the charis, and knyytis of al the oost of Farao, which sueden, and entriden in to the see; sotheli not oon of hem was alyue.

29 Forsothe the sones of Israel yeden thorouy the myddis of the drye see, and the watris weren to hem as for a wal, on the riyt side and left side.

30 And in that dai the Lord delyuerede Israel fro the hond of Egipcians, and thei sien Egipcians deed on the brynke of the see,

31 and thei seiyen the greet hond which the Lord hadde vsid ayens hem; and the puple dredde the Lord, and thei bileueden to the Lord, and to Moises his seruaunt.

CAP 15

1 Thanne Moises song, and the sones of Israel, this song to the Lord; and thei seiden, Synge we to the Lord, for he is magnefied gloriousli; he castide doun the hors and the stiere in to the see.

2 My strengthe and my preisyng is the Lord; and he is maad to me in to heelthe. This is my God, and Y schal glorifie hym; the God of my fadir, and Y schal enhaunse hym.

3 The Lord is as a man fiyter, his name is Almiyti;

4 he castide doun in to the see the charis of Farao, and his oost. Hise chosun princis weren drenchid in the reed see;

5 the depe watris hiliden hem; thei yeden doun in to the depthe as a stoon.

6 Lord, thi riythond is magnyfied in strengthe; Lord, thi riythond smoot the enemye.

7 And in the mychilnesse of thi glorie thou hast put doun alle myn aduersaries; thou sentist thin ire, that deuouride hem as stobil.

8 And watris weren gaderid in the spirit of thi woodnesse; flowinge watir stood, depe watris weren gaderid in the middis of the see.

9 The enemy seide, Y schal pursue, and Y schal take; Y schal departe spuylis, my soule schal be fillid. I schal drawe out my swerde; myn hond schal sle hem.

10 Thi spirit blew, and the see hilide hem; thei weren drenchid as leed in grete watris.

11 Lord, who is lijk thee in stronge men, who is lijk thee? thou art greet doere in hoolynesse; ferdful, and preisable, and doynge myraclis.

12 Thou heldist forth thin hond, and the erthe deuouride hem;

13 thou were ledere in thi merci to thy puple, which thou ayen bouytist; and thou hast bore hym in thi strengthe to thin holi dwellyng place.

14 Puplis stieden, and weren wroothe; sorewis helden the dwelleris of Filistiym.

15 Thanne the pryncis of Edom weren disturblid; tremblyng held the stronge men of Moab.

16 Alle the dwelleris of Canaan 'weren starke; inward drede falle on hem, and outward drede in the greetnesse of thin arm. Be thei maad vnmouable as a stoon, til thi puple passe, Lord; til this thi puple passe, whom thou weldidist.

17 Thou schalt brynge hem in, and thou schalt plaunte in the hil of thin eritage; in the moost stidefast dwellyng place which thou hast wrouyt, Lord; Lord, thi seyntuarie, which thin hondis made stidefast.

18 The Lord schal 'regne in to the world and ferthere.

19 Forsothe Farao, 'a ridere, entride with his charis and knyytis in to the see, and the Lord brouyte the watris of the se on hem; sotheli the sones of Israel yeden bi the drie place, in the myddis of the see.

20 Therfore Marie, profetesse, the 'sistir of Aaron, took a tympan in hir hond, and alle the wymmen yeden out aftir hyr with tympans and cumpanyes;

21 to whiche sche song bifore, and seide, Synge we to the Lord, for he is magnyfied gloriousli; he castide doun in to the see the hors and the stiere of hym.

22 Forsothe Moises took Israel fro the reed see, and thei yeden out in to the deseert of Sur, and thei yeden thre daies bi the wildirnesse, and thei founden not watir.

23 And thei camen in to Marath, and thei miyten not drynk the watris of Marath, for tho weren bittere; wherfor and he puttide a couenable name to the place, and clepide it Mara, that is, bitternesse.

24 And the puple grutchide ayens Moises, and seide, What schulen we drynke?

25 And Moises criede to the Lord, which schewide to hym a tre; and whanne he hadde put that tre in to watris, tho weren turned in to swetnesse. There the Lord ordeynede comaundementis and domes to the puple, and there he asayede the puple,

26 and seide, If thou schalt here the vois of thi Lord God, and schalt do that that is riytful byfore hym, and schalt obeie to his comaundementis, and schalt kepe alle hise heestis, Y schal not brynge yn on thee al the syknesse, which Y puttide in Egipt, for Y am thi Lord Sauyour.

CAP 16

1 Forsothe the sones of Israel camen in to Helym, where weren twelue wellis of watris, and seuenti palm trees, and thei settiden tentis bisidis the watris. And thei yeden forth fro Helym, and al the multitude of the sones of Israel cam in to deseert of Syn, which is bitwixe Helym and Synai, in the fiftenethe dai of the secunde monethe aftir that thei yeden out of the lond of Egipt.

2 And al the congregacioun of the sones of Israel grutchide ayens Moises, and ayens Aaron, in the wildirnesse.

3 And the sones of Israel seiden to hem, We wolden that we hadden be deed bi the 'hoond of the Lord in the lond of Egipt, whanne we saten on the 'pottis of fleisch, and eeten looues in plentee; whi leden ye vs in to this deseert, that ye schulden sle al the multitude with hungur?

4 Forsothe the Lord seide to Moises, Lo! Y schal reyne to you looues fro heuene; the puple go out, that it gadere tho thingis that sufficen bi ech day; that Y asaie the puple, whethir it goith in my lawe, ether nai.

5 Sotheli in the sixte dai make thei redi that that thei schulen bere yn, and be it double ouer that thei weren wont to gadere bi ech dai.

6 And Moises and Aaron seiden to alle the sones of Israel, At euentid ye schulen wite that the Lord ledde you out of the lond of Egipt;

7 and in the morewetid ye schulen se the glorie of the Lord; for Y herde youre grutchyng ayens the Lord; sotheli what ben we, for ye grutchen ayens us?

8 And Moises seide, The Lord schal yyue to you at euentid fleischis to ete, and looues in the morewetid in plentee, for he herde youre grutchyngis, bi which ye grutchiden ayens hym; for whi, what ben we? youre grutchyng is not ayens vs but ayens the Lord.

9 And Moises seide to Aaron, Seie thou to al the congrega- cioun of the sones of Israel, Neiye ye bifore the Lord, for he herde youre grutchyng.

10 And whanne Aaron spak to al the cumpeny of the sones of Israel, thei bihelden to the wildirnesse, and lo! the glorie of the Lord apperide in a cloude.

11 Forsothe the Lord spak to Moises,

12 and seide, Y herde the grutchyngis of the sones of Israel; spek thou to hem, At euentid ye schulen ete fleischis, and in the morewtid ye schulen be fillid with looues, and ye schulen wite that Y am 'youre Lord God.

13 Therfor euentid was maad, and 'curlewes stieden and hiliden the castels; and in the morewtid deew cam bi the face of the castels.

14 And whanne it hadde hilid the erthe, a litil thing, and as powned with a pestel, in the licnesse of an hoorfrost on erthe, apperide in the wildirnesse.

15 And whanne the sones of Israel hadden seyn that, thei seiden to gidere, Man hu? which signyfieth, what is this? for thei wisten not what it was. To whiche Moises seide, This is the breed, which the Lord hath youe to you to ete.

16 This is the word which the Lord comaundide, Ech man gadere therof as myche as suffisith to be etun, gomor bi ech heed, bi the noumbre of youre soulis that dwellen in the taber- nacle, so ye schulen take.

17 And the sones of Israel diden so, and thei gaderiden oon more, another lesse;

18 and thei metiden at the mesure gomor; nethir he that gade- ride more had more, nethir he that made redi lesse fond lesse, but alle gaderiden bi that that thei myyten ete.

19 And Moises seide to hem, Noon leeue therof in to the morewtid; whiche herden not him,

20 but summe of hem leften til to the morewtid, and it bigan to buyle with wormes, and it was rotun; and Moises was wrooth ayens hem.

21 Forsothe alle gaderiden in the morewtid as myche as 'miyte suffice to be eten; and whanne the sunne was hoot, it was moltun.

22 Sotheli in the sixte dai thei gaderiden double metis, that is, 'twei gomor by ech man. Forsothe alle the princis of the mul- titude camen, and telden to Moises, which seide to hem,

23 This it is that the Lord spak, The reste of the sabot is hale- wid to the Lord, do ye what euer thing schal be wrouyt to morewe, and sethe ye tho thingis that schulen be sodun; sotheli what euer thing is residue, kepe ye til in to the morewe.

24 And thei diden so as Moises comaundide, and it was not rotun, nether a worm was foundun ther ynne.

25 And Moises seide, Ete ye that in this dai, for it is the sabat of the Lord, it schal not be foundun to dai in the feeld; gadere ye in sixe daies,

26 forsothe the sabat of the Lord is in the seuenthe dai, therfor it schal not be foundun.

27 The seuenthe dai cam, and summe of the puple yeden out 'to gadire, and thei founden not.

28 Forsothe the Lord seide to Moises, Hou long 'nylen ye kepe my comaundementis, and my lawe?

29 Se ye that the Lord yaf to you the sabat, and for this he yaf to you in the sixte dai double meetis; ech man dwelle at him silf, noon go out of his place in the seuenthe dai.

30 And the puple kepte sabat in the seuenthe dai.

31 And the hous of Israel clepide the name therof man, which was whijt as the seed of coriandre, and the taast therof was as of flour with hony.

32 Forsothe Moises seide, This is the word which the Lord comaundide, Fille thou a gomor therof, and be it kept in to generaciouns to comynge aftirward, that thei knowe the breed bi which Y fedde you in the wildirnesse, whanne ye weren led out of the lond of Egipt.

33 And Moises seide to Aaron, Take thou o vessel, and putte therinne man, as myche as gomor mai take, and putte bifore the Lord, to be kept in to youre generaciouns,

34 as the Lord comaundide to Moises; and Aaron puttide that to be kept in the tabernacle.

35 Forsothe the sones of Israel eeten manna in fourti yeer, til thei camen in to the lond abitable; thei weren fed with this mete til thei touchiden the endis of the lond of Canaan.

36 Forsothe gomor is the tenthe part of efy.

CAP 17

1 Therfor al the multitude of the sones of Israel yede forth fro the deseert of Syn, bi her dwellyngis, bi the word of the Lord, and settiden tentis in Rafidym, where was not watir to the puple to drynke.

2 Whiche puple chidde ayens Moises, and seide, Yyue thou water to vs, that we drynke. To whiche Moises answeride, What chiden ye ayens me, and whi tempten ye the Lord?

3 Therfor the puple thristide there for the scarsnesse of watir, and grutchiden ayens Moises, and seide, Whi madist thou vs to go out of Egipt, to sle vs, and oure fre children, and beestis, for thrist?

4 Forsothe Moises criede to the Lord, and seide, What schal Y do to this puple? yit a litil, also it schal stone me.

5 The Lord seide to Moises, Go thou bifore the puple, and take with thee of the eldre men of Israel, and take in thin hond the yerde, 'bi which thou hast smyte the flood, and go; lo!

6 Y schal stonde there before thee, aboue the stoon of Oreb, and thou schalt smyte the stoon, and water schal go out therof, that the puple drynke. Moises dide so byfore the eldre men of Israel;

7 and he clepide the name of that place Temptacioun, for the chidyng of the sones of Israel, and for thei temptiden the Lord, and seiden, Whether the Lord is in vs, ether nay?

8 Forsothe Amalech cam, and fauyt ayens Israel in Rafidym.

9 And Moises seide to Josue, Chese thou men, and go out, and fiyte to morewe ayens men of Amalech; lo! Y schal stonde in the cop of the hil, and Y schal haue 'the yerde of God in myn hond.

10 Josue dide as Moises spak, and fauyt ayens Amalech. Forsothe Moises, and Aaron, and Hur stieden on the cop of the hil;

11 and whanne Moises reiside the hondis, Israel ouercam; forsothe if he let down a litil, Amalech ouercam.

12 Sotheli 'the hondis of Moises weren heuy, therfor thei token a stoon, and puttide vndir hym, in which stoon he sat. Forsothe Aaron and Hur susteyneden hise hondis, on euer eithir side; and it was don, that hise hondis weren not maad weri, til to the goyng down of the sunne.

13 And Josue droof a wey Amalech and his puple, in 'the mouth of swerd, that is, bi the scharpnesse of the swerd.

14 Forsothe the Lord seide to Moises, Wryte thou this in a book, for mynde, and take in the eeris of Josue; for Y schal do a wei the mynde of Amalech fro vndur heuene.

15 And Moises bildide an auter, and clepide the name therof The Lord myn enhaunsere,

16 and seide, For the hond of the Lord aloone, and the bateil of God schal be ayens Amalech, fro generacioun in to generacioun.

CAP 18

1 And whanne Jetro, the prest of Madian, 'the alye of Moises, hadde herd alle thingis which God hadde do to Moises, and to Israel his puple, for the Lord hadde led Israel out of the lond of Egipt,

2 he took Sefora, 'the wijf of Moises, whom he hadde sent ayen,

3 and hise twei sones, of which oon was clepid Gersan, for the fadir seide, Y was a comelyng in alien lond,

4 forsothe the tother was clepid Eliezer, for Moises seide, God of my fadir is myn helpere, and he delyuerede me fro the swerd of Farao.

5 Therfor Jetro, 'alie of Moises, cam, and the sones of Moises and his wijf camen to Moises, in to deseert, where Jetro settide tentis bisidis the hil of God;

6 and sente to Moises, and seide, Y Jetro, thin alie, come to thee, and thi wijf, and thi twei sones with hir.

7 And Moises yede out into the comyng of his alie, and worschipide, and kiste hym, and thei gretten hem silf to gidere with pesible wordis.

8 And whanne he hadde entrid in to the tabernacle, Moises tolde to 'his alie alle thingis whiche God hadde do to Farao, and to Egipcians, for Israel, and he tolde al the trauel which bifelle to hem in the weie, of which the Lord delyuerede hem.

9 And Jetro was glad on alle the goodis whiche the Lord hadde do to Israel, for he delyuerede Israel fro the hond of Egipcians.

10 And Jetro seide, Blessid be 'the Lord, that delyuerede you fro the hond of Egipcians, and fro 'the hond of Farao, which Lord delyuered his puple fro the hond of Egipt;

11 now Y knowe that the Lord is greet aboue alle goddis, for 'thei diden proudli ayens hem.

12 Therfor Jetro, 'alie of Moises, offride brent sacrifices and offryngis to God; and Aaron, and alle the eldere men of Israel, camen to ete breed with hym bifore God.

13 Forsothe in the tother dai Moises sat that he schulde deme the puple, that stood niy Moises, fro the morewtid til to euentid.

14 And whanne 'his alie hadde seyn this, that is, alle thingis 'whiche he dide in the puple, he seide, What is this that thou doist in the puple? whi sittist thou aloone, and al the puple abidith fro the morewtid til to euentid?

15 To whom Moises answeride, The puple cometh to me, and axith the sentence of God;

16 and whanne ony strijf bifallith to hem, thei comen to me, that Y deme bitwixe hem, and schewe 'the comaundementis of God, and hise lawis.

17 And Jetro seide, Thou doist a thing not good,

18 thou art wastid with a fonned trauel, bothe thou and this puple which is with thee; the werk is a boue thi strengthis, thou aloone maist not suffre it.

19 But here thou my wordis and counseils, and the Lord schal be with thee; be thou to the puple in these thingis that perteynen to God, that thou telle the thingis that ben seid to the puple;

20 and schewe to the puple the cerymonyes, and custom of worschipyng, and the weie bi which 'thei owen to go, and the werk which 'thei owen to do.

21 Forsothe puruey thou of al the puple myyti men, and dredynge God, in whiche is treuthe, and whiche haten auarice; and ordeyne thou of hem tribunes, and centuriouns, and quinquagenaries, and deenys,

22 whiche schulen deme the puple in al tyme; sotheli what euer thing is grettere, telle thei to thee, and deme thei ooneli lesse thingis, and be it esiere to thee, whanne the burthun is departid in to othere men.

23 If thou schalt do this, thou schalt fille the comaundement of God, and thou schalt mowe bere hise comaundementis; and al this puple schal turne ayen with pees to her places.

24 And whanne these thingis weren herd, Moises dide alle thingis whiche Jetro counselide.

25 And whanne noble men of al Israel weren chosun Moises ordeynede hem princis of the puple, tribunes, and centuriouns, and quinquagenaries, and denes,

26 whiche demeden the puple in al tyme; forsothe, whateuer thing was hardere, thei telden to Moises, and thei demeden esiere thingis oneli.

27 And Moises lefte 'his alie, which turnede ayen, and yede in to his lond.

CAP 19

1 In the thridde monethe of the goyng 'of Israel out of the lond of Egipt, in this dai thei camen in to the wildirnesse of Synai;

2 for thei yeden forth fro Rafidym, and camen til in to deseert of Synai, and settiden tentis in the same place; and there Israel settide tentis, euen ayens the hil.

3 Forsothe Moises stiede in to the hil to God; and the Lord clepide hym fro the mount, and seide, Thou schalt seie these thingis to the hows of Jacob, and thou schalt telle to the sones of Israel,

4 Ye silf han seyn what thingis Y haue do to Egipcians, how Y bar you on the wengis of eglis, and took to me.

5 Therfor if ye schulen here my vois, and schulen kepe my couenaunt, ye schulen be to me in to a specialte of alle puplis; for al the lond is myn;

6 and ye schulen be to me in to a rewme of preesthod, and 'ye schulen be an hooli folk; these ben the wordis whiche thou schalt speke to the sones of Israel.

7 Moyses cam, and whanne the gretter men in birthe of the puple weren clepid to gidere, he expownede alle the wordis whiche the Lord comaundide.

8 And alle the puple answeride to gidere, We schulen do alle thingis whiche the Lord spak. And whanne Moises hadde teld the wordis of the puple to the Lord,

9 the Lord seide to hym, Riyt now Y schal come to thee in a derknesse of a cloude, that the puple here me spekynge to thee, and bileue to thee withouten ende. Therfor Moises telde the wordis of the puple to the Lord,

10 which seide to Moises, Go thou to the puple, and make hem holi to dai and to morewe, and waische thei her clothis,

11 and be thei redi in to the thridde dai; for in the thridde dai the Lord schal come doun bifore al the puple on the hil of Synai.

12 And thou schalt sette termes to the puple, bi cumpas; and thou schalt seie to hem, Be ye war, that ye 'stie not in to the hil, nether touche ye the endis therof; ech man that schal touche the hil, schal die bi deeth.

13 Hondis schulen not touche hym, but he schal be oppressid with stoonus, ethir he shall be persid with dartis; whether it schal be a beest, ethir a man, it schal not lyue; whanne a clarioun schal bigynne to sowne, thanne 'stie thei in to the hil.

14 And Moises cam doun fro the hil to the puple, and halewide it; and whanne thei hadden waischun her clothis,

15 he seide to hem, Be ye redi in to the thridde dai, neiye ye not to youre wyues.

16 And now the thridde day was comun, and the morewetid was cleer; and, lo! thundris bigunnen to be herd, and leitis to schyne, and a moost thicke cloude to hile the mounteyn; and 'the sownyng of a clarioun made noise ful greetli, and the puple dredde, that was in the castels.

17 And whanne Moises hadde led hem out in to the comyng of God, fro the place of castels, thei stoden at the rootis of the hil.

18 Forsothe al the hil of Synai smokide, for the Lord hadde come doun theronne in fier; and smoke stiede therof as of a furneis, and al the hil was ferdful;

19 and the 'sown of a clarioun encreesside litil and litil, and was holdun forth lengere. Moises spak, and the Lord answeride to hym,

20 and the Lord cam doun on the hil of Synay, in thilke cop of the hil, and clepide Moises to the cop therof. And whanne he hadde stied thidur,

21 the Lord seide to hym, Go thou doun, and witnesse thou to the puple, lest perauenture it wole passe the termes to se the Lord, and ful greet multitude therof perische;

22 also preestis, that neiyen to the Lord, be halewid, lest Y smyte hem.

23 And Moises seide to the Lord, The comyn puple may not stie in to the hil of Synai; for thou hast witnessid, and hast comaundid, seiyinge, Sette thou termes aboute the hil, and halewe it.

24 To whom the Lord seide, Go thou doun, and thou schalt stie, and Aaron with thee; forsothe the preestis and the puple passe not the termes, nethir stie thei to the Lord, lest perauenture he sle hem.

25 Moises yede doun to the puple, and telde alle thingis to hem.

CAP 20

1 And the Lord spak alle these wordis, Y am thi Lord God,

2 that ladde thee out of the lond of Egipt, fro the hous of seruage.

3 Thou schalt not haue alien goddis bifore me.

4 Thou schalt not make to thee a grauun ymage, nethir ony licnesse of thing which is in heuene aboue, and which is in erthe bynethe, nether of tho thingis, that ben in watris vndur erthe; thou schalt not 'herie tho,

5 nether 'thou schalt worschipe; for Y am thi Lord God, a stronge gelouse louyere; and Y visite the wickidnesse of fadris in to the thridde and the fourthe generacioun of hem that haten me,

6 and Y do mercy in to 'a thousynde, to hem that louen me, and kepen myn heestis.

7 Thou schalt not take in veyn the name of thi Lord God, for the Lord schal not haue hym giltles, that takith in veyn the name of his Lord God.

8 Haue thou mynde, that thou halowe the 'dai of the sabat;

9 in sixe daies thou schalt worche and schalt do alle thi werkis;

10 forsothe in the seuenthe day is the sabat of thi Lord God; thou schalt not do ony werk, thou, and thi sone, and thi douytir, and thi seruaunt, and thin handmaide, thi werk beeste, and the comelyng which is withynne thi yatis;

11 for in sixe dayes God made heuene and erthe, the see, and alle thingis that ben in tho, and restide in the seuenthe dai; herfor the Lord blesside the 'dai of the sabat, and halewide it.

12 Onoure thi fadir and thi moder, that thou be long lyuyng on the lond, which thi Lord God schal yyue to thee.

13 Thou schalt not sle.

14 Thou schalt 'do no letcherie.

15 Thou schalt 'do no theft.

16 Thou schalt not speke fals witnessyng ayens thi neiybore.

17 Thou schalt not coueyte 'the hous of thi neiybore, nether thou schalt desyre his wijf, not seruaunt, not handmaide, not oxe, not asse, nether alle thingis that ben hise.

18 Forsothe al the puple herde voices, and siy laumpis, and the sowne of a clarioun, and the hil smokynge; and thei weren afeerd, and schakun with inward drede, and stoden afer,

19 and seiden to Moises, Speke thou to vs, and we schulen here; the Lord speke not to vs, lest perauenture we dien.

20 And Moises seide to the puple, Nyle ye drede, for God cam to proue you, and that his drede schulde be in you, and that ye schulden not do synne.

21 And the puple stood afer; forsothe Moises neiyede to the derknesse, wherynne God was.

22 And the Lord seide ferthermore to Moises, Thou schalt seie these thingis to the sones of Israel, Ye seiyen that fro heuene Y spak to you;

23 ye schulen not make goddis of silver, nethir ye schulen make to you goddis of gold.

24 Ye schulen make an auter of erthe to me, and ye schulen offre theronne youre brent sacrifices, and pesible sacrifices, youre scheep, and oxun, in ech place in which the mynde of my name schal be; Y schal come to thee, and Y schal blesse thee.

25 That if thou schalt make an auter of stoon to me, thou schalt not bilde it of stoonys hewun; for if thou schalt reise thi knyf theronne, it schal be 'pollutid, ether defoulid.

26 Thou schalt not stye bi grees to myn auter, lest thi filthe be schewid.

CAP 21

1 These ben the domes, whiche thou schalt sette forth to hem.

2 If thou biest an Ebrew seruaunt, he schal serue thee sixe yeer; in the seuenthe yeer he schal go out fre,

3 with out prijs; with what maner clooth he entride, with siche clooth go he out; if he entride hauynge a wijf, and the wijf schal go out to gidere.

4 But if the lord of the servaunt yaf a wijf to hym, and sche childide sones and douytris, the womman and hir children schulen be hir lordis; sotheli the seruaunt schal go out with his owne clooth.

5 That if the seruaunt seith, Y loue my lord, and wijf, and children, Y schal not go out fre;

6 the lord brynge hym to goddis, that is, iugis; and he schal be set to the dore, and postis; and the lord schal perse his eere with a nal, and he schal be seruaunt to hym til in to the world.

7 If ony man sillith his douyter in to seruauntesse, sche schal not go out as handmaidis weren wont to go out;

8 if sche displesith in the iyen of hir lord, to whom sche was bitakun, he schal delyuere hir; sotheli he schal not haue power to sille hir to an alien puple, if he forsakith hir.

9 Forsothe if he weddith hir to his sonne, he schal do to hir 'bi the custom of douytris;

10 that if he takith another womman to hym, he schal puruey to the damysele weddingis, and clothis, and he schal not denye the prijs of chastite.

11 If he doith not these thre, sche schal go out freli without money.

12 He that smytith a man, and wole sle, die bi deeth;

13 forsothe if a man settide not aspies, but God 'bitook hym in to hise hondis, Y schal ordeyne a place to thee, whidur he owith to fle.

14 If ony man sleeth his neiybore bi biforecastyng, and bi aspies, drawe thou hym awey fro myn auter, that he die.

15 He that smytith his fadir, ether modir, die by deeth.

16 He that cursith his fadir, ether modir, die bi deeth.

17 He that stelith a man, and sillith hym, if he is conuyt of the gilt, die bi deeth.

18 If men chiden, and the tother smyte his neiybore with a stoon, ether with the fist, and he is not deed, but liggith in the bed,

19 if he risith, and goith forth on his staf, he that smoot schal be innocent; so netheles that he restore hise trauelis, and costis in lechis.

20 He that smytith his seruaunt, ether handmayde, with a yerde, and thei ben deed in hise hondis, schal be gilti of cryme.

21 Sotheli if the seruaunt ouerlyueth o dai, ether tweyne, he schal not be suget to peyne, 'that is of deeth, for the seruaunt is his catel.

22 If men chiden, and a man smytith a womman with childe, and sotheli makith the child deed borun, but the womman ouerlyueth, he schal be suget to the harm, as myche as the 'hosebonde of the womman axith, and the iugis demen.

23 But if the deeth of hir sueth,

24 he schal yelde lijf for lijf, iye for iye, tooth for tooth, hond for hond, foot for foot,

25 brennyng for brennyng, wounde 'with schedyng of blood for wounde 'with schedyng of blood, 'a wan wounde for a wan wounde.

26 If a man smytith the iye of his seruaunt, ethir of handmaide, and makith hem oon iyed, he schal delyuere hem fre for 'the iye which he puttide out.

27 Also if he smytith out a tooth fro his seruaunt, ethir handmaide, in lijk maner he schal delyuere hem fre.

28 If an oxe smytith with horn a man, ether a womman, and thei ben deed, the oxe schal be oppressid with stoonus, and hise fleischis schulen not be etun, and the lord of the oxe schal be innocent.

29 That if the oxe was 'a pultere with horn fro yisterdai and the thridde dai ago, and men warneden 'the lord of hym, nether the lord closide hym, and he sleeth a man, ethir womman, bothe the oxe schal be oppressid with stoonus, and thei schulen sle 'the lord of hym;

30 that if prijs is put to the lord, he schal yyue for his lijf what euer he is axide.

31 And if he smytith with horn a son, and a douytir, he schal be suget to lijk sentence.

32 If the oxe asailith a seruaunt, and handmaide, the lord of the oxe schal yyue thretti siclis of siluer to 'his lord; forsothe the oxe schal be oppressid with stoonus.

33 If ony man openeth a cisterne, and diggith, and hilith it not, and an oxe ether asse fallith in to it,

34 the lord of the cisterne schal yelde the prijs of the werk beestis; forsothe that that is deed schal be his.

35 If another mannus oxe woundith the oxe of another man, and he is deed, thei schulen sille the quyke oxe, and thei schulen departe the prijs; forsothe thei schulen departe bitwixe hem the karkeis of the deed oxe.

36 Forsothe if his lord wiste, that the oxe was a puttere fro yistirdai and the thridde dai ago, and kepte not him, he schal yelde oxe for oxe, and he schal take the hool carkeys.

CAP 22

1 If ony man stelith a scheep, ether oxe, and sleeth, ether sillith, he schal restore fiue oxen for oon oxe, and foure scheep for o scheep.

2 And if a nyyt theef brekynge an hows, ether vndurmynynge, is foundun, and is deed bi a wounde takun, the smytere schal not be gilti of blood;

3 that if he dide this whanne the sunne was rysun, he dide man sleyng, and he schal die. If a theef hath not that, that he schal yelde for thefte, he schal be seeld;

4 if that thing that he staal, is foundun quyk at hym, ether oxe, ether asse, ether scheep, he schal restore the double.

5 If a man harmeth a feeld, ethir vyner, and suffrith his beeste, that it waaste othere mennus thingis, he schal restore for the valu of harm, 'what euer beste thing he hath in his feeld, ethir vyner.

6 If fier goith out, and fyndith eeris of corn, and catchith heepis of corn, ethir cornes stondynge in feeldis, he that kyndlide the fier schal yeelde the harm.

7 If a man bitakith in to kepyng monei to a freend, ether a vessel 'in to keping, and it is takun awey bi thefte fro hym that resseyuede, if the theef is foundun, he schal restore double.

8 If the theef is hid, the lord of the hows schal be brouyt to goddis, 'that is, iugis, and he schal swere, that he helde not forth the hond in to 'the thing of his neiybore,

9 to 'do fraude; as wel in oxe, as in asse, and in scheep, and in clooth; and what euer thing may brynge in harm, the cause of euer eithir schal come to goddis, and if thei demen, he schal restore the double to his neiybore.

10 If ony man bitakith to his neiybore oxe, asse, scheep, and al werk beeste to kepyng, and it is deed, ether is maad feble, ethir is takun of enemyes, and no man seeth this,

11 an ooth schal be in the myddis, that he helde not forth the hond to the 'thing of his neiybore; and the lord schal resseyue the ooth, and he schal not be compellid to yelde.

12 That if it is takun awei bi thefte, he schal restore the harm to the lord;

13 if it is etun of a beeste, he schal brynge to the lord that that is slayn, and he schal not restore.

14 He that axith of his neiybore ony thing of these bi borewyng, and it is feblid, ether deed, while the lord is not present, he schal be constreyned to yelde; that if the lord is in presence,

15 he schal not restore, moost if it cam hirid, for the meede of his werk.

16 If a man disseyueth a virgyn not yit weddid, and slepith with hir, he schal yyue dower to hir, and schal haue hir wijf.

17 If the fadir of the virgyn nyle yyue, he schal yelde money, bi the maner of dower, which virgyns weren wont to take.

18 Thou schalt not suffre witchis to lyue.

19 He that doith letcherie with a beeste, die by deeth.

20 He that offrith to goddis, out takun to the Lord aloone, be he slayn.

21 Thou schalt not make sory a comelyng, nether thou schalt turmente hym; for also ye weren comelyngis in the lond of Egipt.

22 Ye schulen not anoye a widewe, and a fadirles ethir modirles child.

23 If ye hirten hem, thei schulen crye to me, and Y schal here the cry of hem,

24 and my greet veniaunce schal haue indignacioun, and Y schal smyte you with swerd, and youre wyues schulen be widewis, and youre sones schulen be fadirles.

25 If thou yyuest money to loone to my pore puple, that dwellith with thee, thou schalt not constreyne hym, as an extorsioner doith, nether thou schalt oppresse hym by vsuris.

26 If thou takist of thi neiybore 'a wed a clooth, thou schalt yelde to hym bifore the goyng doun of the sunne;

27 for that aloone is the cloothing of his fleisch, with which he is hilid, nether he hath another, in which he slepith; if he crieth to me, Y schal here hym; for Y am mercyful.

28 Thou schalt not bacbyte goddis, and thou schalt not curse the prince of thi puple.

29 Thou schalt not tarye to offre to the Lord thi tithis, and firste fruytis. Thou schalt yyue to me the firste gendrid of thi sones;

30 also of oxen, and of scheep thou schalt do in lijk maner; seuene daies be he with his modir, in the eiytithe dai thou schalt yelde hym to me.

31 Ye schulen be holi men to me; ye schulen not ete fleisch which is bifore taastid of beestis, but ye schulen caste forth to houndis.

CAP 23

1 Thou schalt not resseyue a vois of leesyng, nether thou schalt ioyne thin hond, that thou seie fals witnessyng for a wickid man.

2 Thou schalt not sue the cumpanye to do yuel, nether thou schalt ascente to the sentence of ful many men in doom, that thou go awey fro treuthe.

3 Also thou schalt not haue mercy of a pore man in a 'cause, ethir doom.

4 If thou meetist 'the oxe of thin enemye, ethir the asse errynge, lede thou ayen to hym.

5 If thou seest that the asse of hym that hatith thee liggyth vndir a burthun, thou schalt not passe, but thou schalt reise with hym.

6 Thou schalt not bowe in the doom of a pore man.

7 Thou schalt fle a lesyng. Thou schalt not sle an innocent man, and iust; for Y am aduersarie to a wickid man.

8 Take thou not yiftis, that blynden also prudent men, and destryen the wordys of iust men.

9 Thou schalt not be diseseful to a pilgrym, for ye knowen the soulis of comelyngis, for also ye weren pilgryms in the lond of Egipt.

10 Sixe yeer thou schalt sowe thi lond, and thou schalt gadre fruytis therof;

11 forsothe in the seuenthe yeer thou schalt leeue it, and schalt make to reste, that the pore men of thi puple ete, and what euer is residue, the beestis of the feeld ete; so thou schalt do in thi vyner, and in place of olyue trees.

12 Sixe daies thou schalt worche, in the seuenthe dai thou schalt ceesse, that thin oxe and asse reste, and the sone of thin handmaide, and the comelyng be refreischid.

13 Kepe ye alle thingis, whiche Y seide to you; and ye schulen not swere bi the name of alien goddis, nether it schal be herd of youre mouth.

14 In thre tymes bi alle yeeris ye schulen halewe feestis to me.

15 Thou schalt kepe the solempnyte of therf looues; seuene daies thou schalt ete therf breed, as Y comaundide to thee, in the tyme of monethe of newe thingis, whanne thou yedist out of Egipt; thou schalt not appere voide in my siyt.

16 And thou schalt kepe the solempnete of the monethe of the firste thingis of thi werk, what euer thingis thou hast sowe in the feeld. Also thou schalt kepe the solempnyte in the goyng out of the yeer, whanne thou hast gaderid all thi fruytis of the feeld.

17 Thries in the yeer al thi male kynde schal appere bifore thi Lord God.

18 Thou schalt not offre the blood of thi slayn sacrifice on sour douy; nether the fatnesse of my solempnete schal dwelle til to the morewtid.

19 Thou schalt bere the firste thingis of the fruytis of thi lond in to the hows of thi Lord God. Thou schalt not sethe a kide in the mylke of his modir.

20 Lo! Y schal sende myn aungel, that schal go bifore thee, and schal kepe in the weie, and schal lede to the place which Y haue maad redi to thee.

21 Take thou hede to hym, and here thou his vois, nether gesse thou hym to be dispisid; for he schal not foryyue, whanne thou synnest, and my name is in him.

22 For if thou herest his vois, and doist alle thingis whiche Y speke, Y schal be enemy to thin enemyes, and Y schal turment hem, that turmenten thee;

23 and myn aungel schal go bifore thee, and he schal lede yn thee to Amorrei, and Ethei, and Ferezei, and Cananey, and Euey, and Jebusei, whiche Y schal breke.

24 Thou schalt not onoure 'the goddis of hem, nether thou schalt worschipe hem; thou schalt not do the werkis of hem, but thou schalt destrie the goddis, and thou schalt breke the ymagis of hem.

25 And ye schulen serue to youre Lord God, that Y blesse thi looues, and watris, and do awei sikenesse fro the myddis of thee;

26 neithir a womman vnfruytful, neither bareyn, schal be in thi lond; Y schal fille the noumbre of thi daies.

27 Y schal sende my drede in to thi biforgoyng, and Y schal sle al the puple, to which thou schalt entre, and Y schal turne the backis of alle thin enemyes bifore thee;

28 and Y schal sende out bifore scrabrouns, that schulen dryue awei Euey, and Cananey, and Ethei, bifore that thou entre.

29 Y schal not caste hem out fro thi face in o yeer, lest the lond be turned in to wildirnesse, and beestis encreesse ayens thee;

30 litil and litil I schal caste hem out fro thi siyt, til thou be encreessid, and welde the loond.

31 Forsothe Y schal sette thi termys fro the reed see til to the see of Palestyns, and fro desert til to the flood. Y schal yyue to youre hondis the dwelleris of the lond, and Y schal caste hem out fro youre siyt;

32 thou schalt not make boond of pees with hem, nethir with 'the goddis of hem.

33 Dwelle thei not in thi lond, lest perauenture thei make thee to do synne ayens me, yf thou seruest her goddis, which thing certis schal be to thee in to sclaundir.

CAP 24

1 Also he seide to Moises, 'Stie thou to the Lord, thou, and Aaron, and Nadab, and Abyu, and seuenti eldere men of Israel; and ye schulen worschipe afer,

2 and Moises aloone stie to the Lord, and thei schulen not neiye, nether the puple schal stie with hym.

3 Therfore Moises cam, and telde to the puple alle the wordis and domes of the Lord; and al the puple answeride with o vois, We schulen do alle the wordis of the Lord, whiche he spak.

4 Forsothe Moises wroot alle the wordis of the Lord; and he roos eerli, and bildide an auter to the Lord at the rootis of the hil, and he bildide twelue titlis bi twelue lynagis of Israel.

5 And he sente yonge men of the sones of Israel, and thei offriden brent sacrifices, and 'thei offriden pesible sacrifices 'to the Lord, twelue calues.

6 And so Moises took half the part of the blood, and sente in to grete cuppis; forsothe he schedde the residue part on the auter.

7 And he took the book of the boond of pees, and redde, while the puple herde; whiche seiden, We schulen do alle thingis which the Lord spak, and we schulen be obedient.

8 Forsothe he took, and sprengide 'the blood on the puple, and seide, This is the blood of the boond of pees, which the Lord couenauntide with yow on alle these wordis.

9 And Moises, and Aaron, and Nadab, and Abyu, and seuenti of the eldere men of Israel stieden,

10 and seiyen God of Israel, vndur hise feet, as the werk of safire stoon, and as heuene whanne it is cleer.

11 And he sente not his hond on hem of the sones of Israel, that hadden go fer awei; and thei sien God, and eeten and drunkun.

12 Forsothe the Lord seide to Moises, 'Stie thou to me in to the hil, and be thou there, and Y schal yyue to thee tablis of stoon, and the lawe, and comaundementis, whiche Y haue write, that thou teche the children of Israel.

13 Moises and Josue his mynystre risen, and Moises stiede in to the hil of God,

14 and seide to the eldere men, Abide ye here, til we turnen ayen to you; ye han Aaron and Hur with you, if ony thing of questioun is maad, ye schulen telle to hem.

15 And whanne Moises hadde stied,

16 a cloude hilide the hil, and the glorie of the Lord dwellide on Synai, and kyueride it with a cloude sixe daies; forsothe in the seuenthe dai the Lord clepide hym fro the myddis of the cloude; forsothe the licnesse of glorie of the Lord

17 was as fier brennynge on the cop of the hil in the siyt of the sones of Israel.

18 And Moises entride into the myddis of the cloude, and stiede in to the hil, and he was there fourti daies and fourti nyytis.

CAP 25

1 And the Lord spak to Moises, and seide, Speke thou to the sones of Israel,

2 that thei take to me the firste fruytis; of ech man that offrith wilfuli, ye schulen take tho.

3 Forsothe these thingis it ben, whiche ye schulen take, gold, and siluer, and bras, iacynt,

4 and purpur, and reed silk twies died, and bijs, heeris of geet, and 'skynnes of wetheris maad reed,

5 and skynnes of iacynt,

6 and trees of Sechym, and oile to liytis to be ordeyned, swete smellynge spiceries in to oynement, and encensis of good odour,

7 onochym stoonys, and gemmes to ourne ephod, and the racional.

8 And thei schulen make a seyntuarie to me, and Y schal dwelle in the myddis of hem, bi al the licnesse of the tabernacle,

9 which Y schal schewe to thee, and of alle the vessels of ournyng therof.

10 And thus ye schulen make it; ioyne ye to gidere an arke of the trees of Sechym, whos lengthe haue twey cubitis and an half, the broodnesse haue a cubit and half, the hiynesse haue 'in lijk maner a cubit and half.

11 And thou schalt ouergilde it with clenneste gold with ynne and with out forth; and thou schalt make a goldun crowne aboue 'bi cumpas,

12 and foure goldun cerclis, whiche thou schalt sette bi foure corneris of the arke; twei ceerclis be in o syde, and twei cerclis in the tother side.

13 Also thou schalt make barris of the trees of Sechym, and thou schalt hile tho with gold,

14 and thou schalt brynge yn bi the cerclis that ben in the sidis of the arke,

15 that it be borun in tho, whiche schulen euere be in the ceerclis, nether schulen ony tyme be drawun out of thoo.

16 And thou schalt putte in to the arke the witnessing, which Y schal yyue to thee.

17 And thou schalt make a propiciatorie of clenneste gold; 'that is a table hilinge the arke; the lengthe therof schal holde twei cubitis and an half, the broodnesse schal holde a cubit and half.

18 Also thou schalt make on euer eithir side of 'Goddis answeryng place twei cherubyns of gold, and betun out with hamer;

19 o cherub be in o syde of 'Goddis answeryng place, and the tother in the tother side;

20 hele thei euer either side of the propiciatorie, and holde thei forth wyngis, and hile thei 'Goddis answeryng place; and

biholde thei hem silf to gidere, while the faces ben turned in to the propiciatorie, with which the arke of the Lord schal be hilid,

21 in which arke thou schalt putte the 'witnessyng, which Y schal yyue to thee.

22 Fro thennus Y schal comaunde, and schal speke to thee aboue the propiciatorie, that is, fro the myddis of twei cherubyns, that schulen be on the arke of witnessyng, alle thingis whiche Y schal comaunde 'bi thee to the sones of Israel.

23 Also thou schalt make a boord of the trees of Sechym, hauinge twei cubitis of lengthe, and a cubit in broodnesse, and a cubit and half in hiyenesse.

24 And thou schalt ouergilde the bord with purest gold, and thou schalt make to it a goldun brynke 'bi cumpas;

25 and 'thou schalt make to that brynke a coroun rasid bit-wixe foure fyngris hiy, and 'thou schalt make on that another lytil goldun coroun.

26 And thou schalt make redi foure goldun cerclis, and thou schalt put thoo in foure corners of the same boord, bi alle feet.

27 Vndur the coroun schulen be goldun cerclis, that the barris be put thorou tho, and that the boord may be borun.

28 Thou schalt make tho barris of the trees of Sechym, and thou schalt cumpas with gold to bere the boord.

29 And thou schalt make redi vessels of vynegre, and viols, cenceris, and cuppis of pureste gold, in whiche fletynge sacri-fices schulen be offrid.

30 And thou schalt sette on the boord looues of proposicioun, in my siyt euere.

31 And thou schalt make a candilstike 'betun forth with hamer, of clenneste gold, and thou schalt make the schaft therof, and yerdis, cuppis, and litle rundelis, and lilies comy-nge forth therof.

32 Sixe yerdis schulen go out of the sidis, thre of o side, and thre of the tother.

33 Thre cuppis as in the maner of a note bi ech yerde, and litle rundelis to gidere, and a lilie, and in lijk maner thre cuppis at the licnesse of a note in the tother, and litle rundelis togidere, and a lilie; this schal be the werk of sixe yerdis, that schulen be brouyt forth of the schaft.

34 Forsothe in thilke candilstik e schulen be foure cuppis in the maner of a note, and litle rundels and lilies by ech cuppe;

35 and litle rundelis schulen be vndir twey yerdis bi thre places, whiche yerdis to gidere ben maad sixe, comynge forth of o schaft; and therfor the litle rundelis and yerdis

36 therof schulen be alle betun out with hamer, of clenneste gold.

37 And thou schalt make seuene lanternes, and thou schalt sette tho on the candilstike, that tho schyne euene ayens.

38 Also tongis to 'do out the snottis, and where tho thingis, that ben snottid out, ben quenchid, be maad of clenneste gold.

39 Al the weiyt of the candilstike with alle hise vesselis schal haue a talent of clennest gold.

40 Biholde thou, and make bi the saumpler, which ys sche-wide to thee in the hil.

CAP 26

1 Forsothe the tabernacle schal be maad thus; thou schalt make ten curtyns of bijs foldyd ayen, and of iacynt, of purpur, and of reed silk twies died, dyuersid bi broidery werk.

2 The lengthe of o curteyn schal haue eiyte and twenti cubitis, the broodnesse schal be of foure cubitis; alle tentis schulen be maad of o mesure.

3 Fyue curtyns schulen be ioyned to hem silf to gidere, and othere fiue cleue to gidere bi lijk boond.

4 Thou schalt make handels of iacynt in the sidis, and hiynes-sis of curtyns, that tho moun be couplid to gidere.

5 A curteyn schal haue fyfti handlis in euer eithir part, so set yn, that 'an handle come ayen an handle, and the toon may be schappid to the tothir.

6 And thou schalt make fifti goldun ryngis, bi whiche the 'veilis of curteyns schulen be ioyned, that o tabernacle be maad.

7 Also thou schalt make enleuene saies to kyuere the hilyng of the tabernacle;

8 the lengthe of o say schal haue thretti cubitis, and the breed schal haue foure cubitis; euene mesure schal be of alle saies.

9 Of which thou schalt ioyne fyue by hem silf, and thou schalt couple sixe to hem silf togidere, so that thou double the sixte say in the frount of the roof.

10 And thou schalt make fifti handles in the hemme of o say, that it may be ioyned with the tother; and 'thou schalt make fifti handles in the hemme of the tothir say, that it be couplid with the tothir;

11 thou schalt make fifti fastnyngis of bras, bi whiche the handles schulen be ioyned to gidere, that oon hylyng be maad of alle.

12 Sotheli that that is residue in the saies, that ben maad redi to the hilyng, that is, o sai whych is more, of the myddis therof thou schalt hile the hyndrere part of the tabernacle; and a cubit schal hange on o part,

13 and the tother cubit on the tother part, which cubit is more in the lengthe of saies, and schal hile euer either syde of the tabernacle.

14 And thou schalt make another hilyng to the roof, of 'skynnes of wetheres maad reed, and ouer this thou schalt make eft anothir hilyng of 'skynnes of iacynt.

15 Also thou schalt make stondynge tablis of the tabernacle, of the trees of Sechym,

16 whiche tablis schulen haue ech bi hem silf ten cubitis in lengthe, and in brede a cubit and half.

17 Forsothe twei dentyngis schulen be in the sidis of a table, bi which a table schal be ioyned to another table; and in this maner alle the tablis schulen be maad redi.

18 Of whiche tablis twenti schulen be in the myddai side, that goith to the south;

19 to whiche tablis thou schalt yete fourti silueren founde-mentis, that twei foundementis be set vndir ech table, bi twei corneris.

20 In the secounde side of the tabernacle, that goith to the north, schulen be twenti tablis, hauynge fourti silueren foun-dementis; twei foundementis schulen be set vndir ech table.

21 Sotheli at the west coost of the tabernacle thou schalt make sixe tablis;

22 and eft thou schalt make tweine othere tablis,

23 that schulen be reisid in the corneris 'bihynde the bak of the taberancle;

24 and the tablis schulen be ioyned to hem silf fro bynethe til to aboue, and o ioynyng schal withholde alle the tablis. And lijk ioynyng schal be kept to the twei tablis, that schulen be set in the corneris,

25 and tho schulen be eiyte tablis to gidere; the siluerne foun-dementis of tho schulen be sixtene, while twei foundementis ben rikenyd bi o table.

26 Thou schalt make also fyue barris of 'trees of Sechym, to holde togidere the tablis in o side of the tabernacle,

27 and fyue othere barris in the tother side, and of the same noumbre at the west coost;

28 whiche barris schulen be put thorou the myddil tablis fro the toon ende til to the tothir.

29 And thou schalt ouergilde tho tablis, and thou schalt yete goldun ryngis in tho, bi whiche ryngis, the barris schulen holde togidere the werk of tablis, whyche barris thou schalt hile with goldun platis.

30 And thou schalt reise the tabernacle, bi the saumpler that was schewid to thee in the hil.

31 Thou schalt make also a veil of iacynt, and purpur, and of reed silk twies died, and of bijs foldid ayen bi broideri werk, and wouun to gidere bi fair dyuersite;

32 which veil thou schalt hange bifor foure pileris of 'the trees of Sechym; and sotheli tho pileris schulen be ouergildid; and tho schulen haue goldun heedis, but foundementis of siluer.

33 Forsothe the veil schal be set in bi the cerclis, with ynne which veil thou schalt sette the arke of witnessyng, wherbi the seyntuarye and the seyntuaries of seyntuarie schulen be departid.

34 And thou schalt sette the propiciatorie on the arke of witnessyng, in to the hooli of hooli thingis;

35 and thou schalt sette a boord with out the veil, and ayens the boord 'thou schalt sette the candilstike in the south side of the tabernacle; for the bord schal stonde in the north side.

36 Thou schalt make also a tente in the entryng of the tabernacle, of iacynt, and purpur, and of reed selk twies died, and of bijs foldid ayen bi broidery werk.

37 And thou schalt ouergilde fyue pileris of 'trees of Sechym, bifor whiche pileris the tente schal be led, of whiche pileris the heedis schulen be of gold, and the foundementis of bras.

CAP 27

1 Also thou schalt make an auter of the trees of Sechym, which schal haue fyue cubitis in lengthe, and so many in brede, that is, sqware, and thre cubitis in heiythe.

2 Forsothe hornes schulen be bi foure corneris therof; and thou schalt hile it with bras.

3 And thou schalt make in to the vsis of the auter pannes, to resseyue aischis, and tongis, and fleisch hookis, and resettis of fyris; thou schalt make alle vessilis of bras.

4 And thou schalt make a brasun gridele in the maner of a net, and bi four corneris therof schulen be foure brasun ryngis,

5 whiche thou schalt putte vndur the yrun panne of the auter; and the gridele schal be til to the myddis of the auter.

6 And thou schalt make twey barris of the auter, of the trees of Sechym, whiche barris thou schalt hile with platis of bras;

7 and thou schalt lede yn 'the barris bi the cerclis, and tho schulen be on euer eithir side of the auter, to bere.

8 Thou schalt make that auter not massif, but voide, and holowe with ynne, as it was schewid to thee in the hil.

9 Also thou schalt make a large street of the tabernacle, 'in the maner of a chirche yeerd, in whos mydday coost ayens the south schulen be tentis of bijs foldid ayen; o side schal holde an hundrid cubitis in lengthe,

10 and twenti pileris, with so many brasun foundementis, whiche pileris schulen haue silueren heedis with her grauyngis.

11 In lijk maner in the north side, bi the lengthe, schulen be tentis of an hundrid cubitis, twenti pileris, and brasun foundementis of the same noumbre; and the heedis of tho pileris with her grauyngis schulen be of siluer.

12 Forsothe in the breede of the large street, that biholdith to the west, schulen be tentis bi fifti cubitis, and ten pileris schulen be, and so many foundementis.

13 In that breede of the large street, that biholdith to the eest, schulen be fifti cubitis,

14 in whiche the tentis of fiftene cubitis schulen be assigned to o side, and thre pileris, and so many foundementis;

15 and in the tother side schulen be tentis holdynge fiftene cubitis, and thre pileris, and so many foundementis.

16 Forsothe in the entryng of the 'greet strete schal be maad a tente of twenti cubitis, of iacynt, and purpur, and of reed selk twies died, and of bijs foldid ayen bi broideri werk; it schal haue four pileris, with so many foundementis.

17 Alle the pileris of the grete street bi cumpas schulen be clothid with platis of siluer, with hedis of siluer, and with foundementis of bras.

18 The greet street schal ocupie an hundrid cubitis in lengthe, fifti in breede; the hiyenesse of the tente schal be of fiue cubitis; and it schal be maad of bijs foldid ayen; and it schal haue brasun foundementis.

19 Thou schalt make of bras alle the vesselis of the tabernacle, in to alle vsis and cerymonyes, as wel stakis therof, as of the greet street.

20 Comaunde thou to the sones of Israel, that thei brynge to thee the clenneste oile of 'the trees of olyues, and powned with a pestel, that a lanterne

21 brenne euere in the tabernacle of witnessyng with out the veil, which is hangid in the tabernacle of witnessyng; and Aaron and hise sones schulen sette it, that it schyne bifore the Lord til the morewtid; it schal be euerlastynge worschiping bi her successiouns of the sones of Israel.

CAP 28

1 Also applie thou to thee Aaron, thi brother, with hise sones, fro the myddis of the sones of Israel, that Aaron, Nadab, and Abyu, Eleazar, and Ythamar, be set in preesthod to me.

2 And thou schalt make an hooli clooth to Aaron, thi brother, in to glorie and fairenesse.

3 And thou schalt speke to alle wise men in herte, whiche Y haue fillid with the spirit of prudence, that thei make clothis to Aaron, in whiche he schal be halewid, and schal mynystre to me.

4 Forsothe these schulen be the clothis, whiche thei schulen make; 'thei schulen make racional, and a clooth on the schuldris, a coote, and a streyt lynnun clooth, a mytre, and a girdil; hooli cloothis to Aaron, thi brother, and to hise sones, that thei be set in preesthod to me.

5 And thei schulen take gold, and iacynt, and purpur, and 'reed selk twies died, and bijs;

6 forsothe thei schulen make the clooth on the schuldris of gold, and of iacynt, and purpur, and of 'reed selk twies died, and of bijs foldid ayen, bi broyderi werk of dyuerse colours.

7 It schal haue twey hemmes ioyned in euer either side of hiynessis, that tho go ayen in to oon.

8 Thilke weuyng, and al dyuersite of the werk schal be of gold, and iacynt, and purpur, and of 'reed selk twies died, and bijs foldis ayen.

9 And thou schalt take twei stoonys of onychym, and thou schalt graue in tho the names of the sones of Israel,

10 sixe names in o stoon, and sixe othere in the tother stoon, bi the ordre of her birthe;

11 bi the werk of a grauere, and bi the peyntyng of a man that ourneth with gemmes thou schalt graue tho stoonys, with the

names of the sones of Israel; and thou schalt enclose and cumpasse in gold.

12 And thou schalt sette tho stoonus in euer either side of the cloth on the schuldris, a memorial to the sones of Israel; and Aaron schal bere the names of hem bifor the Lord on euer either schuldre, for remembryng.

13 And thou schalt make hookis of gold,

14 and twey litil chaynes of clenneste gold, cleuynge to hem silf togidere, whiche litil chaynes thou schalt sette in the hookis.

15 Also thou schalt make the racional of doom by werk of dyuerse colours, bi the weuyng of the cloth on the schuldre, of gold, iacynt, and purpur, of 'reed silk twies died, and of bijs foldid ayen.

16 It schal be foure cornerid, and double; it schal haue the mesure of a pawme of the hond, as wel in lengthe, as in breede.

17 And thou schalt sette ther ynne foure ordris of stoonys; in the firste ordre schal be the stoon sardius, and topazyus, and smaragdus;

18 in the secunde ordre schal be charbuncle, safir, and iaspis; in the thridde ordre schal be ligurie,

19 achates, and ametiste;

20 in the fourthe ordre schal be crisolitus, onochyn, and berille; tho schulen be closid in gold, bi her ordris,

21 and schulen haue the names of the sones of Israel: tho schulen be graven with twelue names; al stonus bi hem silf, with the names of the sones 'of Israel bi hem silf, bi twelue lynagis.

22 Thou schalt make in the racional chaynes cleuynge to hem silf togidere of pureste gold,

23 and thou schalt make twei goldun ryngis, whiche thou schalt sette in euer either hiynesse of racional.

24 And thou schalt ioyne the goldun chaynes with the ryngis that ben in the brynkis therof,

25 and thou schalt couple the 'last thingis of tho chaynes to twey hookis in euer either side of the 'cloth on the schuldur, that biholdith the racional.

26 And thou schalt make twei goldun ryngis, whiche thou schalt sette in the hiynesses of the racional, and in the hemmes of the cloth on the schuldur, that ben euene ayens, and biholden the lattere thingis therof.

27 Also and thou schalt make tweyne othere goldun ryngis, that schulen be set in euer either side of the clooth on the schuldur bynethe, that biholdith ayens the face of the lowere ioynyng, that it may be set couenabli with the 'cloth on the schuldre.

28 And the racional be boundun bi hise ryngis with the ryngis of the 'cloth on the schuldre, with a lace of iacynt, that the ioyning maad craftili dwelle, and that the racional and 'cloth on the schuldre moun not be departid ech fro other.

29 And Aaron schal bere the names of the sones of Israel in the racional of doom on his brest, whanne he entrith in to the seyntuarie, a memorial bifor the Lord with outen ende.

30 Forsothe thou schalt sette in the racional of doom, techyng, and treuthe, whiche schulen be in the brest of Aaron, whanne he entrith bifor the Lord, and he schal bere the doom of the sones of Israel in his brest in the siyt of the Lord euere.

31 And thou schalt make the coote of the 'cloth on the schuldre al of iacynt,

32 in whos myddil aboue schal be an hood, and a wouun hemme 'bi cumpas therof, as it is wont to be don in the hemmes of clothis, lest it be brokun liytli.

33 Forsothe bynethe at the feet of the same coote, bi cumpas, thou schalt make as 'piyn applis, of iacynt, and purpur, of 'reed selk twies died, and of biis foldid ayen; while smale bellis ben medlid in the myddis,

34 so that a litil 'belle of gold be and a 'piyn appil, and eft another litel belle of gold and a 'pyn appil.

35 And Aaron schal be clothid with that coote in the office of seruyce, that sown be herd, whanne he entrith in to the seyntuarie, and goith out, in the siyt of the Lord; and that he die not.

36 And thou schalt make a plate of pureste gold, in which thou schalt graue bi the werk of a grauere, the holi to the Lord.

37 And thou schalt bynde that plate with a lace of iacynt, and it schal be on the mytre,

38 and schal neiye the forheed of the bischop. And Aaron schal bere the wickidnessis of hem whiche the sones of Israel 'offeriden, and halewiden in alle her yiftis and fre yiftis; forsothe the plate schal euere be in 'his forhed, that the Lord be plesid to him.

39 And thou schalt bynde the coot of biis, and the myter of bijs, and thou schalt make also a girdil, 'bi werk of broiderye.

40 Forsothe thou schalt make redi to 'the sones of Aaron linnun cootis, and girdlis, and mytris, in to glorie and fairnesse.

41 And thou schalt clothe Aaron, thi brother, with alle these, and hise sones with hym. And thou schalt sacre the hondis of alle; and thou schalt halewe hem, that thei be set in preesthood to me.

42 Also thou schalt make lynnun brechis, that thei hile the fleisch of her filthe fro the reynes 'til to the hipis.

43 And Aaron and hise sones schulen vse tho, whanne thei schulen entre in to the tabernacle of witnessyng, ether whanne thei neiyen to the auter, that thei mynystren in the seyntuarie, lest thei ben gilti of wickidnesse, and dien; it schal be a lawful thing euerlastynge to Aaron, and to his seed after hym.

CAP 29

1 But also thou schalt do this, that thei be sacrid to me in preesthod; take thou a calf of the droue, and twei rammes with out wem,

2 and therf looues, and a cake with out sour dow, whiche be spreynt to gidere with oile, and therf paast sodun in watir, 'bawmed, ether fried, with oile; thou schalt make alle thingis of whete flour,

3 and thou schalt offre tho put in a panyere. Forsothe thou schal presente the calfe,

4 and twey rammes, and Aaron and his sones, at the dore of tabernacle of witnessyng; and whanne thou hast waische the fadir and the sones in watir,

5 thou schalt clothe Aaron with hise clothis, that is, the lynnen cloth, 'and coote, and the cloth on the schuldris, 'and the racional, which thou schalt bynde with a girdil.

6 And thou schalt sette the mytre on his heed, and the hooli plate on the mytre,

7 and thou schalt schede the oile of anoyntyng on his heed; and bi this custom he schal be sacrid.

8 Also thou schalt presente hise sones, and thou schalt clothe with lynnun cootis,

9 and thou schalt girde Aaron and hise sones with a girdil; and thou schalt sette mytris on hem; and thei schulen be my preestis bi euerlastynge religioun. After that thou hast halewid 'the hondis of hem,

10 also thou schalt presente the calf bifore the tabernacle of witnessyng; and Aaron and hise sones schulen sette hondis 'on the heed therof;

11 and thou schalt sle it in the siyt of the Lord, bisidis the dore of the tabernacle of witnessyng.

12 And thou schalt take the blood of the calf, and schalt putte with thi fyngur on the corneris of the auter. Forsothe thou schalt schede the 'tothir blood bisidis the foundement therof.

13 And thou schalt take al the fatnesse that hilith the entrailis, and the calle of the mawe, and twey kidneris, and the fatnesse which is on hem; and thou schalt offre encense on the auter.

14 Forsothe thou schalt brenne with out the castels the 'fleischis of the calf, and the skyn, and the dung, for it is for synne.

15 Also thou schalt take a ram, on whos heed Aaron and hise sones schulen sette hondis;

16 and whanne thou hast slayn that ram, thou schalt take of 'his blood, and schalt schede aboute the auter.

17 Forsothe thou schalt kitte thilk ram in to smale gobetis, and thou schalt putte hise entrailis waischun, and feet on the fleischis koruun, and on his heed;

18 and thou schalt offre al the ram in to encence on the auter; it is an offryng to the Lord, the swettest odour of the slayn sacrifice of the Lord.

19 And thou schalt take the tothir ram, on whos heed Aaron and hise sones schulen sette hondis;

20 and whanne thou hast offrid that ram, thou schalt take of his blood, and schalt 'putte on the last part of the riyt eere of Aaron, and of hise sones, and on the thombis of her hond; and of her riyt foot; and thou schalt schede the blood on the auter, 'bi cumpas.

21 And whanne thou hast take of the blood, which is on the auter, and of oile of anoynting, thou schalt sprenge Aaron and hise clothis, the sones and her clothis. And whanne thei and the clothis ben sacrid,

22 thou schalt take the ynnere fatnesse of the ram, and the tayl, and the fatnesse that hilith the entrailis, and the calle of the mawe, and twey kideneris, and the fatnesse that is on tho; and thou schalt take the riyt schuldur, for it is the ram of consecracioun;

23 and thou schalt take a tendur cake of o loof, spreynd with oile, paast sodun in watir, and after fried in oile, of the panyer of therf looues, which is set in 'the siyt of the Lord.

24 And thou schalt putte alle 'thingis on the hondis of Aaron and of hise sones, and schalt halewe hem, and reise bifor the Lord.

25 And thou schalt take alle thingis fro 'the hondis of hem, and schalt brenne on the autir, in to brent sacrifice, 'swettist odour in the siyt of the Lord, for it is the offryng of the Lord.

26 Also thou schalt take the brest of the ram, bi which Aaron was halewid, and thou schalt halewe it reisid bifor the Lord; and it schal turne in to thi part.

27 And thou schalt halewe also the brest sacrid, and the schuldur which thou departidist fro the ram,

28 bi which Aaron was halewid, and hise sones; and tho schulen turne in to the part of Aaron, and of hise sones, bi euerlastinge riyt, of the sones of Israel; for tho ben the firste thingis, and the bigynnyngis of the pesible sacrifices of hem, whiche thei offren to the Lord.

29 Forsothe the sones of Aaron schulen haue aftir hym the hooli cloth, which Aaron schal vse, that thei be anoyntid ther ynne, and her hondis be sacrid.

30 'Thilke, that of hise sones schal be maad bischop for hym, schal vse that cloth seuene daies, and which sone schal entre

in to the tabernacle of witnessyng, that he mynystre in the seyntuarie.

31 Sotheli thou schalt take the ram of consecracioun, and thou schalt sethe hise fleischis in the hooli place,

32 whiche fleischis Aaron and his sones schulen ete, and thei schulen ete the looues, that ben in the panyere, in the porche of the tabernacle of witnessyng,

33 that it be a pleasaunt sacrifice, and that the hondis of the offreris be halewid. An alien schal not ete of tho, for tho ben hooli.

34 That if ony thing leeueth of the fleischis halewid, ether of the looues, til the morewtid, thou schalt brenne the relifs by fier, thou schulen not be etun, for tho ben halewid.

35 Thou schalt do on Aaron, and hise sones, alle thingis whiche I comaunde to thee. Seuene daies thou schalt sacre 'the hondis of hem,

36 and thou schalt offre a calf for synne bi ech day to clense; and thou schalt clense the auter, whanne thou hast offrid the sacrifice of clensyng, and thou schalt anoynte the auter in to halewyng.

37 Seuene daies thou shalt clense and halewe the auter, and it schal be the hooli of hooli thingis; ech man that schal touche it schal be halewid.

38 This it is, that thou schalt do in the auter, twei lambren of o yeer contynueli bi ech dai,

39 o lomb in the morewtid, and the tothir in the euentid;

40 'thou schalt do in o lomb the tenthe part of flour spreynt with oyle, powned, that schal haue a mesure, the fourthe part of hyn, and wyn of the same mesure, to make sacrifice.

41 Sotheli thou schalt offre the tother lomb at euentid, bi the custom of the offryng at the morewtid, and bi tho thingis, whiche we seiden, in to the odour of swetnesse;

42 it is a sacrifice to the Lord bi euerlastynge offryng in to youre generaciouns, at the dore of the tabernacle of witnessyng bifor the Lord, where Y schal ordeyne that Y speke to thee;

44 and there Y schal comaunde to the sones of Israel; and the auter schal be halewid in my glorie. Y schal halewe also the tabernacle of witnessyng with the auter, and Aaron with hise sones, that thei be set in presthod to me.

45 And Y schal dwelle in the myddis of the sones of Israel, and Y schal be God to hem;

46 and thei schulen wite, that Y am her Lord God, which ledde hem out of the lond of Egipt, that Y schulde dwelle among hem; for Y am her Lord God.

CAP 30

1 Also thou schalt make an auter of the trees of Sechym, to brenne encense;

2 and the auter schal haue a cubit of lengthe, and another cubit of brede, that is foure cornerid, and twei cubitis in heiythe; corneris schulen come forth of the auter.

3 And thou schalt clothe it with clennest gold, as wel the gridil therof, as the wallis and corneris bi cumpas therof; and thou schalt make to the auter a litil goldun coroun,

4 'bi cumpas, and twei goldun serclis vndur the coroun by alle sidis, that barris be put in to the serclis, and the auter be borun.

5 Also thou schalt make tho barris of the trees of Sechym, and thou schalt ouergilde;

6 and thou schalt sette the auter ayens the veil, which veil hangith bifor the ark of witnessyng bifor the propiciatorie, bi which the witnessyng is hilid, where Y schal speke to thee.

7 And Aaron schal brenne theronne encense smellynge swetly eerli; whanne he schal araye the lanternes, he schal brenne it;

8 and whanne he settith the lanternes at euentid, he schal brenne euerlastynge encense bifor the Lord, in to youre generaciouns.

9 Ye schulen not offre theronne encense of other makyng, nethir offryng, and slayn sacrifice, nether ye schulen offre fletynge offryngis thereonne.

10 And Aaron schal preie on the corneres therof onis bi the yeer, in the blood which is offrid for synne, and he schal plese theronne in youre generaciouns; it schal be the hooli of hooli thingis to the Lord.

11 And the Lord spak to Moises,

12 and seide, Whanne thou schalt take the summe of the sones of Israel, alle bi hem silf schulen yyue 'bi the noumbre prijs for her soulis to the Lord, and veniaunce schal not be in hem, whanne thei ben noumbrid.

13 Sotheli ech that passith to the name, schal yyue this, half a sicle bi the mesure of the temple; a sicle hath twenti halpens; the myddil part of a cicle schal be offrid to the Lord.

14 He that is hadde in noumbre, fro twenti yeer and aboue,

15 schal yyue prijs; a riche man schal not adde to the myddil of cicle, and a pore man schal no thing abate.

16 And thou schalt bitake in to vsis of the tabernacle of witnessyng the money takun, which is gaderid of the sones of Israel, that it be the mynde of hem bifor the Lord, and he schal be merciful to 'the soulis of hem.

17 And the Lord spak to Moises,

18 and seide, Also thou schalt make a greet vessil of bras with his foundement to waische, and thou schalt sette it bitwixe the tabernacle of witnessyng and the auter 'of brent sacrifices; and whanne watir is put therynne,

19 Aaron and hise sones schulen waische therynne her hondis and feet,

20 whanne thei schulen entre in to the tabernacle of witnessyng, and whanne thei schulen neiye to the auter that thei offre therynne encense to the Lord,

21 lest perauenture thei dien; it schal be a lawful thing euerlastinge to hym and to his seed bi successiouns.

22 And the Lord spak to Moises,

23 and seide, Take to thee swete smellynge spiceries, of the firste and chosun myrre, fyue hundrid siclis; and of canel the half, that is, twei hundrid and fifti siclis;

24 in lijk maner of calamy twei hundrid and fifti siclis; also of casia fyue hundrid siclis, in the weiyte of seyntuarie; oile of olyue trees, the mesure hyn;

25 and thou schalt make the hooly oile of anoyntyng, an oynement maad bi the werk of a 'makere of oynement.

26 And thou schal anoynte therof the tabernacle of witnessyng, and the ark of testament, and the boord with hise vessels,

27 the candilstike, and the purtenaunces therof, the auteris of encense,

28 and of brent sacrifice, and al the purtenaunce, that perteyneth to the ournyng of tho.

29 And thou schalt halewe alle thingis, and tho schulen be the hooli of holi thingis; he that schal touche tho, schal be halewid.

30 Thou schalt anoynte Aaron, and hise sones, and thou schalt halewe hem, that thei be set in presthod to me.

31 And thou schalt seie to the sones of Israel, This oile of anoyntyng schal be hooli to me in to youre generaciouns.

32 The fleisch of man schal not be anoyntid therof, and bi the makyng therof ye schulen not make another, for it is halewid, and it schal be hooli to you.

33 What euer man makith sich oile, and yyueth therof to an alien, he schal be 'destried fro his puple.

34 Forsothe the Lord seide to Moises, Take to thee swete smellynge spyceries, stacten, and onyca, galban of good odour, and pureste encense, alle schulen be of euene weiyte.

35 And thou schal make encence, maad by werk of oynement makere, meddlid diligentli, and pure, and moost worthi of halewyng.

36 And whanne thou hast powned alle thingis in to smalleste poudre, thou schalt putte therof bifor the tabernacle of witnessyng, in which place Y schal appere to thee; encense schal be to you the hooli of hooli thingis.

37 Ye schulen not make siche a makyng in to youre vsis, for it is hooli to the Lord.

38 What euer man makith a lijk thing, that he vse the odour therof, he schal perische fro his puple.

CAP 31

1 And the Lord spak to Moyses, 'and seide, Lo!

2 Y haue clepid Beseleel bi name, the sone of Hury, sone of Hur, of the lynage of Juda;

3 and Y haue fillid hym with the spirit of God, with wisdom, and vndirstondyng, and kunnyng in al werk,

4 to fynde out what euer thing may be maad suteli, of gold, and siluer, and bras, and marbil,

5 and gemmes, and dyuersite of trees.

6 And Y haue youe to hym a felowe, Ooliab, the sone of Achisameth, of the kynrede of Dan; and Y haue put in 'the herte of hem the wisdom of ech lerned man, that thei make alle thingis, whiche Y comaundide to thee;

7 the tabernacle of boond of pees, and the arke of witnessyng, and the propiciatorie, ether table, which is theronne, and alle the vessels of the tabernacle;

8 also the bord, and vessels therof, the clenneste candilstike with hise vessels, and the auteris of encence,

9 and of brent sacrifice, and alle the vessels of hem; the greet 'waischyng vessel with his foundement;

10 hooli clothis in seruyce to Aaron prest, and to hise sones, that thei be set in her office in hooli thingis;

11 the oile of anoyntyng, and encence of swete smellynge spiceryes in the seyntuarie; thei schulen make alle thingis whiche Y comaundide to thee.

12 And the Lord spak to Moises, 'and seide, Speke thou to the sones of Israel,

13 and thou schalt seie to hem, Se ye that ye kepe my sabat, for it is a signe bytwixe me and you in youre generaciouns; that ye wite, that Y am the Lord, which halewe you.

14 Kepe ye my sabat, for it is hooli to you; he that defoulith it, schal die bi deeth, the soule of hym, that doith werk in the sabat, schal perische fro the myddis of his puple.

15 Sixe daies ye schulen do werk; in the seuenthe dai is sabat, hooli reste to the Lord; ech man that doith werk in this dai schal die.

16 The sones of Israel kepe sabat, and halewe it in her generaciouns;

17 it is a couenaunt euerlastinge bitwixe me and the sones of Israel, and it is 'a signe euerlastynge; for in sixe daies God made heuene and erthe, and in the seuenthe day he ceessid of werk.

18 And whanne siche wordis weren fillid, the Lord yaf to Moises, in the hil of Synay, twei stonun tablis of witnessyng, writun with the fyngur of God.

CAP 32

1 Forsothe the puple siy, that Moises made tariyng to come doun fro the hil, and it was gaderid ayens Aaron, and seide, Rise thou, and make goddis to vs, that schulen go bifore vs, for we witen not what bifelde to this Moises, that ladde vs out of the lond of Egipt.

2 And Aaron seide to hem, Take ye the goldun eere ryngis fro the eeris of youre wyues, and of sones and douytris, and brynge ye to me.

3 The puple dide tho thingis, that he comaundide, and brouyte eere ryngis to Aaron;

4 and whanne he hadde take tho, he formede bi 'werk of yetyng, and made of tho a yotun calf. And thei seiden, Israel, these ben thi goddis, that ladde thee out of the lond of Egipt.

5 And whanne Aaron had seyn this thing, he bildide an auter bifore hym, and he criede bi the vois of a criere, and seide, To morewe is the solempnete of the Lord.

6 And thei rysen eerli, and offeriden brent sacrifyces, and pesible sacrifices; and the puple sat to ete and drynke, and thei risen to pley.

7 Forsothe the Lord spak to Moises, and seide, Go thou, go doun, thi puple hath synned, 'whom thou leddist out of the lond of Egipt.

8 Thei yeden awei soone fro the weie which thou schewidst to hem, and thei maden to hem a yotun calf, and worschipyden it, and thei offeriden sacrifices to it, and seiden, Israel, these ben thi goddis, that ledden thee out of the lond of Egipt.

9 And eft the Lord seide to Moises, Y se, that this puple is of hard nol;

10 suffre thou me, that my woodnesse be wrooth ayens hem, and that Y do awey hem; and Y schal make thee in to a greet folk.

11 Forsothe Moises preiede 'his Lord God, and seide, Lord, whi is thi veniaunce wrooth ayens thi puple, whom thou leddist out of the lond of Egipt in greet strengthe and in stronge hond?

12 Y biseche, that Egipcians seie not, he ledde hem out felli, 'that he schulde sle in the hillis, and to do awei fro erthe, thin ire ceesse, and be thou quemeful on the wickidnesse of thi puple.

13 Haue thou mynde of Abraham, of Ysaac, and of Israel, thi seruauntis, to whiche thou hast swore bi thi silf, and seidist, Y schal multiplie youre seed as the sterris of heuene, and Y schal yyue to youre seed al this lond of which Y spak, and ye schulen welde it euere.

14 And the Lord was plesid, that he dide not the yuel which he spak ayens his puple.

15 And Moises turnede ayen fro the hil, and bar in his hond twei tablis of witnessyng, writun in euer either side,

16 and maad bi the werk of God; and the writyng of God was grauun in tablis.

17 Forsothe Josue herde the noise of the puple criynge, and seide to Moyses, Yellyng of fiytyng is herd in the castels.

18 To whom Moises answeride, It is not cry of men exitynge to batel, nether the cry of men compellynge to fleyng, but Y here the vois of syngeris.

19 And whanne he hadde neiyid to the castels, he siy the calf, and dauncis; and he was wrooth greetli, and 'castide forth the tablis fro the hond, and brak tho at the rootis of the hil.

20 And he took the calf, which thei hadden maad, and brente, and brak 'til to poudur, which he spreynte in to watir, and yaf therof drynke to the sones of Israel.

21 And Moises seide to Aaron, What dide this puple to thee, that thou brouytist in on hym the gretteste synne?

22 To whom he answeride, My lord, be not wrooth, for thou knowist this puple, that it is enclynaunt to yuel;

23 thei seiden to me, Make thou goddis to vs, that schulen go bifore vs, for we witen not, what bifelde to this Moises, that ladde vs out of the lond of Egipt.

24 To whiche Y seide, Who of you hath gold? Thei token, and yauen to me, and Y castide it forth in to the fier, and this calf yede out.

25 Therfor Moyses siy the puple, that it was maad bare; for Aaron hadde spuylid it for the schenschip of filthe, and hadde maad the puple nakid among enemyes.

26 And Moises stood in the yate of the castels, and seide, If ony man is of the Lord, be he ioyned to me; and alle the sones of Leuy weren gaderid to hym.

27 To whiche he seide, The Lord God of Israel seith these thingis, A man putte swerd on his hipe, go ye, and 'go ye ayen fro yate 'til to yate bi the myddil of the castels, and ech man sle his brother, freend, and neiybore.

28 The sones of Leuy diden bi the word of Moises, and as thre and twenti thousynd of men felden doun in that day.

29 And Moises seide, Ye han halewid youre hondis to dai to the Lord, ech man in his sone, and brother, that blessyng be youun to you.

30 Sotheli whanne 'the tother day was maad, Moises spak to the puple, Ye han synned the moost synne; Y schal stie to the Lord, if in ony maner Y schal mowe biseche hym for youre felony.

31 And he turnede ayen to the Lord, and seide, Lord, Y biseche, this puple hath synned a greet synne, and thei han maad goldun goddis to hem; ethir foryyue thou this gilt to hem,

32 ether if thou doist not, do awey me fro thi book, which thou hast write.

33 To whom the Lord answeride, Y schal do awey fro my book hym that synneth ayens me;

34 forsothe go thou, and lede this puple, whydur Y spak to thee; myn aungel schal go bifore thee; forsothe in the day of veniaunce Y schal visite also this synne of hem.

35 Therfor the Lord smoot the puple for the gilt of the calf, which calf Aaron made.

CAP 33

1 And the Lord spak to Moyses, and seide, Go and stie fro this place, thou, and the puple, whom thou leddist out of the lond of Egipt, in to the lond, which Y haue swore to Abraham, and to Ysaac, and to Jacob, 'and Y seide, Y schal yyue it to thi seed.

2 And Y schal sende thi bifore goere an aungel, that Y caste out Cananey, and Amorei, and Ethei, and Ferezei, and Euey, and Jebusey;

3 and that thou entre in to the lond flowynge with mylk and hony; for Y schal not stye with thee, for 'thou art a puple of hard nol, lest perauenture Y leese thee in the weie.

4 The puple herde this worste word, and morenyde, and noon was clothid with his ournyng bi custom.

5 And the Lord seide to Moises, Spek thou to the sones of Israel, Thou art a puple of hard nol; onys Y schal stie in the

myddis of thee, and Y schal do awey thee; riyt now putte awei thin ournyng, that Y wite, what Y schal do to thee.

6 Therfor the sones of Israel puttiden awey her ournyng fro the hil of Oreb.

7 And Moises took the tabernacle, and settide fer with out the castels, and he clepide the name therof the tabernacle of boond of pees. And al the puple that hadde ony questioun, yede out to the tabernacle of boond of pees, with out the castels.

8 And whanne Moises yede out to the tabernacle, al the puple roos, and ech man stood in the dore of his tente, and thei bihelden 'the bak of Moises, til he entride in to the tente.

9 Sotheli whanne he entride in to the tabernacle of boond of pees, a piler of cloude cam doun, and stood at the dore; and the Lord spak with Moises,

10 while alle men sien that the piler of cloude stood at the 'dore of tabernacle; and thei stoden, and worschipiden bi the dores of her tabernaclis.

11 Forsothe the Lord spak to Moises face to face, as a man is wont to speke to his freend; and whanne he turnede ayen in to 'the castels, Josue, his mynystre, the sone of Nun, a child, yede not awey fro the tabernacle.

12 Forsothe Moises seide to the Lord, Thou comaundist, that Y lede out this puple, and thou 'schewist not to me, whom thou schalt sende with me, 'most sithen thou seidist, Y knewe thee bi name, and thou hast founde grace bifore me.

13 Therfore if Y haue founde grace in thi siyt, schewe thi face to me, that Y knowe thee, and fynde grace bifor thin iyen; biholde thi puple, and this folk.

14 And God seide, My face schal go bifor thee, and Y schal yyue reste to thee.

15 And Moises seide, If thi silf schalt not go bifore, 'lede not vs out of this place;

16 for in what thing moun we wite, Y and thi puple, that we han founde grace in thi siyt, if thou schalt not go with vs, that we be glorified of alle puplis that dwellen on erthe?

17 Forsothe the Lord seide to Moises, Y schal do also this word, which thou hast spoke; for thou hast founde grace bifor me, and Y knewe thi silf bi name.

18 And Moises seide, Schewe thou thi glorie to me.

19 God answeride, Y schal schewe al good to thee, and Y schal clepe in the 'name of the Lord bifor thee, and Y schal do merci to whom Y wole, and Y schal be merciful on whom it plesith to me.

20 And eft God seide, Thou maist not se my face, for a man schal not se me, and schal lyue.

21 And eft God seide, A place is anentis me, and thou schalt stonde on a stoon;

22 and whanne my glorie schal passe, Y schal sette thee in the hoole of the stoon, and Y schal kyuere with my riyt hond, til Y passe; and Y schal take awey myn hond,

23 and thou schalt se myn hyndrere partis, forsothe thou mayst not se my face.

CAP 34

1 And aftirward God seide, Hewe to thee twey tablis of stoon at the licnesse of the formere, and Y schal write on tho tablis thilke wordis, whiche the tablis, that thou 'hast broke, hadden.

2 Be thou redi in the morewtid, that thou stie anoon in to the hil of Synai; and thou schalt stonde with me on the cop of the hil;

3 no man stie with thee, nether ony man be seyn bi al the hil, and oxun and scheep be not fed ayens 'the hil.

4 Therfor Moises hewide twey tablis of stoon, whiche manere tablis weren bifore, and he roos bi nyyt, and stiede in to the hil of Synay, as the Lord comaundide to hym; and he bar with hym the tablis.

5 And whanne the Lord hadde come doun bi a cloude, Moises stood with hym, and clepide inwardli 'the name of the Lord;

6 and whanne the Lord passide bifore hym, he seide, Lordschipere, Lord God, mercyful, and pitouse, pacient, and of myche mersiful doyng, and sothefast,

7 which kepist couenaunt and mercy in to 'a thousande, which doist awey wickidnesse, and trespassis, and synnes, and noon bi hym silf is innocent anentis thee, which yeldist the wickidnesse of fadris to sones and to sones of sones, into the thridde and fourthe generacioun.

8 And hastili Moises was bowid low 'in to erthe, and worschipide,

9 and seide, Lord, if Y haue founde grace in thi siyt, Y biseche that thou go with vs, for the puple is of hard nol, and that thou do awey oure wickidnesses and synnes, and welde vs.

10 The Lord answeride, Y schal make couenaunt, and in siyt of alle men Y schal make signes, that weren neuer seyn on erthe, nether in ony folkis, that this puple, in whos myddis thou art, se the ferdful werk of the Lord, which Y schal make.

11 Kepe thou alle thingis, whiche Y comaundide to thee to dai; I my silf schal caste out bifor thi face Amorrey, and Cananey, and Ethei, and Ferezei, and Euey, and Jebusei.

12 Be war, lest ony tyme thou ioyne frendschipis with the dwelleris of that lond, whiche frenschipis be in to fallyng to thee.

13 But also distrie thou 'the auteris of hem, breke the ymagis, and kitte doun the woodis;

14 'nyl thou worschipe an alien God; 'the Lord a gelous louyere is his name, God is a feruent louyere;

15 make thou not couenaunt with the men of tho cuntreis, lest whanne thei han do fornycacioun with her goddis, and han worschipid the symylacris of hem, ony man clepe thee, that thou ete of thingis offrid to an ydol.

16 Nether thou schalt take a wyif of her douytris to thi sones, lest aftir that tho douytris han do fornycacioun, thei make also thi sones to do fornicacioun in to her goddis.

17 Thou schalt not make to thee yotun goddis.

18 Thou schalt kepe the solempynyte of therf looues; seuene daies thou schalt ete therf looues, as Y comaundide to thee, in the time of the monethe of newe fruytis; for in the monethe of veer tyme thou yedist out of Egipt.

19 Al thing of male kynde that openeth the wombe schal be myn, of alle lyuynge beestis, as wel of oxun, as of scheep, it schal be myn.

20 Thou schalt ayenbie with a scheep the firste gendrid of an asse, ellis if thou yyuest not prijs therfor, it schal be slayn. Thou schalt ayenbie the firste gendrid of thi sones; nether thou schalt appere voide in my siyt.

21 Sixe daies thou schalt worche, the seuenthe day thou schalt ceesse to ere and repe.

22 Thou schalt make to thee the solempnyte of woukis in the firste thingis of fruytis of thi ripe corn of wheete, and the solempnyte, whanne alle thingis ben gadrid in to bernes, whanne the tyme 'of yeer cometh ayen.

23 Ech male kynde of thee schal appere in thre tymes of the yeer in the siyt of the Lord Almyyti, thi God of Israel.

24 For whanne Y schal take awei folkis fro thi face, and Y schal alarge thi termes, noon schal sette tresouns to thi lond, while thou stiest and apperist in the siyt of thi Lord God, thries in the yeer.

25 Thou schalt not offre on sour dow the blood of my sacrifice, nethir ony thing of the slayn sacrifice of the solempnyte of fase schal abide in the morewtid.

26 Thou schalt offre in the hows of thi Lord God the firste of the fruytis of thi lond. Thou schalt not sethe a kide in the mylk of his modir.

27 And the Lord seide to Moises, Write thou these wordis, bi whiche Y smoot a boond of pees, bothe with thee and with Israel.

28 Therfor Moises was there with the Lord bi fourti daies and bi fourti nyytis, he eet not breed, and drank not watir; and he wroot in tablys ten wordis of the boond of pees.

29 And whanne Moises cam doun fro the hil of Synai, he helde twei tablis of witnessyng, and he wiste not that his face was horned of the felouschipe of Goddis word.

30 Forsothe Aaron and the sones of Israel sien Moises face horned,

31 and thei dredden to neiye niy, and thei weren clepid of hym, 'and thei turneden ayen, as wel Aaron as the princis of the synagoge; and after that Moises spak, thei camen to hym,

32 yhe alle the sones of Israel; to whiche Moises comaundide alle thingis, whiche he hadde herd of the Lord in the hil of Synai.

33 And whanne the wordis weren fillid, he puttide a veil on his face;

34 and he entride to the Lord, and spak with hym, and dide awey that veil, til he yede out; and thanne he spak to the sones of Israel alle thingis, that weren comaundid to hym;

35 whiche sien that the face of Moyses goynge out was horned, but eft he hilide his face, if ony tyme he spak to hem.

CAP 35

1 Therfor whanne al the cumpanye of the sones of Israel was gaderid, Moises seide to hem, These thingis it ben, whiche the Lord comaundide to be doon.

2 Sixe daies ye schulen do werk, the seuenthe dai schal be hooli to you, the sabat and reste of the Lord; he that doith werk in the sabat schal be slayn.

3 Ye schulen not kyndle fier in alle youre dwellyng places bi the 'dai of sabat.

4 And Moises seide to al the cumpeny of the sones of Israel, This is the word which the Lord comaundide, and seide,

5 Departe ye at you the firste fruytis to the Lord; ech wilful man and of redi wille offre tho to the Lord, gold, and siluer, and bras,

6 and iacynct, and purpur, and reed selk twies died, and bijs, heeris of geet,

7 and skynnys of rammes maad reed, and of iacynt,

8 trees of Sechym, and oile to liytis to be ordeyned, and that the oynement be maad, and encense moost swete,

9 stoonus of onochyn and gemmes, to the ournyng of the 'cloth on the schuldris, and of the racional.

10 Who euer of you is wijs, come he, and make that, that the Lord comaundide,

11 that is, the tabernacle, and the roof therof, and the hilyng; ryngis, and bildyngis of tablis, with barris, stakis, and foundementis;

12 the arke, and barris; the propiciatorie, and the veil, which is hangid byfore it;

13 the bord with barris, and vesselis, and with looues of settyng forth;

14 the candilstike to susteyne liytis, the vesselis, and lanternes therof, and oile to the nurschyngis of fyris; the auter of encense, and the barris;

15 the oile of anoyntyng, and encense of swete smellynge spiceries; the tente at the dore of the tabernacle;

16 the auter of brent sacrifice, and his brasun gridele, with hise barris, and vessels; the 'greet waischyng vessel, and 'his foundement;

17 the curteyns of the large street, with pileris and foundementis; the tente in the doris of the porche;

18 the stakis of the tabernacle and of the large street, with her coordis;

19 the clothis, whose vss is in 'the seruyce of seyntuarie; the clothis of Aaron bischop, and of hise sones, that thei be set in preesthod to me.

20 And al the multitude of the sones of Israel yede out of 'the siyt of Moises,

21 and offride with moost redi soule and deuout the firste thingis to the Lord, to make the werk of the tabernacle of witnessyng, what euer was nedeful to the ournyng, and to hooli clothis.

22 Men and wymmen yauen bies of the armes, and eeryngis, ryngis, and ournementis of 'the arm niy the hond; ech goldun vessel was departid in to the yiftis of the Lord.

23 If ony man hadde iacynt, and purpur, and 'reed selk twies died, bijs, and the heeris of geet, skynnes of rammes maad reed, and of iacynt,

24 metals of siluer, and of bras, thei offeryden to the Lord, and trees of Sechym in to dyuerse vsis.

25 But also wymmen tauyt yauen tho thingis, whiche thei hadden spunne, iacynt, purpur, and vermyloun,

26 and bijs, and the heeris of geet; and yauen alle thingis by her owne fre wille.

27 Forsothe princes offeriden stoonys of onychyn and iemmes, to the 'cloth on the schuldris, and to the racional, and swete smellynge spiceries,

28 and oyle to the liytis to be ordeyned, and to make redi oynement, and to make the encense of swettist odour.

29 Alle men and wymmen offeriden yiftis with deuout soule, that the werkis schulden be maad, whiche the Lord comaundide bi the hond of Moyses; alle the sones of Israel halewiden wilful thingis to the Lord.

30 And Moises seide to the sones of Israel, Lo! the Lord hath clepid Beseleel bi name, the sone of Hury, sone of Hur, of the lynage of Juda;

31 and the Lord hath fillid hym with the spirit of God, of wisdom, and of vndurstondyng, and of kunnyng, and with al doctryn,

32 to fynde out and to make werk in gold, and siluer, and bras, and in stoonys to be grauun,

33 and in werk of carpentrie; what euer thing may be foundun craftili, the Lord yaf in his herte; and the Lord clepide Ooliab, the sone of Achymasech, of the lynage of Dan; the Lord tauyte bothe 'with wisdom, that thei make the werkis of carpenter, of steynour, and of broiderere, of iacynt, and purpur, and of 'reed selk, and of bijs, and that thei make alle thingis, and fynde alle newe thingis.

CAP 36

1 Therfor Beseleel, and Ooliab, and ech wijs man, to whiche the Lord yaf wisdom and vndurstondyng, that thei kouden

worche crafteli, maden thingis that weren nedeful in to vsis of seyntuarie, and whiche the Lord comaundide to be maad.

2 And whanne Moises hadde clepid hem, and ech lerned man, to whom the Lord hadde youe wisdom and kunnyng, and whiche profriden hem bi her wille to make werk,

3 he bitook to hem alle the yiftis of the sones of Israel. And whanne thei weren bisi in the werk ech dai, the puple offride auowis eerli.

4 Wherfor the werkmen weren compellid to come,

5 and thei seiden to Moises, The puple offrith more than is nedeful.

6 Therfor Moises comaundide to be cried bi the vois of a criere, Nether man nether womman offre more ony thing in the werk of seyntuarie; and so it was ceessid fro yiftis to be offrid, for the thingis offrid sufficiden,

7 and weren ouer abundant.

8 And alle wise men in herte to fille the werk of the tabernacle maden ten curteyns of bijs foldid ayen, and of iacynct, and purpur, and of reed selk twies died, bi dyuerse werk, and bi the craft of many colouris.

9 Of whiche curteyns oon hadde in lengthe eiyte and twenti cubitis, and foure cubitis in breede; o mesure was of alle curteyns.

10 And he ioynede fyue curteyns oon to anothir, and he couplide othere fyue to hem silf to gidere;

11 and he made handlis of iacynt in the hemme of o curteyn on euer either side,

12 and in lijk maner in the hemme of the tother curteyn, that the handlis schulen comen to gidere ayens hem silf, and schulen be ioyned togider;

13 wherfor he yettide also fifti goldun serclis, that schulen 'bite the handlis of curteyns; and o tabernacle was maad.

14 'He made also enleuene saies of the heeris of geet, to hile the roof of the tabernacle;

15 o saie hadde thretti cubitis in lengthe, foure cubitis in breede; alle the saies weren of o mesure;

16 of whiche saies he ioynede fyue bi hem silf, and sixe othere bi hem silf.

17 And he made fifti handlis in the hemme of o say, and fifti in the hemme of the tother say, that tho schulden be ioyned to hem silf to gidere; and he made fifti bokelis of bras bi whiche

18 the roof was fastned to gidere, that oon hilyng were maad of alle the saies.

19 He made also an hilyng of the tabernacle of the skynnes of rammes maad reed, and another veil aboue of skynnes of iacynt.

20 He made also stondynge tablis of the tabernacle of the trees of Sechym;

21 the lengthe of o table was of ten cubitis, and the breede helde o cubit and an half.

22 Twey dentyngis weren bi ech table, that the oon schulde be ioyned to the tother; so he made in al the tablis of the tabernacle.

23 Of whiche tablis twenti weren at the mydday coost ayens the south,

24 with fourti foundementis of siluer; twey foundementis weren set vndur o table on euer either side of the corneris, where the dentyngis of the sidis weren endid in the corneris.

25 And at the coost of the tabernacle that biholdith to the north he made twenti tablis,

26 with fourti foundementis of siluer, twei foundementis bi ech table.

27 Forsothe ayens the west he made sixe tablis,

28 and tweyne othere tablis bi ech corner of the tabernacle bihinde,

29 whiche weren ioyned fro bynethe til to aboue, and weren borun in to o ioynyng to gidere; so he made on euer either part bi the corneris,

30 that tho weren eiyte tablis to gidere, and hadden sixtene foundementis of siluer, that is, twei foundementis vndur ech table.

31 He made also barris of the trees of Sechym, fyue barris to holde to gidere the tablis of o side of the tabernacle,

32 and fyue othere barris to schappe to gidere the tablis of the tother side; and without these, he made fyue othere barris at the west coost of the tabernacle ayens the see.

33 He made also another barre, that schulde come bi the myddil tables fro corner til to corner.

34 Forsothe he ouergildide tho wallis of tablis, and yetide the siluerne foundementis 'of tho, and he made the goldun serclis 'of tho, bi whiche the barris myyten be brouyt in, and be hilide the same barris with goldun platis.

35 He made also a veil dyuerse and departid, of iacynt, and purpur, and reed selk, and bijs foldid ayen bi werk of broiderie.

36 He made also foure pileris of 'the trees of Sechym, whyche pileris with the heedis he ouergildide, and yetide the siluerne foundementis 'of tho.

37 He made also in the entryng of the tabernacle a tent of iacynt, and purpur, and reed selk 'and bijs foldid ayen bi the werk of a broydreie.

38 And he made fyue pileris with her heedis, whiche he hilide with gold, and yetide the brasun foundementis 'of tho, whiche he hilide with gold.

CAP 37

1 Forsothe Beseleel made also an arke of the trees of Sechym, hauynge twey cubitis and an half in lengthe, and a cubit and an half in breede; forsothe the hiynesse was of o cubit and an half; and he clothide the arke with purest gold, with ynne and without forth.

2 And he made to it a goldun coroun 'bi cumpas,

3 and yetide foure goldun ryngis, bi foure corneris therof, twey ryngis in o side, and twei ryngis in the tother side.

4 And he made barris of the trees of Sechym, whiche barris he clothide with gold,

5 and whiche barris he putte into the ryngis that weren in the sidis of the arke, to bere it.

6 He made also a propiciatorie, that is, Goddis answeryng place, of pureste gold, of twei cubitis and an half in lengthe, and of o cubit and an half in breede.

7 Also he made twei cherubyns of gold, betun out with hamer, whiche he settide on euer eithir side of the propiciatorie,

8 o cherub in the hiynesse of o part, and the tother cherub in the hiynesse of the tothir part; twei cherubyns, oon in ech hiynesse of the propiciatorie, stretchynge out the wengis,

9 and hilynge the propiciatorie, and biholdynge hem silf togidere and that.

10 He made also a boord of 'the trees of Sechym, in the lengthe of twey cubitis, and in the breede of o cubit, whiche boord hadde 'a cubit and an half in heiythe.

11 And he cumpaside the boord with clenneste gold, and made to it a goldun brynke bi cumpas;

12 and he made to that brynke a goldun coroun, rasid bitwixe of foure fyngris; and on the same coroun he made anothir goldun coroun.

13 Also he yetide foure goldun serclis whiche he settide in foure corneris,

14 bi alle the feet of the boord ayens the coroun, and he puttide barris in to the serclis, that the 'boord may be borun.

15 And he made tho barris of the trees of Sechym, and cumpasside tho with gold.

16 And he made vesselis to dyuerse vsis of the boord, vessels of vynegre, violis, and litle cuppis, and censeris of pure gold, in whiche the fletynge sacrifices schulen be offrid.

17 And he made a candilstike, betun out with hamer, of clenneste gold, of whos barre yerdis, cuppis, and litle rundelis and lilies camen forth;

18 sixe in euer eithir side, thre yerdis on o side, and thre on the tother side; thre cuppis in the maner of a note bi ech yerde, and litle rundels to gidere, and lilies;

19 and thre cuppis at the licnesse of a note in the tother yerde, and litle rundels to gidere, and lilies; forsothe the werk of sixe schaftis, that camen forth of the 'stok of the candilstike, was euene.

20 Sotheli in that barre weren foure cuppis, in the maner of a note, and litle rundels and lilies weren bi alle cuppis;

21 and litle rundels vndur twei schaftis, bi thre placis, whiche to gidre be maad sixe schaftis comynge forth of o barre;

22 therfor and the litle rundels, and schaftis therof, weren alle betun out with hamer, of pureste gold.

23 He made also seuene lanternes, with her 'snytyng tongis, and the vessels where 'tho thingis, that ben snytid out, ben quenchid, of clennest gold.

24 The candilstike with alle his vessels weiyede a talent of gold.

25 He made also the auter of encense, of trees of Sechym, hauynge a cubit bi square, and twei cubitis in heiythe, of whos corneris camen forth hornes.

26 And he clothide it with clenneste gold, and the gridele, and wallis, and hornes;

27 and he made to it a litil goldun coroun bi cumpas, and twei goldun ryngis vndur the coroun, bi ech syde, that barris be put in to tho, and the auter mow be borun.

28 Forsothe he made tho barris of the trees of Sechym, and hilide with goldun platis.

29 He made also oile to the oynement of halewyng, and encense of swete smellynge spiceries, moost clene, bi the werk of 'a makere of oynement.

CAP 38

1 He made also the auter of brent sacrifice of the trees of Sechym, of fyue cubitis bi square, and of thre cubitis in heiythe;

2 whose hornes camen forth of the corneris, and he hilide it with platis of bras.

3 And in to vsis therof he made redi of bras dyuerse vessels, caudruns, tongis, fleischhokis, hokis, and 'resseittis of firis.

4 He made also the brasun gridile therof, 'bi the maner of a net, and a 'panne for colis vndur it, in the myddis of the auter.

5 And he yetide foure ryngis, by so many endis of the gridele, to putte in the barris to bere;

6 and he made tho same barris of the trees of Sechym, and hilide with platis of bras.

7 And ledde in to the serclis that stonden forth in the sidis of the auter. Forsothe thilke auter was not sad, but holowe of the bildyngis of tablis, and voide with ynne.

8 He made also a 'greet waischyng vessel of bras, with his foundement, of the myrours of wymmen that wakiden in the 'greet street of the tabernacle.

9 And he made the greet street, in whose south coost weren tentis of bijs foldid ayen, of an hundrid cubitis, twenti brasun pilers with her foundementis,

10 the heedis of pilers, and al the grauyng of the werk, weren of siluer;

11 euenli at the north coost the tentis, pilers, and foundementis and heedis of pilers, weren of the same mesure, and werk, and metal.

12 Forsothe in that coost that biholdith the west weren tentis of fyfty cubitis, ten brasun pilers with her foundementis, and the 'heedis of pilers, and al the grauyng of werk, weren of siluer.

13 Sotheli ayens the eest he made redi tentis of fifti cubitis,

14 of whiche tentis o side helde fiftene cubitis of thre pilers with her foundementis; and in the tother side,

15 for he made the entryng of the tabernacle bitwixe euer either, weren tentis euenli of fiftene cubitis, thre pilers, and so many foundementis.

16 Bijs foldid ayen hilide alle the tentis of the greet street.

17 The foundementis of pilers weren of bras; forsothe the heedis of tho pilers, with alle her grauyngis, weren of siluer; but also he clothide with siluer tho pilers of the greet street.

18 And in the entryng therof he made a tente, bi 'werk of broiderie, of iacynt, purpur, vermyloun, and of bijs foldid ayen, which tente hadde twenti cubitis in lengthe, and the heiythe was of fyue cubitis, bi the mesure which alle the tentis of the greet street hadden.

19 Forsothe the pylers in the entryng weren foure, with brasun foundementis, and the heedis of tho pilers and grauyngis weren of siluer;

20 and he made brasun stakis of the tabernacle, and of the greet street, bi cumpas.

21 These ben the instrumentis of the tabernacle of witnessyng, that ben noumbrid, bi the comaundement of Moises, in the cerymonyes of Leuytis, bi the hond of Ithamar, sone of Aaron, preest.

22 Whiche instrumentis Beseleel, sone of Huri, sone of Hur, of the lynage of Juda, fillide; for the Lord comaundide bi Moises,

23 while Ooliab, sone of Achysameth, of the lynage of Dan, was ioyned felowe to hym, and he hym silf was a noble crafti man of trees, and a tapesere and a broderere of iacynt, purpur, vermyloun and bijs.

24 Al the gold that was spendid in the werk of seyntuarie, and that was offrid in yiftis, was of 'nyne and twenti talentis, and of seuene hundrid and thretti siclis, at the mesure of seyntuarie.

25 Forsothe it was offrid of hem that passiden to noumbre fro twenti yeer and aboue, of sixe hundrid and thre thousand, and fyue hundrid and fifty of armed men.

26 Ferthermore, an hundrid talentis of siluer weren, of whiche the foundementis of the seyntuarie weren yotun togidere, and of the entryng, where the veil hangith;

27 an hundrid foundementis weren maad of an hundrid talentis, and for ech foundement was ordeyned o talent.

28 Forsothe of a thousynde seuene hundrid and 'thre scoor and fiftene siclis he made the heedis of pilers, and he 'clothide tho same pilers with siluer.

29 Also of bras weren offrid 'thre scoor and twelue thousynde talentis, and foure hundrid siclis ouer.

30 Of whiche the foundementis in the entryng of the tabernacle of witnessyng weren yotun, and the brasun auter, with his gridele, and al the vessels that perteynen to the vss therof,

31 and the foundementis of the greet street, as wel in the cumpas, as in the entryng therof, and the stakis of the tabernacle, and of the greet street bi cumpas.

CAP 39

1 Forsothe of iacynt, and purpur, vermyloun, and bijs, he made clothis, in whiche Aaron was clothid, whanne he mynystride in hooli thingis, as the Lord comaundide to Moises.

2 Therfor he made the 'cloth on the schuldris of gold, iacynt, and purpur, and of reed selk twies died,

3 and of bijs foldid ayen, bi werk of broiderie; also he kittide thinne goldun platis, and made thinne in to threedis, that tho moun be foldid ayen, with the warp of the formere colouris;

4 and he made tweyne hemmes couplid to hem silf to gidere, in euer either side of the endis; and 'he made a girdil of the same colouris,

5 as the Lord comaundide to Moises.

6 And he made redi twei 'stonys of onychyn, boundun and closid in gold, and grauun bi the craft of worchere in iemmys, with the names of the sones of Israel; sixe names in o stoon, and sixe in the tother stoon, bi the ordre of her birthe.

7 And he settide tho stoonus in the sidis of the 'clooth on the schuldris, in to a memorial of the sones of Israel, as the Lord comaundide to Moises.

8 He made also the racional, 'by werk of broiderie, bi the werk of the 'cloth on the schuldris, of gold, iacynt, purpur, and reed selk twies died, and of biis foldid ayen; he made the racional foure cornerid,

9 double, of the mesure of foure fyngris.

10 And settide thereynne foure ordris of iemmes; in the firste ordre was sardius, topazius, smaragdus; in the secounde was carbuncle,

11 safir, iaspis;

12 in the thridde ordre was ligurie, achates, ametiste;

13 in the fourthe ordre was crisolite, onochyn, and berille, cumpassid and enclosid with gold, bi her ordris.

14 And tho twelue stonys weren grauyn with twelue names, of the lynage of Israel, alle stonys bi hem silf, bi the names of alle lynagis bi hem silf.

15 Thei maden also in the racional litle chaynes, cleuynge to hem silf togidre,

16 of pureste gold, and tweyne hokys, and so many ryngis of gold. Forsothe thei settiden the ryngis on euer either side of the racional,

17 of whiche ryngis twei goldun chaynes hangiden, whiche thei settiden in the hokis, that stonden forth in the corneris of the 'cloth on the schuldris.

18 These acordiden so to hem silf, bothe bifore and bihynde, that the 'cloth on the schuldris, and the racional,

19 weren knyt togidere, fastned to the girdil, and couplid ful strongli with ryngis, whiche ryngis a lace of iacynt ioynede togidere, lest tho weren loose, and 'fletiden doun, and weren moued ech from other, as the Lord comaundide to Moises.

20 Thei maden also 'a coote on the schuldris, al of iacynt;

21 and the hood in the hiyere part, aboute the myddis, and a wouun hemme, bi the cumpas of the hood;

22 forsothe bynethe at the feet piyn applis of iacynt, and purpur, and vermyloun, and biys foldid ayen;

23 and litle bellis of pureste gold, whiche thei settiden bitwixe pum garnadis, in the 'lowest part of the coote, bi cumpas;

24 a goldun litle belle, and a piyn apple; with whiche the bischop yede ourned, whanne he 'was set in seruyce, as the Lord comaundide to Moises.

25 Thei maden also cootis of bijs, bi wouun werk, to Aaron and to hise sones,

26 and mytres with smale corouns of biys,

27 and lynnun clothis of bijs;

28 forsothe a girdil of bijs foldid ayen, of iacynt, purpur, and vermyloun, departid bi craft of broyderie, as the Lord comaundide to Moises.

29 Thei maden also a plate of hooli worschipyng, of pureste gold, and thei writeden therynne bi werk of a worchere in iemmes, The hooli of the Lord.

30 And thei bounden it with the mytre bi a lace of iacynt, as the Lord comaundide to Moises.

31 Therfor al the werk of the tabernacle, and the hilyng of the witnessyng, was parformed; and the sones of Israel diden alle thingis whiche the Lord comaundide to Moises.

32 And thei offeriden the tabernacle, and the roof, and al the purtenaunce, ryngis, tablis, barris, pileris, and foundementis;

33 the hilyng of 'skynnes of rammes, maad reed, and another hilyng of skynnys of iacynt;

34 the veil, the arke, barris, propiciatorie;

35 the boord with vessels, and with the looues of settyng forth;

36 the candilstike, lanternes, and the purtenauncis of tho, with oile;

37 the goldun auter, and oynement, and encense of swete smellynge spiceries;

38 and the tente in the entryng of the tabernacle;

39 the brasun auter, gridile, barris, and alle vessels therof; the 'greet waischyng vessel, with his foundement; the tentis of the greet street, and the pilers with her foundementis;

40 the tente in the entring of the greet street, and the coordis, and stakis therof. No thing of the vessels failide, that weren comaundid to be maad in to the seruyce of the tabernacle, and in to the roof of the boond of pees.

41 Also the sones of Israel offriden the clothis whiche the prestis, that is, Aaron and hise sones, vsen in the seyntuarie,

42 as the Lord comaundide.

43 And aftir that Moises siy alle tho thingis fillid, he blesside hem.

CAP 40

1 And the Lord spak to Moises, 'and seide,

2 In the firste monethe, in the firste dai of the monethe, thou schalt reise the tabernacle of witnessyng.

3 And thou schalt sette the arke therynne, and thou schalt leeue a veil bifore it.

4 And whanne the bord is borun yn, thou schalt sette ther onne tho thingis, that ben comaundid iustli. The candilstike schal stonde with hise lanternes,

5 and the goldun auter, where ynne encense is brent bifor the arke of witnessyng. Thou schalt sette a tente in the entryng of the tabernacle;

6 and bifor it the auter of brent sacrifice,

7 the 'waischyng vessel bitwixe the auter and the tabernacle, which 'waischyng vessel thou schalt fille with water.

8 And thou schalt cumpas the greet street, and the entryng ther of with tentis.

9 And whanne thou hast take oyle of anoyntyng, thou schalt anoynte the tabernacle, with hise vessels, that tho be halewid;

10 the auter of brent sacrifice, and alle vessels ther of; the 'waischyng vessel,

11 with his foundement. Thou schalt anoynte alle thingis with the oile of anoyntyng, that tho be hooli of hooli thingis.

12 And thou schalt present Aaron and hise sones to the dore of the tabernacle of witnessyng;

13 and, whanne thei ben 'waischid in water, thou schalt clothe hem with hooli clothis, that thei mynystre to me, and that the anoyntyng of hem profite in to euerlastynge preesthod.

14 And Moises dide alle thingis whiche the Lord comaundide.

15 Therfor in the firste monethe of the secunde yeer, in the firste dai of the monethe, the tabernacle was set.

16 And Moises reiside it, and settide the tablis, and foundementis, and barris, and he ordeynede pilers;

17 and 'spredde abrood the roof on the tabernacle, and puttide an hilyng aboue, as the Lord comaundide.

18 He puttide also the witnessyng in the arke, and he settide barris with ynne, and Goddis answeryng place aboue.

19 And whanne he hadde brouyt the arke in to the tabernacle, he hangide a veil bifor it, that he schulde fille the comaundement of the Lord.

20 He settide also the boord in the tabernacle of witnessyng, at the north coost, without the veil,

21 and he ordeynede the looues of settyng forth bifore, as the Lord comaundide to Moises.

22 He settide also the candilstike in the tabernacle of witnessyng, euene ayens the boord,

23 in the south side, and settide lanternes bi ordre, bi the comaundement of the Lord.

24 He puttide also the goldun auter vndur the roof of witnessyng,

25 ayens the veil, and he brente theronne encense of swete smellynge spiceries, as the Lord comaundide to Moises.

26 He settide also a tente in the entryng of the tabernacle,

27 and the auter of brent sacrifice in the porche of the witnessyng, and he offride therynne brent sacrifice, and sacrifices, as the Lord comaundide.

28 Also he ordeynede the 'waischyng vessel, bitwixe the tabernacle of witnessyng and the auter, and fillide it with watir.

29 And Moises, and Aaron, and his sones, waischiden her hondis and feet,

30 whanne thei entriden into the roof of boond of pees, and neiyeden to the auter, as the Lord comaundide to Moises.

31 He reiside also the greet street, bi the cumpas of the tabernacle and of the auter, and settyde a tente in the entryng therof. Aftir that alle thingis weren perfitli maad,

32 a cloude hilide the tabernacle of witnessyng, and the glorie of the Lord fillide it;

33 nether Moises myyte entre in to the tabernacle of the boond of pees, while the cloude hilide alle thingis, and the maieste of the Lord schynede, for the cloude hilide alle thingis.

34 If ony tyme the cloude lefte the tabernacle, the sones of Israel yeden forth bi her cumpanyes;

35 if the cloude hangide aboue, thei dwelliden in the same place;

36 for the cloude of the Lord restide on the tabernacle bi dai, and fier in the nyyt, in the siyt of the puplis of Israel, bi alle her dwellyngis.

LEVITICUS

CAP 1

1 FORSOTHE the Lord clepide Moyses, and spak to him fro the tabernacle of witnessyng, 'and seide,

2 Speke thou to the sones of Israel, and thou schalt seie to hem, A man of you, that offrith to the Lord a sacrifice of beestis, that is, of oxun and of scheep, and offrith slayn sacrifices, if his offryng is brent sacrifice,

3 and of the droue of oxun, he schal offre a male beeste without wem at the dore of the tabernacle of witnessyng, to make the Lord plesid to hym.

4 And he schal sette hondis on the heed of the sacrifice, and it schal be acceptable, and profityng in to clensyng of hym.

5 And he schal offre a calf bifor the Lord, and the sones of Aaron, preestis, schulen offre the blood ther of, and thei schulen schede bi the cumpas of the auter, which is bifor the dore of the tabernacle.

6 And whanne the skyn of the sacrifice is drawun awei, thei schulen kitte the membris in to gobetis;

7 and thei schulen put vndur in the auter fier, and thei schulen make an heep of wode bifore; and thei schulen ordeyne aboue

8 'the trees tho thingis that ben kit, that is, the heed, and alle thingis that cleuen to the mawe,

9 whanne the entrailis and feet ben waischid with watir; and the preest schal brenne tho on the auter, in to brent sacrifice, and swete odour to the Lord.

10 That if the offryng is of litle beestis, a brent sacrifice of scheep, ethir of geet, he schal offre a male beeste with out wem,

11 and he schal offre at the side of the auter that biholdith to the north, bifore the Lord. Sotheli the sones of Aaron schulen schede the blood therof on the auter 'bi cumpas,

12 and thei schulen departe the membris, the heed, and alle thingis that cleuen to the mawe, and thei schulen putte on the trees, vndur whiche the fier schal be set;

13 sotheli thei schulen waische in watir the entrailis and feet; and the preest schal brenne alle thingis offrid on the auter, in to brent sacrifice, and swettest odour to the Lord.

14 Forsothe if the offryng of brent sacrifice to the Lord is of briddis, of turtlis, and of culuer briddis,

15 the preest schal offre it at the auter; and whanne the heed is writhun to the necke, and the place of the wounde is brokun, he schal make the blood renne doun on the brenke of the auter.

16 Sotheli he schal caste forth the litil bladdir of the throte, and fetheris bisidis the auter, at the eest coost, in the place in which the aischis ben wont to be sched out;

17 and he schal breke the wyngis therof, and he schal not kerue, nether he schal departe it with yrun; and he schal brenne it on the auter, whanne fier is set vndur the trees; it is a brent sacrifice, and an offryng of swete odour to the Lord.

CAP 2

1 Whanne a soule offrith an offryng of sacrifice to the Lord, flour of wheete schal be his offring. And he schal schede oile ther onne,

2 and he schal putte encense, and he schal bere to the sones of Aaron, preest, of whiche sones oon schal take an handful of 'flour of whete, and of oile, and alle the encense; and he schal putte a memorial on the auter, in to swettest odour to the Lord.

3 Forsothe that that 'is residue of the sacrifice schal be Aarons and hise sones, the hooli of hooli thingis of offryngis to the Lord.

4 Forsothe whanne thou offrist a sacrifice bakun in an ouene of whete flour, that is, loouys without sour dow, spreynd with oile, and therf breed sodun in watir, bawmed with oile;

5 if thin offryng is 'of a friyng panne, of wheete flour spreynd with oile and without sour dow,

6 thou schalt departe it in smale partis, and thou schalt schede oile ther onne.

7 Ellis if the sacrifice is of a gridele, euenli the whete flour schal be spreynd with oile;

8 which whete flour thou schalt offre to the Lord, and schalt bitake in the hondis of the preest.

9 And whanne he hath offrid it, he schal take a memorial of the sacrifice, and he schal brenne it on the auter, in to 'odour of swetnesse to the Lord.

10 Sotheli what euer thing 'is residue, it schal be Aarons and hise sones, the hooly of hooli thingis of the offryngis to the Lord.

11 Ech offryng which is offrid to the Lord, schal be without sour dow, nether ony thing of sour dow, and of hony, schal be brent in the sacrifice of the Lord.

12 Ye schulen offre oneli the firste fruytis of tho, and yiftis; sotheli tho schulen not be put on the auter, in to odour of swetnesse.

13 Whateuer thing of sacrifice thou schalt offre, thou schalt make it sauery with salt, nether thou schalt take awey the salt of the boond of pees of thi God fro thi sacrifice; in ech offryng thou schalt offre salt.

14 Forsothe if thou offrist a yifte of the firste thingis of thi fruytis to the Lord, of 'eeris of corn yit grene, thou schalt seenge tho in fier, and thou schalt breke in the maner of seedis; and so thou schalt offre thi firste fruytis to the Lord,

15 and thou schalt schede oyle theronne, and schalt putte encense, for it is the offryng of the Lord.

16 Of which the preest schal brenne, in to mynde of the yifte, a part of the 'seedis brokun, and of oyle, and al the encense.

CAP 3

1 That if his offryng is a sacrifice of pesible thingis, and he wole offre of oxun, he schal offre bifore the Lord a male, ether a female, without wem.

2 And he schal sette hond on the heed of his sacrifice, that schal be offrid in the entryng of the tabernacle; and the sones of Aaron preest schulen schede the blood bi the cumpas of the auter.

3 And thei schulen offre of the sacrifice of pesible thingis in to offryng to the Lord, the fatnesse that hilith the entrailis, and what euer thing of fatnesse is with ynne;

4 thei schulen offre twey kydeneris, with the fatnesse bi which the guttis clepid ylyon ben hilid, and the calle of the lyuer with the litle reynes.

5 And thei schulen brenne tho on the auter, in to brent sacrifice, whanne fier is put vndur the trees, in to offryng of swettest odour to the Lord.

6 Sotheli if his offryng is of scheep, and a sacrifice of pesible thingis, whether he offrith a male ether a female, tho schulen be without wem.

7 If he offrith a lombe bifor the Lord,

8 he schal sette his hond on the heed of his sacrifice, that schal be offrid in the porche of the tabernacle of witnessyng; and the sones of Aaron schulen schede the blood therof bi 'the cumpas of the auter.

9 And thei schulen offre of the sacrifice of pesible thingis a sacrifice to the Lord, the innere fatnesse,

10 and al the tail with the reynes, and the fatnesse that hilith the wombe, and alle the entrailis, and euer eithir litil reyne, with the fatnesse which is bisidis the 'guttis clepid ylion, and the calle of the mawe, with the litle reynes.

11 And the preest schal brenne tho on the auter, in to the fedyng of fier, and of the offryng to the Lord.

12 If his offryng is a geet, and he offrith it to the Lord,

13 he schal sette his hond on the heed therof, and he schal offre it in to the entryng of the tabernacle of witnessyng; and the sones of Aaron schulen schede the blood therof bi the cumpas of the auter.

14 And thei schulen take therof, in to 'the fedyng of the Lordis fier, the fatnesse that hilith the wombe, and that hilith alle the entrailis,

15 and twei litle reynes with the calle which is on tho bisidis ilion, and the fatnesse of the mawe, with the entrails that cleuen to the litle reynes.

16 And the preest schal brenne tho on the auter, in to the fedyng of fier, and of swettest odour; al the fatnesse schal be the Lordis,

17 by euerlastynge riyt in generaciouns, and in alle youre dwellyng placis, nether in ony maner ye schulen ete blood, nethir fatnesse.

CAP 4

1 And the Lord spak to Moises, and seide, Speke thou to the sones of Israel,

2 Whanne a soule hath do synne bi ignoraunce, and hath do ony thing of alle comaundementis 'of the Lord, whiche he comaundide that tho schulen not be don; if a preest which is anoyntid,

3 hath do synne, makynge the puple to trespasse, he schal offre for his synne a calf without wem to the Lord.

4 And he schal brynge it to the dore of the tabernacle of witnessyng, bifor the Lord, and he schal sette hond on the heed therof, and he schal offre it to the Lord.

5 And he schal take vp of the blood 'of the calf, and schal brynge it in to the tabernacle of witnessyng.

6 And whanne he hath dippid the fyngir in to the blood, he schal sprenge it seuen sithis bifor the Lord, ayens the veil of the seyntuarie.

7 And he schal putte of the same blood on the corners of the auter of encense moost acceptable to the Lord, which auter is in the tabernacle of witnessyng; sotheli he schal schede al the 'tother blood in to the foundement of the auter of brent sacrifice in the entryng of the tabernacle.

8 And he schal offre for synne the ynnere fatnesse of the calf, as well it that hilith the entrails, as alle thingis that ben with ynne,

9 twei litle reynes, and the calle, which is on tho bisidis ilion, and the fatnesse of the mawe,

10 with the litle reines, as it is offrid of the calf of the sacrifice of pesible thingis; and he schal brenne tho on the auter of
brent sacrifice.

11 Sotheli he schal bere out of the castels the skyn, and alle
the fleischis, with the heed, and feet, and entrails,

12 and dung, and the 'residue bodi in to a clene place, where
aischis ben wont to be sched out; and he schal brenne tho on
the heep of trees, whiche schulen be brent in the place of aischis sched out.

13 That if al the cumpeny of the sones of Israel knowith not,
and doith by vnkunnyng that that is ayens the comaundement
of the Lord,

14 and aftirward vndirstondith his synne, it schal offre a calf
for synne, and it schal brynge the calf to the dore of the tabernacle.

15 And the eldere men of the puple schulen sette hondis on
the heed therof bifor the Lord; and whanne the calf is offrid in
the siyt of the Lord,

16 the preest which is anoyntid schal bere ynne of his blood
in to the tabernacle of witnessyng;

17 and whanne the fyngur 'is dippid, he schal sprenge seuen
sithis ayens the veil.

18 And he schal putte of the same blood in the hornes of the
auter, which is bifor the Lord in the tabernacle of witnessyng;
sotheli he schal schede the 'residue blood bisidis the foundement of the auter of brent sacrifice, which is in the dore of
tabernacle of witnessyng.

19 And he schal take al the fatnesse therof, and schal brenne
it on the auter;

20 and so he schal do also of this calf, as he dide also bifor;
and whanne the prest schal preye for hem, the Lord schal be
merciful.

21 Forsothe he schal bere out thilke calf, and schal brenne it,
as also the formere calf, for it is for the synne of the multitude.

22 If the prince synneth, and doith bi ignoraunce o thing of
many, which is forbodun in the lawe of the Lord,

23 and aftirward vndirstondith his synne, he schal offre to the
Lord a sacrifice, a 'buk of geet, 'that hath no wem;

24 and he schal sette his hond on the heed therof. And
whanne he hath offrid it in the place, where brent sacrifice is
wont to be slayn, bifor the Lord, for it is for synne;

25 the preest schal dippe the fyngur in the blood of sacrifice
for synne, and he schal touche the corneris of the auter of
brent sacrifice, and he schal schede the 'residue blood at the
foundement therof.

26 Sotheli the preest schal brenne the innere fatnesse aboue
the auter, as it is wont to be doon in the sacrifice of pesible
thingis, and the preest schal preye for hym, and for his synne,
and it schal be foryouun to hym.

27 That if a soule of the puple of the lond synneth bi
ignoraunce, that he do ony thing of these that ben forbodun in
the lawe of the Lord, and trespassith,

28 and knowith his synne, he schal offre a geet without wem;
29 and he schal sette hond on the heed of the sacrifice which
is for synne, and he schal offre it in the place of brent sacrifice.

30 And the preest schal take of the blood on his fyngur, and
he schal touche the hornes of the auter of brent sacryfice, and
he schal schede the residue at the foundement therof.

31 Sotheli he schal take a wei al the ynnere fatnesse, as it is
wont to be don a wei of the sacrifices of pesible thingis, and
he schal brenne it on the auter, in to odour of swetnesse to the
Lord; and the preest schal preye for hym, and it schal be foryouun to hym.

32 Sotheli if he offrith of litle beestis a sacrifice for synne,
that is,

33 a scheep without wem, he schal putte the hond on the heed
therof, and he schal offre it in the place where the beest of
brent sacrifices ben wont to be slayn.

34 And the preest schal take of the blood therof in his fyngur,
and he schal touche the hornes of the autir of brent sacrifice,
and he schal schede the residue at the foundement therof.

35 And he schal do awey al the ynnere fatnesse as the innere
fatnesse of the ram which is offrid for pesible thingis, is wont
to be don a wei, and he schal brenne it on the auter of
encense of the Lord; and the preest schal preye for hym, and
for his synne, and it schal be foryouun to hym.

CAP 5

1 If a soule synneth, and hereth the vois of a swerere, and is
witnesse, 'for ether he siy, ether 'is witynge, if he schewith
not, he schal bere his synne.

2 A persone that touchith ony vnclene thing, ether which is
slayn of a beeste, ether is deed bi it silf, ether touchith ony
other crepynge beeste, and foryetith his vnclennesse, he is
gilti, and trespassith.

3 And if he touchith ony thing of the vnclennesse of man, bi
al the vnclennesse bi which he is wont to be defoulid, and he
foryetith, and knowith afterward, he schal be suget to trespas.
4 A soule that swerith, and bryngith forth with hise lippis, that
it schulde do ether yuel, ether wel, and doith not, and confermeth the same thing with an ooth, ethir with a word, and foryetith, and aftirward vndirstondith his trespas, do it penaunce
for synne,

5 and offre it of the flockis a femal lomb, ethir a goet;
6 and the preest schal preie for hym, and for his synne.
7 But if he may not offre a beeste, offre he twei turtlis, ethir
'briddis of culuers to the Lord, oon for synne, and the tother
in to brent sacrifice.

8 And he schal yyue tho to the preest, which schal offre the
firste for synne, and schal folde ayen the heed therof to the
wengis, so that it cleue to the necke, and be not 'brokyn outirli.

9 And the preest schal sprynge the wal of the auter, of the
blood therof; sotheli what euer 'is residue, he schal make to
droppe doun at the 'foundement of the auter, for it is for
synne.

10 Sotheli he schal brenne the tother brid in to brent sacrifice, as it is wont to be doon; and the preest schal preie for
hym, and for his synne, and it schal be foryouun to hym.

11 That if his hond mai not offre twei turtlis, ethir twei 'briddis of culueris, he schal offre for his synne the tenthe part of
ephi of wheete flour; he schal not putte oile 'in to it, nether he
schal putte ony thing of encense, for it is for synne.

12 And he schal yyue it to the preest, which preest schal take
vp an handful therof, and schal brenne on the auter, in to
mynde of hym that offeride,

13 and the preest schal preie for hym, and schal clense; forsothe he schal have the tother part in yifte.

14 And the Lord spak to Moises,

15 and seide, If a soule brekith cerymonyes bi errour, and
synneth in these thingis that ben halewid to the Lord, it schal
offre for his trespas a ram without wem of the flockis, that
may be bouyt for twey siclis, bi the weiyte of the seyntuarie.

16 And he schal restore that harm that he dide, and he schal putte the fyuethe part aboue, and schal yyue to the preest, which preest schal preye for hym, and offre the ram, and it schal be foryouun to hym.

17 A soule that synneth bi ignoraunce, and doith oon of these thingis that ben forbodun in the lawe of the Lord, and is gilti of synne, and vndirstondith his wickidnesse,

18 it schal offre to the preest a ram without wem of the flockis, bi the mesure of estymacioun of synne; and the preest schal preye for hym, for he dide vnwytynge, and it schal be foryouun to him,

19 for by errour he trespasside ayens the Lord.

CAP 6

1 And the Lord spak to Moises,

2 and seide, A soule that synneth, and dispisith the Lord, and denyeth to his neiybore a thing bitakun to kepyng, that was bitakun to his feith, ethir takith maisterfuli a thing bi violence, ether makith fals chaleng,

3 ether fyndith a thing lost, and denyeth ferthermore and forswerith, and doth ony other thing of manye in whiche thingis men ben wont to do synne,

4 'if it is conuict of the gilt,

5 it schal yelde hool alle thingis whiche it wolde gete bi fraude, and ferthermore the fyuethe part to the lord, to whom it dide harm.

6 Sotheli for his synne it schal offre a ram vnwemmed of the floc, and it schal yyue that ram to the preest, bi the valu and mesure of the trespas;

7 and the preest schal preie for hym bifor the Lord, and it schal be foryouun to hym, for alle thingis whiche he synnede in doyng.

8 And the Lord spak to Moises, and seide,

9 Comaunde thou to Aaron, and to hise sones, This is the lawe of brent sacrifice; it schal be brent in the auter al nyyt til the morewe; fier that is youun fro heuene schal be of the same auter.

10 The preest schal be clothid with a coote, and 'pruuy lynnun clothis; and he schal take awei the aischis, which the fier deuourynge brente, and he schal putte bisidis the auter;

11 and he schal be spuylid of the formere clothis, and he schal be clothid with other, and schal bere aischis out of the castels, and in a moost clene place he schal make tho to be wastid til to a deed sparcle.

12 Forsothe fier schal brenne euere in the auter, which fier the preest schal nurische, puttynge trees vndur, in the morewtid bi ech dai; and whanne brent sacrifice is put aboue, the preest schal brenne the ynnere fatnessis of pesible thingis.

13 This is euerlastynge fier, that schal neuer faile in the auter.

14 This is the lawe of sacrifice, and of fletynge offryngis, whiche 'the sones of Aaron schulen offre bifore the Lord, and bifor the auter.

15 The preest schal take an handful of wheete flour, which is spreynd with oile, and al the encense which is put on the wheete flour, and he schal brenne it in the auter, in to mynde of swettist odour to the Lord.

16 Forsothe Aaron with hise sones schal ete the tother part of wheete flour, without sour dow; and he schal ete in the hooli place of the greet street of the tabernacle.

17 Sotheli herfor it schal not be 'diyt with sour dow, for a part therof is offrid in to encense of the Lord; it schal be hooli 'of the noumbre of holi thingis, as for synne and for trespas.

18 Malis oonli of the kynrede of Aaron schulen ete it; it is a lawful thing and euerlastynge in youre generaciouns, of the sacrifice of the Lord; ech man that touchith tho schal be halewyd.

19 And the Lord spak to Moises,

20 and seide, This is the offryng of Aaron, and of hise sones, which thei owen offre to the Lord in the day of her anoyntyng; thei schulen offre the tenthe part of ephi of wheete flour, in euerlastynge sacrifice, the myddis therof in the morewtid, and the myddis therof in the euentid;

21 which schal be spreynt with oile in the friyng panne, and schal be fried.

22 Sotheli the preest which is successour to the fadir 'bi riyt, schal offre it hoot, in to sweteste odour to the Lord; and al it schal be brent in the auter.

23 For al the sacrifice of preestis schal be wastid with fier, nether ony man schal ete therof.

24 And the Lord spak to Moises, and seide,

25 Spek thou to Aaron and to hise sones, This is the lawe of sacrifice for synne; it schal be offrid bifor the Lord, in the place where brent sacrifice is offrid; it is hooli 'of the noumbre of hooli thingis.

26 The preest that offrith it, schal ete it in the hooli place, in the greet street of the tabernacle.

27 What euer thing schal touche the fleischis therof, it schal be halewid; if a cloth is bispreynt of the blood therof, it schal be waischun in the hooli place.

28 Sotheli the erthun vessel, in which it is sodun, schal be brokun; that if the vessel is of bras, it schal be scourid, and 'schal be waischun with watir.

29 Ech male of preestis kyn schal ete of the fleischis therof; for it is hooli 'of the noumbre of hooli thingis.

30 Sotheli the sacrifice which is slayn for synne, whos blood is borun in to the tabernacle of witnessyng to clense in the seyntuarie, schal not be etun, but it schal be brent in fier.

CAP 7

1 And this is the lawe of sacrifice for trespas; it is hooli 'of the noumbre of hooli thingis.

2 Therfor where brent sacrifice is offrid, also the sacrifice for trespas schal be slayn; the blood therof schal be sched bi the cumpas of the auter.

3 Thei schulen offre the tail therof, and the fatnesse that hilith the entrailis,

4 the twei litle reynes, and the fatnesse which is bisidis ilioun, and the calle of the mawe, with the litle reynes.

5 And the preest schal brenne tho on the auter; it is encense of the Lord, for trespas.

6 Ech male of the preestis kyn schal ete these fleischis in the hooli place, for it is hooli 'of the noumbre of hooli thingis.

7 As a sacrifice is offrid for synne, so and for trespas, o lawe schal be of euer eithir sacrifice; it schal perteyne to the preest, that offrith it.

8 The preest that offrith the beeste of brent sacrifice, schal haue the skyn therof.

9 And ech sacrifice of wheete flour, which is bakun in an ouene, and what euer is maad redi in a gridile, ethir in a friyng panne, it schal be that preestis, of whom it is offrid,

10 whether it is spreynt with oile, ethir is drye. To alle the sones of Aaron euene mesure schal be departyd, 'to ech 'bi hem silf.

11 This is the lawe of 'the sacrifice of pesible thingis, which is offrid to the Lord.

12 If the offryng is for doyng of thankyngis, thei schulen offre looues without sour dow spreynt with oile, and 'therf looues sodun in watir, that ben anoyntid with oile; and thei

schulen offre wheete flour bakun, and thinne looues spreynt to gidere with the medlyng of oile.

13 Also thei schulen offre 'looues diyt with sour dow, with the sacrifice of thankyngis which is offrid for pesible thingis;

14 of whiche o loof schal be offrid to the Lord for the firste fruytis, and it schal be the preestis that schal schede the blood of the sacrifice,

15 whose fleischis schulen be etun in the same dai, nether ony thing of tho schal dwelle til the morewtid.

16 If a man offrith a sacrifice bi a vow, ethir bi fre wille, it schal be etun in lijk maner in the same dai; but also if ony thing dwellith 'in to the morew, it is leueful to ete it;

17 sotheli fier schal waaste, whateuer thing the thridde day schal fynde.

18 If ony man etith in the thridde dai of the fleischis of sacrifice of pesible thingis, his offryng schal be maad voide, nethir it schal profite to the offerere; but rather whateuer soule defoulith hym silf with suche mete, he schal be gilti of 'brekyng of the lawe.

19 Fleisch that touchith ony vnclene thing, schal not be etun, but it schal be brent bi fier; he that is clene, schal ete it.

20 A pollutid soule, that etith of the fleischis of the sacrifice of pesible thingis, which is offrid to the Lord, schal perische fro hise puplis.

21 And he that touchith vnclennesse of man, ether of beeste, ether of alle thing that may defoule, and etith of suche fleischis, schal perische fro hise puplis.

22 And the Lord spak to Moises,

23 and seide, Speke thou to the sones of Israel, Ye schulen not ete the ynnere fatnesse of a scheep, of an oxe, and of a geet;

24 ye schulen haue in to dyuerse vsis the ynnere fatnesse of a carkeis deed by it silf, and of that beeste which is takun of a rauenus beeste.

25 If ony man etith the ynnere fatnesse, that owith to be offrid in to encense of the Lord, he schal perische fro his puple.

26 Also ye schulen not take in mete the blood of ony beeste, as wel of briddis as of beestis;

27 ech man that etith blood schal perische fro his puplis.

28 And the Lord spak to Moises,

29 and seide, Speke thou to the sones of Israel, He that offrith a sacrifice of pesible thingis to the Lord, offre togidere also a sacrifice, that is, fletynge offryngis therof.

30 He schal holde in the hondis the ynnere fatnesse of the sacrifice, and the brest; and whanne he hath halewid bothe offrid to the Lord, he schal yyue to the preest,

31 which schal brenne the ynnere fatnesse on the auter; sotheli the brest schal be Aarons and hise sones;

32 and the riyt schuldur of the sacrifices of pesible thingis schal turne in to the firste fruytis of the preest.

33 He that of Aarons sones offrith the blood, and the ynnere fatnesse, schal haue also the riyt schuldur in his porcioun.

34 For Y haue take fro the sones of Israel the brest of reisyng, and the schuldur of departyng, of the pesible sacrifices 'of hem, and Y haue youe to Aaron the preest and to hise sones, bi euerlastynge lawe, of al the puple of Israel.

35 This is the anoyntyng of Aaron, and of hise sones, in the cerymonyes of the Lord, in the dai where ynne Moises offride hem that thei schulden be set in preesthod,

36 and whiche thingis the Lord comaundide to be youun to hem of the sones of Israel, bi euerlastynge religioun in her generaciouns.

37 This is the lawe of brent sacrifice, and of sacrifice for synne, and for trespas, and for halewyng, and for the sacrifices of pesible thingis;

38 which lawe the Lord ordeynede to Moises in the hil of Synay, whanne he comaundide to the sones of Israel that thei schulden offre her offryngis to the Lord, in the deseert of Synay.

CAP 8

1 And the Lord spak to Moises, and seide, Take thou Aaron with hise sones,

2 'the clothes of hem, and the oile of anoyntyng, a calf for synne, twei rammes, a panyere with therf looues;

3 and thou schalt gedere al the cumpanye to the dore of the tabernacle.

4 Moises dide as the Lord comaundide; and whanne al the company was gaderid bifor the yatis of the tabernacle, he seide,

5 This is the word which the Lord comaundid to be don.

6 And anoon Moises offride Aaron and hise sones; and whanne he hadde waischun hem,

7 he clothide the bischop with a lynnun schirte, 'and girdide 'the bischop with a girdil, and clothide with a coote of iacynt, and 'puttide the cloth on the schuldris aboue,

8 which cloth on the schuldris he boond with a girdil, and 'dresside to the racional, wherynne doctryn and truthe was.

9 And Moises hilide the heed with a mytre, and 'settide theronne, ayens the forhed, the goldun plate halewid in halewyng, as the Lord comaundide to hym.

10 He took also the oile of anoyntyng, with which he anoyntide the tabernacle with al his purtenaunce;

11 and whanne he hadde halewid and hadde spreynt the auter seuen sithes, he anoyntide it, and halewide with oile alle the vessels therof, and the 'greet waischyng vessel with his foundement.

12 Which oile he schedde on 'the heed of Aaron, and anoyntide hym, and halewide.

13 And he clothide with lynnun cootis, and girdide with girdils 'his sones offrid, and settide on mytris, as the Lord comaundide.

14 He offeride also a calf for synne; and whanne Aaron and hise sones hadden put her hondis on 'that calf,

15 he offride it, and drow up blood; and whanne the fyngur was dippid, he touchide the corneris of the auter bi cumpas; whanne the auter was clensid and halewid, he schedde the 'residue blood at the 'foundement therof.

16 Sotheli he brent on the auter the ynnere fatnesse that was on the entrails, and the calle of the mawe, and the twei litle reynes with her litle fatnessis;

17 and he brente without the castels the calf, with the skyn, fleischis, and dung, as the Lord comaundide.

18 He offride also a ram in to brent sacrifice; and whanne Aaron and hise sones hadden set her hondis on the heed therof,

19 he offride it, and schedde the blood therof bi the cumpas of the auter.

20 And he kittide thilke ram in to gobetis, and brente with fier the heed therof, and membris,

21 and ynnere fatnesse, whanne the entrails and feet weren waischun bifore; and he brente al the ram togidere on the auter, for it was the brent sacrifice of swettiste odour to the Lord, as the Lord comaundide to hym.

22 He offride also the secounde ram, in to the halewyng of preestis; and Aaron and hise sones puttiden her hondis on the heed therof.

23 And whanne Moises hadde offrid the ram, he took of the blood, and touchide the laste part of the riyt eere of Aaron, and the thombe of his riyt hond, in lijk maner and of the foot.

24 He offride also 'the sones of Aaron. And whanne he hadde touchid of the blood of the ram offrid the laste part of 'the riyt eeris of alle, and 'the thombis of the riyt hond and foot, he schedde the 'tothir blood on the auter bi cumpas.

25 Sotheli he departide the ynnere fatnesse, and the taile, and al the fatnesse that hilith the entrails, and the calle of the mawe, and the twey reynes with her fatnessis and with the riyt schuldur.

26 Forsothe he took of the panyere of therf looues, that was bifor the Lord, looues without sour dow, and a cake spreynt with oile, and he puttide looues first sodun in watir and aftirward fried in oile on the ynnere fatnesse, and the riyt schuldur; and bitook alle thingis togidere to Aaron,

27 and to hise sones. And aftir that thei 'reisiden tho bifore the Lord,

28 eft 'he brente tho takun of her hondis, on the auter of brent sacrifice, for it was the offryng of halewyng, in to the odour of swetnesse of sacrifice 'into his part to the Lord.

29 He took also the brest of the ram of consecracioun in to his part, and reiside it bifor the Lord, as the Lord comaundide to hym.

30 And he took the oynement, and blood that was in the auter, and 'spreynte on Aaron, and hise clothis, and on 'the sones of hym, and on her clothis.

31 And whanne he hadde halewid hem in her clothing, he comaundide to hem, and seide, Sethe ye fleischis bifor the 'yatis of the tabernacle, and there ete ye tho; also ete ye the looues of halewyng, that ben put in the panyere, as God comaundide to me, 'and seide, Aaron and hise sones schulen ete tho looues;

32 sotheli whateuer thing is residue of the fleisch and looues, fier schal waste.

33 Also ye schulen not go out of the dore of the tabernacle in seuene daies, til to the day in which the tyme of youre halewyng schal be fillid; for the halewyng is endid in seuene dayes,

34 as it is doon in present tyme, that the riytfulnesse of sacrifice were fillid.

35 Ye schulen dwelle dai and nyyt in the tabernacle, and ye schulen kepe the kepyngis of the Lord, that ye die not; for so it is comaundid to me.

36 And Aaron and hise sones diden alle thingis, whiche the Lord spak bi the hond of Moises.

CAP 9

1 Forsothe whanne the eiytithe dai was maad, Moises clepide Aaron, and hise sones, and the grettere men in birthe of Israel;

2 and he seide to Aaron, Take thou of the droue a calf for synne, and a ram 'in to brent sacrifice, euer either with oute wem, and offre tho bifor the Lord.

3 And thou schalt speke to the sones of Israel, Take ye a buk of geet for synne, and a calf, and a lomb of o yeer and with out wem,

4 in to brent sacrifice, an oxe and a ram for pesible thingis; and offre ye tho bifor the Lord, and offre ye whete flour spreynt with oile in the sacrifice of ech; for to dai the Lord schal appere to you.

5 Therfor thei token alle thingis, whiche Moises comaundide, to the dore of the tabernacle, where, whanne al the multitude stood,

6 Moises seide, This is the word, which the Lord comaundide, do ye, and his glorie schal appere to you.

7 And Moises seide to Aaron, Neiye thou to the auter, and offre thou for thi synne; offre thou brent sacrifice, and preye for thee, and for the puple; and whanne thou hast slayn the sacrifice of the puple, preye thou for hem, as the Lord comaundide.

8 And anoon Aaron neiyede to the auter, and offride a calf for his synne;

9 whos blood hise sones offriden to him, in which blood he dippide the fyngur, and touchide the hornes of the auter, and schedde the residue at the foundement therof;

10 and he brente on the auter the ynnere fatnesse, and litle reynes, and the calle of the mawe, as the Lord comaundide to Moises.

11 Forsothe he brente bi fier without the castels the fleischis and skyn therof.

12 And he offride the beeste of brent sacrifice, and hise sones offriden to hym the blood therof, which he schedde bi the cumpas of the auter;

13 thei offriden also thilke sacrifice kit in to gobetis, with the heed, and alle membris; and he brente bi fier alle these thingis on the auter,

14 whanne the entrailis and feet weren waischun bifor with watir.

15 And he offride and killide a buk of geet, for the synne of the puple; and whanne the auter was clensid,

16 he made brent sacrifice,

17 and addide in to the sacrifice fletynge offryngis that ben offrid togidere; and he brente tho on the auter, without cerymonyes of brent sacrifice of the morewtid.

18 He offride also an oxe, and a ram, pesible sacrifices of the puple; and hise sones offriden to hym the blood, which he schedde bi the cumpas of the auter.

19 Forsothe thei puttiden on the brestis the ynnere fatnesse of the oxe, and the tail of the ram, and the litle reynes with her fatnessis, and the calle of the mawe.

20 And whanne the ynnere fatnessis weren brent in the auter,

21 Aaron departide the brestis, and the riyt schuldris of tho, and reiside bifor the Lord, as Moises comaundide.

22 And he streiyte forth hondis to the puple, and blesside it; and so whanne the sacrifices for synne, and brent sacrifices, and pesible sacrifices, weren fillid, he cam doun.

23 Sotheli Moyses and Aaron entriden in to the tabernacle of witnessyng, and yeden out aftirward, and blessiden the puple; and the glorie of the Lord apperide to al the multitude.

24 And lo! fier yede out fro the Lord, and deuouride the brent sacrifice, and the ynnere fatnesses that weren on the auter; and whanne the cumpanyes hadden seyn this thing, thei preiseden the Lord, 'and felden on her faces.

CAP 10

1 And whanne Nadab and Abyu, the sones of Aaron, hadden take censeris, thei puttiden fier and encense aboue, and offriden bifor the Lord alien fier, which thing was not comaundid to hem.

2 And fier yede out fro the Lord, and deuouride hem, and thei weren deed bifor the Lord.

3 And Moises seide to Aaron, This thing it is which the Lord spak, Y schal be halewid in hem that neiyen to me, and Y

schal be glorified in the siyt of al the puple; which thing Aaron herde, and was stille.

4 Sotheli whanne Moises hadde clepid Mysael and Elisaphan, the sones of Oziel, brother of Aaron's fadir, he seide to hem, Go ye, and take awey youre britheren fro the siyt of seyntuarie, and bere ye out of the castels.

5 And anoon thei yeden, and token hem, as thei laien clothid with lynnun cootis, and castiden out, as it was comaundid to hem.

6 And Moises spak to Aaron, and to Eliasar and Ithamar, the sones of Aaron, Nyle ye make nakid youre heedis, and nyle ye reende clothis, lest perauenture ye dien, and indignacioun rise on al the cumpany; youre britheren and all the hows of Israel byweile the brennyng which the Lord reiside.

7 But ye schulen not go out of the yatis of the tabernacle, ellis ye schulen perische; for the oile of hooli anoyntyng is on you. Whiche diden alle thingis bi the comaundement of Moises.

8 Also the Lord seide to Aaron,

9 Thou and thi sones schulen not drynke wyn, and al thing that may make drunkun, whanne ye schulen entre in to the tabernacle of witnessing, lest ye dien; for it is euerlastynge comaundement in to youre generaciouns,

10 that ye haue kunnyng to make doom bytwixe hooli thing and vnhooli, bitwixe pollutid thing and cleene;

11 and that ye teche the sones of Israel alle my lawful thingis, whiche the Lord spak to hem bi the hond of Moyses.

12 And Moises spak to Aaron, and to Eliazar and Ythamar, hise sones, that weren residue, Take ye the sacrifice that lefte of the offryng of the Lord, and ete ye it with out sour dow, bisidis the auter, for it is hooli 'of the noumbre of hooli thingis.

13 Sotheli ye schulen ete in the hooli place that that is youun to thee and to thi sones, of the offryngis of the Lord, as it is comaundid to me Also thou,

14 and thi sones, and thi douytris with thee, schulen ete in the clenneste place the brest which is offrid, and the schuldur which is departid; for tho ben kept to thee and to thi fre sones, of the heelful sacrifices of the sones of Israel;

15 for thei reiseden bifor the Lord the schuldur and brest, and the ynnere fatnessis that ben brent in the auter; and perteynen tho to thee, and to thi sones, bi euerlastynge lawe, as the Lord comaundide.

16 Among these thingis whanne Moises souyte the 'buk of geet that was offrid for synne, he foond it brent, and he was wrooth ayens Eliazar and Ythamar, 'the sones of Aaron that weren left.

17 And he seide, Whi eten not ye the sacrifice for synne in the hooli place, which sacrifice is hooli 'of the noumbre of hooli thingis, and is youun to you, that ye bere the wickydnesse of the multitude, and preye for it in the siyt of the Lord;

18 moost sithen of the blood therof is not borun yn with ynne hooli thingis, and ye ouyten ete it in the seyntuarie, as it is comaundid to me?

19 And Aaron answeride, Sacrifice for synne, and brent sacrifice is offrid to dai bifor the Lord; sotheli this that thou seest, bifelde to me; how myyte Y ete it, ether plese God in cerymonyes with soreuful soule?

20 And whanne Moises hadde herd this, he resseyuede satisfaccioun.

CAP 11

1 And the Lord spak to Moises and Aaron, and seide,

2 Seie ye to the sones of Israel, Kepe ye alle thingis whiche Y wroot to you, that Y be youre God. These ben the beestis, whiche ye schulen ete, of alle lyuynge beestis of erthe;

3 ye schulen ete 'al thing among beestis that hath a clee departid, and chewith code;

4 sotheli what euer thing chewith code, and hath a clee, but departith not it, as a camel and othere beestis doon, ye schulen not ete it, and ye schulen arette among vnclene thingis.

5 A cirogrille, which chewith code, and departith not the clee, is vnclene; and an hare,

6 for also he chewith code, but departith not the clee;

7 and a swiyn, that chewith not code, thouy he departith the clee.

8 Ye schulen not ete the fleischis of these, nether ye schulen touche the deed bodies, for tho ben vnclene to you.

9 Also these thingis ben that ben gendrid in watris, and is leueful to ete;

10 ye schulen ete al thing that hath fynnes and scalis, as wel in the see, as in floodis and stondynge watris; sotheli what euer thing of tho that ben moued and lyuen in watris, hath not fynnes and scalis, schal be abhominable, and wlatsum to you;

11 ye schulen not ete the fleischis of tho, and ye schulen eschewe the bodies deed bi hem silf.

12 Alle thingis in watris that han not fynnes and scalis, schulen be pollutid,

13 These thingis ben of foulis whiche ye schulen not ete, and schulen be eschewid of you; an egle, and a grippe, aliete, and a kyte, and a vultur by his kynde;

14 and al of 'rauyns kynde bi his licnesse;

15 a strucioun,

16 and nyyt crowe, a lare, and an hauke bi his kinde;

17 an owle, and dippere, and ibis;

18 a swan and cormoraunt, and a pellican;

19 a fawcun, a iay bi his kynde; a leepwynke, and a reremows.

20 Al thing of foulis that goith on foure feet, schal be abhomynable to you;

21 sotheli what euer thing goith on foure feet, but hath lengere hipis bihynde, bi whiche it skippith on the erthe, ye schulen ete;

22 as is a bruke in his kynde, and acatus, and opymacus, and a locuste, alle bi her kynde.

23 Forsothe what euer thing of briddis hath foure feet oneli, it schal be abhomynable to you;

24 and who euer touchith her bodies deed bi hem silf, schal be defoulid, and 'schal be vnclene 'til to euentid;

25 and if it is nede, that he bere ony deed thing of these, he schal waische his clothis, and he schal be vnclene til to the goyng doun of the sunne.

26 Sotheli ech beeste that hath a clee, but departith not it, nether chewith code, schal be vnclene; and what euer thing touchith it, schal be defoulid.

27 That that goith on hondis, of alle beestis that gon on foure feet, schal be vnclene; he, that touchith her bodies deed bi hem silf, schal be defoulid 'til to euentid;

28 and he, that berith siche deed bodies, schal waische hise clothis, and he schal be vnclene 'til to euentid; for alle these thingis ben vnclene to you.

29 Also these thingis schulen be arettid among defoulid thingis, of these that ben moued on erthe; a wesele, and mows, and a cocodrille, 'alle bi her kynde;

30 mygal, camelion, and stellio, and lacerta, and a maldewerp.

31 Alle these ben vnclene; he that touchith her bodies deed bi hem silf, schal be vnclene 'til to euentid;

32 and that thing schal be defoulid, on which ony thing of her bodies deed bi hem silf fallith, as wel a vessel of tree, and a cloth, as skynnes 'and heiris; and in what euer thing werk is maad, it schal be dippid in watir, and tho thingis schulen be defoulid 'til to euentid, and so aftirward tho schulen be clensid.

33 Sotheli a vessel of erthe, in which ony thing of these fallith with ynne, schal be defoulid, and therfor it schal be brokun.

34 Ech mete, which ye schulen ete, schal be vnclene, if water is sched thereon; and ech fletynge thing, which is drunkun of ech vessel, 'where ynne vnclene thingis bifelden, schal be vnclene;

35 and what euer thing of siche deed bodies bi hem silf felde theronne, it schal be vnclene, whether furneisis, ethir vessels of thre feet, tho schulen be destried, and schulen be vnclene.

36 Sotheli wellis and cisternes, and al the congregacioun of watris, schal be clene. He that touchith her bodi deed bi it silf, schal be defoulid.

37 If it fallith on seed, it schal not defoule the seed;

38 sotheli if ony man schedith seed with watir, and aftirward the watir is touchid with deed bodies bi hem silf, it schal be defoulid anoon.

39 If a beeste is deed, which it is leueful to you to ete, he that touchith the deed bodi therof schal be vnclene 'til to euentid; and he that etith therof ony thing,

40 ethir berith, schal waische his clothis, and schal be vnclene 'til to euentid.

41 Al thing that crepith on erthe, schal be abhomynable, nether schal be takun in to mete.

42 'What euer thing goith on the brest and foure feet, and hath many feet, ethir drawun bi the erthe, ye schulen not ete, for it is abhomynable.

43 Nyle ye defoule youre soulis, nether touche ye ony thing of tho, lest ye ben vnclene;

44 for Y am youre Lord God; be ye hooli, for Y am hooli. Defoule ye not youre soulis in ech crepynge 'beeste which is moued on erthe; for Y am the Lord,

45 that ladde you out of the lond of Egipt, that Y schulde be to you in to God; ye schulen be hooli, for Y am hooli.

46 This is the lawe of lyuynge beestes, and of foulis, and of ech lyuynge soule which is moued in watir, and crepith in erthe;

47 that ye knowe differences of clene thing and vnclene, and that ye wite what ye schulen ete, and what ye owen forsake.

CAP 12

1 And the Lord spak to Moises, 'and seide, Speke thou to the sones of Israel,

2 and thou schalt seie to hem, If a womman, whanne sche hath resseyued seed, childith a knaue child, sche schal be vnclene bi seuene daies bi the daies of departyng of corrupt blood, that renneth bi monethis;

3 and the yong child schal be circumsidid in the eiytithe dai.

4 Sotheli sche schal dwelle thre and thretti daies in the blood of hir purifiyng; sche schal not touche ony hooli thing, nethir sche schal entre in to the seyntuarie, til the daies of her clensing be fillid.

5 Sotheli if sche childith a female, sche schal be vnclene twei woukis, bi the custom of flowyng of vnclene blood, and 'thre

scoor and sixe daies sche schal dwelle in the blood of her clensyng.

6 And whanne the daies of hir clensyng, for a sone, ether for a douytir, ben fillid, sche schal brynge a lomb of o yeer in to brent sacrifice, and a 'bryd of a culuer, ethir a turtle, for synne, to the dore of the tabernacle of witnessyng;

7 and sche schal yyue to the preest, which schal offre tho bifor the Lord, and schal preye for hir, and so sche schal be clensid fro the fowyng of hir blood. This is the lawe of a womman childynge a male, ethir a female.

8 That if hir hond fyndith not, nethir may offre a lomb, sche schal take twei turtlis, ethir twei 'briddis of culueres, oon in to brent sacrifice, and the tother for synne; and the preest schal preye for hir, and so sche schal be clensid.

CAP 13

1 The Lord spak to Moyses and Aaron, and seide,

2 A man in whos skyn and fleisch rysith dyuerse colour, ether whelke, ethir as 'sum schynynge thing, that is, a wounde of lepre, he schal be brouyt to Aaron preest, ether to oon 'who euer of hise sones;

3 and whanne he seeth lepre in the skyn, and the heeris chaungide in to whijte colour, and that spice of lepre lowere than the tother skyn and fleisch, it is a wounde of lepre, and he schal be departid at the 'doom of the preest.

4 Sotheli if schynyng whijtnesse is in the skyn, nethir is lower than the tother fleisch, and the heeris ben of the formere colour, the preest schal close hym seuene daies;

5 and schal biholde hym in the seuenthe dai, and sotheli if the lepre wexith not ferther, nethir passith the formere termes in the fleisch, eft the preest schal close hym ayen seuene other daies;

6 and schal biholde in the seuenthe day, if the lepre is derkere, and wexith not in the fleisch, the preest schal clense hym, for it is a scabbe; and the man schal waische hise clothis, and he schal be clene.

7 That if the lepre wexith eft, aftir that he is seyn of the preest, and is yoldun to clennesse, he schal be brouyt to the preest, and schal be demed of vnclennesse.

8 If the wounde of lepre is in man, he schal be brouyt to the preest, and he schal se the man;

9 and whanne whijt colour is in the fleisch, and chaungith the siyt of heeris, and thilke fleisch apperith quyk,

10 it schal be demid eldest lepre, and growun to the skyn; therfor the preest schal defoule hym,

11 and he schal not close eft, for it is of opyn vnclennesse.

12 But if lepre rennynge about in the skyn 'flourith out, and hilith al the fleisch, fro the heed til to the feet, what euer thing fallith vndur the siyt of iyen; the preest schal biholde hym,

13 and schal deme 'that he is holdun with clenneste lepre, for all the skyn is turned in to whijtnesse, and therfor the man schal be cleene.

14 Sotheli whanne quyk fleisch apperith in hym,

15 thanne he schal be defoulid bi the doom of the preest, and he schal be arettid among vncleene men; for quyk fleisch is vnclene, if it is spreynt with lepre.

16 That if the fleisch is turned eft in to whijtnesse, and hilith al the man,

17 the preest schal biholde hym, and schal deme, that he is cleene.

18 Fleisch and skyn, in which a botche is bred,

19 and is heelid, and 'a step of wounde apperith whijt, ethir 'sum deel reed, 'in the place of the botche, the man schal be brouyt to the preest;

20 and whanne the preest seeth the place of lepre lowere than the tother fleisch, and the heeris turned in to whijtnesse, the preest schal defoule hym; for the wounde of lepre is bred in the botche.

21 That if the heer is of the former colour, and the signe of wounde is sumdeel derk, and is not lowere than the 'nyy fleisch, the preest schal close the man seuene daies;

22 and sotheli, if it wexith, the preest schal deme the man of lepre;

23 forsothe if it stondith in his place, it is a signe of botche, and the man schal be cleene.

24 Fleisch and skyn, which the fier hath brent, and is heelid, and hath a whijt ethir reed 'signe of wounde,

25 the preest schal biholde it, and lo! if it is turned in to whijtnesse, and the place therof is lowere than the tothir skyn, the preest schal defoule the man, for a wounde of lepre is bred in the 'signe of wounde.

26 That if the colour of heeris is not chaungid, nether the wounde is lowere than the tother fleisch, and thilke spice of lepre is sumdeel derk, the preest schal close the man bi seuene daies;

27 and in the seuenthe dai he schal biholde; if the lepre wexith in the fleisch, the preest schal defoule the man;

28 ellis if the whijtnesse stondith in his place, and is not cleer ynow, it is a wounde of brennyng, and therfor the man schal be clensid, for it is a signe of brennyng.

29 A man ethir womman, in whos heed ether beerd lepre buriounneth, the preest schal se hem;

30 and if the place is lowere than the tothir fleisch, and the heer is whijt, 'and is sotilere, 'ether smallere, than it is wont, the preest schal defoule hem, for it is lepre of the heed, and of the beerd.

31 Ellis if he seeth the place of wem euene with the nyy fleisch, and seeth the here blak, the preest schal close hem bi seuene daies, and schal se in the seuenthe dai;

32 if the wem waxith not, and the heer is of his colour, and the place of wounde is euene with the tother fleisch,

33 the man schal be schauun, without the place of wem, and he schal be closid eft bi seuene othere daies.

34 If in the seuenthe day the wounde is seyn to haue stonde in his place, nether is lowere than the tother fleisch, the preest schal clense the man; and whanne his clothis ben waischun, he schal be cleene.

35 Ellis if aftir the clensyng a spotte wexith eft in the skyn,

36 the preest schal no more enquere, whether the heer is chaungid in to whijt colour, for apeertli he is vncleene.

37 Sotheli if the spotte stondith, and the heeris ben blake, knowe the preest that the man is heelid, and tristili 'pronounce he the man cleene.

38 A man ethir a womman, in whos skyn whijtnesse apperith, the preest schal biholde hem;

39 if he perseyueth, that whijtnesse 'sum deel derk schyneth in the skyn, wite he, that it is no lepre, but a spotte of whijt colour, and that the man is cleene.

40 A man of whos heed heeris fleten awei, is calu, and clene;

41 and if heeris fallen fro the forheed, he is ballid,

42 and is cleene; ellis if in the ballidnesse bifore, ether in the ballidnesse bihynde, whijt ether reed colour is bred, and the preest seeth this,

43 he schal condempne the man without doute of lepre, which is bred in the ballidnesse.

44 Therfor whoeuer is defoulid with lepre, and is departid at the doom of the preest,

45 he schal haue hise clothis vnsewid, bareheed, the mouth hilid with a cloth, he schal crye hym silf defoulid, and viyl;

46 in al tyme in which he is lepre and vnclene, he schal dwelle aloone without the castels.

47 A wollun cloth, ethir lynnun, that hath lepre in the warp,

48 ethir oof, ethir certis a skyn, ether what euer thing is maad of skiyn,

49 if it is corrupt with a whijt spotte, ethir reed, it schal be arettid lepre, and it schal be schewid to the preest;

50 which schal close it biholden bi seuene daies.

51 And eft he schal biholde in the seuenthe dai, and if he perseyueth, that it wexide, it schal be contynuel lepre; he schal deme the cloth defoulid, and al thing in which it is foundun;

52 and therfor the cloth schal be brent in flawmes.

53 That if he seeth that the spotte wexide not, he schal comaunde,

54 and thei schulen waische that thing wherynne the lepre is, and he schal close it ayen bi seuene othere daies;

55 and whanne he seeth the formere face not turned ayen, netheles that nether the lepre wexede, he schal deme that thing vnclene, and he schal brenne it in fier, for lepre is sched in the ouer part of the cloth, ether thorouy al.

56 Ellis if the 'place of lepre is derkere, aftir that the cloth is waischun, he schal breke awey that place, and schal departe fro the hool.

57 That if fleynge lepre and vnstidefast apperith ferthermore in these places, that weren vnwemmed bifore, it owith be brent in fier; if it ceessith,

58 he schal waische the secounde tyme tho thingis that ben cleene, and tho schulen be cleene.

59 This is the lawe of lepre of cloth, wollun and lynnun, of warp and of oof, and of al purtenaunce of skiyn, hou it owith to be clensyd, ethir 'to be defoulid.

CAP 14

1 And the Lord spak to Moises, and seide, This is the custom of a leprouse man,

2 whanne he schal be clensid. He schal be brouyt to the preest,

3 which preest schal go out of the castels, and whanne he schal fynde that the lepre is clensid,

4 he schal comaunde to the man which is clensid, that he offre for hym silf twei quyke sparewis, whiche it is leueful to ete, and a 'tree of cedre, and vermylyoun, and isope.

5 And the preest schal comaunde that oon of the sparewes be offrid in 'a vessel of erthe,

6 on quyke watris; sotheli he schal dippe the tother sparewe quyk with the 'tre of cedre, and with a reed threed and ysope, in the blood of the sparewe offrid,

7 with which he schal sprenge seuensithis hym that schal be clensid, that he be purgid riytfuli; and he schal delyuere the quyk sparewe, that it fle in to the feeld.

8 And whanne the man hath waische hise clothis, he schal schaue alle the heeris of the bodi, and he schal be waischun in watir, and he schal be clensid, and he schal entre in to the castels; so oneli that he dwelle without his tabernacle bi seuene daies;

9 and that in the seuenthe dai he schaue the heeris of the heed, and the beerd, and brewis, and the heeris of al the bodi. And whanne the clothis and bodi ben waischun,

10 eft in the eiyetithe dai he schal take twei lambren without wem, and a scheep of o yeer without wem, and thre dymes of wheete flour, in to sacrifice, which be spreynte with oile, and bi it silf a sextarie of oyle.

11 And whanne the preest, that purgith the man, hath set hym and alle hise thingis bifor the Lord, in the dore of the tabernacle of witnessyng, he schal take a lomb,

12 and schal offre it for trespas, and schal offre the sextarie of oyle; and whanne alle thingis ben offrid bifor the Lord,

13 he schal offre the lomb, where the sacrifice for synne and the brent sacrifice is wont to be offrid, that is, in the hooli place; for as for synne so and for trespas the offryng perteyneth to the preest; it is hooli of the noumbre of hooli thingis.

14 And the preest schal take of the blood of sacrifice which is offrid for trespas, and schal putte on the laste part of the riyt eere 'of hym which is clensid, and on the thumbis of the riyt hond and foot.

15 And he schal putte of the sextarie of oyle in to his left hond,

16 and he schal dippe the riyt fyngur therynne, and schal sprynge seuensithis bifor the Lord.

17 Sotheli he schal schede that that is residue of the oile in the left hond, on the laste part of the riyt eere 'of hym which is clensid, and on the thombis of the riyt hond and foot, and on the blood which is sched for trespas,

18 and on the heed 'of hym.

19 And the preest schal preye for hym bifor the Lord, and schal make sacrifice for synne; thanne he schal offre brent sacrifice,

20 and schal putte it in the auter with hise fletynge sacrifices, and the man schal be clensid riytfuli.

21 That if he is pore, and his hoond may not fynde tho thingis that ben seid, he schal take for trespas a lomb to offryng, that the preest preie for him, and the tenthe part of wheete flour spreynt togidire with oile in to sacrifice, and a sextarie of oile,

22 and twei turtlis, ethir twei 'briddis of culueris, of whiche oon be for synne, and the tothir in to brent sacrifice;

23 and he schal offre tho in the eiytthe dai of his clensyng to the preest, at the dore of tabernacle of witnessyng bifor the Lord.

24 And the preest schal take the lomb for trespas, and the sextarie of oile, and schal reise togidere;

25 and whanne the lomb is offrid, he schal putte of the blood therof on the laste part of the riyt eere 'of hym that is clensid, and on the thumbis of his riyt hond and foot.

26 Sotheli the preest putte the part of oile in to his left hond,

27 in which he schal dippe the fyngur of the riyt hond, and schal sprynge seuensithes ayens the Lord;

28 and the preest schal touche the laste part of the riyt eere 'of hym that is clensid, and the thombe of the riyt hond and foot, in the place of blood which is sched out for trespas.

29 Sotheli he schal putte the tother part of oile, which is in the left hond, on the 'heed of the man clensid, that he plese the Lord for hym.

30 And he schal offre a turtle, ethir a culuer brid,

31 oon for trespas, and the tothir in to brent sacrifice, with her fletynge offryngis.

32 This is the sacrifice of a leprouse man, that may not haue alle thingis in to the clensyng of hym silf.

33 And the Lord spak to Moises and Aaron, and seide,

34 Whanne ye han entrid in to the lond of Canaan, which lond Y schal yyue to you in to possessioun, if the wounde of lepre is in the housis,

35 he schal go, whos the hous is, 'and schal telle to the preest, and schal seie, It semeth to me, that as a wound of lepre is in myn hous.

36 And the preest schal comaunde, 'that thei bere out of the hous alle thingis bifore that he entre in to it, 'and me se where it be lepre, lest alle thingis that ben in the hows, be maad vnclene; and the preest schal entre aftirward, that he se the lepre of the hows.

37 And whanne he seeth in the wallis therof as litle valeis 'foule bi palenesse, ethir bi reednesse, and lowere than the tother hiyere part,

38 he schal go out at the dore of the hows, and anoon he schal close it bi seuene daies.

39 And he schal turne ayen in the seuenthe day, and schal se it; if he fyndith that the lepre encreesside,

40 he schal comaunde that the stoonys be cast out, in whyche the lepre is, and that tho stonys be cast out of the citee in an vncleene place,

41 Sotheli he schal comaunde that thilke hows be rasid with ynne bi cumpas, and that the dust of the rasyng be spreynt without the citee, in an vnclene place,

42 and that othere stoonys be put ayen for these, that ben takun awey, and that the hows be daubid with othir morter.

43 But if aftir that the stoonus ben takun awey, and the dust is borun out,

44 and othere erthe is daubid, the preest entrith, and seeth the lepre turned ayen, and the wallis spreynt with spottis, the lepre is stidfastly dwellynge, and the hows is vnclene;

45 which hows thei schulen destrye anoon, and thei schulen caste out of the citee, in an vnclene place, the stoonys therof, and the trees, and al the dust.

46 He that entrith in to the hous, whanne it is schit, schal be vnclene 'til to euentid,

47 and he that slepith and etith ony thing therynne, schal waische hise clothis.

48 That if the preest entrith, and seeth that the lepre encreesside not in the hows, aftir that it was daubid the secounde tyme, he schal clense it; for heelthe is yoldun.

49 And in the clensyng therof he schal take twey sparewis, and 'a tre of cedre, and 'a reed threed, and isope.

50 And whanne o sparewe is offrid in a vessel of erthe, on quyk watris,

51 he schal take the 'tre of cedre, and ysope, and reed threed, and the quyk sparewe, and he schal dippe alle thingis in the blood of the sparewe offrid, and in lyuynge watris;

52 and he schal sprynge the hows seuen sithis; and he schal clense it as wel in the blood of the sparewe as in lyuynge watris, and in the quyk sparewe, and in the 'tre of cedre, and in ysope, and 'reed threed.

53 And whanne he hath left the sparewe to fle in to the feeld frely, he schal preye for the hows, and it schal be clensid riytfuli.

54 This is the lawe of al lepre,

55 and of smytyng, of lepre of clothis, and of housis,

56 of syngne of wounde, and of litle whelkis brekynge out, of spotte schynynge, and in colours chaungid in to dyuerse spices,

57 that it may be wist, what is cleene, ether uncleene.

CAP 15

1 And the Lord spak to Moises and Aaron, 'and seide,

2 Speke ye to the sones of Israel, and seie ye to hem, A man that suffrith the rennyng out of seed, schal be vncleene;

3 and thanne he schal be demed to be suget to this vice, whanne bi alle momentis foul vmour 'ethir moysture cleueth to his fleisch, and growith togidere.

4 Ech bed in which he slepith schal be vncleene, and where euer he sittith.

5 If ony man touchith his bed, he schal waische his clothis, and he schal be waischun in watir, and schal be vncleene 'til to euentid.

6 If a man sittith where he satt, also thilke man schal waische hise clothis, and he schal be waischun in watir, and schal be vnclene 'til to euentid.

7 He that touchith hise fleischis, schal waische hise clothis, and he schal be waischun in watir, and schal be vncleene 'til to euentid.

8 If sich a man castith out spetyng on hym that is cleene, he schal waische his clothis, and he schal be waischun in watir, and schal be vncleene 'til to euentid.

9 The sadil on which he sittith,

10 schal be vncleene; and ech man that touchith what euer thing is vndur hym that suffrith the fletyng out of seed, schal be defoulid 'til to euentid. He that berith ony of these thingis, schal waische hise clothis, and he schal be waischun in watir, and schal be vncleene 'til to euentid.

11 Ech man, whom he that is such touchith with hondis not waischun bifore, schal waische hise clothis, and he schal be waischun in watir, and schal be vncleene 'til to euentid.

12 'A vessel of erthe which he touchith, schal be brokun; but a 'vessel of tre schal be waischun in watir.

13 If he that suffrith sich a passioun, is heelid, he schal noumbre seuene daies aftir his clensyng, and whanne the clothis and al 'the bodi ben waischun in lyuynge watris, he schal be clene.

14 Forsothe in the eiytthe dai he schal take twei turtlis, ethir twei 'briddis of a culuer, and he schal come in the 'siyt of the Lord at the dore of tabernacle of witnessyng, and schal yyue tho to the preest;

15 and the preest schal make oon for synne, and the tother in to brent sacrifice; and the preest schal preye for hym bifor the Lord, that he be clensid fro the fletyng out of his seed.

16 A man fro whom the seed of letcherie, 'ethir of fleischli couplyng, goith out, schal waische in watir al his bodi, and he schal be vncleene 'til to euentid.

17 He schal waische in watir the cloth 'and skyn which he hath, and it schal be unclene 'til to euentid.

18 The womman with which he 'is couplid fleischli, schal be waischun in watir, and schal be vncleene 'til to euentid.

19 A womman that suffrith the fletyng out of blood, whanne the moneth cometh ayen, schal be departid bi seuene daies; ech man that touchith hir schal be vncleene 'til to euentid,

20 and the place in which sche slepith ether sittith in the daies of hir departyng, schal be defoulid.

21 He that touchith her bed, schal waische hise clothis, and he schal be waischun in watir, and schal be vncleene 'til to euentid.

22 Who euer touchith ony vessel on which sche sittith, he schal waische hise clothis, and he schal be waischun in watir, and schal be defoulid 'til to euentid.

23 If a man is couplid fleischli with hir in the tyme of blood that renneth bi monethis, he schal be vncleene bi seuene daies, and ech bed in which he slepith schal be defoulid.

24 A womman that suffrith in many daies the 'fletyng out of blood, not in the tyme of monethis, ethir which womman ceessith not to flete out blood aftir the blood of monethis, schal be vncleene as longe as sche 'schal be suget to this passioun, as if sche is in the tyme of monethis.

25 Ech bed in which sche slepith, and 'vessel in which sche sittith, schal be defoulid.

26 Who euer touchith hir schal waische his clothis, and he schal be waischun in watir, and schal be vncleene 'til to euentid.

27 If the blood stondith, and ceessith to flete out, sche schal noumbre seuene daies of hir clensyng,

28 and in the eiytthe dai sche schal offre for hir silf to the preest twei turtlis, ethir twei 'briddis of culueris, at the dore of the tabernacle of witnessyng;

29 and the preest schal make oon for synne, and the tothir in to brent sacrifice; and the preest schal preye for hir bifor the Lord, and for the fletyng out of hir vnclennesse.

30 Therfor ye schulen teche the sones of Israel, that thei eschewe vnclennessis, and that thei die not for her filthis, whanne thei defoulen my tabernacle which is among hem.

31 This is the lawe of hym that suffrith fletyng out of seed, and which is defoulid with fleischly couplyng,

32 and of a womman which is departid in the tymes of monethis, ethir which flowith out in contynuel blood, and of the man that slepith with hir.

CAP 16

1 And the Lord spak to Moises, aftir the deeth of the twei sones of Aaron, whanne thei offriden alien fier, and weren slayn, and comaundide to hym,

2 and seide, Speke thou to Aaron, thi brother, that he entre not in al tyme in to the seyntuarie, which is with ynne the veil bifor the propiciatorie, bi which the arke is hilid, that he die not; for Y schal appere in a cloude on Goddis answeryng place;

3 'no but he do these thingis bifore. He schal offer a calf for synne, and a ram in to brent sacrifice;

4 he schal be clothid with a lynnun coote, he schal hide the schamefast membris with pryuy lynnun clothis; he schal be gird with a lynnun girdil, he schal putte a lynnun mytre on his heed; for these clothis ben hooli, with whiche alle he schal be clothid, whanne he is waischun.

5 And he schal take of al the multitude of the sones of Israel twei kidis for synne, and o ram in to brent sacrifice;

6 and whanne he offrith a calf, and preieth for hym,

7 and for his hows, he schal make twei 'buckis of geet to stonde bifor the Lord, in the dore of the tabernacle of witnessyng;

8 and he schal sende 'on euer eithir, o lot to the Lord, and another lot to the goot that schal be sent out.

9 Whos lot goith out to the Lord, he schal offre it for synne;

10 sotheli whos lot goith out in to goot that schal be sent out, he schal sette hym quyk bifor the Lord, that he sende preyers 'on hym, and sende hym out in to wildirnesse.

11 Whanne these thingis ben doon riytfuli, he schal offre the calf, and 'he schal preye for hym silf, and for his hows, and schal offre the calf.

12 And whanne he hath take the censeer, which he hath fillid of the coolis of the auter, and 'he hath take in hond the 'swete

smellynge spicery maad into encense, he schal entre ouer the veil in to the hooli thingis;

13 that whanne swete smellynge spiceries ben put on the fier, the cloude and 'vapour of tho hile Goddis answeryng place, which is on the witnessyng, and he die not.

14 Also he schal take of the 'blood of the calf, and he schal sprenge seuensithis with the fyngur ayens 'the propiciatorie, 'to the eest.

15 And whanne he hath slayn the 'buk of geet, for synne of the puple, he schal brynge in the blood therof with ynne the veil, as it is comaundid of the 'blood of the calf, that he sprynge euene ayens Goddis answeryng place,

16 and he schal clense the seyntuarie fro vnclennessis of the sones of Israel, and fro her trespassyngis, and alle synnes. Bi this custom he schal do in the tabernacle of witnessyng, which is set among hem, in the myddis of partis of the abitacioun 'of hem.

17 No man be in the tabernacle, whanne the bischop schal entre in to the seyntuarie, that he preye for hym silf, and for his hows, and for al the cumpeny of Israel, til he go out of the tabernacle.

18 Sotheli whanne he hath go out to the auter which is bifor the Lord, preye he for hym silf, and schede he on the hornes therof, bi cumpas, the blood 'that is takun of the calf, and of the 'buk of geet;

19 and sprynge he seuensithis with the fyngur, and clense he, and halewe the autir fro vnclennessis of the sones of Israel.

20 Aftir that he hath clensid the seyntuarie, and tabernacle, and auter, thanne offre he the lyuynge 'buc of geet;

21 and whanne euer eithir hond is set on the heed therof, knowleche the preest alle the wickidnessis of the sones of Israel, and alle the trespassis and synnes 'of hem, whiche the preest schal wische to the heed therof, and schal sende hym out in to deseert bi a man maad redi.

22 And whanne the 'buc of geet hath bore alle the wickidnessis 'of hem in to a deseert lond,

23 and is left 'in deseert, Aaron schal turn ayen in to the tabernacle of witnessyng; and whanne the clothis ben put of, in whiche he was clothid bifore, whanne he entrid in to the seyntuarie of God, and ben left there,

24 he schal waische his fleisch in the hooli place, and he schal be clothid in his owen clothis, and aftir that he hath go out, and hath offrid the brent sacrifice of hym silf, and of the puple, he schal preye as wel for hym silf, as for the puple;

25 and he schal brenne on the auter the innere fatnesse which is offrid for synne.

26 Sotheli he that leet go the 'buk of geet able to be sent out, schal waische hise clothis and bodi with water, and so he schal entre in to the castels.

27 Forsothe thei schulen bere out of the castels the calf and 'buk of geet, that weren offrid for synne, and whos blood was brouyt in to the seyntuarie, that the clensyng were fillid; and thei schulen brenne bi fier as well the skynnys, as the fleischis and dung of tho.

28 And who euer brenneth tho, schal waische hise clothis and fleisch in watir, and so he schal entre in to the castels.

29 And this schal be to you a lawful thing euerlastynge; in the seuenthe monethe, in the tenthe dai of the monethe, ye schulen turment youre soulis, and ye schulen not do ony werk, nethir a man borun in the lond, nether a comelyng which is a pilgrym among you.

30 The delyueryng fro synne, and the clensyng of you schal be in this dai, ye schulen be clensid bifore the Lord fro alle youre synnes;

31 for it is sabat of restyng, and ye schulen turment youre soulis bi euerlastynge religioun.

32 Sotheli the preest schal clense, which is anoyntid, and whos hondis ben halewid, that he be set in preesthod for his fadir; and he schal be clothid in a lynnun stoole, and in hooli clothis,

33 and he schal clense the seyntuarie, and the tabernacle of witnessyng, and the auter, and the preestis, and al the puple.

34 And this schal be to you a lawful thing euerlastynge, that ye preye for the sones of Israel, and for alle the synnes 'of hem, onys in the yeer. Therfor he dide, as the Lord comaundide to Moises.

CAP 17

1 And the Lord spak to Moises, and seide, Speke thou to Aaron,

2 and to hise sones, and to alle the sones of Israel, and seie thou to hem, This is the word which the Lord comaundide,

3 and seide, Ech man of the hows of Israel schal be gilti of blood, if he sleeth an oxe, ether a scheep, ethir a geet in the castels, ethir out of the castels,

4 and offrith not an offryng to the Lord at the dore of the tabernacle; as he schedde mannus blood, so he schal perische fro the myddis of his puple.

5 Therfor the sones of Israel owen to offre her sacrifices to the preest, whiche thei sleen in the feeld, that tho be halewid to the Lord, bifor the dore of the tabernacle of witnessyng, and that thei offre tho pesible sacrifices to the Lord.

6 And the preest schal schede the blood on the auter of the Lord, at the dore of the tabernacle of witnessyng; and he schal brenne the ynnere fatnesse in to odour of swetnesse to the Lord.

7 And thei schulen no more offre her sacrifices to fendis, with whiche thei diden fornycacioun; it schal be a lawful thing euerlastynge to hem, and to the aftircomeris 'of hem.

8 And thou schalt seie to hem, A man of the hows of Israel, and of the comelyngis that ben pilgryms among you, that offrith a brent sacrifice, ethir a slayn sacrifice,

9 and bryngith it not to the dore of the tabernacle of witnessyng, that it be offrid to the Lord, schal perische fro his puple.

10 If ony man of the sones of Israel, and of comelyngis that ben pilgryms among you, etith blood, Y schal sette faste my face ayens 'the soule of hym, and Y schal leese hym fro his puple;

11 for the lijf of fleisch is in blood, and Y yaf that blood to you, that ye clense on myn auter 'for youre soulis, and that the blood be for the synne of soule.

12 Therfor Y seide to the sones of Israel, Ech lyuynge man of you schal not ete blood, nethir of the comelyngis that ben pilgryms among you.

13 What euer man of the sones of Israel, and of the comelyngis that ben pilgryms anentis you, takith a wielde beeste, ethir a brid, whiche it is leueful to ete, whether bi huntyng, whether bi haukyng, schede the blood therof, and hile it with erthe;

14 for the lijf of ech fleisch is in blood. Wherfor Y seide to the sones of Israel, Ye schulen not ete the blood of ony fleisch, for the lijf of fleisch is in blood, and who euer etith blood, schal perische.

15 A man that etith a thing deed bi it silf, ethir takun of a beeste, as wel of men borun in the lond, as of comelyngis, he schal waische hise clothis and hym silf in watir, and he schal be 'defoulid til to euentid; and by this ordre he schal be maad cleene; that if he waischith not his clothis,

16 ether his bodi, he schal bere his wickidnesse.

CAP 18

1 And the Lord spak to Moises, and seide, Speke thou to the sones of Israel,

2 and thou schalt seie to hem, Y am youre Lord God;

3 ye schulen not do by the custom of the lond of Egipt, in which ye dwelliden; ye schulen not do bi the custom of the cuntrei of Canaan, 'to which Y schal brynge you yn, nethir ye schulen go in the lawful thingis of hem.

4 Ye schulen do my domes, and ye schulen kepe myn heestis, and ye schulen go in tho; Y am youre Lord God.

5 Kepe ye my lawis and domes, whiche a man 'schal do, and schal lyue in tho; Y am youre Lord God.

6 Ech man schal not neiy to the nyy womman of his blood, that he schewe 'the filthe of hir; Y am the Lord.

7 Thou schalt not diskyuere the filthe of thi fadir and the filthe of thi modir; sche is thi modir, thou schalt not schewe hir filthe.

8 Thou schalt not vnhile the filthe of the wijf of thi fadir, for it is the filthe of thi fadir.

9 Thou schalt not schewe the filthe of thi sistir, of fadir 'ether of modir, which sister is gendrid at hoome ether without forth.

10 Thou schalt not schewe the filthe of the douyter of thi sone, ether of neece of thi douyter, for it is thi filthe.

11 Thou schalt not schewe the filthe of the douyter of the wijf of thi fadir, which sche childide to thi fadir, and is thi sistir.

12 Thou schalt not opene the filthe of the 'sister of thi fadir, for sche is the fleisch of thi fadir.

13 Thou schalt not schewe the filthe of the sistir of thi modir, for sche is the fleisch of thi modir.

14 Thou schalt not shewe the filthe of the brothir of thi fadir, nethir thou schalt neiye to his wijf, which is ioyned to thee bi affinyte.

15 Thou schalt not schewe the filthe of thi sones wijf, for sche is the wijf of thi sone, nether thou schalt diskiuere hir schenschip; and no man take his brotheris wijf.

16 Thou schalt not schewe the filthe of 'the wijf of thi brother, for it is the filthe of thi brothir.

17 Thou schalt not schewe the filthe of thi wijf, and of hir douyter; thou schalt not take the douytir of hir sone, and the douytir of hir douyter, that thou schewe hir schenschip; thei ben the fleisch of hir, and siche letcherie is incest.

18 Thou schalt not take 'the sister of thi wijf, in to concubynage of hir, nethir thou schalt schewe 'the filthe of hir, while thi wijf lyueth yit.

19 Thou schalt not neiye to a womman that suffrith rennyng of blood of monethe, nethir thou schalt schewe hir filthe.

20 Thou schalt not do letcherie with 'the wijf of thi neiybore, nether thou schalt be defoulid with medlyng of seed.

21 Thou schalt not yyue of thi seed, that it be offrid to the idol Moloch, nether thou schalt defoule the name of thi God; Y am the Lord.

22 Thou schalt not be medlid with a man bi letcherie of womman, for it is abhomynacioun.

23 Thou schalt not do letcherie with ony beeste, nethir thou schalt be defoulid with it. A womman schal not ligge vnder a beeste, nether schal be medlid therwith, for it is greet synne.

24 Be ye not defoulid in alle these thingis, in whiche alle 'folkis, ether hethen men, ben defoulid, whiche folkis Y schal caste out bifor youre siyt,

25 of whiche the lond is defoulid, of which lond Y schal vysyte the grete synnes, that it spewe out hise dwellers.

26 Kepe ye my lawful thingis and domes, that ye do not of alle these abhomynaciouns, as wel a man borun in the lond as a comelyng which is a pilgrym at you.

27 For the dwellers of the lond, that weren bifor you, diden alle these abhomynaciouns, and defouliden that lond.

28 Therfor be ye war, lest it caste out viliche also you in lijk manere, whanne ye han do lijk synnes, as it castide out vileche the folk, that was bifor you.

29 Ech man that doith ony thing of these abhomynaciouns, schal perische fro the myddis of his puple.

30 Kepe ye myn heestis; nyle ye do tho thingis, whiche thei that weren bifor you diden, and be ye not defoulid in tho; Y am youre Lord God.

CAP 19

1 The Lord spak to Moises, and seide,

2 Speke thou to al the cumpenye of the sones of Israel, and thou schalt seie to hem, Be ye hooli, for Y am hooli, youre Lord God.

3 Ech man drede his fadir and his modir. Kepe ye my sabatis; Y am youre Lord God.

4 Nyle ye be turned to ydols, nether ye schulen make to you yotun goddis; Y am youre Lord God.

5 If ye offren a sacrifice of pesible thingis to the Lord, that it be quemeful,

6 ye schulen ete it in that day, in which it is offrid, and in the tother dai; sotheli what euer thing is residue in to the thridde dai, ye schulen brenne in fier.

7 If ony man etith therof aftir twei daes, he schal be vnhooli, and gilti of vnfeithfulnes 'ether wickidnesse; and he schal bere his wickidnesse,

8 for he defoulide the hooli thing of the Lord, and his soule schal perische fro his puple.

9 Whanne thou schalt repe the fruytis of thi lond, thou schalt not kitte 'til to the ground the corn of the lond, nether thou schalt gadere the eeris of corn that ben left;

10 nethir in thi vyner thou schalt gadere reysyns and greynes fallynge doun, but thou schalt leeue to be gaderid of pore men and pilgryms; Y am youre Lord God.

11 Ye schulen not do thefte. Ye schulen not lye, and no man disseyue his neiybour.

12 Thou schalt not forswere in my name, nethir thou schalt defoule the name of thi God; Y am the Lord.

13 Thou schalt not make fals chalenge to thi neiybore, nethir thou schalt oppresse hym bi violence. The werk of thin hirid man schal not dwelle at thee til the morewtid.

14 Thou schalt not curse a deef man, nether thou schalt sette an hurtyng bifor a blynd man; but thou schalt drede thi Lord God, for Y am the Lord.

15 Thou schalt not do that, that is wickid, nether thou schalt deme vniustli; biholde thou not the persoone of a pore man, nethir onoure thou the face of a myyti man; deme thou iustli to thi neiybore.

16 Thou schalt not be a sclaunderere, nether a priuey bacbitere in the puplis; thou schalt not stonde ayens the blood of thi neiybore; Y am the Lord.

17 Thou schalt not hate thi brothir in thin herte, but repreue hym opynly, lest thou haue synne on hym.

18 Thou schalt not seke veniaunce, nether thou schalt be myndeful of the wrong of thi cyteseyns; thou schalt loue thi freend as thi silf; Y am the Lord.

19 Kepe ye my lawis. Thou schalt not make thi beestis to gendre with the lyuynge beestis of another kynde. Thou schalt not sowe the feeld with dyuerse sede. Thou schalt not be clothid in a cloth, which is wouun of twei thingis.

20 If a man slepith with a womman by fleischly knowyng of seed, which womman is an 'hand maide, ye, a noble womman of kyn, and netheles is not ayenbouyt bi prijs, nethir rewardid with fredom, bothe schulen be betun, and thei schulen not die, for sche was not fre.

21 Sotheli the man for his trespas schal offre a ram to the Lord, at the dore of the tabernacle of witnessyng;

22 and the preest schal preye for hym, and for his trespas, bifor the Lord; and the Lord schal be merciful to hym, and the synne schal be foryouun.

23 Whanne ye han entrid in to the lond of biheest, and han plauntid therynne appil trees, ye schulen do awei the firste flouris; the applis whiche tho trees bryngen forth, schulen be vncleene to you, nethir ye schulen ete of tho.

24 Forsothe in the fourthe yeer al the fruyt of tho trees schal be 'halewid preiseful to the Lord;

25 forsothe in the fifthe yeer ye schulen ete fruytis, and schulen gadere applis, whiche tho trees bryngen forth; Y am youre Lord God.

26 Ye schulen not ete fleisch with blood. Ye schulen not make veyn diuynyng, nether ye schulen kepe dremes;

27 nether ye schulen clippe the heer in round, nether ye schulen schaue the beerd;

28 and on deed men ye schulen not kitte youre fleischis, nether ye schulen make to you ony fyguris, ether markis in youre fleisch; Y am the Lord.

29 Sette thou not thi douytir to do leccherie for hire, and the lond be defoulid, and be fillid with synne.

30 Kepe ye my sabatis, and drede ye my seyntuarie; Y 'am the Lord.

31 Bowe ye not to astronomyers, nether axe ye ony thing of fals dyuynours, that ye be defoulid bi hem; Y am youre Lord God.

32 Rise thou bifor an hoor heed, and onoure thou the persoone of an eld man, and drede thou thi Lord God; Y am the Lord.

33 If a comelyng enhabitith in youre lond, and dwellith among you, dispise ye not hym;

34 but be he among you as a man borun in the lond; and ye schulen loue hym as you silf, for also ye weren comelyngis in the lond of Egipt; Y am youre Lord God.

35 Nyle ye do ony wickid thing in doom, in reule, in weiyte, and in mesure; the balance be iust,

36 and the weiytis be euene, the buschel be iust, and the sextarie be euene; Y am youre Lord God, that ladde you out of the lond of Egipt.

37 Kepe ye alle myn heestis, and alle domes, and do ye tho; Y am the Lord.

CAP 20

1 And the Lord spak to Moises, and seide,

2 Speke thou these thingis to the sones of Israel, If eny man of the sones of Israel, and of the comelyngis that dwellen in Israel, yyueth of his seed to the ydol Moloch, die he bi deeth; the puple of the lond schal stone him.

3 And Y schal sette faste my face ayens hym, and Y schal kitte awei him fro the myddis of my puple, for he yaf of his seed to Moloch, and defoulide my seyntuarie, and defoulide myn hooli name.

4 That if the puple of the lond is necgligent, and as litil charg ynge myn heeste, and suffrith the man that yaf of his seed to Moloch, nether wole sle hym, Y schal sette my face on that man,

5 and his kynrede, and Y schal kitte doun hym, and alle that consentiden to him, that thei schulden do fornycacioun with Moloch, fro the myddis of her puple.

6 If a man bowith to astronomyers, and false dyuynours, and doith fornycacioun with hem, Y schal sette my face ayens hym, and Y schal sle hym fro the mydis of hys puple.

7 Be ye halewid, and be ye hooli, for Y am hooli, youre Lord God.

8 Kepe ye myn heestis, and do ye tho, for Y am the Lord that halewe you.

9 He that cursith his fadir, ether modir, die bi deeth; if a man cursith fadir and modir, his blood be on hym.

10 If a man doith leccherie with 'the wijf of another man, and doith auowtrie with 'the wijf of his neiybore, bothe auowter and auowtresse die bi deeth.

11 If a man slepith with hys stepdamme, and schewith 'the schenschip of his fadir, bothe die bi deeth; her blood be on hem.

12 If ony man slepith with 'his sones wijf, euer either die, for thei han wrouyt greet synne; her blood be on hem.

13 If a man slepith with a man, bi letcherie of a womman, euer either hath wrouyt vnleueful thing, die thei bi deeth; her blood be on hem.

14 He that weddith ouer his wijf hir moder, hath wrouyt greet synne; he schal be brent quyk with hem, and so greet vnleueful doynge schal not dwelle in the myddis of you.

15 He that doith letcherie with a greet beeste, ethir a litil beeste die bi deeth, also sle ye the beeste.

16 A womman that liggith vndur ony beeste, be slayn togidere with it; the blood 'of hem be on hem.

17 He that takith his sistir 'the douytir of his fadir, ether the douyter of his modir, and seeth hir filthe, and sche seeth the schenschip of the brothir, thei han wrouyt an vnleueful thing, bothe schulen be slayn in the siyt of her puple; for thei schewiden togidere her filthe, and thei schulen bere her wickidnesse.

18 If a man doith fleischly knowyng with a womman in the flux of monethe, and schewith hir filthe, and sche openeth the welle of hir blood, bothe schulen be slayn fro the myddis of her puple.

19 Thou schalt not diskyuere the filthe of thi modris sistir, and of thi fadris sistir; he, that doith this, schal 'make nakid the schenschip of his fleisch, and bothe schulen bere her wickidnesse.

20 He that doith fleischli knowyng with the wijf of 'his fadris brother, ether of his modris brother, and schewith the filthe of his kyn, bothe schulen bere her synne, thei schulen die without fre children.

21 He that weddith 'the wijf of his brother, doith an vnleueful thing; he schewide 'the filthe of his brother, he schal be without fre children.

22 Kepe ye my lawis and my domes, and do ye tho, lest the lond, in to which ye schulen entre and dwelle, caste out viliche also you.

23 Nyle ye go in the lawful thingis of naciouns, whiche Y schal caste out bifor you, for thei diden alle these thingis, and Y hadde abhomynacioun of hem.

24 Forsothe Y speke to you, Welde ye 'the lond of hem, which Y schal yyue to you in to eritage, the lond flowynge with mylk and hony; Y am youre Lord God, that departide you fro othere puplis.

25 Therfor also ye departe a cleene beeste fro vnclene, and a cleene brid fro vncleene, lest ye defoule youre soulis in a beeste, and in briddis, and in alle thingis that ben moued in erthe, and whiche thingis Y schewide to you to be defoulid.

26 Ye schulen be hooli to me, for 'Y am the hooli Lord, and Y departide you fro othere puplis, that ye schulen be myne.

27 A man ethir a womman, in which is an vncleene spirit spekynge in the 'wombe, ethir 'a spirit of fals dyuynyng, die thei bi deeth; men schulen oppresse hem bi stoonus; her blood be on hem.

CAP 21

1 And the Lord seide to Moyses, Speke thou to preestis, the sones of Aaron, and thou schalt seie to hem, A preest be not defoulid in the deed men of hise citeseyns,

2 no but oneli in kynesmen and niy of blood, that is, on fadir and modir, and sone and douyter,

3 and brother and sister, virgyn, which is not weddid to man;

4 but nether he schal be defoulid in the prince of his puple.

5 Preestis schulen not schaue the heed, nether beerd, nether thei schulen make keruyngis in her fleischis; thei schulen be hooli to her God,

6 and thei schulen not defoule his name; for thei offren encense of the Lord, and the looues of her God, and therfore thei schulen be hooli.

7 A preest schal not wedde a wijf a corrupt womman, and a 'foul hoore, nether he schal wedde 'hir that is forsakun of the hosebonde, for he is halewid to his God,

8 and offrith the looues of settyng forth; therfor be he hooly, for 'Y am the hooli Lord that halewith you.

9 If the 'doutir of a preest is takun in defoulyng of virgynite, and defoulith the name of hir fadir, sche schal be brent in flawmes.

10 The bischop, that is the moost preest among hise britheren, on whose heed the oile of anoyntyng is sched, and whose hondis ben sacrid in preesthod, and he is clothid in hooli clothis, schal not diskyuere his heed, he schal not tere hise clothis,

11 and outirli he schal not entre to ony deed man; and he schal not be defoulid on his fadir and modir,

12 nether he schal go out of hooli thingis, lest he defoule the seyntuarie of the Lord, for the oile of hooli anoyntyng of his God is on hym; Y am the Lord.

13 He schal wedde a wijf virgyn;

14 he schal not take a widewe, and forsakun, and a foul womman, and hoore, but a damesele of his puple;

15 medle he not the generacioun of his kyn to the comyn puple of his folk, for Y am the Lord, that 'halewe hym.

16 And the Lord spak to Moyses,

17 and seide, Speke thou to Aaron; a man of thi seed, bi meynes, that hath a wem, schal not offre breed to his God,

18 nethir schal neiy to his seruyce;

19 if he is blind; if he is crokid; if he is ether of litil, ether of greet, and wrong nose; if he is 'of brokun foot, ethir hond;

20 if he hath a botche; ether if he is blereiyed; if he hath whijt colour in the iye, that lettith the siyt; if he hath contynuel scabbe; if he hath a drye scabbe in the bodi; ethir 'is brokun 'in the pryuy membris.

21 Ech man of the seed of Aaron preest, which man hath a wem, schal not neiye to offre sacrifices to the Lord, nether 'to offre looues to his God;

22 netheles he schal ete the looues that ben offrid in the seyntuarie,

23 so oneli that he entre not with ynne the veil; he schal not neiye to the auter, for he hath a wem, and he schal not defoule my seyntuarie; Y am the Lord that halewe hem.

24 Therfor Moises spak to Aaron, and to hise sones, and to al Israel, alle thingis that weren comaundid to hym.

CAP 22

1 And the Lord spak to Moises, and seide, Speke thou to Aaron and to hise sones,

2 that thei be war of these thingis of the sones of Israel, whiche thingis ben halewid; and that they defoule not the name of thingis halewid to me, whiche thingis thei offren; Y am the Lord.

3 Seie thou to hem, and to the aftir comeris of hem, Ech man of youre kynrede, 'which man neiyeth to tho thingis that ben halewid, and whiche thingis the sones of Israel offreden to the Lord, in 'which man is vnclennesse, schal perische bifor the Lord; Y am the Lord.

4 A man of the seed of Aaron, 'which man is leprouse, ethir suffrith 'fletyng out of seed, schal not ete of these thingis, that ben halewid to me, til he be heelid. He that touchith an vncleene thing on a deed bodi, and fro whom the seed as of leccherie goith out, and which touchith a crepynge beeste,

5 and what euer vncleene thing, whos touchyng is foul,

6 schal be vncleene 'til to euentid, and he schal not ete these thingis, that ben halewid to me; but whanne he hath waische his fleisch in watir,

7 and the sunne hath go doun, thanne he schal be clensid, and schal ete halewid thingis, for it is his mete.

8 He schal not ete a thing deed bi it silf, and takun of a beeste, nethir he schal be defoulid in tho; Y am the Lord.

9 Thei schulen kepe myn heestis, that thei be not suget to synne, and die in the seyntuarye, whanne thei han defoulid it; Y am the Lord that halewe you.

10 Ech alien schal not ete of thingis halewid; the hyne which is a straunger, and the hirid man of the preest, schulen not ete of tho. Sotheli these seruauntis,

11 whom the preest hath bouyt, and which is a borun seruaunt of his hows, schulen ete of tho.

12 If the 'douyter of the preest is weddid to ony of the puple, sche schal not ete of these thingis that ben halewid, and of the firste fruytis;

13 sotheli if sche is a widewe, ether forsakun, and turneth ayen with out fre children to 'the hows of hir fadir, sche schal be susteyned bi the metis of hir fadir, as a damysel was wont; ech alien hath not power to ete of tho.

14 He that etith bi ignoraunce of halewid thingis, schal adde the fyuethe part with that that he eet, and 'schal yyue to the preest in seyntuarie,

15 and thei schulen not defoule the halewid thingis of the sones of Israel, whiche thei offren to the Lord,

16 lest perauenture thei suffren the wickidnesse of her trespas, whanne thei han ete halewid thingis; Y am the Lord that 'halewe hem. The Lord spak to Moises, and seide, Speke thou to Aaron and to hise sones, and to alle the sones of Israel, and thou schalt seie to hem, A man of the hous of Israel and of comelyngis that dwellen at hem, which offrith his offryng to the Lord, and ethir paieth avowis, ethir offrith bi his fre wille, what euer thing he offrith in to brent sacrifice of the Lord, that it be offrid bi you,

19 it schal be a male without wem, of oxen, and of scheep, and of geet; if it hath a wem,

20 ye schulen not offre, nether it schal be acceptable.

21 A man that offrith a sacrifice of pesyble thingis to the Lord, and ethir paieth auowis, ethir offrith bi fre wille, as wel of oxun as of scheep, he schal offre a beeste without wem, that it be acceptable; ech wem schal not be ther ynne.

22 If it is blynd, if it is brokun, if it hath a scar, if it hath whelkis, ether scabbe, ethir drie scabbe, ye schulen not offre tho beestis to the Lord, nether ye schulen brenne of tho beestis on the auter of the Lord.

23 A man may offre wilfuli an oxe and scheep, whanne the eere and tail ben kit of; but avow may not be paied of these beestis.

24 Ye schulen not offre to the Lord ony beeste, whose priuy membris ben brokun, ethir brisid, ether kit, and takun awey, and outerli ye schulen not do these thingis in youre lond.

25 Of 'the hond of an alien ye schulen not offre looues to youre God, and what euer other thing he wole yyue, for alle thingis ben corrupt and defoulid; ye schulen not resseyue tho.

26 And the Lord spak to Moises,

27 and seide, Whanne an oxe, scheep and goet ben brouyt forth 'of the modris wombe, in seuene daies tho schulen be vnder 'the tete of her modir; sotheli in the eiyte dai, and fro thennus forth, tho moun be offrid to the Lord,

28 whether thilke is a cow, whether 'thilke is a scheep; tho schulen not be offrid in o dai with her fruytis.

29 If ye offren to the Lord a sacrifice for the doyng of thankyngis, that it mai be plesaunt,

30 ye schulen ete it in the same dai in which it is offrid; ony thing schal not leeue in the morewtid of the tother dai; Y am the Lord.

31 Kepe ye myn heestis, and do ye tho; Y am the Lord.

32 Defoule ye not myn hooli name, that Y be halewid in the myddis of the sones of Israel; Y am the Lord, that halewe you, and ledde you out of the lond of Egipt,

33 that Y schulde be to you in to God; Y am the Lord.

CAP 23

1 And the Lord spak to Moises and seide, Speke thou to the sones of Israel,

2 and thou schalt seye to hem, These ben the feries of the Lord, whiche ye schulen clepe hooli.

3 Sixe daies ye schulen do werk, the seuenthe dai schal be clepid hooli, for it is the reste of sabat; ye schulen not do ony werk ther ynne; it is the sabat of the Lord in alle youre abitaciouns.

4 These ben the hooli feries of the Lord, whiche ye owen to halewe in her tymes.

5 In the firste monethe, in the fourtenthe dai of the monethe, at euentid, is pask of the Lord;

6 and in the fiftenthe dai of this monethe is the solempnyte of therf looues of the Lord; seuene daies ye schulen ete therf looues;

7 the firste dai schal be moost solempne and hooli to you; ye schulen not do ony 'seruyle werk ther ynne,

8 but ye schulen offre sacrifice in fier to the Lord seuene daies; sotheli the seuenthe dai schal be more solempne and hooliere, 'that is, 'than the formere daies goynge bitwixe, and ye schulen not do ony seruyle werk ther ynne.

9 And the Lord spak to Moises and seide,

10 Speke thou to the sones of Israel, and thou schalt seye to hem, Whanne ye han entrid in to the lond which Y schal yyue to you, and han rope corn, ye schulen bere handfuls of eeris of corn, the firste fruytis of youre rype corn, to the preest;

11 and the preest schal reise a bundel bifor the Lord, that it be acceptable for you, in the tother dai of sabat, that is, of pask; and the preest schal halewe that bundel;

12 and in the same dai, wher ynne the handful is halewid, a lomb of o yeer without wem schal be slayn in to brent sacrifice of the Lord;

13 and fletynge offryngis schulen be offrid ther with, twei tenthe partis of wheete flour spreynt to gidere with oile, in to encense of the Lord, and swettist odour, and fletynge offryngis of wyn, the fourthe part of hyn.

14 Ye schulen not ete a loof, nether a cake, nether podagis of the corn, 'til to the dai in which ye schulen offre therof to youre God; it is a comaundement euerlastynge in youre generaciouns, and alle dwellyng placis.

15 Therfor ye schulen noumbre fro the tother dai of sabat, in which ye offriden handfullis of firste fruytis,

16 seuene fulle woukis, til to the tothir day of fillyng of the seuenthe wouk, that is, fifti dayes; and so ye schulen

17 offre newe sacrifice to the Lord of alle youre dwelling placis, twei looues of the firste fruytis, of twei tenthe partis of flour, 'diyt with soure dow, whiche looues ye schulen bake in to the firste fruytis to the Lord.

18 And ye schulen offre with the looues seuene lambren of o yeer with out wem, and o calf of the droue, and twey rammes, and these schulen be in brent sacrifice, with her fletynge offryngis, in to swettest odour to the Lord.

19 Ye schulen make also a buk of geet for synne, and twey lambren of o yeer, sacrificis of pesible thingis.

20 And whanne the preest hath reisid tho, with the looues of firste fruytys bifor the Lord, tho schulen falle in to his vss.

21 And ye schulen clepe this dai most solempne, and moost hooli; ye schulen not do ther ynne ony seruyle werk; it schal be a lawful thing euerlastynge in alle youre dwellyngis, and generaciouns.

22 Forsothe aftir that ye han rope the corn of youre lond, ye schulen not kitte it 'til to the ground, nether ye schulen gadere the 'eeris of corn abidynge, but ye schulen leeue tho to pore men and pilgrymys; Y am 'youre Lord God.

23 And the Lord spak to Moises, and seide,

24 Speke thou to the sones of Israel, In the seuenthe monethe, in the firste day of the monethe, schal be sabat memorial to yow, sownynge with trumpis, and it schal be clepid hooli;

25 ye schulen not do ony seruyle werk ther ynne, and ye schulen offre brent sacrifice to the Lord.

26 And the Lord spak to Moises, and seide, In the tenthe day of this seuenthe monethe,

27 the day of clensyngis schal be moost solempne, and it schal be clepid hooli; and ye schulen turmente youre soulis to God, and ye schulen offre brent sacrifice to the Lord;

28 ye schulen not do ony werk in the tyme of this day, for it is the day of the clensyng, that youre Lord God be merciful to you.

29 Ech 'man which is not tourmentid in this day, schal perische fro his puplis,

30 and Y schal do a way fro his puple that man that doith eny thing of werk in that dai;

31 therfor ye schulen not do ony thing of werk in that dai; it schal be a lawful thing euerlastynge to you in alle youre generaciouns and abitaciouns;

32 it is the sabat of restyng. Ye schulen turmente youre soulis fro the nynthe day of the monethe; fro euentid 'til to euentid ye schulen halewe youre sabatis.

33 And the Lord spak to Moises,

34 and seide, Speke thou to the sones of Israel, Fro the fiften- the day of this seuenthe monethe schulen be the feries of tab- ernaclis, in seuene daies to the Lord;

35 the firste dai schal be clepid moost solempne and moost hooli, ye schulen not do ony seruyle werk ther ynne;

36 and in seuene daies ye schulen offre brent sacrifices to the Lord, and the eiythe dai schal be moost solempne and moost hooli; and ye schulen offre brent sacrifice to the Lord, for it is the day of cumpany, and of gaderyng; ye schulen not do ony seruyle werk ther ynne.

37 These ben the feries of the Lord, whiche ye schulen clepe moost solempne and moost hooli; and in tho ye schulen offre offryngis to the Lord, brent sacrifices, and fletynge offeryn- gis, bi the custom of ech day,

38 outakun the sabatis of the Lord, and youre yiftys, and whiche ye offren bi avow, ether whiche ye yyuen bi fre wille to the Lord.

39 Therfor fro the fiftenthe day of the seuenthe monethe, whanne ye han gaderid alle the fruytis of youre lond, ye schulen halewe the feries of the Lord seuene daies; in the firste day and the eiyte schal be sabat, that is, reste.

40 And ye schulen take to you in the firste day fruytis of the faireste tree, and braunchis of palm trees, and braunchis of a 'tree of thicke boowis, and salewis of the rennynge streem, and ye schulen be glad bifor youre Lord God;

41 and ye schulen halewe his solempnyte seuene daies bi the yeer; it schal be a lawful thing euerlastynge in youre genera- ciouns. In the seuenthe monethe ye schulen halewe feestis,

42 and ye schulen dwelle in schadewynge placis seuene daies; ech man that is of the kyn of Israel, schal dwelle in tab- ernaclis, that youre aftercomers lerne,

43 that Y made the sones of Israel to dwelle in tabernaculis, whanne Y ledde hem out of the lond of Egipt; Y am youre Lord God.

44 And Moises spak of the solempnytees of the Lord to the sones of Israel.

CAP 24

1 And the Lord spak to Moises, and seide, Comaunde thou to the sones of Israel,

2 that thei brynge to thee oile of olyues, pureste oile, and briyt, to the lanternes to be ordeyned contynueli with out the veil of witnessyng,

3 in the tabernacle of boond of pees; and Aaron schal araye tho lanternes fro euentid 'til to euentid bifor the Lord, bi reli- gioun and custom euerlastynge in youre generaciouns;

4 tho schulen be set euere on a clenneste candilstike in the siyt of the Lord.

5 Also thou schalt take wheete flour, and thou schalt bake therof twelue looues, which schulen haue ech bi hem silf twei tenthe partis,

6 of whiche thou schalt sette sexe on euer eithir side, on a clenneste boord bifor the Lord;

7 and thou schalt sette clereste encense on tho looues, that the looues be in to mynde of offryng of the Lord;

8 bi ech sabat tho schulen be chaungid bifor the Lord, and schulen be takun of the sones of Israel bi euerlastynge boond of pees;

9 and tho schulen be Aarons and hise sones, that thei ete tho in the hooli place, for it is hooli of the noumbre of hooli thingis, of the sacrifices of the Lord, bi euerlastynge lawe.

10 Lo! forsothe the sone of a womman of Israel, whom sche childide of a man Egipcian, yede out among the sones of Israel, and chidde in the castels with a man of Israel,

11 and whanne he hadde blasfemyd the name of the Lord, and hadde cursid the Lord, he was brouyt to Moises; forsothe his modir was clepid Salumyth, the douytir of Dabry, of the lynage of Dan;

12 and thei senten hym to prisoun, til thei wisten what the Lord comaundide.

13 And the Lord spak to Moises and seide,

14 Lede out the blasfemere without the castels, and alle men that herden, sette her hondis on his heed, and al the puple stone hym.

15 And thou schalt speke to the sones of Israel, A man that cursith his God,

16 schal bere his synne, and he that blasfemeth the name of the Lord, die bi deeth; al the multitude of the puple schal oppresse hym with stoonus, whether he that blasfemede the name of the Lord is a citeseyn, whether a pilgrym, die he bi deeth.

17 He that smytith and sleeth a man, die bi deeth;

18 he that smytith a beeste, yelde oon in his stide, that is, lijf for lijf.

19 If a man yyueth a wem to ony of hise citeseyns, as he dide, so be it don to him;

20 he schal restore brekyng for brekyng, iye for iye, tooth for tooth; what maner wem he yaf, he schal be compellid to suf- fre sich a wem.

21 He that smytith werk beeste, yeelde another; he that smytith a man, schal be punyschid.

22 Euene doom be among you, whether a pilgrym ethir a cite- seyn synneth, for Y am youre Lord God.

23 And Moyses spak to the sones of Israel, and thei brouyten forth out of the castels hym that blasfemede, and oppressiden with stoonus. And the sones of Israel diden, as the Lord comaundide to Moyses.

CAP 25

1 And the Lord spak to Moises in the hil of Synai,

2 and seide, Speke thou to the sones of Israel, and thou schalt seye to hem, Whanne ye han entrid in to the lond which Y schal yyue to you, 'the erthe kepe the sabat of the Lord;

3 sixe yeeris thou schalt sowe thi feeld, and sixe yeeris thou schalt kitte thi vyner, and thou schalt gadere the fruytis ther of;

4 forsothe in the seuenthe yeer schal be sabat of the erthe of the restyng of the Lord;

5 thou schalt not sowe the feeld, and thou schalt not kitte the vyner, thou schalt not repe tho thingis whiche the erthe bryn- gith forth 'bi fre wille, and thou schalt not gadere the grapis

of thi firste fruytis, as vyndage; for it is the yeer of restyng of the lond; but tho schulen be to you in to mete,

6 to thee, and to thi seruaunt, to thin handmaide, and to thin hirid man, and to the comelyng which is a pilgrym at thee; alle thingis that 'comen forth,

7 schulen yyue mete to thi werk beestis and smale beestis.

8 Also thou schalt noumbre to thee seuene woukis of yeeris, that is, seuene sithes seuene, whiche togidere maken nyn and fourti yeer;

9 and thou schalt sowne with a clarioun in the seuenthe monethe, in the tenthe dai of the monethe, in the tyme of propiciacioun, 'that is, merci, in al youre lond.

10 And thou schalt halewe the fiftithe yeer, and thou schalt clepe remissioun to alle the dwellers of thi lond; for thilke yeer is iubilee; a man schal turne ayen to hys possessioun, and ech man schal go ayen to the firste meynee,

11 for it is iubilee, and the fiftithe yeer. Ye schulen not sowe, nether ye schulen repe thingis, that comen forth freli in the feeld, and ye schulen not gadere the firste fruytis of vyndage, for the halewyng of iubilee;

12 but anoon ye schulen ete thingis takun awey;

13 in the yeer of iubilee alle men go ayen to her possessiouns.

14 Whanne thou schalt sille ony thing to thi citeseyn, ether schalt bie of hym, make thou not sory thi brother, but bi the noumbre of 'yeeris of iubile thou schalt bie of him,

15 and bi the rekenyng of fruytis he schal sille to thee.

16 Bi as myche as mo yeeris dwellen after the iubilee, by so myche also the prijs schal encreesse, and bi as myche as thou noumbrist lesse of tyme, bi so myche and the biyng schal cost lesse; for he schal sille to thee the time of fruytis.

17 Nyle ye turment men of youre lynagis, but ech man drede his God; for Y am youre Lord God.

18 Do ye my comaundementis, and kepe ye my domes, and fille ye tho, that ye moun dwelle in his lond without ony drede,

19 and that the erthe brynge forth hise fruytis to you, whiche ye schulen ete 'til to fulnesse, and drede not the assailyng of ony man.

20 That if ye seien, what schulen we ete in the seuenthe yeer, if we sowen not, nether gaderen oure fruytis?

21 Y schal yyue my blessyng to you in the sixte yeer, and it schal make fruytis of three yeer;

22 and ye schulen sowe in the eiyte yeer, and ye schulen ete elde fruytis 'til to the nynthe yeer; til newe thingis comen forth ye schulen ete the elde thingis.

23 Also the lond schal not be seeld 'in to with outen ende, for it is myn, and ye ben my comelyngis and tenauntis;

24 wherfor al the cuntre of youre possessioun schal be seeld vndur the condicioun of ayenbiyng.

25 If thi brother is maad pore, and sillith his litil possessioun, and his nyy kynesman wole, he may ayenbie that that he seelde;

26 sotheli if he hath no nyy kynesman, and he may fynde prijs to ayenbie,

27 the fruytis schulen be rekynyd fro that tyme in which he seelde, and he schal yelde 'that that is residue to the biere, and he schal resseyue so his possessioun.

28 That if his hond fynde not, that he yelde the prijs, the biere schal haue that that he bouyte, 'til to the yeer of iubilee; for in that yeer ech sillyng schal go ayen to the lord, and to the firste weldere.

29 He that sillith his hows, with ynne the wallis of a citee, schal haue licence to ayenbie til o yeer be fillid;

30 if he ayenbieth not, and the sercle of the yeer is passid, the biere schal welde it, and his eiris 'in to with outen ende, and it schal not mow be ayenbouyt, ye, in the iubilee.

31 Forsothe if the hows is in a town 'that hath not wallis, it schal be seeld bi the lawe of feeldis; sotheli if it is not ayenbouyt in the iubilee, it schal turne ayen to 'his lord.

32 The howsis of dekenes, that ben in citees, moun euer be ayenbouyt; if tho ben not ayenbouyt,

33 tho schulen turne ayen in the iubilee 'to the lordis; for the 'howsis of the citees of dekenes ben for possessiouns among the sones of Israel;

34 forsothe the suburbabis of hem schulen not be seeld, for it is euerlastynge possessioun.

35 If thi brother is maad pore, and feble in power, and thou resseyuest hym as a comelyng and pilgrym, and he lyueth with thee,

36 take thou not vsuris of hym, nether more than thou hast youe; drede thou thi God, that thi brothir mai lyue anentis thee.

37 Thou schalt not yyue to hym thi money to vsure, and thou schalt not axe ouer 'aboundaunce, ether encrees ouer of fruytis;

38 Y am youre Lord God, that ladde you out of the lond of Egipt, that Y schulde yyue to you the lond of Canaan, and that Y schulde be youre God.

39 If thi brother compellid bi pouert sillith hym silf to thee, thou schalt not oppresse hym bi seruage of seruauntis,

40 but he schal be as an hirid man and tenaunt; 'til to the yeer of iubilee he schal worche at thee,

41 and aftirward he schal go out with his fre children, and he schal turne ayen to the kynrede, and to 'the possessioun of his fadris.

42 For thei ben my seruauntis, and Y ledde hem out of the lond of Egipt; thei schulen not be seeld bi the condicioun of seruauntis;

43 turmente thou not hem bi thi power, but drede thou thi Lord.

44 A seruaunt and handmaide be to you of naciouns that ben in youre cumpas,

45 and of comelyngis that ben pilgrimys at you, ether thei that ben borun of hem in youre lond; ye schulen haue these seruauntis,

46 and bi riyt of eritage ye schulen 'sende ouer to aftir comeris, and ye schulen welde with outen ende; sothely oppresse ye not bi power youre britheren, the sones of Israel.

47 If the hond of a comelyng and of a pilgrim wexith strong at you, and thi brother is maad pore, and sillith hym silf to hym,

48 ether to ony of his kyn, he may be ayenbouyt aftir the sillyng; he that wole of hise britheren, ayenbie hym; bothe 'the brother of fadir,

49 and the sone of 'the fadris brother, and kynesman, and alye. Ellis if also he schal mow, he schal ayenbie hym silf,

50 while the yeeris ben rykenid oneli fro the tyme of his sillyng 'til in to the yeer of iubylee; and while the money, for which he was seeld, is rikenyd bi the noumbre of yeeris, and while the hire of an hirid man is rikenyd.

51 If mo yeeris ben that dwellen 'til to the iubilee, bi these yeeris he schal yelde also the prijs; if fewe yeeris ben,

52 he schal sette rikenyng with hym bi the noumbre of yeeris;

53 and he schal yeelde to the biere that that is residue of yeeris, while tho yeeris, bi whiche he seruyde bifore, ben

rikenyd for hiris; he schal not turmente 'that Ebreu violentli in thi siyt.

54 That if he may not be ayenbouyt bi this, he schal go out with his free children in the 'yeer of iubilee; for the sones of Israel ben myn seruauntis,

55 whiche Y ledde out of the lond of Egipt.

CAP 26

1 Y am youre Lord God; ye schulen not make to you an ydol, and a grauun ymage, nether ye schulen reise titlis, nether ye schulen sette a noble stoon in youre lond, that ye worschipe it; for Y am youre Lord God.

2 Kepe ye my sabatis, and drede ye at my seyntuarie; Y am the Lord.

3 If ye gon in myn heestis, and kepen my comaundementis, and doon tho, Y schal yyue to you reynes in her tymes,

4 and the erthe schal brynge forth his fruyt, and trees schulen be fillid with applis;

5 the threschyng of ripe cornes schal take vyndage, and vyndage schal occupie seed, and ye schulen ete youre breed in fulnesse, and ye schulen dwelle in youre lond without drede.

6 Y schal yyue pees in youre coostis; ye schulen slepe, and noon schal be that schal make you aferd; Y schal do awei yuel beestis fro you, and a swerd schal not passe bi youre termes.

7 Ye schulen pursue youre enemyes, and thei schulen falle bifor you;

8 fyue of youre men schulen pursue an hundrid aliens, and an hundrid of you schulen pursue ten thousande; youre enemyes schulen falle bi swerd in youre siyt.

9 Y schal biholde you, and Y schal make you to encreesse; ye schulen be multiplied; and Y schal make stedfast my couenaunt with you;

10 ye schulen ete the eldest of elde thingis, and ye schulen caste forth elde thingis, whanne newe thingis schulen come aboue;

11 Y schal sette my tabernacle in the myddis of you, and my soule schal not caste you awey;

12 Y schal go among you, and Y schal be youre God, and ye schulen be a puple to me.

13 Y am youre Lord God, that ledde you out of the lond of Egipcians, that ye schulden not serue hem, and which haue broke the chaynes of youre nollis, that ye schulde go vpriyt.

14 That if ye heren not me, nether doon alle myn heestis,

15 and if ye forsaken my lawis, and despisen my domes, that ye doon not tho thingis that ben ordeyned of me, and that ye brengen my couenaunt to auoydyng, also Y schal do these thingis to you;

16 Y schal visyte you swiftly in nedynesse and brennyng, which schal turment youre iyen, and schal waste youre lyues; in veyn ye schulen sowe seed, that schal be deuourid of enemyes;

17 Y schal sette my face ayens you, and ye schulen falle bifor youre enemyes, and ye schulen be sugetis to hem that haten you; ye schulen fle, while no man pursueth.

18 But if nether so ye obeyen to me, Y schal adde youre chastisyngis seuenfold for youre synnes;

19 and Y schal al tobreke the pride of youre hardnesse, and Y schal yyue to you heuene aboue as of yrun, and the erthe as bras;

20 youre trauel schal be wastid in veyn, nether the erthe schal brynge forth fruyt, nethir trees schulen yyue applis.

21 If ye goon contrarie to me, nether wolen here me, Y schal adde youre woundis til in to seuenfold for youre synnes;

22 Y schal sende out in to you cruel beestis of the feeld, that schulen waste you and youre beestis, and schulen brynge alle thingis to fewnesse, and youre weies schulen be forsakun.

23 That if nether so ye wolen resseyue doctryn, but goon contrarie to me,

24 also Y schal go aduersarie ayens you, and Y schal smyte you seuen sithis for youre synnes;

25 and Y schal brynge yn on you the swerd, vengere of my boond of pees; and whanne ye fleen in to citees, Y schal sende pestilence in the myddis of you, and ye schulen be bitakun in the hondis of enemyes,

26 aftir that Y haue broke the staf of youre breed, so that ten wymmen bake looues in oon ouene, and yelde tho looues at weiyte; and ye schulen ete, and ye schulen not be fillid.

27 But if nether bi these thingis ye heren me, but goon ayens me,

28 and Y schal go ayens you in contrarie woodnesse, and Y schal chastise you bi seuene veniaunces for youre synnes,

29 so that ye ete the fleischis of youre sones, and of youre douytris;

30 Y schal destrie youre hiye thingis, and Y schal breke youre symylacris; ye schulen falle bitwixe the fallyngis of your ydols, and my soule schal haue you abhomynable,

31 in so myche that Y turne youre citees in to wildirnesse, and make youre seyntuaries forsakun, nether Y schal resseyue more the swettest odour;

32 and Y schal destrye youre lond, and youre enemyes schulen be astonyed theronne, whanne thei schulen be enhabiters therof;

33 forsothe Y schal scatere you in to folkis, ether hethen men, and Y schal drawe out of the schethe the swerd aftir you, and youre lond schal be forsakun, and youre citees schulen be cast doun.

34 Thanne 'hise sabatis schulen plese the erthe, in alle the daies of his wildirnesse; whanne ye ben in the lond of enemyes,

35 it schal 'kepe sabat, and schal reste in the sabatis of his wildirnesse, for it restide not in youre sabatis, whanne ye dwelliden therynne.

36 And Y schal yyue drede in 'the hertis of hem, whiche schulen abide of you, in the cuntreis of enemyes; the sown of a leef fleynge schal make hem aferd, and so thei schulen fle it as a swerd; thei schulen falle, while noon pursueth,

37 and alle schulen falle on her britheren, as fleynge bateils; no man of you schal be hardi to ayenstonde enemyes;

38 ye schulen perische among hethen men, and the lond of enemyes schal waaste you.

39 That if summe of these Jewes dwellen, thei schulen faile in her wickidnessis, in the lond of her enemyes, and thei schulen be turmentid for the synne of her fadris,

40 and for her owne synnes, til thei knoulechen her wickidnesses, and han mynde of her yuels, bi whiche thei trespassiden ayens me, and yeden contrarie to me.

41 Therfor and Y schal go ayens hem, and Y schal brynge hem in to the lond of enemyes, til the vncircumcidid soule of hem be aschamed; thanne thei schulen preie for her wickidnesses,

42 and Y schal haue mynde of my boond of pees, which Y couenauntide with Jacob, Ysaac, and Abraham; also Y schal be myndeful of the lond,

43 which, whanne it is left of hem, schal plese to it silf in 'his sabatis, and schal suffre wildirnesse for hem; forsothe thei

schulen preye for her synnes, for thei castiden awey my domes, and despyseden my lawis;

44 netheles, yhe, whanne thei weren in 'the lond of enemyes, Y castide not hem awey outirli, nether Y dispiside hem, so that thei weren wastid, and that Y made voide my couenaunt with hem; for Y am the Lord God of hem.

45 And Y schal haue mynde of my formere boond of pees, whanne Y ledde hem out of the lond of Egipt, in the siyt of hethene men, that Y schulde be her God; Y am the Lord God. These ben the comaundementis, and domes, and lawis, whiche the Lord yaf bitwixe hym silf and bitwixe the sones of Israel, in the hil of Synay, bi the hond of Moises.

CAP 27

1 And the Lord spak to Moises and seide, Speke thou to the sones of Israel,

2 and thou schalt seye to hem, A man that makith avow, and bihetith his soule to God, schal yyue the priys vndur valu, ether preisyng.

3 If it is a male, fro the twentithe yeer 'til to the sixtithe yeer, he schal yyue fifti siclis of siluer, at the mesure of seyntuarie, if it is a womman,

4 sche schal yyue thretti siclis;

5 forsothe fro the fifthe yeer 'til to the twentithe yeer, a male schal yyue twenti cyclis, a womman schal yyue ten ciclis;

6 fro o monethe 'til to the fifthe yeer, fyue ciclis schulen be youun for a male, thre ciclis for a womman;

7 a male of sixti yeer and ouer schal yyue fiftene ciclis, a womman schal yyue ten cyclis.

8 If it is a pore man, and may not yelde the valu, he schal stonde bifor the preest, and as myche as the preest preisith, and seeth that the pore man may yelde, so myche he schal yyue.

9 Forsothe if ony man avowith a beeste, that may be offrid to the Lord, it schal be hooli,

10 and schal not mow be chaungid, that is, nethir a betere for 'an yuel, nether 'a worse for a good; and if he chaungith it, bothe that, that is chaungid, and that, for which it is chaungid, schal be halewid to the Lord.

11 Sotheli if ony man avowith an vncleene beeste, that may not be offrid to the Lord, it schal be brouyt bifor the preest,

12 and the preest schal deme whether it is good ether yuel, and schal sette the prijs;

13 which prijs if he that offrith wole yyue, he schal adde the fifthe part ouer the valu.

14 If a man avowith his hows, and halewith it to the Lord, the preest schal biholde, 'whether it is good ether yuel, and bi the prijs, which is ordeyned of hym, it schal be seld;

15 sotheli if he that avowide wole ayen-bie it, he schal yyue the fifthe part of the valu aboue, and he schal haue the hows.

16 That if he avowith the feeld of his possessioun, and halewith to the Lord, the prijs schal be demed bi the mesure of seed; if the feeld is sowun with thritti buyschels of barli, it schal be seeld for fifti siclys of siluer.

17 If he auowith the feeld anoon for the yeer of the iubilee bigynnynge, as myche as it may be worth, bi so myche it schal be preisid;

18 but if it be after 'sum part of tyme, the preest schal rykene the money bi the noumbre of yeeris that ben residue 'til to the iubilee, and it schal be withdrawun of the prijs.

19 That if he that avowide wole ayenbie the feeld, he schal adde the fyuethe part of the money preisid, and he schal welde it;

20 but if he nyle ayenbie, but it is seeld to ony othir man, he that avowide schal 'no more mowe ayenbie it;

21 for whanne the dai of iubilee cometh, it schal be halewid to the Lord, and the possessioun halewid perteyneth to the riyt of preestis.

22 If the feeld is bouyt, and is not of the possessioun of grettere men,

23 and is halewid to the Lord, the preest schal determyne the prijs bi the noumbre of yeeris 'til to the iubilee, and he that avowide the feeld schal yyue the prijs to the Lord;

24 forsothe in the iubilee it schal turne ayen to the formere lord that seelde it, and 'haue he in to the eritage of his possessioun.

25 'Ech preisyng schal be peisid bi the sicle of seyntuarie; a sicle hath twenti halpens.

26 No man may halewe and avowe the firste gendrid thingis that perteynen to the Lord, whether it is oxe, whether scheep, tho ben the Lordis part.

27 That if the beeste is vncleene, he that offride schal ayenbie by his valu, and he schal adde the fyuethe part of prijs; if he nyle ayenbie, it schal be seeld to another man, as myche euer as it is 'set at valu.

28 Al thing which is halewid to the Lord, whether it is man, whether beeste, whether feeld, it schal not be seeld, nether it schal mow be ayenbouyt; whateuer thing is halewid onys, it schal be hooli of the noumbre of hooli thingis to the Lord,

29 and ech halewyng which is offrid of man, schal not be ayenbouyt, but it schal die bi deeth.

30 Alle the tithis of erthe, whether of fruytis, whether of applis of trees, ben the Lordis part, and ben halewid to hym;

31 sotheli if ony man wole ayenbie hise tithis, he schal adde the fyuethe part of tho; of alle tithis,

32 of scheep, and of oxen, and of geet, that passen vndur the 'yerde of scheepherde, whateuer thing cometh to the tenthe part, it schal be halewid to the Lord;

33 it schal not be chosun, nether good, nether yuel; nethir it schal be chaungid for another; if ony man chaungith, bothe that, that is chaungid, and that, for which it is chaungid, schal be halewid to the Lord, and it schal not be ayenbouyt.

34 These ben the comaundementis whiche the Lord comaundide to Moises, and to the sones of Israel, in the hil of Synay.

NUMBERS

CAP 1

1 And the Lord spak to Moises in the deseert of Synay, in the tabernacle of the boond of pees, in the firste day of the secounde monethe, in the tother yeer of her goyng out of Egipt,

2 and seide, Take ye 'the summe of al the congregacioun of the sones of Israel, bi her kynredis, and howsis, and 'the names of alle bi hem silf, what

3 euer thing is of male kynde fro the twentithe yeere and aboue, of alle the stronge men of Israel; and thou and Aaron schulen noumbre hem bi her cumpanies.

4 And the princes of lynagis and of housis, in her kynredis, schulen be with you,

5 of whiche princes these ben the names; of Ruben, Elisur, the sone of Sedeur;

6 of Symeon, Salamyel, the sone of Suri Sadday;

7 of Juda, Naason, the sone of Amynadab; of Ysacar,

8 Nathanael, the sone of Suar;

9 of Zabulon, Eliab, the sone of Elon; sotheli of the sones of Joseph,

10 of Effraym, Elisama, the sone of Amyud; of Manasses, Gamaliel the sone of Phadussur;

11 of Beniamyn, Abidan, the sone of Gedeon;

12 of Dan, Aiezer, the sone of Amysadday;

13 of Aser, Fegiel, the sone of Ochran;

14 of Gad, Elisaphan, the sone of Duel;

15 of Neptalym, Hayra, the sone of Henam.

16 These weren the noblest princes of the multitude, bi her lynagis, and kynredis, and the heedis of the oost of Israel,

17 whiche pryncis Moises and Aaron token, with al the multitude of the comyn puple.

18 And thei gaderiden in the firste dai of the secounde monethe, and telden hem bi kynredis, and housis, and meynees, and heedis, and names of alle by hem silf, fro the twentithe yeer and aboue,

19 as the Lord comaundide to Moises.

20 And of Ruben the firste gendrid of Israel weren noumbrid, in the deseert of Synai, bi her generaciouns, and meynees, and housis, and bi the names of alle heedis, al thing that is of male kynde, fro 'the twentithe yeer and aboue, of men goynge forth to batel,

21 sixe and fourti thousynd and fyue hundrid.

22 Of the sones of Symeon, bi her generaciouns, and meynees, and housis of her kyneredis, weren noumbrid, bi the names and heedis of alle, al that is of male kynde, fro 'the twentithe yeer and aboue, of men goynge forth to batel,

23 nyn and fifty thousand and thre hundrid.

24 Of the sones of Gad, by generaciouns, and meynees, and housis of her kynredis, weren noumbrid, bi the names of alle, fro twenti yeer and aboue, alle men that yeden forth to batels,

25 fyue and fourti thousand sixe hundrid and fifti.

26 Of the sones of Juda, bi generaciouns, and meynees, and housis of her kynredis, by the names of alle, fro 'the twentithe yeer and aboue, alle men that miyten go to batels,

27 weren noumbrid foure and seuenti thousand and sixe hundrid.

28 Of the sones of Ysacar, bi generaciouns, and meynees, and housis of her kynredis, bi the names of alle, fro 'the twentithe yeer and aboue, alle men that yeden forth to batels,

29 weren noumbrid foure and fifti thousande and foure hundrid.

30 Of the sones of Zabulon, bi generaciouns, and meynees, and housis of her kynredis, weren noumbrid, bi the names of alle, fro 'the twentithe yeer and aboue, alle men that myyten go forth to batels,

31 seuene and fifti thousynde and foure hundrid.

32 Of the sones of Joseph, of the sones of Effraym, bi generaciouns, and meynees, and housis of her kynredis, weren noumbrid, bi the names of alle, fro 'the twentithe yeer and aboue, alle men that myyten go forth to batels,

33 fourti thousynde and fyue hundrid.

34 Forsothe of the sones of Manasses, bi generaciouns, and meynees, and housis of her kynredis, weren noumbrid, bi the names of alle, fro the twentithe yeer and aboue, alle men that myyten go forth to batels,

35 two and thretti thousynd and two hundrid.

36 Of the sones of Beniamyn, bi generaciouns, and meynees, and housis of her kynredis, weren noumbrid, bi the names of alle, fro twenti yeer and aboue, alle men that miyten go forth to batels,

37 fyue and thretti thousinde and foure hundrid.

38 Of the sones of Dan, bi generaciouns, and meynees, and housis of her kynredis, weren noumbrid, bi the names of alle,

fro 'the twentithe yere and aboue, alle men that myyten go forth to batels,

39 two and sixti thousynde and seuene hundrid.

40 Of the sones of Aser, bi generaciouns, and meynees, and housis of her kynredis, weren noumbrid, bi the names of alle, fro 'the twentithe yeer and aboue, alle men that myyten go forth to batels,

41 fourti thousynde and a thousynde and fyue hundrid.

42 Of the sones of Neptalym, bi generaciouns, and meynees, and housis of her kynredis, weren noumbrid, bi the names of alle, fro 'the twentithe yeer and aboue, alle men that myyten go forth to batels,

43 thre and fifty thousynde and foure hundrid.

44 These men it ben, whiche Moises and Aaron and the twelue princes of Israel noumbriden, alle bi the housis 'of her kynredis.

45 And alle men of the sones of Israel bi her housis, and meynees, fro 'the twentithe yeer and aboue, that myyten go forth to batels, weren togidere

46 sixe hundrid thousynde and thre thousynde of men, fyue hundrid and fifti.

47 Sotheli the dekenes in the lynage of her meynes weren not noumbrid with hem.

48 And the Lord spak to Moises, and seide, 'Nyle thou noumbre the lynage of Leuy,

49 nether sette thou the summe of hem with the sones of Israel;

50 but thou schalt ordeyne hem on the tabernacle of witnessing, and on alle the vessels therof, and what euer thing perteyneth to cerymonyes ether sacrifices. Thei schulen bere the tabernacle, and alle purtenaunces therof, and thei schulen be in seruyce, and schulen sette tentis bi the cumpas of the tabernacle.

51 Whanne me schal go, the dekenes schulen do doun the tabernacle; whanne the tentis schulen be sette, thei schulen 'reise the tabernacle. Who euer of straungeris neiyeth, he schal be slayn.

52 Sotheli the sones of Israel schulen sette tentis, ech man bi cumpenyes, and gaderyngis, and his oost;

53 forsothe the dekenes schulen sette tentis bi the cumpas of the tabernacle, lest indignacioun be maad on the multitude of the sones of Israel; and thei schulen wake in the kepyngis of the 'tabernacle of witnessyng.

54 Therfor the sones of Israel diden bi alle thingis whiche the Lord comaundide to Moises.

CAP 2

1 And the Lord spak to Moises and to Aaron, and seide, Alle men of the sones of Israel schulen sette tentis bi the cumpenyes, signes, and baneris, and housis of her kynredis, bi the cumpas of the tabernacle of boond of pees.

3 At the est Judas schal sette tentis, bi the cumpenyes of his oost; and Naason, the sone of Amynadab, schal be prince of the sones of Juda;

4 and al the summe of fiyteris of his kynrede, foure and seuenty thousynde and sixe hundrid.

5 Men of the lynage of Ysachar settiden tentis bysydis hym, of whiche the prince was Nathanael, the sone of Suar;

6 and al the noumbre of hise fiyteris, foure and fifti thousynde and foure hundrid.

7 Eliab, the sone of Elon, was prince of the lynage of Zabulon;

8 al the oost of fiyteris of his kynrede, seuene and fifti thousynde and foure hundrid.

9 Alle that weren noumbrid in the castels of Judas, weren an hundrid thousynde 'foure scoore thousynde and sixe and foure hundrid; and thei schulen go out the firste bi her cumpanyes.

10 In the castels of the sones of Ruben, at the south coost, Elisur, the sone of Sedeur, schal be prince; and al the oost of hise fiyteris,

11 that weren noumbrid, sixe and fourti thousynde and fyue hundrid.

12 Men of the lynage of Symeon settiden tentis bisidis hym, of whiche the prince was Salamyhel, the sone of Surisaddai; and al the oost of hise fiyteris,

13 that weren noumbrid, nyne and fifty thousynde and thre hundrid.

14 Eliasaph, sone of Duel, was prince in the lynage of Gad; and al the oost of his fiyteris,

15 that weren noumbrid, fyue and fourti thousynde sixe hundrid and fifti.

16 Alle that weren noumbrid in the castels of Ruben, an hundrid thousynde fifty thousinde and a thousinde foure hundrid and fifty; thei schulen go forth in the secounde place bi her cumpenyes.

17 Sotheli the tabernacle of witnessyng schal be reisid bi the offices of dekenes, and bi the cumpenyes 'of hem; as it schal be reisid, so and it schal be takun doun; alle schulen go forth bi her places and ordris.

18 The castels of the sones of Effraym schulen be at the west coost, of whiche the prince was Elisama, the sone of Amyud;

19 and al the oost of his fiyteris, that weren noumbrid, fourti thousynde and fyue hundrid.

20 And with hem was the lynage of 'the sones of Manasses, of whiche the prince was Gamaliel, the sone of Fadassur;

21 al the oost of hise fiyteris, that weren noumbrid, two and thretti thousande and two hundrid.

22 In the lynage of the sones of Beniamyn the prince was Abidan, the sone of Gedeon;

23 and al the oost of hise fiyteris, that weren noumbrid, fyue and thretti thousynde and foure hundrid.

24 Alle that weren noumbrid in the castels of Effraym weren an hundrid thousynde and eiyte thousynde and oon hundrid; thei schulen go forth 'the thridde bi her cumpenyes.

25 At the 'part of the north the sones of Dan settiden tentis, of whiche the prince was Abiezer, the sone of Amysaddai;

26 al the oost of hise fiyteris, that weren noumbrid, two and sixti thousynde and seuene hundrid.

27 Men of the lynage of Aser settiden tentis bisidis hym, of whiche the prince was Fegiel, the sone of Ochran;

28 and al the oost of hise fiyteris, that weren noumbrid, fourti thousynde 'and a thousynde and fyue hundrid.

29 Of the lynage of the sones of Neptalym the prince was Ahira, the sone of Henam; and al the oost of hise fiyteris,

30 thre and fifti thousynde and foure hundrid.

31 Alle that weren noumbrid in the castels of Dan weren an hundrid thousynde seuene and fifti thousynde and sixe hundrid; thei schulen go forth the laste.

32 This is the noumbre of the sones of Israel, bi the housis of her kynredis, and bi cumpenyes of the oost departid, sixe hundrid thousynde thre thousynde fyue hundrid and fifti.

33 Sotheli the dekenes weren not noumbrid among the sones of Israel; for God comaundide so to Moises.

34 And the sones of Israel diden bi alle thingis whiche the Lord comaundide; thei settiden tentis bi her cumpenyes, and yeden forth bi the meynees, and housis of her fadris.

CAP 3

1 These ben the generaciouns of Aaron and of Moises, in the dai in which the Lord spak to Moises, in the hil of Synay.

2 And these ben the names of 'the sones of Aaron; his first gendrid, Nadab; aftirward, Abyu, and Eleazar, and Ythamar; these ben the names of 'Aarons sones,

3 preestis, that weren anoyntid, and whos hondis weren fillid and halewid, that thei schulden 'be set in preesthod.

4 Nadab and Abyu, whanne thei offeriden alien fier in the 'siyt of the Lord, in the deseert of Synay, weren deed without fre children; and Eleazar and Ythamar 'weren set in preesthod bifor Aaron hir fadir.

5 And the Lord spak to Moises,

6 'and seide, 'Presente thou the lynage of Leuy, and make to stonde in the siyt of Aaron, preest, that thei mynystre to hym;

7 and wake, and that thei kepe what euer thing perteyneth to the religioun of multitude, bifor the tabernacle of witnessyng;

8 and that thei kepe the vessels of the tabernacle, and serue in the seruyce therof.

9 And thou schalt yyue bi fre yifte the Leuytis to Aaron and hise sones, to whiche thei ben youun of the sones of Israel.

10 Sotheli thou schalt ordeyne Aaron and hise sones on the religioun of preesthod; a straungere, that neiyeth for to mynystre, and schal die.

11 And the Lord spak to Moyses, 'and seide,

12 Y haue take the Leuytis of the sones of Israel for ech firste gendrid thing that openeth the womb in the sones of Israel; and the Leuytis schulen be myne,

13 for ech firste gendrid thing is myn; sithen Y smoot the firste gendrid in the lond of Egipt, Y halewide to me what euer thing is borun first in Israel; fro man 'til to beest thei ben myne; Y am the Lord.

14 And the Lord spak to Moises in the deseert

15 of Synay, and seide, Noumbre thou the sones of Leuy bi 'the housis of her fadris, and bi meynees, ech male fro o monethe and aboue.

16 Moises noumbride, as the Lord comaundide.

17 And the sones of Leuy weren foundun, bi her names, Gerson, and Caath, and Merary;

18 the sones of Gerson weren Lebny, and Semey;

19 the sones of Caath weren Amram, and Jessaar, Hebron, and Oziel;

20 and the sones of Merari weren Mooly, and Musi.

21 Of Gerson weren twei meynees, of Lebny, and of Semei;

22 of whiche the puple of male kynde was noumbrid, fro o monethe and aboue, seuene thousynde and fyue hundrid.

23 These schulen sette tentis aftir the tabernacle at the west,

24 vndur the prince Eliasaph, the sone of Jahel.

25 And thei schulen haue kepyngis in the tabernacle of boond of pees, the tabernacle it silf, and the hilyng therof, the tente which is drawun bifor the yatis of the hilyng of the witnessyng of boond of pees;

26 and the curteyns of the greet street, also the tente which is hangid in the entryng of the greet street of the tabernacle, and what euer thing perteyneth to the custom of the auter, the cordis of the tabernacle, and al the purtenaunce therof.

27 The kynrede of Caath schal haue the puplis of Amram, and of Jessaar, and of Ebron, and of Oziel;

28 these ben the meynees of Caathitis, noumbrid bi her names, alle of male kynde, fro o monethe and aboue, eiyte thousynde and sixe hundrid.

29 Thei schulen haue kepyngis of the seyntuarie, and schulen sette tentis at the south coost;

30 and 'the prince of hem schal be Elisaphan, the sone of Oziel.

31 And thei schulen kepe the arke, and the boord, and the candilstike, the auters, and vesselis of the seyntuarie in whiche it is mynystrid, and the veil, and al sich purtenaunce.

32 Sotheli the prince of princis of Leuytis schal be Eleazar, the sone of Aaron, preest; and he schal be on the keperis of the kepyng of the seyntuarie.

33 And sotheli of Merary schulen be the puplis of Mooli, and of Musi,

34 noumbrid bi her names, alle of male kynde fro o monethe and aboue, sixe thousynde and two hundrid;

35 'the prince of hem schal be Suriel, the sone of Abiahiel; thei schulen sette tentis in the north coost.

36 And vndur 'the kepyng of hem schulen be the tablis of the tabernacle, and the barris, and the pileris, and 'the founde-mentis of tho, and alle thingis that perteynen to sich ournyng,

37 and the pileris of the greet street bi cumpas, with her foun-dementis, and the stakis with coordis.

38 Forsothe Moises and Aaron with hise sones schulen sette tentis bifor the tabernacle of boond of pees, that is, at the eest coost, and schulen haue the keping of the seyntuarie, in the myddis of the sones of Israel; what euer alien neiyeth, he schal die.

39 Alle the Leuytis, whiche Moises and Aaron noumbriden, bi comaundement of the Lord, bi her meynees, in male kynde, fro o monethe and aboue, were two and twenti thousynd.

40 And the Lord seide to Moises, Noumbre thou the firste gendrid children of male kynde of the sones of Israel, fro o monethe and aboue; and thou schalt haue the summe of hem; and

41 thou schalt take Leuytis to me for alle the firste gendrid of the sones of Israel; Y am the Lord; and thou schalt take 'the beestis of hem for alle the firste gendrid of the sones of Israel.

42 And as the Lord comaundide, Moises noumbride the firste gendrid children of the sones of Israel; and the males weren bi her names,

43 fro o monethe and aboue, two and twenti thousynde two hundrid and seuenti and thre.

44 And the Lord spak to Moises, and seide,

45 Take thou Leuytis for the firste gendrid children of the sones of Israel, and the beestis of Leuytis for the beestis of hem, and the Leuytis schulen be myne; Y am the Lord.

46 Forsothe in the prijs of two hundrid seuenti and thre, that passen the noumbre of 'Leuytis, of the firste gendrid children of the sones of Israel,

47 thou schalt take fyue ciclis bi ech heed, at the mesure of seyntuarie; a sicle hath xx. halpens;

48 and thou schalt yyue the money to Aaron and to hise sones, the prijs of hem that ben aboue.

49 Therfor Moises took the money of hem that weren aboue, and whiche thei hadden ayenbouyt of the Leuytis, for the firste gendrid of the sones of Israel,

50 a thousand thre hundrid sixti and fyue of siclis, bi the weiyte of seyntuarie;

51 and he yaf that money to Aaron and to hise sones, bi the word which the Lord comaundide to hym.

CAP 4

1 And the Lord spak to Moises and to Aaron,

2 and seide, Take thou the summe of the sones of Caath, fro the myddis of Leuytis,

3 bi her housis and meynees, fro the threttithe yeer and aboue 'til to the fiftithe yeer, of alle that entren, that thei stonde and mynystre in the tabernacle of boond of pees.

4 This is the religioun of the sones of Caath; Aaron and his sones schulen entren in to the tabernacle of boond of pees, and in to the hooli of hooli thingis,

5 whanne the tentis schulen be moued; and thei schulen do doun the veil that hangith bifore the yatis, and thei schulen wlappe in it the arke of witnessyng;

6 and thei schulen hile eft with a veil of 'skynnys of iacynt, and thei schulen stretche forth aboue a mentil al of iacynt, and thei schulen putte in barris 'on the schuldris of the bereris.

7 Also thei schulen wlappe the boord of proposicioun in a mentil of iacynt, and thei schulen putte therwith cenceris, and morteris of gold, litil cuppis, and grete cuppis to fletyng sacri-fices 'to be sched; looues schulen euere be in the boord.

8 And thei schulen strecche forth aboue a reed mentil, which thei schulen hile eft with an hilyng of 'skynnes of iacynt, and thei schulen putte yn barris.

9 Thei schulen take also a mentil of iacynt with which thei schulen hile the candilstike, with hise lanternes, and tongis, and snytels, and alle the 'vessels of oile that ben nedeful to the lanternes to be ordeyned;

10 and on alle thingis thei schulen putte an hilyng of 'skynnys of iacynt, and thei schulen putte in barris.

11 Also and thei schulen wlappe the goldun auter in a clooth of iacynt; and thei schulen stretche forth aboue an hilyng of 'skynnys of iacynt, and thei schulen putte in barris.

12 Thei schulen wlappe in a mentil of iacynt alle the vessels in whiche it is mynystrid in the seyntuarie, and thei schulen strecche forth aboue an hilyng of 'skynnys of iacynt, and thei schulen putte yn barris.

13 But also thei schulen clense the auter fro aische, and thei schulen wlappe it in a clooth of purpur.

14 And thei schulen putte with it alle vessels whiche thei vsen in the seruyce therof, that is, ressettis of firis, tongis, and fleischokis, hokis, and censeris, ether pannys of coolis; thei schulen hile alle the vessels of the auter togidere in a veil of 'skynnes of iacynt, and thei schulen putte in barris.

15 And whanne Aaron and hise sones han wlappid the seyn-tuarie, and alle vessels therof, in the mouyng of tentis, thanne the sones of Caath schulen entre, that thei bere the thingis wlappid, and touche not the vessels of the seyntuarie, lest thei dien.

16 Thes ben the birthuns of the sones of Caath, in the taberna-cle of boond of pees, on whiche Eleazar, the sone of Aaron, preest, schal be; to whois cure 'the oile perteyneth to ordeyne lanternes, and the encense which is maad bi craft, and the sac-rifice which is offrid euere, and the oile of anoyntyng, and what euere thing perteyneth to the ournyng of the tabernacle, and of alle vessels that ben in the seyntuarie.

17 And the Lord spak to Moises and to Aaron, and seide,

18 Nyle ye leese the puple of Caath fro the myddis of Leuytis;

19 but do ye this thing to hem, that thei lyue, and die not, if thei touchen the hooli of hooli thingis. Aaron and hise sones schulen entre, and thei schulen dispose the werkis of alle men, and thei schulen departe 'what who owith to bere.

20 Othere men se not bi ony curiouste tho thingis that ben in the seyntuarie, bifore that tho ben wlappid; ellis thei schulen die.

21 And the Lord spak to Moises,

22 and seide, Take thou the summe also of the sones of Gerson, bi her housis, and meynees, and kynredis; noumbre thou

23 fro thretti yeer and aboue 'til to fifti yeer alle that entren and mynystren in the tabernacle of boond of pees.

24 This is the office of the sones of Gersonytis, that thei bere the curteyns of the tabernacle, and the roof of the boond of pees, an other hilyng,

25 and a veil of iacynt aboue alle thingis, and the tente which hangith in the entryng of the tabernacle of the boond of pees;

26 and the curteyns of the greet street, and the veil in the entryng, 'which veil is bifor the tabernacle.

27 Whanne Aaron comaundith and hise sones, the sones of Gerson schulen bere alle thingis that perteynen to the auter, the coordis, and vessels of seruyce; and alle schulen wite, to what charge thei owen to be boundun.

28 This is the office of the meynee of Gersonytis, in the tabernacle of boond of pees; and thei schulen be vndur the hond of Ythamar, the sone of Aaron, preest.

29 Also thou schalt noumbre the sones of Merary, bi the meynees and housis of her fadris,

30 fro thretti yeer and aboue 'til to fifti yeer, alle that entren to the office of her seruice, and to the ournyng of the boond of pees of witnessyng.

31 These ben 'the chargis of hem; thei schulen bere the tablis of the tabernacle, and the barris therof, the pilers and her foundementis; also the pilers of the greet street bi cumpas,

32 with her foundementis, and her stakis, and coordis; thei schulen take alle instrumentis and purtenaunce at noumbre, and so thei schulen bere.

33 This is the office of 'the meynee of Meraritis, and the seruyce in the tabernacle of boond of pees; and thei schulen be vndur the hond of Ythamar, the sone of Aaron, preest.

34 Therfor Moises and Aaron and the princes of the synagoge noumbriden the sones of Caath, bi the kynredis and housis of her fadris,

35 fro thretti yeer and aboue 'til to the fiftithe yeer, alle that entren to the seruyce of the tabernacle of boond of pees;

36 and thei weren foundun two thousynde seuene hundrid and fifti.

37 This is the noumbre of the puple of Caath, which entrith in to the tabernacle of boond of pees; Moises and Aaron noumbriden these, bi the word of the Lord, bi the hond of Moises.

38 And the sones of Gerson weren noumbrid, bi the kyneredis and housis of her fadris,

39 fro thretti yeer and aboue 'til to 'the fiftithe yeer, alle that entren that thei mynystre in the tabernacle of boond of pees;

40 and thei weren foundun two thousynde sixe hundrid and thretti.

41 This is the puple of Gersonytis, which Moises and Aaron noumbriden, bi the 'word of the Lord.

42 And the sones of Merary weren noumbrid, bi the kynredis and housis of her fadris,

43 fro threttithe yeer and aboue 'til to 'the fiftithe yere, alle that entren to fille the customs, ether seruices, of the tabernacle of boond of pees;

44 'and thei weren foundun thre thousynde and two hundrid.

45 This is the noumbre of the sones of Merari, whiche Moyses and Aaron noumbriden, bi 'the comaundement of the Lord, bi the hoond of Moises.

46 Alle that weren noumbrid of Leuytis, and whiche Moyses and Aaron and the princes of Israel maden to be noumbrid, bi the kynredis and housis of her fadris,

47 fro thretti yeer and aboue 'til to 'the fiftithe yeer, and entriden to the seruyce of the tabernacle, and to bere chargis,

48 weren togidere eiyte thousynde fyue hundrid and foure scoor.

49 By the 'word of the Lord Moises noumbride hem, ech man bi his office and hise chargis, as the Lord comaundide to hym.

CAP 5

1 And the Lord spak to Moises, and seide, Comaunde thou to the sones of Israel,

2 that thei caste out of the castels ech leprouse man, and that fletith out seed, and is defoulid on a deed bodi; caste ye out of the castels,

3 as wel a male as a female, lest thei defoulen tho, whanne thei dwellen with you.

4 And the sones of Israel diden so; and thei castiden hem out of the castels, as the Lord spak to Moises.

5 And the Lord spak to Moises,

6 and seide, Speke thou to the sones of Israel, Whanne a man ethir a womman han do of alle synnes that ben wont to falle to men, and han broke bi necgligence the 'comaundement of the Lord,

7 and han trespassid, thei schulen knowleche her synne, and thei schulen yelde thilke heed, and the fyuethe part aboue, to hym ayens whom thei synneden.

8 But if noon is that schal resseyue thei schulen yyue to the Lord, and it schal be the preestis part, outakun the ram which is offrid for clensyng, that it be a quemeful sacrifice.

9 Also alle the firste fruytis, whiche the sones of Israel offren, perteynen to the preest;

10 and what euer thing is offrid of ech man in the seyntuarie, and is youun to the 'hondis of the preest, it schal be the preestis part.

11 And the Lord spak to Moises,

12 and seide, Speke thou to the sones of Israel, and thou schalt seie to hem, If 'the wijf of a man hath errid, and hath dispisid the hosebonde,

13 and hath slept with another man, and the hosebonde may not take ether preue this, but the auowtrye is hid, and may not be preuyd bi witnessis, for sche is not foundun in leccherie;

14 if the spirit of gelousie stirith the housebonde ayens his wijf, which is ether defoulid, ethir is apechid bi fals suspecioun,

15 the man schal brynge hir to the preest, and he schal offre an offryng for hir 'the tenthe part of a mesure clepid satum of barli meele; he schal not schede oyle ther onne, nethir he schal putte encense, for it is the sacrifice of gelousie, and an offryng enquerynge auowtrye.

16 Therfor the preest schal offre hir, and schal sette bifore the Lord;

17 and he schal take holi watir in 'a vessel of erthe, and he schal putte in to it a litil of the erthe of the pawment of the tabernacle.

18 And whanne the womman stondith in the siyt of the Lord, he schal diskyuere hir heed, and he schal putte 'on the hondis of hir the sacrifice of remembryng, and the offryng of gelousie. Sotheli he schal holde moost bittir watris, in whiche he gaderide togidere cursis with cursyng.

19 And he schal conioure hir, and schal seie, If an alien man slepte not with thee, and if thou art not defoulid in the for-

sakyng the bed of the hosebonde, these bittereste watris schulen not anoye thee, in to whiche Y haue gaderid togidere cursis;

20 ellis if thou bowidst awei fro thin hosebonde, and art defoulid, and hast leyn with another man,

21 thou schalt be suget to these cursyngys; the Lord yyue thee in to cursyng, and in to ensaumple of alle men in his puple; 'the Lord make thin hipe to wexe rotun, and thi wombe swelle, and be brokun;

22 cursid watris entre in to thi wombe, and while the wombe swellith, thin hipe wexe rotun. And the womman schal answere, Amen! amen!

23 And the preest schal write thes cursis in a litil book, and he schal do awey tho cursis with bittereste watris, in to whiche he gaderide cursis,

24 and he schal yyue to hir to drynke. And whanne sche hath drunke tho watris,

25 the preest schal take of hir hond the sacrifice of gelousie, and he schal reise it bifor the Lord, and he schal putte on the auter;

26 so oneli that he take bifore an handful of sacrifice 'of that that is offrid, and brenne on the auter, and so yyue drynke to the womman the moost bittere watris.

27 And whanne sche hath drunke tho watris, if sche is defoulid, and is gilti of auowtrie, for the hosebonde is dispisid, the watris of cursyng schulen passe thorouy hir, and while the wombe is bolnyd, the hipe schal wexe rotun, and the womman schal be in to cursyng and in to ensaumple to al the puple.

28 That if sche is not pollutid, sche schal be harmeles, and schal brynge forth fre children.

29 This is the lawe of gelousie, if a womman bowith awei fro hir hosebonde, and is defoulid,

30 and the hosebonde is stirid with the spirit of gelousye, and bryngith hir in to the 'siyt of the Lord, and the preest doith to hir bi alle thingis that ben writun, the hosebonde schal be with out synne,

31 and sche schal resseyue hir wickidnesse.

CAP 6

1 And the Lord spak to Moises and seide, Speke thou to the sones of Israel,

2 and thou schalt seie to hem, Whanne a man ether a wom- man makith auow, that thei be halewid, and thei wolen halewe hem silf to the Lord,

3 thei schulen absteyne fro wyn and fro al thing that may make drunkun; thei schulen not drynke vynegre of wyn, and of ony other drynkyng, and what euer thing is pressid out of the grape; thei schulen not ete freisch grapis and drie,

4 alle dayes in whiche thei ben halewid bi a vow to the Lord; thei schulen not ete what euer thing may be of the vyner, fro a grape dried 'til to the draf.

5 In al tyme of his departyng a rasour schal not passe on his heed, 'til to the day fillid in which he is halewid to the Lord; he schal be hooli while the heer of his heed 'schal wexe.

6 In al the tyme of his halewing he schal not entre on a deed bodi,

7 and sotheli he schal not be defoulid on the deed bodi of fadir and of moder, of brothir and of sistir, for the halewyng of his God is on his heed;

8 ech dai of his departyng schal be hooli to the Lord.

9 But if ony man is deed sudeynly bifore hym, the heed of his halewyng schal be defoulid, which he schal schaue anoon in the same dai of his clensyng, and eft in the seuenthe dai;

10 forsothe in the eiyte dai he schal offre twei turtlis, ether twei 'briddis of a culuer, to the preest, in the entryng of the boond of pees of witnessyng.

11 And the preest schal make oon for synne, and the tothir in to brent sacrifice; and the preest schal preie for hym, for he synnede on a deed bodi, and he schal halewe his heed in that dai.

12 And he schal halewe to the Lord the daies of his depar- tyng, and he schal offre a lomb of o yeer for synne, so nethe- les that the formere daies be maad voide, for his halewyng is defoulid.

13 This is the lawe of consecracioun. Whanne the daies schulen be fillid, whiche he determynede by a vow, the preest schal brynge hym to the dore of the tabernacle of boond of pees, and schal offre his offryng to the Lord,

14 a lomb of o yeer with out wem, in to brent sacrifice, and a scheep of o yeer with outen wem, for synne, and a ram with out wem, a pesible sacrifice;

15 also a panyere of theerf looues, that ben spreynt togidere with oile, and cakis sodun in watir, and aftir anoyntid with oile, with out sourdow, and fletyng sacrifices of alle bi hem silf;

16 whiche the preest schal offre bifor the Lord, and schal make as wel for synne as in to brent sacrifice.

17 Sotheli he schal offre the ram a pesible sacrifice to the Lord, and he schal offre togidere a panyere of therf looues and fletyng sacryfices, that ben due bi custom.

18 Thanne the Nazarei schal be schauun fro the heer of his consecracioun, bifor the doore of the tabernacle of boond of pees; and the preest schal take hise heeris, and schal putte on the fier, which is put vndur the sacrifice of pesible thingis.

19 And he schal take the schuldur sodun of the ram, and o 'cake of breed with out sourdow fro the panyere, and o theerf caak first sodun in watir and aftirward fried in oile, and he schal bitake in the hondis of the Nazarei, aftir that his heed is schauun.

20 And the preest schal reise in the 'siyt of the Lord the thingis takun eft of hym. And the thingis halewid schulen be the preestis part, as the brest which is comaundid to be departid, and the hipe. Aftir these thingis the Nasarey may drynke wyn.

21 This is the lawe of the Nasarei, whanne he hath avowyd his offryng to the Lord in the tyme of his consecracioun, out- akun these thingis whiche his hond fyndith. By this that he avowide in soule, so he schal do, to the perfeccioun of his halewyng.

22 And the Lord spak to Moyses and seide,

23 Speke thou to Aaron and to hise sones, Thus ye schulen blesse the sones of Israel, and ye schulen seie to hem,

24 The Lord blesse thee, and kepe thee;

25 the Lord schewe his face to thee, and haue mercy on thee;

26 the Lord turne his cheer to thee, and yyue pees to thee.

27 Thei schulen clepe inwardli my name on the sones of Israel, and Y schal blesse hem.

CAP 7

1 Forsothe it was don in the dai in which Moises fillide the tabernacle, and reiside it, and anoyntide and halewide with alle 'hise vessels, the auter in lijk maner and the vessels therof.

2 And the princes of Israel, and the heedis of meynees that weren bi alle lynagis, 'the souereyns of hem that weren noumbrid,

3 offeriden yiftis bifor the Lord, sixe waynes hylid with twelue oxun; twei duykis offeriden o wayn, and ech offeride oon oxe. And thei offeriden tho waynes 'in the siyt of the tabernacle.

4 Forsothe the Lord seide to Moises,

5 Take thou of hem, that tho serue in the seruice of the tabernacle, and bitake thou tho to dekenes bi the ordre of her seruice.

6 And so whanne Moises hadde take the waynes, and the oxun, he bitook tho to the dekenes.

7 He yaf twei waynes and foure oxun to the sones of Gerson, bi that that thei hadden nedeful.

8 He yaf four other waynes and eiyte oxun to the sones of Merari, bi her offices and religioun, vnder the hond of Ythamar, the sone of Aaron, preest.

9 Forsothe he yaf not waynes and oxun to the sones of Caath, for thei seruen in the seyntuarye, and beren chargis with her owne schuldris.

10 Therfor the duykis offeriden, in the halewyng of the auter, in the dai in which it was anoyntid, her offryng to the Lord, bifore the auter.

11 And the Lord seide to Moises, Alle dukis bi hemsilf offre yiftis, bi alle daies bi hem silf, in to the halewyng of the auter.

12 Naason, the sone of Amynadab, of the lynage of Juda, offeride his offryng in the firste day;

13 and a siluerne vessel 'to preue ensense and siche thingis, in the weiyte of an hundrid and thretti siclis, a viol of siluere, hauynge seuenti siclis bi the weiyt of the seyntuarie, 'weren ther ynne, euer eithir ful of flour spreynt togidere with oile, in to sacrifice;

14 a morter, of ten goldun siclis, ful of encence.

15 He offride an oxe of the droue, and a ram, and a lomb of o yeer, in to brent sacrifice;

16 and a 'buk of geet, for synne.

17 And he offeride in the sacrifice of pesible thingis, tweyne oxun, fyue rammys, fyue 'buckis of geet, fyue lambren of o yeer. This is the offryng of Naason, the sone of Amynadab.

18 In the secounde dai Nathanael, the sone of Suar, duyk of the lynage of Isachar,

19 offeride a siluerne vessel 'to preue encense and siche thingis, peisynge an hundrid and thretti siclis, a siluerne viole, hauynge seuenti syclis bi the weiyte of seyntuarie, euer either ful of flour spreynt togidere with oile, in to sacrifice;

20 a goldun morter, hauynge ten siclis, ful of encense;

21 an oxe of the droue, and a ram, and a lomb of o yeer, in to brent sacrifice;

22 and a 'buc of geet, for synne.

23 And in the sacrifice of pesible thingis he offride tweyne oxun, and fyue rammes, fyue 'buckis of geet, fyue lambren of o yeer. This was the offryng of Nathanael the sone of Suar.

24 In the thridde dai Eliab, the sone of Elon, prince of the sones of Zabulon,

25 offeride a siluerne vessel to 'preue encence and siche thingis, peisynge an hundrid and thretti siclis, a siluerne viol, hauynge seuenti siclis at the weiyte of seyntuarie, euer eithir ful of flour spreynt togidere with oile, in to sacrifice; a goldun morter,

26 peisynge ten siclis, ful of encense;

27 an oxe of the droue, and a ram, and a lomb of o yeer, in to brent sacrifice; and a buc of geet, for synne.

28 And in sacrifice of pesible thingis he offride tweyne oxen, fyue rammes, fyue 'buckis of geet, fyue lambren of o yeer.

29 This is the offryng of Eliab, the sone of Helon.

30 In the fourthe dai Helisur, the sone of Sedeur, the prince of the sones of Ruben,

31 offride a siluerne vessel 'to preue encense and siche thingis, peisynge an hundrid and thretti siclis, a siluerne viol, hauynge seuenti syclis at the weiyte of seyntuarie, euer eithir ful of flour spreynt togidere with oile, in to sacrifice;

32 a goldun morter peisynge ten siclis, ful of encense;

33 an oxe of the drooue, and a ram, and a lomb of o yeer in to brent sacrifice,

34 and a 'buc of geet, for synne.

35 And in to sacrifice of pesible thingis he offride tweyne oxun, fyue rammes, fyue 'buckis of geet, fyue lambren of o yeer. This was the offryng of Elisur, the sone of Sedeur.

36 In the fyuethe dai Salamyhel, the sone of Surisaddai, the prince of the sones of Symeon,

37 offeride a siluerne vessel 'to preue encense and siche thingis, peysynge an hundrid and thretti siclis, a siluerne viol, hauynge seuenti siclis at the weiyte of seyntuarie, euer either ful of flour spreynt togidere with oile, in to sacrifice;

38 a goldun morter, peisynge ten siclis, ful of encense;

39 an oxe of the drooue, and a ram, and a lomb of o yeer, in to brent sacrifice;

40 and a 'bucke of geet, for synne.

41 And in to sacrifice of pesible thingis he offeride tweyne oxun, fyue rammes, fyue 'buckis of geet, fyue lambren of o yeer. This was the offring of Salamyhel, the sone of Surisaddai.

42 In the sixte day Elisaphat, the sone of Duel, the prince of the sones of Gad,

43 offride a siluerne vessel 'to preue encense and sich thingis, peisynge an hundrid and thretti siclis, a siluerne viol, hauynge seuenti siclis at the weiyte of seyntuarie, euer eithir ful of flour spreynt togidere with oile in to sacrifice;

44 a goldun morter, peisynge ten siclis, ful of encense;

45 an oxe of the droue, and a ram, and a lomb of o yeer, in to brent sacrifice;

46 and a 'buc of geet, for synne.

47 And in to sacrifice of pesible thingis he offride twei oxun, fyue rammes, fyue 'buckis of geet, fyue lambren of o yeer. This was the offryng of Elisaphat, the sone of Duel.

48 In the seuenthe dai Elisama, the sone of Amyud, the prince of the sones of Effraym,

49 offride a siluerne vessel 'to preue encense and siche thingis, peisynge an hundrid and thretti siclis, a siluerne viol, hauynge seuenti siclis at the weiyte of seyntuarie, euer either ful of flour spreynt togidere with oyle, in to sacrifice; a goldun morter,

50 peisynge ten siclis, ful of encense;

51 an oxe of the drooue, and a ram, and a lomb of o yeer, in to

52 brent sacrifice; and a 'buc of geet, for synne.

53 And in to sacrifices of pesible thingis he offride tweyne oxun, fyue rammes, fyue 'buckis of geet, fyue lambren of o yeer. This was the offryng of Elisama, the sone of Amyud.

54 In the eiytthe dai Gamaliel, the sone of Fadussur, the prince of the sones of Manasses,

55 offride a siluerne vessel 'to preue encense and siche thingis, peisynge an hundrid and thretti syclis, a siluerne viole, hauynge seuenti siclis at the weiyte of seyntuarie, euer eithir ful of flour spreynt togidere with oile, in to sacrifice; a goldun morter,

56 peisynge ten siclis, ful of encense;

57 an oxe of the drooue, and a ram, and a lomb of o yeer, in to brent

58 sacrifice; and a 'buc of geet, for synne.

59 And in to sacrificis of pesible thingis he offride tweyne oxun, fyue rammes, fyue 'buckis of geet, fyue lambren of o yeer. This was the offryng of Gamaliel, the sone of Fadussur.

60 In the nynthe dai Abidan, the sone of Gedeon, the prince of the sones of Beniamyn,

61 offeride a siluerne vessel 'to preue encense and siche thingis, peisynge an hundrid and thretti siclis, a siluerne viol, hauynge seuenti siclis at the weiyte of seyntuarie, euer eithir ful of flour sprent togidere with oile, in to sacrifice;

62 a goldun morter, peisynge ten siclis, ful of encense; an oxe of the drooue,

63 and a ram, and a lomb of o yeer in to brent sacrifice;

64 and a 'buc of geet, for synne.

65 And in to sacrifice of pesible thingis he offride tweyne oxun, fyue rammes, fyue 'buckis of geet, fyue lambren of o yeer. This was the offryng of Abidan, the sone of Gedeon.

66 In the tenthe dai Abiezer, the sone of Amysaddai, the prince of the sones of Dan,

67 offride a siluerne vessel 'to preue encense and siche thingis, peisynge an hundrid and thretti siclis, a siluerne viol, hauynge seuenti siclis at the weiyte of seyntuarie, euer eithir ful of flour spreynt to gidere with oile in to sacrifice;

68 a goldun morter, peisynge ten siclis, ful of encense;

69 an oxe of the drooue, and a ram, and a lomb of o yeer, in to brent sacrifice;

70 and a 'buc of geet, for synne.

71 And in to sacrifices of pesible thingis he offride tweyne oxun, fyue rammes, fyue 'buckis of geet, fyue lambren of o yeer. This was the offryng of Abiezer, the sone of Amysaddai.

72 In the enleuenthe dai Phegiel, the sone of Ocran,

73 the prince of the sones of Aser, offride a siluerne vessel 'to preue encense and siche thingis, peisynge an hundrid and thretti siclis, a siluerne viol, hauynge seuenti siclis at the weiyte of seyntuarie, euer either ful of flour spreynt to gidere with oile, in to sacrifice;

74 a goldun morter, peisynge ten ciclis, ful of encense;

75 an oxe of the drooue, and a ram, and a lomb of o yeer, in to brent sacrifice;

76 and a 'bucke of geet, for synne.

77 And in to sacrifices of pesyble thingis he offride tweyne oxun, fyue rammes, fyue 'buckis of geet, fyue lambren of o yeer. This was the offryng of Phegiel, the sone of Ochran.

78 In the tweluethe dai Ahira, the sone of Enan, the prince of the sones of Neptalym,

79 offride a siluerne vessel 'to preue encense and siche thingis, peisynge an hundrid and thetti siclis, a siluerne viol, hauynge seuenti siclis at the weiyte of seyntuarie, euer eithir ful of flour spreynt to gidere with oile, in to sacrifice;

80 a goldun morter, peisynge ten siclis, ful of encense;

81 an oxe of the drooue, and a ram, and a lomb of o yeer, in to brent sacrifice;

82 and a 'buc of geet, for synne.

83 And in to sacrifices of pesible thingis he offride tweyne oxun, fyue rammes, fyue 'buckis of geet, fyue lambren of o yeer. This was the offryng of Haira, the sone of Henan.

84 These thingis weren offrid of the sones of Israel, in the halewyng of the auter, in the dai in which it was halewid;

siluerne vessels 'to preue, encense and siche thingis twelue, siluerne viols twelue, goldun morteris twelue;

85 so that o vessel 'to preue encense and siche thingis hadde an hundrid and thretti siclis 'of siluer, and o viol hadde seuenti siclis, that is, in comyn, two thousynde and foure hundrid siclis of alle the 'vessels of siluer, bi the weiyte of seyntuarie;

86 goldun morteris twelue, ful of encense, peisynge ten siclis bi the weiyte of seyntuarie, that is to gidere an hundrid and twenti siclis of gold;

87 oxun of the drooue in to brent sacrifice twelue, twelue rammes, twelue lambren of o yeer, and the fletynge sacryfices 'of tho, twelue 'buckis of geet for synne;

88 the sacrifices of pesible thingis, foure and twenti oxun, sexty rammes, sexti 'buckis of geet, sixti lambren of o yeer. These thingis weren offrid in the halewyng of the auter, whanne it was anoyntid.

89 And whanne Moyses entride in to the tabernacle of boond of pees, 'to axe counsel 'of Goddis answeryng place, he herde the vois of God spekynge to hym fro 'the propiciatorie, which was on the arke of witnessyng, bitwixe twei cherubyns, fro whennus also God spak to Moises.

CAP 8

1 And the Lord spak to Moises, and seide, Speke thou to Aaron,

2 and thou schalt seie to hym, Whanne thou hast sett seuene launternes, the candilstike be reisid in the south part; therfor comaunde thou this, that the lanternes biholde euene ayens the north to the boord of looues of 'settyng forth, tho schulen schyne ayenus that part which the candilstike biholdith.

3 And Aaron dide, and puttide lanternes on the candilstike, as the Lord comaundide to Moises.

4 Sotheli this was the makyng of the candilstike; it was of gold betun out with hameris, as wel the myddil stok as alle thingis that camen forth of euer eithir side of the yeerdis; bi the saumple 'whych the Lord schewide to Moises, so he wrouyte the candilstike.

5 And the Lord spak to Moises,

6 and seide, Take thou Leuytis fro the myddis of the sones of Israel;

7 and thou schalt clense hem bi this custom. Be thei spreynt with watir of clensyng, and schaue thei alle the heeris of her fleisch. And whanne thei han waische her clothis and ben clensid, take thei an oxe of drooues,

8 and the fletyng sacrifice therof, flour spreynt to gidere with oile; forsothe thou schalt take another oxe of the drooue for synne;

9 and thou schalt present the Leuytis bifor the tabernacle of boond of pees, whanne al the multitude of the sones of Israel is clepid togidere.

10 And whanne the Leuytis ben bifor the Lord, the sones of Israel schulen sette her hondis on hem;

11 and Aaron schal offre the Leuytis in the siyt of the Lord, a yifte of the sones of Israel, that thei serue in the seruice 'of hym.

12 Also the Leuytis schulen sette her hondis on the heedis of the oxun, of whiche oxun thou schalt make oon for synne, and the tother in to brent sacrifice of the Lord, that thou preye for hem.

13 And thou schalt ordeyne the Leuytis in the siyt of Aaron, and of hise sones, and thou schalt sacre hem offrid to the Lord;

14 and thou schalt departe hem fro the myddis of the sones of Israel, that thei be myne.

15 And aftirward entre thei in to the tabernacle of boond of pees, that thei serue me; and so thou schalt clense and schalt halewe hem, in to an offryng of the Lord, for bi fre yifte thei ben youun to me of the sones of Israel.

16 Y haue take hem for the firste gendrid thingis that openen ech wombe in Israel;

17 for alle the firste gendrid thingis of the sones of Israel ben myne, as wel of men as of beestis, fro the dai in which Y smoot ech firste gendrid thing in the loond of Egipt, Y halewide hem to me.

18 And Y took the Leuytis for alle the firste gendrid children of the sones of Israel;

19 and Y yaf hem bi fre yifte to Aaron and hise sones, fro the myddis of the puple, that thei serue me for Israel, in the tabernacle of boond of pees, and that thei preie for hem, lest veniaunce be in the puple, if thei ben hardi to neiye to the seyntuarye.

20 And Moises and Aaron, and al the multitude of the sones of Israel, diden on the Leuitis tho thingis that the Lord comaundide to Moyses.

21 And thei weren clensid, and thei waischiden her clothis; and Aaron reiside hem in the siyt of the Lord, and preiede for hem,

22 that thei schulen be clensid, and schulden entre to her offices in to the tabernacle of boond of pees, bifor Aaron and hise sones; as the Lord comaundide to Moises of the Leuytis, so it was don.

23 And the Lord spak to Moises, and seide, This is lawe of Leuytis;

24 fro fyue and twentithe yeer and aboue thei schulen entre, for to mynystre in the tabernacle of boond of pees;

25 and whanne thei han fillid the fiftithe yeer of age, thei schulen ceesse to serue.

26 And thei schulen be the mynystris of her bretheren in the tabernacle of boond of pees, that thei kepe tho thingis that ben bitakun to hem; sothely thei schulen not do tho werkis; thus thou schalt dispose Leuytis in her kepyngis.

CAP 9

1 And the Lord spak to Moises, in the deseert of Synay, in the secounde yeer aftir that thei yeden out of the lond of Egipt, in the firste moneth,

2 and seide, The sones of Israel make pask in his tyme,

3 in the fourtenthe day of this monethe, at the euentid, bi alle the cerymonyes and iustifiyngis therof.

4 And Moises comaundide to the sones of Israel, that thei schulden make pask;

5 whiche maden in his tyme, in the fourtenthe dai of the monethe, at euentid, in the hil of Synai; bi alle thingis whiche the Lord comaundide to Moises, the sones of Israel diden.

6 Lo! forsothe summen vncleene on the soule of man, that myyten not make pask in that dai, neiyiden to Moises and Aaron,

7 and seiden to hem, We ben vncleene 'on the soule of man; whi ben we defraudid, that we moun not offre an offryng to the Lord in his tyme, among the sones of Israel?

8 To whiche Moises answeride, Stonde ye, that Y take counseil, what the Lord comaundith of you.

9 And the Lord spak to Moises, and seide,

10 Speke thou to the sones of Israel, A man of youre folk which is vncleene 'on the soule, ether in the weie fer, make he pask to the Lord in the secounde monethe,

11 in the fourtenthe dai of the monethe, at euentid; with therf looues and letusis of the feeld he schal ete it.

12 Thei schulen not leeue ony thing therof til the morewtid, and thei schulen not breke a boon therof; thei schulen kepe al the custom of pask.

13 Forsothe if ony man is bothe cleene, and is not in the weie, and netheles made not pask, thilke man schal be distried fro hise puplis, for he offeride not sacrifice to the Lord in his tyme; he schal bere his synne.

14 Also if a pilgrym and comelyng is anentis you, make he pask to the Lord, bi the cerymonyes and iustifiyngis therof; the same comaundement schal be anentis you, as wel to a comelyng as to a man borun in the loond.

15 Therfore in the dai in which the tabernacle was reisid, a cloude hilide it; sotheli as the licnesse of fier was on the tente fro euentid til the morewtid.

16 Thus it was don continueli, a cloude hilide it bi dai, and as the licnesse of fier bi nyyt.

17 And whanne the cloude that hilide the tabernacle was takun awei, thanne the sones of Israel yeden forth, and in the place where the cloude stood, there thei settiden tentis.

18 At the comaundement of the Lord thei yeden forth, and at his comaundement thei settiden the tabernacle. In alle daies in whiche the cloude stood on the tabernacle, thei dwelliden in the same place.

19 And if it bifelde that it dwellide in myche tyme on the tabernacle, the sones of Israel weren in the watchis of the Lord, and thei yeden not forth,

20 in hou many euer daies the cloude was on the tabernacle. At the comaundement of the Lord thei reisiden tentis, and at his comaundement thei diden doun.

21 If the cloude was fro euentid 'til to the morewtid, and anoon in the morewtid hadde left, thei yeden forth; and if aftir a dai and nyyt it hadde go awei, thei scateriden, 'ether diden doun, tentis.

22 Whether in two monethis, ether in o monethe, ether in lengere tyme, 'the cloude hadde be on the tabernacle, the sones of Israel dwelliden in the same place, and yeden not forth; but anoon as it hadde go awey, thei moueden tentis.

23 Bi the word of the Lord thei settiden tentis, and bi his word thei wenten forth; and thei weren in the watchis of the Lord, bi his comaundement, bi the hond of Moyses.

CAP 10

1 And the Lord spak to Moises, and seide,

2 Make to thee twei siluerne trumpis betun out with hameris, bi whiche thou maist clepe togidere the multitude, whanne the tentis schulen be moued.

3 And whanne thou schalt sowne with trumpis, al the cumpeny schal be gaderid to thee at the dore of the tabernacle of the boond of pees.

4 If thou schalt sowne onys, the princes and the heedis of the multitude of Israel schulen come to thee;

5 but if a lengere and departid trumpyng schal sowne, thei that ben at the eest coost schulen moue tentis first.

6 Forsothe in the secounde sown and lijk noise of the trumpe thei that dwellen at the south schulen reise tentis; and bi this maner othere men schulen do, whanne the trumpis schulen sowne in to goyng forth.

7 Forsothe whanne the puple schal be gederid to gidere, symple cry of trumpis schal be, and tho schulen not sowne departyngli.

8 The sones of Aaron preest schulen sowne with trumpis, and this schal be a lawful thing euerlastynge in youre generaciouns.

9 If ye schulen go out of youre lond to batel ayens enemyes that fiyten ayens you, ye schulen crye with trumpis sownynge, and the bithenkyng of you schal be bifor youre Lord God, that ye be delyuered fro the hondis of youre enemyes.

10 If ony tyme ye schulen haue a feeste, and halidaies, and calendis, ye schulen synge in trumpis on brent sacrifices and pesible sacrifices, that tho be to you in to remembryng of youre God; Y am youre Lord God.

11 In the secounde yeer, in the secounde monethe, in the twentithe dai of the monethe, the cloude was reisid fro the tabernacle of boond of pees.

12 And the sones of Israel yeden forth bi her cumpenyes fro deseert of Synay; and the cloude restide in the wildirnesse of Faran.

13 And the sones of Juda bi her cumpenyes, of whiche the prince was Naason, the sone of Amynadab, moueden first tentis,

14 bi the Lordis comaundement maad in the hond of Moises.

15 In the lynage of the sones of Ysacar the prince was Nathanael, the sone of Suar.

16 In the lynage of Sabulon the prince was Heliab, the sone of Helon.

17 And the tabernacle was takun doun, which the sones of Gerson and of Merary baren, and 'yeden out.

18 And the sones of Ruben yeden forth bi her cumpenyes and ordre, of whiche the prince was Helisur, the sone of Sedeur.

19 Forsothe in the lynage of the sones of Symeon the prince was Salamyel, the sone of Surisaddai.

20 Sotheli in the lynage of Gad the prince was Helisaphath, the sone of Duel.

21 And the sones of Caath yeden forth, and baren the seynturarie; so longe the tabernacle was borun, til thei camen to the place of reisyng therof.

22 Also the sones of Effraym, bi her cumpanyes, moueden tentis, in whos oost the prince was Elisama, the sone of Amyud.

23 Forsothe in the lynage of the sones of Manasses the prince was Gamaliel, the sone of Phadussur.

24 And in the lynage of Beniamyn the duk was Abidan, the sone of Gedeon.

25 The sones of Dan, bi her cumpenyes, yeden forth the laste of alle tentis, in whos oost the prince was Aizer, the sone of Amysaddai.

26 Sotheli in the lynage of the sones of Aser the prince was Phegiel, the sone of Ochran.

27 And in the lynage of the sones of Neptalym the prince was Haira, the sone of Henan.

28 These ben the castels and the goinges forth of the sones of Israel, bi her cumpenyes, whanne thei yeden out.

29 And Moises seide to Heliab, the sone of Raguel, of Madian, his alie 'ethir fadir of his wijf, We goon forth to the place which the Lord schal yyue to vs; come thou with vs, that we do wel to thee, for the Lord bihiyte goode thingis to Israel.

30 To whom he answeride, Y schal not go with thee, but Y schal turne ayen in to my lond, in which Y was borun.

31 And Moises seide, Nyle thou forsake vs, for thou knowist in whiche places we owen to sette tentis, and thou schalt be oure ledere;

32 and whanne thou schalt come with vs, what euer thing schal be the beste of the richessis whiche the Lord schal yyue to vs, we schulen yyue to thee.

33 And therfor thei yeden forth fro the hil of the Lord the weie of thre daies; and the arke of boond of pees of the Lord yede bifor hem, bi thre daies, and purueyde the place of tentis.

34 And the cloude of the Lord was on hem bi day, whanne thei yeden.

35 And whanne the arke was reisid, Moises seide, Ryse thou, Lord, and thin enemyes be scaterid, and thei that haten thee, fle fro thi face;

36 forsothe whanne the arke was put doun, he seide, Lord, turne ayen to the multitude of the oost of Israel.

CAP 11

1 Yn the meene tyme the grutchyng of the puple, as of men sorewynge for trauel, roos ayens the Lord. And whanne Moises hadde herd this thing, he was wrooth; and the fier of the Lord was kyndelid on hem, and deuouride the laste part of the tentis.

2 And whanne the puple hadde cried to Moises, Moises preiede the Lord, and the fier was quenchid.

3 And he clepid the name of that place Brennyng, for the fier of the Lord was kyndlid ayens hem.

4 And the comyn puple of 'malis and femalis, that hadde stied with hem, brent with desire of fleischis, and sat, and wepte with the sones of Israel ioyned togidere to hem, and seide, Who schal yyue to vs fleischis to ete?

5 We thenken on the fischis whiche we eten in Egipt freli; gourdis, and melouns, and lekis, and oyniouns, and garlekis comen in to mynde 'to vs;

6 oure soule is drie; oure iyen byholden noon other thing 'no but manna.

7 Forsothe manna was as the seed of coriaundre, of the colour of bdellyum, which is whijt and briyt as cristal.

8 And the puple yede aboute, and gaderide it, and brak with a queerne stoon, ether pownede in a morter, and sethide in a pot; and made therof litle cakis of the sauour, as of breed maad with oile.

9 And whanne dew cam doun in the niyt on the tentis, also manna cam doun togidere.

10 Therfor Moises herde the puple wepynge bi meynees, and 'alle bi hem silf bi the doris of her tentis; and the woodnesse of the Lord was wrooth greetli, but also the thing was seyn vnsuffrable to Moises.

11 And he seide to the Lord, Whi hast thou turmentid thi seruaunt? whi fynde Y not grace bifor thee? and whi hast thou put on me the burthun of al this puple?

12 whethir Y conseyuede al this multitude, ethir gendride it, that thou seie to me, Bere thou hem in thi bosum as a nurise is wont to bere a litil yong child, and bere thou in to the lond for which thou hast swore to the fadris 'of hem.

13 wherof ben fleischis to me, that Y 'yyue to so greet multitude? Thei wepen bifore me, and seyn, 'Yyue thou fleischis to vs that we ete;

14 I mai not aloone suffre al this puple, for it is greuouse to me.

15 If in other maner it semeth to thee, Y biseche that thou sle me, and that Y fynde grace in thin iyen, that Y be not punyschid bi so grete yuelis.

16 And the Lord seide to Moises, Gadere thou to me seuenti men of the eldre men of Israel, whiche thou knowist, 'that thei ben the elde men and maistris of the puple; and thou schalt lede hem to the dore of the tabernacle of boond of pees, and thou schalt make to stonde there with thee,

17 that Y come doun, and speke to thee; and Y schal take awey of thi spirit, and Y schal yyue to hem, that thei susteyne with thee the birthun of the puple, and not thou aloone be greuyd.

18 And thou schalt seie to the puple, Be ye halewid; to morew ye schulen ete fleischis; for Y herde you seie, Who schal yyue to vs the metis of fleischis? it was wel to vs in Egipt; that the Lord yyue 'fleischis to you,

19 and that ye ete not o dai, ethir tweyne, ethir fyue, ethir ten, sotheli nether twenti,

20 but 'til to a monethe of daies, til it go out bi youre nosethirlis, and turne in to wlatyng; for ye han put awei the Lord, which is in the myddis of you, and ye wepten bifor hym, and seiden, Whi yeden we out of Egipt?

21 And Moises seide to the Lord, Sixe hundrid thousynde of foot men ben of this puple, and thou seist, Y schal yyue to hem 'mete of fleischis an hool monethe.

22 Whether the multitude of scheep and of oxun schal be slayn, that it may suffice to mete, ethir alle the fischis of the see schulen be gaderid to gidere, that tho fille hem?

23 To whom the Lord answeride, Whether the 'hond of the Lord is vnmyyti? riyt now thou schalt se, wher my word schal be fillid in werk.

24 Therfor Moises cam, and telde to the puple the wordis of the Lord; and he gaderide seuenti men of the eldere of Israel, whiche he made stonde aboute the tabernacle.

25 And the Lord cam doun bi a cloude, and spak to Moises, and took a weye of the spirit that was in Moises, and yaf to the seuenti men; and whanne the spirit hadde restid in hem, thei profesieden, and ceessiden not 'aftirward.

26 Forsothe twei men dwelliden stille in the tentis, of whiche men oon was clepid Heldad, and the tothir Medad, on whiche the spirit restide; for also thei weren descryued, and thei yeden not out to the tabernacle.

27 And whanne thei profesieden in the tentis, a child ran, and teld to Moises, and seide, Heldad and Medad profecien in the tentis.

28 Anoon Josue, the sone of Nun, the 'mynystre of Moises, and chosun of manye, seide, My lord Moises, forbede thou hem.

29 And he seide, What hast thou enuye for me? who yyueth that al the puple profesie, and that God yyue his spirit to hem?

30 And Moises turnede ayen, and the eldre men in birthe of Israel in to the tentis.

31 Forsothe a wynde yede forth fro the Lord, and took curlewis, and bar ouer the see, and lefte in to the tentis, in the iurney, as myche as mai be parformed in o day, bi ech part of the tentis bi cumpas; and tho flowen in the eir bi twei cubitis in 'hiynesse ouer the erthe.

32 Therfor the puple roos in al that dai and nyyt and in to the tothir dai, and gaderide the multitude of curlewis; he that gaderide litil, gaderide ten 'mesuris clepid chorus; 'and o chorus conteyneth ten buschels; and thei drieden tho curlewis bi the cumpas of the tentis.

33 Yit 'fleischis weren in the teeth 'of hem, and siche mete failide not; and lo! the woodnesse of the Lord was reisid ayens the puple, and smoot it with a ful greet veniaunce.

34 And thilke place was clepid The sepulcris of coueitise, for there thei birieden the puple that desiride fleischis. Sotheli thei yeden 'out of the sepulcris of coueitise, and camen in to Asseroth, and dwelliden there.

CAP 12

1 And Marie spak and Aaron ayens Moises, for his wijf a womman of Ethiope,

2 and seiden, Whethir God spak oneli by Moises? whethir he spak not also to vs in lijk maner? And whanne the Lord hadde herd this, he was wrooth greetli;

3 for Moises was the myldest man, ouer alle men that dwelliden in erthe.

4 And anoon the Lord spak to Moises and to Aaron and to Marye, Go out ye thre aloone to the tabernacle of boond of pees. And whanne thei weren gon yn,

5 the Lord cam doun in a piler of cloude, and he stood in the entryng of the tabernacle, and clepide Aaron and Marie.

6 And whanne thei hadden go, he seide to hem, Here ye my wordis; if ony among you is a profete of the Lord, Y schal appere to hym in reuelacioun, ethir Y schal speke to hym bi 'a dreem.

7 And he seide, And my seruaunt Moises is not siche, which is moost feithful in al myn hows;

8 for Y speke to hym mouth to mouth, and he seeth God opynli, and not bi derke spechis and figuris. Why therfor dredden ye not to bacbite 'ether depraue my seruaunt Moises?

9 And the Lord was wrooth ayens hem, and he wente a wei.

10 And the cloude yede awei, that was on the tabernacle and lo! Marie apperide whijt with lepre as snow. And whanne Aaron biheelde hir, and siy hir bispreynd with lepre,

11 he seide to Moises, My lord, Y beseche, putte thou not this synne on vs,

12 which we diden folili, that this womman be not maad as deed, and as a deed borun thing which is cast out of the 'wombe of his modir; lo! now the half of hir fleisch is deuourid with lepre.

13 And Moises criede to the Lord, and seide, Lord, Y biseche, heele thou hir.

14 To whom the Lord answerid, If hir fadir hadde spet in to hir face, where sche ouyte not to be fillid with schame, nameli in seuene daies? Therfor be sche departid out of the tentis bi seuen daies, and aftirward sche schal be clepid ayen.

15 And so Marie was excludid out of the tentis bi seuene daies; and the puple was not mouyd fro that place, til Marie was clepid ayen.

CAP 13

1 And the puple yede forth fro Asseroth, whanne the tentis weren set in the deseert of Pharan.

2 And there the Lord spak to Moises,

3 and seide, Sende thou men that schulen biholde the lond of Canaan, which Y schal yyue to the sones of Israel, of ech lynage o man of the princes.

4 Moises dide that that the Lord comaundide, and sente fro the deseert of Pharan princes, men of whiche these ben the names.

5 Of the lynage of Ruben, Semmya, the sone of Zectur.

6 Of the lynage of Symeon, Saphat, the sone of Hury.

7 Of the lynage of Juda, Caleph, the sone of Jephone.

8 Of the lynage of Isachar, Igal, the sone of Joseph.

9 Of the lynage of Effraym, Osee, the sone of Nun.

10 Of the lynage of Beniamyn, Phalti, the sone of Raphu.

11 Of the lynage of Zabulon, Gediel, the sone of Sodi.

12 Of the lynage of Joseph, of the gouernaunce of Manasses, Gaddi, the sone of Susy.

13 Of the lynage of Dan, Amyel, the sone of Gemalli.

14 Of the lynage of Aser, Sur, the sone of Mychael.

15 Of the lynage of Neptalym, Nabdi, the sone of Napsi.

16 Of the lynage of Gad, Guel, the sone of Machi.

17 These ben the names of men, which Moises sente to biholde the lond of Canaan; and he clepide Osee, the sone of Nun, Josue.

18 Therfor Moises sente hem to biholde the lond of Canaan, and seide to hem, 'Stie ye bi the south coost; and whanne ye comen to the hillis,

19 biholde ye the lond, what maner lond it is; and biholde ye the puple which is the dwellere therof, whether it is strong, ethir feble, 'whether thei ben fewe in noumbre, ether manye;

20 whether that lond is good, ethir yuel; what maner citees ben, wallid, ether without wallis;

21 whether the lond is fat, ether bareyn, 'whether it is ful of woodis, ethir without trees. Be ye coumfortid, and 'brynge ye to vs of the fruytis of that lond. Sotheli the tyme was, whanne grapis first ripe myyten be etun thanne.

22 And whanne thei hadden stied, thei aspieden the lond, fro the deseert of Syn 'til to Rohob, as men entryth to Emath.

23 And thei stieden to the south, and camen in to Ebron, where Achyman, and Sisai, and Tholmai, the sones of Enach, weren; for Hebron was maad bi seuen yeer bifor Thamnys, the citee of Egipt.

24 And thei yeden til to the stronde of clustre, and kittiden doun a sioun with his grape, which twei men baren in a barre; also thei token of pumgarnadis, and of the figis of that place which is clepid Nehelescol,

25 that is, the stronde of grape, for the sones of Israel baren a clustre fro thennus.

26 And the aspieris of the lond, whanne thei hadden cump-assid al the cuntrey, after fourti daies camen to Moises and Aaron,

27 and to al the cumpany of the sones of Israel, in to the dese-ert of Pharan which is in Cades. And 'the aspieris spaken to hem, and schewiden the fruytis of the lond to al the multitude, and telden,

28 and seiden, We camen to the lond, to which thou sentest vs, which lond treuli flowith with mylk and hony, as it may be knowun bi these fruytis;

29 but it hath strongeste inhabiteris, and grete cytees, and wallid; we sien there the kynrede of Anachym; Amalech dwellith in the south;

30 Ethei, and Jebusei, and Amorey dwellen in the hilli placis; forsothe Cananey dwellith bisidis the see, and bisidis the floodis of Jordan.

31 Among thes thingis Caleph peeside the grutchyng of the puple, that was maad ayens Moises, and seide, 'Stie we, and welde we the lond, for we moun gete it.

32 Forsothe other aspieris, that weren with hym, seiden, We moun not stie to this puple, for it is strongere than we.

33 And thei deprauyden the lond which thei hadden biholde, anentis the sones of Israel, and seiden, The lond which we cumpassiden deuourith hise dwelleris; the puple which we bihelden is of large stature; there we syen summe wondris ayens kynde,

34 of the sones of Enach, of the kynde of geauntis, to whiche we weren comparisound, and weren seien as locustis.

CAP 14

1 Therfor al the cumpeny criede, and wepte in that nyyt,

2 and alle the sones of Israel grutchiden ayens Moises and Aaron, and seiden,

3 We wolden that we hadden be deed in Egipt, and not in this waast wildirnesse; we wolden that we perischen, and that the Lord lede vs not in to this lond, lest we fallen bi swerd, and oure wyues and fre children ben led prisoneris; whether it is not betere to turne ayen in to Egipt?

4 And thei seiden oon to another, Ordeyne we a duyk to vs, and turne we ayen in to Egipt.

5 And whanne this was herd, Moises and Aaron felden lowe to erthe, bifor al the multitude of the sones of Israel.

6 And sotheli Josue, the sone of Nun, and Caleph, the sone of Jephone, whiche also cumpassiden the lond, to renten her clothis,

7 and spaken to al the multitude of the sones of Israel, The lond which we cumpassiden is ful good;

8 if the Lord is merciful to vs, he schal lede vs in to it, and schal yyue 'to vs the lond flowynge with mylk and hony.

9 Nyle ye be rebel ayens the Lord, nether drede ye the puple of this lond, for we moun deuoure hem so as breed; al her help passide awei fro hem, the Lord is with vs, nyle ye drede.

10 And whanne al the multitude criede, and wolde oppresse hem with stonys, the glorie of the Lord apperide on the roof of the boond of pees, while alle the sones of Israel sien.

11 And the Lord seide to Moises, Hou long schal this puple bacbite me? Hou longe schulen thei not bileue to me in alle 'signes, whiche Y haue do bifor hem?

12 Therfor Y schal smyte hem with pestilence, and Y schal waste hem; forsothe Y schal make thee prince on a greet folk, and strongere than is this.

13 And Moises seide to the Lord, Egipcians 'here not, fro whos myddil thou leddist out this puple,

14 and the dwelleris of this loond, whiche herden that thou, Lord, art in this puple, and art seyn face to face, and that thi cloude defendith hem, and that thou goist bifore hem in a pil-ere of cloude bi dai,

15 and in a piler of fier bi nyyt, that thou hast slayn so greet a multitude as o man,

16 and seie thei, He myyte not brynge this puple in to the lond for whiche he swoor, therfor he killide hem in wildirnesse;

17 therfor the strengthe of the Lord be magnified, as thou hast swore. And Moises seide,

18 Lord pacient, and of myche mercy, doynge awei wickid-nesse and trespassis, and leeuynge no man vngilti, which vis-itist the synnes of fadris in to sones in to the thridde and fourthe generacioun, Y biseche,

19 foryyue thou the synne of this thi puple, aftir the greet-nesse of thi merci, as thou were merciful to men goynge out of Egipt 'til to this place.

20 And the Lord seide, Y haue foryouun to hem, bi thi word.

21 Y lyue; and the glorie of the Lord schal be fillid in al erthe;

22 netheles alle men that sien my mageste, and my signes, whiche Y dide in Egipt and in the wildirnesse, and temptiden me now bi ten sithis, and obeieden not to my vois,

23 schulen not se the lond for which Y swore to her fadris, nethir ony of hem that bacbitide me, schal se it.

24 Y schal lede my seruaunt Caleph, that was ful of anothir spirit, and suede me, in to this lond, which he cumpasside, and his seed schal welde it.

25 For Amalech and Cananei dwellen in the valeis, to morewe moue ye tentis, and turne ye ayen in to wildirnesse bi the weie of the reed see.

26 And the Lord spak to Moises and to Aaron, and seide,

27 Hou long grutchith this werste multitude ayens me? Y haue herd the pleyntis of the sones of Israel.

28 Therfor seie thou to hem, Y lyue, seith the Lord; as ye spaken while Y herde, so Y schal do to you;

29 youre careyns schulen ligge in this wildirnesse. Alle ye that ben noumbrid, fro twenti yeer and aboue, and grutchiden ayens me,

30 schulen not entre in to the lond, on which Y reiside myn hond, that Y schulde make you to dwelle outakun Caleph, the sone of Jephone, and Josue, the sone of Nun.

31 Forsothe Y schal lede in youre litle children, of whiche ye seiden that thei schulden be preyes 'ethir raueyns to enemyes, that thei se the lond which displeside you.

32 Forsothe youre careyns schulen ligge in the wildirnesse;

33 youre sones schulen be walkeris aboute in the deseert bi fourti yeer, and thei schulen bere youre fornycacioun, til the careyns of the fadris ben wastid in the deseert,

34 by the noumbre of fourti daies, in whiche ye bihelden the loond; a yeer schal be arettid for a dai, and bi fourti yeer ye schulen resseyue youre wickidnesse, and ye schulen knowe my veniaunce.

35 For as Y spak, so Y schal do to al this werste multitude, that roos to gidere ayens me; it schal faile, and schal die in this wildirnesse.

36 Therfor alle the men whyche Moises hadde sent to see the lond, and whiche turniden ayen, and maden al the multitude to grutche ayens hym, and depraueden the lond, that it was yuel,

37 weren deed, and smytun in the siyt of the Lord.

38 Sotheli Josue, the sone of Nun, and Caleph, the sone of Jephone, lyueden, of alle men that yeden to se the lond.

39 And Moises spak alle these wordis to alle the sones of Israel, and the puple mourenyde gretli.

40 And, lo! thei riseden in the morewtid first, and 'stieden in to the cop of the hil, and seiden, We ben redi to stie to the place, of which the Lord spak, for we synneden.

41 To whiche Moises seide, Whi passen ye the word of the Lord, that schal not bifalle to you in to prosperite?

42 Nyle ye stie, for the Lord is not with you, lest ye fallen bifor youre enemyes.

43 Amalech and Cananei ben bifor you, bi the swerd of whiche ye schulen falle, for ye nolden assente to the Lord, nether the Lord schal be with you.

44 And thei weren maad derk, and stieden in to the cop of the hil; forsothe the ark of the testament of the Lord and Moises yeden not awey fro the tentis.

45 And Amalech cam doun, and Chananei, that dwelliden in the hil, and he smoot hem, and kittide doun, and pursuede hem til Horma.

CAP 15

1 And the Lord spak to Moises, and seide, Speke thou to the sones of Israel,

2 and thou schalt seie to hem, Whanne ye han entrid in to the lond of youre abitacioun which Y schal yyue to you,

3 and ye make an offryng to the Lord in to brent sacrifice, ether a pesible sacrifice, and ye payen auowis, ethir offren yiftis bi fre wille, ethir in youre solempnytees ye brennen odour of swetnesse to the Lord, of oxun, ether of scheep;

4 who euer offrith the slayn sacrifice, schal offre a sacrifice of flour, the tenthe part of ephi, spreynt togidere with oile, which oil schal haue a mesure the fourthe part of hyn;

5 and he schal yyue wyn to fletynge sacrifices to be sched, of the same mesure, in to brent sacrifice, and slayn sacrifice.

6 Bi ech loomb and ram schal be the sacrifice of flour, of twey tenthe partis, which schal be spreynt togidere with oile, of the thridde part of hyn;

7 and he schal offre wyn to the fletynge sacrifice, of the thridde part of the same mesure, in to odour of swetnesse to the Lord.

8 Forsothe whanne thou makist a brent sacrifice, ethir an offryng of oxun, that thou fille avow, ethir pesible sacrifice, thou schalt yyue,

9 bi ech oxe, thre tenthe partis of flour, spreynt togidere with oile, which schal haue the half of mesure of hyn;

10 and thou schalt yyue wyn to fletynge sacrifices to be sched, of the same mesure, in to offryng of the swettest odour to the Lord.

11 So ye schulen do bi ech oxe, and ram,

12 and lomb, and kide;

13 as wel men borun in the lond,

14 as pilgrymys, schulen offre sacrifices bi the same custom;

15 o comaundement and doom schal be, as wel to you as to comelyngis of the lond.

16 And the Lord spak to Moises,

17 and seide, Speke thou to the sones of Israel, and thou schalt seie to hem,

18 Whanne ye comen in to the lond which Y schal yyue to you,

19 and 'ye eten of the looues of that cuntrey, ye

20 schulen departe the firste fruytis of youre metis to the Lord; as ye schulen departe the firste fruytis of corn flooris,

21 so ye schulen yyue the firste fruytis also of sewis to the Lord.

22 That if bi ignoraunce ye passen ony of tho thingis whiche the Lord spak to Moyses,

23 and comaundide bi hym to you, fro the dai in which he bigan to comaunde,

24 and ouer, and the multitude hath foryete to do, it schal offre a calf of the drooue, brent sacrifice in to swettist odour to the Lord, and the sacrificis therof, and fletynge offryngis, as the cerymonyes therof axen; and it schal offre a 'buc of geet for synne.

25 And the preest schal preie for al the multitude of the sones of Israel, and it schal be foryouun to hem, for thei synneden not wilfuli. And neuerthelesse thei schulen offre encense to the Lord for hemsilf, and for her synne and errour;

26 and it schal be foryouun to al the puple of the sones of Israel, and to comelyngis that ben pilgryms among hem, for it is the synne of al the multitude bi ignoraunce.

27 That if a soule synneth vnwityngli, it schal offre a geet of o yeer for his synne; and the preest schal preye for that soule, for it synnede vnwityngli bifor the Lord;

28 and the preest schal gete foryyuenesse to it, and synne schal be foryouun to it.

29 As wel to men borun in the lond as to comelyngis, o lawe schal be of alle that synnen vnwityngli.

30 Forsothe a man that doith ony synne bi pride, schal perische fro his puple, whether he be a citeseyn, ethir a pilgrym, for he was rebel ayens the Lord;

31 for he dispiside the word of the Lord, and made voide his comaundement; therfor he schal be doon awei, and schal bere his owne wickidnes.

32 Forsothe it was doon, whanne the sones of Israel weren in wildirnesse, and hadde founde a man gaderynge woode in the 'day of sabat,

33 thei brouyten hym to Moises, and to Aaron, and to al the multitude; whiche closiden hym in to prisoun,

34 and wisten not what thei schulden do of hym.

35 And the Lord seide to Moises, This man die bi deeth; al the cumpeny oppresse hym with stoonus with out the tentis.

36 And whanne thei hadden led hym with out forth, thei oppressiden him with stoonus, and he was deed, as the Lord comaundide.

37 Also the Lord seide to Moises,

38 Speke thou to the sones of Israel, and thou schalt seye to hem, that thei make to hem hemmes bi foure corneris of mentils, and sette laces of iacynct 'in tho;

39 and whanne thei seen thoo, haue thei mynde of alle comaundementis of the Lord, lest thei suen her thouytis and iyen, doynge fornycacioun bi dyuerse thingis;

40 but more be thei myndeful of the 'Lordis heestis, and do thei tho, and be thei hooli to her God.

41 Y am youre Lord God, which ledde you out of the lond of Egipt, that Y schulde be youre God.

CAP 16

1 Lo! forsothe Chore, the sone of Isuar, sone of Caath, sone of Leuy, and Dathan and Abiron, the sones of Heliab, and Hon, the sone of Pheleph, of the sones of Ruben, rysen ayens Moises,

2 and othere of the sones of Israel, two hundryd men and fifti, prynces of the synagoge, and whiche weren clepid bi names in the tyme of counsel.

3 And whanne 'thei hadden stonde ayens Moises and Aaron, thei seiden, Suffice it to you, for al the multitude is of hooly men, and the Lord is in hem; whi ben ye reisid on the puple of the Lord?

4 And whanne Moises hadde herd this, he felde lowe on the face.

5 And he spak to Chore, and to al the multitude; he seide, Eerli the Lord schal make knowun whiche perteynen to hym, and he schal applie to hym hooli men; and thei whiche he hath chose, schulen neiye to hym.

6 Therfor do ye this thing; ech man take his cencere, thou Chore, and al thi counsel;

7 and to morewe whanne fier is takun vp, putte ye encense aboue bifor the Lord, and whom euer the Lord chesith, he schal be hooli. Ye sones of Leuy ben myche reisid.

8 And eft Moises seide to Chore, Ye sones of Leuy, here.

9 Whether it is litil to you, that God of Israel departide you fro al the puple, and ioynede you to hym silf, that ye schulden serue hym in the seruyce of tabernacle, and that ye schulden stonde bifor the multitude of puple, and schulden serue hym?

10 Made he therfor thee and alle thi bretheren the sones of Leuy to neiy to hym silf, that ye chalenge to you also preesthod,

11 and al thi gaderyng togidere stonde ayens the Lord? For whi what is Aaron, that ye grutchen ayens hym?

12 Therfor Moises sente to clepe Dathan and Abiron, the sones of Heliab; whiche answeriden, We comen not.

13 Whethir is it litil to thee, that thou leddist vs out of the lond that flowide with mylk and hony, to sle vs in the deseert, no but also thou be lord of vs?

14 Verili thou hast bronyt vs in to the lond that flowith with streemys of mylk and hony, and hast youe to vs possessioun of feeldis, and of vyneris; whethir also thou wolt putte out oure iyen?

15 We comen not. And Moises was wrooth greetli, and seide to the Lord, Biholde thou not the sacrifices of hem; thou wost that Y took neuere of hem, yhe, a litil asse, nethir Y turmentide ony of hem.

16 And Moises seide to Chore, Thou and al thi congregacioun stonde asidis half bifor the Lord, and Aaron to morewe bi hym silf.

17 Take ye alle bi you silf youre censeris, and putte ye encense in tho, and offre ye to the Lord, tweyn hundrid and fifti censeris; and Aaron holde his censer.

18 And whanne thei hadden do this, while Moises and Aaron stoden,

19 and thei hadden gaderid al the multitude to the 'dore of the tabernacle ayens hem, the glorie of the Lord apperide to alle.

20 And the Lord spak to Moises and Aaron,

21 and seide, Be ye departid fro the myddis of this congregacioun, that Y leese hem sodeynli.

22 Whiche felden lowe on the face, and seiden, Strongeste God of the spiritis of al fleisch, whethir 'thin yre schal be fers ayens alle men, for o man synneth?

23 And the Lord seide to Moises,

24 Comaunde thou to al the puple, that it be departid fro the tabernaclis of Chore, and of Dathan, and of Abiron.

25 And Moises roos, and yede to Dathan and Abiron; and while the eldre men of Israel sueden hym,

26 he seide to the cumpeny, Go ye awey fro the tabernaclis of wickid men, and nyle ye touche tho thingis that parteynen to hem, lest ye ben wlappid in the synnes of hem.

27 And whanne thei hadden gon awei fro the tentis 'of hem bi the cumpas, Dathan and Abiron yeden out, and stoden in the entryng of her tentis, with wyues, and fre children, and al the multitude.

28 And Moises seide, In this ye schulen wite that the Lord sente me, that Y schulde do alle thingis whiche ye seen, and Y brouyte not forth tho of myn owne herte.

29 If thei perischen bi customable deeth of men, and wounde visite hem, bi which also othere men ben wont to be visitid,

30 the Lord sente not me; but if the Lord doith a newe thing, that the erthe opene his mouth, and swolewe hem, and alle thingis that perteynen to hem, and thei goen doun quyke in to helle, ye schulen wite that thei blasfemeden the Lord.

31 Therfor anoon as he cesside to speke, the erthe was brokun vndur her feet,

32 and the erthe openyde his mouth, and deuowride hem, with her tabernaclis, and al the catel 'of hem;

33 and thei yeden doun quike in to helle, and weren hilid with erthe, and perischiden fro the myddis of the multitude.

34 And sotheli al Israel that stood bi the cumpas, fledde fro the cry of men perischinge, and seide, Lest perauenture the erthe swolewe also vs.

35 But also fier yede out fro the Lord, and killide tweyn hundrid and fifti men that offriden encense.

36 And the Lord spak to Moises, and seide,

37 Comaunde thou to Eleasar, sone of Aaron, preest, that he take the censeris that liggen in the brennyng, and that he schatere the fier hidur and thidur; for tho ben halewid in the dethis of synneris;

38 and that he bringe forth tho in to platis, and naile to the auter, for encense is offrid in tho to the Lord, and tho ben halewid, that the sonis of Israel se tho for a signe and memorial.

39 Therfor Eleazar, preest, took the brasun senseris, in whiche censeris thei whiche the brennyng deuouride hadden offrid, and he 'brouyt forth tho in to platis, and nailide to the auter;

40 that the sones of Israel schulden haue thingis aftirward, bi whiche thei schulden remembre, lest ony alien, and which is not of the seed of Aaron, neiy to offre encense to the Lord, lest he suffre, as Chore sufferide, and al his multitude, while the Lord spak to Moises.

41 Forsothe al the multitude of the sones of Israel grutchide in the dai suynge ayens Moises and Aaron, and seide, Ye han slayn the puple of the Lord.

42 And whanne discensioun roos,

43 and noise encresside, Moises and Aaron fledden to the tabernacle of the boond of pees; and aftir that thei entriden in to it, a cloude hilide the tabernacle, and the glorie of the Lord apperide.

44 And the Lord seide to Moises and to Aaron,

45 Go ye awey fro the myddis of this multitude, also now Y schal do awey hem. And whanne thei laien in the erthe, Moises seide to Aaron,

46 Take the censer, and whanne fyer is takun vp of the auter, caste encense aboue, and go soone to the puple, that thou preye for hem; for now ire is gon out fro the Lord, and the wounde is feers.

47 And whanne Aaron hadde do this, and hadde runne to the myddis of the multitude, which the brennynge wastid thanne, he offeride encense;

48 and he stood bytwixe the deed men and lyuynge, and bisouyte for the puple, and the wounde ceesside.

49 Sotheli thei that weren smytun weren fourtene thousynde of men and seuene hundrid, with outen hem that perischiden in the discencioun of Chore.

50 And Aaron turnyde ayen to Moyses, to the dore of the tabernacle of boond of pees, aftir that the perischyng restide.

CAP 17

1 And the Lord spak to Moises, 'and seide, Speke thou to the sones of Israel,

2 and take thou yerdis, bi her kynredis, bi ech kynrede o yeerde, take thou of alle the princes of the lynagis twelue yerdis; and thou schalt write the name of each lynage aboue his yerde;

3 forsothe the name of Aaron schal be in the lynage of Leuy, and o yerde schal conteyne alle the meynees of hem.

4 And thou schalt putte tho yerdis in the tabernacle of boond of pees, bifor the witnessyng, where Y schal speke to thee; the yerde of hym schal buriowne, whom Y schal chese of hem;

5 and Y schal refreyne fro me the playnyngis of the sones of Israel, bi whiche thei grutchen ayens you.

6 And Moyses spak to the sones of Israel; and alle princes yauen to hym yerdis, bi alle lynagis; and the yerdis weren twelue, without the yerde of Aaron.

7 And whanne Moises hadde put tho yerdis bifor the Lord, in the tabernacle of witnessyng, he yede ayen in the day suynge,

8 and founde that the yerde of Aaron, 'in the hows of Leuy, buriounnede; and whanne knoppis weren greet, the blossoms 'hadden broke out, whiche weren alargid in leeuys, and weren fourmed in to alemaundis.

9 Therfor Moyses brouyte forth alle the yerdis fro the siyt of the Lord to al the sones of Israel; and thei sien, and resseyueden ech his yerde.

10 And the Lord seide to Moises, Bere ayen the yerde of Aaron in to the tabernacle of witnessyng, that it be kept there in to 'the signe of the rebel sones of Israel, and that her 'playntis reste fro me, lest thei dien.

11 And Moises dide, as the Lord comaundide.

12 Forsothe the sones of Israel seiden to Moises, Lo! we ben wastid, alle we perischiden;

13 who euer neiyeth to the tabernacle of the Lord, he dieth; whethir we schulen be doon awei alle 'til to deeth?

CAP 18

1 And the Lord seide to Aaron, Thou, and thi sones, and the hows of thi fadir with thee, schulen bere the wickidnesse of the seyntuarie; and thou and thi sones togidere schulen suffre the synnes of youre preesthod.

2 But also take thou with thee thi britheren of the lynage of Leuy, and the power of thi fadir, and be thei redi, that thei mynystre to thee. Forsothe thou and thi sones schulen mynystre in the tabernacle of witnessyng;

3 and the dekenes schulen wake at thi comaundementis, and at alle werkis of the tabernacle; so oneli that thei neiye not to the vessels of seyntuarie, and to the autir, lest bothe thei dien, and ye perischen togidere.

4 Forsothe be thei with thee, and wake thei in the kepyngis of the tabernacle, and in alle the cerymonyes therof. An alien schal not be meddlid with you.

5 Wake ye in the kepyng of the seyntuarie, and in the seruyce of the auter, lest indignacioun rise on the sones of Israel.

6 Lo! Y haue youun 'to you youre britheren, dekenes, fro the myddis of the sones of Israel, and Y haue youe a fre yifte to the Lord, that thei serue in the seruyces of his tabernacle.

7 Forsothe thou and thi sones, kepe youre preesthod; and alle thingis that perteynen to the ournyng of the auter, and ben with ynne the veil, schulen be mynystrid bi preestis; if ony straunger neiyeth, he schal be slayn.

8 The Lord spak to Aaron, Lo! Y haue youe to thee the kepyng of my firste fruytis; Y haue youe to thee and to thi sones alle thingis, that ben halewid of the sones of Israel, for preestis office euerlastynge lawful thingis.

9 Therfor thou schalt take these thingis of tho thingis that ben halewid, and ben offrid to the Lord; ech offryng, and sacrifice, and what euer thing is yoldun to me for synne and for trespas, and cometh in to hooli of hooli thingis, schal be thin and thi sones.

10 Thou schalt ete it in the seyntuarie; malis oneli schulen ete therof, for it is halewid to the Lord.

11 Forsothe Y haue youe to thee, and to thi sones and douytris, bi euerlastynge riyt, the firste fruytis whiche the sones of Israel a vowen and offren; he that is clene in thin hous, schal ete tho.

12 Y yaf to thee al the merowe of oile, and of wyn, and of wheete, what euer thing of the firste fruytis thei schulen offre to the Lord.

13 Alle the bigynnyngis of fruytis whiche the erthe bryngith forth, and ben brouyt to the Lord, schulen falle in to thin vsis; he that is cleene in thin hous, schal ete of tho.

14 Al thing which the sones of Israel yelden bi avow, schal be thin.

15 What euer thing 'schal breke out first of the wombe of al fleisch, which fleisch thei offren to the Lord, whether it is of men, ethir of beestis, it schal be of thi riyt; so oneli that thou take prijs for the firste gendrid child of man, and that thou make ech beeste which is vncleene to be bouyt ayen;

16 whos ayenbiyng schal be aftir o monethe, for fyue siclis of siluer, bi the weiyte of seyntuarie; a sicle hath xx. halpens.

17 Forsothe thou schalt not make the firste gendrid of oxe, and of scheep, and of goet, to be ayen bouyt, for tho ben halewid to the Lord; oneli thou schalt schede the blood of tho on the auter, and thou schalt brenne the ynnere fatnesse in to swettist odour to the Lord.

18 Forsothe the fleischis schulen falle in to thin vss, as the brest halewid and the riyt schuldur, schulen be thine.

19 Y yaf to the and to thi sones and douytris, bi euerlastynge riyt, alle the firste fruytis of seyntuarie, whiche the sones of Israel offren to the Lord; it is euerlastynge couenant of salt bifor the Lord, to thee, and to thi sones.

20 And the Lord seide to Aaron, Ye schulen not welde ony thing in the lond of hem, nether ye schulen haue part among hem; Y am thi part and erytage, in the myddis of the sones of Israel.

21 Forsothe Y yaf to the sones of Leuy alle the tithis of Israel in to possessioun, for the seruyce bi whyche thei seruen me in the tabernacle of boond of pees;

22 that the sones of Israel neiye no more to the 'tabernacle of boond of pees, nether do dedli synne.

23 To the sones aloone of Leuy, seruynge me in the tabernacle, and berynge the 'synnes of the puple, it schal be a lawful thing euerlastynge in youre generaciouns.

24 Thei schulen welde noon other thing, and thei schulen be apeied with the offryng of tithis, whiche Y departide in to vsis and necessaries of hem.

25 And the Lord spak to Moises and seide,

26 Comaunde thou, and denounse to the dekenes, Whanne ye han take tithis of the sones of Israel, whiche Y yaf to you, offre ye the firste fruytis of tho to the Lord, that is, the tenthe part of the dyme,

27 that it be arettid to you in to offryng of the firste fruytis, as wel of corn flooris as of pressis;

28 and of alle thingis of whiche ye taken tithis, offre ye the firste fruytis to the Lord, and yyue ye to Aaron, preest.

29 Alle thingis whiche ye schulen offre of tithis, and schulen departe in to the yiftis of the Lord, schulen be the beste, and alle chosun thingis.

30 And thou schalt seye to hem, If ye offren to the Lord alle the clere and betere thingis of tithis, it schal be arettid to you, as if ye yauen the firste fruitis of the corn floor and presse.

31 And ye schulen ete tho tithis in alle youre placis, as wel ye as youre meynees, for it is the prijs for the seruyce, in whiche ye seruen in the tabernacle of witnessyng.

32 And ye schulen not do synne on this thing, 'and resserue noble thingis and fat to you, lest ye defoulen the offryngis of the sones of Israel, and ye dien.

CAP 19

1 And the Lord spak to Moises and to Aaron,

2 and seide, This is the religioun of sacrifice, which the Lord ordeynede. Comaunde thou to the sones of Israel, that thei brynge to thee a reed cow of hool age, in which is no wem, nether sche hath bore yok.

3 And ye schulen bitake hir to Eleazar, preest, which schal offre 'the cow, led out of the tentis, in the siyt of alle men.

4 And he schal dippe his fyngur in the blood therof, and schal sprynge seuene sithis ayens the yatis of the tabernacle.

5 And he schal brenne that cow, while alle men sien; and he schal yyue as wel the skyn and fleischis therof as the blood and dung to flawme.

6 Also the preest schal 'sende a tre of cedre, and ysope, and reed threed died twies, into the flawme that deuourith the cow.

7 And thanne at the laste, whanne hise clothis 'and bodi ben waischun, he schal entre in to the tentis, and he schal be defoulid 'til to euentid.

8 But also he that brente the cow, schal waische hise clothis, and bodi, and he schal be vncleene 'til to euentid.

9 Forsothe a cleene man schal gadere the aischis of the cow, and schal schede out tho with out the tentis, in a place moost cleene, that tho be to the multitude of the sones of Israel in to keping, and in to watir of spryngyng; for the cow is brent for synne.

10 And whanne he that bar the aischis of the cow, hath waische hise clothis, he schal be vncleene 'til to euentid. And the sones of Israel, and comelyngis that dwellen among hem, schulen haue this hooli bi euerlastynge lawe.

11 He that touchith a deed bodi of man, and is vncleene for this bi seuene daies,

12 schal be spreynt of this watir in the thridde, and in the seuenthe dai; and so he schal be clensid. If he is not spreynt in the thridde dai, he schal not mow be clensid in the seuenthe dai.

13 Ech that touchith the deed bodi bi it silf of mannus soule, and is not spreynt with this medlyng, defoulith the 'tabernacle of the Lord, and he schal perische fro Israel; for he is not spreynt with the wateris of clensyng, he schal be vncleene, and his filthe schal dwelle on hym.

14 This is the lawe of a man that dieth in the tabernacle; alle that entren in to his tente, and alle vessels that ben there, schulen be defoulid bi seuene daies.

15 A vessel that hath not an hilyng, nethir a byndyng aboue, schal be vncleene.

16 If ony man touchith the deed bodi of man slayn in the feeld, ether deed bi hym silf, ether a boon, ether the sepulcre 'of hym, he schal be vncleene bi seuene daies.

17 And thei schulen take 'of the aischis of the brennyng, and of the synne, and thei schulen sende quyk watris in to a vessel on tho aischis;

18 in whiche whanne 'a cleene man hath dippid ysope, he schal spreynge therof the tente, and al the purtenaunce of howshold, and men defoulid bi sich defoulyng.

19 And in this maner a cleene man schal clense an vncleene, in the thridde and in the seuenthe dai; and he schal be clensid in the seuenthe dai. And he schal waische hym silf, and hise clothis, and he schal be vncleene 'til to euentid.

20 If ony man is not clensid bi this custom, the soule of hym schal perische fro the myddis of the chirche; for he defoulith the 'seyntuarie of the Lord, and is not spreynt with the watir of clensyng.

21 This comaundement schal be a lawful thing euerlastynge. Also he that schal sprenge the watris schal waische his

clothis; ech man that touchith the watris of clensyng, schal be vncleene 'til to euentid.

22 What euer thing an vncleene man touchith, he schal make it vncleene; and a soule that touchith ony of these thingis 'defoulid so, schal be vncleene 'til to euentid.

CAP 20

1 And the sones of Israel and al the multitude camen in to the deseert of Syn, in the firste monethe. And the puple dwellide in Cades; and Marie was deed there, and biried in the same place.

2 And whanne the puple hadde nede to watir, thei yeden togidere ayens Moises and Aaron; and thei weren turned in to dissensioun,

3 and seiden, We wolden that we hadden perischid among oure britheren bifor the Lord.

4 Whi han ye led out the chirche of the Lord in to wildirnesse, that bothe we and oure beestis die?

5 Whi han ye maad vs to stie from Egipt, and han brouyt vs in to this werste place, which may not be sowun, which nether bryngith forth fige tre, nether vineris, nether pumgranatis, ferthermore and hath not watir to drynke?

6 And whanne the multitude was left, Moises and Aaron entriden in to the tabernacle of boond of pees, and felden lowe to erthe, and crieden to God, and seiden, Lord God, here the cry of this puple, and opene to hem thi tresour, a welle of quyk watir, that whanne thei ben fillid, the grutchyng of hem ceesse. And the glorie of the Lord apperide on hem;

7 and the Lord spak to Moises,

8 and seide, Take the yerde, and gadere the puple, thou, and Aaron thi brother; and speke ye to the stoon bifore hem, and it schal yyue watris. And whanne thou hast led watir out of the stoon, al the multitude schal drynke, and the beestis therof 'schulden drynke.

9 Therfor Moises took the yerde that was in the 'siyt of the Lord, as the Lord comaundide to hym,

10 whanne the multitude was gaderid bifor the stoon; and he seide to hem, Here ye, rebel and vnbileueful; whether we moun brynge out of this stoon watir to you?

11 And whanne Moises hadde reisid the hond, and hadde smyte the flynt twies with the yerde, largeste watris yeden out, so that the puple drank, and the beestis drunken.

12 And the Lord seide to Moises and to Aaron, For ye bileueden not to me, that ye schulden halewe me bifor the sones of Israel, ye schulen not lede these puples in to the lond which Y schal yyue to hem.

13 This is the watir of ayenseiyng; there the sones of Israel stryueden ayens the Lord, and he was halewid in hem.

14 In the meene tyme Moises sente messangeres fro Cades to the kyng of Edom, whiche seiden, Israel thi brother sendith these thinges. Thou knowist al the trauel that took vs,

15 hou oure fadris yeden doun in to Egipt, and we dwelliden there myche tyme, and Egipcians turmentiden vs and oure fadris; and hou we crieden to the Lord,

16 and he herde vs, and sente an aungel that ledde vs out of Egipt. And lo! we ben set in the citee of Cades, which is in thi laste coostis,

17 and we bisechen that it be leueful to vs to passe thorou thi lond; we schulen not go bi feeldis, nether bi vyneris, nether we schulen drynke watris of thi pittis; but we schulen go in the comyn weie, and we schulen not bowe to the riyt side, nether to the left side, til we passen thi termes.

18 To whom Edom answeride, Ye schulen not passe bi me, ellis Y schal be armed, and come ayens thee.

19 And the sones of Israel seiden, We schulen go bi the weie comynli vsid, and if we and oure beestis drynken thi watris, we schulen yyue that that is iust; noon hardnesse schal be in prijs, onely passe we swiftli.

20 And he answeride, Ye schulen not passe. And anoon he yede out ayens Israel, with a multitude without noumbre, and 'strong hond,

21 nether he wolde assente to Israel bisechynge, that he schulde graunte passage bi hise coostis. Wherfor Israel turnede awey fro hym.

22 And whanne thei hadden moued tentis fro Cades, thei camen in to the hil of Hor, which is in the endis of the lond of Edom;

23 where the Lord spak to Moyses and seide, Aaron go to his puples;

24 for he schal not entre in to the lond which Y yaf to the sones of Israel, for he was vnbileueful to my mouth, at the watris of ayenseiyng.

25 Take thou Aaron, and his sone with hym, and thou schalt lede hem in to the hil of Hor;

26 and whanne thou hast maad nakid the fadir of his cloth, thou schalt clothe 'with it Eleazar, his sone, and Aaron schal be gederid, and schal die there.

27 Moises dide as the Lord comaundide; and thei stieden in to the hil of Hor, bifor al the multitude.

28 And whanne he hadde maad nakid Aaron of hise clothis, he clothide with tho Eleazar, his sone.

29 Sotheli whanne Aaron was deed in the 'cop of the hil, Moises cam doun with Eleazar.

30 Sotheli al the multitude siy that Aaron was deed, and wepte on hym thretti daies, bi alle her meyness.

CAP 21

1 And whanne Chananei, the kyng of Arad, that dwellide at the south, hadde herd this, that is, that Israel cam bi the weye of aspieris, he fauyt ayens hem; and Chananei was ouercomere and ledde pray of Israel.

2 And Israel bounde hym sylf bi avow to the Lord, and seide, If thou schalt bitake this puple in myn hond, Y schal do awei 'the citees therof.

3 And the Lord herde the preieris of Israel, and bitook the Chananey; and Israel killid hym, and distruyede hise citees; and clepide the name of that place Horma, that is, cursyng, 'ethir hangyng up.

4 'Forsothe thei yeden forth also fro the hil of Hor, bi the weie that ledith to the reed see, that thei schulden cumpasse the lond of Edom; and it bigan to anoye the puple, of the weie and trauel.

5 And the puple spak ayens the Lord and Moises, and seide, Whi leddist thou vs out of Egipt, that we schulden die in wildirnesse? breed failith, watris ben not; oure soule wlatith now on this 'meete moost liyt.

6 Wherfor the Lord sente 'firid serpentis in to the puple; at the woundis of whiche serpentis, and the dethis of ful many men,

7 thei camen to Moyses, and seiden, We synneden, for we spaken ayens the Lord and thee; preie thou, that he take awey fro vs the serpentis.

8 And Moises preiede for the puple; and the Lord seide to hym, Make thou a serpent of bras, and sette thou it for a signe; he that is smytun and biholdith it, schal lyue.

9 Therfor Moyses made a serpent of bras, and settide for a signe; and men smytun and biholdynge it, weren heelid.

10 And the sones of Israel yeden forth,

11 and settiden tentis in Oboth; fro whennus thei yeden forth, and settiden tentis in Neabarym, in the wildirnesse, that biholdith Moab, ayens the eest coost.

12 And thei moueden fro thennus, and camen to the stronde of Zareth;

13 which thei leften, and settiden tentis ayens Arnon, which is in the deseert, and apperith in the coostis of Amorrei. Forsothe Arnon is the terme of Moab, and departith Moabitis and Ammoreis.

14 Wherfor it is seid in the book of batels of the Lord, As he dide in the reed see, so he schal do in the strondis of Arnon;

15 the harde rochis of the strondis weren bowid, that tho schulen reste in Arnon, and schulden ligge in the coostis of Moabitis.

16 Fro that place the pit apperide, of which the Lord spak to Moyses, Gadere thou the puple, and Y schal yyue watir to it.

17 Thanne Israel soong this song, The pit stie;

18 thei sungen togidere, The pit which the princes diggiden, and the duykis of the multitude maden redi, in the yyuere of the lawe, and in her stauys. And thei yeden forth fro the wildirnesse to Mathana,

19 fro Mathana to Naaliel, fro Naaliel in to Bamoth;

20 Bamoth is a valey in the cuntrey of Moab, in the cop of Phasga, that biholdith ayens the deseert.

21 Forsothe Israel sente messangeris to Seon, kyng of Ammorreis, and seide,

22 Y biseche that it be leueful to me to passe thorou thi loond; we schulen not bowe in to the feeldis and vyneris; we schulen not drynke watris of pittis; we schulen go in the kyngis weie, til we passen thi termes.

23 Which nolde graunte that Israel schulde passe thury hise coostis, but rather, whanne the oost was gaderid, he yede out ayens Israel, in to deseert. And he cam in to Yasa, and fauyt ayens Israel;

24 of whom he was smytun in the scharpnesse of swerd, and his lond was weldid fro Arnon 'til to Jeboth and 'the sones of Amon; for the termes of Amonytis weren holdun bi strong help.

25 Therfor Israel took alle 'the citees of hym, and dwelliden in the citees of Amorrei, that is, in Esebon, and hise townes.

26 The citee of Esebon was Seons, kyng of Ammorei, which Seon fauyt ayens the kyng of Moab, and took al the lond that was of his lordschip, 'til to Arnon.

27 Therfor it is seid in prouerbe, Come ye in to Esebon, be it bildid, and maad the citee of Seon;

28 fier yede out of Esebon, flawme yede out of the citee 'ethir greet castel of Seon, and deuouryde Ar of Moabitis, and the dwelleris of the 'hiye places of Arnon.

29 Moab, wo to thee! thou, puple of Chamos, perischidist; it yaf the sones therof in to fliyt, and the douytris in to caitifte to Seon, kyng of Ammoreis;

30 the yok of hem perischide, fro Esebon 'til to Dibon; the wery men camen in to Jophe, and 'til to Medaba.

31 And so Israel dwellide in the lond of Ammorrey.

32 And Moises sente men that schulden aspie Jaser, whos 'townes thei token, and weldiden the dwelleris.

33 And thei turniden hem silf, and stieden bi the weie of Basan. And Og, the kyng of Basan, with al his puple cam ayens hem, to fiyte in Edray.

34 And the Lord seide to Moises, Drede thou not hym, for Y haue bitake hym, and al his loond, and puple, in thin hoond; and thou schalt do to hym as thou didist to Seon, kyng of Ammorreis, the dwellere of Esebon.

35 Therfor thei smytiden 'bothe hym with hise sones and al his puple, 'til to deeth; and thei weldiden 'the lond of hym.

CAP 22

1 And thei yeden forth, and settiden tentis in the feeldi places of Moab, where Jerico is set ouer Jordan.

2 Forsothe Balach, the sone of Sephor, siy alle thingis whiche Israel hadde do to Ammorrei,

3 and that men of Moab 'hadden dred Israel, and miyten not bere the assailing of him.

4 And he seide to the grettere men in birthe of Madian, So this puple schal do a wei alle men that dwellen in oure coostis, as an oxe is wont to do awei an eerbe 'til to the rootis. Forsothe he, 'that is, Balaac, was kyng in that tyme in Moab.

5 Therfor he sente messangeris to Balaam, the sone of Beor, a fals diuynour, that dwellide on the flood of the lond of the sones of Amon, that thei schulden clepe hym, and schulden seie, Lo! a puple yede out of Egipt, 'which puple hilide the face of erthe, and sittith ayens me.

6 Therfor come thou, and curse this puple, which is strongere than Y, if in ony maner Y may smyte and dryue hym out of my lond; for Y knowe, that he is blissid whom thou blissist, and he is cursid whom thou hast cursid.

7 The eldere men of Moab and the grettere men in birthe of Madian yeden forth, hauynge in hondis the prijs of fals dyuynyng; and whanne thei hadden come to Balaam, and hadden teld to hym alle the wordis of Balaach, he answeride,

8 Dwelle ye here to nyyt, and Y schal answere what euer thing the Lord schal seie to me. Sotheli while thei dwelliden at Balaam, God cam, and seide to hym,

9 What wolen these men at thee 'to hem silf?

10 Balaam answeride, Balaach, the sone of Sephor, kyng of Moabitis, sente to me, and seide, Lo!

11 a puple which is gon out of Egipt hilide the face of erthe; come thou, and curse hem, if in ony maner Y may fiyte, and dryue hym awey.

12 And God seide to Balaam, Nyle thou go with hem, nether curse thou the puple, for it is blessid.

13 Which Balaam roos eerli, and seide to the princes, Go ye in to youre lond, for God forbeed me to come with you.

14 The princes turneden ayen, and seiden to Balaach, Balaam nolde come with vs.

15 Eft Balaach sente many mo and noblere men, than he hadde sent bifore;

16 whiche seiden, whanne thei hadden come to Balaam, Balaach, the sone of Sephor, seith thus, Tarye thou not to come to me, redi to onoure thee;

17 and what euer thing thou wolt, Y schal yyue to thee; come thou, and curse this puple.

18 Balaam answeride, Thouy Balaach schal yyue to me his howsful of siluer and of gold, Y schal not mowe chaunge the word of my God, that Y speke ethir more ethir lesse.

19 Y biseche, that ye dwelle here also in this nyyt, that Y may wite what the Lord schal answere eft to me.

20 Therfor the Lord cam to Balaam in the nyyt, and seide to hym, If these men comen to clepe thee, rise thou, and go with hem, so oneli that thou do that that Y schal comaunde to thee.

21 Balaam roos eerli, and whanne his femal asse was sadelid, he yede forth with hem.

22 And God was wrooth. And the 'aungel of the Lord stood in the weie ayens Balam, that sat on the femal asse, and hadde twei children with hym.

23 The femal asse siy the aungel stondynge in the weie, with swerd drawun, and 'turnede a wei hir silf fro the weie, and yede bi the feeld. And whanne Balaam beet hir, and wolde lede ayen to the path,

24 the aungel stood in the streitnessis of twei wallis, with whiche the vyneris weren cumpassid.

25 And the femal asse siy the aungel, and ioynede hir silf to the wal, and hurtlide the foot of the sittere; and he beet eft 'the asse.

26 And neuer the lesse the aungel yede to the streit place, where me 'myyte not go out of the weie, nether to the riyt side nether to the left side, and stood ayens hym.

27 And whanne the femal asse siy the aungel stondynge, sche felde doun vndir the feet of the sittere, which was wrooth ful greetli, and beet hir sidis with a staaf.

28 And the Lord openyde the 'mouth of the femal asse, and sche spak, What have Y doon to thee? whi smytist thou me, lo! now the thridde tyme?

29 Balaam answeride, For thou hast disserued, and hast scornyd me; Y wolde that Y hadde a swerd to sle thee.

30 And the femal asse seide, Whether Y am not thi beeste on which thou were wont to sitte euere til in to this present dai? seie thou, what lijk thing Y dide euere to thee? And he seide, Neuere.

31 Anoon the Lord openyde 'the iyen of Balaam, and he siy the aungel stondynge in the weie, holdynge a drawun swerd in the hoond; and Balaam worschipide hym lowli in to erthe.

32 To whom the aungel seide, Whi 'betist thou thi femal asse 'the thridde tyme? Y cam to be aduersarie to thee, for thi weie is weiward, and contrarye to me;

33 and if the femal asse hadde not bowid a wey fro the weie, and youe place to ayenstondere, Y hadde slayn thee, and sche schulde lyue.

34 Balaam seide, Y synnede, not witynge that thou stodist ayens me; and now, if it displesith thee that Y go, Y schal turne ayen.

35 The aungel seide, Go thou with these men, but be war that thou speke not other thing than Y schal comaunde to thee. Therfor Balaam yede with the princes.

36 And whanne Balaach hadde herde this, he yede out in to the comyng of hym, in the citee of Moabitis, whiche is set in the laste coostis of Arnon.

37 And he seide to Balaam, Y sente messangeris to clepe thee; whi camest thou not anoon to me? whethir for Y may not yelde meede to thi comyng?

38 To whom Balaam answeride, Lo! Y am present, whethir Y schal mow speke other thing than that, that God schal putte in my mouth?

39 Therfor thei yeden forth to gidere, and camen in to a citee, which was in the laste coost of 'his rewme.

40 And whanne Balaach hadde slayn scheep and oxun, he sente yiftis to Balaam and the princes that weren with hym.

41 Forsothe whanne the morewtid was maad, Balaach ledde Balaam to the hiye placis of Baal, and he bihelde the laste part of the puple, 'that is, al the oost til to the laste part.

CAP 23

1 And Balaam seide to Balaach, Bilde thou here to me seuene auteris, and make redi so many caluys, and rammes of the same noumbre.

2 And whanne he hadde do bi the word of Balaam, thei putti-den a calf and a ram to gidere on the auter.

3 And Balaam seide to Balaach, Stond thou a litil while bisi-dis thi brent sacrifice, while Y go, if in hap the Lord meete me; and Y schal 'speke to thee what euer thing he schal comaunde.

4 And whanne he hadde go swiftli, God cam to hym; and Bal-aam spak to hym, and seide, Y reiside seuene auteris, and Y puttide a calf and a ram aboue.

5 Forsothe the Lord 'puttide a word in his mouth, and seide, Turne ayen to Balaach, and thou schalt speke these thingis.

6 He turnede ayen, and fond Balach stondynge bisidis his brent sacrifice, and alle the princes of Moabitis.

7 And whanne his parable 'was takun, he seide, Balaach, the kyng of Moabitis, brouyte me fro Aran, fro the 'hillis of the eest; and he seide, Come thou and curse Jacob; haaste thou, and greetli curse thou Israel.

8 How schal Y curse whom God cursid not? bi what resoun schal Y 'haue abhomynable whom God 'hath not abhomy-nable?

9 Fro the hiyeste flyntis Y schal se hym, and fro litle hillis Y schal biholde hym; the puple schal dwelle aloone, and it schal not be arettid among hethene men.

10 Who may noumbre the dust, that is, kynrede, of Jacob, and knowe the noumbre of the generacioun of Israel? My lijf die in the deeth of iust men, and my laste thingis be maad lijk hem!

11 And Balaach seide to Balaam, What is this that thou doist? Y clepide thee, that thou schuldist curse myn enemyes, and ayenward thou blessist hem.

12 To whom Balaam answeride, Whether Y may speke othir thing no but that that the Lord comaundith?

13 Therfor Balaach seide to Balaam, Come with me in to anothir place, fro whennus thou se a part of Israel, and mayst not se al; fro thennus curse thou hym.

14 And whanne he hadde led Balaam in to an hiy place, on the cop of the hil of Phasga, he bildide seuene auteris to Bal-aam, and whanne calues and rammes weren put aboue,

15 he seide to Balaach, Stonde here bisidis thi brent sacrifice, while Y go.

16 And whanne the Lord hadde 'come to him, and hadde put 'a word in his mouth, he seide, Turne ayen to Balach, and thou schalt seie these thingis to hym.

17 He turnyde ayen, and foond Balach stondynge bisidis his brent sacrifice, and the princis of Moabitis with hym. To whom Balach seide, What spak the Lord?

18 And whanne his parable 'was takun, he seide, Stonde, Bal-ach, and herkene; here, thou sone of Sephor. God is not 'as a man,

19 that he lye, nethir he is as the sone of a man, that he be chaungid; therfor he seide, and schal he not do? he spak, and schal he not fulfille?

20 Y am brouyt to blesse, Y may not forbede blessyng.

21 Noon idol is in Jacob, nethir symylacre is seyn in Israel; his Lord God is with hym, and the sown of victorie of kyng is in hym.

22 The Lord God ledde hym out of Egipt, whos strengthe is lijk an vnicorn;

23 fals tellyng bi chiteryng of bryddis, 'ethir idolatrie, is not in Jacob, nethir fals dyuynyng is in Israel. In his tymes it schal be seide to Jacob and Israel, What the Lord hath wrought!

24 Lo! the puple schal rise to gidere as a lionesse, and schal be reisid as a lioun; the lioun schal not reste, til he deuoure prey, and drynke the blood of hem that ben slayn.

25 And Balach seide to Balaam, Nether curse thou, nether blesse thou hym.

26 And he seide, Whether Y seide not to thee, that what euer thing that God comaundide to me, Y wolde do this?

27 And Balach seide to hym, Come, and Y schal lede thee to an other place, if in hap it plesith God that fro thennus thou curse hym.

28 And whanne Balaach hadde led hym out on the 'cop of the hil of Phegor, that biholdith the wildirnesse,

29 Balaam seide to hym, Bilde here seuene auteris to me, and make redi so many caluys, and rammes of the same noumbre.

30 Balaach dide as Balaam seide, and he puttide caluys and rammes, bi alle auteris.

CAP 24

1 And whanne Balaam siy that it pleside the Lord that he schulde blesse Israel, he yede not as he 'hadde go bifore, 'that he schulde seke fals dyuynyng 'bi chiteryng of briddis, but he dresside his face ayens the desert,

2 and reiside iyen, and siy Israel dwellynge in tentis bi hise lynagis. And whanne the Spirit of God felde on hym, and whanne a parable was takun,

3 he seide, Balaam, the sone of Beor, seide, a man whois iye is stoppid seide,

4 the herere of Goddis wordis seide, which bihelde the reuelacioun of almyyti God, which fallith doun, and hise iyen ben openyd so, Hou faire ben thi tabernaclis,

5 Jacob, and thi tentis, Israel!

6 as valeys ful of woodis, and moiste gardyns bisidis floodis, as tabernaclis whiche the Lord hath set, as cedris bisidis watris;

7 watir schal flowe of his bokat, and his seed schal be in to many watris, 'that is, puplis. The kyng of hym schal be takun a wei for Agag, and the rewme of hym schal be doon awai.

8 God ledde hym out of Egipt, whos strengthe is lijk an vnicorn; thei schulen deuoure hethene men, enemyes 'of hym, that is, of Israel; and thei schulen breke the boonus of hem, and schulen perse with arowis.

9 He restide and slepte as a lyoun, and as a lionesse, whom no man schal dore reise. He that blessith thee, schal be blessid; he that cursith, schal

10 be arettid in to cursyng And Balaach was wrooth ayens Balaam, and seide, whanne the hondis weren wrungun to gidere, I clepide thee to curse myn enemyes, whiche ayenward thou hast blessid thries.

11 Turne ayen to thi place; forsothe Y demede to onoure thee greetli, but the Lord priuyde thee fro onour disposid.

12 Balaam answeride to Balaach, Whethir Y seide not to thi messangeris, whiche thou sentist to me,

13 Thouy Balaach schal yyue to me his hows ful of siluer and of gold, Y schal not mow passe the word of my Lord God, that Y brynge forth of myn herte ony thing, ethir of good ethir of yuel, but what euer thing the Lord schal seie, Y schal speke this?

14 Netheles Y schal go to my puple, and Y schal yyue counsel to thee, what thi puple schal do in the laste tyme to this puple.

15 Therfor whanne a parable was takun, he seide eft, Balaam, the sone of Beor seide, a man whos iye is stoppid,

16 seide, the herere of Goddis wordis seide, which knowith the doctrine of the hiyeste, and seeth the reuelacioun of almiyti God, which fallith doun and hath opyn iyen,

17 Y schal se hym, but not now; Y schal biholde hym, but not nyy; a sterre schal be borun of Jacob, and a yerde schal rise of Israel; and he schal smyte the duykis of Moab, and he schal waste alle the sones of Seth; and Ydumye schal be hys possessioun,

18 the eritage of Seir schal bifalle to his enemyes; forsothe Israel schal do strongli, of Jacob schal be he that schal be lord,

19 and schal leese the relikis of the citee.

20 And whanne he hadde seyn Amalech, he took a parable, and seide, Amalech is the bigynning of hethene men, whos laste thingis schulen be lost.

21 Also 'he siy Cyney, and whanne a parable was takun, he seide, Forsothe thi dwellyng place is strong, but if thou schalt sette thi nest in a stoon,

22 and schalt be chosun of the generacioun of Cyn, hou longe schalt thou mow dwelle? forsothe Assur schal take thee.

23 And whanne a parable was takun, he spak eft, Alas! who schal lyue, whanne the Lord schal make thes thingis?

24 Thei schulen come in grete schippis fro Ytalie, thei schulen ouercome Assiries, and thei schulen distrie Ebrews, and at the last also thei hem silf schulen perische.

25 And Balaam roos, and turnide ayen in to his place; and Balaach yede ayen bi the weye in which he cam.

CAP 25

1 Forsothe in that tyme Israel dwellide in Sechym; and the puple dide fornycacioun with the douytris of Moab;

2 whiche douytris clepiden hem to her sacrifices, and thei eten, and worschipiden the goddis of tho douytris;

3 and Israel made sacrifice to Belphegor. And the Lord was wrooth,

4 and seide to Moises, Take thou alle the princes of the puple, and hange hem ayens the sunne in iebatis, that my wodnesse, 'that is stronge veniaunce, be turned awai fro Israel.

5 And Moises seide to the iugis of Israel, Ech man sle his neiyboris, that maden sacrifice to Belphagor.

6 And, lo! oon of the sones of Israel entride bifor his britheren to 'an hoore of Madian, in the siyt of Moises, and al the cumpeny of the sones of Israel, whiche wepten bifor the yatis of the tabernacle.

7 And whanne Phynees, the sone of Eleazar, sone of Aaron, preest, hadde seyn this, he roos fro the myddis of the multitude; and whanne he hadde take a swerd,

8 he entride aftir the man of Israel in to the 'hoore hows, and stikide thorou both togidere, that is, the man and the womman, in the places of gendryng. And the veniaunce ceesside fro the sones of Israel,

9 and foure and twenti thousand of men weren slayn.

10 And the Lord seide to Moises,

11 Fynees, the sone of Eleazar, sone of Aaron, preest, turnede away myn yre fro the sones of Israel; for he was stirid ayens hem bi my feruent loue, that Y my silf schulde not do awai the sones of Israel in my greet hete, 'ether strong veniaunce.

12 Therfor speke thou to hym, Lo! Y yyue to hym the pees of my couenaunt,

13 and it schal be an euerlastynge couenaunt of preesthod, as wel to hym silf as to his seed; for he louyde feruentli for his God, and he clenside the greet trespas of the sones of Israel.

14 Forsothe the name of the man of Israel, that was slayn with the womman of Madian, was Zambri, the sone of Salu, duyk of the kynrede and lynage of Symeon.

15 Forsothe the womman of Madian that was slayn togidere, was clepid Cobri, the douyter of Sur, the nobleste prince of Madianytis.

16 And the Lord spak to Moises and seide,

17 'Madianytis feele you enemyes, and smyte ye hem;

18 for also thei diden enemyliche ayens you, and disseyueden thorow tresouns, bi the idol of Phegor, and bi 'the douyter of Corbri, duyk of Madian, her sister, which douyter was sleyn in the dai of veniaunce, for the sacrilege of Phegor.

CAP 26

1 Aftir that the blood of gilti men was sched out, the Lord seide to Moises and to Eleasar,

2 preest, sone of Aaron, Noumbre ye al the summe of the sones of Israel, fro twenti yeer and aboue, bi her housis, and kynredis, alle men that mowen go forth to batels.

3 And so Moises and Eleasar, preest, spaken in the feeldi places of Moab, ouer Jordan, ayens Jerico, to hem that weren of twenti yeer and aboue,

4 as the Lord comaundide; of whiche this is the noumbre.

5 Ruben, the firste gendrid of Israel; the sone of hym was Enoch, of whom was the meynee of Enochitis; and Phallu, of whom the meynee of Phalluytis; and Esrom,

6 of whom the meynee of Esromytis; and Charmy, of whom the meynee of Charmytis.

7 Thes weren the meynees of the generacioun of Ruben, of whiche meynees the noumbre was foundun thre and fourti thousand seuene hundrid and thretti.

8 The sone of Phallu was Heliab;

9 the sones of hym weren Namuel, and Dathan and Abiron. 'These weren Dathan and Abiron, prynces of the puple, that riseden ayens Moises and Aaron, in the rebelte of Chore, whanne thei rebelliden ayens the Lord;

10 and the erthe openyde his mouth, and deuouride Chore, while ful many men dieden, whanne the fier brente two hundrid men and fifti; and a greet myracle was maad,

11 that whanne Chore perischide, hise sones perischiden not.

12 The sones of Symeon bi her kynredis; Namuel, of hym was the meynee of Namuelitis; Jamyn, of hym was the meynee of Jamynytis; Jachin, of hym was the meynee of Jachynytis;

13 Zare, of hym the meynee of Zarenytis; Saul, of hym the meynee of Saulitis.

14 These weren the meynees of Symeon, of whiche all the noumbre was two and twenti thousynde and two hundrid.

15 The sones of Gad bi her kynredis; Sephon, of hym the meynee of Sephonytis; Aggi, of hym the meynee of Aggitis; Sumy, of hym the meynee of Sumytis;

16 Ozny, of hym the meynee of Oznytis; Heri, of hym the meynee of Hereytis;

17 Arod, of hym the meynee of Aroditis; Ariel, of hym the meynee of Arielitis.

18 These weren the meynees of Gad, of whiche al the noumbre was fourti thousynde and fyue hundrid.

19 The sones of Juda weren Her and Onan, whiche bothe weren deed in the lond of Canaan.

20 And the sones of Juda weren bi her kynredis; Sela, of whom the meynee of Selaitis; Phares, of whom the meynee of Pharesitis; Zare, of whom the meynee of Zareitis.

21 Sotheli the sones of Phares weren Esrom, of whom the meynee of Esromytis; and Amul, of whom the meynee of Amulitis.

22 These weren the meynees of Juda, of whiche al the noumbre was seuenty thousynde and fyue hundrid.

23 The sones of Isachar bi her kynredis; Thola, of whom the meynee of Tholaitis; Phua, of whom the meynee of Phuitis;

24 Jasub, of whom the meynee of Jasubitis; Semran, of whom the meynee of Semranytis.

25 These weren the kynredis of Isachar, of whiche the noumbre was foure and sixti thousynd and three hundrid.

26 The sones of Zabulon bi her kinredis; Sarad, of whom the meynee of Sareditis; Helon, of whom the meynee of Helonytis; Jalel, of whom the meynee of Jalelitis.

27 These weren the kynredis of Zabulon, of whiche the noumbre was sixti thousynde and fyue hundrid.

28 The sones of Joseph bi her kynredis weren Manasses and Effraym.

29 Of Manasses was borun Machir, of whom the meynee of Machiritis. Machir gendride Galaad, of whom the meynee of Galaditis.

30 Galaad hadde sones; Hizezer, of whom the meynee of Hizezeritis; and Helech, of whom the meynee of Helechitis;

31 and Ariel, of whom the meynee of Arielitis; and Sechem, of whom the meynee of Sechemytis;

32 and Semyda, of whom the meynee of Semydaitis; and Epher, of whom the meynee of Epheritis.

33 Forsothe Epher was the fadir of Salphath, that hadde not sones, but oneli douytris; of whiche these weren the names; Maala, and Noha, and Egla, and Melcha, and Thersa.

34 These weren the meynees of Manasse, and the noumbre of hem was two and fifty thousynde and seuene hundrid.

35 Forsothe the sones of Effraym bi her kynredis weren these; Suthala, of whom the meynee of Suthalaitis; Bether, of whom the meynee of Betherytis; Tehen, of whom the meynee of Thehenytis.

36 Forsothe the sone of Suthala was Heram, of whom the meynee of Heramytis.

37 These weren the kynredis 'of the sones of Effraym, of whiche the noumbre was two and thretti thousynde and fyue hundrid.

38 These weren the sones of Joseph, bi her meynees. The sones of Beniamyn in her kynredis; Bale, of whom the meynee of Baleytis; Azbel, of whom the meynee of Azbelitis; Ahiram, of whom the meynee of Ahiramitis;

39 Suphan, of whom the meynee of Suphanitis; Huphan, of whom the meynee of Huphanitis.

40 The sones of Bale, Hered and Noeman; of Hered, the meyne of Hereditis; of Noeman, the meynee of Noemanitis.

41 Thes weren the sones of Beniamyn bi her kynredis, of whiche the noumbre was fyue and fourti thousynde and sixe hundrid.

42 The sones of Dan bi her kynredis; Suphan, of whom the meynee of Suphanytis. These weren the kynredis of Dan bi her meynees;

43 alle weren Suphanytis, of whiche the noumbre was foure and sixti thousynde and foure hundrid.

44 The sones of Aser bi her kynredis; Jemma, of whom the meynee of Jemmaytis; Jesuy, of whom the meynee of Jesuytis; Brie, of whom the meynee of Brieitis.

45 The sones of Brie; Haber, of whom the meynee of Haberitis; and Melchiel, of whom the meynee of Melchielitis.

46 Sotheli the name of 'the douytir of Azer was Zara.

47 These weren the kynredis of the sones of Aser, and the noumbre of hem was foure and fifti thousynde and foure hundrid.

48 The sones of Neptalym bi her kynredis; Jesehel, of whom the meynee of Jeselitis; Guny, of whom the meynee of Gunytis;

49 Jeser, of whom the meynee of Jeserytis; Sellem, of whom the meynee of Sellemytis.

50 Thes weren the kynredis of the sones of Neptalym bi her meynees, of whiche the noumbre was fyue and fourti thousynde and foure hundrid.

51 This is the summe of the sones of Israel, that weren noumbrid, sixe hundrid thousynde and a thousynde seuene hundrid and thretti.

52 And the Lord spak to Moises, and seide,

53 The lond schal be departid to these, bi the noumbre of names in to her possessiouns;

54 thou schalt yyue the grettere part to mo men, and the lesse part to fewere men; possessioun schal be youun to alle bi hem silf, as thei ben noumbrid now;

55 so oneli that lot departe the lond to lynagis and meynees.

56 What euer thing bifallith bi lot, ethir mo ether fewere men take this.

57 Also this is the noumbre of the sones of Leuy bi her meynees; Gerson, of whom the meynee of Gersonytis; Caath, of whom the meynee of Caathitis; Merary, of whom the meynee of Meraritis.

58 These weren the meynees of Leuy; the meynee of Lobny, the meynee of Ebron, the meynee of Mooli, the meynee of Musi, the meynee of Chori. And sotheli Caath gendride Amram,

59 which hadde a wijf, Jocabeth, douyter of Leuy, which douyter was borun to hym in Egipt. This Jocabeth gendride to hir hosebonde 'Amram sones, Aaron, and Moyses, and Marie, the sister of hem.

60 Nadab, and Abyu, and Eleazar, and Ithamar weren bigetun of Aaron;

61 of whiche Nadab and Abyu weren deed, whanne thei hadden offrid alien fier bifor the Lord.

62 And alle that weren noumbrid weren thre and twenti thousynde of male kynde, fro o monethe and aboue, whiche weren not noumbrid among the sones of Israel, nether possessioun was youun to hem with othir men.

63 This is the noumbre of the sones of Israel, that weren discryued of Moises and Eleasar, preest, in the feeldi places of Moab, ouer Jordan, ayen Jerico;

64 among whiche noon of hem was that weren noumbrid bifor of Moises and Aaron, in the deseert of Synay,

65 for the Lord bifore seide, that alle schulden die in 'the wildirnesse; and noon of hem dwellide, no but Caleph, 'the sone of Jephone, and Josue, the sone of Nun.

CAP 27

1 Forsothe the douytris of Salphaat, sone of Epher, sone of Galaad, sone of Machir, sone of Manasses, that was 'the sone of Joseph, neiyeden; of whiche douytris these ben the names; Maala, and Noha, and Egla, and Melcha, and Thersa.

2 And thei stoden bifore Moises, and Eleazar, preest, and alle the princes of the puple, at the dore of tabernacle of boond of pees; and seiden;

3 Oure fadir was deed in the deseert, nether he was in the rebelte, that was reisid ayens the Lord, vndur Chore, but he was deed in his synne; he hadde no male sones. Whi is 'the

name of hym takun awei fro his meynee, for he hath no sone? Yif ye possessioun to vs among 'the kynesmen of oure fadir.

4 And Moises telde 'the cause of hem to the doom of the Lord;

5 which seide to Moyses, The douytris of Salphaath axen a iust thing; yyue thou possessioun to hem among 'the kynnysmen of her fadir,

6 and be thei successouris to hym in to eritage.

7 Forsothe thou schalt speke these thingis to the sons of Israel,

8 Whanne a man is deed with out sone, the eritage schal go to his douyter;

9 if he hath not a douyter, he schal haue eiris his britheren;

10 that and if britheren ben not, ye schulen yyue the eritage to 'the britheren of his fadir;

11 forsothe if he hath no britheren of his fadir, the eritage schal be youun to hem that ben next to hym. And this schal be hooli, 'that is, stidefast, bi euerlastynge lawe to the sones of Israel, as the Lord comaundide to Moises.

12 Also the Lord seide to Moises, Stie thou in to this hil of Aberym, and biholde thou fro thennus the lond, which Y schal yyue to the sones of Israel.

13 And whanne thou hast seyn it, also thou schalt go to thi puple, as thi brother Aaron yede;

14 for thou offenddidist me in the deseert of Syn, in the ayen seiyng of the multitude, nether woldist halewe me bifor it, on the watris. These ben the watris of ayen seiyng, in Cades, of the deseert of Syn.

15 To whom Moises answeryde,

16 The Lord God of spiritis of al fleisch puruey a man, that be on this multitude,

17 and may go out, and entre bifor hem, and lede hem out, and lede hem yn, lest the 'puple of the Lord be as scheep with out schepherde.

18 And the Lord seide to hym, Take thou Josue, the sone of Nun, a man in whom the spyrit of God is, and set thin hond on hym; and he schal stonde bifore Eleazar,

19 preest, and bifore al the multitude.

20 And thou schalt yyue to hym comaundementis, in the siyt of alle men, and a part of thi glorie, that al the synagoge of the sones of Israel here hym.

21 If ony thing schal be worthi to be do for this man, Eleasar, preest, schal counseil the Lord; he schal go out, and schal go yn, at the word of Eleazar; he, and alle the sones of Israel with him, and the tother multitude.

22 Moises dide as the Lord comaundide, and whanne he hadde take Josue, he settide hym bifore Eleazar, preest, and bifore al the multitude of the puple;

23 and whanne he hadde set hondis on his heed, he reherside alle thingis whiche the Lord comaundide.

CAP 28

1 Also the Lord seide to Moises, Comaunde thou to the sones of Israel, and thou schalt seie to hem,

2 Offre ye bi her tymes myn offryng, and looues, and encense of swettist odour.

3 These ben the sacrificis whiche ye owen to offre; twey lambren of o yeer, with out wem, ech dai in to euerlastynge brent sacrifice.

4 Ye schulen offre oon eerli, and the tother at euentid.

5 'Ye schulen offre the tenthe part of ephi 'of floure, 'which be spreynt with pureste oile, and haue the fourthe part of hyn.

6 It is continuel brent sacrifice, which ye offriden in the hil of Synai, in to 'odour of swettiste encense to the Lord.

7 And ye schulen offre the fourthe part of hyn of wyn, bi ech lomb, in the seyntuarie of the Lord.

8 And ye schulen offre in lijk maner the tother lomb at euentid, bi al the custom of the morewe sacrifice, and of moist sacrifices therof, an offryng of swettist odour to the Lord.

9 Forsothe in the 'dai of sabat ye schulen offre twey lambren of o yeer, without wem, and twei tenthe partis of flour spreynt togidere with oile, in sacrifice, 'and ye schulen offre moiste sacrificis that ben sched bi custom,

10 bi alle sabatis, in to euerlastynge brent sacrifice.

11 Forsothe in calendis, that is, in the bigynnyngis of monethis, ye schulen offre brent sacrifice to the Lord, tweyne calues of the droue, o ram, seuene lambren of o yeer, without wem,

12 and thre tenthe partis of flour spreynt to gidere with oile, in sacrifice, bi ech calf, and twey tenthe partis of flour spreynt to gidere with oile, bi ech ram;

13 and the tenthe part of 'a dyme of flour of oile in sacrifice, bi ech lomb; it is brent sacrifice of 'swetist odour, and of encense to the Lord.

14 Forsothe the moiste sacrifices of wyn, that schulen be sched bi alle slayn sacrificis, schulen be these; the half part of hyn bi ech calf, the thridde part bi a ram, the fourthe part bi a lomb; this schal be brent sacrifices bi ech monethe, that comen oon aftir anothir while the yeer turneth.

15 Also a 'buc of geet schal be offrid to the Lord for synnes, in to euerlastynge brent sacrifice, with his moiste offryngis.

16 Forsothe in the firste monethe, in the fouretenthe dai of the monethe, schal be phase, 'that is, pask 'ethir passyng, of the Lord;

17 and in the fiftenthe day schal be the solempnyte of the therf looues. Bi seuene daies ye schulen ete therf looues;

18 of whiche the firste dai schal be worschipful and hooli; ye schulen not do ony seruyle werk therynne.

19 And ye schulen offre brent sacrifice to the Lord, twey calues, o ram, seuene lambren of o yeer, without wem;

20 and the sacrifices of ech bi itsilf of flour, which be spreynt to gidere with oile, thre tenthe partis bi ech calf,

21 and twey tenthe partis bi a ram, and the tenthe part of 'a dyme bi ech lomb, that is, bi seuene lambren.

22 'And ye schulen offre o 'buc of geet for synne, that clensyng be maad for you,

23 outakun the brent sacrifice of the morewtid, which ye schulen offre euere.

24 So ye schulen do bi ech dai of seuene daies, into the nurschyng of fier, and in to swettist odour to the Lord, that schal rise of the brent sacrifice, and of moiste sacrifices of ech.

25 Also the seuenthe day schal be moost solempne and hooli to you; ye schulen not do ony seruyle werk ther ynne.

26 Also the dai of the firste fruytis, whanne ye schulen offre newe fruitis to the Lord, whanne the wokis schulen be fillyd, schal be worschipful and hooli; ye schulen not do ony seruyle werk ther ynne.

27 And ye schulen offre brent sacrifice to the Lord, in to 'swettiste odour; twey calues of the droue, o ram, and seuene lambren of o yeer, with out wem;

28 and in the sacrifices of tho ye schulen offre thre tenthe partis of flour spreynt togidere with oile, bi ech calf, twei tenthe partis bi rammes,

29 the tenthe parte of 'a dyme bi the lambren, whiche ben to gidere, seuene lambren. 'And ye schulen offre a 'buc of geet,

which is offrid for clensyng, outakun brent sacrifice euerlastynge, and the moiste sacrifices therof;

31 ye schulen offre alle thingis with out wem, with her moyste sacrifices.

CAP 29

1 Forsothe the firste dai of the seuenthe monethe schal be hooli, and worschipful to you; ye schulen not do ony seruyle werk ther ynne, for it is the day of sownyng, and of trumpis.

2 And ye schulen offre brent sacrifice, in to swettest odour to the Lord, o calf of the droue, o ram, and seuene lambren of o yeer, with out wem;

3 and in the sacrificis of tho 'ye schulen offre thre tenthe partis of flour spreynt togidere with oile, bi ech calfe, twey tenthe partis bi a ram,

4 o tenthe part bi a lomb, whiche togidere ben seuen lambren.

5 And 'ye schulen offre a 'buc of geet, which is offrid for synne, in to the clensyng of the puple,

6 with out the brent sacrifice of kalendis, with hise sacrifices, and without euerlastynge brent sacrifice, with customable fletynge offryngis; and bi the same cerymonyes ye schulen offre encense in to swettiste odour to the Lord.

7 Also the tenthe dai of this seuenthe monethe schal be hooli and worschipful to you, and ye schulen turmente youre soulis; ye schulen not do ony seruyle werk ther ynne.

8 And ye schulen offre brent sacrifice to the Lord, in to swettiste odour; o calf of the droue, o ram, seuene lambren of o yeer with out wem.

9 And in the sacrifices of tho 'ye schulen offre thre tenthe partis of flour spreynt togidere with oyle, bi ech calf, twey tenthe partis bi a ram,

10 the tenthe part of a dyme bi each lomb, that ben togidere seuene lambren.

11 And ye schulen offre a 'buc of geet for synne, with out these thingis that ben wont to be offrid for synne in to clensyng, and 'ye schulen offre euerlastinge brent sacrifice in sacrifice, and fletinge offryngis of tho.

12 Forsothe in the fiftenthe dai of this seuenthe monethe, that schal be hooli and worschipful to you, ye schulen not do ony seruyle werk, but ye schulen halewe solempnyte to the Lord in seuene daies; and ye schulen offre brent sacrifice,

13 in to swetiste odour to the Lord, threttene calues of the droue, twey rammes, fouretene lambren of o yeer, with out wem.

14 And in the moiste sacrifices of tho 'ye schulen offre thre tenthe partis of flour spreynt to gidere with oile bi ech calf, that ben togidere threttene calues, and ye schulen offre twei tenthe partis to twei rammes togidere, that is, o tenthe part to o ram, and 'ye schulen offre the tenthe part of 'a

15 dyme to ech lomb, whiche ben to gidere fourteene lambren.

16 And ye schulen offre a 'buc of geet for synne, with out euerlastynge brent sacrifice, and 'with out the sacrifice and moiste offryng therof.

17 In the tother dai ye schulen offre twelue calues of the droue, twei rammes, fouretene lambren of o yeer without wem.

18 And ye schulen halewe riytfuli sacrifices, and moiste offryngis of alle, bi calues, and rammes, and lambren.

19 And 'ye schulen offre a 'buc of geet for synne, with out euerlastynge brent sacrifice, and 'with out the sacrifice and moist offryng therof.

20 In the thridde dai ye schulen offre euleuen calues, twei rammes, fourtene lambren of o yeer, without wem.

21 And ye schulen halewe riytfuli the sacrifices, and moiste offryngis of alle, bi the caluys, and rammes, and lambren.

22 And ye schulen offre a 'buk of geet for synne, with out euerlastynge brent sacrifice, and with out the sacrifice and moiste offryng therof.

23 In the fourthe day ye schulen offre ten calues, twey rammes, fourtene lambren of o yeer with oute wem.

24 And ye schulen halewe riytfuli the sacrifices, and moiste offryngis of alle, bi the calues, and rammes, and lambren.

25 And ye schulen offre a 'buk of geet for synne, with out euerlastynge brent sacrifice, and 'with out the sacrifice and moiste offryng therof.

26 In the fyuethe dai ye schulen offre nyne calues, twei rammes, fourtene lambren of o yeer, with oute wem.

27 And ye schulen halewe riytfuli the sacrifices, and moiste offryngis 'of alle, bi the calues, and rammes, and lambren.

28 And 'ye schulen offre a 'buc of geet for synne, with out euerlastynge brent sacrifice, and 'with out the sacrifice and moiste offryng therof.

29 In the sixte dai ye schulen offre eiyt calues, and twei rammes, fourtene lambren of o yeer with out wem.

30 And ye schulen halewe riytfuli the sacrifices, and moiste offryngis 'of alle, bi the calues, and rammes, and lambren.

31 And ye schulen offre a 'buk of geet for synne, with out euerlastynge brent sacrifice, and 'with out the sacrifice and moiste offryng therof.

32 In the seuenthe dai ye schulen offre seuene calues, twei rammes, fourtene lambren 'of o yeer with out wem.

33 And ye schulen halewe riytfuli the sacrifices, and moiste offryngis 'of alle, bi the calues, and rammes, and lambren.

34 And 'ye schulen offre a 'buc of geet for synne, with out euerlastynge brent sacrifice, and 'with out the sacrifice and moiste offryng therof.

35 In the eiythe dai, which is moost solempne 'ether hooli; ye schulen not do ony seruyle werk,

36 and ye schulen offre brent sacrifice in to swettest odour to the Lord, o calf, o ram, seuene lambren of o yeer with out wem.

37 And ye schulen halewe riytfuli the sacrifices and moiste offryngis 'of alle, bi the calues, and rammes, and lambren.

38 'And ye schulen offre a 'buc of geet for synne, with out euerlastynge brent sacrifice, and 'with out the sacrifice, and moiste offryng therof.

39 Ye schulen offre these thingis to the Lord, in youre solempnytees, with out avowis, and wilful offryngis, in brent sacrifice, in sacrifice, in moist offryng, and in peesible sacrifices.

CAP 30

1 And Moises telde to the sones of Israel alle thingis whiche the Lord comaundide to hym.

2 And he spak to the princes of the lynagis of the sones of Israel, This is the word, which the Lord comaundide, If ony of men makith a vowe to the Lord,

3 ethir byndith hym silf bi an ooth, he schal not make voide his word, but he schal fille al thing which he bihiyte.

4 If a womman which is in the hows of hir fadir, and is yit in the age of a damysel, 'that is, not yit weddid, avowith ony thing, ethir byndith hir silf bi an ooth, 'if the fadir knowith the avow, which sche bihiyte, and the ooth bi which sche boond

hir soule, and he is stille, sche schal be gilti of the ooth, that is, boundun bi the ooth;

5 what euer thing sche bihiyte and swoor, sche schall fille in werk.

6 Forsothe if the fadir ayenseide anoon as he herde, bothe the vowis and 'oothis of hir schulen be voide, and sche schal not be holdun boundun to the biheeste, for the fadir ayenseide.

7 If sche hath an hosebonde, and avowith ony thing, and a word goynge out of hir mouth onys byndith hir soule with an ooth,

8 in what dai the hosebonde herith, and ayenseith not, sche schal be gilti 'of avow; sche schal yelde, what euer thing sche bihiyte.

9 But if the hosebonde herith, and anoon ayenseith, and makith void alle hir biheestis, and wordis bi whiche sche boond hir soule, the Lord schal be merciful to hir.

10 A widewe, and a womman forsakun of hir hosebonde, schulen yelde, what euer thing thei avowen.

11 Whanne a wijf in 'the hous of hir hosebonde byndith hir silf bi a vow and an ooth,

12 if the hosebonde herith, and is stille and ayenseith not the biheest, sche schal yelde, what euer thing sche bihiyte.

13 Sotheli if the hosebonde ayenseide anoon, sche schal not be holdun gilti of biheest, for the hosebonde ayenseide, and the Lord schal be merciful to hir.

14 If sche avowith, and byndith hir silf bi an ooth, that sche turmente hir soule bi fastyng, ethir bi abstynence of othere thingis, it schal be in the doom of the hosebonde, that sche do, ether do not.

15 That if the hosebonde herith, and is stille, and delaieth the sentence in the tother dai, sche schal yelde what euer thing sche avowide and bihiyte, for he was stille, anoon as he herde.

16 Forsothe if the hosebonde ayenseide aftir that he wiste, he schal bere his wickidnesse. These ben the lawis, which the Lord ordeynede to Moyses bitwixe the hosebonde and the wijf, bitwixe the fadir and the douytir, which is yit in the age of a damysel, 'that is, not yit maried, 'ether which dwellith in 'the hows of the fadir.

CAP 31

1 And the Lord spak to Moyses, and seide,

2 Venge thou firste the sones of Israel of Madianytis, and so thou schalt be gaderid to thi puple.

3 And anoon Moises seide, Arme ye men of you to batel, that moun take of Madianytis the veniaunce of the Lord.

4 Of ech lynage be chosun a thousynde men of Israel, that schulen be sent to batel.

5 And of ech lynage thei yauen a thousynde, that is twelue thousynde of men, redi to batel;

6 whiche Moises sente with Fynees, the sone of Eleazar, preest. And he bitook to hem hooli vesselis, and trumpis to make sown.

7 And whanne thei hadden fouyt ayens Madianytis, and hadden ouercome, thei killiden alle the malis,

8 and 'the kyngis of hem, Euy, and Reem, and Sur, and Hur, and Rebe, fyue princes of 'the folc of hem. Also thei killiden bi swerd Balaam, the sone of Beor.

9 And thei token the wymmen of hem, and the litle children, and alle beestis, and al purtenaunce of howshold; what euer thei myyten haue, thei spuyleden;

10 flawme brente as wel citees, as litle townes and castels.

11 And they token pray, and alle thingis whiche thei hadden take, as wel of men as of beestis, and thei brouyten to Moyses,

12 and to Eleazar, preest, and to al the multitude of the sones of Israel. Forsothe thei baren othere 'thingis perteynynge to vss, to the castels in the feldi places of Moab bisidis Jordan, ayens Jericho.

13 Moises and Eleazar, preest, and alle the princes of the synagoge, yeden out in to the comyng of hem, with out the castels, 'that is, of the tabernacle.

14 And Moises was wrooth to the princes of the oost, to tribunes, and centuriouns, that camen fro batel; and he seide, Whi reserueden ye wymmen?

15

16 whether it be not these that disseyueden the sones of Israel, at the suggestioun of Balaam, and maden you to do trespas ayens the Lord, on the synne of Phegor, wherfor also the puple was slayn?

17 And therfor sle ye alle men, what euer thing is of male kynde, and litle children; and strangle ye the wymmen that knew men fleischli;

18 forsothe reserue ye to you damesels, and alle wymmen virgyns,

19 and dwelle ye with out the castels in seuene daies. He that sleeth a man, ether touchith a slayn man, schal be clensid in the thridde and the seuenthe dai;

20 and of al the pray, whether it is clooth, ether vessel, and ony thing maad redi in to thingis perteynynge to vss, of the skynnys and heeris of geet, and 'of tre, it schal be clensid.

21 And Eleazar, preest, spak thus to the men of the oost that fouyten, This is the comaundement of the lawe, which the Lord comaundide to Moises,

22 The gold, and siluer, and bras, and yrun, and tiyn, and leed, and al thing that may passe by flawme, schal be purgid bi fier;

23 sotheli what euer thing may not suffre fier, schal be halewid bi the watir of clensyng.

24 And ye schulen waische youre clothis in the seuenthe dai, and ye schulen be clensid; and aftirward ye schulen entre in to the castels 'of the tabernacle.

25 And the Lord seide to Moises, Take ye the summe of tho thingis that ben takun, fro man 'til to beeste,

26 thou, and Eleazar, preest, and alle the princes of the comyn puple.

27 And thou schalt departe euenli the prey bytwixe hem that fouyten and yeden out to batel, and bitwixe al the multitude.

28 And thou schalt departe a part to the Lord, of hem that fouyten, and weren in batel, 'o soule of fiue hundrid, as wel of men, as of oxun, and of assis, and of scheep.

29 And thou schalt yyue 'that part to Eleazar, preest, for tho ben the firste fruytis of the Lord.

30 Also of the myddil part of the sones of Israel, thou schalt take the fiftithe heed of men, and of oxun, and of assis, and of scheep, and of alle lyuynge beestis; and thou schalt yyue tho to the dekenes, that waken in the kepyngis of the tabernacle of the Lord.

31 And Moyses and Eleazar diden, as the Lord comaundide.

32 Forsothe the prey which the oost hadde take, was sixe hundrid fyue and seuenti thousynde of scheep,

33 of oxun two and seuenti thousynde, of assis sixti thousynde and a thousynde;

34

35 the soules of persones of femal kynde, that knewen not fleischli men, two and thretti thousynde.

36 And the myddil part was youun to hem that weren in the batel, of scheep thre hundrid seuene and thretti thousynde and fyue hundrid;

37 of whiche sixe hundrid fyue and seuenti scheep weren noumbrid in to the part of the Lord;

38 and of sixe and thretti thousynde oxun,

39 two and seuenti oxun, and of thretti thousynde assis and fyue hundryd, oon and sixti assis;

40 of sixtene thousynde persoones of men, twei and thretti persoones bifelden in to the 'part of the Lord.

41 And Moises bitook the noumbre of the firste fruytis of the Lord to Eleazar, preest, as it was comaundid to hym,

42 of the myddil part of the sones of Israel, which he departide to hem that weren in batel.

43 And of the myddil part that bifelde to the tother multitude, that is, of thre hundrid seuene and thretti thousynde scheep and fyue hundrid,

44 and of sixe and thretti thousynde oxun,

45 and of thretti thousynde assis and fyue hundrid, and of sixtene thousynde wymmen,

46 Moyses took the fyftithe heed,

47 and yaf to the dekenes, that wakiden in the tabernacle of the Lord, as the Lord comaundide.

48 And whanne the princes of the oost, and the tribunes and centuriouns hadden neiyed to Moises,

49 thei seiden, We thi seruauntis han teld the noumbre of fiyters, whiche we hadden vndur oure hoond, and sotheli not oon failide;

50 for which cause we offren 'in the fre yiftis of the Lord, alle bi vs silf, that that we myyten fynde of gold in the pray, girdelis for 'the myddil of wymmen, and bies of the armes, and ryngis, and ournementis of the arm nyy the hond, and bies of the neckis of wymmen, that thou preye the Lord for vs.

51 And Moises and Eleazar, preest, token al the gold in dyuerse spices,

52 'ether kyndis, bi the weiyte of the seyntuarye, sixtene thousynde seuene hundrid and fifti siclis, of the tribunes, and centuriouns.

53 For that that ech man rauyschide in the prey, was his owne;

54 and thei baren the gold taken in to the tabernacle of witnessyng, in to the mynde of the sones of Israel, bifor the Lord.

CAP 32

1 Forsothe the sones of Ruben and of Gad hadden many beestis, and catel with out noumbre was to hem, in werk beestis. And whanne thei hadden seyn Jazer and Galaad, couenable londis to beestis to be fed,

2 thei camen to Moyses and Eleazar, preest, and to the princes of the multitude, and seiden,

3 Astaroth, and Dibon, and Jacer, and Nemra, Esebon, and Eleale, and Sabam,

4 and Nebo, and Beon, the lond which the Lord smoot in the siyt of the sones of Israel, is of moost plenteuous cuntrey to the pasture of beestis; and we thi seruauntis han ful many beestis;

5 and we preyen, if we han founde grace bifor thee, that thou yyue to vs thi seruauntis that cuntrey in to possessioun, and make not vs to passe Jordan.

6 To whiche Moises answeride, Whether youre britheren schulen go to batel, and ye schulen sitte here?

7 Whi peruerten ye the soulis of Israel, that thei doren not passe in to the place, which the Lord schal yyue to hem?

8 Whether youre fadris diden not so, whanne Y sente fro Cades Barne to aspie the lond,

9 and whanne thei camen to the valey of Clustre, whanne al the cuntrey was cumpassid, thei peruertiden the herte of the sones of Israel, that thei entriden not in to the coostis, whiche the Lord yaf to hem.

10 And the Lord was wrooth, and swoor,

11 seiynge, Thes men that stieden fro Egipt, fro twenti yeer and aboue, schulen not se the lond which Y bihiyte vndur an ooth to Abraham, Isaac, and Jacob, and nolden sue me,

12 outakun Caleph, Cenezei, the sone of Jephone, and Josue, the sone of Nun; these tweyne filliden my wille.

13 And the Lord was wrooth ayens Israel, and ledde hym aboute the deseert bi fourti yeer, til al the generacioun was wastid, that hadde do yuel in the 'siyt of the Lord.

14 And Moyses seide, Lo! ye encressyngis, and nurreis, 'ether nurschid children, of synful men, han ryse for youre fadris, that ye schulden encreesse the strong veniaunce of the Lord ayens Israel.

15 That if ye nylen sue the Lord, in 'the wildirnesse he schal forsake the puple, and ye schulen be cause of the deeth of alle men.

16 And thei neiyiden nyy, and seiden, We schulen make foldis of scheep, and the stablis of beestis, and we schulen make strengthid citees to oure litle children.

17 Forsothe we vs silf schulen be armed 'to defence, and schulen be gird 'with armeris to asailyng, and schulen go to batel bifor the sones of Israel, til we bryngen hem in to her places; oure litle children and what euer thing we moun haue, schulen be in strengthid cytees, for the tresouns of the dwelleris.

18 We schulen not turne ayen in to oure housis, til the sones of Israel welden her eritage;

19 and we schulen not axe ony thing ouer Jordan, for we han now oure possessioun in the eest coost therof.

20 To whiche Moises seide, If ye doen that, that ye biheten, be ye maad redi, and go ye to batel bifor the Lord;

21 and ech man fiytere be armed, and passe Jordan, til the Lord distrye hise enemyes,

22 and al the lond be maad suget to hym; thanne ye schulen be giltles anentis God, and anentis Israel, and ye schulen holde the cuntreys, whiche ye wolen, bifor the Lord.

23 But if ye doon not that, that ye seien, it is not doute to ony man, that ne ye synnen ayens God; and wite ye, that youre synne schal take you.

24 Therfor bilde ye citees to youre litle children, and foldis and stablis to scheep, and to beestis; and fille ye that, that ye bihiyten.

25 And the sones of Gad and of Ruben seiden to Moises, We ben thi seruauntis; we schulen do that, that oure lord comaundith.

26 We schulen leeue oure litle children, and wymmen, and scheep, and beestis in the citees of Galaad;

27 forsothe alle we thi seruauntis schulen go redi to batel, as thou, lord, spekist.

28 Therfor Moyses comaundide to Eleazar, preest, and to Josue, the sone of Nun, and to the princes of meynees, bi the lynagis of Israel, and seide to hem,

29 If the sones of Gad, and the sones of Ruben goen alle armed with you, to batel bifor the Lord, and the lond be maad suget to you, yyue ye to hem Galaad in to possessioun;

30 but if thei nylen passe with you in to the lond of Chanaan, take thei places to dwelle among you.

31 And the sones of Gad and the sones of Ruben answeriden, As the Lord spak to hise seruauntis, so we schulen do;

32 we schulen go armed bifor the Lord, in to the lond of Chanaan, and we knowlechen, that we han take now possessioun ouer Jordan.

33 And so Moises yaf to the sones of Gad and of Ruben, and to half the lynage of Manasses, sone of Joseph, the rewme of Seon, kyng of Ammorey, and the rewme of Og, kyng of Basan, and 'the lond of hem, with her citees, bi cumpas.

34 Therfor the sones of Gad bildiden Dibon, and Astaroth, and Aroer,

35 and Roth-Sophan, and Jazer, and Jebaa,

36 and Beeth-Nemra, and Betharan, strengid citees; and foldis to her beestis.

37 Forsothe the sones of Ruben bildiden Esebon, and Eleale, and Cariathiarym, and Nabo,

38 and Balmeon, whanne the names weren turned, and thei bildiden Sabama; and puttiden names to the citees, whiche thei hadden bildid.

39 Forsothe the sones of Machir, sone of Manasses, yeden in to Galaad, and distrieden it, and killiden Ammorei, enhabitere therof.

40 Therfor Moises yaf the lond of Galaad to Machir, sone of Manasses, which Machir dwellide ther ynne.

41 Forsothe Jair, the sone of Manasses, yede, and occupiede the townes therof, whiche he clepide Anochiair, that is, the townes of Jair.

42 Also Nobe yede, and took Canath, with hise townes, and clepide it, bi his name, Nobe.

CAP 33

1 These ben the dwellyngis of the sones of Israel, that yeden out of the lond of Egipt, bi her cumpenyes, in the hond of Moises and of Aaron;

2 whiche dwellyngis Moises discriuede bi the places of tentis, that weren chaungid bi comaundement of the Lord.

3 Therfor the sones of Israel yeden forth in 'an hiy hond fro Ramesses, in the firste monethe, in the fiftenthe dai of the firste monethe, in the tother dai of pask, while alle Egipcians sien,

4 and birieden the firste gendrid children, whiche the Lord hadde slayn; for the Lord hadde take veniaunce also on the goddis 'of hem.

5 'The sones of Israel settiden tentis in Socoth,

6 and fro Sochoth thei camen into Etham, which is in the laste coostis of 'the wildirnesse; fro thennus thei yeden out,

7 and camen ayens Phiayroth, whiche biholdith Beelsephon, and settiden tentis bifor Magdalun.

8 And thei yeden forth fro Phiairoth, and passiden bi the myddil see in to the wildirnesse, and thei yeden thre daies bi the deseert of Ethan, and settiden tentis in Mara.

9 And thei yeden forth fro Mara, and camen in to Helym, where weren twelue wellis of watir, and seuenti palm trees; and there thei settiden tentis.

10 But also thei yeden out fro thennus, and settiden tentis on the Reed See. And thei yeden forth fro the Reed See,

11 and settiden tentis in the deseert of Syn,

12 fro whennus thei yeden out, and camen in to Depheca.

13 And thei yeden forth fro Depheca, and settiden tentis in Haluys.

14 And thei yeden forth fro Haluys, and settiden tentis in Raphidyn, where watir failide to 'the puple to drinke.

15 And thei yeden forth fro Raphidyn, and settiden tentis in the deseert of Synai.

16 But also thei yeden out of the wildirnesse of Synay, and camen to the Sepulcris of Coueitise.

17 And thei yeden forth fro the Sepulcris of Coueytise, and settiden tentis in Asseroth.

18 And fro Asseroth thei camen in to Rethma.

19 And thei yeden forth fro Rethma, and settiden tentis in Remon Phares;

20 fro whennus thei yeden forth, and camen in to Lemphna.

21 And fro Lemphna thei settiden tentis in Ressa.

22 And thei yeden out fro Ressa, and camen into Celatha; fro whennus thei yeden forth, and settiden tentis in the hil of Sepher.

24 Thei yeden out fro the hil of Sepher, and camen in to Arada;

25 fro thennus thei yeden forth, and settiden tentis in Maceloth.

26 And thei yeden forth fro Maceloth, and camen in to Caath.

27 Fro Caath thei settiden tentis in Thare;

28 fro whennus thei yeden out, and settiden tentis in Methcha.

29 And fro Methcha thei settiden tentis in Esmona.

30 And thei yeden forth fro Asmona, and camen in to Moseroth;

31 and fro Moseroth thei settiden tentis in Benalachan.

32 And thei yeden forth fro Benalachan, and camen in to the hil of Galgad;

33 fro whennus thei yeden forth, and settiden tentis in Jethebacha.

34 And fro Jethebacha thei camen in to Ebrona.

35 And thei yeden out fro Ebrona, and settiden tentis in Asiongaber;

36 fro thennus thei yeden forth, and camen in to deseert of Syn; this is Cades.

37 And thei yeden fro Cades, and thei settiden tentis in the hil of Hor, in the laste coostis of the lond of Edom.

38 And Aaron, the preest, stiede in to the hil of Hor, for the Lord comaundide, and there he was deed, in the fourti yeer of the goyng out of the sones of Israel fro Egipt, in the fyuethe monethe, in the firste dai of the monethe;

39 whanne he was of an hundrid and thre and twenti yeer.

40 And Chanaan, kyng of Arad, that dwellide at the south, in the lond of Canaan, herde that the sones of Israel camen.

41 And thei yeden forth fro the hil of Hor, and settiden tentis in Salmona;

42 fro thennus thei yeden forth, and camen in to Phynon.

43 And thei yeden forth fro Phynon, and settiden tentis in Oboth.

44 And fro Oboth thei camen in to Neabarym, 'that is, into the wildirnesse of Abarym, which is in the endis of Moabitis.

45 And thei yeden forth fro Neabarym, and thei settiden tentis in Dibon of Gad;

46 fro whennus thei yeden forth, and settiden tentis in Helmon of Deblathaym.

47 And thei yeden out fro Helmon of Deblathaym, and camen to the hillis of Abarym, ayens Nabo.

48 And thei yeden forth fro the hillis of Abarym, and passiden to the feeldi places of Moab, ouer Jordan, ayens Jericho.

49 And there thei settiden tentis, fro Bethsymon 'til to Belsathym, in the pleynere places of Moabitis,

50 where the Lord spak to Moises,

51 Comaunde thou to the sones of Israel, and seie thou to hem, Whanne ye han passid Jordan, and han entrid in to the lond of Canaan,

52 distrie ye alle the dwelleris of that cuntrey; breke ye the titlis, 'that is, auteris, and dryue ye to poudre the ymagis, and distrie ye alle heiy thingis,

53 and clense ye the lond, and alle men dwellynge thereynne. For Y yaf to

54 you that lond into possessioun whiche ye schulen departe to you bi lot; to mo men ye schulen yyue largere lond, and to fewere men streytere lond, as lot fallith to alle men, so eritage schal be youun; possessioun schal be departid bi lynagis and meynees.

55 But if ye nylen sle the dwelleris of the lond, thei, that abiden, schulen be to you as nailes in the iyen, and speris in the sidis, 'that is, deedli aduersaries; and thei schulen be aduersaries to you in the lond of youre abitacioun;

56 and what euer thing Y thouyte to do 'to hem, Y schal do to you.

CAP 34

1 And the Lord spak to Moises,

2 and seide, Comaunde thou to the sones of Israel, and thou schalt seie to hem, Whanne ye han entrid in to the lond of Canaan, and it bifelde in to possessioun 'to you bi lot, it schal be endid bi these endis.

3 The south part schal bigynne at the wildirnesse of Syn, which is bisidis Edom, and it schal haue termes ayens the eest,

4 the saltiste see, whiche termes schulen cumpasse the south coost bi the 'stiynge of Scorpioun, 'that is, of an hil clepid Scorpioun, so that tho passe in to Senna, and come to the south, 'til to Cades Barne; fro whennus the coostis schulen go out to the town, Abdar bi name, and schulen strecche forth 'til to Asemona;

5 and the terme schal go bi cumpas fro Assemona 'til to the stronde of Egipt, and it schal be endid bi the brynke of the grete see.

6 Forsothe the west coost schal bigynne at the greet see, and schal be closid bi that ende.

7 Sotheli at the north coost, the termes schulen bigynne at the greet see, and schulen come 'til to the hiyeste hil,

8 fro which tho schulen come in to Emath, 'til to the termes of Sedada;

9 and the coostis schulen go 'til to Ephrona, and the town of Enan. These schulen be the termes in the north part.

10 Fro thennus thei schulen mete coostis ayens the eest coost, fro the town Henan 'til to Sephama;

11 and fro Sephama termes schulen go doun in to Reblatha, ayens the welle 'of Daphnyn; fro thennus tho schulen come ayens the eest to the se of Cenereth;

12 and tho schulen strecche forth 'til to Jordan, and at the laste tho schulen be closid with the salteste see. Ye schulen haue this lond bi hise coostis 'in cumpas.

13 And Moises comaundide to the sones of Israel, and seide, This schal be the lond which ye schulen welde bi lot, and which the Lord comaundide to be youun to nyne lynagis and to the half lynage;

14 for the lynage of the sones of Ruben, bi her meynees, and the lynage of the sones of Gad, bi kynrede and noumbre, and half the lynage of Manasses,

15 that is, twey lynagis and an half, han take her part ouer Jordan, ayens Jerico, at the eest coost.

16 And the Lord seide to Moises,

17 These ben the 'names of men that schulen departe the lond to you, Eleazar, preest, and Josue, the sone of Nun, and of each lynage, o prynce;

18 of whiche these ben the names, of the lynage of Juda,

19 Caleph, the sone of Jephone;

20 of the lynage of Symeon, Samuhel, the sone of Amyud;

21 of the lynage of Beniamyn, Heliad, sone of Casselon;

22 of the lynage of the sones of Dan, Bochi, sone of Jogli; of the sones of Joseph,

23 of the lynage of Manasses, Hamyel, sone of Ephoth;

24 of the lynage of Effraym, Camuhel, sone of Septhan;

25 of the lynage of Zabulon, Elisaphan, sone of Pharnat;

26 of the lynage of Isacar, duyk Phaltiel, the sone of Ozan; of the lynage of Azer,

27 Abyud, the sone of Salomy;

28 of the lynage of Neptalym, Fedahel, the sone of Amyud.

29 These men it ben, to whiche the Lord comaundide, that thei schulden departe to the sones of Israel the lond of Chanaan.

CAP 35

1 And the Lord spak these thingis to Moises, in the feeldi places of Moab, aboue Jordan,

2 ayens Jericho, Comaunde thou to the sones of Israel, that thei yyue to dekenes of her possessiouns,

3 citees to dwelle, and the suburbabis of tho bi cumpas, that thei dwelle in 'the citees, and the suburbabis be to beestis, and 'werk beestis;

4 whiche suburbabis schulen be strecchid forth fro the wallis of citees with outforth 'bi cumpas, in the space of a thousynde paacis;

5 ayens the eest schulen be two thousynde cubitis, and ayens the south in lijk manere schulen be two thousynde cubitis, and at the see that biholdith to the west schal be the same mesure, and the north coost schal be endid bi euene terme. And the citees schulen be in the myddis, and the suburbabis with outforth.

6 Forsothe of tho citees whiche ye schulen yyue to dekenes, sixe schulen be departid in to helpis of fugityues, 'ether of fleynge men, that he that schedde blood, fle to tho; and outakun these sixe, ye schulen yyue to dekenes othere two and fourti citees,

7 that is, togidere eiyte and fourti, with her surburbabis.

8 And tho citees that schulen be youun of the possessiouns of sones of Israel, schulen be takun awey, mo fro hem that han more, and fewere 'schulen be takun awey fro hem that han lesse, alle bi hem silf schulen yyue bi the mesure of her eritage, citees to dekenes.

9 The Lord seide to Moises,

10 Spek thou to the sones of Israel, and thou schalt seie to hem, Whanne ye han passid Jordan, in the lond of Canaan,

11 deme ye whiche citees owen to be in to the helpis of fugityues, whiche not wilfuli han sched blood.

12 In whiche whanne the fleere hath fled, the kynesman of hym that is slayn, schal not mow sle hym, til he stonde in the siyt of the multitude, and the cause of hym be demed.

13 Forsothe of tho citees that ben departid to the helpis of fugityues,

14 thre schulen be ouer Jordan, and thre in the lond of Canaan;

15 as wel to the sones of Israel as to comelyngis and pilgryms; that he fle to tho citees, that schedde blood not wilfuli.

16 If ony man smytith a man with yrun, and he that is smytun is deed, 'the smyter schal be gilti of mansleyng, and he schal die.

17 If he castith a stoon, and a man is deed bi the strook, he schal be punyschid in lijk maner.

18 If a man smytun with a staf dieth, he schal be vengid bi 'the blood of the smytere.

19 The niy kynesman of hym that is slayn schal sle the mansleere; anoon as he takith hym, 'that is, the manquellere, he schal sle hym.

20 If bi haterede a man hurtlith, 'ethir schoufith, 'a man, ethir castith ony thing in to hym bi aspiyngis,

21 ether whanne he was enemy, smoot with hond, and he is deed, the smytere schal be gilti of mansleyng. The kynesman 'of him that is slayn, anoon as he findith him, 'that is, the sleere, schal sle hym.

22 That if bi sudeyn caas, and without hatrede and enemytees,

23 he doith ony thing of these;

24 and this is preued in heryng 'of the puple, and the question of blood is discussid bitwixe the smytere and the kynesman,

25 the innocent schal be delyuered fro the hond of the vengere, and bi sentence of iugis he schal be led ayen in to the citee, to which he fledde, and he schal dwelle there, til the grete preest die, which is anoyntid with oile.

26 If the sleere is foundun with out the coostis 'of the citees that ben asigned to exilid men,

27 and is slayn of him that is vengere, he that sleeth him, 'that is, the exilid man, schal be with out gilt;

28 for the exilid man ouyte sitte in the citee 'til to the 'deth of the bischop; forsothe aftir that thilke bischop is deed, the mansleere schal turne ayen in to his lond.

29 These schulen be euerlastynge and lawful thingis in alle youre dwellyngis.

30 A mansleere schal be punyschid vndur witnessis; no man schal 'be dampned at the witnessyng of o man.

31 Ye schulen not take prijs of him which is gilti of blood, anoon and he schal die.

32 Men exilid, and fugityues, schulen not mow turne ayen in ony maner in to her citees, bifore the deeth of the bischop, lest ye defoulen the lond of youre abitacioun,

33 which is defoulid bi the blood of innocent men; and it may not be clensid in other maner, no but bi the blood of hym, that schedde the blood of anothir man.

34 And so youre possessioun schal be clensid, for Y schal dwelle with you; for Y am the Lord, that dwelle among the sones of Israel.

CAP 36

1 Forsothe and the princes of the meynees of Galaad sone of Machir, sone of Manasses, of the generacioun of the sones of Joseph, neiyiden, and spaken to Moises bifor the princes of Israel,

2 and seiden, The Lord comaundide to thee oure lord, that thou schuldist departe the lond bi lot to the sones of Israel, and that thou schuldist yyue to the douytris of Salphaat, oure brothir, possessioun due to the fadir.

3 And if men of anothir lynage schulen take to wyues these douytris, her possessioun schal sue, and it schal be translatid to anothir lynage, and schal be decreessid fro oure eritage;

4 and so it schal be doon, that whanne the iubilee, that is, the fiftithe yeer of remyssioun, cometh, the departyng of lottis be schent, and that the possessioun of othere men passe to othere men.

5 Moises answeride to the sones of Israel, and seide, for the Lord comaundide, The lynage of the sones of Joseph spak riytfuli,

6 and this lawe is denounsid of the Lord on the douytris of Salphaat; be thei weddid to whiche men thei wolen, oneli to the men of her lynage;

7 lest the possessioun of the sones of Joseph be meddlid fro lynage in to lynage. For alle men schulen wedde wyues of her lynage and kynrede;

8 and alle wymmen schulen take hosebondis of the same lynage, that the erytage dwelle in meynees,

9 and lynagis be not meddlid to hem silf, but dwelle so,

10 as tho ben departid of the Lord. And the douytris of Salphaat diden, as it was comaundid to hem.

11 And Maala, and Thersa, and Egla, and Melcha, and Noha, weren weddid to the sones of her fadris brother,

12 of the meynee of Manaasses, that was 'the sone of Joseph, and the possessioun that was youun to hem, dwellide in the lynage and meynee of her fadir.

13 These ben the comaundementis and domes, whiche the Lord comaundide, bi the hond of Moyses, to the sones of Israel, in the feeldi places of Moab, aboue Jordan, ayens Jericho.

DEUTERONOMY

CAP 1

1 These ben the wordis whiche Moyses spak to al Israel ouer Jordan, in the wildirnesse of the feeld, ayens the reed see, bitwix Pharan and Tophel and Laban and Asseroth, where is ful myche gold,

2 by enleuene daies fro Oreb bi the weie of the hil of Seir, til to Cades Barne.

3 In the fortithe yeer, in the enleuenth monethe, in the firste dai of the monethe, Moises spak to the sones of Israel alle thingis whiche the Lord commandide to hym that he schulde seie to hem,

4 after that he smoot Seon, kyng of Ammorreis, that dwellide in Esebon, and Og, the kyng of Basan, that dwelide in Asseroth and in Edray, ouer Jordan, in the lond of Moab.

5 And Moyses bigan to declare the lawe, and to seie,

6 Oure Lord God spak to vs in Oreb, and seide, It suffisith to you that ye han dwellid in this hil;

7 turne ye ayen, and come ye to the hil of Amorreis, and to othere placis that ben next it; to places of feeldis, and of hillis, and to lowere places ayens the south, and bisidis the brenke of the see, to the lond of Cananeys, and of Liban, 'til to the greet flood Eufrates.

8 Lo, 'he seith, Y haue youe to you; entre ye, and 'welde ye 'that lond on which the Lord swoor to youre fadrys, Abraham, Ysaac, and Jacob, that he schulde yyue it to hem, and to her seed after hem.

9 And Y seide to you in that time, Y may not aloone susteyne you, for youre Lord God hath multiplied you,

10 and ye ben ful many to dai, as the sterris of heuene;

11 the Lord God of youre fadris adde to this noumbre many thousyndis, and blesse you, as he spak.

12 Y may not aloone susteyne youre causis, and birthun, and stryues; yyue ye of you men wise 'in dyuyn thingis,

13 and witti 'in mennus thingis worthi to be don, whose conuersacioun is preued in youre lynagis, that Y sette hem princes to you.

14 Thanne ye answeriden to me, The thing is good which thou wolt do.

15 And Y took of youre lynagis men wise and noble, 'in vertues and kyn; and Y ordeynede hem princis, tribunes, and centuryouns, and quynquagenaries, and denys, whiche schulden teche you all thingis.

16 And Y comaundide to hem, and seide, Here ye hem, and deme ye that that is iust, whether he be a citeseyn, whether a pilgrym.

17 No difference schal be of persones; ye schulen here so a litil man, 'that is, pore, as a greet man, nether ye schulen take the persoone of ony man, for it is the doom of God. That if ony thing semeth hard to you, telle ye to me, and Y schal here.

18 And Y comaundide alle thingis whiche ye ouyten to do.

19 Forsothe we yeden forth fro Oreb, and passiden bi a feerdful deseert, and grettiste wildirnesse, which ye sien, bi the weye of the hil of Ammorrey, as oure Lord God comaundide to vs. And whanne we hadden come in to Cades Barne,

20 Y seide to you, Ye ben comen to the hil of Ammorrey, which youre Lord God schal yyue to you;

21 se thou the lond which thi Lord God schal yyue to thee; 'stie thou, and welde it, as oure Lord God spak to thi fadris; 'nyle thou drede, nether 'drede thou in herte ony thing.

22 And alle ye neiyiden to me, and ye seiden, Sende we men, that schulen biholde the lond, and telle to vs bi what weye we owen stie, and to whiche citees we owen to go.

23 And whanne the word pleside to me, Y sente of you twelue men, of ech lynage oon.

24 And whanne thei hadden go, and hadden stied in to the hilli places, thei camen 'til to the valei of Clustre; and whanne thei hadden biholde the lond,

25 thei token of the fruytis therof, to schewe the plentee, and brouyten 'to vs, and seiden, The lond is good which oure Lord God schal yyue to vs.

26 And ye 'nolden stie, but ye weren vnbileueful to the word of oure Lord God.

27 And ye grutchiden in youre tabernaclis, and ye seiden, The Lord hatith vs, and herfor he ledde vs out of the lond of Egipt, that he schulde bitake vs in the hond of Ammorey, and schulde do awei vs.

28 Whidur schulen we stie? the messangeris maden aferd oure herte, and seiden, A grettiste multitude is, and largere in stature than we; the citees ben greete, and wallid 'til to the heuene; we sien there the sones of Enachym, that is, giauntis.

29 And Y seide to you, 'Nyle ye drede 'with ynne, nether 'drede withoutforth; the Lord God hym silf,

30 which is youre ledere, schal fiyte for you, as he dide in Egipt, while alle men sien.

31 And ye sien in the wildirnesse, thi Lord God bar thee, as a man is wont to bere his litil sone, in al the weie bi which ye yeden til ye camen to this place.

32 And sotheli nether so ye bileueden to youre Lord God, that yede bifor you in the weie,

33 and mesuride the place in which ye ouyten to sette tentis, and schewide in nyyt the weie to you bi fier, and in dai bi a piler of cloude.

34 And whanne the Lord hadde herd the vois of youre wordis, he was wrooth,

35 and swoor, and seide, Noon of the men of this werste generacioun schal se the good lond, which Y bihiyte vndur an ooth to youre fadris,

36 outakun Caleph, the sone of Jephone; for he schal se it, and Y schal yyue to hym the lond on which he trad, and to hise sones, for he suede the Lord.

37 Nether the indignacioun ayens the puple is wondirful, sithen the Lord was wrooth also to me for you, and seide,

38 Nether thou schalt entre thidur, but Josue, the sone of Nun, thi mynystre, he schal entre for thee; excyte and strengthe thou him, and he schal departe the lond bi lot to Israel.

39 Youre litle children, of whiche ye seiden, that thei schulden be led prisoneris, and the sones that kunnen not to dai the diuersite of good and of yuel, thei schulen entre; and Y schal yyue to hem the lond, and thei schulen welde it.

40 Sotheli turne ye ayen, and go ye in to the wildirnesse, bi the weie of the Reed See.

41 And ye answeriden to me, We synneden to the Lord; we schulen stie, and we schulen fiyte, as oure Lord God comaundide. And whanne ye weren arayed with armeris, and yeden 'into the hil, the Lord seide to me,

42 Seie thou to hem, 'Nyle ye stye, nether fiyte ye, for Y am not with you, lest ye fallen bifor youre enemyes.

43 Y spak, and ye herden not; but ye 'weren aduersaries to the comaundement of the Lord, and bolnden with prijde, and stieden in to the hil.

44 Therfor Ammorrey yede out, that dwellide in the hillis, and he cam ayens you, and pursuede you, as bees ben wont to pursue, and killide fro Seir til Horma. And whanne ye turneden ayen,

45 and wepten bifor the Lord, he herde not you, nether wolde asente to youre vois;

46 therfor ye saten in Cades Barne bi myche tyme.

CAP 2

1 And we yeden forth fro thennus, and camen in to the wildirnesse that ledith to the Reed See, as the Lord seide to me; and we cumpassiden the hil of Seir in long tyme.

2 And the Lord seide to me, It sufficith to you to cumpasse this hil;

3 go ye ayens the north.

4 And comaunde thou to the puple, and seie, Ye schulen passe bi the termes of youre britheren, the sones of Esau, that dwellen in Seir, and thei schulen drede you.

5 Therfor se ye diligentli, that ye be not moued ayens hem; for Y schal not yyue to you of the land 'of hem as myche as the steppe of o foot may trede, for Y yaf the hil of Seir in to the possessioun of Esau.

6 Ye schulden bie of hem metis for money, and ye schulen ete; ye schulden drawe, and drynke watir bouyt.

7 Thi Lord God blesside thee in al the werk of thin hondis; he knewe thi weye, hou thou passidist this moste wildirnesse, bi fourti yeer; and thi Lord God dwellide with thee, and no thing failide to thee.

8 And whanne we hadden passid bi oure britheren, the sones of Esau, that dwelliden in Seir, bi the weie of the feeld of Elath, and of Asiongaber, we camen to the weie that ledith in to deseert of Moab.

9 And the Lord seide to me, Fiyte thou not ayens Moabitis, nether bigyn thou batel ayens hem, for Y schal not yyue to thee ony thing of the lond 'of hem, for Y yaf Ar in to possessioun to 'the sones of Loth.

10 Emyn, 'that is, griseful men, weren first dwelleris therof, a greet puple, and strong, and so hiy, that thei weren bileued as giantis,

11 of the generacioun of Enachym, and thei weren lijk the sones of Enachym; forsothe Moabitis clepen hem Emyn.

12 Forsothe Horreis dwelliden bifore in Seir, and whanne thei weren put out, and weren doon awey, 'the sones of Esau dwelliden there, as Israel dide in the lond of his possessioun, which the Lord yaf to hym.

13 Therfor we riseden, that we schulden passe the stronde of Zared, and camen to it.

14 Sotheli the tyme in whiche we yeden fro Cades Barne 'til to the passynge of the stronde of Zared, was of eiyte and thretti yeer, til al the generacioun of 'men fiyteris was wastid fro 'the castels, as the Lord hadde swore; whos hond was ayens hem,

15 that thei schulden perische fro the myddis of 'the castels.

16 Forsothe after that alle the fiyteris felden doun,

17 the Lord spak to me, and seide,

18 Thou schalt passe to dai the termes of Moab,

19 the cytee, Ar bi name, and thou schalt neiy in the nyy coost of the sones of Amon; be thou war that thou fiyte not ayens hem, nether be moued to batel; for Y schal not yyue to thee of the lond of the sones of Amon, for Y yaf it to the 'sones of Loth in to possessioun.

20 It is arettid the lond of giauntis, and giauntis enhabitiden therynne sumtyme, whiche giauntis Amonytis clepen Zonym;

21 a myche puple and greet, and of noble lengthe, as Enachym, whiche the Lord dide awey fro the face of hem,

22 and made hem to dwelle for 'tho giauntis, as he dide to the sones of Esau, that dwellen in Seire, 'and dide awai Horreis, and yaf to hem the lond 'of Horreis, which 'the sones of Esau welden 'til in to present tyme.

23 Also men of Capadocie puttiden out Eueys, that dwelliden in Asseryn, 'til to Gaza; which yeden out fro Capadocie, and diden awey Eueis, and dwelliden for hem.

24 Rise ye, and 'passe ye the stronde of Arnon; lo! Y haue bitake in 'thin hond Seon, king of Esebon, of Amorreis; and his lond bigynne thou 'to welde, and smyte thou batel ayens him.

25 To dai Y schal bigynne to sende thi drede and strengthe in to puplis that dwellen vndir al heuene, that whanne thi name is herd, thei drede, and tremble bi the maner of wymmen trauelynge of child, and 'be holdun with sorewe.

26 Therfor Y sente messangeris fro the wildirnesse of Cademoch to Seon, kyng of Esebon; and Y seide with pesible wordis,

27 We schulen passe thorou thi lond, we schulen go in the comyn weie; we schulen not bowe nether to the riyt side, nether to the left side.

28 Sille thow metis 'to vs for prijs, that we ete; yif thow watir for money, and so we schulen drynke. Oneli it is that thou graunte passage to vs,

29 as the sones of Esau diden, that dwellen in Seir, and as Moabitis diden, that dwellen in Ar, til we comen to Jordan, and passen to the lond which oure Lord God schal yyue to vs.

30 And Seon, kyng of Esebon, nolde yyue passage 'to vs; for thi Lord God made hard his spirit, and made sad in yuel 'the herte of hym, that he schulde be bitakun in to thin hondis, as thou seest now.

31 And the Lord seide to me, Lo, Y bigan to bitake to thee Seon, and his lond; bigynne thou to welde it.

32 And Seon yede out ayens vs with al his puple to batel in Jasa.

33 And oure Lord God bitook hym to vs, and we han smyte hym with hise sones, and al his puple.

34 And we token in that tyme alle the citees, whanne the dwelleris of tho citees, men, and wymmen, and children weren slayn; we leften not in hem ony thing,

35 outakun beestis that camen in to the part of men takynge prey, and outakun spuylis of the cytees whiche we tokun.

36 Fro Aroer, which is on the brenke of the stronde of Arnon, fro the toun which is set in the valey, 'til to Galaad, no town was ether citee, that ascapide oure hondis.

37 Oure Lord God bitook alle to vs; outakun the lond of the sones of Amon, to which lond we neiyiden not, and outakun alle thingis that liggen to the stronde of Jeboth, and outakun the citees of the munteyns, and alle places fro whiche oure Lord God forbeed vs.

CAP 3

1 And so we turneden, and stieden bi the weie of Basan; and Og, the kyng of Basan, yede out ayens vs with his puple, to fiyte in Edrai.

2 And the Lord seide to me, Drede thou not hym, for he is bitakun in thin hond, with al his puple, and his lond; and thou schalt do to hym, as thou didist to Seon, kyng of Ammoreis, that dwellide in Esebon.

3 Therfor oure Lord God bitook in oure hondis also Og, kyng of Basan, and al his puple; and we han smyte hym 'til to deeth,

4 and wastiden alle the citees 'of him in o tyme; no town was that ascapide vs; 'we destrieden sixti citees, al the cuntrei of Argob, of the rewme of Og in Basan.

5 Alle the citees weren strengthid with hiyest wallis, and with yatis and barris; with out townes vnnoumbrable, that hadden not wallis.

6 And we diden awey thilke men, as we diden to Seon, kyng of Esebon; and we losten ech citee, and men, and wymmen, and litle children;

7 forsothe we token bi prey beestis, and the spuylis of citees.

8 And we token in that tyme the lond fro the hond of twey kyngis of Ammorreis, that weren biyonde Jordan, fro the stronde of Arnon 'til to the hil of Hermon,

9 'which hil Sidonyes clepen Sarion, and Ammorreis clepen Sanyr.

10 We tooken alle the citees that weren set in the pleyn, and al the lond of Galaad, and of Basan, 'til to Selcha and Edray, citees of the rewme of Og, in Basan.

11 For Og aloone, kyng of Basan, was left of the generacioun of giauntis; and his yrun bed is schewid, which is in Rabath, of the sones of Amon, and hath nyne cubitis of lengthe, and foure cubitis of breede, at the mesure of a cubit of mannus hond.

12 And we weldiden in that tyme the lond, fro Aroer, which is on the 'brynke of the stronde of Arnon, 'til to the myddil paart of the hil of Galaad; and Y yaf the citees 'of hym to Ruben and Gad.

13 Forsothe Y yaf the tother part of Galaad, and al Basan, of the rewme of Og, to the half lynage of Manasses, and al the cuntrei of Argob. Al Basan was clepid the lond of giauntis.

14 Jair, 'sone of Manasses, weldide al the cuntrey of Argob, 'til to the lond of Gesuri and of Machati; and he clepide bi his name Basan Anothiair, that is, the townes of Jair, til in to present dai.

15 Also Y yaf Galaad to Machir; and to the lynagis of Ruben and of Gad Y yaf the lond of Galaad, 'til to the strond of Arnon, the myddil of the stronde,

16 and of the endis 'til to the stronde of Jeboth, which is the terme of 'the sones of Amon.

17 And Y yaf the pleyn of the wildernesse 'til to Jordan, and the termes of Cenereth 'til to the see of deseert, which see is moost salt, at the rotis of the hil of Phasga, ayens the eest.

18 And Y comaundide to you in that tyme, and seide, Youre Lord God yyueth to you this lond in to erytage;

19 alle ye stronge men, without wyues and litle children and beestis, be maad redi, and 'go ye bifor youre brithren, the sones of Israel. For Y knowe that ye han many beestis, and tho schulen dwelle in citees whiche Y yaf to you,

20 til the Lord yyue reste to youre brithren, as he yaf to you, and til thei also welden the lond 'which the Lord schal yyue to hem biyonde Jordan; thanne ech man schal turne ayen in to his possessioun which Y yaf to you.

21 Also Y comaundid to Josue in that tyme, and seide, Thin iyen sien what thingis youre Lord God dide to these twei kyngis; so he schal do to alle rewmes, to whiche thou schalt go; drede thou not hem.

22 And Y preiede the Lord in that tyme,

23 and seide, Lord God, thou hast bigunne to schewe to thi seruaunt thi greetnesse, and strongeste hond,

24 for noon other God is ether in heuene, ether in erthe, that mai do thi werkis, and may be comparisound to thi strengthe.

25 Therfor Y schal passe, and schal se this beeste lond biyende Jordan, and this noble hil and Liban.

26 And the Lord was wrooth to me for you, nethir he herde me, but seide to me, It suffisith to thee; speke thou no more of this thing to me.

27 'Stye thou in to the hiynesse of Phasga, and caste aboute thin iyen to the west, and north, and south, and eest, and biholde, for thou schalt not passe this Jordan.

28 Comaunde thou to Josue, and strengthe thou and coumforte hym; for he schal go bifore this puple, and he schal departe to hem the lond, which thou schalt se.

29 And we dwelliden in the valey ayens the temple of Phegor.

CAP 4

1 And now, thou Israel, here the comaundementis and domes whiche Y teche thee, that thou do tho, and lyue, and that thow entre and welde the lond which the Lord God of youre fadris schal yyue to you.

2 Ye schulen not adde to the word which Y speke to you, nether ye schulen take awei 'fro it; kepe ye the comaundementis of youre Lord God, which Y comaunde to you.

3 Youre iyen sien alle thingis whiche the Lord dide ayens Belphegor; how he alto brak alle the worschiperis 'of hym fro the myddis of you.

4 Forsothe ye that cleuen to youre Lord God lyuen alle 'til in to present day.

5 Ye witen that Y tauyte you the comaundementis and riytfulnessis, as my Lord God comaundide to me; so ye schulen do tho in the lond whiche ye schulen welde,

6 and ye schulen kepe, and schulen fille in werk. For this is youre wisdom and vndurstondyng bifor puplis, that alle men here these comaundementis, and seie, Lo! a wise puple and vnderstondynge! a greet folk!

7 Noon other nacioun is so greet, 'not in noumbre ether in bodili quantite, but in dignite, that hath Goddis neiyynge to it silf, as oure God is redi to alle oure bisechyngis.

8 For whi what other folk is so noble, that it hath cerymonyes and iust domes, and al the lawe which Y schal 'sette forth to dai bifor youre iyen?

9 Therfor kepe thi silf, and thi soule bisili; foryete thou not the wordis whiche thin iyen sien, and falle tho not doun fro thin herte, in alle the daies of thi lijf. Thou schalt teche tho thi sones and thi sones sones.

10 Telle thou the day in which thou stodist bifor thi Lord God in Oreb, whanne the Lord spak to me, and seide, Gadere thou the puple to me, that it here my wordis, and lerne for to drede me in al tyme in which it lyueth in erthe, and teche hise sones.

11 And ye neiyiden to the 'roote of the hille, that brente 'til to heuene; and derknessis, and cloude, and myist weren therynne.

12 And the Lord spak to you fro the myddis of fier; ye herden the vois of hise wordis, and outirli ye sien no fourme.

13 And he schewide to you his couenaunt, which he comaundide, that ye schulden do, and 'he schewide ten wordis, whiche he wroot in two tablis of stoon.

14 And he comaundide to me in that tyme, that Y schulde teche you cerymonyes and domes, whiche ye owen to do in the lond whiche ye schulen welde.

15 Therfor kepe ye bisili youre soulis; ye sien not ony licnesse in the dai in which the Lord spak to you in Oreb, fro the myddis of the fier;

16 lest perauenture ye be disseyued and make to you a grauun licnesse, ether an ymage of male, ether of female;

17 a licnesse of alle beestis that ben on erthe, ether of bridis fleynge vndur heuene,

18 and of crepynge beestis that ben moued in erthe, ether of fischis that dwellen vndur the erthe in watris; lest perauenture,

19 whanne thin iyen ben reisid to heuene, thou se the sonne, and moone, and alle the sterris of heuene, and be disseyued bi errour, and worschipe tho, 'bi outermer reuerence, and onour, 'bi ynner reuerence, 'tho thingis whiche thi Lord God made of nouyt, in to seruyce to alle folkis that ben vndur heuene.

20 Forsothe the Lord took you, and ledde out of the yrun furneys of Egipt, that he schulde haue a puple of eritage, as it is in 'present dai.

21 And the Lord was wrooth ayens me for youre wordis, and swoor that Y schulde not passe Jordan, and schulde not entre in to the beeste lond, which he schal yyue to you.

22 Lo! Y die in this erthe; Y schal not passe Jordan; ye schulen passe, and schulen welde the noble lond.

23 Be thou war, lest ony tyme thou foryete the couenaunt of thi Lord God, which he made with thee, and lest thou make to thee a grauun licness of tho thingis whiche the Lord forbeed to make.

24 For thi Lord God is fier wastynge; 'God, a feruent louyere.

25 If ye gendren sones, and sones of sones, and ye dwellen in the lond, and ye be disceyued, and make to you ony licnesse, and doen yuel bifor youre Lord God, that ye terren hym to greet wrathe,

26 Y clepe witnesses to dai heuene and erthe, 'that is, ech resonable creature beynge in heuene and in erthe, that ye schulen perische soone fro the lond, which ye schulen welde, whanne ye han passid Jordan; ye schulen not dwelle long tyme therynne, but the Lord schal do awey you,

27 and schal scatere 'in to alle hethen men, and ye schulen leeue fewe among naciouns, to whiche the Lord schal lede you.

28 And there ye schulen serue to goddis, that ben maad bi 'the hond of men, to a tre and a stoon, that 'seen not, nether heren, nether eten, nether smellen.

29 And whanne thou hast souyt there thi Lord God, thou schalt fynde hym; if netheles thou sekist with al the herte, and with al the tribulacioun of thi soule.

30 Aftir that alle thingis han founde thee, that ben biforseid, forsothe in the laste tyme, thou schalt turne ayen to thi Lord God, and thou schalt here his vois.

31 For thi Lord God is merciful God; he schal not forsake thee, nethir he schal do awey outirli, nethir he schal foryete the couenaunt, in which he swoor to thi fadris.

32 Axe thou of elde daies that weren bifor thee, fro the day in which thi Lord God made of nouyt man on erthe, axe thou fro that oon ende of heuene 'til to the tother ende therof, if sich a thing was doon ony tyme, ether if it was euere knowun,

33 that a puple herde the vois of God spekynge fro the myddis of the fier, as thou herdist, and siest;

34 if God 'dide, that he entride, and took to him silf a folc fro the middis of naciouns, bi temptaciouns, myraclis, and grete wondris, bi batel, and strong hond, and arm holdun forth, and orrible siytis, bi alle thingis whiche youre Lord God dide for you in Egipt, 'while thin iyen sien;

35 that thou schuldist wite, that the Lord hym silf is God, and noon other is, outakun oon.

36 Fro heuene he made thee to here his vois, that he schulde teche thee; and in erthe he schewide to thee his grettiste fier, and thou herdist the wordis 'of hym fro the myddis of the fier;

37 for he louyde thi fadris, and chees her seed aftir hem. And he ledde thee out of Egipt, and yede bifore in his greet vertu,

38 that he schulde do awei grettiste naciouns, and strongere than thou, in thin entryng, and that he schulde lede thee ynne, and schulde yyue to thee the lond 'of hem in to possessioun, as thou seest in 'present day.

39 Therfor wite thou to dai, and thenke in thin herte, that the Lord him silfe is God in heuene aboue, and in erthe bynethe, and noon other is.

40 Kepe thou hise heestis, and comaundementis, whiche Y comaunde to thee, that it be wel to thee, and to thi sones after thee, and that thou dwelle mych tyme on the lond, which thi Lord God schal yyue to thee.

41 Thanne Moises departide thre citees biyende Jordan at the eest coost,

42 that he fle to tho, that sleeth his neighbore not wilfuli, and was not enemy bifore oon and 'the tother dai, and that he mai fle to summe of these citees;

43 Bosor in the wildirnesse, which is set in the feeldi lond, of the lynage of Ruben; and Ramoth in Galaad, which is in the lynage of Gad; and Golan in Basan, which is in the lynage of Manasses.

44 This is the lawe which Moises 'settide forth bifor the sones of Israel,

45 and these ben the witnessyngis, and cerymonyes, and domes, whiche he spak to the sones of Israel, whanne thei yeden out of Egipt,

46 biyende Jordan, in the valey ayens the temple of Phegor, in the lond of Seon, kyng of Ammorreis, that dwellide in Esebon, whom Moises killide. And the sones of Israel yeden out of Egipt, and weldiden 'the lond of him,

47 and the lond of Og, kyng of Basan, twei kyngis of Ammoreis, that weren biyende Jordan, at the rysyng of the sunne;

48 fro Aroer which is set on the brenke of the stronde of Arnon, 'til to the hil of Seon, which is Hermon;

49 thei weldiden al the pleyn biyende Jordan, at the eest coost, 'til to the see of wildirnesse, and 'til to the rootis of the hil of Phasga.

CAP 5

1 And Moises clepide al Israel, and seide to hym, Here, thou Israel, the cerymonyes and domes, whiche Y speke to dai in youre eeris; lerne ye tho, and 'fille ye in werk.

2 Oure Lord God made a boond of pees with vs in Oreb;

3 he made not couenaunt, 'that is, of lawe writun, with oure fadris, but with vs that ben present, and lyuen.

4 Face to face he spak to vs in the hil, fro the myddis of the fier.

5 Y was recouncelere and mediatour bitwixe God and you in that tyme, that Y schulde telle to you the wordis 'of hym, for ye dredden the fier, and 'stieden not in to the hil. And 'the Lord seide,

6 Y am thi Lord God, that ladde thee out of the lond of Egipt, fro the hows of seruage.

7 Thou schalt not haue alien Goddis in my siyt.

8 Thou schalt not make to thee a grauun ymage, nether a licnesse of alle thingis that ben in heuene aboue, and that ben in erthe bynethe, and that lyuen in watris vndur erthe;

9 thou schalt not herie tho, 'and thou schalt not worschipe tho; for Y am thi Lord God, 'God a feruent louyer; and Y yelde the wickidnesse of fadris, in to sones in to the thridde and the fourthe generacioun to hem that haten me,

10 and Y do mersy in to many thousyndis to hem that louen me, and kepen myn heestis.

11 Thou schalt not mystake the name of thi Lord God in veyn, for he schal not be vnpunyschid, that takith the name of God on a veyn thing.

12 Kepe thou the 'day of sabat that thou halewe it, as thi Lord God comaundide to thee.

13 In sixe daies thou schalt worche, and thou schalt do alle thi werkis;

14 the seventhe day is 'of sabat, that is the reste of thi Lord God. Thou schalt not do therynne ony thing of werk; thou, and thi sone, and douyter, seruaunt, and handmaide, and oxe, and asse, and 'al thi werk beeste, and the pilgrym which is with ynne thi yatis; that thi seruaunt reste and thin handmaide, as also thou.

15 Bithenke thou, that also thou seruedist in Egipt, and thi Lord God ledde thee out fro thennus, in a strong hond, and arm holdun forth; therfor he comaundide to thee, that thou schuldist kepe the 'dai of sabat.

16 Onoure thi fadir and thi modir, as thi Lord God comaundide to thee, that thou lyue in long tyme, and that it be wel to thee, in the lond which thi Lord God schal yyue to thee.

17 Thou schalt not sle.

18 Thou schalt not do letcherie.

19 And thou schalt not do thefte.

20 Thou schalt not speke fals witnessyng ayens thi neiybore.

21 Thou schalt not coueite 'the wijf of thi neiybore, not hows, not feeld, not seruaunt, not handmayde, not oxe, not asse, and alle thingis that ben hise.

22 The Lord spak these wordis to al youre multitude, in the hil, fro the myddis of fier and of cloude and of myist, with greet vois, and addide no thing more; and he wroot tho wordis in two tablis of stoon, whiche he yaf to me.

23 Forsothe after that ye herden the vois fro the myddis of the derknessis, and sien the hil brenne, alle ye princis of lynagis,

and the grettere men in birthe, neiyiden to me, and seiden, Lo!

24 oure Lord God schewide to vs his maieste and greetnesse; we herden his vois fro the myddis of fier, and we preueden to day that a man lyuede, 'while God spak with man.

25 Whi therfor schulen we die, and schal this gretteste fier deuoure vs? For if we heren more the vois of oure Lord God, we schulen die.

26 What is ech man, that he here the vois of God lyuynge, that spekith fro the myddis of fier, as we herden, and that he may lyue?

27 Rathere neiye thou, and here thou alle thingis whiche oure Lord God schal seie to thee; and thou schalt speke to vs, and we schulen here, and schulen do tho wordis.

28 And whanne the Lord hadde herd this, he seide to me, Y herde the vois of the wordis of this puple, whiche thei spaken to thee; thei spaken wel alle thingis.

29 Who schal yyue 'that thei haue siche soule, that thei drede me, and kepe alle my comaundementis in al tyme, that it be wel to hem and to the sones 'of hem, with outen ende?

30 Go thou, and seye to hem, Turne ye ayen in to youre tentis.

31 Sotheli stonde thou here with me, and Y schal speke to thee alle comaundementis, and cerymonyes, and domes, whiche thou schalt teche hem, that thei do tho in the lond which Y schal yyue to hem in to possessioun.

32 Therfor kepe ye, and 'do ye tho thingis, whiche the Lord God comaundide to you; ye schulen not bowe awey, nether to the riyt side nether to the left side,

33 but ye schulen go bi the weie whiche youre Lord God comaundide, that ye lyue, and that it be wel to you, and that youre daies be lengthid in the lond of youre possessioun.

CAP 6

1 These ben the comaundementis, and cerymonyes, and domes, whiche youre Lord God comaundide that Y schulde teche you, and that ye do tho in the lond to which ye passen ouer to welde;

2 that thou drede thi Lord God, and kepe alle hise comaundementis, and heestis, whiche Y comaunde to thee, and to thi sones, and sones of sones, in alle the daies of thi lijf, that thi daies be lengthid.

3 Thou Israel, here, and kepe, that thou do tho thingis whiche the Lord comaundide to thee, and that it be wel to thee, and thou be multiplied more, as the Lord God of thi fadris bihiyte, to yyue to thee a lond flowynge with mylk and hony.

4 Thou Israel, here, thi Lord God is o God.

5 Thou schalt loue thi Lord God of al thin herte, and of al thi soule, and of al thi strengthe.

6 And these wordis whiche Y comaunde to thee to dai, schulen be in thin herte;

7 and thou schalt telle tho to thi sones, and thou schalt thenke on tho, sittynge in thin hows, and goynge in the weie, slepynge, and rysinge.

8 And thou schalt bynde tho as a signe in thin hond; and tho schulen be, and schulen be moued bifor thin iyen; and thou schalt write tho in the lyntel,

9 and in the doris of thin hows.

10 And whanne thi Lord God hath brouyt thee in to the lond, for which he swoor to thi fadris, to Abraham, Isaac, and Jacob, and hath youe to thee grete citees, and beeste, whiche thou bildidist not,

11 housis fulle of alle richessis, whiche thou madist not, and cisternes, which thou diggedist not, 'places of vynes, and 'places of olyues, whiche thou plauntidist not,

12 and thou hast ete, and art fillid,

13 be war diligentli, lest thou foryete the Lord, that ladde thee out of the lond of Egipt, fro the hows of seruage. Thou schalt drede thi Lord God, and thou schalt serue hym aloone, 'bi seruyce due to God onely, and thou schalt swere bi his name.

14 Ye schulen not go aftir alien goddis, of alle hethen men that ben 'in youre cumpas;

15 for God is a feruent louyere, thi Lord God is in the myddis of thee, lest ony tyme the 'strong veniaunce of thi Lord God be wrooth ayens thee, and do awei thee fro 'the face of the erthe.

16 Thou schalt not tempte thi Lord God, as thou temptidist in the place of temptyng.

17 Kepe thou the comaundementis of thi Lord God, and the witnessyngis, and cerymonyes, whiche he comaundide to thee;

18 and do thou that that is plesaunt and good in the siyt of the Lord, that it be wel to thee, and that thou entre, and welde the beste lond, of which the Lord swoor to thi fadris,

19 that he schulde do awey alle thin enemyes bifor thee, as he spak.

20 And whanne thi sone schal axe thee to morewe, that is, in tyme comyng, and schal seie, What wolen these witnessyn-gis, and cerymonyes, and domes to hem silf, whiche oure Lord God comaundide to vs?

21 thou schalt seie to hym, We weren 'seruauntis of Farao in Egipt, and the Lord ledde vs out of Egipt, in strong hond;

22 and he dide myraclis, and grete wondris, and werste, 'that is, moost peyneful veniaunces, in Egipt, ayens Farao and al his hows, in oure siyt.

23 And he ledde vs out therof, that he schulde yyue to vs led yn, the lond of which he swoor to oure fadris.

24 And the Lord comaundide to vs, that we do alle these law-ful thingis, and drede oure Lord God, that it be wel to vs in alle the daies of oure lijf, as it is to dai.

25 And he schal be merciful to vs, if we schulen do and kepe alle hise heestis, bifor oure Lord God, as he comaundide to vs.

CAP 7

1 Whanne thi Lord God hath lad thee in to the lond, in to which thou schalt entre to welde, and hath do awey many folkis bifor thee, Ethei, and Gergesei, and Ammorrey, Cane-nei, and Pherezei, Euey, and Jebusei; seuene folkis, of myche gretter noumbre than thou art, and strengere than thou;

2 and thi Lord God hath bitake hem to thee, thou schalt smyte hem 'til to deeth, thou schalt not make 'with hem a boond of pees, nether thou schalt haue merci on hem,

3 nether thou schalt felowschipe mariagis with him; thou schalt not yyue thi douyter to the sone 'of hym, nether thou schalt take his douytir to thi sone;

4 for sche schal disceyue thi sone, that he sue not me, and that he serue more alien goddis; and the strong veniaunce of the Lord schal be wrooth, and schal do awei thee soone.

5 But rather thou schalt do these thingis to hem; destrie ye the auteris 'of hem, and breke ye ymagis 'of metal, and kitte ye doun wodis, and brenne ye grauun ymagis.

6 For thou art an hooli puple to thi Lord God; thi Lord God chees thee, that thou be a special puple to hym, of alle puplis that ben on erthe.

7 Not for ye ouercamen in noumbre alle folkis, the Lord is ioyned to you, and chees yow, sithen ye ben fewere than alle puplis;

8 but for the Lord louede you, and kepte the ooth which he swoor to youre fadris; and he ledde you out in strong hond, and ayen bouyte you fro the hows of seruage, fro 'the hows of Farao, kyng of Egipt.

9 And thou schalt wite, that thi Lord God hym silf is a strong God, and feithful, and kepith couenaunt and mersi to hem that louen hym, and to hem that kepen hise comaundementis, in to a thousynde generaciouns;

10 and yeldith anoon to hem that haten hym, so that he destrie hem, and differr no lengere; restorynge anoon to hem that that thei disseruen.

11 Therfor kepe thou the comaundementis, and cerymonyes, and domes, whiche Y comaunde to thee to dai, that thou do.

12 If aftir that thou herist these domes, thou kepist, and doist tho, thi Lord God schal kepe to thee couenaunt, and mersi, which he swoor to thi fadris.

13 And he schal loue thee, and schal multiplie thee, and he schal blesse the fruyt of thi wombe, and the fruyt of thi lond, thi wheete, and vindage, oile, and droues of beestis, and the flockis of thi scheep, on the lond for which he swoor to thi fadris, that he schulde yyue it to thee.

14 Thou schalt be blessid among alle puplis; noon bareyn of euer eithir kynde schal be at thee, as well in men, as in thi flockis.

15 The Lord schal do awei fro thee all ache, 'ether sorewe; and he schal not brynge to thee the worste siknessis of Egipt, whiche thou knewist, but to alle thin enemyes.

16 And thou schalt 'deuoure, that is, distrie, alle puplis, whiche thi Lord God schal yyue to thee; thin iye schal not spare hem, nethir thou schalt serue the goddis 'of hem, lest thei ben in to the fallyng of thee.

17 If thou seist in thin herte, These folkis ben mo than Y, hou may Y do awei hem?

18 'nyle thou drede, but haue thou mynde, what thingis thi Lord God dide to Farao, and alle Egipcians;

19 'he dide the gretteste veniaunces, whiche thin iyen sien, and miraclis and grete wondris, and the strong hond, and arm 'holdun forth, that thi Lord God schulde lede thee out; so he schal do to alle puplis whiche thou dredist.

20 Ferthermore and thi Lord God schal sende venemouse flies in to hem, til he do awei, and destrye alle men, that fled-den thee, and thei schulen not mowe be hid.

21 Thou schalt not drede hem, for thi Lord is in the myddis of thee, grete God, and ferdful.

22 He hym silf schal waste these naciouns in thi siyt, litil and litil, and bi partis; thou schalt not mow do awey 'tho naciouns togidere, lest perauenture beestis of erthe be multi-plied ayens thee;

23 and thi Lord God schal yyue hem in thi siyt, and he schal sle hem, til thei be doon awey outerly.

24 And he schal bitake the kyngis 'of hem in to thin hondis, and thou schalt destrie the names 'of hem vndur heuene; noon schal mow ayenstonde thee, til thou al to-breke hem.

25 Thou schalt brenne in fier the grauun ymagis 'of hem; thou schalt not coueite the siluer and gold, of whiche tho ymagis ben maad, nether thou schalt take of tho ony thing to thee, lest thou offende therfor, for it is abhominacioun of thi Lord God.

26 Nether thou schalt brynge ony thing of the idol in to thin hous, lest thou be maad cursid, as also that idol is; thou schalt

wlate it as filthe, and thou schalt haue it as defoulyng, and filthis of abhomynacioun, for it is cursid.

CAP 8

1 Be thou war diligentli, that thou do ech comaundement which Y comaunde to thee to dai, that ye moun lyue, and be multiplied, and that ye entre, and welde the lond, for which the Lord swoor to youre fadris.

2 And thou schalt haue mynde of al the weie, bi which thi Lord God ledde thee by fourti yeer, bi deseert, that he schulde turmente, and schulde tempte thee; and that tho thingis that weren tretid in 'thi soule schulden be knowun, whether thou woldist kepe hise comaundementis, ethir nay.

3 And he turmentide thee with nedynesse, and he yaf to thee meete, manna which thou knewist not, and thi fadris 'knewen not, that he schulde schewe to thee, that a man lyueth not in breed aloone, but in ech word that cometh 'out of the Lordis mouth, 'that is, bi manna, that cam down 'at the heest of the Lord.

4 Thi cloth, bi which thou were hilid, failide not for eldnesse, and thi foot was not brokun undernethe, lo!

5 the fourtith yeer is; that thou thenke in thin herte, for as a man techith his sone,

6 so thi Lord God tauyte thee, that thou kepe the comaundementis of thi Lord God, and go in hise weies, and drede hym.

7 For thi Lord God schal lede thee in to a good lond, in to the lond of ryueris, and of 'stondynge watris, and of wellis, in whos feeldis and mounteyns the depthis of floodis breken out;

8 in to the lond of wheete, of barli, and of vyneris, in which lond fige trees, and pumgranadis, and 'olyue trees comen forth; in to the lond of oile, and of hony;

9 where thow schalt ete thi breed with out nedynesse, and schalt vse the aboundaunce of alle thingis; of which lond the stonys ben yrun, and metals of tyn ben diggid of the hillis therof;

10 that whanne thou hast ete, and art fillid, thou blesse thi Lord God for the beste lond which he yaf to thee.

11 Therfor kepe thou, and be war, lest ony tyme thou foryete thi Lord God, and dispise hise comaundementis, and domes, and cerymonyes, whiche Y comaunde to thee to dai;

12 lest aftir that thou hast ete, and art fillid, hast bildid faire housis, and hast dwellid in tho,

13 and hast droues of oxun, and flockis of scheep, and plente of siluer, and of gold, and of alle thingis, thine herte be reisid,

14 and thenke not on thi Lord God, that ledde thee out of the lond of Egipt, and fro the hous of seruage,

15 and was thi ledere in the greet wildirnesse and ferdful, in which was a serpent brenninge with blast, and scorpioun, and dipsas, and outirli no 'watris; which Lord ledde out stremes of the hardeste stoon,

16 and fedde thee with manna in the wildirnesse, which manna thi fadris knewen not. And after that the Lord turmentid thee, and preuede, at the last he hadd mersi on thee,

17 lest thou woldist seie in thin herte, My strengthe, and the myyt of myn hond yaf alle these thingis to me.

18 But thenke thou on thi Lord God, that he yaf strengthis to thee, that he schulde fille his couenaunt, of whiche he swoor to thi fadris, as present dai schewith.

19 Forsothe if thou foryetist thi Lord God, and suest aliene goddis, and worschipist hem 'in herte, and onourist 'with outforth, lo! now Y biforseie to thee, that thou schalt perische outerli;

20 as hethen men perischiden, whiche the Lord dide awei in thin entryng, so and ye schulen perische, if ye schulen be vnobedient to the vois of youre Lord God.

CAP 9

1 Here thou, Israel; thou schalt passe Jordan to dai, that thou welde mooste naciouns, and strengere than thou; grete citees, and wallid 'til to heuene;

2 a greet puple, and hiy; the sones of Enachym, whiche thi silf 'siest, and herdist, whiche no man may ayenstonde in the contrarie part.

3 Therfor thou schalt wite to dai, that thi Lord God hym silf schal passe bifor thee; he is a fier deuourynge and wastynge, that schal al to breke hem, and schal do awei, and destrie bifor thi face swiftli, as he spak to thee.

4 Seie thou not in thin herte, whanne thi Lord God hath do hem awey in thi siyt, For my riytfulnesse the Lord brouyte me yn, that Y schulde welde this lond; sithen these naciouns ben doon awey for her wickidnessis.

5 For not for thi riytfulnessis, and equyte of thin herte thou schalt entre that thou welde the lond 'of hem; but for thei diden wickidli, thei weren doon awey, whanne thou entridist, and that the Lord schulde fille his word which he bihiyte vndur an ooth to thi fadris, to Abraham, Isaac, and Jacob.

6 Therfor wite thou that not for thi riytfulnesses thi Lord God yaf to thee this beste lond in to possessioun, sithen thou art a puple of hardeste nol.

7 Haue thou mynde, and foryete not, hou in the wildirnesse thou terridist thi Lord God to greet wraththe; fro that dai in which thou yedist out of Egipt 'til to this place, thou striuedist euere ayens the Lord.

8 For whi also in Oreb thou terridist hym, and he was wrooth, and wolde do thee awei, whanne Y stiede in to the hil,

9 that Y schulde take two tablis of stoon, the tablis of couenaunt which the Lord made with you, and Y continuede in the hil fourti daies and nyytis, and Y eet not breed, and Y drank not watir.

10 And the Lord yaf to me, twey tablis of stoon, euer either wrytun with Goddis fyngur, and conteynynge alle the wordis whiche he spak to you in the hil, fro the myddis of the fier, whanne the cumpany of puple was gaderid togidere.

11 And whanne fourti daies and so many nyytis hadden passid, the Lord yaf to me twei tablis of stoon, tablis of boond of pees;

12 and he seide to me, Rise thou, and go doun for hennys soone, for thi puple, which thou leddist out of Egipt, han forsake swiftli the weie which thou schewidist to hem, and thei han maad to hem a yotun calf.

13 And eft the Lord seide to me, 'Y se that this puple is of hard nol;

14 suffre thou me, that I alto breke hym, and do awey the name 'of hym fro vndur heuene; and Y schal ordeyne thee on a folk which is grettere and strongere than this folk.

15 And whanne Y cam doun fro the hil brennynge, and helde with euer either hond twei tablis of boond of pees, and Y seiy,

16 that ye hadde synned to youre Lord God, and hadden maad to you a yotun calf, and hadden forsake swiftli the weie of God which he schewide to you,

17 Y castide doun the tablis fro myn hondis, and brak tho tablis in youre siyt.

18 And Y felde doun bifor the Lord as 'biforto, in fourti daies and fourti nyytis, and Y eet not breed, 'and drank not watir,

for alle youre synnes whiche ye diden ayens the Lord, and terriden hym to 'greet wraththe;

19 for Y dredde the indignacioun and yre of hym, by which he was stirid ayens you, and wolde do you awey. And the Lord herde me also in this tyme.

20 Also the Lord was wrooth greteli ayens Aaron, and wolde alto breke hym, and Y preiede in lijk maner for hym.

21 'Forsothe Y took youre synne which ye maden, that is, the calf, and brente it in fier, and Y alto brak in gobetis, and droof outerli in to dust, and castide forth in to the stronde, that cam doun fro the hil.

22 Also in the brennyng, and in the temptacioun at the watris of ayenseiyng, and in the Sepulcris of Coueytise, ye terriden the Lord;

23 and whanne Y sente you fro Cades Barne, and seide, 'Stye ye, and welde the lond which Y yaf to you, and ye dispisiden the comaundement of youre Lord God, and ye bileueden not to him, nether ye wolden here his vois;

24 but euere ye weren rebel, fro the day in which Y bigan to knowe you.

25 And Y lay byfore the Lord fourti daies and fourti nyytis, in whiche Y bisouyte hym mekeli, that he schulde not 'do awey you, as he manaasside.

26 And Y preiede, and seide, Lord God, distrye not thi puple, and thin eritage, which thou 'ayen bouytist in thi greetnesse, which thou leddist out of Egipt in strong hond.

27 Haue thou mynde of thi seruauntis, of Abraham, Isaac, and Jacob; biholde thou not the hardnesse of this puple, and the wickidnesse, and the synne therof,

28 lest perauenture the dwelleris of the lond, out of which thou leddist vs, seien, The Lord myyte not bryng hem in to the lond which he bihiyte to hem, and he hatide hem; therfor he ledde hem out that he schulde sle hem in wildirnesse;

29 and thei ben thi puple and thin eritage, which thou leddist out in thi greet strengthe, and in thin arm holdun forth.

CAP 10

1 In that tyme the Lord seide to me, Hewe thou twei tablis of stoon to thee, as the formere weren; and stie thou to me 'in to the hil. And thou schalt make an arke,

2 'ether a cofere, of tree, and Y schal write in the tablis, the wordis that weren in these tablis whiche thou brakist bifore; and thou schalt putte tho tablis in to the arke.

3 Therfor Y made an ark of the trees of Sechim, and whanne Y hadde hewe twei tablis of stoon, at the licnesse of the formere tablis, Y stiede in to the hil, and hadde the tablis in the hondis.

4 And he wroot in the tablis, bi that that he 'hadde writun bifore, ten wordis, whiche the Lord spak to you in the hil, fro the myddis of the fyer, whanne the puple was gaderid, and he yaf the tablis to me.

5 And Y turnide ayen fro the hil, and cam doun, and puttide the tablis in to the arke which Y hadde maad, 'whiche tablis ben there hidur to, as the Lord comaundide to me.

6 Forsothe the sones of Israel moueden tentis fro Beroth of the sones of Jachan in to Mosera, where Aaron was deed, and biried, for whom his sone Eleazar was set in preesthod.

7 Fro thennus thei camen in to Galgad; fro which place thei yeden forth, and settiden tentis in Jehabatha, in the lond of watris and of strondis.

8 In that tyme Y departide the lynage of Leuy, that it schulde bere the arke of boond of pees of the Lord, and schulde stonde bifor hym in seruyce, and schulde blesse in his name til in to present dai.

9 For which thing Leuy hadde not part, nether possession with hise brithren, for the Lord hym silf is his possessioun, as thi Lord God bihiyte to hym.

10 Forsothe Y stood in the hil as bifore, fourti daies and fourti niytis, and the Lord herde me also in this tyme, and nolde leese thee.

11 And he seide to me, Go thou, and go bifor this puple, that it entre, and welde the lond which Y swoor to her fadris, that Y schulde yeue to hem.

12 And now, Israel, what axith thi Lord God of thee, no but that thou drede thi Lord, and go in hise weies, and that thou loue hym, and serue thi Lord God in al thin herte, and in al thi soule;

13 and that thou kepe the comaundementis of thi Lord God, and the cerymonyes of hym, whiche Y comaunde to thee to dai, that it be wel to thee.

14 Lo! heuene is of thi Lord God, and heuene of heuene; the erthe and alle thingis that ben ther ynne ben hise;

15 and netheles the Lord was glued to thi fadris, and louede hem, and he chees her seed after hem, and you of alle folkis, as it is preued to dai.

16 Therfor circumcide ye the prepucie, 'ethir vnclennesse, of youre herte, and no more make ye harde youre nol.

17 For youre Lord God hym silf is God of goddis, and Lord of lordis, 'God greet, and miyti, and feerdful, which takith not persoone, nether yiftis.

18 He makith doom to the fadirles, and modirles, and to the widewe; he loueth a pilgrym, and yyueth to hym lyiflode and clothing.

19 And therfor 'loue ye pilgryms, for also ye weren comelyngis in the lond of Egipt.

20 Thou schalt drede thi Lord God, and thou schalt serue hym aloone, and thou schalt cleue to hym, and thou schalt swere in his name.

21 He is thi preisyng, and thi God, that made to thee these grete dedis, and ferdful, whiche thin iyen siyen.

22 In seuenti men thi fadris yeden doun in to Egipt, and lo! now thi Lord God hath multiplied thee as the sterris of heuene.

CAP 11

1 Therfor loue thi Lord God, and kepe thou hise comaundementis and cerymonyes, domes and heestis, in al tyme.

2 Knowe ye to day tho thingis whiche youre sones knowen not, 'whiche sones sien not the doctryn of youre Lord God, hise grete dedis, and strong hond, and 'arm holdun forth,

3 myraclis and werkis, whiche he dide 'in the myddis of Egipt to Farao, kyng, and to al 'the lond of hym, and to al the oost of Egipcians,

4 and to horsis, and carris; hou the watris of the reed see hiliden hem, whanne thei pursueden you, and the Lord 'dide awei hem 'til in to 'present dai;

5 and whiche thingis the Lord dide to you in wildernesse, til ye camen to this place;

6 and to Dathan and Abiron, 'the sones of Heliab, that was 'the sone of Ruben, whiche the erthe swolewide, whanne his mouth was openyd, with 'the housis and tabernaclis, and al the catel 'of hem which thei hadden, in the myddis of Israel.

7 Youre iyen sien alle the grete werkis of the Lord,

8 whiche he dide, that ye kepe alle hise heestis whiche Y comaunde to dai to you, and that ye moun entre, and welde the lond,

9 to which ye schulen entre, and ye lyue therynne in myche time; which lond, flowynge with mylk and hony, the Lord bihiyte vndur an ooth to youre fadris and to 'the seed of hem.

10 For the lond, to which thou schalt entre to welde, is not as the lond of Egipt, 'out of which thou yedist, where whanne the seed is cast in the maner of gardyns, moist waters ben led;

11 but it is hilli, and feldi, and abidith reynes fro heuene,

12 which lond thi Lord God biholdith, and hise iyen ben therynne, fro the bigynnyng of the yeer 'til to the ende therof.

13 Therfor if ye schulen obeie to myn heestis whiche Y comaunde to dai to you, that ye loue youre Lord God, and serue hym in al youre herte, and in al youre soule;

14 he schal yyue to youre lond reyn tymeful and late, that ye gadere wheete, and wyn, and oile,

15 hey of the feeldis to feede beestis, that ye bothe ete and be fillid.

16 Be ye war, lest perauenture youre herte be disseyued, and ye go awei fro the Lord, and serue alien goddis, and worschipe hem;

17 and the Lord be wrooth, and close heuene, and reynes come not doun, nether the erthe yyue his fruyt, and ye perische swiftli fro the beste lond which the Lord schal yyue to you.

18 Putte ye thes wordis in youre hertes and soules, and honge ye 'tho wordis for a signe in the hondis, and sette ye bitwixe youre iyen.

19 Teche youre sones, that thei thenke on tho wordis, whanne thou sittist in thin hows, and goist in the weie, and lyggist doun, and risist.

20 Thou schalt write tho wordis on the postis, and yatis of thin hous,

21 that the daies of thee and of thi sones be multiplied in the lond which the Lord swoor to thi fadris, that he schulde yyue to hem, as long as heuene is aboue erthe.

22 For if ye kepen the heestis whiche Y comaunde to you, and ye do tho, that ye loue youre Lord God, and go in alle hise weies,

23 and cleue to hym, the Lord schal destrie alle these hethen men bifor youre face, and ye schulen welde tho folkis that ben grettere and strongere than ye.

24 Ech place which youre foot schal trede, schal be youre; fro the deseert, and fro the Liban, and fro the greet flood Eufrates 'til to the west see, schulen be youre termes.

25 Noon schal stonde ayens you; youre Lord God schal yiue youre outward drede and inward drede on ech lond which ye schulen trede, as he spak to you.

26 Lo! Y sette forth in youre siyt to day blissyng and cursyng;

27 blessyng, if ye obeien to the heestis of youre Lord God, whiche Y comaunde to you to dai;

28 cursyng, if ye heren not the heestis of youre Lord God, but goen awei fro the weie which Y schewe now to you, and goen after alien goddis whiche ye knowen not.

29 Sotheli whanne thi Lord God hath brouyt thee in to the lond, to which to enhabite thou goist, thou schalt sette blessyng on the hil Garisym, cursyng on the hil Hebal, whiche hillis ben biyende Jordan,

30 aftir the weie that goith to the goyng doun of the sunne, in the lond of Cananey, that dwellith in the feeldi places ayens Galgala, which is bisidis the valey goynge and entrynge fer.

31 For ye schulen passe Jordan, that ye welde the lond which youre Lord God schal yyue to you, and that ye haue and welde that lond.

32 Therfor se ye, 'that ye fille the cerymonyes and domes, whiche I schal sette to dai in youre siyt.

CAP 12

1 These ben the heestis and domes, whiche ye owen to do, in the lond which the Lord God of thi fadrys schal yyue to thee, that thou welde it, in alle daies in whiche thou schalt go on erthe.

2 Distrie ye alle the places wherynne hethen men whiche ye schulen welde, worschipiden her goddis, on hiy mounteyns, and litle hillis, and vndur ech tre ful of bowis.

3 Distrie ye 'the auteris of hem, and 'breke ye the ymagis; brenne ye the wodis with fier, and al to breke ye the idolis; destrie ye 'the names of hem fro the places.

4 Ye schulen not do so to youre Lord God;

5 but ye schulen come to the place which youre Lord God chees of alle youre lynagis, that he putte his name there, and dwelle therynne;

6 and ye schulen come, and schulen offre in that place youre brent sacrifices, and slayn sacrifices, the dymes, and firste fruytis of youre hondis, and avowis and yiftis, the firste gendrid thingis of oxun, and of scheep.

7 And ye and youre housis schulen ete there in the siyt of youre Lord God; and ye schulen be glad in alle thingis to whiche ye putten hond, in whiche youre Lord God blesside you.

8 Ye schulen not do there tho thingis whiche we don here to dai, ech man that semeth riytful to 'hym silf.

9 For 'til in to present tyme ye camen not to reste and possessioun, which the Lord God schal yyue to you.

10 Ye schulen passe Jordan, and ye schulen dwelle in the lond which youre Lord God schal yyue to you, that ye reste fro alle enemyes 'bi cumpas, and dwelle without ony drede.

11 In the place which youre Lord God chees that his name be therynne. Thidur ye schulen bere alle thingis, whiche Y comaunde, brent sacrifices, and sacrifices, and the dymes, and firste fruytis of youre hondis, and what euere is the beste in yiftis, whiche ye auowiden to the Lord.

12 Ther ye schulen ete bifor youre Lord God, ye, and youre sones and douytris, youre seruauntis, and seruauntessis, and the dekenes, that dwellen in youre citees; for thei han not other part and possessioun among you.

13 Be thou war lest thou offre thi brent sacrifices in ech place which thou seest,

14 but in that place which the Lord chees in oon of thi lynagis thou schalt offre sacrifices, and schalt do what euer thingis Y comaunde to thee.

15 Forsothe if thou wolt ete, and the etyng of fleischis delitith thee, sle thou, and ete, bi the blessyng of thi Lord God, which he yaf to thee in thi citees, whether it is vnclene, 'that is, spottid ether wemmed and feble, ether clene, 'that is, hool in membris and with out wem, which is leueful to be offrid, thou schalt ete as a capret and hert; oneli without etyng of blood,

16 which thou schalt schede out as watir on the erthe.

17 Thou schalt not mowe ete in thi citees the tithis of thi wheete, wyn, and oile, the firste gendrid thingis of droues, and of scheep, and alle thingis whiche thou hast avowid and wolt offre bi fre wille, and the firste fruytis of thin hondis;

18 but thou schalt ete tho bifor thi Lord God, in the place which thi Lord God chees, thou, and thi sone, and douyter,

seruaunt, and seruauntesse, and the dekene that dwellith in thi citees; and thou schalt be glad, and schalt be fillid bifor thi Lord God in alle thingis to whiche thou holdist forth thin hond.

19 Be thou war lest thou forsake the dekene in al tyme, 'in which thou lyuest in erthe.

20 Whanne thi Lord God hath alargid thi termes, as he spak to thee, and thou wolt ete fleischis, whiche thi soule desirith,

21 forsothe if the place is fer, which thi Lord God chees, that his name be there, thou schalt sle of thin oxun, and scheep, whiche thou hast, as 'the Lord comaundide to thee; and thou schalt ete in thi citees as it plesith thee.

22 As a capret and hert is etun, so thou schalt ete tho; bothe a cleene man and vncleene schulen ete therof in comyn.

23 Oneli eschewe thou this, that thou ete not blood; for the blood 'of tho beestis is for the lijf, and therfor thou owist not ete the lijf with fleischis,

24 but thou schalt schede as watir 'the blood on the erthe,

25 that it be wel to thee, and to thi sones after thee, whanne thou hast do that, that plesith in the siyt of the Lord.

26 Sotheli thou schalt take that that thou 'auowidist, and hale-widist to the Lord, and thou schalt come to the place which the Lord chees;

27 and thou schalt offre thin offryngis, fleischis, and blood, on the auter of thi Lord God; thou schalt schede in the auter the blood of sacrifices; forsothe thou schalt ete the fleischis.

28 Kepe thou and here alle thingis whiche Y comaunde to thee, that it be wel to thee, and to thi sones after thee, with outen ende, whanne thou hast do that, that is good and ple-saunt in the siyt of thi Lord God.

29 Whanne thi Lord God hath distryed bifor thi face folkis, to whiche thou schalt entre to welde, and thou hast weldid tho folkis, and hast dwellid in 'the lond of hem,

30 be thou war lest thou sue hem, aftir that thei ben distried, whanne thou entrist, and thou seke 'the cerymonyes of hem, and seie, As these folkis worschipyden her goddis, so and Y schal worschipe.

31 Thou schalt not do in lijk manere to thi Lord God; for thei diden to her goddis alle abhomynaciouns whiche the Lord wlatith, and offriden her sones and douytris, and brenten with fier.

32 Do thou to the Lord this thing oneli which Y comaunde to thee, nethir adde thou ony thing, nether abate.

CAP 13

1 If a prophete risith in the myddis of thee, ethir he that seith hym silf to haue seyn a dreem, and he biforseith a signe and a wondur to comynge aftir,

2 and this that he spak bifallith, and he seith to thee, Go we, and sue alien goddis, whiche thou knowist not, and serue we hem,

3 thou schalt not here the wordis of that prophete, ether of dremere; for youre Lord God assaieth you, that he wite opynli whether ye louen hym ether nay, in al youre herte, and in al youre soule.

4 Sue ye youre Lord, and 'drede ye hym; kepe ye his comaun-dementis, and here ye 'the vois of hym; ye schulen serue hym, and ye schulen cleue to hym.

5 Forsothe thilke prophete, ether the feynere of dremes, schal be slayn; for he spak that he schulde turne you awei fro youre Lord God, that ladde you out of the lond of Egipt, and ayen-bouyte you fro the hous of seruage, that 'thilke prophete schulde make thee to erre fro the weie which thi Lord God

comaundide to thee; and thou schalt do awey yuel fro the myddis of thee.

6 If thi brothir, the sone of thi modir, ether thi sone, ethir thi douyter, ether the wijf which is in thi bosum, ethir thi freend whom thou louest as thi soule, wole counsele thee, and seith priueli, Go we and serue alien goddis, whiche thou knowist not,

7 and thi fadris, of alle the folkis 'in cumpas, that ben niy ether fer, fro the bigynnyng 'til to the ende of the lond,

8 assente thou not to hym, nether here thou, nether thin iyen spare hym, that thou haue mercy,

9 and hide hym, but anoon thou schalt sle hym. Thin hond be fyrst on him and aftir thee al the puple putte to hond.

10 He schal be oppressid with stoonus, and 'schal be slayn; for he wolde drawe thee awei fro thi Lord God, that ledde thee out of the lond of Egipt, fro the hous of seruage,

11 that al Israel here and drede, and do no more ony thing lijk this thing.

12 If thou herist ony men seiynge in oon of thi citees, whiche thi Lord God schal yyue to thee to enhabite,

13 The sones of Belial yeden out fro the myddis of thee, and turneden awei the dwelleris of the citee, and seiden, Go we, and serue alien goddis whiche ye knowen not,

14 enquere thou bisili, and whanne the treuthe of the thing is biholdun diligentli, if thou fyndist that this thing is certeyn, which is seid, and that this abhominacioun is doon in werk,

15 anoon thou schalt smyte the dwelleris of that citee bi the scharpnesse of swerd, and thou schalt 'do it awey, and alle thingis that ben ther ynne, 'til to beestis.

16 Also what euer thing of purtenaunce of houshold is, thou schalt gadere in the myddis of the stretis therof, and thou schalt brenne with that citee, so that thou waste alle thingis to thi Lord God, and it be a biriel euerlastynge; it schal no more be bildid.

17 And no thing of that cursyng schal cleue in thin hond, that the Lord be turned awei fro the yre of his strong veniaunce, and haue mercy on thee, and multiplie thee, as he swoor to thi fadris.

18 Whanne thou hast herd the vois of thi Lord God, thou schalt kepe alle hise heestis whiche Y comaunde to thee to day, that thou do that that is plesaunt in the siyt of thi Lord God.

CAP 14

1 Be ye the sones of youre Lord God; ye schulen not kitte you, nether ye schulen make ballidnesse,

2 on a deed man, for thou art an hooli puple to thi Lord God, and he chees thee that thou be to hym in to a special puple, of alle folkis that ben on erthe.

3 Ete ye not tho thingis that ben vncleene.

4 This is a beeste which ye schulen ete; an oxe, and a scheep, and a goet, an hert,

5 a capret, a 'wielde oxe, tregelafun, 'that is, a beeste in parti lijk 'a buk of geet, and in parti liik an hert, a figarde, an ostrich, a camelioun, 'that is, a beeste lijk in the heed to a camel, and hath white spottis in the bodi as a parde, and 'is lijk an hors in the necke, and in the feet is lijc a 'wilde oxe, and a parde.

6 Ye schulen ete ech beeste that departith the clee 'in to twei partis, and chewith code.

7 Sotheli ye schulen not ete these beestis, of these that che-wen code, and departen not the clee; a camel, an hare, and a cirogrille, 'that is, a beeste ful of prickis, and is more than an

irchoun; for tho chewen code, and departen not the clee, tho schulen be vncleene to you;

8 also a swyn, for it departith the clee, and chewith not code, schal be vncleene; ye schulen not ete the fleischis of tho, and ye schulen not touche the deed bodies.

9 Ye schulen ete these thingis, of alle that dwellen in watris; ete ye tho thingis that han fynnes and scalis;

10 ete ye not tho thingis that ben with out fynnes and scalis, for tho ben vncleene.

11 Ete ye alle clene briddis;

12 ete ye not vncleene briddis, that is, an egle, and a gripe,

13 and an aliete, ixon, 'that is, a whijt brid lesse than a vultur, and is of the 'kynde of vultris, and a vultur, and a kite bi his kynde,

14 and al thing of rauenys kynde,

15 and a strucioun, and a nyyt crowe, and a lare,

16 and an hauk bi his kynde, a fawcun,

17 and a swan, and a siconye, and a dippere, a pursirioun, and a reremous, a cormeraunt,

18 and a caladrie, alle in her kynde; also a lapwynke and a backe.

19 And al thing that crepith, and hath fynnes, schal be vncleene, and schal not be etun.

20 Ete ye al thing that is cleene; sotheli what euer thing is deed bi it silf, ete ye not therof.

21 Yyue thou to the pilgrym which is with ynne thi yatis, that he ete, ether sille thou to hym, for thou art the hooli puple of thi Lord God. Thou schalt not sethe a kyde in 'the mylk of his modir.

22 Thou schalt departe the tenthe part of alle thi fruytis that comen forth in the lond bi ech yeer;

23 and thou schal ete in the siyt of thi Lord God, in the place which he chees, that his name be clepid therynne; thou schalt offre the tithe of thi wheete, wyn, and oile, and the firste gendryd thingis of thi droues, and scheep, that thou lerne to drede thi Lord God in al tyme.

24 Sotheli whanne the wei is lengere, and the place which thi Lord God chees is fer, and he hath blessid thee, and thou maist not bere alle these thingis to that place,

25 thou schalt sille alle thingis, and schalt turne in to prijs, and thou schalt bere in thin hond, and thou schalt go to the place which thi Lord God chees;

26 and thou schalt bie of the same money what euer thing plesith to thee, ethir of droues, ether of scheep; also thou schalt bie wyn, and sidur, and al thing that thi soule desirith; and thou schalt ete bifor thi Lord God, and thou schalt make feeste,

27 thou, and thin hows, and the dekene which is withynne thi yatis; be thou war lest thou forsake hym, for he hath not other part in possessioun.

28 In the thridde yeer thou schalt departe another dyme of alle thingis that growen to thee in that yeer, and thou schalt kepe withynne thi yatis.

29 And the dekene schal come, whych hath noon other part nether possessioun with thee, and the pilgrym, and the fadirles, ether modirles child, and widue, that ben withynne thi yatis, 'schulen come, and schulen ete, and be fillid, that thi Lord God blesse thee, in alle werkis of thin hondis whiche thou schalt do.

CAP 15

1 In the seuenthe yeer thou schalt make remyssioun,

2 that schal be fillid bi this ordre. To whom ony thing is 'dettid, ethir owid of his freend, ether neiybore, and brother, he schal not mowe axe, for it is the yeer of remyssioun of the Lord.

3 Thou schalt axe of a pilgrym and comelyng; thou hast not power to axe of a citeseyn and neiybore;

4 and outerli a nedi man and begger schal not be among you, that thi Lord God blesse thee, in the lond which he schal yyue to thee in to the possessioun.

5 If netheles thou schalt here the vois of thi Lord God, and schalt kepe alle thingis whiche he comaundide, and whiche Y comaunde to dai to thee, he schal blesse thee, as he bihiyte.

6 Thou schalt leene to many folkis, and thou schalt not take borewyng of ony man; thou schalt be lord of ful many naciouns, and no man schal be lord of thee.

7 If oon of thi britheren that dwellen with ynne the yatis of thi citee, in the lond which thi Lord God schal yyue to thee, cometh to pouert, thou schalt not make hard thin herte, nether thou schalt 'drawe to gydere the hond,

8 but thou schalt opene it to the pore man, and thou schalt 'yyue loone to which thou siest hym haue nede.

9 Be thou war lest perauenture wickid thouyt crepe priueli to thee, and thou seie in thin herte, The seuenthe yeer of remyssioun neiyeth; and thou turne awey the iyen fro thi pore brother, and thou nyle yyue to hym the loone that he axith; lest he crie ayens thee to the Lord, and it be maad to thee in to synne.

10 But thou schalt yyue to hym, and thou schalt 'not do ony thing falsly in releuynge 'hise nedis, that thi Lord God blesse thee in al tyme, and in alle thingis to whiche thou schalt sette to hond.

11 Pore men schulen not faile in the lond of 'thin habitacioun; therfor Y comaunde to thee, that thou opene the hond to thi brother nedi and pore, that lyuen with thee in the lond.

12 Whanne thi brothir an Ebrew man, ethir an Ebrew womman, is seeld to thee, and hath serued thee sixe yeer, in the seuenthe yeer thou schalt delyuere hym fre.

13 And thou schalt not suffre hym go awey voide, to whom thou hast yyue fredom;

14 but thou schalt yyue lijflode in the weye, of flockis, and of cornfloor, and of thi pressour, in whiche thi Lord God hath blessid thee.

15 Haue thou mynde that also thou seruedist in the lond of Egipt, and thi Lord God delyurede thee, 'ether made thee free, and therfor Y comaunde now to thee.

16 Forsothe if 'the seruaunt seith, Y nyle go out, for he loueth thee, and thin hows, and feelith that it is wel to hym at thee, thou schalt take 'a nal,

17 and thou schalt peerse his eere in the yate of thin hous, and he schal serue thee til in to the world, 'that is til to the iubilee, ethir fiftithe yeer; also thou schalt do in lijk maner to the handmayde.

18 Thou schalt not turne awei fro hem thin iyen, whanne thou schalt delyure hem fre, for bi the hire of an hirid man thei serueden thee bi sixe yeer; that thi Lord God blesse thee, in alle the werkis whiche thou doist.

19 Of the first gendrid thingis that ben borun in thi droues, and scheep, what euer is of male kynde, thou schalt halewe to thi Lord God. Thou schalt not worche in the firste gendrid thing 'of oxe, and thou schalt not clippe the firste gendrid thinges of scheep.

20 Thou schalt ete tho bi alle yeeris in the siyt of thi Lord God, thou, and thin hows, in the place 'which the Lord chees.

21 Sotheli if it hath a wem, ethir is crokid, ethir is blynd, ethir is foul, ethir feble in ony part, it schal not be offrid to thi Lord God;

22 but thou schalt ete it with ynne the yatis of thi citee, bothe a cleene man and vncleene schulen ete tho in lijk maner, as a capret and an hert.

23 Onely thou schalt kepe this, that thou ete not the blood of tho, but schede out as watir in to erthe.

CAP 16

1 Kepe thou the monethe of newe fruytis, and of the bigyn-nyng of somer, that thou make pask to thi Lord God; for in this monethe thi Lord God ledde thee out of Egipt in the nyyt.

2 And thou schalt offre pask to thi Lord God, of scheep and of oxun, in the place which thi Lord God chees, that his name dwelle there.

3 Thou schalt not ete 'ther ynne breed 'diyt with sourdouy; in seuene daies thou schalt ete breed of affliccioun, with out sourdouy, for in drede thou yedist out of Egipt, that thou haue mynde of the dai of thi goyng out of Egipt, in alle the daies of thi lijf.

4 No thing 'diyt with sourdouy schal appere in alle thi termes by seuene daies, and of the fleischis of that that is offrid in the euentid, schal not dwelle in the firste dai in the morewtid.

5 Thou schalt not mow offre pask in ech of thi citees whiche thi Lord God schal yyue to thee,

6 but in the place which thi Lord God chees, that his name dwelle there; thou schalt offre pask in the euentid, at the goyng doun of the sunne, whanne thou yedist out of Egipt.

7 And thou schalt sethe, and ete, in the place which thi Lord God hath chose, and thou schalt rise in the morewtid of the secunde dai, and thou schalt go in to thi tabernaclis.

8 Bi sixe daies thou schalt ete therf breed; and in the seuenthe dai, for it is the gaderyng of thi Lord God, thou schalt not do werk.

9 Thou schalt noumbre to thee seuene woukis, fro that dai in which thou settidist a sikil in to the corn;

10 and thou schalt halewe the feeste dai of woukis to thi Lord God, a wilful offryng of thyn hond, which thou schalt offre by the blessing of thi Lord God.

11 And thou schalt ete bifore thi Lord God, thou, and thi sone, and thi douytir, and thi seruaunt, and thin handmayde, and the dekene which is with ynne thi yatis, and the come-lynge, and the fadirles ethir modirles child, and the widue, that dwellen with you, in the place 'which thi Lord God chees that his name dwelle there.

12 And thou schalt haue mynde for thou were seruaunt in Egipt, and thou schalt kepe and do tho thingis that ben comaundid.

13 And thou schalt halewe the solempnytee of tabernaclis bi seuene daies, whanne thou hast gaderid thi fruytis of the corn-floor, and pressour.

14 And thou schalt ete in thi feeste dai, thou, and thi sone, and douytir, and thi seruaunt, and handmayde, also the dek-ene, and comelyng, and the fadirles ether modirles child, and the widewe, that ben with ynne thi yatis, 'schulen ete.

15 Bi seuene daies thou schalt halewe feestis to thi Lord God, in the place which the Lord chees; and thi Lord God schal blesse thee, in alle thi fruytis, and in al the werk of thin hon-dis, and thou schalt be in gladnesse.

16 In thre tymes bi the yeer al thi male kynde schal appere in the siyt of thi Lord, in the place which he chees, in the solempnyte of therf looues, and in the solempnyte of woukis, and in the solempnyte of tabernaclis. A man schal not appere voide bifor the Lord;

17 but ech man schal offre vpe this that he hath, bi the blessyng of his Lord God, which he yaf to 'that man.

18 Thou schalt ordeyne 'iugis, and maystris, in alle thi yatis whiche thi Lord God schal yyue to thee, bi ech of thi lynagis, that thei deme the puple bi iust doom,

19 and bowe not in 'to the tother part for fauour, ethir yifte 'ayens equete. Thou schalt not take persoone nether yiftis, for whi yiftis blynden the iyen of wise men, 'and chaungen the wordis of iust men.

20 Thou schalt pursue iustli that that is iust, that thou lyue and welde the lond which thi Lord God schal yyue to thee.

21 Thou schalt not plaunte a wode, and ech tre bi the auter of thi Lord God;

22 nether thou schalt make to thee, and ordeyne an ymage; whiche thingis thi Lord God hatith.

CAP 17

1 Thou schalt not offre to thi Lord God an oxe and a scheep in which is a wem, ether ony thing of vice, for it is abhomina-cioun to thi Lord God.

2 And whanne a man ether a womman, that doon yuel in the siyte of thi Lord God, ben foundun at thee, with ynne oon of thi yatis whiche thi Lord God schal yyue to thee, and thei breken the couenaunt of God,

3 that thei go and serue alien goddis, and worschipe hem, the sunne, and moone, and al the knyythod of heuene, whiche thingis Y comaundide not;

4 and this is teld to thee, and thou herist, and 'enquerist dili-gentli, and fyndist that it is soth, and abhomynacioun is doon in Israel;

5 thou schalt lede out the man and the womman, that diden a moost cursid thing, to the yatis of thy citee, and thei schulen be oppressid with stoonus.

6 He that schal be slayn, schal perische in the mouth of tweyne, ethir of thre witnessis; no man be slayn, for o man seith witnessyng ayens hym.

7 The hond of witnessis schal first sle hym, and the last hond of the tothir puple schal be sent, that thou do awei yuel fro the myddis of thee.

8 If thou perseyuest, that hard and douteful doom is at thee, bitwixe blood and blood, cause and cause, lepre and not lepre, and thou seest that the wordis of iugis with ynne thi yatis ben dyuerse; rise thou, and stie to the place which thi Lord God hath choose;

9 and thou schalt come to the preestis of the kyn of Leuy, and to the iuge which is in that tyme, and thou schalt axe of hem, whiche schulen schewe to thee the treuthe of doom.

10 And thou schalt do, what euer thing thei seien, that ben souereyns in the place which the Lord chees, and techen thee bi the lawe of the Lord;

11 thou schalt sue the sentence of hem; thou schalt not bowe to the riyt side, ether to the lefte.

12 Forsothe that man schal die, which is proud, and nyle obeie to the comaundement of the preest, 'that mynystrith in that tyme to thi Lord God, and to the sentence of iuge, and thou schalt do awei yuel fro the myddis of Israel;

13 and al the puple schal here, and drede, that no man fro thennus forth bolne with pride.

14 Whanne thou hast entrid in to the lond, which thi Lord God schal yyue to thee, and weldist it, and dwellist therynne,

and seist, Y schal ordeyne a kyng on me, as alle naciouns 'bi cumpas han;

15 thou schalt ordeyne hym, whom thi Lord God chesith of the noumbre of thi brethren. Thou schalt not mow make king a man of anothir folk, which man is not thi brother.

16 And whanne the king is ordeyned, he schal not multiplie horsis to hym, nethir he schal lede ayen the puple in to Egipt, nethir he schal be reisid bi the noumbre of knyytis, moost sithen the Lord comaundide to you, that ye turne no more ayen bi the same weie.

17 The kyng schal not haue ful many wyues, that drawen his soule 'to ouer myche fleischlynesse, nether 'he schal haue grete burthuns of siluer and of gold.

18 Forsothe after that he hath sete in the trone of his rewme, he schal write to himsilf the deuteronomy of this lawe in a 'volym ether book, and he schal take 'a saumpler at preestis of 'the kyn of Leuy;

19 and he schal haue it with hym, and he schal rede it in alle the daies of his lijf, that he lerne to drede his Lord God, and to kepe hise wordis and cerymonyes, that ben comaundid in the lawe;

20 nether his herte be reisid in to pride on hise brithren, nether bowe he in to the riyt side, ether left side, that he regne long tyme, he and hise sones on Israel.

CAP 18

1 Preestis and dekenes, and alle men that ben of the same lynage, schulen 'not haue part and eritage with the tother puple of Israel, for thei schulen ete the sacrifices of the Lord, and the offryngis of hym;

2 and thei schulen not take ony othir thing of the possessioun of her britheren; for the Lord hym silf is the 'eritage of hem, as he spak to hem.

3 This schal be the doom of preestis of the puple, and of hem that offren sacrifices; whether 'thei offren an oxe, ether a scheep, thei schulen yyue to the preest the schuldre, and the paunche, the firste fruytis of wheete,

4 and of wyn, and of oile, and a part of wollis of the scheryng of scheep.

5 For thi Lord God chees hym of alle thi lynagis, that he stonde and mynystre to 'the name of the Lord, he and hise sones, with outen ende.

6 If a dekene goith out of oon of thi citees of al Israel, in which he dwellith, 'and wole come and desirith the place which the Lord chees,

7 he schal mynystre in the name of his Lord God as alle hise britheren dekenes, that schulen stonde in that tyme byfore the Lord.

8 He schal take the same part of meetis, 'which and othere dekenes schulen take; outakun that that is due to hym in his citee, bi 'successioun ethir eritage 'of fadir.

9 Whanne thou hast entrid in to the lond which thi Lord God schal yyue to thee, be thou war lest thou wole sue abhomynaciouns of tho folkis;

10 noon be foundun in thee that clensith his sone, ether his douytir, 'and ledith bi the fier, ethir that axith questiouns of dyuynouris 'that dyuynen aboute the auteris, and that taketh hede to dremes and chiteryng of bryddis; nethir ony wicche be,

11 nethir an enchauntere, 'that is, that disseyueth mennus iyen that a thing seme that is not; nether a man take counsel at hem that han a feend spekynge 'in the wombe, nether take

counsel at false dyuynouris nethir seke of deed men the treuthe.

12 For the Lord hath abhomynacioun of alle these thingis, and for siche wickidnessis he schal do awei hem in thin entryng.

13 Thou schalt be perfit and without filthe, with thi Lord God.

14 These hethen men, 'the lond of whiche thou schalt welde, heren hem that worchen bi chiteryng of briddis, and false dyuynouris; forsothe thou art tauyt in other maner of thi Lord God.

15 Thi Lord God schal reise a prophete of thi folk and of thi britheren as me, thou schalt here hym;

16 as thou axidist of thi Lord God in Oreb, whanne the cumpany was gaderid, and thou seidist, Y schal no more here the vois of my Lord God, and Y schal no more se 'this grettiste fier, lest Y die.

17 And the Lord seide to me, Thei spaken wel alle thingis.

18 Y schal reise to hem a prophete, lijk thee, of the myddis of her britheren, and Y schal putte my wordis in his mouth, and he schal speke to hem alle thingis, whiche I schal comaunde to him.

19 Forsothe Y schal be vengere of 'that man, that nyle here the wordis 'of hym, whiche he schal speke in my name.

20 'Sotheli a prophete 'schal be slayn, which is bischrewid with pride, and wole speke in my name tho thingis, whiche Y comaundide not to hym, that he schulde seie, ethir bi the name of alien goddis.

21 That if thou answerist bi pryuy thouyt, Hou may Y vndirstonde the word, which the Lord spak not? thou schalt haue this signe,

22 'The Lord spak not this thing which thilke prophete biforseid in the name of the Lord, 'and it bifallith not, but 'the prophete feynede bi the pride of his soule, and therfor thou schalt not drede hym.

CAP 19

1 Whanne thi Lord God hath distried the folkis, whose lond he schal yyue to thee, and thou hast weldid it, and hast dwellid in the citees and housis therof;

2 thou schalt departe thre citees to thee 'in the myddis of the lond which thi Lord God schal yyue to thee into possessioun.

3 Thou schalt make redi diligentli the weye, and thou schalt departe euenly in to thre partis al the prouynce of thi lond, that he that is exilid for mansleyng, haue 'of nyy whidur he may ascape.

4 This schal be the lawe of a mansleere fleynge, whos lijf schal be kept. If a man smytith vnwityngli his neiybore, and which is preuyd to haue not had ony hatered ayens hym yistirdai and the thridde dai agoon,

5 but to haue go sympli with hym in to the wode to hewe doun trees, and in the fellyng doun of trees the axe fleeth fro the hond, and the yrun slidith fro the helue, and smytith, and sleeth his freend; this man schal flee to oon of the forseid citees, and schal lyue;

6 lest perauenture the next kynesman of hym, whos blood is sched out, be prickid with sorewe, and 'pursue, and take hym, if the weie is lengere, and smyte 'the lijf of hym which is not gilti of deeth; for it is schewid that he hadde not ony hatered bifore ayens hym that is slayn.

7 Therfor Y comaunde to thee, that thou departe thre citees of euene space bitwixe hem silf.

8 Forsothe whanne thi Lord God hath alargid thi termes, as he swoor to thi fadris, and hath youe to thee al the lond which he bihiyte to hem; if netheles thou kepist hise comaundementis,

9 and doist tho thingis whiche Y comaunde to thee to day, that thou loue thi Lord God, and go in hise weies in al tyme, thou schalt adde to thee thre othere citees, and thou schalt double the noumbre of the forseid citees,

10 that gilteles blood be not sched out in the myddis of the lond which thi Lord God schal yyue to thee to haue in possessioun, lest thou be gilti of blood.

11 Forsothe if ony man hatith his neiybore, and settith aspies, 'ether tresours, to his lijf, and risith, and smytith him, and he is deed, and he fleeth to oon of the forseid citees,

12 the eldere men of that citee schulen sende, and 'thei schulen take hym fro the place of refuyt; and thei schulen bitake hym in to the hond of the nexte kynesman of hym, whos blood is sched out,

13 and he schal die, and thou schalt not haue mercy on hym; and thou schalt do awey gilti blood fro Israel, that it be wel to thee.

14 Thou schalt not take, and turne ouer the termes of thi neiybore, which the formere men settiden in thi possessioun, which thi Lord God schal yyue to thee in the lond, 'which lond thou schalt take 'to be weldid.

15 O witnesse schal not stonde ayens ony man, what euer thing it is of synne and of wickidnesse; but ech word schal stonde in the mouth of tweyne ethir of thre witnessis.

16 If a fals witnesse stondith ayens a man, and accusith hym of brekyng of the lawe, bothe,

17 of whiche the cause is, schulen stonde bifor the Lord, in the siyt of preestis, and of iugis, that ben in tho daies.

18 And whanne thei sekynge moost diligentli han founde that the fals witnesse seide a leesyng ayens his brothir,

19 thei schulen yelde to hym, as he thouyte to do to his brother; and thou schalt do awey yuel fro the myddis of thee, that othere men here,

20 and haue drede, and be no more hardi to do siche thingis.

21 Thou schalt not haue mercy on hym, but thou schalt axe lijf for lijf, iye for iye, tooth for tooth, hond for hond, foot for foot.

CAP 20

1 If thou goist out to batel ayens thin enemyes, and seest multitude of knyytis, and charis, and grettere multitude of the aduersarie oost than thou hast, thou schalt not drede hem; for thi Lord God is with thee, that ledde thee out of the lond of Egipt.

2 Sotheli whanne the batel neiyeth now, the preest schal stonde bifor the scheltrun, and thus he schal speke to the puple,

3 Thou, Israel, here to dai, ye han batel ayens youre enemyes; youre herte drede not, 'nyle ye drede; nyle ye yyue stede, drede ye not hem;

4 for youre Lord God is in the myddis of you, and he schal fiyte for you ayens aduersaries, that he delyuere you fro perel.

5 'Also the duykis schulen crie bi alle cumpanyes, 'while the oost schal here, Who is a man that bildide a newe hows, and halewide not it? go he and turne ayen into his hows, lest perauenture he die in batel, and another man halewe it.

6 Who is a man that plauntide a vyner, and not yit made it to be comyn, and of which it is leeueful to alle men to ete? go he, and turne ayen in to his hows, lest perauenture he die in batel, and anothir man be set in his office.

7 Who is a man that spowside a wijf, and 'took not hir 'bi fleischli knowyng? go he, and turne ayen in to his hows, lest perauenture he die in batel, and anothir man take hir.

8 Whanne these thingis ben seid, thei schulen adde othere thingis, and schulen speke to the peple, Who is a ferdful man, and of gastful herte? go he, and turne ayen in to his hows, lest he make 'the hertis of his britheren for to drede, as he is agast bi drede.

9 And whanne the duykis of the oost ben stille, and han maad ende of speking, ech 'of the princis and cheuenteyns of the oost schal make redie his cumpeneyes to batel.

10 If ony tyme thou schalt go to a citee to ouercome it, first thou schalt profire pees to it.

11 If the citee resseyueth, and openeth to thee the yatis, al the puple that is ther ynne schal be saued, and schal serue thee vndur tribut.

12 Sotheli if they nylen make boond of pees, and bigynnen batel ayens thee, thou schalt fiyte ayens it.

13 And whanne thi Lord God hath bitake it in thin hond, thou schalt smyte bi the scharpnesse of swerd al thing of male kynde which is ther ynne,

14 with out wymmen, and yonge children, beestis and othere thingis that ben in the citee. Thou schalt departe al the prey to the oost, and thou schalt ete of the spuylis of thin enemyes, whiche spuylis thi Lord God yaf to thee.

15 Thus thou schalt do to alle the citees, that ben ful fer fro thee, and ben not of these citees which thou schalt take in to possessioun.

16 Sotheli of these citees that schulen be youun to thee, thou schalt not suffre eny to lyue,

17 but thou schalt sle bi the scharpnesse of swerd; that is to seie, Ethei, and Ammorrey, and Cananei, Ferezei, Euey, and Jebusei, as 'thi Lord God comaundide to thee;

18 lest perauenture thei techen you to do alle abhomynaciouns, whiche thei wrouyten to her goddis, and ye doon synne ayens youre Lord God.

19 Whanne thou hast bisegid a citee 'in myche tyme, and hast cumpassid with strengthingis that thou ouercome it, thou schalt not kitte doun trees, of whiche 'me may ete, nether thou schalt waste the cuntrey 'bi cumpas with axis; for it is 'a tree, and not man, nether it may encresse the noumbre of fiyteris ayens thee.

20 Forsothe if onye ben not appil trees, but 'of the feeld, and ben able in to othere vsis, kitte doun, and make thou engynes, til thou take the citee that fiytith ayens thee.

CAP 21

1 Whanne the careyn of a man slayn is foundun in the lond which thi Lord God schal yyue to thee, and 'the gilti of sleyng is vnknowun,

2 the grettere men in birthe and thi iugis schulen go out, and schulen mete fro the place of the careyn the spaces of alle citees 'bi cumpas;

3 and the eldre men of that citee, 'which thei seen to be neer than othere, schulen take of the droue a cow calf, that 'drow not yok, nether kittide the erthe with a schar;

4 and thei schulen lede that cow calf to a scharp 'valey, and ful of stoonys, that was neuere erid, nether resseyuede seed; and in that valey thei schulen kitte the heed of the cow calf.

5 And the preestis, the sones of Leuy, schulen neiye, whiche thi Lord God chees, that thei mynystre to hym, and blesse in his name, and al the cause hange at 'the word of hem; and what euer thing is cleene ethir vncleene, be demed.

6 And the grettere men in birthe of that citee schulen come to the slayn man, and thei schulen waische her hondis on the cow calf, that was slayn in the valei;

7 and thei schulen seie, Oure hondis schedden not out this blood, nether oure iyen sien.

8 Lord, be mercyful to thi puple Israel, whom thou 'ayen brouytist, and arette thou not innocent blood in the myddis of thi puple Israel. And the gilt of blood schal be don awey fro hem.

9 Forsothe thou schalt be alien fro the blood of the innocent which is sched, whanne thou hast do that that the Lord comaundide.

10 If thou goist out to batel ayens thin enemyes, that thi Lord God bitakith hem in thin hond, and thou ledist prisoneris,

11 and thou seest in the noumbre of prisounneris a fair wom- man, and thou louest hir, and wole haue hir to wijf,

12 thou schalt brynge hir in to thin hows; 'which womman schal schaue the heer, and schal kitte the nailes aboute, and sche schal putte awei the clooth,

13 wher ynne sche was takun, and sche schal sitte in thin hows, and schal biwepe hir fadir and modir o monethe; and aftirward thou schalt entre to hir, and schalt sleepe with hir, and sche schal be thi wijf.

14 But if aftirward sche sittith not in thi soule, 'that is, plesith not thi wille, thou schalt delyuere hir fre, nethir thou schalt mowe sille hir for money, nether oppresse bi power, for thou 'madist hir lowe.

15 If a man hath twey wyues, oon loued, and 'the tothir hate- ful, and he gendrith of hir fre children, and the sone of the hateful wijf is the firste gendrid,

16 and the man wole departe the catel bitwixe hise sones, he schal not mowe make the sone of the loued wijf the firste gendrid, and sette bifor the sone of the hateful wijf,

17 but he schal knowe the sone of the hateful wijf the firste gendrid, and he schal yyue to that sone alle thingis double of tho thingis that he hath; for this sone is the begynnyng of his fre children, and the firste gendrid thingis ben due to hym.

18 If a man gendrith a sone rebel, and ouerthewert, which herith not the comaundement of fadir and modir, and he is chastisid,

19 and dispisith to obei, thei schulen take hym, and schulen lede to the eldre men of that citee, and to the yate of doom;

20 and thei schulen seie to hem, This oure sone is ouerthewert and rebel; he dispisith to here oure monestyngis, 'ethir hees- tis, he yyueth tent to glotonyes, and letcherie, and feestis.

21 The puple of the citee schal oppresse hym with stoonus, and he schal die, that ye do awei yuel fro the myddis of you, and that al Israel here, and drede.

22 Whanne a man doith a synne which is worthi to be puny- schid bi deeth, and he is demed to deeth, and is hangid in a iebat,

23 his careyn schal not dwelle in the tre, but it schal be biried in the same dai; for he that hangith in the cros is cursid of God, and thou schalt not defoule thi lond which thi Lord God yaf thee in to possessioun.

CAP 22

1 Thou schalt not se 'thi brotheris oxe, ethir scheep, errynge, and schalt passe, but thou schalt brynge ayen to thi brother.

2 And if thi brother is not nyy, nether thou knowist hym, thou schalt lede tho beestis in to thin hows, and tho schulen be at thee, as long as thi brother sekith tho, and til he resseyue hem.

3 In lijk maner thou schalt do of 'the asse, and clooth, and of ech thing of thi brother, that was lost; if thou fyndist it, be thou not necgligent as of an alien thing.

4 If thou seest that the asse, ethir oxe of thi brothir felde in the weye, thou schalt not dispise, but thou schalt 'reise with hym.

5 A womman schal not be clothid in a mannys clooth, nether a man schal vse a wommannys cloth; for he that doith thes thingis is abhomynable bifor God. If thou goist in the weie,

6 and fyndist a 'nest of a brid in a tree, ethir in the erthe, and fyndist the modir sittynge on the briddis ethir eyrun, thou schalt not holde the modir with 'the children, but thou schalt suffre 'the modir go,

7 and schalt holde the sones takun, that it be wel to thee, and thou lyue in long tyme. Whanne thou bildist a newe hows,

8 thou schalt make a wal of the roof bi cumpas, lest blood be sched out in thin hows, and thou be gilti, if another man slidith, and falle in to a dich.

9 Thou schalt not sowe thi vyner 'of another seed, lest bothe the seed which thou hast sowe, and tho thingis that 'comen forth of the vyner, ben halewid togidere.

10 Thou schalt not ere with an oxe and asse togidere.

11 Thou schalt not be clothid in a cloth, which is wouun togidir of wolle and 'of flex.

12 Thou schalt make litle cordis bi foure corneris in the hem- mys of thi mentil, 'with which thou art hilid.

13 If a man weddith a wijf, and aftirward hatith hir,

14 and sekith occasiouns bi which he 'schal forsake hir, and puttith ayens hir 'the werste name, and seith, Y haue take this wijf, and Y entride to hir, and Y foond not hir virgyn; the fadir and modir of hir schulen take

15 hir, and thei schulen bere with hem the signes of her virgy- nyte to the eldre men of the citee, that ben in the yate;

16 and the fadir schal seie, Y yaf my douytir wijf to this man, and for he hatith hir, he puttith to hir 'the werste name,

17 that he seye, Y foond not thi douytir virgyn; and lo! these ben the signes of virgynyte of my douytir; thei schulen sprede forth a cloth bifor the eldre men of the citee. And the eldere men of that citee schulen

18 take the man, and schulen bete hym,

19 and ferthermore thei schulen condempne hym in an hun- drid siclis of siluer, whiche he schal yyue to the 'fadir of the damysel, for he diffamide the werste name on a virgyn of Israel; and he schal haue hir wijf, and he schal not mowe for- sake hir, in al 'the tyme of his lijf.

20 That if it is soth, that he puttith ayens hir, and virgynyte is not foundun in the damysel, thei schulen caste hir 'out of 'the yatis of

21 the hous of hir fadir; and men of that citee schulen oppresse hir with stoonys, and sche schal die, for sche dide vnleueful thing in Israel, that sche dide fornycacioun in 'the hows of hir fadir; and thou schalt do awey yuel fro the myddis of thee.

22 If a man slepith with 'the wijf of another man, euer eithir schal die, that is, auowter and auowtresse; and thou schalt do awey yuel fro Israel.

23 If a man spousith a damysel virgyn, and a man fyndith hir in the citee, and doith letcherie with hir,

24 thou schalt lede euer eithir to the yate of that citee, and thei schulen be oppressid with stoonus; the damysel schal be stonyd, for sche criede not, whanne sche was in the citee; the man schal 'be stonyd, for he 'made low the wijf of his neiy- bore; and thou schalt do awei yuel fro the myddis of thee.

25 Forsothe if a man fyndith in the feeld a 'damysel, which is spousid, and he takith, and doith letcherie with hir, he aloone schal die;

26 the damysel schal suffre no thing of yuel, nethir is gilti of deeth; for as a theef risith ayens his brothir, and sleeth 'his lijf, so and the damysel suffride; sche was aloone in the feeld,

27 sche criede, and noon was present, that schulde delyuer hir.

28 If a man fyndith a damysel virgyn that hath no spowse, and takith, and doith letcherie with hir, and the thing cometh to the doom,

29 he that slepte with hir schal yyue to 'the fadir of the damysel fifti siclis of siluer, and he schal haue hir wijf, for he 'made hir low; he schal not mow forsake hir, in alle the daies of his lijf.

30 A man schal not take 'the wijf of his fadir, nethir he schal schewe 'the hilyng of hir.

CAP 23

1 A geldyng whanne hise stoonys ben brokun, ethir kit awey, and his yerde is kit awei, schal not entre in to the chirche of the Lord.

2 A child borun of hordom schal not entre in to the chirche of the Lord, 'til to the tenthe generacioun;

3 Ammonytis and Moabitis, yhe aftir the tenthe generacioun, schulen not entre into the 'chirche of the Lord with outen ende;

4 for thei nolden come to you with breed and watir in the weie, whanne ye yeden out of Egipt; and for thei hireden ayens thee Balaam, the sone of Beor, fro Mesopotanye of Sirye, that he schulde curse thee;

5 and thi Lord God nolde here Balaam, and God turnede 'the cursyng of Balaam in to thi blessyng, for he louyde thee.

6 Thou schalt not make pees with hem, nethir thou schalt seke goodis to hem, in alle the daies of thi lijf in to with outen ende.

7 Thou schalt not 'haue abhomynacioun of a man of Ydumye, for he is thi brothir, nethir of a man of Egipt, for thou were a comelyng in the lond of hym.

8 Thei that ben borun of hem, schulen entre in the thridde generacioun in to the 'chirche of the Lord.

9 Whanne thou schalt go out 'in to batel ayens thin enemyes, thou schalt kepe thee fro al yuel thing.

10 If a man is among you, which is defoulid in 'sleep of nyyt, he schal go out of 'the castels;

11 and he schal not turne ayen bifore that he be waischun in watir at euentid, and aftir the goyng doun of the sunne he schal go ayen in to the castels.

12 Thou schalt haue a place without the castels, to which thou schalt go out to nedeful thingis of kynde;

13 and thou schalt bere a litil stake in the girdil; and whanne thou hast sete, thou schalt digge 'bi cumpas, and 'thou schalt hile with erthe thingis 'defied out,

14 where thou art releuyd. For thi Lord God goeth in the myddis of castels, that he diliuere thee, and bitake thin enemyes to thee, that thi castels be hooli, and no thing of filthe appere in tho, lest he forsake thee.

15 Thou schalt not bitake a seruaunt to his lord, which seruaunt fleeth to thee;

16 he schal dwelle with thee in the place that plesith hym, and he schal reste in oon of thi citees; and make thou not hym sori.

17 Noon hoore schal be of the douytris of Israel, nether a letchour of the sones of Israel.

18 Thou schalt not offre the hire of 'an hoore hows, nether the prijs of a dogge, in the hows of thi Lord God, what euer thing it is that thou hast avowid; for euer eithir is abhomynacioun bifor thi Lord God.

19 Thou schalt not leene to thi brothir to vsure money, neither fruytis,

20 nethir ony othir thing, but to an alien. Forsothe thou schalt leene to thi brothir without vsure that that he nedith, that thi Lord God blesse thee in al thi werk, in the lond to which thou schalt entre to welde.

21 Whanne thou makist auow to thi Lord God, thou schalt not tarie to yelde, for thi Lord God schal 'requyre, ether axe, that; and if thou tariest, it schal be arretid to thee in to synne.

22 If thou 'nylt bihete, thou schalt be with out synne.

23 Forsothe thou schalt kepe, and 'do that that yede out onys of thi lippis, as thou bihiytist to thi Lord God, and hast spoke with thin owne wille and thi mouth.

24 If thou entrist in to the vynere of thi neiybore, ete thou grapis, as myche as plesith thee; but bere thou not out with thee.

25 If thou entrist in to 'the corn of thi freend, thou schalt breke 'eeris of corn, and frote togidere with 'the hond; but thou schalt not repe with a sikil.

CAP 24

1 If a man takith a wijf, and hath hir, and sche fyndith not grace bifor hise iyen for sum vilite, he schal write a 'libel, ethir litil book, of forsakyng, and he schal yyue in 'the hond of hir, and he schal delyuere hir fro his hows.

2 And whanne sche goith out, and weddith anothir hosebonde,

3 and he also hatith hir, and yyueth to hir a 'litil booke of forsakyng, and delyuereth hir fro his hows, ethir certis he is deed,

4 the formere hosebonde schal not mow resseyue hir in to wijf, for sche is defoulid, and maad abhomynable bifore the Lord; lest thou make thi lond to do synne, which lond thi Lord God yaf to thee to welde.

5 Whanne a man hath take late a wijf, he schal not go forth to batel, nethir ony thing of comyn nede schal be enioyned to hym, but he schal yyue tent with out blame to his hows, that he be glad in o yeer with his wijf.

6 Thou schalt not take in the stide of wed the lowere and the hiyere queerne stoon of thi brothir, for he puttide his lijf to thee.

7 If a man is takun, 'that is, conuyct in doom, bisili aspiynge to stele his brothir of the sones of Israel, and whanne he hath seeld hym, takith prijs, he schal be slayn; and thou schalt do awey yuel fro the myddis of thee.

8 Kepe thou diligentli, lest thou renne in to the sijknesse of lepre, but thou schalt do what euer thingis the preestis of the kyn of Leuy techen thee, bi that that Y comaundide to hem, and 'fille thou diligentli.

9 Haue ye mynde what thingis youre Lord God dide to Marie, in the weie, whanne ye yede 'out of Egipt.

10 Whanne thou schalt axe of thi neiyebore ony thing which he owith to thee, thou schalt not entre in to his hows, that thou take awei a wed;

11 but thou schalt stonde with out forth, and he schal brynge forth that that he hath.

12 Sotheli if he is pore, the wed schal not dwelle bi nyyt at thee,

13 but anoon thou schalt yelde to hym bifor the goyng doun of the sunne, that he slepe in his cloth, and blesse thee, and thou haue riytfulnesse bifor thi Lord God.

14 Thou schalt not denye the hire of thi brother nedi and pore, ethir of the comelyng that dwellith with thee in thi lond, and is with ynne thi yatis;

15 but in the same dai thou schalt yelde to hym the prijs of his trauel, bifor the goyng doun of the sunne, for he is pore, and susteyneth therof his lijf; lest he crye ayens thee to the Lord, and it be arettid to thee into synne.

16 The fadris schulen not be slayn for the sones, nether the sones for the fadris, but ech man schal die for hys owne synne.

17 Thou schalt not 'peruerte, ethir waiwardli turne, the doom of the comelyng, and of fadirles ethir modirles; nethir thou schalt take awei in the stide of wed the cloth of a widewe.

18 Haue thou mynde, that thou seruedist in Egipt, and thi Lord God delyuerede thee fro thennus; therfor Y comaunde to thee that thou do this thing.

19 Whanne thou repist corn in the feeld, and foryetist, and leeuest a repe, thou schalt not turne ayen to take it, but thou schalt suffre that a comelyng, and fadirles, ethir modirles, and a widewe take awei, that thi Lord God blesse thee in al the werk of thin hondis.

20 If thou gaderist fruytis of olyues, what euer thing leeueth in trees, thou schalt not turne ayen to gadere, but thou schalt leeue to a comelyng, fadirles, ether modirles, and to a widewe.

21 If thou gaderist grapis of the vyner, thou schalt not gadere raisyns that leeuen, but tho schulen falle in to the vsis of the comelyng, of the fadirles, ethir modirles, and of the wydewe.

22 Haue thou mynde that also thou seruedist in Egipt, and therfor Y comaunde to thee, that thou do this thing.

CAP 25

1 If cause is bitwixe ony men, and thei axen iugis, thei schulen yyue the victorie of riytfulnesse to him, whom thei perseyuen to be iust, thei schulen condempne hym of wickidnesse, whom thei perseyuen to be wickid.

2 Sotheli if thei seen hym that synnede, worthi of betyngis, thei schulen caste him doun, and make to be betun bifor hem; also the maner of betyngis schal be for the mesure of synne,

3 so oneli that tho passe not the noumbre of fourti, lest thi brother be to-rent viliche bifore thin iyen, and go awei.

4 Thou schalt not bynde the 'mouth of the oxe tredynge thi fruytis in the corn floor.

5 Whanne britheren dwellen to gidere, and oon of hem is deed with out fre children, the wijf of the deed brother schal not be weddid to anothir man, but his brothir schal take hir, and schal reise seed of his brother.

6 And he schal clepe the firste gendrid sone 'of hir bi the name 'of hym, 'that is, of the deed brothir, that his name be not don awei fro Israel.

7 Forsothe if he nyle take the wijf of his brother, which is due to hym bi lawe, the womman schal go to the yate of the citee; and sche schal axe the grettere men in birthe, and sche schal seie, 'The brother of myn hosebonde nyle reise seed of his brother in Israel, nethir wole take me in to mariage.

8 And anoon thei schulen make hym to be clepid, and thei schulen axe. If he answerith, Y nyle take hir to wijf;

9 the womman schal go to hym bifor the eldre men of Israel, and sche schal take awei the schoo, and sche schal spete in to his face, and schal seie, So it schal be doon to the man, that bildith not 'the hows of his brother;

10 and 'the name of hym schal be clepid in Israel, The hows of the man vnschood.

11 If twei men han strijf bitwixe hem silf, and oon bigynneth to stryue ayens another, and the wijf of 'the tother man wole delyuere hir hosebonde fro the hond of the strongere man, and puttith hond, and 'takith the schamefast membris 'of hym,

12 thou schalt kitte awei 'the hond of hir, nether thou schalt be bowid on hir bi ony mercy.

13 Thou schalt not haue in the bagge dyuerse weiytis,

14 a grettere and a lesse, nether a buyschel more and lesse schal be in thin hows.

15 Thou schalt haue a iust weiyte and trewe, and an euene buyschel 'and trewe schal be to thee, that thou lyue in myche tyme on the lond which thi Lord God schal yyue to thee.

16 For the Lord schal haue hym abhomynable that doith these thingis, and he wlatith, 'ethir cursith, al vnriytfulnesse.

17 Haue thou mynde what thingis Amalech dide to thee in the weie, whanne thou yedist out of Egipt;

18 hou he cam to thee, and killide the laste men of thin oost, that saten wery, whanne thou were disesid with hungur and trauel, and he dredde not God.

19 Therfor whanne thi Lord God hath youe reste to thee, and hath maad suget alle naciouns 'bi cumpas, in the lond which he bihiyte to thee, thou schalt do awei 'the name of hym vndur heuene; be thou war lest thou foryete.

CAP 26

1 And whanne thou hast entrid in to the lond which thi Lord God schal yyue to thee to welde, and thou hast gete it, and hast dwellid therynne,

2 thou schalt take the firste fruytis of alle thi fruytis, and thou schalt putte in a panyere; and thou schalt go to the place which thi Lord God chees, that his name be inwardly clepid there.

3 And thou schalt go to the preest, that schal be in tho daies, and thou schalt seie to hym, Y knowleche to dai bifor thi Lord God, that Y entride in to the lond, for which he swoor to oure fadris, that he schulde yyue it to vs.

4 And the preest schal take the panyere of thin hond, and schal sette bifor the auter of thi Lord God.

5 And thou schalt speke in the siyt of thi Lord God, Sirus pursuede my fadir, 'which fadir yede doun in to Egipt, and was a pilgrym there in feweste noumbre; and he encreesside in to a greet folk, and strong, and of multitude without noumbre.

6 And Egipcians turmentiden vs, and pursueden, and puttiden greuouseste birthuns.

7 And we crieden to the Lord God of oure fadris, which herde vs, and bihelde oure mekenesse, and trauel, and angwischis;

8 and he ledde vs out of Egipt in myyti hond, and arm holdun forth, in grete drede, in myraclis, and grete wondris,

9 and ledde vs in to this place; and yaf to vs a lond flowynge with mylk and hony.

10 And therfor Y offre now to thee the fyrste fruytis of the fruitis of the lond which the Lord yaf to me. And thou schalt leeue tho in the siyt of thi Lord God. And whanne thi Lord God is worchipid,

11 thou schalt ete in alle the goodis whiche thi Lord God yaf to thee and to thin hows, thou, and the dekene, and the comelyng which is with thee.

12 Whanne thou hast fillid the tithe of alle thi fruytis, in the thridde yeer of tithis, thou schalt yyue to the dekene, and to the comelyng, and to the fadirles, ether modirles child, and to widewe, that thei ete with ynne thi yatis, and be fillid.

13 And thou schalt speke in the siyt of thi Lord God, Y haue take awai that that is halewid of myn hows, and Y yaf it to the dekene, and to the comelyng, to the fadirles, ethir modirles child, and to the widewe, as thou comaundidist to me; Y passide not thi comaundementis, Y foryat not thin heest.

14 Y ete not of tho thingis in my morenyng, nether Y departide tho in ony vnclennesse, nethir Y spendide of tho ony thing in biriyng of deed body, 'that is, in makynge feestis therof in biryynge of deed men. Y obeiede to the vois of my Lord God, and Y dide alle thingis as thou comaundidist to me.

15 Bihold thou fro thi seyntuarie, fro the hiy dwellyng place of heuene, and blesse thou thi puple Israel, and the lond which thou hast youe to vs, as thou 'hast swoore to oure fadris; the lond flowynge with mylk and hony.

16 To dai thi Lord God comaundide to thee, that thou do these comaundementis and domes, that thou kepe and fille of al thin herte, and of al thi soule.

17 Thou hast chose the Lord to day, that he be God to thee, and thou go in hise weies, and thou kepe hise cerymonyes, and heestis, and domes, and obeie to his comaundement.

18 Lo! the Lord chees thee to day, that thou be a special puple to hym, as he spak to thee, and that thou kepe alle hise comaundementis;

19 and he schal make thee hiyere than alle folkis, whiche he made in to his preisyng, and name, and glorie; that thou be an holi puple of thi Lord God, as he spak to thee.

CAP 27

1 Forsothe Moyses comaundide, and the eldre men, to the puple of Israel, and seiden, Kepe ye ech 'comaundement which Y comaunde to you to dai.

2 And whanne ye han passid Jordan, in to the lond which thi Lord God schal yyue to thee, thou schalt reyse grete stoonus, and thou schalt make tho pleyn with chalk,

3 that thou mow write in tho alle the wordis of this lawe, whanne Jordan is passid, that thou entre in to the lond which thi Lord God schal yyue to thee, the lond flowynge with mylke and hony, as he swoor to thi fadris.

4 Therfor whanne thou hast passid Jordan, reise thou the stonus whiche Y comaunde to dai to thee, in the hil of Hebal; and thou schalt make tho pleyn with chalk.

5 And there thou schalt bilde an auter to thi Lord God, of stoonys whiche yrun touchide not,

6 and of stonys vnformed and vnpolischid; and thou schalt offre theron brent sacrifices to thi Lord God; and thou schalt offre pesible sacrifices,

7 and thou schalt ete there, and thou schalt make feeste bifor thi Lord God.

8 And thou schalt write pleynli and clereli on the stoonys alle the wordis of this lawe.

9 And Moises and the preestis of the kynde of Leuy seiden to al Israel, Israel, perseyue thou, and here; to day thou art maad the puple of thi Lord God;

10 thou schalt here his vois, and thou schalt do 'the comaundementis, and riytfulnessis, whiche Y comaunde to thee to dai.

11 And Moises comaundide to the puple in that day,

12 and seide, These men schulen stonde on the hil of Garizym to blesse the Lord, whanne Jordan 'is passid; Symeon, Leuy, Judas, Isachar, Joseph, and Benjamyn.

13 And euene ayens these men schulen stonde in the hil of Hebal to curse, Ruben, Gad, and Aser, Zabulon, Dan, and Neptalym.

14 And the dekenes schulen pronounce, and schulen seie 'with hiy vois to alle the men of Israel,

15 Cursid is the man that makith a grauun ymage and yotun togidere, abhomynacioun of the Lord, the werk of 'hondis of crafti men, and schal sette it in priuey place; and al the puple schal answere, and schal seie, Amen!

16 He is cursid that onoureth not his fadir and modir; and al the puple schal seie, Amen!

17 Cursid is he that 'berith ouer the termes of his neiybore; and al the puple schal seie, Amen!

18 Cursid is he that makith a blynde man to erre in the weie; and al the puple schal seie, Amen!

19 He is cursid that peruertith the doom of a comelyng, of a fadirles, ethir modirles child, and of a widewe; and al the puple schal seie, Amen!

20 Cursid is he that slepith with 'the wijf of his fadir, and schewith the hiling of his bed; and al the puple schal seie, Amen!

21 Cursid is he that slepith with ony beeste; and al the puple schal seie, Amen!

22 Cursid is he that slepith with his sistir, the douytir of his fadir, ethir of his modir; and al the puple schal seie, Amen!

23 Cursid is he that slepith with his wyues modir; and al the puple schal seye, Amen!

24 Cursid is he that sleeth pryueli his neiybore; and al the puple schal seie, Amen!

25 Cursid is he that slepith with 'the wijf of his neiybore; and al the puple schal seie, Amen!

26 Cursid is he that takith yiftis, that he smyte the lijf of innocent blood; and al the puple schal seie, Amen!

27 Cursid is he that dwellith not in the wordis of this lawe, nethir 'parfourmeth tho in werk; and al the puple schal seie, Amen!

CAP 28

1 Forsothe if thou herist the vois of thi Lord God, that thou do and kepe alle hise comaundementis, whiche Y comaunde to thee to dai, thi Lord God schal make the hiyere than alle folkis that lyuen in erthe.

2 And alle these blessyngis schulen come on thee, and schulen take thee; if netheles thou herist hise comaundementis.

3 Thou schalt be blessid in citee, and blessid in feeld;

4 blessid schal be the fruyt of thi wombe, and the fruyt of thi lond, and the fruit of thi beestis; 'blessid schulen be the flockis of thi grete beestis, and the fooldis of thi scheep;

5 blessid schulen be thi bernes, and 'blessid schulen be 'thi relifs;

6 thou schalt be blessid entrynge, and goynge out.

7 The Lord schal yyue thin enemyes fallynge in thi siyt, that schulen rise ayens thee; bi o weie thei schulen come ayens thee, and by seuene weies thei schulen fle fro thi face.

8 The Lord schal sende out blessyng on thi celeris, and on alle the werkis of thin hondis; and he schal blesse thee in the lond which thou hast take.

9 The Lord schal reise thee to hym silf in to an hooli puple, as he swoor to thee, if thou kepist the heestis of thi Lord God, and goist in his weies.

10 And alle the puples of londis schulen se, that the name of the Lord is inwardli clepid on thee, and thei schulen drede thee.

11 The Lord schal make thee to be plenteuouse in alle goodis, in fruyt of thi wombe, and in fruyt of thi beestis, in the fruyt of thi lond, which the Lord swoor to thi fadris, that he schulde yyue to thee.

12 The Lord schal opene his beste tresour, heuene, that he yyue reyn to thi lond in his tyme; and he schal blesse alle the werkis of thin hondis; and thou schalt leene to many folkis, and of no man thou schalt take borewyng.

13 The Lord God schal sette thee in to the heed, and not in to the tail, and euere thou schalt be aboue, and not bynethe; if netheles thou herist the comaundementis of thi Lord God, whiche Y comaunde to thee to day, and kepist,

14 and doist, and bowist not awey fro tho, nether to the riyt side nether to the lefte side, nether suest alien goddis, nethir worschipist hem.

15 That if thou nylt here the vois of thi Lord God, that thou kepe and do alle hise heestis, and cerymonyes, whiche Y comaunde to thee to day, alle these cursyngis schulen come on thee, and schulen take thee.

16 Thou schalt be cursid in citee, cursid in feeld.

17 Cursid 'schal be thi berne, and cursid schulen be thi relifs.

18 Cursid schal be the fruit of thi wombe, and the fruyt of thi lond; 'cursid schulen be the drooues of thin oxun, and the flockis of thi scheep.

19 Thou schalt be cursid goynge in, and 'thou schalt be cursid goynge out.

20 The Lord schal sende on thee hungur, and thurst, and blamyng in to alle thi werkis whiche thou schalt do, til he al to-breke thee, and leese swiftli, for thi werste fyndyngis, in whiche thou hast forsake me.

21 The Lord ioyne pestilence to thee, til he waaste thee fro the lond, to which thou schalt entre to welde.

22 The Lord smyte thee with nedynesse, feuyr, and coold, brennynge, and heete, and with corrupt eir, and rust; and pursue thee til thou perische.

23 Heuene which is aboue thee be brasun; and the erthe which thou tredist be yrun.

24 The Lord yyue dust for reyn to thi lond, and aysche come doun fro heuene on thee, til thou be al to-brokun.

25 The Lord yyue thee fallynge bifor thin enemyes; bi o weie go thou ayens hem, and bi seuene weies fle thou, and be thou scaterid bi alle the rewmes of erthe;

26 and thi deed bodi be in to mete to alle volatils of heuene, and to beestis of erthe, and noon be that dryue hem awai.

27 The Lord smyte thee with the botche of Egipt, and 'the Lord smyte the part of bodi wherbi 'ordures ben voyded; also 'the Lord smyte thee with scabbe, and yicchyng, so that thou mayst not be curid.

28 The Lord smyte thee with madnesse, and blyndnesse, and woodnesse of thouyt;

29 and grope thou in mydday, as a blynd man is wont to grope in derknessis; and dresse he not thi weies; in al tyme suffre thou fals chaleng, and be thou oppressid bi violence, nethir haue thou ony that schal delyuere thee.

30 Take thou a wijf, and anothir man sleepe with hir; bilde thou an hows, and dwelle thou not ther ynne; plaunte thou a vyner, and gadere thou not grapis therof.

31 Thin oxe be offrid bifor thee, and ete thou not therof; thin asse be rauyschid in thi siyt, and be not yoldun to thee; thi scheep be youun to thin enemyes, and noon be that helpe thee.

32 Thi sones and thi douytris be youun to another puple, 'while thin iyen seen, and failen at the siyt of hem al day; and no strengthe be in thin hond.

33 A puple whom thou knowist not ete the fruytis of thi lond, and alle thi trauels; and euere be thou suffrynge fals calengis, and be thou oppressid in alle daies,

34 and wondrynge at the ferdfulnesse of tho thingis whiche thin iyen schulen se.

35 The Lord smyte thee with the worste botche in the knees, and in the hyndere partes of the leg; and thou mow not be heelid fro the sole of the foot 'til to the top.

36 And the Lord schal lede thee, and thi kyng, whom thou schalt ordeyne on thee, in to a folc which thou knowist not, thou, and thi fadris; and thou schalt serue there to alien goddis, to a tre, and stoon.

37 And thou schalt be lost in to prouerbe, and fable to alle puplis, to whiche the Lord schal brynge thee yn.

38 Thou schalt caste myche seed in to the erthe, and thou schalt gadere litil; for locustis schulen deuoure alle thingis.

39 Thou schalt plaunte, and schalt digge a vyner, and thou schalt not drynke wyn, nether thou schalt gadere therof ony thing; for it schal be wastid with wormes.

40 Thou schalt haue olyue trees in alle thi termes, and thou schalt not be anoyntid with oile; for tho schulen falle doun, and schulen perische.

41 Thou schalt gendre sones and douytris, and thou schalt not vse hem; for thei schulen be led in to caitifte.

42 Rust schal waaste alle thi trees and fruytis of thi lond.

43 A comelyng, that dwellith with thee in the lond, schal stie on thee, and he schal be the hiyere; forsothe thou schalt go doun, and schalt be the lowere.

44 He schal leene to thee, and thou schalt not leene to hym; he schal be in to the heed, and thou schalt be in to the tail.

45 And alle these cursyngis schulen come on thee, and schulen pursue, and schulen take thee, til thou perische; for thou herdist not the vois of thi Lord God, nether kepist hise comaundementis and cerymonyes, whiche he comaundide to thee.

46 And signes, and grete wondris schulen be in thee, and in thi seed, til in to withouten ende;

47 for thou seruedist not thi Lord God in the ioye and gladnesse of herte, for the abundaunce of alle thingis.

48 Thou schalt serue thin enemye, whom God schal sende to thee in hungur, and thirst, and nakidnesse, and in pouert of alle thingis; and he schal putte an yrun yok on thi nol, til he al to-breke thee.

49 The Lord schal brynge on thee a folk fro fer place, and fro the laste endis of erthe, in to the licnesse of an egle fleynge with bire, of which folc thou maist not vnderstonde the langage;

50 a folk moost greedi axere, that schal not yyue reuerence to an elde man, nethir haue mercy on a litil child.

51 And schal deuoure the fruyt of thi beestis, and the fruytis of thi lond, til thou perischist, and schal not leeue to thee wheete, wyn, and oile, droues of oxun, and flockis of scheep,

52 til he leese thee, and al to-breke in alle thi citees, and til thi sadde and hiye wallis be distried, in whiche thou haddist trust in al thi lond. Thou schalt be bisegid withynne thi yatis in al thi lond, which thi Lord God schal yyue to thee.

53 And thou schalt ete the fruyt of thi wombe, and the fleis-chis of thi sones, and of thi douytris, whiche thi Lord God schal yyue to thee, in the angwisch and distriyng, bi which thin enemye schal oppresse thee.

54 A man delicat of lijf, and 'ful letcherouse, schal haue enuye to his brother, and wijf that liggith in his bosum,

55 lest he yyue to hem of the fleischis of hise sones whiche he schal ete; for he hath noon other thing in biseging and pouert, bi which thin enemyes schulen waaste thee with ynne alle thi yatis.

56 A tendur womman and delicat, that myyte not go on the erthe, nether set a step of foot, for most softnesse and tendirnesse, schal haue enuye to hir hosebonde that liggith in hir bosum, on the fleischis of sone and douyter,

57 and on the filthe of skynnes, wherynne the child is wlappid in the wombe, that gon out of the myddis of hir 'scharis, ethir hipe bonys, and on fre children that ben borun in the same our. Thei schulen ete 'tho children priueli, for the scarsete of alle thingis in bisegyng and distriyng, bi which thin enemy schal oppresse thee with ynne thi yatis.

58 No but thou schalt kepe and do alle the wordis of this lawe, that ben writun in this volym, 'ether book, and schalt drede his gloriouse name and ferdful, that is thi Lord God,

59 the Lord schal encreese thi woundis, and the woundis of thi seed; grete woundis and contynuel, sikenessis worste and euerlestinge.

60 And he schal turne in to thee alle the turmentyngis of Egipt, whiche thou dreddist, and tho schulen cleue to thee.

61 Ferthermore the Lord schal brynge on thee also alle the sorewis and woundis, that ben not writun in the volym of this lawe, til he al to-breke thee.

62 And ye schulen dwelle fewe in noumbre, that weren bifore as the sterris of heuene for multitude, for thou herdist not the vois of thi Lord God.

63 And as the Lord was glad bifore on you, and dide wel to you, and multipliede you; so he schal be glad, 'and schal leese, and distrie you, that ye be takun awei fro the lond, to which thou schalt entre to welde.

64 The Lord schal leese thee in to alle puplis, fro the hiynesse of erthe 'til to the termes therof; and thou schalt serue there to alien goddis, whiche thou knowist not, and thi fadris 'knowen not, to trees and stoonys.

65 Also thou schalt not reste in tho folkis, nether rest schal be to the step of thi foot. For the Lord schal yyue to thee there a ferdful herte, and iyen failynge, and lijf waastyd with morenyng.

66 And thi lijf schal be as hangynge bifore thee; thou schalt drede in nyyt and dai, and thou schal not bileue to thi lijf.

67 In the morewtid thou schalt seie, Who schal yyue the euentid to me? and in the euentid 'thou schalt seie, Who schal yyue the morewtid to me? for the drede of thin herte, bi which thou schalt be maad aferd, and for tho thingis whiche thou schalt see with thin iyen.

68 The Lord schal lede thee ayen bi schipis in to Egipt, by the weie of which he seide to thee, that thou schuldist no more se it. There thou schalt be seeld to thin enemyes, in to seruauntis and 'hand maidis; and noon schal be that schal delyuere thee.

CAP 29

1 These ben the wordis of boond of pees, which the Lord comaundide to Moyses, that he schulde smyte with the sones of Israel in the lond of Moab, outakun that bond of pees, which he couenauntide with hem in Oreb.

2 And Moises clepid al Israel, and seide to hem, Ye sien alle thingis whiche the Lord dide bifor you in the lond of Egipt, to Farao and alle hise seruauntis, and to al his lond;

3 the greet temptaciouns whiche thin iyen sien, 'tho signes, and grete wondris.

4 And the Lord yaf not to you an herte vndurstondynge, and iyen seynge, and eeris that moun here, til in to present dai.

5 He ledde you bi fourti yeer thoruy deseert; youre clothis weren not brokun, nether the schoon of youre feet weren waastid bi eldnesse;

6 ye eetun not breed, ye drunken not wyn and sidur, that ye schulden wite that he is youre Lord God.

7 And ye camen to this place; and Seon, the kyng of Esebon yede out, and Og, the kyng of Basan, and camen to us to batel. And we han smyte hem,

8 and we token awey the lond 'of hem, and we yauen 'the lond to possessioun, to Ruben, and to Gad, and to the half lynage of Manasses.

9 Therfor kepe ye the wordis of this couenaunt, and fille ye tho, that ye vndirstonde all thingis whiche ye schulen do.

10 Alle ye stonden to day bifor youre Lord God, youre princes, and lynagis, and the grettere men in birthe, and tech-eris, al the puple of Israel,

11 fre children, and youre wyues, and comelyngis that dwellen with thee in castels, outakun the heweris of stonus, and outakun hem that beren watris;

12 that thou go in the boond of pees of thi Lord God, and in the ooth which thi Lord God smytith with thee,

13 that he reise thee in to a puple to hym silf, and that he be thi Lord God, as he spak to thee, and as he swoor to thi fadris, to Abraham, Ysaac, and Jacob.

14 And not to you aloone Y smyte this loond of pees, and conferme these othis,

15 but to alle men, present and absent.

16 For ye witen hou we dwelliden in the lond of Egipt, and how we passiden bi the myddis of naciouns; whiche ye passiden,

17 and siyen abhomynaciouns and filthis, that is, idols 'of hem, tre and stoon, siluer and gold, whiche thei worschipiden.

18 Lest perauenture among you be man ether womman, meyne ether lynage, whos herte is turned away to dai fro youre Lord God, that he go, and serue the goddis of tho folkis; and a roote buriounnynge galle and bitternesse be among you;

19 and whanne he hath herd the wordis of this ooth, he blesse hym silf in his herte, and seie, Pees schal be to me, and Y schal go in the schrewidnesse of myn herte; and lest the drunkun take the thirsti,

20 and the Lord forgyue not to hym, but thanne ful greetli his strong veniaunce be feers, and the feruour ayens that man, and alle the cursis that ben writun in this book 'sitte on hym; and 'the Lord do away his name vndur heuene,

21 and waaste hym in to perdicioun fro alle the lynagis of Israel, bi the cursis that ben conteyned in the book of this lawe and of boond of pees.

22 And the generacioun suynge schal seie, and the sones that schulen be borun aftirward, and pilgrimys that schulen come fro fer, seynge the veniauncis of that lond, and the sikenessis bi whiche the Lord turmentide that lond,

23 brennynge 'that lond with brymston and heete of the sunne, so that it be no more sowun, nether bringe forth ony grene thing, in to ensaumple of destriyng of Sodom and of

Gommorre, of Adama and of Seboym, whiche the Lord destriede in his ire and stronge veniaunce.

24 And alle folkis schulen seie, Whi dide the Lord so to this lond? What is the greet ire of his stronge veniaunce?

25 and thei schulen answere, For thei forsoken the couenaunt of the Lord, whiche he couenauntide with her fadris, whanne he ledde hem out of the lond of Egipt,

26 and thei serueden alien goddis, and worschipiden hem, whiche thei knewen not, and to whiche thei weren not youun;

27 therfor the strong veniaunce of the Lord was wrooth ayens this lond, that he brouyte yn on it alle the cursis that ben writun in this book;

28 and he castide hem out of her lond, in ire and strong veniaunce, and in gretteste indignacioun; and he castide forth in to an alien lond, as it is preued to dai.

29 Thingis ben hid of oure Lord God, 'that is, in his bifor-knowing, whiche thingis ben schewid to us, and to oure sones with outen ende, that we do alle the wordis of this lawe.

CAP 30

1 Therfor whanne alle these wordis comen on thee, blessyng ether cursing, which Y settide forth in thi siyt, and thou art led bi repentaunce of thin herte among alle folkis, in to whiche thi Lord God hath scaterid thee,

2 and turnest ayen to hym, and obeiest to hise comaundemen-tis, as Y comaundide to thee to dai, with thi sones, in al thin herte and in al thi soule,

3 thi Lord God schal lede thee ayen fro thi caitifte, and schal haue mercy on thee, and eft he schal gadre thee from alle pup-lis, in to whiche he scateride the bifore.

4 If thou art scaterid to the endis of heuene, fro thennus thi Lord God schal withdrawe thee;

5 and he schal take and schal bringe thee in to the lond which thi fadris weldiden; and thou schalt holde it, and he schal blesse thee, and schal make thee to be of more noumbre than thi fadris weren.

6 Thi Lord God schal circumcide thin herte, and the herte of thi seed, that thou loue thi Lord God in al thin herte and in al thi soule, and maist liue.

7 Forsothe the Lord schal turne alle these cursyngis on thin enemyes, and on hem that haten and pursuen thee.

8 Sotheli thou schalt turne ayen, and schalt here the vois of thi Lord God, and schalt do alle the heestis whiche Y comaunde to thee to dai;

9 and thi Lord God schal make thee to be plenteuouse, in alle the workis of thin hondis, in the children of thi wombe, and in the fruyt of thi beestis, in abundaunce of thi lond, and in largenesse of alle thingis. For the Lord schal turne ayen, that he haue ioye on thee in alle goodis, as he ioyede in thi fadris;

10 if netheles thou herist the voys of thi Lord God, and kepist hise heestis and cerymonys, that ben writun in this lawe, and thou turne ayen to thi Lord God in al thin herte, and in al thi soule.

11 This comaundement whiche Y comaunde to thee to day,

12 is not aboue thee, nethir is set fer, nethir is set in heuene, that thou maist seie, Who of vs may stie to heuene, that he brynge it to vs, and we here, and fille in werk?

13 nether it is set biyende the see, 'that thou pleyne, and seye, Who of vs may passe ouer the see, and brynge it til to vs, that we moun here and do that that is comaundid?

14 But the word is ful nyy thee, in thi mouth and in thin herte, that thou do it.

15 Biholde thou, that to day Y haue set forth in thi siyt lijf and good, and ayenward deeth and yuel;

16 that thou loue thi Lord God, and go in hise weies, and kepe hise heestis, and cerymonyes, and domes; and that thou lyue, and he multiplie thee, and blesse thee in the lond to which thou schalt entre to welde.

17 But if thin herte is turned awey, and thou nylt here, and thou art disseyued bi errour, and worschipist alien goddis,

18 and seruest hem, Y biforseie to thee to dai, that thou schalt perische, and schalt dwelle litil tyme in the lond to which thou schalt entre to welde, whanne thou schalt passe Jordan.

19 Y clepe to day heuene and erthe witnesses, that is, aungels and men, that Y haue set forth to you lijf and deeth, good and yuel, blessyng and cursyng; therfor chese thou lijf, that bothe thou lyue and thi seed,

20 and that thou loue thi Lord God, and obeie to his vois, and cleue to hym, for he is thi lijf, and the lengthe of thi daies; that thou dwelle in the lond, for which the Lord swoor to thi fadris, to Abraham, Isaac, and Jacob, that he schulde yyue it to hem.

CAP 31

1 And so Moises yede, and spak alle these wordis to al Israel,

2 and seide to hem, Y am to dai of an hundrid and twenti yeer, Y may no ferthere go out and go yn, moost sithen also the Lord seide to me, Thou schalt not passe this Jordan.

3 Therfor thi Lord God schal passe bifore thee; he schal do awei these folkis in thi siyt, and thou schalt welde hem; and this Josue schal go bifor thee, as the Lord spak.

4 And the Lord schal do to hem as he dide to Seon, and Og kyng of Ammorreis, and to 'the lond of hem; and he schal do hem awey.

5 Therfor whanne the Lord hath bitake to you also hem, ye schulen do in lijk maner to hem, as Y comaundide to you.

6 Do ye manli, and be ye coumfortid; nyle ye drede in herte, nethir drede ye at the siyt of hem, for thi Lord God hym silf is thi ledere, and he schal not leeue, nether schal forsake thee.

7 And Moyses clepid Josue, and seide to hym bifor al the multitude of the sones of Israel, Be thou coumfortid, and be thou strong; for thou schalt lede this puple in to the lond which the Lord swoor that he schal yyue to 'the fadris of hem; and thou schalt departe it bi lot.

8 And the Lord hym silf whiche is youre ledere, schal be with thee, he schal not leeue, nether schal forsake thee; nyle thou drede, nether drede thou in herte.

9 Therfor Moyses wroot this lawe, and bitook it to the prees-tis, sones of Leuy, that baren the arke of the bond of pees of the Lord, and to alle the eldere men of Israel.

10 And Moyses comaundide to hem, and seide, Aftir seuen yeer, in the yeer of remyssioun, in the solempnete of taberna-clis,

11 whanne alle men of Israel schulen come togidere, that thei appere in the siyt of her Lord God, in the place 'which the Lord chees, thou schalt rede the wordis of this lawe bifor al Israel,

12 while thei heren, and while al the puple is gaderid to gidere, as wel to men, as to wymmen, to litle children, and comelyngis that ben with ynne thi yatis; that thei here, and lerne, and drede youre Lord God, and kepe and fille alle the wordis of this lawe;

13 also that the sones of hem, that now knowen not, moun here, and that thei drede her Lord God in alle daies in whiche

thei lyuen in the lond to whiche ye schulen go to gete, whanne Jordan is passid.

14 And the Lord seide to Moises, Lo! the daies of thi deeth ben nyy; clepe thou Josue, and stonde ye in the tabernacle of witnessyng, that Y comaunde to hym. Therfor Moises and Josue yeden, and stooden in the tabernacle of witnessyng;

15 and the Lord apperide there in a pilere of cloude, that stood in the entryng of the tabernacle.

16 And the Lord seide to Moises, Lo! thou schalt slepe with thi fadris, and this puple schal rise, and schal do fornycacioun aftir alien goddis in the lond, to which lond it schal entre, that it dwelle ther ynne; there it schal forsake me, and schal make void the boond of pees, which Y couenauntide with it.

17 And my strong veniaunce schal be wrooth ayens that puple in that dai, and Y schal forsake it, and Y schal hide my face fro it, and it schal be in to deuouryng; alle yuels and turment- yngis schulen fynde it, so that it seie in that dai, Verili for the Lord is not with me, these yuelis han founde me.

18 Forsothe Y schal hide, and schal hile 'my face in that dai, for alle the yuels 'whiche it dide, for it suede alien goddis.

19 Now therfor write ye to you this song, and 'teche ye the sones of Israel, that thei holde it in mynde, and synge bi mouth; and that this song be to me for a witnessyng among the sones of Israel.

20 For Y schal lede hym in to the lond, for which Y swoor to hise fadris, flowynge with mylk and hony; and whanne thei han ete, and ben fillid, and ben maad fat, thei schulen turne to alien goddis, and thei schulen serue hem; and thei schulen bacbite me, and schulen make voide my couenaunt.

21 Aftir that many yuels and turmentyngis han founde hym, this song schal answere hym for witnessing, which song no foryetyng schal do awey fro the mouth of thi seed. For Y knowe the thouytis therof to day, what thingis it schal do, bifore that Y bringe it in to the lond which Y bihiyte to it.

22 Therfor Moises wroot the song, and tauyte the sones of Israel.

23 And the Lord comaundide to Josue, the sone of Nun, and seide, Be thou coumfortid, and be thou strong; for thou schalt lede the sones of Israel in to the lond which Y bihiyte, and Y schal be with thee.

24 Therfor aftir that Moises wroot the wordis of this lawe in a book, and fillide,

25 he comaundide to Leuytis that baren the ark of boond of pees of the Lord,

26 and seide, Take ye this book, and putte ye it in the side of the arke of boond of pees of youre Lord God, that it be there ayens thee in to witnessyng.

27 For Y knowe thi stryuyng, and thin hardest nol; yit while Y lyuede and entride with you, ye diden euere stryuyngli ayens the Lord; hou myche more whanne Y schal be deed.

28 Gadere ye to me all the grettere men in birthe, and tech- eris, bi youre lynagis, and Y schal speke to hem, herynge these wordis, and Y schal clepe ayens hem heuene and erthe.

29 For Y knowe, that aftir my deeth ye schulen do wickidli, and schulen bowe awei soone fro the weie which Y comaun- dide to you; and yuels schulen come to you in the laste tyme, whanne ye 'han do yuel in the siyt of the Lord, that ye terre hym to ire bi the werkis of youre hondis.

30 Therfor while al the cumpeny of the sones of Israel herde, Moises spak the wordis of this song, and fillide 'til to the ende.

CAP 32

1 Ye heuenes, here what thingis Y schal speke; the erthe here the wordis of my mouth.

2 My techyng wexe togidere as reyn; my speche flete out as dew, as lytil reyn on eerbe, and as dropis on gras.

3 For Y schal inwardli clepe the name of the Lord; yyue ye glorie to oure God.

4 The werkis of God ben perfit, and alle hise weies ben domes; God is feithful, and without ony wickidnesse; God is iust and riytful.

5 Thei synneden ayens hym, and not hise sones in filthis, 'that is, of idolatrie; schrewid and waiward generacioun.

6 Whether thou yeldist these thingis to the Lord, thou fonned puple and vnwijs? Whether he is not thi fadir, that weldide thee, and made, 'and made thee of nouyt?

7 Haue thou minde of elde daies, thenke thou alle genera- ciouns; axe thi fadir, and he schal telle to thee, axe thi grettere men, and thei schulen seie to thee.

8 Whanne the hiyeste departide folkis, whanne he departide the sones of Adam, he ordeynede the termes of puplis bi the noumbre of the sones of Israel.

9 Forsothe the part of the Lord is his puple; Jacob is the litil part of his eritage.

10 The Lord foond hym in a deseert lond, 'that is, priued of Goddis religioun, in the place of orrour 'ethir hidousnesse, and of wast wildirnesse; the Lord ledde hym aboute, and tauyte hym, and kepte as the apple of his iye.

11 As an egle stirynge his briddis to fle, and fleynge on hem, he spredde forth his wyngis, and took hem, and bar in hise schuldris.

12 The Lord aloone was his ledere, and noon alien god was with hym.

13 The Lord ordeynede hym on an hiy lond, that he schulde ete the fruytis of feeldis, that he schulde souke hony of a stoon, and oile of the hardeste roche;

14 botere of the droue, and mylke of scheep, with the fatnesse of lambren and of rammes, of the sones of Basan; and that he schulde ete kydis with the merowe of wheete, and schulde drynke the cleereste blood of grape.

15 The louede puple was 'maad fat, and kikide ayen; maad fat withoutforth, maad fat with ynne, and alargid; he forsook God his makere, and yede awei fro 'God his helthe.

16 Thei terriden hym to ire in alien goddis, and thei excitiden to wrathfulnesse in abhomynaciouns.

17 Thei offriden to feendis, and not to God, to goddis whiche thei knewen not, newe goddis, and freische camen, whiche 'the fadris of hem worschipiden not.

18 Thou hast forsake God that gendride thee, and thou hast foryete 'thi Lord creatour.

19 The Lord siy, and was stirid to wrathfulnesse; for hise sones and douytris terriden hym.

20 And the Lord seide, Y schal hyde my face fro hem, and Y schal biholde 'the laste thingis of hem; for it is a waiward generacioun, and vnfeithful sones.

21 Thei terriden me in hym that was not God, and thei 'ter- riden to ire in her vanytees; and Y schal terre hem in hym, that is not a puple, and Y schal terre hem 'to yre in a fonned folk.

22 Fier, that is, peyne maad redi to hem, is kyndlid in my stronge veniaunce, and it schal brenne 'til to the laste thingis of helle; and it schal deuoure the lond with his fruyt, and it schal brenne the foundementis of hillis.

23 Y schal gadere 'yuels on hem, and Y schal fille myn are-wis in hem.

24 Thei schulen be waastid with hungur, and briddis schulen deuoure hem with bitteriste bityng; Y schal sende in to hem the teeth of beestis, with the woodnesse of wormes drawynge on erthe, and of serpentis.

25 Swerd with outforth and drede with ynne schal waaste hem; a yong man and a virgyn togidre, a soukynge child with an elde man.

26 And Y seide, Where ben thei? Y schal make the mynde of hem to ceesse of men.

27 But Y delayede for the yre of enemyes, lest perauenture 'the enemyes of hem shulden be proude, and seie, Oure hiy hond, and not the Lord, dide alle these thingis.

28 It is a folk with out counsel, and with out prudence;

29 Y wolde that thei saueriden, and 'vnderstoden, and purueiden the laste thingis.

30 How pursuede oon of enemyes a thousynde of Jewis, and tweyne dryuen awey ten thousynde? Whether not therfore for her God selde hem, and the Lord closide hem togidere?

31 For oure God is not as the goddis of hem, and oure ene-myes ben iugis.

32 The vyner of hem is of the vyner of Sodom, and of the subarbis of Gomorre; the grape of hem is the grape of galle, and the clustre is most bittir.

33 The galle of dragouns is the wyn of hem, and the venym of eddris, that may not be heelid.

34 Whether these thingis ben not hid at me, and ben seelid in myn tresouris?

35 Veniaunce is myn, and Y schal yelde to hem in tyme, that the foot of hem slide; the dai of perdicioun is nyy, and tymes hasten to be present.

36 The Lord schal deme his puple, and he schal do merci in hise seruauntis; the puple schal se that the hond of fiyteres is sijk, and also men closid failiden, and the residues ben waas-tid.

37 And thei schulen seie, Where ben 'the goddis of hem, in whiche thei hadden trust?

38 Of whos sacrifices thei eeten fatnessis, and drunkun the wyn of fletynge sacrifices, rise thei and helpe you, and defende thei you in nede.

39 Se ye that Y am aloone, and noon other God is outakun me; Y schal sle, and Y schal make to lyue; Y schal smyte, and Y schal make hool; and noon is that may delyuere fro myn hond.

40 And Y schal reise myn hond to heuene, and Y schal seie, Y lyue with outen ende.

41 If Y schal whette my swerd as leit, and myn hond schal take doom, Y schal yelde veniaunce to myn enemyes, and Y schal quyte to hem that haten me.

42 Y schal fille myn arewis with blood, and my swerd schal deuoure fleischis of the blood of hem that ben slayn, and of the caitifte of the heed of enemyes maad nakid.

43 Folkis, preise ye the puplis of hym, for he schal venie the blood of hise seruauntis, and he schal yelde veniaunce in to the enemyes of hem; and he schal be merciful to the lond of his puple.

44 Therfor Moises cam, and spak alle the wordis of this song in the eeris of the puple; bothe he and Josue, the sone of Nun.

45 And 'he fillide alle these wordis, and spak to alle Israel, and seide to hem,

46 Putte ye youre hertis in to alle the wordis whiche Y wit-nesse to you to day, that ye comaunde to youre sones, to kepe,

and do tho, and to fulfille alle thingis that ben writun in the book of this lawe;

47 for not in veyn tho ben comaundid to you, but that alle men schulden lyue in tho; whiche wordis ye schulen do, and schulen contynue in long tyme in the lond, to which ye schulen entre to welde, whanne Jordan is passid.

48 And the Lord spak to Moises in the same day,

49 and seide, Stie thou in to this hil Abirym, that is, passyng, in to the hil of Nebo, which is in the lond of Moab, ayens Jer-ico; and se thou the lond of Canaan, which Y schal yyue to the sones of Israel to holde, and die thou in the hil.

50 In to which hil thou schalt stie, and schalt be ioyned to thi puplis, as Aaron, thi brother, was deed in the hil of Hor, and was put to his puplis.

51 For ye trespassiden ayens me, in the myddis of the sones of Israel, at the Watris of Ayenseiyng, in Cades of deseert of Syn; and ye halewiden not me among the sones of Israel.

52 Ayenward thou schalt se the lond, and schalt not entre in to it, which Y schal yyue to the sones of Israel.

CAP 33

1 This is the blessing, bi which Moises, the man of God, blesside the sones of Israel bifor his deeth;

2 and seide, The Lord cam fro Syna, and he roos to us fro Seir; he apperide fro the hil of Pharan, and thousandis of sey-ntis with hym; a lawe of fier in his riythond.

3 He louede puplis; alle seyntis ben in his hond, and thei that neiyen to hise feet schulen take of his doctryn.

4 Moisis comaundide lawe 'to vs, eritage of the multitude of Jacob.

5 And the king schal be at the moost riytful, whanne princes of the puple schulen be gaderid togidere with the lynagis of Israel.

6 Ruben lyue, and die not, and be he litil in noumbre.

7 This is the blessyng of Juda; Lord, here thou the vois of Juda, and brynge in hym to his puple; hise hondis schulen fiyte for hym, and the helpere of hym schal be ayens hise adu-ersaries.

8 Also he seide to Leuy, Thi perfeccioun and thi techyng is of an hooly man, whom thou preuedist in temptacioun, and demedist at the Watris of Ayenseiynge;

9 which Leuy seide to his fadir and to his modir, Y knowe not you, and to hise britheren, Y knowe not hem; and knewen not her sones. These kepten thi speche, and these kepten thi couenaunt; A!

10 Jacob, thei kepten thi domes, and 'thou, Israel, thei kepten thi lawe; thei schulen putte encense in thi strong veniaunce, and brent sacrifice on thin auter.

11 Lord, blesse thou the strengthe of hym, and resseyue thou the werkis of his hondis; smyte thou the backis of hise ene-myes, and thei that haten hym, rise not.

12 And he seide to Benjamyn, The moost loued of the Lord schal dwelle tristili in hym, 'that is, in the Lord; he schal dwelle al day as in a chaumbur, and he schal reste bitwixe the schuldris of hym.

13 Also he seide to Joseph, 'His lond is of the Lordis blessyng; of the applis of heuene, and of the dewe, and of watir liggynge bynethe;

14 of the applis of fruytis of the sunne and moone; of the coppe of elde munteyns,

15 and of the applis of euerlastynge litle hillis;

16 and of the fruytis of the lond, and of the fulnesse therof. The blessyng of hym that apperide in the busch come on the

heed of Joseph, and on the cop of Nazarey, 'that is, hooli, among hise britheren.

17 As the first gendrid of a bole is the feirnesse of hym; the hornes of an vnicorn ben the hornes of hym; in tho he schal wyndewe folkis, 'til to the termes of erthe. These ben the multitudis of Effraym, and these ben the thousyndis of Manasses.

18 And he seide to Zabulon, Zabulon, be thou glad in thi goyng out, and, Ysacar, in thi tabernaclis.

19 Thei schulen clepe puplis to the hil, there thei schulen offre sacrifices of riytfulnesse; whiche schulen souke the flowing of the see as mylk, and hid tresours of grauel.

20 And he seide to Gad, Gad is blessid in broodnesse; he restide as a lioun, and he took the arm and the nol.

21 And he siy his prinshed, that 'the techere was kept in his part; which Gad was with the princes of the puple, and dide the riytfulnesses of the Lord, and his doom with Israel.

22 Also he seide to Dan, Dan, a whelp of a lioun, schal flowe largeli fro Basan.

23 And he seide to Neptalym, Neptalym schal vse abundaunce, and he schal be ful with blessyngis of the Lord; and he schal welde the see and the south.

24 Also he seide to Aser, Aser, be blessid in sones, and plese he hise britheren; dippe he his foot in oile.

25 Yrun and bras the scho of hym; as the dai of thi youthe so and thin eelde.

26 Noon other god is as the God of the moost riytful, that is, 'as the God 'of the puple of Israel, gouerned bi moost riytful lawe; the stiere of heuene is thin helpere; cloudis rennen aboute bi the glorie of hym.

27 His dwellynge place is aboue, and armes euerlastynge ben bynethe; he schal caste out fro thi face the enemy, and he schal seie, Be thou al to-brokun.

28 Israel schal dwelle trustili and aloone; the iye of Jacob in the lond of whete, and of wyn; and heuenes schulen be derk with dew.

29 Blessed art thou, Israel; thou puple that art saued in the Lord, who is lijk thee? The scheld of thin help and the swerd of thi glorie is thi God; thin enemyes schulen denye thee, and thou schalt trede her neckis.

CAP 34

1 Therfor Moyses stiede fro the feeldi places of Moab on the hil of Nebo, in to the cop of Fasga, ayens Gerico. And the Lord schewide to hym al the lond of Galaad 'til to Dan,

2 and al Neptalym, and the lond of Effraym and of Manasses, and al the lond of Juda, 'til to the laste see; and the south part,

3 and the breede of the feeld of Jerico, of the citee of Palmes 'til to Segor.

4 And the Lord seide to hym, This is the lond for which Y swoor to Abraham, Isaac, and Jacob; and Y seide, Y schal yyue it to thi seed; thou hast seyn it with thin iyen, and thou schalt not passe 'to it.

5 And Moyses, the seruaunt of the Lord, was deed there, in the lond of Moab, 'for the Lord comaundide.

6 And the Lord biriede hym in a valey of the lond of Moab, ayens Fegor, and no man knewe his sepulcre 'til in to present day.

7 Moises was of an hundrid and twenti yeer whanne he diede; his iye dasewide not, nethir hise teeth weren stirid.

8 And the sones of Israel biwepten hym thretti daies in the feeldi places of Moab; and the daies of weilyng of men 'bymorenynge Moises weren fillid.

9 Forsothe Josue, the sone of Nun, was fillid with 'the spyrit of wisdom, for Moises settide hise hondis on hym; and the sones of Israel obeieden to Josue, and diden as the Lord comaundide to Moises.

10 And 'a profete roos no more in Israel 'as Moises, whom the Lord knewe face to face,

11 in alle myraclis, and grete wondris, whiche the Lord sente bi hym, that he schulde do in the lond of Egipt to Farao, and alle hise seruauntis, and to al the lond 'of hym,

12 and al strong hond, and the 'grete merueylis, whiche Moyses dide bifor al Israel.

JOSHUA

CAP 1

1 And it was doon aftir the deeth of Moyses, seruaunt of the Lord, that the Lord spak to Josue, sone of Nun, the mynystre of Moyses, and seide to hym, Moises, my seruaunt, is deed;

2 rise thou, and passe this Jordan, thou, and al the puple with thee, in to the lond which Y schal yyue to the sones of Israel.

3 Y schal yyue to you ech place which the step of youre foot schal trede, as Y spak to Moyses,

4 fro the deseert and Liban til to the greet flood Eufrates; al the lond of Etheis, 'til to the greet see ayens the goyng doun of the sunne, schal be youre terme.

5 Noon schal mow ayenstonde you in alle the daies of thi lijf; as Y was with Moises, so Y schal be with thee; Y schal not leeue, nether Y schal forsake thee.

6 Be thou coumfortid, and be thou strong; for thou schalt departe bi lot to this puple the lond, for which Y swoor to thi fadris, that Y schulde yyue it to hem.

7 Therfor be thou coumfortid, and be thou ful strong, that thou kepe and do al the lawe, which Moyses, my seruaunt, comaundide to thee; bowe thou not fro it to the riyt side, ether to the left side, that thou vndirstonde alle thingis whiche thou doist.

8 The book of this lawe departe not fro thi mouth, but thou schalt thenke therynne in daies and nyytis, that thou kepe and do alle thingis that ben writun therynne; thanne thou schalt dresse thi weie, and schalt vndirstonde it.

9 Lo! Y comaunde to thee; be thou coumfortid, and be thou strong; nyle thou drede 'withoutforth, and nyle thou drede withynne; for thi Lord God is with thee in alle thingis, to whiche thou goost.

10 And Josue comaundide to the princis of the puple, and seide, Passe ye thoruy the myddis of the castels; and comaunde 'ye to the puple, and seie ye, Make ye redi metis to you,

11 for after the thridde dai ye schulen passe Jordan, and ye schulen entre to welde the lond, which youre Lord God schal yyue to you.

12 Also he seide to men of Ruben, and 'to men of Gad, and to the half lynage of Manasses, Haue ye mynde of the word which Moises,

13 the 'seruaunt of the Lord, comaundide to you, and seide, Youre Lord God hath youe to you reste and al the lond;

14 youre wyues and youre sones and beestis schulen dwelle in the lond which Moises yaf to you biyende Jordan; but passe ye armed, 'alle strong in hond, bifor youre britheren; and fiyte ye for hem,

15 til the Lord yyue reste to youre britheren, as 'he yaf also to you, and 'til also thei welden the lond which youre Lord God schal yyue to hem; and so turne ye ayen in to the lond of

youre possessioun, and ye schulen dwelle in that lond which Moises, 'seruaunt of the Lord, yaf to you ouer Jordan, ayens the 'rysyng of the sunne.

16 And thei answeriden to Josue, and seiden, We schulen do alle thingis whiche thou comaundidist to vs, and we schulen go, whidir euer thou sendist vs;

17 as we obeieden in alle thingis to Moises, so we schulen obeie also to thee; oneli thi Lord God be with thee, as he was with Moyses.

18 Die he that ayenseith thi mouth, and obeieth not to alle thi wordis, whiche thou comaundist to hym; oneli be thou coumfortid, and do thou manli.

CAP 2

1 Therfor Josue, the sone of Nun, sente fro Sethym twei men, aspieris in hiddlis, and seide to hem, Go ye, and biholde ye the lond, and the citee of Jerico. Whiche yeden, and entriden into the hous of a womman hoore, 'Raab bi name, and restiden at hir.

2 And it was teld, 'and seid to the kyng of Jerico, Lo! men of the sones of Israel entriden hidir bi nyyt, to aspie the lond.

3 Therfor the kyng of Jerico sente to Raab the hoore, and seide, Brynge out the men, that camen to thee, and entriden in to thin hous; for thei ben aspieris, and thei camen to biholde al the lond.

4 And the womman took the men, and hidde hem, and seide, Y knowleche, thei camen to me, but Y wiste not of whenus thei weren;

5 and whanne the yate was closid in derknessis, and thei yeden out to gidire, Y noot whidur thei yeden; pursue ye soone, and ye schulen take hem.

6 Forsothe sche made the men to stie in to the soler of hir hows, and hilide hem with stobil of flex, that was there.

7 Sotheli thei, that weren sent, sueden hem bi the weie that ledith to the fordis of Jordan; and whanne thei weren goon out, anoon the yate was closid.

8 Thei that weren hid, slepten not yit, and lo! the womman stiede to hem, and seide,

9 Y knowe that the Lord hath bitake to you this lond; for youre feerdfulnesse felde in to vs, and alle the dwelleris of the lond 'weren sike.

10 We herden, that the Lord driede the watris of the Reed See at youre entryng, whanne ye yeden out of Egipt; and what thingis ye diden to twei kyngis of Ammorreis, that weren biyende Jordan, to Seon and Og, whiche ye killiden;

11 and we herden these thingis, and we dredden, and oure herte 'was sike, and spirit dwellide not in vs at youre entryng; for youre Lord God hym silf is God in heuene aboue, and in erthe bynethe.

12 Now therfor swere ye to me bi the Lord God, that as Y dide merci with you, so and ye do with the hows of my fadir; and yyue ye to me a veri signe,

13 that ye saue my fadir and modir, and my britheren and sistris, and alle thingis that ben herne, and dilyuere oure lyues fro deeth.

14 Whiche answeriden to hir, Oure lijf be for you in to deeth, if netheles thou bitraiest not vs; and whanne the Lord hath bitake to vs the lond, we schulen do mercy and treuthe in thee.

15 Therfor sche let hem doun fro the wyndow bi a corde; for hir hows cleuyde to the wal.

16 And sche seide to hem, Stie ye to the hilli places, lest perauenture men turnynge ayen meete you; and be ye hidde there three daies, til thei comen ayen; and so ye schulen go bi youre weie.

17 Whiche seiden to hir, We schulen be giltles of this ooth, bi which thou hast chargid vs,

18 if, whanne we entren in to the lond, this reed corde is not a signe, and thou byndist it not in the wyndow, bi which thou lettist vs doun; and thou gaderist not in to thi hows thi fadir and modir, and britheren, and al thi kynrede; the blood of hym schal be on his heed,

19 that goith out at the dore of thin hows, and we schulen be alien, that is, giltles; forsothe the blood of alle men that ben in the hows with thee, schal turne in to oure heed, if ony man touchith hem.

20 'That if thou wolt betraie vs, and brynge forth in to the myddis this word, we schulen be cleene of this ooth, bi which thou hast chargid vs.

21 And sche answeride, As ye han spoke, so be it doon. And sche lefte hem, that thei schulden go, and sche hangide a reed corde in her wyndow.

22 Sotheli thei yeden, and camen to the hilli places, and dwelliden there three daies, til thei turneden ayen that pursueden; for thei souyten bi ech weie, and founden not hem.

23 And whanne the sekeris entriden in to the citee, the spieris turneden ayen, and camen doun fro the hille; and whanne thei hadde passid Jordan, thei camen to Josue, the sone of Nun;

24 and thei telden to hym alle thingis that bifelden to hem, and seiden, The Lord hath bitake al the lond in to oure hondis, and alle the dwelleris thereof ben casten doun bi drede.

CAP 3

1 Therfor Josue roos bi nyyt, and mouede tentis; and thei yeden out of Sechym, and camen to Jordan, he and alle the sones of Israel, and dwelliden there thre daies.

2 And whanne tho daies weren passid, crieris yeden thorouy the myddis of tentis,

3 and bigunnen to crie, Whanne ye seen the arke of boond of pees of youre Lord God, and the preestis of the generacioun of Leuy berynge it, also rise ye, and sue the biforgoeris;

4 and a space of twey thousynde cubitis be bitwixe you and the arke, that ye moun se fer, and knowe bi what weie ye schulen entre, for ye 'yeden not bifore bi it; and be ye war, that ye neiye not to the arke.

5 And Josue seide to the puple, Be ye halewid, for to morew the Lord schal make merueilis among you.

6 And Josue seide to the preestis, Take ye the arke of the boond of pees 'of the Lord, and go ye bifor the puple. Whiche filliden the heestis, and tooken the arke, and yeden bifor hem.

7 And the Lord seide to Josue, To dai Y schal bigynne to enhaunse thee bifor al Israel, that thei wite, that as Y was with Moises, so Y am also with thee.

8 Forsothe comaunde thou to preestis, that beren the arke of bond of pees, and seie thou to hem, Whanne ye han entrid in to a part of the watir of Jordan, stonde ye therynne.

9 And Josue seide to the sones of Israel, Neiye ye hidur, and here ye the word of youre Lord God.

10 And eft he seide, In this ye schulen wite that the Lord God lyuynge is in the myddis of you; and he schal distrye in youre siyt Cananey, Ethei, Euey, and Feresei, and Gergesei, and Jebusei, and Amorrei.

11 Lo! the arke of boond of pees of the Lord of al erthe schal go bifor you thorouy Jordan.

12 Make ye redi twelue men of the twelue lynagis of Israel, bi ech lynage o man.

13 And whanne the preestis, that beren the arke of boond of pees of the Lord God of al erthe, han set the steppis of her feet in the watris of Jordan, the watris that ben lowere schulen renne doun, and schulen faile; forsothe the watris that comen fro aboue schulen stonde togidere in o gobet.

14 Therfor the puple yede out of her tabernaclis to passe Jordan; and the preestis that baren the arke of boond of pees yeden bifor the puple.

15 And whanne the preestis entriden in to Jordan, and her feet weren dippid in the part of watir; forsothe Jordan 'hadde fillid the brynkis of his trow in the tyme of 'ripe corn;

16 the watris yeden doun, and stoden in o place, and wexiden grete at the licnesse of an hil, and apperiden fer fro the citee that was clepid Edom, 'til to the place of Sarthan; sotheli the watris that weren lowere yeden doun in to the see of wildirnesse, which is now clepid the deed see, 'til the watris failiden outirli.

17 Forsothe the puple yede thorouy Jordan; and the preestis, that baren the arke of the boond of pees of the Lord, stoden gird on the drie erthe in the myddis of Jordan, and al the puple passide thorouy the drie trow.

CAP 4

1 And whanne thei weren passid ouer, the Lord seide to Josue,

2 Chese thou twelue men,

3 by ech lynage o man, and comaunde thou to hem, that thei take fro the myddis of the trow of Jordan, where the 'feet of preestis stoden, twelue hardiste stoonys; whiche thou schalt sette in the place of castels, where ye schulen sette tentis in this nyyt.

4 And Josue clepide twelue men, whiche he hadde chose of the sones of Israel, of ech lynage o man;

5 and he seide to hem, Go ye bifore the arke of youre Lord God to the myddis of Jordan, and bere ye fro thennus in youre schuldris ech man o stoon, bi the noumbre of the sones of Israel,

6 that it be a signe bitwixe you. And whanne youre sones schulen axe you to morewe, that is, in tyme 'to comynge, and schulen seie, What wolen these stonus 'to hem silf?

7 ye schulen answere to hem, The watris of Jordan failiden bifor the arke of boond of pees of the Lord, whanne the arke passide Jordan; therfor these stoonus ben set in to mynde of the sones of Israel, til in to withouten ende.

8 Therfor the sones of Israel diden as Josue comaundide to hem, and baren fro the myddis of the trow of Jordan twelue stoonys, as the Lord comaundide to hem, bi the noumbre of the sones of Israel, 'til to the place in which thei settiden tentis; and there thei puttiden tho stonys.

9 Also Josue puttide othire twelue stoonys in the myddis of the trow of Jordan, where the preestis stoden, that baren the arke of boond of pees of the Lord; and tho stoonys ben there 'til in to present dai.

10 Forsothe the preestis, that baren the arke, stoden in the myddis of Jordan, til alle thingis weren fillid, whiche the Lord comaundide, that Josue schulde speke to the puple, as Moises hadde seide to hym. And the puple hastide, and passide.

11 And whanne alle men hadden passid, also the arke of the Lord passide, and the preestis yeden bifor the puple.

12 Also the sones of Ruben, and of Gad, and half the lynage of Manasse, yeden armed bifor the sones of Israel, as Moyses comaundide to hem.

13 And fourti thousynde of fiyters yeden bi her cumpanyes and gaderyngis on the pleyn and feeldi places of the citee of Jerico.

14 In that day the Lord magnyfiede Josue bifor al Israel, that thei schulden drede hym, as thei dreden Moises, while he lyuede yit.

15 And the Lord seide to Josue,

16 Comaunde thou to the preestis that beren the arke of boond of pees, that thei stie fro Jordan.

17 And Josue comaundide to hem, and seide, Stie ye fro Jordan.

18 And whanne thei hadden stied, berynge the arke of boond of pees of the Lord, and hadde bigunne to trede on the drie erthe, the watris turneden ayen in to her trowe, and flowiden, as tho weren wont before.

19 Forsothe the puple stiede fro Jordan in the tenthe dai of the firste monethe, and thei settiden tentis in Galgalis, ayens the eest coost of the citee of Jerico.

20 Also Josue puttide in Galgalis the twelue stonys, whiche thei hadden take fro the trow of Jordan.

21 And he seide to the sones of Israel, Whanne youre sones schulen axe to morewe her fadris, and schulen seie to hem, What wolen these stoonys 'to hem silf?

22 ye schulen teche hem, and ye schulen seie, We passiden this Jordan bi the drie botme,

23 for oure Lord God driede the watris therof in oure siyt, til we passiden,

24 as he dide bifore in the Reed See, which he driede while we passiden,

25 that alle the puplis of londis lurne the strongeste hond of the Lord, that also ye drede youre Lord God in al tyme.

CAP 5

1 Therfor aftir that alle kyngis of Ammorreys herden, that dwelliden ouer Jordan at the west coost, and alle the kyngis of Canaan, that weldiden nyy places of the greet see, that the Lord hadden dried the flowyngis of Jordan bifor the sones of Israel, til thei passiden, the herte of hem was failid, and spirit dwellide not in hem, dredynge the entring of the sones of Israel.

2 In that tyme the Lord seide to Josue, Make to thee knyues of stoon, and circumside thou the sones of Israel, in the secunde tyme.

3 Josue dide tho thingis whiche the Lord comaundide, and he circumside the sones of Israel in the 'hil of prepucies.

4 Sotheli this is the cause of the secunde circumcisioun; al the puple of male kynde, that yede out of Egipt, alle men fiyteris, weren deed in deseert bi the lengeste cumpassis of weie,

5 whiche alle weren circumsidid. Sotheli the puple

6 that was borun in deseert bi fourti yeer, in the weie of broddeste wildirnesse, was vncircumsidid til thei weren waastid, that herden not the 'vois of the Lord, and to whiche he swoor bifore, that he schulde schewe to hem the lond flowynge with mylk and hony.

7 The sones of hem camen aftirward in to the place of fadris, and thei weren circumsidid of Josue; whiche, as thei weren borun, weren in prepucie, nether ony man hadde circumsidid hem in the weie.

8 Forsothe aftir that alle weren circumsidid, thei dwelliden in the same place of tentis, til thei weren heelid.

9 And the Lord seide to Josue, To dai Y haue take awei fro you the schenschip of Egipt. And the name of that place was clepid Galgala, 'til in to present dai.

10 And the sones of Israel dwelliden in Galgalis, and maden pask in the fourtenthe dai of the monethe at euentide, in the feeldi places of Jerico;

11 And 'thei eten of the fruytis of the lond 'in the tothir day, therf looues, and potage of the same yeer, 'ether cornys seengid and frotid in the hond.

12 And manna failide aftir that thei eten of the fruytis of the lond; and the sones of Israel vsiden no more that mete, but thei eten of the fruytis of present yeer of the lond of Canaan.

13 Sothely whanne Josue was in the feeld of the cite of Jerico, he reiside the iyen, and siy a man stondynge ayens hym, and holdynge a drawun swerd; and Josue yede out to hym, and seide, Art thou oure, ethir 'of aduersaries?

14 To whom he answeride, Nay, but Y am prince of the 'hoost of the Lord, and now Y come.

15 Josue felde lowe to erthe, and worschipide, and seide, What spekith my Lord to his seruaunt?

16 He seide, Vnlace thi schoo fro thi feet, for the place, in which thou stondist, is hooli. And Josue dide, as it was comaundid to hym.

CAP 6

1 Forsothe Jerico was closid and wardid, for the drede of the sones of Israel, and no man durste entre, ethir go out.

2 And the Lord seide to Josue, Lo! Y yaf in to thin hondis Jerico, and the king therof, and alle strong men.

3 Alle ye fiyteris, cumpasse the citee onys bi the day; so ye schulen do in sixe daies.

4 Forsothe in the seuenthe dai the preestis schulen take seuene clariouns, of whiche 'the vss is in iubile; and thei schulen go bifor the arke of boond of pees; and seuen sithes ye schulen cumpasse the citee, and the preestis schulen trumpe with clariouns.

5 And whanne the vois of the trumpe schal sowne lengere, and more bi whiles, and schal sowne in youre eeris, al the puple schal crie togidere with gretteste cry; and the wallis of the citee schulen falle alle doun, and alle men schulen entre bi the place, ayens which thei stonden.

6 Therfor Josue, the sone of Nun, clepide preestis, and seide to hem, Take ye the ark of boond of pees, and seuene othere preestis take seuene clariouns of iubile yeeris, and go thei bifor the arke of the Lord.

7 Also Josue seide to the puple, Go ye, and cumpasse ye the citee, and go ye armed bifor the arke of the Lord.

8 And whanne Josue hadde endid the wordis, and seuene preestis trumpiden with seuen clariouns bifor the arke of boond of pees of the Lord,

9 and al the puple armed yede bifore, the tothir comyn puple of fiyteris suede the arke, and alle thingis sowneden with clariouns.

10 Sotheli Josue comaundide to the puple, and seide, Ye schulen not crye, nethir youre vois schal be herd, nethir ony word schal go out of youre mouth, til the dai come, in which Y schal seie to you, Crye ye, and make ye noyse.

11 Therfor the arke of the Lord cumpasside the citee onys bi day, and turnede ayen in to the castels, and dwellide there.

12 Therfor while Josue roos bi nyyt, preestis tooken the arke of the Lord;

13 and seuene of the preestis token seuen clariouns, of whiche 'the vss is in iubilee, and yeden bifor the arke of the Lord, 'and yeden, and trumpiden; and the puple yede armed bifor hem. Sotheli the tother comyn puple suede the arke, and sownede with clariouns.

14 And thei cumpassiden the citee in the secunde dai onys, and turneden ayen in to the castels; so thei dyden in sixe daies.

15 Sotheli in the seuenthe dai thei risiden eerli, and cumpassiden the citee, as it was disposid, seuen sithis.

16 And whanne in the seuenthe cumpas preestis sowneden with clariouns, Josue seide to al Israel, Crie ye, for the Lord hath bitake the citee to vs;

17 and this citee be cursid, ethir distried, and alle thingis that ben therynne be halewid to the Lord. Raab the hoor aloone lyue, with alle men that ben with hir in the hows; for sche hidde the messangeris whiche we senten.

18 Forsothe be ye war, lest ye touchen ony thing of these that ben comaundid to you, and ye ben gilti of trespassyng; and alle the castels of Israel be vndur synne, and be troblid.

19 Sotheli what euer thing is of gold, and of siluer, and of brasun vessels, and of yrun, be halewid to the Lord, and be kept in hise tresoris.

20 Therfor while al the puple criede, and the trumpis sowneden, aftir that the sowne sownede in the eeris of the multitude, the walles felden doun anoon; and ech man stiede bi the place that was ayens hym. And thei token the citee,

21 and killiden alle thingis that weren therynne, fro man 'til to womman, fro yong child 'til to eld man; also thei smytiden bi the scharpnesse of swerd, oxun, and scheep, and assis.

22 Forsothe Josue seide to twei men, that weren sent aspieris, Entre ye in to the hows of the womman hoore, and brynge ye forth hir, and alle thingis that ben herne, as ye maden stedfast to hir bi an ooth.

23 And the yonge men entriden, and ledden out Raab, and her fadir, and modir, and britheren, and al the purtenaunce of houshold, and the kynrede 'of hir; and maden to dwelle without the castels of Israel.

24 Sotheli thei brenten the citee, and alle thingis that weren foundun therynne, without gold, and siluer, and brasun vesselis, and yrun, which thei halewiden in to the 'treserie of the Lord.

25 Sotheli Josue made Raab the hoore to lyue, and 'the hows of hir fadir, and alle thingis that sche hadde; and thei dwelliden in the myddis of Israel, 'til in to present dai; for sche hidde the messangeris, whiche he sente to asspie Jerico. In that tyme Josue preiede hertli,

26 and seide, Cursid bifor the Lord be the man, that reisith and bildith the citee of Jerico! Leie he the foundementis therof in his firste gendrid sone, and putte he the yatis therof in the laste of fre children.

27 Therfor the Lord was with Josue, and his name was pupplischid in ech lond.

CAP 7

1 Forsothe the sones of Israel braken 'the comaundement, and mystoken of the halewid thing; for Achar, the son of Charmy, sone of Zabdi, sone of Zare, of the lynage of Juda, toke sum thing of the halewid thing; and the Lord was wrooth ayens the sones of Israel.

2 And whanne Josue sente men fro Jerico ayens Hai, which is bisidis Bethauen, at the eest coost of the citee Bethel, he seide to hem, Stie ye, and aspie ye the lond. Whiche filliden 'the comaundementis, and aspieden Hay;

3 and thei turneden ayen, and seiden to hym, 'Not al the puple stie, but twey ether thre thousynde of men go, and do awei the citee; whi schal al the puple be trauelid in veyn ayens feweste enemyes?

4 Therfor thre thousynde of fiyteris stieden, whiche turneden the backis anoon,

5 and weren smytun of the men of Hay; and sixe and thretti men of hem 'felden doun; and aduersaries pursueden hem fro the yate til to Saberym; and thei felden doun fleynge bi lowe places. And the herte of the puple dredde, and was maad vnstidefast at the licnesse of watir.

6 Sotheli Josue torente hise clothis, and felde lowe to the erthe bifor the arke of the Lord, 'til to euentid, as wel he, as alle the elde men of Israel; and thei castiden powdir on her heedis.

7 And Josue seide, Alas! alas! Lord God, what woldist thou lede this puple ouer the flood Jordan, that thou schuldist bitake vs in the hond of Ammorrey, and schulde leese vs? Y wolde, that as we bygunnen, we hadden dwellid biyondis Jordan.

8 My Lord God, what schal Y seie, seynge Israel turnynge the backis to hise enemyes?

9 Cananeys, and alle dwelleris of the lond schulen here, and thei schulen be gaderid togidere, and schulen cumpas vs, and schulen do awei oure name fro erthe; and what schalt thou do to thi grete name?

10 And the Lord seide to Josue, Rise thou; whi liggist thou low in the erthe?

11 Israel synnede, and brak my couenaunt; and thei token of the halewid thing, and thei han stole, and lieden, and hidden among her vessels.

12 And Israel may not stonde bifore hise enemyes, and Israel schal fle hem, for it is defoulid with cursyng; Y schal no more be with you, til ye al to breke hym which is gilti of this trespas.

13 Rise thou, halewe the puple, and seie thou to hem, Be ye halewid ayens to morewe; for the Lord God of Israel seith these thingis, A! Israel! cursyng is in the myddis of thee; thou schalt not mowe stonde bifor thin enemyes, til he that is defoulyd bi this trespas, be doon awei fro thee.

14 And ye schulen come eerli, alle men bi youre lynagis; and whateuer lynage the lot schal fynde, it schal come bi hise meynees; and the meynee schal come bi housis, and the hous schal come bi men.

15 And whoeuer schal be takun with this trespas, he schal be brent bi fier with al his catel, for he brak the couenaunt of the Lord, and dide vnleueful thing in Israel.

16 Therfor Josue roos eerly, and settide in ordre Israel, bi hise lynagis; and the lynage of Juda was foundun;

17 and whanne that lynage was brouyt forth bi hise meynees, the meyne of Zare was foundun. And Josue brouyte forth it bi men, ethir housis, and foond Zabdi;

18 whos hows he departide in to alle men bi hemsilf; and he foond Achar, the sone of Charmy, sone of Zabdi, sone of Zare, of the lynage of Juda.

19 And he seide to Achar, My sone, yyue thou glorie to the Lord God of Israel, and knowleche thou, and schew to me what thou hast do; hide thou not.

20 And Achar answeryde to Josue, and seide to hym, Verily, Y synnede bifor the Lord God of Israel, and Y dide 'so and so;

21 for among the spuylis Y siy a reed mentil ful good, and two hundrid siclis of siluer, and a goldun reule of fifti siclis;

and Y coueytide, and took awei, and hidde in the erthe, ayens the myddis of my tabernacle; and Y hilide the siluer with erthe doluun.

22 Therfor Josue sente mynystris, whyche runnen to his tabernacle, and foundun alle thingis hid in the same place, and the siluer togidere; and thei token awei fro the tente,

23 and brouyten 'tho thingis to Josue, and to alle the sones of Israel; and thei castiden forth bifor the Lord.

24 Therfor Josue took Achar, the sone of Zare, and the siluer, and the mentil, and the goldun reule, and hise sones, and douytris, oxun, assis, and scheep, and the tabernacle 'it silf, and al the purtenaunce of household, and al Israel with Josue; and thei ledden hem to the valei of Achar;

25 where Josue seide, For thou disturblidist vs, the Lord schal disturble thee in this dai. And al Israel stonyde hym; and alle thingis that weren hise, weren wastid bi fier.

26 And thei gaderiden on hym a greet heep of stoonys, whiche dwellen til in to present day. And the strong veniaunce of the Lord was turned awei fro hem; and the name of that place was clepid the valey of Achar 'til to day.

CAP 8

1 Forsothe the Lord seide to Josue, Nether drede thou 'withoutforth, 'nether drede thou withynne; take with thee al the multitude of fiyteris, and rise thou, and stie in to the citee of Hay; lo, Y haue bitake in thin hond the king therof, and the puple, and the citee, and the lond.

2 And thou schalt do to the citee of Hay, and to the king therof, as thou didist to Gerico, and to the king therof; sotheli ye schulen take to you the prey, and alle lyuynge beestis; sette thou 'aspies, ethir buyschementis, to the citee bihynde it.

3 And Josue roos, and al the oost of fiyteris with hym, to stie in to Hay; and bi nyytte he sente thretti chosen thousynde of stronge men;

4 and comaundide to hem, and seide, Sette ye buyschementis bihynde the citee, and go ye not ferthere; and alle ye schulen be redi;

5 forsothe Y, and the tothir multitude which is with me, schulen come on the contrarie side ayens the citee; and whanne thei schulen go out ayens vs, as we diden bifore, we schulen fle, and turne the backis,

6 til thei pursuen, and ben drawun away ferthir fro the citee; for thei schulen gesse, that we schulen fle as bifore.

7 Therfor while we schulen fle, and thei pursue, ye schulen ryse fro the buyschementis, and schulen waste the citee; and youre Lord God schal bitake it in to youre hondis.

8 And whanne ye han take it, 'brenne ye it; 'so ye schulen do alle thingis, as Y comaundide.

9 And Josue lefte hem, and thei yeden to the place of buyschementis, and saten bitwixe Bethel and Hay, at the west coost of the citee of Hay. Forsothe Josue dwellide 'in that nyyt in the myddis of the puple.

10 And he roos eerli, and noumbride felowis, and stiede with the eldere in the frount of the oost, and was cumpassid with the helpe of fiyteris.

11 And whanne thei hadden come, and hadden stied ayens the citee, thei stoden at the north coost of the citee, bitwixe which citee and hem the valei was in the myddis.

12 'Sotheli he hadde chose fyue thousynde men, and hadde sette in buyschementis bitwixe Bethauen and Hay, in the west part of the same citee.

13 Sotheli al the tothir oost dresside scheltroun to the north, so that the laste men of the multitude touchiden the west coost

of the citee. Therfor Josue yede in that nyyt, and stood in the myddis of the valei;

14 and whanne the kyng of Hai had seyn that, he hastide eerli, and yede out with al the oost of the citee, and he dresside scheltrun ayens the deseert; and wiste not that buyschementis weren hid bihinde the bak.

15 Forsothe Josue and al the multitude 'of Israel yauen place, feynynge drede, and fleynge bi the weie of wildirnesse; and thei crieden togidere,

16 and excitiden hem silf togidere, and pursueden hem. And whanne thei hadden go awey fro the citee,

17 and sothely not oon hadde left in the citee of Hai and Bethauen, that 'pursuede not Israel, and thei leften the citees opyn, as thei hadden broke out,

18 the Lord seide to Josue, 'Reise thou the scheeld which is in thin hond, ayens the citee of Hay; for Y schal yyue it to thee.

19 And whanne he hadde reisid the scheld ayens the citee, buyschementis, that weren hid, riseden anoon; and thei yeden to the citee, and token, and brenten it.

20 Forsothe the men of the citee, that pursueden Josue, bihelden, and siyen the smoke of the citee stie 'til to heuene; and thei myyten no more fle hidur and thidur; most sithen thei that hadden feyned fliyt, and yeden to wildirnesse, withstoden stronglieste 'ayens the pursueris.

21 And Josue siy, and al Israel, that the citee was takun, and the smoke of the citee stiede; and he turnede ayen, and smoot the men of Hay.

22 Sotheli also thei that hadden take and brent the citee, yeden out of the cytee ayens her men, and bigunnen to smyte the myddil men of enemyes; and whanne aduersaries weren slayn 'on euer ethir part, so that no man of so greet multitude was sauyd,

23 thei tokun also the kyng of Hay lyuynge, and brouyten to Josue.

24 Therfor, whanne alle men weren slayn, that pursueden Israel goynge to deseert, and felden bi swerd in the same place, the sones of Israel turneden ayen, and smytiden the citee.

25 Forsothe thei that 'felden doun in the same dai, fro man 'til to womman, weren twelue thousynde of men, alle men of the citee of Hay.

26 Sotheli Josue withdrow not the hond, which he hadde dressid an hiy holdynge 'the scheld, til alle the dwelleris of Hay weren slayn.

27 Forsothe the sones of Israel departiden to hem silf the werk beestis, and the preye of the citee, as the Lord comaundide to Josue;

28 which brente the citee, and made it an euerlastynge biriel.

29 And he hangide the king therof in a iebat, 'til to the euentid and the goynge doun of the sunne. And Josue comaundide, and thei puttiden doun his deed bodi fro the cros; and thei 'castiden forth him in thilke entryng of the citee, and gaderiden on hym a greet heep of stoonus, which heep dwellith 'til in to present dai.

30 Thanne Josue bildide an auter to the Lord God of Israel in the hil of Hebal,

31 as Moises, the 'seruaunt of the Lord, comaundide to the sones of Israel, and it is writun in the book of Moises lawe, an auter of stoonys vnpolischid, whiche yrun touchide not. And he offride theron brent sacrifice to the Lord, and he offride pesible sacrifices;

32 and he wroot on the stoonys the Deutronomye of Moises lawe, 'which he hadde declarid bifor the sones of Israel.

33 Sotheli al the puple, and the grettere men in birthe, and the duykis, and iugis stoden on 'euer either side of the arke, in the siyt of preestis and dekenes, that baren the arke of boond of pees of the Lord; as a comeling, so and a man borun in the lond; the mydil part of hem stood bisidis the hil Garasym, and the myddil part stood bisidis the hil Hebal, as Moises, the 'seruaunt of the Lord, comaundide. And first 'sotheli he blesside the puple of Israel.

34 Aftir these thingis he redde alle the wordis of blessyng and of cursyng, and alle thingis that weren writun in the book of lawe.

35 He lefte no thing vntouchid of these thingis that Moises comaundide; but he declaride alle thingis bifor al the multitude of Israel, to wymmen, and litle children, and to comelyngis that dwelliden among hem.

CAP 9

1 And whanne these thingis weren herd, alle the kyngis biyende Jordan, that lyueden in the hilly places, and in 'the feeldi places, in the coostis of the see, and in the brynke of the greet see, and thei that dwellen bisidis Liban, Ethei, and Ammorrei, Cananei, and Feresey, Euey, and Jebusey,

2 weren gaderid togidere to fiyte ayens Josue and Israel, with o wille, and the same sentence.

3 And thei that dwelten in Gabaon, herden alle thingis whiche Josue hadde do to Jerico, and to Hay; and thei thouyten felli,

4 and token to hem silf metis, and puttyden elde sackis on assis, and wyn botels brokun and sewid, and ful elde schoon,

5 whiche weren sewid togidere with patchis, to 'the schewyng of eldenesse; and thei weren clothid with elde clothis; also looues, whiche thei baren for lijflode in the weie, weren harde and brokun in to gobetis.

6 And thei yeden to Josue, that dwellide thanne in tentis in Galgala; and thei seiden to hym, and to al Israel togidere, We comen fro a fer lond, and coueyten to make pees with you. And the men of Israel answeriden to hem,

7 and seiden, Lest perauenture ye dwellen in the lond, which is due to vs bi eritage, and we moun not make bond of pees with you.

8 And thei seiden to Josue, We ben thi seruauntis. To whiche Josue seide, What men ben ye, and fro whennus camen ye?

9 Thei answeriden, Thi seruauntis camen fro a ful fer lond in the name of thi Lord God, for we herden the fame of his power, alle thingis whiche he dide in Egipt,

10 and to twei kyngis of Ammorreis biyendis Jordan; to Seon king of Esebon, and to Og kyng of Basan, that weren in Astroth.

11 And the eldere men and alle the dwelleris of oure lond seiden to vs, Take ye metis in youre hondis, for lengeste weie; and go ye to hem, and seie ye, We ben youre seruauntis; make ye boond of pees with vs.

12 And we token hoote looues, whanne we yeden out of oure housis to come to you; now tho ben maad drye and brokun, for greet eldenesse;

13 we filliden newe botels of wyn; now tho ben brokun and vndoon; the clothis and schoon, with whiche we ben clothid, and whiche we han 'in the feet, ben brokun and almost wastid, fro the lengthe of lengere weie.

14 Therfor 'the sones of Israel token of the metis of hem, and thei axiden not 'the mouth of the Lord.

15 And Josue made pees with hem. And whanne the boond of pees was maad, he bihiyte, that thei schulden not be slayn; and the princes of the multitude sworen to hem.

16 Forsothe aftir thre daies of the boond of pees maad, thei herden, that thei dwelliden in nyy place, and that thei schulden be among hem.

17 And the sones of Israel mouyden tentis, and camen in the thridde dai in to the citees of hem, of whiche citees these ben the names; Gabaon, and Caphira, and Beroth, and Cariathiarym.

18 And thei smytiden not hem, for the princis of the multitude hadden swore to hem in the name of the Lord God of Israel. Therfor al the comyn puple grutchide ayens the princis of Israel;

19 whiche answeriden to hem, We sworen to hem in the name of the Lord God of Israel, and therfor we moun not touche hem;

20 but we schulen do this thing to hem, sotheli be thei reserued that thei lyue, lest the ire of the Lord be stirid ayens vs, if we forsweren to hem;

21 but so lyue thei, that thei hewe trees, and bere watris, in to the vsis of al the multitude. And while thei spaken these thingis,

22 Josue clepide Gabonytis, and seide to hem, Whi wolden ye disseyue vs bi fraude, 'that ye seiden, We dwellen ful fer fro you, sithen ye ben in the myddis of vs?

23 Therfor ye schulen be 'vndur cursyng, and noon schal faile of youre generacioun, hewynge trees and berynge watris, in to the hows of my God.

24 Whiche answeryden, It was told to vs thi seruauntis, that thi Lord God bihiyte to Moises, his seruaunt, that he schulde bitake to you al the lond, and schulde leese alle the dwelleris therof; therfor we dredden greetli, and purueiden to oure lyues, and weren compellid bi youre drede, and we token this counsel.

25 'Now forsothe we ben in 'thin hond; do thou to vs that, that semeth riytful and good to thee.

26 Therfor Josue dide, as he seide, and delyuerede hem fro the hondis of the sones of Israel, that thei schulden not be slayn.

27 And in that dai Josue demyde hem to be in to the seruyce of al the puple, and of the auter of the Lord, and to hewe trees, and to bere watris, 'til in to present tyme, in the place which the Lord hadde chose.

CAP 10

1 And whanne Adonysedech, kyng of Jerusalem, hadde herde these thingis, that is, that Josue hadde take Hai, and hadde destried it; for as Josue hadde do to Jerico and to the kyng therof, so he dide to Hay, and to the kyng therof; and that Gabaonytis hadden fled to Israel, and weren boundun in pees with hem,

2 Adonysedech dredde greetli; for Gabaon was a greet citee, and oon of the kyngis citees, and grettere than the citee of Hai, and alle the fiyteris therof weren most stronge.

3 Therfor Adonysedech, kyng of Jerusalem, sente to Ocham, kyng of Ebron, and to Pharam, kyng of Herymoth, and to Japhie, kyng of Lachis, and to Dabir, kyng of Eglon, and seide,

4 Stie ye to me, and helpe ye, that we fiyte ayens Gabaon, for it was yoldun to Josue, and to the sones of Israel.

5 Therfor fyue kyngis of Ammorreis, the kyng of Jerusalem, the kyng of Ebron, the kyng of Herymoth, the kyng of Lachis, the kyng of Eglon, weren gaderid, and stieden togidere with her oostis; and settiden tentis ayens Gabaon, and fouyten ayens it.

6 Sotheli the dwelleris of the citee of Gabaon, 'that weren bisegid, senten to Josue, that dwellide than in tentis at Galgala, and seide to hym, Withdrawe not thin hondis fro the help of thi seruauntis; 'stie thou soone, and delyuere vs, and helpe thou; for alle the kyngis of Amorreis, that dwelliden in the hilli places, camen togidere ayens vs.

7 And Josue stiede fro Galgala, and al the oost of fiyters, 'the strengeste men, 'with hym.

8 And the Lord seide to Josue, Drede thou not hem, for Y yaf hem in to thin hondis; noon of hem schal mow ayenstonde thee.

9 Therfor Josue felde sodenli on hem, and stiede in al the nyyt fro Galgala;

10 and the Lord 'disturblide hem fro the face of Israel, and al to-brak with greet veniaunce in Gabaon. And Josue pursuede hem bi the weie of the stiyng of Betheron, and smoot 'til to Azecha and Maceda.

11 And whanne thei fledden the sones of Israel, and weren in the goyng doun of Betheron, the Lord sente grete stoonus on hem fro heuene, til to Azecha; and many mo weren deed bi the 'stoonys of hail, than thei whiche the sones of Israel 'smytiden bi swerd.

12 Thanne Josue spak to the Lord, in the dai in which he bitook Amorrey in the siyt of the sones of Israel; and Josue seide bifore hem, Sunne, be thou not mouyd ayens Gabaon, and the moone ayens the valei of Hailon.

13 And the sunne and the moone stoden, til the folc of God vengide it silf of hise enemyes. Whether this is not writun in the book of iust men? And so the sunne stood in the myddis of heuene, and hastide not to go doun in the space of o dai; so long a dai was not bifore and aftirward;

14 for the Lord obeiede to the vois of man, and fauyt for Israel.

15 And Josue turnede ayen, with al Israel, in to the tentis of Galgala.

16 Forsothe fyue kyngis fledden, and hidden hem silf in the denne of the citee of Maceda.

17 And it was teld to Josue, that fyue kyngis weren foundun hid in the denne of the citee of Maceda.

18 Which Josue comaundide to felowis, and seide, Walewe ye grete stoonus to the 'mouth of the denne, and putte ye witti men, that schulen kepe the closid kyngis; sotheli nyle ye stonde,

19 but pursue ye the enemyes, and slee ye alle the laste of fleeris; and suffre ye not hem entre in to the strengthis of her citees, whiche enemyes youre Lord God bitook in to youre hondis.

20 Therfor whanne the aduersaries weren betun with greet veniaunce, and weren almost wastid 'til to deeth, thei that myyten fle Israel, entriden in to the strengthid citees.

21 And al the oost turnede ayen hoole, and in hoole noumbre to Josue, in to Maceda, where the tentis weren thanne; and no man was hardi to grutche, 'ether to make priuy noise, ayens the sones of Israel.

22 And Josue comaundide, and seide, Opene ye the 'mouth of the denne, and brynge forth to me the fyue kyngis that ben hid therynne.

23 And the mynystris diden, as it was comaundid to hem; and thei brouyten forth to Josue fyue kyngis fro the denne; the kyng of Jerusalem, the kyng of Ebron, the kyng of Herymoth, the kyng of Lachis, the kyng of Eglon.

24 And whanne thei weren led out to Josue, he clepide alle the men of Israel, and seide to the princes of the oost, that weren with hym, Go ye, and sette youre feet on the neckis of these kyngis. And whanne thei hadden go, and trediden the neckis of 'the kyngis suget 'to her feet,

25 eft Josue seide to hem, Nyle ye drede, nethir 'drede ye with ynne, be ye coumfortid, and be ye stronge; for the Lord schal do so to alle youre enemyes, ayens whiche ye schulen fiyte.

26 And Josue smoot, and killide hem, and hangide on fyue trees; and thei weren hangid 'til to euentid.

27 And whanne the sunne yede doun, he comaundide to felowis, that thei schulden put hem doun fro the iebatis; and whanne thei weren put doun, thei 'castiden forth hem in to the denne, in which thei weren hid; and thei puttiden grete stoonus on the mouth therof, whiche stoonus dwellen 'til to present tyme.

28 In the same dai Josue took also Maceda, and smoot bi the scharpnesse of swerd, and killide the kyng therof, and alle the dwelleris therof; he lefte not therynne, nameli, litle relikis; and he dide to the kyng of Maceda as he hadde do to the kyng of Jerico.

29 Forsothe Josue passide with al Israel fro Maceda in to Lempna, and fauyt ayens it,

30 which the Lord bitook, with the kyng therof, in the hond of Israel; and thei smytiden the citee bi the scharpnesse of swerd, and alle the dwelleris therof, and leften not ony relikis therynne; and thei diden to the kyng of Lempna as thei hadden do to the kyng of Jerico.

31 Fro Lempna he passide with al Israel in to Lachis; and whanne the oost was disposid bi cumpas, he fauyt ayens it.

32 And the Lord bitook Lachis in the hond of the sones of Israel; and he took it in the tothir dai, and smoot bi the scharpnesse of swerd, and ech man, that was therynne, as he hadde do to Lempna.

33 In that time Yram, kyng of Gazar, stiede to helpe Lachis; whom Josue smoot, with al his puple, til to deeth.

34 And he passide fro Lachis in to Eglon,

35 and cumpasside, and ouercam it in the same dai; and he smoot bi the scharpnesse of swerd alle men that weren therynne, bi alle thingis whiche he hadde do to Lachis.

36 Also he stiede with al Israel fro Eglon in to Ebron, and fauyt ayens it,

37 and took, and smoot bi the scharpnesse of swerd; and the kyng therof, and alle citees of that cuntrey, and alle men that dwelliden therynne; he lefte not ony relikis therynne; as he hadde do to Eglon so he dide also to Ebron, and wastide bi swerd alle thingis that weren therynne.

38 Fro thennus he turnyde in to Dabir, and took it, and wastide;

39 and he smoot bi the scharpnesse of swerd the kyng therof, and alle tounnes 'bi cumpas; he lefte not ony relikis therynne; as he hadde do to Ebron, and to Lempna, and to 'the kyngis of tho, so he dide to Dabir, and to the kyng therof.

40 And so Josue smoot al the 'lond of the hillis, and of the south, and 'of the feeld, and Asedoch with her kyngis; he lefte not therynne ony relikis, but he killide al thing that myyte brethe, as the Lord God of Israel comaundide to hym;

41 fro Cades Barne 'til to Gazan, and al the lond of Jesson, 'til to Gabaon Josue took,

42 and wastide with o fersnesse alle the kyngis, and 'cuntreis of hem; for the Lord God of Israel fauyt for hym.

43 And he turnede ayen with al Israel to the place of tentis in Galgala.

CAP 11

1 And whanne Jabyn, kyng of Asor, hadde herd these thingis, he sente to Jobab, kyng of Madian, and to the kyng of Semeron, and to the kyng of Acsaph; forsothe to the kyngis of the north,

2 that dwelliden in the hilli places, and in the pleyn ayens the south of Seneroth, and in the feeldi places, and cuntreis of Dor, bisidis the see,

3 and 'to Cananei fro the eest and west, and to Ammorrey, and Ethei, and Feresei, and Jebusei, in the 'hilli places, and to Euey, that dwellide at the rootis of Hermon, in the lond of Maspha.

4 And alle yeden out with her cumpanyes, a ful myche puple, as the grauel which is in the 'brynk of the see, and horsis, and charis, of greet multitude.

5 And alle these kyngis camen togidere at the watris of Meron, to fiyte ayens Israel.

6 And the Lord seyde to Josue, Drede thou not hem, for to morewe, in this same our, Y schal bitake alle these men to be woundid in the siyt of Israel; thou schalt hoxe 'the horsis of hem, and thou schalt brenne 'the charis bi fier.

7 And Josue cam, and al his oost with hym, ayens hem sodenli, at the watris of Meron, 'and felden on hem.

8 And the Lord bitook hem in to the hondis of Israel; whiche smytiden hem, 'that is, the hethen kyngis and her oostes, and pursueden 'til to grete Sidon, and the watris of Maserophoth, and to the feeld of Maspha, which is at the eest part therof. Josue smoot so alle men, that he lefte no relikis of hem;

9 and he dide as the Lord comaundide to hym; he hoxide 'the horsis of hem, and brente the charis.

10 And he turnede ayen anoon, and took Asor, and 'smoot bi swerd the kyng therof; for Asor helde bi eld tyme the prinsehed among alle these rewmes.

11 And 'he smoot alle persoones that dwelliden there, he lefte not ony relikys therynne, but he wastide alle thingis 'til to deeth; also he distriede thilke citee bi brennyng.

12 And he took alle 'citees bi cumpas, and 'the kyngis of hem, and smoot, and dide awei, as Moises, the 'seruaunt of the Lord,

13 comaundide to hym, without citees that weren set in the grete hillis, and in litle hillis; and Israel brente the othere citees; flawme wastide oneli o citee, Asor, the strongeste.

14 And the sones of Israel departiden to hem silf al the prei, and werk beestis of these citees, whanne alle men weren slayn.

15 As the Lord comaundide to his seruaunt Moises, so Moises comaundide to Josue, and 'he fillide alle thingis; he passide not of alle comaundementis, 'nether o word sotheli, which the Lord comaundide to Moises.

16 And so Josue took al the 'lond of the hillis, and of the south, the lond of Gosen, and the pleyn, and the west coost, and the hil of Israel, and the feeldi places therof;

17 and the part of the hil that stieth to Seir 'til to Baalgath, bi the pleyn of Liban vndur the hil of Hermon; Josue took, and smoot, and killide alle the kyngis of tho places.

18 Josue fauyt myche tyme ayens these kyngis;

19 'no citee was, which bitook not it silf to the sones of Israel, out takun Euey that dwellide in Gabaon; he took alle bi batel.

20 For it was the sentence of the Lord, that 'the hertis of hem schulde be maad hard, and that thei schulden fiyte ayens

Israel, and schulden falle, and schulden not disserue ony mercy, and schulden perische, as the Lord comaundide to Moises.

21 Josue cam in that tyme, and killide Enachym, that is, giauntis, fro the 'hilli placis of Ebron, and of Dabir, and of Anab, and fro al the hil of Juda, and of Israel, and dide awei 'the citees of hem.

22 He lefte not ony man of the generacioun of Enachim in the lond of the sones of Israel, without the citees of Gasa, and Geth, and Azotus, in whiche aloone thei weren left.

23 Therfor Josue took al the lond, as the Lord spak to Moyses, and he yaf it in to possessioun to the sones of Israel, bi her partis and lynagis; and the lond restide fro batels.

CAP 12

1 These ben the kyngis whiche the sones of Israel han smyte, and weldiden 'the lond of hem, biyende Jordan, at the 'risyng of the sunne, fro the stronde of Arnon 'til to the hil of Hermon, and al the eest coost that biholdith the wildirnesse.

2 Seon, the kyng of Amorreis, that dwellide in Esebon, was lord fro Aroer, which is set on the brenke of the stronde of Arnon, and of the myddil part in the valey, and of half Galaad, til to the stronde of Jaboth, which is the terme of the sones of Amon, and fro the wildirnesse 'til to the see of Ceneroth,

3 ayens the eest, and 'til to the see of deseert, which is the saltist see at the eest coost, bi the weie that ledith to Bethessymoth, and fro the south part that liggith vndur Assedoch, 'til to Phasga.

4 The terme of Og, kyng of Basan, of the relikis of Raphaym, 'that is, giauntis, that dwelliden in Astoroth and in Edraym, and he was lord in the hil of Hermon, and in Salacha, and in al Basan, 'til to the termes of Gessuri and Machati,

5 and of the half part of Galaad, and to the terme of Seon, kyng of Esebon.

6 Moyses, the 'seruaunt of the Lord, and the sones of Israel 'smytiden hem; and Moises yaf 'the lond of hem in to possessioun to Rubenytis and 'to Gadditis and to half the lynage of Manaasses.

7 These ben the kyngis of the lond, whiche Josue and the sones of Israel smytiden biyende Jordan, at the west coost, fro Algad in the feeld of Liban, 'til to the hil whos part stieth in to Seir; and Josue yaf it in to possessioun to the lynagis of Israel, to ech his owne part,

8 as wel in 'hilli placis as in pleyn and feeldi placis; in Asseroth, and in wildirnesse, and in the south was Ethei, and Ammorrei, Cananie, and Pheresei, Euey, and Jebusei.

9 The kyng of Jerico oon; the kyng of Hai, which is at the side of Bethel, oon;

10 the kyng of Jerusalem, oon; the kyng of Ebron, oon;

11 the kyng of Herymoth, oon; the kyng of Lachis, oon; the kyng of Eglon, oon;

12 the kyng of Gazer, oon;

13 the kyng of Dabir, oon; the kyng of Gader, oon;

14 the kyng of Herma, oon;

15 the kyng of Hedreth, oon; the kyng of Lempna, oon; the kyng of Odollam, oon;

16 the kyng of Maceda, oon; the kyng of Bethel, oon;

17 the kyng of Thaphua, oon;

18 the kyng of Affer, oon; the kyng of Affeth, oon; the kyng of Saron, oon; the kyng of Madon, oon;

19 the king of Asor, oon;

20 the kyng of Semeron, oon; the kyng of Axaph, oon;

21 the kyng of Thenach, oon; the kyng of Magedo, oon; the kyng of Cetes, oon;

22 the kyng of Jachanaem of Carmele, oon;

23 the kyng of Dor and of the prouince of Dor, oon; the kyng of folkis of Galgal, oon;

24 the kyng of Thersa, oon; alle the kyngis, oon and thretti.

CAP 13

1 Josue was eld and of greet age; and the Lord seide to him, Thou hast woxe eld, and art of long tyme; and largeste lond is left, which is not yit departid bi lot;

2 that is, al Galile, Filistiym, and al Gessuri,

3 fro the troblid flood that moistith Egipt, 'til to the termes of Acaron ayenus the north; the lond of Chanaan, which is departid 'in to fyue litle kyngis of Filistym, of Gaza, and of Azotus, of Ascolon, of Geth, and of Accaron.

4 Forsothe at the south ben Eueis, al the lond of Canaan, and Maara of Sidonyes, 'til to Affetha, and to the termes of Amorrei, and the coostis of hym;

5 and the cuntrei of Liban ayens the eest, fro Baalgath, vndur the hil of Hermon, til thou entrist into Emath,

6 of alle men that dwelliden in the hil, fro the Liban 'til to the watris of Masserephoth, and alle men of Sidon; Y am, that schal do awei hem fro the face of the sones of Israel; therfor come it in to the part of eritage of Israel, as Y comaundide to thee.

7 And thou now departe the lond in to possessioun to the nyne lynagis, and to the half lynage of Manasses,

8 with which lynage Ruben and Gad weldiden the lond, which lond Moises, the 'seruaunt of the Lord, yaf to hem biyende the flowyngis of Jordan, at the eest coost;

9 fro Aroer, which is set in the brynke of the stronde of Arnon, in the middis of the valei, and alle the feeldi places of Medaba,

10 'til to Dibon, and alle the citees of Seon, kyng of Amorreis, that regnyde in Esebon, 'til to the termes of the sones of Amon,

11 and of Galaad, and to the termes of Gessuri, and of Machati, and al the hil of Hermon, and al Basan, 'til to Salecha;

12 al the rewme of Og in Basan, that regnede in Astoroth, and in Edraym; 'he was of the relikis of Rafaym, 'that is, of giauntis; and Moises smoot hem and dide awey hem.

13 And the sones of Israel nolden destrye Gessurri and Machati; and thei dwelliden in the myddis of Israel, 'til in to present dai.

14 Sotheli he yaf not possessioun to the lynage of Leuy, but sacrifices, and slayn sacrifices of the Lord God of Israel; that is 'his eritage, as God spak to hym.

15 Therfor Moises yaf possessioun to the lynage of the sones of Ruben, bi her kynredis;

16 and 'the term of hem was fro Aroer, which is set in the brenke of the stronde of Arnon, and in the myddil valei of the same stronde, al the pleyn that ledith to Medaba,

17 and Esebon, and alle the townes of tho, that ben in the feeldi places; and Dibon, and Baal Bamoth, and the citee of Baal Meon,

18 and Gesa, and Sedymoth, and Mephe,

19 and Cariathaym, and Sabana, and Sarathaphar, in the hil of the valey of Betheroeth,

20 and of Asedoch, Phasca, and Bethaissymoth;

21 alle the feeldi citees, and alle the rewmes of Seon, kyng of Amorrey, that regnede in Esebon, whom Moyses smoot, with

hise princes, Madian, Euey and Recten, and Sur, and Hur, and Rebee, duykis of Seon, enhabiters of the lond.

22 And the sones of Israel killiden bi swerd Balaam, the fals diuynour, the sone of Beor, with othere men slayn.

23 And the terme of the sones of Ruben was maad the flood of Jordan; this is the possessioun of Rubenytis bi her kynredis of citees and of townes.

24 And Moises yaf to the lynage of Gad, and to the sones therof, bi her kynredis, possessioun, of which this is departyng;

25 he yaf the termes of Jazer, and alle the citees of Galaad, and the half part of the lond of the sones of Amon, 'til to Aroer which is ayens Tabba;

26 and fro Esebon 'til to Ramoth of Masphe, and Bethamyn, and Manayn, 'til to the termes of Dabir;

27 and in the valei he yaf Betharan, and Bethneuar, and Socoth, and Saphan, the tother part of the rewme of Seon, kyng of Esebon; and the ende of this is Jordan, 'til to the laste part of the see of Cenereth ouer Jordan, at the eest coost.

28 This is the possessioun of the sones of Gad, bi her meynees, the citees and townes of tho.

29 He yaf also possessioun to the half lynage of Manasses, and to hise sones, bi her kynredis,

30 of which possessioun this is the bigynnyng; he yaf Ammaym, and al Basan, and alle the rewmes of Og, kyng of Basan, and alle the townes of Jair, that ben in Basan, sixti citees;

31 and half the part of Galaad, and Astoroth, and Edray, the citees of the rewme of Og, kyng of Basan; to the sones of Machir, sones of Manasses, and to half the part of the sones of Machir, bi her kynredis.

32 Moises departide this possessioun in the feeldi placis of Moab ouer Jordan, ayens Jericho, at the eest coost.

33 Forsothe he yaf not possessioun to the lynage of Leuy; for the Lord God himself of Israel is the possessioun of Leuy, as the Lord spak to hym.

CAP 14

1 This 'thing it is, which the sones of Israel weldiden in the lond of Canaan, which lond Eleazar the preest, and Josue, the sone of Nun, and the princes of meynees bi the lynagis of Israel yauen to hem,

2 and departiden alle thingis bi lot, as the Lord comaundide in the hond of Moises, to nyne lynagis and the half lynage.

3 For Moises hadde youe to 'the twey lynagis and to the half lynage 'possessioun ouer Jordan; without the Leuytis, that token no thing of the lond among her britheren;

4 but the sones of Joseph weren departid in to twei lynagis, of Manasses and of Effraym, and 'weren eiris in to the place of hem. And 'the Leuytis token noon other part in the lond, no but citees to dwelle, and the subarbis of tho to werke beestis and her scheep to be fed.

5 As the Lord comaundide to Moises, so the sones of Israel diden, and departiden the lond.

6 And so the sones of Juda neiyiden to Josue in Galgalis; and Caleph, the sone of Jephone, of Ceneth, spak to him, Thou knowist, what the Lord spak to Moises, the man of God, of me and of thee in Cades Barne.

7 Y was of fourti yeer, whanne Moises, 'seruaunt of the Lord, sente me fro Cades Barne, that Y schulde biholde the lond, and Y teelde to hym that, that semyde soth to me.

8 Forsothe my britheren, thats tieden with me, discoumfortiden the herte of the puple, and neuertheles Y suede my Lord God.

9 And Moises swoor in that dai, and seide, The lond, which thi foot trad, schal be thi possessioun, and of thi sones withouten ende; for thou suedist thi Lord God.

10 Sotheli the Lord grauntide lijf to me, as he bihiyte, 'til in to present dai. Fourti yeer and fyue ben, sithen the Lord spak this word to Moises, whanne Israel yede bi the wildirnesse. To dai Y am of 'foure scoor yeer and fyue,

11 and Y am as myyti, as Y was myyti in that time, whanne Y was sent to aspie; the strengthe 'of that tyme dwellith stabli in me 'til to dai, as wel to fiyte, as to go.

12 Therfor yyue thou to me this hil, which the Lord bihiyte to me, while also thou herdist, in which hil ben Enachym, and grete 'citees, and strengthid; if in hap the Lord is with me, and Y mai do hem awei, as he bihiyte to me.

13 And Josue blesside hym, and yaf to hym Ebron in to possessioun.

14 And fro that tyme Ebron was to Caleph, sone of Jephone, of Cenez, 'til in to present dai; for he suede the Lord God of Israel.

15 The name of Ebron was clepid bifore Cariatharbe. Adam, the gretteste, was set there in the lond of Enachym; and the lond ceesside fro batels.

CAP 15

1 Therfor this was the part of the sones of Juda, bi her kynredis; fro the terme of Edom 'til to deseert of Syn ayens the south, and 'til to the laste part of the south coost,

2 the bigynnyng therof fro the hiynesse of the saltist see, and fro the arm therof, that bihooldith to the south.

3 And it goith out ayens the stiyng of Scorpioun, and passith in to Syna; and it stieth in to Cades Barne, and cometh in to Ephron, and it stieth to Daran, and cumpassith Cariacaa;

4 and fro thennus it passith in to Asemona, and cometh to the stronde of Egipt; and the termes therof schulen be the greet see; this schal be the ende of the south coost.

5 Sotheli the eest the bigynnyng schal be the saltiste see, 'til to the laste partis of Jordan, and tho partis, that biholden the north, fro the arm of the see 'til to the same flood of Jordan.

6 And the terme stieth in to Bethaegla, and passith fro the north in to Betharaba; and it stieth to the stoon of Boen,

7 sone of Ruben, and goith 'til to the termes of Debera, fro the valei of Achar ayens the north; and it biholdith Galgala, which is 'on the contrarie part of the stiyng of Adomyn, fro the south part of the stronde; and it passith the watris, that ben clepid the welle of the sunne; and the outgoyngis therof schulen be to the welle of Rogel.

8 And it stieth bi the valei of the sone of Ennon, bi the side of Jebusei, at the south; this is Jerusalem; and fro thennus it reisith it silf to the cop of the hil, which is ayens Jehennon at the west, in the hiynesse of the valei of Raphaym, ayens the north;

9 and it passith fro the 'cop of the hil til to the wel of the watir Nepthoa, and cometh 'til to the tounes of the hil of Ephron; and it is bowid in to Baala, which is Cariathiarym, that is, the citee of woodis;

10 and it cumpassith fro Baala ayens the west, 'til to the hil of Seir, and it passith bi the side of the hil Jarym to the north in Selbon, and goith doun in to Bethsamys; and it passith in to Thanna,

11 and cometh ayens the partis of the north bi the side of Accaron; and it is bowid to Secrona, and passith the hil of Baala; and it cometh in to Gebneel, and it is closid with the ende of the grete see, ayens the west.

12 These ben the termes of the sones of Juda, bi cumpas in her meynees.

13 Sotheli Josue yaf to Caleph, sone of Jephone, part in the myddis of the sones of Juda, as the Lord comaundide to hym, Cariatharbe, of the fadir of Enach; thilke is Ebron.

14 And Caleph dide awei fro it thre sones of Enach, Sisai, and Achyman, and Tholmai, of the generacioun of Enach.

15 And Caleph stiede fro thennus, and cam to the dwelleris of Dabir, that was clepid bifore Cariathsepher, that is, the citee of lettris.

16 And Caleph seide, Y schal yyue Axa, my douyter, wijf to hym that schal smyte Cariathsepher, and schal take it.

17 And Othynyel, sone of Ceneth, the yongere brother of Caleph, took that citee; and Caleph yaf Axa, his douytir, wijf to hym.

18 And whanne 'sche yede togidere, hir hosebonde counseilide hir, that sche schulde axe of hir fadir a feeld; and sche siyyide, as sche sat on the asse;

19 'to whom Caleph seide, What hast thou? And sche answeride, Yyue thou blessyng to me; thou hast youe to me the south lond and drye; ioyne thou also the moist lond. And Caleph yaf to hir the moist lond, aboue and bynethe.

20 This is the possessioun of the lynage of the sones of Juda, bi her meynees.

21 And the citees weren fro the laste partis of the sones of Juda, bisidis the termes of Edom, fro the south; Capsahel, and Edel, and Jagur, Ectyna,

22 and Dymona, Edada,

23 and Cades, and Alor,

24 and Jethnan, and Ipheth, and Thelon,

25 and Balaoth, and Asor, Nobua, and Cariath, Effron;

26 this is Asseromam; Same,

27 and Molida, and Aser, Gabda, and Assemoth,

28 Bethfelech, and Asertual, and Bersabee,

29 and Baiohia, and Baala, and Hymesen,

30 and Betholad, and Exul, and Herma,

31 and Sichelech, and Meacdemana, and Sensena,

32 Lebeoth, and Selymetem Remmoth; alle 'the citees, nyn and thretti, and the townes 'of tho.

33 Sotheli in the feeldi places, Escoal, and Sama,

34 and Asena, and Azanoe, and Engannem, and Taphua,

35 and Enaym, and Jecemoth, Adulam, Socco, and Azecha, and Sarym,

36 Adytaym, and Gedam, and Giderothaym; fourtene citees, and 'the townes of tho;

37 Sanam, and Aseba, and Magdalgad,

38 Delen, and Melcha, Bethel, Lachis,

39 and Baschat, and Esglon,

40 Esbon, and Leemas,

41 and Cethlis, and Gideroth, and Bethdagon, and Neuma, and Maceda; sixtene citees, and 'the townes of tho; 'Jambane,

42 and Ether, and Asam,

43 Jepta, and Jesua,

44 and Nesib, and Ceila, and Azib, and Mareza, nyn citees, and 'the townes of tho;

45 'Accaron with hise townes and vilagis;

46 fro Accaron til to the see, alle thingis that gon to Azotus, and the townes therof;

47 Azotus with hise townes and vilagis; Gaza with hise townes and villagis, til to the stronde of Egipt; and the grete see is the terme therof;

48 and in the hil, Samyr,

49 and Jeccher, and Socco, and Edema, Cariath Senna;

50 this is Dabir; Anab, and Ischemo,

51 and Ammygosen, and Olom, and Gilo, enleuene 'citees, and the townes of tho;

52 'Arab, and Roma,

53 and Esaam, and Amum,

54 and Bethfasua, and Afecha, Ammacha, and Cariatharbe; this is Ebron; and Sior, nyn citees, and 'the townes of tho;

55 'Maon, and Hermen, and Ziph, and Jothae,

56 Zerahel, and Zocadamer, and Anoe, and Chaym,

57 Gabaa, and Kanna, ten citees, and 'the citees of tho;

58 'Alul, and Bethsur,

59 and Jodor, Mareth, and Bethanoth, and Bethecen, sixe citees, and the townes of tho;

60 Cariathbaal; this is Cariathiarym, the citee of woodis; and Rebda, twei citees, and 'the townes of tho;

61 in deseert, 'Betharaba, Medyn, and Siriacha, Nepsan,

62 and the citee of salt, and Engaddi, sixe citees, and 'the townes of tho; 'the citees weren togidere an hundrid and fiftene.

63 Sotheli the sones of Juda myyten not do awei Jebusei, the dwellere of Jerusalem; and Jebusei dwellide with the sones of Juda in Jerusalem 'til in to present day.

CAP 16

1 And the lot, 'ethir part, of the sones of Joseph felde fro Jordan ayens Jerico, and at the watris therof, fro the eest; is the wildirnesse, that stieth fro Jerico to the hil of Bethel,

2 and it goith out fro Bethel 'in to Luzan, and passith the terme of Architaroth,

3 and it goith doun to the west, bisidis the terme of Jefleti, 'til to the termes of the lowere Bethoron, and of Gazer; and the cuntrees therof ben endid with the greet see,

4 whiche cuntreis Manasses and Effraym, the sones of Joseph, weldiden.

5 And the terme of the sones of Effraym, bi her meynees, and 'the possessioun of hem was maad ayens the eest, Accarothaddar 'til to the hiyere Bethoron.

6 And the coostis goon out in to the see; sotheli Mathmetath biholdith the north, and cumpassith the termes ayens the eest in Tharnarselo,

7 and passith fro the stronde of Janee; and it goith doun fro Janee in to Atharoth and Noathara, and cometh in to Jerico; and it goith out to Jordan fro Taphua,

8 and passith ayens the see in to the valey of 'the place of rehedis; and the goyngis out therof ben to the salteste see. This is the possessioun of the sones of Effraym, bi her meynees;

9 and citees and the townes of tho ben departid to the sones of Effraym, in the myddis of the possessioun of the sones of Manasses.

10 And the sones of Effraym killiden not Cananey, that dwellide in Gazer; and Cananey dwellide tributarie in the myddis of Effraym til in to this day.

CAP 17

1 Forsothe lot felde in to the lynage of Manasse, for he is the firste gendrid sone of Joseph; lot felde to Machir, the firste

gendrid sone of Manasses, to the fadir of Galaad, that was a werriour, and he hadde possessioun Galaad and Basan.

2 And lot felde to the othere of the sones of Manasses, bi her meynees; to the sones of Abiezer, and to the sones of Heleth, and to the sones of Hesriel, and to the sones of Sichen, and to the sones of Epher, and to the sones of Semyda; these ben the sones of Manasse, sone of Joseph, the male children, bi her meynees.

3 Sotheli to Salphaat, the sone of Epher, sone of Galaad, sone of Machir, sone of Manasses, weren not sones, but douytris aloone; of whiche these ben the names, Maala, and Noa, and Eegla, and Melcha, and Thersa.

4 And thei camen in the siyt of Eleazar, preest, and of Josue, sone of Nun, and of the princes, and seiden, The Lord comaundide bi the hond of Moises, that possessioun should be youun to vs in the myddis of oure britheren. And Josue yaf to hem possessioun, bi comaundement of the Lord, in the myddis of the britheren of her fadir.

5 And ten cordis, 'that is, londis mesurid bi ten cordis, felden to Manasses, without the lond of Galaad and of Basan biyende Jordan;

6 for the douytris of Manasses weldiden eritage in the myddis of the sones of hym. Sotheli the lond of Galaad felde in to the part of the sones of Manasses, that weren residue.

7 And the terme of Manasses was fro Azer Machynathath, that biholdeth Sichem, and goith out to the riyt side, bisidis the dwelleris of the welle Taphue;

8 for the lond of Thaphue, which is bisidis the terme of Manasses, and of the sones of Effraym, felde in the lot of Manasses.

9 And the terme of the valey of place of rehedis goith doun in the south of the stronde of the citees of Effraym, that ben in the myddis of the citees of Manasses. The terme of Manasses is fro the north of the stronde, and the goyng out therof goith to the see;

10 so that the possessioun of Effraym is fro the south, and the possessioun of Manasses fro the north, and the see closith euer either; and tho ben ioyned to hem silf in the linage of Aser fro the north, and in the lynage of Isachar fro the eest.

11 And the eritage of Manasses was in Isachar and in Aser, Bersan, and the townes therof, and Jeblaan, with hise townes, and the dwellers of Dor, with her citees; and the dwelleris of Endor, with her townes, and also the dwelleris of Thanath, with her townes, and the dwelleris of Maiedo, with her townes, and the thridde part of the citee Nophet.

12 And the sones of Manasses miyten not distrie these citees, but Cananei bigan to dwelle in this lond.

13 Sotheli aftir that the sones of Israel weren stronge, thei maden suget Cananeis, and maden tributaries to hem silf, and killiden not Cananeis.

14 And the sones of Joseph spaken to Josue, and seiden, Whi hast thou youe to me lond in to possessioun of o lot and part, sithen Y am of so greet multitude, and the Lord hath blesside me, 'that is, hath alargid me in children?

15 To whiche Josue seide, If thou art myche puple, stie thou into the wode, and kitte doun to thee spaces in the lond of Feresei, and of Raphaym, for the possessioun of the hil of Effraym is streiyt to thee.

16 To whom the sones of Joseph answerden, We moun not stie to the hilli places, sithen Cananeis, that dwellen in the 'lond of the feeld, vsen ironne charis; in which lond Bersan, with hise townes, and Jesrael, weldynge the myddil valey, ben set.

17 And Josue seide to the hows of Joseph, and of Effraym, and of Manasses, Thou art myche puple, and of greet strengthe; thou schalt not haue o lot,

18 but thou schalt passe to the hil, and thou schalt kitte doun to thee; and thou schalt clense spaces to dwelle. And thou schalt mow go forth ferthere, whanne thou hast distried Cananei, whom thou seist to haue irone charis, and to be moost strong.

CAP 18

1 And alle the sones of Israel weren gaderid in Silo, and there thei 'settiden faste the tabernacle of witnessing; and the lond was suget to hem.

2 Sotheli seuene linagis of the sones of Israel dwelliden, that hadden not yit takun her possessiouns.

3 To whiche Josue seide, Hou longe faden ye 'bi cowardise, 'ethir slouthe, and entren not to welde the lond, which the Lord God of youre fadris yaf to you?

4 Chese ye of ech lynage thre men, that Y sende hem, and thei go, and cumpasse the lond; and that thei discryue 'the lond bi the noumbre of ech multitude, and brynge to me that, that ye han discriued.

5 Departe ye the lond to you in to seuene partis; Judas be in hise termes at the south coost, and 'the hows of Joseph at the north;

6 discryue ye 'the myddil lond bitwixe hem in to seuene partis; and thanne ye schulen come to me, that Y sende lot to you here bifor youre Lord God;

7 for the part of Leuytis is not among you, but the preesthod of the Lord, this is the eritage 'of hem. Forsothe Gad, and Ruben, and the half lynage of Manasses hadden take now her possessiouns ouer Jordan, at the eest coost, whiche possessiouns Moises, the 'seruaunt of the Lord, yaf to hem.

8 And whanne the men hadden rise to go, to discryue the lond, Josue comaundide to hem, and seide, Cumpasse ye the lond, and discryue it, and turne ayen to me, that Y sende lot to you here in Silo, bifore youre Lord God.

9 And so thei yeden, and cumpassiden that lond, and departiden 'in to seuene partis, writynge in a book; and thei turneden ayen to Josue, in to the castels in Silo.

10 Which Josue sente lottis bifor the Lord God in Silo, and departide the lond to the sones of Israel, in to seuene partis.

11 And the firste lot of the sones of Beniamyn, bi her meynees, stiede, that thei schulden welde the lond bitwixe the sones of Juda and the sones of Joseph.

12 And the terme of hem was ayens the north fro Jordan, and passide bi the side of Jerico of the north coost; and it stiede fro thennus ayens the west to the hilli places, and it cam to the wildirnesse of Bethauen;

13 and it passide bisidis Luza to the south; thilke is Bethel; and it goith doun in to Astoroth Adar, in to the hil which is at the south of lowere Betheron; and is bowid,

14 and cumpassith ayens the see, at the south of the hil that biholdith Betheron ayens the north; and the outgoyngis therof ben in to Cariathbaal, which is clepid also Cariathiarym, the citee of the sones of Juda; this is the greet coost ayens the see, at the west.

15 Sotheli fro the south, bi the part of Cariathiarym, the terme goith out ayens the see, and cometh til to the wel of watris of Nepthoa;

16 and it goith doun in to the part of the hil that biholdith the valei of the sones of Ennon, and is ayens the north coost, in

the laste part of the valey of Raphaym; and Jehennon, that is, the valei of Ennon, goith doun bi the side of Jebusei, at the south, and cometh to the welle of Rogel,

17 and passith to the north, and goith out to Emsemes, that is, the welle of the sunne,

18 and passith to the litle hillis that ben ayens the stiyng of Adomyn; and it goith doun to Taben Boen, that is, the stoon of Boen, sone of Ruben, and passide bi the side of the north to the feeldi places; and it goith doun in to the pleyn,

19 and passith forth ayens the north to Bethagala; and the out-goyngis therof ben ayens the arm of the salteste see, fro the north, in the ende of Jordan at the south coost,

20 which is the terme therof fro the eest. This is the posses-sioun of the sones of Beniamyn, bi her termes in cumpas, and bi her meynees;

21 and the citees therof weren Jerico, and Bethagla, and the valei of Casis,

22 Betharacha, and Samaraym,

23 and Bethel, and Anym, and Affara,

24 and Offira, the toun of Hesmona, and Offym, and Gabee, twelue citees, and 'the townes of tho;

25 Gabaon, and Rama,

26 and Beroth, and Mesphe, and Caphera, and Ammosa,

27 and Recem, Jarephel, and Tharela,

28 and Sela, Heleph, and Jebus, which is Jerusalem, Gabaath, and Cariath, fouretene citees and 'the townes of tho; this is the possessioun of the sones of Beniamyn, bi her meynees.

CAP 19

1 And the secounde lot of the sones of Symeon yede out, bi her meynees; and the eritage of hem,

2 in the myddis of possessioun of the sones of Juda, was Ber-sabee, and Sabee,

3 and Melada, and Asersua, Bala,

4 and Asem, and Betholaad, Bethularma, and Siceleth,

5 and Bethmarchaboth, and Asersua,

6 and Bethelebaoth, and Saroem, threttene citees, and 'the townes of tho;

7 Aym, and Remmon, and Athar, and Asam, foure citees, and 'the townes of tho; alle the townes bi cumpas of these citees,

8 'til to Balath Brameth, ayens the south coost, weren seuent-ene citees. This is the eritage of the sones of Symeon, bi her meynees,

9 in the possessioun and part of the sones of Juda, for it was more; and therfor the sones of Symeon hadden possessioun in the myddis of the eritage therof.

10 And the thridde lot of the sones of Zabulon felde, bi her meynees; and the terme of possessioun of the sones of Zabu-lon was maad 'til to Sarith;

11 and it stieth fro the see, and Medala; and it cometh in to Debbaseth, 'til to the stronde which is ayens Jecenam;

12 and it turneth ayen fro Sarith, ayens the eest, in to the coostis of Sechelech Tabor; and goith out to Daberth; and it stieth ayens Jasie;

13 and fro thennus it passith to the eest coost to Gethefer, and Thacasym; and it goith out in to Remmon, Amphar, and Noa; and cumpassith to the north, and Nachon;

14 and the goyngis out therof ben the valei of Jeptael,

15 and Cathel, and Neamai, and Semrom, and Jedaba, and Bethleem, twelue citees, and 'the townes of tho.

16 This is the eritage of the lynage of the sones of Zabulon, bi her meynees, and the citees and 'townes of tho.

17 The fourthe lot yede out to Isacar, bi hise meynees; and the eritage therof was Jezrael,

18 and Casseloth,

19 and Symen, and Affraym, and Seon,

20 and Anaarath, and Cabith, and Cesion, Hames,

21 and Ramech, and Enganym, and Enadda, and Bethfeses.

22 And the terme therof cometh 'til to Tabor, and Seesyma, and Hethsemes; and the outgoyngis therof weren Jordan, six-tene citees, and 'the townes of tho.

23 This is the possessioun of the sones of Ysachar, bi her meynees, the citees and the townes of tho.

24 And the fiuethe lot felde to the lynage of the sones of Aser, by her meynees;

25 and the terme of hem was Alchat, and Adi, and Bethen,

26 and Mesaph, and Elmelech, and Amaad, and Messal; and it cometh 'til to Carmel of the see, and Sior, and Labanath; and it turneth ayen,

27 ayens the eest, to Bethdagan; and passith 'til to Zabulon, and to the valei of Jeptael, ayens the north, in Bethemeth, and Neyel; and it goith out to the left side to Gabul,

28 and Acran, and Roob, and Omynon, and Chane, 'til to grete Sidon;

29 and it turneth ayen in to Horma, 'til to the strongeste citee Tire, and 'til to Ossam; and the outgoyngis therof schulen be in to the see, fro the part of Aczyma,

30 and Affeth, and Roob; two and twenti citees, and 'the townes of tho.

31 This is the possessioun of the sones of Aser, bi her mey-nees, 'the citees, and 'townes of tho.

32 The sixte lot of the sones of Neptalym felde, bi her mey-nees;

33 and the terme bigan of Heleth, and Helon, and Sannaira, and Adarny, 'which is Neceb, and Jebnael, 'til to Letum; and the outgoyng of hem til to Jordan;

34 and the terme turneth ayen, ayens the west, in to Arnoth of Thabor; and fro thennus it goith out in to Hucota, and passith in to Zabulon, ayens the south, and in to Asor, ayens the west, and in to Juda, at Jordan, ayens the risyng of the sunne;

35 of the strongeste citee Assydym, Ser, and Amraath,

36 and Rechath, Cenereth, and Edema,

37 and Arama, Asor, and Cedes, and Edrai,

38 Nason, and Jeron, and Magdael, Horem, and Bethanath, and Bethsemes; nyntene citees, and 'the townes of tho.

39 This is the possessioun of the lynage of the sones of Nep-talym, bi her meynees, the citees, and the townes of tho.

40 The seuenthe lot yede out to the lynage of the sones of Dan, bi her meynees;

41 and the terme of the possessioun therof was Saraa, and Ascahol, and Darsemes, that is, the citee of the sunne,

42 Selenym, and Hailon, and Jethala,

43 Helom, and Thenna, and Acrom,

44 Helthecem, Jebtom, and Baalath, Lud,

45 and Benebarach, and 'Jethremmon, and Ihercon,

46 and Arecon, with the terme that biholdith Joppen,

47 and is closid with that ende. And the sones of Dan stieden, and fouyten ayens Lesem; and thei token it, and smytiden it bi the scharpnes of swerd, and hadden in possessioun, and dwelliden therynne; and thei clepiden the name therof Lesan Dan, by the name of Dan, her fadir.

48 This is the possessioun of the lynage of Dan, bi her mey-nees, the citees, and townes of tho.

49 And whanne thei hadden fillid to departe the lond bi lot to alle men bi her lynagis, the sones of Israel yauen possessioun to Josue, sone of Nun,

50 in the myddis of hem, bi the comaundement of the Lord, the citee which he axide, Thannath Sara, in the hil of Effraym; and he bildide the citee, and dwellide therynne.

51 These ben the possessiouns whiche Eleazar, preest, and Josue, sone of Nun, and the princis of meynees, and of the lynagis of the sones of Israel, departiden bi lot in Silo, bifor the Lord, at the dore of tabernacle of witnessing, and departiden the lond.

CAP 20

1 And the Lord spak to Josue, and seide, Spek thou to the sones of Israel, and seie thou to hem,

2 Departe ye the citees of fugytyues, 'ether of men exilid for vnwilful schedyng of blood, of whiche citees Y spak to you bi the hond of Moises,

3 that whoeuer sleeth vnwytyngli a man, fle to tho citees;

4 that whanne he hath fled to oon of these citees, he may ascape the ire of the neiybore, which is veniere of blood. And he schal stonde bifor the yatis of the citee, and he schal speke to the eldre men of that citee tho thingis that schulen preue hym innocent; and so thei schulen reseyue hym, and schulen yyue to hym place to dwelle.

5 And whanne the vengere of blood pursueth hym, thei schulen not bitake hym in to the hondis of the vengere; for vnwityngli he killide his neiybore, and is not preued his enemy bifor the secounde dai ethir the thridde dai.

6 And he schal dwelle in that citee, til he stonde bifor the doom, and yelde cause of his dede. And he that killide a man, dwelle 'in that citee, til the grete preest die, which is in that tyme; thanne the mansleere schal turne ayen, and he schal entre in to his citee and hows, 'fro which he fledde.

7 And thei ordeyneden Cedes in Galilee, of the hil of Neptalym, and Sichem in the hil of Effraym, and Cariatharbe, thilke is Ebron, in the hil of Juda.

8 And biyende Jordan, ayens the eest coost of Jerico, thei ordeyneden Bosor, which is set in the feeldi wildirnesse of the lynage of Ruben, and Ramoth in Galaad, of the lynage of Gad, and Gaulon in Basan, of the lynage of Manasses.

9 These citees weren ordeyned to alle the sones of Israel, and to comelyngis that dwellen among hem, that he that killide vnwityngli a man, schulde fle to tho citees; and he schulde not die in the hond of neiybore, coueitynge to venge the blood sched out, til he stood bifor the puple, to declare his cause.

CAP 21

1 And the princes of meynees of Leuy neiyiden to Eleazar, preest, and to Josue, sone of Nun, and to the duykis of kynredis, bi alle the lynagis of the sones of Israel;

2 and the Leuytis spaken to hem in Sylo, of the lond of Canaan, and seiden, The Lord comaundide bi the honde of Moises, that citees schulden be youun to vs to dwelle ynne, and the subarbis of tho to werk beestis to be fed.

3 And the sones of Israel yauen 'of her possessiouns, bi comaundement of the Lord, citees and the subarbis of tho.

4 And the lot yede out in to the meynee of Caath, of the sones of Aaron, preest, of the lynages of Juda, and of Symeon, and of Beniamyn, threttene citees;

5 and to the othere of the sones of Caath, that is, to dekenes that weren left, of the lynagis of Effraym, and of Dan, and of the half lynage of Manasse, ten citees.

6 Sotheli lot yede out to the sones of Gerson, that thei schulden take of the lynagis of Isachar, and of Aser, and of Neptalym, and of the half lynage of Manasses 'in Basan, threttene citees in noumbre;

7 and to the sones of Merari, bi her meynees, of the lynagis of Ruben, and of Gad, and of Zabulon, twelue citees.

8 And the sones of Israel yauen to dekenes cytees, and the subarbis 'of tho, as the Lord comaundide bi the hond of Moises; and alle yauen bi lot.

9 Of the lynagis of the sones of Juda, and of Symeon, Josue yaf citees;

10 to the sones of Aaron, bi the meynees of Caath, of the kyn of Leuy, of whiche citees these ben the names; for the firste lot yede out to hem;

11 Cariatharbe, of the fadir of Enach, which is clepid Ebron, in the hil of Juda, and the subarbis therof bi cumpas;

12 sotheli he hadde youe the feeldis and townes therof to Caleph, sone of Jephone, to haue in possessioun.

13 Therfor Josue yaf to the sones of Aaron, preest, Ebron, a citee of refuyt, and the subarbis 'of it, and Lebnam with hise subarbis,

14 and Jether, and Yschymon,

15 and Elon, and Dabir, and Ayn, and Lethan,

16 and Bethsames, with her subarbis; nyne citees, of twei lynagis, as it is seid.

17 Sotheli of the lynage of the sones of Beniamyn, he yaf Gabaon, and Gabee, and Anatoth, and Almon, with her subarbis;

18 'foure citees.

19 Alle the citees togidere of the sones of Aaron, preest, weren threttene, with her subarbis.

20 Forsothe to 'the othere, bi the meynees of the sones of Caath, of the kyn of Leuy, this possessioun was youun;

21 of the lynage of Effraym, the citee of refuyt, Sichen, with hise subarbis, in the hil of Effraym, and Gazer,

22 and Sebsam, and Bethoron, with her subarbis;

23 'foure citees; also of the lynage of Dan, Helthece, and Gebethon, and Haialon,

24 and Gethremmon, with her subarbis;

25 'foure citees; sotheli of the half lynage of Manasses, Thanach, and Gethremon, with her subarbis; 'twei citees.

26 Alle the citees ten, and the subarbis 'of tho weren youun to the sones of Caath, of the lowere degree.

27 Also to the sones of Gerson, of the kyn of Leuy, Josue yaf of the half lynage of Manasses, citees of refuyt, Gaulon in Basan, and Bosra, with her subarbis, 'twei citees.

28 Forsothe of the lynage of Isachar, he yaf Cesion, and Daberath,

29 and Jerimoth, and Engannym, with her subarbis; 'foure citees.

30 Of the lynage of Aser, he yaf Masal, and Abdon,

31 and Elecath, and Roob, with her subarbis; 'foure citees.

32 Also of the lynage of Neptalym, 'he yaf the citee of refuyt, Cedes in Galile, and Amodor, and Carthan, with her subarbis; 'thre citees.

33 Alle the citees of the meynees of Gerson weren threttene, with her subarbis.

34 Sotheli to the sones of Merary, dekenes of the lowere degree, bi her meynees, was youun Getheran, of the linage of Zabulon, and Charcha, and Demna, and Nalol;

35 'foure citees, with her subarbis.

36 And of the lynage of Gad, he yaf the citee of refuyt, Ramoth in Galaad, and Manaym, and Esebon, and Jaser; 'foure citees, with her subarbis.

37 And of the lynage of Ruben, biyende Jordan, ayens Jerico, he yaf 'the citee of refuyt, Bosor in the wildirnesse of Mysor, and Jazer, and Jecson, and Maspha; 'foure citees, with her subarbis.

38 Alle the citees of Merary, bi her meynees and kynredis, weren twelue.

39 And so alle the citees of Leuytis, in the myddis of possessioun of the sones of Israel, weren eiyte and fourti, with her subarbis;

40 and alle citees weren departid by meynees.

41 And the Lord yaf to Israel al the lond which he swoor hym silf to yyue to the fadris 'of hem, and thei hadden it in possessioun, and dwelliden therynne.

42 And pees was youun of hym in to alle naciouns 'by cumpas; and noon of enemyes was hardi to withstonde hem, but alle weren dryuen in to the lordschip 'of hem.

43 Forsothe nether o word, which he bihiyte him silf to yyue to hem, was voide, but alle wordis weren fillid in werkis.

CAP 22

1 In the same tyme Josue clepide men of Ruben, and men of Gad, and half the lynage of Manasses,

2 and seide to hem, Ye han do alle thingis whiche Moises, 'seruaunt of the Lord, comaundide to you, also ye obeieden to me in alle thingis;

3 nether ye han lefte youre britheren in mych tyme til in to present dai, and ye kepten the comaundement of youre Lord God.

4 Therfor for youre Lord God yaf reste and pees to youre britheren, as he bihiyte, turne ye ayen, and go ye in to youre tabernaclis, and in to the loond of youre possessioun, which lond Moyses, the 'seruaunt of the Lord, yaf to you biyende Jordan;

5 so onely that ye kepe bisili, and fille in werk the comaundement and lawe, 'which lawe Moises, the 'seruaunt of the Lord, comaundide to you; that ye loue youre Lord God, and go in alle hise weies, and kepe hise heestis, and cleue to hym and serue him in al youre herte, and in al youre soule.

6 And Josue blesside hem, and lefte hem, whiche turneden ayen in to her tabernaclis.

7 Sotheli Moyses hadde youe possessioun in Basan to the half lynage of Manasses; and therfor to the half lynage that lefte Josue yaf part among her othere britheren biyendis Jordan, at the west coost therof. And whanne Josue leet hem go in to her tabernaclis, and hadde blessid hem,

8 he seyde to hem, With myche catel and richessis turne ye ayen to youre seetis; with siluer and gold, and bras, and yrun, and myche clothing; departe ye the prey of enemyes with youre britheren.

9 And the sones of Ruben, and the sones of Gad, and 'half the lynage of Manasses turneden ayen, and yeden fro the sones of Israel fro Silo, which is set in the lond of Canaan, that thei schulden entre in to Galaad, the lond of her possessioun, which thei gaten bi 'comaundement of the Lord in the hond of Moises.

10 And whanne thei hadden come to the litle hillis of Jordan, in to the lond of Canaan, thei bildiden bisidis Jordan an auter of greetnesse ouer comyn mesure.

11 And whanne the sones of Israel hadden herd this, and certeyn messangeris hadden teld to hem, that the sones of Ruben, and of Gad, and the half lynage of Manasses hadden

bildid an auter in the lond of Canaan, on the heepis of Jordan, ayens the sones of Israel,

12 alle camen togidir in Silo, that thei schulden stie, and fiyte ayens hem.

13 And in the meene tyme thei senten to hem in to the lond of Galaad, Fynees, preest,

14 the sone of Eleazar, and ten princes with hym; of ech lynage o prince.

15 Whiche camen to the sones of Ruben, and of Gad, and of the half lynage of Manasses, in to the lond of Galaad, and seiden to hem,

16 Al the puple of the Lord sendith these thingis; What is this trespassyng? Whi han ye forsake the Lord God of Israel, and han bildid a cursid auter, and han go awei fro the worschiping of hym?

17 Whether it is litil to you that ye synneden in Belfegor, and the wem of this trespas dwellith in you til in to present dai, and many of the puple felden doun?

18 And to day ye han forsake the Lord, and to morewe, that is, in tyme to comynge, the ire of hym schal be feers ayens al Israel.

19 That if ye gessen, that the lond of youre possessioun is vncleene, passe to the lond, 'in which the tabernacle of the Lord is, and dwelle ye among vs, oneli that ye go not awei fro the Lord, and fro oure felouschipe, bi an auter bildid outakun the auter of oure Lord God.

20 Whether not Achar, the sone of Zare, passide the comaundement of the Lord, and his ire felde on al the puple of Israel? And he was o man; and we wolden that he aloone hadde perischid in his trespas.

21 And the sones of Ruben, and of Gad, and of half the lynage of Manasses, answeriden to the princes of the message of Israel,

22 The strongeste Lord God hym silf of Israel knowith, and Israel schal vndirstonde togidere; if we bildiden this auter for entent of trespassyng, 'that is, of ydolatrye, he kepe not vs, but punysche in present time;

23 and if we diden bi that mynde, that we schulden putte theronne brent sacrifice, and sacrifice, and pesible sacrifices, he seke, and deme;

24 and not more 'bi that thouyt and tretyng that we seiden, Youre sones schulen seie 'to morew to oure sones, What is to you and to the Lord God of Israel? Ye sones of Ruben,

25 and ye sones of Gad, the Lord hath set a terme, the flood Jordan, bitwixe vs and you; and therfor ye han not part in the Lord; and bi this occasioun youre sones schulen turne awei oure sones fro the drede of the Lord. Therfor we gessiden betere,

26 and seiden, Bilde we an auter to vs, not in to brent sacrifices, nethir to sacrifices to be offrid,

27 but in to witnessyng bitwixe vs and you, and bitwixe oure children and youre generacioun, that we serue the Lord, and that it be of oure riyt to offre brent sacrifices, and sacrifices, and pesible sacrifices; and that youre sones seie not to morewe to oure sones, No part in the Lord is to you.

28 And if 'youre sones wolen seie this, 'oure sones schulen answere hem, Lo! the auter of the Lord, which oure fadris maden, not in to brent sacrifices, nether in to sacrifice, but in to oure and your witnessing euerlastinge.

29 Fer be this trespas fro vs, that we go awei fro the Lord, and forsake hise steppis, bi an auter bildid to brent sacrifices, and sacrifices, and sacrifices of preisyng to be offrid, outakun the auter of oure 'Lord God, which is bildid bifore his tabernacle.

30 And whanne these thingis weren herd, Fynees, preest, and the princes of message of Israel, that weren with hym, weren plesyd; and thei resseyueden gladli the wordis of the sones of Ruben, and of Gad, and of the half lynage of Manasses.

31 And Finees, preest, the sone of Eleazar, seide to hem, Now we wyten, that the Lord is with you; for ye ben alien fro this trespassyng, and ye han delyuered the sones of Israel fro the hond, 'that is, punyschyng, of the Lord.

32 And Fynees turnede ayen with the princes fro the sones of Ruben and of Gad, fro the lond of Galaad to the coost of Canaan, to the sones of Israel; and he telde to hem.

33 And the word pleside to alle men herynge; and the sones of Israel preisiden God, and seiden, that no more 'thei schulden stie ayens hem, and fiyte, and do awei the lond of her possessioun.

34 And the sones of Ruben and the sones of Gad clepiden the auter, which thei hadden bildid, Oure Witnessyng, that the Lord hym silf is God.

CAP 23

1 Forsothe whanne myche tyme was passid after that the Lord had youe pees to Israel, for alle naciouns 'in cumpas weren suget; and whanne Josue was thanne of long lijf, and 'of ful eld age, Josue clepide al Israel,

2 and the grettere men in birthe, and the princes, and dukis, and maistris, and seide to hem, Y 'wexide elde, and Y am of grettere age;

3 and ye seen alle thingis whiche youre Lord God hath do to alle naciouns 'bi cumpas, hou he fauyt for you.

4 And now for he departide to you bi lot al the lond, fro the eest part of Jordan 'til to the grete see, and many naciouns ben left yit,

5 youre Lord God 'schal distrie hem, and schal take awei fro youre face; and ye schulen welde the lond, as he bihiyte to you.

6 Oneli be ye coumfortid, and be ye bisy, that ye kepe alle thingis that ben writun in the book of Moises lawe, and bowe not awei fro tho, nether to the riyt side nether to the left side,

7 lest aftir that ye han entrid to the hethene men, that schulen be among you, ye swere in the name of 'the goddis of hem, and ye serue tho goddis, and worschipe hem.

8 But cleue ye to youre Lord God, which thing ye han do 'til in to this dai;

9 and thanne the Lord God schal do awei in youre siyt grete folkis, and strongeste; and noon schal mow ayenstonde you.

10 Oon of you schal pursue a thousynde men of enemyes, for youre Lord God schal fiyte for you, as he bihiyte.

11 Be ye war bifore moost diligentli of this thing oneli, that ye loue youre Lord God.

12 That if ye wolen cleue to the errouris of these folkis that dwellen among you, and wolen medle mariagis with hem, and couple frenschipis,

13 wite ye riyt now, that 'youre Lord God schal not do awei hem bifor youre face, but thei schulen be to you in to a dich, and a snare, and in to hirtyng of youre side, and in to stakis in youre iyen, til youre Lord God take awei you, and distrie fro this beste loond, which he yaf to you.

14 Lo! Y entre to dai in to the weye of al erthe; and ye schulen knowe 'with al soule, that of al wordis whiche the Lord bihiyte hym silf to yyue to you, not oon passide in veyn.

15 Therfor as he fillide in werk that, that he bihiyte, and alle thingis bifelden 'bi prosperite, so he schal brynge on you whateuer thing of yuelis he manaasside, til he take awei you, and distrie fro this beste lond, which he yaf to you.

16 For ye braken the couenaunt of 'youre Lord God, which he made with you, and serueden alien goddis, and worschipeden hem, sone and swiftli the strong veniaunce of the Lord schal rise 'on to you; and ye schulen be takun awei fro this beste lond, which he yaf to you.

CAP 24

1 And Josue gaderide alle the lynagis of Israel in to Sechem; and he clepide the grettere men in birthe, and the princes, and iugis, and maistris; and thei stoden in the siyt of the Lord.

2 And he spak thus to the puple, The Lord God of Israel seith these thingis, Youre fadris dwelliden at the bigynnyng biyende the flood Eufrates, Thare, the fadir of Abraham, and Nachor, and thei serueden alien goddis.

3 Therfor Y took youre fadir Abraham fro the coostis of Mesopotanye, and Y brouyte hym in to the lond of Canaan; and Y multipliede 'the seed of hym,

4 and Y yaf Isaac to hym; and eft Y yaf to Isaac, Jacob, and Esau, of whiche Y yaf to Esau the hil of Seir, to 'haue in possessioun; forsothe Jacob and hise sones yeden doun in to Egipt.

5 And Y sente Moises and Aaron, and Y smoot Egipt with many signes and wondris,

6 and Y ledde you and youre fadris out of Egipt. And ye camen to the see, and Egipcians pursueden youre fadris with charis, and multitude of knyytis, 'til to the Reed See.

7 Forsothe the sones of Israel crieden to the Lord, and he settide derknessis bitwixe you and Egipcians; and he brouyte the see on hem, and hilide hem. Youre iyen sien alle thingis, whiche Y dide in Egipt. And ye dwelliden in wildirnesse in myche tyme.

8 And Y brouyte you in to the lond of Ammorrei, that dwellide biyende Jordan; and whanne thei fouyten ayens you, Y bitook hem in to youre hondis, and ye hadden in possessioun 'the lond of hem, and ye killiden hem.

9 Sotheli Balach, the sone of Sephor, the king of Moab, roos, and fauyt ayens Israel; and he sente, and clepide Balaam, the sone of Beor, that he schulde curse you.

10 And Y nolde here hym, but ayenward bi hym Y blesside you, and delyuerede you fro hise hondis.

11 And ye passiden Jordan, and camen to Jerico; and men of that citee fouyten ayens you, Ammorrei, and Feresei, and Cananei, Ethei, and Gergesei, and Euei, and Jebusei; and Y bitook hem in to youre hondis.

12 And Y sente flies with venemouse tongis bifor you, and Y castide hem out of her places; Y kyllide twei kyngis of Ammorreis, not in thi swerd and bowe.

13 And Y yaf to you the lond in which ye traueiliden not, and citees whiche ye bildiden not, that ye schulden dwelle in tho, and vyneris, and places of olyue trees, whiche ye plauntiden not.

14 Now therfor drede ye the Lord, and serue ye hym with perfite herte and moost trewe; and do ye awei the goddis, to whiche youre fadris seruyden in Mesopotanye, and in Egipt; and serue ye the Lord.

15 But if it semeth yuel to you, 'that ye serue the Lord, chesyng is youun to you; chese ye to you to dai that, that plesith, whom ye owen most to serue; whether to goddis, whiche youre fadris serueden in Mesopotanye, whether to the goddis of Ammorreis, in whose lond ye dwellen; forsothe Y, and myn hows schulen serue the Lord.

16 And al the puple answeride and seide, Fer be it fro vs that we forsake the Lord, and serue alien goddis.

17 'Oure Lord God hym silf ledde vs and oure fadris out of the lond of Egipt, fro the hows of seruage, and dide grete signes in oure siyt; and he kepte vs in al the weie, bi which we yeden, and in alle puplis, bi whiche we passiden; and he castide out alle folkis,

18 Ammorrei, the dwellere of the lond, in to which we entriden. Therfor we schulen serue the Lord, for he is 'oure Lord God.

19 And Josue seide to the puple, Ye moun not serue the Lord; for God is hooli, and a strong feruent louyere, and he foryyueth not youre trespassis and synnes.

20 If ye forsaken the Lord, and seruen alien goddis, the Lord schal turne 'hym silf, and schal turment you, and schal distrie, after that he hath youe goodis to you.

21 And the puple seide to Josue, It schal not be so, as thou spekist, but we schulen serue the Lord.

22 And Josue seide to the puple, Ye ben witnessis, that ye han chose the Lord to you, that ye serue him. And thei answeriden, We ben witnessis.

23 Therfor, he seide, Now do ye awei alien goddis fro the myddis of you, and bowe ye youre hertis to the Lord God of Israel.

24 And the puple seide to Josue, We schulen serue 'oure Lord God, and we schulen be obedient to hise heestis.

25 Therfor Josue smoot a boond of pees in that dai, and settide forth to the puple comaundementis and domes in Sichen.

26 And he wroot alle these wordis in the book of Goddis lawe. And he took a greet stoon, and puttide it vndur an ook, that was in the seyntuarie of the Lord.

27 And he seide to al the puple, Lo! this stoon schal be to you in to witnessing, that ye herden alle the wordis of the Lord, whiche he spak to you, lest perauenture ye wolden denye aftirward, and lye to youre Lord God.

28 And he lefte the puple, ech man in to his possessioun.

29 And after these thingis Josue, the sone of Nun, the 'seruaunt of the Lord, diede, an hundride yeer eld and ten.

30 And thei birieden hym in the costis of his possessioun, in Thannath of Sare, which is set in the hil of Effraym, fro the north part of the hil Gaas.

31 And Israel seruede the Lord in alle the daies of Josue, and of the eldre men, that lyueden in long tyme aftir Josue, and whiche eldre men knewen alle the werkis of the Lord, whiche he hadde do in Israel.

32 Also 'the sones of Israel birieden the boonys of Joseph, whiche thei baren fro Egipt in Sichen, in the part of the feeld, which feeld Jacob bouyte of the sones of Emor, fadir of Sichen, for an hundrid yonge scheep; and it was in to possessioun of the sones of Joseph.

33 Also Eliazar, sone of Aaron, preest, diede; and Fynees and hise sones biryden hym in Gabaa, which was youun to hym in the hil of Efraym.

JUDGES

CAP 1

1 Aftir the deeth of Josue the sones of Israel counseliden the Lord, and seiden, Who schal stie bifor vs ayens Cananei, and schal be duik of the batel?

2 And the Lord seide, Judas schal stie; lo! Y haue youe the lond in to hise hondis.

3 And Juda seide to Symeon, his brother, Stie thou with me in my lot, and fiyte thou ayens Cananei, that Y go with thee in thi lot.

4 And Symeon yede with hym; and Judas stiede. And the Lord bitook Cananey and Feresei in to 'the hondis of hem, and thei killiden in Besech ten thousynde of men.

5 And thei founden Adonybozech in Besech, and thei fouyten ayens hym, and smytiden Cananei, and Feresey.

6 Forsothe Adonybozech fledde, whom thei pursueden, and token, and kittiden the endis of hise hondis and feet.

7 And Adonybozech seide, Seuenti kyngis, whanne the endis of hondis and feet weren kit awey, gaderiden relifs of metis vndur my bord; as Y dide, so God hath yolde to me. And thei brouyten hym in to Jerusalem, and there he diede.

8 Therfor the sones of Juda fouyten ayens Jerusalem, and token it, and smytiden bi the scharpnesse of swerd, and bitoken al the cytee to brennyng.

9 And aftirward thei yeden doun, and fouyten ayens Cananey, that dwellide in the hilli places, and at the south, in 'feeldi places.

10 And Judas yede ayens Cananei, that dwellide in Ebron, whos name was bi eld tyme Cariatharbe; and Judas killide Sisay, and Achyman, and Tholmai.

11 And fro thennus he yede forth, and yede to the dwelleris of Dabir, whos eld name was Cariathsepher, that is, the citee of lettris.

12 And Caleph seide, Y schal yyue Axa, my douyter, wijf to hym that schal smyte Cariathsepher, and schal waste it.

13 And whanne Othonyel, sone of Seneth, the lesse brother of Caleph, hadde take it, Caleph yaf Axa, his douyter, wijf to hym.

14 And hir hosebonde stiride hir, goynge in the weie, that sche schulde axe of hir fadir a feeld; and whanne sche hadde siyid, sittynge on the asse, Caleph seide to hir, What hast thou?

15 And sche answeride, Yiue thou blessyng to me, for thou hast youe a drye lond to me; yyue thou also a moyst lond with watris. And Caleph yaf to hir the moist lond aboue, and the moist lond bynethe.

16 Forsothe the sones of Cyney, 'alye of Moyses, stieden fro the citee of palmes with the sones of Juda, in to the desert of his lot, which desert is at the south of Arath; and dwelliden with hym.

17 Sotheli Judas yede with Symeon, his brother; and thei smytiden togidere Cananei, that dwellide in Sephar, and killiden hym; and the name of that citee was clepid Horma, that is, cursyng, 'ether perfit distriyng, for thilke citee was distried outerly.

18 And Judas took Gaza with hise coostis, and Ascolon, and Accaron with hise termes.

19 And the Lord was with Judas, and he 'hadde in possessioun the hilli places; and he myyte not do awey the dwelleris of the valei, for thei weren plenteuouse in 'yrun charis, scharpe as sithis.

20 And 'the sones of Israel yauen Ebron to Caleph, as Moises hadde seid, which Caleph dide awei for it thre sones of Enach.

21 Forsothe the sones of Beniamyn diden not awei Jebusei, the dwellere of Jerusalem; and Jebusei dwellide with the sones of Beniamyn in Jerusalem 'til in to present dai.

22 Also the hows of Joseph stiede in to Bethel, and the Lord was with hem.

23 For whanne thei bisegiden the citee, that was clepid Lusa bifore,

24 thei sien a man goynge out of the citee, and thei seiden to hym, Schewe thou to vs the entrynge of the cytee, and we schulen do mercy with thee.

25 And whanne he hadde schewid to hem, thei smytiden the citee bi scharpnes of swerd; sotheli thei delyueriden that man and al his kynrede.

26 And he was delyuerede, and yede in to the lond of Sethym, and bildide there a citee, and clepid it Luzam; which is clepid so til in to present dai.

27 Also Manasses dide not awei Bethsan and Thanael with her townes, and the dwelleris of Endor, and Geblaam and Magedo with her townes; and Cananei bigan to dwelle with hem.

28 Sotheli after that Israel was coumfortid, he made hem tributaries, 'ethir to paye tribute, and nolde do awey hem.

29 Sotheli Effraym killide not Cananei that dwellyde in Gaser, but dwellide with hym.

30 Zabulon dide not awey the dwelleris of Cethron, and of Naalon; but Cananei dwellide in the myddis of hym, and was maad tributarie to him.

31 Also Aser dide not awey the dwelleris of Acho, and of Sidon, of Alab, and of Azazib, and of Alba, and Aphech, and of Aloa, and of Pha, and of Roob; and he dwellide in the myddis of Cananey,

32 dwellere of that lond, and killide not hym.

33 Neptalym dide not awei the dwelleris of Bethsames, and of Bethanach; and he dwellide among Cananey, dwellere of the lond; and Bethsamytis and Bethanytis weren tributarie to hym.

34 And Ammorrey helde streit the sones of Dan in the hil, and yaf not place to hem to go doun to pleynere places;

35 and he dwellide in the hil of Hares, 'which is interpretid, Witnessyng, in Hailon, and in Salabym. And the hond of the hows of Joseph was maad heuy, and he was maad tributarie to hym.

36 And the terme of Ammorrei was fro the stiyng of Scorpioun, and the stoon, and hiyere places.

CAP 2

1 And the aungel of the Lord stiede fro Galgala to the place of weperis, and seide, Y ledde you out of Egipt, and Y brouyte you in to the lond, 'for which Y swoor to youre fadris, and bihiyte, that Y schulde not make void my couenaunt with you in to with outen ende;

2 so oneli that ye schulde not smyte boond of pees with the dwelleris of this lond, and schulden distrie 'the auteris of hem; and ye nolden here my vois. Whi diden ye these thingis?

3 Wherfore Y nolde do hem awei fro youre face, that ye haue enemyes, and that 'the goddis of hem be to you in to fallyng.

4 And whanne the 'aungel of the Lord spak these wordis to alle the sones of Israel, thei reisiden her vois, and wepten; and the name of that place was clepid,

5 of weperis, ether of teeris; and thei offriden there sacrifices to the Lord.

6 Therfor Josue lefte the puple; and the sones of Israel wenten forth, ech man in to his possessioun, that thei schulden gete it.

7 And thei serueden the Lord in alle the daies of Josue, and of eldere men that lyueden aftir hym in long tyme, and knewen alle the grete werkis of the Lord, whiche he hadde do with Israel.

8 Forsothe Josue, sone of Nun, 'seruaunt of the Lord, 'was deed of an hundrid yeer and ten;

9 and thei birieden hym in the endis of his possessioun, in Thannath of Sare, in the hil of Effraym, at the north coost of the hil Gaas.

10 And al that generacioun was gaderid to her fadris; and othere men riseden, that knewen not the Lord, and the werkis whiche he 'hadde do with Israel.

11 And the sones of Israel diden yuel in the siyt of the Lord, and thei serueden Baalym and Astaroth;

12 and forsoken the Lord God of her fadris, that ledden hem out of the lond of Egipt; and thei sueden alien goddis, the goddis of puplis, that dwelliden in 'the cumpasse of hem, and worschipeden tho goddis, and excitiden the Lord to greet wraththe, and forsoken hym,

13 and serueden Baal and Astoroth.

14 And the Lord was wrooth ayens Israel, and bitook hem in to the hondis of rauyscheris, whiche rauyscheris token hem, and seelden to enemyes, that dwelliden 'bi cumpas; and thei myyten not ayenstonde her aduersaries;

15 but whidir euer thei wolden go, the hond of the Lord was on hem, as he spak and swoor to hem; and thei weren turmentid greetli.

16 And the Lord reiside iugis, that 'delyueriden hem fro the hondis of destrieris, but thei nolden here hem,

17 and thei diden fornycacioun, 'that is, idolatrie, with alien goddis, and worschipiden hem. Soone thei forsoken the weie, bi which 'the fadris of hem entriden; and thei herden the 'comaundementis of the Lord, and diden alle thingis contrarie.

18 And whanne the Lord reiside iugis in 'the daies of hem, he was bowid bi mercy, and he herde the weilyngis of hem turmentid, and he delyuerede hem fro the sleyng of wasteris.

19 Sotheli aftir that the iuge was deed, thei turneden ayen, and diden many thingis grettere 'in yuel than her fadris diden; and thei sueden alien goddis, and serueden hem, and worschipiden hem; thei leften not her owne fyndyngis, and the hardeste weie 'bi which thei weren wont to go.

20 And the strong veniaunce of the Lord was wrooth ayens Israel, and he seide, For this puple hath maad voide my couenaunt which Y couenauntide with her fadris, and dispiside to here my vois; also Y schal not do a wey folkis,

21 whiche Josue 'lefte, and was deed;

22 that in hem Y asaie Israel, whether thei kepen the weie of the Lord, and goen ther ynne, as her fadris kepten, ether nay.

23 Therfor the Lord lefte alle these naciouns, and nolde destrie soone, nethir bitook in to the hondis of Josue.

CAP 3

1 These ben the folkis whiche the Lord lefte, that in hem he schulde teche Israel, and alle men that knewen not the batels of Cananeis;

2 and that aftirward 'the sones of hem schulden lerne to fiyte with enemyes,

3 and to haue custom of batel He lefte fyue princes of Filistees, and al Cananei, and the puple of Sidon, and Euey that dwelliden in the hil Liban, fro the hil Baal Hermon 'til to the entryng of Emath.

4 And he lefte hem, that in hem he schulde asaie Israel, whethir thei wolden here the 'heestis of the Lord, whiche he comaundide to her fadris bi the hond of Moises, ethir nai.

5 And so the sones of Israel dwelliden in the myddis of Cananei, of Ethei, and of Ammorrei, and of Feresei, and of Euey,

6 and of Jebusey, and weddiden wyues, the douytris of hem; and the sones of Israel yauen her douytris to 'the sones of hem, and serueden 'the goddis of hem.

7 And the sones of Israel diden yuel in the 'siyt of the Lord, and foryaten her Lord God, and serueden Baalym, and Astaroth.

8 And the Lord was wrooth ayens Israel, and bitook hem in to the hondis of Cusanrasathaym, kyng of Mesopotanye, and thei serueden hym eiyte yeer.

9 And thei crieden to the Lord, and he reiside to hem a sauy-our, and delyuerede hem, that is, Othonyel, sone of Ceneth, 'the lesse brothir of Caleph.

10 And the spirit of the Lord was in hym, and he demyde Israel. And he yede out to batel, and the Lord bitook in to hise hondis Cusanrathaym, kyng of Sirie; and Othonyel oppres-side hym.

11 And the lond restide fourti yeer; and Othonyel, sone of Ceneth, diede.

12 Forsothe the sones of Israel addiden to do yuel in the 'siyt of the Lord; and he coumfortide ayens hem Eglon, the kyng of Moab, for 'thei diden yuel in the 'siyt of the Lord.

13 And the Lord couplide to hym the sones of Amon and Amalech; and he yede, and smoot Israel, and hadde in posses-sioun the citee of Palmes.

14 And the sones of Israel serueden Eglon, kyng of Moab, eiytene yeer.

15 And aftirward thei crieden to the Lord; and he reiside to hem a sauyour, Aioth bi name, the sone of Gera, sone of Gemyny, which Aioth vside euer either hond for the riyt hond. And the sones of Israel senten bi him yiftis, 'that is, tribute, to Eglon, kyng of Moab;

16 which Aioth made to hym a swerd keruynge on euer either side, hauynge in the myddis a pomel of the lengthe of the pawm of an hond; and he was gird therwith vndir 'the sai, 'that is, a knyytis mentil, 'in the riyt hipe.

17 And he brouyte yiftis to Eglon, the kyng of Moab; forsothe Eglon was ful fat.

18 And whanne he hadde youe yiftis to the kyng, he pursuede felowis that camen with hym; and he turnede ayen fro Galga-lis,

19 where idolis weren, and he seide to the kyng, A kyng, Y haue a priuei word to thee. And he comaundide silence. And whanne alle men weren goon out, that weren aboute hym, Aioth entride to hym;

20 forsothe he sat aloone in a somer parlour. And Aioth seide, Y haue the word of God to thee.

21 Which roos anoon fro the trone. And Aioth helde forth the left hond, and took the swerd fro his riyt hype; and he

22 fastnede in to the 'wombe of the kyng so strongli, that the pomel, 'ether hilte, suede the yrun in the wounde, and was holdun streite 'in the thickeste fatnesse with ynne; and he drow not out the swerd, but so as he hadde smyte, he lefte in the bodi; and anoon bi the priuetees of kynde the tordis of the wombe braste out.

23 Forsothe whanne the doris of the parlour weren closid moost diligentli, and fastned with lok,

24 Aioth yede out bi a posterne. And the 'seruauntis of the king entriden, not in the parlour, but in the porche, and thei sien the doris of the parlour closid, and seiden, In hap he pur-gith the wombe in the somer parlour.

25 And thei abididen longe, til thei weren aschamed; and thei sien that no man openede, and thei token the keie, and thei openyden, and founden her lord liggynge deed in the erthe.

26 Sotheli while thei weren disturblid, Aioth fledde out, and passide the place of idols, fro whennus he turnede ayen; and he cam in to Seirath.

27 And anoon he sownede with a clarioun in the hil of Effraym; and the sones of Israel camen doun with hym, and he yede in the frount.

28 Which seide to hem, Sue ye me, for the Lord hath bitake oure enemyes, Moabitis, in to oure hondis. And thei camen doun after hym, and ocupieden the forthis of Jordan, that ledde ouer in to Moab.

29 And thei suffriden not ony man to passe, but thei smytiden Moabitis in that tyme aboute ten thousande, alle myyti men and stronge; no man of hem myyte ascape.

30 And Moab was maad low in that dai vndur the hond of Israel, and the lond restide fourescoor yeer.

31 Aftir hym was Samgar, the sone of Anath, that smoot of Filisteis sixe hundrid men with a schar; and he also defendide Israel.

CAP 4

1 And the sones of Israel addiden to do yuel in the 'siyt of the Lord, aftir the deeth of Aioth.

2 And the Lord bitook hem in to the hondis of Jabyn, kyng of Canaan, that regnede in Asor; and he hadde a duyk of his oost, Sisara bi name; and he dwellide in Aroseth of hethene men.

3 And the sones of Israel crieden to the Lord; for he hadde nyn hundrid yrone charis, keruynge as sithis, and twenti yeer he oppresside hem greetli.

4 Forsothe Delbora was a prophetesse, the wijf of Lapidoth, which Delbora demyde the puple in that tyme;

5 and sche sat vndur a palm tree, that was clepid bi her name, bitwixe Rama and Bethel, in the hil of Effraym; and the sones of Israel stieden to hir at ech dom. And sche sente, and clepide Barach, the sone of Abynoen, of Cedes of Neptalym, and sche seide to hym, The Lord God of Israel comaundide to thee, Go thou, and lede an oost in to the hil of Thabor, and thou schalt take with thee ten thousande 'of fiyteris of the sones of Neptalym and of the sones of Zabulon.

7 Sotheli Y schal brynge to thee, in the place of the stronde of Cison, Sisara, prince of 'the oost of Jabyn, and his charis, and al the multitude; and Y schal bitake hem in thin hond.

8 And Barach seide to hir, If thou comest with me, Y schal go; if thou nylt come with me, Y schal not go.

9 And sche seyde to hym, Sotheli Y schal go with thee; but in this tyme the victorie schal not be arettide to thee; for Sisara schal be bitakun in the hond of a womman. Therfor Delbora roos, and yede with Barach in to Cedes.

10 And whanne Zabulon and Neptalym weren clepid, he stiede with ten thousynde of fiyteris, and hadde Delbora in his felouschipe.

11 Forsothe Aber of Cyneth hadde departid sum tyme fro oth-ere Cyneys hise britheren, sones of Obab, 'alie of Moises; and he hadde set forth tabernaclis 'til to the valei, which is clepid Sennym, and was bisidis Cedes.

12 And it was teld to Sisara, that Barach, sone of Abynoen, hadde stiede in to the hil of Thabor.

13 And he gaderide nyn hundrid yronne charis, keruynge as sithis, and al the oost fro Aroseth of hethene men to the stronde of Cison.

14 And Delbora seide to Barach, Rise thou, for this is the day, in which the Lord bitook Sisara in to thin hondis; lo! the Lord

is thi ledere. And so Barach cam doun fro the hil of Thabor, and ten thousynde of fyyteris with hym.

15 And the Lord made aferd Sisara, and alle 'the charis of hym, and al the multitude, bi the scharpnesse of swerd, at the siyt of Barach, in so myche that Sisara lippide doun of the chare, and fledde 'a foote. And Barach pursuede the charis fleynge and the oost 'til to Aroseth of hethene men; and al the multitude of enemyes felde doun 'til to deeth.

17 Sotheli Sisara fledde, and cam to the tente of Jahel, the wijf of Aber Cyney; forsothe pees waas bitwixe Jabyn, kyng of Asor, and bitwixe the hows of Aber Cyney.

18 Therfor Jahel yede out in to the comyng of Sisara, and seide to hym, My lord, entre thou to me, entre thou to me; drede thou not. And he entride in to 'the tabernacle of hir, and was hilid of hir with a mentil.

19 And he seide to hir, Y biseche, yyue 'thou to me a litil of watir, for Y thirste greetli. And sche openyde a 'botel of mylk, and yaf to hym to drynke, and hilide hym.

20 And Sisara seide to hir, Stonde thou bifor the dore of the tabernacle, and whanne ony man cometh, and axith thee, and seith, Whether ony man is here? thou schalt answere, No man is here.

21 And so Jahel, the wijf of Aber, took a nayl of the tabernacle, and sche took also an hamer; and sche entride pryueli, and puttide with silence the nail on the temple of his heed, and sche fastnede the nail smytun with the hamer in to the brayn, 'til to the erthe; and he slepte, and diede to gidere, and failide, and was deed.

22 And lo! Barach suede Sisara, 'and cam; and Jahel yede out in to his comyng, and seide to hym, Come, and Y schal schewe to thee the man, whom thou sekist. And whanne he hadde entrid to hir, he siy Sisara liggynge deed, and a nail fastnede in to hise templis.

23 Therfor in that day God 'made low Jabyn, the kyng of Canaan, bifor the sones of Israel; whiche encresiden ech dai, and with strong hond oppressiden Jabyn, the kyng of Canaan, til thei diden hym awey.

CAP 5

1 And Delbora and Barach, sone of Abynoen, sungen in that dai, and seiden,

2 Ye men of Israel, that 'offriden wilfuli youre lyues to perel, blesse the Lord.

3 Ye kingis, here, ye princes, perceyueth with eeris; Y am, Y am the womman, that schal synge to the Lord; Y schal synge to the Lord God of Israel.

4 Lord, whanne thou yedist out fro Seir, and passidist bi the cuntrees of Edom, the erthe was moued, and heuenes and cloudis droppiden with watris; hillis flowiden fro the 'face of the Lord,

5 and Synai fro the face of the Lord God of Israel.

6 In the daies of Sangar, sone of Anach, in the daies of Jahel, paththis restiden, and thei that entriden bi tho yeden bi paththis out of the weie.

7 Stronge men in Israel cessiden, and restiden, til Delbora roos, a modir in Israel.

8 The Lord chees newe batels, and he destriede the yatis of enemyes; scheeld and spere apperiden not in fourti thousynde of Israel.

9 Myn herte loueth the princes of Israel; ye that offriden you to perel bi youre owyn wille,

10 blesse ye the Lord; speke ye, that stien on schynynge assis, and sitten aboue in doom, and goen in the wey.

11 Where the charis weren hurtlid doun to gidere, and the oost of enemyes was straunglid, there the 'riytfulnessis of the Lord be teld, and mercy among the stronge of Israel; thanne the 'puple of the Lord cam doun to the yatis, and gat prinsehod.

12 Rise, rise thou, Delbora, rise thou, and speke a song; rise thou, Barach, and thou, sone of Abynoen, take thi prisoneris.

13 The relikis of the puple ben sauyd; the Lord fauyt ayens stronge men of Effraym.

14 He dide awei hem in Amalech, and aftir hym of Beniamyn in to thi puplis, thou Amalech. Princes of Machir and of Zabulon yeden doun, that ledden oost to fiyte.

15 The duykis of Isachar weren with Delbora, and sueden the steppis of Barach, which yaf hym silf to perel, as in to a dich, and in to helle. While Ruben was departid ayens hym silf; the strijf of greet hertyd men was foundun.

16 Whi dwellist thou bitwixe 'tweyne endis, that thou here the hissyngis of flockis? While Ruben was departid ayens hym silf, the strijf of greet hertid men was foundun.

17 Gad restide biyendis Jordan, and Dan yaf tent to schippis. Aser dwellide in the 'brenke of the see, and dwellide in hauenes.

18 Forsothe Zabulon and Neptalym offriden her lyues to deeth, in the cuntre of Morema, 'that is interpretid, hiy.

19 Kyngis camen, and fouyten; kyngis of Canaan fouyten in Thanath, bisidis the watris of Magedon; and netheles thei token no thing bi prey.

20 Fro heuene 'me fauyt ayens hem; sterris dwelliden in her ordre and cours, and fouyten ayens Sisara.

21 The stronde of Cyson drow 'the deed bodies of hem, the stronde of Cadymyn, the stronde of Cyson. My soule, to-trede thou stronge men.

22 The hors howis felden, while the strongeste of enemyes fledden with bire, and felden heedli.

23 Curse ye the lond of Meroth, seide the 'aungel of the Lord, curse ye 'the dwelleris of hym, for thei camen not to the help of the Lord, 'in to the help of the strongeste of hym.

24 Blessyd among wymmen be Jahel, the wijf of Aber Cyney; blessid be sche in hir tabernacle.

25 To Sisara axynge watir sche yaf mylk, and in a viol of princes sche yaf botere.

26 Sche puttide the left hond to a nail, and the riyt hond to the 'hameris of smyythis; and sche smoot Sisara, and souyte in the heed a place of wounde, and perside strongli the temple.

27 He felde bitwixe 'the feet of hir, he failide, and diede; he was waltryd bifor hir feet, and he lay with out soule, and wretchidful.

28 His modir bihelde bi a wyndow, and yellide; and sche spak fro the soler, Whi tarieth his chaar to come ayen? Whi tarieden the feet of his foure horsid cartis?

29 Oon wisere than 'othere wyues of hym answeride these wordis to the modir of hir hosebonde,

30 In hap now he departith spuylis, and the faireste of wymmen is chosun to hym; clothis of dyuerse colouris ben youun to Sisara in to prey, and dyuerse aray of houshold is gaderid to ourne neckis.

31 Lord, alle thin enemyes perische so; sotheli, thei that louen thee, schyne so, as the sunne schyneth in his risyng.

32 And the lond restide fourti yeer.

CAP 6

1 Forsothe the sones of Israel diden yuel in the 'siyt of the Lord, and he bitook hem in the hond of Madian seuene yeer.

2 And thei weren oppressid of hem greetly; and 'thei maden dichis, and dennes to hem silf in hillis, and strongeste places to fiyte ayen.

3 And whanne Israel hadde sowe, Madian stiede, and Amalech, and othere of the 'naciouns of the eest;

4 and thei settiden tentis at the sones of Israel, and wastiden alle thingis 'as tho weren in eerbis, ethir grene corn, 'til to the entryng of Gaza, and outirli thei leften not in Israel ony thing perteynynge to lijf, not scheep, not oxun, not assis.

5 For thei and alle her flockis camen with her tabernaclis, and at the licnesse of locustus thei filliden alle thingis, and a multitude of men and of camels was with out noumbre, and wastiden what euer thing thei touchiden.

6 And Israel was 'maad low greetli in the siyt of Madian.

7 And Israel criede to the Lord, 'and axyde help ayens Madianytis; and he sente to hem a man,

8 a profete, and he spak, The Lord God of Israel seith these thingis, Y made you to stie fro Egipt, and Y ledde you out of the hows of seruage,

9 and Y delyueride you fro the hond of Egipcians, and of alle enemyes that turmentiden you; and Y castide hem out at youre entryng, and Y yaf to you 'the lond of hem;

10 and Y seide, Y am 'youre Lord God; drede ye not the goddis of Ammorreis, in whose lond ye dwellen; and ye nolden here my vois.

11 Forsothe an aungel of the Lord cam, and sat undur an ook, that was in Effra, and perteynede to Joas, fadir of the meinee of Ezri. And whanne Gedeon, 'his sone, threischide out, and purgide wheetis in a pressour,

12 that he schulde fle Madian, an aungel of the Lord apperide to hym, and seide, The Lord be with thee, thou strongeste of men.

13 And Gedeon seide to hym, My lord, Y biseche, if the Lord is with vs, whi therfor han alle these yuels take vs? Where ben the merueils of hym, whiche oure fadris telden, and seiden, The Lord ledde vs out of Egipt? 'Now forsothe he hath forsake vs, and hath bitake vs in the hond of Madian.

14 And the Lord bihelde to hym, and seide, Go thou in this strengthe of thee, and thou schalt delyuere Israel fro the hond of Madian; wite thou, that Y sente thee.

15 Which Gedeon answeride, and seide, My lord, Y biseche, in what thing schal Y delyuere Israel? Lo! my meynee is the loweste in Manasses, and Y am the leeste in the hows of my fadir.

16 And the Lord seide to hym, Y schal be with thee, and thou schalt smyte Madian as o man.

17 And Gedeon seide, If Y haue foundun grace bifor thee, yyue to me a signe, that thou, that spekist to me, art sente of Goddis part;

18 go thou not 'awei fro hennus, til Y turne ayen to thee, and brynge sacrifice, and offre to thee. Whiche answeride, Y schal abide thi comyng.

19 And so Gedeon entride, and sethide a kide, and took therf looues of a buyschel of mell, and fleischis in a panyere; and he sente the broth of fleischis in a pot, and bar alle thingis vndur an ook, and offride to hym.

20 To whom the aungel of the Lord seide, Take thou the fleischis, and therf looues, and putte on that stoon, and schede the broth aboue. And whanne he hadde do so,

21 the aungel of the Lord helde forth the 'ende of the yerde which he helde in the hond, and he touchide the fleischis, and the therf looues; and fier stiede fro the stoon, and wastide the fleischis, and therf looues. Forsothe the aungel of the Lord vanyschide fro hise iyen.

22 And Gedeon siy that he was 'an aungel of the Lord, and seide, Lord God, alas to me, for Y siy the aungel of the Lord face to face.

23 And the Lord seide to hym, Pees be with thee; drede thou not, thou schalt not die.

24 Therfor Gedeon bildide there an auter to the Lord, and he clepide it the Pees of the Lord, 'til in to present dai. And whanne he was yit in Effra, which is of the meynee of Ezri, the Lord seide to hym in that nyyt,

25 Take thou 'the bole of thy fadir, and anothir bole of seuene yeer, and thou schalt distrie the auter of Baal, which is thi fadris, and kitte thou doun the wode, which is aboute the auter;

26 and thou schalt bilde an auter to thi Lord God in the hiynesse of this stoon, on which thou puttidist sacrifice bifore; and thou schalt take the secounde bole, and thou schalt offre brent sacrifice on the heep of trees, whiche thou kittidist doun of the wode.

27 Therfore Gedeon took ten men of hise seruauntis, and dide as the Lord comaundide to hym. Sotheli Gedeon dredde the hows of his fadir, and the men of that citee, and nolde do bi dai, but fillide alle thingis bi nyyt.

28 And whanne men of that citee hadde rise eerly, thei sien the auter of Baal distried, and the wode kit doun, and the tothir bole put on the auter, that was bildid thanne.

29 And thei seiden togidere, Who hath do this? And whanne thei enqueriden the doer of the deed, it was seid, Gedeon, the sone of Joas, dide alle these thingis.

30 And thei seiden to Joas, Brynge forth thi sone hidur, that he die, for he distriede the auter of Baal, and kittide doun the wode.

31 To whiche he answeride, Whether ye ben the venieris of Baal, that ye fiyte for hym? he that is aduersarie of hym, die, bifor that the 'liyt of the morew dai come; if he is God, venge he hym silf of hym that castide doun his auter.

32 Fro that dai Gedeon was clepid Gerobaal, for Joas hadde seid, Baal take veniaunce of hym that castide doun his auter.

33 Therfor al Madian, and Amalech, and the puplis of the eest weren gadirid to gidere, and passiden Jordan, and settiden tentis in the valey of Jezrael.

34 Forsothe the spirit of the Lord clothide Gedeon; 'and he sownede with a clarioun, and clepide to gidere the hows of Abiezer, that it schulde sue hym.

35 And he sente messangeris in to al Manasses, and he suede Gedeon; and he sente othere messangeris in to Aser, and Zabulon, and Neptalym, whiche camen to hym.

36 And Gedeon seide to the Lord, If thou makist saaf Israel bi myn hond, as thou hast spoke,

37 Y schal putte this flees of wolle in the corn floor; if dew is in the flees aloone, and drynesse is in al the erthe, Y schal wite, that thou schalt delyuere Israel bi myn hond, as thou hast spoke.

38 And it was don so. And he roos bi nyyt, and whanne the flees was wrongun out, he fillide a pot with deew;

39 and he seide eft to the Lord, Thi strong veniaunce be not wrooth ayens me, if Y asaie, 'that is, axe a signe, yit onys, and seke a signe in the flees; Y preye, that the flees aloone be drie, and al the erthe be moist with deew.

40 And the Lord dide in that nyyt, as Gedeon axide; and drynesse was in the flees aloone, and deew was in al the erthe.

CAP 7

1 Therfor Jerobaal, which also Gedeon, roos bi nyyt, and al
the puple with hym, and cam to the welle which is clepid
Arad. Sotheli the tentis of Madian weren in the valey, at the
north coost of the hiy hil.

2 And the Lord seide to Gedeon, Myche puple is with thee,
and Madian schal not be bitakun in to the hondis 'ther of, lest
Israel haue glorie ayens me, and seie, Y am delyuerid bi my
strengthis.

3 Speke thou to the puple, and preche thou, while alle men
heren, He that is ferdful 'in herte, and dredeful 'with outforth,
turne ayen. And thei yeden awei fro the hil of Galaad, and
two and twenti thousynde of men turniden ayen fro the puple;
and oneli ten thousynde dwelliden.

4 And the Lord seide to Gedeon, Yet the puple is myche; lede
thou hem to the watris, and there Y schal preue hem, and he
go, of whom Y schal seye, that he go; turne he ayen, whom Y
schal forbede to go.

5 And whanne the puple hadde go doun to watris, the Lord
seide to Gedeon, Thou schalt departe hem bi hem silf, that
lapen watris with hond and tunge, as doggis ben wont to
lape; sotheli thei, that drynken with knees bowid, schulen be
in the tothir part.

6 And so the noumbre of hem, that lapiden watris bi hond
castynge to the mouth, was thre hundrid men; forsothe al the
tothir multitude drank knelynge.

7 And the Lord seide to Gedeon, In thre hundrid men, that
lapiden watris, Y schal delyuere you, and Y schal bitake
Madian in thin hond; but al the tothir multitude turne ayen in
to her place.

8 And so whanne thei hadden take meetis and trumpis for the
noumbre, he comaundide al the tothir multitude to go to her
tabernaclis; and he, with thre hundrid men, yaf hym silf to
batel. Sothely the tentis of Madian weren bynethe in the
valey.

9 In the same nyyt the Lord seyde to hym, Ryse thou, and go
doun in to 'the castels of Madian, for Y haue bitake hem in
thin hond;

10 sotheli if thou dredist to go aloon, Phara, thi child, go doun
with thee.

11 And whanne thou schalt here what thei speken, thanne thin
hondis schulen be coumfortid, and thou schalt do down siker-
ere to the tentis of enemyes. Therfor he yede doun, and Phara,
his child, in to the part of tentis, where the watchis of armed
men weren.

12 Forsothe Madian, and Amalech, and alle the puplis of the
eest layen spred in the valey, as the multitude of locustis;
sotheli the camelis weren vnnoumbrable, as grauel that liggith in the 'brenke of the see.

13 And whanne Gedeon hadde come, a man tolde a dreem to
his neiybore, and telde bi this maner that, that he hadde seyn,
I siy a dreem, and it semyde to me, that as 'o loof of barly
bakun vndur the aischis was walewid, and cam doun in to the
tentis of Madian; and whanne it hadde come to a tabernacle, it
smoot and distriede 'that tabernacle, and made euene outirly
to the erthe.

14 That man answeride, to whom he spak, This is noon other
thing, no but the swerd of Gedeon, 'sone of Joas, a man of
Israel; for the Lord hath bitake Madian and alle 'tentis therof
in to the hondis of Gedeon.

15 And whanne Gedeon had herd the dreem, and 'the interpretyng therof, he worschypide the Lord, and turnede ayen to
the tentis of Israel, and seide, Ryse ye; for the Lord hath
bitake in to oure hondis the tentis of Madian.

16 And he departide thre hundrid men in to thre partis, and he
yaf trumpis in her hondis, and voyde pottis, and laumpis in
the myddis of the pottis.

17 And he seide to hem, Do ye this thing which ye seen me
do; Y schal entre in to a part of the tentis, and sue ye that, that
Y do.

18 Whanne the trumpe in myn hond schal sowne, sowne ye
also 'bi the cumpas of tentis, and crye ye togidere, To the
Lord and to Gedeon.

19 And Gedeon entride, and thre hundrid men that weren
with hym, 'in to a part of the tentis, whanne the watchis of
mydnyyt bigunnen; and whanne the keperis weren reysid,
thei bigunnen to sowne with trumpis, and to bete togidere the
pottis among hem silf.

20 And whanne thei sowneden in thre places bi cumpas, and
hadden broke the pottis, thei helden laumpis in the left hondis, and sownynge trumpis in the riyt hondis; and thei
crieden, The swerd of the Lord and of Gedeon; and stoden
alle in her place,

21 'bi the cumpas of the tentis of enemyes. And so alle 'the
tentis weren troblid; and thei crieden, and yelliden, and fledden;

22 and neuertheles the thre hundrid men contynueden,
sownynge with trumpis. And the Lord sente swerd in alle the
castels, and thei killiden hem silf bi deeth ech other;

23 and thei fledden 'til to Bethsecha, and bi the side, fro
Elmonla in to Thebbath. Sotheli men of Israel crieden
togidere, of Neptalym, and of Aser, and of alle Manasses, and
pursueden Madian; and the Lord yaf victorie to the puple of
Israel in that day.

24 And Gedeon sente messangeris in to al the hil of Effraym,
and seide, Come ye doun ayens the comyng of Madian, and
ocupie ye the watris 'til to Bethbera and Jordan. And al
Effraym criede, and bifore ocupide the watris and Jordan 'til
to Bethbera.

25 And Effraym killide twei men of Madian, Oreb and Zeb;
he killide Oreb in the ston of Oreb, forsothe 'he killide Zeb in
the pressour of Zeb; and 'thei pursueden Madian, and baren
the heedis of Oreb and of Zeb to Gedeon, ouer the flodis of
Jordan.

CAP 8

1 And the men of Effraym seiden to hym, What is this thing,
which thou woldist do, that thou clepidist not vs, whanne thou
yedist to batel ayens Madian? And thei chidden strongli, and
almest diden violence.

2 To whiche he answeride, 'What sotheli siche thing myyte Y
do, what maner thing ye diden? Whethir a reisyn of Effraym
is not betere than the vindagis of Abiezer?

3 And the Lord bitook in to youre hondis the princes of
Madian, Oreb and Zeb. What sich thing myyte Y do, what
maner thing ye diden? And whanne he hadde spoke this
thing, the spirit of hem restide, bi which thei bolneden ayens
hym.

4 And whanne Gedeon hadde come to Jordan, he passide it
with thre hundrid men, that weren with hym; and for weery-
nesse thei myyten not pursue hem that fledden.

5 And he seide to the men of Socoth, Y biseche, yyue ye looues to the puple, which is with me; for thei failiden greetli, that we moun pursue Zebee and Salmana, kyngis of Madian.

6 The princes of Socoth answeriden in scorne, In hap the pawmes of the hondis of Zebee and of Salmana ben in thin hond, and therfor thou axist, that we yyue looues to thin oost.

7 To whiche he seide, Therfor, whanne the Lord schal bitake Zebee and Salmana in to myn hondis, and whanne Y schal turne ayen ouercomere in pees, Y schal to-reende youre fleischis with the thornes and breris of deseert.

8 And he stiede fro thennus, and cam in to Phanuel; and he spak lijk thingis to men of that place, to whom also thei answeriden, as the men of Socoth hadden answerid.

9 And so he seide to hem, Whanne Y schal turne ayen ouercomere in pees, Y schal distrie this tour.

10 Forsothe Zebee and Salmana restiden with al her oost; for fiftene thousynde men leften of alle the cumpenyes of the 'puplis of the eest, whanne an hundrid and twenti thousynde of 'fiyteris and of men drawynge out swerd weren slayn.

11 And Gedeon stiede bi the weye of hem that dwelliden in tabernaclis at the eest coost of Nobe and of Lethoa, and smoot the 'tentis of enemyes, that weren sikur, and supposiden not ony thing of aduersite.

12 And Zebee and Salmana fledden, whiche Gedeon pursuede and took, whanne al 'the oost of hem was disturblid.

13 And he turnede ayen fro batel bifor the 'risyng of the sunne,

14 and took a child of the men of Socoth; and he axide hym the names of the princes and eldere men of Socoth; and he descryuede seuene and seuenti men in noumbre.

15 And he cam to Socoth, and seide to hem, Lo Zebee and Salmana! of whiche ye vpbreideden me, and seiden, In hap the hondis of Zebee and of Salmana ben in thin hondis, and therfor thou axist, that we yyue looues to men, that ben weeri and failiden.

16 Therfor Gedeon took the eldere men of the citee, and thornes and breris of deseert, and he to-rente with tho, and al to-brak the men of Socoth; also he destriede the tour of Phanuel,

17 whanne the dwelleris of the citee weren slayn.

18 And he seide to Zebee and Salmana, What maner men weren thei, whiche ye killiden in Thabor? Whiche answeriden, Thei weren lijk thee, and oon of hem was as the sone of a kyng.

19 To whiche he seide, Thei weren my britheren, the sones of my modir; the Lord lyueth, if ye hadden saued hem, Y 'nolde sle you.

20 And he seide to Jepther, his firste gendrid sone, Rise thou, and sle hem. Which drow not swerd; for he dredde, for he was yit a child.

21 And Zebee and Salmana seiden, Ryse thou, and falle on vs; for thou art bi the age and strengthe of man. Gedeon roos, and killide Zebee and Salmana, and took the ournementis, and bellis, with whiche the neckis of kyngis camels ben wont to be maad fair.

22 And alle the men of Israel seiden to Gedeon, Be thou lord of vs, thou, and thi sone, and the sone of thi sone; for thou deliueridist vs fro the hond of Madian.

23 To whiche he seide, Y schal not be lord of you, nethir my sone schal be lord on you, but the Lord schal be lord.

24 And he seide to hem, Y axe oon axyng of you, yyue ye to me the eere ryngis of youre prey; for Ismaelitis weren wont to haue goldun eere ryngis.

25 Whiche answeriden, We schulen yyue moost gladli. And thei spredden forth a mentil on the erthe, and castiden forth therynne 'eere ryngis of the prey;

26 and the weiyte of 'eere ryngis axid was a thousynde and seuene hundrid siclis of gold, with out ournementis and brochis and cloth of purpur, whiche the kyngis of Madian weren wont to vse, and outakun goldun bies of camels.

27 And Gedeon made therof ephot, that is, a preestis cloth, 'and propir cloth of the hiyeste preest, and he puttide it in his citee Ephra; and al Israel diden fornycacioun, 'that is ydolatrye, ther ynne; and it was maad to Gedeon and to al his hows in to fallyng.

28 Forsothe Madian was maad low bifor the sones of Israel, and thei myyten no more reise nollis; but the lond restide fourti yeer, in whiche Gedeon was souereyn.

29 And so Jerobaal, sone of Joas, yede, and dwellide in his hows;

30 and he hadde seuenti sones, that yeden out of his thiy, for he hadde many wyues.

31 Forsothe a concubyn, 'that is, secoundarie wijf, of hym, whom he hadde in Sichem, gendride to hym a sone, Abymelech bi name.

32 And Gedeon, sone of Joas, diede in good elde, and was biried in the sepulcre of Joas, his fadir, in Ephra, of the meynee of Ezri.

33 Forsothe aftir that Gedeon was deed, the sones of Israel turneden awey 'fro Goddis religioun, and diden fornycacioun, 'that is, idolatrie, with Baalym; and thei smytiden boond of pees with Baal, that he schulde be to hem in to God,

34 nether thei hadden mynde of her Lord God, that delyuerede hem fro the hond of alle her enemyes 'bi cumpas;

35 nether thei diden merci with the hous of Gerobaal Gedeon, bi alle the goodis whiche he 'hadde do to Israel.

CAP 9

1 Forsothe Abymelech, the sone of Gerobaal, yede in to Sichem to the britheren of his modir; and he spak to hem, and to al the kynrede of 'the hows of his modir, and seide,

2 Speke ye to alle the men of Sichem, What is betere to you, that seuenti men, alle the sones of Gerobaal, be lordis of you, whether that o man be lord to you? and also biholde, for Y am youre boon, and youre fleisch.

3 And the britheren of his modir spaken of hym alle these wordis to alle the men of Sichem; and bowiden her hertis aftir Abymelech, and seiden, He is oure brother.

4 And thei yauen to hym seuenti weiytis of siluer of the temple of Baal Berith; and he hiride to hym therof men pore and hauynge no certeyn dwellynge, and thei sueden hym.

5 And he cam to 'the hows of his fadir in Ephra, and killide hise britheren the sones of Gerobaal, 'seuenti men, on o stoon. And Joathan, the leste sone of Gerobaal, lefte, and was hid.

6 Forsothe alle the men of Sichem, and alle the meynees of the citee of Mello, weren gadirid to gydere, and thei yeden, and maden Abymelech kyng, bysidis the ook that stood in Sichem.

7 And whanne this thing was teld to Joathan, he yede, and stood in the cop of the hil Garisym, and cried with 'vois reisid, and seide, Ye men of Sichem, here me, so that God here you.

8 Trees yeden to anoynte a kyng on hem; and tho seiden to the olyue tre, Comaunde thou to vs.

9 Whiche answeride, Whether Y may forsake my fatnesse, which bothe Goddis and men vsen, and come, that Y be auaunsid among trees?

10 And the trees seiden to the fige tree, Come thou, and take the rewme on vs.

11 Which answeride to hem, Whether Y may forsake my swetnesse and swetteste fruytis, and go that Y be auaunsid among othere trees?

12 Also 'the trees spaken to the vyne, Come thou, and comaunde to vs.

13 Which answeride, Whether Y may forsake my wyn, that gladith God and men, and be auaunsid among othere trees?

14 And alle trees seiden to the ramne, ether theue thorn, Come thou, and be lord on vs.

15 Whiche answeride to hem, If ye maken me verili kyng to you, come ye, and reste vndur my schadewe; sotheli, if ye nylen, fier go out of the ramne, and deuoure the cedris of the Liban.

16 Now therfor if riytfuli and without synne 'ye han maad Abymelech kyng on you, and ye han do wel with Jerobaal, and with his hows, and ye han yolde while to the benefices of hym,

17 that fauyt for you, and yaf his lijf to perelis, that he schulde delyuere you fro the hond of Madian;

18 and ye han rise now ayens the hows of my fadir, and han slayn hyse sones, seuenti men, on o stoon, and 'han maad Abymelech, sone of his handmayde, kyng on the dwelleris of Sichem, for he is youre brother;

19 therfor if ye han do riytfuli, and with out synne with Gerobaal and his hows, to dai be ye glad in Abymelech, and be he glad in you; but if ye han do weiwardli,

20 fier go out 'of hym, and waste the dwelleris of Sichem, and the citee of Mello; and fier go out of the men of Sichem, and of the citee of Mello, and deuoure Abymelech.

21 And whanne he hadde seide these thingis, he fledde, and yede in to Berara, and dwellide there, for drede of Abymelech, his brother.

22 And Abymelech regnede on Israel thre yeer.

23 And the Lord sente the worste spirit bitwixe Abymelech and the dwelleris of Sichem, whiche bigynnen to holde hym abomynable,

24 and to arette the felony of sleyng of seuenti sones of Gerobaal, and the schedyng out of her blood, in to Abymelech her brother, and to othere princes of Sichem, that hadden helpid hym.

25 And thei settiden buyschementis ayens hym in the hiynesse of hillis; and the while thei abideden 'the comyng of hym, thei hauntiden theftis, and token preies of men passynge forth; and it was teld to Abymelech.

26 Forsothe Gaal, 'the sone of Obed, cam with his britheren, and passide in to Siccima; at whos entryng the dwelleris of Sichem weren reisid, and yeden out 'in to feeldis,

27 and wastiden vyneris, and 'to-traden grapis; and with cumpeneys of syngeris maad thei entriden in to 'the temple of her God, and among metis and drynkis thei cursiden Abymalech, while Gaal,

28 the sone of Obed, criede, Who is this Abymelech? And what is Sichem, that we serue hym? Whether he is not the sone of Jerobaal, and made Zebul his seruaunt prince on the men of Emor, fadir of Sichem? Whi therfor schulen we serue hym?

29 'Y wolde, that sum man yaf this puple vndur myn hond, that Y schulde take awei Abimelech fro the myddis. And it

was seid to Abymelech, Gadere thou the multitude of oost, and come thou.

30 For whanne the wordis of Gaal, sone of Obed, weren herd, Zebul, the prynce of the citee, was ful wrooth;

31 and he sente priueli messangeris to Abymelech, and seide, Lo! Gaal, sone of Obed, cam in to Siccymam, with hise britheren, and he excitith the citee to fiyte ayens thee;

32 therfor rise thou bi niyt with the puple, which is with thee, and be thou hid in the feeld;

33 and first in the morewtid, whanne the sunne rysith, falle on the citee; forsothe whanne he goth out with his puple ayens thee, do thou to hym that that thou maist.

34 Therfor Abymelech roos with al his oost bi nyyt, and settide buyschementis bisidis Siccimam, in foure placis.

35 And Gaal, the sone of Obed, yede out, and stood in the entryng of 'the yate of the citee. Forsothe Abymelech and al the oost with hym roos fro the place of buyschementis.

36 And whanne Gaal hadde seyn the puple, he seide to Zebul, Lo! multitude cometh doun fro the hillis. To whom he answeride, Thou seest the schadewis of hillis as the 'heedis of men, and thou art disseyued bi this errour.

37 And eft Gaal seide, Lo! a puple cometh doun fro the myddis of erthe, 'that is, fro the hiynesse of hillis, and o cumpeny cometh bi the weie that biholdith the ook.

38 To whom Zebul seide, Where is now thi mouth, bi which thou spekist, Who is Abymelech, that we serue hym? Whether this is not the puple, whom thou dispisidist? Go thou out, and fiyte ayens hym.

39 Therfor Gaal yede, while the puple of Sichen abood; and he fauyt ayens Abymelech.

40 Which pursuede Gaal fleynge, and constreynede to go in to the citee; and ful many of his part felde doun 'til to the yate of the citee.

41 And Abymelech sat in Ranna; sotheli Zebul puttide Gaal and hise felowis out of the citee, and suffride not to dwelle ther ynne.

42 Therfor in the dai suynge the puple yede out in to the feeld; and whanne this thing was teld to Abymelech,

43 he took his oost, and departide 'in to thre cumpenyes, and settide buyschementis in the feeldis; and he siy that the puple yede out of the citee, and he roos,

44 and felde on hem with his cumpeny, and enpugnyde and bisegide the citee. Sothely twei cumpenyes yeden aboute opynli bi the feeld, and pursueden aduersaries.

45 Certis Abymelech fauyt ayens the citee in al that dai, which he took, whanne the dwelleris weren slayn, and that citee was destried, so that he spreynte abrood salt ther ynne.

46 And whanne thei, that dwelliden in the tour of Sichem, hadde herd this, thei entriden in to the temple of her god Berith, where thei hadden maad boond of pees with hym; and of that the place took name, which place was ful strong.

47 And Abymelech herde the men of the tour of Sichem gaderid to gidere,

48 and he stiede in to the hil Selmon with al his puple; and with an axe takun he kittide doun a boow of a tre, and he bar it, put on the schuldur, and seide to felowis, Do ye this thing, which ye seen me do.

49 Therfor with strijf thei kittiden doun bowis of the trees, and sueden the duyk; whiche cumpassiden and brenten 'the tour; and so it was doon, that with smooke and fier a thousynde of men weren slayn, men togidere and wymmen, of the dwelleris of the tour of Sichem.

50 Forsothe Abymelech wente forth fro thennus, and cam to the citee of Thebes, which he cumpasside, and bisegide with an oost.

51 Forsothe the tour was hiy in the myddis of the citee, to which men togidere and wymmen fledden, and alle the princes of the citee, while the yate was closid stronglieste; and thei stoden on the roof of the tour bi toretis.

52 And Abymelech cam bisidis the tour, and fauyt strongli, and he neiyede to the dore, and enforside to putte fier vndur; and lo!

53 o womman castide fro aboue a gobet of a mylnestoon, and hurtlide to 'the heed of Abymelech, and brak his brayn.

54 And he clepide soone his squyer, and seide to hym, Drawe out thi swerd, and sle me, lest perauenture it be seid, that Y am slan of a womman. Which performede 'the comaundementis, and 'killide Abymelech;

55 and whanne he was deed, alle men of Israel that weren with hym turneden ayen to her seetis.

56 And God yeldide to Abymelech the yuel that he dide ayens his fadir, for he killide hise seuenti britheren.

57 Also that thing was yoldun to men of Sichem, which thei wrouyten, and the curs of Joathan, sone of Jerobaal, cam on hem.

CAP 10

1 Aftir Abymelech roos a duyk in Israel, Thola, the sone of Phua, brother of 'the fadir of Abymelech; Thola was a man of Ysachar, that dwelliden in Sanyr, of the hil of Effraym;

2 and he demyde Israel thre and twenti yeer, and he 'was deed, and biriede in Sanyr.

3 His successour was Jair, a man of Galaad, that demyde Israel bi two and twenti yeer;

4 and he hadde thretti sones, sittynge aboue thretti coltis of femal assis, and thretti princes of citees, whiche ben clepid bi 'his name, Anoth Jair, that is, the citees of Jair, 'til in to present day, in the lond of Galaad.

5 And Jair 'was deed, and biriede in a place 'to which the name is Camon.

6 Forsothe the sones of Israel ioyneden newe synnes to elde synnes, and diden yuels in the 'siyt of the Lord, and serueden to the idols of Baalym, and of Astoroth, and to the goddis of Sirie, and of Sidon, and of Moab, and of the sones of Amon, and of Filistiym; and thei leften the Lord, and worschipiden not hym.

7 And the Lord was wrooth ayens hem, and he bitook hem in to the hondis of Filistiym, and of the sones of Amon.

8 And alle that dwelliden ouer Jordan in the lond of Ammorrey, which is in Galaad, weren turmentid and oppressid greetli bi eiytene yeer,

9 in so myche that the sones of Amon, whanne thei hadden passid Jordan, wastiden Juda and Benjamyn and Effraym; and Israel was turmentid greetli.

10 And thei crieden to the Lord, and seiden, We han synned to thee, for we forsoken oure God, and seruyden Baalym.

11 To whiche the Lord spak, Whether not Egipcians, and Ammorreis, and the sones of Amon, and of Filistiym, and Sidonyes,

12 and Amalech, and Canaan, oppressiden you, and ye crieden to me, and Y delyuerede you fro 'the hondis of hem?

13 And netheles ye forsoken me, and worschipiden alien goddis; therfor Y schal not adde, that Y delyuere you more.

14 Go ye, and clepe goddis whiche ye han chose; delyuere thei you in the tyme of angwisch.

15 And the sones of Israel seiden to the Lord, We han synned; yelde thou to vs what euer thing plesith thee; oneli delyuere vs now.

16 And thei seiden these thingis, and castiden forth fro her coostis alle the idols of alien goddis, and serueden the Lord; which hadde 'rewthe, ether compassioun, on the 'wretchidnessis of hem.

17 And so the sones of Amon crieden togidere, that is, clepyden hem silf togidere to batel, and excitiden ayens Israel, and settiden tentis in Galaad, 'ayens whiche the sones of Israel weren gaderid, and settiden tentis in Masphat.

18 And the princes of Galaad seiden ech to hise neiyboris, He, that bigynneth first of vs to fiyte ayens the sones of Amon, schal be duyk of the puple of Galaad.

CAP 11

1 And so in that tyme Jepte, a man of Galaad, was a ful strong man, and fiytere, the sone of a womman hoore, which Jepte was borun of Galaad.

2 Forsothe Galaad hadde a wijf, of which he hadde sones, whiche aftir that thei encressiden, castiden out Jepte, and seiden, Thou maist not be eir in the hows of oure fadir, for thou art born of a modir auoutresse.

3 'Whiche britheren he fledde, and eschewide, and dwellide in the lond of Tob; and pore men and 'doynge thefte weren gaderid to hym, and sueden as a prince.

4 In tho daies the sones of Amon fouyten ayens Israel;

5 and whanne thei contynueden scharpli, the grettere men in birthe of Galaad, yeden to take in to 'the help of hem silf Jepte fro the lond of Tob;

6 and thei seiden to hym, Come thou, and be oure prince, and fiyte ayens the sones of Amon.

7 To whiche he answeride, Whethir not ye it ben, that haten me, and castiden me out of the hows of mi fadir, and now ye camen to me, and weren compellid bi nede?

8 And the princes of Galaad seiden to Jepte, Therfor for this cause we camen now to thee, that thou go with vs, and fiyt ayens the sones of Amon; and that thou be the duyk of alle men that dwellen in Galaad.

9 And Jepte seide to hem, Whether ye camen verili to me, that Y fiyte for you ayens the sones of Amon, and if the Lord schal bitake hem in to myn hondis, schal Y be youre prince?

10 Whiche answeriden to hym, The Lord hym silf, that herith these thingis, is mediatour and witnesse, that we schulen do oure biheestis.

11 And so Jepte wente with the princes of Galaad, and al the puple made hym her prince; and Jepte spak alle hise wordis bifor the Lord in Maspha.

12 And he sente messangeris to the kyng of the sones of Amon, whiche messangeris schulden seie 'of his persoone, What is to me and to thee, for thou hast come 'ayens me to waaste my lond?

13 To whiche the kyng answeride, For Israel whanne he stiede fro Egipt took awei my lond, fro the coostis of Arnon 'til to Jaboch and to Jordan, now therfor yeelde it to me with pees.

14 Bi whiche massangeris Jepte sente eft, and comaundide to hem, that thei schulden seie to the kyng of Amon,

15 Jepte seith these thingis, Israel took not the lond of Moab, nether the lond of the sones of Amon;

16 but whanne thei stieden fro Egipt, 'he yede bi the wildirnesse 'til to the Reed See, and cam in to Cades;

17 and he sente messangeris to the kyng of Edom, and seide, Suffre thou me, that Y go thoruy thi lond; which kyng nolde assente to his preyeres. Also Israel sente to the kyng of Moab, and he dispiside to yyue passage;

18 and so Israel dwellyde in Cades, and cumpasside bi the side the lond of Edom, and the lond of Moab; and he cam to the eest coost of the lond of Moab, and settide tentis biyende Arnon, nether he wolde entre in to the termes of Moab; for Arnon is the ende of the lond of Moab.

19 And so Israel sente messangeris to Seon, kyng of Ammorreis, that dwellide in Esebon; and thei seiden to hym, Suffre thou, that Y passe thorouy thi lond 'til to the ryuer.

20 And he dispiside the wordis of Israel, and suffride not hym passe bi hise termes, but with a multitude with out noumbre gaderid to gidere he yede out ayens Israel, and ayenstood strongli.

21 And the Lord bitook hym with al his oost in to the hondis of Israel; and Israel smoot hym, and hadde in possessioun al the lond of Ammorrey,

22 dwellere of that cuntrey, and al the coostis therof fro Arnon 'til to Jaboch, and fro the wildirnesse 'til to Jordan.

23 Therfor the Lord God of Israel distriede Ammorrey, fiytynge ayens hym for his puple Israel. And wolt thou now haue in possessioun 'his lond? Whether not tho thingis whiche Chamos, thi god, hadde in possessioun, ben due to thee bi riyt?

24 Forsothe tho thingis whiche 'oure Lord God ouercomere gat, schulen falle in to oure possessioun;

25 no but in hap thou art betere than Balach, the sone of Sephor, kyng of Moab, ether thou maist preue, that he stryuede ayens Israel, and fauyt ayens hym,

26 whanne he dwellide in Esebon, and in townes therof, and in Aroer, and in townes therof, and in alle citees biyende Jordan, bi thre hundrid yeer. Whi in so myche time assaieden ye no thing on this axyng ayen?

27 Therfor not Y do synne ayens thee, but thou doist yuel ayens me, and bryngist in batels not iust to me; the Lord, iuge of this dai, deme bitwixe the sones of Israel and bitwixe the sones of Amon.

28 And the kyng of the sones of Amon nolde assente to the wordis of Jepte, whiche he sente bi messangeris.

29 Therfor the spirit of the Lord was maad on Jepte, and he cumpasside Galaad and Manasses, Maspha and Galaad; and he passide fro thennus to the sones of Amon,

30 and made a vow to the Lord, and seide, If thou schalt bitake the sones of Amon in to myn hondis,

31 who euer goith out first of the dores of myn hows, and cometh ayens me turnynge ayen with pees fro the sones of Amon, Y schal offre hym brent sacrifice to the Lord.

32 And Jepte yede to the sones of Amon, to fiyte ayens hem, whiche the Lord bitook in to hise hondis;

33 and he smoot fro Aroer 'til to thou comest in to Mennyth, twenti citees, and 'til to Abel, which is set aboute with vyneris, with ful greet veniaunce; and the sones of Amon weren maad low of the sones of Israel.

34 Forsothe whanne Jepte turnede ayen in to Maspha, his hows, his oon gendrid douyter cam to hym with tympanys and croudis; for he hadde not othere fre children.

35 And whanne 'sche was seyn, he to-rente his clothis, and seide, Allas! my douytir, thou hast disseyued me, and thou art disseyued; for Y openyde my mouth to the Lord, and Y may do noon other thing.

36 To whom sche answeride, My fadir, if thou openydist thi mouth to the Lord, do to me what euer thing thou bihiytist, while veniaunce and victorie of thin enemyes is grauntid to thee.

37 And sche seide to the fadir, Yyue thou to me oneli this thing, which Y biseche; suffre thou me that in two monethis Y cumpasse hillis, and biweile my maidynhed with my felowis.

38 To whom he answeride, Go thou. And he sufferide hir in two monethis. And whanne sche hadde go with hir felowis and pleiferis, sche biwepte hir maydynhed in the hillis.

39 And whanne twey monethis weren fillid, sche turnede ayen to hir fadir, and he dide to hir as he avowide; and sche knew not fleischli a man. Fro thennus a custom cam in Israel,

40 and the custom is kept, that aftir the 'ende of the yeer the douytris of Israel come togidere, and biweile 'the douytir of Jepte of Galaad 'foure daies.

CAP 12

1 'Lo! forsothe discencioun roos in Effraym; for whi thei, that passiden ayens the north, seiden to Jepte, Whi yedist thou to batel ayens the sones of Amon, and noldist clepe vs, that we schulden go with thee? Therfor we schulen brenne thin hows.

2 To whiche he answeride, Greet strijf was to me and to my puple ayens the sones of Amon, and Y clepide you, that ye schulden 'yyue help to me, and ye nolden do.

3 'Which thing Y siy, and puttide my lijf in myn hondis; and Y passide to the sones of Amon, and 'the Lord bitook hem in to myn hondis; what haue Y disseruyd, that ye ryse togidere ayens me in to batel?

4 Therfor whanne alle the men of Galaad weren clepid to hym, he fauyt ayens Effraym; and the men of Galaad smytiden Effraym; for he seide, Galaad is 'fugitif ether exilid fro Effraym, and dwellith in the myddis of Effraym and of Manasses.

5 And the men of Galaad ocupieden the forthis of Jordan, bi whiche Effraym schulden turne ayen. And whanne a man fleynge of the noumbre of Effraym hadde come to tho forthis, and hadde seid, Y biseche, that thou suffre me passe; men of Galaad seiden to hym, Whether thou art a man of Effraym? And whanne he seide, Y am not,

6 thei axiden hym, Seie thou therfor Sebolech, 'whiche is interpretid, 'an eer of corn. Which answeride, Thebolech, and myyte not brynge forth an eer of corn bi the same lettre. And anoon thei strangeliden hym takun in thilke passyng of Jordan; and two and fourti thousynde of Effraym felden doun in that tyme.

7 And so Jepte, 'a man of Galaad, demyde Israel sixe yeer; and he 'was deed, and biried in his citee Galaad.

8 Abethsan of Bethleem, that hadde thretti sones, and so many douytris, demyde Israel aftir Jepte;

9 whiche douytris he sente out, and yaf to hosebondis, and he took wyues to hise sones of the same noumbre, and brouyte in to hys hows; which demyde Israel seuene yeer;

10 and he 'was deed, and biried in Bethleem.

11 Whos successour was Hailon of Zabulon; and he demyde Israel ten yeer;

12 and he was deed, and biried in Zabulon.

13 Aftir hym Abdon, the sone of Ellel, of Pharaton, demyde Israel;

14 which Abdon hadde fourti sones, and of hem thretti sones, stiynge on seuenti coltis of femal assis, 'that is, mulis, and he demyde Israel eiyte yeer;

15 and he 'was deed, and biried in Pharaton, in the loond of Effraym, in the hil of Amalech.

CAP 13

1 And eft the sones of Israel diden yuel in the 'siyt of the Lord, which bitook hem in to the hondis of Filisteis fourti yeer.

2 Forsothe a man was of Saraa, and of the kynrede of Dan, 'Manue bi name, and he hadde a bareyn wijf.

3 To 'which wijf an aungel of the Lord apperide, and seide to hir, Thou art bareyn, and with out fre children; but thou schalt conseyue, and schalt bere a sone.

4 Therfor be thou war, lest thou drynke wyn, and sydur, nethir ete thou ony vnclene thing;

5 for thou schalt conceyue and schalt bere a sone, whos heed a rasour schal not towche; for he schal be a Nazarei of God fro his yong age, and fro the modris wombe; and he schal bigynne to delyuere Israel fro the hond of Filisteis.

6 And whanne sche hadde come to hir hosebonde, sche seide to hym, The man of God cam to me, and hadde an aungel cheer, and he was ful ferdful, 'that is, worschipful 'and reuerent; and whanne Y hadde axide hym, who he was, and fro whannus he cam, and bi what name he was clepid, he nolde seie to me;

7 but he answeride this, Lo! thou schalt conseyue, and schalt bere a sone; be thou war, that thou drynke not wyn ne sidur, nether ete ony vncleene thing; for the child schal be a Nazarey, 'that is, hooli of the Lord, fro his yonge age and fro the modris wombe 'til to the dai of his deeth.

8 Therfor Manue preide the Lord, and seide, Lord, Y biseche, that the man of God, whom thou sentist, come eft, and teche vs, what we owen to do of the child, that schal be borun.

9 And the Lord herde Manue preiynge; and the aungel of the Lord apperide eft to his wijf sittynge in the feeld; forsothe Manue, hir hosebonde, was not with hir. And whanne sche hadde seyn the aungel,

10 sche hastide, and ran to hir hosebonde, and telde to hym, and seide, Lo! the man whom Y siy bifore, apperide to me.

11 Which roos, and suede his wijf; and he cam to the man, and seide to hym, Art thou he, that hast spoke to the womman? And he answeride, Y am.

12 To whom Manue seide, Whanne thi word schal be fillid, what wolt thou, that the child do, ethir fro what thing schal he kepe hym silf?

13 And the 'aungel of the Lord seide to Manue, Absteyne he hym silf fro alle thingis which Y spak to thi wijf.

14 And ete he not what euer thing cometh forth of the vyner, drynke he not wyn, and sidur, ete he not ony vncleene thing and fille he; and kepe that, that Y comaundide to hym.

15 Therfor Manue seide to the 'aungel of the Lord, Y biseche, that thou assente to my preieris, and we aray to thee a 'kide of the geet.

16 To whom the aungel of the Lord answeride, Thouy thou constreynest me, Y schal not ete thi looues; forsothe if thou wolt make brent sacrifice, offre thou it to the Lord. And Manue wiste not, that it was 'an aungel of the Lord.

17 And Manue seide to hym, What name is to thee, that if thi word be fillid, we onoure thee?

18 To whom he answeride, Whi axist thou my name, which is wondurful?

19 Therfor Manue took a 'kide of the geet, and fletynge sacrifices, and puttide on the stoon, and offryde to the Lord that doith wondirful thingis. Forsothe he and his wijf bihelden.

20 And whanne the flawme of the auter stiede in to heuene, the aungel of the Lord stiede togidere in the flawme. And whanne Manue and his wijf hadden seyn this, thei felden lowe to erthe.

21 And the aungel of the Lord apperide no more to hem. And anoon Manue vndurstood, that he was an aungel of the Lord.

22 And he seide to his wijf, We schulen die bi deeth, for we sien the Lord.

23 To whom the womman answeride, If the Lord wolde sle vs, he schulde not haue take of oure hondis brent sacrifices, and moiste sacrifices, but nether he schulde haue schewid alle thingis to vs, nether 'he schulde haue seid tho thingis, that schulen come.

24 Therfor sche childide a sone, and clepide his name Sampson; and the child encreesside, and the Lord blesside hym.

25 And the spirit of the Lord bigan to be with hym in the castels of Dan, bitwixe Saraa and Escahol.

CAP 14

1 Therfor Sampson yede doun in to Thannatha, and he siy there a womman of 'the douytris of Filisteis;

2 and he stiede, and telde to his fadir and 'to his modir, and seide, Y siy a womman in Thannatha of the 'douytris of Filistees, and Y biseche, that ye take hir a wijf to me.

3 To whom his fadir and modir seiden, Whether no womman is among the douytris of thi britheren and in al my puple, for thou wolt take a wijf of Filisteis, that ben vncircumcidid? And Sampson seide to his fadir, Take thou this wijf to me, for sche pleside myn iyen.

4 Forsothe his fadir and modir wisten not, that the thing was don of the Lord; and that he souyte occasiouns ayens Filisteis; for in that tyme Filisteis weren lordis of Israel.

5 Therfor Sampson yede doun with his fadir and modir in to Thannatha; and whanne thei hadden come to the vyneris of the citee, a fers and rorynge 'whelp of a lioun apperide, and ran to Sampson.

6 Forsothe the spirit of the Lord felde in to Sampson, and he to-rente the lioun, as if he 'to-rendide a kide 'in to gobetis, and outerli he hadde no thing in the hond; and he nolde schewe this to the fadir and modir.

7 And he yede doun, and spak to the womman, that pleside hise iyen.

8 And aftir summe daies he turnede ayen to take hir 'in to matrimonye; and he 'bowide awey to se the 'careyn of the lioun; and lo! a gaderyng of bees was in the 'mouth of the lioun, and 'a coomb of hony.

9 And whanne he hadde take it in hondis, he eet in the weie; and he cam to his fadir and modir, and yaf part 'to hem, and thei eeten; netheles he nolde schewe to hem, that he hadde take hony of the 'mouth of the lioun.

10 And so his fadir yede doun to the womman, and made a feeste to his sone Sampson; for yonge men weren wont to do so.

11 Therfor whanne the citeseyns of that place hadden seyn hym, thei yauen to hym thretti felowis, whiche schulen be with hym.

12 To whiche Sampson spak, Y schal putte forth to you a probleme, 'that is, a douyteful word and priuy, and if ye 'asoilen it to me with ynne seuen daies of the feeste, Y schal yyue to you thretti lynnun clothis, and cootis 'of the same noumbre; sotheli if ye moun not soyle,

13 ye schulen yyue to me thretti lynnun clothis, and cootis 'of the same noumbre. Whiche answeriden to hym, Sette forth the probleme, that we here it.

14 And he seide to hem, Mete yede out of the etere, and swetnesse yede out of the stronge. And bi thre daies thei myyten not assoile the 'proposicioun, that is, the resoun set forth.

15 And whanne the seuenthe dai cam, thei seiden to 'the wijf of Sampson, Glose thin hosebonde, and counseile hym, that he schewe to thee what the probleme signyfieth. That if thou nylt do, we schulen brenne thee and 'the hous of thi fadir. Whether herfor ye clepiden vs to weddyngis, that ye schulden robbe vs?

16 And sche schedde teerys at Sampson, and pleynede, and seide, Thou hatist me, and louest not, therfor thou nylt expowne to me the probleme, which thou settidist forth to the sones of my puple. And he answeride, Y nolde seie to my fadir and modir, and schal Y mow schewe to thee?

17 Therfor bi seuene dayes of the feest sche wepte at hym; at the laste 'he expownede in the seuenthe dai, whanne sche was diseseful to hym. And anoon sche telde to hir citeseyns.

18 And thei seiden to hym in the seuenthe dai bifor the goyng doun of the sunne, What is swettere than hony, and what is strengere than a lioun? And he seide to hem, If ye hadden not erid in my cow calf, 'that is, my wijf, ye hadden not founde my proposicioun.

19 Therfor the spirit of the Lord felde in to hym; and he yede doun to Ascalon, and killyde there thretti men, whose clothis he took awey, and he yaf to hem that soiliden the probleme; and he was ful wrooth, and stiede in to 'the hows of his fadir.

20 Forsothe his wijf took an hosebonde, oon of the frendis and keperis 'of hir.

CAP 15

1 'Forsothe aftir sum del of tyme, whanne the daies of wheete heruest neiyiden, Sampson cam, and wolde visite his wijf, and he brouyte to hir a 'kide of geet; and when he wolde entre in to hir bed bi custom, 'the fadir of hir forbeed hym, and seide,

2 Y gesside that thou haddist hatid hir, and therfor Y yaf hir to thi freend; but sche hath a sistir, which is yongere and fairere than sche, be sche 'wijf to thee for hir.

3 To whom Sampson answeride, Fro this day no blame schal be in me ayens Filistees, for Y schal do yuels to you.

4 And he yede, and took thre hundrid foxis, and ioynede 'the tailis of hem to tailis, and boond brondis in the myddis,

5 whiche he kyndlid with fier, and leet hem, that thei schulden renne aboute hidur and thidur; 'which yeden anoon in to the cornes of Filisteis, bi whiche kyndlid, bothe cornes 'borun now to gidere, and yit stondynge in the stobil, weren brent, in so myche that the flawme wastide vyneris, and 'places of olyue trees.

6 And Filisteis seiden, Who dide this thing? To whiche it was seid, Sampson, hosebonde of the 'douytir of Thannathei, for he took awey Sampsones wijf, and yaf to another man, 'wrouyte this thing. And Filisteis stieden, and brenten bothe the womman and hir fadir.

7 To whiche Sampson seide, Thouy ye han do this, netheles yit Y schal axe veniaunce of you, and than Y schal reste.

8 And he smoot hem with greet wounde, so that thei wondriden, and 'puttiden the hyndrere part of the hipe on the thiy; and he yede doun, and dwellide in the denne of the stoon of Ethan.

9 Therfor Filisteis stieden in to the lond of Juda, and settiden tentis in the place, that was clepid aftirward Lethi, that is, a cheke, wher 'the oost of hem was spred a brood.

10 And men of the lynage of Juda seiden to hem, Whi 'stieden ye ayens vs? Whiche answeriden, We comen that we bynde Sampson, and yelde to hym tho thingis whiche he wrouyte in vs.

11 Therfor thre thousynde of men of Juda yeden doun to the denne of the flynt of Ethan; and thei seiden to Sampson, Woost thou not, that Filisteis comaunden to vs? Why woldist thou do this thing? To whiche he seide.

12 As thei diden to me, Y dide to hem. Thei seien, We comen to bynde thee, and to bitake thee in to the 'hondis of Filisteis. To whiche Sampson answeride, Swere ye, and 'biheete ye to me, that ye sle not me.

13 And thei seiden, We schulen not sle thee, but we schulen bitake thee boundun. And thei bounden him with twei newe cordis, and token fro the stoon of Ethan.

14 And whanne thei hadden come to the place of cheke, and Filisteis criynge hadden runne to hym, the spirit of the Lord felde in to hym, and as stikis ben wont to be wastid at the odour of fier, so and the bondis, with whiche he was boundun, weren scaterid and vnboundun.

15 And he took a cheke foundun, that is, the lowere cheke boon of an asse, that lay, 'and he killyde 'with it a thousinde men; and seide,

16 With the cheke of an asse, that is, with the lowere cheke of a colt of femal assis, Y dide hem awey, and Y killide a thousynde men.

17 And whanne he songe these wordis, and 'hadde fillid, he castide forth fro the hond the lowere cheke; and he clepide the name of that place Ramath Lethi, 'which is interpretid, the reisyng of a cheke.

18 And he thristide greetly, and criede to the Lord, and seide, Thou hast youe in the hond of thi seruaunt this grettest helthe and victory; and lo! Y die for thyrst, and Y schal falle in to the hondis of vncircumcidid men.

19 Therfor the Lord openyde a wang tooth in the cheke boon of the asse, and watris yeden out therof, 'bi whiche drunkun he refreischide the spirit, and resseuede strengthis; therfor the name of that place was clepid the Welle of the clepere of the cheke 'til to present dai.

20 And he demyde Israel in the daies of Filistiym twenti yeer.

CAP 16

1 Also Sampson yede in to Gazam, and he siy there a womman hoore, and he entride to hir.

2 And whanne Filisteis hadden seyn this, and it was pupplischid at hem, that Sampson entride in to the citee, thei cumpassiden hym, whanne keperis weren set in the yate of the citee; and thei abididen there al nyyt 'with silence, that in the morewtid thei schulen kille Sampson goynge out.

3 Forsothe Sampson slepte til to 'the myddis of the nyyt; and 'fro thennus he roos, and took bothe the closyngis, ethir leeues, of the yate, with hise postis and lok; and he bar tho leeues, put on the schuldris, to the cop of the hil that biholdith Ebron.

4 After these thingis Sampson louyde a womman that dwellide in the valey of Soreth, and sche was clepid Dalida.

5 And the princes of Filisteis camen to hir, and seiden, Disseyue thou hym, and lerne thou of hym, in what thing he hath so greet strengthe, and how we mowen ouercome hym, and

turmente hym boundun; that if thou doist, we schulen yyue to thee ech man a thousynde and an hundrid platis of siluer.

6 Therfor Dalida spak to Sampson, Y biseche, seie thou to me, wher ynne is thi gretteste strengthe, and what is that thing, with which thou boundun maist not breke?

7 To whom Sampson answeride, If Y be boundun with seuene coordis of senewis not yit drye 'and yit moiste, Y schal be feble as othere men.

8 And the princis of Filisteis brouyten 'to hir seuene coordis, as he hadde seide; with whiche sche boond him,

9 while buyschementis weren hid at hir, and abididen in a closet the ende of the thing. And sche criede to hym, Sampson, Filisteis ben on thee! Which brak the boondis, as if a man brekith a threed of herdis, writhun with spotle, whanne it hath take the odour of fier; and it was not knowun wher ynne his strengthe was.

10 And Dalida seide to hym, Lo! thou hast scorned me, and thou hast spok fals; nameli now schewe thou to me, with what thing thou schuldist be boundun.

11 To whom he answeride, If Y be boundun with newe coordis, that weren not yit in werk, I schal be feble, and lijk othere men.

12 With whiche Dalida boond him eft, and criede, Sampson, Filistees ben on thee! the while buyschementis weren maad redi in closet. Which brak 'so the boondis as thredis of webbis.

13 And Dalida seide eft to hym, Hou long schalt thou disseyue me, and schalt speke fals? Schew thou to me, with what thing thou schalt be boundun. To whom Sampson answeryde, he seide, If thou plattist seuene heeris of myn heed with a strong boond, and fastnest to the erthe a naile boundun a boute with these, Y schal be feble.

14 And whanne Dalida hadde do this, sche seide to hym, Sampson, Filisteis ben on thee! And he roos fro sleep, and drow out the nail, with the heeris and strong boond.

15 And Dalida seide to hym, Hou seist thou, that thou louest me, sithen thi soule is not with me? Bi thre tymes thou liedist to me, and noldist seie to me, wher ynne is thi moost strengthe.

16 And whanne sche was diseseful to hym, and cleuyde to hym contynueli bi many daies, and yaf not space to reste, his lijf failide, and was maad wery 'til to deeth.

17 Thanne he openyde the treuthe of the thing, and seide to hir, Yrun stiede neuere on myn heed, for Y am a Nazarei, that is, halewid to the Lord, fro 'the wombe of my modir; if myn heed be schauun, my strengthe schal go awei fro me, and Y schal faile, and Y schal be as othere men.

18 And sche siy that he knowlechide to hir al his wille, 'ether herte; and sche sente to the princes of Filisteis, and comaundide, Stie ye yit onys, for now he openyde his herte to me. Whiche stieden, with the money takun which thei bihiyten.

19 And sche made hym slepe on hir knees, and 'bowe the heed in hir bosum; and sche clepide a barbour, and schauede seuene heeris of hym; and sche bigan to caste hym awei, and to put fro hir; for anoon the strengthe yede awei fro him.

20 And sche seide, Sampson, Filisteis ben on thee! And he roos fro sleep, and seide to his soule, Y schal go out, as and Y dide bifore, and Y schal schake me fro boondis; and he wiste not, that the Lord hadde goon awei fro hym.

21 And whanne Filisteis hadden take hym, anoon thei diden out hise iyen, and ledden hym boundun with chaynes to Gaza, and 'maden hym closid in prisoun to grynde.

22 And now hise heeris bigunnen to growe ayen;

23 and the princes of Filisteis camen togidere to offre grete sacrifices to Dagon, her god, and 'to ete, seiynge, Oure god hath bitake oure enemy Sampson in to oure hondis.

24 And the puple seynge also this thing preiside her god, and seide the same thingis, Our god hath bitake oure aduersarie in to oure hondis, which dide awey oure lond, and killide ful many men.

25 And thei weren glad bi feestis, for thei hadden ete thanne; and thei comaundiden, that Sampson schulde be clepid, and schulde pleie bifor hem; which was led out of prisoun, and pleiede bifor hem; and thei maden hym stonde bitwixe twei pileris.

26 And he seide to the 'child gouernynge hise steppis, Suffre thou me, that Y touche the pilers on whiche al the hows stondith, that Y be bowid on tho, and reste a litil.

27 Sotheli the hows was ful of men and of wymmen, and the princes of the Filisteis weren there, and aboute thre thousynde of 'euer either kynde, biholdynge fro the roof and the soler Sampson pleynge.

28 And whanne the Lord 'was inwardli clepid, he seide, My Lord God, haue mynde on me, and, my God, yelde thou now to me the formere strengthe, that Y venge me of myn enemyes, and that Y resseyue o veniaunce for the los of tweyne iyen.

29 And he took bothe pilers, on whiche the hows stood, and he helde the oon of tho in the riythond, and the tother in the left hond; and seide,

30 My lijf die with Filesteis! And whanne the pileris weren schakun togidere strongli, the hows felde on alle the princes, and on the tother multitude, that was there; and he diynge killide many moo, than he quyk hadde slayn bifore.

31 Forsothe hise britheren and al the kinrede camen doun, and token his bodi, and birieden bitwixe Saraa and Escahol, in the sepulcre of his fadir Manue; and he demyde Israel twenti yeer.

CAP 17

1 In that tyme was a man, 'Mycas bi name, of the hil of Effraym.

2 And he seide to his modir, Lo! Y haue a thousynde 'and an hundrid platis of siluer, whiche thou departidist to thee, and on whiche thou sworist, while Y herde, and tho ben at me. To whom sche answeride, Blessid be my sone of the Lord.

3 Therefor he yeldide tho to his modir; and sche seide to hym, Y halewide and avowide this siluer to the Lord, that my sone resseyue of myn hond, and make a grauun ymage and a yotun ymage; and now I 'yyue it to thee.

4 Therfor he yeldide to his modir; and sche took twei hundryd platis of siluer, and yaf tho to a werk man of siluer, that he schulde make of tho a grauun 'ymage and yotun, that was in 'the hows of Mycas.

5 Which departide also a litil hous ther ynne to God; and made ephod, and theraphym, that is, a preestis cloth, and ydols; and he fillide the hond of oon of his sones, and he was maad a preest to hym.

6 In tho daies was no kyng in Israel, but ech man dide this, that semyde riytful to hym silf.

7 Also another yonge wexynge man was of Bethleem of Juda, of the kynrede therof, 'that is, of Juda, and he was a dekene, and dwellide there.

8 And he yede out of the citee of Bethleem, and wolde be a pilgrim, where euere he foond profitable to hym silf. And

whanne he made iourney, and 'hadde come in to the hil of Effraym, and hadde bowid a litil in to 'the hows of Mycha, 9 'he was axid of hym, Fro whennus comest thou? Which answeride, Y am a dekene of Bethleem of Juda, and Y go, that Y dwelle where Y may, and se that it is profitable to me. 10 Micha seide, Dwelle thou at me, and be thou fadir and preest 'to me; and Y schal yyue to thee bi ech yeer ten platis of siluer, and double cloth, and tho thingis that ben nedeful to lijflode.

11 He assentide, and dwellide 'at the man; and he was to the man as oon of sones.

12 And Mycha fillide his hond, and hadde the child preest at hym,

13 and seide, Now Y woot, that God schal do wel to me, hauynge a preest of the kyn of Leuy.

CAP 18

1 In tho daies was no kyng in Israel; and the lynage of Dan souyte possessioun to it silf, to dwelle ther ynne; for 'til to that dai it hadde not take eritage among other lynagis.

2 Therfor the sones of Dan senten fyue the strongeste men of her generacioun and meynee fro Saraa and Escahol, that thei schulden aspie the lond, and biholde diligentli. And thei seiden to hem, Go ye, and biholde the lond. And whanne thei goynge hadden come in to the hil of Effraym, and hadden entrid in to the hows of Mycha, thei restiden there.

3 And thei knewen the voys of the yong wexynge dekene; and thei restiden in 'the yn of hym, and seiden to hym, Who brouyte thee hidur? What doist thou here? For what cause woldist thou come hidur?

4 Which answeride 'to hem, Mychas yaf to me these and these thingis, and hiride me for meede, that Y be preest to hym.

5 Forsothe thei preieden hym, that he schulde counsele the Lord, and thei myyten wite, whether thei yeden in weie of prosperite, and the thing schulde haue effect.

6 Which answeride to hem, Go ye with pees, the Lord biholdith youre weie, and the iourney whidur ye goon.

7 Therfor the fyue men yeden, and camen to Lachys; and thei siyen the puple dwellynge ther ynne with outen ony drede, bi the custom of Sidonyis, sikur and resteful, for no man outirli ayenstood hem, and 'of grete richessis, and fer fro Sidon, and departid fro alle men.

8 And thei turneden ayen to her britheren in Saraa and Escahol; and thei answeriden to 'britheren axynge what thei hadden do,

9 Rise ye, and stie we to hem, for we siyen the lond ful riche and plenteuous; nyle ye be necgligent, nil ye ceesse, go we, and haue it in possessioun;

10 no trauel schal be; we schulen entre to sikir men, in to a largeste cuntrey; and the Lord schal bitake to vs a place, wher ynne is not pouert of ony thing of tho that ben brouyt forth in erthe.

11 Therfor sixe hundrid men gird with armeris of batel yeden forth 'of the kynrede of Dan, that is, fro Saraa and Escahol.

12 And thei stieden, and dwelliden in Cariathiarym of Juda, which place took fro that tyme the name of Castels of Dan, and is bihyndis the bak of Cariathiarym.

13 Fro thennus thei passiden in to the hil of Effraym; and whanne thei hadden come to the hows of Mychas, the fyue men,

14 that weren sent bifore to biholde the lond of Lachis, seiden to her other britheren, Ye knowen, that ephod, and theraphyn, and a grauun ymage and yotun is in these housis; se ye what plesith you.

15 And whanne thei hadden bowid a litil, thei entriden in to the hows of the yong dekene, that was in the hows of Mychas, and thei gretten hym with pesible wordis.

16 Forsothe sixe hundrid men stoden bifore the dore, so as thei weren armed. And thei, that entriden in to the 'hows of the yong man, enforsiden to take awey the grauun ymage, and the ephod, and theraphin, and the yotun ymage; and the preest stood bifore the dore,

17 while sixe hundrid strongeste men abideden not fer.

18 Therfor thei that entriden token the grauun ymage, ephod, and idols, and the yotun ymage; to whiche the preest seide, What doen ye?

19 To whom thei answeriden, Be thou stille, and putte the fyngur on thi mouth, and come with vs, that we haue thee fadir and preest. What is betere to thee, that thou be preest in the hows of o man, whether in o lynage and meynee in Israel?

20 And whanne he hadde herd this, he assentide to 'the wordis of hem, and he took the ephod, and ydols, and the grauun ymage, and yede forth with hem.

21 And whanne thei yeden, and hadden maad the litle children, and werk beestis, and al thing that was preciouse, to go bifor hem;

22 and whanne thei weren now fer fro 'the hows of Mychas, men that dwelliden in the housis of Mychas, crieden togidere, and sueden,

23 and bigunnun to crye 'aftir the bak. Whiche whanne thei hadden biholde, seiden to Mychas, What wolt thou to thee? whi criest thou?

24 Which answeride, Ye han take awey my goddis whiche Y made to me, and the preest, and alle thingis whiche Y haue; and ye seien, What is to thee?

25 And the sones of Dan seiden to hym, Be war, lest thou speke more to vs, and men styrid in soule come to thee, and thou perische with al thin hows.

26 And so thei yeden forth in the iourney bigunnun. Forsothe Mychas siy, that thei weren strongere than he, and turnede ayen in to his hows.

27 Forsothe sixe hundrid men token the preest, and the thingis whiche we biforseiden, and camen in to Lachis to the puple restynge and sikur; and thei smytiden hem bi the scharpnesse of swerd, and bitoken the citee to brennyng,

28 while no man outirli yaf help, for thei dwelliden fer fro Sydon, and hadden not ony thing of felouschipe and cause with ony of men. Forsothe the citee was set in the cuntrei of Roob; which citee thei bildiden eft, and dwelliden ther ynne;

29 while the name of the citee was clepid Dan, bi the name of her fadir, whom Israel hadde gendrid, which citee was seid Lachis bifore.

30 And 'thei settiden there the grauun ymage, and Jonathas, sone of Jerson, sone of Moises, and 'Jonathas sones, preestis, in the lynage of Dan, til in to the dai of her caitifte.

31 And the idol of Mychas dwellide at hem, in al the tyme 'in which the hows of God was in Silo. In tho daies was no kyng in Israel.

CAP 19

1 A man was a dekene dwellinge in the side of the hil of Effraym, which dekene took a wijf of Bethleem of Juda.

2 And sche lefte hym, and turnede ayen in to the hows of hir fadir in Bethleem, and sche dwellide at hym foure monethis.

3 And hir hosebonde suede hir, and wolde be recounselid to hir, and speke faire, and lede hir ayen with him; and he hadde in cumpany a child, and tweyne assis. And sche resseyuede hym, and brouyte him in to 'the hows of hir fadir; and whanne hise wyues fadir hadde herd this, and 'hadde seyn hym, he ran gladli to hym, and kisside the man.

4 And the hosebonde of the douytir dwellide in 'the hows of his wyues fadir in three daies, and eet and drank hoomli with hym.

5 Sotheli in the fourthe dai he roos bi nyyt, and wolde go forth; whom 'the fadir of his wijf helde, and seide to hym, Taaste thou first a litil of breed, and coumforte thi stomak, and so thou schalt go forth.

6 And thei saten togidere, and eeten, and drunkun. And the fadir of the damysele seide to 'the hosebonde of his douytir, Y beseche thee, that thou dwelle here to dai, and that we be glad togidere.

7 And he roos, and bigan to wilne to go; and neuertheles 'the fadir of his wijf helde hym mekeli, and made to dwelle at hym.

8 Forsothe whanne the morewtid was maad, the dekene made redi weie; to whom 'the fadir of his wijf seide eft, Y biseche, that thow take a litil of mete, and make thee strong til the dai encreesse, and aftirward go forth. Therfor thei eten togidere.

9 And the yong man roos to go with his wijf and child; to whom the fadir of his wijf spak eft, Biholde thou, that the dai is 'lowere to the goynge doun, and it neiyeth to euentid; dwelle thou at me also to dai, and lede a glad dai, and to morewe thou schalt go forth, that thou go in to thin hows.

10 The 'hosebonde of the douytir nolde assente to hise wordis; but he yede forth anoon, and cam ayens Jebus, which bi another name is clepid Jerusalem; and he ledde with hym twei assis chargid, and the wijf.

11 And now thei weren bisidis Jebus, and the day was chaungid in to nyyt. And the child seide to his lord, Come thou, Y biseche, bowe we to the citee of Jebus, and dwelle we therynne.

12 To whom the lord answeride, Y schal not entre in to the citee of an alien folc, which is not of the sones of Israel, but Y schal passe 'til to Gabaa;

13 and whanne Y schal come thidur, we schulen dwelle therynne, 'ether certis in the citee of Rama.

14 Therfor thei passiden Jebus, and token the weie bigunnun. And the sunne yede doun to hem bisidis Gabaa, which is in the lynage of Beniamyn;

15 and thei turneden to it, that thei schulden dwelle there. Whidur whanne thei hadden entrid, thei saten in the street of the citee, and no man wolde resseyue hem to herbore.

16 And lo! an eld man turnede ayen fro the feeld, and fro his werk in the euentid, and apperide to hem, which also hym silf was of the hil of Effraym, and he dwellide a pilgrym in Gabaa. Therfor men of that cuntrey weren the sones of Gemyny.

17 And whanne the eld man reiside his iyen, he siy a man sittynge with hise fardels in the street of the citee; and he seide to 'that man, Fro whennus comest thou? and whidur goist thou?

18 Which answeride to hym, We yeden forth fro Bethleem of Juda, and we gon to oure place, which is in the side of the hil of Effraym, fro whennus we yeden to Bethleem; and now we gon to the hows of God, and no man wole resseyue vs vndur his roof,

19 and we han prouendre and hey in to mete of assis, and breed and wyn in to myn vsis, and of thin handmayde, and of the child which is with me; we han no nede to ony thing, no but to herbore.

20 To whom the eld man answeride, Pees be with thee; Y schal yyue alle 'thingis, that ben nedeful; oneli, Y biseche, dwelle thou not in the street.

21 And he brouyte hym in to his hows, and yaf 'mete to the assis; and after that thei waischiden her feet, he resseyuede hem 'in to feeste.

22 While thei eeten, and refreischiden the bodies with mete and drynk after the trauel of weie, men of that citee camen, the sones of Belial, that is, with out yok, and thei cumpassiden the 'hows of the elde man, and bigunnun to knocke the doris; and thei crieden to the lord of the hows, and seiden, Lede out the man that entride in to thin hows, that we mysuse him.

23 And the elde man yede out to hem, and seide, Nyle ye, britheren, nyle ye do this yuel; for the man entride in to myn herbore; and ceesse ye of this foli.

24 Y haue a douyter virgyn, and this man hath a wijf; Y schal lede out hem to you, that ye make lowe hem, and fille youre lust; oneli, Y biseche, that ye worche not this cursidnesse ayens kynde 'ayens the man.

25 Thei nolden assente to hise wordis; which thing the man siy, and ledde out his wijf to hem, and bitook to hem hir to be defoulid. And whanne thei hadden misusid hir al niyt, thei leften hir in the morewtid.

26 And whanne the derknessis departiden, the womman cam to the dore of the hows, where hir lord dwellide, and there sche felde doun.

27 Whanne the morewtid was maad, the man roos, and openyde the dore, 'that he schulde fille the weie bigunnun; and lo! his wijf lay bifor the dore, with hondis spred in the threischfold.

28 And he gesside 'hir to reste, 'and spak to hir, Rise thou, and go we. 'And whanne sche answeride no thing, he vndirstode that sche was deed; and he took hir, and puttide on the asse, and turnede ayen in to his hows.

29 And whanne he entride in 'to that hows, he took a swerd, and departide in to twelue partis and gobetis the deed body of the wijf, and sente in to alle the termes of Israel.

30 And whanne alle 'men hadden herde this, thei crieden, Neuere siche a thing was don in Israel, fro that dai 'in which oure fadris stieden fro Egipt 'til in to 'present tyme; seie ye sentence, and deme ye in comyn, what is nede to be doon.

CAP 20

1 Therfor alle the sones of Israel yeden, and weren gaderid togidere as o man, fro Dan 'til to Bersabee, and fro the lond of Galaad to the Lord in Maspha; and alle the 'corneris of puplis;

2 and alle the lynagis of Israel camen to gidere in to the chirche of 'the puple of God, foure hundrid thousynde of 'foot men fiyters.

3 And it was not 'hid fro the sones of Beniamyn, that the sones of Israel hadden stied in to Maspha. And the dekene, hosebonde of the 'wijf that was slayn, was axid, 'how so greet felonye was doon;

4 and he answeride, Y cam with my wijf in to Gabaa of Beniamyn, and Y turnede thidur.

5 And lo! men of that citee cumpassiden in nyyt the hows, in which Y dwellide, and thei wolden sle me, and thei bitraueliden my wijf with vnbileueful woodnesse of letcherie; at the last sche was deed.

6 And Y took, and Y kittide hir in to gobetis, and Y sente partis in to alle the termes of youre possessioun; for so greet felonye and so greuouse synne was neuere doon in Israel.

7 Alle ye sones of Israel ben present; deme ye, what ye owen do.

8 And al the puple stood, and answeride as bi word of o man, 'that is acordyngli, with out ayenseiyng and with out delay, We schulen not go awei in to oure tabernaclis, nethir ony man schal entre in to his hows;

9 but we schulen do this in comyn ayens Gabaa.

10 'Ten men be chosun of an hundrid, of alle the lynagis of Israel, and an hundrid of a thousynde, and a thousynde of ten thousynde, that thei bere metis to the oost, and that we, fiytynge ayens Gabaa of Beniamyn, moun yelde to it 'for the trespas that that it deserueth.

11 And al the puple, 'as o man, cam togidere to the citee bi the same thouyt and o counsel.

12 And 'thei senten messangeris to al the lynage of Beniamyn, 'whiche messangeris seiden, Whi so greet felony is foundun in you?

13 Bitake ye the men of Gabaa, that diden this wickidnesse, that thei die, and yuel be doon awey fro Israel. 'Whiche nolden here the comaundement of her britheren, the sones of Israel,

14 but of alle the citees, that weren of 'her part, thei camen togidere in to Gabaa, to helpe hem, and to fiyte ayens al the puple of Israel.

15 And fyue and twenti thousynde weren foundun of Beniamyn, of men drawynge out swerd, outakun the dwelleris of Gabaa,

16 whiche weren seuen hundrid strongeste men, fiytynge so with the lefthond as with the riythond, and castynge so stoonus with slyngis at a certeyn thing, that thei myyten smyte also an heer, and the strook of the stoon schulde not be borun in to 'the tother part.

17 Also of the men of Israel, with out the sones of Beniamin, weren foundun foure hundrid thousynd 'of men drawynge swerd and redi to batel.

18 Whiche riseden and camen in to the hows of God, that is in Silo; and thei counceliden God, and seiden, Who schal be prince in oure oost of the batel ayens the sones of Beniamyn? To whiche the Lord answeride, Judas be youre duyk.

19 And anoon the sones of Israel risiden eerli, and settiden tentis ayens Gabaa.

20 And fro thennus thei yeden forth to batel ayens Beniamyn, and bigunnen to fiyte ayens 'the citee.

21 And the sones of Beniamyn yeden out of Gabaa, and killiden of the sones of Israel in that dai two and twenti thousynde of men.

22 And eft the sones of Israel tristiden in strengthe and noumbre, and dressiden schiltrun, in the same place in which thei fouyten bifore;

23 so netheles that thei stieden bifore, and wepten bifor the Lord 'til to nyyt, and counseliden hym, and seiden, Owe Y go forth more to fiyte ayens the sones of Beniamyn, my britheren, ether nay? To whiche he answeride, Stie ye to hem, and bigynne ye batel.

24 And whanne the sones of Israel hadden go forth to batel in the tother dai ayens Beniamyn,

25 the sones of Beniamyn braken out of the yates of Gabaa, and camen to hem; and the sones of Beniamyn weren wood ayens hem bi so greet sleyng, that thei castiden doun eiytene thousynde of men drawynge swerd.

26 Wherfor alle the sones of Israel camen in to the hows of God, and saten, and wepten bifore the Lord, and thei fastiden in that dai 'til to euentid; and thei offeriden to the Lord brent sacrifices and pesible sacrifices,

27 and axiden of her staat. In that tyme the arke of boond of pees of God was there in Silo;

28 and Fynees, the sone of Eleazar, sone of Aaron, was souereyn of the hows. Therfor thei counseliden the Lord, and seiden, Owen we go out more to batel ayens the sones of Beniamyn, oure britheren, ethir reste? To whiche the Lord seide, Stie ye, for to morewe Y schal bytake hem in to youre hondis.

29 And the sones of Israel settiden buyschementis bi the cumpas of the citee of Gabaa;

30 and the thridde tyme as onys and tweis thei brouyten forth oost ayens Beniamyn.

31 But also the sones of Beniamyn braken out of the citee booldli, and pursueden ferthere the aduersaryes fleynge, so that thei woundiden of hem, as in the firste dai and the secounde, and killiden bi twey paththis 'the aduersaries turnynge backis; of whiche paththis oon was borun in to Bethel, the tother in to Gabaa. And thei castiden doun aboute thretti men;

32 for thei gessiden to sle hem 'bi customable maner; whiche 'feyneden fliyt bi craft, and token counsel, that thei schulden drawe hem fro the citee, and that thei as fleynge schulden brynge to the forseid paththis.

33 Therfor alle the sones of Israel risiden of her seetis, and settiden schiltrun in the place which is clepid Baalthamar. And the buschementis, that weren aboute the citee, bigunnen to opene hem silf litil and litil,

34 and to go forth fro the west part of the citee. But also othere ten thousynde of men of al Israel excitiden the dwelleris of the cite to batels; and the batel was maad greuous ayens the sones of Beniamyn, and thei vndurstoden not, that perisching neiyede to hem on eche part.

35 And the Lord smoot hem in the siyt of the sones of Israel, and 'thei killiden of hem in that dai fyue and twenti thousynde and an hundrid men, alle the werryours and drawynge swerd.

36 Sotheli the sones of Beniamyn bigunnen to fle, 'whanne thei sien, that thei weren the lowere. And the sones of Israel sien this, and 'yauen to hem place to fle, that thei schulden come to the buyschementis maad redi, whiche thei hadden set bisidis the citee.

37 And whanne thei hadden rise sudenli fro hid places, and Beniamyn yaf backis to the sleeris, thei entriden in to the citee, and smytiden it by the scharpnesse of swerd.

38 Sotheli the sones of Israel hadden youe a signe to hem whiche thei hadden set in buyschementis, that aftir that thei hadden take the citee, thei schulden kyndle fier, and that bi smook stiynge an hiy, thei schulden schewe the citee takun.

39 And whanne the sones of Israel set in thilke batel sien this; for the sones of Beniamyn gessiden hem to fle, and thei sueden bisiliere, whanne thretti men of her oost weren slayn;

40 and 'the sones of Israel sien as a piler of smoke stie fro the citee; also Beniamyn bihelde bihynde, whanne he siy the citee takun, and flawmes borun in hiye,

41 thei that feyneden fliyt bifore, 'ayenstoden strongliere with face turned. And whanne the sones of Beniamyn hadden seyn this, thei weren turned in to fliyt,

42 and thei bigunnen to go to the weie of deseert; while also aduersaries pursueden hem there, but also thei, that hadden brent the citee, camen ayens hem.

43 And so it was doon, that thei weren slayn of enemyes on ech part, nether ony reste of men diynge was; and thei felden, and weren cast doun at the eest coost of the citee of Gabaa.

44 Forsothe thei, that weren slayn in the same place, weren eiytene thousynde of 'men, alle strongeste fiyteris.

45 And whanne thei that leften of Beniamyn hadden seyn this, thei fledden in to wildirnesse, and thei yeden to the stoon, whos name is Remmon. And in that fliyt the sones of Israel yeden opynli, 'and yeden in to dyuerse places, and killiden fyue thousynde men; and whanne thei yeden ferther, thei pursueden hem, and killiden also othere twei thousynde.

46 And so it was doon, that alle that felden doun of Beniamyn in diuerse places, weren fyue and twenti thousynde, 'fiyterys moost redi to batels.

47 And so sixe hundrid men leften of al the noumbre of Beniamyn, that myyten ascape, and fle in to wildirnesse; and thei saten in the stoon of Remmon foure monethis.

48 Forsothe the sones of Israel yeden out, and smytiden with swerd alle the remenauntis of the citee, fro men 'til to werk beestis; and deuourynge flawme wastide alle the citees and townes of Beniamyn.

CAP 21

1 Also the sones of Israel sworen in Maspha, and seiden, Noon of vs schal yyue to the sones of Beniamyn a wijf of his douytris.

2 And 'alle camen to the hows of God in Silo, and thei saten in the 'siyt of hym 'til to euentid, and thei reisiden the vois, and bigunnen to wepe with greet yellyng,

3 and seiden, Lord God of Israel, whi is this yuel don in thi puple, that to dai o lynage be takun awey of vs?

4 Sotheli in the tother day thei risiden eerli, and bildyden an auter, and offriden there brent sacrifices and pesible sacrifices, and seiden,

5 Who of alle the lynagis of Israel stiede not in to the oost of the Lord? For whanne thei weren in Maspha, thei 'hadden bounde hem silf with a greuouse ooth, that thei that failiden schulden be slayn.

6 And the sones of Israel weren led bi penaunce on her brother Beniamyn, and bigunnen to seie, O lynage of Israel is takun awey;

7 wherof schulen thei take wyues? for alle we sworen in comyn, that we schulen not yyue oure douytris to hem.

8 Therfor thei seiden, Who is of alle the lynagis of Israel, that stiede not to the Lord in Maspha? And lo! the dwelleris of Jabes of Galaad weren foundun, that thei weren not in the oost.

9 Also in that tyme, whanne thei weren in Silo, noon of hem was foundun there.

10 Therfor thei senten ten thousynde strongeste men, and comaundiden to hem, Go ye, and smyte the dwelleris of Jabes of Galaad bi the scharpnesse of swerd, as wel the wyues as 'the litle children of hem.

11 And this thing schal be, which ye 'owen to kepe, sle ye alle of male kynde, and the wymmen, that knewen men fleischli; reserue ye the virgyns.

12 And foure hundrid virgyns, that knewen not the bed of man, weren foundun of Jabes of Galaad; and thei brouyten hem to the castels in Silo, in to the lond of Chanaan.

13 And 'thei senten messangeris to the sones of Beniamyn, that weren in the stoon of Remmon; and thei comaundiden to hem, that thei schulden resseyue tho wymmen in pees.

14 And the sones of Beniamyn camen in that tyme, and the douytris of Jabes of Galaad weren youun to hem to wyues; forsothe thei founden not othere wymmen, whiche thei schulden yyue in lijk maner.

15 And al Israel sorewide greetly, and dide penaunce on the sleyng of o lynage of Israel.

16 And the grettere men in birthe seiden, What schulen we do to the othere men, that han not take wyues? Alle the wymmen in Beniamyn felden doun,

17 and it 'is to vs to puruey 'with greet cure and greet studie, that o lynage be not don awey fro Israel.

18 We moun not yyue oure douytris to hem, for we ben boundun with an ooth and cursyng, bi which we seiden, Be he cursid that yyueth of hise douytris a wijf to Beniamyn.

19 And thei token a counsel, and seiden, Lo! annyuersarie solempnyte of the Lord is in Silo, whych is set at the north of the citee of Bethel, and at the eest coost of the weie that goith from Bethel to Siccyma, and at the south of the citee of Lebona.

20 And thei comaundiden to the sones of Beniamyn, and seiden, Go ye, be ye hid in the vyneris;

21 and whanne ye seen douytris of Silo go forth bi custom to lede daunsis, go ye out of the vyneris sudeynli, and rauysche ye hem, eche man o wijf, and go ye in to the lond of Beniamyn.

22 And whanne the fadris and britheren of hem schulen come, and bigynne to pleyne and plete ayens you, we schulen seie to hem, Haue ye mercy of hem; for thei rauyschiden not hem bi riyt of fiyteris and ouercomeris, but ye 'yauen not to hem preiynge that thei schulden take; and the synne is of youre part.

23 And the sones of Beniamyn diden as it was comaundid to hem, and bi her noumbre thei rauyschiden wyues to hem, ech man o wijf, of hem that ledden daunsis. And thei yeden in to her possessioun, and bildiden citees, and dwelliden in tho.

24 And the sones of Israel turneden ayen, bi lynagis and meynees, in to her tabernaclis. In tho dayes was no kyng in Israel, but ech man dide this, that semyde ryytful to hym silf.

RUTH

CAP 1

1 In the daies of o iuge, whanne iugis weren souereynes, hungur was maad in the lond; and a man of Bethleem of Juda yede to be a pylgrym in the cuntrei of Moab, with his wijf and twey fre sones.

2 He was clepid Elymelech, and his wijf Noemy, and the twey sones, 'the oon was clepid Maalon, and the tother Chelion, Effrateis of Bethleem of Juda; and thei entriden in to the cuntrey of Moab, and dwelliden there.

3 And Elymelech, the hosebonde of Noemy, diede, and sche lefte with the sones;

4 and thei token wyues of Moab, of whiche wyues oon was clepid Orpha, the tother Ruth. And the sones dwelliden there ten yeer,

5 and bothe dieden, that is, Maalon and Chelion; and the womman lefte, and was maad bare of twey fre sones, and hosebonde.

6 And sche roos to go with euer eithir wijf of hir sones in to hir cuntrey fro the cuntrey of Moab; for sche hadde herd, that the Lord hadde biholde his puple, and hadde youe 'metis to hem.

7 Therfor sche yede out of the place of hir pilgrymage with euer either wijf of hir sones; and now sche was set in the weie of turnyng ayen in to the lond of Juda,

8 and sche seide to hem, Go ye in to 'the hows of youre modir; the Lord do mercy with you, as ye diden with the deed men, and with me;

9 the Lord yyue to you to fynde reste in the howsis of hosebondis, whiche ye schulen take. And sche kiste hem. Whiche bigunnen to wepe with 'vois reisid,

10 and to seie, We schulen go with thee to thi puple.

11 To whiche sche answeride, My douytris, turne ye ayen, whi comen ye with me? Y haue no more sones in my wombe, that ye moun hope hosebondis of me; my douytris of Moab, turne ye ayen, and go;

12 for now Y am maad eeld, and Y am not able to boond of mariage; yhe, thouy Y myyte conseyue in this nyyt,

13 and bere sones, if ye wolen abide til thei wexen, and fillen the yeris of mariage, 'ye schulen sunner be eld wymmen than ye schulen be weddid; I biseche, 'nyle ye, my douytris, for youre angwische oppressith me more, and the hond of the Lord yede out ayens me.

14 Therfor, whanne the vois was reisid, eft thei bigunnen to wepe. Orpha kisside 'the modir of hir hosebonde, and turnede ayen, and Ruth 'cleuyde to 'the modir of hir hosebonde.

15 To whom Noemy seide, Lo! thi kyneswomman turnede ayen to hir puple, and to hir goddis; go thou with hir.

16 And sche answeride, Be thou not 'aduersarye to me, that Y forsake thee, and go awei; whidur euer thou schalt go, Y schal go, and where thou schalt dwelle, and Y schal dwelle togidere; thi puple is my puple, and thi God is my God;

17 what lond schal resseyue thee diynge, Y schal die ther ynne, and there Y schal take place of biriyng; God do to me these thingis, and adde these thingis, if deeth aloone schal not departe me and thee.

18 Therfor Noemy siy, that Ruth hadde demyde with stidefast soule to go with hir, and sche nolde be ayens hir, nether counseile ferthere turnynge ayen 'to her cuntrei men.

19 And thei yeden forth togidere, and camen in to Bethleem; and whanne thei entriden in to the citee, swift fame roos anentis alle men, and wymmen seiden, This is thilke Noemy.

20 To whiche sche seide, Clepe ye not me Noemy, that is, fair, but 'clepe ye me Mara, that is, bittere; for Almyyti God hath fillid me greetli with bitternesse.

21 Y yede out ful, and the Lord ledde me ayen voide; whi therfor clepen ye me Noemy, whom the Lord hath 'maad low, and Almyyti God hath turmentid?

22 Therfor Noemy cam with Ruth of Moab, 'the wijf of hir sone, fro the lond of hir pilgrimage, and turnede ayen in to Bethleem, whanne barli was ropun first.

CAP 2

1 Forsothe a myyti man and a man 'of grete richessis, 'Booz bi name, 'was kynysman of Elymelech.

2 And Ruth of Moab seide to hir modir in lawe, If thou comaundist, Y schal go in to the feeld, and Y schal gadere eeris of corn that fleen the hondis of reperis, where euer Y

schal fynde grace of an hosebonde man merciful in me. To whom sche answeride, Go, my douyter.

3 Therfor 'sche yede, and gaderide eeris of corn after the backis of reperis. Forsothe it bifelde, that 'thilke feeld hadde a lord, Booz bi name, that was of the kynrede of Elymelech.

4 And lo! he cam fro Bethleem. And he seide to the reperis, The Lord be with you. Whiche answeriden to hym, The Lord blesse thee.

5 And Booz seide to the yong man that was souereyn to the reperis, Who is this damysel?

6 Whiche answeride, This is the womman of Moab, that cam with Noemy fro the cuntrey of Moab; and sche preiede,

7 that sche schulde gedere eeris of corn leeuynge bihynde, and sue the 'steppis of reperis; and fro the morewtid til now sche stondith in the feeld, and sotheli nethir at a moment sche turnede ayen hoom.

8 And Booz seide to Ruth, Douytir, here thou; go thou not in to anothir feelde to gadere, nether go awei fro this place, but be thou ioyned to my dameselis,

9 and sue thou where thei repen; for Y comaundide to my children, that 'no man be diseseful to thee; but also if thou thirstist, go to the fardels, and drynke 'watris, of whiche my children drynken.

10 And sche felde on hir face, and worschipide on the erthe; and seide to hym, Wherof is this to me, that Y schulde fynde grace bifor thin iyen, that thou woldist knowe me a straunge womman?

11 To whom he answeride, Alle thingis ben teld to me, whiche thou didist to thi modir in lawe after the deeth of thin hosebonde, and that thou hast forsake thi fadir and modir, and the lond 'in which thou were borun, and hast come to a puple, whom thou 'knowist not bifore.

12 The Lord yelde to thee for thi werk, and resseyue thou ful mede of the Lord God of Israel, to whom thou camest, and vndir whose wengis thou fleddist.

13 And sche seide, My lord, Y haue founde grace bifor thin iyen, which hast coumfortid me, and hast spoke to the herte of thin handmaide, which am not lijk oon of thi dameselis.

14 And Booz seide to hir, Whanne the our of etyng is, come thou hidur, and ete breed, and wete thi mussel in vynegre. Therfor sche sat at the 'side of reperis; and he dresside to hir potage, and sche eet, and was fillid; and sche took the relifs.

15 And sche roos fro thennus to gadere eeris of corn bi custom. Forsothe Booz comaundide to hise children, and seide, Also if sche wole repe with you,

16 forbede ye not hir, and also 'of youre handfuls caste ye forth of purpos, and suffre ye to abide, that sche gadere with out schame; and no man repreue hir gaderynge.

17 Therfor sche gaderide in the feeld 'til to euentid; and sche beet with a yerde, and schook out tho thingis that sche hadde gaderid; and sche foond of barly as the mesure of ephi, that is, thre buschels.

18 Which sche bar, and turnede ayen in to the citee, and schewide to hir modir in lawe; ferthermore sche brouyte forth, 'and yaf to hir the relifs of hir mete, with which mete sche was fillid.

19 And the modir in lawe seide to hir, Where 'gaderidist thou to dai, and where 'didist thou werk? Blessid be he, that hadde mercy on thee. And sche telde to hir, at whom sche wrouyte; and sche seide the name 'of the man, that he was clepid Booz.

20 To whom Noemy answeride, Blessid be he of the Lord, for he kepte also to deed men the same grace, which he yaf to the quike. And eft sche seide, He is oure kynysman.

21 And Ruth seide, Also he comaundide this to me, that so longe Y schulde be ioyned to hise reperis, til alle the cornes weren repid.

22 To whom hir modir in lawe seide, My douyter, it is betere that thou go 'out to repe with hise damysels, lest in another feeld ony man ayenstonde thee.

23 'Therfor sche was ioyned to the damesels of Booz; and so longe sche rap with hem, til bothe barli and wheete weren closid in the bernys.

CAP 3

1 Forsothe aftir that Ruth turnede ayen to hir modir in lawe, Ruth herde of hir, My douytir, Y schal seke reste to thee, and Y schal purueye that it be wel to thee.

2 This Booz, to whose damesels thou were ioyned in the feeld, is oure kynesman, and in this niyt he wyndewith the corn floor of barli.

3 Therfor be thou waischun, and anoyntid, and be thou clothid with onestere clothis, and go doun in to the corn floor; the man, 'that is, Booz, se not thee, til he haue endid the mete and drynke.

4 Forsothe whanne he goth to slepe, marke thou the place 'in which he slepith; and thou schalt come and vnhile the cloth, 'with which he is hilid, fro the part of the feet, and thou schalt caste thee doun, and thou schalt ly there. Forsothe he schal seie to thee, what thou 'owist to do.

5 Which answeride, What euer thing thou comaundist, Y schal do.

6 And sche yede doun in to the corn floor, and dide alle thingis whiche hir modir in lawe comaundide to hir.

7 And whanne Booz hadde ete and drunke, and was maad gladere, and hadde go to slepe bisidis the 'heep of handfuls, sche cam, and hidde hir silf; and whanne the cloth was vnhilid fro 'hise feet, sche castide doun hir silf.

8 And lo! now at mydnyyt 'the man dredde, and was troblid; and he siy a womman lyggynge at hise feet;

9 and he seide to hir, Who art thou? Sche answeride, Y am Ruth, thin handmayde; stretche forth thi cloth on thi seruauntesse, for thou art nyy of kyn.

10 And he seide, Douytir, thou art blessid of the Lord, and thou hast ouercome the formere mercy with the lattere; for thou 'suedist not yonge men, pore ethir riche.

11 Therfor 'nyle thou drede, but what euer thing thou schalt seie to me, Y schal do to thee; for al the puple that dwellith with ynne the yatis of my cytee woot, that thou art a womman of vertu.

12 And Y forsake not, that Y am of nyy kyn, but another man is neer than Y;

13 reste thou in this nyyt, and whanne the morewtid is maad, if he wole holde thee bi riyt of nyy kyn, the thing is wel doon; forsothe if he nyle, Y schal take thee with outen ony doute, the Lord lyueth, 'that is, bi the Lord lyuynge; slepe thou til the morewtid.

14 Therfore sche slepte at 'hise feet til to the goyng awey of nyyt, and so sche roos bifor that men knewen 'hem silf togidere. And Booz seide to hir, Be thou war lest ony man knowe, that thou camest hidir.

15 And eft he seide, Stretche forth thi mentil 'with which thou 'art hilid, and holde thou with euer either hond. And while sche stretchide forth and helde, he mete sixe buyschels of barly, and 'puttide on hir; and sche bar, and entride in to the citee,

16 and cam to hir modir in lawe. Which seide to Ruth, What hast thou do, douyter? And Ruth telde to hir alle thingis, whyche 'the man hadde do to hir.

17 And Ruth seide, Lo! he yaf to me sixe buyschels of barly; and he seide, Y nyle that thou turne ayen voide to thi modir in lawe.

18 And Noemy seide, Abide, douyter, til we sien what issu the thing schal haue; for the man schal not ceesse, no but he fille tho thingis whiche he spak.

CAP 4

1 Therfor Booz stiede to the yate, and sat there; and whanne he hadde seyn the kynesman passe forth, of whom the word was had, Booz seide to hym, Bowe thou a litil, and sitte here; and he clepide hym bi his name. And he turnede, and sat.

2 Forsothe Booz took ten 'men of the eldere men of the citee, and seide to hem, Sitte ye here.

3 And while thei saten, Booz spak to the kynesman, Noemy, that turnede ayen fro the cuntrey of Moab, seelde the part of the feeld of oure brother Elymelech,

4 which thing Y wolde that thou here; and Y wolde seie to thee bifor alle 'men syttynge and grettere in birthe of my puple. If thou wolt haue in possessioun the feeld bi riyt of nyy kyn, bye thou, and 'haue thou in possessioun; sotheli if it displesith thee, schewe thou this same thing to me, that Y wyte what Y 'owe to do; for noon is niy in kyn, outakun thee which art the formere, and outakun me which am the secunde. And he answeride, Y schal bie the feeld.

5 To whom Booz seide, Whanne thou hast bouyte the feeld of the 'hond of the womman, thou owist 'to take also Ruth of Moab, that was the wijf of the deed man, that thou reise the name of thi kynesman in his eritage.

6 Which answeride, Y forsake the ryyt of nyy kyn; for Y owe not to do awei the eritage of my meynee; vse thou my priuelegie, which priuelegie Y knowleche me to wante gladli.

7 Forsothe this was the custom bi eld tyme in Israel among kynesmen, that if a man yaf his riyt to anothir man, that the grauntyng were stidefast, the man vnlaase his scho, and yaf to his kynesman; this was the witnessyng of the yift in Israel.

8 Therfor Booz seide to his kynesman, Take the scho fro thee; 'which scho he vnlaside anoon fro his foot.

9 And Booz seide to the grettere men in birthe and to al the puple, Ye ben witnessis to dai, that Y haue take in possessioun alle thingis that weren of Elymelech, and of Chelion, and of Maalon, bi the yifte of Noemy;

10 and that Y haue take in to wedlok Ruth of Moab, the wijf of Maalon, that Y reise the name of the deed man in his erytage; lest his name be doon awey fro his meynee and britheren and puple. Ye, he seide, ben witnessis of this thing.

11 Al the puple, that was in the yate, answeride, and the grettere men in birthe answeriden, We ben witnessis; the Lord make this womman, that entrith in to thin hows, as Rachel and Lia, that bildiden the hows of Israel, that sche be ensaumple of vertu in Effrata, and haue a solempne name in Bethleem;

12 and thin hows be maad as the hows of Fares, whom Thamar childide to Judas, of the seed which the Lord schal yyue to thee of this damesel.

13 Therfor Booz took Ruth, and took hir to wijf; and he entride to hir, and the Lord yaf to hir, that sche conseyuede, 'and childide a sone.

14 And wymmen seiden to Noemy, Blessid be the Lord, which 'suffride not, that an eir failide to thi meynee, and his name were clepid in Israel;

15 and that thou haue 'a man, that schal coumforte thi soule, and nursche elde age. For a child is borun of thi douytir in lawe, 'which child schal loue thee, and he is myche betere to thee, than if thou haddist seuene sones.

16 And Noemy puttide the child resseyued in hir bosum; and sche dide the office of a nurische, and of a berere.

17 Forsothe wymmen neiyboris thankiden hir, and seiden, A sone is borun to Noemy, and clepide his name Obeth. This is the fadir of Ysay, fadir of Dauid.

18 These ben the generaciouns of Fares; Fares gendride Esrom;

19 Esrom gendride Aram; Aram gendride Amynadab;

20 Amynadab gendride Naason; Naason gendride Salmon; Salmon gendride Booz;

21 Booz gendride Obeth;

22 Obeth gendride Isay; Isay gendride Dauid the kyng.

1 KINGS

CAP 1

1 'A man was of 'Ramathym of Sophym, of the hil of Effraym, and his name was Elchana, the sone of Jeroboam, sone of Elyud, sone of Thau, sone of Suph, of Effraym.

2 And Helchana hadde twei wyues; the name 'to oon was Anna, and the 'name of the secounde was Fenenna; and sones weren to Feuenna; forsothe fre children 'weren not to Anna.

3 And thilke man styede fro his citee in daies ordeyned, to worschipe and offre sacrifice to the Lord of oostis in Silo. Forsothe twei sones of Heli weren there, Ophym and Fynees, preestis of the Lord.

4 Therfor the dai cam, and Helcana offride, and yaf partis to Fenenna, his wijf, and to alle hise sones and douytris;

5 forsothe he yaf soreufuly o part to Anna, for he louyde Anna; forsothe the Lord hadde closid hir wombe.

6 And hir enemy turmentide 'hir, and angwischide greetly, in so myche that sche vpbreidide, that the Lord hadde closid hir wombe.

7 And so sche dide 'bi alle yeeris, whanne 'in tyme comynge ayen, thei stieden in to the hows of the Lord; and so sche terride Anna. Forsothe Anna wepte, and took not mete.

8 Therfor Helcana, hir hosebonde, seide to hir, Anna, whi wepist thou, and whi etist thou not, and whi is thin herte turmentid? Whether Y am not betere to thee than ben ten sones?

9 'Sotheli Anna roos, aftir that sche hadde ete and drunke in Silo. 'And the while Hely was on his greet seete, bifor the postis of the 'hows of the Lord,

10 whanne Anna was in bittere soule, sche preyede the Lord, and wepte largeli;

11 and made a vow, and seide, Lord God of oostis, if thou biholdist, and seest the turment of thi seruauntesse, and hast mynde of me, and foryetis not thin handmayde, and yyuest to thi seruauntesse 'a male kynde, Y schal yyue hym to the Lord in alle daies of his lijf, and a rasour schal not stie on his heed.

12 Forsothe it was doon, whanne sche multipliede preieris bifor the Lord, that Ely aspiede hir mouth.

13 Forsothe Anna spak in hir herte, and oneli hir lippis weren mouyd, and outerly hir vois was not herd. Therfor Hely gesside hir drunkun,

14 and he seide to hyr, Hou longe schalt thou be drunkun? Difye thou a litil the wyn, 'bi which thou art moist.

15 Anna answeride, and seide, Nay, my lord, for Y am 'a wretchid womman greetli; Y 'drank not wyn 'and al thing that may make drunkun, but Y schedde out my soule in the 'siyt of the Lord;

16 gesse thou not thin handmaide as oon of the douytris of Belyal, for of the multitude of my sorewe and morenyng Y spak 'til in to present tyme.

17 Thanne Hely seide to hir, Go thou in pees, and God of Israel yyue to thee the axyng which thou preiedist hym.

18 And sche seide, 'Y wolde that thin hondmayde fynde grace in thin iyen. And the womman yede in to hir weie, and eet; and hir cheris weren no more chaungid dyuersly.

19 And 'thei ryseden eerly, and worschipiden bifore the Lord; and thei turneden ayen, and camen in to hir hows in Ramatha. Forsothe Helchana knew fleischli Anna, his wijf; and the Lord thouyte on hir.

20 And it was doon after the cumpas of daies, Anna conseyuede, and childide a sone, and sche clepide his name Samuel; for sche hadde axid hym of the Lord.

21 Forsothe hir hosebonde Helcana stiede, and al his hows, to offre a solempne sacrifice, and his avow to the Lord.

22 And Anna stiede not, for sche hadde seid to hir hosebonde, Y schal not go, til the yonge child be wenyd, and til Y lede hym, and he appere bifor the 'siyt of the Lord, and dwelle there contynueli.

23 And Helcana, hir hosebonde, seide to hir, Do thou that that semeth good to thee, and dwelle thou til thou wene hym; and Y biseche, that the Lord fille his word. Therfor the womman dwellide, and yaf mylk to hir sone, til sche remouyde hym fro mylk.

24 And sche brouyte hym with hir, aftir that sche hadde wened hym, with thre caluys, and thre buyschelis of mele, and amfore, 'ether a pot, of wyn; and sche brouyte hym to the hows of the Lord in Silo. Forsothe the child was yit ful yonge.

25 And thei sacrifieden a calf, and thei offriden the child to Hely.

26 And Anna seide, My lord, Y biseche, that is, that this child be thi 'disciple and seruaunt, thi soule lyueth; Y am that womman, that stood bifor thee here, and preiede the Lord;

27 for this child Y preiede, and the Lord yaf to me myn axyng which Y axide hym;

28 therfor Y haue youe hym to the Lord 'in alle daies, in whiche he is youun to the Lord. And thei worschypiden there the Lord.

CAP 2

1 And Anna worschipide, and seide, Myn herte fulli ioiede in the Lord, and myn horn is reisid in my God; my mouth is alargid on myn enemyes, for Y was glad in thin helthe.

2 Noon is hooli as the Lord is; 'for noon other is, outakun thee, and noon is strong as oure God.

3 Nyle ye multiplie to speke hiye thingis, and haue glorie; elde thingis go awey fro youre mouth; for God is Lord of kunnyngis, and thouytis ben maad redi to hym.

4 The bouwe of strong men is ouercomun, and sijk men ben gird with strengthe.

5 Men fillid bifore settiden hem silf to hire for looues, and hungri men ben fillid; while the bareyn womman childide ful manye, and sche that hadde many sones, was sijke.

6 The Lord sleeth, and quikeneth; he ledith forth to hellis, and bryngith ayen.

7 The Lord makith pore, and makith riche; he makith low, and reisith.

8 He reisith a nedi man fro poudur, and 'he reisith a pore man fro dryt, that he sitte with princes, and holde the seete of glorie; for the endis of erthe ben of the Lord, and he hath set the world on tho.

9 He schal kepe 'the feet of hise seyntis, and wickid men schulen be stille to gidere in derknessis; for a man schal not be maad strong in his owne strengthe.

10 Aduersaries of the Lord schulen drede hym, and in heuenes he schal thundre on hem; the Lord schal deme the endis of erthe, and he schal yyue lordschip to his kyng, and he schal enhaunse the horn, 'that is, power, of his Crist.

11 And Helcana yede in to Ramatha, in to his hows; forsothe the child was seruaunt in the siyt of the Lord bifor the face of Ely the preest.

12 Forsothe the sones of Hely weren sones of Belial,

13 and knewen not the Lord, nether the office of preestis to the puple; but who euer hadde offrid sacrifice, the child of the preest cam, while the fleischis weren in sething, and he hadde a fleischhook with thre teeth in his hond;

14 and he sente it in to the 'grete vessel of stoon, ethir in to the caudrun, ethir in to the pot, ethir in to the panne; and what euer thing the fleischhook reiside, the preest took to hym silf; so thei diden to al Israel of men comynge in to Silo.

15 Yhe bifor that 'the sones of Hely brenten the ynnere fatnesse, the 'child of the preest cam, and seyde to the offerere, Yyue 'thou fleisch to me, that Y sethe to the preest; for Y schal not take of thee sodun fleisch, but raw.

16 And 'the offrere seide to hym, The ynnere fatnesse be brent first to day bi the custom, and take thou to thee hou myche euer thi soule desirith. Whiche answeride, and seide to hym, Nay, for thou schalt yyue now; ellis Y schal take bi violence.

17 Therfor the synne of the children was ful greuouse bifor the Lord; for thei withdrowen men fro the 'sacrifice of the Lord.

18 'Forsothe Samuel, a child gird with a lynnun clooth, mynystride bifor the face of the Lord.

19 And his moder made to hym a litil coote, which sche brouyte in daies ordeyned, and stiede with hir hosebonde, that he schulde offre a solempne offryng, and his auow.

20 And Heli blesside Helcana and his wijf; and Heli seide 'to hym, The Lord yelde to thee seed of this womman, for the yifte which thou hast youe to the Lord. And thei yeden in to her place.

21 Therfor the Lord visitide Anna, and sche conseyuede, and childide thre sones and twei douytris. And the child Samuel was 'magnyfied at the Lord.

22 Forsothe Hely was ful eld, and he herde alle 'thingis whiche hise sones diden in al Israel, and hou thei slepten with wymmen, that awaitiden at the dore of the tabernacle.

23 And he seide to hem, Whi doen ye siche thingis, the worste thingis whiche Y here of al the puple?

24 Nyle ye, my sones; it is not good fame, which Y here, that ye make the 'puple of the Lord to do trespas.

25 If a man synneth ayens a man, God may be plesid to him; forsothe if a man synneth ayens the Lord, who schal preye for hym? And thei herden not the vois of her fadir, for God wolde sle hem.

26 Forsothe the child Samuel profitide, and encreessyde, and pleside bothe God and men.

27 Sotheli a man of God cam to Hely, and seide to hym, The Lord seith these thingis, Whether Y was not schewid apertli to the hows of thi fadir, whanne he was in Egipt, in the hows of Farao?

28 And Y chees hym of alle lynagis of Israel 'in to preest to me, that he schulde stie to myn auter, and schulde brenne encense to me, and that he schulde bere bifor me preestis cloth; and Y yaf to 'the hows of thi fadir alle thingis of the sacrifices of the sones of Israel.

29 Whi hast thou cast awey with the heele my sacrifice, and my yiftis, whiche Y comaundide to be offrid in the temple; and thou onouridst more thi sones than me, that ye eeten the principal partis of ech sacrifice of 'Israel, my puple?

30 Therfor the Lord God of Israel seith these thingis, Y spekynge spak, that thin hows and 'the hows of thi fadir schulde mynystre in my siyt til in to with outen ende; 'now forsothe the Lord seith, Fer be this fro me; but who euere onourith me, Y schal glorifie hym; forsothe thei that dispisen me, schulen be vnnoble.

31 Lo! daies comen, and Y schal kitte awei thin arm, and the arm of the hows of thi fadir, that an eld man be not in thin hows.

32 And thou schalt se thin enemy in the temple, in alle prosperitees of Israel; and an eld man schal not be in thin hows in alle daies.

33 Netheles Y schal not outerli take awei of thee a man fro myn auter, but that thin iyen faile, and thi soule faile; and greet part of thin hows schal die, whanne it schal come to mannus age.

34 Forsothe this schal be signe, that schal come to thi twei sones Ophym and Fynees, bothe schulen die in o dai.

35 And Y schal reise to me a feithful preest, that schal do bi myn herte and my soule; and Y schal bilde to hym a feithful hows, and he schal go bifore my Crist in alle daies.

36 Forsothe it schal come, that who euer dwellith in thin hows, he come that 'me preie for him, and that he offre a peny of siluer, and a cake of breed, and seie, Y biseche, suffre thou me to o 'part of the preest, that Y ete a mussel of breed.

CAP 3

1 Forsothe the child Samuel 'mynystride to the Lord bifor Heli, and the word of the Lord was preciouse; in tho daies was noon opyn reuelacioun.

2 Therfor it was doon in a dai, Heli lay in his bed, and hise iyen dasewiden, and he myyte not se the lanterne of God, bifor that it was quenchid.

3 Forsothe Samuel slepte in the temple of the Lord, where the ark of God was.

4 And the Lord clepide Samuel; and he answeride and seide, Lo!

5 Y. And he ran to Hely, and seide to hym, Lo! Y; for thou clepidist me. Which Hely seide, Y clepide not thee; turne thou ayen and slepe.

6 And he yede and slepte. And the Lord addide eft to clepe Samuel; and Samuel roos, and yede to Hely, and seide, Lo! Y; for thou clepidist me. And Heli answeride, Y clepide not thee, my sone; turne thou ayen and slepe.

7 Forsothe Samuel knew not yit the Lord, nether the 'word of the Lord was shewid to hym.

8 And the Lord addide, and clepide yit Samuel the thridde tyme; 'which Samuel roos and yede to Heli,

9 and seide, Lo! Y; for thou clepidist me. Therfor Heli vndirstood, that the Lord clepide the child; and Heli seide to Samuel, Go and slepe; and if he clepith thee aftirward, thou schalt

seie, Speke thou, Lord, for thi seruaunt herith. Therfor Samuel yede and slepte in his place.

10 And the Lord cam, and stood, and clepide as he hadde clepid the secunde tyme, Samuel, Samuel. And Samuel seide, Speke thou, Lord, for thi seruaunt herith.

11 And the Lord seide to Samuel, Lo! Y make a word in Israel, which word who euer schal here, bothe hise eeris schulen rynge.

12 In that dai Y schal reise ayens Heli alle thingis, whiche Y spak on his hows; Y schal bigynne, and Y schal ende.

13 For Y biforseide to hym, that Y schulde deme his hows with outen ende for wickidnesse; for he knew, that hise sones diden vnworthili, and he chastiside not hem.

14 Therfor Y swoor to the hows of Heli, that the wickidnesse of his hows schal not be clensid bi sacrifices and yiftis til in to with outen ende.

15 Forsothe Samuel slepte til the morewtid, and he openyde the doris of the hows of the Lord; and Samuel dredde to schewe the reuelacioun to Heli.

16 Therfor Heli clepide Samuel, and seide, Samuel, my sone. And he answeride and seide, Y am redi.

17 And Heli axide hym, What is the word which the Lord spak to thee? Y preye thee, hide thou not fro me; God do to thee 'these thingis, and encreesse these thingis, if thou hidist fro me a word of alle wordis that ben seid to thee.

18 And Samuel schewide to hym alle the wordis, and 'hidde not fro hym. And Heli answeride, He is the Lord; do he that, that is good in hise iyen.

19 Forsothe Samuel encreeside, and the Lord was with hym, and noon of alle hise wordis felde in to erthe.

20 And al Israel fro Dan to Bersabee knew, that feithful Samuel was a profete of the Lord.

21 And the Lord addide 'that he schulde appere in Silo, for the Lord was schewid to Samuel in Silo bi the 'word of the Lord; and the word of Samuel cam to al Israel.

CAP 4

1 And it was doon in tho daies Filisteis camen to gidere in to batel; for Israel yede out ayens Filisteis in to batel, and settiden tentis bisidis the stoon of help. Forsothe Filisteis camen in to Aphet,

2 and maden redi scheltrun ayens Israel. Sotheli whanne the batel was bigunnun, Israel turned backis to Filisteis; and as foure thousynde of men weren slayn in that batel 'euery where bi feeldis; and the puple of Israel turnede ayen to tentis. And the grettere men in birthe of Israel seiden, Whi hath the Lord smyte vs to dai bifore Filisteis? Brynge we to vs fro Silo the arke of boond of pees of the Lord, and come it in to the myddis of vs, that it saue vs fro the hond of oure enemyes.

4 Therfor the puple sente in to Silo, and thei token fro thennus the arke of boond of pees of the Lord of oostis, 'that sat on cherubyn. And Ophym and Fynees, twei sones of Heli, weren with the arke of boond of pees of the Lord.

5 And whanne the arke of boond of pees of the Lord hadde come in to the castels, al Israel criede with grete cry, and the erthe sownede.

6 And Filisteis herden the vois of cry, and seiden, What is this vois of greet cry in the castels of Ebrews? And thei knewen, that the arke of boond of pees of the Lord hadde come in to castels.

7 And Filisteis dredden, and seiden, God is come in to 'the castels; and thei weiliden, and seiden, Wo to vs!

8 for so greet ful ioiyng was not yistirdai, and the thridde day passid; wo to vs! who schal kepe vs fro the hond of 'these hiye goddis? these ben the goddis, that smytiden Egipt with al veniaunce in deseert.

9 Filisteis, be ye coumfortid, and be ye men, serue ye not Ebrews, as thei serueden vs; be ye coumfortid, and fiyte ye.

10 Therfor Filisteis fouyten, and Israel was slayn, and ech man flei in to his tabernacle; and a ful greet veniaunce was maad, and thretti thousynde of foot men of Israel felden doun.

11 And the arke of God was takun; and, twei sones of Heli, Ophym and Fynees, weren deed.

12 Sotheli a man of Beniamyn ran fro the scheltrun, and cam in to Silo in that dai, with his cloth torent and his heed bispreynt with dust; and whanne he was comen,

13 Heli sat 'on an hiye seete, 'and bihelde ayens the weie; for his herte was dredyng for the arke of the Lord. Sotheli aftir that thilke man entride, he telde to the citee, and al the citee yellide.

14 And Heli herde the soun of cry, and seide, What is this sown of this noise? And he hastide, and cam, and telde to Heli.

15 Forsothe Heli was of foure score yeer and eiytene, and hise iyen dasiwiden, and he myyte not se.

16 And he seide to Heli, Y am that cam fro batel, and Y am that flei to dai fro the scheltrun. To whom Ely seide, My sone, what is doon?

17 Forsothe he that telde answeride, and seide, Israel flei bifor Filisteis, and a greet fal is maad in the puple; ferthermore and thi twey sones, Ophym and Fynees, ben deed, and the arke of God is takun.

18 And whanne he hadde nemyd the arke of God, Hely felde fro 'the hiye seete bacward bisidis the dore, and 'was deed; for the nollis weren brokun. For he was an eld man, and of greet age; and he demyde Israel bi fourti yeer.

19 Forsothe his douyter in lawe, 'the wijf of Finees, was with childe, and niy the child bering; and whanne 'the message was herd that the arke of God was takun, and that hir fadir in lawe was deed, and hir hosebonde, sche bowide hir silf, and childide; for sodeyn sorewis felden in to hir.

20 Sotheli in that moment of hir deeth, wymmen that stoden aboute hir, seiden to hir, Drede thou not, for thou hast childid a sone. And sche answeride not to hem, for nether 'sche perseyuede.

21 And sche clepide the child Ichaboth, and seide, The glorie of the Lord is translatid fro Israel, for the arke of God is takun; and for hir fadir in lawe and for hir hosebonde sche seide,

22 The glorie of God is translatid fro Israel, for the arke of God is takun.

CAP 5

1 Forsothe Filisteis token the arke of God, and baren awey it fro the stoon of help in to Azotus.

2 And Filisteis tokun the arke of God, and brouyten it to the temple of Dagon, and settiden it bisidis Dagon.

3 And whanne men of Azotus hadden rise eerli in the todir dai, lo! Dagon lay low in the erthe bifor the arke of the Lord. And thei token Dagon, and restoriden hym in his place.

4 And eft thei risiden eerli in the tothir day, and founden Dagon liggynge on his face on the erthe bifor the arke of the Lord. Forsothe the heed of Dagon, and twei pawmes of his hondis weren kit of on the threisfold;

5 certis the stok aloone of Dagon lefte in his place. For this cause the preestis of Dagon, and alle that entren in to his temple, treden not on the threisfold of Dagon in Azotus til in to this dai.

6 Forsothe the hond of the Lord was maad greuouse on men of Azotus, and he distriede hem, and he smoot Azotus and the coostis therof in the priuyere part of buttokis; and townes and feeldis in the myddis of that cuntrey buyliden out, and myis camen forth; and greet confusioun of deth was maad in the citee.

7 Sotheli men of Azotus sien siche a veniaunce, and seiden, The arke of God of Israel dwelle not at vs; for his hond is hard on vs, and on Dagon oure god.

8 And thei senten, and gaderiden alle the wise men, 'ether princes, of Filisteis 'to hem, and seiden, What schulen we do of the arke of God of Israel? And men of Geth answeriden, The arke of God of Israel be led aboute; and thei ledden aboute the arke of God of Israel.

9 Forsothe while thei ledden it aboute, the hond of the Lord 'of ful greet sleyng was maad on alle citees; and he smoot men of ech citee fro a litil man til to 'the more, and the lowere entraylis 'of hem wexiden rotun, and camen forth; and men of Geth token counsel, and maden to hem seetis of skynnes, ethir cuyschuns.

10 Therfor thei senten the arke of the Lord in to Accoron. And whanne the arke of the Lord hadde come in to Accoron, men of Accoron crieden, and seiden, Thei han brought to vs the arke of God of Israel, that he sle vs and oure puple.

11 Therfor thei senten, and gaderiden alle the wise men, 'ethir princes, of Filisteis; whiche seiden, Delyuere ye the arke of God of Israel, and turne it ayen in to his place, and sle not vs with oure puple.

12 For dreed of deeth was maad in alle citees, and the hond of the Lord was 'greuouse greetli. Also the men, that weren not deed, weren smytun in the priuy part of buttokis, and the yelling of ech citee stiede in to heuene.

CAP 6

1 Therfor the arke of the Lord was in the cuntrei of Filisteis bi seuene monethis;

2 and aftir these thingis Filisteis clepiden preestis and false dyuynours, and seiden, What schulen we do of the arke of God? Shewe ye to vs, hou we schulen sende it in to his place.

3 Whiche seiden, If ye senden ayen the arke of God of Israel, nyle ye delyuere it voide, but yelde ye to hym that, that ye owen for synne; and thanne ye schulen be heelid, and ye schulen wite, whi 'his hond goith not awei fro you.

4 And thei seiden, What is it, that we owen to yelde to hym for trespas?

5 And thei answeriden to hem, Bi the noumbre of prouynces of Filisteis ye schulen make fyue goldun ersis, and fyue goldun myis; for o veniaunce was to alle you and to youre 'wise men, ether princes. And ye schulen make the licnesse of youre ersis, and the licnesse of myis that distriede youre lond; and ye schulen yyue glorie to God of Israel, if in hap he withdrawe his hond fro you, and fro youre goddis, and fro youre lond.

6 Whi maken ye heuy youre hertis, as Egipt, and Farao 'made heuy his herte? Whether not after that he was smytun, thanne he delyuerede hem, and thei yeden forth?

7 Now therfor take ye, and make o newe wayn, and ioyne ye twei kien hauynge caluys, on whiche kyen no yok was put; and close ye her calues at hoome.

8 And ye schulen take the arke of the Lord, and ye schulen sette in the wayn; and ye schulen put in a panyere at the side therof the goldun vessels, whiche ye payeden to hym for trespas; and delyuere ye the arke, that it go.

9 And ye schulen biholde, and sotheli if it stieth ayens Bethsames bi the weie 'hise coostis, 'he dide to you this greet yuel; but if nay, we schulen wite 'for his hond touchide not vs, but 'if it bifelde bi hap.

10 Therfor thei diden in this manere; and thei token twei kien that yauen mylk to caluys, and ioyneden to the wayn; and thei closiden her caluys at hoome.

11 And thei puttiden the arke of God on the wayn, and 'thei puttiden the panyere, that hadde the goldun myis, and the licnesse of ersis 'on the wayn.

12 Sotheli the kien yeden streiytli bi the weie that ledith to Bethsames; and tho yeden in o weie goynge and lowynge, and bowiden not nether to the riyt side nether to the left side; but the wise men of Filisteis sueden 'til to the termes of Bethsames.

13 Forsothe men of Bethsames repiden whete in the valey, and thei reisiden the iyen, and sien the arke, and thei weren ioyful, whanne thei hadden sien 'the arke.

14 And the wayn cam in to the feelde of Josue of Bethsames, and stood there. Forsothe a greet stoon was there; and thei kittiden 'the trees of the wayn, and puttiden the kien 'on tho trees, a brent sacrifice to the Lord.

15 Sotheli dekenes token doun the arke of God, and the panyere, that was bisidis it, whare ynne the goldun vessels weren; and thei settiden on the greet stoon. Forsothe the men of Bethsames offriden brent sacrifices, and offriden slayn sacrifices in that dai 'to the Lord.

16 And fyue princes of Filisteis sien, and turneden ayen in to Accoron in that dai.

17 Sotheli these ben the goldun ersis, whiche the Filisteis yeldiden to the Lord for trespas; Azotus yeldide oon; Gaza yeldide oon; Ascolon yeldide oon; Geth yeldide oon; Accaron yeldide oon;

18 and Filisteis yeldiden golden myis bi the noumbre of 'citees of Filisteis of fyue prouynces, fro a wallid citee 'til to 'a town that was with out wal, and 'til to the greet Abel, 'on which thei puttiden the arke of the Lord, that was there 'til in that dai in the feeld of Josue of Bethsames.

19 Forsothe the Lord smoot of the men of Bethsames, for thei hadden seyn the arke of the Lord, and he smoot of the puple seuenti men, and fifty thousynde of the porail. And the puple morenyde, for the Lord hadde smyte 'the puple with greet veniaunce.

20 And men of Bethsames seiden, Who schal now stonde in the siyt of the Lord God of this hooli thing, and to whom schal it stie fro vs?

21 And thei senten messangeris to the dwelleris of Cariathiarym, and seiden, Filisteis han brouyt ayen the arke of the Lord; come ye doun, and lede it ayen to you.

CAP 7

1 Therfor men of Cariathiarym camen, and ledden ayen the arke of the Lord, and brouyten it in to the hows of Amynadab in Gabaa. Sotheli thei halewiden Eleazar his sone, that he schulde kepe the ark of the Lord.

2 And it was doon, fro which dai 'the arke of the Lord dwellide in Caryathiarym, daies weren multiplied; for the twentithe yeer was now, after that Samuel bigan to teche the puple; and al Israel restide aftir the Lord.

3 Forsothe Samuel spak to al the hows of Israel, and seide, If in al youre herte ye turnen ayen to the Lord, do ye awei alien goddis, Balym and Astaroth, fro the myddis of you; and make ye redi youre hertis to the Lord, and serue ye hym aloone; and he schal delyuere you fro the hond of Filisteis.

4 Therfor the sones of Israel diden awey Baalym and Astoroth, and serueden the Lord aloone.

5 Forsothe Samuel seide, Gadere ye al Israel in to Masphat, that Y preie the Lord for you.

6 And thei camen togidere in to Masphat, and thei drowen watir, and shedden out in the 'siyt of the Lord; and thei fastiden in that day, and seiden, Lord, we synneden to thee. And Samuel demyde the sones of Israel in Masphat.

7 And Filisteis herden that the sones of Israel weren gaderid in Masphat; and the princes of Filisteis stieden to Israel. And whanne the sones of Israel hadden herd this, thei dredden of the face of Filisteis.

8 And 'thei seiden to Samuel, Ceesse thou not to crye for vs to oure Lord God, that he saue vs fro the 'hoond of Filisteis.

9 Forsothe Samuel took o soukynge lomb, and offride that hool in to brent sacrifice to the Lord. And Samuel criede to the Lord for Israel; and the Lord herde hym.

10 Forsothe it was doon, whanne Samuel offryde brent sacrifice, that Filisteis bigunnen batel ayens Israel. Sotheli the Lord thundride with greet thundur in that dai on Filisteis, and made hem aferd; and thei weren slayn of the sones of Israel.

11 And the sones of Israel yeden out of Masphat, and pursueden Filisteis, and smytiden hem 'til to the place that was vndur Bethachar.

12 Forsothe Samuel took o stoon, and puttide it bitwixe Masphat, and bitwixe Sen; and he clepide the name of that place The stoon of help. And he seide, Hidir to the Lord helpide vs.

13 And Filisteis weren maad low, and addiden no more to come in to the termes of Israel. And so the 'hond of the Lord was maad on Filisteis in alle the daies of Samuel.

14 And the citees whiche the Filisteis token fro Israel, weren yoldun to Israel, fro Accaron 'til to Geth and 'hise termes; and the Lord delyuerede Israel fro the hond of Filisteis; and pees was bitwixe Israel and Ammorrey.

15 Also Samuel demyde Israel in alle the daies of his lijf, that is, 'til to the ordeynyng 'and confermyng of Saul;

16 and he yede bi 'alle yeeris, and cumpasside Bethel, and Galgal, and Masphat, and he demyde Israel in the forseid places.

17 And he turnede ayen in to Ramatha, for his hows was there; and he demyde Israel there, and he bildide there also an auter to the Lord.

CAP 8

1 Forsothe it was don, whanne Samuel hadde wexide eld, he settide hise sones iugis on Israel.

2 And the name of his firste gendrid sone was Johel, and the name of the secounde was Abia, iugis in Bersabee.

3 And hise sones yeden not in 'the weies of hym, but thei bowiden after aueryce, and thei token yiftis, and peruertiden doom.

4 Therfor alle the grettere men in birthe of Israel weren gaderid, and camen to Samuel in to Ramatha.

5 And thei seiden to hym, Lo! thou hast wexid eld, and thi sones goen not in thi weies; ordeyne thou a kyng to vs, 'that he deme vs, as also alle naciouns han.

6 And the word displeside in the iyen of Samuel, for thei hadden seid, Yyue thou to vs a kyng, that he deme vs. And Samuel preiede to the Lord.

7 Forsothe the Lord seide to Samuel, Here thou the vois of the puple in alle thingis whiche thei speken to thee; for thei han not caste awey thee, but me, that Y regne not on hem.

8 Bi alle her werkis whiche thei diden, fro the day in whiche Y ledde hem out of Egipt 'til to this dai, as thei forsoken me, and seruyden alien goddis, so thei doon also to thee.

9 Now therfor here thou her vois; netheles witnesse thou to hem; biforseie thou to hem the riyt of the kyng, that schal regne on hem.

10 Therfor Samuel seide alle the wordis of the Lord to the puple, that hadde axid of him a king; and he seide,

11 This schal be the 'riyt of the kyng, that schal comaunde to you; he schal take youre sones, and schal sette in hise charis;

12 and he schal make hem 'to hym silf rideris, and biforegoeris of hise cartis; and he schal ordeyne to hym tribunes, 'that is, souereyns of a thousynd, and centuriouns, 'that is, souereyns of an hundrid, and eereris of hise feeldis, and reperis of cornes, and smythis of hise armeris, and charis.

13 Also he schal make youre douytris makeris of 'oynementis to hym silf, and fueris, and bakeris.

14 And he schal take youre feeldis and vyneris and the beste places of olyues, and schal yyue to hise seruauntis.

15 But also he schal take the tenthe part of youre cornes, and rentis of vyneris, that he yyue to his chaumberleyns and seruauntis.

16 Sotheli he schal take awey youre seruauntis and handmaydes, and beste yong men, and assis, and schal sette in his werk.

17 Also he schal take the tenthe part of youre flockis, and ye schulen be 'seruauntis to hym.

18 And ye schulen crye in that dai fro the face of youre kyng, whom ye han chose to you; and the Lord schal not here you in that dai; for ye axiden a kyng to you.

19 Sotheli the puple nolde here the vois of Samuel, but thei seiden, Nay for a kyng schal be on vs;

20 and we also schulen be as alle folkis, and oure kyng schal deme vs, and he schal go out bifor vs, and he schal fiyte oure batel for vs.

21 And Samuel herde alle the wordis of the puple, and 'spak tho in the eeris of the Lord.

22 Forsothe the Lord seide to Samuel, Here thou 'the vois of hem, and ordeyne thou a kyng on hem. And Samuel seide to the men of Israel, Ech man go in to his citee.

CAP 9

1 And 'a man was of Beniamyn, 'Cys bi name, the sone of Abiel, sone of Seor, sone of Bethor, sone of Aphia, sone of the man Gemyny, strong in bodili myyt.

2 And to hym was a sone, Saul bi name, chosun and good; and no man of the sones of Israel was betere than he; fro the schuldur and aboue he apperide ouer al the puple.

3 Sotheli the femal assis of Cys, the fadir of Saul, perischyden. And Cys seide to Saul his sone, Take with thee oon of the children, and rise thou, and go, and seke the femal assis. And whanne thei hadden go bi the hil of Effraym,

4 and bi the lond of Salisa, and hadden not foundun, thei passiden also bi the lond of Salym, and tho weren not there; but also 'thei passiden bi the lond of Gemyny, and founden not.

5 Sotheli whanne thei hadden come in to the lond of Suph, and hadden not founde, Saul seide to his child that was with

hym, Come thou, and turne we ayen; lest perauenture my fadir hath lefte the femal assis, and is bisy for vs.

6 Which child seide to hym, Lo! the man of God is in this citee, a noble man; al thing that he spekith, cometh with out doute. Now therfor go we thidir, if perauenture he schewe to vs of oure weie, for which we camen.

7 And Saul seide to his child, Lo! we schulen go; what schulen we bere to the man of God? Breede failide in oure scrippis, and we han no present, that we yyue to the man of God, 'nether ony othir thing.

8 Eft the child answeride to Saul, and seide, Lo! the fourthe part of 'a stater, that is, a cicle, of siluer is foundun in myn hond; yyue we to the man of God, that he schewe to vs oure weie.

9 Sumtyme in Israel ech man goynge to counsel God spak thus, Come ye, and go we to the seere; for he, that is seid 'to dai a profete, was clepid sumtyme a seere.

10 And Saul seide to his child, 'Thi word is the beste; come thou, go we. And thei yeden in to the citee, 'in which the man of God was.

11 And whanne thei stieden in to the hiynesse of the citee, thei founden damesels goynge out to drawe watir, and thei seiden to the dameselis, Whether the seere is here?

12 Whiche dameselis answeriden, and seiden to hem, He is here; lo! he is bifor thee; 'haste thou now, for to day he cam in to the citee; for to dai is sacrifice of the puple in the hiy place.

13 Ye schulen entre in to the citee, and anoon ye schulen fynde hym, bifor that he stie in to the hiy place to ete; for the puple schal not ete til he come, for he schal blesse the sacrifice, and afterward thei schulen ete that ben clepid. Now therfor stie ye, for to day ye schulen fynde hym.

14 And thei stieden in to the citee. And whanne thei yeden in the myddis of the citee, Samuel apperide goynge out ayens hem, that he schulde stie in to the hiy place.

15 Forsothe the Lord 'hadde maad reuelacioun in the eere of Samuel 'bifor o dai, that Saul cam, and seide,

16 In this same our which is now to morewe, Y schal sende to thee a man of the lond of Beniamyn, and thou schalt anoynte hym duyk on my puple Israel, and he schal saue my puple fro the hond of Filisteis; for Y haue biholde my puple, for 'the cry of hem cam to me.

17 And whanne Samuel hadde biholde Saul, the Lord seide to Samuel, Lo! the man, whom Y seide to thee; this man schal be lord of my puple.

18 Forsothe Saul neiyede to Samuel in the myddis of the yate, and seide, Y preye, schewe thou to me, where is the hows of the seere?

19 And Samuel answeride to Saul, and seide, Y am the seere; stie thou bifor me in to the hiy place, that thou ete with me to dai, and Y schal delyuere thee in the morewtid, and Y schal schewe to thee alle thingis that ben in thin herte.

20 And be thou not bisy of the femal assis, whiche thou lostist the thridde dai agoon, for tho ben foundun; and whose schulen be alle the beste thingis of Israel, whether not to thee, and to al the hows of thi fader?

21 Sotheli Saul answeride, and seide, Whether Y am not a sone of Gemyny, of the leeste lynage of Israel, and my kynrede is the laste among alle the meynees of the lynage of Beniamyn? Whi therfor hast thou spoke to me this word?

22 Therfor Samuel took Saul, and his child, and ledde hem in to the chaumbur of thre ordris, and he yaf to hem a place in the bigynnyng of hem that weren clepid; for thei weren as thretti men.

23 And Samuel seide to the cook, Yyue thou the part, which Y yaf to thee, and comaundide, that thou schuldist kepe bi it silf anentis thee.

24 Sotheli the cook reiside the schuldir, and settide bifor Saul. And Samuel seide, Lo! that, that lefte, 'sette thou bifor thee, and ete; for of purpos it was kept to thee, whanne Y clepide the puple. And Saul eet with Samuel in that dai.

25 And thei camen doun fro the hiy place in to the citee; and Samuel spak with Saul in the soler, and Saul 'araiede a bed in the soler, and slepte.

26 And whanne thei hadden rise eerli, and 'now it bigan to be cleer, Samuel clepide Saul in to the soler, and seide, Rise thou, that Y delyuere thee. And Saul roos, and bothe yeden out, that is, he, and Samuel.

27 And whanne thei yeden doun in the laste part of the citee, Samuel seide to Saul, Seie thou to the child, that he go bifor vs, and passe; forsothe stonde thou a litil, that Y schewe to thee the word of the Lord.

CAP 10

1 Forsothe Samuel took 'a vessel of oyle, and schedde out on the heed of Saul, and kisside hym, and seide, Lo! the Lord hath anoyntid thee in to prince on hys eritage; and thou schalt delyuere his puple fro the hond of his enemyes, that ben 'in his cumpas. And this a tokene to thee, that the Lord hath anoyntid thee in to prince;

2 whanne thou schalt go fro me to day, thou schalt fynde twei men bisidis 'the sepulcre of Rachel, in 'the endis of Beniamyn, in myddai, clensynge grete dichis; and thei schulen seie to thee, The femel assis ben foundun, whiche thou yedist to seke; and while the assis ben lefte, thi fadir is bisy for you, and seith, What schal Y do of my sone?

3 And whanne thou hast go fro thennus, and hast passid ferthere, and hast come to the ook of Tabor, thre men, stiynge to God in to Bethel, schulen fynde thee there, o man berynge thre kydis, and another man berynge thre kakis of breed, and an other man berynge a galoun of wyn.

4 And whanne thei han gret thee, thei schulen yyue to thee twei loues, and thou schalt take of 'the hond of hem.

5 After these thingis thou schalt come in to the 'hil of the Lord, where is the stondyng, that is, forselet, of Filisteis; and whanne thou schalt entre in to the citee, there thou schalt haue metynge thee the flok of prophetis comynge doun fro the hiy place, and a sautree, and tympane, and pipe, and harpe bifor hem, and hem prophesiynge.

6 And the Spirit of the Lord schal skippe in to thee, and thou schalt prophecie with hem, and thou schalt be chaungid in to another man.

7 Therfor whanne alle thesse signes bifallen to thee, do thou, what euer thingis thin hond fyndith, 'that is, dispose thee to regne comelili and myytily, for the Lord is with thee.

8 And thou schalt go doun bifor me in to Galgala; for Y schal come doun to thee, that thou offre an offryng, and offre pesible sacrifices; bi seuene daies thou schalt abide, til I come to thee, and shewe to thee what thou schal do.

9 Therfor whanne Saul hadde turnede awei his schuldre to go fro Samuel, God chaungide another herte to Saul, and alle these signes camen in that dai.

10 And thei camen to the forseid hil, and lo! a cumpeny of prophetis metynge hym; and the Spirit of the Lord 'scippide on hym, and he propheciede in the myddis of hem.

11 Sotheli alle men, that knewen hym yisterdai and the thrid dai ago, sien that he was with the prophetis, and that he prophesiede, and thei seiden togidere, What thing bifelde to the sone of Cys? Whether also Saul is among prophetis?

12 And o man answeride to another man, and seide, And who is 'his fadir? Therfor it was turned in to a prouerbe, Whether also Saul is among prophetis?

13 Forsothe Saul ceside to prophesie, and he cam to an hiy place.

14 And the brothir of 'the fadir of Saul seide to hym, and to his child, Whidur yeden ye? And thei answeriden, To seke the femal assis; and whanne we founden 'not thoo, we camen to Samuel.

15 And the brother of his fadir seide to hym, Schewe thou to me what Samuel seide to thee.

16 And Saul seide to 'the brother of hys fadir, He schewide to vs, that the femal assis weren foundun. Sotheli Saul schewide not to hym of the word of rewme, 'which word Samuel spak to hym.

17 And Samuel clepide togidere the puple to the Lord in Masphat;

18 and he seide to the sones of Israel, The Lord God of Israel seith these thingis, Y ledde Israel out of the lond of Egipt, and Y delyuerede you fro the hond of Egipcians, and fro the hond of alle kyngis that turmentiden you.

19 Forsothe to day ye han caste awei youre Lord God, which aloone sauyde you fro alle youre yuelis and tribulaciouns; and ye seiden, Nay, but ordeyne thou a kyng on vs. Now therfor stonde ye bifor the Lord bi youre lynagis, and bi meynees.

20 And Samuel settide to gidere alle the lynages of Israel, and lot felde on the lynage of Beniamyn.

21 And he settide togidere the lynage of Beniamyn, and the meynees therof; and lot felde on the meynees of Mathri, and it cam 'til to Saul, the son of Cys. Therfor thei souyten hym, and he was not foundun there.

22 And aftir these thingis thei counseliden the Lord, whether Saul schulde come thidur. And the Lord answeride, Lo! he is hid at hoom.

23 Therfor thei runnen, and token hym fro thennus; and he stood in the myddil of the puple, and was hiyere than al the puple fro the schulder and 'aboue.

24 And Samuel seide to al the puple, Certis ye seen whom the Lord hath chose; for noon in al the puple is lijk hym. And al the puple cryede, and seide, Lyue the kyng!

25 Forsothe Samuel spak to the puple the lawe of rewme, and wroot in a book, and puttide vp bifor the Lord. And Samuel dilyuerede al the puple, ech man in to his hows;

26 but also Saul yede in to his hous in to Gabaath; and the part of the oost yede with hym, whose hertis God hadde touchid.

27 Forsothe the sones of Belyal seiden, Whether this man may saue vs? And thei dispisiden hym, and brouyten not yiftis, 'that is, preisyngis, to him; forsothe he 'dissymelide hym to here.

CAP 11

1 And it was don as aftir a monethe, Naas of Amon stiede, and bigan to fiyte ayens Jabes of Galaad. And alle the men of Jabes seiden to Naas, Haue thou vs boundun in pees, and we schulen serue thee.

2 And Naas of Amon answeride to hem, In this Y schal smyte boond of pees with you, that Y putte out the riyt iyen of alle you, and that Y sette you schenschip in al Israel.

3 And the eldere men of Jabes seiden to him, Graunte thou to vs seuene daies, that we senden messangeris to alle the termes of Israel; and if noon be that defende vs, we schulen go out to thee.

4 Therfor messangeris camen in to Gabaad of Saul, and spaken these wordis, 'while the puple herde; and al the puple reiside her vois, and wepte.

5 And lo! Saul cam, 'and suede oxis fro the feeld; and he seide, What hath the puple, for it wepith? And thei telden to hym the wordis of men of Jabes.

6 And the Spirit of the Lord skippide in to Saul, whanne he hadde herd these wordis, and his woodnesse was 'wrooth greetli.

7 And he took euer either oxe, and kittide in to gobetis, and sente in to alle the termes of Israel, bi the hondis of messangeris; and seide, Who euer goith not out, and sueth not Saul and Samuel, so it schal be don to hise oxun. Therfor the drede of the Lord asailide the puple, and thei yeden out as o man.

8 And he noumbride hem in Besech; and thre hundrid thousynd weren of the sones of Israel; forsothe of the men of Juda weren thretti thousynde.

9 And thei seiden to the messangeris that camen, Thus ye schulen seie to the men that ben in Jabes of Galaad, To morew schal be helthe to you, whanne the sunne is hoot. Therfor the messangeris camen, and telden to the men of Jabes; whiche weren glad,

10 and seiden, Eerli we schulen go out to you, and ye schulen do to vs al that plesith you.

11 And it was don, whanne the morewe dai cam, Saul ordeynede the puple in to thre partis; and he entride in to the myddil tentis 'in the wakyng of the morewtid, and he smoot Amon til the dai 'was hoot; 'forsothe the residues weren scaterid, so that tweyne togidere weren not left in hem.

12 And the puple seide to Samuel, Who is this, that seide, Saul schal not regne on vs? Yyue ye the men, and we schulen sle hem.

13 And Saul seide, No man schal be slayn in this dai, for to dai the Lord made helthe in Israel.

14 Forsothe Samuel seide to the puple, Come ye, and go we in to Galgala, and renule we there the rewme.

15 And al the puple yede in to Galgala, and there thei maden Saul kyng bifor the Lord 'in Galgala; and thei offriden pesible sacrifices bifor the Lord. And Saul was glad there, and alle the men of Israel greetli.

CAP 12

1 Forsothe Samuel seide to al Israel, Lo! Y herde youre vois bi alle thingis whiche ye spaken to me, and Y ordeynede a kyng on you;

2 and now the king goith bifor you. Sotheli Y wexide eld and hoor; forsothe my sones ben with you; therfor Y lyuyde bifor you fro my yong wexynge age 'til to this dai. And lo!

3 Y am redi; speke ye to me bifor the Lord, and bifor 'the crist of hym; whether Y took 'the oxe of ony man, ether the asse; if Y falsly chalengide ony mon; yf Y oppresside ony man; if Y took yifte of 'the hond of ony man; and Y schal 'dispise it to dai, and Y schal restore to you.

4 And thei seiden, Thou hast not falsly chalengid vs, nether hast oppressid vs, nether hast take ony thing of 'the hond of ony man.

5 And he seide to hem, The Lord is witnesse ayens you, and his crist is witnesse in this day; for ye han not founde ony thing in myn hond. And thei seiden, Witnesse.

6 And Samuel seide to the puple, The Lord, that made Moises and Aaron, and ledde youre fadris out of the lond of Egipt, is present;

7 now therfor stonde ye, that Y stryue bi doom ayens you bifor the Lord, of alle the mercyes of the Lord, whiche he dide with you, and with youre fadris.

8 Hou Jacob entride in to Egipt, and youre fadris crieden to the Lord; and the Lord sente Moises and Aaron, and ledde youre fadris out of Egipt, and settide hem in this place.

9 Whiche foryaten her Lord God; and he bitook hem in the hond of Sisara, maystir of the chyualrie of Asor, and in the hond of Filisteis, and in the hond of the kyng of Moab; and thei fouyten ayens hem.

10 Sotheli afterward thei crieden to the Lord, and seiden, We synneden, for we forsoken the Lord, and seruyden Baalym and Astroth; now therfor delyuere thou vs fro 'the hond of oure enemyes, and we schulen serue thee.

11 And the Lord sente Gerobaal, and 'Bedan, that is, Sampson, and Barach, and Jepte, and Samuel, and delyuerede you fro the hond of youre enemyes bi cumpass; and ye dwelliden tristili.

12 Forsothe ye sien, that Naas, kyng of the sones of Amon, cam ayens you; and ye seiden to me, counseilynge to axe noon other kyng than God, Nay, but a kyng schal comaunde to vs; whanne 'youre Lord God regnede in you.

13 Now therfor youre kyng is redi, whom ye han chose and axid; lo! the Lord yaf to you a kyng.

14 If ye dreden the Lord, and seruen hym, and heren his vois, and wraththen not the 'mouth of the Lord; ye and youre kyng, that comaundith to you, schulen sue youre Lord God.

15 Forsothe if ye heren not the vois of 'the Lord, but wraththen his word, the hond of the Lord schal be on you, and on youre fadris.

16 But also now stonde ye, and se this gret thing which the Lord schal make in youre siyt.

17 Whether heruest of whete is not 'to dai? I schal inwardli clepe the Lord, and he schal yyue voices, 'that is, thundris, and reynes; and ye schulen wite, and schulen se, for ye axynge a kyng on you han do greuouse yuel to you in the siyt of the Lord.

18 And Samuel criede to the Lord, and the Lord yaf voices and reynes in that dai.

19 And al the puple dredde greetli the Lord and Samuel; and al the puple seide to Samuel, Preye thou for thi seruauntis to thi Lord God, that we die not; for we addiden yuel to alle oure synnes, that we axiden a kyng to vs.

20 Forsothe Samuel seide to the puple, 'Nyle ye drede; ye han do al this yuel; netheles 'nyle ye go awey fro the bak of the Lord, but serue ye the Lord in al youre herte;

21 and nyle ye bowe aftir veyn thingis, that schulen not profite to you, nether schulen delyuere you; for tho ben veyn thingis.

22 And the Lord schal not forsake his puple for his grete name; for the Lord swoor to make you a puple to hym silf.

23 Forsothe this synne be fer fro me in the Lord, that Y ceesse to preye for you; and Y schal teche you a riytful weie and good.

24 Therfor drede ye the Lord, and 'serue ye hym in treuthe, and of al youre herte; for ye sien tho grete thingis, whiche he 'dide in you;

25 that if ye contynuen in malice, bothe ye and youre kyng schulen perische to gidere.

CAP 13

1 Saul was a child of o yeer whanne he bigan to regne; forsothe he regnede on Israel twei yeer.

2 And Saul chees to hym thre thousynde of Israel, and twei thousynde weren with Saul in Machynas, in the hil of Bethel; forsothe a thousynde weren with Jonathas in Gabaath of Beniamyn; sotheli he sente ayen the tother puple ech man in to 'hise tabernaclis.

3 And Jonathas smoot the stacioun of Filisteis, that was in Gabaa. And whanne Filisteis hadden herd this, Saul sownede with a clarioun in al the lond, and seide, Ebreys here.

4 And al Israel herde siche a fame, Saul smoot the stacioun of Filisteis; and Israel reiside hym silf ayens Filisteis; therfor the puple criede after Saul in Galgala.

5 And Filisteis weren gaderid to fiyte ayens Israel; 'of Filisteis weren thretti thousynde of charis, and sixe thousynde of knyytis, and the tother comyn puple, as grauel 'which is ful myche in the brynke of the see; and thei stieden, and settiden tentis in Machynas, at the eest of Bethauen.

6 And whanne men of Israel hadden seyn this, that thei weren set in streiytnesse, for the puple was turmentid, thei hidden hem silf in dennes, and in priuey places, and in stonys, and in dychis, and in cisternes.

7 Sotheli Ebreis passiden Jordan in to the lond of Gad and of Galaad. And whanne Saul was yit in Galgala, al the puple was aferd that suede hym.

8 And seuene daies he abood Samuel bi couenaunt, and Samuel cam not in to Galgala; and the puple yede a wei fro Saul.

9 Therfor Saul seide, Brynge ye to me brent sacrifice, and pesible sacrifices; and he offride brent sacrifice.

10 And whanne he hadde endid offrynge brent sacrifice, lo! Samuel cam; and Saul yede out ayens hym, to greete Samuel.

11 And Samuel spak to hym, What hast thou do? Saul answeride, For Y siy that the puple yede awei fro me, and thou camest not bi the daies of couenaunt; certis Filisteis weren gaderid in Machynas;

12 Y seide, Now Filisteis schulen come doun to me in to Galgala, and Y haue not plesyd the face of the Lord; Y was compellid bi nede, and Y offryde brent sacrifice to the Lord.

13 And Samuel seide to Saul, Thou hast do folili, and thou 'keptist not the heestis of thi Lord God, whiche he comaundide to thee; and if thou haddist not do this thing, riyt now the Lord hadde maad redi thi rewme on Israel with outen ende;

14 but thi rewme schal not rise ferthere. The Lord hath souyt a man to hym silf after his herte; and the Lord comaundide to hym, that he schulde be duyk on his puple, for thou keptist not tho thingis whiche the Lord comaundide.

15 Forsothe Samuel roos, and stiede fro Galgala in to Gabaa of Beniamyn; and the 'residue puplis stieden after Saul ayens the puple which fouyten ayens hem; and thei camen fro Galgala in to Gabaa, in the hil of Beniamyn. And Saul noumbride the puple, that weren foundun with hym as sixe hundrid men.

16 And Saul, and Jonathas his sone, and the puple that was foundun with hem, was in Gabaa of Beniamyn; forsothe Filisteis saten togidere in Machynas.

17 And thre cumpanyes yeden out of the 'castels of Filisteis to take prey; o cumpany yede ayens the weie of Effraym to the lond of Saul;

18 sothely an other cumpeny entride bi the weie of Bethoron; forsothe the thridde cumpenye turnede it silf to the weie of the terme in the lond of Sabaa; and that terme neiyeth to the valey of Seboym ayens the deseert.

19 Forsothe 'no smyyth of yrun was foundun in al the lond of Israel; for Filisteis 'weren war, ether eschewiden, lest perauenture Ebreis maden a swerd ether a spere.

20 Therfor al Israel yede doun to Filisteis, that ech man schulde scharpe his schar, and picoise, and ax, 'and sarpe;

21 'and so alle egis weren bluntid 'of scharris, and of picoisis, and of 'forkis of thre teeth, and of axis, 'til to a pricke to be amendid.

22 And whanne the dai of batel cam, no swerd and spere was foundun in the hond of al the puple that was with Saul and Jonathas, outakun Saul, and Jonathas his sone.

23 Forsothe the stacioun of Filisteis yede out, that it schulde passe in to Machynas.

CAP 14

1 And it bifelde in a day, that Jonathas, the sone of Saul, seide to his squyer, a yong man, Come thou, and passe we to the staciouns of the Filisteis, which is biyende that place; 'sotheli he schewide not this same thing to his fadir.

2 Sotheli Saul dwellide in the laste part of Gabaa, vndur a pumgarnarde tre, that was in the feeld of Gabaa; and the puple as of sixe hundrid men was with hym.

3 And Achias, sone of Achitob, brother of Icaboth, sone of Fynees, that was gendrid of Ely, preest of the Lord in Silo, bar ephod, 'that is, the preestis cloth; but also the puple wiste not whidur Jonathas hadde go.

4 Sotheli bitwixe the stiyngis, bi whiche Jonathas enforside to passe to the stacioun of Filisteis, weren stonys stondynge forth on euer either side, and scarris brokun bifore bi the maner of teeth on ech syde; name to oon was Boses, and name to 'the tother was Sene;

5 o scarre was stondynge forth to the north ayens Machynas, and the tother scarre to the south ayens Gabaa.

6 Forsothe Jonathas seide to his yong squyer, Come thou, passe we to the stacioun of these vncircumcisid men, if in hap the Lord do for vs; for it is not hard to the Lord to saue, ethir in manye ethir in fewe.

7 And his squyer seide to hym, Do thou alle thingis that plesen thi soule; go whidur thou coueitist, Y schal be with thee, where euer thou wolt.

8 And Jonathas seide, Lo! we passen to these men; and whanne we apperen to hem,

9 if thei speken thus to vs, Dwelle ye, til we comen to you; stonde we in oure place, and stie we not to hem.

10 Sotheli if thei seien, Stye ye to vs; stie we, for the Lord hath bitake hem in oure hondis; this schal be a signe to vs.

11 'Therfor euer either apperide to the stacioun of Filisteis; and Filisteis seiden, Lo! Ebreis goen out of caues, in whiche thei weren hid.

12 And men of the stacioun spaken to Jonathas and to his squyer, and seiden, Stie ye to vs, and we schulen schewe to you a thing. And Jonathas seide to his squyer, 'Stie we, sue thou me; for the Lord hath bitake hem in to the hondis of Israel.

13 Forsothe Jonathas stiede crepynge on hondis and feet, and his squyer after hym; and whanne thei hadden seyn the face of Jonathas, summe felden doun bifor Jonathas, his squier killed othere, and suede hym.

14 And the firste wounde was maad, which Jonathas and his squyer smoot, as of twenti men, in 'the myddil part of lond which a peire of oxun was wont to ere in the dai.

15 And a myracle was don in the castels, and bi the feeldis, but also al the puple of the 'stacioun of hem that yeden out to take prey, dredde, and 'the castels weren disturblid; and it bifelde as a myracle of God.

16 And aspyeris of Saul bihelden, that weren in Gabaa of Beniamyn, and lo! a multitude cast doun, and fleynge awei hidur and thidur.

17 And Saul seide to the puple that weren with hym, Seke ye, and se ye, who yede awei fro vs. And whanne thei hadden souyt, it was foundun, that Jonathas and his squyer weren not present.

18 And Saul seide to Achias, Brynge the arke of the Lord; for the arke of God was there in that dai with the sones of Israel.

19 And whanne Saul spak to the preest, a grete noise roos in the castelis of Filisteis; and it encresside litil and litil, and sownede cleerliere. And Saul seide to the preest, Withdraw thin hond.

20 Therfor Saul criede, and al the puple that was with hym; and thei camen 'til to the place of batel, and, lo! the swerd of ech man was turned to his neiybore, and a ful grete sleynge was.

21 But also Ebreis that weren with Filisteis yistirday and the thridde dai ago, and hadde stied with hem in castels, turneden ayen to be with Israel, that weren with Saul and Jonathas.

22 Also alle men of Israel, that hadden hid hem silf in the hil of Effraym, herden that Filisteis hadden fled; and thei felouschipiden hem silf with her men in batel, and as ten thousynde of men weren with Saul.

23 And the Lord sauyde Israel in that day. Sotheli the batel cam til to Bethauen.

24 And men of Israel weren felouschipid to hem silf in that dai; forsothe Saul swoor to the puple, and seide, Cursid be the man, that etith breed 'til to euentid, til 'Y venge me of myn enemyes.

25 And al the puple ete not breed. And al the comyn puple of the lond cam in to a forest, in which was hony on the 'face of erthe.

26 And so the puple entride in to the forest, and flowynge hony apperide; and no man puttide hond to his mouth, for the puple dredde the ooth.

27 Forsothe Jonathas herde not, whanne his fadir swoor to the puple; and he helde forth the ende of a litil yerde, whiche he hadde in the hond, and dippide in to 'a coomb of hony; and he turnede his hond to his mouth, and hise iyen weren liytned.

28 And oon of the puple answeride, and seide, Thi fader boond the puple with an ooth, and seide, Cursid be the man that etith breed to dai. Forsothe the puple was feynt.

29 And Jonathas seide, My fadir hath disturblid the lond; ye sien, that myn iyen ben liytned, for Y tastide a litil of this hony;

30 hou myche more if the puple hadde ete the prey of hise enemyes, which 'prey it foond; whether not gretter veniaunce hadde be maad in Filisteis?

31 Therfore thei smytiden Filisteis in that dai fro Machynas 'til in to Hailon. Forsothe the puple was maad ful wery;

32 and the puple turnede to prey, and took scheep and oxun, and calues; and thei killiden in the erthe; and the puple eet with blood.

33 And thei telden to Saul, and seiden, that the puple etynge with blood hadde synned to the Lord. And Saul seide, Ye han trespassid; walewe ye to me 'riyt now a greet stoon.

34 And Saul seyde, 'Be ye spred abrood in to the comyn puple, and seie ye to hem, that ech man brynge to me his oxe and ram; and sle ye on this stoon, and ete ye, and ye schulen not do synne to the Lord, 'and ete with blood. Therfor al the

puple brouyte ech man an oxe in his hond 'til to nyyt, and thei killiden there.

35 Sotheli Saul bildide an auter to the Lord; and thanne firste he bigan to bilde an auter to the Lord.

36 And Saul seide, Falle we on the Filisteis in the nyyt, and waste we hem til the morewtid schyne; and leeue we not of hem a man. And the puple seide, Do thou al thing that semeth good to thee in thin iyen. And the preest seide, Neiye we hidur to God.

37 And Saul counselide the Lord, and seide, Whether Y schal pursue Filisteis? whether thou schalt bitake hem in to the hondis of Israel? And the Lord answeride not to him in that dai.

38 And Saul seide, Brynge ye hidur alle the corneris of the puple, and wite ye, and se, bi whom this synne bifelde to dai.

39 The Lord sauyour of Israel lyueth; for if 'it is don bi Jonathas my sone, he schal die with out ayen drawyng. At which ooth no man of al the puple ayenseide hym.

40 And he seide to al Israel, Be ye departid in to o part, and Y with my sone Jonathas schal be in the tothir part. And the puple answeride to Saul, Do thou that, that semeth good in thin iyen.

41 And Saul seide to the Lord God of Israel, Lord God of Israel, yyue thou doom, what is, that thou answerist not to dai to thi seruaunt? If this wickidnesse is in me, ether in Jonathas my sone, yyue thou schewyng; ether if this wickidnesse is in thi puple, yyue thou hoolynesse. And Jonathas was takun, and Saul; forsothe the puple yede out.

42 And Saule seide, Sende ye lot bitwixe me and Jonathas my sone. And Jonathas was takun 'bi lot.

43 Forsothe Saul seide to Jonathas, Schewe thou to me, what thou didist. And Jonathas schewide to hym, and seide, Y tastynge tastide a litil of hony 'in the ende of the yerde, that was in myn hond; and lo!

44 Y die. And Saul seide, God do to me these thingis, and adde 'these thingis, for thou, Jonathas, schalt die bi deeth.

45 And the puple seide to Saul, 'Therfor whethir Jonathas schal die, that dide this greet helthe in Israel? this is vnleueful; the Lord lyueth; noon heer of his heed schal falle in to erthe; for he wrouyte with God to dai. Therfor the puple delyuerede Jonathas, that he diede not.

46 And Saul yede a wey, and pursuede not Filisteis; sotheli Filisteys yeden in to her places.

47 And Saul, whanne the rewme was 'confermyd on Israel, fauyt bi cumpas ayens alle hise enemyes, ayens Moab, and the sones of Amon, and Edom, and ayens the kyngis of Soba, and ayens Filisteis; and whidur euer he turnede hym, he ouercam.

48 And whanne the oost was gaderid, he smoot Amalech; and delyuerede Israel fro the hond of hise distrieris.

49 Forsothe the sones of Saul weren Jonathas, and Jesuy, and Melchisua; the names of hise twei douytris, name of the firste gendrid douyter was Merob, and name 'of the lesse douyter was Mycol.

50 And name of 'the wijf of Saul was Achynoem, the douytir of Achymaas; and the name of the prince of his chyualrye was Abner, sone of Ner, brother of the fadir of Saul.

51 Forsothe Cys was the fadir of Saul; and Ner, the sone of Abiel, was fadir of Abner.

52 Sotheli myyti batel was ayens Filisteis in alle the daies of Saul; for whom euere Saul siy a strong man and schapli to batel, Saul felouschipide to him silf that man.

CAP 15

1 And Samuel seide to Saul, The Lord sente me, that Y schulde anoynte thee in to 'kyng on his puple Israel; now therfor here thou the vois 'of the Lord.

2 The Lord of oostis seith thes thingis, Y haue rikenyd what euer thingis Amalech dide to Israel; hou Amalech ayenstood Israel in the weie, whanne he stiede from Egipt.

3 Now therfor go thou, and sle Amalech, and distruye thou alle 'thingis of hym; spare thou not hym, and coueyte thou not ony thing of hise thingis; but sle thou fro man 'til to womman, and a litil child, and soukynge, an oxe, and scheep, and camel, and asse.

4 Therfor Saul comaundide to the puple, and he noumbride hem as lambren twei hundrid thousynde of foot men, and ten thousynde of men of Juda.

5 And whanne Saul cam to the citee of Amalech, he made redi buyschementis in the stronde.

6 And Saul seide to Cyney, Go ye, departe ye, and go ye awei fro Amalech, lest perauenture Y wlappe thee in with hem; for thou didist mercy with alle the sones of Israel, whanne thei stieden fro Egipt. And Cyney departide fro the myddis of Amalech.

7 And Saul smoot Amalech fro Euila, til thou come to Sur, which is ayens Egipt.

8 And he took Agag quyke, the kyng of Amalech; sotheli he killide bi the scharpnesse of swerd alle the comyn puple.

9 And Saul and the puple sparide Agag, and the beste flockis of scheep, and of grete beestis, and clothis, and rammes, and alle thingis that weren faire; and thei nolden destrie tho; sotheli what euer thing was vijl, and repreuable, thei distrieden this.

10 Forsothe the word of the Lord was maad to Samuel,

11 and seide, It repentith me, that Y made Saul kyng; for he forsook me, and fillide not my wordis in werk. And Samuel was sory, and he criede to the Lord in al the nyyt.

12 And whanne Samuel hadde rise bi nyyt to go eerly to Saul, it was told to Samuel, that Saul hadde come in to Carmel, and hadde reisid to hym a signe of victorye; and that he hadde turned ayen, and hadde passid, and hadde go doun in to Galgala. Therfor Samuel cam to Saul, and Saul offride brent sacrifice to the Lord of the cheef thingis of preies, whiche he hadde brouyt fro Amalech.

13 And the while Samuel cam to Saul, Saul seide to hym, Blessid be thou of the Lord, Y haue fillid the 'word of the Lord.

14 And Samuel seide, And what is the vois of flockis, that sowneth in myn eeris, and of grete beestis, whiche Y here?

15 And Saul seide, Thei brouyten tho fro Amalech, for the puple sparide the betere scheep and grete beestis, that tho schulden be offrid to thi Lord God; sotheli we killiden the tothere beestis.

16 Forsothe Samuel seide to Saul, Suffre thou me, and Y schal schewe to thee what thingis the Lord spak to me in the nyyt. And he seide to Samuel, Speke thou.

17 And Samuel seide, Whether not, whanne thou were litil in thin iyen, thou were maade heed in the lynages of Israel, and the Lord anoyntide thee in to kyng on Israel;

18 and the Lord sente thee in to the weie, and seide, Go thou, and sle the synneris of Amalech, and thou schalt fiyte ayens hem 'til to sleyng of hem.

19 Whi therfor herdist thou not the vois of the Lord, but thou were turned to prey, and didist yuel in the 'iyen of the Lord?

20 And Saul seide to Samuel, Yhis, Y herde the 'vois of the Lord, and Y yede in the weie, bi which the Lord sente me, and Y haue brouyt Agag, the kyng of Amalech, and Y killide Amalech.

21 Forsothe the puple took of the prey, scheep and oxun, the firste fruytis of tho thingis, that ben slayn, that thei make sacrifice to her Lord God in Galgalis.

22 And Samuel seide, Whether the Lord wole brent sacrifices, ethir slayn sacrifices, and not more that me obeie to the vois of the Lord? For obedience is betere than sacrifices, and to 'herkene Goddis word is more than to offre the ynnere fatnesse of rammes;

23 for it is as the synne of mawmetrie to 'fiyte ayens Goddis heest, and it is as the wickidnesse of ydolatrie to nyle 'ascente to Goddis heest. Therfor for that, that thou castidist awey the word of the Lord, the Lord castide thee awei, that thou be not kyng.

24 And Saul seide to Samuel, Y synnede, for Y brak the word of the Lord, and thi wordis; 'and Y dredde the puple, 'and obeiede to 'the vois of hem; but now,

25 Y biseche, bere thou my synne, and turne thou ayen with me, that Y worschipe the Lord.

26 And Samuel seide to Saul, Y schal not turne ayen with thee, for thou castidist awey the word of the Lord, and the Lord castide awei thee, that thou be not king on Israel.

27 And Samuel turnede to go a wey; sotheli Saul took the ende of the mentil of Samuel, which also was to-rent.

28 And Samuel seide to hym, The Lord hath kit the rewme of Israel fro thee to dai, and yaf it to thi neiybore betere than thou;

29 certis the ouercomere in Israel schal not spare, and he schal not be bowid bi repentaunce; for he is not man, 'that is, chaungeable, that he do repentaunce.

30 And Saul seide, Y synnede; but now onoure thou me bifor the eldere men of my puple, and bifor Israel, and turne thou ayen with me, that Y worschipe thi Lord God.

31 Therfor Samuel turnede ayen, and suede Saul, and Saul worschipide the Lord.

32 And Samuel seide, Brynge ye to me Agag, the kyng of Amalech. And Agag 'moost fat tremblynge was brouyt to hym. And Agag seide, Whether thus departith bitter deeth?

33 And Samuel seide, As thi swerd made wymmen with out fre children, so thi modir schal be with out fre children among wymmen. And Samuel kittide hym in to gobetis bifor the Lord in Galgalis.

34 Forsothe Samuel yede in to Ramatha; sotheli Saul stiede in to his hows in Gabaa.

35 And Samuel siy no more Saul 'til to the dai of his deeth; netheles Samuel biweilide Saul, for it repentide the Lord, that he hadde ordeyned Saul kyng on Israel.

CAP 16

1 And the Lord seide to Samuel, Hou long biweilist thou Saul, sithen Y castide hym awey, that he regne not on Israel; fille thin horn with oile, and come, that Y sende thee to Ysay of Bethleem; for among hise sones Y haue purueide a king to me.

2 And Samuel seide, Hou schal Y go? for Saul schal here, and he schal sle me. And the Lord seide, Thou schalt take a calf of the droue in thi hond, and thou schalt seye, Y cam to make sacrifice to the Lord.

3 And thou schalt clepe Ysay to the sacrifice, and Y schal schewe to thee, what thou schalt do; and thou schalt anoynte, whom euere Y schal schewe to thee.

4 Therfor Samuel dide, as the Lord spak to hym; and he cam in to Bethleem, and the eldere men of the citee wondriden, and camen to hym, and seiden, Whether thin entryng is pesible?

5 And he seide, It is pesible; Y cam to make sacrifice to the Lord; be ye halewid, and come ye with me, that Y make sacrifice. Therfor he halewide Ysai, and hise sones, and clepide hem to the sacrifice.

6 And whanne thei hadden entrid, he siy Eliab, and seide, Whether bifor the Lord is his crist?

7 And the Lord seide to Samuel, Biholde thou not his cheer, nethir hiynesse of his stature; for Y castide hym awei, and Y demyde not bi 'the siyt of man; for a man seeth tho thingis that ben opyn, but the Lord biholdith the herte.

8 And Ysai clepide Amynadab, and brouyte hym bifor Samuel; which seide, Nether the Lord hath chose this.

9 Forsothe Isay brouyte Samma; of whom Samuel seide, Also the Lord hath not chose this.

10 Therfor Isai brouyte hise seuene sones bifor Samuel; and Samuel seide to Ysai, The Lord hath 'not chose of these.

11 And Samuel seide to Isai, Whether thi sones ben now fillid? And Isai answeride, Yit 'another is, a litil child, and lisewith scheep. And Samuel seide to Isai, Sende thou, and brynge hym; for we schulen not sitte to mete, bifor that he come hidur.

12 Therfor Ysai sente, and brouyte hym; sotheli he was rodi, and fair in siyt, and of semely face. And the Lord seide, Rise thou, and anoynte hym; for it is he.

13 Therfor Samuel took the horn of oyle, and anoyntid hym in the myddis of his britheren; and the Spirit of the Lord was dressid in to Dauid fro that day 'and afterward. And Samuel roos, and yede in to Ramatha.

14 And so the Spirit of the Lord yede awei fro Saul, and a wickid spirit of the Lord trauelide Saul.

15 And the seruauntis of Saul seiden to hym, Lo! an yuel spirit of the Lord traueilith thee;

16 oure lord the kyng comaunde, and thi seruauntis that ben bifore thee, schulen seke a man, that kan synge with an harpe, that whanne the yuel spirit of the Lord takith thee, he harpe with his hond, and thou bere esiliere. And Saul seide to hise seruauntis, Puruey ye to me sum man syngynge wel, and brynge ye hym to me.

18 And oon of the children answeride and seide, Lo! Y siy the sone of Ysai of Bethleem, kunnynge to synge, and 'strongeste in myyt, and 'a man able to batel, and prudent in wordis, and a feir man; and the Lord is with hym.

19 Therfor Saul sente messangeris to Ysay, and seide, Sende thou to me Dauid thi sone, 'which is in the lesewis.

20 Therfor Isai took an asse 'ful of looues, and a galoun of wyn, and a 'kyde of geet; and sente bi the hond of Dauid his sone to Saul.

21 And Dauid cam to Saul, and stood bifor hym; and Saul louyde hym greetli, and he was maad 'his squyer.

22 And Saul sente to Isay, and seide, Dauid stonde in my siyt, for he foond grace in myn iyen.

23 Therfor whanne euer the wickid spirit of the Lord took Saul, Dauid took the harpe, and smoot with his hond, and Saul was coumfortid, and he hadde liytere; for the wickid spirit yede awey fro hym.

1 Forsothe Filisteis gaderiden her cumpenyes in to batel, and camen togidere in Socoth of Juda, and settiden tentis bitwixe Socoth and Azecha, in the coostis of Domyn.

2 Sotheli Saul and the men of Israel weren gaderid, and camen in to the valey of Terebynte, and dressiden scheltrun to fiyte ayens Filisteis.

3 And Filisteis stoden aboue the hil on this part, and Israel stood on the hil on the tother part of the valey, that was bitwixe hem. And a man, 'sone of a widewe, whos fadir was vncerteyn, yede out of the 'castels of Filisteis, Goliath bi name of Geth, of sixe cubitis heiy and a spanne; and a brasun basynet on his heed;

5 and he was clothid with 'an haburioun hokid, ether mailid; forsothe the weiyte of his haburioun was fyue thousynde siclis of bras;

6 and he hadde 'bootis of bras in the hipis, and a 'scheld of bras hilide hise schuldris.

7 Forsothe 'the schaft of his spere was as the beem of webbis; forsothe thilke yrun of his spere hadde sixe hundrid siclis of yrun; and his squier yede bifor hym.

8 And he stood, and cried ayens the cumpenyes of armed men of Israel, and seide to hem, Why camen ye redi to batel? Whether Y am not a Filistei, and ye ben the seruauntis of Saul? Chese ye a man of you, and come he doun to syngulere batel;

9 if he may fiyte with me, and sleeth me, we schulen be 'seruauntis to you; forsothe if Y haue the maystry, and sle hym, ye schulen be boonde, and 'ye schulen serue vs.

10 And 'the Filistei seide, Y haue 'seyd schenschip to dai to the cumpenyes of Israel; yyue ye a man, and bigynne he 'synguler batel with me.

11 Sotheli Saul and alle men of Israel herden siche wordis of 'the Filistey, and thei weren astonyed, and dredden greetli.

12 Forsothe Dauid was 'the sone of a man of Effrata, of whom it is 'biforseid, of Bethleem of Juda, to 'which man the name was Isay, which hadde eiyte sones; and 'the man was eld in the daies of Saul, and of greet age among men.

13 Sotheli thre grettere sones of Ysai yeden after Saul in to batel; and the names of hise thre sones, that yeden to batel, Heliab, the firste gendryd, and the secounde, Amynadab, and the thridde, Samma.

14 Forsothe Dauid was the leeste. Therfor while thre grettere sueden Saul, Dauid yede,

15 and turnede ayen fro Saul, that he schulde kepe the floc of his fadir in Bethleem.

16 Forsothe the Filistey cam forth in the morewtid, and euentid; and stood 'bi fourti daies.

17 Sotheli Ysai seide to Dauid his sone, Take thou to thi britheren meete maad of meele, the mesure of ephi, and these ten looues, and renne thou in to the castels to thi britheren;

18 and thou schalt bere to the tribune these ten 'litil formes of chese; and thou schalt visite thi britheren, whether thei doon riytli, and lurne thou, with whiche men thei ben ordeyned.

19 Forsothe Saul, and thei, and alle the sones of Israel in the valei of Terebynte fouyten ayens Filisteis.

20 Therfor Dauid roos eerli, and bitook the floc to the kepere, and he yede chargid, as Ysai 'hadde comaundid to hym; and he cam to the place Magala, and to the oost, which oost yede out to the batel, and criede in 'the batel.

21 For Israel hadde dressid scheltrun; 'but also Filisteis weren maad redi 'euen ayens.

22 Therfor Dauid lefte the vessels, whiche he hadde brouyt, vndur the hond of a kepere 'at the fardels, and he ran to the place of batel, and he axyde, if alle thingis weren 'doon riytli anentis hise britheren.

23 And whanne he spak yit to hem, thilke bastard apperide, Goliath bi name, a Filisti of Geth, and stiede fro the castels of Filisteis; and 'while he spak these same wordis, Dauid herde.

24 And whanne alle men of Israel hadden seyn 'the man, thei fledden fro his face, and dredden hym greetli.

25 And ech man of Israel seide, Whether thou hast seyn this man that stiede? for he stiede to seie schenship to Israel; therfor the kyng schal make riche with greet richessis 'the man that sleeth thilke Filistei; and the kyng schal yyue his douyter to that man, and schal make the hows of his fader with out 'tribut in Israel.

26 And Dauyd spak to the men that stoden with hym, and seide, What schal be youun to the man that sleeth this Filistei, and doith awei schenschip fro Israel? for who is this Filistei vncircumcidid, that dispiside the scheltruns of God lyuynge?

27 Forsothe the puple tolde to hym the same word, and seide, These thingis schulen be youun to the man that sleeth hym.

28 And whanne Heliab, 'his more brother, had herd this, while he spak with othere men, he was wrooth ayens Dauid, and seide, Whi camest thou, and whi 'leftist thou tho fewe scheep in deseert? Y knowe thi pride, and the wewardnesse of thin herte; for thou camest doun to se the batel.

29 And Dauid seide, What haue Y do? Whether it is not a word?

30 And Dauid bowide a litil fro hym to another man; and Dauid seide the same word, and the puple answeride to hym al word as bifore.

31 Forsothe these wordis weren herd, whiche Dauid spak, and weren teld 'in the siyt of Saul.

32 And whanne Dauyd was brouyt to Saul, Dauyd spak to hym, The herte of ony man falle not doun for 'that Filistei, Y thi seruaunt schal go, and 'Y schal fiyte ayens the Filistei.

33 And Saul seide to Dauid, Thou maist not ayenstonde this Filistei, nether fiyte ayens hym, for thou art a child; forsothe this man is a werriour fro his yong wexynge age.

34 And Dauid seide to Saul, Thi seruaunt kepte 'the floc of his fadir, and a lioun cam, ether a bere, and took awei a ram fro the myddis of the floc;

35 Y pursuede, and killide hem, and rauyschide fro 'the mouth of hem; and thei risiden ayens me, and I took the nether chaule 'of hem, and Y stranglide, and killide hem.

36 For Y thi seruaunt killide bothe a lioun and a bere; therfor and this Filistei vncircumcidid schal be as oon of hem. Now Y schal go, and Y schal do awey the schenschip of the puple; for who is this Filistei vncircumcidid, that was hardi to curse the oost of God lyuynge?

37 And Dauid seide, The Lord that delyuerede me fro the 'mouth of the lioun, and fro the 'hond, that is, power, of the bere, he schal delyuere me fro the hond of this Filistei. Forsothe Saul seide to Dauid, Go thou, and the Lord be with thee.

38 And Saul clothide Dauid with hise clothis, and puttide a brasun basynet on his heed, and clothide hym with an haburioun.

39 Therfor Dauid was gird with his swerd on his cloth, and bigan to asaie if he myyte go armed; for he hadde not custom. And Dauid seide to Saul, Y may not go so, for Y haue not vss. And Dauid puttide awei tho,

40 and he took his staaf, which he hadde euere in the hondis. And he chees to hym fyue clereste stonys, that is, harde, pleyn, and rounde, of the stronde; and he sente tho in to the schepherdis scrippe, which he hadde with hym; and he took the slynge in the hond, and yede forth ayens the Filistei.

41 Sotheli the Filistei yede, 'goynge and neiyyng ayens Dauid; and his squyer yede bifor hym.

42 And whanne 'the Filistei hadde biholde Dauid, and hadde seyn hym, he dispiside Dauid; forsothe Dauid was a yong wexynge man, rodi, and feir in siyt.

43 And 'the Filistei, seide to Dauid, Whether Y am a dogge, for thou comest to me with a staf? And 'the Filistei curside Dauid in hise goddis; and he seide to Dauid,

44 Come thou to me, and Y schal yyue thi fleischis to the 'volatilis of heuene, and to the beestis of erthe.

45 Sotheli Dauid seide to 'the Filistei, Thou comest to me with swerd, and spere, and scheeld; but Y come to thee in the name of the Lord God of oostis, of God of the cumpanyes of Israel, to whiche thou seidist schenschip to dai.

46 And the Lord schal yyue thee in myn hond, and Y schal sle thee, and Y schal take awey thin heed fro thee; and I schal yyue the deed bodies of the castels of Filisteis 'to day to the volatils of heuene, and to the beestis of erthe; that al the erthe wite, that the Lord God is in Israel,

47 and that al this chirche knowe, that the Lord saueth not in swerd nether in spere; for the batel is his, and he schal bitake you in to oure hondis.

48 Therfor whanne the Filistei hadde rise, and cam, and neiyede ayens Dauid, Dauid hastide, and ran to batel ayens 'the Filistei.

49 And Dauid putte his hond 'in to his scrippe, and he took o stoon, and he castide with the slynge, 'and ledde aboute, and smoot 'the Filistei in the forheed; and the stoon was fastned in his forheed, and he felde doun in to his face on the erthe.

50 And Dauid hadde the maistrie ayens 'the Filistei 'in a slyng and stoon, and he killide 'the Filistei smytun. And whanne Dauid hadde no swerd in the hond,

51 he ran, and stood on 'the Filistei, and took his swerd; and Dauid drow out the swerd of his schethe, and 'killide him, and kittide awei his heed. Forsothe the Filisteis sien, that the strongeste of hem was deed, and thei fledden.

52 And the sones of Israel and of Juda risiden to gidere, and crieden, and pursueden Filisteis, 'til the while thei camen in to the valei, and 'til to the yate of Accaron. And woundid men of Filisteis felden in the weye of Sarym, and 'til to Geth, and 'til to Accaron.

53 And the sones of Israel turneden ayen, aftir that thei hadden pursuede Filisteis, and thei assailiden 'the tentis of hem.

54 Forsothe Dauid took the heed of 'the Filistei, and brouyte it in to Jerusalem; sotheli he puttide hise armeris in the 'tabernacle of the Lord.

55 Forsothe in that tyme in which Saul siy Dauid goynge out ayens 'the Filistei, he seide to Abner, prince of his chiualrie, Abner, of what generacioun 'cam forth this yong waxynge man? And Abner seide, Kyng, thi soule lyueth, I knowe not.

56 And the kyng seide, Axe thou, whos sone this child is.

57 And whanne Dauid hadde come ayen, whanne 'the Filistei was slayn, Abner took Dauid, and brouyte hym in, hauynge in the hond the heed of 'the Filistei, 'bifor Saul.

58 And Saul seide to hym, Of what generacioun art thou, yong waxynge man? And Dauid seide, Y am the sone of thi seruaunt, Isai of Bethleem.

CAP 18

1 And it was doon, whanne Dauid 'hadde endid to speke to Saul, the soule of Jonathas was glued togidre to the soule of Dauid, and Jonathas louyde hym as his owne soule.

2 And Saul took Dauid in that dai, and grauntide not 'to hym, 'that he schulde turne ayen in to 'the hows of his fadir.

3 Forsothe Jonathas and Dauid maden boond of pees, 'that is, swerynge euerlastynge frenschip; for Jonathas louyde Dauid as his owne soule;

4 for whi Jonathas dispuylide him silf fro the coote 'in which he was clothid, and yaf it to Dauid, and hise othere clothis, 'til to his swerd and bouwe, and 'til to the girdil.

5 Also Dauid yede out to alle thingis, to what euer thingis Saul 'hadde sent hym, and he gouernede hym silf prudentli; and Saul settide hym ouer the men of batel, and 'he was acceptid, 'ether plesaunt, in the iyen of al the puple, and moost in the siyt of 'the seruauntis of Saul.

6 Forsothe whanne Dauid turnede ayen, whanne 'the Filistei was slayn, and bar the heed of 'the Filistei in to Jerusalem, wymmen yeden out of alle the citees of Israel, and sungen, and ledden queris, ayens the comyng of king Saul, in tympans of gladnesse, and in trumpis.

7 And the wymmen sungen, pleiynge, and seiynge, Saul smoot a thousynde, and Dauid smoot ten thousynde.

8 Saul was wrooth greetli, and this word displeside 'in his iyen; and he seide, Thei yauen ten thousynde to Dauid, and 'thei yauen a thousynde to me; what leeueth to hym, no but the rewme aloone?

9 Therfor Saul bihelde Dauid not with 'riytful iyen, 'fro that dai and afterward.

10 Sotheli aftir the tother dai a wickid spirit of God asailide Saul, and he propheciede in the myddis of his hows.

11 Forsothe Dauid harpide with his hond, as bi alle daies; and Saul helde a spere, and caste it, and gesside that he myyte prene Dauid with the wal, that is, perse with the spere, so that it schulde passe til to the wal; and Dauid bowide 'fro his face the secounde tyme.

12 And Saul dredde Dauid, for the Lord was with hym, and hadde go awei fro him silf.

13 Therfor Saul remouide Dauid fro hym silf, and made hym tribune on a thousynde men; and Dauid yede out and entride in 'the siyt of the puple.

14 And Dauid dide warli in alle hise weies, and the Lord was with hym;

15 and so Saul siy that Dauid was ful prudent, and he bigan to be war of Dauid.

16 Forsothe al Israel and Juda louyden Dauid; for he entride and yede out bifor hem.

17 And Saul seide to Dauid, Lo! 'my more douytir Merob, Y schal yiue her wijf to thee; oneli be thou a strong man, and fiyte thou the 'batels of the Lord. Forsothe Saul 'arettide, and seide, Myn hond be not in hym, but the hond of Filisteis be on hym.

18 Sotheli Dauid seide to Saul, Who am Y, ether what is my lijf, ether the meynee of my fadir in Israel, that Y be maad the 'sone in lawe of the kyng?

19 Forsothe the tyme 'was maad whanne Merob, the douyter of Saul, 'ouyte to be youun to Dauid, sche was youun wijf to Hadriel Molatite.

20 Forsothe Dauid louide Mychol, the douytir of Saul; and it was teld to Saul, and it pleside hym.

21 And Saul seide, Y schal yyue hir to hym, that it be to hym in to sclaundir, and the hond of Filisteis be on hym. Therfor

Saul seide to Dauid, In 'twei douytris thou schalt be my sone in lawe to dai.

22 And Saul comaundide to hise seruauntis, Speke ye to Dauid, while it 'is hid fro me, and seie ye, Lo! thou plesist the king, and alle hise seruauntis louen thee; now therfor be thou hosebonde of the 'douytir of the kyng.

23 And the seruauntis of Saul spaken alle these wordis in the eeris of Dauid. And Dauid seide, Whether it semeth litil to you 'to be sone in lawe of the kyng? Forsothe Y am a pore man, and a feble.

24 And the seruauntis telden to Saul, and seiden, Dauid spak siche wordis.

25 Sotheli Saul seide, Thus speke ye to Dauid, The kyng hath no nede to yiftis for spowsails, no but onely to an hundrid prepucies, 'that is, mennus yerdis vncircumcidid, 'of Filisteis, that veniaunce be maad of the kyngis enemyes. Certis Saul thouyte to bitake Dauid in to the hondis of Filisteis.

26 And whanne the seruauntis of Saul hadden teld to Dauid the wordis, whiche Saul hadde seid, the word pleside 'in the iyen of Dauid, that he schulde be maad the kyngis son in lawe.

27 And aftir a fewe daies Dauid roos, and yede in to Acharon, with the men that weren with hym, and he killide of Filisteis twei hundrid men; and brouyte 'the prepucies of hem, and noumbride tho to the kyng, that he schulde be the kyngis sone in lawe. And so Saul yaf Mycol, his douyter, wiif to hym.

28 And Saul siy, and vndirstood, that the Lord was with Dauid.

29 Forsothe Mychol, 'the douyter of Saul, louide Dauid, and Saul bigan more to drede Dauid; and Saul was maad enemye to Dauid in alle daies.

30 And the princes of Filisteis yeden out; forsothe fro the big-ynnyng of her goyng out Dauyd bar hym silf more warli than alle the men of Saul; and the name of Dauid was maad ful solempne.

CAP 19

1 Forsothe Saul spak to Jonathas, his sone, and to alle hise seruauntis, that thei schulden sle Dauid; certis Jonathas, the sone of Saul, louyde Dauid greetli.

2 And Jonathas schewide to Dauid, and seide, Saul, my fadir, sekith to sle thee, wherfor, Y biseche, kepe 'thou thee eerli; and thou schalt dwelle priueli, and thou schalt be hid.

3 Sotheli Y schal go out, and stonde bisidis my fadir in the feeld, where euer he schal be; and Y schal speke of thee to my fadir, and what euer thing Y shal se, Y schal telle to thee.

4 Therfor Jonathas spak good thingis of Dauid to Saul, his fadir, and seide to hym, Kyng, do thou not synne ayens thi seruaunt Dauid, for he 'synnede not to thee, and hise werkis ben ful good to thee;

5 and he puttide his lijf in his hond, and he killide the Filistei. And the Lord made greet heelthe to al Israel; thou siy, and were glad; whi therfor synnest thou in giltles blood, and sleest Dauid, which is with out gilt?

6 And whanne Saul hadde herd this, he was plesid with the vois of Jonathas, and swoor, 'The Lord lyueth, 'that is, bi the Lord lyuynge, for Dauid schal not be slayn.

7 Therfor Jonathas clepide Dauid, and schewide to hym alle these wordis. And Jonathas brouyte in Dauid to Saul, and he was bifor hym as 'yistirdai and the thridde dai ago.

8 Forsothe batel was moued eft; and Dauyd yede out, and fauyt ayens Filisteis, and he smoot hem with a greet wounde, and thei fledden fro his face.

9 And the yuel spirit of the Lord was maad on Saul; sotheli he sat in his hows, and helde a spere; certis Dauid harpide in his hond.

10 And Saul enforside to prene with the spere Dauid in the wal; and Dauid bowide fro 'the face of Saul; forsothe the spere 'with voide wounde was borun in to the wal; and Dauid fledde, and was saued in that niyt.

11 Therfor Saul sente hise knyytis in the nyyt in to the hows of Dauid, that thei schulden kepe hym, and that he 'schulde be slayn in the morewtide. And whanne Mychol, the wijf of Dauid, hadde teld this to Dauid, and seide, If thou sauest not thee in this nyyt, thou schalt die to morew;

12 sche puttide hym doun bi a wyndow. Forsothe he yede, and fledde, and was sauyd.

13 Sotheli Mychol took an ymage, and puttide it on the bed, and puttide 'an heeri skyn of geet at the heed therof, and hilide it with clothis.

14 Forsothe Saul sente sergeauntis, 'that schulden rauysche Dauid, and it was answeride, that he was sijk.

15 And eft Saul sente messangeris, that thei schulden se Dauid, and he seide, Brynge ye hym to me in the bed, that he be slayn.

16 And whanne the messangeris hadden come, 'a symylacre was foundun on the bed, and 'skynnes of geet at the heed therof.

17 And Saul seide to Mychol, Whi scornedist thou me so, and 'delyueredist myn enemy, that he fledde? And Mychol answeride to Saul, For he spak to me, and seide, Delyuere thou me, ellis Y schal slee thee.

18 Forsothe Dauid fledde, and was sauyd; and he cam to Samuel in to Ramatha, and telde to hym alle thingis which Saul hadde do to hym; and he and Samuel yeden, and dwell-iden in Naioth.

19 Forsothe it was teld to Saul of men, seiynge, Lo! Dauid is in Naioth in Ramatha.

20 Therfor Saul sente sleeris, that thei schulden rauysche Dauid; and whanne thei hadden seyn the cumpeny of profetis profeciynge, and Samuel stondynge ouer hem, the Spirit of the Lord, 'that is, the spirit of deuocioun, was maad in hem, and thei also bigunnen to prophecie.

21 And whanne this was told to Saul, he sente also othere messangeris; 'sotheli and thei profesieden. And eft Saul sente the thridde messangeris, and thei prophecieden. And Saul was wrooth 'with irefulnesse;

22 and he also yede in to Ramatha, and he cam 'til to the greet cisterne, which is in Socoth, and he axide, and seide, In what place ben Samuel and Dauid? And it was seid to hym, Lo! thei ben in Naioth in Ramatha.

23 And he yede in 'to Naioth in Ramatha; and the Spirit of the Lord was maad also on him; and he 'yede, and entride, and propheciede, 'til the while he cam 'in to Naioth in Ramatha.

24 And 'he also dispuylide him silf of hise clothis, and proph-eciede with othere men bifor Samuel, and he profeciede nakid in al that dai and nyyt. Wherfor 'a prouerbe, that is, a comyn word, yede out, Whether and Saul among prophetis?

CAP 20

1 Forsothe Dauid fledde fro Naioth, which is in Ramatha, and cam and spak bifor Jonathas, What haue Y do? what is my wickidnesse, and what is my synne ayens thi fadir, for he sekith my lijf?

2 And Jonathas seide to hym, Fer be it fro thee, thou schalt not die, for my fadir schal not do ony thing greet ether litil, 'no but he schewe firste to me; therfor my fadir kepte preuy fro me this word oneli, forsothe it schal not be.

3 And eft he swoor to Dauid. And Dauid seide, Treuli thi fadir woot, that Y haue founde grace 'in thin iyen, and he schal seie, Jonathas wite not this, lest perauenture he be sory; certis the Lord lyueth, 'and thi soule lyueth, for, that Y seie so, Y and deeth ben departid oneli bi o degree.

4 And Jonathas seide to Dauid, What euer thing thi soule schal seie to me, Y schal do to thee.

5 And Dauid seide to Jonathas, Lo! calendis ben to morewe, and bi custom Y am wont to sitte bi the kyng to ete; therfor suffre thou me, 'that Y be hid in the feeld 'til to euentid of the thridde dai.

6 If thi fadir biholdith, and axith me, thou schalt answere to hym, Dauid preiede me, that he schulde go swiftli into Bethleem, his citee, for solempne sacrifices ben there to alle the men of his lynage.

7 If he seith, Wel, pees schal be to thi seruaunt; forsothe if he is wrooth, wite thou, that his malice is fillid.

8 Therfor do thou mercy in to thi seruaunt, for thou madist me thi seruaunt to make with thee the boond of pees of the Lord; sotheli if ony wickidnesse is in me, sle thou me, and brynge thou not in me to thi fadir.

9 And Jonathas seide, Fer be this fro me, for it mai not be doon, that Y telle not to thee, if Y knowe certeynli, that the malice of my fadir is fillid ayens thee.

10 And Dauid seide to Jonathas, Who schal telle to me, if in caas thi fadir answerith harde ony thing of me?

11 And Jonathas seide to Dauid, Come thou, and go we forth in to the feeld. And whanne bothe hadden go in to the feeld,

12 Jonathas seide to Dauid, Lord God of Israel, if Y enquere the sentence of my fadir to morewe, ether in the nexte dai aftir, and ony 'thing of good is of Dauid, and Y sende not anoon to thee,

13 and make knowun to thee, God do these thingis to Jonathas, and 'adde these thingis. Forsothe if the malice of my fadir contynueth ayens thee, Y schal schewe to thin eere, and Y schal delyuere thee, that thou go in pees; and the Lord be with thee, as he was with my fadir.

14 And if Y lyue, do thou the mercies of the Lord to me;

15 forsothe if Y am deed, 'thou schalt not take awei thi mercy fro myn hows 'til in to with outen ende; 'and yif Y do it not, whanne the Lord schal drawe out bi the roote the enemyes of Dauid, ech man fro the lond, take he awei Jonathas fro his hows, and seke the Lord of the hond of the enemyes of Dauid.

16 Therfor Jonathas made boond of pees with the hows of Dauid, and the Lord souyte of the hond of enemyes of Dauid.

17 And Jonathas addide to swere stedfastli to Dauid, for he louyde Dauid; for he louyde so Dauid, as his owne soule.

18 And Jonathas seide to hym, 'Calendis ben to morewe, and thou schalt be souyt;

19 for thi sittyng schal be souyt til after to morewe. Therfor thou schalt go doun hastili, and thou schalt come in to the place, where thou schalt be hid in the day, whanne it is leueful to worche; and thou schalt sitte bisidis the stoon, 'to which the name is Ezel.

20 And Y schal sende thre arowis bisidis that stoon, and Y schal caste as 'excercisynge ether pleiynge me at a signe.

21 Y schal sende also and my child, and Y schal seie to hym, Go thou, and brynge to me the arewis.

22 If Y seie to the child, Lo! the arewis ben 'with ynne thee, take thou tho; come thou to me, for pees is to thee, and no thing is of yuel, the Lord lyueth. Sotheli if Y speke thus to the child, Lo! the arowis ben biyende thee; go thou in pees, for the Lord deliuerede thee.

23 Forsothe of the word, which thou and Y han spoke, the Lord be bitwixe me and thee til in to with outen ende.

24 Therfor Dauid was hid in the feeld; and the 'calendis camen, and the kyng sat to ete breed.

25 And whanne the kyng hadde seete on his chaier bi custom, 'which chaier was bisidis the wal, Jonathas roos, and sat 'aftir Abner, and Abner sat at the side of Saul, and the place of Dauid apperide voide.

26 And Saul spak not ony thing in that dai; for he thouyte, that 'in hap it bifelde to hym, that he was not clene 'nether purified.

27 And whanne the secounde dai aftir the calendis hadde schyned, eft the place of Dauid apperide voide. And Saul seide to Jonathas his sone, Whi cometh not the sone of Isai, nether yisterdai, nether to dai to ete?

28 And Jonathas answeride to Saul, He preiede me mekeli, that he schulde go in to Bethleem;

29 and he seide, Suffre thou me, for solempne sacrifice is in my citee; oon of my britheren clepide me; now therfor if Y foond grace 'in thin iyen, Y schal go soone, and 'Y schal se my britheren; for this cause he cometh not to the 'table of the kyng.

30 Forsothe Saul was wrooth ayens Jonathas, and seide to hym, Thou sone of a womman 'rauyschynge at her owne wille a man, whether Y woot not, that thou louest the sone of Ysay in to thi confusioun, and in to the confusioun of thi schendful modir?

31 For in alle the daies in whiche the sone of Isai lyueth on erthe, thou schalt not be stablischid, nether thi rewme; therfor 'riyt now sende thou, and brynge hym to me, for he is the sone of deeth.

32 Sotheli Jonathas answeride to Saul his fadir, and seide, Whi schal he die? what hath he do?

33 And Saul took the spere, that he schulde smyte hym, and Jonathas vndirstood, that it was determynd of his fadir, that Dauid schulde be slayn.

34 Therfor Jonathas roos fro the table in 'the ire of woodnesse, and he ete not breed in the secounde dai of calendis; for he was sori on Dauid, for his fadir hadde schent him.

35 And whanne the morewtid 'hadde schyned, Jonathas cam in to the feeld, and a litil child with hym, bi the couenaunt of Dauid.

36 And Jonathas seide to his child, Go thou, and brynge to me the arowis whiche Y caste. And whanne the child hadde runne, he castide another arowe biyende the child.

37 Therfor the child cam to the place of the arowe which Jonathas hadde sent; and Jonathas criede bihynde the 'bak of the child, and seide, Lo! the arowe is not there, certis it is biyende thee.

38 And Jonathas criede eft bihynde the bak of the child, 'and seide, Haste thou swiftli, stonde thou not. Therfor the child gaderide the arowis of Jonathas, and brouyte to his lord,

39 and outerli he wiste not what was doon; for oonli Jonathas and Dauid knewen the thing.

40 Therfor Jonathas yaf hise armeris to the child, and seide to hym, Go thou, bere in to the citee.

41 And whanne the child hadde go, Dauid roos fro the place that 'yede to the south; and he felde low 'in to the erthe, and

worschipide the thridde tyme, and thei kissiden hem silf to gidere, and 'wepten to gidere; forsothe Dauid wepte more.
42 Therfor Jonathas seide to Dauid, Go thou in pees; what euer thingis we bothe han swoore in the 'name of the Lord, 'and seiden, 'The Lord be bitwixe me and thee, and bitwixe my seed and thi seed til in to with outen ende, 'be stidfast. And Dauid roos, and yede, but also Jonathas entride in to the citee.

CAP 21

1 Forsothe Dauid cam in to Nobe to Achimelech preest; and Achymelech wondrid, for Dauid 'hadde come; and he seide to Dauid, Whi art thou aloone, and no man is with thee?
2 And Dauid seide to Achymelech preest, The kyng comaundide to me a word, and seide, No man wite the thing, for which thou art sent fro me, and what maner comaundementis Y yaf to thee; for Y seide also to children, that thei schulden go in to that 'and that place;
3 now therfor if thou hast ony thing at hond, ether fyue looues, yyue thou to me, ether what euer thing thou fyndist.
4 And the preest answeride to Dauid, and seide to hym, Y haue 'not lewid, 'that is, comyn, looues at hoond, but oneli hooli breed; whether the children ben clene, and moost of wymmen?
5 And Dauid answeride to the preest, and seide to hym, And sotheli if it is doon of wymmen, we absteyneden vs fro yistirdai and the thridde dai ago, whanne we yeden out, and the 'vessels, that is, bodies, of the children weren cleene; forsothe this weie is defoulyd, but also that schal be halewid to dai in the vessels.
6 Therfor the preest yaf to hym halewid breed, for noon other breed was there, no but oneli looues of settyng forth, that weren takun awey fro the face of the Lord, that hoote looues schulen be set.
7 Forsothe sum man of the seruauntis of Saul was there with ynne in the tabernacle of the Lord; and his name was Doech of Ydumee, the myytiest of the scheepherdis, 'that is, iugis, of Saul.
8 Forsothe Dauid seide to Achymelech, If thou hast 'here at hond spere, ether swerd, yyue to me; for Y took not with me my swerd and myn armeris; for the 'word of the kyng constreynede me.
9 And the preest seide, Lo! here the swerd of Goliath Filistei, whom thou killidst in the valey of Terebynte, is wlappid in a cloth aftir ephoth; if thou wolt take this, take thou; for here is noon other outakun that. And Dauid seide, Noon other is lijk this, yyue thou it to me.
10 Therfor Dauid roos, 'and fledde in that dai fro the face of Saul, and cam to Achis, the kyng of Geth.
11 And the seruauntis of Achis seiden to hym, whanne thei hadden seyn Dauid, Whether this is not Dauid, kyng of the lond? Whether thei sungen not to hym bi queeris, and seiden, Saul smoot a thousynde, and Dauid smoot ten thousynde?
12 Sotheli Dauid puttide these wordis 'in his herte, and he dredde greetli of the face of Achis, kyng of Geth.
13 And Dauid chaungide his mouth bifor Achis, and felde doun bitwixe her hondis, and he hurtlide ayens the doris of the yate, and his drauelis, 'that is, spotelis, flowiden doun in to the beerd.
14 And Achis seide to hise seruauntis, Seen ye the wood man? why brouyten ye hym to me? whether wood men failen to vs? whi han ye brouyt in hym, that he schulde be wood,

while Y am present? Delyuere ye hym fro hennus, lest he entre in to myn hows.

CAP 22

1 Therfor Dauid yede fro thennus, and fledde in to the denne of Odollam; and whanne hise britheren, and al the hows of his fadir hadden herd this, thei camen doun thidur to hym.
2 And alle men that weren set in angwisch, and oppressid with othere mennus dette, and in bittir soule, camen togidere to hym; and he was maad the prince 'of hem, and as foure hundrid men weren with hym.
3 And Dauid yede forth fro thennus in to Masphat, which is of Moab; and he seide to the kyng of Moab, Y preye, dwelle my fadir and my modir with you, til Y wite what thing God schal do to me.
4 And he lefte hem bifor the face of the kyng of Moab; and thei dwelliden at hym in alle daies, 'in whiche Dauid was in 'the forselet, ether stronghold.
5 And Gad, the profete, seide to Dauid, Nyle thou dwelle in 'the forselet; go thou forth, and go in to the lond of Juda. And Dauid yede forth, and cam in to the forest of Areth.
6 And Saul herde, that Dauid apperide, and the men that weren with hym. Forsothe whanne Saul dwellide in Gabaa, and was in the wode which is in Rama, and 'helde a spere in the hond, and alle hise seruauntis stoden aboute hym,
7 he seide to hise seruauntis that stoden nyy hym, The sones of Gemyny, here me now; whether the sone of Ysai schal yyue to alle you feeldis and vyneris, and schal make alle you tribunes and centuriouns?
8 For alle ye han swore, ether conspirid, togidere ayens me, and noon is that tellith to me; moost sithen also my sone hath ioyned boond of pees with the sone of Ysai; noon is of you, that sorewith 'for my stide, nether that tellith to me, for my sone hath reisid my seruaunt ayens me, settynge tresoun to me 'til to dai.
9 Sotheli Doech of Ydumye answeride, that stood nyy, and was the firste among 'the seruauntis of Saul, and seide, Y siy 'the sone of Ysai in Nobe, at Achymelech, preest, the sone of Achitob;
10 which counseilide the Lord for Dauid, and yaf meetis 'to hym, but also he yaf to Dauid the swerd of Goliath Filistei.
11 Therfor the kyng sente to clepe Achymelech, the preest, 'the sone of Achitob, and al the hows of his fadir, of preestis that weren in Nobe; whiche alle camen to the kyng.
12 And Saul seide to Achymelech, Here, thou sone of Achitob.
13 Which answeride, Lord, Y am redi. And Saul seide to hym, Whi hast thou conspirid ayens me, thou, and the sone of Ysai, and yauest looues and a swerd to hym, and councelidist the Lord for hym, that he schulde rise ayens me, and he dwellith a tretour 'til to dai?
14 And Achymelech answeride to the kyng, and seide, And who among alle thi seruauntis is as Dauid feithful, and the sone in lawe 'of the kyng, and goynge at thi comaundement, and gloriouse in thin hows?
15 Whether Y bigan to dai to counsele the Lord for hym? Fer be this fro me; suppose not the kyng ayens his seruaunt 'siche a thing in al 'the hows of my fadir; for thi seruaunt knew not ony thing, ether litil ethir greet, of this cause.
16 And the kyng seide, Achymelech, thou schalt die bi deeth, thou, and al the hows of thi fadir.
17 And the kyng seide to men able to be sent out, that stoden aboute hym, Turne ye, and sle the preestis of the Lord, for the

hond of hem is with Dauid; and thei wisten that he fledde, and thei schewiden not to me. Sotheli the seruauntis of the kyng nolden holde forth her hond in to the preestis of the Lord.

18 And the kyng seide to Doech, Turne thou, and hurle in to the preestis of the Lord. And Doech of Ydumee turnede, and hurlide in to the preestis, and stranglide in that dai foure score and fyue men, clothid with 'ephoth of lynnun cloth.

19 Forsothe he smoot Nobe, the citee of preestis, by the scharpnesse of swerd, men and wymmen, litle children and soukynge, and oxe, and asse, and sheep, bi the scharpnesse of swerd.

20 Forsothe o sone of Achymelech, sone of Achitob, ascapide, of which sone the name was Abiathar; and he fledde to Dauid,

21 and telde to hym that Saul hadde slayn the preestis of the Lord.

22 And Dauid seide to Abiathar, Sotheli Y wiste, 'that is, Y coniectide, ether dredde, in that dai, that whanne Doech of Ydumee was there, he wolde telle with out doute to Saul; Y am gilti of alle the lyues of thi fadir.

23 Dwelle thou with me, drede thou not; if ony man sekith thi lijf, he schal seke also my lijf, and thou schalt be kept with me.

CAP 23

1 And thei telden to Dauid, and seiden, Lo! Filisteis fiyten ayens Seila, and rauyschen the corn floris.

2 Therfor Dauid councelide the Lord, and seide, Whether Y schal go, and smyte Filisteis? And the Lord seide to Dauid, Go thou, and thou schalt smyte Filisteis, and thou schalt saue Seila.

3 And men, that weren with Dauid, seiden to him, Lo! we ben heere in Judee, and dredden; hou myche more, if we schulen go in to Seila ayens the cumpanyes of Filisteis.

4 Therfor eft Dauid councelide the Lord; which answeride, and seide to Dauid, Rise thou, and go 'in to Seila; for Y schal bitake Filisteis in thin hond.

5 Therfor Dauid yede, and hise men, in to Seila, and fauyt ayens Filisteis; and he droof awey her werk beestis, and smoot hem with greet wounde; and Dauid sauyde the dwelleris of Seila.

6 Forsothe in that tyme, 'wher ynne Abiathar, sone of Achymelech, fledde to Dauid in to Seile, he cam doun, and hadde with hym 'ephoth, that is, the cloth of the hiyeste preest.

7 Forsothe it was teld to Saul, that Dauid hadde come in to Seila; and Saul seide, The Lord hath take hym in to myn hondis, and he 'is closid, and entride in to a citee, in which ben yatis and lockis.

8 And Saul comaundide to al the puple, that it schulde go doun to batel in to Seila, and bisege Dauid and hise men.

9 And whanne Dauid perceyuede, that Saul made redi yuel priueli to hym, he seide to Abiathar, preest, Brynge hidur ephoth.

10 And Dauid seide, Lord God of Israel, thi seruaunt 'herde fame, that Saul disposith to come to Seila, that he distrie the citee for me;

11 if the men of Seila schulen bitake me in to hise hondis, and if Saul schal come doun, as thi seruaunt herde, thou Lord God of Israel schewe to thi seruaunt? And the Lord seide, He schal come doun.

12 And Dauid seide eft, Whether the men of Seila schulen bitake me, and the men that ben with me, in to the hondis of Saul? And the Lord seide, Thei schulen bitake, 'that is, if thou dwellist in the citee, and Saul come thidur.

13 Therfor Dauid roos, and hise men, as sixe hundrid; and thei yeden out of Seila, and wandriden vncerteyn hidur and thidur. And it was telde to Saul, that Dauid hadde fledde fro Seila, and was saued; wherfor Saul dissymylide to go out.

14 Forsothe Dauid dwellide in the deseert, in strongeste places, and he dwellide in the hil of wildirnesse of Ziph, in a derk hil; netheles Saul souyte hym in alle daies, and the Lord bitook not hym in to the hondis of Saul.

15 And Dauid siy, that Saul yede out, that he schulde seke his lijf. Forsothe Dauid was in the deseert of Ziph, in a wode.

16 And Jonathas, the sone of Saul, roos, and yede to Dauid in to the wode, and coumfortide hise hondis in God.

17 And he seide to Dauid, Drede thou not; for the hond of Saul my fadir schal not fynde thee, and thou schalt regne on Israel, and Y schal be the secounde to thee; but also Saul my father woot this.

18 Therfor euer eithir smoot boond of pees bifor the Lord. And Dauid dwellide in the wode; forsothe Jonathas turnede ayen in to his hows.

19 Forsothe men of Ziph stieden to Saul in Gabaa, and seiden, Lo! whether not Dauid is hid at vs in the sikireste places of the wode, in the hille of Achille, which is at the riyt syde of deseert?

20 Now therfor come thou doun, as thi soule desiride, that thou schuldist come doun; forsothe it schal be oure, that we bitake hym in to the hondis of the kyng.

21 And Saul seide, Blessid be ye of the Lord, for ye sorewiden 'for my stide.

22 Therfor, Y preie, go ye, and make redi more diligentli, and do ye more curiousli ether intentifli, and biholde ye swiftly, where his foot is, ethir who siy hym there, where ye seiden; for he thenkith on me, that felli Y aspie hym.

23 Biholde ye, and se alle his hidyng places, in whiche he is hid, and turne ye ayen to me at a certeyn thing, that Y go with you; that if he closith hym silf yhe in to erthe, Y schal seke hym with alle the thousyndis of Juda.

24 And thei risiden, and yeden in to Ziph bifor Saul. Forsothe Dauid and hise men weren in the deseert of Maon, in the feldi places, at the riyt half of Jesymyth.

25 Therfor Saul yede and hise felowis to seke Dauid, and it was told to Dauid; and anoon he yede doun to the stoon, and lyuyde in the deseert of Maon; and whanne Saul hadde herd this, he pursuede Dauid in the deseert of Maon.

26 And Saul yede and hise men at the side of the hil 'on o part; forsothe Dauid and hise men weren in the side of the hil on the tother part; sotheli Dauid dispeiride, that he myyte ascape fro the face of Saul. And so Saul and hise men cumpassiden bi the maner of a coroun Dauid and hise men, that thei schulden take hem.

27 And a messanger cam to Saul, and seide, Haste thou, and come, for Filisteis han spred hem silf on the lond.

28 Therfor Saul turnede ayen, and ceesside to pursue Dauid; and yede ayens the comyng of Filisteis. For this thing thei clepen that place the Stoon Departynge.

CAP 24

1 Therfor Dauid stiede fro thennus, and dwellide in the sykireste places of Engaddi.

2 And whanne Saul turnede ayen, aftir that he pursuede Filisteis, thei telden to hym, and seiden, Lo! Dauid is in the deseert of Engaddi.

3 Therfor Saul took three thousinde of chosun men of al Israel, and yede to seke Dauid and hise men, yhe on moost brokun rochis, that ben 'able to weie to wield geet aloone.

4 And he cam to the fooldis of scheep, that offriden hem silf to the wei goere. And there was a denne, in to which denne Saul entride, that he schulde purge the wombe; forsothe Dauid and hise men weren hid in the ynnere part of the denne.

5 And the seruauntis of Dauid seiden to hym, Lo! the dai of which the Lord spak to the, Y schal bitake to thee thin enemy, that thou do to hym as it plesith in thin iyen. Therfor Dauid roos, and kittide the hemme of the mentil of Saul priuely.

6 Aftir these thingis Dauid smoot his herte, for he hadde kit awei the hemme of the mentil of Saul.

7 And Dauid seide to hise men, The Lord be merciful to me, lest Y do this thing to my lord, the crist of the Lord, that Y sende myn hond 'in to hym, for he is the crist of the Lord. The Lord lyueth, for no but the Lord smyte hym, ether his dai come, that he die, ether he go doun in to batel and perische, the Lord be merciful to me, that Y sende not myn hond in to the crist of the Lord.

8 Forsothe Saul roos out of the denne, and yede in the weie bigunnun.

9 Sotheli Dauid roos aftir hym, and he yede out of the denne, and criede aftir the bak of Saul, and seide, My lord, the kyng! And Saul bihelde bihinde him silf; and Dauid bowide hym silf lowe to the erthe, and worschipide.

10 And he seide to Saul, Whi herist thou the wordis of men spekynge, Dauid sekith yuel ayens thee?

11 Lo! to dai thin iyen siyen, that the Lord bitook thee in myn hond in the denne, and Y thouyte that Y wolde sle thee, but myn iye sparide thee; for Y seide, Y schal not holde forth myn hond in to my lord, which is the crist, 'that is, anoyntid, of the Lord.

12 But rathere, my fadir, se thou, and knowe the hemme of thi mentil in myn hond, for whanne Y kittide aweie the hemme of thi mentil, Y nolde holde forth myn hond in thee; perseyue thou, and see, for nether yuel nether wickidnesse is in myn hond, nether Y synnede ayens thee; but thou aspiest my lijf, that thou do it awei.

13 The Lord deme bitwixe me and thee, and the Lord venge me of thee; but myn hond be not in thee,

14 as it is seid also in eld prouerbe, Wickidnesse schal go out of wickid men; therfor myn hond be not in thee.

15 'Whom pursuest thou, kyng of Israel, whom pursuest thou? Thou pursuest a deed hound, and a quyk fle.

16 The Lord be iuge, and the Lord deme bitwixe me and thee, and se, and deme my cause, and delyuere me fro thin hond.

17 Sotheli whanne Dauid hadde fillid spekynge siche wordis to Saul, Saul seide, Whether this is thi vois, my sone Dauid? And Saul reiside his vois, and wepte.

18 And he seide to Dauid, Thou art more iust than Y; for thou yauest goodis to me; forsothe Y yeldide yuelis to thee.

19 And thou schewidist to me to dai, what goodis thou hast do to me, how the Lord bitook me in thin hond, and thou killidist not me.

20 For who, 'whanne he fyndith his enemy, schal delyuere hym in good weie? But the Lord yelde to thee this while, for that, that thou wrouytist to dai in me.

21 And now, for Y woot, that thou schalt regne moost certeynli, and schalt haue in thin hond the rewme of Israel, swere thou to me in the Lord,

22 that thou do not a wei my seed aftir me, nether take a wey my name fro the hows of my fadir.

23 And Dauid swoor to Saul. Therfor Saul yede in to his hows, and Dauid and hise men stieden to sikire placis.

CAP 25

1 Forsothe Samuel was deed; and al Israel was gaderid to gidere, and thei biweiliden hym greetly, and birieden hym in his hows in Ramatha. And Dauid roos, and yede doun in to deseert of Faran.

2 Forsothe a 'man was in Maon, and his possessioun was in Carmele, and thilke man was ful greet, and thre thousynde scheep and a thousynde geet 'weren to hym; and it bifelde that his flocke was clippid in Carmele.

3 Forsothe the name of that man was Nabal, and the name of his wijf was Abigail; and thilke womman was moost prudent and fair; forsothe hir hosebond was hard and ful wickid and malicious; sotheli he was of the kyn of Caleph.

4 Therfor whanne Dauid hadde herde in deseert, that Nabal clippide his floc,

5 he sente ten yonge men, and seide to hem, Stie ye in to Carmele, and ye schulen come to Nabal, and ye schulen grete hym of my name pesibli;

6 and ye schulen seie thus, Pees be to my britheren and to thee, and pees be to thin hows, and pees be to alle thingis, 'what euer thingis thou hast.

7 Y herde that thi scheepherdis, that weren with vs in deseert, clippiden thi flockis; we weren neuere dieseful to hem, nether ony tyme ony thing of the floc failide to hem, in al time in which thei weren with vs in Carmele;

8 axe thi children, and thei schulen schewe to thee. Now therfor thi children fynde grace in thin iyen; for in a good dai we camen to thee; what euer thing thin hond fyndith, yyue to thi seruauntis, and to thi sone Dauid.

9 And whanne the children of Dauid hadden come, thei spaken to Nabal alle these wordis in the name of Dauid, and helden pees.

10 Forsoth Nabal answeride to the children of Dauid, and seide, Who is Dauith? and who is the sone of Isai? To dai seruauntis encreesiden that fleen her lords.

11 Therfor schal Y take my looues and my watris, and the fleischis of beestis, whiche Y haue slayn to my schereris, and schal Y yyue to men, whiche Y knowe not of whennus thei ben?

12 Therfor the children of Dauid yeden ayen bi her weie; and thei turneden ayen, and camen, and telden to hym alle wordis whiche Nabal hadde seid.

13 Thanne Dauid seide to hise children, Ech man be gird with his swerd. And alle men weren gird with her swerdis, and Dauid also was gird with his swerd; and as foure hundrid men sueden Dauid, forsothe two hundrid leften at the fardels.

14 Forsothe oon of hise children telde to Abigail, wijf of Nabal, and seide, Lo! Dauid sente messangeris fro deseert, that thei schulden blesse oure lord, and he turnede hem awey;

15 these men weren good ynow, and not dieseful to vs, and no thing perischide 'in ony tyme in al the tyme in which we lyueden with hem in deseert;

16 thei weren to vs for a wal, bothe in niyt and in dai, in alle daies in whiche we lesewiden flockis at hem.

17 Wherfor biholde thou, and thenke, what thou schalt do; for malice is fillid ayens thin hosebonde, and ayens 'thin hows; and he is the sone of Belial, so that no man may speke to him.

18 Therfor Abigail hastide, and took two hundrid looues, and two vessels of wyn, and fyue whetheris sodun, and seuene buyschelis and an half of flour, and an hundrid bundles of

dried grape, and two hundrid gobetis of dried figus; and puttide on assis,

19 and seide to hir children, Go ye bifor me; lo! Y schal sue you 'aftir the bak. Forsothe sche schewide not to hir hosebonde Nabal.

20 Therfor whanne sche hadde stied on the asse, and cam doun 'at the roote of the hil, and Dauid and hise men camen doun in to the comyng 'of hir; whiche also sche mette.

21 And Dauid seide, Verili in veyn Y haue kept alle thingis that weren of this Nabal in the deseert, and no thing perischide of alle thingis that perteyneden to hym, and he hath yolde to me yuel for good.

22 The Lord do these thingis, and adde these thingis to the enemyes of Dauid, if Y schal leeue of alle thingis that perteynen to him til the morewe a pisser to the wal.

23 Sotheli whanne Abigail siy Dauid, sche hastide, and yede doun of the asse; and sche fel doun bifor Dauid on hir face, and worschipide on the erthe.

24 And sche felde doun to hise feet, and seide, My lord the kyng, this wickydnesse be in me; Y biseche, speke thin handmayden in thin eeris, and here thou the wordis of thi seruauntesse;

25 Y preie, my lord the kyng, sette not his herte on this wickid man Nabal, for bi his name he is a fool, and foli is with hym; but, my lord, Y thin handmayde siy not thi children, whiche thou sentist.

26 Now therfor, my lord, the Lord lyueth, and thi soule lyueth, which Lord forbeed thee, lest thou schuldist come in to blood, and he sauede thi soule to thee; and now thin enemyes, and thei that seken yuel to my lord, be maad as Nabal.

27 Wherfor resseyue thou this blessyng, which thin handmaide brouyte to thee, my lord, and yyue thou to the children that suen thee, my lord.

28 Do thou awey the wickidnesse of thi seruauntesse; for the Lord makynge schal make a feithful hows to thee, my lord, for thou, my lord, fiytist the batels of the Lord; therfor malice be not foundun in thee in alle dais of thi lijf.

29 For if a man risith ony tyme, and pursueth thee, and sekith thi lijf, the lijf of my lord schal be kept as in a bundel of lyuynge trees, at thi Lord God; forsothe the soule of thin enemyes schal be hurlid round aboute as in feersnesse, and sercle of a slynge.

30 Therfor whanne the Lord hath do to thee, my lord, alle these goode thingis, whiche he spak of thee, and hath ordeyned thee duyk on Israel,

31 this schal not be in to siyyng and in to doute of herte to thee, my lord, that thou hast sched out giltles blood, ether that thou hast vengid thee. And whanne the Lord hath do wel to thee, my lord, thou schalt haue mynde on thin handmaide, and thou schalt do wel to hir.

32 And Dauid seide to Abigail, Blessid be the Lord God of Israel, that sente thee to dai in to my comyng, and blessid be thi speche;

33 and blessid be thou, that hast forbede me, lest Y yede to blood, and vengide me with myn hond;

34 ellis the Lord God of Israel lyueth, which forbeed me, 'lest Y dide yuel to thee, if thou haddist not soone come in to 'metyng to me, a pissere to the wal schulde not haue left to Nabal til to the morewe liyt.

35 Therfor Dauid resseyuede of hir hond alle thingis whiche sche hadde brouyt to hym; and he seide to hir, Go thou in pees in to thin hows; lo! Y herde thi vois, and Y onouride thi face.

36 Forsothe Abigail cam to Nabal; and, lo! a feeste was to him in his hows, as the feeste of a kyng; and the herte of Nabal was iocounde, for he was 'drunkun greetli; and sche schewide not to hym a word litil ether greet til the morewe.

37 Forsothe in the morewtid, whanne Nabal hadde defied the wiyn, his wijf schewide to hym alle these wordis; and his herte was almest deed with ynne, and he was maad as a stoon.

38 And whanne ten daies hadden passid, the Lord smoot Nabal, and he was deed.

39 Which thing whanne Dauid hadde herd, Nabal deed, he seide, Blessid be the Lord God, that vengide the cause of my schenschip of the hond of Nabal, and kepte his seruaunt fro yuel, and the Lord yeldide the malice of Nabal in to the heed of hym. Therfor Dauid sente, and spak to Abigail, that he wolde take hir wijf to hym.

40 And the children of Dauid camen to Abigail in to Carmele, and spaken to hir, and seiden, Dauid sente vs to thee, that he take thee in to wijf to hym.

41 And sche roos, and worschipide lowe to erthe, and seide, Lo! thi seruauntesse be in to an handmayde, that sche waische the feet of the seruauntis of my lord.

42 And Abigail hastide, and roos, and stiede on an asse; and fyue damesels, sueris of hir feet, yeden with hir, and sche suede the messangeris of Dauid, and was maad wijf to hym.

43 But also Dauid took Achynoem of Jezrael, and euer eithir was wijf to hym;

44 forsothe Saul yaf Mycol his douytir, wijf of Dauid, to Phalti, the sone of Lais, that was of Gallym.

CAP 26

1 And Zipheis camen to Saul in to Gabaa, and seiden, Lo! Dauid is hidde in the hille of Achille, which is 'euene ayens the wildirnesse.

2 And Saul roos, and yede doun in to deseert of Ziph, and with hym thre thousynde of men of the chosun of Israel, that he schulde seke Dauid in the desert of Ziph.

3 And Saul settide tentis in Gabaa of Achille, that was euen ayens the wildirnesse in the weie. Sotheli Dauid dwellide in deseert. Forsothe Dauid siy that Saul hadde come aftir hym in to deseert;

4 and Dauid sente aspieris, and lernede moost certeynli, that Saul hadde come thidur.

5 And Dauid roos priueli, and cam to the place where Saul was. And whanne Dauid hadde seyn the place, wher ynne Saul slepte, and Abner, the sone of Ner, the prince of his chyualrye, and Saul slepynge in the tente, and the tother comyn puple bi his cumpas, Dauid seide to Achymelech,

6 Ethey, and to Abisai, sone of Saruye, the brother of Joab, 'and seide, Who schal go doun with me to Saul in to 'the castels? And Abisai seide, Y schal go doun with thee.

7 Therfor Dauid and Abisai camen to the puple in the nyyt, and thei founden Saul lyggynge and slepynge in 'the tente, and a spere sette faste in the erthe at his heed; 'forsothe thei founden Abner and the puple slepynge in his cumpas.

8 And Abisay seide to Dauid, God hath closid to dai thin enemy in to thin hondis; now therfor Y schal peerse hym with a spere onys in the erthe, and 'no nede schal be the secounde tyme.

9 And Dauid seide to Abysai, Sle thou not hym, for who schal holde forth his hond into the crist of the Lord, and schal be innocent?

10 And Dauid seide, The Lord lyueth, for no but the Lord smyte hym, ether his dai come that he die, ether he go doun in to batel and perische;

11 the Lord be merciful to me, that Y holde not forth myn hond in to the crist of the Lord; now therfor take thou the spere, which is at his heed, and 'take thou the cuppe of watir, and go we awei.

12 Dauid took the spere, and the cuppe of watir, that was at the heed of Saul, and thei yeden forth, and no man was that siy, and vndirstood, and wakide, but alle men slepten; for the sleep of the Lord 'hadde feld on hem.

13 And whanne Dauid hadde passid euene ayens, and hadde stonde on the cop of the hil afer, and a greet space was bit-wixe hem,

14 Dauid criede to the puple, and to Abner, the sone of Ner, and seide, Abner, whether thou schalt not answere? And Abner answeride, and seide, Who art thou, that criest, and disesist the kyng?

15 And Dauith seide to Abner, Whether thou art not a man, and what other man is lijk thee in Israel? whi therfor 'kepist thou not thi lord the kyng? 'For o man of the cumpanye entride, that he schulde sle thi lord the kyng;

16 this that thou hast doon, is not good; the Lord lyueth, for ye ben sones of deeth, that kepten not youre lord, the crist of the Lord. Now therfor se thou, where is the spere of the kyng, and where is the cuppe of watir, that weren at his heed.

17 Forsothe Saul knew the vois of Dauid, and seide, Whether this vois is thin, my sone Dauid? And Dauid seide, My lord the kyng, it is my vois.

18 And Dauid seide, For what cause pursueth my lord his seruaunt? What haue Y do, ether what yuel is in myn hond? Now therfor,

19 my lord the kyng, Y preye, here the wordis of thi seruaunt; if the Lord stirith thee ayens me, the sacrifice be smellid; for-sothe if sones of men stiren thee, thei ben cursid in the siyt of the Lord, whiche han cast me out 'to dai, that Y dwelle not in the erytage of the Lord, and seien, Go thou, serue thou alien goddis.

20 And now my blood be not sched out in the erthe bifor the Lord; for the kyng of Israel yede out, that he seke a quike fle, as a partrich is pursuede in hillis.

21 And Saul seide, Y synnede; turne ayen, my sone Dauid, for Y schal no more do yuel to thee, for my lijf was precious to day in thin iyen; for it semeth, that Y dide folili, and Y vnknew ful many thingis.

22 And Dauid answeride and seide, Lo! the spere of the kyng, oon of the 'children of the kyng passe, and take it; forsothe the Lord schal yelde to ech man bi his riytfulnesse and feith;

23 for the Lord bitook thee to dai in to myn hond, and Y nolde holde forth myn hond in to the crist of the Lord;

24 and as thi lijf is magnified to dai in myn iyen, so my lijf be magnyfied in the iyen of the Lord, and delyuere he me fro al angwisch.

25 Therfor Saul seide to Dauid, Blessid be thou, my sone Dauid; and sotheli thou doynge schalt do, and thou myyti schalt be myyti. Therfor Dauid yede in to his weie, and Saul turnede ayen in to his place.

CAP 27

1 And Dauid seide in his herte, Sumtyme Y schal falle in o dai in the hond of Saul; whether it is not betere, that Y fle, and be sauyd in the lond of Filisteis, that Saul dispeire, and

cesse to seke me in alle the endis of Israel; therfor fle we hise hondis.

2 And Dauid roos, and yede, he and sixe hundrid men with hym, to Achis, the sone of Maoth, kyng of Geth.

3 And Dauid dwellide with Achis in Geth, he, and hise men, and his hows; Dauid, and hise twei wyues, Achynoem of Jezrael, and Abigail, the wijf of Nabal of Carmele.

4 And it was teld to Saul, that Dauid fledde in to Geth; and he addide no more 'that he schulde seke Dauid.

5 Forsothe Dauid seide to Achis, If Y haue founden grace in thin iyen, a place be youun to me in oon of the citees of this cuntrey, that Y dwelle there; for whi dwellith thi seruaunt in the citee of the kyng with thee?

6 Therfor Achis yaf to hym Sichelech in that dai, for which cause Sichelech was maad in to the possessioun of the kyngis of Juda 'til in to this dai.

7 Forsothe the noumbre of daies, in whiche Dauid dwellide in the cuntrei of Filisteis, was of foure monethis.

8 And Dauid stiede, and hise men, and token preies of Geth-suri, and of Gethri, and of men of Amalech; for these townes weren enhabitid bi eld tyme in the lond, to men goynge to Sur, 'til to the lond of Egipt.

9 And Dauid smoot al the lond of hem, and lefte not man 'lyuynge and womman; and he took scheep, and oxun, and assis, and camels, and clothis, and turnede ayen, and cam to Achis.

10 Sotheli Achis seide to hym, 'In to whom 'hurliden ye to dai? Dauid answeride, Ayens the south of Juda, and ayens the south of Hiramel, and ayens the south of Ceney.

11 Dauid left not quik man and womman, nether brouyte 'in to Geth, and se ide, Lest perauenture thei speken ayens vs. Dauid dide these thingis, and this was his doom, in alle daies in whiche he dwellide in the cuntrei of Filisteis.

12 Therfor Achis bileuyde to Dauid, and seide, Forsothe he wrouyte many yuelis ayens his puple Israel, therfor he schal be euerlastynge seruaunt to me.

CAP 28

1 Forsothe it was doon in tho daies, Filisteis gaderiden her cumpenyes, that thei schulden be maad redi ayens Israel to batel. And Achis seide to Dauid, Thou witynge 'wite now, for thou schalt go out with me in castels, thou and thi men.

2 And Dauid seide to Achis, Now thou schalt wyte what thingis thi seruaunt schal do. And Achis seide to Dauid, And Y schal sette thee kepere of myn heed in alle dayes.

3 Forsothe Samuel was deed, and al Israel biweilide hym, and thei birieden hym in Ramatha, his citee. And Saul dide awey fro the lond witchis and fals dyuynours, 'and he slouy hem that hadden 'charmers of deuelis 'in her wombe.

4 And Filisteis weren gaderid, and camen, and settiden tentis in Sunam; sotheli and Saul gaderide al Israel, and cam in to Gelboe.

5 And Saul siy the castels of Filisteis, and he dredde, and his herte dredde greetli.

6 And he counselide the Lord; and the Lord answeride not to hym, nether bi preestis, nether bi dremes, nether bi profetis.

7 And Saul seide to hise seruauntis, Seke ye to me a womman hauynge a feend spekynge in the wombe; and Y schal go to hir, and Y schal axe bi hir. And hise seruauntis seiden to hym, A womman hauynge a feend spekynge in the wombe is in Endor.

8 Therfor Saul chaungide his clothing, and he was clothid with othere clothis; and he yede, and twei men with hym; and

thei camen to the womman in the nyyt. And he seyde, Dyuyne thou to me in a fend spekynge in the wombe, and reise thou to me whom Y schal seie to thee.

9 And the womman seide to hym, Lo! thou woost hou grete thingis Saul hath do, and hou he dide awei fro the lond witchis, and fals dyuynours; whi therfor settist thou tresoun to my lijf, that Y be slayn?

10 And Saul swoor to hir in the Lord, and seide, The Lord lyueth; for no thing of yuel schal come to thee for this thing.

11 And the womman seide to hym, Whom schal Y reise to thee? And he seide, Reise thou Samuel to me.

12 Sotheli whanne the womman hadde seyn Samuel, sche criede with greet vois, and seide to Saul, Whi hast thou disseyued me? for thou art Saul.

13 And the kyng seide to hir, Nyl thou drede; what hast thou seyn? And the womman seide to Saul, Y siy goddis stiynge fro erthe.

14 And Saul seide to hir, What maner forme is of hym? And sche seide, An eld man stieth, and he is clothid with a mentil. And Saul vndirstood that it was Samuel; and Saul bowide hym silf on his face to the erthe, and worschipide.

15 Sotheli Samuel seide to Saul, Whi hast thou disesid me, that Y schulde be reisid? And Saul seide, Y am constreyned greetli; for Filisteis fiyten ayens me, and God yede awei fro me, and he nolde here me, nether bi the hond of profetis, nether bi dremes; therfor Y clepide thee, that thou schuldist schewe to me what Y schal do.

16 And Samuel seide, What axist thou me, whanne God hath go awei fro thee, and passide to thin enemy?

17 For the Lord schal do to thee as he spak in myn hond, and he schal kitte awey thi rewme fro thin hond, and he schal yyue it to Dauid, thi neiybore;

18 for thou obeiedist not to the vois of the Lord, nether didist the 'ire of hys strong veniaunce in Amalech. Therfor the Lord hath do to thee to day that that thou suffrist;

19 and the Lord schal yyue also Israel with thee in the hond of Filisteis. Forsothe to morewe thou and thi sones schulen be with me; but also the Lord schal bitake the castels of Israel in the hond of Filistiym.

20 And anoon Saul felde stretchid forth to erthe; for he dredde the wordis of Samuel, and strengthe was not in hym, for he hadde not ete breed in al that dai and al nyyt.

21 Therfor thilke womman entride to Saul, and seide; for he was disturblid greetli; and sche seide to hym, Lo! thin hand-mayde obeiede to thi vois, and Y haue put my lijf in myn hond, and Y herde thi wordis, whiche thou spakist to me.

22 Now therfor and thou here the vois of thin handmaide, and Y schal sette a mussel of breed bifor thee, and that thou etynge wexe strong, and maist do the iourney.

23 And he forsook, and seide, Y schal not ete. Sothely hise seruauntis and the womman compelliden hym; and at the laste, whanne the vois of hem was herd, he roos fro the erthe, and sat on the bed.

24 Sotheli thilke womman hadde a fat calf in the hows, and 'sche hastide, and killide hym; and sche took mele, and med-dlide it, and made therf breed;

25 and settide bifor Saul and bifor hise seruauntis, and whanne thei hadden ete, thei risiden, and walkiden bi al that nyyt.

CAP 29

1 Therfor alle the cumpenyes of Filisteis weren gaderid in Aphec, but also Israel settide tentis aboue the welle that was in Jezrael.

2 And sotheli the princis of Filisteis yeden in cumpenyes of an hundrid, and in thousyndis; forsothe Dauid and hise men weren in the laste cumpenye with Achis.

3 And the princes of Filisteis seiden to Achis, What wolen these Ebreis to hem silf? And Achis seide to the princes of Filisteis, Whether ye knowen not Dauid, that was the seruaunt of Saul, kyng of Israel? and he was with me in many daies, 'ether yeeris, and Y foond not in hym ony thing, fro the dai, in which he fledde to me 'til to this dai.

4 Sotheli the princes of Filisteis weren wrooth ayens hym, and seiden to hym, The man turne ayen, and sitte in his place, in which thou hast ordened hym, and come he not doun with vs in to batel, lest he be maad aduersarie to vs, whanne we han bigunne to fiyte; for hou mai he plese his lord in other maner, no but in oure heedis?

5 Whether this is not Dauid, to whom thei sungen in daunsis, and seiden, Saul smoot in thousyndis, and Dauid smoot in hise ten thousyndis?

6 Therfor Achis clepide Dauid, and seide to hym, The Lord lyueth; for thou art riytful, and good in my siyt, and thi goyng out and 'thin entryng is with me in castels, and Y 'foond not in thee ony thing of yuel, fro the day in which thou camest to me til to this dai; but thou plesist not the princis.

7 Therfor turne thou ayen, and go in pees, and offende thou not the iyen of princis of Filisteis.

8 And Dauid seide to Achis, Forsothe what 'dide Y, and what hast thou founde in me thi seruaunt, fro the dai in which Y was in thi siyt til in to this dai, that Y come not, and fiyte ayens the enemyes of my lord the kyng?

9 Forsothe Achis answeride, and spak to Dauid, Y woot that thou art good, and as the aungel of God in my iyen; but the princes of Filisteis seyden, He schal not stie with vs in to batel.

10 Therfor rise thou eerli, thou, and thi seruauntis that camen with thee; and whanne ye han ryse bi nyyt, and it bigynneth to be cleer, go ye.

11 Therfor Dauid roos bi nyyt, he and hise men, that thei schulden go forth eerli, and turne ayen to the lond of Fylisteis; sotheli Filisteis stieden in to Jezrael.

CAP 30

1 And whanne Dauid and hise men hadden come 'in to Sichelech in the thridde dai, men of Amalech hadden maad asauyt on the south part in Sichelech; and thei smytiden Sichelech, and brenten it bi fier.

2 And thei ledden the wymmen prisoneris fro thennus, fro the leeste 'til to the grete; and thei hadden not slayn ony, but thei ledden with hem, and yeden in her weie.

3 Therfor whanne Dauid and hise men hadde come to the citee, and hadden founde it brent bi fier, and that her wyues, and her sones, and douytris weren led prisoneris,

4 Dauid and the puple that was with hym reisiden her voices, and weiliden, til teeris failiden in hem.

5 Forsothe also twei wyues of Dauid weren led prisoneris, Achynoem of Jezrael, and Abigail, the wijf of Nabal of Car-mele.

6 And Dauid was ful sori; forsothe al the puple wold stone hym, for the soule of ech man was bittir on her sones and douytris. Forsothe Dauid was coumfortid in his Lord God.

7 And he seide to Abiathar, preest, the sone of Achymelech, Bringe thou ephoth to me. And Abiathar brouyte ephoth to Dauid; and Dauid councelide the Lord,

8 and seide, Schal Y pursue, ether nay, 'these theues? and schal Y take hem? And the Lord seide to hym, Pursue thou; for with out doute thou schalt take hem, and thou schalt take awey the prey.

9 Therfor Dauid yede, he and sixe hundrid men that weren with hym, and thei camen 'til to the stronde of Besor; and sotheli the wery men abididen.

10 Forsothe Dauid pursuede, he and foure hundrid men; for twei hundrid abididen, that weren weeri, and myyten not passe the stronde of Besor.

11 And thei founden a man of Egipte in the feeld, and thei brouyten hym to Dauid; and thei yauen 'breed to hym, that he schulde ete, and 'schulde drynke watir;

12 but also thei yauen to hym a gobet of a bundel of drye figis, and twei byndyngis of dried grapis. And whanne he hadde ete tho, his spirit turnede ayen, and he was coumfortid; for he hadde not ete breed, nether hadde drunk watir in thre daies and thre nyytis.

13 Therfor Dauid seide to hym, Whos man art thou, ethir fro whennus and whidur goist thou? And he seide, Y am a child of Egipt, the seruaunt of a man of Amalech; forsothe my lord forsook me, for Y bigan to be sijk the thridde dai ago.

14 Sotheli we braken out to the south coost of Cerethi, and ayens Juda, and to the south of Caleb, and we brenten Sichelech bi fier.

15 And Dauid seide to hym, Maist thou lede me to this cumpeny? Which seide, Swere thou to me bi God, that thou schalt not sle me, and schalt not bitake me in to the hondis of my lord; and Y schal lede thee to this cumpeny. And Dauid swoor to hym.

16 And whanne the child hadde ledde hym, lo! thei saten at the mete, on the face of al the erthe, etynge and drynkynge, and as halewynge a feeste, for al the prey and spuylis whiche thei hadden take of the lond of Filisteis, and of the lond of Juda.

17 And Dauid smoot hem fro euentid 'til to euentid of the tothir dai, and not ony of hem escapide, no but foure hundrid yonge men, that stieden on camels, and fledden.

18 Forsothe Dauid delyuerede alle thingis whiche the men of Amalech token, and he delyuerede hise twei wyues;

19 nether ony of hem failide fro litil 'til to greet, as wel of sones as of douytris, and of spuylis; and what euer thingis thei hadden rauyschid, Dauid ledde ayen alle thingis;

20 and he took alle flockis and grete beestis, and droof bifor his face. And thei seiden, This is the prey of Dauid.

21 Forsothe Dauid cam to twei hundrid men, that weren weeri, and abididen, and myyten not sue Dauid; and he hadde comaundid hem to sitte in the stronde of Besor; whiche yeden out ayens Dauid, and the puple that was with hym. Forsothe Dauid neiyede to the puple, and grette it pesibli.

22 And o man, the werste and vniust of the men that weren with Dauid, answeride, and seide, For thei camen not with vs, we schulen not yyue to hem ony thing of the prey, which we rauyschiden, but his wijf and children 'suffice to ech man; and whanne thei han take hem, go thei awei.

23 Forsothe Dauid seide, My britheren, ye schulen not do so of these thingis, whiche the Lord yaf to vs, and kepte vs, and yaf the theues, that braken out ayens vs, in to oure hondis;

24 nether ony man schal here vs on this word. For euene part schal be of him that goith doun to batel, and of hym that dwellith at the fardelis; and in lijk maner thei schulen departe.

25 And this was maad a constitucioun and doom fro that dai and afterward, and as a lawe in Israel til in to this dai.

26 Therfor Dauid cam in to Sichelech, and sente yiftis of the prey to the eldere men of Juda, hise neiyboris, and seide, Take ye blessyng of the prey of enemyes of the Lord;

27 to hem that weren in Bethel, and that weren in Ramoth, at the south,

28 and that weren in Jether, and that weren in Aroer, and that weren in Sephamoth, and that weren in Escama, and that weren in Rethala,

29 and that weren in the citees of Jeramel, and that weren in the citees of Ceny,

30 and that weren in Arama, and that weren in Lautuasam, and that weren in Athec,

31 and that weren in Ebron, and to othere men, that weren in these places, in whiche Dauid dwellide and hise men.

CAP 31

1 Forsothe Filisteis fouyten ayens Israel, and the men of Israel fledden bifor the face of Filisteis, and felden slayn in the hil of Gelboe.

2 And Filisteis hurliden on Saul, and on hise sones, and smytiden Jonathas, and Amynadab, and Melchisua, sones of Saul.

3 And al the weiyte of batel was turned 'in to Saul; and men archeris pursueden hym, and he was woundid greetli of the archeris.

4 And Saul seide to his squyer, Drawe out thi swerd, and sle me, lest perauenture these vncircumcidid men come, and sle me, and scorne me. And his squyer nolde, for he was aferd bi ful grete drede; therfor Saul took his swerd, and felde theronne.

5 And whanne his squyer hadde seyn this, 'that is, that Saul was deed, also he felde on his swerd and was deed with hym.

6 Therfor Saul was deed, and hise thre sones, and his squyer, and alle his men in that dai togidere.

7 Forsothe the sones of Israel, that weren biyendis the valei, and biyendis Jordan, sien that the men of Israel hadden fled, and that Saul was deed, and hise sones, and thei leften her citees and fledden; and Filisteis camen, and dwelliden there.

8 Forsothe in 'the tother dai maad, Filisteis camen, that thei schulden dispuyle the slayn men, and thei founden Saul, and hise thre sones, liggynge in the hil of Gelboe; and thei kittiden awei the heed of Saul,

9 and dispuyliden hym of armeris; and senten in to the lond of Filisteis bi cumpas, that it schulde be teld in the temple of idols, and in the puplis.

10 And thei puttiden hise armeris in the temple of Astoroth; sotheli thei hangiden his bodi in the wal of Bethsan.

11 And whanne the dwellers of Jabes of Galaad hadden herd this, what euer thingis Filisteis hadden do to Saul,

12 alle the strongeste men risiden, and yeden in al that nyyt, and token the deed bodi of Saul, and the deed bodies of hise sones fro the wal of Bethsan; and the men of Jabes of Galaad camen, and brenten tho deed bodies bi fier.

13 And thei token the boonus of hem, and birieden in the wode of Jabes, and fastiden bi seuene daies.

2 KINGS

CAP 1

1 Forsothe it was doon, after that Saul was deed, that Dauid turnede ayen fro the sleyng of Amalech, and dwellide twei daies in Sichelech.

2 Forsothe in the thridde dai a man apperide, comynge fro the castels of Saul with the cloth to-rent, and his heed spreynt with dust; and as he cam to Dauid, he felde on his face, and worschipide.

3 And Dauid seide to hym, Fro whennus comest thou? Which seide to Dauid, Y fledde fro the castels of Israel.

4 And Dauid seide to hym, What is the word which is doon; schewe thou to me. And he seide, The puple fledde fro the batel, and many of the puple felden, and ben deed; but also Saul, and Jonathas, his sonne, perischyden.

5 And Dauid seide to the yong man, that telde to hym, Wherof woost thou, that Saul is deed, and Jonathas, his sonne?

6 And the yong man seide, that telde to hym, Bi hap Y cam in to the hil of Gelboe, and Saul lenyde on his spere; forsothe charis and knyytis neiyiden to hym;

7 and he turnede bihynde his bak, 'and siy me, and clepide. To whom whanne Y hadde answeride, Y am present; he seide to me, Who art thou?

8 And Y seide to hym, Y am a man of Amalech.

9 And he spak to me, Stonde thou on me, and sle me; for angwischis holden me, and yit al my lijf is in me.

10 And Y stood on hym, and Y killide hym; for Y wiste that he myyte not lyue aftir the fallyng; and Y took the diademe, that was in his heed, and the bye fro his arm, and Y brouyte hidur to thee, my lord.

11 Forsothe Dauid took and to-rente hise clothis, and the men that weren with hym;

12 and thei weiliden, and wepten, and fastiden 'til to euentid, on Saul, and Jonathas, his sone, and on the puple of the Lord, and on the hows of Israel, for thei hadden feld bi swerd.

13 And Dauid seide to the yong man, that telde to him, Of whennus art thou? And he answeride, Y am the sone of a man comelyng, of a man of Amalech.

14 And Dauid seide to him, Whi dreddist thou not to sende thine hond, that thou schuldist sle the crist of the Lord?

15 And Dauid clepide oon of hise children, and seide, Go thou, and falle on hym. Which smoot that yong man, and he was deed.

16 And Dauid seide to hym, Thi blood be on thin heed; for thi mouth spak ayens thee, and seide, Y killide the crist of the Lord.

17 Forsooth Dauid biweilide sych a weilyng on Saul, and on Jonathas, his sone;

18 and comaundide, that thei schulden teche the sones of Juda weilyng, as it is writun in the Book of Just Men. And Dauid seyde, Israel, biholde thou, for these men that ben deed, woundid on thin hiye placis;

19 the noble men of Israel ben slayn on thin hillis.

20 Hou felden stronge men? nyle ye telle in Geth, nether telle ye in the weilottis of Ascolon; lest perauenture the douytris of Filisteis be glad, lest the douytris of vncircumcidid men 'be glad.

21 Hillis of Gelboe, neither dew nethir reyn come on you, nether the feeldis of firste fruytis be; for the scheeld of stronge men was cast awey there, the scheeld of Saul, as 'if he were not anoyntid with oile.

22 Of the blood of slayn men, of the fatnesse of strong men, the arewe of Jonathas yede neuer abak, and the swerd of Saul turnede not ayen void.

23 Saul and Jonathas amyable, and fair in her lijf, weren not departid also in deeth; thei weren swiftere than eglis, strongere than liouns.

24 Douytris of Israel, wepe ye on Saul, that clothide you with fyn reed colourid in delicis, that yaf goldun ournementis to youre atyre.

25 Hou 'felden doun stronge men in batel?

26 Jonathas was slayn in the hiye places. Y make sorewe on thee, my brother Jonathas, ful fair, 'and amyable more than the loue of wymmen; as a modir loueth oon aloone sone, so Y louyde thee.

27 Hou therfor 'felden doun stronge men, and armeris of batel perischide?

CAP 2

1 Therfor aftir these thingis Dauid counseilide the Lord, and seide, Whether Y schal stie in to oon of the citees of Juda? And the Lord seide to hym, Stie thou. And Dauid seide to the Lord, Whidur schal Y stie? And the Lord answeride to hym, In to Ebron.

2 Therfor Dauid stiede, and hise twei wyues, Achynoem of Jezrael, and Abigail, the wijf of Nabal of Carmele.

3 But also Dauid ledde the men that weren with hym, ech man with his hows; and thei dwelliden in the townes of Ebron.

4 And the men of Juda camen, and anoyntiden there Dauid, that he schulde regne on the hows of Juda. And it was teld to Dauid, that men of Jabes of Galaad hadden biried Saul.

5 Therfor Dauid sente messangeris to the men of Jabes of Galaad, and seide to hem, Blessid be ye of the Lord, that diden this mercy with your lord Saul, and birieden hym.

6 And now sotheli the Lord schal yelde to you merci and treuthe, but also Y schal yelde thankyng, for ye diden this word.

7 Youre hondis be coumfortid, and be ye sones of strengthe; for thouy youre lord Saul is deed, netheles the hows of Juda anoyntide me kyng to 'hym silf.

8 Forsothe Abner, the sone of Ner, prince of the oost of Saul, took Isbosech, the sone of Saul, and ledde hym aboute bi the castels,

9 and made him kyng on Galaad, and on Gethsury, and on Jezrael, and on Effraym, and on Beniamyn, and on al Israel.

10 Isbosech, the sone of Saul, was of fourti yeer, whanne he began to regne on Israel; and he regnede twei yeer. Sotheli the hous aloone of Juda suede Dauid.

11 And the noumbre of daies, bi whiche Dauid dwellide regnynge in Ebron on the hows of Juda, was of seuene yeer and sixe monethis.

12 And Abner, the sone of Ner, yede out, and the children of Isbosech, sone of Saul, fro the castels in Gabaon.

13 Forsothe Joab, the sone of Saruye, and the children of Dauid yeden out, and camen to hem bisidis the cisterne in Gabaon. And whanne thei hadden come togidere in to o place euene ayens, these saten on o part of the cisterne, and thei on the tother.

14 And Abner seide to Joab, 'The children rise, and plei befor us. And Joab answeride, Rise thei.

15 Therfor thei risiden, and passiden twelue in noumbre of Beniamyn, of the part of Isbosech, sone of Saul; and twelue of the children of Dauid.

16 And ech man, whanne 'the heed of his felowe was takun, fastnede the swerde in to the side of 'the contrarye; and thei felden doun togidere. And the name of that place was clepid The Feeld of stronge men in Gabaon.

17 And 'batel hard ynow roos in that dai; and Abner and the sones of Israel 'weren dryuun of the children of Dauid.

18 Forsothe thre sones of Saruye weren there, Joab, and Abisai, and Asahel; forsothe Asahel was a 'rennere moost swift, as oon of the capretis that dwellen in woodis.

19 Forsothe Asahel pursuede Abner, and bowide not, nether to the riyt side nether to the left side, ceessynge to pursue Abner.

20 Therfor Abner bihelde bihynde his bac, and seide, Whether thou art Asahel?

21 Which answeride, Y am. And Abner seide to hym, Go to the riytside, ether to the lefte side; and take oon of the yonge men, and take to thee hise spuylis. Sotheli Asahel nolde ceesse, that ne he pursuede hym.

22 And eft Abner spak to Asahel, Go thou awei; nyle thou pursue me, lest Y be compellid to peerse thee in to erthe, and Y schal not mowe reise my face to Joab, thi brother.

23 And Asahel dispiside to here, and nolde bowe awey. Therfor Abner smoot him 'with the spere turned awei in the schar, and roof thorouy, and he was deed in the same place; and alle men that passiden bi the place, in which place Asahel felde doun, and was deed, stoden stille.

24 Forsothe while Joab and Abisai pursueden Abner fleynge, the sunne yede doun; and thei camen til to the litil hil of the water cundiyt, which is euene ayens the valey, and the weie of deseert in Gabaon.

25 And the sones of Beniamyn weren gaderid to Abner, and thei weren gaderid togidere in to o cumpeny, and stoden in the hiynesse of oon heep of erthe.

26 And Abner criede to Joab, and seide, Whether thi swerd schal be feers 'til to sleyng? Whether thou knowist not, that dispeir is perelouse? Hou longe seist thou not to the puple, that it ceesse to pursue hise britheren?

27 And Joab seyde, The Lord lyueth, for if thou haddist spoke eerli, the puple pursuynge his brother hadde go awey.

28 And Joab sownede with a clarioun, and al the oost stood; and thei pursueden no ferthere Israel, nether bigunnen batel.

29 Forsothe Abner and hise men yeden by the feeldi places of Moab in al that nyyt, and passiden Jordan; and whanne al Bethoron was compassid, thei camen to the castels.

30 Sotheli whanne Abner was left, Joab turnede ayen, and gaderide togidere al the puple; and ten men and nyne, outakun Asahel, failiden of the children of Dauid.

31 Forsothe the seruauntis of Dauid smytiden of Beniamyn, and of the men that weren with Abner, thre hundrid men and sixti, whiche also weren deed.

32 And thei token Asahel, and birieden hym in the sepulcre of his fadir in Bethleem. And Joab, and the men that weren with hym, yeden in al that nyyt, and in thilke morewtid thei camen in to Ebron.

CAP 3

1 Therfor long strijf was maad bitwixe the hows of Dauid and 'bitwixe the hows of Saul; and Dauid profitide and euere was strongere than hym silf, forsothe the hows of Saul decreesside ech dai.

2 And sones weren borne to Dauid in Ebron; and his firste gendrid sone was Amon, of Achynoem of Jezrael;

3 and aftir hym was Celeab, of Abigail, wijf of Nabal of Carmele; sotheli the thrydde was Absolon, the sone of Maacha, douytir of Tholomay, kyng of Gessur;

4 forsothe the fourthe was Adonyas, the sone of Agith; and the fyuethe was Saphacias, the sone of Abitail; and the sixte was Gethraam of Egla,

5 the wijf of Dauid. These weren borne to Dauid in Ebron.

6 Therfor whanne batel was bytwixe the hows of Saul and the hows of Dauid, Abner, the sone of Ner, gouernyde the hows of Saul.

7 Sotheli a concubyn, that is, a secoundarie wijf, Respha bi name, the douytir of Achia, 'was to Saul; and Abner entride to hir.

8 And Isbosech seide to Abner, Whi 'entridist thou to the concubyn of my fadir? Which was wrooth greetli for the wordis of Isbosech, and seide, Whether Y am the heed of a dogge ayens Juda to dai, and Y have do merci on the hous of Saul, thi fadir, and on hise britheren, and neiyboris, and Y bitook not thee in to the hondis of David, and thou hast souyt in me that, that thou schuldist repreue me for a womman to dai?

9 God do these thingis to Abner, and adde these thingis to hym, no but as the Lord swoor to Dauid, 'so Y do with hym,

10 that the rewme be translatid fro the hous of Saul, and the trone of Dauid be reisid on Israel and on Juda, fro Dan 'til to Bersabee.

11 And Isbosech myyte not answere ony thing to Abner, for he dredde Abner.

12 Therfor Abner sente messangeris to Dauid, and thei seiden 'for hym, Whos is the lond? and that the messangeris schulden speke, Make thou frenschipis with me, and myn hond schal be with thee, and Y schal brynge al Israel to thee.

13 And Dauid seide, Best Y schal make frenschipis with thee, but Y axe of thee o thing, and seie, Thou schalt not se my face, bifore that thou brynge Mycol, the douyter of Saul, and so thou schalt come, and schalt se me.

14 Therfor Dauid sente messangeris to Isbosech, the sone of Saul, and seide, Yelde thou my wijf Mycol, whom Y spouside to me for an hundryd prepucies of Filisteis.

15 Therfor Isbosech sente, and took hir fro hir hosebonde, Faltiel, son of Lais;

16 and hir hosebonde suede hir and wepte til Bahurym. And Abner seide to hym, Go thou, and turne ayen; and he turnede ayen.

17 Also Abner brouyte in a word to the eldere men of Israel, and seide, Bothe yistirdai and the thridde dai ago ye souyten Dauid, that he schulde regne on you.

18 Now therfor do ye; for the Lord spak to Dauid, and seide, In the hond of my seruaunt Dauid Y schal saue my puple Israel fro the hond of Filisteis, and of alle his enemyes.

19 Forsothe Abner spak also to Beniamyn, and he yede, that he schulde speke to Dauid, in Ebron, alle thingis that plesiden Israel and al Beniamin.

20 And he cam to Dauid in Ebron with twenti men. And Dauid made a feeste to Abner, and to the men that camen with hym.

21 And Abner seide to Dauid, Y schal rise, that Y gadere al Israel to thee, my lord the kyng, and that Y make boond of pees with thee, and that thou regne on alle, as thi soule desirith. Therfor whanne Dauid hadde ledde forth Abner, and he hadde go in pees,

22 anoon the children of Dauid and Joab camen with a ful grete prey, whanne theues weren slayn; sotheli Abner was not

with Dauid, in Ebron, for Dauid hadde left hym, and he yede forth in pees.

23 And Joab, and the oostis that weren with hym, camen aftirward; therfor it was teld to Joab of telleris, Abner, the sone of Ner, cam to the kyng, and the kyng lefte hym, and he yede in pees.

24 And Joab entride to the kyng, and seide, What hast thou do? Lo! Abner cam to thee; whi leftist thou hym, and he yede, and departide?

25 Knowist thou not Abner, the sone of Ner, for herto he cam to thee, that he schulde disseyue thee, and that he schulde knowe thi going out and thin entryng, and schulde knowe alle thingis whiche thou doist?

26 Therfor Joab yede out fro Dauid, and sente messangeris aftir Abner; and 'ledde hym ayen fro the cisterne of Cyrie, 'while Dauid knew not.

27 And whanne Abner hadde come ayen in to Ebron, Joab ledde hym asidis half to 'the myddil of the yate, that he schulde speke to hym in gile; and he smoot Abner there in the schar, and he was deed, in to the veniaunce of the blood of his brother Asahel.

28 That whanne Dauid hadde herd the thing doon, he seide, Y am clene and my rewme anentis God til in to with outen ende fro the blood of Abner, sone of Ner;

29 and come it on the heed of Joab, and on al the hows of his fadir; a man suffrynge flux of seed, and a leprouse man, holdynge spyndil, and fallynge bi swerd, and hauynge nede to breed, 'that is, suffrynge hungur, 'faile not of the hows of Joab.

30 Therfor Joab, and Abisay, his brother, killiden Abner, for he hadde slayn Asahel, her brother, in Gabaon, in batel.

31 Forsothe Dauid seide to Joab, and to al the puple that was with hym, To rende ye your clothis, and be ye gird with sackis, and biweile ye bifor the heersis, 'ether dirige, of Abner. Forsothe kyng Dauid suede the beere.

32 And whanne thei hadden biried Abner in Ebron, kyng Dauid reiside his vois, and wepte on the biriel of Abner; 'forsothe and al the puple wepte.

33 And the kyng biweilide, and bymorenyde Abner, and seide, Abner, thou diedist not as dredeful men, 'ethir cowardis, ben wont to die.

34 Thin hondis weren not boundun, and thi feet weren not greuyd with stockis, but thou feldist doun, as men ben wont to falle bifor the sones of wickidnesse. And al the puple doublide togidere, and wepte on hym.

35 And whanne al the multitude cam to take mete with Dauid, while the dai was yit cleer, Dauid swoor, and seide, God do to me these thingis, and adde these thingis, if Y schal taast breed ethir ony othir thing bifor the going doun of the sune.

36 And al the puple herde; and alle thingis which the kyng dide in the siyt of al the puple plesiden hem;

37 and al the comyn puple and al Israel knewe in that day, that it was not doon of the kyng, that Abner, the sone of Ner, was slayn.

38 Also the kyng seide to hise seruauntis, Whether ye witen not, that the prince and gretteste felde doun to dai in Israel?

39 Forsothe Y am 'delicat, ether tendir, yit and anoyntid kyng; sotheli these sones of Saruye ben hard to me; the Lord yelde to hym that doith yuel bi his malice.

CAP 4

1 Forsothe Isbosech, the sone of Saul, herde that Abner hadde falde doun in Ebron; and 'hise hondis weren discoumfortid, and al Israel was disturblid.

2 Forsothe twei men, princes of theues, weren to the sone of Saul; name to oon was Baana, and name to the tother was Rechab, the sones of Remmon Berothite, of the sones of Beniamyn; for also Beroth is arettid in Beniamyn.

3 And men of Beroth fledden in to Gethaym; and thei weren comelyngis there 'til to that tyme.

4 Forsothe a sone feble in feet was to Jonathas, the sone of Saul; forsothe he was fyue yeer eld, whanne the messanger cam fro Saul and Jonathas, fro Jezrael. Therfor his nurse took hym, and fledde; and whanne sche hastide to fle, sche felde doun, and the child was maad lame; and 'he hadde a name Myphibosech.

5 Therfor Rechab and Baana, sones of Remmon of Beroth, camen, and entriden in the hoot dai in to the hows of Isbosech, that slepte on his bed in myd dai, 'and the womman oischer of the hous clensynge wheete, slepte strongli.

6 Forsothe thei entriden into the hows pryueli, and token eeris of whete; and Rechab, and Baana, his brother, smytiden Isbosech in the schar, and fledden.

7 Sotheli whanne thei hadden entrid in to the hous, he slepte on his bedde in a closet; and thei smytiden and killiden hym; and whanne 'his heed was takun, thei yeden bi the weie of deseert in al the nyyt.

8 And thei brouyten the heed of Isbosech to Dauid, in Ebron, and thei seiden to the kyng, Lo! the heed of Isbosech, sone of Saul, thin enemy, that souyte thi lijf; and the Lord yaf to dai to oure lord the kyng veniaunce of Saul and of his seed.

9 Forsothe Dauid answeride to Rechab, and Baana, his brother, the sones of Remmon of Beroth, and seide to hem, The Lord lyueth, that delyueride my lijf fro al angwisch;

10 for Y helde hym that telde to me, and seide, Saul is deed, which man gesside hym silf to telle prosperitees, and Y killide hym in Sichelech, to whom it bihofte me yyue meede for message;

11 hou myche more now, whanne wickid men han slayn a giltles man in his hows on his bed, schal I not seke his blood of youre hond, and schal Y do awey you fro erthe?

12 Therfor Dauid comaundide to his children, and thei killiden hem; and thei kittiden awei the hondis and 'feet of hem, and hangiden hem ouer the cisterne in Ebron. Forsothe thei token the heed of Isbosech, and birieden in the sepulcre of Abner, in Ebron.

CAP 5

1 And alle the lynagis of Israel camen to Dauid, in Ebron, and seiden, Lo! we ben thi boon and thi fleisch.

2 But also yistirdai and the thridde day ago, whanne Saul was kyng on vs, thou leddist out, and leddist ayen Israel; forsothe the Lord seide to thee, Thou schalt fede my puple Israel, and thou schalt be duyk on Israel.

3 Also and the eldere men of Israel camen to the kyng, in Ebron; and kyng Dauid smoot with hem boond of pees in Ebron, bifor the Lord; and thei anoyntiden Dauid in to kyng on Israel.

4 Dauid was a sone of thretti yeer, whanne he bigan to regne, and he regnyde fourti yeer in Ebron;

5 he regnede on Juda seuene yeer and sixe monethis; forsothe in Jerusalem he regnede thretti and thre yeer, on al Israel and Juda.

6 And the kyng yede, and alle men that weren with hym, in to Jerusalem, to Jebusey, dweller of the lond. And it was seide of hem to Dauid, Thou schalt not entre hidur, no but thou do awei blynde men and lame, seiynge, Dauid schal not entre hydur.

7 Forsothe Dauid took the tour of Syon; this is the citee of Dauid.

8 For Dauid hadde 'sette forth meede in that dai to hym, that hadde smyte Jebusei, and hadde touchid the goteris of roouys, and hadde take awey lame men and blynde, hatynge the lijf of Dauid. Therfor it is seid in prouerbe, A blynde man and lame schulen not entre in to the temple.

9 Forsothe Dauid dwellide in the tour, and clepide it the citee of Dauid; and he bildide bi cumpas fro Mello, and with ynne.

10 And he entride profitynge and encreessynge; and the Lord God of oostis was with hym.

11 Also Hyram, kyng of Tire, sent messangeris to Dauid, and cedre trees, and crafti men of trees, and crafti men of stoonus to wallis; and thei bildiden the hows of Dauid.

12 And Dauid knew, that the Lord hadde confermed hym kyng on Israel, and that he hadde enhaunsid his rewme on his puple Israel.

13 Therfor Dauid took yit concubyns, and wyues of Jerusalem, after that he cam fro Ebron; and also othere sones and douytris weren borun to Dauid.

14 And these ben the names of hem that weren borun to hym in Jerusalem; Samua, and Sobab, and Nathan,

15 and Salomon, and Jobaar, and Helisua,

16 and Repheg, and Japhia, and Helysama, and Holida, and Heliphelech.

17 Therfor Filisteis herden, that thei hadden anoyntid Dauid kyng on Israel, and alle Filisteis stieden to seke Dauid. And whanne Dauid hadde herd this, he yede doun into a strong hold.

18 Forsothe Filisteis camen, and weren spred abroad in the valei of Raphaym.

19 And Dauid counseilide the Lord, and seide, Whether Y schal stie to Filisties, and whether thou schalt yyue hem in myn hond? And the Lord seide to Dauid, Stie thou, for Y schal bitake, and Y schal yyue Filisteis in thin hond.

20 Therfor Dauid cam in to Baal Farasym, and smoot hem there, and seide, The Lord departide myn enemyes bifor me, as watris ben departid. Therfor the name of that place was clepid Baal Farasym.

21 And thei leften there her sculptils, whiche Dauid took, and hise men.

22 And Filisteis addiden yit, that thei schulden stie, and thei weren spred abroad in the valey of Raphaym.

23 Sotheli Dauid councelide the Lord, and seide, Whether Y schal stie agens Filistis, and whether thou schalt bitake hem in to myn hondis? Which answeride, Thou schalt not stie ayens hem, but cumpasse thou bihynde her bak, and thou schalt come to hem on the contrarie side of the pere trees.

24 And whanne thou schalt here the sown of cry goynge in the cop of 'pere trees, thanne thou schalt biginne batel; for thanne the Lord schal go out befor thi face, that he smyte the castels of Filisteis.

25 Therfor Dauid dide as the Lord comaundide to hym; and he smoot Filisteys fro Gabaa til 'the while thei camen to Jezer.

CAP 6

1 Forsothe Dauid gaderide eft alle the chosun men of Israel, thritti thousynde.

2 And Dauid roos, and yede, and al the puple that was with hym of the men of Juda, to brynge the arke of God, on which the name of the Lord of oostis, sittynge in cherubyn on that arke, was clepid.

3 And thei puttiden the arke of God on a newe wayn, and thei token it fro the hows of Amynadab, that was in Gabaa. Forsothe Oza and Haio, the sons of Amynadab, dryueden the newe wayn.

4 And whanne thei hadden take it fro the hows of Amynadab, that was in Gabaa, and kepte the arke of God, Haio yede bifor the arke.

5 Forsothe Dauid and al Israel pleieden byfor the Lord, in alle 'trees maad craftili, and harpis, and sitols, and tympans, and trumpis, and cymbalis.

6 Forsothe after that thei camen to the corn floor of Nachor, Oza helde forth the hond to the arke of God, and helde it, for the oxun kikiden, and bowiden it.

7 And the Lord was wrooth bi indignacioun ayens Oza, and smoot hym on 'the foli; and he was deed there bisidis the arke of God.

8 Forsothe Dauid was sori, for the Lord hadde smyte Oza; and the name of that place was clepid the Smytyng of Oza 'til in to this dai.

9 And Dauid dredde the Lord in that dai, and seide, Hou schal the arke of the Lord entre to me?

10 And he nolde turne the arke of the Lord to hym silf in to the citee of Dauid, but he turnede it in to the hows of Obethedom of Geth.

11 And the arke of the Lord dwellide in the hows of Obethedom

3of Geth thre monethis; and the Lord blessid Obethedom, and al his hows.

12 And it was told to kyng Dauid, that the Lord hadde blessid Obethedom, and alle 'thingis of hym, for the arke of God. And Dauid seide, Y schal go, and brynge the arke with blessyng in to myn hows. Therfor Dauid yede, and brouyte the arke of God fro the hows of Obethedom in to the citee of Dauid with ioye; and ther weren with Dauid seuen cumpanyes, and the slain sacrifice of a calff.

13 And whanne thei, that baren the arke of the Lord, hadden stied six paaces, thei offriden an oxe and a ram. And Dauid smoot in organs boundun to the arm;

14 and daunside with alle strengthis bifor the Lord; sotheli Dauid was clothid with a lynnun surplis.

15 And Dauid, and al the men of Israel, ledden forth the arke of testament of the Lord in hertli song, and in sown of trumpe.

16 And whanne the arke of the Lord hadde entride in to the citee of Dauid, Mychol, the douytir of Saul, bihelde bi a wyndow, and sche siy the kyng skippynge and daunsynge bifor the Lord; and sche dispiside hym in hir herte.

17 And thei brouyten in the arke of the Lord, and settiden it in his place, in the myddis of tabernacle, which tabernacle Dauid hadde maad 'redy therto; and Dauid offride brent sacrifices and pesible bifor the Lord.

18 And whanne Dauid hadde endid tho, and hadde offrid brent sacrifices and pesible, he blesside the puple in the name of the Lord of oostis.

19 And he yaf to al the multitude of Israel, as wel to man as to womman, to ech 'o thinne loof, and o part rostid of bugle

fleisch, and flour of wheete fried with oile; and al the puple yede, ech man in to his hows.

20 And Dauid turnede ayen to blesse his hows, and Mychol, the douytir of Saul, yede out in to the comyng of Dauid, and seide, Hou glorious was the kyng of Israel to day vnhilynge hym silf bifor the handmaidis of hise seruauntis, and he was maad nakid, as if oon of the harlotis be maad nakid?

21 And Dauid seide to Mychol, The Lord lyueth, for Y schal pley bifor the Lord, that chees me rathere than thi fadir, and than al the hows of hym, and comaundide to me, that Y schulde be duyk on the puple 'of the Lord of Israel;

22 and Y schal pleie, and Y schal be maad 'vilere more than Y am maad, and Y schal be meke in myn iyen, and Y schal appere gloriousere with the handmaydys, of whiche thou spakist.

23 Therfor a sone was not borun to Mychol, the douytir of Saul, til in to the dai of hir deeth.

CAP 7

1 Forsothe it was doon, whanne the kyng Dauid hadde sete in his hows, and the Lord hadde youe reste to hym on ech side fro alle hise enemyes,

2 he seyde to Nathan the prophete, Seest thou not, that Y dwelle in an hows of cedre, and the arke of God is put in the myddis of skynnys?

3 And Nathan seide to the kyng, Go thou, and do al thing which is in thin herte, for the Lord is with thee.

4 Forsothe it was don in that niyt, and lo! the word of the Lord, seiynge to Nathan, Go thou,

5 and speke to my servaunt Dauid, The Lord seith these thingis, Whether thou schalt bilde to me an hows to dwelle ynne?

6 For Y 'dwellide not in an hows fro the dai in which Y ledde the sones of Israel out of the lond of Egipt til in to this dai; but Y yede in tabernacle and in tent,

7 bi alle places, to whiche Y passyde with alle the sones of Israel? Whether Y spekynge spak to oon of the lynagis of Israel, to whom Y comaundyde, that he schulde feede my puple Israel, and seide, Whi 'bildidist thou not an hows of cedre to me?

8 And now thou schalt seie these thingis to my seruaunt Dauid, The Lord of oostis seith these thingis, Y took thee fro lesewis suynge flockis, that thou schuldist be duyk on my puple Israel, and Y was with thee in alle thingis,

9 where euere thou yedist, and Y killide alle thin enemyes fro thi face, and Y made to thee a greet name bi the name of grete men that ben in erthe;

10 and Y schall sette a place to my puple Israel, and Y schal plaunte hym, and Y schal dwelle with hym, and he schal no more be troblid, and the sones of wickidnesse schulen not adde, that thei turmente hym as bifor,

11 fro the dai in which Y ordenede iugis on my puple Israel; and Y schal yyue reste to thee fro alle thin enemyes. And the Lord biforseith to thee, that 'the Lord schal mak an hows to thee;

12 and whanne thi daies be fillid, and thou hast slept with thi fadris, Y schal reyse thi seed aftir thee, which schal go out of thi wombe, and Y schal make 'stidfast his rewme.

13 He schal bilde an hows to my name, and Y schal make stable the troone of his rewme til in to with outen ende;

14 Y schal be to hym in to fadir, and he schal be to me in to a sone; and if he schal do ony thing wickidli, Y schal chastise

hym in the yerde of men, and in the woundis of the sones of men.

15 Forsothe Y schal not do awey my mercy fro hym, as Y dide awei fro Saul, whom Y remouede fro my face.

16 And thin hows schal be feithful, and thi rewme schal be til in to with outen ende bifor my face, and thi trone schal be stidfast contynueli.

17 By alle these wordys, and bi al this reuelacioun, so Nathan spak to Dauid.

18 Forsothe Dauid the kyng entride, and satt bifor the Lord, and seide, Who am Y, my Lord God, and what is myn hows, that thou brouytist me hidur to?

19 But also this is seyn litil in thi siyt, my Lord God; no but thou schuldist speke also of the hows of thi seruaunt in to long tyme. Forsothe this is the lawe of Adam, Lord God;

20 what therfor may Dauid adde yit, that he speke to thee? For thou, Lord God, knowist thi seruaunt; thou hast do alle these grete thingis,

21 for thi word, and bi thin herte, so that thou madist knowun to thi seruaunt.

22 Herfor, Lord God, thou art magnyfied, for noon is lijk thee, ne there is no God outakun thee, in alle thingis whiche we herden with oure eeris.

23 Sotheli what folk in erthe is as the puple of Israel, for which the Lord God yede, that he schulde ayenbie it to him in to a puple, and schulde sette to hym silf a name, and schulde do to it grete thingis, and orible on erthe, in castinge out therof the folk and 'goddis therof fro the face of thi puple, which thou 'ayen bouytist to thee fro Egipt?

24 And thou confermidist to thee thi puple Israel in to a puple euerlastynge, and thou, Lord, art maad in to God to hem.

25 Now therfor, Lord God, reise thou withouten ende the word that thou hast spoke on thi seruaunt and on his hows, and do as thou hast spoke;

26 and thy name be magnyfied til in to withouten ende, and be it seid, The Lord of oostis is God on Israel; and the hows of thi seruaunt Dauid schal be stablischid byfor the Lord;

27 for thou, Lord of oostis, God of Israel, hast maad reuelacioun to the eere of thi seruaunt, and seidist, Y schal bilde an hows to thee; therfor thi seruaunt foond his herte, that he schulde preie thee bi this preier.

28 Now therfor, Lord God, thou art veri God, and thi wordis schulen be trewe; for thou hast spoke these goodis to thi seruaunt;

29 therfor bigynne thou, and blesse the hows of thi seruaunt, that it be withouten ende bifor thee; for thou, Lord God, hast spoke these thingis, and bi thi blessyng the hows of thi seruaunt schal be blessid withouten ende.

CAP 8

1 Forsothe it was doon aftir these thingis, Dauid smoot Filisteis, and made low hem; and Dauid took awei the bridil of tribute fro the hond of Filisteis.

2 And Dauid smoot Moab, and mat hem with a coorde, and made euene to the erthe; forsothe 'he mat twey cordis, oon to sle, and oon to quikene. And Moab seruyde Dauid vndur tribute.

3 And Dauid smoot Adadezer, sone of Roob, kyng of Soba, whanne he yede forth to be lord ouer the flood Eufrates.

4 And whanne a thousynde and seuene hundrid kniytis of his part weren takun, and twenti thousynde of foot men, Dauid hoxide alle 'drawynge beestis in charis; but Dauid lefte of tho an hundrid charis, that is, the horsis of an hundrid charis.

5 Also Sirie of Damask cam, that it schulde bere help to Adadezer, kyng of Soba; and Dauid smoot of Sirie two and twenti thousynde of men.

6 And Dauid settide strengthe in Sirie of Damask, and Sirie was maad seruynge Dauid vndur tribute. And the Lord kepte Dauid in alle thingis, to what euer thingis he yede forth.

7 And Dauid took goldun armeris and bies, whiche the seruauntis of Adadezer hadden, and he brouyte tho in to Jerusalem.

8 And of Bethe, and of Beroth, citees of Adadezer, Dauith the kyng took ful myche metal; 'of the whiche Salomon made alle the brasen vessels in the temple, and the brasen see, and the pilers, and the auter.

9 Forsothe Thou, kyng of Emath, herde that Dauid hadde smyte al the strengthe of Adadezer.

10 And Thou sente Joram, his sone, to 'kyng Dauid, that he schulde grete hym, and thanke, and do thankyngis, for he hadde ouercome Adadezer, and hadde smyte hym; for Thou was enemy to Adadeser; and vessels of silver, and vessels of gold, and vessels of bras weren in his hond.

11 And the same vessels kyng Dauid halewid 'to the Lord, with the siluer and gold, whiche he hadde halewid of alle hethene men, whiche 'hethene men he made suget of Sirye,

12 and Moab, and the sones of Amon, and Filisteis, and Amalech, and of the spuylis of Adadezer, sone of Roob, kyng of Soba.

13 Also Dauid made to hym a name, whanne he turnede ayen, whanne Sirie was takun, for eiytene thousynde weren slayn in the valey, where salt is maad, and in Gebelem, to thre and twenti thousynde.

14 And he settide keperis in Ydumee, and ordeinede strong hold, and al Ydumee was maad seruynge to Dauid; and the Lord kepte Dauid in alle thingis, to whateuer thingis he yede forth.

15 And Dauid regnede on al Israel, and Dauid dide doom, and riytfulnesse to al his puple.

16 Forsothe Joab, the sone of Saruy, was ouer the oost; sotheli Josaphat, sone of Achilud, was chaunceler; and Sadoch,

17 sone of Achitob, and Achymelech, sone of Abiathar, weren preestis; and Saraye was scryuyn.

18 Forsothe Bananye, sone of Joiada, was ouer Cerethi and Pherethi, that is, ouer archeris and arblasteris; sotheli the sones of Dauid weren prestis.

CAP 9

1 And Dauid seide, Whether ony man is, that lefte of the hows of Saul, that Y do mercy with hym for Jonathas?

2 Forsothe a seruaunt, Siba bi name, was of the hous of Saul; whom whanne the kyng hadde clepid to hym silf, 'the kyng seide to hym, Whethir thou art not Siba? And he answeride, Y am thi seruaunt.

3 And the kyng seide, Whether ony man lyeth of the hows of Saul, that Y do with hym the mercy of God? And Siba seide to the kyng, A sone of Jonathas lyeth, feble in the feet.

4 The kyng seide, Where is he? And Siba seide to the kyng, Lo! he is in the hows of Machir, sone of Amyel, in Lodabar.

5 Therfor 'Dauid the kyng sente, and took hym fro the hows of Machir, sone of Amyel, fro Lodobar.

6 Forsothe whanne Myphibosech, the sone of Jonathas, sone of Saul, hadde come to Dauid, he felde in to his face, and

worschipide. And Dauid seide, Myphibosech! Which answeride, Y am present, thi seruaunt.

7 And Dauid seide to hym, Drede thou not, for Y doynge schal do mersi to thee for Jonathas, thi fadir; and Y schal restore to thee alle the feeldis of Saul, thi fadir, and thou schalt ete breed in my boord euere.

8 Which worschipide him, and seide, Who am Y, thi seruaunt, for thou hast biholde on a deed dogge lijk me?

9 Therfor the kyng clepide Siba, the child of Saul; and seide to hym, Y haue youe to the sone of thi lord alle thingis, which euer weren of Saul, and al the hows of hym;

10 therfor worche thou the lond to hym, thou, and thi sones, and thi seruauntis, and thou schalt brynge in meetis to the sone of thi lord, that he be fed; forsothe Myphibosech, sone of thi lord, schal ete euer breed on my bord. Sotheli fiftene sones and twenti seruauntis weren to Siba.

11 And Siba seyde to the kyng, As thou, my lord kyng, hast comaundid to thi seruaunt, so thi seruaunt schal do; and Myphibosech, as oon of the sones of the kyng, schal ete on thi boord.

12 Forsothe Myphibosech hadde a litil sone, Mycha bi name; sotheli al the meyne of the hows of Siba seruyde Myphibosech.

13 Forsothe Myphibosech dwellide in Jerusalem; for he eet contynueli of the kingis boord, and was crokid on either foot.

CAP 10

1 Forsothe it was doon aftir these thingis, that Naas, kyng of the sones of Amon, diede; and Anoon, his sone, regnede for hym. And Dauid seide,

2 Y schal do mercy with Anon, the sone of Naas, as his fadir dide mercy with me. Therfor Dauid sente coumfortynge hym by hise seruauntis on the deeth of the fadir. Sotheli whanne the seruauntis of Dauid hadden come in to the lond of the sones of Amon,

3 princes of the sones of Amon seiden to Anon, her lord, Gessist thou that for the onour of thi fadir Dauid sente coumfortouris to thee; and not herfor Dauid sente hise seruauntis to thee, that he schulde aspie, and enserche the citee, and distrie it?

4 Therfor Anoon took the seruauntis of Dauid, and schauyde half the part of 'the beerd of hem, and he kittide awey the myddil clothis of hem 'til to the buttokis; and lefte hem.

5 And whanne this was teld to Dauid, he sente in to the comyng of hem, for the men weren schent ful vilensly. And Dauid comaundide to hem, Dwelle ye in Jerico, til youre beerd wexe, and thanne turne ye ayen.

6 Sotheli the sones of Amon sien, that thei hadden do wrong to Dauid, and thei senten, and hiriden bi meede Roob of Sirye, and Soba of Sirie, twenti thousynde of foot men, and of kyng Maacha, a thousynde men, and of Istob twelue thousynde of men.

7 And whanne Dauid hadde herd this, he sent Joab and al the oost of fiyteris.

8 Therfor the sones of Amon yeden out, and dressiden scheltrun bifor hem in the entryng of the yate. Forsothe Soba, and Roob of Sirie, and Istob, and Maacha weren asidis half in the feeld.

9 Therfor Joab siy, that batel was maad redi ayens hym, bothe euene ayens and bihynde the bak; and he chees to hym silf of alle the chosun men of Israel, and ordeynede scheltrun ayens Sirus.

10 Forsothe he bitook to Abisai, his brothir, the tother part of the puple, which dresside scheltrun ayens the sones of Amon.

11 And Joab seide, If men of Sirie han the maistrie ayens me, thou schalt be to me in to help; sotheli if the sones of Amon han the maistrie ayens thee, Y schal helpe thee;

12 be thou a strong man, and fiyte we for oure puple, and for the citee of oure God; forsothe the Lord schal do that, that is good in his siyt.

13 Therfor Joab and his puple that was with hym, bigan batel ayens men of Sirie, whiche fledden anoon fro his face.

14 Forsothe the sones of Amon sien, that men of Sirie hadden fled; and thei fledden also fro the face of Abisai, and entriden in to the citee; and Joab turnede ayen fro the sones of Amon, and cam in to Jerusalem.

15 Forsothe men of Sirye sien that thei hadden feld bifor Israel, and thei weren gaderid to gidere.

16 And Adadezer sente, and ledde out men of Sirie that weren biyende the flood, and he brouyte the oost of hem; sotheli Sobach, mayster of the chyualrie of Adadezer, was the prince of hem.

17 And whanne this was teld to Dauid, he drow togidere al Israel, and passide Jordan, and cam in to Helama. And men of Sirie dressiden scheltrun ayens Dauid, and fouyten ayens hym.

18 And Sireis fledden fro the face of Israel; and Dauid killide of Sireis seuene hundrid charis, and fourti thousynde of knyytis; and he smoot Sobach, the prince of chyualrie, which was deed anoon.

19 Forsothe alle kyngis, that weren in the help of Adadezer, siyen that thei weren ouercomun of Israel, and thei maden pees with Israel, and serueden hem; and Sireis dredden to yyue help to the sones of Amon.

CAP 11

1 Forsothe it was doon, whanne the yeer turnede ayen in that tyme wherynne kyngis ben wont to go forth to batels, Dauid sente Joab, and with hym hise seruauntis, and al Israel; and thei distrieden the sones of Amon, and bisegiden Rabath; forsothe Dauid dwellide in Jerusalem.

2 While these thingis weren doon, it befelde, that Dauid roos in a dai fro his bed after mydday, and walkide in the soler of the kyngis hows; and he siy a womman waischynge hir silf euen ayens on hir soler; sotheli the womman was ful fair.

3 Therfor the kyng sente, and enqueride, what womman it was; and it was teld to hym, that sche was Bersabee, the douytir of Heliam, and was the wijf of Vrye Ethei.

4 Therfor bi messangeris sent Dauid took hir; and whanne sche entride to hym, he slepte with hir, and anoon sche was halewid fro hir vnclenesse.

5 And sche turnede ayen in to hir hows, with child conseyued; and sche sente, and telde to Dauid, and seide, Y haue conseyued.

6 Forsothe Dauid sente to Joab, and seide, Sende thou Vrye Ethei to me; and Joab sente Vrye to Dauid.

7 And Vrie cam to Dauid; and Dauid axide, hou riytfuli Joab dide and the puple, and hou the batel was mynystrid.

8 And Dauid seide to Vrye, Go in to thin hows, and waische thi feet. Vrye yede out fro the hows of the kyng, and the kyngis mete suede hym.

9 Sotheli Vrye slepte bifor the yate of the kyngis hows with othere seruauntis of his lord, and yede not doun to his hows.

10 And it was teld to Dauid of men, seiynge, Vrye 'yede not to his hows. And Dauid seide to Vrye, Whether thou camest not fro the weye? whi yedist thou not doun in to thin hows?

11 And Vrie seide to Dauid, The arke of God, Israel and Juda dwellen in tentis, and my lord Joab, and the seruauntis of my lord dwellen on the face of erthe, and schal Y go in to myn hows, to ete and drynke, and slepe with my wijf? Bi thin helthe, and bi the helthe of thi soule, Y schal not do this thing.

12 Therfor Dauid seide to Vrye, Dwelle thou here also to dai, and to morewe Y schal delyuere thee. Vrie dwellide in Jerusalem in that day and the tothir.

13 And Dauid clepide hym, that he schulde ete and drynke bifor hym, and Dauid made drunkun Vrye; and he yede out in the euentid, and slepte in his bed with the seruauntes of his lord; and yede not doun in to his hows.

14 Therfor the morewtid was maad, and Dauid wroot epistle to Joab, and sente bi the hond of Vrye,

15 and wroot in the pistle, Sette ye Vrye euene ayens the batel, where the batel is strongeste, 'that is, where the aduersaries ben stronge, and forsake ye hym, that he be smitun and perische.

16 Therfor whanne Joab bisegide the citee, he settide Vrie in the place where he wiste that strongeste men weren.

17 And men yeden out of the citee, and fouyten ayens Joab, and thei killiden of the puple of seruauntis of Dauid, and also Vrye Ethei was deed.

18 Therfor Joab sente, and telde alle the wordis of the batel;

19 and he comaundyde to the messanger, and seide, Whanne thou hast fillid alle wordis of the batel to the kyng,

20 if thou seest, that he is wrooth, and seith, Whi neiyiden ye to the wal to fiyte? whether ye wisten not, that many dartis ben sent 'fro aboue fro the wal?

21 who smoot Abymelech, sone of Gerobaal? whether not a womman sente on hym a gobet of a mylnestoon fro the wal, and killide hym in Thebes? whi neiyiden ye bisidis the wal? thou schalt seie, Also thi seruaunt, Vrye Ethei, diede.

22 Therfor the messanger yede, and telde to Dauid alle thingis whiche Joab hadde comaundid to hym.

23 And the messanger seide to Dauid, 'Men hadden the maistri ayens us, and thei yeden out to vs in to the feeld; sotheli bi 'fersnesse maad we pursueden hem 'til to the yate of the citee.

24 And archeris senten dartis to thi seruauntis fro the wal aboue, and summe of the 'kyngis seruauntis ben deed; forsothe also thi seruaunt, Vrye Ethei, is deed.

25 And Dauid seide to the messanger, Thou schalt seie these thingis to Joab, This thing breke not thee; for the bifallyng of batel is dyuerse, and swerd wastith now this man, now that man; coumforte thi fiyteris ayens the citee, that thou distrye it, and excite thou hem.

26 Forsothe the wijf of Vrye herde, that Vrye hir hosebond was deed, and sche biweilide hym.

27 And whanne the morenyng was passid, Dauid sente, and brouyte hir in to his hows; and sche was maad wijf to hym, and sche childide a sone to hym. And this word which Dauid hadde do displeside bifor the Lord.

CAP 12

1 Therfor the Lord sente Nathan to Dauid; and whanne he hadde come to Dauid, he seide to Dauid, Answere thou doom to me; twei men weren in o citee; o man was riche, and the tother was pore.

2 The riche man hadde ful many scheep, and oxun;

3 sotheli the pore man hadde vttirli no thing, outakun o litil scheep, which he hadde bouyt, and nurschid, and which 'hadde wexid at hym with hise sones, and eet togidere of his breed, and drank of his cuppe, and slepte in his bosum; and it was as a douyter to hym.

4 Forsothe whanne a pilgrym 'hadde come to the riche man, he sparide to take of hise scheep and oxun, that he schulde make a feeste to that pilgrym, that cam to hym; and he took the scheep of the pore man, and 'made redi metis to the man that cam to hym.

5 Forsothe Dauid was ful wrooth with indignacioun ayens that man, and seide to Nathan, The Lord lyueth, for the man that dide this is the sone of deeth;

6 he schal yelde the scheep in to foure folde, for he dide this word, and sparide not.

7 Forsothe Nathan seide to Dauid, Thou art thilke man, that hast do this thing. The Lord God of Israel seith these thingis, Y anoyntide thee 'in to kyng on Israel, and Y delyuerede thee fro the hond of Saul,

8 and Y yaf to thee the hows of thi lord, and the wyues of thi lord in thi bosum, and Y yaf to thee the hows of Israel, and of Juda; and if these thingis ben litil, Y schal adde to thee myche grettere thingis.

9 Whi therfor hast thou dispisid the word of the Lord, that thou didist yuels in my siyt? Thou hast smyte by swerd Vrye Ethei, and thou hast take his wijf in to wijf to thee, and thou hast slayn hym with the swerd of the sones of Amon.

10 Wherfor swerd schal not go awey fro thin hows til in to with outen ende; for thou dispysidist me, and tokist the wijf of Vrye Ethei, that sche schulde be thi wijf.

11 Therfor the Lord seith these thingis, Lo! Y schal reise on thee yuel of thin hows, and Y schal take thi wyues in 'thin iyen, and Y schal yyue to thi neiybore, and he schal slepe with thi wyues in the iyen of this sunne, 'that is, opynli bifor alle men, as in xv. chapitre.

12 For thou hast do priueli; forsothe Y schal do this word in the siyt of al Israel, and in the siyt of this sunne.

13 And Dauid seide to Nathan, Y haue synned to the Lord. And Nathan seide to Dauid, Also the Lord hath turned awei thi synne; thou schalt not die.

14 Netheles for thou madist enemyes to blasfeme the name of the Lord, for this word the child which is borun to thee schal die bi deeth.

15 And Nathan turnede ayen in to his hows. And the Lord smoot the litil child, whom the wijf of Vrye childide to Dauid, and he dispeiride.

16 And Dauid preiede the Lord for the litil child; and Dauid fastide bi fastyng, and entride asidis half, and lai on the erthe.

17 Sotheli the eldere men of his hows camen, and con-streyneden hym 'bi meke preieris, that he schulde rise fro the erthe; and he nolde, nethir he eet mete with hem.

18 Forsothe it bifelde in the seuenthe dai, that the yong child diede; and the seruauntis of Dauid dredde to telle to hym, that the litil child was deed; for thei seiden, Lo! whanne the litil child lyuede yit, we spaken to hym, and he herde not oure vois; hou myche more, if we seien the child is deed, he schal turment himsilf?

19 Therfore whanne Dauid hadde herd his seruauntis spe-kynge priueli, 'ether moterynge, he understood that the yong child was deed; 'and he seyde to his seruauntis, Whether the child is deed? Whiche answeriden to hym, He is deed.

20 Therfor Dauid roos fro the erthe, and was waischid, and anoyntid; and whanne he hadde chaungid cloth, he entride in to the hows of the Lord, and worschipide, and cam in to his hows; and he axide, that thei schulden sette breed to hym, and he eet.

21 Sothely his seruauntis seiden to hym, What is the word which thou hast do? Thou fastidist, and weptist for the yong child, whanne he lyuede yit; sotheli whanne the child was deed, thou risidist and etist breed?

22 And Dauid seide, Y fastide and wepte for the yong child, whanne he lyuyde yit; for Y seide, Who woot, if perauenture the Lord yyue hym to me, and the yong child lyue?

23 'Now forsothe for he is deed, whi 'fast Y? whether Y schal mow ayen clepe hym more? Y schal 'go more to hym, but he schal not turne ayen to me.

24 And Dauid coumfortid Bersabee, his wijf; and he entride to hir, and slepte with hir. And sche gendride a sone, and Dauid clepide his name Salomon; and the Lord louyde hym.

25 And he sente Salomon in the hond of Nathan, the proph-ete; and he clepide his name Amyable to the Lord, for the Lord louyde hym.

26 Therfor Joab fauyt ayens Rabath, of the sones of Amon, and he fauyt ayens the 'kyngis citee.

27 And Joab sente messangeris to Dauid, and seide, Y fauyte ayens Rabath, and the citee of watris schal be takun.

28 Now therfor gadere thou the tother part of the puple, and bisege thou the citee, and take thou it, lest whanne the citee is wastid of me, the victorie be arettid to my name.

29 Therfor Dauid gaderide al the puple, and he yede forth ayens Rabath; and whanne he hadde fouyte, he took it.

30 And he took the diademe of the kyng of hem fro his heed, bi weiyte a talent of gold, hauynge preciouseste peerlis; and it was put on the heed of Dauid, 'that is, aftir that it was weldid and purgid bi fier; but also Dauid bar awey ful myche prey of the citee.

31 Also he ledde forth the puple therof, and sawide, and 'dide aboute hem 'yrun instrumentis of turment, and departide with knyues, and 'ledde ouer bi the licnesse of tijl stoonus; so he dide to alle the citees of the sones of Amon. And Dauid turnede ayen, and al his oost, in to Jerusalem.

CAP 13

1 Forsothe it was doon aftir these thingis, that Amon, the sone of Dauid, louyde the faireste sistir, Thamar bi name, of Abso-lon, sone of Dauid.

2 And Amon perischide greetli for hir, so that he was sijk for 'the loue of hir. For whanne she was a virgyn, it semyde hard to hym, that he schulde do ony thing vnonestli with hir.

3 Forsothe a freend, Jonadab bi name, sone of Semmaa, brother of Dauid, 'was to Amon; Jonadab was a ful prudent man.

4 Which seide to Amon, Sone of the kyng, whi art thou maad feble so bi leenesse bi alle daies? whi schewist thou not to me? And Amon seide to him, Y loue Thamar, the sister of my brother Absolon.

5 And Jonadab answeride to hym, Li thou on thi bed, and feyne thou sikenesse; and whanne thi fadir cometh, that he visyte thee, seie thou to hym, Y preye, come Thamar, my sis-ter, that sche yyue mete to me, and make a seew, that Y ete of hir hond.

6 Therfor Amon lay doun, and 'bigan as to be sijk. And whanne the kyng hadde come to visite him, Amon seide to the kyng, Y biseche, come Thamar, my sistir, that sche make twei soupyngis bifor my iyen, and that Y take of hir hond meete maad redi.

7 Therfor Dauid sente to the hows of Thamar, and seide, Come thou in to the hows of Amon, thi brother, and make thou seew to hym.

8 And Thamar cam in to the hows of Amon, hir brother. Sotheli he lai; and sche took mele, and medlide, and made moist bifor hise iyen, and sethide soupyngis;

9 and sche took that, that sche hadde sode, and helde out, and settide byfor hym, and he nolde ete. And Amon seide, Putte ye out alle men fro me. And whanne thei hadden put out alle men,

10 Amon seide to Thamar, Bere the mete in to the closet, that Y ete of thin hond. Therfor Thamar took the soupingis whiche sche hadde maad, and brouyte in to Amon, hir brother, in the closet.

11 And whanne sche hadde proferid mete to hym, he took hir, and seide, Come thou, my sistir, li thou with me.

12 And sche answeride to hym, My brother, nyle thou, nyle thou oppresse me, for this is not leueful in Israel; nyle thou do this foli.

13 For Y schal not mow bere my schenschip, and thou schalt be as oon of the vnwise men in Israel; but rather speke thou to the kyng, and he schal not denye me to thee.

14 Sotheli he nolde assente to hir preieris; but he was strengere in myytis, and oppresside hir, and lay with hir.

15 And 'Amon hadde hir hateful bi ful grete haterede, so that the hatrede was gretter, bi which he hatide hir, than the loue bi which he louyde hir bifor. And Amon seide to hir, Rise thou, and go.

16 And sche answeride to hym, This yuel is more which thou doist now ayens me, and puttist me out, than that, that thou didist bifore. And he nolde here hir; but whanne the child was clepide,

17 that mynystride to hym, he seide, Putte thou out this womman fro me, and close thou the dore aftir hir.

18 And sche was clothid with a coote doun to the heele; for the kyngis douytris virgyns vsiden siche clothis. Therfor the mynystre of Amon puttide hir out, and closide the dore aftir hir.

19 And sche spreynte aische to hir heed, whanne the coote to 'the heele was to-rent, and whanne the hondis weren put on hir heed, and sche yede entrynge and criynge.

20 Forsothe Absolon, hir brother, seide to hir, Whether Amon, thi brothir, hath leyn with thee? But 'now, sister, be stille; he is thi brother, and turmente not thin herte for this thing. Therfor Thamar dwellide morenynge in the hows of Absolon, hir brothir.

21 Forsothe whanne 'kyng Dauid hadde herd these wordis, he was ful sori, and he nolde make sore the spyrit of Amon, his sone; for he louyde Amon, for he was the firste gendrid 'to hym.

22 Forsothe Absolon spak not to Amon, nether yuel nether good; for Absolon hatide Amon, for he hadde defoulid Thamar, his sistir.

23 Forsothe it was doon aftir the tyme of twei yeer, that the scheep of Absolon weren shorun in Baalasor, which is bisidis Effraym. And Absolon clepide alle the sones of the kyng.

24 And he cam to the kyng, and seide to hym, Lo! the scheep of thi seruaunt ben schorun; Y preye, come the king with hise seruauntis to his seruaunt.

25 And the kyng seide to Absolon, Nyle thou, my sone, nyle thou preye, that alle we come, and greeue thee. Forsothe whanne he constreynede Dauid, and he nolde go, he blesside Absolon.

26 And Absolon seide to Dauid, If thou nylt come, Y byseche, come nameli Amon, my brother, with vs. And the kyng seide to hym, It is no nede, that he go with thee.

27 Therfor Absolon constreynede hym; and he delyuerede with him Amon, and alle the sones of the kyng. And Absolon hadde maad a feeste as the feeste of a kyng.

28 Sotheli Absolon comaundide to hise children, and seide, Aspie ye, whanne Amon is drunkun of wyn, and Y seie to you, Smyte ye, and sle hym. Nyle ye drede, for Y am that comaunde to you; be ye strengthid, and be ye stronge men.

29 Therfor the children of Absolon diden ayens Amon, as Absolon hadde comaundide to hem; and alle the sones of the kyng risiden, and stieden ech on his mule, and fledden.

30 And whanne thei yeden yit in the weie, fame cam to the kyng, and seide, Absolon hath kild alle the sones of the king, and 'nameli not oon lefte of hem.

31 Therfor the kyng roos, and to-rente hise clothis, and felde doun on the erthe; and alle hise seruauntis that stoden nyy to hym, to-renten her clothis.

32 Sotheli Jonadab, sone of Semmaa, brother of Dauid, answeride and seide, My lord the kyng, gesse not, that alle the children, and sones of the kyng, ben slayn; Amon aloone is deed, for he was set in hatrede to Absolon, fro the day in which he oppresside Thamar, his sistir.

33 Now therfor, my lord the kyng, set not this word on his herte, and seie, Alle the sones of the kyng ben slayn; for Amon aloone is deed.

34 Forsothe Absolon fledde. And a child aspiere reiside hise iyen, and bihelde, and lo! myche puple cam bi a weye out of the comyn weie bi the side of the hil.

35 And Jonadab seide to the kyng, Lo! the sones of the kyng comen; bi the word of thi seruaunt, so it is doon.

36 And whanne he hadde ceessid to speke, also the sones of the kyng apperiden; and thei entriden, and reisiden her vois, and wepten; but also the kyng and alle his seruauntis wepten bi ful greet wepyng.

37 Forsothe Absolon fledde, and yede to Tholmai, sone of Amyur, the kyng of Gessur. Therfor Dauid biweilide his sone Amon in many daies.

38 Forsothe Absolon, whanne he hadde fled, and hadde come in to Gessur, was there thre yeer.

39 And Dauid ceesside to pursue Absolon, for he was coumfortid on the deeth of Amon.

CAP 14

1 Forsothe Joab, the sone of Saruye, vndirstood, that the herte of the kyng was turned to Absolon;

2 and he sente to Thecua, and took fro thennus a wise womman, and he seide to hir, Feyne thee to morene, and be thou clothid with clooth of duyl, and be thou anoyntid with oile, that thou be as a womman by morenynge 'now in ful myche tyme a deed man.

3 And thou schalt entre to the kyng, and thou schalt speke to hym siche wordis. Sotheli Joab puttide the wordis in hir mouth.

4 Therfor whanne the womman of Thecua hadde entrid to the kyng, sche felde bifor hym on the erthe, and worschipide, and seide, A! kyng, kepe me.

5 And the kyng seide to hir, What hast thou of cause? And sche answeride, Alas! Y am a womman widewe, for myn hosebonde is deed;

6 and tweyne sones weren of thin handmayde, whiche debati-
den ayens hem silf in the feeld, and 'noon was that myyte
forbede hem, and oon smoot 'the tother, and killide hym.
7 And lo! al the kynrede risith ayens thin handmayde, and
seith, Yyue thou hym that killide his brothir, that we sle hym
for the lijf of his brother whom he killide, and that we do awei
the eir; and thei seken to quenche my sparcle whych is lefte,
that name dwelle not to myn hosebonde, and relikis, 'ethir
remenauntis, be not to him on erthe.
8 And the kyng seide to the womman, Go in to thin hows, and
Y schal comaunde for thee.
9 And the womman of Thecua seide to the kyng, My lord the
kyng, this wickidnesse be on me, and on the hows of my
fadir; forsothe the kyng and his trone be innocent.
10 And the kyng seide, Brynge thou hym to me, that
ayenseith thee, and he schal no more adde that he touche thee.
11 And sche seide, The kyng haue mynde on his Lord God,
and the nexte men of blood to take veniaunce be not multiplied, and 'thei schulen not sle my sone. And the kyng seide,
The Lord lyueth, for noon of the heeris of thi sone schal falle
on the erthe.
12 Therfor the womman seide, Thin handmayde speke a word
to my lord the kyng. And the kyng seide, Speke thou.
13 And the womman seide, Whi 'thouytist thou sich a thing
ayens the puple of God? and the kyng spak this word, that he
do synne, and brynge not ayen his sone cast out?
14 Alle we dyen, and as watris that schulen not turne ayen,
we sliden in to erthe; and God nyl that a soule perische, but he
withdrawith, and thenkith lest he perische outirly, which is
cast awey.
15 Now therfor come thou, that Y speke to my lord the kyng
this word, while the puple is present; and thin handmaide
seide, Y schal speke to the kyng, if in ony maner the kyng do
the word of his handmayde.
16 And the kyng herde the wordis, that he schulde delyuere
his handmayde fro the hondis of alle men, that wolden do
awei me, and my sone to gidere, fro the eritage of the Lord.
17 Therfor thin hand mayde seie, that the word of my lord the
kyng be maad as sacrifice, 'that is, that the sentence youun of
hym be plesaunt to God, as sacrifice plesith God; for as an
aungel of the Lord, so is my lord the kyng, that he be not
mouyd bi blessyng nether bi cursyng. Wherfor and thi Lord
God is with thee.
18 And the kyng answeride, and seide to the womman, Hide
thou not fro me the word which Y axe thee. And the womman
seide to hym, Speke thou, my lord the kyng.
19 And the kyng seide, Whether the hond of Joab is with thee
in alle these thingis? The womman answeride, and seide, Bi
the helthe of this soule, my lord the kyng, nether to the left
side nether to the riyt side is ony thing of alle these thingis,
whiche my lord the kyng spak. For thi seruaunt Joab hym silf
comaundide to me, and he puttide alle these wordis in to the
mouth of thin handmaide,
20 that Y schulde turne the figure of this word; for thi seruaunt Joab comaundide this thing. Forsothe thou, my lord the
kyng, art wijs, as an aungel of God hath wisdom, that thou
vnderstonde alle thingis on erthe.
21 And the kyng seide to Joab, Lo! Y am plesid, and Y haue
do thi word; therfor go thou, and ayen clepe thou the child
Absolon.
22 And Joab felde on his face to erthe, and worschipide, and
blesside the kyng; and Joab seide, Thi seruaunt hath vndir-

stonde to dai, that Y foond grace in thin iyen, my lord the
kyng, for thou hast do the word of thi seruaunt.
23 Therfor Joab roos, and yede in to Gessur, and brouyte
Absolon in to Jerusalem.
24 Forsothe the kyng seide, Turne he ayen in to his hows, and
se not he my face.
25 Therfor Absolon turnede ayen in to his hows, and siy not
the face of the kyng. Sotheli no man in al Israel was so fair as
Absolon, and ful comeli; fro the step of the foot 'til to the top,
'no wem was in hym;
26 and in as myche as 'he clippide more the heeris, bi so
myche thei wexiden more; forsothe he was clippid onys in the
yeer, for the heer greuede him. And whanne he clippide the
heeris, he weiyide 'the heeris of his heed bi twei hundrid
siclis with comyn weiyte.
27 Forsothe thre sones, and a douyter, Thamar bi name, of
'excellent forme weren borun to Absolon.
28 And Absolon dwellide in Jerusalem twei yeer, and he siy
not the face of the kyng.
29 Therfor he sente to Joab, that he schulde sende hym to the
kyng; which Joab nolde come to hym. And whanne he hadde
sent the secounde tyme, and Joab nolde come,
30 Absolon seide to hise seruauntis, Ye knowen the feeld of
Joab bisidis my feeld hauynge ripe barli; therfor go ye, and
brenne ye it with fier. Therfor the seruauntis of Absolon
brenten the corn with fier. And the seruauntis of Joab camen
with her clothis to-rent, and seiden, The seruauntis
31 of Absolon han brent the part of feeld bi fier. And Joab
roos, and cam to Absolon in to his hows, and seide, Whi
32 han thi seruauntis brent my corn bi fier? And Absolon
answeride to Joab, Y sente to thee, and bisouyte that thou
schuldist come to me, and that Y schulde sende thee to the
kyng, that thou schuldist seie to hym, Whi cam Y fro Gessur?
It was betere to me to be there; therfor Y biseche, that Y se
the face of the kyng, that if he is myndeful of my wickidnesse, sle he me.
33 Joab entride to the kyng, and telde to hym. And Absolon
was clepid, and entryde to the kyng, and worschipide on the
face of erthe bifor hym, and the kyng kisside Absolon.

CAP 15

1 Therfor aftir these thingis Absolon made a chaar to hym,
and knyytis, and fifti men, that schulden go bifor hym.
2 And Absolon roos eerli, and stood bisidis the entryng of the
yate in the weie; and Absolon clepide to hym ech man, that
hadde a cause that he schulde come to the doom of the kyng,
and Absolon seide, Of what citee art thou? Which answeride,
and seide, Of o lynage of Israel Y am, thi seruaunt.
3 And Absolon answeride to hym, Thi wordis semen to me
good and iust, but noon is ordeyned of the kyng to here thee.
And Absolon seide, Who schal ordeyne me iuge on the lond,
4 that alle men that han cause come to me, and Y deme
iustly?
5 But whanne a man cam to Absolon to greete hym, he helde
forth the hond, and took, and kisside that man;
6 and Absolon dide this to al Israel, that cam to doom to be
herd of the kyng; and Absolon drow awei the hertis of men of
Israel.
7 Forsothe aftir foure yeer Absolon seide to kyng Dauid, Y
schal go, and Y schal yelde my vowis, whiche Y vowide to
the Lord in Ebron;

8 for thi seruaunt vowynge vowide, whanne he was in Gessur of Sirie, and seide, If the Lord bryngith ayen me in to Jerusalem, Y schal make sacrifice to the Lord.

9 And the kyng seide to hym, Go thou in pees. And Absolon roos, and yede in to Ebron.

10 Forsothe Absolon sente aspieris in to al the lynage of Israel, and seide, Anoon as ye heren the sown of clarioun, seye ye, Absolon schal regne in Ebron.

11 Forsothe twei hundrid men clepid of Jerusalem yeden with Absolon, and yede with symple herte, and outirli thei knewen not the cause.

12 Also Absolon clepide Achitofel of Gilo, the councelour of Dauid, fro his citee Gilo. And whanne he offride sacrifices a strong swerynge togidere was maad, and the puple rennynge togidere was encreessid with Absolon.

13 Therfor a messanger cam to Dauid, and seide, With al herte al Israel sueth Absolon.

14 And Dauid seide to hise seruauntis that weren with hym in Jerusalem, Rise ye, and flee we; for noon ascaping schal be to us fro the face of Absolon; therfor haste ye to go out, lest he come, and ocupie vs, and fille on vs fallynge, and smyte the citee bi the scharpnesse of swerd.

15 And the seruauntis of the kyng seiden to hym, We thi seruauntis schulen performe gladli alle thingis, what euer thingis oure lord the kyng schal comaunde.

16 Therfor the kyng yede out, and al his hous, on her feet; and the king lefte ten wymmen concubyns, 'that is, secundarie wyues, to kepe the hous.

17 And the king yede out, and al Israel, on her feet, and the kyng stood fer fro the hous.

18 And alle hise seruauntis yeden bisidis him, and the legiouns of Cerethi and of Ferethi, and alle men of Geth 'strong fiyters, sixe hundrid men, that sueden him fro Geth, yeden on foote bifor the kyng.

19 Forsothe the kyng seide to Ethai of Geth, Whi comest thou with vs? Turne thou ayen, and dwelle with the kyng, for thou art a pilgrym, and thou yedist out fro thi place.

20 Thou camest yistirdai, and to dai thou art compellid to go out with vs. Sotheli Y schal go, whidur Y schal go; turne ayen, and lede ayen thi britheren with thee, and the Lord do mercy and treuthe with thee, for thou schewidist grace and feith.

21 And Ethai answeride to the kyng, and seide, The Lord lyueth, and my lord the kyng lyueth, for in what euer place thou schalt be, my lord the kyng, ether in deeth ethir in lijf, there thi seruaunt schal be.

22 And Dauid seide to Ethay, Come thou, and passe. And Ethai of Geth passide, and the kyng, and alle men that weren with hym, and the tother multitude.

23 And alle men wepten with greet vois, and al the puple passide; and the kyng yede ouer the strond of Cedron, and al the puple yede ayens the weie of the olyue tree, that biholdith to deseert.

24 Forsothe and Sadoch the preest cam, and alle the dekenes with hym, and thei baren the arke of boond of pees of God, and thei diden doun the arke of God; and Abiathar stiede, til al the puple was passid that yede out of the citee.

25 And the kyng seide to Sadoch, Bere ayen the arke of God in to the citee; if Y schal fynde grace in the iyen of the Lord, he schal lede me ayen, and he schal schewe to me that arke and his tabernacle.

26 Sotheli if the Lord seith, Thou plesist not me; Y am redi, do he that, that is good bifor hym silf.

27 And the kyng seide to Sadoch, preest, A! thou seere, 'that is, profete, turne ayen in to the citee, with pees; and Achymaas, thi sone, and Jonathas, the sone of Abiathar, youre twei sones, be with you.

28 Lo! Y schal be hid in the feeldi places of deseert, til word come fro you, and schewe to me.

29 Therfor Sadoch and Abiathar baren ayen the arke of God in to Jerusalem, and dwelliden there.

30 Forsothe Dauid stiede on the hil of olyue trees, stiynge and wepynge, with the heed hilyd, and 'goynge with nakid feet; but also al the puple that was with hym, stiede with the heed hilid, and wepte.

31 Forsothe it was teld to Dauid, that Achitofel was in the sweryng togidere with Absolon; and Dauid seide, Lord, Y byseche, make thou fonned the counsel of Achitofel.

32 And whanne Dauid stiede in to the hiyenesse of the hil, in which he schulde worschipe the Lord, lo! Cusi of Arath, with the cloth to-rent, and with the heed ful of erthe, cam to hym.

33 And Dauid seide to hym, If thou comest with me, thou schalt be to me to charge; sotheli if thou turnest ayen in to the citee,

34 and seist to Absolon, Y am thi seruaunt, kyng, suffre thou me to lyue; as Y was the seruaunt of thi fadir, so Y schal be thi seruaunt; thou schalt distrye the counsel of Achitofel.

35 Forsothe thou hast with thee Sadoch and Abiathar, preestis; and 'thou schalt schewe ech word, what euer word thou schalt here in the hows of the kyng, to Sadoch and Abiathar, preestis.

36 Sotheli twei sones 'of hem ben with hem, Achymaas, sone of Sadoch, and Jonathan, sone of Abiathar; and ye schulen sende bi hem to me ech word which ye schulen here.

37 Therfor whanne Chusi, freend of Dauid, cam in to the citee, also Absolon entryde in to Jerusalem.

CAP 16

1 And whanne Dauid hadde passid a litil the cop of the hil, Siba, the child of Mysphoboseth, apperide in to his comyng, with tweyne assis, that weren chargid with twei hundrid looues, and with an hundrid bundels of dried grapis, and with an hundrid gobetis of pressid figus, and with twei vessels of wyn.

2 And the kyng seide to Siba, What wolen these thingis to hem silf? And Siba answeride, My lord the kyng, the assis ben to the meyneals of the kyng, that thei sitte; the looues and 'figis pressid ben to thi children to ete; forsothe the wyn is, that if ony man faile in deseert, he drynke.

3 And the kyng seide, Where is the sone of thi lord? And Siba answeride to the kyng, He dwellide in Jerusalem, 'and seide, To dai the Lord of the hows of Israel schal restore to me the rewme of my fadir.

4 And the kyng seide to Siba, Alle thingis that weren of Mysphibosech ben thine. And Siba seide, Y preye, fynde Y grace bifor thee, my lord the kyng.

5 Therfor kyng Dauid cam 'til to Bahurym, and lo! a man of the meynee of the hows of Saul, Semey bi name, sone of Gera, yede out fro thennus; he yede forth goynge out, and curside.

6 And he sente stoonys ayens Dauid, and ayens alle seruauntis of kyng Dauid; forsothe al the puple, and alle fiyteris yeden at the riytside and at the left side of the king.

7 Sotheli Semey spak so, whanne he curside the kyng, Go out, go out, thou man of bloodis, and man of Belial!

8 The Lord hath yolde to thee al the blood of the hows of
Saul, for thou rauyschedist the rewme fro hym; and the Lord
yaf the rewme in to the hond of Absolon, thi sone; and lo!
thin yuels oppressen thee, for thou art a man of blodis.

9 Forsothe Abisay, the sone of Saruye, seide to the kyng, Whi
cursith this dogge, that schal die, my lord the kyng? Y schal
go, and Y schal girde of his heed.

10 And the kyng seide, Ye sones of Saruye, what is to me and
to you? Suffre ye hym, that he curse; for the Lord comaundide to hym, that he schulde curse Dauid; and who is he that
dare seie, Whi dide he so?

11 And the kyng seide to Abysay, and to alle hise seruauntis,
Lo! my sone, that yede out of my wombe, sekith my lijf; hou
myche more now this sone of Gemyny? Suffre ye hym, that
he curse bi comaundement of the Lord;

12 if in hap the Lord biholde my turmentyng, and yelde good
to me for this 'cursyng of this dai.

13 Therfor Dauid yede, and hise felowis, bi the weie with
hym; forsothe Semey yede bi the slade of the hil 'bi the side
ayens hym; and curside, and sente stoonus ayens him, and
spreynte erthe.

14 And so 'Dauid the king cam, and al the puple weery with
hym, and thei weren refreischid there.

15 Forsothe Absolon, and al the puple of Israel entriden in to
Jerusalem, but also Achitofel with hym.

16 Sotheli whanne Chusi of Arath, the frend of Dauid, hadde
come to Absolon, he spak to Absolon, Heil, kyng! heil, kyng!

17 To whom Absolon seide, This is thi grace to thi freend;
whi yedist thou not with thi freend?

18 And Chusi answeride to Absolon, Nay, for Y shal be seruaunt of hym, whom the Lord hath chose, and al this puple,
and al Israel; and Y schal dwelle with him.

19 But that Y seie also this, to whom schal Y serue? whethir
not to the sone of the kyng? as Y obeiede to thi fadir, so Y
schal obeie to thee.

20 Forsothe Absolon seide to Achitofel, Take ye counsel,
what we owen to do.

21 And Achytofel seide to Absolon, Entre thou to the concubyns of thi fadir, whiche he lefte to kepe the hows; that
whanne al Israel herith, that thou hast defoulid thi fadir, the
hondis of hem be strengthid with thee.

22 Therfor thei tildeden Absolon a tabernacle in the soler, and
he entride to the concubyns of his fadir bifor al Israel.

23 Sotheli the counsel of Achitofel, which he yaf in tho daies,
was as if a man counselide God; so was al the counsel of
Achitofel, bothe whanne he was with Dauid, and whanne he
was with Absolon.

CAP 17

1 Therfor Achitofel seide to Absolon, Y schal chese twelue
thousynde of men 'to me, and Y schal rise, and pursue Dauid
in this nyyt.

2 And Y schal falle on hym, for he is wery, and with vnboundun hondis Y schal smyte hym. And whanne al the puple
fleeth which is with hym, Y schal smyte the kyng 'desolat,
ether left aloone.

3 And Y schal lede ayen al the puple, as o man is wont to
turne ayen; for thou sekist o man, and al the puple schal be in
pees.

4 And the word of him plesyde Absolon, and alle the grete
men in birthe of Israel.

5 Forsothe Absolon seide, Clepe ye also Chusy of Arath, and
here we what also he seith.

6 And whanne Chusi hadde come to Absolon, Absolon seide
to hym. Achitofel spak siche a word; owen we do, ethir nay?
what counsel yyuest thou?

7 And Chusi seide to Absolon, This is not good counsel,
which Achitofel yaf in this tyme.

8 And eft Chusi seide, Thou knowist, that thi fadir, and the
men that ben with him, ben moost stronge, and in bitter soule,
as if a femal bere is fers in the forest, whanne the whelpis ben
rauyschid; but also thi fader is a man werriour, and he schal
not dwelle with the puple.

9 In hap now he is hid in the dichis, ethir in o place, in which
he wole; and whanne ony man fallith in the bigynnyng, who
euer schal here, he schal here, and schal seie, Wounde is
maad in the puple that suede Absolon.

10 And ech strongeste man, whos herte is as 'the herte of a
lioun, schal be discoumfortid for drede; for al the puple of
Israel knowith, that thi fadir is strong, and that alle men ben
stronge, that ben with him.

11 But this semeth to me to be riytful counsel; al Israel be
gaderid to thee, fro Dan 'til to Bersabee, vnnoumbrable as the
soond of the see; and thou schalt be in the myddis of hem.

12 And we schulen falle on hym, in what euer place he is
foundun, and we schulen hile hym, as dew is wont to falle on
the erthe; and we schulen not leeue of the men that ben with
hym, 'sotheli not oon.

13 'That if he entrith in to ony citee, al Israel schal cumpasse
that citee with roopis, and we schulen drawe it in to the
stronde, that no thing be foundun, sotheli not a litil stoon
therof.

14 And Absolon seide, and alle the men of Israel, The counsel
of Chusi of Arath is betere than the counsel of Achitofel;
sotheli the profitable counsel of Achitofel was destried bi
Goddis wille, that the Lord schulde brynge in yuel on Absolon.

15 And Chusi seide to Sadoch and to Abiathar, preestis,
Achitofel yaf counsel to Absolon, and to the eldere men of
Israel in this and this maner, and Y yaf sich and sich counsel.

16 Now therfor sende ye soone, and telle ye to Dauid, and
seie ye, Dwelle thou not this nyyt in the feeldi places of deseert, but passe thou with out delay; lest perauenture the kyng
be destried, and al the puple which is with hym.

17 Forsothe Jonathas and Achymaas stoden bisidis the welle
of Rogel; an handmaide yede, and telde to hem, and thei
yeden forth to telle the message to kyng Dauid; for thei
myyten not be seyn, nether entre in to the citee.

18 Forsothe a child siy hem, and he schewide to Absolon;
sotheli thei entriden with swift goyng in to the hows of 'sum
man in Bahurym, that hadde a pit in his place, and thei yeden
doun in to that pit.

19 Forsothe a womman took, and spred abrood an hilyng of
the mouth of the pit as driynge 'barli with the pile takun a
wey, and so the thing was hid.

20 And whanne the seruauntis of Absolon hadde come in to
the hows, thei seiden to the womman, Where is Achymaas
and Jonathas? And the womman answeride to hem, Thei
passiden hastili, whanne 'watir was tastid a litil. And whanne
thei that souyten hem hadden not founde, thei turneden ayen
in to Jerusalem.

21 And whanne thei 'that souyten hadden go, thei stieden fro
the pit; and thei yeden, and telden to kyng Dauid, and seiden,
Rise ye, passe ye soone the flood, for Achitofel yaf sich counsel ayens you.

22 Therfor Dauid roos, and al the puple that was with hym, and thei passiden Jordan, til it was cleer dai, bifor that the word was pupplischid; and sotheli not oon was left, that 'passide not the flood.

23 Forsothe Achitofel siy, that his counsel was not doon, and he sadlide his asse, and roos, and yede in to his hows, and in to his citee; and whanne his hows was disposid, he perischide bi hangyng, and he was biried in the sepulcre of his fadir.

24 Sotheli Dauid cam in to the castels, and Absolon passide Jordan, he and alle the men of Israel with hym.

25 Forsothe Absolon ordeynede Amasan for Joab on the oost; forsothe Amasan was the sone of a man that was clepid Jethra of Jeyrael, which entride to Abigail, douyter of Naas, the sistir of Saruye, that was the modir of Joab.

26 And Israel settide tentis with Absolon in the lond of Galaad.

27 And whanne Dauid hadde come in to castels, Sobi, the sone of Naas of Rabath, of the sones of Amon, and Machir, the sone of Amyel, of Lodobar, and Berzellai, of Galaad,

28 of Rogelym, brouyten to hym beddyngis, and tapitis, and erthun vessels, wheete, and barli, and mele, and flour, and benys, and lente, and fried chichis, and hony,

29 and botere, and scheep, and fatte calues. And thei yauen to Dauid, and to the puple that weren with hym, to ete; for thei supposiden the puple to be maad feynt for hungur and thirst in deseert.

CAP 18

1 Therfor Dauid, whanne the puple 'was biholdun, ordeynede tribunes and centuriouns on hem.

2 And he yaf the thridde part of the puple vndur the hond of Joab; and the thridde part vndur the hond of Abisai, sone of Saruye, brother of Joab; and the thridde part vndur the hond of Ethai, that was of Geth. And the kyng seide to the puple, Also Y schal go out with you.

3 And the puple answeride, Thou schalt not go out; for whether we fleen, it schal not perteyne to hem bi greet werk of vs; whether half the part fallith doun of vs, thei schulen not recke ynow, for thou art rekynyd for ten thousynde; therfor it is betere, that thou be to vs in the citee in stronge hold.

4 'To whiche the kyng seide, Y schal do this, that semeth riytful to you. Therfor the kyng stood bisidis the yate, and the puple yede out bi her cumpenyes, bi hundridis and bi thousyndis.

5 And the king comaundide to Joab, and to Abisai, and Ethai, and seyde, Kepe ye to me the child Absolon. And al the puple herde the kyng comaundinge to alle the princes for Absolon.

6 Therfor the puple yede out in to the feeld ayens Israel; and the batel was maad in the forest of Effraym.

7 And the puple of Israel was slayn there of the oost of Dauid, and a greet sleyng of twenti thousynde was maad in that dai.

8 Forsothe the batel was scaterid there on the face of al erthe, and many mo weren of the puple whiche the forest wastide, than thei whiche the swerd deuourid in that dai.

9 Sotheli it bifeld, that Absalon sittinge on a mule, cam ayens the seruauntis of Dauid; and whanne the mule hadde entrid vndur a thicke ook, and greet, the heed of Absolon cleuyde to the ook; and whanne he was hangid bitwixe heuene and erthe, the mule, on which he sat, passide.

10 Sotheli 'sum man siy this, and telde to Joab, and seide, Y siy Absolon hange on an ook.

11 And Joab seide to the man that 'hadde telde to hym, If thou siyest, whi persidist thou not hym to the erthe, and Y schulde haue youe 'to thee ten siclis of siluer, and a girdil?

12 And he seide to Joab, Thouy thou paiedist in myn hondis a thousynde platis of siluer, Y nolde sende myn hond in to the sone of the king; for the while we herden, the kyng comaundide to thee, and to Abisai, and to Ethai, and seide, Kepe ye to me the child Absolon.

13 But and if Y hadde do ayens my lijf hardili, this myyte not be hid fro the kyng, and thou woldist stonde on the contrarye side.

14 And Joab seide, Not as thou wolt, 'Absolon schal be kept, but Y schal asaile hym bifor thee. Therfore Joab took thre speris in his hond, and fitchide tho in the herte of Absolon. And whanne he spraulide, yit cleuynge in the ook,

15 ten yonge squieris of Joab runnen, and smytiden, and killiden hym.

16 Sotheli Joab sownede with a clarioun, and withhelde the puple, lest it pursuede Israel fleynge, and he wolde spare the multitude.

17 And thei token Absolon, and castiden forth him in to a greet dich in the forest, and baren togidere a ful greet heep of stoonys on hym; forsothe al Israel fledde in to his tabernaclis.

18 Forsothe Absolon, while he lyuyde yit, hadde reisid to hym a memorial, which is in the valey of the kyng; for he seide, Y haue no sone, and this schal be the mynde of my name; and he clepide 'the memorial bi his name, and it is clepid the Hond, 'that is, werk, of Absolon 'til to this dai.

19 Forsothe Achymaas, sone of Sadoch, seide, Y schal renne, and Y schal telle to the kyng, that the Lord hath maad doom to hym of the hond of hise enemyes.

20 To whom Joab seide, Thou schalt not be messanger in this dai, but thou schalt telle in another dai; I nyle that thou telle to dai, for the sone of the kyng is deed.

21 And Joab seide to Chusi, Go thou, and telle to the kyng tho thingis that thou hast seyn. Chusi worschypide Joab, and ran.

22 Eft Achymaas, sone of Sadoch, seide to Joab, What lettith, if also Y renne aftir Chusi? And Joab seide to hym, What wolt thou renne, my sone? Come thou hidur, thou schalt not be a berere of good message.

23 Which answeride, 'What sotheli if Y schal renne? And Joab seide to hym, Renn thou. Therfor Achymaas ran bi the weie of schortnesse, 'and sped, and passide Chusi.

24 Forsothe Dauid sat bitwixe twei yatis; sotheli the spiere, that was in the hiynesse of the yate on the wal, reiside the iyen, and siy a man aloone rennynge;

25 and the spiere criede, and schewide to the kyng. And the kyng seide to hym, If he is aloone, good message is in his mouth.

26 Sotheli while he hastide, and neiyede neer, the spiere siy another man rennynge; and the spiere criede 'in the hiynesse, and seide, Another man rennynge aloone apperith to me. And the kyng seide to hym, And this man is a good messanger.

27 Sotheli the spiere seide, Y biholde the rennyng of the formere, as the rennyng of Achymaas, sone of Sadoch. And the kyng seide, He is a good man, and he cometh bryngynge a good message.

28 Forsothe Achymaas criede, and seide to the kyng, Heil kyng! And he worschipide the kyng lowli bifor hym to erthe, and seide, Blessid be thi Lord God, that closide togidere the men, that reisyden her hondis ayens my lord the kyng.

29 And the kyng seide, Whether pees is to the child Absolon? And Achymaas seide, Y siy, 'that is, Y herde, a great noise,

whanne Joab, thi seruaunt, thou kyng, sente me thi seruaunt; Y kan noon othir thing.

30 To whom the kyng seide, Passe thou, and stonde here. And whanne he hadde passid, and stood, Chusi apperide;

31 and he cam and seide, My lord the kyng, Y brynge good message; for the Lord hath demed to dai for thee of the hond of alle men that risiden ayens thee.

32 Forsothe the kyng seide to Chusi, Whether pees is to the child Absolon? To whom Chusi answeride, and seide, The enemyes of my lord the kyng, and alle men that risiden ayens hym in to yuel, be maad as the child.

33 Therfor the kyng was sory, and stiede in to the soler of the yate, and wepte, and spak thus goynge, My sone, Absolon! Absolon, my sone! who yyueth to me, that Y die for thee? Absolon, my sone! my sone, Absolon!

CAP 19

1 Forsothe it was teld to Joab, that the kyng wepte, and biweilide his sone;

2 and the victorie in that dai was turned in to morenyng to al the puple; for the puple herde, that it was seid in that dai, The kyng makith sorewe on his sone.

3 And the puple eschewide to entre in to the citee in that dai, as the puple turned and fleynge fro batel is wont to bowe awey.

4 Sotheli the kyng hilide his heed, and criede with greet vois, My sone, Absolon!

5 Absolon, my sone! Therfor Joab entride to the kyng in to the hows, and seide, Thou hast schent to dai the cheris of alle thi seruauntis, that han maad saaf thi lijf, and the lijf of thi sones and of thi douytris, and the lijf of thi wyues, and the lijf of thi secoundarie wyues.

6 Thou louest hem that haten thee, and thou hatist hem that louen thee; and thou schewidist to dai that thou reckist not of thi duykis and of thi seruauntis; and verily Y haue knowe now, that if Absolon lyuede, and alle we hadden be deed, thanne it schulde plese thee.

7 Now therfor ryse thou, and go forth, and speke thou, and make satisfaccioun to this eruauntis; for Y swere to thee bi the Lord, that if thou schalt not go out, sotheli not o man schal dwelle with thee in this nyyt; and this schal be worse to thee, than alle yuels that camen on thee fro thi yong wexynge age til in to present tyme.

8 Therfor the kyng roos, and sat in the yate; and it was teld to al the puple, that the kyng sat in the yate, and al the multitude cam bifor the kyng. Forsothe Israel fledde in to hise tabernaclis.

9 And al the puple stryuede in al the lynagis of Israel, and seide, The kyng delyuerede vs fro the hond of alle oure enemyes, and he sauide vs fro the hond of Filisteis; and now 'he fleeth fro the lond for Absolon.

10 Forsothe Absolon, whom we anoyntiden on vs, is deed in batel; hou longe ben ye stille, 'that is, fro knowlechyng of synne, and fro axyng of foryyuenesse, and bryngen not ayen the kyng? And the counsel of al Israel cam to the kyng.

11 Forsothe kyng Dauid sente to Sadoch and to Abiathar, preestis, and seide, Speke ye to the grettere men in birthe of Juda, and seie ye, Whi camen ye the laste to brynge ayen the kyng in to his hows? Sotheli the word of al Israel cam to the kyng, that thei wolden brynge hym ayen in to his hows. For the kyng seide, Ye schulen seie these thingis to the puple,

12 Ye ben my britheren, ye ben my boon and my fleisch; whi the laste bryngen ye ayens the kyng?

13 And seie ye to Amasa, Whether thou art not my boon and my fleisch? God do these thingis to me, and adde these thingis, if thou schalt not be maistir of chyualrye bifore me in al tyme aftir Joab.

14 And Dauid bowide the herte of alle men of Juda as of o man; and thei senten to the kyng, and seiden, Turne thou ayen, and alle thi seruauntis.

15 And the kyng turnede ayen, and cam 'til to Jordan; and al Juda cam til in to Galgala to mete the kyng, and lede hym ouer Jordan.

16 Forsothe Semei, the sone of Gera, sone of Gemyny, of Bahurym, hastide, and cam doun with the men of Juda in to the metyng of kyng Dauid,

17 with a thousynde men of Beniamyn; and Siba, a child of the hows of Saul, and fiftene sones of hym, and twenti seruauntis weren with hym; and thei braken in to Jordan, bifor the kyng,

18 and passide the forthis, that thei schulden lede ouer the hows of the kyng, and schulden do bi the comaundement of the kyng. Sotheli Semei, the sone of Gera, knelide bifor the king, whanne he hadde passid now Jordan, and seide to the kyng,

19 My lord the kyng, arette thou not wickidnesse to me, nether haue thou mynde of the wrongis of thi seruaunt in the dai, in which thou, my lord the kyng, yedist out of Jerusalem, nether sette thou, kyng, in thin herte; for Y thi seruaunt knoleche my synne;

20 and therfor to dai Y cam the firste of al the hows of Joseph, and Y cam doun in to the meetyng of my lord the kyng.

21 Forsothe Abisai, the sone of Saruye, answeride and seide, Whether Semei, that curside the crist of the Lord, schal not be slayn for these wordis?

22 And Dauid seide, What is to me and to you, ye sones of Saruye? Whi ben ye maad to me to dai in to Sathan? Therfor whether a man schal be slayn to dai in Israel? Whether Y knowe not me maad kyng to dai on Israel?

23 And the kyng seide to Semey, Thou schalt not die; and the kyng swoor to hym.

24 Also Myphibosech, sone of Jonathas, sone of Saul, cam doun with vnwaischun feet, and with berd vnclippid, in to the comyng of the kyng. And Mysphibosech hadde not waische hise clothis, fro the dai in which the kyng yede out of Jerusalem til to the dai of his turnyng ayen in pees.

25 And whanne at Jerusalem he hadde come to the kyng, the kyng seide to him, Myphibosech, whi camest thou not with me?

26 And he answeride and seide, My lord the kyng, my seruaunt dispiside me; and Y thi seruaunt seide to hym, that he schulde sadle the asse to me, and Y schulde stie, and Y schulde go with the king; for Y thi seruaunt am crokid.

27 More ouer and he accuside me, thi seruaunt, to thee, my lord the kyng; forsothe thou, my lord 'the kyng, art as the aungel of God; do thou that, that is plesaunt to thee.

28 For the hows of my fadir was not no but gilti of deeth to my lord the kyng; sotheli thou hast set me thi seruaunt among the gestis of thi boord; what therfor haue Y of iust pleynt, ether what may Y more crye to the kyng?

29 Sotheli the kyng seide to hym, What spekist thou more? that that Y haue spoke is stidefast; thou and Siba depart possessyouns.

30 And Myphibosech answeride to the kyng, Yhe, take he alle thingis, aftir that my lord the kyng turnede ayen pesibli in to his hows.

31 Also Berzellai of Galaad, a ful eld man, cam doun fro Rogelym, and ledde the kyng ouer Jordan, redi also to sue hym ouer the flood.

32 Forsothe Berzellai of Galaad was ful eld, that is, of foure score yeer, and he yaf metis to the kyng, whanne the kyng dwellyde in castels; for Berzellai was a ful riche man.

33 Therfor the kyng seide to Berzellai, Come thou with me, that thou reste sikirli with me in Jerusalem.

34 And Berzellai seide to the kyng, Hou manye ben the daiest of yeeres of my lijf, that Y stie with the kyng in to Jerusalem?

35 Y am of foure score yeer to dai; whether my wittis ben quike to deme swete thing ethir bittir, ether mete and drynk may delite thi seruaunt, ether may Y here more the vois of syngeris ether of syngsters? Whi is thi seruaunt to charge to my lord the kyng?

36 Y thi seruaunt schal go forth a litil fro Jordan with thee, Y haue no nede to this yeldyng;

37 but Y biseche, that Y thi seruaunt turne ayen, and die in my citee, and be biried bisidis the sepulcre of my fadir and of my modir; forsothe Chamaam is thi seruaunt, my lord the kyng, go he with thee, and do thou to hym that that semeth good to thee.

38 Therfor the kyng seide to hym, Chamaam passe with me; and Y schal do to hym what euer thing plesith thee, and thou schalt gete al thing, which thou axist of me.

39 And whanne al the puple and the kyng hadden passid Jordan, the kyng abood; and 'the kyng kisside Berzellai, and blesside hym; and he turnede ayen in to his place.

40 Therfor the kyng passide in to Galgala, and Chamaam with hym. Sotheli al the puple of Juda hadde ledde the kyng ouer, and the half part oneli of the puple of Israel was present.

41 Therfor alle the men of Israel camen togidere to the king, and seiden to hym, Whi han oure britheren, the men of Juda, stole thee, and han led the kyng and his hows ouer Jordan, and alle the men of Dauid with hym?

42 And ech man of Juda answeride to the men of Israel, For the kyng is neer to me; whi art thou wrooth on this thing? Whether we han ete ony thing of the kyng, ether yiftis ben youun to vs?

43 And a man of Israel answeride to the men of Juda, and seide, Y am grettere bi ten partis at the kyng, and Dauith perteyneth more to me than to thee; whi hast thou do wrong to me, and 'it was not teld to 'me the formere, that Y schulde brynge ayen my kyng? Forsothe the men of Juda answeryden hardere to the men of Israel.

CAP 20

1 Also it bifelde, that a man of Belial was there, Siba bi name, the sone of Bothri, a man of the generacioun of Gemyny; and he sownede with a clarioun, and seide, No part is to vs in Dauid, nether eritage in the sone of Ysai; thou, Israel, turne ayen in to thi tabernaclis.

2 And al Israel was departid fro Dauid, and suede Siba, the sone of Bothri; forsothe the men of Juda cleuyden to her kyng, fro Jordan 'til to Jerusalem.

3 And whanne the kyng hadde come in to his hows in Jerusalem, he took ten wymmen, hise secundarie wyues, whiche he hadde left to kepe the hous, and he bitook hem in to keping, and yaf mete to hem; and he entride not to hem; but thei weren closid 'til to the dai of her deeth, and lyueden in widewehed.

4 Forsothe Dauid seide to Amasa, Clepe thou to gidere to me alle the men of Juda in to the thridde dai, and be thou present.

5 Therfor Amasa yede, that he clepe to gidere the puple of Juda; and he dwellide ouer the couenaunt, which the kyng hadde set to hym.

6 Sotheli Dauid seide to Abisai, Now Siba, the sone of Botri, schal turmente vs more than Absolon dide; therfor take the seruauntis of thi lord, and pursue hym, lest in hap he fynde strengthid citees, and ascape vs.

7 Therfor the men of Joab yeden out with Abisai, and Cerethi and Ferethi, and alle stronge men yeden out of Jerusalem to pursue Siba, the sone of Bochry.

8 And whanne thei weren bisidis the greet stoon, which is in Gabaon, Amasa cam, and ran to hem; forsothe Joab was clothid with a streit coote at the mesure of his abit, and was gird aboue with a swerd, 'ether dagger, hangynge doun 'til to the entrayls in a schethe, 'which swerd maad 'craftili myyte go out bi liyt touchyng, and smyte. Therfor Joab seide to Amasa,

9 Heil, my brother! And he helde with the riyt hond the chyn of Amasa, as kissinge him.

10 Forsothe Amasa took not kepe of the swerd, 'which swerd Joab hadde, and Joab smoot Amasa in the side, and schedde out his entrailis in to the erthe, and Amasa was deed; and Joab addide not 'the secounde wounde. Forsothe Joab and Abisai, his brother, pursueden Siba, the sone of Bochri.

11 In the meene tyme whanne 'sum men of the children of Dauid, of the felowis of Joab, hadden stonde bisidis the deed bodi of Amasa, thei seiden, Lo! he that wolde be the felowe of Dauid for Joab.

12 Forsothe Amasa was bispreynt with blood, and lay in the myddil of the weie. Sum man siy this, that al the puple abood to se Amasa, and he remouyde Amasa fro the weie in to the feeld, and he hilide Amasa with a cloth, lest men passynge schulden abide for hym.

13 Therfor whanne he was remouyd fro the weie, ech man passide suynge Joab to pursue Siba, the sone of Bochri.

14 Forsothe Siba hadde passide bi alle the lynagis of Israel til in to Habela, and in to Bethmacha; and alle chosun men weren gaderid to hym.

15 Therfor thei camen, and fouyten ayens hym in Habela, and in Bethmacha, and cumpassiden the citee with strengthingis; and the citee was bisegid. Sotheli al the cumpany, that was with Joab, enforside to distrie the wallis.

16 And a wijs womman of the citee criede an hiy, Here ye! here ye! seie ye to Joab, Neiye thou hidur, and Y schal speke with thee.

17 And whanne he hadde neiyed to hir, sche seide to hym, Art thou Joab? And he answeride, Y am. To whom sche spak thus, Here thou the wordis of thin handmayde. Which Joab answeride, Y here.

18 And eft sche seide, A word was seid in eld prouerbe, Thei that axen, axe in Habela; and so thei profitiden.

19 Whethir Y am not, that answere treuthe to Israel? and sekist thou to distrie a citee, and to distrie a modir citee in Israel? whi castidist thou doun the eritage of the Lord?

20 And Joab answeride, and seide, Fer be, fer be this fro me; Y 'caste not doun, nether Y distrye.

21 The thing hath not so it silf; but a man of the hil of Effraym, Siba, sone of Bochri, bi surname, reiside his hond ayens kyng Dauid; bitake ye him aloone, and we schulen go

awei fro the citee. And the womman seide to Joab, Lo! his heed schal be sent to thee bi the wal.

22 Therfor the womman entride to al the puple, and sche spak to hem wiseli; whiche 'castiden forth to Joab the heed of Siba, sone of Bochri, gird of. And Joab sownede with a trumpe, and thei departiden fro the citee, ech man in to hise tabernaclis; forsothe Joab turnede ayen to Jerusalem to the kyng.

23 Therfor Joab was on al the oost of Israel; forsothe Benanye, sone of Joiada, was on Cerethi and Ferethi;

24 forsothe Adhuram was on tributis; forsothe Josaphat, sone of Achilud, was chaunceler; forsothe Siba was scryueyn;

25 forsothe Sadoch and Abiathar weren preestis;

26 forsothe Hira of Hiarith was preest of Dauid.

CAP 21

1 Also hungur was maad in the lond of Israel in the daies of Dauid, bi thre yeer contynueli. And Dauid counselide the answere of the Lord; and the Lord seide, For Saul, and his hows, and blood, for he killide men of Gabaon.

2 Therfor whanne Gabaonytis weren clepid, the kyng seide to hem; sotheli Gabaonytis ben not of the sones of Israel, but thei ben the relikys of Ammorreis; and the sones of Israel hadden swore to hem, 'that is, that thei schulden not 'be slayn, and Saul wolde smyte hem for feruent loue, as for the sones of Israel and of Juda;

3 therfor Dauid seide to Gabaonytis, What schal Y do to you, and what schal be youre amendis, that ye blesse the eritage of the Lord?

4 And Gabaonytis seiden to hym, No questioun is to vs on gold and siluer, but ayens Saul, and ayens his hows; nether we wolen, that a man of Israel be slayn. To whiche the kyng seide, What therfor wolen ye, that Y do to you?

5 Whiche seiden to the king, We owen to do awei so the man, that 'al to brak ethir defoulide vs, and oppresside wickidli, that not oon sotheli be residue of his generacioun in alle the coostis of Israel.

6 Seuene men of hise sones be youun to vs, that we 'crucifie hem to the Lord in Gabaa of Saul, sum tyme the chosun man of the Lord. And the kyng seide, Y schal yyue.

7 And the kyng sparide Myphibosech, sone of Jonathas, sone of Saul, for the ooth of the Lord, that was bitwixe Dauid and bitwixe Jonathas, sone of Saul.

8 Therfor the kyng took twei sones of Respha, douyter of Ahira, whiche sche childide to Saul, Armony, and Mysphibosech; and he took fyue sones of Mychol, douyter of Saul, whiche sche gendride to Adriel, sone of Berzellai, that was of Molaty.

9 And he yaf hem in to the hondis of Gabaonytis, whiche crucifieden tho sones in the hil bifor the Lord; and these seuene felden slayn togidere in the daies of the firste rep, whanne the repyng of barli bigan.

10 Forsothe Respha, douytir of Ahia, took an heire, and 'araiede to hir silf a place aboue the stoon, fro the bigynnyng of heruest til watir droppide 'on hem fro heuene; and sche suffride not briddis to tere hem bi dai, nether beestis bi nytt.

11 And tho thingis whiche Respha, secoundarie wijf of Saul, douytir of Ahia, hadde do, weren teld to Dauid.

12 And Dauid yede, and took the boonys of Saul, and the boonys of Jonathas, his sone, of the men of Jabes of Galaad; that hadden stole tho boonys fro the street of Bethsan, in which street the Filisteis hadden hangid hem, whanne thei hadden slayn Saul in Gelboe.

13 And Dauid bar out fro thennus the boonys of Saul, and the boonys of Jonathas, his sone; and thei gaderiden the boonys of hem that weren crucified, and birieden tho with the boonys of Saul and of Jonathas, his sone, in the lond of Beniamyn, in the side of the sepulcre of Cys, fadir of Saul.

14 And thei diden al thingis, what euer thingis the kyng comaundide; and the Lord dide mercy to the lond aftir these thingis.

15 Forsothe batel of Filisteis was maad eft ayens Israel; and Dauid yede doun, and hise seruauntis with hym, and fouyten ayen Filisteis.

16 Sotheli whanne Dauid failide, Jesbydenob, that was of the kyn of Arapha, that is, of giauntis, and the yrun of his spere peiside thre hundrid ouncis, and he was gird with a newe swerd, enforside to smyte Dauid.

17 And Abisai, sone of Saruye, was in help to Dauid; and he smoot and killide the Filistei. Than the men of Dauid sworen, and seiden, Now thou schalt not go out with vs in to batel, lest thou quenche the lanterne of Israel.

18 Also the secounde batel was in Gob ayens Filisteis; thanne Sobothai of Osothai smoot Zephi, of the generacioun of Arapha, of the kyn of giauntis.

19 Also the thridde batel was in Gob ayens Filisteis; in which batel a man youun of God, the sone of forest, a broiderer, a man of Bethleem, smoot Golyath of Geth, whos 'schaft of spere was as a beem of webbis.

20 The fourthe batel was in Geth; where ynne was an hiy man, that hadde sixe fyngris in the hondis and feet, that is, foure and twenti; and he was of the kyn of Arapha;

21 and he blasfemyde Israel; sotheli Jonathan, sone of Samaa, brother of Dauid, killide hym.

22 These foure weren borun of Arapha in Geth, and thei felden doun in the hond of Dauid, and of hise seruauntis.

CAP 22

1 Forsothe Dauid spak to the Lord the wordis of this song, in the dai in which the Lord delyuerede hym fro the hond of alle hise enemyes, and fro the hond of Saul.

2 And Dauid seide, The Lord is my stoon, and my strengthe, and my sauyour;

3 my God, my stronge, I schal hope in to hym; my scheeld, and the horn of myn helthe, 'my reisere, and my refuyt; my sauyour, thou schalt delyuere me fro wickidnesse.

4 Y schal inwardly clepe the Lord worthi to be preisid; and Y schal be saaf fro myn enemyes.

5 For the sorewis of deeth cumpasside me; the strondis of Belial maden me aferd.

6 The coordis of helle cumpassiden me; the snaris of deeth camen bifor me.

7 In tribulacioun Y schal clepe, 'that is, Y clepide thee, Lord, and Y schal crie to my God; and he herd fro his holi temple my vois, and my crye schal come to hise eeris.

8 The erthe was mouyd, and tremblide; the foundementis of hillis weren smytun and schakun togidere, for the Lord was wrooth to hem.

9 Smoke stiede fro hise nosethirlis, and fier of his mouth schal deuoure; colis weren kyndlid of it.

10 And he bowide heuenes, and cam doun; and myist vndur hise feet.

11 And he stiede on cherubyn, and fliy; and he slood on the pennys of wynd.

12 He puttide derknessis hidyng place in his cumpas, and riddlide watris fro the cloudis of heuenes;

13 for briytnesse in his siyt colis of fier weren kyndelid.

14 The Lord schal thundur fro heuene; and hiy God schal yyue his vois.

15 He sente hise arowis, and scateride hem; he sente leitis, and wastide hem.

16 And the schedyngis out of the see apperiden, and the foundementis of the world weren schewid; fro the blamyng of the Lord, fro the brething of the spirit of his strong veniaunce.

17 He sente fro heuene, and took me; and drow me out of manye watris.

18 He delyuerede me fro my myytiest enemy, and fro hem that hatiden me; for thei weren strongere than Y.

19 Thei camen bifore me in the dai of my turmentyng; and the Lord was maad my stidfastnesse.

20 And he ledde me out in to largenesse, and he delyuerede me; for Y pleside hym.

21 The Lord schal yelde to me vp my riytfulnesse; and he schal yelde to me vp, 'ethir aftir, the clennesse of myn hondis.

22 For Y kepte the weies of the Lord; and Y dide not wickidli fro my God.

23 For alle hise domes weren in my siyt; and Y dide not awei fro me hise heestis.

24 And Y schal be perfit with hym; and Y schal kepe me fro my wickidnesse.

25 And the Lord schal restore to me vpe my riytfulnesse; and vp the clennesse of myn hondis in the siyt of hise iyen.

26 With the hooli thou schalt be hooli, and with the stronge, 'that is, to suffre aduersitees pacientli, thou schalt be perfit;

27 and with a chosun man 'to blis thou schalt be chosun, and with a weiward man thou schalt be maad weiward, 'that is, in yeldynge iustli peyne to hym vpe his weiwardnesse.

28 And thou schalt make saaf a pore puple; and with thin iyen thou schalt make lowe hem that ben hiye.

29 For thou, Lord, art my lanterne, and thou, Lord, schalt liytne my derknessis.

30 For Y gird, 'that is, maad redi to batel, schal renne in thee, 'that is, in thi vertu; and in my God Y schal 'scippe ouer the wal.

31 'God his weie is 'with out wem; the speche of the Lord is examynyd bi fier, 'that is, is pure and clene as metal preuyd in the furneys; he is a scheeld of alle men hopynge in hym.

32 For who is God, outakun the Lord; and who is strong, outakun oure God?

33 God, that hath gird me with strengthe, and hath maad pleyn my perfit weie;

34 and he made euene my feet with hertis, and settide me on myn hiye thingis;

35 and he tauyte myn hondis to batel, and made myn armes as a brasun bouwe.

36 Thou hast youe to me the sheeld of thin heelthe; and my myldenesse multipliede me.

37 Thou schalt alarge my steppis vndur me; and myn heelis schulen not faile.

38 Y schal pursue myn enemyes, and Y schal al to-breke hem; and Y schal not turne ayen, til Y waste hem.

39 Y schal waste hem, and Y schal breke, that thei rise not; thei schulen falle vndur my feet.

40 Thou hast gird me with strengthe to batel; thou hast bowid vnder me hem that ayenstoden me.

41 Thou hast youe myn enemyes abac to me, men hatynge me; and Y schal distrie hem.

42 Thei schulen crye, 'that is, to ydols ether to mennus help, and noon schal be that schal saue; 'thei schulen crie to the Lord, and he schal not here hem.

43 Y schal do awei hem as the dust of erthe; Y schal 'powne hem, and Y schal do awei as the clei of stretis.

44 Thou schalt saue me fro ayenseiyngis of my puple; thou schalt kepe me in to the heed of folkis; the puple, whom Y knowe not, schal serue me.

45 Alien sones schulen ayenstonde me; bi heryng of eere thei schulen obeie to me.

46 Alien sones fletiden awei; and thei schulen be drawun togidere in her angwischis.

47 The Lord lyueth, and my God is blessid; and the stronge God of myn helthe schal be enhaunsid.

48 God, that yyuest veniauncis to me; and hast cast doun puplis vndur me.

49 Which ledist me out fro myn enemyes, and reisist me fro men ayenstondinge me; thou schalt deliuere me fro the wickid man.

50 Therfor, Lord, Y schal knowleche to thee in hethene men; and Y schal synge to thi name.

51 And he magnyfieth the helthis of his kyng; and doith mercyes to his crist Dauid, and to his seed til in to withouten ende.

CAP 23

1 Forsothe these ben the laste wordis, whiche Dauid, the sone of Ysai, seide. The man seide, to whom it is ordeyned of Crist, of the God of Jacob, the noble salm makere of Israel;

2 The spiryt of the Lord spak bi me, and his word bi my tunge.

3 Dauid seide, God of Israel spak to me, the stronge of Israel, the 'iust Lord of men, 'is Lord in the drede of God.

4 As the liyt of the morewtid, whanne the sunne risith eerli, is briyt with out cloudis; and as an erbe cometh forth of the erthe bi reynes.

5 And myn hows is not so greet anentis God, that he schulde make with me euerlastynge couenaunt, stidefast and maad strong in alle thingis; for al myn helthe hangith of him, and al the wille 'that is, al my desir, goith in to hym, and no thing is therof, that makith not fruyt.

6 Forsothe alle trespassouris schulen be drawun out as thornes, that ben not takun with hondis.

7 And if ony man wole touche tho, he schal be armed with irun, and with tre formed in to spere; and the thornes schulen be kyndlid, and schulen be brent 'til to nouyt.

8 These ben the names of the stronge men of Dauid. Dauid sittith in the chaier, the wiseste prince among thre; he is as a moost tendir worm of tree, that killide eiyte hundrid with o fersnesse.

9 Aftir hym was Eleazar, the sone of his fadirs brother Abohi; among thre stronge men, that weren with Dauid, whanne thei seiden schenschip to Filisteis, and weren gaderid thidir in to batel.

10 And whanne the men of Israel hadden stied, he stood, and smoot Filistiis, til his hond failide, and was starke with the swerd. And the Lord made greet helthe in that dai; and the puple that fledde turnedc ayen to drawe awei the spuylis of slayn men.

11 And aftir hym was Semma, the sone of Age, of Arari. And Filisteis weren gaderid in the stacioun; forsothe there was a feeld ful of lente; and whanne the puple fledde fro the face of Filisteis,

12 he stood in the myddis of the feeld, and bihelde it; and he smoot Filisteis, and the Lord made greet helthe.

13 Also and thre men yeden doun bifore, that weren princes among thretti, and camen to Dauid in the tyme of reep in to the denne of Odollam. Forsothe the castels of Filisteis weren set in the valei of giauntis.

14 And Dauid was in a strong hold; sotheli the stacioun of Filisteis was thanne in Bethleem.

15 Therfor Dauid desiride water of the lake, and seide, If ony man wolde yyue to me drynk of watir of the cisterne, which is in Bethleem, bisidis the yate.

16 Therfor thre stronge men braken in to the castels of Filisteis, and drowen watir of the cisterne of Bethleem, that was bisidis the yate, and brouyten to Dauid; and he nolde drinke,

17 but offride it to the Lord, and seide, The Lord be merciful to me, that Y do not this; whether Y schal drynke the blood of these men, that yeden forth, and the perel of soulis? Therfor he nolde drynke. Thre strongeste men diden thes thingis.

18 Also Abisay, brother of Joab, the sone of Saruye, was prince of thre; he it is that reiside his schaft ayens thre hundrid men, whiche he killide; 'he was nemid among thre,

19 and was the noblere among thre, and he was the prince of hem; but he cam not to the thre firste men.

20 And Banaye, the sone of Joiada, strongeste man of grete werkis, of Capseel, he smoot twei liouns of Moab, 'that is, twei knyytis hardi as liouns; and he yede doun, and smoot a lioun in the myddil cisterne in the daies of snow.

21 Also he killide a man of Egipt, a man worthi of spectacle, hauynge a spere in the hond; therfor whanne he hadde come doun with a yerde to that man, bi miyt he wrooth out the spere fro the hond of the man of Egipt, and killide hym with his owne spere.

22 Banaye, sone of Joiada, dide these thingis;

23 and he was nemyed among thre stronge men, that weren among the thretti noblere men; netheles he cam not til to the thre. And Dauid made hym a counselour of priuyte to hym silf.

24 Asahel, the brother of Joab, was among thretti men; Eleanan, the sone of his fadris brother, of Bethleem; Semma, of Arari;

25 Elcha, of Arodi; Helas, of Phelti;

26 Hira, sone of Aches, of Thecua; Abiezer, of Amatoth;

27 Mobannoy, of Cosathi; Selmon, of Achotes;

28 Macharai, of Nethopath;

29 Heled, the sone of Baana, and he was of Netophath; Hiray, sone of Rabai, of Gebeeth, of the sones of Beniamyn; Banay, of Effrata;

30 Hedday, of the stronde of Gaas;

31 Abiadon, of Arbath; Asmaneth, of Berromy;

32 Eliaba, of Sabony; sones of Assen, Jonathan, and Jasan; Semma, of Herodi;

33 Hayam, sone of Sarai, of Zaroth;

34 Eliphelech, the sone of Saalbai, the sone of Maachati; Heliam, sone of Achitofel, of Gilo;

35 Esrai, of Carmele; Pharai, of Arbi;

36 Ygaal, sone of Nathan, of Soba;

37 Bonny, of Gaddi; Silech, of Ammony; Naarai, of Beroth, the squyer of Joab, the sone of Saruye;

38 Haray, of Jethri; Gareb, and he was of Gethri;

39 Vrye, of Ethei; alle weren seuene and thretti men.

CAP 24

1 And the strong veniaunce of the Lord addide to be wrooth ayens Israel [Note: of this that the Lord wolde punysche the puple, he suffride Dauyth to be reisid bi pride to the noumbring of the puple; wherfor the gloss of Gregre on this place seith thus, The dedis of gouernours ben disposid for the maneris of sugetis, that ofte for the yuel of the floc, the liyf yhe of a good schepparde trespassith, for Dauyth was preisid bi God witnesse, and he was blowun with the bolnyng of sudeyn pride, and synnede in noumbringe puple, and the puple resseyuede peyne; for the hertis of gouernours ben disposid, vp the meritis of the puplis. The synne of the puple for which it was punyschid, is not expressid in the text, but in the book of Ebreu questiouns it is seid, that this was herfor, for the puple ayen stood not Dauyth as it ouyte, in the dede of Vrie, but for this dede was priuy til it was al doon; the puple myyte not withstonde Dauyth in the synne to be lettid, and aftir that this synne cam in to the knowing of the puple, the puple ouyte not to punysche it, for the peyne was determynd thanne of God, as it is opin in xii. co. bi the wordis of Nathan, therfor it is seid betere, that the synne of the puple, was the rebelte therof ayenus Dauyth in suynge Siba, sone of Bothry, that was the worste man and ful of dissencioun, and Siba aloone was punyschid for this rebelte.], and he stiride in hem Dauid, seiynge to Joab, Go thou, and noumbre thou Israel and Juda.

2 And the kyng seide to Joab, the prince of his oost, Go thou bi alle lynagis of Israel fro Dan 'til to Bersabee, and noumbre thou the puple, that Y wite the noumbre therof.

3 And Joab seide to the kyng, Thi Lord God encresse to this puple, 'hou greet it is now, and eft multiplie he an hundrid fold in the siyt of my lord the kyng; but what wole my lord the kyng to hym silf in sich a thing?

4 Sotheli the word of the kyng ouer cam the wordis of Joab, and of the princes of the oost; and Joab yede out, and the princes of the knyytis, fro the face of the kyng, that thei schulden noumbre the puple of Israel.

5 And whanne thei hadden passid Jordan, thei camen in to Aroer, to the riyt side of the citee which is in the valei of Gad;

6 and thei passiden bi Jazer in to Galaad, and in to the lowere lond of Odsi, and camen in to the wodi places of Dan; and thei cumpassiden bisidis Sidon,

7 and passiden nyy the wallis of Tire, and nyy al the lond of Euei, and of Chananei; and thei camen to the south of Juda, in Bersabee.

8 And whanne al the lond was cumpassid, thei camen aftir nyne monethis and twenti daies in to Jerusalem.

9 Therfor Joab yaf the noumbre of discriuyng of the puple to the kyng. And of Israel weren foundun nyne hundryd thousynd [Note: in I. book of Paralip. xxi. co. is a thousinde, and an hundrid thousinde; here is set the lesse noumbre, and there the gretter noumbre, and of Juda is set there the lesse noumbre, and here the gretter.] of stronge men, that drewen out swerd; and of Juda fyue hundrid thousynde of fiyteris.

10 Forsothe the herte of Dauid smoot hym, 'that is, his concience repreuyde hym, aftir that the puple was noumbrid; and Dauid seide to the Lord, Y synnede greetli [Note: in pride, and in breking of Goddis heest, for in xxxi. co. of Exody, whanne the sones of Israel weren noumbrid, ech man schulde [offre] to the Lord half a sicle, and this was not doon here.] in this dede; but, Lord, Y preye that thou turne awei the wickidnesse of thi seruaunt, for Y dide ful folili.

11 Therfor Dauid roos eerli, and the word of the Lord was maad to Gad, the prophete and seere, and seide, Go thou,

12 and speke to Dauid, The Lord seith these thingis, The chesyng of thre thingis is youun to thee; chese thou oon, which thou wolt of these, that Y do to thee.

13 And whanne Gad hadde come to Dauid, he telde to Dauid, and seide, Ether hungur schal come to thee in thi lond seuene yeer; ethir thre monethis thou schalt fle thin aduersaries, and thei schulen pursue thee; ether certis thre daies pestilence schal be in thi lond; now therfor delyuere thou, 'ether auyse thou, and se, what word Y schal answere to hym that sente me.

14 Forsothe Dauid seide to Gad, Y am constreyned on ech side greetli; but it is betere that Y falle in to the hondis of the Lord [Note: if Dauyth hadde chose huugur of vii. yeer, he and riche men wolden haue purueyed to hem silf of liyflode, and pore men schulden haue be turmentid gretly; and if he hadde chose fliyt bifor enemyes, he and myyty men schulden haue be defendid and pore men slayn, therfor he chees pestilence, comyn peyne to alle, for he tristide in Goddis mersi.], for his emercies ben manye, than in the hondis of men.

15 And the Lord sente pestilence in to Israel fro the morewtid 'til to the tyme ordeyned [Note: that is, til to the oure of sacrifice of euentid; the ii. laste dayes of pestilence, weren seid bi manassing, and weren releessid for the penaunce of Dauyth.]; and seuenti thousynde of men weren deed of the puple fro Dan 'til to Bersabee.

16 And whanne the aungel of the Lord hadde holde forth his hond ouer Jerusalem, that he schulde distrie it, the Lord hadde mercy on the turmentyng; and seide to the aungel smytynge the puple, It sufficith now; withholde thin hond. Forsothe the aungel of the Lord was bisidis the corn floor of Areuna Jebusey.

17 And Dauid seide to the Lord, whanne he hadde seyn the aungel sleynge the puple, Y am he that 'haue synned, and Y dide wickidli; what han these do, that ben scheep? Y biseche, thin hond be turned ayens me, and ayens the hows of my fadir.

18 Forsothe Gad, the prophete, cam to Dauid in that dai, and seide to hym, Stie thou, and ordeyne an auter to the Lord in the corn floor of Areuna Jebusei.

19 And Dauid stiede, vpe the word of Gad, which the Lord hadde comaundid to hym.

20 And Areuna bihelde, and perseyuede, that the kyng and hise seruauntis passiden to hym;

21 and he yede out, and worschipide the kyng bi low cheer to the erthe; and seide, What 'cause is, that my lord the kyng cometh to his seruaunt? To whom Dauid seide, That Y bie of thee the corn floor, and bilde an auter to the Lord, and the sleynge ceesse, which is cruel in the puple.

22 And Areuna seide to Dauid, My lord the kyng take, and offre, as it plesith hym; thou hast oxis in to brent sacrifice, and a wayn and yockis of oxis in to vss of wode.

23 Areuna yaf alle thingis [Note: that is, wolde yyue.] to the king. And Areuna seide to the king, Thi Lord God reseyue thi vow.

24 To whom the king answeride, and seide, Not as thou wolt, but Y schal bie of thee for prijs, and Y schal not offre to 'my Lord God brent sacrifices youun freli. Therfor Dauid bouyte the corn floor [Note: for vi. hundrid siclis of gold, in the firste book of Paralip. xxi. co.], and 'he bouyte oxis for fifti siclis of siluer.

25 And Dauid bildide there an auter to the Lord, and offride brent sacrifices and pesible sacrifices; and the Lord dide merci to the lond, and the veniaunce was refreyned fro Israel.

3 KINGS

CAP 1

1 And kyng Dauid wax eld, and hadde ful many daies of age; and whanne he was hilid with clothis, he was not maad hoot.

2 Therfor hise seruauntis seiden to hym, Seke we to oure lord the kyng a yong wexynge virgyn; and stonde sche bifor the kyng, and nursche sche hym, and slepe in his bosum, and make hoot oure lord the kyng.

3 Therfor thei souyten a yong wexyng virgyn, fair in alle the coostis of Israel; and thei founden Abisag of Sunam, and thei brouyten hir to the kyng.

4 Forsothe the damysel was ful fair, and sche slepte with the kyng, and mynystride to hym; forsothe the king knew not hir fleischli.

5 Sotheli Adonye, sone of Agith, was reisid, and seide, Y schal regne. And he made to hym a chare, and knyytis, and fifti men, that runnen bifor hym.

6 Nether his fadir repreuyde hym ony tyme, and seide, Whi 'didist thou this? Forsothe also he was ful fair, the secounde child aftir Absolon; and his word was with Joab,

7 sone of Saruye, and with 'Abiathar, preest, that helpiden the partis of Adonye.

8 Sotheli Sadoch, the preest, and Banaie, sone of Joiada, and Nathan, the prophete, and Semey, and Cerethi, and Ferethi, and al the strengthe of the oost of Dauid, weren not with Adonye.

9 Therfor whanne rammes weren offrid, and caluys, and alle fatte thingis, bisidis the stoon Zoelech, that was nyy the welle of Rogel, Adonye clepide alle hise britheren, sones of the kyng, and alle the men of Juda, seruauntis of the kyng.

10 Sotheli 'he clepide not Nathan, the profete, and Banaie, and alle stronge men, and Salomon, his brothir.

11 Therfor Nathan seide to Bersabee, modir of Salomon, Whether thou herdist, that Adonye, sone of Agith, regnede, and oure lord Dauid knoweth not this?

12 Now therfor come thou, take thou counsel of me, and saue thi lijf, and of Salomon thi sone.

13 Go thou, and entre to kyng Dauid, and seie thou to hym, Whether not thou, my lord the kyng, hast swore to me, thin handmaide, and seidist, that Salomon thi sone schal regne aftir me, and he schal sitte in my trone?

14 Whi therfor regneth Adonye? And yit while thou schalt speke there with the kyng, Y schal come aftir thee, and 'Y schal fille thi wordis.

15 Therfor Bersabee entride to the kyng in the closet; forsothe the kyng was ful eeld, and Abisag of Sunam 'mynystride to hym.

16 Bersabee bowide hir silf, and worschipide the kyng; to whom the kyng seide, What wolt thou to thee?

17 And sche answeride, and seide, My lord the kyng, thou hast swore to thin handmaide bi thi Lord God, Salomon thy sone schal regne aftir me, and he schal sitte in my trone;

18 and lo! Adonye hath regnede now, 'while thou, my lord the kyng, knowist not;

19 he hath slayn oxis, and alle fatte thingis, and ful many rammes; and he clepide alle the sones of the king, also 'Abiathar preest, and Joab, the prince of chyualri; but he clepide not Salomon, thi seruaunt.

20 Netheles, my lord the kyng, the iyen of al Israel biholden in to thee, that thou schewe to hem, who owith to sitte in thi trone, my lord the kyng, aftir thee;

21 and it schal be, whanne my lord the kyng hath slepte with hise fadris, Y and my sone Salomon schulen be synneris.

22 'While sche spak yit with the king, Nathan, the prophete, cam.

23 And thei telden to the kyng, and seiden, Nathan, the prophete, is present. And whanne he hadde entrid in the siyt of the kyng, and hadde worschipide hym lowli to erthe,

24 Nathan seide, My lord the kyng, seidist thou, Adonye regne aftir me, and sitte he on my trone?

25 For he cam doun to dai, and offride oxis, and fatte thingis, and ful many wetheris; and he clepide alle the sones of the kyng, also Abiathar, preest; and whanne thei eten, and drunken bifor hym, and seiden, Kyng Adonye lyue;

26 he clepide not me, thi seruaunt, and Sadoch, preest, and Banaie, sone of Joiada, and Salomon, thi sone.

27 Whether this word yede out fro my lord the kyng, and thou schewidist not to me, thi seruaunt, who schulde sitte on the trone of my lord the king after hym?

28 And kyng Dauid answeride, and seide, Clepe ye Bersabee to me. And whanne sche hadde entrid bifor the kyng, and hadde stonde bifor hym, the kyng swoor,

29 and seide, The Lord lyueth, that delyueryde my lijf fro al angwisch;

30 for as Y swore to thee bi the Lord God of Israel, and seide, Salomon, thi sone, schal regne after me, and he schal sitte on my trone for me, so Y schal do to dai.

31 And Bersabee, with the cheer cast doun in to erthe, worschipide the kyng, and seide, My lord the kyng Dauid lyue with outen ende.

32 And kyng Dauid seide, Clepe ye Sadoch, the preest, to me, and Nathan, the prophete, and Banaie, sone of Joiada. And whanne thei hadden entrid bifor the kyng,

33 the kyng seide to hem, Take with you the seruauntis of youre lord, and putte ye my sone Salomon on my mule, and lede ye hym in to Gyon.

34 And Sadoch, the preest, and Nathan, the profete, anoynte hym in to kyng on Israel and Juda; and ye schulen synge with a clarioun, and ye schulen seie, Lyue kyng Salomon!

35 Ye schulen stie aftir hym, and ye schulen come to Jerusalem; and he schal sitte on my trone, and he schal regne for me; and Y schal comaunde to hym, that he be duyk on Israel and on Juda.

36 And Banaie, sone of Joiada, answeride to the kyng, and seide, Amen, 'that is, so be it, ether verili, ether feithfuli; so speke the Lord God of my lord the kyng.

37 As the Lord was with my lord the kyng, so be he with Salomon, and make he the trone of Salomon heiyere than the trone of my lord the kyng Dauid.

38 Therfor Sadoch, the preest, yede doun, and Nathan, the prophete, and Banaie, sone of Joiada, and Cerethi, and Ferethi; and thei puttiden Salomon on the mule of Dauid, the kyng, and thei brouyten hym in to Gion.

39 And Sadoch, the preest, took an horn of oile of the tabernacle, and anoyntide Salomon; and thei sungen with a clarioun; and al the puple seide, Lyue kyng Salomon!

40 And al the multitude stiede after hym, and the puple of men syngynge with pipis, and 'of men beynge glad with greet ioye, 'stiede aftir hym; and the erthe sownede of the cry of hem.

41 Forsothe Adonye herde, and alle that weren clepid of hym to feeste; and thanne the feeste was endid. But also Joab seide, whanne the vois of trumpe was herd, What wole it to it silf the cry of the citee makynge noise?

42 Yit the while he spak, Jonathan, sone of Abiathar, the preest, cam; to whom Adonye seide, Entre thou, for thou art a strong man, and tellynge goode thingis.

43 And Jonathan answeride to Adonye, Nay; for oure lord the kyng Dauid hath ordeyned Salomon kyng;

44 and Dauid sente with Salomon Sadoch, the preest, and Nathan, the prophete, and Banaie, sone of Joiada, and Cerethi, and Ferethi; and thei puttiden Salomon on the mule of the kyng.

45 And Sadoch, the preest, and Nathan, the prophete, anoyntiden hym kyng in Gion; and thei camen doun fro thennus beynge glad, and the citee sownede; this is the vois which ye herden.

46 But also Salomon sittith on the trone of rewme;

47 and the seruauntis of the kyng entriden, and blessiden oure lord the kyng Dauid, and seiden, God make large the name of Salomon aboue thi name, and magnyfye his trone aboue thi trone. And kyng Dauid worschipide in his bed;

48 and ferthermore he spak these thingis, Blessid be the Lord God of Israel, that yaf to dai a sittere in my trone, while myn iyen seen.

49 Therfor alle, that weren clepid of Adonye to feeste, weren aferd, and risiden, and ech man yede in to his weie.

50 Sotheli Adonye dredde Salomon, and roos, and yede in to the tabernacle of the Lord, and helde the horn of the auter.

51 And thei telden to Salomon, and seiden, Lo! Adonye dredith the kyng Salomon, and holdith the horn of the auter, and seith, Kyng Salomon swere to me to dai, that he schal not sle his seruaunt bi swerd.

52 And Salomon seide, If he is a good man, sotheli not oon heer of hym schal falle in to erthe; but if yuel be foundun in hym, he schal die.

53 Therfor kyng Salomon sente, and ledde 'hym out fro the auter; and he entride, and worschipide kyng Salomon; and Salomon seide to hym, Go in to thin hows.

CAP 2

1 Forsothe the daies of Dauid neiyiden, that he schulde die; and he comaundide to Salomon, his sone, and seide, Lo!

2 Y entre in to the weie of al erthe; be thou coumfortid, and be thou a strong man.

3 And kepe thou the kepyngis and heestis of thi Lord God, that thou go in hise weies, and kepe hise cerymonyes, and hise heestis, and hise domes, and witnessyngis, as it is writun in the lawe of Moises; that thou vndurstonde alle thingis whiche thou doist, and whidur euer thou schalt turne thee.

4 That the Lord conferme hise wordis, whiche the Lord spak of me, and seide, If thi sones kepen my weies, and goen bifor me in treuthe, in al her herte, and in al her soule, a man schal not be takun awei of thee fro the trone of Israel.

5 Also thou knowist what thingis Joab, the sone of Saruye, dide to me; what thingis he dide to twey princis of the oost of Israel, to Abner, sone of Ner, and to Amasa, sone of Jether, whiche he killide, and schedde the blood of batel in pees; and puttide the blood of batel in his girdil, that was aboute hise leendis, and in his scho, that was in hise feet.

6 Therfor thou schalt do by thi wisdom, and thou schalt not lede forth his hoornesse pesibli to hellis.

7 But also thou schalt yelde grace to the sones of Bersellai of Galaad, and thei schulen be eetynge in thi boord; for thei metten me, whanne Y fledde fro the face of Absolon, thi brother.

8 Also thou hast anentis thee Semey, sone of Gera, sone of Gemyny, of Bahurym, which Semei curside me bi the worste cursyng, whanne Y yede to 'the castels; but for he cam doun to me in to metyng, whanne Y passide Jordan, and Y swoor to him bi the Lord, and seide, Y schal not slee thee bi swerd,

9 nyle thou suffre hym to be vnpunyschid; forsothe thou art a wise man, and thou schalt wite what thou schalt do to hym, and thou schalt lede forth hise hoor heeris with blood to hellis.

10 Sotheli Dauid slepte with hise fadris, and was biriede in the citee of Dauid.

11 Forsothe the daies, in whiche Dauid regnede on Israel, ben fourti yeer; in Ebron he regned seuene yeer, in Jerusalem thre and thretti yeer.

12 Forsothe Salomon sat on the trone of Dauid, his fadir, and his rewme was maad stidfast greetli.

13 And Adonye, sone of Agith, entride to Bersabee, modir of Salomon; and sche seide to hym, Whether thin entryng is pesible? And he answeride, It is pesible.

14 And he addide, A word of me is to thee. 'To whom sche seide, Speke thou.

15 And he seide, Thou knowist that the rewme was myn, and al Israel purposide to make me in to king to hem; but the rewme is translatid, and is maad my brotheris; for of the Lord it is ordeyned to hym.

16 Now therfor Y preye of the oon axyng; schende thou not my face. And sche seide to hym, Speke thou. And he seide, Y preie,

17 that thou seie to Salomon the king; for he may not denye ony thing to thee; that he yyue to me Abisag of Sunam wijf.

18 And Bersabee seide, Wel, Y schal speke for thee to the kyng.

19 Therfor Bersabee cam to kyng Salomon, to speke to hym for Adonye; and the kyng roos ayens the comyng of hir, and worschipide hir, and 'sat on his trone; and a trone was set to the modir of the kyng, and sche sat at his riyt side.

20 And sche seide to hym, Y preie of thee o litil axyng; schende thou not my face. And the kyng seide to hir, My modir, axe thou; for it is not leueful that Y turne awei thi face.

21 And sche seide, Abisag of Sunam be youun wijf to Adonye, thi brother.

22 And kyng Salomon answeride, and seide to his modir, Whi axist thou Abisag of Sunam to Adonye? Axe thou to hym also the rewme; for he is 'my gretter brothir, and he hath Abiathar, preest, and Joab, sone of Saruye.

23 Therfor kyng Salomon swoor bi the Lord, and seide, God do to me these thingis, and adde these thinges, for Adonie spak this word ayens his lijf.

24 And now the Lord lyueth, that confermede me, and hath set me on the trone of my fadir, and that hath maad to me an hows, as he spak, for Adonye schal be slayn to dai.

25 And kyng Salomon sente bi the hond of Banaie, sone of Joiada; which Banaie killide Adonye, and he was deed.

26 Also the kyng seide to Abiathar, preest, Go thou in to Ana-tot, to thi feeld; and sotheli thou art a man of deeth, 'that is, worthi the deeth, for conspiryng ayens me, and the ordy-naunce of God, and of my fadir; but to dai Y schal not sle thee, for thou barist the arke of the Lord God bifor Dauid, my fadir, and thou suffridist trauele in alle thingis, in whiche my fadir trauelide.

27 Therfor Salomon puttide out Abiathar, that he schulde not be preest of the Lord, that the word of the Lord were fillid, which he spak on the hows of Heli, in Silo.

28 Forsothe a messanger cam to Salomon, that Joab hadde bowid aftir Adonye, and that he hadde not bowid after Salomon. Therfor Joab fledde in to the tabernacle of the Lord, and took the horn of the auter.

29 And it was told to kyng Salomon, that Joab hadde fledde in to the tabernacle of the Lord, and was bisidis the auter; and Salomon sente Banaie, sone of Joiada, and seide, Go thou, and sle hym.

30 And Banaie cam to the tabernacle of the Lord, and seide to Joab, The kyng seith these thingis, Go thou out. And he seide, Y schal not go out, but Y schal die here. Banaie telde the word to the kyng, and seide, Joab spak thes thingis, and answeride these thingis to me.

31 And the kyng seide to Banaie, Do thou as he spak, and sle thou hym, and birie him; and thou schalt remoue the innocent blood, that was sched out of Joab, fro me, and fro the hows of my fadir.

32 And the Lord yelde on his heed his blood, for he killide twei iust men, and betere than hym silf, and he killide hem bi swerd, while Dauid, my fadir, 'wiste not, Abner, the sone of Ner, the prince of the chyualrie of Israel, and Amasa, sone of Jether, the prince of the oost of Juda.

33 And the blood of hem schal turne ayen in to the heed of Joab, and in to the heed of his seed with outen ende; forsothe pees be of the Lord til in to with outen ende to Dauid, and to his seed, and to the hous and trone of hym.

34 Therfor Banaie, sone of Joiada, stiede, and asailide, and killide Joab; and Joab was biried in his hows in deseert.

35 And the kyng ordeynede Banaie, sone of Joiada, on the oost for hym; and the kyng puttide Sadoch preest for Abia-thar.

36 Also the kyng sente, and clepide Semey, and seide to hym, Bilde to thee an hows in Jerusalem, and dwelle thou there, and thou schalt not go out fro thennus hidur and thidur;

37 sotheli in what euer dai thou goist out, and passist the stronde of Cedron, wite thou thee worthi to be slayn; thi blood schal be on thin heed.

38 And Semei seide to the kyng, The word of the kyng is good; as my lord the kyng spak, so thi seruaunt schal do. Therfor Semey dwellide in Jerusalem in many daies.

39 Forsothe it was doon after thre yeer, that the seruauntis of Semei fledden to Achis, sone of Maacha, the kyng of Geth; and it was told to Semey, that hise seruauntis hadden go in to Geth.

40 And Semey roos, and sadlide his asse, and yede to Achis, in to Geth, to seke hise seruauntis; and brouyte hem ayen fro Geth.

41 Forsothe it was told to kyng Salomon, that Semey hadde go to Geth fro Jerusalem, and hadde come ayen.

42 And Salomon sente, and clepide hym, and seide to hym, Whether Y witnessede not to thee bi the Lord, and bifor seide to thee, In what euer dai thou schalt go out hidur and thidur, wite thou that thou schalt die; and thou answeridist to me, The word is good, which Y herde?

43 Whi therfor keptist thou not the ooth of the Lord, and the comaundement which Y comaundide to thee?

44 And the kyng seide to Semei, Thou knowist al the yuel, of which thin herte is gilti to thee, which yuel thou didist to my fadir; the Lord hath yolde thi malice in to thin heed.

45 And kyng Salomon schal be blessid; and the trone of Dauid schal be stable bifor the Lord til in to with outen ende.

46 Therfor the kyng comaundide to Banaie, sone of Joiada; and he assailide, and smoot Semey, and he was deed.

CAP 3

1 Therfor the rewme was confermyd in to the hondis of Salomon; and bi affynyte, 'ether aliaunce, he was ioyned to Pharao, kyng of Egipt; for he took the douyter of Farao, and brouyte in to the citee of Dauid, til he 'fillide bildynge his hows, and the hows of the Lord, and the wal of Jerusalem bi cumpas.

2 Netheles the puple offride in hiye places; for the temple was not bildid to the name of the Lord til in to that dai.

3 Forsothe Salomon louyde the Lord, and yede in the comaundementis of Dauid, his fadir, out takun that Salomon offride in hiye placis, and brente encense 'in hiye places.

4 Therfor Salomon yede in to Gabaon, to offre there; for thilke was the moost hiy place. Salomon offride on that auter in Gabaon a thousynde offryngis in to brent sacrifice.

5 Sotheli the Lord apperide to Salomon bi sleep in the nyyt, and seide, Axe thou 'that, that thou wolt, that Y yyue to thee.

6 And Salomon seide, Thou hast do greet merci with thi seruaunt Dauid, my fadir, as he yede in thi siyt, in treuthe, and riytfulnesse, and riytful herte with thee; thou hast kepte to hym thi greet merci, and hast youun to hym a sone, sittynge on his trone, as it is to dai.

7 And now, Lord God, thou hast maad thi seruaunt to regne for Dauid, my fadir; forsothe Y am a litil child, and not knowynge myn outgoynge and entryng.

8 And thi seruaunt is in the myddis of the puple, which thou hast chose, of puple with outen noumbre, that may not be noumbrid and rikened, for multitude.

9 Therfor thou schalt yyue to thi seruaunt an herte able to be tauyt, 'that is, liytned of thee, that he may deme the puple, and iuge bitwixe good and yuel; for who may deme this puple, thi puple, this miche puple?

10 Therfor the world pleside bifore the Lord, that Salomon hadde axid sich a thing.

11 And the Lord seide to Salomon, For thou axidist this word, and axidist not to thee many daies, nether richessis, nether the lyues of thin enemyes, but thou axidist to thee wisdom to deme doom, lo!

12 Y haue do to thee vpe thi wordis, and Y haue youe to thee a wyse herte and vndirstondynge, in so myche that no man bifor thee was lijk thee, nether schal rise aftir thee.

13 But also Y haue youe to thee these thingis, whiche thou axidist not, that is, richessis, and glorie, that no man be lijk thee in kyngis in alle tymes aftirward.

14 Forsothe if thou goist in my weies, and kepist my biddyngis and comaundementis, as thi fadir yede, Y schal make thi daies long.

15 Therfor Salomon wakide, and vndirstood what the sweuen was. And whanne he hadde come to Jerusalem, he stood bifor the arke of boond of pees of the Lord, and he offride brent sacrifices, and made pesible sacrifices, and a greet feeste to alle hise meynees.

16 Thanne twei wymmen hooris camen to the kyng, and stoden bifor hym;

17 of whiche oon seide, My lord, Y biseche, Y and this womman dwelliden in oon hows, and Y childide at hir in a couche.

18 Sotheli in the thridde dai aftir that Y childide, also this womman childide; and we weren togidere in the hows, and noon other was with vs in the hows, outakun vs tweyne.

19 Forsothe the sone of this womman was deed in the nyyt, for sche slepte, and oppresside hym;

20 and sche roos in the fourthe part of the nyyt in silence, and took my sone fro the side of me, thin handmaide slepynge, and settide in hir bosum; forsothe sche puttide in my bosum hir sone, that was deed.

21 And whanne Y hadde ryse eerli, to yyue mylk to my sone, he apperide deed; whom Y bihelde diligentlier bi cleer liyt, and Y perseyuede, that he was not myn, whom Y hadde gendrid.

22 The tother womman answeride, It is not so as thou seist, but thi sone is deed; forsothe 'my sone lyueth. Ayenward sche seide, Thou liest; for my sone lyueth, and thi sone is deed. And bi this maner thei stryueden bifore the kyng.

23 Thanne the kyng seide, This womman seith, My sone lyueth, and thi sone is deed; and this womman answerith, Nay, but thi sone is deed; forsothe my sone lyueth.

24 Therfor the kyng seide, Brynge ye to me a swerd. And whanne thei hadden brouyt a swerd bifor the kyng,

25 he seide, Departe ye the quyk yong child in to twei partis, and yyue ye the half part to oon, and the half part to the tother.

26 Forsothe the womman, whos sone was quik, seide to the kyng; for her entrailis weren mouyd on hir sone; Lord, Y biseche, yyue ye to hir the quik child, and nyle ye sle hym. Ayenward sche seide, Be he nethir to me, nether to thee, but be he departid.

27 The kyng answeride, and seide, Yyue ye to this womman the yong child quyk, and be he not slayn; forsothe this is 'his modir.

28 Therfor al Israel herde the doom, which the kyng hadde demyd; and thei dredden the kyng, and sien, that the wisdom of God was in hym, to make doom.

CAP 4

1 'Forsothe kyng Salomon was regnynge on al Israel.

2 And these weren the princes which he hadde; Azarie, sone of Sadoch, preest;

3 Helioreb, and Haia, sones of Sila, 'weren scryueyns; Josophat, sone of Achilud, was chaunseler;

4 Banaie, sone of Joiada, was on the oost; forsothe Sadoch and Abiathar weren preestis;

5 Azarie, sone of Nathan, was on hem that stoden niy the kyng; Zabul, the sone of Nathan, was preest, 'that is, greet and worschipful, a freend of the kyng;

6 and Ahiasar was stiward of the hows; and Adonyram, sone of Adda, was on the tributis.

7 Forsothe Salomon hadde twelue 'prefectis, ether cheef minystrys, on al Israel, that yauen lijflode to the kyng, and to his hows; sotheli bi ech monethe bi it silf in the yeer, ech prefect bi hym silf mynystride necessaries.

8 And these ben the names of hem; Benhur, in the hil of Effraym;

9 Bendechar, in Macces, and in Salebbym, and in Bethsames, and in Helon, and in Bethanan;

10 Beneseth, in Araboth; forsothe Socco, and al the lond of Epher was his;

11 Benabidanab, whos was al Neptad, hadde Dortaphaed, 'Solomons douyter, to wijf.

12 Bena, sone of Achilud, gouernyde Thaneth, and Mageddo, and al Bethsan, which is bisidis Sarthana, vndur Jezrael, fro Bethsan 'til to Abelmeula, euene ayens Zelmaan.

13 Bengaber in Ramoth of Galaad hadde Anothiair, of the sone of Manasses, in Galaad; he was souereyn in al the cun-

trey of Argob, which is in Basan, to sixti greet citees and wallid, that hadden brasun lockis.

14 Achymadab, sone of Addo, was souereyn in Manaym;

15 Achymaas was in Neptalym, but also he hadde Bachsemath, douyter of Salomon, in wedloc;

16 Banaa, sone of Husy, was in Aser, and in Balod;

17 Josephat, sone of Pharue, was in Ysachar; Semey, sone of Hela, was in Beniamyn;

18 Gaber,

19 sone of Sury, was in the lond of Galaad, and in the lond of Seon, kyng of Amorrey, and of Og, kyng of Basan, on alle thingis, that weren in that lond.

20 Juda and Israel weren vnnoumbrable, as the soond of the see in multitude, etynge, and drynkynge, and beynge glad.

21 Forsothe Solomon was in his lordschip, and hadde alle rewmes, as fro the flood of the lond of Filisteis 'til to the laste part of Egipt, of men offrynge yiftis to hym, and seruynge to hym, in alle the daies of his lijf.

22 Forsothe the mete of Salomon was bi ech day, thritti chorus of clene flour of whete, and sixti chorus of mele,

23 ten fatte oxis, and twenti oxis of lesewe, and an hundrid wetheris, outakun huntyng of hertys, of geet, and of buglis, and of briddis maad fat.

24 For he helde al the cuntrei that was biyende the flood, as fro Caphsa 'til to Gasa, and alle the kyngis of tho cuntreis; and he hadde pees bi ech part in cumpas.

25 And Juda and Israel dwelliden withouten ony drede, ech man vndur his vyne, and vndur his fige tree, fro Dan 'til to Bersabe, in alle the daies of Salomon.

26 And Salomon hadde fourty thousynd cratchis of horsis for charis, and twelue thousynde of roode horsis; and the forseid prefectis nurshiden tho horsis.

27 But also with greet bisynesse thei yauen necessaries to the boord of kyng Salomon in her tyme;

28 also thei brouyten barli, and forage of horsis and werk beestis, in to the place where the king was, 'bi ordenaunce to hem.

29 Also God yaf to Salomon wisdom, and prudence ful myche, and largenesse of herte, as the soond which is in the brenke of the see.

30 And the wisdom of Solomon passide the wisdom of alle eest men, and Egipcians;

31 and he was wisere than alle men; he was wisere than Ethan Esraite, and than Eman, and than Cacal, and than Dorda, the sones of Maol; and he was named among alle folkis bi cumpas.

32 And Salomon spak thre thousynde parablis, and hise songis weren fyue thousynde;

33 and he disputide of trees fro a cedre which is in the Lyban, 'til to the ysope that goith out of the wal; he disputide of werk beestis, and briddis, and crepynge beestis, and fischis.

34 And thei camen fro alle puplis to here the wisdom of Salomon, and fro alle kyngis of erthe, that herden his wisdom.

CAP 5

1 Also Hiram, kyng of Tire, sente hise seruauntis to Salomon; for he herde that thei hadden anoyntide hym kyng for his fadir; for Hiram was frend of Dauid in al time.

2 Sotheli also Salomon sente to Hiram,

3 and seide, Thou knowist the wille of Dauid, my fadir, and for he miyte not bilde an hows to the name of his God, for

batels neiyynge bi cumpas, til the Lord yaf hem vndur the step of hise feet.

4 Now forsothe my Lord God yaf reste to me bi cumpas, and noon aduersarie is, nethir yuel asailyng;

5 wherfor Y thenke to buylde a temple to the name of my Lord God, as God spak to Dauid, my fadir, and seide, Thi sone, whom Y schal yyue to thee for thee on thi trone, he schal bilde an hows to my name.

6 Therfor comaunde thou, that thi seruauntis hewe doun to me cedris of the Liban; and my seruauntis be with thi seruauntis; sotheli Y schal yyue to thee the meede of thi seruauntis, what euere meede thou schalt axe; for thou woost, that in my puple is not a man that kan hewe trees, as Sidonyes kunnen.

7 Therfor whanne Hiram hadde herde the wordis of Salomon, he was ful glad, and seide, Blessid be the Lord God to dai, that yaf to Dauid a sone moost wijs on this puple ful myche.

8 And Hiram sente to Salomon, and seide, Y haue herde what euer thingis thou sentist to me; Y schal do al thi wille, in trees of cedres, and of beechis.

9 My seruauntis schulen putte doun tho trees fro the Liban to the see, and Y schal araye tho trees in schippis in the see, 'til to the place which thou schalt signyfie to me; and Y schal dresse tho there, that thou take tho; and thou schalt yyue necessaries to me, that mete be youun to myn hows.

10 Therfor Hiram yaf to Salomon 'trees of cedres, and 'trees of beechis, bi al his wille;

11 forsothe Salomon yaf to Hiram twenti thousynde chorus of wheete, in to meete to his hows, and twenti chorus of pureste oile; Salomon yaf these thingis to Hiram bi alle yeeris.

12 Also the Lord yaf wisdom to Salomon, as he spak to hym; and pees was bitwixe Hiram and Salomon, and bothe smytiden boond of pees.

13 And kyng Salomon chees werk men of al Israel; and the summe was thretti thousynde of men.

14 And 'Salomon sente hem in to the Liban, ten thousynde bi ech monethe bi whilis, so that in twei monethis bi whilis thei weren in her howsis; and Adonyram was on sich a summe.

15 Therfor seuenti thousynde of hem, that baren burthuns, weren to Salomon, and foure score thousynde of masouns in the hil, with out the souereyns,

16 that weren maistris of alle werkis, bi the noumbre of thre thousynde and thre hundrid, comaundynge to the puple, and to hem that maden werk.

17 And the kyng comaundide, that thei schulden take greete stonys, 'and preciouse stonys, in to the foundement of the temple, and that thei schulden make tho square;

18 whiche stoonys the masouns of Salomon, and the masouns of Hyram, hewiden. Forsothe Biblies maden redi trees and stonus, to the hows to be bildid.

CAP 6

1 Forsothe it was doon in the fourthe hundrid and fourescore yeer of the goynge out of the sones of Israel fro the lond of Egipt, in the fourthe yeer, in the monethe Zio; thilke is the secounde monethe of the rewme of Salomon on Israel; he bigan to bilde an hows to the Lord.

2 Forsothe the hows which kyng Salomon bildide to the Lord, hadde sexti cubitis in lengthe, and twenti cubitis in breede, and thretti cubitis in heiythe.

3 And a porche was bifor the temple of twenti cubitis of lengthe, by the mesure of the breed of the temple; and the

porche hadde ten cubitis of breede, bifor the face of the temple.

4 And Salomon made in the temple 'wyndows streyte withoutforth, and large with ynne.

5 And he bildide on the wal of the temple bildyngis of tablis bi cumpas, in the wallis of the hows, 'bi cumpas of the temple, and of Goddis answeryng place; and he made sidis in the cumpas.

6 The bildyng of tablis, that was vndur, hadde fyue cubitis of breede; and the myddil bildyng of tablis was of sixe cubits of breede; and the thridde bildyng of tablis was hauynge seuene cubitis of breede. Sotheli he puttide beemys in the hous bi cumpas with outforth, that tho cleuiden not to the wallis of the temple.

7 Forsothe whanne the hows was bildid, it was bildid of 'stoonys hewid and perfit; and an hamer, and ax, and al thing maad of yrun, weren not herd in the hows, while it was in bildyng.

8 The dore of the myddil side was in the wal of the riythalf hows; and bi a vijs thei stieden in to the myddil soler, and fro the myddil soler in to the thridde soler.

9 And Salomon bildide the hows, and endide it. Also Salomon hilide the hows with couplis of cedre,

10 and bildide a bildyng of tablis ouer al the hows, bi fyue cubitis of heiythe, and hilide the hows with 'trees of cedre.

11 And the word of the Lord was maad to Salomon, and seide,

12 This is the hows, which thou bildist; if thou gost in myn heestis, and dost my domes, and kepist alle my comaundementis, and goist bi tho, Y schal make stidefast my word to thee, 'which word Y spak to Dauid, thi fadir;

13 and Y schal dwelle in the myddis of the sones of Israel, and Y schal not forsake my puple Israel.

14 Therfor Salomon bildide the hows, and endide it;

15 and he bildide the wallis of the hows with ynne with tablis of cedre, fro the pawment of the hows 'til to the heiynesse of the wal, and 'til to the couplis; and hilide with trees of cedre with ynne; and he hilide the pawment of the hows with tablis of beeche.

16 And he bildide a wal of tablis of cedre of twenti cubitis at the hyndrere part of the temple, fro the pawment 'til to the hiyere partis; and he made the ynnere hows of Goddis answeryng place, in to the hooli of hooli thingis.

17 Sotheli thilke temple bifor the doris of Goddis answering place was of fourti cubitis.

18 And al the hows with ynne was clothid with cedre, and hadde hise smethenessis, and hise ioynyngis maad suteli, and grauyngis apperynge aboue; alle thingis weren clothid with tablis of cedre, and outirli a stoon miyte not appere in the wal.

19 Forsothe Salomon made Goddis answeryng place in the myddis of the hows, in the ynnere part, that he schulde sette there the arke of boond of pees of the Lord.

20 Sotheli Goddis answeryng place hadde twenti cubitis of lengthe, and twenti cubitis of breede, and twenti cubitis of hiyte; and he hilide, and clothide it with pureste gold; but also he clothide the auter with cedre.

21 Also he hilide with pureste gold the hows bifor 'Goddis answeryng place, and fastnyde platis with goldun nailis.

22 No thing was in the temple, 'which thing was not hilid with gold; but also he hilid with gold al the auter of Goddis answeryng place.

23 And he made in 'Goddis answeryng place twey cherubyns of the trees of olyues, of ten cubits of heiyte;

24 o wynge of cherub was of fyue cubitis, and the tother wynge of cherub was of fyue cubitis, that is, hauynge ten cubitis, fro the heiynesse of 'the o wynge 'til to the hiynesse of the tother wynge.

25 And the secunde cherub was of ten cubitis in euene mesure; and o werk was in the twey cherubyns,

26 that is, o cherub hadde the hiythe of ten cubitis, and in lijk maner the tother cherub.

27 And he settide cherubyns in the myddis of the ynnere temple; forsothe the cherubyns helden forth her wyngis, and o wenge touchide the wal, and the wynge of the secunde cherub touchide the tother wal; forsothe the othere wyngis in the middil part of the temple touchiden hem silf togidere.

28 And he hilide the cherubyns with gold,

29 and alle the wallis of the temple 'bi cumpas; and grauyde with dyuerse grauyngis and smethenesse; and he made in tho wallys cherubyns, and palmes, and dyuerse peynturis, as stondinge forth and goynge out of the wal.

30 But also he hilide with gold the pawment of the hows, withynne and with outforthe.

31 And in the entryng of 'Goddis answering place he made twei litil doris of the trees of olyues; and he made postis of fyue corneris,

32 and twei doris of the trees of olyues; and grauyde in tho the peynture of cherubyns, and the licnessis of palmes, and grauyngis aboue stondynge forth gretli; and he hilide tho with gold; and he hilide as wel the cherubyns, as palmes, and othere thingis with gold.

33 And in the entring of the temple he made postis foure cornerid of the trees of olyues;

34 and he made twei doris of the trees of beech, ech ayens other; and euer either dore was double, and it was openyd holdynge it silf togidere.

35 And he grauyde cherubyns, and palmes, and grauyngis apperynge greetli; and he hilide alle thingis with goldun platis, bi square werk at reule.

36 And he bildide a large street with ynne, bi thre ordris of stoonys maad fair, and bi oon ordre of trees of cedre.

37 The hows of the Lord was foundid in the fourthe yeer, in the monethe Zio;

38 and the hows was maad perfit in al his werk, and in alle vessels, ether 'purtenauncis, in the eleuenthe yeer, in the monethe Zebul; thilke is the eiythe monethe; and he bildide that hows in seuene yeer.

CAP 7

1 Forsothe Salomon bildide his owne hows in thrittene yeer, and brouyte it til to perfeccioun.

2 He bildide an hows of the forest of Liban, of an hundrid cubitis of lengthe, and of fifti cubitis of breede, and of thretti cubitis of hiythe; and he bildide foure aleis bitwixe the pilers of cedre; for he hadde hewe doun trees of cedres in to pilers.

3 And he clothide al the chaumbir with wallis of cedris; which chaumbir was susteyned with fyue and fourti pileris. Sotheli oon ordre hadde fiftene pileris, set ayens hem silf togidere,

4 and biholdynge hem silf euene ayens, bi euene space bitwixe the pilers;

5 and on the pilers weren foure square trees, euene in alle thingis.

6 And he made a porche of pilers of fifti cubitis of lengthe, and of thritti cubitis of breede; and 'he made an other porche

in the face of the gretter porche; and he made pileris, and pomels on the pileris.

7 Also he maad a porche of the kyngis seete, in which the seete of doom was; and he hilide with trees of cedre, fro the pawment 'til to the hiynesse.

8 And a litil hows, in which he sat to deme, was in the myddil porche, bi lijk werk. Also Salomon made an hows to the douyter of Farao, whom he hadde weddid, bi sich werk, bi what maner werk he made and this porche.

9 He made alle thingis of precious stoonys, that weren sawid at sum reule and mesure, bothe with ynne and with outforth, fro the foundement 'til to the hiynesse of wallis, and with ynne and 'til to the gretter street, ethir court.

10 Sotheli the foundementis weren of precious stoonys, grete stoonys of ten, ethir of eiyte cubitis;

11 and preciouse stoonys hewun of euene mesure weren aboue; in lijk maner and of cedre.

12 And the gretter court, 'ethir voide space, was round, of thre ordris of hewun stonus, and of oon ordre of hewun cedre; also and in the ynnere large strete of the hows of the Lord, and in the porche of the hows of the Lord.

13 Also kyng Salomon sente, and brouyte fro Tire Hiram, the sone of a womman widewe,

14 of the lynage of Neptalym, of the fadir a man of Tyre, Hiram, a crafty man of brasse, and ful of wisdom, and vndirstondynge, and doctryn, to make al werk of bras. And whanne he hadde come to kyng Salomon, he made al hys werk.

15 And he made twey pilers of bras, o piler of eiytene cubitis of hiythe; and a lyne of twelue cubitis cumpasside euer either piler.

16 Also he made twei pomels, yotun of bras, that weren set on the heedis of the pilers; o pomel of fyue cubitis of hiythe, and the tothir pomel of fyue cubitis of heiythe; and bi the maner of a net,

17 and of chaynes knyt to gidere to hem, bi wonderful werk. Euer either pomel of the pilers was yotun; seuen werkis lijk nettis of orders weren in o pomel, and seuen werkis lijk nettis weren in the tother pomel.

18 And he made perfitli the pilers, and twei ordris 'bi cumpas of alle werkis lijk nettis, that tho schulden hile the pomels, that weren on the hiynesse of pumgarnadis; in the same maner he dide also to the secounde pomel.

19 Sotheli the pomels, that weren on the heedis of the pilers in the porche, weren maad as bi the werk of lilye, of foure cubitis;

20 and eft othere pomels in the hiynesse of pilers aboue, bi the mesure of the piler, ayens the werkis lijk nettis; forsothe twey hundrid ordris of pumgarnadis weren in the cumpas of the secounde pomel.

21 And he settide the twey pilers in the porche of the temple; and whanne he hadde set the riythalf pilere, he clepide it bi name Jachym; in lijk maner he reiside the secounde pilere, and he clepide the name therof Booz.

22 And he settide on the heedis of the pilers a werk bi the maner of a lilie; and the werk of the pilers was maad perfit.

23 Also he made a yotun see, that is, a waisching vessel for preestis, round in cumpas, of ten cubitis fro brynke til to the brinke; the heiynesse therof was of fyue cubitis; and a corde of thretti cubitis yede aboute it bi cumpas.

24 And grauyng vndir the brynke cumpasside it, and cumpasside the see bi ten cubitis; tweyne ordris of grauyngis conteynynge summe stories weren yotun, and stoden on twelue oxis;

25 of whiche oxis thre bihelden to the north, and thre to the west, and thre to the south, and three to the eest; and the see was aboue on tho oxis, of whiche alle the hyndere thingis weren hid 'with ynne.

26 Sotheli the thicknesse of the see was of thre ounces, and the brynke therof was as the brynke of a cuppe, and as the leef of a lilie crokid ayen; the see took twei thousynde bathis, thre thousynde metretis.

27 And he made ten brasun foundementes, ech foundement of foure cubites of lengthe, and of foure cubitis of brede, and of thre cubitis of hiynes.

28 And thilke werk of foundementis was rasid bitwixe; and grauyngis weren bitwixe the ioynturis.

29 And bitwixe the litil corouns and serclis weren lions, oxis, and cherubyns; and in the ioynturis lijk maner aboue; and vndir the lyouns and oxis weren as reynes of bridels of bras hangynge doun.

30 And bi ech foundement weren foure wheelis, and brasun extrees; and bi foure partis weren as litle schuldryngis vndir the waischyng vessel, 'the schuldryngis yotun, and biholdynge ayens hemsilf togidere.

31 And the mouth of the waischyng vessel with ynne was in the hiynesse of the heed, and that, that apperide with outforth, was of o cubit, and it was al round, and hadde togidere o cubit and an half; sotheli dyuerse grauyngis weren in the corneris of pilers, and the mydil piler bitwixe was square, not round.

32 And the foure wheelis, that weren bi foure corneris of the foundement, cleuyden togidere to hem silf vndir the foundement; o wheele hadde o cubit and an half of hiythe.

33 Sotheli the wheelis weren siche, whiche maner wheelis ben wont to be maad in a chare; and the extrees, and the 'naue stockis, and the spokis, and dowlis of tho wheelis, alle thingis weren yotun.

34 For also the foure litle schuldryngis, bi alle the corners of o foundement, weren ioyned to gidere, and yotun of that foundement.

35 Sotheli in the hiynesse of the foundement was sum roundenesse, of o cubite and an half, so maad craftili, that the waischyng vessel myyte be set aboue, hauynge his purtreiyngis, and dyuerse grauyngis of it silf.

36 Also he grauyde in tho wallis, that weren of bras, and in the corneris, cherubyns, and liouns, and palmes, as bi the licnesse of a man stondynge, that tho semeden not grauun, but put to bi cumpas.

37 Bi this maner he made ten foundementis, bi o yetyng and mesure, and lijk grauyng.

38 Also he made ten waischyng vessels of bras; o waischyng vessel took fourti bathis, and it was of foure cubitis; and he puttide ech waischyng vessel bi it silf bi ech foundement bi it silf, that is, ten.

39 And he made ten foundementis, fyue at the riyt half of the temple, and fyue at the left half; sotheli he settide the see at the riyt half of the temple, ayens the eest, at the south.

40 Also Hiram made cawdrouns, and pannes, and wyn vessels; and he made perfitli al the werk of kyng Salomon in the temple of the Lord.

41 He made twey pilers, and twei cordis of pomels on the pomels of pilers, and twei werkis lijk nettis, that tho schulden hile twey cordis, that weren on the heedis of pileris.

42 And 'he made pumgarnadis foure hundrid in twey werkis lijk nettis; 'he made tweyne ordris of pumgarnadis in ech werk lijk a net, to hile the cordis of the pomels, that weren on the heedis of pilers.

43 And he made ten foundementis, and ten waischyng vessels on the foundementis;

44 and o se, 'that is, a waischyng vessel for preestis, and twelue oxis vndur the see;

45 and 'he made cawdruns, and pannys, and wyn vessels. Alle vessels, whiche Hiram made to kyng Salomon in the hows of the Lord, weren of latoun.

46 And the kyng yetide tho vessels in the feeldi cuntrey of Jordan, in cleyi lond, bitwixe Sochot and Sarcham.

47 And Salomon settide alle the vessels; forsothe for greet multitude no weiyte was of bras, 'that is, it passide al comyn weiyte.

48 And Salomon made alle vessels in the hows of the Lord; sotheli he made the golden auter, 'that is, the auter of encense, that was with ynne the temple, and the goldun boord, on whych the loouys of settynge forth weren set;

49 and he made goldun candilstikis, fyue at the riyt half, and fyue at the left half, ayens Goddis answerynge place, 'of purest gold; and he made as the flouris of a lilie, and goldun lanterns aboue, and goldun tongis; and pottis,

50 and hokis, and violis, and morteris, and censeris of pureste gold; and the herris, ether heengis, of the doris of the ynnere hows of the hooli of hooli thingis, and of the doris of the hows of the temple weren of gold.

51 And Salomon performyde al the werk, which he made in the hows of the Lord; and he brouyte ynne the thingis, whiche Dauid, his fadir, hadde halewid; siluer, and gold, and vessels; and he kepte in the tresours of the hows of the Lord.

CAP 8

1 Thanne alle the gretter men in birthe in Israel, with the princes of lynagis, and the duykis of meynees of the sones of Israel, weren gaderid to kyng Salomon, in to Jerusalem, that thei schulden bere the arke of boond of pees of the Lord fro the citee of Dauid, that is, fro Syon.

2 And al Israel cam to gidere in the moneth Bethanym, in the solempne dai; thilke is the seuenthe moneth.

3 And alle the elde men of Israel camen; and the preestis token the arke,

4 and baren the arke of the Lord, and the tabernacle of boond of pees, and alle vessels of the seyntuarye, that weren in the tabernacle; and the preestis and dekenes baren tho.

5 Sotheli kyng Salomon, and al the multitude of Israel, that camen togidere to hym, yede with hym bifor the arke; and thei offriden scheep and oxis, with out gessyng and noumbre.

6 And prestis brouyten the arke of boond of pees of the Lord in to his place, in to Goddis answerynge place of the temple, in to the hooli of hooli thingis, vndur the wengis of cherubyns.

7 Forsothe cherubyns spredden forth wengis ouer the place of the arke; and hiliden the arke, and the barris therof aboue.

8 And whanne the barris stoden forth, and the hiynesse of tho apperiden with out the seyntuarye, bifor 'Goddis answerynge place, tho apperyden no ferther with outforth; whiche barris also weren there 'til in to present day.

9 Forsothe in the arke is noon other thing, no but twei tablis of stoon, whiche tablis Moyses in Oreb hadde put in the ark, whanne the Lord made boond of pees with the sones of Israel, whanne thei yeden out of the loond of Egipt.

10 Forsothe it was doon whanne the preestis hadden go out of the seyntuarie, a cloude fillide the hows of the Lord;

11 and the preestis myyten not stonde and mynystre, for the cloude; for whi the glorye of the Lord hadde fillid the hows of the Lord.

12 Thanne Salomon seide, The Lord seide, that he wolde dwelle in a cloude.

13 Y bildynge haue bildid an hows in to thi dwelling place, in to thi moost stidefast trone with outen ende.

14 And the kyng turnede his face, and blesside al the chirche in Israel; for al the chirche of Israel stood.

15 And Salomon seide, Blessid be the Lord God of Israel, that spak with his mouth to Dauid, my fadir, and performyde in hise hondis, and seide,

16 Fro the dai in which Y ledde my puple Israel out of Egipt, Y chees not a citee of alle the lynagis of Israel, that an hows schulde be bildid, and my name schulde be there; but Y chees Dauid, that he schulde be ouer my puple Israel.

17 And Dauid, my fadir, wolde bilde an hows to the name of the Lord God of Israel.

18 And the Lord seide to Dauid, my fadir, That thou thouytist in thin herte to bilde an hows to my name, thou didist wel, tretynge this same thing in soule;

19 netheles thou schalt not bilde an hows to me, but thi sone, that schal go out of thi reynes, he schal bilde an hows to my name.

20 The Lord hath confermyd his word, which he spak; and Y stood for Dauid, my fadir, and Y sat on the trone of Israel, as the Lord spak; and Y haue bildid an hows to the name of the Lord God of Israel.

21 And Y haue ordeyned there a place of the arke, in which arke the boond of pees of the Lord is, which he smoot with oure fadris, whanne thei yeden out of the lond of Egipt.

22 Forsothe Salomon stood bifoor the auter of the Lord, in the siyt of the chirch of Israel; and he helde forth hise hondis ayens heuene,

23 and seide, Lord God of Israel, no God in heuene aboue, nether on erthe bynethe, is lijk thee, which kepist couenaunt and mercy to thi seruauntis, that goon bifor thee in al her herte;

24 and thou kepist to Dauid, my fadir, thi seruaunt, tho thingis whiche thou hast spoke to him; bi mouth thou hast spoke, and bi hondis thou hast fillid, as this day preueth.

25 Now therfor, Lord God of Israel, kepe thou to thi seruaunt Dauid, my fadir, tho thingis whiche thou spakist to hym, and seidist, A man of thee schal not be taken awei bifor me, which man schal sitte on the trone of Israel, so netheles if thi sones kepen thi weye, that thei go bifor me, as thou yedist in my siyt.

26 And now, Lord God of Israel, thi wordis be maad stidfast, whiche thou spakist to thi seruaunt Dauid, my fadir.

27 Therfor whether it is to gesse, that God dwellith verily on erthe; for if heuene, and heuene of heuenes moun not take thee, how myche more this hows, which Y bildid to thee, 'mai not take thee.

28 But, my Lord God, biholde thou to the preiere of thi seruaunt, and to the bisechyngis of hym; here thou the 'ympne, ether preysing, and preiere, which thi seruaunt preieth bifor thee to day;

29 that thin iyen be openyd on this hows bi niyt and dai, on the hows, of which thou seidist, My name schal be there; that thou here the preier, which thi seruaunt preieth to thee in this place; that thou here the bisechyng of thi seruaunt,

30 and of thi puple Israel, what euer thing he preieth in this place, and here thou in the place of thi dwellyng in heuene; and whanne thou hast herd, thou schalt be mercyful.

31 If a man synneth ayens a man, and hath ony ooth, bi which he is holdun boundun, and cometh for the ooth in to thin hows, bifor thin auter, thou schalt here in heuene,

32 and thou schalt do, and thou schalt deme thi seruauntis; and thou schalt condempne the wickid man, and schalt yelde his weie on his heed, and thou schalt iustifie the iust man, and schalt yelde to hym vp his riytfulnesse.

33 If thi puple Israel fleeth hise enemyes, for he schal do synne to thee, and thei doen penaunce, and knoulechen to thi greet name, and comen, and worschipen, and bisechen thee in this hows,

34 here thou in heuene, and foryyue thou the synne of thi puple; and thou schalt lede hem ayen in to the lond, which thou hast youe to the fadris of hem.

35 If heuene is closid, and reyneth not for the synnes of hem, and thei preyen in this place, and doen penaunce to thi name, and ben conuertid fro her synnes for her turment,

36 here thou hem in heuene, and foryyue thou the synnes of thi seruauntis, and of thi puple Israel, and schewe thou to hem good weie, bi which thei schulen go, and yyue thou reyn to hem on the lond, which thou hast youe to hem in to possessioun.

37 If hungur risith in the lond, ether pestilence is, ether corrupt eyr is, ether rust, ether locuste, ether myldew, and his enemy turmentith hym, and bisegith the yatis, al wounde, al sikenesse, al cursyng,

38 and wichyng of yuel, that bifallith to ech man of thi puple Israel, if ony man knowith the wounde of his herte, and holdith forth hise hondis in this hows,

39 thou schalt here in heuene, in the place of thi dwellyng, and thou schalt do mercy, and thou schalt do that thou yyue to ech man vpe alle hise weies, as thou seest his herte; for thou aloone knowist the herte of alle the sones of men,

40 that thei drede thee in alle daies in whiche thei lyuen on the face of the lond, which thou hast youe to oure fadrys.

41 Ferthermore and whanne an alien, which is not of thi puple Israel, cometh fro a fer lond for thi name; for thi grete name, and thi strong hond,

42 and thin arm 'holdun forth schal be herd euery where; therfor whanne he cometh, and preieth in this place,

43 thou schalt here in heuene, in the firmament of thi dwellyng place, and thou schalt do alle thingis, for whiche the alien clepith thee, that alle puplis of londis lerne to drede thi name, as thi puple Israel doith, and preue, that thi name is clepid on this hows, which Y bildide.

44 If thi puple goith out to batel ayens hise enemyes, bi the weie whidir euer thou sendist hem, thei schulen preye thee ayens the weie of the citee which thou hast chose, and ayens the hows which Y bildide to thi name,

45 and thou schalt here in heuene the preyeris of hem, and the bisechyngis of hem, and thou schalt make the doom of hem.

46 That if thei synnen to thee, for no man is that synneth not, and thou art wrooth, and bitakist hem to her enemyes, and thei ben led prisoneris in to the lond of enemyes,

47 fer ether nyy, and thei doon penaunce in her herte in the place of prisonyng, and ben conuertid, and bisechen in her prisonyng, and seien, We han synned, we han do wickidli, we han do vnfeithfuli;

48 and thei turnen ayen to thee in al her herte and al her soule, in the lond of her enemyes, to which thei ben led prisoneris,

and thei preyen thee ayens the weie of her lond which thou hast youe to her fadris, and of the citee which thou hast chose, and of the temple which Y bildide to thi name, thou schalt here in heuene,

49 in the firmament of thi seete, the preiers of hem, and the bisechingis of hem, and thou schalt make the doom of hem;

50 and thou schalt be merciful to thi puple, that synnede to thee, and to alle the wickidnessis, bi whiche thei trespassiden ayens thee; and thou schalt do merci bifor tho men, that hadden hem prisoneris, that tho men do mercy to hem.

51 For it is thi puple, and thin erytage, whiche thou leddist out of the lond of Egipt, fro the myddis of yrone furneis;

52 that thin yyen be opyn to the bisechyng of thi seruaunt, and of thi puple Israel; and thou schalt here hem in alle thingis, for whiche thei clepen thee.

53 For thou hast departid hem to thee in to heritage fro alle the puplis of erthe, as thou spakist bi Moyses, thi seruaunt, whanne thou, Lord God, leddist oure fadris out of Egipt.

54 Forsothe it was don, whanne Salomon, preiynge the Lord, hadde fillid al this preier and bisechyng, he roos fro the siyt of the auter of the Lord; for he hadde set fast euer either kne to the erthe, and hadde holde forth the hondis to heuene.

55 Therfor he stood, and blesside al the chirche of Israel, and seide with greet vois,

56 Blessid be the Lord God of Israel, that yaf reste to his puple Israel, bi alle thingis whiche he spak; a word felde not doun, sotheli nether oon, of alle goodis whiche he spak bi Moises, his seruaunt.

57 Oure Lord God be with vs, as he was with oure fadris, and forsake not vs, nether caste awey;

58 but bowe he oure hertis to hym silf, that we go in alle hise weies, and kepe hise comaundementis, and cerymonyes, and domes, whiche euere he comaundide to oure fadris.

59 And these wordis of me, bi whiche Y preiede bifor the Lord, be neiyynge to oure Lord God bi dai and niyt, that he make doom to his seruaunt, and to his puple Israel bi alle daies;

60 and alle the puplis of erthe wite, that the Lord hym silf is God, and noon 'is ouer 'with out hym.

61 Also oure herte be perfit with oure Lord God, that we go in hise domes, and kepe hise comaundementis, as and to dai.

62 Therfor the kyng, and al Israel with hym, offriden sacrifices bifor the Lord.

63 And Salomon killide pesible sacrifices, whiche he offride to the Lord; of oxis two and twenti thousynde, and of scheep sixe score thousynde; and the king and the sones of Israel halewiden the temple of the Lord.

64 In that dai the kyng halewide the myddil of the greet street, that was bifor the hows of the Lord; for he made there brent sacrifice, and sacrifice, and the innere fatnesse of pesible thingis; for the brasun auter that was bifor the Lord, was to litil, and myyte not take the brent sacrifice, and the sacrifice, and the ynnere fatnesse of pesible thingis.

65 Therfor Salomon made in that tyme a solempne feeste, and al Israel with hym, a grete multitude, fro the entryng of Emath 'til to the stronde of Egipt, bifor oure Lord God, in seuene daies and seuene daies, that is, fourtene daies.

66 And in the eiythe day he delyueryde the puplis, whiche blessiden the kyng, and yeden forth in to her tabernaclis, and weren glade and of ioyful herte on alle the goodis whiche God hadde do to Dauid, his seruaunt, and to Israel, his puple.

CAP 9

1 Forsothe it was doon, whanne Salomon had perfourmed the bildyng of the hows of the Lord, and the bildyng of the kyng, and al thing that he coueitide, and wolde make,

2 the Lord apperide to Salomon the secunde tyme, as he apperide to hym in Gabaon.

3 And the Lord seide to hym, Y haue herd thi preier, and thi bisechyng, which thou bisouytist bifor me; Y haue halewid this hows, which thou bildidist, that Y schulde sette there my name with outen ende; and myn iyen and myn herte schulen be there in alle daies.

4 Also if thou goist bifore me, as thi fadir yede, in simplenesse of herte, and in equite, and doist alle thingis whiche Y comaundide to thee, and kepist my domes, and my lawful thingis,

5 Y schal sette the trone of thi rewme on Israel with outen ende, as Y spak to Dauid, thi fadir, and seide, A man of thi kyn schal not be takun awei fro the trone of Israel.

6 Forsothe if bi turnyng awei ye and youre sones turnen awey, and suen not me, and kepen not myn hestis and cerymonyes, whiche Y settide forth to you, but ye goen, and worschipen alien goddis, and onouren hem 'bi outward reuerence,

7 Y schal do awei Israel fro the face of the lond which Y yaue to hem; and Y schal caste awei fro my siyt the temple, which Y halewid to my name; and Israel schal be in to a prouerbe and in to a fable, to alle puplis.

8 And this hows schal be in to ensaumple of Goddis offence; ech man that schal passe bi it, schal wondre, and schal hisse, and schal seye, Whi hath the Lord do thus to this lond, and to this hows?

9 And thei schulen answere, For thei forsoken her Lord God, that ladde the fadris of hem out of Egipt; and thei sueden alien goddis, and worschipiden hem, and onouriden hem; therfor the Lord brouyte in on hem al this yuel.

10 Sotheli whanne twenti yeer weren fillid, aftir that Salomon hadde bildid tweyne housis, that is, the hows of the Lord, and the hows of the kyng, while Hiram,

11 kyng of Tire, yaf to Salomon trees of cedre, and of beech, and gold, bi al thing that he hadde nedeful; thanne Salomon yaf to Hiram twenti citees in the lond of Galile.

12 And Hiram yede out of Tyre that he schulde se the citees, whiche Salomon hadde youe to hym, and tho plesiden not hym;

13 and he seide, Whethir thes ben the citees, whiche thou, brother, hast youe to me? And he clepide tho citees the lond of Chabul, 'til to this dai.

14 Also Hiram sente to king Salomon sixe score talentis of gold.

15 This is the summe of 'costis, which summe Salomon the kyng yaf to bilde the hows of the Lord, and his house Mello, and the wal of Jerusalem, and Ezer, and Maggeddo, and Gazer.

16 Farao, kyng of Egipt, stiede, and took Gazer, and brente it bi fier; and he killide Chananei, that dwellide in the citee, and yaf it in to dower to his douytir, the wijf of Salomon.

17 Therfor Salomon bildide Gazer, and the lower Bethoron,

18 and Balaath, and Palmyra in the lond of wildirnesse;

19 and he made strong alle the townes, that perteyneden to hym, and weren with out wal, and the citees of chaaris, and the citees of knyytis, and what euer thing pleside hym to bilde in Jerusalem, and in the Liban, and in al the lond of his power.

20 Salomon made tributaries 'til to this dai al the puple, that lefte of Ammorreis, Etheis, and Fereseis, and Eueys, and Jebuseys, that ben not of the sones of Israel,

21 the sones of these hethen men, that dwelliden in the lond, that is, whiche the sones of Israel myyten not distrye.

22 Sotheli kyng Salomon ordeynede not ony man of the sones of Israel to serue, but thei weren men werriours, and mynystris of him, and princes, and dukis, and prefectis of his chares and horsis.

23 Sotheli fyue hundrid and fifti 'souereynes weren princes ouer alle the werkis of Salomon, whiche princes hadden the puple suget, and comaundiden to werkis ordeyned.

24 Sotheli the douyter of Farao stiede fro the citee of Dauid in to hir hows, 'which hows Salomon hadde bildid to hir; thanne he bildide Mello.

25 Also Salomon offride in thre tymes bi alle yeeris brent sacrifices and pesible sacrifices, on the auter which he hadde bildid to the Lord; and he brente encense bifor the Lord, and the temple was performed.

26 Also king Salomon made 'o schip in Asiongaber, which is bisidis Haila, in the brenke of the Reed sea, and in the lond of Idumee.

27 And Iram sente in that schip hise seruauntis, schipmen, and kunnynge of the see, with the seruauntis of Salomon;

28 and whanne thei hadden come in to Ophir, thei brouyten fro thennus gold of foure hundrid and twenti talentis to kyng Salomon.

CAP 10

1 But also the queen of Saba, whanne the fame of Salomon was herd, cam in the name of the Lord to tempte hym in derk and douti questiouns.

2 And sche entride with myche felouschipe and richessis in to Jerusalem, and with camels berynge swete smellynge thingis, and gold greetli with out noumbre, and precious stoonys; and sche cam to king Salomon, and spak to hym alle thingis whiche sche hadde in hir herte.

3 And Salomon tauyte hir alle wordis whiche sche hadde put forth; no word was, that myyte be hid fro the kyng, and which he answeryde not to hir.

4 Forsothe the queen of Saba siy al the wisdom of Salomon, and the hows which he hadde bildid,

5 and the metis of his table, and the dwellyng places of hise seruauntis, and the ordris of mynystris, and the clothis of hem, and the boteleris, and the brent sacrifices whiche he offride in the hows of the Lord; and sche hadde no more spirite.

6 And sche seide to the kyng, The word is trewe, which Y herde in my lond, of thi wordis, and of thi wisdom;

7 and Y bileuyde not to men tellynge to me, til Y my silf cam, and siy with myn iyen, and preuede that the half part was not teld to me; thi wisdom is more and thi werkis, than the tale which Y herde.

8 Thi men ben blessid, and thi seruauntis ben blessid, these that stonden bifor thee euere, and heren thi wisdom.

9 Blessid be thi Lord God, whom thou plesedist, and hath set thee on the trone of Israel; for the Lord louyde Israel with outen ende, and hath ordeynyd thee kyng, that thou schuldist do doom and riytfulnesse.

10 Therfor sche yaf to the kyng sixe score talentis of gold, and ful many swete smellynge thingis, and precious stoonus; so many swete smellynge thingis weren no more brouyt, as tho which the queen of Saba yaf to kyng Salomon.

11 But also the schip of Hiram, that brouyte gold fro Ophir, brouyte fro Ophir ful many trees of tyme, and preciouse stoonys.

12 And kyng Salomon made of the trees of tyme vndir settyngis of the hows of the Lord, and of the kyngis hows, and harpis, and sitols to syngeris; siche trees of tyme weren not brouyt nether seyn, til in to present dai.

13 Sotheli kyng Salomon yaf to the queen of Saba alle thingis whiche sche wolde, and axide of hym, outakun these thingis whiche he hadde youe to hir bi the kyngis yifte wilfuli; and sche turnede ayen, and yede in to hir lond with hir seruauntis.

14 Forsothe the weyte of gold, that was offrid to Salomon bi ech yeer, was of sixe hundrid and sixe and sixti talentis of gold,

15 outakun that which men that weren on the talagis, 'that is, rentis for thingis borun aboute in the lond, and marchauntis, and alle men sillynge scheeldys, and alle the kyngis of Arabie, and dukis of erthe yauen.

16 And kyng Salomon made two hundrid scheeldis of pureste gold; he yaf sixe hundrid siclis of gold in to the platis of oo scheeld;

17 and he made thre hundrid of bokeleris of preued gold; thre hundrid talentis of gold clothiden o bokeler. And the kyng puttide tho in the hows of the forest of Lyban.

18 Also kyng Salomon made a greet trone of yuer, and clothide it with ful fyn gold;

19 which trone hadde sixe grees; and the hiynesse of the trone was round in the hynderere part; and tweine hondis on this side and on that side, holdynge the seete, and twei lyouns stoden bisidis ech hond;

20 and twelue litil liouns stondynge on sixe grees on this side and on that side; siche a werk was not maad in alle rewmes.

21 But also alle the vessels, of which kyng Salomon drank, weren of gold, and alle the purtenaunce of the hows of the forest of Liban was of pureste gold; siluer was not, nether it was arettid of ony prijs in the daies of Salomon.

22 For the schip of 'the kyng wente onys bi thre yeer with the schip of Hiram in to Tharsis, and brouyte fro thennus gold, and siluer, and teeth of olifauntis, and apis, and pokokis.

23 Therfor kyng Salomon was magnified aboue alle kyngis of erthe in richessis and wisdom.

24 And al erthe desiride to se the cheer of Salomon, to here the wisdom of him, which wisdom God hadde youe in his herte.

25 And alle men brouyten yiftis to hym, vessels of gold, and of siluer, clothis, and armeris of batel, and swete smellynge thingis, and horsis, and mulis, bi ech yeer.

26 And Salomon gaderide togidere charis, and knyytis; and a thousinde and foure hundrid charis weren maad to hym, and twelue thousynde 'of knyytis; and he disposide hem bi strengthid citees, and with the kyng in Jerusalem.

27 And he made, that so greet aboundaunce of siluer was in Jerusalem, how greet was also of stoonys; and he yaf the multitude of cedris as sicomoris, that growen in feeldly places.

28 And the horsis of Salomon weren led out of Egipt, and of Coa; for the marchauntis of the kyng bouyten of Coa, and brouyten for prijs ordeyned.

29 Forsothe a chare yede out of Egipt for sixe hundrid siclis of siluer, and an hors for an hundrid and fifti siclis; and bi this maner alle the kyngis of Etheis and of Sirye seelden horsis.

CAP 11

1 Forsothe kyng Salomon louyde brennyngli many alien wymmen, and the douytir of Pharao, and wymmen of Moab, and Amonytis, and Ydumeis, and Sydoneis, and Etheis;

2 of the folkis of whiche the Lord seide to the sones of Israel, Ye schulen not entre to tho folkis, nether ony of hem schulen entre to you; for most certeynli thei schulen turne awei youre hertis, that ye sue the goddis of hem. Therfor kyng Salomon was couplid to these wymmen, bi moost brennyng loue.

3 And wyues as queenys weren seuene hundrid to hym, and thre hundrid secundarie wyues; and the wymmen turneden awey his herte.

4 And whanne he was thanne eld, his herte was bischrewid bi wymmen, that he suede alien goddis; and his herte was not perfit with his Lord God, as the herte of Dauid, his fadir, 'was perfit.

5 But Salomon worschipide Astartes

1, the goddesse of Sidoneis, and Chamos, the god of Moabitis, and Moloch, the idol of Amonytis;

6 and Salomon dide that, that pleside not bifor the Lord, and he fillide not that he suede the Lord, as Dauid, his fadir, dide.

7 Thanne Salomon bildide a temple to Chamos, the idol of Moab, in the hil which is ayens Jerusalem, and to Moloch, the idol of the sones of Amon.

8 And bi this maner he dide to alle hise alien wyues, that brenten encencis, and offriden to her goddis.

9 Therfor the Lord was wrooth to Salomon, for his soule was turned awei fro the Lord God of Israel; that apperide to Salomon the secounde tyme,

10 and comaundide of this word, that he schulde not sue alien goddis; and he kepte not tho thingis, whiche the Lord comaundide to hym.

11 Therfor the Lord seide to Salomon, For thou haddist this thing anentis thee, and keptist not my couenaunt, and myn heestis, whiche Y comaundide to thee, Y schal breke, and Y schal departe thi rewme, and Y schal yyue it to thi seruaunt.

12 Netheles Y schal not do in thi daies, for Dauid, thi fadir; Y schal kitte it fro the hond of thi sone;

13 nether Y schal do a wey al the rewme, but Y schal yyue o lynage to thi sone, for Dauid, my seruaunt, and for Jerusalem, which Y chess.

14 Forsothe the Lord reiside to Solomon an aduersarie, Adad Ydumey, of the kyngis seed, that was in Edom.

15 For whanne Dauid was in Ydumee, and Joab, the prince of chyualrie, hadde stied to birie hem that weren slayn, and he hadde slayn ech male kynde in Ydumee;

16 for Joab, and al Israel dwelliden there bi sixe monethis, til thei killiden ech male kynde in Ydumee; Adad hym silf fledde,

17 and men of Ydumee, of 'the seruauntis of his fadir, with hym, that he schulde entre in to Egipt; sotheli Adad was a litil child.

18 And whanne thei hadden rise fro Madian, thei camen in to Faran; and thei token with hem men of Faran, and entriden in to Egipt, to Pharao, kyng of Egipt; which Farao yaf an hows to hym, and ordeynede metis, and assignede lond.

19 And Adad foond grace bifor Farao greetli, in so myche that Farao yaf to hym a wijf, the sister of his wijf, sister of the queen, of Taphnes.

20 And the sistir of Taphnes gendrid to hym a sone, Genebath; and Taphnes nurschide hym in the hows of Farao; and Genebath dwellide bifor Farao, with hise sones.

21 And whanne Adad hadde herd in Egipt, that Dauid slepte with hise fadris, and that Joab, the prince of chyualrie, was deed, he seide to Farao, Suffre thou me, that Y go in to my lond.

22 And Farao seide to hym, For of what thing hast thou nede at me, that thou sekist to go to thi lond? And he answeride, Of no thing; but Y biseche thee, that thou 'delyuere me.

23 Also God reiside an aduersarie to Salomon, Rason, sone of Eliadam, that fledde Adadezer, kyng of Soba, his lord;

24 and gaderide men ayens hym, and was maad the prince of theuys, whanne Dauid killide hem; and thei yeden to Damask, and dwelliden there; and thei maden hym kyng in Damask.

25 And he was aduersarie of Israel in alle the daies of Salomon; and this is the yuel of Adad, and the hatrede ayens Israel; and he regnede in Sirie.

26 Also Jeroboam, sone of Nabath, of Effraym of Saredera, the seruaunt of Salomon, of which Jeroboam, a womman widewe, Serua bi name, was modir, reisyde hond ayens the kyng.

27 And this was cause of rebelte ayens the kyng; for Salomon bildide Mello, and made euene the swolowe of the citee of Dauid, his fadir.

28 Forsothe Jeroboam was a miyti man and strong; and Salomon siy the yong wexynge man of good kynrede, and witti in thingis to be doon, and Salomon made hym 'prefect, ether souereyn, on the tributis of al the hows of Joseph.

29 Therfor it was doon in that tyme, that Jeroboam yede out of Jerusalem; and Ahias of Sylo, a profete, hilid with a newe mentil, foond hym in the weie; sotheli thei tweyne weren oneli in the feeld.

30 And Ahias took his newe mentil, with which he was hilid, and kittide in to twelue partis;

31 and seide to Jeroboam, Take to thee ten kyttyngis; for the Lord God of Israel seith these thingis, Lo! Y schal kytte the rewme fro the hond of Salomon, and Y schal yyue to thee ten lynagis;

32 forsothe o lynage schal dwelle to hym, for Dauid, my seruaunt, and for Jerusalem, the citee which Y chees of alle the lynagis of Israel;

33 this kittyng schal be; for Salomon forsook me, and worschipide Astartes, goddesse of Sidoneis, and Chamos, the god of Moab, and Moloch, the god of the sones of Amon; and yede not in my weies, that he dide riytwisnesse bifor me, and myn heestis, and my domes, as Dauid, his fadir, dide.

34 And Y schal not take awey al the rewme fro 'his hond, but Y schal putte hym duyk in alle the daies of his lijf, for Dauid, my seruaunt, whom Y chees, which Dauid kepte myn heestis, and my comaundementis.

35 Sotheli Y schal take awey the rewme fro the hond of 'his sone, and Y schal yyue ten lynagis to thee;

36 forsothe Y schal yyue o lynage to 'his sone, that a lanterne dwelle to Dauid, my seruaunt, in alle daies bifor me in Jerusalem, the citee which Y chees, that my name schulde be there.

37 Forsothe Y schal take thee, and thou schalt regne on alle thingis whiche thi soule desirith, and thou schalt be kyng on Israel.

38 Therfor if thou schalt here alle thingis whiche Y schal comaunde to thee, and if thou schalt go in my weies, and if thou schalt do that, that is riytful bifore me, and if thou schalt kepe my comaundementis, and myn heestis, as Dauid, my seruaunt, dide, Y schal be with thee, and Y schal bilde a feithful hows to thee, as Y bildide an hows to Dauid, and Y schal yyue Israel to thee;

39 and Y schal turmente the seed of Dauid on this thing, netheles not in alle daies.

40 Therfor Salomon wolde sle Jeroboam, which roos, and fledde in to Egipt, to Susach, kyng of Egipt; and he was in Egipt 'til to the deeth of Salomon.

41 Forsothe the residue of the wordis of Salomon, and alle thingis whiche he dide, and his wisdom, lo! alle thingis ben writun in the book of wordis of daies of Salomon.

42 Sotheli the daies bi whiche Salomon regnede in Jerusalem on al Israel, ben fourti yeer.

43 And Salomon slepte with hise fadris, and was biriede in the citee of Dauid, his fadir; and Roboam, his sone, regnede for hym.

CAP 12

1 Forsothe Roboam cam in to Sichem; for al Israel was gaderid thidur to make hym kyng.

2 'And sotheli Jeroboam, sone of Nabath, whanne he was yit in Egipt, and fledde fro the face of kyng Salomon, turnede ayen fro Egipt, for the deeth of Salomon was herd;

3 and thei senten, and clepiden hym. Therfor Jeroboam cam, and al the multitude of Israel, and thei spaken to Roboam,

4 and seiden, Thi fadir puttide hardeste yok on vs, therfor abate thou a litil now of the hardest comaundement of thi fadir, and of the greuousiste yok which he puttide on vs, and we schulen serue to thee.

5 Which Roboam seide to hem, Go ye 'til to the thridde dai, and turne ye ayen to me.

6 And whanne the puple hadde go, kyng Roboam took counsel with the eldere men, that stoden bifor Salomon, his fadir, while he lyuyde yit; and Roboam seide, What counsel yyue ye to me, that Y answere to the puple?

7 Whiche seiden to hym, If thou obeiest to dai to this puple, and seruest this puple, and yyuest stide to her axyng, and spekist to hem liyte wordis, thei schulen be seruauntis to thee in alle daies.

8 Which Roboam forsook the counsel of elde men, which thei yauen to hym, and took yonge men, that weren nurschid with hym, and stoden nyy him;

9 and he seide to hem, What counsel yyue ye to me, that Y answere to this puple, that seiden to me, Make thou esyere the yok which thi fadir puttide on vs?

10 And the yonge men, that weren nurschid with hym, seiden to hym, Thus speke thou to this puple, that spaken to thee, and seiden, Thi fadir made greuouse oure yok, releeue thou vs; thus thou schalt speke to hem, My leest fyngur is grettere than the bak of my fader;

11 and now my fadir puttide on you a greuouse yok, forsothe Y schal adde on youre yok; my fadir beet you with scourgis, forsothe Y schal bete you with scorpiouns.

12 Therfor Jeroboam, and al the puple, cam to Roboam, in the thridde dai, as the kyng spak, seiynge, Turne ye ayen to me in the thridde dai.

13 And the kyng answeride harde thingis to the puple, while the counsel of eldere men was forsakun, which thei hadden youe to hym;

14 and he spak to hem bi the counsel of yonge men, and seide, My fadir made greuouse youre yok, forsothe Y schal adde to youre yok; my fadir beet you with scourgis, forsothe Y schal bete you with scorpiouns.

15 And the kyng assentide not to the puple, for the Lord hadde turned awey, 'ether hadde wlatid hym, that the Lord

schulde reise his word, which he hadde spoke in the hond of Ahias of Silo to Jeroboam, sone of Nabath.

16 Therfor the puple siy, that the kyng nolde here hem; and the puple answeride to the kyng, and seide, What part is to vs in Dauid, ether what eritage in the sone of Ysay? Israel, turne thou ayen in to thi tabernaclis; now, Dauid, se thou thin hows. And Israel yede in to hise tabernaclis.

17 Forsothe Roboam regnede on the sones of Israel, whiche euere dwelliden in the citees of Juda.

18 Therfore kyng Roboam sente Adhuram, that was on the tributis; and al the puple of Israel stonyde hym, and he was deed.

19 Forsothe kyng Roboam stiede hastili on the chare, and fledde in to Jerusalem; and Israel departide fro the hows of Dauid, til in to present dai.

20 Forsothe it was doon, whanne al Israel hadde herd that Jeroboam turnede ayen, thei senten, and clepiden hym, whanne the cumpany was gaderid togidere, and thei maden hym kyng on al Israel; and no man suede the hows of Dauid, outakun the lynage aloone of Juda.

21 Forsothe Roboam cam to Jerusalem, and gaderide al the hows of Juda, and the lynage of Beniamyn, an hundrid and fourescore thousynde of chosun men and weriours, that thei schulden fiyte ayens the hows of Israel, and schulden brynge ayen the rewme to Roboam, sone of Solomon.

22 Forsothe the word of God was made to Semeia, the man of God, and seide,

23 Speke thou to Roboam, sone of Salomon, the kyng of Juda, and to al the hows of Juda and of Beniamyn, and to the residue of the puple, and seie thou, The Lord seith thes thingis,

24 Ye schulen not stie, nether ye schulen fiyte ayens youre britheren, the sones of Israel; 'a man turne ayen in to his hows, for this word is doon of me. Thei herden the word of the Lord, and thei turneden ayen fro the iurney, as the Lord comaundide to hem.

25 Forsothe Jeroboam bildide Sichem, in the hil of Effraym, and dwellide there; and he yede out fro thennus, and bildide Phanuel.

26 And Jeroboam seide in his herte, Now the rewme schal turne ayen to the hows of Dauid,

27 if this puple stieth to Jerusalem, that it make sacrifices in the hows of the Lord in Jerusalem; and the herte of this puple schal turne to her lord, Roboam, kyng of Juda; and thei schulen sle me, and schulen turne ayen to hym.

28 And by counsel thouyt out, he made tweyne goldun caluys, and seide to hem, Nyle ye stie more in to Jerusalem; Israel, lo! thi goddis, that ledden thee out of the lond of Egipt.

29 And he settide oon in Bethel, and the tother in Dan.

30 And this word was maad to Israel in to synne; for the puple yede til in to Dan, to worschipe the calf.

31 And Jeroboam made templis in hiye placis, and 'he made preestis of the laste men of the puple, that weren not of the sones of Leuy.

32 And he ordeynede a solempne dai in the eiythe monethe, in the fiftenthe dai of the monethe, bi the licnesse of solempnyte which was halewid in Juda. And he stiede, and made in lijk maner an auter in Bethel, that he schulde offre to the calues, whiche he hadde maad; and he ordeynede in Bethel preestis of the hiye places, whiche he hadde maad.

33 And he styede on the auter, which he hadde bildid in Bethel, in the fiftenthe day of the eiythe monethe, which he hadde feyned of his herte; and he made solempnyte to the sones of Israel, and he stiede on the auter, that he schulde brenne encence.

CAP 13

1 And lo! a man of God cam fro Juda, bi the word of the Lord, in to Bethel, while Jeroboam stood on the auter, 'and castide encence.

2 And 'the man of God criede ayens the auter, bi the word of the Lord, and seide, Auter! auter! the Lord seith these thingis, Lo! a sone, Josias by name, shal be borun to the hows of Dauid; and he schal offre on thee the preestis of hiye thingis, that brennen now encensis yn thee, and he schal brenne the bonys of men on thee.

3 And he yaf a signe in that dai, 'and seide, This schal be 'the signe that the Lord spak, Lo! the auter schal be kit, and the aische which is 'there ynne, schal be sched out.

4 And whanne the kyng hadde herd the word of the man of God, which word he hadde cried ayens the auter in Bethel, the kyng helde forth his hond fro the auter, and seide, Take ye hym. And his hond driede, which he hadde holde forth, and he myyte not drawe it ayen to hym silf.

5 Also the auter was kit, and the aische was sched out of the auter, bi the signe which the man of God bifor seide, in the word of the Lord.

6 And the kyng seide to the man of God, Biseche thou the face of thi Lord God, and preie thou for me, that myn hond be restorid to me. And the man of God preiede the face of God; and the hond of the king turnede ayen to hym, and it was maad as it was bifore.

7 Sotheli the kyng spak to the man of God, Come thou hoom with me, that thou ete, and Y schal yyue yiftis to thee.

8 And the man of God seide to the kyng, Thouy thou schalt yyue to me the half part of thin hows, Y schal not come with thee, nether Y schal ete breed, nether Y schal drynke watir in this place;

9 'for so it is comaundid to me bi the word of the Lord, comaundinge, Thou schalt not ete breed, nether thou schalt drynke water, nether thou schalt turne ayen bi the weie bi which thou camest.

10 Therfor he yede bi another weie, and turnede not ayen bi the weie, bi which he cam in to Bethel.

11 Forsothe sum elde profete dwellide in Bethel, to whom hise sones camen, and telden to hym alle the werkis whiche the man of God hadde do in that dai in Bethel; and thei telden to her fader the wordis whiche he spak to the kyng.

12 And the fadir of hem seide to hem, Bi what weie yede he? Hise sones schewiden to hym the weie, bi which the man of God yede, that cam fro Juda.

13 And he seide to hise sones, Sadle ye an asse to me. And whanne thei hadden sadlid,

14 he stiede, and yede after the man of God, and foond hym sittyng vndur a terebynte. And he seide to the man of God, Whether thou art the man of God, that camest fro Juda? He answeride, Y am.

15 And he seide to hym, Come thou with me hoom, that thou ete breed.

16 And he seide, Y may not turne ayen, nether come with thee, nether Y schal ete breed, nether Y schal drynke water in this place;

17 for the Lord spak to me in the word of the Lord, and seide, Thou schalt not ete breed, and thou schalt not drynke water there, nether thou schalt turne ayen bi the weie bi which thou yedist.

18 Which seide to hym, And Y am a profete lijk thee; and an aungel spak to me bi the word of the Lord, and seide, Lede ayen hym in to thin hows, that he ete breed, and drynke watir. He disseyuede the man of God,

19 and brouyte him ayen with hym. Therfor he ete breed in his hows, and drank watir.

20 And whanne he sat at the table, the word of the Lord was maad to the prophete that brouyte hym ayen;

21 and he criede to the man of God that cam fro Juda, and seide, The Lord seith these thingis, For thou obeidist not to the mouth of the Lord, and keptist not the comaundement which thi Lord God comaundide to thee,

22 and thou turnedist ayen, and etist breed, and drankist watir in the place in which Y comaundide to thee, that thou schuld-ist not ete breed, nether schuldist drynke watir, thi deed bodi schal not be borun in to the sepulcre of thi fadris,

23 And whanne he hadde ete and drunke, the prophete, whom he hadde brouyt ayen, sadlide his asse.

24 And whanne he hadde go, a lioun foond hym in the weye, and killide hym. And his deed bodi was cast forth in the weie; sotheli the asse stood bisydis hym, and the lioun stood bisidis the deed bodi.

25 And lo! men passynge sien the deed bodi cast forth in the weye, and the lyoun stondynge bisidis the deed bodi; and thei camen, and pupplischiden in the citee, in which thilke eeld prophete dwellide.

26 And whanne thilke prophete, that brouyte hym ayen fro the weye, hadde herd this, he seide, It is the man of God, that was vnobedient to the mouth of God; and the Lord bitook hym to the lioun, that brak hym, and killide hym, bi the word of the Lord which he spak to hym.

27 And he seide to hise sones, Sadle ye an asse to me.

28 And whanne thei hadden sadlid, and he hadde go, he foond his deed bodi cast forth in the weie, and the asse and the lioun stondinge bisidis the deed bodi; and the lioun eet not the deed bodi, nether hirtide the asse.

29 Therfor the profete took the deed bodi of the man of God, and puttide it on the asse; and he turnede ayen, and brouyte it in to the cyte of the eeld prophete, that he schulde biweile hym.

30 And he puttide his deed bodi in his sepulcre, and thei biweiliden him, Alas! alas! my brother!

31 And whanne thei hadden biweilid hym, he seide to hise sones, Whanne Y schal be deed, birie ye me in the sepulcre, in which the man of God is biried; putte ye my bonys bisidis hise bonys.

32 For sotheli the word schal come, which he bifor seide in the word of the Lord, ayens the auter which is in Bethel, and ayens alle the templis of hiy placis, that ben in the citees of Samarie. After these wordis Jeroboam turnede not ayen fro his werste weie, but ayenward of the laste puplis he made pre-estis of hiye places; who euer wolde, fillide his hond, and he was maad preest of hiy placis.

33 And for this cause the hows of Jeroboam synnede, and it was distried, and doon awey fro the face of erthe.

CAP 14

1 In that tyme Abia, sone of Jeroboam, was sijk.

2 And Jeroboam seide to his wijf, Rise thou, and chaunge clothing, that thou be not knowun, that thou art the wijf of Jeroboam; and go thou in to Silo, where Ahia, the prophete, is, which spak to me, that Y schulde regne on this puple.

3 Also take thou in the hond ten looues, and a cake, and a ves-sil of hony, and go thou to hym; for he schal schewe to thee, what schal bifalle to this child.

4 The wijf of Jeroboam dide as he seide, and sche roos, and yede in to Silo, and cam in to the hows of Ahia; and he miyte not se, for hise iyen dasewiden for eelde.

5 Forsothe the Lord seide to Ahia, Lo! the wijf of Jeroboam entrith, that sche counsele thee on hir sone, which is sijk; thou schalt speke these and these thingis to hir. Therfor whanne sche hadde entrid, and hadde feyned hir silf to be that 'wom-man which sche was not,

6 Ahia herde the soune of the feet of hir entrynge bi the dore, and he seide, Entre thou, the wijf of Jeroboam; whi feynest thou thee to bee an other womman? Forsothe Y am sent an hard messanger to thee.

7 Go thou, and seie to Jeroboam, The Lord God of Israel seith these thingis, For Y enhaunside thee fro the myddis of the puple, and Y yaf thee duyk on my puple Israel,

8 and Y kittide the rewme of the hows of Dauid, and Y yaf it to thee, and thou were not as my seruaunt Dauid, that kepte myn heestis, and suede me in al his herte, and dide that that was plesaunt in my siyt;

9 but thou wrouytist yuel, ouer alle men that weren bifore thee, and madist to thee alien goddis, and wellid to gidere, that thou schuldist excite me to wrathfulnesse, sotheli thou hast cast forth me bihyndis thi bak.

10 Therfor lo! Y schal brynge in yuels on the hows of Jero-boam, and Y schal smyte of Jeroboam 'til to a pissere to the wal, and prisoned, and the laste in Israel; and Y schal clense the relikis of the hows of Jeroboam, as dung is wont to be clensid 'til to the purete, 'ether clennesse;

11 sotheli doggis schulen ete hem, that schulen die of the hows of Jeroboam in citee; forsothe briddis of the eyr schulen deuoure hem, that schulen die in the feeld; for the Lord spak.

12 Therfor rise thou, and go in to thin hows; and in thilke entryng of thi feet in to the citee the child schal die.

13 And al Israel schal biweile him, and schal birie; for this child aloone of Jeroboam schal be borun in to sepulcre, for a good word is foundun on hym of the Lord God of Israel, in the hows of Jeroboam.

14 Forsothe the Lord schal ordeyne to hym a kyng on Israel, that schal smyte the hows of Jeroboam, in this dai and in this tyme;

15 and the Lord God of Israel schal smyte, as a reed in the water is wont to be mouyd; and he schal drawe out Israel fro this good lond, which he yaf to her fadris, and he schal wyndewe hem ouer the flood, for thei maden to hem woodis, that thei schulden terre the Lord to ire.

16 And the Lord God schal bitake Israel to hise enemyes, for the synnes of Jeroboam, that synnede, and made Israel to do synne.

17 Therfor the wijf of Jeroboam roos, and yede, and cam in to Thersa; whanne sche entride in to the threschfold of the hows, the child was deed.

18 And thei birieden hym; and al Israel biweilide hym, bi the word of the Lord, which he spak in the hoond of his seruaunt, Ahia the prophet.

19 Forsothe, lo! the residue of wordis of Jeroboam, how he fauyt, and how he regnede, ben writun in the book of wordis of the daies of kyngis of Israel.

20 Forsothe the daies, in whiche Jeroboam regnede, ben two and twenti yeer; and Jeroboam slepte with hise fadris, and Nadab, his sone, regnede for hym.

21 Forsothe Roboam, the sone of Salomon, regnede in Juda; Roboam was of oon and fourti yeer, whanne he bigan to regne, and he regnede seuentene yeer in Jerusalem, the citee which the Lord chees of alle the lynagis of Israel, that he schulde sette his name there. Sotheli the name of his moder was Naama Amanyte.

22 And Juda dide yuel bifor the Lord, and thei terriden hym to ire on alle thingis, whiche her fadris diden in her synnes, bi whiche thei synneden.

23 For also thei bildiden to hem silf auters, and ymagis, and wodis, on eche hiy hil, and vndur ech tree ful of bowis.

24 But also 'men of wymmens condiciouns weren in the lond, and thei diden alle abhominaciouns of hethene men, whiche the Lord al to-brak bifor the face of the sones of Israel.

25 Forsothe in the fifthe yeer of the rewme of Roboam, Sesach, the kyng of Egipt, styede in to Jerusalem;

26 and he took the tresouris of the hows of the Lord, and the kyngis tresouris, and he rauischide alle thingis; also 'he rauischide the goldun scheeldis, whiche Salomon made.

27 For whiche kyng Roboam made brasun scheeldis, and yaf tho in the hondis of duykis of scheeld makeris, and of hem that wakiden bifor the dore of the hows of the Lord.

28 And whanne the kyng entride in to the hows of the Lord, thei that hadden office to go bifore, baren tho, and baren ayen to the place of armer of scheeld makeris.

29 Forsothe, lo! the residue of wordis of Roboam, and alle thingis whiche he dide, ben writun in the book of wordis of daies of kyngis of Juda.

30 And batel was bitwixe Roboam and Jeroboam, in alle daies.

31 And Roboam slepte with hise fadris, and was biried with hem in the citee of Dauid. Forsothe the name of his modir was Naama Amanyte; and Abia, his sone, regnede for hym.

CAP 15

1 Therfor in the eiytenthe yeer of the rewme of Jeroboam, sone of Nabath, Abia regnede on Juda.

2 Thre yeer he regnede in Jerusalem; the name of his modir was Maacha, douyter of Abessalon.

3 And he yede in alle the synnes of his fadir, which he dide bifor hym; and his herte was not perfit with his Lord God, as the herte of Dauid, his fadir, 'was perfit.

4 But for Dauid his Lord God yaf to hym a lanterne in Jerusalem, that he schulde reise his sone after hym, and that he schulde stonde in Jerusalem;

5 for Dauid hadde do riytfulnesse in the iyen of the Lord, and hadde not bowid fro alle thingis whiche the Lord hadde comaundid to him, in alle the daies of his lijf, outakun the word of Urie Ethei.

6 Netheles batel was bitwix Abia and Jeroboam, in al the tyme of his lijf.

7 Sotheli the residue of wordis of Abia, and alle thinges whiche he dide, whether these ben not writun in the book of wordis of daies of the kyngys of Juda? And batel was bitwixe Abia and Jeroboam.

8 And Abia slepte with his fadris; and thei birieden hym in the citee of Dauid; and Asa, his sone, regnede for hym.

9 Sotheli Asa, king of Jude, regnede in the twentithe yeer of Jeroboam, kyng of Israel;

10 and Asa regnede oon and fourti yeer in Jerusalem. The name of his modir was Maacha, douyter of Abessalon.

11 And Asa dide riytfulnesse in the siyt of the Lord, as Dauid, his fadir, dide;

12 and he took awey fro the loond men of wymmens condiciouns, and he purgide alle the filthis of idols, whiche his fadris maden.

13 Ferthermore and he remouyde Maacha, his modir, that sche schulde not be princesse in the solempne thingis of Priapus, and in his wode which sche hadde halewid; and he distriede the denne of hym, and he brak the foulest symylacre, and brente in the stronde of Cedron;

14 sotheli he dide not awei hiy thingis; netheles the herte of Asa was perfit with hys Lord God, in alle hise daies.

15 And he brouyte in to the hous of the Lord tho thingis, whiche his fadir hadde halewid and auowid, siluer, and gold, and vessel.

16 Forsothe batel was bitwixe Asa and Baasa, kyng of Israel, in alle the daies of hem.

17 And Baasa, kyng of Israel, stiede in to Juda, and bildide Rama, that no man of the part of Aza, kyng of Juda, myyte go out, ether go yn.

18 Therfor Asa took al the siluer and gold, that lefte in the tresouris of the hows of the Lord, and in the tresouris of the kyngis hows, and yaf it in to the hondis of hise seruauntis; and sente to Benadab, sone of Tabrennon, sone of Ozion, the kyng of Sirie, that dwellide in Damask, and seide,

19 Boond of pees is bitwixe me and thee, and bitwixe my fadir and thi fadir, and therfor Y sente to thee yiftis, gold, and siluer; and Y axe, that thou come, and make voide the boond of pees, which thou hast with Baasa, kyng of Israel, and that he go awey fro me.

20 Benadab assentide to kyng Asa, and sente the princes of his oost in to the citees of Israel; and thei smytiden Ahion, and Dan, and Abel, the hows of Maacha, and al Cenoroth, that is, al the lond of Neptalym.

21 And whanne Baasa hadde herd this thing, he lefte to bilde Rama, and turnede ayen in to Thersa.

22 Forsothe kyng Asa sente message in to al Juda, and seide, No man be excusid. And thei token the stoonys of Rama, and the trees therof, bi whiche Baasa hadde bildid; and kyng Asa bildide of the same 'stoonys and trees Gabaa of Beniamyn, and Maspha.

23 Sotheli the residue of alle wordis of Asa, and of al his strengthe, and alle thingis whiche he dide, and the citees whiche he bildide, whether these ben not writun in the book of wordis of daies of kingis of Juda? Netheles Asa hadde ache in feet

11, in the tyme of his eelde.

24 And Asa slepte with hise fadris, and he was biried with hem in the citee of Dauid, his fader; and Josophat, his sone, regnede for him.

25 Forsothe Nadab, the sone of Jeroboam, regnede on Israel, in the secunde yeer of Asa, king of Juda; and he regnede on Israel two yeer.

26 And he dide that, that was yuel in the siyt of the Lord, and he yede in the weies of his fadir, and in the synnes of hym, in whiche he made Israel to do synne.

27 Forsothe Baasa, the sone of Ahia, of the hows of Ysachar, settide tresoun to hym, and smoot him in Gebethon, which is a citee of Filisteis; sothely Nadab and al Israel bisegiden Gebethon.

28 Therfor Baasa killide hym, in the thridde yeer of Asa, king of Juda, and regnede for hym.

29 And whanne he hadde regnede, he smoot al the hows of Jeroboam; he lefte not sotheli not o man of his seed, til he

dide awei hym, bi the word of the Lord, which he spak in the hond of his seruaunt, Ahia of Silo, a profete,

30 for the synnes of Jeroboam whiche he synnede, and in whiche he made Israel to do synne, and for the trespas, bi which he wraththide the Lord God of Israel.

31 Sotheli the residue of wordis of Nadab, and alle thingis whiche he wrouyte, whether these ben not writun in the book of wordis of daies of the kyngis of Israel?

32 And batel was bitwixe Asa and Baasa, kyng of Israel, in al the daies of hem.

33 In the thridde yeer of Asa, kyng of Juda, Baasa, sone of Ahia, regnede on al Israel, in Thersa, foure and twenti yeer.

34 And he dide yuel bifor the Lord, and he yede in the weies of Jeroboam, and in hise synnes, bi whiche he made Israel to do synne.

CAP 16

1 Forsothe the word of the Lord was maad to Hieu, sone of Anany, ayens Baasa, and seide,

2 For that that Y reiside thee fro dust, and settide thee duyk on Israel, my puple; sotheli thou yedist in the weie of Jeroboam, and madist my puple Israel to do synne, that thou schuldist terre me to ire, in the synnes of hem; lo!

3 Y schal kitte awey the hyndrere thingis of Baasa, and the hyndrere thingis of 'his hows, and Y schal make thin hows as the hows of Jeroboam, sone of Nabath.

4 Doggis schulen ete that man of Baasa, that schal be deed in citee, and briddis of the eyr schulen ete that man of Baasa, that schal die in the feeld.

5 Sotheli the residue of wordis of Baasa, and what euer thingis he dide, and hise batels, whether these ben not writun in the book of wordis of daies of the kynges of Israel?

6 Therfor Baasa slepte with hise fadris, and he was biried in Thersa; and Hela, his sone, regnede for hym.

7 Forsothe whanne the word of the Lord was maad in the hond of Hieu, sone of Anany, ayens Baasa, and ayens his hows, and ayens al yuel which he dide bifor the Lord, to terre hym to ire in the werkis of hise hondis, that he schulde be as the hows of Jeroboam, for this cause he killide hym, that is, Hieu, the prophete, the sone of Anany.

8 In the sixe and twentithe yeer of Aza, kyng of Juda, Hela, the sone of Baasa, regnyde on Israel, in Thersa, twei yeer.

9 And Zamry, 'his seruaunt, duyk of the half part of knyytis, rebellide ayens hym; sotheli Hela was in Thersa, and drank, and was drunkun in the hows of Arsa, prefect of Thersa.

10 Therfor Zamri felde in, and smoot, and killide hym, in the seuene and twentithe yeer of Asa, kyng of Juda; and regnede for hym.

11 And whanne he hadde regned, and hadde setun on his trone, he smoot al the hows of Baasa, and he lefte not therof a pissere to the wal, and hise kynnesmen, and frendis.

12 And Zamri dide awey al the hows of Baasa, bi the word of the Lord, which he spak to Baasa, in the hond of Hieu, the prophete, for alle the synnes of Baasa,

13 and for the synnes of Hela, his sone, whiche synneden, and maden Israel to do synne, and wraththiden the Lord God of Israel in her vanytees.

14 Sotheli the residue of the wordis of Hela, and alle thingis whiche he dide, whether these ben not writun in the book of wordis of daies of the kyngis of Israel?

15 In the seuene and twentithe yeer of Aza, kyng of Juda, Zamri regnede seuene daies in Tharsa; forsothe the oost bisegide Gebethon, the citee of Philisteis.

16 And whanne it hadde herd, that Zamri hadde rebellid, and hadde slayn the kyng, al Israel made Amry kyng to hem, that was prince of the chyualrye, on Israel, in that dai, in 'the castels.

17 Therfor Amry stiede, and al Israel with hym, fro Gebethon, and bisegide Thersa.

18 Sothely Zamri siy, that the citee schulde be ouercomun, and he entride in to the palis, and brente hym silf with the kyngis hows;

19 and he was deed in hise synnes whiche he synnede, doynge yuel bifor the Lord, and goynge in the weie of Jeroboam, and in hise synnes, bi whiche he made Israel to do synne.

20 Sotheli the residue of wordis of Zamri, and of his tresouns, and tyrauntrie, whether these ben not writun in the book of wordis of daies of the kyngis of Israel?

21 Thanne the puple of Israel was departid in to twei partis; the half part of the puple suede Thebny, sone of Geneth, to make hym kyng, and the half part suede Amry.

22 Sotheli the puple that was with Amry, hadde maystry ouer the puple that suede Thebny, the sone of Geneth; and Thebny was deed, and Amri regnede.

23 In the oon and thrittithe yeer of Aza, kyng of Juda, Amri regnede on Israel, twelue yeer; in Thersa he regnede sixe yeer.

24 And he bouyte of Soomeer, for twei talentis of siluer, the hil of Samarie, and 'bildide that hil; and he clepide the name of the citee, which he hadde bildid, bi the name of Soomer, lord of the hil of Samarie.

25 Forsothe Amry dide yuel in the siyt of the Lord, and wrouyte weiwardli, ouer alle men that weren bifor hym.

26 And he yede in al the weie of Jeroboam, sone of Nabath, and in hise synnes, bi whiche he made Israel to do synne, that he schulde terre to ire, in his vanytees, the Lord God of Israel.

27 Forsothe the residue of wordis of Amry, and hise batels, which he dide, whether these ben not writun in the book of wordis of daies of the kyngis of Israel?

28 And Amry slepte with hise fadris, and was biried in Samarie; and Achab, his sone, regnede for hym.

29 Forsothe Achab, the sone of Amry, regnede on Israel, in the 'eiyte and thrittithe yeer of Asa, kyng of Juda; and Achab, sone of Amry, regnede on Israel, in Samarie, two and twenti yeer.

30 And Achab, sone of Amry, dide yuel in the siyte of the Lord, ouer alle men that weren bifor hym;

31 and it suffiside not to hym that he yede in the synnes of Jeroboam, sone of Nabath, ferthermore and he weddide a wijf, Jezabel, the douyter of Methaal, kyng of Sydoneis; and he yede, and seruyde Baal, and worschipide hym.

32 And he settide an auter to Baal in the temple of Baal, which he hadde bildid in Samarie, and he plauntide a wode;

33 and Achab addide in his werk, and terride to ire the Lord God of Israel, more thanne alle kyngis of Israel that weren bifor hym.

34 Forsothe in hise daies Ahiel of Bethel bildide Jerico; in Abiram, his firste sone, he foundide it, in Segub, his laste sone, he settide yatis therof, bi the word of the Lord, which he hadde spoke in the hond of Josue, sone of Nun.

CAP 17

1 And Elie 'of Thesbi, of the dwelleris of Galaad, seide to Achab, The Lord God of Israel lyueth, in whos siyt Y stonde,

deeu and reyn schal not be in these yeeris, no but bi the wordis of my mouth.

2 And the word of the Lord was maad to hym, and seide,
3 Go thou awey fro hennus, and go ayens the eest, and be thou hid in the stronde of Carith, which is ayens Jordan,
4 and there thou schalt drynke of the stronde; and Y comaundide to crowis, that thei feede thee there.
5 Therfor he yede, and dide bi the word of the Lord; and whanne he hadde go, he sat in the stronde of Carith, which is ayens Jordan.
6 And crowis baren to hym breed and fleisch eerli; in lijk maner in the euentid; and he drank of the stronde.
7 Forsothe after summe daies the stronde was dried; for it hadde not reynede on the erthe.
8 Therfor the word of the Lord was maad to hym, and seide,
9 Rise thou, and go in to Serepta of Sydoneis, and thou schalt dwelle there; for Y comaundide to a womman, widewe there, that sche feede thee.
10 He roos, and yede in to Sarepta of Sidoneis; and whanne he hadde come to the yate of the citee, a womman widewe gaderynge stickis apperide to hym; and he clepide hir, and seide to hir, Yyue thou to me a litil of water in a vessel, that Y drynke.
11 And whanne sche yede to bringe, he criede bihynde hir bac, and seide, Y biseche, bringe thou to me also a mussel of breed in thin hond.
12 And sche answeride, Thi Lord God lyueth, for Y haue no breed, no but as myche of mele in a pot, as a fist may take, and a litil of oile in a vessel; lo! Y gadere twei stickis, that Y entre, and make it to me, and to my sone, that we ete and die.
13 And Elie seide to hir, Nyle thou drede, but go, and make as thou seidist; netheles make thou firste to me of that litil mele a litil loof, bakun vndur the aischis, and brynge thou to me; sotheli thou schalt make afterward to thee and to thi sone.
14 Forsothe the Lord God of Israel seith thes thingis, The pot of mele schal not faile, and the vessel of oile schal not be abatid, til to the dai in which the Lord schal yyue reyn on the face of erthe.
15 And sche yede, and dide bi the word of Elie; and he eet, and sche, and hir hows.
16 And fro that dai the pot of mele failide not, and the vessel of oile was not abatid, bi the word of the Lord, which he hadde spoke in the hond of Elie.
17 Forsothe it was doon aftir these wordis, the sone of a womman hosewijf was sijk, and the sijknesse was moost strong, so that breeth dwellide not in hym.
18 Therfor sche seide to Elie, What to me and to thee, thou man of God? Entridist thou to me, that my wickidnessis schulden be remembrid, and that thou schuldist sle my sone?
19 And Elie seide to hir, Yyue thi sone to me. And he took 'that sone fro hir bosum, and bar in to the soler, where he dwellide; and he puttide hym on his bed.
20 And he criede to the Lord, and seide, My Lord God, whether thou hast turmentid also the widewe, at whom Y am susteyned in al maner, that thou killidist hir sone?
21 He sprad abrood hym silf, and mat on the child bi thre tymes; and he cryede to the Lord, and seide, My Lord God, Y biseche, the soule of this child turne ayen in to the entrailis of hym.
22 The Lord herde the vois of Elie, and the soule of the child turnede ayen with ynne hym, and he lyuede ayen.

23 And Elie took the child, and puttide hym doun of the soler in to the lower hows, and bitook him to his modir; and he seide to hir, Lo! thi sone lyueth.
24 And the womman seide to Elie, Now in this Y haue knowe, that thou art the man of God, and the word of God is soth in thi mouth.

CAP 18

1 Aftir many daies the word of the Lord was maad to Elie, in the thridde yeer, and seide, Go, and schewe thee to Achab, that Y yyue reyn on the face of erthe.
2 Therfor Elie yede to schewe hym silf to Achab; forsothe greet hungur was in Samarie.
3 And Achab clepide Abdie, dispendere, ether stiward, of his hows; forsothe Abdie dredde greetli the Lord God of Israel.
4 For whanne Jezabel killide the prophetis of the Lord, he took an hundrid prophetis, and hidde hem, bi fifties and fifties, in dennes, and fedde hem with breed and watir.
5 Therfor Achab seide to Abdie, Go thou in to the lond, to alle wellis of watris, and in to alle valeis, if in hap we moun fynde gras, and saue horsis and mulis; and werk beestis perische not outirli.
6 Therfor thei departiden the cuntreis to hem silf, that thei schulden cumpasse tho; Achab yede bi o weye, and Abdie yede bi another weie, 'bi hym silf.
7 And whanne Abdie was in the weie, Elie mette hym; and whanne he hadde knowe Elie, he felde on his face, and seide, Whethir thou art my lord Elie?
8 To whom he answeride, Y am. And Elie seide, Go thou, and seie to thi lord, Elie is present.
9 And Abdie seide, What 'synnede Y, for thou bitakist me in the hond of Achab, that he sle me?
10 Thi Lord God lyueth, for no folk ethir rewme is, whidur my lord, sekynge thee, sente not; and whanne alle men answeriden, He is not here, he chargide greetli alle rewmes and folkis, for thou were not foundun; and now thou seist to me,
11 Go, and seie to thi lord, Elie is present.
12 And whanne Y schal departe fro thee, the Spirit of the Lord schal bere thee awey in to a place which Y knowe not; and Y schal entre, and 'Y schal telle to Achab, and he schal not fynde thee, and he schal sle me; forsothe thi seruaunt dredith the Lord fro his yong childhod.
13 Whether it is not schewid to thee, my lord, what Y dide, whanne Jesabel killide the prophetis of the Lord, that Y hidde of the prophetis of the Lord an hundrid men, bi fifty and bi fifti, in dennes, and Y fedde hem with breed and watir?
14 And now thou seist, Go, and seie to thi lord, Elie is present, that he sle me.
15 And Elie seide, The Lord of oostis lyueth, bifor whos siyt Y stonde, for to dai Y schal appere to hym.
16 Therfor Abdie yede in to the metyng of Achab, and schewide to hym; and Achab cam in to the meetyng of Elie.
17 And whanne he hadde seyn Elie, he seide, Whether thou art he, that disturblist Israel?
18 And he seide, Not Y disturble Israel, but thou, and the hows of thi fadir, whiche han forsake the comaundementis of the Lord, and sueden Baalym, 'disturbliden Israel.
19 Netheles now sende thou, and gadere to me al Israel, in the hil of Carmele, and foure hundrid and fifti prophetis of Baal, and foure hundrid prophetis of woodis, that eten of the table of Jezabel.

20 Achab sente to alle the sones of Israel, and gaderide prophetis in the hil of Carmele.

21 Forsothe Elie neiyede to al the puple of Israel, and seide, Hou long halten ye in to twey partis? If the Lord is God, sue ye hym; forsothe if Baal is God, sue ye hym. And the puple answeride not o word to hym.

22 And Elie seide eft to the puple, Y dwellide aloone a prophete of the Lord; sotheli the prophetis of Baal ben foure hundrid and fifti, and the prophetis of woodis ben foure hundrid men.

23 Tweyne oxis be youun to us; and chese thei oon oxe, and thei schulen kitte in to gobetis, and schulen putte on trees, but putte thei not fier vndur; and Y schal make the tother oxe in to sacrifice, and Y schal putte on the trees, and Y schal not putte fier vnder.

24 Clepe ye the name of youre goddis, and Y schal clepe the name of my God; and the God that herith bi fier, be he God. And al the puple answeride, and seide, The resoun is best, 'which resoun Elie spak.

25 Therfor Elie seide to the prophetis of Baal, Chese ye oon oxe to you, and make ye first, for ye ben the mo; and clepe ye the names of youre goddis, and putte ye not fier vnder.

26 And whanne thei hadden take the oxe, whom Elie yaf to hem, thei maden sacrifice, and clepiden the name of Baal, fro the morewtid 'til to myddai, and seiden, Baal, here vs! And no vois was, nether ony that answerd; and thei skippiden ouer the auter, which thei hadden maad.

27 And whanne it was thanne myddai, Elie scornede hem, and seide, Crie ye with gretter vois, for Baal is youre god, and in hap he spekith with an other, ethir he is in a herborgerie, ether in weie, ether certis he slepith, that he be reisid.

28 Therfor thei crieden with greet vois, and thei kerueden hem silf with knyues and launcetis, bi her custom, til thei weren bisched with blood.

29 Sotheli after that myddday passide, and while thei prophesieden, the tyme cam, in which the sacrifice is wont to be offrid, nether vois was herd 'of her goddis, nether ony answeride, nether perceyuede hem preiynge.

30 Elie seide to al the puple, Come ye to me. And whanne the puple cam to him, he arrayede the auter of the Lord, that was distried.

31 And he took twelue stonys, bi the noumbre of lynagis of sones of Jacob, to which Jacob the word of the Lord was maad, and seide, Israel schal be thi name.

32 And he bildide an auter of stonys, in the name of the Lord, and he made a ledyng to of watir, 'ether a dich, as bi twei litle dichis in the cumpas of the auter.

33 And he dresside trees, and he departide the oxe bi membris, and puttide on the trees,

34 and seide, Fille ye foure pottis with watir, and schede ye on the brent sacrifice, and on the trees. And eft he seide, Also the secounde tyme do ye this. 'And thei diden the secounde tyme. And he seide, Do ye the same thing the thridde tyme; and thei diden the thridde tyme.

35 And the watris runnen aboute the auter, and the dich of ledyng to 'of watir was fillid.

36 And whanne the tyme was thanne, that the brent sacrifice schulde be offrid, Elye the prophete neiyede, and seide, Lord God of Abraham, of Isaac, and of Israel, schewe thou to dai that thou art God of Israel, and that Y am thi seruaunt, and haue do alle these wordis bi thi comaundement.

37 Lord, here thou me; Lord, here thou me; that this puple lerne, that thou art the Lord God, and that thou hast conuertid eft the herte of hem.

38 Sotheli fier of the Lord felde doun, and deuouride brent sacrifice, and trees, and stonus, and lickide vp also the poudre, and the water that was in the 'leding of water.

39 And whanne al the puple hadde seyn this, it felde in to his face, and seide, The Lord he is God; the Lord he is God.

40 And Elie seide to hem, Take ye the prophetis of Baal; not oon sotheli ascape of hem. And whanne thei hadden take hem, Elie ledde hem to the stronde of Cison, and killide hem there.

41 And Elie seide to Achab, Stie thou, ete, and drynke, for the sown of myche reyn is.

42 Achab stiede to ete and drynke; forsothe Elie stiede in to the hil of Carmele, and he settide lowli his face to the erthe, bitwixe hise knees;

43 and seide to his child, Stie thou, and biholde ayens the see. And whanne he hadde stied, and hadde biholde, he seide, No thing is. And eft Elie seide to hym, Turne thou ayen bi seuene tymes.

44 Sotheli in the seuenthe tyme, lo! a litil cloude as the step of a man stiede fro the see. And Elie seide, Stie thou, and seie to Achab, Ioyne thi chare, and go doun, lest the reyn byfor ocupie thee.

45 And whanne thei turneden hem hidur and thidur, lo! heuenes weren maad derk, and cloud, and wynd, and greet reyn was maad. Therfor Achab stiede, and yede in to Jezrael;

46 and the hond of the Lord was maad on Elie, and whanne the leendis weren gird, he ran bifor Achab, til he cam in to Jezrael.

CAP 19

1 Forsothe Achab telde to Jezabel alle thingis whiche Elie hadde do, and how he hadde slayn by swerd alle the prophetis of Baal.

2 And Jezabel sente a messanger to Elie, and seide, Goddis do these thingis to me, and adde these thingis, no but to morewe in this our Y schal putte thi lijf as the lijf of oon of hem.

3 Therfor Elie dredde, and roos, and yede whidur euer wille bar hym; and he cam in to Bersabe of Juda, and he lefte there his child;

4 and yede in to deseert, the weie of o dai. And whanne he cam, and sat vndir o iunypere tre, he axide to his soule, that he schulde die; and he seide, Lord, it suffisith to me, take my soule; for Y am not betere than my fadris.

5 And he castide forth hym silf, and slepte in the schadewe of the iunypere tree. And lo! the aungel of the Lord touchide hym, and seide to hym, Rise thou, and ete.

6 He bihelde, and, lo! at his heed was a loof bakun vndur aischis, and a vessel of watir. Therfor he ete, and drank, and slepte eft.

7 And the aungel of the Lord turnede ayen the secounde tyme, and touchide hym; and 'the aungel seide to hym, Rise thou, and ete; for a greet weie is to thee.

8 And whanne he hadde rise, he ete, and drank; and he yede in the strengthe of that mete bi fourti dayes and fourti nyytis, 'til to Oreb, the hil of God.

9 And whanne he hadde come thidur, he dwellide in a denne; and lo! the word of the Lord 'was maad to him, and seide to hym, Elie, what doist thou here?

10 And he answeride, Bi feruent loue Y louede feruentli, for the Lord God of oostis; for the sones of Israel forsoken the

couenaunt of the Lord; thei destrieden thin auters, and killiden bi swerd thi prophetis; and Y am left aloone, and thei seken my lijf, that thei do it awei.

11 And he seide to Elie, Go thou out, and stonde in the hil, bifor the Lord. And lo! the Lord passith, and a greet wynde, and strong, turnynge vpsodoun hillis, and al to brekinge stonys bifor the Lord; not in the wynde ys the Lord. And aftir the wynd is a stirynge; not in the stiryng is the Lord.

12 And aftir the stiryng is fier; not in the fier is the Lord. And aftir the fier is the issyng of thinne wynd; there is the Lord.

13 And whanne Elie hadde herd this, he hilide his face with a mentil, and he yede out, and stood in the dore of the denne. And a vois spak to hym, and seide, Elie, what doist thou here?

14 And he answeride, Bi feruent loue Y louede feruentli, for the Lord God of oostis; for the sones of Israel forsoken thi couenaunt; thei distrieden thin auteris, and thei killiden bi swerd thi prophetis; and Y am left aloone, and thei seken my lijf, that thei do it awey.

15 And the Lord seide to hym, Go, and turne ayen in to thi weie, bi the deseert, in to Damask; and whanne thou schalt come thidur, thou schalt anoynte Asahel kyng on Sirie;

16 and thou schalt anoynte kyng on Israel Hieu, the sone of Namsi; sotheli thou schalt anoynte prophete for thee, Elise, sone of Saphat, which is of Abelmeula.

17 And it schal be, who euer schal fle the swerd of Asahel, Hieu schal sle hym; and who euer schal fle the swerd of Hieu, Elise schal sle hym.

18 And Y schal leeue to me in Israel seuene thousynde of men, of whiche the knees ben not bowid bifor Baal, and ech mouth that worschipide not hym, and kisside hond.

19 Therfor Elie yede forth fro thennus, and foond Elise, sone of Saphat, erynge in twelue yockis of oxis; and he was oon in the twelue yockis of oxys, erynge. And whanne Elie hadde come to hym, Elie castide his mentil on hym.

20 Which ran anoon after Elie, whanne the oxis weren left, and seide, Y preie thee, kysse Y my fadir and my modir, and so Y schal sue thee. And Elie seide to hym, Go thou, and turne ayen, for Y haue do to thee that that was myn.

21 'Sotheli he turnede ayen fro Elie, and took tweine oxis, and killide hem; and with the plow of oxis he sethide the fleischis, and yaf to the puple, and thei eeten; and he roos, and yede, and suede Elie, and 'mynystride to hym.

CAP 20

1 Forsothe Benadab, kyng of Sirye, gaderide al his oost, and two and thritti kyngis with hym, and horsis, and charis; and he stiede ayens Samarie, and fauyt, and bisegide it.

2 And he sente messangeris to Achab, kyng of Israel, in to the citee,

3 and seide, Benadab seith these thingis, Thi siluer and thi gold is myn, and thi wyues, and thi beste sones ben myn.

4 And the kyng of Israel answeride, Bi thi word, my lord the kyng, Y am thin, and alle my thingis 'ben thine.

5 And the messangeris turneden ayen, and seiden, Benadab, that sente vs to thee, seith these thingis, Thou schalt yyue to me thi siluer, and thi gold, and thi wyues, and thi sones.

6 Therfor to morewe, in this same our, Y schal sende my seruauntis to thee, and thei schulen seke thin hows, and the hows of thi seruauntis; and thei schulen putte in her hondis, and take awey al thing that schal plese hem.

7 Forsothe the kyng of Israel clepide alle the eldere men of the lond, and seide, Perseyue ye, and se, that he settith tresoun

to vs; for he sente to me for my wyues, and sones, and for siluer, and gold, and Y forsook not.

8 And alle the gretter men in birthe, and al the puple seiden to hym, Here thou not, nether assente thou to hym.

9 And he answeride to the messangeris of Benadab, Seie ye to my lord the kyng, Y schal do alle thingis, for whiche thou sentist in the bigynnyng to me, thi seruaunt; forsothe Y may not do this thing.

10 And the messangeris turneden ayen, and telden alle thingis to hym. Which sente ayen, and seide, Goddis do these thingis to me, and adde these thingis, if the dust of Samarie schal suffice to the fistis of al the puple that sueth me.

11 And the kyng of Israel answeride, and seide, Seie ye to hym, A gird man, 'that is, he that goith to batel, haue not glorie euenli as a man vngird.

12 Forsothe it was doon, whanne Benadab hadde herd this word, he drank, and the kyngis, in schadewyng places; and he seide to hise seruauntis, Cumpasse ye the citee.

13 And thei cumpassiden it. And lo! o prophete neiyede to Acab, kyng of Israel, and seide to hym, The Lord God seith these thingis, Certis thou hast seyn al this multitude ful greet; lo! Y schal bitake it in to thin hond to dai, that thou wite that Y am the Lord.

14 And Achab seide, Bi whom? And he seide to Achab, The Lord seith these thingis, Bi the squyeris of the princes of prouynces. And Achab seide, Who schal bigynne to fiyte? And the prophete seide, Thou.

15 Therfor he noumbryde the children of the princes of prouynces, and he foond the noumbre of twei hundrid and two and thretti; and aftir hem he noumbride the puple, alle the sones of Israel, seuene thousynde.

16 And thei yeden out in myddai. Forsothe Benadab drank, and was drunkun in his schadewyng place, and two and thretti kyngis with hym, that camen to the help of hym.

17 Sotheli the children of princes of prouynces yeden out in the firste frount. Therfor Benadab sente men, whiche telden to hym, and seide, Men yeden out of Samarie.

18 And he seide, Whether thei comen for pees, take ye hem quyke; whether to fiyte, take ye hem quyke.

19 Therfor the children of prynces of prouynces yeden out,

20 and the residue oost suede; and ech smoot the man that cam ayens hym. And men of Sirie fledden, and Israel pursuede hem; also Benadab, kyng of Sirie, fledde on an hors with his kniytis.

21 Also the king of Israel yede out, and smoot horsis and charis, and he smoot Sirie with a ful greet veniaunce.

22 Forsothe a prophete neiyede to the kyng of Israel, and seide, Go thou, and be coumfortid, and wyte, and se, what thou schalt do; for the kyng of Sirie schal stie ayens thee in the yeer suynge.

23 Sotheli the seruauntis of the kyng of Sirie seiden to hym, The Goddis of hillis ben the Goddis of the sones of Israel, therfor thei ouercamen vs; but it is betere that we fiyte ayens hem in feeldi placis, and we schulen geet hem.

24 Therfor do thou this word; remoue thou alle kyngis fro thin oost, and sette thou princis for hem;

25 and restore thou the noumbre of knyytis, that felden of thine, and horsis bi the formere horsis, and restore thou charis, bi the charis whiche thou haddist bifore; and we schulen fiyte ayens hem in feeldy places, and thou schalt se, that we schulen gete hem. He bileuyde to the counsel of hem, and dide so.

26 Therfor after that the yeer hadde passid, Benadab noumbride men of Sirie, and he stiede in to Affech, to fiyte ayens Israel.

27 Forsothe the sones of Israel weren noumbrid; and whanne meetis weren takun, thei yeden forth euene ayens, and thei, as twey litle flockis of geet, settiden tentis ayens men of Sirie. Forsothe men of Sirie filliden the erthe.

28 And o prophete of God neiyede, and seide to the kyng of Israel, The Lord God seith these thingis, For men of Sirie seiden, God of hillis is the Lord of hem, and he is not God of valeis, Y schal yyue al this greet multitude in thin hond, and ye schulen wite that Y am the Lord.

29 In seuene daies these and thei dressiden scheltruns euene ayens; forsothe in the seuenthe dai the batel was joyned togidere, and the sones of Israel smytiden of men of Syrie an hundrid thousynde of foot men in o dai.

30 Forsothe thei that leften fledden in to the citee of Affech, and the wal felde doun on seuene and twenti thousynde of men that leften. Forsothe Benadab fledde, and entride in to the citee, in to a closet that was with ynne a closet;

31 and hise seruauntis seiden to him, We herden that the kyngis of the hows of Israel ben merciful, therfor putte we sackis in oure leendis, and cordis in oure heedis, and go we out to the kyng of Israel; in hap he schal saue oure lyues.

32 Thei girdiden her leendis with sackis, and puttiden coordis in her heedis, and thei camen to the kyng of Israel, and seiden to hym, Thi seruaunt Benadab seith, Y preye thee, lete 'my soule lyue. And he seide, If Benadab lyueth yit, he is my brother.

33 Which thing the men of Sirie token for a graciouse word, and rauyschiden hastily the word of his mouth, and seiden, Thi brother Benadab lyueth. And Achab seide to hem, Go ye, and brynge ye hym to me. Therfor Benadab yede out to hym, and he reiside Benadab in to his chare.

34 'Which Benadab seide to hym, Y schal yelde the citees whiche my fadir took fro thi fadir, and make thou stretis to thee in Damask, as my fadir made in Samarie; and Y schal be boundun to pees, and Y schal departe fro thee. Therfor he made boond of pees, and delyuerede hym.

35 Thanne sum man of the sones of prophetis seide to his felowe, in the word of the Lord, Smyte thou me. And he nolde smyte.

36 To 'whiche felowe he seide, For thou noldist here the vois of the Lord, lo! thou schalt go fro me, and a lioun schal smyte thee. And whanne he hadde go a litil fro hym, a lioun foond hym, and slowy hym.

37 But also the prophete foond another man, and he seide to that man, Smyte thou me. Which smoot him, and woundide him.

38 Therfor the prophete yede, and mette the kyng in the weie; and he chaungide his mouth and iyen, by sprynging of dust.

39 And whanne the kyng hadde passid, he criede to the kyng, and seide, Thi seruaunt yede out to fiyte anoon, and whanne o man hadde fledde, sum man brouyte hym to me, and seide, Kepe thou this man; and if he aschapith, thi lijf schal be for his lijf, ether thou schalt paye a talent of siluere.

40 Sotheli while Y was troblid, and turnede me hidur and thidur, sodeynly he apperide not. And the kyng of Israel seide to hym, This is thi doom which thou hast demed.

41 And anoon he wipide awey the dust fro his face, and the kyng of Israel knew him, that he was of the prophetis.

42 Which seide to the kyng, The Lord seith these thingis, For thou deliueridist fro thin hond a man worthi the deeth, thi lijf schal be for his lijf, and thi puple 'schal be for his puple.

43 Therfor the kyng of Israel turnede ayen in to his hows, and dispiside to here, and cam wod in to Samarie.

CAP 21

1 Forsothe after these wordis, in that tyme, the vyner of Naboth of Jezrael, 'that was in Jezrael, was bisidis the paleis of Achab, kyng of Samarye.

2 Therfor Achab spak to Naboth, and seide, Yyue thou to me the vyner, that Y make to me a gardyn of wortis, for it is nyy, and nyy myn hows; and Y schal yyue to thee a betere vyner for it; ethir if thou gessist it more profitable to thee, Y schall yyue the prijs of siluer, as myche as it is worth.

3 To whom Naboth answeride, The Lord be merciful to me, that Y yyue not to thee the eritage of my fadris.

4 Therfor Acab cam in to his hows, hauynge indignacioun, and gnastyng on the word which Naboth of Jezrael hadde spoke to him, and seide, Y schal not yyue to thee the eritage of my fadirs. And Achab castide doun him silf in to his bed, and turnede awei his face to the wal, and ete not breed.

5 Forsothe Jezabel, his wijf, entride to hym, and seide to hym, What is this thing, wherof thi soule is maad sory? and whi etist thou not breed?

6 Which answeride to hir, Y spak to Naboth of Jezrael, and Y seide to hym, Yyue thi vyner to me for money takun, ethir if it plesith thee, Y schal yyue to thee a betere vyner for it. And he seide, Y schal not yyue to thee my vyner.

7 Therfor Jezabel, his wijf, seide to hym, Thou art of greet auctorite, and thou gouernest wel Israel; rise thou, and ete breed, and be thou 'pacient, ethir coumfortid; Y schal yyue to thee the vyner of Naboth of Jezrael.

8 Therfor sche wroot lettris in the name of Achab, and seelide tho with the ryng of hym; and sche sente to the grettere men in birthe, and to the beste men, that weren in the citee of hym, and dwelliden with Naboth.

9 Sotheli this was the sentence of the lettre; Preche ye fastyng, and make ye Naboth to sitte among the firste men of the puple;

10 and sende ye priueli twei men, the sones of Belial, ayens hym, and sey thei fals witnessyng, Naboth blesside God and the kyng; and lede ye out hym, and stoon ye him, and die he so.

11 Therfor hise citeseyns, the grettere men in birthe, and the beste men that dwelliden with hym in the citee, diden as Jezabel hadde comaundid, and as it was writun in the lettris, whiche sche hadde sent to hem.

12 Thei prechiden fastyng, and maden Naboth to sitte among the firste men of the puple;

13 and whanne twey men, sones of the deuel, weren brouyt, thei maden hem to sitte ayens hym, and thei, that is, as men of the deuel, seiden witnessyng ayens him bifor al the multitude, Naboth blesside God and the kyng; for which thing thei ledden hym with out the citee, and killiden him with stoonys.

14 And thei senten to Jezabel, and seiden, Naboth is stoonyd, and is deed.

15 Forsothe it was doon, whanne Jezabel hadde herd Naboth stonyd and deed, sche spak to Achab, Rise thou, take thou in possessioun the vyner of Naboth of Jezrael, which nolde assente to thee, and yyue it for money takun; for Naboth lyueth not, but is deed.

16 And whanne Achab hadde herd this, that is, Naboth deed, he roos, and yede doun in to the vyner of Naboth of Jezrael, to haue it in possessioun.

17 Therfor the word of the Lord was maad to Elie of Thesbi, 18 and seide, Rise thou, go doun in to the comyng of Achab, kyng of Israel, which is in Samarie; lo! he goith doun to the vyner of Naboth, that he haue it in possessioun.

19 And thou schalt speke to hym, and 'thou schalt seie, The Lord God seith these thingis, Thou hast slayn, ferthermore and thou hast take in possessioun; and aftir these thingis thou schalt adde, In this place, wherynne doggis lickiden the blood of Naboth, thei schulen licke also thi blood.

20 And Achab seyde to Elie, Whether thou hast founde me thin enemy? Which Elie seide, Y haue founde, for thou art seeld that thou schuldist do yuel in the siyt of the Lord.

21 Therfor the Lord seith these thingis, Lo! Y schal brynge yn on thee yuel, and Y schal kitte awey thin hyndrere thingis, and Y schal sle of Achab a pissere to the wal, and prisoned, and the laste in Israel;

22 and Y schal yyue thin hows as the hows of Jeroboam, sone of Naboth, and as the hows of Baasa, sone of Ahia; for thou didist to excite me to wrathfulnesse, and madist Israel to do synne.

23 But also the Lord spak of Jezabel, and seide, Doggis schulen ete Jezabel in the feeld of Jesrael;

24 if Achab schal die in the citee, doggis schulen ete hym; sotheli if he schal die in the feeld, briddis of the eyr schulen ete hym.

25 Therfor noon other was sich as Achab, that was seeld to do yuel in the siyt of the Lord; for Jezabel his wijf excitide hym; 26 and he was maad abhomynable, in so myche that he suede the ydols that Ammorreis maden, which Ammorreis the Lord wastide fro the face of the sones of Israel.

27 Therfor whanne Achab hadde herd these wordis, he torente his cloth, and hilide his fleisch with an hayre, and he fastide, and slepte in a sak, and yede with the heed cast doun.

28 The word of the Lord was maad to Elie of Thesbi, and seide, Whethir thou hast not seyn Achab maad low bifor me? Therfor for he is maad low for the cause of me, Y schal not brynge yn yuel in hise daies, but in the daies of his sone Y schal bryng yn yuel to his hows.

CAP 22

1 Therfor thre yeeris passiden with out batel bitwixe Sirie and Israel.

2 Forsothe in the thridde yeer Josephat, king of Juda, yede doun to the kyng of Israel.

3 And the kyng of Israel seide to hise seruauntis, Witen ye not, that Ramoth of Galaad is oure, and we ben necgligent to take it fro the hoond of the kyng of Sirie?

4 And he seide to Josaphat, Whether thou schalt come with me to fiyte in to Ramoth of Galaad?

5 And Josophat seide to the kyng of Israel, As Y am, so and thou; my puple and thi puple ben oon; and my knyytis and thy knyytis 'ben oon. And Josephat seide to the kyng of Israel, Y preie thee, axe thou to dai the word of the Lord.

6 Therfor the kyng of Israel gaderide prophetis aboute foure hundrid men, and he seide to hem, Owe Y to go in to Ramoth of Galaad to fiyte, ethir to reste? Whiche answeriden, Stie thou, and the Lord schal yyue it in the hond of the kyng.

7 Forsothe Josephat seide, Is not here ony profete of the Lord, that we axe bi hym?

8 And the kyng of Israel seide to Josephat, O man, Mychee, sone of Hiemla, is left, bi whom we moun axe the Lord; but Y hate hym, for he prophesieth not good to me, but yuel. To whome Josephat seide, Kyng, spek thou not so.

9 Therfor the kyng of Israel clepide summe chaumburleyn, and seide to hym, Haste thou to brynge Mychee, sone of Hiemla.

10 Forsothe the kyng of Israel, and Josephat, kyng of Juda, saten, ech in his trone, clothid with kyngis ournement, in the large hows bisidis the dore of the yate of Samarie; and alle prophetis prophecieden in the siyt of hem.

11 Also Sedechie, sone of Chanaan, made to hym silf hornes of yrun, and seide, The Lord God seith these thingis, With these thou schalt scatere Sirye, til thou do awei it.

12 And alle prophetis prophecieden in lijk maner, and seiden, Stye thou in to Ramoth of Galaad, and go thou with prosperite; and the Lord schal bitake thin enemyes in the hond of the kyng.

13 Sotheli the messanger, that yede to clepe Mychee, spak to hym, and seide, Lo! the wordis of prophetis with o mouth prechen goodis to the kyng; therfor thi word be lijk hem, and speke thou goodis.

14 To whom Mychee seide, The Lord lyueth, for what euer thing the Lord schal seie to me, Y schal speke this.

15 Therfor he cam to the kyng. And the kyng seide to hym, Mychee, owen we go in to Ramoth of Galaad to fiyte, ether ceesse? To which kyng he answeride, Stie thou, and go in prosperite; and the Lord schal bitake it 'in to the hond of the kyng.

16 Forsothe the kyng seide to hym, Eft and eft Y coniure thee, that thou speke not to me, not but that that is soth in the name of the Lord.

17 And he seide, Y siy al Israel scaterid in the hillis, as scheep not hauynge a scheepherde; and the Lord seide, These han no lord, ech man turne ayen in to his hows in pees.

18 Therfor the kyng of Israel seide to Josaphat, Whethir Y seide not to thee, that he prophecieth not good to me, but euere yuel?

19 Sotheli thilke Mychee addide, and seide, Therefore here thou the word of the Lord; Y siy the Lord sittynge on his trone, and Y siy al the oost of heuene stondynge nyy hym, on the riyt side and on the left side.

20 And the Lord seide, Who schal disseyue Achab, kyng of Israel, that he stye, and falle in Ramoth of Galaad? And oon seide siche wordis, and another in anothir maner.

21 Sotheli a spirit yede out, and stood bifor the Lord, and seide, Y schal disseyue hym. To whom the Lord spak, In what thing?

22 And he seide, Y schal go out, and Y schal be a spirit of leesyng in the mouth of alle hise prophetis. And the Lord seide, Thou schalt disseyue, and schalt haue the maystry; go thou out, and do so.

23 Now therfor, lo! the Lord yaf a spirit of leesyng in the mouth of alle prophetis that ben here; and the Lord spak yuel ayens thee.

24 Forsothe Sedechie, sone of Canaan, neiyede, and smoot Mychee on the cheke, and seide, Whether the Spirit of the Lord forsook me, and spak to thee?

25 And Mychee seide, Thou schalt se in that dai, whanne thou schalt go in to closet with ynne closet, that thou be hid.

26 And the kyng of Israel seide, Take ye Mychee, and dwelle he at Amon, prince of the citee, and at Joas, the sone of Amalech;

27 and seie ye to hem, The kyng seith these thingis, Sende ye this man in to prisoun, and susteyne ye hym with breed of tribulacioun, and with watir of angwisch, til Y turne ayen in pees.

28 And Mychee seide, If thou schalt turne ayen in pees, the Lord spak not in me. And he seide, Here ye, alle puplis.

29 Therfor the kyng of Israel stiede, and Josaphat, kyng of Juda, in to Ramoth of Galaad.

30 Therfor the kyng of Israel seide to Josephat, Take thou armeris, and entre thou in to batel, and be thou clothid in thi clothis, that is, noble signes of the kyng. Certis the kyng of Israel chaungide hise clothing, and entride in to batel.

31 Sotheli the kyng of Sirie hadde comaundid to two and thritti princes of charis, and seide, Ye schulen not fiyte ayens ony man lesse, ethir more, no but ayens the kyng of Israel oonli.

32 Therfor whanne the princes of charis hadden seyn Josephat, thei suposiden that he was king of Israel, and bi feersnesse maad thei fouyten ayens hym.

33 And Josephat criede; and the princis of charis vndurstoden, that it was not the king of Israel, and thei ceessiden fro hym.

34 Sotheli sum man bente a bowe, and dresside an arowe in to vncerteyn, and bi hap he smoot the kyng of Israel bitwixe the lunge and the stomak. And the kyng seide to his charietere, Turne thin hond, and cast me out of the oost, for Y am woundid greuousli.

35 Therfor batel was ioyned in that dai, and the kyng of Israel stood in his chare ayens men of Sirie, and he was deed at euentid. Forsothe the blood of the wounde fletide doun in to the bothome of the chare.

36 And a criere sownede in al the oost, before that the sunne yede doun, and seide, Ech man turne ayen in to his citee, and in to his lond.

37 Forsothe the kyng was deed, and was borun in to Samarie; and thei birieden the kyng of Samarie.

38 And thei waischiden his chare in the cisterne of Samarie, and doggis lickiden his blood, and thei wayschiden the reynes, bi the word of the Lord whiche he hadde spoke.

39 Sotheli the residue of wordis of Achab, and alle thingis whiche he dide, and the hows of yuer which he bildide, and of alle citees whiche he bildide, whether these ben not writun in the book of wordis of daies of the kyngis of Israel?

40 Therfor Achab slepte with hise fadris, and Ocozie, his sone, regnede for hym.

41 Forsothe Josephat, sone of Asa, bigan to regne on Juda in the fourthe yeer of Achab, kyng of Israel.

42 Josephat was of fyue and thretti yeer, whanne he bigan to regne, and he regnede fyue and twenti yeer in Jerusalem; the name of his modir was Azuba, douyter of Salai.

43 And he yede in al the weye of Asa, his fadir, and bowide not fro it; and he dide that, that was riytful in the siyt of the Lord.

44 Netheles he dide not awey hiy thingis, for yit the puple made sacrifice, and brente encense in hiy places.

45 And Josephat hadde pees with the king of Israel.

46 Sotheli the residue of wordis of Josephat, and the werkis and batels, whiche he dide, whethir these ben not writun in the book of wordis of daies of the kyngis of Juda?

47 But also he took awey fro the loond the relikis of men turned in to wymmens condiciouns, that leften in the daies of Aza, his fadir.

48 Nethir a kyng was ordeyned thanne in Edom.

49 Forsothe king Josephat made schippis in the see, that schulden seile in to Ophir for gold, and tho myyten not go, for thei weren brokun in Asiongaber.

50 Thanne Ocozie, sone of Achab, seide to Josephat, My seruauntis go with thine in schippis.

51 And Josephat nolde. And Josephat slepte with hise fadris, and was biried with hem in the citee of Dauid, his fadir; and Joram, his sone, regnede for hym.

52 Forsothe Ocozie, sone of Achab, bigan to regne on Israel, in Samarie, in the seuenetenthe yeer of Josephat, kyng of Juda; and Ocozie regnede on Israel twei yeer.

53 And he dide yuel in the siyt of the Lord, and yede in the wey of his fadir, and of his modir, and in the weie of Jeroboam, sone of Nabath, that made Israel to do synne.

54 And he seruyde Baal, and worschipide hym, and wraththide the Lord God of Israel, bi alle thingis whiche his fadir hadde do.

4 KINGS

CAP 1

1 Forsothe Moab trespasside ayens Israel, after that Achab was deed.

2 And Ocozie felde thorou the aleris of his soler, which he hadde in Samarie, and was sijk; and he sente messangeris, and seide to hem, Go ye, and councele Belzebub, god of Acharon, whether Y may lyue after this sijknesse of me.

3 Forsothe the aungel of the Lord spak to Elye of Thesbi, and seide, Rise thou, and go doun into the metynge of the messangeris of the kyng of Samarie; and thou schalt seie to hem, Whether God is not in Israel, that ye go to counsel Belzebub, god of Acharon?

4 For which thing the Lord seith these thingis, Thou schalt not go doun of the bed, on which thou stiedist.

5 And Elie yede. And the messangeris turneden ayen to Ocozie. And he seide to hem, Whi turneden ye ayen?

6 And thei answeriden to hym, A man mette vs, and seide to vs, Go ye, turne ye ayen to the kyng, that sente you; and ye schulen seie to him, The Lord seith these thingis, Whether for God was not in Israel, thou sendist, that Belzebub, god of Acharon, be counselid? Therfor thou schalt not go doun of the bed, on which thou stiedist, but thou schalt die bi deeth.

7 Which Ocozie seide to hem, Of what figure and abite is that man, that mette you, and spak to you these wordis?

8 And thei seiden, An heeri man, and gird with a girdil of skyn in the reynes. Which seide to hem, It is Elie of Thesbi.

9 And he sente to Elie a prince of fifti, and fifti men that weren vndur hym. Which prince stiede to hym, and seide to hym, sittynge in the cop of the hil, Man of God, the kyng comaundith, that thou come doun.

10 And Elie answeride, and seide to the prince of fifti men, If Y am the man of God, fier come doun fro heuene, and deuoure thee and thi fifti men. Therfor fier cam doun fro heuene, and deuouride hym, and the fifti men that weren with hym.

11 Eft he sente to Elie another prince of fifti, and fifti men with hym, which spak to Helye, Man of God, the kyng seith these thingis, Haste thou, come thou doun.

12 Elie answeride, and seide, If Y am the man of God, fier come doun fro heuene, and deuoure thee and thi fifti men. Therfor the fier of God cam doun fro heuene, and deuouride hym and hise fifti men.

13 Eft he sente the thridde prince of fifti men, and fifti men that weren with hym. And whanne this prynce hadde come,

he bowide the knees ayens Elie, and preiede hym, and seide, Man of God, nyle thou dispise my lijf, and the lyues of thi seruauntis that ben with me.

14 Lo! fier cam doun fro heuene, and deuouride tweyne, the firste princis of fifti men, and the fifti men that weren with hem; but now, Y biseche, that thou haue mercy on my lijf.

15 Forsothe the aungel of the Lord spak to Helie of Thesbi, and seide, Go thou doun with hym; drede thou not. Therfor Elie roos, and cam doun with hym to the kyng;

16 and he spak to the kyng, The Lord seith thes thingis, For thou sentist messangeris to counsele Belzebub, god of Acharon, as if no God were in Israel, of whom thow myytist axe a word; therfor thou schalt not go doun of the bed, on which thou stiedist, but thou schalt die bi deeth.

17 Therfor he was deed bi the word of the Lord, which word Elie spak; and Joram, hys brothir, regnyde for hym, in the secounde yeer of Joram, the sone of Josephat, kyng of Juda; for Ocozie hadde no sone.

18 Sotheli the residue of wordis of Ocozie, whiche he wrouyte, whether these ben not writun in the book of wordis of daies of the kyngis of Israel?

CAP 2

1 Forsothe it was don, whanne the Lord wolde reise Elie bi a whirlewynd in to heuene, Elie and Elisee yeden fro Galgalis.

2 And Elie seide to Elisee, Sitte thou here, for the Lord sente me til into Bethel. To whom Elisee seide, The Lord lyueth and thi soule lyueth, for Y schal not forsake thee. And whanne thei hadden come doun to Bethel,

3 the sones of prophetis, that weren in Bethel, yeden out to Elisee, and seiden to hym, Whether thou knowist, that the Lord schal take awey thi lord to dai fro thee? Which answeride, And I knowe; be ye stille.

4 Forsothe Elie seide to Elisee, Sitte thou here, for the Lord sente me into Jerico. And he seide, The Lord lyueth and thi soule lyueth, for Y schal not forsake thee. And whanne thei hadden come to Jerico,

5 the sones of prophetis, that weren in Jerico, neiyiden to Elisee, and seiden to hym, Whether thou knowist, that the Lord schal take awei thi lord to dai fro thee? And he seide, Y knowe; be ye stille.

6 Forsothe Elie seide to Elisee, Sitte thou here, for the Lord sente me 'til to Jordan. Which seide, The Lord lyueth and thi soule lyueth, for Y schal not forsake thee. Therfor bothe yeden togidere;

7 and fifti men of the sones of prophetis sueden, which also stoden fer euen ayens; sothely thei bothe stoden ouer Jordan.

8 And Elie took his mentil, and wlappide it, and smoot the watris; whiche weren departid 'into euer ethir part, and bothe yeden bi the drie.

9 And whanne thei hadden passid, Elie seide to Elisee, Axe thou that, that thou wolt that Y do to thee, bifor that Y be takun awey fro thee. And Elisee seide, Y biseche, that thi double spirit be 'maad in me.

10 Which Elie answeride, Thou axist an hard thing; netheles if thou schalt se me, whanne Y schal be takun awey fro thee, that that thou axidist schal be; sotheli, if thou schalt not se, it schal not be.

11 And whanne thei yeden, and spaken goynge, lo! a chare of fier and horsys of fier departiden euer either; and Elie stiede bi a whirlewynd in to heuene.

12 Forsothe Elise siy, and criede, My fadir! my fadir! the chare of Israel, and the charietere therof. And he siy no more

Elie. And he took hise clothis, and to-rente tho in to twei partis.

13 And he reiside the mentil of Elie, that felde doun to hym; and he turnede ayen, and stood ouer the ryuer of Jordan.

14 And with the mentil of Elie, that felde doun to hym, he smoot the watris, whiche weren not departid. And he seide, Where is God of Elie also now? And he smoot the watris, and tho weren departid hidur and thidur; and Elisee passide.

15 Sotheli the sones of prophetis, that weren in Jerico euene ayens, siyen, and seiden, The spirit of Elie restide on Elisee. And thei camen in to the meetyng of hym, and worschipiden hym lowli to erthe.

16 And thei seiden to hym, Lo! with thi seruauntis ben fifti stronge men, that moun go, and seke thi lord, lest perauenture the Spirit of the Lord hath take hym, and hath cast forth hym in oon of the hillis, ethir in oon of the valeys.

17 Which seide, 'Nyle ye sende. And thei constreyneden hym, til he assentide to hem, and seide, Sende ye. And thei senten fifti men; and whanne thei hadden souyt bi thre daies, thei founden not.

18 And thei turneden ayen to hym; and he dwelide in Jerico. And he seide to hem, Whether Y seide not to you, Nyle ye sende?

19 Therfor the men of the citee seiden to Elisee, Lo! the dwellyng of this cite is ful good, as thou thi silf, lord, seest; but the watris ben ful yuele, and the lond is bareyn.

20 And he seide, Brynge ye to me a newe vessel, and sende ye salt in to it. And whanne thei hadden brouyt it,

21 he yede out to the welle of watris, and sente salt in to it, and seide, The Lord seith these thingis, Y haue helid these watris, and nethir deeth, nether bareynesse, schal be more in tho.

22 Therfor the watris weren heelid til in to this dai, bi the word of Elisee, which he spak.

23 Forsothe Elisee stiede fro thennus in to Bethel; and whanne he stiede bi the weie, litle children yeden out of the citee, and scorneden hym, and seiden, Stie, thou ballard! stie, thou ballard!

24 And whanne he hadde biholde, he siy hem, and curside hem in the name of the Lord. And twey beeris yeden out of the forest, and to-rente fourti children of hem.

25 Sotheli Elisee wente fro thennus in to the hil of Carmele, and fro thennus he turnede 'ayen to Samarie.

CAP 3

1 Forsothe Joram, sone of Achab, regnede on Israel, in Samarie, in the eiytenthe yeer of Josephat, kyng of Juda. And he regnede twelue yeer,

2 and he dide yuel bifor the Lord, but not as his fader and modir;

3 for he took awei the ymagis of Baal, whiche his fadir hadde maad, netheles in the synnes of Jeroboam, sone of Nabath, that made Israel to do synne, 'he cleuyde, and yede not awei fro tho.

4 Forsothe Mesa, kyng of Moab, nurschide many beestis, and paiede to the kyng of Israel an hundrid thousynde of lambren, and an hundrid thousynde of wetheris, with her fleesis.

5 And whanne Achab was deed, he brak the boond of pees, which he hadde with the kyng of Israel.

6 Therfor kyng Joram yede out of Samarie in that dai, and noumbride al Israel.

7 And he sente to Josephat, kyng of Juda, and seide, The kyng of Moab yede awei fro me; come thou with me ayens him to

batel. Which Josephat answeride, Y schal stie; he that is myn, is thin; my puple is thi puple; and myn horsis ben thin horsis.

8 And he seide, Bi what weie schulen we stie? And he answeride, Bi the deseert of Ydumee.

9 Therfor the kyng of Israel, and the kyng of Juda, and the kyng of Edom, yeden forth, and cumpassiden bi the weie of seuene daies; and 'watir was not to the oost, and to the beestis, that sueden hem.

10 And the kyng of Israel seide, Alas! alas! alas! the Lord hath gaderide vs thre kyngis to bitake vs in the hond of Moab.

11 And Josephat seide, Whether ony prophete of the Lord is here, that we biseche the Lord bi hym? And oon of the seruauntis of the kyng of Israel answeride, Elisee, the sone of Saphat, is here, that schedde watir on the hondis of Elie.

12 And Josephat seide, Is the word of the Lord at hym? Whiche seiden, 'It is. And the kyng of Israel, and Josephat, kyng of Juda, and the kyng of Edom, yeden doun to hym.

13 Forsothe Elise seide to the kyng of Israel, What is to me and to thee? Go thou to the prophetis of thi fadir and of thi modir. And the kyng of Israel seide to hym, Whi hath the Lord gaderid these thre kyngis, to bitake hem into the hondis of Moab?

14 And Elisee seide to hym, The Lord of oostis lyueth, in whos siyt Y stonde, if Y were not aschamed of the cheer of Josephat, king of Juda, treuli Y hadde not perseyued, nethir Y hadde biholde thee.

15 Now forsothe brynge ye to me a sautrere. And whanne the sautrere song, the hond of the Lord was maad on hym, and he seide, The Lord seith these thingis,

16 Make ye the wombe, ether depthe, of this stronde dichis and dichis.

17 For the Lord seith these thingis, Ye schulen not se wynd, nethir reyn, and this depthe schal be fillid with watris, and ye schulen drynke, and youre meynees, and youre beestis.

18 And this is litil in the siyt of the Lord. Ferthermore also he schal bitake Moab in to youre hondis;

19 and ye schulen smyte ech strengthid citee, and ech chosun citee, and ye schulen kitte doun ech tre berynge fruyt, and ye schulen stoppe alle the wellis of watris, and ye schulen hile with stonys ech noble feeld.

20 Therfor it was doon eerli, whanne sacrifice is wont to be offrid, and, lo! watris camen bi the weie of Edom, and the lond was fillid with watris.

21 Sotheli alle men of Moab herden, that kyngis hadden stied to fiyte ayens hem; 'and men of Moab clepiden togidere alle men, that weren gird with girdil aboue, and thei stoden in the termes.

22 And men of Moab risiden ful eerli, and whanne the sunne was risun thanne euen ayens the watris, thei sien the watris reed as blood euene ayens.

23 And thei seiden, It is the blood of swerd, 'that is, sched out bi swerd; kyngis fouyten ayens hem silf, and thei ben slayn togider; now go thou, Moab, to the prey.

24 And thei yeden in to the castels of Israel; forsothe Israel roos, and smoot Moab, and thei fledden bifor men of Israel. Therfor thei that hadden ouercome, camen, and smytiden Moab, and destrieden cytees;

25 and alle men sendynge stoonys filliden ech beste feeld, and stoppiden alle the wellis of watris, and kittiden doun alle trees berynge fruyt, so that oneli 'wallis maad of erthe weren left; and the citee was cumpassid of men settynge engynes, and was smytun bi greet part.

26 And whanne the kyng of Moab hadde seyn this, that is, that the enemyes hadden the maistrie, he took with hym seuene hundrid men drawynge swerdis, that thei shulden breke in to the kyng of Edom; and thei myyten not.

27 And he took his firste gendrid sone, that schulde regne for hym, and offride brent sacrifice on the wal; and greet indignacioun was maad in Israel; and anoon thei yeden awei fro hym, and turneden ayen in to her lond.

CAP 4

1 Forsothe sum womman of the wyues of prophetys criede to Elisee, and seide, Thi seruaunt, myn hosebonde, is deed, and thou knowist that thi seruaunt dredde God; and lo! the creaunser, 'that is, he to whom the dette is owid, cometh to take my two sones to serue hym.

2 To whom Elisee seide, What wolt thou that Y do to thee? seie thou to me, what hast thou in thin hows? And she answeride, Y thin handmayde haue not ony thing in myn hows, no but a litil of oile, bi which Y schal be anoyntid.

3 To whom he seide, Go thou, and axe bi borewyng of alle thi neiyboris voide vessels not fewe.

4 And entre, and close thi dore, whanne thou art with ynne, thou and thi sones; and putte ye therof in to alle these vessels; and whanne tho schulen be ful, thou schalt take awei.

5 Therfor the womman yede, and closide the dore on hir silf and on hir sones, thei brouyten vessels, and sche 'heldide in.

6 And whanne the vessels weren fulle, sche seide to hir sone, Brynge thou yit a vessel to me. And he answeride, Y haue not. And the oyle stood.

7 Forsothe sche cam, and schewide to the man of God; and he seide, Go thou, sil thou the oile, and yelde to thi creauncer; forsothe thou and thi children lyue of the residue.

8 Forsothe sum day was maad, and Elisee passide bi a citee, Sunam; sotheli a greet womman was there, which helde hym, that he schulde ete breed. And whanne he passide ofte therbi, 'he turnede to hir, that he schulde ete breed.

9 'Which womman seide to hir hosebonde, Y perseyue that this is an hooli man of God, that passith ofte bi vs;

10 therfor make we a litil soler to hym, and putte we therynne a litil bed to hym, and a boord, and a chaier, and a candilstike; that whanne he cometh to vs, he dwelle there.

11 Therfor sum dai was maad, and he cam, and turnede in to the soler, and restide there.

12 And he seide to Giezi, his child, Clepe thou this Sunamyte. And whanne he hadde clepid hir, and sche hadde stonde

13 bifor hym, he seide to his child, Speke thou to hir, Lo! thou hast mynystride to vs bisili in alle thingis; what wolt thou that Y do to thee? Whether thou hast a cause, and wolt that Y speke to the kyng, ether to the prince of the chyualrye? And sche answeride, I dwelle in the myddis of my puple.

14 And he seide, What therfor wole sche that Y do to hir? Giezi seide to hym, Axe thou not, for she hath no sone, and hir hosebonde is eeld.

15 Therfor Elisee comaundide, that he schulde clepe hir. And whanne sche was clepid, and stood bifor the dore,

16 he seide to hir, In this tyme and in this same our, if lijf schal be felow, thou schalt haue a sone in the wombe. And sche answeride, Nyle thou, my lord, the man of God, Y biseche, nyle thou lye to thin hondmaide.

17 And the womman conseyuede, and childide a sone in the tyme, and in the same our, in which Elisee hadde seid.

18 Sotheli the child encreeside; and whanne sum day was, and the child was goon out, and yede to his fadir,

19 and to the repers, he seide to his fadir, Myn heed akith, myn heed akith. And he seide to a child, Take, and lede hym to his modir.

20 And whanne he hadde take, and hadde brouyt hym to his modir, sche settide hym on hir knees 'til to myddai, and he was deed.

21 Sotheli she stiede, and leide hym on the litil bed of the man of God, and closide the dore.

22 And sche yede out, and clepide hir hosebonde, and seide, Y biseche, sende thou with me oon of the children, and an asse, and Y schal renne out 'til to the man of God, and Y schal turne ayen.

23 And he seide to hir, For what cause goist thou to hym? to dai ben not calendis, nether sabat. And she answeride, Y schal go.

24 And sche sadlide the asse, and comaundide to the child, Dryue thou, and haaste; make thou not tariyng to me in goyng, and do thou this thing which Y comaunde to thee.

25 Therfor sche yede forth, and cam to the man of God, in to the hil of Carmele. And whanne the man of God hadde seyn hir euene ayen, he seide to Giezi, his child, Lo! thilke Sunamyte; go thou therfor in to the metyng of hir,

26 and seie thou to hir, Whether it is doon riytfuli aboute thee, and aboute thin hosebonde, and aboute thi sone? And sche answeride, Riytfuli.

27 And whanne sche hadde come to the man of God, in to the hil, sche took his feet; and Giezi neiyede, that he schulde remoue hir. And the man of God seide, Suffre thou hir; for hir soule is in bitternesse, and the Lord helde priuy fro me, and schewide not to me.

28 And sche seide to hym, Whether I axide my sone of my lord? Whether Y seide not to thee, Scorne thou not me?

29 And he seide to Giezi, Girde thi leendis, and take my staf in thin hond, and go; if a man metith thee, grete thou not hym; and if ony man gretith thee, answere thou not hym; and putte thou my staf on the face of the child.

30 Forsothe the 'modir of the child seide, The Lord lyueth and thi soule lyueth, Y schal not leeue, 'ether forsake, thee. Therfor he roos, and suede hir.

31 Sotheli Giezi yede bifor hem, and puttide the staaf on the face of the child; and 'vois was not, nether wit. And Giezi turnede ayen to the meetyng of hym; and telde to him, and seyde, The child 'roos not.

32 Therfor Elisee entride in to the hows, and, lo! the deed child lai in his bed.

33 And he entride, and closide the dore on hym silf, and on the child; and preiede to the Lord.

34 And he stiede, and lay on the child; and he puttide his mouth on the mouth of the child, and hise iyen on the iyen of the child, and hise hondis on the hondis of the child. And he bouwide hym silf on the child; and the fleisch of the child was maad hoot.

35 And he turnede ayen, and walkide in the hows onys hidur and thidur; and Elisee stiede, and lai on the child, and the child yoxide seuene sithis, and openyde the iyen.

36 And he clepide Giezi, and seide to hym, Clepe thou this Sunamyte. And sche was clepid, and entride to hym. And he seide, Take thi sone.

37 She cam, and felde doun to his feet, and worschipide on erthe; and sche took hir sone, and yede out.

38 And Elisee turnede ayen in to Galgala. Forsothe hungur was in the lond, and the sones of prophetis dwelliden bifor

hym. And Elisee seide to oon of his children, Set thou a greet pot, and sethe thou potage to the sones of prophetis.

39 And oon yede out in to the feeld to gadere eerbis of the feeld; and he foond as a wilde vyne, and he gaderide therof gourdis of the feeld. And he fillide his mentil, and he turnede ayen, and schredde in to the pot of potage; for he wiste not what it was.

40 Therfor thei helden yn to felowis to ete; and whanne thei hadden taastid of the sething, thei crieden out, and seiden, Deth in the pot! deeth in the pot! thou man of God. And thei miyten not ete. And he seide, Brynge ye meele.

41 And whanne thei hadden brouyt, he puttide in to the pot, and seide, Helde ye to the cumpany, that thei ete; and ony thing of bitternesse was nomore in the pot.

42 Forsothe sum man cam fro the pleyn of Salisa, and bar to the man of God looues of the firste fruytis, ten looues of barli, and newe wheete, in his scrippe. And the man of God seide, Yyue thou to the puple, that it ete.

43 And his mynystre answeride to hym, 'Hou myche is this, that Y sette bifor an hundrid men? Eft Elisee seide, Yyue thou to the puple, that it ete; for the Lord seith these thingis, Thei schulen ete, and it shal leeue.

44 Therfor he puttide bifor hem, whiche eeten; and it lefte, bi the word of the Lord.

CAP 5

1 Naaman, prince of the chyualrye of the kyng of Syrie, was a greet man, and worschipid anentis his lord; for bi hym the Lord yaf helthe to Sirie; sotheli he was a strong man and riche, but leprouse.

2 Forsothe theues yede out of Sirie, and ledden prisonere fro the lond of Israel a litil damysele, that was in the seruyce of the wijf of Naaman.

3 'Which damysele seide to hir ladi, 'Y wolde, that my lord hadde be at the prophete which is in Samarie; sotheli the prophete schulde haue curid hym of the lepre which he hath.

4 Therfor Naaman entride to his lord, and telde to hym, and seide, A damysel of the lond of Israel spak so and so.

5 Therfor the kyng of Syrie seide to hym, Go thou, and Y schal sende lettris to the kyng of Israel. And whanne he hadde go forth, and hadde take with hym ten talentis of siluer, and sixe thousynde goldun platis, 'ether floreyns, and ten chaung-yngis of clothis,

6 he brouyte lettris to the kyng of Israel bi these wordis; Whanne thou hast take this pistle, wite thou, that Y haue sent to thee Naaman, my seruaunt, that thou cure hym of his lepre.

7 And whanne the kyng of Israel hadde red the lettris, he to-rente his clothis, and seide, Whether Y am God, that may sle and quykene, for this kyng sente to me, that Y cure a man of his lepre? Perseyue ye, and se, that he sekith occasiouns ayens me.

8 And whanne Elisee, the man of God, hadde herd this, that is, that the kyng of Israel hadde to-rente hise clothis, he sente to the kyng, and seide, Whi to-rentist thou thi clothis? come he to me, and wite he, that a prophete is in Israel.

9 Therfor Naaman cam with horsis and charis, and stood at the dore of the hows of Elisee.

10 And Elisee sente to hym a messanger, and seide, Go thou, and be thou waischun seuensithis in Jordan; and thi fleisch shal resseyue helthe, and thou schalt be clensid.

11 Naaman was wrooth, and yede awei, and seide, Y gesside, that he schulde go out to me, and that he schulde stonde, and

clepe the name of 'the Lord his God, and that he schulde touche with his hond the place of lepre, and schulde cure me.

12 Whether Abana and Pharphar, floodis of Damask, ben not betere than alle the watris of Israel, that Y be waischun in tho, and be clensid?

13 Therfor whanne he hadde turned hym silf, and yede awei, hauynge indignacioun, hise seruauntis neiyiden to hym, and spaken to hym, Fadir, thouy the prophete hadde seid to thee a greet thing, certis thou owist to do; hou myche more for now he seide to thee, Be thou waischun, and thou schalt be clensid.

14 He yede doun, and waischide hym seuensithis in Jordan, bi the word of the man of God; and his fleisch was restored as the fleisch of a litil child, and he was clensid.

15 And he turnede ayen with al his felouschipe to the man of God, and cam, and stood bifor hym; and seide, Verili Y knowe, that noon other God is in al erthe, no but oneli God of Israel; therfor, Y biseche, that thou take blessyng of thi seruaunt.

16 And he answeride, The Lord lyueth bifor whom Y stonde, for Y schal not take. And whanne he made 'strengthe, that is, greet preier, Elisee assentide not outirli.

17 Therfor Naaman seide, As thou wolt; but, I biseche, graunte thou to me, thi seruaunt, that Y take of 'the lond the birthun of twei burdones; for thi seruaunt schal no more make brent sacrifice, ether slayn sacrifice, to alien goddis, no but to the Lord.

18 Forsothe this thing is oneli, of which thou schalt preie the Lord for thi seruaunt, whanne my lord shal entre into the temple of Remmon, that he worschipe, and while he 'schal lene on myn hond, if Y worschipe in the temple of Remmon, while he worschipith in the same place, that the Lord foryyue to thi seruaunt for this thing.

19 Which Elisee seide to hym, Go thou in pees. 'Therfor he yede fro Elisee in a chosun tyme of the lond.

20 And Giezi, the child of the man of God, seide, My lord sparide this Naaman of Syrie, that he took not of hym that, that he brouyte; the Lord lyueth, for Y schal renne aftir hym, and Y schal take of hym sum thing.

21 And Giezi suede aftir the bak of Naaman; and whanne Naaman hadde seyn Giezi rennynge to hym, he skippide doun of the chare in to the metyng of Giezi; and seide, Whether alle thingis ben riytfuli?

22 And he seide, Riytfuli; my lord sente me to thee, and seide, Twey yonge men of the hille of Effraym, of the sones of prophetis, camen now to me; yyue thou to hem a talent of siluer, and double chaungyng clothis.

23 And Naaman seide, It is betere that thou take twei talentis. And Naaman constreynede hym; and Naaman boond twei talentis of siluer in twei sackis, and double clothis, and puttide on his twey children, 'that is, seruauntis, whiche also baren bifor Giezi.

24 And whanne he hadde come thanne in the euentid, he took fro the hond of hem, and leide vp in the hows; and he delyuerede the men, and thei yeden.

25 Forsothe Giezi entride, and stood bifor his lord. And Elise seide, Giezi, fro whennus comest thou? Which answeride, Thi seruaunt yede not to ony place.

26 And Elise seide, Whether myn herte was not in present, whanne the man turnede ayen fro his chare in to the metyng of thee? Now therfor thou hast take siluer, and thou hast take clothis, that thou bie places of olyues, and vyneris, and scheep, and oxis, and seruauntis, and handmaydis;

27 but also the lepre of Naaman schal cleue to thee, and to thi seed withouten ende. And Giezi yede leprouse as snow, 'fro hym.

CAP 6

1 Forsothe the sones of prophetis seiden to Elisee, Lo! the place in which we dwellen bifor thee, is streiyt to vs;

2 go we 'til to Jordan, and ech man take of the wode 'a mater for hym silf, that we bild to vs here a place to dwelle.

3 Which Elisee seide, Go ye. And oon of hem seide, Therfor 'and thou come with thi seruauntis. He answeride, Y schal come. And he yede with hem.

4 And whanne thei 'hadden come to Jordan, thei hewiden trees.

5 Sotheli it bifelde, that whanne 'o man hadde kit doun mater, the yrun of the axe felde in to the watir; and he criede, and seide, Alas! alas! alas! my lord, and Y hadde take this same thing bi borewing.

6 Sotheli the man of God seide, Where felde it? And he schewide to hym the place. Therfor he kittide doun a tree, and sente thidur; and the yrun fletide.

7 And he seide, Take thou. Which helde forth the hond, and took it.

8 Forsothe the kyng of Syrie fauyte ayens Israel; and he took counseil with hise seruauntis, and seide, Sette we buschementis in this place and that.

9 Therfor the man of God sente to the kyng of Israel, and seide, Be war, lest thou passe to that place, for men of Sirie ben there in buschementis.

10 Therfor the kyng of Israel sente to the place, which the man of God hadde seid to him, and bifor ocupiede it, and kepte hym silf there not onys, nether twies.

11 And the herte of the kyng of Sirie was disturblid for this thing; and whanne hise seruauntis weren clepide togidere, he seide, Whi schewen ye not to me, who is my tretour anentis the kyng of Israel?

12 And oon of hise seruauntis seide, Nay, my lord the kyng, but Elisee, the prophete, which is in Israel, schewith to the kyng of Israel alle thingis, what euer thingis thou spekist in thi closet.

13 And the kyng seide to hem, 'Go ye, and se, where he is, that Y sende, and take hym. And thei telden to him, and seiden, Lo! he dwellith in Dothaym.

14 And the kyng sente thidur horsis, and charis, and the strengthe of the oost; whiche, whanne thei hadden come bi nyyt, cumpassiden the citee.

15 Sotheli the mynystre of the man of God roos eerli, and yede out, and he siy an oost in the cumpas of the citee, and horsis, and charis. And he telde to the man of God, and seide, Alas! alas! alas! my lord, what schulen we do?

16 And he answeride, Nile thou drede; for mo ben with vs than with hem.

17 And whanne Elisee hadde preied, he seide, Lord, opene thou the iyen of this child, that he se. And the Lord openyde the iyen of the child, and he siy. And, lo! the hil ful of horsis, and of charis of fier, in the cumpas of Elisee.

18 Sotheli the enemyes camen doun to hym; forsothe Elisee preiede to the Lord, and seide, Y biseche, smyte thou this folc with blyndenesse. And the Lord smoot hem, that thei sien not, bi the word of Elisee.

19 Forsothe Elisee seide to hem, This is not the weie, nether this is the citee; sue ye me, and Y schal schewe to you the man, whom ye seken. And he ledde hem into Samarie.

20 And whanne thei hadden entrid into Samarie, Elisee seide, Lord, opene thou the iyen of these men, that thei see. And the Lord openyde her iyen, and thei siyen, that thei weren in the myddis of Samarie.

21 And the kyng of Israel, whanne he hadde seyn hem, seide to Elisee, My fadir, whether Y schal smyte hem?

22 And he seide, Thou schalt not smyte hem, for thou hast not take hem bi thi swerd and bouwe, that thou smyte hem; but sette thou breed and watir bifor hem, that thei ete and drynke, and go to her lord.

23 And 'greet makyng redi of metis was set forth to hem; and thei eten, and drunken. And the kyng lefte hem, and thei yeden to her lord; and theues of Sirie camen no more in to the lond of Israel.

24 Forsothe it was don after these thingis, Benadab, king of Sirie, gaderide alle his oost, and stiede, and bisegide Samarie.

25 And greet hungur was maad in Samarie; and so long it was bisegid, til the heed of an asse were seeld for fourescore platis of siluer, and the fourthe part of a mesure clepid cabus of the crawe of culueris was seeld for fyue platis of siluer.

26 And whanne the kyng of Israel passide bi the wal, sum womman criede to hym, and seide, My lord the kyng, saue thou me.

27 Which seide, Nai, the Lord saue thee; wherof may Y saue thee? of cornfloor, ethir of pressour? And the kyng seide to hir, What wolt thou to thee?

28 And sche answeride, This womman seide to me, Yyue thi sone, that we ete hym to dai, and we schulen ete my sone to morewe.

29 Therfor we setheden my sone, and eten him. And Y seide to hir in the tother day, Yyue thi sone, that we ete hym; and she hidde hir sone.

30 And whanne the kyng hadde herd this, he to-rente hise clothis, and passide bi the wal; and al the puple siy the heire, 'with which the kyng was clothid at the fleisch with ynne.

31 And the kyng seide, God do to me these thingis, and adde these thingis, if the heed of Elise, sone of Saphat, schal stonde on hym to dai.

32 Sotheli Elisee sat in his hows, and elde men saten with hym; 'therfor he biforsente a man, and bifor that thilke mes- sanger cam, Elisee seide to the elde men, Whether ye witen, that the sone of manquellere sente hidur, that myn heed be gird of? Therfor se ye, whanne the messanger cometh, close ye the dore, and 'suffre ye not hym to entre; for, lo! the sown of the feet of his lord is bihynde hym.

33 And yit 'while he spak to hem, the messanger that cam to hym apperide; and the kyng seide, Lo! so greet yuel is of the Lord; sotheli what more schal Y abide of the Lord?

CAP 7

1 Forsothe Elisee seide, Here ye the word of the Lord; the Lord seith these thingis, In this tyme to morewe a buschel of flour schal be for a stater, and twei buschels of barli for a stater, in the yate of Samarie.

2 And oon of the duykis, on whos hond the kyng lenyde, answeride to the man of God, and seide, Thouy 'also the Lord make the goteris of heuene to be openyd, whether that, that thou spekist, mai be? Which Elisee seide, Thou schalt se with thin iyen, and thou schalt not ete therof.

3 Therfor foure leprouse men weren bisidis the entryng of the yate, whiche seiden togidere, What wolen we be here, til we dien?

4 Whether we wolen entre in to the citee, we schulen die for hungur; whether we dwellen here, we schulen die. Therfor come ye, and fle we ouer to the castels of Sirie; if thei schulen spare vs, we schulen lyue; sotheli if thei wolen sle, netheles we schulen die.

5 Therfor thei risiden in the euentide to come to the castels of Sirie; and whanne thei hadden come to the bigynnyng of the castels of Sirie, thei founden not ony man there.

6 Forsothe the Lord hadde maad a sown of charis, and of horsis, and of ful myche oost to be herd in the castels of Sirie; and thei seiden togidere, Lo! the kyng of Israel hath hirid bi meede ayens vs the kyngis of Etheis and of Egipcians; and thei camen on vs.

7 Therfor thei risiden, and fledden in derknessis, and leften her tentis, and horsis, and mulis, and assis, in the castels; and thei fledden, couetynge to saue her lyues oonli.

8 Therfor whanne thilke leprouse men hadden come to the bigynnyng of the castels, thei entriden into o tabernacle, and eetun, and drunken; and thei token fro thennus siluer, and gold, and clothis; and yeden, and hidden; and eft thei turneden ayen to anothir tabernacle, and in lijk maner thei token awei fro thennus, and hidden.

9 And thei seiden togidere, We doen not riytfuli, for this is a dai of good message; if we holden stille, and nylen telle til the morewtid, we schulen be repreued of trespassyng; come ye, go we, and telle in the 'halle of the kyng.

10 And whanne thei hadden come to the yate of the citee, thei telden to hem, and seiden, We yeden to the castels of Sirie, and we founden not ony man there, no but horsis and assis tied, and tentis fastned.

11 Therfor the porteris yeden, and telden in the paleis of the kyng with ynne.

12 Which king roos bi niyt, and seide to hise seruauntis, Y seie to you, what the men of Sirie han do to vs; thei witen, that we trauelen with hungur, therfor thei yeden out of the castels, and ben hid in the feeldis, and seien, Whanne thei schulen go out of the citee, we schulen take hem quyk, and thanne we schulen mowe entre in to the citee.

13 Forsothe oon of his seruauntis answeride, Take we fyue horsis, that leften in the citee; for tho ben oonli in al the mul- titude of Israel, for othere horsis ben wastid; and we sendynge moun aspie.

14 Therfor thei brouyten forth twei horsis; and the kyng sente in to the castels of men of Sirie, and seide, Go ye, and se.

15 Whiche yeden after hem 'til to Jordan; lo! forsothe al the weie was ful of clothis, and of vessels, whiche the men of Sirie castiden forth, whanne thei weren disturblid. And the messangeris turneden ayen, and schewiden to the kyng.

16 And the puple yede out, and rauyschide the castels of Sirie; and a buyschel of flour was maad for o stater, and twei buyschels of barli for o stater, bi the word of the Lord.

17 Forsothe the kyng ordeynede at the yate that duyk, in whos hond the kyng lenyde; whom the cumpeny to-trad with her feet, and he was deed, bi the word, which the man of God spak, whanne the kyng cam doun to hym.

18 And it was doon bi the word of the man of God, which he seide to the kyng, whanne he seide, Twei buyschels of barli shulen be for a statir, and a buyschel of wheete flour for a stater, in this same tyme to morewe in the yate of Samarie;

19 whanne thilke duyk answeride to the man of God, and seide, Yhe, thouy the Lord schal make the goteris in heuene to be openyd, whether this that thou spekist may be? and the

man of God seide, Thou schalt se with thin iyen, and thou schalt not ete therof.

20 Therfore it bifelde to hym, as it was biforseid; and the puple to-trad hym with feet in the yate, and he was deed.

CAP 8

1 Forsothe Elisee spak to the womman, whose sone he made to lyue, and he seide, Rise thou, and go, bothe thou and thin hows, and 'go in pilgrimage, where euer thou schalt fynde; for the Lord schal clepe hungur, and it schal come on the lond bi seuene yeer.

2 And sche roos, and dide bi the word of the man of God; and sche yede with hir hows, and was in pilgrimage in the lond of Philistym many daies.

3 And whanne seuene yeer weren endid, the womman turnede ayen fro the lond of Philisteis; and sche yede out, to axe the kyng for her hows, and hir feeldis.

4 Sotheli the kyng spak with Giezi, child of the man of God, and seide, Telle thou to me alle the grete dedis whiche Elisee dide.

5 And whanne he telde to the kyng, hou Elisee hadde reiside a deed man, the womman apperide, whos sone he hadde maad to lyue, and sche criede to the kyng for hir hows, and for hir feeldis. And Giesi seide, My lord the king, this is the wom-man, and this is hir sone, whom Elisee reiside.

6 And the kyng axide the womman, and sche tolde to hym, that the thingis weren sothe. And the kyng yaf to hir o chaum-burleyn, and seide, Restore thou to hir alle thingis that ben hern, and alle fruytis of the feeldis, fro the dai in which she left the lond 'til to present tyme.

7 Also Elisee cam to Damask, and Benadab, kyng of Sirie, was sijk; and thei telden to hym, and seiden, The man of God cam hidur.

8 And the kyng seide to Azael, Take with thee yiftis, and go thou in to the meetyng of the man of God, and 'counsele thou bi hym the Lord, and seie thou, Whether Y may ascape fro this 'sikenesse of me?

9 Therfor Azael yede in to the meetyng of hym, and hadde with hym silf yiftis, and alle the goodis of Damask, the burthuns of fourti camels. And whanne he hadde stonde bifor Elisee, he seide, Thi sone, Benadab, kyng of Sirie, sente me to thee, and seide, Whether Y may be helid of this 'sikenesse of me?

10 And Elisee seide, Go thou, and seye to hym, Thou schalt be heelid; forsothe the Lord schewide to me that he schal die bi deth.

11 And he stood with hym, and he was disturblid, 'til to the castyng doun of cheer; and the man of God wepte.

12 'To whom Azael seide, Whi wepith my lord? And he answeride, For Y woot what yuelis thou schalt do to the sones of Israel; thou schalt brenne bi fier the strengthid citees of hem, and thou schalt sle bi swerd the yonge men of hem, and thou schalt hurtle doun the litle children of hem, and thou schalt departe the women with childe.

13 And Azael seide, What sotheli am Y, thi seruaunt, a dogge, that Y do this grete thing? And Elisee seide, The Lord schewide to me that thou schalt be kyng of Sirie.

14 And whanne he hadde departid fro Elisee, he cam to his lord; which seide to Azael, What seide Elisee to thee? And he answeride, Elisee seide to me, Thou schalt resseyue helthe.

15 And whanne 'the tother day hadde come, Azael took the cloth on the bed, and bischedde with watir, and spredde

abrood on the face of hym; and whanne he was deed, Azael regnede for hym.

16 In the fyuethe yeer of Joram, sone of Achab, kyng of Israel, and of Josephat, kyng of Juda, Joram, sone of Josephat, kyng of Juda, regnede.

17 He was of two and thretti yeer whanne he bigan to regne, and he regnede eiyte yeer in Jerusalem.

18 And he yede in the weies of the kyngis of Israel, as the hows of Achab hadde go; for the douyter of Achab was his wijf; and he dide that, that is yuel in the siyt of the Lord.

19 Forsothe the Lord nolde distrie Juda, for Dauid, his seru-aunt, as he 'hadde bihiyt to Dauid, that he schulde yyue to hym a lanterne, and to hise sones in alle daies.

20 In tho daies Edom, 'that is, Ydumee, yede awei, that it schulde not be vndur Juda; and made a kyng to it silf.

21 And Joram cam to Seira, and alle the charis with hym; and he roos bi nyyt, and smoot Ydumeis, that cumpassiden hym, and the princis of charis; sotheli the puple fledde in to her tab-ernaclis.

22 Therfor Edom yede awei, that it was not vndur Juda 'til to this day; thanne also Lobna yede awey in that tyme.

23 Forsothe the residues of wordis of Joram, and alle thingis whiche he dide, whether these ben not writun in the book of wordis of daies of the kingis of Juda?

24 And Joram slepte with hise fadris, and was biried with hem in the citee of Dauid; and Ocozie, his sone, regnede for hym.

25 In the tweluethe yeer of Joram, sone of Achab, kyng of Israel, Ocozie, sone of Joram, kyng of Juda, regnede.

26 Ocozie, the sone of Joram, was of two and twenti yeer whanne he bigan to regne, and he regnede o yeer in Jerusa-lem; the name of his moder was Athalia, the douyter of Amry, kyng of Israel.

27 And he yede in the waies of the hows of Achab, and dide that, that is yuel, bifor the Lord, as the hows of Achab dide; for he was hosebonde of a douyter of the hows of Achab.

28 Also he yede with Joram, sone of Achab, to fiyt ayens Azael, kyng of Sirie, in Ramoth of Galaad; and men of Sirie woundiden Joram.

29 Which turnede ayen, to be heelid in Jezrael; for men of Sirie woundiden hym in Ramoth, fiytynge ayens Azael, kyng of Sirye. Forsothe Ocozie, sone of Joram, the kyng of Juda, cam doun to se Joram, sone of Achab, in to Jezrael, that was sijk there.

CAP 9

1 Forsothe Elisee, the prophete, clepide oon of the sones of prophetis, and seide to hym, Girde thi leendis, and take this vessel of oile in thin hond, and go in to Ramoth of Galaad.

2 And whanne thou schalt come thidur, thou schalt se Hieu, sone of Josephat, sone of Namsi; and thou schalt entre, and schalt reise hym fro the myddis of hise britheren, and thou schalt lede hym in to the ynnere closet.

3 And thou schalt holde the vessel of oile, and schalt schede on his heed, and schalt seie, The Lord seith these thingis, I haue anoyntid thee in to kyng on Israel; and thou schalt opene the dore, and schalt flee, and schalt not abide there.

4 Therfor the yong wexynge man, the child of the prophete, yede in to Ramoth of Galaad, and entride thidur.

5 Lo! sotheli the princes of the oost saten; and he seide, A! prince, Y haue a word to thee. And Hieu seide, To whom of alle vs? And he seide, To thee, thou prince.

6 And he roos, and entride into the closet. And thilk child schedde oile on the heed of hym, and seide, The Lord God of Israel seith these thingis, Y haue anointid thee in to kyng on the puple of the Lord of Israel; and thou schalt smyte the hows of Achab,

7 thi lord, that Y venge the blood of my seruauntis prophetis, and the blood of alle the seruauntis of the Lord, of the hond of Jezabel.

8 And Y schal lese al the hows of Achab, and Y schal sle of the hows of Achab a pissere to the wal, and closid, and the laste in Israel.

9 And Y schal yyue the hows of Achab as the hows of Jeroboam, sone of Nabat, and as the hous of Baasa, sone of Ahia.

10 Also doggis schulen ete Jezabel in the feeld of Jezrael; and 'noon schal be that schal birie hir. And 'the child openyde the dore, and fledde.

11 Forsothe Hieu yede out to the seruauntis of his lord, whiche seiden to hym, Whether alle thingis ben riytfuli? What cam this wood man to thee? Which seide to hem, Ye knowen the man, and what he spak.

12 And thei answeriden, It is fals; but more telle thou to vs. Which seide to hem, He spak these and these thingis to me, and seide, The Lord seith these thingis, Y haue anoyntid thee kyng on Israel.

13 Therfor thei hastiden, and ech man took his mentil, and puttide vndir hise feet bi the licnesse of a trone. And thei sungen with a trumpe, and seiden, Hieu schal regne.

14 Therfor Hieu, sone of Josephat, sone of Namsi, swoor to gidere ayens Joram. Forsothe Joram hadde bisegid Ramoth of Galaad, he and al Israel, ayens Azael, kyng of Sirie.

15 And he turnede ayen to be heelid in Jezrael for woundis; for men of Sirie hadden smyte hym fiytynge ayens Azael, kyng of Sirie. And Hieu seide, If it plesith you, no man go out fleynge fro the citee, lest he go, and telle in Jezrael.

16 And he stiede, and yede forth in to Jezrael; for Joram was sijk there, and Ocozie, kyng of Juda, cam doun to visite Joram.

17 Therfor a spiere, that stood aboue a tour of Jezrael, siy the multitude of Hieu comynge, and he seide, Y se a multitude. And Joram seide, Take thou a chare, and sende in to the metyng of hem; and seie the goere, Whether alle thingis ben riytfuli?

18 Therfor he, that stiede on the chare, yede in to the meetyng of hym, and seide, The kyng seith these thingis, Whether alle thingis ben peesid? And Hieu seide to hym, What to thee and to pees? Passe thou, and sue me. And the aspiere telde, and seide, the messanger cam to hem, and he turneth not ayen.

19 Also the kyng sente the secounde chare of horsis, and he cam to hem, and seide, The kyng seith these thingis, Whether pees is? And Hieu seide, What to thee and to pees? Passe thou, and sue me.

20 Sotheli the aspiere telde, and seide, He cam 'til to hem, and he turneth not ayen; forsothe the goyng is as the goyng of Hieu, sone of Namsi; sothely he goith faste.

21 And Joram seide, Ioyn ye a chare. And thei ioyneden his chare. And Joram, kyng of Israel, yede out, and Ocozie, kyng of Juda, yede out, ech in his chare; and thei yeden out in to the meetyng of Hieu, and thei founden hym in the feeld of Naboth of Jezrael.

22 And whanne Joram hadde seyn Hieu, he seide, Hieu, 'is pees? And he answeride, What pees? Yit the fornycaciouns of Jezabel, thi modir, and many poisenyngis of hir ben in strengthe.

23 Forsothe Joram turnede his hond, and fledde, and seide to Ocozie, Tresouns! tresouns!

24 Ocozie. Forsothe Hieu bente a bouwe with the hond, and smoot Joram bitwixe the schuldris, and the arowe yede out thoruy his herte; and anoon he felde doun in his chare.

25 And Hieu seide to Badacher duyk, Take thou awei, cast forth hym in the feeld of Naboth of Jezrael; for Y haue mynde, whanne Y and thou saten in the chare, and suede Achab, the fadir of hym, that the Lord reiside on hym this birthun, and seide, If not for the blood of Naboth,

26 and for the blood of hise sones, which Y siy yistirdai, seith the Lord, Y schal yeeld to thee in this feeld, seith the Lord. Now therfor do awei him, and cast forth him in the feeld, bi the word of the Lord.

27 Forsothe Ocozie, king of Juda, siy this, and fledde bi the weie of the hows of the gardyn; and Hieu pursuede hym, and seide, Also smyte ye this man in his chare. And thei smytiden hym in the stiyng of Gaber, which is bisidis Jeblaam; and he fledde into Mageddo, and was deed there.

28 And hise seruauntis puttiden hym on his chare, and brouyten hym in to Jerusalem; and thei birieden hym in a sepulcre with hise fadris, in the citee of Dauid.

29 In the eleuenthe yeer of Joram, sone of Achab, kyng of Israel, Ocozie regnede on Juda.

30 And Hieu cam in to Jezrael. Forsothe whanne his entryng was herd, Jezabel peyntide hir iyen with oynement of wymmen, and ournede hir heed;

31 and sche bihelde bi a wyndow Hieu entrynge bi the yate, and sche seide, Whether pees may be to Zamri, that kyllide his lord?

32 And Hieu reiside his face to the wyndow, and seide, What womman is this? And tweyne ether thre chaumbirleyns bowiden hem silf to hym, and seiden to hym, This is thilke Jezabel.

33 And he seide to hem, Caste ye hir doun. And thei 'castiden doun hir; and the wal was bispreynt with blood, and the howues of horsis, that 'to tredden hir.

34 And whanne he hadde entrid to ete and drynke, he seide, Go ye, and se thilke cursid womman, and birie ye hir, for sche is a kyngis douyter.

35 And whanne thei hadden go to birie hir, thei founden not, no but the sculle, and the feet, and the endis of hondis;

36 and thei turneden ayen, and telden to hym. And Hieu seide, It is the word of the Lord, which he spak bi his seruaunt, Elie 'of Thesbi, and seide, Doggis schulen ete the fleisch of Jezabel in the feeld of Jezrael;

37 and the fleischis of Jezabel schulen be as 'a toord on the face of erthe in the feeld of Jezrael, so that men passynge forth seie, Lo! this is thilke Jezabel.

CAP 10

1 Forsothe seuenti sones in Samarie weren to Achab. Therfor Hieu wroot lettris, and sente in to Samarie to the beste men of the citee, and to the gretter men in birthe, and to alle the nurschis of Achab, and seide,

2 Anoon as ye han take these lettris, ye that han the sones of youre lord, and the charis, and horsis, and stronge citees, and armeris,

3 chese the beste, and hym that plesith to you of the sones of youre lord, and sette ye him on the trone of his fadir, and fiyte ye for the hows of youre lord.

4 And thei dredden greetli, and seiden, Lo! twei kyngis myyten not stonde bifor hym, and how schulen we mowe ayenstonde hym?

5 Therfor the souereyns of the hows, and the prefect of the citee, and the grettere men in birthe, and the nurchis senten to Hieu, and seiden, We ben thi seruauntis; what euer thingis thou comaundist, we schulen do, and we schulen not make a kyng to vs; do thou what euer thing plesith thee.

6 Forsothe he wroot ayen to hem lettris the secunde tyme, and seide, If ye ben myne, and obeien to me, take ye the heedis of the sones of youre lord, and come ye to me in this same our to morewe in to Jezrael. Sotheli the sones of the kyng, seuenti men, weren nurschid at the beste men of the citee.

7 And whanne the lettris hadden come to hem, thei token the sones of the kyng, and killiden seuenti men, and puttiden the heedis of hem in coffyns; and senten to hym in to Jezrael.

8 Forsothe a messanger cam to hym, and schewide to hym, and seide, Thei han brouyt the heedis of the sones of the king. Which answeride, Putte ye tho heedis to tweyne hepis, bisidis the entring of the yate, til the morewtid.

9 And whanne it was cleer dai, he yede out, and stood, and seide to al the puple, Ye ben iust men; if Y conspiride ayens my lord, and killide hym, who killide alle these?

10 Therfor se ye now, that noon of the wordis of the Lord felde doun in to the erthe, whiche the Lord spak on the hows of Achab; and the Lord hath do that, that he spak in the hond of his seruaunt, Elie.

11 Therfor Hieu smoot alle that weren residue of the hows of Achab in Jezrael, and alle the beste men of hym, and knowun men, and preestis, til no relikis of hym leften.

12 And he roos, and cam in to Samarie; and whanne he hadde come to the chaumbir of schepherdis in the weie,

13 he foond the britheren of Ocozie, kyng of Juda; and he seide to hem, Who ben ye? And thei answeriden, We ben the britheren of Ocozie, and we comen doun to grete the sones of the kyng and the sones of the queen.

14 Which Hieu seide, Take ye hem quyke. And whanne thei hadden take hem quyke, thei strangliden hem in the cisterne, bisidis the chaumbre, two and fourti men; and he lefte not ony of hem.

15 And whanne he hadde go fro thennus, he foond Jonadab, the sone of Rechab, in to meetyng of hym; and he blesside hym. And Hieu seide to hym, Whether thin herte is riytful with myn herte, as myn herte is with thin herte? And Jonadab seide, It is. Hieu seide, If 'it is, yyue thin hond. Which yaf his hond to hym; and he reiside hym to hym silf in to the chare.

16 And he seide to hym, Come thou with me, and se my feruent loue for the Lord.

17 And he ledde hym, put in hys chare, in to Samarie. And he killide alle men that weren residue of Achab in Samarie 'til to oon, bi the word of the Lord, which he spak bi Elie.

18 Therfor Hieu gaderide to gidere alle the puple, and seide to hem, Achab worschipide Baal a litil, but Y schal worschipe hym more.

19 Now therfor clepe ye to me alle the prophetis of Baal, and alle hise seruauntis, and alle hise preestis; 'noon be that come not, for grete sacrifice is of me to Baal; who euer schal faile, he schal not lyue. Forsothe Hieu dide this bi tresoun, that he schulde distrie alle the worschipers of Baal.

20 And he seide, Halewe ye a solempne day to Baal.

21 And he clepide, and sente in to alle the termes of Israel; and alle the seruauntis of Baal camen, 'noon was residue, and sotheli 'not oon was that cam not. And thei entriden in to the temple of Baal; and the hows of Baal was fillid, fro oon ende 'til to 'the tothir.

22 And he seide to hem that weren souereyns ouer the clothis, Bringe ye forth clothis to alle the seruauntis of Baal; and thei brouyten forth clothis to hem.

23 And Hieu entride, and Jonadab, the sone of Rechab, in to the temple of Baal. And Hieu seide to the worschiperis of Baal, Enquere ye, and se, lest perauenture ony of the seruauntis of the Lord be with you; but that the seruauntis be aloone of Baal.

24 Therfor thei entriden, to make slayn sacrifices, and brent sacrifices. Sotheli Hieu hadde maad redi to hym with outforth foure scoore men, and hadde seid to hem, Who euer schal fle of alle these, whiche Y schal brynge in to youre hondis, the lijf of hym schal be for the lijf of hym that ascapith.

25 Forsothe it was don, whanne the brent sacrifice was fillid, Hieu comaundide to hise knyytis and duykis, Entre ye, and sle hem, that noon ascape. And the knyytis and duykis smytiden 'hem bi the scharpnesse of swerd, and castiden forth. And 'thei yeden into the citee of the temple of Baal,

26 and thei brouyten forth the ymage fro the temple of Baal,

27 and brenten it, and al to braken it. Also thei destrieden the hows of Baal, and maden priuyes for it 'til in to this dai.

28 Therfor Hieu dide awei Baal fro Israel;

29 netheles he yede not awei fro the synnes of Jeroboam, sone of Nabath, that made Israel to do synne, nether he forsook the goldun caluys, that weren in Bethel and in Dan.

30 Forsothe the Lord seide to Hieu, For thou didist bisili that that was riytful, and pleside in myn yyen, and hast do ayens the hows of Achab alle thingis that weren in myn herte, thi sones 'til to the fourthe generacioun schulen sitte on the trone of Israel.

31 Forsothe Hieu kepte not, that he yede in the lawe of the Lord God of Israel in al his herte; for he yede not awei fro the synnes of Jeroboam, that made Israel to do synne.

32 In tho daies the Lord bigan to be anoyed on Israel; and Asahel smoot hem in alle the coostis of Israel,

33 fro Jordan ayens the eest coost, al the lond of Galaad, and of Gad, and of Ruben, and of Manasses, fro Aroer which is on the stronde of Arnon, and Galaad, and Baasan.

34 Forsothe the residue of wordis of Hieu, and alle thingis whiche he dide, and his strengthe, whether these ben not writun in the book of wordis of daies of the kyngis of Israel?

35 And Hieu slepte with hise fadris; and thei birieden hym in Samarie; and Joachaz, his sone, regnyde for hym.

36 Forsothe the daies, in whiche Hieu regnede on Israel in Samarie, ben eiyte and twenti yeer.

CAP 11

1 Forsothe Athalie, modir of Ocozie, siy hir sone deed, and sche roos, and killide al the seed of the kyng.

2 Sotheli Josaba, douyter of kyng Joram, the sistir of Ocozie, took Joas, sone of Ocozie, and stal him fro the myddis of the sones of the kyng, that weren slayn; and sche took the nursche of hym fro the hows of thre stagis; and sche hidde hym fro the face of Athalie, that he were not slayn.

3 And he was with hir in the hows of the Lord priueli sixe yeer. Forsothe Athalia regnede on the lond sixe yeer.

4 Forsothe in the seuenthe yeer Joiada sente, and took centuriouns, and knyytis, and brouyte to hym in to the temple of the Lord; and couenauntide with hem boond of pees, and he made hem to swere in the temple of the Lord, and schewide to hem the sone of the kyng.

5 And he comaundide to hem, and seide, This is the word, which ye owen to do;

6 the thridde part of you entre in the sabat, and kepe the wakyngis of the 'hows of the kyng; sothely the thridde part be at the yate of Seir; and the thridde part be at the yate which is bihynde the dwellyng place of the makeris of scheeldis; and ye schulen kepe the wakyngis of the hows of Messa.

7 Forsothe twei partis of you alle goynge out in the sabat, kepe ye the wakyngis of the hows of the Lord aboute the kyng.

8 And ye schulen cumpasse hym, and ye schulen haue armeris in youre hondis; forsothe if ony man entrith in to the closyng of the temple, be he slayn; and ye schulen be with the kyng goynge in and goynge out.

9 And the centuriouns diden bi alle thingis whiche Joiada, the preest, hadde comaundid to hem; and alle takynge her men that entriden to the sabat, with hem that yeden out fro the sabat, camen to Joiada, the preest.

10 Which yaf to hem speris, and armeris of kyng Dauid, that weren in the hows of the Lord.

11 And alle stoden hauynge armeris in her hond, fro the riyt side of the temple 'til to the left side of the auter and of the hows, aboute the kyng.

12 And he brouyte forth the sone of the kyng, and puttide on hym a diademe, and witnessyng; and thei maden hym kyng, and anoyntiden hym; and thei beeten with the hoond, and seiden, The kyng lyue!

13 Forsothe Athalia herde the vois of the puple rennynge, and sche entride to the cumpenyes in to the temple of the Lord,

14 and sche siy the kyng stondynge on the trone bi custom, and syngeris, and cumpenyes nyy hym, and al the puple of the lond beynge glad, and syngynge with trumpis. And sche torente hir clothis, and criede, 'Swerynge togidere! swerynge togidere! ether tresoun.

15 Forsothe Joiada comaundide to the centuriouns, that weren on the oost, and seide to hem, Lede ye hir out of the closyngis of the temple; and who euer sueth hir, be smytun with swerd. Forsothe the preest seide, Be sche not slayn in the temple of the Lord.

16 And thei puttiden hondis on hir, and hurliden hir bi the weie of the entryng of horsis bisidis the paleis; and sche was slayn there.

17 Therfor Joiada made boond of pees bitwixe the Lord and the kyng, and bitwixe the puple, that it schulde be the puple of the Lord; and bitwixe the kyng and the puple.

18 Al the puple of the lond entride in to the temple of Baal; and thei distrieden the auteris of hym, and al tobraken strongli the ymagis; and thei killiden bifore the auter Mathan, the preest of Baal. And the preest settide kepyngis in the hows of the Lord; and he took centuriouns, and the legiouns of Cerethi and Pherethi, and al the puple of the lond.

19 And thei ledden forth the kyng fro the hows of the Lord; and thei camen bi the weie of the yate of makeris of scheldis in to the paleis; and he sat on the trone of kyngis.

20 And al the puple of the lond was glad, and the citee restide. Forsothe Athalia was slayn bi swerd in the hows of the kyng.

21 And Joas was of seuen yeer, whanne he bigan to regne.

CAP 12

1 Joas regnede in the seuenthe yeer of Hieu; Joas regnede fourti yeer in Jerusalem; the name of his modir was Sebia of Bersabee.

2 And Joas dide riytfulnesse bifor the Lord in alle the daies, in whiche Joiada, the preest, tauyte hym.

3 Netheles he dide noyt awey hiy thingis; for yit the puple made sacrifice, and brente encense in hiye thingis.

4 And Joas seide to the preestis, 'Preestis bi her ordre take al that money of hooli thingis, which is brouyt of men passyng forth in to the temple of the Lord, 'which money is offrid for the prijs of soule, and 'which money thei bryngen wilfuli, and bi the fredom of her herte, in to the temple of the Lord.

5 And 'the preestis reparele the hilyngis of the hows, if thei seen ony thing nedeful in reparelyng.

6 Therfor the preestis reparaeliden not the hilyngis of the temple, 'til to the thre and twentithe yeer of kyng Joas.

7 And Joas, the kyng, clepide Joiada, the bischop, and the prestis, and seide to hem, Whi han ye not reparelid the hilyngis of the temple? Therfor nyle ye more take money bi youre ordre, but yelde it to the reparacioun of the temple.

8 And the prestis weren forbodun to take more the money of the puple, and to reparele the hilyngis of the hows.

9 And Joiada, the bischop, took a cofere of tresorie, and openyde an hole aboue, and settide it bisidis the auter, at the riytside of men entrynge in to the hows of the Lord; and preestis, that kepten the doris, senten in it al the money that was brouyt to the temple of the Lord.

10 And whanne thei sien that ful myche money was in the tresorie, the scryuen of the kyng and the bischop stieden, and schedden it out, and thei noumbriden the money that was founden in the hous of the Lord.

11 And thei yauen it bi noumbre and mesure in the hond of hem, that weren souereyns to the masouns of the hows of the Lord, whiche 'spendiden that money in 'crafti men of trees, and in these masouns, that wrouyten in the hous of the Lord,

12 and maden the hilyngis, and in these men that hewiden stoonys; and that thei schulden bie trees and stoonys, that weren hewid doun; so that the reparacioun of the hows of the Lord was fillid in alle thingis, that nediden cost to make strong the hows.

13 Netheles water pottis of the temple of the Lord weren not maad of the same money, and fleischokis, and censeris, and trumpis; ech vessel of gold and of siluer weren not maad of the money, that was brouyt in to the temple of the Lord.

14 For it was youun to hem that maden werk, that the temple of the Lord schulde be reparelid.

15 And rekenyng was not maad to these men that token monei, that thei schulden deele it to crafti men; but thei tretiden it in feith.

16 Sotheli thei brouyten not in to the temple of the Lord the money for trespas, and the money for synnes, for it was the preestis.

17 Thanne Asael, kyng of Sirie, stiede, and fauyte ayen Geth; and he took it, and dresside his face, that he schulde stie in to Jerusalem.

18 Wherfor Joas, kyng of Juda, took alle 'thingis halewid, whiche Josephat hadde halewid, and Joram, and Ocozie, fadris of hym, kyngis of Juda, and whiche thingis he hadde offrid, and al the siluer, that myyte be foundun in the tresours of the temple of the Lord, and in the paleis of the kyng.

19 And he sente to Asael, kyng of Sirie; and he yede awei fro Jerusalem. Sotheli the residue of wordis of Joas, and alle thingis whiche he dide, whether these ben not writun in the book of wordis of daies of the kyngis of Juda?

20 Forsothe hise seruauntis risiden, and sworen togidere bitwixe hem silf, and smytiden Joas in the hows Mello, and in the goyng doun of Sela.

21 For Jozachat, sone of Semath, and Joiadath, sone of Soomer, hise seruauntis, smytiden him, and he was deed; and thei birieden hym with hise fadris in the citee of Dauid; and Amasie, his sone, regnyde for hym.

CAP 13

1 In the thre and twentithe yeer of Joas, sone of Ocozie, kyng of Juda, Joachaz, sone of Hieu, regnede on Israel, in Samarie seuentene yeer.

2 And he dide yuel bifor the Lord, and he suede the synnes of Jeroboam, sone of Nabath, that made Israel to do synne; and he bowide not awei fro tho.

3 And the strong veniaunce of the Lord was wrooth ayens Israel, and he bitook hem in to the hondis of Azael, kyng of Sirie, and in the hond of Benadab, sone of Asael, in alle daies.

4 Forsothe Joachaz bisouyte the face of the Lord, and the Lord herde hym; for he siy the anguysch of Israel, for the kyng of Sirie hadde al to brokun hem.

5 And the Lord yaf a sauyour to Israel, and he was delyuered fro the hond of the kyng of Sirie; and the sones of Israel dwelliden in her tabernaclis, as yistirdai and the thridde dai ago.

6 Netheles thei departiden not fro the synnes of the hows of Jeroboam, that made Israel to do synne; thei yeden in tho synnes; sotheli also the wode dwellide in Samarie.

7 And to Joacham weren not left of the puple, no but fyue hundrid kniytis, and ten charis, and ten thousynde of foot men; for the kyng of Sirie hadde slayn hem, and hadde dryue hem as in to poudur in the threischyng of a cornfloor.

8 Forsothe the residue of wordis of Joachaz, and alle thingis whiche he dide, and the strength of hym, whether these ben not wrytun in the book of wordis of daies of the kyngis of Israel?

9 And Joachaz slepte with hise fadris, and thei birieden hym in Samarie; and Joas, his sone, regnyde for hym.

10 In the seuenthe and threttithe yeer of Joas, king of Juda, Joas, sone of Joachaz, regnede on Israel in Samarie sixtene yeer.

11 And he dide that, that is yuel in the siyt of the Lord; for he bowide not awei fro alle the synnes of Jeroboam, sone of Nabath, that made Israel to do synne; he yede in tho synnes.

12 Forsothe the residue of wordis of Joas, and alle thingis whiche he dide, but also his strengthe, hou he fauyt ayens Amasie, kyng of Juda, whether these ben not writun in the book of wordis of daies of the kyngis of Israel?

13 And Joas slepte with hise fadris; forsothe Jeroboam sat on his trone. Sotheli Joas was biried in Samarie with the kyngis of Israel.

14 Forsothe Elisee was sijk in sikenesse, bi which and he was deed; and Joas, kyng of Israel, yede doun to hym, and wepte bifor hym, and seide, My fadir! my fadir! the chare of Israel, and the charietere therof!

15 And Elisee seide to hym, Brynge thou a bouwe and arowis. And whanne he hadde brouyte to Elisee a bouwe and arowis,

16 he seide to the kyng of Israel, Set thin hond on the bouwe. And whanne he hadde set his hond, Elisee settide his hondis on the hondis of the

17 kyng, and seide, Opene thou the eest wyndow. And whanne he hadde openyd, Elisee seide, Schete thou an arewe;

and he schete. And Elisee seide, It is an arewe of helthe of the Lord, and an arowe of helthe ayens Sirie; and thou schalt smyte Sirie in Affeth, til thou waste it.

18 And Elisee seide, Take awei the arowis. And whanne he hadde take awei, Elisee seide eft to him, Smyte thou the erthe with a dart. And whanne he hadde smyte thre tymes,

19 and hadde stonde, the man of God was wrooth ayens hym, and seide, If thou haddist smyte fyue sithis, ether sixe sithis, ethir seuen sithis, thou schuldist haue smyte Sirie 'til to the endyng; now forsothe thou schalt smyte it thre sithis.

20 Therfor Elisee was deed, and thei birieden hym. And the theuys of Moab camen in to the lond in that yeer.

21 Forsothe sum men birieden a man, and thei siyen the theues, and thei castiden forth the deed bodi in the sepulcre of Elisee; and whanne it hadde touchid the bonys of Elisee, the man lyuede ayen, and stood on his feet.

22 Therfor Azael, kyng of Sirie, turmentide Israel in alle the daies of Joachaz.

23 And the Lord hadde merci on hem, and turnede ayen to hem for his couenaunt, which he hadde with Abraham, Isaac, and Jacob; and he nolde distrie hem, nether cast awei outirli, til in to present tyme.

24 Forsothe Azael, kyng of Sirie, diede; and Benadad, his sone, regnede for hym.

25 Forsothe Joas, sone of Joachas, took awei citees fro the hond of Benadad, sone of Asael, which he hadde take bi the riyt of batel fro the hoond of Joachaz, his fadir; Joas smoot hym thre tymes, and he yeldide the citees of Israel.

CAP 14

1 Yn the secounde yeer of Joas, sone of Joachas, kyng of Israel, Amasie, sone of Joas, kyng of Juda, regnyde.

2 Amasie was of fyue and twenti yeer, whanne he bigan to regne; forsothe he regnyde in Jerusalem nyne and twenti yeer; the name of his modir was Joade of Jerusalem.

3 And he dide riytfulnesse bifor the Lord, netheles not as Dauid, his fadir; he dide bi alle thingis whiche Joas, his fadir, dide, no but this oonli,

4 that he dide not awei hiy thingis; for yit the puple made sacrifice, and brent encence in hiy thingis.

5 And whanne he hadde gete the rewme, he smoot hise seruauntis, that hadden killid the kyng, his fadir;

6 but he killide not the sones of hem that hadden slayn 'the kyng, bi that that is writun in the book of the lawe of Moyses, as the Lord comaundide to Moises, and seide, Fadris schulen not die for the sones, nethir the sones for the fadris, but eche man schal die in his owne synne.

7 He smoot Edom in the valey of makyngis of salt, 'he smoot ten thousynde, and took 'the Stoon in batel; and he clepide the name therof Jethel, 'til in to present dai.

8 Thanne Amasie sente messangeris to Joas, sone of Joachaz, sone of Hieu, kyng of Israel, and seide, Come thou, and se we vs 'in batel.

9 And Joas, kyng of Israel, sente ayen to Amasie, kyng of Juda, and seide, The cardue, 'that is, a low eerbe, and ful of thornes, of the Liban sente to the cedre, which is in the Liban, and seide, Yyue thi douytir wijf to my sone; and the beestis of the forest, that ben in the Liban, passiden, and tredden doun the cardue.

10 Thou hast smyte, and haddist the maistri on Edom, and thin herte hath reisid thee; be thou apaied with glorie, and sitte in thin hows; whi excitist thou yuel, that thou falle, and Juda with thee?

11 And Amasie assentide not 'to be in pees; and Joas, kyng of Israel, stiede, and he and Amasie, kyng of Juda, sien hem silf in Bethsames, a citee of Juda.

12 And Juda was smytun bifor Israel; and thei fledden ech man in to his tabernaclis.

13 Sotheli Joas, kyng of Israel, took in Bethsames Amasie, kyng of Juda, the sone of Joas, sone of Ocozie, and brouyte hym in to Jerusalem; and he brak the wal of Jerusalem, fro the yate of Effraym 'til to the yate of the corner, bi foure hundrid cubitis.

14 And he took al the gold and siluer, and alle vessels, that weren foundun in the hows of the Lord, and in the tresours of the kyng; and he took ostagis, and turnede ayen in to Samarie.

15 Sotheli the resydue of wordis of Joas, whiche he dide, and his strengthe, bi which he fauyt ayens Amasie, kyng of Juda, whether these ben not writun in the book of wordis of dayes of the kyngis of Israel?

16 And Joas slepte with hise fadris, and was biried in Samarie with the kyngis of Israel; and Jeroboam, his sone, regnede for hym.

17 Forsothe Amasie, sone of Joas, kyng of Juda, lyuede fyue and twenti yeer, after that Joas, sone of Joachaz, kyng of Israel, was deed.

18 Forsothe the residue of wordis of Amasie, whether these ben not writun in the book of wordis of daies of the kyngis of Juda?

19 And 'sweryng togidir in Jerusalem was maad ayens hym, and he fledde in to Lachis; and thei senten aftir hym in to Lachis, and killiden hym there.

20 And thei baren out hym in horsis, and he was biried in Jerusalem with hise fadris, in the citee of Dauid.

21 Forsothe al the puple of Juda took Azarie, hauynge sixtene yeer; and maden hym king for his fadir Amasie.

22 And he bildide Ahila, and restoride it to Juda, after that 'the kyng slepte with hise fadris.

23 In the fiftenethe yeer of Amasie, sone of Joas, kyng of Juda, Jeroboam, sone of Joas, kyng of Israel, regnyde in Samarie oon and fourti yeer;

24 and dide that, that is yuel bifor the Lord; he yede not awei fro alle the synnes of Jeroboam, sone of Nabath, that made Israel to do synne.

25 He restoride the termes of Israel, fro the entryng of Emath 'til to the see of wildirnesse, bi the word of the Lord God of Israel, which he spak bi his seruaunt Jonas, sone of Amathi, bi Jonas, the prophete, that was of Jeth, 'which Jeth is in Ophir.

26 For the Lord siy the ful bittir turment of Israel, and that thei weren wastid 'til to the closid men of prisoun, and the laste men, and 'noon was that helpide Israel.

27 And the Lord spak not, that he schulde do awei Israel fro vndur heuene, but he sauyde hem in the hond of Jeroboam, sone of Joas.

28 Forsothe the residue of wordis of Jeroboam, and alle thingis whiche he dide, and the strengthe of hym, bi which he fauyt, and hou he restoride Damask, and Emath of Juda, in Israel, whether these ben not wrytun in the book of wordis of daies of the kyngis of Israel?

29 And Jeroboam slepte with hise fadris, the kyngis of Israel; and Azarie, his sone, regnede for hym.

CAP 15

1 In the seuenthe and twentithe yeer of Jeroboam, king of Israel, Azarie, sone of Amasie, kyng of Juda, regnede;

2 he was of sixtene yeer, whanne he bigan to regne, and he regnede two and fifti yeer in Jerusalem; the name of his modir was Jecelia of Jerusalem.

3 And he dide that, that was plesaunt bifor the Lord, bi alle thingis which Amasie, his fadir, hadde do;

4 netheles he distriede not hiy thingis; yit the puple made sacrifice, and brente encense in hiye thingis.

5 Forsothe the Lord smoot the kyng, and he was leprouse til in to the day of his deeth; and he dwellide in an hous freli bi hym silf. Sotheli Joathas, sone of the kyng, gouernde the palis, and demyde the puple of the lond.

6 Forsothe the residue of the wordis of Azarie, and alle thingis whiche he dide, whether these ben not writun in the book of wordis of daies of the kyngis of Juda?

7 And Azarie slepte with hise fadris; and thei birieden hym with hise eldre men in the citee of Dauid; and Joathas, his sone, regnede for hym.

8 In the eiyte and threttithe yeer of Azarie, kyng of Juda, Zacharie, sone of Jeroboam, regnede on Israel in Samarie sixe monethis.

9 And he dide that, that was yuel bifor the Lord, as his fadris diden; he departide not fro the synnes of Jeroboam, sone of Nabath, that made Israel to do synne.

10 Forsothe Sellum, the sone of Jabes, conspiride ayens hym in Samarie; and Sellum smoot hym opynli, and killide hym, and regnede for hym.

11 Sotheli the residue of the wordis of Zacharie, whethir these ben not writun in the book of wordis of daies of the kyngis of Israel?

12 Thilke is the word of the Lord, which he spak to Hieu, and seide, 'Thi sones 'til to the fourthe generacioun schulen sitte 'of thee on the trone of Israel; and it was doon so.

13 Sellum, sone of Jabes, regnede in the nynthe and thritty yeer of Azarie, kyng of Juda; sotheli he regnyde o monethe in Samarie.

14 And Manaheu, the sone of Gaddi, styede fro Thersa, and cam in to Samarie; and he smoot Sellum, sone of Jabes, in Samarie, and killide hym, and regnede for hym.

15 Sotheli the residue of wordis of Sellum, and his conspirasie, bi which he settide tresouns, whether these ben not writun in the book of wordis of daies of the kyngis of Israel.

16 Thanne Manaheu smoot Capham, and alle men that weren thereynne, and the termes therof fro Thersa, for thei nolden opyn to hym; and he killide alle wymmen therof with child, and karf hem.

17 In the nynthe and thrittithe yeer of Azarie, kyng of Juda, Manaheu, sone of Gaddi, regnede on Israel ten yeer in Samarie.

18 And he dide that, that was yuel bifor the Lord; he departide not fro the synnes of Jeroboam, sone of Nabath, that made Israel to do synne.

19 In alle the daies of hym Phul, the kyng of Assiries, cam in to Thersa. And Manaheu yaf to Phul a thousynde talentis of siluer, that he schulde be to hym in to help, and schulde make stidefast his rewme;

20 and Manaheu settide taliage of siluer on Israel to alle myyti men and riche, that he schulde yyue to the kyng of Assiries; he settide fifti siclis of siluer bi alle men; and the king of Assiries turnede ayen, and dwellide not in Thersa.

21 Forsothe the residue of wordis of Manaheu, and alle thingis whiche he dide, whether these ben not wrytun in the book of wordis of daies of the kyngis of Israel?

22 And Manaheu slepte with hise fadris; and Phaceia, his sone, regnyde for hym.

23 In the fiftithe yeer of Azarie, kyng of Juda, Phaceia, sone of Manaheu, regnede on Israel in Samarie twei yeer.

24 And he dide that, that was yuel bifor the Lord; he departide not fro the synnes of Jeroboam, sone of Nabath, that made Israel to do synne.

25 Forsothe Phacee, sone of Romelie, duyk of his oost, conspiride ayens hym, and smoot hym in Samarie, in the tour of the kyngis hous, bisidis Argob, and bisidis Arib; 'and he smoot hym with fifti men of the sones of Galaditis; and Phacee killide hym, and regnede for hym.

26 Sotheli the residue of wordis of Phacee, and alle thingis whiche he dide, whether these ben not writun in the book of wordis of daies of the kyngis of Israel?

27 In the two and fiftithe yeer of Azarie, kyng of Juda, Phasee, sone of Romelie, regnyde in Samarie twenti yeer.

28 And he dide that, that was yuel bifor the Lord; and he departide not fro the synnes of Jeroboam, sone of Nabath, that made Israel to do synne.

29 In the daies of Phacee, kyng of Israel, Teglat Phalasar, kyng of Assur, cam, and took Aion, and Aibel, the hows of Maacha, and Janoe, and Cedes, and Asor, and Galaad, and Galilee, and al the lond of Neptalym; and translatide hem in to Assiriens.

30 Forsothe Osee, sone of Hela, conspiride, and settide tresouns ayens Phasee, sone of Romelie, and smoot hym, and killide hym; and he regnyde for hym, in the twentithe yeer of Joathan, sone of Ozie.

31 Forsothe the residue of wordis of Phacee, and alle thingis whiche he dide, whether these ben not writun in the book of wordis of daies of the kyngis of Israel?

32 In the secounde yeer of Phacee, sone of Romelie, kyng of Israel, Joathan, sone of Ozie, kyng of Juda, regnyde;

33 he was of fyue and twenti yeer, whanne he bigan to regne, and he regnede sixtene yeer in Jerusalem; the name of his modir was Jerusa, the douyter of Sadoch.

34 And he dide that, that was plesaunt bifor the Lord; he wrouyte bi alle thingis, whiche his fadir Ozie hadde do;

35 netheles he dide not awey hiy thingis; yit the puple made sacrifice, and brente incense in hiy thingis; he bildide the hiyeste yate of the hows of the Lord.

36 Forsothe the residue of wordis of Joathan, and alle thingis whiche he dide, whether these ben not writun in the book of wordis of daies of the kyngis of Juda?

37 In tho daies the Lord bigan to sende in to Juda Rasyn, the kyng of Sirie, and Phacee, the sone of Romelie.

38 And Joathan slepte with hise fadris, and was biried with hem in the citee of Dauid, his fadir; and Achaz, his sone, regnyde for hym.

CAP 16

1 In the seuententhe yeer of Phacee, sone of Romelie, Achaz, the sone of Joathan, kyng of Juda, regnyde.

2 Achaz was of twenti yeer, whanne he bigan to regne, and he regnyde sixtene yeer in Jerusalem; he dide not that, that was plesaunt in the siyt of his Lord God, as Dauid, his fadir dide, but he yede in the weie of the kyngis of Israel.

3 Ferthermore and he halewide his sone, and bar thorouy the fier, bi the idols of hethene men, whiche the Lord distriede bifore the sones of Israel.

4 And he offride sacrifices, and brente encense in hiy placis, and in hillis, and vndur ech tree ful of bowis.

5 Thanne Rasyn, kyng of Sirye, and Phacee, sone of Romelie, kyng of Israel, stiede in to Jerusalem to fiyte; and whanne thei bisegide Achaz, thei miyten not ouercome hym.

6 In that tyme Rasyn, kyng of Sirie, restoride Ahila to Sirie, and castide out Jewis fro Ahila; and Ydumeis and men of Sirie camen into Ahila, and dwelliden there til in to this dai.

7 Forsothe Achaz sente messangeris to Teglat Phalasar, kyng of Assiriens, and seide, Y am thi seruaunt and thi sone; stie thou, and make me saaf fro the hond of the kyng of Sirie, and fro the hond of the kyng of Israel, that han rise togidere ayens me.

8 And whanne Achaz hadde gaderide togidere siluer and gold, that myyte be foundun in the hows of the Lord, and in the tresours of the kyng, he sente yiftis to the kyng of Assiriens;

9 whiche assentide to his wille. Sotheli the kyng of Asseriens stiede in to Damask, and wastide it, and translatide the dwelleris therof to Sirenen; sotheli he killide Rasyn.

10 And kyng Achaz yede in to metyng to Teglat Phalasaar, kyng of Assiriens; and whanne kyng Achaz hadde seyn the auter of Damask, he sent to Vrie, the preest, the saumpler and licnesse therof, bi al the werk therof.

11 And Vrie, the preest, bildide an auter bi alle thingis whiche king Achaz hadde comaundid fro Damask, so dide the preest Vrie, til kyng Achaz cam fro Damask.

12 And whanne the king cam fro Damask, he siy the auter, and worschipide it; and he stiede, and offride brent sacrifices, and his sacrifice;

13 and he offride moist sacrifices, and he schedde the blood of pesible thingis, which he hadde offrid on the auter.

14 Forsothe he dide awei the brasun auter, that was bifor the Lord, fro the face of the temple, and fro the place of the auter, and fro the place of the temple of the Lord; and settide it on the side of the auter 'at the north.

15 Also kyng Achaz comaundide to Vrie, the preest, and seide, Offre thou on the more auter the brent sacrifice of the morewtid, and the sacrifice of euentid, and the brent sacrifice of the king, and the sacrifice of hym, and the brent sacrifice of al the puple of the lond, and the sacrifices of hem, and the moist sacrifices of hem; and thou schalt schede out on that al the blood of brent sacrifice, and al the blood of slayn sacrifice; sotheli the brasun auter schal be redi at my wille.

16 Therfor Vrie, the preest, dide bi alle thingis whiche kyng Achaz hadde comaundid to hym.

17 Forsothe kyng Achaz took the peyntid foundementis, and the waischyng vessel, that was aboue, and he puttide doun the see, that is, the waischung vessel 'for preestis, fro the brasun oxis, that susteyneden it, and he settide on the pawment araied with stoon.

18 Also he turnede the tresorie of sabat, which he hadde bildid in the temple, and 'he turnede the entryng of the kyng with outforth, in to the temple of the Lord for the kyng of Assiriens.

19 Forsothe the residue of wordis of Achaz, and alle thingis whiche he dide, whether these ben not writun in the book of wordis of daies of the kyngis of Juda?

20 And Achaz slepte with hise fadris, and was biried with hem in the citee of Dauid; and Ezechie, his sone, regnede for hym.

CAP 17

1 Yn the tweluethe yeer of Achaz, kyng of Juda, Osee, sone of Hela, regnyde in Samarie on Israel nyne yeer.

2 And he dide yuel bifor the Lord, but not as the kyngis of Israel, that weren bifor hym.

3 Salmanasar, kyng of Assiriens, stiede ayens this Osee, and Osee was maad seruaunt to hym, and yildide tributis to hym.

4 And whanne the kyng of Assiriens hadde perseyued, that Osee he enforside to be rebelle, and hadde sent messangeris to Sua, kyng of Egipt, that he schulde not yyue tributis to the kyng of Assiriens, as he was wont bi alle yeeris, 'the kyng of Assiriens bisegide hym, and sente him boundun in to prisoun.

5 And he yede thoruy al the lond, and he stiede to Samarie, and bisegide it bi thre yeer.

6 Forsothe in the nynthe yeer of Osee, the kyng of Assiriens took Samarie, and translatide Israel in to Assiriens; and he puttide hem in Hela, and in Thabor, bisidis the flood Gozam, in the citee of Medeis.

7 Forsothe it was don, whanne the sones of Israel hadden synned bifor her Lord God, that ledde hem out of the lond of Egipt, fro the hond of Farao, kyng of Egipt, thei worschipeden alien goddis;

8 and yeden bi the custom of hethene men, whiche the Lord hadde wastid in the siyt of the sones of Israel, and of the kyngis of Israel, for thei hadden do in lijk maner.

9 And the sones of Israel offendiden her Lord God bi wordis not riytful, and thei bildiden to hem silf hiy thingis in alle her citees, fro the tour of keperis 'til to a strengthid citee.

10 And thei maden to hem ymagis, and wodis, in ech hiy hil, and vndur ech tree ful of bowis;

11 and thei brenten there encence on the auteris bi the custom of hethene men, whiche the Lord hadde translatid fro the face of hem. And thei diden werste wordis, and thei wraththiden the Lord;

12 and worschipiden vnclenesses, of whiche the Lord comaundide to hem, that thei schulden not do this word.

13 And the Lord witnesside in Israel and in Juda, bi the hond of alle prophetis and seeris, and seide, Turne ye ayen fro youre werste weies, and kepe ye my comaundementis, and ceremonyes, bi al the lawe whiche Y comaundide to youre fadris, and as Y sente to you in the hond of my seruauntis prophetis.

14 Whiche herden not, but maden hard her nol bi the nol of her fadris, that nolden obeie to her Lord God.

15 And thei castiden, awei the lawful thingis of hym, and the couenaunt which he couenauntide with her fadris, and the witnessyngis bi whiche he witnesside to hem; and thei sueden vanytees, 'that is, idols, and diden veynli; and sueden hethene men, that weren 'bi the cumpas of hem; of whiche vanytees the Lord comaundide to hem, that thei schulden not do as also tho hethene men diden.

16 And thei forsoken alle the comaundementis of her Lord God, and thei maden to hem twei yotun calues, and wodis, and worschipiden al the knyythod of heuene; and thei seruyden Baal, and halewiden to hym her sones,

17 and her douytris thoruy fier, and thei seruyden to fals dyuynyng, and to dyuynyng bi chiterynge of briddis; and thei yauen hem silf to do yuel bifor the Lord, and thei wraththiden hym.

18 And the Lord was wrooth greetli to Israel; and he took awei hem fro his siyt, and noon lefte, no but the lynage of Juda oneli.

19 But nether Juda hym silf kepte the heestis of 'his Lord God, netheles he erride, and yede in the errour of Israel, whiche it wrouyte.

20 And the Lord castide awei al the seed of Israel, and turmentide hem, and bitook hem in the hond of rauynouris; til he castide awei hem fro his face,

21 fro that tyme in which Israel was departid fro the hous of Dauid, and maden to hem a kyng, Jeroboam, sone of Nabath. For Jeroboam departide Israel fro the Lord, and made hem to do a greet synne.

22 And the sones of Israel yeden in alle the synnes of Jeroboam, whiche he hadde do; and thei departiden not fro tho synnes,

23 til the Lord dide awei Israel fro his face, as he spak in the hond of alle hise seruauntis prophetis; and Israel was translatid fro his lond in to Assiriens til in to this dai.

24 Forsothe the kyng of Assiriens brouyte puple fro Babiloyne, and fro Cutha, and fro Hailath, and fro Emath, and fro Sepharuaym, and settide hem in the citees of Samarie for the sones of Israel; whiche hadden in possessioun Samarie, and dwelliden in the citees therof.

25 And whanne thei bigunnen to dwelle there, thei dredden not the Lord; and the Lord sente to hem liouns, that killiden hem.

26 And it was teld to the kyng of Assiriens, and was seid, The folkis whiche thou translatidist, and madist to dwelle in the citees of Samarie, kunnen not the lawful thingis of God of the lond; and the Lord sente liouns in to hem, and lo! liouns sleen hem; for thei kunnen not the custom of God of the lond.

27 Sotheli the kyng of Assiriens comaundide, and seide, Lede ye thidur oon of the preestis, whiche ye brouyten prisoneris fro thennus, that he go, and dwelle with hem, and teche hem the lawful thingis of God of the lond.

28 Therfor whanne oon of these preestis had come, that weren led prisoneris fro Samarie, he dwellide in Bethel, and tauyte hem, how thei schulden worschipe the Lord.

29 And ech folk made his god, and thei settiden tho goddis in the hiy templis, whiche the men of Samarie hadden maad, folk and folk in her citees, in whiche thei dwelliden.

30 For men of Babiloyne maden Socoth Benoth; forsothe men of Cutha maden Vergel; and men of Emath maden Asyma;

31 forsothe Eueis maden Nabaath and Tharcha; sotheli thei that weren of Sepharuaym brenten her sones in fier to Adramelech and Anamelech, goddis of Sepharuaym.

32 And netheles thei worschipiden the Lord; forsothe of the laste men thei maden preestis of the hiye thingis, and settiden hem in hiye templis.

33 And whanne thei worschipiden God, thei serueden also her goddis, bi the custom of hethene men, fro whiche thei weren translatid to Samarie;

34 'til in to present dai thei suen the eld custom; thei dredden not the Lord, nethir thei kepen hise cerymonyes, and domes, and lawe, and comaundement, which the Lord comaundide to the sones of Jacob, whom he nemyde Israel;

35 and he smoot a couenaunt with hem, and comaundide to hem, and seide, Nyle ye drede alien goddis, and onoure ye not outwardli hem, nethir worschipe ye inwardli hem, and make ye not sacrifice to hem;

36 but youre Lord God, that ledde you out of the lond of Egipt in greet strengthe, and in arm holdun forth, drede ye hym, and worschipe ye hym, and make ye sacrifice to hym.

37 And kepe ye the cerymonyes, and domes, and the lawe, and comaundement, which he wroot to you, that ye do in alle daies; and drede ye not alien goddis.

38 And nyle ye foryete the couenaunt, which he smoot with you, nether worschipe ye alien goddis;

39 but drede ye youre Lord God, and he schal delyuere you fro the hond of alle youre enemyes.

40 Forsothe thei herden not, but diden bi her formere custom.

41 Therfor these hethene men dredden sotheli God; but nethe-les thei serueden also her idols, for bothe her sones and the sones of sones doen so, til in to present dai, as her fadris diden.

CAP 18

1 In the thridde yeer of Osee, sone of Hela, kyng of Israel, regnyde Ezechie, sone of Achaz, kyng of Juda.

2 He was of fyue and twenti yeer, whanne he bigan to regne, and he regnyde in Jerusalem nyne and twenti yeer; the name of his modir was Abisa, douyter of Zacharie.

3 And he dide that, that was good bifor the Lord, bi alle thingis, which Dauid, his fadir, hadde do.

4 And he distriede hiye places, and al to-brak ymagis, and kit-tide doun wodis, and he brak the brasun serpent, whom Moy-ses hadde maad; for 'til to that tyme the sones of Israel brenten encense to it; and he clepide the name therof Noes-tam.

5 And he hopide in the Lord God of Israel; therfor aftir hym noon was lijk hym of alle the kyngis of Juda, but 'and nether in tho kyngis that weren bifor hym.

6 And he cleuyde to the Lord, and yede not awei fro hise step-pis, and he dide the comaundementis of the Lord, whiche the Lord comaundide to Moises;

7 wherfor and the Lord was with hym, and he gouernede wiseli hym silf in alle thingis, to whiche he yede forth. Also he rebellide ayens the kyng of Assiriens, and therfor he seruede not to 'that kyng of Asseriens;

8 and he smoot Philisteis 'til to Gazam, and alle the termes of hem, fro the tour of keperis 'til to a citee maad strong.

9 In the fourthe yeer of kyng Ezechie, that was the seuenthe yeer of Osee, sone of Hela, kyng of Israel, Salmanazar, kyng of Assiriens, stiede to Samarie,

10 and fauyt ayens it, and took it. For after thre yeer, in the sixte yeer of Ezechie, that is, in the nynthe yeer of Osee, kyng of Israel, Samarie was takun;

11 and the kyng of Assiriens translatide Israel in to Assiriens, and settyde hem in Haila, and in Habor, ryueris of Gozam, in the citees of Medeis;

12 for thei herden not the vois of her Lord God, but thei braken his couenaunt; thei herden not, nether diden alle thingis, whiche Moises, the seruaunt of the Lord, comaun-dide.

13 In the fourtenthe yeer of kyng Ezechie, Senacherub, kyng of Assiryens, stiede to alle the strengthide citees of Juda, and took tho.

14 Thanne Ezechie, kyng of Juda, sente messangeris to the kyng of Assiriens in to Lachis, and seide, Y haue synned; go awei fro me, and Y schal bere 'al thing, which thou schalt putte to me. Therfor the kyng of Asseriens puttide on Ezechie, kyng of Juda, thre hundrid talentis of siluer, and thretti talentis of gold.

15 And Ezechie yaf al the siluer, that was foundun in the hows of the Lord, and in the kyngis tresories.

16 In that tyme Ezechie brak the yatis of the temple of the Lord, and the platis of gold, whiche he hadde fastned, and he yaf tho to the kyng of Assiriens.

17 Forsothe the kyng of Assiriens sente Thercha and Rab-saces fro Lachis to kyng Ezechie, with strong hond to Jerusa-lem; and whanne thei hadden stied, thei camen to Jerusalem, and stoden bisidis the water cundijt of the hiyere cisterne, which is in the weie of the fullere, 'ethir toukere.

18 And thei clepiden the kyng; sotheli Eliachym, sone of Elchie, the souereyn of the hows, and Sobna, scryueyn, and Joahe, chaunseler, the sone of Asaph, yeden out to hem.

19 And Rabsaces seide to hem, Speke ye to Ezechie, The grete kyng, the kyng of Assiriens, seith these thingis, What is this trist, in which thou enforsist?

20 In hap thou hast take counsel, that thou woldist make thee redi to batel. In whom tristist thou, that thou be hardi to rebelle?

21 Whethir thou hopist in a 'staf of rehed and brokun, Egipt, on which, if a man lenith, it schal be brokun, and schal entre in to hys hond, and schal peerse it? So is Farao, kyng of Egipt, to alle men that tristen on hym.

22 That if thou seist to me, We han trist in 'oure Lord God; whether this is not he, whos hiye thingis and auteris Ezechie took awei, and comaundide to Juda and to Jerusalem, Ye schulen worschipe bifor this auter in Jerusalem?

23 Now therfor passe ye to my lord, the kyng of Assiriens, and Y schal yyue to you twei thousynde of horsis, and se ye, whether ye moun haue rideris of 'tho horsis?

24 And hou moun ye withstonde bifor o prince of the leste seruauntis of my lord? Whether thou hast trist in Egipt, for charis and knyytis?

25 Whether Y stiede with outen 'Goddis wille to this place, that Y schulde distrie it? 'The Lord seide to me, 'Stie thou to this lond, and distrie thou it.

26 Forsothe Eliachym, sone of Elchie, and Sobna, and Joahe, seiden to Rabsaces, We preien, that thou speke bi the langage of Sirie to vs, thi seruauntis; for we vndirstondun this lan-gage; and that thou speke not to vs bi the langage of Juwis, while the puple herith, which is on the wal.

27 And Rabsaces answeride, 'and seide, Whethir my lord sente me to thi lord and to thee, that Y schulde speke these wordis, and not rather to the men 'that sitten on the wal, that thei ete her toordis, and drynke her pisse with you?

28 Therfor Rabsaces stood, and criede with greet vois bi lan-gage of Jewis, and seide, Here ye the wordis of the greet kyng, the kyng of Assiriens.

29 The kyng seith these thingis, Ezechie disceyue not you, for he may not delyuere you fro myn hond;

30 nether yyue he trist to you on the Lord, and seie, The Lord delyuerynge schal delyuere vs, and this citee shal not be bitakun in the hond of the kyng of Assiriens;

31 nyle ye here Ezechie. For the kyng of Assiriens seith these thingis, Do ye with me that, that is profitable to you, and go ye out to me; and eche man schal ete of his vyner, and of his fige tree, and ye schulen drynke watris of youre cisternes,

32 til Y come, and translate you in to a lond which is lijk youre lond, in to a fruytful lond, and plenteuouse of wyn, a lond of breed, and of vineris, a lond of olyue trees, and of oile, and of hony; and ye schulen lyue, and ye schulen not die. Nyle ye here Ezechie, that disseyueth you, and seith, The Lord schal delyuere yow.

33 Whether the goddis of hethene men delyueriden her lond fro the hond of the kyng of Assiriens?

34 Where is god of Emath, and of Arphat? Where is god of Sapharuaym, of Ana, and of Aua? Whether thei delyueriden Samarie fro myn hond?

35 For who ben thei in alle goddis of londis, that delyueriden her cuntrey fro myn hond, that the Lord may delyuere Jerusalem fro myn hoond?

36 Therfor the puple was stille, and answeride not ony thing to hym; for thei hadden take comaundement of the kyng, that thei schulden not answere to hym.

37 And Eliachym, sone of Elchie, the souereyn of the hows, and Sobna, scryuen, and Joahe, chaunceler, the sone of Asaph, camen with to-rent clothis to Ezechie; and telden to hym the wordis of Rabsaces.

CAP 19

1 And whanne kyng Ezechie hadde herd these thingis, he torente his clothis, and was hilid with a sak; and he entride in to the hous of the Lord.

2 And he sente Eliachym, souereyn of the hous, and Sobna, scryueyn, and elde men of the preestis, hilid with sackis, to Ysaie, the prophete, sone of Amos.

3 Whiche seiden, Ezechie seith these thingis, This dai is a dai of tribulacioun, and of blamyng, and of blasfemye; sones camen 'til to the childberyng, and the 'traueler of childe hath not strengthis.

4 If perauenture thi Lord God here alle the wordis of Rabsaces, whom the kyng of Assiryens, his lord sente, that he schulde dispise the Lord lyuynge, and repreue bi wordis, whiche thi Lord God herde; and make thou preier for these relikis, that ben foundun.

5 Therfor the seruauntis of kyng Ezechie camen to Isaie;

6 and Isaie seide to hem, Seie ye these thingis to youre lord, The Lord seith these thingis, Nyle thou drede of the face of wordis whiche thou herdist, bi whiche the children of the kyng of Assiriens blasfemeden me.

7 Lo! Y schal sende to hym a spirit, and he schal here a messanger, and he schal turne ayen in to his lond; and Y schal caste hym doun bi swerd in his owne lond.

8 Therfor Rabsaces turnede ayen, and foond the kyng of Assiriens fiytynge ayens Lobna; for he hadde herd, that the kyng hadde go awei fro Lachis.

9 And whanne he hadde herd of Theracha, kyng of Ethiope, 'men seyynge, Lo! he yede out, that he fiyte ayens thee; that he schulde go ayens 'that kyng, he sente messangeris to Ezechie,

10 and seide, Seie ye these thingis to Ezechie, kyng of Juda, Thi Lord God, in whom thou hast trist, disseyue not thee, nether seie thou, Jerusalem schal not be 'bitakun in to the hondis of the kyng of Assiriens;

11 for thou thi silf herdist what thingis the kyngis of Assiriens diden in alle londis, hou thei wastiden tho; whether therfor thou aloone maist be delyuered?

12 Whether the goddis of hethene men delyueriden alle men whiche my fadris distrieden, that is, Gozam, and Aran, and Reseph, and the sones of Eden, that weren in Thelassar?

13 Where is the kyng of Emath, and the kyng of Arphat? and the kyng of the cytee of Sepharuaym, of Ana, and of Aua?

14 Therfor whanne Ezechie hadde take the lettris fro the hond of messangeris, and hadde red tho, he stiede in to the hows of the Lord, and spredde abrood tho bifor the Lord;

15 and preiede in his siyt, and seide, Lord God of Israel, that sittist on cherubym, thou art God aloone of alle kyngis of erthe; thou madist heuene and erthe.

16 Bowe thin eere, and here; opyn thin iyen, Lord, and se; and here alle the wordis of Senacherib, which sente, that he schulde dispise 'to vs 'God lyuynge.

17 Verili, Lord, the kynges of Assiriens distrieden hethene men, and the londis of alle men,

18 and senten the goddis of hem in to fier; for thei weren not goddis, but werkis of 'hondis of men, of tre and stoon; and thei losten 'tho goddis.

19 Now therfor, oure Lord God, make vs saaf fro the hond of hem, that alle rewmes of erthe wite that thou art the Lord God aloone.

20 Forsothe Isaie, sone of Amos, sente to Ezechie, and seide, The Lord God of Israel seith these thingis, Y haue herd tho thingis, whiche thou preidist me on Sennacherib, king of Assiriens.

21 This is the word, which the Lord spak of hym, Thou virgyn douytir of Syon, he dispiside thee, and scornyde thee; thou douyter of Jerusalem, he mouyde his heed aftir thi bak.

22 Sennacherib, whom 'dispisidist thou, and whom 'blasfemedist thou? Ayens whom hast thou reisid thi vois, and hast reisid thin iyen an hiye? Ayens the hooli of Israel.

23 Bi the hond of thi seruauntis thou dispisidist the Lord, and seidist, In the multitude of my charys Y stiede in to the hiye thingis of hillis, in the hiynesse of Liban, and kittide doun the hiye cedris therof, and the chosyn beechis therof; and Y entride 'til to the termes therof,

24 and Y kittide doun the forest of Carmele therof; and Y drank alien watris, and Y made drie with the steppis of 'the feet of myn 'alle watris closid.

25 Whether thou herdist not, what Y made at the bigynnyng? Fro elde daies Y made it, and now Y haue brouyt forth; and strengthid citees of fiyteris schulen be in to fallyng of hillis.

26 And thei that sitten meke of hond in tho, trembliden togidere, and ben schent; thei ben maad as the hei of the feeld, and as grene eerbe of roouys, which is dried, bifor that it cam to ripenesse.

27 And Y bifor knew thi dwellyng, and thi goyng out, and thin entryng, and thi weie, and thi woodnesse ayens me.

28 Thou were wood ayens me, and thi pride stide in to myn eeris; therfor Y schal putte a cercle in thi nosethirlis, and a bernacle in thi lippis, and Y schal lede thee ayen in to the weie bi which thou camest.

29 Forsothe, Ezechie, this schal be a signe 'to thee; ete thou in this yeer that, that thou fyndist; forsothe in the secounde yeer tho thingis, that growen bi her owne wille; sotheli in the thridde yeer sowe ye, and repe ye, plaunte ye vyneris, and ete the fruytis of tho.

30 And what euer thing schal be residue of the hows of Juda, it schal sende root dounward, and schal make fruyt vpward.

31 For relikis schulen go out of Jerusalem, and that, that schal be sauyd, 'schal go out of the hil of Syon; the feruent loue of the Lord of oostis schal do this.

32 Wherfor the Lord seith these thingis of the kyng of Assiriens, He schal not entre in to this citee, nethir he schal sende an arowe in to it, nether scheeld shal occupie it, nether strengthing, ethir bisegyng, schal cumpasse it.

33 He schal turne ayen bi the weie 'bi which he cam, and he schal not entre in to this citee, seith the Lord;

34 and Y schal defende this citee, and Y schal saue it for me, and for Dauid, my seruaunt.

35 Therfor it was don, in that niyt the aungel of the Lord cam, and smoot in the castels of Assiryens an hundrid foure score and fyue thousynde. And whanne Sennacherib hadde rise eerli, he siy alle bodies of deed men; and he departide, and yede awei.

36 And Sennacherib, the kyng of Assiriens, turnede ayen, and dwellide in Nynyue.

37 And whanne he worschipide in the temple Nestrach his god, Adramelech and Sirasar, his sones, killide hym with swerd; and thei fledden in to the lond of Armenyes; and Asaradon, his sone, regnyde for hym.

CAP 20

1 In tho daies Ezechie was sijk 'til to the deeth; and Isaie, the prophete, sone of Amos, cam to hym, and seide to hym, The Lord God seith these thingis, Comaunde to thin hows, for thou schalt die, and thou schalt not lyue.

2 Which Ezechie turnyde his face to the wal, and worschipide the Lord,

3 and seide, Y biseche, Lord, haue mynde, hou Y yede bifor thee in treuthe, and in a parfit herte, and Y dide that, that was plesaunt bifor thee. Therfor Ezechie wepte bi greet wepyng.

4 And bifor that Ysaie yede out half the part of the court, the word of the Lord was maad to Isaie, and seide,

5 Turne thou ayen, and seie to Ezechie, duyk of my puple, The Lord God of Dauid, thi fadir, seith thes thingis, Y herde thi preiere, and Y siy thi teer, and, lo! Y heelide thee. In the thridde dai thou schalt stie in to the temple of the Lord,

6 and Y schal adde fiftene yeer to thi daies; but also Y schal delyuere thee and this citee fro the hond of the kyng of Assiriens, and Y schal defende this citee for me, and for Dauid, my seruaunt.

7 And Ysaie seide, Brynge ye to me a gobet of figis. And whanne thei hadden brouyte it, and hadde putte on 'his botche, he was heelid.

8 Forsothe Ezechie seide to Isaie, What schal be the signe, that the Lord schal heele me, and that in the thridde dai Y schal stie in to the temple of the Lord?

9 To whom Ysaie seide, This schal be 'a signe of the Lord, that the Lord schal do the word which he spak; wolt thou, that the schadewe stie by ten lynes, ethir turne ayen bi so many degrees?

10 And Ezechie seide, It is esy that the schadewe encreesse bi ten lynes, nethir Y wole that this be doon, but that it turne ayen bacward bi ten degrees.

11 Therfor Ysaie, the prophete, clepide inwardli the Lord, and brouyte ayen bacward bi ten degrees the schadewe bi lynes, bi whiche it hadde go doun thanne in the orologie of Achaz.

12 In that tyme Beradacbaladan, sone of Baladam, the kyng of Babiloyne, sente lettris and yiftis to Ezechie; for he hadde herd that Ezechie was sijk, and hadde couerid.

13 Forsothe Ezechie was glad in the comyng of hem, and he schewide to hem the hows of spyceries, and gold, and siluer, and dyuerse pymentis, also oynementis, and the hows of hise vessels, and alle thingis whiche he myyte haue in hise tresouris; 'no word was, 'which Ezechie schewide not to hem in his hows, and in al his power.

14 Sotheli Ysaie, the prophete, cam to the kyng Ezechie, and seide to hym, What seiden these men, ether fro whennus camen thei to the? To whom Ezechie seide, Thei camen to me fro a fer lond, fro Babiloyne.

15 And he answeride, What 'sien thei in thin hows? Ezechie seide, Thei sien alle thingis, what euer thingis ben in myn hows; no thing is in my tresouris, which Y schewide not to hem.

16 Therfor Isaie seide to Ezechie, Here thou the word of the Lord.

17 Lo! dayes comen, and alle thingis that ben in thin hows, and 'whiche thingis thi fadris maden til in to this dai, schulen be takun awey into Babiloyne; 'not ony thing schal dwelle, seith the Lord.

18 But also of thi sones, that schulen go out of thee, whiche thou schalt gendere, schulen be takun, and thei schulen be geldyngis in the paleis of the king of Babiloyne.

19 Ezechie seide to Isaie, The word of the Lord, 'which he spak, is good; ooneli pees and treuthe be in my daies.

20 Forsothe the residue of wordis of Ezechie, and al his strengthe, and hou he made a cisterne, and a watir cundijt, and brouyte watris, 'in to the citee, whether these ben not writun in the book of wordis of daies of the kyngis of Juda?

CAP 21

21 And Ezechie slepte with hise fadris, and Manasses, his sone, regnyde for hym.

1 Manasses was of twelue yeer, whanne he bigan to regne, and he regnyde fyue and fifti yeer in Jerusalem; the name of his modir was Asiba.

2 And he dide yuel in the siyt of the Lord, bi the idols of hethene men, whiche hethene men the Lord dide awei fro the face of the sones of Israel.

3 And he was turned, and bildide hiye thingis, whiche Ezechie, his fadir, distriede; and he reiside auteris of Baal, and he made woodis, as Achab kyng of Israel hadde do; and he worschipide 'with out forth al the knyythod of heuene, and worschipide it in herte.

4 And he bildide auteris in the hows of the Lord, of which the Lord seide, Y schal sette my name in Jerusalem.

5 And he bildide auteris to al the knyythod of heuene in the twei large places of the temple of the Lord;

6 and he 'ledde ouer his sone thorouy the fier; and he vside false dyuynyngis in auteris, on whiche sacrifice was maad to feendis, and he kepte false dyuynyngis bi chiteryng of bryddis; and he made men to haue yuele spiritis spekynge in the wombe, and he multipliede false dyuynours in entraylis of beestis sacrified to feendis, that he schulde do yuel bifor the Lord, and terre hym to ire.

7 And he settide an ydol of wode, which he hadde maad, in the temple of the Lord, 'of which temple the Lord spak to Dauid, and to Salomon, his sone, Y schal sette my name withouten ende in this temple, and in Jerusalem which Y chees of alle the lynagis of Israel.

8 And Y schal nomore make the foot of Israel to be moued fro the lond which Y yaf to the fadris of hem; so netheles if thei kepen in werk alle thingis whiche Y comaundide to hem, and al the lawe whiche Moises, my seruaunt, comaundide to hem.

9 Sotheli thei herden not, but weren disseyued of Manasses, that thei diden yuel ouer hethene men, whiche the Lord al tobrak fro the face of the sones of Israel.

10 And the Lord spak in the hond of his seruauntis prophetis, and seide,

11 For Manasses, kyng of Juda, dide these worste abhomynaciouns ouer alle thingis which Ammorreis diden bifor hym, and maden also the puple of Juda to do synne in hise vnclennessis;

12 therfor the Lord God of Israel seith these thingis, Lo! Y schal brynge in yuelis on Jerusalem and Juda, that who euer herith, bothe hise eeris tyngle;

13 and Y schal holde forth on Jerusalem the corde of Samarie, and the birthun of the hows of Achab, and Y schal do awei Jerusalem, as tablis ben wont to be doon awei; and Y

schal do awey and turne it, and Y schal lede ful ofte the poyntel on the face therof.

14 Forsothe Y schal leeue relikis of myn eritage, and Y schal bitake hem in to the hond of enemyes therof; and thei schulen be in distriynge, and in raueyn to alle her aduersaries;

15 for thei diden yuel bifor me, and thei continueden terrynge me to ire, fro the dai in which her fadris yeden out of the lond of Egipt 'til to this day.

16 Ferthermore also Manasses schedde ful myche ynnocent blood, til he fillide Jerusalem 'til to the mouth, with outen hise synnes bi whiche he made Juda to do synne, to do yuel bifor the Lord.

17 Forsothe the residue of the wordis of Manasses, and alle thingis whiche he dide, and his synne whiche he synnede, whether these ben not writun in the book of wordis of daies of the kyngis of Juda?

18 And Manasses slepte with hise fadris, and was biried in the gardyn of his hows, in the gardyn of Azam; and Amon, his sone, regnyde for hym.

19 He was of two and twenti yeer, whanne he bigan to regne; and he regnede twei yeer in Jerusalem; the name of his modir was Mesalamech, the douyter of Arus of Gethela.

20 And he dide yuel in the siyt of the Lord, as Manasses, his fader, hadde do.

21 And he yede in al the weie, bi which his fader hadde go, and he seruide to vnclennessis, to whiche his fadir hadde seruyd, and he worschipide tho; and he forsook the Lord God of hise fadris,

22 and he yede not in the weye of the Lord.

23 And hise seruauntis settiden tresouns to hym, and killiden the kyng in hise hows.

24 Sothely the puple of the Lord smoot alle men, that hadden conspirid ayens kyng Amon, and thei ordeyneden to hem a kyng, Josias, 'his sone, for hym.

25 Forsothe the residue of wordis of Amon, whiche he dide, whether these ben not writun in the book of wordis of daies of the kyngis of Juda?

26 And he slepte with hise fadris, and thei birieden hym in his sepulcre in the gardyn of Azam; and Josias, his sone, regnede for him.

CAP 22

1 Josias was of eiyte yeer, whanne he bigan to regne, and he regnyde oon and thritti yeer in Jerusalem; the name of his modir was Ydida, the douytir of Phadaia of Besechath.

2 And he dide that, that was plesaunt bifor the Lord, and he yede be alle the wayes of Dauid, his fadir; he bowide not, nethir to the riytside, nethir of the leftside.

3 Forsothe in the eiytenthe yeer of kyng Josias, the kyng sente Saphan, sone of Asua, the sone of Mesulam, scryueyn, ethir doctour, of the temple of the Lord,

4 and seide to him, Go thou to Elchie, the grete preest, that the money, which is borun in to the temple of the Lord, be spendid, which money the porteris of the temple han gaderid of the puple;

5 and that it be youun to crafti men bi the souereyns of the hows of the Lord; which also departide that money to hem that worchen in the temple of the Lord, to reparele the rooues of the temple of the Lord,

6 that is, to carpenteris, and to masouns, and to hem that maken brokun thingis, and that trees and stoonus of quarieris be bouyt, to reparele the temple of the Lord;

7 netheles siluer, which thei taken, be not rekynyd to hem, but haue thei in power, and in feith.

8 Forsothe Helchie, the bischop, seide to Saphan, the scryuen, Y haue founde the book of the lawe in the hows of the Lord. And Elchie yaf the book to Saphan, the scryuen, which also redde it.

9 Also Saphan, the scryuen, cam to the kyng, and telde to hym tho thingis, whiche Elchie hadde comaundid, and he seide, Thi seruauntis han spendid the monei, which was foundun in the hows of the Lord, and yauen, that it schulde be departid to crafti men of the souereyns of werkis of the temple of the Lord.

10 Also Saphan, the scriueyn, telde to the kyng, and seide, Helchie, the preest of God, yaf to me a book; and whanne Saphan hadde red that book bifor the kyng,

11 and the kyng hadde herd the wordis of the book of the lawe of the Lord, he to-rente hise clothis.

12 And he comaundide to Elchie, the preest, and to Aicham, sone of Saphan, and to Achabor, sone of Mycha, and to Saphan, the scryuen, and to Achia, seruaunt of the kyng,

13 and seide, Go ye, and 'counsele ye the Lord on me, and on the puple, and on al Juda, of the wordis of this book, which is foundun; for greet ire of the Lord is kyndlid ayens vs, for oure fadris herden not the wordis of this book, to do al thing which is writun to vs.

14 Therfor Helchie, the preest, and Aicham, and Achabor, and Saphan, and Asia, yeden to Olda, the prophetesse, the wijf of Sellum, sone of Thecue, sone of Aras, kepere of the clothis, which Olda dwellide in Jerusalem, in the secounde dwellyng; and thei spaken to hir.

15 And sche answeride to hem, The Lord God of Israel seith these thingis, Seie ye to the man,

16 that sente you to me, The Lord God of Israel seith these thingis, Lo! Y schal brynge yuelis on this place, and on the dwelleris therof, alle the wordis 'of the lawe, whiche the kyng of Juda redde;

17 for thei forsoken me, and maden sacrifice to alien goddis, and terriden me to ire in alle the werkis of her hondis; and myn indignacioun schal be kyndlid in this place, and schal not be quenchid.

18 Sotheli to the kyng of Juda, that sente you, that ye schulen 'counsele the Lord, ye schulen seie thus, The Lord God of Israel seith these thingis, For thou herdist the wordis of the book,

19 and thin herte was aferd, and thou were maad meke bifor the Lord, whanne the wordis weren herd ayens this place and ayens the dwelleris therof, that is, that thei schulden be maad in to wondryng, and in to cursyng, and thou to-rentist thi clothis, and weptist bifor me, and Y herde, seith the Lord;

20 herfor Y schal gadere thee to thi fadris, and thou schalt be gaderid to thi sepulcre in pees; that thin iyen se not alle the yuelis, whiche Y schal brynge yn on this place.

CAP 23

1 And thei telden to the kyng that, that sche seide; 'which kyng sente, and alle the elde men of Juda, and of Jerusalem, weren gaderid to hym.

2 And the kyng stiede in to the temple of the Lord, and alle the men of Juda, and alle men that dwelliden in Jerusalem with hym, the preestis, and the prophetis, and al the puple, fro litil 'til to greet; and he redde, while alle men herden, alle the wordis of the book of boond of pees of the Lord, which book was foundun in the hows of the Lord.

3 And the kyng stood on the grees; and he smoot boond of pees bifor the Lord, that thei schulden go aftir the Lord, and kepe hise comaundementis and witnessyngis and cerymonyes in al the herte and in al the soule, that thei schulden reise the wordis of this boond of pees, that weren writun in that book; and the puple assentide to the couenaunt.

4 And the kyng comaundide to Helchie, the bischop, and to the preestis of the secounde ordre, and to the porteris, that thei schulden caste out of the temple alle the vesselis, that weren maad to Baal, and in the wode, and to al the knyythod of heuene; and he brente tho vessels with out Jerusalem, in the euene valey of Cedron, and he bar the poudir of tho 'vessels in to Bethel.

5 And he dide awei false dyuynours 'that dyuynyden in the entrailis of beestis sacrified to idols, whiche the kingis of Juda hadden sett to make sacrifice in hiy thingis bi the citees of Juda, and in the cumpas of Jerusalem; and he dide awey hem that brenten encense to Baal, and to the sunne, and to the moone, and to twelue signes, and to al the knyythod of heuene.

6 And he made the wode to be borun out of the hows of the Lord without Jerusalem in the euene valey of Cedron, and he brente it there; and he droof it in to poudir, and castide it forth on the sepulcris of the comyn puple.

7 Also he distriede the litle housis of 'men turnyd into wommens condiciouns, whiche housis weren in the hows of the Lord; for whiche the wymmen 'maden as litil howsis of the wode.

8 And he gaderide alle the preestis fro the citees of Juda, and he defoulide the hiye thingis, where the preestis maden sacrifice, fro Gabaa 'til to Bersabee; and he distriede the auters of yatis in the entryng of the dore of Josie, prince of a citee, which dore was at the lift half of the yate of the cytee.

9 Netheles the preestis of hiye thingis stieden not to the auter of the Lord in Jerusalem, but oneli thei eten therf looues in the myddis of her britheren.

10 Also he defoulide Tophet, which is in the euene valey of the sone of Ennon, that no man schulde halewe his sone ether his douytir bi fier to Moloch.

11 Also he dide awei horsis, whiche the kyngis of Juda hadden youe to the sunne, in the entryng of the temple of the Lord, bisidis the chaumbir of Nathanmalech, geldyng, that was in Pharurym; forsothe he brente bi fier the charis of the sunne.

12 Also the kyng distriede the auteris, that weren on the roouys of the soler of Achaz, whiche auteris the kyngis of Juda hadden maad; and the kyng distriede the auteris, whiche Manasses hadde maad in the twei grete placis of the temple of the Lord; and he ran fro thennus, and scateride the askis of tho in to the strond of Cedron.

13 Also the kyng defoulide the hiye thingis, that weren in Jerusalem at the riyt part of the hil of offencioun, whiche Salomon, kyng of Israel, hadde bildid to Astroth, the ydol of Sidoneis, and to Chamos, the offencioun of Moab, and to Melchon, abhominacioun of the sones of Amon;

14 and he al to-brak ymagis, and kittide doun wodis, and fillide the places of tho with the boonys of deed men.

15 Ferthermore also he distriede the auter that was in Bethel, and 'he distriede the hiye thing, which Jeroboam, sone of Nabath, hadde maad, that made Israel to do synne; and he distriede that hiy autir, and brente it, and al to brak it in to poudir, and kittide doun also the wode.

16 And Josias turnyde, and siy there sepulcris that weren in the hil; and he sente, and took the boonys fro the sepulcris, and brente tho on the auter, and defoulide it bi the word of the Lord, which word the man of God spak, that biforseide these wordis.

17 And the kyng seide, What is this biriel, which Y se? And the citeseyns of that citee answeriden to hym, It is the sepulcre of the man of God, that cam fro Juda, and biforseide these wordis, whiche thou hast doon on the auter of Bethel.

18 And the kyng seide, Suffre ye hym; no man moue hise boonys. And hise boonys dwelliden vntouchid with the boones of the prophete, that cam fro Samarie.

19 Ferthermore also Josias dide awei alle the templis of hiye thingis, that weren in the citees of Samarie, whiche the kyngis of Israel hadden maad to terre the Lord to ire; and he dide to tho templis bi alle thingis whiche he hadde do in Bethel.

20 And he killide alle the preestis of hiye thingis, that weren there on the auteris, and he brente mennus boonus on tho auteris; and he turnede ayen to Jerusalem;

21 and comaundide to al the puple, and seide, Make ye pask to 'youre Lord God, vp that, that is writun in the book of this boond of pees.

22 Forsothe sich pask was not maad, fro the daies of iugis that demyden Israel, and of alle daies of the kyngis of Israel and of Juda,

23 as this pask was maad to the Lord in Jerusalem in the eiytenthe yeer of kyng Josias.

24 But also Josias dide awei men hauynge fendis spekinge in her wombis, and false diuinouris in auteris, and 'he dide awei the figuris of idols, and alle vnclennessis, and abhomynaciouns, that weren in the lond of Juda and in Jerusalem, that he schulde do the wordis of the lawe, that weren writun in the book, 'which book Elchie, the preest, foond in the temple of the Lord.

25 No kyng bifor him was lijk hym, 'that turnede ayen to the Lord in al his herte, and in al his soule, and in al his vertu, bi al the lawe of Moises; nether aftir hym roos ony lijk hym.

26 Netheles the Lord was not turned awei fro the ire of his greet veniaunce, bi which his strong veniaunce was wrooth ayens Juda, for the terryngis to ire by whiche Manasses hadde terrid hym to ire.

27 Therfor the Lord seide, Y schal do awei also Juda fro my face, as Y dide awei Israel; and Y schal caste awei this citee, which Y chees, Jerusalem, and the hows 'of which Y seide, My name schal be there.

28 Forsothe the residue of wordis of Josias, and alle thingis whiche he dide, whether these ben not writun in the book of wordis of daies of the kyngis of Juda?

29 In the daies of hym Farao Nechao, kyng of Egipt, stiede ayens the kyng of Assiriens, to the flood Eufrates; and Josias, kyng of Juda, yede in to metyng of hym, and Josias was slayn in Magedo, whanne he hadde seyn hym.

30 And 'hise seruauntis baren hym deed fro Magedo, and brouyte him in to Jerusalem, and birieden hym in his sepulcre; and the puple of the lond took Joachaz, sone of Josias, and anoyntiden hym, and maden hym kyng for his fadir.

31 Joachaz was of thre and twenti yeer, whanne he bigan to regne, and he regnede thre monethis in Jerusalem; the name of his modir was Amychal, douyter of Jeremye of Lobna.

32 And he dide yuel bifor the Lord, bi alle thingis which hise fadris hadden do.

33 And Farao Nechao boond hym in Reblatha, which is in the lond of Emath, that he schulde not regne in Jerusalem; and he

settide 'peyne, ether raunsum, to the lond, in an hundrid talentis of siluer, and in a talent of gold.

34 And Farao Nechao made kyng Eliachim, sone of Josias, for Josias, his fadir; and he turnede the name of hym Joachym; forsothe Farao took Joachaz, and ledde hym in to Egipt.

35 Sotheli Joachym yaf siluer and gold to Farao, whanne he hadde comaundid to the lond bi alle yeeris, that it schulde be brouyt, bi the comaundement of Farao; and he reiside of ech man bi hise myytis bothe siluer and gold, of the puple of the lond, that he schulde yyue to Pharao Nechao.

36 Joachym was of fyue and twenti yeer, whanne he bigan to regne, and he regnede eleuene yeer in Jerusalem; the name of his modir was Zebida, douyter of Phadaia of Ruma.

37 And he dide yuel bifor the Lord, bi alle thingis which hise fadris hadden do.

CAP 24

1 In the daies of hym Nabugodonosor, kyng of Babiloyne, stiede, and Joachym was maad seruaunt to hym by thre yeeris; and eft Joachym rebellide ayens hym.

2 And the Lord sente to hym theuys of Caldeis, and theuys of Sirie, and theuys of Moab, and theuys of the sones of Amon; and he sente hem 'in to Juda, that he schulde destrie it, bi the word of the Lord, which he spak bi hise seruauntis prophetis.

3 Forsothe this was doon bi the word of the Lord ayens Juda, that he schulde do awei it bifor him silf, for the synnes of Manasses, and alle thingis whiche he dide,

4 and for the giltles blood which he sched out; and he fillide Jerusalem with the blood of innocentis; and for this thing the Lord nolde do mercy.

5 Forsothe the residue of wordis of Joachim, and alle thingis whiche he dide, whether these ben not writun in the book of wordis of daies of the kyngis of Juda?

6 And Joachym slept with hise fadris, and Joakyn, his sone, regnyde for him.

7 And the kyng of Egipt addide no more to go out of hys lond; for the kyng of Babiloyne hadde take alle thingis that weren the kyngis of Egipt, fro the strond of Egipt 'til to the flood Eufrates.

8 Joakyn was of eiytene yeer, whanne he bigan to regne, and he regnyde thre monethis in Jerusalem; the name of his modir was Nahesta, douytir of Helnathan of Jerusalem.

9 And he dide yuel bifor the Lord, bi alle thingis whiche hise fadir hadde do.

10 In that tyme the seruauntis of Nabugodonosor, kyng of Babiloyne, stieden 'in to Jerusalem, and the citee was cumpassid with bisegyngis.

11 And Nabugodonosor, kyng of Babiloyne, cam to the citee with hise seruauntis, that he schulde fiyte ayens it.

12 And Joakyn, kyng of Juda, yede out to the king of Babiloyne, he, and his modir, and hise seruauntis, and hise princis, and hise chaumburleyns; and the king of Babiloyne resseyuede him, in the eiythe yeer of 'his rewme.

13 And he brouyte forth fro thens alle the tresours of the 'hous of the Lord, and the tresours of the kingis hous; and he beet togider alle the goldun vessels, whiche Salomon, king of Israel, hadde maad in the temple of the Lord, bi the 'word of the Lord.

14 And he translatide al Jerusalem, and alle the princis, and alle the strong men of the oost, ten thousynde, in to caitiftee, and ech crafti man, and goldsmyyt; and no thing was left, outakun the pore puplis of the lond.

15 Also he translatide Joakyn in to Babiloyne, and the moder of the king, 'the wyues of the king, and the chaumburleyns of the king; and he ledde the iugis of the lond in to caitifte fro Jerusalem in to Babiloyne;

16 and alle stronge men, seuene thousynde; and crafti men and goldsmyythis, a thousynde; alle stronge men and werriouris; and the king of Babiloyne ledde hem prisoners in to Babiloyne.

17 And he ordeynede Mathanye, the brother of his fadir, for hym; and puttide to hym the name Sedechie.

18 Sedechie hadde the oon and twentithe yeer of age, whanne he bigan to regne, and he regnyde eleuene yeer in Jerusalem; the name of his modir was Amychal, douyter of Jeremye of Lobna.

19 And he dide yuel bifor the Lord, bi alle thingis which Joachym hadde do.

20 For the Lord was wrooth ayens Jerusalem, and ayens Juda, til he caste hem awey fro his face; and Sedechie yede awei fro the king of Babiloyne.

CAP 25

1 Forsothe it was don in the nynthe yeer of his rewme, in the tenthe moneth, in the tenthe dai of the moneth, Nabugodonosor, kyng of Babiloyne, cam, he, and al his oost, in to Jerusalem; and thei cumpassiden it, and bildiden 'stronge thingis in the cumpass therof.

2 And the citee was closid, and cumpassid, 'til to the eleuenthe yeer of king Sedechie,

3 in the nynthe day of the monethe; and hungur 'hadde maistrie in the citee, and 'breed was not to the puple of the lond.

4 And the citee was brokun, and alle men werriours fledden in the niyt bi the weie of the yate, which is bitwixe the double wal, to the gardyn of the kyng; sotheli Caldeis bisegiden the citee 'bi cumpas. Therfor Sedechie fledde bi the weie that ledith to the feeldi placis of the wildirnesse;

5 and the oost of Caldeis pursuede the king, and it took him in the pleyn of Jerico; and alle the werriours, that weren with him, weren scaterid, and leften him.

6 Therfor thei ledden the king takun to the king of Babiloyne, in to Reblatha, which spak dom with him, 'that is, with Sedechie.

7 Sotheli he killide the sones of Sedechie bifor him, and puttide out his iyen, and boond him with chaynes, and ledde him in to Babiloyne.

8 In the fifthe monethe, in the seuenthe dai of the monethe, thilke is the nyntenthe yeer of the king of Babiloyne, Nabuzardan, prince of the oost, seruaunt of the king of Babiloyne, cam in to Jerusalem;

9 and he brente the hows of the Lord, and the hows of the king, and the housis of Jerusalem, and he brente bi fier ech hows;

10 and al the oost of Caldeis, that was with the prince of knyytis, distriede the wallis of Jerusalem 'in cumpas.

11 Forsothe Nabuzardan, prince of the chyyualrie, translatide the tother part of the puple, that dwellide in the citee, and the fleeris, that hadden fled ouer to the king of Babiloyne, and the residue comyn puple;

12 and he lefte of the pore men of the lond vyntilieris, and erthe tilieris.

13 Sotheli Caldeis braken the brasun pilers, that weren in the temple, and the foundementis, and the see of bras, that was in the hous of the Lord; and thei translatiden al the metal in to Babiloyne.

14 And thei token the pottis of bras, and trullis, and fleisch hokis, and cuppis, and morteris, and alle brasun vessels, in whiche thei mynystriden;

15 also and censeris, and violis. The prince of the chyualrie took tho that weren of gold, and tho that weren of siluer,

16 that is, twei pileris, o see, and the foundementis, whiche king Salomon hadde maad 'in to the temple of the Lord; and no weiyte was of metal of alle the vessels.

17 O piler hadde eiyten cubitis of hiyte, and a brasun pomel on it of the heiyte of thre cubitis, and a werk lijk a net, and pomgarnadis on the pomel of the piler, alle thingis of bras; and the secounde piler hadde lijk ournyng.

18 Also the prince of the chyualrie took Saraie, the firste pre-est, and Sophony, the secunde prest,

19 and thre porteris, and oon onest seruaunt of the citee, that was a souereyn ouer men werriours, and fyue men 'of hem that stoden bifor the king, whiche he foond in the citee; and he took Sopher, the prince of the oost, that preuide yonge knyytis, 'ether men able to batel, of the puple of the lond, and sixe men of the comyns, that weren foundyn in the citee;

20 whiche Nabuzardan, prince of the chyualrie, took, and ledde to the king of Babiloyne, in to Reblatha.

21 And the kyng of Babiloyne smoot hem, and killide hem in Reblatha, in the lond of Emath; and Juda was translatid fro his lond.

22 Sotheli he made souereyn Godolie, sone of Aicham, sone of Saphan, to the puple that was left in the lond of Juda; which puple Nabugodonosor, king of Babiloyne, hadde left.

23 And whanne alle the duykis of knyytis hadde herd these thingis, thei, and the men that weren with hem, that is, that the king of Babiloyne hadde ordeyned Godolie, thei camen 'to Godolie, in Maspha, Ismael, sone of Nathanye, and Johannan, sone of Charee, and Saraie, sone of Thenameth of Nechophat, and Jeconye, sone of Machati, thei, and Machat, and the felowis of hem.

24 And Godolie swoor to hem, and to the felowis of hem, and seide, Nyle ye drede to serue the Caldeis; dwelle ye in the lond, and serue ye the king of Babiloyne, and it schal be wel to you.

25 Forsothe it was don in the seuenthe monethe, 'that is, sithen Godolie was maad souereyn, Hismael, the sone of Nathanye, sone of Elysama, of the 'kyngis seed, cam, and ten men with hym, and thei smytiden Godolie, which diede; but also thei smytiden Jewis and Caldeis, that weren with hym in Maspha.

26 And al the puple roos fro litil 'til to greet, and the prynces of knyytis, and camen in to Egipt, and dredden Caldeis.

27 Therfor it was doon in the seuenthe and threttithe yeer of transmigracioun, 'ether passyng ouer, of Joakyn, kyng of Juda, in the tweluethe monethe, in the seuene and twentithe dai of the monethe, Euylmeradach, kyng of Babiloyne, in the yeer in which he bigan to regne, reiside the heed of Joakyn, kyng of Juda,

28 fro prisoun, and spak to hym benygneli; and he settide the trone of Joakyn aboue the trone of kyngis, that weren with hym in Babilonye.

29 And he chaungide 'hise clothis, whiche he hadde in prisoun; and he eet breed euer in the siyt of Euylmeradach, in alle the daies of his lijf.

30 Also Euylmeradach ordeynede sustenaunce 'to hym with out ceessyng; which sustenaunce also was youun of the kyng to hym bi alle daies, and in alle the daies of his lijf.

1 PARALIPOMENON

CAP 1

1 Adam gendride Seth; Enos,

2 Chaynan, Malaleel, Jared,

3 Enoch, Matussale, Lameth;

4 Noe gendride Sem, Cham, and Japhet.

5 The sones of Japhat weren Gomer, Magog, Magdai, and Jauan, Tubal, Mosoch, and Tiras.

6 Forsothe the sones of Gomer weren Asceneth, and Riphat, and Thogorma.

7 Sotheli the sones of Jauan weren Helisa, and Tharsis, Cethym, and Dodanym.

8 The sones of Cham weren Chus, and Mesraym, Phuth, and Chanaan.

9 Sotheli the sones of Chus weren Saba, and Euila, Sabatha, and Regma, and Sabathaca. Forsothe the sones of Regma weren Saba, and Dadan.

10 Sotheli Chus gendride Nemroth; this Nemroth bigan to be myyti in erthe.

11 Forsothe Mesraym gendride Ludym, and Ananyn, and Labaym,

12 and Neptoym, and Phetrusym, and Casluym, of whiche the Philisteis and Capthureis yeden out.

13 Sotheli Chanaan gendride Sidon his first gendrid sone,

14 and Ethei, and Jebusei, and Ammorrei, and Gergesei,

15 and Euei, and Arachei, and Synei,

16 and Aradye, and Samathei, and Emathei.

17 The sones of Sem weren Elam, and Assur, and Arphaxat, and Luth, and Aram. Forsothe the sones of Aram weren Hus, and Hul, and Gothor, and Mosoch.

18 Forsothe Arphaxat gendride Sale; which hym silf gendride Heber.

19 Sotheli to Heber weren borun twei sones; name of oon was Phaleg, for the lond was departid in hise daies; and the name of his brother was Jectan.

20 Forsothe Jectan gendride Elmodad, and Salech, and Aselmod,

21 and Jare, and Adoram, and Vzal,

22 and Deda, Hebal, and Ameth, and Abymael,

23 and Saba, also and Ophir, and Euila, and Jobab; alle these weren the sones of Jectan.

24 Sem, Arphaxat, Sale,

25 Heber, Phalech, Ragau,

26 Seruth, Nachor, Thare, Abram;

27 forsothe this is Abraham.

28 The sones of Abraham weren Isaac and Ismael.

29 And these the generaciouns of hem; the firste gendrid of Ismael Nabioth, and Cedar, and Abdahel, and Mapsam,

30 and Masma, and Duma, and Massa, Adad, and Themar, Jahur, Naphis, Cedma;

31 these ben the sones of Ismael.

32 Forsothe the sones of Cethure, secoundarie wijf of Abraham, whiche sche gendride, weren Zamram, Jersan, Madan, Madian, Jelboe, Sue. Sotheli the sones of Jersan weren Saba, and Dadan. Forsothe the sones of Dadan weren Assurym, and Latusym, and Laomym.

33 Sotheli the sones of Madian weren Epha, Ethei, and Enoch, and Abdia, and Heldaa. Alle these weren the sones of Cethure.

34 Forsothe Abraham gendride Isaac; whose sones weren Esau and Israel.

35 The sones of Esau weren Eliphat, Rahuel, Semyaus, and Elam, and Chore.

36 The sones of Eliphath weren Theman, Omer, Sephi, Gethem, Genez, Cenez, Thanna, Amalech.

37 The sones of Rahuel weren Naab, Gazara, Samma, Masa.

38 The sones of Seir weren Lothan, Sobal, Sebeon, Ana, Dison, Eser, Disan.

39 The sones of Lothan weren Horry, Huma; sotheli the sistir of Lothan was Thanna.

40 The sones of Sobal weren Alian, and Manaath, and Ebal, and Sephi, and Onam. The sones of Sebeon weren Ana, and Anna. The sone of Ana was Dison.

41 The sones of Dison weren Amaram, and Hesabam, and Lecram, and Caram.

42 The sones of Eser weren Balaam, and Jaban, and Jesan. The sones of Disan weren Hus and Aram.

43 These ben the kyngis that regneden in the lond of Edom, bifor that a kyng was on the sones of Israel. Bale, the sone of Beor; and the name of his citee was Danaba.

44 Sotheli Bale was deed; and Jobab, sone of Zare of Basra, regnyde for hym.

45 And whanne Jobab was deed, Husam of the lond of The-mayns regnede for hym.

46 And Husam diede; and Adad, sone of Badad, that smoot Madian in the lond of Moab, regnyde for hym; and the name of the citee of 'hym, that is, of Adad, was Abyud.

47 And whanne Adad was deed, Semela of Maserecha, regnede for hym.

48 But also Semela was deed, and Saul of Robooth, which is set bisidis the ryuer, regnyde for hym.

49 Also whanne Saul was deed, Balanam, the sone of Acha-bor, regnyde for him.

50 But also he was deed, and Adad, the name of whos citee was Phou, regnede for hym; and his wijf was clepid Methe-sael, the douyter of Mathred, douyter of Mezaab.

51 Forsothe whanne Adad was deed, dukis bigunnen to be in Edom for kyngis; duyk Thanna, duyk Alia, duyk Jetheth,

52 duyk Olibama, duyk Ela, duyk Phynon,

53 duik Ceneth, duyk Theman, duyk Mabsar,

54 duyk Magdiel, duyk Iram. These weren the duykis of Edom.

CAP 2

1 Forsothe the sones of Israel weren Ruben, Symeon, Leuy, Juda, Isachar, and Zabulon,

2 Dan, Joseph, Beniamyn, Neptalym, Gad, Aser.

3 The sones of Juda weren Her, Onam, Sela; these thre weren borun to hym of Sue, a douyter of Canaan. Sotheli Her, the first gendrid sone of Juda, was yuel bifor the Lord, and he killide hym.

4 Forsothe Thamar, wijf of the sone of Judas, childide to hym Phares, and Zaram; therfor alle the sones of Judas weren fyue.

5 Sotheli the sones of Phares weren Esrom, and Chamul.

6 And the sones of Zare weren Zamry, and Ethen, and Eman, and Calchab, and Dardan; fyue togidere.

7 The sone of Charmy was Achar, that disturblide Israel, and synnede in the theft of thing halewid to the Lord.

8 The sone of Ethan was Azarie.

9 Sotheli the sones of Esrom, that weren borun to hym, weren Jeramael, and Aram, and Calubi.

10 Forsothe Aram gendryde Amynadab. Sotheli Amynadab gendride Naason, the prince of the sones of Juda.

11 And Naason gendride Salmon; of which Salmon Booz was borun.

12 Sotheli Booz gendride Obeth; which hym silf gendride Ysay.

13 Forsothe Ysai gendride the firste gendride sone, Elyab, the secounde, Amynadab; the thridde, Samaa;

14 the fourthe, Nathanael;

15 the fyuethe, Sadai; the sixte, Asom;

16 the seuenthe, Dauyd; whose sistris weren Saruya, and Abigail. The sones of Saruye weren thre, Abisai, Joab, and Asahel.

17 Forsothe Abigail childide Amasa, whos fadir was Gether Hismaelite.

18 Sotheli Caleph, sone of Esrom, took a wijf, Azuba bi name, of whom he gendride Jerioth; and hise sones weren Jesar, and Sobab, and Ardon.

19 And whanne Azuba was deed, Caleph took a wijf Effrata, whiche childide Hur to hym.

20 Forsothe Hur gendride Hury; Hury gendride Beseleel.

21 After these thingis Esrom entride to the douytir of Machir, fadir of Galaad, and he took hir, whanne he was of sixti yeer; and sche childide Segub to hym.

22 But also Segub gendride Jair; and he hadde in possessioun thre and twenti citees in the lond of Galaad;

23 and he took Gessur, and Aran, the citees of Jair, and Cha-nath, and the townes therof of seuenti citees. Alle these weren the sones of Machir, fadir of Galaad.

24 Sotheli whanne Esrom was deed, Caleph entride in to Effrata. And Esrom hadde a wijf Abia, which childide to hym Assir, fadir of Thecue.

25 Forsothe sones weren borun of Jezrameel, the firste gend-rid of Esrom; Ram, the first gendrid of hym, and Aran, and Ason, and Achia.

26 Also Jezrameel weddide anothir wijf, Athara bi name, that was the modir of Onam.

27 But and the sones of Ram, the firste gendrid of Jezrameel, weren Mohas, and Jamyn, and Achaz.

28 Forsothe Onam gendride sones, Semey, and Juda. Sotheli the sones of Semei weren Nadab, and Abisur;

29 forsothe the name of the wijf of Abisur was Abigail, that childide to hym Haaobban, and Molid.

30 Sotheli the sones of Nadab weren Saled and Apphaym; forsothe Saled diede without children.

31 Sotheli the sone of Apphaym was Jesi, which Jesi gend-ride Sesan; sotheli Sesan gendride Oholi.

32 Forsothe the sones of Jada, brother of Semei, weren Jether and Jonathan; but Jether diede with out sones; treuli Jonathan gendride Phalech,

33 and Ziza. These ben the sones of Jerameel.

34 Forsothe Sesan hadde not sones, but douytris, and a seru-aunt of Egipt, Jeraa bi name;

35 and he yaf his douyter to wijf to Jeraa, whiche childide Ethei to hym.

36 Forsothe Ethei gendride Nathan, and Nathan gendride Zadab.

37 Also Zadab gendride Ophial, and Ophial gendride Obed.

38 Obed gendride Yeu, Yeu gendride Azarie,

39 Azarie gendride Helles, Helles gendride Elasa,

40 Elasa gendride Sesamoy, Sesamoy gendride Sellum,

41 Sellum gendride Jecamya, Jecamia gendride Elisama.

42 Forsothe the sones of Caleph, brothir of Jerameel, weren Mosa, the firste gendrid sone of hym; thilke is the fadir of Ziph; and the sones of Maresa, the fadir of Hebron.

43 Certis the sones of Ebron weren Chore, and Raphu, Recem, and Samma.

44 Forsothe Samma gendride Raam, the fadir of Jerechaam; and Recem gendride Semei.

45 The sone of Semei was Maon; and Maon was the fadir of Bethsur.

46 Sotheli Epha, the secundarie wijf of Caleph, childide Aram, and Musa, and Theser; forsothe Aram gendride Jezen.

47 The sones of Jadai weren Regon, and Jethon, and Zesum, Phalez, and Epha, and Saaph.

48 Matha, the secoundarie wijf of Caleph, childide Zaber, and Tharana.

49 Forsothe Saaph, the fadir of Madmenas, gendride Sue, the fadir of Magbena, and the fader of Gabaa; sotheli the douyter of Caleph was Axa.

50 These weren the sones of Caleph. The sones of Hur, the firste gendrid sone of Effrata, weren Sobal, the fader of Cariathiarim;

51 Salma, the fader of Bethleem; Ariph, the fader of Bethgader.

52 Sotheli the sones of Sobal, fader of Cariatiarim, that siy the myddil of restingis,

53 and was of the kynrede of Caryathiarym, weren Jethrey, and Aphutei, and Samathei, and Maserathei. Of these weren borun Sarytis, and Eschaolitis.

54 The sones of Salma, fadir of Bethleem, and of Netophati, weren the corouns of the hows of Joab, and the half of restyng of Sarai.

55 And the kynredis of scryuens, dwellynge in Jabes, syngynge, and sownynge, and dwellynge in tabernaclis. These ben Cyneis, that camen of the heete of the fadir of the hows of Rechab.

CAP 3

1 Forsothe Dauid hadde these sones, that weren borun to hym in Ebron; the firste gendrid sone, Amon, of Achynoem of Jezrael; the secounde sone, Danyel, of Abigail of Carmele;

2 the thridde, Absolon, the sone of Maacha, douyter of Tolomei, kyng of Gessuri; the fourthe, Adonye, sone of Agith;

3 the fyuethe, Saphacie, of Abithal; the sixte, Jethraan, of Egla his wijf.

4 Therfor sixe sones weren borun to hym in Ebron, where he regnede seuene yeer and sixe monethis; sotheli he regnyde thre and thritti yeer in Jerusalem.

5 Forsothe foure sones, Sama, and Sobab, and Nathan, and Salomon, weren borun of Bersabee, the douyter of Amyhel, to hym in Jerusalem;

6 also Jabaar, and Elisama, and Eliphalech,

7 and Noge, and Napheth, and Japhie,

8 also and Elisama, and Eliade, and Eliphalech, nyne.

9 Alle these weren the sones of David, with out the sones of secoundarie wyues; and thei hadden a sistir, Thamar.

10 Sotheli the sone of Salomon was Roboam, whos sone Abia gendride Asa;

11 and Josephat, the fadir of Joram, was borun of this Asa; which Joram gendride Ocozie, of whom Joas was borun.

12 And Amasie, the sone of this Joas, gendride Azarie; sotheli Azarie, the sone of Joathan,

13 gendride Achaz, the fadir of Ezechie; of whom Manasses was borun.

14 But also Manasses gendride Amon, the fadir of Josias.

15 Forsothe the sones of Josias weren, the firste gendrid sone, Johannan; the secounde, Joachym; the thridde, Sedechie; the fourthe, Sellum.

16 Of Joachym was borun Jechonye, and Sedechie.

17 The sones of Jechonye weren Asir,

18 Salatiel, Melchiram, Phadaie, Sennaser, and Jech, Semma, Sama, and Nadabia.

19 Of Phadaie weren borun Zorobabel, and Semey. Zorobabel gendryde Mosolla, Ananye, and Salomyth, the sister of hem; and Asaba,

20 and Ochol, and Barachie, and Asadaie, and Josabesed, fyue.

21 Forsothe the sone of Ananye was Falcias, the fadir of Jeseie, whose sone was Raphaie. And the sone of him was Arnan, of whom was borun Abdia, whos sone was Sechema.

22 The sone of Sechema was Semeia, whose sones weren Archus, and Gegal, and Baaria, and Naaria, and Saphat, and Sela; sixe in noumbre.

23 The sones of Naaria weren thre, Helionai, and Ezechie, and Zichram.

24 The sones of Helionai weren seuene, Odyna, and Eliasub, and Pheleia, and Accub, and Johannan, and Dalaia, and Anani.

CAP 4

1 The sones of Juda weren Phares, and Esrom, and Carmy, and Hur, and Sobal.

2 Forsothe Reaia, the sone of Sobal, gendride Geth; of whom weren borun Achymai, and Laed. These weren the kynredis of Sarathi.

3 And this is the generacioun of Ethan; Jesrael, Jezema, and Jedebos; and the name of the sistir of hem was Asaelphumy.

4 Sotheli Phunyel was the fadir of Gedor, and Ezer was the fadir of Osa; these ben the sones of Hur, the firste gendrid sone of Effrata, the fadir of Bethleem.

5 Sotheli Assur, the fadir of Thecue, hadde twei wyues, Haala, and Naara;

6 forsothe Naara childide to hym Oozam, and Epher, and Theman, and Aschari; these ben the sones of Naara.

7 Forsothe the sones of Haala weren Sereth, Isaar, and Ethan.

8 Forsothe Chus gendride Anob, and Sobala, and the kynredis of Arab, sone of Arym.

9 Forsothe Jabes was noble byfor alle hise britheren; and his modir clepide his name Jabes, and seide, For Y childide hym in sorewe.

10 Sotheli Jabes clepide inwardli God of Israel, and seide, Yf thou blessynge schal blesse me, and schalt alarge my termes, and if thin hond schal be with me, and thou schalt make me to be not oppressid of malice. And God yaf to hym that thing, that he preiede.

11 Forsothe Caleph, the brother of Sua, gendride Machir, that was the fadir of Eston;

12 sotheli Eston gendride Beth, Rapha, and Phese, and Thena, the fadir of the citee Naas. These ben the sones of Recha.

13 Forsothe the sones of Cenez weren Othonyel, and Saraia.

14 Sotheli the sones of Othonyel weren Athiath, and Maonaththa, that gendride Opham. Forsothe Saraia gendride Joab, the fadir of the valey of crafti men; for there weren crafti men.

15 Sotheli the sones of Caleph, sone of Jephone, weren Hyn, and Helam, and Nahemi. And the sones of Helam weren Cenez.

16 Also the sones of Jaleel weren Zeph, and Zipha, Tiria, and Asrael.

17 And the sones of Esra weren Chether, and Merid, and Epher, and Jalon; and he gendride Marie, and Semmai, and Jesba, the fadir of Eschamo.

18 Also Judaia, hys wijf, childide Jared, the fadir of Gedor; and Heber, the fadir of Zocho; and Hieutihel, the fadir of Janon. Sotheli these weren the sones of Bethie, the douyter of Pharao, whom Mered took to wijf.

19 And the sones of the wijf of Odoie, sister of Nathan, fadir of Ceila, weren Garmy, and Escamo, that was of Machati.

20 Also the sones of Symeon weren Amon and Rena; the sone of Anam was Chilon; and the sones of Gesi weren Zoeth, and Benzoeth.

21 The sones of Cela, sone of Juda, weren Her, the fadir of Lecha, and Laada, the fadir of Marasa; and these weren the kynredis of the hows of men worchynge biys in the hows of an ooth,

22 and which made the sunne to stonde, and the men of leesyng, sikir, and goynge, that weren princes in Moab, and that turneden ayen in to Bethleem; forsothe these ben elde wordis.

23 These ben potteris dwellinge in plauntyngis, and in heggis, anentis kyngis in her werkis; and thei dwelliden there.

24 The sones of Symeon weren Namyhel, and Jamyn, Jarib, Zara, Saul.

25 Sellum was his sone; Mapsan was his sone; Masma was his sone.

26 The sones of Masma; Amuel, his sone; and Zaccur, his sone; Semey, his sone.

27 The sones of Semey weren sixtene, and sixe douytris; sotheli hise britheren hadden not many sones, and al the kynrede myyte not be euene to the summe of the sones of Juda.

28 Forsothe thei dwelliden in Bersabee, and in Molada, and in Asarsual,

29 and in Balaa, and in Aason, and in Tholat,

30 and in Bathuel, and in Horma,

31 and in Sicheloch, and in Betmarchaboth, and in Archasusym, and in Bethbaray, and in Saarym; these weren the citees of hem, 'til to the kyng Dauid.

32 Also the townes of hem weren Ethan, and Aen, and Remmon, and Techen, and Asan; fyue citees.

33 And alle the vilagis of hem bi the cumpas of these citees, 'til to Baal; this is the dwellyng of hem, and the departyng of seetis.

34 Also Mosobaly, and Jemlech, and Josa, the sone of Amasie,

35 and Johel, and Jehu, the sone of Josabie, and the sones of Saraie, the sones of Asiel,

36 and Helioneai, and Jacoba, and Sucua, and Asaia, and Adihel, and Hisemeel, and Banaia;

37 and Ziza, the sone of Sephei, the sone of Allon, sone of Abdaia, sone of Semry, sone of Samaia.

38 These ben princis nemyd in her kynredis, and ben multiplied greetli in the hows of her alies.

39 And thei yeden forth to entre in to Gador, 'til to the eest of the valei, and to seke pasturis to her scheep.

40 And thei fonden pasturis ful plenteuouse, and ful goode, and a ful large lond, and restful, and plenteuouse, wherynne men of the generacioun of Cham hadden dwellid bifore.

41 Therfor these men, whiche we discryueden bifore 'bi name, camen in the daies of Ezechie, kyng of Juda; and smytiden the tabernaclis of hem, and the dwelleris that weren foundun there; and thei 'diden awei hem 'til in to present dai; and thei dwelliden for hem, for thei founden there ful plenteuouse pasturis.

42 Also fyue hundrid men of the sones of Symeon yeden in to the hil of Seir, and thei hadden princes Faltias, and Narias, and Raphaias, and Oziel, the sones of Jesi;

43 and thei smytiden the relifs of Amalechites, that myyten ascape; and thei dwelliden there for hem 'til to this day.

CAP 5

1 Also the sones of Ruben, the firste gendrid sone of Israel; for he was the first gendrid sone of Israel, but whanne he hadde defoulid the bed of his fadir, the dignitye of his firste gendryng was youun to the sones of Joseph, the sone of Israel; and Ruben was not arettid in to the firste gendrid sone.

2 Forsothe Judas, that was the strongeste among hise britheren, prynces weren gaderid of his generacioun; forsothe the 'riyt of firste gendryng was arettid to Joseph.

3 Therfor the sones of Ruben, the firste gendrid sone of Israel, weren Enoch, and Phallu, Esrom, and Charmy.

4 The sones of Johel weren Samaie; his sone, Gog; his sone, Semey;

5 his sone, Mycha; his sone, Rema; his sone, Baal;

6 his sone, Bera; whom Theglatphalassar, kyng of Assyriens, ledde prisoner; and he was prince in the lynage of Ruben.

7 Sotheli hise britheren, and al the kynrede, whanne thei weren noumbrid bi her meynees, hadden princes Jehiel, and Zacharie.

8 Forsothe Bala, the sone of Achaz, sone of Sama, sone of Johel, he dwellide in Aroer til to Nebo and Beelmoon;

9 and he dwellide ayens the eest coost, til to the ende of deseert, 'and to the flood Eufrates. And he hadde in possessioun myche noumbre of beestis in the lond of Galaad.

10 Forsothe in the daies of Saul the sones of Ruben fouyten ayens Agarenus, and killide hem; and dwelliden for hem in the tabernaclis of hem, in al the coost that biholdith to the eest of Galaad.

11 Sotheli the sones of Gad euene ayens hem dwelliden in the lond of Basan til to Selca;

12 Johel was in the bygynnyng, and Saphan was the secounde; also Janahi and Saphan weren in Basan.

13 Also her britheren bi the housis of her kynredis, Mychael, and Mosollam, and Sebe, and Jore, and Jachan, and Zie, and Heber, seuene.

14 These weren the sones of Abiahel, the sone of Vry, sone of Jaro, sone of Galaad, sone of Mychael, sone of Esesi, sone of Jeddo, sone of Buz.

15 Also the britheren of the sone of Abdiel, sone of Gumy, was prince of the hows in hise meynees.

16 And thei dwelliden in Galaad, and in Basan, and in the townes therof, in alle the subarbis of Arnon, til to the endis.

17 Alle these weren noumbrid in the daies of Joathan, kyng of Juda, and in the daies of Jeroboam, kyng of Israel.

18 The sones of Ruben, and of Gad, and of half the lynage of Manasses, weren men werriours, berynge scheeldis and swerdis, and beendynge bouwe, and tauyt to batels, foure and fourti thousynde seuene hundrid and sixti,

19 and thei yeden forth to batel, and fouyten ayens Agarenus. Forsothe Ethureis, and Napheis,

20 and Nadab, yauen help to hem; and Agarenus, and alle men that weren with hem, weren bitakun in to the hondis of Ruben, and Gad, and Manasses; for thei clepiden inwardli the

Lord, while thei fouyten, and the Lord herde hem, for thei 'hadden bileuyd in to him.

21 And thei token alle thingis whiche Agarenus hadden in possessioun, fifti thousynde of camels, and twei hundrid and fifty thousynde of scheep, twei thousynde of assis, and an hundrid thousynde persoones of men;

22 for many men weren woundid and felden doun; for it was the batel of the Lord. And thei dwelliden for Agarenus til to the conquest.

23 Also the sones of the half lynage of Manasses hadden in possessioun the lond, fro the endis of Basan til to Baal Hermon, and Sanyr, and the hil of Hermon; for it was a greet noumbre.

24 And these weren the princes of the hows of her kynrede; Epher, and Jesi, and Heliel, and Esryel, and Jeremye, and Odoie, and Jedihel, strongeste men and myyti, and nemyd duykis in her meynees.

25 Forsothe thei forsoken the God of her fadris, and diden fornycacioun after the goddis of puplis of the lond, whiche the Lord took awei bifor hem.

26 And the Lord God of Israel reiside the spirit of Phul, kyng of Assiriens, and the spirit of Theglatphalasser, kyng of Assur; and he translatide Ruben, and Gad, and the half lynage of Manasses, and brouyte hem in to Ale, and Abor, and Aram, and in to the ryuer of Gozam, til to this dai.

CAP 6

1 The sones of Leuy weren Gerson, Caath, and Merary.

2 The sones of Chaath weren Amram, Isaar, Ebron, and Oziel.

3 The sones of Amram weren Aaron, Moyses, and Marie. The sones of Aaron weren Nadab,

4 and Abyu, Eleazar, and Ythamar. Eleazar gendride Phynees, and Phynees gendride Abisue,

5 Abisue gendride Bocci, and Bocci gendride Ozi,

6 Ozi gendride Zaraie, and Zaraie gendride Meraioth.

7 Forsothe Meraioth gendride Amarie, Amarie gendride Achitob,

8 Achitob gendride Sadoch, Sadoch gendride Achymaas, Achymaas gendride Azarie,

9 Azarie gendride Johannam,

10 Johannam gendride Azarie; he it is that was set in pre-esthod, in the hows which Salomon bildide in Jerusalem.

11 Forsothe Azarie gendride Amarye, and Amarie gendride Achitob,

12 Achitob gendride Sadoch, Sadoch gendride Sellum,

13 Sellum gendride Helchie,

14 Helchie gendride Azarie, Azarie gendride Saraie, Saraie gendride Josedech.

15 Forsothe Josedech yede out, whanne the Lord translatide Juda and Jerusalem bi the hondis of Nabugodonosor kyng.

16 Therfor the sones of Leuy weren Gerson, Caath, and Merary.

17 And these weren the names of the sones of Gerson; Lobeni, and Semei.

18 The sones of Caath weren Amram, and Isaar, and Ebron, and Oziel.

19 The sones of Merari weren Moli, and Musi. Sotheli these weren the kynredis of Leuy bi the meynees of hem;

20 Gerson; Lobony, his sone; Jaath, his sone; Zama, his sone;

21 Joaith, his sone; Addo, his sone; Zara, his sone; Jethrai, his sone.

22 The sones of Caath; Amynadab, his sone; Chore, his sone;

23 Azyra, his sone; Helcana, his sone; Abiasaph, his sone;

24 Aser, his sone; Caath, his sone; Vriel, his sone; Azias, his sone; Saul, his sone.

25 The sones of Helchana weren Amasay, and Achymoth, and Helcana.

26 The sones of Helcana; Saphay, his sone;

27 Naath, his sone; Heliab, his sone; Heroam, his sone; Helcana, his sone.

28 The sones of Samuel; the firste gendrid Nasen, and Abia.

29 Sotheli the sones of Merari; Moli, his sone; Lobeny, his sone; Semey, his sone;

30 Oza, his sone; Sama, his sone; Aggias, his sone; Azaya, his sone;

31 These it ben whiche Dauid ordeynede on the syngeris of the hows of the Lord, sithen the arke of the Lord was set;

32 and thei mynystriden bifor the tabernacle of witnessyng, and sungun, til Salomon bildide the hows of the Lord in Jerusalem; forsothe thei stoden bi her ordre in seruyce.

33 Sotheli thes it ben that stoden nyy with her sones. Of the sones of Caath; Heman the chauntor, the sone of Joel, sone of Samuel,

34 sone of Helcana, sone of Joroam, sone of Heliel,

35 sone of Thou, sone of Suph,

36 sone of Helcana, sone of Mabath, sone of Amasi, sone of Helcana, sone of Joel, sone of Azarie, sone of Sophonye, sone of Caath,

37 sone of Asyr, sone of Abiasaph,

38 sone of Chore, sone of Isaar, sone of Caath, sone of Leuy, sone of Israel.

39 And hise britheren; Asaph, that stood at the riythalf of hym, Asaph, the sone of Barachie,

40 sone of Samaa, sone of Mychael, sone of Basye, sone of Melchie, sone of Atthay,

41 sone of Zara, sone of Adala,

42 sone of Edan, sone of Zama, sone of Semey,

43 sone of Geth, sone of Gerson, sone of Leuy.

44 Forsothe the sones of Merary, the britheren of hem, weren at the leftside; Ethan, the sone of Chusi, sone of Abdi, sone of Moloch, sone of Asabie,

45 sone of Amasie, sone of Helchie,

46 sone of Amasay, sone of Bonny, sone of Soomer,

47 sone of Moli, sone of Musi, sone of Merarie, sone of Leuy.

48 And dekenes, the britheren of hem, that weren ordeyned in to al the seruyce of the tabernacle of the hows of the Lord.

49 Forsothe Aaron and hise sones brenten encense on the auter of brent sacrifices, and on the auter of encense, in to al the werk 'of the hooli of hooli thingis; and that thei schulden preie for Israel, by alle thingis whiche Moises, the seruaunt of God, comaundide.

50 Sotheli these ben the sones of Aaron; Eleazar, his sone; Phynes, his sone;

51 Abisue, his sone; Bocci, his sone; Ogzi, his sone; Zara, his sone; Meraioth, his sone;

52 Amarias, his sone; Achitob, his sone;

53 Sadoch, his sone; Achimaas, his sone.

54 And these weren the dwelling places, bi the townes and coostis of hem, that is, of the sones of Aaron, bi the kynredis of Caathitis; for tho bifelden to hem bi lot.

55 Therfor the children of Israel yauen to hem Ebron in the lond of Juda, and the subarbis therof bi cumpas;

56 sotheli thei yauen the feeldis and townes of the citees to Caleph, sone of Jephone.

57 Forsothe thei yauen citees to the sones of Aaron, Ebron to refuyt; and thei yauen Lobna,

58 with hise subarbis, and Jether, and Escamo, with her subarbis, but also Helon, and Dabir, with her subarbis; also thei yauen Asan,

59 and Bethsames, and the subarbis of tho.

60 Sotheli of the lynage of Beniamyn thei yauen Gabee, and the subarbis therof, and Alamach with hise subarbis, Anathot also with hise subarbis; alle the citees weren threttene with her subarbis, bi the kynredis of hem.

61 Forsothe to the sones of Caath, residues of her kynrede, thei yauen of the half lynage of Manasses ten citees 'in to possessioun.

62 Sotheli to the sones of Gerson bi her kynredis thei yauen fourtene citees in Basan, of the lynage of Ysacar, and of the lynage of Aser, and of the lynage of Neptalym, and of the lynage of Manasses.

63 Forsothe to the sones of Merary by her kynredis thei yauen bi lottis twelue citees, of the lynage of Ruben, of the lynage of Gad, and of the lynage of Zabulon.

64 And the sones of Israel yauen to dekenes citees and subarbis of tho;

65 and thei yauen bi lot, of the sones of the lynage of Juda, and of the lynage of the sones of Symeon, and of the lynage of the sones of Beniamyn, these citees, which the dekenes clepiden bi her names;

66 and of hem that weren of the kynrede of the sones of Caath, and in the termes of hem weren the citees of the lynage of Effraym.

67 And the sones of Israel yauen to hem citees of refuyt; Sichem with hise subarbis in the hil of Effraym, and Gazer with hise subarbis, also Hicmaan with hise subarbis,

68 and Betheron also.

69 Also of the lynage of Dan thei yauen Ebethe, Gebethor, and Heialan, and Helon, with her subarbis, and Gethremon bi the same maner.

70 Forsothe of the half lynage of Manasses thei yauen Aner, and the subarbis therof, Balaam, and the subarbis therof; that is, to hem that weren residue of the kynrede of the sones of Caath.

71 Sotheli to the sones of Gerson thei yauen of the kynrede of half the lynage of Manasses, Gaulon in Basan, and the subarbis therof, and Astoroth with hise subarbis.

72 Of the lynage of Isachar thei yauen Cedes, and the subarbis therof, and Daberith with hise subarbis; also Samoth,

73 and his subarbis, 'and Anem with hise subarbis.

74 Also of the linage of Aser thei yauen Masal with hise subarbis, and Abdon also,

75 and Asach, and the subarbis therof, and Roob with hise subarbis.

76 Sotheli of the lynage of Neptalym thei yauen Cedes in Galilee, and the subarbis therof, Amon with hise subarbis, and Cariathiarym, and subarbis therof.

77 Sotheli to the residue sones of Merary thei yauen of the lynage of Zabulon, Remon, and subarbis therof, and Thabor with hise subarbis.

78 Also biyende Jordan, euene ayens Jerico, ayens the eest of Jordan, thei yauen of the lynage of Ruben, Bosor in the wildirnesse with hise subarbis, and Jasa with hise subarbis,

79 also Cademoth, and hise subarbis, and Myphaat with hise subarbis.

80 Also and of the lynage of Gad thei yauen Ramoth in Galaath, and the subarbis therof, Manaym with hise subarbis,

81 but also Esebon with hise subarbis, and Jezer with hise subarbis.

CAP 7

1 Forsothe the sones of Isachar weren foure; Thola, and Phua, Jasub, and Sameron.

2 The sones of Thola weren Ozi, and Raphaia, and Jerihel, and Jemay, and Jepsen, and Samuel, princis bi the housis of her kynredis. Of the generacioun of Thola, weren noumbrid strongeste men in the daies of Dauid, two and twenti thousynde and sixe hundrid.

3 The sones of Ozi weren Jezraie; of whom weren borun Mychael, and Obadia, and Johel, and Jezray, fyue, alle princes.

4 And with hem weren bi her meynees and puplis, sixe and thretti thousynde strongeste men gird to batel; for thei hadden many wyues and sones.

5 And her britheren by alle the kynredis of Isachar 'moost stronge to fiyte weren noumbrid foure scoore and seuene thousynde.

6 The sones of Beniamyn weren Bale, and Bothor, and Adiel, thre.

7 The sones of Bale weren Esbon, and Ozi, and Oziel, and Jerymoth, and Vray, fyue, princes of meynees, mooste stronge to fiyte; for the noumbre of hem was two and twenti thousynde and foure and thretti.

8 Forsothe the sones of Bochor weren Samara, and Joas, and Eliezer, and Elioenai, and Zamri, and Jerimoth, and Abia, and Anathoth, and Almachan; alle these weren the sones of Bochor.

9 Sotheli the princes of kynredis weren noumbrid bi her meynees twenti thousynde and two hundrid moost stronge men to batels.

10 Forsothe the sones of Ledihel weren Balan; sotheli the sones of Balan weren Jheus, and Beniamyn, and Aoth, and Camana, and Jothan, and Tharsis, and Thasaar.

11 Alle these the sones of Ledihel weren princes of her meynees, seuentene thousynde and two hundrid, strongeste men goynge forth to batel.

12 Also Saphan and Apham weren the sones of Hir; and Basym was the sone of Aser.

13 Forsothe the sones of Neptalym weren Jasiel, and Guny, and Aser, and Sellum; the sones of Bale.

14 Sotheli the sone of Manasses was Esriel; and Sira his secundarie wijf childide Machir, the fadir of Galaad.

15 And Machir took wyues to hise sones Huphyn and Suphyn; and he hadde a sister Maacha bi name; and the name of the secounde sone was Salphaath, and douytris weren borun to Salphaath.

16 And Maacha, the wijf of Machir, childide a sone, and clepide his name Phares; forsothe the name of his brothir was Sares; and hise sones weren Vlam and Recem.

17 Sotheli the sone of Vlam was Baldan. These weren the sones of Galaad, sone of Machir, sone of Manasses;

18 forsothe Regma his sistir childide a feir man, Abiezer, and Mola.

19 Forsothe the sones of Semyda weren Abym, and Sichem, and Liey, and Amany.

20 Sotheli the sones of Effraym weren Suchaba; Bareth, his sone; Caath, his sone; Elda, his sone; and Thaath, his sone; and Zadaba, his sone;

21 and Suthala, his sone; and Ezer, and Elad, his sones. For-sothe men of Geth borun in the lond killiden hem, for thei yeden doun to assaile her possessiouns.

22 Therfor Effraym, the fadir of hem, weilide bi many daies; and hise britheren camen to coumforte hym.

23 And he entride to his wijf, which conseyuede, and childide a sone; and he clepide his name Beria, for he was borun in the yuelis of his hows.

24 Sotheli his douytir was Sara; that bildide Betheron, the lowere and the hiyere, and Ozen, and Sara.

25 Forsothe his sone was Rapha, and Reseph, and Thale;

26 of whom was borun Thaan, that gendride Laodon; and Amyud, the sone of hym, gendride Elysama;

27 of whom was borun Nun; that hadde a sone Josue.

28 Sotheli the possessioun and 'dwellyng place of hem was Bethil with hise villagis, and ayens the eest, Noram; at the west coost, Gazer, and hise villagis, also Sichem with hise villagis, and Aza with hise villagis.

29 Also bisidis the sones of Manasses, Bethsan, and hise townes, Thanach and hise townes, Maggeddo, and hise townes, Dor, and hise townes; the sones of Joseph sone of Israel dwelliden in these townes.

30 The sones of Aser weren Sona, and Jesua, and Isuy, and Baria; and Sara was the sister of hem.

31 Sotheli the sones of Baria weren Heber, and Melchiel; he is the fadir of Barsath.

32 Sotheli Heber gendride Ephiath, and Soomer, and Otham, and Sua, the sister of hem.

33 Forsothe the sones of Jephiath weren Phosech, and Camaal, and Jasoph; these weren the sones of Jephiath.

34 Sotheli the sones of Soomer weren Achi, and Roaga, and Jaba, and Aram.

35 Sotheli the sones of Helem, his brother, weren Supha, and Jema, and Selles, and Amal.

36 The sones of Supha weren Sue, Arnapheth, and Sual, and Bery,

37 and Jamra, and Bosor, and Ador, and Sama, and Salusa, and Jethram, and Beram.

38 The sones of Ether weren Jephone, and Phaspha, and Ara.

39 Sotheli the sones of Ollaa weren Areth, and Aniel, and Resia.

40 Alle these weren the sones of Aser, princes of kynredis, chosun men and strongeste duykis of duykis; forsothe the noumbre, of the age of hem that weren abel to batel, was sixe and twenti thousynde.

CAP 8

1 Forsothe Beniamyn gendride Bale his firste gendrid sone, Asbaal the secounde, Othora the thridde,

2 Naua the fourthe, and Rapha the fyuethe.

3 And the sones of Bale weren Addoar, and Jera, and Abyud, and Abisue,

4 and Noemany, and Acte,

5 but also Gera, and Sophupham, and Vram.

6 These ben the sones of Haoth, princes of kynredis dwellynge in Gabaa, that weren translatid in to Manath.

7 Forsothe Noaman, and Achia, and Jera, 'he translatide hem, and gendride Oza and Abyud;

8 forsothe 'Saarym gendride in the cuntrey of Moab, aftir that he lefte Vrym and Bara, hise wyues;

9 sotheli he gendride of Edes, his wijf, Jodab, and Sebia, and Mosa, and Molchon, also Jebus, and Sechia, and Maryna;

10 tho ben the sones of hym, prynces in her meynees.

11 Forsothe Musyn gendride Achitob, and Elphaal.

12 Sotheli the sones of Elphaal weren Heber, and Musaam, and Samaath; he bildide Ono, and Lod, and hise villagis;

13 forsothe Bara and Sama weren princes of kynredis dwellynge in Hailon; these dryueden awei the dwelleris of Geth;

14 and Haio, and Sesath, and Jerymoth,

15 and Zadabia, and Arod, and Heder,

16 and Mychael, and Jespha helpiden hem 'ayens men of Geth; the sones of Abaria,

17 and Zadabia, and Mosollam, and Ezethi,

18 and Heber, and Jesamary, and Jezlia, and Jobab helpiden 'in this iurney ayens men of Geth. The sones of Elphaal weren Jachym,

19 and Jechri,

20 and Zabdi, and Helioenay, and Selettay,

21 and Henelech, and Adaia, and Barasa, and Samarath; the sones of Semey weren Jesphan,

22 and Heber, and Esiel, and Abdon,

23 and Zechry, and Canaan, and Anany, and Jalam,

24 and Anathotia, and Jephdaia, and Phanuel;

25 the sones of Sesac weren Sampsaray,

26 and Scoria, and Otholia, and Jersia,

27 and Helia, and Zechri, the sones of Jeream.

28 These weren patriarkis and princes of kynredis, that dwelliden in Jerusalem.

29 Forsothe in Gabaon dwelliden Abigabaon, and Maacha the name of his wijf;

30 and his firste gendrid sone Abdon, and Sur, and Cys, and Baal, and Ner, and Nadab,

31 and Geddo, and Haio, and Zacher, and Macelloth.

32 Forsothe Marcelloth gendride Samaa; and thei dwelliden euene ayens her britheren in Jerusalem with her britheren.

33 Forsothe Ner gendride Cys, and Cys gendride Saul; for-sothe Saul gendride Jonathan, and Melchisue, and Abynadab, and Isbaal.

34 Sotheli the sone of Jonathan was Myphibaal; and Myphib-aal gendride Micha.

35 The sones of Micha weren Phiton, and Melech, and Thara, and Ahaz.

36 And Ahaz gendride Joiada; and Joiada gendride Almoth, and Azimoth, and Zamry.

37 Forsothe Zamri gendride Moosa, and Moosa gendride Banaa, whos sone was Raphaia, of whom was gendrid Elesa, that gendride Asel.

38 Sotheli Asel hadde sixe sones bi these names, Esricham, Bochru, Ismael, Saria, Abadia, Aman; alle these weren the sones of Asel.

39 Forsothe the sones of Asa, his brothir, weren Vlam, the firste gendride sone, and Hus, the secounde, and Eliphales, the thridde.

40 And the sones of Vlam weren strongeste men, and been-dynge a bouwe with greet strength, and hauynge many sones, and sones of sones, til to an hundrid and fifti. Alle these weren the sones of Beniamyn.

CAP 9

1 Therfor al Israel was noumbrid, and the summe of hem was writun in the book of kyngis of Israel and of Juda; and thei weren translatid in to Babiloyne for her synne.

2 Sotheli thei that dwelliden first in her citees, and in the pos-sessiouns of Israel, and the preestis, and the dekenes, and Natyneys, dwelliden in Jerusalem.

3 Of the sones of Juda, and of the sones of Beniamyn, also of the sones of Effraym, and of Manasses;

4 Othi, the sone of Amyud, sone of Semry, sone of Omroy, sone of Bonny, of the sones of Phares, the sone of Juda;

5 and of Sylom, Asia, the firste gendrid, and his sones;

6 sotheli of the sones of Zaray, Heuel, and hise britheren; sixe hundrid fourescore and ten.

7 Forsothe of the sones of Beniamyn; Salo, the sone of Mosollam, the sones of Odoia, the sones of Asana,

8 and Jobanya, the sone of Jerobam, and Ela, the sone of Ozi, the sones of Mochozi, and Mosollam, the sone of Saphacie, sone of Rahuel, sone of Jebanye, and the britheren of hem,

9 bi her meynees; nyne hundrid sixe and fifti. Alle these weren princes of her kynredis by the housis of her fadris.

10 Forsothe of the preestis, Joiada, Jozarib, and Jachym;

11 and Azarie, the sone of Helchie, sone of Mosollam, sone of Sadoch, sone of Maraioth, sone of Achitob, was bischop of the hows of the Lord.

12 Forsothe Adaias, sone of Jeroam, sone of Phasor, sone of Melchia, and Masaia, sone of Adihel, sone of Jezra, sone of Mosollam, sone of Mosselamoth, sone of Emyner,

13 also her britheren, prynces bi her meynees, weren a thousynde seuene hundrid and fourescoore, men strongeste in bodili myyt, to make the werk of seruyce in the hows of the Lord.

14 Forsothe of dekenes, Semeya, the sone of Assub, sone of Ezricam, sone of Asebyn, of the sones of Merary;

15 also Balthasar the carpenter, and Galebeth, and Machama, sone of Mycha, sone of Zechri, sone of Asaph,

16 and Obdias, sone of Semey, sone of Calaal, sone of Idithum, and Barachie, the sone of Asa, sone of Helcana, that dwellide in the porchis of Methophati.

17 Sotheli the porteris weren Sellum, and Achub, and Thelmon, and Achyman, and the britheren of hem; Sellum was the prince;

18 til to that tyme thei kepten bi her whilis in the yate of the kyng at the eest, of the sones of Leuy.

19 Sellum forsothe, the sone of Chore, sone of Abiasaph, sone of Chore, with hise britheren, and with the hows of his fadir; these ben the sones of Chore on the werkis of the seruyce, keperis of the porchis of the tabernacle, and the meynees of hem kepten bi whilis the entryng of the castelis of the Lord.

20 Forsothe Phynees, the sone of Eleazar, was the duyk of hem bifor the Lord.

21 Sotheli Zacarie, the sone of Mosollam, was porter of the yate of the tabernacle of witnessyng.

22 Alle these chosun in to porteris bi yatis weren twei hundrid and twelue, and weren discryued in her owne townes, which dekenes Dauid and Samuel, the prophete, ordeyneden in her feith,

23 both hem and the sones of hem in the doris of the hows of the Lord, and in the tabernacle of witnessyng, bi her whiles.

24 Porteris weren bi foure coostis, that is, at the eest, and at the west, and at the north, and at the south.

25 Forsothe her britheren dwelliden in townes, and camen in her sabatis fro tyme til to tyme.

26 Al the noumbre of porteris was bitakun to these foure dekenes, and thei kepten the chaumbris, and the tresours of the hows of the Lord.

27 Also thei dwelliden in her kepyngis bi the cumpas of the temple of the Lord, that whanne tyme were, thei schulden opene the yatis eerli.

28 Men of her kyn weren also on the vessels of seruyce; for the vessels weren borun in at noumbre, and weren borun out of hem.

29 And thei that hadden the vesselis of seyntuarie bitakun to her kepyng, weren souereyns on flour, and wyn, and oile, and encense, and swete smellinge spyceries.

30 Sotheli the sones of preestis maden oynementis of swete smellynge spiceries.

31 And Mathatias dekene, the firste gendrid sone of Sellum of the kynrede of Chore, was the souereyn of alle thingis that weren fried in the friyng panne.

32 Sotheli men of the sones of Caath, the britheren of hem, weren on the looues of settyng forth, that thei schulden make redi euere newe looues bi ech sabat.

33 These ben the princis of chauntouris bi the meynees of Leuytis, that dwelliden in chaumbris, so that thei schulden serue contynueli dai and nyyt in her seruyce.

34 The heedis of Leuitis bi her meynees, the princes, dwelliden in Jerusalem.

35 Forsothe there dwelliden in Gabaon; Jaiel, the fadir of Gabaon, and the name of his wijf Maacha;

36 Abdon, his firste gendrid sone, and Sur, and Cys, and Baal,

37 and Ner, and Nadab, and Gedor, and Ahaio, and Zacharie, and Macelloth; forsothe Macelloth gendride Semmaa;

38 these dwelliden euene ayens her britheren in Jerusalem, with her britheren.

39 Sotheli Ner gendride Cys, and Cys gendride Saul, and Saul gendride Jonathan, and Melchisue, and Abynadab, and Hisbaal.

40 Forsothe the sone of Jonathan was Myribaal, and Myribaal gendride Mycha.

41 Sotheli the sones of Micha weren Phiton, and Malech, and Thara;

42 forsothe Aaz gendride Jara, and Jara gendride Alamath, and Azmoth, and Zamri; and Zamri gendride Moosa,

43 sotheli Moosa gendride Baana, whose sone Raphaia gendride Elisa, of whom Esel was gendrid.

44 Forsothe Esel hadde sixe sones bi these names, Ezricam, Bochru, Hismael, Saria, Obdia, Anan; these weren the sones of Hesel.

CAP 10

1 Forsothe Filisteis fouyten ayens Israel, and the sones of Israel fledden Palestyns, and felden doun woundid in the hil of Gelboe.

2 And whanne Filisteis hadde neiyed pursuynge Saul and hise sones, thei killiden Jonathan, and Abynadab, and Melchisue, the sones of Saul.

3 And the batel was agreggid ayens Saul; and men archeris foundun hym, and woundiden hym with dartis.

4 And Saul seide to his squiere, Drawe out thi swerd, and sle me, leste these vncircumcidid men come, and scorne me. Sothli his squyer was aferd bi drede, and nolde do this; therfor Saul took a swerd, and felde on it.

5 And whanne his squyer hadde seyn this, that is, that Saul was deed, he felde also on his swerd, and was deed.

6 Therfor Saul perischide, and hise thre sones, and al his hows felde doun togidere.

7 And whanne the men of Israel, that dwelliden in feeldi places, hadden seyn this, thei fledden; and whanne Saul and hise sones weren deed, thei forsoken her citees, and weren

scaterid hidur and thidur; and Filisteis camen, and dwelliden in tho.

8 Therfor in the tother day Filisteis drowen awei the spuylis of slayn men, and founden Saul and hise sones liggynge in the hil of Gelboe.

9 And whanne thei hadden spuylid hym, and hadden gird of the heed, and hadden maad hym nakid of armeris, thei senten in to her lond, that it schulde be borun aboute, and schulde be schewid in the templis of idols and to puplis;

10 forsothe thei halewiden his armeris in the temple of her god, and thei settiden the heed in the temple of Dagon.

11 Whanne men of Jabes of Galad hadden herd this, that is, alle thingis whiche the Filisteis diden on Saul,

12 alle stronge men risiden togidere, and took the deed bodies of Saul and of hise sones, and brouyten tho in to Jabes; and thei birieden the boonus of hem vndur an ook, that was in Jabes; and thei fastiden seuene daies.

13 Therfor Saul was deed for hise wickidnessis, for he brak the comaundement of the Lord, whiche he comaundide, and kepte not it, but ferthirmore also he took counsel at a womman hauynge a feend spekynge in the wombe, and he hopide not in the Lord;

14 for which thing both the Lord killide hym, and translatide his rewme to Dauid, sone of Ysay.

CAP 11

1 Therfor al Israel was gaderid to Dauid in Ebron, and seide, We ben thi boon and thi fleisch;

2 also yisterdai and the thridde dai ago, whanne Saul regnede yit on Israel, thou it were that leddist out and leddist in Israel; for 'thi Lord God seide to thee, Thou schalt fede my puple Israel, and thou schalt be prince on it.

3 Therfor alle the gretter in birthe of Israel camen to the kyng in Ebron; and Dauid maad with hem a boond of pees bifor the Lord, and thei anoyntiden hym kyng on Israel, bi the word of the Lord, which he spak in the hond of Samuel.

4 Therfor Dauid yede, and al Israel, in to Jerusalem; this Jerusalem is Jebus, where Jebuseis enhabiteris of the lond weren.

5 And thei that dwelliden at Jebus seiden to Dauid, Thou schalt not entre hidur. Forsothe Dauid took the hiy tour of Syon, which is the citee of Dauid;

6 and he seide, Ech man that 'sleeth first Jebusei, schal be prince and duyk. Therfor Joab, sone of Saruye, stiede first, and was maad prince.

7 Sotheli Dauid dwellide in the hiy tour, and therfor it was clepid the cytee of Dauid;

8 and he bildide the citee in cumpas fro Mello til to the cumpas; forsothe Joab bildide the tother part of the citee.

9 And Dauid profitide goynge and wexynge, and the Lord of oostis was with hym.

10 These ben the princes of the stronge men of Dauid, that helpiden hym, that he schulde be kyng on al Israel, bi the word of the Lord which he spak to Israel.

11 And this is the noumbre of the stronge men of Dauid; Jesbaam, the sone of Achamony, was prince among thretti; this reiside his schaft ethir spere on thre hundrid woundid men in o tyme.

12 And after hym was Eleazar, the sone of his fadris brothir, and was 'a man of Ahoit, which Eleazar was among thre miyti men.

13 This was with Dauid in Aphesdomyn, whanne Filisteis weren gaderid to o place in to batel; and a feeld of that cun-

trey was ful of barli, and the puple fledde fro the face of Filisteis.

14 This Eleazar stood in the myddis of the feeld, and defendide it; and whanne he hadde slayn Filisteis, the Lord yaf greet helthe to his puple.

15 Sotheli thre of thritti princes yeden doun to the stoon, wher ynne Dauid was, to the denne of Odolla, whanne Filisteis settiden tentis in the valey of Raphaym.

16 Forsothe Dauid was in a strong hold, and the stacioun, 'that is, the oost gaderid, of Filisteis was in Bethleem.

17 Therfor Dauid desiride watir, and seide, Y wolde, that sum man yaf to me water of the cisterne of Bethleem, which is in the yate.

18 Therfor these thre yeden thoruy the myddil of the castelis of Filisteis, and drowen watir of the cisterne of Bethleem, that was in the yate, and thei brouyten to Dauid, that he schulde drynke; and Dauid nolde 'drynke it, but rather he offride it to the Lord, and seide, Fer be it,

19 that Y do this thing in the siyt of my God, and that Y drynke the blood of these men, for in the perel of her lyues thei brouyten watir to me; and for this cause he nolde drynke. Thre strongeste men diden these thingis.

20 Also Abisai, the brother of Joab, he was the prince of thre men, and he reiside his schaft ayens thre hundrid woundid men; and he was moost named among thre,

21 among the secounde thre he was noble, and the prince of hem; netheles he cam not til to the firste thre.

22 Banaye, the sone of Joiada, strongest man of Capsael, that dide many werkis; he killide two stronge men of Moab; and he yede doun, and killide a lioun in the myddil of a cisterne, in the tyme of snow;

23 and he killide a man of Egipt, whos stature was of fyue cubitis, and he hadde a spere as the beem of webbis; therfor Banaye yede doun to hym with a yerde, and rauyschide the spere, which he held in the hond, and killide hym with his owne spere.

24 Banaye, the sone of Joiada, dide these thingis, that was moost named among thre stronge men, and was the firste among thretti;

25 netheles he cam not til to the thre; sotheli Dauid settide hym at his eere.

26 Forsothe the strongeste men 'in the oost weren Asael, the brother of Joab, and Eleanan, the sone of his fadris brothir of Bethleem,

27 Semynoth Arorites, Helles Phallonytes, Iras,

28 the sone of Acces of Thecue, Abieser of Anathot,

29 Sobochay Sochites, Ylai Achoytes,

30 Maray Nethophatithes, Heles, the sone of Banaa, Nethophatithes, Ethaa,

31 the sone of Rabai, of Gabaath of the sones of Beniamyn; Banaye Pharatonythes, men of the stronde Gaas,

32 Abihel Arabatithes, Azmoth Baruanythes, Eliaba Salaonythes,

33 the sones of Assem Gesonythes, Jonathan, the sone of Saga, Ararithes, Achiam,

34 the sone of Achar, Ararites,

35 Eliphal, the sone of Mapher,

36 Mechoratithes, Ahya Phellonythes,

37 Asrahi Carmelites, Neoray,

38 the sone of Thasbi, Johel, the brother of Nathan, Mabar, the sone of Aggaray, Selech Ammonythes,

39 Nooray Berothites, the squyer of Joab, sone of Saruye,

40 Iras Jetreus, Gareb Jethreus,

41 Vrie Ethei, Sabab,

42 the sone of Ooli, Adyna, the sone of Segar Rubenytes,
prince of Rubenytis, and thritti men with hym;

43 Hanan, the sone of Macha, and Josaphath Mathanythes,
Ozias Astarothites,

44 Semma and Jahel, the sones of Hotayn Aroerites,

45 Ledihel, the sone of Zamri, and Joha, his brother, Thosay-
thes,

46 Hehiel Maanytes, Jerybay and Josia, the sones of Helnaen,
Jethma Moabites, Heliel, and Obed, and Jasihel of Masobia.

CAP 12

1 Also these camen to Dauid in Sichelech, whanne he fledde
yit fro Saul, the sone of Cys; whiche weren strongeste men
and noble fiyterys,

2 beendynge bouwe, and castynge stoonys with slyngis with
euer either hond, and dressynge arowis; of the britheren of
Saul of Beniamyn,

3 the prince Achieser, and Joas, the sones of Samaa of
Gabaath, and Jazachel, and Phallech, the sones of Azmod,
and Barachie, and Jehu of Anathot;

4 also Samay of Gabaon was the strongeste among thretti and
aboue thretti; Jeremy, and Jezihel, and Johannan, and
Zebadga Zerothites,

5 Elusay, and Jerymoth, and Baalia, and Samaria, and Saphia
Araphites,

6 Elchana, and Jesia, and Azrahel, and Jezer, and Jesbaam of
Taremy,

7 and Joelam, and Sabadia, the sones of Jeroam of Jedor.

8 But also of Gaddi strongeste men, and beste fiyteris, holdynge scheld and spere, fledden ouer to Dauid, whanne he was
hid in deseert; the faces of hem as the face of a lioun, and thei
weren swift as capretis in hillis.

9 Ozer was the prince, Obdias the secounde, Eliab the
thridde,

10 Masmana the fourthe, Jeremye the fyuethe,

11 Becchi the sixte, Heliel the seuenthe,

12 Johannan the eiythe, Helzedad the nynthe,

13 Jeremye the tenthe, Bachana the euleuenthe;

14 these of the sones of Gad weren princes of the oost; the
laste was souereyn ouer an hundrid knyytis, and the moost
was souereyn ouer a thousynde.

15 These it ben that passiden ouer Jordan in the firste monethe, whanne it was wont to flowe ouer hise brynkis; and thei
dryueden awei alle men that dwelliden in the valeis at the eest
coost and west coost.

16 Sotheli also men of Beniamyn and of Juda camen to the
stronge hoold, whereyn Dauid dwellide.

17 And Dauid yede out ayens hem, and seide, If ye 'ben
comyn pesible to me, for to helpe me, myn herte be ioyned to
you; forsothe if ye setten aspies to me for myn aduersaries,
sithen Y haue not wickidnesse in the hondis, God of our
fadris se and deme.

18 Forsothe the spirit clothide Amasay, the prynce among
thritti, and he seide, A! Dauid, we ben thin, and thou, sone of
Ysai, we schulen be with thee; pees, pees to thee, and pees to
thin helperis, for thi Lord God helpith thee. Therfor Dauid
resseyuede hem, and made princes of the cumpeny.

19 Forsothe men of Manasses fledden ouer to Dauid, whanne
he cam with Filisteis to fiyte ayens Saul, and he fauyte not
with hem, for after that the princes of Filisteis hadden take
counsel, thei senten hym ayen, and seiden, With perel of oure
heed he schal turne ayen to Saul his lord.

20 Therfor whanne Dauid turnede ayen in to Sichelech, men
of Manasses fledden ouer to hym, Eduas, and Jozabad, Jedihel, and Mychael, and Naas, and Jozabath, and Helyu, and
Salathi, princes of knyytis in Manasses.

21 These men yauen help to Dauid ayens theues; for alle
weren strongeste men, and thei weren maad prynces in the
oost.

22 But also bi ech dai men camen to Dauid, for to helpe hym,
til that the noumbre was maad greet as the oost of God.

23 Also this is the noumbre of princes of the oost that camen
to Dauid, whanne he was in Ebron, that thei schulden translate the rewme of Saul to hym, bi the word of the Lord; the
sones of Juda,

24 berynge scheeld and spere, sixe thousynde and eiyte hundrid, redi to batel;

25 of the sones of Simeon, seuene thousinde and an hundrid,
of strongeste men to fiyte;

26 of the sones of Leuy, foure thousynde and sixe hundrid;

27 also Joiada, prince of the generacioun of Aaron, and thre
thousynd and seuene hundrid with hym;

28 also Sadoch, a child of noble wit, and the hows of his
fadir, twei and twenti princes;

29 forsothe of the sones of Beniamyn, britheren of Saul, thre
thousynde; for a greet part of hem suede yit the hows of Saul;

30 forsothe of the sones of Effraym, twenti thousynde and
eiyte hundrid, strongeste men in bodili myyt, men named in
her meynees;

31 and of the half part of the lynage of Manasses, eiytene
thousynde; alle camen bi her names, to make Dauid kyng;

32 also of the sones of Ysacar, two hundrid princes, lernd
men, that knewen ech tyme to comaunde what the puple of
Israel ouyt to do; sotheli al the residue lynage suede the counseils of hem;

33 forsothe of Zabulon camen fifti thousynde in to helpe, not
in double herte, which yeden out to batel, and stoden in the
scheltrun, and weren maad redi with armuris of batel;

34 and of Neptalym a thousynde pryncis, and with hem
camen seuene and thritti thousynde men, arayed with scheeld
and speere;

35 also of Dan, eiyte and twenti thousynde and sixe hundrid
men, maad redi to batel;

36 and of Aser fourti thousynde men, goynge out to batel, and
stirynge to batel in the scheltrun.

37 Forsothe biyende Jordan, of the sones of Ruben, and of
Gad, and of the half part of the lynage of Manasses, sixe scoore thousynde men, araied with armuris of batel.

38 Alle these men werriouris and redi to batel camen with
perfit herte in to Ebron, to make Dauid kyng on al Israel; but
also alle the residue of Israel weren of oon herte, that Dauid
schulde be maad king on al Israel.

39 And thei weren ther at Dauid thre daies, and eten and
drunken; for her britheren hadden maad redi to hem;

40 but also thei that weren niy hem, til to Isacar and Zabulon
and Neptalym, brouyten looues on assis, and camelis, and
mulis, and oxis, for to ete; mele, bundelis of pressid figis,
dried grapis, wyn, oile, oxis and wetheres, to al plentee; for
ioy was in Israel.

CAP 13

1 Forsothe Dauid took counsel with tribunes, and centuriouns, and alle princes;

2 and seide to alle the cumpeny of the sones of Israel, If it
plesith you, and if the word which Y speke goith out fro oure

Lord God, sende we to 'oure residue britheren to alle the cuntrees of Israel, and to preestis and dekenes that dwellen in the subarbis of citees, that thei be gaderid to vs,

3 and that we brynge ayen to vs the arke of oure God; for we souyten not it in the daies of Saul.

4 And al the multitude answeride, that it schulde be don so; for the word pleside al the puple.

5 Therfor Dauid gaderide togidere al Israel, fro Sior of Egipt til thou entre in to Emath, that he schulde brynge the arke of God fro Cariathiarim.

6 And Dauid stiede, and alle the men of Israel, to the hil of Cariathiarym, which is in Juda, that he schulde brynge fro thennus the arke of the Lord God sittynge on cherubyn, where his name was clepid.

7 And thei puttiden the arke of the Lord God on a newe wayn fro the hous of Amynadab; forsothe Oza and hise britheren driueden the wayn.

8 Forsothe Dauid and al Israel pleieden bifor the Lord, with al miyt, in songis, and in harpis, and sautries, and tympans, and cymbalis, and trumpis.

9 Forsothe whanne thei hadden come to the cornfloor of Chidon, Oza strechide forth his hond to susteyne the arke; for the oxe wexynge wielde hadde bowid it a litil.

10 Therfor the Lord was wrooth ayens Oza, and smoot hym, for he hadde touchide the ark; and he was deed there bifor the Lord.

11 And Dauid was sori, for the Lord hadde departid Oza; and he clepide that place The Departyng of Oza 'til in to present dai.

12 And Dauid dredde the Lord in that tyme, and seide, How may Y brynge in to me the arke of the Lord?

13 And for this cause he brouyte not it to hym, that is, in to the citee of Dauid, but he turnede it in to the hows of Obededom of Geth.

14 Therfor the arke of God dwellide in the hous of Obededom of Geth thre monethis; and the Lord blessid his hows, and 'alle thingis that he hadde.

CAP 14

1 And Iram, the kyng of Tyre, sente messageris to Dauid, and 'he sente trees of cedre, and werk men of wallis and of trees, that thei schulden bilde to hym an hows.

2 And Dauid knewe that the Lord hadde confermyd hym in to kyng on Israel; and that his rewme was reisid on his puple Israel.

3 And Dauid took othere wyues in Jerusalem, and gendride sones and douytris.

4 And these ben the names of hem that weren borun to hym in Jerusalem; Sammu, and Sobab, Nathan, and Salomon,

5 Jeber, and Elisu, and Heli, and Eliphalech,

6 and Noga, and Napheg, and Japhie,

7 and Elisama, and Baliada, and Eliphelech.

8 Forsothe the Filisteis herden that Dauid was anoyntid 'in to kyng on al Israel, and alle stieden to seke Dauid. And whanne Dauid hadde herd this thing, he yede out ayens hem.

9 Forsothe Filisteis camen, and weren spred abroad in the valey of Raphaym;

10 and Dauid counselide the Lord, and seide, Whether Y schal stie to Filisteis? and whether thou schalt bitake hem in to myn hondis? And the Lord seide to hym, Stie thou, and Y schal bitake hem in thin hond.

11 And whanne thei hadden styed in to Baal Pharasym, Dauid smoot hem there, and seide, God hath departid myn enemyes

bi myn hond, as watris ben departid. And therfor the name of that place was clepid Baal Pharasym; and thei leften there her goddis,

12 which Dauid comaundide to be brent.

13 Forsothe another tyme Filisteis felden in, and weren spred abrood in the valei;

14 and eft Dauid counseilide the Lord, and the Lord seide to hym, Thou schalt not stie aftir hem; go awei fro hem, and thou schalt come ayens hem euen ayens the pere trees.

15 And whanne thou schalt here the sowun of a goere in the cop of the pere trees, thanne thou schalt go out to batel; for the Lord is go out byfor thee, to smyte the castels of Filisteis.

16 Therfor Dauid dide as God comaundide to hym, and he smoot the castels of Filisteis fro Gabaon 'til to Gazara.

17 And the name of Dauid was puplischid in alle cuntreis, and the Lord yaf his drede on alle folkis.

CAP 15

1 And he made to hym housis in the citee of Dauid, and he bildide 'a place to the arke of the Lord, and araiede a tabernacle to it.

2 Thanne Dauid seide, It is vnleueful, that the arke of God be borun of 'ony thing no but of the dekenes, whiche the Lord chees to bere it, and 'for to mynystre to hym 'til in to with outen ende.

3 And he gaderide togidere al Israel in to Jerusalem, that the arke of God schulde be brouyt in to 'his place, which he hadde maad redy to it;

4 also and he gaderide togidere the sones of Aaron, and the dekenes;

5 of the sones of Caath Vriel was prince, and hise britheren two hundrid and twenti;

6 of the sones of Merari Asaya was prince, and hise britheren two hundrid and thritti;

7 of the sones of Gerson the prince was Johel, and hise britheren an hundrid and thretti;

8 of the sones of Elisaphan Semei was prynce, and hise britheren two hundrid;

9 of the sones of Ebroun Heliel was prince, and hise britheren foure score;

10 of the sones of Oziel Amynadab was prince, and hise britheren an hundrid and twelue.

11 And Dauid clepide Sadoch and Abiathar preestis, and the dekenes Vriel, Asaie, Johel, Semeie, Eliel, and Amynadab; and seide to hem,

12 Ye that ben princes of the meynees of Leuy, be halewid with youre britheren, and brynge ye the arke of the Lord God of Israel to the place, which is maad redi to it;

13 lest, as at the bigynnyng, for ye weren not present, the Lord smoot vs, and now it be don, if we don ony vnleueful thing.

14 Therfor the preestis and dekenes weren halewid, that thei schulden bere the arke of the Lord God of Israel.

15 And the sones of Leuy token the arke of God with barris on her schuldris, as Moises comaundide bi the word of the Lord.

16 And Dauid seide to the princes of dekenes, that thei schulden ordeyne of her britheren syngeris in orguns of musikis, that is, in giternes, and harpis, and symbalis; that the sown of gladnesse schulde sowne an hiy.

17 And thei ordeyneden dekenes, Heman, the sone of Johel, and of hise britheren, Asaph, the sone of Barachie; sotheli of

the sones of Merary, britheren of hem, thei ordeyneden
Ethan,

18 the sone of Casaye, and the britheren of hem with hem; in
the secunde ordre 'thei ordeyneden Zacarie, and Ben, and
Jazihel, and Semyramoth, and Jahiel, 'and Am, Heliab, and
Benaye, and Maasie, and Mathathie, and Eliphalu, and
Mathenye, and Obededon, and Jehiel, porteris;

19 forsothe 'thei ordeyneden the syngeris Eman, Asaph, and
Ethan, sownynge in brasun cymbalis;

20 sotheli Zacarie, and Oziel, and Semyramoth, and Jahihel,
and Ham, and Eliab, and Maasie, and Banaie, sungun pryuetees in giternes; forsothe Mathathie,

21 and Eliphalu, and Mathenye, and Obededom, and Jehiel,
and Ozazym, sungen in harpis for the eiytithe, and epyny-
chion, 'that is, victorie 'be to God ouercomere;

22 forsothe Chinonye, the prince of dekenes, and of profecie,
was souereyn to biforsynge melodie, for he was ful wijs;

23 and Barachie, and Elchana, weren porters of the arke; forsothe Sebenye,

24 and Josaphath, and Mathanael, and Amasaye, and Zacarie,
and Banaye, and Eliezer, preestis, sowneden with trumpis
bifor the arke of the Lord; and Obededom, and Achymaas,
weren porteris of the arke.

25 Therfor Dauid, and the grettere men in birthe of Israel, and
the tribunes, yeden to brynge the arke of boond of pees of the
Lord fro the hows of Obededom with gladnesse.

26 And whanne God hadde helpid the dekenes that baren the
arke of boond of pees of the Lord, seuene bolis and seuene
rammes weren offrid.

27 Forsothe Dauid was clothid with a white stole, and alle the
dekenes that baren the arke, and the syngeris, and Chononye,
the prince of profecie among syngeris, weren clothid in white
stolis; forsothe also Dauid was clothid with a lynun surplijs.

28 And al Israel ledden forth the arke of boond of pees of the
Lord, and sowneden in ioiful song, and in sown of clariouns,
and in trumpis, and cymbalis, and giternis, and harpis.

29 And whanne the arke of boond of pees of the Lord hadde
come to the citee of Dauid, Mychol, the douytir of Saul,
bihelde forth bi a wyndowe, and sche siy king Dauyd daunsynge and pleiynge; and sche dispiside hym in hir herte.

CAP 16

1 Therfor thei brouyten the arke of God, and settiden it in the
myddis of the tabernacle, that Dauid hadde araied therto; and
thei offriden brent sacrifices and pesible sacrifices bifor the
Lord.

2 And whanne Dauid offrynge brent sacrifices and pesible
sacrifices hadde fillid, he blesside the puple in the name of
the Lord;

3 and departide to alle to ech bi hym silf fro a man til to a
womman o cake of breed, and a part of rostid fleisch of a
bugle, and flour fried in oile.

4 And he ordeynede bifor the arke of the Lord, of the Leuytis,
that schulden mynystre, and haue mynde of the werkis of the
Lord, and glorifie and preyse the Lord God of Israel;

5 'he ordeynede Asaph the prince, and Zacharie his secounde;
forsothe 'he ordeynede Jahiel, and Semiramoth, and Jahel,
and Mathathie, and Eliab, and Banaye, and Obededom, and
Jehiel, on the orguns, on the sautrie, and on the harpis; but he
ordeynede Asaph to sowne with cymbalis;

6 sotheli he ordeynede Banaye and Aziel, preestis, bifor the
arke of the boond of pees of the Lord, for to trumpe contynueli.

7 In that dai Dauid made Asaph prince, and hise britheren, for
to knowleche 'to the Lord.

8 Knowleche ye to the Lord, and inwardli clepe ye his name;
make ye hise fyndyngis knowun among puplis.

9 Synge ye to hym, and seie ye salm to hym, and telle ye alle
his merueylis.

10 Preise ye his hooli name; the herte of men sekynge the
Lord be glad.

11 Seke ye the Lord and his vertu; seke ye euere his face.

12 Haue ye mynde of hise merueilis whiche he dide; of hise
signes, and of the domes of his mouth.

13 The seed of Israel, his seruaunt, preise thou God; the sones
of Jacob, his chosun, preise ye God.

14 He is 'oure Lord God; hise domes ben in ech lond.

15 Haue ye mynde with outen ende of his couenaunt; of the
word whiche he couenauntide 'in to a thousynde generaciouns.

16 Which word he couenauntide with Abraham; and of his
ooth to Ysaac.

17 And he ordeynede that to Jacob in to a comaundement;
and to Israel in to euerlastynge couenaunt.

18 And seide, To thee Y schal yyue the lond of Canaan; the
part of youre erytage.

19 Whanne thei weren fewe in noumbre; litle, and pilgrims
therof.

20 And thei passiden fro folk in to the folk; and fro a rewme
to another puple.

21 He suffride not ony man falseli chalenge hem; but he
blamyde kyngis for hem.

22 Nyle ye touche my cristis; and nyle ye do wickidli ayens
my prophetis.

23 Al erthe, singe ye to the Lord; telle ye fro dai into dai his
helthe.

24 Telle ye among hethen men his glorie; hise merueylis
among alle puplis.

25 For the Lord is greet, and worthi to be preisid ful myche;
and he is orible, 'ethir griseful, ouer alle goddis.

26 For alle the goddis of puplis ben idols; but the Lord made
heuenes.

27 Knoulechyng and greet doyng ben bifor hym; strengthe
and ioy ben in the place of hym.

28 Ye meynees of puplis, 'bringe ye to the Lord; brynge ye to
the Lord glorie and empire.

29 Yyue ye glorie to his name, reise ye sacrifice, and come ye
in his siyt; and worschipe ye the Lord in hooli fairnesse.

30 Al erthe be mouyd fro his face; for he foundide the world
vnmouable.

31 Heuenes be glad, and the erthe 'ioy fulli; and seie thei
among naciouns, The Lord schal regne.

32 The see thundre, and his fulnesse; the feeldis fulli ioye,
and alle thingis that ben in tho.

33 Thanne the trees of the forest schulen preyse bifor the
Lord; for he cometh to deme the erthe.

34 Knouleche ye to the Lord, for he is good; for his mersi is
withouten ende.

35 And seie ye, Thou God oure sauyour, saue vs, and gadere
vs, and delyuere vs fro hethen men; that we knowleche to thin
hooli name, and be fulli glade in thi songis.

36 Blessid be the Lord God of Israel fro with oute bigynnyng
and til 'in to with outen ende; and al the puple seie, Amen,
and seie heriyng to God.

37 Therfor Dauid lefte there, bifor the arke of boond of pees of the Lord, Asaph and hise britheren, for to mynystre in the siyt of the arke contynueli bi alle daies and her whilis.

38 Forsothe he ordeynede porteris, Obededom and hise britheren, eiyte and sixti, and Obededom, the sone of Idithum, and Oza.

39 Sotheli 'he ordeynede Sadoch preest, and hise britheren, preestis bifor the tabernacle of the Lord, in the hiy place that was in Gabaon,

40 for to offre brent sacrifices to the Lord on the auter of brent sacrifice contynueli, in the morwetid and euentid, bi alle thingis that ben writun in the lawe of the Lord, which he comaundide to Israel.

41 And aftir hym Dauyd ordeynede Eman, and Idithum, and other chosene, ech man bi his name, for to knowleche to the Lord; for his mercy is withouten ende.

42 Also he ordeynede Eman, and Idithum, trumpynge, and schakynge cymbalis, and alle orguns of musikis, for to synge to God; forsothe he made the sones of Idithum to be portours, 'ether bereris.

43 And al the puple turnede ayen in to her hows, and Dauid turnede ayen, to blesse also his hows.

CAP 17

1 Forsothe whanne Dauid dwellide in his hows, he seide to Nathan, the prophete, Lo! Y dwelle in an hows of cedris; sotheli the arke of boond of pees of the Lord is vndur skynnys.

2 And Nathan seide to Dauid, Do thou alle thingis that ben in thin herte, for God is with thee.

3 Therfor in that nyyt the word of the Lord was maad to Nathan,

4 and seide, Go thou, and speke to Dauid, my seruaunt, The Lord seith these thingis, Thou schalt not bilde to me an hows to dwelle in;

5 for Y 'dwellide not in an hows, fro that tyme in which Y ledde Israel out of the lond of Egipt til to this dai, but euere Y chaungide places of tabernacle, and dwellide in a tente with al Israel.

6 Where I spak nameli to oon of the iugis of Israel, to which I comaundide that thei schulde fede my puple, and seide, Whi 'bildidist thou not to me an hous of cedre?

7 Now therfor thou schalt speke thus to my seruaunt Dauid, The Lord of oostis seith these thingis, Y took thee, whanne thou suedist the floc in the lesewis, that thou schuldist be duyk on my puple Israel;

8 and Y was with thee whidur euere thou yedist, and Y killide alle thin enemyes bifor thee, and Y made to thee an name as of oon of the grete men that ben maad worschipful, ether 'famouse, in erthe.

9 And Y yaf a place to my puple Israel; it schal be plauntid, and schal dwelle there ynne, and it schal no more be moued, and the sones of wickydnesse schulen not defoule hem,

10 as fro the bigynnyng, fro the daies in whiche Y yaf iugis to my puple Israel; and Y made lowe alle thin enemyes. Therfor Y telle to thee, that the Lord schal bilde an hows to thee.

11 And whanne thou hast fillid thi daies, that thou go to thi fadris, Y schal reise thi seed after thee, that schal be of thi sones, and Y schal stablische his rewme;

12 he schal bilde to me an hows, and Y schal make stidefast his seete til in to with outen ende.

13 Y schal be to hym in to a fadir, and he schal be to me in to a sone; and Y schal not do my mersi fro hym, as Y took awei fro hym that was bifore thee;

14 and Y schal ordeyne hym in myn hows and in my rewme til in to with outen ende; and his trone schal be moost stidefast with outen ende.

15 Bi alle these wordis, and bi al this reuelacioun, so Nathan spak to Dauid.

16 And whanne kyng Dauid hadde come, and hadde sete bifore the Lord, he seide, Lord God, who am Y, and what is myn hows, that thou schuldist yyue siche thingis to me?

17 But also this is seyn litil in thi siyt, and therfor thou spakest on the hows of thi seruaunt, yhe, in to tyme to comynge; and hast maad me worthi to be biholdun ouer alle men.

18 My Lord God, what may Dauid adde more, sithen thou hast so glorified thi seruaunt, and hast knowe hym?

19 Lord, for thi seruaunt thou hast do bi thin herte al this grete doyng, and woldist that alle grete thingis be knowun.

20 Lord, noon is lijk thee, and noon other God is with oute thee, of alle whiche we herden with oure eeris.

21 For who is anothir as thi puple Israel, o folc in erthe, to whom God yede, to delyuere and make a puple to hym silf, and to caste out bi his greetnesse and dredis naciouns fro the face therof, which he delyuerede fro Egipt?

22 And thou hast set thi puple Israel in to a puple to thee til in to with outen ende, and thou, Lord, art maad the God therof.

23 Now therfor, Lord, the word which thou hast spoke to thi seruaunt, and on his hows, be confermed with outen ende, and do, as thou spake;

24 and thi name dwelle, and be magnefied 'with outen ende; and be it seid, The Lord of oostis is God of Israel, and the hous of Dauid, his seruaunt, dwellynge bifor hym.

25 For thou, my Lord God, hast maad reuelacioun to the eere of thi seruaunt, that thou woldist bilde to hym an hous; and therfor thi seruaunt foond trist, that he preie bifor thee.

26 Now therfor, Lord, thou art God, and hast spoke to thi seruaunt so grete benefices;

27 and thou hast bigunne to blesse the hous of thi seruaunt, that it be euer bifore thee; for, Lord, for thou blessist, it schal be blessid with outen ende.

CAP 18

1 Forsothe it was doon aftir these thingis, that Dauid smoot Filisteis, and made hem lowe, and took awey Geth and vilagis therof fro the hond of Filisteis;

2 and that he smoot Moab; and Moabitis weren maad seruauntis of Dauid, and brouyten yiftis to hym.

3 In that tyme Dauid smoot also Adadezer, kyng of Soba, of the cuntrey of Emath, whanne he yede for to alarge his empire til to the flood Eufrates.

4 Therfor Dauid took a thousynde foure horsid cartis of his, and seuene thousynde of horsmen, and twenti thousynde of foot men; and he hoxide alle the horsis of charis, outakun an hundrid foure horsid cartis, whiche he kepte to hym silf.

5 Forsothe also Sirus of Damask cam aboue, to yyue help to Adadezer, kyng of Soba, but Dauid smoot also of hise two and twenti thousynde of men;

6 and he settide kniytis in Damask, that Sirie also schulde serue hym, and brynge yiftis. And the Lord helpide hym in alle thingis to whiche he yede.

7 And Dauid took goldun arowe caasis, whiche the seruauntis of Adadezer hadden, and he brouyte tho in to Jerusalem;

8 also and of Thebath and of Chum, the citees of Adadezer, he took ful myche of bras, wherof Salomon made the brasun see, 'that is, waischynge vessel, and pileris, and brasun vessels.

9 And whanne Thou, kyng of Emath, hadde herd this thing, 'that is, that Dauid hadde smyte al the oost of Adadezer, kyng of Soba,

10 he sente Aduram, his sone, to Dauid the kyng, for to axe of hym pees, and for to thanke hym, for he hadde ouercome and hadde smyte Adadezer; for whi king Adadezer was aduersarie of Thou.

11 But also kyng Dauid halewide to the Lord alle the vessels of gold, and of siluer, and of bras; and the siluer, and the gold, which the kyng hadde take of alle folkis, as wel of Idumee and Moab, and of the sones of Amon, as of Filisteis and Amalech.

12 Forsothe Abisai, the sone of Saruye, smoot Edom in the valei of salt pittis, 'ten and eiyte thousynde.

13 And he settide strong hold in Edom, that Ydumei schulde serue Dauid. And the Lord sauide Dauid in alle thingis, to whiche he yede.

14 Therfor Dauid regnede on al Israel, and dide doom and riytwisnesse to al his puple.

15 Forsothe Joab, the sone of Saruye, was 'on the oost; and Josaphat, the sone of Ayluth, was chaunceler;

16 forsothe Sadoch, the sone of Achitob, and Achymalech, the sone of Abyathar, weren preestis; and Susa was scribe;

17 and Banaye, the sone of Joiada, was on the legiouns Cerethi and Phelethi; sotheli the sones of Dauid weren the firste at the hond of the kyng.

CAP 19

1 Forsothe it bifelde, that Naas, kyng of the sones of Amon, diede, and his sone regnyde for him.

2 And Dauid seide, Y schal do mercy with Anoon, the sone of Naas; for his fadir yaf merci to me. And Dauid sente messageris, to coumforte hym on the deeth of his fadir. And whanne thei weren comen in to the lond of the sones of Amon,

3 for to coumforte Anon, the princes of the sones of Amon seiden to Anon, In hap thou gessist, that Dauid for cause of onour in to thi fadir sente men, that schulden coumforte thee; and thou perseyuest not, that hise seruauntis ben comen to thee to aspie, and enquere, and seche thi lond.

4 Therfor Anoon made ballid and schauyde the children of Dauid, and kittide the cootis of hem fro the buttokis of hem til to the feet; and lefte hem.

5 And whanne thei hadden go, and hadden sent this to Dauid, he sente in to the meting of hem; for thei hadden suffrid greet dispit; and he comaundide, that thei schulden dwelle in Gerico, til her berde wexide, and thanne thei schulden turne ayen.

6 Forsothe the sones of Amon sien, that thei hadden do wrong to Dauid, bothe Anoon and the tother puple, and thei senten a thousynde talentis of siluer, for to hire to hem charis and horsmen of Mesopotanye and Sirie, of Maacha and of Soba;

7 and thei hiriden to hem two and thretti thousynde of charis, and the kyng of Maacha with his puple. And whanne thei weren comen, thei settiden tentis euene ayens Medaba; and the sones of Amon weren gaderid fro her citees, and camen to batel.

8 And whanne Dauid 'hadde herd this, he sente Joab, and al the oost of stronge men.

9 And the sones of Amon yeden out, and dressiden scheltrun bisidis the yate of the citee; but the kyngis, that weren comen to helpe, stoden asidis half in the feeld.

10 Therfor Joab vndurstood, that batel was maad ayens hym 'euene ayens and bihynde the bak, and he chees the strongeste men of al Israel, and yede ayens Sirus;

11 sotheli he yaf the residue part of the puple vnder the hond of Abisai, his brother; and thei yeden ayens the sones of Amon.

12 And Joab seide, If Sirus schal ouercome me, thou schalt helpe me; sotheli if the sones of Amon schulen ouercome thee, Y schal helpe thee; be thou coumfortid,

13 and do we manli for oure puple, and for the citees of oure God; forsothe the Lord do that, that is good in his siyt.

14 Therfor Joab yede, and the puple that was with hym, ayens Sirus to batel, and he droof hem awei.

15 Sotheli the sones of Amon sien, that Sirus hadde fled, and thei fledden fro Abisay, his brother, and entriden in to the citee; and Joab turnede ayen in to Jerusalem.

16 Forsothe Sirus siy, that he felde doun bifor Israel, and he sente messageris, and brouyte Sirus, that was biyende the flood; sotheli Sophath, the prynce of chyualrie of Adadezer, was the duyk of hem.

17 And whanne this was teld to Dauid, he gaderide al Israel, and passide Jordan; and he felde in on hem, and dresside scheltrun euene ayens hem, fiytynge ayenward.

18 'Forsothe Sirus fledde fro Israel, and Dauid killide of men of Sirie seuene thousynde of charis, and fourti thousynde of foot men, and Sophath, the prince of the oost.

19 Sotheli the seruauntis of Adadezer siyen, that thei weren ouercomun of Israel, and thei fledden ouer to Dauid, and seruiden hym; and Sirie wolde no more yyue helpe to the sones of Amon.

CAP 20

1 Forsothe it was doon after the ende of a yeer, in that tyme wherinne kyngis ben wont to go forth to batels, Joab gederide the oost, and the strengthe of chyualrie, and he wastide the lond of the sones of Amon, and yede, and bisegide Rabath; forsothe Dauid dwellide in Jerusalem, whanne Joab smoot Rabath, and distriede it.

2 Forsothe Dauid took the coroun of Melchon fro his heed, and foond therynne the weiyt of gold a talent, and moost precious iemmes, and he made therof a diademe to hym silf; also he took ful many spuylis of the citee.

3 Sotheli he ledde out the puple that was therynne, and made breris, 'ethir instrumentis bi whiche cornes ben brokun, and sleddis, and irone charis, to passe on hem, so that alle men weren kit in to dyuerse partis, and weren al to-brokun; Dauid dide thus to alle the 'cytees of the sones of Amon, and turnede ayen with al his puple in to Jerusalem.

4 Aftir these thingis a batel was maad in Gazer ayens Filisteis, wherynne Sobochai Vsachites slow Saphai of the kyn of Raphym, and mekide hem.

5 Also another batel was don ayens Filisteis, in which a man youun of God, the sone of forest, a man of Bethleem, killide Goliath of Geth, the brother of giauntis, of whos schaft the tre was as the beem of webbis.

6 But also another batel bifelde in Geth, in which a ful long man was, hauynge sixe fyngris, that is, togidere foure and twenti, and he was gendrid of the generacioun of Raphaym;

7 he blasfemyde Israel, and Jonathan, the sone of Samaa, brother of Dauid, killide hym. These ben the sones of

Raphaym in Geth, that felden doun in the hond of Dauid and of hise seruauntis.

CAP 21

1 Sotheli Sathan roos ayens Israel, and stiride Dauid for to noumbre Israel.

2 And Dauid seide to Joab, and to the princes of the puple, Go ye, and noumbre Israel fro Bersabe til to Dan, and brynge ye the noumbre to me, that Y wite.

3 And Joab answeride, The Lord encresse his puple an hundrid fold more than thei ben; my lord the kyng, whether alle ben not thi seruauntis? Whi sekith my lord this thing, that schal be arettid in to synne to Israel?

4 But the word of the kyng hadde more the maistrie; and Joab yede out, and cumpasside al Israel, and turnede ayen in to Jerusalem.

5 And he yaf to Dauid the noumbre of hem, which he hadde cumpassid; and al the noumbre of Israel was foundun a thousynde thousande, and an hundrid thousynde of men, drawynge out swerd; forsothe of Juda weren thre hundrid thousynde, and seuenti thousynde of werriouris.

6 For Joab noumbride not Leuy and Beniamyn, for ayens his wille he dide the comaundement of the kyng.

7 Forsothe that that was comaundid displeside the Lord, and he smoot Israel.

8 And Dauid seide to God, Y synnede greetli that Y wolde do this; Y biseche, do thou awey the wickidnesse of thi seruaunt, for Y dide folili.

9 And the Lord spak to Gad, the profete of Dauid,

10 and seide, Go thou, and speke to Dauid, and seie to him, The Lord seith these thingis, Y yeue to thee the chesyng of thre thingis; chese thou oon which thou wolt, that Y do to thee.

11 And whanne Gad was comen to Dauid, he seide to Dauid, The Lord seith these thingis, Chese thou that that thou wolt, ether pestilence thre yeer,

12 ether that thre monethis thou fle thin enemyes and mow not ascape her swerd, ether that the swerd of the Lord and deeth regne thre daies in the lond, and that the aungel of the Lord slee in alle the coostis of Israel. Now therfor se thou, what Y schal answere to hym that sente me.

13 And Dauid seide to Gad, Angwischis oppresse me on ech part, but it is betere to me, that Y falle in to the hondis of the Lord, for his merciful doynges ben manye, than in to the hondis of men.

14 Therfor the Lord sente pestilence in to Israel, and seuenti thousynde of men felden doun of Israel.

15 Also he sente an aungel in to Jerusalem, that he schulde smyte it; and whanne it was smytun, the Lord siy, and hadde merci on the greetnesse of yuel; and comaundide to the aungel that smoot, It suffisith, now thin hond ceesse. Forsothe the aungel of the Lord stood bisidis the cornfloor of Ornam Jebusey.

16 And Dauid reiside hise iyen, and siy the aungel of the Lord stondynge bitwixe heuene and erthe, and a drawun swerd in his hond, and turnede ayens Jerusalem. And bothe he and the grettere men in birthe weren clothid with heiris, and felden doun lowe on the erthe.

17 And Dauid seide to the Lord, Whether Y am not that comaundide that the puple schulde be noumbrid? Y it am that synnede, Y it am that dide yuel; what disseruid this floc? My Lord God, Y biseche, thin hond be turned 'in to me, and 'in to the hows of my fadir; but thi puple be not smytun.

18 Forsothe an aungel of the Lord comaundide Gad, that he schulde seie to Dauid, 'that he schulde stie, and bilde an auter to the Lord God in the cornfloor of Ornam Jebusei.

19 Therfor Dauid stiede bi the word of Gad, which he spak to hym bi the word of the Lord.

20 Forsothe whanne Ornam hadde 'biholde, and hadde seyn the aungel, and hise foure sones 'with hym 'hadde seyn, thei hidden hem, for in that tyme he threischide whete in the cornfloor.

21 Therfor whanne Dauid cam to Ornam, Ornam bihelde Dauid, and yede forth fro the cornfloor ayens hym, and worschipide hym, lowli on the ground.

22 And Dauid seide to hym, Yyue the place of thi cornfloor to me, that Y bilde ther ynne an auter to the Lord; so that thou take as myche siluer as it is worth, and that the veniaunce ceesse fro the puple.

23 Forsothe Ornam seide to Dauid, Take thou, and my lord the kyng do what euer thing plesith hym; but also Y yyue oxis in to brent sacrifice, and instrumentis of tree, wherbi cornes ben throischun, in to trees, and wheete in to sacrifice; Y yyue alle thingis wilfully.

24 And 'Dauid the kyng seide to hym, It schal not be don so, but Y schal yyue siluer as myche as it is worth; for Y owe not take awei fro thee, and offre so to the Lord brent sacrifices freli youun.

25 Therfor Dauid yaf to Ornam for the place sixe hundrid siclis of gold of most iust weiyte.

26 And he bildide there an auter to the Lord, and he offride brent sacrifice and pesible sacrifices, and he inwardli clepide God; and God herde hym in fier fro heuene on the auter of brent sacrifice.

27 And the Lord comaundide to the aungel, and he turnede his swerd in to the schethe.

28 Therfor anoon Dauid siy, that the Lord hadde herd hym in the corn floor of Ornam Jebusey, and he offride there slayn sacrifices.

29 Forsothe the tabernacle of the Lord, that Moyses hadde maad in the deseert, and the auter of brent sacrifices, was in that tempest in the hiy place of Gabaon;

30 and Dauid myyte not go to the auter, to biseche God there, for he was aferd bi ful greet drede, seynge the swerd of the 'aungel of the Lord.

CAP 22

1 And Dauid seide, This is the hows of God, and this auter is in to brent sacrifice of Israel.

2 And he comaundide that alle conuersis fro hethenesse to the lawe of Israel 'schulden be gaderid 'of the lond of Israel; and he ordeynede of hem masouns for to kytte stoonys and for to polische, that the hows of the Lord schulde be bildid;

3 also Dauid made redy ful myche yrun to the nailes of the yatis, and to the medlyngis and ioyntouris, and vnnoumbrable weiyte of bras;

4 also the trees of cedre myyten not be gessid, whiche the men of Sidonye and the men of Tyre brouyten to Dauid.

5 And Dauid seide, Salomon, my sone, is a litil child and delicat; sotheli the hows, which Y wole be bildid to the Lord, owith to be sich, that it be named in alle cuntrees; therfor Y schal make redi necessaries to hym. And for this cause Dauid bifor his deeth made redi alle costis.

6 And he clepide Salomon, his sone, and comaundide to hym, that he schulde bilde an hows to the Lord God of Israel.

7 And Dauid seide to Salomon, My sone, it was my wille to bilde an hows to the name of 'my Lord God;

8 but the word of the Lord was made to me, and seide, Thou hast sched out myche blood, and thou hast fouyt ful many batels; thou mayst not bilde an hows to my name, for thou hast sched out so myche blood bifor me;

9 the sone that schal be borun to thee, schal be a man most pesible, for Y schal make hym to haue reste of alle hise enemyes bi cumpas, and for this cause he schal be clepid pesible, and Y schal yyue pees and reste in Israel in alle hise daies.

10 He schal bilde an hows to my name; he schal be to me in to a sone, and Y schal be to hym in to a fadir, and Y schal make stidefast the seete of his rewme on Israel withouten ende.

11 Now therfor, my sone, the Lord be with thee, and haue thou prosperite, and bilde thou an hows to 'thi Lord God, as he spak of thee.

12 And the Lord yyue to thee prudence and wit, that thou mow gouerne Israel, and kepe the lawe of 'thi Lord God.

13 For thanne thou maist profite, if thou kepist the comaundementis and domes, whiche the Lord comaundide to Moises, that he schulde teche Israel; be thou coumfortid, and do manli, drede thou not 'with outforth, nether drede thou 'with ynne.

14 Lo! in my pouert Y haue maad redi the costis of the hows of the Lord; an hundrid thousinde talentis of gold, and a thousynde thousynde talentis of siluer; sotheli of bras and irun is no weiyte, for the noumbre is ouercomun bi greetnesse; Y haue maad redi trees and stoonys to alle costis.

15 Also thou hast ful many crafti men, masouns, and leggeris of stonys, and crafti men of trees, and of alle craftis,

16 most prudent to make werk, in gold, and siluer, and bras, and in yrun, of which is no noumbre; therfor rise thou, and make, and the Lord schal be with thee.

17 Also Dauid comaundide to alle the princis of Israel, that thei schulden helpe Salomon,

18 his sone, and seide, Ye seen, that 'youre Lord God is with you, and hath youe to you reste 'by cumpas, and hath bitake alle enemyes in youre hoond, and the erthe is suget bifor the Lord, and bifor his puple.

19 Therfor yyue youre hertis and youre soulis, that ye seke 'youre Lord God; and rise ye togidere, and bilde ye a seyntuarie to 'youre Lord God, that the arke of boond of pees of the Lord be brouyt in, and that vessels halewid to the Lord be brouyt in to the hows, which is bildid to the name of the Lord.

CAP 23

1 Therfor Dauid was eld and ful of daies, and ordeynede Salomon, his sone, kyng on Israel.

2 And he gaderide togidere alle the princes of Israel, and the preestis, and dekenes;

3 and the dekenes weren noumbrid fro twenti yeer and aboue, and eiyte and thretti thousynde of men weren foundun.

4 And foure and twenty thousynde men weren chosun of hem, and weren departid in to the seruyce of the hows of the Lord; sotheli of souereyns, and iugis, sixe thousynde;

5 forsothe foure thousynde 'porteris weren, and so many syngeris, syngynge to the Lord in orguns, whiche Dauid hadde maad for to synge.

6 And Dauid departide hem bi the whilis of the sones of Leuy, that is, of Gerson, and of Caath, and Merary.

7 And the sones of Gerson weren Leedan and Semeye.

8 The sones of Leedan weren thre, the prince Jehiel, and Ethan, and Johel.

9 The sones of Semei weren thre, Salamyth, and Oziel, and Aram; these weren the princes of the meynees of Leedan.

10 Forsothe the sones of Semeye weren Leeth, and Ziza, and Yaus, and Baria, these foure weren the sones of Semei.

11 Sotheli Leeth was the formere, and Ziza the secounde; forsothe Yaus and Baria hadden not ful many sones, and therfor thei weren rikenyd in o meynee and oon hows.

12 The sones of Caath weren foure, Amram, and Ysaac, Ebron, and Oziel.

13 The sones of Amram weren Aaron and Moyses; and Aaron was departid, that he schulde mynystre in the hooli thing of hooli thingis, he and hise sones with outen ende, and to brenne encense to the Lord bi his custom, and to blesse his name with outen ende.

14 Also the sones of Moyses, man of God, weren noumbrid in the lynage of Leuy.

15 The sones of Moises weren Gerson and Elieser.

16 The sones of Gerson; 'Subuhel the firste.

17 Sotheli the sones of Eliezer weren Roboya the firste, and othere sones weren not to Eliezer; forsothe the sones of Roboia weren multipliede ful miche.

18 The sones of Isaar; 'Salumuth the firste.

19 The sones of Ebron; 'Jerian the firste, Amarias the secounde, Jaziel the thridde, Jethamaan the fourthe.

20 The sones of Oziel; 'Mycha the firste, Jesia the secounde.

21 The sones of Merari weren Mooli and Musi. The sones of Mooli weren Eleazar, and Cys.

22 Sotheli Eleazar was deed, and hadde not sones, but douytris; and the sones of Cys, the britheren of hem, weddiden hem.

23 The sones of Musi weren thre, Mooli, and Heder, and Jerymuth.

24 These weren the sones of Leuy in her kynredis and meynees, prynces bi whilis, and noumbre of alle heedis, that diden the trauel of the seruyce of the hows of the Lord, fro twenti yeer and aboue.

25 For Dauid seide, The Lord God of Israel hath youe reste to his puple, and a dwellyng in Jerusalem til in to with outen ende;

26 and it schal not be the office of dekenes for to bere more the tabernacle, and alle vessels therof for to mynystre.

27 Also bi the laste comaundementis of Dauid the noumbre of the sones of Leuy schulen be rikened fro twenti yeer and aboue;

28 and thei schulen be vndir the hond of the sones of Aaron in to the worschipe of the hows of the Lord, in porchis, and in chaumbris, and in the place of clensyng, and in the seyntuarie, and in alle werkis of the seruyce of the temple of the Lord.

29 Forsothe preestis schulen be ouer the looues of proposicioun, and to the sacrifice of flour, and to the pastis sodun in watir, and to the therf looues, and friyng panne, and to hoot flour, and to seenge, and ouer al weiyte and mesure.

30 Forsothe the dekenes schulen be, that thei stonde eerli, for to knowleche and synge to the Lord, and lijk maner at euentide,

31 as wel in the offryng of brent sacrifices of the Lord, as in sabatis, and kalendis, and othere solempnytees, bi the noumbre and cerymonyes of eche thing contynueli bifor the Lord;

32 and that thei kepe the obseruaunces of the tabernacle of the boond of pees of the Lord, and the custum of the seyntuarie,

and the obseruaunce of the sones of Aaron, her britheren, that thei mynystre in the hows of the Lord.

CAP 24

1 Forsothe to the sones of Aaron these porciouns schulen be; the sones of Aaron weren Nadab, and Abyud, Eleazar, and Ythamar;

2 but Nadab and Abyud weren deed with out fre children bifor her fadir, and Eleazar and Ythamar weren set in presthod.

3 And Dauith departide hem, that is, Sadoch, of the sones of Eleazar, and Achymelech, of the sones of Ithamar, by her whiles and seruyce;

4 and the sones of Eleazar weren founden many mo in the men princes, than the sones of Ythamar. Forsothe he departide to hem, that is, to the sones of Eleazar, sixtene prynces bi meynees; and to the sones of Ythamar eiyte prynces bi her meynees and howsis.

5 Sotheli he departide euer eithir meynees among hem silf bi lottis; for there weren princes of the seyntuarye, and princes of the hows of God, as wel of the sones of Eleazar as of the sones of Ithamar.

6 And Semeye, the sone of Nathanael, a scribe of the lynage of Leuy, discriuede hem bifore the king and pryncis, and bifor Sadoch, the preest, and Achymelech, the sone of Abiathar, and to the prynces of meynees of the preestis and of the dekenes; he discriuyde oon hows of Eleazar, that was souereyn to othere, and 'the tother hows of Ithamar, that hadde othere vndir hym.

7 Forsothe the firste lot yede out to Joiarib, the secounde to Jedeie,

8 the thridde to Aharym, the fourthe to Seorym,

9 the fyuethe to Melchie,

10 the sixte to Maynan, the seuenthe to Accos,

11 the eiythe to Abia, the nynthe to Hieusu, the tenthe to Sechema, the elleuenthe to Eliasib,

12 the tweluethe to Jacyn,

13 the thrittenthe to Opha, the fourtenthe to Isbaal,

14 the fiftenthe to Abelga, the sixtenthe to Emmer,

15 the seuententhe to Ezir, the eiytenthe to Ahapses, the nyntenthe to Pheseye,

16 the twentithe to Jezechel,

17 the oon and twentithe to Jachym, the two and twentithe to Gamul, the thre and twentithe to Dalayam,

18 the foure and twentithe to Mazzian.

19 These weren the whilis of hem bi her mynysteries, that thei entre in to the hows of God, and bi her custom vndur the hond of Aaron, her fadir, as the Lord God of Israel comaundide.

20 Forsothe Sebahel was prince of the sones of Leuy that weren resydue, of the sones of Amram; and the sone of Sebahel was Jedeie;

21 also Jesie was prince of the sones of Roobie.

22 Sotheli Salomoth was prince of Isaaris; and the sone of Salamoth was Janadiath;

23 and his firste sone was Jeriuans, 'Amarie the secounde, Azihel the thridde, 'Jethmoan the fourthe.

24 The sone of Ozihel was Mycha; the sone of Mycha was Samyr;

25 The brother of Mycha was Jesia; and the sone of Jesia was Zacharie.

26 The sones of Merary weren Mooli and Musi; the sone of Josyan was Bennon;

27 and the sone of Merarie was Ozian, and Soen, and Zaccur, and Hebri.

28 Sotheli the sone of Mooli was Eleazar, that hadde not fre sones; forsothe the sone of Cys was Jeremyhel;

29 the sones of Musy weren Mooli,

30 Eder, Jerymuth. These weren the sones of Leuy, bi the housis of her meynees.

31 Also and thei senten lottis ayens her britheren, the sones of Aaron, bifor Dauid the kyng, and bifor Sadoch, and Achymelech, and the princes of meynees of preestis and of dekenes; lot departide euenli alle, bothe the gretter and the lesse.

CAP 25

1 Therfor Dauid, and the magestratis of the oost, departiden in to the seruyce the sones of Asaph, and of Eman, and of Idithum, whiche schulden profecye in harpis, and sawtrees, and cymbalis, bi her noumbre, and serue the office halewid to hem.

2 Of the sones of Asaph; Zaccur, and Joseph, and Nathania, and Asarela; sotheli the sones of Asaph vndir the hond of Asaph profesieden bisidis the kyng.

3 Forsothe the sones of Idithum weren these; Idithum, Godolie, Sori, Jesie, and Sabaie, and Mathatie, sixe; vndur the hond of hir fadir Idithum, that profesiede in an harpe on men knoulechynge and preysynge the Lord.

4 Also the sones of Heman weren Heman, Boccia, Mathanya, Oziel, Subuhel, and Jerymoth, Ananye, Anan, Elyatha, Gaeldothi, and Romenthi, Ezer, and Jesbacasi, Melothy, Othir, Mazioth;

5 alle these sones of Heman weren profetis of the kyng in the wordis of God, that he schulde enhaunse the horn. And God yaf to Heman fourtene sones, and thre douytris.

6 Alle vndur the hond of her fadir weren 'delid, ethir asigned, to synge in the temple of the Lord, in cymbalis, and sawtrees, and harpis, in to the seruyces of the hows of the Lord nyy the kyng, that is to seie, Asaph, and Idithum, and Heman.

7 Sotheli the noumbre of hem with her britheren, that tauyten the songe of the Lord, alle the techeris, was twey hundrid 'foure scoor and eiyte.

8 And thei senten lottis bi her whiles euenli, as wel the gretter as the lesse, also a wijs man and vnwijs.

9 And the firste lot yede out to Joseph, that was of Asaph; the secounde to Godolie, to hym, and hise sones and hise britheren twelue;

10 the thridde to Zaccur, to hise sones and hise bretheren twelue;

11 the fourthe to Isary, to hise sones and hise britheren twelue; the fyuethe to Nathanye,

12 to hise sones and hise britheren twelue;

13 the sixte to Boccian, to hise sones and hise britheren twelue;

14 the seuenthe to Israhela, to hise sones and britheren twelue;

15 the eiythe to Isaie, to his sones and britheren twelue;

16 the nynthe to Mathany, to his sones and britheren twelue;

17 the tenthe to Semei, to his sones and britheren twelue;

18 the elleuenthe to Ezrahel, to hise sones and britheren twelue;

19 the tweluethe to Asabie, to his sones and britheren twelue;

20 the thrittenthe to Subahel, to hise sones and britheren twelue;

21 the fourtenthe to Mathathatie, to hise sones and britheren twelue; the fiftenthe to Jerymoth,

22 to hise sones and britheren twelue;

23 the sixtenthe to Ananye, to hise sones and britheren twelue;

24 the seuententhe to Jesbocase, to hise sones and britheren twelue;

25 the eiytenthe to Annam, to hise sones and britheren twelue;

26 the nyntenthe to Mollothi, to hise sones and britheren twelue; the twentithe to Eliatha,

27 to hise sones and britheren twelue;

28 the oon and twentithe to Othir, to hise sones and britheren twelue;

29 the two and twentithe to Godoliathi, to hise sones and britheren twelue; the thre and twentithe to Mazioth,

30 to hise sones and britheren twelue;

31 the foure and twentithe to Romonathiezer, to his sones and britheren twelue.

CAP 26

1 Forsothe these weren the departingis of porteris; of the sones of Chore, Mellesemye was the sone of Chore, of the sones of Asaph.

2 The sones of Mellesemie weren Zacharie the firste gendrid, Jedihel the secounde, Zabadie the thridde, Yathanyel the fourthe,

3 Aylam the fifthe, Johannan the sixte, Helioenay the seuenthe.

4 Forsothe the sones of Ebededom weren these; Semey the firste gendrid, Jozabab the secounde, Joaha the thridde, Seccar the fourthe, Nathanael the fyuethe,

5 Amyhel the sixte, Isachar the seuenthe, Pollathi the eiythe, for the Lord blesside hym.

6 Forsothe to Semeye, his sone, weren borun sones, souereyns of her meynees; for thei weren ful stronge men.

7 Therfor the sones of Semeye weren Othyn, and Raphael, and Obediel, and Zadab; and hise britheren, ful stronge men; also Helyu, and Samathie.

8 Alle these weren of the sones of Obededom; thei and her sones and britheren, ful stronge men for to serue, two and sixti of Obededom.

9 Sotheli of Mellesemeye, the sones and britheren, ful stronge, ʼweren eiytene.

10 Forsothe of Oza, that is, of the sones of Merarie, Sechri was prince; for he hadde no firste gendrid, and therfor his fadir settide hym in to prince;

11 and Elchias the secounde, Thebelias the thridde, Zacarie the fourthe; alle these threttene weren the sones and britheren of Osa.

12 These weren departid in to porteris, that euere the princes of kepyngis, as also her britheren, schulden mynystre in the hows of the Lord.

13 Therfor lottis weren sent euenly, bothe to the litle and to the grete, bi her meyneeis, in to ech of the yatis.

14 Therfor the lot of the eest bifelde to Semelie; forsothe the north coost bifelde bi lot to Zacarie, his sone, a ful prudent man and lernd;

15 sotheli to Obededom and hise sones at the southe, in which part of the hows the counsel of the eldre men was;

16 Sephyma and Thosa weren at the west, bisidis the yate that ledith to the weie of stiyng, kepyng ayens kepyng.

17 Sotheli at the eest weren sixe dekenes, and at the north weren foure bi dai; and at the south also weren foure at the myddai; and, where the counsel was, weren tweyne and tweyne.

18 And in the sellis, ethir ʼlitle housis, of porteris at the west, weren foure in the weie, and tweyne bi the sellis.

19 These weren the departyngis of porteris, of the sones of Chore and of Merary.

20 Forsothe Achias was ouer the tresours of the hows of the Lord, and ouer the vessels of hooli thingis.

21 The sones of Leedan, the sone of Gerson; of Leedan weren the princis of meynees of Leedan, and of Gerson, and of Jehiel.

22 The sones of Jehiel weren, Zethan, and Johel, his brother, ouer the tresours of the hows of the Lord,

23 Amramytis, and Isaaritis, and Ebronytis, and Ezielitis.

24 Forsothe Subahel, the sone of Gerson, sone of Moises, was souereyn of the tresour;

25 and his brother, Eliezer; whos sone was Raabia; and his sone was Asaye; his sone was Joram; and his sone was Zechry; but and his sone was Selemith.

26 Thilke Selemith, and his britheren, weren ouer the tresours of hooli thingis, whiche ʼDauid the kyng halewide, and the princes of meynees, and the tribunes, and the centuriouns, and the duykis of the oost,

27 of the batels, and of the spuylis of batels, whiche thei halewiden to the reparacioun and purtenaunce of the temple of the Lord.

28 Forsothe Samuel, the prophete, halewide alle these thingis, and Saul, the sone of Cys, and Abner, the sone of Ner, and Joab, the sone of Saruye; and alle halewiden tho thingis bi the hond of Salemyth, and of his britheren.

29 Sotheli Chonenye was souereyn and hise sones to Isaaritis, to the werkis with outforth on Israel, to teche and to deme hem.

30 Sotheli of Ebronytis, Asabie, and Sabie, and hise britheren, ful stronge men, a thousynde and seuene hundrid, weren souereyns on Israel biyende Jordan ayens the weste, in alle the werkis of the Lord, and in to the seruyce of the kyng.

31 Forsothe Herie was prynce of Ebronytis, bi her meynees and kynredis. In the fourtithe yeer of the rewme of Dauid there weren noumbred and foundun ful stronge men in Jazer Galaad;

32 and hise britheren, of strongere age, twei thousynde and seuene hundrid, princes of meynees. Sotheli ʼDauid the kyng made hem souereyns of Rubenytis and Gaditis, and of the half lynage of Manasses, ʼin to al the seruyce of God and of the kyng.

CAP 27

1 Forsothe the sones of Israel bi her noumbre, the princes of meynees, the tribunes, and centuriouns, and prefectis, that mynystriden to the kyng bi her cumpenyes, entrynge and goynge out bi ech monethe in the yeer, weren souereyns, ech bi hym silf, on foure and twenti thousynde.

2 Isiboam, the sone of Zabdihel, was souereyn of the firste cumpenye in the firste monethe, and vndur hym weren foure and twenti thousynde;

3 of the sones of Fares was the prince of alle princes in the oost, in the firste monethe.

4 Dudi Achoites hadde the cumpany of the secounde monethe, and aftir hym silf he hadde another man, Macelloth bi

name, that gouernede a part of the oost of foure and twenti thousynde.

5 And Bananye, the sone of Joiada, the preest, was duyk of the thridde cumpenye in the thridde monethe, and four and twenti thousynde in his departyng;

6 thilke is Bananye, the strongest among thritti, and aboue thritti; forsothe Amyzadath, his sone, was souereyn of his cumpenye.

7 In the fourthe monethe, the fourthe prince was Asahel, the brother of Joab, and Zabadie, his sone, aftir hym, and foure and twenti thousynde in his cumpeny.

8 In the fifthe monethe, the fifthe prince was Samoth Jezarites, and foure and twenti thousynde in his cumpenye.

9 In the sixte monethe, the sixte prince was Ira, the sone of Actes, Techuytes, and foure and twenti thousynde in his cumpeny.

10 In the seuenthe monethe, the seuenthe prince was Helles Phallonites, of the sones of Effraym, and foure and twenti thousynde in his cumpeny.

11 In the eiythe monethe, the eiythe prince was Sobothai Assothites, of the generacioun of Zarai, and foure and twenti thousynde in his cumpeny.

12 In the nynthe monethe, the nynthe prince was Abiezer Anathotites, of the generacioun of Gemyny, and foure and tweynti thousynde in his cumpeny.

13 In the tenthe monethe, the tenthe prince was Maray, and he was Neophatites, of the generacioun of Zaray, and foure and twenti thousynde in his cumpany.

14 In the elleuenthe monethe, the elleuenthe prince was Banaas Pharonytes, of the sones of Effraym, and foure and twenti thousynde in his cumpeny.

15 In the tweluethe monethe, the tweluethe prince was Holdia Nethophatites, of the generacioun of Gothonyel, and foure and twenti thousynde in his cumpeny.

16 Forsothe these weren souereyns of the lynages of Israel; duyk Eliezer, sone of Zechri, was souereyn to Rubenytis; duyk Saphacie, sone of Maacha, was souereyn to Symeonytis;

17 Asabie, the sone of Chamuel, was souereyn to Leuytis; Sadoch 'was souereyn to Aaronytis;

18 Elyu, the brothir of Dauid, 'was souereyn to the lynage of Juda; Amry, the sone of Mychael, 'was souereyn to Isacharitis;

19 Jesmaye, the sone of Abdie, was souereyn to Zabulonytis; Jerymuth, the sone of Oziel, 'was souereyn to Neptalitis;

20 Ozee, the sone of Ozazym, 'was souereyn to the sones of Effraym; Johel, the sone of Phatae, was souereyn to the half lynage of Manasses;

21 and Jaddo, the sone of Zacarie, 'was souereyn to the half lynage of Manasses in Galaad; sotheli Jasihel, the sone of Abner, 'was souereyn to Beniamyn; forsothe Ezriel,

22 the sone of Jeroam, was souereyn to Dan; these weren the princes of the sones of Israel.

23 Forsothe Dauid nolde noumbre hem with ynne twenti yeer, for the Lord seide, that he wolde multiplie Israel as the sterris of heuene.

24 Joab, the sone of Saruye, bigan for to noumbre, and he fillide not; for ire fel on Israel for this thing, and therfor the noumbre of hem, that weren noumbrid, was not teld in to the bookis of cronyclis of kyng Dauid.

25 Forsothe Azymoth, the sone of Adihel, was on the tresouris of the kyng; but Jonathan, the sone of Ozie, was souereyn of these tresours, that weren in cytees, and in townes, and in touris.

26 Sotheli Ezri, the sone of Chelub, was souereyn on the werk of hosebondrie, and on erthe tiliers, that tiliden the lond;

27 and Semeye Ramathites was souereyn on tilieris of vyneris; sotheli Zabdie Aphonytes was souereyn on the wyn celeris;

28 for Balanam Gadaritis was on the olyue placis, and fige places, that weren in the feeldi places; sotheli Joas was on the schoppis, 'ether celeris, of oile;

29 forsothe Cethray Saronytis 'was souereyn of the droues, that weren lesewid in Sarena; and Saphat, the sone of Abdi, was ouer the oxis in valeys;

30 sotheli Vbil of Ismael was ouer the camelis; and Jadye Meronathites was ouer the assis; and Jazir Aggarene was ouer the scheep;

31 alle these weren princes of the catel of kyng Dauid.

32 Forsothe Jonathas, brother of 'Dauithis fader, was a councelour, a myyti man, and prudent, and lettrid; he and Jahiel, the sone of Achamony, weren with the sones of the kyng.

33 Also Achitofel was a counselour of the kyng; and Chusi Arachites was a frend of the kyng.

34 Aftir Achitofel was Joiada, the sone of Banaye, and Abyathar; but Joab was prince of the oost of the kyng.

CAP 28

1 Therfor Dauid clepide togidere alle the princes of Israel, the duykis of lynagis, and the souereyns of cumpenyes, that 'mynystriden to the kyng, also the tribunes, and centuriouns, and hem that weren souereyns ouer the catel and possessiouns of the kyng, and hise sones, with 'nurchis, and techeris, and alle the myyti and strongeste men in the oost of Jerusalem.

2 And whanne the kyng hadde rise, and 'hadde stonde, he seide, My britheren and my puple, here ye me. Y thouyte for to bilde an hows, wherynne the arke of boond of pees of the Lord, and the stool of the feet of oure God schulde reste; and Y made redi alle thingis to bilde.

3 But God seide to me, Thou schalt not bilde an hows to my name, for thou art a man werriour, and hast sched blood.

4 But the Lord God of Israel chees me of al the hows of my fadir, that Y schulde be kyng on Israel with outen ende; for of Juda he chees princes, sotheli of the hows of Juda he chees the hows of my fadir, and of the sones of my fadir it pleside hym to chese me kyng on al Israel.

5 But also of my sones, for the Lord yaf to me many sones, he chees Salomon, my sone, that he schulde sitte in the troone of the rewme of the Lord on Israel.

6 And he seide to me, Salomon, thi sone, schal bilde myn hows, and myn auters; for Y haue chose hym to me in to a sone, and Y schal be to hym in to a fadir;

7 and Y schal make stidefast his rewme til in to with outen ende, if he schal contynue to do myn heestis and domes, as and to dai.

8 Now therfor bifor al the cumpeny of Israel, 'Y seie these thingis that suen in the heryng of God, kepe ye and seke ye alle the comaundementis of 'youre Lord God, that ye haue in possessioun a good lond, and that ye leeue it to youre sones aftir you til in to with outen ende.

9 But thou, Salomon, my sone, knowe the God of thi fadir, and serue thou hym with perfit herte, and wilful soule; for the Lord serchith alle hertis, and vndirstondith alle thouytis of soulis; if thou sekist hym, thou schalt fynde hym; forsothe if thou forsakist hym, he schal caste thee awei with outen ende.

10 Now therfor, for the Lord chees thee, for to bilde the hows of seyntuarie, be thou coumfortid, and parforme.

11 Forsothe Dauid yaf to Salomon, his sone, the discryuyng, 'ether ensaumple, of the porche, and of the temple, and of celeris, and of the soler, and of closetis in pryuy places, and of the hows of propiciacioun, 'that is, of mersi;

12 also and of alle thingis whiche he thouyte of the large places, and of chaumbris bi cumpas, in to the tresours of the hows of the Lord, and 'in to the tresours of holi thingis,

13 and of the departyngis of preestis and of dekenes, in to alle the werkis of the hows of the Lord, and alle vessels of the seruyce of the temple of the Lord.

14 Of gold in weiyte bi ech vessel of the seruyce, and of siluer, for dyuersitee of vessels, and of werkis;

15 but also to goldun candilstikis, and to her lanternes, he yaf gold, for the mesure of ech candilstike and lanternes; also and in silueren candilstikis, and in her lanternes, he bitook the weiyte of siluer, for the dyuersite of mesure.

16 Also and he yaf gold in to the bord of settyng forth, for the dyuersite of mesure, also and he yaf siluer in to othere siluerne boordis;

17 also to fleisch hookis, and viols, and censeris of pureste gold; and to litle goldun lyouns, for the maner of mesure, he departide a weiyte in to a litil lyoun and a litil lioun; also and in to siluerne liouns he departide dyuerse weiyte of siluer.

18 Forsothe he yaf pureste gold to the auter, wherynne encense was brent, that a lickenesse of the cart of cherubyns, holdinge forth wyngis, and hilynge the arke of boond of pees of the Lord, schulde be maad therof.

19 Dauid seide, Alle thingis camen writun bi the hond of the Lord to me, that Y schulde vndirstonde alle the werkis of the saumpler.

20 And Dauid seide to Salomon, his sone, Do thou manli, and be thou coumfortid, and make; drede thou not 'with outforth, nether drede thou 'with ynne; for 'my Lord God schal be with thee, and he schal not leeue thee, nether schal forsake thee, til thou performe al the werk of the seruyce of the hows of the Lord.

21 Lo! the departyngis of prestis and of dekenes, in to al the werk of the seruyce of the hows of the Lord, schulen stonde niy thee; and thei ben redi, and bothe the princes and the puple kunnen do alle thi comaundementis.

CAP 29

1 And kyng Dauid spak to al the chirche, God hath chose Salomon, my sone, yit a child and tendre; forsothe the werk is greet, and a dwellyng is not maad redi to man but to God.

2 Sotheli Y in alle my myytis haue maad redi the costis of the hows of my God; gold to goldun vessels, siluer in to siluerne vessels, bras in to brasun vessels, irun in to irun vessels, tre in to trenun vessels, onychyn stonys, and stonys as of the colour of wymmens oynement, and ech precious stoon of dyuerse colouris, and marbil of dyuerse colouris, most plenteuously.

3 And ouer these thingis Y yyue gold and siluer in to the temple of my God, whiche Y offride of my propir catel in to the hows of my God, outakun these thingis whiche Y made redi in to the hooli hows,

4 thre thousynde talentis of gold, of the gold of Ophir, and seuene thousynde of talentis of siluer most preuyd, to ouergilde the wallis of the temple;

5 and werkis be maad bi the hondis of crafti men, where euere gold is nedeful, of gold, and where euere siluer is nedeful, of

siluer; and if ony man offrith bi his fre wille, fille he his hond to dai, and offre he that that he wole to the Lord.

6 Therfor the princes of meynees, and the duykis of the lynagis of Israel, and the tribunes, and the centuriouns, and the princes of the possessiouns of the kyng, bihiyten;

7 and thei yauen in to the werkis of the hows of the Lord, fyue thousynde talentis of gold, and ten thousynde schyllyngis; ten thousynde talentis of siluer, and eiytene thousynde talentis of bras, and an hundrid thousynde of talentis of irun.

8 And at whom euere stoonys were foundun, thei yauen in to the tresour of the hows of the Lord, bi the hond of Jehiel Gersonyte.

9 And the puple was glad, whanne thei bihiyten avowis bi her fre wille, for with al the herte thei offriden tho to the Lord. But also kyng Dauid was glad with greet ioye, and blesside the Lord bifor al the multitude,

10 and seide, Lord God of Israel, oure fadir, thou art blessid fro with outen bigynnyng in to with outen ende;

11 Lord, worthi doyng is thin, and power, and glorie, and victorie, and heriyng is to thee; for alle thingis that ben in heuene and in erthe ben thine; Lord, the rewme is thin, and thou art ouer alle princes; ritchessis ben thin, and glorie is thin;

12 thou art Lord of alle; in thin hond is vertu, and power, and in thin hond is greetnesse, and lordschipe of alle.

13 Now therfor, oure God, we knoulechen to thee, and we herien thi noble name.

14 Who am Y, and who is my puple, that we moun bihete alle these thingis to thee? Alle thingis ben thine, and we han youe to thee tho thingis, whiche we token of thin hond.

15 For we ben pilgrimes and comelyngis bifor thee, as alle oure fadris; oure daies ben as schadewe on the erthe, and 'no dwellyng is.

16 Oure Lord God, al this plentee which we han maad redi, that an hows schulde be byldid to thin hooli name, is of thin hond; and alle thingis ben thin.

17 My God, Y woot, that thou preuest hertis, and louest symplenesse of herte; wherfor and Y, in the symplenesse of myn herte, haue offrid gladli alle these thingis; and Y siy with greet ioye thi puple, which is foundun here, offre yiftis to thee.

18 Lord God of Abraham, and of Ysaac, and of Israel, oure fadris, kepe thou with outen ende this wille of her hertis; and this mynde dwelle euere in to the worschipyng of thee.

19 Also yyue thou to Salomon, my sone, a perfit herte, that he kepe thin heestis, and witnessyngis, and thi ceremonyes; and do alle thingis, and that he bilde the hows, whose costis Y haue maad redi.

20 Forsothe Dauid comaundide to al the chirche, Blesse ye 'oure Lord God. And al the chirche blesside the Lord God of her fadris, and thei bowiden hem silf, and worschipiden God, aftirward the kyng.

21 And thei offriden slayn sacrifices to the Lord, and thei offriden brent sacrifices in the dai suynge; a thousynde boolis, and a thousynde rammes, and a thousynde lambren, with her fletynge sacrifices, and al the custom, most plenteuously, in to al Israel.

22 And thei eten and drunken bifor the Lord in that dai, with greet gladnesse. And thei anoyntiden the secounde tyme Salomon, the sone of Dauid; and thei anoyntiden hym in to prince to the Lord, and Sadoch in to bischop.

23 And Salomon sat on the trone of the Lord in to kyng, for Dauid, his fadir; and it pleside alle men, and al Israel obeiede to hym.

24 But also alle princes, and myyti men, and alle the sones of kyng Dauid, yauen hond, and weren suget to 'Salomon the kyng.

25 Therfor the Lord magnefiede Salomon on al Israel, and yaue to hym glorie of the rewme, what maner glorie no kyng of Israel hadde bifor hym.

26 Therfor Dauid, the sone of Ysai, regnede on al Israel;

27 and the daies in whiche he regnede on Israel weren fourti yeer; in Ebron he regnede seuene yeer, and in Jerusalem thre and thretti yeer.

28 And he diede in good eelde, and was ful of daies, and richessis, and glorie; and Salomon, his sone, regnede for hym.

29 Forsothe the formere and the laste dedis of Dauid ben writun in the book of Samuel, the prophete, and in the book of Nathan, prophete, and in the book of Gad, the prophete;

30 and of al his rewme, and strengthe, and tymes, that passiden vndur hym, ethir in Israel, ethir in alle rewmes of londis.

2 PARALIPOMENON

CAP 1

1 Therfor Salomon, the sone of Dauid, was coumfortid in his rewme, and the Lord was with hym, and magnefiede hym an hiy.

2 And Salomon comaundide to al Israel, to tribunes, and centuriouns, and to duykis, and domesmen of al Israel, and to the princes of meynees;

3 and he yede with al the multitude in to the hiy place of Gabaon, where the tabernacle of boond of pees of the Lord was, which tabernacle Moyses, the seruaunt of the Lord, made in wildirnesse.

4 Forsothe Dauid hadde brouyt the arke of God fro Cariathiarym in to the place which he hadde maad redy to it, and where he hadde set a tabernacle to it, that is, in to Jerusalem.

5 And the brasun auter, which Beseleel, the sone of Vri, sone of Vr, hadde maad, was there bifor the tabernacle of the Lord; whiche also Salomon and al the chirche souyte.

6 And Salomon stiede to the brasun autir, bifor the tabernacle of boond of pees of the Lord, and offride in it a thousynde sacrifices.

7 Lo! 'forsothe in that nyyt God apperide to hym, 'and seide, Axe that that thou wolt, that Y yyue to thee.

8 And Salomon seide to God, Thou hast do greet mersi with Dauid, my fadir, and hast ordeyned me kyng for hym.

9 Now therfor, Lord God, thi word be fillid, which thou bihiytist to Dauid, my fadir; for thou hast maad me kyng on thi greet puple, which is so vnnoumbrable as the dust of erthe.

10 Yiue thou to me wisdom and vndurstondyng, that Y go in and go out bifor thi puple; for who may deme worthili this thi puple, which is so greet?

11 Sotheli God seide to Salomon, For this thing pleside more thin herte, and thou axidist not richessis, and catel, and glorie, nether the lyues of them that hatiden thee, but nether ful many daies of lijf; but thou axidist wisdom and kunnyng, that thou maist deme my puple, on which Y ordeynede thee kyng,

12 wisdom and kunnyng ben youun to thee; forsothe Y schal yyue to thee richessis, and catel, and glorie, so that noon among kyngis, nether bifor thee nethir aftir thee, be lijk thee.

13 Therfor Salomon cam fro the hiy place of Gabaon in to Jerusalem, bifor the tabernacle of boond of pees, and he regnede on Israel.

14 And he gaderide to hym chaaris and knyytis, and a thousynde and foure hundrid charis weren maad to hym, and twelue thousynde of knyytis; and he made hem to be in the citees of cartis, and with the kyng in Jerusalem.

15 And the kyng yaf in Jerusalem gold and siluer as stoonys, and cedris as sicomoris, that comen forth in feeldi places in greet multitude.

16 Forsothe horsis weren brouyt to hym fro Egipt, and fro Choa, bi the marchauntis of the kyng, whiche yeden, and bouyten bi prijs,

17 'a foure 'horsid carte for sixe hundrid platis of siluer, and an hors for an hundrid and fifti. In lijk maner biyng was maad of alle the rewmes of citees, and of the kingis of Sirie.

CAP 2

1 Forsothe Salomon demyde to bilde an hows to the name of the Lord, and a paleis to hym silf.

2 And he noumbride seuenti thousynde of men berynge in schuldris, and fourescore thousynde that schulden kitte stoonys in hillis; and the souereyns of hem thre thousynde and sixe hundrid.

3 And he sente to Iram, kyng of Tire, and seide, As thou didist with my fadir Dauid, and sentist to hym trees of cedre, that he schulde bilde to hym an hows, in which also he dwellide;

4 so do thou with me, that Y bilde an hows to the name of 'my Lord God, and that Y halewe it, to brenne encense bifor hym, and to make odour of swete smellynge spiceries, and to euerlastynge settynge forth of looues, and to brent sacrifices in the morewtid and euentid, and in sabatis, and neomenyes, and solempnytees of 'oure Lord God in to with outen ende, that ben comaundid to Israel.

5 For the hows which Y coueyte to bilde is greet; for 'oure Lord God is greet ouer alle goddis.

6 Who therfor may haue myyt to bilde a worthi hows to hym? For if heuene and the heuenes of heuenes moun not take hym, hou greet am Y, that Y may bilde 'an hows to hym, but to this thing oonli, that encense be brent bifor hym?

7 Therfor sende thou to me a lernd man, that can worche in gold, and siluer, bras, and yrun, purpur, rede silke, and iacynct; and that can graue in grauyng with these crafti men, which Y haue with me in Judee and Jerusalem, whiche Dauid, my fadir, made redi.

8 But also sende thou to me cedre trees, and pyne trees, and thyne trees of the Liban; for Y woot, that thi seruauntis kunnen kitte trees of the Liban; and my seruauntis schulen be with thi seruauntis,

9 that ful many trees be maad redi to me; for the hows which Y coueyte to bilde is ful greet and noble.

10 Ferthermore to thi seruauntis, werk men that schulen kitte trees, Y schal yyue in to meetis twenti thousynde chorus of whete, and so many chorus of barli, and twenti thousynde mesuris of oile, that ben clepid sata.

11 Forsothe Iram, king of Tire, seide bi lettris whiche he sente to Salomon, For the Lord louyde his puple, therfor he made thee to regne on it.

12 And he addide, seiynge, Blessid be the Lord God of Israel, that made heuene and erthe, which yaf to 'Dauid the kyng a wijs sone, and lernd, and witti, and prudent, that he schulde bilde an hows to the Lord, and a paleis to hym silf.

13 Therfor Y sente to thee a prudent man and moost kunnynge, Iram,

14 my fadir, the sone of a womman of the lynage of Dan, whos fadir was a man of Tire; whiche Iram can worche in

gold, and siluer, bras, and irun, and marble, and trees, also in purpur, and iacynct, and bijs, and rede silke; and which Iram can graue al grauyng, and fynde prudentli, what euer thing is nedeful in werk with thi crafti men, and with the crafti men of my lord Dauid, thi fadir.

15 Therfor, my lord, sende thou to thi seruauntis the whete, and barli, and oyle, and wyn, whiche thou bihiytist.

16 Sotheli we schulen kitte trees of the Liban, how many euere thou hast nedeful; and we schulen brynge tho in schippis bi the see in to Joppe; forsothe it schal be thin to lede tho ouer in to Jerusalem.

17 Therfor Salomon noumbride alle men conuertid fro hethenesse, that weren in the lond of Israel, aftir the noumbryng which Dauid, his fadir, noumbride; and an hundrid thousynde and thre and fifti thousynde and sixe hundrid weren foundun.

18 And he made of hem seuenti thousynde, that schulden bere birthuns in schuldris, and 'foure score thousynde, that schulden kitte stonys in hillis; sotheli he made thre thousynde and sixe hundrid souereyns of werkis of the puple.

CAP 3

1 And Salomon bigan to bilde the hows of the Lord in Jerusalem, in the hil of Moria, that was schewid to Dauid, his fadir, in the place which Dauid hadde maad redi in the corn floor of Ornam Jebusei.

2 Forsothe he bigan to bilde in the secounde monethe, in the fourthe yeer of his rewme.

3 And these weren the foundementis, whiche Salomon settide, that he schulde bilde the hous of God; sixti cubitis of lengthe in the firste mesure, twenti cubitis of breede.

4 Forsothe he bildide a porche bifor the frount, that was stretchid forth along bisidis the mesure of the breede of the hows, of twenti cubitis, sotheli the hiynesse was of an hundrid and twenti cubitis; and he ouergilde it with inne with clennest gold.

5 Also he hilide the gretter hows with tablis of beech, and he fastnede platis of gold of beste colour al aboute; and he grauyde therynne palmtrees, and as smale chaynes biclipynge hem silf togidere.

6 And he arayede the pawment of the temple with most preciouse marble, in myche fairenesse.

7 Forsothe the gold was moost preued, of whose platis he hilide the hows, and the beemys therof, and the postis, and the wallis, and the doris; and he grauyde cherubyns in the wallis.

8 Also he made an hows to the holi of holi thingis, in lengthe bi the breede of the hows, of twenti cubitis, and the breed also of twenti cubitis; and he hilide it with goldun platis, as with sixe hundrid talentis.

9 But also he made goldun nailis, so that ech nail peiside fifti siclis; and he hilide the solers with gold.

10 Also he made in the hows of the hooli of hooli thingis twei cherubyns bi the werk of an ymage makere, and hilide hem with gold.

11 The wyngis of cherubyns weren holdun forth bi twenti cubitis, so that o wynge hadde fyue cubitis, and touchide the wal of the hows; and the tother wynge hadde fyue cubitis, and touchide the wynge of the tother cherub.

12 In lijk maner the wynge of the tother cherub hadde fyue cubitis, and touchide the wal, and the tother wynge therof of fyue cubitis touchide the wynge of the tothir cherub.

13 Therfor the wyngis of euer eithir cherub weren spred abrood, and weren holdun forth bi twenti cubitis; sotheli

thilke cherubyns stoden on the feet reisid, and her faces weren turned to the outermere hows.

14 Also he made a veil of iacynct and purpur, of reed seelk and bijs; and weuyde cherubyns therynne.

15 Also bifor the yate of the temple he made twei pilers, that hadden fyue and thretti cubitis of heiythe; forsothe the heedis of tho weren of fyue cubitis.

16 Also he made and as litle chaynes in Goddis answeryng place, and puttide tho on the heedis of the pilers; also he made an hundrid pumgarnadis, whiche he settide bitwixe the litle chaynes.

17 And he settide tho pilers in the porche of the temple, oon at the riytside, and the tother at the leftside; he clepide that that was at the riytside Jachym, and that that was at the leftside he clepide Booz.

CAP 4

1 Also he made a brasun auter of twenti cubitis of lengthe, and of twenti cubitis of breede, and of ten cubitis of heiythe;

2 he made also a yotun see of ten cubitis fro brynke til to brynke, round bi cumpas; it hadde fyue cubitis of heiythe; and a coorde of thritti cubitis cumpasside the cumpas therof.

3 And the licnesse of oxis was vndur it, and bi ten cubitis summe grauyngis with outforth cumpassiden the brynke of the see as with tweyne ordris; sotheli the oxis weren yotun.

4 And thilke see was set on twelue oxis, of whiche oxis thre bihelden to the north, and othere thre to the west, sotheli thre othere bihelden the south, and thre 'that weren residue bihelden the eest, and hadden the see set aboue; but the hyndrere partis of the oxis weren with ynne vndur the see.

5 Sotheli the thicknesse therof hadde the mesure of a pawm of the hond, and the brynke therof was as the brynke of a cuppe, ethir of a lilie crokid ayen, and it took thre thousynde metretis of mesure.

6 Also he made ten holowe vessels, and settide fyue at the riytside, and fyue at the leftside, that thei schulden waische in tho alle thingis, whiche thei schulden offre in to brent sacrifice; sotheli the preestis weren waischun in the see.

7 Sotheli he made ten goldun candilstikis bi the licknesse which he hadde comaundid to be maad; and he settide tho in the temple, fyue at the riytside and fyue at the leftsid.

8 And he made also ten boordis, and settide tho in the temple, fyue at the riytside and fyue at the leftside.

9 Also he made an hundrid goldun viols. 'Also he made a large place of preestis, and a greet hows, and doris in the greet hows, which he hilide with bras.

10 Forsothe he settide the see in the riytsyde ayens the eest at the south.

11 Also Iram made cawdruns, and fleischokis, and viols, and he fillide al the werk of the kyng in the hows of God,

12 that is, twei pilers, and pomels, and heedis, and as summe nettis, that hiliden the heedis aboue the pomels;

13 also he made fourti pumgarnadis, and twei werkis lijk nettis, so that two ordris of pumgarnadis weren ioyned to ech werk like nettis, which hiliden the pomels, and heedis of the pilers.

14 He made also foundementis, and holow vessels, whiche he settide on the foundementis;

15 he made o see, and twelue oxis vndur the see,

16 and caudruns, and fleischookis, and viols. Iram, the fadir of Salomon, made to hym alle vessels in the hows of the Lord of clennest bras.

17 The kyng yetide tho in the cuntrey of Jordan, in cleiy lond bitwixe Socoth and Saredata.

18 Forsothe the multitude of vessels was vnnoumbrable, so that the weiyte of bras was not knowun.

19 And Salomon made alle the vessels of Goddis hows, the goldun auter, 'and bordis, and loouys of settyng forth on tho;

20 and candilstikis of purest gold, with her lanternes, that tho schulden schyne bifor Goddis answering place bi the custom;

21 and he made summe werkis lijk flouris, and lanternes, and goldun tongis; alle thingis weren maad of clennest gold;

22 also he made pannes for colis to brenne encense, and censeris, and viols, and morters, of pureste gold. And he grauyde doris of the ynnere temple, that is, in the hooli of hooli thingis, and the goldun doris of the temple with out forth; and so al the werk was fillid that Salomon made in the hows of the Lord.

CAP 5

1 Therfor Salomon brouyte in alle thingis, siluer and gold, whiche Dauid, his fadir, hadde avowid; and he puttide alle vesselis in the tresouris of the hows of the Lord.

2 After whiche thingis he gaderide togidere alle the grettere men in birthe of Israel, and alle the princes of lynagis, and the heedis of meynees, of the sones of Israel, in to Jerusalem, that thei schulden brynge the arke of boond of pees of the Lord fro the citee of Dauid, which is Syon.

3 Therfor alle men of Israel camen to the kyng, in the solempne dai of the seuenthe monethe.

4 And whanne alle the eldre men of Israel 'weren comen, the dekenes baren the arke,

5 and brouyten it in, and al the aray of the tabernacle. Forsothe the preestis with the dekenes baren the vessels of seyntuarie, that weren in the tabernacle.

6 Sotheli kyng Salomon, and alle the cumpenyes of Israel, and alle that weren gaderid to gidere, offriden bifor the arke wetheris and oxis with outen ony noumbre; for the multitude of slayn sacrificees was 'so greet.

7 And preestis brouyten the arke of boond of pees of the Lord in to his place, that is, to Goddis answeryng place of the temple, in to the hooli of hooli thingis, vndur the wyngis of cherubyns;

8 so that cherubyns spredden forth her wyngis ouer the place, in which the arke was put, and hiliden thilke arke with hise barris.

9 Sotheli the heedis, by which the arke was borun, weren opyn bifor Goddis answeryng place, for tho heedis weren a litil lengere; but if a man hadde be a litil with out forth, he myyt not se tho barris. Therfor the arke was there til in to present dai;

10 and noon other thing was in the arke, no but twei tablis, whiche Moyses hadde put in Oreb, whanne the Lord yaf the lawe to the sones of Israel goynge out of Egipt.

11 Forsothe the prestis yeden out of the seyntuarie, for alle preestis, that myyten be foundun there, weren halewid, and the whiles, and the ordre of seruyces among hem was not departid yit in that tyme;

12 bothe dekenes and syngeris, that is, bothe thei that weren vndur Asaph, and thei that weren vndur Eman, and thei that weren vndur Idithum, her sones and britheren, clothid with white lynun clothis, sownyden with cymbalis and sautrees and harpis, and stoden at the west coost of the auter, and with hem weren sixe score preestis trumpynge.

13 Therfor whanne alle sungen togidur both with trumpis, and vois, and cymbalis, and orguns, and of dyuerse kynde of musikis, and reisiden the vois an hiy, the sown was herd fer, so that whanne thei hadden bigunne to preyse the Lord, and to seie, Knouleche ye to the Lord, for he is good, for his mercy is in to the world, 'ether, with outen ende; the hows of God was fillid with a cloude,

14 and the preestis miyten not stonde and serue for the derknesse; for the glorie of the Lord hadde fillid the hows of the Lord.

CAP 6

1 Thanne Salomon seide, The Lord bihiyte, that he wolde dwelle in derknesse;

2 forsothe I haue bilde an hows to his name, that he schulde dwelle there with outen ende.

3 And Salomon turnede his face, and blesside al the multitude of Israel; for al the cumpeny stood ententif; and he seide,

4 Blessid be the Lord God of Israel, for he fillide in werk that thing, that he spak to Dauid, my fadir, and seide,

5 Fro the dai in which Y ledde my puple out of the lond of Egipt, Y chees not a citee of alle the lynagis of Israel, that an hows schulde be bildid therynne to my name, nether Y chees ony other man, that he schulde be duyk on my puple Israel;

6 but Y chees Jerusalem, that my name be therynne, and Y chees Dauid, to ordeyne hym on my puple Israel.

7 And whanne it was of the wille of Dauid, my fadir, to bilde an hows to the name of the Lord God of Israel,

8 the Lord seide to hym, For this was thi wille, 'that thou woldist bilde an hows to my name, sotheli thou didist wel,

9 hauynge suche a wil, but thou schalt not bilde an hows to me; netheles the sone, that schal go out of thi leendis, he schal bilde an hows to my name.

10 Therfor the Lord hath fillid his word, which he spak; and Y roos for Dauid, my fader, and Y sat on the trone of Israel, as the Lord spak, and Y bildide an hous to the name of the Lord God of Israel;

11 and I haue put therynne the arke, in which is the couenaunt of the Lord, which he 'couenauntide with the sones of Israel.

12 Therfor Salomon stood bifor the auter of the Lord euene ayens al the multitude of Israel, and stretchide forth his hondis.

13 For Salomon hadde maad a brasun foundement, and hadde set it in the myddis of the greet hows, and it hadde fyue cubitis of lengthe, and fyue of breede, and thre cubitis of heiythe, and he stood theron; and fro that tyme he knelide ayens al the multitude of Israel, and reiside the hondis in to heuene,

14 and seide, Lord God of Israel, noon is lijk thee; 'thou art God in heuene and in erthe, which kepist couenaunt and mercy with thi seruauntis, that goon bifor thee in al her herte;

15 which hast youe to Dauid thi seruaunt, my fadir, what euer thingis thou hast spoke to hym, and thow hast fillid in werk tho thingis, whiche thou bihiytist bi mouth, as also present tyme preueth.

16 Now therfor, Lord God of Israel, fille thou to thi seruaunt my fadir Dauid, what euer thingis thou hast spoke, seiynge, A man of thee schal not faile bifor me, that schal sitte on the trone of Israel; so netheles if thi sones kepen my weies, and goon in my lawe, as and thou hast go bifor me.

17 And now, Lord God of Israel, thi word be maad stidefast, which thou spakist to thi seruaunt Dauid.

18 Therfor whether it is leueful, that the Lord dwelle with men on erthe? If heuene and the heuenes of heuenes 'taken not thee, how myche more this hows, which Y haue bildid?
19 But herto oneli it is maad, that thou, my Lord God, biholde the preier of thi seruaunt, and the bisechyng of hym, and that thou here the preieris, whiche thi seruaunt schedith bifor thee;
20 that thou opyne thin iyen on this hows bi dayes and nyytis, on the place in which thou bihiytist, that thi name schulde be clepid,
21 and that thou woldist here the preier, which thi seruaunt preieth therynne. Here thou the preieris of thi seruaunt, and of thi puple Israel; who euer preieth in this place, here thou fro thi dwellyng place, that is, fro heuenes, and do thou merci.
22 If ony man synneth ayens his neiybore, and cometh redi to swere ayens him, and byndith hym silf with cursyng bifor the auter in this hows,
23 thou schalt here fro heuene, and schalt do the doom of thi seruauntis; so that thou yelde to the wickid man his weie in to his owne heed, and that thou venge the iust man, and yelde to hym after his riytfulnesse.
24 If thi puple Israel is ouercomen of enemyes, for thei schulen do synne ayens thee, and if thei conuertid doen penaunce, and bisechen thi name, and preien in this place,
25 thou schalt here fro heuene, and do thou mercy to the synne of thi puple Israel, and brynge hem ayen 'in to the lond, which thou hast youe to hem, and to 'the fadris of hem.
26 If whanne heuene is closid, reyn come not doun for the synne of thi puple, and thei bisechen thee in this place, and knowlechen to thi name, and ben turned fro her synnes, whanne thou hast turmentid hem,
27 here thou, Lord, fro heuene, and foryyue thou synnes to thi seruauntis, and to thi puple Israel, and teche thou hem a good weie, bi which thei schulen entre, and yyue thou reyn to the lond, which thou hast youe to thi puple to haue in possessioun.
28 If hungur risith in the lond, and pestilence, and rust, and wynd distriynge cornes, and a locuste, and bruke cometh, and if enemyes bisegen the yatis of the citee, aftir that the cuntreis ben distried, and al veniaunce and sikenesse oppressith;
29 if ony of thi puple Israel bisechith, and knowith his veniaunce and sikenesse, and if he spredith abrood hise hondis in this hows,
30 thou schalt here fro heuene, that is, fro thin hiye dwellyng place, and do thou mercy, and yelde thou to ech man aftir hise weies, whiche thou knowist, that he hath in his herte; for thou aloone knowist the hertis of the sones of men;
31 that thei drede thee, and go in thi weies in alle daies, in which thei lyuen on the face of erthe, which thou hast youe to oure fadris.
32 Also thou schalt here fro heuene, thi moost stidfast dwellyng place, a straunger, which is not of thi puple Israel, if he cometh fro a fer lond for thi greet name, and for thi stronge hond, and arm holdun forth, 'and preye in this place;
33 and thou schalt do alle thingis, for which thilke pilgrym 'inwardli clepith thee, that alle the puplis of erthe knowe thi name, and drede thee, as thi puple Israel doith; and that thei knowe, that thi name is clepid on this hows, which Y haue bildid to thi name.
34 If thi puple goith out to batel ayens hise aduersaries, bi the weie in which thou sendist hem, thei schulen worschipe thee ayens the weie in which this citee is, which thou hast chose, and the hows which Y bildide to thi name,

35 that thou here fro heuene her preieris and bisechyng, and do veniaunce.
36 Forsothe if thei synnen ayens thee, for no man is that synneth not, and if thou art wrooth to hem, and bitakist hem to enemyes; and enemyes leden hem prisoneris in to a fer lond, ether certis which lond is nyy;
37 and if thei ben conuertid in her herte in the lond, to which thei ben led prisoneris, and thei don penaunce, and bisechen thee in the lond of her caitifte, and seien, We han synned, we han do wickidly, we diden vniustli;
38 and if thei turnen ayen to thee in al her herte, and in al her soule, in the lond of her caitifte, to which thei ben led, thei schulen worschipe thee ayens the weie of her lond, which thou hast youe to the fadris of hem, and of the citee which thou hast chose, and of the hows which Y bildide to thi name; that thou here fro heuene,
39 that is, fro thi stidefast dwellyng place, the preieris of hem, and that thou make dom, and foryyue to thi puple, thouy 'it be synful; for thou art my God;
40 Y biseche, be thin iyen openyd, and thin eeris be ententif to the preier which is maad in this place.
41 Now therfor, Lord God, rise in to thi reste, thou and the arke of thi strengthe; Lord God, thi preestis be clothid with helthe, and thi hooli men be glad in goodis.
42 Lord God, turne thou not a weie the face of thi crist; haue thou mynde on the mercyes of Dauid thi seruaunt.

CAP 7

1 And whanne Salomon schedynge preyeris hadde fillid, fier cam doun fro heuene, and deuouride brent sacrifices, and slayn sacrifices; and the maieste of the Lord fillide the hows.
2 And preestis myyten not entre in to the temple of the Lord; for the maieste of the Lord hadde fillid the temple of the Lord.
3 But also alle the sones of Israel sien fier comynge doun, and the glorie of the Lord on the hows, and thei felden down lowe to the erthe on the pawment araied with stoon, and thei worschipiden, and preisiden the Lord, For he is good, for his merci is in to al the world.
4 Forsothe the kyng and al the puple offriden slayn sacrifices bifor the Lord.
5 Therfor king Salomon killide sacrifices of oxis two and twenti thousynd, of wetheris six score thousynde; and the kyng and al the puple halewiden the hows of God.
6 Forsothe the preestis stoden in her offices, and dekenes in orguns of songis of the Lord, whiche kyng Dauid made to preise the Lord, For his merci is in to the world; and thei sungen the ympnes of Dauid bi her hondis; sotheli the prestis sungen with trumpis bifor hem, and al the puple of Israel stood.
7 Therfor Salomon halewide the myddil of the large place bifor the temple of the Lord; for he hadde offrid there brent sacrifices, and the ynnere fatnesses of pesible sacrifices, for the brasun auter which he hadde maad myyte not susteyne the brent sacrifices, and sacrifices, and the innere fatnessis of pesible sacrifices.
8 Therfor Salomon made a solempnyte in that tyme in seuene dayes, and al Israel with hym, a ful greete chirche, fro the entryng of Emath 'til to the stronde of Egipt.
9 And in the eiythe dai he made a gaderyng of money, 'that is, for necessaries of the temple, for he hadde halewid the auter in seuene daies, and 'hadde maad solempnytee in seuene daies.

10 Therfor in the thre and twentithe dai of the seuenthe monethe he lete the puplis go to her tabernaclis, ioiynge and gladynge on the good that God hadde do to Dauid, and to Salomon, and to his puple Israel.

11 And Salomon parformyde the hows of the Lord, and the hows of the kyng, and alle thingis which he hadde disposid in his herte for to do in the hows of the Lord and in his owne hows; and he hadde prosperite.

12 Forsothe the Lord aperide to hym in the nyyt, and seide, Y haue herd thi preiere, and Y haue chose this place to me in to an hows of sacrifice.

13 If Y close heuene, and reyn cometh not doun, and if Y sende, and comaunde to a locuste, that he deuoure the lond, and if Y send pestilence in to my puple;

14 forsothe if my puple is conuertid, on whiche my name is clepid, and if it bisechith me, and sekith my face, and doith penaunce of hise werste weies, Y schal here fro heuene, and Y schal be merciful to the synnes of hem, and Y schal heele the lond of hem.

15 And myn iyen schulen be openyd, and myn eeren schulen be reisid to the preiere of hym, that preieth in this place;

16 for Y haue chose, and halewid this place, that my name be there with outen ende, and that myn iyen and myn herte dwelle there in alle daies.

17 Also if thou gost bifore me, as Dauid thi fadir yede, and doist bi alle thingis whiche Y comaundide to thee, and kepist my riytwisnessis and domes, Y schal reise the trone of thi rewme,

18 as Y bihiyte to Dauid thi fadir, and seide, A man of thi generacioun schal not be takun awei, that schal be prince in Israel.

19 But if ye turnen awey, and forsake my riytwisnessis and my comaundementis whiche Y settide forth to you, and ye goen, and seruen alien goddis, and worschipen hem,

20 Y schal drawe you awey fro my lond, which Y yaf to you, and Y schal caste awey fro my face this hows which Y haue bildid to my name, and Y schal yyue it in to a parable, and in to ensaumple to alle puplis.

21 And this hows schal be in to a prouerbe to alle men passynge forth; and thei schulen seie, wondringe, Whi dide the Lord so to this lond, and to this hows?

22 And thei schulen answere, For thei forsoken the Lord God of her fadris, that ledde hem out of the lond of Egipt, and thei token alien goddis, and worschipiden, and herieden hem; therfor alle these yuelis camen on hem.

CAP 8

1 Forsothe whanne twenti yeer weren fillid, aftir that Salomon bildide the hows of the Lord,

2 and his owne hows, he bildide the citees, whiche Iram hadde youe to Salomon; and he made the sones of Israel to dwelle there.

3 Also he yede in to Emath of Suba, and gat it.

4 And he bildide Palmyram in deseert, and he bildide othere 'citees maad ful stronge in Emath.

5 And he bildide the hiyere Betheron and the lowere Betheron, wallid citees, hauynge yatis and lockis and barris;

6 also he bildide Balaath, and alle 'citees ful stronge that weren of Salomon; and alle the citees of cartis, and the citees of knyytis kyng Salomon bildide, and disposide alle thingis whiche euere he wolde, in Jerusalem, and in the Liban, and in al the lond of his power.

7 Salomon made suget in to tributaries til in to this dai al the puple that was left of Etheis, and Amorreis, and Phereseis, and Eueis, and of Jebuseis, that weren not of the generacioun of Israel, and of the sones of hem,

8 and of the aftircomers of hem, whiche the sones of Israel hadden not slayn.

9 Sotheli of the sones of Israel he settide not, that thei schulden serue the werkis of the kyng; for thei weren men werriours, and the firste duykis, and princes of charis, and of hise knyytis;

10 forsothe alle the princes of the oost of kyng Salomon weren two hundrid and fifti, that tauyten the puple.

11 Sotheli he translatide the douyter of Farao fro the citee of Dauid in to the hows, which he hadde bildid to hir; for the kyng seide, My wijf schal not dwelle in the hows of Dauid, kyng of Israel, for it is halewid, for the arke of the Lord entride in to that hows.

12 Thanne Salomon offride brent sacrifices to the Lord on the auter of the Lord, which he hadde bildid bifor the porche,

13 that bi alle daies me schulde offre in it, bi the comaundement of Moises, in sabatis, and in kalendis, and in feeste daies, thries bi the yeer, that is, in the solempnyte of the therflooues, and in the solempnyte of woukis, and in the solempnyte of tabernaclis.

14 And he ordeynede bi the ordynaunce of Dauid, his fadir, the officis of preestis in her seruyces, and the dekenes in her ordre, that thei schulden preise and mynystre bifor preestis bi the custom of ech dai; and he ordeynede porteris in her departyngis bi yate and yate. For Dauid, the man of God, hadde comaundid so;

15 and bothe preestis and dekenes passiden not fro the comaundementis of the kyng of alle thingis whiche he hadde comaundid.

16 And Salomon hadde alle costis maad redi in the kepingis of tresouris, fro that dai in whiche he foundide the hows of the Lord til in to the dai in which he perfourmyde it.

17 Thanne Salomon yede in to Asiongaber, and in to Hailath, at the brynke of the reed see, which is in the lond of Edom.

18 Therfor Iram sente to hym, by the hondis of his seruauntis, schippis, and schippe men kynnyng of the see, and thei yeden with the seruauntis of Salomon in to Ophir, and thei token fro thennus foure hundrid and fifti talentis of gold, and brouyten to kyng Salomon.

CAP 9

1 Also the queen of Saba, whanne sche hadde herd the fame of Salomon, cam to tempte hym in derk figuris 'in to Jerusalem, with grete ritchessis, and camels, that baren swete smellynge spices, and ful myche of gold, and preciouse iemmes, 'ether peerlis. And whanne sche was comun to Salomon, sche spak to hym what euer thingis weren in hir herte.

2 And Salomon expownede to hir alle thingis whiche sche hadde put forth, and no thing was, which he made not opyn to hir.

3 And aftir that sche siy these thingis, that is, the wisdom of Salomon, and the hows which he hadde bildid,

4 also and the metis of his boord, and the dwellyng places of seruauntis, and the offices of hise mynystris, and the clothis of hem, and the boteleris, and her clothis, and the sacrifices whiche he offride in the hows of the Lord, spirit was no more in hir for wondryng.

5 And sche seide to the kyng, The word 'is trewe, which Y herde in my lond, of thi vertues and wisdom;

6 Y bileuyde not to telleris, til Y my silf hadde come, and myn yyen hadden seyn, and Y hadde preued that vnnethis the half of thi wisdom was teld to me; thou hast ouercome the fame bi thi vertues.

7 Blessid ben thi men, and blessid ben thi seruauntis, these that stonden bifor thee in al tyme, and heren thi wisdom.

8 Blessid be 'thi Lord God, that wolde ordeyne thee on his trone kyng of the puple of 'thi Lord God; treuli for God loueth Israel, and wole saue hym with outen ende, therfor he hath set thee kyng on hym, that thou do domes and riytfulnesse.

9 Forsothe sche yaf to the kyng sixe scoore talentis of gold, and ful many swete smellynge spices, and moost preciouse iemmes; ther weren not siche swete smellynge spices, as these whiche the queen of Saba yaf 'to kyng Salomon.

10 But also the seruauntis of Iram with the seruauntis of Salomon brouyten gold fro Ophir, and trees of thyne, and most preciouse iemmes; of whiche,

11 that is, of the trees of thyne, the kyng made grees in the hows of the Lord, and in the hows of the kyng, 'harpis also, and sautrees to syngeris; siche trees weren neuere seyn in the lond of Juda.

12 Forsothe Salomon yaf to the queen of Saba alle thingis whiche sche wolde, and whiche sche axide, many moo than sche hadde brouyt to hym. And sche turnede ayen, and yede in to hir lond with hir seruauntis.

13 Forsothe the weiyt of gold, that was brouyt to Salomon bi ech yeer, was sixe hundrid and sixe and sixti talentis of gold,

14 outakun that summe whiche the legatis of dyuerse folkis, and marchauntis weren wont to brynge, and alle the kyngis of Arabie, and the princes of londis, that brouyten togidere gold and siluer to Salomon.

15 Therfor kyng Salomon made two hundrid goldun speris of the summe of sixe hundrid 'floreyns, ether peesis of gold, that weren spendid in ech spere;

16 and he made thre hundrid goldun scheeldis of thre hundrid floreyns, with whiche ech scheeld was hilid; and the kyng puttide tho in the armure place, that was set in the wode.

17 Also the kyng made a greet seete of yuer, and clothide it with clennest gold;

18 and he made sixe grees, bi whiche me stiede to the seete, and a goldun stool, and tweyne armes, oon ayens 'the tother, and twei liouns stondynge bisidis the armes;

19 but also he made twelue othere litle liouns stondynge on sixe grees on euer either side. Siche a seete was not in alle rewmes.

20 And alle the vessels of the feeste of the kyng weren of gold, and the vessels of the hows of the forest of the Liban weren of pureste gold; for siluer in tho daies was arettid for nouyt.

21 For also the schippis of the kyng yeden in to Tharsis with the seruauntis of Iram onys in thre yeer, and brouyten fro thennus gold, and siluer, and yuer, and apis, and pokokis.

22 Therfor kyng Salomon was magnyfied ouer alle kyngis of erthe for richessis and glorie.

23 And alle the kyngis of londis desireden to se the face of Salomon, for to here the wisdom which God hadde youe in his herte; and thei brouyten to hym yiftis,

24 vessels of siluer and of gold, clothis and armuris, and swete smellynge spices, horsis and mulis, bi ech yeer.

25 Also Salomon hadde fourti thousynde of horsis in stablis, and twelue thousynde of charis and of knyytis; and 'he ordeynede hem in the citees of charis, and where the kyng was in Jerusalem.

26 Forsothe he vside power on alle the kyngis, fro the flood Eufrates 'til to the lond of Filisteis, and 'til to the termes of Egipt.

27 And he yaf so greet plente of siluer in Jerusalem, as of stoonys, and so greet multitude of cedris, as of sycomoris that growen in feeldi places.

28 Forsothe horsis weren brouyt fro Egipt, and fro alle cuntreis.

29 Sotheli the residue of the formere werkis and the laste of Salomon ben writun in the wordis of Nathan, the prophete, and in the wordis of Achie of Silo, and in the visioun, 'ether prophesie, of Addo, the prophete, ayens Jeroboam, sone of Nabath.

30 Sotheli Salomon regnede in Jerusalem on al Israel fourti yeer, and he slepte with his fadris; and thei birieden hym in the citee of Dauid, and Roboam, his sone, regnyde for hym.

CAP 10

1 Forsothe Roboam yede forth in to Sichem; for al Israel came togidere thidur to make hym kyng.

2 And whanne Jeroboam, the sone of Nabath, that was in Egipt, 'for he fledde thidur bifor Salomon, hadde herd this, he turnyde ayen anoon.

3 And thei clepiden hym, and he cam with al Israel, and thei spaken to Roboam, and seiden,

4 Thi fadir oppresside vs with ful hard yok; comaunde thou liytere thingis than thi fader, that settide on vs a greuouse seruage; and releese thou a litil of 'the birthun, that we serue thee. And he seide,

5 After thre daies turne ye ayen to me. And whanne the puple was goon, he took counsel with elde men,

6 that stoden bifor his fadir Salomon, while he lyuyde yit, and seide, What counsel yyuen ye, that Y answere to the puple?

7 And thei seiden to hym, If thou plesist this puple, and makist hem softe bi meke wordis, thei schulen serue thee in al tyme.

8 And he forsook the counsel of elde men, and bigan to trete with yonge men, that weren nurischid with hym, and weren in his cumpenye.

9 And he seide to hem, What semeth to you? ether what owe Y answere to this puple, that seide to me, Releese thou the yok, which thi fadir puttide on vs?

10 And thei answeriden, as yonge men and nurschyd with hym in delicis, and seiden, Thus thou schalt speke to the puple that seide to thee, Thi fadir made greuouse oure yok, releese thou; and thus thou schalt answere to hem, My leeste fyngur is gretter than the leendis of my fader;

11 my fadir puttide on you a greuouse yok, and Y schal leie to a gretter birthun; my fadir beet you with scourgis, forsothe Y schal bete you with 'scorpiouns, that is, hard knottid roopis.

12 Therfor Jeroboam and al the puple cam to Roboam in the thridde dai, as he hadde comaundid to hem.

13 And 'the kyng answeride harde thingis, after that he hadde forsake the counsel of the eldere men,

14 and he spak bi the wille of the yonge men, My fadir puttide on you a greuouse yok, which Y schal make greuousere; my fadir beet you with scourgis, sotheli Y schal bete you with scorpiouns.

15 And he assentide not to the preieris of the puple; for it was the wille of God, that his word schulde be fillid, which he hadde spoke bi the hond of Ahie of Silo to Jeroboam, sone of Nabath.

16 Sotheli whanne the kyng seide hardere thingis, al the puple spak thus to hym, No part is to vs in Dauid, nether eritage in the sone of Isai; Israel, turne thou ayen in to thi tabernaclis, sotheli thou, Dauid, feede thin hows. And Israel yede in to hise tabernaclis.

17 Forsothe Roboam regnede on the sones of Israel, that dwelliden in the citees of Juda.

18 And kyng Roboam sente Adhuram, that was souereyn ouer the tributis; and the sones of Israel stonyden hym, and he was deed. Certis kyng Roboam hastide to stie in to the chare, and fledde in to Jerusalem.

19 And Israel yede awei fro the hows of Dauid 'til to this dai. Forsothe it was doon, whanne al Israel hadde herd, that Jeroboam turnede ayen, thei senten, and clepiden hym, whanne the cumpeny was gaderid, and thei ordeyneden him king on al Israel; and no man, outakun the lynage of Juda aloone, suede 'the hows of Dauid.

CAP 11

1 Forsothe Roboam cam in to Jerusalem, and clepide togidere al the hows of Juda and of Beniamyn, 'til to nyne scoore thousynde of chosen men and werriouris, for to fiyte ayens Israel, and for to turne his rewme to hym.

2 And the word of the Lord was maad to Semeye, the man of God,

3 and seide, Speke thou to Roboam, the sone of Salomon, kyng of Juda, and to al Israel, which is in Juda and Beniamyn; The Lord seith these thingis,

4 Ye schulen not stie, nethir ye schulen fiyte ayens youre britheren; ech man turne ayen in to his hows, for this thing is doon bi my wille. And whanne thei hadden herd the word of the Lord, thei turneden ayen, and yeden not ayens kyng Jeroboam.

5 Forsothe Roboam dwellide in Jerusalem, and he bildide wallid citees in Juda;

6 and bildide Bethleem, and Ethan, and Thecue, and Bethsur; 7 and Sochot, and Odollam;

8 also and Jeth, and Maresa, and Ziph;

9 but also Huram, and Lachis, and Azecha;

10 and Saraa, and Hailon, and Ebron, that weren in Juda and Beniamyn, ful strong citees.

11 And whanne he hadde closid tho with wallis, he settide 'in tho citees princes, and bernes of metis, that is, of oile, and of wyn.

12 But also in ech citee he made placis of armuris of scheeldis, and speris, and he made tho strong with most diligence; and he regnyde on Juda and Beniamyn.

13 Sotheli the preestis and dekenes, that weren in al Israel, camen to hym fro alle her seetis,

14 and forsoken her subarbis and possessiouns, and thei passiden to Juda and to Jerusalem; for Jeroboam and hise aftir comeris hadden cast hem a wey, that thei schulden not be set in preesthod of the Lord;

15 which Jeroboam made to hym preestis of hiye places, and of feendis, and of caluys, which he hadde maad.

16 But also of alle the linagis of Israel, whiche euer yauen her herte to seke the Lord God of Israel, thei camen to Jerusalem for to offre her sacrifices bifor the Lord God of her fadris.

17 And thei strengthiden the rewme of Juda, and strengthiden Roboam, the sone of Salomon, bi thre yeer; for thei yeden in the weies of Dauid, and of Salomon, oneli bi thre yeer.

18 Forsothe Roboam weddide a wijf Malaoth, the douytir of Jerymuth, sone of Dauid, and Abiail, the douytir of Heliab, sone of Ysaye;

19 and sche childide to hym sones, Yeus, and Somorie, and Zerei.

20 Also after this wijf he took Maacha, the douyter of Abissalon, and sche childide to hym Abia, and Thai, and Ziza, and Salomyth.

21 Forsothe Roboam louyde Maacha, the douytir of Abissalon, aboue alle hise wyues and secundarie wyues. Forsothe he hadde weddid eiytene wyues, sotheli sixti secundarie wyues; and he gendride eiyte and twenti sones, and sixti douytris.

22 Sotheli he ordeynede Abia, the sone of Maacha, in the heed, duyk ouer alle hise britheren; for he thouyte to make Abia kyng,

23 for he was wisere and myytiere ouer alle hise sones, and in alle the coostis of Juda and of Beniamyn, and in alle wallid citees; and he yaf to hem ful many metis, and he had many wyues.

CAP 12

1 And whanne the rewme of Roboam was maad strong and coumfortid, he forsook the lawe of the Lord, and al Israel with hym.

2 Sotheli in the fyuethe yeer of the rewme of Roboam Sesach, the kyng of Egipt, stiede in to Jerusalem, for thei synneden ayens the Lord;

3 and he stiede with a thousynde and two hundrid charys, and with sixti thousynde of horse men, and no noumbre was of the comyn puple, that cam with hym fro Egipt, that is, Libiens, and Trogoditis, and Ethiopiens.

4 And he took ful stronge citees in Juda, and he cam 'til to Jerusalem.

5 Forsothe Semei, the prophete, entride to Roboam, and to the princes of Juda, whiche fleynge fro Sesach weren gaderid togidere 'in to Jerusalem. And he seide to hem, The Lord seith these thingis, Ye han forsake me, and Y haue forsake you in the hond of Sesach.

6 And the princes of Israel and the kyng weren astonyed, and seiden, The Lord is iust.

7 And whanne the Lord hadde seyn that thei weren mekid, the word of the Lord was maad to Semey, and seide, For thei ben mekid, Y schal not distrie hem, and Y schal yyue to hem a litil help, and my stronge veniaunce schal not droppe on Jerusalem bi the hond of Sesach.

8 Netheles thei schulen serue hym, that thei knowe the dyuersitee of my seruyce and of the seruyce of the rewme of londis.

9 Therfor Sesach, the kyng of Egipt, yede a wey fro Jerusalem, aftir that he hadde take awei the tresouris of the hows of the Lord, and of the kyngis hows; and he took alle thingis with hym, and the goldun scheeldis whiche Salomon hadde maad,

10 for whiche the kyng made brasun scheeldis, and took tho to the princes of scheeld makeris, that kepten the porche of the paleis.

11 And whanne the kyng entride in to the hows of the Lord, the scheeldmakeris camen, and token tho, and eft brouyten tho to his armure place.

12 Netheles for thei weren mekid, the ire of the Lord was turned a wei fro hem, and thei weren not don a wei outirli; for good werkis weren foundyn also in Juda.

13 Therfor kyng Roboam was coumfortid in Jerusalem, and regnede. Forsothe he was of oon and fourti yeer, whanne he

bigan to regne, and he regnyde seuentene yeer in Jerusalem, the citee which the Lord chees of alle the lynagis of Israel, that he schulde conferme his name there. Forsothe the name of hise modir was Naama Amanytis.

14 And he dide yuel, and he made not redi his herte to seke God.

15 Sotheli the firste and the laste werkis of Roboam ben writun, and diligentli declarid in the bookis of Semei the profete, and of Abdo the profete.

16 And Roboam and Jeroboam fouyten in alle daies ayens hem silf. And Roboam slepte with hise fadris, and was biried in the citee of Dauid; and Abia, his sone, regnede for hym.

CAP 13

1 Yn the eiytenthe yeer of kyng Jeroboam Abia regnede on Juda;

2 he regnede thre yeer in Jerusalem; and the name of hise modir was Mychaie, the douyter of Vriel of Gabaa. And batel was bitwixe Abia and Jeroboam.

3 And whanne Abia hadde bigunne batel, and hadde most chyualrouse men, and four hundrid thousynde of chosun men, Jeroboam arayede ayenward the scheltroun with eiyte hundrid thousynde of men, and thei weren chosun men and most stronge to batels.

4 Therfor Abia stood on the hil Semeron, that was in Effraym, and seide, Here thou, Jeroboam and al Israel;

5 whether ye knowen not, that the Lord God of Israel yaf to Dauid the rewme on Israel with outen ende, to hym and to hise sones in to the couenaunt of salt, 'that is, stidefast and stable?

6 And Jeroboam, the sone of Nabath, the seruaunt of Salomon, sone of Dauid, roos, and rebellide ayens his lord.

7 And most veyn men and the sones of Belial weren gaderid to hym, and thei hadden myyt ayens Roboam, the sone of Salomon. Certis Roboam was buystuouse, 'ether fonne, and of feerdful herte, and myyte not ayenstonde hem.

8 Now therfor ye seien, that ye moun ayenstonde the rewme of the Lord, which he holdith in possessioun bi the sones of Dauid; and ye han a greet multitude of puple, and goldun caluys, whiche Jeroboam made in to goddis to you.

9 And ye han caste a wei the preestis of the Lord, the sones of Aaron, and dekenes, and ye han maad preestis to you, as alle the puplis of londis han preestis; who euer cometh and hale-with his hond in a bole, in oxis, and in seuene wetheris, anoon he is maad preest of hem that ben not goddis.

10 But oure Lord is God, whom we forsaken not; and preestis of the sones of Aaron mynystren to the Lord, and dekenes ben in her ordre;

11 and thei offren brent sacrifices to the Lord bi ech dai in the morewtid and euentid, and encense maad bi comaundementis of the lawe; and loues ben set forth in a moost clene boord; and at vs is the goldun candilstik and his lanterne, that it be teendid euere at euentid; forsothe we kepen the comaunde-mentis of our God, whom ye han forsake.

12 Therfor God is duyk in oure oost, and hise preestis, that trumpen and sownen ayens you; nyle ye, sones of Israel, fiyte ayens the Lord God of youre fadris, for it spedith not to you.

13 While he spak these thingis, Jeroboam made redi tresouns bihynde; and whanne he stood euene ayens the enemyes, he cumpasside with his oost Juda vnwitynge.

14 And Juda bihelde, and siy batel neiy euene ayens, and bihynde the bak; and he criede to the Lord, and preestis big-unnen for to trumpe.

15 And alle the men of Juda crieden, and, lo! while thei crieden, God made aferd Jeroboam and al Israel, that stood euen ayens Juda and Abia.

16 And the men of Israel fledden fro Juda, and God bitook hem in to the hondis of men of Juda.

17 Therfor Abia and his puple smoot hem with a greet wounde, and there felden doun of hem fyue hundrid thousynde of stronge men woundid.

18 And the sones of Israel weren maad lowe in that tyme, and the sones of Juda weren coumfortid ful greetli, for thei had-den hopid in the Lord God of her fadris.

19 Forsothe Abia pursuede Jeroboam fleynge, and took hise cytees, Bethel and hise vilagis, and Jesana with hise vilagis, and Ephron and hise vilagis;

20 and Jeroboam miyte no more ayenstonde in the daies of Juda, whom the Lord smoot, and he was deed.

21 Therfor Abia, whanne his empire was coumfortid, took fourtene wyues, and he gendride two and twenti sones, and sixtene douytris.

22 The residue of wordis of Abia and of his weyes and werkis, ben writun ful diligentli in the book of Abdo, the pro-fete.

CAP 14

1 Forsothe Abia slepte with hise fadris, and thei birieden hym in the citee of Dauid; and Asa, his sone, regnede for hym. In whos daies the lond restide ten yeer.

2 And Asa dide that, that was good and plesaunt in the siyt of his God, and he destriede the auteris of straunge wors-chipyng, and 'he destriede hiy places,

3 and brak ymagis, and kittide doun woodis;

4 and he comaundide Juda to seke the Lord God of her fadris, and to do the lawe and alle comaundementis.

5 And he took awei fro alle the citees of Juda auteris and tem-plis of idols, and he regnede in pees.

6 And he bildide stronge cytees in Juda; for he was in reste, and no batels risiden in his tymes, for the Lord yaf pees.

7 Forsothe he seide to Juda, Bilde we these cytees, and cump-asse we with wallis, and strengthe we with touris and yatis and lockis, as longe as alle thingis ben restful fro batel; for we han souyte the Lord God of oure fadris, and he hath youe to vs pees bi cumpas. Therfor thei bildiden, and no lettyng was in bildyng.

8 Sotheli Asa hadde in his oost thre hundrid thousynde of men of Juda berynge scheldis and speris, sotheli of Beniamyn he hadde two hundrid thousynde and fourscoore thousynde of scheeld beeris and of archeris; alle these weren ful stronge men.

9 Forsothe Zara of Ethiop yede out ayens hem with his oost ten 'sithis an hundrid thousynde, and with thre hundrid charis, and cam 'til to Masera.

10 Certis Aza yede ayens hem, and araiede scheltrun to batel in the valei Sephata, which is bisidis Masera. And he inwardli clepide the Lord God,

11 and seide, Lord, no dyuersitee is anentis thee, whether thou helpe in fewe, ethir in manye; oure Lord God, helpe thou vs, for we han trist in thee and in thi name, and camen ayens this multitude; Lord, thou art oure God, a man haue not the maistrye ayens thee.

12 Therfor the Lord made aferd Ethiopens bifor Asa and Juda, and Ethiopens fledden; and Asa and his puple,

13 that was with hym, pursuede hem 'til to Gerare. And Ethi-opens felden doun 'til to deeth, for thei weren al to-brokun bi

the Lord sleynge, and bi his oost fiytynge. Therfor thei token many spuylis,

14 and smitiden alle the citees 'bi the cumpas of Gerare; for greet drede hadde assailid alle men. And thei rifliden cytees, and baren a weye myche prey;

15 but also thei destrieden the fooldis of scheep, and token multitude without noumbre of scheep and of camels, and turneden ayen in to Jerusalem.

CAP 15

1 Forsothe Azarie, the sone of Obeth, whanne the spirit of the Lord was comyn in to hym,

2 yede out in to the metyng of Asa; and seide to hym, Asa and al Juda and Beniamyn, here ye me; the Lord is with you, for ye weren with hym; if ye seken hym, ye schulen fynde hym; sotheli if ye forsaken hym, he schal forsake you.

3 Forsothe many daies schulen passe in Israel with outen veri God, and without preest, and without techere, and without lawe.

4 And whanne thei turnen ayen in her angwisch, and crien to the Lord God of Israel, and seken hym, thei schulen fynde hym.

5 In that tyme schal not be pees to go out and to go in, but dredis on al side on alle the dwelleris of londis.

6 For a folk schal fiyte ayens folk, and a citee ayens a citee, for the Lord schal disturble hem in al anguysch;

7 but be ye coumfortid, and youre hondis be not slakid; for mede schal be to youre werk.

8 And whanne Asa hadde herd this thing, that is, the wordis and profesye of Asarie, the sone of Obed, the profete, he was coumfortid, and he dide a wei alle the idols fro al the lond of Juda and of Beniamyn, and fro the citees whiche he hadde take of the hil of Effraym. And he halewide the auter of the Lord, that was bifor the porche of the hows of the Lord.

9 And he gaderide togidere al Juda and Beniamyn, and with hem the comelyngis of Effraym, and of Manasses, and of Symeon; for manye of Israel, seynge that his Lord God was with hym, fledden ouer to hym.

10 And whanne thei hadden comun in to Jerusalem, in the thridde monethe, in the fiftenthe yeer of the rewme of Asa,

11 thei offriden 'to the Lord in that dai, bothe of the spuylis and of the prey, which thei hadden brouyt, seuene hundrid oxis, and seuene thousynde wetheris.

12 And Asa entride bi custom to make strong the boond of pees, that thei schulden seke the Lord God of her fadris in al her herte, and in al her soule.

13 Sotheli he seide, If ony man sekith not the Lord God of Israel, die he, fro the leeste 'til to the mooste, fro man 'til to womman.

14 And alle that weren in Juda sworen with cursyng to the Lord, with greet vois, in hertli song, and in sown of trumpe, and in sown of clariouns;

15 for thei sworen in al her herte, and in al the wille thei souyten hym, and founden hym; and the Lord yaf to hem reste bi cumpas.

16 But also he puttide doun Maacha, the modir of 'Asa the kyng, fro the streit empire, for sche hadde made in a wode the symylacre, 'ether licnesse, of a mannus yerde; and he al to-brak al 'that symylacre, and pownede it in to gobetis, and 'brente it in the stronde of Cedron.

17 But hiy places weren left in Israel; netheles the herte of Asa was riytful in alle hise daies.

18 And he brouyte in to the hows of the Lord tho thingis that his fadir avowide, siluer and gold, and dyuerse purtenaunce of vessels;

19 sotheli batel was not 'til to the threttithe yeer of the rewme of Asa.

CAP 16

1 Forsothe in the sixe and thrittithe yeer of his rewme Baasa, the kyng of Israel, stiede in to Juda, and cumpasside Rama with a wal, that no man of the rewme of Asa myyte go out ether entre sikirli.

2 Sotheli Asa brouyte forth gold and siluer fro the tresours of the hows of the Lord, and fro the kyngis tresouris; and sente to Benadab, kyng of Sirie, that dwellide in Damask,

3 and seide, Boond of pees is bitwixe me and thee, and my fadir and thi fadir hadden acordyng; wherfor Y sente to thee siluer and gold, that whanne thou hast broke the boond of pees, which thou hast with Baasa, king of Israel, thou make hym to go awei fro me.

4 And whanne this was foundun, Benadab sente princes of hise oostis to the citees of Israel, whiche smytiden Ahion, and Dan, and Abelmaym, and alle the wallid citees of Neptalym.

5 And whanne Baasa hadde herd this, he ceesside to bilde Rama, and left his werk.

6 Forsothe kyng Asa took al Juda, and thei token fro Rama the stonys and trees, whiche Baasa hadde maad redi to bil- dyng; and he bildide of tho Gabaa, and Maspha.

7 In that tyme Anany, the profete, cam to Asa, kyng of Juda, and seide to hym, For thou haddist trist in the kyng of Sirie, and not in 'thi Lord God, herfor the oost of 'the kyng of Sirie aschapide fro thin hond.

8 Whether 'Ethiopiens and Libiens weren not many mo in charis, and knyytis, and ful greet multitude; whiche whanne thou haddist bileuyd to the Lord, he bitook in to thin hondis?

9 For the iyen of the Lord biholden al the erthe, and yyuen strengthe to hem, that with perfit herte bileuen in to hym. Therfor thou hast do folili, and for this, yhe, in present tyme batels schulen rise ayens thee.

10 And Asa was wrooth ayens the prophete, and comaundide hym to be sent in to stockis. Forsothe the Lord hadde indigna- cioun greetli on this thing, and killide ful many of the puple in that tyme.

11 Sotheli the firste and the laste werkis of Asa ben writun in the book of kyngis of Juda and of Israel.

12 Forsothe Asa was sijk ful gretli in the akynge of feet, in the nyne and thrittithe yeer of his rewme; and nether in his sikenesse he souyte the Lord, but tristide more in the craft of lechis.

13 And Asa slepte with hise fadris, and he was deed in the oon and fourtithe yeer of his rewme.

14 And thei birieden him in his sepulcre, which he hadde maad to hym silf in the cytee of Dauid; and thei puttiden hym on his bed ful of swete smellynge spices and oynementis of hooris, that weren 'maad togidere bi the craft of oynement makeris, and thei brenten on hym with ful greet cost.

CAP 17

1 Forsothe Josaphat, his sone, regnyde for hym; and he hadde the maistrye ayens Israel.

2 And he settide noumbris of knyytis in alle the citees of Juda, that weren cumpassid with wallis, and he disposide strong holdis in the lond of Juda, and in the citees of Effraym, whiche Asa, his fadir, hadde take.

3 And the Lord was with Josaphat, whiche yede in the firste weies of Dauid, his fadir; he hopide not in Baalym,

4 but in the Lord God of Dauid, his fadir, and he yede in the comaundementis of God, and not bi the synnes of Israel.

5 And the Lord confermyde the rewme in his hond; and al Juda yaf yiftis to Josaphat, and ritchessis with outen noumbre, and myche glorie weren maad to hym.

6 And whanne his herte hadde take hardynesse for the weies of the Lord, he took awei also hiy placis and wodis fro Juda.

7 Forsothe in the thridde yeer of his rewme he sente of hise princes Benail, and Abdie, and Zacarie, and Nathanael, and Mychee, that thei schulden teche in the citees of Juda;

8 and with hem he sente dekenes Semeye, and Nathanye, and Zabadie, and Azahel, and Semyramoth, and Jonathan, and Adonye, and Thobie, and Abadonye, dekenes; and with hem 'he sente Elisama and Joram, preestis;

9 and thei tauyten the puple in Juda, and hadden the book of the lawe of the Lord; and thei cumpassiden alle the citees of Juda, and tauyten al the puple.

10 Therfor the drede of the Lord was maad on al the rewmes of londis, that weren 'bi cumpas of Juda; and tho dursten not fiyte ayens Josaphat.

11 But also Filisteis brouyten yiftis to Josaphat, and tol of siluer; and men of Arabie brouyten scheep seuene thousynde, and seuene hundrid of wetheris, and so many buckis of geet.

12 Therfor Josaphat encreesside, and was magnified 'til in to an hiy; and he bildide in Juda housis at the licnesse of touris, and stronge citees;

13 and he made redi many werkis in the citees of Juda. Also men werriouris and stronge men weren in Jerusalem;

14 of whiche this is the noumbre, 'bi the housis and meynees of alle in Juda. Duyk Eduas was prince of the oost, and with hym weren thre hundrid thousynde ful stronge men.

15 Aftir hym was Johannan prince, and with hym weren two hundrid thousynde and foure scoore thousynde.

16 After this also Amasye, the sone of Zechri, was halewid to the Lord, and with hym weren two hundrid thousynde of stronge men.

17 Eliada myyti to batels suede this Amasie, and with hym weren two hundrid thousynde of men holdynge bouwe and scheeld.

18 Aftir this was also Josaphat, and with hym weren an hundrid thousynde and foure scoore thousynde of redi knyytis.

19 Alle these weren at the hond of the kyng, outakun othere, whiche he hadde put in wallid cytees and in al Juda.

CAP 18

1 Therfor Josaphat was riche and ful noble, and bi affynyte, 'ethir alie, he was ioyned to Achab.

2 And aftir yeeris he cam doun to hym in to Samarie; at whos comyng Achab killide ful many wetheris and oxis, and to the puple that cam with hym; and he counseilide hym to stie in to Ramoth of Galaad.

3 And Achab, the kyng of Israel, seide to Josaphat, kyng of Juda, Come thou with me in to Ramoth of Galaad. To whom he answeride, As and Y am, thou art; as thi puple, so and my puple; and we schulen be with thee in batel.

4 And Josaphat seide to the kyng of Israel, Y biseche, counsele thou in present tyme the word of the Lord.

5 Therfor the kyng of Israel gaderide togidere foure hundrid 'men of prophetis, and seide to hem, Owen we to go in to Ramath of Galaad for to fiyte, ethir 'take reste? And thei seiden, Stie ye, and God schal bitake in the hond of the king.

6 And Josaphat seide, Whether no profete of the Lord is here, that we 'axe also of hym?

7 And the kyng of Israel seide to Josaphat, O man is, of whom we 'moun axe the wille of the Lord, but and Y hate hym, for he prophecieth not good, but yuel to me in al tyme; sothely it is Mychee, the sone of Jebla. And Josaphat seide to hym, Kyng, speke thou not in this maner.

8 Therfor the kyng of Israel clepide oon of the geldyngis, and seide to hym, Clepe thou soone Mychee, the sone of Jebla.

9 Forsothe the kyng of Israel and Josaphat, the kyng of Juda, saten euer eithir in his seete, and weren clothid in kyngis aray; forsothe thei saten in the cornfloor, 'ether large hows, bisidis the yate of Samarie; and alle the prophetis profesieden bifor hem.

10 Forsothe Sedechie, the sone of Cananee, made to hym yrone hornes, and seide, The Lord seith these thingis, With these thou schalt wyndewe Sirie, til thou al to-brake it.

11 And alle prophetis profesieden in lijk maner, and seiden, Stie thou in to Ramoth of Galaad, and thou schalt haue prosperite; and the Lord schal bitake hem in to the hondis of the kyng.

12 Forsothe the messanger, that yede to clepe Mychee, seide to hym, Lo! the wordis of alle prophetis tellen with o mouth goodis to the kyng; therfor, Y preye thee, that thi word disente not fro hem, and that thou speke prosperitees.

13 To whom Mychee answeride, The Lord lyueth, for what euer thingis my Lord spekith to me, Y schal speke these thingis. Therfor he cam to the kyng.

14 To whom the kyng seide, Mychee, owen we go in to Ramoth of Galaad to fiyte, ether take reste? To whom he answeride, Stie ye, for alle prosperitees schulen come, and enemyes schulen be bitakun in to youre hondis.

15 And the kyng seide, Eft and eft Y charge thee, that thou speke not to me no but that that is soth in the name of the Lord.

16 And he seide, Y siy al Israel scaterid in the hillis, as scheep with out scheepherde. And the Lord seide, These men han not lordis; ech man turne ayen in to his hows in pees.

17 The kyng of Israel seide to Josaphat, Whether Y seide not to thee, that he profesiede not ony good to me, but tho thingis that ben yuele?

18 And therfor Mychee seide, Here ye the word of the Lord. Y siy the Lord sittynge in his trone, and al the oost of heuene stondynge nyy him at the riytside and 'leftside.

19 And the Lord seide, Who schal disseyue Achab, the kyng of Israel, that he stie, and falle doun in Ramoth of Galaad? And whanne oon seide in this maner, and another seide in another maner, a spirit cam forth,

20 and stood bifor the Lord, and seide, Y schal disseyue hym. To whom the Lord seide, 'Wherynne, therfor schalt thou disseyue?

21 And he answeride, Y schal go out, and Y schal be a 'fals spirit in the mouth of alle hise profetis. And the Lord seide, Thou schalt disseyue, and thou schalt haue the maystri; go thou out, and do so.

22 Now therfor, lo! the Lord hath youe a spirit of leesyng in the mouth of alle thi prophetis, and the Lord spak yuels of thee.

23 Forsothe Sedechie, the sone of Chananee, neiyide, and smoot 'the cheke of Mychee, and seide, Bi what weye passide the Spirit of the Lord fro me to speke to thee?

24 And Mychee seide, Thou thi silf schalt se in that dai, whanne thou schalt entre fro closet in to closet, that thou be hid.

25 Sotheli the kyng of Israel comaundide, seiynge, Take ye Mychee, and lede ye hym to Amon, prince of the citee, and to Joas, the sone of Amalech;

26 and ye schulen seie, The kyng seith these thingis, Sende ye this man in to prisoun, and yyue ye to hym a litil of breed, and a litil of watir, til Y turne ayen in pees.

27 And Mychee seide, If thou turnest ayen in pees, the Lord spak not in me. And he seide, Alle 'puplis here ye.

28 Therfor the kyng of Israel, and Josaphat, the kyng of Juda, stieden in to Ramoth of Galaad.

29 And the kyng of Israel seide to Josaphat, Y schal chaunge clothing, and so Y schal go to fiyte; but be thou clothid in thi clothis. Therfor whanne the kyng of Israel hadde chaungid clothing, he cam to batel.

30 Forsothe the kyng of Sirie comaundide to the duykis of his multitude of knyytis, and seide, Fiyte ye not ayens the leeste, nether ayens the mooste; no but ayens the kyng aloone of Israel.

31 Therfor whanne the princes of the multitude of knyytis hadden seyn Josaphat, thei seiden, This is the kyng of Israel; and thei cumpassiden hym, and fouyten. And he criede to the Lord; and the Lord helpide hym, and turnede hem awey fro hym.

32 Sotheli whanne the duykis of the multitude of knyytis hadden herd, that it was not the kyng of Israel, thei leften hym.

33 Forsothe it bifelde, that oon of the puple schette an arewe in to vncerteyn, and smoot the kyng of Israel bitwixe the necke and the schuldris. And he seide to his charietere, Turne thin hond, and lede me out of the scheltrun; for Y am woundid.

34 And the batel was endid in that dai. Certis the kyng of Israel stood in his chare ayens men of Sirye 'til to euentid, and he diede, whanne the sunne yede doun.

CAP 19

1 Forsothe Josaphat, kyng of Juda, turnede ayen pesibli in to his hows in to Jerusalem.

2 Whom the profete Hieu, the sone of Ananye, mette, and seide to hym, Thou yyuest help to a wickid man, and thou art ioyned bi frendschip to hem that haten the Lord; and therfor sotheli thou deseruedist the wraththe of the Lord;

3 but good werkis ben foundyn in thee, for thou didist awey wodis fro the lond of Juda, and thou hast maad redi thin herte, for to seke the Lord God of thi fadris.

4 Therfor Josaphat dwellide in Jerusalem; and eft he yede out to the puple fro Bersabee til to the hil of Effraym, and he clepide hem ayen to the Lord God of her fadris.

5 And he ordeynede iugis of the lond in alle the strengthid citees of Juda, bi ech place.

6 And he comaundide to the iugis, and seide, Se ye, what ye doen; for ye vsen not the doom of man, but of the Lord; and what euere thing ye demen, schal turne 'in to you;

7 the drede of the Lord be with you, and do ye alle thingis with diligence; for anentis 'youre Lord God is no wickidnesse, nether takynge of persoones, nether coueitise of yiftis.

8 Also in Jerusalem Josaphat ordeynede dekenes, and preestis, and the princes of meynees of Israel, that thei schulden deme the doom and cause of the Lord to the dwellers of it.

9 And he comaundide to hem, and seide, Thus ye schulen do in the drede of the Lord, feithfuli and in perfite herte.

10 Ech cause that cometh to you of youre britheren, that dwellen in her citees, bitwixe kynrede and kynrede, where euere is questioun of the lawe, of 'the comaundement, of cerymonyes, 'ether sacrifices, of iustifyingis, schewe ye to hem, that thei do not synne ayens the Lord, and that wraththe com not on you and on youre britheren. Therfor ye doynge thus schulen not do synne.

11 Forsothe Amarie, youre preest and bischop, schal be souereyn in these thingis, that perteynen to God. Sotheli Zabadie, the sone of Ismael, which is duyk in the hows of Juda, schal be on tho werkis that perteynen to the office of the kyng, and ye han maistris dekenes bifor you; be ye coumfortid, and do ye diligentli, and the Lord schal be with you in goodis.

CAP 20

1 Aftir these thingis the sones of Moab, and the sones of Amon, and with hem of Idumeis, weren gaderid togidere to Josaphat, for to fiyte ayens hym.

2 And messangeris camen, and schewiden to Josaphat, seiden, A greet multitude of tho placis that ben biyondis the see, and of Sirie, is comun ayens thee; and, lo! thei stonden in Asasonthamar, which is Engaddi.

3 Forsothe Josaphat was aferd by drede, and 'yaf hym silf al for to preye 'the Lord, and prechide fastynge to al Juda.

4 And Juda was gaderid togidere for to preye the Lord, but also alle men camen fro her citees for to biseche hym.

5 And whanne Josaphat hadde stonde in the myddis of the cumpeny of Juda and of Jerusalem, in the hows of the Lord, bifor the newe large place,

6 he seide, Lord God of oure fadris, thou art God in heuene, and thou art lord of alle rewmes of folkis; strengthe and power ben in thin hond, 'and noon may ayenstonde thee.

7 Whether not thou, oure God, hast slayn alle the dwelleris of this lond bifor thi puple Israel, and hast youe it to the seed of Abraham, thi freend, withouten ende?

8 And thei dwelliden therynne, and bildiden therinne a seyntuarie to thi name, and seiden,

9 If yuelis comen on vs, the swerd of doom, pestilence, and hungur, we schulen stonde bifor this hows withouten ende in thi siyt, in which hows thi name is clepid, and we schulen crie to thee in oure tribulaciouns; and thou schalt here vs, and schalt make vs saaf.

10 Now therfor lo! the sones of Amon and of Moab and the hil of Seir, bi whiche thou grauntidist not to the sones of Israel for to passe, whanne thei yeden out of Egipt, but thei bowiden awei fro hem, and killiden not hem,

11 thei doon ayenward, and enforsen to caste vs out of the possessioun, which thou, oure God, hast youe to vs;

12 therfor whether thou schalt not deme hem? Treuli in vs is not so greet strengthe, that we moun ayenstonde this multitude, that felde yn on vs; but sithen we witen not what we owen to do, we 'han oneli this residue, that we dresse oure iyen to thee.

13 Sotheli al Juda stood bifor the Lord, with her litle children and wyues and fre children.

14 Forsothe Hiaziel, the sone of Zacarie, sone of Ananye, sone of Hieyel, sone of Machanye, was a dekene, and of the sones of Asaph, on whom the Spirit of the Lord was maad in the myddis of the cumpeny,

15 and he seide, Al Juda, and ye that dwellen in Jerusalem, and thou, king Josaphat, perseyue ye, the Lord seith these

thingis to you, Nyle ye drede, nether be ye aferd of this multitude, for it is not youre batel, but Goddis batel.

16 To morewe ye schulen stie 'ayens hem; for thei schulen stie bi the side of the hil, 'bi name Seys, and ye schulen fynde hem in the hiynesse of the stronde, which is ayens the wildirnesse of Jheruhel.

17 For it schulen not be ye, that schulen fiyte; but oneli stonde ye trustili, and ye schulen se the help of the Lord on you. A! Juda and Jerusalem, nyle ye drede, nether be ye aferd; to morewe ye schulen go out ayens hem, and the Lord schal be with you.

18 Therfor Josaphat, and Juda, and alle the dwelleris of Jerusalem, felden lowli on the erthe bifor the Lord, and worschypiden hym.

19 Forsothe the dekenes of the sones of Caath, and of the sones of Chore, herieden the Lord God of Israel with greet vois an hiy.

20 And whanne thei hadden rise eerli, thei yeden not bi the deseert of Thecue; and whanne thei 'hadden gon forth, Josaphat stood in the myddis of hem, and seide, Juda and alle the dwelleris of Jerusalem, here ye me; bileue ye in 'youre Lord God, and ye schulen be sikur; bileue ye to hise prophetis, and alle prosperitees schulen come.

21 And he yaf counsel to the puple, and he ordeynede the syngeris of the Lord, that thei schulden herye hym in her cumpanyes, and that thei schulden go bifor the oost, and seie with acordynge vois, Knouleche ye to the Lord, for he is good; for his merci is 'in to the world.

22 And whanne thei bigunnen to synge heriyngis, the Lord turnede the buyschementis of hem 'in to hem silf, that is, of the sones of Amon and of Moab and of the hil of Seir, that yeden out to fiyte ayens Juda; and thei weren slayn.

23 For whi the sones of Amon and of Moab risiden togidere ayens the dwelleris of the hil of Seir, to sle, and to do awey hem; and whanne thei hadden do this in werk, thei weren 'turned also 'in to hem silf, and felden doun togidere bi woundis ech of othere.

24 Certis whanne Juda was comun to the denne, that biholdith the wildirnesse, he siy afer al the large cuntrei ful of deed bodies, and that noon was left, that miyte ascape deeth.

25 Therfor Josaphat cam, and al the puple with hym, to drawe awey the spuylis of deed men, and thei founden among the deed bodies dyuerse purtenaunce of houshold, and clothis, and ful preciouse vessels; and thei rauyischiden in dyuerse maneres, so that thei myyten not bere alle thingis, nether thei myyten take awei the spuylis bi thre daies, for the greetnesse of prey.

26 Sotheli in the fourthe dai thei weren gaderid togidere in the valey of Blessyng; 'forsothe for thei blessiden the Lord there, thei clepiden that place the valei of Blessyng 'til in to present dai.

27 And ech man of Juda turnede ayen, and the dwelleris of Jerusalem, and Josaphat bifor hem, in to Jerusalem with greet gladnesse; for the Lord God hadde youe to hem ioye of her enemyes.

28 And thei entriden in to Jerusalem with sawtrees, and harpis, and trumpis, in to the hows of the Lord.

29 Forsothe the drede of the Lord felde on alle the rewmes of londis, whanne thei hadden herd, that the Lord hadde fouyte ayens the enemies of Israel.

30 And the rewme of Josaphat restide; and the Lord yaf 'pees to hym 'bi cumpas.

31 Therfor Josaphat regnede on Juda; and he was of fyue and thritti yeer, whanne he bigan to regne; sotheli he regnede fyue and twenti yeer in Jerusalem; and the name of his modir was Azuba, the douytir of Selathi.

32 And he yede in the weie of Asa his fadir, and bowide not fro it, and he dide what euer thingis weren plesaunt bifor the Lord.

33 Netheles he dide not awei hiy thingis; yit the puple hadde not dressid her herte to the Lord God of her fadris.

34 Forsothe the residue of the formere and the laste dedis of Josaphat ben writun in the book of Hieu, the sone of Anany, which he ordeynede in the book of kyngis of Israel.

35 After these thingis Josaphat, kyng of Juda, made frendschipis with Ocozie, kyng of Israel, whose werkis weren ful yuele;

36 and he was parcener that thei maden schippis, that schulden go in to Tharsis; and thei maden o schip in to Asiongaber.

37 Sotheli Eliezer, sone of Dodan, of Maresa, profesiede to Josaphat, and seide, For thou haddist boond of pees with Ocozie, the Lord smoot thi werkis; and the schippis ben brokun, and myyten not go in to Tharsis.

CAP 21

1 Forsothe Josaphat slepte with hise fadris, and was biried with hem in the citee of Dauid; and Joram, his sone, regnede for hym.

2 And he hadde britheren, the sones of Josaphat, Azarie, Jahiel, and Zacarie, Anany, and Mychael, and Saphatie; alle these weren the sones of Josaphat, kyng of Juda.

3 And her fadir yaf to hem many yiftis of gold and of siluer, and rentis, with strongeste citees in Juda; but he yaf the rewme to Joram, for he was the firste gendrid.

4 Forsothe Joram roos on the rewme of his fadir; and whanne he hadde confermyd hym silf, he killide alle hise britheren bi swerd, and summe of the princes of Juda.

5 Joram was of two and thritti yeer, whanne he bigan to regne; and he regnede eiyte yeer in Jerusalem.

6 And he yede in the weies of the kyngis of Israel, as the hows of Achab hadde do, for the douyter of Achab was his wijf; and he dide yuel in the siyt of the Lord.

7 But the Lord nolde distrie the hows of Dauid, for the couenaunt which he 'hadde maad with Dauid, and for he 'hadde bihiyte to yyue to hym a lanterne, and to hise sones in al tyme.

8 In tho daies Edom rebellide, that it was not suget to Juda, and it ordeynede a kyng to it silf.

9 And whanne Joram hadde passide with hise princes, and al the multitude of knyytis, that was with hym, he roos bi niyt, and smoot Edom, that cumpasside him, and alle hise duykis of his multitude of knyytis.

10 Netheles Edom rebellide, that it was not vndir the lordschip of Juda 'til to this dai. In that tyme also Lobna yede awei, that it was not vndur the hond of hym; for he hadde forsake the Lord God of hise fadris.

11 Ferthermore he made hiye places in the citees of Juda, and made the dwelleris of Jerusalem to do fornycacioun, 'that is, idolatrie, and Juda to breke the lawe.

12 Forsothe lettris weren brouyt to hym fro Elie, the prophete, in whiche it was writun, The Lord God of Dauid,

13 thi fadir, seith these thingis, For thou 'yedist not in the weies of Josaphat, thi fadir, and in the weie of Asa, kyng of Juda, but thou yedist bi the weie of the kyngis of Israel, and madist Juda and the dwelleris of Jerusalem to do fornica-

cioun, and suedist the fornicacioun of the hows of Achab; ferthermore and thou hast slayn thi britheren and the hows of thi fadir, 'that weren betere than thou; lo!

14 the Lord schal smyte thee with a greet veniaunce, and thi puple, and thi sones, and wyues, and al thi catel;

15 sotheli thou schalt be sijk 'with the worste sorewe of wombe, til thin entrailis go out litil and litil bi ech dai.

16 Therfor the Lord reiside ayens Joram the spirit of Filisteis and Arabeis, that marchen with Ethiopiens; and thei stieden in to the lond of Juda,

17 and wastiden it, and thei token awei al the catel, that was foundun in the hows of the kyng, ferthermore and hise sones, and wyues; and no sone was left to hym, no but Joachaz, that was the leeste in birthe.

18 And ouer alle these thingis the Lord smoot hym with vncurable sorewe of the wombe.

19 And whanne dai cam aftir a dai, and the spaces of tymes weren turned aboute, the cours of twey yeer was fillid; and so he was wastid 'bi long rot, so that he castide out also his entrailis, and so he wantide sorewe and liyf togidere, and he was deed in the werste sikenesse. And the puple dide not to hym seruyce of deed men bi the custom of brennyng, as it hadde do to hise grettere, 'ether auncetris.

20 He was of two and thritti yeer whanne he bigan to regne, and he regnede eiyte yeer in Jerusalem, and he yede not riytfuli; and thei birieden hym in the citee of Dauid, netheles not in the sepulcre of kingis.

CAP 22

1 Forsothe the dwelleris of Jerusalem ordeyneden Ocozie, 'his leeste sone, kyng for hym; for theues of Arabeis, that felden in to the castels, hadden slayn alle the grettere 'in birthe, that weren bifor hym. And Ocozie, the sone of Joram, kyng of Juda, regnede.

2 Ocozie was of two and fourti yeer, whanne he bigan to regne, and he regnede o yeer in Jerusalem; the name of his modir was Athalia, the douyter of Amry.

3 But he entride bi the weie of the hows of Achab; for his modir compellide hym to do yuele.

4 Therfor he dide yuel in the siyt of the Lord, as the hows of Achab; for thei weren counselouris to hym in to his perischyng, aftir the deth of his fadir;

5 and he yede in the counsele of hem. And he yede with Joram, the sone of Achab, kyng of Israel, in to batel ayens Azahel, kyng of Sirye, in to Ramoth of Galaad. And men of Sirie woundiden Joram;

6 which turnede ayen for to be heelid in Jezrahel; for he hadde take many woundis in the forseid batel. Therfor Ocozie, kyng of Juda, the sone of Joram, yede doun to visite Joram, the sone of Achab, sijk in Jezrahel;

7 for it was Goddis wille ayens Ocozie, that he cam to Joram. And whanne he was comun, he yede out with hym ayens Hieu, the sone of Namsi, whom God anoyntide, that he schulde do awey the hows of Achab.

8 Therfor whanne Hieu destriede the hows of Achab, he foond the princis of Juda, and the sones of the britheren of Ocozie, that 'mynystriden to hym; and he killide hem.

9 And he souyte thilke Ocozie, and cauyte him hid in Samarie, and after that he was brouyt to Hieu, Hieu killide hym; and thei birieden hym, for he was the sone of Josaphat, that hadde souyt God in al his herte. And noon hope was more, that ony of the generacioun of Ocozie schulde regne.

10 For Athalia, his modir, siy, that hir sone was deed, and sche roos, and killide alle the kyngis generacioun of the hows of Joram.

11 Forsothe Josabeth, the douyter of the kyng, took Joas, the sone of Ocozie, and stal hym fro the myddis of the sones of the kyng, whanne thei weren slayn; and sche hidde hym with his nurse in the closet of beddis. Forsothe Josabeth, that 'hadde hid hym, was the douytir of kyng Joram, and wijf of Joiada, the bischop, and the sister of Ocozie; and therfor Athalia killide not hir.

12 Therfor he was hid with hem in the hows of God sixe yeer, in whiche Athalia regnede on the lond.

CAP 23

1 Forsothe in the seuenthe yeer Joiada was coumfortid, and took centuriouns, that is, Azarie, sone of Jeroboam, and Ismael, the sone of Johannam, and Azarie, the sone of Obeth, and Maasie, the sone of Adaie, and Elisaphat, the sone of Zechri; and he made with hem a counsel and a boond of pees.

2 Which cumpassiden Juda, and gaderiden togidere dekenes of alle the citees of Juda, and the princes of the meynees of Israel, and camen in to Jerusalem.

3 Therfor al the multitude made couenaunt in the hows of the Lord with the kyng. And Joiada seide to hem, Lo! the sone of the kyng schal regne, as the Lord spak on the sones of Dauid.

4 Therfor this is the word, which ye schulen do.

5 The thridde part of you that ben comun to the sabat, of preestis, and of dekenes, and of porterys, schal be in the yatis; sotheli the thridde part schal be at the hows of the kyng; and the thridde part schal be at the yate, which is clepid of the foundement. Forsothe al the tother comyn puple be in the large places of the hows of the Lord;

6 and noon other man entre in to the hows of the Lord, no but preestis, and thei that mynystren of the dekenes; oneli entre thei, that ben halewid, and al the tother comyn puple kepe the kepyngis of the Lord.

7 Forsothe the dekenes cumpasse the kyng, and ech man haue hise armuris; and if ony othere man entrith in to the temple, be he slayn; and be thei with the kyng entrynge and goynge out.

8 Therfor the dekenes and al Juda diden bi alle thingis, which Joiada, the bischop, hadde comaundid; and alle token the men, that weren with hem, and camen bi the ordre of sabat with hem, that hadden 'fillid now the sabat, and schulen go out.

9 For Joiada, the bischop, suffride not the cumpenyes to go awei, that weren wont to come oon after 'the tother bi ech wouke. And Joiada, the preest, yaf to the centuriouns speris, and scheeldis, and bokeleris of kyng Dauid, whiche he hadde halewid in to the hows of the Lord.

10 And he ordeynede al the puple, of hem 'that helden swerdis, at the riyt side of the temple 'til to the left side of the temple, bifor the auter and the temple, bi cumpas of the king.

11 And thei ledden out the sone of the kyng, and settiden a diademe on hym; and thei yauen to hym in his hond the lawe to be holdun, and thei maden hym kyng. And Joiada, the bischop, and his sones anoyntiden hym; and thei preiden hertli, and seiden, The kyng lyue!

12 And whanne Athalia hadde herd this thing, that is, the vois of men rennynge and preisynge the kyng, sche entride to the puple, in to the temple of the Lord.

13 And whanne sche hadde seyn the kyng stondynge on the grees in the entryng, and the princes and cumpenyes of knyy-

tis aboute hym, and al the puple of the lond ioiynge, and sownynge with trumpis, and syngynge togidere with orguns of dyuerse kynde, and the vois of men preisynge, sche torente hir clothis, and seide, Tresouns! tresouns!

14 Sotheli Joiada, the bischop, yede out to the centuriouns, and princes of the oost, and seide to hem, Lede ye hir with out the 'purseyntis, ethir closyngis, of the temple, and be sche slayn with outforth bi swerd; and the preest comaundide, that sche schulde not be slayn in the hows of the Lord.

15 And thei settiden hondis on hir nol; and whanne she hadde entrid in to the yate of the horsis, of the kyngis hows, thei killiden hir there.

16 Forsothe Joiada couenauntide a boond of pees bitwixe him silf and al the puple and the kyng, that it schulde be the puple of the Lord.

17 Therfor al the puple entride in to the hows of Baal, and distrieden it, and braken the auteris and symylacris therof; but thei killiden bifor the auteris Mathan, the preest of Baal.

18 Forsothe Joiada ordeynede souereyns in the hows of the Lord, that vndur the hondis of preestis, and of dekenes, whiche Dauid departide in the hows of the Lord, thei schulden offre brent sacrifices to the Lord, as it is writun in the book of Moises, in ioie and songis, by the ordynaunce of Dauid.

19 Also he ordeynede porteris in the yatis of the hows of the Lord, that an vnclene man in ony thing schulde not entre in to it.

20 And he took the centuriouns, and strongeste men, and princes of the puple, and al the comyn puple of the lond. And thei maden the kyng to go doun fro the hows of the Lord, and to entre bi the myddis of the hiyere yate in to the hows of the kyng; and thei settiden hym in the kyngis trone.

21 And al the puple of the lond was glad, and the citee restide; forsothe Athalia was slayn bi swerd.

CAP 24

1 Joas was of seuene yeer, whanne he bigan to regne, and he regnyde fourti yeer in Jerusalem; the name of his modir was Sebia of Bersabee.

2 And he dide that, that was good bifor the Lord, in alle the daies of Joiada, the preest.

3 Sotheli and Joas took twei wyues, of whyche he gendride sones and douytris.

4 After whiche thingis it pleside Joas to reparele the hows of the Lord.

5 And he gaderide togidere preestis and dekenes, and seide to hem, Go ye out to the citees of Juda, and gadere ye of al Israel money, to the reparelyng of the temple of 'youre Lord God, bi ech yeer; and do ye this hiyyngli.

6 Certis the dekenes diden necgligentli. And the kyng clepide Joiada, the prince, and seide to hym, Whi was it not charge to thee, to constreyne the dekenes to brynge yn money of Juda and of Jerusalem, which money was ordeyned of Moises, the seruaunt of 'the Lord, that al the multitude of Israel schulde brynge it in to the tabernacle of witnessyng?

7 For the worste Athalia, and hir sones, distrieden the hows of God; and of alle thingis, that weren halewid to the temple of the Lord, thei ourneden the temple of Baalym.

8 Therfor the kyng comaundide, and thei maden an arke, and settiden it bisidis the yate of the Lord with out forth.

9 And it was prechid in Juda and Jerusalem, that ech man schulde brynge to the Lord the prijs, which Moyses, the seruaunt of God, ordeynede on al Israel, in deseert.

10 And alle the princes and al the puple weren glad, and thei entriden, and brouyten, and senten in to the arke of the Lord, so that it was fillid.

11 And whanne it was tyme, that thei schulden bere the arke bifor the kyng bi the hondis of dekenes, for thei sien myche money, the clerk of the kyng entride, and he whom the firste preest hadde ordeynede, and thei schedden out the money, that was in the arke; sotheli thei baren ayen the arke to 'his place. And so thei diden bi alle daies, and money with out noumbre was gaderid togidere;

12 which the kyng and Joiada yauen to hem that weren souereyns of the werkis of the hows of the Lord. And thei hiriden therof kitteris of stonys, and crafti men of alle werkis, that thei schulden reparele the hows of the Lord; also thei hiriden smythis of yrun, and of bras, that that thing schulde be vndurset, that bigan to falle.

13 Thei that wrouyten diden craftili, and the crasyng of the wallis was stoppid bi the hondis of hem; and thei reisiden the hows of the Lord in to the formere staat, and maden it to stonde stidfastli.

14 And whanne thei hadden fillid alle werkis, thei brouyten bifor the kyng and Joiada the tother part of the money, of which money vessels weren maad in to the seruyce of the temple, and to brent sacrifices; also viols, and othere vessels of gold and of siluer 'weren maad therof. And brent sacrifices weren offrid in the hows of the Lord contynueli, in alle the daies of Joiada.

15 Forsothe Joiada ful of daies wexide eld, and he was deed, whanne he was of an hundrid yeer and thritti;

16 and thei birieden hym in the citee of Dauid with kyngis; for he hadde do good with Israel, and with his hows.

17 But aftir that Joiada diede, the princes of Juda entriden, and worschipiden the kyng, which was flaterid with her seruices, and assentide to hem.

18 And thei forsoken the temple of the Lord God of her fadris, and seruyden idols in wodis, and grauen ymagis; and the ire of the Lord was maad ayens Juda and Jerusalem for this synne.

19 And he sente to hem profetis, that thei schulen turne ayen to the Lord; whiche profetis witnessynge thei nolden here.

20 Therfor the Spirit of the Lord clothide Zacharie, the preest, the sone of Joiada; and he stood in the siyt of the puple, and seide to hem, The Lord seith these thingis, Whi breken ye the comaundement of the Lord, 'which thing schal not profite to you, and ye han forsake the Lord, that he schulde forsake you?

21 Whiche weren gaderide togidere ayens hym, and senten stonys, bi comaundement 'of the kyng, in the large place of the hows of the Lord.

22 And kyng Joas hadde not mynde on the merci which Joiada, the fadir of Zacharie, hadde doon with hym; but he killide the sone of Joiada. And whanne Zacharie diede, he seide, The Lord se, and seke.

23 And whanne a yeer was turned aboute, 'ether endid, the oost of Sirie stiede ayens Joas, and it cam in to Juda and in to Jerusalem, and it killide alle the princes of the puple; and thei senten al the prey to the kyng, to Damask.

24 And certeyn, whanne a ful litle noumbre of men of Sirie was comun, the Lord bitook in her hondis a multitude with out noumbre, for thei hadden forsake the Lord God of her fadris. Also thei vsiden schameful domes in Joas;

25 and thei yeden awei, and leften hym in grete sorewis. Sotheli hise seruauntis risiden ayens hym, in to veniaunce of

the blood of the sone of Joiada, preest; and killiden hym in his bed, and he was deed. And thei birieden hym in the citee of Dauid, but not in the sepulcris of kyngis.

26 Forsothe Sabath, the sone of Semath of Amon, and Josabeth, the sone of Semarith of Moab, settiden tresouns to hym.

27 Sotheli hise sones, and the summe of money that was gaderid vndur hym, and the reparelyng of the hows of God, ben writun diligentli in the book of Kyngis.

CAP 25

1 Forsothe Amasie, 'his sone, regnede for hym; Amasie was of fyue and twenti yeer, whanne he bigan to regne, and he regnyde nyne and twenti yeer in Jerusalem; the name of his modir was Joiaden, of Jerusalem.

2 And he dide good in the siyt of the Lord, netheles not in perfit herte.

3 And whanne he siy the empire strengthid to hym silf, he stranglide the seruauntis, that killiden the kyng, his fadir;

4 but he killide not the sones of hem; as it is writun in the book of the lawe of Moises, where the Lord comaundide, seiynge, Fadris schulen not be slayn for the sones, nether the sones for her fadris; but ech man schal die in his owne synne.

5 Therfor Amasie gaderide togidere Juda, and ordeynede hem bi meynees and tribunes and centuriouns, in al Juda and Beniamyn; and he noumbride fro twenti yeer and aboue, and he foonde thritti thousynde of yonge men, that yeden out to batel, and helden spere and scheeld.

6 Also for mede he hiride of Israel an hundrid thousynde of stronge men, for an hundrid talentis of siluer, that thei schulden fiyte ayens the sones of Edom.

7 Forsothe a man of God cam to hym, and seide, A! kyng, the oost of Israel go not out with thee, for the Lord is not with Israel and with alle the sones of Effraym;

8 for if thou gessist that batels stonden in the myyt of oost, the Lord schal make thee to be ouercomun of enemyes, for it is of God for to helpe, and to turne in to fliyt.

9 And Amasie seide to the man of God, What therfor schal be doon of the hundrid talentis, which Y yaf to the knyytis of Israel? And the man of God answeride to hym, The Lord hath, wherof he may yelde to thee myche mo thingis than these.

10 Therfor Amasie departide the oost that cam to hym fro Effraym, that it schulde turne ayen in to his place; and thei weren wrooth greetli ayens Juda, and turneden ayen in to her cuntrei.

11 Forsothe Amasie ledde out tristili his puple, and yede in to the valei of makyngis of salt, and he killide of the sones of Seir ten thousynde.

12 And the sones of Juda token othere ten thousynde of men, and brouyten to the hiy scarre of summe stoon; and castiden hem doun fro the hiyeste in to the pit; whiche alle braken.

13 And thilke oost whom Amasie hadde sent ayen, that it schulde not go with him to batel, was spred abroad in the citees of Juda fro Samarie 'til to Betheron; and aftir 'that it hadde slayn thre thousynde, it took awey a greet preie.

14 And Amasie, after the sleyng of Idumeis, and after that he hadde brouyt the goddis of the sones of Seir, ordeynede hem 'in to goddis to hym silf, and worschipide hem, and brente encense to hem.

15 Wherfor the Lord was wrooth ayens Amasie, and sente to hym a profete, that seide to hym, Whi worschipist thou goddis that 'delyueriden not her puple fro thin hond?

16 Whanne the profete spak these thingis, Amasie answeride to hym, Whether thou art a counselour of the king? ceesse thou, lest perauenture Y sle thee. Therfor the profete yede awei, and seide, Y woot, that the Lord thouyte to sle thee; for thou didist this yuel, and ferthermore thou assentidist not to my counsel.

17 Therfor Amasie, the king of Juda, whanne he hadde take a ful yuel counsel, sente to the kyng of Israel Joas, the sone of Joachaz, the sone of Hieu, and seide, Come thou, se we vs togidere.

18 And he sente ayen messangeris, and seide, A 'cardue, ether a tasil, which is in the Liban sente to the cedre of the Liban, and seide, Yyue thi douyter a wijf to my sone; and lo! beestis that weren in the wode of the Liban yeden and defouliden the cardue.

19 Thou seidist, Y haue smyte Edom, and therfor thin herte is reysid in to pride; sitte thou in thin hows; whi stirist thou yuel ayens thee, that thou falle, and Juda with thee?

20 Amasie nolde here, for it was the wille of the Lord, that he schulde be bitakun in to the hondis of enemyes, for the goddis of Edom.

21 Therfor Joas, kyng of Israel, stiede, and thei siyen hem silf togidere. Sotheli Amasie, the kyng of Juda, was in Bethsames of Juda;

22 and Juda felde doun bifor Israel, and fledde in to his tabernaclis.

23 Certis the kyng of Israel took in Bethsames Amasie, the kyng of Juda, the sone of Joas, sone of Joachaz, and brouyte in to Jerusalem; and he destriede the wallis therof fro the yate of Effraym 'til to the yate of the corner, bi foure hundrid cubitis.

24 And be ledde ayen in to Samarie al the gold and siluer, and alle vessels whiche he foond in the hows of the Lord, and at Obededom, in the tresouris also of the kyngis hows, also and the sones of ostagis.

25 Forsothe Amasie, kyng of Juda, the sone of Joas, lyuede fiftene yeer aftir that Joas, kyng of Israel, the sone of Joachaz, was deed.

26 Sotheli the residue of the formere and the laste wordis of Amasie ben writun in the book of kyngis of Juda and of Israel.

27 And aftir that he yede awei fro the Lord, thei settiden to hym tresouns in Jerusalem; and whanne he hadde fledde to Lachis, thei senten and killiden hym there;

28 and thei brouyten ayen on horsis, and birieden hym with his fadris in the citee of Dauid.

CAP 26

1 Forsothe al the puple of Juda made kyng, Ozie, his sone, 'of sixtene yeer, for his fader Amasie.

2 He bildide Hailath, and restoride it to the lordschipe of Juda, after that the kyng slepte with hise fadris.

3 Ozie was of sixtene yeer, whanne he bigan to regne; and he regnede two and fifti yeer in Jerusalem; the name of his modir was Hiechelia, of Jerusalem.

4 And he dide that, that was riytful in the siyt of the Lord, bi alle thingis whiche Amasie, his fadir, hadde do.

5 And he souyte the Lord in the daies of Zacarie, vndurstondynge and seynge God; and whanne he souyte God, God reulide hym in alle thingis.

6 Forsothe he yede out, and fauyt ayens Filisteis, and distriede the wal of Geth, and the wal of Jabyne, and the wal of

Azotus; and he bildide stronge places in Azotus and in Filistiym.

7 And the Lord helpide hym bothe ayens Filisteis, and ayens
Arabeis that dwelliden in Garbahal, and ayenus Amonytis.

8 Amonytis paieden yiftis to Ozie, and his name was pupplischid 'til to the entryng of Egipt for ofte victories.

9 And Ozie bildide touris in Jerusalem ouer the yate of the
corner, and ouer the yate of the valey, and othere touris in the
same side of the wal; and made tho stidefast.

10 Also he bildide touris in the wildirnesse, and he diggide
ful many cisternes; for he hadde many beestis as wel in the
feeldi places as in the wastnesse of deseert. Also he hadde
vyneris and tiliers of vynes in the hilles, and in Carmele; for
he was a man youun to erthetilthe.

11 Forsothe the oost of hise werriours, that yeden forth to
batels, vndur the hond of Heiel, scribe, and of Masie, techere,
and vndur the hond of Ananye that was of the duykis of the
kyng; and al the noumbre of princes, by her meynees, was of
stronge men two thousynde and sixe hundrid.

13 And vndur hem was al the oost, thre hundrid thousynde
and seuen thousynde and fyue hundrid, that weren able to
batel, and fouyten for the king ayens aduersaries.

14 And Ozie made redi to hem, that is, to al the oost, scheldis,
and speris, and basynetis, and haburiouns, and bouwis, and
slyngis to caste stonys.

15 And he made in Jerusalem engynes of dyuerse kynde,
which he settide in touris, and in the corneris of wallis, that
tho schulden caste arowis and grete stoonys; and his name
yede out fer, for the Lord helpide hym, and hadde maad him
strong.

16 But whanne he was maad strong, his herte was reisid in to
his perischyng; and he dispiside 'his Lord God; and he entride
in to the temple of the Lord, and wolde brenne encense on the
auter of encense.

17 And anoon Azarie, the preest, entride after hym, and with
hym the preestis of the Lord, seuenti 'men ful noble;

18 whiche ayenstoden the kyng, and seiden, Ozie, it is not of
thin office, that thou brenne encense to the Lord, but of the
preestis of the Lord, that is, of the sones of Aaron, that ben
halewid to siche seruyce; go thou out of the seyntuarye;
dispise thou not; for this thing schal not be arettid of the Lord
God to thee in to glorie.

19 And Ozie was wrooth, and he helde in the hond the censere for to offre encence, and manaasside the preestis; and
anoon lepre was sprungun forth in his forheed, bifor the preestis in the hows of the Lord on the auter of encense.

20 And whanne Azarie, the bischop, hadde biholde hym, and
alle othere preestis 'hadden biholde him, thei sien lepre in his
forheed, and hiyngli thei puttiden hym out; but also he was
aferd, and hastide to go out; for he feelide anoon the
veniaunce of the Lord.

21 Therfor kyng Ozie was leprouse 'til to the dai of his deeth,
and dwellide in an hows bi it silf, and he was ful of lepre; 'for
which he was cast out of the hows of the Lord. Forsothe
Joathan, his sone, gouernyde the hows of the kyng, and
demyde the puple of the lond.

22 Sotheli Ysaie, the prophete, the sone of Amos, wroot the
residue 'of the formere and of the laste wordis of Ozie.

23 And Ozie slepte with hise fadris, and thei birieden not hym
in the feeld of the kyngis sepulcris, for he was leprouse; and
Joathan, his sone, regnyde for hym.

CAP 27

1 Joathan was of fyue and twenti yeer, whanne he bigan to
regne, and he regnede sixtene yeer in Jerusalem; the name of
his modir was Jerusa, the douyter of Sadoch.

2 He dide that, that was riytful bifor the Lord, bi alle thingis
whiche Ozie, his fadir, hadde do; outakun that he entride not
in to the temple of the Lord, and the puple trespasside yit.

3 He bildide the hiy yate of the hous of the Lord, and he bildide manye thingis in the wal of Ophel;

4 also he bildide citees in the hillis of Juda, and he bildide
castels and touris in forestis.

5 He fauyt ayens the kyng of the sones of Amon, and ouercam hym; and the sones of Amon yauen to hym in that tyme
an hundrid talentis of siluer, and ten thousynde choris of barli,
and so many of wheete; the sones of Amon yauen these
thingis to hym in the secounde and in the thridde yeer.

6 And Joathan was maad strong, for he hadde dressid hise
weies bifor 'his Lord God.

7 Forsothe the residue of wordis of Joathan, and alle hise
batels, and werkis, ben writun in the book of kyngis of Israel
and of Juda.

8 He was of fyue and twenti yeer, whanne he bigan to regne,
and he regnede sixtene yeer in Jerusalem.

9 And Joathan slepte with hise fadris, and thei birieden hym
in the citee of Dauid; and Achaz, his sone, regnede for him.

CAP 28

1 Achaz was of twenti yeer, whanne he bigan to regne, and he
regnede sixtene yeer in Jerusalem; he dide not riytfulnesse in
the siyt of the Lord, as Dauid, his fadir, dide;

2 but he yede in the weies of the kyngis of Israel. Ferthermore
and he yetyde ymagis to Baalym.

3 He it is that brente encense in the valey of Beennon, and
purgide hise sones bi fier bi the custom of hethene men,
whiche the Lord killide in the comyng of the sones of Israel.

4 Also he made sacrifice, and brente encense in hiy places,
and in hillis, and vndur ech tree ful of bowis.

5 And 'his Lord God bitook hym in the hond of the kyng of
Sirie, which smoot Achaz, and took a greet preie of his
empire, and brouyten in to Damask. Also Achaz was bitakun
to the hondis of the kyng of Israel, and was smytun with a
greet wounde.

6 And Facee, the sone of Romelie, killide of Juda sixe scoore
thousynde in o dai, alle the men werriours; for thei hadden
forsake the Lord God of her fadris.

7 In the same tyme Zechry, a myyti man of Effraym, killide
Maasie, the sone of Rogloth, the kyng; and 'he killide Ezrica,
the duyk of his hows, and Elcana, the secounde fro the kyng.

8 And the sones of Israel token of her britheren two hundrid
thousynde of wymmen and of children and of damysels, and
prey with out noumbre; and baren it in to Samarie.

9 In that tempest a profete of the Lord, Obed bi name, was
there, which yede out ayens the oost comynge in to Samarie,
and seide to hem, Lo! the Lord God of youre fadris was
wrooth ayens Juda, and bitook hem in youre hondis; and ye
han slayn hem crueli, so that youre cruelte stretchide forth in
to heuene.

10 Ferthermore ye wolen make suget to you the sones of Juda
and of Jerusalem in to seruauntis and handmaidis; which
thing is not nedeful to be doon; for ye han synned on this
thing to 'youre Lord God.

11 But here ye my councel, and lede ayen the prisounneris, whyche ye han brouyt of youre britheren; for greet veniaunce of the Lord neiyith to you.

12 Therfor men of the princes of the sones of Effraym, Azarie, the sone of Johannan, Barachie, the sone of Mosollamoth, Jesechie, the sone of Sellum, and Amasie, the sone of Adali, stoden ayens hem that camen fro the batel;

13 and seiden to hem, Ye schulen not brynge in hidur the prisoneris, lest we doen synne ayens the Lord; whi wolen ye 'ley to on youre synnes, and heepe elde trespassis? For it is greet synne; the ire of the strong veniaunce of the Lord neiyeth on Israel.

14 And the men werriouris leften the prey, and alle thingis whiche thei hadden take, bifor the princes and al the multitude.

15 And the men stoden, whiche we remembriden bifore, and thei token the prisounneris, and clothiden of the spuylis alle that weren nakid; and whanne thei hadden clothid hem, and hadden schod, and hadden refreschid with mete and drynke, and hadden anoyntid for trauel, and hadden youe cure, 'ether medecyn, to hem; 'thei puttiden hem on horsis, whiche euere 'myyten not go, and weren feble 'of bodi, and brouyten to Jerico, a citee of palmes, to 'the britheren of hem; and thei turneden ayen in to Samarie.

16 In that tyme kyng Achaz sente to the kyng of Assiriens, and axide help.

17 And Ydumeis camen, and killiden many men of Juda, and token greet prey.

18 Also Filisteis weren spred abrood bi citees of the feeldis, and at the south of Juda; and thei token Bethsames, and Hailon, and Gaderoth, and Socoth, and Thannan, and Zamro, with her villagis; and dwelliden in tho.

19 For the Lord made low Juda for Achaz, the kyng of Juda; for he hadde maad him nakid of help, and hadde dispisid the Lord.

20 And the Lord brouyte ayens him Teglat Phalasar, kyng of Assiriens, that turmentide hym, and waastide hym, while no man ayenstood.

21 Therfor Achaz, after that he hadde spuylid the hows of the Lord, and the hows of the kyng and of princes, yaf yiftis to the kyng of Assiriens, and netheles it profitide 'no thing to hym.

22 Ferthermore also in the tyme of his angwisch he encreesside dispit ayens God; thilke kyng Achaz bi

23 hym silf offride sacrifices to the goddis of Damask, hise smyteris, and seide, The goddis of the kyngis of Sirie helpen hem, whiche goddis Y schal plese bi sacrifices, and thei schulen help me; whanne ayenward thei weren fallyng to hym, and to al Israel.

24 Therfor aftir that Achaz hadde take awei, and broke alle the vessels of the hows of God, he closide the yatis of Goddis temple, and made auteris to hym silf in alle the corneris of Jerusalem.

25 And in alle citees of Juda he bildide auteris to brenne encence, and he stiride the Lord God of hise fadris to wrathfulnesse.

26 Sotheli the residue of hise wordis and of alle hise werkis, the formere and the laste, ben writun in the book of kyngis of Juda and of Israel.

27 And Achaz slepte with hise fadris, and thei birieden hym in the citee of Jerusalem; for thei resseyueden not hym in the sepulcris of the kyngis of Israel; and Ezechie, his sone, regnede for hym.

CAP 29

1 Therfor Ezechie bigan to regne, whanne he was of fyue and twenti yeer, and he regnede in Jerusalem nyne and twenti yeer; the name of his modir was Abia, the douytir of Zacharie.

2 And he dide that, that was pleasaunt in the siyt of the Lord, bi alle thingis whiche Dauid, his fadir, hadde do.

3 In that yeer and the firste monethe of his rewme he openyde the yatis of the hows of the Lord, and restoride tho;

4 and he brouyte the preestis and dekenes, and gaderide hem in to the eest strete,

5 and seide to hem, Sones of Leuy, here ye me, and be ye halewid; clense ye the hows of the Lord God of youre fadris; do ye awei al vnclennesse fro the seyntuarie.

6 Oure fadris synneden, and diden yuel in the siyt of 'oure Lord God, and forsoken hym; thei turneden awei her faces fro the tabernacle of 'oure Lord God, and yauen the bak.

7 Thei closiden the doris that weren in the porche, and quenchiden the lanternes; and thei brenten not encense, and thei offriden not brent sacrifices in the seyntuarie of God of Israel.

8 Therfor the stronge veniaunce of the Lord was reisid on Juda and Jerusalem; and he yaf hem in to stiryng, and in to perischyng, and in to 'hisshing, ether scornyng, as ye seen with youre iyen.

9 Lo! oure fadris felden doun bi swerdis; oure sones, and oure douytris, and wyues ben led prisouneris for this greet trespas.

10 Now therfor it plesith me, that we make a boond of pees with the Lord God of Israel, and that he turne fro vs the stronge veniaunce of his ire.

11 My sones, nyle ye be reccheles; the Lord hath chose you, that ye stonde bifor hym, and serue hym, that ye herie hym, and brenne encense to hym.

12 Therfor the dekenes risiden, Mahat, the sone of Amasie, and Johel, the sone of Azarie, of the sones of Caath; sotheli of the sones of Merarye, Cys, the sone of Abdai, and Azarie, the sone of Jelaleel; forsothe of the sones of Jerson, Joha, the sone of Zemma, and Hedem, the sone of Johaa;

13 and sotheli of the sones of Elisaphan, Samri, and Jahiel; and of the sones of Asaph, Zacharie, and Mathanye;

14 also of the sones of Heman, Jahiel, and Semei; but also of the sones of Iditum, Semei, and Oziel.

15 And thei gaderiden to gidere her britheren, and weren halewid; and thei entriden bi comaundement of the kyng, and bi comaundement of the Lord, for to clense the hows of the Lord.

16 Also preestis entriden in to the temple of the Lord, for to halewe it, and thei baren out al vnclennesse, which thei founden ther ynne in the porche, 'ethir large place, of the hows of the Lord; which vnclennesse the dekenes token, and baren out to the stronde of Cedron with outforth.

17 Sotheli thei bigunnen to clense in the firste dai of the firste monethe, and in the eiyte dai of the same monethe thei entriden in to the porche of the hows of the Lord, and thei clensiden the temple eiyte daies; and in the sixtenthe dai of the same monethe thei filliden that, that thei hadden bigunne.

18 And thei entriden to Ezechie, the king, and seiden to hym, We han halewid al the hows of the Lord, and the auter of brent sacrifice therof, and the vessels therof, also and the boord of settyngforth with alle hise vessels,

19 and al the purtenaunce of the temple, 'which purtenaunce king Achaz hadde defoulid in his rewme, aftir that he brak the

lawe; and lo! alle thingis ben set forth bifor the auter of the Lord.

20 And Ezechie, the kyng, roos in the morwetid, and gaderide togidere alle the princes of the citee, and stiede in to the hows of the Lord;

21 and thei offriden togidere seuene bolis, and seuene rammes, seuene lambren, and seuene buckis of geet, for synne, for the rewme, for the seyntuarye, and for Juda. And he seide to preestis, the sones of Aaron, that thei schulden offre on the auter of the Lord.

22 Therfor thei killiden bolis, and 'the preestis tooken the blood, and schedden it on the auter; also thei killiden rammes, and 'the preestis schedden the blood of tho on the auter; thei offriden lambren, and 'the preestis schedden the blood on the auter.

23 And thei brouyten buckis of geet 'for synne bifor the kyng and al the multitude, and thei settiden her hondis on tho;

24 and the preestis offriden tho, and spreynten the blood of tho bifor the auter, for the clensyng of al Israel. For the king comaundide, that brent sacrifice shulde be made for al Israel, and for synne.

25 Also he ordeynede dekenes in the hows of the Lord, with cymbalis, and sawtrees, and harpis, bi the ordenaunce of 'Dauid the kyng, and of Gad, the profete, and of Nathan, the profete; for it was the comaundement of the Lord bi the hond of hise prophetis.

26 And the dekenes stoden, and helden the orguns of Dauid; and preestis helden trumpis.

27 And Ezechie comaundide, that thei schulden offre brent sacrifices on the auter; and whanne brent sacrifices weren offrid, thei bigunnen to synge preisyngis to the Lord, and to sowne with trumpis, and in dyuerse orguns, whiche Dauid, the kyng of Israel, hadde maad redi for to sowne.

28 Forsothe whanne al the cumpenye worschipide, syngeris and thei that helden trumpis weren in her office, til the brent sacrifice was fillid.

29 And whanne the offryng was endid, the kyng was bowid, and alle that weren with hym, and thei worschipiden God.

30 And Ezechie and the princes comaundiden to the dekenes, that thei schulden preise the Lord with the wordis of Dauith, and of Asaph, the profete; whiche preisiden hym with greet gladnesse, and kneliden, and worschipiden.

31 Sothely Ezechie addide also these thingis, Ye han fillid youre hondis to the Lord; neiye ye, and offre sacrifices and preisyngis in the hows of the Lord.

32 Therfor al the multitude offride with deuoute soule sacrifices, and preisyngis, and brent sacrifices. Sotheli this was the noumbre of brent sacrifices, whiche the multitude offride; seuenti bolis, and an hundrid rammes, two hundrid lambren.

33 Also thei halewiden to the Lord sixe hundrid oxis, and thre thousynde sheep.

34 Forsothe the preestis weren fewe, and myyten not suffice for to 'drawe awei the skynnes of brent sacrifices; wherfor and the dekenes her britheren helpiden hem, til the werk was fillid, and the preestis weren halewid; for the dekenes ben halewid bi liytere custom than the preestis.

35 Therfor there weren ful many brent sacrifices, ynnere fatnessis of pesible sacrifices, and the moyste sacrifices of brent sacrifices, and the worschip, 'ethir ournyng, of the 'Lordis hows was fillid.

36 And Ezechie was glad, and al the puple, for the seruyce of the Lord was fillid; for it pleiside, that this was doon sodeynly.

CAP 30

1 And Ezechie sente to al Israel and to Juda, and he wroot pistlis to Effraym and to Manasses, that thei schulden come in to the hous of the Lord in Jerusalem, and make paske to the Lord God of Israel.

2 Therfor whanne counseil was takun of the kyng, and of princes, and of al the cumpeny of Jerusalem, thei demyden to make paske in the secounde moneth.

3 For thei demyden not to do in his tyme; for the preestis that myyten suffice weren not halewid, and the puple was not yit gaderid in to Jerusalem.

4 And the word pleside the king, and al the multitude.

5 And thei demyden to sende messangeris in to al Israel, fro Bersabee 'til to Dan, that thei schulden come, and make pask to the Lord God of Israel in Jerusalem; for many men hadden not do, as it is bifor writun in the lawe.

6 And corouris yeden forth with pistlis, bi comaundement of the kyng and of hise princis, in to al Israel and Juda, and prechiden bi that, that the kyng hadde comaundid, Sones of Israel, turne ye ayen to the Lord God of Abraham, and of Isaac, and of Israel; and he schal turne ayen to the residue men, that ascapiden the hondis of the kyng of Assiriens.

7 Nyle ye be maad as youre fadris and britheren, that yeden awei fro the Lord God of her fadris; and he yaue hem in to perischyng, as ye seen.

8 Nyle ye make hard youre nollis, as youre fadris diden; yyue ye hondis to the Lord, and come ye to his seyntuarie, which he halewide withouten ende; serue ye the Lord God of youre fadris, and the ire of his strong veniaunce schal 'be turned awey fro you.

9 For if ye turnen ayen to the Lord, youre britheren and youre sones schulen haue mercy, bifor her lordis that ledden hem prisoneris; and thei schulen turne ayen in to this lond. For 'oure Lord God is pitouse, 'ethir benygne, and merciful; and he schal not turne awey his face fro you, if ye turne ayen to hym.

10 Therfor the corours yeden swiftli fro cytee in to citee thorou the lond of Effraym and of Manasses 'til to Zabulon, while thei scorniden and bimowiden hem.

11 Netheles sum men of Aser, and of Manasses, and of Zabulon, assentiden to the counsel, and camen in to Jerusalem.

12 Forsothe the hond of the Lord was maad in Juda, that he yaf to hem oon herte, and that thei diden the word of the Lord, bi the comaundement of the kyng and of the princes.

13 And many puplis weren gaderid in to Jerusalem, for to make the solempnyte of therf looues in the secounde monethe.

14 And thei risiden, and destrieden the auteris, that weren in Jerusalem; and 'thei destriynge alle thingis in whiche encense was brent to idols, castiden forth in to the stronde of Cedron.

15 Forsothe thei offriden pask in the fourtenthe dai of the secounde monethe; also the preestis and the dekenes weren halewid at the laste, and offriden brent sacrifices in the hows of the Lord.

16 And thei stoden in her ordre, bi the ordynaunce and lawe of Moises, the man of God. Sothely the preestis token of the hondis of dekenes the blood to be sched out,

17 for myche cumpeny was not halewid; and therfor the dekenes offriden pask for hem, that myyten not be halewid to the Lord.

18 Also a greet part of the puple of Effraym, and Manasses, and of Ysachar, and of Zabulon, that was not halewid, eet

pask not bi that that is writun. And Ezechie preyde for hem, and seide, The good Lord schal do mercy to alle men,

19 that seken in al the herte the Lord God of her fadris; and it schal not be arettid to hem, that thei ben not halewid.

20 And the Lord herde hym, and was plesid to the puple.

21 And the sones of Israel, that weren founden in Jerusalem, maden solempnyte of therf looues seuene daies in greet gladnesse, and herieden the Lord bi ech dai; and dekenes and preestis 'preisiden the Lord bi orguns, that acordiden to her offices.

22 And Ezechie spak to the herte of alle the dekenes, that hadden good vndurstondyng of the Lord; and thei eeten bi seuene daies of the solempnyte, offrynge sacrifices of pesible thingis, and heriynge the Lord God of her fadris.

23 And it pleside al the multitude to halewe also othere seuene daies; which thing also thei diden with greet ioye.

24 Forsothe Ezechie, kyng of Juda, yaf to the multitude a thousynde bolis, and seuene thousynde of scheep; sotheli the princes yauen to the puple a thousynde bolis, and ten thousynde scheep. Therfor ful greet multitude of preestis was halewid;

25 and al the cumpany of Juda was fillid with gladnesse, as wel of preestis and dekenes, as of al the multitude, that camen fro Israel, and 'of conuersis of the lond of Israel, and of dwelleris in Juda.

26 And greet solempnytee was maad in Jerusalem, which maner solempnyte was not in that citee fro the daies of Salomon, sone of Dauid, kyng of Israel.

27 Sotheli preestis and dekenes rysyden, and blessiden the puple; and the vois of hem was herd, and the preier cam in to the hooli dwelling place of heuene.

CAP 31

1 And whanne these thingis weren doon riytfuli, al Israel yede out, that was foundun in the citees of Juda; and thei braken symylacris, and kittiden doun woodis, and wastiden hiy places, and distrieden auteris, not oneli of al Juda and Beniamyn, but also and of Effraym and Manasses, til thei distrieden outirli. And alle the sones of Israel turneden ayen in to her possessiouns and citees.

2 Forsothe Ezechie ordeynede cumpenyes of preestis and of dekenes bi her departyngis, ech man in his owne office, that is, as wel of preestis as of dekenes, to brent sacrifices and pesible sacrifices, that thei schulden mynystre, and knowleche, and synge in the yatis of the castels of the Lord.

3 Sotheli the part of the kyng was, that of his owne catel brent sacrifice schulde be offrid euere in the morewtid and euentide, also in sabatis, and calendis, and othere solempnytees, as it is writun in the lawe of Moises.

4 Also he comaundide to the puple of hem that dwelliden in Jerusalem, to yyue partis to the preestis and dekenes, that thei myyten yyue tent to the lawe of the Lord.

5 And whanne this was knowun in the eeris of the multitude, the sones of Israel offriden ful many firste fruytis of wheete, of wyn, of oyle, and of hony; and of alle thingis whiche the erthe bringith forth, thei offriden tithis.

6 But also the sones of Israel and of Juda, that dwelliden in the citees of Juda, offriden tithis of oxis and of scheep, and the tithis of holi thingis, whiche thei avowiden to 'her Lord God, and thei brouyten alle thingis, and maden ful many heepis.

7 In the thridde monethe thei bigunnen to leie the foundementis of the heepis, and in the seuenthe monethe thei filliden tho heepis.

8 And whanne Ezechie and hise princes hadden entrid, thei siyen the heepis, and blessiden the Lord, and the puple of Israel.

9 And Ezechie axide the preestis and dekenes, whi the heepis laien so.

10 Azarie, the firste preest of the generacioun of Sadoch, answeride to hym, and seide, Sithen the firste fruytis bigunnen to be offrid in the hows of the Lord, we han ete and ben fillid, and ful many thingis ben left; for the Lord hath blessid his puple; sotheli this plentee, which thou seest, is of the relifs.

11 Therfor Ezechie comaundide, that thei schulden make redi bernes in the hows of the Lord; and whanne thei hadden do this thing,

12 thei brouyten in feithfuly bothe the firste fruytis, and tithis, and what euere thingis thei hadden avowid. Forsothe Chonenye, the dekene, was the souereyn of tho; and Semei his brother was the secounde;

13 aftir whom Jehiel, and Azarie, and Nabath, and Asahel, and Jerimoth, 'and Jozabad, and Helyel, and Jesmahie, and Maath, and Banaie, weren souereyns vndur the hondis of Chonenye and Semei, his brother, bi the comaundement of 'Ezechie the kyng, and of Azarie, the bischop of the hows of the Lord, to whiche alle thingis perteyneden.

14 But Chore, the sone of Jemnya, dekene and portere of the eest yate, was souereyn of tho thingis that weren offrid bi fre wille to the Lord, and of the firste fruytis, and of thingis halewid in to hooli thingis of the noumbre of hooli thingis;

15 and vndur his cure weren Eden, and Beniamyn, Jesue, and Semeye, and Amarie, and Sechenye, in the citees of preestis, that thei schulden departe feithfuli to her britheren the partis, to the lesse and the grettere,

16 outakun malis fro three yeer and aboue, these thingis to alle that entriden in to the temple of the Lord, and what euer thing bi ech dai was hirid in the seruyce and obseruaunces bi her departyngis.

17 To preestis bi meynees, and to dekenes fro 'the twentithe yeer and aboue bi her ordris and cumpenyes, and to alle the multitude,

18 bothe to the wyues and fre children of hem of euer either kynde, metis weren youun feithfuli of these thingis that weren halewid.

19 But also men of the sones of Aaron weren ordeyned bi the feeldis and subarbis of alle citees, whyche men schulden dele partis to al the male kynde of preestis and dekenes.

20 Therfor Ezechie dide alle thingis, whiche we seiden, in al Juda, and he wrouyte that, that was riytful and good and trewe bifor 'his Lord God,

21 in al the religioun of the seruyce of the hows of the Lord, bi the lawe and cerymonyes; and he wolde seke his Lord God in al his herte, and he dide, and hadde prosperite.

CAP 32

1 Aftir whiche thingis and sich treuthe, Senacherib, the kyng of Assiriens, cam and entride in to Juda; and he bisegide stronge citees, and wolde take tho.

2 And whanne Ezechie hadde herd this thing, that is, that Senacherib was comun, and that al the fersnesse of batel was turned ayens Jerusalem,

3 he took counsel with the princes and strongest men, that
thei schulden stoppe the heedis of wellis, that weren without
the citee; and whanne the sentence of alle men demyde this,
4 he gaderide togidere a ful greet multitude, and thei stoppiden alle the wellis, and the ryuer, that flowide in the myddis
of the lond; and seiden, Lest the kyngis of Assiriens comen,
and fynden abundance of watris.
5 Also he dide wittili, and bildide al the wal that was distride,
and he bildide touris aboue, and an other wal withoutforth.
And he reparilide Mello in the citee of Dauid; and made
armure of al kynde, and scheldis.
6 And he ordeynede princes of werriouris in the oost; and he
clepide togidere alle men in the street of the yate of the citee,
and spake to the herte of hem,
7 and seide, Do ye manli, and be ye coumfortid; nyle ye
drede, nether be ye aferd of the kyng of Assiriens, and of al
the multitude which is with him; for many mo ben with vs
than with him.
8 Fleischli arm is with him; 'oure Lord God is with vs, which
is oure helpere, and schal fiyte for vs. And the puple was
coumfortid with sich wordis of Ezechie, kyng of Juda.
9 And aftir that these thingis weren doon, Sennacherib sente
hise seruauntis to Jerusalem; for he 'with al the oost bisegide
Lachis. He sente to Ezechie, kyng of Juda, and to al the puple
that was in the citee,
10 and seide, Sennacherib, the kyng of Assiriens, seith these
thingis, In whom han ye trist, and sitten bisegid in Jerusalem?
11 Whether Ezechie disseyueth you, that he bitake you to
deeth in hungur and thirst, and affermeth, that 'youre Lord
God schal delyuere you fro the hond of the kyng of Assyriens?
12 Whether not this is Ezechie, that distriede hiy places, and
auteris of hym, and comaundide to Juda and to Jerusalem, and
seide, Ye schulen worschipe bifor oon auter, and therynne ye
schulen brenne encense?
13 Whether ye witen not what thingis Y haue do, and my
fadir, to alle the puplis of londis? Whether the goddis of
folkis and of alle londis myyten delyuere her cuntrei fro myn
hond?
14 Who is of alle goddis of folkis, whiche my fadris distrieden, that myyte delyuere his puple fro myn hond, that also
youre God may delyuere you fro this hond?
15 Therfor Ezechie disseyue not you, nether scorne bi veyn
counselyng, nethir bileue ye to hym; for if no god of alle
folkis and cuntreis myyte delyuere his puple fro myn hond,
and fro the hond of my fadris, suyngli nether youre God schal
mowe delyuere you fro this myn hond.
16 But also hise seruauntis spaken many othir thingis ayenus
the Lord God, and ayens Ezechie, his seruaunte.
17 Also he wroot epistlis ful of blasfemye ayens the Lord
God of Israel, and he spak ayens God, As the goddis of othere
folkis myyten not delyuere her puple fro myn hond, so and
the God of Ezechie may not delyuere his puple fro myn hond.
18 Ferthermore and with greet cry in the langage of Jewis he
sownede ayens the puple, that sat on the wallis of Jerusalem,
to make hem aferd, and to take the citee.
19 And he spake ayens God of Israel, as ayens the goddis of
the puplis of erthe, the werkis of mennus hondis.
20 Therfor Ezechie, the kyng, and Ysaie, the profete, the sone
of Amos, preieden ayens this blasfemye, and crieden til in to
heuene.
21 And the Lord sente his aungel, that killide ech strong man
and werriour, and the prince of the oost of the kyng of Assir-

iens; and he turnede ayen with schenship 'in to his lond. And
whanne he hadde entrid in to the hows of his god, the sones,
that yeden out of his wombe, killiden hym with swerd.
22 And the Lord sauyde Ezechie, and the dwelleris of Jerusalem, fro the hond of Senacherib, kyng of Assiriens, and fro
the hond of alle men; and yaf to hem reste bi cumpas.
23 Also many men brouyten offryngis and sacrifices to the
Lord in to Jerusalem, and yiftis to Ezechie, kyng of Juda;
which was enhaunsid aftir these thingis bifor alle folkis.
24 In tho daies Ezechie was sijk 'til to the deth, and he
preiede the Lord; and he herde hym, and yaf to hym a signe;
25 but he yeldide not bi the benefices whiche he hadde take,
for his herte was reisid; and ire was maad ayens hym, and
ayens Juda, and ayens Jerusalem.
26 And he was mekid aftirward, for his herte was reisid;
bothe he was mekid, and the dwelleris of Jerusalem; and therfor the ire of the Lord cam not on hem in the daies of Ezechie.
27 Forsothe Ezechie was riche, and ful noble, and gaderide to
hym silf ful many tresours of siluer, of gold, and of preciouse
stoon, of swete smellynge spices, and of armuris of al kynde,
and of vessels of greet prijs.
28 Also he bildide large housis of wheete, of wyn, and of oile,
and cratchis of alle beestis,
29 and fooldis to scheep, and sixe citees. For he hadde
vnnoumbrable flockis of scheep and of grete beestis; for the
Lord hadde youe to hym ful myche catel.
30 Thilke is Ezechie, that stoppide the hiyere welle of the
watris of Gion, and turnede tho awei vndur the erthe at the
west of the citee of Dauid; in alle hise werkis he dide 'bi prosperite, what euer thing he wolde.
31 Netheles in the message of the princes of Babiloyne, that
weren sent to hym for to axe of the grete wondir, that bifelde
on the lond, God forsook hym, that he were temptid, and that
alle thingis weren knowun that weren in his herte.
32 Sotheli the residue of wordis of Ezechie, and of hise mercies, ben writun in the profesie of Ysaie, the profete, sone of
Amos, and in the book of kyngis of Juda and of Israel.
33 And Ezechie slepte with hise fadris, and thei birieden hym
aboue the sepulcris of the sones of Dauid. And al Juda and
alle the dwelleris of Jerusalem maden solempne the seruyces
of his biriyng; and Manasses, his sone, regnide for him.

CAP 33

1 Manasses was of twelue yeer, whanne he bygan to regne,
and he regnyde in Jerusalem fyue and fifti yeer.
2 Forsothe he dide yuel bifor the Lord bi abhomynaciouns of
hethene men, whiche the Lord destriede bifor the sones of
Israel.
3 And he turnede, and restoride the hiye places, whiche
Ezechie, his fadir, hadde destried. And he bildide auteris to
Baalym, and made wodis, and worschipide al the knyythod of
heuene, and heriede it.
4 And he bildide auteris in the hows of the Lord, of which the
Lord hadde seid, My name schal be in Jerusalem with outen
ende.
5 Sotheli he bildide tho auteris to al the knyythod of heuene
in the twei large places of the hows of the Lord.
6 And he made hise sones to passe thorouy the fier in the
valei of Beennon; he kepte dremes; he suede fals diuynyng bi
chiteryng of briddis; he seruyde witche craftis; he hadde with
hym astronomyeris and enchaunteris, 'ethir trigetours, that
disseyuen mennus wittis, and he wrouyte many yuelis bifor
the Lord to terre hym to wraththe.

7 Also he settide a grauun signe and a yotun signe in the hows of the Lord, of which hows God spak to Dauid, and to Salomon, his sone, and seide, Y schal sette my name with outen ende in this hows and in Jerusalem, which Y chees of alle the lynagis of Israel;

8 and Y schal not make the foot of Israel to moue fro the lond which Y yaf to her fadris, so oneli if thei kepen to do tho thingis whiche Y comaundide to hem, and al the lawe, and cerymonyes, and domes, bi the hond of Moises.

9 Therfor Manasses disseyuede Juda, and the dwelleris of Jerusalem, that thei diden yuel, more than alle hethene men, whiche the Lord hadde distriede fro the face of the sones of Israel.

10 And the Lord spak to hym, and to his puple; and thei nolden take heed.

11 Therfor the Lord brouyte on hem the princes of the oost of the kyng of Assiriens; and thei token Manasses, and bounden hym with chaynes, and stockis, and ledden hym in to Babiloyne.

12 And aftir that he was angwischid, he preiede 'his Lord God, and dide penaunce gretli bifor the God of hise fadris.

13 And he preiede God, and bisechide ententifli; and God herde his preier, and brouyte hym ayen 'in to Jerusalem in to his rewme; and Manasses knew, that the Lord hym silf is God.

14 Aftir these thingis he bildide the wal with out the citee of Dauid, at the west of Gion, in the valei, fro the entryng of the yate of fischis, bi cumpas 'til to Ophel; and he reiside it gretli; and he ordeynede princes of the oost in alle the stronge citees of Juda.

15 And he dide awei alien goddis and symylacris fro the hows of the Lord; and he dide awei the auteris, whiche he hadde maad in the hil of the hows of the Lord, and in Jerusalem, and he castide awei alle with out the citee.

16 Certis he restoride the auter of the Lord, and offride theronne slayn sacrifices, and pesible sacrifices, and preisyng; and he comaundide Juda to serue the Lord God of Israel.

17 Netheles the puple offride yit in hiy places to 'her Lord God.

18 Forsothe the residue of dedis of Manasses, and his bisechyng to 'his Lord God, and the wordis of profetis, that spaken to hym in the name of the Lord God of Israel, ben conteyned in the wordis of the kyngis of Israel.

19 And his preier, and the heryng, and alle synnes, and dispisyng, also the places in whiche he bildide hiy thingis, and made wodis and ymagis, bifor that he dide penaunce, ben writun in the bokis of Ozai.

20 Forsothe Manasses slepte with hise fadris, and thei birieden hym in his hows; and Amon, his sone, regnyde for hym.

21 Amon was of two and twenti yeer, whanne he bigan to regne; and he regnyde twei yeer in Jerusalem.

22 And he dide yuel in the siyt of the Lord, as Manasses, his fadir, hadde do; and he offride, and seruyde to alle the idols, whiche Manasses hadde maad.

23 And he reuerenside not the face of the Lord, as Manasses, 'his fadir, reuerenside; and he dide mych gretter trespassis.

24 And whanne his seruauntis 'hadden swore to gyder ayens hym, thei killiden hym in his hows.

25 Sotheli the residue multitude of the puple, aftir that thei hadden slayn hem that 'hadden slayn Amon, ordeyneden Josie, his sone, kyng for hym.

CAP 34

1 Josie was of eiyte yeer, whanne he bigan to regne, and he regnede in Jerusalem oon and thritti yeer.

2 And he dide that, that was riytful in the siyt of the Lord; and yede in the waies of Dauid, his fadir, and bowide not to the riyt side nether to the left side.

3 Forsothe in the eiytethe yeer of the rewme of his empire, whanne he was yit a child, he bigan to seke God of his fadir Dauid; and in the tweluethe yeer after that he bigan, he clenside Juda and Jerusalem fro hiy places, and wodis, and similacris, and grauun ymagis.

4 And thei destrieden bifor hym the auteris of Baalym, and thei destrieden the symylacris, that weren put aboue. Also he hewide doun the wodis, and grauun ymagis, and brak to smale gobetis; and scateride abrood 'the smale gobetis on the birielis of hem, that weren wont to offre 'to tho.

5 Ferthermore he brente the boonys of preestis in the auteris of idols, and he clenside Juda and Jerusalem.

6 But also he destriede alle idols in the citees of Manasses, and of Effraym, and of Symeon, 'til to Neptalym.

7 And whanne he hadde scateride the auteris, and hadde al tobroke in to gobetis the wodis, and grauun ymagis, and hadde destried alle templis of ydols fro al the lond of Israel, he turnede ayen in to Jerusalem.

8 Therfor in the eiytenthe yeer of his rewme, whanne the lond and temple 'of the Lord was clensid nowe, he sente Saphan, the sone of Helchie, and Masie, the prince of the citee, and Joa, the sone of Joachaz, chaunceler, that thei schulden reparele the hous 'of his Lord God.

9 Whiche camen to Helchie, the grete preest; and whanne thei hadden take of hym the money, which was brouyt in to the hows of the Lord; and which monei the dekenes and porteris hadden gaderid of Manasses, and of Effraym, and of alle the residue men of Israel, and of al Juda and Beniamyn, and of the dwelleris of Jerusalem,

10 thei yauen it in the hondis of hem that weren souereyns of the werk men in the hows of the Lord, that thei schulden restore the temple, and reparele alle feble thingis.

11 And thei yauen that monei to the crafti men and masouns, for to bie stoonys hewid out of the 'delues, ether quarreris, and trees to the ioynyngis of the bildyng, and to the coupling of housis, whiche the kingis of Juda hadden destried.

12 Whiche men diden feithfuli alle thingis. Sotheli the souereyns of worcheris weren Jabath, and Abdie, of the sones of Merari; Zacarie, and Mosallam, of the sones of Caath; whiche hastiden the werk; alle weren dekenes, kunnynge to synge with orguns.

13 Sotheli ouer them that baren birthuns to dyuerse vsis weren the scribis, and maistris of the dekenes, and porteris.

14 And whanne thei baren out the monei, that was borun in to the temple of the Lord, Helchie, 'the preest, foond the book of the lawe of the Lord bi the hond of Moises.

15 And he seide to Saphan, the writere, Y haue founde the book of the lawe in the hows of the Lord.

16 And Helchie took to Saphan, and he bar in the book to the king; and telde to hym, and seide, Lo! alle thingis ben fillid, whiche thou hast youe in to the hondis of thi seruauntis.

17 Thei han wellyd togidere the siluere, which is foundun in the hous of the Lord; and it is youun to the souereyns of the crafti men, and makynge dyuerse werkis;

18 ferthermore Helchie, the preest, took to me this book. And whanne he hadde rehersid this book in the presence of the kyng,

19 and he hadde herd the wordis of the lawe, he to-rente hise clothis; and he comaundide to Helchie,

20 and to Aichan, the sone of Saphan, and to Abdon, the sone of Mycha, and to Saphan, the scryuen, and to Asaie, the seruaunt of the kyng,

21 and seide, Go ye, and preie the Lord for me, and for the resydue men of Israel and of Juda, on alle the wordis of this book, which is foundun. For greet veniaunce of the Lord hath droppid on vs, for oure fadris kepten not the wordis of the Lord, to do alle thingis that ben writun in this book.

22 Therfor Helchie yede, and thei that weren sent togidere of the king, to Olda, the prophetesse, the wijf of Sellum, sone of Thecuath, sone of Asra, kepere of clothis, which Olda dwellide in Jerusalem in the secounde warde; and thei spaken to hir the wordis, whiche we telden bifore.

23 And sche answeride to hem, The Lord God of Israel seith these thingis, Seie ye to the man, that sente you to me,

24 The Lord seith these thingis, Lo! Y schal brynge ynne yuels on this place, and on the dwelleris therof, and alle the cursyngis that ben writun in this book, which thei redden bifor the kyng of Juda.

25 For thei han forsake me, and han sacrified to alien goddis, for to terre me to wrathfulnesse in alle the werkis of her hondis; therfor my strong veniaunce schal droppe on this place, and it schal not be quenchid.

26 But speke ye thus to the kyng of Juda, that sente you to preye the Lord, The Lord God of Israel seith these thingis, For thou herdist the wordis of the book,

27 and thin herte is maad neisch, and thou art mekid in the siyt of the Lord of these thingis that ben seide ayens this place and the dwelleris of Jerusalem, and thou hast reuerensid my face, and hast to-rente thi clothis, and hast wepte bifor me; also Y haue herd thee, seith the Lord.

28 For now Y schal gadere thee to thi fadris, and thou schalt be borun in to thi sepulcre in pees; and thin iyen schulen not se al yuel, which Y schal brynge yn on this place, and on the dwelleris therof. Therfor thei telden to the king alle thingis, whiche Olda hadde seid.

29 And aftir that he hadde clepid togidere alle the eldere men of Juda and of Jerusalem,

30 he stiede in to the hows of the Lord, and togidere alle the men of Juda, 'and the dwelleris of Jerusalem, preestis, and dekenes, and al the puple, fro the leeste 'til to the moste; to whiche herynge in the hows of the Lord, the kyng redde alle the wordis of the book.

31 And he stood in his trone, and smoot a boond of pees bifor the Lord, for to 'go aftir hym, and to kepe the comaundementis, and witnessyngis, and iustifiyngis of hym, in al his herte and in al his soule; and to do tho thingis that weren writun in that book, which he hadde red.

32 And he chargide greetli on this thing alle men, that weren foundun in Jerusalem and Beniamyn; and the dwellers of Jerusalem diden aftir the couenaunt of the Lord God of her fadris.

33 Therfor Josie dide awei alle abhomynaciouns fro alle the cuntreis of the sones of Israel; and he made alle men, that weren residue in Israel, to serue her Lord God; in alle the daies of his lijf thei yeden not awei fro the Lord God of her fadris.

CAP 35

1 Forsothe Josie made pask to the Lord in Jerusalem, that was offrid in the fourtenthe dai of the firste monethe;

2 and he ordeynede prestis in her offices; and he comaundide hem for to mynystre in the hows of the Lord.

3 And he spak to the dekenes, at whos techyng al Israel was halewid to the Lord, Sette ye the arke in the seyntuarie of the temple, which Salomon, kyng of Israel, the sone of Dauid, bildide; for ye schulen no more bere it. But now serue 'youre Lord God and his puple Israel,

4 and make you redi bi youre housis and meynees in the departyngis of ech bi hym silf, as Dauid, king of Israel, comaundide, and Salomon, his sone, discryuede;

5 and serue ye in the seyntuarie bi the meynees and cumpenyes of dekenes,

6 and be ye halewid, and offre ye pask; also 'make redi youre britheren, that thei moun 'do bi the wordis, whiche the Lord spak in the hond of Moyses.

7 Ferthermore Josie yaf to al the puple, that was foundun there in the solempnytee of pask, lambren, and kidis of the flockis, and of residue scheep 'he yaf thritti thousynde, and of oxis thre thousynde; these thingis of al the catel of the kyng.

8 And hise duykis offriden tho thingis whiche thei avowiden bi fre wille, as wel to the puple as to prestis and dekenes. Forsothe Elchie, and Zacharie, and Jehiel, princes of the hows of the Lord, yauen to preestis, to make pask in comyn, two thousynde and sixe hundrid scheep, and thre hundrid oxis.

9 Forsothe Chononye, and Semei, and Nathanael and hise britheren, also Asabie, Jahiel, and Josabaz, princis of dekenes, yauen to othere dekenes, to make pask, fyue thousynde of scheep, and fyue hundrid oxis.

10 And the seruyce was maad redi; and preestis stoden in her office, and dekenes in cumpenyes, bi comaundement of the kyng; and pask was offrid.

11 And preestis spreynten her hondis with blood, and dekenes drowen of the skynnes of sacrifices, and departiden tho sacrificis,

12 for to yyue bi the housis and meyneis of alle men; and that tho schulden be offrid to the Lord, as it is writun in the book of Moises; and of oxis thei diden in lijk maner.

13 And thei rostiden pask on the fier, bi that that is writun in the lawe. Sotheli thei sethiden pesible sacrifices in pannes, and cawdruns, and pottis, and in haste thei deliden to al the puple;

14 but thei maden redi aftirward to hem silf, and to prestis; for preestis weren occupied 'til to nyyt in the offryng of brent sacrifices and of ynnere fatnessis. Wherfor dekenes maden redi to hem silf and to preestis, the sones of Aaron, 'the laste.

15 Forsothe syngeris, the sones of Asaph, stoden in her ordre, bi the comaundement of Dauid, and of Asaph, and of Eman, and of Yditum, the profetis of the kyng; but the porteris kepten bi ech yate, so that thei yeden not awei fro the seruice, sotheli in a poynt; wherfor and dekenes, her britheren, maden redi metis to hem.

16 Therfor al the religioun of the Lord was fillid riytfuli in that day, that thei maden pask, and offriden brent sacrifices on the auter of the Lord, bi the comaundement of kyng Josie.

17 And the sones of Israel, that weren foundun there, maden pask in that tyme, and the solempnite of therf looues seuene daies.

18 No pask was lijk this in Israel, fro the daies of Samuel, the prophete; but nethir ony of the kyngis of Israel made pask as Josie dide, to preestis and dekenes, and to al Juda and Israel, that was foundun, and to the dwelleris of Jerusalem.

19 This pask was halewid in the eiytenthe yeer of 'the rewme of Josie.

20 Aftir that Josie hadde reparelid the temple, Nechao, the kyng of Egipt, stiede to fiyte in Carcamys bisidis Eufrates; and Josie yede forth in to his metyng.

21 And he seide bi messangeris sent to hym, Kyng of Juda, what is to me and to thee? Y come not ayens thee to dai, but Y fiyte ayens another hows, to which God bad me go in haste; ceesse thou to do ayens God, which is with me, lest he sle thee.

22 Josie nolde turne ayen, but made redi batel ayens hym; and he assentide not to the wordis of Nechao, bi Goddis mouth, but he yede for to fiyte in the feeld of Magedo.

23 And there he was woundide of archeris, and seide to hise children, 'Lede ye me out of the batel, for Y am woundid greetli.

24 Whiche baren hym ouer fro the chare in to an other chare, that suede hym, bi custom of the kyng, and 'baren out hym in to Jerusalem; and he diede, and was biried in the sepulcre of hise fadris. And al Juda and Jerusalem biweiliden hym,

25 Jeremye moost, of whom alle syngeris and syngeressis 'til in to present dai rehersen 'lamentaciouns, ether weilyngis, on Josie; and it cam forth as a lawe in Israel, Lo! it is seid writun in Lamentaciouns. Forsothe the residue of wordis of Josie, and of hise mercies, that ben comaundid in the lawe of the Lord, and hise werkis, 'the firste and the laste, ben wryten in the book of kyngis of Israel and of Juda.

CAP 36

1 Therfor the puple of the lond took Joachaz, the sone of Josie, and ordeynede hym kyng for his fadir in Jerusalem.

2 Joachaz was of thre and twenti yeer, whanne he bigan to regne, and he regnede thre monethis in Jerusalem.

3 Sotheli the kyng of Egipt, 'whan he hadde come to Jerusalem, remouyde hym, and condempnede the lond in an hundrid talentis of siluer and in a talent of gold.

4 And he ordeynede for hym Eliachim, his brother, kyng on Juda and Jerusalem; and turnede his name Joakym. Sotheli he took thilk Joachaz with hym silf, and brouyte in to Egipt.

5 Joakym was of fyue and twenti yeer, whanne he bigan to regne, and he regnyde eleuene yeer in Jerusalem, and he dide yuel bifor 'his Lord God.

6 Nabugodonosor, kyng of Caldeis, styede ayens this Joakym, and ledde hym boundun with chaynes in to Babiloyne.

7 To which Babiloyne he translatide also the vessels of the Lord, and settide tho in his temple.

8 Sotheli the residue of wordis of Joakym, and of hise abhomynaciouns whiche he wrouyte, and that weren foundun in hym, ben conteyned in the book of kyngis of Israel and of Juda. Therfor Joachym, his sone, regnede for hym.

9 Joachym was of eiyte yeer, whanne he bigan to regne, and he regnede thre monethis and ten daies in Jerusalem, and he dide yuel in the siyt of the Lord.

10 And whanne the cercle of the yeer was turned aboute, Nabugodonosor the kynge sente men, whiche also brouyten hym in to Babiloyne, whanne the moost preciouse vessels of the hows of the Lord weren borun out togidir. Sotheli he ordeynede Sedechie, his fadris brother, kyng on Juda and Jerusalem.

11 Sedechie was of oon and twenti yeer, whanne he bigan to regne, and he regnede eleuene yeer in Jerusalem.

12 And he dide yuel in the siyt of 'his Lord God, and he was not aschamed of the face of Jeremye, the prophete, spekynge to hym bi the mouth of the Lord.

13 Also he yede awey fro the kyng Nabugodonosor, that hadde made hym to swere bi God; and he made hard his nol and herte, that he nolde turne ayen to the Lord of Israel.

14 But also alle the princes of preestis and the puple trespassiden wickidli, bi alle abhomynaciouns of hethene men; and thei defouliden the hows of the Lord, which he halewide to hym silf in Jerusalem.

15 Forsothe the Lord God of her fadris sente to hem bi the hond of hise messangeris, and roos bi nyyt, and amonestide ech day; for he sparide his puple and dwellyng place.

16 And thei scorneden the messangeris of God, and dispisiden hise wordis, and scorneden hise prophetis; til the greet veniaunce of the Lord stiede on his puple, and noon heelyng were.

17 And he brouyte on hem the kyng of Caldeis; and killide the yonge men of hem 'bi swerd in the hows of seyntuarie; 'he hadde not merci of a yong 'man, and of a vergyn, and of an eld man, and sotheli nether of a man niy the deth for eldnesse, but he bitook alle in the hond of that king of Caldeis.

18 And he translatide in to Babiloyne alle the vessels of the hows of the Lord, bothe the grettere and the lasse vessels, and the tresours of the temple, and of the kyng, and of the princes.

19 Enemyes brenten the hows of the Lord; thei distrieden the wal of Jerusalem; thei brenten alle the touris; and thei distrieden what euer thing was preciouse.

20 If ony man ascapide the swerd, he was led in to Babiloyne, and seruyde the kyng and hise sones; til the kyng of Peersis regnyde,

21 and the word of the Lord bi the mouth of Jeremye was fillid, and til the lond halewide hise sabatis. For in alle the daies of desolacioun it made sabat, til that seuenti yeer weren fillid.

22 Forsothe in the firste yeer of Cyrus, kyng of Persis, to fille the word of the Lord, which he hadde spoke bi the mouth of Jeremye, the Lord reiside the spirit of Cirus, king of Persis, that comaundide to be prechid in al his rewme, yhe, bi scripture, and seide, Cirus,

23 the king of Persis, seith these thingis, The Lord God of heuene yaf to me alle the rewmes of erthe, and he comaundide to me, that Y schulde bilde to hym an hows in Jerusalem, which is in Judee. Who of you is in al his puple? 'his Lord God be with hym, and stie he 'in to Jerusalem.

CAP 37

1 Lord God Almyyti of our fadris, Abraham, Isaac, and Jacob, and of her iust seed, which madist heuene and erthe with al the ournyng of tho, which hast markid the see bi the word of 'thi comaundement, which hast closid to gidere the depthe of watris, and hast markid to thi ferdful and preysable name, which alle men dreden, 'and tremblen of the cheer of thi vertu, and the ire of thi manassyng on synneris 'is vnsuffrable, 'ether may not be susteyned. Sotheli the merci of thi biheest is fulgreet and 'vnserchable, ether may not be comprehendid 'bi mannus wit; for 'thou art the Lord moost hiy ouer al erthe; thou art pacient, and myche merciful, and 'doynge penaunce on the malices of men. Treuli, Lord, thou bi thi goodnesse hast bihiyt penaunce of foryyuenesse of synnes; and thou, God of iust men, hast not set penaunce to iust men, to Abraham, Ysaac, and Jacob, to hem that synneden not ayens thee. For Y haue synned more than the noumbre is of the grauel of the see; my wickidnessis ben multiplied. Y am bowid with myche boond of yrun, and no breth-

ing is to me; for Y haue stirid thi wrathfulnesse, and Y haue doon yuel bifor thee, 'and Y haue set abhomynaciouns, and 'Y haue multiplied offensiouns. And now Y bowe the knees of myn herte, and biseche goodnesse of thee, Lord. Y haue synned, Lord; Y haue synned, and Y knowleche my wickidnesse. Y axe, and preye thee, Lord; foryyue thou to me, foryyue thou to me; leese thou me not togidire with my wickidnessis, nether reserue thou yuels to me withouten ende. For, Lord, bi thi greet merci thou schalt saue me vnworthi, and Y schal herie thee euere in alle the daies of my lijf; for al the vertu of heuenes herieth thee, and to thee is glorie in to worldis of worldis. Amen.

1 ESDRAS

CAP 1

1 In the firste yeer of Cirus, kyng of Persis, that the word of the Lord bi the mouth of Jeremye schulde be fillid, the Lord reiside the spirit of Cyrus, kyng of Persis; and he pupplischide a vois in al his rewme, ye, bi the scripture, and seide, Cirus,

2 the kyng of Persis, seith these thingis, The Lord God of heuene yaf to me alle the rewmes of erthe, and he comaundide to me, that Y schulde bilde to hym an hows in Jerusalem, which is in Judee.

3 Who is among you of al his puple? his God be with hym; stie he in to Jerusalem, which is in Judee, and bilde he the hows of the Lord God of Israel; he is God, which is in Jerusalem.

4 And alle othere men, 'that dwellen where euere in alle places, helpe hym; the men of her place helpe in siluer, and gold, and catel, and scheep, outakun that that thei offren wilfulli to the temple of God, which is in Jerusalem.

5 And the princis of fadris of Juda and of Beniamyn risiden, and the preestis, and dekenes, and ech man whos spirit God reiside, for to stie to bilde the temple of the Lord, that was in Jerusalem.

6 And alle men that weren 'in cumpas helpiden the hondis of hem, in vesselis of siluer, and of gold, 'in catel, in purtenaunce of houshold, and in alle werk beestis, outakun these thingis which thei offriden bi fre wille.

7 Forsothe kyng Cyrus brouyte forth the vessels of the temple of the Lord, whiche Nabugodonosor hadde take fro Jerusalem, and hadde set tho in the temple of his god.

8 Sotheli Cyrus, the kyng of Persis, brouyte forth tho bi the hond of Mytridatis, sone of Gazabar; and noumbride tho to Sasabazar, the prince of Juda.

9 And this is the noumbre of tho vessels; goldun violis, thritti; siluerne viols, a thousynde; 'grete knyues, nyne and twenti; goldun cuppis, thritti; siluerne cuppis,

10 two thousynde foure hundrid and ten; othere vessels, a thousynde;

11 alle the vessels of gold and siluere weren fyue thousynde foure hundrid. Sasabazar took alle vessels, with hem that stieden fro the transmygracioun of Babiloyne, in to Jerusalem.

CAP 2

1 Forsothe these ben the sones of prouynce, that stieden fro the caitifte, which Nabugodonosor, kyng of Babiloyne, hadde translatid in to Babiloyne; and thei turneden ayen in to Jerusalem and in to Juda, ech man in to his citee, that camen with Zorobabel;

2 Jesua, Neemie, Saray, Rahelaie, Mardochaa, Belsan, Mesfar, Begnay, Reum, Baana. This is the noumbre of men of the sones of Israel; the sones of Phares,

3 two thousynde an hundrid and two and seuenti; the sones of Arethi, seuene hundrid and fyue and seuenti;

4 the sones of Sephezie, thre hundrid and two and seuenti;

5 the sones of Area, seuene hundrid and fyue and seuenti;

6 the sones of Phe and of Moab, sones of Josue and of Joab, twei thousynde nyne hundrid and twelue;

7 the sones of Helam, a thousynde two hundrid and foure and fifti;

8 the sones of Zechua, nyne hundrid and fyue and fourti;

9 the sones of Zahai, seuene hundrid and sixti;

10 the sones of Bany, sixe hundrid and two and fourti;

11 the sones of Bebai, sixe hundrid and thre and twenti; the sones of Azgad,

12 a thousynde two hundrid and two and twenti;

13 the sones of Adonycam, sixe hundrid and sixe and sixti;

14 the sones of Beguai, two thousynde two hundrid and sixe and fifti; the sones of Adyn,

15 foure hundrid and foure and fifti;

16 the sones of Ather, that weren of Ezechie, nynti and eiyte;

17 the sones of Besai, thre hundrid and thre and twenti;

18 the sones of Jora, an hundrid and twelue;

19 the sones of Asom, two hundrid and thre and thritti;

20 the sones of Gebar weren nynti and fyue;

21 the sones of Bethleem weren an hundrid and eiyte and twenti;

22 the men of Nechopha, sixe and fifti;

23 the men of Anathot, an hundrid and eiyte and twenti;

24 the sones of Asmaneth, two and fourti;

25 the sones of Cariathiarym, Cephiara, and Berhoc, seuene hundrid and thre and fourti;

26 the sones of Arama and of Gaba, sixe hundrid and oon and twenti;

27 men of 'Mathmas, an hundrid and two and twenti; men of Bethel and of Gay,

28 two hundrid and thre and twenti;

29 the sones of Nebo, two and fifti;

30 the sones of Nebgis, an hundrid and sixe and fifti;

31 the sones of the tother Helam, a thousynde two hundrid and foure and fifti;

32 the sones of Arym, thre hundrid and twenti;

33 the sones of Loradid and of Ono, seuene hundrid and fyue and twenti;

34 the sones of Jerico, thre hundrid and fyue and fourti;

35 the sones of Sanaa, thre thousynde sixe hundrid and thritti;

36 preestis, the sones of Idaie, in the hows of Jesue, nyne hundrid and thre and seuenti;

37 the sones of Emmeor, a thousynde and two and fifti; the sones of Phesur,

38 a thousynde two hundrid and seuene and fourti;

39 the sones of Arym, a thousynde and seuentene; dekenes,

40 the sones of Jesue and of Cedynyel, sones of Odonye, foure and seuenti; syngeris,

41 the sones of Asaph, an hundrid and eiyte and twenti;

42 the sones of porteris, sones of Sellum, sones of Ather, sones of Thelmon, sones of Accub, sones of Aritha, sones of Sobar, sones of Sobai, alle weren an hundrid and eiyte and thritty;

43 Nathynneis, the sones of Osai, sones of Asupha, sones of Thebaoth, sones of Ceros,

44 sones of Sisaa, sones of Phadon,

45 sones of Jebana, sones of Agaba, sones of Accub,

46 sones of Accab, sones of Selmai,

47 sones of Annam, sones of Gaddel, sones of Gaer,

48 sones of Rahaia, sones of Rasyn, sones of Nethoda, sones of Gazem, sones of Asa,

49 sones of Phasea, sones of Besee,

50 sones of Asennaa, sones of Numyn, sones of Nethusym,

51 sones of Bethuth, sones of Acupha, sones of Aryn, sones of Besluth,

52 sones of Maida, sones of Arsa,

53 sones of Bercos, sones of Sisara, sones of Thema,

54 sones of Nasia, sones of Acupha,

55 the sones of the seruauntis of Salomon, the sones of Sothelthei, the sones of Soforeth, the sones of Pharuda, the sones of Asa,

56 the sones of Delcon, the sones of Gedeb,

57 the sones of Saphata, the sones of Atil, the sones of Phecerethi, that weren of Asebam, the sones of Ammy;

58 alle the Nathyneis, and the sones of the seruauntis of Salomon weren thre hundrid nynti and tweyne.

59 And thei that stieden fro Thelmela, Thelersa, Cherub, and Don, and Mey, and myyten not schewe the hows of her fadris and her seed, whether thei weren of Israel;

60 the sones of Delaya, the sones of Thobie, the sones of Nethoda, sixe hundrid and two and fifti;

61 and of the sones of prestis, the sones of Obia, sones of Accos, sones of Berzellai, which took a wijf of the douytris of Bersellai Galadite, and was clepid bi the name of hem;

62 these souyten the scripture of her genologie, and founden not, and thei weren cast out of preesthod.

63 And Attersatha seide to hem, that thei schulden not ete of the hooli of hooli thingis, til a wijs preest and perfit roos.

64 Al the multitude as o man, two and fourti thousynde thre hundrid and sixti,

65 outakun the seruauntis of hem and 'the handmaydis, that weren seuene thousynde thre hundrid and seuene and thretti; and among hem weren syngeris and syngeressis twei hundrid.

66 The horsis of hem weren sixe hundrid and sixe and thritti; the mulis of hem weren foure hundrid and fyue and fourti;

67 the camels of hem weren foure hundrid and fyue and thritti; the assis of hem weren sixe thousynde seuene hundrid and twenti.

68 And of the princes of fadris, whanne thei entriden in to the temple of the Lord, which is in Jerusalem, thei offriden of fre wille in to the hows of God, to bilde it in his place;

69 thei yauen 'bi her myytes the costis of the werk, oon and fourti thousynde platis of gold; fyue thousynde besauntis of siluer; and preestis clothis an hundrid.

70 Therfor preestis and dekenes of the puple, and syngeris, and porteris, and Nathynneis dwelliden in her citees, and al Israel in her cytees.

CAP 3

1 And thanne the seuenthe monethe was comun, and the sones of Israel weren in her citees.

2 Therfor the puple was gaderid as o man in to Jerusalem. And Josue, the sone of Josedech, roos, and hise britheren, prestis, and Zorobabel, the sone of Salatiel, and hise britheren, and thei bildiden the auter of God of Israel for to offre therynne brent sacrifices, as it is writun in the lawe of Moises, the man of God.

3 Forsothe thei settiden the auter on his foundementis, while the puplis of londis bi cumpas maden hem aferd, and thei offriden on that auter brent sacrifice to the Lord in the morewtid and euentid.

4 And thei maden solempnytee of tabernaclis, as it is writun, and brent sacrifice ech dai bi ordre, 'bi the werk of the dai comaundid in his dai.

5 And after this thei offriden contynuel brent sacrifice, bothe in calendis and in alle solempnytees of the Lord, that weren halewid, and in alle solempnytees, in which yifte was offrid to the Lord bi fre wille.

6 In the firste dai of the seuenthe monethe thei bigunnen to offre brent sacrifice to the Lord; certis the temple of God was not foundid yit.

7 But thei yauen monei to heweris of stoon, and to liggeris of stoon, and thei yauen mete, and drynke, and oile, to men of Sidon, and 'to men of Tire, that thei schulden brynge cedre trees fro the Liban to the see of Joppe, bi that that Cirus, kyng of Persis, hadde comaundid to hem.

8 Forsothe in the secounde yeer of her comyng to the temple of God in Jerusalem, in the secounde monethe, Zorobabel, the sone of Salatiel, and Josue,

9 the sone of Josedech, and othere of her britheren, preestis and dekenes, and alle that camen fro the caitifte in to Jerusalem, bigunnen; and thei ordeyneden dekenes, fro twenti yeer and aboue, for to haste the werk of the Lord; and Josue stood, and hise sones, and hise britheren, Cedynyel and hise sones, and the sones of Juda, as o man, to be bisi ouer hem that maden the werk in the temple of God; the sones of Benadab, her sones and her britheren, dekenes, 'weren bisy.

10 Therfor whanne the temple 'of the Lord was foundid of stoon leggeris, prestis stoden in her ournement with trumpis, and dekenes, the sones of Asaph, in cymbalis, for to herie God bi the hond of Dauid, kyng of Israel.

11 And thei sungen togidere in ympnes and knoulechyng to the Lord, For he is good, for his merci is with outen ende on Israel. And al the puple criede with greet cry, in preisynge the Lord, for the temple of the Lord was foundid.

12 Also ful manye of the preestis, and of the dekenes, and the princes of fadris, and the eldre men, that hadden seyn the formere temple, whanne it was foundid, and this temple bifor her iyen, wepten with greet vois, and many men criynge in gladnesse reisiden the vois;

13 and no man myyte knowe the vois of cry of men beynge glad, and the vois of wepyng of the puple; for the puple criede togidere with greet cry, and the vois was herd afer.

CAP 4

1 Forsothe the enemyes of Juda and of Beniamyn herden, that the sones of caitifte bildiden a temple to the Lord God of Israel;

2 and thei neiyeden to Zorobabel, and to the princes of fadris, and seiden to hem, Bilde we with you, for so as ye, we seken youre God; lo! we han offrid sacrificis fro the daies of Assoraddon, kyng of Assur, that brouyte vs hidur.

3 And Zorobabel, and Josue, and the othere princes of the fadris of Israel, seiden to hem, It is not to vs and to you, that we bilde an hows to oure God; but we vs silf aloone schulen bilde to 'oure Lord God, as Cirus, the kyng of Persis, comaundide to vs.

4 Forsothe it was doon, that the puple of the lond lettide the hondis of the puple of Juda, and trobliden hem in bildyng.

5 And thei hiriden counselouris ayens the Jewis, that thei schulden destrie the counseil of the Jewis, in alle the daies of

Cirus, king of Persis, and 'til to the rewme of Darius, king of Persis.

6 Forsothe in the rewme of Assueris, he is Artaxersis, in the bigynnyng of his rewme, thei writiden accusing ayens the dwellers of Juda and of Jerusalem;

7 and in the daies of Artaxarses, Besellam wroot, Mytridates, and Thabel, and othere, that weren in the counsel of hem, to Artaxarses, kyng of Persis. For the pistle of accusyng was writun in langage of Sirie, and was red in word of Sirie.

8 Reum, Beel, Theem, and Samsai, the scryuen, writen sich oon epistle fro Jerusalem to the kyng Artaxerses; Reum,

9 Beel, Theem, and Samsai, the writere, and othere counselouris of hem, Dyney, Pharsathei, and Therphalei, Arphasei, Harthuei, men of Babiloyne, Susanne, Thanei, Dacei, men of Helam,

10 and othere of hethene men, whiche the grete and gloriouse Asennaphar translatide, and made hem to dwelle in the citees of Samarie, and in othere cuntrees biyonde the flood, 'in pees.

11 This is the saumplere of the pistle, which thei senten to the kyng. 'To Artaxerses, king, thi seruauntis, men 'that ben biyende the flood, seyn helthe.

12 Be it knowun to the kyng, that the Jewis, that stieden fro thee, ben comun to vs 'in to Jerusalem, the rebel and worste citee, which thei bilden, and thei maken the ground wallis therof, and arayen the wallis aboue.

13 Nou therfor be it knowun to the kyng, that if thilke citee be bildid, and the wallis therof be restorid, thei schulen not yyue tribut, and tol, and annuel rentis, and this trespas schal come 'til to the kyng.

14 Therfor we ben myndeful of the salt, which we eeten in the paleis, and for we holden it vnleueful to se the harmes of the kyng, therfor we han sent and told to the kyng;

15 that thou acounte in the bokis of stories of thi fadris, and thou schalt fynde writun in cronyclis, and thou schalt wite, that thilke citee is a rebel citee, and that it anoieth kyngis and prouynces, and batels ben reisid therynne of elde daies; wherfor also thilke citee was distried.

16 We tellen to the kyng, that if thilke citee be bildid, and the wallis therof be restorid, thou schalt not haue possessioun biyende the flood.

17 The kyng sente word to Reum, Beel, Theem, and to Samsai, the scryuen, and to othere that weren in the counsel of hem, to the dwelleris of Samarie, and to othere biyendis the flood, and seide, Helthe and pees.

18 The accusyng, which ye senten to vs, was red opynli bifor me;

19 and it was comaundid of me, and thei rekenyden, and thei foundun, that thilke citee rebellith of elde daies ayens kyngis, and dissenciouns and batels ben reisid therynne;

20 for whi 'and ful stronge kyngis weren in Jerusalem, which also weren lordis of al the cuntrei which is biyende the flood; also thei token tribut, and tol, and rentis.

21 Now therfor here ye the sentence, that ye forbede tho men, and that thilke citee be not bildid, til if perauenture it be comaundid of me.

22 Se ye, that this be not fillid necgligentli, and yuel encreesse litil 'and litil ayens kyngis.

23 Therfor the saumple of the comaundement of kyng Artaxarses was red bifor Reum, Beel, Theem, and Samsai, the scryueyn, and her counseleris; and thei yeden hastili in to Jerusalem to the Jewis, and forbediden hem with arm and myyt.

24 Thanne the werk of Goddis hows in Jerusalem was left, and it was not maad til to the secounde yeer of Darius, king of Persis.

CAP 5

1 Forsothe Aggei, the prophete, and Zacharie, the prophete, the sone of Ado, prophesieden, prophesiynge in the name of God of Israel, to the Jewis that weren in Juda and Jerusalem.

2 Thanne Zorobabel, the sone of Salatiel, and Josue, the sone of Josedech, risiden, and bigunnen to bilde the temple of God in Jerusalem; and with hem rysyden the prophetis of God, helpynge hem.

3 Forsothe in that tyme Tatannai, that was duyk biyende the flood, and Starbusannay, and the counselouris of hem, camen to hem, and seiden thus to hem, Who yaf counsel to you to bilde this hows, and to restore these wallis?

4 To which thing we answeriden to hem, whiche weren the names of men, autours of that bildyng.

5 Forsothe the iye of God of hem was maad on the elde men of Jewis, and thei myyten not forbede the Jewis; and it pleside that the thing schulde be teld to Darius, and thanne thei schulden make satisfaccioun ayens that accusyng.

6 This is the saumpler of the pistle, which Tathannai, duyk of the cuntrey biyende the flood, and Starbursannai, and hise counselouris, Arphasacei, that weren biyende the flood, senten to kyng Darius.

7 The word which thei senten to hym was writun thus; Al pees be to the kyng Darius.

8 Be it knowun to the kyng, that we yeden to the prouince of Judee, to the hows of greet God, which is bildid with stoon vnpolischid, and trees ben set in the wallis, and thilke werk is bildid diligentli, and encreessith in the hondis of hem.

9 Therfor we axiden tho elde men, and thus we seiden to hem, Who yaf to you power to bilde this hows, and to restore these wallis?

10 But also we axiden of hem the names 'of hem, that we schulden telle to thee; and we han write the names of men, whiche thei ben, that ben princes among hem.

11 Sotheli thei answeriden bi sich word, and seiden, We ben the seruauntis of God of heuene and of erthe; and we bilden the temple that was bildid bifor these many yeeris, and 'which temple the greet kyng of Israel 'hadde bildid, and maad.

12 But aftir that oure fadris stiryden God of heuene and of erthe to wrathfulnesse, bothe he bitook hem in the hond of Nabugodonosor, Caldey, kyng of Babiloyne; and he distriede this hows, and translatide the puple therof in to Babiloyne.

13 Forsothe in the firste yeer of Cirus, king of Babiloyne, Cirus, the king of Babiloyne, settide forth 'a comaundement, that the hows of God schulde be bildid.

14 For whi kyng Cirus brouyte forth 'fro the temple of Babiloyne also the goldun and siluerne vessels of Goddis temple, whiche Nabugodonosor hadde take fro the temple, that was in Jerusalem, and hadde bore tho awei in to the temple of Babiloyne; and tho vessels weren youun to Sasabazar bi name, whom 'he made also prince. And Cirus seide to hym, Take these vessels,

15 and go, and sette tho in the temple, which is in Jerusalem; and the hows of God be bildid in 'his place.

16 Therfor thanne thilke Sasabazar cam, and settide the foundementis of Goddis temple in Jerusalem; and fro that tyme 'til to now it is bildid, and is not yit fillid.

17 Now therfor if it 'semeth good to the king, rikene he in the biblet of the kyng, which is in Babiloyne, whether it be comaundid of kyng Cyrus, that Goddis hows schulde be bildid in Jerusalem; and sende he to vs the wille of the kyng 'on this thing.

CAP 6

1 Thanne kyng Darius comaundide, and thei rekenyden in the biblet of bokis, that weren kept in Babiloyne.

2 And o book was foundun in Egbatanys, which is a castel in the prouynce of Medena, and sich a sentence of the kyng was writun therynne.

3 In the first yeer of kyng Cirus, Cirus the kyng demyde, that, 'Goddis hows, which is in Jerusalem, schulde be bildid in the place where thei offren sacrifices, and that thei sette foundementis supportynge the heiythe of sixti cubitis, and the lengthe of sixti cubitis, thre ordris of stonys vnpolischid,

4 and so ordris of newe trees. Sotheli costis schulen be youun of the kyngis hows.

5 But also the goldun and siluerne vessels of Goddis temple, whiche Nabugodonosor took fro the temple of Jerusalem, and brouyte tho in to Babiloyne, be yoldun, and borun ayen in to the temple of Jerusalem, and in to her place, whiche also be set in the temple of God.

6 Now therfor Tathannai, duyk of the cuntrei which is biyende the flood, and Starbusannai, and youre counseleris, Arphasacei, that ben byyende the flood, departe ye fer fro hem;

7 and suffre ye, that thilke temple of God be maad of the duyk of Jewis, and of the eldre men of hem; and that thei bilde that hows of God in his place.

8 But also it is comaundid of me, that that bihoueth to be maad of tho preestis of Jewys, that the hows of God be bildid, that is, that costis be youun bisili to tho men of the arke of the kyng, that is, of tributis, that ben youun of the contrei biyende the flood, lest the werk be lettid.

9 That if it be nede, yyue thei bothe calues, and lambren, and kidis in to brent sacrifice to God of heuene; wheete, salt, and wyn, and oile, bi the custom of preestis that ben in Jerusalem, be youun to hem bi ech dai, that no pleynt be in ony thing.

10 And offre thei offryngis to God of heuene; and preye thei for the lijf of the kyng and of hise sones.

11 Therfor the sentence is set of me, that if ony man chaungith this comaundement, a tre be takun of his hows, and be reisid, and be he hangid therynne; sotheli his hows be forfetid.

12 Forsothe God, that makith his name to dwelle there, distrie alle rewmes and puple, that holdith forth her hond to impugne and destrie thilke hows of God, which is in Jerusalem. I Darius haue demyd the sentence, which Y wole be fillid diligentli.

13 Therfor Tathannai, duyk of the 'cuntrei biyende the flood, and Starbusannai, and hise counseleris, diden execucioun, 'ether filliden, so diligentli, bi that that kyng Darius hadde comaundid.

14 Sotheli the eldre men of Jewis bildiden, and hadden prosperite, bi the profesie of Aggey, the profete, and of Zacarie, the sone of Ado; and thei bildiden, and maden, for God of Israel comaundide, and for Cirus, and Darius, and Artaxerces, kyngis of Persis, comaundiden;

15 and thei performyden this hows of God 'til to the thridde dai of the monethe Adar, which is the sixte yeer of the rewme of king Darius.

16 Forsothe the sones of Israel, the preestis and dekenes, and the othere of the sones of transmygracioun, 'that is, that camen fro transmigracioun, 'ether caitifte, maden the halewyng of Goddis hows in ioie;

17 and offriden, 'in the halewyng of Goddis hows, an hundrid caluys, twei hundryd wetheris, foure hundrid lambren, twelue buckis of geet for the synne of al Israel, bi the noumbre of lynagis of Israel.

18 And thei ordeyneden preestis in her ordris, and dekenes in her whilis, on the werkis of God in Jerusalem, as it is writun in the book of Moises.

19 Forsothe the sones of transmygracioun maden pask, in the fourtenthe dai of the firste monethe.

20 For the preestis and dekenes as o man weren clensid, alle weren clene for to offre pask to alle the sones of transmygracioun, and to her britheren preestis, and to hem silf.

21 And the sones of Israel eeten, that turneden ayen fro transmygracioun, and ech man eet, that hadde departid hym silf fro al the defoulyng of hethene men of the lond, for to seke the Lord God of Israel.

22 And thei maden solempnyte of therf looues seuene daies in gladnesse; for the Lord hadde maad hem glad, and hadde turned the herte of the kyng of Assur to hem, that he wolde helpe 'her hondis in the werk of the hows of the Lord God of Israel.

CAP 7

1 Forsothe aftir these wordis Esdras, the sone of Saraie, sone of Azarie, sone of Helchie,

2 sone of Sellum, sone of Sadoch, sone of Achitob,

3 sone of Amarie, sone of Azarie,

4 sone of Maraioth, sone of Saraie, sone of Ozi,

5 sone of Bocci, sone of Abisue, sone of Phynees, sone of Eleazar, sone of Aaron, preest at the bigynnyng, was in the rewme of Artaxerses, king of Persis; thilke Esdras stiede fro Babiloyne,

6 and he was a swift writere in the lawe of Moises, which the Lord God of Israel yaf; and the kyng yaf to hym al his axyng, by the goode hoond of his Lord God on hym.

7 And there stieden of the sones of Israel, and of the sones of preestis, and of the sones of dekenes, and of the syngeris, and of the porteris, and of Nathyneis, 'in to Jerusalem in the seuenthe yeer of Artaxerses, kyng.

8 And thei camen in to Jerusalem in the fyuethe monethe; thilke is the seuenthe of the kyng.

9 For in the firste dai of the firste monethe he bigan to stie fro Babiloyne, and in the firste dai of the fyuethe monethe he cam in to Jerusalem, bi the good hond of his God on hym. Forsothe

10 Esdras made redi his herte to enquere the lawe of the Lord, and to do, and teche in Israel the comaundement and doom.

11 Sotheli this is the saumpler of the pistle of the comaundement, which the kyng Artaxerses yaf to Esdras, preest, writere lerud in the wordis and comaundementis of the Lord, and in hise cerymonyes in Israel.

12 Artaxerses, kyng of kyngis, desirith helthe to Esdras, the preest, moost wijs writere of the lawe of God of heuene.

13 It is demyd of me, that whom euer it plesith in my rewme of the puple of Israel, and of hise preestis, and dekenes, to go in to Jerusalem, go he with thee.

14 For thou art sent fro the face of the kyng and of hise seuene counseleris, that thou visite Judee and Jerusalem in the lawe of thi God, which is in thin hond;

15 and that thou bere siluer and gold, which the kyng and hise counseleris han offrid bi fre wille to God of Israel, whos tabernacle is in Jerusalem.

16 And take thou freli al siluer and gold, which euer thou fyndist in al the prouynce of Babiloyne, and the puple wole offre, and of preestis that offriden bi fre wille to the hows of her God, which is in Jerusalem;

17 and bie thou bisili of this monei calues, rammes, lambren, and sacrifices, and moiste sacrifices of tho; and offre thou tho on the auter of the temple of youre God, which temple is in Jerusalem.

18 But also if ony thing plesith to thee, and to thi britheren, for to do of the residue siluer and gold, do ye bi the wille of youre God;

19 also bitake thou in the siyt of God in Jerusalem the vessels, that ben youun in to the seruyce of the hows of thi God.

20 But also thou schalt yyue of the tresouris of the kyng, and of the comyn arke, 'ethir purse, and of me 'othere thingis, that ben nedeful in the hows of thi God, as myche euere as is nedeful, that thou spende.

21 Y Artaxerses, kyng, haue ordeyned, and demyd to alle the keperis of the comyn arke, that ben biyende the flood, that what euer thing Esdras, the preest, writere of the lawe of God of heuene, axith of you, ye yyue with out tariyng,

22 'til to an hundrid talentis of siluer, and to an hundrid 'mesuris clepid chorus of wheete, and til an hundrid mesuris clepid bathus of wyn, and 'til to an hundrid 'mesuris clepid bathus of oile, salt forsothe without mesure.

23 Al thing that perteyneth to the custom, 'ethir religioun, of God of heuene, be youun diligentli in the hows of God of heuene, lest perauenture he be wrooth ayens the rewme of the kyng and of hise sones.

24 Also we make knowun to you of alle the preestis, and dekenes, syngeris, and porteris, and Nathyneis, and mynystris of the hows of this God, 'that ye han not power to put on hem tol, and tribute, and costis for keperis of the lond.

25 Forsothe thou, Esdras, bi the wisdom of thi God, which is in thin hond, ordeyne iugis and gouernouris, that thei deme to the puple, which is biyende the flood, that is, to hem that kunnen the lawe of thi God, and the lawe of the kyng; but also teche ye freli vnkunnynge men.

26 And ech man, that doth not the lawe of thi God, and the lawe of the kyng diligentli, doom schal be of hym, ethir in to the deeth, ethir in to exilyng, ethir in to condempnyng of his catel, ethir certis in to prisoun. And Esdras, the writere, seide, Blissid be the Lord God of oure fadris,

27 that yaf this thing in the herte of the kyng, that he schulde glorifie the hows of the Lord,

28 which is in Jerusalem, and bowide his mercy in to me bifor the kyng, and hise counseleris, and bifore alle the myyti princes of the kyng. And Y was coumfortid bi the hond of 'my Lord God, that was in me, and Y gederide of the sones of Israel princes, that stieden with me.

CAP 8

1 Therfor these ben the princes of meynees, and this is the genologie of hem, whiche beynge in the rewme of Artaxerses, kyng, stieden with me fro Babiloyne.

2 Of the sones of Phynees, Gerson; of the sones of Ythamar, Danyel; of the sones of Dauid, Arcus;

3 of the sones of Sechemye and of the sones of Pharos, Zacarie, and with hym weren noumbrid an hundrid and fifti men;

4 of the sones of Phet, Moab, and Elioneay, the sone of Zacharie, and with hym two hundrid men;

5 of the sones of Sechemye, the sone of Ezechiel, and with hym thre hundrid men;

6 of the sones of Addam, Nabeth, the sone of Jonathan, and with hym fifti men;

7 of the sones of Elam, Ysaie, the sone of Italie, and with him seuenti men;

8 of the sones of Saphacie, Zebedie, the sone of Mycael, and with him fourescore men;

9 of the sones of Joab, Obedie, the sone of Jehiel, and with him two hundrid and eiytene men;

10 of the sones of Salomyth, the sone of Josphie, and with hym an hundrid and sixti men; of the sones of Belbai,

11 Zacarie, the sone of Belbai, and with hym twenti and eiyte men;

12 of the sones of Ezead, Johannam, the sone of Ezethan, and with hym an hundrid and ten men;

13 of the sones of Adonycam, that weren the laste, and these ben the names of hem, Eliphelech, and Eihel, and Samaie, and with hem weren sexti men;

14 of the sones of Beguy, Vtai, and Zaccur, and with hem weren seuenti men.

15 Forsothe Y gaderide hem togidere at the flood, that renneth doun to Hanna; and we dwelliden there thre daies. And 'Y souyte in the puple, and in the prestis of the sonus of Leuy, and Y fonde not there.

16 Therfor Y sente Eliezer, and Ariehel, and Semeam, and Helnathan, and Jaubeth, and an other Helnathan, and Nathan, and Zacharie, and Mesollam, princes; and Joarib, and Elnathan, wise men;

17 and Y sente hem to Heldo, which is 'the firste in the place of Casphie, and Y puttide in the mouth of hem wordis, whiche thei schulden speke to Heldo, and to hise britheren, Natynneis, in the place of Casphie, for to brynge to vs the mynystris of the hows of oure God.

18 And 'thei brouyten to vs, bi the good hoond of oure God on vs, a ful wijs man of the sones of Mooli, the sone of Leuy, sone of Israel; and Sarabie, and his sones twenti, and his britheren eiytene;

19 and Azabie, and Isaie, with him of the sones of Merari, thei brouyten his britheren, and his sones, twenti;

20 and of Nathynneis, whiche Dauid and the princis hadden youe to the seruyces of dekenes, thei brouyten two hundrid and twenti Nathynneis; alle these weren clepid bi her names.

21 And 'Y prechide there fastyng bisidis the flood of Hanna, that we schulden be turmentid bifor 'oure Lord God, and that we schulden axe of him the riytful weie to vs, and to oure sones, and to al oure catel.

22 For Y schamede to axe of the kyng help, and horse men, that schulden defende vs fro enemyes in the weie, for we hadden seid to the king, The hond of oure God is on alle men that seken hym in goodnesse; and his lordschip, and his strengthe, and strong veniaunce ben on alle men that forsaken hym.

23 Forsothe we fastiden, and preieden oure God for this thing, and it bifelde to vs 'bi prosperite.

24 And 'Y departide twelue of the princes of prestis, Sarabie, and Asabie, and ten of her britheren with hem;

25 and Y bitook vndur certeyn weiyte and noumbre to hem the siluer and gold, and the halewid vessels of the hows of oure God, whiche the kyng hadde offrid, and hise counseleris, and hise princes, and 'al Israel, of hem that weren foundun.

26 And Y bitook vndur certeyn weiyte and noumbre in the hondis of hem sixe hundrid and fifti talentis of siluer, and an hundrid siluerne vessels; an hundrid talentis of gold,

27 and twenti goldun cuppis, that hadden a thousynde peesis of gold; and twei faire vessels of best bras, schynynge as gold.

28 And Y seide to hem, Ye ben the hooli men of the Lord,

29 and wake ye, and kepe the hooli vessels, and siluer and gold, which is offrid bi fre wille to the Lord God of oure fadris, til ye yelde vndur certeyn weiyte and noumbre bifor th princes of prestis, and of dekenes, and bifor the duykis of meynees of Israel in Jerusalem, in to the tresour of Goddis hows.

30 Sotheli the preestis and dekenes token the weiyte of siluer, and of gold, and of vessels, for to bere in to Jerusalem, in to the hows of oure God.

31 Therfor we mouyden forth fro the flood of Hanna, in the tweluethe dai of the firste monethe, for to go in to Jerusalem; and the hond of oure God was on vs, and delyuerde vs fro the hond of enemye and of aspiere in the weie.

32 And we camen to Jerusalem, and we dwelliden there thre daies.

33 Forsothe in the fourthe dai the siluer was yoldun vndur certeyn weiyte and noumbre, and the gold, and the vessels, 'in the hows of oure God, by the noumbre and weiyte of alle thingis, bi the hond of Remmoth, 'sone of Vrie, preest; and with him was Eleazar, the sone of Phynees, and with him weren Jozaded, the sone of Josue, and Noadaie, the sone of Bennoy, dekenes;

34 and al the weiyte was discriued in that tyme.

35 But also the sones of transmygracioun, that camen fro caitifte, offriden brent sacrifices to the Lord God of Israel, 'twelue calues for al the puple of Israel, nynti and sixe rammes, seuene and seuenti lambren, twelue buckis of geet for synne; alle thingis in to brent sacrifice to the Lord.

36 Forsothe thei yauen the comaundementis of the kyng to the princes, that weren of the siyt of the king, and to the duykis biyende the flood; and thei reisiden the puple, and the hows of God.

CAP 9

1 Forsothe after that these thingis weren fillid, the princes neiyeden to me, and seiden, The puple of Israel, and the prestis, and dekenes, ben not depertid fro the 'puplis of londis, and fro abhominaciouns of hem, that is, of Cananei, of Ethei, and of Pheresei, and of Jebusei, and of Amonytis, and of Moabitis, and of Egipcians, and of Ammorreis.

2 For thei han take 'of her douytris wyues to hem silf, and to her sones, and thei han medlid hooli seed with the puplis of londis; also the hond of princes and of magistratis was the firste in this trespassyng.

3 And whanne Y hadde herd this word, Y torente my mentil and coote, and Y pullide awei the heeris of myn heed and berd, and Y sat morenynge.

4 Forsothe alle that dredden the word of God of Israel camen togidere to me, for the trespassyng of hem that weren comun fro caitifte; and Y sat sori 'til to the sacrifice of euentid.

5 And in the sacrifice of euentid Y roos fro myn afflicioun, and aftir that Y to-rente the mentil and coote, Y bowide my knees, and I spredde abrood myn hondis to 'my Lord God,

6 and Y seide, My God, Y am confoundid and aschamed to reise my face to thee, for oure wickidnessis ben multiplied 'on myn heed, and oure trespassis encreessiden 'til to heuene,

7 fro the daies of oure fadris; but also we vs silf han synned greuousli 'til to this dai, and for our wickidnessis we, and oure kyngis, and oure prestis ben bitakun in the hondis of kyngis of londis, bothe in to swerd, and in to caitifte, in to raueyn, and in to schenship of cheer, as also in this dai.

8 And now as at a litil and at a moment oure preier is maad anentis 'oure Lord God, that relikis schulden be left to vs, and that 'his pees schulde be youun in his hooli place, and that oure God schulde liytne oure iyen, and yyue to vs a litil lijf in oure seruage.

9 For we ben seruauntis, and oure God forsoke vs not in oure seruage; and he bowide merci on vs bifor the king of Persis, that he schulde yyue lijf to vs, and enhaunse the hows of oure God, and that he schulde bilde the wildernessis therof, and yyue to vs hope in Juda and in Jerusalem.

10 And now, 'oure Lord God, what schulen we seie after these thingis? For we han forsake thi comaundementis,

11 whiche thou comaundidist in the hond of thi seruauntis profetis, and seidist, The lond, to which ye schulen entre, to holde it in possessioun, is an vnclene lond, bi the vnclennesse of puplis, and of othere londis, in the abhomynaciouns of hem, that filliden it with her defoulyng, fro the mouth 'til to the mouth.

12 Now therfor yiue ye not youre douytris to her sones, and take ye not her douytris to youre sones; and seke ye not the pees of hem and the prosperite 'of hem 'til in to with outen ende; that ye be coumfortid, and ete the goodis, that ben of the lond, and that ye haue eiris, youre sones, 'til in to 'the world.

13 And after alle thingis that camen on vs in oure werste werkis, and in oure grete trespas, for thou, oure God, hast delyuered vs fro oure wickidnesse, and hast youe helthe to vs,

14 as 'it is to dai, that we schulden not be turned, and make voide thi comaundementis, and that we schulden not ioyne matrimonyes with the puplis of these abhomynacouns. Whether thou art wrooth to vs 'til to the endyng, that thou schuldist not leeue to us remenauntis, and helthe?

15 Lord God of Israel, thou art iust; for we ben left, that schulden be sauyd as in this day, lo! we ben bifor thee in oure synne; for me may 'not stonde bifor thee on this thing.

CAP 10

1 Therfor while Esdras preiede so, and bisouyte God, and wepte, and lai bifor the temple of God, a ful greet cumpenye of Israel, of men, and of wymmen, and of children, was gaderid to him; and the puple wepte bi myche weping.

2 And Sechenye, the sone of Jehiel, of the sones of Helam, answeride, and seide to Esdras, We han trespasside ayens oure God, and han weddid wyues, alien wymmen, of 'the puplis of the lond. And now, for penaunce is in Israel on this thing,

3 smyte we boond of pees with 'oure Lord God, and caste we awei alle 'wyues aliens, and hem that ben borun of tho wyues, bi the wille of the Lord; and of hem that dreden the comaundement of oure God, 'be it don bi the lawe.

4 Rise thou, it 'is thin office to deme, and we schulen be with thee; be thou coumfortid, and do.

5 Therfor Esdras roos, and chargide greetli the princes of prestis, and of dekenes, and of al Israel, to do after this word; and thei sworen.

6 And Esdras roos bifor the hows of God, and he yede to the bed of Johannan, sone of Eliasiph, and entride thidur; he eet

not breed, and drank not watir; for he biweilide the trespassing of hem, that weren comun fro the caitifte.

7 And a vois of hem was sent in to Juda and Jerusalem, to alle the sones of transmygracioun, that thei schulden be gaderid in to Jerusalem;

8 and ech man that cometh not in thre daies, bi the counsel of the princes and of eldre men, al his catel schal be takun awey fro him, and he schal be cast awei fro the cumpeny of transmygracioun.

9 Therfor alle the men of Juda and of Beniamyn camen togidere in to Jerusalem in thre daies; thilke is the nynthe monethe, in the twentithe dai of the monethe; and al the puple sat in 'the street of Goddis hows, and trembliden for synne and reyn.

10 And Esdras, the preest, roos, and seide to hem, Ye han trespassid, and han weddid wyues, alien wymmen, that ye schulden 'leie to on the trespas of Israel.

11 And now yyue ye knowlechyng to the Lord God of oure fadris, and do ye his pleasaunce, and be ye departid fro the puplis of the lond, and fro 'wyues aliens.

12 And al the multitude answeride, and seide with greet vois, Bi thi word to vs, so be it doon.

13 Netheles for the puple is myche, and the tyme of reyn is, and we suffren not to stonde withoutforth, and it is not werk of o dai, nether of tweyne; for we han synned greetli in this word;

14 'princes be ordeyned in al the multitude, and alle men in oure citees, that han weddid 'wyues aliens, come in tymes ordeyned, and with hem come the eldere men, bi citee and citee, and the iugis therof, til the ire of oure God be turned awei fro vs on this synne.

15 Therfor Jonathan, the sone of Asahel, and Jaazie, the sone of Thecue, stoden on this thing; and Mosollam, and Sebethai, dekenes, helpiden hem.

16 And the sones of transmygracioun diden so. And Esdras, the prest, and men, princes of meynees, yeden into the howsis of her fadris, and alle men bi her names; and thei saten in the firste dai of the tenthe monethe, for to seke the thing.

17 And alle men weren endid, that hadden weddid 'wyues aliens, 'til to the firste dai of the firste monethe.

18 And there weren foundun of the sones of preestis, that weddiden 'wyues aliens; of the sones of Josue, the sone of Josedech, and hise britheren, Maasie, and Eliezer, and Jarib, and Godolie.

19 And thei yauen her hondis, that thei schulden caste out her wyues, and offre for her trespas a ram of the scheep.

20 And of the sones of Semmer; Anam, and Zebedie.

21 And of the sones of Serym; Maasie, and Helie, and Semeie, and Jehiel, and Ozie.

22 And of the sones of Phessur; Helioneai, Maasie, Hismael, Nathanael, and Jozabet, and Elasa.

23 And of the sones of dekenes; Josabeth, and Semey, and Elaie; he is Calithaphataie; Juda, and Elezer.

24 And of syngeris, Eliazub; and of porteris, Sellum, and Thellem, and Vry.

25 And of Israel, of the sones of Pharos; Remea, and Ezia, and Melchia, and Vnanym, and Eliezer, and Melchia, and Banea.

26 And of the sones of Elam; Mathanye, and Zacharie, and Jehil, and Abdi, and Rymoth, and Helia.

27 And of the sones of Zechua; Helioneay, Heliasib, Mathanye, and Jerymuth, and Zaeth, and Aziza.

28 And of the sones of Bebai; Johannan, Ananye, Zabbai, Athalia.

29 And of the sones of Beny; Mosallam, and Melue, and Azaie, Jasub, and Saal, and Ramoth.

30 And of the sones of Phaeth; Moab, Edua, and Calal, Banaie, and Massie, Mathanye, Beseleel, and Bennun, and Manasse.

31 And of the sones of Erem; Elieer, Jesue, Melchie, Semeye, Symeon, Beniamyn, Maloth, Samarie.

32 And of the sones of Asom; Mathanai, Mathetha,

33 Zabeth, Eliphelech, Jermai, Manasse, Semei.

34 Of the sones of Bany; Maddi, Amram,

35 and Huel, Baneas, and Badaie, Cheilian,

36 Biamna, Marymuth, and Eliasiph, Mathanye,

37 and Jasy, and Bany, and Bennan,

39 and Semei, and Salymas, and Nathan, and Daias,

40 Metuedabai, Sisai, Sarai, Ezrel,

41 and Seloman, Semerie, Sellum,

42 Amarie, Joseph.

43 Of the sones of Nebny; Aiel, Mathatie, Zabed, Zabina, Jebdu, and Johel, Banai.

44 Alle these hadden take 'wyues aliens, and of hem weren wymmen, that hadden bore children.

2 ESDRAS

CAP 1

1 The wordis of Neemye, the sone of Helchie. And it was doon in the monethe Casleu, in the twentithe yeer, and Y was in the castel Susis;

2 and Ananye, oon of my britheren, cam to me, he and men of Juda; and Y axide hem of the Jewis, that weren left, and weren alyue of the caitifte, and of Jerusalem.

3 And thei seiden to me, Thei that 'dwelliden, and ben left of the caitifte there in the prouynce, ben in greet turment, and in schenship; and the wal of Jerusalem is destried, and the yatis therof ben brent with fier.

4 And whanne Y hadde herd siche wordis, Y sat and wepte, and morenede many daies, and Y fastide, and preiede bifor the face of God of heuene;

5 and Y seide, Y biseche, Lord God of heuene, strong, greet, and ferdful, which kepist couenaunt and merci with hem, that louen thee, and kepen thin heestis;

6 thin eere be maad herknynge, and thin iyen openyd, that thou here the preier of thi seruaunt, bi which Y preie bifor thee 'to dai, bi nyyt and dai, for the sones of Israel, thi seruauntis, and 'Y knouleche for the synnes of the sones of Israel, bi which thei han synned to thee; bothe Y and the hows of my fadir han synned; we weren disseyued bi vanyte,

7 and we 'kepten not 'thi comaundement, and cerymonyes, and domes, which thou comaundidist to Moises, thi seruaunt.

8 Haue mynde of the word, which thou comaundidist to thi seruaunt Moises, and seidist, Whanne ye han trespassid, Y schal scatere you in to puplis;

9 and if ye turnen ayen to me, that ye kepe myn heestis, and do tho, yhe, thouy ye ben led awei to the fertheste thingis of heuene, fro thennus Y schal gadere you togidere, and Y schal brynge you in to the place, which Y chees, that my name schulde dwelle there.

10 And we ben thi seruauntis, and thi puple, whiche thou 'ayen bouytist in thi greet strengthe, and in thi strong hond.

11 Lord, Y biseche, 'thin eere be ententif to the preier of thi seruaunt, and to the preier of thi seruauntis, that wolen drede

thi name; and dresse thi seruaunt to dai, and yiue thou merci to him bifor this man. For Y was the boteler of the kyng.

CAP 2

1 Forsothe it was doon in the monethe Nysan, in the twentithe yeer of Artaxerses, kyng, and wyn was bifor hym, and Y rey-side the wyn, and yaf to the kyng, and Y was as langwis-chynge bifor his face.

2 And the kyng seide to me, Whi is thi cheer sory, sithen Y se not thee sijk? This is not without cause; but 'yuel, Y not what, is in thin herte. And Y dredde ful greetli;

3 and seide to the kyng, Kyng, lyue thou withouten ende; whi moreneth not my cheer? for the citee of the hows of the sepul-cris of my fadir is desert, 'ether forsakun, and the yatis therof ben brent with fier.

4 And the kyng seide to me, For what thing axist thou? And Y preiede God of heuene,

5 and seide to the kyng, If it semeth good to the kyng, and if it plesith thi seruauntis bifor thi face, Y biseche, that thou sende me in to Judee, to the citee of the sepulcre of my fadir, and Y schal bilde it.

6 And the kyng seide to me, and the queen sat bisidis him, 'Til to what tyme schal thi weie be, and whanne schalt thou turne ayen? And Y pleside 'bifor the cheer of the kyng, and he sente me, and Y ordeynede to hym a time;

7 and Y seide to 'the kyng, If it semeth good to kyng, yyue he pistlis to me to the duykis of the cuntrey biyende the flood, that thei lede me ouer, til Y come in to Judee;

8 'and a pistle to Asaph, kepere of the kyngis forest, that he yyue trees to me, that Y may hile the yatis of the tour of the hows, and of the wal of the citee, and the hows, into which Y schal entre. And 'the kyng yaf to me, bi the good hond of my God with me.

9 And Y cam to the duykis of the cuntrei biyende the flood, and Y yaf to hem the pistlis of the kyng. Sotheli the kyng 'hadde sent with me the princes of knyytis, and horsemen.

10 And Sanaballath Oronythes, and Tobie, the seruaunt Amanytes, herden, and thei weren soreuful bi greet turment, for a man was comun, that souyte prosperite of the sones of Israel.

11 And Y cam in to Jerusalem, and Y was there thre daies.

12 And Y roos bi nyyt, Y and a fewe men with me, and Y schewide not to ony man, what thing God hadde youe in myn herte, that Y wolde do in Jerusalem; and no werk beest was with me, no but the beeste, 'on which Y sat.

13 And Y yede out bi the yate of the valei bi nyyt, and bifor the welle of dragoun, and to the yat of drit; and Y bihelde the wal of Jerusalem distried, and the yatis therof wastid bi fier.

14 And Y passid to the yate of the welle, and to the watir cun-dit of the kyng, and no place was to the hors, 'on which Y sat 'for to passe;

15 and Y stiede bi the stronde 'in nyyt, and Y bihelde the wal, and Y turnede ayen, and cam to the yate of the valei, and Y yede ayen.

16 Forsothe the magistratis wisten not, whidir Y hadde go, ethir what Y wolde do; but also Y hadde not schewid ony thing to the Jewis, and prestis, and to the best men, and mag-estratis, and to othere men that maden the werk, 'til to that 'place, that is, til to that tyme.

17 And Y seide to hem, Ye knowen the turment, in which we ben, for Jerusalem is deseert, and the yatis therof ben wastid with fier; come ye, bilde we the wallis of Jerusalem, and be we no more schenship.

18 And Y schewide to hem the hond of my God, that it was good with me, and the wordis of the kyng, whiche he spak to me; and Y seide, Rise we, and bilde we; and the hondis of hem weren coumfortid in good.

19 Forsothe Sanballath Oronytes, and Tobie, the seruaunt Amanytes, and Gosem Arabs, herden, and scorneden vs, and dispisiden; and seiden, What is this thing, which ye doon? whether ye rebellen ayens the kyng?

20 And Y yeldide to hem a word, and seide to hem, God hym silf of heuene helpith vs, and we ben hise seruauntis; rise we, and bilde; forsothe part and riytfulnesse and mynde in Jerusa-lem is not to you.

CAP 3

1 And Eliasiph, the greet preest, roos, and hise britheren, and prestis, and thei bildiden the yate of the floc; thei maden it stidfast; and settiden the yatis therof, and 'til to the tour of an hundrid cubitis, thei maden it stidfast, 'til to the tour of Ananehel.

2 And bisidis hym the men of Jerico bildiden; and bisidis hem Zaccur, the sone of Amry, bildide.

3 Forsothe the sones of Asamaa bildiden the yatis of fischis; thei hiliden it, and settiden the yatis therof, and lockis, and barris. And Marymuth, sone of Vrye, the sone of Accus, bil-dide bisidis hem.

4 And Mosolla, sone of Barachie, the sone of Meseze, bildide bisidis hym. And Sadoch, the sone of Baana, bildide bisidis him.

5 And men of Thecue bildiden bisidis hym; but the principal men of hem puttiden not her neckis vndur in the werk of her Lord God.

6 And Joiada, the sone of Phasea, and Mosollam, the sone of Besoyda, bildiden the elde yate; thei hiliden it, and settiden the yatis therof, and lockis, and barris.

7 And Melchie Gabaonyte, and Jaddon Methonatite, men of Gabaon and of Maspha, bildiden bisidis hem, for the duyk that was in the cuntrei biyende the flood.

8 And Eziel, goldsmyyt, the sone of Araie, bildide bisidis hym; and Annany, the sone of 'a makere of oynement, bildide bisidis him; and thei leften Jerusalem 'til to the wal of the largere street.

9 And Raphaie, the sone of Hahul, prince of a street of Jerus-alem, bildide bisidis him.

10 And Jeieda, the sone of Aramath, bildide bisidis him ayens his owne hous; and Accus, the sone of Asebonye, bildide bisi-dis hym.

11 Forsothe Melchie, the sone of Herem, and Asub, the sone of Phet Moab, bildiden the half part of the street, and the tour of ouenys.

12 Sellum, the sone of Aloes, prince of the half part of a street of Jerusalem, bildide bisidis hym, he and hise sones.

13 And Amram, and the dwelleris of Zanoe, bildiden the yate of the valei; thei bildiden it, and settiden the yatis therof, and lockis, and barris therof; and thei bildiden a thousynde cubitis in the wal 'til to the yate of the dunghil.

14 And Melchie, the sone of Rechab, prynce of a street of Bethacarem, bildide the yate of the dunghil; he bildide it, and settide, and hilide the yatis therof, and lockis, and barris.

15 And Sellum, the sone of Colozai, prince of a toun Maspha, bildide the yate of the welle; he bildide it, and hilide, and set-tide the yatis therof, and lockis, and barris; and he bildide the wallis of the cisterne of Ciloe 'til in to the orchard of the

kyng, and 'til to the greces of the kyng, that comen doun fro the citee of Dauid.

16 Nemye, the sone of Azboch, prince of the half part of the street of Bethsury, bildide after hym til ayens the sepulcre of Dauid, and 'til to the cisterne, which is bildide with greet werk, and 'til to the hous of stronge men.

17 Dekenes bildiden after hym; and Reum, the sone of Beny, bildide aftir hem. Asebie, the prince of half part of the street of Cheile, bildide in his street aftir hym.

18 The britheren of hem, Bethyn, the sone of Enadab, prince of the half part of Cheyla, bildiden after hym.

19 And Aser, the sone of Josue, prince of Maspha, bildide bisidis hym the secounde mesure ayens the stiyng of the 'moost stidefast corner.

20 Baruch, the sone of Zachay, bildide aftir hym in the hil the secounde mesure fro the corner 'til to the yate of the hows of Eliasiph, the greet prest.

21 Marymuth, the sone of Vrie, sone of Zaccur, bildide after hym the secounde mesure fro the yate of Eliasiph, as fer as the hows of Eliasiph was stretchid forth.

22 And prestis, men of the feeldi places of Jordan, bildiden aftir hym.

23 Beniamyn and Asub bildiden after hem ayens her hows; and Azarie, the sone of Maasie, sone of Ananye, bildide aftir hym ayens his owne hows.

24 Bennuy, the sone of Senadad, bildide after hym the secounde mesure fro the hows of Azarie 'til to the bowyng and 'til to the corner.

25 Phalel, the sone of Ozi, bildide ayens the bowyng, and the tour that stondith forth, fro the hiy hows of the kyng, that is in the large place of the prisoun; Phadaie, the sone of Pheros, bildide after hym.

26 Forsothe Nathynneis dwelliden in Ophel til ayens the yate of watris at the eest, and the tour that apperide.

27 Aftir hym men of Thecue bildiden the secounde mesure euene ayens, fro the greet tour and apperynge 'til to the wal of the temple.

28 Forsothe prestis bildiden aboue at the yate of horsis, ech man ayens his hows. Seddo, the sone of Enner, bildide ayens his hows aftir hem.

29 And Semeie, the sone of Sechenye, the kepere of the eest yate, bildide after hym.

30 Ananye, the sone of Selemye, and Anon, the sixte sone of Selon, bildide aftir hym the secounde mesure. Mosallam, the sone of Barachie, bildide ayenus his tresorie after hym. Melchie, the sone of a goldsmiyt, bildide aftir hym 'til to the hows of Nathynneis, and of men sillynge scheldis ayens the yate of iugis, and 'til to the soler of the corner.

31 And crafti men and marchauntis bildiden with ynne the soler of the corner and the yate of the kyng.

CAP 4

1 Forsothe it was doon, whanne Sanaballath hadde herd, that we bildiden the wal, he was ful wrooth, and he was stirid greetli, and scornede the Jewis.

2 And he seide bifor hise britheren, and the multitude of Samaritans, What doen the feble Jewis? Whether hethene men schulen suffre hem? Whether thei schulen fille, and make sacrifice in o dai? Whether thei moun bilde stonys of the heepis of the dust, that ben brent?

3 But also Tobie Amanytes, his neiybore, seide, Bilde thei; if a fox stieth, he schal 'skippe ouer the stony wal 'of hem.

4 And Neemye seide, Oure God, here thou, for we ben maad dispising; turne thou the schenschip on her heed, and yyue thou hem in to dispisyng in the lond of caytifte;

5 hile thou not the wickidnesse of hem, and her synnes be not doon awei bifor thi face; for thei scorneden bilderis.

6 Therfor we bildiden the wal, and ioyneden togidere al 'til to the half part, and the herte of the puple was exitid to worche.

7 Forsothe it was doon, whanne Sanaballat 'hadde herd, and Tobie, and Arabiens, and Amanytys, and men of Azotus hadden herd, that the brekyng of the wal of Jerusalem was stoppid, and that the crasyngis hadden bigunne to be closid togidere, thei weren ful wrothe.

8 And alle weren gaderid togidere to come and fiyte ayens Jerusalem, and to caste tresouns.

9 And we preieden oure Lord God, and we settiden keperis on the wal bi dai and niyt ayens hem.

10 Forsothe Juda seide, The strengthe of the berere is maad feble, and the erthe is ful myche, and we moun not bilde the wal.

11 And oure enemyes seiden, Wite thei not, and knowe thei not, til we comen in to the myddil of hem, and sleen hem, and maken the werk to ceesse.

12 Forsothe it was doon, whanne Jewis came, that dwelliden bisidis hem, and seiden to vs 'bi ten tymes, fro alle places fro whiche thei camen to vs,

13 Y ordeynede the puple in ordre, with her swerdis, and speris, and bouwis, in a place bihynde the wal bi cumpas.

14 Y bihelde, and roos, and seide to the principal men, and magistratis, and to 'the tother part of the comyn puple, Nyle ye drede of her face; haue ye mynde of the greet Lord, and ferdful, and fiyte ye for youre britheren, and youre sones, and youre douytris, for youre wyues, and housis.

15 Forsothe it was doon, whanne oure enemyes hadden herd that it was teld to vs, God distriede her counsel; and alle we turneden ayen to the wallis, ech man to his werk.

16 And it was doon fro that dai, the half part of yonge men made werk, and the half part was redi to batel; 'and speris, and scheldis, and bouwis, and harburiouns, and princes aftir hem, in al the hows of men of Juda,

17 bildynge in the wal, and berynge birthuns, and puttynge on; with her oon hond thei maden werk, and with the tother thei helden swerd.

18 For ech of the bilderis was gird with the swerd on the reynes; and thei bildiden, and sowneden with clariouns bisidis me.

19 And Y seide to the principal men, and magistratis, and to the tothir part of the comyn puple, The werk is greet and brood, and we ben departid fer in the wal, oon from anothir;

20 in what euer place ye heren the sown of the trumpe, renne ye togidere thidur to vs; for oure God schal fiyte for vs.

21 And we 'vs silf schal make the werk, and the half part of vs holde speris, fro 'the stiyng of the moreutid til that sterris go out.

22 And 'in that tyme Y seide to the puple, Ech man with his child dwelle in the myddil of Jerusalem, and whilis be to vs 'bi nyyt and dai to worche.

23 But Y, and my britheren, and my keperis, and children, that weren after me, diden not of oure clothis; ech man was maad nakid oneli to waischyng.

CAP 5

1 And greet cry of the puple and of her wyues was maad ayens her britheren Jewis.

2 And there weren that seiden, Oure sones and oure douytris ben ful manye; take we wheete for the prijs of hem, and ete we, and lyue.

3 And there weren that seiden, Sette we forth oure feeldis, and vyneris, and oure howsis, and take we wheete in hungur.

4 And othere men seiden, Take we money bi borewyng in to the tributis of the kyng, and yyue oure feeldis and vyneris.

5 And now as the fleischis of oure britheren ben, so and oure fleischis ben; and as ben the sones of hem, so and oure sones ben; lo! we han maad suget oure sones and oure douytris in to seruage, and seruauntissis ben of oure douytris, and we han not wherof thei moun be ayenbouyt; and othere men han in possessioun oure feeldis, and oure vyneris.

6 And Y was ful wrooth, whanne Y hadde herde the cry of hem bi these wordis.

7 And myn herte thouyte with me, and Y blamede the principal men and magistratis; and Y seide to hem, Axe ye not vsuris, 'ech man of youre britheren. And Y gaderide togidire a greet cumpeny ayens hem,

8 and Y seide to hem, As ye witen, we bi oure power ayenbouyten oure britheren Jewis, that weren seeld to hethene men; and ye therfor sillen youre britheren, and schulen we ayenbie hem? And thei holden silence, and founden not what thei schulen answere.

9 And Y seide to hem, It is not good thing, which ye doon; whi goen ye not in the drede of oure God, and repreef be not seid to vs of hethene men, oure enemyes?

10 Bothe Y and my britheren, and my children, han lent to ful many men monei and wheete; in comyn axe we not this ayen; foryyue we alien money, which is due to vs.

11 Yelde ye to hem to dai her feeldis, and her vyneris, her olyue places, and her housis; but rather yyue ye for hem bothe the hundrid part 'of money of wheete, of wyn, and of oile, which we weren wont to take of hem.

12 And thei seiden, We schulen yelde, and we schulen axe no thing of hem; and we schulen do so as thou spekist. And Y clepide the preestis, and Y made hem to swere, that thei schulden do aftir that, that Y hadde seid.

13 Ferthermore Y schook my bosum, and Y seide, So God schake awei ech man, 'that fillith not this word fro his hows, and hise trauels; and be he schakun awei, and be he maad voide. And al the multitude seide, Amen; and thei herieden God. Therfor the puple dide, as it was seid.

14 Forsothe fro that dai in which the kyng hadde comaundid to me, that Y schulde be duyk in the lond of Juda, fro the twentithe yeer 'til to the two and threttithe yeer of Artaxerses kyng, bi twelue yeer, Y and my britheren eeten not sustenauncis, that weren due to duykis.

15 But the firste duykis, that weren bifor me, greuyden the puple, and token of hem in breed, and in wiyn, and in monei, ech dai fourti siclis; but also her mynistris oppressiden the puple. Forsothe Y dide not so, for the drede of God;

16 but rather Y bildide in the werk of the wal, and Y bouyte no feeld, and alle my children weren gaderid to the werk.

17 Also 'Jewis and the magistratis of hem, an hundrid and fifti men; and thei that camen to me fro hethene men, that ben in oure cumpas, weren in my table.

18 Forsothe bi ech dai oon oxe was maad redi to me, sixe chosun wetheris, outakun volatils, and withynne ten daies dyuerse wynes; and Y yaf many othere thingis; ferthermore and Y axide not the sustenauncis of my duchee; for the puple was maad ful pore.

19 My God, haue thou mynde of me in to good, bi alle thingis whiche Y dide to this puple.

CAP 6

1 Forsothe it was doon, whanne Sanaballath hadde herd, and Tobie, and Gosem of Arabie, and oure other enemyes, that Y hadde bildide the wal, and nomore brekyng was therynne; sotheli 'til to that tyme Y hadde not set leeuys of schittyng in the yatis;

2 Sanaballath, and Tobie, and Gosem of Arabie senten to me, and seiden, Come thou, and smyte we boond of pees in calues, 'in o feeld; forsothe thei thouyten for to do yuel to me.

3 Therfor Y sente messangeris to hem, and Y seide, Y make a greet werk, and Y mai not go doun, lest perauenture it be doon retchelesli, whanne Y come, and go doun to you.

4 Sotheli thei senten to me 'bi this word bi foure tymes, and Y answeride to hem by the formere word.

5 And Sanaballath sente to me the fyuethe tyme bi the formere word his child; and he hadde in his hond a pistle writun in this maner;

6 It is herd among hethene men, and Gosem seide, that thou and the Jewis thenken for to rebelle, and therfor ye bilden, and thou wolt 'reise thee king on hem;

7 for which cause also thou hast set profetis, that prechen of thee in Jerusalem, and seien, A king is in Jerusalem; the king schal here these wordis; therfor come thou now, that we take counsel togidere.

8 And Y sente to hem, and seide, It is not doon bi these wordis whiche thou spekist; for of thin herte thou makist these thingis.

9 Alle these men maden vs aferd, and thouyten that oure hondis schulden ceesse fro werkis, that we schulden reste; for which cause Y coumfortide more myn hond.

10 And Y entride priueli in to the hows of Samaie, sone of Dalie, the sone of Methabehel, which seide, Trete we with vs silf in the hows of God, in the myddis of the temple, and close we the yatis of the hows; for thei schulen come to sle thee, 'and thei schulen come 'bi niyt to sle thee.

11 And Y seide, Whether ony man lijk me fledde, and who as Y schal entre in to the temple, and schal lyue?

12 Y schal not entre. And Y vndurstood that God 'hadde not sent hym, but 'he spak as profesiynge to me; and Tobie and Sanaballath 'hadden hirid hym for meede.

13 For he hadde take prijs, that Y schulde be aferd, and do, and that Y schulde do synne; and thei schulden haue yuel, which thei schulden putte to me with schenschip.

14 Lord, haue mynde of me, for Tobye and Sanaballath, bi siche werkis 'of hem; but also of Noadie, the profete, and of othere profetis, that maden me aferd.

15 Forsothe the wal was fillid in the fyue and twentithe dai of the monethe Ebul, in two and fifti daies.

16 Sotheli it was doon, whanne alle oure enemyes hadden herd, that alle hethene men dredden, that weren in oure cumpas, and thei felden doun with ynne hem silf, and wiste, that this work was maad of God.

17 But also in tho daies many pistlis of the principal men of Jewis weren sent to Tobie, and camen fro Tobie to hem.

18 For many men weren in Judee, and hadden his ooth; for he hadde weddid the douyter of Sechenye, the sone of Rotel; and Johannam, his sone, hadde take the douyter of Mosallam, sone of Barachie.

19 But also thei preisiden hym bifor me, and telden my wordis to hym; and Tobie sente lettris, for to make me aferd.

CAP 7

1 Forsothe aftir that the wal of Jerusalem was bildid, and Y hadde set yatis, and Y hadde noumbrid porters, and syngeris,
2 and dekenys, Y comaundide to Aneny, my brother, and to Ananye, the prince of the hows of Jerusalem; for he semyde a sothefast man, and dredynge God more than othere men diden;
3 'and Y seide 'to hem, The yatis of Jerusalem ben not openyd 'til to the heete of the sunne; and, whanne Y was yit present, the yatis weren closid, and lockid. And Y settide keperis of the dwelleris of Jerusalem, alle men bi her whilis, and ech man ayens his hows.
4 Sotheli the citee was ful brood and greet, and litil puple was in myddis therof, and housis weren not bildid.
5 Forsothe God yaf in myn herte, and Y gaderide togidere the principal men, and magistratis, and the comyn puple, for to noumbre hem; and Y foond the book of the noumbre of hem, that hadden stied first. And it was foundun writun ther ynne,
6 These ben the sones of the prouynce, 'that stieden fro the caitifte of men passynge ouer, whiche Nabugodonosor, the kyng of Babiloyne, hadde 'translatid, ether led ouer;
7 and thei that weren comun with Zorobabel turneden ayen in to Jerusalem and in to Judee, ech man in to his citee; Josue, Neemye, Azarie, Raanye, Naanum, Mardochee, Bethsar, Mespharath, Beggaay, Naum, Baana. The noumbre of men of the puple of Israel;
8 the sones of Pharos, two thousynde an hundrid and two and seuenti; the sones of Saphaie,
9 thre hundrid and two and seuenti;
10 the sones of Area, sixe hundrid and two and fifti; the sones of Phaeth Moab,
11 of the sones of Josue and of Joab, two thousynde eiyte hundrid and eiytene;
12 the sones of Helam, a thousynde eiyte hundrid and foure and fifti;
13 the sones of Ezecua, eiyte hundrid and fyue and fourti;
14 the sones of Zachai, seuene hundrid and sixti;
15 the sones of Bennuy, sixe hundrid and eiyte and fourti;
16 the sones of Hebahi, sixe hundrid and eiyte and twenti;
17 the sones of Degad, two thousynde thre hundrid and two and twenti;
18 the sones of Azonicam, sixe hundrid and seuene and sixti;
19 the sones of Bagoamy, two thousynde and seuene and sixti;
20 the sones of Adyn, sixe hundrid and fiue and fifti;
21 the sones of Azer, sone of Ezechie, eiyte and twenti;
22 the sones of Asem, thre hundrid and eiyte and twenti; the sones of Bethsai,
23 thre hundrid and foure and twenti;
24 the sones of Areph, an hundrid and seuene and twenti;
25 the sones of Zabaon, fyue and twenti;
26 the men of Bethleem and of Necupha, an hundrid foure score and eiyte;
27 the men of Anatoth, an hundrid and eiyte and twenti;
28 the men of Bethamoth, two and fourti;
29 the men of Cariathiarym, of Cephura, and Beroth, seuene hundrid and thre and fourti;
30 the men of Rama and of Gabaa, sixe hundrid and oon and twenti; the men of Machimas,
31 two hundrid and two and twenti;
32 the men of Bethel and of Hay, an hundrid and thre and twenti; the men of the tother Nebo,
33 two and fifti;
34 the men of the tother Helam, a thousynde two hundrid and foure and fifti;
35 the sones of Arem, thre hundrid and twenti;
36 the sones of Jerico, thre hundrid and fyue and fourti;
37 the sones of Joiadid and Anon, seuene hundrid and oon and twenti;
38 the sones of Senaa, thre thousynde nyne hundrid and thritti; preestis,
39 the sones of Idaie, in the hous of Josua, nyne hundrid and foure and seuenti; the sones of Emmer,
40 a thousynde and two and fifti;
41 the sones of Phassur, a thousynd two hundrid and 'seuene and fourti;
42 the sones of Arem, a thousynde and eiytene;
43 dekenes, the sones of Josue and of Gadymel,
44 sones of Odyna, foure and seuenti;
45 syngeris, the sones of Asaph, an hundrid and seuene and fourti;
46 porteris, the sones of Sellum, sones of Ater, sones of Thelmon, sones of Accub, sones of Accita, sones of Sobai, an hundrid and eiyte and thretti;
47 Nathynneis, sones of Soa, sones of Aspha, sones of Thebaoth, sones of Cheros,
48 sones of Sicca, sones of Phado, sones of Lebana, sones of Agaba, sones of Selmon,
49 sones of Anan, sones of Geddel,
50 sones of Gaer, sones of Raaie, sones of Rasym,
51 sones of Necuda, sones of Jezem, sones of Asa, sones of Phascha, sones of Besai,
52 sones of Mynum, sones of Nephusym,
53 sones of Bechue, sones of Acupha, sones of Assur,
54 sones of Belloth, sones of Meida,
55 sones of Arsa, sones of Berchos, sones of Sisara,
56 sones of Thema, sones of Nesia,
57 sones of Atipha, sones of the seruauntis of Salomon, sones of Sothai, sones of Sophoreth,
58 sones of Pherida, sones of Jacala, sones of Dalcon, sones of Geddel, sones of Saphatie,
59 sones of Atthal, the sones of Phetereth, 'that was borun of Abaim, sone of Amon;
60 alle Natynneis, and the sones of the seruauntis of Salomon, weren thre hundrid and two and twenti.
61 Forsothe these it ben that stieden, Dethemel, Mela, Thelarsa, Cherub, Addo, and Emmer, and myyten not schewe the hows of her fadris, and her seed, whether thei weren of Israel; the sones of Dalaie,
62 the sones of Tobie, the sones of Nethoda, sixe hundrid and two and fourti;
63 and of prestis, the sones of Abia, the sones of Achos, the sones of Berzellai, that took a wijf of the douytris of Berzellai of Galaad, and was clepid bi the name of hem;
64 these souyten the scripture of her genelogie, and founden not, and weren cast out of presthod.
65 And Athersata seide to hem, that thei schulden not eete of the hooli thingis of hooli men, til a wijs prest 'and lerud roos.
66 Al the multitude as o man, two and fourti thousynde sixe hundrid and sixti,
67 outakun the seruauntis and handmaidis of hem, that weren seuene thousynde thre hundrid and seuene and thretti; and among the syngeris and syngeressis, sixe hundrid and fyue and fourti.

68 The horsis of hem, sixe hundrid and sixe and thritti; the mulis of hem, two hundrid and fyue and fourti;

69 the camels of hem, foure hundrid and fyue and thritti; the assis of hem, sixe thousynde eiyte hundrid and thritti.

70 Forsothe summe of the princes of meynees yauen costis in to the werk of God; Athersata yaf in to the tresour, a thousynde dragmes of gold, fifti viols, fyue hundrid and thritti cootis of prestis.

71 And of the prynces of meynees thei yauen in to the tresour of the werk, twenti thousynde dragmes of gold, and two thousynde and two hundrid besauntis of siluer.

72 And that that the residue puple yaf, twenti thousynde dragmes of gold, and two thousynde besauntis of siluer, and seuene and sixti cootis of prestis. Sotheli prestis, and dekenes, and porteris, and syngeris, and the residue puple, and Natynneis, and al Israel dwelliden in her citees.

CAP 8

1 And the seuenthe monethe 'was comun vndur Esdras and Neemye; sotheli the sones of Israel weren in her cytees. And al the puple was gaderid togydere as o man, to the street which is bifor the yate of watris. And thei seiden to Esdras, the scribe, that he schulde brynge the book of the lawe of Moises, which the Lord hadde comaundid to Israel.

2 Therfor Esdras, the preest, brouyte the lawe bifor the multitude of men and of wymmen, and bifor alle that myyten vndurstonde, 'in the firste day of the seuenth monethe.

3 And he redde in it opynli in the street that was bifor the yate of watris, fro the morewtid 'til to myddai, in the siyt of men and of wymmen and of wise men; and the eeris of al the puple weren reisid to the book.

4 Forsothe Esdras the writere stood on the grees of tree, which he hadde maad to speke theron; and Mathatie, and Semma, and Ananye, and Vrie, and Elchie, and Maasie stoden bisidis hym at his riyt half; and Phadaie, Mysael, and Melchie, Assum, and Aseph, Dana, and Zacharie, and Mosollam stoden at the left half.

5 And Esdras openyde the book bifor al the puple; for he apperide ouer al the puple; and whanne he hadde openyd the book, al the puple stood.

6 And Esdras blesside the Lord God with greet vois; and al the puple answeride, Amen, Amen, reisynge her hondis. And thei weren bowid, and thei worschipiden God, lowli on the erthe.

7 Forsothe Josue, and Baany, and Serebie, Jamyn, Acub, Septhai, Odia, Maasie, Celitha, Ayarie, Jozabeth, Anan, Phallaie, dekenes, maden silence in the puple for to here the lawe. Sotheli the puple stood in her degree.

8 And thei redden in the book of Goddis lawe distinctli, 'ether atreet, and opynli to vndurstonde; 'and thei vndurstoden, whanne it was red.

9 Forsothe Neemye seide, he is Athersata, and Esdras, the preest and writere, and the dekenes, expownynge to al the puple, It is a dai halewid to 'oure Lord God; nyle ye morne, and nyle ye wepe. For al the puple wepte, whanne it herde the wordis of the lawe.

10 And he seide to hem, Go ye, and 'ete ye fatte thingis, and drynke ye wiyn 'maad swete with hony, and sende ye partis to hem, that maden not redi to hem silf, for it is an hooli dai of the Lord; 'nyle ye be sory, for the ioye of the Lord is youre strengthe.

11 Sotheli the dekenes maden silence in al the puple, and seiden, Be ye stille, for it is an hooli dai; and 'nyle ye make sorewe.

12 Therfor al the puple yede for to ete, and drynke, and to sende partis, and 'to make greet gladnesse; for thei vndurstoden the wordis, whiche he hadde tauyt hem.

13 And in the secound dai the princes of meynees, alle the puplis, prestis, and dekenes, weren gaderid togidere to Esdras, the writere, that he schulde expowne to hem the wordis of the lawe.

14 And thei foundun writun in the lawe, that the Lord comaundide 'in the hond of Moyses, that the sones of Israel dwelle in tabernaclis in the solempne dai, in the seuenthe moneth;

15 and that thei preche, and pupplische a vois in alle her citees, and in Jerusalem; and seie, Go ye out in to the hil, and brynge ye bowis of olyue, and bowis of the faireste tree, the bowis of a myrte tree, and the braunchis of a palm tree, and the bowis of a 'tree ful of wode, that tabernaclis be maad, as it is writun.

16 And al the puple yede out, and thei brouyten, and maden to hem silf tabernaclis, 'ech man in 'his hows roof, and in her stretis, 'ether foryerdis, and in the large placis of Goddis hows, and in the street of the yate of watris, and in the street of the yate of Effraym.

17 Therfor al the chirche of hem, that camen ayen fro caytifte, made tabernaclis, and thei dwelliden in tabernaclis. For the sones of Israel hadden not do siche thingis fro the daies of Josue, sone of Nun, 'til to that dai; and ful greet gladnesse was.

18 Forsothe Esdras radde in the book of Goddis lawe bi alle daies, fro the firste dai 'til to the laste dai; and thei maden solempnytee bi seuene daies, and in the eiyte day thei maden a gaderyng of siluer, 'bi the custom.

CAP 9

1 Forsothe in the foure and twentithe dai of this monethe, the sones of Israel camen togidere in fastyng,

2 and in sackis, and 'erthe was on hem. And the seed of the sones of Israel was departid fro ech alien sone. And thei stoden bifor the Lord, and knoulechiden her synnes, and the wickidnessis of her fadris.

3 And thei risiden togidere to stonde; and thei redden in the book of the lawe of 'her Lord God fouresithis in the dai, and fouresithis in the niyt; thei knoulechiden, and herieden 'her Lord God.

4 Forsothe 'thei risiden on the degree, of dekenes, Jesuy, and Bany, Cedynyel, Remmy, Abany, Sarabie, Bany, and Chanany.

5 And the dekenes crieden with grete vois to her Lord God. And Jesue, and Cedyniel, Bonny, Assebie, Serebie, Arabie, Odaie, Sebua, and Facaia, seiden, Rise ye, and blesse ye 'youre Lord God fro without bigynnyng and til in to with outen ende; and blesse thei the hiye name of thi glorie in al blessyng and preysyng.

6 And Esdras seide, Thou thi silf, Lord, art aloone; thou madist heuene and the heuene of heuenes, and al the oost of tho heuenes; thou madist the erthe and alle thingis that ben there ynne; 'thou madist the sees and alle thingis that ben in tho; and thou quikenyst alle these thingis; and the oost of heuene worschipith thee.

7 Thou thi silf art the Lord God, that chesidist Abram, and leddist hym out of the fier of Caldeis, and settidist his name Abraham;

8 and foundist his herte feithful bifor thee, and thou hast smyte with hym a boond of pees, that thou woldist yyue to hym the lond of Cananei, of Ethei, of Euey, and of Ammorrei, and of Pherezei, and of Jebuzei, and of Gergesei, that thou woldist yyue it to his seed; and thou hast fillid thi wordis, for thou art iust.

9 And thou hast seyn the turment of oure fadris in Egipt, and thou herdist the cry of hem on the reed see.

10 And thou hast youe signes and grete wondris in Farao, and in alle hise seruauntis, and in al the puple of that lond; for thou knowist, that thei diden proudli ayens oure fadris; and thou madist to thee a name, as also in this dai.

11 And thou departidist the see bifor hem, and thei passiden thorou the 'myddis of the see in the drie place; forsothe thou castidist doun the pursueris of hem into depthe, as a stoon in strong watris.

12 And in a piler of cloude thou were the ledere of hem bi dai, and in a piler of fier bi nyyt, that the weie, bi which thei entriden, schulde appere to hem.

13 Also thou camest doun at the hil of Synai, and spakist with hem fro heuene, and thou yauest to hem riytful domes, and the lawe of trewthe, cerymonyes, and goode comaundementis.

14 And thou schewidist to hem an halewid sabat; and thou comaundidist 'to hem comaundementis, and cerymonyes, and lawe, in the hond of Moises, thi seruaunt.

15 Also thou yauest to hem breed fro heuene in her hungur; and thou leddist out of the stoon watir to hem thirstinge; and thou seidist to hem, that thei schulden entre, and haue in possessioun the lond, on which lond thou reisidist thin hond, that thou schuldist yyue it to hem.

16 But 'thei and oure fadris diden proudli, and maden hard her nollis, and herden not thi comaundementis.

17 And thei nolden here; and thei hadden not mynde of thi merueils, which thou haddist do to hem; and thei maden hard her nollis; and thei yauen the heed, that thei 'weren al turned to her seruage as bi strijf; but thou art God helpful, meke, and merciful, abidynge longe, 'ether pacient, and of myche merciful doyng, and forsokist not hem;

18 and sotheli whanne thei hadden maad to hem a yotun calf, as bi strijf, and hadden seid, This is thi God, that 'ledde thee out of Egipt, and thei diden grete blasfemyes.

19 But thou in thi many mercyes leftist not hem in deseert; for a piler of cloude yede not awei fro hem bi the dai, that it schulde lede hem in to the weie; and a piler of fier yede not awei 'fro hem bi nyyt, that it schulde schewe to hem the weie, bi which thei schulden entre.

20 And thou yauest to hem thi good Spirit, that tauyte hem; and thou forbedist not thin aungels mete fro her mouth, and thou yauest to hem water in thirst.

21 Fourti yeer thou feddist hem in deseert, and no thing failide to hem; her clothis wexiden not elde, and her feet weren not hirt.

22 And thou yauest to hem rewmes, and puplis; and thou departidist lottis, 'ether eritagis, to hem, and thei hadden in possessioun the lond of Seon, and the lond of the kyng of Esebon, and the lond of Og, kyng of Basan.

23 And thou multipliedist the sones of hem, as the sterris of heuene; and thou brouytist hem to the lond, of which thou sei-

dist to her fadris, that thei schulden entre, and holde it in possessioun.

24 And the sones of Israel camen, and hadden the lond in possessioun; and bifor hem thou madist low the dwellers of the lond, Cananeis; and thou yauest hem in to the hondis of the sones of Israel, and the kyngis of hem, and the puplis of the lond, that thei diden to hem, as it pleside hem.

25 And thei token citees maad strong, and fat erthe; and thei hadden in possessioun housis fulle of alle goodis, cisternes maad of othere men, vineris, and places of olyues, and many apple trees. And thei eeten, and weren fillid, and weren maad fat; and hadden plentee of ritchessis 'in thi greet goodnesse.

26 Sotheli thei terriden thee to wrathfulnesse, and yeden awei fro thee, and castiden awei thi lawe bihynde her backis; and thei killiden thi prophetis, that witnessiden to hem, that thei schulden turne ayen to thee; and thei diden grete blasfemyes.

27 And thou yauest hem in to the hond of her enemyes; and thei turmentiden hem; and in the tyme of her tribulacioun thei crieden to thee; and thou herdist them fro heuyn, and bi thi many merciful doyngis thou yauest hem sauyours, that sauyden hem fro the hond of her enemyes.

28 And whanne thei hadden restid, thei turneden ayen to do yuel in thi siyt; and thou forsokist hem in the hond of her enemyes, and enemyes hadden hem in possessioun; and thei weren conuertid, and thei crieden to thee; forsothe thou herdist hem fro heuene, and delyueridist hem 'in thi mercies in many tymes.

29 And thou witnessidist to hem, that thei schulden turne ayen to thi lawe; but thei diden proudli, and herden not thin heestis, and synneden in thi domes, whiche a man that schal do schal lyue in tho; and thei yauen the schuldre goynge awei, and thei maden hard her nol.

3 And thou drowist along many yeeris on hem, and thou witnessidist to hem in thi Spirit bi the hond of thi prophetis; and thei herden not; and thou yauest hem in to the hond of the puplis of londis.

31 But in thi mercies ful manye thou madist not hem in to wastyng, nethir thou forsokist hem; for thou art God of merciful doynges, and meke.

32 Now therfor, oure Lord God, greet God, strong, and ferdful, kepynge couenaunt and merci, turne thou not awei thi face in al the trauel that foond vs, oure kyngis, and oure princes, and oure fadris, and oure preestis, and oure profetis, and al thi puple, fro the daies of kyng Assur til to this dai.

33 And thou art iust in alle thingis, that camen on vs, for thou didist trewthe to vs; but we han do wickidli.

34 Oure kyngis, and oure princes, oure prestis, and fadris 'diden not thi lawe; and thei perseyueden not thin heestis and witnessyngis, whiche thou witnessidist in hem.

35 And thei in her good rewmes, and in thi myche goodnesse, which thou yauest to hem, and in the largest lond and fat, whych thou haddist youe in the siyt of hem, serueden not thee, nether turneden ayen fro her werste studies.

36 Lo! we 'vs silf ben thrallis to dai; and the lond which thou yauest to oure fadris, that thei schulden ete the breed therof, and the goodis that ben therof, 'is thral; and we 'vs silf ben thrallis, 'ethir boonde men, in that lond.

37 And the fruytis therof ben multiplied to kyngis, whiche thou hast set on vs for oure synnes; and thei ben lordis of oure bodies, and of oure beestis, bi her wille, and we ben in greet tribulacioun.

CAP 10

38 Therfor on alle these thingis we 'vs silf smyten and writen boond of pees, and oure princes, oure dekenes, and oure prestis aseelen.

1 Forsothe the seeleris weren Neemye, Athersata, the sone of Achilai,

2 and Sedechie, Saraie, Azarie, Jeremye, Phasur,

3 Amarie, Melchie,

4 Accus, Sebenye,

5 Mellucarem, Nerymuth, Oddie, Danyel,

6 Genton, Baruc, Mosollam, Abia,

7 Mianymy, Mazie, Belga, and Semeie;

8 these weren prestis.

9 Forsothe the dekenes weren Josue, the sone of Azarie, Bennuy, of the sones of Ennadab,

10 Cedinyel, and hise britheren, Sethenye, Odenmye, Telita, Phalaie, Anam,

11 Myca, Roob, Asebie

12 Zaccur, Serebie, Sabanye,

13 Odias, Bany, Hamyn.

14 The heedis of the puple, Phetos, Moab, Elam,

15 Zecu, Banny, Bonny, Azgad, Bebay,

16 Donai, Bogoia, Adyn,

17 Ather, Azochie, Azur,

18 Odenye, Assuyn, Bessaie,

19 Ares, Anatoth, Nebai,

20 Methpie, Mosollam, Azir,

21 Meizabel, Sadoch, Reddua,

22 Pheltie, Ananye, Osee,

23 Anaie, Azub, Aloes,

24 Phaleam, Sobeth,

25 Reu, Asebyne, Mathsie,

26 Ethaie, Anam,

27 Mellucarem, Baana;

28 and othere of the puple, prestis, dekenes, porteris, and syngeris, Natynneis, and alle men that departiden hem silf fro the puplis of londis to the lawe of God, the wyues of hem, and 'the sones of hem, and the douytris of hem;

29 alle that myyten vndurstonde, bihetynge for her britheren, the principal men of hem, 'and thei that camen to biheete, and to swere, that thei schulden go in the lawe of the Lord, which he 'hadde youe bi the hond of Moyses, his seruaunt, that thei schulden do and kepe alle the heestis of 'oure Lord God, and hise domes, and hise cerymonyes; and that we schulden not yyue

30 oure douytris to the puple of the lond, and that we schulden not take her douytris to oure sones.

31 Also the puplis of the lond, 'that bryngen in thingis set to sale, and alle thingis to vss, bi the dai of sabat, for to sille, we schulen not take of hem in the sabat, and in a dai halewid; and we schulen leeue the seuenthe yeer, and the axynge of al hond.

32 And we schulen ordeyne comaundementis 'on vs, that we yyue the thridde part of a sicle 'bi the yeer to the werk of 'oure Lord God,

33 to the looues of settyngforth, and to the euerlastynge sacrifice, 'and in to brent sacrifice euerlastynge, in sabatis, in calendis, 'that is, bigynnyngis of monethis, in solempnytees, in halewid daies, and for synne, that 'me preie for Israel, and in to al the vss of the hows of oure God.

34 'Therfor we senten 'lottis on the offryng of trees, bitwixe prestis and dekenes and the puple, that tho schulden be brouyt in to the hows of oure God, bi the housis of oure fadris bi

tymes, fro the tymes of a yeer 'til to a yeer, that 'tho schulden brenne on the auter of 'oure Lord God, as it is writun in the lawe of Moyses;

35 and that we bringe the firste gendrid thingis of oure lond, and the firste fruytis of al fruyt of ech tree, fro yeer in to yeer,

36 in to the hows of the Lord, and the firste gendrid thingis of oure sones, and of oure beestis, as it is writun in the lawe, and the firste gendrid thingis of oure oxis, and of oure scheep, that tho be offrid in the hows of oure God, to prestis that mynystren in the hows of oure God;

37 and we schulen brynge the firste fruytis of oure metis, and of oure moiste sacrifices, and the applis of ech tre, and of vendage, and of oile, to 'prestis, at the treserie of the Lord, and the tenthe part of oure lond to dekenes; thilke dekenes schulen take tithis of alle the citees of oure werkis.

38 Sotheli a prest, the sone of Aaron, schal be with the dekenes in the tithis of dekenes; and the dekenes schulen offre the tenthe part of her tithe in the hows of oure God, 'at the tresorie, in the hows of tresour.

39 For the sones of Israel and the sones of Leuy schulen brynge the firste fruytis of wheete, of wiyn, and of oile; and halewid vessels schulen be there, and prestis, and syngeris, and porteris, and mynystris; and we schulen not forsake the hows of 'oure God.

CAP 11

1 Forsothe the princis of the puple dwelliden in Jerusalem; the principal men dwelliden in the myddis of the puple with out lot; but the residue puple sente lot, for to take o part of ten, 'whiche schulden dwelle in Jerusalem, in the hooli citee; the tenthe part of the puple is chosun for to dwelle in Jerusalem, for the citee was voide; forsothe the nyne partis dwelliden in citees.

2 Forsothe the puple blesside alle men, that profriden hem silf bi fre wille to dwelle in Jerusalem.

3 And so these ben the princes of prouynce, that dwelliden in Jerusalem, and in the citees of Juda; sotheli ech man dwellide in his possessioun, in her citees of Israel, prestis, dekenes, Nathynneis, and the sones of the seruauntis of Salomon.

4 And men of the sones of Juda, and of the sones of Beniamyn dwelliden in Jerusalem; of the sones of Juda, Athaie, the sone of Aziam, sone of Zacarie, sone of Amarie, sone of Saphie, sone of Malaleel;

5 of the sones of Phares, Amasie, the sone of Baruch, the sone of Colozay, the sone of Azie, the sone of Adaie, the sone of Jozarib, the sone of Zacarie, the sone of Salonytes; alle the sones of Phares,

6 that dwelliden in Jerusalem, weren foure hundrid eiyte and sixti, stronge men.

7 Sotheli these ben the sones of Beniamyn; Sellum, the sone of Mosollam, the sone of Joedi, the sone of Sadaie, the sone of Colaie, the sone of Masie, the sone of Ethel, the sone of Saie;

8 and aftir hym Gabai, Sellai, nynti and eiyte and twenti; and Johel, the sone of Zechri, was the souereyn of hem, and Judas, the sone of Semyna, was the secounde man on the citee.

10 And of prestis; Idaie,

11 sone of Joarib, Jachyn, Saraie, the sone of Helchie, the sone of Mossollam, the sone of Sadoch, the sone of Meraioth, the sone of Achitob, 'the princis of 'Goddis hows,

12 and her britheren, makynge the werkis of the temple, weren eiyte hundrid and two and twenti. And Adaie, the sone

of Jeroam, the sone of Pheler, the sone of Amsi, the sone of Zacarie, the sone of Phessur,

13 the sone of Melchie, and the britheren of hem, the princes of fadris, weren two hundrid and two and fourti. And Amasie, the sone of Azrihel, the sone of Azi, the sone of Mosollamoth, the sone of Semyner,

14 and her britheren, ful myyti men, weren an hundrid and eiyte and twenti; and the souereyn of hem was Zebdiel, the sone of myyty men.

15 And of dekenes; Sechenye, the sone of Azab, the sone of Azarie, the sone of Azabie, the sone of Bone, and Sabathai;

16 and Jozabed was ordened of the princes of dekenes, on alle the werkis that weren with out forth in Goddis hows.

17 And Mathanye, the sone of Mycha, the sone of Zebdai, the sone of Asaph, was prince, to herie and to knowleche in preier; and Bethechie was the secounde of hise britheren, and Abdie, the sone of Sammya, the sone of Galal, the sone of Iditum.

18 Alle the dekenes in the hooli citee, weren two hundrid and foure score and foure.

19 And the porteris, Accub, Thelmon, and the britheren of hem, that kepten the doris, weren an hundrid 'and two and seuenti.

20 And othere men of Israel, prestis, and dekenes, in alle the citees of Juda, ech man in his possessioun.

21 And Natynneis, that dwelliden in Ophel, and Siacha, and Gaspha; of Natynneis.

22 And bischopis of dekenes in Jerusalem; Azi, the sone of Bany, the sone of Asabie, the sone of Mathanye, the sone of Mychee. Of the sones of Asaph, syngeris in the seruyce of Goddis hows.

23 For the comaundement of the kyng was on hem, and ordre was in syngeris bi alle daies;

24 and Aphataie, the sone of Mosezehel, of the sones of Zara, sone of Juda, in the hond of the kyng, bi ech word of the puple;

25 and in the housis bi alle the cuntreis of hem. Of the sones of Juda dwelliden in Cariatharbe, and in the vilagis therof, and in Dibon, and in the vilagis therof, and in Capseel, and in the townes therof;

26 and in Jesue, and in Molada, and in Bethpheleth,

27 and in Asersual, and in Bersabee, and in the vilagis therof;

28 and in Sicheleg, and in Mochone, and in the vilagis therof;

29 and in Remmon, and in Sara,

30 and in Jerymuth, Zonocha, Odollam, and in the townes 'of tho; in Lachis, and in the cuntreis therof; in Azecha and the vilagis therof; and thei dwelliden in Bersabee 'til to the valei of Ennon.

31 Forsothe the sones of Beniamyn dwelliden in Areba, Mechynas, and Aia, and Bethel and vilagis therof;

32 in Anatoth, Nob, Ananya,

33 Asor, Rama, Jethaym,

34 Adid, Soboym,

35 Nebollaloth, and in Onam, the valei of crafti men.

36 And of dekenes, 'the porciouns of Juda and of Beniamyn.

CAP 12

1 Sotheli these weren prestis and dekenes, that stieden with Zorobabel, the sone of Salatiel, and with Josue; Saraie, Jeremye,

2 Esdras, Amarie, Melluch, Accus,

3 Sechenye, Reum, Merymucth,

4 Addo, Jethon, Myomyn,

5 Abia, Meldaa, Belga, Semeie, and Joarib,

6 Adaie, Sellum, Amoe, Elceia, and Jadie;

7 these weren the princes of prestis 'and her britheren, in the daies of Josue.

8 Certis dekenes; Jesua, Bennuy, Cedynyel, Serabie, Juda, Mathanye, 'weren ouer the ympnes, 'thei and her britheren;

9 and Bezechie, and Ezanny, and the britheren of hem, ech man in his office.

10 Sotheli Josue gendride Joachym, and Joachym gendride Eliasib, and Eliasib gendride Joiada,

11 and Joiada gendride Jonathan, and Jonathan gendride Jeddaia.

12 Forsothe in the daies of Joachym weren prestis, and princis of meynees of prestis, Saraie, Amarie, Jeremye, Ananye, Esdre,

13 Mosollam, Amarie, Johannam,

14 Mylico, Jonathan, Sebenye,

15 Joseph, Aram, Edua,

16 Maraioth, Elchie, Addaie, Zacharie, Genthon,

17 Mosollam, Abie, Zecherie, Myamyn, and Moadie,

18 Phelti, Belge, Sannya, Semeie,

19 Jonathan, Joarib, Mathanye, Jodaie, Azi,

20 Sellaye, Mochebor, Helchie,

21 Asebie, Idaie, Nathanael.

22 Dekenes in the daies of Eliasib, and of Joiada, and of Jonam, and of Jedda, weren writun princes of meynees, 'and prestis in the rewme of Darius of Persis.

23 The sones of Leuy, princes of meynees, weren writun in the book of wordis of daies, and 'til to the daies of Jonathan, sone of Eliasib.

24 'And the princes of dekenes weren Asebie, Serebie, and Jesue, the sone of Cedynyel; and the britheren of hem bi her whiles, that thei schulden herie and knowleche bi the comaundement of kyng Dauid, the man of God, and thei schulden kepe euenli bi ordre.

25 Mathanye, and Bethbecie, and Obedie, Mosollam, Thelmon, Accub, weren keperis of the yatis, and of the porchis bifor the yatis.

26 These weren in the daies of Joachym, sone of Josue, sone of Josedech, and in the daies of Neemye, duyk, and of Esdras, the prest and writere.

27 Forsothe in the halewyng of the wal of Jerusalem thei souyten dekenes of alle her places, to bryng hem in to Jerusalem, and to make the halewyng in gladnesse, in the doyng of thankyngis, and in song, and in cymbalis, and in sautrees, and in harpis.

28 Sotheli the sones of syngeris weren gaderid bothe fro the feeldi places aboute Jerusalem, and fro the townes of Nethophati,

29 and fro the hows of Galgal, and fro the cuntreis of Gebez, and of Amanech; for syngeris hadden bildid townes to hem silf in the cumpas of Jerusalem.

30 And prestis and dekenes weren clensid, and thei clensiden the puple, and the yatis, and the wal.

31 Forsothe Y made the princes of Juda to stie on the wal, and Y ordeynede twei greete queris of men heriynge; and thei yeden to the riyt side on the wal, to the yate of the dunghil.

32 And Osaie yede aftir hem, and the half part of prynces of Juda,

33 and Azarie, Esdras, and Mosollam, Juda, and Beniamyn, and Semeye, and Jeremye 'yeden aftir hem.

34 And of the sones of prestis syngynge in trumpis; Zacharie, the sone of Jonathan, the sone of Semeie, the sone of Math-

anye, the sone of Machaie, the sone of Zeccur, the sone of Asaph.

35 And hise britheren; Semeie, and Azarel, Malalai, Galalai, Maai, Nathanael, and Juda, and Amany, in the instrumentis of song of Dauid, the man of God; and Esdras, the wrytere, bifor hem, in the yate of the welle.

36 And thei stieden ayens hem in the greis of the citee of Dauid, in the stiyng of the wal, on the hows of Dauid, and 'til to the yate of watris at the eest.

37 And the secounde queer of men tellynge thankyngis yede euene ayens, and Y aftir hym; and the half part of the puple was on the wal, and on the tour of ouenys, and 'til to the broddeste wal;

38 and on the yate of Effraym, and on the elde yate, and on the yate of fischis, and on the toure of Ananeel, and on the tour of Emath, and thei camen 'til to the yate of the floc;

39 and thei stoden in the yate of kepyng. And twei queeris of men heriynge stoden in the hows of God, and Y and the half part of magistratis with me.

40 And the prestis, Eliachym, Maasie, Myamyn, Mychea, Helioneai, Zacharie, Ananye, in trumpis;

41 and Maasie, and Senea, and Eleazar, and Azi, and Johannan, and Melchia, and Elam, and Ezer; and the syngeris sungen clereli, and Jezraie, the souereyn.

42 And thei offriden in that dai grete sacrifices, and weren glad; 'for God 'hadde maad hem glad with grete gladnesse. But also her wyues and lawful childre weren ioiful, and the gladnesse of Jerusalem is herd fer.

43 Also thei noumbriden in that dai men ouer the keping places of tresour, to moiste sacrifices, and to the firste fruytis, and to tithis, that the princes of the citee schulden brynge in bi hem, 'in the fairenesse of doyng of thankyngis, prestis and dekenes; for Juda was glad in prestis and dekenes present.

44 And thei kepten the kepyng of her God, the kepyng of clensyng; and syngeris, and porteris, bi the comaundement of Dauid and of Salomon, his sone;

45 for in the daies of Dauid and of Asaph fro the bigynnyng princes of syngeris weren ordeyned, heriyng in song, and knoulechynge to God.

46 And al Israel, in the daies of Zorobabel, and in the daies of Neemye, yauen partis to syngeris and to porteris bi alle 'the daies; and thei halewiden dekenes, and the dekenes halewiden the sones of Aaron.

CAP 13

1 Forsothe in that dai it was red in the book of Moises, in heryng of the puple; and it was foundun writun ther ynne, that Amonytis and Moabitis owen not entre in to the chirche of God til in to with outen ende;

2 for thei metten not the sones of Israel with breed and watir, and thei hiriden ayens the sones of Israel Balaam, for to curse hem; and oure God turnede the cursyng in to blessyng.

3 Sotheli it was doon, whanne 'thei hadden herd the lawe, thei departiden ech alien fro Israel.

4 And upon these thingis Eliasib, the prest, 'was blameful, that was the souereyn in the tresorie of the hows of oure God, and was the neiybore of Tobie.

5 Therfor he made to him a grete treserie, 'that is, in the hows of God; and men kepynge yiftis, and encence, and vessels, and the tithe of wheete, of wyn, and of oile, the partis of dekenes, and of syngeris, and of porteris, and the firste fruytis of prestis, 'weren there bifor him.

6 Forsothe in alle these thingis Y was not in Jerusalem; for in the two and thrittithe yeer of Artaxerses, kyng of Babiloyne, Y cam to the kyng, and in the ende of daies Y preiede the kyng.

7 And Y cam in to Jerusalem, and Y vndurstood the yuel, which Eliasib hadde do to Tobie, to make to hym a tresour in the porchis of Goddis hows; and to me it semede ful yuel.

8 And Y castide forth the vessels of the hows of Tobie out of the tresorie;

9 and Y comaundide, and thei clensiden the tresories; and Y brouyte ayen there the vessels of Goddis hous, sacrifice, and encence.

10 And Y knew that the partes of dekenes weren not youun, and that ech man of the dekenes and of the syngeris, and of hem that mynystriden hadde fledde in to his cuntrei;

11 and Y dide the cause ayens magistratis, and Y seide, Whi 'forsaken we the hous of God? And Y gaderide hem togidere, 'that is, dekenes and mynystris 'that hadden go awei, and Y made hem to stonde in her stondyngis.

12 And al Juda brouyte the tithe of wheete, of wiyn, and of oile, in to bernes.

13 And we ordeyneden on the bernes, Selemye, the prest, and Sadoch, the writere, and Phadaie, of the dekenes, and bisidis hem, Anan, the sone of Zaccur, the sone of Mathanye; for thei weren preued feithful men, and the partis of her britheren weren bitakun to hem.

14 My God, haue mynde of me for this thing, and do thou not awei my merciful doyngis, whiche Y dide in the hows of my God, and in hise cerymonyes.

15 Yn tho daies Y siy in Juda men tredinge pressours in the sabat, 'men bryngynge hepis, and chargynge on assis wiyn, and grapis, and figis, and al birthun, and 'bringynge in to Jerusalem in the dai of sabat; and Y witnesside to hem, that thei schulden sille in the dai, in which it was leueful to sille.

16 And men of Tire dwelliden 'in it, and brouyten in fischis, and alle thingis set to sale, and thei selden 'in the sabatis to the sones of Juda and of Jerusalem.

17 And Y rebuykide the principal men of Juda, and Y seide to hem, What is this yuel thing which ye doen, and maken vnhooli the daie of the sabat?

18 Whether oure fadris diden not these thingis, and oure God brouyte on vs al this yuel, and on this citee? and 'ye encreessen wrathfulnesse on Israel, in defoulynge the sabat.

19 Forsothe it was doon, whanne the yatis of Jerusalem hadden restid in the dai of sabat, Y seide, Schitte ye the yatis; and thei schittiden the yatis; and I comaundide, that thei schuden not opene tho yatis til aftir the sabat. And of my children Y ordeynede noumbris on the yatis, that no man schulde brynge in a birthun in the dai of sabat.

20 And marchauntis, and men sillinge alle thingis set to sale dwelliden with out Jerusalem onys and twies.

21 And Y aresonyde hem, and Y seide to hem, Whi dwellen ye euene ayens the wal? If ye doon this the secounde tyme, Y schal sette hond on you. Therfor fro that tyme thei camen not in the sabat.

22 Also Y seide to dekenes, that thei schulden be clensid, and that thei schulden come to kepe the yatis, and to halowe the dai of sabat. And therfor for this thing, my God, haue mynde of me, and spare me bi the mychilnesse of thi merciful doyngis.

23 But also in tho daies Y siy Jewys weddinge wyues, wymmen of Azotus, and wymmen of Amonytis, and wymmen of Moabitis.

24 And her children spaken half part bi the speche of Ayotus, and kouden not speke bi the speche of Jewis, and thei spaken bi the langage of puple and of puple.

25 And Y rebuykide hem, and Y curside; and Y beet the men 'of hem, and Y made hem ballid, and Y made hem to swere bi the Lord, that thei schulden not yyue her douytris to the sones of 'tho aliens, and that thei schulden not take of the douytris of 'tho aliens to her sones, and to hem silf;

26 and Y seide, Whether Salomon, the kyng of Israel, synnede not in siche a thing? And certis in many folkis was no kyng lijk hym, and he was loued of his God, and God set-tide hym kyng on al Israel, and therfor alien wymmen brouyten hym to synne.

27 Whether also we vnobedient schulden do al this grete yuel, that we trespasse ayens 'oure Lord God, and wedde alien wyues?

28 Forsothe Sanabalath Horonyte hadde weddid a douyter of the sones of Joiada, sone of Eliasib, the grete prest, which Sanaballath Y droof awei fro me.

29 My Lord God, haue mynde ayens hem, that defoulen presthod, and the riyt of prestis and of dekenes. Therfor I clenside hem fro alle aliens, and I ordeynede ordris of prestis and of dekenes,

30 ech man in his seruice, and in the offring,

31 that is, dressing, of trees in tymes ordeyned, and in the firste fruytis. My God, haue mynde of me in to good.

3 ESDRAS

CAP 1

1 And Josias made pask in Jerusalem to the Lord, and he offride pask the fourtenthe day of the monthe of the first monthe,

2 ordeynynge prestis bi her whiles of daies, clothid in stolis, or longe clothis, in the temple of the Lord.

3 And he seide to the dekens, the holy seruauntis of Israel, that thei schulden halewe hem self to the Lord, in settynge of the holy arke of the Lord in the hous, that kyng Salomon, the sone of Dauid, bildide;

4 It schal not be to you no more to take it upon schuldris; and now serueth to oure Lord, and do ye cure of that folk of Israel, of the part aftir townes,

5 and her lynagis, aftir the writyng of Dauid, kyng of Israel, and aftir the greet wirschipful doyng of Salomon, his sone, in al the temple, and aftir youre litil fadris part of princehood of hem, that stonden in the siyt of the bretheren of the sones of Israel.

6 Offre ye pask, and maketh redy the sacrifices to youre bretheren; and do ye aftir the heest of the Lord, that is youen to Moyses.

7 And Josias yaf to the folc that was founden there, scheep, of lombis, and of kides, and of sche geet, thritti thousynd; cal-ues, thre thousynd.

8 Thes yiftis ben youen of the kingis owne thingis aftir the heest of the Lord to the peple, and to prestis, in to pask; scheep in noumbre two thousynd, and calues an hundrid.

9 And Jechonyas, and Semeias, and Nathanael, his brother, and Azabias, and Oziel, and Coroba, yauen in to pask, fyue thousynd scheep, and fyue hundrid calues.

10 And whanne thes thingis weren nobly don, the prestis and dekens stoden, hauynge therf looues bi lynages.

11 And aftir the partis of the princehood of fadris thei offriden to the Lord in the siyt of the peple, after tho thingis that ben writen in the book of Moyses.

12 And thei rostiden the pask with fijr, as it bihouyde; and thei soden oostis in sethinge vessels and in pottis, with wel willyng.

13 And thei brouyten it to alle that ther weren of the folk; and aftir thes thingis thei maden redy to hem self and to prestis.

14 Forsothe the prestis offriden ynner fatnesse, vnto the hour was endid; and dekens greythiden to hem self, and to her bretheren, and to the sones of Aaron.

15 And men sacrifiynge offriden her douytris, aftir the oordre and the heestis of Dauid; and Azaph, and Zacharie, and Jed-dynus, that was of the king;

16 and the porters bi alle the yatis offriden, so that noon pas-side his yate. Forsothe her bretheren greythiden to hem.

17 And so tho thingis, that perteynyden to the sacrifice of the Lord, ben endid.

18 In that day thei diden pask, and offriden ostis upon the sac-rifice of the Lord, aftir the heest of kyng Josie.

19 And the sones of Israel, that weren founden present, diden in that tyme pask, and the feest day of therf looues bi seuen daies.

20 And ther was not solempnyzed sich a paske in Israel, fro the tymes of Samuel, the prophet.

21 And alle the kyngis of Israel halewiden not sich a pask, as diden Josias, and the prestis, and dekens, and Jewis, and al Israel, that weren founden in the commemoracioun, or mynde making, at Jerusalem.

22 In the eiytenthe yer, Josie regnynge, this pask was hale-wid.

23 And the werkis of Josie ben maad riyt in the siyt of his Lord, in ful dredynge herte;

24 and tho thingis forsothe that weren aboute him ben writen, in the rathere tymes of hem that synnyden, and the whiche weren vnreligious ayen the Lord, bifore or more than al hethen folk, and the whiche synners souyten not the wordis of the Lord upon Israel.

25 And aftir al this deede of Josie, Pharao, king of Egipt, yede up, comynge to casten awey in Carcamys upon Eufraten; and Josias wente in to metyng to him.

26 And the king of Egipt sente to Josiam, seiynge, What is to me and to thee, kyng of Jude?

27 I am not sent of the Lord, upon Eufraten forsothe is my bataile; hastily therfor go doun.

28 And Josias was not turned ayen upon the chare, but he enforside him self to ouercome Pharao, not takinge hede to the word of the prophet, fro the mouth of the Lord;

29 but he sette to him bataile in the feeld of Mecedan; and princis camen doun to kyng Josiam.

30 And thanne the king seide to his children, or seruauntes, Moueth me awey fro the bataile; forsothe I am gretly maad sijk. And anoon his children moueden him awey fro the scheltrun.

31 And he stiede upon his secoundarie chare; and comynge to Jerusalem, he diede, and was biried in his fadris sepulcre.

32 And in al Jude thei biweiliden Josie, and thei that bifore seten with wyues, weiliden him vnto this day; and this is grauntid to be don euer more in al the kynrede of Israel.

33 Thes thingis forsothe ben writen in the book of stories of kyngis of Juda, and the glorie of Josie, and his vndirstonding in the lawe of God, bi alle dedes of the doyng of him; for

euenly tho weren don of hym, and the whiche ben not writun in the book of kingis of Israel and of Juda.

34 And thei that weren of the kynrede token Jeconye, the sone of Josie, and setten him king for Josie, his fadir, whanne he was of thre and thritty yeer.

35 And he regnyde upon Israel thre monthis; and thanne the kyng of Egipt putte him awey, that he regnyde not in Jerusalem.

36 And he pilide the folk of an hundrid talentis of siluer, and of a talent of gold.

37 And the kyng of Egipt sette Joachim, his brother, kyng of Jude and of Jerusalem; and he bonde the maistir iuges of Joachim, and takynge Saracel, his brother, he brouyte him ayen to Egipt.

39 Joachim was of fyue and twenty yeer, whanne he regnyde in the loond of Juda and of Jerusalem; and he dide yuel thing in the siyt of the Lord.

40 Aftir this forsothe Nabugodonosor, kyng of Babiloyne, stiede up, and byndynge Joachim in a strong boond, brouyte him in to Babiloyne;

41 and Nabugodonosor toke and brouyte the holy vessels of God, and sacride tho in his temple in Babiloyne.

42 Forsothe of his vnclennesse and his vnreligioustee it is writen in the book of the tymes of kyngis.

43 And Joachim, his sone, regnyde for him; whanne forsothe he was ordeyned king, he was of eiyte yeer.

44 Forsothe he regnyde thre monthis and ten daies in Jerusalem; and dide yuel in siyt of the Lord.

45 And aftir a yer Nabugodonosor sente, and brouyte him ouer in to Babiloyne, togidre with the sacrid vessels of the Lord.

46 And he sette Sedechie kyng of Juda and of Jerusalem, whanne he was of oon and twenti yeer.

47 Forsothe he regnyde elleuen yeer; and he dide yuel in siyt of the Lord, and was not adred of the wordis that ben seid of Jeremye, the prophet, fro the mouth of the Lord.

48 And he adiurid, or chargid bi ooth, of kyng Nabugodonosor, forsworn wente awey, and his noll made hard, he ouerpasside the laweful thingis of the Lord God of Israel.

49 And the duykis of the Lordis peple baren hem wickidly many thingis, and thei diden vnpitously ouer alle the wickidnessis of Gentiles; and thei defouliden the temple of the Lord, that was hooly in Jerusalem.

50 And God of her fadris sente bi his aungel to ayenclepe hem, for the whiche thing he sparide to hem, and to her tabernaclis.

51 Thei forsothe scornyden in her corners, and that dai that the Lord spake, thei weren bobbynge his prophetis.

52 The whiche Lord is stirid to wraththe upon his folk, for their irreligiositee. And the kyngis of Caldeis comaundiden, and stiyeden up,

53 thei slowen the younge men of hem with swerd, aboute the hooly temple of hem; and thei spariden not to yonge man, ne to maiden, ne to old man, and to ful woxen man;

54 but also alle thei ben taken in to the hondis of hem; and thei token alle the sacrid vessels of the Lord, and the kyngis coffres, and brouyten tho in to Babiloyne.

55 And thei brenden up the hous of the Lord, and destroieden the wallis of Jerusalem, and thei brenden his touris with fijr.

56 And thei wastiden alle the wurschipful thingis, and brouyten hem to nouyt; and thei brouyten the peple lefte of the swerd in to Babiloyne.

57 And thei weren his thrallis, vn to the tyme that Peersis regnyden, in the fulfillynge of the word of the Lord, in the mouth of Jeremye;

58 til that the loond wolde do benyngnely their sabotis, he sabatisede al the tyme of their forsakyng, in the appliynge of seuenti yer.

CAP 2

1 Regnynge Cyro, kyng of Peersis, in the fulfillyng of the word of the Lord, in the mouth of Jeremye,

2 the Lord reiside up the spirit of Ciry, kyng of Persis; and he prechide in al his rewme togidre bi scripture, seiynge,

3 Thes thingis seith Cirus, kyng of Persis, The Lord of Israel, the hiye Lord, hath ordeyned me kyng to the world of erthis;

4 and he signyfiede to me to bilde to him an hous in Jerusalem, that is in Juda.

5 If ther is ony man of youre kynrede, his Lord stie up with him in to Jerusalem.

6 Therfor hou many euer dwellen in places aboute, helpe thei hem that dwellen in that place, in gold and siluer,

7 in yiftis, with hors, and bestis, and with othere thingis, the whiche aftir vowes ben leid up in to the hous of the Lord, that is in Jerusalem.

8 And the stondynge princis of lynages of townes of Jude, of the lynage of Beniamyn, and prestis and dekens, whom the Lord stiride to wende up, and to bilde up the hous of the Lord, that is in Jerusalem; and thei, that weren in the enuyroun, or in cumpas, of hem, schulden helpe in al siluer and gold of it,

9 and in bestis, and in many vowis; and many othere, of whom the witt is stirid, helpe thei also.

10 And kyng Cirus brouyte forth the sacrid vessels of the Lord, the whiche Nabugodonosor translatide fro Jerusalem, and sacride hem in his mawmett.

11 And Cirus, king of Persis, bryngynge hem forth, toke tho to Mitridate, that was upon the tresours of him.

12 Forsothe bi him thei ben taken to Salmanasar, gouernour of Jude.

13 Of thes thinges forsothe this is the noumbre; silueren halewid vessels of licours, two thousynd and foure hundrid; thritti silueren drinkynge vessels; thritty goldene violes; and two thousynd and foure hundrid silueren violes; and a thousynd othere vessels.

14 Forsothe alle the golden and silueren vessels weren foure thousynd and foure hundrid and eiyt and sixty.

15 And thei ben delyuered out to Salmanasar, togidere with hem, that weren comen in to Jerusalem of the caytiftee or thraldom of Babiloyne.

16 Forsothe in the tyme of Artaxerses, kyng of Persis, ther wreten to him, of thes that dwelliden in Judee and in Jerusalem, Balsamus, and Mitridatus, and Sabelius, and Ratymus, Baltheneus, and Samelius, the scribe, and othere dwellinge in Samarie, and in othere placis, thei writen this subiect lettre to the kyng Artaxersy.

17 Lord, thi children, Ratymus, and Sabelius, the scribe, and othere domes men of thi court, of thingis that fallen in Coelem Siriem, and Fenycen.

18 And now be it knowen to the lord the kyng, that Jewis, the whiche stieden up fro you to us, comynge in to Jerusalem, a citee of fleers awei, and a ful yuel citee, thei bilden up the ouenes of it, and thei setten the wallis, and reren the temple.

19 That if this citee and wallis weren maad up, thei shul not suffre to yelde tributis, but also thei shul ayenstonde to kyngis.

20 And for cause that that thing is done aboute the temple, to haue it riytly we haue demed to not despise that same thing,
21 but to make knowen to the lord kyng, that if it schal be seen plesyng to the king, be it souyt in the bookis of thi fadris;
22 and thou schalt fynde in remembrauncis writen of hem, and thou schalt knowe, that thilke citee was ayen flowun, and kyngis and citees smytinge togidre,
23 and Jewis fleynge ayen, and makinge bateilis in it alwey; for the whiche cause this citee was forsake.
24 Now therfor we maken knowen to the lord king, that if this citee were bild up, and the wallis of it weren arerid, ther schal be no comyng doun to thee in to Choelem Cyriem and Fenycen.
25 Thanne the kyng wroot ayen to Ratimym, that wroot tho thingis that bifellen, and to Bellumym, and to Sabellio, the scribe, and to othere ordeyned souereyns, and dwellinge in Cirye and in Fenyce, he wrot to hem thes thingis that ben sett vndir.
26 I haue rad the lettre, that thou sentist to me. Therfor I comaundide it to be souyt; and it was founden, that thilke citee was alwey withstondynge to kyngis,
27 and men ayen fugitijf, and makynge bateilis in it; and moost stronge kingis han ben lordschipinge in Jerusalem, and askinge tributis of Chole Cirie and Fenycem.
28 Now therfore I comaunde to forfende tho men to bilde up the citee, and to loke, that ony thing be not maad her aftir;
29 but that thei passe not in to ful myche, sith thei ben of malice, so that greuauncis be not brouyt ther to kinges.

CAP 3

30 Thanne aftir thes thingis weren rehersid, that weren writen of Artaxerses, the kyng, Rathinus, and Sabellius, the scribe, and thei that weren with hem ordeyned, ioynynge, hyingly camen in to Jerusalem, with horse men, and peple, and with cumpanye;
31 and thei bigunnen to forfende the buylders. And thei voididen thanne fro the bildyng of the temple, vnto the secounde yeer of the rewme of Darij, kyng of Persis.
1 Kyng Darius made a gret soper to alle his seruauntis, and to alle the maister iuges of Medes and of Persis,
2 and to alle that wereden purpre, and to gouernours, and to counselers, and to prefectis vndir him, fro Ynde vn to Ethiope, to an hundrid and seuen and twenty prouyncis.
3 And whanne thei hadden eten and drunken, and weren fulfillid, thei turneden ayen. Thanne kyng Darius stiede vp in his litil bed place, and slepte, and was waken.
4 Thanne thilke thre younge men, kepers of the bodi, the whiche kepten the bodi of the kyng, seiden oon to an oother,
5 Sey we ech of us a word, that bifore passe in kunnyng; and whos euer word seme wiser than of an oother, kyng Darius schal yiue to him grete yiftis,
6 and to be kouered with purpre, and to drynke in gold, and to slepe upon gold; and he schal yiue him a golden chare, with the bridil, and a mytre of bijs, and a bie aboute the necke;
7 and he schal sitte in the secounde place fro Darius, for his wisdom; and he schal be clepid Daryus cosyn.
8 Thanne ech of hem thre writinge his word, seleden, and putten tho vndir the pelewe of kyng Daryus;
9 and seiden, Whanne the king hath risen, thei wil take to him her thingis writen, and what euer thing the kyng shall deme of thre, and the maistir iuges of Persis, forsothe the word of him is wiser than of the othere, to him schal be youen the victorie, as it is writen.

10 Oon wrot, Wyn is strong.
11 An oother wrot, The kyng is strenger.
12 The thridde wrot, Wymmen ben strengiste; treuthe ouercomith forsothe ouer alle thingis.
13 And whanne the kyng had resen up, thei token her thingis writen, and youen tho to him, and he radde.
14 And he sende and clepede alle the maistre iuges of Persis, and of the lond Medis, and the clothid men in purpre, and the rewlers of prouynces, and prefectis;
15 and thei seten in counsel, and the writingis weren red bifore hem.
16 And the kyng seide, Clepeth the younge men, and thei schul schewe her wordis. And thei weren clepid, and thei camen yn.
17 And Darius seide to hem, Schewe ye to us of thes thingis that ben writen. And the firste, that had seid of the strengthe of wyn, he biganne, and seide to hem, Men!
18 ful passynge strong is wyn; to alle men that drynken it it berith doun the mynde; also it makith the mynde veyn,
19 bothe of kyng and of the fadirles child; also of seruaunt and of fre men, of pore and of riche; and it turnith al the mynde in to sikirnesse,
20 and to gladnesse; and it remembrith not ony serewe and dette;
21 and it makith alle the entrailes honest; and it remembrith not kyng, ne maistir iuge; and alle thingis it makith speke bi talent;
22 and whanne thei han drunken, thei remembren not frendschip ne brotherhed, and not longe aftir thei taken swerdis;
23 and whanne thei han be drowned of wyn, and rijsen, thei han no mynde what thinges thei diden.
24 O men! whether wyn is not passyngly strong, that thus constreynith men to do? And this thing seid, he hilde his pes.

CAP 4

1 And the nexte folewer biganne to sey, that seide of the strengthe of a kyng,
2 O men! whether men ben not passyngly stronge, the whiche holden loond and see, and alle thingis that ben in hem?
3 The kyng forsothe passith aboue alle thingis, and he hath lordschip of hem, and thei don al thing, what euer he wil sey to hem.
4 And if he sende hem to fiyters, thei gon, and destroyen hillis, and walles, and toures; thei ben sleyn,
5 and slen, and thei passen not the word of the kyng; for if thei ouercomen, thei bryngen to the king alle thingis, what euer thingis thei han spoiled euermore, and all othere thingis.
6 And hou fele euer beren not knyythod, ne fiyten, but eren the loond, eftsone whanne thei schul repe, thei bringen tributis to the king.
7 And he is oon aloone; and if he bidde to sle, thei sleen; and if he bidde hem to foryiue, thei foryiuen;
8 and if he sey hem to smyten, thei smyten; if he sey to outlawe, thei outlawen; if he bidde hem to bilden, thei bilden;
9 if he bidde to throwe doun, thei throwen adoun; if he bidde to plaunte, thei plaunten;
10 and alle folk and vertues obeishen to him; and ouer alle thes thingis he schal sitte, and drynke, and slepe.
11 Thes forsothe kepen him aboute, and moun not gon echoon, and do her owne werkis, but in his word men obeishen to him.
12 What maner wise passith not the kyng bifore oothere, that thus is loosid?

13 And he helde his pes. The thridde, that had seid of wymmen, and of treuthe; this is seid Sorobabel; he biganne to speke, O men!

14 the kyng is not greet, neither many othere men, ne wyn passith biforn; who is it thanne that hath lordschip of hem?

15 Whether not wymmen, that han goten kyngis, and al the peple, the whiche kingis han lordschip bothe of see and of loond, and of wymmen thei ben born?

16 And thei brouyten forth hem that plauntiden vynes, of the whiche wyn is maad.

17 And thei maken the stoles, or longe clothis, of alle men, and thei don glorie to men, and men moun not be seuered fro wymmen.

18 If thei gedere togidere gold and siluer, and al fair thing, and seen a womman in good aray, and in good fairnesse,

19 thei, forsakynge alle thes thingis, taken heede to here, and the mouth opened, thei biholden hir, and thei drawen more to hir than to gold and siluer, or ony precious thing.

20 A man schal forsake his fadir, that norishide him, and his owne loond, and to a womman he ioynith him togidre,

21 and with a womman he lyuith his lijf, and noither remembrith fadir, ne modir, ne the lond of his birthe.

22 And therfor it bihouith us to knowen, that wymmen han lordschip of us. Whether ye serewen not?

23 And also a man takith his swerd, and goth in the wey to don theftis, and man slauytris, and to seilen ouer the see, and ouer flodes;

24 and he seeth a lioun, and he goth in derkenessis; and whanne he hath don his thefte, and gijles, and raueynes, he bringith it to his leef.

25 And efte a man louith his wijf more than fadir or modir;

26 and many men ben maad woode for their wyues, and many ben maad thrallis for hem;

27 and many perischiden, and weren stranglid, and many han synned for wymmen.

28 And now leeueth me; forsothe a kyng is greet, and his power, for alle regiouns, or kingdoms aboute, ben aferd to touche him.

29 I sawye neuer the latter Apeemen, the douyter of Besacis, the wondirful man, the secoundarie wijf of the kyng, sittynge biside the kyng at the riyt side;

30 and takynge awey the diademe fro his heed, and puttynge it on hir self, and with the pawme of hir lift hoond she smote the kyng.

31 And ouer thes thingis, the mouth opened, he bihilde hir, and if sche lowye to him, he lowye, and if sche were wrooth to him, he glosith or plesith, vnto the tyme that he be recounsilid to grace.

32 O men! whi ben not wymmen strengist? Greet is the erthe, and heuen is hiy, that don thes thingis.

33 Thanne the kyng and the purpred men bihelden either in to oothere; and he biganne to speke of treuthe.

34 O men! wher wymmen ben not stronge? Greet is the eerthe, and heuen is hiy, and the cours of the sunne is swift; it is turned in the cumpas of heuen, and eft it renneth ayen in to the same place in a day.

35 Wher he is not a greet doer, that makith thes thingis? and treuthe greet, and strenger biforn alle thingis?

36 All erthe clepith inwardly trouthe, also it blessith heuene, and alle werkis ben moued and dreden it; and ther is no wickid thing with it.

37 Wickid kyng, and wickid wymmen, and alle the sones of men ben wickid, and ther is not treuthe in hem, and in her wickidnesse thei schul perische;

38 and treuthe dwellith, and wexith in to withouten ende, and it lyuith, and weldith, into worldus of worldis.

39 It is not anentis treuthe to outtake persoones, and differencis; but it doth tho thingis that ben riytful, to alle vnriytwise and yuel men; and alle men ben maad benyngne in his werkis.

40 And ther is not wickidnesse in his doom, but ther is strengthe, and rewme, and power, and magestee of alle duryngis aboue tyme.

41 Blessid be the God of treuthe! And thanne he lefte in spekynge. And alle the peplis crieden, and seiden, Greet is treuthe, and it passith bifore alle othere.

42 Thanne the kyng seide to him, Aske, if thou wilt, ony thing more ouer, than ther ben writen, and I schal yiue to thee, aftir that thou art founden wiser; and next to me thou schalt sitte, and thou schalt be clepid my cosyn.

43 Thanne seide he to the king, Be thou myndeful of the vowy, that thou vowidist, to bilden up Jerusalem, in the day in whiche thou toke the rewme; and to senden ayen alle the vessels,

44 that ben taken fro Jerusalem, the whiche Cyrus departide, whanne he slouy Babiloyne, and wolde sende ayen thoo thingis thidere.

45 And thou woldist bilde up the temple, that Ydumes brenden, for Judee is put out of her termes, or marchis, of the Caldeis.

46 And now, lord, this it is that I aske, and that I bidde; this is the mageste that I aske of thee, that thou do the vow that thou vowidist to the kyng of heuen, of thi mouth.

47 Thanne Darius, the kyng, risynge kisside him, and wroot epistlis to alle the dispensatours, and prefectis, and to men clothid in purpre, that thei schulden lede him forth, and hem that weren with him, alle wendynge up to bilde Jerusalem.

48 And to alle the prefectis that weren in Sirie, and Fenyce, and Liban, he wroot epistles, that thei schulden drawe cedre trees fro the hill Liban in to Jerusalem, that thei bilde up the citee with hem.

49 And he wroot to alle the Jewis, that steyden up fro the rewme in Judee, for fredam, that ony man of power, or maistir iuge, and prefect, schulden not come ouer to the yatis of hem,

50 and eche regioun, that thei hadden holde, to be fre fro hem; and that Ydumeis leue up the castels of Jewis, that thei withholden,

51 and to yiue yer bi yer twenty talentis, in to making of the temple, vnto the tyme that it be ful bildid;

52 and ech day to offre ostis upon the place of sacrid thingis, as thei ben comaundid; to offre, bi alle yeris, othere ten talentis; and to alle men,

53 that gon forth fro Babiloyne, to make the citee, as fredom were, bothe to hem, and to the sones of hem, and to the prestis that gon bifore.

54 Forsothe also he wroot the quantitee; and he comaundide the sacrid stole, or vestyment, to be youen, in whiche thei schulden serue;

55 and he wroot wagis to be youen to the dekens, vnto the day that the hous schulde be fully endid, and Jerusalem maad out; and he wrot to alle men kepinge the citee,

56 to yiue to the bilders lottis and wagis.

57 And he lefte hem alle the vessels, that Cirus had partid fro Babiloyn; and alle thingis, what euer Cyrus seide, he comaundide it to be don, and to be sent to Jerusalem.

58 And whanne that younge man had gon forth, reisynge his face toward Jerusalem, he blesside the kyng of heuen, and seide,

59 Of thee, Lord, is victorie, and of thee is wisdom, and clernesse, and I am thi seruaunt.

60 Thou art blessid, for thou hast youen to me wisdom, and I knowleche to thee, Lord of oure fadris.

61 And he toke the epistlis, or lettres, and wente forth in to Babiloyne; and he came, and tolde to alle his bretheren, that weren in Babyloyne.

62 And thei blessiden the God of her fadris, that yaf to hem foryiuenesse and refreschyng,

63 that thei schulden stye up, and bilde Jerusalem, and the temple, where his name is nemned in it; and thei ioyeden with musikis and with gladnesse seuen daies.

CAP 5

1 Aftir thes thingis forsothe ther weren pryncis chosen of townus, that thei schulden wende up, bi housis, bi her lynagis, and the wyues of hem, and the sonus and douytris of hem, and seruauntis and hand maydens of hem, and her bestis.

2 And kyng Darye sende togidre with hem a thousynd hors men, to the tyme that thei brouyte hem in to Jerusalem, with pees, and with musikis, and tymbres, and trumpis; and alle the britheren weren pleiynge.

3 And he made hem to stie up togidre with hem.

4 And thes ben the names of the men, that yeden up, bi her tounnes, in to lynagis, and in to part of the princehod of hem.

5 Prestis; the sones of Fynees, the sones of Aaron, Jesus, the sone of Josedech, Joachim, the sone of Sorobabel, sone of Salathiel, of the hous of Dauid, of the progenye of Phares, of the lynage forsothe of Juda,

6 that spac vndir Darij, king of Persis, merueylous doynge wordis, in the secounde yeer of his rewme, in Aprel, the firste monthe.

7 Forsothe thes it ben, that stieden up of Juda fro the caitiftee, or thraldom, of the transmygracioun, whom Nabugodonosor, kyng of Babiloyne, translatide in to Babiloyne; and ech is turned ayen in to Jerusalem,

8 and in to alle the citees of Judee, ech in to his owne citee, that camen with Sorobabel, and with Jesu; Neemyas, Ariores, and Elymeo, Emmanyo, Mardocheo, Beelsuro, Methsatothor, Olioro, Eboma, oon of the princis of hem.

9 And the noumbre fro the Gentiles of hem, fro the prouostis, or reeuys, of hem; the sones of Phares, two thousynd an hundrid seuenty and two;

10 the sones of Ares, thre thousynd and fifty and seuen;

11 the sones of Phemo, an hundrid and two and fourty; the sones of Jesu and of Joabes, a thousynd thre hundrid and two;

12 the sones of Denny, two thousynd foure hundrid and seuenty; the sones of Choroba, two hundrid and fyue; the sones of Banycha, an hundrid and sixty and eiyte;

13 the sones of Bebeth, foure hundrid and thre; the sones of Arcad, foure hundrid and seuen and twenty;

14 the sones of Thau, seuen and thritty; the sonis of Zozaar, two thousynd sixty and seuen; the sones of Adymy, foure hundrid and oon and sixty;

15 the sones of Azeroectis, an hundrid and eiyte; the sonus of Ziazo and Zelas, an hundrid and seuene; the sones of Azoroch, foure hundrid and nyne and thritty;

16 the sones of Jebdarbone, an hundrid and two and thritty; the sones of Ananye, an hundrid and thritty;

17 the sones of Arsom; the sones of Marsar, foure hundrid and two and twenty; the sones of Saberus, nynty and fyue; the sones of Sophelemon, an hundrid and thre and twenty;

18 the sones of Nepobai, fyue and fifty; the sones of Ecbanatus, an hundrid and eiyt and fifty; the sones of Ebethamus, an hundrid and two and thritty;

19 the sones of Octatarpatros, the whiche weren clepid Enochadies and Modie, foure hundrid and two and twenti; thei that weren of Gramas and Gabia, an hundrid and oon and twenti; the whiche weren of Besellon and of Agie,

20 fyue and sixty; thei that weren of Bascharo, an hundrid and two and twenty; the whiche of Bethonobes, fyue and fifty;

21 the sones of Lippis, an hundrid and fyue and fifty; the sones of Jabomy, thre hundrid and seuen and fifty;

22 the sones of Sichem, thre hundrid and seuenty; the sones of Sanadon and of Chamus, thre hundrid and seuenty and eiyte;

23 the sones of Ericus, two thousynd an hundrid and fyue and fifty; the sones of Anaas, thre hundrid and seuenty.

24 Prestis; the sones of Jeddus, the sones of Enytem, the sones of Eliazib, thre hundrid and two and seuenty; the sones of Emmechus, two hundrid and two and fifty;

25 the sones of Sasurij, thre hundrid and seuen and fifty; the sones of Charee, two hundrid and seuen and twenty.

26 Dekens; the sonus of Jesu, in Caduel, and Banus, and Serebias, and Edias, foure and seuenty; al the noumbre fro the two and twenty yeer, thritti thousynd foure hundrid and two and sixty; sones,

27 and douytris, and wyues, al the noumbryng, sixty thousynd two hundrid and two and fourty.

28 The sones of prestis, that sungen in the temple; the sones of Asaph, an hundrid and eiyt and twenty.

29 Vschers forsothe; the sones of Esueum, the sones of Ather, the sones of Amon, the sones of Accuba Copa, the sones of Thoby, alle an hundrid and nyne and thritty.

30 Prestis, seruynge in the temple; sones of Sel, the sones of Gasipa, the sones of Tabloth, the sones of Carie, the sones of Su, the sones of Phellu, the sones of Labana, the sones of Acmathi, the sones of Accub, the sones of Vta, the sones of Cetha, the sones of Agab, the sones of Obay, the sones of Anan, the sones of Chayma, the sones of Jeddu,

31 the sones of An, the sones of Radyn, the sones of Desamyn, the sones of Nechoba, the sones of Caseba, the sones of Gase, the sones of Osyn, the sones of Phynoe, the sones of Atren, the sones of Bascem, the sones of Aziana, the sones of Manay, the sones of Naphisym, the sones of Accuphu, the sones of Agista, the sonus of Aria Phausym, the sones of Phasaluon, the sones of Meeda,

32 the sones of Phusia, the sones of Careth, the sones of Barthus, the sones of Caree, the sones of Thoesy, the sones of Nasith, the sones of Agisty, the sones of Pedon.

33 Salmon, the sones of hym, the sones of Asophoth, the sones of Pharida, the sones of Thely, the sones of Dedon, the sones of Gaddahel, the sones of Cephegy,

34 the sones of Aggya, the sones of Phacareth, the sones of Sabathan, the sones of Saroneth, the sones of Malcie, the sones of Ame, the sones of Saphuy, the sones of Addus, the sones of Suba, the sones of Eirra, the sones of Rabatis, the sones of Phasophat, the sonus of Malmon.

35 Alle thes weren in holy seruyng; and the children of Salmon weren foure hundrid foure score and two.

36 These ben the sones that yeden up to Athemel and Thersas; the princis of hem weren Carmellam and Careth; and thei myyten not telle out her citees,

37 and her progenyes, what manere thei ben; and of Israel, the sones of Dalarij, the sones of Tubam, the sones of Nechodaicy.

38 And of the prestis, that vsiden presthod, and weren founden; the sones of Obia, the sones of Achisos, the sones of Addyn, that token Vmyn wijf, of the douytris of Phargelen,

39 and thei ben clepid bi the name of hir; and of thes is souyt the genologie writen of the kynrede, and thei ben forfendid to vsen presthode.

40 And Neemye seide to hem, and Astaras, that thei take not part of the hooly thingis, til the tyme that ther arijse a tauyt bischop, in to schewyng and treuthe.

41 Al Israel forsothe was twelff thousynd, out take seruauntis and hand maidens, two and fourty thousynd thre hundrid and sixti.

42 The seruauntis of hand maidens weren seuen thousynd thre hundrid and seuen and thritty; syngers and singsters, two hundrid and fyue and sixty;

43 cameils, foure hundrid and fyue and thritty; horsis, seuen thousind sixe and thritti; mules, two hundrid thousynd and fyue and fourty; bestis vndir yok, fyue thousynd and fyue and twenty.

44 And of tho prouostis, or reeues, bi tounnes, while thei schulden come in to the temple of God, that was in Jerusalem, to ben avowid to rere up the temple in his place, aftir her vertue;

45 and the hooly tresorie to be youen in to the temple of werkis, weren elleuen thousynd besauntis, and an hundrid prestis stolis.

46 And ther dwelliden prestis, and dekens, and othere, that weren of the peple, in Jerusalem, and in the rewme; and the hooly syngers, and vsshers, and al Israel, in her regiouns.

47 While the seuenthe monthe yitt lastide, and whanne the sonus of Israel weren ech in his owne thingis, thei camen togidre of oon accord in to the porche, that was bifore the eest yate.

48 And while Jesus, the sone of Josedech, and his bretheren, prestis, stoden, and Sorobabel, the sone of Salatiel, and his bretheren, thei maden redy an auter, that thei wolden offre on it brent sacrifices,

49 aftir tho thingis that ben writen in the book of Moyses, the man of God.

50 And ther camen to hem of othere naciouns of the loond, and reriden the holy tresorie in his place, alle the folk of the lond; and thei offriden oostis, and brent sacrifises of the morutijd to the Lord.

51 And thei diden the feest of tabernaclis, and a solempne dai, as it is writen in the lawe, and sacrifises ech day, as it bihouyde.

52 And aftir thes thinges thei ordeyneden offryngis, and oostis of sabotis, and of newe mones, and of alle solempne daies halewid.

53 And hou many euere vowiden to the Lord, fro the tyme of the newe moone of the seuenthe monthe, thei token oostis to offren to God; and the temple of the Lord was not yitt bildid up.

54 And thei yauen money to masouns, and to wriytis, and drynkis and metis with ioye.

55 And thei yauen carris to Sydonyes and to Tyres, that thei schulden carie ouer to hem fro Lyban wode cedre beemes, and to make a nauee in to the haauen of Joppe, aftir the decree that was writen to hem fro Cyro, kyng of Persis.

56 And in the secounde yeer thei camen in to the temple of God, in to Jerusalem; the secunde monthe Sorobabel biganne, the sone of Salatiel, and Jesus, the sone of Josedech, and the bretheren of hem, and prestis, and Leuytis, and alle thei that camen fro the caitiftee in to Jerusalem; and founden the temple of God,

57 in the newe moone of the secunde monthe of the secunde yeer, whanne thei hadden come in to Judee and to Jerusalem;

58 and setten dekens fro the age of twenty yeer upon the werkis of the Lord. And Jesus stode, his sone, and his bretheren, alle the dekens togidre castynge, and executours, or folewers, of the lawe, and doynge werkis in the hous of the Lord.

59 And ther stoden prestis, hauynge stoles, or longe clothis, with trumpis, and Leuytis, the sones of Asaph,

60 hauynge cymbals, togidre preisyng the Lord, and blessynge him, aftir the maner of Dauid, kyng of Israel.

61 And thei sungen a song to the Lord, for his swetnesse and his worschip in to worldis, or euer, upon al Israel.

62 And al the peple sungen with trumpe, and crieden with gret vois, preisynge togidre the Lord, in the rerynge of the Lordus hous.

63 And ther camen many of the prestis, and of dekens, and of presidentis aftir tounnes, to the eldris that hadden seen the rather hous,

64 and at the bildyng up of this hous, with cry, and with greet weilyng; and many with trumpis,

65 and gret ioye, so that the peple herde not the trumpis, for the gret weilyng of the peple. Forsothe ther was a cumpeny syngynge wirschipfully in trumpe, so that it was herd a ferr.

66 And the enmyes herden the lynagis of Juda and of Beniamyn, and camen to wite, what was this vois of trumpis.

67 And thei knewen, that thei that weren of the caitiftee bildiden the temple to the Lord God of Israel.

68 And the enmyes comynge niy to Sorobabel, and to Jesu, and to the reeues of tounnes, thei seiden to hem, We schul bilde togidre with you.

69 In lijk maner forsothe we haue herd oure Lord, and we haue gon togidre from the daies of Asbasareth, kyng of Assiriens, that ouer passide fro hennes.

70 And Sorobabel, and Jesus, and the princis of the tounnus of Israel seiden to hem,

71 It longith not to us and to you togidere to bilde up the hous of oure God; forsothe we aloone shul bilde the hous of oure God, aftir tho thingis, that Cyrus, kyng of Persis, comaundide.

72 The Gentiles forsothe of the loond leuynge with hem that ben in Judee, and rerynge up the werk of bildyng, and bringynge forth bothe aspies and peple, thei forfendiden hem to bilden up;

73 and thei lettiden men, hauntynge the goynges to, that the bildyng shulde not be endid in al the tyme of the lijf of the kyng Ciry; and thei drowen along the makyng up bi two yeer, vnto the regne of Darij.

CAP 6

1 Forsothe in the secounde yeer of the rewme of Darij, Agge propheciede, and Zacharias, the sone of Addyn, a prophete,

anentis Judee and in Jerusalem, in the name of the Lord God of Israel, upon hem.

2 Thanne stondynge Sorobabel, the sone of Salathiel, and Jesus, the sone of Josedech, thei bigunnen to bilde up the hous of the Lord, that is in Jerusalem;

3 whanne ther weren niy to hem prophetis of the Lord, and helpiden hem. In that tyme came to hem Cysennes, the vndir litil kyng of Cirye and of Fenycis, and Satrabozanes, and her felawis.

4 And thei seiden to hem, Who comaundide to you, that ye bilden this hows, and this roof, and many othere thingis ye perfourmen? and who ben tho bilders, that bilden up thes thingis?

5 And the eldre men of Israel hadden grace of the Lord, whanne the visitacioun of hem was maad upon hem that weren of the caitifte;

6 and thei weren not lettid to bilden up, to the tyme that it were signified to Darij of alle thes thingis, and an answere were taken ayen.

7 This is the ensaumple of the lettre, that Cysennes, the vndir kyng of Cyrie and of Fenyces, and Satrobosanes, and her felawis, rewlers in Sirye and in Fenyce, senden to the king. To kyng Darye, gretyng.

8 Alle thingis be thei knowen to the lord the kyng; forsothe whanne we camen in to the regioun of Judee, and wenten in to Jerusalem, we founden men bildynge a greet hous of God,

9 and a temple of gret polishid stones, and of precious maters in the wallis;

10 and tho werkis besily in makynge, and to help, and to make welsum in the hondis of hem, and in al glorie, ful diligently to be perfourmyd.

11 Thanne we askiden the eldre men, seiynge, Who suffride you to bilde this hous, and to bilde thes werkis?

12 Therfor forsothe we askiden hem, that we myyten make knowen to thee the men, and the prouostis, or reuys; and we askiden hem the writyng of the names of the maistris of the werk.

13 And thei answeriden to vs, seiynge, We ben seruauntis of the Lord, that made bothe heuen and erthe;

14 and this hous was bild bifore thes many yeris of the kyng of Israel, that was greet, and a ful strong kyng, and it was destried ayen.

15 And for oure fadris terriden and synneden ayen God of Israel, he bitook hem in to the hondis of Nabugodonosor, kyng of Babiloyne, kyng of Caldeis;

16 and thei destrieden and brenden up this hous, and thei brouyten the peple maad thral in to Babiloyne.

17 In the first yeer regnynge Cyro, kyng of Babiloyne, kyng Cyrus wroot to bilden up this hous;

18 and tho hooly golden vessels and silueren, that Nabugodonosor had born awey fro the hous of God, that is in Jerusalem, and had sacrid hem in his temple, efte kyng Cyrus brouyte hem forth fro the temple that was in Babiloyn, and thei weren bitake to Sorobabel, and to Salmanasar, the vndir litil kyng.

19 And it was comaundid to hem, that thei offre thes vessels, and thei schulde ley hem up in the temple, that was in Jerusalem, and to bilde up that temple of God in that place.

20 Thanne Salmanasar vndirleide the foundementis of the hous of the Lord, that is in Jerusalem; and fro thennes vn to now is a bildynge, and hath take no ful endyng.

21 Now thanne, O kyng! if it is demed of thee, that it be perfitly souyt in the kyngis libraries of kyng Cyry, that ben in Babiloyne;

22 and if it were founden in the counseil of kyng Ciry, the makyng of the hous of the Lord, that is in Jerusalem, to be bigunnen, and if it schal be schewid of the lord oure kyng, write he to vs of thes thingis.

23 Thanne kyng Darie comaundid to ben ynwardly souyt in the libraries; and ther was founden in Egbathanys, a borouy town, that is in the myddil regioun, a place, in the whiche weren wreten thes thingis.

24 The firste yer regnynge Cyro kyng, Cyrus comaundide to bilden up the hous of the Lord, that is in Jerusalem, where thei brenden with contynuel fijr; whos heiyt was maad of lx. cubitis,

25 and the brede of sixty cubitis, squarid with thre polischid stones, and with soler tree of the same regioun, and with o newe soler; and costis to be youen of the hous of king Cyrus;

26 and the holy vessels of the hous of the Lord, bothe golden and silueren, that Nabugodonosor bare awey, that tho be putt thidere in to the hous, that is in Jerusalem, where thei weren put.

27 And he comaundide Cysennem, the vndir litil kyng of Cyrie and Fenyce, and Satrabusanam, and his felawis, to do her bisynesse, and thei that weren in Sirie and Fenyce ordeyneden rewlers, that thei schulden absteyne them fro the same place.

28 And I also comaundide to make it up al, and I lokide forth, that thei help them that ben of the caitiftee of Jewis, vnto the tyme that the temple of the hous of the Lord be full endid;

29 and a quantitee to be youen diligently to these men of the traueile of the tributis of Sirye Choles and Fenyces, to the sacrifice of the Lord, to Sorobabel, the prefect, to bolis, and wetheris, and to lombis;

30 also forsothe bothe whete, and salt, wyn, and oile, bisily bi alle yeris, as the prestis, that ben in Jerusalem, ordeyneden to be fulfillid eche day, withoute ony delay;

31 also that ther be offrid offryngis of licours to the hiyest God, for the kyng, and for his children, and preie thei for the lijf of hem.

32 And be it denounsid, that who so euer ouer passen ony thing of these thingis that ben wreten, outher despisen, be ther taken a tree of her owne, and be thei hangid theron, and her goodes be ethchetid to the kyng.

33 Therfor also the Lord, whos name is ynwardly clepid there, outlawe he eche kyng and folk, that strecchen out her hoond to offende, or to yuele trete that hous of the Lord, that is in Jerusalem.

34 I, kyng Darie, haue maad a decree, to be don as moost diligently after thes thingis.

CAP 7

1 Thanne Cysennes, the litil vndir kyng of Choelem Cyrie and Fenycen, and Satrabusanes, and her felawis, obeisheden to these thingis, that weren demyd of kyng Darie,

2 and stoden ful diligently in to the hooly werkis, wirchinge togidre with the eldre men of Jewis, princis of Cirie.

3 And the hooly werkis ben maad welsum, as the prophetes Agge and Zacharie prophecieden.

4 And thei fulfilliden alle thingis, aftir the heest of the Lord God of Israel, and aftir the counseil of Cyri, and of Darij, and of Artaxersis, kyng of Persis.

5 And oure hous is endid, in the three and twentithe dai of the monthe of Marche, in the sixte yeer of kyng Darij.

6 And the sones of Israel, and the prestis, and dekens, and othere that weren of the caitiftee, the whiche ben sett to, diden aftir thoo thingis that ben writen in the book of Moyses.

7 And thei offreden in to the dedicatioun of the temple of the Lord, an hundrid bolis, two hundrid wetheris, foure hundrid lambren,

8 twelue kides, for the synnes of al Israel, after the noumbre of the xij. lynages of Israel.

9 And the prestis and dekens stoden, clothid with the stolis, bi her lynagis, upon the werkis of the Lord God of Israel, aftir the book of Moyses; and ther weren porters bi alle the yatis.

10 And the sones of Israel diden that pask, with hem that weren of the caitiftee, in the moone of the first monthe, the fourtenthe day, whanne the prestis and dekens ben halewid.

11 And alle the sones of caitiftee thei ben not halewid togidre, for alle the Leuytis ben halewid togidere.

12 And thei offreden pask to alle the sones of caitiftee, and to her bretheren, prestis, and to them selff.

13 And the sonus of Israel, the whiche weren of the caitiftee, alle thei that hadden left fro alle the cursidnessis of Gentiles, or hethen folk, of the eerthe, eeten, and souyten the Lord;

14 and thei halewiden the feest day of therff looues, seuene daies etynge in siyt of the Lord;

15 for he conuertide the counseil of the kyng of Assirijs in hem, to coumforte the hondis of hem to the werkis of the Lord God of Israel.

1 And aftir this, while Artaxerse, kyng of Persis, regnyde, ther wente to Esdras, a man that was the sone of Azarie, sone of Elchie, sone of Salome, sone of Sadduch,

2 sone of Achitob, sone of Amarie, sone of Aza, sone of Bocce, sone of Abisae, sone of Phynees, sone of Eleazar, sone of Aaron, the first preest.

3 This Esdras stiede up fro Babiloyne, whanne he was scribe, and witty in the lawe of Moyses, the whiche was youen of the Lord of Israel, to sey it and do it.

4 And the kyng yaaf to him glorie, that he hadde founden grace in al dignytee, and in desijr, in the siyt of him.

5 And ther stiede up with him in to Jerusalem of the sones of Israel, bothe prestis, and dekens, and holy syngers of the temple, and vsshers, and seruauntis of the temple.

6 In the seuenthe yeer regnynge Artaxerse, in the fifthe monthe, this is the seuenthe yeer of the rewme, goynge out forsothe fro Babiloyne in the newe moone of the fifte monthe,

7 thei camen to Jerusalem, aftir the heestis of him, whanne the prosperitee of the wey was grauntid to hem of that Lord.

8 In these thingis forsothe Esdras weldide greet discipline, lest he passide ony thing of tho thingis that weren of the lawe of the Lord, and of the heestis, and in techynge al Israel al riytwisnesse and doom.

9 Thei forsothe that writen the writyngis of kyng Artaxerses, comynge niy, token writen that, that came from kyng Artaxerses to Esdras, the prest, and redere of the lawe of the Lord, the ensaumple of the whiche thing writen is sett next aftir.

10 Kyng Artaxerses to Esdre, the prest, and redere of the lawe of the Lord, sendith gretyng.

11 More benygne I demynge also to benefetis, comaundide to hem that desiren of the folke of Jewis their owne thingis wilfully, and of the prestis, and of dekens, that ben in my rewme, to felawschipe with thee in to Jerusalem.

12 Thanne if ony coueiten to gon with thee, come thei togidre, and go thei forth, as it plesith to me, and to my seuene frendis counseilers; that thei visite tho thingis,

13 that ben don aftir Jude and Jerusalem, kepinge the lawe, as thou hast in the lawe of the Lord:

14 and bere thei yiftis to the Lord of Israel, whom I knew, and the frendis of Jerusalem, and al the gold and the siluer, that weren founde in the rewme of Babiloyne, be it born to the Lord in Jerusalem,

15 with that that is youen of thilke folk in the temple of the Lord, of hem that is in Jerusalem; that this gold be gederid and siluer, to bolis, and wetheris, and to lambis, and kides, and that to these ben couenable; that thei offren oostes to the Lord,

16 upon the auter of the Lord of hem, that is in Jerusalem.

17 And alle thingis what euer thou wilt do with thi bretheren, perfourme it with gold and siluer, for thi will, aftir the heest of the Lord thi God.

18 And the sacrid hooly vessels, the whiche weren youen to thee, to the werkis of the Lordis hous,

19 thi God, that is in Jerusalem, and othere thingis, what euere woln helpe to the werkis of the temple of thi God, thou schalt yiuen it of the kyngis tresorie,

20 whanne thou wilt maken the werk with thi bretheren, with gold and siluer; and parfourme thou al thing aftir the will of thi Lord.

21 And I, kyng Artaxerses, haue comaundid to kepers of the tresours of Cirye and of Fenyce, that what euer thingis Esdras, the preest, and redere of the lawe of the Lord, wrijte fore, bisily be it youen to him, vn to an hundrid talentis of siluer, also and of gold;

22 and vnto an hundrid busshelis of whete, and an hundrid vessels of wyn, and othere thingis, what euer abounden, withoute taxynge.

23 Alle thingis be don to the hiest God, aftir the lawe of God, lest perauenture wraththe arijse up in the rewme of the kyng, and of his sone, and of the sones of him.

24 To you forsothe it was seid, that to alle the prestis, and dekens, and to holy syngers, and seruauntis of the temple, and to scribis of this temple,

25 no tribute, no ony oother forfendyng be born to hem, ne haue ther ony man power to ayen caste ony thing to hem.

26 Thou forsothe, Esdras, aftir the wisdom of God ordeyne domesmen and arbitrours, in al Cirye and Fenyce, and teche alle that knowen the lawe of thi God;

27 that hou fele euere passen the lawe, thei be besely punyshid, or bi deth, or bi tourment, or also bi multyng, or punysching, of money, or bi departyng awey.

28 And Esdras, the scribe, seide, Blessid be the Lord God of oure fadris, that yaaf this will in to the herte of the kyng, to clarifie his hous, that is in Jerusalem;

29 and hath wirschipid me in siyt of the kyng, and of hise counselours, and of hise frendis, and of hise purpred men.

30 And I am maad stidefast in inwitt, aftir the helpyng of the Lord oure God; and I gadride of Israel men, that thei schulden stie up togidre with me.

31 And these ben the prouostis, aftir their cuntrees, and porcionel princehedis of hem, that with me stieden up fro Babiloyne, in the rewme of Artaxerses.

32 Of the sones of Phares was Jersomus; of the sones of Cyemarith, Amenus; of the sones of Dauid, Accus, the sone of Cecelie;

33 of the sones of Phares, Zacharie, and with him ben turned ayen an hundrid men and fifty;

34 of the sonus of Ductor, Moabilonys, Zaraey, and with him two hundrid men and fifty;

35 of the sonus of Sacues, Jechonye, Thetheely, and with him two hundrid men and fifty;

36 of the sones of Salomosias, Gotholie, and with him seuenty men;

37 of the sones of Saphacye, Zarias, Mychely, and with him foure score men;

38 of the sones of Jobab, Dias, Jesely, and with him two hundrid men and twelue;

39 of the sones of Banye, Salymoth, the sone of Josaphie, and with him an hundrid men and sixty;

40 of the sones of Beer, Zacharie, Bebey, and with him two hundrid men and eiyte;

41 of the sones of Azachie, Channes, Acharie, and with him an hundrid men and ten;

42 of the sones of Adonycam, that ben the laste, and thes ben the names of hem, Elyphalam, the sone of Jebel, and Semeas, and with him seuenty men.

43 And I gedride hem to the flood, that is seid Thia and Methaty; there we weren thre daies, and I knewe hem.

44 And of the sones of prestis and of Leuytis I fonde not there.

45 And I sente to Eleazar, and to Eccelom, and Masman, and Malolan, and Enaathan, and Samea, and Joribum, Nathan, Ennagan, Zacharie, Mosollamym, the whiche weren leders and wise men.

46 And I seide to hem, that thei schulden come to Luddium, that was at the place of the tresorie.

47 And I sente to hem, that they schulden sey to Luddyum, and his bretheren, and to hem that weren in the tresorie, that thei schulden sende to vs hem that schulden vse presthod in the hous of the Lord oure God.

48 And thei brouyten to us, aftir the strong hoond of the Lord oure God, wise men of the sones of Mooly, sone of Leuy, sone of Israel, Sebebian, and sones, and bretheren, that weren eiytene;

49 Asbiam, and Ammum, of the sones of Chananey; and the sonus of hem weren twenti men.

50 And of hem that seruyden in the temple, the whiche Dauid and thei princis yauen, to the wirching to the Leuytis, to the temple, of men seruynge, two hundrid and twenty. The names of alle ben signyfied in scripturis.

51 And I vowide there fastyng to yonge men, in the siyt of the Lord, that I schulde seche of hym a good wey to us, and to hem that weren with us, of sones, and bestis, for aspies.

52 Forsothe I schamyde to aske of the kyng foot men and hors men, in felauschipe of grace, of keping ayen oure aduersaries.

53 Forsothe we seiden to the kyng, For the vertue of the Lord schal be with hem, that inwardly sechen him in al effect.

54 And efte we preieden the Lord oure God, aftir thes thingis, whom also we hadden benyngly; and we ben maad hool to oure God.

55 And I departide of the prouostis of the folc, and of the prestis of the temple, xij men, and Sedebian, and Affamyan, and ten men with hem of her bretheren.

56 And I weiede to hem siluer and gold, and prestis vessels, of the hous of the Lord oure God, the whiche the kyng had youen, and his counseilers, and princis, and al Israel.

57 And whanne I hadde peisid it, I toke an hundrid talentis of siluer and fifty, and silueren vessels of an hundrid talentis, and of gold an hundrid talentis,

58 and of golden vessels seuen score, and twelue brasen vessels of good schynynge metal, yeldinge the liknesse of gold.

59 And we seide to hem, Bothe ye ben holy to the Lord, and the vessels ben holy, and the gold and the siluer is of the avowe to the Lord God of oure fadris.

60 Wake ye, and kepe it, til the tyme that ye take it of the prouostes of the peple, and of the prestis, and of the dekens, and of princis of the citees of Israel and Jerusalem, in the priuey chaumbre of the hous of oure God.

61 And thes prestis and dekens, that token gold and siluer, and vessels, that weren in Jerusalem, thei broyten thoo in to the temple of the Lord.

62 And we moeueden forth fro the flood of Thya, the twelfthe day of the firste monthe, til that we yeden in to Jerusalem.

63 And whanne the thrid day was don, the firthe day forsothe the peisid gold and siluer was bitaken in to the hous of the Lord oure God, to Marymoth, the sone of Jory, the prest;

64 and with him was Eleazar, the sone of Phynees; and ther weren with him Josabdus, the sone of Jesu, and Medias, and Banny, the sone of a deken; alle thingis at noumbre and weiyt.

65 And the weiyt of hem is writen in the same hour.

66 Thoo forsothe, that camen fro the caitifte, offriden sacrifice of the Lord of Israel, twelue bolis for alle Israel, foure score wetheris and sixe,

67 two and seuenty lambren, twelue geet for synne, and twelue kiyn for helthe; alle in to the sacrifice of the Lord.

68 And eft thei redden the hestis of the kyng to the kyngis dispensatours, and to the litle vndir kyngis of Choele, and of Cirye, and of Fenyce; and thei wirschipiden the folc and the temple of the Lord.

69 And aftir thes thingis weren endid, thei camen to me, seiynge, The kynrede of Israel, and the princis, and the prestis,

70 and Leuytis, and alien folkis, and naciouns of the lond, han not partid awey her vnclennessis fro the Chananeis, and Etheis, and fro Pheriseis, and Jebuseis, and fro the Moabitis, and Egipcians, and Ydumeis;

71 forsothe thei weren ioyned to the douytris of hem, bothe thei and their sones; and the hooly seed was mengid togidre with the hethene folk of the loond; and the prouostis and maistre iuges weren parceners of this wickidnesse, fro the bigynnyng of that rewme.

72 And anoon as I herde thes thingis, I kitte my clothis, and the halewid coote, and I taar the heris of myn hed, and the berd, and I sate serewynge, and drury.

73 And ther camen to me thanne as many as euer weren moued in the word of the Lord God of Israel, weilynge me upon this wickidnesse; and I saat serewful vnto the euentijd sacrifice.

74 And thanne I risynge fro fastyng, hauynge my clothis kitt, knelide myche, and strecchinge out myn hondis to the Lord,

75 I seide, Lord, I am confoundid, and I am adred bifore thi face.

76 Forsothe oure synnes ben multiplied upon oure hedis, and oure wickidnessis ben enhaunsid vnto heuen;

77 for fro the tyme of oure fadris we haue be in gret synne vnto this dai.

78 And for oure owne synnes, and for the synne of oure fadris we ben taken, with oure bretheren, and with oure prestis, and

with kyngis of the loond, in to swerd, and caitiftee, and in to prey, with confusion, vnto the dai that is now.

79 And now hou myche is it, that the mercy of thee, Lord God, fallith to us; leue thou to us a roote and a name, in to the place of thin halewyng,

80 to vnkoueren oure yyuere of liyt in the hous of the Lord oure God, to yiue to us mete in the tyme of oure seruage.

81 And whanne we seruyden, we weren not forsaken of the Lord oure God; but he sette us in grace, puttynge to us kyngis of Persis to yiue us mete,

82 and to clarifie the temple of the Lord oure God, and to bilde the deseertis of Syon, and to yiue to us stablenesse in Judee and in Jerusalem.

83 And now, Lord, what sey we, hauynge thes thingis? We haue ouerpassid thin hestis, the whiche thou yiue in to the hondis of thi children,

84 prophetis, that seiden, Forsothe the lond, in whiche ye haue entrid, to welde the heritage of it, is a defoulid lond with the filthis of hethen men of the lond, and the vnclennessis of hem han fulfillid al it in his vnclennesse.

85 And now therfor ye schul not ioyne youre douytris to her sones, and her douytris ye schul not take to youre sones;

86 and ye schul not seche to haue pes with hem al tyme, that comynge aboue ye ete the beste thingis of the lond, and that ye dele the heritage to youre sones, for euere.

87 And thoo thingis that fallen to us, be thei alle don for oure schrewid werkis, and oure grete synnes.

88 And thou hast youen to us sich a roote, and eft we ben turned ayen to ouerpasse thi laweful thingis, that the vnclennessis of the hethen folc of this lond weren mengid.

89 Whether thou schalt not wraththen to us, to lese us, for til the roote be forsaken, and oure seed?

90 Lord God of Israel, thou art sothfast; forsothe the root is forsaken, vnto the day that is now.

91 Lo! now we ben in thi siyt in oure wickidnessis; forsothe it is not yitt to stonde bifore thee in thes thingis.

92 And whanne Esdras honouringe knowlechide, wepinge, he fel doun to the erthe bifore the temple, ther ben gederid bifore him a ful gret multitude of Jerusalem, men, and wymmen, and younge men, and younge wymmen; forsothe the wepynge was gret in that multitude.

93 And whanne Jechonyas, the sone of Jeely, of the sones of Israel, hadde cried, Esdras seide, We haue synned ayen the Lord, for that we haue sett with us in to matrimonye hethen wymmen, of the Gentiles of the lond.

94 And now who so euer is ouer al Israel in thes thingis, be ther to vs an ooth of the Lord, to putten awey alle oure wyues, that ben, with her sones, of the hethene folk;

95 as it is demed to thee of the grettere men, aftir the lawe of the Lord. Arijse now up, and schewe thi will;

96 forsothe to thee abijdith this nede, and we ben with thee; do manly.

97 And Esdras arisynge up, made the princis of prestes, and the dekens, and al Israel, to swere to do aftir alle thes thingis; and thei sworen.

CAP 8

1 And Esdras risynge up fro the fore porche of the temple, wente in to the celle of Jonathe, the sone of Nazaby.

2 And he herbowrewid there, tastide no bred, ne dronke watir, for the wickidnessis of the multitude.

3 And ther was maad a prechyng in al Judee and in Jerusalem, to alle that weren of the caitiftee gederid in Jerusalem,

4 Who so euer ayen comith not to the secounde or the thrid day, aftir the doom of the eldre men sittynge, his facultees schul be taken awey, and he be demed alien fro the multitude of the caitiftee.

5 And alle, that weren of the lynage of Judee and of Beniamyn, weren gedrid togidre, thre daies in Jerusalem; this is the nynthe monthe, the twentithe day of the monthe.

6 And al the multitude saat in the floor of the temple, tremblynge for wyntir thanne beynge.

7 And Esdras risynge up, seide to Israel, Ye han do wickidly, settynge to you in to matrimonye hethen wyues, that ye adde to the synnes of Israel.

8 And now yiue ye to the Lord God of oure fadris confessioun, and gret worthynesse;

9 and perfourme ye his will, and goth awey fro the hethene folc of the lond, and fro hethene wyues.

10 And al the multitude criede, and thei seiden with a gret voice, We schul do, as thou hast seid.

11 But for the multitude is gret, and the tyme is wyntir, and we mowen not stonde vnholpen, and this werk is not to us of oo day, ne of two; myche we haue synned in thes thingis;

12 therfor stonde the prouostis of the multitude, and alle that dwellen with us, and hou many euere han anentis hem hethen wijues;

13 and stonde thei nyy in the tyme that is take, prestis, and domesmen, til that thei lousen the wraththe of the Lord, of this nede.

14 Jonathas forsothe, the sone of Ezely, and Ozias, Thethan, token aftir thes thingis, and Bosoramus, and Leuys, and Satheus wrouyten togidre with hem.

15 And alle that weren of the caitiftee stoden there, aftir alle thes thingis.

16 And Esdras, prest, chees to him men, grete princis, of the fadris of hem, aftir the names; and thei seten togidre, in the newe moone of the tenthe monthe, to examyne this nede.

17 And it is determyned of the men, that hadden hethen wyues, vnto the newe mones of the firste monthe.

18 And ther ben founden mengid among of the prestis, that hadden hethen wiues;

19 of the sones of Jesu, the sone of Josedech, and of his bretheren, Maseas, and Eleeserus, and Joribus, and Joadeus.

20 And thei leiden her hoondis, that thei schuldn putte awey their wyues, and for to sacrifie a ram, in to preier for their ignoraunce.

21 And of the sones of Semmery, Masseas, and Esses, and Geley, Azarias;

22 and of the sonus of Phosore, Leomasias, Hismaenis, and Nathanae, Jussio, Jeddus, and Talsas.

23 And of the dekens, Josabdus, and Semeis, and Cholitus, and Calitas, and Phacceas, and Coluas, and Elionas.

24 And of the halewid syngers, Eliazub, Zacturus.

25 And of the vsschers, Salumus, and Thosbanes.

26 And of Israel, of the sones of Phorcosy, and Remyas, and Jeddias, and Melchias, and Mychelus, and Eleazarus, and Jemebias, and Bannas.

27 And of the sones of Jolamani, Anias, and Zacharias, Jerselus, and Jobdius, and Erymath, and Elias.

28 And of the sonus of Sachon, Eleadas, and Eleasumus, and Othias, and Jarymoth, and Zabdis, and Thebedias.

29 And of the sones of Bedo, Johannes, and Amanyas, and Zabdias, and Emetis.

30 And of the sonus of Banny, Olamus, and Mallucus, and Jeddeus, and Jazub, and Azabus, and Jerymoth.

31 And of the sones of Addyn, Naathus, and Moosias, and Calemus, and Raanas, and Baseas, Mathatias, and Bethsel, and Bonnus, and Manasses.

32 And of the sones of Myaie, Nenyas, and Apheas, and Melcheas, and Sameas, and Symon, Beniamyn, and Malchus, and Marias.

33 Of the sones of Azom, Cartaneus, Mathatias, and Bannus, and Eliphalath, and Manasses, and Semey.

34 Of the sones of Banny, Jeremias, and Moodias, and Abramus, and Johel, and Baneas, and Pelias, and Jonas, and Marymoth, and Eliazub, and Mathaneus, and Eleazis, and Ozias, and Dielus, and Samedius, and Zambris, and Josephus.

35 And of the sones of Nobey, Ydelus, and Mathatias, and Zaladus, and Setheda, Sedym, and Jessei, Baneas.

36 Alle these ioyneden to hem hethen wyues, and leften hem, with her sones.

37 And prestis, and dekens, and thei that weren of Israel, dwelliden in Jerusalem in an oo regioun, the newe moone of the seuenthe monthe; and the sones of Israel weren in their abidyngis.

38 And al the multitude gedride togidre in the floor, that is fro the eest of the halewid yate.

39 And thei seiden to Esdre, bisschop and reder, that he schulde brynge forth the lawe of Moises, that was youen of the Lord God of Israel.

40 And Esdras, the bisschop, brouyte forth the lawe to al the multitude of hem, fro man vn to womman, and to alle the prestis, to here the lawe, in the newe moone of the seuenthe monthe.

41 And he radde in the floor, that is bifore the hooly yate of the temple, fro the firste liyt of the daie vnto euyn, bifore men and wymmen; and alle thei yauen witt to the lawe.

42 And Esdras, the prest, and redere of the lawe, stood upon the treen chaier, that was maad therfore.

43 And ther stoden with him Mathatias, and Samus, and Ananyas, Azarias, Vrias, Ezechias, and Balsamus, at the riyt side;

44 and at the left side, Phaleleus, Mysael, Malachias, Abustas, Sabus, Nabadias, and Zacharias.

45 And Esdras took a book bifore al the multitude; forsothe he sate bifore in worschip, in the siyt of alle.

46 And whanne he hadde assoilid the lawe, alle thei stoden upright. And Esdras blesside the Lord God, alther hiyest God of Sabaoth, al myyti.

47 And al the peple answeride, Amen. And efte thei reisyden up her hondis, and fallynge doun vnto the erthe, thei honouriden the Lord.

48 And Esdras comaundide, that these schulden teche the lawe, Jesus, and Banaeus, and Sarabias, and Jadmus, and Accubus, and Sabatheus, and Calithes, and Azarias, and Joradus, and Ananyas, and Philas, dekens.

49 The whiche tauyten the lawe of the Lord, and in the multitude thei radden the lawe of the Lord; and eche bi him self, that vndirstoden the lesson, tolde it before hem.

50 And Atharathes seide to Esdre, the bisschop and redere, and to the Leuytis that tauyten the multitude,

51 seiynge, This day is hooly to the Lord. And alle thei wepten, whanne thei hadden herd the lawe.

52 And Esdras seide, Ye therfore, aftir ye ben gon atwynne, eteth alle moost fatte thingis, and drynketh alle mooste swete, and sende ye yiftis to hem that han not;

53 forsothe this day of the Lord is hooly; and be ye not sory, the Lord forsothe schal clarifie vs.

54 And the dekens denounciden, or schewiden, openly to alle men, seiynge, This day is hooly; wille ye not be sory.

55 And thanne alle thei wenten awey, to ete, and to drynke, and to haue plentee of mete, and to yiue yiftis to hem that han not, wheroff to ete plenteuously. Gretly forsothe thei ben enhaunsid in the wordis, with the whiche thei ben tauyt.

56 And alle thei weren gadrid in to Jerusalem, to make solempne the gladnesse, aftir the testament of the Lord God of Israel.

TOBIT

CAP 1

1 Tobie was of the lynage and citee of Neptalym, which is in the hiyere partis of Galilee, aboue Naason, bihynde the weie that ledith to the west, and hath in the lefte side the citee of Sapheth,

2 whanne he was takun in the daies of Salmanazar, kyng of Assiriens, netheles he set in caytifte, 'ether takun prisoner, forsook not the weie of treuthe,

3 so that he departide ech dai alle thingis whiche he myyte haue, with caitif britheren that weren of his kyn.

4 And whanne he was yongere than alle in the lynage of Neptalym, netheles he dide no childische thing in werk.

5 Forsothe whanne alle Jewis yeden to the goldun calues, whiche Jeroboam, the kyng of Israel, made, this Tobie aloone fledde the cumpenyes of alle men;

6 and he yede to Jerusalem, to the temple of the Lord, and there he worschipide the Lord God of Israel; and he offride feithfuly alle hise firste fruytis, and hise tithis;

7 so that in the thridde yeer he mynystride al the tithe to conuersis and comlyngis.

8 The yonge man kepte these thingis, and thingis lijk these, bi the lawe of God of heuene.

9 Sotheli whanne he was maad a man, he took a wijf, Anne, of his lynage; and he gendride of hir a sone, and puttide his owne name to hym;

10 whom he tauyte fro yong childhed for to drede God, and for to absteyne fro al synne.

11 Therfor whanne bi caitifte he was comun, with his wijf and sone, in to the citee Nynyue,

12 with al his lynage, and alle men eeten of the meetis of hethene men, this Tobie kepte his soule, and was neuere defoulid in the metis of hem.

13 And for he was myndeful of the Lord in al his herte, God yaf grace to hym in the siyt of Salamanazar, the kyng;

14 and he yaf to Tobie power to go whidur euer he wolde, and he hadde fredom to do what euer thingis he wolde.

15 Therfor he yede bi alle men that weren in caitifte, and yaf to hem the heestis of helthe.

16 Sotheli whanne he was comyn in to Rages, a citee of Medeis, and hadde ten talentis of siluer, of these thingis bi whiche he was onourid of the kyng;

17 and siy Gabelus nedi, that was of his lynage, with myche cumpeny of his kyn, Tobie yaf to hym, vndur an obligacioun, the forseid weiyte of siluer.

18 Forsothe after myche tyme, aftir that Salamanazar, the kyng, was deed, whanne Senacherib, his sone, regnyde for hym, and hadde the sones of Israel hateful in his siyt,

19 Tobie yede ech dai bi al his kynrede, and coumfortide hem, and departide of hise catels to ech man, as he myyte;

20 he fedde hungri men, and yaf clothis to nakid men, and he 'yaf bisili sepulture to deed men and slayn.

21 Sotheli whanne the kyng Senacherib turnede ayen, fleynge fro Judee the veniaunce that God 'hadde do aboute hym for his blasfemye, and he was wrooth, and killide many of the sones of Israel, Tobie biriede 'the bodies of hem.

22 And aftir that it was teld to the kyng, he comaundide Tobie to be slayn, and he took awei al his catel.

23 Sotheli Tobie fledde with his sone and with his wijf, and was hid nakid, for many men loueden hym.

24 Forsothe after fyue and fourti daies, the sones of the kyng kyilliden the kyng; and Tobie turnede ayen to his hows,

25 and al his catel was restorid to hym.

CAP 2

1 Forsothe aftir these thingis, whanne a feeste dai of the Lord was, and a good meete was maad in the hows of Tobie, he seide to his sone,

2 Go thou, and brynge sum men of oure lynage, 'that dreden God, that thei ete with vs.

3 And whanne he was goon, he turnede ayen, and telde to hym, that oon of the sones of Israel lai stranglid in the street; and anoon 'he skippide fro his sittyng place, and lefte the mete, and cam fastynge to the bodi; and he took it,

4 and bar to his hows pryuely, for to birie hym warli, whanne the sunne was go doun.

5 And whanne he hadde hid the bodi, he eet breed with morenyng and tremblyng,

6 and remembride that word, which the Lord seide bi Amos, the prophete, Youre feeste daies schulen be turned in to morenyng and 'lamentacioun, ether weilyng.

7 Sotheli whanne the sunne was go doun, Tobie yede, and biriede hym.

8 Forsothe alle hise neiyboris blameden hym, and seiden, Now for the cause of this thing thou were comaundid to be slayn, and vnnethis thou ascapidist the comaundement of deeth, and eft 'biriest thou deed men?

9 But Tobie dredde more God than the kyng, and took awei the bodies of slayn men, and hidde in his hows, and biriede tho in the myddil of nyytis.

10 Sotheli it bifelde, that in sum day he was maad wery of biriyng; and he cam hoom, and leide hym silf bisidis a wal, and slepte;

11 and while he slepte, hoote ordures 'fellen doun fro the nest of swalewis on hise iyen; and he was maad blynd.

12 Forsothe herfor the Lord suffride this temptacioun bifalle to hym, that the saumple of his pacience, 'as also of seynt Job, schulde be youun to 'after comeris.

13 For whi whanne he dredde God euere fro his yong child-hed, and kepte hise comaundementis, he was not sory ayens God, for the sikenesse of blyndnesse cam to hym;

14 but he dwellide vnmouable in the drede of God, and dide thankyngis to God in alle the dais of his lijf.

15 For whi as kyngis vpbreididen seynt Job, so it bifelde to this Tobie, hise eldris and kynesmen scorneden his lijf,

16 and seiden, Where is thin hope, for which thou didist almes dedis and biriyngis?

17 Sotheli Tobie blamyde hem, and seide,

18 Nyle ye speke so, for we ben the sones of hooli men, and we abiden that lijf, which God schal yyue to hem that chaungen neuere her feith fro hym.

19 Forsothe Anne, his wijf, yede ech dai to the 'werk of weuyng, and brouyte lyuelode, which sche myyte gete of the trauel of hir hondis.

20 Wherof it 'was doon, that sche took a kide of geet, and brouyte hoom.

21 And whanne hir hosebonde hadde herd the vois of this kide bletynge, he seide, Se ye, lest perauenture it be of thefte, but 'yelde ye it to 'hise lordis; for it is not leueful 'to vs, ethir to ete ether to touche ony thing of thefte.

22 At these thingis his wijf was wrooth, and answeride, Opynli thin hope is maad veyn, and thin almes dedis apperiden now.

23 And bi these and 'othere siche wordis sche seide schens-chip to hym.

CAP 3

1 Thanne Tobie inwardli sorewide, and bigan to preye with teeris, and seide, Lord,

2 thou art iust, and alle thi domes ben iust, and alle thi weies ben mercy, and treuthe, and doom.

3 And now, Lord, haue thou mynde of me, and take thou not veniaunce of my synnes, nether haue thou mynde of my tres-passis, ethir of my fadris.

4 For we 'obeieden not to 'thi comaundementis, and we ben takun in to rifelyng, and in to caitifte, and in to deth, and in to 'a fable, and in to schenschip to alle naciouns, among whiche thou hast scaterid vs.

5 And now, Lord, thi domes ben grete; for we han not do aftir 'thi comaundementis, and we han not go clenli bifor thee.

6 And now, Lord, bi thi wille do thou merci with me, and comaunde thou my spirit to be resseyued in pees; for it spedith more to me to die than to lyue.

7 And so it bifelde in the same dai, that Sare, the douyter of Raguel, was in Rages, a citee of Medeis, and sche herd schens-chip of oon of the handmaidis of hir fadir;

8 for sche was youun to seuene hosebondis, and a feend, Asmodeus bi name, killide hem, anoon as thei hadden entrid to hir.

9 Therfor whanne sche blamyde 'the damysele for her gilt, the damisele answeride to hir, and seide, Thou sleeresse of thin hosebondis, se we 'no more a sone ether a douyter of thee 'on erthe;

10 whether also thou wolt sle me, as also thou hast slayn seuene men? At this vois sche yede in to the hiyere closet of hir hows, and thre daies and thre nyytis sche eet not, nether drank;

11 but sche contynuede in preier with teeris, and bisouyte God, that he schulde delyuere hir fro this schenschip.

12 Forsothe it was doon in the thridde dai, while sche hadde fillid the preier,

13 sche blesside the Lord, and seide, God of oure fadris, thi name is blessid, which whanne thou hast be wrooth, schalt do merci, and in tyme of tribulacioun foryyuest synnes to hem, that inwardli clepen thee.

14 Lord, to thee Y turne togidere my face; to thee 'Y reise 'myn iyen.

15 Lord, Y axe, that thou assoile me fro the boond of this schenschip, ether certis that thou take me awei fro aboue the erthe.

16 Lord, thou wost, that Y neuere coueitide man, and Y haue kept my soule cleene fro al coueitise.

17 Y medlide me neuere with pleieris, nether Y yaf me parce-ner with hem that goon in vnstablenesse.

18 But Y consentide to take an hosebonde with thi drede, not with my lust.

19 And ether Y was vnworthi to hem, ether thei perauenture weren not worthi to me; for in hap thou hast kept me to another hosebonde.

20 For thi councel is not in the power of man.

21 Forsothe ech that worschipith thee hath this for a certeyn, that if his lijf is in preuyng, he schal be corowned; sotheli if he is in tribulacioun, he schal be delyuerid; and if he is in chastisyng, it schal be leueful to come to thi merci.

22 For thou delitist not in oure lossis; for after tempest thou makist pesible, and after morenyng and wepyng thou bryngist yn ful ioye.

23 God of Israel, thi name be blessid 'in to worldis, that is, til in to withouten ende.

24 In that tyme the preieris of bothe weren herd in the siyt of glorie of hiyeste God; and Raphael,

25 the hooli aungel of the Lord, was sent for to heele hem bothe, whose preyeris weren rehersid in o tyme in the siyt of the Lord.

CAP 4

1 Therfor whanne Tobie gesside his preier to be herd, that he myyte die, he clepide Tobie,

2 his sone, to hym silf, and seide to hym, My sone, here thou the wordis of my mouth, and bilde thou tho as foundementis in thin herte.

3 Whanne God hath take my soule, byrie thou my bodi; and 'thou schal haue onour to thi modir in alle the daies of hir lijf;

4 for thou owist to be myndeful, what perels and how grete sche suffride for thee in hir wombe.

5 Forsothe whanne also sche hath fillid the tyme of hir lijf, thou schalt birie hir bisidis me.

6 Sotheli in alle the daies of thi lijf haue thou God in mynde, and be thou war, lest ony tyme thou consente to synne, and forsake the heestis of oure God.

7 Of thi catel do thou almes, and nyle thou turne awei thi face fro ony pore man; for so it schal be doon, that the face of the Lord be not turned awei fro thee.

8 As thou maist, so be thou merciful.

9 If thou hast myche, yyue thou plenteuousli; if thou hast a litil, also be thou bisi to departe wilfuli a litil.

10 For thou tresorist to thee a good meede in the dai of nede;

11 for whi almes delyuereth fro al synne and fro deeth, and schal not suffre the soule to go in to derknessis.

12 Almes schal be grete trist bifor the hiyeste God to alle men doynge it.

13 Sone, take heede to thi silf, and fle fro al fornicacioun, and, 'outakun thi wijf, suffre thou neuere to know synne.

14 Suffre thou neuere pride to haue lordschip in thi wit, nether in thi word; for al 'los, ether dampnacioun, took biginnyng in that pride.

15 Who euere worchith ony thing to thee, yelde thou anoon his mede, and outirli the hire of 'thin hirid man dwelle not at thee.

16 That that thou hatist to be doon to thee of another man, se thou, lest ony tyme thou do to another man.

17 Ete thi breed with hungri men and nedi, and with thi clothis hile thou nakid men.

18 Ordeyne thi breed and thi wiyn on the sepulture of a iust man, and nyle thou ete and drynke therof with synneris.

19 Euere seke thou perfitli a counsel of a wijs man.

20 Al tyme blesse thou God, and axe thou of hym, that he dresse thi weies, and alle thi counsels dwelle in hym.

21 Also, my sone, Y schewe to thee, that the while thou were yit a litil child, Y yaf ten talentis of siluer to Gabelus, in Rages, a citee of Medeis; and Y haue his obligacioun anentis me;

22 and therfor perfitli enquere thou, hou thou schalt come to hym, and resseyue of hym the forseid weiyte of siluer, and restore to hym his obligacioun.

23 My sone, nyle thou drede; forsothe we leden a pore lijf, but we schulen haue many goodis, if we dreden God, and goen awei fro al synne, and doen wel.

CAP 5

1 Thanne Tobie answeride to his fadir, and seide, Fadir, Y schal do alle thingis, which euer thou comaundidist to me;

2 but Y noot, hou Y schal gete this money; he knowith not me, and Y knowe not him; what tokyn schal Y yyue to hym? but nether Y knew ony tyme the weie, bi which me goith thidur.

3 Thanne his fadir answerid to hym, and seide, Sotheli Y haue this obligacioun at me, which the while thou schewist to him, he schal restore anoon the monei.

4 But go now, and enquere to thee sum feithful man, that schal go with thee for his hire saf, 'the while Y lyue yit, that thou resseyue that monei.

5 Thanne Tobie yede out, and foond a yong oon stondynge, 'schynynge, and gird, and as redi to go;

6 and he wiste not, that it was the angel of God. And he grette the yong oon, and seide, Of whennus han we thee, goode yonge man?

7 And he answeride, Of the sones of Israel. And Tobie seide to hym, Knowist thou the weie, that ledith in to the cuntrei of Medeis?

8 To whom he answeride, Y knowe, and Y haue go ofte alle the weies therof, and Y haue dwellid at Gabelus, youre brother, that dwellith in Rages, a citee of Medeis, which is set in 'the hil of Echbathanis.

9 To whom Tobie seide, Y biseche, abide thou me, til Y telle these thingis to my fader.

10 Thanne Tobie entride, and telde alle these thingis to his fader; on which thingis the fader wondride, and preiede, that he wolde entre to him.

11 Therfor he entride, and grette Tobie, and seide, Ioie be euere to thee!

12 And Tobie seide, What maner ioie schal be to me, that sitte in derknessis, and se not 'the liyt of heuene?

13 To whom the yong oon seide, Be thou of strong wit; it is in the nexte that thou be heelid of God.

14 Therfor Tobie seide to hym, Whether thou maist lede my sone to Gabelus in to Rages, the citee of Medeis, and whanne thou comest ayen, Y schal restore thi mede to thee?

15 And the aungel seide to hym, Y schal lede, and bringe ayen him hool to thee.

16 To whom Tobie answeride, Y preie thee, schewe to me, of what hows, ether of what lynage thou art?

17 To whom Raphael, the aungel, seide, Axist thou the kyn of the hirid man, ethir the hirid man hym silf, that schal go with thi sone?

18 But lest perauenture Y make thee douteful, Y am Azarie, the sone of grete Ananye.

19 And Tobie answeride, Thou art of greet kyn; but Y axe, that thou be not wrooth, that Y wolde knowe thi kyn.

20 Forsothe the aungel seide to hym, Y schal lede thi sone hool, and Y schal bring ayen to thee 'thi sone hool.

21 Sotheli Tobie answeride, and seide, Wel 'go ye, and the Lord be in youre weie, and his aungel go with you.

22 Thanne whanne alle thingis weren redi, that schulden be borun in the weie, Tobie made 'farewel to his fadir and his modir; and 'bothe yeden togidere.

23 And whanne thei weren goon forth, his modir bigan to wepe, and to seie, Thou hast take the staf of oure eelde, and hast sent awey fro vs;

24 'Y wolde thilke monei were neuere, 'for which thou sentist him;

25 oure pouert sufficide to vs, that we schulden arette this richessis, that we sien oure sone.

26 And Tobie seide to hir, 'Nyle thou wepe; oure sone schal come saaf, and he schal turne ayen saaf to vs, and thin iyen schulen se hym.

27 For Y bileue, that the good aungel of God goith with him, and he schal dispose wel alle thingis, that ben doon aboute hym, so that he turne ayen with ioie to vs.

28 At this vois his moder ceesside to wepe, and was stille.

CAP 6

1 Forsothe Tobie yede forth, and 'a dogge suede hym, and he dwellide in the firste dwellyng bisidis the flood of Tigrys.

2 And he 'yede out to waische hise feet; and lo! a greet fisch yede out to deuoure hym.

3 Which fisch Tobie dredde, and criede with greet vois, and seide, Sire, he assailith me.

4 And the aungel seide to hym, Take 'thou his gile, 'ether iowe, and drawe hym to thee. And whanne he hadde do this thing, he drow it in to the drie place, and it bigan to spraule bifor hise feet.

5 Thanne the aungel seide to hym, Drawe out the entrails of this fisch, and kepe to thee his herte and galle and mawe; for these thingis ben nedeful to medicyns profitabli.

6 And whanne he hadde do this thing, he rostide 'hise fleischis, and thei token 'with hem in the weie; thei saltiden othere thingis, that schulde suffice to hem in the weie, til thei camen in to Rages, the citee of Medeis.

7 Thanne Tobie axide the aungel, and seide to hym, Azarie, brother, Y biseche thee, that thou seie to me, what remedie these thingis schulen haue, whiche thou comaundidist to be kept of the fisch.

8 And the aungel answeride, and seide to hym, If thou puttist a lytil part of his herte on the coolis, the smoke therof dryueth awei al the kynde of feendis, ethir fro man ether fro womman, so that it neiye no more to hem.

9 And the galle is myche worth to anoynte iyen, in whiche is a web, and tho schulen be heelid.

10 And Tobie seide to him, Where wolt thou, that we dwelle?

11 And the aungel answeride, and seide, Here is a man, Raguel bi name, a nyy man of thi lynage, and he hath a douytir, Sare bi name; but nether he hath male nethir ony other femal, outakun hir.

12 Al his catel is due to thee; and it bihoueth thee haue hir to wijf.

13 Therfor axe thou hir of hir fadir; and he schal yyue 'hir a wijf to thee.

14 Thanne Tobie answeride, and seide, Y haue herd, that sche was youun to seuene hosebondis, and thei ben deed; but also Y herde this, that a fend killide hem.

15 Therfor Y dredde, lest perauenture also these thingis bifalle to me; and sithen Y am oon aloone to my fadir and modir, Y putte doun 'with sorewe her eelde to hellis.

16 Thanne the aungel Raphael seide to hym, Here thou me, and Y schal schewe to thee, 'whiche it ben, ouer whiche the fend hath maistrie; ouer hem,

17 that taken so weddyngys, that thei close out God fro hem and fro her mynde; 'the fend hath power ouer hem, that yyuen so tent to her letcherie, as an hors and mule doon, 'that han noon vndurstondyng.

18 But whanne thou hast take hir, entre thou in to the bed, and bi thre daies be thou continent 'fro hir, and to noon other thing thou schalt yyue tent with hir, no but to preieris.

19 Forsothe in that firste niyt, whanne the mawe of the fisch is brent, the fend schal be dryuun awei.

20 Sotheli in the secounde nyyt thou schalt be resseyued in the couplyng of hooli patriarkis.

21 Forsothe in the thridde nyyt thou schalt gete blessyng, that hoole sones be gendrid of you.

22 But whanne the thridde niyt is passid, thou schalt take the virgyn with the drede of the Lord, and thou schalt be led more bi the loue of children than of lust, that in the seed of Abraham thou gete blessyng in sones.

CAP 7

1 'Forsothe thei entriden to Raguel; and Raguel resseyuede hem with ioie.

2 And Raguel bihelde Tobie, and seide to Anne, his wijf, This yong man is ful lijk my sister sone.

3 And whanne he hadde seid these thingis, he seide, Of whennus ben ye, yonge men, oure britheren? And thei seiden, We ben of the lynage of Neptalym, of the caitifte of Nynyue.

4 And Raguel seide to hem, Knowen ye Tobi, my brother? Whiche answeriden, We knowen him.

5 And 'whanne he spak manye good thingis of Tobie, the aungel seide to Raguel, Tobie, of whom thou axist, is the fadir of this man.

6 Thanne Raguel bowede doun hym silf, and with teeris he kisside Tobie, and he wepte on his necke,

7 and seide, My sone, blessyng be to thee; for thou art the sone of a good and 'a ful noble man.

8 And Anne, 'his wijf, and Sare, 'the douytir of hem, wepten.

9 Forsothe after that thei hadden spoke, Raguel comaundide a wethir to be slayn, and a feeste to be maad redi. And whanne he excitide hem to sitte doun to mete, Tobie seide,

10 Y schal not ete, nethir drynke here to dai, no but thou conferme first myn axyng, and biheete to yyue to me Sare, thi douyter.

11 And whanne this word was herd, Raguel dredde, witynge what bifelde to tho seuene men; and he bigan for to drede, lest perauenture it schulde bifalle in lijk maner to this Tobie. And whanne he doutide, and yaf noon answere to the axere,

12 the aungel seide to hym, Nyle thou drede to yyue hir to this man; for thi douyter 'is due wiyf to this man dredynge God; therfor another man myyte not haue hir.

13 Thanne Raguel seide, Y doute not, that God hath resseyued my preieris and teeris in his siyt.

14 And Y bileue, that herfor the Lord made you come to me, that also this womman schulde be ioyned to her kynrede bi the lawe of Moises; and now nyle thou bere doute, that Y schal yyue hir to thee.

15 And he took the riyt hond of his douyter, and yaf to the riyt hond of Tobie, and seide, God of Abraham, and God of Isaac, and God of Jacob, be with you, and he ioyne you togidere, and 'he fille his blessyng in you.

16 And whanne a chartere 'was takun, thei maden 'writyng togidere of the mariage.

17 And aftir these thingis thei eten, and blessiden God.

18 And Raguel clepide to hym Anne, his wijf, and comaundide hir to make redi another bed.

19 And sche ledde Sare, hir douytir, in to it, and sche wepte; and Anne seide to hir, My douyter, be thou of strong wit; the Lord of heuene yyue to thee ioie, for the anoie that thou suffridist.

CAP 8

1 Forsothe aftir that thei hadden soupid, thei brouyten in the yong man to hir.

2 Therfor Tobie bithouyte of the wordis of the aungel, and 'brouyte forth of his scrippe a part of the mawe, and puttide it on quike coolis.

3 Thanne Raphael, the aungel, took the fend, and boond hym in the desert of hiyere Egipte.

4 Thanne Tobie monestide the virgyn, and seide to hir, Sare, rise vp, and preye we God to dai, and to morewe, and 'the secounde morewe; for in these thre nyytis we ben ioyned to God; sotheli whanne the thridde nyyt is passid, we schulen be in oure mariage;

5 for we ben the children of hooli men, and we moun not so be ioyned togidere as also hethene men, that knowen not God.

6 Sotheli thei risiden togidere, and bothe preyeden togidere bisili, that helthe schulde be youun to hem.

7 And Tobie seide, Lord God of oure fadris, heuenes, and londis, and the see, and wellis, and floodis, and ech creature of thin, which is in tho, blesse thee; thou madist Adam of the sliym of erthe,

8 and yauest to hym an help, Eue.

9 And now, Lord, thou woost, that Y take my sistir not for cause of letcherie, but for loue aloone of eeris, in whiche thi name be blessid in to worldis of worldis.

10 Therfor Sare seide, Lord, haue thou mercy on vs, haue thou merci on vs, and waxe we bothe eelde togidere hoole.

11 And it was doon aboute the 'cockis crowyng, Raguel made hise seruauntis to be clepid, and thei yeden with hym to digge a sepulcre.

12 For he dredde, lest it bifelde in lijk maner to hym, that bifelde also to 'seuene othere men, that entriden to hir.

13 And whanne thei hadden maad redi a pit, Raguel yede ayen to his wijf, and seide to hir,

14 Sende oon of thin handmaydis, and se sche, whether 'he is deed, that Y byrie hym, bifor that the liyt come.

15 And sche sente oon of hir handmaidis, which entride in to the closet, and foond hem saaf and sounde, slepynge togidir with hem silf.

16 And sche turnede ayen, and teld good massage. And thei blessiden the Lord, that is, Raguel and Anne,

17 his wijf, and seiden, Lord God of Israel, we blessen thee, for it 'bifelde not to vs, as we gessiden;

18 for thou hast do thi merci with vs, and hast schit out fro vs the enemy pursuynge vs.

19 Sotheli thou hast do merci 'to tweyne aloone. My Lord, make thou hem to blesse thee fulliere, and for to offre to thee the sacrifice of thi preisyng, and of her helthe, that the vnyuersite of folkis knowe, that thou art God aloone in al erthe.

20 And anoon Raguel comaundide hise seruauntis to fille the pit, which thei hadden maad, bifor that the liyt cam.

21 'Forsothe he seide to his wijf, that sche schulde araie a feeste, and make redi alle thingis, that weren nedeful to men makynge iournei.

22 Also he made to be slayn twei fatte kien, and foure wetheris, and metis to be maad redi to alle hise neiyboris, and alle hise frendis.

23 And Raguel made Tobie to swere, that he schulde 'dwelle twei woukis at Raguel.

24 Sotheli of alle thingis, whiche Raguel hadde in possessioun, he yaf the half part to Tobie; and he made this scripture, that the half part, that was left, schulde come to the lordschip of Tobie aftir the deeth of hem.

CAP 9

1 Thanne Tobie clepide to hym the aungel, whom sotheli he gesside a man. And Tobie seide to hym, Azarie, brother, Y axe, that thou herkne my wordis.

2 Thouy Y bitake my silf seruaunt to thee, Y schal not be euene worthi to thi puruyaunce.

3 Netheles Y biseche thee, that thou take to thee beestis, ethir seruyces, and go thou to Gabelus 'in to Rages, a citee of Medeis, and yelde to hym his obligacioun; and take of hym the money, and preie hym to come to my weddyngis.

4 For thou woost, that my fadir noumbrith the daies, and yf Y tarie o dai more, his soule schal be maad sorie.

5 And certis thou seest, hou Raguel hath chargid me, whos chargyng Y mai not dispise.

6 Thanne Raphael took foure of the seruauntis of Raguel, and twei camels, and yede in to Rages, a citee of Medeis, and he foond Gabelus, and yaf to hym his obligacioun, and resseyuede of hym al the monei;

7 and he schewide to hym of Tobie, the sone of Tobie, alle thingis that weren doon. And he made Gabelus come with hym to the weddyngis.

8 And whanne he entride in to the hows of Raguel, he foond Tobie sittynge at the mete; and 'he skippide vp, and thei kissiden hem silf togidere.

9 And Gabelus wepte, and blesside God, and seide, The Lord God of Israel blesse thee, for thou art the sone of a ful good man, and iust, and dredynge God, and doynge almesdedis;

10 and blessing be seid on thi wijf, and on youre fadris and modris,

11 and se ye youre sones, and the sones of youre sones, til in to the thridde and the fourthe generacioun; and youre seed be blessid of God of Israel, that regneth in 'to the worldis of worldis.

12 And whanne alle men hadden seid Amen, thei yeden to 'the feeste; but also thei vsiden the feeste of weddyngis with the drede of the Lord.

CAP 10

1 Sotheli whanne Tobie made tariyngis for 'the cause of weddyngis, 'Tobie his fadir was angwisched, seiynge, Gessist thou, whi my sone tarieth, ethir whi he is 'witholdun there?

2 Gessist thou, whether Gabelus is deed, and no man yeldith to hym the monei?

3 'Forsothe he bigan to be 'sorie ful myche, and Anne, his wijf, with hym; and bothe bigunnen to wepe togidere, for her sone turnede not ayen to hem 'in the dai set.

4 Therfor his modir wepte with teeris withouten remedie, and seide, Alas to me! my sone, whi senten we thee a pilgrimage, the liyt of oure iyen, the staf of oure eelde, the solace of oure lijf, the hope of oure eiris?

5 We hadden alle thingis togidere in thee oon, and ouyte not leete thee go fro vs.

6 To whom Tobie seide, Be stille, and nyle thou be troblid; oure sone is hool; thilke man is feithful ynow, with whom we senten hym.

7 Forsothe sche myyte not be coumfortid in ony maner, but ech dai sche 'skippide forthe, and lokide aboute, and cumpasside alle the weies, bi whiche the hope of 'comyng ayen was seyn, to se hym comynge afer, if it myyte be doon.

8 And sotheli Raguel seide to 'the hosebonde of his douytir, Dwelle thou here, and Y schal sende a messanger of helthe 'of thee to Tobie, thi fadir.

9 To whom Tobie seide, Y knowe, that my fadir and my modir rekynen now the daies, and her spirit is turmentid in hem.

10 And whanne Raguel preiede Tobie with many wordis, and he 'nolde here Raguel bi ony resoun, Raguel bitook to hym Sare, and half 'the part of al his catel, in children and damysels, in the scheep and camels, and in kiyn, and in myche monei; and he delyueride fro hym silf Tobie saaf and ioiynge,

11 and seide, The hooli aungel of the Lord be in youre weie, and brynge you sounde, and fynde ye alle thingis riytfuli aboute youre fadir and modir,

12 and myn iyen se youre sones, bifor that Y die. And the fadir and modir token 'her douyter, and kissiden hir,

13 and leeten hir go, and monestiden hir to onour the fader and modir of hir hosebonde, to loue the hosebonde, to reule the meynee, to gouerne the hows, and to schewe hir self vnrepreuable.

CAP 11

1 And whanne 'thei turneden ayen, thei camen to Carram, which is in the myddil of the weie ayens Nynyue, 'in the eleuenthe dai.

2 And the aungel seide, Tobie brother, thou woost, hou thou leftist thi fadir.

3 Therfor if it plesith thee, go we bifore; and the meineis, with thi wijf togidere and with the beestis, sue oure weie with soft goynge.

4 And whanne this pleside, that thei schulden go, Raphael seide to Tobie, Take with thee of the galle of the fisch, for it schal be nedeful. Therfor Tobie took of that galle, and thei yeden forth.

5 Forsothe Anne sat bisidis the weie ech dai in the cop of the hil, fro whennus sche myyte biholde fro afer.

6 And while sche biheelde fro the same place the comyng of hym, sche siy a fer, and knew anoon hir sone comynge; and sche ran, and telde to hir hosebonde, and seide, Lo! thi sone cometh.

7 And Raphael seide to Tobie, And whanne thou hast entrid in to thin hows, anoon worschipe 'thi Lord God, and do thou thankyngis to hym, and neiye to thi fadir, and kisse hym.

8 And anoon anoynte on hise iyen of this galle of the fisch, which galle thou berist with thee; for 'whi wite thou, that anoon hise iyen schulen be openyd, and 'thi fadir schal se the liyt of heuene, and he schal be ioiful in thi siyt.

9 Thanne the dogge 'ran bifore, 'that was togidere in the weie, and made ioie with the faunyng of his tail, as a messanger comynge.

10 And his blynde fadir roos vp, and bigan to renne, hirtynge 'in the feet, and whanne he hadde youe hond to a child, he ran ayens his sone.

11 And he resseyuede and kisside hym, 'with his wijf, and bothe bigunnen to wepe for ioie.

12 And whanne thei hadden worschipid God, and hadden do thankyngis, thei saten togidere.

13 Thanne Tobie took of the galle of the fisch, and anoyntide the iyen of his fadir.

14 And he abood as half an our almest, and the web, as the litil skyn of an ey, bigan to go out of hise iyen.

15 Which web Tobie took, and drow fro hise iyen, and anoon he resseyuede siyt.

16 And thei glorifieden God, that is, he, and his wijf, and alle that knewen hym.

17 And Tobie seide, Lord God of Israel, Y blesse thee, for thou hast chastisid me, and thou hast saued me; and lo! Y se Tobie, my sone.

18 Also Sare, the wijf of his sone, entride aftir seuene daies, and alle the meynees, and the beestis hoole, and camels, and miche monei of the wijf, but also the money which 'he hadde resseyued of Gabelus.

19 And he telde to his fadir and modir alle the benefices of God, whiche he hadde do aboute hym bi the man, that hadde led hym.

20 And Achior and Nabath, the 'sistir sones of Tobie, camen ioiful to Tobie, and thankiden hym of alle the 'goodis, whiche God hadde schewid aboute hym.

21 And bi seuene daies thei eeten, and ioyden with greet ioye.

CAP 12

1 Thanne Tobie clepide to hym his sone, and seide to hym, What moun we yyue to this hooli man, that cam with thee?

2 Tobie answeride, and seide to his fadir, Fadir, what meede schulen we yyue to hym, ether what mai be worthi to hise benefices?

3 He ledde, and 'brouyte me hool ayen; he resseyuede of Gabelus the monei; he made me to haue a wijf, and he droof awei the feend fro hir; he made ioie to hir fadir and moder; he delyuerede 'my silf fro the deuouryng of a fisch; and he made thee to se the liyt of heuene; and we ben fillid with alle goodis bi hym; what thing worthi to these thingis moun we yyue to hym?

4 But, fadir, Y axe thee, that thou preie hym, if perauenture he schal vouche saaf to take to hym the half of alle thingis, what euer thingis ben brouyt.

5 And the fadir and the sone clepiden hym, and token hym asidis half, and bigunnen to preie, that he wolde vouche saaf to haue acceptable the half part of alle thingis, whiche thei hadden brouyt.

6 Thanne he seide to hem priueli, Blesse ye God of heuene, and knouleche ye to hym bifor alle men lyuynge, for he hath do his merci with you.

7 For it is good to hide the priuyte of a kyng; but it is worschipful to schewe and knowleche the werkis of God.

8 Preier is good with fastyng, and almes, more than to hide tresouris of gold;

9 for whi almes delyuereth fro deth, and thilke almes it is that purgith synnes, and makith to fynde euerlastynge lijf.

10 Forsothe thei that doon synne and wickidnesse, ben enemyes of her soule.

11 Therfor Y schewe trewthe to you, and Y schal not hide fro you a pryuy word.

12 Whane thou preyedist with teeris, and biryedist deed men, and 'forsokist the meete, and hiddist deed men bi dai in thin

hows, and biriedist 'in the nyyt, Y offride thi preier to the Lord.

13 And for thou were acceptable to God, it was nedeful that temptacioun schulde preue thee.

14 And now the Lord sente me 'for to cure thee, and to delyuere Sare, the wijf of thi sone, fro the fend.

15 For Y am Raphael, the aungel, oon of the seuene that ben present bifor the Lord.

16 And whanne thei hadden herd this, thei weren disturblid, and felden tremblynge on her face.

17 And the aungel seide to hem, Pees be to you, nyle ye drede;

18 for whanne Y was with you, Y was bi Goddis wille. Blesse ye hym, and synge ye to hym.

19 Sotheli Y semyde to ete and drynke with you; but Y vse vnuysible meete, and drynk that mai not be seyn of men.

20 Therfor it is tyme, that Y turne ayen to hym, that sente me; but blesse ye God, and telle ye out alle hise merueils; blesse ye hym, and synge ye to hym.

21 And whanne he hadde seide these thingis, he was takun awei fro her siyt; and thei myyten no more se hym.

22 Thanne thei felden doun 'bi thre ouris on the face, and blessiden God; and thei risynge vp telden alle hise merueils.

CAP 13

1 Forsothe the eldere Tobie openyde his mouth, and blesside God, and seide, Lord, thou art greet with outen ende, and thi rewme is in to 'alle worldis;

2 for thou betist, and makist saaf; thou ledist doun to hellis, and 'ledist ayen; and noon is that ascapith thin hoond.

3 Sones of Israel, knowleche ye to the Lord, and herye ye hym in the siyt of hethene men;

4 for herfor he scateride you among hethene men, that knowen not God, that ye telle out his merueils, and make hem to wite, that noon othere God is almyyti outakun hym.

5 He chastiside vs for oure wickidnessis; and he schal saue vs for his mercy.

6 Therfor biholde ye, what thingis he hath do with you, and knouleche ye to hym with drede and tremblyng; and enhaunse ye the kyng of worldis in youre werkis.

7 Forsothe Y in the lond of my caitifte schal knouleche to hym; for he schewide his maieste on a synful folc.

8 Therfor, synneris, be ye conuertid, and do ye riytfulnesse bifor God, and bileue ye, that he schal do his merci with you.

9 Sotheli Y and my soule schulen be glad in hym.

10 Alle chosun of the Lord, blesse ye hym; make ye the daies of gladnesse, and knouleche ye to hym.

11 Jerusalem, the citee of God, the Lord hath chastisid thee for the werkis of thin hondis.

12 Knouleche thou to God in thi goodis, and blesse thou God of worldis, that he bilde ayen in thee his tabernacle, and ayen clepe to thee alle thi prisoneris; and that thou haue ioie in to alle worldis of worldis.

13 Thou schalt schyne with briyt liyt, and alle the coostis of erthe schulen worschipe thee.

14 Naciouns schulen come fro fer to thee, and thei schulen brynge yiftis, and schulen worschipe the Lord in thee, and thei schulen haue thi lond in to halewyng;

15 for thei schulen 'clepe in thee the grete name.

16 And thei schulen be cursid, that dispisen thee, and thei schulen be dampned, that blasfemen thee; and thei schulen be blessid, that bilden thee.

17 Forsothe thou schalt be glad in thi sones, for alle schulen be blessid, and schulen be gaderid togidere to the Lord.

18 Blessid ben alle that louen thee, and that han ioie on thi pees.

19 My soule, blesse thou the Lord, for 'oure Lord God hath delyuered Jerusalem, his citee, fro alle tribulaciouns therof.

20 Y schal be blessid, if the relikis of my seed schulen be to se the clerenesse of Jerusalem.

21 The yatis of Jerusalem schulen be bildid of saphire and smaragde, and of preciouse stoon; al the cumpas of wallis therof schal be of white and clene stoon.

22 Alle the stretis therof schulen be strewid; and alleluya, 'that is, the heriyng of God, schal be sungun bi the stretis therof.

23 Blessid be the Lord, that enhaunside it, that his rewme be on it in to worldis of worldis. Amen.

CAP 14

1 And the wordis of Tobie [Note: Tobie The preisable knowleching of Tobie, and his profecie of heuenli Jerusalem.] weren endid; and aftir that he was liytned, he lyuede two and fourti yeer, and siy the sones of hise sones sones.

2 For whanne an hundrid yeer and tweyn weren fillid, he was biried worschipfuli in Nynyue.

3 'For he of sixe and fifti yeer loste the liyt of iyen; sotheli he sixti yeer eeld resseyuede 'that liyt.

4 Forsothe the residue of his lijf was in ioie, and he yede in pees with good encresyng of Goddis drede.

5 Forsothe in the our of his deeth he clepide to hym Tobie, his sone, and seuene yonge sones of hym, hise sones sones,

6 and seide to hem, The perischyng of Nynyue schal be niy, for the word of God schal not falle doun [Note: sum is profesie of manaas, and this is chaungid, as the meritis of men chaungen; and in this maner Jonas profeciede the distriyng of Nynyue, but for thei diden penaunce, this peyne was delayed; and whanne thei turneden ayen to her synnes, God yaf ful doom of distriynge of Nynyue bi profesie of predestynacioun ether of ful doom, as it is in Goddis knowyng, and this profesie ether doom is neuere chaungid.]; and youre britheren, that ben scaterid fro the lond of Israel, schulen turne ayen to it.

7 Sotheli al deseert lond therof schal be fillid, and the hows of God, which is brent ther ynne, schal be bildid ayen, and alle that dreden God schulen turne ayen thidur.

8 And hethene men schulen forsake her idols [Note: this profesie was fillid in part, whanne the Jewis turneden ayen fro Babiloyne; but more perfitly it was fillid in the tyme of Crist and hise apostlis, whanne hethen men forsoken her idols, and camen to cristen feith, and serueden Crist truly, King of Israel.], and schulen come to Jerusalem, and schulen 'enhabite it.

9 And alle the kyngis of erthe schulen haue ioie ther ynne, and schulen worschipe the kyng of Israel.

10 Therfor, my sones, here ye youre fadir; serue ye the Lord in drede and treuthe; and enquere ye to do tho thingis that ben plesaunt to hym.

11 And comaunde ye youre sones to do riytfulnessis and almesdedis; that thei be myndeful of God, and blesse God in al tyme, in treuthe and in al her vertu.

12 Now therfor, my sones, here ye me, and nyle ye dwelle here, but in what euer dai ye han biried youre modir biside me in o sepulcre, fro that dai dresse ye youre steppis, that ye go out fro hennus;

13 for Y se that the wickidnesse therof schal 'yyue an ende therto.

14 Forsothe it was doon aftir the deeth of his modir, Tobie yede awei fro Nynyue, with his wijf, and sones, and with the sones of sones, and turnede ayen to the fadir and modir of his wijf.

15 And he foond hem sounde in good eelde. And he dide the cure of hem, and he closide her iyen; and he took al the erytage of the hows of Raguel, and he siy the fyuethe generacioun, the sones of hise sones.

16 And whanne nynti yeer and nyne weren fillid in the drede of the Lord, thei birieden hym with ioie.

17 Forsothe al his kynrede, and al his generacioun, dwellide perfitli in good lijf, and in hooli conuersacioun, so that thei weren acceptable bothe to God and to men, and to alle enhabitynge the erthe.

JUDITH

CAP 1

1 'And so Arphaxat, kyng of Medeis, hadde maad suget many folkis to his empire; and he bildide a ful myyti citee, which he clepide Egbathanys.

2 Of squarid stonys and korfe he made the wallis therof, in the heiythe of thre score cubitis and ten, and in the breede of thritti cubitis. Sotheli he settide the touris therof in the heiythe of an hundrid cubitis.

3 Forsothe bi the square of tho touris euer either side was stretchid forth, bi the space of twenti feet; and he settide the yatis of that citee in the heiythe of the touris.

4 And he hadde glorie, as miyti in the power of his oost, and in the glorie of hise charis.

5 Therfor Nabugodonosor, kyng of Assyriens, that regnede in the grete citee Nynyue, fauyt in the tweluethe yeer of his rewme ayens Arphaxat, and gat him in the greet feeld,

6 'which is clepid Ragau, bisidis Eufrates, and Tigris, and Jadasa, in the feeld of Erioch, kyng of Elichoris.

7 Thanne the rewme of Nabugodonosor was enhaunsid, and his herte was reisid; and he sente to alle men, that dwelliden in Cilicie, and in Damask, and in Liban,

8 and to folkis, that weren in Carmele, and in Cedar, and to men dwellynge in Galile, and in the grete feeld of Esdrolon, and to alle men,

9 that weren in Samarie, and biyende the flood Jordan, 'til to Jerusalem; and to al the lond of Jesse, til me come to the hillis of Ethiope.

10 Nabugodonosor, kyng of Assiriens, sente messangeris 'to alle these men; 'which alle ayenseiden with o wille, and senten ayen hem voide, and castiden awei with out onour.

12 Thanne kyng Nabugodonosor was wrooth to al that lond, and swoor bi his rewme and trone, that he wolde defende him fro alle these cuntreis.

CAP 2

1 In the thrittenthe yeer of kyng Nabugodonosor, in the two and twentithe dai of the firste monethe, a word was maad in the hows of Nabugodonosor, kyng of Assiriens, that he wolde defende hym.

2 And he clepide to hym alle the eldere men, and alle duykis, hise werriouris; and hadde with hem the priuete of his counsel.

3 And he seide, that his thouyte was in that thing, to make suget ech lond to his empire.

4 And whanne this seiyng hadde plesid alle men, 'kyng Nabugodonosor clepide Holofernes, prince of his chyualrie,

5 and seide to hym, Go thou out ayens ech rewme of the west, and ayens hem principali, that dispisiden 'my comaundement.

6 Thin iyen schal not spare ony rewme, and thou schalt make suget to me ech strengthid citee.

7 Thanne Holofernes clepide the duykis and magistratis of the vertu of Assiriens, and he noumbride men in to the makyng redi, as the kyng 'comaundide to hym, sixe score thousynde of foot men fiyteris, and twelue thousynde horse men and archeris.

8 And he made al his puruyaunce to go bifore in multitude of vnnoumbrable camels, with these thingis that suffisiden plenteuousli to the oostis, and droues of oxis, and flockis of scheep, of which was noon noumbre.

9 He ordeynede whete to be maad redi of al Sirie 'in his passage.

10 And he took ful myche gold and siluer of the kyngis hows.

11 And he, and al his oost, yede forth with charis, and horse men, and archeris, whiche hiliden the face of the erthe, as locustis doon.

12 And whanne he hadde passid the endis of Assiriens, he came to the grete hillis Auge, that ben at the lift half of Cilicie; and he stiede in to alle the castels of hem, and he gat ech strong place.

13 Forsothe he brak the richeste, ethir famouse, citee Melothi, and robbide alle the sones of Tharsis, and the sones of Ismael, that weren ayens the face of desert, and at the south of the lond Celeon.

14 And he passide Eufrates, and cam in to Mesopotanye, and he brak alle hiye citees that weren there, fro the stronde Manbre til 'me come to the see.

15 And he occupiede the endis therof fro Cilicie 'til to the endis of Japhet, that ben at the south.

16 And he brouyte alle the sones of Madian, and he 'robbide al the richessis of hem; and he killide 'bi the scharpnesse of swerd alle men ayenstondynge hym.

17 And after these thingis he cam doun in to the feeldis of Damask, in the daies of ripe corn, and he brente alle cornes, and he made alle trees and vynes to be kit doun;

18 and his drede 'felde on alle men 'enhabitynge the lond.

CAP 3

1 Thanne kyngis and princes of alle citees and prouynces, that is, of Cirie, of Mesopotanye, and of Sirie Sobal, and of Libie, and of Cilicie, sente her messangeris. 'Whiche comynge to Holofernes, seiden,

2 Thin indignacioun ceesse aboute vs; for it is betere, that we lyue and serue Nabugodonosor, the grete kyng, and be suget to thee, than that we die, and suffre with oure perischyng the harmes of oure seruage.

3 Ech citee of oure, al possessioun, alle munteyns, and litle hillis, and feeldis, and droues of oxes, and flockis of scheep, and of geet,

4 and of horsis, and of camels, and alle oure richessis and meyneis ben in thi siyt; alle thingis be vndur thi lawe.

5 Also we and oure children ben thi seruauntis.

6 Come thou a pesible lord to vs, and vse thou oure seruyce, as it plesith thee.

7 Thanne he cam doun fro the hillis, with knyytis in greet 'vertu, that is, strengthe, and gat ech citee, and ech man 'enhabitynge the lond.

8 Forsothe of alle citees he took to hym helperis, stronge men and chosun to batel.

9 And so grete drede lay on alle prouynces, that enhabiteris of alle citees, princes and 'onourid men, yeden togidere out with puplis to meete hym comynge,

10 and 'resseyueden hym with corouns and laumpis, and ledden daunsis with pipis and tympans.

11 Netheles thei doynge these thingis myyten not swage the fersnesse of his herte;

12 for whi bothe he distriede her citees, and hew doun her wodis.

13 For kyng Nabugodonosor hadde comaundid to hym, that he schulde distrie alle the goddis of erthe, that is, that he aloone schulde be seid god of alle these naciouns, that myyten be maad suget bi the power of Holofernes.

14 Forsothe he passide al Sirie Sobal, and al Appanye, and al Mesopotanye, and cam to Idumeis 'in to the lond of Gabaa;

15 and he took the citees of hem, and dwellide there bi thritti daies, in whiche daies he comaundide al the oost of his power to be gaderid togidere.

CAP 4

1 Thanne the sones of Israel, that dwelliden in the lond of Juda, herden these thingis, and dredden greetli of 'his face.

2 Also tremblyng and hidousnesse asailide the wittis of hem, lest he schulde do this thing to Jerusalem and to the temple of the Lord, which thing he hadde do to othere citees and templis of tho.

3 And thei senten in to al Samarie, bi cumpas 'til to Jerico, and bifore ocupieden alle the coppis of hillis;

4 and thei cumpassiden her townes with wallis, and gaderiden togidere wheete in to making redi of batel.

5 Also the prest Eliachym wroot to alle men, 'that weren ayenus Esdrelon, which is ayenus the face of the grete feeld bisidis Dotaym, and to alle men bi whiche passage myyte be,

6 that thei schulden holde the stiyngis of hillis, bi whiche weie myyte be to Jerusalem, and that thei schulden kepe there, where streyt weie miyte be among hillis.

7 And the sones of Israel diden aftir this, that Eliachym, prest of the Lord, hadde ordeyned to hem.

8 And al the puple criede to the Lord with greet instaunce, and thei and the wymmen of hem mekiden her soulis in fastyngis.

9 And the prestis clothiden hem silf with heyris, and yonge children boweden hem silf ayens the face of the temple of the Lord, and thei hiliden the auter of the Lord with an heire.

10 And thei crieden togidere to the Lord God of Israel, lest the children of hem schulden be youun in to prey, and the wyues of hem in to departyng, and her citees in to distriyng, and her hooli thingis in to defoulyng.

11 Thanne Eliachym, the grete prest of the Lord, cumpasside al Israel,

12 and spak to hem, and seide, Wite ye, that the Lord schal here youre preieris, if ye dwellinge dwellen perfitli in fastyngis and preieris in the siyt of the Lord.

13 Be ye myndful of Moises, the seruaunt of the Lord, which not in fiytynge with irun, but in preiynge with hooli preieris, castide doun Amalech tristinge in his vertu, and in his power, and in his oost, and in hise scheldis, and in hise charis, and in hise knyytis;

14 so alle the enemyes of Israel schulen be cast doun, if ye continuen in this werk, which ye han bigunne.

15 Therfor at this excityng of hym thei preieden hertli the Lord, 'and dwelliden in the siyt of the Lord, so that also thei,

16 that offriden brent sacrifices to the Lord, weren gird with heiris, and thei offriden sacrifices to the Lord, and 'aische was on her heedis.

17 And alle men of al her herte preieden God, that he wolde visite his puple Israel.

CAP 5

1 And it was teld to Holofernes, prince of the chiualrie of Assiriens, that the children of Israel maden redi hem silf to ayenstonde, and that thei hadden closid togidere the weies of hillis.

2 And bi ouer greet woodnesse he brente out in to greet wrathfulnesse; and he clepide alle the princes of Moab, and the duykis of Amon,

3 and seide to hem, Seie ye to me, who this puple is, that bisegith the hilli places; ethir whiche, and what maner, and hou grete ben her citees; also what is the vertu of hem, ether what is the multitude of hem, ethir who is the kyng of her chyualrie;

4 and whi bifor alle men, that dwellen in the eest, han these men dispisid me, and thei han not go out to resseyue vs with pees?

5 Than Achior, duyk of alle the sones of Amon, answerde and seide, My lord, if thou vouchist saaf to here, Y schal seie treuthe in thi siyt of this puple that dwellith in the hilli places, and a fals word schal not go out of my mouth.

6 This puple is of the generacioun of Caldeis;

7 this puple dwellide firste in Mesopotanye; for thei nolden sue the goddis of her fadris, that weren in the lond of Caldeis.

8 Therfor thei forsoken the cerymonyes of her fadris, that weren with the multitude of goddis,

9 and worschipiden o God of heuene, which also comaundide to hem to go out fro thennus, and to dwelle in Carram. And whanne hungur hadde hilid al the lond, thei yeden doun in to Egipt, and there thei weren so multiplied bi foure hundrid yeer, that the oost of hem myyte not be noumbrid.

10 And whanne the kyng of Egipt hadde greuyd hem, and hadde maad hem sugetis in the bildyngis of hise citees in cley and tijl stoon, thei crieden to her God, and he smoot al the lond of Egipt with dyuerse veniaunces.

11 And whanne Egipcians hadden castid out 'hem fro hem silf, and the veniaunce hadde ceessid fro hem, and efte wolden take hem, and ayen clepe to her seruyce,

12 God of heuene openyde the see to these men fleynge, so that on this side and that side the watris weren maad sad as wallis, and these men with dry foot passiden 'in walkynge bi the depthe of the see.

13 In which place the while vnnoumbrable oost of Egipcians pursuede hem, it was so kyueryd with watris, that there dwellide not nameli oon, that schulde telle the dede to aftir comeris.

14 Also thei yeden out of the Reed See, and ocupieden the desertis of the hil Sina, in whiche 'neuere man myyte dwelle, nethir the sone of man restyde.

15 There bittir wellis weren maad swete to hem for to drynke; and bi fourti yeer thei gaten lyuelode fro heuene.

16 Where euere thei entriden, her God fauyt for hem, and ouer cam with out bouwe and arowe, and without scheld and swerd.

17 And 'noon was that castide doun this puple, no but whanne it yede awey fro the worschipyng of her Lord God.

18 Sotheli as ofte euere as thei worschipiden an other outakun thilke her God, thei weren youun in to preye, and in to swerd, and in to schenschip.

19 But as ofte euere as thei repentiden that thei hadden go awei fro the worschipyng of her God, God of heuene yaf to hem vertue to ayenstonde.

20 Forsothe thei castiden doun the kyng Cananei, and Jebusei, and Pheresei, and Ethei, and Euey, and Ammorrei, and alle the myyti men of Esebon, and thei hadden in possessioun the londis of hem, and the citees of hem;

21 and til that thei hadden synned in the siyt of her God, good thingis weren with hem, for the God of hem hatith wickidnesse.

22 For whi and bifor these yeeris, whanne thei hadden go awei fro the weie which God hadde youe to hem, that thei schulden go ther ynne, thei weren distried of naciouns bi many batels, and ful many of hem weren led prisoneris in to a lond not hern.

23 Forsothe a while agoon thei turneden ayen to 'her Lord God, and weren gaderid togidere fro the scateryng, in which thei weren scaterid; and thei stieden in to alle these hilli places, and eft thei han Jerusalem in possessioun, where the hooli of hooli thingis ben.

24 Now therfor, my lord, enquere thou perfitli, if ony wickidnesse of hem is in the siyt of her God, and stie we to hem; for her God bitakynge schal bitake hem to thee, and thei schulen be maad suget vndur the yok of thi myyt.

25 Trewli if noon offense of this puple is bifor her God, we moun not ayenstonde hem; for the God of hem schal defende hem, and we schulen be in to schenschip to al erthe.

26 And it was doon, whanne Achior hadde ceessid to speke these wordis, alle the grete men of Holofernes weren wrothe, and thei thouyten to sle hym,

27 and seiden togidere, Who is this that seith, that the sones of Israel, men with outen armure, and with out vertu, and with out kunnyng of the craft of fiytynge, moun ayenstonde kyng Nabugodonosor and hise oostis?

28 Therfor that Achior knowe, that he disseyueth vs, stie we in to the hilli places; and whanne the myyti men of hem ben takun, thanne he schal be persid with swerd with the same men;

29 'that ech folk knowe, that Nabugodonosor is god of erthe, and outakun hym 'noon other is.

CAP 6

1 Forsothe it was doon, whanne thei hadden ceessid to speke, Holofernes hadde dedeyn gretli,

2 and seide to Achior, For thou propheciedist to vs, and seidist, that the folk of Israel is defendid of her God, that Y schewe to thee, that no god is no but Nabugodonosor;

3 whanne we han slayn 'hem alle as o man, thanne also thou schalt perische with hem bi the swerd of Assiriens, and al Israel schal perische dyuerseli with thee in perdicioun; and thou schalt preue,

4 that Nabugodonosor is lord of al erthe; and thanne the swerd of my chyualrie schal passe thorouy thi sidis, and thou schalt be persid, and schalt falle among the woundid men of Israel, and thou schalt no more brethe ayen, til thou be distried with hem.

5 But certis if thou gessist thi profecie sothe, thi cheer falle not doun; and the palenesse that hath gete thi face, go awey fro thee, if thou gessist that these my wordis moun not 'be fillid.

6 But that thou knowe, that thou schalt feele this thing togidere with hem, lo! fro this our thou schalt be felouschipid to the puple of hem, that whanne thei han take worthi peynes of my swerd, thou be suget to lijk veniaunce.

7 Thanne Olofernes comaundide hise seruauntis to take Achior, and to lede hym in to Bethulia, and to bitake hym in to the hondis of the sones of Israel.

8 And the seruauntis of Olofernes token him, and yeden forth bi the feeldi places, but whanne thei hadden neiyid to the hilli places, slingeris yeden out ayens hem.

9 Sotheli thei turneden awei fro the side of the hil, and bounden Achior to a tre bi hondis and feet, and so thei leften hym boundun with withthis, and turneden ayen to her lord.

10 Certis the sones of Israel yeden doun fro Bethulia, and camen to hym, whom thei vnbounden, and ledden to Bethulia, and thei settiden hym in to the myddis of the puple, and axiden, what manere of thinges bifel, that Assiriens hadden left hym boundun.

11 In tho daies princes weren there, Ozias, the sone of Mycha, of the lynage of Symeon, and Charmy, which is also Gothonyel.

12 Therfor in the myddis of eldere men, and in the siyt of alle men, Achior seide alle thingis, whiche he was axid of Holofernes, and hadde spoke, and hou the puple of Holofernes wolde sle hym for this word,

13 and hou Holofernes hym silf was wrooth, and comaundide hym to be bitakun for this cause to men of Israel, that the while he ouercam the sones of Israel, thanne he comaundide that also thilk Achior perische bi dyuerse turmentis, for this that he hadde seid, God of heuene is the defendere of hem.

14 And whanne Achior hadde expowned alle thingis, al the puple felde doun on the face, and worschipide the Lord; and with comyn weilyng and wepyng thei schedden out to the Lord her preyeris of o wille,

15 seiynge, Lord God of heuene and of erthe, biholde the pride of hem, and biholde thou to oure mekenesse, and perseyue the face of thi seyntis, and schewe that thou forsakist not men tristynge of thee, and thou makist low men tristynge of hem silf, and 'men hauynge glorie of her vertu.

16 Therfor whanne the wepyng was endid, and the preier of the puple bi al the dai was fillid,

17 thei coumfortiden Achior, and seiden, God of oure fadris, whos vertu thou prechidist, he is rewardere, and schal yyue to thee this while, that thou se more the perischyng of hem.

18 Forsothe whanne 'oure Lord God hath youe this fredom to hise seruauntis, also the Lord be with thee in the myddis of vs, that as it plesith thee, so thou lyue with 'alle thi thingis.

19 Thanne after that the counsel was endid, Ozias resseyuede hym in to his hows, and made a greet soper to hym.

20 And whanne alle the prestis weren clepid togidere, aftir that the fastyng was fillid, thei refreischiden Achior 'and hem silf.

21 Forsothe aftirward al the puple was clepid togidere, and thei preieden bi al the niyt with ynne the chirche, and axiden help of God of Israel.

CAP 7

1 Forsothe in 'the tother dai Holofernes comaundide hise oostis to stie ayens Bethulia.

2 Forsothe there weren six score thousynde 'foot men of fiyteris, and twelue thousynde knyytis, 'outakun the makyng redi of tho men, whiche caitifte hadde ocupied, and weren brouyt fro prouynces and citees, of alle yongthe.

3 Alle togidere maden hem redi to batel ayens the sones of Israel; and thei camen bi the side of the hil 'til to the cop, that biholdith Dothaym, fro the place which is seid Belma 'til to Selmon, which is ayens Esdrolon.

4 Forsothe the sones of Israel, as thei sien the multitude of hem, bowiden doun hem silf on the erthe, and senten aische on her heedis, and preiden with o wille, that God of Israel schulde schewe his merci on his puple.

5 And thei token her armuris of batel, and saten bi the places 'that dressen the path of streyt weie bitwixe hilli places, and thei kepten tho places al the dai and nyyt.

6 Certis Holofernes, the while he yede aboute bi cumpas, foonde that the welle, that flowide in to the watir cundit of hem, was dressid at the south part with out the citee, and he comaundide her watir cundit to be kit.

7 Netheles wellis weren not fer fro the wallis, of whiche wellis thei weren seyn to drawe watir bi thefte, rather to refreische than to drynke.

8 But the sones of Amon and of Moab neiyiden to Holofernes, and seiden, The sones of Israel tristen not in spere and arowe, but hillis defenden hem, and litle hillis set in the rooche of stoon maken hem stronge.

9 Therfor that thou maist ouercome hem without asailyng of batel, sette thou keperis of wellis, that thei drawe not of tho; and thou schalt sle hem without swerd, ethir certis thei maad feynt schulen bitake her citee, which thei gessen 'to mow not be ouercomun 'in the hillis.

10 And these wordis plesiden bifor Holofernes, and bifor alle hise knyytis; and he ordeynede bi cumpas bi ech welle an hundrid men.

11 And whanne 'this kepyng was fillid bi twenti daies, cisternes and gaderyngis of watris fayliden to alle men dwellynge in Bethulia, so that there was not with ynne the citee, wherof thei schulden be fillid, nameli o dai, for the watir was youun at mesure to the puplis ech dai.

12 Thanne alle men and wymmen, yonge men and elde, and litle children, weren gaderid togidere to Ozie, and alle thei seiden to gidere with o vois,

13 The Lord deme bitwixe vs and thee, for thou, not wyllynge speke pesibli with Assiriens, hast 'do yuels ayenus vs, and for this thing God hath seld vs in the hondis of hem.

14 And therfor 'noon is that helpith, whanne we ben cast doun in thirst, and in greet los bifor her iyen.

15 And now gadere ye togidere alle men, that ben in the citee, that alle we puplis bitake vs bi fre wille to Holofernes.

16 It is betere that we prisoneris blesse God and lyue, than that we die, and be schenschip to ech man, sithen we seen that oure wyues and oure yonge children dien bifor oure iyen.

17 We clepen in to witnessyng to dai heuene and erthe, and the God of oure fadris, that punischith vs aftir oure synnes, that nowe ye bitake the citee in to the hondis of the chyualrie of Holofernes, and oure ende be schort in the scharpnesse of swerd, which ende is maad lengere in the drynesse of thirst.

18 And whanne thei hadden seid these thingis, greet wepyng and yellyng was maad of alle men in the grete chirche, and bi many ouris thei crieden 'with o vois to the Lord,

19 and seiden, We and oure fadris han synned, we han do vniustli, we diden wickidnesse.

20 Thou, for thou art mercyful, haue mercy on vs, and venge oure wickidnessis in thi scourge; and nyle thou bitake men knoulechynge thee to a puple that knowith not thee,

21 that thei seie not amonge hethene men, Where is the God of hem?

22 And whanne thei weren maad feynt with these cries, and weren maad wery with these wepyngis, and weren stille,

23 Ozie roos up, bisched with teeris, and seide, Britheren, be ye pacient, and bi these fyue daies abide we mercy of the Lord;

24 for in hap he schal kitte a wei his indignacioun, and schal yyue glorie to his name.

25 Sotheli if whanne these fyue daies ben passid, help cometh not, we schulen do these wordis whiche ye han spoke.

CAP 8

1 And it was doon, whanne Judith, the widowe, had herd these wordis, whiche Judith was the douyter of Merary, the sone of Idor, the sone of Joseph, the sone of Ozie, the sone of Elai, the sone of Jamnor, the sone of Jedeon, the sone of Raphony, the sone of Achitob, the sone of Melchie, the sone of Euam, the sone of Mathanye, the sone of Salatiel, the sone of Symeon, the sone of Ruben.

2 And hir hosebonde was Manasses, that was deed in the daies of barli heruest;

3 for he stood bisili ouer men byndynge togidere reepis in the feeld, and heete cam on his heed, and he was deed in Bethulia his citee, and was biried there with hise fadris.

4 Sotheli Judith left of hym was widewe thanne thre yeer and sixe monethis. And in the hiyere partis of hir hows sche made to hir a priuy closet, in which sche dwellide cloos with hir damesels;

5 and sche hadde an heire on her leendis, and fastide alle the daies of hir lijf, outakun sabatis, and the 'bigynnyngis of monethis, and the feestis of the hows of Israel.

6 Sotheli sche was of ful semeli biholdyng, to whom hir hosebonde hadde left many richessis, and plenteuouse meynee, and possessiouns ful of droues of oxis, and of flockis of scheep.

7 And this Judith was moost famouse among alle men; for sche dredde God greetli, nethir ony was that spak of hir an yuel word.

8 Therfor whanne this Judith hadde herd, that Ozie hadde bihiyte, that whanne the fyuethe day was passid, he wolde bitake the citee, sche sente to the prestis Cambri and Carmy.

9 And thei camen to hir; and sche seide to hem, What is this word, in which Ozie consentide to bitake the citee to Assiriens, if with ynne fyue daies help cometh not to vs?

10 And who ben ye that tempten the Lord?

11 This 'word is not that stirith merci; but rather that stirith ire, and kyndlith woodnesse.

12 Han ye set tyme of the merciful doynge of the Lord, and in youre wille 'ye han set a dai to hym?

13 But for the Lord is pacient, do we penaunce for this synne, and axe we with teeris his foryyuenesse;

14 for God schal not manaasse so as man, nethir as 'a sone of man he schal be enflawmed to wrathfulnesse.

15 And therfor meke we oure soulis to hym, and in contrit spirit and maad meke serue we hym;

16 and seie we wepynge to the Lord, that aftir his wille so he do his merci with vs; and as oure herte is troblid in the pride of hem, so haue we glorie 'also of oure mekenesse.

17 For we 'sueden not the synnes of oure fadris, that forsoken her God, and worschipiden alien goddis;

18 for which greet trespas thei weren youun to her enemyes in to swerd, and in to raueyn, and in to confusioun; but we knowen not an othir God outakun hym.

20 'Abide we meke his coumfort, and he schal seke oure blood of the turmentis of oure enemies; and he schal make meke alle folkis, whiche euer risen ayens vs; and oure Lord God schal make hem without onour.

21 And now, britheren, for ye ben prestis in the puple of God, and the soule of hem hangith of you, reise ye her hertis at youre speche, that thei be myndeful, that oure fadris weren temptid, that thei schulden be preued, whethir thei worschipiden God verili.

22 Thei owen to be myndeful, hou oure fadir Abraham was temptid, and he was preuyd bi many tribulaciouns, and was maad the frend of God.

23 So Isaac, so Jacob, so Moyses, and alle that plesiden 'the Lord, passiden feithful bi many tribulaciouns.

24 Sotheli thei that resseyueden not temptaciouns with the drede of the Lord, and brouyten forth her vnpacience, and the schenschip of her grutchyng 'ayens the Lord,

25 weren distried of a distriere, and perischiden of serpentis.

26 And therfor venge we not vs for these thingis whiche we suffren;

27 but arette we, that these same turmentis ben lesse than oure synnes, and bileue we, as seruauntis of the Lord that ben chastisid, that the betyngis of the Lord ben comun to amendyng, and not to oure perdicioun.

28 And Ozie and the prestis seiden to hir, Alle thingis, whiche thou hast spoke, ben sothe, and no repreuyng is in thi wordis.

29 Now therfor preie thou for vs, for thou art an hooli womman, and dredynge God.

30 And Judith seide to hem, As ye knowen, that this, that Y myyte speke, is of God,

31 so preue ye, if this that Y purposide to do, is of God; and preie ye, that God make stidfast my counsel.

32 Ye schulen stonde at the yate this niyt, and Y schal go out with my fre handmayde; and preie ye, that, as ye seiden, the Lord biholde his puple Israel in fyue daies.

33 But Y nyle, that ye enquere my doyng, and til that Y telle to you, 'noon othir thing be doon, no but preier for me to oure Lord God.

34 And Ozie, the prince of Juda, seide to hir, Go thou in pees, and the Lord be with thee in the veniaunce of oure enemyes. And thei turneden ayen, and yeden awey.

CAP 9

1 And while thei yeden awei, Judith entride in to hir oratorie, and sche clothide hir silf with an heire, and puttide aische on hir heed; and sche bowide doun hir silf to the Lord, and criede to the Lord, and seide,

2 Lord God of my fadir Symeon, which yauest to hym a swerd in to defence of aliens, that weren defouleris in her defoulyng, and maden nakid the hipe of a virgyn in to confusioun;

3 and thou yauest the wymmen of hem in to prey, the douytris of hem in to caitifte, and al the prey in to departyng to thi seruauntis, that loueden feruentli thi feruent loue; Lord, Y biseche, helpe thou me a widewe.

4 For thou madist the formere thingis, and thouytist tho thingis aftir tho, and this thing is maad, which thou woldist.

5 For alle thi weies ben redi, and thou has set thi domes in thi puruyaunce.

6 Biholde thou the castels of Assiriens now, as thou vouchidist saaf to biholde thanne the castels of Egipcians, whanne thei runnen armed after thi seruauntis, and tristiden in charis, and in multitude of her knyytis, and in multitude of werriours.

7 But thou biheldist on the castels of hem, and derknessis maden hem feynt; the botme of the see helde her feet,

8 and watris hiliden hem.

9 Lord, 'also these men be maad so, that tristen in her multitude, and in her charis, and in scharp schaftis with oute irun, and in her arowis; and han glorie in her speris;

10 and witen not, that thou thi silf art oure God, that 'al tobrekist batels fro the bigynnyng, and the Lord is name to thee.

11 Reise thin arm as at the bigynnyng, and hurle doun the power of hem 'in thi vertu; the power of hem falle doun in thi wrathfulnesse, whiche biheten hem to defoule 'thin hooli thingis, and to defoule the tabernacle of thi name, and to cast doun with her swerd the horn of thin auter.

12 Lord, make thou that the pride of hem be kit of with her owne swerd;

13 be he takun with the snare of hise iyen in me; and thou schalt smyte hym with the lippis of my charite.

14 Yyue thou to me stidfastnesse in soule, that Y dispise hym and his vertu, and distrie hym.

15 For it schal be a memorial of thi name, whanne the hondis of a womman han cast hym doun.

16 For whi, Lord, thi vertu is not in multitude, nether thi wille is in the strengthis of horsis; and proude spiritis plesiden not thee at the bigynnyng, but the preier of meke men and mylde 'pleside euere thee.

17 God of heuenes, the creatour of watris, and Lord of alle creature, here thou me wretchid womman preiynge and tristynge of thi merci.

18 Lord, haue thou mynde of thi testament, and yyue thou a word in my mouth, and make thou strong the counsel in myn herte, that thin hows dwelle perfitly in thin halewyng;

19 and that alle folkis knowe, that thou art God, and noon other is outakun thee.

CAP 10

1 Forsothe it was doon, whanne sche hadde ceessid to crie to the Lord, sche roos fro the place, in which sche lay bowid doun to the Lord.

2 And sche clepide hir fre handmaide, and cam doun in to hir hows; and sche took awei fro hir the heire, and vnclothide hir silf fro the clothing of hir widewehod.

3 And sche waischide hir bodi, and anoyntide hir with beste myrre, and sche schedide the heer of hir heed, and settide a mytre on hir heed, and sche clothide hir with the clothis of hyr gladnesse, and clothide hir feet with sandalies; and sche took ournementis of the armes, and lilies, and eeryngis, and ryngis, and ournede hir silf with alle hir ournementis.

4 To whom also the Lord yaf briytnesse, for al this ourenement hangide not of letcherie, but of vertu; and therfor the Lord 'made large this fairnesse on hir, that bi 'vncomparable fairnesse sche apperide to the iyen of alle men.

5 Therfor sche puttide on hir fre handmaide a botel of wyn, and a vessel of oile, and meet maad of meele, and dried figus, and looues, and cheese, and yeden forth.

6 And whanne thei weren comen to the yate of the citee, thei founden Ozie and the prestis of the citee abidynge hir.

7 And whanne thei hadden seyn hir, thei weren astonyed, and wondriden ful myche on hir fairnesse.

8 Netheles thei axiden hir no thing, and leeten passe, and seiden, The God of oure fadris yyue grace to thee, and make strong with his vertu al the counsel of thin herte, and Jerusalem haue glorie on thee, and thi name be in the noumbre of hooli and iust men.

9 And alle thei, that weren there, seiden with o vois, Be it doon! be it doon!

10 Therfor Judith preiede the Lord, and passide thorouy the yatis, sche and hir fre handmayde.

11 Forsothe it was doon, whanne sche cam doun of the hil aboute the risynge of the dai, the aspieris of Assiriens metten hir, and helden hir, and seiden, Fro whennus comest thou, ether whidur goist thou?

12 And sche answeride, Y am a douyter of Ebreis, and therfor Y fledde fro the face of hem, for Y knew, that it schal come, that thei schulen be youun to you in to prey, for thei dispisiden you, and nolde bitake hem silf wilfuli, that thei schulden fynde grace in youre siyt.

13 For this cause Y thouyte with me, and seide, Y schal go to the face of the prynce Holofernes, for to schewe to hym the priuytees of hem, and Y schal schewe to hym, bi what entryng he mai gete hem, so that not o man of his oost falle doun.

14 And whanne tho men hadden herd the wordis of hir, thei bihelden hir face, and wondryng was in her iyen, for thei wondriden greetli on hir fairnesse.

15 And thei seiden to hir, Thou hast kept thi lijf, for thou hast founde sich a counsel, that thou woldist come doun to oure lord.

16 Sotheli wite thou this, that, whanne thou 'hast stonde in his siyt, he schal do wel to thee, and thou schalt be moost acceptable in his herte. And thei ledden hir to the tabernacle of Holofernes, and thei schewiden hir to hym.

17 And whanne sche hadde entrid bifor his face, anoon Holofernes was takun bi hise iyen.

18 And hise knyytis seiden to hym, Who schal dispise the puple of Jewis, whiche han so faire wymmen, that we owen not to fiyte skilfuli ayenus hem for these wymmen?

19 Therfor Judith siy Holofernes sittynge in a curteyn, round bynethe and scharp aboue, that was wouun of purpur, and gold, and smaragde, and moost precelour stoonys,

20 and whanne sche hadde lokid in to his face, sche worschipide hym, and bowide doun hir silf on the erthe; and the seruauntis of Holofernes reisiden hir, for her lord comaundide.

CAP 11

1 Thanne Holofernes seide to hir, Be thou coumfortid, and nyle thou drede in thin herte, for Y neuere anoyede man, that wolde serue Nabugodonosor, the kyng.

2 Sotheli if thi puple hadde not dispisid me, Y hadde not reisid 'myn hond on it.

3 But 'now seie to me, for what cause yedist thou awei fro hem, and it pleside thee to come to vs.

4 And Judith seide, Take thou the wordis of thin handmaide; for, if thou suest the wordis of thin handmaide, the Lord schal make a perfit thing with thee.

5 Forsothe Nabugodonosor, the kyng of erthe, lyueth, and his vertu lyueth, which is in thee to the chastisyng of alle soulis errynge; for not oneli men schulen serue hym 'bi thee, but also beestis of the feeld obeien to hym.

6 For the prudence of thi soule is teld to alle folkis; and it is schewid to al the world, that thou aloon art good and myyti in al his rewme; and thi techyng is prechid in alle prouyncis.

7 Nether this thing is hid, which Achior spak, nether that thing is vnknowun, which thou comaundidist to bifalle to hym.

8 For it is knowun, that oure God is so offendid bi synnes, that he sente bi hise profetis to the puple, that he wolde bitake hem for her synnes.

9 And for the sones of Israel witen, that thei han offendid 'her Lord God, the tremblyng of hym is on hem.

10 Ferthermore also hungur hath asailid hem, and for drynesse of watir thei ben rikenyd now among deed men.

11 Forsothe thei ordeynen this, that thei sle her beestis, and drynke her blood;

12 and thei thouyten to yyue these hooli thingis 'of her Lord in wheete, wyn, and oile, whiche God comaundide to be not touchid, and thei wolen waste the thingis, which thei ouyten not touche with hondis; therfor for thei doen these thingis, it is certeyn that thei schulen be youun in to perdicioun.

13 Which thing Y, thin handmaide, knew, and fledde fro hem, and the Lord sente me to telle these same thingis to thee.

14 For Y, thin handmaide, worschipe God, also now at thee; and thin handmaide schal go out, and Y schal preie God;

15 and he schal seie to me, whanne he schal yelde to hem her synne; and Y schal come, and telle to thee, so that Y brynge thee thorouy the myddis of Jerusalem, and thou schalt haue al the puple of Israel as scheep 'to whiche is no scheepherde, and ther schal not berke ayens thee nameli oon;

16 for these thingis ben seid to me bi the puruyaunce of God.

17 And for God is wrooth to hem, Y am sente to telle to thee these same thingis.

18 Sotheli alle these wordis plesiden bifor Holofernes, and bifore hise children; and thei wondriden at the wisdom of hir; and oon seide to another,

19 Ther is not sich a womman on erthe in siyt, in fairenesse, and in wit of wordis.

20 And Holofernes seide to hir, God dide wel, that sente thee bifor the puple, that thou yyue it in myn hondis;

21 and for thi biheest is good, if thi God doith these thingis to me, he schal be also my God, and thow schalt be greet in the hows of Nabugodonosor, and thi name schal be nemyd in al erthe.

CAP 12

1 Thanne Holofernes comaundide hir to entre, where his tresouris weren kept, and he comaundide hir to dwelle there; and he ordeynede, what schulde be youun to hir of his feeste.

2 To whom Judith answeride, and seide, Now Y may not ete of these thingis, which thou comaundidist to be youun to me, lest offence come on me; but Y schal ete of these thingis, whiche Y brouyte with me.

3 To whom Holofernes seide, If these thingis failen, whiche thou brouytist with thee, what schulen we do to thee?

4 And Judith seide, Lord, thi soule lyueth, for thin handmaide schal not spende alle these thingis, til God schal do in myn hondis these thingis which Y thouyte. And hise seruauntis ledden hir in to the tabernacle, whidur he hadde comaundid.

5 And sche axide, the while sche entride, that fredom schulde be youun to hir to go out to preier, in the nyyt, and bifor the liyt, and to biseche the Lord.

6 And he comaundide to his chaumberleyns, that, as it pleside hir, sche schulde go out, and entre, for to preie hir God bi thre daies.

7 And sche yede out in nyytis in to the valei of Bethulia, and waischide hir silf in the welle of watir.

8 And as sche stiede, sche preiede the Lord God of Israel, that he wolde dresse hir weie to the delyueraunce of his puple.

9 And sche entride, and dwellide clene in the tabernacle, til that sche took hir mete in the euentid.

10 And it was doon in the fourthe dai, Holofernes made a soper to hise seruauntis, and he seide to Vagao, the chaumburleyn, Go thou, and councele that Ebrew womman, that sche consente wilfuli to dwelle with me.

11 For it is foul anentis Assiriens, if a womman scorne a man, in doynge that sche passe 'with out part fro hym.

12 Thanne Vagao entride to Judith, and seide, A good damesele be not aschamed to entre to my lord, that sche be onourid bifor his face, and that sche eete with hym, and drynke wiyn with gladnesse.

13 To whom Judith answeryde, Who am Y, that Y ayenseie my lord?

14 Y schal do al thing, that schal be good and best bifor hise iyen. Sotheli what euer thing plesith hym, this schal be best to me in alle the daies of my lijf.

15 And sche roos, and ournede hir silf with hir clothis, and entride, and stood bifor 'his face.

16 Forsothe the herte of Holofernes was stirid; for he was brennynge in the coueitise of hir.

17 And Holofernes seide to hir, Drynke thou now, and take mete in gladnesse; for thou hast founde grace bifor me.

18 And Judith seide, Lord, Y schal drynke, for my soule is magnyfied to dai bifor alle the daies of my lijf.

19 And sche took, and eet, and drank bifor hym tho thingis, whiche hir handmayde hadde maad redi to hir.

20 And Holofernes was maad glad 'to hir, and he drank ful myche wiyn, hou myche he hadde neuere drank in o dai in his lijf.

CAP 13

1 Forsothe as euentid was maad, hise seruauntis hastiden to her ynnes; and Vagao closid togidere the doris of the closet, and yede forth.

2 For alle men weren maad feynt of wiyn;

3 and Judith aloone was in the closet.

4 Certis Holofernes lai in the bed, aslepid with ful myche drunkenesse.

5 And Judith seide to hir damesele, that sche schulde stonde with outforth bifor the dore of the closet, and aspie.

6 And Judith stood bifor the bed, preiynge with teeris, and with stiryng of lippis 'in silence,

7 seiynge, Lord God of Israel, conferme me, and biholde in this our to the werkis of myn hondis, that, as thou bihiytist, thou reise Jerusalem thi citee; and that Y performe this thing, which thing Y bileuynge thouyte to mow be doon bi thee.

8 And whanne sche hadde seid this, sche neiyede to the piler that was at the heed of his bed, and sche loside his swerd, that hangide boundun 'ther ynne.

9 And whanne sche hadde drawe out of the scheeth thilke swerd, sche took the heer of his heed; and seide, Lord God of Israel, conferme me in this our.

10 And sche smoot twies on his necke, and kittide awei his heed; and sche took awei his curteyn fro the pileris, and walewide awei his bodi heedles.

11 And aftir a litil sche yede out, and bitook the heed of Holofernes to hir handmaide, and comaundide, that sche schulde putte it in to hir scrippe.

12 And the twei wymmen yeden out 'bi her custom as to preier, and passiden the castels of Assiriens, and thei cumpassiden the valei, and camen to the yate of the citee.

13 And Judith seide afer to the keperis of the wallis, 'Opene ye the yatis, for God is with vs, that hath do greet vertu in Israel.

14 And it was doon, whanne the men hadden herd 'her vois, thei clepiden the prestis of the citee.

15 And alle men fro the leest 'til to the mooste runnen to hir; for thei hopiden not, that sche schulde come now.

16 And thei teendiden liytis, and alle men cumpassiden aboute hir. Sotheli sche stiede in to an hiyere place, and comaundide silence to be maad. And whanne alle men weren stille,

17 Judith seide, Herie ye 'oure Lord God, that hath not forsake hem that hopen in hym,

18 and bi me, his handmaide, he hath fillid his merci, which he bihiyte to the hows of Israel, and hath slayn in myn hond the enemye of his puple 'in this niyt.

19 And sche 'brouyte forth of the scrippe the heed of Holofernes, and schewide it to hem, and seide, Lo! the heed of Holofernes, prince of the chiualrie of Assiriens; and, lo! his curteyn, in which he lay in his drunkenesse, where also oure Lord God killide hym bi the hond of a womman.

20 Forsothe the Lord God lyueth, for his aungel kepte me, bothe goynge fro hennus, and dwellynge there, and turnynge ayen fro thennus hidur; and the Lord 'suffride not his handmaide to be defoulid, but with out defoulyng of synne he ayen clepid me to you, and Y haue ioie in his victorie, and in 'my scapyng, and in youre delyueraunce.

21 Knouleche ye alle to hym, for he is good, for his mercy is in to 'the world.

22 Sotheli alle men worschipiden the Lord, and seiden to hir, The Lord hath blessid thee in his vertu, for bi thee he hath brouyt to nouyt oure enemyes.

23 Certis Ozie, prince of the puple of Israel, seide to hir, Douytir, thou art blessid of the hiy Lord God, bifor alle wymmen on erthe.

24 Blessid be the Lord, that made heuene and erthe, and that dresside thee in to the woundis of the heed of the prince of oure enemyes;

25 for to dai he hath magnefied so thi name, that thi preisyng go not awei fro the mouth of men, that schulen be myndeful of the vertu of the Lord with outen ende; for whiche thou sparidist not thi lijf for the angwischis and tribulaciouns of thi kyn, but helpidist the fallinge bifor the siyt of oure God.

26 And al the puple seide, 'Be it! be it!

27 Forsothe Achior was clepid, and cam; and Judith seide to hym, Thilke God of Israel, to whom thou yauest witnessyng, that he auengith hym of hise enemyes, hath kit of the heed of alle vnbileueful men in this niyt bi myn hond.

28 And that thou preue that it is so, lo! the heed of Holofernes, which in the dispit of his pride dispiside God of Israel, and manaasside deth to thee, and seide, Whanne the puple of Israel is takun, Y schal comaunde thi sidis to be persid with a swerd.

29 Sotheli Achior siy the heed of Holofernes, and was angwischid for drede, and felde doun on his face on the erthe, and his soule suffride eneyntisyng.

30 Sotheli aftir that he hadde take ayen spirit, and was coumfortid, he felde doun at 'hir feet, and worschipide hir,

31 and seide, Blessid art thou of thi God in al the tabernacle of Jacob; for in ech folk, that schal here thi name, God of Israel schal be magnyfied in thee.

CAP 14

1 Forsothe Judith seide to al the puple, Britheren, here ye; hang ye this heed on youre wallis.

2 And it schal be, whanne the sunne 'goith out, ech man take hise armuris, and go ye out with feersnesse, not that ye go doun binethe, but as makyng asauyt.

3 Thanne it schal be nede, that the spieris of the lond fle to reise her prynce to batel.

4 And whanne the duykis of hem rennen togidere to the tabernacle of Holofernes, and fynden hym heedles, waltrid in his blood, dreed schal falle doun on hem.

5 And whanne ye knowen that thei fleen, go ye sikirli aftir hem, for God schal al to-breke hem vndur youre feet.

6 Thanne Achior siy the vertu that God of Israel hadde do, and he forsook the custom of hethenesse, and bileuede to God; and he circumcidede the fleisch of his yerde, and he was put to the puple of Israel, and al the aftircomyng of his kyn 'til in to this dai.

7 Forsothe anoon as the dai roos, thei hangiden the heed of Holofernes on the wallis; and ech man took his armuris, and thei yeden out with grete noise and yellyng.

8 Which thing the aspieris sien, and runnen to the tabernacle of Holofernes.

9 Certis thei, that weren in the tabernacle, camen, and maden noise bifore the entryng of the bed, and ymagyneden by craft vnrestfulnesse for cause of reisyng, that Holofernes schulde awake not of the reiseris, but of sowneris.

10 For no man was hardi to opene the tabernacle of the vertu of Assiriens bi knockyng ethir bi entryng.

11 But whanne hise duykis, and tribunes, and alle the grettere men of the oost of the kyng of Assiriens weren comen, thei seiden to the chaumburleyns, Entre ye, and reise ye hym;

12 for myis ben goon out of her caues, and doren excite vs to batel.

13 Thanne Vagao entride in to his closet, and stood bifor the curtyn, and made betyng togidere with hise hondis; for he supposide hym to slepe with Judith.

14 But whanne he perseyuede not 'with wit of eeris ony stiryng of Holofernes liggynge, he cam neiyynge to the curtyn, and he 'reiside it, and siy the deed bodi with out the heed 'of Holofernes 'maad slow in his blood ligge on the erthe, and he criede bi grete vois with weping, and to-rente hise clothis.

15 And he entride in to the tabernacle of Judith, and foond not hir, and he skippide out to the puple,

16 and seide, Oon Ebrew womman hath maad confusioun in the hows of kyng Nabugodonosor; for lo! Holofernes liggith in the erthe, and his heed is not in hym.

17 And whanne the prynces of the vertu of Assiriens hadden herd this thing, alle thei to-renten her clothis, and vnsuffrable drede and tremblyng felde doun on hem, and her soulis weren troblid greetli.

18 And 'vncomparable cry was maad 'bi the myddil of her tentis.

CAP 15

1 And whanne al the oost hadde herd Holofernes biheedid, mynde and councel fledde fro hem, and thei 'schakun bi tremblyng and drede aloone token the help of fliyt,

2 so that no man spak with his neiybore; but 'whanne the heed was bowid doun, and alle thingis 'weren forsakun, thei weren bisy to ascape Ebreis, which thei hadden herd to come armed on hem; and thei fledden bi the weies of feeldis, and bi the pathis of litle hillis.

3 Therfor the sones of Israel siyen Assiriens fleynge, and sueden hem, and camen doun, and sowneden with trumpis, and yelliden aftir hem.

4 And for Assiriens not gaderid togidere yeden heedlyng in to fliyt, forsothe the sones of Israel pursuynge with o cumpeny maden feble alle, whiche thei myyten fynde.

5 And Ozie sente messangeris bi alle the citees and cuntreis of Israel.

6 Therfor ech cuntrei and ech citee sente chosun yonge men armed after hem; and thei pursueden 'thilke Assiriens with the scharpnesse of swerd, til thei camen to the laste part of her coostis.

7 Forsothe the residue men, that weren in Bethulia, entriden in to the tentis of Assiriens, and token awey with hem the prey, which Assiriens fleynge hadden left, and thei weren chargid gretli.

8 But thei that weren ouercomerys, turneden ayen to Bethulia, and thei token awei with hem alle thingis which euer weren of tho Assiriens, so that no noumbre was in scheep, and beestis, and in alle mouable thingis of hem, that fro the leeste 'til to the mooste alle men weren maad riche of her preies.

9 Forsothe Joachym, the hiyeste bischop, cam fro Jerusalem in to Bethulia with alle the prestis, to se Judith.

10 And whanne sche hadde goon out to hym, alle blessiden hir with o vois, and seiden, Thou art the glorie of Jerusalem, and thou art the gladnesse of Israel, thou art the onour of oure puple,

11 which hast do manli, and thin herte was coumfortid, for thou louedist chastite, and aftir thin hosebonde thou knowist not another; therfor and the hond of the Lord coumfortide thee, and therfor thou schalt be blessid with outen ende.

12 And al the puple seide, 'Be it! be it!

13 Forsothe bi thritti daies vnnethis the spuylis of Assiriens weren gaderid of the puple of Israel.

14 Certis thei yauen to Judith alle thingis, that weren preued to be propir, 'ether synguler, of Holofernes, in gold, and siluer, and in clothis, and in gemmes, and in alle purtenaunce of houshold; and alle thingis weren youun to hir of the puple.

15 And alle puplis 'maden ioye, with wymmen, and vergynes, and yonge men, in organs and harpis.

CAP 16

1 Thanne Judith song 'this song to the Lord, and seide, Bigynne ye in tympans;

2 synge ye to the Lord in cymbalis; synge ye swetli a newe salm to hym; fulli make ye ioye, and inwardli clepe ye his name.

3 The Lord al to-brekith batels, the Lord is name to hym;

4 that hath set hise castels in the myddis of his puple, for to deliuere vs fro the hond of alle oure enemyes.

5 Assur cam fro the hillis, fro the north, in the multitude of his strengthe; whose multitude stoppide strondis, and the horsis of hem hiliden valeis.

6 And he seide, that he schulde brenne my coostis, and sle my yonge men bi swerd, to yiue my yonge children in to prei, virgyns in to caitifte.

7 But the Lord Almyyti anoiede hym, and bitook hym in to the hondis of a womman, and schente hym.

8 For the myyti of hem felde not doun of yonge men, nether the sones of giauntis killiden hym, nether hiye giauntis puttiden hem silf to hym; but Judith, the douytir of Merari, ouercam hym bi the fairnesse of hir face.

9 For sche vnclothide hir fro the cloth of widewehod, and clothide hir with the cloth of gladnesse, in the ful ioiyng of the sones of Israel.

10 Sche anoyntide hir face with oynement, and boond togidere the tressis of hir heeris with a coronal, to disseyue hym.

11 'Hir sandalies rauyschiden hise iyen, hir fairnesse made his soule caitif; with a swerd sche kittide of his necke.

12 Men of Persis hadden hidousnesse of hir stidfastnesse, and Medeis of hyr hardynesse.

13 Thanne the castels of Assiriens yelliden, whanne my meke men, wexinge drie for thirst, apperiden.

14 The sones of damesels prickiden hem, and killiden hem as children fleynge; thei perischiden in batel fro the face of my God.

15 'Synge we an ympne to the Lord, synge we a newe ympne to oure God.

16 Lord, Lord God, thou art grete, and ful cleer in thi vertu, and whom no man may ouercome.

17 Ech creature of thin serue thee, for thou seidist, and thingis weren maad; thou sentist thi spirit, and thingis weren maad of nouyt; and noon is that ayenstondith thi comaundement.

18 Hillis schulen be moued fro foundementis with watris; stonys schulen flete a brood as wex bifor thi face.

19 Sotheli thei that dreden thee, schulen be grete anentis thee bi alle thingis.

20 Woo to the folk rysynge on my kyn; for the Lord Almyyti schal take veniaunce in hem, in the dai of doom he schal visite hem.

21 For he schal yyue fier and wormes in the fleischis of hem, that thei be brent, and lyue, and feele til in to with outen ende.

22 And it was doon aftir these thingis, al the puple aftir the victorie cam to Jerusalem to worschipe the Lord; and anoon as thei weren clensid, alle men offriden brent sacrifices, and a vowis, and her biheestis.

23 Certis Judith yaf in to the cursyng of foryetyng alle the armuris of batel of Holofernes, whiche the puple yaf to hir, and the curteyn, which sche hadde take awei.

24 Forsothe al the puple was myrie aftir the face of hooli men; and bi thre monethis the ioye of this victorie was halewid with Judith.

25 Sotheli aftir tho daies ech man yede ayen in to his owne; and Judith was maad greet in Bethulia, and sche was more cleer thanne alle wymmen of the lond of Israel.

26 For chastite was ioyned to hir vertu, so that sche knewe not man alle the daies of hir lijf, sithen Manasses, hir hosebonde, was deed.

27 Sotheli in 'feeste daies sche cam forth with greet glorie.

28 Forsothe sche dwellide in the hows of hir hosebonde an hundrid yeer and fyue; and sche lefte hir handmaide fre. And sche was deed, and biried with hir hosebonde in Bethulia; 29 and al the puple biweilide hir seuene daies.

30 Forsothe in al the space of her lijf noon 'was disturblide Israel, and many yeeris aftir hir deeth.

31 Sotheli the day of the victorie of this feeste is takun of Ebreis in the noumbre of hooli daies, and it is worschipid of the Jewis fro that tyme til in to present day.

ESTHER

CAP 1

1 In the daies of kyng Assuerus, that regnede fro Ynde 'til to Ethiopie, on an hundrid and seuene and twenti prouynces, whanne he sat in the seete of his rewme,

2 the citee Susa was the bigynnyng of his rewme.

3 Therfor in the thridde yeer of his empire he made a greet feeste to alle hise princes and children, the strongeste men of Persis, and to the noble men of Medeis, and to the prefectis of prouynces, bifor him silf,

4 to schewe the richessis of the glorie of his rewme, and the gretnesse, and boost of his power in myche tyme, that is, an hundrid and 'foure scoor daies.

5 And whanne the daies of the feeste weren fillid, he clepide to feeste al the puple that was foundun in Susa, fro the moost 'til to the leeste; and he comaundide the feeste to be maad redi bi seuene daies in the porche of the orcherd and wode, that was set with the kyngis ournement and hond.

6 And tentis of 'the colour of the eir, and of gold, and of iacynct, susteyned with coordis of bijs, and of purpur, hangiden on ech side, whiche weren set in cerclis of yuer, and weren vndur set with pilers of marble; also seetis at the maner of beddis of gold and of siluer 'weren disposid on the pawment arayede with smaragde and dyuerse stoon; which pawment peynture made fair bi wonderful dyuersite.

7 Sotheli thei, that weren clepid to meet, drunkun in goldun cuppis, and metes weren borun in with othere 'and othere vessels; also plenteuouse wiyn, and 'the best was set, as it was worthi to the greet doyng of the kyng.

8 And 'noon was that constreynede 'men not willynge to drynke; but so the kyng hadde ordeyned, 'makynge souereyns of hise princes 'to alle boordis, that ech man schulde take that, that he wolde.

9 Also Vasthi, the queen, made a feeste of wymmen in the paleis, where kyng Assuerus was wont to dwelle.

10 Therfor in the seuenthe dai, whanne the kyng was gladdere, and was hoot of wiyn aftir ful myche drinkyng, he comaundide Nauman, and Baracha, and Arbana, and Gabatha, and Zarath, and Abgatha, and Charchas, seuene oneste and chast seruauntis, 'that mynistriden in his siyt,

11 that thei schulden brynge in bifor the kyng the queen Vasti, with a diademe set on hir heed, to schewe hir fairnesse to alle the puplis and prynces; for sche was ful fair.

12 And sche forsook, and dispiside to come at the comaundement of the kyng, which he hadde sent bi the oneste and chast seruauntes. Wherfor the kyng was wrooth, and kyndlid bi fulgreet woodnesse; and he axide the wise men,

13 whiche bi the 'kyngis custom weren euere with hym, and he dide alle thingis bi the counsel of hem, kunnynge the lawis and ritis of grettere men;

14 forsothe the firste and the nexte weren Carsena, and Sechaaba, Admatha, and Tharsis, and Mares, and Marsana, and Manucha, seuene duykis of Persis and of Medeis, that sien the face of the kyng, and weren wont to sitte the firste aftir hym;

15 'the kyng axide hem, to what sentence the queen Vasthi schulde be suget, that nolde do the comaundement of kyng Assuerus, which he hadde sent bi the onest and chast seruauntis.

16 And Manucha answeride, in audience of the kyng and of the pryncis, The queen Vasthi hath not oneli dispisid the kyng, but alle the pryncis and puplis, that ben in alle prouynces of kyng Assuerus.

17 For the word of the queen schal go out to alle wymmen, that thei dispise her hosebondis, and seie, Kyng Assuerus comaundide, that the queen Vasthi schulde entre to hym, and sche nolde.

18 And bi this saumple alle the wyues of prynces of Persis and of Medeis schulen dispise the comaundementis of hosebondis; wherfor the indignacioun of the kyng is iust.

19 If it plesith to thee, 'a comaundement go out fro thi face, and 'be writun bi the lawe of Persis and of Medeis, which it is vnleueful to be passid, that Vasthi entre no more to the kyng, but anothir womman, which is betere than sche, take 'the rewme of hir.

20 And be this puplischid in to al the empire of thi prouynces, which is ful large, that alle wyues, both of grettere men and of lesse, yyue onour to her hosebondis.

21 His counsel pleside the kyng and the prynces, and the kyng dide bi the counsel of Manucha;

22 and he sente pistlis bi alle the prouyncis of his rewme, as ech folk myyte here and rede, in dyuerse langagis and lettris, that hosebondis ben prynces and the grettere in her housis; and 'he sente, that this be pupplischid bi alle puplis.

CAP 2

1 Therfor whanne these thingis weren doon, aftir that the indignacioun of kyng Assuerus was coold, he bithouyte of Vasthi, and what thingis sche hadde do, ethir what thingis sche suffride.

2 And the children and the mynystris of the kyng seiden to 'the kyng, Damyselis, virgyns 'and faire, be souyt to the kyng; and 'men ben sent,

3 that schulen biholde bi alle prouinces damesels faire and virgyns; and brynge thei hem to the citee Susa, and bitake thei in to the hows of wymmen, vndur the hond of Egei, the onest seruaunt and chast, which is the souereyn and kepere of the kyngis wymmen; and take the damesels ournement of wymmen, and other thingis nedeful to vsis.

4 And which euer damesele among alle plesith the iyen of the kyng, regne sche for Vasti. The word pleside the kyng; and he comaundide to be don so, as thei counceliden.

5 Forsothe a man, a Jew, was in the citee Susa, Mardoche bi name, the sone of Jair, sone of Semei, sone of Cys, of the generacioun of Gemyny;

6 that was translatid fro Jerusalem in that tyme, wherynne Nabugodonosor, kyng of Babiloyne, hadde translatid Jechonye, kyng of Juda;

7 which Mardoche was the nurschere of Edissa, the douyter of his brothir, which douytir was clepid Hester bi anothir name, and sche hadde lost bothe fadir and modir; sche was ful fair, and semeli of face; and whanne hir fadir and modir weren deed, Mardoche 'purchaside hir in to a douyter to hymsilf.

8 And whanne the comaundement of the kyng was ofte pupplischid, and bi his comaundement many faire virgyns weren brouyt to Susa, and weren bitakun to Egey, the onest seruaunt and chast, also Hester among othere damesels was bytakun to hym, that sche schulde be kept in the noumbre of wymmen.

9 And sche pleside hym, and foond grace in his siyt, that he hastide the ournement of wymmen, and bitook to hir her partis, and seuene the faireste damesels of the kyngis hows; and he ournede and araiede bothe hir and damesels suynge hir feet.

10 And 'sche nolde schewe to hym hir puple and hir cuntrei; for Mardoche hadde comaundid to hir, that in al maner sche schulde be stille of this thing.

11 And he walkide ech dai bifor the porche of the dore, in which the chosun virgyns weren kept, and he dide the cure of the helthe of Hester, and wolde wite, what bifelde to hyr.

12 And whanne the tyme of alle damesels bi ordre was comun, that thei schulden entre to the kyng, whanne alle thingis weren fillid that perteyneden to wymmens atire, the tweluethe monethe was turned; so oneli that thei weren anoyntid with oile of 'myrte tre bi sixe monethis, and bi othere sixe monethis 'thei vsiden summe pymentis and swetesmellynge oynementis.

13 And thei entriden to the kyng, and what euer thing perteynynge to ournement thei axiden, thei token; and thei weren araied as it pleside hem, and passiden fro the chaumbre of wymmen to the kyngis bed.

14 And sche that hadde entrid in the euentid, yede out in the morwetid; and fro thennus thei weren led forth in to the secounde housis, that weren vndur the hond of Sagazi, onest seruaunt and chast, that was gouernour of the kyngis concubyns; and sche hadde not power to go ayen more to the kyng, no but the kyng wolde, 'and had comaundid hir to come bi name.

15 Sotheli whanne the tyme was turned aboute bi ordre, the dai neiyede, wherynne Hester, the douyter of Abiahel, brother of Mardoche, 'whom he hadde purchasid in to a douyter to hym silf, ouyte entre to the kyng; and sche axide not wymmenus ournement, but what euer thingis Egei, the onest seruaunt and chast, kepere of virgyns, wolde, he yaf these thingis to hir to ournement; for sche was ful schapli, and of fairnesse that may not liytli be bileuyd, and sche semyde graciouse and amyable to the iyen of alle men.

16 Therfor sche was lad to the bed of kyng Assuerus, in the tenthe monethe, which is clepid Cebeth, in the seuenthe yeer of his rewme.

17 And the kyng feruentli louyde hir more than alle wymmen, and sche hadde grace and mercy bifor hym ouer alle wymmen; and he settide the diademe of rewme 'on hir heed, and he made hir to regne in the stide of Vasthi.

18 And he comaundide a ful worschipful feeste to be maad redi to alle hise princes and seruauntis, for the ioynyng togidere and the weddyngis of Hester; and he yaf rest to alle prouynces, and yaf yiftis aftir the worschipful doyng of a prynce.

19 And whanne virgyns weren souyt also the secounde tyme, and weren gaderid togidere, Mardochee dwellide at the yate of the kyng.

20 Hester hadde not yit schewid hir cuntrei and puple, bi comaundement of hym; for whi what euer thing he comaundide, Hester kepte, and sche dide so alle thingis, as sche was wont in that tyme, in which he nurschide hir a litil child.

21 Therfor in that tyme, wherynne Mardochee dwellide at the 'yate of the king, Bagathan and Thares, twei seruauntis of the kyng, weren wrothe, 'that weren porteris, and saten in the first threisfold of the paleis; and thei wolden rise ayens the kyng, and sle hym.

22 Which thing was not hid fro Mardochee, and anoon he telde to the queen Hester, and sche to the kyng, bi the name of Mardochee, that hadde teld the thing to hir.

23 It was souyt, and it was foundun, and ech of hem was hangid in a iebat; and 'it was sent to storyes, and was bitakun to bookis of yeeris, 'bifor the kyng.

CAP 3

1 Aftir these thingis kyng Assuerus enhaunside Aaman, the sone of Amadathi, that was of the kynrede of Agag, and settide his trone aboue alle the princes whiche he hadde.
2 And alle the seruauntis of the kyng, that lyuyden in the yatis of the paleis, kneliden, and worschipiden Aaman; for the emperour hadde comaundid so to hem; Mardochee aloone bowide not the knees, nethir worschipide hym.
3 'To whom the children of the kyng seiden, that saten bifore at the yatis of the paleis, Whi kepist 'thou not the comaundementis of the kyng, othere wise than othere men?
4 And whanne thei seiden ful ofte these thingis, and he nolde here, thei tolden to Aaman, 'and wolden wite, whether he contynuede in sentence; for he hadde seid to hem, that he was a Jew.
5 And whanne Aaman hadde herd this thing, and hadde preued 'bi experience, that Mardochee bowide not the kne to hym, nethir worschipide hym, he was ful wrooth,
6 and he ledde for nouyt to sette hise hondis on Mardochee aloone; for he hadde herd, that Mardochee was of the folc of Jewis, and more he wolde leese al the nacioun of Jewis, that weren in the rewme of Assuerus.
7 In the firste monethe, whos nam is Nysan, in the tweluethe yeer of the rewme of Assuerus, lot was sent in to a vessel, which lot is seid in Ebrew phur, 'bifor Aaman, in what dai and in what monethe the folk of Jewis ouyte to be slayn; and the tweluethe monethe yede out, which is clepid Adar.
8 And Aaman seide to the king Assuerus, A puple is scaterid bi alle the prouynces of thi rewme, and is departid fro it silf togidere, and vsith newe lawis and cerymonyes, and farthermore it dispisith also the comaundementis of the kyng; and thou knowest best, that it spedith not to thi rewme, 'that it encreesse in malice bi licence.
9 If it plesith thee, 'deme thou that it perisch, and Y schal paie ten thousynde of talentis to the keperis of thi tresour.
10 Therfor the kyng took 'fro his hond the ryng which he vside, and yaf it to Aaman, the sone of Amadathi, of the kynrede of Agag, to the enemy of Jewis.
11 And the kyng seide to hym, The siluer, which thou bihiytist, be thin; do thou of the puple that, that plesith thee.
12 And the scryuens of the kyng weren clepid in the firste monethe Nysan, in the threttenthe dai of the same monethe; and it was writun, as Aaman hadde comaundid, to alle prynces of the kyng, and to domesmen of prouynces and of dyuerse folkis, that ech folk myyte rede and here, 'for dyuersite of langagis, bi the name of kyng Assuerus. And lettris aseelid with
13 the ring of the kyng weren sent bi the corouris of the kyng to alle hise prouynces, that thei schulden sle, and 'do awei alle Jewis, fro a child to an eld man, litle children and wymmen, in o dai, that is, in the thrittenthe dai of the tweluethe monethe, which is clepid Adar; and that thei schulden take awei the goodis of Jewis.
14 Forsothe the sentence 'in schort of the pistlis was this, that alle prouyncis schulden wite, and make hem redi to the forseid dai. And the coroures, that weren sent, hastiden to fille the comaundement of the kyng; and anoon the comaundement hangide in Susa, 'while the kyng and Aaman maden feeste, and 'the while that alle Jewis wepten, that weren in the citee.

CAP 4

1 And whanne Mardochee hadde herd these thingis, he torente hise clothis, and he was clothid in a sak, and spreynt aische on the heed, and he criede with greet vois in the street of the myddis of the citee, and schewide the bitternesse of his soule,
2 and he yede with this yellyng 'til to the yatis of the paleis; for it was not leueful a man clothid with a sak to entre in to the halle of the kyng.
3 Also in alle prouynces, citees, and places, to which the cruel sentence of the king was comun, was greet weilyng, fastyng, yellyng, and wepyng anentis the Jewis, and many Jewis vsiden sak and aische for bed.
4 Sotheli the dameselis and onest seruauntis and chast of Hester entriden, and telden to hir; which thing sche herde, and was astonyed; and sche sente a cloth to Mardochee, that whanne the sak was takun a wei, he schulde clothe hym therynne; which cloth he nolde take.
5 And aftir that Athac, the onest seruaunt and chast, 'was clepid, whom the kyng hadde youe a mynystre to hir, sche comaundide, that he schulde go to Mardochee, and lerne of hym, whi he dide this thing.
6 And Athac yede out, and yede to Mardochee stondynge in the street of the citee, bifor the dore of the paleis;
7 which schewide to Athac alle thingis that bifelden, hou Aaman hadde bihiyt to bryng siluer in to tresours of the kyng for the deeth of Jewis.
8 Also he yaf to Athac the copie of the comaundement, that hangide in Susa, to schewe to the queen, and to moneste hir for to entre to the kyng, and to biseche hym for hir puple.
9 And Athac yede ayen, and telde to Hester alle thingis, whiche Mardochee hadde seid.
10 And sche answeryde to hym, and seide, that he schulde seie to Mardochee, Alle the seruauntis of the kyng,
11 and alle prouyncis that ben vndur his lordschip, knowen, that whether a man ether a womman not clepid entrith in to the ynnere halle of the kyng, he schal be slayn anoon with outen ony tariyng, no but in hap the kyng holdith forth the goldun yerde 'to hym for 'the signe of merci, and he mai lyue so; therfor hou mai Y entre to the kyng, which am not clepid to hym now bi thritti daies?
12 And whanne Mardochee hadde herd 'this thing, he sente efte to Hester,
13 and seide, Gesse thou not, that thou schalt delyuer oonli thi lijf, for thou art in the hows of the kyng, bifor alle Jewis;
14 for if thou art stille now, Jewis schulen be delyuered bi another occasioun, and thou and the hows of thi fadir schulen perische; and who knowith, whether herfor thou camist to the rewme, that thou schuldist be maad redi in sich a tyme?
15 And eft Hester sente these wordis to Mardochee,
16 Go thou, and gadere togidere alle Jewis, whiche thou fyndist in Susa, and preie ye for me; ete ye not, nether drynke ye in thre daies and thre nyytis, and Y with myn handmaydis schal fast in lijk maner; and thanne Y not clepid schal entre to the kyng, and Y schal do ayens the lawe, and Y schal bitake me to deth and to perel.
17 Therfor Mardochee yede, and dide alle thingis, whiche Hester hadde comaundid to hym.

CAP 5

1 Forsothe in the thridde dai Hester was clothid in 'the kyngis clothis, and stood in the porche of the kyngis hows, that was

'the ynnere ayens the kyngis halle; and he sat on his trone, in the consistorie of the paleis, ayens the dore of the hows.

2 And whanne he hadde seyn Hester, the queen, stondynge, sche pleside hise iyen, and he helde forth ayens hir the goldun yerde, which he helde in the hond; and sche neiyide, and kisside the hiynesse of his yerde.

3 And the king seide to hir, Hester, the queen, what 'wolt thou? what is thin axyng? Yhe, thouy thou axist the half part of my rewme, it schal be youun to thee.

4 And sche answeride, If it plesith the kyng, Y biseche, that thou come to me to dai, and Aaman with thee, to the feeste, which Y haue maad redi.

5 And anoon the king seide, Clepe ye Aaman soone, that he obeie to the wille of Hester. Therfor the kyng and Aaman camen to the feeste, which the queen hadde maad redi to hem.

6 And the king seide to hir, aftir that he hadde drunk wiyn plenteuousli, What axist thou, that it be youun to thee, and for what thing axist thou? Yhe, thouy thou axist the half part of my rewme, thou schalt gete.

7 To whom Hester answeride, My axyng and preieris ben these.

8 If Y haue founde grace in the siyt of the kyng, and if it plesith the kyng, that he yyue to me that, that Y axe, and that he fille myn axyng, the kyng and Aaman come to the feeste, which Y haue maad redi to hem; and to morewe Y schal opene my wille to the kyng.

9 Therfor Aaman yede out glad and swift 'in that dai. And whanne he hadde seyn Mardochee sittynge bifor the yatis of the paleys, and not oneli to haue not rise to hym, but sotheli nether moued fro the place of his sittyng, he was ful wrooth;

10 and 'whanne the ire was dissymelid, he turnede ayen in to his hows, and he clepide togidire 'to him silf frendis, and Zares, his wijf;

11 and he declaride to hem the greetnesse of his richessis, and the cumpeny of children, and with hou greet glorie the kyng hadde enhaunsid hym aboue alle hise princis and seruauntis.

12 And he seide after these thinges, Also the queen Hester clepide noon other man with the kyng to the feeste, outakun me, anentis 'which queen Y schal ete also to morewe with the kyng.

13 And whanne Y haue alle these thingis, Y gesse that Y haue no thing, as long as Y se Mardochee, Jew, sittynge bifor the 'kyngis yatis.

14 And Zares, his wijf, and othere frendis answeriden to hym, Comaunde thou an hiy beem to be maad redi, hauynge fifti cubitis of heiythe; and seie thou eerly to the kyng, that Mardochee be hangid theronne; and so thou schalt go glad with the kyng to the feeste.

15 And the counsel plesyde him, and he comaundide an hiy cros to be maad redi.

CAP 6

1 The kyng ledde that nyyt with out sleep, and he comaundide the stories and the bookis of yeeris 'of formere tymes to be brouyt to hym. And whanne tho weren red in his presense,

2 me cam to the place, where it was writun, hou Mardochee hadde teld the tresouns of Gabathan and Thares, oneste seruauntis, couetynge to strangle kyng Assuerus.

3 And whanne the kyng hadde herd this, he seide, What onour and meede gat Mardochee for this feithfulnesse? And hise seruauntis and mynystris seiden to hym, Outirli he took no meede.

4 And anoon the kyng seide, Who is in the halle? Sotheli Aaman hadde entrid in to the ynnere halle of the kyngis hows, to make suggestioun to the kyng, that he schulde comaunde Mardochee to be hangid on the iebat, which was maad redi to him.

5 And the children answeriden, Aaman stondith in the halle.

6 And the kyng seide, Entre he. And whanne he was comun yn, the kyng seide to hym, What owith to be don to the man, whom the kyng desirith onoure? Aaman thouyte in his herte, and gesside, that the kyng wolde onoure noon othere man no but hym silf;

7 and he answeride, The man, whom the kyng couetith to onoure,

8 owith to be clothid with the kyngis clothis, and to be set on the hors which is of the kyngis sadel, and to take the kyngis diademe on his heed;

9 and the firste of the princes and stronge men of the kyng holde his hors, and go bi the stretis of the citee, and crie, and seie, Thus he schal be onourid, whom euer the kyng wole onoure.

10 Therfor the kyng seide to hym, Haste thou, and whanne 'a stoole and hors is takun, do thou, as thou hast spoke, to Mardochee the Jew, that sittith bifor the yatis of the paleis; be thou war, that thou leeue not out ony thing of these, whiche thou hast spoke.

11 Therfor Aaman took 'a stoole and hors, and yede, and criede bifor Mardochee clothid in the strete of the citee, and set on 'the hors, He is worthi this onour, whom euer the kyng wole onoure.

12 And Mardochee turnede ayen to the yate of the paleis, and Aaman hastide to go in to his hows, morenynge, and with the heed hilid.

13 And he teld to Zares, his wijf, and to frendis alle thingis that hadden bifelde to hym. To whom the wise men, whiche he hadde in counsel, and his wijf, answeriden, If Mardochee, bifor whom thou hast bigunne to falle, is of the seed of Jewis, thou schalt not mowe ayenstonde hym, but thou schalt falle in his siyt.

14 Yit while thei spaken, the oneste seruauntis and chast of the kyng camen, and compelliden hym to go soone to the feeste, which the queen hadde maad redi.

CAP 7

1 Therfor the kyng and Aaman entriden to the feeste, to drynke with the queen.

2 And the kyng seide to hir, yhe, in the secounde dai, aftir that he was hoot of the wiyn, Hester, what is thin axyng, that it be youun to thee, and what wolt thou be doon? Yhe, thouy thou axist the half part of my rewme, thou schalt gete.

3 To whom sche answeride, A! king, if Y haue founde grace in thin iyen, and if it plesith thee, yyue thou my lijf to me, for which Y preie, and my puple, for which Y biseche.

4 For Y and my puple ben youun, that we be defoulid, and stranglid, and that we perische; 'and Y wolde, that we weren seeld in to seruauntis and seruauntessis, 'and the yuel 'were suffrable, and Y 'were stille weilynge; but now oure enemy is, whos cruelte turneth 'in to the kyng.

5 And kyng Assuerus answeride, and seide, Who is this, and of what power, that he be hardi to do these thingis?

6 And Hester seide, Oure worste aduersarie and enemy is this Aaman. Which thing he herde, and was astonyde anoon, and 'suffride not to bere the semelaunt of the kyng and of the queen.

7 Forsothe the kyng roos wrooth, and fro the place of the feeste he entride in to a gardyn biset with trees. And Aaman roos for to preie Hester, the queen, for his lijf; for he vndurstood yuel maad redi of the kyng to hym.

8 And whanne the kyng turnede ayen fro the gardyn 'biset with wode, and hadde entrid in to the place of feeste he foond that Aaman felde doun on the bed, wherynne Hester lai. And the king seide, 'Also he wole oppresse the queen, while Y am present, in myn hows. The word was not yit goon out of the kyngis mouth, and anoon thei hiliden his face.

9 And Arbona seide, oon of the onest seruauntis and chast, that stoden in the seruyce of the kyng, Lo! the tre hauynge fifti cubitis of heiythe stondith in the hows of Aaman, which tre he hadde maad redi to Mardochee, that spak for the kyng. To whom the kyng seide, Hange ye Aaman in that tre.

10 Therfor Aaman was hangid in the iebat, which he hadde maad redi to Mardochee, and the ire of the kyng restide.

CAP 8

1 In that dai kyng Assuerus yaf to Hester, the queen, the hows of Aaman, aduersarie of Jewis. And Mardochee entride bifor the face of the kyng; for Hester knoulechide to hym, that he was 'hir fadris brother.

2 Therfor the kyng took the ryng, which he hadde comaundid to be resseyued fro Aaman, and yaf to Mardochee. Forsothe Hester ordeynede Mardochee ouer hir hows.

3 And Hester was not appaied with these thingis, and felde doun to the feet of the kyng, and wepte, and spak to hym, and preiede, that he schulde comaunde the malice of Aaman of Agag, and hise worste castis, whiche he hadde thouyte out ayens Jewis, 'to be maad voide.

4 And the kyng bi custom helde forth the goldun yerde of the kyng with his hond, bi which the signe of merci was schewid. 'Therfor sche roos vp,

5 and stood bifor hym, and seide, If it plesith the kyng, and if Y haue founde grace bifor hise iyen, and if my preier is not seyn 'to be contrarie to hym, Y biseche, that the elde lettris of Aaman, traitour and enemy of Jewis, by whiche he hadde comaundid hem to perische in alle the prouynces of the kyng, be amendid bi newe pistlis;

6 for hou schal Y mowe suffre the deth, and the sleyng of my puple?

7 And kyng Assuerus answeride to Hester, the queen, and to Mardochee, Jew, Y grauntide the hows of Aaman to Hester, the queen, and Y comaundide hym to be hangid 'on the cros, for he was hardi to sette hond ayens the Jewis.

8 Therfor write ye to Jewis, as it plesith to you, 'bi the name of the kyng, and aseele ye the lettris with my ring. For this was the custom, that no man durste ayenseie the pistlis, that weren sente in the kyngis name, and weren aseelid with his ryng.

9 And whanne the dyteris and 'writeris of the kyng weren clepid; 'sotheli it was the tyme of the thridde monethe, which is clepid Siban, in the thre and twentithe dai of that monethe; pistlis weren writun, as Mardochee wolde, to Jewis, and to princes, and to procuratouris, and to iugis, that weren souereyns of an hundrid and seuene and twenti prouynces, fro Iynde 'til to Ethiope, to prouynce and to prouynce, to puple and to puple, bi her langagis and lettris, and to Jewis, that thei myyten rede and here.

10 And tho pistlis, that weren sent 'bi the kyngis name, weren aseelid with his ryng, and sent bi messangeris, whiche runnen aboute bi alle prouynces, and camen with newe messagis bifor the elde lettris.

11 To whiche the kyng comaundide, that thei schulden clepe togidere the Jewis bi alle citees, 'and comaunde to be gaderid togidere, that thei schulden stonde for her lyues; and schulden sle, and do awei alle her enemyes, with her wyues and children, and alle howsis.

12 And o dai of veniaunce, that is, in the thrittenthe dai of the tweluethe monethe Adar, was ordeined bi alle prouynces.

13 And the schort sentence of the pistle was this, that it were maad knowun in alle londis and puplis, that weren suget to the empire of kyng Assuerus, that the Jewis ben redi to take veniaunce of her enemyes.

14 And the messangeris yeden out, bifor berynge swift messages; and the comaundement of the kyng hangide in Susa.

15 Sotheli Mardochee yede out of the paleis and of the kyngis siyt, and schynede in the kyngis clothis, that is, of iacynct and of colour of the eir, and he bar a goldun coroun in his heed, and was clothid with a mentil of selk and of purpur; and al the citee fulli ioiede, and was glad.

16 Forsothe a newe liyt semede to rise to the Jewis,

17 ioie, onour, and daunsyng, at alle puplis, citees, and alle prouynces, whidur euere the comaundementis of the kyng camen, a wondurful ioie, metis, and feestis, and an hooli dai, in so myche, that many of an other folk and sect weren ioyned to the religioun and cerymonyes of hem; for the greet drede of the name of Jewis 'hadde asaylid alle hem.

CAP 9

1 Therfor in the thrittenthe dai of the tweluethe monethe, which we seiden now bifore to be clepid Adar, whanne sleyng was maad redi to alle Jewis, and her enemyes settiden tresoun to blood, ayenward Jewes bigunnen to be the hiyere, and to venge hem of aduersaries.

2 And thei weren gaderid togidere bi alle citees, castels, and places, to stretche forth hond ayens her enemyes and pursueris; and no man was hardi to ayenstonde, for the drede of her gretnesse hadde persid alle puplis.

3 For whi bothe the iugis, duykis, and procuratouris of prouynces, and ech dignyte, that weren souereyns of alle places and werkis, enhaunsiden Jewis, for the drede of Mardochee,

4 whom thei knewen to be prince of the paleis, and to mow do ful myche; and the fame of his name encreeside ech dai, and flei bi the mouthis of alle men.

5 Therfor the Jewis smytiden her enemyes with greet veniaunce, and killiden hem, and yeldiden to tho enemyes that, that thei hadden maad redi to do to 'the Jewis,

6 in so myche, that also in Susa thei killiden fyue hundrid men, with out the ten sones of Aaman of Agag, the enemye of Jewis, of whiche these ben the names;

7 Phasandatha, Delphon, and Esphata,

8 and Phorata, and Adalia, and Aridatha,

9 and Ephermesta, and Arisai, and Aridai, and Vaizatha.

10 And whanne the Jewis hadden slayn hem, thei nolden take preies of the catels of hem.

11 And anoon the noumbre of hem, that weren slayn in Susa, was teld to the kyng.

12 Which seide to the queen, Jewis han slayn fyue hundrid men in the citee of Susa, and othere ten sones of Aaman; hou grete sleyng gessist thou, that thei haunten in alle prouynces? what axist thou more? and what wolt thou, that Y comaunde to be doon?

13 To whom sche answeride, If it plesith the kyng, power be youun to the Jewis, that as thei han do to dai in Susa, so do thei also to morewe, and that the ten sones of Aaman be hangid vp in iebatis.

14 And the kyng comaundide, that it schulde be doon so; and anoon the comaundement hangide in Susa, and the ten sones of Aaman weren hangid.

15 Therfor whanne the Jewis weren gaderid togidere, in the fourtenthe dai of the monethe Adar, thre hundrid men weren slayn in Susa, and the Jewis token not awei the catel of tho men.

16 But also bi alle the prouynces, that weren suget to the lord-schip of the kyng, Jewis stoden for her lyues, whanne her ene-myes and pursueris weren slayn, in so myche, that fyue and seuenti thousynde of slayn men 'weren fillid, and no man touchide ony thing of the catelis of hem.

17 Forsothe the thrittenthe dai of the monethe Adar was o dai of sleyng at alle Jewis, and in the fourtenthe dai thei ceessiden to sle; which thei ordeyneden to be solempne, that therynne in ech tyme aftirward thei schulden yyue tent to metis, to ioye, and to feestis.

18 And thei, that hauntiden sleyng in the citee of Susa, 'lyueden in sleyng in the thrittenthe and fourtenthe dai of the same monethe. But in the fiftenthe dai thei ceessiden to sle; and therfor thei ordeyneden the same dai solempne of feestis and of gladnesse.

19 Forsothe these Jewis, that dwelliden in borow townes not wallid and vilagis, demeden the fourtenthe dai of the monethe Adar of feestis, and of ioie, so that thei be ioiful therynne, and sende ech to other partis of feestis and of metis.

20 Therfor Mardochee wroot alle these thingis, and sente these thingis comprehendid bi lettris to the Jewis, that dwell-iden in alle prouynces of the kyng, as wel to Jewis set nyy as fer,

21 that thei schulden resseyue the fourtenthe and the fiftenthe dai of the monethe Adar 'for feestis, and euer whanne the yeer turneth ayen, 'thei schulden halowe with solempne onour;

22 for in tho daies the Jewis vengiden hem silf of her ene-myes, and morenyng and sorewe weren turned in to gladnesse and ioie; and these daies schulden be daies of feestis, and of gladnesse, and 'that thei schulden sende ech to other partis of metis, and 'yyue litle yiftis to pore men.

23 Forsothe the Jewis resseyueden in to solempne custom alle thingis, whiche thei bigunnen to do in that tyme, and whiche thingis Mardochee hadde comaundid bi lettris to be doon.

24 Sotheli Aaman, the sone of Amadathi, of the kynrede of Agag, the enemy and aduersarie of Jewis, thouyte yuel ayens hem, to sle hem and to do awei, and he sente phur, which is interpretid in oure langage 'in to lot.

25 And afterward Hester entride to the kyng, and bisouyte, that 'hise enforsyngis schulden be maad voide bi the lettris of the kyng, and that the yuel, which he hadde thouyt ayenus the Jewis, schulde turne ayen in to his heed. 'Forsothe thei hangiden on the cros 'bothe hym and hise sones.

26 And fro that tyme these daies weren clepid 'Phurym, that is, of lottis, for 'phur, that is, lot, was sent in to a vessel; and the Jewis resseyueden on hem silf, and on her seed, and on alle men that wolden be couplid to her religioun, alle thingis that weren doon, and ben conteyned in the volym of the pis-tle, 'that is, of this book,

27 and whiche thingis thei suffriden, and whiche thingis weren chaungid aftirward, that it be not leueful to ony man to passe with out solempnyte these 'daies, which the scripture witnessith, and certeyn tymes axen, while the yeeris comen contynuely oon aftir an other.

28 These ben the daies, whiche neuer ony foryetyng schal do awei, and bi alle generaciouns alle prouynces, that ben in al the world, schulen halewe; nether 'ony citee is, in which the daies of Phurym, that is, of lottis, schulen not be kept of Jewis, and of the generacioun of hem, which is bounden to these cerymonyes.

29 And Hester, the queen, the douyter of Abiahel, and Mar-dochee, the Jew, writiden also the secounde pistle, that this solempne dai schulde be halewid aftirward with al bisynesse.

30 And thei senten to tho Jewis, that dwelliden in an hundrid and seuene and twenti prouynces of kyng Assuerus, that thei schulden haue pees, and resseyue the trewthe,

31 and kepe the daies of lottis, and halewe with ioie in her tyme, as Mardochee and Hester hadden ordeyned; and thei resseiueden the fastyngis, and the cries, and the daies of lottis, to be kept of hem silf and of her seed,

32 and 'that thei schulden resseyue among hooli bookis alle thingis that ben conteyned in the storie of this book, which is clepid Hester.

CAP 10

1 Forsothe kyng Assuerus made tributarye ech lond, and alle the ilis of the see;

2 whos strengthe and empire and dignyte and hiynesse, by which he enhaunside Mardochee, ben writun in the bookis of Medeis and of Persis;

3 and how Mardochee of the kyn of Jewis was the secounde fro king Assuerus, and was greet anentis Jewis, and accept-able to the puple of hise britheren, and he souyte goodis to his puple, and spak tho thingis, that perteyneden to the pees of his seed.

4 And Mardochee seide, These thingis ben doon of God.

5 Y haue mynde on the dreem, which 'Y siy, signifiynge these same thingis, and no thing of tho was voide.

6 A litil welle, that wexide in to a flood, and was turned in to the liyt and sunne, and turnede ayen in to ful many watris, is Hester, whom the kyng took in to wijf, and wolde that sche were his queen.

7 Sotheli twei dragouns, Y am and Aaman;

8 folkis that camen togidere, ben these, that enforsiden to do a wei the name of Jewis.

9 Sotheli my folk Israel it is, that criede to the Lord; and the Lord made saaf his puple, and delyueride vs fro alle yuels, and dide grete signes and wondris among hethene men;

10 and he comaundide twei lottis to be, oon of Goddis puple, and the tother of alle hethene men.

11 And euer either lot cam in to 'determynd dai thanne fro that tyme bifor God and alle folkis.

12 And the Lord hadde mynde on his puple, and hadde merci on his eritage.

13 And these daies schulen be kept in the monethe Adar, in the fourtenthe 'and the fiftenthe dai of the same monethe, with al bisynesse and ioie of the puple gaderid in to o cumpenye, in to alle generaciouns of the puple of Israel aftir-ward.

CAP 11

1 In the fourthe yeer, whanne Ptolome and Cleopatra regneden, Dositheus, that seide hym silf to be a prest and of the kyn of Leuy, and Ptolome, his sone, brouyten this pistle of

lottis in to Jerusalem, which pistle thei seiden, that Lysimachus, the sone of Ptolome, translatide.

2 In the secounde yeer, whanne Artaxerses the moost regnyde, Mardochee, the sone of Jairy, sone of Semei, sone of Cys, of the lynage of Beniamyn, siy a dreem in the firste dai of the monethe Nysan;

3 and Mardochee was a man Jew, that dwellide in the citee of Susa, a grete man, and amonge the firste men of the kyngis halle.

4 Sotheli he was of that noumbre of prisoneris, which Nabugodonosor, the kyng of Babiloyn, hadde translatid fro Jerusalem with Jeconye, kyng of Judee.

5 And this was 'his dreem. Voices and noises and thundris and erthemouyngis and troblyng apperiden on the erthe.

6 And lo! twei grete dragouns, and maad redi ayens hem silf in to batel;

7 at the cry 'of which alle naciouns weren stirid togidere, to fiyte ayens the folc of iust men.

8 And that was a day of derknessis, and of perel, of tribulacioun, and of angwisch, and grete drede was on erthe.

9 And the folc of iust men dredynge 'her yuels was disturblid, and maad redi to deeth.

10 And thei crieden to God; and whanne thei crieden, a litil welle encreesside in to a ful greet flood, and turnede ayen in to ful many watris.

11 The liyt and the sunne roos; and meke men weren enhaunsid, and deuouriden noble men.

12 And whanne Mardochee hadde seyn this thing, and hadde rise fro the bed, he thouyte, what God wolde do, and he hadde fast set in soule, and couetide to wite, what the dreem signyfiede.

CAP 12

1 Forsothe Mardochee dwellide that tyme in the halle of the kyng, with Bagatha and Thara, oneste seruauntis of the kyng, that weren porteris of the paleis.

2 And whanne he hadde vndurstonde the thouytis of hem, and hadde bifor seyn ful diligentli the bisynessis, he lurnyde that thei enforsiden to set hond on kyng Artaxerses, and he telde of that thing to the kyng.

3 And whanne enqueryng was had of euer eithir, the kyng comaundide hem, 'that knoulechiden, to be led to deth.

4 Forsothe the kyng wroot in bookis that, that was doon, but also Mardochee bitook the mynde of the thing to lettris.

5 And the kyng comaundide hym, that he schulde dwelle in the halle of the paleis, and yaf to hym yiftis for the tellynge.

6 Forsothe Aaman, the sone of Amadathi, a bugei, was moost glorius bifor the kyng, and he wolde anoye Mardochee, and his puple, for the 'tweyne oneste seruauntis of the king 'that weren slayn.

CAP 13

1 The gretteste kyng Artaxerses, fro Iynde 'til to Ethiope, seith helthe to the princes and duykys of an hundrid and seuene and twenti prouynces, whiche princes and duykis ben suget to his empire.

2 Whanne Y was lord of ful many folkis, and Y hadde maad suget al the world to my lordschip, Y wolde not mysuse the greetnesse of power, but gouerne sugetis bi merci and softnesse, that thei, ledynge lijf in silence with outen ony drede, schulden vse pees couetid of alle deedli men.

3 Sotheli whanne Y axide of my counselours, hou this myyte be fillid, oon, Aaman bi name, that passide othere men in wisdom and 'feithfulnesse, and was the secounde aftir the kyng,

4 schewide to me, that a puple was scaterid in al the roundnesse of londis, which puple vside newe lawis, and dide ayens the custom of alle folkis, and dispiside the comaundementis of kyngis, and defoulide bi his discencioun the acordyng of alle naciouns.

5 And whanne we hadden lerned this thing, and sien, that o folk rebel ayens al the kynde of men vside weiward lawis, and was contrarie to oure comaundementis, and disturblide the pees and acording of prouynces suget to vs,

6 'we comaundiden, that whiche euere Aaman 'schewide, which is souereyn of alle prouynces, and is the secounde fro the kyng, and whom we onouren in 'the place of fadir, thei with her wiues and children be doon awei of her enemyes, and noon haue merci on hem, in the fourtenthe dai of the twelfithe monethe Adar, of present yeer;

7 that cursid men go doun to hellis in o dai, and yelde pees to oure empire, which thei hadden troblid.

8 Forsothe Mardochee bisouyte the Lord, and was myndeful of alle 'hise werkys, and seide,

9 Lord God, kyng almyyti, alle thingis ben set in thi lordschip, 'ethir power, and 'noon is, that may ayenstonde thi wille; if thou demest for to saue Israel, we schulen be delyuered anoon.

10 Thou madist heuene and erthe, and what euer thing is conteyned in the cumpas of heuene.

11 Thou art Lord of alle thingis, and 'noon is that ayenstondith thi maieste.

12 Thou knowist alle thingis, and woost, that not for pride and dispit and ony coueytise of glorie Y dide this thing, that Y worschipide not Aaman moost proud;

13 for Y was redi 'wilfuli to kisse, yhe, the steppis of hise feet for the helthe of Israel, but Y dredde,

14 lest Y schulde bere ouere to a man the onour of my God, and lest Y schulde worschipe ony man outakun my God.

15 And now, Lord kyng, God of Abraham, haue thou merci on thi puple, for oure enemyes wolen leese vs, and do awei thin eritage;

16 dispise not thi part, which thou ayenbouytist fro Egipt.

17 Here thou my preier, and be thou merciful to the lot, and the part of thin eritage; and turne thou oure morenyng in to ioie, that we lyuynge herie thi name, Lord; and close thou not the mouthis of men heriynge thee.

18 And al Israel with lijk mynde and bisechyng criede to the Lord, for certeyn deeth neiyede to hem.

CAP 14

1 Also the queen Hester fledde to the Lord, and dredde the perel, that neiyede.

2 And whanne sche hadde put awei the kyngis clothis, sche took clothis couenable to wepyngis and morenyng; and for dyuerse oynementis sche 'fillide the heed with aische and dust, and 'made meke hir bodi with fastyngys; and with tobreidyng awei of heeris, sche fillide alle places, in which sche was wont to be glad;

3 and bisouyte the Lord God of Israel, and seide, My Lord, which aloone art oure kyng, helpe me a womman left aloone, and of whom noon othere helpere is outakun thee;

4 my perel is in my hondis.

5 Y haue herd of my fadir, that thou, Lord, tokist awei Israel fro alle folkis, and oure fadris fro alle her grettere men bifore,

that thou schuldist welde euerlastynge eritage; and thou hast do to hem, as thou hast spoke.

6 We synneden in thi siyt, and therfor thou hast bitake vs in to the hondis of oure enemyes;

7 for we worschipiden the goddis of hem.

8 Lord, thou art iust; and now it suffisith not to hem, that thei oppressen vs with hardeste seruage, but thei aretten the strengthe of her hondis to the power of idols,

9 and wolen chaunge thi biheestis, and do awei thin eritage, and close the mouthis of men heriynge thee, and quenche the glorie of thi temple and auter,

10 that thei opene the mouthis of hethene men, and preise the strengthe of ydols, and preche a fleischli kyng with outen ende.

11 Lord, yyue thou not thi kyngis yerde to hem, that ben noyt, lest thei leiyen at oure fallyng; but turne thou the councel of hem on hem, and distrie thou hym, that bigan to be cruel ayens vs.

12 Lord, haue thou mynde, and schewe thee to vs in the tyme of tribulacioun; and, Lord, kyng of goddis and of al power, yyue thou trist to me;

13 yyue thou a word wel dressid in my mouth in the siyt of the lioun, and turne ouer his herte in to the hatrede of oure enemy, that bothe he perische, and othere men that consenten to hym.

14 But delyuere vs in thin hond, and helpe me, hauynge noon othere help no but thee, Lord, that hast the kunnyng of alle thingis;

15 and knowist that Y hate the glorie of wickid men, and that Y wlate the bed of vncircumcidid men, and of ech alien.

16 Thou knowist my freelte and nede, that Y holde abhomynable the signe of my pride and glorie, which is on myn heed in the daies of my schewyng, and that Y wlate it 'as the cloth of a womman hauynge vncleene blood, and Y bere not in the daies of my stillenesse,

17 and that Y eet not in the boord of Aaman, nether the feeste of the kyng pleside me, and Y drank not the wiyn of moiste sacrifices,

18 and that thin handmayde 'was neuere glad, sithen Y was translatid hidur til in to present dai, no but in thee, Lord God of Abraham.

19 'God stronge aboue alle, here thou the vois of hem, that han noon othere hope, and delyuere thou vs fro the hond of wickid men, and delyuere thou me fro my drede.

CAP 15

1 And 'he sente to hir, no doute that ne Mardochee sente to Hester, that sche schulde entre to the kyng, and preie for hir puple, and for hir cuntrei.

2 He seide, Be thou myndeful of the daies of thi mekenesse, hou thou were nurschid in myn hond; for Aaman, ordeyned the secounde fro the kyng, spak ayens vs in to deth;

3 and thou inwardli clepe the Lord, and speke to the kyng for vs, and delyuere vs fro deeth.

4 Forsothe in the thridde dai sche 'puttide of the clothis of hir ournyng, and was cumpassid with hir glorie.

5 And whanne sche 'schinede in the kyngis clothing, and hadde inwardli clepid the Gouernour of alle thingis and the sauyour God, sche took twei seruauntis,

6 and sotheli sche leenyde on oon, as not susteynynge to bere hir body, for delices and ful greet tendirnesse;

7 but the tother 'of the seruauntessis suede the ladi, and bar vp the clothis fletinge doun 'in to the erthe.

8 'Sotheli sche was bisched with 'colour of roosis 'in the cheer, and with pleasaunt and schynynge iyen sche hilide the soreuful soule, and drawun togidere with ful myche drede.

9 Therfor sche entride thorouy alle the doris bi ordre, and stood ayens the kyng, where he sat on the seete of his rewme, and was clothid in the kyngis clothis, and schynyde in gold and preciouse stoonys, and was dredeful in siyt.

10 And whanne he hadde reisid the face, and hadde schewid the woodnesse of herte with brennynge iyen, the queen felde doun; and whanne the colour was chaungid in to palenesse, sche restide the heed slidun on the handmaide.

11 And God turnede the spirit of the kyng in to myldenesse, and he hastide, and dredde, 'and skippyde out of the seete; and he 'susteynede hir with hise armes, til sche cam ayen to hir self; and he spak faire bi these wordis,

12 Hester, what hast thou? Y am thi brother; nyle thou drede, thou schalt not die;

13 for this lawe is not maad for thee, but for alle men.

14 Therfor neiye thou, and touche the ceptre, 'that is, the kyngis yerde.

15 And whanne sche was stille, he took the goldun yerde, and 'puttide on hir necke; and he kisside hir, and seide, Why spekist thou not to me?

16 And sche answeride, Lord, Y siy thee as an aungel of God, and myn herte was troblid for the drede of thi glorye;

17 for, lord, thou art ful wondurful, and thi face is ful of graces.

18 And whanne sche spak, eft sche felde doun, and was almest deed.

19 Sotheli the kyng was troblid, and alle hise mynystris coumfortiden hir.

CAP 16

1 The grete kyng Artaxerses, fro Yinde 'til to Ethiopie, seith helthe to the duykis and pryncis of an hundrid and seuene and twenti prouynces, that obeien to oure comaundement.

2 Many men mysusen in to pride the goodnesse and onour of princes, which is youun to hem;

3 and not oneli thei enforsen to oppresse sugetis to kyngis, but thei beren not glorie youun to hem, and maken redy tresouns ayens hem, that yauen the glorie.

4 And thei ben not apaied to do not thankyngis for benefices, and to defoule in hem silf the lawis of curtesie; but also thei demen, that thei moun fle the sentence of God seynge alle thingis.

5 And thei breken out in to so mych woodnesse, that thei enforsen with the roopis of leesyngis to distrie hem, that kepen diligentli offices bitakun to hem, and doen so alle thingis, that thei ben worthi the preisyng of alle men;

6 while bi sutil fraude 'false men disseyuen the symple eeris of kyngis, 'and gessynge othere men bi her owne kynde.

7 Which thing is preuyd bothe bi elde stories, and bi these thingis that ben doen ech dai; hou the studies of kyngis ben maad schrewid bi yuele suggestiouns of summen.

8 Wherfor it is to purueye for the pees of alle prouynces.

9 And thouy we comaunden dyuerse thingis, ye owen not to gesse, that it cometh of the vnstablenesse of oure soule; but that we yyuen sentence for the maner and nede of tymes, as the profit of the comyn thing axith.

10 And that ye vndurstonde opynliere that, that we seyen; Aaman, the sone of Amadathi, a man of Macedoyne bi soule and folk, and an alien fro the blood of Persis, and defoulynge

oure pitee with his cruelte, was a pilgrym, ethir a straunger, and was resseyued of vs;

11 and he feelide in hym silf so grete curtesie of vs, that he was clepid oure fadir, and was worschipid of alle men the secounde aftir the kyng;

12 which Aaman was reisid in to so greet bolnyng of pride, that he enforside to pryue us of the rewme and spirit.

13 For bi summe newe and vnherd castis he axide in to deeth Mardochee, bi whos feith and benefices we liuen, and the felowe of oure rewme Hester, with al hir folk;

14 and he thouyte these thingis, that whanne thei weren slayn, he schulde sette tresoun to 'oure aloonenesse, and that he schulde translate the rewme of Persis in to Macedoynes.

15 Forsothe we founden not the Jewis in ony gilt outirli, that weren ordeyned to deth by the worste of deedli men; but ayenward that thei vsen iust lawis,

16 and þen the sones of the hiyeste and moste God, and 'euere lyuynge, bi whos benefice the rewme was youun bothe to oure fadris and to vs, and is kept 'til to dai.

17 Wherfor wyte ye, that tho lettris ben voide, whiche thilke Aaman sente vndur oure name.

18 For which greet trespas bothe he that ymagynede, and al his kynrede, hangith in iebatis bifor the yatis of this citee, 'that is, Susa; for not we, but God yeldide to hym that, that he desseruyde.

19 Forsothe this comaundement, which we senden now, be set forth in alle citees, that it be leueful to Jewis to vse her lawis.

20 'Whyche Jewis ye owen helpe, that thei moun sle hem, that maden hem silf redi to the deeth of Jewis, in the thrittenthe dai of the tweluethe monethe, which is clepyd Adar;

21 for Almyyti God turneth this dai of weilyng and morenyng in to ioye to hem.

22 Wherfor and ye han this dai among othere feeste daies, and halowe it with al gladnesse; that it be knowun aftirward,

23 that alle men, that obeien feithfuli to Persis, resseyuen worthi meed for feith; sotheli thei thei, that setten tresoun to the rewme of hem, perischen for the felony.

24 Forsothe ech prouynce and citee, that wole not be parcenere of this solempnytee, perische bi swerd and fier; and be it 'doon awey so, that not oneli it be with out weie to men but also to beestis with outen ende, for ensaumple of dispisyng and vnobedience.

JOB

CAP. I.

1 'A man, Joob bi name, was in the lond of Hus; and thilke man was symple, and riytful, and dredynge God, and goynge awey fro yuel.

2 And seuene sones and thre douytris weren borun to hym;

3 and his possessioun was seuene thousynde of scheep, and thre thousynde of camels, and fyue hundrid yockis of oxis, and fyue hundrid of femal assis, and ful myche meynee; and 'thilke man was grete among alle men of the eest.

4 And hise sones yeden, and maden feestis bi housis, ech man in his day; and thei senten, and clepiden her thre sistris, 'that thei schulden ete, and drynke wiyn with hem.

5 And whanne the daies of feeste hadden passid in to the world, Joob sente to hem, and halewide hem, and he roos eerli, and offride brent sacrifices 'bi alle. For he seide, Lest perauenture my sones do synne, and curse God in her hertis. Joob dide so in alle daies.

6 Forsothe in sum day, whanne the sones of God 'weren comun to be present bifor the Lord, also Sathan cam among hem.

7 To whom the Lord seide, Fro whennus comest thou? Which answeride, and seide, Y haue cumpassid the erthe, and Y haue walkid thorouy it.

8 And the Lord seide to hym, Whether thou hast biholde my seruaunt Joob, that noon in erthe is lyik hym; he is a symple man, and riytful, and dredynge God, and goynge awei fro yuel?

9 To whom Sathan answeride, Whether Joob dredith God veynli?

10 Whethir thou hast not cumpassid hym, and his hows, and al his catel bi cumpas? Thou hast blessid the werkis of hise hondis, and hise possessioun encreesside in erthe.

11 But stretche forth thin hond a litil, and touche thou alle thingis whiche he hath in possessioun; if he cursith not thee 'in the face, 'bileue not to me.

12 Therfor the Lord seide to Sathan, Lo! alle thingis, whiche he hath, ben in thin hond; oneli stretche thou not forth thin hond in to hym. And Sathan yede out fro the face of the Lord.

13 Sotheli whanne in sum dai 'hise sones and douytris eeten, and drunken wiyn in the hows of her firste gendrid brothir,

14 a messanger cam to Job, 'whiche messanger seide, Oxis eriden, and femal assis 'weren lesewid bisidis tho;

15 and Sabeis felden yn, and token awey alle thingis, and 'smytiden the children with swerd; and Y aloone ascapide for to telle to thee.

16 And whanne he spak yit, anothir cam, and seide, Fier of God cam doun fro heuene, and wastide scheep, and 'children touchid; and Y aloone ascapide for to telle 'to thee.

17 But yit the while he spak, also anothir cam, and seide, Caldeis maden thre cumpenyes, and assailiden the camels, and token tho awei, and thei smytiden 'also the children with swerd; and Y aloone ascapide to telle to thee.

18 And yit he spak, and, lo! anothir entride, and seide, While thi sones and douytris eeten, and drunken wiyn in the hows of her firste gendrid brothir,

19 a greet wynde felde yn sudenli fro the coost of desert, and schook foure corneris of the hows, 'which felde doun, and oppresside thi children, and thei ben deed; and Y aloone fledde to telle to thee.

20 Thanne Joob roos, and to-rente hise clothis, and 'with pollid heed he felde doun on the erthe, and worschipide God,

21 and seide, Y yede nakid out of the wombe of my modir, Y schal turne ayen nakid thidur; the Lord yaf, the Lord took awei; as it pleside the Lord, so 'it is doon; the name of the Lord be blessid.

22 In alle these thingis Joob synnede not in hise lippis, nether spak ony fonned thing ayens God.

CAP 2

1 Forsothe it was doon, whanne in sum dai the sones of God 'weren comun, and stoden bifor the Lord, and Sathan 'was comun among hem, and stood in his siyt,

2 that the Lord seide to Sathan, Fro whennus comest thou? Which answeride, and seide, Y haue cumpassid the erthe, 'and Y haue go thury it.

3 And the Lord seide to Sathan, Whethir thou hast biholde my seruaunt Joob, that noon in erthe is lijk hym; he is a symple man, and riytful, and dredynge God, and goynge awei fro yuel, and yit holdynge innocence? 'But thou hast moued me ayens him, that 'Y schulde turmente hym in veyn.

4 To whom Sathan answeride, and seide, 'A man schal yyue skyn for skyn, and alle thingis that he hath for his lijf;
5 'ellis sende thin hond, and touche his boon and fleisch, and thanne thou schalt se, that he schal curse thee in the face.
6 Therfor the Lord seide to Sathan, Lo! he is in 'thin hond; netheles kepe thou his lijf.
7 Therfor Sathan yede out fro the face of the Lord, and smoot Joob with 'a ful wickid botche fro the sole of the foot 'til to his top;
8 which Joob schauyde the quytere with a schelle, 'and sat in the dunghil.
9 Forsothe his wijf seide to hym, Dwellist thou yit in thi symplenesse? Curse thou God, and die.
10 And Joob seide, Thou hast spoke as oon of the fonned wymmen; if we han take goodis of the hond of the Lord, whi forsothe suffren we not yuels? In alle these thingis Joob synnede not in hise lippis.
11 Therfor thre frendis of Joob herden al the yuel, that hadde bifelde to hym, and camen ech man fro his place, Eliphath Temanytes, and Baldach Suythes, and Sophar Naamathites; for thei 'hadden seide togidere to hem silf, that thei wolden come togidere, and visite hym, and coumforte.
12 And whanne thei hadden reisid afer 'her iyen, thei knewen not hym; and thei crieden, and wepten, and to-renten her clothis, and spreynten dust on her heed 'in to heuene.
13 And thei saten with hym in the erthe seuene daies and seuene nyytis, and no man spak a word to hym; for thei sien, that his sorewe was greet.

CAP 3

1 Aftir these thingis Joob openyde his mouth,
2 and curside his dai, and seide, Perische the dai in which Y was borun,
3 and the nyyt in which it was seid, The man is conceyued.
4 Thilke dai be turnede in to derknessis; God seke not it aboue, and be it not in mynde, nethir be it liytned with liyt.
5 Derknessis make it derk, and the schadewe of deeth and myist occupie it; and be it wlappid with bittirnesse.
6 Derk whirlwynde holde that niyt; be it not rikynyd among the daies of the yeer, nethir be it noumbrid among the monethes.
7 Thilke nyyt be soleyn, and not worthi of preisyng.
8 Curse thei it, that cursen the dai, that ben redi to reise Leuyathan.
9 Sterris be maad derk with the derknesse therof; abide it liyt, and se it not, nethir the bigynnyng of the morwetid risyng vp.
10 For it closide not the doris of the wombe, that bar me, nethir took awei yuels fro min iyen.
11 Whi was not Y deed in the wombe? whi yede Y out of the wombe, and perischide not anoon?
12 Whi was Y takun on knees? whi was Y suclid with teetis?
13 For now Y slepynge schulde be stille, and schulde reste in my sleep,
14 with kyngis, and consuls of erthe, that bilden to hem soleyn places;
15 ethir with prynces that han gold in possessioun, and fillen her housis with siluer;
16 ethir as a 'thing hid not borun Y schulde not stonde, ethir whiche conseyued sien not liyt.
17 There wickid men ceessiden of noise, and there men maad wery of strengthe restiden.
18 And sum tyme boundun togidere with out disese thei herden not the voys of the wrongful axere.

19 A litil man and greet man be there, and a seruaunt free fro his lord.
20 Whi is liyt youun to the wretche, and lijf to hem that ben in bitternesse of soule?
21 Whiche abiden deeth, and it cometh not;
22 as men diggynge out tresour and ioien greetly, whanne thei han founde a sepulcre?
23 Whi is liyt youun to a man, whos weie is hid, and God hath cumpassid hym with derknessis?
24 Bifore that Y ete, Y siyhe; and as of watir flowynge, so is my roryng.
25 For the drede, which Y dredde, cam to me; and that, that Y schamede, bifelde.
26 Whether Y dissymilide not? whether Y was not stille? whether Y restide not? and indignacioun cometh on me.

CAP 4

1 Forsothe Eliphat Themanytes answeride, and seide,
2 If we bigynnen to speke to thee, in hap thou schalt take it heuyli; but who may holde a word conseyued?
3 Lo! thou hast tauyt ful many men, and thou hast strengthid hondis maad feynt.
4 Thi wordis confermyden men doutynge, and thou coumfortidist knees tremblynge.
5 But now a wounde is comun on thee, and thou hast failid; it touchide thee, and thou art disturblid.
6 Where is thi drede, thi strengthe, and thi pacience, and the perfeccioun of thi weies?
7 Y biseche thee, haue thou mynde, what innocent man perischide euere, ethir whanne riytful men weren doon awei?
8 Certis rathir Y siy hem, that worchen wickidnesse, and sowen sorewis,
9 and repen tho, to haue perischid bi God blowynge, and to be wastid bi the spirit of his ire.
10 The roryng of a lioun, and the vois of a lionesse, and the teeth of 'whelpis of liouns ben al to-brokun.
11 Tigris perischide, for sche hadde not prey; and the whelpis of a lioun ben distried.
12 Certis an hid word was seid to me, and myn eere took as theueli the veynes of priuy noise therof.
13 In the hidousnesse of 'nyytis siyt, whanne heuy sleep is wont to occupie men,
14 drede and tremblyng helde me; and alle my boonys weren aferd.
15 And whanne the spirit 'yede in my presence, the heiris of 'my fleisch hadden hidousnesse.
16 Oon stood, whos chere Y knewe not, an ymage bifor myn iyen; and Y herde a vois as of softe wynd.
17 Whether a man schal be maad iust in comparisoun of God? ethir whethir a man schal be clennere than his Makere?
18 Lo! thei that seruen hym ben not stidefast; and he findith schrewidnesse in hise aungels.
19 Hou myche more thei that dwellen in housis of cley, that han an ertheli foundement, schulen be wastyd as of a mouyte.
20 Fro morewtid til to euentid thei schulen be kit doun; and for no man vndurstondith, thei schulen perische with outen ende.
21 Sotheli thei, that ben residue, schulen be takun awei; thei schulen die, and not in wisdom.

CAP 5

1 Therfor clepe thou, if 'ony is that schal answere thee, and turne thou to summe of seyntis.

2 Wrathfulnesse sleeth 'a fonned man, and enuye sleeth a litil child.

3 Y siy a fool with stidefast rote, and Y curside his feirnesse anoon.

4 Hise sones schulen be maad fer fro helthe, and thei schulen be defoulid in the yate, and 'noon schal be that schal delyuere hem.

5 Whos ripe corn an hungri man schal ete, and an armed man schal rauysche hym, and thei, that thirsten, schulen drynke hise richessis.

6 No thing is doon in erthe with out cause, and sorewe schal not go out of the erthe.

7 A man is borun to labour, and a brid to fliyt.

8 Wherfor Y schal biseche the Lord, and Y schal sette my speche to my God.

9 That makith grete thingis, and that moun not be souyt out, and wondurful thingis with out noumbre.

10 Which yyueth reyn on the face of erthe, and moistith alle thingis with watris.

11 Which settith meke men an hiy, and reisith with helthe hem that morenen.

12 Which distrieth the thouytis of yuel willid men, that her hondis moun not fille tho thingis that thei bigunnen.

13 Which takith cautelouse men in the felnesse 'of hem, and distrieth the counsel of schrewis.

14 Bi dai thei schulen renne in to derknessis, and as in nyyt so thei schulen grope in myddai.

15 Certis God schal make saaf a nedi man fro the swerd of her mouth, and a pore man fro the hond of the violent, 'ethir rauynour.

16 And hope schal be to a nedi man, but wickidnesse schal drawe togidere his mouth.

17 Blessid is the man, which is chastisid of the Lord; therfor repreue thou not the blamyng of the Lord.

18 For he woundith, and doith medicyn; he smytith, and hise hondis schulen make hool.

19 In sixe tribulaciouns he schal delyuere thee, and in the seuenthe tribulacioun yuel schal not touche thee.

20 In hungur he schal delyuere thee fro deeth, and in batel fro the power of swerd.

21 Thou schalt be hid fro the scourge of tunge, and thou schalt not drede myseiste, 'ethir wretchidnesse, whanne it cometh.

22 In distriyng maad of enemyes and in hungur thou schalt leiye, and thou schalt not drede the beestis of erthe.

23 But thi couenaunt schal be with the stonys of erthe, and beestis of erthe schulen be pesible to thee.

24 And thou schalt wite, that thi tabernacle hath pees, and thou visitynge thi fairnesse schalt not do synne.

25 And thou schalt wite also, that thi seed schal be many fold, and thi generacioun schal be as an erbe of erthe.

26 In abundaunce thou schalt go in to the sepulcre, as an heep of wheete is borun in his tyme.

27 Lo! this is so, as we han souyt; which thing herd, trete thou in minde.

CAP 6

1 Forsothe Joob answeride, and seide,

2 Y wolde, that my synnes, bi whiche Y 'desseruede ire, and the wretchidnesse which Y suffre, weren peisid in a balaunce.

3 As the grauel of the see, this wretchidnesse schulde appere greuousere; wherfor and my wordis ben ful of sorewe.

4 For the arowis of the Lord ben in me, the indignacioun of whiche drynkith vp my spirit; and the dredis of the Lord fiyten ayens me.

5 Whether a feeld asse schal rore, whanne he hath gras? Ethir whether an oxe schal lowe, whanne he stondith byfor a 'ful cratche?

6 Ether whethir a thing vnsauery may be etun, which is not maad sauery bi salt? Ether whether ony man may taaste a thing, which tastid bryngith deeth? For whi to an hungri soule, yhe, bittir thingis semen to be swete; tho thingis whiche my soule nolde touche bifore, ben now my meetis for angwisch.

8 Who yyueth, that myn axyng come; and that God yyue to me that, that Y abide?

9 And he that bigan, al to-breke me; releesse he his hond, and kitte me doun?

10 And 'this be coumfort to me, that he turmente me with sorewe, and spare not, and that Y ayenseie not the wordis of the hooli.

11 For whi, what is my strengthe, that Y suffre? ethir which is myn ende, that Y do pacientli?

12 Nethir my strengthe is the strengthe of stoonus, nether my fleisch is of bras.

13 Lo! noon help is to me in me; also my meyneal frendis 'yeden awey fro me.

14 He that takith awei merci fro his frend, forsakith the drede of the Lord.

15 My britheren passiden me, as a stronde doith, that passith ruschyngli in grete valeis.

16 Snow schal come on hem, that dreden frost.

17 In the tyme wherynne thei ben scaterid, thei schulen perische; and as thei ben hoote, thei schulen be vnknyt fro her place.

18 The pathis of her steppis ben wlappid; thei schulen go in veyn, and schulen perische.

19 Biholde ye the pathis of Theman, and the weies of Saba; and abide ye a litil.

20 Thei ben schent, for Y hopide; and thei camen 'til to me, and thei ben hilid with schame.

21 Now ye ben comun, and now ye seen my wounde, and dreden.

22 Whether Y seide, Brynge ye to me, and yiue ye of youre catel to me? ethir,

23 Delyuere ye me fro the hond of enemy, and rauysche ye me fro the hond of stronge men?

24 Teche ye me, and Y schal be stille; and if in hap Y vnknew ony thing, teche ye me.

25 Whi han ye depraued the wordis of trewthe? sithen noon is of you, that may repreue me.

26 Ye maken redi spechis oneli for to blame, and ye bryngen forth wordis in to wynde.

27 Ye fallen in on a fadirles child, and enforsen to peruerte youre frend.

28 Netheles fille ye that, that ye han bigunne; yyue ye the eere, and se ye, whether Y lie.

29 Y biseche, answere ye with out strijf, and speke ye, and deme ye that, that is iust.

30 And ye schulen not fynde wickidnesse in my tunge, nethir foli schal sowne in my chekis.

CAP 7

1 Knyythod is lijf of man on erthe, and his daies ben as the daies of an hired man.

2 As an hert desireth schadowe, and as an hirede man abideth the ende of his werk;

3 so and Y hadde voide monethis, and Y noumbrede trauailous niytes to me.

4 If Y schal slepe, Y schal seie, Whanne schal Y rise? and eft Y schal abide the euentid, and Y schal be fillid with sorewis 'til to derknessis.

5 Mi fleisch is clothid with rot, and filthis of dust; my skyn driede vp, and is drawun togidere.

6 My daies passiden swiftliere thanne a web is kit doun 'of a webstere; and tho daies ben wastid with outen ony hope.

7 God, haue thou mynde, for my lijf is wynde, and myn iye schal not turne ayen, that it se goodis.

8 Nethir the siyt of man schal biholde me; but thin iyen ben in me, and Y schal not 'be in deedli lijf.

9 As a cloude is wastid, and passith, so he that goith doun to helle, schal not stie;

10 nether schal turne ayen more in to his hows, and his place schal no more knowe hym.

11 Wherfor and Y schal not spare my mouth; Y schal speke in the tribulacioun of my spirit, Y schal talke togidere with the bitternesse of my soule.

12 Whether Y am the see, ethir a whal, for thou hast cump-assid me with prisoun?

13 If Y seie, My bed schal coumfort me, and Y schal be releeuyd, spekynge with me in my bed;

14 thou schalt make me aferd bi dremys, and thou schalt schake me with 'orrour, ethir hidousnesse, 'bi siytis.

15 Wherfor my soule 'chees hangyng, and my boonys cheesi-den deth.

16 'Y dispeiride, now Y schal no more lyue; Lord, spare thou me, for my daies ben nouyt.

17 What is a man, for thou 'magnifiest hym? ether what set-tist thou thin herte toward hym?

18 Thou visitist hym eerly, and sudeynli thou preuest hym.

19 Hou long sparist thou not me, nether suffrist me, that Y swolowe my spotele?

20 Y haue synned; A! thou kepere of men, what schal Y do to thee? Whi hast thou set me contrarie to thee, and I am maad greuouse to my silf?

21 Whi doist thou not awei my sinne, and whi takist thou not awei my wickidnesse? Lo! now Y schal slepe in dust, and if thou sekist me eerli, Y schal not abide.

CAP 8

1 Sotheli Baldath Suytes answeride, and seide,

2 Hou longe schalt thou speke siche thingis? The spirit of the word of thi mouth is manyfold.

3 Whether God supplauntith, 'ethir disseyueth, doom, and whether Almyyti God distrieth that, that is iust?

4 Yhe, thouy thi sones synneden ayens hym, and he lefte hem in the hond of her wickidnesse;

5 netheles, if thou risist eerli to God, and bisechist 'Almyyti God, if thou goist clene and riytful,

6 anoon he schal wake fulli to thee, and schal make pesible the dwellyng place of thi ryytfulnesse;

7 in so miche that thi formere thingis weren litil, and that thi laste thingis be multiplied greetli.

8 For whi, axe thou the formere generacioun, and seke thou diligentli the mynde of fadris. For we ben men of yistirdai, and 'kunnen not; for oure daies ben as schadewe on the erthe.

10 And thei schulen teche thee, thei schulen speke to thee, and of her herte thei schulen bring forth spechis.

11 Whether a rusche may lyue with out moysture? ethir a spier 'may wexe with out watir?

12 Whanne it is yit in the flour, nethir is takun with hond, it wexeth drie bifor alle erbis.

13 So the weies of alle men, that foryeten God; and the hope of an ypocrite schal perische.

14 His cowardise schal not plese hym, and his trist schal be as a web of yreyns.

15 He schal leene, 'ether reste, on his hows, and it schal not stonde; he schal vndursette it, and it schal not rise togidere.

16 The rusche semeth moist, bifor that the sunne come; and in the risyng of the sunne the seed therof schal go out.

17 Rootis therof schulen be maad thicke on an heep of stoonys, and it schal dwelle among stoonys.

18 If a man drawith it out of 'his place, his place schal denye it, and schal seie, Y knowe thee not.

19 For this is the gladnesse of his weie, that eft othere ruschis springe out of the erthe.

20 Forsothe God schal not caste a wei a symple man, nethir schal dresse hond to wickid men;

21 til thi mouth be fillid with leiytir, and thi lippis with hertli song.

22 Thei that haten thee schulen be clothid with schenschip; and the tabernacle of wickid men schal not stonde.

CAP 9

1 Joob answeride, and seide, Verili Y woot, that it is so,

2 and that a man comparisound to God schal not be maad iust.

3 If he wole stryue with God, he may not answere to God oon for a thousynde.

4 He is wiys in herte, and strong in myyt; who ayenstood hym, and hadde pees?

5 Which bar hillis fro o place to anothir, and thei wisten not; whiche he distriede in his strong veniaunce.

6 Which stirith the erthe fro his place, and the pilers therof schulen 'be schakun togidere.

7 Which comaundith to the sunne, and it risith not; and he closith the sterris, as vndur a signet.

8 Which aloone stretchith forth heuenes, and goith on the wawis of the see.

9 Which makith Ariture, and Orionas, and Hiadas, 'that is, seuene sterris, and the innere thingis of the south.

10 Which makith grete thingis, and that moun not be souyt out, and wondurful thingis, of whiche is noon noumbre.

11 If he cometh to me, 'that is, bi his grace, Y schal not se hym; if he goith awey, 'that is, in withdrawynge his grace, Y schal not vndurstonde.

12 If he axith sodeynli, who schal answere to hym? ethir who may seie to hym, Whi doist thou so?

13 'God is he, whos wraththe no man may withstonde; and vndur whom thei ben bowid, that beren the world.

14 Hou greet am Y, that Y answere to hym, and speke bi my wordis with hym?

15 Which also schal not answere, thouy Y haue ony thing iust; but Y schal biseche my iuge.

16 And whanne he hath herd me inwardli clepynge, Y bileue not, that he hath herd my vois.

17 For in a whirlewynd he schal al to-breke me, and he schal multiplie my woundis, yhe, without cause.

18 He grauntith not, that my spirit haue reste, and he fillith me with bittirnesses.

19 If strengthe is souyt, 'he is moost strong; if equyte of doom is souyt, no man dar yelde witnessynge for me.

20 If Y wole make me iust, my mouth schal dampne me; if Y schal schewe me innocent, he schal preue me a schrewe.

21 Yhe, thouy Y am symple, my soule schal not knowe this same thing; and it schal anoye me of my lijf.

22 O thing is, which Y spak, he schal waste 'bi deth also the innocent and wickid man.

23 If he betith, sle he onys, and leiye he not of the peynes of innocent men.

24 The erthe is youun in to the hondis of the wickid; he hilith the face of iugis; that if he is not, who therfor is?

25 Mi daies weren swiftere than a corour; thei fledden, and sien not good.

26 Thei passiden as schippis berynge applis, as an egle fleynge to mete.

27 Whanne Y seie, Y schal not speke so; Y chaunge my face, and Y am turmentid with sorewe.

28 Y drede alle my werkis, witynge that thou 'woldist not spare the trespassour.

29 Sotheli if Y am also thus wickid, whi haue Y trauelid in veyn?

30 Thouy Y am waischun as with watris of snow, and thouy myn hondis schynen as moost cleene,

31 netheles thou schalt dippe me in filthis, and my clothis, 'that is, werkis, schulen holde me abhomynable.

32 Trewli Y schal not answere a man, which is lijk me; nether that may be herd euenli with me in doom.

33 'Noon is, that may repreue euer eithir, and sette his hond in bothe.

34 Do he awei his yerde fro me, and his drede make not me aferd.

35 Y schal speke, and Y schal not drede hym; for Y may not answere dredynge.

CAP 10

1 Yt anoieth my soule of my lijf; Y schal lete my speche ayens me, Y schal speke in the bitternesse of my soule.

2 Y schal seie to God, Nyle thou condempne me; schewe thou to me, whi thou demest me so.

3 Whether it semeth good to thee, if thou 'falsli chalengist and oppressist me, the werk of thin hondis; and if thou helpist the counsel of wickid men?

4 Whethir fleischli iyen ben to thee, ethir, as a man seeth, also thou schalt se?

5 Whether thi daies ben as the daies of man, and 'thi yeeris ben as mannus tymes;

6 that thou enquere my wickidnesse, and enserche my synne?

7 And wite, that Y haue do no 'wickid thing; sithen no man is, that may delyuere fro thin hond?

8 Thin hondis han maad me, and han formed me al in cumpas; and thou castist me doun so sodeynli.

9 Y preye, haue thou mynde, that thou madist me as cley, and schalt brynge me ayen in to dust.

10 Whether thou hast not mylkid me as mylk, and hast cruddid me togidere as cheese?

11 Thou clothidist me with skyn and fleisch; thou hast ioyned me togidere with boonys and senewis.

12 Thou hast youe lijf and mercy to me, and thi visiting hath kept my spirit.

13 Thouy thou helist these thingis in thin herte, netheles Y woot, that thou hast mynde of alle thingis.

14 If Y dide synne, and thou sparidist me at an our; whi suffrist thou not me to be cleene of my wickidnesse?

15 And if Y was wickid, wo is to me; and if Y was iust, Y fillid with turment and wretchidnesse 'schal not reise the heed.

16 And if Y reise 'the heed for pride, thou schalt take me as a lionesse; and thou turnest ayen, and turmentist me wondirli.

17 Thou gaderist in store thi witnessis ayens me, and thou multipliest thin yre, 'that is, veniaunce, ayens me; and peynes holden knyythod in me.

18 Whi hast thou led me out of the wombe? 'And Y wolde, that Y were wastid, lest an iye 'schulde se me.

19 That Y hadde be, as if Y were not, and 'were translatid, ethir borun ouer, fro the wombe to the sepulcre.

20 Whether the fewnesse of my daies schal not be endid in schort? Therfor suffre thou me, that Y biweile 'a litil my sorewe,

21 bifor that Y go, and turne not ayen, to the derk lond, and hilid with the derknesse of deth, to the lond of wrecchidnesse and of derknessis;

22 where is schadewe of deeth, and noon ordre, but euerlastynge hidousnesse dwellith.

CAP 11

1 Forsothe Sophar Naamathites answeride, and seide,

2 Whether he, that spekith many thingis, schal not also here? ether whethir a man ful of wordis schal be maad iust?

3 Schulen men be stille to thee aloone? whanne thou hast scorned othere men, schalt thou not be ouercomun of ony man?

4 For thou seidist, My word is cleene, and Y am cleene in thi siyt.

5 And 'Y wolde, that God spak with thee, and openyde hise lippis to thee;

6 to schewe to thee the priuetees of wisdom, and that his lawe is manyfold, and thou schuldist vndurstonde, that thou art requirid of hym to paie myche lesse thingis, than thi wickidnesse disserueth.

7 In hap thou schalt comprehende the steppis of God, and thou schalt fynde Almyyti God 'til to perfeccioun.

8 He is hiyere than heuene, and what schalt thou do? he is deppere than helle, and wherof schalt thou knowe?

9 His mesure is lengere than erthe, and brodere than the see.

10 If he distrieth alle thingis, ethir dryueth streitli 'in to oon, who schal ayenseie hym? Ethir who may seie to hym, Whi doest thou so?

11 For he knowith the vanyte of men; and whether he seynge byholdith not wickidnesse?

12 A veyn man is reisid in to pride; and gessith hym silf borun fre, as the colt of a wilde asse.

13 But thou hast maad stidefast thin herte, and hast spred abrood thin hondis to hym.

14 If thou doest awei 'fro thee the wickidnesse, which is in thin hond, and vnriytfulnesse dwellith not in thi tabernacle,

15 thanne thou schalt mowe reise thi face with out wem, and thou schalt be stidefast, and thou schalt not drede.

16 And thou schalt foryete wretchidnesse, and thou schalt not thenke of it, as of watris that han passid.

17 And as myddai schynynge it schal reise to thee at euentid; and whanne thou gessist thee wastid, thou schalt rise vp as the dai sterre.

18 And thou schalt haue trist, while hope schal be set forth to thee; and thou biried schalt slepe sikurli.

19 Thou schalt reste, and 'noon schal be that schal make thee aferd; and ful many men schulen biseche thi face.

20 But the iyen of wickid men schulen faile; and socour schal perische fro hem, and the hope of hem schal be abhominacyioun of soule.

CAP 12

1 Sotheli Joob answeride, and seide,

2 Therfor ben ye men aloone, that wisdom dwelle with you?

3 And to me is an herte, as and to you, and Y am not lowere than ye; for who knowith not these thingis, whiche ye knowen?

4 He that is scorned of his frend, as Y am, schal inwardli clepe God, and God schal here hym; for the symplenesse of a iust man is scorned.

5 A laumpe is dispisid at the thouytis of riche men, and the laumpe is maad redi to a tyme ordeyned.

6 The tabernaclis of robberis ben plenteuouse, 'ether ful of goodis; and boldli thei terren God to wraththe, whanne he hath youe alle thingis in to her hondis.

7 No wondur, ax thou beestis, and tho schulen teche thee; and axe thou volatilis of the eir, and tho schulen schewe to thee.

8 Speke thou to the erthe, and it schal answere thee; and the fischis of the see schulen telle tho thingis.

9 Who knowith not that the hond of the Lord made alle these thingis?

10 In whos hond the soule is of ech lyuynge thing, and the spirit, 'that is, resonable soule, of ech fleisch of man.

11 Whether the eere demeth not wordis, and the chekis of the etere demen sauour?

12 Wisdom is in elde men, and prudence is in myche tyme.

13 Wisdom and strengthe is at God; he hath counsel and vndurstondyng.

14 If he distrieth, no man is that bildith; if he schittith in a man, 'noon is that openith.

15 If he holdith togidere watris, alle thingis schulen be maad drie; if he sendith out tho watris, tho schulen distrie the erthe.

16 Strengthe and wisdom is at God; he knowith bothe hym that disseyueth and hym that is disseyued.

17 And he bryngith conselours in to a fonned eende, and iugis in to wondryng, ethir astonying.

18 He vnbindith the girdil of kyngis, and girdith her reynes with a coorde.

19 He ledith her prestis with out glorie, and he disseyueth the principal men, 'ethir counselours;

20 and he chaungith the lippis of sothefast men, and takith awei the doctrine of elde men.

21 He schedith out dispisyng on princes, and releeueth hem, that weren oppressid.

22 Which schewith depe thingis fro derknessis; and bryngith forth in to liyt the schadewe of deeth.

23 Which multiplieth folkis, and leesith hem, and restorith hem destried in to the hool.

24 Which chaungith the herte of princes of the puple of erthe; and disseyueth hem, that thei go in veyn out of the weie.

25 Thei schulen grope, as in derknessis, and not in liyt; and he schal make hem to erre as drunken men.

CAP 13

1 Lo! myn iye siy alle thingis, and myn eere herde; and Y vndurstood alle thingis.

2 Euene with youre kunnyng also Y kan, and Y am not lowere than ye.

3 But netheles Y schal speke to Almyyti God, and Y coueite to dispute with God;

4 and firste Y schewe you makeris of leesyng, and louyeris of weyward techyngis.

5 And 'Y wolde that ye weren stille, that ye weren gessid to be wise men.

6 Therfor here ye my chastisyngis; and perseyue ye the doom of my lippis.

7 Whether God hath nede to youre leesyng, that ye speke gilis for hym?

8 Whether ye taken his face, and enforsen to deme for God?

9 Ethir it schal plese hym, fro whom no thing mai be hid? Whether he as a man schal be disseyued with youre falsnessis?

10 He schal repreue you; for ye taken his face in hiddlis.

11 Anoon as he schal stire hym, he schal disturble you; and his drede schal falle on you.

12 Youre mynde schal be comparisound to aische; and youre nollis schulen be dryuun in to clei.

13 Be ye stille a litil, that Y speke, what euer thing the mynde hath schewid to me.

14 Whi to-rende Y my fleischis with my teeth, and bere my lijf in myn hondis?

15 Yhe, thouy God sleeth me, Y schal hope in hym; netheles Y schal preue my weies in his siyt.

16 And he schal be my sauyour; for whi ech ypocrite schal not come in his siyt.

17 Here ye my word, and perseyue ye with eeris derke and harde figuratif spechis.

18 Yf Y schal be demed, Y woot that Y schal be foundun iust.

19 Who is he that is demed with me? Come he; whi am Y stille, and am wastid?

20 Do thou not to me twei thingis oneli; and thanne Y schal not be hid fro thi face.

21 Make thin hond fer fro me; and thi drede make not me aferd.

22 Clepe thou me, and Y schal answere thee; ethir certis Y schal speke, and thou schalt answere me.

23 Hou grete synnes and wickidnessis haue Y? Schewe thou to me my felonyes, and trespassis.

24 Whi hidist thou thi face, and demest me thin enemy?

25 Thou schewist thi myyt ayens a leef, which is rauyschid with the wynd; and thou pursuest drye stobil.

26 For thou writist bitternessis ayens me; and wolt waste me with the synnes of my yong wexynge age.

27 Thou hast set my foot in a stok, and thou hast kept alle my pathis; and thou hast biholde the steppis of my feet.

28 And Y schal be wastid as rot, and as a cloth, which is etun of a mouyte.

CAP 14

1 A man is borun of a womman, and lyueth schort tyme, and is fillid with many wretchidnessis.

2 Which goith out, and is defoulid as a flour; and fleeth as schadewe, and dwellith neuere perfitli in the same staat.

3 And gessist thou it worthi to opene thin iyen on siche a man; and to brynge hym in to doom with thee?

4 Who may make a man clene conseyued of vnclene seed? Whether not thou, which art aloone?

5 The daies of man ben schorte, the noumbre of his monethis is at thee; thou hast set, ethir ordeyned, hise termes, whiche moun not be passid.

6 Therfor go thou awey fro hym a litil, 'that is, bi withdrawyng of bodili lijf, that he haue reste; til the meede coueitid come, and his dai is as the dai of an hirid man.

7 A tree hath hope, if it is kit doun; and eft it wexith greene, and hise braunches spreden forth.

8 If the roote therof is eeld in the erthe, and the stok therof is nyy deed in dust;

9 it schal buriowne at the odour of watir, and it schal make heer, as whanne it was plauntid first.

10 But whanne a man is deed, and maad nakid, and wastid; Y preye, where is he?

11 As if watris goen awei fro the see, and a ryuer maad voide wexe drie,

12 so a man, whanne he hath slept, 'that is, deed, he schal not rise ayen, til heuene be brokun, 'that is, be maad newe; he schal not wake, nether he schal ryse togidere fro his sleep.

13 Who yiueth this to me, that thou defende me in helle, and that thou hide me, til thi greet veniaunce passe; and thou sette to me a tyme, in which thou haue mynde on me?

14 Gessist thou, whethir a deed man schal lyue ayen? In alle the daies, in whiche Y holde knyythod, now Y abide, til my chaungyng come.

15 Thou schalt clepe me, and Y schal answere thee; thou schalt dresse the riyt half, 'that is, blis, to the werk of thin hondis.

16 Sotheli thou hast noumbrid my steppis; but spare thou my synnes.

17 Thou hast seelid as in a bagge my trespassis, but thou hast curid my wickidnesse.

18 An hil fallynge droppith doun; and a rooche of stoon is borun ouer fro his place.

19 Watris maken stoonys holowe, and the erthe is wastid litil and litil bi waischyng a wey of watir; and therfor thou schalt leese men in lijk maner.

20 Thou madist a man strong a litil, that he schulde passe with outen ende; thou schalt chaunge his face, and schalt sende hym out.

21 Whether hise sones ben noble, ether vnnoble, he schal not vndurstonde.

22 Netheles his fleisch, while he lyueth, schal haue sorewe, and his soule schal morne on hym silf.

CAP 15

1 Forsothe Eliphat Themanytes answeride, and seide,

2 Whether a wise man schal answere, as spekynge ayens the wynd, and schal fille his stomac with brennyng, 'that is, ire?

3 For thou repreuest hym bi wordis, which is not lijk thee, and thou spekist that, that spedith not to thee.

4 As myche as is in thee, thou hast avoidid drede; and thou hast take awey preyeris bifor God.

5 For wickidnesse hath tauyt thi mouth, and thou suest the tunge of blasfemeris.

6 Thi tunge, and not Y, schal condempne thee, and thi lippis schulen answere thee.

7 Whether thou art borun the firste man, and art formed bifor alle little hillis?

8 Whether thou herdist the counsel of God, and his wisdom is lower than thou?

9 What thing knowist thou, whiche we knowen not? What thing vndurstondist thou, whiche we witen not?

10 Bothe wise men and elde, myche eldre than thi fadris, ben among vs.

11 Whether it is greet, that God coumforte thee? But thi schrewid wordis forbeden this.

12 What reisith thin herte thee, and thou as thenkynge grete thingis hast iyen astonyed?

13 What bolneth thi spirit ayens God, that thou brynge forth of thi mouth siche wordis?

14 What is a man, that he be with out wem, and that he borun of a womman appere iust?

15 Lo! noon among hise seyntis is vnchaungable, and heuenes ben not cleene in his siyt.

16 How myche more a man abhomynable and vnprofitable, that drynkith wickidnesse as water?

17 I schal schewe to thee, here thou me; Y schal telle to thee that, that Y siy.

18 Wise men knoulechen, and hiden not her fadris.

19 To whiche aloone the erthe is youun, and an alien schal not passe bi hem.

20 A wickid man is proud in alle hise daies; and the noumbre of hise yeeris and of his tirauntrie is vncerteyn.

21 The sown of drede is euere in hise eeris, and whanne pees is, he supposith euere tresouns.

22 He bileueth not that he may turne ayen fro derknessis to liyt; and biholdith aboute on ech side a swerd.

23 Whanne he stirith hym to seke breed, he woot, that the dai of derknessis is maad redi in his hond.

24 Tribulacioun schal make hym aferd, and angwisch schal cumpas hym, as a kyng which is maad redi to batel.

25 For he helde forth his hond ayens God, and he was maad strong ayens Almyyti God.

26 He ran with neck reisid ayens God, and he was armed with fat nol.

27 Fatnesse, that is, pride 'comyng forth of temporal aboundaunce, hilide his face, 'that is, the knowyng of vndurstondyng, and outward fatnesse hangith doun of his sidis.

28 He schal dwelle in desolat citees, and in deseert, 'ethir forsakun, housis, that ben turned in to biriels.

29 He schal not be maad riche, nether his catel schal dwelle stidefastli; nether he schal sende his roote in the erthe,

30 nether he schal go awei fro derknessis. Flawme schal make drie hise braunchis, and he schal be takun a wey bi the spirit of his mouth.

31 Bileue he not veynli disseyued bi errour, that he schal be ayenbouyt bi ony prijs.

32 Bifor that hise daies ben fillid, he schal perische, and hise hondis schulen wexe drye;

33 he schal be hirt as a vyne in the firste flour of his grape, and as an olyue tre castinge awei his flour.

34 For the gaderyng togidere of an ipocrite is bareyn, and fier schal deuoure the tabernaclis of hem, that taken yiftis wilfuli.

35 He conseyuede sorewe, and childide wickidnesse, and his wombe makith redi tretcheries.

CAP 16

1 Forsothe Joob answeride, and seide, Y 'herde ofte siche thingis;

2 alle ye ben heuy coumfortouris.

3 Whether wordis ful of wynd schulen haue an ende? ether ony thing is diseseful to thee, if thou spekist?

4 Also Y myyte speke thingis lijk to you, and 'Y wolde, that youre soule were for my soule;

5 and Y wolde coumfort you by wordis, and Y wolde moue myn heed on you;

6 Y wolde make you stronge bi my mouth, and Y wolde moue lippis as sparynge you.

7 But what schal Y do? If Y speke, my sorewe restith not; and if Y am stille, it goith not awei fro me.

8 But now my sorewe hath oppressid me, and alle my lymes ben dryuun in to nouyt.

9 My ryuelyngis seien witnessyng ayens me, and a fals spekere is reisid ayens my face, and ayenseith me.

10 He gaderide togidere his woodnesse in me, and he manaasside me, and gnastide ayens me with his teeth; myn enemye bihelde me with ferdful iyen.

11 Thei openyden her mouthis on me, and thei seiden schenschip, and smytiden my cheke; and thei ben fillid with my peynes.

12 God hath closid me togidere at the wickid, and hath youe me to the hondis of wickid men.

13 Y thilke riche man and famouse sum tyme, am al to brokun sudeynli; 'he helde my nol; he hath broke me, and hath set me as in to a signe.

14 He hath cumpasside me with hise speris, he woundide togidere my leendis; he sparide not, and schedde out myn entrails in to the erthe.

15 He beet me with wounde on wounde; he as a giaunt felde in on me.

16 Y sewide togidere a sak on my skyn; and Y hilide my fleisch with aische.

17 My face bolnyde of wepynge, and myn iyeliddis wexiden derke.

18 Y suffride these thingis with out wickidnesse of myn hond, 'that is, werk, whanne Y hadde cleene preieris to God.

19 Erthe, hile thou not my blood, and my cry fynde not in thee a place of hidyng.

20 'For, lo! my witnesse is in heuene; and the knowere of my consience is in hiye places.

21 A! my frendis, ful of wordis, myn iye droppith to God.

22 And 'Y wolde, that a man were demed so with God, as the sone of man is demed with his felowe.

23 'For lo! schorte yeeris passen, and Y go a path, bi which Y schal not turne ayen.

CAP 17

1 Mi spirit schal be maad feble; my daies schulen be maad schort, and oneli the sepulcre is left to me.

2 Y have not synned, and myn iye dwellith in bittirnessis.

3 Lord, delyuere thou me, and sette thou me bisidis thee; and the hond of ech fiyte ayens me.

4 Thou hast maad the herte of hem fer fro doctryn, 'ethir knowyng of treuthe; therfor thei schulen not be enhaunsid.

5 He bihetith prey to felowis, and the iyen of hise sones schulen faile.

6 He hath set as in to a prouerbe of the comyn puple, and his saumple bifor hem.

7 Myn 'iye dasewide at indignacioun; and my membris ben dryuun as in to nouyt.

8 Iust men schulen wondre on this thing; and an innocent schal be reisid ayens an ypocrite.

9 And a iust man schal holde his weie, and he schal adde strengthe to clene hondis.

10 Therfor alle 'ye be conuertid, and come ye; and Y schal not fynde in you ony wiys man.

11 My daies ben passid; my thouytis ben scaterid, turmentynge myn herte.

12 Tho han turned the nyyt 'in to day; and eft aftir derknessis hope liyt.

13 If Y 'susteyne, ether suffre pacientli, helle is myn hous; and Y haue arayede my bed in derknessis.

14 Y seide to rot, Thou art my fadur; and to wormes, Ye ben my modir and my sister.

15 Therfor where is now myn abidyng? and who biholdith my pacience?

16 Alle my thingis schulen go doun in to deppeste helle; gessist thou, whether reste schal be to me, nameli there.

CAP 18

1 Forsothe Baldach Suythes answeride, and seide,

2 'Til to what ende schalt thou booste with wordis? Vndurstonde thou first, and so speke we.

3 Whi ben we arettid as beestis, and han we be foule bifor thee?

4 What leesist thou thi soule in thi woodnes? Whether the erthe schal be forsakun 'for thee, and hard stoonys schulen be borun ouer fro her place?

5 Whethir the liyt of a wickid man schal not be quenchid; and the flawme of his fier schal not schyne?

6 Liyt schal wexe derke in his tabernacle; and the lanterne, which is on hym, schal be quenchid.

7 The steppis of his vertu schulen be maad streit; and his counsel schal caste hym doun.

8 For he hath sent hise feet in to a net; and he goith in the meschis therof.

9 His foot schal be holdun with a snare; and thirst schal brenne out ayens hym.

10 The foot trappe of hym is hid in the erthe, and his snare on the path.

11 Dredis schulen make hym aferd on ech side, and schulen biwlappe hise feet.

12 His strengthe be maad feble bi hungur; and pouert asaile hise ribbis.

13 Deuoure it the fairnesse of his skyn; the firste gendrid deth waste hise armes.

14 His trist be takun awei fro his tabernacle; and perischyng, as a kyng, aboue trede on hym.

15 The felowis of hym that is not, dwelle in his tabernacle; brymston be spreynt in his tabernacle.

16 The rootis of hym be maad drie bynethe; sotheli his ripe corn be al to-brokun aboue.

17 His mynde perische fro the erthe; and his name be not maad solempne in stretis.

18 He schal put hym out fro 'liyt in to derknessis; and he schal bere hym ouer fro the world.

19 Nethir his seed nether kynrede schal be in his puple, nether ony relifs in hise cuntreis.

20 The laste men schulen wondre in hise daies; and hidousnesse schal asaile the firste men.

21 Therfor these ben the tabernaclis of a wickid man; and this is the place of hym, that knowith not God.

CAP 19

1 Forsothe Joob answeride, and seide, Hou long turmente ye my soule,

2 and al to-breken me with wordis?

3 Lo! ten sithis ye schenden me, and ye ben not aschamed, oppressynge me.

4 Forsothe and if Y 'koude not, myn vnkynnyng schal be with me.

5 And ye ben reisid ayens me, and repreuen me with my schenschipis.

6 Nameli now vndurstonde ye, that God hath turmentid me not bi euene doom, and hath cumpassid me with hise betyngis.

7 Lo! Y suffrynge violence schal crye, and no man schal here; Y schal crye loude, and 'noon is that demeth.

8 He bisette aboute my path, and Y may not go; and he settide derknessis in my weie.

9 He hath spuylid me of my glorye, and hath take awey the coroun fro myn heed.

10 He hath distried me on ech side, and Y perischide; and he hath take awei myn hope, as fro a tre pullid vp bi the roote.

11 His stronge veniaunce was wrooth ayens me; and he hadde me so as his enemye.

12 Hise theues camen togidere, and 'maden to hem a wei bi me; and bisegiden my tabernacle in cumpas.

13 He made fer my britheren fro me; and my knowun as aliens yeden awei fro me.

14 My neiyboris forsoken me; and thei that knewen me han foryete me.

15 The tenauntis of myn hows, and myn handmaydis hadden me as a straunger; and Y was as a pilgrym bifor her iyen.

16 Y clepide my seruaunt, and he answeride not to me; with myn owne mouth Y preiede hym.

17 My wijf wlatide my breeth; and Y preiede the sones of my wombe.

18 Also foolis dispisiden me; and whanne Y was goon awei fro hem, thei bacbitiden me.

19 Thei, that weren my counselouris sum tyme, hadden abhomynacioun of me; and he, whom Y louede moost, was aduersarie to me.

20 Whanne fleischis weren wastid, my boon cleuyde to my skyn; and 'oneli lippis ben left aboute my teeth.

21 Haue ye merci on me, haue ye merci on me, nameli, ye my frendis; for the hond of the Lord hath touchid me.

22 Whi pursuen ye me, as God pursueth; and ben fillid with my fleischis?

23 Who yyueth to me, that my wordis be writun? Who yyueth to me,

24 that tho be writun in a book with an yrun poyntil, ethir with a plate of leed; ethir with a chisel be grauun in a flynt?

25 For Y woot, that myn ayenbiere lyueth, and in the laste dai Y schal rise fro the erthe;

26 and eft Y schal be cumpassid with my skyn, and in my fleisch Y schal se God, my sauyour.

27 Whom Y my silf schal se, and myn iyen schulen biholde, and not an other man. This myn hope is kept in my bosum.

28 Whi therfor seien ye now, Pursue we hym, and fynde we the roote of a word ayens hym?

29 Therfor fle ye fro the face of the swerd; for the swerd is the vengere of wickidnessis, and wite ye, that doom schal be.

CAP 20

1 Forsothe Sophar Naamathites answeride, and seide,

2 Therfor my thouytis dyuerse comen oon aftir anothir; and the mynde is rauyischid in to dyuerse thingis.

3 Y schal here the techyng, bi which thou repreuest me; and the spirit of myn vndurstondyng schal answere me.

4 Y woot this fro the bigynnyng, sithen man was set on erthe,

5 that the preisyng of wickid men is schort, and the ioie of an ypocrite is at the licnesse of a poynt.

6 Thouy his pride 'stieth in to heuene, and his heed touchith the cloudis,

7 he schal be lost in the ende, as a dunghil; and, thei that sien hym, schulen seie, Where is he?

8 As a dreem fleynge awei he schal not be foundun; he schal passe as 'a nyytis siyt.

9 The iye that siy hym schal not se; and his place schal no more biholde him.

10 Hise sones schulen be 'al to-brokun with nedynesse; and hise hondis schulen yelde to hym his sorewe.

11 Hise boonys schulen be fillid with the vices of his yong wexynge age; and schulen slepe with hym in dust.

12 For whanne yuel was swete in his mouth, he hidde it vndur his tunge.

13 He schal spare it, and schal not forsake it; and schal hide in his throte.

14 His breed in his wombe schal be turned in to galle of snakis withynne.

15 He schal spue out the richessis, whiche he deuouride; and God schal drawe tho ritchessis out of his wombe.

16 He schal souke the heed of snakis; and the tunge of an addre schal sle hym.

17 Se he not the stremys of the flood of the stronde, of hony, and of botere.

18 He schal suffre peyne for alle thingis whiche he hath do, netheles he schal not be wastid; aftir the multitude of his fyndyngis, so and 'he schal suffre.

19 For he brake, and made nakid the hows of a pore man; he rauyschide, and bildide it not.

20 And his wombe was not fillid; and whanne he hath that, that he couetide, he may not holde in possessioun.

21 'No thing lefte of his mete; and therfor no thing schal dwelle of his goodis.

22 Whanne he is fillid, he schal be maad streit; he schal 'be hoot, and alle sorewe schal falle in on hym.

23 'Y wolde, that his wombe be fillid, that he sende out in to hym the ire of his strong veniaunce, and reyne his batel on hym.

24 He schal fle yrun armuris, and he schal falle in to a brasun boowe.

25 Led out, and goynge out 'of his schethe, and schynynge, 'ether smytinge with leit, 'in to his bittirnesse; orrible fendis schulen go, and schulen come on hym.

26 Alle derknessis ben hid in hise priuytees; fier, which is not teendid, schal deuoure hym; he schal be turmentid left in his tabernacle.

27 Heuenes schulen schewe his wickidnesse; and erthe schal rise togidere ayens hym.

28 The seed of his hows schal be opyn; it schal be drawun doun in the dai of the strong veniaunce of the Lord.

29 This is the part of a wickid man, 'which part is youun of God, and the eritage of hise wordis of the Lord.

CAP 21

1 Forsothe Joob answeride, and seide,

2 Y preye, here ye my wordis, and do ye penaunce.

3 Suffre ye me, that Y speke; and leiye ye aftir my wordis, if it schal seme worthi.

4 Whether my disputyng is ayens man, that skilfuli Y owe not to be sori?

5 Perseyue ye me, and be ye astonyed; and sette ye fyngur on youre mouth.

6 And whanne Y bithenke, Y drede, and tremblyng schakith my fleisch.

7 Whi therfor lyuen wickid men? Thei ben enhaunsid, and coumfortid with richessis.

8 Her seed dwellith bifor hem; the cumpeny of kynesmen, and of sones of sones dwellith in her siyt.

9 Her housis ben sikur, and pesible; and the yerde of God is not on hem.

10 The cow of hem conseyuede, and caluede not a deed calf; the cow caluyde, and is not priued of hir calf.

11 Her litle children goen out as flockis; and her yonge children 'maken fulli ioye with pleies.

12 Thei holden tympan, and harpe; and ioien at the soun of orgun.

13 Thei leden in goodis her daies; and in a point thei goen doun to hellis.

14 Whiche men seiden to God, Go thou awei fro us; we nylen the kunnyng of thi weies.

15 Who is Almiyti God, that we serue him? and what profitith it to vs, if we preien him?

16 Netheles for her goodis ben not in her hond, 'that is, power, the counsel of wickid men be fer fro me.

17 Hou ofte schal the lanterne of wickid men be quenchid, and flowing schal come on hem, and God schal departe the sorewis of his stronge veniaunce?

18 Thei schulen be as chaffis bifor the face of the wynd; and as a deed sparcle, whiche the whirlewynd scaterith abrood.

19 God schal kepe the sorewe of the fadir to hise sones; and whanne he hath yoldun, thanne he schal wite.

20 Hise iyen schulen se her sleyng; and he schal drynke of the stronge veniaunce of Almyyti God.

21 For whi what perteyneth it to hym of his hows aftir hym, thouy the noumbre of his monethis be half takun awey?

22 Whether ony man schal teche God kunnyng, which demeth hem that ben hiye?

23 This yuel man dieth strong and hool, riche and blesful, 'that is, myrie.

24 Hise entrails ben ful of fatnesse; and hise boonys ben moistid with merowis.

25 Sotheli anothir wickid man dieth in the bittirnesse of his soule, and with outen ony richessis.

26 And netheles thei schulen slepe togidere in dust, and wormes schulen hile hem.

27 Certis Y knowe youre wickid thouytis, and sentensis ayens me.

28 For ye seien, Where is the hows of the prince? and where ben the tabernaclis of wickid men?

29 Axe ye ech of 'the weie goeris; and ye schulen knowe, that he vndurstondith these same thingis,

30 that an yuel man schal be kept in to the dai of perdicioun, and schal be led to the dai of woodnesse.

31 Who schal repreue hise weies bifor hym? and who schal yelde to hym tho thingis, whiche he hath doon?

32 He schal be led to the sepulcris; and he schal wake in the heep of deed men.

33 He was swete to the 'stoonys, ether filthis, of helle; and drawith ech man aftir hym, and vnnoumbrable men bifor him.

34 Hou therfor coumforten ye me in veyn, sithen youre answeris ben schewid to 'repugne to treuthe?

CAP 22

1 Forsothe Eliphat Themanytes answeride, and seide,

2 Whether a man, yhe, whanne he is of perfit kunnyng, mai be comparisound to God?

3 What profitith it to God, if thou art iust? ethir what schalt thou yyue to hym, if thi lijf is without wem?

4 Whether he schal drede, and schal repreue thee, and schal come with thee in to doom,

5 and not for thi ful myche malice, and thi wickidnessis with out noumbre, 'these peynes bifelden iustli to thee?

6 For thou hast take awei with out cause the wed of thi britheren; and hast spuylid nakid men of clothis.

7 Thou yauest not watir to the feynt man; and thou withdrowist breed fro the hungri man.

8 In the strengthe of thin arm thou haddist the lond in possessioun; and thou moost myyti heldist it.

9 Thou leftist widewis voide; and al to-brakist the schuldris of fadirles children.

10 Therfor thou art cumpassid with snaris; and sodeyn drede disturblith thee.

11 And thou gessidist, that thou schuldist not se derknessis; and that thou schuldist not be oppressid with the fersnesse of watris flowyng.

12 Whether thou thenkist, that God is hiyere than heuene, and is enhaunsid aboue the coppe of sterris?

13 And thou seist, What sotheli knowith God? and, He demeth as bi derknesse.

14 A cloude is his hidyng place, and he biholdith not oure thingis, and he 'goith aboute the herris of heuene.

15 Whether thou coueitist to kepe the path of worldis, which wickid men han ofte go?

16 Whiche weren takun awei bifor her tyme, and the flood distriede the foundement of hem.

17 Whiche seiden to God, Go thou awei fro vs; and as if Almyyti God may do no thing, thei gessiden hym,

18 whanne he hadde fillid her housis with goodis; the sentence of whiche men be fer fro me.

19 Iust men schulen se, and schulen be glad; and an innocent man schal scorne hem.

20 Whether the reisyng of hem is not kit doun, and fier schal deuoure the relifs of hem?

21 Therfor assente thou to God, and haue thou pees; and bi these thingis thou schalt haue best fruytis.

22 Take thou the lawe of his mouth, and sette thou hise wordis in thin herte.

23 If thou turnest ayen to Almyyti God, thou schalt be bildid; and thou schalt make wickidnesse fer fro thi tabernacle.

24 He schal yyue a flynt for erthe, and goldun strondis for a flynt.

25 And Almyyti God schal be ayens thin enemyes; and siluer schal be gaderid togidere to thee.

26 Thanne on Almyyti God thou schalt flowe with delicis; and thou schalt reise thi face to God.

27 Thou schalt preye hym, and he schal here thee; and thou schalt yelde thi vowis.

28 Thou schalt deme a thing, and it schal come to thee; and lyyt schal schyne in thi weies.

29 For he that is mekid, schal be in glorie; and he that bowith doun hise iyen, schal be saued.

30 An innocent schal be saued; sotheli he schal be saued in the clennesse of hise hondis.

CAP 23

1 Sotheli Joob answeride, and seide,

2 Now also my word is in bitternesse, and the hond of my wounde is agreggid on my weilyng.

3 Who yyueth to me, that Y knowe, and fynde hym, and come 'til to his trone?

4 Y schal sette doom bifor hym, and Y schal fille my mouth with blamyngis;

5 that Y kunne the wordis, whiche he schal answere to me, and that Y vnderstonde, what he schal speke to me.

6 Y nyle, that he stryue with me bi greet strengthe, nether oppresse me with the heuynesse of his greetnesse.

7 Sette he forth equite ayens me, and my doom come perfitli to victorie.

8 If Y go to the eest, God apperith not; if Y go to the west, Y schal not vndurstonde hym; if Y go to the left side,

9 what schal Y do? Y schal not take hym; if Y turne me to the riyt side, Y schal not se hym.

10 But he knowith my weie, and he schal preue me as gold, that passith thorouy fier.

11 My foot suede hise steppis; Y kepte his weie, and Y bowide not awey fro it.

12 Y yede not awei fro the comaundementis of hise lippis; and Y hidde in my bosum the wordis of his mouth.

13 For he is aloone, and no man may turne awei hise thouytis; and what euer thing he wolde, his wille dide this thing.

14 Whanne he hath fillid his wille in me, also many othere lijk thingis ben redi to hym.

15 And therfor Y am disturblid of his face, and Y biholdynge hym am anguyschid for drede.

16 God hath maad neische myn herte, and Almyyti God hath disturblid me.

17 For Y perischide not for derknessis neiyynge; nethir myist hilide my face.

CAP 24

1 Tymes ben not hid fro Almyyti God; sotheli thei that knowen hym, knowen not hise daies.

2 Othere men turneden ouer the termes of neiyboris eritage, thei token awei flockis, and fedden tho.

3 Thei driueden awei the asse of fadirlesse children, and token awei the cow of a widewe for a wed.

4 Thei distrieden the weie of pore men, and thei oppressiden togidere the mylde men of erthe.

5 Othere men as wielde assis in deseert goon out to her werk; and thei waken to prey, and bifor maken redy breed to her children.

6 Thei kitten doun a feeld not hern, and thei gaderen grapis of his vyner, whom thei han oppressid bi violence.

7 Thei leeuen men nakid, and taken awei the clothis, to whiche men is noon hiling in coold;

8 whiche men the reynes of munteyns weeten, and thei han noon hilyng, and biclippen stoonys.

9 Thei diden violence, and robbiden fadirles and modirles children; and thei spuyliden, 'ether robbiden, the comynte of pore men.

10 Thei token awey eeris of corn fro nakid men, and goynge with out cloth, and fro hungry men.

11 Thei weren hid in myddai among the heepis of tho men, that thirsten, whanne the presses ben trodun.

12 Thei maden men of citees to weile, and the soulis of woundid men schulen crye; and God suffrith it not to go awei vnpunyschid.

13 Thei weren rebel to liyt; thei knewen not the weyes therof, nether thei turneden ayen bi the pathis therof.

14 A mansleere risith ful eerli, and sleeth a nedi man, and a pore man; sotheli bi nyyt he schal be as a nyyt theef.

15 The iye of avouter kepith derknesse, and seith, An yye schal not se me; and he schal hile his face.

16 Thei mynen housis in derknessis, as thei seiden togidere to hem silf in the dai; and thei knewen not liyt.

17 If the morewtid apperith sudeynli, thei demen the schadewe of deth; and so thei goon in derknessis as in liyt.

18 He is vnstablere than the face of the water; his part in erthe be cursid, and go he not bi the weie of vyneris.

19 Passe he to ful greet heete fro the watris of snowis, and the synne of hym 'til to hellis.

20 Merci foryete hym; his swetnesse be a worm; be he not in mynde, but be he al to-brokun as 'a tre vnfruytful.

21 For he fedde the bareyn, and hir that childith not, and he dide not wel to the widewe.

22 He drow doun stronge men in his strengthe; and whanne he stondith in 'greet state, he schal not bileue to his lijf.

23 God yaf to hym place of penaunce, and he mysusith that in to pride; for the iyen of God ben in the weies of that man.

24 Thei ben reisid at a litil, and thei schulen not stonde; and thei schulen be maad low as alle thingis, and thei schulen be takun awei; and as the hyynessis of eeris of corn thei schulen be al to-brokun.

25 That if it is not so, who may repreue me, that Y liede, and putte my wordis bifor God?

CAP 25

1 Forsothe Baldach Suytes answeride, and seide,

2 Power and drede is anentis hym, that is, God, that makith acordyng in hise hiye thingis.

3 Whether noumbre is of hise knyytis? and on whom schyneth not his liyt?

4 Whether a man comparisound to God mai be iustified, ether borun of a womman mai appere cleene?

5 Lo! also the moone schyneth not, and sterris ben not cleene in 'his siyt;

6 hou miche more a man rot, and the sone of a man a worm, is vncleene 'and vile, if he is comparisound to God.

CAP 26

1 Forsothe Joob answeride, and seide, Whos helpere art thou?

2 whether 'of the feble, and susteyneste the arm of hym, which is not strong?

3 To whom hast thou youe counsel? In hap to hym that hath not wisdom; and thou hast schewid ful myche prudence.

4 Ether whom woldist thou teche? whether not hym, that made brething?

5 Lo! giauntis weilen vnder watris, and thei that dwellen with hem.

6 Helle is nakid bifor hym, and noon hilyng is to perdicioun.

7 Which God stretchith forth the north on voide thing, and hangith the erthe on nouyt.

8 'Which God byndith watris in her cloudis, that tho breke not out togidere dounward.

9 'Whych God holdith the cheer of his seete, and spredith abrood theron his cloude.

10 He hath cumpassid a terme to watris, til that liyt and derknessis be endid.

11 The pilers of heuene tremblen, and dreden at his wille.

12 In the strengthe of hym the sees weren gaderid togidere sudeynly, and his prudence smoot the proude.

13 His spiryt ournede heuenes, and the crokid serpent was led out bi his hond, ledynge out as a mydwijf ledith out a child.

14 Lo! these thingis ben seid in partie of 'hise weyes; and whanne we han herd vnnethis a litil drope of his word, who may se the thundur of his greetnesse?

CAP 27

1 Also Joob addide, takynge his parable, and seide,

2 God lyueth, that hath take awey my doom, and Almyyti God, that hath brouyt my soule to bitternesse.

3 For as long as breeth is in me, and the spirit of God is in my nose thirlis,

4 my lippis schulen not speke wickidnesse, nether my tunge schal thenke a leesyng.

5 Fer be it fro me, that Y deme you iust; til Y faile, Y schal not go awei fro myn innocence.

6 Y schal not forsake my iustifiyng, which Y bigan to holde; for myn herte repreueth me not in al my lijf.

7 As my wickid enemy doth; myn aduersarie is as wickid.

8 For what is the hope of an ypocrite, if he rauyschith gredili, and God delyuerith not his soule?

9 Whether God schal here the cry of hym, whanne angwisch schal come on hym?

10 ether whether he may delite in Almyyti God, and inwardli clepe God in al tyme?

11 Y schal teche you bi the hond of God, what thingis Almyyti God hath; and Y schal not hide.

12 Lo! alle ye knowen, and what speken ye veyn thingis with out cause?

13 This is the part of a wickid man anentis God, and the eritage of violent men, ether rauenours, whiche thei schulen take of Almyyti God.

14 If hise children ben multiplied, thei schulen be slayn in swerd; and hise sones sones schulen not be fillid with breed.

15 Thei, that ben residue of hym, schulen be biried in perischyng; and the widewis of hym schulen not wepe.

16 If he gaderith togidere siluer as erthe, and makith redi clothis as cley;

17 sotheli he made redi, but a iust man schal be clothid in tho, and an innocent man schal departe the siluer.

18 As a mouyte he hath bildid his hous, and as a kepere he made a schadewyng place.

19 A riche man, whanne he schal die, schal bere no thing with hym; he schal opene hise iyen, and he schal fynde no thing.

20 Pouert as water schal take hym; and tempeste schal oppresse hym in the nyyt.

21 Brennynge wynd schal take hym, and schal do awei; and as a whirlewynd it schal rauysche hym fro his place.

22 He schal sende out turmentis on hym, and schal not spare; he fleynge schal 'fle fro his hond.

23 He schal streyne hise hondis on him, and he schal hisse on hym, and schal biholde his place.

CAP 28

1 Siluer hath bigynnyngis of his veynes; and a place is to gold, in which it is wellid togidere.

2 Irun is takun fro erthe, and a stoon resolued, 'ethir meltid, bi heete, is turned in to money.

3 God hath set tyme to derknessis, and he biholdith the ende of alle thingis.

4 Also a stronde departith a stoon of derknesse, and the schadewe of deth, fro the puple goynge in pilgrymage; it departith tho hillis, whiche the foot of a nedi man foryat, and hillis with out weie.

5 The erthe, wher of breed cam forth in his place, is destried bi fier.

6 The place of saphir ben stoonys therof, and the clottis therof ben gold.

7 A brid knewe not the weie, and the iye of a vultur, ethir rauenouse brid, bihelde it not.

8 The sones of marchauntis tretiden not on it, and a lyonesse passide not therbi.

9 God stretchide forth his hond to a flynt; he distriede hillis fro the rootis.

10 He hewide doun ryuers in stoonys; and his iye siy al precious thing.

11 And he souyte out the depthis of floodis; and he brouyte forth hid thingis in to liyt.

12 But where is wisdom foundun, and which is the place of vndurstondyng?

13 A man noot the prijs therof, nether it is foundun in the lond of men lyuynge swetli, 'ether delicatli.

14 The depthe of watris seith, It is not in me; and the see spekith, It is not with me.

15 Gold ful cleene schal not be youun for wisdom, nether siluer schal be weied in the chaungyng therof.

16 It schal not be comparysound to the died colours of Ynde, not to the moost precioue stoon of sardius, nether to saphir.

17 Nether gold, nether glas schal be maad euene worth therto;

18 and hiye and fer apperynge vessels of gold schulen not be chaungid for wisdom, nether schulen be had in mynde in comparisoun therof. Forsothe wisdom is drawun of pryuy thingis;

19 topasie of Ethiope schal not be maad euene worth to wisdom, and moost precioue diyngis schulen not be set togidere in prijs, 'ether comparisound, therto.

20 Therfor wherof cometh wisdom, and which is the place of vndurstondyng?

21 It is hid fro the iyen of alle lyuynge men; also it is hid fro briddis of heuene.

22 Perdicioun and deeth seiden, With oure eeris we herden the fame therof.

23 God vndurstondith the weye therof, and he knowith the place therof.

24 For he biholdith the endis of the world, and biholdith alle thingis that ben vndur heuene.

25 'Which God made weiyte to wyndis, and weiede watris in mesure.

26 Whanne he settide lawe to reyn, and weie to tempestis sownynge;

27 thanne he siy wisdom, and telde out, and made redi, and souyte out.

28 And he seide to man, Lo! the drede of the Lord, thilke is wisdom; and to go awei fro yuel, is vndurstondyng.

CAP 29

1 Also Joob addide, takynge his parable, and seide,

2 Who yyueth to me, that I be bisidis the elde monethis, bi the daies in whiche God kepte me?

3 Whanne his lanterne schynede on myn heed, and Y yede in derknessis at his liyt.

4 As Y was in the daies of my yongthe, whanne in priuete God was in my tabernacle.

5 Whanne Almyyti God was with me, and my children weren in my cumpas;

6 whanne Y waischide my feet in botere, and the stoon schedde out to me the stremes of oile;

7 whanne Y yede forth to the yate of the citee, and in the street thei maden redi a chaier to me.

8 Yonge men, 'that is, wantoun, sien me, and weren hid, and elde men risynge vp stoden;

9 princes ceessiden to speke, and puttiden the fyngur on her mouth;

10 duykis refreyneden her vois, and her tunge cleuyde to her throte.

11 An eere herynge blesside me, and an iye seynge yeldide witnessyng to me;

12 for Y hadde delyueride a pore man criynge, and a fadirles child, that hadde noon helpere.

13 The blessyng of a man 'to perische cam on me, and Y coumfortide the herte of a widewe.

14 Y was clothid with riytfulnesse; and Y clothide me as with a cloth, and with my 'doom a diademe.

15 Y was iye 'to a blynde man, and foot to a crokyd man.

16 Y was a fadir of pore men; and Y enqueride most diligentli the cause, which Y knew not.

17 Y al tobrak the grete teeth of the wickid man, and Y took awei prey fro hise teeth.

18 And Y seide, Y schal die in my nest; and as a palm tre Y schal multiplie daies.

19 My roote is openyde bisidis watris, and deew schal dwelle in my repyng.

20 My glorie schal euere be renulid, and my bouwe schal be astorid in myn hond.

21 Thei, that herden me, abiden my sentence; and thei weren ententif, and weren stille to my counsel.

22 Thei dursten no thing adde to my wordis; and my speche droppide on hem.

23 Thei abididen me as reyn; and thei openyden her mouth as to the softe reyn 'comynge late.

24 If ony tyme Y leiyide to hem, thei bileueden not; and the liyt of my cheer felde not doun in to erthe.

25 If Y wolde go to hem, Y sat the firste; and whanne Y sat as kyng, while the oost stood aboute, netheles Y was comfortour of hem that morenyden.

CAP 30

1 But now yongere men in tyme scornen me, whos fadris Y deynede not to sette with the doggis of my flok.

2 Of whiche men the vertu of hondis was for nouyt to me, and thei weren gessid vnworthi to that lijf.

3 Thei weren bareyn for nedynesse and hungur; that gnaw-iden in wildirnesse, and weren pale for pouert and wretchid-nesse;

4 and eeten eerbis, aud the ryndis of trees; and the roote of iunyperis was her mete.

5 Whiche men rauyschiden these thingis fro grete valeis; and whanne thei hadden foundun ony of alle, thei runnen with cry to tho.

6 Thei dwelliden in deseertis of strondis, and in caues of erthe, ethir on grauel, 'ethir on cley.

7 Whiche weren glad among siche thingis, and arettiden deli-ces to be vndur buschis.

8 The sones of foolis and of vnnoble men, and outirli appe-rynge not in erthe.

9 But now Y am turned in to the song of hem, and Y am maad a prouerbe to hem.

10 Thei holden me abhomynable, and fleen fer fro me, and dreden not to spete on my face.

11 For God hath openyd his arowe caas, and hath turmentid me, and hath set a bridil in to my mouth.

12 At the riytside of the eest my wretchidnessis risiden anoon; thei turneden vpsedoun my feet, and oppressiden with her pathis as with floodis.

13 Thei destrieden my weies; thei settiden tresoun to me, and hadden the maistri; and 'noon was that helpide.

14 Thei felden in on me as bi a brokun wal, and bi yate openyd, and weren stretchid forth to my wretchidnessis.

15 Y am dryuun in to nouyt; he took awei my desir as wynd, and myn helpe passide awei as a cloude.

16 But now my soule fadith in my silf, and daies of turment holden me stidfastly.

17 In nyyt my boon is persid with sorewis; and thei, that eten me, slepen not.

18 In the multitude of tho my cloth is wastid, and thei han gird me as with coler of a coote.

19 Y am comparisound to cley, and Y am maad lijk to a deed sparcle and aisch.

20 Y schal cry to thee, and thou schalt not here me; Y stonde, and thou biholdist not me.

21 Thou art chaungid in to cruel to me, and in the hardnesse of thin hond thou art aduersarie to me.

22 Thou hast reisid me, and hast set as on wynd; and hast hurtlid me doun strongli.

23 Y woot, that thow schalt bitake me to deeth, where an hows is ordeyned to ech lyuynge man.

24 Netheles thou sendist not out thin hond to the wastyng of hem; and if thei fallen doun, thou schalt saue.

25 Y wepte sum tyme on him, that was turmentid, and my soule hadde compassioun on a pore man.

26 Y abood goodis, and yuelis ben comun to me; Y abood liyt, and derknessis braken out.

27 Myn ynnere thingis buyliden out with outen my reste; daies of turment camen bifor me.

28 Y yede morenynge, and Y roos with out woodnesse in the cumpenye, and criede.

29 Y was the brother of dragouns, and the felow of ostrigis.

30 My skyn was maad blak on me, and my boonys drieden for heete.

31 Myn harpe is turned in to morenyng, and myn orgun in to the vois of weperis.

CAP 31

1 I made couenaunt with myn iyen, that Y schulde not thenke of a virgyn.

2 For what part schulde God aboue haue in me, and eritage Almyyti God of hiye thingis?

3 Whether perdicioun is not to a wickid man, and alienacioun of God is to men worchynge wickidnesse?

4 Whether he biholdith not my weies, and noumbrith alle my goyngis?

5 If Y yede in vanyte, and my foot hastide in gile,

6 God weie me in a iust balaunce, and knowe my symple-nesse.

7 If my step bowide fro the weie; if myn iye suede myn herte, and a spotte cleuede to myn hondis;

8 sowe Y, and another ete, and my generacioun be drawun out bi the root.

9 If myn herte was disseyued on a womman, and if Y settide aspies at the dore of my frend; my wijf be the hoore of anothir man,

10 and othir men be bowid doun on hir.

11 For this is vnleueful, and the moost wickidnesse.

12 Fier is deourynge 'til to wastyng, and drawynge vp bi the roote alle generaciouns.

13 If Y dispiside to take doom with my seruaunt and myn hand mayde, whanne thei stryueden ayens me.

14 What sotheli schal Y do, whanne God schal rise to deme? and whanne he schal axe, what schal Y answere to hym?

15 Whether he, that wrouyte also hym, made not me in the wombe, and o God formede me in the wombe?

16 If Y denyede to pore men that, that thei wolden, and if Y made the iyen of a wydewe to abide;

17 if Y aloone eet my mussel, and a faderles child eet not therof;

18 for merciful doyng encreesside with me fro my yong childhed, and yede out of my modris wombe with me;

19 if Y dispiside a man passynge forth, for he hadde not a cloth, and a pore man with out hilyng;

20 if hise sidis blessiden not me, and was not maad hoot of the fleeces of my scheep;

21 if Y reiside myn hond on a fadirles child, yhe, whanne Y siy me the hiyere in the yate;

22 my schuldre falle fro his ioynt, and myn arm with hise boonys be al to-brokun.

23 For euere Y dredde God, as wawis wexynge gret on me; and 'Y myyte not bere his birthun.

24 If Y gesside gold my strengthe, and if Y seide to purid gold, Thou art my trist;

25 if Y was glad on my many ritchessis, and for myn hond foond ful many thingis;

26 if Y siy the sunne, whanne it schynede, and the moone goynge clereli;

27 and if myn herte was glad in priuyte, and if Y kisside myn hond with my mouth;

28 which is the moost wickidnesse, and deniyng ayens hiyeste God;

29 if Y hadde ioye at the fallyng of hym, that hatide me, and if Y ioide fulli, that yuel hadde founde hym;

30 for Y yaf not my throte to do synne, that Y schulde asaile and curse his soule;

31 if the men of my tabernacle seiden not, Who yyueth, that we be fillid of hise fleischis? a pilgryme dwellide not with outforth;

32 my dore was opyn to a weiegoere;

33 if Y as man hidde my synne, and helide my wickidnesse in my bosum;

34 if Y dredde at ful greet multitude, and if dispisyng of neyyboris made me aferd; and not more Y was stille, and yede not out of the dore;

35 who yyueth an helpere to me, that Almyyti God here my desire? that he that demeth,

36 write a book, that Y bere it in my schuldre, and cumpasse it as a coroun to me?

37 Bi alle my degrees Y schal pronounce it, and Y schal as offre it to the prynce.

38 If my lond crieth ayens me, and hise forewis wepen with it;

39 if Y eet fruytis therof with out money, and Y turmentide the soule of erthetileris of it;

40 a brere growe to me for wheete, and a thorn for barli.

CAP 32

1 Forsothe these thre men leften of to answere Joob, for he semyde a iust man to hem.

2 And Helyu, the sone of Barachel Buzites, of the kynrede of Ram, was wrooth, and hadde indignacioun; forsothe he was wrooth ayens Joob, for he seide hym silf to be iust bifor God.

3 Sotheli Helyu hadde indignacioun ayens the thre frendis of hym, for thei hadden not founde resonable answere, but oneli hadde condempned Joob.

4 Therfor Helyu abood Joob spekynge, for thei, that spaken, weren eldere men.

5 But whanne he hadde seyn, that thre men myyten not answere, he was wrooth greetly.

6 And Helyu, the sone of Barachel Buzites, answeride, and seyde, Y am yongere in tyme, sotheli ye ben eldere; therfor with heed holdun doun Y dredde to schewe to you my sentence.

7 For Y hopide that lengere age schulde speke, and that the multitude of yeeris schulden teche wisdom.

8 But as Y se, spirit is in men, and the enspiryng 'ether reuelacioun, of Almyyti God yyueth vndurstondyng.

9 Men of long lijf ben not wise, and elde men vndurstonden not doom.

10 Therfor Y schal seie, Here ye me, and Y also schal schewe my kunnyng to you.

11 For Y abood youre wordis, Y herde youre prudence, as long as ye dispuytiden in youre wordis.

12 And as long as Y gesside you to seie ony thing, Y bihelde; but as Y se, 'noon is of you, that may repreue Joob, and answere to hise wordis;

13 lest perauenture ye seien, We han founde wisdom; God, and not man, hath cast hym awei.

14 Joob spak no thing to me, and Y not bi youre wordis schal answere hym.

15 Thei dredden, and answeriden no more, and token awei speche fro hem silf.

16 Therfor for Y abood, and thei spaken not, thei stoden, and answeriden no more; also Y schal answere my part,

17 and Y schal schewe my kunnyng.

18 For Y am ful of wordis, and the spirit of my wombe, 'that is, mynde, constreyneth me.

19 Lo! my wombe is as must with out 'spigot, ether a ventyng, that brekith newe vessels.

20 Y schal speke, and brethe ayen a litil; Y schal opene my lippis, and Y schal answere.

21 Y schal not take the persoone of man, and Y schal not make God euene to man.

22 For Y woot not hou long Y schal abide, and if my Makere take me awei 'after a litil tyme.

CAP 33

1 Therfor, Joob, here thou my spechis, and herkene alle my wordis.

2 Lo! Y haue openyd my mouth, my tunge schal speke in my chekis.

3 Of symple herte ben my wordis, and my lippis schulen speke clene sentence.

4 The spirit of God made me, and the brething of Almyyti God quykenyde me.

5 If thou maist, answere thou to me, and stoonde thou ayens my face.

6 Lo! God made me as and thee; and also Y am formyd of the same cley.

7 Netheles my myracle make thee not aferd, and myn eloquence be not greuouse to thee.

8 Therfor thou seidist in myn eeris, and Y herde the vois of thi wordis;

9 Y am cleene, and with out gilt, and vnwemmed, and wickidnesse is not in me.

10 'For God foond querels in me, therfor he demyde me enemy to hym silf.

11 He hath set my feet in a stok; he kepte alle my pathis.

12 Therfor this thing it is, in which thou art not maad iust; Y schal answere to thee, that God is more than man.

13 Thou stryuest ayenus God, that not at alle wordis he answeride to thee.

14 God spekith onys, and the secounde tyme he rehersith not the same thing.

15 God spekith bi a dreem in the visioun of nyyt, whanne sleep fallith on men, and thei slepen in the bed.

16 Thanne he openith the eeris of men, and he techith hem, 'and techith prudence;

17 that he turne awei a man fro these thingis whiche he made, and delyuere hym fro pride; delyuerynge his soule fro corrupcioun,

18 and his lijf, that it go not in to swerd.

19 Also God blameth a synnere bi sorewe in the bed, and makith alle the boonys of hym 'to fade.

20 Breed is maad abhomynable to hym in his lijf, and mete desirable 'bifor to his soule.

21 His fleisch schal faile for rot, and hise boonys, that weren hilid, schulen be maad nakid.

22 His soule schal neiye to corrupcioun, and his lijf to thingis 'bryngynge deeth.

23 If an aungel, oon of a thousynde, is spekynge for hym, that he telle the equyte of man, God schal haue mercy on hym,

24 and schal seie, Delyuere thou hym, that he go not doun in to corrupcioun; Y haue founde in what thing Y schal do merci to hym.

25 His fleisch is wastid of turmentis; turne he ayen to the daies of his yonge wexynge age.

26 He schal biseche God, and he schal be quemeful to hym; and he schal se his face in hertly ioye, and he schal yelde to man his riytfulnesse.

27 He schal biholde men, and he schal seie, Y haue synned, and verili Y haue trespassid; and Y haue not resseyued, as Y was worthi.

28 For he delyueride his soule, that it schulde not go in to perischyng, but that he lyuynge schulde se liyt.

29 Lo! God worchith alle these thingis in thre tymes bi alle men;

30 that he ayen clepe her soulis fro corrupcioun, and liytne in the liyt of lyuynge men.

31 Thou, Joob, perseyue, and here me, and be thou stille, the while Y speke.

32 Sotheli if thou hast what thou schalt speke, answere thou to me, speke thou; for Y wole, that thou appere iust.

33 That if thou hast not, here thou me; be thou stille, and Y schal teche thee wisdom.

CAP 34

1 And Helyu pronounside, and spak also these thingis,

2 Wise men, here ye my wordis, and lerned men, herkne ye me; for the eere preueth wordis,

3 and the throte demeth metis bi taast.

4 Chese we doom to vs; and se we among vs, what is the betere.

5 For Job seide, Y am iust, and God hath distried my doom.

6 For whi lesynge is in demynge me, and myn arowe is violent with out ony synne.

7 Who is a man, as Joob is, that drynkith scornyng as watir?

8 that goith with men worchynge wickidnesse, and goith with vnfeithful men?

9 For he seide, A man schal not plese God, yhe, thouy he renneth with God.

10 Therfor ye men hertid, 'that is, vndurstonde, here ye me; vnpite, 'ethir cruelte, be fer fro God, and wickidnesse fro Almyyti God.

11 For he schal yelde the werk of man to hym; and bi the weies of ech man he schal restore to hym.

12 For verili God schal not condempne with out cause; nether Almyyti God schal distrie doom.

13 What othere man hath he ordeyned on the lond? ether whom hath he set on the world, which he made?

14 If God dressith his herte to hym, he schal drawe to hym silf his spirit and blast.

15 Ech fleisch schal faile togidere; 'and a man schal turne ayen in to aisch.

16 Therfor if thou hast vndurstondyng, here thou that that is seid, and herkne the vois of my speche.

17 Whether he that loueth not doom may be maad hool? and hou condempnest thou so myche him, that is iust?

18 Which seith to the kyng, Thou art apostata; which clepith the duykis vnpitouse, 'ethir vnfeithful.

19 'Which takith not the persoones of princes, nether knew a tyraunt, whanne he stryuede ayens a pore man; for alle men ben the werk of hise hondis.

20 Thei schulen die sudeynli, and at mydnyyt puplis schulen be troblid, 'ethir schulen be bowid, as othere bookis han; and schulen passe, and schulen take 'awei 'a violent man with out hond.

21 For the iyen of God ben on the weies of men, and biholdith alle goyngis of hem.

22 No derknessis ben, and no schadewe of deeth is, that thei, that worchen wickidnesse, be hid there;

23 for it is 'no more in the power of man, that he come to God in to doom.

24 God schal al to-breke many men and vnnoumbrable; and schal make othere men to stonde for hem.

25 For he knowith the werkis of hem; therfor he schal brynge yn niyt, and thei schulen be al to-brokun.

26 He smoot hem, as vnpitouse men, in the place of seinge men.

27 Whiche yeden awei fro hym bi 'castyng afore, and nolden vndurstonde alle hise weies.

28 That thei schulden make the cry of a nedi man to come to hym, and that he schulde here the vois of pore men.

29 For whanne he grauntith pees, who is that condempneth? Sithen he hidith his cheer, who is that seeth hym? And on folkis and on alle men 'he hath power 'to do siche thingis.

30 Which makith 'a man ypocrite to regne, for the synnes of the puple.

31 Therfor for Y haue spoke to God, also Y schal not forbede thee.

32 If Y erride, teche thou me; if Y spak wickidnesse, Y schal no more adde.

33 Whether God axith that wickidnesse of thee, for it displeside thee? For thou hast bigunne to speke, and not Y; that if thou knowist ony thing betere, speke thou.

34 Men vndurstondynge, speke to me; and a wise man, here me.

35 Forsothe Joob spak folili, and hise wordis sownen not techyng.

36 My fadir, be Joob preuede 'til to the ende; ceesse thou not fro the man of wickidnesse,

37 'that addith blasfemye ouer hise synnes. Be he constreyned among vs in the meene tyme; and thanne bi hise wordis stire he God to the doom.

CAP 35

1 Therfor Helyu spak eft these thingis, Whethir thi thouyt semeth euene,

2 'ether riytful, to thee, that thou schuldist seie, Y am riytfulere than God?

3 For thou seidist, That, that is good, plesith not thee; ethir what profitith it to thee, if Y do synne?

4 Therfor Y schal answere to thi wordis, and to thi frendis with thee.

5 Se thou, and biholde heuene, and biholde thou the eir, that God is hiyere than thou.

6 If thou synnest 'ayens hym, what schalt thou anoye hym? and if thi wickidnessis ben multiplied, what schalt thou do ayens hym?

7 Certis if thou doist iustli, what schalt thou yyue to hym; ether what schal he take of thin hond?

8 Thi wickidnesse schal anoie a man, which is lijk thee; and thi riytfulnesse schal helpe the sone of a man.

9 Thei schulen cry for the multitude of fals chalengeris, and thei schulen weile for the violence of the arm of tirauntis.

10 And Joob seide not, Where is God, that made me, and that yaf songis in the nyyt?

11 Which God techith vs aboue the beestis of erthe, and he schal teche vs aboue the briddis of heuene.

12 There thei schulen crye, and God schal not here, for the pride of yuele men.

13 For God schal not here with out cause, and Almyyti God schal biholde the causis of ech man.

14 Yhe, whanne thou seist, He biholdith not; be thou demed bifor hym, and abide thou hym.

15 For now he bryngith not in his strong veniaunce, nether vengith 'greetli felonye.

16 Therfor Joob openith his mouth in veyn, and multiplieth wordis with out kunnyng.

CAP 36

1 Also Helyu addide, and spak these thingis,

2 Suffre thou me a litil, and Y schal schewe to thee; for yit Y haue that, that Y schal speke for God.

3 Y schal reherse my kunnyng fro the bigynnyng; and Y schal preue my worchere iust.

4 For verili my wordis ben with out leesyng, and perfit kunnyng schal be preued to thee.

5 God castith not awei myyti men, sithen he is myyti;

6 but he saueth not wickid men, and he yyueth dom to pore men.

7 He takith not awei hise iyen fro a iust man; and he settith kyngis in seete with out ende, and thei ben reisid there.

8 And if thei ben in chaynes, and ben boundun with the roopis of pouert,

9 he schal schewe to hem her werkis, and her grete trespassis; for thei weren violent, 'ethir rauenours.

10 Also he schal opene her eere, that he chastise; and he schal speke, that thei turne ayen fro wickidnesse.

11 If thei heren, and kepen, thei schulen fille her daies in good, and her yeris in glorie.

12 Sotheli if thei heren not, thei schulen passe bi swerd, and thei schulen be wastid in foli.

13 Feyneris and false men stiren the ire of God; and thei schulen not crye, whanne thei ben boundun.

14 The soule of hem schal die in tempest; and the lijf of hem among 'men of wymmens condiciouns.

15 He schal delyuere a pore man fro his angwisch; and he schal opene 'the eere of hym in tribulacioun.

16 Therfor he schal saue thee fro the streit mouth of the broddeste tribulacioun, and not hauynge a foundement vndur it; sotheli the rest of thi table schal be ful of fatnesse.

17 Thi cause is demed as the cause of a wickid man; forsothe thou schalt resseyue thi cause and doom.

18 Therfor ire ouercome thee not, that thou oppresse ony man; and the multitude of yiftis bowe thee not.

19 Putte doun thi greetnesse with out tribulacioun, and putte doun alle stronge men bi strengthe.

20 Dilaie thou not nyyt, that puplis stie for hem.

21 Be thou war, that thou bowe not to wickidnesse; for thou hast bigunne to sue this wickidnesse aftir wretchidnesse.

22 Lo! God is hiy in his strengthe, and noon is lijk hym among the yyueris of lawe.

23 Who mai seke out the weies of God? ethir who dar seie to hym, Thou hast wrouyt wickidnesse?

24 Haue thou mynde, that thou knowist not his werk, of whom men sungun.

25 Alle men seen God; ech man biholdith afer.

26 Lo! God is greet, ouercomynge oure kunnyng; the noumbre of hise yeeris is with out noumbre.

27 Which takith awei the dropis of reyn; and schedith out reynes at the licnesse of floodyatis,

28 whiche comen doun of the cloudis, that hilen alle thingis aboue.

29 If he wole stretche forthe cloudis as his tente,

30 and leite with his liyt fro aboue, he schal hile, yhe,

31 the herris of the see. For bi these thingis he demeth puplis, and yyueth mete to many deedli men.

CAP 37

32 In hondis he hidith liyt; and comaundith it, that it come eft.

33 He tellith of it to his freend, that it is his possessioun; and that he may stie to it.

1 Myn herte dredde of this thing, and is moued out of his place.

2 It schal here an heryng in the feerdfulnesse of his vois, and a sown comynge forth of his mouth.

3 He biholdith ouere alle heuenes; and his liyt is ouere the termes of erthe.

4 Sown schal rore aftir hym, he schal thundre with the vois of his greetnesse; and it schal not be souyt out, whanne his vois is herd.

5 God schal thundre in his vois wondurfulli, that makith grete thingis and that moun not be souyt out.

6 Which comaundith to the snow to come doun on erthe, and to the reynes of wijntir, and to the reynes of his strengthe.

7 Which markith in the hond of alle men, that alle men knowe her werkis.

8 An vnresonable beeste schal go in to his denne, and schal dwelle in his caue, 'ethir derke place.

9 Tempestis schulen go out fro the ynnere thingis, and coold fro Arturus.

10 Whanne God makith blowyng, frost wexith togidere; and eft ful brood watris ben sched out.

11 Whete desirith cloudis, and cloudis spreeden abrood her liyt.

12 Whiche cloudes cumpassen alle thingis bi cumpas, whidur euere the wil of the gouernour ledith tho, to al thing which he comaundith 'to tho on the face of the world;

13 whether in o lynage, ethir in his lond, ether in what euer place of his merci he comaundith tho to be foundun.

14 Joob, herkene thou these thingis; stonde thou, and biholde the meruels of God.

15 Whethir thou woost, whanne God comaundide to the reynes, that tho schulen schewe the liyt of hise cloudis?

16 Whether thou knowist the grete weies of cloudis, and perfit kunnyngis?

17 Whether thi cloothis ben not hoote, whanne the erthe is blowun with the south?

18 In hap thou madist with hym heuenes, which moost sad ben foundid, as of bras.

19 Schewe thou to vs, what we schulen seie to hym; for we ben wlappid in derknessis.

20 Who schal telle to hym, what thingis Y speke? yhe, if he spekith, a man schal be deuourid.

21 And now men seen not liyt; the eir schal be maad thicke sudenli in to cloudis, and wynd passynge schal dryue awei tho.

22 Gold schal come fro the north, and ferdful preisyng of God.

23 For we moun not fynde him worthili; he is greet in strengthe, and in doom, and in riytfulnesse, and may not be teld out.

24 Therfor men schulen drede hym; and alle men, that semen to hem silf to be wise, schulen not be hardi to biholde.

CAP 38

1 Forsothe the Lord answeride fro the whirlewynd to Joob,

2 and seide, Who is this man, wlappynge sentences with vnwise wordis?

3 Girde thou as a man thi leendis; Y schal axe thee, and answere thou to me.

4 Where were thou, whanne Y settide the foundementis of erthe? schewe thou to me, if thou hast vndurstondyng.

5 Who settide mesures therof, if thou knowist? ethir who stretchide forth a lyne theronne?

6 On what thing ben the foundementis therof maad fast? ether who sente doun the corner stoon therof,

7 whanne the morew sterris herieden me togidere, and alle the sones of God sungun ioyfuli?

8 Who closide togidere the see with doris, whanne it brak out comynge forth as of the wombe?

9 Whanne Y settide a cloude the hilyng therof, and Y wlappide it with derknesse, as with clothis of yong childhed.

10 Y cumpasside it with my termes, and Y settide a barre, and doris;

11 and Y seide, 'Til hidur thou schalt come, and thou schalt not go forth ferthere; and here thou schalt breke togidere thi bolnynge wawis.

12 Whethir aftir thi birthe thou comaundist to the bigynnyng of dai, and schewidist to the morewtid his place?

13 Whethir thou heldist schakynge togidere the laste partis of erthe, and schakedist awei wickid men therfro?

14 A seeling schal be restorid as cley, and it schal stonde as a cloth.

15 The liyt of wickid men schal be takun awey fro hem, and an hiy arm schal be brokun.

16 Whethir thou entridist in to the depthe of the see, and walkidist in the laste partis of the occian?

17 Whether the yatis of deeth ben openyd to thee, and 'siest thou the derk doris?

18 Whethir thou hast biholde the brede of erthe? Schewe thou to me, if thou knowist alle thingis,

19 in what weie the liyt dwellith, and which is the place of derknesse;

20 that thou lede ech thing to hise termes, and thou vndurstonde the weies of his hows.

21 Wistist thou thanne, that thou schuldist be borun, and knew thou the noumbre of thi daies?

22 Whethir thou entridist in to the tresours of snow, ether biheldist thou the tresours of hail?

23 whiche thingis Y made redy in to the tyme of an enemy, in to the dai of fiytyng and of batel.

24 Bi what weie is the liyt spred abrood, heete is departid on erthe?

25 Who yaf cours to the strongeste reyn,

26 and weie of the thundur sownynge? That it schulde reyne on the erthe with out man in desert, where noon of deedli men dwellith?

27 That it schulde fille a lond with out weie and desolat, and schulde brynge forth greene eerbis?

28 Who is fadir of reyn, ether who gendride the dropis of deew?

29 Of whos wombe yede out iys, and who gendride frost fro heuene?

30 Watris ben maad hard in the licnesse of stoon, and the ouer part of occian is streyned togidere.

31 Whether thou schalt mowe ioyne togidere schynynge sterris Pliades, ethir thou schalt mowe distrie the cumpas of Arturis?

32 Whether thou bryngist forth Lucifer, 'that is, dai sterre, in his tyme, and makist euene sterre to rise on the sones of erthe?

33 Whether thou knowist the ordre of heuene, and schalt sette the resoun therof in erthe?

34 Whethir thou schalt reise thi vois in to a cloude, and the fersnesse of watris schal hile thee?

35 Whethir thou schalt sende leitis, and tho schulen go, and tho schulen turne ayen, and schulen seie to thee, We ben present?

36 Who puttide wisdoom in the entrailis of man, ethir who yaf vndurstondyng to the cok?

37 Who schal telle out the resoun of heuenes, and who schal make acordyng of heuene to sleep?

38 Whanne dust was foundid in the erthe, and clottis weren ioyned togidere?

39 Whether thou schalt take prey to the lionesse, and schalt fille the soulis of hir whelpis,

40 whanne tho liggen in caues, and aspien in dennes?

41 Who makith redi for the crowe his mete, whanne hise briddis crien to God, and wandren aboute, for tho han not meetis?

CAP 39

1 Whethir thou knowist the tyme of birthe of wielde geet in stoonys, ethir hast thou aspied hyndis bryngynge forth calues?

2 Hast thou noumbrid the monethis of her conseyuyng, and hast thou knowe the tyme of her caluyng?

3 Tho ben bowid to the calf, and caluen; and senden out roryngis.

4 Her calues ben departid, and goen to pasture; tho goen out, and turnen not ayen to 'tho hyndis.

5 Who let go the wielde asse fre, and who loside the boondis of hym?

6 To whom Y haue youe an hows in wildirnesse, and the tabernacles of hym in the lond of saltnesse.

7 He dispisith the multitude of citee; he herith not the cry of an axere.

8 He lokith aboute the hillis of his lesewe, and he sekith alle greene thingis.

9 Whether an vnycorn schal wilne serue thee, ethir schal dwelle at thi cratche?

10 Whether thou schalt bynde the vnicorn with thi chayne, for to ere, ethir schal he breke the clottis of valeis aftir thee?

11 Whether thou schalt haue trist in his grete strengthe, and schalt thou leeue to hym thi traueils?

12 Whether thou schalt bileue to hym, that he schal yelde seed to thee, and schal gadere togidere thi cornfloor?

13 The fethere of an ostriche is lijk the fetheris of a gerfawcun, and of an hauk;

14 which ostrige forsakith hise eirun in the erthe, in hap thou schalt make tho hoot in the dust.

15 He foryetith, that a foot tredith tho, ethir that a beeste of the feeld al tobrekith tho.

16 He is maad hard to hise briddis, as if thei ben not hise; he traueilide in veyn, while no drede constreynede.

17 For God hath priued hym fro wisdom, and 'yaf not vnderstondyng to hym.

18 Whanne tyme is, he reisith the wengis an hiy; he scorneth the hors, and his ridere.

19 Whether thou schalt yyue strengthe to an hors, ether schal yyue neiyng 'aboute his necke?

20 Whether thou schalt reyse hym as locustis? The glorie of hise nosethirlis is drede.

21 He diggith erthe with the foot, he 'fulli ioieth booldli; he goith ayens armed men.

22 He dispisith ferdfulnesse, and he yyueth not stide to swerd.

23 An arowe caas schal sowne on hym; a spere and scheeld schal florische.

24 He is hoot, and gnastith, and swolewith the erthe; and he arettith not that the crie of the trumpe sowneth.

25 Whanne he herith a clarioun, he 'seith, Joie! he smellith batel afer; the excityng of duykis, and the yellyng of the oost.

26 Whether an hauk spredinge abrood hise wyngis to the south, bigynneth to haue fetheris bi thi wisdom?

27 Whether an egle schal be reisid at thi comaundement, and schal sette his nest in hiy places?

28 He dwellith in stoonys, and he dwellith in flyntis brokun bifor, and in rochis, to whiche 'me may not neiye.

29 Fro thennus he biholdith mete, and hise iyen loken fro fer.

30 Hise briddis souken blood, and where euere a careyn is, anoon he is present.

31 And the Lord addide, and spak to Joob,

32 Whether he, that stryueth with God, schal haue rest so liytli? Sotheli he, that repreueth God, owith for to answere to hym.

33 Forsothe Joob answeride to the Lord,

34 and seide, What may Y answere, which haue spoke liytli? Y schal putte myn hond on my mouth.

35 Y spak o thing, which thing Y wold, that Y hadde not seid; and Y spak anothir thing, to which Y schal no more adde.

CAP 40

1 Forsothe the Lord answeride to Joob fro the whirlewynd,

2 and seide, Girde thou as a man thi leendis, and Y schal axe thee, and schewe thou to me.

3 Whether thou schalt make voide my doom, and schalt condempne me, that thou be maad iust?

4 And if thou hast an arm, as God hath, and if thou thundrist with lijk vois, 'take thou fairnesse aboute thee,

5 and be thou reisid an hiy, and be thou gloriouse, and be thou clothid 'in faire clothis.

6 Distrie thou proude men in thi woodnesse, and biholde thou, and make lowe ech bostere.

7 Biholde thou alle proude men, and schende thou hem; and al to-breke thou wickid men in her place.

8 Hide thou hem in dust togidere, and drenche doun her faces in to a diche.

9 And Y schal knowleche, that thi riyt hond may saue thee.

10 Lo! behemot, whom Y made with thee, schal as an oxe ete hey.

11 His strengthe is in hise leendis, and his vertu is in the nawle of his wombe.

12 He streyneth his tail as a cedre; the senewis of his 'stones of gendrure ben foldid togidere.

13 Hise boonys ben as the pipis of bras; the gristil of hym is as platis of yrun.

14 He is the bigynnyng of the weies of God; he, that made hym, schal sette his swerd to hym.

15 Hillis beren eerbis to this behemot; alle the beestis of the feeld pleien there.

16 He slepith vndur schadewe, in the pryuete of rehed, in moiste places.

17 Schadewis hilen his schadewe; the salewis of the ryuer cumpassen hym.

18 He schal soupe vp the flood, and he schal not wondre; he hath trist, that Jordan schal flowe in to his mouth.

19 He schal take hem bi 'the iyen of hym, as bi an hook; and bi scharpe schaftis he schal perse hise nosethirlis.

20 Whether thou schalt mowe drawe out leuyathan with an hook, and schalt bynde with a roop his tunge?

21 Whethir thou schalt putte a ryng in hise nosethirlis, ethir schalt perse hyse cheke with 'an hook?

22 Whether he schal multiplie preieris to thee, ether schal speke softe thingis to thee?

23 Whether he schal make couenaunt with thee, and 'thou schalt take him a seruaunt euerlastinge?

24 Whether thou schalt scorne hym as a brid, ethir schalt bynde hym to thin handmaidis?

25 Schulen frendis 'kerue hym, schulen marchauntis departe hym?

26 Whether thou schalt fille nettis with his skyn, and a 'leep of fischis with his heed?

27 Schalt thou putte thin hond on hym? haue thou mynde of the batel, and adde no more to speke.

28 Lo! his hope schal disseyue hym; and in the siyt of alle men he schal be cast doun.

CAP 41

1 I not as cruel schal reise hym; for who may ayenstonde my face?

2 And who 'yaf to me bifore, that Y yelde to hym? Alle thingis, that ben vndur heuene, ben myne.

3 Y schal not spare hym for myyti wordis, and maad faire to biseche.

4 Who schal schewe the face of his clothing, and who schal entre in to the myddis of his mouth?

5 Who schal opene the yatis of his cheer? ferdfulnesse is bi the cumpas of hise teeth.

6 His bodi is as yotun scheldys of bras, and ioyned togidere with scalis ouerleiynge hem silf.

7 Oon is ioyned to another; and sotheli brething goith not thorouy tho.

8 Oon schal cleue to anothir, and tho holdynge hem silf schulen not be departid.

9 His fnesynge is as schynynge of fier, and hise iyen ben as iyelidis of the morewtid.

10 Laumpis comen forth of his mouth, as trees of fier, that ben kyndlid.

11 Smoke cometh forth of hise nosethirlis, as of a pot set on the fier 'and boilynge.

12 His breeth makith colis to brenne, and flawme goith out of his mouth.

13 Strengthe schal dwelle in his necke, and nedynesse schal go bifor his face.

14 The membris of hise fleischis ben cleuynge togidere to hem silf; God schal sende floodis ayens hym, and tho schulen not be borun to an other place.

15 His herte schal be maad hard as a stoon; and it schal be streyned togidere as the anefeld of a smith.

16 Whanne he schal be takun awei, aungels schulen drede; and thei aferd schulen be purgid.

17 Whanne swerd takith hym, it may not stonde, nethir spere, nether haburioun.

18 For he schal arette irun as chaffis, and bras as rotun tre.

19 A man archere schal not dryue hym awei; stoonys of a slynge ben turned in to stobil to hym.

20 He schal arette an hamer as stobil; and he schal scorne a florischynge spere.

21 The beemys of the sunne schulen be vndur hym; and he schal strewe to hym silf gold as cley.

22 He schal make the depe se to buyle as a pot; and he schal putte, as whanne oynementis buylen.

23 A path schal schyne aftir hym; he schal gesse the greet occian as wexynge eld.

24 No power is on erthe, that schal be comparisound to hym; which is maad, that he schulde drede noon.

25 He seeth al hiy thing; he is kyng ouer alle the sones of pride.

CAP 42

1 Forsothe Joob answeride to the Lord, and seide,

2 Y woot, that thou maist alle thingis, and no thouyt is hid fro thee [Note: Joob wiste wel, that in remembringe his riytfulnesse he suffride sum stiring of veynglorie, which is wont to come liytly in siche thingis, yhe, in men that ben perfit. in preisinge my riytfulnesse. in enqueringe ouer myche the resouns of Goddis domes.].

3 Who is this, that helith counsel with out kunnyng? Therfor Y spak vnwiseli, and tho thingis that passiden ouer mesure my kunnyng.

4 Here thou, and Y schal speke; Y schal axe thee, and answere thou to me.

5 Bi heryng of eere Y herde thee, but now myn iye seeth thee.

6 Therfor Y repreue me, and do penaunce in deed sparcle and aische.

7 Forsothe aftir that the Lord spak these wordis to Joob, he seide to Eliphat Themanytes, My stronge veniaunce is wrooth ayens thee, and ayens thi twey frendis [Note: God seith not ayenus Helyu, ether ayenus Joob; for whi to do synne bi presumpcioun, ether bi vnwar speking, as Helyu and Joob diden, is not so greuouse synne as to do synne bi afermyng of falsnesse, which bifelde to these thre men. for he synnede liytly, and dide penaunce therfor perfitly.]; for ye 'spaken not bifor me riytful thing, as my seruaunt Joob dide.

8 Therfor take ye to you seuene bolis, and seuene rammes; and go ye to my seruaunt Joob, and offre ye brent sacrifice for you. Forsothe Joob, my seruaunt, schal preie for you; Y schal resseyue his face, that foli be not arettid to you [Note: to euerlastinge peyne.]; for ye 'spaken not bifor me riytful thing, as my seruaunt Joob dide.

9 Therfor Eliphat Themanytes, and Baldach Suythes, and Sophar Naamathites, yeden, and diden, as the Lord hedde spoke to hem; and the Lord resseyuede the face of Joob.

10 Also the Lord was conuertid to the penaunce of Joob, whanne he preiede for hise frendis. And the Lord addide alle thingis double, whiche euere weren of Joob.

11 Sotheli alle hise britheren, and alle hise sistris, and alle that knewen hym bifore, camen to hym; and thei eeten breed with hym in his hows, and moueden the heed on hym; and thei coumfortiden hym of al the yuel, which the Lord hadde brouyt in on hym; and thei yauen to hym ech man o scheep, and o goldun eere ring.

12 Forsothe the Lord blesside the laste thingis of Joob, more than the bigynnyng of hym; and fouretene thousynde of scheep weren maad to hym, and sixe thousinde of camels, and a thousynde yockis of oxis, and a thousynde femal assis.

13 And he hadde seuene sones [Note: the formere sones and douytris weren in the weye of saluacioun, and so not deed outirly.], and thre douytris; and he clepide the name of o douytir Dai, and the name of the secounde douytir Cassia, and the name of the thridde douytir 'An horn of wymmens oynement.

14 'Sotheli no wymmen weren foundun so faire in al erthe, as the douytris of Joob; and her fadir yaf eritage to hem among her britheren.

15 Forsothe Joob lyuede aftir these betyngis an hundrid and fourti yeer, and 'siy hise sones, and the sones of hise sones, 'til to the fourthe generacioun; and he was deed eld, and ful of daies.

PSALMS

PSALM 1

1 Blessid is the man, that yede not in the councel of wickid men; and stood not in the weie of synneris, and sat not in the chaier of pestilence.

2 But his wille is in the lawe of the Lord; and he schal bithenke in the lawe of hym dai and nyyt.

3 And he schal be as a tree, which is plauntid bisidis the rennyngis of watris; which tre schal yyue his fruyt in his tyme. And his leef schal not falle doun; and alle thingis which euere he schal do schulen haue prosperite.

4 Not so wickid men, not so; but thei ben as dust, which the wynd castith awei fro the face of erthe.

5 Therfor wickid men risen not ayen in doom; nethir synneres in the councel of iust men.

6 For the Lord knowith the weie of iust men; and the weie of wickid men schal perische.

PSALM 2

1 Whi gnastiden with teeth hethene men; and puplis thouyten veyn thingis?

2 The kyngis of erthe stoden togidere; and princes camen togidere ayens the Lord, and ayens his Crist?

3 Breke we the bondis of hem; and cast we awei the yok of hem fro vs.

4 He that dwellith in heuenes schal scorne hem; and the Lord schal bimowe hem.

5 Thanne he schal speke to hem in his ire; and he schal disturble hem in his stronge veniaunce.

6 Forsothe Y am maad of hym a kyng on Syon, his hooli hil; prechynge his comaundement.

7 The Lord seide to me, Thou art my sone; Y haue gendrid thee to dai.

8 Axe thou of me, and Y schal yyue to thee hethene men thin eritage; and thi possessioun the termes of erthe.

9 Thou schalt gouerne hem in an yrun yerde; and thou schalt breke hem as the vessel of a pottere.

10 And now, ye kyngis, vndurstonde; ye that demen the erthe, be lerud.

11 Serue ye the Lord with drede; and make ye ful ioye to hym with tremblyng.

12 Take ye lore; lest the Lord be wrooth sumtyme, and lest ye perischen fro iust waie.

13 Whanne his 'ire brenneth out in schort tyme; blessed ben alle thei, that tristen in hym.

PSALM 3

1 The title of the thridde salm. 'The salm of Dauid, whanne he fledde fro the face of Absolon, his sone.

2 Lord, whi ben thei multiplied that disturblen me?

3 many men rysen ayens me. Many men seien of my soule, Noon helthe is to hym in his God.

4 But thou, Lord, art myn vptakere; my glorye, and enhaunsyng myn heed.

5 With my vois Y criede to the Lord; and he herde me fro his hooli hil.

6 I slepte, and 'was quenchid, and Y roos vp; for the Lord resseyuede me.

7 I schal not drede thousyndis of puple cumpassynge me; Lord, rise thou vp; my God, make thou me saaf.

8 For thou hast smyte alle men beynge aduersaries to me with out cause; thou hast al to-broke the teeth of synneris.

9 Helthe is of the Lord; and thi blessyng, Lord, is on thi puple.

PSALM 4

1 The title of the fourthe salm. 'To the victorie in orguns; the salm of Dauid.

2 Whanne Y inwardli clepid, God of my riytwisnesse herde me; in tribulacioun thou hast alargid to me.

3 Haue thou mercy on me; and here thou my preier. Sones of men, hou long ben ye of heuy herte? whi louen ye vanite, and seken a leesyng?

4 And wite ye, that the Lord hath maad merueilous his hooli man; the Lord schal here me, whanne Y schal crye to hym.

5 Be ye wrothe, and nyle ye do synne; 'and for tho thingis whiche ye seien in youre hertis and in youre beddis, be ye compunct.

6 Sacrifie ye 'the sacrifice of riytfulnesse, and hope ye in the Lord; many seien, Who schewide goodis to vs?

7 Lord, the liyt of thi cheer is markid on vs; thou hast youe gladnesse in myn herte.

8 Thei ben multiplied of the fruit of whete, and of wyn; and of her oile.

9 In pees in the same thing; Y schal slepe, and take reste.

10 For thou, Lord; hast set me syngulerli in hope.

PSALM 5

1 The title of the fyuethe salm. To the ouercomere on the eritagis, the song of Dauid.

2 Lord, perseyue thou my wordis with eeris; vndurstonde thou my cry.

3 Mi kyng, and my God; yyue thou tent to the vois of my preier.

4 For, Lord, Y schal preie to thee; here thou eerly my vois.

5 Eerli Y schal stonde nyy thee, and Y schal se; for thou art God not willynge wickidnesse.

6 Nethir an yuel willid man schal dwelle bisidis thee; nethir vniust men schulen dwelle bifor thin iyen.

7 Thou hatist alle that worchen wickidnesse; thou schalt leese alle that speken leesyng. The Lord schal holde abhomynable a manquellere, and gileful man.

8 But, Lord, in the multitude of thi merci Y schal entre in to thin hows; Y schal worschipe to thin hooli temple in thi drede.

9 Lord, lede thou forth me in thi riytfulnesse for myn enemyes; dresse thou my weie in thi siyt.

10 For whi treuthe is not in her mouth; her herte is veyn.

11 Her throte is an opyn sepulcre, thei diden gilefuli with her tungis; God, deme thou hem. Falle thei doun fro her thouytis, vp the multitude of her wickidnessis caste thou hem doun; for, Lord, thei han terrid thee to ire. And alle that hopen in thee, be glad; thei schulen make fulli ioye with outen ende, and thou schalt dwelle in hem.

12 And alle that louen thi name schulen haue glorie in thee;

13 for thou schalt blesse a iust man. Lord, thou hast corouned vs, as with the scheeld of thi good wille.

PSALM 6

1 The title of the sixte salm. To the ouercomere in salmes, the salm of Dauid, 'on the eiythe.

2 Lord, repreue thou not me in thi stronge veniaunce; nether chastice thou me in thin ire.

3 Lord, haue thou merci on me, for Y am sijk; Lord, make thou me hool, for alle my boonys ben troblid.

4 And my soule is troblid greetli; but thou, Lord, hou long?

5 Lord, be thou conuertid, and delyuere my soule; make thou me saaf, for thi merci.

6 For noon is in deeth, which is myndful of thee; but in helle who schal knouleche to thee?

7 I traueilide in my weilyng, Y schal waische my bed bi ech nyyt; Y schal moiste, 'ether make weet, my bedstre with my teeris.

8 Myn iye is disturblid of woodnesse; Y waxe eld among alle myn enemyes.

9 Alle ye that worchen wickidnesse, departe fro me; for the Lord hath herd the vois of my wepyng.

10 The Lord hath herd my bisechyng; the Lord hath resseyued my preier.

11 Alle my enemyes be aschamed, and be disturblid greetli; be thei turned togidere, and be thei aschamed ful swiftli.

PSALM 7

1 The title of the seuenthe salm. For the ignoraunce of Dauid, which he songe to the Lord on the wordis of Ethiopien, the sone of Gemyny.

2 Mi Lord God, Y haue hopid in thee; make thou me saaf fro alle that pursuen me, and delyuere thou me.

3 Lest ony tyme he as a lioun rauysche my soule; the while noon is that ayenbieth, nether that makith saaf.

4 Mi Lord God, if Y dide this thing, if wickidnesse is in myn hondis;

5 if Y 'yeldide to men yeldynge to me yuels, falle Y 'bi disse-ruyng voide fro myn enemyes;

6 myn enemy pursue my soule, and take, and defoule my lijf in erthe; and brynge my glorie in to dust.

7 Lord, rise thou vp in thin ire; and be thou reysid in the coos-tis of myn enemyes.

8 And, my Lord God, rise thou in the comaundement, which thou 'hast comaundid; and the synagoge of puplis schal cum-passe thee.

9 And for this go thou ayen an hiy; the Lord demeth puplis. Lord, deme thou me bi my riytfulnesse; and bi myn inno-cence on me.

10 The wickidnesse of synneris be endid; and thou, God, sekyng the hertis and reynes, schalt dresse a iust man.

11 Mi iust help is of the Lord; that makith saaf riytful men in herte.

12 The Lord is a iust iuge, stronge and pacient; whether he is wrooth bi alle daies?

13 If ye ben 'not conuertid, he schal florische his swerd; he hath bent his bouwe, and made it redi.

14 And therynne he hath maad redi the vessels of deth; he hath fulli maad his arewis with brennynge thingis.

15 Lo! he conseyuede sorewe; he peynfuli brouyte forth vnriytfulnesse, and childide wickidnesse.

16 He openide a lake, and diggide it out; and he felde in to the dich which he made.

17 His sorewe schal be turned in to his heed; and his wickid-nesse schal come doun in to his necke.

18 I schal knouleche to the Lord bi his riytfulnesse; and Y schal synge to the name of the hiyeste Lord.

PSALM 8

1 The title of the eiythe salm. To the ouercomere, for pres-sours, the salm of Dauid.

2 Lord, thou art oure Lord; thi name is ful wonderful in al erthe. For thi greet doyng is reisid, aboue heuenes.

3 Of the mouth of yonge children, not spekynge and soukynge mylk, thou madist perfitli heriyng, for thin ene-myes; that thou destrie the enemy and avengere.

4 For Y schal se thin heuenes, the werkis of thi fyngris; the moone and sterris, whiche thou hast foundid.

5 What is a man, that thou art myndeful of hym; ethir the sone of a virgyn, for thou visitist hym?

6 Thou hast maad hym a litil lesse than aungels; thou hast corouned hym with glorie and onour,

7 and hast ordeyned hym aboue the werkis of thin hondis.

8 Thou hast maad suget alle thingis vndur hise feet; alle scheep and oxis, ferthermore and the beestis of the feeld;

9 the briddis of the eir, and the fischis of the see; that passen bi the pathis of the see.

10 Lord, 'thou art oure Lord; thi name 'is wondurful in al erthe.

PALM 9

1 The title of the nynthe salm. In to the ende, for the pryuy-tees of the sone, the salm of Dauid.

2 Lord, Y schal knouleche to thee in al myn herte; Y schal telle alle thi merueils.

3 Thou hiyeste, Y schal be glad, and Y schal be fulli ioieful in thee; Y schal synge to thi name.

4 For thou turnest myn enemy abac; thei schulen be maad feble, and schulen perische fro thi face.

5 For thou hast maad my doom and my cause; thou, that demest riytfulnesse, 'hast set on the trone.

6 Thou blamedist hethene men, and the wickid perischide; thou hast do awei the name of hem in to the world, and in to the world of world.

7 The swerdis of the enemy failiden in to the ende; and thou hast distried the citees of hem. The mynde of hem perischide with sown;

8 and the Lord dwellith with outen ende. He made redi his trone in doom; and he schal deme the world in equite,

9 he schal deme puplis in riytfulnesse.

10 And the Lord is maad refuyt, 'ether help, 'to a pore man; an helpere in couenable tymes in tribulacioun.

11 And thei, that knowen thi name, haue hope in thee; for thou, Lord, hast not forsake hem that seken thee.

12 Synge ye to the Lord, that dwellith in Syon; telle ye hise studyes among hethene men.

13 God foryetith not the cry of pore men; for he hath mynde, and sekith the blood of hem.

14 Lord, haue thou merci on me; se thou my mekenesse of myn enemyes.

15 Which enhaunsist me fro the yatis of deeth; that Y telle alle thi preisyngis in the yatis of the douyter of Syon.

16 Y schal 'be fulli ioyeful in thin helthe; hethene men ben fast set in the perisching, which thei maden. In this snare, which thei hidden, the foot of hem is kauyt.

17 The Lord makynge domes schal be knowun; the synnere is takun in the werkis of hise hondis.

18 Synneris be turned togidere in to helle; alle folkis, that foryeten God.

19 For the foryetyng of a pore man schal not be in to the ende; the pacience of pore men schal not perische in to the ende.

20 Lord, rise thou vp, a man be not coumfortid; folkis be demyd in thi siyt.

21 Lord, ordeine thou a lawe makere on hem; wite folkis, that thei ben men.

1 Lord, whi hast thou go fer awei? thou dispisist 'in couen-able tymes in tribulacioun.

2 While the wickid is proud, the pore man is brent; thei ben taken in the counsels, bi whiche thei thenken.

3 Forwhi the synnere is preisid in the desiris of his soule; and the wickid is blessid.

4 The synnere 'wraththide the Lord; vp the multitude of his ire he schal not seke.

5 God is not in his siyt; hise weies ben defoulid in al tyme. God, thi domes ben takun awei fro his face; he schal be lord of alle hise enemyes.

6 For he seide in his herte, Y schal not be moued, fro genera-cioun in to generacioun without yuel.

7 'Whos mouth is ful of cursyng, and of bitternesse, and of gyle; trauel and sorewe is vndur his tunge.

8 He sittith in aspies with ryche men in priuytees; to sle the innocent man.

9 Hise iyen biholden on a pore man; he settith aspies in hid place, as a lioun in his denne. He settith aspies, for to rauysche a pore man; for to rauysche a pore man, while he drawith the pore man.

10 In his snare he schal make meke the pore man; he schal bowe hym silf, and schal falle doun, whanne he hath be lord of pore men.

11 For he seide in his herte, God hath foryete; he hath turned awei his face, that he se not in to the ende.

12 Lord God, rise thou vp, and thin hond be enhaunsid; foryete thou not pore men.

13 For what thing terride the wickid man God to wraththe? for he seide in his herte, God schal not seke.

14 Thou seest, for thou biholdist trauel and sorewe; that thou take hem in to thin hondis. The pore man is left to thee; thou schalt be an helpere to the fadirles and modirles.

15 Al to-breke thou the arme of the synnere, and yuel willid; his synne schal be souyt, and it schal not be foundun.

16 The Lord schal regne with outen ende, and in to the world of world; folkis, ye schulen perische fro the lond of hym.

17 The Lord hath herd the desir of pore men; thin eere hath herd the makyng redi of her herte.

18 To deme for the modirles 'and meke; that a man 'leie to no more to 'magnyfie hym silf on erthe.

PSALM 10

1 The title of the tenthe salm. To the victorie of Dauid.

2 I triste in the Lord; hou seien ye to my soule, Passe thou ouere in to an hil, as a sparowe doith?

3 For lo! synneris han bent a bouwe; thei han maad redi her arowis in an arowe caas; 'for to schete in derknesse riytful men in herte.

4 For thei han distryed, whom thou hast maad perfit; but what dide the riytful man?

5 The Lord is in his hooli temple; he is Lord, his seete is in heuene. Hise iyen biholden on a pore man; hise iyelidis axen the sones of men.

6 The Lord axith a iust man, and vnfeithful man; but he, that loueth wickidnesse, hatith his soule.

7 He schal reyne snaris on 'synful men; fier, brymston, and the spirit of tempestis ben the part of the cuppe of hem.

8 For the Lord is riytful, and louede riytfulnessis; his cheer siy equite, 'ethir euennesse.

PSALM 11

1 The title of the eleuenthe salm. To the victorie on the eiyte, the song of Dauid.

2 Lord, make thou me saaf, for the hooli failide; for treuthis ben maad litle fro the sones of men.

3 Thei spaken veyn thingis, ech man to hys neiybore; thei han gileful lippis, thei spaken in herte and herte.

4 The Lord destrie alle gileful lippis; and the greet spekynge tunge.

5 Whiche seiden, We schulen magnyfie oure tunge, our lippis ben of vs; who is oure lord?

6 For the wretchednesse of nedy men, and for the weilyng of pore men; now Y schal ryse vp, seith the Lord. I schal sette inhelt he; Y schal do tristili in hym.

7 The spechis of the Lord ben chast spechis; siluer examynyd bi fier, preued fro erthe, purgid seuen fold.

8 Thou, Lord, schalt kepe vs; and thou 'schalt kepe vs fro this generacioun with outen ende.

9 Wickid men goen in cumpas; bi thin hiynesse thou hast multiplied the sones of men.

PSALM 12

1 The title of the twelfthe salm. To the victorie of Dauid. Lord, hou long foryetist thou me in to the ende? hou long turnest thou awei thi face fro me?

2 Hou long schal Y sette counsels in my soule; sorewe in my herte bi dai?

3 Hou long schal myn enemy be reisid on me?

4 My Lord God, biholde thou, and here thou me. Liytne thou myn iyen, lest ony tyme Y slepe in deth;

5 lest ony tyme myn enemye seie, Y hadde the maistri ayens hym. Thei, that troblen me, schulen haue ioie, if Y schal be stirid; forsothe Y hopide in thi merci.

6 Myn herte schal fulli haue ioie in thin helthe; Y schal synge to the Lord, that yyueth goodis to me, and Y schal seie salm to the name of the hiyeste Lord.

PSALM 13

1 The 'title of the threttenthe salm. To the victorie of Dauid. The vnwise man seide in his herte, God is not. Thei ben corrupt, and ben maad abhomynable in her studies; noon is that doith good, noon is til to oon.

2 The Lord bihelde fro heuene on the sones of men; that he se, if ony is vndurstondynge, ethir sekynge God.

3 Alle bowiden awei, togidere thei ben maad vnprofitable; noon is that doth good, noon is 'til to oon. The throte of hem is an open sepulcre, thei diden gilefuli with her tungis; the venym of snakis is vndur her lippis. Whos mouth is ful of cursyng and bittirnesse; her feet ben swift to schede out blood. Sorewe and cursidnesse is in the weies of hem, and thei knewen not the weie of pees; the drede of God is not bifor her iyen.

4 Whether alle men that worchen wickidnesse schulen not knowe; that deuowren my puple, as mete of breed?

5 Thei clepeden not the Lord; thei trembliden there for dreed, where was no drede;

6 for the Lord is in a riytful generacioun. Thou hast schent the counsel of a pore man; for the Lord is his hope.

7 Who schal yyue fro Syon helthe to Israel? Whanne the Lord hath turned awei the caitifte of his puple; Jacob schal 'fulli be ioiful, and Israel schal be glad.

PSALM 14

1 Lord, who schal dwelle in thi tabernacle; ether who schal reste in thin hooli hil?

2 He that entrith with out wem; and worchith riytfulnesse.

3 Which spekith treuthe in his herte; which dide not gile in his tunge. Nethir dide yuel to his neiybore; and took not schenschip ayens hise neiyboris.

4 A wickid man is brouyt to nouyt in his siyt; but he glorifieth hem that dreden the Lord. Which swerith to his neiybore, and disseyueth not;

5 which yaf not his money to vsure; and took not yiftis on the innocent. He, that doith these thingis, schal not be moued with outen ende.

PSALM 15

1 The title of the fiuetenthe salm. 'Of the meke and symple, the salm of Dauid. Lord, kepe thou me, for Y haue hopid in thee;

2 Y seide to the Lord, Thou art my God, for thou hast no nede of my goodis.

3 To the seyntis that ben in the lond of hym; he made wondurful alle my willis in hem.

4 The sikenessis of hem ben multiplied; aftirward thei hastiden. I schal not gadire togidere the conuenticulis, 'ethir litle couentis, of hem of bloodis; and Y schal not be myndeful of her names bi my lippis.

5 The Lord is part of myn eritage, and of my passion; thou art, that schalt restore myn eritage to me.

6 Coordis felden to me in ful clere thingis; for myn eritage is ful cleer to me.

7 I schal blesse the Lord, that yaf vndurstondyng to me; ferthermore and my reynes blameden me 'til to nyyt.

8 I purueide euere the Lord in my siyt; for he is on the riythalf to me, that Y be not moued.

9 For this thing myn herte was glad, and my tunge ioyede fulli; ferthermore and my fleisch schal reste in hope.

10 For thou schalt not forsake my soule in helle; nether thou schalt yyue thin hooli to se corrupcioun. Thou hast maad knowun to me the weies of lijf; thou schalt fille me of gladnesse with thi cheer; delityngis ben in thi riythalf 'til in to the ende.

PSALM 16

1 The title of the sixtenthe salm. The preier of Dauid. Lord, here thou my riytfulnesse; biholde thou my preier. Perseuye thou with eeris my preier; not maad in gileful lippis.

2 Mi doom come 'forth of thi cheer; thin iyen se equite.

3 Thou hast preued myn herte, and hast visitid in niyt; thou hast examynyd me bi fier, and wickidnesse is not foundun in me.

4 That my mouth speke not the werkis of men; for the wordis of thi lippis Y haue kept harde weies.

5 Make thou perfit my goyngis in thi pathis; that my steppis be not moued.

6 I criede, for thou, God, herdist me; bowe doun thin eere to me, and here thou my wordis.

7 Make wondurful thi mercies; that makist saaf 'men hopynge in thee.

8 Kepe thou me as the appil of the iye; fro 'men ayenstondynge thi riyt hond. Keuere thou me vndur the schadewe of thi wyngis;

9 fro the face of vnpitouse men, that han turmentid me. Myn enemyes han cumpassid my soule;

10 thei han closide togidere her fatnesse; the mouth of hem spak pride.

11 Thei castiden me forth, and han cumpassid me now; thei ordeyneden to bowe doun her iyen in to erthe.

12 Thei, as a lioun maad redi to prey, han take me; and as the whelp of a lioun dwellynge in hid places.

13 Lord, rise thou vp, bifor come thou hym, and disseyue thou hym; delyuere thou my lijf fro the 'vnpitouse,

14 delyuere thou thi swerd fro the enemyes of thin hond. Lord, departe thou hem fro a fewe men of 'the lond in the lijf of hem; her wombe is fillid of thin hid thingis. Thei ben fillid with sones; and thei leften her relifis to her litle children.

15 But Y in riytfulnesse schal appere to thi siyt; Y schal be fillid, whanne thi glorie schal appere.

PSALM 17

1 The title of the seuenetenthe salm. To victorie, the word of the Lord to Dauid; which spak the wordis of this song, in the dai in which the Lord delyuerede hym fro the hond of alle hise enemyes, and fro the hond of Saul; and he seide:

2 Lord, my strengthe, Y schal loue thee; the Lord is my stidfastnesse, and my refuyt, and mi deliuerere.

3 Mi God is myn helpere; and Y schal hope in to hym. My defendere, and the horn of myn helthe; and myn vptakere.

4 I schal preise, and ynwardli clepe the Lord; and Y schal be saaf fro myn enemyes.

5 The sorewis of deth cumpassiden me; and the strondis of wickidnesse disturbliden me.

6 The sorewis of helle cumpassiden me; the snaris of deeth 'bifor ocupieden me.

7 In my tribulacioun Y inwardli clepide the Lord; and Y criede to my God. And he herde my vois fro his hooli temple; and my cry in his siyt entride in to hise eeris.

8 And the erthe was mouede togidere, and tremblede togidere; the foundementis of hillis weren troblid togidere, and weren moued togidere; for he was wrooth to hem.

9 Smoke stiede in the ire of hym, and fier brente out fro his face; coolis weren kyndlid of hym.

10 He bowide doun heuenes, and cam doun; and derknesse was vndur hise feet.

11 And he stiede on cherubym, and flei; he fley ouer the pennes of wyndis.

12 And he settide derknesses his hidyng place, his tabernacle 'in his cumpas; derk water was in the cloudes of the lowere eir.

13 Ful cleer cloudis passiden in his siyt; hail and the coolis of fier.

14 And the Lord thundrid fro heuene; and the hiyeste yaf his vois, hail and the coolis of fier 'camen doun.

15 And he sente hise arowis, and distriede tho men; he multipliede leytis, and disturblide tho men.

16 And the wellis of watris apperiden; and the foundementis of the erthe weren schewid. Lord, of thi blamyng; of the brething of the spirit of thin ire.

17 He sente fro the hiyeste place, and took me; and he took me fro many watris.

18 He delyuerede me fro my strongeste enemyes; and fro hem that hatiden me, fro thei weren coumfortid on me.

19 Thei camen bifor me in the dai of my turment; and the Lord was maad my defendere.

20 And he ledde out me in to breede; he maad me saaf, for he wolde me.

21 And the Lord schal yelde to me bi my riytfulnesse; and he schal yelde to me bi the clennesse of myn hondis.

22 For Y kepte the weies of the Lord; and Y dide not vnfeithfuli fro my God.

23 For alle hise domes ben in my siyt; and Y puttide not awei fro me hise riytfulnessis.

24 And Y schal be vnwemmed with hym; and Y schal kepe me fro my wickidnesse.

25 And the Lord schal yelde to me bi my riytfulnesse; and bi the clennesse of myn hondis in the siyt of hise iyen.

26 With the hooli, thou schalt be hooli; and with 'a man innocent, thou schalt be innocent.

27 And with a chosun man, thou schalt be chosun; and with a weiward man, thou schalt be weiward.

28 For thou schalt make saaf a meke puple; and thou schalt make meke the iyen of proude men.

29 For thou, Lord, liytnest my lanterne; my God, liytne thou my derknessis.

30 For bi thee Y schal be delyuered fro temptacioun; and in my God Y schal 'go ouer the wal.

31 Mi God, his weie is vndefoulid, the speches of the Lord ben examyned bi fier; he is defendere of alle men hopynge in hym.

32 For whi, who is God out takun the Lord? ethir who is God outakun oure God?

33 God that hath gird me with vertu; and hath set my weie vnwemmed.

34 Which made perfit my feet as of hertis; and ordeynynge me on hiye thingis.

35 Which techith myn hondis to batel; and thou hast set myn armys as a brasun bouwe.

36 And thou hast youe to me the kyueryng of thin helthe; and thi riythond hath vptake me. And thi chastisyng amendide me in to the ende; and thilke chastisyng of thee schal teche me.

37 Thou alargidist my paaces vndur me; and my steppis ben not maad vnstidefast.

38 Y schal pursue myn enemyes, and Y schal take hem; and Y schal not turne til thei failen.

39 I schal al to-breke hem, and thei schulen not mowe stonde; thei schulen falle vndur my feet.

40 And thou hast gird me with vertu to batel; and thou hast 'supplauntid, ether disseyued, vndur me men risynge ayens me.

41 And thou hast youe myn enemyes abac to me; and thou hast distried 'men hatynge me.

42 Thei crieden, and noon was that maad hem saaf; 'thei crieden to the Lord, and he herde not hem.

43 And Y schal al to-breke hem, as dust bifor the face of wynd; Y schal do hem awei, as the cley of stretis.

44 Thou schalt delyuere me fro ayenseiyngis of the puple; thou schalt sette me in to the heed of folkis.

45 The puple, which Y knewe not, seruede me; in the herynge of eere it obeiede to me.

46 Alien sones lieden to me, alien sones wexiden elde; and crokiden fro thi pathis.

47 The Lord lyueth, and my God be blessid; and the God of myn helthe be enhaunsid.

48 God, that yauest veniaunces to me, and makist suget puplis vndur me; my delyuerere fro my wrathful enemyes.

49 And thou schalt enhaunse me fro hem, that risen ayens me; thou schalt delyuere me fro a wickid man.

50 Therfor, Lord, Y schal knouleche to thee among naciouns; and Y schal seie salm to thi name.

51 Magnyfiynge the helthis of his kyng; and doynge merci to his crist Dauid, and to his seed til in to the world.

PSALM 18

1 The title of the eiytenthe salm. To victorie, the salm of Dauid.

2 Heuenes tellen out the glorie of God; and the firmament tellith the werkis of hise hondis.

3 The dai tellith out to the dai a word; and the nyyt schewith kunnyng to the nyyt.

4 No langagis ben, nether wordis; of whiche the voices of hem ben not herd.

5 The soun of hem yede out in to al erthe; and the wordis of hem 'yeden out in to the endis of the world.

6 In the sunne he hath set his tabernacle; and he as a spouse comynge forth of his chaumbre. He fulli ioyede, as a giaunt, to renne his weie;

7 his goynge out was fro hiyeste heuene. And his goyng ayen was to the hiyeste therof; and noon is that hidith hym silf fro his heet.

8 The lawe of the Lord is with out wem, and conuertith soulis; the witnessyng of the Lord is feithful, and yyueth wisdom to litle children.

9 The riytfulnessis of the Lord ben riytful, gladdynge hertis; the comaundement of the Lord is cleere, liytnynge iyen.

10 The hooli drede of the Lord dwellith in to world of world; the domes of the Lord ben trewe, iustified in to hem silf.

11 Desirable more than gold, and a stoon myche preciouse; and swettere than hony and honycoomb.

12 'Forwhi thi seruaunt kepith thoo; myche yeldyng is in tho to be kept.

13 Who vndurstondith trespassis? make thou me cleene fro my priuy synnes;

14 and of alien synnes spare thi seruaunt. 'If the forseid defautis ben not, Lord, of me, than Y schal be with out wem; and Y schal be clensid of the mooste synne.

15 And the spechis of my mouth schulen be, that tho plese; and the thenkynge of myn herte euere in thi siyt. Lord, myn helpere; and myn ayenbiere.

PSALM 19

1 The title of the nyntenthe salm. To victorie, the salm of Dauid.

2 The Lord here thee in the dai of tribulacioun; the name of God of Jacob defende thee.

3 Sende he helpe to thee fro the hooli place; and fro Syon defende he thee.

4 Be he myndeful of al thi sacrifice; and thi brent sacrifice be maad fat.

5 Yyue he to thee aftir thin herte; and conferme he al thi counsel.

6 We schulen be glad in thin helthe; and we schulen be magnyfied in the name of oure God.

7 The Lord fille alle thin axyngis; nowe Y haue knowe, that the Lord hath maad saaf his crist. He schal here hym fro his hooly heuene; the helthe of his riyt hond is in poweris.

8 Thes in charis, and these in horsis; but we schulen inwardli clepe in the name of oure Lord God.

9 Thei ben boundun, and felden doun; but we han rise, and ben reisid.

10 Lord, make thou saaf the kyng; and here thou vs in the dai in which we inwardli clepen thee.

PSALM 20

1 The title of the twentithe salm. To victorie, the salm of Dauid.

2 Lord, the kyng schal be glad in thi vertu; and he schal ful out haue ioye greetli on thin helthe.

3 Thou hast youe to hym the desire of his herte; and thou hast not defraudid hym of the wille of hise lippis.

4 For thou hast bifor come hym in the blessyngis of swetnesse; thou hast set on his heed a coroun of preciouse stoon.

5 He axide of thee lijf, and thou yauest to hym; the lengthe of daies in to the world, 'and in to the world of world.

6 His glorie is greet in thin helthe; thou schalt putte glorie, and greet fayrnesse on hym.

7 For thou schalt yyue hym in to blessing in to the world of world; thou schalt make hym glad in ioye with thi cheer.

8 For the kyng hopith in the Lord; and in the merci of the hiyeste he schal not be moued.

9 Thyn hond be foundun to alle thin enemyes; thi riythond fynde alle hem that haten thee.

10 Thou schalt putte hem as a furneis of fier in the tyme of thi cheer; the Lord schal disturble hem in his ire, and fier schal deuoure hem.

11 Thou schalt leese the fruyt of hem fro erthe; and 'thou schalt leese the seed of hem fro the sones of men.

12 For thei bowiden yuels ayens thee; thei thouyten counseils, whiche thei myyten not stablische.

13 For thou schalt putte hem abac; in thi relifs thou schalt make redi the cheer of hem.

14 Lord, be thou enhaunsid in thi vertu; we schulen synge, and seie opinly thi vertues.

PSALM 21

1 The 'title of the oon and twentithe salm. To ouercome, for 'the morewtid hynd; the salm of Dauid.

2 God, my God, biholde thou on me, whi hast thou forsake me? the wordis of my trespassis ben fer fro myn helthe.

3 Mi God, Y schal crye bi dai, and thou schalt not here; and bi nyyt, and not to vnwisdom to me.

4 Forsothe thou, the preisyng of Israel, dwellist in holynesse;

5 oure fadris hopiden in thee, thei hopiden, and thou delyueridist hem.

6 Thei crieden to thee, and thei weren maad saaf; thei hopiden in thee, and thei weren not schent.

7 But Y am a worm, and not man; the schenschip of men, and the outcastyng of the puple.

8 Alle men seynge me scorneden me; thei spaken with lippis, and stiriden the heed.

9 He hopide in the Lord, delyuere he hym; make he hym saaf, for he wole hym.

10 For thou it art that drowist me out of the wombe, thou art myn hope fro the tetis of my modir;

11 in to thee Y am cast forth fro the wombe. Fro the wombe of my modir thou art my God; departe thou not fro me.

12 For tribulacioun is next; for noon is that helpith.

13 Many calues cumpassiden me; fatte bolis bisegiden me.

14 Thei openyden her mouth on me; as doith a lioun rauyschynge and rorynge.

15 I am sched out as watir; and alle my boonys ben scaterid. Myn herte is maad, as wex fletynge abrood; in the myddis of my wombe.

16 Mi vertu driede as a tiyl stoon, and my tunge cleuede to my chekis; and thou hast brouyt forth me in to the dust of deth.

17 For many doggis cumpassiden me; the counsel of wickid men bisegide me. Thei delueden myn hondis and my feet;

18 thei noumbriden alle my boonys. Sotheli thei lokiden, and bihelden me;

19 thei departiden my clothis to hem silf, and thei senten lot on my cloth.

20 But thou, Lord, delaie not thin help fro me; biholde thou to my defence.

21 God, delyuere thou my lijf fro swerd; and delyuere thou myn oon aloone fro the hond of the dogge.

22 Make thou me saaf fro the mouth of a lioun; and my mekenesse fro the hornes of vnycornes.

23 I schal telle thi name to my britheren; Y schal preise thee in the myddis of the chirche.

24 Ye that dreden the Lord, herie hym; alle the seed of Jacob, glorifie ye hym.

25 Al the seed of Israel drede hym; for he forsook not, nethir dispiside the preier of a pore man. Nethir he turnede awei his face fro me; and whanne Y criede to hym, he herde me.

26 Mi preisyng is at thee in a greet chirche; Y schal yelde my vowis in the siyt of men dredynge hym.

27 Pore men schulen ete, and schulen be fillid, and thei schulen herie the Lord, that seken hym; the hertis of hem schulen lyue in to the world of world.

28 Alle the endis of erthe schulen bithenke; and schulen be conuertid to the Lord. And alle the meynees of hethene men; schulen worschipe in his siyt.

29 For the rewme is the Lordis; and he schal be Lord of hethene men.

30 Alle the fatte men of erthe eeten and worschipiden; alle men, that goen doun in to erthe, schulen falle doun in his siyt.

31 And my soule schal lyue to hym; and my seed schal serue him.

32 A generacioun to comyng schal be teld to the Lord; and heuenes schulen telle his riytfulnesse to the puple that schal be borun, whom the Lord made.

PSALM 22

1 The title of the two and twentithe salm. 'The salm, ether the song of Dauid. The Lord gouerneth me, and no thing schal faile to me;

2 in the place of pasture there he hath set me. He nurschide me on the watir of refreischyng;

3 he conuertide my soule. He ledde me forth on the pathis of riytfulnesse; for his name.

4 For whi thouy Y schal go in the myddis of schadewe of deeth; Y schal not drede yuels, for thou art with me. Thi yerde and thi staf; tho han coumfortid me.

5 Thou hast maad redi a boord in my siyt; ayens hem that troblen me. Thou hast maad fat myn heed with oyle; and my cuppe, 'fillinge greetli, is ful cleer.

6 And thi merci schal sue me; in alle the daies of my lijf. And that Y dwelle in the hows of the Lord; in to the lengthe of daies.

PSALM 23

1 The title of the 'thre and twentithe salm. The song of Dauid. The erthe and the fulnesse therof is 'the Lordis; the world, and alle that dwellen therynne 'is the Lordis.

2 For he foundide it on the sees; and made it redi on floodis.

3 Who schal stie in to the hil of the Lord; ethir who schal stonde in the hooli place of hym?

4 The innocent in hondis, and in cleene herte; whiche took not his soule in veyn, nether swoor in gile to his neiybore.

5 'This man schal take blessyng of the Lord; and mercy of God his helthe.

6 This is the generacioun of men sekynge hym; of men sekynge the face of God of Jacob.

7 Ye princes, take vp youre yatis, and ye euerelastynge yatis, be reisid; and the kyng of glorie schal entre.

8 Who is this kyng of glorie? the Lord strong and myyti, the Lord myyti in batel.

9 Ye princes, take vp youre yatis, and ye euerlastynge yatis, be reisid; and the kyng of glorie schal entre.

10 Who is this kyng of glorie? the Lord of vertues, he is the kyng of glorie.

PSALM 24

1 The title of the foure and twentithe salm. To Dauid.

2 Lord, to thee Y haue reisid my soule; my God, Y truste in thee, be Y not aschamed.

3 Nethir myn enemyes scorne me; for alle men that suffren thee schulen not be schent.

4 Alle men doynge wickyd thingis superfluli; be schent. Lord, schewe thou thi weies to me; and teche thou me thi pathis.

5 Dresse thou me in thi treuthe, and teche thou me, for thou art God my sauyour; and Y suffride thee al dai.

6 Lord, haue thou mynde of thi merciful doyngis; and of thi mercies that ben fro the world.

7 Haue thou not mynde on the trespassis of my yongthe; and on myn vnkunnyngis. Thou, Lord, haue mynde on me bi thi merci; for thi goodnesse.

8 The Lord is swete and riytful; for this he schal yyue a lawe to men trespassynge in the weie.

9 He schal dresse deboner men in doom; he schal teche mylde men hise weies.

10 Alle the weies of the Lord ben mercy and treuthe; to men sekynge his testament, and hise witnessyngis.

11 Lord, for thi name thou schalt do merci to my synne; for it is myche.

12 Who is a man, that dredith the Lord? he ordeyneth to hym a lawe in the weie which he chees.

13 His soule schal dwelle in goodis; and his seed schal enerite the lond.

14 The Lord is a sadnesse to men dredynge hym; and his testament is, that it be schewid to hem.

15 Myn iyen ben euere to the Lord; for he schal breide awey my feet fro the snare.

16 Biholde thou on me, and haue thou mercy on me; for Y am 17 oon aloone and pore The tribulaciouns of myn herte ben multiplied; delyuere thou me of my nedis.

18 Se thou my mekenesse and my trauel; and foryyue thou alle my trespassis.

19 Bihold thou myn enemyes, for thei ben multiplied; and thei haten me bi wickid hatrede.

20 Kepe thou my soule, and delyuere thou me; be Y not aschamed, for Y hopide in thee.

21 Innocent men and riytful cleuyden to me; for Y suffride thee.

22 God, delyuere thou Israel; fro alle hise tribulaciouns.

PSALM 25

1 The title of the fyue and twentithe salm. 'To Dauid. Lord, deme thou me, for Y entride in myn innocens; and Y hopynge in the Lord schal not be made vnstidfast.

2 Lord, preue thou me, and asaie me; brenne thou my reynes, and myn herte.

3 For whi thi merci is bifor myn iyen; and Y pleside in thi treuthe.

4 I sat not with the counsel of vanyte; and Y schal not entre with men doynge wickid thingis.

5 I hatide the chirche of yuele men; and Y schal not sitte with wickid men.

6 I schal waische myn hondis among innocentis; and, Lord, Y schal cumpasse thin auter.

7 That Y here the vois of heriyng; and that Y telle out alle thi merueils.

8 Lord, Y haue loued the fairnesse of thin hows; and the place of the dwellyng of thi glorie.

9 God, leese thou not my soule with vnfeithful men; and my lijf with men of bloodis.

10 In whose hondis wyckidnessis ben; the riythond of hem is fillid with yiftis.

11 But Y entride in myn innocens; ayenbie thou me, and haue merci on me.

12 Mi foot stood in riytfulnesse; Lord, Y schal blesse thee in chirchis.

PSALM 26

1 The title of the sixe and twentithe salm. To Dauid. The Lord is my liytnyng, and myn helthe; whom schal Y drede? The Lord is defendere of my lijf; for whom schal Y tremble?

2 The while noiful men neiyen on me; for to ete my fleischis. Myn enemyes, that trobliden me; thei weren maad sijk and felden doun.

3 Thouy castels stonden togidere ayens me; myn herte schal not drede. Thouy batel risith ayens me; in this thing Y schal haue hope.

4 I axide of the Lord o thing; Y schal seke this thing; that Y dwelle in the hows of the Lord alle the daies of my lijf. That Y se the wille of the Lord; and that Y visite his temple.

5 For he hidde me in his tabernacle in the dai of yuelis; he defendide me in the hid place of his tabernacle.

6 He enhaunside me in a stoon; and now he enhaunside myn heed ouer myn enemyes. I cumpasside, and offride in his tabernacle a sacrifice of criyng; Y schal synge, and Y schal seie salm to the Lord.

7 Lord, here thou my vois, bi which Y criede to thee; haue thou merci on me, and here me.

8 Myn herte seide to thee, My face souyte thee; Lord, Y schal seke eft thi face.

9 Turne thou not awei thi face fro me; bouwe thou not awei in ire fro thi seruaunt. Lord, be thou myn helpere, forsake thou not me; and, God, myn helthe, dispise thou not me.

10 For my fadir and my modir han forsake me; but the Lord hath take me.

11 Lord, sette thou a lawe to me in thi weie; and dresse thou me in thi path for myn enemyes.

12 Bitake thou not me in to the soules of hem, that troblen me; for wickid witnessis han rise ayens me, and wickydnesse liede to it silf.

13 I bileue to see the goodis of the Lord; in the lond of 'hem that lyuen.

14 Abide thou the Lord, do thou manli; and thin herte be coumfortid, and suffre thou the Lord.

PSALM 27

1 The title of the seuen and twentithe salm. To Dauid. Lord, Y schal crye to thee; my God, be thou not stille fro me, be thou not stille 'ony tyme fro me; and Y schal be maad lijk to hem, that goen doun in to the lake.

2 Lord, here thou the vois of my bisechyng, while Y preie to thee; whyle Y reise myn hondis to thin hooli temple.

3 Bitake thou not me togidere with synneris; and leese thou not me with hem that worchen wickidnesse. Whyche speken pees with her neiybore; but yuels ben in her hertis.

4 Yyue thou to hem vpe the werkis of hem; and vpe the wickidnesse of her fyndyngis. Yyue thou to hem vpe the werkis of her hondis; yelde thou her yeldyng to hem.

5 For thei vndurstoden not the werkis of the Lord, and bi the werkis of hise hondis thou schalt destrie hem; and thou schalt not bilde hem.

6 Blissid be the Lord; for he herde the vois of my bisechyng.

7 The Lord is myn helpere and my defendere; and myn herte hopide in hym, and Y am helpid. And my fleisch flouride ayen; and of my wille Y schal knowleche to hym.

8 The Lord is the strengthe of his puple; and he is defendere of the sauyngis of his crist.

9 Lord, make thou saaf thi puple, and blesse thou thin eritage; and reule thou hem, and enhaunse thou hem til in to with outen ende.

PSALM 28

1 The title of the eiyt and twentithe salm. The salm, ethir song of Dauid. Ye sones of God, brynge to the Lord; brynge ye to the Lord the sones of rammes.

2 Brynge ye to the Lord glorie and onour; brynge ye to the Lord glorie to his name; herie ye the Lord in his hooli large place.

3 The vois of the Lord on watris, God of mageste thundride; the Lord on many watris.

4 The vois of the Lord in vertu; the vois of the Lord in greet doyng.

5 The vois of the Lord brekynge cedris; and the Lord schal breke the cedris of the Liban.

6 And he schal al to-breke hem to dust as a calf of the Liban; and the derling was as the sone of an vnycorn.

7 The vois of the Lord departynge the flawme of fier;

8 the vois of the Lord schakynge desert; and the Lord schal stire togidere the desert of Cades.

9 The vois of the Lord makynge redi hertis, and he schal schewe thicke thingis; and in his temple alle men schulen seie glorie.

10 The Lord makith to enhabite the greet flood; and the Lord schal sitte kyng with outen ende.

11 The Lord schal yyue vertu to his puple; the Lord schal blesse his puple in pees.

PSALM 29

1 The title of the nyne and twentithe salm. The salm of song, for the halewyng of the hows of Dauid.

2 Lord, Y schal enhaunse thee, for thou hast vp take me; and thou delitidist not myn enemyes on me.

3 Mi Lord God, Y criede to thee; and thou madist me hool.

4 Lord, thou leddist out my soule fro helle; thou sauedist me fro hem that goen doun into the lake.

5 Ye seyntis of the Lord, synge to the Lord; and knowleche ye to the mynde of his hoolynesse.

6 For ire is in his indignacioun; and lijf is in his wille. Wepyng schal dwelle at euentid; and gladnesse at the morewtid.

7 Forsothe Y seide in my plentee; Y schal not be moued with outen ende.

8 Lord, in thi wille; thou hast youe vertu to my fairnesse. Thou turnedist awei thi face fro me; and Y am maad disturblid.

9 Lord, Y schal crye to thee; and Y schal preye to my God.

10 What profit is in my blood; while Y go doun in to corrupcioun? Whether dust schal knouleche to thee; ethir schal telle thi treuthe?

11 The Lord herde, and hadde merci on me; the Lord is maad myn helpere.

12 Thou hast turned my weilyng in to ioye to me; thou hast to-rent my sak, and hast cumpassid me with gladnesse.

13 That my glorie synge to thee, and Y be not compunct; my Lord God, Y schal knouleche to thee with outen ende.

PSALM 30

1 The title of the thrittithe salm. To victorie, the salm of Dauid.

2 Lord, Y hopide in thee, be Y not schent with outen ende; delyuere thou me in thi riytfulnesse.

3 Bouwe doun thin eere to me; haaste thou to delyuere me. Be thou to me in to God defendere, and in to an hows of refuyt; that thou make me saaf.

4 For thou art my strengthe and my refuyt; and for thi name thou schalt lede me forth, and schalt nurische me.

5 Thou schalt lede me out of the snare, which thei hidden to me; for thou art my defendere.

6 I bitake my spirit in to thin hondis; Lord God of treuthe, thou hast ayen bouyt me.

7 Thou hatist hem that kepen vanytees superfluli.

8 Forsothe Y hopide in the Lord; Y schal haue fulli ioie, and schal be glad in thi merci. For thou byheldist my mekenesse; thou sauedist my lijf fro nedis.

9 And thou closidist not me togidere withynne the hondis of the enemy; thou hast sett my feet in a large place.

10 Lord, haue thou merci on me, for Y am troblid; myn iye is troblid in ire, my soule and my wombe 'ben troblid.

11 For whi my lijf failide in sorewe; and my yeeris in weilynges. Mi vertu is maad feble in pouert; and my boonys ben disturblid.

12 Ouer alle myn enemyes Y am maad schenship greetli to my neiyboris; and drede to my knowun. Thei that sien me with outforth, fledden fro me; Y am youun to foryetyng,

13 as a deed man fro herte. I am maad as a lorun vessel;

14 for Y herde dispisyng of many men dwellynge in cumpas. In that thing the while thei camen togidere ayens me; thei counceliden to take my lijf.

15 But, Lord, Y hopide in thee; Y seide, Thou art my God; my tymes ben in thin hondis.

16 Delyuer thou me fro the hondis of mynen enemyes; and fro hem that pursuen me.

17 Make thou cleer thi face on thi seruaunt; Lord, make thou me saaf in thi merci;

18 be Y not schent, for Y inwardli clepide thee. Unpitouse men be aschamed, and be led forth in to helle;

19 gileful lippys be maad doumbe. That speken wickidnesse ayens a iust man; in pride, and in mysusyng.

20 Lord, the multitude of thi swetnesse is ful greet; which thou hast hid to men dredynge thee. Thou hast maad a perfit thing to hem, that hopen in thee; in the siyt of the sones of men.

21 Thou schalt hide hem in the priuyte of thi face; fro disturblyng of men. Thou schalt defende hem in thi tabernacle; fro ayenseiyng of tungis.

22 Blessid be the Lord; for he hath maad wondurful his merci to me in a strengthid citee.

23 Forsothe Y seide in the passyng of my soule; Y am cast out fro the face of thin iyen. Therfor thou herdist the vois of my preier; while Y criede to thee.

24 Alle ye hooli men of the Lord, loue hym; for the Lord schal seke treuthe, and he schal yelde plenteuousli to hem that doen pride.

25 Alle ye that hopen in the Lord, do manli; and youre herte be coumfortid.

PSALM 31

1 The title of the oon and thrittithe salm. Lernyng to Dauid. Blessid ben thei, whose wickidnessis ben foryouun; and whose synnes ben hilid.

2 Blessid is the man, to whom the Lord arrettide not synne; nethir gile is in his spirit.

3 For Y was stille, my boonys wexiden elde; while Y criede al dai.

4 For bi dai and nyyt thin 'hond was maad greuouse on me; Y am turned in my wretchednesse, while the thorn is set in.

5 I made my synne knowun to thee; and Y hidde not my vnriytfulnesse. I seide, Y schal knouleche ayens me myn vnriytfulnesse to the Lord; and thou hast foryoue the wickidnesse of my synne.

6 For this thing ech hooli man schal preye to thee; in couenable tyme. Netheles in the greet flood of many watris; tho schulen not neiye to thee.

7 Thou art my refuyt fro tribulacioun, that cumpasside me; thou, my fulli ioiyng, delyuere me fro hem that cumpassen me.

8 Y schal yyue vnderstondyng to thee, and Y schal teche thee; in this weie in which thou schalt go, Y schal make stidefast myn iyen on thee.

9 Nile ye be maad as an hors and mule; to whiche is noon vndurstondyng. Lord, constreyne thou the chekis of hem with a bernacle and bridil; that neiyen not to thee.

10 Many betyngis ben of the synnere; but merci schal cumpasse hym that hopith in the Lord.

11 Ye iust men, be glad, and make fulli ioie in the Lord; and alle ye riytful of herte, haue glorie.

PSALM 32

1 The two and threttithe salm hath no title. Ye iust men, haue fulli ioye in the Lord; presyng togidere bicometh riytful men.

2 Knouleche ye to the Lord in an harpe; synge ye to hym in a sautre of ten strengis.

3 Synge ye to hym a newe song; seie ye wel salm to hym in criyng.

4 For the word of the Lord is riytful; and alle hise werkis ben in feithfulnesse.

5 He loueth merci and doom; the erthe is ful of the merci of the Lord.

6 Heuenes ben maad stidfast bi the word of the Lord; and 'al the vertu of tho bi the spirit of his mouth.

7 And he gaderith togidere the watris of the see as in a bowge; and settith depe watris in tresours.

8 Al erthe drede the Lord; sotheli alle men enhabitynge the world ben mouyd of hym.

9 For he seide, and thingis weren maad; he comaundide, and thingis weren maad of nouyt.

10 The Lord distrieth the counsels of folkis, forsothe he repreueth the thouytis of puplis; and he repreueth the counsels of pryncis.

11 But the counsel of the Lord dwellith with outen ende; the thouytis of his herte dwellen in generacioun and into generacioun.

12 Blessid is the folk, whose Lord is his God; the puple which he chees into eritage to hym silf.

13 The Lord bihelde fro heuene; he siy alle the sones of men.

14 Fro his dwellyng place maad redi bifor; he bihelde on alle men, that enhabiten the erthe.

15 Which made syngulerli the soules of hem; which vndurstondith all the werkis of hem.

16 A kyng is not sauyd bi myche vertu; and a giaunt schal not be sauyd in the mychilnesse of his vertu.

17 An hors is false to helthe; forsothe he schal not be sauyd in the habundaunce, 'ether plentee, of his vertu.

18 Lo! the iyen of the Lord ben on men dredynge hym; and in hem that hopen on his merci.

19 That he delyuere her soules fro deth; and feede hem in hungur.

20 Oure soule suffreth the Lord; for he is oure helpere and defendere.

21 For oure herte schal be glad in him; and we schulen haue hope in his hooli name.

22 Lord, thi merci be maad on vs; as we hopiden in thee.

PSALM 33

1 The title of the thre and thrittithe salm. To Dauid, whanne he chaungide his mouth bifor Abymalech, and he 'droof out Dauid, 'and he yede forth.

2 I schal blesse the Lord in al tyme; euere his heriyng is in my mouth.

3 Mi soule schal be preisid in the Lord; mylde men here, and be glad.

4 Magnyfie ye the Lord with me; and enhaunse we his name into it silf.

5 I souyte the Lord, and he herde me; and he delyueride me fro alle my tribulaciouns.

6 Neiye ye to him, and be ye liytned; and youre faces schulen not be schent.

7 This pore man criede, and the Lord herde hym; and sauyde hym fro alle hise tribulaciouns.

8 The aungel of the Lord sendith in the cumpas of men dredynge hym; and he schal delyuere hem.

9 Taaste ye, and se, for the Lord is swete; blessid is the man, that hopith in hym.

10 Alle ye hooli men of the Lord, drede hym; for no nedynesse is to men dredynge hym.

11 Riche men weren nedi, and weren hungri; but men that seken the Lord schulen not faile of al good.

12 Come, ye sones, here ye me; Y schal teche you the drede of the Lord.

13 Who is a man, that wole lijf; loueth to se good daies?

14 Forbede thi tunge fro yuel; and thi lippis speke not gile.

15 Turne thou awei fro yuel, and do good; seke thou pees, and perfitli sue thou it.

16 The iyen of the Lord ben on iust men; and hise eeren ben to her preiers.

17 But the cheer of the Lord is on men doynge yuels; that he leese the mynde of hem fro erthe.

18 Just men cryeden, and the Lord herde hem; and delyueride hem fro alle her tribulaciouns.

19 The Lord is nyy hem that ben of troblid herte; and he schal saue meke men in spirit.

20 Many tribulaciouns ben of iust men; and the Lord schal delyuere hem fro alle these.

21 The Lord kepith alle the boonys of hem; oon of tho schal not be brokun.

22 The deth of synneris is werst; and thei that haten a iust man schulen trespasse.

23 The Lord schal ayenbie the soulis of hise seruauntis; and alle, that hopen in him, schulen not trespasse.

PSALM 34

1 The title of the foure and thrittithe salm. 'To Dauid. Lord, deme thou hem, that anoien me; ouercome thou hem, that fiyten ayens me.

2 Take thou armeris and scheeld; and rise vp into help to me.

3 Schede out the swerd, and close togidere ayens hem that pursuen me; seie thou to my soule, Y am thin helthe.

4 Thei that seken my lijf; be schent, and aschamed. Thei that thenken yuels to me; be turned awei bacward, and be schent.

5 Be thei maad as dust bifor the face of the wynd; and the aungel of the Lord make hem streit.

6 Her weie be maad derknesse, and slydirnesse; and the aungel of the Lord pursue hem.

7 For with out cause thei hidden to me the deth of her snare; in veyn thei dispisiden my soule.

8 The snare which he knoweth not come to hym, and the takyng which he hidde take hym; and fall he in to the snare in that thing.

9 But my soule schal fulli haue ioye in the Lord; and schal delite on his helthe.

10 Alle my boonys schulen seie, Lord, who is lijk thee? Thou delyuerist a pore man fro the hond of his strengere; a nedi man and pore fro hem that diuersely rauischen hym.

11 Wickid witnessis risynge axiden me thingis, whiche Y knewe not.

12 Thei yeldiden to me yuels for goodis; bareynnesse to my soule.

13 But whanne thei weren diseseful to me; Y was clothid in an heire. I mekide my soule in fastyng; and my preier schal be turned 'with ynne my bosum.

14 I pleside so as oure neiybore, as oure brother; Y was 'maad meke so as morenynge and sorewful.

15 And thei weren glad, and camen togidere ayens me; turmentis weren gaderid on me, and Y knew not.

16 Thei weren scaterid, and not compunct, thei temptiden me, thei scornyden me with mowyng; thei gnastiden on me with her teeth.

17 Lord, whanne thou schalt biholde, restore thou my soule fro the wickidnesse of hem; 'restore thou myn oon aloone fro liouns.

18 I schal knowleche to thee in a greet chirche; Y schal herie thee in a sad puple.

19 Thei that ben aduersaries wickidli to me, haue not ioye on me; that haten me with out cause, and bikenen with iyen.

20 For sotheli thei spaken pesibli to me; and thei spekynge in wrathfulnesse of erthe thouyten giles.

21 And thei maden large her mouth on me; thei seiden, Wel, wel! oure iyen han sien.

22 Lord, thou hast seen, be thou not stille; Lord, departe thou not fro me.

23 Rise vp, and yyue tent to my doom; my God and my Lord, biholde in to my cause.

24 Mi Lord God, deme thou me bi thi riytfulnesse; and haue thei not ioye on me.

25 Seie thei not in her hertis, Wel, wel, to oure soule; nether seie thei, We schulen deuoure hym.

26 Shame thei, and drede thei togidere; that thanken for myn yuels. Be thei clothid with schame and drede; that speken yuele thingis on me.

27 Haue thei ful ioie, and be thei glad that wolen my riytfulnesse; and seie thei euere, The Lord be magnyfied, whiche wolen the pees of his seruaunt.

28 And my tunge schal bithenke thi riytfulnesse; al day thin heriyng.

PSALM 35

1 'The title of the fyue and thrittithe salm. 'To victorie, to Dauid, 'the seruaunt of the Lord.

2 The vniust man seide, that he trespasse in hym silf; the drede of God is not bifor hise iyen.

3 For he dide gilefuli in the siyt of God; that his wickidnesse be foundun to hatrede.

4 The wordis of his mouth ben wickidnesse and gile, he nolde vndirstonde to do wel.

5 He thouyte wickidnesse in his bed, he stood nyy al weie not good; forsothe he hatide not malice.

6 Lord, thi merci is in heuene; and thi treuthe is 'til to cloudis.

7 Thi riytfulnesse is as the hillis of God; thi domes ben myche depthe of watris. Lord, thou schalt saue men and beestis;

8 as thou, God, hast multiplied thi merci. But the sones of men; schulen hope in the hilyng of thi wyngis.

9 Thei schulen be fillid gretli of the plentee of thin hows; and thou schalt yyue drynke to hem with the steef streem of thi likyng.

10 For the wel of life is at thee; and in thi liyt we schulen se liyt.

11 Lord, sette forth thi mercy to hem, that knowen thee; and thi ryytfulnesse to hem that ben of riytful herte.

12 The foot of pryde come not to me; and the hond of the synnere moue me not.

13 There thei felden doun, that worchen wickidnesse; thei ben cast out, and myyten not stonde.

PSALM 36

1 The title of the sixe and thrittithe salm. To Dauith. Nile thou sue wickid men; nether loue thou men doynge wickidnesse.

2 For thei schulen wexe drie swiftli as hey; and thei schulen falle doun soone as the wortis of eerbis.

3 Hope thou in the Lord, and do thou goodnesse; and enhabite thou the lond, and thou schalt be fed with hise richessis.

4 Delite thou in the Lord; and he schal yyue to thee the axyngis of thin herte.

5 Schewe thi weie to the Lord; and hope thou in hym, and he schal do.

6 And he schal lede out thi riytfulnesse as liyt, and thi doom as myddai;

7 be thou suget to the Lord, and preye thou hym. Nile thou sue hym, that hath prosperite in his weie; a man doynge vnriytfulnessis.

8 Ceese thou of ire, and forsake woodnesse; nyle thou sue, that thou do wickidli.

9 For thei, that doen wickidli, schulen be distried; but thei that suffren the Lord, schulen enerite the lond.

10 And yit a litil, and a synnere schal not be; and thou schalt seke his place, and schalt not fynde.

11 But mylde men schulen enerite the lond; and schulen delite in the multitude of pees.

12 A synnere schal aspie a riytful man; and he schal gnaste with hise teeth on hym.

13 But the Lord schal scorne the synnere; for he biholdith that his day cometh.

14 Synners drowen out swerd; thei benten her bouwe. To disseyue a pore man and nedi; to strangle riytful men of herte.

15 Her swerd entre in to the herte of hem silf; and her bouwe be brokun.

16 Betere is a litil thing to a iust man; than many richessis of synneris.

17 For the armes of synneris schal be al to-brokun; but the Lord confermeth iust men.

18 The Lord knowith the daies of vnwemmed; and her heritage schal be withouten ende.

19 Thei schulen not be schent in the yuel tyme, and thei schulen be fillid in the dayes of hungur;

20 for synneris schulen perische. Forsothe anoon as the enemyes of the Lord ben onourid, and enhaunsid; thei failynge schulen faile as smoke.

21 A synnere schal borewe, and schal not paie; but a iust man hath merci, and schal yyue.

22 For thei that blessen the Lord schulen enerite the lond; but thei that cursen hym schulen perische.

23 The goyng of a man schal be dressid anentis the Lord; and he schal wilne his weie.

24 Whanne he fallith, he schal not be hurtlid doun; for the Lord vndursettith his hond.

25 I was yongere, and sotheli Y wexide eld, and Y siy not a iust man forsakun; nethir his seed sekynge breed.

26 Al dai he hath merci, and leeneth; and his seed schal be in blessyng.

27 Bouwe thou awei fro yuel, and do good; and dwelle thou in to the world of world.

28 For the Lord loueth doom, and schal not forsake hise seyntis; thei schulen be kept with outen ende. Vniust men schulen be punyschid; and the seed of wickid men schal perische.

29 But iust men schulen enerite the lond; and schulen enabite theronne in to the world of world.

30 The mouth of a iust man schal bithenke wisdom; and his tunge schal speke doom.

31 The lawe of his God is in his herte; and hise steppis schulen not be disseyued.

32 A synnere biholdith a iust man; and sekith to sle hym.

33 But the Lord schal not forsake hym in hise hondis; nethir schal dampne hym, whanne it schal be demed ayens hym.

34 Abide thou the Lord, and kepe thou his weie, and he schal enhaunse thee, that bi eritage thou take the lond; whanne synneris schulen perische, thou schalt se.

35 I siy a wickid man enhaunsid aboue; and reisid vp as the cedris of Liban.

36 And Y passide, and lo! he was not; Y souyte hym, and his place is not foundun.

37 Kepe thou innocence, and se equite; for tho ben relikis to a pesible man.

38 Forsothe vniust men schulen perische; the relifs of wickid men schulen perische togidere.

39 But the helthe of iust men is of the Lord; and he is her defendere in the tyme of tribulacioun.

40 And the Lord schal helpe hem, and schal make hem fre, and he schal delyuere hem fro synneris; and he schal saue hem, for thei hopiden in hym.

PSALM 37

1 The title of the seuene and thrittithe salm. 'The salm of Dauid, to bythenke on the sabat.

2 Lord, repreue thou not me in thi strong veniaunce; nether chastice thou me in thin ire.

3 For thin arowis ben fitchid in me; and thou hast confermed thin hond on me.

4 Noon helthe is in my fleisch fro the face of thin ire; no pees is to my boonys fro the face of my synnes.

5 For my wickidnessis ben goon ouer myn heed; as an heuy birthun, tho ben maad heuy on me.

6 Myn heelid woundis weren rotun, and ben brokun; fro the face of myn vnwisdom.

7 I am maad a wretche, and Y am bowid doun til in to the ende; al dai Y entride sorewful.

8 For my leendis ben fillid with scornyngis; and helthe is not in my fleisch.

9 I am turmentid, and maad low ful greetli; Y roride for the weilyng of myn herte.

10 Lord, al my desire is bifor thee; and my weilyng is not hid fro thee.

11 Myn herte is disturblid in me, my vertu forsook me; and the liyt of myn iyen 'forsook me, and it is not with me.

12 My frendis and my neiyboris neiyiden; and stoden ayens me. And thei that weren bisidis me stoden afer;

13 and thei diden violence, that souyten my lijf. And thei that souyten yuels to me, spaken vanytees; and thouyten gilis al dai.

14 But Y as a deef man herde not; and as a doumb man not openynge his mouth.

15 And Y am maad as a man not herynge; and not hauynge repreuyngis in his mouth.

16 For, Lord, Y hopide in thee; my Lord God, thou schalt here me.

17 For Y seide, Lest ony tyme myn enemyes haue ioye on me; and the while my feet ben mouyd, thei spaken grete thingis on me.

18 For Y am redi to betyngis; and my sorewe is euere in my siyt.

19 For Y schal telle my wickidnesse; and Y schal thenke for my synne.

20 But myn enemyes lyuen, and ben confermed on me; and thei ben multiplyed, that haten me wickidli.

21 Thei that yelden yuels for goodis, backbitiden me; for Y suede goodnesse.

22 My Lord God, forsake thou not me; go thou not awei fro me.

23 Lord God of myn helthe; biholde thou in to myn help.

PSALM 38

1 The title of the eiyte and threttithe salm. For victorie, to Iditum, the song of Dauid.

2 I seide, Y schal kepe my weies; that Y trespasse not in my tunge. I settide kepyng to my mouth; whanne a synnere stood ayens me.

3 I was doumb, and was mekid ful gretli, and was stille fro goodis; and my sorewe was renulid.

4 Myn herte was hoot with ynne me; and fier schal brenne out in my thenkyng.

5 I spak in my tunge; Lord, make thou myn eende knowun to me. And the noumbre of my daies what it is; that Y wite, what failith to me.

6 Lo! thou hast set my daies mesurable; and my substaunce is as nouyt bifor thee. Netheles al vanytee; ech man lyuynge.

7 Netheles a man passith in ymage; but also he is disturblid veynli. He tresorith; and he noot, to whom he 'schal gadere tho thingis.

8 And now which is myn abiding? whether not the Lord? and my substaunce is at thee.

9 Delyuere thou me fro alle my wickidnessis; thou hast youe me schenschip to the vnkunnynge.

10 I was doumbe, and openyde not my mouth; for thou hast maad,

11 remoue thou thi woundis fro me.

12 Fro the strengthe of thin hond Y failide in blamyngis; for wickidnesse thou hast chastisid man. And thou madist his lijf to faile as an vreyne; netheles ech man is disturblid in veyn.

13 Lord, here thou my preier and my bisechyng; perseyue thou with eeris my teeris.

14 Be thou not stille, for Y am a comelyng at thee; and a pilgrime, as alle my fadris.

15 Foryyue thou to me, that Y be refreischid, bifor that Y go; and Y schal no more be.

PSALM 39

1 The title of the nyne and threttithe salm. For victorie, the song of Dauid.

2 Y abidynge abood the Lord; and he yaf tent to me.

3 And he herde my preieris; and he ledde out me fro the lake of wretchidnesse, and fro the filthe of draft. And he ordeynede my feet on a stoon; and he dresside my goyngis.

4 And he sente in to my mouth a newe song; a song to oure God. Many men schulen se, and schulen drede; and schulen haue hope in the Lord.

5 Blessid is the man, of whom the name of the Lord is his hope; and he bihelde not in to vanitees, and in to false woodnesses.

6 Mi Lord God, thou hast maad thi merueils manye; and in thi thouytis noon is, that is lijk thee. I teld, and Y spak; and thei ben multiplied aboue noumbre.

7 Thou noldist sacrifice and offryng; but thou madist perfitli eeris to me. Thou axidist not brent sacrifice, and sacrifice for synne;

8 thanne Y seide, Lo! Y come. In the heed of the book it is writun of me,

9 that Y schulde do thi wille; my God, Y wolde; and thi lawe in the myddis of myn herte.

10 I telde thi riytfulnesse in a greet chirche; lo! Y schal not refreine my lippis, Lord, thou wistist.

11 I hidde not thi riytfulnesse in myn herte; Y seide thi treuthe and thin helthe. I hidde not thi mercy and thi treuthe; fro a myche counsel.

12 But thou, Lord, make not fer thi merciful doyngis fro me; thi mercy and treuthe euere token me vp.

13 For whi yuels, of whiche is no noumbre, cumpassiden me; my wickidnessis token me, and y myyte not, that Y schulde se. Tho ben multiplied aboue the heeris of myn heed; and myn herte forsook me.

14 Lord, plese it to thee, that thou delyuere me; Lord, biholde thou to helpe me.

15 Be thei schent, and aschamed togidere; that seken my lijf, to take awei it. Be thei turned abac, and be thei schamed; that wolen yuels to me.

16 Bere thei her confusioun anoon; that seien to me, Wel! wel! 'that is, in scorn.

17 Alle men that seken thee, be fulli ioyful, and be glad on thee; and seie thei, that louen thin helthe, The Lord be magnyfied euere.

18 Forsothe Y am a beggere and pore; the Lord is bisi of me. Thou arte myn helpere and my defendere; my God, tarie thou not.

PSALM 40

1 The title of the fourtithe salm. For victorie, the song of Dauid.

2 Blessid is he that vndurstondith 'on a nedi man and pore; the Lord schal delyuere hym in the yuel dai.

3 The Lord kepe hym, and quykene hym, and make hym blesful in the lond; and bitake not hym in to the wille of his enemyes.

4 The Lord bere help to hym on the bed of his sorewe; thou hast ofte turned al his bed stre in his sijknesse.

5 I seide, Lord, haue thou mercy on me; heele thou my soule, for Y synnede ayens thee.

6 Myn enemyes seiden yuels to me; Whanne schal he die, and his name schal perische?

7 And if he entride for to se, he spak veyn thingis; his herte gaderide wickidnesse to hym silf.

8 He yede with out forth; and spak to the same thing. Alle myn enemyes bacbitiden pryuyli ayens me; ayens me thei thouyten yuels to me.

9 Thei ordeineden an yuel word ayens me; Whether he that slepith, schal not leie to, that he rise ayen?

10 For whi the man of my pees, in whom Y hopide, he that eet my looues; made greet disseit on me.

11 But thou, Lord, haue merci on me, and reise me ayen; and Y schal yelde to hem.

12 In this thing Y knew, that thou woldist me; for myn enemye schal not haue ioye on me.

13 Forsothe thou hast take me vp for ynnocence; and hast confermed me in thi siyt with outen ende.

14 Blessid be the Lord God of Israel, fro the world and in to the world; be it doon, be it doon.

PSALM 41

1 The title of the oon and fourtithe salm. To victorie, to the sones of Chore.

2 As an hert desirith to the wellis of watris; so thou, God, my soule desirith to thee.

3 Mi soule thirstide to God, 'that is a 'quik welle; whanne schal Y come, and appere bifor the face of God?

4 Mi teeris weren looues to me bi dai and nyyt; while it is seid to me ech dai, Where is thi God?

5 I bithouyte of these thingis, and Y schedde out in me my soule; for Y schal passe in to the place of the wondurful tabernacle, til to the hows of God. In the vois of ful out ioiyng and knoulechyng; is the sown of the etere.

6 Mi soule, whi art thou sory; and whi disturblist thou me? Hope thou in God, for yit Y schal knouleche to hym; he is the helthe of my cheer,

7 and my God. My soule is disturblid at my silf; therfor, God, Y schal be myndeful of thee fro the lond of Jordan, and fro the litil hil Hermonyim.

8 Depthe clepith depthe; in the vois of thi wyndows. Alle thin hiye thingis and thi wawis; passiden ouer me.

9 The Lord sente his merci in the dai; and his song in the nyyt.

10 At me is a preier to the God of my lijf; Y schal seie to God, Thou art my 'takere vp. Whi foryetist thou me; and whi go Y sorewful, while the enemy turmentith me?

11 While my boonys ben brokun togidere; myn enemyes, that troblen me, dispiseden me. While thei seien to me, bi alle daies; Where is thi God?

12 Mi soule, whi art thou sori; and whi disturblist thou me? Hope thou in God, for yit Y schal knouleche to hym; 'he is the helthe of my cheer, and my God.

PSALM 42

1 'The two and fourtithe salm. God, deme thou me, and departe thou my cause fro a folc not hooli; delyuere thou me fro a wickid man, and gileful.

2 For thou art God, my strengthe; whi hast thou put me abac, and whi go Y soreuful, while the enemy turmentith me?

3 Sende out thi liyt, and thi treuthe; tho ledden me forth, and brouyten in to thin hooli hil, and in to thi tabernaclis.

4 And Y schal entre to the auter of God; to God, that gladith my yongthe. God, my God, Y schal knowleche to thee in an harpe; my soule,

5 whi art thou sory, and whi troblist thou me? Hope thou in God, for yit Y schal knouleche to hym; he is the helthe of my cheer, and my God.

PSALM 43

1 The title of the thre and fourtithe salm. 'To victorie, lernyng to the sones of Chore.

2 God, we herden with oure eeris; oure fadris telden to vs. The werk, which thou wrouytist in the daies of hem; and in elde daies.

3 Thin hond lost hethene men, and thou plauntidist hem; thou turmentidist puplis, and castidist hem out.

4 For the children of Israel weldiden the lond not bi her swerd; and the arm of hem sauyde not hem. But thi riyt hond, and thin arm, and the liytnyng of thi cheer; for thou were plesid in hem.

5 Thou art thi silf, my kyng and my God; that sendist helthis to Jacob.

6 Bi thee we schulen wyndewe oure enemyes with horn; and in thi name we schulen dispise hem, that risen ayen vs.

7 For Y schal not hope in my bouwe; and my swerd schal not saue me.

8 For thou hast saued vs fro men turmentinge vs; and thou hast schent men hatinge vs.

9 We schulen be preisid in God al dai; and in thi name we schulen knouleche to thee in to the world.

10 But now thou hast put vs abac, and hast schent vs; and thou, God, schalt not go out in oure vertues.

11 Thou hast turned vs awei bihynde aftir oure enemyes; and thei, that hatiden vs, rauyschiden dyuerseli to hem silf.

12 Thou hast youe vs as scheep of meetis; and among hethene men thou hast scaterid vs.

13 Thou hast seeld thi puple with out prijs; and multitude was not in the chaungyngis of hem.

14 Thou hast set vs schenschip to oure neiyboris; mouwyng and scorn to hem that ben in oure cumpas.

15 Thou hast set vs into licnesse to hethene me; stiryng of heed among puplis.

16 Al dai my schame is ayens me; and the schenschipe of my face hilide me.

17 Fro the vois of dispisere, and yuele spekere; fro the face of enemy, and pursuere.

18 Alle these thingis camen on vs, and we han not foryete thee; and we diden not wickidli in thi testament.

19 And oure herte yede not awei bihynde; and thou hast bowid awei oure pathis fro thi weie.

20 For thou hast maad vs lowe in the place of turment; and the schadewe of deth hilide vs.

21 If we foryaten the name of oure God; and if we helden forth oure hondis to an alien God.

22 Whether God schal not seke these thingis? for he knowith the hid thingis of herte. For whi we ben slayn al dai for thee; we ben demed as scheep of sleyng.

23 Lord, rise vp, whi slepist thou? rise vp, and putte not awei in to the ende.

24 Whi turnest thou awei thi face? thou foryetist oure pouert, and oure tribulacioun.

25 For oure lijf is maad low in dust; oure wombe is glued togidere in the erthe.

26 Lord, rise vp thou, and helpe vs; and ayenbie vs for thi name.

PSALM 44

1 The title of the foure and fourtithe salm. To the ouercomere for the lilies, the most loued song of lernyng of the sones of Chore.

2 Myn herte hath teld out a good word; Y seie my workis 'to the kyng. Mi tunge is 'a penne of a writere; writynge swiftli.

3 Crist, thou art fairer in schap than the sones of men; grace is spred abrood in thi lippis; therfor God blessid thee withouten ende.

4 Be thou gird with thi swerd; on thi hipe most myytili.

5 Biholde thou in thi schaplynesse and thi fairnesse; come thou forth with prosperite, and regne thou. For treuthe, and myldenesse, and riytfulnesse; and thi riyt hond schal lede forth thee wondurfuli.

6 Thi scharpe arowis schulen falle in to the hertis of the enemyes of the kyng; puplis schulen be vndur thee.

7 God, thi seete is in to the world of world; the yerde of thi rewme is a yerde of riyt reulyng, 'ethir of equite.

8 Thou louedist riytfulnesse, and hatidist wickidnesse; therfor thou, God, thi God, anoyntide thee with the oile of gladnesse, more than thi felowis.

9 Mirre, and gumme, and cassia, of thi clothis, of the 'housis yuer;

10 of whiche the douytris of kyngis delitiden thee. A queen stood nyy on thi riyt side in clothing ouergildid; cumpassid with dyuersitee.

11 Douyter, here thou, and se, and bowe doun thin eere; and foryete thi puple, and the hows of thi fadir.

12 And the kyng schal coueyte thi fairnesse; for he is thi Lord God, and thei schulen worschipe hym.

13 And the douytris of Tire in yiftis; alle the riche men of the puple schulen biseche thi cheer.

14 Al the glorye of that douyter of the kyng is with ynne in goldun hemmes;

15 sche is clothid aboute with dyuersitees. Virgyns schulen be brouyt to the kyng aftir hir; hir neiyboressis schulen be brouyt to thee.

16 Thei schulen be brouyt in gladnesse, and ful out ioiyng; thei schulen be brouyt in to the temple of the kyng.

17 Sones ben borun to thee, for thi fadris; thou schalt ordeyne hem princes on al erthe.

18 Lord, thei schulen be myndeful of thi name; in ech generacioun, and in to generacioun. Therfor puplis schulen knouleche to thee withouten ende; and in to the world of world.

PSALM 45

1 The title of the five and fourtithe salm. To the ouercomere, the song of the sones 'of Chore, 'for yongthis.

2 Oure God, thou art refuyt, and vertu; helpere in tribula-cions, that han founde vs greetly.

3 Therfor we schulen not drede, while the erthe schal be troblid; and the hillis schulen be borun ouer in to the herte of the see.

4 The watris of hem sowneden, and weren troblid; hillis weren troblid togidere in the strengthe of hym.

5 The feersnesse of flood makith glad the citee of God; the hiyeste God hath halewid his tabernacle.

6 God in the myddis therof schal not be moued; God schal helpe it eerli in the grey morewtid.

7 Hethene men weren disturblid togidere, and rewmes weren bowid doun; God yaf his vois, the erthe was moued.

8 The Lord of vertues is with vs; God of Jacob is oure vptak-ere.

9 Come ye, and se the werkis of the Lord; whiche wondris he hath set on the erthe.

10 He doynge awei batels til to the ende of the lond; schal al to-brese bouwe, and schal breke togidere armuris, and schal brenne scheldis bi fier.

11 Yyue ye tent, and se ye, that Y am God; Y schal be enhaunsid among hethene men; and Y schal be enhaunsid in erthe.

12 The Lord of vertues is with vs; God of Jacob is oure vptak-ere.

PSALM 46

1 The title of the sixte and fourtithe salm. To victorie, a salm to the sones of Chore.

2 Alle ye folkis, make ioie with hondis; synge ye hertli to God in the vois of ful out ioiyng.

3 For the Lord is hiy and ferdful; a greet kyng on al erthe.

4 He made puplis suget to vs; and hethene men vndur oure feet.

5 He chees his eritage to vs; the fairnesse of Jacob, whom he louyde.

6 God stiede in hertli song; and the Lord in the vois of a trumpe.

7 Synge ye to oure God, synge ye; synge ye to oure kyng, synge ye.

8 For God is kyng of al erthe; synge ye wiseli.

9 God schal regne on hethene men; God sittith on his hooli seete.

10 The princes of puplis ben gaderid togidere with God of Abraham; for the stronge goddis of erthe ben reisid greetli.

PSALM 47

1 The title of the seuene and fourtithe salm. The song of salm, of the sones of Chore.

2 The Lord is greet, and worthi to be preisid ful myche; in the citee of oure God, in the hooli hil of hym.

3 It is foundid in the ful out ioiyng of al erthe; the hil of Syon; the sidis of the north, the citee of the greet kyng.

4 God schal be knowun in the housis therof; whanne he schal take it.

5 For lo! the kyngis of erthe weren gaderid togidere; thei camen into o place.

6 Thei seynge so wondriden; thei weren disturblid, thei weren mouyd togidere, tremblyng took hem.

7 There sorewis as of a womman trauelynge of child;

8 in a greet spirit thou schalt al to-breke the schippis of Thar-sis.

9 As we herden, so we sien, in the citee of the Lord of ver-tues, in the citee of oure God; God hath foundid that citee with outen ende.

10 God, we han resseyued thi mercy; in the myddis of thi temple.

11 Aftir thi name, God, so thin heriyng is spred abrood in to the endis of erthe; thi riyt hond is ful of riytfulnesse.

12 The hil of Sion be glad, and the douytris of Judee be fulli ioiful; for thi domes, Lord.

13 Cumpasse ye Syon, and biclippe ye it; telle ye in the touris therof.

14 Sette ye youre hertis in the vertu of him; and departe ye the housis of hym, that ye telle out in an other generacioun.

15 For this is God, oure God, in to withouten ende, and in to the world of world; he schal gouerne vs in to worldis.

PSALM 48

1 The title of the eiyte and fourtithe salm. To victorie, a salm to the sones of Chore.

2 Alle ye folkis, here these thingis; alle ye that dwellen in the world, perseyue with eeris.

3 Alle the sones of erthe and the sones of men; togidere the riche man and the pore in to oon.

4 Mi mouth schal speke wisdom; and the thenkyng of myn herte schal speke prudence.

5 I schal bouwe doun myn eere in to a parable; Y schal opene my resoun set forth in a sautree.

6 Whi schal Y drede in the yuel dai? the wickidnesse of myn heele schal cumpasse me.

7 Whiche tristen in her owne vertu; and han glorie in the mul-titude of her richessis.

8 A brother ayenbieth not, schal a man ayenbie? and he schal not yyue to God his plesyng.

9 And he schal not yyue the prijs of raunsum of his soule; and he schal trauele with outen ende,

10 and he schal lyue yit in to the ende.

11 He schal not se perischyng, whanne he schal se wise men diynge; the vnwise man and fool schulen perische togidere. And thei schulen leeue her richessis to aliens;

12 and the sepulcris of hem ben the housis of hem with outen ende. The tabernaclis of hem ben in generacioun and genera-cioun; thei clepiden her names in her londis.

13 A man, whanne he was in honour, vndurstood not; he is comparisound to vnwise beestis, and he is maad lijk to tho.

14 This weie of hem is sclaundir to hem; and aftirward thei schulen plese togidere in her mouth.

15 As scheep thei ben set in helle; deth schal gnawe hem. And iust men schulen be lordis of hem in the morewtid; and the helpe of hem schal wexe eld in helle, for the glorie of hem.

16 Netheles God schal ayenbie my soule from the power of helle; whanne he schal take me.

17 Drede thou not, whanne a man is maad riche; and the glo-rie of his hows is multiplied.

18 For whanne he schal die, he schal not take alle thingis; and his glorie schal not go doun with him.

19 For his soule schal be blessid in his lijf; he schal knouleche to thee, whanne thou hast do wel to hym.

20 He schal entre til in to the generaciouns of hise fadris; and til in to with outen ende he schal not se liyt.

21 A man, whanne he was in honour, vndurstood not; he is comparisound to vnwise beestis, and is maad lijk to tho.

PSALM 49

1 The title of the nyne and fourtithe salm. The salm of Asaph. God, the Lord of goddis, spak; and clepide the erthe,

2 fro the risynge of the sunne til to the goyng doun. The schap of his fairnesse fro Syon,

3 God schal come opynli; oure God, and he schal not be stille. Fier schal brenne an hiye in his siyt; and a strong tempest in his cumpas.

4 He clepide heuene aboue; and the erthe, to deme his puple.

5 Gadere ye to hym hise seyntis; that ordeynen his testament aboue sacrifices.

6 'And heuenes schulen schewe his riytfulnesse; for God is the iuge.

7 Mi puple, here thou, and Y schal speke to Israel; and Y schal witnesse to thee, Y am God, thi God.

8 I schal not repreue thee in thi sacrifices; and thi brent sacrifices ben euere bifor me.

9 I schal not take calues of thin hows; nethir geet buckis of thi flockis.

10 For alle the wyelde beestis of wodis ben myne; werk beestis, and oxis in hillis.

11 I haue knowe alle the volatils of heuene; and the fairnesse of the feeld is with me.

12 If Y schal be hungry, Y schal not seie to thee; for the world and the fulnesse therof is myn.

13 Whether Y schal eete the fleischis of boolis? ethir schal Y drynke the blood of geet buckis?

14 Offre thou to God the sacrifice of heriyng; and yelde thin avowis to the hiyeste God.

15 And inwardli clepe thou me in the dai of tribulacioun; and Y schal delyuere thee, and thou schalt onoure me.

16 But God seide to the synnere, Whi tellist thou out my riytfulnessis; and takist my testament bi thi mouth?

17 Sotheli thou hatidist lore; and hast cast awey my wordis bihynde.

18 If thou siyest a theef, thou 'hast runne with hym; and thou settidist thi part with avowtreris.

19 Thi mouth was plenteuouse of malice; and thi tunge medlide togidere giles.

20 Thou sittynge spakist ayens thi brother, and thou settidist sclaundir ayens the sone of thi modir;

21 thou didist these thingis, and Y was stille. Thou gessidist wickidli, that Y schal be lijk thee; Y schal repreue thee, and Y schal sette ayens thi face.

22 Ye that foryeten God, vndurstonde these thingis; lest sum tyme he rauysche, and noon be that schal delyuere.

23 The sacrifice of heriyng schal onoure me; and there is the weie, where ynne Y schal schewe to hym the helthe of God.

PSALM 50

1 The title of the fiftithe salm. To victorie, the salm of Dauid;

2 'whanne Nathan the prophete cam to hym, whanne he entride to Bersabee.

3 God, haue thou merci on me; bi thi greet merci. And bi the mychilnesse of thi merciful doyngis; do thou awei my wickidnesse.

4 More waische thou me fro my wickidnesse; and clense thou me fro my synne.

5 For Y knouleche my wickidnesse; and my synne is euere ayens me.

6 I haue synned to thee aloone, and Y haue do yuel bifor thee; that thou be iustified in thi wordis, and ouercome whanne thou art demed. For lo!

7 Y was conseyued in wickednessis; and my modir conceyuede me in synnes.

8 For lo! thou louedist treuthe; thou hast schewid to me the vncerteyn thingis, and pryuy thingis of thi wisdom.

9 Lord, sprenge thou me with ysope, and Y schal be clensid; waische thou me, and Y schal be maad whijt more than snow.

10 Yyue thou ioie, and gladnesse to myn heryng; and boonys maad meke schulen ful out make ioye.

11 Turne awei thi face fro my synnes; and do awei alle my wickidnesses.

12 God, make thou a clene herte in me; and make thou newe a riytful spirit in my entrailis.

13 Caste thou me not awei fro thi face; and take thou not awei fro me thin hooli spirit.

14 Yiue thou to me the gladnesse of thyn helthe; and conferme thou me with the principal spirit.

15 I schal teche wickid men thi weies; and vnfeithful men schulen be conuertid to thee.

16 God, the God of myn helthe, delyuere thou me fro bloodis; and my tunge schal ioyfuli synge thi riytfulnesse.

17 Lord, 'opene thou my lippis; and my mouth schal telle thi preysyng.

18 For if thou haddist wold sacrifice, Y hadde youe; treuli thou schalt not delite in brent sacrifices.

19 A sacrifice to God is a spirit troblid; God, thou schalt not dispise a contrit herte and 'maad meke.

20 Lord, do thou benygneli in thi good wille to Syon; that the wallis of Jerusalem be bildid.

21 Thanne thou schalt take plesauntli the sacrifice of riytfulnesse, offryngis, and brent sacrifices; thanne thei schulen putte calues on thin auter.

PSALM 51

1 The title of the oon and fiftithe salm. To victorie, the salm of Dauid,

2 'whanne Doech Idumei cam, and telde to Saul, and seide to him, Dauid cam in to the hows of Abymelech.

3 What hast thou glorie in malice; which art miyti in wickidnesse?

4 Al dai thi tunge thouyte vnriytfulnesse; as a scharp rasour thou hast do gile.

5 Thou louedist malice more than benygnite; 'thou louedist wickidnesse more than to speke equite.

6 Thou louedist alle wordis of casting doun; with a gileful tunge.

7 Therfor God schal distrie thee in to the ende, he schal drawe thee out bi the roote, and he schal make thee to passe awei fro thi tabernacle; and thi roote fro the lond of lyuynge men.

8 Iust men schulen se, and schulen drede; and thei schulen leiye on hym, and thei schulen seie, Lo!

9 the man that settide not God his helpere. But he hopide in the multitude of his richessis; and hadde maistrie in his vanite.

10 Forsothe Y, as a fruytful olyue tre in the hous of God; hopide in the merci of God with outen ende, and in to the world of world.

11 Y schal knowleche to thee in to the world, for thou hast do mercy to me; and Y schal abide thi name, for it is good in the siyt of thi seyntis.

PSALM 52

1 The title of the two and fiftithe salm. To the ouercomer bi the quere, the lernyng of Dauid. The vnwise man seide in his herte; God is not.

2 Thei ben 'corrupt, and maad abhomynable in her wickidnessis; noon is that doith good.

3 God bihelde fro heuene on the sones of men; that he se, if 'ony is vndurstondynge, ether sekynge God.

4 Alle boweden awei, thei ben maad vnprofitable togidre; noon is that doith good, ther is not til to oon.

5 Whether alle men, that worchen wickidnesse, schulen not wite; whiche deuouren my puple as the mete of breed?

6 Thei clepiden not God; there thei trembliden for drede, where no drede was. For God hath scaterid the boones of hem, that plesen men; thei ben schent, for God hath forsake hem.

7 Who schal yyue fro Syon helthe to Israel? whanne the Lord hath turned the caitifte of his puple, Jacob schal 'ful out make ioie, and Israel schal be glad.

PSALM 53

1 The title of the thre and fiftithe salm. To victorie in orguns, ether in salmes, the lernyng of Dauid,

2 'whanne Zyfeys camen, and seiden to Saul, Whethir Dauid is not hid at vs?

3 God, in thi name make thou me saaf; and in thi vertu deme thou me.

4 God, here thou my preier; with eeris perseyue thou the wordis of my mouth.

5 For aliens han rise ayens me, and stronge men souyten my lijf; and thei settiden not God bifor her siyt.

6 For, lo! God helpith me; and the Lord is vptaker of my soule.

7 Turne thou awei yuelis to myn enemyes; and leese thou hem in thi treuthe.

8 Wilfuli Y schal make sacrifice to thee; and, Lord, Y schal knouleche to thi name, for it is good.

9 For thou delyueridist me fro al tribulacioun; and myn iye dispiside on myn enemyes.

PSALM 54

1 The title of the foure and fiftithe salm. 'In Ebreu thus, To victorie in orguns, the lernyng of Dauid. 'In Jeroms translacioun thus, To the ouercomer in salmes of Dauid lernid.

2 God, here thou my preier, and dispise thou not my bisechyng;

3 yyue thou tent to me, and here thou me. I am sorewful in myn exercising; and Y am disturblid of the face of the enemye,

4 and of the tribulacioun of the synner. For thei bowiden wickidnessis in to me; and in ire thei weren dieseful to me.

5 Myn herte was disturblid in me; and the drede of deth felde on me.

6 Drede and trembling camen on me; and derknessis hiliden me.

7 And Y seide, Who schal yyue to me fetheris, as of a culuer; and Y schal fle, and schal take rest?

8 Lo! Y yede fer awei, and fledde; and Y dwellide in wildirnesse.

9 I abood hym, that made me saaf fro the litilnesse, 'ether drede, of spirit; and fro tempest.

10 Lord, caste thou doun, departe thou the tungis of hem; for Y siy wickidnesse and ayenseiyng in the citee.

11 Bi dai and nyyt wickidnesse schal cumpasse it on the wallis therof;

12 and trauel and vnriytfulnesse ben in the myddis therof. And vsure and gile failide not; fro the stretis therof.

13 For if myn enemye hadde cursid me; sotheli Y hadde suffride. And if he, that hatide me, hadde spoke greet thingis on me; in hap Y hadde hid me fro hym.

14 But thou art a man of o wille; my leeder, and my knowun.

15 Which tokist togidere swete meetis with me; we yeden with consent in the hous of God.

16 Deth come on hem; and go thei doun quyk in to helle. For weiwardnessis ben in the dwelling places of hem; in the myddis of hem.

17 But Y criede to thee, Lord; and the Lord sauede me.

18 In the euentid and morewtid and in myddai Y schal telle, and schewe; and he schal here my vois.

19 He schal ayenbie my soule in pees fro hem, that neiyen to me; for among manye thei weren with me.

20 God schal here; and he that is bifore the worldis schal make hem low. For chaungyng is not to hem, and thei dredden not God;

21 he holdith forth his hoond in yelding. Thei defouliden his testament,

22 the cheris therof weren departid fro ire; and his herte neiyede. The wordis therof weren softer than oyle; and tho ben dartis.

23 Caste thi cure on the Lord, and he schal fulli nurische thee; and he schal not yyue with outen ende flotering to a iust man.

24 But thou, God, schalt lede hem forth; in to the pit of deth. Menquelleris and gilours schulen not haue half her daies; but, Lord, Y schal hope in thee.

PSALM 55

1 The title of the fyue and fiftithe salm. 'In Ebreu thus, To the ouercomyng on the doumb culuer of fer drawing awei, the comely song of Dauid, whanne Filisteis helden hym in Geth. 'In Jeroms translacioun thus, To the ouercomer for the doumb culuer, for it yede awei fer. Dauid meke and symple made this salm, whanne Palesteyns helden hym in Geth.

2 God, haue thou merci on me, for a man hath defoulid me; al dai he impugnyde, and troublide me.

3 Myn enemyes defouliden me al dai; for manye fiyteris weren ayens me.

4 Of the hiynesse of dai Y schal drede; but God Y schal hope in thee.

5 In God Y schal preise my wordis; Y hopide in God, Y schal not drede what thing fleisch schal do to me.

6 Al dai thei cursiden my wordis; ayens me alle her thouytis weren in to yuel.

7 Thei schulen dwelle, and schulen hide; thei schulen aspie myn heele.

8 As thei abiden my lijf, for nouyt schalt thou make hem saaf; in ire thou schalt breke togidre puplis.

9 God, Y schewide my lijf to thee; thou hast set my teeris in thi siyt. As and in thi biheest, Lord;

10 thanne myn enemyes schulen be turned abak. In what euere dai Y schal inwardli clepe thee; lo! Y haue knowe, that thou art my God.

11 In God Y schal preise a word; in the Lord Y schal preyse a word. Y schal hope in God; Y schal not drede what thing a man schal do to me.

12 God, thin auowis ben in me; whiche Y schal yelde heriyngis to thee.

13 For thou hast delyuerid my lijf fro deth, and my feet fro slidyng; that Y pleese bifore God in the liyt of hem that lyuen.

PSALM 56

1 The title of the sixte and fiftithe salm. 'In Ebreu thus, To the victorie, lese thou not the semeli song, 'ether the 'swete song of Dauid, 'whanne he fledde fro the face of Saul in to the denne. 'In Jeroms translacioun thus, For victorie, that thou lese not Dauid, meke and simple, whanne he fledde fro the face of Saul in to the denne.

2 God, haue thou merci on me, haue thou merci on me; for my soule tristith in thee. And Y schal hope in the schadewe of thi wyngis; til wickidnesse passe.

3 I schal crye to God altherhiyeste; to God that dide wel to me.

4 He sente fro heuene, and delyuerede me; he yaf in to schenschip hem that defoulen me. God sente his merci and his treuthe,

5 and delyuerede my soule fro the myddis of whelpis of liouns; Y slepte disturblid. The sones of men, the teeth of hem ben armuris and arowis; and her tunge is a scharp swerd.

6 God, be thou enhaunsid aboue heuenes; and thi glorie aboue al erthe.

7 Thei maden redi a snare to my feet; and thei greetly boweden my lijf. Thei delueden a diche bifore my face; and thei felden doun in to it.

8 God, myn herte is redi, myn herte is redi; Y schal singe, and Y schal seie salm.

9 Mi glorie, rise thou vp; sautrie and harpe, rise thou vp; Y schal rise vp eerli.

10 Lord, Y schal knouleche to thee among puplis; and Y schal seie salm among hethene men.

11 For thi merci is magnified til to heuenes; and thi treuthe til to cloudis.

12 God, be thou enhaunsid aboue heuenes; and thi glorie ouer al erthe.

PSALM 57

1 The title of the seuene and fiftithe salm. 'In Ebreu thus, To victorie; 'lese thou not the swete song, ether the semely salm, of Dauid. 'In Jeroms translacioun thus, To the ouercomere, that thou lese not Dauid, meke and simple.

2 Forsothe if ye speken riytfulnesse verili; ye sones of men, deme riytfuli.

3 For in herte ye worchen wickidnesse in erthe; youre hondis maken redi vnriytfulnessis.

4 Synneris weren maad aliens fro the wombe; thei erriden fro the wombe, thei spaken false thingis.

5 Woodnesse is to hem, bi the licnesse of a serpent; as of a deef snake, and stoppynge hise eeris.

6 Which schal not here the vois of charmeris; and of a venym makere charmynge wiseli.

7 God schal al to-breke the teeth of hem in her mouth; the Lord schal breke togidere the greet teeth of liouns.

8 Thei schulen come to nouyt, as water rennynge awei; he bente his bouwe, til thei ben maad sijk.

9 As wexe that fletith awei, thei schulen be takun awei; fier felle aboue, and thei siyen not the sunne.

10 Bifore that youre thornes vndurstoden the ramne; he swolewith hem so in ire, as lyuynge men.

11 The iust man schal be glad, whanne he schal se veniaunce; he schal waische hise hondis in the blood of a synner.

12 And a man schal seie treuli, For fruyt is to a iust man; treuli God is demynge hem in erthe.

PSALM 58

1 The title of the eiyte and fiftithe salm. 'In Jeroms translacioun thus, To the ouercomer, that thou lese not Dauid, meke and simple, 'whanne Saul sente and kepte the hous, to slee hym. 'In Ebreu thus, To the ouercomyng, leese thou not the semeli song of Dauid, and so forth.

2 Mi God, delyuer thou me fro myn enemyes; and delyuer thou me fro hem that risen ayens me.

3 Delyuer thou me fro hem that worchen wickidnesse; and saue thou me fro menquelleris.

4 For lo! thei han take my soule; stronge men fellen in on me.

5 Nethir my wickidnesse, nether my synne; Lord, Y ran with out wickidnesse, and dresside 'my werkis.

6 Rise vp thou in to my meetyng, and se; and thou, Lord God of vertues, art God of Israel. Yyue thou tent to visite alle folkis; do thou not merci to alle that worchen wickidnesse.

7 Thei schulen be turned at euentid, and thei as doggis schulen suffre hungir; and thei schulen cumpas the citee.

8 Lo! thei schulen speke in her mouth, and a swerd in her lippis; for who herde?

9 And thou, Lord, schalt scorne hem; thou schalt bringe alle folkis to nouyt.

10 I schal kepe my strengthe to thee;

11 for God is myn vptaker, my God, his mercy schal come byfore me.

12 God schewide to me on myn enemyes, slee thou not hem; lest ony tyme my puples foryete. Scatere thou hem in thi vertu; and, Lord, my defender, putte thou hem doun.

13 Putte thou doun the trespas of her mouth, and the word of her lippis; and be thei takun in her pride. And of cursyng and of leesyng; thei schulen be schewid in the endyng.

14 In the ire of ending, and thei schulen not be; and thei schulen wite, that the Lord schal be Lord of Jacob, and of the endis of erthe.

15 Thei schulen be turned at euentid, and thei as doggis schulen suffre hungir; and thei schulen cumpas the citee.

16 Thei schulen be scaterid abrood, for to eete; sotheli if thei ben not fillid, and thei schulen grutche.

17 But Y schal synge thi strengthe; and eerli Y schal enhaunse thi merci. For thou art maad myn vptaker; and my refuyt, in the dai of my tribulacioun.

18 Myn helper, Y schal synge to thee; for thou art God, myn vptaker, my God, my mercy.

PSALM 59

1 The title of the nyne and fiftithe salm. 'In Ebreu thus, To victorie, on the witnessyng of roose, the swete song of Dauid, to teche, 'whanne he fauyte ayens Aram of floodis, and Sirie of Soba; and Joab turnede ayen, and smoot Edom in the 'valei of salt pittis, twelue thousynde. 'In Jeroms translacioun thus, 2 To the ouercomer for lilies, the witnessing of meke and parfit Dauid, to teche, whanne he fauyte ayens Sirie of Mesopotamye, and Soba, and so forth.

3 God, thou hast put awei vs, and thou hast distried vs; thou were wrooth, and thou hast do merci to vs.

4 Thou mouedist the erthe, and thou disturblidist it; make thou hool the sorewis therof, for it is moued.

5 Thou schewidist harde thingis to thi puple; thou yauest drynk to vs with the wyn of compunccioun.

6 Thou hast youe a signefiyng to hem that dreden thee; that thei fle fro the face of the bouwe. That thi derlyngis be delyuered;

7 make thou saaf with thi riyt hond 'the puple of Israel, and here thou me.

8 God spak bi his hooli; Y schal be glad, and Y schal departe Siccimam, and Y schal meete the greet valei of tabernaclis.

9 Galaad is myn, and Manasses is myn; and Effraym is the strengthe of myn heed.

10 Juda is my king; Moab is the pot of myn hope. In to Idumee Y schal stretche forth my scho; aliens ben maad suget to me.

11 Who schal lede me in to a citee maad strong; who schal leede me til in to Ydumee?

12 Whether not thou, God, that hast put awei vs; and schalt thou not, God, go out in oure vertues?

13 Lord, yyue thou to vs help of tribulacioun; for the heelthe of man is veyn.

14 In God we schulen make vertu; and he schal bringe to nouyt hem that disturblen vs.

PSALM 60

1 The titil of the sixtithe salm. To the victorie on orgun, to Dauid hym silf.

2 God, here thou my biseching; yyue thou tent to my preyer.

3 Fro the endis of the lond Y criede to thee; the while myn herte was angwischid, thou enhaunsidist me in a stoon.

4 Thou laddest me forth, for thou art maad myn hope; a tour of strengthe fro the face of the enemye.

5 I schal dwelle in thi tabernacle in to worldis; Y schal be keuered in the hilyng of thi wengis.

6 For thou, my God, hast herd my preier; thou hast youe eritage to hem that dreden thi name.

7 Thou schalt adde daies on the daies of the king; hise yeeris til in to the dai of generacioun and of generacioun.

8 He dwellith with outen ende in the siyt of God; who schal seke the merci and treuthe of hym?

9 So Y schal seie salm to thi name in to the world of world; that Y yelde my vowis fro dai in to dai.

PSALM 61

1 The titil of the oon and sixtithe salm. To the victorie on Iditum, the salm of Dauid.

2 Whether my soule schal not be suget to God; for myn heelthe is of hym.

3 For whi he is bothe my God, and myn heelthe; my 'taker vp, Y schal no more be moued.

4 Hou longe fallen ye on a man? alle ye sleen; as to a wal bowid, and a wal of stoon with out morter cast doun.

5 Netheles thei thouyten to putte awei my prijs, Y ran in thirst; with her mouth thei blessiden, and in her herte thei cursiden.

6 Netheles, my soule, be thou suget to God; for my pacience is of hym.

7 For he is my God, and my saueour; myn helpere, Y schal not passe out.

8 Myn helthe, and my glorie is in God; God is the yyuer of myn help, and myn hope is in God.

9 Al the gaderyng togidere of the puple, hope ye in God, schede ye out youre hertis bifore hym; God is oure helpere with outen ende.

10 Netheles the sones of men ben veyne; the sones of men ben liers in balauncis, that thei disseyue of vanytee in to the same thing.

11 Nile ye haue hope in wickidnesse, and nyle ye coueyte raueyns; if ritchessis be plenteuouse, nyle ye sette the herte therto.

12 God spak onys, Y herde these twei thingis, that power is of God, and, thou Lord, mercy is to thee;

13 for thou schalt yelde to ech man bi hise werkis.

PSALM 62

1 The titil of the two and sixtithe salm. 'The salm of Dauid, 'whanne he was in the desert of Judee.

2 God, my God, Y wake to thee ful eerli. Mi soule thirstide to thee; my fleisch thirstide to thee ful many foold.

3 In a lond forsakun with out wei, and with out water, so Y apperide to thee in hooli; that Y schulde se thi vertu, and thi glorie.

4 For thi merci is betere than lyues; my lippis schulen herie thee.

5 So Y schal blesse thee in my lijf; and in thi name Y schal reise myn hondis.

6 Mi soule be fillid as with inner fatnesse and vttermere fatnesse; and my mouth schal herie with lippis of ful out ioiyng.

7 So Y hadde mynde on thee on my bed, in morewtidis Y shal thenke of thee;

8 for thou were myn helpere. And in the keueryng of thi wyngis Y schal make 'ful out ioye, my soule cleuede after thee;

9 thi riythond took me vp.

10 Forsothe thei souyten in veyn my lijf, thei schulen entre in to the lower thingis of erthe;

11 thei schulen be bitakun in to the hondis of swerd, thei schulen be maad the partis of foxis.

12 But the king schal be glad in God; and alle men schulen be preysid that sweren in hym, for the mouth of hem, that speken wickid thingis, is stoppid.

PSALM 63

1 The titil of the thre and sixtithe salm. 'In Ebrewe thus, To the victorie, the salm of Dauid. 'In Jerom 'thus, To the ouercomer, the song of Dauid.

2 God, here thou my preier, whanne Y biseche; delyuere thou my soule fro the drede of the enemy.

3 Thou hast defendid me fro the couent of yuele doers; fro the multitude of hem that worchen wickidnesse.

4 For thei scharpiden her tungis as a swerd, thei benten a bowe, a bittir thing;

5 for to schete in priuetees hym that is vnwemmed.

6 Sodeynli thei schulen schete hym, and thei schulen not drede; thei maden stidefast to hem silf a wickid word. Thei telden, that thei schulden hide snaris; thei seiden, Who schal se hem?

7 Thei souyten wickidnessis; thei souyten, and failiden in sekinge. A man neiyhe to deep herte;

8 and God schal be enhaunsid. The arowis of 'litle men ben maad the woundis of hem;

9 and the tungis of hem ben maad sijk ayens hem. Alle men ben disturblid, that sien hem;

10 and ech man dredde. And thei telden the werkis of God; and vndurstoden the dedis of God.

11 The iust man schal be glad in the Lord, and schal hope in hym; and alle men of riytful herte schulen be preisid.

PSALM 64

1 The titil of the foure and sixtithe salm. 'To victorie, 'the salm of the song of Dauid.

2 God, heriyng bicometh thee in Syon; and a vow schal be yolden to thee in Jerusalem.

3 Here thou my preier; ech man schal come to thee.

4 The wordis of wickid men hadden the maistrye ouer vs; and thou schalt do merci to oure wickidnessis.

5 Blessid is he, whom thou hast chose, and hast take; he schal dwelle in thin hallis. We schulen be fillid with the goodis of thin hous;

6 thi temple is hooli, wondurful in equite. God, oure heelthe, here thou vs; thou art hope of alle coostis of erthe, and in the see afer.

7 And thou makest redi hillis in thi vertu, and art gird with power;

8 which disturblist the depthe of the see, the soun of the wawis therof.

9 Folkis schulen be disturblid, and thei that dwellen in the endis schulen drede of thi signes; thou schalt delite the outgo-ingis of the morewtid and euentid.

10 Thou hast visitid the lond, and hast greetli fillid it; thou hast multiplied to make it riche. The flood of God was fillid with watris; thou madist redi the mete of hem, for the makyng redi therof is so.

11 Thou fillynge greetli the stremes therof, multiplie the fruy-tis therof; the lond bringinge forth fruytis schal be glad in got-eris of it.

12 Thou schalt blesse the coroun of the yeer of thi good wille; and thi feeldis schulen be fillid with plentee of fruytis.

13 The feire thingis of desert schulen wexe fatte; and litle hil-lis schulen be cumpassid with ful out ioiyng.

14 The wetheris of scheep ben clothid, and valeis schulen be plenteuouse of wheete; thei schulen crye, and sotheli thei schulen seye salm.

PSALM 65

1 The titil of the fyue and sixtithe salm. To the victorie, the song of salm.

2 Al the erthe, make ye ioie hertli to God, seie ye salm to his name; yyue ye glorie to his heriyng.

3 Seie ye to God, Lord, thi werkis ben dredeful; in the multi-tude of thi vertu thin enemyes schulen lie to thee.

4 God, al the erthe worschipe thee, and synge to thee; seie it salm to thi name.

5 Come ye and se ye the werkis of God; ferdful in counseils on the sones of men.

6 Which turnede the see in to drie lond; in the flood thei schulen passe with foot, there we schulen be glad in hym.

7 Which is Lord in his vertu withouten ende, hise iyen biholden on folkis; thei that maken scharp be not enhaunsid in hem silf.

8 Ye hethen men, blesse oure God; and make ye herd the vois of his preising.

9 That hath set my soule to lijf, and yaf not my feet in to stiryng.

10 For thou, God, hast preued vs; thou hast examyned vs bi fier, as siluer is examyned.

11 Thou leddist vs in to a snare, thou puttidist tribulaciouns in oure bak;

12 thou settidist men on oure heedis. We passiden bi fier and water; and thou leddist vs out in to refreschyng.

13 I schal entre in to thin hous in brent sacrifices; Y schal yelde to thee my vowis,

14 which my lippis spaken distinctly. And my mouth spake in my tribulacioun;

15 Y shal offre to thee brent sacrificis ful of merowy, with the brennyng of rammes; Y schal offre to thee oxis with buckis of geet.

16 Alle ye that dreden God, come and here, and Y schal telle; hou grete thingis he hath do to my soule.

17 I criede to hym with my mouth; and Y ioyede fulli vndir my tunge.

18 If Y bihelde wickidnesse in myn herte; the Lord schal not here.

19 Therfor God herde; and perseyuede the vois of my bisechyng.

20 Blessid be God; that remeued not my preyer, and 'took not awei his merci fro me.

PSALM 66

1 The titil of the sixe and sixtithe salm. 'In Ebreu thus, To the victorie in orguns, the salm of the song. 'In Jerom 'thus, To the ouercomer in salmes, the song of writing of a delitable thing with metre.

2 God haue merci on vs, and blesse vs; liytne he his cheer on vs, and haue merci on vs.

3 That we knowe thi weie on erthe; thin heelthe in alle folkis.

4 God, puplis knowleche to thee; alle puplis knouleche to thee.

5 Hethen men be glad, and make fulli ioye, for thou demest puplis in equite; and dressist hethene men in erthe.

6 God, puplis knouleche to thee, alle puplis knouleche to thee;

7 the erthe yaf his fruyt. God, oure God blesse vs, God blesse vs; and alle the coostis of erthe drede hym.

PSALM 67

1 The titil of the seuene and sixtithe salm. To the victorie, the salm 'of the song 'of Dauid.

2 God rise vp, and hise enemyes be scaterid; and thei that haten hym fle fro his face.

3 As smoke failith, faile thei; as wax fletith fro the face of fier, so perische synneris fro the face of God.

4 And iust men eete, and make fulli ioye in the siyt of God; and delite thei in gladnesse.

5 Synge ye to God, seie ye salm to his name; make ye weie to hym, that stieth on the goyng doun, the Lord is name to hym. Make ye fulli ioye in his siyt, enemyes schulen be disturblid fro the face of hym,

6 which is the fadir of fadirles and modirles children; and the iuge of widewis.

7 God is in his hooli place; God that makith men of o wille to dwelle in the hous. Which leedith out bi strengthe hem that ben boundun; in lijk maner hem that maken scharp, that dwellen in sepulcris.

8 God, whanne thou yedist out in the siyt of thi puple; whanne thou passidist forth in the desert.

9 The erthe was moued, for heuenes droppiden doun fro the face of God of Synay; fro the face of God of Israel.

10 God, thou schalt departe wilful reyn to thin eritage, and it was sijk; but thou madist it parfit.

11 Thi beestis schulen dwelle therynne; God, thou hast maad redi in thi swetnesse to the pore man.

12 The Lord schal yyue a word; to hem that prechen the gospel with myche vertu.

13 The kyngis of vertues ben maad loued of the derlyng; and to the fairnesse of the hous to departe spuylis.

14 If ye slepen among the myddil of eritagis, the fetheris of the culuer ben of siluer; and the hyndrere thingis of the bak therof ben in the shynyng of gold.

15 While the king of heuene demeth kyngis theronne, thei schulen be maad whitter then snow in Selmon;

16 the hille of God is a fat hille. The cruddid hil is a fat hil;

17 wherto bileuen ye falsli, cruddid hillis? The hil in which it plesith wel God to dwelle ther ynne; for the Lord schal dwelle 'in to the ende.

18 The chare of God is manyfoold with ten thousynde, a thousynde of hem that ben glad; the Lord was in hem, in Syna, in the hooli.

19 Thou stiedist an hiy, thou tokist caitiftee; thou resseyuedist yiftis among men. For whi thou tokist hem that bileueden not; for to dwelle in the Lord God.

20 Blessid be the Lord ech dai; the God of oure heelthis schal make an eesie wei to vs.

21 Oure God is God to make men saaf; and outgoyng fro deeth is of the Lord God.

22 Netheles God schal breke the heedis of hise enemyes; the cop of the heere of hem that goen in her trespassis.

23 The Lord seide, Y schal turne fro Basan; Y schal turne in to the depthe of the see.

24 That thi foot be deppid in blood; the tunge of thi doggis be dippid in blood of the enemyes of hym.

25 God, thei sien thi goyngis yn; the goyngis yn of my God, of my king, which is in the hooli.

26 Prynces ioyned with syngeris camen bifore; in the myddil of yonge dameselis syngynge in tympans.

27 In chirchis blesse ye God; blesse ye the Lord fro the wellis of Israel.

28 There Beniamyn, a yonge man; in the rauyschyng of mynde. The princis of Juda weren the duykis of hem; the princis of Zabulon, the princis of Neptalym.

29 God, comaunde thou to thi vertu; God, conferme thou this thing, which thou hast wrouyt in vs.

30 Fro thi temple, which is in Jerusalem; kyngis schulen offre yiftis to thee.

31 Blame thou the wielde beestis of the reheed, the gaderyng togidere of bolis is among the kien of puplis; that thei exclude hem that ben preuyd bi siluer. Distrie thou folkis that wolen batels,

32 legatis schulen come fro Egipt; Ethiopie schal come bifore the hondis therof to God.

33 Rewmes of the erthe, synge ye to God; seie ye salm to the Lord.

34 Singe ye to God; that stiede on the heuene of heuene at the eest. Lo! he schal yyue to his vois the vois of vertu, yyue ye glorie to God on Israel;

35 his greet doyng and his vertu is in the cloudis.

36 God is wondirful in hise seyntis; God of Israel, he schal yyue vertu, and strengthe to his puple; blessid be God.

PSALM 68

1 The title of the eiyte and sixtithe salm. 'In Ebreu thus, To the victorie, on the roosis of Dauid. 'In Jerom thus, To the ouercomer, for the sones of Dauid.

2 God, make thou me saaf; for watris 'entriden til to my soule.

3 I am set in the sliym of the depthe; and 'substaunce is not. I cam in to the depthe of the see; and the tempest drenchide me.

4 I traueilide criynge, my cheekis weren maad hoose; myn iyen failiden, the while Y hope in to my God.

5 Thei that hatiden me with out cause; weren multiplied aboue the heeris of myn heed. Myn enemyes that pursueden me vniustli weren coumfortid; Y paiede thanne tho thingis, whiche Y rauischide not.

6 God, thou knowist myn vnkunnyng; and my trespassis ben not hid fro thee.

7 Lord, Lord of vertues; thei, that abiden thee, be not aschamed in me. God of Israel; thei, that seken thee, be not schent on me.

8 For Y suffride schenschipe for thee; schame hilide my face.

9 I am maad a straunger to my britheren; and a pilgryme to the sones of my modir.

10 For the feruent loue of thin hous eet me; and the schenschipis of men seiynge schenschipis to thee fellen on me.

11 And Y hilide my soule with fastyng; and it was maad in to schenschip to me.

12 And Y puttide my cloth an heire; and Y am maad to hem in to a parable.

13 Thei, that saten in the yate, spaken ayens me; and thei, that drunken wien, sungen of me.

14 But Lord, Y dresse my preier to thee; God, Y abide the tyme of good plesaunce. Here thou me in the multitude of thi mercy; in the treuthe of thin heelthe.

15 Delyuer thou me fro the cley, that Y be not faste set in; delyuere thou me fro hem that haten me, and fro depthe of watris.

16 The tempest of watir drenche not me, nethir the depthe swolowe me; nethir the pit make streit his mouth on me.

17 Lord, here thou me, for thi merci is benygne; vp the multitude of thi merciful doyngis biholde thou in to me.

18 And turne not awei thi face fro thi child; for Y am in tribulacioun, here thou me swiftli.

19 Yyue thou tente to my soule, and delyuer thou it; for myn enemyes delyuere thou me.

20 Thou knowist my schenschip, and my dispysyng; and my schame.

21 Alle that troblen me ben in thi siyt; myn herte abood schendschipe, and wretchidnesse. And Y abood hym, that was sory togidere, and noon was; and that schulde coumforte, and Y foond not.

22 And thei yauen galle in to my meete; and in my thirst thei yauen 'to me drinke with vynegre.

23 The boord of hem be maad bifore hem in to a snare; and in to yeldyngis, and in to sclaundir.

24 Her iyen be maad derk, that thei se not; and euere bouwe doun the bak of hem.

25 Schede out thin ire on hem; and the strong veniaunce of thin ire take hem.

26 The habitacioun of hem be maad forsakun; and 'noon be that dwelle in the tabernaclis of hem.

27 For thei pursueden hym, whom thou hast smyte; and thei addiden on the sorewe of my woundis.

28 Adde thou wickidnesse on the wickidnesse of hem; and entre thei not in to thi riytwisnesse.

29 Be thei don awei fro the book of lyuynge men; and be thei not writun with iust men.

30 I am pore and sorewful; God, thin heelthe took me vp.

31 I schal herye the name of God with song; and Y schal magnefye hym in heriyng.

32 And it schal plese God more than a newe calf; bryngynge forth hornes and clees.

33 Pore men se, and be glad; seke ye God, and youre soule schal lyue.

34 For the Lord herde pore men; and dispiside not hise boundun men.

35 Heuenes and erthe, herye hym; the se, and alle crepynge bestis in tho, herye hym.

36 For God schal make saaf Syon; and the citees of Juda schulen be bildid. And thei schulen dwelle there; and thei schulen gete it bi eritage.

37 And the seed of hise seruauntis schal haue it in possessioun; and thei that louen his name, schulen dwelle ther ynne.

PSALM 69

1 The titil of the nyne and sixtithe salm. To the victorie 'of Dauid, 'to haue mynde.

2 God, biholde thou in to myn heelp; Lord, hast thou to helpe me.

3 Be thei schent, and aschamed; that seken my lijf. Be thei turned a bak; and schame thei, that wolen yuels to me.

4 Be thei turned awei anoon, and schame thei; that seien to me, Wel! wel!

5 Alle men that seken thee, make fulli ioie, and be glad in thee; and thei that louen thin heelthe, seie euere, The Lord be magnyfied.

6 Forsothe Y am a nedi man, and pore; God, helpe thou me. Thou art myn helper and my delyuerere; Lord, tarye thou not.

PSALM 70

1 The seuentithe salm hath no title. Lord, Y hopide in thee, be Y not schent with outen ende;

2 in thi riytwisnesse delyuere thou me, and rauysche me out. Bowe doun thin eere to me; and make me saaf.

3 Be thou to me in to God a defendere; and in to a strengthid place, that thou make me saaf. For thou art my stidefastnesse; and my refuit.

4 My God, delyuere thou me fro the hoond of the synner; and fro the hoond of a man doynge ayens the lawe, and of the wickid man.

5 For thou, Lord, art my pacience; Lord, thou art myn hope fro my yongthe.

6 In thee Y am confermyd fro the wombe; thou art my defendere fro the wombe of my modir.

7 My syngyng is euere in thee; Y am maad as a greet wonder to many men; and thou art a strong helpere.

8 My mouth be fillid with heriyng; that Y synge thi glorie, al dai thi greetnesse.

9 Caste thou not awei me in the tyme of eldnesse; whanne my vertu failith, forsake thou not me.

10 For myn enemyes seiden of me; and thei that kepten my lijf maden counsel togidere.

11 Seiynge, God hath forsake hym; pursue ye, and take hym; for noon is that schal delyuere.

12 God, be thou not maad afer fro me; my God, biholde thou in to myn help.

13 Men that bacbiten my soule, be schent, and faile thei; and be thei hilid with schenschip and schame, that seken yuels to me.

14 But Y schal hope euere; and Y schal adde euere ouer al thi preising.

15 Mi mouth schal telle thi riytfulnesse; al dai thin helthe. For Y knewe not lettrure, Y schal entre in to the poweres of the Lord;

16 Lord, Y schal bithenke on thi riytfulnesse aloone.

17 God, thou hast tauyt me fro my yongthe, and 'til to now; Y schal telle out thi merueilis.

18 And til in to 'the eldnesse and the laste age; God, forsake thou not me. Til Y telle thin arm; to eche generacioun, that schal come. Til Y telle thi myyt,

19 and thi riytfulnesse, God, til in to the hiyeste grete dedis which thou hast do; God, who is lijk thee?

20 Hou grete tribulaciouns many and yuele hast thou schewid to me; and thou conuertid hast quykenyd me, and hast eft brouyt me ayen fro the depthis of erthe.

21 Thou hast multiplied thi greet doyng; and thou conuertid hast coumfortid me.

22 For whi and Y schal knowleche to thee, thou God, thi treuthe in the instrumentis of salm; Y schal synge in an harpe to thee, that art the hooli of Israel.

23 Mi lippis schulen make fulli ioye, whanne Y schal synge to thee; and my soule, which thou ayen bouytist.

24 But and my tunge schal thenke al dai on thi riytfulnesse; whanne thei schulen be schent and aschamed, that seken yuelis to me.

PSALM 71

1 The title of the oon and seuentithe salm. 'To Salomon.

2 God, yyue thi doom to the king; and thi riytfulnesse to the sone of a king. To deme thi puple in riytfulnesse; and thi pore men in doom.

3 Mounteyns resseyue pees to the puple; and litle hillis resseyue riytfulnesse.

4 He schal deme the pore men of the puple, and he schal make saaf the sones of pore men; and he schal make low the false chalengere.

5 And he schal dwelle with the sunne, and bifore the moone; in generacioun and in to generacioun.

6 He schal come doun as reyn in to a flees; and as goteris droppinge on the erthe.

7 Riytfulnesse schal come forth in hise dayes, and the aboundaunce of pees; til the moone be takun awei.

8 And he schal be lord fro the-see 'til to the see; and fro the flood til to the endis of the world.

9 Ethiopiens schulen falle doun bifore hym; and hise enemyes schulen licke the erthe.

10 The kyngis of Tarsis and ilis schulen offre yiftis; the kyngis of Arabie and of Saba schulen brynge yiftis.

11 And alle kyngis schulen worschipe hym; alle folkis schulen serue hym.

12 For he schal delyuer a pore man fro the miyti; and a pore man to whom was noon helpere.

13 He schal spare a pore man and nedi; and he schal make saaf the soulis of pore men.

14 He schal ayen bie the soulis of hem fro vsuris, and wickidnesse; and the name of hem is onourable bifor hym.

15 And he schal lyue, and me schal yyue to hym of the gold of Arabie; and thei schulen euere worschipe of hym, al dai thei schulen blesse hym.

16 Stidefastnesse schal be in the erthe, in the hiyeste places of mounteyns; the fruyt therof schal be enhaunsid aboue the Liban; and thei schulen blosme fro the citee, as the hey of erthe doith.

17 His name be blessid in to worldis; his name dwelle bifore the sunne. And all the lynagis of erthe schulen be blessid in hym; alle folkis schulen magnyfie hym.

18 Blessid be the Lord God of Israel; which aloone makith merueiylis.

19 Blessid be the name of his maieste with outen ende; and al erthe schal be fillid with his maieste; be it doon, be it doon.

20 'The preieris of Dauid, the sone of Ysay, ben endid.

PSALM 72

1 The 'title of the two and seuentithe salm. 'The salm of Asaph. God of Israel is ful good; to hem that ben of riytful herte.

2 But my feet weren moued almeest; my steppis weren sched out almeest.

3 For Y louede feruentli on wickid men; seynge the pees of synneris.

4 For biholdyng is not to the deth of hem; and stidefastnesse in the sikenesse of hem.

5 Thei ben not in the trauel of men; and thei schulen not be betun with men.

6 Therfore pride helde hem; thei weren hilid with her wickidnesse and vnfeithfulnesse.

7 The wickidnesse of hem cam forth as of fatnesse; thei yeden in to desire of herte.

8 Thei thouyten and spaken weiwardnesse; thei spaken wickidnesse an hiy.

9 Thei puttiden her mouth in to heuene; and her tunge passide in erthe.

10 Therfor my puple schal be conuertid here; and fulle daies schulen be foundun in hem.

11 And thei seiden, How woot God; and whether kunnyng is an heiye, 'that is, in heuene?

12 Lo! thilke synneris and hauynge aboundance in the world; helden richessis.

13 And Y seide, Therfor without cause Y iustifiede myn herte; and waischide myn hoondis among innocentis.

14 And Y was betun al dai; and my chastisyng was in morutidis.

15 If Y seide, Y schal telle thus; lo! Y repreuede the nacioun of thi sones.

16 I gesside, that Y schulde knowe this; trauel is bifore me.

17 Til Y entre in to the seyntuarie of God; and vndurstonde in the last thingis of hem.

18 Netheles for gilis thou hast put to hem; thou castidist hem doun, while thei weren reisid.

19 Hou ben thei maad into desolacioun; thei failiden sodeynli, thei perischiden for her wickidnesse.

20 As the dreem of men that risen; Lord, thou schalt dryue her ymage to nouyt in thi citee.

21 For myn herte is enflaumed, and my reynes ben chaungid; 22 and Y am dryuun to nouyt, and Y wiste not.

23 As a werk beeste Y am maad at thee; and Y am euere with thee.

24 Thou heldist my riythond, and in thi wille thou leddist me forth; and with glorie thou tokist me vp.

25 For whi what is to me in heuene; and what wolde Y of thee on erthe?

26 Mi fleische and myn herte failide; God of myn herte, and my part is God withouten ende.

27 For lo! thei that drawen awei fer hem silf fro thee, 'bi deedli synne, schulen perische; thou hast lost alle men that doen fornycacioun fro thee.

28 But it is good to me to cleue to God; and to sette myn hope in the Lord God. That Y telle alle thi prechyngis; in the yatis of the douyter of Syon.

PSALM 73

1 The title of the thre and seuentithe salm. The lernyng of Asaph. God, whi hast thou put awei in to the ende; thi strong veniaunce is wrooth on the scheep of thi leesewe?

2 Be thou myndeful of thi gadering togidere; which thou haddist in possessioun fro the bigynnyng. Thou ayenbouytist the yerde of thin eritage; the hille of Syon in which thou dwellidist ther ynne.

3 Reise thin hondis in to the prides of hem; hou grete thingis the enemy dide wickidli in the hooli.

4 And thei that hatiden thee; hadden glorie in the myddis of thi solempnete.

5 Thei settiden her signes, 'ethir baneris, signes on the hiyeste, as in the outgoing; and thei knewen not.

6 As in a wode of trees thei heweden doun with axis the yatis therof in to it silf; thei castiden doun it with an ax, and a brood fallinge ax.

7 Thei brenten with fier thi seyntuarie; thei defouliden the tabernacle of thi name in erthe.

8 The kynrede of hem seiden togidere in her herte; Make we alle the feest daies of God to ceesse fro the erthe.

9 We han not seyn oure signes, now 'no profete is; and he schal no more knowe vs.

10 God, hou long schal the enemye seie dispit? the aduersarie territh to ire thi name in to the ende.

11 Whi turnest thou awei thin hoond, and 'to drawe out thi riythond fro the myddis of thi bosum, til in to the ende?

12 Forsothe God oure kyng bifore worldis; wrouyte heelthe in the mydis of erthe.

13 Thou madist sad the see bi thi vertu; thou hast troblid the heedis of dragouns in watris.

14 Thou hast broke the heedis of 'the dragoun; thou hast youe hym to mete to the puplis of Ethiopiens.

15 Thou hast broke wellis, and strondis; thou madist drie the flodis of Ethan.

16 The dai is thin, and the niyt is thin; thou madist the moreutid and the sunne.

17 Thou madist alle the endis of erthe; somer and veer tyme, thou fourmedist tho.

18 Be thou myndeful of this thing, the enemye hath seid schenschip to the Lord; and the vnwijs puple hath excitid to ire thi name.

19 Bitake thou not to beestis men knoulechenge to thee; and foryete thou not in to the ende the soulis of thi pore men.

20 Biholde in to thi testament; for thei that ben maad derk of erthe, ben fillid with the housis of wickidnessis.

21 A meke man be not turned awei maad aschamed; a pore man and nedi schulen herie thi name.

22 God, rise vp, deme thou thi cause; be thou myndeful of thin vpbreidyngis, of tho that ben al dai of the vnwise man.

23 Foryete thou not the voices of thin enemyes; the pride of hem that haten thee, stieth euere.

PSALM 74

1 The title of the foure and seuentithe salm. 'To the ouercomere; leese thou not the salm of the song of Asaph.

2 God, we schulen knouleche to thee, 'we schulen knouleche; and we schulen inwardli clepe thi name.

3 We schulen telle thi merueilis; whanne Y schal take tyme, Y schal deme riytfulnesses.

4 The erthe is meltid, and alle that duellen ther ynne; Y confermede the pileris therof.

5 I seide to wickid men, Nyle ye do wickidli; and to trespassouris, Nyle ye enhaunce the horn.

6 Nyle ye reise an hiy youre horn; nyle ye speke wickidnesse ayens God.

7 For nether fro the eest, nethir fro the west, nethir fro desert hillis; for God is the iuge.

8 He mekith this man, and enhaunsith hym; for a cuppe of cleene wyn ful of meddling is in the hoond of the Lord.

9 And he bowide of this in to that; netheles the drast therof is not anyntischid; alle synneris of erthe schulen drinke therof.

10 Forsothe Y schal telle in to the world; Y schal synge to God of Jacob.

11 And Y schal breke alle the hornes of synneris; and the hornes of the iust man schulen be enhaunsid.

PSALM 75

1 The title of the fyue and seuentithe salm. To the victorie in orguns, 'the salm of the song of Asaph.

2 God is knowun in Judee; his name is greet in Israel.

3 And his place is maad in pees; and his dwellyng is in Syon.

4 Ther he brak poweris; bowe, scheeld, swerd, and batel.

5 And thou, God, liytnest wondirfuli fro euerlastynge hillis;

6 alle vnwise men of herte weren troblid. Thei slepten her sleep; and alle men founden no thing of richessis in her hondis.

7 Thei that stieden on horsis; slepten for thi blamyng, thou God of Jacob.

8 Thou art feerful, and who schal ayenstonde thee? fro that tyme thin ire.

9 Fro heuene thou madist doom herd; the erthe tremblide, and restide.

10 Whanne God roos vp in to doom; to make saaf al the mylde men of erthe.

11 For the thouyt of man schal knouleche to thee; and the relifs of thouyt schulen make a feeste dai to thee.

12 Make ye a vow, and yelde ye to youre Lord God; alle that bringen yiftis in the cumpas of it.

13 To God ferdful, and to him that takith awei the spirit of prynces; to the ferdful at the kyngis of erthe.

PSALM 76

1 The 'title of the sixte and seuentithe salm. 'To the ouercomere on Yditum, 'the salm of Asaph.

2 With my vois Y criede to the Lord; with my vois to God, and he yaf tent to me.

3 In the dai of my tribulacioun Y souyte God with myn hondis; in the nyyt 'to fore hym, and Y am not disseyued. Mi soule forsook to be coumfortid;

4 Y was myndeful of God, and Y delitide, and Y was exercisid; and my spirit failide.

5 Myn iyen bifore took wakyngis; Y was disturblid, and Y spak not.

6 I thouyte elde daies; and Y hadde in mynde euerlastinge yeeris.

7 And Y thouyte in the nyyt with myn herte; and Y was exercisid, and Y clensid my spirit.

8 Whether God schal caste awei with outen ende; ether schal he not lei to, that he be more plesid yit?

9 Ethir schal he kitte awei his merci into the ende; fro generacioun in to generacioun?

10 Ethir schal God foryete to do mercy; ethir schal he withholde his mercies in his ire?

11 And Y seide, Now Y bigan; this is the chaunging of the riythond of 'the hiye God.

12 I hadde mynde on the werkis of the Lord; for Y schal haue mynde fro the bigynnyng of thi merueilis.

13 And Y schal thenke in alle thi werkis; and Y schal be occupied in thi fyndyngis.

14 God, thi weie was in the hooli; what God is greet as oure God?

15 thou art God, that doist merueilis. Thou madist thi vertu knowun among puplis;

16 thou ayenbouytist in thi arm thi puple, the sones of Jacob and of Joseph.

17 God, watris sien thee, watris sien thee, and dredden; and depthis of watris weren disturblid.

18 The multitude of the soun of watris; cloudis yauen vois.

19 For whi thin arewis passen; the vois of thi thundir was in a wheel. Thi liytnyngis schyneden to the world; the erthe was moued, and tremblid.

20 Thi weie in the see, and thi pathis in many watris; and thi steppis schulen not be knowun.

21 Thou leddist forth thi puple as scheep; in the hond of Moyses and of Aaron.

PSALM 77

1 The 'title of the seuene and seuentithe salm. The lernyng of Asaph. Mi puple, perseyue ye my lawe; bowe youre eere in to the wordis of my mouth.

2 I schal opene my mouth in parablis; Y schal speke perfite resouns fro the bigynnyng.

3 Hou grete thingis han we herd, aud we han knowe tho; and oure fadris. telden to vs.

4 Tho ben not hid fro the sones of hem; in anothir generacioun. And thei telden the heriyngis of the Lord, and the vertues of hym; and hise merueilis, whyche he dide.

5 And he reiside witnessyng in Jacob; and he settide lawe in Israel. Hou grete thingis comaundide he to oure fadris, to make tho knowun to her sones;

6 that another generacioun knowe. Sones, that schulen be born, and schulen rise vp; schulen telle out to her sones.

7 That thei sette her hope in God, and foryete not the werkis of God; and that thei seke hise comaundementis.

8 Lest thei be maad a schrewid generacioun; and terrynge to wraththe, as the fadris of hem. A generacioun that dresside not his herte; and his spirit was not bileued with God.

9 The sones of Effraym, bendinge a bouwe and sendynge arowis; weren turned in the dai of batel.

10 Thei kepten not the testament of God; and thei nolden go in his lawe.

11 And thei foryaten hise benefices; and hise merueils, whiche he schewide to hem.

12 He dide merueils bifore the fadris of hem in the loond of Egipt; in the feeld of Taphneos.

13 He brak the see, and ledde hem thorou; and he ordeynede the watris as in a bouge.

14 And he ledde hem forth in a cloude of the dai; and al niyt in the liytnyng of fier.

15 He brak a stoon in deseert; and he yaf watir to hem as in a myche depthe.

16 And he ledde watir out of the stoon; and he ledde forth watris as floodis.

17 And thei 'leiden to yit to do synne ayens hym; thei exciti- den hiye God in to ire, in a place with out water.

18 And thei temptiden God in her hertis; that thei axiden mee- tis to her lyues.

19 And thei spaken yuel of God; thei seiden, Whether God may make redi a bord in desert?

20 For he smoot a stoon, and watris flowiden; and streemys yeden out in aboundaunce. Whether also he may yyue breed; ether make redi a bord to his puple?

21 Therfor the Lord herde, and delaiede; and fier was kin- delid in Jacob, and the ire of God stiede on Israel.

22 For thei bileueden not in God; nether hopiden in his heelthe.

23 And he comaundide to the cloudis aboue; and he openyde the yatis of heuene.

24 And he reynede to hem manna for to eete; and he yaf to hem breed of heuene.

25 Man eet the breed of aungels; he sent to hem meetis in aboundance.

26 He turnede ouere the south wynde fro heuene; and he brouyte in bi his vertu the weste wynde.

27 And he reynede fleischis as dust on hem; and 'he reinede volatils fethered, as the grauel of the see.

28 And tho felden doun in the myddis of her castels; aboute the tabernaclis of hem.

29 And thei eeten, and weren fillid greetli, and he brouyte her desire to hem;

30 thei weren not defraudid of her desier. Yit her metis weren in her mouth;

31 and the ire of God stiede on hem. And he killide the fatte men of hem; and he lettide the chosene men of Israel.

32 In alle these thingis thei synneden yit; and bileuede not in the merueils of God.

33 And the daies of hem failiden in vanytee; and the yeeris of hem faileden with haste.

34 Whanne he killide hem, thei souyten hym; and turneden ayen, and eerli thei camen to hym.

35 And thei bithouyten, that God is the helper of hem; and 'the hiy God is the ayenbier of hem.

36 And thei loueden hym in her mouth; and with her tunge thei lieden to hym.

37 Forsothe the herte of hem was not riytful with hym; nethir thei weren had feithful in his testament.

38 But he is merciful, and he schal be maad merciful to the synnes of hem; and he schal not destrie hem. And he dide greetli, to turne awei his yre; and he kyndelide not al his ire.

39 And he bithouyte, that thei ben fleische; a spirit goynge, and not turnynge ayen.

40 Hou oft maden thei hym wrooth in desert; thei stireden hym in to ire in a place with out watir.

41 And thei weren turned, and temptiden God; and thei wraththiden the hooli of Israel.

42 Thei bithouyten not on his hond; in the dai in the which he ayen bouyte hem fro the hond of the trobler.

43 As he settide hise signes in Egipt; and hise grete wondris in the feeld of Taphneos.

44 And he turnede the flodis of hem and the reynes of hem in to blood; that thei schulden not drynke.

45 He sente a fleisch flie in to hem, and it eet hem; and he sente a paddok, and it loste hem.

46 And he yaf the fruytis of hem to rust; and he yaf the trauels of hem to locustis.

47 And he killide the vynes of hem bi hail; and the moore trees of hem bi a frost.

48 And he bitook the beestis of hem to hail; and the posses- sioun of hem to fier.

49 He sente in to hem the ire of his indignacioun; indigna- cioun, and ire, and tribulacioun, sendingis in bi iuel aungels.

50 He made weie to the path of his ire, and he sparide not fro the deth of her lyues; and he closide togidere in deth the bees- tis of hem.

51 And he smoot al the first gendrid thing in the lond of Egipt; the first fruytis of alle the trauel of hem in the taberna- clis of Cham.

52 And he took awei his puple as scheep; and he ledde hem forth as a flok in desert.

53 And he ledde hem forth in hope, and thei dredden not; and the see hilide the enemyes of hem.

54 And he brouyte hem in to the hil of his halewyng; in to the hil which his riythond gat. And he castide out hethene men fro the face of hem; and bi lot he departide to hem the lond in a cord of delyng.

55 And he made the lynagis of Israel to dwelle in the taberna- clis of hem.

56 And thei temptiden, and wraththiden heiy God; and thei kepten not hise witnessyngis.

57 And thei turneden awei hem silf, and thei kepten not couenaunt; as her fadris weren turned in to a schrewid bouwe.

58 Thei stiriden him in to ire in her litle hillis; and thei ter- riden hym to indignacioun of her grauen ymagis.

59 God herde, and forsook; and brouyte to nouyt Israel gree- tli.

60 And he puttide awei the tabernacle of Sylo; his tabernacle where he dwellide among men.

61 And he bitook the vertu of hem in to caitiftee; and the fairnesse of hem in to the hondis of the enemye.

62 And he closide togidere his puple in swerd; and he dispi- side his erytage.

63 Fier eet the yonge men of hem; and the virgyns of hem weren not biweilid.

64 The prestis of hem fellen doun bi swerd; and the widewis of hem weren not biwept.

65 And the Lord was reisid, as slepynge; as miyti greetli fillid of wiyn.

66 And he smoot hise enemyes on the hynderere partis; he yaf to hem euerlastyng schenschipe.

67 And he puttide awei the tabernacle of Joseph; and he chees not the lynage of Effraym.

68 But he chees the lynage of Juda; he chees the hil of Syon, which he louede.

69 And he as an vnicorn bildide his hooli place; in the lond, which he foundide in to worldis.

70 And he chees Dauid his seruaunt, and took hym vp fro the flockis of scheep; he took hym fro bihynde scheep with lam- bren.

71 To feed Jacob his seruaunt; and Israel his eritage.

72 And he fedde hem in the innocens of his herte; and he ledde hem forth in the vndurstondyngis of his hondis.

PSALM 78

1 The 'title of the eiyte and seuentithe salm. Of Asaph.

God, hethene men cam in to thin eritage; thei defouliden thin hooli temple, thei settiden Jerusalem in to the keping of applis.

2 Thei settiden the slayn bodies of thi seruauntis, meetis to the volatilis of heuenes; the fleischis of thi seyntis to the beestis of the erthe.

3 Thei schedden out the blood of hem, as watir in the cumpas of Jerusalem; and noon was that biriede.

4 We ben maad schenschipe to oure neiyboris; mowynge and scornynge to hem, that ben in oure cumpas.

5 Lord, hou longe schalt thou be wrooth in to the ende? schal thi veniaunce be kyndelid as fier?

6 Schede out thin ire in to hethene men, that knowen not thee; and in to rewmes, that clepiden not thi name.

7 For thei eeten Jacob; and maden desolat his place.

8 Haue thou not mynde on oure elde wickidnesses; thi mercies bifore take vs soone, for we ben maad pore greetli.

9 God, oure heelthe, helpe thou vs, and, Lord, for the glorie of thi name delyuer thou vs; and be thou merciful to oure synnes for thi name.

10 Lest perauenture thei seie among hethene men, Where is the God of hem? and be he knowun among naciouns bifore oure iyen. The veniaunce of the blood of thi seruauntis, which is sched out; the weilyng of feterid men entre in thi siyt.

11 Vpe the greetnesse of thin arm; welde thou the sones of slayn men.

12 And yelde thou to oure neiyboris seuenfoold in the bosum of hem; the schenschip of hem, which thei diden schenschipfuli to thee, thou Lord.

13 But we that ben thi puple, and the scheep of thi leesewe; schulen knouleche to thee in to the world. In generacioun and in to generacioun; we schulen telle thin heriyng.

PSALM 79

1 The title of the nyne and seuentithe salm. To victorie; this salm is witnessing of Asaph for lilies.

2 Thou that gouernest Israel, yyue tent; that leedist forth Joseph as a scheep. Thou that sittist on cherubym; be schewid bifore Effraym,

3 Beniamyn, and Manasses. Stire thi power, and come thou; that thou make vs saaf.

4 God of vertues, turne thou vs; and schewe thi face, and we schulen be saaf.

5 Lord God of vertues; hou longe schalt thou be wrooth on the preier of thi seruaunt?

6 Hou longe schalt thou feede vs with the breed of teeris; and schalt yyue drynke to vs with teeris in mesure?

7 Thou hast set vs in to ayenseiyng to oure neiyboris; and oure enemyes han scornyde vs.

8 God of vertues, turne thou vs; and schewe thi face, and we schulen be saaf.

9 Thou translatidist a vyne fro Egipt; thou castidist out hethene men, and plauntidist it.

10 Thou were leeder of the weie in the siyt therof; and thou plauntidist the rootis therof, and it fillide the lond.

11 The schadewe therof hilide hillis; and the braunchis therof filliden the cedris of God.

12 It streiyte forth hise siouns til to the see, and the generacioun ther of 'til to the flood.

13 Whi hast thou destried the wal therof; and alle men that goen forth bi the weie gaderiden awei the grapis therof?

14 A boor of the wode distriede it; and a singuler wielde beeste deuouride it.

15 God of vertues, be thou turned; biholde thou fro heuene, and se, and visite this vyne.

16 And make thou it perfit, which thi riythond plauntide; and biholde thou on the sone of man, which thou hast confermyd to thee.

17 Thingis brent with fier, and vndurmyned; schulen perische for the blamyng of thi cheer.

18 Thin hond be maad on the man of thi riythond; and on the sone of man, whom thou hast confermed to thee.

19 And we departiden not fro thee; thou schalt quykene vs, and we schulen inwardli clepe thi name.

20 Lord God of vertues, turne thou vs; and schewe thi face, and we schulen be saaf.

PSALM 80

1 The title of the eiytetithe salm. To the ouercomer in the pressours of Asaph.

2 Make ye fulli ioye to God, oure helpere; synge ye hertli to God of Jacob.

3 Take ye a salm, and yyue ye a tympan; a myrie sautere with an harpe.

4 Blowe ye with a trumpe in Neomenye; in the noble dai of youre solempnite.

5 For whi comaundement is in Israel; and doom is to God of Jacob.

6 He settide that witnessing in Joseph; whanne he yede out of the lond of Egipt, he herde a langage, which he knew not.

7 He turnede a wei his bak fro birthens; hise hondis serueden in a coffyn.

8 In tribulacioun thou inwardli clepidist me, and Y delyuerede thee; Y herde thee in the hid place of tempest, Y preuede thee at the water of ayenseiyng.

9 My puple, here thou, and Y schal be witnesse ayens thee;

10 Israel, if thou herist me, a fresche God schal not be in thee, and thou schalt not worschipe an alien god.

11 For Y am thi Lord God, that ladde thee out of the lond of Egipt; make large thi mouth, and Y schal fille it.

12 And my puple herde not my vois; and Israel yaue not tente to me.

13 And Y lefte hem aftir the desiris of her herte; thei schulen go in her fyndyngis.

14 If my puple hadde herde me; if Israel hadde go in my weies.

15 For nouyt in hap Y hadde maad low her enemyes; and Y hadde send myn hond on men doynge tribulacioun to hem.

16 The enemyes of the Lord lieden to hym; and her tyme schal be in to worldis.

17 And he fedde hem of the fatnesse of whete; and he fillide hem with hony of the stoon.

PSALM 81

1 The title of the oon and eiytetithe salm. Of Asaph. God stood in the synagoge of goddis; forsothe he demeth goddis in the myddil.

2 Hou longe demen ye wickidnesse; and taken the faces of synneris?

3 Deme ye to the nedi man, and to the modirles child; iustifie ye the meke man and pore.

4 Raueische ye out a pore man; and delyuere ye the nedi man fro the hond of the synner.

5 Thei knewen not, nether vndirstoden, thei goen in derknessis; alle the foundementis of erthe schulen be moued.

6 I seide, Ye ben goddis; and alle ye ben the sones of hiy God.

7 But ye schulen die as men; and ye schulen falle doun as oon of the princis.

8 Ryse, thou God, deme thou the erthe; for thou schalt haue eritage in alle folkis.

PSALM 82

1 The title of the two and eiytetithe salm. The song of the salm of Asaph.

2 God, who schal be lijk thee? God, be thou not stille, nether be thou peesid.

3 For lo! thin enemyes sowneden; and thei that haten thee reisiden the heed.

4 Thei maden a wickid counsel on thi puple; and thei thouyten ayens thi seyntis.

5 Thei seiden, Come ye, and leese we hem fro the folk; and the name of Israel be no more hadde in mynde.

6 For thei thouyten with oon acord;

7 the tabernaclis of Ydumeys, and men of Ismael disposiden a testament togidere ayens thee. Moab, and Agarenus, Jebal, and Amon, and Amalech;

8 alienys with hem that dwellen in Tyre.

9 For Assur cometh with hem; thei ben maad in to help to the sones of Loth.

10 Make thou to hem as to Madian, and Sisara; as to Jabyn in the stronde of Sison.

11 Thei perischiden in Endor; thei weren maad as a toord of erthe.

12 Putte thou the prynces of hem as Oreb and Zeb; and Zebee and Salmana. Alle the princis of hem, that seiden;

13 Holde we bi eritage the seyntuarie of God.

14 My God, putte thou hem as a whele; and as stobil bifor the face of the wynde.

15 As fier that brenneth a wode; and as flawme brynnynge hillis.

16 So thou schalt pursue hem in thi tempeste; and thou schalt disturble hem in thin ire.

17 Lord, fille thou the faces of hem with schenschipe; and thei schulen seke thi name.

18 Be thei aschamed, and be thei disturblid in to world of world; and be thei schent and perische thei.

19 And knowe thei, that the Lord is name to thee; thou aloone art the hiyeste in ech lond.

PSALM 83

1 The title of the thre and eiytetithe salm. The salm of the sones of Chore.

2 Lord of vertues, thi tabernaclis ben greetli loued;

3 my soule coueitith, and failith in to the porchis of the Lord. Myn herte and my fleische; ful out ioyeden in to quyk God.

4 For whi a sparewe fyndith an hous to it silf; and a turtle fyndith a neste to it silf, where it 'schal kepe hise bryddis. Lord of vertues, thin auteris; my king, and my God.

5 Lord, blessid ben thei that dwellen in thin hous; thei schulen preise thee in to the worldis of worldis.

6 Blessid is the man, whos help is of thee; he hath disposid stiyngis in his herte,

7 in the valei of teeris, in the place which he hath set.

8 For the yyuer of the lawe schal yyue blessyng, thei schulen go fro vertu in to vertu; God of goddis schal be seyn in Sion.

9 Lord God of vertues, here thou my preier; God of Jacob, perseyue thou with eeris.

10 God, oure defender, biholde thou; and biholde in to the face of thi crist.

11 For whi o dai in thin hallis is bettere; than a thousynde. I chees to be 'an out cast in the hous of my God; more than to dwelle in the tabernaclis of synneris.

12 For God loueth merci and treuthe; the Lord schal yyue grace and glorie.

13 He schal not depriue hem fro goodis, that gon in innocence; Lord of vertues, blessid is the man, that hopith in thee.

PSALM 84

1 The title of the foure and eiytetithe salm. Of the sones of Chore.

2 Lord, thou hast blessid thi lond; thou hast turned awei the caitifte of Jacob.

3 Thou hast foryoue the wickidnesse of thi puple; thou hast hilid alle the synnes of hem.

4 Thou hast aswagid al thin ire; thou hast turned awei fro the ire of thin indignacioun.

5 God, oure helthe, conuerte thou vs; and turne awei thin ire fro vs.

6 Whether thou schalt be wrooth to vs withouten ende; ether schalt thou holde forth thin ire fro generacioun in to generacioun?

7 God, thou conuertid schalt quykene vs; and thi puple schal be glad in thee.

8 Lord, schewe thi merci to vs; and yyue thin helthe to vs.

9 I schal here what the Lord God schal speke in me; for he schal speke pees on his puple. And on hise hooli men; and on hem that ben turned to herte.

10 Netheles his helthe is niy men dredynge him; that glorie dwelle in oure lond.

11 Merci and treuthe metten hem silf; riytwisnesse and pees weren kissid.

12 Treuthe cam forth of erthe; and riytfulnesse bihelde fro heuene.

13 For the Lord schal yyue benignyte; and oure erthe schal yyue his fruyt.

14 Riytfulnesse schal go bifore him; and schal sette hise steppis in the weie.

PSALM 85

1 The 'title of the fyue and eiytetithe salm. The preier of Dauid. Lord, bowe doun thin eere, and here me; for Y am nedi and pore.

2 Kepe thou my lijf, for Y am holi; my God, make thou saaf thi seruaunt hopynge in thee.

3 Lord, haue thou merci on me, for Y criede al day to thee;

4 make thou glad the soule of thi seruaunt, for whi, Lord, Y haue reisid my soule to thee.

5 For thou, Lord, art swete and mylde; and of myche merci to alle men inwardli clepynge thee.

6 Lord, perseyue thou my preier with eeris; and yyue thou tente to the vois of my bisechyng.

7 In the dai of my tribulacioun Y criede to thee; for thou herdist me.

8 Lord, noon among goddis is lijk thee; and noon is euene to thi werkis.

9 Lord, alle folkis, whiche euere thou madist, schulen come, and worschipe bifore thee; and thei schulen glorifie thi name.

10 For thou art ful greet, and makinge merueils; thou art God aloone.

11 Lord, lede thou me forth in thi weie, and Y schal entre in thi treuthe; myn herte be glad, that it drede thi name.

12 Mi Lord God, Y schal knouleche to thee in al myn herte; and Y schal glorifie thi name withouten ende.

13 For thi merci is greet on me; and thou deliueridist my soule fro the lower helle.

14 God, wickid men han rise vp on me; and the synagoge of myyti men han souyt my lijf; and thei han not set forth thee in her siyt.

15 And thou, Lord God, doynge merci, and merciful; pacient, and of myche merci, and sothefast.

16 Biholde on me, and haue mercy on me, yyue thou the empire to thi child; and make thou saaf the sone of thin hand-mayden.

17 Make thou with me a signe in good, that thei se, that haten me, and be aschamed; for thou, Lord, hast helpid me, and hast coumfortid me.

PSALM 86

1 The title of the sixte and eiytetithe salm. 'The salm of the song of the sones of Chore.

The foundementis therof ben in hooli hillis;

2 the Lord loueth the yatis of Sion, more than alle the tabernaclis of Jacob.

3 Thou citee of God, with outen ende; gloriouse thingis ben seide of thee.

4 I schal be myndeful of Raab, and Babiloyne; knowynge me. Lo! aliens, and Tyre, and the puple of Ethiopiens; thei weren there.

5 Whether a man schal seie to Sion, And a man is born ther ynne; and that man altherhiyeste foundide it?

6 The Lord schal telle in the scripturis of puplis; and of these princis, that weren ther ynne.

7 As the dwellyng 'of alle that ben glad; is in thee.

PSALM 87

1 The title of the seuene and eiytetithe salm. The song of salm, to the sones of Chore, to victorie on Mahalat, for to answere, the lernyng of Heman Ezraite.

2 Lord God of myn helthe; Y criede in dai and nyyt bifore thee.

3 Mi preier entre bifore thi siyt; bowe doun thin eere to my preier.

4 For my soule is fillid with yuels; and my lijf neiyede to helle.

5 I am gessid with hem that goon doun in to the lake; Y am maad as a man with outen help,

6 and fre among deed men. As men woundid slepinge in sepulcris, of whiche men noon is myndeful aftir; and thei ben put awei fro thin hond.

7 Thei han put me in the lower lake; in derke places, and in the schadewe of deth.

8 Thi strong veniaunce is confermed on me; and thou hast brouyt in alle thi wawis on me.

9 Thou hast maad fer fro me my knowun; thei han set me abhomynacioun to hem silf. I am takun, and Y yede not out;

10 myn iyen weren sijk for pouert. Lord, Y criede to thee; al dai Y spredde abrood myn hondis to thee.

11 Whethir thou schalt do merueils to deed men; ether leechis schulen reise, and thei schulen knouleche to thee?

12 Whether ony man in sepulcre schal telle thi merci; and thi treuthe in perdicioun?

13 Whether thi merueilis schulen be knowun in derknessis; and thi riytfulnesse in the lond of foryetyng?

14 And, Lord, Y criede to thee; and erli my preier schal bifor come to thee.

15 Lord, whi puttist thou awei my preier; turnest awei thi face fro me?

16 I am pore, and in traueils fro my yongthe; sotheli Y am enhaunsid, and Y am maad low, and disturblid.

17 Thi wraththis passiden on me; and thi dredis disturbliden me.

18 Thei cumpassiden me as watir al dai; thei cumpassiden me togidere.

19 Thou madist fer fro me a frend and neiybore; and my knowun fro wretchidnesse.

PSALM 88

1 The title of the eiyte and eiytetithe salm. The lernyng of Ethan, Ezraite.

2 I schal synge with outen ende; the mercies of the Lord. In generacioun and in to generacioun; Y schal telle thi treuthe with my mouth.

3 For thou seidist, With outen ende merci schal be bildid in heuenes; thi treuthe schal be maad redi in tho.

4 I disposide a testament to my chosun men; Y swoor to Dauid, my seruaunt,

5 Til in to with outen ende I schal make redi thi seed. And Y schal bilde thi seete; in generacioun, and in to generacioun.

6 Lord, heuenes schulen knouleche thi merueilis; and thi treuthe in the chirche of seyntis.

7 For who in the cloudis schal be maad euene to the Lord; schal be lijk God among the sones of God?

8 God, which is glorified in the counsel of seyntis; is greet, and dreedful ouere alle that ben in his cumpas.

9 Lord God of vertues, who is lijk thee? Lord, thou art miyti, and thi treuthe is in thi cumpas.

10 Thou art Lord of the power of the see; forsothe thou aswagist the stiryng of the wawis therof.

11 Thou madist lowe the proude, as woundid; in the arm of thi vertu thou hast scaterid thin enemyes.

12 Heuenes ben thin, and erthe is thin; thou hast foundid the world, and the fulnesse therof;

13 thou madist of nouyt the north and the see. Thabor and Hermon schulen make ful out ioye in thi name;

14 thin arm with power. Thin hond be maad stidefast, and thi riythond be enhaunsid;

15 riytfulnesse and doom is the makyng redy of thi seete. Merci and treuthe schulen go bifore thi face;

16 blessid is the puple that kan hertli song. Lord, thei schulen go in the liyt of thi cheer;

17 and in thi name thei schulen make ful out ioye al dai; and thei schulen be enhaunsid in thi riytfulnesse.

18 For thou art the glorie of the vertu of hem; and in thi good plesaunce oure horn schal be enhaunsid.

19 For oure takyng vp is of the Lord; and of the hooli of Israel oure kyng.

20 Thanne thou spakist in reuelacioun to thi seyntis, and seidist, Y haue set help in the myyti; and Y haue enhaunsid the chosun man of my puple.

21 I foond Dauid, my seruaunt; Y anoyntide hym with myn hooli oile.

22 For myn hond schal helpe him; and myn arm schal conferme hym.

23 The enemye schal no thing profite in him; and the sone of wickidnesse schal not 'ley to, for to anoye him.

24 And Y schal sle hise enemyes fro his face; and Y schal turne in to fliyt hem that haten hym.

25 And my treuthe and mercy schal be with him; and his horn schal be enhaunsid in my name.

26 And Y schal sette his hond in the see; and his riyt hoond in flodis.

27 He schal inwardli clepe me, Thou art my fadir; my God, and the vptaker of myn heelthe.

28 And Y schal sette him the firste gendrid sone; hiyer than the kyngis of erthe.

29 With outen ende Y schal kepe my merci to hym; and my testament feithful to him.

30 And Y schal sette his seed in to the world of world; and his trone as the daies of heuene.

31 Forsothe if hise sones forsaken my lawe; and goen not in my domes.

32 If thei maken vnhooli my riytfulnessis; and kepen not my comaundementis.

33 I schal visite in a yerde the wickidnessis of hem; and in betyngis the synnes of hem.

34 But Y schal not scatere my mercy fro hym; and in my treuthe Y schal not anoye hym.

35 Nethir Y schal make vnhooli my testament; and Y schal not make voide tho thingis that comen forth of my lippis.

36 Onys Y swoor in myn hooli;

37 Y schal not lie to Dauid, his seed schal dwelle with outen ende.

38 And his trone as sunne in my siyt, and as a perfit mone with outen ende; and a feithful witnesse in heuene.

39 But thou hast put awei, and hast dispisid; and hast dilaied thi crist.

40 Thou hast turned awei the testament of thi seruaunt; thou madist vnhooli his seyntuarie in erthe.

41 Thou distriedist alle the heggis therof; thou hast set the stidefastnesse therof drede.

42 Alle men passynge bi the weie rauyschiden him; he is maad schenschipe to hise neiyboris.

43 Thou hast enhaunsid the riythond of men oppressinge him; thou hast gladid alle hise enemyes.

44 Thou hast turned awei the help of his swerd; and thou helpidist not hym in batel.

45 Thou destriedist him fro clensing; and thou hast hurtlid doun his seete in erthe.

46 Thou hast maad lesse the daies of his time; thou hast bisched him with schenschip.

47 Lord, hou longe turnest thou awei in to the ende; schal thin ire brenne out as fier?

48 Bithenke thou what is my substaunce; for whether thou hast ordeyned veynli alle the sones of men?

49 Who is a man, that schal lyue, and schal not se deth; schal delyuere his soule fro the hond of helle?

50 Lord, where ben thin elde mercies; as thou hast swore to Dauid in thi treuthe?

51 Lord, be thou myndeful of the schenschipe of thi seruauntis, of many hethene men; whiche Y helde togidere in my bosum.

52 Whiche thin enemyes, Lord, diden schenschipfuli; for thei dispisiden the chaungyng of thi crist.

53 Blessid be the Lord with outen ende; be it don, be it don.

PSALM 89

1 The title of the nyne and eiytetithe salm. The preier of Moises, the man of God. Lord, thou art maad help to vs; fro generacioun in to generacioun.

2 Bifore that hillis weren maad, ether the erthe and the world was formed; fro the world and in to the world thou art God.

3 Turne thou not awei a man in to lownesse; and thou seidist, Ye sones of men, be conuertid.

4 For a thousynde yeer ben bifore thin iyen; as yistirdai, which is passid, and as keping in the niyt.

5 The yeeris of hem schulen be; that ben had for nouyt.

6 Eerli passe he, as an eerbe, eerli florische he, and passe; in the euentid falle he doun, be he hard, and wexe drie.

7 For we han failid in thin ire; and we ben disturblid in thi strong veniaunce.

8 Thou hast set oure wickidnessis in thi siyt; oure world in the liytning of thi cheer.

9 For alle oure daies han failid; and we han failid in thin ire. Oure yeris schulen bithenke, as an yreyn;

10 the daies of oure yeeris ben in tho seuenti yeeris. Forsothe, if fourescoor yeer ben in myyti men; and the more tyme of hem is trauel and sorewe. For myldenesse cam aboue; and we schulen be chastisid.

11 Who knew the power of thin ire; and durste noumbre thin ire for thi drede?

12 Make thi riythond so knowun; and make men lerned in herte bi wisdom.

13 Lord, be thou conuertid sumdeel; and be thou able to be preied on thi seruauntis.

14 We weren fillid eerli with thi merci; we maden ful out ioye, and we delitiden in alle oure daies.

15 We weren glad for the daies in whiche thou madist vs meke; for the yeeris in whiche we siyen yuels.

16 Lord, biholde thou into thi seruauntis, and in to thi werkis; and dresse thou the sones of hem.

17 And the schynyng of oure Lord God be on vs; and dresse thou the werkis of oure hondis on vs, and dresse thou the werk of oure hondis.

PSALM 90

1 'The nyntithe salm. He that dwellith in the help of the hiyeste God; schal dwelle in the proteccioun of God of heuene.

2 He schal seie to the Lord, Thou art myn vptaker, and my refuit; my God, Y schal hope in him.

3 For he delyuered me fro the snare of hunteris; and fro a scharp word.

4 With hise schuldris he schal make schadowe to thee; and thou schalt haue hope vnder hise fetheris.

5 His treuthe schal cumpasse thee with a scheld; thou schalt not drede of nyytis drede.

6 Of an arowe fliynge in the dai, of a gobelyn goynge in derknessis; of asailing, and a myddai feend.

7 A thousynde schulen falle doun fro thi side, and ten thousynde fro thi riytside; forsothe it schal not neiye to thee.

8 Netheles thou schalt biholde with thin iyen; and thou schalt se the yelding of synneris.

9 For thou, Lord, art myn hope; thou hast set thin help altherhiyeste.

10 Yuel schal not come to thee; and a scourge schal not neiye to thi tabernacle.

11 For God hath comaundid to hise aungels of thee; that thei kepe thee in alle thi weies.

12 Thei schulen beere thee in the hondis; leste perauenture thou hirte thi foot at a stoon.

13 Thou schalt go on a snake, and a cocatrice; and thou schalt defoule a lioun and a dragoun.

14 For he hopide in me, Y schal delyuere hym; Y schal defende him, for he knew my name.

15 He criede to me, and Y schal here him, Y am with him in tribulacioun; Y schal delyuere him, and Y schal glorifie hym.

16 I schal fille hym with the lengthe of daies; and Y schal schewe myn helthe to him.

PSALM 91

1 The 'title of the oon and nyntithe salm. 'The salm of 'song, in the dai of sabath.

2 It is good to knouleche to the Lord; and to synge to thi name, thou hiyeste.

3 To schewe eerli thi merci; and thi treuthe bi nyyt.

4 In a sautrie of ten cordis; with song in harpe.

5 For thou, Lord, hast delitid me in thi makyng; and Y schal make ful out ioye in the werkis of thin hondis.

6 Lord, thi werkis ben magnefied greetli; thi thouytis ben maad ful depe.

7 An vnwise man schal not knowe; and a fool schal not vndirstonde these thingis.

8 Whanne synneris comen forth, as hey; and alle thei apperen, that worchen wickidnesse.

9 That thei perische in to the world of world; forsothe thou, Lord, art the hiyest, withouten ende. For lo!

10 Lord, thin enemyes, for lo! thin enemyes schulen perische; and alle schulen be scaterid that worchen wickidnesse.

11 And myn horn schal be reisid as an vnicorn; and myn eelde in plenteuouse merci.

12 And myn iye dispiside myn enemyes; and whanne wickid men rysen ayens me, myn eere schal here.

13 A iust man schal floure as a palm tree; he schal be multiplied as a cedre of Liban.

14 Men plauntid in the hous of the Lord; schulen floure in the porchis of the hous of oure God.

15 Yit thei schulen be multiplied in plenteuouse elde; and thei schulen be suffryng wel. That thei telle, that oure Lord God is riytful; and no wickidnesse is in hym.

PSALM 92

1 The two and nyntithe salm. The Lord hath regned, he is clothid with fairnesse; the Lord is clothid with strengthe, and hath gird hym silf.

2 For he made stidefast the world; that schal not be moued.

3 God, thi seete was maad redi fro that tyme; thou art fro the world. Lord, the flodis han reisid; the flodis han reisid her vois. Flodis reisiden her wawis; of the voicis of many watris.

4 The reisyngis of the see ben wondurful; the Lord is wondurful in hiye thingis.

5 Thi witnessingis ben maad able to be bileued greetli; Lord, holynesse bicometh thin hous, in to the lengthe of daies.

PSALM 93

1 The thre and nyntithe salm. God is Lord of veniauncis; God of veniauncis dide freli.

2 Be thou enhaunsid that demest the erthe; yelde thou yeldinge to proude men.

3 Lord, hou longe synneris; hou longe schulen synneris haue glorie?

4 Thei schulen telle out, and schulen speke wickidnesse; alle men schulen speke that worchen vnriytfulnesse.

5 Lord, thei han maad lowe thi puple; and thei han disesid thin eritage.

6 Thei killiden a widowe and a comelyng; and thei han slayn fadirles children and modirles.

7 And thei seiden, The Lord schal not se; and God of Jacob schal not vndurstonde.

8 Ye vnwise men in the puple, vndirstonde; and, ye foolis, lerne sum tyme.

9 Schal not he here, that plauntide the eere; ethere biholdith not he, that made the iye?

10 Schal not he repreue, that chastisith folkis; which techith man kunnyng?

11 The Lord knowith the thouytis of men; that tho ben veyne.

12 Blessid is the man, whom thou, Lord, hast lerned; and hast tauyt him of thi lawe.

13 That thou aswage hym fro yuele daies; til a diche be diggid to the synner.

14 For the Lord schal not putte awei his puple; and he schal not forsake his eritage.

15 Til riytfulnesse be turned in to dom; and who ben niy it, alle that ben of riytful herte.

16 Who schal rise with me ayens mysdoeris; ether who schal stonde with me ayens hem that worchen wickidnesse?

17 No but for the Lord helpide me; almest my soule hadde dwellid in helle.

18 If Y seide, My foot was stirid; Lord, thi merci helpide me.

19 Aftir the multitude of my sorewis in myn herte; thi coumfortis maden glad my soule.

20 Whether the seete of wickidnesse cleueth to thee; that makist trauel in comaundement?

21 Thei schulen take ayens the soule of a iust man; and thei schulen condempne innocent blood.

22 And the Lord was maad to me in to refuyt; and my God was maad in to the help of myn hope.

23 And he schal yelde to hem the wickidnesse of hem; and in the malice of hem he schal lese hem, oure Lord God schal lese hem.

PSALM 94

1 The foure and nyntithe salm. Come ye, make we ful out ioie to the Lord; hertli synge we to God, oure heelthe.

2 Bifore ocupie we his face in knowleching; and hertli synge we to him in salmes.

3 For God is a greet Lord, and a greet king aboue alle goddis; for the Lord schal not putte awei his puple.

4 For alle the endis of erthe ben in his hond; and the hiynesses of hillis ben hise.

5 For the see is his, and he made it; and hise hondis formeden the drie lond.

6 Come ye, herie we, and falle we doun bifore God, wepe we bifore the Lord that made vs;

7 for he is oure Lord God. And we ben the puple of his lesewe; and the scheep of his hond.

8 If ye han herd his vois to dai; nyle ye make hard youre hertis.

9 As in the terryng to wraththe; bi the dai of temptacioun in desert. Where youre fadris temptiden me; thei preueden and sien my werkis.

10 Fourti yeer I was offendid to this generacioun; and Y seide, Euere thei erren in herte.

11 And these men knewen not my weies; to whiche Y swoor in myn ire, thei schulen not entre in to my reste.

PSALM 95

1 The fyue and nyntithe salm hath no title. Singe ye a newe song to the Lord; al erthe, synge ye to the Lord.

2 Synge ye to the Lord, and blesse ye his name; telle ye his heelthe fro dai in to dai.

3 Telle ye his glorie among hethene men; hise merueilis among alle puplis.

4 For the Lord is greet, and worthi to be preisid ful myche; he is ferdful aboue alle goddis.

5 For alle the goddis of hethene men ben feendis; but the Lord made heuenes.

6 Knouleching and fairnesse is in his siyt; hoolynesse and worthi doyng is in his halewing.

7 Ye cuntrees of hethene men, brynge to the Lord, bringe ye glorye and onour to the Lord;

8 bringe ye to the Lord glorie to hys name. Take ye sacrificis, and entre ye in to the hallis of hym;

9 herie ye the Lord in his hooli halle. Al erthe be moued of his face;

10 seie ye among hethene men, that the Lord hath regned. And he hath amendid the world, that schal not be moued; he schal deme puplis in equite.

11 Heuenes be glad, and the erthe make ful out ioye, the see and the fulnesse therof be moued togidere; feeldis schulen make ioye,

12 and alle thingis that ben in tho. Thanne alle the trees of wodis schulen make ful out ioye, for the face of the Lord, for he cometh;

13 for he cometh to deme the erthe. He schal deme the world in equite; and puplis in his treuthe.

PSALM 96

1 The sixe and nyntithe salm. The Lord hath regned, the erthe make ful out ioye; many ilis be glad.

2 Cloude and derknesse in his cumpas; riytfulnesse and doom is amending of his seete.

3 Fier schal go bifore him; and schal enflawme hise enemyes in cumpas.

4 Hise leitis schyneden to the world; the erthe siy, and was moued.

5 Hillis as wax fletiden doun fro the face of the Lord; al erthe fro the face of the Lord.

6 Heuenes telden his riytfulnesse; and alle puplis sien his glorie.

7 Alle that worschipen sculptilis be schent, and thei that han glorie in her symelacris; alle ye aungels of the Lord, worschipe him.

8 Sion herde, and was glad, and the douytris of Juda maden ful out ioye; for 'thi domes, Lord.

9 For thou, Lord, art the hiyeste on al erthe; thou art greetli enhaunsid ouere alle goddis.

10 Ye that louen the Lord, hate yuel; the Lord kepith the soulis of hise seyntis; he schal delyuer hem fro the hond of the synner.

11 Liyt is risun to the riytful man; and gladnesse to riytful men of herte.

12 Juste men, be ye glad in the Lord; and knouleche ye to the mynde of his halewyng.

PSALM 97

1 The seuen and nyntithe salm hath no title. Singe ye a newe song to the Lord; for he hath do merueils. His riyt hond and his hooli arm; hath maad heelthe to hym.

2 The Lord hath maad knowun his heelthe; in the siyt of hethene men he hath schewid his riytfulnesse.

3 He bithouyte on his merci; and on his treuthe, to the hous of Israel. Alle the endis of erthe; sien the heelthe of oure God.

4 Al erthe, make ye hertli ioye to God; synge ye, and make ye ful out ioye, and seie ye salm.

5 Singe ye to the Lord in an harpe, in harpe and vois of salm;

6 in trumpis betun out with hamer, and in vois of a trumpe of horn. Hertli synge ye in the siyt of the Lord, the king; the see and the fulnesse therof be moued;

7 the world, and thei that dwellen therynne.

8 Flodis schulen make ioie with hond, togidere hillis schulen make ful out ioye, for siyt of the Lord;

9 for he cometh to deme the erthe. He schal deme the world in riytfulnesse; and puplis in equite.

PSALM 98

1 The eiyte and nyntithe salm. The Lord hath regned, puplis ben wrooth; thou that sittist on cherubyn, the erthe be moued.

2 The Lord is greet in Sion; and hiy aboue alle puplis.

3 Knouleche thei to thi greet name, for it is ferdful and hooli;

4 and the onour of the king loueth doom. Thou hast maad redi dressyngis; thou hast maad doom and riytfulnesse in Jacob.

5 Enhaunse ye oure Lord God; and worschipe ye the stool of hise feet, for it is hooli.

6 Moises and Aaron weren among hise preestis; and Samuel was among hem that inwardli clepen his name. Thei inwardli clepiden the Lord, and he herde hem;

7 in a piler of cloude he spak to hem. Thei kepten hise witnessyngis; and the comaundement which he yaf to hem.

8 Oure Lord God, thou herdist hem; God, thou were merciful to hem, and thou tokist veniaunce on al her fyndyngis.

9 Enhaunse ye oure Lord God, and worschipe ye in his hooli hil; for oure Lord God is hooli.

PSALM 99

1 The titil of the nyne and nyntithe salm. 'A salm to knouleche; 'in Ebrew 'thus, A salm for knouleching.

2 Al erthe, singe ye hertli to God; serue ye the Lord in gladnesse. Entre ye in his siyt; in ful out ioiyng.

3 Wite ye, that the Lord hym silf is God; he made vs, and not we maden vs. His puple, and the scheep of his lesewe,

4 entre ye in to hise yatis in knoulechyng; entre ye in to hise porchis, 'knouleche ye to him in ympnes.

5 Herye ye his name, for the Lord is swete, his merci is with outen ende; and his treuthe is in generacioun and in to generacioun.

PSALM 100

1 The titil of the hundrid salm. 'The salm of Dauid. Lord, Y schal synge to thee; merci and doom.

2 I schal synge, and Y schal vndurstonde in a weie with out wem; whanne thou schalt come to me. I yede perfitli in the innocence of myn herte; in the myddil of myn hous.

3 I settide not forth bifore myn iyen an vniust thing; Y hatide hem that maden trespassyngis.

4 A schrewide herte cleuede not to me; Y knewe not a wickid man bowynge awei fro me.

5 I pursuede hym; that bacbitide priueli his neiybore. With the proude iye and an herte vnable to be fillid; Y eet not with this.

6 Myn iyen weren to the feithful men of erthe, that thei sitte with me; he that yede in a weie with out wem, mynystride to me.

7 He that doith pride, schal not dwelle in the myddil of myn hous; he that spekith wickid thingis, seruede not in the siyt of myn iyen.

8 In the morutid Y killide alle the synners of erthe; that Y schulde leese fro the citee of the Lord alle men worchynge wickidnesse.

PSALM 101

1 The title of the 'hundrid and o salm. The preier of a pore man, whanne he was angwishid, and schedde out his speche bifore the Lord.

2 Lord, here thou my preier; and my crie come to thee.

3 Turne not awei thi face fro me; in what euere dai Y am troblid, bowe doun thin eere to me. In what euere day Y schal inwardli clepe thee; here thou me swiftli.

4 For my daies han failid as smoke; and my boonus han dried vp as critouns.

5 I am smytun as hei, and myn herte dried vp; for Y haue foryete to eete my breed.

6 Of the vois of my weilyng; my boon cleuede to my fleische.

7 I am maad lijk a pellican of wildirnesse; Y am maad as a niyt crowe in an hous.

8 I wakide; and Y am maad as a solitarie sparowe in the roof.

9 Al dai myn enemyes dispisiden me; and thei that preisiden me sworen ayens me.

10 For Y eet aschis as breed; and Y meddlide my drinke with weping.

11 Fro the face of the ire of thin indignacioun; for thou reisinge me hast hurtlid me doun.

12 Mi daies boweden awei as a schadewe; and Y wexede drie as hei.

13 But, Lord, thou dwellist with outen ende; and thi memorial in generacioun and in to generacioun.

14 Lord, thou risinge vp schalt haue merci on Sion; for the tyme 'to haue merci therof cometh, for the tyme cometh.

15 For the stones therof plesiden thi seruauntis; and thei schulen haue merci on the lond therof.

16 And, Lord, hethen men schulen drede thi name; and alle kingis of erthe schulen drede thi glori.

17 For the Lord hath bildid Sion; and he schal be seen in his glorie.

18 He bihelde on the preier of meke men; and he dispiside not the preier of hem.

19 Be these thingis writun in an othere generacioun; and the puple that schal be maad schal preise the Lord.

20 For he bihelde fro his hiye hooli place; the Lord lokide fro heuene in to erthe.

21 For to here the weilingis of feterid men; and for to vnbynde the sones of slayn men.

22 That thei telle in Sion the name of the Lord; and his preising in Jerusalem.

23 In gaderinge togidere puplis in to oon; and kingis, that thei serue the Lord.

24 It answeride to hym in the weie of his vertu; Telle thou to me the fewnesse of my daies.

25 Ayenclepe thou not me in the myddil of my daies; thi yeris ben in generacioun and in to generacioun.

26 Lord, thou foundidist the erthe in the bigynnyng; and heuenes ben the werkis of thin hondis.

27 Tho schulen perische, but thou dwellist perfitli; and alle schulen wexe eelde as a clooth. And thou schalt chaunge hem as an hiling, and tho schulen be chaungid;

28 but thou art the same thi silf, and thi yeeris schulen not faile.

29 The sones of thi seruauntis schulen dwelle; and the seed of hem schal be dressid in to the world.

PSALM 102

1 The title of 'hundred and secounde salm. 'Of Dauid. Mi soule, blesse thou the Lord; and alle thingis that ben with ynne me, blesse his hooli name.

2 Mi soule, blesse thou the Lord; and nyle thou foryete alle the yeldyngis of him.

3 Which doith merci to alle thi wickidnessis; which heelith alle thi sijknessis.

4 Which ayenbieth thi lijf fro deth; which corowneth thee in merci and merciful doyngis.

5 Which fillith thi desijr in goodis; thi yongthe schal be renulid as the yongthe of an egle.

6 The Lord doynge mercies; and doom to alle men suffringe wrong.

7 He made hise weies knowun to Moises; hise willis to the sones of Israel.

8 The Lord is merciful doer, and merciful in wille; longe abidinge, and myche merciful.

9 He schal not be wrooth with outen ende; and he schal not thretne with outen ende.

10 He dide not to vs aftir oure synnes; nether he yeldide to vs aftir oure wickidnessis.

11 For bi the hiynesse of heuene fro erthe; he made strong his merci on men dredynge hym.

12 As myche as the eest is fer fro the west; he made fer oure wickidnessis fro vs.

13 As a fadir hath merci on sones, the Lord hadde merci on men dredynge him;

14 for he knewe oure makyng.

15 He bithouyte that we ben dust, a man is as hey; his dai schal flowre out so as a flour of the feeld.

16 For the spirit schal passe in hym, and schal not abide; and schal no more knowe his place.

17 But the merci of the Lord is fro with out bigynnyng, and til in to with outen ende; on men dredinge hym. And his riytfulnesse is in to the sones of sones;

18 to hem that kepen his testament. And ben myndeful of hise comaundementis; to do tho.

19 The Lord hath maad redi his seete in heuene; and his rewme schal be lord of alle.

20 Aungels of the Lord, blesse ye the Lord; ye myyti in vertu, doynge his word, to here the vois of hise wordis.

21 Alle vertues of the Lord, blesse ye the Lord; ye mynystris of hym that doen his wille.

22 Alle werkis of the Lord, blesse ye the Lord, in ech place of his lordschipe; my soule, blesse thou the Lord.

PSALM 103

1 The hundrid and thridde salm. Mi soule, blesse thou the Lord; my Lord God, thou art magnyfied greetli. Thou hast clothid knouleching and fairnesse; and thou art clothid with liyt,

2 as with a cloth. And thou stretchist forth heuene as a skyn;

3 and thou hilist with watris the hiyer partis therof. Which settist a cloude thi stiyng; which goest on the fetheris of wyndis.

4 Which makist spiritis thin aungels; and thi mynystris brennynge fier.

5 Which hast foundid the erthe on his stablenesse; it schal not be bowid in to the world of world.

6 The depthe of watris as a cloth is the clothing therof; watris schulen stonde on hillis.

7 Tho schulen fle fro thi blamyng; men schulen be aferd of the vois of thi thundur.

8 Hillis stien vp, and feeldis goen doun; in to the place which thou hast foundid to tho.

9 Thou hast set a terme, which tho schulen not passe; nether tho schulen be turned, for to hile the erthe.

10 And thou sendist out wellis in grete valeis; watris schulen passe bitwix the myddil of hillis.

11 Alle the beestis of the feeld schulen drynke; wielde assis schulen abide in her thirst.

12 Briddis of the eir schulen dwelle on tho; fro the myddis of stoonys thei schulen yyue voices.

13 And thou moistist hillis of her hiyer thingis; the erthe schal be fillid of the fruyt of thi werkis.

14 And thou bringist forth hei to beestis; and eerbe to the seruyce of men. That thou bringe forth breed of the erthe; 15 and that wiyn make glad the herte of men. That he make glad the face with oile; and that breed make stidefast the herte of man.

16 The trees of the feeld schulen be fillid, and the cedris of the Liban, whiche he plauntide;

17 sparewis schulen make nest there. The hous of the gerfaukun is the leeder of tho;

18 hiye hillis ben refute to hertis; a stoon is refutt to irchouns.

19 He made the moone in to tymes; the sunne knewe his goyng doun.

20 Thou hast set derknessis, and nyyt is maad; alle beestis of the wode schulen go ther ynne.

21 Liouns whelpis rorynge for to rauysche; and to seke of God meete to hem silf.

22 The sunne is risun, and tho ben gaderid togidere; and tho schulen be set in her couchis.

23 A man schal go out to his werk; and to his worching, til to the euentid.

24 Lord, thi werkis ben magnefiede ful myche, thou hast maad alle thingis in wisdom; the erthe is fillid with thi possessioun.

25 This see is greet and large to hondis; there ben crepinge beestis, of which is noon noumbre. Litil beestis with grete; 26 schippis schulen passe there. This dragoun which thou hast formyd; for to scorne hym.

27 Alle thingis abiden of thee; that thou yyue to hem meete in tyme.

28 Whanne thou schalt yyue to hem, thei schulen gadere; whanne thou schalt opene thin hond, alle thingis schulen be fillid with goodnesse.

29 But whanne thou schalt turne awey the face, thei schulen be disturblid; thou schalt take awei the spirit of them, and thei schulen faile; and thei schulen turne ayen in to her dust.

30 Sende out thi spirit, and thei schulen be formed of the newe; and thou schalt renule the face of the erthe.

31 The glorie of the Lord be in to the world; the Lord schal be glad in hise werkis.

32 Which biholdith the erthe, and makith it to tremble; which touchith hillis, and tho smoken.

33 I schal singe to the Lord in my lijf; Y schal seie salm to my God, as longe as Y am.

34 Mi speche be myrie to him; forsothe Y schal delite in the Lord.

35 Synneris faile fro the erthe, and wickid men faile, so that thei be not; my soule, blesse thou the Lord.

PSALM 104

1 The title of the hundrid and fourthe salm. Alleluya. Knouleche ye to the Lord, and inwardli clepe ye his name; telle ye hise werkis among hethen men.

2 Synge ye to hym, and seie ye salm to him, and telle ye alle hise merueylis;

3 be ye preisid in his hooli name. The herte of men sekynge the Lord be glad;

4 seke ye the Lord, and be ye confermed; seke ye euere his face.

5 Haue ye mynde on hise merueilis, whiche he dide; on his grete wondris, and domes of his mouth.

6 The seed of Abraham, his seruaunt; the sones of Jacob, his chosun man.

7 He is oure Lord God; hise domes ben in al the erthe.

8 He was myndeful of his testament in to the world; of the word which he comaundide in to a thousynde generaciouns.

9 Which he disposide to Abraham; and of his ooth to Isaac.

10 And he ordeynede it to Jacob in to a comaundement; and to Israel in to euerlastinge testament.

11 And he seide, I shal yiue to thee the lond of Canaan; the cord of youre eritage.

12 Whanne thei weren in a litil noumbre; and the comelingis of hem weren ful fewe.

13 And thei passiden fro folk in to folk; and fro a rewme in to another puple.

14 He lefte not a man to anoye hem; and he chastiside kyngis for hem.

15 Nile ye touche my cristis; and nyle ye do wickidli among my prophetis.

16 And God clepide hungir on erthe; and he wastide al the stidefastnesse of breed.

17 He sente a man bifore hem; Joseph was seeld in to a seruaunt.

18 Thei maden lowe hise feet in stockis, irun passide by his soule; til the word of him cam.

19 The speche of the Lord enflawmede him;

20 the king sente and vnbond hym; the prince of puplis sente and delyuerede him.

21 He ordeynede him the lord of his hous; and the prince of al his possessioun.

22 That he schulde lerne hise princis as him silf; and that he schulde teche hise elde men prudence.

23 And Israel entride in to Egipt; and Jacob was a comeling in the lond of Cham.

24 And God encreesside his puple greetli; and made hym stidefast on hise enemyes.

25 He turnede the herte of hem, that thei hatiden his puple; and diden gile ayens hise seruauntis.

26 He sent Moises, his seruaunt; thilke Aaron, whom he chees.

27 He puttide in hem the wordis of hise myraclis; and of hise grete wondris in the lond of Cham.

28 He sente derknessis, and made derk; and he made not bitter hise wordis.

29 He turnede the watris of hem in to blood; and he killide the fischis of hem.

30 And the lond of hem yaf paddoks; in the priue places of the kyngis of hem.

31 God seide, and a fleische flie cam; and gnattis in alle the coostis of hem.

32 He settide her reynes hail; fier brennynge in the lond of hem.

33 And he smoot the vynes of hem, and the fige trees of hem; and al to-brak the tree of the coostis of hem.

34 He seide, and a locuste cam; and a bruk of which was noon noumbre.

35 And it eet al the hey in the lond of hem; and it eet al the fruyt of the lond of hem.

36 And he killide ech the firste gendrid thing in the lond of hem; the firste fruitis of alle the trauel of hem.

37 And he ledde out hem with siluer and gold; and noon was sijk in the lynagis of hem.

38 Egipt was glad in the goyng forth of hem; for the drede of hem lai on Egipcians.

39 He spredde abrood a cloude, in to the hiling of hem; and fier, that it schynede to hem bi nyyt.

40 Thei axiden, and a curlew cam; and he fillide hem with the breed of heuene.

41 He brak a stoon, and watris flowiden; floodis yeden forth in the drye place.

42 For he was myndeful of his hooli word; which he hadde to Abraham, his child.

43 And he ledde out his puple in ful out ioiyng; and hise chosun men in gladnesse.

44 And he yaf to hem the cuntreis of hethen men; and thei hadden in possessioun the trauels of puplis.

45 That thei kepe hise iustifiyngis; and seke his lawe.

PSALM 105

1 The 'title of the hundrid and fifthe salm. Alleluya. Kouleche ye to the Lord, for he is good; for his mercy is with outen ende.

2 Who schal speke the powers of the Lord; schal make knowun alle hise preisyngis?

3 Blessid ben thei that kepen dom; and doon riytfulnesse in al tyme.

4 Lord, haue thou mynde on vs in the good plesaunce of thi puple; visite thou vs in thin heelthe.

5 To se in the goodnesse of thi chosun men, to be glad in the gladnes of thi folk; that thou be heried with thin eritage.

6 We han synned with oure fadris; we han do vniustli, we han do wickidnesse.

7 Oure fadris in Egipt vndirstoden not thi merueils; thei weren not myndeful of the multitude of thi merci. And thei stiynge in to the see, in to the reed see, terreden to wraththe;

8 and he sauede hem for his name, that 'he schulde make knowun his power.

9 And he departide the reed see, and it was dried; and he lede forth hem in the depthis of watris as in deseert.

10 And he sauede hem fro the hond of hateris; and he ayen bouyte hem fro the hond of the enemye.

11 And the watir hilide men troublynge hem; oon of hem abood not.

12 And thei bileueden to hise wordis; and thei preisiden the heriynge of hym.

13 Thei hadden 'soone do, thei foryaten hise werkis; and thei abididen not his councel.

14 And thei coueitiden coueitise in deseert; and temptiden God in a place with out watir.

15 And he yaf to hem the axyng of hem; and he sente fulnesse in to the soulis of hem.

16 And thei wraththiden Moyses in the castels; Aaron, the hooli of the Lord.

17 The erthe was opened, and swolewid Datan; and hilide on the congregacioun of Abiron.

18 And fier brente an hiye in the synagoge of hem; flawme brente synneris.

19 And thei maden a calf in Oreb; and worschipiden a yotun ymage.

20 And thei chaungiden her glorie; in to the liknesse of a calf etynge hei.

21 Thei foryaten God, that sauede hem, that dide grete werkis in Egipt,

22 merueils in the lond of Cham; feerdful thingis in the reed see.

23 And God seide, that he wolde leese hem; if Moises, his chosun man, hadde not stonde in the brekyng of his siyt. That he schulde turne awei his ire; lest he loste hem.

24 And thei hadden the desirable lond for nouyt, thei bileueden not to his word, and thei grutchiden in her tabernaclis;

25 thei herden not the vois of the Lord.

26 And he reiside his hond on hem; to caste doun hem in desert.

27 And to caste awei her seed in naciouns; and to leese hem in cuntreis.

28 And thei maden sacrifice to Belfagor; and thei eeten the sacrificis of deed beestis.

29 And thei wraththiden God in her fyndyngis; and fallyng was multiplied in hem.

30 And Fynees stood, and pleeside God; and the veniaunce ceesside.

31 And it was arrettid to hym to riytfulnesse; in generacioun and in to generacioun, til in to with outen ende.

32 And thei wraththiden God at the watris of ayenseiyng; and Moises was trauelid for hem, for thei maden bittere his spirit,

33 and he departide in his lippis.

34 Thei losten not hethen men; whiche the Lord seide to hem.

35 And thei weren meddlid among hethene men, and lerneden the werkis of hem,

36 and serueden the grauen ymagis of hem; and it was maad to hem in to sclaundre.

37 And thei offriden her sones; and her douytris to feendis.

38 And thei schedden out innocent blood, the blood of her sones and of her douytris; whiche thei sacrificiden to the grauun ymagis of Chanaan.

39 And the erthe was slayn in bloodis, and was defoulid in the werkis of hem; and thei diden fornicacioun in her fyndyngis.

40 And the Lord was wrooth bi strong veniaunce ayens his puple; and hadde abhominacioun of his eritage.

41 And he bitook hem in to the hondis of hethene men; and thei that hatiden hem, weren lordis of hem.

42 And her enemyes diden tribulacioun to hem, and thei weren mekid vndir the hondis of enemyes;

43 ofte he delyuerede hem. But thei wraththiden hym in her counsel; and thei weren maad low in her wickidnessis.

44 And he siye, whanne thei weren set in tribulacioun; and he herde the preyer of hem.

45 And he was myndeful of his testament; and it repentide hym bi the multitude of his merci.

46 And he yaf hem in to mercies; in the siyt of alle men, that hadden take hem.

47 Oure Lord God, make thou vs saaf; and gadere togidere vs fro naciouns. That we knouleche to thin hooli name; and haue glorie in thi preisyng.

48 Blessid be the Lord God of Israel fro the world and til in to the world; and al the puple schal seye, Be it don, be it don.

PSALM 106

1 The 'title of the hundrid and sixte salm. Alleluya. Knouleche ye to the Lord, for he is good; for his merci is in to the world.

2 Sei thei, that ben ayen bouyt of the Lord; whiche he ayen bouyte fro the hond of the enemye, fro cuntreis he gaderide hem togidere.

3 Fro the risyng of the sunne, and fro the goyng doun; fro the north, and fro the see.

4 Thei erriden in wildirnesse, in a place with out watir; thei founden not weie of the citee of dwellyng place.

5 Thei weren hungri and thirsti; her soule failide in hem.

6 And thei crieden to the Lord, whanne thei weren set in tribulacioun; and he delyuerede hem fro her nedynesses.

7 And he ledde forth hem in to the riyt weie; that thei schulden go in to the citee of dwelling.

8 The mercies of the Lord knouleche to hym; and hise merueilis knouleche to the sones of men.

9 For he fillide a voide man; and he fillide with goodis an hungry man.

10 God delyuerede men sittynge in derknessis, and in the schadowe of deth; and men prisoned in beggerye and in yrun.

11 For thei maden bitter the spechis of God; and wraththiden the councel of the hiyeste.

12 And the herte of hem was maad meke in trauelis; and thei weren sijk, and noon was that helpide.

13 And thei crieden to the Lord, whanne thei weren set in tribulacioun; and he delyuerede hem from her nedynesses.

14 And he ledde hem out of derknessis, and schadowe of deth; and brak the boondis of hem.

15 The mercies of the Lord knouleche to hym; and hise merueils knouleche to the sones of men.

16 For he al to-brak brasun yatis; and he brak yrun barris.

17 He vptook hem fro the weie of her wickidnesse; for thei weren maad lowe for her vnriytfulnesses.

18 The soule of hem wlatide al mete; and thei neiyeden 'til to the yatis of deth.

19 And thei crieden to the Lord, whanne thei weren set in tribulacioun; and he delyuerede hem fro her nedynessis.

20 He sente his word, and heelide hem; and delyuerede hem fro the perischingis of hem.

21 The mercies of the Lord knouleche to hym; and hise merueils to the sones of men.

22 And offre thei the sacrifice of heriyng; and telle thei hise werkis in ful out ioiyng.

23 Thei that gon doun in to the see in schippis; and maken worching in many watris.

24 Thei sien the werkis of the Lord; and hise merueilis in the depthe.

25 He seide, and the spirit of tempest stood; and the wawis therof weren arerid.

26 Thei stien til to heuenes, and goen doun 'til to the depthis; the soule of hem failide in yuelis.

27 Thei weren troblid, and thei weren moued as a drunkun man; and al the wisdom of hem was deuourid.

28 And thei crieden to the Lord, whanne thei weren set in tribulacioun; and he ledde hem out of her nedynessis.

29 And he ordeynede the tempest therof in to a soft wynde; and the wawis therof weren stille.

30 And thei weren glad, for tho weren stille; and he ladde hem forth in to the hauene of her wille.

31 The mercies of the Lord knouleche to hym; and hise merueilis to the sones of men.

32 And enhaunse thei him in the chirche of the puple; and preise thei him in the chaier of eldre men.

33 He hath set floodis in to deseert; and the out goingis of watris in to thirst.

34 He hath set fruytful lond in to saltnesse; for the malice of men dwellyng ther ynne.

35 He hath set deseert in to pondis of watris; and erthe with out watir in to outgoyngis of watris.

36 And he settide there hungri men; and thei maden a citee of dwelling.

37 And thei sowiden feeldis, and plauntiden vynes; and maden fruyt of birthe.

38 And he blesside hem, and thei weren multiplied greetli; and he made not lesse her werk beestis.

39 And thei weren maad fewe; and thei weren trauelid of tribulacioun of yuelis and of sorewis.

40 Strijf was sched out on princes; and he made hem for to erre without the weie, and not in the weie.

41 And he helpide the pore man fro pouert; and settide meynees as a scheep bringynge forth lambren.

42 Riytful men schulen se, and schulen be glad; and al wickidnesse schal stoppe his mouth.

43 Who is wijs, and schal kepe these thingis; and schal vndirstonde the mercies of the Lord?

PSALM 107

1 The 'title of the hundrid and seuenthe salm. The song of 'the salm of Dauid.

2 Min herte is redi, God, myn herte is redi; Y schal singe, and Y schal seie salm in my glorie.

3 My glorie, ryse thou vp, sautrie and harp, rise thou vp; Y schal rise vp eerli.

4 Lord, Y schal knouleche to thee among puplis; and Y schal seie salm to thee among naciouns.

5 For whi, God, thi merci is greet on heuenes; and thi treuthe is til to the cloudis.

6 God, be thou enhaunsid aboue heuenes; and thi glorie ouer al erthe.

7 That thi derlingis be delyuerid, make thou saaf with thi riythond, and here me; God spak in his hooli.

8 I schal make ful out ioye, and Y schal departe Siccimam; and Y schal mete the grete valei of tabernaclis.

9 Galaad is myn, and Manasses is myn; and Effraym is the vptaking of myn heed. Juda is my king; Moab is the caudron of myn hope.

10 In to Ydume Y schal stretche forth my scho; aliens ben maad frendis to me.

11 Who schal lede me forth in to a stronge citee; who schal lede me forth til in to Idume?

12 Whether not thou, God, that hast put vs awei; and, God, schalt thou not go out in oure vertues?

13 Yyue thou help to vs of tribulacioun; for the heelthe of man is veyn.

14 We schulen make vertu in God; and he schal bringe oure enemyes to nouyt.

PSALM 108

1 The title of the hundrid and eiytthe salm. To victorye, the salm of Dauid.

2 God, holde thou not stille my preisyng; for the mouth of the synner, and the mouth of the gileful man is openyd on me.

3 Thei spaken ayens me with a gileful tunge, and thei cumpassiden me with wordis of hatrede; and fouyten ayens me with out cause.

4 For that thing that thei schulden loue me, thei bacbitiden me; but Y preiede.

5 And thei settiden ayens me yuelis for goodis; and hatrede for my loue.

6 Ordeyne thou a synner on him; and the deuel stonde on his riyt half.

7 Whanne he is demed, go he out condempned; and his preier 'be maad in to synne.

8 Hise daies be maad fewe; and another take his bischopriche.

9 Hise sones be maad faderles; and his wijf a widewe.

10 Hise sones tremblinge be born ouer, and begge; and be cast out of her habitaciouns.

11 An vsurere seke al his catel; and aliens rauysche hise trauelis.

12 Noon helpere be to him; nether ony be that haue mercy on hise modirles children.

13 Hise sones be maad in to perisching; the name of him be don awei in oon generacioun.

14 The wickidnesse of hise fadris come ayen in to mynde in the siyt of the Lord; and the synne of his modir be not don awei.

15 Be thei maad euere ayens the Lord; and the mynde of hem perische fro erthe.

16 For that thing that he thouyte not to do merci,

17 and he pursuede a pore man and beggere; and to slee a man compunct in herte.

18 And he louede cursing, and it schal come to hym; and he nolde blessing, and it schal be maad fer fro him. And he clothide cursing as a cloth, and it entride as water in to hise ynnere thingis; and as oile in hise boonus.

19 Be it maad to him as a cloth, with which he is hilyd; and as a girdil, with which he is euere gird.

20 This is the werk of hem that bacbiten me anentis the Lord; and that speke yuels ayens my lijf.

21 And thou, Lord, Lord, do with me for thi name; for thi merci is swete.

22 Delyuere thou me, for Y am nedi and pore; and myn herte is disturblid with ynne me.

23 I am takun awei as a schadowe, whanne it bowith awei; and Y am schakun awei as locustis.

24 Mi knees ben maad feble of fasting; and my fleische was chaungid for oile.

25 And Y am maad schenschipe to hem; thei sien me, and moueden her heedis.

26 Mi Lord God, helpe thou me; make thou me saaf bi thi merci.

27 And thei schulen wite, that this is thin hond; and thou, Lord, hast do it.

28 Thei schulen curse, and thou schalt blesse, thei that risen ayens me, be schent; but thi seruaunt schal be glad.

29 Thei that bacbiten me, be clothid with schame; and be thei hilid with her schenschipe as with a double cloth.

30 I schal knouleche to the Lord greetli with my mouth; and Y schal herie hym in the myddil of many men.

31 Which stood nyy on the riyt half of a pore man; to make saaf my soule fro pursueris.

PSALM 109

1 The 'title of the hundrid and nynthe salm. 'The salm of Dauith. The Lord seide to my Lord; Sitte thou on my riyt side. Til Y putte thin enemyes; a stool of thi feet.

2 The Lord schal sende out fro Syon the yerde of thi vertu; be thou lord in the myddis of thin enemyes.

3 The bigynnyng is with thee in the dai of thi vertu, in the briytnessis of seyntis; Y gendride thee of the wombe before the dai sterre.

4 The Lord swoor, and it schal not repente him; Thou art a preest with outen ende, bi the ordre of Melchisedech.

5 The Lord on thi riyt side; hath broke kyngis in the dai of his veniaunce.

6 He schal deme among naciouns, he schal fille fallyngis; he schal schake heedis in the lond of many men.

7 He dranke of the stronde in the weie; therfor he enhaunside the heed.

PSALM 110

1 The 'title of the hundrid and tenthe salm. Alleluya. Lord, Y schal knouleche to thee in al myn herte; in the counsel and congregacioun of iust men.

2 The werkis of the Lord ben greete; souyt out in to alle hise willis.

3 His werk is knoulechyng and grete doyng; and his riytfulnesse dwellith in to the world of world.

4 The Lord merciful in wille, and a merciful doere, hath maad a mynde of hise merueilis;

5 he hath youe meete to men dredynge hym. He schal be myndeful of his testament in to the world;

6 he schal telle to his puple the vertu of hise werkis.

7 That he yyue to hem the eritage of folkis; the werkis of hise hondis ben treuthe and doom.

8 Alle hise comaundementis ben feithful, conformed in to the world of world; maad in treuthe and equite.

9 The Lord sente redempcioun to hys puple; he comaundide his testament with outen ende. His name is hooli and dreedful;

10 the bigynnyng of wisdom is the drede of the Lord. Good vndirstondyng is to alle that doen it; his preising dwellith in to the world of world.

PSALM 111

1 The 'title of the hundrid and enleuenthe salm. Alleluya. Blissid is the man that dredith the Lord; he schal wilne ful myche in hise comaundementis.

2 His seed schal be myyti in erthe; the generacioun of riytful men schal be blessid.

3 Glorie and richessis ben in his hous; and his riytfulnesse dwellith in to the world of world.

4 Liyt is risun vp in derknessis to riytful men; the Lord is merciful in wille, and a merciful doere, and riytful.

5 The man is merye, that doith merci, and leeneth; he disposith hise wordis in dom;

6 for he schal not be moued with outen ende.

7 A iust man schal be in euerlastinge mynde; he schal not drede of an yuel heryng. His herte is redi for to hope in the Lord;

8 his herte is confermed, he schal not be moued, til he dispise hise enemyes.

9 He spredde abrood, he yaf to pore men; his riytwisnesse dwellith in to the world of world; his horn schal be reisid in glorie.

10 A synner schal se, and schal be wrooth; he schal gnaste with hise teeth, and schal faile; the desijr of synneris schal perische.

PSALM 112

1 The 'title of the hundrid and twelfthe salm. Alleluya. Children, preise ye the Lord; preise ye the name of the Lord.

2 The name of the Lord be blessid; fro this tyme now and til in to the world.

3 Fro the risyng of the sunne til to the goyng doun; the name of the Lord is worthi to be preisid.

4 The Lord is hiy aboue alle folkis; and his glorie is aboue heuenes.

5 Who is as oure Lord God, that dwellith in hiye thingis;

6 and biholdith meke thingis in heuene and in erthe?

7 Reisynge a nedi man fro the erthe; and enhaunsinge a pore man fro drit.

8 That he sette hym with princes; with the princes of his puple.

9 Which makith a bareyn womman dwelle in the hous; a glad modir of sones.

PSALM 113

1 The titil of the hundrid and thrittenthe salm. Alleluya. In the goyng out of Israel fro Egipt; of the hous of Jacob fro the hethene puple.

2 Judee was maad the halewyng of hym; Israel the power of hym.

3 The see siy, and fledde; Jordan was turned abac.

4 Munteyns ful out ioyeden as rammes; and litle hillis as the lambren of scheep.

5 Thou see, what was to thee, for thou fleddist; and thou, Jordan, for thou were turned abak?

6 Munteyns, ye maden ful out ioye as rammes; and litle hillis, as the lambren of scheep.

7 The erthe was moued fro the face of 'the Lord; fro the face of God of Jacob.

8 Which turnede a stoon in to pondis of watris; and an hard rooch in to wellis of watris.

9 Lord, not to vs, not to vs; but yyue thou glorie to thi name.

10 On thi merci and thi treuthe; lest ony tyme hethene men seien, Where is the God of hem?

11 Forsothe oure God in heuene; dide alle thingis, whiche euere he wolde.

12 The symulacris of hethene men ben siluer and gold; the werkis of mennus hondis.

13 Tho han mouth, and schulen not speke; tho han iyen, and schulen not se.

14 Tho han eeris, and schulen not here; tho han nose thurls, and schulen not smelle.

15 Tho han hondis, and schulen not grope; tho han feet, and schulen not go; tho schulen not crye in her throte.

16 Thei that maken tho ben maad lijk tho; and alle that triste in tho.

17 The hous of Israel hopide in the Lord; he is the helpere 'of hem, and the defendere of hem.

18 The hous of Aaron hopide in the Lord; he is the helpere of hem, and the defendere of hem.

19 Thei that dreden the Lord, hopiden in the Lord; he is the helpere of hem, and the defendere of hem.

20 The Lord was myndeful of vs; and blesside vs. He blesside the hous of Israel; he blesside the hous of Aaron.

21 He blesside alle men that dreden the Lord; 'he blesside litle 'men with the grettere.

22 The Lord encreesse on you; on you and on youre sones.

23 Blessid be ye of the Lord; that made heuene and erthe.

24 Heuene of 'heuene is to the Lord; but he yaf erthe to the sones of men.

25 Lord, not deed men schulen herie thee; nether alle men that goen doun in to helle.

26 But we that lyuen, blessen the Lord; fro this tyme now and til in to the world.

PSALM 114

1 The titil of the hundrid and fourtenthe salm. Alleluia. I louede 'the Lord; for the Lord schal here the vois of my preier.

2 For he bowide doun his eere to me; and Y schal inwardli clepe in my daies.

3 The sorewis of deth cumpassiden me; and the perelis of helle founden me.

4 I foond tribulacioun and sorewe; and Y clepide inwardli the name of the Lord. Thou, Lord, delyuere my soule;

5 the Lord is merciful, and iust; and oure God doith merci.

6 And the Lord kepith litle children; Y was mekid, and he delyuerede me.

7 Mi soule, turne thou in to thi reste; for the Lord hath do wel to thee.

8 For he hath delyuered my soule fro deth; myn iyen fro wepingis, my feet fro fallyng doun.

9 I schal plese the Lord; in the cuntrei of hem that lyuen.

PSALM 115

1 I bileuede, for which thing Y spak; forsoth Y was maad low ful myche.

2 I seide in my passing; Ech man is a lier.

3 What schal Y yelde to the Lord; for alle thingis which he yeldide to me?

4 I schal take the cuppe of heelthe; and Y schal inwardli clepe the name of the Lord.

5 I schal yelde my vowis to the Lord bifor al his puple;

6 the deth of seyntis of the Lord is precious in his siyt.

7 O! Lord, for Y am thi seruant; Y am thi seruaunt, and the sone of thi handmaide. Thou hast broke my bondys,

8 to thee Y schal offre a sacrifice of heriyng; and Y schal inwardli clepe the name of the Lord.

9 I schal yelde my vowis to the Lord, in the siyt of al his puple;

10 in the porchis of the hous of the Lord, in the myddil of thee, Jerusalem.

PSALM 116

1 The title of the hundrid and sixtenthe salm. Alleluya. Alle hethen men, herie ye the Lord; alle puplis, herie ye hym.

2 For his merci is confermyd on vs; and the treuthe of the Lord dwellith with outen ende.

PSALM 117

1 The titil of the hundrid and seuententhe salm. Alleluia. Knouleche ye to the Lord, for he is good; for his merci is with outen ende.

2 Israel seie now, for he is good; for his merci is with outen ende.

3 The hous of Aaron seie now; for his merci is with outen ende.

4 Thei that dreden the Lord, seie now; for his merci is withouten ende.

5 Of tribulacioun Y inwardli clepide the Lord; and the Lord herde me in largenesse.

6 The Lord is an helpere to me; Y schal not drede what a man schal do to me.

7 The Lord is an helpere to me; and Y schal dispise myn enemyes.

8 It is betere for to trist in the Lord; than for to triste in man.

9 It is betere for to hope in the Lord; than for to hope in princes.

10 Alle folkis cumpassiden me; and in the name of the Lord it bifelde, for Y am auengide on hem.

11 Thei cumpassinge cumpassiden me; and in the name of the Lord, for Y am auengid on hem.

12 Thei cumpassiden me as been, and thei brenten out as fier doith among thornes; and in the name of the Lord, for Y am avengid on hem.

13 I was hurlid, and turnede vpsedoun, that Y schulde falle doun; and the Lord took me vp.

14 The Lord is my strengthe, and my heryyng; and he is maad to me in to heelthe.

15 The vois of ful out ioiyng and of heelthe; be in the tabernaclis of iust men.

16 The riyt hond of the Lord hath do vertu, the riyt hond of the Lord enhaunside me; the riyt hond of the Lord hath do vertu.

17 I schal not die, but Y schal lyue; and Y schal telle the werkis of the Lord.

18 The Lord chastisinge hath chastisid me; and he yaf not me to deth.

19 Opene ye to me the yatis of riytfulnesse, and Y schal entre bi tho, and Y schal knouleche to the Lord;

20 this yate is of the Lord, and iust men schulen entre bi it.

21 I schal knouleche to thee, for thou herdist me; and art maad to me in to heelthe.

22 The stoon which the bilderis repreueden; this is maad in to the heed of the corner.

23 This thing is maad of the Lord; and it is wonderful bifore oure iyen.

24 This is the dai which the Lord made; make we ful out ioye, and be we glad ther ynne.

25 O! Lord, make thou me saaf, O! Lord, make thou wel prosperite;

26 blessid is he that cometh in the name of the Lord. We blesseden you of the hous of the Lord;

27 God is Lord, and hath youe liyt to vs. Ordeyne ye a solempne dai in thicke puplis; til to the horn of the auter.

28 Thou art my God, and Y schal knouleche to thee; thou art my God, and Y schal enhaunse thee. I schal knouleche to thee, for thou herdist me; and thou art maad to me in to heelthe.

29 Knouleche ye to the Lord, for he is good; for his merci is with outen ende.

PSALM 118

1 'The titil of the hundrid and eiytenthe salm. Alleluia. Blessid ben men with out wem in the weie; that gon in the lawe of the Lord.

2 Blessid ben thei, that seken hise witnessingis; seken him in al the herte.

3 For thei that worchen wickidnesse; yeden not in hise weies.

4 Thou hast comaundid; that thin heestis be kept greetly.

5 I wolde that my weies be dressid; to kepe thi iustifiyngis.

6 Thanne Y schal not be schent; whanne Y schal biholde perfitli in alle thin heestis.

7 I schal knouleche to thee in the dressing of herte; in that that Y lernyde the domes of thi riytfulnesse.

8 I schal kepe thi iustifiyngis; forsake thou not me on ech side.

9 In what thing amendith a yong waxinge man his weie? in keping thi wordis.

10 In al myn herte Y souyte thee; putte thou me not awei fro thin heestis.

11 In myn herte Y hidde thi spechis; that Y do not synne ayens thee.

12 Lord, thou art blessid; teche thou me thi iustifiyngis.

13 In my lippis Y haue pronounsid; alle the domes of thi mouth.

14 I delitide in the weie of thi witnessingis; as in alle richessis.

15 I schal be ocupied in thin heestis; and Y schal biholde thi weies.

16 I schal bithenke in thi iustifiyngis; Y schal not foryete thi wordis.

17 Yelde to thi seruaunt; quiken thou me, and Y schal kepe thi wordis.

18 Liytne thou myn iyen; and Y schal biholde the merueils of thi lawe.

19 I am a comeling in erthe; hide thou not thin heestis fro me.

20 Mi soule coueitide to desire thi iustifiyngis; in al tyme.

21 Thou blamedist the proude; thei ben cursid, that bowen awei fro thin heestis.

22 Do thou awei 'fro me schenschipe and dispising; for Y souyte thi witnessingis.

23 For whi princis saten, and spaken ayens me; but thi seruaunt was exercisid in thi iustifiyngis.

24 For whi and thi witnessyngis is my thenkyng; and my counsel is thi iustifiyngis.

25 Mi soule cleuede to the pawment; quykine thou me bi thi word.

26 I telde out my weies, and thou herdist me; teche thou me thi iustifiyngis.

27 Lerne thou me the weie of thi iustifiyngis; and Y schal be exercisid in thi merueils.

28 Mi soule nappide for anoye; conferme thou me in thi wordis.

29 Remoue thou fro me the weie of wickidnesse; and in thi lawe haue thou merci on me.

30 I chees the weie of treuthe; Y foryat not thi domes.

31 Lord, Y cleuede to thi witnessyngis; nyle thou schende me.

32 I ran the weie of thi comaundementis; whanne thou alargidist myn herte.

33 Lord, sette thou to me a lawe, the weie of thi iustifiyngis; and Y schal seke it euere.

34 Yyue thou vndurstonding to me, and Y schal seke thi lawe; and Y schal kepe it in al myn herte.

35 Lede me forth in the path of thin heestis; for Y wolde it.

36 'Bowe thou myn herte in to thi witnessingus; and not in to aueryce.

37 Turne thou awei myn iyen, that 'tho seen not vanyte; quykene thou me in thi weie.

38 Ordeyne thi speche to thi seruaunt; in thi drede.

39 Kitte awey my schenschip, which Y supposide; for thi domes ben myrie.

40 Lo! Y coueitide thi comaundementis; quikene thou me in thin equite.

41 And, Lord, thi merci come on me; thin heelthe come bi thi speche.

42 And Y schal answere a word to men seiynge schenschipe to me; for Y hopide in thi wordis.

43 And take thou not awei fro my mouth the word of treuthe outerli; for Y hopide aboue in thi domes.

44 And Y schal kepe thi lawe euere; in to the world, and in to the world of world.

45 And Y yede in largenesse; for Y souyte thi comaundementis.

46 And Y spak of thi witnessyngis in the siyt of kingis; and Y was not schent.

47 And Y bithouyte in thin heestis; whiche Y louede.

48 And Y reiside myn hondis to thi comaundementis, whiche Y louede; and Y schal be excercisid in thi iustifiyngis.

49 Lord, haue thou mynde on thi word to thi seruaunt; in which word thou hast youe hope to me.

50 This coumfortide me in my lownesse; for thi word quikenede me.

51 Proude men diden wickidli bi alle thingis; but Y bowide not awei fro thi lawe.

52 Lord, Y was myndeful on thi domes fro the world; and Y was coumfortid.

53 Failing helde me; for synneris forsakinge thi lawe.

54 Thi iustifiyngis weren delitable to me to be sungun; in the place of my pilgrimage.

55 Lord, Y hadde mynde of thi name bi niyt; and Y kepte thi lawe.

56 This thing was maad to me; for Y souyte thi iustifiyngis.

57 Lord, my part; Y seide to kepe thi lawe.

58 I bisouyte thi face in al myn herte; haue thou merci on me bi thi speche.

59 I bithouyte my weies; and Y turnede my feet in to thi witnessyngis.

60 I am redi, and Y am not disturblid; to kepe thi comaundementis.

61 The coordis of synneris han biclippid me; and Y haue not foryete thi lawe.

62 At mydnyyt Y roos to knouleche to thee; on the domes of thi iustifiyngis.

63 I am parcener of alle that dreden thee; and kepen thin heestis.

64 Lord, the erthe is ful of thi merci; teche thou me thi iustifiyngis.

65 Lord, thou hast do goodnesse with thi seruaunt; bi thi word.

66 Teche thou me goodnesse, and loore, and kunnyng; for Y bileuede to thin heestis.

67 Bifor that Y was maad meke, Y trespasside; therfor Y kepte thi speche.

68 Thou art good; and in thi goodnesse teche thou me thi iustifiyngis.

69 The wickidnesse of hem that ben proude, is multiplied on me; but in al myn herte Y schal seke thin heestis.

70 The herte of hem is cruddid as mylk; but Y bithouyte thi lawe.

71 It is good to me, that thou hast maad me meke; that Y lerne thi iustifiyngis.

72 The lawe of thi mouth is betere to me; than thousyndis of gold and of siluer.

73 Thin hondis maden me, and fourmeden me; yyue thou vndurstondyng to me, that Y lerne thin heestis.

74 Thei that dreden thee schulen se me, and schulen be glad; for Y hopide more on thi wordis.

75 Lord, Y knewe, that thi domes ben equite; and in thi treuth thou hast maad me meke.

76 Thi merci be maad, that it coumforte me; bi thi speche to thi seruaunt.

77 Thi merciful doyngis come to me, and Y schal lyue; for thi lawe is my thenkyng.

78 Thei that ben proude be schent, for vniustli thei diden wickidnesse ayens me; but Y schal be exercisid in thin heestis.

79 Thei that dreden thee be turned to me; and thei that knowen thi witnessyngis.

80 Myn herte be maad vnwemmed in thi iustifiyngis; that Y be not schent.

81 Mi soule failide in to thin helthe; and Y hopide more on thi word.

82 Myn iyen failiden in to thi speche; seiynge, Whanne schalt thou coumforte me?

83 For Y am maad as a bowge in frost; Y haue not foryete thi iustifiyngis.

84 Hou many ben the daies of thi seruaunt; whanne thou schalt make doom of hem that pursuen me?

85 Wickid men telden to me ianglyngis; but not as thi lawe.

86 Alle thi comaundementis ben treuthe; wickid men han pursued me, helpe thou me.

87 Almeest thei endiden me in erthe; but I forsook not thi comaundementis.

88 Bi thi mersi quikene thou me; and Y schal kepe the witnessingis of thi mouth.

89 Lord, thi word dwellith in heuene; with outen ende.

90 Thi treuthe dwellith in generacioun, and in to generacioun; thou hast foundid the erthe, and it dwellith.

91 The dai lastith contynueli bi thi ordynaunce; for alle thingis seruen to thee.

92 No but that thi lawe was my thenking; thanne perauenture Y hadde perischid in my lownesse.

93 With outen ende Y schal not foryete thi iustifiyngis; for in tho thou hast quikened me.

94 I am thin, make thou me saaf; for Y haue souyt thi iustifiyngis.

95 Synneris aboden me, for to leese me; Y vndurstood thi witnessingis.

96 I siy the ende of al ende; thi comaundement is ful large.

97 Lord, hou louede Y thi lawe; al dai it is my thenking.

98 Aboue myn enemyes thou madist me prudent bi thi comaundement; for it is to me with outen ende.

99 I vndurstood aboue alle men techinge me; for thi witnessingis is my thenking.

100 I vndirstood aboue eelde men; for Y souyte thi comaundementis.

101 I forbeed my feet fro al euel weie; that Y kepe thi wordis.

102 I bowide not fro thi domes; for thou hast set lawe to me.

103 Thi spechis ben ful swete to my cheekis; aboue hony to my mouth.

104 I vnderstood of thin heestis; therfor Y hatide al the weie of wickidnesse.

105 Thi word is a lanterne to my feet; and liyt to my pathis.

106 I swoor, and purposide stidefastli; to kepe the domes of thi riytfulnesse.

107 I am maad low bi alle thingis; Lord, quykene thou me bi thi word.

108 Lord, make thou wel plesinge the wilful thingis of my mouth; and teche thou me thi domes.

109 Mi soule is euere in myn hondis; and Y foryat not thi lawe.

110 Synneris settiden a snare to me; and Y erride not fro thi comaundementis.

111 I purchasside thi witnessyngis bi eritage with outen ende; for tho ben the ful ioiyng of myn herte.

112 I bowide myn herte to do thi iustifiyngis with outen ende; for reward.

113 I hatide wickid men; and Y louede thi lawe.

114 Thou art myn helpere, and my 'taker vp; and Y hopide more on thi word.

115 Ye wickide men, bowe awei fro me; and Y schal seke the comaundementis of my God.

116 Vp take thou me bi thi word, and Y schal lyue; and schende thou not me fro myn abydyng.

117 Helpe thou me, and Y schal be saaf; and Y schal bithenke euere in thi iustifiyngis.

118 Thou hast forsake alle men goynge awey fro thi domes; for the thouyt of hem is vniust.

119 I arettide alle the synneris of erthe brekeris of the lawe; therfor Y louede thi witnessyngis.

120 Naile thou my fleischis with thi drede; for Y dredde of thi domes.

121 I dide doom and riytwisnesse; bitake thou not me to hem that falsli chalengen me.

122 Take vp thi seruaunt in to goodnesse; thei that ben proude chalenge not me.

123 Myn iyen failiden in to thin helthe; and in to the speche of thi riytfulnesse.

124 Do thou with thi seruaunt bi thi merci; and teche thou me thi iustifiyngis.

125 I am thi seruaunt, yyue thou vndurstondyng to me; that Y kunne thi witnessingis.

126 Lord, it is tyme to do; thei han distried thi lawe.

127 Therfor Y louede thi comaundementis; more than gold and topazion.

128 Therfor Y was dressid to alle thin heestis; Y hatide al wickid weie.

129 Lord, thi witnessingis ben wondirful; therfor my soule souyte tho.

130 Declaring of thi wordis liytneth; and yyueth vnderstond-ing to meke men.

131 I openede my mouth, and drouy the spirit; for Y desiride thi comaundementis.

132 Biholde thou on me, and haue merci on me; bi the dom of hem that louen thi name.

133 Dresse thou my goyingis bi thi speche; that al vnriytful-nesse haue not lordschip on me.

134 Ayeyn bie thou me fro the false chalengis of men; that Y kepe thin heestis.

135 Liytne thi face on thi seruaunt; and teche thou me thi ius-tifiyngis.

136 Myn iyen ledden forth the outgoynges of watris; for thei kepten not thi lawe.

137 Lord, thou art iust; and thi dom is riytful.

138 Thou hast comaundid riytfulnesse, thi witnessingis; and thi treuthe greetli to be kept.

139 Mi feruent loue made me to be meltid; for myn enemys foryaten thi wordis.

140 Thi speche is greetli enflawmed; and thi seruaunt louede it.

141 I am yong, and dispisid; Y foryat not thi iustifiyngis.

142 Lord, thi riytfulnesse is riytfulnesse with outen ende; and thi lawe is treuthe.

143 Tribulacioun and angwische founden me; thin heestis is my thenking.

144 Thi witnessyngis is equite with outen ende; yyue thou vndirstondyng to me, and Y schal lyue.

145 I criede in al myn herte, Lord, here thou me; and Y schal seke thi iustifiyngis.

146 I criede to thee, make thou me saaf; that Y kepe thi comaundementis.

147 I bifor cam in ripenesse, and Y criede; Y hopide aboue on thi wordis.

148 Myn iyen bifor camen to thee ful eerli; that Y schulde bithenke thi speches.

149 Lord, here thou my vois bi thi merci; and quykene thou me bi thi doom.

150 Thei that pursuen me neiyden to wickidnesse; forsothe thei ben maad fer fro thi lawe.

151 Lord, thou art nyy; and alle thi weies ben treuthe.

152 In the bigynnyng Y knewe of thi witnessingis; for thou hast foundid tho with outen ende.

153 Se thou my mekenesse, and delyuere thou me; for Y foryat not thi lawe.

154 Deme thou my dom, and ayenbie thou me; quikene thou me for thi speche.

155 Heelthe is fer fro synners; for thei souyten not thi iustifi-yngis.

156 Lord, thi mercies ben manye; quykene thou me bi thi dom.

157 Thei ben manye that pursuen me, and doen tribulacioun to me; Y bowide not awei fro thi witnessingis.

158 I siy brekers of the lawe, and Y was meltid; for thei kepten not thi spechis.

159 Lord, se thou, for Y louede thi comaundementis; quikene thou me in thi merci.

160 The bigynnyng of thi wordis is treuthe; alle the domes of thi riytwisnesse ben withouten ende.

161 Princes pursueden me with outen cause; and my herte dredde of thi wordis.

162 I schal be glad on thi spechis; as he that fyndith many spuylis.

163 I hatide and wlatide wickidnesse; forsothe Y louede thi lawe.

164 I seide heriyngis to thee seuene sithis in the dai; on the domes of thi riytfulnesse.

165 Miche pees is to hem that louen thi lawe; and no sclaun-dir is to hem.

166 Lord, Y abood thin heelthe; and Y louede thin heestis.

167 Mi soule kepte thi witnessyngis; and louede tho greetli.

168 I kepte thi 'comaundementis, and thi witnessingis; for alle my weies ben in thi siyt.

169 Lord, my biseching come niy in thi siyt; bi thi speche yyue thou vndurstonding to me.

170 Myn axing entre in thi siyt; bi thi speche delyuere thou me.

171 Mi lippis schulen telle out an ympne; whanne thou hast tauyte me thi iustifiyngis.

172 Mi tunge schal pronounce thi speche; for whi alle thi comaundementis ben equite.

173 Thin hond be maad, that it saue me; for Y haue chose thin heestis.

174 Lord, Y coueitide thin heelthe; and thi lawe is my thenking.

175 Mi soule schal lyue, and schal herie thee; and thi domes schulen helpe me.

176 I erride as a scheep that perischide; Lord, seke thi seruaunt, for Y foryat not thi comaundementis.

PSALM 119

1 The 'title of the hundrid and nyntenthe salm. The song of greces. Whanne Y was set in tribulacioun, Y criede to the Lord; and he herde me.

2 Lord, delyuere thou my soule fro wickid lippis; and fro a gileful tunge.

3 What schal be youun to thee, ether what schal be leid to thee; to a gileful tunge?

4 Scharpe arowis of the myyti; with colis that maken desolat.

5 Allas to me! for my dwelling in an alien lond is maad long, Y dwellide with men dwellinge in Cedar; my soule was myche a comelyng.

6 I was pesible with hem that hatiden pees;

7 whanne Y spak to hem, thei ayenseiden me with outen cause.

PSALM 120

1 The 'title of the hundrid and twentithe salm. The song of greces. I reiside myn iyen to the hillis; fro whannus help schal come to me.

2 Myn help is of the Lord; that made heuene and erthe.

3 The Lord yyue not thi foot in to mouyng; nether he nappe, that kepith thee.

4 Lo! he schal not nappe, nether slepe; that kepith Israel.

5 The Lord kepith thee; the Lord is thi proteccioun aboue thi riythond.

6 The sunne schal not brenne thee bi dai; nether the moone bi nyyt.

7 The Lord kepe thee fro al yuel; the Lord kepe thi soule.

8 The Lord kepe thi goyng in and thi goyng out; fro this tyme now and in to the world.

PSALM 121

1 The 'title of the hundrid and oon and twentithe salm. The song of the grecis of Dauid. I am glad in these thingis, that ben seid to me; We schulen go in to the hous of the Lord.

2 Oure feet weren stondynge; in thi hallis, thou Jerusalem.

3 Jerusalem, which is bildid as a citee; whos part taking therof is in to the same thing.

4 For the lynagis, the lynagis of the Lord stieden thidir, the witnessing of Israel; to knouleche to the name of the Lord.

5 For thei saten there on seetis in doom; seetis on the hous of Dauid.

6 Preie ye tho thingis, that ben to the pees of Jerusalem; and abundaunce be to hem that louen thee.

7 Pees be maad in thi vertu; and abundaunce in thi touris.

8 For my britheren and my neiyboris; Y spak pees of thee.

9 For the hous of oure Lord God; Y souyte goodis to thee.

PSALM 122

1 The 'title of the hundrid and two and twentithe salm. 'The song of grecis. To thee Y haue reisid myn iyen; that dwellist in heuenes.

2 Lo! as the iyen of seruauntis; ben in the hondis of her lordis. As the iyen of the handmaide ben in the hondis of her ladi; so oure iyen ben to oure Lord God, til he haue mercy on vs.

3 Lord, haue thou merci on vs, haue thou merci on vs; for we ben myche fillid with dispisyng.

4 For oure soule is myche fillid; we ben schenschipe to hem that ben abundaunte with richessis, and dispising to proude men.

PSALM 123

1 The 'title of the hundrid and thre and twentithe 'salm. The song of grecis 'of Dauith. Israel seie now, No but for the Lord was in vs;

2 no but for 'the Lord was in vs. Whanne men risiden vp ayens vs;

3 in hap thei hadden swalewid vs quike. Whanne the woodnesse of hem was wrooth ayens vs;

4 in hap watir hadde sope vs vp.

5 Oure soule passide thoruy a stronde; in hap oure soule hadde passide thoruy a watir vnsuffrable.

6 Blessid be the Lord; that 'yaf not vs in taking to the teeth of hem.

7 Oure soule, as a sparowe, is delyuered; fro the snare of hunters. The snare is al to-brokun; and we ben delyuered.

8 Oure helpe is in the name of the Lord; that made heuene and erthe.

PSALM 124

1 The 'title of the hundrid and foure and twentithe salm. 'The song of greces. Thei that tristen in the Lord ben as the hil of Syon; he schal not be moued with outen ende,

2 that dwellith in Jerusalem. Hillis ben in the cumpas of it, and the Lord is in the cumpas of his puple; fro this tyme now and in to the world.

3 For the Lord schal not leeue the yerde of synneris on the part of iust men; that iust men holde not forth her hondis to wickidnesse.

4 Lord, do thou wel; to good men, and of riytful herte.

5 But the Lord schal lede them that bowen in to obligaciouns, with hem that worchen wickidnesse; pees be on Israel.

PSALM 125

1 The 'title of the hundrid and fyue and twentithe 'salm. The song of grecis. Whanne the Lord turnede the caitifte of Sion; we weren maad as coumfortid.

2 Thanne oure mouth was fillid with ioye; and oure tunge with ful out ioiyng. Thanne thei schulen seie among hethene men; The Lord magnefiede to do with hem.

3 The Lord magnefiede to do with vs; we ben maad glad.

4 Lord, turne thou oure caitifte; as a stronde in the south.

5 Thei that sowen in teeris; schulen repe in ful out ioiyng.

6 Thei goynge yeden, and wepten; sendynge her seedis. But thei comynge schulen come with ful out ioiyng; berynge her handfullis.

PSALM 126

1 The 'title of the hundrid and sixe and twentithe 'salm. The song of greces of Salomon. 'No but the Lord bilde the hous;

thei that bilden it han trauelid in veyn. No but the Lord kepith the citee; he wakith in veyn that kepith it.

2 It is veyn to you to rise bifore the liyt; rise ye after that ye han sete, that eten the breed of sorewe. Whanne he schal yyue sleep to his loued; lo!

3 the eritage of the Lord 'is sones, the mede is the fruyt of wombe.

4 As arowis ben in the hond of the miyti; so the sones of hem that ben schakun out.

5 Blessid is the man, that hath fillid his desier of tho; he schal not be schent, whanne he schal speke to hise enemyes in the yate.

PSALM 127

1 The title of the hundrid and seuene and twentithe salm. The song of greces. Blessid ben alle men, that dreden the Lord; that gon in hise weies.

2 For thou schalt ete the trauels of thin hondis; thou art blessid, and it schal be wel to thee.

3 Thi wijf as a plenteous vyne; in the sidis of thin hous. Thi sones as the newe sprenges of olyue trees; in the cumpas of thi bord.

4 Lo! so a man schal be blessid; that dredith the Lord.

5 The Lord blesse thee fro Syon; and se thou the goodis of Jerusalem in alle the daies of thi lijf.

6 And se thou the sones of thi sones; se thou pees on Israel.

PSALM 128

1 The 'title of the hundrid and eiyte and twentithe 'salm. The song of greces. Israel seie now; Ofte thei fouyten ayens me fro my yongth.

2 Ofte thei fouyten ayens me fro my yongthe; and sotheli thei miyten not to me.

3 Synneris forgeden on my bak; thei maden long her wickidnesse.

4 The 'iust Lord schal beete the nollis of synneris;

5 alle that haten Sion be schent, and turned abak.

6 Be thei maad as the hey of hous coppis; that driede vp, bifore that it be drawun vp.

7 Of which hei he that schal repe, schal not fille his hond; and he that schal gadere hondfullis, schal not fille his bosum.

8 And thei that passiden forth seiden not, The blessing of the Lord be on you; we blessiden you in the name of the Lord.

PSALM 129

1 The 'title of the hundrid and nyne and twentithe 'salm. The song of greces. Lord, Y criede to thee fro depthes; Lord, here thou mi vois.

2 Thin eeris be maad ententif; in to the vois of my biseching.

3 Lord, if thou kepist wickidnessis; Lord, who schal susteyne?

4 For merci is at thee; and, Lord, for thi lawe Y abood thee. Mi soule susteynede in his word; my soule hopide in the Lord.

5 Fro the morewtid keping til to niyt;

6 Israel hope in the Lord.

7 For whi merci is at the Lord; and plenteous redempcioun is at hym.

8 And he schal ayen bie Israel; fro alle the wickidnessis therof.

PSALM 130

1 The title of the hundrid and thrittithe salm. The song of greces, 'to Dauith himself. Lord, myn herte is not enhaunsid; nether myn iyen ben reisid. Nether Y yede in the grete thingis; nether in merueilis aboue me.

2 If Y feelide not mekely; but enhaunside my soule. As a childe wenyde on his modir; so yelding be in my soule.

3 Israel hope in the Lord; fro this tyme now and in to the world.

PSALM 131

1 The title of the hundrid and oon and thrittithe salm. The song of greces. Lord, haue thou mynde on Dauid; and of al his myldenesse.

2 As he swoor to the Lord; he made a vowe to God of Jacob.

3 I schal not entre in to the tabernacle of myn hous; Y schal not stie in to the bed of mi restyng.

4 I schal not yyue sleep to myn iyen; and napping to myn iye liddis.

5 And rest to my templis, til Y fynde a place to the Lord; a tabernacle to God of Jacob.

6 Lo! we herden that arke of testament in Effrata, 'that is, in Silo; we founden it in the feeldis of the wode.

7 We schulen entre in to the tabernacle of hym; we schulen worschipe in the place, where hise feet stoden.

8 Lord, rise thou in to thi reste; thou and the ark of thin halewing.

9 Thi prestis be clothid with riytfulnesse; and thi seyntis make ful out ioye.

10 For Dauid, thi seruaunt; turne thou not awei the face of thi crist.

11 The Lord swoor treuthe to Dauid, and he schal not make hym veyn; of the fruyt of thi wombe Y schal sette on thi seete.

12 If thi sones schulen kepe my testament; and my witness-ingis, these whiche Y schal teche hem. And the sones of hem til in to the world; thei schulen sette on thi seete.

13 For the Lord chees Sion; he chees it in to dwelling to hym silf.

14 This is my reste in to the world of world; Y schal dwelle here, for Y chees it.

15 I blessynge schal blesse the widewe of it; Y schal fille with looues the pore men of it.

16 I schal clothe with heelthe the preestis therof; and the hooli men therof schulen make ful out ioye in ful reioisinge.

17 Thidir Y schal bringe forth the horn of Dauid; Y made redi a lanterne to my crist.

18 I schal clothe hise enemyes with schame; but myn halewing schal floure out on hym.

PSALM 132

1 The 'title of the hundrid and two and thrittithe salm. The song of grecis. Lo! hou good and hou myrie it is; that brith-eren dwelle togidere.

2 As oynement in the heed; that goith doun in to the beerd, in to the beerd of Aaron. That goith doun in to the coler of his cloth; as the dew of Ermon,

3 that goith doun in to the hil of Sion. For there the Lord sente blessing; and lijf til in to the world.

PSALM 133

1 The 'title of the hundrid and thre and thrittithe salm. The song of greces. Lo! now blesse ye the Lord; alle the seruaun-

tis of the Lord. Ye that stonden in the hous of the Lord; in the hallis of 'the hous of oure God.

2 In nyytis reise youre hondis in to hooli thingis; and blesse ye the Lord.

3 The Lord blesse thee fro Syon; which Lord made heuene and erthe.

PSALM 134

1 The title of the hundrid and foure and thrittithe salm. Alleluya. Herie ye the name of the Lord; ye seruauntis of the Lord, herie ye.

2 Ye that stonden in the hous of the Lord; in the hallis of 'the hous of oure God.

3 Herie ye the Lord, for the Lord is good; singe ye to his name, for it is swete.

4 For the Lord chees Jacob to him silf; Israel in to possessioun to him silf.

5 For Y haue knowe, that the Lord is greet; and oure God bifore alle goddis.

6 The Lord made alle thingis, what euere thingis he wolde, in heuene and in erthe; in the see, and in alle depthis of watris.

7 He ledde out cloudis fro the ferthest part of erthe; and made leitis in to reyn. Which bringith forth wyndis fro hise tresours;

8 which killide the firste gendrid thingis of Egipt, fro man 'til to beeste.

9 He sente out signes and grete wondris, in the myddil of thee, thou Egipt; in to Farao and in to alle hise seruauntis.

10 Which smoot many folkis; and killide stronge kingis.

11 Seon, the king of Ammorreis, and Og, the king of Basan; and alle the rewmes of Chanaan.

12 And he yaf the lond of hem eritage; eritage to Israel, his puple.

13 Lord, thi name is with outen ende; Lord, thi memorial be in generacioun and in to generacioun.

14 For the Lord schal deme his puple; and he schal be preied in hise seruauntis.

15 The symulacris of hethene men ben siluer and gold; the werkis of the hondis of men.

16 Tho han a mouth, and schulen not speke; tho han iyen, and schulen not se.

17 Tho han eeris, and schulen not here; for 'nether spirit is in the mouth of tho.

18 Thei that maken tho, be maad lijk tho; and alle that tristen in tho.

19 The hous of Israel, blesse ye the Lord; the hous of Aaron, blesse ye the Lord.

20 The hous of Leuy, blesse ye the Lord; ye that dreden the Lord, 'blesse ye the Lord.

21 Blessid be the Lord of Syon; that dwellith in Jerusalem.

PSALM 135

1 The title of the hundrid and fyue and thrittithe salm. Alleluya. Knouleche ye to the Lord, for he is good, for his merci is withouten ende.

2 Knouleche ye to the God of goddis.

3 Knouleche ye to the Lord of lordis.

4 Which aloone makith grete merueils.

5 Which made heuenes bi vndurstondyng.

6 Which made stidefast erthe on watris.

7 Which made grete liytis.

8 The sunne in to the power of the dai.

9 The moone and sterris in to the power of the niyt.

10 Which smoot Egipt with the firste gendrid thingis of hem.

11 Which ledde out Israel fro the myddil of hem.

12 In a miyti hond and in an hiy arm.

13 Whiche departide the reed see in to departyngis.

14 And ledde out Israel thoruy the myddil therof.

15 And he 'caste a down Farao and his pouer in the reed see.

16 Which ledde ouer his puple thoruy desert.

17 Which smoot grete kingis.

18 And killide strong kingis.

19 Seon, the king of Amorreis.

20 And Og, the king of Baasan.

21 And he yaf the lond of hem eritage.

22 Eritage to Israel, his seruaunt.

23 For in oure lownesse he hadde mynde on vs.

24 And he ayenbouyte vs fro oure enemyes.

25 Which yyueth mete to ech fleisch. Knouleche ye to God of heuene.

26 Knouleche ye to the Lord of lordis; for his merci is with outen ende.

PSALM 136

1 The hundrid and sixe and thrittithe salm. On the floodis of Babiloyne there we saten, and wepten; while we bithouyten on Syon.

2 In salewis in the myddil therof; we hangiden vp oure orguns.

3 For thei that ledden vs prisoners; axiden vs there the wordis of songis. And thei that ledden awei vs seiden; Synge ye to vs an ympne of the songis of Syon.

4 Hou schulen we singe a songe of the Lord; in an alien lond?

5 If Y foryete thee, Jerusalem; my riyt hond be youun to foryeting.

6 Mi tunge cleue to my chekis; if Y bithenke not on thee. If Y purposide not of thee, Jerusalem; in the bigynnyng of my gladnesse.

7 Lord, haue thou mynde on the sones of Edom; for the dai of Jerusalem. Whiche seien, Anyntische ye, anyntische ye; 'til to the foundement ther ynne.

8 Thou wretchid douyter of Babiloyne; he is blessid, that 'schal yelde to thee thi yelding, which thou yeldidist to vs.

9 He is blessid, that schal holde; and hurtle doun hise litle children at a stoon.

PSALM 137

1 The 'title of the hundrid and seuene and thrittithe salm. 'To Dauith him silf. Lord, Y schal knouleche to thee in al myn herte; for thou herdist the wordis of my mouth. Mi God, Y schal singe to thee in the siyt of aungels;

2 Y schal worschipe to thin hooli temple, and Y schal knouleche to thi name. On thi merci and thi treuthe; for thou hast magnefied thin hooli name aboue al thing.

3 In what euere dai Y schal inwardli clepe thee, here thou me; thou schalt multipli vertu in my soule.

4 Lord, alle the kingis of erthe knouleche to thee; for thei herden alle the wordis of thi mouth.

5 And singe thei in the weies of the Lord; for the glorie of the Lord is greet.

6 For the Lord is hiy, and biholdith meke thingis; and knowith afer hiy thingis.

7 If Y schal go in the myddil of tribulacioun, thou schalt quikene me; and thou stretchidist forth thin hond on the ire of myn enemyes, and thi riyt hond made me saaf.

8 The Lord schal yelde for me, Lord, thi merci is with outen ende; dispise thou not the werkis of thin hondis.

PSALM 138

1 The 'title of the hundrid and eiyte and thrittithe salm. 'To victorie, the salm of Dauith. Lord, thou hast preued me, and hast knowe me;

2 thou hast knowe my sitting, and my rising ayen.

3 Thou hast vndirstonde my thouytis fro fer; thou hast enquerid my path and my corde.

4 And thou hast bifor seien alle my weies; for no word is in my tunge.

5 Lo! Lord, thou hast knowe alle thingis, the laste thingis and elde; thou hast formed me, and hast set thin hond on me.

6 Thi kunnyng is maad wondirful of me; it is coumfortid, and Y schal not mowe to it.

7 Whidir schal Y go fro thi spirit; and whider schal Y fle fro thi face?

8 If Y schal stie in to heuene, thou art there; if Y schal go doun to helle, thou art present.

9 If Y schal take my fetheris ful eerli; and schal dwelle in the last partis of the see.

10 And sotheli thider thin hond schal leede me forth; and thi riyt hond schal holde me.

11 And Y seide, In hap derknessis schulen defoule me; and the nyyt is my liytnyng in my delicis.

12 For whi derknessis schulen not be maad derk fro thee, aud the niyt schal be liytned as the dai; as the derknessis therof, so and the liyt therof.

13 For thou haddist in possessioun my reines; thou tokist me vp fro the wombe of my modir.

14 I schal knouleche to thee, for thou art magnefied dreedfuli; thi werkis ben wondirful, and my soule schal knouleche ful miche.

15 Mi boon, which thou madist in priuete, is not hyd fro thee; and my substaunce in the lower partis of erthe.

16 Thin iyen sien myn vnperfit thing, and alle men schulen be writun in thi book; daies schulen be formed, and no man is in tho.

17 Forsothe, God, thi frendis ben maad onourable ful myche to me; the princeheed of hem is coumfortid ful myche.

18 I schal noumbre hem, and thei schulen be multiplied aboue grauel; Y roos vp, and yit Y am with thee.

19 For thou, God, schalt slee synneris; ye menquelleris, bowe awei fro me.

20 For ye seien in thouyt; Take thei her citees in vanite.

21 Lord, whether Y hatide not hem that hatiden thee; and Y failide on thin enemyes?

22 Bi perfite haterede Y hatide hem; thei weren maad enemyes to me.

23 God, preue thou me, and knowe thou myn herte; axe thou me, and knowe thou my pathis.

24 And se thou, if weie of wickidnesse is in me; and lede thou me forth in euerlastinge wei.

PSALM 139

1 The 'title of the hundrid and nyne and thrittithe 'salm. To victorie, the salm of Dauith.

2 Lord, delyuere thou me fro an yuel man; delyuere thou me fro a wickid man.

3 Whiche thouyten wickidnesses in the herte; al dai thei ordeyneden batels.

4 Thei scharpiden her tungis as serpentis; the venym of snakis vndir the lippis of hem.

5 Lord, kepe thou me fro the hond of the synnere; and delyuere thou me fro wickid men. Which thouyten to disseyue my goyngis;

6 proude men hidden a snare to me. And thei leiden forth cordis in to a snare; thei settiden sclaundir to me bisidis the weie.

7 I seide to the Lord, Thou art mi God; Lord, here thou the vois of my biseching.

8 Lord, Lord, the vertu of myn heelthe; thou madist schadowe on myn heed in the dai of batel.

9 Lord, bitake thou not me fro my desire to the synnere; thei thouyten ayens me, forsake thou not me, lest perauenture thei ben enhaunsid.

10 The heed of the cumpas of hem; the trauel of her lippis schal hile hem.

11 Colis schulen falle on hem, thou schalt caste hem doun in to fier; in wretchidnessis thei schulen not stonde.

12 A man a greet ianglere schal not be dressid in erthe; yuels schulen take an vniust man in perisching.

13 I haue knowe, that the Lord schal make dom of a nedi man; and the veniaunce of pore men.

14 Netheles iust men schulen knouleche to thi name; and riytful men schulen dwelle with thi cheer.

PSALM 140

1 The 'title of the hundrid and fourtithe salm. 'The salm 'of Dauith. Lord, Y criede to thee, here thou me; yyue thou tent to my vois, whanne Y schal crye to thee.

2 Mi preier be dressid as encense in thi siyt; the reisyng of myn hondis be as the euentid sacrifice.

3 Lord, sette thou a keping to my mouth; and a dore of stonding aboute to my lippis.

4 Bowe thou not myn herte in to wordis of malice; to excuse excusingis in synne. With men worchinge wickidnesse; and Y schal not comyne with the chosun men of hem.

5 A iust man schal repreue me in mersi, and schal blame me; but the oile of a synner make not fat myn heed. For whi and yit my preier is in the wel plesaunt thingis of hem;

6 for the domesmen of hem ioyned to the stoon weren sopun vp. Here thei my wordis,

7 for tho weren myyti. As fatnesse is brokun out on the erthe; oure bonys ben scatered niy helle. Lord, Lord,

8 for myn iyen ben to thee, Y hopide in thee; take thou not awei my soule.

9 Kepe thou me fro the snare which thei ordeyneden to me; and fro the sclaundris of hem that worchen wickidnesse. Synneris schulen falle in the nett therof;

10 Y am aloone til Y passe.

PSALM 141

1 The 'title of the hundrid and oon and fourtithe salm. The lernyng of Dauid; 'his preier, 'whanne he was in the denne.

2 With my vois Y criede to the Lord; with my vois Y preiede hertli to the Lord.

3 I schede out my preier in his siyt; and Y pronounce my tribulacioun bifor him.

4 While my spirit failith of me; and thou hast knowe my pathis. In this weie in which Y yede; proude men hidden a snare to me.

5 I bihelde to the riyt side, and Y siy; and noon was that knew me. Fliyt perischide fro me; and noon is that sekith my soule.

6 Lord, Y criede to thee, Y seide, Thou art myn hope; my part in the lond of lyueris.

7 Yyue thou tent to my biseching; for Y am maad low ful greetli. Delyuere thou me fro hem that pursuen me; for thei ben coumfortid on me.

8 Lede my soule out of keping to knouleche to thi name; iust men abiden me, til thou yelde to me.

PSALM 142

1 The 'title of the hundrid and two and fourtithe salm. The salm of Dauid. Lord, here thou my preier, with eeris perseyue thou my biseching; in thi treuthe here thou me, in thi riytwisnesse.

2 And entre thou not in to dom with thi seruaunt; for ech man lyuynge schal not be maad iust in thi siyt.

3 For the enemy pursuede my soule; he made lowe my lijf in erthe. He hath set me in derk placis, as the deed men of the world,

4 and my spirit was angwischid on me; myn herte was disturblid in me.

5 I was myndeful of elde daies, Y bithouyte in alle thi werkis; Y bithouyte in the dedis of thin hondis.

6 I helde forth myn hondis to thee; my soule as erthe with out water to thee.

7 Lord, here thou me swiftli; my spirit failide. Turne thou not a wei thi face fro me; and Y schal be lijk to hem that gon doun in to the lake.

8 Make thou erli thi merci herd to me; for Y hopide in thee. Make thou knowun to me the weie in which Y schal go; for Y reiside my soule to thee.

9 Delyuere thou me fro myn enemyes, Lord, Y fledde to thee; 10 teche thou me to do thi wille, for thou art my God. Thi good spirit schal lede me forth in to a riytful lond;

11 Lord, for thi name thou schalt quikene me in thin equite. Thou schalt lede my soule out of tribulacioun;

12 and in thi merci thou schalt scatere alle myn enemyes. And thou schalt leese alle them, that troublen my soule; for Y am thi seruaunt.

PSALM 143

1 The title of the hundrid and thre and fourtithe salm. 'A salm. Blessid be my Lord God, that techith myn hondis to werre; and my fyngris to batel.

2 Mi merci, and my refuyt; my takere vp, and my delyuerer. Mi defender, and Y hopide in him; and thou makist suget my puple vnder me.

3 Lord, what is a man, for thou hast maad knowun to him; ether the sone of man, for thou arettist him of sum valu?

4 A man is maad lijk vanyte; hise daies passen as schadow.

5 Lord, bowe doun thin heuenes, and come thou doun; touche thou hillis, and thei schulen make smoke.

6 Leite thou schynyng, and thou schalt scatere hem; sende thou out thin arowis, and thou schalt disturble hem.

7 Sende out thin hond fro an hiy, rauysche thou me out, and delyuere thou me fro many watris; and fro the hond of alien sones.

8 The mouth of which spak vanite; and the riythond of hem is the riyt hond of wickidnesse.

9 God, Y schal synge to thee a new song; I schal seie salm to thee in a sautre of ten stringis.

10 Which yyuest heelthe to kingis; which ayen bouytist Dauid, thi seruaunt, fro the wickid swerd rauische thou out me.

11 And delyuere thou me fro 'the hond of alien sones; the mouth of whiche spak vanyte, and the riythond of hem is the riyt hond of wickidnesse.

12 Whose sones ben; as new plauntingis in her yongthe. The douytris of hem ben arayed; ourned about as the licnesse of the temple.

13 The selers of hem ben fulle; bringinge out fro this vessel in to that. The scheep of hem ben with lambre, plenteuouse in her goingis out;

14 her kien ben fatte. 'No falling of wal is, nether passing ouere; nether cry is in the stretis of hem.

15 Thei seiden, 'The puple is blessid, that hath these thingis; blessid is the puple, whos Lord is the God of it.

PSALM 144

1 The title of the hundrid and foure and fourtithe salm. 'The ympne of Dauith. Mi God king, Y schal enhaunse thee; and Y schal blesse thi name in to the world, and in to the world of world.

2 Bi alle daies Y schal blesse thee; and Y schal herie thi name in to the world, and in to the world of the world.

3 The Lord is greet, and worthi to be preisid ful myche; and noon ende is of his greetnesse.

4 Generacioun and generacioun schal preise thi werkis; and thei schulen pronounse thi power.

5 Thei schulen speke 'the greet doyng of the glorie of thin holynesse; and thei schulen telle thi merueils.

6 And thei schulen seye the vertu of thi ferdful thingis; and thei schulen telle thi greetnesse.

7 Thei schulen bringe forth the mynde of the abundaunce of thi swetnesse; and thei schulen telle with ful out ioiyng thi riytfulnesse.

8 The Lord is a merciful doere, and merciful in wille; paciente, and myche merciful.

9 The Lord is swete in alle thingis; and hise merciful doyngis ben on alle hise werkis.

10 Lord, alle thi werkis knouleche to thee; and thi seyntis blesse thee.

11 Thei schulen seie the glorie of thi rewme; and thei schulen speke thi power.

12 That thei make thi power knowun to the sones of men; and the glorie of the greetnesse of thi rewme.

13 Thi rewme is the rewme of alle worldis; and thi lordschipe is in al generacioun and in to generacioun. The Lord is feithful in alle hise wordis; and hooli in alle hise werkis.

14 The Lord liftith vp alle that fallen doun; and reisith alle men hurtlid doun.

15 Lord, the iyen of alle beestis hopen in thee; and thou yyuest the mete of hem in couenable tyme.

16 Thou openest thin hond; and thou fillist ech beeste with blessing.

17 The Lord is iust in alle hise weies; and hooli in alle hise werkis.

18 The Lord is niy to alle that inwardli clepen him; to alle that inwardli clepen him in treuthe.

19 He schal do the wille of hem, that dreden him, and he schal here the biseching of hem; and he schal make hem saaf.

20 The Lord kepith alle men louynge him; and he schal leese alle synners.

21 Mi mouth schal speke the heriyng of the Lord; and ech man blesse his hooli name in to the world, and in to the world of world.

PSALM 145

1 The 'title of the hundred and fyue and fourtithe 'salm. Alleluya.

2 Mi soule, herie thou the Lord; Y schal herie the Lord in my lijf, Y schal synge to my God as longe as Y schal be. Nile ye triste in princis;

3 nether in the sones of men, in whiche is noon helthe.

4 The spirit of hym schal go out, and he schal turne ayen in to his erthe; in that dai alle the thouytis of hem schulen perische.

5 He is blessid, of whom the God of Jacob is his helpere, his hope is in his Lord God, that made heuene and erthe;

6 the see, and alle thingis that ben in tho.

7 Which kepith treuthe in to the world, makith dom to hem that suffren wrong; yyueth mete to hem that ben hungri. The Lord vnbyndith feterid men;

8 the Lord liytneth blynde men. The Lord reisith men hurtlid doun; the Lord loueth iust men.

9 The Lord kepith comelyngis, he schal take vp a modirles child, and widewe; and he schal distrie the weies of synners.

10 The Lord schal regne in to the worldis; Syon, thi God schal regne in generacioun and in to generacioun.

PSALM 146

1 The 'title of the hundrid and sixe and fourtithe salm. Alleluya. Herie ye the Lord, for the salm is good; heriyng be myrie, and fair to oure God.

2 The Lord schal bilde Jerusalem; and schal gadere togidere the scateryngis of Israel.

3 Which Lord makith hool men contrit in herte; and byndith togidere the sorewes of hem.

4 Which noumbrith the multitude of sterris; and clepith names to alle tho.

5 Oure Lord is greet, and his vertu is greet; and of his wisdom is no noumbre.

6 The Lord takith vp mylde men; forsothe he makith low synneris 'til to the erthe.

7 Bifore synge ye to the Lord in knoulechyng; seye ye salm to oure God in an harpe.

8 Which hilith heuene with cloudis; and makith redi reyn to the erthe. Which bryngith forth hei in hillis; and eerbe to the seruice of men.

9 Which yyueth mete to her werk beestis; and to the briddys of crowis clepinge hym.

10 He schal not haue wille in the strengthe of an hors; nether it schal be wel plesaunt to hym in the leggis of a man.

PSALM 147

1 It is wel plesaunt to the Lord on men that dreden hym; and in hem that hopen on his mercy.

2 Jerusalem, herie thou the Lord; Syon, herie thou thi God.

3 For he hath coumfortid the lockis of thi yatis; he hath blessid thi sones in thee.

4 Which hath set thi coostis pees; and fillith thee with the fatnesse of wheete.

5 Which sendith out his speche to the erthe; his word renneth swiftli.

6 Which yyueth snow as wolle; spredith abrood a cloude as aische.

7 He sendith his cristal as mussels; who schal suffre bifore the face of his cooldnesse?

8 He schal sende out his word, and schal melte tho; his spirit schal blowe, and watris schulen flowe.

9 Which tellith his word to Jacob; and hise riytfulnessis and domes to Israel.

10 He dide not so to ech nacioun; and he schewide not hise domes to hem.

PSALM 148

1 The 'title of the hundrid and eiyte and fourtithe salm. Alleluya. Ye of heuenes, herie the Lord; herie ye hym in hiye thingis.

2 Alle hise aungels, herie ye hym; alle hise vertues, herye ye hym.

3 Sunne and moone, herie ye hym; alle sterris and liyt, herie ye hym.

4 Heuenes of heuenes, herie ye hym; and the watris that ben aboue heuenes,

5 herie ye the name of the Lord.

6 For he seide, and thingis weren maad; he comaundide, and thingis weren maad of nouyt. He ordeynede tho thingis in to the world, and in to the world of world; he settide a comaundement, and it schal not passe.

7 Ye of erthe, herie ye the Lord; dragouns, and alle depthis of watris.

8 Fier, hail, snow, iys, spiritis of tempestis; that don his word.

9 Mounteyns, and alle litle hillis; trees berynge fruyt, and alle cedris.

10 Wielde beestis, and alle tame beestis; serpentis, and fetherid briddis.

11 The kingis of erthe, and alle puplis; the princis, and alle iugis of erthe.

12 Yonge men, and virgyns, elde men with yongere, herie ye the name of the Lord;

13 for the name of hym aloone is enhaunsid.

14 His knouleching be on heuene and erthe; and he hath enhaunsid the horn of his puple. An ympne be to alle hise seyntis; to the children of Israel, to a puple neiyynge to hym.

PSALM 149

1 The 'title of the hundrid and nyne and fourtithe salm. Alleluya. Synge ye to the Lord a newe song; hise heriyng be in the chirche of seyntis.

2 Israel be glad in hym that made hym; and the douytris of Syon make ful out ioye in her king.

3 Herie thei his name in a queer; seie thei salm to hym in a tympan, and sautre.

4 For the Lord is wel plesid in his puple; and he hath reisid mylde men in to heelthe.

5 Seyntis schulen make ful out ioye in glorie; thei schulen be glad in her beddis.

6 The ful out ioiyngis of God in the throte of hem; and swerdis scharp on 'ech side in the hondis of hem.

7 To do veniaunce in naciouns; blamyngis in puplis.

8 To bynde the kyngis of hem in stockis; and the noble men of hem in yrun manaclis.

9 That thei make in hem doom writun; this is glorye to alle hise seyntis.

PSALM 150

1 The title of the hundrid and fiftithe salm. Alleluya. Herie ye the Lord in hise seyntis; herie ye hym in the firmament of his vertu.

2 Herie ye hym in hise vertues; herie ye hym bi the multitude of his greetnesse.

3 Herie ye hym in the soun of trumpe; herie ye hym in a sautre and harpe.

4 Herie ye hym in a tympane and queer; herie ye hym in strengis and orgun.

5 Herie ye hym in cymbalis sownynge wel, herye ye hym in cymbalis of iubilacioun;

6 ech spirit, herye the Lord.

PROVERBS

CAP 1

1 The parablis of Salomon, the sone of Dauid, king of Israel;
2 to kunne wisdom and kunnyng;

3 to vndurstonde the wordis of prudence; and to take the lernyng of teching; to take riytfulnesse, and dom, and equyte;

4 that felnesse be youun to litle children, and kunnyng, and vndurstonding to a yong wexynge man.

5 A wise man heringe schal be wisere; and a man vndurstondinge schal holde gouernails.

6 He schal perseyue a parable, and expownyng; the wordis of wise men, and the derk figuratif spechis of hem.

7 The drede of the Lord is the bigynning of wisdom; foolis dispisen wisdom and teching.

8 My sone, here thou the teching of thi fadir, and forsake thou not the lawe of thi modir;

9 that grace be addid, ethir encreessid, to thin heed, and a bie to thi necke.

10 Mi sone, if synneris flateren thee, assente thou not to hem.

11 If thei seien, Come thou with vs, sette we aspies to blood, hide we snaris of disseitis ayens an innocent without cause;

12 swolowe we him, as helle swolowith a man lyuynge; and al hool, as goynge doun in to a lake; we schulen fynde al preciouse catel,

13 we schulen fille oure housis with spuylis; sende thou lot with vs,

14 o purs be of vs alle;

15 my sone, go thou not with hem; forbede thi foot fro the pathis of hem.

16 For the feet of hem rennen to yuel; and thei hasten to schede out blood.

17 But a net is leid in veyn bifore the iyen of briddis, that han wengis.

18 Also 'thilke wickid disseyueris setten aspies ayens her owne blood; and maken redi fraudis ayens her soulis.

19 So the pathis of ech auerouse man rauyschen the soulis of hem that welden.

20 Wisdom prechith with outforth; in stretis it yyueth his vois.

21 It crieth ofte in the heed of cumpenyes; in the leeues of yatis of the citee it bringith forth hise wordis,

22 and seith, Hou long, ye litle men in wit, louen yong childhod, and foolis schulen coueyte tho thingis, that ben harmful to hem silf, and vnprudent men schulen hate kunnyng?

23 Be ye conuertid at my repreuyng; lo, Y schal profre forth to you my spirit, and Y schal schewe my wordis.

24 For Y clepide, and ye forsoken; Y helde forth myn hond, and noon was that bihelde.

25 Ye dispisiden al my councel; and chargiden not my blamyngis.

26 And Y schal leiye in youre perisching; and Y schal scorne you, whanne that, that ye dreden, cometh to you.

27 Whanne sodeyne wretchidnesse fallith in, and perisching bifallith as tempest; whanne tribulacioun and angwisch cometh on you.

28 Thanne thei schulen clepe me, and Y schal not here; thei schulen rise eerli, and thei schulen not fynde me.

29 For thei hatiden teching, and thei token not the drede of the Lord,

30 nether assentiden to my councel, and depraueden al myn amendyng.

31 Therfor thei schulen ete the fruytis of her weie; and thei schulen be fillid with her counseils.

32 The turnyng awei of litle men in wit schal sle hem; and the prosperite of foolis schal leese hem.

33 But he that herith me, schal reste with outen drede; and he schal vse abundaunce, whanne the drede of yuels is takun awei.

CAP 2

1 Mi sone, if thou resseyuest my wordis, 'and hidist myn heestis anentis thee;

2 that thin eere here wisdom, bowe thin herte to knowe prudence.

3 For if thou inwardli clepist wisdom, and bowist thin herte to prudence;

4 if thou sekist it as money, and diggist it out as tresours;

5 thanne thou schalt vndirstonde the drede of the Lord, and schalt fynde the kunnyng of God.

6 For the Lord yyueth wisdom; and prudence and kunnyng is of his mouth.

7 He schal kepe the heelthe of riytful men, and he schal defende hem that goen sympli.

8 And he schal kepe the pathis of riytfulnesse, and he schal kepe the weies of hooli men.

9 Thanne thou schalt vndirstonde riytfulnesse, and dom, and equytee, and ech good path.

10 If wysdom entrith in to thin herte, and kunnyng plesith thi soule,

11 good councel schal kepe thee, and prudence schal kepe thee; that thou be delyuered fro an yuel weie,

12 and fro a man that spekith weiward thingis.

13 Whiche forsaken a riytful weie, and goen bi derk weies;

14 whiche ben glad, whanne thei han do yuel, and maken ful out ioye in worste thingis;

15 whose weies ben weywerd, and her goyingis ben of yuel fame.

16 That thou be delyuered fro an alien womman, and fro a straunge womman, that makith soft hir wordis;

17 and forsakith the duyk of hir tyme of mariage,

18 and hath foryete the couenaunt of hir God. For the hous of hir is bowid to deeth, and hir pathis to helle.

19 Alle that entren to hir, schulen not turne ayen, nether schulen catche the pathis of lijf.

20 That thou go in a good weie, and kepe the pathis of iust men.

21 Forsothe thei that ben riytful, schulen dwelle in the lond; and symple men schulen perfitli dwelle ther ynne.

22 But vnfeithful men schulen be lost fro the loond; and thei that doen wickidli, schulen be takun awey fro it.

CAP 3

1 Mi sone, foryete thou not my lawe; and thyn herte kepe my comaundementis.

2 For tho schulen sette to thee the lengthe of daies, and the yeeris of lijf, and pees.

3 Merci and treuthe forsake thee not; bynde thou tho to thi throte, and write in the tablis of thin herte.

4 And thou schalt fynde grace, and good teching bifore God and men.

5 Haue thou trist in the Lord, of al thin herte; and triste thou not to thi prudence.

6 In alle thi weies thenke thou on hym, and he schal dresse thi goyngis.

7 Be thou not wijs anentis thi silf; drede thou God, and go awei fro yuel.

8 For whi helthe schal be in thi nawle, and moisting of thi boonys.

9 Onoure thou the Lord of thi catel, and of the beste of alle thi fruytis yyue thou to pore men;

10 and thi bernes schulen be fillid with abundaunce, and pressours schulen flowe with wiyn.

11 My sone, caste thou not awei the teching of the Lord; and faile thou not, whanne thou art chastisid of him.

12 For the Lord chastisith hym, whom he loueth; and as a fadir in the sone he plesith hym.

13 Blessid is the man that fyndith wisdom, and which flowith with prudence.

14 The geting therof is betere than the marchaundie of gold and of siluer; the fruytis therof ben the firste and clenneste.

15 It is preciousere than alle richessis; and alle thingis that ben desirid, moun not be comparisound to this.

16 Lengthe of daies is in the riythalf therof, and richessis and glorie ben in the lifthalf therof.

17 The weies therof ben feire weies, and alle the pathis therof ben pesible.

18 It is a tre of lijf to hem that taken it; and he that holdith it, is blessid.

19 The Lord foundide the erthe bi wisdom; he stablischide heuenes bi prudence.

20 The depthis of watris braken out bi his wisdom; and cloudis wexen togidere bi dewe.

21 My sone, these thingis flete not awei fro thin iyen; kepe thou my lawe, and my counsel;

22 and lijf schal be to thi soule, and grace 'schal be to thi chekis.

23 Thanne thou schalt go tristili in thi weie; and thi foot schal not snapere.

24 If thou schalt slepe, thou schalt not drede; thou schalt reste, and thi sleep schal be soft.

25 Drede thou not bi sudeyne feer, and the powers of wickid men fallynge in on thee.

26 For the Lord schal be at thi side; and he schal kepe thi foot, that thou be not takun.

27 Nil thou forbede to do wel him that mai; if thou maist, and do thou wel.

28 Seie thou not to thi frend, Go, and turne thou ayen, and to morewe Y schal yyue to thee; whanne thou maist yyue anoon.

29 Ymagyne thou not yuel to thi freend, whanne he hath trist in thee.

30 Stryue thou not ayens a man with out cause, whanne he doith noon yuel to thee.

31 Sue thou not an vniust man, sue thou not hise weies.

32 For ech disseyuer is abhomynacioun of the Lord; and his speking is with simple men.

33 Nedinesse is sent of the Lord in the hous of a wickid man; but the dwelling places of iust men schulen be blessid.

34 He schal scorne scorneris; and he schal yyue grace to mylde men.

35 Wise men schulen haue glorie; enhaunsing of foolis is schenschipe.

CAP 4

1 Sones, here ye the teching of the fadir; and perseiue ye, that ye kunne prudence.

2 Y schal yyue to you a good yifte; forsake ye not my lawe.

3 For whi and Y was the sone of my fadir, a tendir sone, and oon 'gendride bifore my modir.

4 And my fadir tauyte me, and seide, Thin herte resseyue my wordis; kepe thou myn heestis, and thou schalt lyue.

5 Welde thou wisdom, welde thou prudence; foryete thou not, nethir bowe thou awey fro the wordis of my mouth.

6 Forsake thou not it, and it schal kepe thee; loue thou it, and it schal kepe thee.

7 The bigynnyng of wisdom, welde thou wisdom; and in al thi possessioun gete thou prudence.

8 Take thou it, and it schal enhaunse thee; thou schalt be glorified of it, whanne thou hast biclippid it.

9 It schal yyue encresyngis of graces to thin heed; and a noble coroun schal defende thee.

10 Mi sone, here thou, and take my wordis; that the yeris of lijf be multiplied to thee.

11 Y schal schewe to thee the weie of wisdom; and Y schal lede thee bi the pathis of equyte.

12 In to whiche whanne thou hast entrid, thi goyngis schulen not be maad streit; and thou schalt rennen, and schalt not haue hirtyng.

13 Holde thou teching, and forsake it not; kepe thou it, for it is thi lijf.

14 Delite thou not in the pathis of wyckid men; and the weie of yuele men plese not thee.

15 Fle thou fro it, and passe thou not therbi; bowe thou awei, and forsake it.

16 For thei slepen not, 'no but thei han do yuele; and sleep is rauyschid fro hem, no but thei han disseyued.

17 Thei eten the breed of vnpite, and drinken the wyn of wickidnesse.

18 But the path of iust men goith forth as liyt schynynge, and encreessith til to perfit dai.

19 The weie of wickid men is derk; thei witen not where thei schulen falle.

20 Mi sone, herkene thou my wordis; and bowe doun thin eeris to my spechis.

21 Go not tho awei fro thyn iyen; kepe thou hem in the myddil of thin herte.

22 For tho ben lijf to men fyndynge thoo, and heelthe 'of al fleisch.

23 With al keping kepe thin herte, for lijf cometh forth of it.

24 Remoue thou a schrewid mouth fro thee; and backbitynge lippis be fer fro thee.

25 Thin iyen se riytful thingis; and thin iyeliddis go bifore thi steppis.

26 Dresse thou pathis to thi feet, and alle thi weies schulen be stablischid.

27 Bowe thou not to the riytside, nether to the leftside; turne awei thi foot fro yuel. For the Lord knowith the weies that ben at the riytside; but the weies ben weiward, that ben at the leftside. Forsothe he schal make thi goyngis riytful; and thi weies schulen be brouyt forth in pees.

CAP 5

1 Mi sone, perseyue thou my wisdom, and bowe doun thin eere to my prudence; that thou kepe thi thouytis,

2 and thi lippis kepe teching. Yyue thou not tent to the falsnesse of a womman;

3 for the lippis of an hoore ben an hony coomb droppinge, and hir throte is clerere than oile;

4 but the last thingis ben bittir as wormod, and hir tunge is scharp as a swerd keruynge on ech side.

5 Hir feet gon doun in to deeth; and hir steppis persen to hellis.

6 Tho goon not bi the path of lijf; hir steppis ben vncerteyn, and moun not be souyt out.

7 Now therfor, my sone, here thou me, and go not awei fro the wordis of my mouth.

8 Make fer thi weie fro hir, and neiye thou not to the doris of hir hous.

9 Yyue thou not thin onour to aliens, and thi yeeris to the cruel;

10 lest perauenture straungeris be fillid with thi strengthis, and lest thi trauels be in an alien hous;

11 and thou biweile in the laste daies, whanne thou hast wastid thi fleschis, and thi bodi; and thou seie,

12 Whi wlatide Y teching, and myn herte assentide not to blamyngis;

13 nether Y herde the voys of men techinge me, and Y bowide not doun myn eere to maistris?

14 Almest Y was in al yuel, in the myddis of the chirche, and of the synagoge.

15 Drinke thou watir of thi cisterne, and the floodis of thi pit.

16 Thi wellis be stremed forth; and departe thi watris in stretis.

17 Haue thou aloone 'tho watris; and aliens be not thi parceneris.

18 Thi veyne be blessid; and be thou glad with the womman of thi yong wexynge age.

19 An hynde moost dereworthe; and an hert calf moost acceptable. Hir teetis fille thee in al tyme; and delite thou contynueli in the loue of hir.

20 Mi sone, whi art thou disseyued of an alien womman; and art fostrid in the bosum of an othere?

21 The Lord seeth the weie of a man; and biholdith alle hise steppis.

22 The wickidnessis of a wyckid man taken hym; and he is boundun with the roopis of hise synnes.

23 He schal die, for he hadde not lernyng; and he schal be disseyued in the mychilnesse of his fooli.

CAP 6

1 Mi sone, if thou hast bihiyt for thi freend; thou hast fastned thin hoond at a straunger.

2 Thou art boundun bi the wordis of thi mouth; and thou art takun with thin owne wordis.

3 Therfor, my sone, do thou that that Y seie, and delyuere thi silf; for thou hast fallun in to the hond of thi neiybore. Renne thou aboute, haste thou, reise thi freend;

4 yyue thou not sleep to thin iyen, nether thin iyeliddis nappe.

5 Be thou rauyschid as a doo fro the hond; and as a bridde fro aspiyngis of the foulere.

6 O! thou slowe man, go to the 'amte, ether pissemyre; and biholde thou hise weies, and lerne thou wisdom.

7 Which whanne he hath no duyk, nethir comaundour, nether prince;

8 makith redi in somer mete to hym silf, and gaderith togidere in heruest that, that he schal ete.

9 Hou long schalt thou, slow man, slepe? whanne schalt thou rise fro thi sleep?

10 A litil thou schalt slepe, a litil thou schalt nappe; a litil thou schalt ioyne togidere thin hondis, that thou slepe.

11 And nedynesse, as a weigoere, schal come to thee; and pouert, as an armed man. Forsothe if thou art not slow, thi ripe corn schal come as a welle; and nedynesse schal fle fer fro thee.

12 A man apostata, a man vnprofitable, he goith with a weiward mouth;

13 he bekeneth with iyen, he trampith with the foot, he spekith with the fyngur,

14 bi schrewid herte he ymagyneth yuel, and in al tyme he sowith dissenciouns.

15 His perdicioun schal come to hym anoon, and he schal be brokun sodeynli; and he schal no more haue medecyn.

16 Sixe thingis ben, whyche the Lord hatith; and hise soule cursith the seuenthe thing.

17 Hiye iyen, a tunge liere, hondis schedinge out innocent blood,

18 an herte ymagynynge worste thouytis, feet swifte to renne in to yuel,

19 a man bringynge forth lesingis, a fals witnesse; and him that sowith discordis among britheren.

20 Mi sone, kepe the comaundementis of thi fadir; and forsake not the lawe of thi modir.

21 Bynde thou tho continueli in thin herte; and cumpasse 'to thi throte.

22 Whanne thou goist, go tho with thee; whanne thou slepist, kepe tho thee; and thou wakynge speke with tho.

23 For the comaundement of God is a lanterne, and the lawe is liyt, and the blamyng of techyng is the weie of lijf;

24 'that the comaundementis kepe thee fro an yuel womman, and fro a flaterynge tunge of a straunge womman.

25 Thin herte coueite not the fairnesse of hir; nether be thou takun bi the signes of hir.

26 For the prijs of an hoore is vnnethe of o loof; but a womman takith the preciouse soule of a man.

27 Whether a man mai hide fier in his bosum, that hise clothis brenne not;

28 ethir go on colis, and hise feet be not brent?

29 So he that entrith to the wijf of his neiybore; schal not be cleene, whanne he hath touchid hir.

30 It is not greet synne, whanne a man stelith; for he stelith to fille an hungri soule.

31 And he takun schal yelde the seuenthe fold; and he schal yyue al the catel of his hous, and schal delyuere hym silf.

32 But he that is avouter; schal leese his soule, for the pouert of herte.

33 He gaderith filthe, and sclaundrith to hym silf; and his schenschip schal not be don awei.

34 For the feruent loue and strong veniaunce of the man schal not spare in the dai of veniaunce,

35 nether schal assente to the preieris of ony; nether schal take ful many yiftis for raunsum.

CAP 7

1 Mi sone, kepe thou my wordis; and kepe myn heestis to thee. Sone, onoure thou the Lord, and thou schalt be 'myyti; but outakun hym drede thou not an alien.

2 Kepe thou myn heestis, and thou schalt lyue; and my lawe as the appil of thin iyen.

3 Bynde thou it in thi fyngris; write thou it in the tablis of thin herte.

4 Seie thou to wisdom, Thou art my sistir; and clepe thou prudence thi frendesse.

5 That it kepe thee fro a straunge womman; and fro an alien womman, that makith hir wordis swete.

6 For whi fro the wyndow of myn hous bi the latijs Y bihelde; and Y se litle children.

7 I biholde a yong man coward,

8 that passith bi the stretis, bisidis the corner; and he

9 goith niy the weie of hir hous in derk tyme, whanne the dai drawith to niyt, in the derknessis and myst of the nyyt.

10 And lo! a womman, maad redi with ournement of an hoore to disseyue soulis, meetith hym, and sche is a ianglere, and goynge about,

11 and vnpacient of reste, and mai not stonde in the hous with hir feet;

12 and now without forth, now in stretis, now bisidis corneris sche 'aspieth.

13 And sche takith, and kissith the yong man; and flaterith with wowynge cheer, and seith, Y ouyte sacrifices for heelthe;

14 to dai Y haue yolde my vowis.

15 Therfor Y yede out in to thi meetyng, and Y desiride to se thee; and Y haue founde thee.

16 Y haue maad my bed with coordis, Y haue arayed with tapetis peyntid of Egipt;

17 Y haue bispreynt my bed with myrre, and aloes, and canel.

18 Come thou, be we fillid with tetis, and vse we collyngis that ben coueitid; til the dai bigynne to be cleer.

19 For myn hosebonde is not in his hows; he is goon a ful long weie.

20 He took with hym a bagge of money; he schal turne ayen in to his hous in the dai of ful moone.

21 Sche boonde hym with many wordis; and sche drow forth hym with flateryngis of lippis.

22 Anoon he as an oxe led to slayn sacrifice sueth hir, and as a ioli lomb and vnkunnynge; and the fool woot not, that he is drawun to bondys,

23 til an arowe perse his mawe. As if a brid hastith to the snare; and woot not, that it is don of the perel of his lijf.

24 Now therfor, my sone, here thou me; and perseyue the wordis of my mouth.

25 Lest thi soule be drawun awei in the weies of hir; nether be thou disseyued in the pathis of hir.

26 For sche castide doun many woundid men; and alle strongeste men weren slayn of hir.

27 The weies of helle is hir hous; and persen in to ynnere thingis of deeth.

CAP 8

1 Whether wisdom crieth not ofte; and prudence yyueth his vois?

2 In souereyneste and hiy coppis, aboue the weie, in the myddis of pathis,

3 and it stondith bisidis the yate of the citee, in thilke closyngis, and spekith, and seith, A!

4 ye men, Y crie ofte to you; and my vois is to the sones of men.

5 Litle children, vndirstonde ye wisdom; and ye vnwise men, 'perseyue wisdom.

6 Here ye, for Y schal speke of grete thingis; and my lippis schulen be openyd, to preche riytful thingis.

7 My throte schal bithenke treuthe; and my lippis schulen curse a wickid man.

8 My wordis ben iust; no schrewid thing, nether weiward is in tho.

9 'My wordis ben riytful to hem that vndurstonden; and ben euene to hem that fynden kunnyng.

10 Take ye my chastisyng, and not money; chese ye teching more than tresour.

11 For wisdom is betere than alle richessis moost preciouse; and al desirable thing mai not be comparisound therto.

12 Y, wisdom, dwelle in counsel; and Y am among lernyd thouytis.

13 The drede of the Lord hatith yuel; Y curse boost, and pride, and a schrewid weie, and a double tungid mouth.

14 Counseil is myn, and equyte 'is myn; prudence is myn, and strengthe 'is myn.

15 Kyngis regnen bi me; and the makeris of lawis demen iust thingis bi me.

16 Princis comaunden bi me; and myyti men demen riytfulnesse bi me.

17 I loue hem that louen me; and thei that waken eerli to me, schulen fynde me.

18 With me ben rychessis, and glorie; souereyn richessis, and riytfulnesse.

19 My fruyt is betere than gold, and precyouse stoon; and my seedis ben betere than chosun siluer.

20 Y go in the weies of riytfulnesse, in the myddis of pathis of doom;

21 that Y make riche hem that louen me, and that Y fille her tresouris.

22 The Lord weldide me in the bigynnyng of hise weies; bifore that he made ony thing, at the bigynnyng.

23 Fro with out bigynnyng Y was ordeined; and fro elde tymes, bifor that the erthe was maad.

24 Depthis of watris weren not yit; and Y was conseyued thanne. The wellis of watris hadden not brokun out yit,

25 and hillis stoden not togidere yit bi sad heuynesse; bifor litil hillis Y was born.

26 Yit he hadde not maad erthe; and floodis, and the herris of the world.

27 Whanne he made redi heuenes, Y was present; whanne he cumpasside the depthis of watris bi certeyn lawe and cumpas.

28 Whanne he made stidfast the eir aboue; and weiede the wellis of watris.

29 Whanne he cumpasside to the see his marke; and settide lawe to watris, that tho schulden not passe her coostis. Whanne he peiside the foundementis of erthe;

30 Y was making alle thingis with him. And Y delitide bi alle daies, and pleiede bifore hym in al tyme,

31 and Y pleiede in the world; and my delices ben to be with the sones of men.

32 Now therfor, sones, here ye me; blessid ben thei that kepen my weies.

33 Here ye teching, and be ye wise men; and nile ye caste it awei.

34 Blessid is the man that herith me, and that wakith at my yatis al dai; and kepith at the postis of my dore.

35 He that fyndith me, schal fynde lijf; and schal drawe helthe of the Lord.

36 But he that synneth ayens me, schal hurte his soule; alle that haten me, louen deeth.

CAP 9

1 Wisdom bildide an hous to him silf; he hewide out seuene pileris,

2 he offride his slayn sacrifices, he medlide wijn, and settide forth his table.

3 He sente hise handmaides, that thei schulden clepe to the tour; and to the wallis of the citee.

4 If ony man is litil; come he to me. And wisdom spak to vnwise men,

5 Come ye, ete ye my breed; and drynke ye the wiyn, which Y haue medlid to you.

6 Forsake ye yong childhed, and lyue ye; and go ye bi the weyes of prudence.

7 He that techith a scornere, doith wrong to him silf; and he that vndirnymmeth a wickid man, gendrith a wem to him silf.

8 Nile thou vndirnyme a scornere; lest he hate thee. Vndirnyme thou a wise man; and he schal loue thee.

9 Yyue thou occasioun to a wise man; and wisdom schal be encreessid to hym. Teche thou a iust man; and he schal haste to take.

10 The bigynnyng of wisdom is the dreed of the Lord; and prudence is the kunnyng of seyntis.

11 For thi daies schulen be multiplied bi me; and yeeris of lijf schulen be encreessid to thee.

12 If thou art wijs; thou schalt be to thi silf, and to thi neiyboris. Forsothe if thou art a scornere; thou aloone schalt bere yuel.

13 A fonned womman, and ful of cry, and ful of vnleueful lustis, and that kan no thing outirli,

14 sittith in the doris of hir hous, on a seete, in an hiy place of the cite;

15 to clepe men passinge bi the weie, and men goynge in her iournei.

16 Who is a litil man 'of wit; bowe he to me. And sche spak to a coward,

17 Watris of thefte ben swettere, and breed hid is swettere.

18 And wiste not that giauntis ben there; and the gestis 'of hir ben in the depthis of helle. Sotheli he that schal be applied, ether fastned, to hir; schal go doun to hellis. For whi he that goith awei fro hir; schal be saued.

CAP 10

1 The parablis of Salomon. A wijs sone makith glad the fadir; but a fonned sone is the sorewe of his modir.

2 Tresouris of wickidnesse schulen not profite; but riytfulnesse schal delyuere fro deth.

3 The Lord schal not turmente the soule of a iust man with hungur; and he schal distrie the tresouns of vnpitouse men.

4 A slow hond hath wrouyt nedynesse; but the hond of stronge men makith redi richessis. Forsothe he that enforsith to gete 'ony thing bi leesyngis, fedith the wyndis; sotheli the same man sueth briddis fleynge.

5 He that gaderith togidere in heruest, is a wijs sone; but he that slepith in sommer, is a sone of confusioun.

6 The blessing of God is ouer the heed of a iust man; but wickidnesse hilith the mouth of wickid men.

7 The mynde of a iust man schal be with preisingis; and the name of wickid men schal wexe rotun.

8 A wijs man schal resseyue comaundementis with herte; a fool is betun with lippis.

9 He that goith simpli, goith tristili; but he that makith schrewid hise weies, schal be opyn.

10 He that bekeneth with the iye, schal yyue sorewe; a fool schal be betun with lippis.

11 The veyne of lijf is the mouth of a iust man; but the mouth of wickid men hilith wickidnesse.

12 Hatrede reisith chidingis; and charite hilith alle synnes.

13 Wisdom is foundun in the lippis of a wise man; and a yerd in the bak of him that is nedi of herte.

14 Wise men hiden kunnyng; but the mouth of a fool is nexte to confusioun.

15 The catel of a riche man is the citee of his strengthe; the drede of pore men is the nedynesse of hem.

16 The werk of a iust man is to lijf; but the fruyt of a wickid man is to synne.

17 The weie of lijf is to him that kepith chastising; but he that forsakith blamyngis, errith.

18 False lippis hiden hatrede; he that bringith forth dispisinge is vnwijs.

19 Synne schal not faile in myche spekyng; but he that mesurith hise lippis, is moost prudent.

20 Chosun siluer is the tunge of a iust man; the herte of wickid men is for nouyt.

21 The lippis of a iust man techen ful manye men; but thei that ben vnlerned, schulen die in nedinesse of herte.

22 The blessing of the Lord makith riche men; and turment schal not be felowschipid to hem.

23 A fool worchith wickidnesse as bi leiyyng; but 'wisdom is prudence to a man.

24 That that a wickid man dredith, schal come on hym; the desire of iust men schalbe youun to hem.

25 As a tempeste passynge, a wickid man schal not be; but a iust man schal be as an euerlastynge foundement.

26 As vynegre noieth the teeth, and smoke noieth the iyen; so a slow man noieth hem that senten hym in the weie.

27 The drede of the Lord encreesith daies; and the yeeris of wickid men schulen be maad schort.

28 Abiding of iust men is gladnesse; but the hope of wickid men schal perische.

29 The strengthe of a symple man is the weie of the Lord; and drede to hem that worchen yuel.

30 A iust man schal not be moued with outen ende; but wickid men schulen not dwelle on the erthe.

31 The mouth of a iust man schal bringe forth wisdom; the tunge of schrewis schal perische.

32 The lippis of a iust man biholden pleasaunt thingis; and the mouth of wickid men byholdith weiward thingis.

CAP 11

1 A gileful balaunce is abhominacioun anentis God; and an euene weiyte is his wille.

2 Where pride is, there also dispising schal be; but where meeknesse is, there also is wisdom.

3 The simplenesse of iust men schal dresse hem; and the disseyuyng of weiward men schal destrie hem.

4 Richessis schulen not profite in the dai of veniaunce; but riytfulnesse schal delyuere fro deth.

5 The riytfulnesse of a simple man schal dresse his weie; and a wickid man schal falle in his wickidnesse.

6 The riytfulnesse of riytful men schal delyuere hem; and wickid men schulen be takun in her aspiyngis.

7 Whanne a wickid man is deed, noon hope schal be ferther; and abidyng of bisy men schal perische.

8 A iust man is delyuered from angwisch; and a wickid man schal be youun for hym.

9 A feynere bi mouth disseyueth his freend; but iust men schulen be deliuered bi kunnyng.

10 A citee schal be enhaunsid in the goodis of iust men; and preysyng schal be in the perdicioun of wickid men.

11 A citee schal be enhaunsid bi blessing of iust men; and it schal be distried bi the mouth of wickid men.

12 He that dispisith his freend, is nedi in herte; but a prudent man schal be stille.

13 He that goith gilefuli, schewith priuetees; but he that is feithful, helith the priuetee of a freend.

14 Where a gouernour is not, the puple schal falle; but helthe 'of the puple is, where ben many counsels.

15 He that makith feith for a straunger, schal be turmentid with yuel; but he that eschewith snaris, schal be sikur.

16 A graciouse womman schal fynde glorie; and stronge men schulen haue richessis.

17 A merciful man doith wel to his soule; but he that is cruel, castith awei, yhe, kynnesmen.

18 A wickid man makith vnstable werk; but feithful mede is to hym, that sowith riytfulnesse.

19 Merci schal make redi lijf; and the suyng of yuels 'schal make redi deth.

20 A schrewid herte is abhomynable to the Lord; and his wille is in hem, that goen symply.

21 Thouy hond be in the hond, an yuel man schal not be innocent; but the seed of iust men schal be sauyd.

22 A goldun 'sercle, ether ryng, in the 'nose thrillis of a sowe, a womman fair and fool.

23 The desir of iust men is al good; abiding of wickid men is woodnesse.

24 Sum men departen her owne thingis, and ben maad richere; other men rauyschen thingis, that ben not hern, and ben euere in nedynesse.

25 A soule that blessith, schal be maad fat; and he that fillith, schal be fillid also.

26 He that hidith wheete 'in tyme, schal be cursid among the puplis; but blessyng schal come on the heed of silleris.

27 Wel he risith eerli, that sekith good thingis; but he that is a serchere of yuels, schal be oppressid of tho.

28 He that tristith in hise richessis, schal falle; but iust men schulen buriowne as a greene leef.

29 He that disturblith his hows, schal haue wyndis in possessioun; and he that is a fool, schal serue a wijs man.

30 The fruyt of a riytful man is the tre of lijf; and he that takith soulis, is a wijs man.

31 If a iust man receyueth in erthe, how miche more an vnfeithful man, and synnere.

CAP 12

1 He that loueth chastisyng, loueth kunnyng; but he that hatith blamyngis, is vnwijs.

2 He that is good, schal drawe to hym silf grace of the Lord; but he that tristith in hise thouytis, doith wickidli.

3 A man schal not be maad strong by wyckidnesse; and the root of iust men schal not be moued.

4 A diligent womman is a coroun to hir hosebond; and rot is in the boonys of that womman, that doith thingis worthi of confusioun.

5 The thouytis of iust men ben domes; and the counselis of wickid men ben gileful.

6 The wordis of wickid men setten tresoun to blood; the mouth of iust men schal delyuere hem.

7 Turne thou wickid men, and thei schulen not be; but the housis of iust men schulen dwelle perfitli.

8 A man schal be knowun bi his teching; but he that is veyn and hertles, schal be open to dispising.

9 Betere is a pore man, and sufficient to him silf, than a gloriouse man, and nedi of breed.

10 A iust man knowith the soulis of hise werk beestis; but the entrailis of wickid men ben cruel.

11 He that worchith his lond, schal be fillid with looues; but he that sueth idilnesse, is moost fool. He that is swete, lyueth in temperaunces; and in hise monestyngis he forsakith dispisyngis.

12 The desir of a wickid man is the memorial of worste thingis; but the roote of iust men schal encreesse.

13 For the synnes of lippis 'falling doun neiyeth to an yuel man; but a iust man schal scape fro angwisch.

14 Of the fruyt of his mouth ech man schal be fillid with goodis; and bi the werkis of hise hondis it schal be yoldun to him.

15 The weie of a fool is riytful in hise iyen; but he that is wijs, herith counsels.

16 A fool schewith anoon his ire; but he that dissymelith wrongis, is wijs.

17 He that spekith that, that he knowith, is a iuge of riytfulnesse; but he that lieth, is a gileful witnesse.

18 A man is that bihetith, and he is prickid as with the swerd of conscience; but the tunge of wise men is helthe.

19 The lippe of treuthe schal be stidfast with outen ende; but he that is a sudeyn witnesse, makith redi the tunge of leesyng.

20 Gile is in the herte of hem that thenken yuels; but ioye sueth hem, that maken counsels of pees.

21 What euere bifallith to a iust man, it schal not make hym sori; but wickid men schulen be fillid with yuel.

22 False lippis is abhominacioun to the Lord; but thei that don feithfuli, plesen him.

23 A fel man hilith kunnyng; and the herte of vnwise men stirith foli.

24 The hond of stronge men schal haue lordschip; but the hond that is slow, schal serue to tributis.

25 Morenynge in the herte of a iust man schal make hym meke; and he schal be maad glad bi a good word.

26 He that dispisith harm for a frend, is a iust man; but the weie of wickid men schal disseyue hem.

27 A gileful man schal not fynde wynnyng; and the substaunce of man schal be the prijs of gold.

28 Lijf is in the path of riytfulnesse; but the wrong weie leedith to deeth.

CAP 13

1 A wijs sone is the teching of the fadir; but he that is a scornere, herith not, whanne he is repreuyd.

2 A man schal be fillid with goodis of the fruit of his mouth; but the soule of vnpitouse men is wickid.

3 He that kepith his mouth, kepith his soule; but he that is vnwar to speke, schal feel yuels.

4 A slow man wole, and wole not; but the soule of hem that worchen schal be maad fat.

5 A iust man schal wlate a fals word; but a wickid man schendith, and schal be schent.

6 Riytfulnesse kepith the weie of an innocent man; but wickidnesse disseyueth a synnere.

7 A man is as riche, whanne he hath no thing; and a man is as pore, whanne he is in many richessis.

8 Redempcioun of the soule of man is hise richessis; but he that is pore, suffrith not blamyng.

9 The liyt of iust men makith glad; but the lanterne of wickid men schal be quenchid.

10 Stryues ben euere a mong proude men; but thei that don alle thingis with counsel, ben gouerned bi wisdom.

11 Hastid catel schal be maad lesse; but that that is gaderid litil and litil with hond, schal be multiplied.

12 Hope which is dilaied, turmentith the soule; a tre of lijf is desir comyng.

13 He that bacbitith ony thing, byndith hym silf in to tyme to comynge; but he that dredith the comaundement, schal lyue in pees.

14 The lawe of a wise man is a welle of lijf; that he bowe awei fro the falling of deth.

15 Good teching schal yyue grace; a swolowe is in the weie of dispiseris.

16 A fel man doith alle thingis with counsel; but he that is a fool, schal opene foli.

17 The messanger of a wickid man schal falle in to yuel; a feithful messanger is helthe.

18 Nedynesse and schenschip is to him that forsakith techyng; but he that assentith to a blamere, schal be glorified.

19 Desir, if it is fillid, delitith the soule; foolis wlaten hem that fleen yuels.

20 He that goith with wijs men, schal be wijs; the freend of foolis schal be maad lijk hem.

21 Yuel pursueth synneris; and goodis schulen be yoldun to iust men.

22 A good man schal leeue aftir him eiris, sones, and the sones of sones; and the catel of a synnere is kept to a iust man.

23 Many meetis ben in the new tilid feeldis of fadris; and ben gaderid to othere men with out doom.

24 He that sparith the yerde, hatith his sone; but he that loueth him, techith bisili.

25 A iust man etith, and fillith his soule; but the wombe of wickid men is vnable to be fillid.

CAP 14

1 A wijs womman bildith hir hous; and an unwijs womman schal distrie with hondis an hous bildid.

2 A man goynge in riytful weie, and dredinge God, is dispisid of hym, that goith in a weie of yuel fame.

3 The yerde of pride is in the mouth of a fool; the lippis of wijs men kepen hem.

4 Where oxis ben not, the cratche is void; but where ful many cornes apperen, there the strengthe of oxe is opyn.

5 A feithful witnesse schal not lie; a gileful witnesse bringith forth a leesing.

6 A scornere sekith wisdom, and he fyndith not; the teching of prudent men is esy.

7 Go thou ayens a man a fool; and he schal not knowe the lippis of prudence.

8 The wisdom of a fel man is to vndirstonde his weie; and the vnwarnesse of foolis errith.

9 A fool scorneth synne; grace schal dwelle among iust men.

10 The herte that knowith the bittirnesse of his soule; a straunger schal not be meddlid in the ioie therof.

11 The hous of wickid men schal be don awei; the tabernaclis of iust men schulen buriowne.

12 Sotheli a weie is, that semeth iust to a man; but the laste thingis therof leden forth to deth.

13 Leiyyng schal be medlid with sorewe; and morenyng ocupieth the laste thingis of ioye.

14 A fool schal be fillid with hise weies; and a good man schal be aboue hym.

15 An innocent man bileueth to eche word; a felle man biholdith hise goyngis.

16 A wijs man dredith, and bowith awei fro yuel; a fool skippith ouer, and tristith.

17 A man vnpacient schal worche foli; and a gileful man is odiouse.

18 Litle men of wit schulen holde foli; and felle men schulen abide kunnyng.

19 Yuel men schulen ligge bifor goode men; and vnpitouse men bifor the yatis of iust men.

20 A pore man schal be hateful, yhe, to his neiybore; but many men ben frendis of riche men.

21 He that dispisith his neiybore, doith synne; but he that doith merci to a pore man, schal be blessid. He that bileueth in the Lord, loueth merci;

22 thei erren that worchen yuel. Merci and treuthe maken redi goodis;

23 abundaunce 'schal be in ech good werk. Sotheli where ful many wordis ben, there nedynesse is ofte.

24 The coroun of wise men is the richessis of hem; the fooli of foolis is vnwarnesse.

25 A feithful witnesse delyuereth soulis; and a fals man bringith forth leesyngis.

26 In the drede of the Lord is triste of strengthe; and hope schal be to the sones of it.

27 The drede of the Lord is a welle of lijf; that it bowe awei fro the fallyng of deth.

28 The dignite of the king is in the multitude of puple; and the schenschipe of a prince is in the fewnesse of puple.

29 He that is pacient, is gouerned bi myche wisdom; but he that is vnpacient, enhaunsith his foli.

30 Helthe of herte is the lijf of fleischis; enuye is rot of boonys.

31 He that falsli chalengith a nedi man, dispisith his maker; but he that hath merci on a pore man, onourith that makere.

32 A wickid man is put out for his malice; but a iust man hopith in his deth.

33 Wisdom restith in the herte of a wijs man; and he schal teche alle vnlerned men.

34 Riytfulnesse reisith a folc; synne makith puplis wretchis.

35 A mynystre vndurstondynge is acceptable to a kyng; a mynystre vnprofitable schal suffre the wrathfulnesse of him.

CAP 15

1 A soft answere brekith ire; an hard word reisith woodnesse.

2 The tunge of wise men ourneth kunnyng; the mouth of foolis buylith out foli.

3 In ech place the iyen of the Lord biholden good men, and yuel men.

4 A plesaunt tunge is the tre of lijf; but the tunge which is vnmesurable, schal defoule the spirit.

5 A fool scorneth the techyng of his fadir; but he that kepith blamyngis, schal be maad wisere. Moost vertu schal be in plenteuouse riytfulnesse; but the thouytis of wickid men schulen be drawun vp bi the roote.

6 The hous of a iust man is moost strengthe; and disturbling is in the fruitis of a wickid man.

7 The lippis of wise men schulen sowe abrood kunnyng; the herte of foolis schal be vnlijc.

8 The sacrifices of wickyd men ben abhomynable to the Lord; avowis of iust men ben plesaunt.

9 The lijf of the vnpitouse man is abhomynacioun to the Lord; he that sueth riytfulnesse, schal be loued of the Lord.

10 Yuel teching is of men forsakinge the weie of lijf; he that hatith blamyngis, schal die.

11 Helle and perdicioun ben open bifor the Lord; hou myche more the hertis of sones of men.

12 A man ful of pestilence loueth not hym that repreueth him; and he goith not to wyse men.

13 A ioiful herte makith glad the face; the spirit is cast doun in the morenyng of soule.

14 The herte of a wijs man sekith techyng; and the mouth of foolis is fed with vnkunnyng.

15 Alle the daies of a pore man ben yuele; a sikir soule is a contynuel feeste.

16 Betere is a litil with the drede of the Lord, than many tresouris and vnfillable.

17 It is betere to be clepid to wortis with charite, than with hatrede to a calf maad fat.

18 A wrathful man reisith chidyngis; he that is pacient, swagith chidyngis reisid.

19 The weie of slow men is an hegge of thornes; the weie of iust men is with out hirtyng.

20 A wise sone makith glad the fadir; and a fonned man dispisith his modir.

21 Foli is ioye to a fool; and a prudent man schal dresse hise steppis.

22 Thouytis ben distried, where no counsel is; but where many counseleris ben, tho ben confermyd.

23 A man is glad in the sentence of his mouth; and a couenable word is best.

24 The path of lijf is on a lernyd man; that he bowe awei fro the laste helle.

25 The Lord schal distrie the hows of proude men; and he schal make stidefast the coostis of a widewe.

26 Iuele thouytis is abhomynacioun of the Lord; and a cleene word moost fair schal be maad stidfast of hym.

27 He that sueth aueryce, disturblith his hous; but he that hatith yiftis schal lyue. Synnes ben purgid bi merci and feith; ech man bowith awei fro yuel bi the drede of the Lord.

28 The soule of a iust man bithenkith obedience; the mouth of wickid men is ful of yuelis.

29 The Lord is fer fro wickid men; and he schal here the preyers of iust men.

30 The liyt of iyen makith glad the soule; good fame makith fat the boonys.

31 The eere that herith the blamyngis of lijf, schal dwelle in the myddis of wise men.

32 He that castith awei chastisyng, dispisith his soule; but he that assentith to blamyngis, is pesible holdere of the herte.

33 The drede of the Lord is teching of wisdom; and mekenesse goith bifore glorie.

CAP 16

1 It perteyneth to man to make redi the soule; and it perteyneth to the Lord to gouerne the tunge.

2 Alle the weies of men ben opyn to the iyen of God; the Lord is a weiere of spiritis.

3 Schewe thi werkys to the Lord; and thi thouytis schulen be dressid.

4 The Lord wrouyte alle thingis for hym silf; and he made redi a wickid man to the yuel dai.

5 Abhomynacioun of the Lord is ech proude man; yhe, thouy the hond is to the hond, he schal not be innocent. The bigynnyng of good weie is to do riytwisnesse; forsothe it is more acceptable at God, than to offre sacrifices.

6 Wickidnesse is ayen bouyt bi merci and treuthe; and me bowith awei fro yuel bi the drede of the Lord.

7 Whanne the weyes of man plesen the Lord, he schal conuerte, yhe, hise enemyes to pees.

8 Betere is a litil with riytfulnesse, than many fruytis with wickidnesse.

9 The herte of a man schal dispose his weie; but it perteyneth to the Lord to dresse hise steppis.

10 Dyuynyng is in the lippis of a king; his mouth schal not erre in doom.

11 The domes of the Lord ben weiyte and a balaunce; and hise werkis ben alle the stoonys of the world.

12 Thei that don wickidli ben abhomynable to the king; for the trone of the rewme is maad stidfast bi riytfulnesse.

13 The wille of kyngis is iust lippis; he that spekith riytful thingis, schal be dressid.

14 Indignacioun of the kyng is messangeris of deth; and a wijs man schal plese him.

15 Lijf is in the gladnesse of the 'cheer of the king; and his merci is as a reyn comynge late.

16 Welde thou wisdom, for it is betere than gold; and gete thou prudence, for it is precyousere than siluer.

17 The path of iust men bowith awei yuelis; the kepere of his soule kepith his weie.

18 Pride goith bifore sorewe; and the spirit schal be enhaunsid byfor fallyng.

19 It is betere to be maad meke with mylde men, than to departe spuylis with proude men.

20 A lerned man in word schal fynde goodis; and he that hopith in the Lord is blessid.

21 He that is wijs in herte, schal be clepid prudent; and he that is swete in speche, schal fynde grettere thingis.

22 The welle of lijf is the lernyng of him that weldith; the techyng of foolis is foli.

23 The herte of a wijs man schal teche his mouth; and schal encreesse grace to hise lippis.

24 Wordis wel set togidere is a coomb of hony; helthe of boonys is the swetnesse of soule.

25 A weye is that semeth riytful to a man; and the laste thingis therof leden to deth.

26 The soule of a man trauelinge trauelith to hym silf; for his mouth compellide hym.

27 An vnwijs man diggith yuel; and fier brenneth in hise lippis.

28 A weiward man reisith stryues; and a man ful of wordis departith princis.

29 A wickid man flaterith his frend; and ledith hym bi a weie not good.

30 He that thenkith schrewid thingis with iyen astonyed, bitith hise lippis, and parformeth yuel.

31 A coroun of dignyte is eelde, that schal be foundun in the weies of riytfulnesse.

32 A pacient man is betere than a stronge man; and he that 'is lord of his soule, is betere than an ouercomere of citees.

33 Lottis ben sent into the bosum; but tho ben temperid of the Lord.

CAP 17

1 Betere is a drie mussel with ioye, than an hous ful of sacrifices with chidyng.

2 A wijs seruaunt schal be lord of fonned sones; and he schal departe eritage among britheren.

3 As siluer is preued bi fier, and gold is preued bi a chymnei, so the Lord preueth hertis.

4 An yuel man obeieth to a wickid tunge; and a fals man obeieth to false lippis.

5 He that dispisith a pore man, repreueth his maker; and he that is glad in the fallyng of another man, schal not be vnpunyschid.

6 The coroun of elde men is the sones of sones; and the glorie of sones is the fadris of hem.

7 Wordis wel set togidere bisemen not a fool; and a liynge lippe bicometh not a prince.

8 A preciouse stoon moost acceptable is the abiding of hym that sekith; whidur euere he turneth hym silf, he vndurstondith prudentli.

9 He that helith trespas, sekith frenschipis; he that rehersith bi an hiy word, departith hem, that ben knyt togidere in pees.

10 A blamyng profitith more at a prudent man, than an hundryd woundis at a fool.

11 Euere an yuel man sekith stryues; forsothe a cruel aungel schal be sent ayens hym.

12 It spedith more to meete a femal bere, whanne the whelpis ben rauyschid, than a fool tristynge to hym silf in his foli.

13 Yuel schal not go a wei fro the hous of hym, that yeldith yuels for goodis.

14 He that leeueth watir, is heed of stryues; and bifor that he suffrith wrong, he forsakith dom.

15 Bothe he that iustifieth a wickid man, and he that condempneth a iust man, euer ethir is abhomynable at God.

16 What profitith it to a fool to haue richessis, sithen he mai not bie wisdom? He that makith his hous hiy, sekith falling; and he that eschewith to lerne, schal falle in to yuels.

17 He that is a frend, loueth in al tyme; and a brother is preuyd in angwischis.

18 A fonned man schal make ioie with hondis, whanne he hath bihiyt for his frend.

19 He that bithenkith discordis, loueth chidingis; and he that enhaunsith his mouth, sekith fallyng.

20 He that is of weiward herte, schal not fynde good; and he that turneth the tunge, schal falle in to yuel.

21 A fool is borun in his schenschipe; but nether the fadir schal be glad in a fool.

22 A ioiful soule makith likinge age; a sorewful spirit makith drie boonys.

23 A wickid man takith yiftis fro the bosum, to mys turne the pathis of doom.

24 Wisdom schyneth in the face of a prudent man; the iyen of foolis ben in the endis of erthe.

25 A fonned sone is the ire of the fadir, and the sorewe of the modir that gendride hym.

26 It is not good to brynge in harm to a iust man; nether to smyte the prince that demeth riytfuli.

27 He that mesurith his wordis, is wijs and prudent; and a lerud man is of preciouse spirit.

28 Also a foole, if he is stille, schal be gessid a wijs man; and, if he pressith togidre hise lippis, he 'schal be gessid an vndurstondynge man.

CAP 18

1 He that wole go a wei fro a frend, sekith occasiouns; in al tyme he schal be dispisable.

2 A fool resseyueth not the wordis of prudence; 'no but thou seie tho thingis, that ben turned in his herte.

3 A wickid man, whanne he cometh in to depthe of synnes, dispisith; but sclaundre and schenschipe sueth hym.

4 Deep watir is the wordis of the mouth of a man; and a stronde fletinge ouer is the welle of wisdom.

5 It is not good to take the persoone of a wickid man in doom, that thou bowe awei fro the treuthe of dom.

6 The lippis of a fool medlen hem silf with chidyngis; and his mouth excitith stryues.

7 The mouth of a fool is defoulyng of hym; and hise lippis ben the fallynge of his soule.

8 The wordis of a double tungid man ben as symple; and tho comen 'til to the ynnere thingis of the wombe. Drede castith doun a slowe man; forsothe the soulis of men turned in to wymmens condicioun schulen haue hungur.

9 He that is neisch, and vnstidfast in his werk, is the brother of a man distriynge hise werkis.

10 A strongeste tour is the name of the Lord; a iust man renneth to hym, and schal be enhaunsid.

11 The catel of a riche man is the citee of his strengthe; and as a stronge wal cumpassinge hym.

12 The herte of man is enhaunsid, bifor that it be brokun; and it is maad meke, bifore that it be glorified.

13 He that answerith bifore that he herith, shewith hym silf to be a fool; and worthi of schenschipe.

14 The spirit of a man susteyneth his feblenesse; but who may susteyne a spirit liyt to be wrooth?

15 The herte of a prudent man schal holde stidfastli kunnyng; and the eere of wise men sekith techyng.

16 The yift of a man alargith his weie; and makith space to hym bifore princes.

17 A iust man is the first accusere of hym silf; his frend cometh, and schal serche hym.

18 Lot ceessith ayenseiyngis; and demeth also among miyti men.

19 A brother that is helpid of a brothir, is as a stidfast citee; and domes ben as the barris of citees.

20 A mannus wombe schal be fillid of the fruit of his mouth; and the seedis of hise lippis schulen fille hym.

21 Deth and lijf ben in the werkis of tunge; thei that louen it, schulen ete the fruytis therof.

22 He that fyndith a good womman, fyndith a good thing; and of the Lord he schal drawe vp myrthe. He that puttith a wey a good womman, puttith awei a good thing; but he that holdith auowtresse, is a fool and vnwijs.

23 A pore man schal speke with bisechingis; and a riche man schal speke sterneli.

24 A man freendli to felouschipe schal more be a frend, than a brothir.

CAP 19

1 Betere is a pore man, that goith in his simplenesse, than a riche man bitynge hise lippis, and vnwijs.

2 Where is not kunnyng of the soule, is not good; and he that is hasti, in feet hirtith.

3 The foli of a man disseyueth hise steppis; and he brenneth in his soule ayens God.

4 Richessis encreessen ful many freendis; forsothe also thei ben departid fro a pore man, whiche he hadde.

5 A fals witnesse schal not be vnpunyschid; and he that spekith leesingis, schal not ascape.

6 Many men onouren the persoone of a myyti man; and ben frendis of hym that deelith yiftis.

7 The britheren of a pore man haten hym; ferthermore and the freendis yeden awei fer fro hym. He that sueth wordis oonli, schal haue no thing;

8 but he that holdith stabli the mynde, loueth his soule, and the kepere of prudence schal fynde goodis.

9 A fals witnesse schal not be vnpunyschid; and he that spekith leesyngis, schal perische.

10 Delices bicomen not a fool; nether 'it bicometh a seruaunt to be lord of princes.

11 The teching of a man is knowun bi pacience; and his glorie is to passe ouere wickid thingis.

12 As the gnasting of a lioun, so and the ire of the king; and as deewe on eerbe, so and the gladnesse of the kyng.

13 The sorewe of the fadir is a fonned sone; and roofes droppynge contynueli is a womman ful of chiding.

14 Housis and richessis ben youun of fadir and modir; but a prudent wijf is youun propirli of the Lord.

15 Slouth bringith in sleep; and a negligent soule schal haue hungur.

16 He that kepith the comaundement of God, kepith his soule; but he that chargith not his weie, schal be slayn.

17 He that hath mercy on a pore man, leeneth to the Lord; and he schal yelde his while to hym.

18 Teche thi sone, and dispeire thou not; but sette thou not thi soule to the sleyng of hym.

19 Forsothe he that is vnpacient, schal suffre harm; and whanne he hath rauyschid, he schal leie to anothir thing.

20 Here thou counsel, and take thou doctryn; that thou be wijs in thi laste thingis.

21 Many thouytis ben in the herte of a man; but the wille of the Lord schal dwelle.

22 A nedi man is merciful; and betere is a pore iust man, than a man liere.

23 The drede of the Lord ledith to lijf 'of blis; and he 'that dredith God schal dwelle in plentee, with outen visityng 'of the worste.

24 A slow man hidith his hond vndur the armpit; and putteth it not to his mouth.

25 Whanne a man ful of pestilence is betun, a fool schal be wisere. If thou blamist a wijs man, he schal vndurstonde techyng.

26 He that turmentith the fadir, and fleeth fro the modir, schal be ful of yuel fame, and schal be cursid.

27 Sone, ceesse thou not to here techyng; and knowe thou the wordis of kunnyng.

28 A wickid witnesse scorneth doom; and the mouth of vnpitouse men deuourith wickidnesse.

29 Domes ben maad redi to scorneris; and hameris smytynge ben maad redi to the bodies of foolis.

CAP 20

1 Wiyn is a letcherouse thing and drunkenesse is ful of noise; who euere delitith in these, schal not be wijs.

2 As the roryng of a lioun, so and the drede of the kyng; he that territh hym to ire, synneth ayens his owne lijf.

3 It is onour to a man that departith hym silf fro stryuyngis; but fonned men ben medlid with dispisyngis.

4 A slow man nolde ere for coold; therfor he schal begge in somer, and me schal not yyue to hym.

5 As deep watir, so counsel is in the herte of a man; but a wijs man schal drawe it out.

6 Many men ben clepid merciful; but who schal fynde a feithful man?

7 Forsothe a iust man that goith in his simplenesse, schal leeue blessid sones aftir hym.

8 A king that sittith in the seete of doom, distrieth al yuel bi his lokyng.

9 Who may seie, Myn herte is clene; Y am clene of synne?

10 A weiyte and a weiyte, a mesure and a mesure, euer eithir is abhomynable at God.

11 A child is vndurstondun bi hise studies, yf his werkis ben riytful and cleene.

12 An eere heringe, and an iye seynge, God made euere eithir.

13 Nyle thou loue sleep, lest nedynesse oppresse thee; opene thin iyen, and be thou fillid with looues.

14 Ech biere seith, It is yuel, it is yuel; and whanne he hath go awey, thanne he schal haue glorie.

15 Gold, and the multitude of iemmes, and a preciouse vessel, ben the lippis of kunnyng.

16 Take thou awei the cloth of hym, that was borewe of an othere man; and for straungeris take thou awei a wed fro hym.

17 The breed of a leesing is sweet to a man; and aftirward his mouth schal be fillid with rikenyng.

18 Thouytis ben maad strong bi counselis; and bateils schulen be tretid bi gouernals.

19 Be thou not medlid with him that schewith pryuetees, and goith gylefulli, and alargith hise lippis.

20 The liyt of hym that cursith his fadir and modir, schal be quenchid in the myddis of derknessis.

21 Eritage to which me haastith in the bigynnyng, schal wante blessing in the laste tyme.

22 Seie thou not, Y schal yelde yuel for yuel; abide thou the Lord, and he schal delyuere thee.

23 Abhomynacioun at God is weiyte and weiyte; a gileful balaunce is not good.

24 The steppis of man ben dressid of the Lord; who forsothe of men mai vndurstonde his weie?

25 Falling of man is to make auow to seyntis, and aftirward to withdrawe the vowis.

26 A wijs kyng scaterith wickid men; and bowith a bouwe of victorie ouer hem.

27 The lanterne of the Lord is the spirit of man, that sekith out alle the priuetees of the wombe.

28 Merci and treuthe kepen a kyng; and his trone is maad strong bi mekenesse.

29 The ful out ioiyng of yonge men is the strengthe of hem; and the dignyte of elde men is hoornesse.

30 The wannesse of wounde schal wipe aweie yuels, and woundis in the priuyere thingis of the wombe.

CAP 21

1 As departyngis of watris, so the herte of the kyng is in the power of the Lord; whidur euer he wole, he schal bowe it.

2 Ech weye of a man semeth riytful to hym silf; but the Lord peisith the hertis.

3 To do merci and doom plesith more the Lord, than sacrifices doen.

4 Enhaunsyng of iyen is alargyng of the herte; the lanterne of wickid men is synne.

5 The thouytis of a stronge man ben euere in abundaunce; but ech slow man is euere in nedynesse.

6 He that gaderith tresours bi the tunge of a leesing, is veyne, and with outen herte; and he schal be hurtlid to the snaris of deth.

7 The raueyns of vnpitouse men schulen drawe hem doun; for thei nolden do doom.

8 The weiward weie of a man is alien fro God; but the werk of hym that is cleene, is riytful.

9 It is betere to sitte in the corner of an hous with oute roof, than with a womman ful of chydyng, and in a comyn hous.

10 The soule of an vnpitouse man desirith yuel; he schal not haue merci on his neiybore.

11 Whanne a man ful of pestilence is punyschid, a litil man of wit schal be the wisere; and if he sueth a wijs man, he schal take kunnyng.

12 A iust man of the hous of a wickid man thenkith, to withdrawe wickid men fro yuel.

13 He that stoppith his eere at the cry of a pore man, schal crye also, and schal not be herd.

14 A yift hid quenchith chidyngis; and a yift in bosum quenchith the moost indignacioun.

15 It is ioye to a iust man to make doom; and it is drede to hem that worchen wickidnesse.

16 A man that errith fro the weie of doctryn, schal dwelle in the cumpany of giauntis.

17 He that loueth metis, schal be in nedynesse; he that loueth wiyn and fatte thingis, schal not be maad riche.

18 An vnpitouse man schal be youun for a iust man; and a wickid man schal be youun for a riytful man.

19 It is betere to dwelle in a desert lond, than with a womman ful of chidyng, and wrathful.

20 Desirable tresoure and oile is in the dwelling places of a iust man; and an vnprudent man schal distrie it.

21 He that sueth riytfulnesse and mercy, schal fynde lijf and glorie.

22 A wijs man stiede 'in to the citee of stronge men, and distriede the strengthe of trist therof.

23 He that kepith his mouth and his tunge, kepith his soule from angwischis.

24 A proude man and boosteere is clepid a fool, that worchith pride in ire.

25 Desiris sleen a slow man; for hise hondis nolden worche ony thing.

26 Al dai he coueitith and desirith; but he that is a iust man, schal yyue, and schal not ceesse.

27 The offringis of wickid men, that ben offrid of greet trespas, ben abhomynable.

28 A fals witnesse schal perische; a man obedient schal speke victorie.

29 A wickid man makith sad his cheer vnschamefastli; but he that is riytful, amendith his weie.

30 No wisdom is, no prudence is, no counsel is ayens the Lord.

31 An hors is maad redi to the dai of batel; but the Lord schal yyue helthe.

CAP 22

1 Betere is a good name, than many richessis; for good grace is aboue siluer and gold.

2 A riche man and a pore man metten hem silf; the Lord is worchere of euer eithir.

3 A felle man seeth yuel, and hidith him silf; and an innocent man passid, and he was turmentid bi harm.

4 The ende of temperaunce is the drede of the Lord; richessis, and glorye, and lijf.

5 Armuris and swerdis ben in the weie of a weiward man; but the kepere of his soule goith awey fer fro tho.

6 It is a prouerbe, A yong wexynge man bisidis his weie, and whanne he hath wexe elde, he schal not go awei fro it.

7 A riche man comaundith to pore men; and he that takith borewyng, is the seruaunt of the leenere.

8 He that sowith wickidnes, schal repe yuels; and the yerde of his yre schal be endid.

9 He that is redi to merci, schal be blessid; for of his looues he yaf to a pore man. He that yyueth yiftis, schal gete victorie and onour; forsothe he takith awei the soule of the takeris.

10 Caste thou out a scornere, and strijf schal go out with hym; and causis and dispisyngis schulen ceesse.

11 He that loueth the clennesse of herte, schal haue the kyng a freend, for the grace of hise lippis.

12 The iyen of the Lord kepen kunnyng; and the wordis of a wickid man ben disseyued.

13 A slow man schal seie, A lioun is withoutforth; Y schal be slayn in the myddis of the stretis.

14 The mouth of an alien womman is a deep diche; he to whom the Lord is wrooth, schal falle in to it.

15 Foli is boundun togidere in the herte of a child; and a yerde of chastisyng schal dryue it awey.

16 He that falsli chalengith a pore man, to encreesse hise owne richessis, schal yyue to a richere man, and schal be nedi.

17 My sone, bowe doun thin eere, and here thou the wordis of wise men; but sette thou the herte to my techyng.

18 That schal be fair to thee, whanne thou hast kept it in thin herte, and it schal flowe ayen in thi lippis.

19 That thi trist be in the Lord; wherfor and Y haue schewid it to thee to dai.

20 Lo! Y haue discryued it in thre maneres, in thouytis and kunnyng,

21 that Y schulde schewe to thee the sadnesse and spechis of trewthe; to answere of these thingis to hem, that senten thee.

22 Do thou not violence to a pore man, for he is pore; nethir defoule thou a nedi man in the yate.

23 For the Lord schal deme his cause, and he schal turmente hem, that turmentiden his soule.

24 Nyle thou be freend to a wrathful man, nether go thou with a wood man;

25 lest perauenture thou lerne hise weies, and take sclaundir to thi soule.

26 Nyle thou be with hem that oblischen her hondis, and that proferen hem silf borewis for dettis; for if he hath not wherof he schal restore,

27 what of cause is, that thou take awei hilyng fro thi bed?

28 Go thou not ouer the elde markis, whiche thi faders han set.

29 Thou hast seyn a man smert in his werk; he schal stonde bifore kyngis, and he schal not be bifor vnnoble men.

CAP 23

1 Whanne thou sittist, to ete with the prince, perseyue thou diligentli what thingis ben set bifore thi face,

2 and sette thou a withholding in thi throte. If netheles thou hast power on thi soule,

3 desire thou not of his metis, in whom is the breed of 'a leesing.

4 Nyle thou trauele to be maad riche, but sette thou mesure to thi prudence.

5 Reise not thin iyen to richessis, whiche thou maist not haue; for tho schulen make to hem silf pennes, as of an egle, and tho schulen flee in to heuene.

6 Ete thou not with an enuyouse man, and desire thou not hise metis;

7 for at the licnesse of a fals dyuynour and of a coniectere, he gessith that, that he knowith not. He schal seie to thee, Ete thou and drinke; and his soule is not with thee.

8 Thou schalt brake out the metis, whiche thou hast ete; and thou schalt leese thi faire wordis.

9 Speke thou not in the eeris of vnwise men; for thei schulen dispise the teching of thi speche.

10 Touche thou not the termes of litle children; and entre thou not in to the feeld of fadirles and modirles children.

11 For the neiybore of hem is strong, and he schal deme her cause ayens thee.

12 Thin herte entre to techyng, and thin eeris 'be redi to the wordis of kunnyng.

13 Nile thou withdrawe chastisyng fro a child; for thouy thou smyte hym with a yerde, he schal not die.

14 Thou schalt smyte hym with a yerde, and thou schalt delyuere his soule fro helle.

15 Mi sone, if thi soule is wijs, myn herte schal haue ioye with thee;

16 and my reynes schulen make ful out ioye, whanne thi lippis speken riytful thing.

17 Thin herte sue not synneris; but be thou in the drede of the Lord al dai.

18 For thou schalt haue hope at the laste, and thin abidyng schal not be don awei.

19 Mi sone, here thou, and be thou wijs, and dresse thi soule in the weie.

20 Nyle thou be in the feestis of drinkeris, nether in the ofte etyngis of hem, that bryngen togidere fleischis to ete.

21 For men yyuynge tent to drinkis, and yyuyng mussels togidere, schulen be waastid, and napping schal be clothid with clothis.

22 Here thi fadir, that gendride thee; and dispise not thi modir, whanne sche is eld.

23 Bie thou treuthe, and nyle thou sille wisdom, and doctryn, and vndurstonding.

24 The fadir of a iust man ioieth ful out with ioie; he that gendride a wijs man, schal be glad in hym.

25 Thi fadir and thi modir haue ioye, and he that gendride thee, make ful out ioye.

26 My sone, yyue thin herte to me, and thin iyen kepe my weyes.

27 For an hoore is a deep diche, and an alien womman is a streit pit.

28 Sche settith aspie in the weie, as a theef; and sche schal sle hem, whiche sche schal se vnwar.

29 To whom is wo? to whos fadir is wo? to whom ben chidingis? to whom ben dichis? to whom ben woundis with out cause? to whom is puttyng out of iyen?

30 Whether not to hem, that dwellen in wyn, and studien to drynke al of cuppis?

31 Biholde thou not wyn, whanne it sparclith, whanne the colour therof schyneth in a ver.

32 It entrith swetli, but at the laste it schal bite as an eddre doith, and as a cocatrice it schal schede abroad venyms.

33 Thin iyen schulen se straunge wymmen, and thi herte schal speke weiwerd thingis.

34 And thou schalt be as a man slepinge in the myddis of the see, and as a gouernour aslepid, whanne the steere is lost.

35 And thou schalt seie, Thei beeten me, but Y hadde not sorewe; thei drowen me, and Y feelide not; whanne schal Y wake out, and Y schal fynde wynes eft?

CAP 24

1 Sue thou not yuele men, desire thou not to be with hem.

2 For the soule of hem bithenkith raueyns, and her lippis speken fraudis.

3 An hous schal be bildid bi wisdom, and schal be maad strong bi prudence.

4 Celeris schulen be fillid in teching, al riches preciouse and ful fair.

5 A wijs man is strong, and a lerned man is stalworth and miyti.

6 For whi batel is bigunnun with ordenaunce, and helthe schal be, where many counsels ben.

7 Wisdom is hiy to a fool; in the yate he schal not opene his mouth.

8 He that thenkith to do yuels, schal be clepid a fool.

9 The thouyte of a fool is synne; and a bacbitere is abhomynacioun of men.

10 If thou that hast slide, dispeirist in the dai of angwisch, thi strengthe schal be maad lesse.

11 Delyuere thou hem, that ben led to deth; and ceesse thou not to delyuere hem, that ben drawun to deth.

12 If thou seist, Strengthis suffisen not; he that is biholdere of the herte, vndirstondith, and no thing disseyueth the kepere of thi soule, and he schal yelde to a man bi hise werkis.

13 Mi sone, ete thou hony, for it is good; and an honycomb ful swete to thi throte.

14 'So and the techyng of wisdom is good to thi soule; and whanne thou hast founde it, thou schalt haue hope in the laste thingis, and thin hope schal not perische.

15 Aspie thou not, and seke not wickidnesse in the hous of a iust man, nether waste thou his reste.

16 For a iust man schal falle seuene sithis in the dai, and schal rise ayen; but wickid men schulen falle in to yuele.

17 Whanne thin enemye fallith, haue thou not ioye; and thin herte haue not ful out ioiyng in his fal;

18 lest perauenture the Lord se, and it displese hym, and he take awei his ire fro hym.

19 Stryue thou not with 'the worste men, nether sue thou wickid men.

20 For whi yuele men han not hope of thingis to comynge, and the lanterne of wickid men schal be quenchid.

21 My sone, drede thou God, and the kyng; and be thou not medlid with bacbiteris.

22 For her perdicioun schal rise togidere sudenli, and who knowith the fal of euer either?

23 Also these thingis that suen ben to wise men. It is not good to knowe a persoone in doom.

24 Puplis schulen curse hem, that seien to a wickid man, Thou art iust; and lynagis schulen holde hem abhomynable.

25 Thei that repreuen iustli synners, schulen be preisid; and blessing schal come on hem.

26 He that answerith riytful wordis, schal kisse lippis.

27 Make redi thi werk with outforth, and worche thi feelde dilygentli, that thou bilde thin hous aftirward.

28 Be thou not a witnesse with out resonable cause ayens thi neiybore; nether flatere thou ony man with thi lippis.

29 Seie thou not, As he dide to me, so Y schal do to him, and Y schal yelde to ech man aftir his werk.

30 I passide bi the feeld of a slow man, and bi the vyner of a fonned man; and, lo!

31 nettlis hadden fillid al, thornes hadden hilid the hiyere part therof, and the wal of stoonys with out morter was distried.

32 And whanne Y hadde seyn this thing, Y settide in myn herte, and bi ensaumple Y lernyde techyng.

33 Hou longe slepist thou, slow man? whanne schalt thou ryse fro sleep? Sotheli thou schalt slepe a litil, thou schalt nappe a litil, thou schalt ioyne togidere the hondis a litil, to take reste;

34 and thi nedynesse as a currour schal come to thee, and thi beggerie as an armed man.

CAP 25

1 Also these ben the Parablis of Salomon, whiche the men of Ezechie, kyng of Juda, translatiden.

2 The glorie of God is to hele a word; and the glorie of kyngis is to seke out a word.

3 Heuene aboue, and the erthe bynethe, and the herte of kyngis is vnserchable.

4 Do thou a wei rust fro siluer, and a ful cleene vessel schal go out.

5 Do thou awei vnpite fro the cheer of the kyng, and his trone schal be maad stidfast bi riytfulnesse.

6 Appere thou not gloriouse bifore the kyng, and stonde thou not in the place of grete men.

7 For it is betere, that it be seid to thee, Stie thou hidur, than that thou be maad low bifore the prince.

8 Brynge thou not forth soone tho thingis in strijf, whiche thin iyen sien; lest aftirward thou maist not amende, whanne thou hast maad thi frend vnhonest.

9 Trete thou thi cause with thi frend, and schewe thou not priuyte to a straunge man;

10 lest perauenture he haue ioye of thi fal, whanne he hath herde, and ceesse not to do schenschipe to thee. Grace and frenschip delyueren, whiche kepe thou to thee, that thou be not maad repreuable.

11 A goldun pomel in beddis of siluer is he, that spekith a word in his time.

12 A goldun eere ryng, and a schinynge peerle is he, that repreueth a wijs man, and an eere obeiynge.

13 As the coold of snow in the dai of heruest, so a feithful messanger to hym that sente 'thilke messanger, makith his soule to haue reste.

14 A cloude and wind, and reyn not suynge, is a gloriouse man, and not fillynge biheestis.

15 A prince schal be maad soft bi pacience; and a soft tunge schal breke hardnesse.

16 Thou hast founde hony, ete thou that that suffisith to thee; lest perauenture thou be fillid, and brake it out.

17 Withdrawe thi foot fro the hous of thi neiybore; lest sum tyme he be fillid, and hate thee.

18 A dart, and a swerd, and a scharp arowe, a man that spekith fals witnessing ayens his neiybore.

19 A rotun tooth, and a feynt foot is he, that hopith on an vnfeithful man in the dai of angwisch,

20 and leesith his mentil in the dai of coold. Vynegre in a vessel of salt is he, that singith songis to the worste herte. As a

mouyte noieth a cloth, and a worm noieth a tree, so the sorewe of a man noieth the herte.

21 If thin enemy hungrith, feede thou him; if he thirstith, yyue thou watir to hym to drinke;

22 for thou schalt gadere togidere coolis on his heed; and the Lord schal yelde to thee.

23 The north wind scatereth reynes; and a sorewful face distrieth a tunge bacbitinge.

24 It is betere to sitte in the corner of an hous without roof, than with a womman ful of chidyng, and in a comyn hous.

25 Coold watir to a thirsti man; and a good messanger fro a fer lond.

26 A welle disturblid with foot, and a veyne brokun, a iust man fallinge bifore a wickid man.

27 As it is not good to hym that etith myche hony; so he that is a serchere of maieste, schal be put doun fro glorie.

28 As a citee opyn, and with out cumpas of wallis; so is a man that mai not refreyne his spirit in speking.

CAP 26

1 As snow in somer, and reyn in heruest; so glorie is vnsemeli to a fool.

2 For whi as a brid fliynge ouer to hiy thingis, and a sparowe goynge in to vncerteyn; so cursing brouyt forth with out resonable cause schal come aboue in to sum man.

3 Beting to an hors, and a bernacle to an asse; and a yerde in the bak of vnprudent men.

4 Answere thou not to a fool bi his foli, lest thou be maad lijk hym.

5 Answere thou a fool bi his fooli, lest he seme to him silf to be wijs.

6 An haltinge man in feet, and drinkinge wickidnesse, he that sendith wordis by a fonned messanger.

7 As an haltinge man hath faire leggis in veyn; so a parable is vnsemeli in the mouth of foolis.

8 As he that casteth a stoon in to an heep of mercurie; so he that yyueth onour to an vnwijs man.

9 As if a thorn growith in the hond of a drunkun man; so a parable in the mouth of foolis.

10 Doom determyneth causis; and he that settith silence to a fool, swagith iris.

11 As a dogge that turneth ayen to his spuyng; so is an vnprudent man, that rehersith his fooli.

12 Thou hast seyn a man seme wijs to hym silf; an vnkunnyng man schal haue hope more than he.

13 A slow man seith, A lioun is in the weie, a liounnesse is in the foot pathis.

14 As a dore is turned in his hengis; so a slow man in his bed.

15 A slow man hidith hise hondis vndur his armpit; and he trauelith, if he turneth tho to his mouth.

16 A slow man semeth wysere to hym silf, than seuene men spekynge sentensis.

17 As he that takith a dogge bi the eeris; so he that passith, and is vnpacient, and is meddlid with the chiding of anothir man.

18 As he is gilti, that sendith speris and arowis in to deth;

19 so a man that anoieth gilefuli his frend, and whanne he is takun, he schal seie, Y dide pleiynge.

20 Whanne trees failen, the fier schal be quenchid; and whanne a priuy bacbitere is withdrawun, stryues resten.

21 As deed coolis at quic coolis, and trees at the fier; so a wrathful man reisith chidyngis.

22 The wordis of a pryuei bacbitere ben as symple; and tho comen til to the ynneste thingis of the herte.

23 As if thou wolt ourne a vessel of erthe with foul siluer; so ben bolnynge lippis felouschipid with 'the werste herte.

24 An enemy is vndirstondun bi hise lippis, whanne he tretith giles in the herte.

25 Whanne he 'makith low his vois, bileue thou not to hym; for seuene wickidnessis ben in his herte.

26 The malice of hym that hilith hatrede gilefuli, schal be schewid in a counsel.

27 He that delueth a diche, schal falle in to it; and if a man walewith a stoon, it schal turne ayen to hym.

28 A fals tunge loueth not treuth; and a slidir mouth worchith fallyngis.

CAP 27

1 Haue thou not glorie on the morewe, 'not knowynge what thing the dai to comynge schal bringe forth.

2 Another man, and not thi mouth preise thee; a straunger, and not thi lippis 'preise thee.

3 A stoon is heuy, and grauel is chariouse; but the ire of a fool is heuyere than euer eithir.

4 Ire hath no merci, and woodnesse brekynge out 'hath no merci; and who mai suffre the fersnesse of a spirit stirid?

5 Betere is opyn repreuyng, than loue hid.

6 Betere ben the woundis of hym that loueth, than the gileful cossis of hym that hatith.

7 A man fillid schal dispise an hony coomb; but an hungri man schal take, yhe, bittir thing for swete.

8 As a brid passinge ouer fro his nest, so is a man that forsakith his place.

9 The herte delitith in oynement, and dyuerse odours; and a soule is maad swete bi the good counsels of a frend.

10 Forsake thou not thi frend, and the frend of thi fadir; and entre thou not in to the hous of thi brothir, in the dai of thi turment. Betere is a neiybore nyy, than a brothir afer.

11 Mi sone, studie thou a boute wisdom, and make thou glad myn herte; that thou maist answere a word to a dispisere.

12 A fel man seynge yuel was hid; litle men of wit passinge forth suffriden harmes.

13 Take thou awei his clooth, that bihiyte for a straunger; and take thou awei a wed fro hym for an alien man.

14 He that blessith his neiybore with greet vois; and risith bi niyt, schal be lijk hym that cursith.

15 Roouys droppynge in the dai of coold, and a womman ful of chidyng ben comparisond.

16 He that withholdith hir, as if he holdith wynd; and auoidith the oile of his riyt hond.

17 Yrun is whettid bi irun; and a man whettith the face of his frend.

18 He that kepith a fige tre, schal ete the fruytis therof; and he that is a kepere of his lord, schal be glorified.

19 As the cheris of men biholdinge schynen in watris; so the hertis of men ben opyn to prudent men.

20 Helle and perdicioun schulen not be fillid; so and the iyen of men moun not be fillid.

21 As siluer is preuyd in a wellyng place, and gold 'is preued in a furneys; so a man is preued bi the mouth of preyseris. The herte of a wickid man sekith out yuels; but a riytful herte sekith out kunnyng.

22 Thouy thou beetist a fool in a morter, as with a pestel smytynge aboue dried barli; his foli schal not be don awei fro him.

23 Knowe thou diligentli the cheere of thi beeste; and biholde thou thi flockis.

24 For thou schalt not haue power contynueli; but a coroun schal be youun to thee in generacioun and in to generacioun.

25 Medewis ben openyd, and greene eerbis apperiden; and hey is gaderid fro hillis.

26 Lambren be to thi clothing; and kidis be to the prijs of feeld.

27 The mylke of geete suffice to thee for thi meetis; in to the necessarie thingis of thin hous, and to lijflode to thin handmaidis.

CAP 28

1 A wickid man fleeth, whanne no man pursueth; but a iust man as a lioun tristynge schal be with out ferdfulnesse.

2 For the synnes of the lond ben many princis therof; and for the wisdom of a man, and for the kunnyng of these thingis that ben seid, the lijf of the duyk schal be lengere.

3 A pore man falsli calengynge pore men, is lijk a grete reyn, wherynne hungur is maad redi.

4 Thei that forsaken the lawe, preisen a wickid man; thei that kepen 'the lawe, ben kyndlid ayens hym.

5 Wickid men thenken not doom; but thei that seken the Lord, perseyuen alle thingis.

6 Betere is a pore man goynge in his sympilnesse, than a riche man in schrewid weies.

7 He that kepith the lawe, is a wijs sone; but he that fedith glotouns, schendith his fadir.

8 He that gaderith togidere richessis bi vsuris, and fre encrees, gaderith tho togidere ayens pore men.

9 His preyer schal be maad cursid, that bowith awei his eere; that he here not the lawe.

10 He that disseyueth iust men in an yuel weye, schal falle in his perisching; and iuste men schulen welde hise goodis.

11 A ryche man semeth wijs to him silf; but a pore man prudent schal serche him.

12 In enhaunsing of iust men is miche glorie; whanne wickid men regnen, fallyngis of men ben.

13 He that hidith hise grete trespassis, schal not be maad riytful; but he that knoulechith and forsakith tho, schal gete merci.

14 Blessid is the man, which is euere dredeful; but he that is 'harde of soule, schal falle in to yuel.

15 A rorynge lioun, and an hungry bere, is a wickid prince on a pore puple.

16 A duyk nedi of prudence schal oppresse many men bi fals chalenge; but the daies of hym that hatith aueryce, schulen be maad longe.

17 No man susteyneth a man that falsly chalengith the blood of a man, if he fleeth 'til to the lake.

18 He that goith simpli, schal be saaf; he that goith bi weiward weies, schal falle doun onys.

19 He that worchith his lond, schal be fillid with looues; he that sueth ydelnesse, schal be fillid with nedynesse.

20 A feithful man schal be preisid myche; but he that hastith to be maad riche, schal not be innocent.

21 He that knowith a face in doom, doith not wel; this man forsakith treuthe, yhe, for a mussel of breed.

22 A man that hastith to be maad riche, and hath enuye to othere men; woot not that nedinesse schal come on hym.

23 He that repreueth a man, schal fynde grace aftirward at hym; more than he that disseyueth bi flateryngis of tunge.

24 He that withdrawith ony thing fro his fadir and fro his modir, and seith that this is no synne, is parcener of a man-quellere.

25 He that auauntith hym silf, and alargith, reisith stryues; but he that hopith in the Lord, schal be sauyd.

26 He that tristith in his herte, is a fool; but he that goith wiseli,

27 schal be preysid. He that yyueth to a pore man, schal not be nedi; he that dispisith 'a pore man bisechynge, schal suffre nedynesse.

28 Whanne vnpitouse men risen, men schulen be hid; whanne tho 'vnpitouse men han perischid, iust men schulen be multi-plied.

CAP 29

1 Sodeyn perischyng schal come on that man, that with hard nol dispisith a blamere; and helth schal not sue hym.

2 The comynalte schal be glad in the multipliyng of iust men; whanne wickid men han take prinshod, the puple schal weyle.

3 A man that loueth wisdom, makith glad his fadir; but he that nurschith 'an hoore, schal leese catel.

4 A iust king reisith the lond; an auerouse man schal distrie it.

5 A man that spekith bi flaterynge and feyned wordis to his frend; spredith abrood a net to hise steppis.

6 A snare schal wlappe a wickid man doynge synne; and a iust man schal preise, and schal make ioye.

7 A iust man knowith the cause of pore men; an vnpitouse man knowith not kunnyng.

8 Men ful of pestilence distryen a citee; but wise men turnen awei woodnesse.

9 If a wijs man stryueth with a fool; whether he be wrooth, 'ether he leiyith, he schal not fynde reste.

10 Menquelleris haten a simple man; but iust men seken his soule.

11 A fool bringith forth al his spirit; a wise man dilaieth, and reserueth in to tyme comynge afterward.

12 A prince that herith wilfuli the wordis of a leesyng; schal haue alle mynystris vnfeithful.

13 A pore man and a leenere metten hem silf; the Lord is liytnere of euer ethir.

14 If a kyng demeth pore men in treuthe; his trone schal be maad stidfast with outen ende.

15 A yerde and chastisyng schal yyue wisdom; but a child, which is left to his wille, schendith his modir.

16 Grete trespassis schulen be multiplied in the multipliyng of wickid men; and iust men schulen se the fallyngis of hem.

17 Teche thi sone, and he schal coumforte thee; and he schal yyue delicis to thi soule.

18 Whanne prophesie faylith, the puple schal be distried; but he that kepith the lawe, is blessid.

19 A seruaunt mai not be tauyt bi wordis; for he vndirstondith that that thou seist, and dispisith for to answere.

20 Thou hast seyn a man swift to speke; foli schal be hopid more than his amendyng.

21 He that nurschith his seruaunt delicatli fro childhod; schal fynde hym rebel aftirward.

22 A wrathful man territh chidingis; and he that is liyt to haue indignacioun, schal be more enclynaunt to synnes.

23 Lownesse sueth a proude man; and glorie schal vp take a meke man of spirit.

24 He that takith part with a theef, hatith his soule; he herith a man chargynge greetli, and schewith not.

25 He that dredith a man, schal falle soon; he that hopith in the Lord, shal be reisid.

26 Many men seken the face of the prince; and the doom of alle men schal go forth of the Lord.

27 Iust men han abhomynacioun of a wickid man; and wickid men han abhomynacioun of hem, that ben in a riytful weye. A sone kepynge a word, schal be out of perdicioun.

CAP 30

1 The wordis of hym that gaderith, of the sone spuynge. The prophesie which a man spak, with whom God was, and which man was coumfortid bi God dwellyng with hym,

2 and seide, Y am the moost fool of men; and the wisdom of men is not with me.

3 Y lernede not wisdom; and Y knew not the kunnyng of hooli men.

4 Who stiede in to heuene, and cam doun? Who helde togidere the spirit in hise hondis? who bonde togidere watris as in a cloth? Who reiside alle the endis of erthe? What is name of hym? and what is the name of his sone, if thou know-ist?

5 Ech word of God is a scheld set a fiere, to alle that hopen in hym.

6 Adde thou not ony thing to the wordis of hym, and thou be repreued, and be foundun a liere.

7 I preiede thee twei thingis; denye not thou to me, bifor that Y die.

8 Make thou fer fro me vanyte and wordis of leesyng; yyue thou not to me beggery and richessis; yyue thou oneli neces-saries to my lijflode;

9 lest perauenture Y be fillid, and be drawun to denye, and seie, Who is the Lord? and lest Y compellid bi nedynesse, stele, and forswere the name of my God.

10 Accuse thou not a seruaunt to his lord, lest perauenture he curse thee, and thou falle doun.

11 A generacioun that cursith his fadir, and that blessith not his modir.

12 A generacioun that semeth cleene to it silf, and netheles is not waischun fro hise filthis.

13 A generacioun whose iyen ben hiy, and the iye liddis therof ben reisid in to hiy thingis.

14 A generacioun that hath swerdis for teeth, and etith with hise wank teeth; that it ete nedi men of erthe, and the porails of men.

15 The watir leche hath twei douytris, seiynge, Brynge, bringe. Thre thingis ben vnable to be fillid, and the fourthe, that seith neuere, It suffisith;

16 helle, and the mouth of the wombe, and the erthe which is neuere fillid with water; but fier seith neuere, It suffisith.

17 Crowis of the stronde picke out thilke iye, that scorneth the fadir, and that dispisith the child beryng of his modir; and the briddis of an egle ete that iye.

18 Thre thingis ben hard to me, and outirli Y knowe not the fourthe thing;

19 the weye of an egle in heuene, the weie of a serpent on a stoon, the weie of a schip in the myddil of the see, and the weie of a man in yong wexynge age.

20 Siche is the weie of a womman auowtresse, which etith, and wipith hir mouth, and seith, Y wrouyte not yuel.

21 The erthe is moued bi thre thingis, and the fourthe thing, which it may not susteyne;

22 bi a seruaunt, whanne he regneth; bi a fool, whanne he is fillid with mete;

23 bi an hateful womman, whanne sche is takun in matrymonye; and bi an handmaide, whanne sche is eir of hir ladi.

24 Foure ben the leeste thingis of erthe, and tho ben wisere than wise men;

25 amtis, a feble puple, that maken redi mete in heruest to hem silf;

26 a hare, a puple vnmyyti, that settith his bed in a stoon;

27 a locust hath no kyng, and al goith out bi cumpanyes; an euete enforsith with hondis,

28 and dwellith in the housis of kingis.

29 Thre thingis ben, that goon wel, and the fourthe thing, that goith richeli.

30 A lioun, strongeste of beestis, schal not drede at the meetyng of ony man;

31 a cok gird the leendis, and a ram, and noon is that schal ayenstonde him.

32 He that apperith a fool, aftir that he is reisid an hiy; for if he hadde vndurstonde, he hadde sett hond on his mouth.

33 Forsothe he that thristith strongli teetis, to drawe out mylk, thristith out botere; and he that smytith greetli, drawith out blood; and he that stirith iris, bringith forth discordis.

CAP 31

1 The wordis of Lamuel, the king; the visioun bi which his modir tauyte hym.

2 What my derlyng? what the derlyng of my wombe? what the derlyng of my desiris?

3 Yyue thou not thi catel to wymmen, and thi richessis to do awei kyngis.

4 A! Lamuel, nyle thou yiue wyn to kingis; for no pryuete is, where drunkenesse regneth.

5 Lest perauenture thei drynke, and foryete domes, and chaunge the cause of the sones of a pore man.

6 Yyue ye sidur to hem that morenen, and wyn to hem that ben of bitter soule.

7 Drinke thei, and foryete thei her nedinesse; and thenke thei no more on her sorewe.

8 Opene thi mouth for a doumb man,

9 and opene thi mouth for the causes of alle sones that passen forth. Deme thou that that is iust, and deme thou a nedi man and a pore man.

10 Who schal fynde a stronge womman? the prijs of her is fer, and fro the laste endis.

11 The herte of hir hosebond tristith in hir; and sche schal not haue nede to spuylis.

12 Sche schal yelde to hym good, and not yuel, in alle the daies of hir lijf.

13 Sche souyte wolle and flex, and wrouyte bi the counsel of hir hondis.

14 Sche is maad as the schip of a marchaunt, that berith his breed fro fer.

15 And sche roos bi nyyt, and yaf prey to hir meyneals, and metis to hir handmaidis.

16 Sche bihelde a feeld, and bouyte it; of the fruyt of hir hondis sche plauntide a vyner.

17 Sche girde hir leendis with strengthe, and made strong hir arm.

18 Sche taastide, and siy, that hir marchaundie was good; hir lanterne schal not be quenchid in the niyt.

19 Sche putte hir hondis to stronge thingis, and hir fyngris token the spyndil.

20 Sche openyde hir hond to a nedi man, and stretchide forth hir hondis to a pore man.

21 Sche schal not drede for hir hous of the cooldis of snow; for alle hir meyneals ben clothid with double clothis.

22 Sche made to hir a ray cloth; bijs and purpur is the cloth of hir.

23 Hir hosebonde is noble in the yatis, whanne he sittith with the senatours of erthe.

24 Sche made lynnun cloth, and selde; and yaf a girdil to a Chananei.

25 Strengthe and fairnesse is the clothing of hir; and sche schal leiye in the laste dai.

26 Sche openyde hir mouth to wisdom; and the lawe of merci is in hir tunge.

27 Sche bihelde the pathis of hir hous; and sche eet not breed idili.

28 Hir sones risiden, and prechiden hir moost blessid; hir hosebonde roos, and preiside hir.

29 Many douytris gaderiden richessis; thou passidist alle.

30 Fairnesse is disseiuable grace, and veyn; thilke womman, that dredith the Lord, schal be preisid.

31 Yyue ye to hir of the fruyt of hir hondis; and hir werkis preise hir in the yatis.

ECCLESIASTES

CAP 1

1 The wordis of Ecclesiastes, sone of Dauid, the kyng of Jerusalem.

2 The vanyte of vanytees, seide Ecclesiastes; the vanyte of vanytees, and alle thingis ben vanite.

3 What hath a man more of alle his trauel, bi which he traueilith vndur the sunne?

4 Generacioun passith awei, and generacioun cometh; but the erthe stondith with outen ende.

5 The sunne risith, and goith doun, and turneth ayen to his place;

6 and there it risith ayen, and cumpassith bi the south, and turneth ayen to the north. The spirit cumpassynge alle thingis goith 'in cumpas, and turneth ayen in to hise cerclis.

7 Alle floodis entren in to the see, and the see fletith not ouer the markis set of God; the floodis turnen ayen to the place fro whennus tho comen forth, that tho flowe eft.

8 Alle thingis ben hard; a man may not declare tho thingis bi word; the iye is not fillid bi siyt, nether the eere is fillid bi hering.

9 What is that thing that was, that that schal come? What is that thing that is maad, that that schal be maad?

10 No thing vndir the sunne is newe, nether ony man may seie, Lo! this thing is newe; for now it yede bifore in worldis, that weren bifore vs.

11 Mynde of the formere thingis is not, but sotheli nether thenkyng of tho thingis, that schulen come afterward, schal be at hem that schulen come in the last tyme.

12 I Ecclesiastes was king of Israel in Jerusalem;

13 and Y purposide in my soule to seke and enserche wiseli of alle thingis, that ben maad vndur the sunne. God yaf this werste ocupacioun to the sones of men, that thei schulden be ocupied therynne.

14 I siy alle thingis that ben maad vndur the sunne, and lo! alle thingis ben vanyte and turment of spirit.

15 Weiward men ben amendid of hard; and the noumbre of foolis is greet with outen ende.

16 I spak in myn herte, and Y seide, Lo! Y am made greet, and Y passide in wisdom alle men, that weren bifore me in

Jerusalem; and my soule siy many thingis wiseli, and Y lernede.

17 And Y yaf myn herte, that Y schulde knowe prudence and doctryn, and errours and foli. And Y knew that in these thingis also was trauel and turment of spirit;

18 for in myche wisdom is myche indignacioun, and he that encressith kunnyng, encreessith also trauel.

CAP 2

1 Therfor Y seide in myn hertez, Y schal go, and Y schal flowe in delicis, and Y schal vse goodis; and Y siy also that this was vanyte.

2 And leiyyng Y arrettide errour, and Y seide to ioye, What art thou disseyued in veyn?

3 I thouyte in myn herte to withdrawe my fleisch fro wyn, that Y schulde lede ouer my soule to wisdom, and that Y schulde eschewe foli, til Y schulde se, what were profitable to the sones of men; in which dede the noumbre of daies of her lijf vndur the sunne is nedeful.

4 Y magnefiede my werkis, Y bildide housis to me, and Y plauntide vynes; Y made yerdis and orcherdis,

5 and Y settide tho with the trees of al kynde;

6 and Y made cisternes of watris, for to watre the wode of trees growynge.

7 I hadde in possessioun seruauntis and handmaidis; and Y hadde myche meynee, and droues of grete beestis, and grete flockis of scheep, ouer alle men that weren bifore me in Jerusalem.

8 Y gaderide togidere to me siluer and gold, and the castels of kingis and of prouyncis; Y made to me syngeris and synger-essis, and delicis of the sones of men, and cuppis and vessels in seruyce, to helde out wynes;

9 and Y passide in richessis alle men, that weren bifor me in Jerusalem. Also wisdom dwellide stabli with me,

10 and alle thingis whiche myn iyen desiriden, Y denyede not to hem; nether Y refreynede myn herte, that ne it vside al lust, and delitide it silf in these thingis whiche I hadde maad redi; and Y demyde this my part, if Y vside my trauel.

11 And whanne Y hadde turned me to alle werkis whiche myn hondys hadden maad, and to the trauels in whiche Y hadde swet in veyn, Y siy in alle thingis vanyte and turment of the soule, and that no thing vndir sunne dwellith stabli.

12 I passide to biholde wisdom, errours, and foli; Y seide, What is a man, that he may sue the king, his maker?

13 And Y siy, that wisdom yede so mych bifor foli, as miche as liyt is dyuerse fro derknessis.

14 The iyen of a wijs man ben in his heed, a fool goith in derknessis; and Y lernede, that o perisching was of euer either.

15 And Y seide in myn herte, If o deth schal be bothe of the fool and of me, what profitith it to me, that Y yaf more bisy-nesse to wisdom? And Y spak with my soule, and per-seyuede, that this also was vanyte.

16 For mynde of a wijs man schal not be, in lijk maner as nether of a fool with outen ende, and tymes to comynge schulen hile alle thingis togidere with foryetyng; a lerned man dieth in lijk maner and an vnlerned man.

17 And therfor it anoiede me of my lijf, seynge that alle thingis vndur sunne ben yuele, and that alle thingis ben vanyte and turment of the spirit.

18 Eft Y curside al my bisynesse, bi which Y trauelide moost studiousli vndur sunne, and Y schal haue an eir after me,

19 whom Y knowe not, whether he schal be wijs ether a fool; and he schal be lord in my trauels, for whiche Y swatte gree-tli, and was bisi; and is ony thing so veyn?

20 Wherfor Y ceesside, and myn herte forsook for to trauele ferthere vnder sunne.

21 For whi whanne another man trauelith in wisdom, and techyng, and bisynesse, he leeueth thingis getun to an idel man; and therfor this is vanyte, and greet yuel.

22 For whi what schal it profite to a man of al his trauel, and turment of spirit, bi which he was turmentid vndur sunne?

23 Alle hise daies ben ful of sorewis and meschefs, and bi nyyt he restith not in soule; and whether this is not vanyte?

24 Whether it is not betere to ete and drynke, and to schewe to hise soule goodis of hise trauels? and this thing is of the hond of God.

25 Who schal deuoure so, and schal flowe in delicis, as Y dide?

26 God yaf wisdom, and kunnyng, and gladnesse to a good man in his siyt; but he yaf turment, and superflu bisynesse to a synnere, that he encreesse, and gadere togidere, and yyue to hym that plesith God; but also this is vanyte, and veyn bisy-nesse of soule.

CAP 3

1 Alle thingis han tyme, and alle thingis vndur sunne passen bi her spaces.

2 Tyme of birthe, and time of diyng; tyme to plaunte, and tyme to drawe vp that that is plauntid.

3 Tyme to sle, and tyme to make hool; tyme to distrie, and tyme to bilde.

4 Tyme to wepe, and tyme to leiye; tyme to biweile, and tyme to daunse.

5 Tyme to scatere stoonys, and tyme to gadere togidere; tyme to colle, and tyme to be fer fro collyngis.

6 Tyme to wynne, and tyme to leese; tyme to kepe, and tyme to caste awei.

7 Tyme to kitte, and tyme to sewe togidere; tyme to be stille, and tyme to speke.

8 Tyme of loue, and tyme of hatrede; tyme of batel, and tyme of pees.

9 What hath a man more of his trauel?

10 I siy the turment, which God yaf to the sones of men, that thei be occupied therynne.

11 God made alle thingis good in her tyme, and yaf the world to disputyng of hem, that a man fynde not the werk which God hath wrouyt fro the bigynnyng 'til in to the ende.

12 And Y knew that no thing was betere 'to a man, 'no but to be glad, and to do good werkis in his lijf.

13 For whi ech man that etith and drinkith, and seeth good of his trauel; this is the yifte of God.

14 I haue lerned that alle werkis, whiche God made, lasten stidfastli 'til in to with outen ende; we moun not adde ony thing to tho, nether take awei fro tho thingis, whiche God made, that he be dred.

15 That thing that is maad, dwellith perfitli; tho thingis that schulen come, weren bifore; and God restorith that, that is goon.

16 I siy vndur sunne vnfeithfulnesse in the place of doom; and wickidnesse in the place of riytfulnesse.

17 And Y seide in myn herte, The Lord schal deme a iust man, and an vnfeithful man; and the tyme of ech thing schal be thanne.

18 I seide in myn herte of the sones of men, that God schulde preue hem, and schewe that thei ben lijk vnresonable beestis.

19 Therfor oon is the perisching of man and of beestis, and euene condicioun is of euer eithir; as a man dieth, 'so and tho beestis dien; alle beestis brethen in lijk maner, and a man hath no thing more than a beeste.

20 Alle thingis ben suget to vanyte, and alle thingis goen to o place; tho ben maad of erthe, and tho turnen ayen togidere in to erthe.

21 Who knowith, if the spirit of the sones of Adam stieth vpward, and if the spirit of beestis goith dounward?

22 And Y perseyuede that no thing is betere, than that a man be glad in his werk, and that this be his part; for who schal brynge hym, that he knowe thingis that schulen come after hym?

CAP 4

1 I turnede me to othere thingis, and Y siy fals chalengis, that ben don vndur the sunne, and the teeris of innocentis, and no man coumfortour; and that thei forsakun of the help of alle men, moun not ayenstonde the violence of hem.

2 And Y preiside more deed men than lyuynge men;

3 and Y demyde hym, that was not borun yit, and siy not the yuels that ben don vndur the sunne, to be blisfulere than euer eithir.

4 Eft Y bihelde alle the trauelis of men, and bisynesses; and Y perseyuede that tho ben opyn to the enuye of neiybore; and therfor in this is vanyte, and superflu bisynesse.

5 A fool foldith togidere hise hondis, and etith hise fleischis,

6 and seith, Betere is an handful with reste, than euer either hondful with trauel and turment of soule.

7 I bihelde and foond also another vanytee vndir the sunne;

8 oon is, and he hath not a secounde; not a sone, not a brother; and netheles he ceesith not for to trauele, nether hise iyen ben fillid with richessis; nether he bithenkith, and seith, To whom trauele Y, and disseyue my soule in goodis? In this also is vanyte, and the worste turment.

9 Therfor it is betere, that tweyne be togidere than oon; for thei han profite of her felouschipe.

10 If oon fallith doun, he schal be vndurset of the tothere; wo to hym that is aloone, for whanne he fallith, he hath noon reisynge him.

11 And if tweyne slepen, thei schulen be nurschid togidere; hou schal oon be maad hoot?

12 And if ony man hath maistri ayens oon, tweyne ayen stonden hym; a threfolde corde is brokun of hard.

13 A pore man and wijs is betere than an eld kyng and fool, that kan not bifore se in to tyme to comynge.

14 For sum tyme a man goith out bothe fro prysoun and chaynes to a rewme; and anothir borun in to a rewme is wastid bi nedynesse.

15 I siy alle men lyuynge that goen vndur the sunne, with the secounde yong wexynge man, that schal rise for hym.

16 The noumbre of puple, of alle that weren bifore hym, is greet with outen mesure, and thei that schulen come aftirward, schulen not be glad in hym; but also this is vanyte and turment of the spirit.

17 Thou that entrist in to the hous of God, kepe thi foot, and neiye thou for to here; for whi myche betere is obedience than the sacrifices of foolis, that witen not what yuel thei don.

1 Speke thou not ony thing folily, nether thin herte be swift to brynge forth a word bifore God; for God is in heuene, and thou art on erthe, therfor thi wordis be fewe.

2 Dremes suen many bisynessis, and foli schal be foundun in many wordis.

3 If thou hast avowid ony thing to God, tarie thou not to yelde; for an vnfeithful and fonned biheest displesith hym; but 'yelde thou what euer thing thou hast avowid;

4 and it is myche betere to make not a vowe, than aftir a vowe to yelde not biheestis.

5 Yyue thou not thi mouth, that thou make thi fleisch to do synne; nether seie thou bifor an aungel, No puruyaunce is; lest perauenture the Lord be wrooth on thi wordis, and distruye alle the werkis of thin hondis.

6 Where ben many dremes, ben ful many vanytees, and wordis with out noumbre; but drede thou God.

7 If thou seest false chalengis of nedi men, and violent domes, and that riytfulnesse is distried in the prouynce, wondre thou not on this doyng; for another is hiyere than an hiy man, and also othere men ben more hiye aboue these men;

8 and ferthermore the kyng of al erthe comaundith to the seruaunt.

CAP 5

9 An auerouse man schal not be fillid of monei; and he that loueth richessis schal not take fruytis of tho; and therfor this is vanyte.

10 Where ben many richessis, also many men ben, that eten tho; and what profitith it to the haldere, no but that he seeth richessis with hise iyen?

11 Slepe is swete to hym that worchith, whether he etith litil ether myche; but the fulnesse of a ryche man suffrith not hym to slepe.

12 Also anothir sijknesse is ful yuel, which Y siy vndur the sunne; richessis ben kept in to the yuel of her lord.

13 For thei perischen in the worste turment; he gendride a sone, that schal be in souereyn nedynesse.

14 As he yede nakid out of his modris wombe, so he schal turne ayen; and he schal take awei with hym no thing of his trauel.

15 Outirli it is a wretchid sijknesse; as he cam, so he schal turne ayen. What therfor profitith it to hym, that he trauelide in to the wynde?

16 In alle the daies of his lijf he eet in derknessis, and in many bisinessis, and in nedynesse, and sorewe.

17 Therfor this semyde good to me, that a man ete, and drynke, and vse gladnesse of his trauel, in which he trauelide vndir the sunne, in the noumbre of daies of his lijf, which God yaf to hym; and this is his part.

18 And to ech man, to whom God yaf richessis, and catel, and yaf power to hym to ete of tho, and to vse his part, and to be glad of his trauel; this is the yifte of God.

19 For he schal not bithenke miche on the daies of his lijf, for God ocupieth his herte with delicis.

CAP 6

1 Also another yuel is, which Y siy vndur the sunne; and certis it is oft vsid anentis men.

2 A man is, to whom God yaf richessis, and catel, and onour; and no thing failith to his soule of alle thingis which he desirith; and God yyueth not power to hym, that he ete therof, but a straunge man shal deuoure it. This is vanyte, and a greet wretchidnesse.

3 If a man gendrith an hundrid fre sones, and lyueth many yeris, and hath many daies of age, and his soule vsith not the

goodis of his catel, and wantith biriyng; Y pronounce of this man, that a deed borun child is betere than he.

4 For he cometh in veyn, and goith to derknessis; and his name schal be don a wei bi foryetyng.

5 He siy not the sunne, nether knew dyuersyte of good and of yuel;

6 also thouy he lyueth twei thousynde yeeris, and vsith not goodis; whether alle thingis hasten not to o place?

7 Al the trauel of a man is in his mouth, but the soule of hym schal not be fillid with goodis.

8 What hath a wijs man more than a fool? and what hath a pore man, no but that he go thidur, where is lijf?

9 It is betere to se that, that thou coueitist, than to desire that, that thou knowist not; but also this is vanyte, and presumpcioun of spirit.

10 The name of hym that schal come, is clepid now, and it is knowun, that he is a man, and he mai not stryue in doom ayens a strongere than hym silf.

11 Wordis ben ful manye, and han myche vanyte in disputyinge.

1 What nede is it to a man to seke grettere thingis than hym silf; sithen he knowith not, what schal bifalle to hym in his lijf, in the noumbre of daies of his pilgrimage, and in the tyme that passith as schadowe? ether who may schewe to hym, what thing vndur sunne schal come aftir hym?

CAP 7

2 A good name is betere than preciouse oynementis; and the dai of deth is betere than the dai of birthe.

3 It is betere to go to the hous of morenyng, than to the hous of a feeste; for in that hous 'of morenyng the ende of alle men is monestid, and a man lyuynge thenkith, what is to comynge.

4 Yre is betere than leiyyng; for the soule of a trespassour is amendid bi the heuynesse of cheer.

5 The herte of wise men is where sorewe is; and the herte of foolis is where gladnesse is.

6 It is betere to be repreued of a wijs man, than to be disseyued bi the flateryng of foolis;

7 for as the sown of thornes brennynge vndur a pot, so is the leiyyng of a fool. But also this is vanyte.

8 Fals chalenge disturblith a wijs man, and it schal leese the strengthe of his herte.

9 Forsothe the ende of preyer is betere than the bigynnyng. A pacient man is betere than a proud man.

10 Be thou not swift to be wrooth; for ire restith in the bosum of a fool.

11 Seie thou not, What gessist thou is of cause, that the formere tymes weren betere than ben now? for whi siche axyng is fonned.

12 Forsothe wisdom with richessis is more profitable, and profitith more to men seynge the sunne.

13 For as wisdom defendith, so money defendith; but lernyng and wisdom hath this more, that tho yyuen lijf to 'her weldere.

14 Biholde thou the werkis of God, that no man may amende hym, whom God hath dispisid.

15 In a good day vse thou goodis, and bifore eschewe thou an yuel day; for God made so this dai as that dai, that a man fynde not iust playnyngis ayens hym.

16 Also Y siy these thingis in the daies of my natyuyte; a iust man perischith in his riytfulnesse, and a wickid man lyueth myche tyme in his malice.

17 Nyle thou be iust myche, nether vndurstonde thou more than is nedeful; lest thou be astonyed.

18 Do thou not wickidli myche, and nyle thou be a fool; lest thou die in a tyme not thin.

19 It is good, that thou susteyne a iust man; but also withdrawe thou not thin hond from hym; for he that dredith God, is not necligent of ony thing.

20 Wisdom hath coumfortid a wise man, ouer ten pryncis of a citee.

21 Forsothe no iust man is in erthe, that doith good, and synneth not.

22 But also yyue thou not thin herte to alle wordis, that ben seid; lest perauenture thou here thi seruaunt cursynge thee;

23 for thi conscience woot, that also thou hast cursid ofte othere men.

24 I asayede alle thingis in wisdom; Y seide, I schal be maad wijs, and it yede awei ferthere fro me, myche more than it was;

25 and the depthe is hiy, who schal fynde it?

26 I cumpasside alle thingis in my soule, to kunne, and biholde, and seke wisdom and resoun, and to knowe the wickidnesse of a fool, and the errour of vnprudent men.

27 And Y foond a womman bitterere than deth, which is the snare of hunteris, and hir herte is a net, and hir hondis ben boondis; he that plesith God schal ascape hir, but he that is a synnere, schal be takun of hir.

28 Lo! Y foond this, seide Ecclesiastes, oon and other, that Y schulde fynde resoun, which my soule sekith yit;

29 and Y foond not. I foond o man of a thousynde; Y foond not a womman of alle.

30 I foond this oonli, that God made a man riytful; and he medlide hym silf with questiouns with out noumbre. Who is siche as a wijs man? and who knowith the expownyng of a word?

1 The wisdom of a man schyneth in his cheer; and the myytieste schal chaunge his face.

CAP 8

2 I kepe the mouth of the kyng, and the comaundementis and sweryngis of God.

3 Haste thou not to go awei fro his face, and dwelle thou not in yuel werk. For he schal do al thing, that he wole;

4 and his word is ful of power, and no man mai seie to hym, Whi doist thou so?

5 He that kepith the comaundement of God 'in this lijf, schal not feele ony thing of yuel; the herte of a wijs man vndurstondith tyme and answer.

6 Tyme and cesoun is to ech werk; and myche turment is of a man,

7 for he knowith not thingis passid, and he mai not knowe bi ony messanger thingis to comynge.

8 It is not in the power of man to forbede the spirit, nethir he hath power in the dai of deth, nethir he is suffrid to haue reste, whanne the batel neiyeth; nethir wickidnesse schal saue a wickid man.

9 I bihelde alle thes thingis, and Y yaf myn herte in alle werkis, that ben don vndur the sunne. Sum tyme a man is lord of a man, to his yuel.

10 Y siy wickid men biryed, which, whanne thei lyueden yit, weren in hooli place; and thei weren preisid in the citee, as men of iust werkis; but also this is vanyte.

11 Forsothe for the sentence is not brouyt forth soone ayens yuele men, the sones of men doon yuels with outen ony drede.

12 Netheles of that, that a synnere doith yuel an hundrid sithis, and is suffrid bi pacience, Y knew that good schal be to men dredynge God, that reuerensen his face.

13 Good be not to the wickid man, nethir hise daies be maad longe; but passe thei as schadewe, that dreden not the face of the Lord.

14 Also another vanyte is, which is don on erthe. Iust men ben, to whiche yuels comen, as if thei diden the werkis of wickid men; and wickid men ben, that ben so sikur, as if thei han the dedis of iust men; but Y deme also this moost veyn.

15 Therfor Y preysid gladnesse, that no good was to a man vndur the sunne, no but to ete, and drynke, and to be ioiful; and that he schulde bere awei with hym silf oneli this of his trauel, in the daies of his lijf, whiche God yaf to hym vndur the sunne.

16 And Y settide myn herte to knowe wisdom, and to vndirstonde the departing, which is turned in erthe. A man is, that bi daies and niytis takith not sleep with iyen.

17 And Y vndurstood, that of alle the werkis of God, a man may fynde no resoun of tho thingis, that ben don vndur the sunne; and in as myche as he traueilith more to seke, bi so myche he schal fynde lesse; yhe, thouy a wijs man seith that he knowith, he schal not mow fynde.

CAP 9

1 I tretide alle these thingis in myn herte, to vndirstonde diligentli. Iust men, and wise men ben, and her werkis ben in the hond of God; and netheles a man noot, whether he is worthi of loue or of hatrede.

2 But alle thingis ben kept vncerteyn in to tyme to comynge; for alle thingis bifallen euenli to a iust man and to a wickid man, to a good man and to an yuel man, to a cleene man and to an vnclene man, to a man offrynge offryngis and sacrifices, and to a man dispisynge sacrifices; as a good man, so and a synnere; as a forswerun man, so and he that greetli swerith treuthe.

3 This thing is the worste among alle thingis, that ben don vndur the sunne, that the same thingis bifallen to alle men; wherfor and the hertis of the sones of men ben fillid with malice and dispisyng in her lijf; and aftir these thingis thei schulen be led doun to hellis.

4 No man is, that lyueth euere, and that hath trist of this thing; betere is a quik dogge than a deed lioun.

5 For thei that lyuen witen that thei schulen die; but deed men knowen no thing more, nether han meede ferthere; for her mynde is youun to foryetyng.

6 Also the loue, and hatrede, and enuye perischiden togidere; and thei han no part in this world, and in the werk that is don vndur the sunne.

7 Therfor go thou, iust man, and ete thi breed in gladnesse, and drynke thi wiyn with ioie; for thi werkis plesen God.

8 In ech tyme thi clothis be white, and oile faile not fro thin heed.

9 Vse thou lijf with the wijf which thou louest, in alle the daies of lijf of thin vnstablenesse, that ben youun to thee vndur sunne, in al the tyme of thi vanyte; for this is thi part in thi lijf and trauel, bi which thou trauelist vndur the sunne.

10 Worche thou bisili, what euer thing thin hond mai do; for nether werk, nether resoun, nethir kunnyng, nether wisdom schulen be at hellis, whidir thou haastist.

11 I turnede me to another thing, and Y siy vndur sunne, that rennyng is not of swift men, nethir batel is of stronge men,

nether breed is of wise men, nether richessis ben of techeris, ne grace is of crafti men; but tyme and hap is in alle thingis.

12 A man knowith not his ende; but as fischis ben takun with an hook, and as briddis ben takun with a snare, so men ben takun in yuel tyme, whanne it cometh sudeynli on hem.

13 Also Y siy this wisdom vndur the sunne, and Y preuede it the mooste.

14 A litil citee, and a fewe men ther ynne; a greet kyng cam ayens it, and cumpasside it with palis, and he bildide strengthis bi cumpas; and bisegyng was maad perfit.

15 And a pore man and a wijs was foundun ther ynne; and he delyuerede the citee bi his wisdom, and no man bithouyte aftirward on that pore man.

16 And Y seide, that wisdom is betere than strengthe; hou therfor is the wisdom of a pore man dispisid, and hise wordis ben not herd?

17 The wordis of wise men ben herd in silence, more than the cry of a prince among foolis.

CAP 10

18 Betere is wisdom than armuris of batel; and he that synneth in o thing, schal leese many goodis.

1 Flies 'that dien, leesen the swetnesse of oynement. Litil foli at a tyme is preciousere than wisdom and glorie.

2 The herte of a wijs man is in his riyt side; and the herte of a fool is in his left side.

3 But also a fool goynge in the weie, whanne he is vnwijs, gessith alle men foolis.

4 If the spirit of hym, that hath power, stieth on thee, forsake thou not thi place; for heeling schal make gretteste synnes to ceesse.

5 An yuel is, which Y siy vndur the sunne, and goith out as bi errour fro the face of the prince; a fool set in hiy dignyte,

6 and riche men sitte bynethe.

7 I siy seruauntis on horsis, and princes as seruauntis goynge on the erthe.

8 He that diggith a diche, schal falle in to it; and an eddre schal bite hym, that distrieth an hegge.

9 He that berith ouer stoonys, schal be turmentid in tho; and he that kittith trees, schal be woundid of tho.

10 If yrun is foldid ayen, and this is not as bifore, but is maad blunt, it schal be maad scharp with myche trauel; and wisdom schal sue aftir bisynesse.

11 If a serpent bitith, it bitith in silence; he that bacbitith priueli, hath no thing lesse than it.

12 The wordis of the mouth of a wijs man is grace; and the lippis of an vnwijs man schulen caste hym doun.

13 The bigynnyng of hise wordis is foli; and the laste thing of his mouth is the worste errour.

14 A fool multiplieth wordis; a man noot, what was bifore hym, and who mai schewe to hym that, that schal come aftir hym?

15 The trauel of foolis shal turment hem, that kunnen not go in to the citee.

16 Lond, wo to thee, whos kyng is a child, and whose princes eten eerli.

17 Blessid is the lond, whos kyng is noble; and whose princis eten in her tyme, to susteyne the kynde, and not to waste.

18 The hiynesse of housis schal be maad low in slouthis; and the hous schal droppe in the feblenesse of hondis.

19 In leiyyng thei disposen breed and wyn, that thei drynkynge ete largeli; and alle thingis obeien to monei.

20 In thi thouyt bacbite thou not the kyng, and in the priuete of thi bed, curse thou not a riche man; for the briddis of heuene schulen bere thi vois, and he that hath pennys, schal telle the sentence.

CAP 11

1 Sende thi breed on watris passynge forth, for aftir many tymes thou schalt fynde it.

2 Yyue thou partis seuene, and also eiyte; for thou woost not, what yuel schal come on erthe.

3 If cloudis ben filled, tho schulen schede out reyn on the erthe; if a tre fallith doun to the south, ether to the north, in what euer place it fallith doun, there it schal be.

4 He that aspieth the wynd, sowith not; and he that biholdith the cloudis, schal neuere repe.

5 As thou knowist not, which is the weye of the spirit, and bi what resoun boonys ben ioyned togidere in the wombe of a womman with childe, so thou knowist not the werkis of God, which is makere of alle thingis.

6 Eerli sowe thi seed, and thin hond ceesse not in the euentid; for thou woost not, what schal come forth more, this ethir that; and if euer eithir cometh forth togidere, it schal be the betere.

7 The liyt is sweet, and delitable to the iyen to se the sunne.

8 If a man lyueth many yeeris, and is glad in alle these, he owith to haue mynde of derk tyme, and of many daies; and whanne tho schulen come, thingis passid schulen be repreued of vanyte.

9 Therfor, thou yonge man, be glad in thi yongthe, and thin herte be in good in the daies of thi yongthe, and go thou in the weies of thin herte, and in the biholdyng of thin iyen; and wite thou, that for alle these thingis God shal brynge thee in to doom.

10 Do thou awei ire fro thin herte, and remoue thou malice fro thi fleisch; for whi yongthe and lust ben veyne thingis.

CAP 12

1 Haue thou mynde on thi creatour in the daies of thi yongthe, bifore that the tyme of thi turment come, and the yeris of thi deth neiye, of whiche thou schalt seie, Tho plesen not me.

2 'Haue thou mynde on thi creatour, bifor that the sunne be derk, and the liyt, and sterrys, and the mone; and cloude turne ayen after reyn.

3 Whanne the keperis of the hous schulen be mouyd, and strongeste men schulen tremble; and grynderis schulen be idel, whanne the noumbre schal be maad lesse, and seeris bi the hoolis schulen wexe derk;

4 and schulen close the doris in the street, in the lownesse of vois of a gryndere; and thei schulen rise at the vois of a brid, and alle the douytris of song schulen wexe deef.

5 And hiy thingis schulen drede, and schulen be aferd in the weie; an alemaunde tre schal floure, a locuste schal be maad fat, and capparis schal be distried; for a man schal go in to the hous of his euerlastyngnesse, and weileris schulen go aboute in the street.

6 Haue thou mynde on thi creatour, byfore that a siluerne roop be brokun, and a goldun lace renne ayen, and a watir pot be al to-brokun on the welle, and a wheele be brokun togidere on the cisterne;

7 and dust turne ayen in to his erthe, wherof it was, and the spirit turne ayen to God, that yaf it.

8 The vanyte of vanytees, seide Ecclesiastes, the vanyte of vanytees, and alle thingis ben vanyte.

9 And whanne Ecclesiastes was moost wijs, he tauyte the puple, and he telde out the thingis whiche he dide,

10 and he souyte out wisdom, and made many parablis; he souyte profitable wordis, and he wroot moost riytful wordis, and ful of treuthe.

11 The wordis of wise men ben as prickis, and as nailis fastned deepe, whiche ben youun of o scheepherde bi the counsels of maistris.

12 My sone, seke thou no more than these; noon ende is to make many bookis, and ofte thenkyng is turment of fleisch.

13 Alle we here togydere the ende of spekyng. Drede thou God, and kepe hise heestis; 'that is to seie, ech man.

14 God schal brynge alle thingis in to dom, that ben don; for ech thing don bi errour, whether it be good, ether yuel.

SONGES OF SONGES

CAP 1

1 Kisse he me with the cos of his mouth.

2 For thi tetis ben betere than wyn, and yyuen odour with beste oynementis. Thi name is oile sched out; therfor yonge damesels loueden thee.

3 Drawe thou me after thee; we schulen renne in to the odour of thin oynementis. The kyng ledde me in to hise celeris; we myndeful of thi teetis aboue wyn, schulen make ful out ioye, and schulen be glad in thee; riytful men louen thee.

4 Ye douytris of Jerusalem, Y am blak, but fair, as the tabernaclis of Cedar, as the skynnes of Salomon.

5 Nyle ye biholde me, that Y am blak, for the sunne hath discolourid me; the sones of my modir fouyten ayens me, thei settiden me a kepere in vyners; Y kepte not my vyner.

6 Thou spouse, whom my soule loueth, schewe to me, where thou lesewist, where thou restist in myddai; lest Y bigynne to wandre, aftir the flockis of thi felowis.

7 A! thou fairest among wymmen, if thou knowist not thi silf, go thou out, and go forth aftir the steppis of thi flockis; and feede thi kidis, bisidis the tabernaclis of scheepherdis.

8 Mi frendesse, Y licnede thee to myn oost of knyytis in the charis of Farao.

9 Thi chekis ben feire, as of a turtle; thi necke is as brochis.

10 We schulen make to thee goldun ournementis, departid and maad dyuerse with silver.

11 Whanne the kyng was in his restyng place, my narde yaf his odour.

12 My derlyng is a bundel of myrre to me; he schal dwelle bitwixe my tetis.

13 My derlyng is to me a cluster of cipre tre, among the vyneres of Engaddi.

14 Lo! my frendesse, thou art fair; lo! thou art fair, thin iyen ben the iyen of culueris.

15 Lo, my derling, thou art fair, and schapli; oure bed is fair as flouris.

16 The trees of oure housis ben of cedre; oure couplis ben of cipresse.

1 I am a flour of the feeld, and a lilye of grete valeis.

2 As a lilie among thornes, so is my frendesse among douytris.

3 As an apple tre among the trees of wodis, so my derlyng among sones.

CAP 2

I sat vndur the shadewe of hym, whom Y desiride; and his fruyt was swete to my throte.

4 The king ledde me in to the wyn celer; he ordeynede charite in me.

5 Bisette ye me with flouris, cumpasse ye me with applis; for Y am sijk for loue.

6 His left hond is vndur myn heed; and his riyt hond schal biclippe me.

7 Ye douytris of Jerusalem, Y charge you greetli, bi capretis, and hertis of feeldis, that ye reise not, nether make to awake the dereworthe spousesse, til sche wole. The vois of my derlyng; lo!

8 this derlyng cometh leepynge in mounteyns, and skippynge ouer litle hillis.

9 My derlyng is lijk a capret, and a calf of hertis; lo! he stondith bihynde oure wal, and biholdith bi the wyndows, and lokith thorouy the latisis.

10 Lo! my derlyng spekith to me, My frendesse, my culuer, my faire spousesse, rise thou, haaste thou, and come thou;

11 for wyntir is passid now, reyn is goon, and is departid awei.

12 Flouris apperiden in oure lond, the tyme of schridyng is comun; the vois of a turtle is herd in oure lond,

13 the fige tre hath brouyt forth hise buddis; vyneris flourynge han youe her odour. My frendesse, my fayre spousesse, rise thou, haaste thou, and come thou.

14 My culuer is in the hoolis of stoon, in the chyne of a wal with out morter. Schewe thi face to me, thi vois sowne in myn eeris; for thi vois is swete, and thi face is fair.

15 Catche ye litle foxis to vs, that destrien the vyneris; for oure vyner hath flourid.

16 My derlyng is to me, and Y am to hym, which is fed among lilies;

17 til the dai sprynge, and schadewis be bowid doun. My derlyng, turne thou ayen; be thou lijk a capret, and a calf of hertis, on the hillis of Betel.

CAP 3

1 In my litle bed Y souyte hym bi niytis, whom my soule loueth; Y souyte hym, and Y foond not.

2 I shal rise, and Y schal cumpasse the citee, bi litle stretis and large stretis; Y schal seke hym, whom my soule loueth; I souyte hym, and Y foond not.

3 Wakeris, that kepen the citee, founden me. Whether ye sien hym, whom my soule loueth?

4 A litil whanne Y hadde passid hem, Y foond hym, whom my soule loueth; Y helde hym, and Y schal not leeue hym, til Y brynge him in to the hous of my modir, and in to the closet of my modir.

5 Ye douytris of Jerusalem, Y charge you greetli, bi the capretis, and hertis of feeldis, that ye reise not, nether make to awake the dereworthe spousesse, til sche wole.

6 Who is this womman, that stieth bi the deseert, as a yerde of smoke of swete smellynge spices, of mirre, and of encence, and of al poudur of an oynement makere?

7 Lo! sixti stronge men of the strongeste men of Israel cumpassen the bed of Salomon; and alle thei holden swerdis,

8 and ben moost witti to batels; the swerd of ech man is on his hipe, for the drede of nyytis.

9 Kyng Salomon made to hym a seete, of the trees of Liban;

10 he made the pilers therof of siluer; he made a goldun restyng place, a stiyng of purpur; and he arayede the myddil thingis with charite, for the douytris of Jerusalem.

11 Ye douytris of Sion, go out, and se kyng Salomon in the diademe, bi which his modir crownede hym, in the dai of his spousyng, and in the dai of the gladnesse of his herte.

CAP 4

1 Mi frendesse, thou art ful fair; thin iyen ben of culueris, with outen that that is hid with ynne; thin heeris ben as the flockis of geete, that stieden fro the hil of Galaad.

2 Thi teeth ben as the flockis of clippid sheep, that stieden fro waischyng; alle ben with double lambren, and no bareyn is among tho.

3 Thi lippis ben as a reed lace, and thi speche is swete; as the relif of an appil of Punyk, so ben thi chekis, with outen that, that is hid with ynne.

4 Thi necke is as the tour of Dauid, which is bildid with strengthis maad bifore for defense; a thousynde scheldis hangen on it, al armure of stronge men.

5 Thi twei tetis ben as twey kidis, twynnes of a capret, that ben fed in lilies,

6 til the dai sprynge, and shadewis ben bowid doun. Y schal go to the mounteyn of myrre, and to the litil hil of encense.

7 My frendesse, thou art al faire, and no wem is in thee.

8 My spousesse, come thou fro the Liban; come thou fro the Liban, come thou; thou schalt be corowned fro the heed of Amana, fro the cop of Sanyr and Hermon, fro the dennys of liouns, fro the hillis of pardis.

9 My sister spousesse, thou hast woundid myn herte; thou hast woundid myn herte, in oon of thin iyen, and in oon heer of thi necke.

10 My sistir spousesse, thi tetis ben ful faire; thi tetis ben feirere than wyn, and the odour of thi clothis is aboue alle swete smellynge oynementis.

11 Spousesse, thi lippis ben an hony coomb droppynge; hony and mylk ben vndur thi tunge, and the odour of thi clothis is as the odour of encence.

12 Mi sister spousesse, a gardyn closid togidere; a gardyn closid togidere, a welle aseelid.

13 Thi sendingis out ben paradis of applis of Punyk, with the fruytis of applis, cipre trees, with narde;

14 narde, and saffrun, an erbe clepid fistula, and canel, with alle trees of the Liban, myrre, and aloes, with alle the beste oynementis.

15 A welle of gardyns, a pit of wallynge watris, that flowen with fersnesse fro the Liban.

16 Rise thou north wynd, and come thou, south wynd; blowe thou thorouy my gardyn, and the swete smellynge oynementis therof schulen flete.

CAP 5

1 Mi derlyng, come in to his gardyn, to ete the fruyt of hise applis. Mi sister spousesse, come thou in to my gardyn. Y have rope my myrre, with my swete smellynge spices; Y haue ete an hony combe, with myn hony; Y haue drunke my wyn, with my mylk. Frendis, ete ye, and drynke; and dereworthest frendis, be ye fillid greetli.

2 Y slepe, and myn herte wakith. The vois of my derlyng knockynge; my sister, my frendesse, my culuer, my spousesse vnwemmed, opene thou to me; for myn heed is ful of dew, and myn heeris ben ful of dropis of niytis.

3 I have vnclothid me of my coote; hou schal Y be clothid ther ynne? I haue waische my feet; hou schal Y defoule tho?

4 Mi derlyng putte his hond bi an hoole; and my wombe tremblide at the touchyng therof.

5 Y roos, for to opene to my derlyng; myn hondis droppiden myrre, and my fyngris weren ful of myrre moost preued.

6 Y openede the wiket of my dore to my derlyng; and he hadde bowid awei, and hadde passid. My soule was meltid, as the derlyng spak; Y souyte, and Y foond not hym; Y clepide, and he answerde not to me.

7 Keperis that cumpassiden the citee founden me; thei smytiden me, and woundiden me; the keperis of wallis token awey my mentil.

8 Ye douytris of Jerusalem, Y biseche you bi an hooli thing, if ye han founde my derlyng, that ye telle to hym, that Y am sijk for loue.

9 A! thou faireste of wymmen, of what manner condicioun is thi derlyng 'of the louede? of what manner condicioun is thi derling of a derling? for thou hast bisouyt vs bi an hooli thing.

10 My derling is whyt and rodi; chosun of thousyndis.

11 His heed is best gold; hise heeris ben as the bowis of palm trees, and ben blake as a crowe.

12 Hise iyen ben as culueris on the strondis of watris, that ben waischid in mylk, and sitten besidis fulleste ryueris.

13 Hise chekis ben as gardyns of swete smellynge spices, set of oynement makeris; hise lippis ben lilies, droppynge doun the best myrre.

14 Hise hondis ben able to turne aboute, goldun, and ful of iacynctis; his wombe is of yuer, ourned with safiris.

15 Hise lippis ben pilers of marble, that ben foundid on foundementis of gold; his schapplinesse is as of the Liban, he is chosun as cedris.

16 His throte is moost swete, and he is al desirable. Ye douytris of Jerusalem, siche is my derlyng, and this is my freend.

17 Thou faireste of wymmen, whidur yede thi derlyng? whidur bowide thi derlyng? and we schulen seke hym with thee.

CAP 6

1 My derlyng yede doun in to his orcherd, to the gardyn of swete smellynge spices, that he be fed there in orcherdis, and gadere lilyes.

2 Y to my derlyng; and my derlyng, that is fed among the lilies, be to me.

3 Mi frendesse, thou art fair, swete and schappli as Jerusalem, thou art ferdful as the scheltrun of oostis set in good ordre.

4 Turne awei thin iyen fro me, for tho maden me to fle awei; thin heeris ben as the flockis of geet, that apperiden fro Galaad.

5 Thi teeth as a flok of scheep, that stieden fro waischyng; alle ben with double lambren, 'ether twynnes, and no bareyn is among tho. As the rynde of a pumgranate, so ben thi chekis, without thi priuytees.

6 Sixti ben queenys, and eiyti ben secundarie wyues; and of yong damesels is noon noumbre.

7 Oon is my culuer, my perfit spousesse, oon is to hir modir, and is the chosun of hir modir; the douytris of Syon sien hir, and prechiden hir moost blessid; queenys, and secundarie wyues preisiden hir.

8 Who is this, that goith forth, as the moreutid risynge, fair as the moone, chosun as the sunne, ferdful as the scheltrun of oostis set in good ordre?

10 Y cam doun in to myn orcherd, to se the applis of grete valeis, and to biholde, if vyneris hadden flourid, and if pumgranate trees hadden buriowned.

11 Y knew not; my soule disturblide me, for the charis of Amynadab.

12 Turne ayen, turne ayen, thou Sunamyte; turne ayen, turne ayen, that we biholde thee. What schalt thou se in the Sunamyte, no but cumpenyes of oostis?

CAP 7

1 Douytir of the prince, thi goyngis ben ful faire in schoon; the ioyncturis of thi heppis ben as brochis, that ben maad bi the hond of a crafti man.

2 Thi nawle is as a round cuppe, and wel formed, that hath neuere nede to drynkis; thi wombe is as an heep of whete, biset aboute with lilies.

3 Thi twei teetis ben as twei kidis, twynnes of a capret.

4 Thi necke is as a tour of yuer; thin iyen ben as cisternes in Esebon, that ben in the yate of the douyter of multitude; thi nose is as the tour of Liban, that biholdith ayens Damask.

5 Thin heed is as Carmele; and the heeres of thin heed ben as the kyngis purpur, ioyned to trowyis.

6 Dereworthe spousesse, thou art ful fair, and ful schappli in delices.

7 Thi stature is licned to a palm tree, and thi tetis to clustris of grapis.

8 I seide, Y schal stie in to a palm tree, and Y schal take the fruytis therof. And thi tetis schulen be as the clustris of grapis of a vyner; and the odour of thi mouth as the odour of pumgranatis;

9 thi throte schal be as beste wyn. Worthi to my derlyng for to drynke, and to hise lippis and teeth to chewe.

10 Y schal cleue by loue to my derlyng, and his turnyng schal be to me.

11 Come thou, my derlyng, go we out in to the feeld; dwelle we togidere in townes.

12 Ryse we eerli to the vyner; se we, if the vyner hath flourid, if the flouris bryngen forth fruytis, if pumgranatis han flourid; there I schal yyue to thee my tetis.

13 Mandrogoris han youe her odour in oure yatis; my derlyng, Y haue kept to thee alle applis, new and elde.

CAP 8

1 Who 'mai grante to me thee, my brother, soukynge the tetis of my modir, that Y fynde thee aloone without forth, and that Y kisse thee, and no man dispise me thanne?

2 Y schal take thee, and Y schal lede thee in to the hous of my modir, and in to the closet of my modir; there thou schalt teche me, and Y schal yyue to thee drink of wyn maad swete, and of the must of my pumgranatis.

3 His lefthond vndur myn heed, and his riythond schal biclippe me.

4 Ye douytris of Jerusalem, Y charge you greetli, that ye reise not, nether make the dereworthe spousesse to awake, til sche wole.

5 Who is this spousesse, that stieth fro desert, and flowith in delices, and restith on hir derlynge? Y reiside thee vndur a pumgranate tre; there thi modir was corrupt, there thi modir was defoulid.

6 Set thou me as a signet on thin herte, as a signet on thin arm; for loue is strong as deth, enuy is hard as helle; the laumpis therof ben laumpis of fier, and of flawmes.

7 Many watris moun not quenche charite, nether floodis schulen oppresse it. Thouy a man yyue al the catel of his hous for loue, he schal dispise 'that catel as nouyt.

8 Oure sistir is litil, and hath no tetys; what schulen we do to oure sistir, in the dai whanne sche schal be spokun to?

9 If it is a wal, bilde we theronne siluerne touris; if it is a dore, ioyne we it togidere with tablis of cedre.

10 I am a wal, and my tetis ben as a tour; sithen Y am maad as fyndynge pees bifore hym.

11 A vyner was to the pesible; in that citee, that hath puplis, he bitook it to keperis; a man bryngith a thousynde platis of siluer for the fruyt therof.

12 The vyner is bifore me; a thousynde ben of thee pesible, and two hundrid to hem that kepen the fruytis therof.

13 Frendis herkene thee, that dwellist in orchertis; make thou me to here thi vois.

14 My derlyng, fle thou; be thou maad lijk a capret, and a calf of hertis, on the hillis of swete smellynge spices.

WISDOM

CAP 1

1 Ye that demen the erthe, loue riytfulnesse; feele ye of the Lord in goodnesse, and seke ye hym in the symplenesse of herte.

2 For he is foundun of hem, that tempten not hym; forsothe he apperith to hem, that han feith in to hym.

3 For whi weiward thouytis departen fro God; but preued vertu repreueth vnwise men.

4 For whi wisdom schal not entre in to an yuel willid soule; nethir schal dwelle in a bodi suget to synnes.

5 Forsothe the Hooli Goost of wisdom schal fle awei fro 'a feyned man, and he schal take awei hym silf fro thouytis, that ben with out vnderstondyng; and the man schal be punyschid of wyckidnesse comynge aboue.

6 For the spirit of wisdom is benyngne, and he schal not delyuere a cursid man fro hise lippis; for whi God is witnesse of hise reynes, and the serchere of his herte is trewe, and the herere of his tunge.

7 For whi the Spirit of the Lord hath fillid the world; and this thing, that conteyneth alle thingis, hath the kunnyng of vois.

8 For this he that spekith wickid thingis, may not be hid; and doom punyschynge schal not passe hym.

9 For whi axyng schal be in the thouytis of a wickid man.

10 Forsothe the heryng of hise wordis schal come to God, and to the punyschyng of hise wickidnessis; for the eere of feruent loue herith alle thingis, and the noise of grutchyngis schal not be hyd.

11 Therfor kepe ye you fro grutchyng, that profitith no thing, and fro bacbityng spare ye the tunge; for a derk word schal not go in to veyn; forsothe the mouth that lieth, sleeth the soule.

12 Nyle ye coueyte deth, in the errour of youre lijf, nether gete ye perdicioun in the werkis of youre hondis; for God made not deth,

13 nether is glad in the perdicioun of lyuynge men.

14 For whi God made of nouyt alle thingis, that tho schulden be; and he made the naciouns of the world able to be heelid. Forwhi medecyn of distriyng is not in tho men, nether the rewme of hellis is in erthe.

15 For riytfulnesse is euerlastynge, and vndeedli; but vnriytfulnesse is getyng of deeth.

16 Forsothe wickid men clepiden that vnriytfulnesse bi hondis and wordis, and thei gessiden it a frendesse, and fletiden awei, and thei puttiden biheestis to it; for thei ben worthi the deth, that ben of the part therof.

CAP 2

1 Forsothe wickid men seiden, thenkynge anentis hem silf not riytfuli, The tyme of oure lijf is litil, and with anoye; no refreisching is in the ende of a man, and noon is, that is knowun, that turnede ayen fro hellis.

2 For we weren borun of nouyt, and aftir this tyme we schulen be, as if we hadden not be; forwhi smoke is blowun out in oure nose thirlis, and a word of sparcle to stire oure herte.

3 For oure bodi schal be quenchid aische, and the spirit schal be scaterid abrood as soft eir; and oure lijf schal passe as the step of a cloude, and it schal be departid as a myst, which is dryuun awey of the beemys of the sunne, and is greued of the heete therof.

4 And oure name schal take foryeting bi tyme; and no man schal haue mynde of oure werkis.

5 Forwhi oure tyme is the passyng of a schadewe, and no turnyng ayen of oure ende is; for it is aseelid, and no man turneth ayen.

6 Therfor come ye, and vse we the goodis that ben, and vse we a creature, as in yongthe, swiftli.

7 Fille we vs with preciouse wyn and oynementis; and the flour of tyme passe not vs.

8 Corowne we vs with roosis, bifor that tho welewen; no medewe be, 'bi which oure letcherie passe not.

9 No man of vs be with out part of oure letcherie; euery where leeue we the signes of gladnesse; for this is oure part, and this is oure eritage.

10 Oppresse we a pore iust man, and spare we not a widewe, nether reuerence we hoor heeris of an old man of myche tyme.

11 But oure strengthe be the lawe of riytfulnesse; forwhi that that is feble, is foundun vnprofitable.

12 Therfor disseyue we a iust man, for he is vnprofitable to vs, and he is contrarie to oure werkis; and he vpbreidith to vs the synnes of lawe, and he defameth on vs the synnes of oure techyng.

13 He biheetith that he hath the kunnyng of God, and he nemeth hym silf the sone of God.

14 He is maad to us in to schewyng of oure thouytis.

15 He is greuouse to vs, yhe, to se; forwhi his lyf is vnlijk to other men, and hise weies ben chaungid.

16 We ben gessid of hym to be triffleris, and he absteyneth hym silf fro oure weies, as fro vnclenessis; and he bifore settith the laste thingis of iust men, and he hath glorie, that he hath God a fadir.

17 Therfor se we, if hise wordis ben trewe; and asaie we, what thingis schulen come to hym; and we schulen wite, what schulen be the laste thingis of hym.

18 For if he is the very sone of God, he schal vp take hym, and schal delyuere hym fro the hondis of hem that ben contrarie.

19 Axe we hym bi dispisyng and turment, that we knowe his reuerence, and that we preue his pacience.

20 Bi fouleste deth condempne we hym; for whi biholdyng schal be of hise wordis.

21 Thei thouyten these thingis, and thei erriden; for whi her malice blyndide hem.

22 And thei knewen not the sacramentis of God, nethir thei hopiden the meede of riytfulnesse, nether thei demyden the onour of hooli soulis.

23 For whi God made man vnable to be distried, and God made man to the ymage of his licnesse.

24 But bi enuye of the deuel deth entride in to the world;
25 for sothe thei suen hym, that ben of his part.

CAP 3

1 Forsothe the soulis of iust men ben in the hond of God; and the turment of deth schal not touche hem.

2 Thei semyden to the iyen of vnwise men to die; and turment was demed the outgoyng of hem.

3 And fro iust weie thei yeden in to distriyng, and that that is of vs the weie of distriyng; but thei ben in pees.

4 Thouy thei sufriden turmentis bifore men, the hope of hem is ful of vndeedlynesse.

5 Thei weren trauelid in a fewe thingis, and thei schulen be disposid wel in many thingis; for whi God asaiede hem, and foond hem worthi to hym silf.

6 He preuede hem as gold in a furneis, and he took hem as the offryng of brent sacrifice; and the biholdyng of hem schal be in tyme of yelding.

7 Iust men schulen schyne, and schulen renne aboute as sparclis in a place of rehed.

8 Thei schulen deme naciouns, and schulen be lordis of puplis; and the Lord of hem schal regne with outen ende.

9 Thei that trusten on hym, schulen vnderstonde treuthe; and feithful men in loue schulen assente to hym; for whi yifte and pees is to hise chosun men.

10 But wickid men, bi tho thingis that thei thouyten, schulen haue punyschyng; whiche dispisiden iust thing, and yeden awei fro the Lord.

11 For he that castith awei wisdom and lore, is cursid; and the hope of wickid men is voide, and her trauels ben without fruyt, and her werkis ben vnhabitable, and vnprofitable.

12 The wymmen of hem ben vnwitti, and the sones of hem ben ful weiward.

13 The creature of hem is cursid; for whi a womman bareyn and vndefoulid is blessid, that 'knew not bed in trespas; sche schal haue fruyt in the biholdyng of holy soulis.

14 And a man vnmyyti to gendre is blessid, that 'wrouyte not wickidnesse bi hise hondis, nether thouyte moost weiward thingis ayens the Lord; for whi a chosun yifte of feith schal be youun to hym, and a most acceptable eritage in the temple of God.

15 For whi the fruyt of good trauels is gloriouse, and the roote of wisdom that fallith not doun.

16 But the sones of avowtreris schulen be in distriyng, and the seed of a wickid bed schal be destried.

17 And sotheli thouy thei schulen be of long lijf, thei schulen be arettid in to nouyt; and the laste eelde of hem schal be withouten onour.

18 And if thei ben deed swiftliere, thei schulen not haue hope, nether alowyng in the dai of knowyng.

19 Forsothe wickide naciouns ben of hard ending.

CAP 4

1 A! hou fair is chast generacioun with clerenesse; for the mynde therof is vndeedli, for it is knowun, both anentis God, and anentis men.

2 Whanne it is present, thei suen it; and thei desiren it, whanne it hath led out it silf, and it ouercomyng getith bi victorie the mede of batels vndefoulid, and is corouned with outen ende.

3 But the many fold gendrid multitude of wickid men schal not be profitable; and plauntyngis of auoutrie schulen not yyue deepe rootis, nether schulen sette stable stidfastnesse.

4 Thouy thei buriounen in bowis in time, thei set vnstidfastli schulen be moued of the wynd, and schulen be drawun out bi the roote of the greetnesse of wyndys.

5 For whi bowis vnperfit schulen be brokun togidere; and the fruytis of hem ben vnprofitable, and soure to ete, and couenable to no thing.

6 For whi alle sones, that ben borun of wickid men, ben witnessis of wickidnesse ayens fadirs and modris, in her axyng.

7 But a iust man, thouy he be bifore ocupied bi deth, schal be in refreischyng.

8 For whi worschipful eelde is not of long tyme, nether is rikened bi the noumbre of yeeris; the wittis of a man ben hoore,

9 and the age of eelde is lijf withouten wem.

10 He pleside God, and was maad dereworth, and he lyuynge among synneris was 'borun ouer; he was rauyschid,

11 lest malice schulde chaunge his vnderstondyng, ethir lest feynyng schulde disseyue his soule.

12 For whi disseyuyng of trifelyng makith derk goode thingis, and the vnstablenesse of coueitise turneth ouer the wit without malice.

13 He was endid in schort tyme, and fillide many tymes;

14 for whi his soule was plesant to God; for this thing God hastide to lede hym out fro the myddis of wickidnesses; but puplis sien and vndurstoden not, nether settiden siche thingis in 'the inwardnesses.

15 For whi the grace and merci of God is on hise seyntis, and biholdyng of 'Goddis coumfort is on hise chosun men.

16 Forsothe a iust man deed condempneth quyke wickid men; and yongthe endid swiftliere condempneth long lijf of an vniust man.

17 For thei schulen se the ende of a wise man, and thei schulen not vndurstonde, what thing God thouyte of hym, and whi the Lord made hym lesse.

18 For thei schulen se, and schulen dispise hym; but the Lord schal scorne hem.

19 And aftir these thingis thei schulen be fallynge doun withouten onour, and in dispisyng among deed men with outen ende. For he schal al to-breke hem bolnyd with out vois, and he schal moue hem fro the foundementis; and thei schulen be desolat til to the laste thing. And thei schulen be weilynge, and the mynde of hem schal perische.

20 Thei schulen come ferdful in the thouyt of her synnes; and her wickidnessis on the contrarie side schulen lede hem ouer.

CAP 5

1 Thanne iust men schulen stonde in greet stidfastnesse ayens hem that angwischiden 'iust men, and whiche token awei her trauelis.

2 Thei schulen se, and schulen be disturblyd with orrible drede, and thei schulen wondre in the sudeynte of heelthe vnhopid; and thei schulen weile for angwisch of spirit,

3 and thei schulen seie, doynge penaunce withynne hem silf, and weilyng for the angwysch of spirit, These men it ben, whiche we hadden sum tyme in to scorn, and in to licnesse of vpbreidyng.

4 We woode men gessiden her lijf woodnesse, and the ende of hem with oute onour;

5 hou therfor ben thei rekened among the sones of God, and her part is among seyntis?

6 Therfor we erriden fro the weie of treuthe, and the liyt of riytfulnesse schynede not to us, and the sunne of vndurstondyng roos not vp to us.

7 We weren maad weri in the weie of wickidnesse and of perdicioun; and we yeden hard weies.

8 But we knewen not the weie of the Lord; what profitide pride to vs, ethir what brouyte the boost of richessis to vs?

9 All tho thingis passiden as schadewe, and as a messanger bifore rennynge.

10 And as a schip, that passith thorou the flowynge watir, of which whanne it hath passid, it is not to fynde a step, nethir the path of the botme therof in wawys.

11 Ethir as a bryd, that flieth ouer in the eir, of which no preef is foundun of the weie therof, but oneli the sown of wengis betynge liyt wynde, and keruynge the eir by the myyt of weie, and with wyngis moued togidere it flei ouer, and aftir this no signe is foundun of the weie therof.

12 Ethir as an arowe shot out in to a place ordeyned, the eir is departid, and is closid ayen anoon, that the passyng therof be not knowun.

13 'So and we borun ceessiden anoon to be, and sotheli we myyten schewe no signe of vertu; but we weren wastid in oure malice.

14 Thei that synneden, seiden siche thingis in helle.

15 For the hope of a wickid man is as the flour of a brere which is takun awei of the wynd, and as smal froth which is scaterid of a tempest, and as smoke which is spred abrood of wynd, and as the mynde of 'an herborid man of o dai, that passith forth.

16 But iust men schulen lyue withouten ende, and the meede of hem is anentis the Lord; and the thouyt of hem is anentis the hiyeste.

17 Therfor thei schulen take of the hond of the Lord the rewme of fairnesse, and the diademe of comelynesse; for he schal gouerne hem with his riythond, and he schal defende hem with his hooli arm.

18 And his feruent loue schal take armure, and he schal arme the creature to the venieaunce of enemyes.

19 He schal clothe riytfulnesse for an haburioun, and he schal take certeyn doom for a basynet;

20 he schal take a scheeld that may not be ouercomun, equyte;

21 forsothe he schal whette hard wraththe in to a spere, and the world schal fiyte with him ayens vnwitti men.

22 Streiyte sendyngis out of leytis schulen go, and as the sidis of a reynbouwe, whanne the bouwe of cloudis is crokid, thei schulen be destried; and thei schulen skippe in to a certeyn place.

23 And fulle hailstones schulen be sent fro a stony wreththe, and the watir of the see schal wexe whijt ayens hem, and floodis schulen renne togider harde.

24 The spirit of vertu schal stonde ayens hem, and as the whirlyng of wind it schal departe hem; and the wickidnesse of hem schal brynge al the lond to desert, and malice schal distrye the seetis of myyti men.

CAP 6

1 Wisdom is beter than strengthis, and a prudent man doith more than a strong man.

2 Therfor, ye kyngis, here, and vndurstonde; and ye iugis of the coostis of erthe, lerne.

3 Ye that holden togidere multitudis, and plesen you in the cumpenyes of naciouns, yyue eeris;

4 forwhi power is youun of the Lord to you, and vertu is youun of the hiyeste, that schal axe youre werkis, and schal serche thouytis.

5 For whanne ye weren mynystris of his rewme, ye demeden not riytfuli, nether ye kepten the lawe of riytfulnesse, nether ye yeden bi the wille of God.

6 Hidousli and soone he schal appere to you; forwhi hardeste doom schal be maad in hem, that ben souereyns.

7 Forsothe merci is grauntid to a litil man; but miyti men schulen suffre turmentis miytili.

8 For the Lord, which is lord of alle thingis, schal not withdrawe the persoone of ony man, nether he schal drede the greetnesse of ony man; for he made the litil man and the greet man, and charge is to hym euenli of alle men.

9 But strongere turment neiyeth to strongere men.

10 Therfor, ye kyngis, these my wordis ben to you, that ye lerne wisdom, and that ye falle not doun.

11 For thei that kepen riytfulnesse, schulen be deemed riytfuli; and thei, that lernen iust thingis, schulen fynde, what thei schulen answere.

12 Therfor coueite ye my wordis, and loue ye tho; and ye schulen haue techyng.

13 Wisdom is cleer, and that schal neuer fade; and it is seyn liytli of hem that louen it, and it is foundun of hem that seken it.

14 It bifore ocupieth hem that coueyten it, that it schewe it silf the formere to hem.

15 He that wakith bi liyt to it, schal not trauele; forsothe he schal fynde it sittynge nyy hise yatis.

16 Therfor to thenke on wisdom is parfit wit, and he that wakith for it, schal soone be sikir.

17 For whi it goith aboute, and sekith men worthi to it; and in her weies it schal schewe it silf gladli to hem, and in al puruyaunce it schal meete hem.

18 For whi the bigynnyng of wisdom is the verieste coueytise of lernyng.

19 Therfor the bisynesse of lernyng is loue; and loue is the kepyng of lawis therof. Sotheli the kepyng of lawis is perfeccioun of vncorrupcioun;

20 forsothe vncorrupcioun makith to be next to God.

21 Therfor the coueitise of wisdom schal brynge to euerlastynge rewme.

22 Therfor if ye, kyngis of the puple, deliten in seetis, and in kyngis yerdis, 'ether regaltees, loue ye wisdom, that ye regne with outen ende.

23 Alle ye, that ben souereyns to puplis, loue the liyt of wisdom.

24 Sotheli what is wisdom, and hou it is maad, Y schal telle; and Y schal not hide fro you the sacramentis of God; but fro the bigynnyng of birthe Y schal seke, and Y schal sette in to the liyt the kunnyng therof, and Y schal not passe treuthe.

25 And Y schal not haue weye with enuye wexynge rotun; for siche a man schal not be parcener of wisdom.

26 Forsothe the multitude of wise men is the helthe of the world; and a wijs kyng is the stablischyng of the puple.

27 Therfor take ye techyng bi my wordis, and it schal profite to you.

CAP 7

1 Forsothe and Y am a deedli man, lijk men, and of erthli kynde of hym that was maad first, and in the wombe of the modir Y was fourmed fleische.

2 In the time of ten monethis Y was cruddid togidere in blood, of the seed of man, and bi acordynge delit of sleep.

3 And Y was borun, and took comyn eir, and in lijk maner Y felle doun in to the erthe maad; and Y wepynge sente out the firste vois, lijk alle men.

4 Y was nurschid in wrappyngis, and in greet bisynesses;

5 for whi no man of kyngis hadde othere bigynnyng of birthe.

6 Therfor oon entryng to lijf is to alle men, and lijk goyng out.

7 Herfor Y desiride, and wit was youun to me; and Y inwardli clepide, and the spirit of wisdom cam in to me.

8 And Y settide wisdom bifore rewmes, and seetis; and Y seide, that richessis ben nouyt in comparisoun therof,

9 and Y comparisonede not a preciouse stoon to it; forwhi al gold in comparisoun therof is a litil grauel, and siluer schal be arettid as cley in the siyt therof.

10 Y louyde wisdom more than helthe and fairnesse; and Y purposide to haue it for liyt, for the liyt therof may not be quenchid.

11 Forsothe alle goodis camen togidere to me with it; and vnnoumbrable oneste is by the werkys therof.

12 And Y was glad in alle thingis; for this wisdom yede bifore me, and Y knew not, for it is the modir of alle goodis.

13 Which wisdom Y lernyde with out feynyng, and Y comyne without enuye; and Y hide not the oneste therof.

14 For it is tresour with out noumbre to men, and thei, that vsiden that tresour, weren maad parceneris of Goddis frenschip, and weren preisid for the yiftis of kunnyng.

15 Forsothe God yaf to me to seie of sentence, and to bifore take worthi thingis of these thingis that ben youun to me; for he is the ledere of wisdom, and amendere of wise men.

16 For whi bothe we, and oure wordis, and al wisdom, and lernyng of kunnyng of werkis ben in his hond.

17 Forsothe he yaf to me the veri kunnyng of these thingis that ben, that Y knowe the disposicioun of the world, and the vertues of elementis;

18 the bigynnyng, and the endyng, and the myddil of tymes; the chaungyngis of whilis, and the endyngis of tymes; the chaungyngis of maneres, and departyngis of tymes; the coursis of the yeer,

19 and the disposiciouns of sterris;

20 the kyndis of beestis, and the wraththis of wielde beestis; the strengthe of wyndis, and the thouytis of men; the differences of trees, and the vertues of rootis.

21 And Y lernede what euer thingis ben hid and vnpurueyed; for whi wisdom, the crafti maker of alle thingis, tauyte me.

22 For in that wisdom vnmaad is the spirit of vndurstonding, hooli, many fold, oon aloone, sutil, temperat, wijs, mouable, vndefoulid, certeyn, swete, louynge a good dede, which spirit forbedith no thing to do wel;

23 curteis, benynge, stable, sikur, hauynge al vertu, biholdynge alle thingis, and which takith alle spiritis able to vndurstonde, and he is clene, and sutil.

24 For whi wisdom is more mouable than alle mouable thingis; forsothe it stretchith forth euery where, for his clennesse.

25 For it is a brething of Goddis vertu, and it is sum cleene comyngforth of the clerenesse of Almiyti God;

26 and therfor no defoulid thing renneth in to it. For it is briytnesse of euerlastynge liyt, and it is a myrrour with out wem of Goddis maieste, and it is an ymage of his goodnesse.

27 And whanne it is oon, it may alle thingis; and it dwellith in it silf, and renulith alle thingis, and bi naciouns it berith ouer it silf in to hooli soulis; it makith the frendis of God and profetis.

28 For God loueth no man, no but hym that dwellith with wisdom.

29 Forwhi this wisdom is fairere than the sunne, and is aboue al the disposicioun of sterris; wisdom comparisound to liyt, is foundun the formere.

30 Forwhi niyt cometh aftir that liyt; but wysdom ouercometh malice.

1 Therfor wisdom stretchith forth fro the ende til to the ende strongli, and disposith alle thingis swetly.

CAP 8

2 I louede this wisdom maad, and Y souyte it out fro my yongthe; and Y souyte to take it a spousesse to me, and Y am maad a louyere of the fairnesse therof.

3 He that hath the felouschip of God, glorifieth the gentilnesse therof; but also the Lord of alle thingis louede it.

4 For it is the techeresse of the lernyng of God, and cheseresse of hise werkis.

5 And if richessis ben coueitid in lijf, what is richere than wisdom, that worchith alle thingis?

6 Sotheli if wit worchith, who is a crafti maker more than wisdom, of these thingis that ben?

7 And if a man loueth riytfulnesse, the trauels of this wisdom han grete vertues; for it techith sobrenesse, and prudence, and riytfulnesse, and vertu; and no thing is profitablere than these in lijf to men.

8 And if a man desirith multitude of kunnyng, wisdom knowith thingis passid, and gessith of thingis to comynge; it kan the felnessis of wordis, and asoilyngis of argumentis; it kan signes and schewyngis of thingis to comynge, bifore that tho ben maad; and the bifallyngis of tymes and of worldus.

9 Therfor Y purposide to brynge to me this wisdom, to lyue togidere; witynge that it schal comyne with me of goodis, and spekyng togidere of my thouyt, and of myn anoi schal be.

10 For this wisdom Y schal haue clerenesse at cumpenyes, and onour at eldre men;

11 Y schal be foundun yong and scharp in doom, and in the siyt of myyti men Y schal be wondurful, and the faces of princes schulen worschipe me.

12 Thei schulen abide me, beynge stille, and thei schulen biholde me, spekynge; and the while I speke many thingis, thei schulen sette hondis on her mouth.

13 Ferthermore bi this wisdom Y schal haue vndedlynesse; and Y schal leeue euerlastynge mynde to hem, that schulen come aftir me.

14 I schal dispose puplis; and naciouns schulen be suget to me.

15 Hidouse kyngis herynge me schulen drede; and in multitude Y schal be seyn good, and strong in batel.

16 Y schal entre in to myn hous, and Y schal reste with wisdom; for the conuersacioun therof hath no bitternesse, and the dwellynge togidere therof hath noon anoye, but gladnesse and ioye.

17 Y thouyte these thingis at me, and Y remembride in myn herte; forwhi wisdom is vndeedli in thouyt,

18 and good delityng is in the frendschipe therof; and onestee without defaute is in the werkis of hondis therof; and wisdom is in the strijf of speche therof; and greet clerenesse is in the comyning of wordis therof; Y yede aboute, sekinge to take wisdom to me.

19 Forsothe Y was a witti child, and Y gat a good soule.

20 And whanne Y was more good, Y cam to a bodi vndefoulid.

21 And as Y knew, that ellis Y mai not be chaste, no but God yyue, and this same thing was wisdom, to wite whos this yifte was; Y yede to the Lord, and Y bisouyte hym, and Y seide, of alle myn entralis.

CAP 9

1 God of my fadris, and Lord of merci, that madist alle thingis bi thi word,

2 and ordeynedist man bi thi wisdom, that he schulde be lord of creature, which is maad of thee,

3 that he dispose the world in equite and riytfulnesse, and deme doom in riyt reulyng of herte;

4 yyue thou to me wisdom, that stondith nyy thi seetis; and nyle thou repreue me fro thi children.

5 For Y am thi seruaunt, and the sone of thin hand mayde; Y am a sijk man, and of litil tyme, and lesse to the vndurstondyng of doom and of lawis.

6 And if ony man is perfit among the sones of men, if thi wisdom fleeth awei fro hym, he schal be rikenyd in to nouyt.

7 Forsothe thou hast chose me kyng to thi puple, and a iuge of thi sones and douytris;

8 and thou seidist, that Y schulde bilde a temple in thin holi hil, and an auter in the citee of thi dwellyng place; the licnesse of thin hooli tabernacle, which thou madist redi at the bigynnyng.

9 And thi wisdom is with thee, that knowith thi werkis, which also was present thanne, whanne thou madist the world, and wiste what was plesaunt to thin iyen, and what was dressid in thi comaundementis.

10 Sende thou that wisdom fro thin hooli heuenes, and fro the seete of thi greetnesse, that it be with me, and trauele with me; and that Y wyte what is acceptable anentis thee.

11 Forwhi thilke wisdom knowith and vndirstondith alle thingis; and it schal lede me forth in my werkis sobrely, and it schal kepe me in his power.

12 And my werkis schulen be acceptable, and Y schal dispose thi puple iustli, and Y schal be worthi of the seetis of my fadir.

13 For who of men mai knowe the counsel of God? ether who mai thenke, what wole God?

14 For whi the thouytis of deedli men ben dreedful, and oure puruyaunces ben vncerteyn.

15 For whi the bodi that is corrupt, greueth the soule; and ertheli dwellyng pressith doun the wit, thenkynge many thingis.

16 And of hard we gessen tho thingis, that ben in erthe; and we fynden with trauel tho thingis, that ben in biholdyng.

17 But who schal serche tho thingis, that ben in heuenes? But who schal knowe thi wit, 'no but thou yyue wisdom, and sende thin Hooli Spirit fro hiyeste thingis?

18 And if the pathis of hem, that ben in londis, ben amendid, and if men han lernyd tho thingis, that plesen thee.

19 For whi, Lord, whiche euer plesiden thee fro the bigynnyng, weren maad hool bi wisdom.

CAP 10

1 This wisdom 'of God kepte hym, that was formed first of God, the fadir of the world, whanne he aloone was maad of nouyt.

2 And 'this wisdom ledde hym out of his trespas, and ledde hym out of the sliym of erthe, and yaf to hym vertu to holde togider alle thingis.

3 As the vnjust man in his ire yede awei fro this wisdom, brotherhed perischide bi the ire of manquellyng.

4 For which thing whanne watir dide awei the erthe, wisdom heelide eft; gouernynge a iust man bi a dispisable tre.

5 This wisdom also in the consent of pride, whanne naciouns hadden reisid hem silf, knew a iust man, and kept with out playnt to God; and this wisdom kepte strong merci in sones.

6 'This wisdom deliuerede a iust man fleynge fro wickid men perischinge, whanne fier cam doun in to the place of fyue cytees.

7 For whiche wickid men the lond smokynge is maad deseert, in to witnessyng of weiwardnesse, and trees hauynge fruytis in vncerteyn tyme; and the mynde of an vnbileueful soule stondynge an ymage of salt.

8 For whi men passynge wisdom, not oneli fellen in this, that thei knewen not goodis, but also thei leften to men the mynde of her vnwisdom, that in these synnes, whiche thei diden, thei miyten not be hid.

9 Forsothe wisdom delyuerede hem fro sorewis, that kepen it.

10 Sotheli this wisdom ledde forth a iust man bi riytful weies, that fledde fro the ire of his brother; and it schewide to hym the rewme of God, and yaf to hym the kunnyng of seyntis; it made hym onest in trauels, and fillide hise trauelis.

11 It helpide hym in the fraude of disseyueris, and made hym onest.

12 It kepte hym fro enemyes and defendide hym fro disseyueris; and it yaf to him a strong batel, that he schulde ouercome, and wite, that wisdom is the myytieste of alle.

13 This wisdom forsook not a iust man seeld, but delyuerede hym fro synneris;

14 and it yede doun with hym in to a diche; and it forsook not hym in boondis, til it brouyte to hym the ceptre of the rewme, and power ayens hem that oppressiden hym; and it schewide hem lieris, that defouliden hym, and it yaf to hym euerlastynge clerenesse.

15 This wisdom delyuerede a iust puple, and hooli without pleynt, fro naciouns that oppressiden it.

16 Wisdom entride in to the soule of Goddis seruaunt, and he stood ayens hidouse kyngis, in grete wondris and myraclis.

17 And it yeldide to iust men the meede of her trauelis, and ledde hem forth in a wondurful weie; and it was to hem in hilyng of the dai, and in the liyt of sterris bi nyyt.

18 And it 'ledde ouer hem thorouy the reede see; and bar hem ouer thoruy ful myche watir.

19 But it drenchide doun the enemyes of hem in to the see; and ledde hem out fro the depthe of hellis. Therfor iust men taken awei the spuylis of wickid men;

20 and, Lord, thei magnefieden in song thin hooli name, and preyseden togidere thin hond ouercomer.

21 Forwhi wisdom openyde the mouth of doumbe men, and made the tungis of yonge children not spekynge to be wise.

1 He dresside the werkis of hem, in the hondis of an hooli profete.

CAP 11

2 Thei maden iourney bi desertis, that weren not enhabitid; and thei maden litle housis in desert places.

3 Thei stoden ayens kyngis, and vengiden hem of enemyes.

4 Thei thirstiden, and thei inwardli clepiden thee; and watir of a ful hiy stoon was youun to hem, and reste of thirst was youun to hem of an hard stoon.

5 For bi whiche thingis the enemyes of hem suffriden peynes, for defaute of her drink, and the sones of Israel weren glad, whanne thei hadden plentee;

6 bi these thingis, whanne these failiden to tho enemyes, it was don wel with hem.

7 For sotheli for the welle of euerlastynge flood, thou yauest mannus blood to vniust men.

8 And whanne thei weren maad lesse, in the leding awei of yonge children slayn, thou yauest sudeynli plenteuouse watir to hem; and schewidist bi the thirst,

9 that was thanne, hou thou woldist enhaunse thi seruauntis, and woldist sle the aduersaries of hem.

10 For whanne thei weren asaied, sotheli thei token chastisyng with merci; thei wisten, hou wickid men demed with ire, schulden suffre turmentis.

11 Sotheli thou amonestynge as a fadir, preuedist these men; but thou as an hard kyng axynge condempnedist hem.

12 For whi men absent and men present weren turmentid in lijk maner.

13 For whi double anoye hadde take hem, and weilyng with the mynde of thingis passid.

14 Sotheli whanne thei herden, that it was don wel with hem silf bi her turmentis, thei bithouyten on the Lord, and wondriden on the ende of the out goyng.

15 For at the ende of the bifallyng, thei worschipiden him, whom thei scorneden cast out in schrewid puttyng forth; and thou didist not in lijk maner to iust men.

16 Forsothe for vnwise thouytis the wickidnessis of hem weren punyschid; for summen errynge worschipiden doumbe serpentis, and superflu beestis, thou sentist in to hem a multitude of doumbe beestis, in to veniaunce; that thei schulden wite,

17 that bi what thingis a man synneth, he is turmentid also bi these thingis.

18 For whi thin hond almyyti, that made the world of mater vnseyn, was not vnmyyti to sende in to hem a multitude of beeris, ether hardi liouns,

19 ether beestis of newe kynde ful of ire, and vnknowun beestis, ether beestis frothinge heete of firis, ethir bryngynge forth the odour of smoke, ethir sendynge out fro the iyen hidouse sparclis;

20 of whiche beestis not oneli the hirtyng myyte distrie hem, but also the siyt myyte sle bi drede.

21 For whi and with oute these beestis thei myyten be slayn bi o spirit, and suffre persecucioun of tho her owne dedis, and be scaterid by the spirit of thi vertu. But and thou hast disposid alle thingis in mesure, and in noumbre, and in weiyte;

22 for it was left euere to thee aloone to mow do myche; and who schal ayenstonde the vertu of thin arm?

23 For as the tunge of a balaunce, so is the world bifore thee; and as a drope of dew rysynge bifore the liyt, that cometh doun in to erthe.

24 And thou hast merci of alle thingis, for thou maist alle thingis; and thou dissymelist the synnes of men, for penaunce.

25 For thou louest alle thingis that ben, and thou hatist no thing of tho, that thou madist; for thou not hatynge ony thing ordeynedist, ether madist.

26 But hou myyte ony thing dwelle, 'no but thou woldist? ether hou schulde a thing be kept, that were not clepid of thee?

27 But, Lord, that louest soulis, thou sparist alle thingis; for tho thingis ben thine.

CAP 12

1 Lord, hou good, and hou swete is thi Spirit in alle thingis;

2 and therfor thou chastisist bi partis these men that erren; and thou monestist; of whiche thingis thei synnen, and thou spekist to hem, that whanne thei han forsake malice, thei bileue in thee, Lord.

3 For thou woldist leese thilke elde dwelleris of thin hooli lond, whiche thou wlatidist;

4 for thei diden werkis hateful to thee, bi medicynes, and vniust sacrifices;

5 and the slears of her sones, with out merci, and eteris of entrailis of men,

6 and deuowreris of blood; and bi the hondis of oure fadris thou woldist leese fro thi myddil sacrament fadris and modris, autours of soulis vnhelpid;

7 that oure fadris schulden take the worthi pilgrymage of Goddis children, which is to thee the derewortheste lond of alle.

8 But also thou sparidist these as men, and thou sentist waspis, the bifore goeris of thin oost, that tho schulden destrie hem litil and litil.

9 Not for thou were vnmyyti to make wickid men suget to iust men in batel;

10 but thou demydist bi partis, and yauest place to penaunce, and wistist, that the nacioun of hem was weiward, and her malice was kyndli, and that her thouyt myyte not be chaungid with outen ende.

11 For it was a cursid seed at the bigynnyng. And thou not dredynge ony man, yauest foryyuenesse to the synnes of hem.

12 For whi who schal seie to thee, What hast thou do? ether who schal stonde ayens thi doom? ethir who schal come in thi siyt, to be auengere of wickid men? ether who schal arette to thee, if naciouns perischen, whiche thou madist?

13 For whi noon other than thou is God, to whom is charge of alle thingis, that thou schewe, that thou demest doom not vniustli.

14 Nether king nether tiraunt in thi siyt schulen enquere of these men, whiche thou hast lost.

15 Therfor sithen thou art iust, thou disposist iustli alle thingis; also, fadir, thou condempnest hym, that owith not to be punyschid, and thou gessist hym a straunger fro thi vertu.

16 For whi thi vertu is the bigynnyng of riytfulnesse; and for this, that thou art lord of alle men, thou makist thee to spare alle men.

17 For thou, that art not bileued to be perfit in vertu, schewist vertu; and thou ledist ouer these men, that knowen not thee, in hardynesse.

18 But thou, lord of vertu, demest with pesiblenesse, and disposist vs with greet reuerence; for it is suget to thee to mow, whanne thou wolt.

19 Forsothe thou hast tauyt thi puple bi siche werkis, that it bihoueth a iuge to be iust, and benygne; and thou madist thi sones of good hope, for thou demest, and yyuest place to penaunce in synnes.

20 For if thou turmentidist the enemyes of thi seruauntis, and men due to deth with so greet perseyuyng, and delyueridist, and yauest tyme and place, bi which thei myyten be chaungid fro malice;

21 with hou greet diligence demest thou thi sones, to whos fadris thou yauest othis and couenauntis of good biheestis?

22 Therfor whanne thou yyuest chastisyng to vs, thou betist many fold oure enemyes, that we demynge thenke thi goodnesse; and whanne it is demyd of vs, that we hope thi merci.
23 Wherfor and to hem, that lyueden vnwiseli, and vniustli in her lijf, thou yauest souereyn turmentis, bi these thingis whiche thei worschipiden.
24 For thei erriden ful longe in the weie of errour, and gessiden goddis these thingis that ben superflu in beestis, and lyueden bi custom of yonge children vnwitti.
25 For this thing thou yauest doom, in to scorn, as to children vnwitti;
26 but thei, that weren not amendid bi scornyngis and blamyngis, feeliden the worthi doom of God.
27 For thei baren heuyli in these thingis, whiche thei suffriden, in whiche thingis thei suffrynge hadden indignacioun; thei seynge hym, whom thei denyeden sum tyme hem to knowe, knewen hym veri God, bi these thingis whiche thei gessiden goddis among hem, whanne tho weren destried; for which thing and the ende of her condempnacioun schal come on hem.

CAP 13

1 Forsothe alle men ben veyn, in whiche the kunnyng of God is not; and of these thingis that ben seyn goode, thei myyten not vndurstonde him, that is, and thei perseyuynge the werkis knewen not, who was the worchere;
2 but thei gessiden goddis gouernours of the world, ethir the fier, ether the wynd, ethir the eir maad swift, ether the cumpas of sterris, ether ful myche watir, ethir the sunne and moone;
3 and if thei delitiden in the fairnesse of tho thingis, and gessiden tho goddis, wite thei, hou myche the lord of tho is fairere than tho; for whi the gendrere of fairnesse made alle these thingis.
4 Ethir if thei wondriden on the vertu and werkis of tho thingis, vndurstonde thei of tho, that he that made these thingis, is strongere than tho;
5 for bi the greetnesse of fairnesse and of creature the creatour of these thingis myyte be seyn knowyngli.
6 But netheles yit in these men is lesse playnt; for thei erren, in hap sekynge God, and willynge to fynde.
7 For whanne thei lyuen in hise werkis, thei seken, and holden for a soth, that tho thingis ben goode, that ben seyn.
8 Eft sotheli it owith not to be foryouun to these men.
9 For if thei miyten wite so myche, that thei miyten gesse the world, hou founden thei not liytliere the lord therof?
10 forsothe thei ben cursid, and the hope of hem is among deed men, that clepiden goddis the werkis of mennus hondis, gold, and siluer, the fyndyng of craft, and licnessis of beestis, ether a stoon vnprofitable, the werk of an eld hond.
11 Ethir if ony crafti man, a carpenter, hewith doun of the wode a streiyt tre, and rasith awei perfitli al the riynde therof, and vsith his craft diligentli, and makith a vessel ful profitable in to conuersacioun of lijf;
12 sotheli he vsith the relifs of this werk to the makyng redi of mete; and the residue of these thingis,
13 which he makith to no werk, a crokid tre, and ful of knottis, he graueth diligentli bi his voidnesse, and bi the kunnyng of his craft he figurith it, and licneth it to the ymage of a man,
14 ether makith it lijk to sum of beestis, and anoyntith with reed colour, and makith the colour therof rodi with peynture, and anoyntith eche spotte which is in it,
15 and makith to it a worthi dwellyng place, and settith it in the wal, and he fastneth it with irun,

16 lest perauenture it falle doun; and he purueyeth for it, and woot, that it may not helpe it silf; for it is an ymage, and help is nedeful therto.
17 And he makith auowe, and enquerith of his catel, and of hise sones, and of weddyngis; he is not aschamed to speke with hym, that is with out soule;
18 and sotheli for helthe he bisechith a thing vnmyyti, and for lijf he preieth a thing with out lijf, and he clepith an vnprofitable thing in to help.
19 And for iourney he axith of that thing, that mai not go; and of getyng, and of worchyng, and of bifallyng of alle thingis he axith of hym, which is vnprofitable in alle thingis.

CAP 14

1 Eft an other man thenkynge to seile in schip, and bigynnynge to make iournei thorouy ferse wawis, inwardli clepith a tre frelere than the tre that berith hym.
2 For whi couetise to gete money foond that idol; and a crafti man made it bi his wisdom.
3 But thou, fadir, gouernest bi puruyaunce, for thou yauest weie in the see, and a most stidfast path among wawis;
4 schewynge that thou art miyti to make hool of alle thingis, yhe, if a man goith to the see with out schip;
5 but that the werkis of thi wisdom schulden not be voide, for this thing men bitaken her lyues, yhe, to a litil tre, and thei passen the see, and ben delyuered bi a schip.
6 But at the bigynnyng, whanne proude giauntis perischiden, the hope of the world fledde to a schip, and sente efte seed of birthe to the world, which was gouerned bi thin hond.
7 For whi blessid is the tree, bi which riytfulnesse was maad.
8 But the idol which is maad bi hond is cursid, bothe it, and he that made it, for sotheli he wrouyte grete trespas; sotheli that idol, whanne it was freel, was nemyd God.
9 Forsothe in lijk maner the wickid man and his wickidnesse ben hateful to God.
10 For whi that that is maad schal suffre turmentis, with hym that made it.
11 For this thing and to the idols of naciouns schal not be biholdyng; for the creaturis of God ben maad in to hatrede, and in to temptacioun to the soule of men, and in to a trappe to the feet of vnwise men.
12 For the bigynnyng of fornycacioun is the sekyng out of idols, and the fynding of tho idols is the corrupcioun of lijf.
13 Forsothe tho weren not at the bigynnyng, nethir tho schulen be with out ende.
14 For whi the voidnesse of men foond these idols in to the world; and therfor the ende of tho is foundun schort.
15 For whi the fadir makinge sorewe with bittir morenyng, made soone to hym an ymage of the sone 'that was rauyschid; and bigan to worschipe hym now as a god, that was deed thanne as a man; and he ordeynede hooli thingis and sacrifices among hise seruauntis.
16 Aftirward in tyme comynge bitwixe, whanne the wickid custom was strong, this errour was kept as a lawe, and ymagis weren worschipid bi lordschip of tirauntis.
17 The figure of hem was brouyt fro fer, whiche the men miyten not onoure in opyn, for thei weren fer; and thei maden an opyn ymage of the kyng, whom thei wolden onoure; that bi her bisynesse thei schulden worschipe hym as present, that was absent.
18 Forsothe the noble diligence of a crafti man brouyte in also hem, that knewen not, to the worschipyng of thes kyngis.

19 For he willynge more to plese that kyng, that took hym, trauelide perfitli bi his craft, to make a licnesse in to betere.

20 Sotheli the multitude of men, disseyued bi the fairnesse of werk, gessiden hym now a god, that was onourid as a man bifore that tyme.

21 And this was the disseit of mannys lijf; for whi men seruynge greetli, ethir to affeccioun, ethir to kyngis, puttiden to stoonys and trees the name that mai not be comynyd.

22 And it suffiside not, that thei erriden aboute the kunnyng of God; but also thei lyuynge in greet batel of vnkunnyng, clepen so many and so grete yuels pees.

23 For ethir thei sleynge her sones in sacrifice, ethir makynge derk sacrifices, ethir hauynge wakyngis ful of woodnesse, 24 kepen now nether cleene lijf, nether cleene weddyngis; but also o man sleeth another man bi enuye, ethir doynge auowt-rie makith sory his neiybore.

25 And alle thingis ben medlid togidere, blood, mansleyng, thefte, and feynyng, corrupcioun, vnfeithfulnesse, distur-blyng, and forsweryng,

26 noise, foryetyng of goodis of the Lord, defoulyng of sou-lis, chaungyng of birthe, vnstidfastnesse of weddyngis, vnor-deynyng of letcherie and of vnchastite.

27 For whi the worschipyng of cursid idols is the cause, and the bigynnyng, and the ende of al yuel.

28 For whi ethir thei wexen woode, while thei ben glad; ether certis thei profecien false thingis, ethir thei lyuen vniustli, ethir thei forsweren soone.

29 For the while thei tristen in idols, that ben with out soule, thei sweren yuele, and hopen not, that thei schulen be anoyed.

30 Therfor euer eithir schulen come to hem worthili; for thei demeden yuele of God, and yauen tent to idols, and thei sworen vniustli in an idol, and thei dispisiden riytfulnesse.

31 For whi an ooth is not vertu, but the peyne of synneris goith forth euere, in to the breking of iust thingis.

CAP 15

1 Forsothe thou, oure God, art swete, and trewe, and pacient, and disposist alle thingis in merci.

2 For if we synnen, we ben thin, and knowen thi greetnesse; and if we synnen not, we witen, that we ben acountid at thee.

3 For whi to knowe thee, is parfit riytfulnesse; and to kunne thi riytfulnesse and vertu, is the root of vndedlynesse.

4 Forsothe the thenkyng out of yuel craft of men brouyte not vs in to errour, nether the schadewe of peynture trauel with-out fruyt, an ymage gravun bi dyuerse colours;

5 whos biholdyng yyueth coueytise to an vnwise man, and he loueth the licnesse of a deed ymage with out soule.

6 The louyers of yuels ben worthi the deeth, that han hope in siche; and thei that maken tho, and thei that louen, and thei that worschipen ben worthi the deth.

7 But also a pottere, thristynge neische erthe, bi greet trauel makith ech vessel to oure vsis; and of the same clei he makith vessels that ben clene to vss, and in lijk maner tho that ben contrarie to these; forsothe what vss is of these vessels, the pottere is iuge.

8 And he that was maad of erthe a litil bifore, makith a god of the same clei with veyn trauel; and the pottere, axid to yelde the dette of soule which he hadde, ledith hym silf aftir a litil tyme to the erthe, fro whennus he was takun.

9 But he hath care, not for he schal trauele, nether for his lijf is schort, but he stryueth with gold smythis and siluer smythis; but also he sueth worcheris of bras, and settith bifore glorie; for he makith superflu thingis.

10 For the herte of hym is aische, and superflu erthe is his hope, and his lijf is vilere than clei.

11 For he knew not God, that made him, and that enspiride a soule to hym; and he loueth tho thingis whiche he hath wrouyt; and he knew not God, that blowide in hym a spirit of lijf.

12 But thei gessiden fleischli delityng to be oure lijf, and the conuersacioun of lijf to be maad to wynnyng, and that it bihoueth to gete on ech side, yhe, of yuel.

13 Forsothe this man that makith freele vessels, and grauun ymagis of the mater of erthe, woot that he trespassith aboue alle men.

14 Forsothe, Lord, alle vnwise men and cursid ben proude ouer the mesure of her soule, and ben enemyes of thi puple, and vpbreyden it;

15 for thei gessiden alle the idols of naciouns to be goddis, that han nethir siyt of iyen to se, nethir nose thirlis to per-seyue a spirit, ethir wynd, nether eeris to here, nethir fyngris of hondis to touche, but also her feet ben slowe to go.

16 For whi a man made tho, and he that borewide a spirit, made tho; forwhi no man mai make a god lijk hym silf.

17 For sithen he is deedli, bi wickid hondis he makith a deed idol; for he is betere than these goddis, whiche he worschip-ith; for sotheli he liuyde, whanne he was deedli, but thei lyueden neuere.

18 But also moost wretchid men worschipen beestis; for whi vnresonable beestis, comparisound to these men, ben worse than thei.

19 But nether bi siyt ony man mai of these beestis biholde goodis; forsothe thei han dryue awei the heriyng of God, and his blessyng.

CAP 16

1 For these thingis, and thingis lijk these, thei suffriden tur-mentis worthili, and thei weren destried bi multitude of bees-tis.

2 For whiche turmentis thou disposidist wel thi puple, to whiche thou yauest coueitise of her delityng a new sauour, makynge redi mete to hem a curlew.

3 That sotheli thei coueitynge mete, weren turned awei, yhe, fro nedeful coueityng, for tho thingis that weren schewid, and sent to hem; but these men maad pore in schort tyme, tastiden newe mete.

4 For sotheli it bihofte perischyng to come on hem with outen excusyng, vsynge tirauntri; but to schewe oneli to these Ebries, hou her enemyes weren destried.

5 Forsothe whanne the feers ire of beestis cam on hem, thei weren destried bi the bityngis of weiward serpentis.

6 But, Lord, thin ire dwellide not with outen ende; but thei weren troblid in schort time to amendyng, and hadden a signe of helthe, to remembryng of the comaundement of thi lawe.

7 For he that was conuertid, was heelid not bi that he siy, but bi thee, sauyour of alle men.

8 Forsothe in this thou schewidist to oure enemyes, that thou it art, that delyuerist fro al yuel.

9 Forsothe the bityngis of locustis and of flies killiden hem, and heelthe of her lijf was not foundun; for thei weren worthi to be destried of siche thingis.

10 But nether the teeth of dragouns, nethir of venemouse beestis ouercamen thi children; for whi thi merci cam, and heelide hem.

11 For thei weren turmentid in mynde of thi wordis, and thei weren heelid swiftli; lest thei fallynge in to deep foryetyng of God, miyten not vse thin help.

12 For nethir eerbe, nethir plastere heelide hem; but, Lord, thi word, that heelith alle thingis.

13 Lord, thou art, that hast power of lijf and of deth; and ledist forth to the yatis of deth, and ledist ayen.

14 But sotheli a man sleeth his soule bi malice; and whanne the spirit is goen out, it schal not turne ayen, nether the bodi schal ayen clepe the soule, which is resseyued;

15 but it is vnpossible to ascape thin hond.

16 Forwhi wickid men, denying to knowe thee, weren turmentid bi strengthe of thin arm; thei suffriden persecusioun bi newe watris, and hailis, and reines, and weren wastid bi fier.

17 For whi that was wondurful, the fier hadde more miyt in the watir, that quenchith alle thingis; for whi the world was veniere of iust men.

18 For whi sum tyme the fier was mylde, lest the beestis schulden be brent, that weren sent to wickid men; but that thei seynge schulden wite, that thei suffren persecucioun bi the doom of God.

19 And sum tyme the fier brente an hiy on ech side in the water, aboue the vertu of fier, to destrie the wickid nacioun of the lond.

20 For whiche thingis thou nurischidist thi puple with mete of aungels, and thou yauest fro heuene breed maad redi to hem, with out trauel; hauynge al delityng in it silf, and the swetnesse of al sauour.

21 For thou schewidist thi catel, and thi swetnesse, which thou hast, to sones; and the breed seruynge to the wille of eche man, was turned to that, that ech man wolde.

22 Forsothe snow and iys suffriden the miyt of fier, and meltiden not; that thei schulden wite, that fier brennynge, in hail and reyn leytynge, destryede the fruytis of enemyes.

23 Sotheli eft this was wondirful, also fier foryat his vertu, that iust men schulden be nurschid.

24 For whi the creature seruynge to thee the makere, wexith whijt in to turment ayens vniust men, and is maad liytere to do wel, for hem that tristen in thee.

25 For this thing and alle thingis transfigurid thanne seruyden to thi grace, nurischere of alle thingis, to the wille of hem, that ben desirid of thee;

26 that, Lord, thi sones schulden wite, whiche thou louedist, that not the fruytis of birthe feeden men, but thi word kepeth hem, that bileuen in thee.

27 For whi that that miyte not be distried of fier, meltide anoon as it was maad hoot of a litil beem of the sunne;

28 that it were knowun to alle men, that it bihoueth to come bifore the sunne to thi blessing, and to worschipe thee at the risyng of the liyt.

29 Forsothe the hope of an vnkynde man schal melte awei as iys of wyntir, and schal perische as superflu watir.

CAP 17

1 Forsothe, Lord, thi domes ben greet, and thi wordis moun not be fulli teld out; vnlerned soulis erriden for these.

2 For the while wickid men holden for stidfast, that thei moun be lordis of hooli nacioun, thei weren feterid with boondis of derknessis, and of long niyt, and weren closid vndur rooues; and thei fugityues weren suget to euerlastinge puruyaunce.

3 And the while thei gessen hem to be hid in derk synnes, thei weren scaterid bi derk hidyng of foryetyng, dredynge hidousli, and disturblid with ful greet wondryng.

4 For the denne that withhelde hem, kepte not with out drede; for whi sown comynge doun disturblide hem, and soreuful persoones apperynge to hem, yauen drede to hem.

5 And sotheli no myyt of fier myyte yyue liyt to hem, and the cleer flawmes of sterris myyten not liytne that hidouse nyyt.

6 Sotheli sodeyn fier ful of drede apperide to hem; and thei weren smytun with the drede of that face, that was not seyn, and gessiden tho thingis to be worse, that weren seyn.

7 And scornes of whitche craft weren leid to, and the glorie of wisdom was chastisyng with dispisyng.

8 For thei, that bihiyten hem silf to putte awei dredis and disturblyngis fro a sijk soule, weren ful with scorn, and weren sijk for drede.

9 For whi thouy no thing of the wondris ayens kynde disturblide hem, thei weren mouyd bi the passyng of beestis, and bi the hissyng of eddris, and trembliden, and perischiden; and denyeden, that thei sien the eyr, which a man myyte not ascape bi ony resoun; for whi worste thingis bifore ocupien ofte, while the conscience repreueth.

10 For sithen wickidnesse is dreedful, it is youun in to condempnacioun of alle men; for whi a conscience disturblid presumeth euere wickid thingis.

11 For whi drede is no thing, no but help of presumpcioun, and schewyng of thouyt of helpis.

12 And the while lesse abydyng is fro with ynne, it gessith gretter power of that cause, of which it yyueth turment.

13 Forsothe thei, that camen in to a myyti niyt, and comynge aboue fro loweste thingis, and fro hiyeste thingis, thei slepynge the same sleep,

14 weren hurlid sum tyme bi drede of wondris ayens kynde, sum tyme the soulis failiden bi ledyng ouer; for why sudeyn drede and vnhopid, cam on hem.

15 Afterward if ony of hem hadde fel doun, he was kept closid in prisoun, with out yrun;

16 for if ony cheerl was, ethir scheepherd, ethir a werk man of feeldis, and was bifore ocupied, he suffride nede that miyte not be ascapid.

17 For whi alle men weren boundun togidere bi o chayne of derknessis; ether a wynd hissynge, ether swete sown of briddis bitwixe the thicke bowis of trees, ethir the feersnesse of watir rennynge doun greetli,

18 ethir a strong soun of stoonys cast doun, ethir the rennyng vnseyn of beestis pleiynge, ethir the strong vois of beestis lowynge, ethir ecco sownynge ayen fro hiyeste hillis, maden hem failynge for drede.

19 Forsothe al the world was liytned with cleer liyt, and was not withholdun in werkis lettid.

20 But a greuouse niyt, the ymage of derknessis, that was to comyng on hem, was set on hem aloone; therfor thei weren greuousere to hem silf than the derknessis.

CAP 18

1 But ful greet liyt was to thin hooli seruauntis, and sotheli enemyes herden the vois of hem, but thei sien not the figure, ethir schap; and for also thei suffriden not bi the same thingis, thei magnefieden thee.

2 And for thei weren hirt bifore, thei diden thankyngis to thee, for thei weren not hirt; and that difference schulde be bitwixe hem and Egipcians, thei axiden thee, God.

3 For which thing thei hadden a brennynge piler of fier, the ledere of vnknowun weie; and thou yauest the sunne, with out hirtyng of good herbore.

4 Forsothe thei weren worthi to wante liyt, and to suffre the prisoun of derknessis, whiche helden thi sones enclosid; bi whiche sones the vncorrupt lijt of lawe bigan to be youun to the world.

5 Whanne thei thouyten to sle the yonge children of iust men; and whanne o sone was put forth, and delyuered, thou tokist awei the multitude of sones, for the ledyng ouer of hem, and thou lostist hem togidere in strong watir.

6 Forsothe thilke nyyt was knowun bifore of oure fadris, that thei witynge verili to whiche othis thei bileuyden, schulden be more paciente.

7 Forsothe helthe of iust men was resseyued verili of thi puple, 'and also distriyng of vniust men.

8 For as thou hirtidist oure aduersaries, so thou excitidist also vs, and magnefiedist vs.

9 For whi iust children of goode men maden sacrifice priueli, and disposiden the lawe of riytfulnesse in to acordyng; thei disposiden iust men to resseyue goodis and yuels in lijk maner, and sungen heriyngis to the fadir of alle men.

10 But vnsemeli vois of enemyes sownede, and wepeful weilyng of biweperis of yonge children was herd.

11 Forsothe the seruaunt was turmentid bi lijk peyne with the lord; and a man of the puple suffride thingis lijk the kyng.

12 Therfor in lijk maner alle men bi o name of deth hadden deed men vnnoumbrable, for nether quyke men suffiseden to birie; for whi the nacioun of hem, that was clerere than othere, was destried in o moment.

13 Forsothe of alle Egipcians men not bileuynge for benefices, bihiyten hem thanne to be Goddis puple, whanne the distriyng of the firste gendryd thingis was first.

14 Forsothe whanne alle thingis helden restful silence, and the nyyt hadde the myddil weie in his cours,

15 Lord, thi word almyyti comynge swiftli fro heuene, cam fro the kyngis seetis;

16 a scharp swerd berynge thi comaundement not feyned, cam forth, ouercomere in to the myddil of the lond of destriyng; and it stood, and fillide alle thingis with deeth, and it stood in erthe, and stretchide forth til to heuene.

17 Thanne anoon the siytis of yuel dremes disturbliden hem, and dredis not hopid camen aboue.

18 And another man cast forth half quyk in an other place, schewide for what cause of deth he diede.

19 For whi siytis that disturbliden hem, bifore warneden these thingis, that thei schulden perische not vnwityngli, why thei suffriden yuels.

20 Forsothe temptacioun of deth touchide thanne also iust men, and mouyng togidere of multitude was maad in desert; but thin ire dwellide not longe.

21 For a man without pleynt hastide to biseche for puplis, and he brouyte forth preier the scheld of his seruyce, and he aleggide preier bi encence, and ayen stood ire; and he settide an ende to the nede, and schewide that he was thi seruaunt.

22 Forsothe he ouercam cumpenyes, not bi vertu of bodi, nether bi armure of power; but he remembride the othis, and the testament of fadris, and bi word he made hym suget, that trauelide hym silf.

23 For whanne deed men fellen doun bi heepis, ech on other, he stood bitwixe 'deed men and lyuynge, and kittide awei the feersnesse of brennyng, and departide that weie, that ledde to quyke men.

24 For whi al the world was in the cloth lastynge to the heelis, which he hadde; and the grete thingis of fadris weren grauun

in foure ordris of stoonys; and, Lord, thi magnyficence was writun in the diademe of his heed.

25 Forsothe he that distriede, yaf stide to these thingis, and dredde these thingis; for whi the temptacioun aloone was sufficient to ire.

CAP 19

1 Forsothe ire with out merci cam on wickid men til in to the laste; forwhi God bifore knew also the thingis to comynge of hem.

2 For whanne thei weren turned, and hadden suffrid, that thei schulden lede out hem, and hadden bifor sent hem with greet bysynesse, the dedis of repentyng sueden hem.

3 For thei hauynge yit morenyng bitwixe the hondis, and thei biwepynge at the sepulcris of deed men, token to hem anothir thouyt of vnkunnyng; and thei pursueden tho Ebreis, as fleeris awei, whiche thei preiynge hadden sent forth.

4 For whi worthi nede ledde hem to this ende, and thei losten remembryng of these thingis, that hadden bifeld, that punyschyng schulde fille tho thingis, that failiden of turmentis,

5 and that sotheli thi puple schulde passe wondurfuli; forsothe that thei schulden fynde a newe deth.

6 For whi ech creature seruynge to thin heestis, was refourmed to his kynde at the bigynnyng, that thi children schulden be kept vnhirt.

7 For whi a cloude bischadewide the castels of hem, and drie erthe apperide in watir that was bifore; and a weie with out letting apperide in the reed see, and a feeld buriownynge fro ful greet depthe; bi which feeld al the nacioun passide,

8 that was hilid with thin hond; forsothe thei sien thi merueilis and wondris.

9 For thei as horsis deuouriden mete, and as lambren thei maden ful out ioye, magnefiynge thee, Lord, that delyueredist hem.

10 For thei weren myndeful yit of tho thingis, that weren don in the dwellyng of hem among Egipcians; hou the lond brouyte forth flies, for the nacioun of beestis, and the flood brouyte forth multitude of paddokis, for fischis.

11 Forsothe at the last thei sien a newe creature of briddis, whanne thei weren led bi coueitise, and axiden metis of feeste.

12 For in the spekynge to of her desir, a curlew stiede to hem fro the see; and diseesis camen on synneris, and not with out preuyngis of tho thingis, that weren don bifor bi the feersnesse of floodis. For thei suffriden iustli, bi her wickidnessis;

13 for thei ordeyneden more abhomynable vnospitalite. Sotheli summe resseyueden not vnknowun comelyngis; sotheli othere token good men herborid in to thraldom.

14 And not oneli thei diden these thingis, but sotheli also another biholding of hem was, that thei ayens her wille resseyueden straungeris.

15 Forsothe thei that vsiden the same ordynaunces, turmentiden with cruelest sorewis hem, that resseyueden with gladnesse.

16 Forsothe thei weren smytun with blyndnesse, as thei in the yatis of the iust man, whanne thei weren hilid with sudeyne derknessis; ech man souyte the passyng of his dore.

17 Forsothe while elementis ben turned in to hem silf, as the sown of maner is chaungid in orgun, and alle thingis kepen her sown; wherfor it mai be gessid of that certeyn siyt.

18 Beestis of the feeld weren turned in to beestis of watir; what euer weren swymmynge thingis, yeden in the lond.

19 Fier in watir hadde power aboue his vertu; and water foryat the kynde quenchynge.

20 Ayenward flawmes of corruptible beestis disesiden not the fleischis of Ebreis goynge togidere; nethir departiden that good mete, that was departid liytly as iys. Forsothe, Lord, thou magnefiedist thi puple in alle thingis, and onouridist; and dispisidist not, and helpidist hem in ech tyme and in ech place.

SYRACH

CAP 1

1 Al wisdom is of the Lord God, and was euere with hym, and is bifore the world.

2 Who noumbride the grauel of the see, and the dropis of reyn, and the daies of the world? Who mesuride the hiynesse of heuene, and the breed of erthe, and the depthe of the see?

3 Who enserchide the wisdom of God, that goith bifore alle thingis?

4 Wisdom was formed firste of alle thingis, and the vndurstonding of prudence, fro the world.

5 The welle of wisdom is the sone of God in hiy thingis; and the entryng of that wisdom is euerlastynge comaundementis.

6 To whom was the roote of wisdom schewid? and who knewe the sutilites therof?

7 To whom was the lore of wisdom shewid, and maad opyn? and who vndurstood the multipliyng of the entryng therof?

8 Oon is the hiyeste creatour of alle thingis, almyyti, and a myyti kyng, and worthi to be dred ful miche, sittynge on the trone of that wisdom, and God hauynge lordschipe.

9 He fourmyde 'that wisdom in the Hooli Ghost, and he siy, and noumbride, and he mesuride.

10 And he schedde out it on alle hise werkis, and on ech fleisch bi his yifte; he yyueth it to hem that louen hym.

11 The drede of the Lord is glorie, and gloriyng, and gladnesse, and a coroun of ful out ioiyng.

12 The drede of the Lord schal delite the herte; and schal yyue gladnesse and ioie in to lengthe of daies.

13 To hym that dredith God, it schal be wel in the laste thingis; and he schal be blessid in the dai of his deth.

14 Forsothe thei to whiche wisdom apperith in siyt, louen it in siyt, and in knowyng of hise grete thingis.

15 The loue of God is onourable wisdom.

16 The bigynnyng of wisdom is the drede of the Lord; and it is formyd togidere in the wombe with feithful men, and it goith with chosun wymmen, and is knowun with iust men and feithful.

17 The drede of the Lord is religiouste of kunnyng.

18 Religiouste schal kepe, and schal iustifie the herte; and schal yyue myrthe and ioie.

19 It schal be wel to hym that dredith God; and he schal be blessid in the daies of his coumfort.

20 The fulnesse of wisdom is for to drede God; and fulnesse is of the fruytis therof.

21 It schal fille ech yifte of hym of generaciouns, and reseitis of the tresouris therof.

22 The coroun of wisdom is the drede of the Lord, and fillith pees, and the fruyt of heelthe.

23 And he siy, and noumbride it; forsothe euer eithir ben the yiftis of God.

24 Wisdom schal departe the kunnyng and vndurstondyng of prudence; and it enhaunsith the glorie of hem, that holden it.

25 The roote of wisdom is for to drede God; forsothe the braunchis therof ben longe durynge.

26 Vndurstonding, and religiouste of kunnyng ben in the tresouris of wisdom; but wisdom is abhomynacioun to synners.

27 The drede of the Lord puttith awei synne,

28 for he that is with out drede, mai not be iustified; for whi the wrathfulnesse of his pride is the destriyng of hym.

29 A pacient man schal suffre til in to tyme; and aftirward schal be yelding of mirthe.

30 Good wit schal hide the wordis of hym til in to a tyme; and the lippis of many men schulen telle out the wit of hym.

31 In the tresouris of wisdom is signefiyng of kunnyng;

32 but the worschipyng of God is abhomynacioun to a synnere.

33 A! sone, coueitynge wisdom, kepe thou riytfulnesse, and God schal yyue it to thee.

34 For whi the drede of the Lord is wisdom, and kunnyng, and that

35 that is wel plesaunt to hym is feith and myldenesse; and God schal fille the tressours of hym.

36 Be thou not rebel, and vnbileueful to the drede of the Lord; and neiye thou not to hym in double herte.

37 Be thou not an ypocrite in the siyt of men; and be thou not sclaundrid in thi lippis.

38 Take thou kepe to tho, lest thou falle, and brynge disonour to thi soule; and lest God schewe thi priuytees,

39 and hurtle thee doun in the myddis of the synagoge;

40 for thou neiyidist wickidli to the Lord, and thin herte was ful of gile and of falsnesse.

CAP 2

1 Sone, neiyynge to the seruyce of God, stonde thou in riytfulnesse, and drede; and make redi thi soule to temptacioun.

2 Bere doun thin herte, and suffre, and bowe doun thin eere, and take the wordis of vndirstonding, and haaste thou not in to the tyme of deeth.

3 Suffre thou the susteynyngis of God; be thou ioyned to God, and abide thou, that thi lijf wexe in the last tyme.

4 Take thou alle thing that is set to thee, and suffre thou in sorewe, and haue thou pacience in thi lownesse.

5 For whi gold and siluer is preued in fier; forsothe men worthi to be resseyued ben preued in the chymeney of lownesse.

6 Bileue thou to God, and he schal rekeuere thee; and dresse thou thi weie, and hope thou in to hym. Kepe thou his drede, and wexe thou eld ther ynne.

7 Ye that dreden the Lord, abide his merci, and boowe ye not awei fro hym, lest ye falle doun.

8 Ye that dreden the Lord, bileue to hym, and youre mede schal not be auoidid.

9 Ye that dreden the Lord, hope into hym, and merci schal come to you into delityng.

10 Ye that dreden the Lord, loue hym, and youre hertis schulen be liytned.

11 Sones, biholde ye the naciouns of men, and wite ye, that no man hopide in the Lord, and was schent;

12 noon dwellide in hise heestis, and was forsakun; ether who inwardli clepide hym, and he despiside hym 'that clepide?

13 For whi God is pitouse, and merciful, and he schal foryyue synnes in the dai of tribulacioun; and he is defendere to alle men, that seken hym in treuthe.

14 Woo to the 'man with double herte, and with cursid lippis, and misdoynge hondys; and to a synnere entrynge in to the lond bi twei weies.

15 Wo to hem that ben dissolute of herte, that bileuen not to God; and therfor thei schulen not be defendid of him.

16 Wo to hem that han lost pacience, and that han forsake riytful weies, and han turned awei in to schrewid weies.

17 And what schulen thei do, whanne the Lord schal bigynne to biholde?

18 Thei that dreden the Lord, schulen not be vnbileueful to his word; and thei that louen hym, schulen kepe his weie.

19 Thei that dreden the Lord, schulen enquere tho thingis, that ben wel plesaunt to hym; and thei that louen him, schulen be fillid with his lawe.

20 Thei that dreden the Lord, schulen make redi her hertis, and schulen halewe her soulis in his siyt.

21 Thei that dreden the Lord, schulen kepe hise comaunde-mentis, and schulen haue pacience til to the biholdyng of hym;

22 and schulen seie, If we doon not penaunce, we schulen falle in to the hondis of the Lord, and not in to the hondis of men.

23 For bi the greetnesse of hym, so and his merci is with hym.

CAP 3

1 The sones of wisdom ben the chirche of iust men, and the nacioun of hem is obedience and loue.

2 Dereworthe sones, here ye the doom of the fadir; and do ye so, that ye be saaf.

3 For whi God onouride the fadir in sones, and he sekith, and hath maad stidfast the doom of the modir in to sones.

4 He that loueth God, schal preie for synnes, and he schal absteyne hym silf fro tho, and he schal be herd in the preier of daies.

5 And as he that tresourith, so and he that onourith his modir.

6 He that onourith his fadir, schal be maad myrie in sones, and he schal be herd in the dai of his preier.

7 He that onourith his fadir, schal lyue bi lengere lijf; and he that obeieth to the fader, schal refreische the modir.

8 He that dredith the Lord, onourith fadir and modir; and he schal serue in werk, and word,

9 and al pacience to hem that gendriden hym as to lordis.

10 Onoure thi fadir, that the blessyng of God come to thee; and his blessing dwellith in the laste.

11 The blessyng of the fadir makith stidfast the housis of sones; but the cursyng of the modir drawith out the founde-mentis.

12 Haue thou not glorie in the dispisyng of thi fadir; for it is not glorie to thee, but confusioun.

13 For whi the glorie of a man is of the onour of his fadir; and the schenschip of the sone is a fadir with out onour.

14 Sone, resseyue the elde of thi fadir, and make thou not hym sori in his lijf;

15 and if he failith in wit, yyue thou foryyuenesse, and dispise thou not hym in thi vertu; for whi the almes of the fadir schal not be foryetyng.

16 For whi good schal be restorid to thee for the synne of the modir,

17 and bildyng schal be maad to thee in riytfulnesse; and it schal remembre of thee in dai of tribulacioun, and thi synnes schulen be releessid, as iys in clerenesse of the sunne.

18 He is of ful yuel fame, that forsakith the fadir; and he that wraththith the modir, is cursid of God.

19 Sone, performe thi werkis in myldenesse, and thou schalt be loued ouer the glorie of men.

20 In as myche as thou art greet, make thee meke in alle thingis, and thou schalt fynde grace bifore God; for whi the power of God aloon is greet,

21 and he is onourid of meke men.

22 Seke thou not hiyere thingis than thou, and enquere thou not strongere thingis than thou; but euere thenke thou tho thingis, whiche God comaundide to thee; and be thou not curiouse in ful many werkis of hym.

23 For it is not nedeful to thee to se with thin iyen tho thingis, that ben hid.

24 In superflu thingis nyle thou seke manyfold; and be thou not curiouse in many werkis of hym;

25 for whi ful many thingis aboue the wit of men ben schewid to thee.

26 For the suspecioun of many men hath disseyued hem, and withhelde her wittis in vanytee.

27 And hard herte schal haue yuel in the laste tyme; and he that loueth perel, schal perische ther ynne.

28 An herte that entrith bi tweie weies, schal not haue pros-peritees, ether reste; and a man of schrewid herte schal be sclaundrid in tho.

29 A wickid herte schal be greuyd in sorewis; and a synnere schal 'hepe to do synne.

30 Helthe schal not be to the synagoge of proude men; for whi the thicke wode of synne schal be drawun out bi the roote in hem, and it schal not be vndurstondun.

31 The herte of a wise man is vndurstondun in wisdom, and a good eere schal here wisdom with al coueitise.

32 A wijs herte and able to vndurstonde schal absteyne it silf fro synnes, and schal haue prosperitees in the werkis of riyt-fulnesse.

33 Watir quenchith fier brennynge, and almes ayenstondith synnes.

34 And God, the biholdere of hym that yeldith grace, hath mynde aftirward; and he schal fynde stidefastnesse in the tyme of his fal.

CAP 4

1 Sone, defraude thou not the almes of a pore man, and turne not ouere thin iyen fro a pore man.

2 Dispise thou not an hungri man, and wraththe thou not a pore man in his nedynesse.

3 Turmente thou not the herte of a nedi man, and tarie thou not the yifte to a man that is set in angwisch.

4 Caste thou not awei the preiyng of a man set in tribulacioun, and turne not awei thi face fro a nedi man.

5 Turne not awei thi iyen fro a pore man for ire, and yyue not occasioun to men axynge to curse thee byhynde.

6 For the preyer of hym that cursith thee in the bitternesse of soule, schal be herd; forsothe he that made hym, schal here hym.

7 Make thee eesi to speke to the congregacioun of pore men, and make meke thi soule to a preest, and make meke thin heed to a greet man.

8 Boowe doun with out sorewe thin eere to a pore man, and yelde thi debt, and answere thou pesibli in myldenesse.

9 Delyuere thou hym that suffrith wrong fro the hond of a proude man, and bere thou not heuyli in thi soule.

10 In demynge be thou merciful as a fadir to fadirles children, and be thou for an hosebonde to the modir of hem;

11 and thou schalt be as an obedient sone of the hiyeste, and he schal haue merci on thee more than a modir 'hath merci on hir child.

12 Wisdom enspirith lijf to hise sones, and resseyueth men sekinge hym, and schal go bifore in the wei of riytfulnesse; and he that loueth that wisdom,

13 loueth lijf, and thei that waken to it, schulen biclipe the pesiblenesse, ether swetnesse, therof.

14 Thei that holden it, schulen enherite lijf; and whidir it schal entre, God schal blesse.

15 Thei that seruen it, schulen be obeiynge to the hooli; and God loueth hem, that louen it.

16 He that herith it, demeth folkis; and he that biholdith it, schal dwelle tristili.

17 If a man bileueth to it, he schal dwelle, and enherite it; and the creaturis of hem schulen be in confermyng.

18 For in temptacioun it goith with hym, and among the firste it chesith hym.

19 It schal brynge in on hym drede, and feer, and preuyng, and it schal turmente hym in the tribulacioun of his doctryn, til it tempte hym in hise thouytis, and bileue to his soule.

20 And it schal make hym stidefast, and schal brynge riyt weie to hym, and it schal make hym glad;

21 and schal make nakid hise priuytees to hym, and schal tresore on hym kunnyng, and vndurstondyng of riytfulnesse.

22 Forsothe if he errith, God schal forsake hym, and schal bitake hym in to the hondis of his enemy.

23 Sone, kepe thou tyme, and eschewe thou fro yuel.

24 Be thou not aschamed for thi lijf to seie treuthe; for whi ther is schame that bryngith synne,

25 and ther is schame that bryngith glorie and grace.

26 Take thou not a face ayens thi face, nethir a leesyng ayens thi soule.

27 Schame thou not thi neiybore in his fal,

28 nether withholde thou a word in the tyme of helthe. Hide not thi wisdom in the fairnesse therof;

29 for whi wisdom is knowun in tunge, and wit, and kunnyng, and techyng in the word of a wijs man; and stidfastnesse is in the werkis of riytfulnesse.

30 Ayenseie thou not the word of treuthe in ony maner; and be thou aschamed of the leesyng of thi mislernyng.

31 Be thou not aschamed to knouleche thi synnes; and make thee not suget to ech man for synne.

32 Nyle thou stonde ayens the face of the myyti, nethir enforse thou ayens the strok of the flood.

33 For riytfulnesse fiyte thou for thi soule, and til to the deth stryue thou for riytfulnesse; and God schal ouercome thin enemyes for thee.

34 Nyle thou be swift in thi tunge, and vnprofitable and slak in thi werkis.

35 Nyle thou be as a lioun in thin hous, turnynge vpsedoun thi meneals, and oppressynge hem that ben sugetis to thee.

36 Thin hond be not redi to take, and closid togidere to yyue.

CAP 5

1 Nile thou take heed to wickid possessiouns, and seie thou not, Sufficient lijf is to me; for it schal no thing profite in the tyme of veniaunce, and of failynge, ether deth.

2 Sue thou not the coueitise of thin herte in thi strengthe,

3 and seie thou not, As Y myyte, ether who schal make me suget for my dedis? For whi God vengynge schal venge.

4 Seie thou not, Y haue synned, and what sorewful thing bifelle to me? For the hiyeste is a pacient yeldere.

5 Of the foryyuenesse of synnes, nyle thou be without drede, nether heepe thou synne on synne.

6 And seie thou not, The merciful doyng of God is greet; he schal haue merci on the multitude of my synnes.

7 For whi merci and ire neiyeth soone fro hym, and his ire biholdith on synneris.

8 Tarie thou not to be conuertid to the Lord, and dilaie thou not fro dai in to dai.

9 For whi his ire schal come sodeynli, and he schal leese thee in the time of veniaunce.

10 Nyle thou be angwischid in vniust richessis; for tho schulen not profite in the dai of failing, ether of deth, and of veniaunce.

11 Wyndewe thee not in to ech wynd, and go thou not in to ech weie; for so a synnere is preued in double tunge.

12 Be thou stidfast in the weie of the Lord, and in treuthe and kunnyng of thi wit; and the word of pees and riytfulnesse sue thee perfitli.

13 Be thou mylde to here the word of God, that thou vndurstonde, and with wisdom brynge thou forth a trewe answere.

14 If thou hast vndirstondyng, answere thi neiybore; ellis thin hond be on thi mouth, lest thou be takun in a word vnwiseli tauyt, and be aschamed.

15 Onour and glorie is in the word of a wijs man; but the tunge of an vnprudent man is his distriyng.

16 Be thou not clepid a preuy yuel spekere in thi lijf, and be thou not takun in thi tunge, and be aschamed.

17 Schame and penaunce is on a theef, and worst schenschip is on a man of double tunge. Forsothe hatrede and enemytee and dispisyng is to a preuy bacbitere.

18 Iustifie thou a litil man and a greet man in lijk maner.

CAP 6

1 Nile thou for a freend be maad enemye to the neiybore; for whi an yuele man schal enherite vpbreidyng and dispisyng, and ech synnere enuyouse and double tungid.

2 Enhaunse thee not in the thouyt of thi soule, as a bole doith; lest thi vertu be hurtlid doun bi foli,

3 and it ete thi leeues, and leese thi fruytis, and thou be left as a drye tree in deseert.

4 Forsothe a wickid soule schal leese hym that hath it, and it yyueth hym in to the ioie of the enemye, and it schal leede forth in to the part of wickid men.

5 A swete word multiplieth frendis, and swagith enemyes; and a tunge wel graciouse schal be plenteuouse in a good man.

6 Many pesible men be to thee, and oon of a thousynde be a counselour to thee.

7 If thou hast a frend, haue hym in temptacioun, and bitake not liytli thi silf to hym.

8 For ther is a frend bi his time, and he schal not dwelle in the dai of tribulacioun.

9 And ther is a frend which is turned to enemytee; and ther is a freend, that schal schewe opynli hatrede, and chiding, and dispisyngis.

10 Forsothe ther is a frend, felowe of table, and dwellith not in the dai of nede.

11 If a frend dwellith stidfast, he schal be as a man euene with thee, and he schal do tristili in thi meyneal thingis.

12 If he mekith hym silf bifore thee, and hidith hym fro thi face, thou schalt haue good frendschip of oon acord.

13 Be thou departid fro thin enemyes, and take heede of thi frendis.

14 A feithful frend is a strong defendyng; forsothe he that fyndith him, fyndith tresour.

15 No comparisoun is to a feithful frend; weiyng of gold and of siluer is not worthi ayens the goodnesse of his feithful-nesse.

16 A feithful frend is medicyn of lijf, and of vndeedlynesse; and thei that dreden the Lord, schulen fynde hym.

17 He that dredith the Lord, schal haue euenli good frends-chip; for whi his frend schal be at the licnesse of hym.

18 Sone, fro thi yongthe take thou doctryn, and til to hoor heeris thou schalt fynde wisdom.

19 As he that erith, and that sowith, neiye thou to it, and abide thou the goode fruytis therof.

20 For thou schalt trauele a litil in the werk therof, and thou schalt ete soone of the generaciouns therof.

21 Wisdom is ouer scharp to vntauyt men, and an hertles man schal not dwelle there ynne.

22 As the vertu of a stoon, preuyng schal be in hem; and thei schulen not tarie to caste awei it.

23 Forsothe the wisdom of techyng is bi the name therof, and it is not opyn to many men; but it dwellith with hem, of whiche it is knowun, til to the siyt of God.

24 Sone, here thou, and take the counsel of vndurstondyng, and caste thou not awei my counsel.

25 Set in thi foot in to the stockis therof, and thi necke in to the bies therof.

26 Make suget thi schuldir, and bere it, and be thou not anoied in the boondis therof.

27 In al thi wille go to it, and in al thi vertu kepe the weies therof.

28 Enquere thou it, and it schal be maad opyn to thee; and thou made holdinge wisdom forsake not it.

29 For in the laste thingis thou schalt fynde reste ther ynne, and it schal turne to thee in to deliting.

30 And the stockis therof schulen be to thee in defence of strengthe, and the foundementis of vertu, and the bie therof in a stoole of glorie.

31 For whi the fairnesse of lijf is in wisdom, and the boondis therof ben heelful byndyng.

32 Thou schalt 'were it as a stoole of glorie, and thou schalt sette on thee a coroun of thankyng.

33 Sone, if thou takist heede to me, thou schalt lerne wisdom; and if thou yyuest thi wille, thou schalt be wijs.

34 If thou bowist doun thin eere, thou schalt take teching; and if thou louest for to here, thou schalt be wijs.

35 Stonde thou in the multitude of prudent preestis, and be thou ioyned of herte to the wisdom of hem; that thou maist here ech telling of God, and the prouerbis of preisyng fle not awey fro thee.

36 And if thou seest a wijs man, wake thou to hym, and thi foot trede on the greeces of his doris.

37 Haue thou thouyt in the comaundementis of God, and be thou most bisi in his heestis; and he schal yyue to thee herte, and coueitise of wisdom schal be youun to thee.

CAP 7

1 Nile thou do yuels, and tho schulen not take thee.

2 Departe thou fro wickidnesse, and yuels schulen faile fro thee.

3 Sowe thou not yuels in the forewis of vnriytfulnesse, and thou schalt not repe tho in seuene fold.

4 Nyle thou seke of a man ledyng, nethir of a kyng the chaier of onour.

5 Iustifie thou not thee bifore God, for he is the knowere of the herte; and nyle thou wilne to be seyn wijs anentis the king.

6 Nile thou seke to be maad a iuge, no but thou maist breke wickidnessis bi vertu; lest thou drede the face of a myyti man, and sette sclaundre in thi swiftnesse.

7 Do thou not synne in the multitude of a cytee, nether sende thee in to the puple;

8 nether bynde thou double synnes, for thou schalt not be giltles in oon.

9 Nyle thou be a coward in thi soule, to preie;

10 and dispise thou not to do almes.

11 Seie thou not, God schal biholde in the multitude of my yiftis; and whanne Y schal offre to God alther hiyeste, he schal take my yiftis.

12 Scorne thou not a man in the bitternesse of soule; for whi God is the biholdere, that makith meke, and enhaunsith.

13 Nyle thou loue a leesyng ayens thi brother; nether do thou in lijk maner ayens a frend.

14 Nyle thou wilne to lie ony leesing; for whi the contynu-aunce therof is not good.

15 Nyle thou be a ianglere in the multitude of preestis; and reherse thou not a word in thi preier.

16 Haate thou not trauelouse werkis, and erthetilthe maad of the hiyeste.

17 Arette thou not thee in the multitude of vnlernyd men.

18 Haue thou mynde on ire, for it schal not tarie.

19 Make thou meke greetli thi spirit, for whi the veniaunce of the fleisch of an vnpitouse man is fier, and worm.

20 Nyle thou trespasse ayens thi frend dilaiynge monei; nether dispise thou a ful dereworth brother for gold.

21 Nyle thou departe fro a wijs womman, and good, whom thou hast gete in the drede of the Lord; for whi the grace of hir schamefastnesse is aboue gold.

22 Hirte thou not a seruaunt worchynge in treuthe, nether an hirid man yyuynge his lijf.

23 A witti seruaunt be dereworthe to thee as thi soule; defraude thou not hym of fredom, nether forsake thou hym nedi.

24 Beestis ben to thee? take thou heede to tho; and if tho ben profitable, dwelle tho stille at thee.

25 Sones ben to thee? teche thou hem, and bowe thou hem fro her childheed.

26 Douytris ben to thee? kepe thou the bodi of hem, and schewe thou not glad face to hem.

27 Yyue thi douyter to mariage, and thou doist a greet werk; and yyue thou hir to a wijs man.

28 If a womman is to thee aftir thi soule, caste hir not awei; and bitake thou not thee in alle thin herte to an hateful wom-man.

29 Onoure thi fadir; and foryete thou not the weilyngis of thi modir.

30 Haue thou mynde that thou haddist not be, no but bi hem, and yelde thou to hem as and thei diden to thee.

31 In al thi soule drede thou God, and halewe thou hise prees-tis.

32 In al thi vertu loue thou him that made thee; and forsake thou not hise mynystris.

33 Onoure thou God of al thi soule; and onoure thou preestis, and clense thee with armes.

34 Yyue thou to hem the part of the firste fruytis, and of purg-yng, as also it is comaundid to thee; and of thi negligence purge thou thee with fewe men.

35 Thou schalt offre to the Lord the yyfte of thin armes, and the sacrifice of halewyng, the bigynnyngis of hooli men.
36 And dresse thin hond to a pore man, that thi merci and blessyng be performyd.
37 Grace is youun in the siyt of ech that lyueth; and forbede thou not grace to a deed man.
38 Faile thou not in coumfort to hem that wepen; and go thou with hem that morenen.
39 Be thou not slow to visite a sijk man; for bi these thingis thou schalt be maad stidfast in loue.
40 In alle thi werkis haue thou mynde on thi laste thingis; and thou schalt not do synne withouten ende.

CAP 8

1 Chide thou not with a miyti man, leste thou falle in to hise hondis.
2 Stryue thou not with a riche man, lest perauenture he make ple ayenward to thee.
3 For whi gold and siluer hath lost many men; and it stret-chith forth til to the herte of kyngis, and turneth.
4 Chide thou not with a man, a ianglere, and leie thou not trees in to his fier.
5 Comyne thou not with an vntauyt man, lest he speke yuele of thi kynrede.
6 Dispise thou not a man turnynge awei hym silf fro synne, nether vpbreide thou hym; haue thou mynde, that alle we ben in corrupcioun.
7 Dispise thou not a man in his eelde; for whi of vs men wexen eld.
8 Nyle thou make ioye of thin enemy deed, witynge that alle we dien, and wolen not come in to ioie of oure enemys.
9 Dispise thou not the tellyng of wise preestes, and be thou conuersaunt in the prouerbis of hem;
10 for of hem thou schalt lerne wisdom, and techyng of vndurstondyng, and to serue without pleynt to grete men.
11 The tellyng of eldere men passe not thee; for thei han lerned of her fadris.
12 For of hem thou schalt lerne vndurstondyng; and in the tyme of nede thou schalt yyue answere.
13 Kyndle thou not the coolis of synneris, and repreue hem; and be thou not brent with the flawme of fier of her synnes.
14 Stonde thou not ayens the face of a man ful of dispisyng; lest he sitte as a spiere to thi mouth.
15 Nyle thou leene to a man strongere than thou; that if thou hast lent, haue thou it as lost.
16 Biheete thou not aboue thi power; that if thou hast bihiyt, bithenke thou as yeldynge.
17 Deme thou not ayens a iuge; for he demeth vp that, that is iust.
18 Go thou not in the weie with an hardi man, lest perauen-ture he agregge hise yuels in thee; for he goith aftir his wille, and thou schalt perische togidere with his foli.
19 Make thou not chidyng with a wrathful man, and go thou not in to desert with an hardi man; for whi blood is as nouyt bifore hym, and where noon help is, he schal hurtle thee doun.
20 Haue thou not councel with foolis; for thei moun not loue, no but tho thingis that plesen hem.
21 Make thou not a counsel bifore a straunger; for thou noost, what he schal bringe forth. Make not thin herte knowun to ech man; lest perauenture he brynge to thee fals grace, and dispise thee.

CAP 9

1 Loue thou not gelousli the womman of thi bosum; lest sche schewe on thee the malice of yuel doctryn.
2 Yyue thou not to a womman the power of thi soule; lest sche entre in thi vertu, and thou be schent.
3 Biholde thou not a womman of many willis; lest perauen-ture thou falle in to the snaris of hir.
4 Be thou not customable with a daunseresse, nethir here thou hir; lest perauenture thou perische in the spedi werk of hir.
5 Biholde thou not a virgyn; lest perauenture thou be sclaun-drid in the feirnesse of hir.
6 Yyue not thi soule to hooris in ony thing; lest thou leese thee, and thi soule, and thin eritage.
7 Nyle thou biholde aboute in the lanys of the cytee; nethir erre thou in the large streetis therof.
8 Turne awei thi face fro a womman 'wel arayed; and biholde thou not aboute the fairnesse of othere.
9 Many men han perischid for the fairnesse of a womman; and 'herbi couetise brenneth 'an hiy as fier.
10 Ech womman which is an hoore, ethir customable to fornycacioun, schal be defoulid as a fen in the weie.
11 Many men wondrynge on the fairnesse of an alien wom-man weren maad repreuable, for whi the speche of hir bren-neth an hiy as fier.
12 Sitte thou not in ony maner with an alien womman, nether reste thou with hir on a bed;
13 and iangle thou not with hir in wyn, lest perauenture thin herte boowe in to hir, and thou falle in to perdicioun bi thi blood.
14 Forsake thou not an eld frend; for a newe frend schal not be lijk hym.
15 Newe wijn is a newe frend; it schal wexe eld, and thou schalt drinke it with swetnesse.
16 Coueyte thou not the glorie and richessis of a synnere; for thou noost, what distriyng of hym schal come.
17 The wrong of vniust men plese not thee, and wite thou that a wickid man schal not plese til to hellis.
18 Be thou fer fro a man that hath power to sle, and thou schalt not haue suspicioun of the drede of deth;
19 and if thou neiyest to hym, nyle thou do ony trespasse, lest perauenture he take awei thi lijf.
20 Knowe thou the comynyng of deth; for thou schalt entre in to the myddis of snaris, and thou schalt go on the armuris of hem that sorewen.
21 Bi thi vertu kepe thee fro thi neiybore; and trete thou with wise men and prudent men.
22 Just men be gestis, ethir mete feris, to thee; and gloriyng be 'to thee in the dreed of God.
23 And the thouyt of God be to thee in wit; and al thi tellynge be in the heestis of the hiyeste.
24 Werkis schulen be preisid in the hond of crafti men, and the prince of the puple in the wisdom of his word; forsothe in the wit of eldere men a word.
25 A man, a ianglere, is dredeful in his citee; and a fool hardi man in his word schal be hateful.

CAP 10

1 A wijs iuge schal deme his puple; and the prinshed of a witti man schal be stidfast.
2 Aftir the iuge of the puple, so and hise mynystris; and what maner man is the gouernour of the citee, siche ben also men dwellinge ther ynne.

3 An vnwijs king schal leese his puple; and citees schulen be enhabitid bi the wit of prudent men.

4 The power of erthe is in the hond of God, and al the wickidnesse of hethene men is abhomynable; and he schal reise a profitable gouernour at a tyme on it.

5 The power of man is in the hond of God; and he schal sette his onour on the face of a wijs man in the lawe.

6 Haue thou not mynde on al the wrong of the neiybore; and do thou no thing in the werkis of wrong.

7 Pride is hateful bifore God and men; and al the wickidnesse of hethene men is abhomynable.

8 A rewme is translatid fro a folk in to folk, for vnriytfulnessis, and wrongis, and dispisyngis, and dyuerse gilis.

9 No thing is cursidere than an auerouse man. What art thou proude, thou erthe and aische?

10 No thing is worse, than for to loue monei; for whi this man hath also his soule set to sale, for in his lijf he hath cast awei hise ynneste thingis.

11 Ech power is schort lijf; lengere siknesse greueth the leche.

12 A leche kittith awei schort siknesse; so and a king is to dai, and to morewe he schal die.

13 Forsothe whanne a man schal die, he schal enherite serpentis, and beestis, and wormes.

14 The bigynnyng of pride of man was to be apostata fro God;

15 for his herte yede awei fro hym that made hym. For whi pride is the bigynnyng of al synne; he that holdith it, schal be fillid with cursyngis, and it schal distrye hym in to the ende.

16 Therfor the Lord hath schent the couentis of yuele men, and hath destried hem til 'in to the ende.

17 God destriede the seetis of proude duykis; and made mylde men to sitte for hem.

18 God made drie the rootis of proude folkis; and plauntide meke men of tho folkis.

19 The Lord destriede the londis of folkis; and loste tho 'til to the foundement.

20 He made drie the rootis of hem, and loste hem; and made the mynde of hem to ceesse fro the erthe.

21 God loste the mynde of proude men; and lefte the mynde of meke men in wit.

22 Pride was not maad to men; nether wrathfulnesse to the nacioun of wymmen.

23 This seed of men that dredith God, schal be onourid; but this seed schal be disonourid, that passith the comaundementis of the Lord.

24 In the myddis of britheren the gouernour of hem is in onour; and thei that dreden God, schulen be in hise iyen.

25 The glorie of riche men onourid and of pore men is the drede of God.

26 Nyle thou dispise a iust pore man; and nyle thou magnefie a riche synful man.

27 The iuge is greet, and is myyti in onour; and he is not grettere than that man that dredith God.

28 Fre children seruen a witti seruaunt; and a prudent man and lerned schal not grutche, whanne he is blamed, and an vnkunnynge man schal not be onourid.

29 Nyle thou enhaunse thee in thi werk to be don; and nyle thou be slow in the tyme of angwisch.

30 He is betere that worchith, and hath plente in alle thingis, than he that hath glorie, and nedith breed.

31 Sone, kepe thi soule in myldenesse; and yyue thou onour to it, aftir his merit.

32 Who schal iustifie hym that synneth ayens his soule? and who schal onoure hym that disonourith his soule?

33 A pore man hath glorie bi his lernyng and drede; and ther is a man that is onourid for his catel.

34 Forsothe if a man hath glorie in pouert, hou myche more in catel? and he that hath glorie in catel, drede pouerte.

CAP 11

1 The wisdom of a man maad meke schal enhaunse his heed; and schal make hym to sitte in the middis of grete men.

2 Preise thou not a man in his fairnesse; nether dispise thou a man in his siyt.

3 A bee is litil among briddis; and his fruyt hath the bigynnyng of swetnesse.

4 Haue thou neuere glorie in clothing, and be thou not enhaunsid in the dai of thin onour; for whi the werkis of the hiyeste aloon ben wondurful, and hise werkis ben gloriouse, and hid, and vnseyn.

5 Many tyrauntis han sete in trone; and a man of whom was no supposyng bar the diademe.

6 Many myyty men ben oppressid strongli; and gloriouse men ben youun in to the hondis of othere men.

7 Bifore that thou axe, blame thou not ony man; and whanne thou hast axid, blame thou iustli.

8 Bifor that thou here, answere thou not a word; and in the myddis of eldere men adde thou not to speke.

9 Stryue thou not, of that thing that disesith not thee; and stonde thou not in the dom of synnes.

10 Sone, thi dedis be not in many thingis; and if thou art riche, thou schalt not be with out part of gilt. For if thou suest, thou schalt not take; and thou schalt not ascape, if thou rennist bifore.

11 Ther is a man trauelynge, and hastynge, and sorewynge, and vnpitouse; and bi so myche more he schal not haue plentee.

12 Ther is a man fade, nedi of rekyueryng, failynge more in vertu, and plenteuouse in pouert;

13 and the iye of God bihelde hym in good, and reiside hym fro his lownesse, and enhaunsid his heed; and many men wondriden in him, and onouriden God.

14 Goodis and yuels, lijf and deth, pouert and oneste, ben of God.

15 Wisdom, and lernyng, and kunnyng of the lawe ben anentis the Lord; loue and the weies of goode men ben at him.

16 Errour and derknessis ben maad togidere to synneris; forsothe thei that maken ful out ioye in yuel, wexen eld togidere in to yuels.

17 The yifte of God dwellith to iust men; and encreessyngis of hym schulen haue prosperitees without ende.

18 A man is that is maad riche in doynge scarsli, and this is the part of his mede,

19 in that that he seith, Y haue founden reste to me, and now Y aloone schal ete of my goodis.

20 And he noot that tyme passith hym, and deth neiyeth, and he schal leeue alle thingis to othere men, and schal die.

21 Stonde thou in thi testament, and speke thou togidere in it; and wexe thou eld in the werk of thin heestis.

22 Dwelle thou not in the werkis of synneris; but triste thou in God, and dwelle in thi place.

23 For it is esy in the iyen of God, sudeynli to make onest a pore man.

24 The blessing of God haastith in to the meede of a iust man; and the going forth of hym makith fruyt in swift onour.

25 Seie thou not, What is nede to me? and what goodis schulen be me her aftir?

26 Seie thou not, Y am sufficient, and what schal Y be maad worse heraftir?

27 In the dai of goodis be thou not vnmyndeful of yuels, and in the dai of yuels be thou not vnmyndeful of goodis;

28 for it is esi bifor God to yelde in the dai of deth to ech man aftir hise weies.

29 The malice of oon our makith foryeting of moost letcherie; and in the ende of a man is makyng nakid of hise werkis.

30 Preise thou not ony man bifore his deth; for whi a man is knowun in hise sones.

31 Brynge thou not ech man in to thin hous; for whi many tresouns ben of a gileful man.

32 For whi as the entrailis of stynkynge thingis breken out, and as a partrich is led in to a trap, ether net, and as a capret is led in to a snare, so and the herte of proude men; and as a biholdere seynge the fal of his neiybore.

33 For he turneth goodis in to yuels, and settith tresouns, and puttith a wem on chosun men.

34 Fier is encreessid of a sparcle, and blood is encreessid of a gileful man; for whi a synful man settith tresoun to blood.

35 Take heede to thee fro a gileful man, for he makith yuels; lest perauenture he bringe yn on thee scornyng with outen ende.

36 Resseyue thou an alien to thee, and he schal distrie thee in whirlwynd, and he schal make thee alien fro thin owne weies.

CAP 12

1 If thou doist wel, wite thou to whom thou doist; and miche grace schal be to thi goodis.

2 Do thou wel to a iust man, and thou schalt fynde greet yeldyng; thouy not of hym, certis of the Lord.

3 It is not wel to hym that is customable in yuels, and to hym that yyueth not almes; for whi the hiyeste bothe hatith synneris, and doith merci to hem that doen penaunce.

4 Yyue thou to a merciful man, and resseyue thou not a synnere; God schal yelde veniaunce bothe to vnfeithful men and to synneris, kepynge hem in the dai of veniaunce.

5 Yyue thou to a good man, and resseyue thou not a synnere.

6 Do thou good to a meke man, and yyue thou not to an vnpitouse man; forbede thou to yyue looues to hym, lest in tho he be myytiere than thou.

7 For thou schalt fynde double yuels in alle goodis, whiche euere thou doist to hym; for whi the hiyeste bothe hatith synneris, and schal yelde veniaunce to vnfeithful men.

8 A frend schal not be knowun in goodis, and an enemy schal not be hid in yuels.

9 In the goodis of a man hise enemyes ben sori; and a frend is knowun in the sorewe and malice of him.

10 Bileue thou neuer to thin enemy; for his wickidnesse roustith as irun.

11 Thouy he be maad meke, and go lowe, caste awei thi soule, and kepe thee fro him.

12 Sette thou not him bisidis thee, nether sitte he at thi riytside, lest he turne and stonde in thi place; lest perauenture he turne in to thi place, and enquere thi chaier, and in the laste tyme thou know mi wordis, and be prickid in my wordis.

13 Who schal do medecyn to an enchauntere smytun of a serpent, and to alle men that neiyen to beestis, and to him that goith with an yuel man, and is wlappid in the synnes of him?

14 In oon our he schal dwelle with thee; sotheli if thou bowist awei, he schal not bere vp.

15 The enemy makith swete in hise lippis, and in his herte he settith tresoun to ouerturne thee in to the dich.

16 The enemy wepith in hise iyen; and if he fyndith tyme, he schal not be fillid of blood.

17 If yuels bifallen to thee, thou schalt fynde hym the formere there.

18 The enemy schal wepe bifore thin iyen, and he as helpynge schal vndurmyne thi feet.

19 He schal stire his heed, and he schal beete with hond; and he schal speke priuyli many yuels of thee, and schal chaunge his chere.

CAP 13

1 He that touchith pitch, schal be defoulid of it; and he that comyneth with a proude man, schal clothe pride.

2 He reisith a weiyte on hym silf, that comyneth with a more onest man than hym silf; and be thou not felowe to a man richere than thou.

3 What schal a cawdroun comyne to a pot? for whanne tho hirtlen hem silf togidere, the pot schal be brokun.

4 A riche man schal do vniustli, and schal gnaste; but a pore man hirt schal be stille.

5 If thou yyuest, he schal take thee; and if thou hast not, he schal forsake thee.

6 If thou hast, he schal lyue togidere with thee, and schal make thee voide; and he schal not haue sorewe on thee.

7 If thou art nedeful to hym, he schal disseyue thee; and he schal flatere, and schal yyue hope, tellinge to thee alle goodis; and schal seie, What is nede to thee?

8 And he schal schende thee in hise metis, til he anyntische thee twies and thries, and at the laste he schal scorne thee; aftirward he schal se, and schal forsake thee, and he schal moue his heed to thee.

9 Be thou maad meke to God, and abide thou hise hondis.

10 Take heede, lest thou be disseyued, and be maad lowe in foli.

11 Nyle thou be lowe in thi wisdom, lest thou be maad low, and be disseyued in to foli.

12 Whanne thou art clepid of a miytiere man, go thou awei; for bi this he schal more clepe thee.

13 Be thou not greetli pressyng, lest thou be hurtlid doun; and be thou not fer fro hym, lest thou go in to foryetyng.

14 Witholde thou not to speke with hym euenli, and bileue thou not to hise many wordis; for of myche speche he schal tempte thee, and he schal leiye priuyli, and schal axe thee of thin hid thingis.

15 His cruel soule schal kepe thi wordis, and he schal not spare of malice, and of bondis.

16 Be war to thee, and take heede diligentli to thin heryng; for thou goist with thi distriyng.

17 But thou heringe tho thingis, se as in sleep, and thou schalt wake.

18 In al thi lijf loue thou God, and inwardli clepe thou him in thin heelthe.

19 Ech beeste loueth a beeste lijk it silf; so and ech man owith to loue his neiybore.

20 Ech fleisch schal be ioyned to fleisch lijk it silf, and ech man schal be felouschipid to a man lijk hym silf.

21 As a wulf schal comyne sum tyme with a lomb, so a synnere with a iust man.

22 What cominge is of an hooli man to a dogge? ethir what good part is of a riche man to a pore man?

23 The huntyng of a lioun is a wielde asse in desert; so the lesewis of riche men ben pore men.

24 And as mekenesse is abhomynacioun to a proude man, so and a pore man is abhomynacioun of a riche man.

25 A riche man moued is confermed of hise frendis; but a meke man, whanne he fallith, schal be cast out, yhe, of knowun men.

26 Many rekyuereris ben to a riche man disseyued; he spak proudli, and thei iustifieden hym.

27 A meke man is disseiued, ferthermore also he is repreuyd; he spak wiseli, and no place was youun to hym.

28 The riche man spak, and alle men weren stille; and thei schulen brynge his word til to the cloudis.

29 A pore man spak, and thei seien, Who is this? and if he offendith, thei schulen destrye hym.

30 Catel is good to hym, to whom is no synne in conscience; and 'the worste pouert is in the mouth of a wickid man.

31 The herte of a man chaungith his face, ethir in good ethir in yuel.

32 Of hard and with trauel thou schalt fynde the step of a good herte, and a good face.

CAP 14

1 Blessid is the man, that stood not bi the word of his mouth, and was not prickid in the sorewe of trespas.

2 He is blessid, that hath not sorewe of his soule, and fallith not doun fro his hope.

3 Catel is with out resoun to a coueitouse man, and hard nygard; and wherto is gold to an enuyouse man?

4 He that gaderith of his wille vniustli, gaderith to othere men; and another man schal mak wast in hise goodis.

5 To what othere man schal he be good, which is wickid to hym silf? and he schal not be myrye in hise goodis.

6 No thing is worse, than he that hath enuye to hym silf; and this is the yelding of his malice.

7 And if he doith good, he doith vnwityngli, and not wilfuli; and at the laste he schewith his malice.

8 The iye of an enuyouse man is wickid, and turnynge awei the face, and dispisynge his soule.

9 The iye of the coueitouse man is neuere fillid; he schal not be fillid in to the part of wickidnesse, til he performe vnriytfulnesse, and make drie his soule.

10 An yuel iye to yuels, and the nedi man schal not be fillid of breed; and he schal be in sorewe on his table.

11 Sone, if thou hast, do wel with thi silf, and offre thou worthi offryngis to God.

12 Be thou myndeful that deth schal not tarie, and the testament of hellis, which is schewid to thee; for whi the testament of this world schal die bi deth.

13 Bifore deth do thou good to thi frend, and bi thi miytis stretche thou forth, and yyue to a pore man.

14 Be thou not disseyued of a good dai, and a litil part of a good day passe not thee.

15 Whether thou schalt not leeue to othere men thi sorewis, and trauels?

16 In the departyng of lot yyue thou, and take; and iustifie thi soule.

17 Bifore thi deth worche thou riytfulnesse; for at hellis it is not to fynde mete.

18 Ech man schal wexe eld as hey, and as a leef bryngynge fruit in a greene tree.

19 Othere ben gendrid, and othere ben cast doun; so the generacioun of fleisch and blood, another is endid, and another is borun.

20 Ech corruptible werk schal faile in the ende; and he that worchith it, schal go with it.

21 And al chosun werk schal be iustified; and he that worchith it, schal be onourid in it.

22 Blessid is the man, that schal dwelle in wisdom, and that schal bithenke in riytfulnesse, and schal thenke in wit the biholding of God.

23 Which thenkith out, ether fyndith out, the weies of hym in his herte, and schal be vndurstondynge in the hid thingis of hym; goynge as a serchere aftir it, and stondynge in the weies of it.

24 Which biholdith bi the wyndows therof, and herith in the yatis therof;

25 which restith nyy the hous therof, and settith a stak in the wallis therof. He schal sette his litil hous at the hondis of hym, and goodis schulen reste in his litil hous, bi duryng of the world;

26 he schal sette hise sones vndur the hilyng therof, and he schal dwelle vndur the boowis therof;

27 he schal be kyuerid vndur the hilyng therof fro heete, and he schal reste in the glorie therof.

CAP 15

1 He that dredith God, schal do goode werkis; and he that holdith riytfulnesse, schal take it.

2 And it as a modir onourid schal meete hym, and as a womman fro virgynyte it schal take hym.

3 It shal feede hym with the breed of lijf, and of vndurstonding; and it schal yyue drynke to hym with watir of heelful wisdom; it schal be maad stidfast in hym, and he schal not be bowid.

4 And it schal holde hym, and he schal not be schent; and it schal enhaunse hym at his neiyboris.

5 And in the myddis of the chirche he schal opene his mouth; and God schal fille hym with the spirit of wisdom, and of vndurstonding, and schal clothe hym with the stoole of glorie.

6 God schal tresore on hym myrthe, and ful out ioiyng; and schal enherite hym with euerlastynge name.

7 Fonned men schulen not take that wisdom, and witti men schulen meete it. Fonned men schulen not se it; for whi it goith awey fer fro pride, and gile.

8 Men leesyngmongeris schulen not be myndful therof, and sothefast men ben foundun ther ynne; and schulen haue prosperite 'til to the biholding of God.

9 Preisyng is not fair in the mouth of a synnere, for he is not sent of the Lord.

10 For whi wisdom yede forth fro God; forsothe heriyng schal stonde nyy the wisdom of God, and it schal be plenteuouse in a feithful mouth, and the Lord schal yyue it to him.

11 Seie thou not, It goith awei bi God; for whi do thou not tho thingis, whiche God hatith.

12 Seie thou not, He made me for to erre; for whi wickid men ben not nedeful to hym.

13 The Lord hatith al cursidnesse of errour, and it schal not be amyable to hem, that dreden hym.

14 At the bigynnyng God made man, and lefte him in the hond of his councel.

15 He addide hise comaundementis, and lawis;

16 if thou wolt kepe the comaundementis, tho schulen kepe thee, and kepe plesaunt feith with outen ende.

17 He hath set to thee watir and fier; dresse thin hond to that, that thou wolt.

18 Bifor man is lijf and deth, good and yuel; that, that plesith hym, schal be youun to hym.

19 For whi the wisdom of God is myche, and he is strong in power, and seeth alle men without ceessing.

20 The iyen of the Lord ben to hem, that dreden hym; and he knowith al the trauel of man.

21 He comaundide not to ony man to do wickidli; and he yaf not to ony man space to do synne.

22 For he coueytith not the multitude of sones vnfeithful and vnprofitable.

CAP 16

1 Be thou not glad in wickid sones, if thei ben multiplied; nether delite thou on hem, if the drede of God is not in hem.

2 Bileue thou not to the lijf of hem, and biholde thou not in to the trauels of hem.

3 For whi betere is oon dredynge God, than a thousynde wickid sones.

4 And it is more profitable to die with out sones, than to leeue wickid sones.

5 A cuntrei schal be enhabitid of o witti man; and it schal be maad desert of thre wickid men.

6 Myn iye siy many othere thingis, and myn eere herde strongere thingis than these.

7 Fier schal brenne an hiy in the synagoge of synneris, and yre schal brenne an hiy in a folk vnbileuful.

8 Elde giauntis that weren distried, tristynge on her vertu, preieden not for her synnes;

9 and God sparide not the pilgrymage of hem, but he killide hem, and curside hem, for the pride of her word.

10 He hadde not merci on hem, and he loste al the folk enhaunsynge hem silf in her synnes.

11 And as he killide sixe hundrid thousynde of foot men, that weren gaderid togidere in the hardnesse of her herte; and if oon hadde be hard nollid, wondur if he hadde be giltles.

12 For whi merci and ire is with hym; preier is myyti, and schedynge out ire.

13 Bi his merci, so is the chastisyng of ech man; he is demyd bi hise werkis.

14 A synnere in raueyn schal not ascape; and the sufferaunce of hym that doith merci schal not tarie.

15 Al merci schal make place to ech man, aftir the merit of his werkis, and aftir the vndurstonding of his pilgrymage.

16 Seie thou not, Y schal be hid fro God; and fro the hiyeste, who schal haue mynde on me?

17 Seie thou not, Y schal not be knowun in a greet puple; for whi which is my soule in so greet a creature?

18 Lo! heuene, and the heuenes of heuenes, the greet occian, and al erthe, and tho thingis that ben in tho, schulen be mouyd in his siyt;

19 munteyns togidere, and litle hillis, and the foundementis of erthe; and whanne God biholdith tho, tho schulen be schakun togidere with tremblyng.

20 And in alle these thingis the herte is vnwijs, and ech herte is vndurstondun of hym.

21 And who vndurstondith hise weies? and 'who vndurstondith a tempest, which the iye of man siy not?

22 For whi ful many werkis of hym ben 'in hid thingis, but who schal telle out the werkis of his riytfulnesse, ether who schal suffre? For whi the testament is fer fro summe men; and the axyng of men is in the endyng.

23 He that is maad litil in herte, thenkith veyn thingis; and a man vnprudent and a fool thenkith fonned thingis.

24 Sone, here thou me, and lerne thou techyng of wit, and yyue thou tent to my wordis in thin herte; and Y schal seie techyng in equyte, and Y schal seke to telle out wisdom. And yyue thou tent to my wordis in thin herte;

25 and Y seie in equyte of spirit the vertues, whiche God hath set on hise werkis at the bigynnyng, and in treuthe Y telle out the kunnyng of him.

26 In the doom of God ben hise werkis fro the bigynnyng; and in the ordynaunce of tho he departyde the partis of tho, and he departide the bigynnyngis of tho in hise folkis.

27 He ournede with outen ende the werkis of hem; thei hungriden not, nether traueliden, and thei ceessiden not of her werkis.

28 Ech schal not make streit the nexte to hym, til in to with outen ende.

29 Be thou not vnbileueful to the word of him.

30 Aftir these thingis God bihelde 'in to the erthe, and fillide it with hise goodis.

31 Forsothe the soule of ech lyuynge thing teld bifore his face; and thilke soule is eft the turnyng ayen of tho thinges.

CAP 17

1 God formede man of erthe; and aftir his ymage he made man.

2 And eft he turnede man in to that ymage; and aftir hym silf he clothide hym with vertu.

3 He yaf to hym the noumbre of daies, and tyme; and he yaf to him power of tho thingis that ben on erthe.

4 He settide the drede of man on al fleisch, and he was lord of beestis and fliynge briddis.

5 He formyde of man an help lijk hym; he yaf to hem councel, and tunge, and iyen, and eeris, and herte to thenke out; and he fillide hem with techyng of vndurstondyng.

6 He made to hem the kunnyng of spirit, he fillide the herte of hem with wit; and he schewide to hem yuels and goodis.

7 He settide the iye of hem on the hertes of hem, to schewe to hem the grete thingis of hise werkis,

8 that thei preise togidere the name of halewyng; and to haue glorie in hise meruels, that thei telle out the grete thingis of hise werkis.

9 He addide to hem techyng; and he enheritide hem with the lawe of lijf.

10 He ordeynyde an euerlastynge testament with hem; and he schewide to hem hise riytfulnesse, and domes.

11 And the iye of hem siy the grete thingis of his onour, and the eeris of hem herden the onour of vois; and he seide to hem, Take heede to you fro al wickid thing.

12 And he comaundide to hem, to ech man of his neiybore.

13 The weies of hem ben euere bifore hym; tho ben not hid fro hise iyen.

14 On ech folk he made souereyn a gouernour;

15 and Israel was maad the opyn part of God.

16 And alle the werkis of hem ben as the sunne in the siyt of God; and hise iyen biholden with out ceessyng in the weies of hem.

17 Testamentis weren not hid fro the wickidnesse of hem; and alle the wickydnessis of hem weren in the siyt of God.

18 The almes of a man is as a bagge with hym, and it schal kepe the grace of a man as the appil of the iye;

19 and afterward man schal rise ayen, and it schal yelde to hem a yelding, to ech man in to the heed of hem; and schal turne in to the lower partis of erthe.

20 Forsothe it yaf to men repentinge the weie of riytfulnesse, and confermede men failynge to suffre, and ordeynede to hem the part of treuthe.

21 Turne thou to the Lord, and forsake thi synnes;

22 preye thou bifore the face of the Lord, and make thou lesse hirtingis.

23 Turne thou ayen to the Lord, and turne thou awei fro thin vnriytfulnesse, and hate thou greetli cursyng.

24 And knowe thou the riytfulnessis, and domes of God; and stonde thou in the part of good purpos, and of preier of the hiyeste God.

25 Go thou in to the partis of the hooli world, with men lyuynge, and yyuynge knouleching to God.

26 Dwelle thou not in the errour of wickid men. Knouleche thou bifore deth; knouleching perischith fro a deed man, as no thing.

27 Lyuynge thou schalt knouleche, lyuynge and hool thou schalt knowleche, and schalt herie God; and thou schalt haue glorie in the merciful doyngis of hym.

28 The merci of God is ful greet, and his help to hem that conuerten to hym.

29 For whi not alle thingis moun be in men; for whi the sone of man is not vndeedli, and malices plesiden in to vanyte.

30 What is clerere than the sunne? and this schal faile; ethir what is worse than that, that fleisch and blood thouyte out? and of this he schal be repreued.

31 He biholdith the vertu of hiynesse of heuene; and alle men ben erthe and aische.

CAP 18

1 He that lyueth with out bigynnyng and ende, made of nouyt alle thingis togidere; God alone schal be iustified, and he dwellith a king vnouercomun with outen ende.

2 Who schal suffice to telle out his werkis?

3 for whi who schal seke the grete thingis of hym?

4 But who schal telle out the vertu of his greetnesse? ether who schal leie to for to telle out his mercy?

5 It is not to make lesse, nether to leie to; nethir it is to fynde the grete thingis of God.

6 Whanne a man hath endid, thanne he schal bigynne; and whanne he hath restid, he schal worche.

7 What is a man, and what is the glorie of him? and what is good, ether what is the wickid thing of him?

8 The noumbre of the daies of men, that ben comynli an hundrid yeer, ben arettid as the dropis of the watir of the see; and as the stoon of grauel, so a fewe yeeris in the dai of euerlastyngnesse.

9 For this thing God is pacient in hem, and schedith out on hem his merci.

10 He siy the presumpcioun of her herte, for it was yuel; and he knew the distriyng of hem, for it was wickid.

11 Therfor he fillide his merci in hem, and schewide to hem the weie of equite.

12 The merciful doyng of man is aboute his neiybore; but the merci of the Lord is ouer ech fleisch.

13 He that hath merci, and techith, and chastisith as a scheepherde his floc,

14 do merci, takynge the techyng of merciful doyng; and he that hastith in the domes therof.

15 Sone, in goodis yyue thou not pleynt, and in ech yifte yyue thou not heuynesse of an yuel word.

16 Whether dew schal not kele heete? so and a word is betere than yifte.

17 Lo! whether a word is not aboue a good yifte? but euer ethir is with a man iustified.

18 A fool schal vpbreide scharpli; and the yifte of an vntauyt man makith iyen to faile.

19 Bifore the doom make thou redi riytfulnesse to thee; and lerne thou, bifore that thou speke.

20 Bifore sikenesse yyue thou medicyn; and bifore the doom axe thi silf, and thou schalt fynde merci in the siyt of God.

21 Bifore sikenesse make the meke, and in the tyme of sikenesse schewe thi lyuyng.

22 Be thou not lettid to preye euere, and drede thou not to be iustified til to deth; for whi the meede of God dwellith with outen ende.

23 Bifore preier make redi thi soule; and nyle thou be as a man that temptith God.

24 Haue thou mynde of ire in the dai of endyng; and make thou in lyuyng the tyme of yelding.

25 Haue thou mynde of pouert in the dai of abundaunce; and the nede of pouert in the tyme of richessis.

26 Fro the morewtid 'til to the euentid the tyme schal be chaungid; and alle these thingis ben swift in the iyen of God.

27 A wise man schal drede in alle thingis; and in the daies of trespassis he schal fle fro vnkunnyng, ether slouthe.

28 Ech fel man knowith wisdom; and to hym that fyndith it, he schal yyue knouleching.

29 Witti men in wordis also thei diden wiseli, and vndurstoden treuthe, and riytfulnesse; and bisouyten prouerbis and domes.

30 Go thou not aftir thi coueitises; and be thou turned awei fro thi wille.

31 If thou yyuest to thi soule the coueitisis therof, it schal make thee in to ioie to thin enemyes.

32 Delite thou not in cumpenyes, nether in litle cumpenyes; for whi the synnyng of hem is contynuel.

33 Be thou not meene in the stryuyng of looue, and sum thing is to thee in the world; for whi thou schalt be enuyouse to thi soule.

CAP 19

1 A drunkelew werk man schal not be maad riche; and he that chargith not litle synnes, fallith doun litil and litil.

2 Wyn and wymmen maken to be apostataas, yhe, wise men; and thei repreuen witti men.

3 And he that ioyneth hym silf to hooris, schal be wickid; rot and wormes schulen enherite hym, and he schal be set an hiy in to more ensaumple, and his soule schal be takun awei fro noumbre.

4 He that bileueth soone, is vnstable in herte, and schal be maad lesse; and he that trespassith ayens his soule, schal be had ferthermore.

5 He that ioieth in wickidnesse, schal be cursid; and he that hatith blamyng, schal be maad lesse in lijf; and he that hatith ianglyng, quenchith malice.

6 He that synneth ayens his soule, schal repente; and he that is myrie in malice, schal be cursid.

7 Reherse thou not an hard word, and wickid; and thou schalt not be maad lesse.

8 Nyle thou telle thi wit to frend and enemye; and if trespas is to thee, nyle thou make nakid.

9 For he schal here thee, and schal kepe thee, and he as defen-dynge the synne schal hate thee; and so he schal be euere with thee.

10 Thou hast herd a word ayens thi neiybore; die it togidere in thee, and triste thou that it schal not breke thee.

11 A fool trauelith greetli of the face of a word, as the sorewe of beryng of a yong child.

12 An arowe fastned in the hipe of a dogge, so a word in the herte of a fool.

13 Repreue thou a frend, lest perauenture he vndurstonde not, and seie, Y dide not; ether if he hath do, lest he adde to do eft.

14 Repreue thou a neiybore, lest perauenture he seie not; and if he seith, lest perauenture he reherse.

15 Repreue thou a frend, for whi trespassynge is don ofte;

16 and bileue thou not to ech word. Ther is a man that fallith bi his tunge, but not of wille.

17 For 'whi who is he, that trespassith not in his tunge? Repreue thou a neiybore, bifore that thou manaasse;

18 and yyue thou place to the drede of the hiyeste. For whi al wisdom is the drede of God, and in that wisdom for to drede God; and the ordynaunce of lawe is in al wisdom.

19 And the teching of wickidnesse is not wisdom; and the prudence of synnes is not good thouyt.

20 Ther is wickidnesse of prudence, and cursidnesse is ther ynne; and ther is an vnwijs man, which is maad litil in wis-dom.

21 Betere is a man that hath litil in wisdom, and failynge in wit in the drede of God, than he that hath plentee of wit, and brekith the lawe of the hiyeste.

22 Ther is certeyn sutilte, and it is wickid.

23 And ther is a man, that sendith out a certeyn word, tellynge out treuthe. Ther is a man, that mekith hym silf wickidly; and hise ynnere thingis ben ful of gile.

24 And ther is a iust man, that makith low greetli hym silf of myche mekenesse; and ther is a iust man, that bowith the face, and feyneth hym to se not that, that is vnknowun.

25 Thouy he is forbodun of feblenesse of strengthis to do synne; if he fyndith tyme to do yuele, he schal do yuel.

26 A man is knowun bi siyt; and a witti man is knowun bi meetyng of face.

27 The clothing of bodi, and the leiyyng of teeth, and the entring of a man, tellen out of hym.

28 Ther is fals repreuyng in the ire of a man ful of dispisyng; and ther is dom which is not preued to be good; and ther is a stille man, and he is prudent.

CAP 20

1 It is ful good to repreue, more than to be wrooth, and to forbede not a man knoulechyng in preiere.

2 The coueitise of a geldyng hath defoulid the maidynhed of a yong womman,

3 so he that makith wickid dom bi violence.

4 It is ful good, that a man 'that is repreued schewe opynli penaunce; for so thou schalt ascape wilful synne.

5 Ther is a stil man, which is foundun wijs; and he is hateful, which is fool hardi to speke.

6 Sotheli ther is a stille man, not hauynge wit of speche; and ther is a stille man, knowynge the sesoun of couenable tyme.

7 A wijs man schal be stille til to tyme; but a ioli man and vnprudent man schulen not kepe tyme.

8 He that vsith many wordis, hirtith his soule; and he that takith power to hym silf vniustli, schal be hatid.

9 Ther is goyng forth in yuels to a man vnlernyd; and ther is fyndyng in to peiryng.

10 Ther is a yifte, which is not profitable; and ther is a yifte, whos yeldyng is double.

11 Ther is makyng lesse for glorie; and ther is a man, which schal reise the heed fro mekenesse.

12 Ther is a man, that ayen bieth many synnes for litil prijs, and restorith tho in seuenfold.

13 A wijs man in wordis makith hym silf amyable; but the graces of foolis schulen be sched out.

14 The yifte of an vnwijs man schal not be profitable to thee; for hise iyen ben seuenfold.

15 He schal yyue litle thingis, and he schal vpbreide many thingis; and the openyng of his mouth is enflawming.

16 To dai a man leeneth, and to morewe he axith; and siche a man is hateful.

17 A frend schal not be to a fool, and grace schal not be to hise goodis.

18 For thei that eten his breed, ben of fals tunge; hou ofte and hou many men schulen scorne hym?

19 For he departith not bi euene wit that, that was worthi to be had; in lijk maner and that, that was not worthi to be had.

20 The falling of a fals tunge is as he that fallith in the paw-ment; so the fallis of yuele men schulen come hastili.

21 A man with out grace is as a veyn fable; and it schal be customable in the mouth of vnlerned men.

22 A parable schal be repreued of the mouth of a fool; for he seith not it in his tyme. Ther is a man, that is forbodun to do synne, for pouert; and he schal be prickid in his reste.

23 Ther is a man, that schal leese his soule for schame; and for the vnprudence of a persoone he schal leese it.

24 Forsothe he schal leese hym silf for the takyng of a per-soone.

25 Ther is a man, that for schame biheetith to a frend; and he hath gete hym enemy with out cause.

26 Leesyng is a wickid schenschip in a man; and it schal be customabli in the mouth of vnlerned men.

27 Betere is a theef than the customablenesse of a man, a leesyngmongere; forsothe bothe thei schulen enherite perdi-cioun.

28 The maneres of men leesyngmongeris ben with outen onour; and her schenschype is with hem with out ceessyng.

29 A wijs man in wordis schal brynge forth hym silf; and a prudent man schal pleese grete men.

30 He that worchith his lond, shal make hiy the heep of fruy-tis; and he that worchith riytfulnesse, schal be enhaunsid. Sotheli he that plesith grete men, schal ascape wickidnesse.

31 Presentis and yiftis blynden the iyen of iugis; and as doumb in the mouth it turneth awei the chastisyngis of hem.

32 Wisdom hid, and tresour vnseyn, what profit is in euer eithir?

33 He is betere, that hidith his vnwisdom, than a man that hidith his wisdom.

CAP 21

1 Sone, thou hast do synne? adde thou not eft; but biseche thou for the formere synnes, that tho be foryouun to thee.

2 As fro the face of a serpent fle thou synnes; and if thou neiyest to 'tho synnes, tho schulen take thee.

3 The teeth of a lioun ben the teeth therof, that sleen the soulis of men.

4 Al wickidnesse is as a scharp swerd on either syde; heelthe is not to the wounde therof.

5 Chidyngis and wrongis schulen distrie catel; and an houe that is ouer riche, schal be distriede bi pride; so the catel of a proude man schal be drawun vp bi the roote.

6 The preyer of a pore man schal come fro the mouth 'til to eeris; and doom schal come to hym hastili.

7 He that hatith repreuyng, is a step of the synnere; and he that dredith God, schal be turned to his herte.

8 A miyti man with an hardi tunge is knowun afer; and a witti man kan kepe him silf fro that man.

9 He that bildith his hous with othere mennus costis, is as he that gaderith hise stonys in wyntir.

10 Scheuys gaderid togidere is the synagoge of synneris; and the endyng of hem is the flawme of fier.

11 The weie of synneris is set togidere with stoonys; and in the ende of hem ben hellis, and derknessis, and peynes.

12 He that kepith riytfulnesse, schal holde the wit therof.

13 The perfeccioun of Goddis drede is wisdom and wit.

14 He schal not be tauyt, which is not wijs in good.

15 Forsothe vnwisdom is, which is plenteuouse in yuel; and wit is not, where is bittirnesse.

16 The kunnyng of a wijs man schal be plenteuouse as flow-yng; and the councel of hym dwellith as a welle of lijf.

17 The herte of a fool is as a brokun vessel; and it schal not holde ony wisdom.

18 What euer wijs word a kunnynge man herith, he schal pre-ise, and leie to. A letcherouse man herde, and it schal displese hym; and he schal caste it awei bihynde his bak.

19 The tellynge of a fool is as a birthun in the weie; for whi grace schal be foundun in the lippis of a wijs man.

20 The mouth of a prudent man is souyt in the chirche; and men schulen thenke hise wordis in her hertis.

21 As an hous distried, so is wisdom to a fool; and the kun-nyng of an vnwijs man is wordis that moun not be teld out.

22 Stockis in the feet is techyng to a fool; and as bondis of hondis on the riyt hond.

23 A fool enhaunsith his vois in leiyyng; but a wijs man schal leiye vnnethis stilli.

24 Techyng is a goldun ournement to a prudent man; and as an ournement of the arm in the riyt arm.

25 The foot of a fool is liyt in to the hous of a neiybore; and a wijs man schal be aschamed of the persoone of a miyti man.

26 A fool biholdith fro the wyndow in to the hous; but a lerned man schal stonde with out forth.

27 It is foli of a man to herkene bi the dore; and a prudent man schal be greuyd bi dispisyng.

28 The lippis of 'vnprudent men schulen telle fonned thingis; but the wordis of prudent men schulen be weied in a bal-aunce.

29 The herte of foolis is in her mouth; and the mouth of wise men is in her herte.

30 Whanne a wickid man cursith the deuel, he cursith his owne soule.

31 A priuy bacbitere schal defoule his soule, and in alle thingis he schal be hatid, and he that dwellith, schal be hatid; a stil man and wijs schal be onourid.

CAP 22

1 A slow man is stonyd in a stoon of cley; and alle men schulen speke on the dispisyng of him.

2 A slow man is stonyd of the dung of oxis; and ech man that touchith hym, schal schake the hondis.

3 The schame of a fadir is of a sone vnlerned; but a fonned douyter schal be in decreessyng.

4 A prudent douyter is eritage to hir hosebonde; for sche that schendith hir hosebonde, is in dispisyng of the fadir.

5 A 'schameles womman schendith the fadir and hosebonde, and schal not be maad lesse than vnfeithful men; forsothe sche schal not be onourid of euer either.

6 Melodie in morenyng is vncouuenable tellyng; betyngis and techyng in al tyme with wisdom.

7 He that techith a fool, as he that glueth togidere a tiel stoon.

8 He that tellith a word to hym that herith not, is as he that reisith a man slepynge fro a greuouse sleep.

9 He that tellith wisdom to a fool, spekith with a man slepynge; and in the ende of the tellyng he schal seie, Who is this?

10 Wepe thou on a deed man, for whi his liyt failide; and wepe thou on a fool, for he failide of wit.

11 Wepe thou a litil on a deed man, for he hath restid.

12 Forsothe the lijf of a ful wickid man is ful wickid, more than the deth of a fool.

13 The morenyng of a deed man is seuene daies; but the morenyng of a fool and of a wickid man is alle the daies of her lijf.

14 Speke thou not myche with a fool, and go thou not with an vnwijs man.

15 Keep thee fro hym, that thou haue not disese; and thou schalt not be defoulid in the synne of hym.

16 Boowe thou awei fro hym, and thou schalt fynde reste; and be thou not anoied by his foly.

17 What schal be maad heuyere than leed? and what othere name than a fool is to it?

18 It is liytere to bere grauel, and salt, and a gobet of yrun, than a man vnprudent, and a fool, and vnfeithful.

19 As an heep of trees, boundun togidere in the foundement of the bilding, schal not be vnboundun, so and an herte con-fermed in the thouyt of counsel.

20 The thouyt of a wijs man shal not be maad schrewid in ony tyme, nether drede.

21 As chaffis in hiye places, and soond with out medling of hym, set ayens the face of wynd, schulen not dwelle;

22 so and a dreedful herte in the thouyt of a fool ayenstondith not ayens the feersnesse of drede.

23 As ournyng, ether pargetyng, ful of grauel in a cleer wal, so and a ferdful herte in the thouyt of a fool schal not drede in ony tyme; so and he that dwellith euere in the heestis of God.

24 He that prickith the iye, schal leede out teeris; and he that prickith the herte, bryngith forth wit.

25 He that castith a stoon to briddis, schal caste doun tho; so and he that doith wrong to a frend, departith frenschipe.

26 Thouy thou bryngist forth a swerd to a frend, dispeire thou not; for ther is going ayen to the frend.

27 If he openeth a soreuful mouth, drede thou not; for whi ther is acordyng, outakun dispisynge, and schenschipe, and pride, and schewyng of preuyte, and a tretcherouse wounde; in alle these thingis a frend schal fle awei.

28 Haue thou feith with a frend in his pouert, that thou be glad also in hise goodis.

29 In the tyme of his tribulacioun dwelle thou feithful to hym, that also thou be euene eir in the eritage of hym.

30 Heete and smook of fier is maad hiy bifore the fier of a chymenei; so and cursyngis, and dispisyngis, and manaassis, comen bifore blood.

31 I schal not be aschamed for to grete a frend, and Y schal not hide me fro his face; thouy yuels comen to me bi hym, Y schal suffre.

32 Ech man that schal here, schal kepe warli hym silf fro hym.

33 Who schal yyue keping to my mouth, and a certeyn ceelyng on my lippis, that Y falle not bi tho, and that my tunge leese not me?

CAP 23

1 Lord, fadir, and lordli gouernour of my lijf, forsake thou me not in the thouyt and counsel of hem; nether suffre thou me to falle in that schenschipe.

2 Who settith aboue in my thouyt beetyngis, and in myn hert the techyng of wisdom, that in the vnkunnyngis of hem he spare not me, and that the trespassis of hem appere not?

3 Lest myn vnkunnyngis encreesse, and my trespassis be multiplied, and my synnes be plenteuouse; and lest Y falle in the siyt of myn aduersaries, and myn enemy haue ioie.

4 Lord, fadir, and God of my lijf, forsake thou not me in the thouyt of hem.

5 Yyue thou not to me enhaunsyng of myn iyen; and turne thou awei fro me al schrewid desijr.

6 Do thou awei fro me the coueitisis of the wombe, and the coueitisis of letcherie take me not; and yyue thou not 'me to a soule vnreuerent and vndiscreet.

7 Sones, here ye the techyng of mouth; and he that kepith it, schal not perische bi hise lippis, nether schal be

8 sclaundrid in worste werkis A synnere and proude man schal be takun in his vanite; and a cursid man schal be sclaundrid in tho.

9 Thy mouth be not customable to swering; for whi many fallyngis ben ther ynne.

10 Forsothe the nemyng of God be not customable in thi mouth, and be thou not meddlid to the names of seyntis; for thou schalt not be giltles of hem.

11 For as a seruaunt that is axid bisili, schal not wante wannesse; so ech man swerynge and nemynge schal not be purgid of synne in al.

12 A man swerynge myche schal be fillid with wickidnesse; and veniaunce schal not go awei fro his hous.

13 And if he disseyueth a brother, his trespas schal be aboue hym; and if he feyneth, he schal trespasse doubli.

14 And if he swerith in veyn, he schal not be iustified; for whi his hous schal be fillid with worst yelding.

15 Also ayenward another speche is in to deth; be it not found in the eritage of Jacob.

16 For whi alle these thingis schulen be don awei fro merciful men; and thei schulen not delite in trespassis.

17 Thi mouth be not customable to vnreuerent speche; for whi a word of synne is in it.

18 Haue thou mynde on thi fadir and modir; for thou stondist in the myddis of grete men.

19 Lest perauenture God foryete thee in the siyt of hem; and lest thou maad a fool bi thi customablenesse, suffre schenschipe, and haddist leuere to be not borun, and curse the dai of thi birthe.

20 A man customable in the wordis of schenschipe, in alle daies schal not be tauyt.

21 Twei kyndis ben plenteuouse in synnes, and the thridde bringith ire and perdicioun.

22 An hoot soule brennynge as fier schal not be quenchid, til it swolewe sum thing;

23 and a wickid man in the mouth of his fleisch schal not faile, til he kyndle fier.

24 Ech breed is swete to a letcherouse man; he schal not be maad weri, trespassynge 'til to the ende.

25 Ech man that passith his bed, doith dispit ayens his soule, and seith, Who seeth me?

26 Derknessis cumpassen me, and wallis kyueren me, and no man biholdith me. Whom drede Y? The hiyeste schal not haue mynde on my synnes.

27 And he vndirstondith not, that the iye of him seeth alle thingis; for whi the drede of siche a man puttith awei fro him the drede of God, and the iyen of men that dreden hym putten awei fro hym Goddis drede.

28 And he knew not, that the iyen of the Lord ben myche more clerere than the sunne, and biholden alle the weies of men, and the depthe of the see, and biholden the hertis of men in to hid partis.

29 For whi alle thingis weren knowun to the Lord, bifore that thei weren maad of nouyt; so and aftir the makyng he biholdith alle thingis.

30 This man schal be punyschid in the stretis of the citee; he schal be dryuun a wei as an horse colt, and he schal be takun, where he hopith not.

31 And he schal be schenschip to alle men; for he vndurstood not the drede of the Lord.

32 So and ech womman forsakynge hir hosebonde schal do synne, and ordeynynge eritage of an alien matrimonye.

33 For firste sche was vnbileueful in the lawe of the hiyeste; and the secounde tyme sche forsook hir hosebonde; and the thridde tyme sche was defoulid in auowtrie, and ordeynede to hym sones of another man.

34 'This womman schal be brouyt in to the chirche, and me schal biholde on hir sones.

35 Hir sones schulen not yyue rootis, and hir braunchis schulen not yyue fruyt.

36 Thei schulen leeue the mynde of hir in to cursyng, and the schenschipe of hir schal not be don awei.

37 And thei that ben left schulen knowe, that no thing is betere than the drede of God, and nothing is swettere than to biholde in the comaundementis of the Lord.

38 It is greet glorie to sue the Lord; for whi lengthe of daies schulen be takun of hym.

CAP 24

1 Wisdom schal preise his soule, and he schal be onourid in God; and he schal haue glorie in the myddis of his puple.

2 And he schal opene his mouth in the chirchis of the hiyeste; and he schal haue glorie in the siyt of his vertu.

3 And he schal be enhaunsid in the myddis of his puple; and he schal wondre in hooli plentee.

4 And in the multitude of chosun men he schal haue preisyng; and among blessid men he schal be blessid,

5 and seie, I, the firste gendrid bifore ech creature, cam forth fro the mouth of the hiyeste.

6 I made in heuenes, that liyt neuere failynge roos vp, and as a cloude Y hilide al erthe.

7 Y dwellide in hiyeste thingis, and my trone in a piler of cloude.

8 Y aloone yede aboute the cumpas of heuene, and Y perside the depthe of the see; and Y yede in the wawis of the see,

9 and Y stood in al the lond.

10 And Y hadde the firste dignite in ech puple, and in ech folk;

11 and Y trad bi vertu on the neckis of alle excelent men and meke; and in alle these men Y souyte reste, and Y schal dwelle in the eritage of the Lord.

12 Thanne the creatour of alle comaundide, and seide to me; and he that formyde me, restide in my tabernacle; and he seide to me,

13 Dwelle thou in Jacob, and take thou eritage in Israel, and sende thou rootis in my chosun men.

14 Y was gendrid of the bigynnyng and bifore worldis, and Y schal not faile 'til to the world to comynge; and Y mynystride in an hooli dwellyng bifore hym.

15 And so Y was maad stidfast in Syon, and in lijk maner Y restide in a citee halewid, and my power was in Jerusalem.

16 And Y rootid in a puple onourid; and the eritage therof in to the partis of my God, and my witholding in the plentee of seyntis.

17 Y was enhaunsid as a cedre in Liban, and as a cipresse tree in the hil of Syon.

18 Y was enhaunsid as a palm tree in Cades, and as the plauntyng of roose in Jeryco.

19 As a fair olyue tree in feeldis; and Y was enhaunsid as a plane tree bisidis watir in stretis.

20 As canel and bawme yyuynge greet smelle, Y yaf odour; as chosun myrre Y yaf the swetnesse of odour.

21 And as storax, and galban, and vngula, and gumme, and as Liban not kit doun, Y made hoot my dwellyng place; and myn odour as bawme not meddlid.

22 Y as a terebynte stretchide forth my boowis; and my boowis ben boowis of onour, and of glorie.

23 Y as a vyne made fruyt the swetnesse of odour; and my flouris ben the fruytis of onour, and of oneste.

24 I am a modir of fair loue, and of drede, and of knowyng, and of hooli hope.

25 In me is al grace of weie, and of treuthe; in me is al hope of lijf and of vertu.

26 Alle ye that coueiten me, passe to me; and be ye fillid of my generaciouns.

27 For whi my spirit is swete aboue hony; and myn eritage is aboue hony, and hony comb.

28 My mynde is in the generacioun of worldis.

29 Thei that eten me, schulen hungre yit; and thei that drynken me, schulen thirste yit.

30 He that herith me, shal not be schent; and thei that worchen in me, schulen not do synne; and thei that declaren me,

31 schulen haue euere lastynge lijf.

32 Alle these thingis is the book of lijf, and the testament of the hiyeste, and the knowyng of treuthe.

33 Moises comaundide a lawe in the comaundementis of riytfulnessis, and eritage to the hous of Jacob, and biheestis to Israel.

34 He settide to Dauid, his child, to reise of hym a kyng moost strong, and sittynge with outen ende in the trone of onour.

35 Which kyng fillith wisdom, as Phison schedith out watir; and as Tigris in the daies of newe thingis.

36 Which, as Eufrates, fillith wit; which multiplieth, as Jordan in the tyme of heruest.

37 Which sendith techyng as liyt; and is niy alle men, as Gion in the dai of vendage.

38 Which makith perfitli first to knowe that wisdom; and a feblere man schal not enserche it.

39 For whi the thouyt therof schal be plenteuouse of the see; and his counsel in the greet occian.

40 Y wisdom schedde out floodis;

41 Y as a weie of ful greet watir of the flood. Y as the flood Dorix, and as a watir cundit Y yede out of paradis.

42 Y seide, I schal watir my gardyn of plauntyngis; and Y schal greetli fille the fruyt of my child beryng.

43 And lo! a plenteuouse weie of watir is maad to me; and my flood neiyede to the see.

44 For Y liytne techyng as the cheer morewtid to alle men; and Y schal telle out it 'til to fer.

45 Y schal perse alle the lowere partis of erthe, and Y schal biholde alle that slepen; and Y schal liytne alle that hopen in the Lord.

46 Yit Y schal schede out teching as profesie, and Y schal leeue it to hem that seken wisdom; and Y schal not faile in to the generaciouns of hem, til in to the hooli world.

47 Se ye, that Y trauelide not to me aloone, but to alle that seken out treuthe.

CAP 25

1 In thre thingis it is plesid to my spirit, which ben appreued bifore God and men; acordyng of britheren,

2 and loue of neiyboris, a man and womman wel consentynge to hem silf.

3 My soule hatide thre spicis, and Y am greued greetli to the soule of hem;

4 a pore man proud, and a riche man liere, and an eld man a fool and vnwitti.

5 Hou schalt thou fynde in thin eelde tho thingis, whiche thou gaderist not in thi yongthe?

6 Doom is ful fair in hoornesse, and to preestis to knowe councel.

7 Wisdom is ful fair to eelde men, and gloriouse vndirstondyng, and councel.

8 The coroun of eelde men is in myche kunnyng; and the glorie of hem is the drede of God.

9 I magnefiede nyne thingis vnsuspect of the herte; and Y schal seie the tenthe thing bi tunge to men.

10 A man which lyuynge is myrie in sones, and seynge the distriyng of hise enemyes.

11 He is blissid that dwellith with a witty womman, and he that felle not bi his tunge, and he that seruyde not to men vnworthi to hym silf.

12 He is blessid that fyndith a very frend, and he that tellith out riytfulnesse to an eere heringe.

13 He is ful greet that fyndith wisdom and kunnyng; but he is not aboue him that dredith God.

14 The drede of God hath set it silf aboue alle thingis.

15 Blessid is the man to whom it is youun to have the drede of God; to whom schal he be licned, that holdith that drede?

16 The drede of God is the bigynnyng of his loue; forsothe the bigynnyng of feith is to be faste ioyned therto.

17 The sorewe of herte is ech wounde; and the wickidnesse of a womman is al malice.

18 A leche shal se ech wounde, and not the wounde of herte; and al wickidnesse,

19 and not the wickidnesse of a womman;

20 and ech hilyng, and not hilyng of hateris;

21 and ech veniaunce, and not the veniaunce of enemyes.

22 Noon heed is worse than the heed of an eddre dwellynge in schadewe;

23 and noon ire is aboue the ire of a womman. It schal plese more to dwelle with a lioun and a dragoun, than to dwelle with a wickid womman.

24 The wickidnesse of a womman chaungith hir face; and sche blyndide her cheer as a beer doith, and sche schal schewe as a sak in the myddis of neiyboris.

25 Hir hosebonde weilide; and his wickid wijf herde, and siyyide a litil.

26 Al malice is schort on the malice of a womman; the parte of synneris falle on hir.

27 As a stiynge ful of grauel in the feet of an elde man, so is a womman a greet ianglere to a pesible man.

28 Biholde thou not the fairnesse of a womman, and coueyte thou not a womman for fairnesse.

29 The ire and vnreuerence of a womman is grete schens-chipe.

30 If a womman hath the firste dignyte, ethir cheef gouernail, sche is contrarie to hir hosebonde.

31 A low herte, and soreuful face, and wounde of deeth, is a wickid womman.

32 Feble hondis and knees vnboundun, a womman that blessith not hir hosebonde.

33 The bygynnyng of synne was maad of a womman; and alle we dien bi hir.

34 Yyue thou not issu to thi watir, yhe, not a litil issu; nether to a wickid womman fredom of goyng forth.

35 If sche goith not at thin hond, sche schal schende thee in the siyt of enemyes.

36 Kitte hir a wei fro thi fleischis, lest euere sche mysvse thee.

CAP 26

1 The hosebonde of a good womman is blessid; for whi the noumbre of her yeeris is double.

2 A strong womman delitith hir hosebonde; and shal fille in pees the yeeris of his lijf.

3 A good womman is a good part; in the good part of hem that dreden God, sche schal be youun to a man for goode dedis.

4 Forsothe the herte of a riche man and of a pore man is good; in al tyme her cheer is glad.

5 Myn herte dredde of thre thingis, and my face dredde in the fourthe thing.

6 Bitraiyng of a citee, and the gadering togidere of puple,

7 and fals chaleng; alle thingis greuouse on deth.

8 The sorewe of herte, and morenyng is a ielouse womman.

9 In a gelouse womman is betyng of tunge, and sche comyneth with alle men.

10 As a yok of oxis which is mouyd, so and a wickid womman; he that holdith hir, is as he that takith a scorpioun.

11 A drunkelew womman is greet ire, and dispisyng; and hir filthe schal not be hilid.

12 The fornycacioun of a womman is in the reisyng of yyen; and schal be knowun in the iye liddis of hir.

13 Make thou sad kepyng in a douytir not turnynge a wei hir silf; lest sche mysvse hir silf, if sche fyndith occasioun.

14 Be thou war of al vnreuerence of hir iyen; and wondre thou not, if sche dispisith thee.

15 As a weiegoere thirstynge schal opene the mouth at a welle, and schal drynke of ech watir next; and the forseid douytir schal sitte ayens ech pale, and schal opene the arowe caas ayens ech arowe, til sche faile.

16 The grace of a bisi womman schal delite hir hosebonde; and schal make fat hise boonus.

17 The kunnyng of hir is the yifte of God.

18 A wijs womman and stille is not chaungyng of a lernyd soule.

19 Grace on grace is an hooli womman, and schamfast.

20 Forsothe al weiyng is not worth a contynent soule.

21 As the sunne risynge in the world in the hiyeste thingis of God, so the fairnesse of a good womman is in to the ourne-ment of hir hous.

22 A lanterne schynynge on an hooli candilstike, and the fair-nesse of a face on stidfast age.

23 Goldun pileris on siluerne foundementis, and stidfast feet on the soolis of a stidfast womman.

24 Euerlastynge foundementis on a sad stoon, and the heestis of God in the herte of an hooli womman.

CAP 27

25 In twei thingis myn herte was maad sori, and in the thridde thing wrathfulnesse cam to me.

26 A man a werriour failynge bi nedynesse, and a wijs man dispisid.

27 And God hath maad hym redi to the swerd, that passith ouer fro riytfulnesse to synne.

28 Twei spices apperiden harde and perilouse to me; a mar-chaunt is delyuered of hard fro his necgligence, and a tauerner schal not be iustified of synnes of lippis.

1 Many men han trespassid for nedynesse; and he that sekith to be maad riche, turneth a wei his iye.

2 As a stake is fastned in the myddis of a heep of stoonys, so and a man schal be angwischid bi synnes bitwixe the middis of sillyng and biyng.

3 Trespas schal be al to-brokun with hym that trespassith.

4 If thou holdist not thee diligentli in the drede of the Lord, thin hous schal soone be turned vpsedoun.

5 As dust schal dwelle in the hoolis of a riddil, so the ang-wisch of a man schal dwelle in the thouyt of hym.

6 A furneis preueth the vessels of a pottere; and the tempta-cioun of tribulacioun preueth iust men.

7 As cherliche trauel aboute a tree schewith the fruyt therof, so a word of thouyt schewith the herte of man.

8 Preise thou not a man bifore a word; for whi this is the temptacioun of men.

9 If thou suest riytfulnesse, thou schalt take it; thou schalt clothe it as a long cloth of onour, and thou schalt dwelle with it, and it schal defende thee with outen ende, and in the dai of knowing thou shalt fynde stidfastnesse.

10 Volatilis comen togidere to briddis lijk hem silf; and treuthe schal turne ayen to hem that worchen it.

11 A lioun settith aspies euere to huntyng; so synnes to hem that worchen wickidnesse.

12 An hooly man dwellith in wisdom, as the sunne dwellith stabli; for whi a fool is chaungid as the moone.

13 In the myddis of vnwise men kepe thou a word to tyme; but be thou bisi in the myddis of hem that thenken the lawe of God.

14 The tellyng of synneris is hateful; and the leiyyng of hem is in the trespassis of synne.

15 Speche sweringe myche schal make stondyng up of heeris, for astonying, to the heed; and vnreuerence therof is stoppyng of eeris.

16 The schedyng out of blood is in the chidyng of proude men; and the cursyng of hem is greuouse heryng.

17 He that schewith opynli the priuytees of a frend, leesith feithfulnesse; and he schal not fynde a frend to his soule.
18 Loue thou a neiybore, and be thou ioyned with hym in feith.
19 For if thou schewist opynli the priuytees of hym, thou schalt not perfitli sue aftir hym.
20 For as a man that leesith his frend, so he that leesith the frenschipe of his neiybore.
21 And as a man that latith go a brid fro his hond, so thou that hast forsake thi neiybore, and thou schalt not take hym.
22 Thou schalt not sue hym, for he is fer absent; for he ascapid as a capret fro a snare, for the soule of hym is woundid.
23 Thou schalt no more mow bynde hym togidere; but of yuel seiyng is acordyng.
24 Sotheli to schewe opynli the pryuytees of a frend, is dispeir of a soule vnblessid.
25 He that twynclith with the iye, makith wickid thingis;
26 and no man schal caste hym awei. In the siyt of thin iyen he schal defoule his mouth, and he schal wondre on thi wordis; but at the laste he schal turne weiwerdli his mouth, and in his wordis he schal yyue sclaundre.
27 Y herde mani thingis, and Y made not euene to hym; and the Lord schal hate hym.
28 If a man throwith a stoon an hiy, it schal falle on his heed; and the gileful wounde of a gyleful man schal departe woundis.
29 And he that diggith a diche, schal falle in to it; and he that settith a stoon to a neiybore, schal offende therynne; and he that settith a snare to a nother man, schal perische ther ynne.
30 If a man makith worst councel, it schal be turned on hym; and he schal not knowe fro whennus it schal come to him.
31 The scornyng and dispisyng of proude men and veniaunce schal sette a spie to hym, as a lioun doith.
32 Thei that deliten in the fal of iust men, schulen perische bi a snare; forsothe sorewe schal waste hem, bifore that thei dien.
33 Ire and woodnesse, euer either ben abhomynable; and a synful man schal holde tho.

CAP 28

1 He that wole be vengid, schal fynde of the Lord veniaunce; and he kepynge schal kepe hise synnes.
2 Foryyue thou to thi neiybore that anoieth thee, and thanne synnes schulen be releessid to thee preiynge.
3 A man kepith ire to man; and sekith he of God medicyn?
4 He hath no merci on a man lijk hym silf; and bisechith he the hiyeste for hise owne synnes?
5 He the while he is fleisch, reserueth ire; and axith he of God merci? who schal preie for hise synnes?
6 Haue thou mynde on the laste thingis, and ceesse thou to be enemy.
7 For whi failyng and deth neiyen not in the comaundementis of God.
8 Haue thou mynde on the drede of the Lord, and be thou not wrooth to the neiybore.
9 Haue thou mynde on the testament of the hiyeste, and dispise thou the ignoraunce of thi neiybore.
10 Absteyne thee fro strijf, and thou schalt abregge synnes.
11 For whi a wrathful man kyndlith strijf; and a synful man schal disturble frendis, and he schal sende in enemyte in the myddis of men hauynge pees.

12 For whi aftir the trees of the wode, so fier schal brenne an hiy; and after the myyte of a man, so his wrathfulnesse schal be, and aftir his catel he schal enhaunse his ire.
13 Hasti stryuyng schal kyndle fier, and hasti chidyng schal schede out blood; and a tunge berynge witnessing schal brynge deth.
14 If thou blowist, as fier it schal brenne an hiy; and if thou spetist theron, it schal be quenchid; euer either comen forth of the mouth.
15 A preuy bacbiter, and a double tungid man is cursid; for he disturblide many men hauynge pees.
16 The thridde tunge hath stirid many men, and hath scaterid hem fro folc in to folc.
17 It hath distried wallid citees of riche men, and hath myned doun the housis of grete men.
18 It hath kit doun the vertues of puplis, and hath vnknit strong folkis.
19 The thridde tunge hath cast out weddid wymmen, and hath priued hem of her trauelis.
20 He that biholdith the thridde tunge, schal not haue rest; nether schal haue a frend, in whom he schal reste.
21 The wounde of betyng makith wannesse; but the wounde of tunge schal make lesse the boonys.
22 Many men fellen doun bi the scharpnesse of swerd; but not so as thei that perischiden bi her tunge.
23 He is blessid that is kyuerid fro a wickid tunge; and he that passide not in the wrathfulnesse therof, and he that drow not the yok therof, and was not boundun in the bondis therof.
24 For whi the yok therof is an irun yok, and the boond therof is a brasun boond.
25 The deth therof is the worste deth; and helle is more profitable than it.
26 The perseueraunce therof schal not dwelle, but it schal holde the weies of vniust men; in his flawme it schal not brenne iust men.
27 Thei that forsaken God, schulen falle in to it; and it schal brenne greetli in hem, and it schal not be quenchid; and as a lioun it schal be sent in to hem, and as a parde it schal hirte hem.
28 Bisette thin eeris with thornes, and nyle thou here a wickid tunge; and make thou doris to thi mouth, and lockis to thin eeris.
29 Welle thou togidere thi gold, and thi siluer; and make thou a balaunce to thi wordis, and riytful bridels to thi mouth.
30 And take heede, lest perauenture thou slide in tunge, and falle in the siyt of enemyes, settynge tresoun to thee, and thi falle be vncurable in to deth.

CAP 29

1 He that doith merci, leeneth to his neiybore; and he that is ful myyti in hond, kepith the comaundementis.
2 Leene thou to thi neiybore in the tyme of his nede; and eft yelde thou to a neiybore in his tyme.
3 Conferme thou a word, and do thou feithfuli with hym; and in al tyme thou schalt fynde that, that is nedeful to thee.
4 Many men gessiden borewyng as fyndyng, and yauen disese to tho men that helpiden hem.
5 Til thei taken, thei kissen the hondis of the yyuer; and in biheestis thei maken meke her vois.
6 And in the time of yelding he schal axe tyme, and he schal speke wordis of anoie, and of grutchingis, and he schal calenge falsli the tyme.

7 Forsothe if he mai yelde, he schal be aduersarie; of a schilling vnnethis he schal yelde the half, and he schal rekyn that as fyndyng.

8 Ellis he schal defraude him in his monei, and the leenere schal haue him an enemy with outen cause.

9 And he schal yelde to hym, that is, to the leenere, wrongis and cursyngis; and for onour and benefice he schal yelde to hym dispisyng.

10 Many men lenten not 'to pore neiyboris, not for cause of wickidnesse, but thei dredden to be defraudid with outen cause.

11 Netheles on a meke man in soule be thou strongere; and for almes drawe thou not hym.

12 For the comaundement of God take thou a pore man; and for his nedynesse leeue thou not hym voide.

13 Leese thou monei for a brother and frend, and hide thou not it vndur a stoon, in to perdicioun.

14 Putte thi tresour in the comaundementis of the hiyeste; and it schal profite to thee more than gold 'schal profite.

15 Close thou almes in the bosum of a pore man; and this almes schal preye for thee 'to be delyuered of God fro al yuel.

16 The almes of a man is as a bagge with hym; and it schal kepe the grace of man as the appil of the iye.

17 And aftirward it schal rise ayen, and schal yelde to hem a yelding, to ech man in to the heed of hem.

18 Aboue a scheld of the myyti man, and aboue a spere it schal fiyte ayens thin enemye.

19 A good man makith feith to his neiybore; and he that leesith, schal leeue schame to hym.

20 Foryete thou not the grace of the borewe; for he yaf his lijf for thee.

21 A synful man and vncleene fleeth the biheetere.

22 A synnere arretteth to hym silf the goode wordis of the borowe; and the vnkynde man in wit forsakith a man delyuerynge hym.

23 A man biheetith for his neiybore; and whanne 'the neiybore hath lost reuerence, the borew schal be forsakun of hym.

24 Worst biheest hath lost many louynge men, and hath moued hem as the wawis of the see.

25 It goynge in cumpas made myyti men to passe ouer; and thei wandriden aboute among alien folkis.

26 A synnere brekynge the comaundement of the Lord schal falle in to a wickid biheest; and he that enforsith to do many thingis, schal falle in to dom.

27 Rekiuere thi neiybore bi thi vertu; and take heed to thi silf, lest thou falle.

28 The bigynnyng of lijf of a man is watir, and breed, and clothing, and hous hilynge filthe.

29 Betere is the lijflode of a pore man vndur the hilyng of sparris, than schynynge feestis in pilgrymage with outen hous.

30 The leeste thing pleese thee for a greet thing; and thou schalt not here the schenschipe of pilgrymage.

31 It is wickid lijf to seke herbore fro hous in to hous; and where he schal be herborid, he schal not do tristili, nethir he schal opene the mouth.

32 He schal be herborid, and he schal feede, and yyue drinke to vnkynde men; and yit he schal here bittir thingis.

33 Passe, thou that art herborid, and araye a table; and yyue thou meetis to othere men, tho thingis that thou hast in the hond.

34 Go thou out fro the face of the onour of my frendis, for the frendschipe, ethir affinyte, of myn hous; bi herboryng thou art maad a brother to me.

35 These thingis ben greuouse to a man hauynge wit; the repreuyng of hous, and the dispising of the vsurer.

CAP 30

1 He that loueth his sone, yyueth bisili betingis to hym, that he be glad in hise laste thing, and that the sone touche not the doris of neiyboris.

2 He that techith his sone, schal be preisid in hym; and schal haue glorie in hym in the myddis of menyals.

3 He that techith his sone, sendith the enemye in to enuye; and in the myddis of frendis he schal haue glorie in that sone.

4 The fadir of hym is deed, and he is as not deed; for he hath left aftir hym a sone lijk hym.

5 He siy in his lijf, and was glad in hym; and in his deth he was not sori, nether was aschamed bifore enemyes.

6 For he lefte a defendere of the hous ayens enemyes; and yeldynge grace to frendis.

7 For the soulis of sones he schal bynde togidere hise woundis; and hise entrails schulen be disturblid on ech vois.

8 An hors vntemyd, 'ether vnchastisid, schal ascape hard, and a sone vnchastisid schal ascape heedi.

9 Flatere thou the sone, and he schal make thee dredinge; pleie thou with hym, and he schal make thee sory.

10 Leiye thou not with hym, lest thou haue sorewe togidere, and at the laste thi teeth schulen be astonyed.

11 Yyue thou not power to hym in yongthe, and dispise thou not hise thouytis.

12 Boowe thou his necke in yongthe, and bete thou hise sidis, while he is a yong child; lest perauenture he wexe hard, and bileue not to thee, and he schal be sorewe of soule to thee.

13 Teche thi sone, and worche in hym; lest thou offende in to the filthe of hym.

14 Betere is a pore man hool, and strong in myytis, than a riche man feble, and betun with malice.

15 The helthe of soule is in the hoolynesse of riytfulnesse, and it is betere than ony gold and siluer; and a strong bodi is betere than ful myche catel.

16 No catel is aboue the catel of helthe of bodi; and no likyng is aboue the ioie of herte.

17 Betere is deth than bittir lijf, and euerlastinge reste is betere than siknesse dwellynge contynueli.

18 Goodis hid in a closid mouth ben as settyngis forth of metis set aboute a sepulcre.

19 What schal sacrifice profite to an idol? for whi it schal not ete, nether schal smelle.

20 So he that is dryuun awei fro the Lord, and berith the medis of wickidnesse,

21 seynge with iyen and weilynge inwardli, as a geldynge biclippynge a virgyn, and siyyynge.

22 Yyue thou not sorewe to thi soule, and turmente not thi silf in thi counsel.

23 Mirthe of herte, this is the lijf of man, and is tresour of hoolynesse with outen failyng; and ful out ioiyng of a man is long lijf.

24 Haue thou mercy on thi soule, and plese thou God; and holde togidere and gadere togidere thin herte in the hoolynesse of hym, and putte fer awei sorewe fro thee.

25 For whi sorewe hath slayn many men; and noon heelthe is ther ynne.

26 Enuye and wrathfulnesse schulen make lesse daies; and thouytys schulen brynge eldnesse bifore the tyme.

27 A schynynge herte is good in metis; for whi meetis therof ben maad diligentli.

CAP 31

1 Wakyng of oneste schal make fleischis to faile; and thouyt therof schal take awei sleep.

2 Thouyt of bifore knowyng turneth awey wit; and greuouse siknesse makith sobre the soule.

3 A ryche man trauelide in the gaderyng of catel; and in his reste he schal be fillyd with hise goodis.

4 A pore man trauelide in decreessyng of lijflode; and in the ende he is maad nedi.

5 He that loueth gold, schal not be iustified; and he that sueth wastyng, schal be fillid therof.

6 Many men ben youun in to the fallyngis of gold; and the perdicioun of hem was maad in the feirnesse therof.

7 A tre of offencioun is the gold of hem that maken sacrifice; wo to hem that suen it, and ech vnprudent man schal perische ther ynne.

8 Blissid is a riche man, which is foundun with out wem; and that yede not aftir gold, nether hopide in money, and tresouris.

9 Who is this, and we schulen preyse hym? for he dide merueils in his lijf.

10 Which is preued ther ynne, and is foundun perfit, and euerlastynge glorye schal be to hym? which myyte trespasse, and trespasside not, and do yuels, and dide not.

11 Therfor hise goodis ben stablischid in the Lord; and al the chirche of seyntis schal telle out hise almesdedis.

12 Thou hast sete at a greet boord; opene thou not firste thi cheke on it.

13 Seie thou not, whether tho ben many thingis, that ben on it.

14 Haue thou mynde, that an yuel iye is weiward.

15 What thing worse, than an iye is maad? therfor of al his face he schal wepe, whanne he seeth.

16 Stretche thou not forth first thin hond; and thou defoulid bi enuye, be aschamed.

17 Be thou not oppressid of wyn in a feeste.

18 Vnderstonde of thi silf the thingis, that ben of thi neiybore.

19 Vse thou as a discreet and temperat man these thingis that ben set forth to thee; and be thou not hatid, whanne thou etist myche.

20 Ceesse thou first bicause of lernyng, ethir nurture; and nyle thou be outrageouse, lest perauenture thou offende.

21 And if thou hast sete in the myddis of many men, stretche not forth thin hond sunnere than thei; and axe thou not firste for to drynke.

22 A litil wyn is ful sufficient to a lerned man; and in slepynge thou schalt not trauele for that wyn, and thou schalt not feele trauel.

23 Wakyng, and colre, ether bittir moisture, and gnawyng to an vndiscreet 'either vntemperat man.

24 But the sleep of heelthe is in a scars man; he schal slepe 'til to the morewtid, and his soule schal delite with hym.

25 And if thou art constreyned in etyng myche, ryse thou fro the myddis, and brake thou; and it schal refreische thee, and thou schalt not brynge sikenesse to thi bodi.

26 Sone, here thou me, and dispise thou not me; and at the laste thou schalt fynde my wordis.

27 In alle thi werkis be thou swift; and al sikenesse schal not come to thee.

28 The lippis of many men schulen blesse a schynynge man in looues; and the witnessyng of his treuthe is feithful.

29 The citee schal grutche in the worste breed; and the witnessyng of wickidnesse therof is soth.

30 Nyle thou excite hem that ben diligent in wyn; for whi wyn hath distried many men.

31 Fier preueth hard irun; so wyn drunkun in drunkenesse schal repreue the hertis of proude men.

32 Euene lijf to men is wyn drunkun in sobrenesse; if thou drynkist it mesurably, thou schalt be sobre.

33 What is the lijf which is maad lesse bi wyn?

34 What defraudith lijf? deth.

35 Wyn was maad in gladnesse, not in drunkenesse, at the bigynnyng.

36 Wyn drunkun mesurabli is ful out ioiyng of soule and of bodi.

37 Sobre drynk is helthe of soule and of bodi.

38 Wyn drunkun myche makith avoiding, and ire, and many fallyngis.

39 Wyn drunkun myche is bitternesse of soule.

40 Strengthe of drunkenesse and hirting of an vnprudent man makith vertu lesse, and makynge woundis.

41 In the feeste of wyn repreue thou not a neiybore; and dispise thou not hym in his mirthe.

42 Seye thou not wordis of schenschipe to hym; and oppresse thou not hym in axynge.

CAP 32

1 Thei han set thee a gouernour, nyle thou be enhaunsid; be thou among hem as oon of hem.

2 Haue thou cure of hem, and so biholde thou; and whanne al thi cure is fillid, sitte thou to mete.

3 That thou be glad for hem, and take the ournement of grace; and gete coroun, and dignyte of congregacioun.

4 Speke thou the gretter man in birthe;

5 for whi the word of hym that loueth kunnyng bicome thee first; and lette thou not musik.

6 Where heryng is not, schede thou not out a word; and nyle thou be enhaunsid vncouenabli in thi wisdom.

7 A iemme of carbuncle in the ournement of gold; and comparisoun of musikis in the feeste of wyn.

8 As in the makyng of gold is a signe of smaragde, so the noumbre of musikis is in myrie and mesurable wyn.

9 Here thou stille, and good grace schal come to thee for reuerence.

10 Yonge man, speke thou vnnethis in thi cause, whanne nede is.

11 If thou art axid twies, the heed haue thin answere.

12 In many thingis be thou as vnkunnyng, and here thou stille togidere and axynge.

13 And presume thou not to speke in the myddis of grete men; and where elde men ben, speke thou not myche.

14 Leityng schal go bifore hail, and grace schal go bifore schamfastnesse, and good grace schal come to thee for reuerence.

15 And in the our of risyng tifle thee not; forsothe renne thou bifore first in to thin hous, and there clepe thou thee to answer, and there pleie thou.

16 And do thi conseitis, and not in synnes, and in a proud word.

17 On alle these thingis blesse thou the Lord, that made thee, and fillynge thee greetli of alle hise goodis.

18 He that dredith God, schal take his techyng; and thei that waken to hym, schulen fynde blessyng.

19 He that sekith the lawe, schal be fillid therof; and he that doith tretourousli, schal be sclaundrid ther ynne.

20 Thei that dreden God, schulen fynde iust dom; and schulen kyndle riytfulnesse as liyt.

21 A synful man schal eschewe blamyng; and aftir his wille he schal fynde comparisoun.

22 A man of counsel schal not leese vndirstonding; a man alien and proud schal not drede dredyng.

23 Yhe, aftir that he hath do with that drede with out councel, and he schal be repreued bi hise suyngis.

24 Sone, do thou no thing with out councel; and aftir the dede thou schalt not repente.

25 Go thou not in the weie of fallyng, and offende thou not ayens stoonys. Bitake thou not thee to a trauelouse weie, lest thou sette sclaundir to thi soule;

26 and be thou war of thi sones, and perseyue thou of thi meyneals.

27 In al thi werk bileue thou bi feith of thi soule; for whi this is the keping of comaundementis.

28 He that bileueth to God, takith heede to the comaundementis; and he that tristith in hym, schal not be maad lesse.

CAP 33

1 Iuelis schulen not come to hym that dredith God; but God schal kepe hym in temptacioun, and schal delyuere fro yuelis.

2 A wijs man hatith not the comaundementis, and riytfulnessis; and he schal not be hurtlid doun, as in the tempest of a schip.

3 A wijs man bileeueth to the lawe of God, and the lawe is feithful to hym.

4 He that makith opene axyng, schal make redi a word; and so he schal preie, and schal be herd, and he schal kepe techyng, and thanne he schal answere.

5 The entraylis of a fool ben as a wheel of a carte, and his thouytis as an extre able to turne aboute.

6 An hors a staloun, so and a frend a scornere, neiyeth vndur ech sittynge aboue.

7 Whi a dai ouercometh a dai, and eft the liyt ouercometh liyt, and a yeer ouercometh a yeer, the sunne ouercometh the sunne?

8 Tho ben departid of the kunnyng of the Lord, bi the sunne maad, and kepynge the comaundement of God.

9 And it schal chaunge tymes and the feeste daies of hem, and in tho tymes the Jewis halewiden hali daies at an our.

10 God enhaunside and magnyfiede of tho hali daies; and of tho he settide in to the noumbre of daies; and God made alle men of sad erthe, and of neische erthe, whereof Adam was formed.

11 In the multitude of kunnyng of the Lord he departide hem, and chaungide the weies of hem.

12 Of hem God blesside, and enhaunside; and of hem he halewide, and chees to hym silf; of hem he curside, and made lowe, and turnyde hem fro the departyng of hem.

13 As cley of a pottere is in the hond of hym,

14 to make and dispose, that alle the weies therof ben aftir the ordynaunce of hym; so a man is in the hond of hym that made hym; and he schal yelde to hym bi his dom.

15 Ayens yuel is good, and ayens lijf is deth; so and a synnere is ayens a iust man. And so biholde thou in to alle the werkis of the hiyeste; twey thingis ayens tweyne, and o thing ayens oon.

16 And Y the laste wakide, and as he that gaderith draf of grapis, aftir the gadereris of grapis.

17 And Y hopide in the blessyng of God; and as he that gaderith grapis, Y fillide the pressour.

18 Biholde ye, for Y trauelide not to me aloone, but to alle that seken kunnyng.

19 Grete men, and alle puplis, here ye me; and ye gouernouris of the chirche, perseyue with eeris.

20 Yyue thou not power ouer thee in thi lijf to a sone, and to a womman, to a brothir, and to a freend; and yyue thou not thi possessioun to another man, lest perauenture it repente thee, and thou biseche for tho.

21 While thou art alyue, and brethist yit, ech man schal not chaunge thee.

22 For it is betere, that thi sones preye thee, than that thou biholde in to the hondis of thi sones.

23 In alle thi werkis be thou souereyn;

24 yyue thou not a wem in to thi glorie. In the day of endyng of daies of thi lijf, and in tyme of thi goyng out departe thin erytage.

25 Metis, and a yerde, and birthun to an asse; breed, and chastisyng, and werk to a seruaunt.

26 He worchith in chastisyng, and sekith to haue reste; slake thou hondis to hym, and he sekith fredom.

27 A yok and bridil bowen doun an hard necke; and bisi worchingis bowen doun a seruaunt.

28 Turment and stockis to an yuel willid seruaunt; sende thou hym in to worchyng, lest he be ydel;

29 for whi idilnesse hath tauyte miche malice.

30 Ordeyne thou hym in werk, for so it bicometh hym; that if he obeieth not, bowe thou doun hym in stockis, and make thou not hym large ouer ony man, but with out dom do thou no thing greuouse.

31 If a feithful seruaunt is to thee, be he as thi soule to thee; trete thou him so as a brother, for thou hast bouyt hym in the blood of lijf.

32 If thou hurtist hym vniustli, he schal be turned in to fleyng awei;

33 and if he enhaunsynge goith awei, thou noost whom thou schalt seke, and in what weie thou schalt seke hym.

CAP 34

1 Veyn hope and a leesyng to an vnwijs man; and dremes enhaunsen vnprudent men.

2 As he that takith schadewe, and pursueth wynd, so and he that takith heede to leesyngis seyn.

3 Vpe this thing is the siyt of dremes; bifore the face of a man is the licnesse of another man.

4 What schal be clensid of him that is vnclene, and what trewe thing schal be seid of a liere?

5 Fals dyuynyng of errour, and fals dyuynyngis bi chiteryng of briddis, and dremes of witchis, is vanyte.

6 And as the herte of a womman trauelynge of child, thin herte suffrith fantasies; no but visitacioun is sent out of the hiyeste, yyue thou not thin herte in tho dremes.

7 For whi dremes han maad many men for to erre, and men hopynge in tho fellen doun.

8 The word of the lawe 'of God and of hise profetis, schal be maad perfit with out leesyng; and wisdom in the mouth of a feithful man schal be maad pleyn.

9 What kan he, that is not asaied? A man asaied in many thingis, schal thenke many thingis; and he that lernyde many thingis, schal telle out vndirstondyng.

10 He that is not asaied, knowith fewe thingis; forsothe he that is a fool in many thingis, schal multiplie malice.

11 What maner thingis kan he, that is not asaied? He that is not plauntid, schal be plenteuouse in wickidnesse.

12 I siy many thingis in tellyng out, and ful many customs of wordis.

13 Sum tyme Y was in perel 'til to deth, for the cause of these thingis; and Y was delyuered bi the grace of God.

14 The spirit of hem that dreden God is souyt, and schal be blessid in the biholding of hym.

15 For whi the hope of hem is in to God sauynge hem; and the iyen of the Lord ben in to hem, that louen hym.

16 He that dredith God, schal not tremble for ony thing, and he schal not drede; for whi God is his hope.

17 The soule of hym that dredith the Lord, is blessid.

18 To whom biholdith he, and who is his strengthe?

19 The iyen of the Lord ben on hem that dreden hym. God is a defendere of myyt, stidfastnesse of vertu, hilyng of heete, and a schadewyng place of myddai;

20 bisechyng of offendyng, and help of fallyng, enhaunsynge the soule, and liytnynge the iyen, and yyuynge heelthe, and lijf, and blessyng.

21 The offryng of hym that offrith of wickid thing, is defoulid; and the scornyngis of vniust men ben not wel plesaunt.

22 The Lord aloone is to hem that abiden hym in the weie of treuthe, and of riytfulnesse.

23 The hiyeste appreueth not the yiftis of wickid men, nethir biholdith in the offryngis of wickid men, nether in the multitude of her sacrifices he schal do mercy to synnes.

24 He that offrith sacrifice of the catel of pore men, is as he that sleeth the sone in the siyt of his fadir.

25 The breed of nedi men is the lijf of a pore man; he that defraudith hym, is a man of blood.

26 He that takith awei breed in swoot, is as he that sleeth his neiybore.

27 He that schedith out blood, and he that doith fraude to an hirid man, ben britheren.

28 Oon bildynge, and oon distriynge; what profitith it to hem, no but trauel?

29 Oon preiynge, and oon cursynge; whos vois schal the Lord here?

30 What profitith the waischyng of hym, that is waischun for a deed bodi, and touchith eft a deed bodi?

31 So a man that fastith in hise synnes, and eft doynge the same synnes, what profitith he in mekynge hym silf? who schal here his preyer?

CAP 35

1 He that kepith the word, multiplieth preier.

2 Heelful sacrifice is to take heede to the comaundementis, and to departe fro al wickidnesse.

3 And to offre the plesyng of sacrifice for vnriytfulnesses, and bisechyng for synnes, is to go awey fro vnriytfulnesse.

4 He that offrith purest flour of wheete, schal yelde grace; and he that doith merci, offrith a sacrifice.

5 It is wel plesaunt to the Lord, to go awei fro wickidnesse; and preier is to go awei fro vnriytfulnesse.

6 Thou schalt not appere voide bifore the siyt of God;

7 for whi alle these thingis ben doon for the heestis of God.

8 The offryng of a iust man makith fat the auter, and is odour of swetnesse in the siyt of the hiyeste.

9 The sacrifice of a iust man is acceptable, and the Lord schal not foryete the mynde of hym.

10 With good wille yelde thou glorie to God, and make thou not lesse the firste fruytis of thin hondis.

11 In ech yifte make glad thi cheer, and in ful out ioiyng halewe thi tithis.

12 Yyue thou to the hiyeste aftir his yifte; and with good iye make thou the fyndyng of thin hondis.

13 For whi the Lord is a yeldere, and he schal yelde seuene fold so myche to thee.

14 Nyle thou offre schrewid yiftis; for he schal not resseyue tho.

15 And nyle thou biholde an vniust sacrifice; for the Lord is iuge, and glorie of persoone is not at hym.

16 The Lord schal not take a persoone ayens a pore man; and he schal here the preier of hym that is hirt.

17 He schal not dispise the preyeris of a fadirles child, nether a widewe, if sche schedith out speche of weilyng.

18 Whether the teeris of a widew goen not doun to the cheke, and the criyng of hir on hym that ledith forth tho teeris?

19 For whi tho stien fro the cheke 'til to heuene, and the Lord herere schal not delite in tho.

20 He that worschipith God in delityng, schal be resseyued; and his preyer schal neiye 'til to the clowdis.

21 The preier of hym that mekith hym silf perse clowdis, and til it neiyeth, he schal not be coumfortid, and he schal not go awey, til the hiyeste biholde.

22 And the Lord schal not be fer, but he schal iuge iust men, and schal make doom; and the strongeste schal not haue pacience in tho, that he troble the bak of hem.

23 And he schal yelde veniaunce to folkis, til he take awei the fulnesse of proude men, and troble togidere the ceptris of wickid men;

24 til he yelde to men aftir her dedis, and aftir the werkis of Adam, and aftir the presumpcioun of hym;

25 til he deme the dome of his puple, and schal delite iust men in his merci.

26 The merci of God is fair in the tyme of tribulacioun, as clowdis of reyn in the tyme of drynesse.

CAP 36

1 God of alle thingis, haue thou merci on vs; and biholde thou vs, and schewe thou to vs the liyt of thi merciful doyngis.

2 And sende thi drede on hethene men, that souyten not thee, that thei knowe that no God is, no but thou; that thei telle out thi grete dedis.

3 Reise thin hond on hethene men aliens, that thei se thi power.

4 For as thou were halewid in vs in the siyt of hem, so in oure siyt thou schalt be magnefyed in hem;

5 that thei knowe thee, as and we han knowe, that noon othere is God, outakun thee, Lord.

6 Make thou newe signes, and chaunge thou merueilis;

7 glorifie the hond, and the riyt arm.

8 Reise thou stronge veniaunce, and schede out ire;

9 take awei the aduersarie, and turmente the enemye.

10 Haaste thou the tyme, and haue thou mynde on the ende, that thei telle out thi merueils.

11 And he that is sauyd, be deuourid in the ire of flawme; and thei that treten worst thi puple, fynde perdicioun.

12 Al to-breke thou the heed of princis, and of enemyes, seiynge, Noon othere is, outakun vs.

13 Gadere thou togidere alle the lynagis of Jacob, and knowe thei that no God is, no but thou, that thei telle out thi grete dedis; and thou schalt enherite hem, as at the bigynnyng.

14 Haue thou merci on thi puple, on which thi name is clepid in to help; and on Israel, whom thou madist euene to thi firste gendrid sone.

15 Haue thou merci on Jerusalem, the citee of thin halewyng, on the citee of thi reste.

16 Fille thou Syon with thi vertues, that moun not be teld out, and fille thi puple with thi glorie.

17 Yyue thou witnessyng, that at the bigynnyng thei weren thi creaturis; and reise thou preieris, whiche the formere profetis spaken in thi name.

18 Lord, yyue thou meede to hem that abiden thee, that thi prophetis be foundun trewe; and here thou the preier of thi seruauntis.

19 Aftir the blessyng of Aaron yyue thou to thi puple, and dresse thou vs in to the weie of riytfulnesse; that alle men wite, that dwellen in erthe, that thou art God, the biholdere of worldis.

20 The wombe schal ete alle mete, and o mete is betere than another mete.

21 Chekis touchen mete almest, and an vnwise herte resseyueth false wordis.

22 A schrewid herte schal yyue heuynesse, and a wijs man schal ayenstonde it.

23 A womman schal take ech knaue child, and a douytir is betere than a sone.

24 The fairnesse of a womman makith glad the face of hir hosebonde, and sche schal brynge desir ouer al the coueitise of man.

25 If ther is a tunge of heelyng, ther is also of swagyng, and of merci; the hosebonde of hir is not aftir the sones of men.

26 He that hath in possessioun a good womman, bigynneth possessioun; sche is an help lijk hym, and a piler as reste.

27 Where an hegge is not, the possessioun schal be rauyschid awei; and where a womman is not, a nedi man weilith.

28 To whom bileueth he that hath no nest, and bowith doun where euer it is derk, as a theef girt, skippynge out fro citee in to citee?

CAP 37

1 Ech frend schal seie, And Y haue couplid frenschip; but that is a frend, a frend bi name aloone. Whether sorewe is not til to deth?

2 Forsothe a felowe of table and a frend schulen be turned to enemyte.

3 A! the worste presumpcioun, wherof art thou maad to hile drie malice, and the gilefulnesse therof?

4 A felowe of table schal be myrie with a frend in delityngis, and in the dai of tribulacioun he schal be aduersarie.

5 A felowe of table schal haue sorewe with a frend, for cause of the wombe; and he schal take scheeld ayens an enemye.

6 Foryete thou not thi frend in thi soule, and be thou not vnmyndeful of hym in thi werkis.

7 Nyle thou take councel with the fadir of thi wijf; and hide thou councel fro hem that han enuye to thee.

8 Ech councelour schewith councel, but ther is a councelour to hym silf.

9 Kepe thi soule fro an yuel counselour; firste wite thou, what is his nede, and what he schal thenke in his soule;

10 lest perauenture he sende a stake in to the erthe, and seie to thee,

11 Thi weie is good, and he stonde ayenward, to se what schal bifalle to thee.

12 With an vnreligiouse man trete thou of holynesse, and with an vniust man of riytfulnesse, and with a womman of these thingis whiche sche hatith. With a ferdful man trete thou of batel, with a marchaunt, of cariyng ouer of marchaundies to chepyng; with a biere, of sillyng, with an enuyouse man, of graces to be don;

13 with an vnpitouse man, of pytee, with an vnonest man, of oneste, with a werk man of the feeld, of ech werk;

14 with a werk man hirid bi the yeer, of the endyng of the yeer, with a slowe seruaunt, of myche worchyng. Yyue thou not tent to these men in al councel,

15 but be thou bisi with an hooli man, whom euere thou knowist kepynge Goddis drede,

16 whos soule is aftir thi soule. Who euer doutith in derknessis, schal not haue sorewe with thee.

17 And stablische thou the herte of good councel with thee; for whi another thing is not more than it to thee.

18 The soule of an hooli man tellith out treuthis sum tyme; more than seuene biholderis sittynge an hiy for to biholde.

19 And in alle these thingis biseche thou the hiyeste, that he dresse thi weie in treuthe.

20 Bifore alle werkis a sothefast word go bifore thee; and a stidfast councel go bifore ech dede.

21 A wickid word schal chaunge the herte, of which herte foure partis comen forth; good and yuel, lijf and deth; and a bisi tunge is lord of tho.

22 A wijs man hath tauyt many men, and he is swete to his soule.

23 He that spekith 'bi soffym, is hateful; he schal be defraudid in ech thing.

24 For whi grace is not youun of the Lord to hym, for he is defraudid of al wisdom.

25 A wijs man is wijs to his soule, and the fruytis of his wit ben worthi to be preisid.

26 A wijs man techith his puple, and the fruytis of his wit ben feithful.

27 A wijs man schal be fillid with blessyngis, and thei that seen hym schulen preise hym.

28 The lijf of a man is in the noumbre of daies; but the daies of Israel ben vnnoumbrable.

29 A wijs man in the puple schal enherite onour, and his name schal be lyuynge with outen ende.

30 Sone, asaie thi soule in thi lijf; and if it is wickid, yyue thou not power to it;

31 for whi not alle thingis speden to alle men, and not ech kynde plesith ech soule.

32 Nyle thou be gredi in ech etyng, and schede thou not out thee on ech mete.

33 For in many metis schal be sikenesse, and gredynesse schal neiye 'til to colrye.

34 Many men dieden for glotenye; but he that is abstinent, schal encreesse lijf.

CAP 38

1 Onoure thou a leche, for nede; for whi the hiyeste hath maad hym.

2 For whi al medicyn is of God; and he schal take of the kyng a yifte.

3 The kunnyng of a leche schal enhaunse his heed; and he schal be preisid in the siyt of grete men.

4 The hiyeste hath maad of the erthe medicyn; and a prudent man schal not wlate it.

5 Whether bittir watir was not maad swete of a tre?

6 The vertu of tho thingis cam bi experience to the knowing of men; and the hiyeste yaf kunnyng to men, for to be onourid in his merueils.

7 A man heelynge in these thingis schal aswage sorewe, and an oynement makere schal make pymentis of swetnesse, and schal make anoyntyngis of heelthe; and hise werkis schulen not be endid.

8 For whi the pees of God is on the face of erthe.

9 Mi sone, dispise not thi silf in thi sikenesse; but preie thou the Lord, and he schal heele thee.

10 Turne thou awei fro synne, and dresse thin hondis, and clense thin herte fro al synne.

11 Yyue thou swetnesse, and the mynde of cleene flour of wheete, and make thou fat offryng; and yyue thou place to a leche.

12 For the Lord made hym, and departe he not fro thee; for hise werkis ben nedeful to thee.

13 For whi tyme is, whanne thou schalt falle in to the hondis of hem.

14 Forsothe thei schulen biseche the Lord, that he dresse the werk of hem, and helthe for her lyuyng.

15 He that trespassith in the siyt of hym, that made hym, schal falle in to the hondis of the leche.

16 Sone, brynge thou forth teeris on a deed man, and thou as suffrynge hard thingis bigynne to wepe; and bi doom hile thou the bodi of hym, and dispise thou not his biriyng.

17 But for bacbityng bere thou bittirli the morenyng of hym o dai; and be thou coumfortid for sorewe.

18 And make thou morenyng aftir his merit o dai, ether tweyne, for bacbityng.

19 For whi deth hastith of sorewe, and hilith vertu; and the sorewe of herte bowith the heed.

20 Sorewe dwellith in ledyng awei; and the catel of a nedi man is aftir his herte.

21 Yyue thou not thin herte in sorewe, but put it awei fro thee; and haue thou mynde on the laste thingis, and nyle thou foryete.

22 For whi no turning is, and thou schalt no thing profite to this deed man; and thou schalt harme worste thi silf.

23 Be thou myndeful of mi dom; for also thin schal be thus, to me yistirdai, and to thee to dai.

24 In the reste of a deed man make thou hys mynde to haue reste; and coumforte thou hym in the goyng out of his spirit.

25 Write thou wisdom in the tyme of voidenesse; and he that is made lesse in dede, schal perseyue wisdom; for he schal be fillid of wisdom.

26 He that holdith the plow, and he that hath glorie in a gohode, dryueth oxis with a pricke, and he lyueth in the werkis of tho; and his tellyng is in the sones of bolis.

27 He schal yyue his herte to turne forewis; and his wakyng schal be aboute the fatnesse of kien.

28 So ech carpenter, and principal werk man, that passith the niyt as the dai; that graueth ymagis grauun, and the bisynesse of hym dyuersith the peynture; he schal yyue his herte to the licnesse of peynture, and bi his wakyng he perfourmeth the werk.

29 So a smyth sittynge bisidis the anefelt, and biholdynge the werk of yrun, the heete of fier brenneth hise fleischis; and he stryueth in the heete of the furneis.

30 The vois of a hamer makith newe his eere; and his iye is ayens the licnesse of a vessel.

31 He schal yyue his herte in to the perfourmyng of werkis; and bi his wakyng he schal ourne vnperfeccioun.

32 So a potter sittynge at his werk, turnynge a wheel with hise feet, which is put euere in bisynesse for his werk; and al his worchyng is vnnoumbrable.

33 In his arm he schal fourme clei; and bifore hise feet he schal bowe his vertu.

34 He schal yyue his herte to ende perfitli sum thing; and bi his wakyng he schal clense the furneis.

35 Alle these men hopiden in her hondis; and ech man is wijs in his craft.

36 A citee is not bildid with outen alle these men.

37 And thei schulen not dwelle, nether go; and thei schulen not skippe ouer in to the chirche.

38 Thei schulen not sitte on the seete of a iuge; and thei schulen not vndirstonde the testament of doom, nether thei schulen make opyn techyng and doom; and thei schulen not be foundun in parablis.

39 But thei schulen conferme the creature of the world, and her preyer is in the worching of craft; and thei yyuen her soule, and thei axen togidere in the lawe of the hiyeste.

CAP 39

1 A wijs man schal seke out the wisdom of alle elde men; and he schal yyue tent in profetis.

2 He schal kepe the tellyng of named men; and he schal entre togidere in to the hard sentensis of parablis.

3 He schal seke out the pryuy thingis of prouerbis; and he schal be conuersaunt in the hid thingis of parablis.

4 He schal mynystre in the myddis of grete men; and he schal appere in the siyt of the cheef iuge.

5 He schal passe in to the lond of alien folkis; for he schal asaie goodis, and yuels in alle thingis.

6 He schal yyue his herte to wake eerli to the Lord that made hym; and he schal biseche in the siyt of the hiyeste.

7 He schal opene his mouth in preier; and he schal biseche for hise trespassis.

8 For if the grete Lord wole, he schal fille hym with the spirit of vndurstondyng.

9 And he schal sende the wordis of his wisdom, as reynes; and in preier he schal knouleche to the Lord.

10 And he schal dresse his counsel, and techyng; and schal councele in hise hid thingis.

11 He schal make opene the wisdom of his techyng; and he schal haue glorie in the lawe of the testament of the Lord.

12 Many men schulen preyse his wisdom; and it schal not be don awey til in to the world.

13 His mynde schal not go awei; and his name schal be souyt fro generacioun in to generacioun.

14 Folkis schulen telle out his wisdom; and the chirche schal telle his preisyng.

15 If his name dwellith, he schal leeue more than a thousynde; and if he restith, it schal profite to hym.

16 Yit Y schal take councel to telle out, for Y am fillid as with woodnesse;

17 and myn ynnere spirit seith in vois, Ye fruytis of God, here me, and make ye fruyt, as roosis plauntide on the ryuers of watris.

18 Haue ye odour of swetnesse, as the Liban hath.

19 Bringe forth flouris, as a lilee; yyue ye odour, and make ye boowis in to grace. And preise ye togidere a song; and blesse ye the Lord in hise werkis.

20 Yyue ye greet onour to his name, and knouleche ye to him in the vois of youre lippis, in songis of lippis, and in harpis; and thus ye schulen seie in knouleching,

21 Alle the werkis of the Lord ben ful goode.

22 Forsothe watir as an heepe of stoonys stood at his word; and as resettis of watris in the word of his mouth.

23 For whi pesiblenesse is maad in his comaundement; and no defaute is in the heelthe of hym.

24 The werkis of ech fleisch ben bifore hym; and no thing is hid fro hise iyen.

25 He biholdith fro the world til in to the world; and no thing is wondurful in his siyt.

26 It is not to seie, What is this thing, ether, What is that thing? for whi alle thingis schulen be souyt in her tyme.

27 The blessyng of hym schal flowe as a flood;

28 and as the grete flood fillide greteli the erthe, so his yre schal enherite in folkis, that souyten not hym.

29 As he turnede watris in to drynessis, and the erthe was dried, and hise weies weren dressid to the weies of hem; so offenciouns in his ire ben dressid to synneris.

30 Goode thingis weren maad at the bigynnyng to goode men; so goode thingis and yuele ben maad to worste men.

31 The bigynnyng of nedeful thing to the lijf of men, watir, fier, and yrun, and salt, and mylk, and breed of cleene flour of whete, and hony, and a clustre of grape, and oile, and cloth.

32 Alle these thingis schulen turne to hooli men in to goodis; so and to vnfeithful men and synneris in to yuels.

33 Spiritis ben that ben maad to veniaunce; and in her woodnesse thei confermyden her turmentis.

34 And in the tyme of endyng thei schulen schede out vertu; and thei schulen confounde the strong veniaunce of hym that made hem.

35 Fier, hail, hungur, and deth; alle these thingis ben maad to veniaunce; the teeth of beestis,

36 and scorpiouns, and serpentis, and a swerd punyschynge wickid men in to destriyng.

37 In the comaundementis of hym tho schulen ete, and tho schulen be maad redi on the erthe in nede; and in her tymes tho schulen not passe o word.

38 Therfor fro the bigynnyng Y was confermed; and Y counselide, and thouyte, and lefte writun.

39 Alle the werkis of the Lord ben goode; and ech werk schal serue in his our.

40 It is not to seie, This is worse than that; for whi alle thingis schulen be preued in her tyme.

41 And now in al the herte and mouth preise ye togidere, and blesse ye the name of the Lord.

CAP 40

1 Greet occupacioun is maad to alle men, and an heuy yok on the sones of Adam, fro the dai of the goyng out of the wombe of her modir, til in to the dai of biriyng in to the modir of alle men.

2 The thouytis of hem, and the dredis of herte, fyndyngis of abidyng, and the dai of endyng;

3 fro hym that sittith bifore on a gloriouse seete, 'til to a man maad lowe in to erthe and aische;

4 fro hym that vsith iacynct, and berith a coroun, 'til to hym that is hilid with raw lynnun cloth, woodnesse, enuye, noise,

doutyng, and drede of deth, wrathfulnesse dwellynge contynueli, and strijf;

5 and in the tyme of restyng in the bed, the sleep of nyyt chaungith his kunnyng.

6 Forsothe a litil is as nouyt in reste; biholdyng is of hym in sleep as in the dai.

7 He is disturblid in the siyt of his herte, as he that ascapith in the dai of batel. He roos vp in the dai of his helthe, and dredynge not at ony drede, with al fleisch,

8 fro man 'til to beeste, and seuenefold schal come on synneris.

9 At these thingis, deth, blood, stryuyng, and swerd, oppressyngis, hungur, and sorewe, and beetyngis;

10 alle these thingis ben maad on wickid men, and the greet flood was maad for hem.

11 For whi alle thingis that ben of the erthe, schulen turne in to the erthe; and alle watris schulen turne in to the see.

12 Al yifte and wickidnesse schal be don awei; and feith schal stonde in to the world.

13 The richessis of vniust men schulen be maad drie as a flood; and schulen sowne as a greet thundur in reyn.

14 An vniust man schal be glad in openynge hise hondis; so trespassouris schulen faile in the ende.

15 The sones of sones of wickid men schulen not multiplie braunchis; and vncleene rootis sownen on the cop of a stoon.

16 Grenenesse bisidis ech watir; and at the brynk of the flood it schal be drawun out bi the roote bifor al hey.

17 Grace as paradiss in blessyngis; and merci dwellith in to the world.

18 The lijf of a werk man sufficient to hym silf schal be maad swete; and thou schalt fynde tresour ther ynne.

19 Bildyng of a citee schal conferme a name; and a womman with out wem schal be rikenyd aboue this.

20 Wyn and musik maken glad the herte; and loue of wisdom gladith aboue euer either.

21 Pipis and sawtree maken swete melodie; and a swete tunge aboue euer either.

22 An yye schal desire grace and fairnesse; and greene sowyngis aboue these thingis.

23 A frend and felowe comynge togidere in tyme; and a womman with man aboue euer either.

24 Britheren in to help in the tyme of tribulacioun 'coumforten myche; and merci schal delyuere more than thei.

25 Gold and siluer, and settyng of feet; and counsel wel plesing is aboue euer either.

26 Richessis and vertues enhaunsen the herte; and the drede of the Lord more than this.

27 Making lesse is not in the drede of the Lord; and in that drede it is not to seke help.

28 The drede of the Lord is as paradijs of blessyng; and 'the blessyngis of God kyueriden hym aboue al glorie.

29 Sone, in the tyme of thi lijf be thou not nedi; for it is betere to die, than to be nedi.

30 A man biholdinge in to another mannus boord, his lijf is not in the thouyt of lijflode; for he susteyneth his lijf with othere mennus metis.

31 Forsothe a chastisid man and lernd schal kepe him silf.

32 Nedynesse schal be defoulid in the mouth of an vnprudent man; and fier schal brenne in his wombe.

CAP 41

1 A! deth, thi mynde is ful bittir to an vniust man, and hauynge pees in hise richessis;

2 to a restful man, and whose weies ben dressid in alle thingis, and yit myyti to take mete.

3 A! deth, thi doom is good to a nedi man, and which is maad lesse in strengthis,

4 and failith for age, and to whom is care of alle thingis, and vnbileueful, that leesith wisdom.

5 Nyle thou drede the doom of deth; haue thou mynde what thingis weren byfore thee, and what thingis schulen come on thee; this dom is of the Lord to ech man.

6 And tho thingis that schulen come on thee in the good plesaunce of the hiyeste; whethir ten yeer, ether an hundrid, ether a thousynde.

7 For whi noon accusyng of lijf is in helle.

8 The sones of abhomynaciouns ben the sones of synneris; and thei that dwellen bisidis the housis of wickid men.

9 The eritage of the sones of synneris schal perische; and the contynuaunce of schenschipe with the seed of hem.

10 Sones playnen of a wickid fadir; for thei ben in schenschip for hym.

11 Wo to you, ye wickid men, that han forsake the lawe of the hiyeste.

12 And if ye be borun, ye schulen be borun in cursidnesse; and if ye ben deed, youre part schal be in cursidnesse.

13 Alle thingis that ben of the erthe, schulen turne in to the erthe; so wickid men schulen turne fro cursyng in to perdicioun.

14 The morenyng of men is in the bodi of hem; but the name of wickid men schal be doon awei.

15 Haue thou bisynesse of a good name; for whi this schal dwelle more with thee, than a thousynde tresouris grete and preciouse.

16 The noumbre of daies is the terme of good lijf; but a good name schal dwelle with outen ende.

17 Sones, kepe ye techyng in pees; for whi wisdom hid, and tresour vnseyn, what profit is in euer either?

18 Betere is a man that hidith his foli, than a man that hidith his wisdom.

19 Netheles turne ye ayen in these thingis that comen forth of my mouth.

20 For it is not good to kepe alle vnreuerence, and not alle thingis plesen alle men in feith.

21 Be ye aschamed of fornycacioun, bifor fadir, and bifor modir; and of a leesyng, bifore a iustice, and bifore a myyti man;

22 and of trespas, bifor a prince, and bifore a iuge; and of wickidnesse, bifore a synagoge, and a puple; and of vnriytwisnesse,

23 bifore a felow, and a frend;

24 and of thefte, in the place where ynne thou dwellist; of the treuthe and testament of God; of sittyng at the mete in looues, and of the blemyschyng of yifte, and takyng;

25 of stilnesse, bifore hem that greeten; of the biholdyng of a letcherouse womman, and of the turnyng a wey of the cheer of a cosyn.

26 Turne thou not awey the face fro thi neiybore; and be thou war of takyng a wei a part, and not restorynge.

27 Biholde thou not the womman of an othere man; and enserche thou not her hand maide, nether stonde thou at hir bed.

28 Be thou war of frendis, of the wordis of vpbreidyng; and whanne thou hast youe, vpbreide thou not.

CAP 42

1 Double thou not a word of heryng, of the schewyng of an hid word; and thou schalt be verily with out schame, and thou schalt fynde grace in the siyt of alle men. Be thou not schent for alle these thingis; and take thou not a persoone, that thou do trespas.

2 Be thou war of the lawe and testament of the hiyeste, of doom to iustifie a wickid man;

3 of the word of felowis, and of weigoeris, and of the yyuyng of eritage of frendis;

4 of the euennesse of balaunce, and of weiytis, of the getyng of many thingis, and of fewe thingis;

5 of corrupcioun of biyng, and of marchauntis, and of myche chastising of sones; and of a worste seruaunt, to make the side to bleede.

6 A seelyng is good on a wickid man.

7 Where ben many hondis, close thou; and what euer thing thou schalt bitake, noumbre thou, and weie thou; forsothe discryue thou, ether write, ech yifte, and takyng.

8 Absteine thou fro the techyng of an vnwitti man, and fool, and of eldere men that ben demed of yonge men; and thou schalt be lernd in alle thingis, and thou schalt be comendable in the siyt of alle men.

9 An hid douyter of a fadir is wakynge and bisynesse of hym; sche schal take awei sleep; lest perauenture sche be maad auowtresse in hir yong wexynge age, and lest sche dwellynge with the hosebonde, be maad hateful;

10 lest ony tyme sche be defoulid in hir virginytee, and be foundun with child in the kepyng of hir fadir; leste perauenture sche dwellynge with the hosebonde, do trespasse, ether certis be maad bareyn.

11 Ordeyne thou kepyng on a letcherouse douyter, lest ony tyme sche make thee to come in to schenschipe to enemyes, of bacbityng in the citee, and of castyng out of the puple; and sche make thee aschamed in the multitude of puple.

12 Nyle thou take heed to ech man in the fairnesse; and nyle thou dwelle in the myddis of wymmen.

13 For whi a mouyte cometh forth of clothis, and the wickidnesse of a man cometh forth of a womman.

14 For whi the wickidnesse of a man is betere than a womman doynge wel, and a womman schendyng in to schenschipe.

15 Therfor be thou myndeful of the werkis of the Lord; and Y schal telle the werkis of the Lord, whiche Y siy, in the wordis of the Lord.

16 The sunne liytnynge bihelde by alle thingis; and the werk therof is ful of the glorie of the Lord.

17 Whether the Lord made not hooli men to telle out alle hise merueilis, whiche the Lord almyyti stidfast in his glorie schal conferme?

18 He schal enserche the depthe, and the herte of men; and he schal thenke in the felnesse of hem.

19 For the Lord knew al kunnyng, and bihelde in to the signe of the world; tellynge tho thingis that ben passid, and tho thingis that schulen come; schewynge the steppis of hid thingis.

20 And no thouyt passith hym, and no word hidith it silf fro hym.

21 He made fair the grete werkis of his wisdom, which is bifore the world, and til in to the world; nether ony thing is encreessid,

22 nether is decreessid, and he hath no nede to the counsel of ony.

23 Alle hise werkis ben ful desirable, and to biholde, as a sparcle which is.

24 Alle these thingis lyuen, and dwellen in to the world; and alle thingis obeien to hym in al nede.

25 Alle thingis ben double, oon ayens oon; and he made not ony thing to faile. He schal conferme the goodis of ech; and who schal be fillid, seynge his glorie?

CAP 43

1 The firmament of hiynesse is the fairnesse therof; the fairnesse of heuene in the siyt of glorie.

2 The sunne in biholdyng, tellynge in goyng out, is a woundurful vessel, the werk of hiy God.

3 In the tyme of myddai it brenneth the erthe; and who schal mow suffre in the siyt of his heete? Kepynge a furneis in the werkis of heete;

4 the sunne brennynge hillis in thre maneris, sendynge out beemys of fier, and schynynge ayen with hise beemys, blyndith iyen.

5 The Lord is greet, that made it; and in the wordis of hym it hastide iourney.

6 And the moone in alle men in his tyme is shewing of tyme, and a signe of the world.

7 A signe of the feeste dai is takun of the moone; the liyt which is maad litil in the ende.

8 The monethe is encreessynge bi the name therof, wondirfuli in to the ending.

9 A vessel of castels in hiy thingis, schynynge gloriousli in the firmament of heuene.

10 The fairnesse of heuene is the glorie of sterris; the Lord an hiy liytneth the world.

11 In the wordis of the hooli tho schulen stonde at the doom; and tho schulen not faile in her wakyngis.

12 Se thou the bouwe, and blesse thou hym that made it; it is ful fair in his schynyng.

13 It yede aboute heuene in the cumpas of his glorie; the hondis of hiy God openyden it.

14 Bi his comaundement he hastide the snow; and he hastith to sende out the leiytyngis of his dom.

15 Therfor tresouris weren opened, and clowdis fledden out as been.

16 In his greetnesse he settide clowdis; and stoonys of hail weren brokun.

17 Hillis schulen be moued in his siyt; and the south wynd schal blowe in his wille.

18 The vois of his thundur schal beete the erthe; the tempest of the north, and the gaderyng togidere of wynd.

19 And as a brid puttynge doun to sitte sprengith snow, and the comyng doun of that snow is as a locust drenchynge doun.

20 The iye schal wondre on the fairnesse of whitnesse therof; and an herte dredith on the reyn therof.

21 He schal schede out frost as salt on the erthe; and while the wynd blowith, it schal be maad as coppis of a brere.

22 The coold northun wynd blew, and cristal of watir frees togidre; it restith, on al the gedering togidere of watris, and it clothith it silf with watris, as with an haburioun.

23 And it schal deuoure hillis, and it schal brenne the desert; and it schal quenche grene thing as fier.

24 The medicyn of alle thingis is in the haasting of a cloude; a deewe, meetynge the heete comynge of brennyng, schal make it low.

25 The wynd was stille in the word of God; bi his thouyt he made peesible the depthe of watris; and the Lord Jhesu plauntide it.

26 Thei that seilen in the see, tellen out the perels therof; and we heeringe with oure eeris schulen wondre.

27 There ben ful cleer werkis, and wonderful, dyuerse kindis of beestis, and of alle litle beestis, and the creature of wondurful fischis.

28 The ende of weie is confermyd for it; and alle thingis ben maad in the word of hym.

29 We seien many thingis, and we faylen in wordis; forsothe he is the endyng of wordis.

30 To what thing schulen we be myyti, that han glorie in alle thingis? for he is al myyti aboue alle hise werkis.

31 The Lord is ferdful, and ful greet; and his power is wondurful.

32 Glorifie ye the Lord as myche as euere ye moun, yit he schal be myytiere; and his grete doynge is wondurful.

33 Ye blessynge the Lord, enhaunse hym as myche as ye moun; for he is more than al preisyng.

34 Ye enhaunsynge hym schulen be fillid with vertu; trauele ye not, for ye schulen not take perfitli.

35 Who siy hym, and schal telle out? and who schal magnefie hym, as he is fro the bigynnyng?

36 Many thingis gretter than these ben hid fro vs; for we han seyn fewe thingis of hise werkis.

37 Forsothe the Lord made alle thingis; and he yaf wisdom to men doynge feithfuli.

CAP 44

1 Preise we gloriouse men, and oure fadris in her generacioun.

2 The Lord made myche glorie bi his greet doyng, fro the world.

3 Grete men in vertu weren lordis in her poweris, and riche in her prudence; tellynge in profetis the dignete of profetis, and comaundynge in present puple,

4 and tellynge hoolieste wordis to puplis, bi the vertu of prudence.

5 Sekynge maneres of musik in her childhod, and tellynge songis of scripturis.

6 Riche men in vertu, hauynge the studie of fairnesse, makynge pees in her housis.

7 Alle these men gaten glorie in the generaciouns of her folk; and ben had in preysyngis in her daies.

8 Thei that weren borun of hem, leften a name to telle the preisyngis of hem.

9 And summe ben, of whiche is no mynde; thei perischiden as thei that weren not, and thei weren borun as not borun; and her sones perischiden with hem.

10 But also tho men of mercy ben, whose pitees failiden not;

11 and good eritage dwellide contynueli with the seed of hem.

12 And the seed of her sones sones stood in testament,

13 and the eritage of her sones dwellith for hem, til in to with outen ende; the seed of hem, and the glorie of hem, schal not be forsakun.

14 The bodies of hem ben biried in pees; and the name of hem schal lyue in to generaciouns and generaciouns.

15 Puplis tellen the wisdom of hem; and the chirche tellith the preysyng of hem.

16 Enok pleside God, and was translatid in to paradis, that he yyue wisdom to folkis.

17 Noe was foundun parfit and iust, and he was maad recouncelynge in the tyme of wrathfulnesse.

18 Therfor residue seed was left to erthe, whanne the greet flood was maad.

19 Testamentis of the world weren set anentis hym, lest al fleisch myyte be doon awei bi the greet flood.

20 Abraham was the greet fadir of the multitude of folkis; and noon was foundun lijk hym in glorie, which kepte the lawe of hiy God, and was in the testament with hym.

21 He made a testament to stonde in his fleisch; and he was foundun feithful in temptacioun.

22 Therfor God with an ooth yaf to hym glorie in his folk; God made hym to encreesse, as an heep of erthe,

23 and to enhaunse his seed as sterris, and to enherite hem fro the see 'til to the see, and fro the flood 'til to the endis of erthe.

24 And to Isaac God dide in the same maner, for Abraham, his fadir.

25 The Lord yaf to hym the blessing of alle folkis; and confermyde his testament on the heed of Jacob.

26 He knew hym in hise blessyngis, and yaf eritage to hym; and departide to hym a part in twelue lynagis.

27 And he kepte to hym men of merci, fyndynge grace in the siyt of eche man.

CAP 45

1 Moises was loued of God and of men; whose mynde is in blessyng.

2 He made him lijk in the glorie of seyntis, and he magnefiede hym in the drede of enemyes; and in his wordis he made peesible the wondris ayens kynde.

3 He glorifiede hym in the siyt of kyngis, and he 'comaundide to hym bifore his puple, and schewide his glorie to hym.

4 In the feith and myldenesse of hym God made hym hooli; and chees him of alle men.

5 For he herde hym, and his vois; and ledde in hym in a cloude.

6 And yaf to hym an herte to comaundementis, and to the lawe of lijf, and of techyng; to teche Jacob a testament, and Israel hise domes.

7 He made hiy Aaron, his brother, and lijk hym of the lynage of Leuy.

8 He ordeynede to hym euerlastynge testament, and yaf to hym the preesthod of the folk. And he made hym blissful in glorie,

9 and girte hym with a girdil of riytfulnesse; and clothide hym with a stoole of glorie, and crownede hym in the ournementis of vertu.

10 He settide on hym sandalies, and breeches, and a clooth on the schuldur, and girte hym aboute with ful many small goldun bellis in cumpas;

11 to yyue soun in his goyng, to make soun herd in the temple, in to mynde to the sones of his folk.

12 God yaf to hym an hooli stoole, a wouun werk, with gold, and iacynct, and purpur, the werk of a wijs man, maad riche with doom and treuthe;

13 the werk of a crafti man, in writhun reed threed, with preciouse iemmes grauun in the byndyng of gold, and grauun bi the werk of a crafti man of stoonys, in to mynde, bi the noumbre of the lynagis of Israel.

14 A goldun coroun on his mytre, set forth with the signe of hoolynesse, the glorie of onour, and the werk of vertu, ourned to desijr of iyen.

15 Siche thingis so faire weren not bifore hym, 'til to the eest.

16 Noon alien was clothid ther ynne, but oneli hise sones, and hise sones sones aloone, bi al tyme.

17 Hise sacrifices weren endid ech dai bi fyer.

18 Moises fillide hise hondis, and anoyntide hym with hooli oile.

19 It was maad to hym in to euerlastynge testament, and to his seed as the daies of heuene, to vse presthod, and to haue preisyng, and to glorifie his puple in his name.

20 God chees hym of ech lyuynge man, to offre sacrifice to God, encense, and good odour, in to mynde, for to plese for his puple.

21 And he yaf to hym power in hise comaundementis, and in the testamentis of domes, to teche Jacob witnessyngis, and in his lawe to yyue liyt to Israel.

22 For aliens stooden ayens hym, and men that weren with Datan and Abiron, and the congregacioun of Chore, in wrathfulnesse cumpassiden hym for enuye, in desert.

23 The Lord siy, and it pleside not hym; and thei weren wastid in the feersnesse of wrathfulnesse.

24 He made to hem wondris ayens kynde, and in the flawme of fier he wastide hem.

25 And he encreesside glorie to Aaron, and yaf eritage to hym; and he departide to Aaron the firste thingis of fruytis of the erthe.

26 He made redi his breed in the firste thingis, in to fulnesse; for whi and thei shulen ete the sacrifices of the Lord, whiche he yaf to hym, and to his seed.

27 But in the lond of his folk he schal not haue eritage, and no part is to hym among the folk; for whi God is the part and eritage of hym.

28 Fynees, the sone of Eleazarus, was the thridde in glorie, in suynge hym in the drede of God,

29 and to stonde in the reuerence of folk; in the goodnesse and gladnesse of his soule he pleside God of Israel.

30 Therfor God ordeynede to hym the testament of pees, and made hym prince of hooli men, and of his folk; that the dignete of presthod be to hym and to his seed, with outen ende.

31 And the testament of Dauid, the sone of Jesse, of the lynage of Juda, was eritage to hym, and to his seed; that he schulde yyue wisdom in to oure herte, to deme his folk in riytfulnesse, lest her goodis schulen be don awei; and he made the glorie of hem to be euerlastinge, in the folk of hem.

CAP 46

1 Jhesus Naue, the successour of Moises in profetis, was strong in batel, that was greet bi his name.

2 The gretteste in to the helthe of chosun men of God, to ouercome enemyes risynge ayens hem, that he schulde gete the erytage of Israel.

3 Which glorie he gat in reysynge his hondis, and in castynge scharpe arowis ayens citees.

4 Who bifore hym ayenstood so? for whi the Lord hym silf smoot the enemyes.

5 Whether the sunne was not lettid in the wrathfulnesse of hym, and o dai was maad as tweyne?

6 He clepide to help the hiyeste God, myyti in ouercomynge enemyes on ech side; and God, greet and hooli, herde hym, in stoonys of hail of ful greet vertu.

7 He made asauyt ayens the folk enemy, and in the comynge doun he loste the aduersaries;

8 that hethene men knowe the myyt of hym, for it is not esy to fiyte ayens the Lord; and he suede myyti men at the bak.

9 And in the daies of Moises he and Caleph, the sone of Jephone, diden merci; to stonde ayens the enemye, and to forbede the folk fro synnes, and to refreyne the grutchyng of malice.

10 And thei tweyne weren stidfast, and weren delyuered fro perel, of the noumbre of sixe hundrid thousynde 'foot men, to brynge hem in to the eritage, in to the lond that flowith mylk and hony.

11 And the Lord yaf strengthe to thilke Caleph, and til in to elde vertu dwellide perfitli to hym; that he stiede in to the hiy place of the lond, and his seed gat eritage.

12 And alle the children of Israel sien, that it is good to obeie to hooli God.

13 And alle iugis bi her name, the herte of whiche was not corrupt, weren strong in batel, which weren not turned awei fro the Lord;

14 that the mynde of hem be in blessyng, and her boonys apperen fro her place;

15 and her name dwellith with outen ende, for the glorie of hooli men dwellith at the sones of hem.

16 Samuel, the profete of the Lord, that was louyd of his Lord God, made newe the empire, and anoyntide prynces in his folk.

17 In the lawe of the Lord he demyde the congregacioun, and he siy the Lord of Jacob, and in his feith he was preued a profete.

18 And he was knowun feithful in hise wordis, for he siy the Lord of liyt.

19 And he clepide in to help the Lord almyyti, in ouercomynge enemyes stondynge aboute on ech side, in the offrynge of a man vndefoulid.

20 And the Lord thundride fro heuene, and in greet soun he made his vois herd.

21 And he al to-brak the princes of men of Tyre, and alle the duykis of Filisteis.

22 And bifore the tyme of ende of his lijf, and of the world, he yaf witnessyng in the siyt of the Lord, and of Crist; he took not of ony man richessis, yhe, til to schoon; and no man accuside hym.

23 And after this he slepte, and he made knowun to the kyng, and he schewide to hym the ende of his lijf; and he enhaunside his vois fro the erthe in profesie, to do awei the wickidnesse of the folc.

CAP 47

1 Aftir these thingis Nathan, the profete, roos, in the daies of Dauid.

2 And as ynnere fatnesse departide fro the fleisch, so Dauid fro the sones of Israel.

3 He pleiede with liouns, as with lambren; he dide in lijk maner with beris, as with lambren of scheep.

4 Whether in his yongthe he killide not a giaunt, and took awei schenschip fro the folk?

5 In reisynge the hond in a stoon of a slynge, he castide doun the ful out ioiyng of Golias,

6 where he clepide to help the Lord almyyti; and he yaf in his riyt hond to do awei a stronge man in batel, and to enhaunse the horn of his folk.

7 So he glorifiede hym in ten thousynde, and he preiside hym in the blessyngis of the Lord, in offrynge to hym the coroun of glorie.

8 For he al to-brak enemyes on ech side, and drow out bi the roote Filisteis contrarie, 'til in to this dai; he al to-brak the horn of hem, 'til in to with outen ende.

9 Dauid in ech werk yaf knouleching to hooli God, and hiy in the word of glorie.

10 Of al his herte he heriede God, and he louyde the Lord that made hym, and yaf to hym power ayens enemyes.

11 And he made syngeris to stonde ayens the auter; and he made swete motetis in the soun of hem.

12 And he yaf fairnesse in halewyngis, and he ournede tymes 'til to the endyng of lijf; that thei schulden preise the hooli name of the Lord, and make large eerli the hoolynesse of God.

13 Crist purgide the synnes of hym, and enhaunside his horn with outen ende; and he yaf to hym the testament of kyngis, and the seete of glorie in Israel.

14 Aftir hym roos a witti sone; and for hym he castide doun al the power of enemyes.

15 Salomon regnede in the daies of pees, to whom God made suget alle enemyes, that he schulde make an hous in the name of God, and make redi hoolynesse with outen ende, as he was lerned in his yongthe.

16 And he was fillid with wisdom as a flood is fillid; and his soule vnhilide the erthe.

17 And thou, Salomon, fillidist derk figuratif spechis in licnessis; and thi name was pupplischid to ilis afer, and thou were louyde in thi pees.

18 Londis wondriden in songis, and in prouerbis, and in licnessis, and interpretyngis, ether exposiciouns; and in the name of the Lord,

19 to whom the surname is God of Israel.

20 Thou gaderidist togidere gold as latoun, and thou fillidist siluer as leed.

21 And thou bouwidist thi thies to wymmen; thou haddist power in thi bodi.

22 Thou hast youe a wem in thi glorie, and madist vnhooli thi seed, to brynge in wrathfulnesse to thi children, and thi foli in othere men;

23 that thou schuldist make the rewme departid in to tweyne, and of Effrem to comaunde an hard comaundement.

24 But God schal not forsake his merci, and schal not distrie nether do awei hise werkis, nether he schal leese fro generacioun the sones sones of his chosun kyng Dauid; and he schal not distrie the seed of hym that loueth the Lord.

25 Forsothe God yaf remenaunt to Jacob, and to Dauid of that generacioun.

26 And Salomon hadde an ende with hise fadris.

27 And he lefte aftir hym of his seed Roboam,

28 the foli of the folk, and made lesse fro prudence; which Roboam turnede awei the folk bi his councel.

29 And Jeroboam, the sone of Nabath, that made Israel to do synne, and yaf to Effraym weie to do synne; and ful many synnes of hem weren plenteuouse,

30 for thei turneden hem awei greetli fro her lond.

31 And the lynage of Effraym souyte al wickidnessis, til defence cam to hem; and delyuerede hem fro alle synnes.

CAP 48

1 And Elie, the profete, roos as fier; for whi his word brente as a brond.

2 Which brouyte yn hungur on hem, and thei suynge hym weren maad fewe for enuye; for thei myyten not suffre the comaundementis of the Lord.

3 Bi the word of the Lord he held togidere heuene, and castide doun fro it fier to the erthe.

4 So Elie was alargid in his merueils; and who may haue glorie in lijk maner with thee, which tokist awei a deed man fro hellis,

5 fro the eritage of deth, in the word of the Lord God?

6 Which castidist doun kyngis to deth, and hast broke togidere liytli the power of hem, and gloriouse men fro her bed.

7 Which herdist dom in Syna, and in Oreb domes of defence.

8 Which anoyntist kyngis to penaunce, and makist prophetis successouris aftir thee.

9 Which were reseyued in a whirlwynde of fier, in a chare of horsis of fier.

10 Which art writun in the domes of tymes, to plese the wrathfulnesse of the Lord, to recounsele the herte of the fadir to the sone, and to restore the lynagis of Jacob.

11 Thei ben blessid, that siyen thee, and weren maad feir in thi frenschipe;

12 for whi we lyuen oneli in lijf, but after deth oure name schal not be siche.

13 Elie, that was hilid in a whirlewynd; and his spirit was fillid in Elisee. Elisee in hise daies dredde not the prince, and no man ouercam hym bi power;

14 nether ony word ouercam hym, and his deed bodi profesiede.

15 In his lijf he dide wondris ayens kynde; and in deth he wrouyte merueilis.

16 In alle these thingis the puple dide not penaunce, and yeden not awei fro her synnes, til whanne thei weren cast awei fro her lond, and weren scatered in to ech lond.

17 And a ful fewe folk was left, and a prince in the hous of Dauid.

18 Summe of hem diden that, that pleside God; but othere diden many synnes.

19 Ezechie maad strong his citee, and brouyte watir in to the myddis therof; and diggide a rooche with irun, and bildide a pit to watir.

20 In hise daies Senacherib stiede, and sente Rapsaces; and he reiside his hond ayens hem, and he reiside his hond ayens Syon, and was maad proud in his power.

21 Thanne the hertis and hondis of hem weren moued; and thei hadden sorewe as wymmen trauelynge of child.

22 And thei clepiden to help the merciful Lord, and thei spredden abrood the hondis, and reisiden to heuene; and the hooli Lord God herde soone the vois of hem.

23 He hadde not mynde on her synnes, nether yaf hem to her enemyes; but he purgide hem in the hond of Isaie, the hooli profete.

24 The aungel of the Lord castide doun the castels of Assiriens, and al to-brak hem.

25 For whi Ezechie dide that that pleside the Lord, and yede strongli in the weie of Dauith, his fadir; which weie Isaie, the grete profete, and feithful in the siyt of God, comaundide to hym.

26 In the daies of hym the sunne yede ayen abak; and God encreesside lijf to the kyng.

27 With greet spirit Ysaie siy the laste thingis; and he coumfortide the moreneris in Sion, 'in to with outen ende.

28 He schewide thingis to comynge, and hid thingis, bifore that tho camen.

CAP 49

1 The mynde of Josie maad in the makyng of odour, is the werk of a pyment makere.

2 In ech mouth his mynde schal be maad swete as hony, and as musik in the feeste of wyn.

3 He was dressid of God in the penaunce of folk; and he took awei the abhomynaciouns of wickidnesse.

4 And the herte of hym gouernede to the Lord; and in the daies of synnes he strengthide pitee.

5 Outakun Dauid, Ezechie and Josie, alle kyngis diden synne.

6 For whi the kyngis of Juda leften the lawe of myyti God, and dispisiden the drede of God.

7 For thei yauen her rewme to othere men, and her glorie to an alien folk.

8 Thei brenten the chosun citee of hoolynesse; and thei maden the weies therof forsakun in the hond of Jeremye.

9 For thei tretiden yuel hym, which from the wombe of the modir was halewid a profete, to turne vpsedoun, and to leese, and efte to bilde, and make newe.

10 Ezechiel, that siy the siyt of glorie, which the Lord schewide to hym in the chare of cherubyn.

11 For he made mynde of enemyes in reyn, to do wel to hem, that schewiden riytful weies.

12 And the boonys of twelue profetis apperen fro her place; and thei strengthiden Jacob, and ayenbouyten hem in the feith of her vertu.

13 Hou schulen we alarge Zorobabel? for whi and he was a signe in the riyt hond of God to Israel;

14 and Jhesu, the sone of Josedech? whiche in her daies bildiden an hous, and enhaunsiden the hooli temple to the Lord, maad redi in to euerlastynge glorie.

15 And Neemye in the mynde of myche tyme, that reiside to vs the wallis, 'that weren cast doun, and made the yatis and lockis to stonde; which Neemye reiside oure housis.

16 No man borun in erthe was such as Enok; for whi and he was resseyued fro the erthe.

17 And Joseph, that was borun a man, the prince of britheren, the stidfastnesse of folk, the gouernour of britheren, the stablischyng of puple;

18 and his boonys weren visitid, and profesieden after deth.

19 Seth and Sem, these gaten glorie anentis men, and ouer ech man in the generacioun of Adam.

CAP 50

1 Symount, the sone of Onyas, was a greet preest, which in his lijf vndursettide the hous, and in hise daies strengthide the temple.

2 Also the hiynesse of the temple was bildide of hym, the double bildyng, and hiy wallis of the temple.

3 In the daies of hym the pittis of watris camen forth; and as the see tho weren fillid aboue mesure.

4 Which Symount helide his folk, and delyuerede it fro perdicioun.

5 Which was myyti to alarge the citee; which gat glorie in the conuersacioun of folk; and alargide the entryng of the hous, and of the large cumpas aboute.

6 As the dai sterre in the myddis of a cloude, and as a ful moone schyneth in hise daies;

7 and as the sunne schynynge, so he schynede in the temple of God;

8 as a reyn bouwe schynynge among the cloudis of glorie, and as a flour of rosis in the daies of veer, and as lilies, that

ben in the passyng of watir, and as encense smellynge in the daies of somer; as fier schynynge,

9 and ensence brennynge in fier;

10 as a sad vessel of gold, ourned with ech preciouse stoon;

11 as an olyue tree spryngynge forth, and a cipresse tree reisynge it silf an hiy; while he took the stoole of glorie, and was clothid in the perfeccioun of vertu.

12 In the stiyng of the hooli auter, the clothing of hoolynesse yaf glorie.

13 Forsothe in takynge partis of the hoond of prestis, and he stood bisidis the auter. The coroun of britheren, as a plauntyng of cedre in the hil Liban, was aboute hym;

14 so thei stoden aboute hym as boowis of palm tree, and alle the sones of Aaron stoden in her glorie.

15 Sotheli the offryng of the Lord was in the hondis of hem, bifore al the synagoge of Israel; and he vside ful endyng on the auter, to alarge the offryng of the hiy kyng.

16 And he dresside his hond in moiste sacrifice; and sacrifiside in the blood of grape.

17 He schedde out in the foundement of the auter, the odour of God to the hiy prince.

18 Thanne the sones of Aaron crieden lowde; thei sowneden in trumpis betun out with hameris, and maden a grete vois herd in to mynde bifore God.

19 Thanne al the puple hastiden togidere, and fellen doun on the face on the erthe, for to worschipe her Lord God, and to yyue preyers to almyyti God an hiy.

20 And men syngynge in her voices alargiden; and a soun ful of swetnesse was maad in the greet hous.

21 And the puple preiede the hiy Lord in preier, til that the onour of the Lord was doon perfitli, and thei parformeden her yifte.

22 Thanne Symount cam doun, and reiside hise hondis in to al the congregacioun of the sones of Israel, to yyue glorie to God bi hise lippis, and to haue glorie in the name of hym.

23 And he reherside his preier, willynge to schewe the vertu of God.

24 And he preyede more the Lord of alle, that made grete thingis in ech lond; which encreeside oure daies fro the wombe of oure modir, and dide with vs bi his mercy.

25 Yyue he gladnesse of herte to vs, and that pees be maad in Israel bi euerlastynge daies;

26 that Israel bileue, that Goddis merci is with vs, that he delyuere hem in her dayes.

27 Mi soule hatith twei folkis; but the thridde is not a folk, whom Y hate.

28 Thei that sitten in the hil of Seir, and the Filisteis, and the fonned puple, that dwellith in Sichemys.

29 Jhesus, the sone of Sirach, a man of Jerusalem, wroot in this book the techyng of wisdom, and of kunnyng; and he renulide wisdom of his herte.

30 He is blessid, that dwellith in these goodis; he that settith tho in his herte, schal euere be wijs.

31 For if he doith these thingis, he schal be miyti to alle thingis; for whi the liyt of God is the step of hym.

CAP 51

1 Lord kyng, Y schal knouleche to thee; and Y schal togidere herie thee, my sauyour.

2 Y schal knouleche to thi name, for thou art maad an helpere and defendere to me;

3 and thou hast delyuered my bodi fro perdicioun, fro the snare of a wickid tunge, and fro the lippis of hem that

worchen a leesyng; and in the siyt of hem that stonden nyy thou art maad an helpere to me.

4 And thou hast delyuered me, bi the multitude of merci of thi name, fro roreris maad redi to mete;

5 fro the hondis of hem that souyten my soule, and fro many tribulaciouns that cumpassiden me;

6 fro ouerleiyng of flawme that cumpasside me, and in the myddis of fier Y was not brent;

7 fro the depthe of the wombe of helle, and fro a tunge defoulyd, and fro a word of leesyng; fro a wickid kyng, and fro a tunge vniust.

8 'Til to the deth my soule schal preise thee, Lord;

9 and my lijf was neiyynge in helle bynethe.

10 Thei cumpassiden me on ech side, and noon was that helpide; Y was biholdynge to the help of men, and noon was.

11 Lord, Y hadde mynde on thi merci, and on thi worchyng togidere, that ben fro the world;

12 for thou delyuerst hem that abiden thee, and thou delyuerst hem fro the hond of hethene men.

13 Thou enhaunsidist my dwellyng on erthe; and Y bisouyte for deth fletynge doun.

14 Y clepyde to help the Lord, fadir of my Lord, that he forsake not me in the dai of my tribulacioun, and forsake not me with outen help, in the tyme of hem that ben proude.

15 Y schal preise thi name contynueli, and Y schal herie it togidere in knoulechyng; and my preier is herd.

16 And thou hast delyuered me fro perdicioun, and thou hast delyuered me fro the wickid tyme.

17 Therfor Y schal knouleche, and Y schal seie heriyng to thee; and Y schal blesse the name of the Lord.

18 Whanne yit Y was yongere, bifore that Y erride, Y souyte wisdom opynli in my preier.

19 Bifore the tyme of eelde Y axide for it, and 'til in to the laste thingis Y schal enquere it; and it schal flour as a grape ripe bifore othere.

20 Myn herte was glad ther ynne, my foot yede a riytful weye; fro my yongthe Y souyte it.

21 Y bowide doun a litil myn eere, and Y took it.

22 Y foonde myche wisdom in my silf, and Y profitide myche ther ynne.

23 Y schal yyue glorie to hym, that yyueth wisdom to me.

24 For whi Y took councel to do it; Y loued feruentli good, and Y schal not be schent.

25 My soule wrastlide togidere ther ynne; and Y was confermyd in doynge it.

26 Y stretchide forth myn hondis an hiy; and my soule schynede in the wisdom of hym, and he liytnyde myn vnkunnyngis.

27 Y dresside my soule to it; and Y foond it in knowyng.

28 Y hadde pesibli fro the bigynnyng an herte with tho; for this thing Y schal not be forsakun.

29 My soule was disturblid in sekynge it; therfor Y schal haue pesibli a good possessioun.

30 For whi the Lord yaf to me a tunge my meede; and in it Y schal preise hym.

31 Ye vntauyt men, neiye to me; and gadere ye you in to the hous of techyng.

32 What tarien ye yit? and what seien ye in these thingis? youre soules thristen greetli.

33 Y openyde my mouth, and Y spak, Bie ye wisdom to you with out siluer,

34 and make youre necke suget to the yok therof, and youre soule resseyue techyng; for whi it is in the nexte to fynde it.

35 Se ye with youre iyen, that Y trauelide a litil, and Y foond myche reste to me.

36 Take ye techyng in myche noumbre of siluere, and welde ye plenteuouse gold ther ynne.

37 Youre soule be glad in the merci of hym; and ye schulen not be schent in the preysing of hym.

38 Worche ye youre werk bifore the tyme; and he schal yyue to you youre meede in his tyme.

ISAIAH

CAP 1

1 The visioun, ether profesie, of Ysaie, the sone of Amos, which he siy on Juda and Jerusalem, in the daies of Osie, of Joathan, of Achas, and of Ezechie, kyngis of Juda.

2 Ye heuenes, here, and thou erthe, perseyue with eeris, for the Lord spak. Y haue nurschid and Y haue enhaunsid sones; sotheli thei han dispisid me.

3 An oxe knew his lord, and an asse knew the cratche of his lord; but Israel knewe not me, and my puple vndurstood not.

4 Wo to the synful folk, to the puple heuy in wickidnesse, to the weiward seed, to the cursid sones; thei han forsake the Lord, thei han blasfemyd the hooli of Israel, thei ben aliened bacward.

5 On what thing schal Y smyte you more, that encreessen trespassyng? Ech heed is sijk, and ech herte is morenynge.

6 Fro the sole of the foot til to the nol, helthe is not ther ynne; wounde, and wannesse, and betyng bolnynge is not boundun aboute, nether curid bi medicyn, nether nurschid with oile.

7 Youre lond is forsakun, youre citees ben brent bi fier; aliens deuouren youre cuntrei bifore you, and it schal be disolat as in the distriyng of enemyes.

8 And the douytir of Sion, 'that is, Jerusalem, schal be forsakun as a schadewynge place in a vyner, and as an hulke in a place where gourdis wexen, and as a citee which is wastid.

9 If the Lord of oostis hadde not left seed to vs, we hadden be as Sodom, and we hadden be lijk as Gomorre.

10 Ye princes of men of Sodom, here the word of the Lord; and ye puple of Gommorre, perseyue with eeris the lawe of youre God.

11 Wherto offren ye to me the multitude of youre sacrifices? seith the Lord. Y am ful; Y wolde not the brent sacrifices of wetheris, and the ynnere fatnesse of fatte beestis, and the blood of calues, and of lambren, and of buckis of geet.

12 Whanne ye camen bifore my siyt, who axide of youre hondis these thingis, that ye schulden go in myn hallys?

13 Offre ye no more sacrifice in veyn; encense is abhomynacioun to me; Y schal not suffre neomenye, and sabat, and othere feestis.

14 Youre cumpenyes ben wickid; my soule hatith youre calendis and youre solempnytees; tho ben maad diseseful to me, Y trauelide suffrynge.

15 And whanne ye stretchen forth youre hondis, Y schal turne awei myn iyen fro you; and whanne ye multiplien preyer, Y schal not here; for whi youre hondis ben ful of blood.

16 Be ye waischun, be ye clene; do ye awei the yuel of youre thouytis fro myn iyen; ceesse ye to do weiwardli, lerne ye to do wel.

17 Seke ye doom, helpe ye hym that is oppressid, deme ye to the fadirles and modirles child, defende ye a widewe.

18 And come ye, and repreue ye me, seith the Lord. Thouy youre synnes ben as blood reed, tho schulen be maad whijt as snow; and thouy tho ben reed as vermylioun, tho schulen be whijt as wolle.

19 If ye wolen, and heren me, ye schulen ete the goodis of erthe.

20 That if ye nylen, and ye terren me to wrathfulnesse, swerd schal deuoure you; for whi the mouth of the Lord spak.

21 Hou is the feithful citee ful of dom maad an hoore? riytfulnesse dwellide ther ynne; but now menquelleris dwellen ther ynne.

22 Thi siluer is turned in to dros, ether filthe; thi wyn is medlid with watir.

23 Thi princes ben vnfeithful, the felowis of theuys; alle louen yiftis, suen meedis; thei demen not to a fadirles child, and the cause of a widewe entrith not to hem.

24 For this thing, seith the Lord God of oostis, the stronge of Israel, Alas! Y schal be coumfortid on myn enemyes, and Y schal be vengid on myn enemyes.

25 And Y schal turne myn hond to thee, and Y schal sethe out thi filthe to the cleene, and Y schal do awei al thi tyn.

26 And Y schal restore thi iuges, as thei weren bifor to, and thi counselours, as in elde tyme. Aftir these thingis thou schalt be clepid the citee of the riytful, a feithful citee.

27 Sion schal be ayen bouyt in dom, and thei schulen bringe it ayen in to riytfulnesse;

28 and God schal al to-breke cursid men and synneris togidere, and thei that forsoken the Lord, schulen be wastid.

29 For thei schulen be aschamed of idols, to whiche thei maden sacrifice; and ye shulen be aschamid on the orcherdis, whiche ye chesiden.

30 Whanne ye schulen be as an ook, whanne the leeues fallen doun, and as an orcherd with out watir.

31 And youre strengthe schal be as a deed sparcle of bonys, 'ether of herdis of flex, and youre werk schal be as a quyk sparcle; and euer either schal be brent togidere, and noon schal be that schal quenche.

CAP 2

1 The word which Ysaie, the sone of Amos, siy on Juda and Jerusalem.

2 And in the laste daies the hil of the hous of the Lord schal be maad redi in the cop of hillis, and schal be reisid aboue litle hillis. And alle hethene men schulen flowe to hym;

3 and many puplis schulen go, and schulen seie, Come ye, stie we to the hil of the Lord, and to the hous of God of Jacob; and he schal teche vs hise weies, and we schulen go in the pathis of hym. For whi the lawe schal go out of Syon, and the word of the Lord fro Jerusalem.

4 And he schal deme hethene men, and he schal repreue many puplis; and thei schulen welle togidere her swerdes in to scharris, and her speris in to sikelis, ether sithes; folk schal no more reise swerd ayens folk, and thei schulen no more be exercisid to batel.

5 Come ye, the hous of Jacob, and go we in the liyt of the Lord.

6 Forsothe thou hast cast awei thi puple, the hous of Jacob, for thei ben fillid as sum tyme bifore; and thei hadden false dyuynouris bi the chiteryng of briddis, as Filisteis, and thei cleuyden to alien children.

7 The lond is fillid with siluer and gold, and noon ende is of the tresouris therof; and the lond therof is fillid with horsis, and the foure horsid cartis therof ben vnnoumbrable.

8 And the lond therof is fillid with ydols, and thei worschipiden the werk of her hondis, which her fyngris maden;

9 and a man bowide hymsilf, and a man of ful age was maad low. Therfor foryyue thou not to hem.

10 Entre thou, puple of Juda, in to a stoon, be thou hid in a diche in erthe, fro the face of the drede of the Lord, and fro the glorie of his mageste.

11 The iyen of an hiy man ben maad low, and the hiynesse of men schal be bowid doun; forsothe the Lord aloone schal be enhaunsid in that dai.

12 For the dai of the Lord of oostis schal be on ech proud man and hiy, and on ech boostere, and he schal be maad low;

13 and on alle the cedres of the Liban hiye and reisid, and on alle the ookis of Baisan,

14 and on alle hiy munteyns, and on alle litle hillis, 'that ben reisid;

15 and on ech hiy tour, and on ech strong wal;

16 and on alle schippis of Tharsis, and on al thing which is fair in siyt.

17 And al the hiynesse of men schal be bowid doun, and the hiynesse of men schal be maad low; and the Lord aloone schal be reisid in that dai,

18 and idols schulen be brokun togidere outirli.

19 And thei schulen entre in to dennes of stoonys, and in to the swolewis of erthe, fro the face of the inward drede of the Lord, and fro the glorie of his maieste, whanne he schal ryse to smyte the lond.

20 In that dai a man schal caste awei the idols of his siluer, and the symylacris of his gold, whiche he hadde maad to hym silf, for to worschipe moldewarpis and backis, 'ether rere myis.

21 And he schal entre in to chynnis, ethir crasyngis, of stoonys, and in to the caues of hard roochis, fro the face of the inward drede of the Lord, and fro the glorie of his mageste, whanne he schal ryse to smyte the lond.

22 Therfor ceesse ye fro a man, whos spirit is in hise nose thirlis, for he is arettid hiy.

CAP 3

1 For lo! the lordli gouernour, the Lord of oostis, schal take awei fro Jerusalem and fro Juda a myyti man, and strong, and al the strengthe of breed, and al the strengthe of watir;

2 a strong man, and a man a werriour, and a domesman, and a profete, and a false dyuynour in auteris, and an elde man,

3 a prince ouer fifti men, and a worschipful man in cheer, and a counselour, and a wijs man of principal crafti men, and a prudent man of mystik, ethir goostli, speche.

4 And Y schal yyue children the princes of hem, and men of wymmens condiciouns schulen be lordis of hem.

5 And the puple schal falle doun, a man to a man, ech man to his neiybore; a child schal make noyse ayens an eld man, and an vnnoble man ayens a noble man.

6 For a man schal take his brother, the meneal of his fadir, and schal seie, A clooth is to thee, be thou oure prince; forsothe this fallyng be vndur thin hond.

7 And he schal answere in that dai, and seie, Y am no leche, and nether breed, nether cloth is in myn hous; nyle ye make me prince of the puple.

8 For whi Jerusalem felle doun, and Juda felle doun togidere; for the tunge of hem, and the fyndingis of hem weren ayens the Lord, for to terre to wraththe the iyen of his mageste.

9 The knowyng of her cheer schal answere to hem; and thei prechiden her synne, as Sodom dide, and hidden not. Wo to the soule of hem, for whi yuels ben yoldun to hem.

10 Seie ye to the iust man, that it schal be to hym wel; for he schal ete the fruyt of hise fyndyngis.

11 Wo to the wickid man in to yuel; for whi the yeldyng of hise hondis schal be maad to hym.

12 The wrongful axeris of my puple robbiden it, and wymmen weren lordis therof. Mi puple, thei that seien thee blessid, disseyuen thee, and distrien the weie of thi steppis.

13 The Lord stondith for to deme, and 'the Lord stondith for to deme puplis;

14 the Lord schal come to doom, with the eldere men of his puple, and with hise princes; for ye han wastid my vyner, and the raueyn of a pore man is in youre hous.

15 Whi al to-breken ye my puple, and grynden togidere the faces of pore men? seith the Lord God of oostis.

16 And the Lord God seide, For that that the douytris of Syon weren reisid, and yeden with a necke stretchid forth, and yeden bi signes of iyen, and flappiden with hondis, and yeden, and with her feet yeden in wel araied goyng,

17 the Lord schal make ballyd the nol of the douytris of Sion, and the Lord schal make nakid the heer of hem.

18 In that dai the Lord schal take awei the ournement of schoon, and goldun litle bellis lijk the moone,

19 and ribans, and brochis, and ournementis of armes nyy the schuldris, and mytris, ether chapelettis,

20 and coombis, and ournementis of armes niy the hondis, and goldun ourenementis lijk laumpreis, and litil vessels of oynementis,

21 and eere ryngis, and ryngis, and preciouse stoonys hangynge in the forheed,

22 and chaungynge clothis, and mentils, and schetis, ether smockis, and needlis,

23 and myrouris, and smal lynun clothis aboute the schuldris, and kercheues, and roketis.

24 And stynk shal be for swete odour, and a corde for the girdil; ballidnesse schal be for crispe heer, and an heire for a brest girdil.

25 Also thi faireste men schulen falle bi swerd, and thi stronge men schulen falle in batel.

26 And the yatis therof schulen weile, and morene; and it schal sitte desolat in erthe.

CAP 4

1 And seuene wymmen schulen catche o man in that dai, and schulen seie, We schulen ete oure breed, and we schulen be hilid with oure clothis; oneli thi name be clepid on vs, do thou awei oure schenschip.

2 In that dai the buriownyng of the Lord schal be in greet worschip and glorie; and the fruyt of erthe schal be hiy, and ful out ioye 'schal be to hem that schulen be sauyd of Israel.

3 And it schal be, ech that is left in Sion, and is resydue in Jerusalem, schal be clepid hooli; ech that is writun in lijf in Jerusalem;

4 if the Lord waischith awei the filthis of the douytris of Sion, and waischith the blood of Jerusalem fro the myddis therof, in the spirit of doom, and in the spirit of heete.

5 And the Lord made on ech place of the hille of Sion, and where he was clepid to help, a cloude bi dai, and smoke, and briytnesse of fier flawmynge in the niyt; for whi hilyng schal be aboue al glorie.

6 And a tabernacle schal be in to a schadewynge place of the dai, fro heete, and in to sikirnesse and in to hidyng, fro whirlewynd and fro reyn.

CAP 5

1 I schal synge for my derlyng the song of myn vnclis sone, of his vyner. A vyner was maad to my derlyng, in the horne in the sone of oile.

2 And he heggide it, and chees stoonys therof, and plauntide a chosun vyner; and he bildide a tour in the myddis therof, and rerede a presse ther ynne; and he abood, that it schulde bere grapis, and it bare wielde grapis.

3 Now therfor, ye dwelleris of Jerusalem, and ye men of Juda, deme bitwixe me and my viner.

4 What is it that Y ouyt to do more to my vyner, and Y dide not to it? whether that Y aboob, that it schulde bere grapis, and it bare wielde grapis?

5 And now Y schal schewe to you, what Y schal do to my vyner. Y schal take awei the hegge therof, and it schal be in to rauyschyng; Y schal caste doun the wal therof, and it schal be in to defoulyng; and Y schal sette it desert,

6 ether forsakun. It schal not be kit, and it schal not be diggid, and breris and thornes schulen 'growe vp on it; and Y schal comaunde to cloudis, that tho reyne not reyn on it.

7 Forsothe the vyner of the Lord of oostis is the hous of Israel, and the men of Juda ben the delitable buriownyng of hym. Y abood, that it schal make doom, and lo! wickidnesse; and that it schulde do riytfulnesse, and lo! cry.

8 Wo to you that ioynen hows to hous, and couplen feeld to feeld, 'til to the ende of place. Whether ye aloone schulen dwelle in the myddis of the lond?

9 These thingis ben in the eeris of me, the Lord of oostis; if many housis ben not forsakun, grete housis and faire, with outen dwellere, bileue ye not to me.

10 For whi ten acris of vynes schulen make a potel, and thretti buschels of seed schulen make thre buschels.

11 Wo to you that risen togidere eerli to sue drunkennesse, and to drinke 'til to euentid, that ye brenne with wyn.

12 Harpe, and giterne, and tympan, and pipe, and wyn ben in youre feestis; and ye biholden not the werk of the Lord, nether ye biholden the werkis of hise hondis.

13 Therfor my puple is led prisoner, for it hadde not kunnyng; and the noble men therof perischiden in hungur, and the multitude therof was drye in thirst.

14 Therfor helle alargide his soule, and openyde his mouth with outen ony ende; and strong men therof, and the puple therof, and the hiy men, and gloriouse men therof, schulen go doun to it.

15 And a man schal be bowid doun, and a man of age schal be maad low; and the iyen of hiy men schulen be pressid doun.

16 And the Lord of oostis schal be enhaunsid in doom, and hooli God schal be halewid in riytfulnesse.

17 And lambren schulen be fed bi her ordre, and comelyngis schulen ete desert places turned in to plentee.

18 Wo to you that drawen wickydnesse in the cordis of vanyte, and drawen synne as the boond of a wayn; and ye seien,

19 The werk of hym haaste, and come soone, that we se; and the counsel of the hooli of Israel neiy, and come, and we schulen knowe it.

20 Wo to you that seien yuel good, and good yuel; and putten derknessis liyt, and liyt derknessis; and putten bittir thing in to swete, and swete thing in to bittir.

21 Wo to you that ben wise men in youre iyen, and ben prudent bifor you silf.

22 Wo to you that ben myyti to drynke wyn, and ben stronge to meddle drunkenesse;

23 and ye iustifien a wickid man for yiftis, and ye taken awei the riytfulnesse of a iust man fro hym.

24 For this thing, as the tunge of fier deuourith stobil, and the heete of flawme brenneth, so the roote of hem schal be as a deed sparcle, and the seed of hem schal stie as dust; for thei castiden awei the lawe of the Lord of oostis, and blasfemyden the speche of the hooli of Israel.

25 Therfor the strong veniaunce of the Lord was wrooth ayens his puple, and he stretchide forth his hond on it, and smoot it; and hillis weren disturblid, and the deed bodies of hem weren maad as a toord in the myddis of stretis. In alle these thingis the stronge vengeaunce of him was not turned awei, but yit his hond was stretchid forth.

26 And he schal reise a signe among naciouns afer, and he schal hisse to hym fro the endis of erthe; and lo! he schal haaste, and schal come swiftli.

27 Noon is failynge nethir trauelynge in that oost; he schal not nappe, nether slepe, nether the girdil of his reynes schal be vndo, nether the lace of his scho schal be brokun.

28 Hise arowis ben scharpe, and alle hise bowis ben bent; the houys of hise horsis ben as a flynt, and hise wheelis ben as the feersnesse of tempest.

29 His roryng schal be as of lioun; he schal rore as the whelpis of liouns; and he schal gnaste, and schal holde prey, and schal biclippe, and noon schal be, that schal delyuere.

30 And he schal sowne on it in that dai, as doith the soun of the see; we schulen biholde in to the erthe, and lo! derknessis of tribulacioun, and liyt is maad derk in the derknesse therof.

CAP 6

1 In the yeer in which the kyng Osie was deed, Y siy the Lord sittynge on an hiy seete, and reisid; and the hous was ful of his mageste, and tho thingis that weren vndur hym, filliden the temple.

2 Serafyn stoden on it, sixe wyngis weren to oon, and sixe wyngis to the tothir; with twei wyngis thei hiliden the face of hym, and with twei wyngis thei hiliden the feet of hym, and with twei wyngis thei flowen.

3 And thei crieden 'the toon to the tother, and seiden, Hooli, hooli, hooli is the Lord God of oostis; al erthe is ful of his glorie.

4 And the lyntels aboue of the herris were moued togidere of the vois of the criere, and the hous was fillid with smoke.

5 And Y seide, Wo to me, for Y was stille; for Y am a man defoulid in lippis, and Y dwelle in the myddis of the puple hauynge defoulid lippis, and Y siy with myn iyen the kyng Lord of oostis.

6 And oon of serafyn flei to me, and a brennynge cole was in his hond, which cole he hadde take with a tonge fro the auter.

7 And he touchide my mouth, and seide, Lo! Y haue touchid thi lippis with this cole, and thi wickidnesse schal be don awei, and thi synne schal be clensid.

8 And Y herde the vois of the Lord, seiynge, Whom schal Y sende, and who schal go to you? And Y seide, Lo! Y; sende thou me.

9 And he seide, Go thou, and thou schalt seie to this puple, Ye herynge here, and nyle ye vndurstonde; and se ye the profesie, and nyle ye knowe.

10 Make thou blynde the herte of this puple, and aggrege thou the eeris therof, and close thou the iyen therof; lest perauenture it se with hise iyen, and here with hise eeris, and vndurstonde with his herte, and it be conuertid, and Y make it hool.

11 And Y seide, Lord, hou long? And he seide, Til citees ben maad desolat with out dwellere, and housis with out man. And the lond schal be left desert,

12 and the Lord schal make men fer. And that that was forsakun in the myddil of erthe, schal be multiplied, and yit tithing schal be ther ynne;

13 and it schal be conuertid, and it schal be in to schewyng, as a terebynte is, and as an ook, that spredith abrood hise boowis; that schal be hooli seed, that schal stonde ther ynne.

CAP 7

1 And it was don in the daies of Achas, the sone of Joathan, the sone of Osias, kyng of Juda, Rasyn, the kyng of Sirie, and Facee, the sone of Romelie, the kyng of Israel, stieden to Jerusalem, for to fiyte ayens it; and thei myyten not ouercome it.

2 And thei telden to the hous of Dauid, and seiden, Sirie hath restid on Effraym, and the herte of hym and of his puple was mouyd togidere, as the trees of wodis ben mouyd of the face of the wynd.

3 And the Lord seide to Isaie, Go thou out, and Jasub, thi sone, which is left, in to the meetyng of Achas, at the laste ende of the water cundijt of the hiyere cisterne, in the weie of the feeld of the fullere.

4 And thou schalt seie to hym, Se thou, that thou be stille; nyle thou drede, and thin herte be not aferd of twei tailis of these brondis smokynge in the wraththe of woodnesse, of Rasyn, kynge of Sirie, and of the sone of Romelye.

5 For Sirie, and Effraym, and the sone of Romelie, han bigunne yuel councel ayens thee, and seien, Stie we to Juda,

6 and reise we hym, and drawe we hym out to vs; and sette we a kyng in the myddis therof, the sone of Tabeel.

7 The Lord God seith these thingis, This schal not be, and it schal not stonde;

8 but Damask schal be the heed of Sirie, and Rasyn 'schal be the heed of Damask; and yit sixti yeer and fiue, and Effraym schal faile to be a puple;

9 and Samarie shal faile to be the heed of Effraym, and the sone of Romelie 'schal faile to be heed of Samarie. Forsothe if ye schulen not bileue, ye schulen not dwelle.

10 And the Lord addide to speke to Achas,

11 and seide, Axe thou to thee a signe of thi Lord God, in to the depthe of helle, ethir in to heiythe aboue.

12 And Achas seide, Y schal not axe, and Y schal not tempte the Lord.

13 And Ysaie seide, Therfor the hous of Dauid, here ye; whether it is litil to you to be diseseful to men, for ye ben diseseful also to my God?

14 For this thing the Lord hym silf schal yyue a signe to you. Lo! a virgyn schal conseyue, and schal bere a sone; and his name schal be clepid Emanuel.

15 He schal ete botere and hony, that he kunne repreue yuel, and cheese good.

16 For whi bifore that the child kunne repreue yuel, and chese good, the lond, which thou wlatist, schal be forsakun of the face of her twei kyngis.

17 The Lord schal brynge on thee, and on thi puple, and on the hous of thi fadir, daies that camen not fro the daies of departyng of Effraym fro Juda, with the kyng of Assiriens.

18 And it schal be, in that dai the Lord schal hisse to a flie, which is in the laste parte of the floodis of Egipt; and to a bee, which is in the lond of Assur;

19 and 'alle so schulen come, and schulen reste in the strondis of valeis, and in caues of stoonis, and in alle places of buyschis, and in alle hoolis.

20 And in that dai the Lord schal schaue with a scharp rasour in these men, that ben biyendis the flood, in the kyng of Assiriens, the heed, and heeris of the feet, and al the beerd.

21 And it schal be, in that day a man schal nurische a cow of oxis, and twei scheep,

22 and for the plentee of mylk he schal ete botere; for whi ech man that schal be left in the myddis of the lond, schal ete boter and hony.

23 And it schal be, in that dai ech place where a thousand vyneris schulen be worth a thousynde platis of siluer, and schulen be in to thornes and breeris,

24 men schulen entre thidur with bouwis and arowis; for whi breris and thornes schulen be in al the lond.

25 And alle hillis that schulen be purgid with a sarpe, the drede of thornes and of breris schal not come thidir; and it schal be in to lesewe of oxen, and in to treding of scheep.

CAP 8

1 And the Lord seide to me, Take to thee a greet book, and write ther ynne with the poyntil of man, Swiftli drawe thou awei spuylis, take thou prey soone.

2 And Y yaf to me faithful witnessis, Vrie, the prest, and Sacarie, the sone of Barachie.

3 And Y neiyede to the profetesse; and sche conseyuede, and childide a sone. And the Lord seide to me, Clepe thou his name Haste thou to drawe awei spuylis, haaste thou for to take prey.

4 For whi bifor that the child kan clepe his fadir and his modir, the strengthe of Damask schal be doon awei, and the spuylis of Samarie, bifor the kyng of Assiriens.

5 And the Lord addide to speke yit to me, and he seide,

6 For that thing that this puple hath caste awei the watris of Siloe, that goen with silence, and hath take more Rasyn, and the sone of Romelie, for this thing lo!

7 The Lord schal brynge on hem the stronge and many watris of the flood, the king of Assiriens, and al his glorie; and he schal stiye on alle the stremes therof, and he schal flowe on alle the ryueris therof.

8 And he schal go flowynge bi Juda, and he schal passe til to the necke, and schal come; and the spredyng forth of hise wyngis schal be, and schal fille the breede of thi lond, thou Emanuel.

9 Puplis, be ye gaderid togidere, and be ye ouercomun; and alle londis afer, here ye. Be ye coumfortid, and be ye ouercomun; gird ye you, and be ye ouercomun;

10 take ye councel, and it schal be destried; speke ye a word, and it schal not be doon, for God is with vs.

11 For whi the Lord seith these thingis to me, as he tauyte me in a stronge hond, that Y schulde not go in to the weie of this puple,

12 and seide, Seie ye not, It is sweryng togidere, for whi alle thingis which this puple spekith is sweryng togidere; and drede ye not the ferdfulnesse therof, nether be ye aferd.

13 Halowe ye the Lord hym silf of oostis; and he schal be youre inward drede, and he schal be youre ferdfulnesse, and he schal be to you in to halewyng.

14 Forsothe he schal be in to a stoon of hirtyng, and in to a stoon of sclaundre, to tweyne housis of Israel; in to a snare, and in to fallyng, to hem that dwellen in Jerusalem.

15 And ful many of hem schulen offende, and schulen falle, and thei schulen be al to-brokun, and thei schulen be boundun, and schulen be takun.

16 Bynde thou witnessyng, mark thou the lawe in my disciplis.

17 Y schal abide the Lord, that hath hid his face fro the hous of Jacob, and Y schal abide hym.

18 Lo! Y and my children, whiche the Lord yaf to me in to a signe, and greet wondur to Israel, of the Lord of oostis that dwellith in the hil of Sion.

19 And whanne thei seien to you, Axe ye of coniureris, and of false dyuynouris, that gnasten in her enchauntyngis, whether the puple schal not axe of her God a reuelacioun for quyke men and deed?

20 It is to go to the lawe more and to the witnessyng, that if thei seien not after this word, morewtide liyt schal not be to hem.

21 And it schal passe bi that, and it schal falle doun, and it schal hungre. And whanne it schal hungre, it schal be wrooth, and schal curse his kyng and his God, and it schal biholde vpward.

22 And it schal loke to the erthe, and lo! tribulacioun, and derknessis, and vnbyndyng, ether discoumfort, and angwisch, and myist pursuynge; and it schal not mow fle awei fro his angwisch.

CAP 9

1 In the firste tyme the lond of Zabulon and the lond of Neptalym was releessid; and at the laste the weie of the see biyende Jordan of Galile of hethene men was maad heuy.

2 The puple that yede in derknessis siy a greet liyt; whanne men dwelliden in the cuntre of schadewe of deth, liyt roos vp to hem.

3 Thou multipliedist folk, thou magnefiedist not gladnesse; thei schulen be glad bifore thee, as thei that ben glad in heruest, as ouercomeris maken ful out ioie, whanne thei han take a prey, whanne thei departen the spuylis.

4 For thou hast ouercome the yok of his birthun, and the yerde of his schuldre, and the ceptre of his wrongful axere, as in the day of Madian.

5 For whi al violent raueyn with noise, and a cloth meddlid with blood schal be in to brennyng, and 'schal be the mete of fier.

6 Forsothe a litil child is borun to vs, and a sone is youun to vs, and prinsehod is maad on his schuldre; and his name schal be clepid Wondurful, A counselour, God, Strong, A fadir of the world to comynge, A prince of pees.

7 His empire schal be multiplied, and noon ende schal be of his pees; he schal sitte on the seete of Dauid, and on the rewme of hym, that he conferme it, and make stronge in doom and riytfulnesse, fro hennus forth and til in to with outen ende. The feruent loue of the Lord of oostis schal make this.

8 The Lord sente a word in to Jacob, and it felle in Israel.

9 And al the puple of Effraym schal wite, and thei that dwellen in Samarie, seiynge in the pride and greetnesse of herte,

10 Tijl stoonys fellen doun, but we schulen bilde with square stoonys; thei han kit doun sicomoris, but we schulen chaunge cedris.

11 And the Lord schal reise the enemyes of Rasyn on hym, and he schal turne the enemyes of hym in to noyse;

12 God schal make Sirie to come fro the eest, and Filisteis fro the west; and with al the mouth thei schulen deuoure Israel. In alle these thingis the stronge veniaunce of the Lord is not turned awei, but yit his hond is stretchid forth;

13 and the puple is not turned ayen to the Lord smytynge it, and thei souyten not the Lord of oostis.

14 And the Lord schal leese fro Israel the heed and the tail; crokynge and bischrewynge, ether refreynynge, in o dai.

15 An elde man and onourable, he is the heed, and a profete techynge a leesyng, he is the tail.

16 And thei that blessen his puple, schulen be disseyueris, and thei that ben blessid, schulen be cast doun.

17 For this thing the Lord schal not be glad on the yonge men therof, and he schal not haue merci on the fadirles children and widewis therof; for ech man is an ypocrite and weiward, and ech mouth spak foli. In alle these thingis the stronge veniaunce of hym is not turned awei, but yit his hond is stretchid forth;

18 and the puple is not turned ayen to the Lord smytynge it. For whi wickidnesse is kyndlid as fier; it schal deuoure the breris and thornes, and it schal be kyndlid in the thickenesse of the forest, and it schal be wlappid togidere in the pride of smoke.

19 In the wraththe of the Lord of oostis the lond schal be disturblid, and the puple schal be as the mete of fier; a man schal not spare his brothir.

20 And he schal boowe to the riyt half, and he schal hungre, and he schal ete at the left half, and he schal not be fillid; ech man schal deuoure the fleisch of his arm. Manasses schal deuoure Effraym, and Effraym 'schal deuoure Manasses, and thei togidere ayens Juda.

21 In alle these thingis the strong veniaunce of hym is not turned awei, but yit his hoond is stretchid forth.

CAP 10

1 Wo to them that maken wickid lawis, and thei writynge han wryte vnriytfulnesse, for to oppresse pore men in doom,

2 and to do violence to the cause of meke men of my puple; that widewis schulen be the prey of them, and that thei schulden rauysche fadirles children.

3 What schulen ye do in the dai of visitacioun, and of wretchidnesse comynge fro fer? To whos help schulen ye fle? and where schulen ye leeue youre glorie,

4 that ye be not bowid doun vndur boond, and falle not doun with slayn men? On alle these thingis his strong veniaunce is not turned awei, but yit his hond is stretchid forth.

5 Wo to Assur, he is the yerde and staf of my strong veniaunce; myn indignacioun is in the hond of them.

6 Y schal send hym to a fals folk, and Y schal comaunde to hym ayens the puple of my strong veniaunce; that he take awei the spuylis, and departe prey, and that he sette that puple in to defouling, as the fen of stretis.

7 Forsothe he schal not deme so, and his herte schal not gesse so, but his herte schal be for to al to-breke, and to the sleynge of many folkis.

8 For he schal seie, Whether my princes ben not kyngis to gidere?

9 Whether not as Carcamys, so Calanno; and as Arphat, so Emath? whether not as Damask, so Samarie?

10 As myn hond foond the rewmes of idol, so and the symylacris of hem of Jerusalem and of Samarie.

11 Whether not as Y dide to Samarie, and to the idols therof, so Y schal do to Jerusalem, and to the simylacris therof?

12 And it schal be, whanne the Lord hath fillid alle hise werkis in the hil of Syon and in Jerusalem, Y schal visite on the fruit of the greet doynge herte of the kyng of Assur, and on the glorie of the hiynesse of hise iyen.

13 For he seide, Y haue do in the strengthe of myn honde, and Y haue understonde in my wisdom; and Y haue take awei the endis of peplis, and Y haue robbid the princes of them, and Y as a myyti man haue drawun doun them that saten an hiy.

14 And myn hond foond the strengthe of puplis as a nest, and as eirun ben gaderid togidere that ben forsakun, so Y gaderid togidere al erthe; and noon was that mouyde a fethere, and openyde the mouth, and grutchide.

15 Whether an ax schal haue glorie ayens hym that kittith with it? ether a sawe schal be enhaunsid ayens hym of whom it is drawun? as if a yerde is reisid ayens hym that reisith it, and a staf is enhaunsid, which sotheli is a tre.

16 For this thing the lordli gouernour, Lord of oostis, schal sende thinnesse in the fatte men of hym, and his glorie kyndlid vndur schal brenne as 'the brenning of fier.

17 And the liyt of Israel schal be in fier, and the hooli of it in flawme; and the thorn of him and brere schal be kyndlid and deuourid in o dai.

18 And the glorie of his forest and of his Carmele schal be wastid, fro the soule 'til to fleisch; and he schal be fleynge awei for drede.

19 And the relifs of the tree of his forest schulen be noumbrid for fewnesse, and a child schal write hem.

20 And it schal be in that dai, the remenaunt of Israel, and thei that fledden of the house of Jacob, schal not adde for to triste on hym that smytith hem; but it schal triste on the hooli Lord of Israel, in treuthe.

21 The relifs, Y seie, the relifs of Jacob, schulen be conuertid to the stronge Lord.

22 Forwhi, Israel, if thi puple is as the grauel of the see, the relifs schulen be turned therof; an endyng maad schort schal make riytfulnesse to be plenteuouse.

23 For whi the Lord God of oostis schal make an endyng and a breggyng in the myddis of al erthe.

24 For this thing the Lord God of oostis seith these thingis, My puple, the dwellere of Sion, nyle thou drede of Assur, for he schal smite thee in a yerde, and he schal reise his staf on thee in the weie of Egipt.

25 Forwhi yit a litil, and a litil, and myn indignacioun and my strong veniaunce schal be endid on the greet trespas of hem.

26 And the Lord of oostis schal reise a scourge on hym bi the veniaunce of Madian in the stoon of Oreb, and bi his yerde on the see; and he schal reise that yerde in the wei of Egipt.

27 And it schal be in that dai, his birthun schal be takun awei fro thi schuldre, and his yok fro thi necke; and the yok schal wexe rotun fro the face of oile.

28 He schal come in to Aioth, he schal passe in to Magron, at Magynas he schal bitake his vessels to kepyng.

29 Thei passiden swiftli, Gabaa is oure seete, Rama was astonyed, Gabaa of Saul fled.

30 Thou douytir of Gallym, weile with thi vois; thou Laisa, perseyue, thou pore Anatot.

31 Medemena passide; the dwelleris of Gabyn fledden; be ye coumfortid.

32 Yit it is dai, that me stonde in Nobe; he schal dryue his hond on the hil of the douyter of Syon, on the litil hil of Jerusalem.

33 Lo! the lordli gouernour, the Lord of oostis, schal breke a potel in drede, and hiy men of stature schulen be kit doun.

34 And proude men schulen be maade low, and the thicke thingis of the forest schulen be distried bi irun; and the Liban with hiy thingis schal falle doun.

CAP 11

1 And a yerde schal go out of the roote of Jesse, and a flour schal stie of the roote of it.

2 And the Spirit of the Lord schal reste on hym, the spirit of wisdom and of vndurstondyng, the spirit of counsel and of strengthe, the spirit of kunnyng and of pitee;

3 and the spirit of the drede of the Lord schal fille him. He schal deme not bi the siyt of iyen, nether he schal repreue bi the heryng of eeris;

4 but he schal deme in riytfulnesse pore men, and he schal repreue in equyte, for the mylde men of erthe. And he schal smyte the lond with the yerde of his mouth, and bi the spirit of his lippis he schal sle the wickid man.

5 And riytfulnesse schal be the girdil of hise leendis, and feith schal be the girdyng of hise reynes.

6 A wolf schal dwelle with a lombe, and a parde schal reste with a kide; a calf, and a lioun, and a scheep schulen dwelle togidere, and a litil child schal dryue hem.

7 A calf and a beere schulen be lesewid togidere; the whelpis of hem schulen reste, and a lioun as an oxe schal ete stre.

8 And a yonge soukyng child fro the tete schal delite on the hole of a snake, and he that is wenyd schal putte his hond in the caue of a cocatrice.

9 Thei schulen not anoye, and schulen not sle in al myn hooli hil; forwhi the erthe is fillid with the kunnyng of the Lord, as watris of the see hilynge.

10 In that dai the roote of Jesse, that stondith in to the signe of puplis; hethene men schulen biseche hym, and his sepulchre schal be gloriouse.

11 And it schal be in that day, the Lord schal adde the secounde tyme his hond to haue in possessioun the residue of his puple that schal be left, of Assiriens, and of Egipt, and of Fethros, and of Ethiope, and of Elan, and of Sennar, and of Emath, and of ylis of the see.

12 And he schal reise a sygne to naciouns, and schal gadere togidere the fleeris awei of Israel; and he schal gadere togidere the scaterid men of Juda fro foure coostis of erthe.

13 And the enuye of Effraym schal be don awei, and the enemyes of Juda schulen perische; Effraym schal not haue enuye to Juda, and Juda schal not fiyte ayens Effraym.

14 And thei schulen flie in to the schuldris of Filisteis bi the see, thei schulen take prey togidere of the sones of the eest; Ydume and Moab schulen be the comaundement of the hond of hem, and the sones of Amon schulen be obedient.

15 And the Lord schal make desolat the tunge of the see of Egipt, and he schal reise his hond on the flood in the strengthe of his spirit; and he schal smyte, ethir departe, it in seuene ryueris, so that schood men passe bi it.

16 And a weie schal be to my residue puple that schal be left, of Assiriens, as it was to Israel, in the dai in which it stiede fro the lond of Egipt.

CAP 12

1 And thou schalt seie in that dai, Lord, Y schal knouleche to thee, for thou were wrooth to me; thi strong venieaunce is turned, and thou hast coumfortid me.

2 Lo! God is my sauyour, Y schal do feithfuli, and Y schal not drede. For whi the Lord is my strengthe and my preysyng, and he is maad to me in to helthe.

3 Ye schulen drawe watris with ioie of the wellis of the sauyour.

4 And ye schulen seie in that dai, Knouleche ye to the Lord, and clepe ye his name in to help; make ye knowun hise fyndyngis among puplis; haue ye mynde, that his name is hiy.

5 Synge ye to the Lord, for he hath do worschipfuli; telle ye this in al erthe.

6 Thou dwellyng of Syon, make ful out ioie, and preise; for whi the hooli of Israel is greet in the myddis of thee.

CAP 13

1 The birthun of Babiloyne, which birthun Ysaie, the sone of Amos, siy.

2 Reise ye a signe on a myisti hil, and enhaunse ye vois; reise ye the hond, and duykis entre bi the yatis.

3 Y haue comaundid to myn halewid men, and Y clepid my stronge men in my wraththe, that maken ful out ioie in my glorie.

4 The vois of multitude in hillis, as of many puplis; the vois of sown of kyngis, of hethene men gaderit togidere. The Lord of oostis comaundide to the chyualry of batel,

5 to men comynge fro a fer lond. The Lord cometh fro the hiynesse of heuene, and the vessels of his strong veniaunce, that he distrie al the lond.

6 Yelle ye, for the dai of the Lord is niy; as wastyng it schal come of the Lord.

7 For this thing alle hondis schulen be vnmyyti, and eche herte of man schal faile,

8 and schal be al to-brokun. Gnawyngis and sorewis schulen holde Babiloyns; thei schulen haue sorewe, as they that trauelen of child. Ech man schal wondre at his neiybore; her cheris schulen be brent faces.

9 Lo! the dai of the Lord schal come, cruel, and ful of indignacioun, and of wraththe, and of woodnesse; to sette the lond into wildirnesse, and to al to-breke the synneris therof fro that lond.

10 For whi the sterris of heuene and the schynyng of tho schulen not sprede abrood her liyt; the sunne is maade derk in his risyng, and the moone schal not schine in hir liyt.

11 And Y schal visite on the yuels of the world, and Y schal visite ayens wickid men the wickidnesse of hem; and Y schal make the pride of vnfeithful men for to reste, and Y schal make low the boost of stronge men.

12 A man of ful age schal be preciousere than gold, and a man schal be preciousere than pure gold and schynyng.

13 On this thing I schal disturble heuene, and the erthe schal be moued fro his place; for the indignacioun of the Lord of oostis, and for the dai of wraththe of his strong veniaunce.

14 And it schal be as a doo fleynge, and as a scheep, and noon schal be that schal gadere togidere; ech man schal turne to his puple, and alle bi hem silf schulen fle to her lond.

15 Ech man that is foundun, schal be slayn; and ech man that cometh aboue, schal falle doun bi swerd.

16 The yonge children of them schulen be hurtlid doun bifore the iyen of them; her housis schulen be rauischid, and her wyues schulen be defoulid.

17 Lo! Y schal reise on them Medeis, that seken not siluer, nethir wolen gold;

18 but thei shulen sle litle children bi arowis, and thei schulen not haue merci on wombis yyuynge mylk, and the iye of them schal not spare on sones.

19 And Babiloyne, thilke gloriouse citee in rewmes, noble in the pride of Caldeis, schal be destried, as God destried Sodom and Gomore.

20 It shall not be enhabitid til in to the ende, and it schal not be foundid til to generacioun and generacioun; a man of Arabie schal not sette tentis there, and scheepherdis schulen not reste there.

21 But wielde beestis schulen reste there, and the housis of hem schulen be fillid with dragouns; and ostrichis schulen dwelle there, and heeri beestis schulen skippe there.

22 And bitouris schulen answere there in the housis therof, and fliynge serpentis in the templis of lust.

CAP 14

1 It is niy that the tyme therof come, and the daies therof schulen not be maad fer; for whi the Lord schal haue merci of Jacob, and he schal chese yit of Israel, and schal make them for to reste on her lond; a comelyng schal be ioyned to them, and schal cleue to the house of Jacob.

2 And puplis schulen holde hem, and schulen brynge hem in to her place. And the hous of Israel schal haue hem in possessioun in to seruauntis and handmaidis on the lond of the Lord; and thei schulen take tho men that token hem, and thei schulen make suget her wrongful axeris.

3 And it schal be in that dai, whanne God schal yyue to thee reste of thi trauel, and of thi shakyng, and of hard seruage, in which thou seruedist bifore,

4 thou schalt take this parable ayens the kyng of Babiloyne, and thou schalt sei, Hou ceesside the wrongful axere, restide tribute?

5 The Lord hath al to-broke the staf of wickid men, the yerde of lordis,

6 that beet puplis in indignacioun, with vncurable wounde, that sugetide folkis in woodnesse, that pursuede cruely.

7 Ech lond restide, and was stille; it was ioiful, and made ful out ioie.

8 Also fir trees and cedris of the Liban weren glad on thee; sithen thou sleptist, noon stieth that kittith vs doun.

9 Helle vndur thee is disturblid for the meeting of thi comyng; he schal reise giauntis to thee; alle the princes of erthe han rise fro her seetis, alle the princes of naciouns.

10 Alle thei schulen answere, and thei shulen seie to thee, And thou art woundid as and we, thou art maad lijk vs.

11 Thi pride is drawun doun to hellis, thi deed careyn felle doun; a mouyte schal be strewyd vndur thee, and thin hilyng schal be wormes.

12 A! Lucifer, that risidist eerli, hou feldist thou doun fro heuene; thou that woundist folkis, feldist doun togidere in to erthe.

13 Which seidist in thin herte, Y schal stie in to heuene, Y schal enhaunse my seete aboue the staris of heuene; Y schal sitte in the hil of testament, in the sidis of the north.

14 Y schal stie on the hiynesse of cloudis; Y schal be lijk the hiyeste.

15 Netheles thou schalt be drawun doun to helle, in to the depthe of the lake.

16 Thei that schulen se thee, schulen be bowid doun to thee, and schulen biholde thee. Whether this is the man, that disturblid erthe, that schook togidere rewmes?

17 that settide the world desert, and distried the citees therof, and openyde not the prisoun to the boundun men of hym?

18 Alle the kyngis of hethene men, alle slepten in glorie, a man in his hous.

19 But thou art cast out of thi sepulcre, as an vnprofitable stok, as defoulid with rot; and wlappid with hem that ben slayn with swerd, and yeden doun to the foundement of the lake.

20 As a rotun careyn, thou schalt not haue felouschipe, nethir with hem in sepulture, for thou hast lost thi lond, thou hast slayn the puple; the seed of the worst men schal not be clepid with outen ende.

21 Make ye redi hise sones to sleying, for the wickidnesse of her fadris; thei schulen not rise, nether thei schulen enherite the lond, nether thei schulen fille the face of the roundenesse of citees.

22 And Y schal rise on hem, seith the Lord of oostis, and Y schal leese the name of Babyloyne, and the relifs, and generacioun, and seed, seith the Lord.

23 And Y schal sette that Babiloyne in to possessioun of an irchoun, and in to mareisis of watris; and Y schal swepe it with a beesme, and Y schal stampe, seith the Lord of oostis.

24 The Lord of oostis swoor, seiynge, Whether it schal not be so, as Y gesside, and it schal bifalle so, as Y tretide in soule?

25 That Y al to-breke the kyng of Assiriens in my lond, and that Y defoule hym in myn hillis; and his yok schal be takun awei fro hem, and his birthun schal be takun awei fro the schuldur of hem.

26 This is the council which Y thouyte on al the lond, and this is the hond stretchid forth on alle folkis.

27 For whi the Lord of oostis hath demed, and who mai make vnstidfaste? and his hond is stretchid forth, and who schal turne it awei?

28 The birthun of Filisteis. In the yeer wheryne kyng Achas diede, this birthun was maad.

29 Al thou Filistea, be not glad, for the yerde of thi smytere is maad lesse; for whi a cocatrice schal go out of the roote of an eddre, and his seed schal soupe up a brid.

30 And the firste gendrid of pore men schulen be fed, and pore men schulen reste feithfuli; and Y schal make thi throte to perisch in hungur, and Y schal sle thi relifs.

31 Yelle, thou yate; cry, thou citee, al Filistea is cast doun; for whi smoke schal come fro the north, and noon is that schal ascape his oost.

32 And what schal be answerid to the messangeris of folk? for the Lord hath foundid Sion, and the pore men of his puple schulen hope in hym.

CAP 15

1 The birthun of Moab. For Ar was destried in niyt, Moab was stille; for the wal was distried in the niyt, Moab was stille.

2 The kingis hous, and Dybon stieden to hiy places, in to weilyng; on Nabo, and on Medaba Moab schal yelle. In alle hedis therof schal be ballidnesse, and ech beerd schal be schauun.

3 In the meetyng of thre weies therof thei ben gird in a sak, alle yellyng on the housis therof and in the stretis therof; it schal go doun in to wepyng.

4 Esebon schal crie, and Eleale, the vois of hem is herd 'til to Jasa; on this thing the redi men of Moab schulen yelle, the soule therof schal yelle to it silf.

5 Myn herte schal crie to Moab, the barris therof 'til to Segor, a cow calf of thre yeer. For whi a wepere schal stie bi the stiyng of Luith, and in the weie of Oronaym thei schulen reise cry of sorewe.

6 For whi the watris of Nemrym schulen be forsakun; for the eerbe dried up, buriownyng failide, al grenenesse perischide.

7 Bi the greetnesse of werk, and the visityng of hem, to the stronde of salewis thei schulen lede hem.

8 For whi cry cumpasside the ende of Moab; 'til to Galym the yellyng therof, and the cry therof 'til to the pit of Helym.

9 For the watris of Dibon ben fillid with blood; for Y schal sette encreessyngis on Dibon, to tho men of Moab that fledden fro the lioun, and to the relifs of the lond.

CAP 16

1 Lord, sende thou out a lomb, the lordli gouernour of erthe, fro the stoon of desert to the hil of the douyter of Sion.

2 And it schal be as a foule fleynge, and briddis fleynge awei fro the nest, so schulen be the douytris of Moab in the passyng ouer of Arnon.

3 Take thou councel, constreyne thou councel; sette thou as niyt thi schadewe in myddai, hide thou hem that fleen, and bitraye thou not men of vnstidfast dwellyng.

4 My fleeris awei schulen dwelle at thee. Moab, be thou the hidyng place of hem fro the face of distriere. For whi dust is endid, the wretchid is wastid; he that defoulide the lond failude.

5 And the kyngis seete schal be maade redi in merci, and he schal sitte on it in treuthe, in the tabernacle of Dauid, demynge, and sekynge doom, and yeldynge swiftli that that is iust.

6 We han herd the pride of Moab, he is ful proud; his pride, and his boost, and his indignacioun is more than his strengthe.

7 Therfor Moab schal yelle to Moab, al Moab shal yelle to hem that ben glad on the wallis of bakun tijl stoon; speke ye her woundis.

8 For whi the subarbis of Esebon and the vyner of Sabama ben forsakun. The lordis of hethene men han kit doun the siouns therof; thei camen 'til to Jaser, thei erriden in desert. The bowis therof ben forsakun, thei passiden the see.

9 On this thing Y schal wepe in the weping of Jaser, and on the vyner of Sabama. Esebon and Eleale, Y schal fille thee with my teer; for the vois of defouleris fellen on thi vyndage, and on thi heruest.

10 And gladnesse and ful out ioiyng schal be takun awei fro Carmele; and noon schal make ful out ioye, nether schal synge hertli song in vyneris. He that was wont to wringe out, schal not wrynge out wyn in a pressour; Y haue take awei the vois of wryngeris out.

11 On this thing my wombe schal sowne as an harpe to Moab, and myn entrails to the wal of bakun tiel stoon.

12 And it schal be, whanne it schal appere, that Moab hath trauelid on hise places, it schal entre to hise hooli thingis, that it biseche, and it schal not be worth.

13 This is the word which the Lord spak to Moab fro that tyme.

14 And now the Lord spak, seiynge, In thre yeer that weren as the yeeris of an hirid man, the glorie of Moab schal be takun awei on al the myche puple; and ther schal be left in it as a litil rasyn, and a litil, and not myche.

CAP 17

1 The birthun of Damask. Lo! Damask schal faile to be a citee, and it schal be as an heep of stoonys in fallyng.

2 The forsakun citees of Aroer schulen be to flockis; and tho schulen reste there, and noon schal be that schal make aferd.

3 And help schal ceesse fro Effraym, and a rewme fro Damask; and the relifs of Sirie schulen be as the glorie of the sones of Israel, seith the Lord of oostis.

4 And it schal be, in that dai the glorie of Jacob schal be maad thinne, and the fatnesse of his fleisch schal fade.

5 And it schal be as gaderyng togidere that that is left in heruest, and his arm schal gadere eeris of corn, and it schal be as sekynge eeris of corn in the valei of Raphaym.

6 And there schal be left in it as a rasyn, and as the schakyng doun of the fruyt of olyue tre, as of tweyne ether of thre olyue trees in the hiynesse of a braunche, ether of foure ether of fyue; in the cooppis therof schal be the fruyt therof, seith the Lord God of Israel.

7 In that dai a man schal be bowid to his maker, and hise iyen schulen biholde to the hooli of Israel.

8 And he schal not be bowid to the auteris, whiche hise hondis maden, and whiche hise fyngris wrouyten; he schal not biholde wodis, and templis of idols.

9 In that dai the citees of strengthe therof schulen be forsakun as plowis, and cornes that weren forsakun of the face of the sones of Israel; and thou schalt be forsakun.

10 For thou hast foryete God, thi sauyour, and haddist not mynde on thi stronge helpere; therfor thou schalt plaunte a feithful plauntyng, and thou schalt sowe an alien seed.

11 In the dai of thi plauntyng schal be a wielde vyne, and erli thi seed schal floure; ripe corne is takun awei in the dai of eritage, and Israel schal make sorewe greuousli.

12 Wo to the multitude of many puplis, as the multitude of the see sownynge, and the noise of cumpenyes as the sown of many watris.

13 Puplis schulen sowne as the sown of flowynge watris, and God schal blame hym; and he schal fle fer, and he schal be rauyschid as the dust of hillis fro the face of the wynd, and as a whirlewynd bifor tempest.

14 In the time of euentide, and lo! disturbling; in the morewtid, and he schal not abide. This is the part of hem that destrieden vs, and the part of hem that rauyschiden vs.

CAP 18

1 Wo to the lond, the cymbal of wyngis, which is biyende the flood of Ethiopie; that sendith messangeris bi the see,

2 and in vessels of papirus on watris. Go, ye messangeris, to the folk drawun up and to-rent; to a ferdful puple, aftir which is noon other; to the folk abidynge and defoulid, whos lond the flodis han rauyschid; to the hil of the name of the Lord of oostis, to the hil of Sion.

3 Alle ye dwelleris of the world, that dwellen in the lond, schulen se whanne a signe schal be reisid in the hillis, and ye schulen here the cry of a trumpe.

4 For whi the Lord seith these thingis to me, Y schal reste, and Y schal biholde in my place, as the myddai liyt is cleer, and as a cloude of dew in the dai of heruest.

5 For whi al flouride out bifore heruest, aud vnripe perfeccioun buriownede; and the litle braunchis therof schulen be kit doun with sithis, and tho that ben left, schulen be kit awei. Thei schulen be schakun out,

6 and schulen be left togidere to the briddis of hillis, and to the beestis of erthe; and briddis schulen be on hym by a somer euerlastinge, and alle the beestis of erthe schulen dwelle bi wyntir on hym.

7 In that tyme a yifte schal be brouyt to the Lord of oostis, of the puple drawun up and to-rent; of the puple ferdful, aftir which was noon other; of the folk abidynge and defoulid,

whos lond floodis rauyschiden; the yifte schal be brouyt to the place of the name of the Lord of oostis, to the hil of Sion.

CAP 19

1 The birthun of Egipt. Lo! the Lord schal stie on a liyt cloude, and he schal entre in to Egipt; and the symilacris of Egipt schulen be mouyd fro his face, and the herte of Egipt schal faile in the myddis therof.

2 And Y schal make Egipcians to renne togidere ayens Egipcians, and a man schal fiyte ayens his brother, and a man ayens his frend, a citee ayens a citee, and a rewme ayens a rewme.

3 And the spirit of Egipt schal be brokun in the entrailis therof, and Y schal caste doun the councel therof; and thei schulen axe her symylacris, and her false diuinouris, and her men that han vncleene spiritis spekinge in the wombe, and her dyuynouris bi sacrifices maad on auteris to feendis.

4 And Y schal bitake Egipt in to the hond of cruel lordis, and a strong kyng schal be lord of hem, seith the Lord God of oostis.

5 And watir of the see schal wexe drie, and the flood schal be desolat, and schal be dried.

6 And the floodis schulen faile, and the strondis of the feeldis schulen be maad thynne, and schulen be dried; a rehed and spier schal fade.

7 The botme of watir schal be maad nakid, and stremys fro her welle; and the moiste place of al seed schal be dried, schal waxe drie, and schal not be.

8 And fischeris schulen morne, and alle that casten hook in to the flood, schulen weile; and thei that spreden abrood a net on the face of watris, schulen fade.

9 Thei schulen be schent, that wrouyten flex, foldynge and ordeynynge sutil thingis.

10 And the watir places therof schulen be drye; alle that maden poondis to take fischis, schulen be schent.

11 The fonned princes of Tafnys, the wise counselouris of Farao, yauen vnwise counsel; hou schulen ye seie to Farao, Y am the sone of wise men, the sone of elde kyngis?

12 Where ben now thi wise men? Telle thei to thee, and schewe thei, what the Lord of oostis thouyte on Egipt.

13 The princes of Tafnys ben maad foolis; the princes of Memphis fadiden; thei disseyueden Egipt, a corner of the puplis therof.

14 The Lord meddlid a spirit of errour in the myddis therof; and thei maden Egipt for to erre in al his werk, as a drunkun man and spuynge errith.

15 And werk schal not be to Egipt, that it make an heed and tail bowynge and refreynynge.

16 In that dai Egipt schal be as wymmen, and thei schulen be astonyed, and schulen drede of the face of the mouynge of the hoond of the Lord of oostis, which he mouede on it.

17 And the lond of Juda schal be to Egipt in to drede; ech that schal thenke on it, schal drede of the face of the counsel of the Lord of oostis, whiche he thouyte on it.

18 In that dai fyue citees schulen be in the lond of Egipt, and schulen speke with the tunge of Canaan, and schulen swere bi the Lord of oostis; the citee of the sunne schal be clepid oon.

19 In that dai the auter of the Lord schal be in the myddis of the lond of Egipt, and the title of the Lord schal be bisidis the ende therof;

20 and it schal be in to a signe and witnessyng to the Lord of oostis, in the lond of Egipt. For thei schulen crie to the Lord

fro the face of the troblere, and he schal sende a sauyour to
hem, and a forfiytere, that schal delyuere hem.

21 And the Lord schal be knowun of Egipt, and Egipcians
schulen knowe the Lord in that dai; and thei schulen worschipe hym in sacrifices and yiftis, and thei schulen make
vowis to the Lord, and thei schulen paie.

22 And the Lord schal smyte Egipt with a wounde, and schal
make it hool; and Egipcians schulen turne ayen to the Lord,
and he schal be plesid in hem, and he schal make hem hool.

23 In that dai a wei schal be fro Egipt in to Assiriens, and
Egipcians schulen serue Assur; and Assur schal entre in to
Egipt, and Egipt in to Assiriens.

24 In that dai Israel schal be the thridde to Egipt and to Assur,
the blessyng in the myddil of erthe;

25 whom the Lord of oostis blesside, seiynge, Blessid be my
puple of Egipt, and the werk of myn hondis be to Assiriens;
but myne eritage be to Israel.

CAP 20

1 In the yeer wherynne Tharthan entride in to Azotus, whanne
Sargon, the kyng of Assiriens, hadde sent hym, and he hadde
fouyte ayens Azotus, and hadde take it;

2 in that tyme the Lord spak in the hond of Isaye, the sone of
Amos, and seide, Go thou, and vnbynde the sak fro thi leendis, and take awei thi schoon fro thi feet. And he dide so,
goynge nakid and vnschood.

3 And the Lord seide, As my seruaunt Ysaie yede nakid and
vnschood, a signe and greet wondur of thre yeer schal be on
Egipt, and on Ethiopie;

4 so the kyng of Assiriens schal dryue the caitifte of Egipt,
and the passyng ouer of Ethiopie, a yong man and an eld man,
nakid and vnschood, with the buttokis vnhilid, to the schenschipe of Egipt.

5 And thei schulen drede, and schulen be schent of Ethiopie,
her hope, and of Egipt, her glorie.

6 And a dwellere of this ile schal seie in that dai, This was our
hope, to which we fledden for help, that thei schulden delyuere vs fro the face of the kyng of Assiryens; and hou moun
we ascape?

CAP 21

1 The birthun of the forsakun see. As whirlewyndis comen
fro the southwest, it cometh fro desert, fro the orible lond.

2 An hard reuelacioun is teld to me; he that is vnfeithful,
doith vnfeithfuli; and he that is a distriere, distrieth. Thou
Helam, stie, and thou, Meda, biseche; Y made al the weilyng
therof for to ceesse.

3 Therfor my leendis ben fillid with sorewe; angwische weldide me, as the angwisch of a womman trauelynge of child; Y
felle doun, whanne Y herde; Y was disturblid, whanne Y siy.

4 Myn herte fadide, derknessis astonieden me; Babiloyne, my
derlyng, is set to me in to myracle.

5 Sette thou a boord, biholde thou in to a toting place; rise, ye
princes, etynge and drynkynge, take ye scheeld.

6 For whi the Lord seide these thingis to me, Go thou, and
sette a lokere; and telle he, what euer thing he seeth.

7 And he siy the chare of tweyne horse men, the stiere of an
asse, and the stiere of a camel; and he bihelde diligentli with
myche lokyng,

8 and criede as a lioun, Y stonde contynueli bi dai on the
totyng place of the Lord, and Y stonde bi alle nyytis on my
kepyng.

9 Lo! this cometh, a man stiere of a carte of horse men. And
Isaie criede, and seide, Babiloyne felle doun, felle doun; and
alle the grauun ymagis of goddis therof ben al to-brokun in to
erthe.

10 Mi threschyng, and the douyter of my cornfloor, Y haue
teld to you what thingis Y herde of the Lord of oostis, of God
of Israel.

11 The birthun of Duma. It crieth fro Seir to me, Kepere,
what our of the niyt? 'kepere, what our of the niyt?

12 The kepere seide, Morewtid cometh, and niyt; if ye seken,
seke ye, and be ye conuertid, and 'come ye.

13 The birthun in Arabie. In the forest at euentid ye schulen
slepe, in the pathis of Dodanym.

14 Ye that dwellen in the lond of the south, renne, and bere
watir to the thristi; and renne ye with looues to hym that
fleeth.

15 For thei fledden fro the face of swerdis, fro the face of
swerd neiyynge, fro the face of bouwe bent, fro the face of
greuouse batel.

16 For the Lord seith these thingis to me, Yit in o yeer, as in
the yeer of an hirid man, and al the glorie of Cedar schal be
takun awei.

17 And the remenauntis of the noumbre of stronge archeris of
the sones of Cedar schulen be maad lesse; for whi the Lord
God of Israel spak.

CAP 22

1 The birthun of the valei of visioun. What also is to thee, for
and al thou stiedist in to roouys,

2 thou ful of cry, a citee of myche puple, a citee ful out
ioiynge? thi slayn men weren not slayn bi swerd, nether thi
deed men weren deed in batel.

3 Alle thi princes fledden togidere, and weren boundun harde;
alle that weren foundun, weren boundun togidere, thei fledden fer.

4 Therfor Y seide, Go ye awei fro me, Y schal wepe bittirli;
nyle ye be bisie to coumforte me on the distriyng of the
douyter of my puple.

5 For whi a dai of sleyng, and of defoulyng, and of wepyngis,
is ordeined of the Lord God of oostis, in the valei of visioun;
and he serchith the walle, and is worschipful on the hil.

6 And Helam took an arowe caas, and the chare of an horse
man; and the scheeld made nakid the wal.

7 And thi chosun valeis, Jerusalem, schulen be ful of cartis;
and knyytis schulen putte her seetis in the yate.

8 And the hilyng of Juda schal be schewid; and thou schalt se
in that dai the place of armuris of the hous of the forest;

9 and ye schulen se the crasyngis of the citee of Dauid, for tho
ben multiplied. Ye gaderiden togidere the watris of the lowere cisterne,

10 and ye noumbriden the housis of Jerusalem, and ye distrieden housis, to make strong the wal; and ye maden a lake
bitwixe twei wallis,

11 and ye restoriden the watir of the elde sisterne; and ye
biholden not to hym, that made 'thilke Jerusalem, and ye sien
not the worchere therof afer.

12 And the Lord God of oostis schal clepe in that dai to
wepyng, and to morenyng, and to ballidnesse, and to a girdil
of sak; and lo!

13 ioie and gladnesse is to sle caluys, and to strangle wetheris, to ete fleisch, and to drynke wyn; ete we, and drynke we,
for we schulen die to morewe.

14 And the vois of the Lord of oostis is schewid in myn eeris, This wickidnesse schal not be foryouun to you, til ye dien, seith the Lord God of oostis.

15 The Lord God of oostis seith these thingis, Go thou, and entre to hym that dwellith in the tabernacle, to Sobna, the souereyn of the temple; and thou schalt seie to hym,

16 What thou here, ethir as who here? for thou hast hewe to thee a sepulcre here, thou hast hewe a memorial in hiy place diligentli, a tabernacle in a stoon to thee.

17 Lo! the Lord schal make thee to be borun out, as a kapoun is borun out, and as a cloth, so he shal reise thee.

18 He crowninge schal crowne thee with tribulacioun; he schal sende thee as a bal in to a large lond and wijd; there thou schalt die, and there schal be the chare of thi glorie, and the schenschipe of the hous of thi Lord.

19 And Y schal caste thee out of thi stondyng, and Y schal putte thee doun of thi seruyce.

20 And it schal be, in that dai Y schal clepe my seruaunt Eliachim, the sone of Helchie; and Y schal clothe hym in thi coote,

21 and Y schal coumforte hym with thi girdil, and Y shal yyue thi power in to the hondis of hym; and he schal be as a fadir to hem that dwellen in Jerusalem, and to the hous of Juda.

22 And Y schal yyue the keie of the hous of Dauyd on his schuldre; and he schal opene, and noon schal be that schal schitte; and he schal schitte, and noon schal be that schal opene.

23 And Y schal sette hym a stake in a feithful place, and he schal be in to the seete of glorie of the hous of his fadir.

24 And thou schalt hange on hym al the glorie of the hous of his fadir, diuerse kindis of vessels, eche litil vessel, fro the vesselis of cuppis 'til to ech vessel of musikis.

25 In that dai, seith the Lord of oostis, the stake that was set in the feithful place, schal be takun awei, and it schal be brokun, and schal falle doun; and schal perische that hangide therynne, for the Lord spak.

CAP 23

1 The birthun of Tire. Ye schippis of the see, yelle, for the hous is distried, fro whennus coumfort was wont to come; fro the lond of Cethym, and was schewid to hem.

2 Be ye stille, that dwellen in the ile, the marchaundie of Sidon; men passynge the see filliden thee in many watris;

3 the seed of Nylus is heruest, the flood is the corn therof, and it is maad the marchaundie of hethene men.

4 Thou, Sidon, be aschamed, seide the see, the strengthe of the see, and seide, Y trauelide not of child, and Y childide not, and Y nurschide not yonge men, and Y brouyte not fulli virgyns to encreessyng.

5 Whanne it schal be herd in Egipt, thei schulen make sorewe, whanne thei heren of Tire.

6 Passe ye the sees; yelle ye, that dwellen in the ile.

7 Whether this citee is not youre, that hadde glorie fro elde daies in his eldnesse? the feet therof schulen lede it fer, to go in pilgrymage.

8 Who thouyte this thing on Tire sum tyme crownede, whos marchauntis weren princes, the selleris of marchaundie therof weren noble men of erthe?

9 The Lord of oostis thouyte this thing, that he schulde drawe doun the pride of al glorie, and that he schulde bringe to schenschipe alle the noble men of erthe.

10 Thou douyter of the see, passe thi lond as a flood; a girdil is no more to thee.

11 It stretchide forth his hond aboue the see, and disturblide rewmes. The Lord sente ayenes Canaan, for to al to-breke the stronge men therof;

12 and he seide, Thou maide, the douyter of Sidon, that suffrist caleng, schalt no more adde, that thou haue glorie. Rise thou, and passe ouer the see in to Sechym; there also no reste schal be to thee.

13 Lo! the lond of Caldeis, sich a puple was not; Assur foundide that Tyre; thei ledden ouer in to caitifte the strong men therof; thei myneden the housis therof, thei settiden it in to fallyng.

14 Yelle, ye schippis of the see, for youre strengthe is distried.

15 And it schal be, in that dai, thou Tire, schalt be in foryetyng bi seuenti yeer, as the daies of o king; but aftir seuenti yeer, as the song of an hoore schal be to Tyre.

16 Thou hoore, youun to foryetyng, take an harpe, cumpasse the citee; synge thou wel, vse thou ofte a song, that mynde be of thee.

17 And it schal be, aftir seuenti yeer, the Lord schal visite Tire, and schal brynge it ayen to hise hiris; and eft it schal be, whanne it schal do fornycacioun with alle rewmes of erthe, on the face of erthe.

18 And the marchaundies therof and the meedis therof schulen be halewid to the Lord; tho schulen not be hid, nethir schulen be leid vp; for whi the marchaundie therof schal be to hem that dwellen bifore the Lord, that thei ete to fulnesse, and be clothid 'til to eldnesse.

CAP 24

1 Lo! the Lord schal distrie the erthe, and schal make it nakid, and schal turmente the face therof; and he schal scater abrood the dwelleris therof.

2 And it schal be, as the puple, so the preest; as the seruaunt, so his lord; as the handmaide, so the ladi of hir; as a biere, so he that sillith; as the leenere, so he that takith borewyng; as he that axith ayen, so he that owith.

3 Bi distriyng the lond schal be distried, and schal be maad nakid by rauyschyng; for whi the Lord spak this word.

4 The erthe morenyde, and fleet awei, and is maad sijk; the world fleet awei, the hiynesse of the puple of erthe is maad sijk,

5 and the erthe is slayn of hise dwelleris. For thei passiden lawis, chaungiden riyt, distrieden euerlastynge boond of pees.

6 For this thing cursyng schal deuoure the erthe, and the dwelleris therof schulen do synne; and therfor the louyeris therof schulen be woode, and fewe men schulen be left.

7 Vyndage morenyde, the vyne is sijk; alle men that weren glad in herte weiliden.

8 The ioie of tympans ceesside, the sowne of glad men restide; the swetnesse of harpe with song was stille.

9 Thei schulen not drynke wyn; a bittere drynk schal be to hem that schulen drynke it.

10 The citee of vanyte is al to-brokun; ech hous is closid, for no man entrith.

11 Cry schal be on wyn in streetis, al gladnesse is forsakun, the ioie of erthe is 'takun awei.

12 Desolacioun is left in the citee, and wretchidnesse schal oppresse the yatis.

13 For these thingis schulen be in the myddis of erthe, in the myddis of puplis, as if a fewe fruitis of olyue trees that ben

left ben schakun of fro the olyue tre, and racyns, whanne the vyndage is endid.

14 These men schulen reise her vois, and schulen preise, whanne the Lord schal be glorified; thei schulen schewe signes of gladnesse fro the see.

15 For this thing glorifie ye the Lord in techyngis; in the ilis of the see glorifie ye the name of the Lord God of Israel.

16 Fro the endis of erthe we han herd heriyngis, the glorye of the iust. And Y seide, My priuyte to me, my pryuyte to me. Wo to me, trespassours han trespassid, and han trespassid bi trespassyng of brekeris of the lawe.

17 Ferdfulnesse, and a diche, and a snare on thee, that art a dwellere of erthe.

18 And it schal be, he that schal fle fro the face of ferdfulnesse, schal falle in to the diche; and he that schal delyuere hym silf fro the dich, schal be holdun of the snare; for whi the wyndows of hiye thingis ben openyd, and the foundementis of erthe schulen be schakun togidere.

19 The erthe schal be brokun with brekyng,

20 the erthe schal be defoulid with defoulyng, the erthe schal be mouyd with mouyng, the erthe schal be schakun with schakyng, as a drunkun man.

21 And it schal be takun awei, as the tabernacle of o nyyt, and the wickidnesse therof schal greue it; and it schal falle down, and it schal not adde, for to rise ayen. And it schal be, in that dai the Lord schal visite on the knyythod of heuene an hiy, and on the kyngis of erthe, that ben on erthe.

22 And thei schulen be gaderid togidere in the gadering togidere of a bundel in to the lake, and thei schulen be closid there in prisoun; and aftir many daies thei schulen be visited.

23 And the moone schal be aschamed, and the sunne schal be confoundid, whanne the Lord of oostis schal regne in the hil of Sion, and in Jerusalem, and schal be glorified in the siyt of hise eldre men.

CAP 25

1 Lord, thou art my God, Y schal enhaunse thee, and Y schal knouleche to thi name; for thou hast do marueils, thin elde feithful thouytis.

2 Amen. For thou hast set the citee in to a biriel, a strong citee in to fallyng, the hous of aliens, that it be not a citee, and be not bildid with outen ende.

3 For this thyng a strong puple schal herie thee, the citee of strong folkis schal drede thee.

4 For thou art maad strengthe to a pore man, strengthe to a nedi man in his tribulacioun, hope fro whirlwynd, a schadewyng place fro heete; for whi the spirit of stronge men is as a whirlewynd hurlynge the wal.

5 As bi heete in thirst, thou schalt make meke the noise of aliens; and as bi heete vndur a cloude brennynge, thou schalt make the siouns of stronge men to fade.

6 And the Lord of oostis schal make in this hil to alle puplis the feeste of fatte thingis, the feeste of vyndage of fatte thingis ful of merow, of vyndage wel fyned.

7 And he schal caste doun in this hil the face of boond, boundun togidere on alle puplis, and the web which he weuyde on alle naciouns.

8 And he schal caste doun deth with outen ende, and the Lord God schal do awey ech teer fro ech face; and he schal do awei the schenschure of his puple fro ech lond; for the Lord spak.

9 And thei schulen seie in that dai, Lo! this is oure God; we abididen hym, and he schal saue vs; this is the Lord; we suf-

friden him, and we schulen make ful out ioie, and schulen be glad in his helthe.

10 For whi the hond of the Lord schal reste in this hil, and Moab schal be threischid vndur hym, as chaffis ben stampid in a wayn.

11 And he schal stretche forth hise hondis vndur hym, as a swymmere stretchith forth to swymme; and he schal make low the glorye of him with hurtlyng doun of hise hondis.

12 And the strengthingis of thin hiy wallis schulen falle doun, and schulen be maad low, and schulen be drawun doun to the erthe, 'til to the dust.

CAP 26

1 In that dai this song schal be sungun in the lond of Juda. The citee of oure strengthe; the sauyour schal be set ther ynne, the wal and the 'fore wal.

2 Opene ye the yatis, and the iust folk schal entre, kepynge treuthe.

3 The elde errour is gon awei; thou schalt kepe pees, pees, for thou, Lord, we hopiden in thee.

4 Ye han hopid in the Lord, in euerlastynge worldis, in the Lord God, strong with outen ende.

5 For he schal bowe doun hem that dwellen an hiy, and he schal make low an hiy citee; he schal make it low 'til to the erthe; he schal drawe it doun 'til to the dust.

6 The foot of a pore man schal defoule it, and the steppis of nedi men schulen defoule it.

7 The weie of a iust man is riytful, the path of a iust man is riytful to go.

8 And in the weie of thi domes, Lord, we suffriden thee; thi name, and thi memorial is in desir of soule.

9 My soule schal desire thee in the niyt, but also with my spirit in myn entrails; fro the morewtid Y schal wake to thee. Whanne thou schalt make thi domes in erthe, alle dwelleris of the world schulen lerne riytfulnesse.

10 Do we merci to the wickid man, and he schal not lerne to do riytfulnesse; in the lond of seyntis he dide wickid thingis, and he schal not se the glorie of the Lord.

11 Lord, thin hond be enhaunsid, that thei se not; puplis hauynge enuye se, and be schent, and fier deuoure thin enemyes.

12 Lord, thou schalt yyue pees to vs, for thou hast wrouyt alle oure werkis in vs.

13 Oure Lord God, lordis hadden vs in possessioun, withouten thee; oneli in thee haue we mynde of thi name.

14 Thei that dien, lyue not, and giauntis risen not ayen. Therfor thou hast visityd, and hast al-to broke hem, and thou hast lost al the mynde of hem; and Lord, thou hast foryoue to a folc,

15 thou hast foryoue to a folc. Whether thou art glorified? thou hast maad fer fro thee all the endis of erthe.

16 Lord, in angwisch thei souyten thee; in the tribulacioun of grutchyng thi doctryn to hem.

17 As sche that conseyuede, whanne sche neiyeth sorewful to the child beryng, crieth in her sorewis, so we ben maad, Lord, of thi face.

18 We han conseyued, and we han as trauelid of child, and we han childid the spirit of helthe; we diden not riytfulnesse in erthe. Therfor the dwelleris of erthe fellen not doun; thi deed men schulen lyue,

19 and my slayn men schulen rise ayen. Ye that dwellen in dust, awake, and herie; for whi the deew of liyt is thi deew, and thou schalt drawe doun the lond of giauntis in to fallyng.

20 Go thou, my puple, entre in to thi beddis, close thi doris on thee, be thou hid a litil at a moment, til indignacioun passe.
21 For lo! the Lord schal go out of his place, to visite the wickidnesse of the dwellere of erthe ayens hym; and the erthe schal schewe his blood, and schal no more hile hise slayn men.

CAP 27

1 In that dai the Lord schal visite in his hard swerd, and greet, and strong, on leuyathan, serpent, a barre, and on leuyathan, the crookid serpent; and he schal sle the whal, which is in the see.
2 In that dai the vyner of cleen wyn and good schal synge to him.
3 Y am the Lord that kepe that vyner; sudeynli Y schal yyue drynke to it, lest perauenture it be visitid ayens it;
4 nyyt and dai Y kepe it, indignacioun is not to me. Who schal yyue me a thorn and brere? In batel Y schal go on it, Y schal brenne it togidere.
5 Whether rathere Y schal holde my strengthe? It schal make pees to me, it schal make pees to me, for
6 the merit of hem that schulen go out with fersnesse fro Jacob. Israel schal floure and brynge forth seed, and thei schulen fille the face of the world with seed.
7 Whether he smoot it bi the wounde of the puple of Jewis smytynge hym? ether as it killide the slayn men of hym, so it was slayn?
8 In mesure ayens mesure, whanne it schal be cast awei, he schal deme it; he bithouyte in his hard spirit, bi the dai of heete.
9 Therfor on this thing wickidnesse schal be foryouun to the hous of Jacob, and this schal be al the fruyt, that the synne therof be don awei, whanne it hath set all the stoonys of the auter as the stoonys of aische hurtlid doun. Wodis and templis schulen not stonde.
10 Forsothe the strong citee schal be desolat, the fair citee schal be left, and schal be forsakun as a desert; there a calf schal be lesewid, and schal ligge there, and schal waste the hiynessis therof.
11 In the drynesse of ripe corn therof wymmen comynge, and thei that techen it, schulen be al to-brokun. Forsothe it is not a wijs puple, therfor he that made it, schal not haue mercy on it; and he that formyde it, schal not spare it.
12 And it schal be, in that dai the Lord schal smyte thee, fro the botme of the flood 'til to the stronde of Egipt; and ye sones of Israel, schulen be gaderid oon and oon.
13 And it schal be, in that dai me schal come with a greet trumpe, and thei that weren lost, schulen come fro the lond of Assiriens, and thei that weren cast out, schulen come fro the lond of Egipt; and they schulen worschipe the Lord, in the hooli hil in Jerusalem.

CAP 28

1 Wo to the coroun of pride, to the drunkun men of Effraym, and to the flour fallynge doun of the glorie of the ful out ioiyng therof, that weren in the cop of the fatteste valei, and erriden of wyn.
2 Lo! the myyti and strong Lord, as the feersnesse of hail, a whirlwynd brekynge togidere, as the fersnesse of many watris flowynge, and sent out on a large lond.
3 The coroun of pride of the drunken men of Effraym schal be defoulid with feet,

4 and the flour of glorie of the ful out ioiyng of hym, that is on the cop of valei of fat thingis, schal be fallyng doun, as a tymeli thing bifore the ripenesse of heruest; which whanne a man seynge biholdith, anoon as he takith with hond, he schal deuoure it.
5 In that dai the Lord of oostis schal be a coroun of glorie, and a garlond of ful out ioiyng, to the residue of his puple;
6 and a spirit of doom to hym that sittith on the trone, and strengthe to hem that turnen ayen fro batel to the yate.
7 But also thei knewen not for wyn, and erriden for drunkenesse; the preest and profete knewen not for drunkenesse; thei weren sopun up of wyn, thei erriden in drunkenesse; thei knewen not a profete, thei knewen not doom.
8 For whi alle bordis weren fillid with spuyng and filthis, so that ther was no more place.
9 Whom schal he teche kunnyng, and whom schal he make to vndurstonde heryng? Men wenyd fro mylk, men drawun awei fro tetis.
10 For whi comaunde thou, comaunde thou ayen; comaunde thou, comaunde thou ayen; abide thou, abide thou ayen; abide thou, abide thou ayen; a litil there, a litil there.
11 For whi in speche of lippe, and in other langage he schal speke to this puple,
12 to which he seide, This is my reste; refreische ye a weri man, and this is my refreischyng; and thei nolden here.
13 And the word of the Lord schal be to hem, Sende thou, sende thou ayen; send thou, sende thou ayen; abide thou, abide thou ayen; abide thou, abide thou ayen; a litil there, a litil there; that thei go, and falle backward, and be al to-brokun, and be snarid, and be takun.
14 For this thing, ye men scorneris, that ben lordis ouer my puple which is in Jerusalem, here the word of the Lord.
15 For ye seiden, We han smyte a boond of pees with deth, and we han maad couenaunt with helle; a scourge flowynge whanne it schal passe, schal not come on vs, for we han set a leesyng oure hope, and we ben kyuered with a leesyng.
16 Therfor the Lord God seith these thingis, Lo! Y schal sende in the foundementis of Sion a corner stoon preciouse, preuyd, foundid in the foundement; he that bileueth, schal not haaste.
17 And Y schal sette doom in weiyte, and riytfulnesse in mesure; and hail schal distrie the hope of leesyng, and watris schulen flowe on proteccioun. And youre boond of pees with deth schal be don awei,
18 and youre couenaunt with helle schal not stonde; whanne the scourge flowynge schal passe, ye schulen be to it in to defoulyng.
19 Whanne euer it schal passe, it schal take awei yow; for whi erli in the grey morewtid it schal passe, in dai and niyt; and oonli trauel aloone schal yyue vndurstondyng to heryng.
20 Forsothe the bed is streit, so that the tother falle doun; and a schort mentil schal not hile euer either.
21 For as in the hil of departyngis the Lord schal stonde, as in the valei, which is in Gabaon, he schal be wroth, that he do his werk; his werk alien, that he worche his werk; his werk is straunge fro hym.
22 And now nyle ye scorne, lest perauenture youre boondis be maad streit togidere; for Y herde of the Lord God of oostis, endyng and abreggyng on al erthe.
23 Perseyue ye with eeris, and here ye my vois; perseyue ye, and here ye my speche.
24 Whether he that erith, schal ere al dai, for to sowe, and schal be kerue, and purge his londe?

25 Whether whanne he hath maad euene the face therof, schal he not sowe gith, and sprenge abrood comyn? and he schal not sette wheete bi ordre, and barli, and mylium, and fetchis in his coostis?

26 And his God schal teche hym, in doom he schal teche hym.

27 Forsothe gith schal not be threischid in sawis, and a wheel of a wayn schal not cumpasse on comyn; but gith schal be betun out with a yerd, and comyn with a staf.

28 Sotheli breed schal be maad lesse, but he that threischith schal not threische it with outen ende, nether schal trauele it with a wheel of a wayn, nether schal make it lesse with hise clees.

29 And this thing yede out of the Lord God of oostis, that he schulde make wondirful councel, and magnefie riytfulnesse.

CAP 29

1 Wo! Ariel, Ariel, the citee which Dauid ouercam; yeer is addid to yeer, solempnytees ben passyd.

2 And Y schal cumpasse Ariel, and it schal be soreuful and morenynge; and Jerusalem schal be to me as Ariel.

3 And Y schal cumpasse as a round trendil in thi cumpasse, and Y schal caste erthe ayens thee, and Y schal sette engynes in to thi bisegyng.

4 Thou schalt be maad low, thou schalt speke of erthe, and thi speche schal be herd fro the erthe; and thi vois schal be as the vois of a deed man reisid bi coniuring, and thi speche schal ofte grutche of the erthe.

5 And the multitude of hem that wyndewen thee, schal be as thynne dust; and the multitude of hem that hadden the maistrie ayens thee, schal be as a deed sparcle passynge.

6 And it schal be sudenli, anoon it schal be visitid of the Lord of oostis, in thundur, and in mouyng of the erthe, and in greet vois of whirlwynd, and of tempest, and of flawme of fier deuowrynge.

7 And the multitude of alle folkis that fouyten ayens Ariel schal be as the dreem of a nyytis visioun; and alle men that fouyten, and bisegiden, and hadden the maistrie ayens it.

8 And as an hungry man dremyth, and etith, but whanne he is awakid, his soule is voide; and as a thirsti man dremeth, and drynkith, and after that he is awakid, he is weri, and thirstith yit, and his soule is voide, so schal be the multitude of alle folkis, that fouyten ayens the hil of Sion.

9 Be ye astonyed, and wondre; wake ye, and douyte ye; be ye drunken, and not of wyn; be ye moued, and not with drunkenesse.

10 For the Lord hath meddlid to you the spirit of sleep; he schal close youre iyen, and schal hile youre profetis, and princes that sien visiouns.

11 And the visioun of alle profetis schal be to you as the wordis of a book aseelid; which whanne thei schulen yyue to hym that kan lettris, thei schulen seie, Rede thou this book; and he schal answere, Y may not, for it is aseelid.

12 And the book schal be youun to him that kan not lettris, and it schal be seid to hym, Rede thou; and he schal answere, Y kan no lettris.

13 And the Lord seide, For that this puple neiyeth with her mouth, and glorifieth me with her lippis, but her herte is fer fro me; and thei dredden me for the comaundement and techyngis of men, therfor lo!

14 Y schal adde, that Y make wondryng to this puple, in a greet myracle and wondurful; for whi wisdom schal perische

fro wise men therof, and the vndurstondyng of prudent men therof schal be hid.

15 Wo to you that ben hiye of herte, that ye hide counsel fro the Lord; the werkis of whiche ben in derknessis, and thei seien, Who seeth vs, and who knowith vs?

16 This thouyt of you is weiward, as if cley thenke ayens a pottere, and the werk seie to his makere, Thou madist not me; and a thing 'that is maad, seie to his makere, Thou vndurstondist not.

17 Whether not yit in a litil time and schort the Liban schal be turned in to Chermel, and Chermel schal be arettid in to the forest?

18 And in that dai deef men schulen here the wordis of the book, and the iyen of blynde men schulen se fro derknessis and myisty;

19 and mylde men schulen encreesse gladnesse in the Lord, and pore men schulen make ful out ioie in the hooli of Israel.

20 For he that hadde the maistrie, failide, and the scornere is endid, and alle thei ben kit doun that walkiden on wickidnesse;

21 whiche maden men to do synne in word, and disseyueden a repreuere in the yate, and bowiden awey in veyn fro a iust man.

22 For this thing the Lord, that ayen bouyte Abraham, seith these thingis to the hous of Jacob, Jacob schal not be confoundid now, nether now his cheer schal be aschamed; but whanne he schal se hise sones,

23 the werkis of myn hondis, halewynge my name in the myddis of hym. And thei schulen halewe the hooli of Jacob, and thei schulen preche God of Israel;

24 and thei that erren in spirit, schulen knowe vndurstondyng, and idil men schulen lerne the lawe.

CAP 30

1 Wo! sones forsakeris, seith the Lord, that ye schulden make a councel, and not of me; and weue a web, and not bi my spirit, that ye schulden encreesse synne on synne.

2 Whiche goen, to go doun in to Egipt, and ye axiden not my mouth; ye hopynge help in the strengthe of Farao, and ye hauynge trist in the schadewe of Egipt.

3 And the strengthe of Farao schal be to you in to confusioun, and the trist of the schadewe of Egipt in to schenschipe.

4 For whi thi princes weren in Taphnys, and thi messangeris camen til to Anes.

5 Alle thei weren schent on the puple, that myyten not profite to hem; thei weren not in to help, and in to ony profit, but in to schame and schenschip.

6 The birthun of werk beestis of the south. In the lond of tribulacioun and of angwisch, a lionesse, and a lioun, of hem a serpent, and a cocatrice; thei weren berynge her richessis on the schuldris of werk beestis, and her tresours on the botche of camels, to a puple that myyte not profite to hem.

7 For whi Egipt schal helpe in veyn, and idili. Therfor Y criede on this thing, It is pride oneli; ceesse thou.

8 Now therfor entre thou, and write to it on box, and write thou it diligentli in a book; and it schal be in the last dai in to witnessyng, til in to with outen ende.

9 For it is a puple terrynge to wrathfulnesse, and sones lieris, sones that nylen here the lawe of God.

10 Whiche seien to profetis, Nyle ye prophesie; and to biholderis, Nyle ye biholde to vs tho thingis that ben riytful; speke ye thingis plesynge to vs, se ye errouris to vs.

11 Do ye awei fro me the weie, bowe ye awei fro me the path; the hooli of Israel ceesse fro oure face.

12 Therfor the hooli of Israel seith these thingis, For that that ye repreuiden this word, and hopiden on fals caleng, and on noise, and tristiden on it,

13 therfor this wickidnesse schal be to you as a brekyng fallynge doun, and souyt in an hiy wal; for sudeynli while it is not hopid, the brekyng therof schal come.

14 And it schal be maad lesse, as a galoun of a pottere is brokun with ful strong brekyng; and a scherd schal not be foundun of the gobetis therof, in which scherd a litil fier schal be borun of brennyng, ethir a litil of watir schal be drawun of the diche.

15 For whi the Lord God, the hooli of Israel, seith these thingis, If ye turnen ayen, and resten, ye schulen be saaf; in stilnesse and in hope schal be youre strengthe. And ye nolden.

16 And ye seiden, Nai, but we schulen fle to horsis; therfor ye schulen fle. And we schulen stie on swifte horsis; therfor thei schulen be swiftere, that schulen pursue you.

17 A thousynde men schulen fle fro the face of the drede of oon; and ye schulen fle fro the face of drede of fyue, til ye be left as the mast of a schip in the cop of a munteyn, and as a signe on a litil hil.

18 Therfor the Lord abidith, that he haue mercy on you, and therfor he schal be enhaunsid sparynge you; for whi God is Lord of doom, blessid ben alle thei that abiden hym.

19 Forsothe the puple of Sion schal dwelle in Jerusalem; thou wepynge schal not wepe, he doynge merci schal haue merci on thee; at the vois of thi cry, anoon as he herith, he schal answere to thee.

20 And the Lord schal yyue to thee streyt breed, and schort watir, and schal no more make thi techere to fle awei fro thee; and thin iyen schulen be seynge thi comaundour,

21 and thin eeris schulen here a word bihynde the bak of hym that monestith; This is the weie, go ye therynne, nether to the riyt half nether to the left half.

22 And thou schalt defoule the platis of the grauun ymagis of thi siluer, and the cloth of the yotun ymage of thi gold; and thou schalt scatere tho, as the vnclennesse of a womman in vncleene blood; Go thou out, and thou schalt seie to it.

23 And reyn schal be youun to thi seed, where euere thou schalt sowe in erthe, and the breed of fruytis of erthe schal be moost plenteuouse and fat; in that dai a lomb schal be fed largeli in thi possessioun.

24 And thi bolis and coltis of assis, that worchen the lond, schulen ete barli with chaf meynd togidere, as it is wyndewid in the cornfloor.

25 And strondis of rennynge watris schulen be on ech hiy munteyn, and on ech litil hil reisid, in the dai of sleyng of many men, whanne touris fallen doun.

26 And the liyt of the moone schal be as the liyt of the sunne, and the liyt of the sunne schal be seuenfold, as the liyt of seuene daies, in the dai in which the Lord schal bynde togidere the wounde of his puple, and schal make hool the smytynge of the wounde therof.

27 Lo! the name of the Lord cometh doun fro fer; his strong veniaunce is brennynge and greuouse to bere; hise lippis ben fillid of indignacioun, and his tunge is as fier deuouringe.

28 His spirit is as a stef streem, flowynge 'til to the myddis of the necke, to leese folkis in to nouyt, and the bridil of errour, that was in the chekis of puplis.

29 Song schal be to you, as the vois of an halewid solempnyte; and gladnesse of herte, as he that goth with a pipe, for to entre in to the hil of the Lord, to the stronge of Israel.

30 And the Lord schal make herd the glorie of his vois, and he schal schewe the ferdfulnesse of his arm in manassyng of strong veniaunce, and in flawme of fier brennynge; he schal hurtle doun in whirlewynd, and in stoon of hail.

31 For whi Assur smytun with a yerde schal drede of the vois of the Lord;

32 and the passyng of the yerd schal be foundid, which yerde the Lord schal make for to reste on hym. In tympans, and harpis, and in souereyn batels he schal ouercome hem.

33 For whi Tophet, that is, helle, deep and alargid, is maad redi of the kyng fro yistirdai; the nurschyngis therof ben fier and many trees; the blast of the Lord as a streem of brymstoon kyndlith it.

CAP 31

1 Wo to hem that goon doun in to Egipt to help, and hopen in horsis, and han trist on cartis, for tho ben manye, and on knyytis, for thei ben ful stronge; and thei tristiden not on the hooli of Israel, and thei souyten not the Lord.

2 Forsothe he that is wijs, hath brouyt yuel, and took not awei hise wordis; and he schal rise togidere ayens the hous of worste men, and ayens the helpe of hem that worchen wickidnesse.

3 Egipt is a man, and not God; and the horsis of hem ben fleisch, and not spirit; and the Lord schal bowe doun his hond, and the helpere schal falle doun, and he schal falle, to whom help is youun, and alle schulen be wastid togidere.

4 For whi the Lord seith these thingis to me, If a lioun rorith, and a whelp of a lioun on his prey, whanne the multitude of schipherdis cometh ayens hym, he schal not drede of the vois of hem, and he schal not drede of the multitude of hem; so the Lord of oostis schal come doun, for to fiyte on the mounteyn of Sion, and on the litil hil therof.

5 As briddis fleynge, so the Lord of oostis schal defende Jerusalem; he defendynge and delyuerynge, passynge forth and sauynge.

6 Ye sones of Israel, be conuertid, as ye hadden go awei in to depthe.

7 Forsothe in that dai a man schal caste awei the idols of his siluer, and the idols of his gold, whiche youre hondis maden to you in to synne.

8 And Assur schal falle bi swerd, not of man, and a swerd, not of man, schal deuoure hym; and he schal fle, not fro the face of swerd, and hise yonge men schulen be tributaries;

9 and the strengthe of hym schal passe fro ferdfulnesse, and hise princes fleynge schulen drede. The Lord seide, whos fier is in Sion, and his chymeney is in Jerusalem.

CAP 32

1 Lo! the kyng schal regne in riytfulnesse, and princes schulen be souereyns in doom.

2 And a man schal be, as he that is hid fro wynd, and hidith hym silf fro tempest; as stremes of watris in thirst, and the schadewe of a stoon stondynge fer out in a desert lond.

3 The iyen of profetis schulen not dasewe, and the eeris of heereris schulen herke diligentli;

4 and the herte of foolis schal vndurstonde kunnyng, and the tunge of stuttynge men schal speke swiftli, and pleynli.

5 He that is vnwijs, schal no more be clepid prince, and a gileful man schal not be clepid the grettere.

6 Forsothe a fool shal speke foli thingis, and his herte schal do wickidnesse, that he performe feynyng, and speke to the Lord gilefuli; and he schal make voide the soule of an hungry man, and schal take awei drynke fro a thirsti man.

7 The vessels of a gileful man ben worste; for he schal make redi thouytis to leese mylde men in the word of a leesyng, whanne a pore man spak doom.

8 Forsothe a prince schal thenke tho thingis that ben worthi to a prince, and he schal stonde ouer duykis.

9 Riche wymmen, rise ye, and here my vois; douytris tristynge, perseyue ye with eeris my speche.

10 For whi aftir daies and a yeer, and ye that tristen schulen be disturblid; for whi vyndage is endid, gaderyng schal no more come.

11 Ye riche wymmen, be astonyed; ye that tristen, be disturblid; vnclothe ye you, and be ye aschamed;

12 girde youre leendis; weile ye on brestis, on desirable cuntrei, on the plenteuouse vyner.

13 Thornes and breris schulen stie on the erthe of my puple; hou myche more on alle the housis of ioie of the citee makynge ful out ioie?

14 For whi the hous is left, the multitude of the citee is forsakun; derknessis and gropyng ben maad on dennes, 'til in to with outen ende. The ioie of wield assis is the lesewe of flockis;

15 til the spirit be sched out on us fro an hiy, and the desert schal be in to Chermel, and Chermel schal be arettid in to a forest.

16 And doom schal dwelle in wildirnesse, and riytfulnesse schal sitte in Chermel;

17 and the werk of riytfulnesse schal be pees, and the tilthe of riytfulnesse schal be stilnesse and sikirnesse, 'til in to with outen ende.

18 And my puple schal sitte in the fairnesse of pees, and in the tabernaclis of trist, and in riche reste.

19 But hail schal be in the coming doun of the foreste, and bi lownesse the citee schal be maad low.

20 Blessid ben ye, that sowen on alle watris, and putten yn the foot of an oxe and of an asse.

CAP 33

1 Wo to thee, that robbest; whether and thou schalt not be robbid? and that dispisist, whether and thou schalt not be dispisid? Whanne thou hast endid robbyng, thou schalt be robbid; and whanne thou maad weri ceessist to dispise, thou schalt be dispisid.

2 Lord, haue thou merci on vs, for we abiden thee; be thou oure arm in the morewtid, and oure helthe in the tyme of tribulacioun.

3 Puplis fledden fro the vois of the aungel; hethene men ben scaterid fro thin enhaunsyng.

4 And youre spuylis schulen be gaderid togidere, as a bruke is gaderid togidere, as whanne dichis ben ful therof.

5 The Lord is magnefied, for he dwellide an hiy, he fillid Sion with doom and riytfulnesse.

6 And feith schal be in thi tymes; the ritchessis of helthe is wisdom and kunnynge; the drede of the Lord, thilke is the tresour of hym.

7 Lo! seeris withoutenforth schulen crye, aungels of pees schulen wepe bittirli.

8 Weies ben distried, a goere bi the path ceesside; the couenaunt is maad voide, he castide doun citees, he arettide not men.

9 The lond morenyde, and was sijk; the Liban was schent, and was foul; and Saron is maad as desert, and Basan is schakun, and Carmele.

10 Now Y schal ryse, seith the Lord, now I schal be enhaunsid, and now I schal be reisid vp.

11 Ye schulen conseyue heete, ye schulen brynge forth stobil; youre spirit as fier schal deuoure you.

12 And puplis schulen be as aischis of the brennyng; thornes gaderid togidere schulen be brent in fier.

13 Ye that ben fer, here what thingis Y haue do; and, ye neiyboris, knowe my strengthe.

14 Synneris ben al to-brokun in Syon, tremblyng weldide ipocritis; who of you mai dwelle with fier deuowringe? who of you schal dwelle with euerlastinge brennyngis?

15 He that goith in riytfulnessis, and spekith treuthe; he that castith awei aueryce of fals calenge, and schakith awei his hondis fro al yifte; he that stoppith his eeris, that he heere not blood, and closith his iyen, that he se not yuel.

16 This man schal dwelle in hiy thingis, the strengthis of stoonys ben the hiynesse of hym; breed is youun to hym, hise watris ben feithful.

17 Thei schulen se the kyng in his fairnesse; the iyen of hym schulen biholde the londe fro fer.

18 Eliachym, thin herte schal bithenke drede; where is the lettrid man? Where is he that weieth the wordis of the lawe? where is the techere of litle children?

19 Thou schalt not se a puple vnwijs, a puple of hiy word, so that thou maist not vndurstonde the fair speking of his tunge, in which puple is no wisdom.

20 Biholde thou Sion, the citee of youre solempnyte; thin iyen schulen se Jerusalem, a riche citee, a tabernacle that mai not be borun ouer, nether the nailis therof schulen be takun awei withouten ende; and alle the cordis therof schulen not be brokun.

21 For oneli the worschipful doere oure Lord God is there; the place of floodis is strondis ful large and opyn; the schip of roweris schal not entre bi it, nethir a greet schip schal passe ouer it.

22 For whi the Lord is oure iuge, the Lord is oure lawe yyuere, the Lord is oure kyng; he schal saue vs.

23 Thi roopis ben slakid, but tho schulen not auaile; thi mast schal be so, that thou mow not alarge a signe. Thanne the spuylis of many preyes schulen be departid, crokid men schulen rauysche raueyn.

24 And a neiybore schal seie, Y was not sijk; the puple that dwellith in that Jerusalem, wickidnesse schal be takun awei fro it.

CAP 34

1 Neiye, ye hethene men, and here; and ye puplis, perseyue; the erthe, and the fulnesse therof, the world, and al buriownyng therof, here ye.

2 For whi indignacioun of the Lord is on alle folkis, and strong veniaunce on al the chyualrie of hem; he killide hem, and yaf hem in to sleyng.

3 The slayn men of hem schulen be cast forth, and stynk schal stie of the careyns of hem; hillis schulen flete of the blood of hem.

4 And al the chyualrie of heuenys schal faile, and heuenys schulen be foldid togidere as a book, and al the knyythod of tho schal flete doun, as the leef of a vyner and of a fige tre fallith doun.

5 For my swerd is fillid in heuene; lo! it schal come doun on Ydumee, and on the puple of my sleyng, to doom.

6 The swerd of the Lord is fillid of blood, it is maad fat of the ynner fatnesse of the blood of lambren and of buckis of geet, of the blood of rammes ful of merow; for whi the slayn sacrifice of the Lord is in Bosra, and greet sleyng is in the lond of Edom.

7 And vnycornes schulen go doun with hem, and bolis with hem that ben myyti; the lond of hem schal be fillid with blood, and the erthe of hem with ynnere fatnesse of fatte beestis;

8 for it is a dai of veniaunce of the Lord, a yeer of yeldyng of the dom of Sion.

9 And the strondis therof schulen be turned in to pitche, and the erthe therof in to brymstoon; and the lond therof schal be in to brennyng pitch, niyt and dai.

10 It schal not be quenchid withouten ende, the smoke therof schal stie fro generacioun in to generacioun, and it schal be desolat in to worldis of worldis; noon schal passe therbi.

11 And onocrotalus, and an irchoun schulen welde it; and a capret, and a crowe schulen dwelle therynne; and a mesure schal be stretchid forth theronne, that it be dryuun to nouyt, and an hangynge plomet in to desolacyoun.

12 The noble men therof schulen not be there; rathere thei schulen clepe the kyng in to help, and alle the princes therof schulen be in to nouyt.

13 And thornes and nettlis schulen growe in the housis therof, and a tasil in the strengthis therof; and it schal be the couche of dragouns, and the lesewe of ostrichis.

14 And fendis, and wondurful beestis, lijk men in the hiyere part and lijk assis in the nethir part, and an heeri schulen meete; oon schal crie to an other.

15 Lamya schal ligge there, and foond rest there to hir silf; there an irchoun hadde dichis, and nurschide out whelpis, and diggide aboute, and fostride in the schadewe therof; there kitis weren gaderid togidere, oon to another.

16 Seke ye diligentli in the book of the Lord, and rede ye; oon of tho thingis failide not, oon souyte not another; for he comaundide that thing, that goith forth of my mouth, and his spirit he gaderide tho togidere.

17 And he sente to hem eritage, and his hond departide it in mesure; til in to withouten ende tho schulen welde that lond, in generacioun and in to generacioun tho schulen dwelle ther ynne.

CAP 35

1 The forsakun Judee and with outen weie schal be glad, and wildirnesse schal make ful out ioye, and schal floure as a lilie.

2 It buriownynge schal buriowne, and it glad and preisynge schal make ful out ioie. The glorie of Liban is youun to it, the fairnesse of Carmele and of Saron; thei schulen se the glorie of the Lord, and the fairnesse of oure God.

3 Coumforte ye comelid hondis, and make ye strong feble knees.

4 Seie ye, Men of litil coumfort, be ye coumfortid, and nyle ye drede; lo! oure God schal brynge the veniaunce of yel-dyng, God hym silf schal come, and schal saue vs.

5 Thanne the iyen of blynde men schulen be openyd, and the eeris of deef men schulen be opyn.

6 Thanne a crokid man schal skippe as an hert, and the tunge of doumbe men schal be openyd; for whi watris ben brokun out in desert, and stremes in wildirnesse.

7 And that that was drie, is maad in to a poond, and the thirsti is maad in to wellis of watris. Grenenesse of rehed, and of spier schal growe in dennes, in whiche dwelliden dragouns bifore. And a path and a weie schal be there,

8 and it schal be clepid an hooli weie, he that is defoulid schal not passe therbi; and this schal be a streiyt weie to you, so that foolis erre not therbi.

9 A lioun schal not be there, and an yuel beeste schal not stie therbi, nether schal be foundun there.

10 And thei schulen go, that ben delyuered and ayenbouyt of the Lord; and thei schulen be conuertid, and schulen come in to Sion with preisyng; and euerlastynge gladnesse schal be on the heed of hem; thei schulen haue ioie and gladnesse, and sorewe and weilyng schulen fle awei.

CAP 36

1 And it was don in the fourtenthe yeer of kyng Ezechie, Sennacherib, the kyng of Assiriens, stiede on alle the stronge citees of Juda, and took tho.

2 And the kyng of Assiriens sente Rapsases fro Lachis to Jerusalem, to kyng Ezechie, with greet power; and he stood at the watir cundit of the hiyere sisterne, in the weie of the feeld of a fullere.

3 And Eliachym, the sone of Elchie, that was on the hous, yede out to hym, and Sobna, the scryuen, and Joae, the sone of Asaph, the chaunceler.

4 And Rapsases seide to hem, Seie ye to Ezechie, The greet king, the king of Assiriens, seith these thingis, What is the trist, in which thou tristist?

5 ethir bi what councele ether strengthe disposist thou for to rebelle? on whom hast thou trist, for thou hast go awei fro me?

6 Lo! thou tristist on this brokun staf of rehed, on Egipt, on which if a man restith, it schal entre in to his hoond, and schal perse it; so doith Farao, the kyng of Egipt, to alle men that tristen in hym.

7 That if thou answerist to me, We tristen in oure Lord God; whether it is not he, whose hiye places and auteris Esechie dide awei, and he seide to Juda and to Jerusalem, Ye schulen worschipe bifore this auter?

8 And now bitake thee to my lord, the kyng of Assiriens, and Y schal yyue to thee twei thousynde of horsis, and thou maist not yyue of thee stieris of tho horsis.

9 And hou schalt thou abide the face of the iuge of o place of the lesse seruauntis of my lord? That if thou tristist in Egipt, and in cartis, and in knyytis;

10 and now whethir Y stiede to this lond with out the Lord, that Y schulde distrie it? The Lord seide to me, Stie thou on this lond, and distrie thou it.

11 And Eliachym, and Sobna, and Joae, seiden to Rapsaces, Speke thou to thi seruauntis bi the langage of Sirie, for we vndurstonden; speke thou not to vs bi the langage of Jewis in the eeris of the puple, which is on the wal.

12 And Rapsaces seide to hem, Whether mi lord sente me to thi lord, and to thee, that Y schulde speke alle these wordis, and not rathere to the men that sitten on the wal, that thei ete her toordis, and drynke the pisse of her feet with you?

13 And Rapsaces stood, and criede with greet vois in the langage of Jewis, and seide, Here ye the wordis of the greet kyng, the kyng of Assiriens.

14 The kyng seith these thingis, Esechie disseyue not you, for he may not delyuere you;

15 and Ezechie yyue not to you trist on the Lord, and seie, The Lord delyuerynge schal delyuere vs; this citee schal not be youun in to the hoond of the kyng of Assiriens.

16 Nyle ye here Ezechie. For whi the kyng of Assiriens seith these thingis, Make ye blessyng with me, and go ye out to me; and ete ye ech man his vyner, and ech man his fige tre, and drynke ye ech man the water of his cisterne,

17 til Y come, and take awei you to a lond which is as youre lond; to a lond of whete and of wyn, to a lond of looues and of vyneris.

18 Ezechie disturble not you, and seie, The Lord schal delyuere vs. Whether the goddis of folkis delyuereden ech his lond fro the hond of the kyng of Assiriens?

19 Where is the god of Emath, and of Arphat? Where is the god of Sepharuaym? Whethir thei delyueriden Samarie fro myn hond?

20 Who is of alle goddis of these londis, that delyueride his lond fro myn hond, that the Lord delyuere Jerusalem fro myn hond?

21 And thei weren stille, and answeriden not to hym a word. For whi the kyng comaundide to hem, and seide, Answere ye not to him.

22 And Eliachym, the sone of Elchie, that was on the hous, and Sobna, the scryueyn, and Joae, the sone of Asaph, chaunceler, entriden with to-rent clothis to Ezechie, and telde to hym the wordis of Rapsaces.

CAP 37

1 And it was don, whanne kyng Ezechie hadde herd, he to-rente hise clothis, and he was wlappid in a sak, and entride in to the hous of the Lord.

2 And he sente Eliachym, that was on the hous, and Sobna, the scryuen, and the eldre men of prestis, hilid with sackis, to Isaie, the prophete, the sone of Amos.

3 And thei seiden to hym, Ezechie seith these thingis, A dai of tribulacioun, and of angwisch, and of chastisyng, and of blasfemye is this dai; for children camen 'til to childberyng, and vertu of childberyng is not.

4 Therfor reise thou preier for the relifs that ben foundun, if in ony maner thi Lord God here the wordis of Rapsaces, whom the king of Assiriens, his lord, sente, for to blasfeme lyuynge God, and to dispise bi the wordis, whiche thi Lord God herde.

5 And the seruauntis of kyng Esechie camen to Isaie;

6 and Isaie seide to hem, Ye schulen seie these thingis to youre lord, The Lord seith these thingis, Drede thou not of the face of wordis whiche thou herdist, bi whiche the children of the kyng of Assiriens blasfemyden me.

7 Lo! Y schal yyue to hym a spirit, and he schal here a messanger; and he schal turne ayen to his londe, and Y schal make hym to falle doun bi swerd in his lond.

8 Forsothe Rapsaces turnede ayen, and foond the kyng of Assiriens fiytynge ayens Lobna; for he hadde herd, that the kyng was gon fro Lachis.

9 And the kyng herde messangeris seiynge of Theracha, kyng of Ethiopiens, He is gon out to fiyte ayens thee. And whanne he hadde herd this thing, he sente messangeris to Ezechie, and seide, Ye schulen seie,

10 spekynge these thingis to Ezechye, kyng of Juda, Thi God disseyue not thee, in whom thou tristist, and seist, Jerusalem schal not be youun in to the hond of the kyng of Assiriens.

11 Lo! thou herdist alle thingis whiche the kynges of Assiriens diden to alle londis whiche thei distrieden; and maist thou be delyuered?

12 Whethir the goddis of folkis delyuereden hem, whiche my fadris distrieden; Gosan, and Aran, and Reseph, and the sones of Eden, that weren in Thalasar?

13 Where is the kyng of Emath, and the kyng of Arphath, and the kyng of the citee of Sepharuaym, and of Ana, and of Aua?

14 And Ezechie took the bookis fro the hond of messangeris, and redde tho; and he stiede in to the hous of the Lord, and spredde abrood tho bifore the Lord;

15 and preiede to the Lord,

16 and seide, Lord of oostis, God of Israel, that sittist on cherubyn, thou art God aloone of alle the rewmes of erthe; thou madist heuene and erthe.

17 Lord, bowe doun thin eere, and here; Lord, open thin iyen, and se; and here thou alle the wordis of Sennacherib, whiche he sente for to blasfeme lyuynge God.

18 For verili, Lord, the kyngis of Assiriens maden londis dissert, and the cuntreis of tho, and yauen the goddis of tho to fier;

19 for thei weren not goddis, but the werkis of mennus hondis, trees and stoonys; and thei al to-braken tho goddis.

20 And now, oure Lord God, saue thou vs fro the hond of hym; and alle rewmes of erthe knowe, that thou art Lord God aloone.

21 And Isaie, the sone of Amos, sente to Ezechie, and seide, The Lord God of Israel seith these thingis, For whiche thingis thou preidist me of Sennacherib, the kyng of Assiriens,

22 this is the word which the Lord spak on hym, Thou virgyn, the douyter of Sion, he dispiside thee, he scornede thee; thou virgyn, the douyter of Jerusalem, he moued his heed aftir thee.

23 Whom despisist thou, and whom blasfemedist thou? and on whom reisidist thou thi vois, and reisidist the hiynesse of thin iyen?

24 To the hooli of Israel. Bi the hond of thi seruauntis thou dispisidist the Lord, and seidist, In the multitude of my cartis Y stiede on the hiynesses of hillis, on the yockis of Liban; and Y schal kitte doun the hiy thingis of cedris therof, and the chosun beechis therof; and Y schal entre in to the hiynesse of the cop therof, in to the forest of Carmele therof.

25 Y diggide, and drank watir; and Y made drie with the step of my foot all the strondis of feeldis.

26 Whether thou, Sennacherib, herdist not what thingis Y dide sum tyme? Fro elde daies Y fourmyde that thing, and now Y haue brouyt; and it is maad in to drawyng vp bi the roote of litle hillis fiytynge togidere, and of strong citees.

27 The dwelleris of tho citees trembliden togidere with hond maad schort, and ben aschamed; thei ben maad as hei of the feeld, and the gras of lesewe, and as erbe of roouys, that driede vp bifore that it wexide ripe.

28 Y knew thi dwellyng, and thi goyng out, and thin entryng, and thi woodnesse ayens me.

29 Whanne thou were wood ayens me, thi pride stiede in to myn eeris; therfor Y schal sette a ryng in thi nosethirlis, and a bridil in thi lippis; and Y schal lede thee ayen in to the weie, bi which thou camest.

30 Forsothe to thee, Ezechie, this schal be a signe; ete thou in this yeer tho thingis that growen bi her fre wille, and in the secunde yeer ete thou applis; but in the thridde yeer sowe ye, and repe ye, and plaunte ye vyneris, and ete ye the fruyt of tho.

31 And that that is sauyd of the hous of Juda, and that, that is left, schal sende roote bynethe, and schal make fruyt aboue;

32 for whi relifs schulen go out of Jerusalem, and saluacioun fro the hil of Sion; the feruent loue of the Lord of oostis schal do this thing.

33 Therfor the Lord seith these thingis of the kyng of Assiriens, He schal not entre in to this citee, and he schal not schete there an arowe; and a scheeld schal not ocupie it, and he schal not sende erthe in the cumpas therof.

34 In the weie in which he cam, he schal turne ayen bi it; and he schal not entre in to this citee, seith the Lord.

35 And Y schal defende this citee, that Y saue it, for me, and for Dauid, my seruaunt.

36 Forsothe the aungel of the Lord yede out, and killide an hundride thousynde and fourscoor and fyue thousynde in the tentis of Assiriens; and thei risen eerli, and lo! alle men weren careyns of deed men.

37 And Sennacherib yede out of Jude, and wente awei. And Sennacherib, the kyng of Assiriens, turnede ayen, and dwellide in Nynyue.

38 And it was don, whanne he worschipide Mesrach, his god, in the temple, Aramalech and Sarasar, hise sones, killiden hym with swerd, and fledden in to the lond of Ararath; and Asaradon, his sone, regnyde for hym.

CAP 38

1 In tho daies Esechie was sijk 'til to the deth; and Isaie, the profete, the sone of Amos, entride to hym, and seide to hym, The Lord seith these thingis, Dispose thi hous, for thou schalt die, and thou schalt not lyue.

2 And Esechie turnede his face to the wal, and preiede the Lord, and seide, Lord, Y biseche;

3 haue thou mynde, Y biseche, hou Y yede bifore thee in treuthe, and in perfit herte, and Y dide that that was good bifore thin iyen. And Ezechye wept with greet wepyng.

4 And the word of the Lord was maad to Isaie, and seide,

5 Go thou, and seie to Ezechye, The Lord God of Dauid, thi fadir, seith these thingis, I haue herd thi preier, and Y siy thi teeris. Lo! Y schal adde on thi daies fiftene yeer;

6 and Y schal delyuere thee and this citee fro the hond of the kyng of Assiriens, and Y schal defende it.

7 Forsothe this schal be to thee a signe of the Lord, that the Lord schal do this word, which he spak.

8 Lo! Y schal make the schadewe of lynes, bi which it yede doun in the orologie of Achas, in the sunne, to turne ayen backward bi ten lynes. And the sunne turnede ayen bi ten lynes, bi degrees bi whiche it hadde go doun.

9 The scripture of Ezechie, kyng of Juda, whanne he hadde be sijk, and hadde rekyuered of his sikenesse.

10 I seide, in the myddil of my daies Y schal go to the yatis of helle.

11 Y souyte the residue of my yeeris; Y seide, Y schal not se the Lord God in the lond of lyueris; Y schal no more biholde a man, and a dwellere of reste.

12 My generacioun is takun awei, and is foldid togidere fro me, as the tabernacle of scheepherdis is foldid togidere. Mi lijf is kit doun as of a webbe; he kittide doun me, the while Y was wouun yit. Fro the morewtid 'til to the euentid thou schalt ende me;

13 Y hopide til to the morewtid; as a lioun, so he al to-brak alle my boonys. Fro the morewtid til to the euentid thou schalt ende me; as the brid of a swalewe, so Y schal crie;

14 Y schal bithenke as a culuer. Myn iyen biholdynge an hiy, ben maad feble. Lord, Y suffre violence, answere thou for me; what schal Y seie,

15 ether what schal answere to me, whanne 'I mysilf haue do? Y schal bithenke to thee alle my yeeris, in the bitternisse of my soule.

16 Lord, if me lyueth so, and the lijf of my spirit is in siche thingis, thou schalt chastise me, and schalt quykene me.

17 Lo! my bitternesse is moost bittir in pees; forsothe thou hast delyuered my soule, that it perischide not; thou hast caste awey bihynde thi bak alle my synnes.

18 For not helle schal knowleche to thee, nethir deth schal herie thee; thei that goon doun in to the lake, schulen not abide thi treuthe.

19 A lyuynge man, a lyuynge man, he schal knouleche to thee, as and Y to dai; the fadir schal make knowun thi treuthe to sones.

20 Lord, make thou me saaf, and we schulen synge oure salmes in all the daies of oure lijf in the hous of the Lord.

21 And Ysaie comaundide, that thei schulden take a gobet of figus, and make a plaster on the wounde; and it schulde be heelid.

22 And Ezechie seide, What signe schal be, that Y schal stie in to the hous of the Lord?

CAP 39

1 In that tyme Marodach Baladan, the sone of Baladam, the kyng of Babiloyne, sente bookis and yiftis to Ezechie; for he hadde herd, that Ezechie hadde be sijk, and was rekyuerid.

2 Forsothe Ezechie was glad on hem, and schewide to hem the selle of swete smellynge spices, and of siluer, and of gold, and of smellynge thingis, and of best oynement, and alle the schoppis of his purtenaunce of houshold, and alle thingis that weren foundun in hise tresours; no word was, which Ezechie schewide not to hem in his hous, and in al his power.

3 Sotheli Ysaie, the prophete, entride to kyng Ezechie, and seide to hym, What seiden thes men, and fro whennus camen thei to thee? And Ezechie seide, Fro a fer lond thei camen to me, fro Babiloyne.

4 And Ysaie seide, What siyen thei in thin hous? And Ezechie seide, Thei sien alle thingis that ben in myn hous; no thing was in my tresours, which Y schewide not to hem.

5 And Ysaie seide to Ezechie, Here thou the word of the Lord of oostis.

6 Lo! daies schulen come, and alle thingis that ben in thin hous, and whiche thingis thi fadris tresoriden til to this dai, schulen be takun awei in to Babiloyne; not ony thing schal be left, seith the Lord.

7 And thei schulen take of thi sones, that schulen go out of thee, whiche thou schalt gendre; and thei schulen be onest seruauntis and chast in the paleis of the kyng of Babiloyne.

8 And Ezechie seide to Ysaie, The word of the Lord is good, which he spak. And Ezechie seide, Pees and treuthe be maad oneli in my daies.

CAP 40

1 My puple, be ye coumfortid, be ye coumfortid, seith youre Lord God.

2 Speke ye to the herte of Jerusalem, and clepe ye it, for the malice therof is fillid, the wickidnesse therof is foryouun; it hath resseyued of the hond of the Lord double thingis for alle hise synnes.

3 The vois of a crier in desert, Make ye redi the weie of the Lord, make ye riytful the pathis of oure God in wildirnesse.

4 Ech valey schal be enhaunsid, and ech mounteyn and litil hil schal be maad low; and schrewid thingis schulen be in to

streiyt thingis, and scharpe thingis schulen be in to pleyn weies.

5 And the glorie of the Lord schal be schewid, and ech man schal se togidere, that the mouth of the Lord hath spoke.

6 The vois of God, seiynge, Crie thou. And Y seide, What schal Y crie? Ech fleisch is hei, and al the glorie therof is as the flour of the feeld.

7 The hei is dried vp, and the flour felle doun, for the spirit of the Lord bleew therynne.

8 Verely the puple is hey; the hey is dried vp, and the flour felle doun; but the word of the Lord dwellith with outen ende.

9 Thou that prechist to Sion, stie on an hiy hil; thou that prechist to Jerusalem, enhaunse thi vois in strengthe; enhaunse thou, nyle thou drede; seie thou to the citees of Juda, Lo! youre God.

10 Lo! the Lord God schal come in strengthe, and his arm schal holde lordschipe; lo! his mede is with hym, and his werk is bifore hym.

11 As a scheepherd he schal fede his flok, he schal gadere lambreen in his arm, and he schal reise in his bosom; he schal bere scheep 'with lomb.

12 Who mat watris in a fist, and peiside heuenes with a spanne? Who peiside the heuynesse of the erthe with thre fyngris, and weide mounteyns in a weihe, and litle hillis in a balaunce?

13 Who helpide the Spirit of the Lord, ether who was his councelour, and schewide to hym?

14 With whom took he councel, and who lernyde hym, and tauyte hym the path of riytfulnesse, and lernyde hym in kunnyng, and schewyde to him the weie of prudence?

15 Lo! folkis ben as a drope of a boket, and ben arettid as the tunge of a balaunce; lo!

16 ylis ben as a litil dust, and the Liban schal not suffice to brenne his sacrifice, and the beestis therof schulen not suffice to brent sacrifice.

17 Alle folkis ben so bifore hym, as if thei ben not; and thei ben rettid as no thing and veyn thing to hym.

18 To whom therfor maden ye God lijk? ether what ymage schulen ye sette to hym?

19 Whether a smyth schal welle togidere an ymage, ether a gold smyth schal figure it in gold, and a worchere in siluer schal diyte it with platis of siluer?

20 A wijs crafti man chees a strong tre, and vnable to be rotun; he sekith how he schal ordeyne a symylacre, that schal not be mouyd.

21 Whether ye witen not? whether ye herden not? whether it was not teld to you fro the begynnynge? whether ye vndurstoden not the foundementis of erthe?

22 Which sittith on the cumpas of erthe, and the dwelleris therof ben as locustis; which stretchith forth heuenes as nouyt, and spredith abrood tho as a tabernacle to dwelle.

23 Which yyueth the sercheris of priuytees, as if thei be not, and made the iugis of erthe as a veyn thing.

24 And sotheli whanne the stok of hem is nether plauntid, nether is sowun, nether is rootid in erthe, he bleew sudenli on hem, and thei drieden vp, and a whirle wynd schal take hem awei as stobil.

25 And to what thing 'ye han licned me, and han maad euene? seith the hooli.

26 Reise youre iyen an hiy, and se ye, who made these thingis of nouyt; which ledith out in noumbre the kniythod of tho, and clepith alle bi name, for the multitude of his strengthe, and stalworthnesse, and vertu; nether o residue thing was.

27 Whi seist thou, Jacob, and spekist thou, Israel, My weie is hid fro the Lord, and my doom passide fro my God?

28 Whether thou knowist not, ether herdist thou not? God, euerlastynge Lord, that made of nouyt the endis of erthe, schal not faile, nether schal trauele, nether enserchyng of his wisdom is.

29 That yyueth vertu to the weeri, and strengthe to hem that ben not, and multiplieth stalworthnesse.

30 Children schulen faile, and schulen trauele, and yonge men schulen falle doun in her sikenesse.

31 But thei that hopen in the Lord, schulen chaunge strengthe, thei schulen take fetheris as eglis; thei schulen renne, and schulen not trauele; thei schulen go, and schulen not faile.

CAP 41

1 Iles, be stille to me, and folkis chaunge strengthe; neiye thei, and thanne speke thei; neiye we togidere to doom.

2 Who reiside the iust man fro the eest, and clepide hym to sue hym silf? He schal yyue folkis in his siyt, and he schal welde kyngis; he schal yyue as dust to his swerd, and as stobil 'that is rauyschid of the wynd, to his bowe.

3 He schal pursue hem, he schal go in pees; a path schal not appere in hise feet.

4 Who wrouyte and dide these thingis? clepynge generaciouns at the bigynnyng. Y am the Lord; and Y am the firste and the laste.

5 Ilis sien, and dredden; the laste partis of erthe were astonyed; thei camen niy, and neiyiden.

6 Ech man schal helpe his neiybore, and schal seie to his brother, Be thou coumfortid.

7 A smyth of metal smytynge with an hamer coumfortide him that polischyde, ethir made fair, in that tyme, seiynge, It is good, to glu; and he fastenede hym with nailis, that he schulde not be mouyd.

8 And thou, Israel, my seruaunte, Jacob, whom Y chees, the seed of Abraham, my frend, in whom Y took thee;

9 fro the laste partis of erthe, and fro the fer partis therof Y clepide thee; and Y seide to thee, Thou art my seruaunt; Y chees thee, and castide not awei thee.

10 Drede thou not, for Y am with thee; boowe thou not awei, for Y am thi God. Y coumfortide thee, and helpide thee; and the riythond of my iust man vp took thee.

11 Lo! alle men schulen be schent, and schulen be aschamed, that fiyten ayens thee; thei schulen be as if thei ben not, and men schulen perische, that ayen seien thee.

12 Thou schalt seke hem, and thou schalt not fynde thi rebel men; thei schulen be, as if thei ben not, and as the wastyng of a man fiytynge ayens thee.

13 For Y am thi Lord God, takynge thin hond, and seiynge to thee, Drede thou not, Y helpide thee.

14 Nyle thou, worm of Jacob, drede, ye that ben deed of Israel. Y helpide thee, seith the Lord, and thin ayen biere, the hooli of Israel.

15 Y haue set thee as a newe wayn threischynge, hauynge sawynge bilis; thou schalt threische mounteyns, and schalt make smal, and thou schalt sette litle hillis as dust.

16 Thou schalt wyndewe hem, and the wynd schal take hem awei, and a whirlewynd schal scatere hem; and thou schalt make ful out ioie in the Lord, and thou schalt be glad in the hooli of Israel.

17 Nedi men and pore seken watris, and tho ben not; the tunge of hem driede for thirst. Y the Lord schal here hem, I God of Israel schal not forsake hem.

18 Y schal opene floodis in hiy hillis, and wellis in the myddis of feeldis; Y schal sette the desert in to poondis of watris, and the lond without weie in to ryuers of watris.

19 Y schal yyue in wildirnesse a cedre, and a thorn, and a myrte tre, and the tre of an olyue; Y schal sette in the desert a fir tre, an elm, and a box tre togidere.

20 That thei se, and knowe, and bithenke, and vndurstonde togidere; that the hond of the Lord dide this thing, and the hooli of Israel made that of nouyt.

21 Make ye niy youre doom, seith the Lord; brynge ye, if in hap ye han ony thing, seith the kyng of Jacob.

22 Neiy tho, and telle to vs, what euer thingis schulen come; telle ye the formere thingis that weren, and we schulen sette oure herte, and schulen wite; schewe ye to vs the laste thingis of hem, and tho thingis that schulen come.

23 Telle ye what thingis schulen come in tyme to comynge, and we schulen wite, that ye ben goddis; al so do ye wel, ethir yuele, if ye moun; and speke we, and see we togidere.

24 Lo! ye ben of nouyt, and youre werk is of that that is not; he that chees you, is abhomynacioun.

25 I reiside fro the north, and he schal come fro the risyng of the sunne; he schal clepe my name. And he schal brynge magistratis as cley, and as a pottere defoulynge erthe.

26 Who tolde fro the bigynnyng, that we wite, and fro the bigynnyng, that we seie, Thou art iust? noon is tellynge, nether biforseiynge, nether herynge youre wordis.

27 The firste schal seie to Sion, Lo! Y am present; and Y schal yyue a gospellere to Jerusalem.

28 And Y siy, and noon was of these, that token councel, and he that was axid, answeride a word.

29 Lo! alle men ben vniust, and her werkis ben wynd and veyn; the symylacris of hem ben wynd, and voide thing.

CAP 42

1 Lo! my seruaunt, Y schal vptake hym, my chosun, my soule pleside to it silf in hym. I yaf my spirit on hym, he schal brynge forth doom to hethene men.

2 He schal not crie, nether he schal take a persoone, nether his vois schal be herd withoutforth.

3 He schal not breke a schakun rehed, and he schal not quenche smokynge flax; he schal brynge out doom in treuthe.

4 He schal not be sorewful, nether troblid, til he sette doom in erthe, and ilis schulen abide his lawe.

5 The Lord God seith these thingis, makynge heuenes of noyt, and stretchynge forth tho, makynge stidfast the erthe, and tho thingis that buriownen of it, yyuynge breeth to the puple, that is on it, and yyuynge spirit to hem that treden on it.

6 Y the Lord haue clepid thee in riytfulnesse, and Y took thin hond, and kepte thee, and Y yaf thee in to a boond of pees of the puple, and in to liyt of folkis;

7 That thou schuldist opene the iyen of blynde men; that thou schuldist lede out of closyng togidere a boundun man, fro the hous of prisoun men sittynge in derknessis.

8 Y am the Lord, this is my name; Y schal not yyue my glorie to an othere, and my preisyng to grauun ymagis.

9 Lo! tho thingis that weren the firste, ben comun, and Y telle newe thingis; Y schal make herd to you, bifore that tho bigynnen to be maad.

10 Synge ye a newe song to the Lord; his heriyng is fro the laste partis of erthe; ye that goon doun in to the see, and the fulnesse therof, ilis, and the dwelleris of tho.

11 The desert be reisid, and the citees therof; he schal dwelle in the housis of Cedar; ye dwelleris of the stoon, herie ye; thei schulen crie fro the cop of hillis.

12 Thei schulen sette glorie to the Lord, and they schulen telle his heriyng in ilis.

13 The Lord as a strong man schal go out, as a man a werryour he schal reise feruent loue; he schal speke, and schal crie; he schal be coumfortid on hise enemyes.

14 Y was stille, euere Y helde silence; Y was pacient, Y schal speke as a womman trauelynge of child; Y schal scatere, and Y schal swolowe togidere.

15 Y schal make desert hiy mounteyns and litle hillis, and Y schal drie vp al the buriownyng of tho; and Y schal sette floodis in to ilis, and Y schal make poondis drie.

16 And Y schal lede out blynde men in to the weie, which thei knowen not, and Y schal make hem to go in pathis, whiche thei knewen not; Y schal sette the derknessis of hem bifore hem in to liyt, and schrewid thingis in to riytful thingis; Y dide these wordis to hem, and Y forsook not hem.

17 Thei ben turned abac; be thei schent with schenschipe, that trusten in a grauun ymage; whiche seien to a yotun ymage, Ye ben oure goddis.

18 Ye deef men, here; and ye blynde men, biholde to se.

19 Who is blynd, no but my seruaunt? and deef, no but he to whom Y sente my messangeris? Who is blynd, no but he that is seeld? and who is blynd, no but the seruaunt of the Lord?

20 Whether thou that seest many thingis, schalt not kepe? Whether thou that hast open eeris, schalt not here?

21 And the Lord wolde, that he schulde halewe it, and magnefie the lawe, and enhaunse it.

22 But thilke puple was rauyschid, and wastid; alle thei ben the snare of yonge men, and ben hid in the housis of prisouns. Thei ben maad in to raueyn, and noon is that delyuereth; in to rauyschyng, and noon is that seith, Yelde thou.

23 Who is among you, that herith this, perseyueth, and herkneth thingis to comynge?

24 Who yaf Jacob in to rauyschyng, and Israel to distrieris? Whether not the Lord? He it is, ayens whom thei synneden; and thei nolden go in hise weies, and thei herden not his lawe.

25 And he schedde out on hem the indignacioun of his strong veniaunce, and strong batel; and thei brenten it in cumpas, and it knewe not; and he brente it, and it vndurstood not.

CAP 43

1 And now the Lord God, makynge of nouyt thee, Jacob, and formynge thee, Israel, seith these thingis, Nyle thou drede, for Y ayenbouyte thee, and Y clepide thee bi thi name; thou art my seruaunt.

2 Whanne thou schalt go bi watris, Y schal be with thee, and floodis schulen not hile thee; whanne thou schalt go in fier, thou schalt not be brent, and flawme schal not brenne in thee.

3 For Y am thi Lord God, the hooli of Israel, thi sauyour. I yaf thi merci Egipt; Ethiopie and Saba for thee.

4 Sithen thou art maad onourable, and glorious in myn iyen; Y louyde thee, and Y schal yyue men for thee, and puplis for thi soule.

5 Nyle thou drede, for Y am with thee; Y schal brynge thi seed fro the eest, and Y schal gadere thee togidere fro the west.

6 Y schal seie to the north, Yyue thou, and to the south, Nyle thou forbede; brynge thou my sones fro afer, and my douytris fro the laste partis of erthe.

7 And ech that clepith my name to help, in to my glorie Y made hym of nouyt; Y fourmyde hym, and made hym.

8 Lede thou forth the blynde puple, and hauynge iyen; the deef puple, and eeris ben to it.

9 Alle hethene men ben gaderid togidere, and lynagis be gaderid togidere. Who among you, who schal telle this, and schal make you to here tho thingis, that ben the firste? yyue thei witnessis of hem, and be thei iustified, and here thei, and seie.

10 Verili ye ben my witnessis, seith the Lord, and my seruaunt, whom Y chees; that ye wite, and bileue to me, and vndurstonde, for Y mysilf am; bifore me is no God formere, and after me schal noon be.

11 Y am, Y am the Lord, and with out me is no sauyour.

12 I telde, and sauyde; Y made heryng, and noon alien God was among you. Ye ben my witnessis, seith the Lord;

13 and Y am God fro the bigynnyng, Y my silf am, and noon is that delyuerith fro myn hoond; Y schal worche, and who schal distrie it?

14 The Lord, youre ayenbiere, the hooli of Israel, seith these thingis, For you Y sente out in to Babiloyne, and Y drow doun alle barris, and Caldeis hauynge glorie in her schippis.

15 Y am the Lord, youre hooli, youre king, makynge Israel of nouyt.

16 The Lord seith these thingis, that yaf weie in the see, and a path in rennynge watris;

17 which ledde out a carte, and hors, a cumpany, and strong man; thei slepten togidere, nether thei schulen rise ayen; thei ben al tobrokun as flex, and ben quenchid.

18 Thenke ye not on the formere thingis, and biholde ye not olde thingis.

19 Lo! Y make newe thingis, and now tho schulen bigynne to be maad; sotheli ye schulen know tho. Y schal sette weie in desert, and floodis in a lond without weie.

20 And a beeste of the feelde schal glorifie me, dragouns and ostrigis schulen glorifie me; for Y yaf watris in desert, and floodis in the lond without weie, that Y schulde yyue drynk to my puple, to my chosun puple.

21 Y fourmyde this puple to me, it schal telle my preysyng.

22 Jacob, thou clepidist not me to help; and thou, Israel, trauelidist not for me.

23 Thou offridist not to me the ram of thi brent sacrifice, and thou glorifiedist not me with thi slayn sacrifices. Y made not thee to serue in offryng, nethir Y yaf to thee trauel in encense.

24 Thou bouytist not to me swete smellynge spicerie for siluer, and thou fillidist not me with fatnesse of thi slayn sacrifices; netheles thou madist me to serue in thi synnes, thou yauest trauel to me in thi wickidnessis.

25 Y am, Y my silf am, that do awei thi wickidnessis for me, and Y schal not haue mynde on thy synnes.

26 Brynge me ayen in to mynde, and be we demyd togidere; telle thou, if thou hast ony thing, that thou be iustified.

27 Thi firste fadir synnede, and thin interpretours trespassiden ayens me.

28 And Y made foul hooli princes, and Y yaf Jacob to deth, and Israel in to blasfemye.

CAP 44

1 And now, Jacob, my seruaunt, here thou, and Israel, whom I chees.

2 The Lord makynge and foryyuynge thee, thin helpere fro the wombe, seith these thingis, My seruaunt, Jacob, nyle thou drede, and thou moost riytful, whom Y chees.

3 For Y schal schede out watris on the thirsti, and floodis on the dry lond; Y schal schede out my spirit on thi seed, and my blessyng on thi generacioun.

4 And thei schulen buriowne among erbis, as salewis bisidis rennynge watris.

5 This man schal seie, Y am of the Lord, and he schal clepe in the name of Jacob; and this man schal write with his hoond to the Lord, and schal be licned in the name of Israel.

6 The Lord, kyng of Israel, and ayenbiere therof, the Lord of oostis seith these thingis, Y am the firste and Y am the laste, and with outen me is no God.

7 Who is lijk me? clepe he, and telle, and declare ordre to me, sithen Y made elde puple; telle he to hem thingis to comynge, and that schulen be.

8 Nyle ye drede, nether be ye disturblid; fro that tyme Y made thee for to here, and Y telde; ye ben my witnessis. Whethir a God is with out me, and a formere, whom Y knew not?

9 Alle the fourmeris of an idol ben no thing, and the moost louyd thingis of hem schulen not profite; thei ben witnessis of tho, that tho seen not, nether vndurstonden, that thei be schent.

10 Who fourmyde a god, and yetide an ymage, not profitable to ony thing?

11 Lo! alle the parteneris therof schulen be schent; for the smythis ben of men. Whanne alle schulen come, thei schulen stonde, and schulen drede, and schulen be schent togidere.

12 A smith wrouyte with a file; he fourmyde it in coolis, and in hameris, and he wrouyte with the arm of his strengthe. He schal be hungri, and he schal faile; he schal not drynke watre, and he schal be feynt.

13 A carpenter stretchide forth a reule, he fourmyde it with an adese; he made it in the corner places, and he turnede it in cumpas; and he made the ymage of a man, as a fair man, dwellynge in the hous.

14 He kittide doun cedris, he took an hawthorn, and an ook, that stood among the trees of the forest; he plauntide a pyne apple tre, which he nurschide with reyn,

15 and it was maad in to fier to men. He took of tho, and was warmed, and he brente, and bakide looues; but of the residue he wrouyte a god, and worschipide it, and he made a grauun ymage, and he was bowid bifore that.

16 He brente the myddil therof with fier, and of the myddil therof he sethide fleischis, and eet; he sethide potage, and was fillid; and he was warmed, and he seide, Wel!

17 Y am warmed; Y siy fier. Forsothe the residue therof he made a god, and a grauun ymage to hym silf; he is bowide bifore that, and worschipith that, and bisechith, and seith, Delyuere thou me, for thou art my god.

18 Thei knewen not, nether vndurstoden, for thei han foryete, that her iye se not, and that thei vndurstonde not with her herte.

19 Thei bythenken not in her soule, nether thei knowen, nether thei feelen, that thei seie, Y brente the myddil therof in fier, and Y bakide looues on the coolis therof, and Y sethide fleischis, and eet; and of the residue therof schal Y make an idol? schal Y falle doun bifore the stok of a tree?

20 A part therof is aische; an vnwijs herte schal worschipe it, and he schal not delyuere his soule, nether he schal seie, A strong leesyng is in my riythond.

21 Thou, Jacob, and Israel, haue mynde of these thingis, for thou art my seruaunt; Y formyde thee, Israel, thou art my seruaunt; thou schalt not foryete me.

22 Y dide awei thi wickidnessis as a cloude, and thi synnes as a myist; turne thou ayen to me, for Y ayenbouyte thee.

23 Ye heuenes, herie, for the Lord hath do merci; the laste partis of erth, synge ye hertli song; hillis, sowne ye preisyng; the forest and ech tre therof, herie God; for the Lord ayenbouyte Jacob, and Israel schal haue glorie.

24 The Lord, thin ayenbiere, and thi fourmere fro the wombe, seith these thingis, Y am the Lord, makynge alle thingis, and Y aloone stretche forth heuenes, and stablische the erthe, and noon is with me;

25 and Y make voide the signes of false dyuynours, and Y turne in to woodnesse dyuynours, that dyuynen by sacrifices offrid to feendis; and Y turne wise men bacward, and Y make her science fonned.

26 And the Lord reisith the word of his seruaunt, and fillith the councel of hise messangeris; and Y seie, Jerusalem, thou schalt be enhabitid; and to the citees of Juda, Ye schulen be bildid, and Y schal reise the desertis therof;

27 and Y seie to the depthe, Be thou desolat, and Y shal make drie thi floodis;

28 and Y seie to Cirus, Thou art my scheepherde, and thou schalt fille al my wille; and Y seie to Jerusalem, Thou schalt be bildid; and to the temple, Thou schalt be foundid.

CAP 45

1 The Lord seith these thingis to my crist, Cirus, whos riythond Y took, that Y make suget folkis bifor his face, and turne the backis of kyngis; and Y schal opene yatis bifore hym, and yatis schulen not be closid.

2 Y schal go bifore thee, and Y schal make lowe the gloriouse men of erthe; Y schal al to-breke brasun yatis, and Y schal breke togidere irun barris.

3 And Y schal yyue hid tresours to thee, and the priuy thingis of priuytees, that thou wite, that Y am the Lord, that clepe thi name, God of Israel,

4 for my seruaunt Jacob, and Israel my chosun, and Y clepide thee bi thi name; Y licnyde thee, and thou knewist not me.

5 Y am the Lord, and ther is no more; with out me is no God. Y haue gird thee, and thou knewist not me.

6 That thei that ben at the risyng of the sunne, and thei that ben at the west, know, that with out me is no God.

7 Y am the Lord, and noon other God is; fourmynge liyt, and makynge derknessis, makynge pees, and fourmynge yuel; Y am the Lord, doynge alle these thingis.

8 Heuenes, sende ye out deew fro aboue, and cloudis, reyne a iust man; the erthe be openyde, and brynge forth the sauyour, and riytfulnesse be borun togidere; Y the Lord haue maad hym of nouyt.

9 Wo to hym that ayen seith his maker, a tiel stoon of erthe of Sannys. Whether clei seith to his pottere, What makist thou, and thi werk is withouten hondis?

10 Wo to hym that seith to the fadir, What gendrist thou? and to a womman, What childist thou?

11 The Lord, the hooli of Israel, the fourmere therof, seith these thingis, Axe ye me thingis to comynge on my sones, and sende ye to me on the werkis of myn hondis.

12 Y made erthe, and Y made a man on it; myn hondis helden abrood heuenes, and Y comaundide to al the knyythod of tho.

13 Y reiside hym to riytfulnesse, and Y schal dresse alle hise weies; he schal bilde my citee, and he schal delyuere my prisoneris, not in prijs, nether in yiftis, seith the Lord of oostis.

14 The Lord God seith these thingis, The trauel of Egipt, and the marchaundie of Ethiopie, and of Sabaym; hiy men

schulen go to thee, and schulen be thine; thei schulen go aftir thee, thei schulen go boundun in manyclis, and schulen worschipe thee, and schulen biseche thee. God is oneli in thee, and with out thee is no God.

15 Verili thou art God hid, God, the sauyour of Israel.

16 Alle makeris of errours ben schent, and weren aschamed; thei yeden togidere in to confusioun.

17 Israel is sauyde in the Lord, bi euerlastynge helthe; ye schulen not be schent, and ye schulen not be aschamed, til in to the world of world.

18 For whi the Lord makynge heuenes of nouyt, seith these thingis; he is God fourmynge erthe, and makinge it, he is the makere therof; he made it of noyt, not in veyn, but he formyde it, that it be enhabitid; Y am the Lord, and noon other is.

19 Y spak not in hid place, not in a derk place of erthe; I seide not to the seed of Jacob, Seke ye me in veyn. Y am the Lord spekynge riytfulnesse, tellynge riytful thingis.

20 Be ye gaderid, and come ye, and neiye ye togidere, that ben sauyd of hethene men; thei that reisen a signe of her grauyng, knewen not, and thei preien a god that saueth not.

21 Telle ye, and come ye, and take ye councel togidere. Who made this herd fro the bigynnyng? fro that tyme Y bifor seide it. Whether Y am not the Lord, and no God is ferthere with out me? God riytful and sauynge is noon, outakun me.

22 Alle the coostis of erthe, be ye conuertid to me, and ye schulen be saaf; for Y am the Lord, and noon other is.

23 Y swoor in my silf, a word of riytfulnesse schal go out of my mouth, and it schal not turne ayen;

24 for ech kne schal be bowid to me, and ech tunge schal swere.

25 Therfor thei schulen sei in the Lord, Riytfulnessis and empire ben myne; alle that fiyten ayens hym schulen come to hym, and schulen be aschamed.

26 Al the seed of Israel schal be iustified and preysid in the Lord.

CAP 46

1 Bel is brokun, Nabo is al to-brokun; her symylacris lijk to wielde beestis and werk beestis ben brokun; youre birthuns

2 with heuy charge 'til to werynesse weren rotun, and ben al to-brokun togidere; tho miyten not saue the berere, and the soule of hem schal go in to caitifte.

3 The hous of Jacob, and al the residue of the hous of Israel, here ye me, whiche ben borun of my wombe, whiche ben borun of my wombe.

4 Til to eelde Y my silf, and til to hoor heeris Y schal bere; Y made, and Y schal bere, and Y schal saue.

5 To whom han ye licned me, and maad euene, and han comparisound me, and han maad lijk?

6 Whiche beren togidere gold fro the bagge, and peisen siluer with a balaunce, and hiren a goldsmyth to make a god, and thei fallen doun, and worschipen; thei berynge beren in schuldris,

7 and settynge in his place; and he schal stonde, and schal not be mouyd fro his place; but also whanne thei crien to hym, he schal not here, and he schal not saue hem fro tribulacioun.

8 Haue ye mynde of this, and be ye aschamed; ye trespassouris, go ayen to the herte.

9 Bithenke ye on the formere world, for Y am God, and no God is ouer me, nether is lijk me.

10 And Y telle fro the bigynnyng the laste thing, and fro the bigynnyng tho thingis that ben not maad yit; and Y seie, My councel schal stonde, and al my wille schal be don.

11 And Y clepe a brid fro the eest, and the man of my wille fro a ferr lond; and Y spak, and Y schal brynge that thing; Y haue maad of nouyt, and Y schal make that thing.

12 Ye of hard herte, here me, that ben fer fro riytfulnesse.

13 Y made nyy myn riytfulnesse, it schal not be drawun afer, and myn helthe shal not tarie; Y schal yyue helthe in Sion, and my glorie in Israel.

CAP 47

1 Thou virgyn, the douytir Babiloyne, go doun, sitte thou in dust, sitte thou in erthe; a kyngis seete is not to the douyter of Caldeis, for thou schalt no more be clepid soft and tendir.

2 Take thou a queerne stoon, and grynde thou mele; make thou nakid thi filthe, diskeuere the schuldur, schewe the hippis, passe thou floodis.

3 Thi schame schal be schewid, and thi schenschipe schal be seen; Y schal take veniaunce, and no man schal ayenstonde me.

4 Oure ayen biere, the Lord of oostis is his name, the hooli of Israel.

5 Douyter of Caldeis, sitte thou, be thou stille, and entre in to derknessis, for thou schalt no more be clepid the ladi of rewmes.

6 I was wrooth on my puple, Y defoulid myn eritage, and Y yaf hem in thin hond, and thou settidist not mercies to hem; thou madist greuouse the yok greetli on an eld man,

7 and thou seidist, With outen ende Y schal be ladi; thou puttidist not these thingis on thin herte, nether thou bithouytist on thi laste thing.

8 And now, thou delicat, and dwellynge tristili, here these thingis, which seist in thin herte, Y am, and outakun me ther is no more; Y schal not sitte widewe, and Y schal not knowe bareynesse.

9 These twei thingis, bareynesse and widewhod schulen come to thee sudenli in o dai; alle thingis camen on thee for the multitude of thi witchecraftis, and for the greet hardnesse of thin enchauntours, ether tregetours.

10 And thou haddist trist in thi malice, and seidist, Noon is that seeth me; this thi wisdom and thi kunnyng disseyuede thee; and thou seidist in thin herte,

11 Y am, and outakun me ther is noon other. Yuel schal come on thee, and thou schalt not knowe the bigynning therof; and wrecchidnesse schal falle on thee, which thou schalt not mowe clense; wretchidnesse which thou knowist not, schal come on thee sudenly.

12 Stonde thou with thin enchauntours, and with the multitude of thi witchis, in whiche thou trauelidist fro thi yongthe; if in hap thei profiten ony thing to thee, ether if thou maist be maad the strongere.

13 Thou failidist in the multitude of thi councels; the false dyuynours of heuene stonde, and saue thee, whiche bihelden staris, and noumbriden monethis, that thei schulden telle bi tho thingis to comynge to thee.

14 Lo! thei ben maad as stobil, the fier hath brent hem; thei schulen not delyuere her lijf fro the power of flawme; colis ben not, bi whiche thei schulen be warmed, nether fier, that thei sitte at it.

15 So tho thingis ben maad to thee in whiche euere thou trauelidist; thi marchauntis fro thi yongthe erriden, ech man in his weie; noon is, that schal saue thee.

CAP 48

1 The hows of Jacob, that ben clepid bi the name of Israel, and yeden out of the watris of Juda, here these thingis, whiche sweren in the name of the Lord, and han mynde on God of Israel, not in treuthe, nether in riytfulnesse.

2 For thei ben clepid of the hooli citee, and ben stablischid on the God of Israel, the Lord of oostis is his name.

3 Fro that tyme Y telde the former thingis, and tho yeden out of my mouth; and Y made tho knowun; sudenli Y wrouyte, and tho thingis camen.

4 For Y wiste that thou art hard, and thi nol is a senewe of irun, and thi forhed is of bras.

5 Y biforseide to thee fro that tyme, bifore that tho thingis camen, Y schewide to thee, lest perauenture thou woldist seie, Myn idols diden these thingis, and my grauun ymagis and my yotun

6 ymagis senten these thingis whiche thou herdist. Se thou alle thingis, but ye telden not. Y made herd newe thyngis to thee fro that tyme, and thingis ben kept whiche thou knowist not;

7 now tho ben maad of nouyt, and not fro that tyme, and bifor the dai, and thou herdist not tho thingis; lest perauenture thou seie, Lo! Y knew tho thingis.

8 Nether thou herdist, nether thou knewist, nether thin eere was openyd fro that tyme; for Y woot, that thou trespassynge schal trespasse, and Y clepide thee a trespassour fro the wombe.

9 For my name Y schal make fer my strong veniaunce, and with my preysyng Y schal refreyne thee, lest thou perische.

10 Lo! Y haue sode thee, but not as siluer; Y chees thee in the chymeney of pouert.

11 Y schal do for me, that Y be not blasfemyd, and Y schal not yyue my glorie to another.

12 Jacob and Israel, whom Y clepe, here thou me; Y my silf, Y am the firste and Y am the laste.

13 And myn hond foundide the erthe, and my riyt hond mat heuenes; Y schal clepe tho, and tho schulen stonde togidere.

14 Alle ye be gaderid togidere, and here; who of hem telde these thingis? The Lord louyde hym, he schal do his wille in Babiloyne, and his arm in Caldeis.

15 Y, Y spak, and clepide hym; Y brouyte hym, and his weie was dressid.

16 Neiye ye to me, and here ye these thingis; at the bigynnyng Y spak not in priuete; fro tyme, bifore that thingis weren maad, Y was there, and now the Lord God and his Spirit sente me.

17 The Lord, thin ayen biere, the hooli of Israel, seith these thingis, Y am thi Lord God, techynge thee profitable thingis, and Y gouerne thee in the weie, wher ynne thou goist.

18 Y wolde that thou haddist perseyued my comaundementis, thi pees hadde be maad as flood, and thi riytfulnesse as the swolowis of the see;

19 and thi seed hadde be as grauel, and the generacioun of thi wombe, as the litle stoonys therof; the name of it hadde not perischid, and hadde not be al to-brokun fro my face.

20 Go ye out of Babiloyne, fle ye fro Caldeis; telle ye in the vois of ful out ioiying; make ye this herd, and bere ye it 'til to the laste partis of erthe; seie ye, The Lord ayenbouyte his seruaunt Jacob.

21 Thei thirstiden not in desert, whanne he ladde hem out; he brouyte forth to hem watir of a stoon, and he departide the stoon, and watris flowiden.

22 Pees is not to wickid men, seith the Lord.

CAP 49

1 Ilis, here ye, and puplis afer, perseyue ye; the Lord clepide me fro the wombe, he thouyte on my name fro the wombe of my modir.

2 And he hath set my mouth as a scharp swerd, he defendide me in the schadewe of his hond, and settide me as a chosun arowe; he hidde me in his arowe caas,

3 and seide to me, Israel, thou art my seruaunt, for Y schal haue glorie in thee.

4 And Y seide, Y trauelide in veyn, Y wastide my strengthe with out cause, and veynli; therfor my doom is with the Lord, and my werk is with my God.

5 And now the Lord, formynge me a seruaunt to hym silf fro the wombe, seith these thingis, that Y brynge ayen Jacob to hym. And Israel schal not be gaderid togidere; and Y am glorified in the iyen of the Lord, and my God is maad my strengthe.

6 And he seyde, It is litil, that thou be a seruaunt to me, to reise the lynages of Jacob, and to conuerte the drastis of Israel; Y yaf thee in to the liyt of hethene men, that thou be myn helthe 'til to the laste part of erthe.

7 The Lord, ayenbiere of Israel, the hooli therof, seith these thingis to a dispisable soule, and to a folk had in abhomynacioun, to the seruaunt of lordis, Kyngis schulen se, and princes schulen rise togidere, and schulen worschipe, for the Lord, for he is feithful, and for the hooli of Israel, that chees thee.

8 The Lord seith these thingis, In a plesaunt tyme Y herde thee, and in the dai of helthe Y helpide thee; and Y kepte thee, and yaf thee in to a bonde of pees of the puple, that thou schuldist reise the erthe, and haue in possessioun eritagis, 'that ben distried;

9 that thou schuldist seie to hem that ben boundun, Go ye out, and to hem that ben in derknessis, Be ye schewid. Thei schulen be fed on weies, and the lesewis of hem schulen be in alle pleyn thingis.

10 Thei schulen not hungre, and thei schulen no more thirste, and heete, and the sunne schal not smyte hem; for the merciful doere of hem schal gouerne hem, and schal yyue drynk to hem at the wellis of watris.

11 And Y schal sette alle myn hillis in to weie, and my pathis schulen be enhaunsid.

12 Lo! these men schulen come fro fer, and lo! thei schulen come fro the north, and see, and these fro the south lond.

13 Heuenes, herie ye, and, thou erthe, make ful out ioie; hillis, synge ye hertli heriyng; for the Lord coumfortide his puple, and schal haue merci on hise pore men.

14 And Syon seide, The Lord hath forsake me, and the Lord hath foryete me.

15 Whether a womman may foryete hir yonge child, that sche haue not merci on the sone of hir wombe? thouy sche foryetith, netheles Y schal not foryete thee.

16 Lo! Y haue write thee in myn hondis; thi wallis ben euer bifore myn iyen.

17 The bilderis ben comun; thei that distrien thee, and scateren, schulen go awei fro thee.

18 Reise thin iyen in cumpas, and se; alle these men ben gaderid togidere, thei ben comun to thee. Y lyue, seith the Lord, for thou schalt be clothid with alle these as with an ournement, and thou as a spousesse schalt bynde hem to thee.

19 For whi thi desertis, and thi wildirnessis, and the lond of thi fallyng now schulen be streit for enhabiteris; and thei schulen be dryuun awei fer, that swolewiden thee.

20 Yit the sones of thi bareynesse schulen seie in thin eeris, The place is streit to me, make thou a space to me for to dwelle.

21 And thou schalt seie in thin herte, Who gendride these sones to me? Y am bareyn, not berynge child; Y am led ouer, and prisoner; and who nurschide these sones? Y am destitute, and aloone; and where weren these?

22 The Lord God seith these thingis, Lo! Y reise myn hond to hethene men, and Y schal enhaunce my signe to puplis; and thei schulen brynge thi sones in armes, and thei schulen bere thi douytris on shuldris.

23 And kingis schulen be thi nurseris, and quenys schulen be thi nursis; with cheer cast doun in to erthe thei schulen worschipe thee, and thei schulen licke the dust of thi feet; and thou schalt wite, that Y am the Lord, on whom thei schulen not be schent, that abiden hym.

24 Whether prey schal be takun awei fro a strong man? ether that that is takun of a stalworthe man, mai be saaf?

25 For the Lord seith these thingis, Sotheli and caitifte schal be takun awey fro the stronge man, and that that is takun awei of a stalworthe man, schal be saued. Forsothe Y schal deme hem, that demyden thee, and Y schal saue thi sones.

26 And Y schal fede thin enemyes with her fleischis, and thei schulen be greetli fillid with her blood as with must; and eche man schal wite, that Y am the Lord, sauynge thee, and thin ayenbiere, the strong of Jacob.

CAP 50

1 The Lord seith these thingis, What is this book of forsakyng of youre modir, bi which Y lefte her? ether who is he, to whom Y owe, to whom Y seeld you? For lo! ye ben seeld for youre wickidnessis, and for youre grete trespassis Y lefte youre modir.

2 For Y cam, and no man was; Y clepide, and noon was that herde. Whether myn hond is abreggid, and maad litil, that Y mai not ayenbie? ether vertu is not in me for to delyuere? Lo! in my blamyng Y schal make the see forsakun, 'ether desert, Y schal sette floodis in the drie place; fischis without watir schulen wexe rotun, and schulen dye for thirst.

3 Y schal clothe heuenes with derknessis, and Y schal sette a sak the hilyng of tho.

4 The Lord yaf to me a lerned tunge, that Y kunne susteyne hym bi word that failide; erli the fadir reisith, erli he reisith an eere to me, that Y here as a maister.

5 The Lord God openede an eere to me; forsothe Y ayenseie not, Y yede not abak.

6 I yaf my bodi to smyteris, and my chekis to pulleris; Y turnede not a wei my face fro men blamynge, and spetynge on me.

7 The Lord God is myn helpere, and therfor Y am not schent; therfor Y haue set my face as a stoon maad hard, and Y woot that Y schal not be schent.

8 He is niy, that iustifieth me; who ayenseith me? stonde we togidere. Who is myn aduersarie? neiye he to me.

9 Lo! the Lord God is myn helpere; who therfor is he that condempneth me? Lo! alle schulen be defoulid as a cloth, and a mouyte schal ete hem.

10 Who of you dredith the Lord, and herith the vois of his seruaunt? Who yede in dercnessis and liyt is not to hym, hope he in the name of the Lord, and triste he on his God.

11 Lo! alle ye kyndlynge fier, and gird with flawmes, go in the liyt of youre fier, and in the flawmes whiche ye han kyndlid to you. This is maad of myn hond to you, ye schulen slepe in sorewis.

CAP 51

1 Here ye me, that suen that that is iust, and seken the Lord. Take ye hede to the stoon, fro whennys ye ben hewun doun, and to the caue of the lake, fro which ye ben kit doun.

2 Take ye heede to Abraham, youre fadir, and to Sare, that childide you; for Y clepide hym oon, and Y blesside hym, and Y multipliede hym.

3 Therfor the Lord schal coumforte Sion, and he schal coumforte alle the fallyngis therof; and he schal sette the desert therof as delices, and the wildirnesse therof as a gardyn of the Lord; ioie and gladnesse schal be foundun therynne, the doyng of thankyngis and the vois of heriyng.

4 Mi puple, take ye heede to me, and, my lynage, here ye me; for whi a lawe schal go out fro me, and my doom schal reste in to the liyt of puplis.

5 My iust man is nyy, my sauyour is gon out, and myn armes schulen deme puplis; ilis schulen abide me, and schulen suffre myn arm.

6 Reise youre iyen to heuene, and se ye vndur erthe bynethe; for whi heuenes schulen melte awei as smoke, and the erthe schal be al to-brokun as a cloth, and the dwelleris therof schulen perische as these thingis; but myn helthe schal be withouten ende, and my riytfulnesse schal not fayle.

7 Ye puple, that knowen the iust man, here me, my lawe is in the herte of hem; nyle ye drede the schenschipe of men, and drede ye not the blasfemyes of hem.

8 For whi a worm schal ete hem so as a cloth, and a mouyte schal deuoure hem so as wolle; but myn helthe schal be withouten ende, and my riytfulnesse in to generaciouns of generaciouns.

9 Rise thou, rise thou, arm of the Lord, be thou clothyd in strengthe; rise thou, as in elde daies, in generaciouns of worldis. Whether thou smytidist not the proude man, woundidist not the dragoun?

10 Whether thou driedist not the see, the watir of the greet depthe, which settidist the depthe of the see a weie, that men 'that weren delyuered, schulden passe?

11 And now thei that ben ayenbouyt of the Lord schulen turne ayen, and schulen come heriynge in to Syon, and euerlastynge gladnesse on the heedis of hem; thei schulen holde ioie and gladnesse, sorewe and weilyng schal fle awei.

12 'Y my silf schal coumforte you; what art thou, that thou drede of a deedli man, and of the sone of man, that schal wexe drie so as hei?

13 And thou hast foryete 'the Lord, thi creatour, that stretchide abrood heuenes, and foundide the erthe; and thou dreddist contynueli al dai of the face of his woodnesse, that dide tribulacioun to thee, and made redi for to leese. Where is now the woodnesse of the troblere?

14 Soone he schal come, goynge for to opene; and he schal not sle til to deth, nether his breed schal faile.

15 Forsothe Y am thi Lord God, that disturble the see, and the wawis therof wexen greet; the Lord of oostis is my name.

16 Y haue put my wordis in thi mouth, and Y defendide thee in the schadewe of myn hond; that thou plaunte heuenes, and founde the erthe, and seie to Sion, Thou art my puple.

17 Be thou reisid, be thou reisid, rise thou, Jerusalem, that hast drunke of the hond of the Lord the cuppe of his wraththe; thou hast drunke 'til to the botme of the cuppe of sleep, thou hast drunke of 'til to the drastis.

18 Noon is that susteyneth it, of alle the sones whiche it gendride; and noon is that takith the hond therof, of alle the sones whiche it nurshide.

19 Twei thingis ben that camen to thee; who schal be sori on thee? distriyng, and defoulyng, and hungur, and swerd. Who schal coumforte thee?

20 Thi sones ben cast forth, thei slepten in the heed of alle weies, as the beeste orix, takun bi a snare; thei ben ful of indignacioun of the Lord, of blamyng of thi God.

21 Therfor, thou pore, and drunkun, not of wyn, here these thingis.

22 Thi lordli gouernour, the Lord, and thi God, that fauyt for his puple, seith these thingis, Lo! Y haue take fro thyn hond the cuppe of sleep, the botme of the cuppe of myn indignacioun; Y schal not leie to, that thou drynke it ony more.

23 And Y schal sette it in the hond of hem that maden thee low, and seiden to thi soule, Be thou bowid that we passe; and thou hast set thi bodi as erthe, and as a weye to hem that goen forth.

CAP 52

1 Rise thou, Sion, rise thou, be thou clothid in thi strengthe; Jerusalem, the citee of the hooli, be thou clothid in the clothis of thi glorie; for a man vncircumcidid and a man vncleene schal no more leie to, that he passe by thee.

2 Jerusalem, be thou schakun out of dust; rise thou, sitte thou; thou douyter of Sion, prisoner, vnbynde the boondis of thi necke.

3 For the Lord seith these thingis, Ye ben seeld without cause, and ye schulen be ayenbouyt with out siluer.

4 For the Lord God seith these thingis, Mi puple in the bigynnyng yede doun in to Egipt, that it schulde be there 'an erthe tiliere, and Assur falsli calengide it with out ony cause.

5 And now what is to me here? seith the Lord; for my puple is takun awei with out cause; the lordis therof doen wickidli, seith the Lord, and my name is blasfemyd contynueli al dai.

6 For this thing my puple schal knowe my name in that day, for lo! Y my silf that spak, am present.

7 Ful faire ben the feet of hym that tellith, and prechith pees on hillis, of hym that tellith good, of hym that prechith helthe, and seith, Sion, thi God schal regne.

8 The vois of thi biholderis; thei reisiden the vois, thei schulen herie togidere; for thei schulen se with iye to iye, whanne the Lord hath conuertid Sion.

9 The forsakun thingis of Jerusalem, make ye ioie, and herie ye togidere; for the Lord hath coumfortid his puple, he hath ayenbouyt Jerusalem.

10 The Lord hath maad redi his hooli arm in the iyen of alle folkis, and alle the endis of the erthe schulen se the helthe of oure God.

11 Go ye awei, go ye awei, go ye out fro thennus; nyle ye touche defoulid thing, go ye out fro the myddis therof; be ye clensid, that beren the vessels of the Lord.

12 For ye schulen not go out in noyse, nether ye schulen haaste in fleynge awei; for whi the Lord schal go bifore you, and the God of Israel schal gadere you togidere.

13 Lo! my seruaunt schal vndirstonde, and he schal be enhaunsid, and he schal be reisid, and he schal be ful hiy.

14 As many men wondriden on hym, so his biholdyng schal be with out glorie among men, and the fourme of hym among the sones of men.

15 He schal bisprenge many folkis; kyngis schulen holde togidere her mouth on him; for thei schulen se, to whiche it was not teld of hym, and thei that herden not, bihelden.

CAP 53

1 Who bileuyde to oure heryng? and to whom is the arm of the Lord schewide?

2 And he schal stie as a yerde bifore hym, and as a roote fro thirsti lond. And nether schap nether fairnesse was to hym; and we sien hym, and no biholdyng was;

3 and we desiriden hym, dispisid, and the laste of men, a man of sorewis, and knowynge sikenesse. And his cheer was as hid and dispisid; wherfor and we arettiden not hym.

4 Verili he suffride oure sikenessis, and he bar oure sorewis; and we arettiden hym as a mesel, and smytun of God, and maad low.

5 Forsothe he was woundid for oure wickidnessis, he was defoulid for oure greet trespassis; the lernyng of oure pees was on hym, and we ben maad hool bi his wannesse.

6 Alle we erriden as scheep, ech man bowide in to his owne weie, and the Lord puttide in hym the wickidnesse of vs alle.

7 He was offrid, for he wolde, and he openyde not his mouth; as a scheep he schal be led to sleyng, and he schal be doumb as a lomb bifore hym that clippith it, and he schal not opene his mouth.

8 He is takun awey fro angwisch and fro doom; who schal telle out the generacioun of hym? For he was kit doun fro the lond of lyueris. Y smoot hym for the greet trespas of my puple.

9 And he schal yyue vnfeithful men for biriyng, and riche men for his deth; for he dide not wickidnesse, nether gile was in his mouth;

10 and the Lord wolde defoule hym in sikenesse. If he puttith his lijf for synne, he schal se seed long durynge, and the wille of the Lord schal be dressid in his hond.

11 For that that his soule trauelide, he schal se, and schal be fillid. Thilke my iust seruaunt schal iustifie many men in his kunnyng, and he schal bere the wickidnessis of hem.

12 Therfor Y schal yelde, ethir dele, to hym ful many men, and he schal departe the spuilis of the stronge feendis; for that that he yaf his lijf in to deth, and was arettid with felenouse men; and he dide a wei the synne of many men, and he preiede for trespassouris.

CAP 54

1 Thou bareyn, that childist not, herie; thou that childist not, synge heriyng, and make ioie; for whi many sones ben of the forsakun 'womman more than of hir that hadde hosebonde, seith the Lord.

2 Alarge thou the place of thi tente, and stretche forth the skynnes of thi tabernaclis; spare thou not, make longe thi roopis, and make sad thi nailis.

3 For thou schalt perse to the riytside and to the leftside; and thi seed schal enherite hethene men, and schal dwelle in forsakun citees.

4 Nile thou drede, for thou schal not be schent, nether thou schalt be aschamed. For it schal not schame thee; for thou schalt foryete the schenschipe of thi yongthe, and thou schalt no more thenke on the schenschipe of thi widewehod.

5 For he that made thee, schal be lord of thee; the Lord of oostis is his name; and thin ayenbiere, the hooli of Israel, schal be clepid God of al erthe.

6 For the Lord hath clepid thee as a womman forsakun and morenynge in spirit, and a wijf, 'that is cast awei fro yongthe.

7 Thi Lord God seide, At a poynt in litil tyme Y forsook thee, and Y schal gadere thee togidere in greete merciful doyngis.

8 In a moment of indignacioun Y hidde my face a litil fro thee, and in merci euerlastynge Y hadde merci on thee, seide thin ayenbiere, the Lord.

9 As in the daies of Noe, this thing is to me, to whom Y swoor, that Y schulde no more bringe watris of the greet flood on the erthe; so Y swoor, that Y be no more wrooth to thee, and that Y blame not thee.

10 Forsothe hillis schulen be mouyd togidere, and litle hillis schulen tremble togidere; but my merci schal not go a wei fro thee, and the boond of my pees schal not be mouyd, seide the merciful doere, the Lord.

11 Thou litle and pore, drawun out bi tempest, with outen ony coumfort, lo! Y schal strewe thi stoonys bi ordre, and Y schal founde thee in safiris;

12 and Y schal sette iaspis thi touris, and thi yatis in to grauun stoonys, and alle thin eendis in to desirable stoonys.

13 'Y schal make alle thi sones tauyt of the Lord; and the multitude of pees to thi sones,

14 and thou schalt be foundid in riytfulnesse. Go thou awei fer fro fals caleng, for thou schalt not drede; and fro drede, for it schal not neiye to thee.

15 Lo! a straunger schal come, that was not with me; he, that was sum tyme thi comelyng, schal be ioyned to thee.

16 Lo! Y made a smyth blowynge coolis in fier, and bringynge forth a vessel in to his werk; and Y haue maad a sleere, for to leese.

17 Ech vessel which is maad ayens thee, schal not be dressid; and in the doom thou schalt deme ech tunge ayenstondynge thee. This is the eritage of the seruauntis of the Lord, and the riytfulnesse of hem at me, seith the Lord.

CAP 55

1 Alle that thirsten, come ye to watris, and ye han not siluer, haaste, bie ye, and ete ye; come ye, bie ye, with out siluer and with outen ony chaungyng, wyn and mylk.

2 Whi peisen ye siluer, and not in looues, and youre trauel, not in fulnesse? Ye herynge here me, and ete ye good, and youre soule schal delite in fatnesse.

3 Bowe ye youre eere, and 'come ye to me; here ye, and youre soule schal lyue; and Y schal smyte with you a couenaunt euerlastynge, the feithful mercies of Dauid.

4 Lo! Y yaf hym a witnesse to puplis, a duyk and a comaundour to folkis.

5 Lo! thou schalt clepe folkis, whiche thou knewist not; and folkis, that knewen not thee, schulen renne to thee; for thi Lord God, and the hooli of Israel, for he glorifiede thee.

6 Seke ye the Lord, while he mai be foundun; clepe ye hym to help, while he is niy.

7 An vnfeithful man forsake his weie, and a wickid man forsake hise thouytis; and turne he ayen to the Lord, and he schal haue merci on hym, and to oure God, for he is myche to foryyue.

8 For why my thouytis ben not youre thouytis, and my weies ben not youre weies, seith the Lord.

9 For as heuenys ben reisid fro erthe, so my weies ben reisid fro youre weies, and my thouytis fro youre thouytis.

10 And as reyn and snow cometh doun fro heuene, and turneth no more ayen thidur, but it fillith the erthe, and bis-

chedith it, and makith it to buriowne, and yyueth seed to hym that sowith, and breed to hym that etith,

11 so schal be my word, that schal go out of my mouth. It schal not turne ayen voide to me, but it schal do what euer thingis Y wolde, and it schal haue prosperite in these thingis to whiche Y sente it.

12 For ye schulen go out in gladnesse, and ye schulen be led forth in pees; mounteyns and litil hillis schulen synge heriynge bifore you, and alle the trees of the cuntrei schulen make ioie with hond.

13 A fir tre schal grow for a firse, and a mirte tre schal wexe for a nettil; and the Lord schal be nemyd in to a signe euerlastynge, that schal not be doon awei.

CAP 56

1 The Lord seith these thingis, Kepe ye doom, and do ye riytfulnesse, for whi myn helthe is niy, that it come, and my riytfulnesse, that it be schewid.

2 Blessid is the man, that doith this, and the sone of man, that schal take this; kepynge the sabat, that he defoule not it, kepynge hise hondis, that he do not ony yuel.

3 And seie not the sone of a comelyng, that cleueth faste to the Lord, seiynge, Bi departyng the Lord schal departe me fro his puple; and a geldyng, ether a chast man, seie not, Lo! Y am a drie tree.

4 For the Lord seith these thingis to geldingis, that kepen my sabatis, and chesen what thingis Y wolde, and holden my boond of pees.

5 Y schal yyue to hem a place in myn hous, and in my wallis, and the beste name of sones and douytris; Y schal yyue to hem a name euerlastynge, that schal not perische.

6 And Y schal brynge in to blis the sones of a comelyng, that cleuen faste to the Lord, that thei worschipe hym, and loue his name, that thei be to hym in to seruauntis; ech man kepynge the sabat, that he defoule it not, and holdynge my boond of pees;

7 Y schal brynge hem in to myn hooli hil, and Y schal make hem glad in the hous of my preier; her brent sacrifices and her slayn sacrifices schulen plese me on my auter; for whi myn hous schal be clepid an hous of preier to alle puplis,

8 seith the Lord God, that gaderith togidere the scaterid men of Israel. Yit Y schal gadere togidere to hym alle the gaderid men therof.

9 Alle beestis of the feeld, come ye to deuoure, alle beestis of the forest.

10 Alle the biholderis therof ben blinde, alle thei knewen not; doumbe doggis, that moun not berke, seynge veyn thingis, slepynge, and louynge dremes;

11 and moost vnschamefast doggis knewen not fulnesse. Tho scheepherdis knewen not vndurstondyng; alle thei bowyden in to her weie, ech man to his aueryce, fro the hiyeste 'til to the laste.

12 Come ye, take we wyn, and be we fillid of drunkenesse; and it schal be as to dai, so and to morewe, and myche more.

CAP 57

1 A iust man perischith, and noon is, that thenkith in his herte; and men of merci ben gaderid togidere, for noon is that vndurstondith; for whi a iust man is gaderid fro the face of malice.

2 Pees come, reste he in his bed, that yede in his dressyng.

3 But ye, sones of the sekere of fals dyuynyng bi chiteryng of briddys, neiye hidur, the seed of auowtresse, and of an hoore.

4 On whom scorneden ye? on whom maden ye greet the mouth, and puttiden out the tunge? Whethir ye ben not cursid sones, a seed of leesyngis?

5 which ben coumfortid in goddis, vndur ech tree ful of bowis, and offren litle children in strondis, vndur hiye stoonys.

6 Thi part is in the partis of the stronde, this is thi part; and to tho thou scheddist out moist offryng, thou offridist sacrifice. Whether Y schal not haue indignacioun on these thingis?

7 Thou puttidist thi bed on an hiy hil and enhaunsid, and thidur thou stiedist to offre sacrifices;

8 and thou settidist thi memorial bihynde the dore, and bihynde the post. For bisidis me thou vnhilidist, and tokist auouter; thou alargidist thi bed, and madist a boond of pees with hem; thou louedist the bed of hem with openyd hond,

9 and ournedist thee with kyngis oynement, and thou multipliedist thi pymentis; thou sentist fer thi messangeris, and thou art maad low 'til to hellis.

10 Thou trauelidist in the multitude of thi weie, and seidist not, Y schal reste; thou hast founde the weie of thin hond,

11 therfor thou preiedist not. For what thing dreddist thou bisy, for thou liedist, and thouytist not on me? And thou thouytist not in thin herte, that Y am stille, and as not seynge; and thou hast foryete me.

12 Y schal telle thi riytfulnesse, and thi werkis schulen not profite to thee.

13 Whanne thou schalt crie, thi gaderid tresours delyuere thee; and the wynd schal take awei alle tho, a blast schal do awei hem; but he that hath trist on me, schal enherite the lond, and schal haue in possessioun myn hooli hil.

14 And Y schal seie, Make ye weie, yyue ye iurney, bowe ye fro the path, do ye awei hirtyngis fro the weie of my puple.

15 For the Lord hiy, and enhaunsid, seith these thingis, that dwellith in euerlastyngnesse, and his hooli name in hiy place, and that dwellith in hooli, and with a contrite and meke spirit, that he quykene the spirit of meke men, and quykene the herte of contrit men.

16 For Y schal not stryue with outen ende, nether Y schal be wrooth 'til to the ende; for whi a spirit schal go out fro my face, and Y schal make blastis.

17 Y was wrooth for the wickidnesse of his aueryce, and Y smoot hym. Y hidde my face fro thee, and Y hadde indignacioun; and he yede with out stidfast dwellyng, in the weie of his herte.

18 Y siy hise weies, and Y helide hym, and Y brouyte hym ayen; and Y yaf coumfortyngis to hym, and to the moreneris of hym.

19 Y made the fruyt of lippis pees, pees to hym that is fer, and to hym that is niy, seide the Lord; and Y heelide hym.

20 But wickid men ben as the buyling see, that may not reste; and the wawis therof fleten ayen in to defoulyng, and fen.

21 The Lord God seide, Pees is not to wickid men.

CAP 58

1 Crye thou, ceesse thou not; as a trumpe enhaunse thi vois, and schewe thou to my puple her grete trespassis, and to the hous of Jacob her synnes.

2 For thei seken me fro dai in to dai, and thei wolen knowe my weies; as a folk, that hath do riytfulnesse, and that hath not forsake the doom of her God; thei preien me domes of riytfulnesse, and wolen neiy to God.

3 Whi fastiden we, and thou biheldist not; we mekiden oure soulis, and thou knewist not? Lo! youre wille is foundun in the dai of youre fastyng, and ye axen alle youre dettouris.

4 Lo! ye fasten to chidyngis and stryuyngis, and smyten with the fist wickidli. Nyl ye fast, as 'til to this dai, that youre cry be herd an hiy.

5 Whether sich is the fastyng which Y chees, a man to turmente his soule bi dai? whether to bynde his heed as a sercle, and to make redi a sak and aische? Whethir thou schalt clepe this a fastyng, and a dai acceptable to the Lord?

6 Whether not this is more the fastyng, which Y chees? Vnbynde thou the byndingis togidere of vnpitee, releesse thou birthuns pressynge doun; delyuere thou hem free, that ben brokun, and breke thou ech birthun.

7 Breke thi breed to an hungri man, and brynge in to thin hous nedi men and herborles; whanne thou seest a nakid man, hile thou hym, and dispise not thi fleisch.

8 Thanne thi liyt schal breke out as the morewtid, and thin helthe schal rise ful soone; and thi riytfulnesse schal go bifore thi face, and the glorie of the Lord schal gadere thee.

9 Thanne thou schalt clepe to help, and the Lord schal here; thou schalt crie, and he schal seie, Lo! Y am present, for Y am merciful, thi Lord God. If thou takist awei a chayne fro the myddis of thee, and ceessist to holde forth the fyngur, and to speke that profitith not;

10 whanne thou schedist out thi soule to an hungri man, and fillist a soule, 'that is turmentid, thi liyt schal rise in derknessis, and thi derknessis schulen be as myddai.

11 And the Lord thi God schal yyue euere reste to thee, and schal fille thi soule with schynyngis, and schal delyuere thi boonys; and thou schalt be as a watri gardyn, and as a welle of watris, whose waters schulen not faile.

12 And the forsakun thingis of worldis schulen be bildid in thee, and thou schalt reise the foundementis of generacioun and generacioun; and thou schalt be clepid a bildere of heggis, turnynge awei the pathis of wickidnessis.

13 If thou turnest awei thi foot fro the sabat, to do thi wille in myn hooli dai, and clepist the sabat delicat, and hooli, the gloriouse of the Lord, and glorifiest him, while thou doist not thi weies, and thi wille is not foundun, that thou speke a word;

14 thanne thou schalt delite on the Lord, and Y schal reise thee on the hiynesse of erthe, and Y schal fede thee with the eritage of Jacob, thi fadir; for whi the mouth of the Lord spak.

CAP 59

1 Lo! the hoond of the Lord is not abreggid, that he mai not saue, nether his eere is maad hard, that he here not;

2 but youre wickidnessis han departid bitwixe you and youre God, and youre synnes han hid his face fro you, that he schulde not here.

3 For whi youre hondis ben defoulid with blood, and youre fyngris with wickidnesse; youre lippis spaken leesyng, and youre tunge spekith wickidnesse.

4 Noon is, that clepith riytfulnesse to help, and noon is, that demeth verili; but thei tristen in nouyt, and speken vanytees; thei conseyueden trauel, and childiden wickidnesse.

5 Thei han broke eiren of snakis, and maden webbis of an yreyn; he that etith of the eiren of hem, schal die, and that that is nurschid, ether brouyt forth, schal breke out in to a cocatrice.

6 The webbis of hem schulen not be in to cloth, nethir thei schulen be hilid with her werkis; the werkis of hem ben

vnprofitable werkis, and the werk of wickidnesse is in the hondis of hem.

7 The feet of hem rennen to yuel, and haasten to schede out innocent blood; the thouytis of hem ben vnprofitable thouytis; distriyng and defouling ben in the weies of hem.

8 Thei knewen not the weie of pees, and doom is not in the goyngis of hem; the pathis of hem ben bowid to hem; ech that tredith in tho, knowith not pees.

9 Therfor doom is made fer fro vs, and riytfulnesse schal not take vs; we abididen liyt, and lo! derknessis ben; we abididen schynyng, and we yeden in derknessis.

10 We gropiden as blynde men the wal, and we as with outen iyen touchiden; we stumbliden in myddai, as in derknessis, in derk places, as deed men.

11 Alle we schulen rore as beeris, and we schulen weile thenkynge as culueris; we abididen doom, and noon is; we abididen helthe, and it is maad fer fro vs.

12 For whi oure wickidnessis ben multiplied bifore thee, and oure synnes answeriden to vs; for our grete trespassis ben with vs, and we knewen oure wickidnessis,

13 to do synne, and to lie ayens the Lord. And we ben turned awei, that we yeden not aftir the bak of oure God, that we speken fals caleng, and trespassyng. We conseyueden, and spaken of herte wordis of leesyng; and doom was turned abak,

14 and riytfulnesse stood fer; for whi treuthe felle doun in the street, and equite miyt not entre.

15 And treuthe was maad in to foryetyng, and he that yede awei fro yuel, was opyn to robbyng. And the Lord siy, and it apperide yuel in hise iyen, for ther is no doom.

16 And God siy, that a man is not, and he was angwischid, for noon is that renneth to. And his arm schal saue to hym silf, and his riytfulnesse it silf schal conferme hym.

17 He is clothid with riytfulnesse as with an harburioun, and the helm of helthe is in his heed; he is clothid with clothis of veniaunce, and he is hilid as with a mentil of feruent worchyng.

18 As to veniaunce, as to yeldyng of indignacioun to hise enemyes, and to quityng of tyme to hise aduersaries, he schal yelde while to ylis.

19 And thei that ben at the west, schulen drede the name of the Lord, and thei that ben at the risyng of the sunne, schulen drede the glorie of hym; whanne he schal come as a violent flood, whom the spirit of the Lord compellith.

20 Whan ayen biere schal come to Syon, and to hem that goen ayen fro wickidnesse in Jacob, seith the Lord.

21 This is my boond of pees with hem, seith the Lord; My spirit which is in thee, and my wordis whiche Y haue set in thi mouth, schulen not go awei fro thi mouth, and fro the mouth of thi seed, seith the Lord, fro hennus forth and til into with outen ende.

CAP 60

1 Rise thou, Jerusalem, be thou liytned, for thi liyt is comun, and the glorie of the Lord is risun on thee.

2 For lo! derknessis schulen hile the erthe, and myist schal hile puplis; but the Lord schal rise on thee, and his glorie schal be seyn in thee.

3 And hethene men schulen go in thi liyt, and kyngis 'schulen go in the schynyng of thi risyng.

4 Reise thin iyen in cumpas, and se; alle these men ben gaderid togidere, thei ben comun to thee; thi sones schulen come fro fer, and thi douytris schulen rise fro the side.

5 Thanne thou schalt se, and schalt flowe; and thin herte schal wondre, and schal be alargid, whanne the multitude of the see is conuertid to thee, the strengthe of hethene men is comun to thee;

6 the flowyng of camels schal hile thee, the lederis of dromedis of Madian and of Effa; alle men of Saba schulen come, bryngynge gold and encense, and tellynge heriyng to the Lord.

7 Ech scheep of Cedar schal be gaderid to thee, the rammes of Nabaioth schulen mynystre to thee; thei schulen be offrid on myn acceptable auter, and Y schal glorifie the hous of my maieste.

8 Who ben these, that fleen as cloudis, and as culueris at her wyndowis?

9 Forsothe ilis abiden me, and the schippis of the see in the bigynnyng; that Y brynge thi sones fro fer, the siluer of hem, and the gold of hem is with hem, to the name of thi Lord God, and to the hooli of Israel; for he schal glorifie thee.

10 And the sones of pilgrymes schulen bilde thi wallis, and the kyngis of hem schulen mynystre to thee. For Y smoot thee in myn indignacioun, and in my recounselyng Y hadde merci on thee.

11 And thi yatis schulen be openyd contynueli, day and niyt tho schulen not be closid; that the strengthe of hethene men be brouyt to thee, and the kyngis of hem be brouyt.

12 For whi the folk and rewme that serueth not thee, schal perische, and hethene men schulen be distried bi wildirnesse.

13 The glorie of the Liban schal come to thee, a fir tre, and box tre, and pyne appil tre togidere, to ourne the place of myn halewyng; and Y schal glorifie the place of my feet.

14 And the sones of hem that maden thee lowe, schulen come lowe to thee, and alle that bacbitiden thee, schulen worschipe the steppis of thi feet; and schulen clepe thee A citee of the Lord of Sion, of the hooli of Israel.

15 For that that thou were forsakun, and hatid, and noon was that passide bi thee, Y schal sette thee in to pryde of worldis, ioie in generacioun and in to generacioun.

16 And thou schalt souke the mylke of folkis, and thou schalt be soclid with the tete of kyngis; and thou schalt wite that Y am the Lord, sauynge thee, and thin ayen biere, the stronge of Jacob.

17 For bras Y schal brynge gold, and for irun Y schal brynge siluer; and bras for trees, and yrun for stoonys; and Y schal sette thi visitacioun pees, and thi prelatis riytfulnesse.

18 Wickidnesse schal no more be herd in thi lond, nether distriyng and defoulyng in thi coostis; and helthe schal ocupie thi wallis, and heriyng schal ocupie thi yatis.

19 The sunne schal no more be to thee for to schyne bi dai, nether the briytnesse of the moone schal liytne thee; but the Lord schal be in to euerlastynge liyt to thee, and thi God schal be in to thi glorie.

20 Thi sunne schal no more go doun, and thi moone schal not be decreessid; for the Lord schal be in to euerlastynge liyt to thee, and the daies of thi mourenyng schulen be fillid.

21 Forsothe thi puple alle iust men, withouten ende schulen enherite the lond, the seed of my plauntyng, the werk of myn hond for to be glorified.

22 The leeste schal be in to a thousynde, and a litil man schal be in to a ful stronge folk. Y, the Lord, schal make this thing sudenli, in the tyme therof.

CAP 61

1 The spirit of the Lord is on me, for the Lord anoyntide me; he sente me to telle to mylde men, that Y schulde heele men contrite in herte, and preche foryyuenesse to caitifs, and openyng to prisoneris; and preche a plesaunt yeer to the Lord, 2 and a dai of veniaunce to oure God; that Y schulde coumforte alle that mourenen;

3 that Y schulde sette coumfort to the moureneris of Sion, and that Y schulde yyue to them a coroun for aische, oile of ioie for mourenyng, a mentil of preysyng for the spirit of weilyng. And stronge men of riytfulnesse schulen be clepid ther ynne, the plauntyng of the Lord for to glorifie.

4 And thei schulen bilde thingis 'that ben forsakun fro the world, and thei schulen reise elde fallyngis, and thei schulen restore citees 'that ben forsakun and distried, in generacioun and in to generacioun.

5 And aliens schulen stonde, and fede youre beestis; and the sones of pilgrymes schulen be youre erthe tilieris and vyn tilieris.

6 But ye schulen be clepid the preestis of the Lord; it schal be seid to you, Ye ben mynystris of oure God. Ye schulen ete the strengthe of hethene men, and ye schulen be onourid in the glorie of hem.

7 For youre double schenschip and schame thei schulen preise the part of hem; for this thing thei schulen haue pesibli double thingis in her lond, and euerlastynge gladnesse schal be to hem.

8 For Y am the Lord, louynge doom, and hatynge raueyn in brent sacrifice. And Y schal yyue the werk of hem in treuthe, and Y schal smyte to hem an euerlastynge boond of pees.

9 And the seed of hem schal be knowun among folkis, and the buriownyng of hem in the myddis of puplis. Alle men that seen hem, schulen knowe hem, for these ben the seed, whom the Lord blesside.

10 I ioiynge schal haue ioie in the Lord, and my soule schal make ful out ioiyng in my God. For he hath clothid me with clothis of helthe, and he hath compassid me with clothis of riytfulnesse, as a spouse made feir with a coroun, and as a spousesse ourned with her brochis.

11 For as the erthe bryngith forth his fruyt, and as a gardyn buriowneth his seed, so the Lord God schal make to growe riytfulnesse, and preysyng bifore alle folkis.

CAP 62

1 For Sion Y schal not be stille, and for Jerusalem Y schal not reste, til the iust man therof go out as schynyng, and the sauyour therof be teendid as a laumpe.

2 And hethene men schulen se thi iust man, and alle kyngis schulen se thi noble man; and a newe name, which the mouth of the Lord nemyde, schal be clepid to thee.

3 And thou schalt be a coroun of glorie in the hond of the Lord, and a diademe of the rewme in the hond of thi God.

4 Thou schalt no more be clepid forsakun, and thi lond schal no more be clepid desolat; but thou schalt be clepid My wille in that, and thi lond schal be enhabitid; for it plesid the Lord in thee, and thi lond schal be enhabited.

5 For a yong man schal dwelle with a virgyn, and thi sones schulen dwelle in thee; and the spouse schal haue ioie on the spousesse, and thi God schal haue ioie on thee.

6 Jerusalem, Y haue ordeyned keperis on thi wallis, al dai and al niyt with outen ende thei schulen not be stille. Ye that thenken on the Lord, be not stille,

7 and yyue ye not silence to him, til he stablische, and til he sette Jerusalem 'preisyng in erthe.

8 The Lord swoor in his riyt hond and in the arm of his strengthe, Y schal no more yyue thi wheete mete to thin enemyes, and alien sones schulen not drynke thi wyn, in which thou hast trauelid.

9 For thei that schulen gadere it togidere, schulen ete it, and schulen herie the Lord; and thei that beren it togidere, schulen drynke in myn hooli hallis.

10 Passe ye, passe ye bi the yatis; make ye redi weie to the puple, make ye a playn path; and chese ye stoonys, and reise ye a signe to puplis.

11 Lo! the Lord made herd in the laste partis of the erthe. Seie ye to the douytir of Sion, Lo! thi sauyour cometh; lo! his meede is with hym, and his werk is bifore hym.

12 And thei schulen clepe hem the hooli puple, ayenbouyt of the Lord. Forsothe thou schalt be clepid a citee souyt, and not forsakun.

CAP 63

1 Who is this that cometh fro Edom, in died clothis fro Bosra? this fair man in his 'long cloth, goynge in the multitude of his vertu? Y that speke riytfulnesse, and am a forfiytere for to saue.

2 Whi therfor is thi clothing reed? and thi clothis ben as of men stampynge in a pressour?

3 Y aloone stampide the presse, and of folkis no man is with me; Y stampide hem in my stronge veniaunce, and Y defoulide hem in my wraththe; and her blood is spreynt on my clothis, and Y made foul alle my clothis.

4 For whi a dai of veniaunce is in myn herte, and the yeer of my yeldyng cometh.

5 I lokide aboute, and noon helpere was; Y souyte, and noon was that helpide; and myn arm sauyde to me, and myn indignacioun, that helpide me.

6 And Y defoulide puplis in my stronge veniaunce; and Y made hem drunkun in myn indignacioun, and Y drow doun her vertu in to erthe.

7 I schal haue mynde on the merciful doyngis of the Lord, Y schal preche the heriyng of the Lord on alle thingis whiche the Lord yeldide to vs, and on the multitude 'of goodis of the hous of Israel, whiche he yaf to hem bi his foryyuenesse, and bi the multitude of hise mercies.

8 And the Lord seide, Netheles it is my puple, sones not denyynge, and he was maad a sauyour to hem in al the tribulacioun of hem.

9 It was not set in tribulacioun, and the aungel of his face sauyde hem. In his loue and in his foryyuenesse he ayenbouyte hem, and he bar hem, and reiside hem in alle daies of the world.

10 Forsothe thei exciten hym to wrathfulnesse, and turmentiden the spirit of his hooli; and he was turned in to an enemye to hem, and he ouercam hem in batel.

11 And he hadde mynde on the daies of the world, of Moises, and of his puple. Where is he, that ledde hem out of the see, with the scheepherdis of his floc? Where is he, that settide the spirit of his holi in the myddil therof;

12 whiche ledde out Moises to the riyt half in the arm of his maieste? which departide watris bifore hem, that he schulde make to hym silf a name euerlastynge;

13 whiche ledde hem out thoruy depthis of watris, as an hors not stumblynge in desert,

14 as a beeste goynge doun in the feeld? The Spirit of the Lord was the ledere therof; so thou leddist thi puple, that thou madist to thee a name of glorie.

15 Biholde thou fro heuene, and se fro thin hooli dwellyng place, and fro the seete of thi glorie. Where is thi feruent loue, and thi strengthe, the multitude of thin entrailis, and of thi merciful doyngis?

16 Tho withelden hem silf on me. Forsothe thou art oure fadir, and Abraham knew not vs, and Israel knew not vs.

17 Thou, Lord, art oure fadir, and oure ayenbiere; thi name is fro the world. Lord, whi hast thou maad vs to erre fro thi weies? thou hast made hard oure herte, that we dredden not thee? be thou conuertid, for thi seruauntis, the lynages of thin eritage.

18 Thei hadden as nouyt thin hooli puple in possessioun, and oure enemyes defouliden thin halewyng.

19 We ben maad as in the bigynnyng, whanne thou were not Lord of vs, nethir thi name was clepid to help on vs.

CAP 64

1 I wolde that thou brakist heuenes, and camest doun, that hillis fletiden awei fro thi face,

2 and failiden as brennyng of fier, and brente in fier; that thi name were made knowun to thin enemyes, and folkis weren disturblid of thi face.

3 Whanne thou schalt do merueils, we schulen not abide. Thou camest doun, and hillis fletiden awei fro thi face.

4 Fro the world thei herden not, nethir perseyueden with eeris; God, non iye siy, withouten thee, what thingis thou hast maad redi to hem that abiden thee.

5 Thou mettist hym that is glad, and doith riytfulnesse; in thi weies thei schulen bithenke on thee. Lo! thou art wrooth, and we synneden; in tho synnes we weren euere, and we schulen be saued.

6 And alle we ben maad as an vncleene man; alle oure riytfulnessis ben as the cloth of a womman in vncleene blood; and alle we fellen doun as a leef, and our wickidnessis as wynd han take awei vs.

7 Noon is, that clepith thi name to help, that risith, and holdith thee; thou hast hid thi face fro vs, and thou hast hurtlid doun vs in the hond of oure wickidnesse.

8 And now, Lord, thou art oure fadir; forsothe we ben cley, and thou art oure maker, and alle we ben the werkis of thin hondis.

9 Lord, be thou not wrooth ynow, and haue thou no more mynde on oure wickidnesse. Lo! Lord, biholde thou, alle we ben thi puple.

10 The citee of thi seyntuarie is forsakun, Sion is maad deseert, Jerusalem is desolat.

11 the hous of oure halewyng and of oure glorie, where oure fadris herieden thee, is maad in to brennyng of fier; and alle oure desirable thingis ben turned in to fallyngis.

12 Lord, whether on these thingis thou schalt witholde thee? schalt thou be stille, and schalt thou turmente vs greetli?

CAP 65

1 Thei souyten me, that axiden not bifore; thei that souyten not me, founden me. Y seide, Lo! Y, lo! Y, to hethene men that knewen not me, and that clepiden not mi name to help.

2 I stretchide forth myn hondis al dai to a puple vnbileueful, that goith in a weie not good, aftir her thouytis.

3 It is a puple that stirith me to wrathfulnesse, euere bifore my face; whiche offren in gardyns, and maken sacrifice on tiel stoonys;

4 whiche dwellen in sepulcris, and slepen in the templis of idols; whiche eten swynes fleisch, and vnhooli iwisch is in the vessels of hem;

5 whiche seien to an hethene man, Go thou awei fro me, neiy thou not to me, for thou art vncleene; these schulen be smoke in my stronge veniaunce, fier brennynge al dai.

6 Lo! it is writun bifore me; Y schal not be stille, but Y schal yelde, and Y schal quyte in to the bosum of hem youre wickidnessis,

7 and the wickidnessis of youre fadris togidere, seith the Lord, whiche maden sacrifice on mounteyns, and diden schenschipe to me on litle hillis; and Y schal mete ayen the firste werk of hem in her bosum.

8 The Lord seith thes thingis, As if a grape be foundun in a clustre, and it be seid, Distrie thou not it, for it is blessyng; so Y schal do for my seruantis, that Y leese not al.

9 And Y schal lede out of Jacob seed, and of Juda a man hauynge in possessioun myn hooli hillis; and my chosun men schulen enherite it, and my seruauntis schulen dwelle there.

10 And the feeldi places schulen be into floodis of flockis, and the valei of Achar in to a restyng place of droues of neet, to my puple that souyten me.

11 And Y schal noumbre you in swerd, that forsoken the Lord, that foryaten myn hooli hil, whiche setten a boord to fortune, and maken sacrifice theronne,

12 and alle ye schulen falle bi sleyng; for that that Y clepide, and ye answeriden not; Y spak, and ye herden not; and ye diden yuel bifor myn iyen, and ye chesiden tho thingis whiche Y nolde.

13 For these thingis, the Lord God seith these thingis, Lo! my seruauntis schulen ete, and ye schulen haue hungur; lo! my seruauntis schulen drynke, and ye schulen be thirsti;

14 lo! my seruauntis schulen be glad, and ye schulen be aschamed; lo! my seruauntis schulen herie, for the ful ioie of herte, and ye schulen crie, for the sorewe of herte, and ye schulen yelle, for desolacioun of spirit.

15 And ye schulen leeue youre name in to an ooth to my chosun men; and the Lord God schal sle thee, and he schal clepe hise seruauntis bi another name.

16 In which he that is blessid on erthe, schal be blessid in God amen; and he that swerith in erthe, shal swere in God feithfuli; for the formere angwischis ben youun to foryetyng, and for tho ben hid fro youre iyen.

17 For lo! Y make newe heuenes and a newe erthe, and the formere thingis schulen not be in mynde, and schulen not stie on the herte.

18 But ye schulen haue ioie, and make ful out ioiyng til in to with outen ende, in these thingis whiche Y make; for lo! Y make Jerusalem ful out ioiynge, and the puple therof ioie.

19 And Y schal make ful out ioiyng in Jerusalem, and Y schal haue ioie in my puple; and the vois of weping and the vois of cry schal no more be herd ther ynne.

20 A yong child of daies schal no more be there, and an eld man that fillith not hise daies; for whi a child of an hundrid yeer schal die, and a synnere of an hundrid yeer schal be cursid.

21 And thei schulen bilde housis, and schulen enhabite hem, and thei schulen plaunte vynes, and schulen ete the fruytis of tho.

22 Thei schulen not bilde housis, and an othir schal enhabite hem, thei schulen not plaunte, and an othir schal ete; for whi the daies of my puple schulen be after the daies of the tree, and the werkis of

23 her hondis schulen be elde to my chosun men. Thei schulen not trauele in veyn, nether thei schulen gendre in disturblyng; for it is the seed of hem that ben blessid of the Lord, and the cosyns of hem ben with hem.

24 And it schal be, bifor that thei crien, Y schal here; yit while thei speken, Y schal here.

25 A wolf and a lomb schulen be fed togidere, and a lioun and an oxe schulen ete stree, and to a serpent dust schal be his breed; thei schulen not anoie, nether schulen sle, in al myn hooli hil, seith the Lord.

CAP 66

1 The Lord seith these thingis, Heuene is my seete, and the erthe is the stool of my feet. Which is this hous, which ye schulen bilde to me, and which is this place of my reste?

2 Myn hond made alle these thingis, and alle these thingis ben maad, seith the Lord; but to whom schal Y biholde, no but to a pore man and contrit in spirit, and greetli dredynge my wordis?

3 He that offrith an oxe, is as he that sleeth a man; he that sleeth a scheep, is as he that brayneth a dogge; he that offrith an offryng, is as he that offrith swynes blood; he that thenketh on encense, is as he that blessith an idol; thei chesiden alle thes thingis in her weies, and her soule delitide in her abhomynaciouns.

4 Wherfor and Y schal chese the scornyngis of hem, and Y schal brynge to hem tho thingis whiche thei dredden; for Y clepide, and noon was that answeride; Y spak, and thei herden not; and thei diden yuel bifor myn iyen, and chesiden tho thingis whiche Y nolde.

5 Here ye the word of the Lord, whiche quaken at his word; youre britheren hatynge you, and castynge a wey for my name, seiden, The Lord be glorified, and we schulen se in youre gladnesse; forsothe thei schulen be schent.

6 The vois of the puple fro the citee, the vois fro the temple, the vois of the Lord yeldynge a reward to hise enemyes.

7 Bifor that sche trauelide of child, sche childide; bifor that the sorewe of hir child beryng cam, sche childide a sone.

8 Who herde euere suche a thing, and who siy a thing lijk this? Whether the erthe schal trauele of child in o dai, ether whether a folk schal be childide togidere? For whi Sion trauelede of child, and childide hir sones.

9 Whether that Y 'my silf that make othere to bere child, schal not ber child? seith the Lord. Whether Y that yyue generacioun to othere men, schal be bareyn? seith thi Lord God.

10 Be ye glad with Jerusalem, and alle ye that louen that, make ful out ioye ther ynne; alle ye that mourenen on that Jerusalem, make ye ioye with it in ioie;

11 that bothe ye souke, and be fillid of the tetis and coumfort therof, that ye mylke, and flowe in delicis, of al maner glorie therof.

12 For whi the Lord seith these thingis, Lo! Y schal bowe doun on it, as a flood of pees, and as a flowynge streem the glorie of hethene men, which ye schulen souke; ye schulen be borun at tetis, and on knees thei schulen speke plesauntly to you.

13 As if a modir spekith faire to ony child, so Y schal coumforte you, and ye schulen be coumfortid in Jerusalem.

14 Ye schulen se, and youre herte schal haue ioie, and youre boonys schulen buriowne as an erbe. And the hond of the Lord schal be knowun in hise seruauntis, and he schal haue indignacioun to hise enemyes.

15 For lo! the Lord schal come in fier, and as a whirlwynd hise charis, to yelde in indignacioun hise strong veniaunce, and his blamyng in the flawme of fier.

16 For whi the Lord schal deme in fier, and in hys swerd to ech fleisch; and slayn men of the Lord schulen be multiplied,

17 that weren halewid, and gessiden hem cleene, in gardyns aftir o yate with ynne; that eten swynes fleisch, and abhomy-nacioun, and a mows, thei schulen be waastid togidere, seith the Lord.

18 Forsothe Y come to gadere togidere the werkis of hem, and the thouytis of hem, with alle folkis and langagis; and thei schulen come, and schulen se my glorie.

19 And Y schal sette a signe in hem, and Y schal sende of hem that ben sauyd to hethene men, in to the see, in to Affrik, and in to Liddia, and to hem that holden arowe, in to Italie, and Greek lond, to ilis fer, to hem that herden not of me, and sien not my glorie. And thei schulen telle my glorie to heth-ene men,

20 and thei schulen brynge alle youre britheren of alle folkis a yifte to the Lord, in horsis, and charis, and in literis, and in mulis, and in cartis, to myn hooli hil, Jerusalem, seith the Lord; as if the sones of Israel bryngen a yifte in a cleene ves-sel in to the hous of the Lord.

21 And Y schal take of hem in to preestis and dekenes, seith the Lord.

22 For as newe heuenes and newe erthe, whiche Y make to stonde bifore me, seith the Lord, so youre seed schal stonde, and youre name.

23 And a monethe schal be of monethe, and a sabat of sabat; ech man schal come for to worschipe bifore my face, seith the Lord.

24 And thei schulen go out, and schulen se the careyns of men, that trespassiden ayens me; the worm of hem schal not die, and the fier of hem schal not be quenchid; and thei schulen be 'til to fillyng of siyt to ech man.

JEREMIAH

CAP 1

1 The wordis of Jeremye, sone of Helchie, of the preestis that weren in Anathot, in the lond of Beniamyn.

2 For the word of the Lord was maad to hym in the daies of Josie, the sone of Amon, kyng of Juda, in the threttenethe yeer of his rewme.

3 And it was don in the daies of Joachym, the sone of Josie, the king of Juda, til to the endyng of the enleuenthe yeer of Sedechie, sone of Josie, kyng of Juda, til the passyng ouer, ether caitifte, of Jerusalem, in the fyuethe monethe.

4 And the word of the Lord was maad to me,

5 and seide, Bifor that Y fourmede thee in the wombe, Y knewe thee; and bifor that thou yedist out of the wombe, Y halewide thee; and Y yaf thee a profete among folkis.

6 And Y seide, A! A! A! Lord God, lo! Y kan not speke, for Y am a child.

7 And the Lord seide to me, Nyle thou seie, that Y am a child; for thou schalt go to alle thingis, to whiche Y schal sende thee, and thou schalt speke alle thingis, what euer thingis Y schal comaunde to thee.

8 Drede thou not of the face of hem, for Y am with thee, to delyuere thee, seith the Lord.

9 And the Lord sente his hond, and touchide my mouth; and the Lord seide to me, Lo! Y haue youe my wordis in thi mouth; lo!

10 Y haue ordeynede thee to day on folkis, and on rewmes, that thou drawe vp, and distrie, and leese, and scatere, and bilde, and plaunte.

11 And the word of the Lord was maad to me, and seide, What seest thou, Jeremye?

12 And Y seide, Y se a yerde wakynge. And the Lord seide to me, Thou hast seen wel, for Y schal wake on my word, to do it.

13 And the word of the Lord was maad the secounde tyme to me, and seide, What seest thou? Y se a pot buylynge, and the face therof fro the face of the north.

14 And the Lord seide to me, Fro the north schal be schewid al yuel on alle the dwelleris of the lond.

15 For lo! Y schal clepe togidere alle the naciouns of rewmes of the north, seith the Lord, and thei schulen come, and sette ech man his seete in the entryng of the yatis of Jerusalem, and on alle the wallis therof in cumpas, and on alle the citees of Juda.

16 And Y schal speke my domes with hem on al the malice of hem, that forsoken me, and maden sacrifice to alien goddis, and worschipiden the werk of her hondis.

17 Therfor girde thou thi leendis, and rise thou, and speke to hem alle thingis whiche Y comaunde to thee; drede thou not of the face of hem, for Y schal not make thee for to drede the cheer of hem.

18 For Y yaf thee to dai in to a strong citee, and in to an yrun piler, and in to a brasun wal, on al the lond, to the kyngis of Juda, and to the princis therof, and to the preestis therof, and to al the puple of the lond.

19 And thei schulen fiyte ayens thee, and thei schulen not haue the maistrie; for Y am with thee, seith the Lord, that Y delyuere thee.

CAP 2

1 And the word of the Lord was maad to me,

2 and seide, Go thou, and crye in the eeris of Jerusalem, and seie, The Lord seith these thingis, Y hadde mynde on thee, and Y hadde merci on thee in thi yong wexynge age, and on the charite of thi spousyng, whanne thou suedist me in desert, in the lond which is not sowun.

3 Israel was hooli to the Lord, the firste of fruytis of hym; alle men that deuouren that Israel, trespassen; yuelis schulen come on hem, seith the Lord.

4 The hous of Jacob, and alle the lynagis of the hous of Israel, here ye the word of the Lord.

5 The Lord seith these thingis, What of wickidnesse foundun youre fadris in me, for thei yeden fer awey fro me, and yeden after vanyte, and weren maad veyn?

6 And thei seiden not, Where is the Lord, that made vs to stie fro the lond of Egipt, that ledde vs ouer thorou desert, bi the lond vnabitable and with out weie, bi the lond of thirst, and bi the ymage of deeth, bi the lond in whiche a man yede not, nether a man dwellide.

7 And Y brouyte you in to the lond of Carmele, that ye schul-den ete the fruyt therof, and the goodis therof; and ye entriden, and defouliden my lond, and settiden myn eritage in to abhomynacioun.

8 Preestis seiden not, Where is the Lord? and thei that helden the lawe, knewen not me; and scheepherdis trespassiden ayens me, and profetis profesieden in Baal, and sueden idols.

9 Therfor yit Y schal stryue with you in doom, seith the Lord, and Y schal dispute with youre sones.

10 Go ye to the ilis of Cethym, and se ye; and sende ye in to Cedar, and biholde ye greetli; and se ye,

11 if siche a thing is doon, if a folk chaungide hise goddis; and certeynli thei ben no goddis; but my puple chaungide hise glorie in to an ydol.

12 Heuenes, be ye astonyed on this thing, and, ye yatis of heuene, be ye desolat greetli, seith the Lord.

13 For whi my puple hath don tweyne yuels; thei han forsake me, the welle of quyke watir, and han diggid to hem cisternes, 'that weren distried, that moun not holde watris.

14 Whether Israel is a boond man, ether is borun boonde?

15 Whi therfor is he maad in to prey? Liouns roriden on hym, and yauen her vois; thei han set the londe of hym in to wildirnesse, the citees of him ben brent, and noon is that dwellith in tho.

16 Also the sones of Menfis and of Tafnys han defoulid thee, 'til to the cop of the heed.

17 Whether this is not don to thee, for thou forsokist thi Lord God, in that tyme in which he ledde thee bi the weie?

18 And now what wolt thou to thee in the weie of Egipt, that thou drynke troblid watir? And what is to thee with the weie of Assiriens, that thou drynke water of the flood?

19 Thi malice schal repreue thee, and thi turnyng awei schal blame thee; wite thou and se, that it is yuel and bittir that thou hast forsake thi Lord God, and that his drede is not at thee, seith the Lord God of oostis.

20 Fro the world thou hast broke my yok, thou hast broke my bondis, and seidist, Y schal not serue. For thou hoore didist hordom in ech hiy litil hil, and vndur ech tree ful of bowis.

21 Forsothe Y plauntide thee a chosun vyner, al trewe seed; hou therfor art thou, alien vyner, turned to me in to a schrewid thing?

22 Thouy thou waischist thee with fulleris clei, and multypliest to thee the erbe borith, thou art defoulid in thi wickidnesse bifore me, seith the Lord God.

23 Hou seist thou, Y am not defoulid, Y yede not aftir Baalym? Se thi weies in the greet valei, wite thou what thou hast do; a swifte rennere ordeynynge hise weies.

24 A wielde asse customable in wildirnesse drow the wynd of his loue in the desire of his soule; no man schal turne awei it. Alle that seken it, schulen not faile; thei schulen fynde it in the flux of vncleene blood therof.

25 Forbede thi foot fro nakidnesse, and thi throte fro thirst; and thou seidist, Y dispeiride, Y schal not do; for Y louede brennyngli alien goddis, and Y schal go aftir hem.

26 As a theef is schent, whanne he is takun, so the hous of Israel ben schent; thei, and kyngis of hem, the princes, and prestis, and the prophetis of hem,

27 that seien to a tree, Thou art my fadir; and to a stoon, Thou hast gendrid me. Thei turneden to me the bak, and not the face; and in the tyme of her turment thei schulen seie, Ryse thou, and delyuere vs.

28 Where ben thi goddis, whiche thou madist to thee? Rise thei, and delyuere thee in the tyme of thi turment; for aftir the noumbre of thi citees weren thi goddis, thou Juda.

29 What wolen ye stryue with me in doom? Alle ye han forsake me, seith the Lord.

30 In veyn Y smoot youre sones, thei resseyueden not chastisyng; youre swerd deuouride youre prophetis, youre generacioun is distried as a lioun.

31 Se ye the word of the Lord, whether Y am maad a wildirnesse to Israel, ether a lond late bryngynge forth fruyt? Whi therfor seide my puple, We han go awei, we schulen no more come to thee?

32 Whethir a virgyn schal foryete hir ournement? and a spousesse 'schal foryete hir brest girdil? But mi puple hath foryete me bi daies with out noumbre.

33 What enforsist thou to schewe thi weie good to seke loue, which ferthermore bothe hast tauyt thi malices thi weies,

34 and the blood of pore men and innocentis is foundun in thi wyngis? Y fond not hem in dichis, but in alle thingis whiche Y remembride bifore.

35 And thou seidist, Y am with out synne and innocent; and therfor thi stronge veniaunce be turned awei fro me. Lo! Y schal stryue with thee in doom; for thou seidist, Y synnede not.

36 Hou vijl art thou maad, rehersynge thi weies? and thou schalt be schent of Egipt, as thou were schent of Assur.

37 For whi and thou schalt go out of this lond, and thin hondis schulen be on thin heed; for whi the Lord hath al to-broke thi trist, and thou schalt haue no thing to prosperite.

CAP 3

1 It is seid comunli, If a man forsakith his wijf, and sche go awei fro hym, and be weddid to an othere hosebonde, whether he schal turne ayen more to hir? whether thilke womman schal not be defoulid, and maad vncleene? Forsothe thou hast do fornycacioun with many loueris; netheles turne thou ayen to me, 'seith the Lord, and Y schal resseyue thee.

2 Reise thin iyen in to streiyt, and se, where thou art not cast doun. Thou hast setun in weies, abidynge hem as a theef in wildirnesse, and thou hast defoulid the erthe in thi fornicaciouns and in thi malices.

3 Wherfor the dropis of reynes weren forbodun, and no late reyn was. The forhed of a womman hoore is maad to thee; thou noldist be aschamed.

4 Nameli fro this tyme forth clepe thou me, Thou art my fadir, the ledere of my virginyte.

5 Whether thou schalt be wrooth with outen ende, ether schalt contynue in to the ende? Lo! thou hast spoke, and hast do yuels, and thou were myyti. And for wordis of penaunce thou blasfemydist bi wordis of pride; and thou fillidist thin yuel thouyt, and schewidist thi strengthe ayens thi hosebonde, that thou maist do that thing that thou tretidist bi word.

6 And the Lord seide to me, in the daies of Josie, the kyng, Whether thou hast seyn what thing the aduersarie, Israel, hath do? Sche yede hir silf on ech hiy hil, and vndur ech tre ful of boowis, and dide fornycacioun there.

7 And Y seide, whanne sche hadde do alle these thingis, Turne thou ayen to me; and sche turnede not ayen. And hir sistir, Juda, brekere of the lawe,

8 siy, that for the aduersarie, Israel, dide auowtrie, Y hadde left hir, and Y hadde youe to hir a libel of forsakyng; and Juda, hir sistir, brekere of the lawe, dredde not, but also sche yede, and dide fornycacioun.

9 And bi liytnesse of hir fornicacioun sche defoulide the erthe, and dide auowtrie with a stoon, and with a tree.

10 And in alle these thingis hir sistir, Juda, brekere of the lawe, turnede not ayen to me, in al hir herte, but in a leesyng, seith the Lord God.

11 And the Lord seide to me, The aduersarie, Israel, hath iustified hir soule, in comparisoun of Juda, brekere of the lawe.

12 Go thou, and crye these wordis ayens the north; and thou schalt seie, Thou aduersarie, Israel, turne ayen, seith the Lord, and Y schal not turne awei my face fro you; for Y am hooli, seith the Lord, and Y schal not be wrooth with outen ende.

13 Netheles knowe thou thi wickidnesse; for thou hast trespassid ayens thi Lord God, and thou hast spred abrood thi weies to aliens vndur ech tre ful of bowis; and thou herdist not my vois, seith the Lord.

14 Be ye conuertid, sones, turnynge ayen, seith the Lord, for Y am youre hosebonde; and Y schal take you oon of a citee, and tweyne of a kynrede, and Y schal lede you in to Sion;

15 and Y schal yyue to you scheepherdis after myn herte, and thei schulen feede you with kunnyng and teching.

16 And whanne ye schulen be multiplied, and encreesse in the lond, in tho daies, seith the Lord, thei schulen no more seie, The arke of testament of the Lord; nether it schal stie on the herte, nether thei schulen thenke on it, nether it schal be visitid, nether it schal be ferthere.

17 In that tyme thei schulen clepe Jerusalem The seete of the Lord, and alle hethene men schulen be gaderid togidere to it, in the name of the Lord, in Jerusalem; and thei schulen not go aftir the schrewidnesse of her worste herte.

18 In tho daies the hous of Juda schal go to the hous of Israel; and thei schulen come togidere fro the lond of the north to the lond which Y yaf to youre fadris.

19 Forsothe Y seide, Hou schal Y sette thee among sones, and schal yyue to thee a desirable lond, a ful cleer eritage of the oostis of hethene men? And Y seide, Thou schalt clepe me fadir, and thou schalt not ceesse to entre aftir me.

20 But as if a womman dispisith hir louyere, so the hous of Israel dispiside me, seith the Lord.

21 A vois is herd in weies, the weping and yellyng of the sones of Israel; for thei maden wickid her weie, thei foryaten her Lord God.

22 Be ye conuertid, sones, turnynge ayen, and Y schal heele youre turnyngis awei. Lo! we comen to thee; for thou art oure Lord God.

23 Verili litil hillis weren lieris, the multitude of mounteyns was fals; verili in oure Lord God is the helthe of Israel.

24 Schenschipe eete the trauel of oure fadris, fro oure yongthe; schenschipe eet the flockis of hem, and the droues of hem, the sones of hem, and the douytris of hem.

25 We schulen slepe in oure schenschipe, and oure sclaundir schal hile vs; for we synneden to oure Lord God, bothe we and oure fadris, fro oure yongthe 'til to this dai; and we herden not the vois of oure Lord God.

CAP 4

1 Israel, if thou turnest ayen, seith the Lord, turne thou to me; if thou takist awei thin offendyngis fro my face, thou schalt not be mouyd.

2 And thou schalt swere, The Lord lyueth, in treuthe and in doom and in riytfulnesse; and alle folkis schulen blesse hym, and schulen preise hym.

3 For the Lord God seith these thingis to a man of Juda and to a dwellere of Jerusalem, Make ye newe to you a lond tilid of the newe, and nyle ye sowe on thornes.

4 Men of Juda, and dwelleris of Jerusalem, be ye circumcidid to the Lord, and do ye awey the filthis of youre hertis; lest perauenture myn indignacioun go out as fier, and be kyndlid, and noon be that quenche, for the malice of youre thouytis.

5 Telle ye in Juda, and make ye herd in Jerusalem; speke ye, and synge ye with a trumpe in the lond; crye ye strongli, and seie ye, Be ye gaderid togidere, and entre we in to stronge citees.

6 Reise ye a signe in Sion, coumforte ye, and nyle ye stonde; for Y bringe yuel fro the north, and a greet sorewe.

7 A lioun schal 'rise vp fro his denne, and the robbere of folkis schal reise hym silf. He is goon out of his place, to sette thi lond in to wildirnesse; thi citees schulen be distried, abidynge stille with out dwellere.

8 On this thing girde you with heiris; weile ye, and yelle, for the wraththe of the strong veniaunce of the Lord is not turned awei fro you.

9 And it schal be, in that dai, seith the Lord, the herte of the king schal perische, and the herte of princis; and the prestis schulen wondre, and the prophetis schulen be astonyed.

10 And Y seide, Alas! alas! alas! Lord God; therfor whether thou hast disseyued this puple and Jerusalem, seiynge, Pees schal be to you, and lo! a swerd is comun 'til to the soule?

11 In that tyme it schal be seide to this puple and to Jerusalem, A brennynge wynd in the weies that ben in desert, ben the weies of the douytir of my puple, not to wyndewe, and not to purge.

12 A spirit ful of hem schal come to me; and now Y, but Y schal speke my domes with hem.

13 Lo! he schal stie as a cloude, and hise charis as a tempest; hise horsis ben swifter than eglis; wo to vs, for we ben distried.

14 Thou Jerusalem, waische thin herte fro malice, that thou be maad saaf. Hou long schulen noiful thouytis dwelle in thee?

15 For whi the vois of a tellere fro Dan, and makynge knowun an idol fro the hil of Effraym.

16 Reise, ye folkis; lo! it is herd in Jerusalem that keperis ben comun fro a fer lond, and yyuen her vois on the citees of Juda.

17 As the keperis of feeldis thei ben maad on it in cumpas; for it stiride me to wrathfulnesse, seith the Lord.

18 Thi weyes and thi thouytis han maad this to thee; this malice of thee, for it is bittir, for it touchide thin herte.

19 Mi wombe akith, my wombe akith; the wittis of myn herte ben disturblid in me. Y schal not be stille, for my soule herde the vois of a trumpe, the cry of batel.

20 Sorewe is clepid on sorewe, and al the lond is distried; my tabernaclis ben wastid sudeynli, my skynnes ben wastid sudeynli.

21 Hou longe schal Y se hem that fleen, schal Y here the vois of a clarioun?

22 For my fonned puple knew not me; thei ben vnwise sones, and cowardis; thei ben wise to do yuels, but thei kouden not do wel.

23 Y bihelde the lond, and lo! it was void, and nouyt; and Y bihelde heuenes, and no liyt was in tho.

24 Y siy munteyns, and lo! tho weren mouyd, and all litle hillis weren disturblid.

25 Y lokide, and no man was, and ech brid of heuene was gon a wey.

26 Y bihelde, and lo! Carmele is forsakun, and alle citees therof ben distried fro the face of the Lord, and fro the face of the ire of his strong veniaunce.

27 For the Lord seith these thingis, Al the lond schal be forsakun, but netheles Y schal not make an endyng.

28 The erthe schal mourne, and heuenys aboue schulen make sorewe, for that Y spak; Y thouyte, and it repentide not me, nether Y am turned awei fro it.

29 Ech citee fledde fro the vois of a knyyt, and of a man schetynge an arowe; thei entriden in to hard places, and stieden in to roochis of stoon; alle citees ben forsakun, and no man dwellith in tho.

30 But what schalt thou 'destried do? Whanne thou schalt clothe thee with reed scarlet, whanne thou schalt be ourned with a goldun broche, and schalt anoynte thin iyen with wommans oynement, thou schalt be araied in veyn; thi louyeris han dispisid thee, thei schulen seke thi soule.

31 For Y herd a vois as of a womman trauelynge of child, the angwischis as of a womman childynge; the vois of the douyter of Sion among hem that dien, and spreden abrood her hondis; Wo to me, for my soule failide for hem that ben slayn.

CAP 5

1 Cumpasse ye the weies of Jerusalem, and loke, and biholde ye, and seke ye in the stretis therof, whether ye fynden a man doynge doom, and sekynge feith; and Y schal be merciful to hem.

2 That if also thei seien, The Lord lyueth, yhe, thei schulen swere this falsli.

3 Lord, thin iyen biholden feith; thou hast smyte hem, and thei maden not sorewe; thou hast al tobroke hem, and thei forsoken to take chastisyng; thei maden her faces hardere than a stoon, and nolden turne ayen.

4 Forsothe Y seide, In hap thei ben pore men, and foolis, that knowen not the weie of the Lord, and the doom of her God.

5 Therfor Y schal go to the principal men, and Y schal speke to hem; for thei knewen the weie of the Lord, and the doom of her God. And lo! thei han more broke togidere the yok, and han broke boondis.

6 Therfor a lioun of the wode smoot hem; a wolf at euentid wastide hem, a parde wakynge on the citees of hem. Ech man that goith out of hem, schal be takun; for the trespassyngis of hem ben multiplied, the turnyngis awei of hem ben coumfortid.

7 On what thing mai Y be merciful to thee? Thi sones han forsake me, and sweren bi hem that ben not goddis. Y fillide hem, and thei diden auowtrie, and in the hous of an hoore thei diden letcherie.

8 Thei ben maad horsis, and stalouns, louyeris to wymmen; ech man neiyede to the wijf of his neiybore.

9 Whether Y schal not visite on these thingis, seith the Lord, and schal not my soule take veniaunce in siche a folk?

10 Stye ye on the wallis therof, and distrie ye; but nyle ye make an endyng. Do ye awei the siouns therof, for thei ben not seruauntis of the Lord.

11 For whi the hous of Israel and the hous of Juda hath trespassid bi trespassyng ayens me, seith the Lord;

12 thei denyeden the Lord, and seiden, He is not, nether yuel schal come on vs; we schulen not se swerd and hungur.

13 The profetis spaken ayens the wynd, and noon answer was in hem; therfor these thingis schulen come to hem.

14 The Lord God of oostis seith these thingis, For ye spaken this word, lo! Y yyue my wordis in thi mouth in to fier, and this puple in to trees, and it schal deuoure hem.

15 Lo! thou hous of Israel, seith the Lord, Y schal brynge on you a folk fro fer; a strong folk, an eeld folk, 'a folk whos langage thou schalt not knowe, nether schalt vndurstonde what it spekith.

16 The arowe caas therof is as an opyn sepulcre; alle ben stronge men.

17 And it schal ete thi cornes, and it schal deuoure thi breed, thi sones and thi douytris; it schal ete thi flok, and thi droues, it schal ete also thi vyner, and thi fige tre; and it schal al tobreke thi stronge citees bi swerd, in whiche thou hast trist.

18 Netheles in tho daies, seith the Lord, Y schal not make you in to endyng.

19 That if ye seien, Whi hath oure Lord God do alle these thingis to vs? thou schalt seie to hem, As ye forsoken me, and serueden an alien god in youre lond, so ye schulen serue alien goddis in a lond not youre.

20 Telle ye this to the hous of Jacob, and make ye herd in Juda, and seie ye,

21 Here, thou fonned puple, that hast noon herte; whiche han iyen, and seen not, and eeris, and heren not.

22 Therfor schulen not ye drede me, seith the Lord, and schulen not ye make sorewe for my face? Whiche haue set grauel a terme, ether ende, to the see, an euerlastynge comaundement, whiche it schal not passe; and the wawis therof schulen be mouyd, and schulen not haue power; and schulen wexe greet, and schulen not passe it.

23 Forsothe an herte vnbileueful and terrynge to wraththe is maad to this puple; thei departiden,

24 and yeden awei, and thei seiden not in her herte, Drede we oure Lord God, that yiueth to vs reyn tymeful, and lateful in his tyme; that kepith to vs the plente of heruest of the yeer.

25 Youre wickidnessis diden awei these thingis, and youre synnes forbediden good fro you.

26 For ther ben foundun in my puple wickid men, settynge tresoun, as fouleres settynge snaris and trappis, to take men.

27 As a net, ether a trap, ful of briddis, so the housis of hem ben ful of gile. Therfor thei ben magnefied,

28 and maad riche, maad fat with ynne, and maad fat with outforth, and thei passiden worst my wordis; thei demyden not a cause of a widewe, thei dressiden not the cause of a fadirles child, and thei demyden not the doom of pore men.

29 Whether Y schal not visite on these thingis, seith the Lord, ether schal not my soule take veniaunce on sich a folk?

30 Wondur and merueilouse thingis ben maad in the lond;

31 profetis profesieden leesyng, and prestis ioieden with her hondis, and my puple louyde siche thingis. What therfor schal be don in the laste thing therof?

CAP 6

1 Sones of Beniamyn, be ye coumfortid in the myddil of Jerusalem, and make ye noise with a clarioun in Thecua, and reise ye a baner on Bethecarem; for whi yuel and greet sorewe is seyn fro the north.

2 Y haue licned the douytir of Sion to a fair womman and delicat.

3 Scheepherdis and her flockis schulen come to it; thei han piyt tentis in it in cumpas; ech man schal feede hem, that ben vndur his hond.

4 Halewe ye batel on it. Rise ye togidire, and stie we in myddai. Wo to vs, for the dai is bowid doun, for shadewis ben maad lengere in the euentid.

5 Rise ye, and stie we in the niyt, and distry we the housis therof.

6 For the Lord of oostis seith these thingis, Kitte ye doun the tre therof, and schede ye erthe aboute Jerusalem; this is the citee of visitacioun; al fals caleng is in the myddis therof.

7 As a cisterne makith his water coold, so it made his malice coold; wickidnesse and distriyng schal euer be herd ther ynne bifore me, sikenesse and wounde.

8 Jerusalem, be thou tauyt, lest perauenture my soule go awei fro thee; lest perauenture Y sette thee forsakun, a loond vnhabitable.

9 The Lord of oostis seith these thingis, Thei schulen gadere til to a racyn, thei schulen gadere the remenauntis of Israel as in a vyner; turne thin hond, as a gaderer of grapis to the bascat.

10 To whom schal Y speke, and to whom schal Y seie witnessing, that he here? Lo! the eeris of hem ben vncircumcidid, and thei moun not here; lo! the word of the Lord is maad to hem in to dispit, and thei schulen not resseiue it.

11 Therfor Y am ful of the strong veniaunce of the Lord, and Y trauelide suffrynge. Schede thou out on a litil child with outforth, and on the counsel of yonge men togidere; for a man with his wijf schal be takun, and an eeld man with him that is ful of daies.

12 And the housis of hem, the feeldis and wyues togidere, schulen go to othere men; for Y schal stretche forth myn hond on the dwelleris of the lond, seith the Lord.

13 For fro the lesse 'til to the grettere, alle studien to auerise; and alle doon gile, fro the profete 'til to the preest.

14 And thei heeliden the sorewe of the douyter of my puple with yuel fame, seiynge, Pees, pees, and no pees was.

15 Thei ben schent, that diden abhomynacioun; yhe, rathere thei weren not schent bi confusioun, and thei kouden not be aschamed. Wherfor thei schulen falle doun among hem that schulen falle doun; thei schulen falle doun in the tyme of her visitacioun, seith the Lord.

16 The Lord seith these thingis, Stonde ye on weies, and se ye, and axe ye of elde pathis, which is the good weie; and go ye ther ynne, and ye schulen fynde refreischyng to youre soulis. And thei seiden, We schulen not go.

17 And Y ordeynede aspieris on you, and Y seide, Here ye the vois of a trumpe. And thei seiden, We schulen not here.

18 Therfor, hethene men, here ye, and, thou congregacioun, knowe, hou grete thingis Y schal do to hem.

19 Thou erthe, here, lo! Y schal brynge yuels on this puple, the fruit of her thouytis; for thei herden not my wordis, and castiden awei my lawe.

20 Wherto bryngen ye to me encense fro Saba, and a tre of spicerie smellynge swetli fro a fer lond? Youre brent sacrifices ben not acceptid, and youre slayn sacrifices plesiden not me.

21 Therfor the Lord God seith these thingis, Lo! Y schal yyue fallyngis in to this puple, and fadris and sones togidere, a neiybore and kynesman, schulen falle in hem, and schulen perische.

22 The Lord God seith these thingis, Lo! a puple cometh fro the lond of the north, and a greet folk schal rise togidere fro the endis of erthe.

23 It schal take an arowe and scheld; it is cruel, and schal not haue merci; the vois therof schal sowne as the see, and thei maad redi as a man to batel schulen stie on horsis ayens thee, thou douyter of Sion.

24 We herden the fame therof, oure hondis ben 'a clumsid; tribulacioun hath take vs, sorewis han take vs as a womman trauelinge of child.

25 Nyle ye go out to the feeldis, and go ye not in the weie, for the swerd of the enemye, drede in cumpas.

26 The douytir of my puple, be thou gird with heire, and be thou spreynt togidere with aische; make to thee mourenyng of oon aloone gendrid sone, a bitter weilyng, for whi a wastere schal come sodenli on you.

27 I yaf thee a strong preuere in my puple, and thou schalt knowe, and preue the weie of hem.

28 Alle these princis bowynge awei, goynge gilefuli, ben metal and irun; alle ben corrupt.

29 The belu failide, leed is waastid in the fier, the wellere wellide in veyn; for the malices of hem ben not wastid.

30 Clepe ye hem repreuable siluer, for the Lord hath cast hem awei.

CAP 7

1 The word that was maad of the Lord to Jeremye,

2 and seide, Stonde thou in the yate of the hous of the Lord, and preche there this word, and seie, Al Juda, that entren bi these yatis for to worschipe the Lord, here ye the word of the Lord.

3 The Lord of oostis, God of Israel, seith these thingis, Make ye good youre weies, and youre studies, and Y schal dwelle with you in this place.

4 Nyle ye triste in the wordis of leesyng, and seie, The temple of the Lord, the temple of the Lord, the temple of the Lord is.

5 For if ye blessen youre weies, and your studies; if ye doon doom bitwixe a man and his neiybore;

6 if ye maken not fals caleng to a comelyng, and to a fadirles child, and to a widewe; nether scheden out innocent blood in this place, and goen not after alien goddis, in to yuel to you silf,

7 Y schal dwelle with you in this place, in the lond which Y yaf to youre fadris, fro the world and til in to the world.

8 Lo! ye trusten to you in the wordis of leesyng, that shulen not profite to you;

9 to stele, to sle, to do auowtrie, to swere falsli, to make sacrifice to Baalym, and to go aftir alien goddys, whiche ye knowen not.

10 And ye camen, and stoden bifor me in this hous, in which my name is clepid to help; and ye seiden, We ben delyuered, for we han do alle these abhomynaciouns.

11 Whether therfor this hous, wherynne my name is clepid to help bifore youre iyen, is maad a denne of theues? I, Y am, Y siy, seith the Lord.

12 Go ye to my place in Silo, where my name dwellide at the bigynnyng, and se ye what thingis Y dide to it, for the malice of my puple Israel.

13 And now, for ye han do alle these werkis, seith the Lord, and Y spak to you, and roos eerli, and Y spak, and ye herden not, and Y clepide you, and ye answeriden not;

14 Y schal do to this hous, wherynne my name is clepid to help, and in which hous ye han trist, and to the place which Y yaf to you and to youre fadris, as Y dide to Silo.

15 And Y schal caste you forth fro my face, as Y castide forth alle youre britheren, al the seed of Effraym.

16 Therfor nyl thou preie for this puple, nether take thou heriyng and preier for hem; and ayenstonde thou not me, for Y schal not here thee.

17 Whether thou seest not, what these men don in the citees of Juda, and in the stretis of Jerusalem?

18 The sones gaderen stickis, and the fadris kyndlen a fier; and wymmen sprengen togidere ynnere fatnesse, to make kakis to the queen of heuene, to make sacrifice to alien goddis, and to terre me to wrathfulnesse.

19 Whether thei stiren me to wrathfulnesse? seith the Lord; whether thei stiren not hem silf in to schenschip of her cheer?
20 Therfor the Lord God seith these thingis, Lo! my strong veniaunce and myn indignacioun is wellid togidere on this place, on men, and on beestis, and on the tree of the cuntrei, and on the fruitis of erthe; and it schal be kyndlid, and it schal not be quenchid.
21 The Lord of oostis, God of Israel, seith these thingis, Heepe ye youre brent sacrifices to youre slayn sacrifices, and ete ye fleischis.
22 For Y spak not with youre fadris, and Y comaundide not to hem of the word of brent sacrifices, and of slayn sacrifices, in the dai in which Y ledde hem out of the lond of Egipt.
23 But Y comaundide this word to hem, and Y seide, Here ye my vois, and Y schal be God to you, and ye schulen be a puple to me; and go ye in al the weie which Y comaundide to you, that it be wel to you.
24 And thei herden not, nether bowiden doun her eere, but thei yeden in her lustis, and in the schrewidnesse of her yuel herte; and thei ben put bihynde, and not bifore,
25 fro the dai in which her fadris yeden out of the lond of Egipt til to this dai. And Y sente to you alle my seruauntis profetis, and Y roos eerli bi the dai, and Y sente.
26 And thei herden not me, nether bowiden doun her eere; but thei maden hard her nol, and wrouyten worse than the fadris of hem.
27 And thou schalt speke to hem alle these wordis, and thei schulen not heere thee; and thou schalt clepe hem, and thei schul not answere to thee.
28 And thou schalt seie to hem, This is the folc, that herde not the vois of her Lord God, nether resseyuede chastysyng; feith perischide, and is takun awei fro the mouth of hem.
29 Clippe thin heer, and cast awei, and take thou weilyng streiytli; for the Lord hath cast awei, and hath forsake the generacioun of his strong veniaunce.
30 For the sones of Juda han do yuel bifor myn iyen, seith the Lord; thei han set her offendyngis in the hous, in which my name is clepid to help, that thei schulden defoule that hous;
31 and thei bildiden hiye thingis in Tophet, which is in the valei of the sone of Ennon, that thei schulden brenne her sones and her douytris bi fier, whiche thingis Y comaundide not, nether thouyte in myn herte.
32 Therfor lo! daies comen, seith the Lord, and it schal no more be seid Tophet, and the valei of the sone of Ennon, but the valey of sleyng; and thei schulen birie in Tophet, for ther is no place.
33 And the deed careyn of this puple schal be in to mete to the briddis of heuene, and to the beestis of erthe; and noon schal be that schal dryue awei.
34 And Y schal make to ceesse the vois of ioye, and the vois of gladnesse, and the vois of spouse, and the vois of spousesse fro the citees of Juda, and fro the stretis of Jerusalem; for the lond schal be in desolacioun.

CAP 8

1 In that tyme, seith the Lord, thei schulen caste out the boonys of the kingis of Juda, and the boonys of princes therof, and the boonys of prestis, and the boonys of profetis, and the boonys of hem that dwelliden in Jerusalem fro her sepulcris;
2 and thei schulen leie abrood tho boonys to the sunne, and moone, and to al the knyythod of heuene, which thei louyden, and which thei seruyden, and aftir whiche thei yeden, and

whiche thei souyten, and worschipiden; tho schulen not be gaderid, and schulen not be biried; tho schulen be in to a dunghil on the face of erthe.
3 And alle men schulen cheese deth more than lijf, whiche ben left of this worst kynrede, in alle places that ben left, to whiche places Y castide hem out, seith the Lord of oostis.
4 And thou schalt seie to hem, The Lord seith these thingis, Whether he that schal falle, schal not rise ayen? and whether he that is turned awei, schal not turne ayen?
5 Whi therfor is this puple in Jerusalem turned awei bi turnyng awei ful of strijf? Thei han take leesyng, and nolden turne ayen.
6 Y perseyuede, and herknede; no man spekith that that is good, noon is that doith penaunce for his synne, and seith, What haue Y do? Alle ben turnede togidere to her cours, as an hors goynge bi fersnesse to batel.
7 A kite in the eir knew his tyme; a turtle, and a swalewe, and a siconye, kepten the tyme of her comyng; but my puple knew not the doom of the Lord.
8 Hou seien ye, We ben wise men, and the lawe of the Lord is with vs? Verili the fals writyng of scribis wrouyte leesyng.
9 Wise men ben schent, ben maad aferd and takun. For thei castiden awei the word of the Lord, and no wisdom is in hem.
10 Therfor Y schal yyue the wymmen of hem to straungeris, and the feeldis of hem to alien eiris; for fro the leeste 'til to the mooste alle suen aueryce, fro a profete 'til to the preest alle maken leesyng;
11 and thei heeliden the sorowe of the douytir of my puple to schenschipe, seiynge, Pees, pees, whanne no pees was.
12 Thei ben schent, for thei diden abhomynacioun; yhe, rather thei weren not schent bi schenschipe, and kouden not be aschamed. Therfor thei schulen falle among falleris, in the tyme of her visitacioun thei schulen falle, seith the Lord.
13 I gaderynge schal gadere hem, seith the Lord; no grape is in the vynes, and figis ben not in the fige tre; a leef felle doun, and Y yaf to hem tho thingis that ben go out ouer.
14 Whi sitten we? come ye togidere, entre we in to a strong citee, and be we stille there; for oure Lord hath maad vs to be stille, and yaf to vs drynk the watir of galle; for we han synned to the Lord.
15 We abididen pees, and no good was; we abididen tyme of medicyn, and lo! drede is.
16 Gnastyng of horsis therof is herd fro Dan; al the lond is moued of the vois of neiyngis of hise werriours; and thei camen, and deuouriden the lond, and the plente therof, the citee, and the dwelleris therof.
17 For lo! Y schal sende to you the werste serpentis, to whiche is no charmyng; and thei schulen bite you, seith the Lord.
18 My sorewe is on sorewe, myn herte is mourenynge in me.
19 And lo! the vois of cry of the douyter of my puple cometh fro a fer lond. Whether the Lord is not in Sion, ethir the kyng therof is not therynne? Whi therfor stiriden thei me to wrathfulnesse bi her grauun ymagis, and bi alien vanytees?
20 Heruest is passid, somer is endid; and we ben not sauyd.
21 Y am turmentid, and sori on the sorewe of the douyter of my puple; astonying helde me.
22 Whether resyn is not in Galaad, ether a leche is not there? Whi therfor the wounde of the douytir of my puple is not heelid perfitli?

CAP 9

1 Who schal yyue watir to myn heed, and a welle of teeris to myn iyen? And Y schal biwepe dai and niyt the slayn men of the douyter of my puple.

2 Who schal yyue me in to a wildirnesse of dyuerse weigoeris? And I schal forsake my puple, and Y schal go awei fro hem. For whi alle ben auowteris, and the cumpenyes of trespassouris ayens the lawe;

3 and thei helden forth her tunge as a bouwe of leesyng, and not of treuthe Thei ben coumfortid in erthe, for thei yeden out fro yuel to yuel, and thei knewen not me, seith the Lord.

4 Ech man kepe hym fro his neiybore, and haue no trist in ony brother of hym; for whi ech brother disseyuyng schal disseyue, and ech frend schal go gilefuli.

5 And a man schal scorne his brother, and schal not speke treuthe; for thei tauyten her tunge to speke leesyng; thei traueliden to do wickidli.

6 Thi dwellyng is in the myddis of gile; in gile thei forsoken to knowe me, seith the Lord.

7 Therfor the Lord of oostis seith these thingis, Lo! Y schal welle togidere, and Y schal preue hem; for whi what other thing schal Y do fro the face of the douyter of my puple?

8 The tunge of hem is an arowe woundynge, and spak gile; in his mouth he spekith pees with his frend, and priueli he settith tresouns to hym.

9 Whether Y schal not visite on these thingis, seith the Lord, ether schal not my soule take veniaunce on siche a folc?

10 On hillis Y schal take wepyng and mournyng, and weilyng on the faire thingis of desert, for tho ben brent; for no man is passynge forth, and thei herden not the vois of hym that weldith; fro a brid of the eir 'til to scheep, tho passiden ouer, and yeden awei.

11 And Y schal yyue Jerusalem in to heepis of grauel, and in to dennes of dragouns; and Y schal yyue the citees of Juda in to desolacioun, for ther is no dwellere.

12 Who is a wise man that schal vndurstonde these thingis, and to whom the word of the mouth of the Lord schal be maad, that he telle this? Whi the erthe perischide, it is brent as desert, for noon is that passith?

13 And the Lord seide, For thei forsoken my lawe, which Y yaf to hem, and thei herden not my vois, and thei yeden not therynne;

14 and thei yeden aftir the schrewidnesse of her herte, and aftir Baalym, which thei lerneden of her fadris;

15 therfor the Lord of oostis, God of Israel, seith these thingis, Lo! Y schal fede this puple with wermod, and Y schal yyue to hem drynke the watir of galle.

16 And Y schal scatere hem among hethene men, whiche thei and her fadris knewen not; and Y schal sende swerd aftir hem, til thei ben wastid.

17 The Lord of oostis, God of Israel, seith these thingis, Biholde ye, and clepe ye wymmen 'that weilen, and come thei; and sende ye to tho wymmen that ben wise, and haste thei.

18 Haste thei, and take thei weilynge on you; youre iyen brynge doun teeris, and youre iyelidis flowe with watris;

19 for the vois of weilyng is herd fro Sion. Hou ben we distried, and schent greetli? for we han forsake the lond, for oure tabernaclis ben forsakun.

20 Therfor, wymmen, here ye the word of the Lord, and youre eeris take the word of his mouth; and teche ye youre douytris weilyng, and ech womman teche hir neiybore mournyng.

21 For whi deth stiede bi youre wyndows, it entride in to youre housis, to leese litle children with outforth, and yonge men fro the stretis.

22 Speke thou, the Lord seith, these thingis, And the deed bodi of a man schal fal doun as a toord on the face of the cuntrei, and as hei bihynde the bak of the mowere, and noon is that gaderith.

23 The Lord seith these thingis, A wise man haue not glorie in his wisdom, and a strong man haue not glorie in his strengthe, and a riche man haue not glorie in hise richessis; but he that hath glorie,

24 haue glorie in this, to wite and knowe me, for Y am the Lord, that do merci and dom and riytfulnesse in erthe. For whi these thingis plesen me, seith the Lord.

25 Lo! daies comen, seith the Lord, and Y schal visite on ech man that hath prepucie vncircumcidid; on Egipt,

26 and on Juda, and on Edom, and on the sones of Amon, and on Moab, and on alle men that ben clippid on long heer, and dwellen in desert; for whi alle hethene men han prepucie, forsothe al the hous of Israel ben vncircumcidid in herte.

CAP 10

1 The hous of Israel, here ye the word which the Lord spak on you.

2 The Lord seith these thingis, Nyle ye lerne aftir the weies of hethene men, and nyle ye drede of the signes of heuene, whiche signes hethene men dreden.

3 For the lawis of puplis ben veyn, for whi the werk of hondis of a crafti man hath kit doun with an axe a tre of the forest.

4 He made it fair with siluer and gold; with naylis and hameris he ioynede it togidere, that it be not loosid.

5 Idols ben maad in the licnesse of a palm tree, and schulen not speke; tho schulen be takun and be borun, for tho moun not go; therfor nyle ye drede tho, for tho moun nether do yuel, nethir wel.

6 Lord, noon is lijk thee; thou art greet, and thi name is greet in strengthe.

7 A! thou king of folkis, who schal not drede thee? for whi onour is thin among alle wise men of hethene men, and in alle the rewmes of hem noon is lijk thee.

8 Thei schulen be preued, vnwise and foolis togidere; the techyng of her vanyte is a tre.

9 Siluer wlappid is brouyt fro Tharsis, and gold fro Ophaz; it is the werk of a crafti man, and of the hond of a worchere in metel; iacynct and purpur ben the clothing of tho; alle these thingis ben the werk of werk men.

10 Forsothe the Lord is veri God; he is God lyuynge, and a kyng euerlastynge; the erthe schal be mouyd togidere of his indignacioun, and hethene men schulen not suffre the manaassing of hym.

11 Therfor thus ye schulen seie to hem, Goddis that maden not heuene and erthe, perische fro erthe, and fro these thingis that ben vndur heuene.

12 He is God, that makith the erthe in his strengthe, makith redi the world in his wisdom, and stretchith forth heuenes bi his prudence.

13 At his vois he yyueth the multitude of watris in heuene, and he reisith mystis fro the endis of erthe; he makith leitis into reyn, and ledith out wynd of his tresouris.

14 Ech man is maad a fool of kunnyng, ech crafti man is schent in a grauun ymage; for whi that that he wellide togidere is fals, and no spirit is in tho.

15 Tho ben veyn, and a werk worthi of scorn; tho schulen perische in the tyme of her visitacioun.

16 The part of Jacob is not lijk these, for he that formede alle thingis is God of Jacob, and Israel is the yerde of his eritage; the Lord of oostis is name to hym.

17 Thou that dwellist in bisegyng, gadere fro the lond thi schenschipe;

18 for the Lord seith these thingis, Lo! Y schal caste awei fer the dwelleris of the loond in this while; and Y schal yyue tribulacioun to hem, so that thei be not foundun.

19 Wo to me on my sorewe, my wounde is ful yuel; forsothe Y seide, Pleynli this is my sikenesse, and Y schal bere it.

20 My tabernacle is distried, alle my roopis ben brokun; my sones yeden out fro me, and ben not; noon is that schal stretche forth more my tente, and schal reyse my skynnes.

21 For the scheepherdis diden folili, and souyten not the Lord; therfor thei vndurstoden not, and alle the flok of hem is scaterid.

22 Lo! the vois of hering cometh, and a greet mouynge togidere fro the lond of the north, that it sette the citees of Juda in to wildirnesse, and a dwellynge place of dragouns.

23 Lord, Y woot, that the weie of a man is not of hym, nether it is of a man that he go, and dresse hise steppis.

24 Lord, chastise thou me; netheles in doom and not in thi strong veniaunce, lest perauenture thou dryue me to nouyt.

25 Schede out thin indignacioun on hethene men that knewen not thee, and on prouynces that clepiden not thi name to help; for thei eeten Jacob, and deuouriden hym, and wastiden hym, and destrieden the onour of hym.

CAP 11

1 The word that was maad of the Lord to Jeremye,

2 and seide, Here ye the wordis of this couenaunt, and speke ye to the men of Juda, and to the dwelleris of Jerusalem; and thou schalt seie to hem,

3 The Lord God of Israel seith these thingis, Cursid be the man that herith not the wordis of this couenaunt,

4 which Y comaundide to youre fadris, in the dai in which Y ledde hem out of the lond of Egipt, fro the irone furneis; and Y seide, Here ye my vois, and do ye alle thingis whiche Y comaundide to you, and ye schulen be in to a puple to me, and Y schal be in to God to you;

5 that Y reise the ooth which Y swoor to youre fadris, that Y schulde yyue to hem a lond flowynge with mylk and hony, as this dai is. And Y answeride, and seide, Amen, Lord.

6 And the Lord seide to me, Crye thou alle these wordis in the citees of Juda, and with out Jerusalem, and seie thou, Here ye the wordis of this couenaunt, and do ye tho;

7 for Y witnessynge haue witnessid to youre fadris, in the dai in which Y ledde hem out of the lond of Egipt, 'til to this dai; Y roos eerli, and witnesside, and seide, Here ye my vois.

8 And thei herden not, nether bowiden doun her eere, but thei yeden forth ech man in the schrewidnesse of his yuel herte; and Y brouyte in on hem alle the wordis of this couenaunt, which Y comaundide that thei schulden do, and thei diden not.

10 And the Lord seide to me, Sweryng togidere is foundun in the men of Juda, and in the dwelleris of Jerusalem; thei turneden ayen to the formere wickidnessis of her fadris, that nolden here my wordis; and therfor these men yeden aftir alien goddis, for to serue hem; the hous of Israel and the hous of Juda maden voide my couenaunt, which Y made with the fadris of hem.

11 Wherfor the Lord seith these thingis, Lo! Y schal bringe in on hem yuels, of whiche thei schulen not mow go out; and thei schulen crie to me, and Y schal not here hem.

12 And the citees of Juda and the dwellers of Jerusalem schulen go, and schulen crye to hem, to whiche thei offren sacrifices; and thei schulen not saue hem in the tyme of her turment.

13 For thou, Juda, thi goddis weren bi the noumbre of thi citees, and thou settidist auters of schenschipe, bi the noumbre of the weies of Jerusalem, auters to offre sacrifices to Baalym.

14 Therfor nyle thou preie for this puple, and take thou not heriyng and preier for hem; for Y schal not here in the tyme of the cry of hem to me, in the tyme of the turment of hem.

15 What is it, that my derlyng doith many greet trespassis in myn hous? whether hooli fleischis schulen do awei fro thee thi malice, in which thou hast glorie?

16 The Lord clepide thi name an olyue tre, fair, ful of fruyt, schapli; at the vois of a greet speche fier brent an hiy ther ynne, and the buyschis therof ben brent.

17 And the Lord of oostis that plauntide thee, spak yuel on thee, for the yuels of the hous of Israel, and of the hous of Juda, whiche thei diden to hem silf, and offriden to Baalym, to terre me to wraththe.

18 Forsothe, Lord, thou schewidist to me, and Y knew; thou schewidist to me the studies of hem.

19 And Y am as a mylde lomb, which is borun to slayn sacrifice; and Y knew not, that thei thouyten counsels on me, and seiden, Sende we a tre in to the brede of hym, and rase we hym awei fro the lond of lyueris, and his name be no more hadde in mynde.

20 But thou, Lord of oostis, that demest iustli, and preuest reynes and hertis, se Y thi veniaunce of hem; for to thee Y schewide my cause.

21 Therfor the Lord seith these thingis to the men of Anathot, that seken thi lijf, and seien, Thou schalt not prophesie in the name of the Lord, and thou schalt not die in oure hondis.

22 Therfor the Lord of oostis seith these thingis, Lo! Y schal visite on hem; the yonge men of hem schulen die bi swerd, the sones of hem and the douytris of hem schulen die for hungur;

23 and no relifs, ether children abidynge, schulen be of hem; for Y schal bringe ynne yuel on the men of Anathot, the yeer of the visitacioun of hem.

CAP 12

1 Forsothe, Lord, thou art iust; if Y dispute with thee, netheles Y schal speke iust thingis to thee. Whi hath the weie of wickid men prosperite? It is wel to alle men that breken the lawe, and doen wickidli?

2 Thou hast plauntid hem, and thei senten roote; thei encreessen, and maken fruyt; thou art niy to the mouth of hem, and fer fro the reynes of hem.

3 And thou, Lord, hast knowe me, thou hast seyn me, and hast preued myn herte with thee. Gadere thou hem togidere as a flok to slayn sacrifice, and halewe thou hem in the dai of sleyng.

4 Hou long schal the erthe mourne, and ech eerbe of the feeld schal be dried, for the malice of hem that dwellen ther ynne? A beeste is wastid, and a brid, for thei seiden, The Lord schal not se oure laste thingis.

5 If thou trauelist rennynge with foot men, hou schalt thou mow stryue with horsis? but whanne thou art sikur in the lond of pees, what schalt thou do in the pride of Jordan?

6 For whi bothe thi britheren and the hous of thi fadir, yhe, thei fouyten ayens thee, and crieden with ful vois aftir thee; bileue thou not to hem, whanne thei speken goodis to thee.

7 I haue left myn hous, Y haue forsake myn eritage; Y yaf my loued soule in to the hondis of enemyes therof.

8 Myn eritage is maad as a lioun in the wode to me; it yaf vois ayens me, therfor Y hate it.

9 Whether myn eritage is a brid of dyuerse colours to me? whether it is a brid died thorou out? Alle beestis of the feeld, come ye, be ye gaderid togidere; haste ye for to deuoure.

10 Many scheepherdis distrieden my vyner, defouliden my part, yauen my desirable porcioun in to desert of wildirnesse;

11 thei settiden it in to scateryng, and it mourenyde on me; al the lond is desolat bi desolacioun, for noon is that ayenthenkith in herte.

12 Alle distrieris of the lond camen on alle the weies of desert, for the swerd of the Lord schal deuoure fro the laste part of the lond 'til to the laste part therof; no pees is to al fleisch.

13 Thei sowiden wheete, and repiden thornes; thei token erytage, and it schal not profite to hem. Ye schulen be schent of youre fruytis, for the wraththe of the stronge veniaunce of the Lord.

14 The Lord seith these thingis ayens alle my worst neiyboris, that touchen the eritage which Y departide to my puple Israel, Lo! Y schal drawe hem out of her lond, and Y schal drawe the hous of Juda out of the myddis of hem.

15 And whanne Y schal drawe out thilke Jewis, Y schal conuerte, and haue merci on hem; and Y schal lede hem ayen, a man to his eritage, and a man in to his lond.

16 And it schal be, if thei 'that ben tauyt lernen the weies of my puple, that thei swere in my name, The Lord lyueth, as thei tauyten my puple to swere in Baal, thei schulen be bildid in the myddis of my puple.

17 That if thei heren not, Y schal drawe out that folk by drawyng out and perdicioun, seith the Lord.

CAP 13

1 The Lord seith these thingis to me, Go, and take in possessioun to thee a lynnun breigirdil; and thou schalt putte it on thi leendis, and thou schalt not bere it in to watir.

2 And Y took in possessioun a breigirdil, bi the word of the Lord; and Y puttide aboute my leendis.

3 And the word of the Lord was maad to me in the secounde tyme,

4 and seide, Take the brigirdil, which thou haddist in possessioun, which is aboute thi leendis; and rise thou, and go to Eufrates, and hide thou it there, in the hoole of a stoon.

5 And Y yede, and hidde it in Eufrates, as the Lord comaundide to me.

6 And it was don aftir ful many daies, the Lord seide to me, Rise thou, and go to Eufrates, and take fro thennus the brigirdil, whiche Y comaundide to thee, that thou schuldist hide it there.

7 And Y yede to Eufrates, and diggide out, and Y took the breigirdil fro the place, where Y hadde hidde it; and lo! the breigirdil was rotun, so that it was not able to ony vss.

8 And the word of the Lord was maad to me,

9 and seide, The Lord seith these thingis, So Y schal make rotun the pride of Juda, and the myche pride of Jerusalem,

10 and this worste puple, that nylen here my wordis, and goen in the schrewidnesse of her herte; and thei yeden aftir alien goddis, to serue hem, and to worschipe hem; and thei schulen be as this breigirdil, which is not able to ony vss.

11 For as a breigirdil cleueth to the leendis of a man, so Y ioynede faste to me al the hous of Israel, and al the hous of Juda, seith the Lord, that thei schulden be to me in to a puple, and in to name, and in to heriyng, and in to glorie; and thei herden not.

12 Therfor thou schalt seie to hem this word, The Lord God of Israel seith these thingis, Ech potel schal be fillid of wyn. And thei schulen seie to thee, Whether we witen not, that ech potel schal be fillid of wyn?

13 And thou schalt seie to hem, The Lord seith these thingis, Lo! Y schal fille with drunkenesse alle the dwelleris of this lond, and the kyngis of the generacioun of Dauith, that sitten on his trone, and the prestis, and profetis, and alle the dwelleris of Jerusalem.

14 And Y schal scatere hem, a man fro his brother, and the fadris and sones togidere, seith the Lord; Y schal not spare, and Y schal not graunte, nether Y schal do mercy, that I leese not hem.

15 Here ye, and perseyue with eeris; nyle ye be reisid, for the Lord spak.

16 Yyue ye glorie to youre Lord God, bifore that it wexe derk, and bifor that youre feet hirte at derk hillis; ye schulen abide liyt, and he schal sette it in to the schadewe of deeth, and in to derknesse.

17 That if ye heren not this, my soule schal wepe in hid place for the face of pride; it wepynge schal wepe, and myn iye shal caste out a teer, for the floc of the Lord is takun.

18 Seye thou to the kyng, and to the ladi, Be ye mekid, sitte ye, for the coroun of youre glorie schal go doun fro youre heed.

19 The cities of the south ben closid, and noon is that openith; al Juda is translatid bi perfit passyng ouere, ether goynge out of her lond.

20 Reise ye youre iyen, and se ye, what men comen fro the north; where is the floc which is youun to thee, thi noble scheep?

21 What schalt thou seie, whanne he schal visite thee? for thou hast tauyt hem ayens thee, and thou hast tauyt ayens thin heed. Whether sorewis han not take thee, as a womman trauelynge of child?

22 That if thou seist in thin herte, Whi camen these thingis to me? for the multitude of thi wickidnesse thi schamefulere thingis ben schewid, thi feet ben defoulid.

23 If a man of Ethiopie mai chaunge his skyn, ether a pard mai chaunge hise dyuersitees, and ye moun do wel, whanne ye han lerned yuel.

24 And Y schal sowe hem abrood, as stobil which is rauyschid of the wynd in desert.

25 This is thi lot, and the part of thi mesure of me, seith the Lord; for thou foryetidist me, and tristidist in a leesyng.

26 Wherfor and Y made nakid thin hipis ayens thi face, and thi schenschipe apperide,

27 thin auowtries, and thin neyyng, and the felonye of thi fornycacioun on litle hillis in the feeld; Y siy thin abhomynaciouns. Jerusalem, wo to thee, thou schalt not be clensid after me til yit.

CAP 14

1 The word of the Lord, that was maad to Jeremye, of the wordis of dryenesse.

2 Jude weilide, and the yatis therof fellen doun, and ben maad derk in erthe, and the cry of Jerusalem stiede.

3 Grettere men senten her lesse men to water; thei camen to drawe watir, and thei foundun no water, thei brouyten ayen her vessels voide; thei weren schent and turmentid,

4 and thei hiliden her heedis for distriyng of the lond, for reyn cam not in the lond. Erthe tilieris weren schent, thei hiliden her heedis.

5 For whi and an hynde caluyde in the feeld, and lefte her calues, for noon eerbe was;

6 and wield assis stoden in rochis, and drowen wynde as dragouns; her iyen failiden, for noon eerbe was.

7 If oure wickidnessis answeren to vs, Lord, do thou for thi name, for oure turnyngis awei ben manye; we han synned ayens thee.

8 Thou abidyng of Israel, the sauyour therof in the tyme of tribulacioun,

9 whi schalt thou be as a comelyng in the lond, and as a weigoere bowynge to dwelle? whi schalt thou be as a man of vnstable dwellyng, as a strong man that mai not saue? Forsothe, Lord, thou art in vs, and thin hooli name is clepid to help on vs; forsake thou not vs.

10 The Lord seith these thingis to this puple, that louede to stire hise feet, and restide not, and pleside not the Lord; now he schal haue mynde on the wickidnesses of hem, and he schal visite the synnes of hem.

11 And the Lord seide to me, Nyle thou preie for this puple in to good.

12 Whanne thei schulen faste, Y schal not here the preieris of hem; and if thei offren brent sacrifices and slayn sacrifices, Y schal not resseyue tho, for Y schal waste hem bi swerd and hungur and pestilence.

13 And Y seide, A! A! A! Lord God, profetis seien to hem, Ye schulen not se swerd, and hungur schal not be in you, but he schal yyue to you veri pees in this place.

14 And the Lord seide to me, The profetis profesien falsli in my name; Y sente not hem, and Y comaundide not to hem, nether Y spak to hem; thei profesien to you a fals reuelacioun, and a gileful dyuynyng, and the disseyuyng of her herte.

15 Therfor the Lord seith these thingis of the profetis that profesien in my name, whiche Y sente not, and seien, Swerd and hungur schal not be in this lond; Tho profetis schulen be wastid bi swerd and hungur.

16 And the puplis, to whiche thei profesieden, schulen be cast forth in the weies of Jerusalem, for hungur and swerd, and noon schal be, that schal birie hem; they and the wyues of hem, the sones and the douytris of hem 'schulen be cast forth; and Y schal schede out on hem her yuel.

17 And thou schalt seie to hem this word, Myn iyen lede doun a teer bi niyt and dai, and be not stille, for the virgyn, the douyter of my puple, is defoulid bi greet defoulying, with the worste wounde greetli.

18 If Y go out to feeldis, lo! men ben slayn bi swerd; and if Y entre in to the citee, lo! men ben maad leene for hungur; also a profete and a prest yeden in to the lond which thei knewen not.

19 Whether thou castynge awei hast cast awei Juda, ether thi soule hath wlatid Sion? whi therfor hast thou smyte vs, so that noon heelthe is? We abididen pees, and no good is; and we abididen time of heeling, and lo! disturbling is.

20 Lord, we han know oure vnfeithfulnessis, and the wickidnessis of oure fadris, for we han synned to thee.

21 Yyue thou not vs in to schenschip, for thi name, nether do thou dispite to vs; haue thou mynde on the seete of thi glorie, make thou not voide thi boond of pees with vs.

22 Whether in grauun ymagis of hethene men ben thei that reynen, ethir heuenes moun yyue reynes? whether thou art not oure Lord God, whom we abididen? For thou madist alle these thingis.

CAP 15

1 And the Lord seide to me, Thouy Moises and Samuel stoden bifore me, my soule is not to this puple; caste thou hem out fro my face, and go thei out.

2 That if thei seien to thee, Whidur schulen we go out? thou schalt seie to hem, The Lord seith these thingis, Thei that to deth, to deth, and thei that to swerd, to swerd, and thei that to hungur, to hungur, and thei that to caitiftee, to caitifte.

3 Y schal visite on hem foure spices, seith the Lord; a swerd to sleeynge, and doggis for to reende, and volatilis of the eir, and beestis of the erthe to deuoure and to distrie.

4 And Y schal yyue hem in to feruour to alle rewmes of erthe, for Manasses, the sone of Ezechie, king of Juda, on alle thingis whiche he dide in Jerusalem.

5 For whi who schal haue merci on thee, Jerusalem, ethir who schal be sori for thee, ether who schal go to preie for thi pees? 6 Thou hast forsake me, seith the Lord, thou hast go abac; and Y schal stretche forth myn hond on thee, and Y schal sle thee; Y trauelide preiyng.

7 And Y schal scatere hem with a wyndewynge instrument in the yatis of erthe; Y killide, and loste my puple, and netheles thei turneden not ayen fro her weies.

8 The widewis therof ben multiplied to me aboue the grauel of the see; and Y brouyte in to hem a distriere in myddai on the modir of a yonge man, Y sente drede sudeynli on citees.

9 Sche was sijk that childide seuene, hir soule failide; the sunne yede doun to hir, whanne dai was yit. Sche was schent, and was aschamed; and Y schal yyue the residue therof in to swerd in the siyt of her enemyes, seith the Lord.

10 Mi modir, wo to me; whi gendridist thou me a man of chidyng, a man of discord in al the lond? Y lente not, nether ony man lente to me; alle men cursen me, the Lord seith.

11 No man bileue to me, if thi remenauntis be not in to good, if Y ranne not to thee in the tyme of turment, and in the tyme of tribulacioun and of anguysch, ayens the enemye.

12 Whether yrun and metal schal be ioyned bi pees to irun fro the north?

13 And Y schal yyue freli thi ritchessis and thi tresouris in to rauyschyng, for alle thi synnes, and in alle thin endis.

14 And Y schal brynge thin enemyes fro the lond which thou knowist not; for fier is kyndlid in my strong veniaunce, and it schal brenne on you.

15 Lord, thou knowist, haue thou mynde on me, and visite me, and delyuere me fro hem that pursuen me; nyle thou take me in thi pacience, knowe thou, that Y suffride schenschipe for thee.

16 Thi wordis ben foundun, and Y eet tho; and thi word was maad to me in to ioye, and in to gladnesse of myn herte; for thi name, Lord God of oostis, is clepid to help on me.

17 Y sat not in the counsel of pleieris, and Y hadde glorie for the face of thin hond; Y sat aloone, for thou fillidist me with bittirnesse.

18 Whi is my sorewe maad euerlastinge, and my wounde dispeirid forsook to be curid? it is maad to me, as a leesyng of vnfeithful watris.

19 For this thing the Lord seith these thingis, If thou turnest, Y schal turne thee, and thou schalt stonde bifore my face; and if thou departist preciouse thing fro vijl thing, thou schalt be as my mouth; thei schulen be turned to thee, and thou schalt not be turned to hem.

20 And Y schal yyue thee in to a brasun wal and strong to this puple, and thei schulen fiyte ayens thee, and schulen not haue the victorie; for Y am with thee, to saue thee, and to delyuere thee, seith the Lord.

21 And Y schal delyuere thee fro the hond of the worste men, and Y schal ayenbie thee fro the hond of stronge men.

CAP 16

1 And the word of the Lord was maad to me,

2 and seide, Thou schalt not take a wijf, and sones and douytris schulen not be to thee in this place.

3 For the Lord seith these thingis on sones and douytris, that ben gendrid in this place, and on the modris of hem, that gendride hem, and on the fadris of hem, of whos generacioun thei ben borun in this lond.

4 Thei schulen die bi dethis of sikenessis, thei schulen not be biweilid, and thei schulen not be biried; thei schulen be in to a dunghil on the face of erthe, and thei schulen be wastid bi swerd and hungur; and the careyn of hem schal be in to mete to the volatilis of heuene, and to beestis of erthe.

5 For the Lord seith these thingis, Entre thou not in to an hous of feeste, nethir go thou to biweile, nether comfourte thou hem; for Y haue take awei my pees fro this puple, seith the Lord, 'Y haue take awei merci and merciful doyngis.

6 And greete and smalle schulen die in this lond; thei schulen not be biried, nethir schulen be biweilid; and thei schulen not kitte hem silf, nethir ballidnesse schal be maad for hem.

7 And thei schulen not breke breed among hem to hym that mourneth, to coumforte on a deed man, and thei schulen not yyue to hem drynk of a cuppe, to coumforte on her fadir and modir.

8 And thou schalt not entre in to the hous of feeste, that thou sitte with hem, and ete, and drynke.

9 For whi the Lord of oostis, God of Israel, seith these thingis, Lo! Y schal take awei fro this place, bifore youre iyen and in youre daies, the vois of ioie, and the vois of gladnesse, and the vois of spouse, and the vois of spousesse.

10 And whanne thou schalt telle alle these wordis to this puple, and thei schulen seie to thee, Whi spak the Lord al this greet yuel on vs? what is oure wickidnesse, ether what is oure synne which we synneden to oure Lord God?

11 thou schalt seie to hem, For youre fadris forsoken me, seith the Lord, and yeden aftir alien goddis, and seruyden hem, and worschipiden hem, and thei forsoken me, and kepten not my lawe.

12 But also ye wrouyten worse than youre fadris; for lo! ech man goith aftir the schrewidnesse of his yuel herte, that he here not me.

13 And Y schal caste you out of this lond, in to the lond which ye and youre fadris knowen not; and ye schulen serue there to alien goddis dai and niyt, whiche schulen not yiue reste to you.

14 Therfor lo! daies comen, seith the Lord, and it schal no more be seid, The Lord lyueth, that ledde the sones of Israel out of the lond of Egipt;

15 but the Lord lyueth, that ledde the sones of Israel fro the lond of the north, and fro alle londis to whiche Y castide hem out; and Y schal lede hem ayen in to her lond which Y yaf to the fadris of hem.

16 Lo! Y schal sende many fischeris to hem, seith the Lord, and thei schulen fische hem; and aftir these thingis Y schal sende many hunteris to hem, and thei schulen hunte hem fro ech mounteyn, and fro ech litil hil, and fro the caues of stoonys.

17 For myn iyen ben on alle the weies of hem; tho weies ben not hid fro my face, and the wickidnesse of hem was not priuy fro myn iyen.

18 And Y schal yelde first the double wickidnessis and synnes of hem, for thei defouliden my lond in the slayn beestis of her idols, and filliden myn eritage with her abhomynaciouns.

19 Lord, my strengthe, and my stalworthnesse, and my refuyt in the dai of tribulacioun, hethene men schulen come to thee fro the fertheste places of erthe, and schulen seie, Verili oure fadris helden a leesyng in possessioun, vanyte that profitide not to hem.

20 Whether a man schal make goddis to hym silf? and tho ben no goddis.

21 Therfor lo! Y schal schewe to hem bi this while, Y schal schewe to hem myn hond, and my vertu; and thei schulen wite, that the name to me is Lord.

CAP 17

1 The synne of Juda is writun with an irone poyntel, in a nail of adamaunt; it is writun on the breede of the herte of hem, and in the hornes of the auteris of hem.

2 Whanne the sones of hem bithenken on her auteris, and woodis, and on the trees ful of boowis, makynge sacrifice in the feld in hiye munteyns,

3 Y schal yyue thi strengthe and alle thi tresouris in to rauyschyng, thin hiye thingis for synnes in alle thin endis.

4 And thou schalt be left aloone fro thin eritage which Y yaf to thee; and Y schal make thee to serue thin enemyes, in the lond which thou knowist not; for thou hast kyndlid fier in my strong veniaunce, it schal brenne til in to with outen ende.

5 The Lord seith these thingis, Cursid is the man that trestith in man, and settith fleisch his arm, and his herte goith awei fro the Lord.

6 For he schal be as bromes in desert, and he schal not se, whanne good schal come; but he schal dwelle in drynesse in desert, in the lond of saltnesse, and vnabitable.

7 Blessid is the man that tristith in the Lord, and the Lord schal be his trist.

8 And he schal be as a tre, which is plauntid ouer watris, which sendith hise rootis to moisture; and it schal not drede, whanne heete schal come; and the leef therof schal be greene, and it schal not be moued in the tyme of drynesse, nether ony tyme it schal faile to make fruyte.

9 The herte of man is schrewid, and 'may not be souyt; who schal knowe it?

10 Y am the Lord sekynge the herte, and preuynge the reynes, and Y yyue to ech man after his weye, and aftir the fruyt of his fyndyngis.

11 A partriche nurschide tho thingis whiche sche bredde not; he made richessis, and not in doom; in the myddis of hise daies he schal forsake tho, and in hise laste tyme he schal be vnwijs.

12 The seete of glorie of hiynesse was at the bigynnyng the place of oure halewyng, the abidyng of Israel.

13 Lord, alle thei that forsaken thee, schulen be schent; thei that goen aweie fro thee, schulen be writun in erthe, for thei han forsake the Lord, a veyne of quyk watirs.

14 Lord, heele thou me, and Y schal be heelid; make thou me saaf, and Y schal be saaf; for thou art myn heriyng.

15 Lo! thei seien to me, Where is the word of the Lord? come it.

16 And Y am not disturblid, suynge thee scheepherd, and Y desiride not the dai of man, thou woost. That that yede out of my lippis was riytful in thi siyt.

17 Be thou not to drede to me; thou art myn hope in the dai of turment.

18 Be thei schent, that pursuen me, and be Y not schent; drede thei, and drede not Y; brynge in on hem a dai of turment, and defoule thou hem bi double defouling.

19 The Lord seith these thingis to me, Go thou, and stonde in the yate of the sones of the puple, bi whiche the kingis of Juda entren and goen out, and in alle the yatis of Jerusalem.

20 And thou schalt seie to hem, Here the word of the Lord, ye kingis of Juda, and al Judee, and alle the dwelleris of Jerusalem, that entren bi these yatis.

21 The Lord God seith these thingis, Kepe ye youre soulis, and nyle ye bere birthuns in the dai of sabat, nether bringe in bi the yatis of Jerusalem.

22 And nyle ye caste birthuns out of youre housis in the dai of sabat, and ye schulen not do ony werk; halewe ye the dai of sabat, as Y comaundide to youre fadris.

23 And thei herden not, nether bowiden doun her eere, but thei maden hard her nol, that thei schulden not here me, and that thei schulden not take chastisyng.

24 And it schal be, if ye heren me, seith the Lord, that ye bere not in birthuns bi the yatis of this citee in the dai of sabat, and if ye halewen the dai of sabat, that ye do not werk ther ynne,

25 kingis and princes sittynge on the seete of Dauid schulen entre bi the yatis of this citee, and stiynge in charis and horsis; thei, and the princis of hem, the men of Juda, and the dwelleris of Jerusalem; and this citee schal be enhabitid withouten ende.

26 And thei schulen come fro the citees of Juda, and fro the cumpas of Jerusalem, and fro the lond of Beniamyn, and fro feeldi places, and fro hilli places, and fro the south, beringe brent sacrifice, and slayn sacrifice, and encense; and thei schulen bringe offring in to the hous of the Lord.

27 Forsothe if ye heren not me, that ye halewe the dai of sabat, and that ye bere not a birthun, and that ye bringe not in bi the yatis of Jerusalem in the dai of sabat, Y schal kyndle fier in the yatis therof; and it schal deuoure the housis of Jerusalem, and it schal not be quenchid.

CAP 18

1 The word that was maad of the Lord to Jeremye,

2 and seide, Rise thou, and go doun in to the hous of a pottere, and there thou schalt here my wordis.

3 And Y yede doun in to the hous of a pottere, and lo! he made a werk on a wheel.

4 And the vessel was distried, which he made of clei with hise hondis; and he turnede it, and made it another vessel, as it pleside in hise iyen to make.

5 And the word of the Lord was maad to me,

6 and he seide, Whether as this pottere doith, Y mai not do to you, the hous of Israel? seith the Lord. Lo! as cley is in the hond of a pottere, so ye, the hous of Israel, ben in myn hond.

7 Sudenli Y schal speke ayens a folk, and ayens a rewme, that Y drawe out, and distrie, and leese it.

8 If thilke folk doith penaunce of his yuel, which Y spak ayens it, also Y schal do penaunce on the yuel, which Y thouyte to do to it.

9 And Y schal speke sudenli of a folk, and of a rewme, that Y bilde, and plaunte it.

10 If it doith yuel bifore myn iyen, that it here not my vois, Y schal do penaunce on the good which Y spak, that Y schulde do to it.

11 Now therfor seie thou to a man of Juda, and to the dwellere of Jerusalem, and seie, The Lord seith these thingis, Lo! Y make yuel ayens you, and Y thenke a thouyte ayens you; ech man turne ayen fro his yuel weie, and dresse ye youre weies and youre studies.

12 Whiche seiden, We han dispeirid, for we schulen go after oure thouytis, and we schulen do ech man the schrewidnesse of his yuel herte.

13 Therfor the Lord seith these thingis, Axe ye hethene men, who herde siche orible thingis, whiche the virgyn of Israel hath do greetli?

14 Whether snow of the Liban schal fail fro the stoon of the feeld? ether coolde watris brekynge out, and fletynge doun moun be takun awei?

15 For my puple hath foryete me, and offriden sacrifices in veyn, and snaperiden in her weies, and in the pathis of the world, that thei yeden bi tho in a weie not trodun;

16 that the lond of hem schulde be in to desolacioun, and in to an hissyng euerlastinge; for whi ech that passith bi it, schal be astonyed, and schal moue his heed.

17 As a brennynge wynd Y schal scatere hem bifor the enemy; Y schal schewe to hem the bak and not the face, in the dai of the perdicioun of hem.

18 And thei seiden, Come ye, and thenke we thouytis ayens Jeremye; for whi the lawe schal not perische fro a preest, nether councel schal perische fro a wijs man, nether word schal perische fro a profete; come ye, and smyte we hym with tunge, and take we noon heede to alle the wordis of hym.

19 Lord, yyue thou tent to me, and here thou the vois of myn aduersaries.

20 Whether yuel is yoldun for good, for thei han diggid a pit to my soule; haue thou mynde, that Y stoode in thi siyt, to speke good for hem, and to turne awei thin indignacioun fro hem.

21 Therfor yyue thou the sones of hem in to hungur, and lede forth hem in to the hondis of swerd; the wyues of hem be maad with out children, and be maad widewis, and the hosebondis of hem be slayn bi deth; the yonge men of hem be persid togidere bi swerd in batel.

22 Cry be herd of the housis of hem, for thou schalt bringe sudenli a theef on hem; for thei diggiden a pit to take me, and hidden snaris to my feet.

23 But thou, Lord, knowist al the councel of hem ayens me in to deth; do thou not merci to the wickidnesse of hem, and the synne of hem be not doon awei fro thi face; be thei maad fallynge doun in thi siyt, in the tyme of thi stronge veniaunce; vse thou hem to othir thing than thei weren ordeyned.

CAP 19

1 The Lord seith these thingis, Go thou, and take an erthene potel of a pottere, of the eldre men of the puple, and of the eldre men of preestis.

2 And go thou out to the valei of the sones of Ennon, which is bisidis the entring of the erthene yate; and there thou schalt preche the wordis whiche Y schal speke to thee;

3 and thou schalt seie, Kyngis of Juda, and the dwelleris of Jerusalem, here ye the word of the Lord. The Lord of oostis, God of Israel, seith these thingis, Lo! Y schal bringe in turment on this place, so that ech man that herith it, hise eeris tyngle.

4 For thei han forsake me, and maad alien this place, and offriden sacrifices to alien goddis ther ynne, whiche thei, and the fadris of hem, and the kingis of Juda, knewen not; and thei filliden this place with the blood of innocentis,

5 and bildiden hiy thingis to Baalym, to brenne her sones in fier, in to brent sacrifice to Baalym; whiche thingis Y comaundide not, nether spak, nether tho stieden in to myn herte.

6 Therfor the Lord seith, Lo! daies comen, and this place schal no more be clepid Tophet, and the valei of the sone of Ennon, but the valei of sleyng.

7 And Y schal distrie the councel of Juda and of Jerusalem in this place, and Y schal distrie hem bi swerd, in the siyt of her enemyes, and in the hond of men sekynge the lyues of hem; and Y schal yyue her deed bodies mete to the briddis of the eir, and to beestis of erthe.

8 And Y schal sette this citee in to wondring, and in to hissing; ech that passith bi it, schal wondre, and hisse on al the veniaunce therof.

9 And Y schal feede hem with the fleischis of her sones, and with the fleischis of her douytris; and ech man schal ete the fleischis of his frend in the bisegyng and angwisch, in which the enemyes of hem, and thei that seken the lyues of hem, schulen close hem togidere.

10 And thou schalt al to-breke the potel bifore the iyen of the men, that schulen go with thee.

11 And thou schalt seie to hem, The Lord of oostis seith these thingis, So Y schal al to-breke this puple, and this citee, as the vessel of a pottere is al to-brokun, which mai no more be restorid; and thei schulen be biried in Tophet, for noon other place is to birie.

12 So Y schal do to this place, seith the Lord, and to dwelleris therof, that Y sette this citee as Tophet.

13 And the housis of Jerusalem, and the housis of the kingis of Juda, schulen be as the place of Tophet; alle the vncleene housis, in whose roouys thei sacrifieden to al the chyualrie of heuene, and offriden moist sacrifices to alien goddis.

14 Forsothe Jeremye cam fro Tophet, whidur the Lord hadde sente hym for to profesie; and he stood in the porche of the hous of the Lord,

15 and seide to al the puple, The Lord of oostis, God of Israel, seith these thingis, Lo! Y schal bringe in on this citee, and on alle the citees therof, alle the yuelis whiche Y spak ayens it; for thei maden hard her nol, that thei herden not my wordis.

CAP 20

1 And Phassur, the sone of Emyner, the preest, that was ordeyned prince in the hous of the Lord, herde Jeremye profesiynge these wordis.

2 And Phassur smoot Jeremye, the profete, and sente hym in to the stockis, that weren in the hiyere yate of Beniamyn, in the hous of the Lord.

3 And whanne it was cleer in the morewe, Phassur ledde Jeremye out of the stockis. And Jeremye seide to hym, The Lord clepide not Phassur thi name, but Drede on ech side.

4 For the Lord seith these thingis, Lo! Y schal yyue thee and alle thi freendis in to drede, and thei schulen falle doun bi the swerd of her enemyes; and thin iyen schulen se; and Y schal yyue al Juda in the hond of the king of Babiloyne, and he schal lede hem ouer in to Babiloyne, and he schal smyte hem bi swerd.

5 And Y schal yyue al the catel of this citee, and al the trauel therof, and al the prijs; and Y schal yyue alle the tresours of the kingis of Juda in the hond of her enemyes; and thei schulen rauysche tho, and schulen take, and lede forth in to Babiloyne.

6 Forsothe thou, Phassur, and alle the dwelleris of thin hous, schulen go in to caitifte; and thou schalt come in to Babiloyne, and thou schalt die there; and thou schalt be biried there, thou and alle thi freendis, to whiche thou profesiedist a leesyng.

7 Lord, thou disseyuedist me, and Y am disseyued; thou were strongere than Y, and thou haddist the maistrie; Y am maad in to scorn al dai.

8 Alle men bymowen me, for now a while ago Y speke criynge wickidnesse, and Y criede distriynge. And the word of the Lord is maad to me in to schenschip, and in to scorn al dai.

9 And Y seide, Y schal not haue mynde on hym, and Y schal no more speke in his name. And the word of the Lord was maad, as fier swalynge in myn herte, and cloosid in my boonys; and Y failide, not suffryng to bere.

10 For Y herde dispisyngis of many men, and drede in cumpas, Pursue ye, and pursue we hym, of alle men that weren pesible to me, and kepynge my side; if in ony maner he be disseyued, and we haue the maistrie ayens hym, and gete veniaunce of hym.

11 Forsothe the Lord as a stronge werriour is with me, therfor thei that pursuen me schulen falle, and schulen be sijk; and thei schulen be schent greetli, for thei vndurstoden not euerlastynge schenschip, that schal neuere be don awei.

12 And thou, Lord of oostis, the preuere of a iust man, which seest the reynes and herte, Y biseche, se Y thi veniaunce of hem; for Y haue schewid my cause to thee.

13 Synge ye to the Lord, herie ye the Lord, for he delyueride the soule of a pore man fro the hond of yuel men.

14 Cursid be the dai where ynne Y was borun, the dai where ynne my modir childide me, be not blessid.

15 Cursid be the man, that telde to my fadir, and seide, A knaue child is borun to thee, and made hym glad as with ioye.

16 Thilke man be as the citees ben, whiche the Lord distriede, and it repentide not hym;

17 he that killide not me fro the wombe, here cry eerli, and yellynge in the tyme of myddai; that my modir were a sepulcre to me, and hir wombe were euerlastinge conseyuyng.

18 Whi yede Y out of the wombe, that Y schulde se trauel and sorewe, and that mi daies schulen be waastid in schenschipe?

CAP 21

1 The word which was maad of the Lord to Jeremye, whanne king Sedechie sente to hym Phassur, the sone of Helchie, and Sofonye, the preest, the sone of Maasie, and seide,

2 Axe thou the Lord for vs, for Nabugodonosor, the kyng of Babiloyne, fiytith ayens vs; if in hap the Lord do with vs bi alle hise merueilis, and he go awei fro vs.

3 And Jeremye seide to hem, Thus ye schulen seie to Sedechie,

4 The Lord God of Israel seith these thingis, Lo! Y schal turne the instrumentis of batel that ben in youre hondis, and with which ye fiyten ayens the king of Babiloyne, and ayens Caldeis, that bisegen you in the cumpas of wallis; and Y schal gadere tho togidere in the myddis of this citee.

5 And Y schal ouercome you in hond stretchid forth, and in strong arm, and in stronge veniaunce, and indignacioun, and in greet wraththe;

6 and Y schal smyte the dwelleris of this citee, men and beestis schulen die bi greet pestilence.

7 And after these thingis, seith the Lord, Y schal yyue Sedechie, kyng of Juda, and hise seruauntis, and his puple, and that ben left in this citee fro pestilence, and swerd, and hungur, in the hond of Nabugodonosor, kyng of Babiloyne, and in the hond of her enemyes, and in the hond of men sekynge the lijf of hem; and he schal smyte hem bi the scharpnesse of swerd; and he schal not be bowid, nether schal spare, nether schal haue mercy.

8 And thou schalt seie to this puple, The Lord God seith these thingis, Lo! Y yyue bifore you the weie of lijf, and the weie of deth.

9 He that dwellith in this citee, schal die bi swerd, and hungur, and pestilence; but he that goith out, and fleeth ouer to Caldeis that bisegen you, schal lyue, and his lijf schal be as a prey to hym.

10 For Y haue set my face on this citee in to yuel, and not in to good, seith the Lord; it schal be youun in the hond of the king of Babiloyne, and he schal brenne it with fier.

11 And thou schalt seie to the hous of the king of Juda, the hous of Dauid, Here ye the word of the Lord.

12 The Lord seith these thingis, Deme ye eerli doom, and delyuere ye hym that is oppressid bi violence fro the hond of the fals chalenger; lest perauenture myn indignacioun go out as fier, and be kyndlid, and noon be that quenche, for the malice of youre studies.

13 Lo! Y to thee, dwelleresse of the sad valei and pleyn, seith the Lord, which seien, Who schal smyte vs, and who schal entre in to oure housis?

14 And Y schal visite on you bi the fruyt of youre studies, seith the Lord; and Y schal kyndle fier in the forest therof, and it schal deuoure alle thingis in the cumpas therof.

CAP 22

1 The Lord seith these thingis, Go thou doun in to the hous of the kyng of Juda, and thou schalt speke there this word, and schalt seie,

2 Thou kyng of Juda, that sittist on the seete of Dauid, here the word of the Lord, thou, and thi seruauntis, and thi puple, that entren bi these yatis.

3 The Lord seith these thingis, Do ye doom, and riytfulnesse, and delyuere ye hym that is oppressid bi violence fro the hond of the fals chalenger; and nyle ye make sori, nether oppresse ye wickidli a comelyng, and a fadirles child, and a widewe, and schede ye not out innocent blood in this place.

4 For if ye doynge don this word, kyngis of the kyn of Dauid sittynge on his trone schulen entre bi the yatis of this hous, and schulen stie on charis and horsis, thei, and the seruauntis, and the puple of hem.

5 That if ye heren not these wordis, Y swoore in my silf, seith the Lord, that this hous schal be in to wildirnesse.

6 For the Lord seith these thingis on the hous of the kyng of Juda, Galaad, thou art to me the heed of the Liban; credence be not youun to me, if Y sette not thee a wildirnesse, citees vnhabitable.

7 And Y schal halewe on thee a man sleynge, and hise armuris; and thei schulen kitte doun thi chosun cedris, and schulen caste doun in to fier.

8 And many folkis schulen passe bi this citee, and ech man schal seie to his neiybore, Whi dide the Lord thus to this greet citee?

9 And thei schulen answere, For thei forsoken the couenaunt of her Lord God, and worschipiden alien goddis, and serueden hem.

10 Nyle ye biwepe hym that is deed, nether weile ye on hym bi wepyng; biweile ye hym that goith out, for he schal no more turne ayen, nether he schal se the lond of his birthe.

11 For the Lord seith these thingis to Sellum, the sone of Josie, the kyng of Juda, that regnede for Josye, his fadir, He that yede out of this place, schal no more turne ayen hidur;

12 but in the place to which Y translatide him, there he schal die, and he schal no more se this lond.

13 Wo to him that bildith his hous in vnriytfulnesse, and his soleris not in doom; he schal oppresse his freend in veyn, and he schal not yelde his hire to hym.

14 Which seith, Y schal bilde to me a large hous, and wide soleris; which openeth wyndows to hym silf, and makith couplis of cedre, and peyntith with reed colour.

15 Whether thou schalt regne, for thou comparisonest thee to a cedre? whether thi fadir eet not, and drank, and dide doom and riytfulnesse thanne, whanne it was wel to hym?

16 He demyde the cause of a pore man, and nedi, in to his good; whether not therfor for he knew me? seith the Lord.

17 Forsothe thin iyen and herte ben to aueryce, and to schede innocent blood, and to fals caleng, and to the perfourmyng of yuel werk.

18 Therfor the Lord seith these thingis to Joachym, the sone of Josie, the kyng of Juda, Thei schulen not biweile hym, Wo brother! and wo sistir! thei schulen not sowne togidere to hym, Wo lord! and wo noble man!

19 He schal be biried with the biriyng of an asse, he schal be rotun, and cast forth without the yatis of Jerusalem.

20 Stie thou on the Liban, and cry thou, and yyue thi vois in Basan, and cry to hem that passen forth, for alle thi louyeris ben al to-brokun.

21 Y spak to thee in thi plentee, and thou seidist, Y schal not here; this is thi weie fro thi yongthe, for thou herdist not my vois.

22 Wynd schal feede alle thi scheepherdis, and thi louyeris schulen go in to caitifte;

23 and thanne thou that sittist in the Liban, and makist nest in cedris, schalt be schent, and be aschamed of al thi malice. Hou weilidist thou, whanne sorewis weren comun to thee, as the sorew of a womman trauelynge of child?

24 I lyue, seith the Lord, for thouy Jeconye, the sone of Joachym, kyng of Juda, were a ring in my riyt hond, fro thennus Y schal drawe awei hym.

25 And Y schal yyue thee in the hond of hem that seken thi lijf, and in the hond of hem whos face thou dredist, and in the hond of Nabugodonosor, kyng of Babiloyne, and in the hond of Caldeis.

26 And Y schal sende thee, and thi moder that gendride thee, in to an alien lond, in which ye weren not borun, and there ye schulen die;

27 and thei schulen not turne ayen in to the lond, to which thei reisen her soule, that thei turne ayen thidur.

28 Whether this man Jeconye is an erthene vessel, and al to-brokun? whether a vessel withouten al likyng? Whi ben he and his seed cast awei, and cast forth in to a lond which thei knewen not?

29 Erthe, erthe, erthe, here thou the word of the Lord.

30 The Lord seith these thingis, Write thou this man bareyn, a man that schal not haue prosperite in hise daies; for of his seed schal be no man, that schal sitte on the seete of Dauid, and haue powere ferthere in Juda.

CAP 23

1 Wo to the scheepherdis, that scateren and to-drawen the floc of my lesewe, seith the Lord.

2 Therfor the Lord God of Israel seith these thingis to the scheepherdis, that feeden my puple, Ye han scaterid my floc, and han cast hem out, and han not visitid hem; lo! Y schal visite on you the malice of youre studies, seith the Lord.

3 And Y schal gadere togidere the remenauntis of my floc fro alle londis, to whiche Y schal caste hem out thidur; and Y schal turne hem to her feeldis, and thei schulen encreesse, and schulen be multiplied.

4 And Y schal reise schepherdis on hem, and thei schulen feede hem; thei schulen no more drede, and schulen not be aferd; and noon schal be souyt of the noumbre seith the Lord.

5 Lo! daies comen, seith the Lord, and Y schal reise a iust buriownyng to Dauid; and he schal regne a kyng, and he schal be wijs, and he schal make doom and riytfulnesse in erthe.

6 In tho daies Juda schal be sauid, and Israel schal dwelle tristili; and this is the name which thei schulen clepe hym, The Lord oure riytful.

7 For this thing lo! daies comen, seith the Lord, and thei schulen no more seie, The Lord lyueth, that ledde the sones of Israel out of the lond of Egipt;

8 but, The Lord lyueth, that ledde out, and brouyte the seed of the hous of Israel fro the lond of the north, and fro alle londis to whiche Y hadde cast hem out thidur; and thei schulen dwelle in her lond.

9 To the prophetis; Myn herte is contrit in the myddis of me, alle my boonys trembliden togidere; Y am maad as a man drunkun, and as a man weet of wyn, of the face of the Lord, and of the face of the hooli wordis of hym;

10 for the lond is fillid with auowteris. For the erthe mourenede of the face of cursyng; the feeldis of desert ben maad drie, the cours of hem is maad yuel, and her strengthe is vnlijk.

11 For whi the profete and the prest ben defoulid; and in myn hous, seith the Lord, Y foond the yuel of hem.

12 Therfor the weie of hem schal be as slidur in derknessis, for thei schulen be hurtlid, and schulen falle doun therynne; for Y schal bringe on hem yuels, the yeer of visitacioun of hem, seith the Lord.

13 And in the profetis of Samarie Y siy fonnednesse, and thei profesieden in Baal, and disseyueden my puple Israel.

14 And in the profetis of Jerusalem Y siy licnesse, auoutrie, and the weie of leesyng; and thei confortiden the hondis of the worste men, that ech man schulde not conuerte fro his malice; alle thei ben maad as Sodom to me, and alle the dwellers therof 'ben maad as Gommorre.

15 Therfor the Lord of oostis seith these thingis to the prophetis, Lo! Y schal feed hem with wermod, and Y schal yyue drynke to hem with galle; for whi defoulyng is goen out of the profetis of Jerusalem on al the lond.

16 The Lord of oostis seith these thingis, Nyle ye here the wordis of profetis, that profesien to you, and disseyuen you; thei speken the visioun of her herte, not of the mouth of the Lord.

17 Thei seien to hem that blasfemen me, The Lord spak, Pees schal be to you; and thei seiden to ech man that goith in the schrewidnesse of his herte, Yuel schal not come on you.

18 For whi who is present in the councel of the Lord, and siy, and herde his word? who bihelde, and herde the word of hym?

19 Lo! the whirlewynd of the Lordis indignacioun schal go out, and tempest brekynge schal come on the heed of wickid men.

20 The strong veniaunce of the Lord schal not turne ayen, til that he do, and til that he fille the thouyt of his herte. In the laste daies ye schulen vndurstonde the councel of hym.

21 Y sente not the profetis, and thei runnen; Y spak not to hem, and thei profesieden.

22 If thei hadden stonde in my councel, and hadde maad knowun my wordis to my puple, forsothe Y hadde turned hem awei fro her yuel weie, and fro her worste thouytis.

23 Gessist thou, whether Y am God of niy, seith the Lord, and not God afer?

24 A man schal not be priuy in hid places, and Y schal not se hym, seith the Lord. Whether Y fille not heuene and erthe? seith the Lord.

25 Y herde what thingis the profetis seiden, profesiynge a leesyng in my name, and seiynge, Y dremede dremes.

26 Hou longe is this thing in the herte of profetis, profesiynge a leesyng, and profesiynge the disseite of her herte?

27 Whiche wolen make, that my puple foryete my name for the dremes of hem, which ech man tellith to his neiybore, as the fadris of hem foryaten my name for Baal.

28 A profete that hath a dreme, telle a dreem; and he that hath my word, speke verili my word. What is with chaffis to the wheete? seith the Lord.

29 Whether my wordis ben not as fier brennynge, seith the Lord, and as an hamer al to-brekynge a stoon?

30 Therfor lo! Y am redi to the profetis, seith the Lord, that stelen my wordis, ech man fro his neiybore.

31 Lo! Y to the profetis, seith the Lord, that taken her tungis, and seien, The Lord seith.

32 Lo! Y to the profetis, dremynge a leesyng, seith the Lord; which telden tho, and disseyueden my puple in her leesyng, and in her myraclis, whanne Y hadde not sente hem, nether hadde comaundide to hem; whiche profitiden no thing to this puple, seith the Lord.

33 Therfor if this puple, ether profete, ether prest, axith thee, and seith, What is the birthun of the Lord? thou schalt seie to hem, Ye ben the birthun, for Y schal caste you awei, seith the Lord;

34 and a profete, and a prest, and the puple, that seith, The birthun of the Lord, Y schal visite on that man, and on his hous.

35 Ye schulen seie these thingis, ech man to his neiybore, and to his brother, What answeride the Lord? and what spak the Lord?

36 For the birthun of the Lord schal no more be remembrid, and the word of ech man schal be birthun to hym; and ye han

peruertid the wordis of lyuynge God, of the Lord of oostis, youre God.

37 Thou schalt seie these thingis to the profete, What answeride the Lord to thee? and what spak the Lord?

38 Forsothe if ye seien, The birthin of the Lord, for this thing the Lord seith these thingis, For ye seiden this word, The birthun of the Lord, and Y sente to you, and Y seide, Nyle ye seie, The birthun of the Lord; therfor lo!

39 Y schal take you awei, and schal bere, and Y schal forsake you, and the citee which Y yaf to you, and to youre fadris, fro my face.

40 And Y schal yyue you in to euerlastynge schenschipe, and in to euerlastynge sclaundir, that schal neuere be doon awei bi foryetyng.

CAP 24

1 The Lord schewide to me, and lo! twei panyeris ful of figys weren set bifor the temple of the Lord, aftir that Nabug-odonosor, kyng of Babiloyne, translatide Jeconye, the sone of Joachym, the kyng of Juda, and the princes of hym, and a sutil crafti man, and a goldsmith fro Jerusalem, and brouyte hem in to Babiloyne.

2 And o panyere hadde ful good figis, as figis of the firste tyme ben wont to be; and o panyere hadde ful yuel figis, that miyten not be etun, for tho weren yuel figis.

3 And the Lord seide to me, Jeremye, what thing seest thou? And Y seide, Figis, goode figis, ful goode, and yuele figis, ful yuele, that moun not be etun, for tho ben yuele figis.

4 And the word of the Lord was maad to me,

5 and seide, The Lord God of Israel seith these thingis, As these figis ben goode, so Y schal knowe the transmygracioun of Juda, which I sente out fro this place in to the lond of Caldeis, in to good.

6 And Y schal sette myn iyen on hem to plese, and Y schal brynge hem ayen in to this lond; and Y schal bilde hem, and Y schal not distrie hem; and Y schal plaunte hem, and Y schal not drawe vp bi the roote.

7 And Y schal yyue to hem an herte, that thei knowe me, for Y am the Lord; and thei schulen be in to a puple to me, and Y schal be in to God to hem, for thei schulen turne ayen to me in al her herte.

8 And as the worste figis ben, that moun not be etun, for tho ben yuele figis, the Lord seith these thingis, So Y schal yyue Sedechie, the kyng of Juda, and the princes of hym, and other men of Jerusalem, that dwelliden in this citee, and that dwellen in the lond of Egipt.

9 And Y schal yyue hem into trauelyng and turment in alle rewmes of erthe, in to schenschipe, and in to parable, and in to a prouerbe, and in to cursyng, in alle places to whiche Y castide hem out.

10 And Y schal sende in hem a swerd, and hungur, and pesti-lence, til thei be wastid fro the lond which Y yaf to hem, and to the fadris of hem.

CAP 25

1 The word of the Lord, that was maad to Jeremye, of al the puple of Juda, in the fourthe yeer of Joachym, the sone of Josie, the king of Juda, aftir that Jeconye was translatid in to Babiloyne; thilke is the firste yeer of Nabugodonosor, kyng of Babiloyne; which word Jeremy,

2 the prophete, spak to al the puple of Juda, and to alle the dwelleris of Jerusalem, and seide,

3 Fro the threttenthe yeer of the rewme of Josie, the sone of Amon, the kyng of Juda, 'til to this dai, this is the three and twentithe yeer, the word of the Lord was maad to me; and Y spak to you, and Y roos bi niyt and spak, and ye herden not.

4 And the Lord sente to you alle hise seruauntis profetis, and roos ful eerli, and sente, and ye herden not, nether ye bowiden youre eeris, for to here;

5 whanne he seide, Turne ye ayen, ech man fro his yuel weie, and fro youre worste thouytis, and ye schulen dwelle in the lond whiche the Lord yaf to you, and to youre fadris, fro the world and til in to the world.

6 And nyle ye go aftir alien goddis, that ye serue hem, and worschipe hem, nether terre ye me to wrathfulnesse, in the werkis of youre hondis, and Y schal not turmente you.

7 And ye herden not me, seith the Lord, that ye terreden me to wrathfulnesse in the werkis of youre hondis, in to youre yuel.

8 Therfor the Lord of oostis seith these thingis, For that that ye herden not my wordis, lo!

9 Y schal sende, and take alle the kynredis of the north, seith the Lord, and Nabugodonosor, my seruaunt, the kyng of Babiloyne; and Y schal bringe hem on this lond, and on the dwelleris therof, and on alle naciouns, that ben in the cumpas therof; and Y schal sle hem, and Y schal sette hem in to won-dryng, and in to hissyng, and in to euerlastynge wildirnessis.

10 And Y schal leese of hem the vois of ioye, and the vois of gladnesse, the vois of spouse, and the vois of spousesse, the vois of queerne, and the liyt of the lanterne.

11 And al the lond therof schal be in to wildirnesse, and in to wondring; and alle these folkis schulen serue the king of Babiloyne seuenti yeer.

12 And whanne seuenti yeer ben fillid, Y schal visite on the kyng of Babiloyne, and on that folc the wickidnesse of hem, seith the Lord, and on the lond of Caldeis, and Y schal set it in to euerlastynge wildirnesses.

13 And Y schal brynge on that lond alle my wordis whiche Y spak ayens it, al thing that is writun in this book; what euer thingis Jeremye profeside ayens alle folkis;

14 for thei serueden to hem, whanne thei weren many folkis, and grete kingis; and Y schal yelde to hem aftir the werkis of hem, and aftir the dedis of her hondis.

15 For the Lord of oostis, God of Israel, seith thus, Take thou the cuppe of wyn of this woodnesse fro myn hond, and thou schal birle therof to alle hethene men, to whiche Y schal sende thee.

16 And thei schulen drynke, and schulen be disturblid, and schulen be woode of the face of swerd, which Y schal sende among hem.

17 And Y took the cuppe fro the hond of the Lord, and Y birlide to alle folkis, to whiche the Lord sente me;

18 to Jerusalem, and to alle the citees of Juda, and to the kyn-gis therof, and to the princes therof; that Y schulde yyue hem in to wildirnesse, and in to wondring, and in to hissyng, and in to cursing, as this dai is; to Farao,

19 the king of Egipt, and to hise seruauntis, and to hise princes, and to al hise puple;

20 and to alle men generali, to alle the kyngis of the lond Ansitidis, and to alle the kyngis of the lond of Filistiym, and to Ascalon, and to Gaza, and to Acoron, and to the residues of Azotus;

21 to Idumee, and to Moab, and to the sones of Amon;

22 and to alle the kyngis of Tirus, and to alle the kingis of Sidon, and to the kingis of the lond of ilis that ben biyendis the see;

23 and to Dedan, and Theman, and Buz, and to alle men that ben clippid on the long heer;

24 and to alle the kingis of Arabie, and to alle the kingis of the west, that dwellen in desert;

25 and to alle the kingis of Zambri, and to alle the kingis of Elam, and to alle the kyngis of Medeis; and to alle the kingis of the north,

26 of niy and of fer, to ech man ayens his brothir; and to alle the rewmes of erthe, that ben on the face therof; and kyng Sesac schal drynke after hem.

27 And thou schalt seie to hem, The Lord of oostis, God of Israel, seith these thingis, Drynke ye, and be ye drunkun, and spue ye, and falle ye doun, and nyle ye rise fro the face of swerd which Y schal sende among you.

28 And whanne thei nylen take the cuppe fro thin hond, that thei drynke, thou schalt seie to hem, The Lord of oostis seith these thingis, Ye drynkynge schulen drynke;

29 for lo! in the citee in which my name is clepid to help, Y bigynne to turmente, and schulen ye as innocentis be with out peyne? ye schulen not be with out peyne, for Y clepe swerd on alle the dwelleris of erthe, seith the Lord of oostis.

30 And thou schalt profesie to hem alle these wordis, and thou schalt seie to hem, The Lord schal rore fro an hiy, and fro his hooli dwellyng place he schal yyue his vois; he rorynge schal rore on his fairnesse; a myry song, as of men tredynge in pressouris, schal be sungun ayens alle dwelleris of erthe.

31 Sown is comun til to the laste partis of erthe, for whi doom is to the Lord with folkis, he is demed with ech fleisch; the Lord seith, Y haue youe wickid men to the swerd.

32 The Lord of oostis seith these thingis, Lo! turment schal go out fro folk in to folk, and a greet whirlwynd schal go out fro the endis of erthe.

33 And the slayn men of the Lord schulen be in that dai fro the ende of the erthe 'til to the ende therof; thei schulen not be biweilid, nether schulen be gaderid togidere, nether schulen be biried; thei schulen ligge in to a dunghil on the face of erthe.

34 Yelle, ye scheepherdis, and crye, and, ye princypals of the floc, bispreynge you with aische; for youre daies ben fillid, that ye be slayn, and youre scateryngis ben fillid, and ye schulen falle as precious vessels.

35 And fleyng schal perische fro scheepherdis, and sauyng schal perische fro the principals of the floc.

36 The vois of the crye of scheepherdis, and the yellyng of the principals of the floc, for the Lord hath wastid the lesewis of hem.

37 And the feeldis of pees weren stille, for the face of wrath-the of the strong veniaunce of the Lord.

38 He as a lion hath forsake his tabernacle, for the lond of hem is maad in to desolacioun, of the face of wraththe of the culuer, and of the face of wraththe of the strong veniaunce of the Lord.

CAP 26

1 In the bigynnyng of the rewme of Joachym, the sone of Josie, kyng of Juda, this word was maad of the Lord, and seide,

2 The Lord seide these thingis, Stonde thou in the porche of the hous of the Lord, and thou schalt speke to alle the citees of Juda, fro whiche thei comen for to worschipe in the hous of the Lord, alle the wordis whiche Y comaundide to thee, that thou speke to hem; nyle thou withdrawe a word;

3 if perauenture thei heren, and ben conuertid, ech man fro his yuele weie, and it repente me of the yuel which Y thouyte to do to hem for the malices of her studies.

4 And thou schalt seie to hem, The Lord seith these thingis, If ye heren not me, that ye go in my law which Y yaf to you,

5 that ye here the wordis of my seruauntis, profetis, whiche Y risynge bi niyte, and dressynge, sente to you, and ye herden not;

6 Y schal yyue this hous as Silo, and Y schal yyue this citee in to cursyng to alle folkis of erthe.

7 And the prestis, and profetis, and al the puple herden Jere-mye spekynge these wordis in the hous of the Lord.

8 And whanne Jeremye hadde fillid spekynge alle thingis, whiche the Lord hadde comaundid to hym, that he schulde speke to al the puple, the prestis, and profetis, and al the puple token hym, and seiden, Die he bi deeth;

9 whi profesiede he in the name of the Lord, and seide, This hous schal be as Silo, and this citee schal be desolat, for no dwellere is? And al the puple was gaderid togidere ayens Jer-emye, in the hous of the Lord.

10 And the princes of Juda herden alle these wordis; and thei stieden fro the kyngis hous in to the hous of the Lord, and saten in the entryng of the newe yate of the hous of the Lord.

11 And the prestis and profetis spaken to the princes, and to al the puple, and seiden, Doom of deth is to this man, for he pro-fesiede ayens this citee, as ye herden with youre eeris.

12 And Jeremye seide to alle the princes, and to al the puple, 'and seide, The Lord sente me, that Y schulde prophesie to this hous, and to this citee, alle the wordis whiche ye herden.

13 Now therfor make ye good youre weies, and youre studies, and here ye the vois of youre Lord God; and it schal repente the Lord of the yuel which he spak ayens you.

14 Lo! forsothe Y am in youre hondis; do ye to me, as it is good and riytful bifore youre iyen.

15 Netheles wite ye, and knowe, that if ye sleen me, ye schulen bitraie innocent blood ayens you silf, and ayens this citee, and the dwelleris therof; for in trewthe the Lord sente me to you, that Y schulde speke in youre eeris alle these wor-dis.

16 And the princes and al the puple seiden to the preestis and profetis, Doom of deth is not to this man; for he spak to vs in the name of oure Lord God.

17 Therfor men of the eldere men of the lond rysiden vp, and seiden to al the cumpanye of the puple,

18 and spaken, Mychee of Morasten was a profete in the daies of Ezechie, king of Juda; and he seide to al the puple of Juda, and seide, The Lord of oostis seith these thingis, Sion schal be erid as a feeld, and Jerusalem schal be in to an heep of stoonys, and the hil of the hous of the Lord schal be in to hiy thingis of woodis.

19 Whether Ezechie, kyng of Juda, and al Juda condempnede hym bi deth? Whether thei dredden not the Lord, and bisouyten the face of the Lord? and it repentide the Lord of the yuel which he spak ayens hem. Therfor do we not greet yuel ayens oure soulis.

20 Also Vrye, the sone of Semey, of Cariathiarym, was a man profesiynge in the name of the Lord; and he profesiede ayens this citee, and ayens this lond, bi alle the wordis of Jeremye.

21 And kyng Joachym, and alle the myyti men, and princes of hem, herden these wordis; and the kyng souyte to sle hym; and Vrye herde, and dredde, and he fledde, and entride in to Egipt.

22 And kyng Joachym sente men in to Egipt, Elnathan, the sone of Achobor, and men with hym, in to Egipt;

23 and thei ledden Vrye out of Egipt, and brouyten hym to kyng Joachym; and the kyng killide hym bi swerd, and castide forth his careyn in the sepulcris of the comyn puple vnnoble.

24 Therfor the hond of Aicham, sone of Saphan, was with Jeremye, that he was not bitakun in to the hondis of the puple, and that it killide not hym.

CAP 27

1 In the bigynnyng of the rewme of Joachym, the sone of Josie, kyng of Juda, this word was maad of the Lord to Jeremye, and seide,

2 The Lord seith these thingis to me, Make thou to thee boondis and chaynes, and thou schalt putte tho in thi necke;

3 and thou schalt sende tho to the kyng of Edom, and to the kyng of Moab, and to the kyng of the sones of Amon, and to the kyng of Tyre, and to the kyng of Sidon, bi the hond of messangeris that camen to Jerusalem, and to Sedechie, kyng of Juda.

4 And thou schalt comaunde to hem, that thei speke to her lordis, The Lord of oostis, God of Israel, seith these thingis, Ye schulen seie these thingis to youre lordis,

5 Y made erthe, and man, and beestis that ben on the face of al erthe, in my greet strengthe, and in myn arm holdun forth; and Y yaf it to hym that plesyde bifore myn iyen.

6 And now therfor Y yaf alle these londis in the hond of Nabugodonosor, my seruaunt, the kyng of Babiloyne; ferthermore and Y yaf to hym the beestis of the feeld, that thei serue hym.

7 And alle folkis schulen serue hym, and his sone, and the sone of his sone, til the tyme of his lond and of hym come; and many folkis and grete kyngis schulen serue hym.

8 Forsothe the folk and rewme that serueth not Nabugodonosor, kyng of Babiloyne, and whoeuer bowith not his necke vndur the yok of the kyng of Babiloyne, Y schal visite on that folk in swerd, and hungur, and pestilence, seith the Lord, til Y waaste hem in his hond.

9 Therfor nyle ye here youre profetis, and false dyuynouris, and dremeris, and dyuyneris bi chiteryng and fleyng of briddis, and witchis, that seien to you, Ye schulen not serue the kyng of Babiloyne;

10 for thei profesien a lessyng to you, that thei make you fer fro youre lond, and caste out you, and ye perische.

11 Certis the folk that makith suget her nol vndur the yok of the kyng of Babiloyne, and serueth hym, Y schal dismytte it in his lond, seith the Lord; and it schal tile that lond, and schal dwelle therynne.

12 And Y spak bi alle these wordis to Sedechie, kyng of Juda, and Y seide, Make ye suget youre neckis vndur the yok of the kyng of Babiloyne, and serue ye hym, and his puple, and ye schulen lyue.

13 Whi schulen ye die, thou and thi puple, bi swerd, and hungur, and pestilence, as the Lord spak to the folk, that nolde serue to the kyng of Babiloyne?

14 Nyle ye here the wordis of profetis seiynge to you, Ye schulen not serue the kyng of Babiloyne; for thei speken leesyng to you, for Y sente not hem, seith the Lord;

15 and thei profesien falsly in my name, that thei caste out you, and that ye perische, bothe ye and the profetis that profesien to you.

16 And Y spak to the preestis, and to this puple, and Y seide, The Lord God seith these thingis, Nyle ye here the wordis of youre profetis, that profesien to you, and seien, Lo! the vessels of the Lord schulen turne ayen now soone fro Babiloyne; for thei profesien a leesyng to you.

17 Therfor nyle ye here hem, but serue ye to the kyng of Babiloyne, that ye lyue; whi is this citee youun in to wildirnesse?

18 And if thei ben profetis, and if the word of God is in hem, renne thei to the Lord of oostis, that the vessels whiche weren left in the hous of the Lord, and in the hous of the kyng of Juda, and in Jerusalem, come not in to Babiloyne.

19 For the Lord of oostis seith these thingis to the pilers, and to the see, that is, a greet waischyng vessel, and to the foundementis, and to the remenauntis of vessels, that weren left in this citee,

20 whiche Nabugodonosor, king of Babiloyne, took not, whanne he translatide Jeconye, the sone of Joachim, king of Juda, fro Jerusalem in to Babiloyne, and alle the principal men of Juda and of Jerusalem.

21 For the Lord of oostis, God of Israel, seith these thingis to the vessels that ben left in the hous of the Lord, and in the hous of the king of Juda, and in Jerusalem, Tho schulen be translatid in to Babiloyne,

22 and schulen be there 'til to the dai of her visitacioun, seith the Lord; and Y schal make tho to be brouyt, and to be restorid in this place.

CAP 28

1 And it was don in that yeer, in the bigynnyng of the rewme of Sedechie, kyng of Juda, in the fourthe yeer, in the fyuethe monethe, Ananye, the sone of Azur, a profete of Gabaon, seide to me in the hous of the Lord, bifor the preestis, and al the puple,

2 'and seide, The Lord of oostis, God of Israel, seith these thingis, Y haue al to-broke the yok of the kyng of Babiloyne.

3 Yit twei yeeris of daies ben, and Y schal make to be brouyt ayen to this place alle the vessels of the Lord, whiche Nabugodonosor, kyng of Babiloyne, took fro this place, and translatide tho in to Babiloyne.

4 And Y schal turne to this place, seith the Lord, Jeconye, the sone of Joachym, the kyng of Juda, and al the passyng ouer of Juda, that entriden in to Babiloyne; for Y schal al to-breke the yok of the kyng of Babiloyne.

5 And Jeremye, the profete, seide to Ananye, the profete, bifore the iyen of preestis, and bifore the iyen of al the puple that stoden in the hous of the Lord.

6 And Jeremye, the profete, seide to Ananye, Amen! so do the Lord; the Lord reise thi wordis whiche thou profesiedist, that the vessels be brouyt ayen in to the hous of the Lord, and al the passyng ouer fro Babiloyne, to this place.

7 Netheles here thou this word, which Y speke in thin eeris, and in the eeris of al the puple.

8 Profetis that weren bifore me, and bifor thee, fro the bigynnyng, and profesieden on many londis, and on many rewmes, of batel, and of turment, and of hungur.

9 The profete that profesiede pees, whanne his word cometh, shal be knowun the profete whom the Lord sente in treuthe.

10 And Ananye, the profete, took the chayne fro the necke of Jeremye, the profete, and brak it.

11 And Ananye, the profete, seide in the siyt of al the puple, 'and seide, The Lord seith these thingis, So Y schal breke the

yok of Nabugodonosor, kyng of Babiloyne, aftir twei yeeris of daies, fro the necke of alle folkis.

12 And Jeremye, the profete, yede in to his weie. And the word of the Lord was maad to Jeremye, aftir that Ananye, the profete, brak the chayne fro the necke of Jeremye; and the Lord seide,

13 Go thou, and seie to Ananye, The Lord seith these thingis, Thou hast al to-broke the chaynes of tre, and thou schalt make yrun chaynes for tho.

14 For the Lord of oostis, God of Israel, seith these thingis, Y haue set an yrun yok on the necke of alle these folkis, that thei serue Nabugodonosor, the king of Babiloyne, and thei schulen serue hym; ferthermore and Y yaf to hym the beestis of erthe.

15 And Jeremye, the profete, seide to Ananye, the profete, Ananye, here thou; the Lord sente not thee, and thou madist this puple for to triste in a leesyng.

16 Therfor the Lord seith these thingis, Lo! Y schal sende thee out fro the face of erthe; in this yeer thou schalt die, for thou spakest ayens the Lord.

17 And Ananye, the profete, diede in that yeer, in the seuenthe monethe.

CAP 29

1 And these ben the wordis of the book, whiche Jeremye, the profete, sente fro Jerusalem to the residues of eldere men of passyng ouer, and to the preestis, and to the profetis, and to al the puple, whom Nabugodonosor hadde ledde ouer fro Jerusalem in to Babiloyne,

2 after that Jeconye, the kyng, yede out, and the ladi, and the onest seruauntis and chast, and the princis of Juda yeden out of Jerusalem, and a sutel crafti man, and a goldsmyth of Jerusalem,

3 in the hond of Elasa, sone of Saphan, and of Gamalie, the sone of Elchie, whiche Sedechie, the kyng of Juda, sente to Nabugodonosor, the kyng of Babiloyne, in to Babiloyne.

4 And Jeremye seide, The Lord of oostis, God of Israel, seith these thingis to al the passyng ouer, which Y translatide fro Jerusalem in to Babiloyne,

5 Bilde ye housis, and enhabite, and plaunte ye orcherdis, and ete ye fruyt of tho;

6 take ye wyues, and gendre ye sones and douytris, and yyue ye wyues to youre sones, and yyue ye youre douytris to hosebondis, and bere thei sones and douytris; and be ye multiplied there, and nyle ye be fewe in noumbre.

7 And seke ye pees of the citees, to whiche Y made you to passe ouer; and preie ye the Lord for it, for in the pees therof schal be pees to you.

8 The Lord of oostis, God of Israel, seith these thingis, Youre profetis, that ben in the myddis of you, and youre dyuynours disseyue you not; and take ye noon heede to youre dremes, whiche ye dremen;

9 for thei profesien falsli to you in my name, and Y sente not hem, seith the Lord.

10 For the Lord seith thes thingis, Whanne seuenti yeer bigynnen to be fillid in Babiloyne, Y schal visite you, and Y schal reise on you my good word, and Y schal brynge you ayen to this place.

11 For Y knowe the thouytis whiche Y thenke on you, seith the Lord, the thouytis of pees, and not of turment, that Y yyue to you an ende and pacience.

12 And ye schulen clepe me to help, and ye schulen go, and schulen worschipe me, and Y schal here you;

13 ye schulen seke me, and ye schulen fynde, whanne ye seken me in al youre herte.

14 And Y schal be foundun of you, seith the Lord, and Y schal brynge ayen youre caitifte, and Y schal gadere you fro alle folkis, and fro alle places, to whiche Y castide out you, seith the Lord; and Y schal make you to turne ayen fro the place, to which Y made you to passe ouer.

15 For ye seiden, The Lord schal reise profetis to vs in Babiloyne.

16 For the Lord seith these thingis to the kyng, that sittith on the seete of Dauid, and to al the puple, dwellere of this citee, to youre britheren, that yeden not out with you in to the passyng ouer,

17 The Lord of oostis seith these thingis, Lo! Y schal sende among hem swerd, and hungur, and pestilence; and Y schal sette hem as yuele figis, that moun not be etun, for tho ben ful yuele.

18 And Y schal pursue hem in swerd, and in hungur, and in pestilence; and Y schal yyue hem in to trauelyng in alle rewmes of erthe, in to cursyng, and in to wondryng, and in to scornyng, and in to schenschipe to alle folkis, to whiche Y castide hem out.

19 For thei herden not my wordis, seith the Lord, which Y sente to hem bi my seruauntis, profetis, and roos bi nyyt, and sente, and ye herden not, seith the Lord.

20 Therfor al the passyng ouer, which Y sente out fro Jerusalem in to Babiloyne, here ye the word of the Lord.

21 The Lord of oostis, God of Israel, seith these thingis to Achab, the sone of Chulie, and to Sedechie, the sone of Maasie, that profesien to you a leesyng in my name, Lo! Y schal bitake hem in to the hond of Nabugodonosor, kyng of Babiloyne, and he schal smyte hem bifore youre iyen.

22 And cursyng schal be takun of hem to al the passyng ouer of Juda, which is in Babiloyne, of men seiynge, The Lord sette thee as Sedechie, and as Achab, whiche the kyng of Babiloyne friede in fier,

23 for thei diden foli in Israel, and diden auowtrie on the wyues of her frendis; and thei spaken a word falsli in my name, which Y comaundide not to hem; Y am iuge and witnesse, seith the Lord.

24 And thou schalt seie to Semei Neelamyte,

25 The Lord of oostis, God of Israel, seith these thingis, For that that thou sentist bookis in my name to al the puple, which is in Jerusalem, and to Sofony, the sone of Maasie, the preest, and to alle the prestis,

26 and seidist, The Lord yaf thee the preest for Joiada, the preest, that thou be duyk in the hous of the Lord on ech man 'that is trauelid of the fend, and profesiynge, that thou sende hym in to stockis, and in to prisoun.

27 And now whi blamest thou not Jeremye of Anathot, that profesieth to you?

28 For on this thing he sente to vs in to Babiloyne, and seide, It is long; bielde ye housis, and enhabite, and plaunte ye orcherdis, and ete ye the fruit of tho.

29 Therfor Sofonye, the preest, redde this book in the eeris of Jeremye, the prophete.

30 And the word of the Lord was maad to Jeremye,

31 and seide, Sende thou to al the passyng ouer, and seie, The Lord seith these thingis to Semeye Neelamite, For that that Semeye profesiede to you, and Y sente not hym, and he made you to triste in a leesyng;

32 therfor the Lord seith thes thingis, Lo! Y schal visite on Semeye Neelamyte, and on his seed; and no man sittynge in

the myddis of this puple schal be to hym; and he schal not se
the good, which Y schal do to my puple, seith the Lord, for he
spak trespassyng ayens the Lord.

CAP 30

1 This is the word, that was maad of the Lord to Jeremye,
2 and seide, The Lord God of Israel seith these thingis, and
spekith, Write to thee in a book, alle these wordis whiche Y
spak to thee.
3 For lo! daies comen, seith the Lord, and Y schal turne the
turnyng of my puple Israel and Juda, seith the Lord; and Y
schal turne hem to the lond which Y yaf to the fadris of hem,
and thei schulen haue it in possessioun.
4 And these ben the wordis, whiche the Lord spak to Israel,
and to Juda,
5 For the Lord seith these thingis, We herden a word of drede;
inward drede is, and pees is not.
6 Axe ye, and se, if a male berith child; whi therfor siy Y the
hond of ech man on his leende, as of a womman trauelynge of
child, and alle faces ben turned in to yelow colour?
7 Wo! for thilke day is greet, nether ony is lyk it; and it is a
tyme of tribulacioun to Jacob, and of hym schal be sauyd.
8 And it schal be, in that dai, seith the Lord of oostis, Y schal
al to-breke the yok of hym fro thi necke, and Y schal breke
hise boondis; and aliens schulen no more be lordis of it,
9 but thei schulen serue to her Lord God, and to Dauid, her
kyng, whom Y schal reyse for hem.
10 Therfor, Jacob, my seruaunt, drede thou not, seith the
Lord, and Israel, drede thou not; for lo! Y schal saue thee fro
a fer lond, and thi seed fro the lond of the caitiftee of hem.
And Jacob schal turne ayen, and schal reste, and schal flowe
with alle goodis; and noon schal be whom he schal drede.
11 For Y am with thee, seith the Lord, for to saue thee. For Y
schal make endyng in alle folkis, in whiche Y scateride thee;
sotheli Y schal not make thee in to endyng, but Y schal chastise thee in doom, that thou be not seyn to thee to be gilteles.
12 For the Lord seith these thingis, Thi brekyng is vncurable,
thi wounde is the worste.
13 Noon is, that demeth thi doom to bynde togidere; the profit
of heelyngis is not to thee.
14 Alle thi louyeris han foryete thee, thei schulen not seke
thee; for Y haue smyte thee with the wounde of an enemy,
with cruel chastisyng; for the multitude of thi wickidnesse, thi
synnes ben maad hard.
15 What criest thou on thi brekynge? thi sorewe is vncurable;
for the multitude of thi wickidnesse, and for thin hard synnes,
Y haue do these thingis to thee.
16 Therfor alle that eeten thee, schulen be deuourid, and alle
thin enemyes schulen be led in to caitifte; and thei that distrien thee, schulen be distried, and Y schal yyue alle thi robberis in to raueyn.
17 For Y schal heele perfitli thi wounde, and Y schal make
thee hool of thi woundis, seith the Lord; for thou, Sion, thei
clepeden thee cast out; this is it that hadde no sekere.
18 The Lord seith these thingis, Lo! Y schal turne the turnyng
of the tabernaclis of Jacob, and Y schal haue merci on the
housis of hym; and the citee schal be bildid in his hiynesse,
and the temple schal be foundid bi his ordre.
19 And heriyng and the vois of pleiers schal go out of hem,
and Y schal multiplie hem, and thei schulen not be
decreessid; and Y schal glorifie hem, and thei schulen not be
maad thynne.

20 And the sones therof schulen be as at the bigynnyng, and
the cumpeny therof schal dwelle bifore me; and Y schal visite
ayens alle that doon tribulacioun to it.
21 And the duyk therof schal be of it, and a prince schal be
brouyt forth of the myddis therof; and Y schal applie hym,
and he schal neiye to me; for who is this, that schal applie his
herte, that he neiye to me? seith the Lord.
22 And ye schulen be in to a puple to me, and Y schal be in to
God to you.
23 Lo! the whirlewynd of the Lord, a strong veniaunce
goynge out, a tempest fallynge doun, schal reste in the heed
of wickid men.
24 The Lord schal not turne awey the ire of indignacioun, til
he do, and fille the thouyt of his herte; in the laste of daies ye
schulen vndurstonde tho thingis.
1 In that tyme, seith the Lord, Y schal be God to alle the
kynredis of Israel; and thei schulen be in to a puple to me.

CAP 31

2 The Lord seith these thingis, The puple that was left of
swerd, foond grace in desert; Israel schal go to his reste.
3 Fer the Lord apperide to me, and in euerlastynge charite Y
louede thee; therfor Y doynge merci drow thee.
4 And eft Y schal bilde thee, and thou, virgyn Israel, schalt be
bildid; yit thou schalt be ourned with thi tympans, and schalt
go out in the cumpenye of pleieris.
5 Yit thou schalt plaunte vynes in the hillis of Samarie; men
plauntynge schulen plaunte, and til the tyme come, thei
schulen not gadere grapis.
6 For whi a dai schal be, wherynne keperis schulen crye in the
hil of Samarie, and in the hil of Effraym, Rise ye, and stie we
in to Sion, to oure Lord God.
7 For the Lord seith these thingis, Jacob, make ye ful out ioye
in gladnesse, and neye ye ayens the heed of hethene men;
sowne ye, synge ye, and seie ye, Lord, saue thi puple, the residues of Israel.
8 Lo! Y schal brynge hem fro the loond of the north, and Y
schal gadere hem fro the fertheste partis of erthe; among
whiche schulen be a blynd man, and crokid, and a womman
with childe, and trauelynge of child togidere, a greet cumpeny
of hem that schulen turne ayen hidur.
9 Thei schulen come in wepyng, and Y schal brynge hem
ayen in merci; and Y schal brynge hem bi the strondis of
watris in a riytful weie, thei schulen not spurne therynne; for
Y am maad a fadir to Israel, and Effraym is my gendrid sone.
10 Ye hethene men, here ye the word of the Lord, and telle ye
in ylis that ben fer, and seie, He that scateride Israel, schal
gadere it, and schal kepe it, as a scheepherde kepith his floc.
11 For the Lord ayenbouyte Jacob, and delyuerede hym fro
the hond of the myytiere.
12 And thei schulen come, and herye in the hil of Sion; and
thei schulen flowe togidere to the goodis of the Lord, on
wheete, wyn, and oile, and on the fruyt of scheep, and of neet;
and the soule of hem schal be as a watri gardyn, and thei
schulen no more hungre.
13 Thanne a virgyn schal be glad in a cumpenye, yonge men
and elde togidere; and Y schal turne the morenyng of hem in
to ioie, and Y schal coumforte hem, and Y schal make hem
glad of her sorewe.
14 And Y schal greetli fille the soule of prestis with fatnesse,
and my puple schal be fillid with my goodis, seith the Lord.
15 The Lord seith these thingis, A vois of weilyng, and of
wepyng, and of mourenyng, was herd an hiy; the vois of

Rachel biwepynge hir sones, and not willynge to be coumfortid on hem, for thei ben not.

16 The Lord seith these thingis, Thi vois reste of wepyng, and thin iyen reste of teeres; for whi mede is to thi werk, seith the Lord; and thei schulen turne ayen fro the lond of the enemy.

17 And hope is to thi laste thingis, seith the Lord, and thi sones schulen turne ayen to her endis.

18 I heringe herde Effraym passinge ouer; thou chastisidist me, and Y am lerned as a yong oon vntemyd; turne thou me, and Y schal be conuertid, for thou art my Lord God.

19 For aftir that thou conuertidist me, Y dide penaunce; and aftir that thou schewidist to me, Y smoot myn hipe; Y am schent, and Y schamede, for Y suffride the schenschipe of my yongthe.

20 For Effraym is a worschipful sone to me, for he is a delicat child; for sithen Y spak of hym, yit Y schal haue mynde on hym; therfor myn entrails ben disturblid on him, Y doynge merci schal haue merci on hym, seith the Lord.

21 Ordeyne to thee an hiy totyng place, sette to thee bitternesses; dresse thin herte in to a streiyt weie, in which thou yedist; turne ayen, thou virgyn of Israel, turne ayen to these thi citees.

22 Hou longe, douyter of vnstidfast dwellyng, art thou maad dissolut in delices? for the Lord hath maad a newe thing on erthe, a womman schal cumpasse a man.

23 The Lord of oostis, God of Israel, seith these thingis, Yit thei schulen seie this word in the lond of Juda, and in the citees therof, whane Y schal turne the caytifte of hem, The Lord blesse thee, thou fairnesse of riytfulnesse, thou hooli hil.

24 And Juda, and alle citees therof schulen dwelle in it togidere, erthetilieris, and thei that dryuen flockis.

25 For Y fillide greetli a feynt soule, and Y haue fillid ech hungri soule.

26 Therfor Y am as reisid fro sleep, and Y siy; and my sleep was swete to me.

27 Lo! daies comen, seith the Lord, and Y schal sowe the hous of Israel and the hous of Juda with the seed of men, and with the seed of werk beestis.

28 And as Y wakide on hem, to drawe vp bi the roote, and to distrie, and to scatere, and to leese, and to turmente; so Y schal wake on hem, to bilde, and to plaunte, seith the Lord.

29 In tho daies thei schulen no more seie, The fadres eeten a sour grape, and the teeth of sones weren astonyed; but ech man schal die in his wickidnesse,

30 ech man that etith a sour grape, hise teeth schulen be astonyed.

31 Lo! daies comen, seith the Lord, and Y schal smyte a newe boond of pees to the hous of Israel, and to the hous of Juda;

32 not bi the couenaunte which Y made with youre fadris, in the dai in which Y took the hond of hem, to lede hem out of the lond of Egipt, the couenaunte which thei made voide; and Y was Lord of hem, seith the Lord.

33 But this schal be the couenaunte, which Y schal smyte with the hous of Israel aftir tho daies, seith the Lord; Y schal yyue my lawe in the entrails of hem, and Y schal write it in the herte of hem, and Y schal be in to God to hem, and thei schulen be in to a puple to me.

34 And a man schal no more teche his neiybore, and a man his brother, and seie, Knowe thou the Lord; for alle schulen knowe me, fro the leeste of hem 'til to the mooste, seith the Lord; for Y schal be merciful to the wickidnessis of hem, and Y schal no more be myndeful on the synne of hem.

35 The Lord seith these thingis, that yyueth the sunne in the liyt of dai, the ordre of the moone and of sterris in the liyt of the niyt, whiche disturblith the see, and the wawis therof sownen, the Lord of oostis is name to hym.

36 If these lawis failen bifore me, seith the Lord, thanne and the seed of Israel schal faile, that it be not a folk bifore me in alle daies.

37 The Lord seith these thingis, If heuenes aboue moun be mesurid, and the foundementis of erthe bynethe be souyt out, and Y schal caste awei al the seed of Israel, for alle thingis whiche thei diden, seith the Lord.

38 Lo! daies comen, seith the Lord, and a citee schal be bildid to the Lord, fro the tour of Ananeel 'til to the yate of the corner.

39 And it schal go out ouer the reule of mesure, in the siyt therof, on the hil Gareb, and it schal cumpasse Goatha,

40 and al the valei of careyns, and it schal cumpasse aischis, and al the cuntrei of deth, 'til to the stronde of Cedron, and til to the corner of the eest yate of horsis; the hooli thing of the Lord schal not be drawun out, and it schal no more be destried with outen ende.

CAP 32

1 The word that was maad of the Lord to Jeremye, in the tenthe yeer of Sedechie, kyng of Juda; thilke is the eiytenthe yeer of Nabugodonosor.

2 Thanne the oost of the kyng of Babiloyne bisegide Jerusalem; and Jeremye, the profete, was closid in the porche of the prisoun, that was in the hous of the kyng of Juda.

3 For whi Sedechie, the kyng of Juda, hadde closid hym, and seide, Whi profesiest thou, seiynge, The Lord seith these thingis, Lo! Y schal yyue this citee in the hond of the kyng of Babyloyne, and he schal take it; and Sedechie,

4 the kyng of Juda, schal not ascape fro the hond of Caldeis, but he schal be bitake in to the hond of the kyng of Babiloyne; and his mouth schal speke with the mouth of hym, and hise iyen schulen se the iyen of hym;

5 and he schal lede Sedechie in to Babiloyne, and he schal be there, til Y visyte hym, seith the Lord; forsothe if ye fiyten ayens Caldeis, ye schulen haue no thing in prosperite?

6 And Jeremye seide, The word of the Lord was maad to me, and seide, Lo!

7 Ananeel, the sone of Sellum, the sone of thi fadris brothir, schal come to thee, and seie, Bi thou to thee my feeld, which is in Anathot; for it bifallith to thee by niy kynrede, that thou bie it.

8 And Ananeel, the sone of my fadris brothir, cam to me, bi the word of the Lord, to the porche of the prisoun, and seide to me, Welde thou my feeld, which is in Anathot, in the lond of Beniamyn; for whi the erytage bifallith to thee, and thou art the next of blood, that thou welde it. Forsothe Y vndirstood, that it was the word of the Lord.

9 And Y bouyte the feeld, which is in Anathot, of Ananeel, the sone of my fadris brothir. And Y paiede to hym siluer, seuene stateris, and ten platis of siluer;

10 and Y wroot in a book, and Y seelide, and Y yaf witnessis. And Y weiede siluer in a balaunce;

11 and Y took the book aseelid of possessioun, and axingis and answerys of the seller and bier, and couenauntis, and seelis withoutforth.

12 And Y yaf the book of possessioun to Baruc, the sone of Neri, sone of Maasie, bifore the iyen of Ananeel, the sone of my fadris brother, and bifore the iyen of witnessis that weren

writun in the book of biyng, bifore the iyen of alle Jewis, that saten in the porche of the prisoun.

13 And Y comaundide to Baruc bifore hem,

14 and Y seide, The Lord of oostis, God of Israel, seith these thingis, Take thou these bookis, this seelid book of biyng, and this book which is opyn, and putte thou tho in an erthen vessel, that tho moun dwelle bi many daies.

15 For whi the Lord of oostis, God of Israel, seith these thingis, Yit housis, and feeldis, and vynes schulen be weldid in this lond.

16 And Y preiede to the Lord, aftir that Y bitook the book of possessioun to Baruc, the sone of Nery; and Y seide, Alas! 17 alas! alas! Lord God, Lord, thou madist heuene and erthe in thi greet strengthe, and in thin arm stretchid forth; ech word schal not be hard to thee;

18 which doist merci in thousyndis, and yeldist the wickidnesse of fadris in to the bosum of her sones aftir hem. Thou strongeste, greet, myyti, Lord of oostis is name to thee;

19 greet in councel, and vncomprehensible in thouyt, whose iyen ben open on alle the weies of the sones of Adam, that thou yelde to ech aftir hise weies, and aftir the fruyt of hise fyndyngis;

20 which settidist signes and greet woundris in the lond of Egipt, 'til to this dai, bothe in Israel and in men; and madist to thee a name, as this dai is.

21 And thou leddist thi puple Israel out of the lond of Egipt, in signes and in greet woundris, and in a strong hond, and in an arm holdun forth, and in greet dreed; and thou yauest to hem this lond,

22 which thou sworist to the fadris of hem, that thou woldist yyue to hem, a lond flowynge with milk and hony.

23 And thei entriden, and hadden it in possessioun; and thei obeieden not to thi vois, and thei yeden not in thi lawe; alle thingis whiche thou comaundidist to hem to do, thei diden not; and alle these yuels bifellen to hem.

24 Lo! strengthis ben bildid ayens the citee, that it be takun, and the citee is youun in to the hondis of Caldeis, and in to the hondis of the kyng of Babiloyne, that fiyten ayens it, of the face of swerd, and of hungur, and of pestilence; and what euer thingis thou spakest, bifellen, as thou thi silf seest.

25 And Lord God, thou seist to me, Bie thou a feeld for siluer, and yyue thou witnessis, whanne the citee is youun in the hondis of Caldeis.

26 And the word of the Lord was maad to Jeremye, and seide, Lo!

27 Y am the Lord God of 'al fleisch. Whether ony word schal be hard to me?

28 Therfor the Lord seith these thingis, Lo! Y schal bitake this citee in to the hondis of Caldeis, and in to the hond of the kyng of Babiloyne, and he schal take it.

29 And Caldeis schulen come, and fiyte ayens this citee, and thei schulen brenne it with fier, and thei schulen brenne it, and housis, in whose rooues thei sacrifieden to Baal, and offriden moist sacrifices to alien goddis, to terre me to wraththe.

30 For whi the sones of Israel and the sones of Juda diden yuel contynueli, fro her yonge waxynge age, bifore myn iyen, the sones of Israel, whiche 'til to now wraththen me bi the werk of her hondis, seith the Lord.

31 For whi this citee is maad to me in my strong veniaunce and indignacioun, fro the day in which thei bildiden it, 'til to this dai, in which it schal be takun awei fro my siyt;

32 for the malice of the sones of Israel, and of the sones of Juda, which thei diden, terrynge me to wrathfulnesse, thei, and the kyngis of hem, the princes of hem, and the prestis, and profetis of hem, the men of Juda, and the dwelleris of Jerusalem.

33 And thei turneden to me the backis, and not the faces, whanne Y tauyte, and enformede hem erli; and thei nolden here, that thei schulden take techyng.

34 And thei settiden her idols in the hous, in which my name is clepid to help, that thei schulden defoule it.

35 And thei bildiden hiy thingis to Baal, that ben in the valei of the sones of Ennon, that thei schulden halewe her sones and her douytris to Moloc, which thing Y comaundide not to hem, nether it stiede in to myn herte, that thei schulden do this abhomynacioun, and brynge Juda in to synne.

36 And now for these thingis, the Lord God of Israel seith these thingis to this citee, of whiche ye seien, that it schal be bitakun in to the hondis of the kyng of Babiloyne, in swerd, and in hungur, and in pestilence, Lo!

37 Y schal gadere hem fro alle londis, to whiche Y castide hem out in my strong veniaunce, and in my wraththe, and in greet indignacioun; and Y schal brynge hem ayen to this place, and Y schal make hem to dwelle tristili.

38 And thei schulen be in to a puple to me, and Y schal be in to God to hem.

39 And Y schal yyue to hem oon herte and o soule, that thei drede me in alle daies, and that it be wel to hem, and to her sones aftir hem.

40 And Y schal smyte to hem a couenaunt euerlastynge, and Y schal not ceese to do wel to hem, and Y schal yyue my drede in the herte of hem, that thei go not awey fro me.

41 And Y schal be glad on hem, whanne Y schal do wel to hem; and Y schal plaunte hem in this lond in treuthe, in al myn herte, and in al my soule.

42 For the Lord seith these thingis, As Y brouyte on this puple al this greet yuel, so Y schal brynge on hem al the good, which Y schal speke to hem.

43 And feeldis schulen be weldid in this lond, of which ye seien, that it is desert, for no man and beeste is left; and it is youun in to the hondis of Caldeis.

44 Feeldis schulen be bouyt for money, and schulen be writun in a book, and a seel schal be preentid; and witnessis schulen be youun, in the lond of Beniamyn, and in the cumpas of Jerusalem, and in the citees of Juda, and in the citees in hilli places, and in the citees in feeldi places, and in the citees that ben at the south; for Y schal turne the caitiftee of hem, seith the Lord.

CAP 33

1 And the word of the Lord was maad to Jeremye, in the secounde tyme, whanne he was closid yit in the porche of the prisoun, and seide,

2 The Lord seith these thingis, The Lord is name of hym, that schal do, and fourme, and make redi that thing;

3 Crye thou to me, and Y schal here thee, and Y schal telle to thee grete thingis, and stidfast, whiche thou knowist not.

4 For the Lord God of Israel seith these thingis to the housis of this citee, and to the housis of the kyng of Juda, that ben distried, and to the strengthingis,

5 and to the swerd of men comynge to fiyte with Caldeis, and to fille tho housis with careyns of men, which Y smoot in my strong veniaunce, and in myn indignacioun; and Y hidde my face fro this citee, for al the malice of hem.

6 Lo! Y schal close togidere to hem a wounde and helthe, and Y schal make hem hool, and Y schal schewe to hem the bisechyng of pees and of treuthe;

7 and Y schal conuerte the conuersioun of Juda, and Y schal conuerte the conuersioun of Jerusalem, and Y schal bilde hem, as at the bigynnyng.

8 And Y schal clense hem fro al her wickidnesse, in which thei synneden to me, and Y schal be merciful to alle the wickidnessis of hem, in which thei trespassiden to me, and forsoken me.

9 And thei schulen be to me in to a name, and in to ioye, and in to heriyng, and in to ful out ioiyng to alle folkis of erthe, that herden alle the goodis whiche Y schal do to hem; and thei schulen drede, and schulen be disturblid in alle goodis, and in al the pees, which Y schal do to hem.

10 The Lord seith these thingis, Yit in this place, which ye seien to be forsakun, for no man is nether beeste in the citees of Juda, and in the yatis of Jerusalem, that ben desolat, without man, and with out dwellere,

11 and with out beeste, the vois of ioye schal be herd, and the vois of gladnesse, the vois of spouse, and the vois of spousesse, the vois of men, seiynge, Knowleche ye to the Lord of oostis, for the Lord is good, for his merci is with outen ende, and of men berynge vowis in to the hous of the Lord; for Y schal brynge ayen the conuersioun of the lond, as at the bigynnyng, seith the Lord.

12 The Lord of oostis seith these thingis, Yit in this forsakun place, with out man, and with out beeste, and in alle citees therof, schal be a dwellyng place of scheepherdis, of flockis ligynge.

13 And in the citees in hilli places, and in the citees in feeldi places, and in the citees that ben at the south, and in the lond of Beniamyn, and in the cumpas of Jerusalem, and in the citees of Juda, yit flockis schulen passe, at the hond of the noumbrere, seith the Lord.

14 Lo! daies comen, seith the Lord, and Y schal reise the good word, which Y spak to the hous of Israel, and to the hous of Juda.

15 In tho daies, and in that tyme, Y schal make the seed of riytfulnesse to buriowne to Dauid, and he schal make doom and riytfulnesse in erthe.

16 In tho daies Juda schal be sauyd, and Israel schal dwelle tristili; and this is the name which thei schulen clepe hym, Oure riytful Lord.

17 For the Lord seith these thingis, A man of Dauid schal not perische, that shal sitte on the trone of the hous of Israel;

18 and of preestis and dekenes a man schal not perische fro my face, that schal offre brent sacrifices, and brenne sacrifice, and sle sacrifice, in alle daies.

19 And the word of the Lord was maad to Jeremye,

20 and seide, The Lord seith these thingis, If my couenaunt with the dai and my couenaunt with the niyt mai be maad voide, that the dai and the niyt be not in his tyme;

21 and my couenaunt with Dauid, my seruaunt, mai be voide, that of hym be no sone, that schal regne in his trone, and no dekenes, and preestis, my mynistris;

22 as the sterris of heuene moun not be noumbrid, and the grauel of the see mai not be metun, so Y schal multiplie the seed of Dauid, my seruaunt, and dekenes, my mynystris.

23 And the word of the Lord was maad to Jeremye, and seide, Whether thou hast not seyn,

24 that this puple spak, seiynge, Twei kynredis whiche the Lord chees, ben cast awei, and thei dispisiden my puple, for it is no more a folc bifore hem.

25 The Lord seith these thingis, If Y settide not my couenaunt bitwixe dai and niyt, and if Y settide not lawis to heuene and erthe;

26 sotheli and Y schal caste awei the seed of Jacob, and of Dauid, my seruaunt, that Y take not of the seed of hym princes, of the seed of Abraham, of Isaac, and of Jacob; for Y schal brynge ayen the conuersioun of hem, and Y schal haue merci on hem.

CAP 34

1 The word that was maad of the Lord to Jeremye, whanne Nabugodonosor, kyng of Babiloyne, and al his oost, and alle the rewmes of erthe, that weren vndur the power of his hond, and alle puplis fouyten ayens Jerusalem, and ayens alle citees therof; and he seide,

2 The Lord God of Israel seith these thingis, Go thou, and speke to Sedechie, kyng of Juda; and thou schalt seie to hym, The Lord seith these thingis, Lo! Y schal bitake this citee in to the hond of the kyng of Babiloyne, and he schal brenne it bi fier.

3 And thou schalt not ascape fro his hond, but thou schalt be takun bi takyng, and thou schalt be bitakun in to his hond; and thin iyen schulen se the iyen of the kyng of Babiloyne, and his mouth schal speke with thi mouth, and thou schalt entre in to Babiloyne.

4 Netheles Sedechie, the kyng of Juda, here thou the word of the Lord; the Lord seith these thingis to thee, Thou schalt not die bi swerd,

5 but thou schalt die in pees, and bi the brennyngis of thi fadris, the formere kyngis that weren bifore thee, so thei schulen brenne thee, and thei schulen biweile thee, Wo! lord; for Y spak a word, seith the Lord.

6 And Jeremye, the profete, spak to Sedechie, kyng of Juda, alle these wordis in Jerusalem.

7 And the oost of the kyng of Babiloyne fauyt ayens Jerusalem, and ayens alle the citees of Juda, that weren left; ayens Lachis, and ayens Azecha; for whi these strong citees weren left of the citees of Juda.

8 The word that was maad of the Lord to Jeremye, aftir that kyng Sedechie smoot boond of pees with al the puple in Jerusalem,

9 and prechide, that ech man schulde delyuere his seruaunt, and ech man his handmaide, an Ebreu man and an Ebru womman fre, and that thei schulden not be lordis of hem, that is, in a Jew, and her brothir.

10 Therfor alle the princes and al the puple herden, whiche maden couenaunt, that thei schulden delyuere ech man his seruaunt, and ech man his handmaide fre, and schulde no more be lordis of hem; therfor thei herden, and delyueriden;

11 and thei weren turned aftirward, and drowen ayen her seruauntis, and handmaidis, whiche thei hadden left fre, and thei maden suget in to seruauntis, and in to seruauntessis.

12 And the word of the Lord was maad of the Lord to Jeremye, and seide,

13 The Lord God of Israel seith these thingis, Y smoot a boond of pees with youre fadris, in the dai in which Y ledde hem out of the lond of Egipt, out of the hous of seruage; and Y seide, Whanne seuene yeeris ben fillid,

14 ech man delyuere his brother, an Ebreu man, which is seeld to hym, and he schal serue thee sixe yeer, and thou

schalt delyuere hym fro thee; and youre fadris herden not me, nether bowiden her eere.

15 And ye ben conuertid to dai, and ye diden that, that is riytful bifore myn iyen, that ye precheden ech man fredom to his frend, and ye maden couenaunt in my siyt, in the hous wherynne my name is clepid to help on that fredom.

16 And ye turneden ayen, and defouliden my name, and ye brouyten ayen ech man his seruaunt, and ech man his handmaide, whiche ye delyueriden, that thei schulden be fre, and of her owne power; and ye maden hem suget, that thei be seruauntis and haundmaidis to you.

17 Therfor the Lord seith thes thingis, Ye herden not me, that ye prechiden fredom, ech man to his brothir, and ech man to his freend; lo! Y preeche to you fredom, seith the Lord, and to swerd, and to hungur, and to pestilence, and Y schal yyue you in to stiryng to alle rewmes of erthe.

18 And Y schal yyue the men, that breken my boond of pees, and kepten not the wordis of boond of pees, to whiche thei assentiden in my siyt, and kepten not the calf, which thei kittiden in to twei partis; and the princes of Juda,

19 and the princes of Jerusalem, and the onest seruauntis, and preestis yeden bytwixe the partyngis therof, and al the puple of the lond, that yeden bitwixe the departyngis of the calf;

20 and Y schal yyue hem in to the hond of her enemyes, and in to the hond of hem that seken her lijf; and the deed careyn of hem schal be in to mete to the volatilis of the eir, and to the beestis of erthe.

21 And Y schal yyue Sedechie, the kyng of Juda, and hise princes, in to the hond of her enemyes, and in to the hond of hem that seken her lijf, and in to the hond of the oostis of the kyng of Babiloyne, that yeden awei fro you.

22 Lo! Y comaunde, seith the Lord, and Y schal brynge hem ayen in to this citee, and thei schulen fiyte ayens it, and schulen take it, and schulen brenne it with fier; and Y schal yyue the citees of Juda in to wildirnesse, for ther is no dwellere.

CAP 35

1 The word that was maad of the Lord to Jeremye, in the daies of Joachym, sone of Josie,

2 kyng of Juda, and seide, Go thou to the hous of Recabitis, and speke thou to hem; and thou schalt brynge hem in to the hous of the Lord, in to o chaumbre of tresouris, and thou schalt yyue to hem to drynke wyn.

3 And Y took Jeconye, the sone of Jeremye, sone of Absanye, and hise britheren, and alle the sones of hym, and al the hous of Recabitis.

4 And Y ledde hem in to the hous of the Lord, to the treserie of the sones of Eman, sone of Godolie, the man of God; which treserie was bisidis the treserie of princes, aboue the tresour of Maasie, sone of Sellum, that was kepere of the vestiarie.

5 And Y settide bifore the sones of the hous of Recabitis pecis, and grete cowpis ful of wyn; and Y seide to hem, Drinke ye wyn.

6 And thei answeriden, We schulen not drinke wyn; for whi Jonadab, oure fadir, the sone of Recab, comaundide to vs, and seide, Ye schulen not drinke wyn, ye and youre sones, 'til in to withouten ende;

7 and ye schulen not bilde an hous, and ye schulen not sowe seed, and ye schulen not plaunte vynes, nether schulen haue, but ye schulen dwelle in tabernaclis in alle youre daies, that ye lyue many daies on the face of erthe, in which ye goen in pilgrymage.

8 Therfor we obeieden to the vois of Jonadab, oure fadir, the sone of Recab, in alle thingis whiche he comaundide to vs; so that we drunken not wyn in alle oure dayes, we, and oure wymmen, oure sones, and douytris;

9 and we bildiden not housis to dwelle, and we hadden not a vyner, and a feeld, and seed;

10 but we dwelliden in tabernaclis, and weren obeiynge, and diden bi alle thingis, whiche Jonadab, oure fadir, comaundide to vs.

11 But whanne Nabugodonosor, kyng of Babiloyne, hadde stied to this lond, we seiden, Come ye, and entre we in to Jerusalem, fro the face of the oost of Caldeis, and fro the face of the oost of Sirie; and we dwelliden in Jerusalem.

12 And the word of the Lord was maad to Jeremye,

13 and seide, The Lord of oostis, God of Israel, seith these thingis, Go thou, and seie to the men of Juda, and to the dwelleris of Jerusalem, Whether ye schulen not take techyng, that ye obeie to my wordis, seith the Lord?

14 The wordis of Jonadab, sone of Rechab, hadden the maistrie, whiche he comaundide to hise sones, that thei schulden not drynke wyn; and thei drynken not, 'til to this dai; for thei obeieden to the comaundement of her fadir; but Y spak to you, and Y roos ful eerli, and spake, and ye obeieden not to me.

15 And Y sente to you alle my seruauntis profetis, and Y roos ful eerli, and Y sente, and seide, Be ye conuertid, ech man fro his worste weye, and make ye good youre studies, and nyle ye sue alien goddis, nether worschipe ye hem, and ye schulen dwelle in the lond, which Y yaf to you, and to youre fadris; and ye bowiden not youre eere, nether herden me.

16 Therfor the sones of Jonadab, sone of Recab, maden stidfast the comaundement of her fadir, which he comaundide to hem; but this puple obeiede not to me.

17 Therfor the Lord of oostis, God of Israel, seith these thingis, Lo! Y schal bringe on Juda, and on alle the dwelleris of Jerusalem, al the turment which Y spak ayens hem; for Y spak to hem, and thei herden not; Y clepide hem, and thei answeriden not to me.

18 Forsothe Jeremye seide to the hous of Recabitis, The Lord of oostis, God of Israel, seith these thingis, For that that ye obeieden to the comaundement of Jonadab, youre fadir, and kepten alle hise comaundementis, and diden alle thingis, whiche he comaundide to you;

19 therfor the Lord of oostis, God of Israel, seith these thingis, A man of the generacioun of Jonadab, sone of Recab, schal not faile stondynge in my siyt in alle daies.

CAP 36

1 And it was don, in the fourthe yeer of Joachym, sone of Josie, kyng of Juda, this word was maad of the Lord to Jeremye, and seide,

2 Take thou the volym of a book, and thou schalt write therynne alle the wordis, whiche Y spake to thee ayens Israel and Juda, and ayens alle folkis, fro the dai in whiche Y spak to thee, fro the daies of Josie 'til to this dai.

3 If perauenture whanne the hous of Juda herith alle the yuels whiche Y thenke to do to hem, ech man turne ayen fro his worste weye, and Y schal be merciful to the wickidnesse and synne of hem.

4 Therfor Jeremye clepide Baruk, the sone of Nerye; and Baruk wroot of the mouth of Jeremye in the volym of a book alle the wordis of the Lord, whiche he spak to hym.

5 And Jeremye comaundide to Baruk, and seide, Y am closid, and Y may not entre in to the hous of the Lord.

6 Therfor entre thou, and rede of the book, in which thou hast write of my mouth the wordis of the Lord, in hering of the puple, in the hous of the Lord, in the dai of fastyng; ferthermore and in heryng of al Juda, that comen fro her citees, thou schalt rede to hem;

7 if perauenture the preier of hem falle in the siyt of the Lord, and eche man turne ayen fro his worste weie; for whi the strong veniaunce and indignacioun is greet, which the Lord spak ayens this puple.

8 And Baruk, the sone of Nerie, dide aftir alle thingis, which Jeremye, the prophete, comaundide to hym; and he redde of the book the wordis of the Lord, in the hous of the Lord.

9 Forsothe it was doon, in the fyueth yeer of Joachym, sone of Josie, kyng of Juda, in the nynthe monethe, thei prechiden fastynge in the siyt of the Lord, to al the puple in Jerusalem, and to al the multitude, that cam togidere fro the citees of Juda in to Jerusalem.

10 And Baruc redde of the volym the wordis of Jeremye, in the hous of the Lord, in the treserie of Gamarie, sone of Saphan, scryuen, in the hiyere porche, in the entring of the newe yate of the hous of the Lord, in audience of al the puple.

11 And whanne Mychie, the sone of Gamarie, sone of Saphan, hadde herd alle the wordis of the Lord,

12 of the book, he yede doun in to the hous of the kyng, to the treserye of the scryuen. And lo! alle the princes saten there, Elisama, the scryuen, and Dalaie, the sone of Semeye, and Elnathan, the sone of Achabor, and Gamarie, the sone of Saphan, and Sedechie, the sone of Ananye, and alle princes.

13 And Mychee telde to hem alle the wordis, whiche he herde Baruc redynge of the book, in the eeris of the puple.

14 Therfor alle the princes senten to Baruc Judi, the sone of Nathathie, sone of Selemye, sone of Chusi, and seiden, Take in thin hond the book, of which thou reddist in audience of the puple, and come thou. Therfor Baruc, the sone of Nereie, took the book in his hoond, and cam to hem.

15 And thei seiden to hym, Sitte thou, and rede these thingis in oure eeris; and Baruc redde in the eeris of hem.

16 Therfor whanne thei hadden herd alle the wordis, thei wondriden ech man to his neiybore, and thei seiden to Baruc, Owen we to telle to the kyng alle these wordis?

17 And thei axiden hym, and seiden, Schewe thou to vs, hou thou hast write alle these wordis of his mouth.

18 Forsothe Baruc seide to hem, Of his mouth he spak, as redynge to me, alle these wordis; and Y wroot in a book with enke.

19 And alle the princes seiden to Baruc, Go, be thou hid, thou and Jeremye; and no man wite where ye ben.

20 And thei entriden to the kyng, in to the halle; forsothe thei bitoken the book to be kept in to the treserie of Elisame, the scryuen. And thei telden alle the wordis, in audience of the kyng.

21 Therfor the kyng sente Judi, that he schulde take the book. Which took the book fro the treserie of Elysame, the scryuen, and redde in audience of the kyng, and of alle the princes, that stoden aboute the kyng.

22 Forsothe the kyng sat in the wyntir hous, in the nynthe monethe; and a panne ful of coolis was set bifore hym.

23 And whanne Judi hadde red thre pagyns, ethir foure, he kittide it with the knyf of a scryueyn, and castide in to the fier, 'that was in the panne, til al the book was wastid bi the fier, that was on the panne.

24 And the kyng and alle hise seruauntis, that herden alle these wordis, dredden not, nethir to-renten her clothis.

25 Netheles Elnathan, and Dalaie, and Gamarie ayenseiden the kyng, that he schulde not brenne the book; and he herde not hem.

26 And the kyng comaundide to Jeremyel, sone of Amalech, and to Saraie, sone of Esreel, and to Selemye, sone of Abdehel, that thei schulden take Baruc, the writer, and Jeremye, the profete; forsothe the Lord hidde hem.

27 And the word of the Lord was maad to Jeremye, the profete, aftir that the kyng hadde brent the book and wordis, whiche Baruc hadde write of Jeremyes mouth;

28 and he seid, Eft take thou another book, and write therynne alle the former wordis, that weren in the firste book, which Joachym, the kyng of Juda, brente.

29 And thou schalt seie to Joachym, kyng of Juda, The Lord seith these thingis, Thou brentist that book, and seidist, What hast thou write therynne, teliynge, The kyng of Babiloyne schal come hastynge, and schal distrie this lond, and schal make man and beeste to ceesse therof?

30 Therfor the Lord seith these thingis ayens Joachym, king of Juda, Noon schal be of hym, that schal sitte on the seete of Dauid; and his careyn schal be cast forth to the heete bi dai, and to the forst bi niyt.

31 And Y schal visite ayens hym, and ayens his seed, and ayens hise seruauntis, her wickidnessis. And Y schal bryng on hem, and on the dwelleris of Jerusalem, and on the men of Juda, al the yuel which Y spak to hem, and thei herden not.

32 Forsothe Jeremye took an other book, and yaf it to Baruc, the writer, the sone of Nerie, which wroot therynne of Jeremyes mouth alle the wordis of the book, which book Joachym, the kyng of Juda, hadde brent bi fier; and ferthermore many mo wordis weren addid than weren bifore.

CAP 37

1 And kyng Sedechie, the sone of Josie, regnede for Jeconye, the sone of Joachym, whom Nabugodonosor, kyng of Babiloyne, made kyng in the lond of Juda.

2 And he, and hise seruauntis, and his puple obeieden not to the wordis of the Lord, whiche he spak in the hond of Jeremye, the profete.

3 And kyng Sedechie sente Jothal, the sone of Selemye, and Sofonye, the preest, the sone of Maasie, to Jeremye, the profete, and seide, Preie thou for vs oure Lord God.

4 Forsothe Jeremye yede freli in the myddis of the puple; for thei hadden not sente hym in to the kepyng of the prisoun. Therfor the oost of Farao yede out of Egipt, and Caldeis, that bisegiden Jerusalem, herden sich a message, and yeden awei fro Jerusalem.

5 And the word of the Lord was maad to Jeremye, the profete, 6 and seide, The Lord God of Israel seith these thingis, Thus ye schulen seie to the kyng of Juda, that sente you to axe me, Lo! the oost of Farao, which yede out to you in to help, schal turne ayen in to his lond, in to Egipt.

7 And Caldeis schulen come ayen, and schulen fiyte ayens this citee, and schulen take it, and schulen brenne it bi fier.

8 The Lord seith these thingis, Nyle ye disseyue youre soulis, seiynge, Caldeis goynge schulen go a wey, and schulen departe fro vs; for thei schulen not go a wei.

9 But thouy ye sleen al the oost of Caldeis, that fiyten ayens you, and summe woundid men of hem be left, ech man schal rise fro his tente, and thei schulen brenne this citee bi fier.

10 Therfor whanne the oost of Caldeis hadde goon awei fro Jerusalem, for the oost of Farao, Jeremye yede out of Jerusalem,

11 to go in to the lond of Beniamyn, and to departe there the possessioun in the siyt of citeseyns.

12 And whanne he was comun to the yate of Beniamyn, ther was a kepere of the yate bi whiles, Jerie bi name, the sone of Selemye, sone of Ananye; and he took Jeremye, the prophete, and seide, Thou fleest to Caldeis.

13 And Jeremye answeride, It is fals; Y fle not to Caldeis. And he herde not Jeremye, but Jerie took Jeremye, and brouyte hym to the princes.

14 Wherfor the princes weren wrooth ayens Jeremye, and beeten hym, and senten hym in to the prisoun, that was in the hous of Jonathas, the scryuen; for he was souereyn on the prisoun.

15 Therfor Jeremye entride in to the hous of the lake, and in to the prisoun of trauel; and Jeremye sat there manye daies.

16 Therfor kyng Sedechie sente, and took hym a wei, and axide hym priuyli in his hous, and seide, Gessist thou, whether a word is of the Lord? And Jeremye seide, Ther is. And Jeremye seide, Thou schalt be bitakun in to the hond of the kyng of Babiloyne.

17 And Jeremye seide to Sedechie, the kyng, What haue Y synned to thee, and to thi seruauntis, and to thi puple, for thou hast sent me in to the hous of prisoun?

18 Where ben youre profetis, that profesieden to you, and seiden, The king of Babiloyne schal not come on you, and on this lond?

19 Now therfor, my lord the kyng, Y biseche, here thou, my preier be worth in thi siyt, and sende thou not me ayen in to the hous of Jonathas, the scryuen, lest Y die there.

20 Therfor Sedechie comaundide, that Jeremye schulde be bitakun in to the porche of the prisoun, and that a cake of breed schulde be youun to hym ech dai, outakun seew, til alle looues of the citee weren wastid; and Jeremye dwellide in the porche of the prisoun.

CAP 38

1 Forsothe Safacie, sone of Nathan, and Jedelie, sone of Fassur, and Jothal, sone of Selemye, and Fassour, sone of Melchie, herden the wordis whiche Jeremye spak to al the puple,

2 'and seide, The Lord seith these thingis, Who euer dwellith in this citee, schal die bi swerd, and hungur, and pestilence; but he that flieth to Caldeis, shal lyue, and his soule schal be hool and lyuynge.

3 The Lord seith these thingis, This citee to be bitakun schal be bitakun in to the hond of the oost of the kyng of Babiloyne, and he schal take it.

4 And the princes seiden to the kyng, We preien, that this man be slayn; for of bifore castyng he discoumfortith the hondis of men werriours, that dwelliden in this citee, and the hondis of al the puple, and spekith to hem bi alle these wordis. For whi this man sekith not pees to this puple, but yuel.

5 And kyng Sedechie seide, Lo! he is in youre hondis, for it is not leueful that the kyng denye ony thing to you.

6 Therfor thei token Jeremye, and castiden hym doun in to the lake of Elchie, sone of Amalech, which was in the porche of the prisoun; and thei senten doun Jeremye bi cordis in to the lake, wherynne was no watir, but fen; therfor Jeremye yede doun in to the filthe.

7 Forsothe Abdemalech Ethiopien, a chast man and oneste, herde, that was in the kyngis hous, that thei hadden sent Jeremye in to the lake; sotheli the king sat in the yate of Beniamyn.

8 And Abdemalech yede out of the kyngis hous, and spak to the kyng,

9 and seide, My lord the kyng, these men diden yuele alle thingis, what euer thingis thei diden ayens Jeremye, the profete, sendynge hym in to the lake, that he die there for hungur; for whi looues ben no more in the citee.

10 Therfor the kyng comaundide to Abdemelech Ethiopien, and seide, Take with thee thretti men fro hennus, and reise thou Jeremye, the profete, fro the lake, bifor that he die.

11 Therfor whanne Abdemelech hadde take men with hym, he entride in to the hous of the kyng, that was vndur the celer; and he took fro thennus elde clothis, and elde ragges, that weren rotun; and he sente tho doun to Jeremye, in to the lake, bi cordis.

12 And Abdemelech Ethiopien seide to Jeremye, Putte thou elde clothis, and these to-rent and rotun thingis vndur the cubit of thin hondis, and on the cordis. Therfor Jeremye dide so.

13 And thei drowen out Jeremye with cordis, and ledden hym out of the lake. Forsothe Jeremye dwellide in the porche of the prisoun.

14 And kyng Sedechie sente, and took hym Jeremye, the profete, at the thridde dore that was in the hous of the Lord. And the kyng seide to Jeremye, Y axe of thee a word; hide thou not ony thing fro me.

15 Forsothe Jeremye seide to Sedechie, If Y telle to thee, whether thou schalt not sle me? And if Y yyue councel to thee, thou schalt not here me.

16 Therfor Sedechie the king swoor to Jeremye priueli, and seide, The Lord lyueth, that maad to vs this soule, Y schal not sle thee, and Y schal not bitake thee in to the hondis of these men, that seken thi lijf.

17 And Jeremye seide to Sedechie, The Lord of oostis, God of Israel, seith these thingis, If thou goest forth, and goest out to the princes of the kyng of Babiloyne, thi soule schal lyue, and this citee schal not be brent with fier, and thou schalt be saaf, thou and thin hous.

18 Forsothe if thou goest not out to the princes of the kyng of Babiloyne, this citee schal be bitakun in to the hondis of Caldeis; and thei schulen brenne it with fier, and thou schalt not ascape fro the hond of hem.

19 And kyng Sedechie seide to Jeremye, Y am angwischid for the Jewis that fledden ouer to Caldeis, lest perauenture Y be bitakun in to the hondis of hem, and thei scorne me.

20 Forsothe Jeremye answeride, and seide to hym, Thei schulen not bitake thee; Y biseche, here thou the vois of the Lord, which Y schal speke to thee, and it schal be wel to thee, and thi soule schal lyue.

21 That if thou wolt not go out, this is the word which the Lord schewide to me, Lo!

22 alle the wymmen, that weren left in the hous of the kyng of Juda, schulen be led out to the princes of the kyng of Babiloyne; and tho wymmen schulen seie, Thi pesible men disseyueden thee, and hadden the maistrye ayens thee; thei drenchiden thee in filthe, and thi feet in slidirnesse, and yeden awei fro thee.

23 And alle thi wyues and thi sones schulen be led out to Caldeis, and thou schalt not ascape the hondis of hem; but thou schalt be bitakun in to the hondis of the kyng of Babiloyne, and he schal brenne this citee bi fier.

24 Therfore Sedechie seide to Jeremye, No man wite these wordis, and thou schalt not die.

25 Sotheli if the princes heren, that Y spak with thee, and comen to thee, and seien to thee, Schewe thou to vs what thou spakest with the kyng, hide thou not fro vs, and we schulen not sle thee; and what the kyng spak with thee,

26 thou schalt seie to hem, Knelyngli Y puttide forth my preiris bifore the kyng, that he schulde not comaunde me to be led ayen in to the hous of Jonathan, and Y schulde die there.

27 Therfor alle the princes camen to Jeremye, and axiden hym; and he spak to hem bi alle the wordis whiche the kyng hadde comaundid to hym, and thei ceessiden fro hym; for whi no thing was herd.

28 Therfor Jeremye dwellide in the porche of the prisoun, til to the dai wherynne Jerusalem was takun; and it was don, that Jerusalem schulde be takun.

CAP 39

1 In the nynethe yeer of Sedechie, kyng of Juda, in the tenthe monethe, Nabugodonosor, kyng of Babiloyne, and al his oost cam to Jerusalem, and thei bisegiden it.

2 Forsothe in the enleuenthe yeer of Sedechie, in the fourthe monethe, in the fyuethe day of the monethe, the citee was opened;

3 and alle the princes of the kyng of Babiloyne entriden, and saten in the myddil yate, Veregel, Fererer, Semegar, Nabusarrachym, Rapsaces, Neregel, Sereser, Rebynag, and alle othere princes of the kyng of Babiloyne.

4 And whanne Sedechie, the kyng of Juda, and alle the men werriouris hadden seien hem, thei fledden, and yeden out bi niyt fro the citee, bi the weie of the gardyn of the kyng, and bi the yate that was bitwixe twei wallis; and thei yeden out to the weie of desert.

5 Forsothe the oost of Caldeis pursueden hem, and thei token Sedechie in the feeld of wildirnesse of Jericho; and thei token hym, and brouyten to Nabugodonosor, kyng of Babiloyne, in Reblatha, which is in the lond of Emath; and Nabugodonosor spak domes to hym.

6 And the kyng of Babiloyne killide the sones of Sedechye in Reblatha, bifor hise iyen; and the kyng of Babyloyne killide alle the noble men of Juda.

7 Also he puttide out the iyen of Sedechie, and boond hym in feteris, that he schulde be led in to Babiloyne.

8 And Caldeis brenten with fier the hous of the kyng, and the hous of the comun puple, and distrieden the wal of Jerusalem.

9 And Nabusardan, the maister of knyytis, translatide in to Babiloyne the residues of the puple, that dwelliden in the citee, and the fleeris awei, that hadden fled ouer to hym, and the superflue men of the comyn puple, that weren left.

10 And Nabusardan, the maistir of knyytis, lefte in the lond of Juda, of the puple of pore men, and yaf to hem vyneris and cisternes in that dai.

11 Forsothe Nabugodonosor, kyng of Babiloyne, hadde comaundid of Jeremye to Nabusardan, maister of chyualrie, and seide,

12 Take thou him, and sette thin iyen on hym, and do thou no thing of yuel to him; but as he wole, so do thou to hym.

13 Therfor Nabusardan, the prynce of chyualrie, sente Nabu, and Lesban, and Rapsases, and Veregel, and Sereser, and Rebynag, and alle the principal men of the kyng of Babiloyne,

14 senten, and token Jeremye fro the porche of the prisoun, and bitokun hym to Godolie, the sone of Aicham, sone of Saphan, that he schulde entre in to the hous, and dwelle among the puple.

15 Forsothe the word of the Lord was maad to Jeremye, whanne he was closid in the porche of the prisoun, and seide,

16 Go thou, and seie to Abdemelech Ethiopien, and speke thou, The Lord of oostis, God of Israel, seith these thingis, Lo! Y schal brynge my wordis on this citee in to yuel, and not in to good; and tho schulen be in thi siyt in that dai.

17 And Y schal delyuere thee in that day, seith the Lord, and thou schalt not be bitakun in to the hondis of men, whiche thou dreddist;

18 but Y delyuerynge schal delyuere thee, and thou schalt not falle doun bi swerd; but thi soule schal be in to helthe to thee, for thou haddist trist in me, seith the Lord.

CAP 40

1 The word that was maad of the Lord to Jeremye, aftir that he was delyuered of Nabusardan, maister of chyualrie, fro Rama, whanne he took hym boundun with chaynes, in the myddis of alle men that passiden fro Jerusalem, and fro Juda, and weren led in to Babyloyne.

2 Therfor the prince of chyualrie took Jeremye, and seide to hym, Thi Lord God spak this yuel on this place,

3 and the Lord hath brouyt, and hath do, as he spak; for ye synneden to the Lord, and herden not the vois of hym, and this word is doon to you.

4 Now therfor lo! Y haue releessid thee to dai fro the chaynes that ben in thin hondis; if it plesith thee to come with me in to Babiloyne, come thou, and Y schal sette myn iyen on thee; sotheli if it displesith thee to come with me in to Babiloyne, sitte thou here; lo! al the lond is in thi siyt, that that thou chesist, and whidur it plesith thee to go, thidur go thou,

5 and nyle thou come with me. But dwelle thou with Godolie, sone of Aicham, sone of Saphan, whom the kyng of Babiloyne made souereyn to the citees of Juda; therfor dwelle thou with hym in the myddis of the puple, ether go thou, whidir euer it plesith thee to go. And the maister of chyualrie yaf to hym metis, and yiftis, and lefte hym.

6 Forsothe Jeremye cam to Godolie, sone of Aicham, in to Masphat, and dwellide with hym, in the myddis of the puple that was left in the lond.

7 And whanne alle princes of the oost hadden herd, that weren scatered bi cuntreis, thei and the felowis of hem, that the kyng of Babiloyne hadde maad Godolie souereyn of the lond, the sone of Aicham, and that he hadde bitake to Godolie men, and wymmen, and litle children, and of pore men of the lond, that weren not translatid in to Babiloyne,

8 thei camen to Godolie in Masphat; and Ismael, the sone of Nathanye, and Johannan, the sone of Caree, and Jonathan, and Sareas, the sone of Tenoemeth, and the sones of Offi, that weren of Nethophati, and Jeconye, the sone of Machati; bothe thei and her men camen to Godolie.

9 And Godolie, sone of Aicham, sone of Saphan, swoor to hem, and to the felowis of hem, and seide, Nyle ye drede to serue Caldeis; but dwelle ye in the lond, and serue ye the kyng of Babiloyne, and it schal be wel to you.

10 Lo! Y dwelle in Mesphath, for to answere to the comaundement of Caldeis, that ben sent to vs; forsothe gadere ye vyndage, and ripe corn, and oile, and kepe ye in youre vessels, and dwelle ye in youre citees whiche ye holden.

11 But also alle the Jewis, that weren in Moab, and in the oostis of Amon, and in Ydumee, and in alle the cuntreis, whanne it is herd, that the kyng of Babiloyne hadde youe residues, ether remenauntis, in Judee, and that he hadde maad souereyn on hem Godolie, the sone of Aicham, sone of Saphan,

12 sotheli alle Jewis turneden ayen fro alle places, to whiche thei hadden fled; and thei camen in to the lond of Juda, to Godolie in Masphat, and gaderiden wyn and ripe corn ful myche.

13 Forsothe Johannan, the sone of Caree, and alle the princes of the oost, that weren scaterid in the cuntreis, camen to Godolie in Masphath,

14 and seiden to hym, Wite thou, that Bahalis, kyng of the sones of Amon, hath sent Ismael, the sone of Nathanye, to smyte thi lijf. And Godolie, the sone of Aicham, bileuyde not to hem.

15 Forsothe Johannan, the sone of Caree, seide to Godolie asidis half in Masphath, and spak, Y schal go, and sle Ismael, the sone of Nathanye, while no man knowith, lest he sle thi lijf, and alle the Jewis ben scatered, that ben gaderid to thee, and the remenauntis of Juda schulen perische.

16 And Godolie, the sone of Aicham, seide to Johannan, the sone of Caree, Nyle thou do this word, for thou spekist fals of Ismael.

CAP 41

1 And it was don in the seuenthe monethe, Ismael, the sone of Nathanye, sone of Elisama, of the kingis seed, and the principal men of the kyng, and ten men with hym, camen to Godolie, the sone of Aicham, in Masphath; and thei eeten there looues togidere in Masphath.

2 Forsothe Ismael, the sone of Nathanye, and the ten men that weren with hym, risiden vp, and killiden bi swerd Godolie, the sone of Aicham, sone of Saphan; and thei killiden hym, whom the kyng of Babiloyne hadde maad souereyn of the lond.

3 Also Ismael killide alle the Jewis, that weren with Godolie in Masphath, and the Caldeis, that weren foundun there, and the men werriours.

4 Forsothe in the secounde dai, aftir that he hadde slayn Godolie, while no man wiste yit,

5 foure scoor men with schauen beerdis, and to-rent clothis, and pale men, camen fro Sichem, and fro Silo, and fro Samarie; and thei hadden yiftis and encense in the hond, for to offre in the hous of the Lord.

6 Therfor Ismael, the sone of Nathanye, yede out of Masphath in to the metyng of hem; and he yede goynge and wepynge. Sotheli whanne he hadde met hem, he seide to hem, Come ye to Godolie, the sone of Aicham;

7 and whanne thei weren comun to the myddis of the citee, Ismael, the sone of Nathanye, killide hem aboute the myddis of the lake, he and the men that weren with hym 'killiden hem.

8 But ten men weren foundun among hem, that seiden to Ismael, Nyle thou sle vs, for we han tresour of wheete, and of barli, and of oile, and of hony, in the feeld. And he ceesside, and killide not hem with her britheren.

9 Forsothe the lake in to which Ismael castide forth alle the careyns of men, whiche he killide for Godolie, is thilke lake, which kyng Asa made for Baasa, the kyng of Israel; Ismael, the sone of Nathanye, fillide that lake with slayn men.

10 And Ismael ledde prisoneris alle the remenauntis of the puple, that weren in Mesphath, the douytris of the kyng, and al the puple that dwelliden in Masphath, whiche Nabusardan, the prince of chyualrie, hadde bitakun to kepyng to Godolie, the sone of Aicham. And Ismael, the sone of Nathanye, took hem, and yede to passe ouer to the sones of Amon.

11 Forsothe Johannan, the sone of Caree, and alle the princes of werriouris, that weren with hym, herden al the yuel, which Ismael, the sone of Nathanye, hadde do.

12 And whanne thei hadden take alle men, thei yeden forth to fiyte ayens Ismael, the sone of Nathanye; and thei foundun hym at the many watris, that ben in Gabaon.

13 And whanne al the puple, that was with Ismael, hadden seyn Johannan, the sone of Caree, and alle the princes of werriouris, that weren with hym, thei weren glad.

14 And al the puple, whom Ismael hadde take in Masphath, turnede ayen; and it turnede ayen, and yede to Johannan, the sone of Caree.

15 Forsothe Ismael, the sone of Nathanye, fledde with eiyte men fro the face of Johannan, and yede to the sones of Amon.

16 Therfor Johannan, the sone of Caree, and alle the princes of werriours, that weren with hym, token alle the remenauntis of the comyn puple, whiche thei brouyten ayen fro Ismael, the sone of Nathanye, that weren of Masphat, aftir that he killide Godolie, the sone of Aicham; he took strong men to batel, and wymmen, and children, and geldyngis, whiche he hadde brouyt ayen fro Gabaon.

17 And thei yeden, and saten beynge pilgryms in Canaan, which is bisidis Bethleem, that thei schulden go, and entre in to Egipt fro the face of Caldeis;

18 for thei dredden thilke Caldeis, for Ismael, the sone of Nathanye, hadde slayn Godolie, the sone of Aicham, whom the kyng Nabugodonosor hadde maad souereyn in the lond of Juda.

CAP 42

1 And alle the princes of werriours neiyiden, and Johannan, the sone of Caree, and Jeconye, the sone of Josie, and the residue comyn puple, fro a litil man 'til to a greet man.

2 And thei seiden to Jeremye, the profete, Oure preier falle in thi siyt, and preie thou for vs to thi Lord God, for alle these remenauntis; for we ben left a fewe of manye, as thin iyen biholden vs; and thi Lord God telle to vs the weie,

3 bi which we schulen go, and the word which we schulen do.

4 Forsothe Jeremye, the profete, seide to hem, Y haue herd; lo! Y preye to oure Lord God, bi youre wordis; Y schal schewe to you ech word, what euere word the Lord schal answere to me, nether Y schal hide ony thing fro you.

5 And thei seiden to Jeremye, The Lord be witnesse of treuthe and of feith bitwixe vs; if not bi ech word, in which thi Lord God schal sende thee to vs, so we schulen do, whether it be good ether yuel.

6 We schulen obeie to the vois of oure Lord God, to whom we senden thee, that it be wel to vs, whanne we han herd the vois of oure Lord God.

7 Forsothe whanne ten daies weren fillid, the word of the Lord was maad to Jeremye.

8 And he clepide Johannan, the sone of Caree, and alle the princes of werriours, that weren with hym, and al the puple fro the leste 'til to the mooste; and he seide to hem,

9 The Lord God of Israel seith these thingis, to whom ye senten me, that Y schulde mekeli sette forth youre preyeris in his siyt.

10 If ye resten, and dwellen in this lond, Y schal bilde you, and Y schal not distrie; Y schal plaunte, and Y schal not drawe out; for now Y am plesid on the yuel which Y dide to you.

11 Nyle ye drede of the face of the kyng of Babiloyne, whom ye 'that ben ferdful, dreden; nyle ye drede hym, seith the Lord, for Y am with you, to make you saaf, and to delyuere fro his hond.

12 And Y schal yyue mercies to you, and Y schal haue merci on you, and Y schal make you dwelle in youre lond.

13 Forsothe if ye seien, We schulen not dwelle in this lond, nether we schulen here the vois of oure Lord God, and seie,

14 Nai, but we schulen go to the lond of Egipt, where we schulen not se batel, and schulen not here the noise of trumpe, and we schulen not suffre hungur, and there we schulen dwelle;

15 for this thing, ye remenauntis of Juda, here now the word of the Lord. The Lord of oostis, God of Israel, seith these thingis, If ye setten youre face, for to entre in to Egipt, and if ye entren,

16 to dwelle there, the swerd whiche ye dreden schal take you there in the lond of Egipt, and the hungur for which ye ben angwischid schal cleue to you in Egipt; and there ye schulen die.

17 And alle the men that settiden her face, to entre in to Egipt, and to dwelle there, schulen die bi swerd, and hungur, and pestilence; no man of hem schal dwelle stille, nether schal aschape fro the face of yuel, which Y schal brynge on hem.

18 For why the Lord of oostis, God of Israel, seith these thingis, As my strong veniaunce and myn indignacioun is wellid togidere on the dwelleris of Jerusalem, so myn indignacioun schal be wellid togidere on you, whanne ye han entrid in to Egipt; and ye schulen be in to sweryng, and in to wondring, and in to cursyng, and in to schenschipe; and ye schulen no more se this place.

19 The word of the Lord is on you, ye remenauntis of Juda; nyle ye entre in to Egipt; ye witinge schulen wite, that Y haue witnessid to you to dai;

20 for ye han disseyued youre soulis, for ye senten me to youre Lord God, and seiden, Preye thou for vs to oure Lord God, and bi alle thingis what euer thingis oure Lord schal seie to thee, so telle thou to vs, and we schulen do.

21 And Y telde to you to dai, and ye herden not the vois of youre Lord God, on alle thingis for whiche he sente me to you.

22 Now therfor ye witynge schulen wite, for ye schulen die bi swerd, and hungur, and pestilence, in the place to which ye wolden entre, to dwelle there.

CAP 43

1 Forsothe it was don, whanne Jeremye spekinge to the puple hadde fillid alle the wordis of the Lord God of hem, for whiche the Lord God of hem sente hym to hem, alle these wordis,

2 Azarie, the sone of Josie, seide, and Johanna, the sone of Caree, and alle proude men, seiynge to Jeremye, Thou spekist a leesyng; oure Lord God sente not thee, and seide, Entre ye not in to Egipt, to dwelle there;

3 but Baruc, the sone of Nerie, stirith thee ayens vs, that he bitake vs in the hondis of Caldeis, that he sle vs, and make to be led ouer in to Babiloyne.

4 And Johanna, the sone of Caree, and alle the princes of werriours, and al the puple, herden not the vois of the Lord, that thei dwellen in the lond of Juda.

5 But Johanna, the sone of Caree, and alle the princes of werriours, token alle of the remenauntis of Juda, that turneden ayen fro alle folkis, to whiche thei weren scatered bifore, that thei schulden dwelle in the lond of Juda;

6 thei token men, and wymmen, and litle children, and the douytris of the kyng, and ech persoone, whom Nabusardan, the prince of chyualrie, hadde left with Godolie, the sone of Aicham, sone of Saphan. And thei token Jeremye, the profete, and Baruc, the sone of Nerie,

7 and thei entriden in to the lond of Egipt; for thei obeieden not to the vois of the Lord, and thei camen 'til to Taphnys.

8 And the word of the Lord was maad to Jeremye in Taphnys,

9 and seide, Take in thin hond grete stoonys, and hide thou tho in a denne, which is vndur the wal of tiil stoon, in the yate of the hous of Farao, in Taphnys, while alle Jewis seen.

10 And thou schalt seie to hem, The Lord of oostis, God of Israel, seith these thingis, Lo! Y schal sende, and Y schal take Nabugodonosor, my seruaunt, the kyng of Babiloyne; and Y schal sette his trone on these stoonys, whiche Y hidde; and he schal sette his seete on tho stoonys.

11 And he schal come, and smyte the lond of Egipt, whiche in deth in to deth, and whiche in caitiftee in to caitiftee, and whiche in swerd in to swerd.

12 And he schal kindle fier in the templis of goddis of Egipt, and he schal brenne tho templis, and schal lede hem prisoneris; and the lond of Egipt schal be wlappid, as a scheepherd is wlappid in his mentil; and he schal go out fro thennus in pees.

13 And he schal al to-breke the ymagis of the hous of the sunne, that ben in the lond of Egipt; and he schal brenne in fier the templis of the goddis of Egipt.

CAP 44

1 The word that was maad to Jeremye, and to alle the Jewis, that dwelliden in the lond of Egipt, dwellinge in Magdalo, and in Taphnys, and in Memphis, and in the lond of Phatures,

2 and seide, The Lord of oostis, God of Israel, seith these thingis, Ye sien al this yuel, which Y brouyte on Jerusalem, and on alle the citees of Juda; and lo! tho ben forsakun to dai, and no dwellere is in tho;

3 for the malice which thei diden, to terre me to wrathfulnesse, and that thei yeden, and maden sacrifice, and worschipiden alien goddis, whiche thei knewen not, bothe ye, and thei, and youre fadris.

4 And Y sente to you alle my seruauntis profetis; and Y roos bi nyyte, and sente, and seide, Nyle ye do the word of sich abhomynacioun.

5 And thei herden not, nether bowiden doun her eere, that thei schulen be conuertid fro her yuels, and schulden not make sacrifice to alien goddis.

6 And myn indignacioun and my strong veniaunce is wellid togidere, and is kindlid in the citees of Juda, and in the stretis of Jerusalem; and tho ben turned in to wildirnesse, and wastnesse, bi this dai.

7 And now the Lord of oostis, God of Israel, seith these thingis, Whi doon ye this greet yuel ayens youre soulis, that a man of you perische and a womman a litil child and soukynge

perische, fro the myddis of Juda, nether ony residue thing be left in you,

8 that terre me to wraththe bi the werkis of youre hondis, in makynge sacrifice to alien goddis in the lond of Egipt, in to which ye entriden, that ye dwelle there, and that ye perische, and be in to cursyng, and in to schenschipe to alle the folkis of erthe?

9 Whether ye han foryete the yuels of youre fadris, and the yuels of the kingis of Juda, and the yuels of her wiues, and youre yuels, and the yuels of youre wyues, whiche thei diden in the lond of Juda, and in the cuntreis of Jerusalem?

10 Thei ben not clensid 'til to this dai, and thei dredden not, and thei yeden not in the lawe of the Lord, and in myn heestis, whiche Y yaf bifore you, and bifore youre fadris.

11 Therfor the Lord of oostis, God of Israel, seith these thingis, Lo! Y schal sette my face in you in to yuel,

12 and Y schal leese al Juda, and Y schal take the remenauntis of Juda, that settiden her faces, to go in to the lond of Egipt, and to dwelle there; and alle schulen be waastid in the lond of Egipt, thei schulen falle doun bi swerd, and schulen be wastid in hungur, fro the leeste 'til to the mooste, thei schulen die bi swerd and hungur, and schulen be in to swering, and in to myracle, and in to cursyng, and in to schenschipe.

13 And Y schal visite on the dwelleris of Egipt, as Y visitide on Jerusalem, in swerd, and in hungur, and in pestilence.

14 And noon schal be, that schal ascape, and be residue of the remenauntis of Jewis, that goen to be pilgrimys in the lond of Egipt, and to turne ayen to the lond of Juda, to which thei reisen her soulis, that thei turne ayen, and dwelle there; thei schulen not turne ayen thidir, no but thei that fledden.

15 Forsothe alle men answeriden to Jeremye, and wisten, that her wyues maden sacrifice to alien goddis, and alle wymmen, of whiche a greet multitude stood, and alle the puple of dwelleris in the lond of Egipt, in Fatures, and seiden,

16 We schulen not here of thee the word which thou spekist to vs in the name of oure Lord God,

17 but we doynge schulen do ech word that schal go out of oure mouth, that we make sacrifice to the queen of heuene, and that we offre to it moist sacrifices, as we diden, and oure fadris, oure kingis, and oure princes, in the citees of Juda, and in the stretis of Jerusalem; and we weren fillid with looues, and it was wel to vs, and we sien noon yuel.

18 But fro that tyme, in which we ceessiden to make sacrifice to the queen of heuene, and to offre to it moist sacrifices, we hadden nede to alle thingis, and we weren wastid bi swerd and hungur.

19 That if we maken sacrifice to the queen of heuene, and offren to it moist sacrifices, whether withouten oure hosebondis we maden to it cakis, to worschipe it, and looues to be offrid?

20 And Jeremye seide to al the puple, ayens the men, and ayens the wymmen, and ayens al the puple, that answeriden to hym the word, and he seide,

21 Whether not the sacrifice which ye sacrifisiden in the citees of Juda, and in the stretis of Jerusalem, ye, and youre fadris, youre kyngis, and youre princes, and the puple of the lond, terriden God to veniaunce? The Lord hadde mynde on these thingis, and it stiede on his herte;

22 and the Lord myyte no more bere, for the malice of youre studies, and for abhomynaciouns whiche ye diden. And youre lond is maad in to desolacioun, and in to wondryng, and in to curs, for no dwellere is, as this dai is.

23 Therfor for ye maden sacrifice to idols, and synneden to the Lord, and herden not the vois of the Lord, and yeden not in the lawe, and in the comandementis, and in the witnessis of hym, therfor these yuels bifellen to you, as this dai is.

24 Forsothe Jeremye seide to al the puple, and to alle the wymmen, Al Juda, that ben in the lond of Egipt, here ye the word of the Lord.

25 The Lord of oostis, God of Israel, seith these thingis, and spekith, Ye and youre wyues spaken with youre mouth, and filliden with youre hondis, and seiden, Make we oure vowis whiche we vowiden, that we make sacrifice to the queen of heuene, and offre to it moist sacrifices; ye filliden youre vowis, and diden tho in werk.

26 Therfor, al Juda, that dwellen in the lond of Egipt, here ye the word of the Lord; Lo! Y swoor in my greet name, seith the Lord, that my name schal no more be clepid bi the mouth of ech man Jew, seiynge, The Lord God lyueth, in al the lond of Egipt.

27 Lo! Y schal wake on hem in to yuel, and not in to good; and alle the men of Juda, that ben in the lond of Egipt, schulen be waastid, bi swerd and hungur, til thei be wastid outerli.

28 And a fewe men that fledden the swerd, schulen turne ayen fro the lond of Egipt in to the lond of Juda; and alle the remenauntis of Juda, of hem that entren in to the lond of Egipt, to dwelle there, schulen wite, whos word schal be fillid, myn ether hern.

29 And this schal be a signe to you, seith the Lord, that Y schal visite on you in this place, that ye wite, that verili my wordis schulen be fillid ayens you in to yuel.

30 The Lord seith these thingis, Lo! Y schal bitake Farao, the kyng of Egipt, in to the hond of hise enemyes, and in to the hond of hem that seken his lijf, as Y bitook Sedechie, the kyng of Juda, in to the hond of Nabugodonosor, kyng of Babiloyne, his enemye, and sekynge his lijf.

CAP 45

1 The word that Jeremye, the profete, spak to Baruc, the sone of Nerie, whanne he hadde write these wordis in the book, of the mouth of Jeremye, in the fourthe yeer of Joachym, the sone of Josie, kyng of Juda,

2 and seide, The Lord God of Israel seith these thingis to thee, Baruc.

3 Thou seidist, Wo to me wretche, for the Lord encreesside sorewe to my sorewe; Y trauelide in my weilyng, and Y foond not reste.

4 The Lord seith these thingis, Thus thou schalt seye to hym, Lo! Y distrie hem, whiche Y bildide, and Y drawe out hem, whiche Y plauntide, and al this lond.

5 And sekist thou grete thingis to thee? nyle thou seke, for lo! Y schal brynge yuel on ech man, seith the Lord, and Y schal yyue to thee thi lijf in to helthe, in alle places, to whiche euer places thou schalt go.

CAP 46

1 The word of the Lord, that was maad to Jeremye, the profete, ayens hethene men;

2 to Egipt, ayens the oost of Farao Nechao, kyng of Egipt, that was bisidis the flood Eufrates, in Charchamys, whom Nabugodonosor, kyng of Babiloyne, smoot, in the fourthe yeer of Joachym, sone of Josie, kyng of Juda.

3 Make ye redi scheeld and targat, and go ye forth to batel.

4 loyne ye horsis, and stie, ye knyytis; stonde ye in helmes, polische ye speris, clothe ye you in haburiowns.

5 What therfor? Y siy hem dredeful, and turnynge the backis, the stronge men of hem slayn; and thei fledden swiftli, and bihelden not; drede was on ech side, seith the Lord.

6 A swift man schal not fle, and a strong man gesse not hym silf to be saued; at the north, bisidis the flood Eufrates, thei weren ouer comun, and fellen doun.

7 Who is this, that stieth as a flood, and hise swelewis wexen greet as of floodis?

8 Egipte stiede at the licnesse of a flood, and hise wawis schulen be mouyd as floodis; and it schal seie, Y schal stie, and hile the erthe; Y schal leese the citee, and dwelleris therof.

9 Stie ye on horsis, and make ye ful out ioie in charis; and stronge men, come forth, Ethiopie and Libie, holdynge scheeld, and Lidii, takynge and schetynge arowis.

10 Forsothe that dai of the Lord God of oostis is a dai of veniaunce, that he take veniaunce of hise enemyes; the swerd schal deuoure, and schal be fillid, and schal greetli be fillid with the blood of hem; for whi the slayn sacrifice of the Lord of oostis is in the lond of the north, bisidis the flood Eufrates.

11 Thou virgyn, the douyter of Egipt, stie in to Galaad, and take medicyn. In veyn thou schalt multiplie medecyns; helthe schal not be to thee.

12 Hethene men herden thi schenschipe, and thi yellyng fillide the erthe; for a strong man hurtlide ayens a strong man, and bothe fellen doun togidere.

13 The word which the Lord spak to Jeremye, the profete, on that that Nabugodonosor, kyng of Babiloyne, was to comynge, and to smytynge the lond of Egipt.

14 Telle ye to Egipt, and make ye herd in Magdalo, and sowne it in Memphis, and seie ye in Taphnys, Stonde thou, and make thee redi, for a swerd schal deuoure tho thingis that ben bi thi cumpas.

15 Whi hath thi strong man wexe rotun? He stood not, for the Lord vndurturnede hym.

16 He multipliede falleris, and a man felle doun to his neiybore; and thei schulen seie, Rise ye, and turne we ayen to oure puple, and to the lond of oure birthe, fro the face of swerd of the culuer.

17 Clepe ye the name of Farao, kyng of Egipt; the tyme hath brouyt noise.

18 Y lyue, seith the kyng, the Lord of oostis is his name; for it schal come as Thabor in hillis, and as Carmele in the see.

19 Thou dwelleresse, the douyter of Egipt, make to thee vessels of passyng ouer; for whi Memfis schal be in to wildirnesse, and schal be forsakun vnhabitable.

20 Egipt is a schapli cow calf, and fair; a prickere fro the north schal come to it.

21 Also the hirid men therof, that liueden as caluys maad fatte in the myddis therof, ben turned, and fledden togidere, and miyten not stonde; for the dai of sleynge of hem schal come on hem, the tyme of the visityng of hem.

22 The vois of hem schal sowne as of bras, for thei schulen haste with oost, and with axis thei schulen come to it. As men kittynge doun trees thei kittiden doun the forest therof,

23 seith the Lord, which mai not be noumbrid; thei ben multiplied ouer locustis, and no noumbre is in hem.

24 The douytir of Egipt is schent, and bitakun in to the hond of the puple of the north,

25 seide the Lord of oostis, God of Israel. Lo! Y schal visite on the noise of Alisaundre, and on Farao, and on Egipt, and on the goddis therof, and on the kyngis therof, and on hem that tristen in hym.

26 And Y schal yyue hem in to the hondis of men that seken the lijf of hem, and in to the hondis of Nabugodonosor, kyng of Babiloyne, and in to the hondis of hise seruauntis; and aftir these thingis it schal be enhabitid, as in the formere daies, seith the Lord.

27 And thou, Jacob, my seruaunt, drede thou not, and Israel, drede thou not; for lo! Y schal make thee saaf fro fer place, and thi seed fro the lond of his caitiftee; and Jacob schal turne ayen, and schal reste, and schal haue prosperite, and noon schal be, that schal make hym aferd.

28 And Jacob, my seruaunt, nyle thou drede, seith the Lord, for Y am with thee; for Y schal waste alle folkis, to whiche Y castide thee out; but Y schal not waste thee, but Y schal chastise thee in doom, and Y schal not spare thee as innocent.

CAP 47

1 The word of the Lord, that was maad to Jeremye, the profete, ayens Palestyns, bifor that Farao smoot Gaza.

2 The Lord seith these thingis, Lo! watris schulen stie fro the north, and tho schulen be as a stronde flowynge, and tho schulen hile the lond, and the fulnesse therof, the citee, and the dwelleris therof. Men schulen crie, and alle the dwelleris of the lond schulen yelle,

3 for the noise of boost of armed men, and of werriours of hym, and for mouyng of hise cartis, and multitude of hise wheelis. Fadris bihelden not sones with clumsid hondis,

4 for the comyng of the dai in which alle Filisteis schulen be destried; and Tirus schal be destried, and Sidon with alle her othere helpis. For the Lord hath destried Palestyns, the remenauntis of the ile of Capadocie.

5 Ballidnesse cam on Gaza; Ascolon was stille, and the remenauntis of the valei of tho.

6 Hou longe schalt thou falle doun, O! swerd of the Lord, hou long schalt thou not reste? Entre thou in to thi schethe, be thou refreischid, and be stille.

7 Hou schal it reste, whanne the Lord comaundide to it ayens Ascalon, and ayens the see coostis therof, and there hath seide to it?

CAP 48

1 To Moab the Lord of oostis, God of Israel, seith these thingis. Wo on Nabo, for it is destried, and schent; Cariathiarym is takun, the stronge citee is schent, and tremblide.

2 And ful out ioiyng is no more in Moab, thei thouyten yuel ayens Esebon. Come ye, and leese we it fro folk. Therfor thou beynge stille, schalt be stille, and swerd schal sue thee.

3 A vois of cry fro Oronaym, distriynge, and greet sorewe.

4 Moab is defoulid, telle ye cry to litil children therof.

5 For a man wepynge stiede with wepyng bi the stiyng of Luyth, for in the comyng doun of Oronaym enemyes herden the yellyng of sorewe.

6 Fle ye, saue ye youre lyues; and ye schulen be as bromes in desert.

7 For that that thou haddist trist in thi strengthis, and in thi tresouris, also thou schalt be takun. And Chamos schal go in to passyng ouer, the preestis therof and the princes therof togidere.

8 And a robbere schal come to ech citee, and no citee schal be sauyd; and valeis schulen perische, and feeldi places schulen be distried, for the Lord seide.

9 Yyue ye the flour of Moab, for it schal go out flourynge; and the citees therof schulen be forsakun, and vnhabitable.

10 He is cursid, that doith the werk of God gilefuli; and he is cursid, that forbedith his swerd fro blood.

11 Moab was plenteuouse fro his yong wexynge age, and restide in hise drastis, nether was sched out fro vessel in to vessel, and yede not in to passyng ouer; therfor his taaste dwellide in hym, and his odour is not chaungid.

12 Therfor lo! daies comun, seith the Lord, and Y schal sende to it ordeynours, and arayeris of potels; and thei schulen araye it, and thei schulen waste the vessels therof, and hurtle togidere the potels of hem.

13 And Moab schal be schent of Chamos, as the hous of Israel was schent of Bethel, in which it hadde trist.

14 Hou seien ye, We ben stronge, and stalworthe men to fiyte?

15 Moab is distried, and thei han brent the citees therof, and the chosun yonge men therof yeden doun in to sleynge, seith the kyng, the Lord of oostis is his name.

16 The perischyng of Moab is nyy, that it come, and the yuel therof renneth ful swiftli.

17 Alle ye that ben in the cumpas therof, coumforte it; and alle ye that knowen the name therof, seie, Hou is the stronge yerde brokun, the gloriouse staaf?

18 Thou dwellyng of the douytir of Dibon, go doun fro glorie, sitte thou in thirst; for the distriere of Moab schal stie to thee, and he schal destrie thi strengthis.

19 Thou dwellyng of Aroer, stonde in the weie, and biholde; axe thou hym that fleeth, and hym that ascapide; seie thou, What bifelle?

20 Moab is schent, for he is ouercomun; yelle ye, and crye; telle ye in Arnon, that Moab is destried.

21 And doom is comun to the lond of the feeld, on Elon, and on Jesa, and on Mephat, and on Dibon,

22 and on Nabo, and on the hous of Debalthaym,

23 and on Cariathiarym, and on Bethgamul, and on Bethmaon, and on Scarioth,

24 and on Bosra, and on alle the citees of the lond of Moab, that ben fer, and that ben niy.

25 The horn of Moab is kit awei, and the arm therof is al tobrokun, seith the Lord.

26 Fille ye him greetli, for he is reisid ayens the Lord; and he schal hurtle doun the hond of Moab in his spuyng, and he also schal be in to scorn.

27 For whi, Israel, he was in to scorn to thee, as if thou haddist founde hym among theues; therfor for thi wordis whiche thou spakist ayens hym, thou schalt be led prisoner.

28 Ye dwelleris of Moab, forsake citees, and dwelle in the stoon, and be ye as a culuer makynge nest in the hiyeste mouth of an hool.

29 We han herd the pride of Moab; he is ful proud.

30 Y knowe, seith the Lord, the hiynesse therof, and pride in word, and pride in beryng, and the hiynesse of herte, and the boost therof, and that the vertu therof is not niy, ethir lijk it, nethir it enforside to do bi that that it miyte.

31 Therfor Y schal weile on Moab, and Y schal crie to al Moab, to the men of the erthene wal, that weilen.

32 Of the weilyng of Jaser Y schal wepe to thee, thou vyner of Sabama; thi siouns passiden the see, tho camen 'til to the see of Jazer; a robbere felle in on thi ripe corn, and on thi vyndage.

33 Ful out ioye and gladnesse is takun awei fro Carmele, and fro the lond of Moab, and Y haue take awei wyn fro pressou-

ris; a stampere of grape schal not synge a customable myri song.

34 Of the cry of Esebon 'til to Eleale and Jesa thei yauen her vois, fro Segor 'til to Oronaym a cow calf of thre yeer; forsothe the watris of Nemrym schulen be ful yuele.

35 And Y schal take awei fro Moab, seith the Lord, him that offrith in hiy places, and him that makith sacrifice to the goddis therof.

36 Therfor myn herte schal sowne as a pipe of bras to Moab, and myn herte schal yyue sown of pipis to the men of the erthene wal; for it dide more than it myyte, therfor thei perischiden.

37 For whi ech heed schal be ballidnesse, and ech beerd schal be schauun; in alle hondis schal be bindyng togidere, and an heir schal be on ech bak.

38 And al weilyng schal be on alle the roouys of Moab, and in the stretis therof, for Y haue al to-broke Moab as an vnprofitable vessel, seith the Lord.

39 Hou is it ouercomun, and thei yelliden? hou hath Moab cast doun the nol, and is schent? And Moab schal be in to scorn, and in to ensaumple to alle men in his cumpas.

40 The Lord seith these thingis, Lo! as an egle he schal fle out, and he schal stretche forth hise wyngis to Moab.

41 Carioth is takun, and stronge holdis ben takun; and the herte of stronge men of Moab schal be in that dai, as the herte of a womman trauelynge of child.

42 And Moab schal ceesse to be a puple, for it hadde glorie ayens the Lord.

43 Drede, and diche, and snare is on thee, thou dwellere of Moab, seith the Lord.

44 He that fleeth fro the face of drede, schal falle in to a diche; and thei that stien fro the dyche, schulen be takun with a snare. For Y schal brynge on Moab the yeer of the visitacioun of hem, seith the Lord.

45 Men fleynge fro the snare stoden in the schadewe of Esebon, for whi fier yede out of Esebon, and flawme fro the myddis of Seon; and deuouride a part of Moab, and the cop of the sones of noise.

46 Moab, wo to thee; thou puple of Chamos, hast perischid, for whi thi sones and thi douytris ben takun in to caitiftee.

47 And Y schal conuerte the caitiftee of Moab in the laste daies, seith the Lord. Hidur to ben the domes of Moab.

CAP 49

1 'Go ye to the sones of Amon. The Lord seith these thingis. Whether no sones ben of Israel, ether an eir is not to it? whi therfor weldide Melchon the eritage of Gad, and the puple therof dwellide in the citees of Gad?

2 Lo! daies comen, seith the Lord, and Y schal make the gnaistyng of batel herd on Rabath of the sones of Amon; and it schal be distried in to noise, and the vilagis therof schulen be brent with fier, and Israel schal welde hise welderis, seith the Lord.

3 Yelle ye, Esebon, for Hay is distried; crie, ye douytris of Rabath, girde you with heiris, weile ye, and cumpasse bi heggis; for whi Melchon schal be lad in to passyng ouer, the prestis therof and princes therof togidere.

4 What hast thou glorie in valeis? Thi valeis fleet awei, thou delicat douyter, that haddist trist in thi tresours, and seidist, Who schal come to me?

5 Lo! Y schal bringe in drede on thee, seith the Lord God of oostis, God of Israel, of alle men that ben in thi cumpasse;

and ye schulen be scaterid, ech bi hym silf, fro youre siyt, and noon schal be, that gadere hem that fleen.

6 And after these thingis Y schal make the fleeris and prisoneris of the sones of Amon to turne ayen, seith the Lord.

7 To Ydumee the Lord God of oostis seith these thingis. Whether wisdom is no more in Theman? Councel perischide fro sones, the wisdom of hem is maad vnprofitable.

8 Fle ye, and turne ye backis; go doun in to a swolowe, ye dwelleris of Dedan, for Y haue brouyt the perdicioun of Esau on hym, the tyme of his visitacioun.

9 If gadereris of grapis hadden come on thee, thei schulden haue left a clustre; if theues in the niyt, thei schulden haue rauyschid that that suffiside to hem.

10 Forsothe Y haue vnhilid Esau, and Y haue schewid the hid thingis of hym, and he mai not mow be hid; his seed is distried, and hise britheren, and hise neiyboris, and it schal not be.

11 Forsake thi fadirles children, and Y schal make hem to lyue, and thi widewis schulen hope in me.

12 For the Lord seith these thingis, Lo! thei drynkynge schulen drynke, to whiche was no doom, that thei schulden drynke the cuppe. And 'schalt thou be left as innocent? thou schalt not be innocent, but thou drynkynge schalt drynke.

13 For Y swoor bi my silf, seith the Lord, that Bosra schal be in to wildirnesse, and in to schenschipe, and in to forsakyng, and in to cursyng; and alle the citees therof schulen be in to euerlastynge wildirnessis.

14 I herde an heryng of the Lord, and Y am sent a messanger to hethene men; be ye gaderid togidere, and come ye ayens it, and rise we togidere in to batel.

15 For lo! Y haue youe thee a litil oon among hethene men, despisable among men.

16 Thi boost, and the pride of thin herte, hath disseyued thee, that dwellist in the caues of stoon, and enforsist to take the hiynesse of a litil hil; whanne thou as an egle hast reisid thi nest, fro thennus Y schal drawe thee doun, seith the Lord.

17 And Ydumee schal be forsakun; ech man that schal passe bi it, schal wondre, and schal hisse on alle the woundis therof;

18 as Sodom and Gommor is distried, and the niy citees therof, seith the Lord. A man schal not dwelle there, and the sone of man schal not enhabite it.

19 Lo! as a lioun he schal stie, fro the pride of Jordan to the strong fairnesse; for Y schal make hym renne sudenli to it; and who schal be the chosun man, whom Y schal sette bifore hym? For who is lijk to me, and who schal suffre me? and who is this scheepherde, that schal ayenstonde my cheer?

20 Therfor here ye the councel of the Lord, which he took of Edom, and his thouytis, whiche he thouyte of the dwelleris of Theman. If the litle of the floc caste not hem doun, if thei distrien not with hem the dwellyng of hem, ellis no man yyue credence to me.

21 The erthe was mouyd of the vois of fallyng of hem; the cry of vois therof was herd in the reed see.

22 Lo! as an egle he schal stie, and fle out, and he schal sprede abrood hise wynges on Bosra; and the herte of the strong men of Idumee schal be in that dai, as the herte of a womman trauelynge of child.

23 To Damask. Emath is schent, and Arphath, for thei herden a ful wickid heryng; thei weren disturblid in the see, for angwisch thei miyten not haue reste.

24 Damask was discoumfortid, it was turned in to fliyt; tremblyng took it, angwischis and sorewis helden it, as a womman trauelynge of child.

25 How forsoken thei a preisable citee, the citee of gladnesse?

26 Therfor the yonge men therof schulen falle in the stretis therof, and alle men of batel schulen be stille in that dai, seith the Lord of oostis.

27 And Y schal kyndle fier in the wal of Damask, and it schal deuoure the bildyngis of Benadab.

28 To Cedar, and to the rewme of Azor, which Nabugodonosor, kyng of Babiloyne, smoot, the Lord seith these thingis. Rise ye, and stie to Cedar, and distrie ye the sones of the eest.

29 Thei schulen take the tabernaclis of hem, and the flockis of hem; thei schulen take to hem the skynnes of hem, and alle the vessels of hem, and the camels of hem; and thei schulen clepe on hem inward drede in cumpas.

30 Fle ye, go ye awei greetli, ye that dwellen in Asor, sitte in swolewis, seith the Lord. For whi Nabugodonosor, kyng of Babiloyne, hath take councel ayens you, and he thouyte thouytis ayens you.

31 Rise ye togidere, and stie ye to a pesible folk, and dwellinge tristili, seith the Lord; not doris nether barris ben to it, thei dwellen aloone.

32 And the camels of hem schulen be in to rauyschyng, and the multitude of her beestis in to prey; and Y schal schatere hem in to ech wynd, that ben biclippid on the long heer, and bi ech coost of hem Y schal brynge perischyng on hem, seith the Lord.

33 And Asor schal be in to a dwellyng place of dragouns; it schal be forsakun 'til in to withouten ende; a man schal not dwelle there, nether the sone of man schal enhabite it.

34 The word of the Lord that was maad to Jeremye, the profete, ayens Elam, in the bigynnyng of the rewme of Sedechie,

35 kyng of Juda, and seide, The Lord of oostis, God of Israel, seith these thingis, Lo! Y schal breke the bowe of Elam, and Y schal take the strengthe of hem.

36 And I schal bringe on Elam foure wyndis; fro foure coostis of heuene, and Y schal wyndewe hem in to alle these wyndis; and no folc schal be, to which the fleeris of Elam schulen not come.

37 And Y schal make Elam for to drede bifore her enemyes, and in the siyt of men sekynge the lijf of hem; and Y schal brynge on hem yuel, the wraththe of my strong veniaunce, seith the Lord; and Y schal sende after hem a swerd, til Y waste hem.

38 And Y schal sette my kyngis seete in Elam, and Y schal leese therof kyngis, and princes, seith the Lord.

39 But in the laste daies Y schal make the prisoneris of Elam to turne ayen, seith the Lord.

CAP 50

1 The word which the Lord spak of Babiloyne, and of the lond of Caldeis, in the hond of Jeremye, the profete.

2 Telle ye among hethene men, and make ye herd; reise ye a signe; preche ye, and nyle ye holde stille; seie ye, Babiloyne is takun, Bel is schent, Maradach is ouer comun; the grauun ymagis therof ben schent, the idols of hem ben ouer comun.

3 For a folk schal stie fro the north ayenus it, which folk schal sette the lond therof in to wildirnesse; and noon schal be that schal dwelle therynne, fro man 'til to beeste; and thei ben moued, and yeden a wei.

4 In tho daies, and in that tyme, seith the Lord, the sones of Israel schulen come, thei and the sones of Juda togidere,

goynge and wepynge; thei schulen haaste, and seke her Lord God in Sion,

5 and thei schulen axe the weie. Hidur the faces of hem schulen come, and thei schulen be set to the Lord with boond of pees euerlastynge, which schal not be don awei by ony foryetyng.

6 My puple is maad a lost floc, the scheepherdis of hem disseyueden hem, and maden to go vnstabli in hillis; thei passiden fro mounteyn in to a litil hil, thei foryaten her bed.

7 Alle men that founden, eeten hem, and the enemyes of hem seiden, We synneden not, for that thei synneden to the Lord, the fairnesse of riytfulnesse, and to the Lord, the abidyng of her fadris.

8 Go ye awei fro the myddis of Babiloyne, and go ye out of the lond of Caldeis, and be ye as kydis bifore the floc.

9 For lo! Y schal reise, and brynge in to Babiloyne the gaderyng togidere of grete folkis, fro the lond of the north; and thei schulen be maad redi ayens it, and it schal be takun in the dai; the arowe therof as of a strong man a sleere, schal not turne ayen voide.

10 And Caldee schal be in to prey, alle that distrien it, schulen be fillid, seith the Lord.

11 For ye maken ful out ioye, and speken grete thingis, and rauyschen myn eritage; for ye ben sched out as caluys on erbe, and lowiden as bolis.

12 Youre modir is schent greetli, and sche that gendride you, is maad euene to dust; lo! sche schal be the last among folkis, and forsakun, with out weie, and drie.

13 For the wraththe of the Lord it schal not be enhabitid, but it schal be dryuun al in to wildirnesse; ech that schal passe bi Babiloyne, schal wondre, and schal hisse on alle the woundis therof.

14 Alle ye that beenden bowe, be maad redi ayens Babiloyne bi cumpas; ouercome ye it, spare ye not arowis, for it synnede to the Lord.

15 Crye ye ayens it, euery where it yaf hond; the foundementis therof fellen doun, and the wallis therof ben distried; for it is the veniaunce of the Lord. Take ye veniaunce of it; as it dide, do ye to it.

16 Leese ye a sowere of Babiloyne, and hym that holdith a sikil in the tyme of heruest, fro the face of swerd of the culuer; ech man schal be turned to his puple, and ech man schal flee to his lond.

17 Israel is a scaterid flok, liouns castiden out it; first kyng Assur eete it, this laste Nabugodonosor, kyng of Babiloyne, dide awei the bonys therof.

18 Therfor the Lord of oostis, God of Israel, seith these thingis, Lo! Y schal visite the kyng of Babiloyne, and his lond, as Y visitide the kyng of Assur;

19 and Y schal brynge ayen Israel to his dwellyng place. Carmele and Baasan schal be fed, and his soule schal be fillid in the hil of Effraym, and of Galaad.

20 In tho daies, and in that tyme, seith the Lord, the wickidnesse of Israel schal be souyt, and it schal not be; and the synne of Juda schal be souyt, and it schal not be foundun; for Y schal be merciful to hem, whiche Y schal forsake.

21 Stie thou on the lond of lordis, and visite thou on the dwelleris therof; scatere thou, and sle tho thingis, that ben aftir hem, seith the Lord; and do thou bi alle thingis which Y comaundide to thee.

22 The vois of batel and greet sorewe in the lond.

23 Hou is the hamer of al erthe brokun and al defoulid? hou is Babiloyne turned in to desert, among hethene men?

24 Babiloyne, Y haue snarid thee, and thou art takun, and thou wistist not; thou art foundun, and takun, for thou terridist the Lord to wraththe.

25 The Lord openide his tresour, and brouyte forth the vessels of his wraththe; for whi a werk is to the Lord God of oostis in the lond of Caldeis.

26 Come ye to it fro the fertheste endis, opene ye, that thei go out, that schulen defoule it; take ye awei stoonys fro the weie, and dryue ye in to heepis, and sle ye it, and nothing be residue.

27 Distrie ye alle the stronge men therof, go thei doun in to sleynge; wo to hem, for the dai of hem cometh, the tyme of visityng of hem.

28 The vois of fleeris, and of hem that ascapiden fro the lond of Babiloyne, that thei telle in Sion the veniaunce of oure Lord God, the veniaunce of his temple.

29 Telle ye ayens Babiloyne to ful many men, to alle that beenden bowe. Stonde ye togidere ayens it bi cumpas, and noon ascape; yelde ye to it aftir his werk, aftir alle thingis whiche it dide, do ye to it; for it was reisid ayens the Lord, ayens the hooli of Israel.

30 Therfor yonge men therof schulen falle doun in the stretis therof, and alle men werriours therof schulen be stille in that dai, seith the Lord.

31 Lo! thou proude, Y to thee, seith the Lord God of oostis, for thi dai is comun, the tyme of thi visitacioun.

32 And the proude schal falle, and schal falle doun togidere, and noon schal be, that schal reise hym; and Y schal kyndle fier in the citees of hym, and it schal deuoure alle thingis in cumpas of it.

33 The Lord of oostis seith these thingis, The sones of Israel and the sones of Juda togidere suffren fals caleng; alle that token hem, holden, thei nylen delyuere hem.

34 The ayenbyere of hem is strong, the Lord of oostis is his name; bi dom he schal defende the cause of hem, that he make the lond aferd, and stire togidere the dwelleris of Babiloyne.

35 A swerd to Caldeis, seith the Lord, and to the dwelleris of Babiloyne, and to the princes, and to the wise men therof.

36 A swerd to the false dyuynours therof, that schulen be foolis; a swerd to the stronge men therof, that schulen drede.

37 Swerd to the horsis therof, and to the charis therof, and to al the comyn puple whiche is in the myddis therof, and thei schulen be as wymmen; a swerd to the tresours therof, that schulen be rauyschid.

38 Drynesse schal be on the watris therof, and tho schulen be drye; for it is the lond of grauun ymagis, and hath glorie in false feynyngis.

39 Therfor dragouns schulen dwelle with fonned wielde men, and ostrigis schulen dwelle therynne; and it schal no more be enhabitid 'til in to with outen ende, and it schal not be bildid 'til to generacioun and generacioun;

40 as the Lord distriede Sodom and Gomorre, and the niy citees therof, seith the Lord. A man schal not dwelle there, and the sone of man schal not dwelle in it.

41 Lo! a puple cometh fro the north, and a greet folc, and many kyngis schulen rise togidere fro the endis of erthe.

42 Thei schulen take bowe and swerd, thei ben cruel and vnmerciful; the vois of hem schal sowne as the see, and thei schulen stie on horsis as a man maad redi to batel, ayens thee, thou douyter of Babiloyne.

43 The kyng of Babiloyne herde the fame of hem, and hise hondis ben aclumsid; angwisch took hym, sorewe took hym, as a womman trauelynge of child.

44 Lo! as a lioun he schal stie fro the pride of Jordan to the stronge fairnesse, for Y schal make hym to renne sudenli to it; and who schal be the chosun man, whom Y schal sette bifore him? For who is lijk me? and who schal suffre me? and who is this scheepherde, that schal ayenstonde my cheer?

45 Therfore here ye the councel of the Lord, which he conseyuede in mynde ayens Babiloyne, and hise thouytis, whiche he thouyte on the lond of Caldeis, no but the litle of the flockis drawen hem doun, no but the dwellyng place of hem be destried with hem, ellis no man yyue credence to me.

46 The erthe is mouyd of the vois of caitiftee of Babiloyne, and cry is herd among hethene men.

CAP 51

1 The Lord seith these thingis, Lo! Y schal reise on Babiloyne, and on the dwelleris therof, that reisiden her herte ayens me, as a wynd of pestilence.

2 And Y schal sende in to Babiloyne wyndeweris, and thei schulen wyndewe it, and thei schulen destrie the lond of it; for thei camen on it on ech side, in the dai of the turment therof.

3 He that beendith his bowe, beende not, and a man clothid in haburioun, stie not; nyle ye spare the yonge men therof, sle ye al the chyualrie therof.

4 And slayn men schulen falle in the lond of Caldeis, and woundid men in the cuntreis therof.

5 For whi Israel and Juda was not maad widewe fro her God, the Lord of oostis; but the lond of hem was fillid with trespas of the hooli of Israel.

6 Fle ye fro the myddis of Babiloyne, that ech man saue his soule; nyle ye be stille on the wickidnesse therof, for whi tyme of veniaunce therof is to the Lord; he schal yelde while to it.

7 Babiloyne is a goldun cuppe in the hond of the Lord, and fillith al erthe; hethene men drunken of the wyn therof, and therfor thei ben mouyd.

8 Babiloyne felle doun sudenli, and is al to-brokun; yelle ye on it, take ye recyn to the sorewe therof, if perauenture it be heelid.

9 We heeliden Babiloyne, and it is not maad hool; forsake we it and go we ech in to his lond; for the doom therof cam 'til to heuenes, and is reisid 'til to cloudis.

10 The Lord hath brouyt forth oure riytfulnessis; come ye, and telle we in Sion the werk of oure Lord God.

11 Scharpe ye arowis, fille ye arowe caasis; the Lord reiside the spirit of the kyngis of Medeis, and his mynde is ayen Babiloyne, that he leese it, for it is the veniaunce of the Lord, the veniaunce of his temple. The kyng of Medeis is reisid of the Lord ayens Babiloyne.

12 Reise ye a signe on the wallis of Babiloyne, encreesse ye kepyng, reise ye keperis, make ye redi buyschementis; for the Lord thouyte, and dide, what euer thing he spak ayens the dwelleris of Babiloyne.

13 A! thou Babiloyne, that dwellist on many watris, riche in thi tresours, thin ende cometh, the foote mesure of thi kittyng doun.

14 The Lord of oostis swoor bi his soule, that Y schal fille thee with men, as with bruke, and a myry song schal be sungun on thee.

15 The Lord swoor, which made erthe bi his strengthe, made redy the world bi his wisdom, and stretchide forth heuenes bi his prudence.

16 Whanne he yyueth vois, watris ben multiplied in heuene; which Lord reisith cloudis fro the laste of erthe, made leitis in to reyn, and brouyt forth wynd of hise tresouris.

17 Ech man is maad a fool of kunnyng, ech wellere togidere is schent in a grauun ymage; for his wellyng togidere is fals, and a spirit is not in tho.

18 The werkis ben veyn, and worthi of scorn; tho schulen perische in the tyme of her visityng.

19 The part of Jacob is not as these thingis; for he that made alle thingis is the part of Jacob, and Israel is the septre of his eritage; the Lord of oostis is his name.

20 Thou hurtlist doun to me the instrumentis of batel, and Y schal hurtle doun folkis in thee, and Y schal leese rewmes in thee;

21 and Y schal hurtle doun in thee an hors, and the ridere therof; and Y schal hurtle doun in thee a chare, and the stiere therof;

22 and Y schal hurtle doun in thee a man and womman; and Y schal hurtle doun in thee an elde man and a child; and Y schal hurtle doun in thee a yong man and a virgyn;

23 and Y schal hurtle doun in thee a scheepherde and his floc; and Y schal hurtle doun in thee an erthetiliere and his yok beestis; and Y schal hurtle doun in thee duykis and magistratis.

24 And Y schal yelde, seith the Lord, to Babiloyne, and to alle the dwelleris of Caldee, al her yuel, which thei diden in Sion, bifore youre iyen.

25 Lo! Y, seith the Lord, to thee, thou hil berynge pestilence, which corrumpist al erthe. Y schal stretche forth myn hond on thee, and Y schal vnwlappe thee fro stoonys, and Y schal yyue thee in to an hil of brennyng.

26 And Y schal not take of thee a stoon in to a corner, and a stoon in to foundementis; but thou schalt be lost with outen ende, seith the Lord.

27 Reise ye a signe in the lond, sowne ye with a clarioun in hillis; halewe ye folkis on it, telle ye to the kyngis of Ararath, of Menny, and of Ascheneth ayens it; noumbre ye Tapser ayens it, and bringe ye an hors, as a bruke hauynge a pricke.

28 Halowe ye folkis ayens it, the kyngis of Medey, the duykis therof, and alle magistratis therof, and al the lond of his power.

29 And the erthe schal be mouyd, and schal be disturblid; for the thouyt of the Lord schal fulli wake ayens Babiloyne, that he sette the lond of Babiloyne desert, and vnhabitable.

30 The stronge men of Babiloyne ceessiden of batel, thei dwelliden in stronge holdis; the strengthe of hem is deuourid, and thei ben maad as wymmen; the tabernaclis therof ben brent, the barris therof ben al to-brokun.

31 A rennere schal come ayens a rennere, and a messanger ayens a messanger, to telle to the kyng of Babiloyne, that his citee is takun fro the toon ende 'til to the tother ende;

32 and the forthis ben bifore ocupied, and the mareisis ben brent with fier, and the men werryours ben disturblid.

33 For the Lord of oostis, God of Israel, seith these thingis, The douyter of Babiloyne is as a corn floor, the tyme of threischyng therof; yit a litil, and the tyme of repyng therof schal come.

34 Nabugodonosor, the kyng of Babiloyne, eet me, and deuouride me; he made me as a voide vessel, he as a dragoun

swolewide me; he fillide his wombe with my tendirnesse, and he castide me out.

35 Wickidnesse ayens me, and my fleisch on Babiloyne, seith the dwellyng of Sion; and my blood on the dwelleris of Caldee, seith Jerusalem.

36 Therfor the Lord seith these thingis, Lo! Y schal deme thi cause, and Y schal venge thi veniaunce; and Y schal make the see therof forsakun, and Y schal make drie the veyne therof.

37 And Babiloyne schal be in to biriels, it schal be the dwellyng of dragouns, wondryng and hissyng, for that no dwellere is.

38 Thei schulen rore togidere as liouns, and thei schulen schake lockis, as the whelpis of liouns.

39 In the heete of hem Y schal sette the drynkis of hem; and Y schal make hem drunkun, that thei be brouyt asleepe, and that thei slepe euerlastynge sleep, and rise not, seith the Lord.

40 Y schal lede forth hem, as lambren to slayn sacrifice, and as wetheris with kidis. Hou is Sesac takun, and the noble citee of al erthe is takun?

41 Hou is Babiloyne made in to wondre among hethene men?

42 And the see stiede on Babiloyne, it was hilid with the multitude of hise wawis.

43 The citees therof ben maad in to wondryng, the lond is maad vnhabitable and forsakun; the lond wherynne no man dwellith, and the sone of man schal not passe bi it.

44 And Y schal visite on Bel in to Babiloyne, and Y schal caste out of hise mouth that, that he hadde swolewid, and folkis schulen no more flowe to it; for also the wal of Babiloyne schal falle doun.

45 Mi puple, go ye out fro the myddis therof, that ech man saue his soule fro the wraththe of the strong veniaunce of the Lord;

46 and lest perauenture youre herte wexe neische, and lest ye dreden the heryng, that schal be herd in the lond; and heryng schal come in a yeer, and aftir this yeer schal come heryng and wickidnesse in the lond, and a lord on a lord.

47 Therfor lo! daies comen, seith the Lord, and Y schal visite on the grauun ymagis of Babiloyne; and al the lond therof schal be schent, and alle slayn men therof schulen falle doun in the myddis therof.

48 And heuenes, and erthis, and alle thingis that ben in tho, schulen herie on Babiloyne; for rauynours schulen come fro the north to it, seith the Lord.

49 And as Babiloyne dide, that slayn men felle doun in Israel, so of Babiloyne slayn men schulen falle doun and in al the lond.

50 Come ye, that fledden the swerd, nyle ye stonde; haue ye mynde afer on the Lord, and Jerusalem stie on youre herte.

51 We ben schent, for we herden schenschipe; schame hilide oure faces, for aliens comen on the halewyng of the hous of the Lord.

52 Therfor lo! daies comen, seith the Lord, and Y schal visite on the grauun ymagis of Babiloyne, and in al the lond therof a woundid man schal loowe.

53 If Babiloyne stieth in to heuene, and makith stidfast his strengthe an hiy, distrieris therof schulen come on me, seith the Lord.

54 The vois of a criere of Babiloyne, and greet sorewe of the lond of Caldeis,

55 for the Lord distriede Babiloyne, and lost of it a greet vois; and the wawis of hem schulen sowne as many watris. The vois of hem yaf sown,

56 for a rauenour cam on it, that is, on Babiloyne; and the stronge men therof ben takun, and the bouwe of hem welewide, for the stronge vengere the Lord yeldynge schal yelde.

57 And Y schal make drunkun the princis therof, and the wise men therof, the duykis therof, and the magistratis therof, and the stronge men therof; and thei schulen slepe euerlastynge sleep, and thei schulen not be awakid, seith the kyng, the Lord of oostis is name of hym.

58 The Lord God of oostis seith these thingis, Thilke brodeste wal of Babiloyne schal be mynyd with mynyng, and the hiye yatis therof schulen be brent with fier; and the trauels of puples schulen be to nouyt, and the trauels of hethene men schulen be in to fier, and schulen perische.

59 The word which Jeremye, the profete, comaundide to Saraie, sone of Nerie, sone of Maasie, whanne he yede with Sedechie, the kyng, in to Babiloyne, in the fourthe yeer of his rewme; forsothe Saraie was prynce of profesie.

60 And Jeremye wroot al the yuel, that was to comynge on Babiloyne, in a book, alle these wordis that weren writun ayens Babiloyne.

61 And Jeremye seide to Saraie, Whanne thou comest in to Babiloyne, and seest, and redist alle these wordis,

62 thou schalt seie, Lord, thou spakist ayens this place, that thou schuldist leese it, that noon be that dwelle therynne, fro man 'til to beeste, and that it be an euerlastynge wildirnesse.

63 And whanne thou hast fillid to rede this book, thou schalt bynde to it a stoon, and thou schalt caste it forth in to the myddis of Eufrates; and thou schalt seie,

64 So Babiloyne schal be drenchid, and it schal not rise fro the face of turment, which Y brynge on it, and it schal be distried. Hidurto ben the wordis of Jeremye.

CAP 52

1 Sedechie was a sone of oon and twenti yeer, whanne he bigan to regne, and he regnede enleuene yeer in Jerusalem; and the name of his modir was Amychal, the douyter of Jeremye of Lobna.

2 And he dide yuels bifore the iyen of the Lord, bi alle thingis whiche Joachym hadde do.

3 For the stronge veniaunce of the Lord was in Jerusalem, and in Juda, til he castide hem awey fro his face. And Sedechie yede awei fro the kyng of Babiloyne.

4 Forsothe it was don in the nynthe yeer of his rewme, in the tenthe monethe, in the tenthe dai of the monethe, Nabugodonosor, the kyng of Babiloyne, cam, he and al his oost, ayens Jerusalem; and thei bisegiden it, and bildiden ayens it strengthis in cumpas.

5 And the citee was bisegid, til to the enleuenthe yeer of the rewme of Sedechie.

6 Forsothe in the fourthe monethe, in the nynthe dai of the monethe, hungur helde the citee; and foodis weren not to the puple of the lond.

7 And the citee was brokun, and alle men werriouris therof fledden; and thei yeden out of the citee in the niyt, bi the weie of the yate, which is bitwixe twei wallis, and ledith to the gardyn of the kyng, while Caldeis bisegiden the citee in cumpas; and thei yeden forth bi the weie that ledith in to desert.

8 Sotheli the oost of Caldeis pursuede the kyng; and thei token Sedechie in desert, which is bisidis Jerico, and al his felouschipe fledde awei fro hym.

9 And whanne thei hadden take the kyng, thei brouyten hym to the kyng of Babiloyne in Reblatha, which is in the lond of Emath; and the kyng of Babiloyne spak domes to hym.

10 And the kyng of Babiloyne stranglide the sones of Sedechie bifore hise iyen; but also he killide alle the princes of Juda in Rablatha.

11 And he puttide out the iyen of Sedechie, and boond hym in stockis; and the kyng of Babiloyne brouyte hym in to Babiloyne, and puttide hym in the hous of prisoun, til to the dai of his deth.

12 Forsothe in the nynthe monethe, in the tenthe dai of the monethe, thilke is the nyntenthe yeer of the kyng of Babiloyne, Nabusardan, the prince of chyualrie, that stood bifore the kyng of Babiloyne, cam in to Jerusalem.

13 And he brente the hous of the Lord, and the hous of the kyng, and alle the housis of Jerusalem; and he brente with fier ech greet hous.

14 And al the ost of Caldeis, that was with the maistir of chyualrie, distriede al the wal of Jerusalem bi cumpas.

15 Sotheli Nabusardan, the prince of chyualrie, translatide of the pore men of the puple, and of the residue comyn puple, that was left in the citee, and of the fleeris ouer, that fledden ouer to the kyng of Babiloyne; and he translatide other men of the multitude.

16 But Nabusardan, the prince of chyualrie, lefte of the pore men of the lond vyne tilers, and erthe tilers.

17 Also Caldeis brakun the brasun pilers, that weren in the hous of the Lord, and the foundementis, and the brasun waischyng vessel, that was in the hous of the Lord; and thei token al the metal of tho in to Babiloyne.

18 And thei tokun cawdruns, and fleischokis, and sautrees, and violis, and morteris, and alle brasun vessels, that weren in seruyce;

19 thei token also 'watir pottis, and vessels of encense, and pottis, and basyns, and candilstikis, and morters, and litle cuppis; hou manye euere goldun, goldun, and hou manye euere siluerne, siluerne.

20 The maister of chyualrie took twei pilers, and o waischyng vessel, and twelue brasun caluys, that weren vndur the foundementis, whiche kyng Salomon hadde maad in the hous of the Lord. No weiyte was of the metal of alle these vessels.

21 Forsothe of the pilers, eiytene cubitis of heiythe weren in o piler, and a roop of twelue cubitis cumpasside it; certis the thickenesse therof was of foure fyngris, and was holowe withynne.

22 And brasun pomels weren on euer either; and the heiythe of a pomel was of fyue cubitis; and werkis lijk nettis and pumgranatis weren on the coroun 'in cumpas.

23 And the pumgranatis weren nynti and sixe hangynge doun, and alle pumgranatis weren cumpassid with an hundred werkis lijk nettis.

24 And the maister of the chyualrie took Saraie, the firste preest, and Sophonye, the secounde preest, and three keperis of the vestiarie.

25 And of the citee he took o chast seruaunt and onest, that was souereyn on the men werriours; and seuene men of hem that sien the face of the kyng, whiche weren foundun in the citees; and a scryuen, prince of knyytis, that preuyde yonge knyytis; and sixti men of the puple of the lond, that weren foundun in the myddis of the citee.

26 Forsothe Nabusardan, the maistir of chyualrie, took hem, and brouyte hem to the kyng of Babiloyne in Reblatha.

27 And the kyng of Babiloyne smoot hem, and killide hem in Reblatha, in the lond of Emath; and Juda was translatid fro his lond.

28 This is the puple, whom Nabugodonosor translatide in the seuenthe yeer; Jewis, thre thousynde and thre and twenti.

29 In the eiytenthe yeer, Nabugodonosor translatide fro Jerusalem eiyte hundrid and two and thritti persoones.

30 In the thre and twentithe yeer of Nabugodonosor, Nabusardan, the maister of chyualrie, translatide seuene hundrid and fyue and fourti persoones of Jewis. Therfor alle the persoones weren foure thousynde and sixe hundrid.

31 And it was doon, in the seuene and threttithe yeer of the passyng ouer of Joachym, kyng of Juda, in the tweluethe monethe, in the fyue and twentithe dai of the monethe, Euylmerodach, kyng of Babiloyne, reiside in that yeer of his rewme the heed of Joachym, kyng of Juda; and ledde hym out of the hous of the prisoun,

32 and spak good thingis with hym. And he settide the trone of him aboue the trones of kyngis, that weren after hym in Babiloyne,

33 and chaungide the clothis of his prisoun. And Joachym eet breed bifore hym euere, in alle the daies of his lijf;

34 and hise metis, euerlastynge metis weren youun to hym of the kyng of Babiloyne, ordeyned bi ech dai, til to the dai of his deth, in alle the daies of his lijf. And it was don, aftir that Israel was led in to caititee, and Jerusalem was distried, Jeremye, the profete, sat wepinge, and biweilide Jerusalem with this lamentacioun; and he siyyide, and weilide with bitter soule, and seide.

LAMENTATIONS

CAP 1

1 Aleph. Hou sittith aloone the citee ful of puple? the ladi of folkis is maad as a widewe; the prince of prouynces is maad vndir tribute.

2 Beth. It wepynge wepte in the niyt, and the teeris therof ben in 'the chekis therof; 'noon is of alle the dereworthe therof, that coumfortith it; alle the frendis therof forsoken it, and ben maad enemyes to it.

3 Gymel. Juda passide fro turment and multitude of seruage, it dwellide among hethene men, and foond no reste; alle the pursueris therof token it among angwischis.

4 Deleth. The weies of Sion mourenen, for no men comen to the solempnytee; alle the yatis therof ben distried, the prestis therof weilen; the vergyns therof ben defoulid, and it is oppressid with bitternesse.

5 He. The enemyes therof ben maad in the heed, and the enemyes therof ben maad riche, for the Lord spak on it. For the multitude of wickidnessis therof the litle children therof ben led in to caititee, bifore the face of the troblere.

6 Vau. And al the fairnesse of the douyter of Syon yede out fro the douyter of Sion; the princes therof ben maad as rammes not fyndynge lesewis; and yeden forth withouten strengthe bifore the face of the suere.

7 Zai. And Jerusalem bithouyte on the daies of hir affliccioun and of trespassyng, and on alle hir desirable thingis whiche it hadde fro elde daies; whanne the puple therof felle doun in the hond of enemyes, and noon helpere was; enemyes sien it, and scorneden the sabatis therof.

8 Heth. Jerusalem synnede a synne, therfor it was maad vnstidfast; alle that glorifieden it forsoken it, for thei sien the schenschipe therof; forsothe it weilide, and was turned a bak.

9 Theth. The filthis therof ben in the feet therof, and it hadde no mynde of hir ende; it was putte doun greetli, and hadde no

coumfortour; Lord, se thou my turment, for the enemye is reisid.

10 Joth. The enemye putte his hond to alle desirable thingis therof; for it siy hethene men entride in to thi seyntuarie, of which thou haddist comaundid, that thei schulden not entre in to thi chirche.

11 Caph. Al the puple therof was weilinge and sekynge breed, thei yauen alle preciouse thingis for mete, to coumforte the soule; se thou, Lord, and biholde, for Y am maad vijl.

12 Lameth. A! alle ye that passen bi the weie, perseyue, and se, if ony sorewe is as my sorewe; for he gaderide awei grapis fro me, as the Lord spak in the day of wraththe of his strong veniaunce.

13 Men. Fro an hiy he sente fier in my boonys, and tauyte me; he spredde a brood a net to my feet, he turnede me a bak; he settide me desolat, meddlid togidere al dai with mourenyng.

14 Nun. The yok of my wickidnessis wakide in the hond of hym, tho ben foldid togidere, and put on my necke; my vertu is maad feble; the Lord yaf me in the hond, fro which Y schal not mowe rise.

15 Sameth. The Lord took awei alle my worschipful men fro the myddis of me; he clepide tyme ayens me, that he schulde al to-foule my chosun men; the Lord stampide a pressour to the virgyn, the douytir of Juda.

16 Ayn. Therfor Y am wepynge, and myn iye is ledynge doun watir; for a coumfortour, conuertynge my soule, is maad fer fro me; my sones ben maad lost, for the enemye hadde the maistrie.

17 Phe. Sion spredde a brood hise hondis, noon is that coumfortith it; the Lord sente ayenus Jacob enemyes therof, in the cumpas therof; Jerusalem is maad as defoulid with vncleene blood among hem.

18 Sade. The Lord is iust, for Y terride his mouth to wrathfulnesse; alle puplis, Y biseche, here ye, and se my sorewe; my virgyns and my yonge men yeden forth in to caitiftee.

19 Coth. I clepide my frendis, and thei disseyueden me; my prestis and myn elde men in the citee ben wastid; for thei souyten mete to hem silf, to coumforte hir lijf.

20 Res. Se thou, Lord, for Y am troblid, my wombe is disturblid; myn herte is distried in my silf, for Y am ful of bittirnesse; swerd sleeth with outforth, and lijk deth is at hoome.

21 Syn. Thei herden, that Y make ynward weilyng, and noon is that coumfortith me; alle myn enemyes herden myn yuel, thei ben glad, for thou hast do; thou hast brouyt a dai of coumfort, and thei schulen be maad lijk me.

22 Tau. Al the yuel of hem entre byfore thee, and gadere thou grapis awei fro hem, as thou hast gaderid grapis awei fro me; for my wickidnessis, for my weilyngis ben manye, and myn herte is mornynge.

CAP 2

1 Aleph. Hou hath the Lord hilid the douyter of Sion with derknesse in his strong veniaunce? he hath caste doun fro heuene in to erthe the noble citee of Israel; and bithouyte not on the stool of hise feet, in the dai of his strong veniaunce.

2 Beth. The Lord castide doun, and sparide not alle the faire thingis of Jacob; he distried in his strong veniaunce the strengthis of the virgyn of Juda, and castide doun in to erthe; he defoulide the rewme, and the princes therof.

3 Gymel. He brak in the ire of his strong veniaunce al the horn of Israel; he turnede a bak his riyt hond fro the face of the enemy; and he kyndlide in Jacob, as fier of flawme deuowrynge in cumpas.

4 Deleth. He as an enemye bente his bouwe, he as an aduersarie made stidfast his riyt hond; and he killide al thing that was fair in siyt in the tabernacle of the douytir of Sion; he schedde out his indignacioun as fier.

5 He. The Lord is maad as an enemy; he castide doun Israel, he castide doun alle the wallis therof; he destriede the strengthis therof, and fillide in the douyter of Juda a man maad low, and a womman maad low.

6 Vau. And he scateride his tent as a gardyn, he distried his tabernacle; the Lord yaf to foryetyng in Sion a feeste dai, and sabat; and the kyng and prest in to schenschipe, and in to the indignacioun of his strong veniaunce.

7 Zai. The Lord puttide awei his auter, he curside his halewyng; he bitook in to the hondis of enemy the wallis of the touris therof; thei yauen vois in the hous of the Lord, as in a solempne dai.

8 Heth. The Lord thouyte to distrie the wal of the douyter of Sion; he stretchide forth his coorde, and turnede not awei his hond fro perdicioun; the forwal, ether the outerward, mourenyde, and the wal was distried togidere.

9 Teth. The yatis therof ben piyt in the erthe, he loste and al to-brak the barris therof; the kyng therof and the princes therof among hethene men; the lawe is not, and the profetis therof founden not of the Lord a visioun.

10 Joth. Thei saten in erthe, the elde men of the douytir of Sion weren stille; thei bispreynten her heedis with aische, the eldere men of Juda ben girt with hairis; the virgyns of Juda castiden doun to erthe her heedis.

11 Caph. Myn iyen failiden for teeris, myn entrails weren disturblid; my mawe was sched out in erthe on the sorewe of the douyter of my puple; whanne a litil child and soukynge failide in the stretis of the citee.

12 Lameth. Thei seiden to her modris, Where is wheete, and wyn? whanne thei failiden as woundid men in the stretis of the citee; whanne thei senten out her soulis in the bosum of her modris.

13 Men. To whom schal Y comparisoun thee? ether to whom schal Y licne thee, thou douyter of Jerusalem? to whom schal Y make thee euene, and schal Y coumforte thee, thou virgyn, the douyter of Sion? for whi thi sorewe is greet as the see; who schal do medicyn to thee?

14 Nun. Thi profetis sien to thee false thingis, and fonned; and openyden not thi wickidnesse, that thei schulden stire thee to penaunce; but thei sien to thee false takyngis, and castyngis out.

15 Sameth. Alle men passynge on the weie flappiden with hondis on thee; thei hissiden, and mouyden her heed on the douyter of Jerusalem; and seiden, This is the citee of perfit fairnesse, the ioie of al erthe.

16 Ayn. Alle thin enemyes openyden her mouth on thee; thei hissiden, and gnaistiden with her teeth, and seiden, We schulen deuoure; lo! this is the dai which we abididen, we founden, we sien.

17 Phe. The Lord dide tho thingis whiche he thouyte, he fillide hise word which he hadde comaundid fro elde daies; he distriede, and sparide not; and made glad the enemy on thee, and enhaunside the horn of thin enemyes.

18 Sade. The herte of hem criede to the Lord, on the wallis of the douyter of Syon; leede thou forth teeris as a stronde, bi dai and niyt; yyue thou not reste to thee, nether the appil of thin iye be stille.

19 Coph. Rise thou togidere, herie thou in the nyyt, in the begynnyng of wakyngis; schede out thin herte as watir, bifore

the siyt of the Lord; reise thin hondis to hym for the soulis of thi litle children, that failiden for hungur in the heed of alle meetyngis of weies.

20 Res. Se thou, Lord, and byholde, whom thou hast maad so bare; therfor whether wymmen schulen ete her fruyt, litle children at the mesure of an hond? for a prest and profete is slayn in the seyntuarie of the Lord.

21 Syn. A child and an elde man laien on the erthe without-forth; my virgyns and my yonge men fellen doun bi swerd; thou hast slayn hem in the dai of thi strong veniaunce, thou smotist 'and didist no merci.

22 Thau. Thou clepidist, as to a solempne dai, hem that maden me aferd of cumpas; and noon was that ascapide in the dai of the strong veniaunce of the Lord, and was left; myn enemy wastide hem, whiche Y fedde, and nurschide up.

CAP 3

1 Aleph. I am a man seynge my pouert in the yerde of his indignacioun.

2 Aleph. He droof me, and brouyte in to derknessis, and not in to liyt.

3 Aleph. Oneli he turnede in to me, and turnede togidere his hond al dai.

4 Beth. He made eld my skyn, and my fleisch; he al to-brak my boonys.

5 Beth. He bildid in my cumpas, and he cumpasside me with galle and trauel.

6 Beth. He settide me in derk places, as euerlastynge deed men.

7 Gymel. He bildide aboute ayens me, that Y go not out; he aggregide my gyues.

8 Gymel. But and whanne Y crie and preye, he hath excludid my preier.

9 Gymel. He closide togidere my weies with square stoonus; he distriede my pathis.

10 Deleth. He is maad a bere settinge aspies to me, a lioun in hid places.

11 Deleth. He distriede my pathis, and brak me; he settide me desolat.

12 Deleth. He bente his bowe, and settide me as a signe to an arowe.

13 He. He sente in my reynes the douytris of his arowe caas.

14 He. Y am maad in to scorn to al the puple, the song of hem al dai.

15 He. He fillide me with bitternesses; he gretli fillide me with wermod.

16 Vau. He brak at noumbre my teeth; he fedde me with aische.

17 Vau. And my soule is putte awei; Y haue foryete goodis.

18 Vau. And Y seide, Myn ende perischide, and myn hope fro the Lord.

19 Zai. Haue thou mynde on my pouert and goyng ouer, and on wermod and galle.

20 Zai. Bi mynde Y schal be myndeful; and my soule schal faile in me.

21 Zai. Y bithenkynge these thingis in myn herte, schal hope in God.

22 Heth. The mercies of the Lord ben manye, for we ben not wastid; for whi hise merciful doyngis failiden not.

23 Heth. Y knew in the morewtid; thi feith is miche.

24 Heth. My soule seide, The Lord is my part; therfor Y schal abide hym.

25 Teth. The Lord is good to hem that hopen in to hym, to a soule sekynge hym.

26 Teth. It is good to abide with stilnesse the helthe of God.

27 Teth. It is good to a man, whanne he hath bore the yok fro his yongthe.

28 Joth. He schal sitte aloone, and he schal be stille; for he reiside hym silf aboue hym silf.

29 Joth. He schal sette his mouth in dust, if perauenture hope is.

30 Joth. He schal yyue the cheke to a man that smytith hym; he schal be fillid with schenschipis.

31 Caph. For the Lord schal not putte awei with outen ende.

32 Caph. For if he castide awei, and he schal do merci bi the multitude of hise mercies.

33 Caph. For he makide not low of his herte; and castide not awei the sones of men. Lameth.

34 That he schulde al to-foule vndur hise feet alle the boun-dun men of erthe. Lameth.

35 That he schulde bowe doun the dom of man, in the siyt of the cheer of the hiyeste.

36 Lameth. That he schulde peruerte a man in his dom, the Lord knew not.

37 Men. Who is this that seide, that a thing schulde be don, whanne the Lord comaundide not?

38 Men. Nether goodis nether yuels schulen go out of the mouth of the hiyeste.

39 Men. What grutchide a man lyuynge, a man for hise synnes?

40 Nun. Serche we oure weies, and seke we, and turne we ayen to the Lord.

41 Nun. Reise we oure hertis with hondis, to the Lord in to heuenes.

42 Nun. We han do wickidli, and han terrid thee to wraththe; therfor thou art not able to be preied.

43 Sameth. Thou hilidist in stronge veniaunce, and smitidist vs; thou killidist, and sparidist not.

44 Sameth. Thou settidist a clowde to thee, that preier passe not.

45 Sameth. Thou settidist me, drawing vp bi the roote, and castynge out, in the myddis of puplis.

46 Ayn. Alle enemyes openyden her mouth on vs.

47 Ayn. Inward drede and snare is maad to vs, profesie and defoulyng.

48 Ayn. Myn iyen ledden doun departyngis of watris, for the defoulyng of the douyter of my puple.

49 Phe. Myn iye was turmentid, and was not stille; for no reste was.

50 Phe. Vntil the Lord bihelde, and siy fro heuenes.

51 Phe. Myn iye robbide my soule in alle the douytris of my citee.

52 Sade. Myn enemyes token me with out cause, bi huntyng as a brid.

53 Sade. My lijf slood in to a lake; and thei puttiden a stoon on me.

54 Sade. Watris flowiden ouer myn heed; Y seide, Y perischide.

55 Coph. Lord, Y clepide to help thi name, fro the laste lake.

56 Coph. Thou herdist my vois; turne thou not awei thin eere fro my sobbyng and cries.

57 Coph. Thou neiyidist to me in the dai, wherynne Y clepide thee to help; thou seidist, Drede thou not.

58 Res. Lord, ayenbiere of my lijf, thou demydist the cause of my soule.

59 Res. Lord, thou siest the wickidnesse
59 of hem ayens me; deme thou my doom.
60 Res. Thou siest al the woodnesse, alle the thouytis of hem
ayenus me.
61 Syn. Lord, thou herdist the schenshipis of hem; alle the
thouytis of hem ayens me.
62 Syn. The lippis of men risynge ayens me, and the thouytis
of hem ayens me al dai.
63 Syn. Se thou the sittynge and risyng ayen of hem; Y am
the salm of hem.
64 Thau. Lord, thou schalt yelde while to hem, bi the werkis
of her hondis.
65 Tau. Thou schalt yyue to hem the scheeld of herte, thi
trauel.
66 Tau. Lord, thou schalt pursue hem in thi strong veniaunce,
and thou schalt defoule hem vndur heuenes.

CAP 4

1 Aleph. How is gold maad derk, the beste colour is
chaungid? the stonys of the seyntuarie ben scaterid in the
heed of alle stretis.
2 Beth. The noble sones of Sion, and clothid with the best
gold, hou ben thei arettid in to erthene vessels, in to the werk
of the hondis of a pottere?
3 Gimel. But also lamyes maden nakid her tetis, yauen mylk
to her whelpis; the douyter of my puple is cruel, as an ostrig
in desert.
4 Deleth. The tonge of the soukynge childe cleued to his palat
in thirst; litle children axiden breed, and noon was that brak to
hem.
5 He. Thei that eeten lustfuli, perischiden in weies; thei that
weren nurschid in cradels, biclippiden toordis.
6 Vau. And the wickidnesse of the douyter of my puple is
maad more than the synne of men of Sodom, that was distried
in a moment, and hondis token not therynne.
7 Zai. Nazareis therof weren whitere than snow, schynyngere
than mylk; rodier than elde yuer, fairere than safire.
8 Heth. The face of hem was maad blackere than coolis, and
thei weren not knowun in stretis; the skyn cleuyde to her
boonys, it driede, and was maad as a tre.
9 Teth. It was betere to men slayn with swerd, than to men
slayn with hungur; for these men wexiden rotun, thei weren
wastid of the bareynesse of erthe.
10 Joth. The hondis of merciful wymmen sethiden her children; thei weren maad the metis of tho wymmen in the
sorewe of the douyter of my puple.
11 Caph. The Lord fillide his strong veniaunce, he schedde
out the ire of his indignacioun; and the Lord kyndlide a fier in
Sion, and it deuouride the foundementis therof.
12 Lamet. The kyngis of erthe, and alle dwelleris of the world
bileueden not, that an aduersarie and enemy schulde entre bi
the yatis of Jerusalem.
13 Men. For the synnes of the profetis therof, and for wickidnessis of preestis therof, that schedden out the blood of iust
men in the myddis therof.
14 Nun. Blynde men erryden in stretis, thei weren defoulid in
blood; and whanne thei miyten not go, thei helden her
hemmes.
15 Samet. Thei crieden to hem, Departe awei, ye defoulide
men, departe ye, go ye awei, nyle ye touche; forsothe thei
chidden, and weren stirid; thei seiden among hethene men,
God schal no more leie to, that he dwelle among hem.

16 Ayn. The face of the Lord departide hem, he schal no more
leie to, that he biholde hem; thei weren not aschamed of the
faces of preestis, nether thei hadden merci on eld men.
17 Phe. The while we stoden yit, oure iyen failiden to oure
veyn help; whanne we bihelden ententif to a folc, that myyte
not saue vs.
18 Sade. Oure steppis weren slidir in the weie of oure stretis;
oure ende neiyede, oure daies weren fillid, for oure ende cam.
19 Coph. Oure pursueris weren swiftere than the eglis of
heuene; thei pursueden vs on hillis, thei settiden buschementis to vs in desert.
20 Res. The spirit of oure mouth, Crist the Lord, was takun in
oure synnes; to whom we seiden, We schulen lyue in thi
schadewe among hethene men.
21 Syn. Thou douyter of Edom, make ioye, and be glad, that
dwellist in the lond of Hus; the cuppe schal come also to thee,
thou schalt be maad drunkun, and schalt be maad bare.
22 Thau. Thou douyter of Sion, thi wickidnesse is fillid; he
schal not adde more, that he make thee to passe ouer; thou
douyter of Edom, he schal visite thi wickidnesse, he schal
vnhile thi synnes.

CAP 5

1 Lord, haue thou mynde what bifelle to vs; se thou, and
biholde oure schenschipe.
2 Oure eritage is turned to aliens, oure housis ben turned to
straungers.
3 We ben maad fadirles children with out fadir; oure modris
ben as widewis.
4 We drunken oure watir for monei, we bouyten oure trees for
siluer.
5 We weren dryuun bi oure heedis, and reste was not youun
to feynt men.
6 We yauen hond to Egipt, and to Assiriens, that we schulden
be fillid with breed.
7 Oure fadris synneden, and ben not, and we baren the wickidnessis of hem.
8 Seruauntis weren lordis of vs, and noon was, that ayenbouyte fro the hond of hem.
9 In oure lyues we brouyten breed to vs, fro the face of swerd
in desert.
10 Oure skynne is brent as a furneis, of the face of tempestis
of hungur.
11 Thei maden low wymmen in Sion, and virgyns in the citees of Juda.
12 Princes weren hangid bi the hond; thei weren not
aschamed of the faces of elde men.
13 Thei mysusiden yonge wexynge men vnchastli, and children fellen doun in tree.
14 Elde men failiden fro yatis; yonge men failiden of the
queer of singeris.
15 The ioie of oure herte failide; oure song is turned in to
mourenyng.
16 The coroun of oure heed fellen doun; wo to vs! for we
synneden.
17 Therfor oure herte is maad soreuful, therfor oure iyen ben
maad derk.
18 For the hil of Sion, for it perischide; foxis yeden in it.
19 But thou, Lord, schal dwelle with outen ende; thi seete
schal dwelle in generacioun and in to generacioun.
20 Whi schalt thou foryete vs with outen ende, schalt thou
forsake vs in to lengthe of daies?

21 Lord, conuerte thou vs to thee, and we schal be conuertid; make thou newe oure daies, as at the bigynnyng.

22 But thou castynge awei hast cast awei vs; thou art wrooth ayens vs greetli.

PREIER OF JEREMYE

CAP 1

1 For the synnes which ye synneden bifor God, ye schulen be led prisoneris in to Babiloyne, of Nabugodonosor, kyng of Babiloynes.

2 Therfor ye schulen entre in to Babiloyne, and ye schulen be there ful many yeeris, and in to long tyme, til to seuene generaciouns; forsothe after this Y schal lede out you fro thennus with pees.

3 But now ye schulen se in Babiloyne goddis of gold, and of siluer, and of stoon, and of tree, to be borun on schuldris, schewynge drede to hethene men.

4 Therfor se ye, lest also ye be maad lijk alien dedis, and lest ye dreden, and drede take you in hem.

5 Therfor whanne ye seen a cumpeny bihynde and bifore, worschipe ye God, and seie in youre hertes, Lord God, it bihoueth that thou be worschipid.

6 Forsothe myn aungel is with you, but Y schal seke youre soulis.

7 For whi the trees of hem ben polischid of a carpenter; also tho ben araied with gold, and araied with siluer, and ben false, and moun not speke.

8 And as to a virgyn louynge ournementis, so, whanne gold is takun, ourenementis ben maad to idols.

9 Certis the goddis of hem han goldun corouns on her heedis; wherfor prestis withdrawen fro tho goddis gold and siluer, and spenden it in hem silf.

10 Sotheli thei yyuen also of that to hooris, and araien hooris; and eft whanne thei resseyuen that of hooris, thei araien her goddis.

11 But tho goddis ben not delyuered fro rust and mouyte.

12 Forsothe whanne 'tho goddis ben hilid with a cloth of purpure, preestis schulen wipe the face of tho, for dust of the hous, which is ful myche among tho goddis.

13 Forsothe idols han a septre, as a man hath; as the iuge of a cuntrei, that sleeth not a man synnynge ayens him silf.

14 Also tho han in the hond a swerd, and ax; but tho delyueren not hem silf fro batel and fro theues. Wherfor be it knowun to you, that tho ben not goddis;

15 therfor worschipe ye not tho. For as a brokun vessel of a man is maad vnprofitable, siche also ben the goddis of hem.

16 Whanne tho ben set in the hous, the iyen of tho ben ful of dust of the feet of men entrynge.

17 And as yatis ben set aboute a man that offendide the kyng, ether as whanne a deed man is brouyt to the sepulcre, so preestis kepen sikirli the doris with closyngis and lockis, lest tho be robbid of theuys.

18 Thei teenden lanternes to tho, and sotheli many lanternes, of which tho moun se noon; forsothe tho ben as beemes in an hous.

19 Sotheli men seien that serpentis, that ben of erthe, licken out the hertis of tho; while the serpentis eten tho, and her cloth, and tho feelen not.

20 The faces of tho ben blake of the smoke, which is maad in the hous.

21 Nyyt crowis and swalewis fleen aboue the bodi of tho, and aboue the heed of tho, and briddis also, and cattis in lijk maner.

22 Wherfor wite ye, that tho ben not goddis; therfor drede ye not tho.

23 Also the gold which tho han, is to fairnesse; no but summan wipe awei the rust, tho schulen not schyne. For tho feliden not, the while tho weren wellid togidere.

24 Tho ben bouyt of al prijs, in which no spirit is in tho.

25 Tho without feet ben borun on schuldris of men, and schewen opynli her vnnoblei to men; be thei schent also that worschipen tho.

26 Therfor if tho fallen doun to erthe, tho schulen not rise of hem silf; and if ony man settith that idol upriyt, it schal not stonde bi it silf, but as to deed thingis schuldris schulen be put to tho.

27 The prestis of tho sillen the sacrifices of tho, and mysvsen; in lijk maner and the wymmen of hem rauyschen awei, nether to a sijk man, nether to a begger tho yyuen ony thing.

28 Of her sacrifices foule wymmen, and in vncleene blood, touchen. Therfor wite ye bi these thingis, that tho ben not goddis, and drede ye not tho.

29 For wherof ben tho clepid goddis? For wymmen setten sacrifices to goddis of siluer, and of gold, and of tre;

30 and preestis that han cootis to-rent, and heedis and berd schauun, whos heedis ben nakid, sitten in the housis of tho.

31 Sotheli thei roren and crien ayens her goddis, as in the soper of a deed man.

32 Prestis taken awei the clothis of tho, and clothen her wyues, and her children. And if tho suffren ony thing of yuel of ony man,

33 ether if tho suffren ony thing of good, tho moun not yelde. Nether tho moun ordeyne a kyng, nethir do awei.

34 In lijk maner tho moun nether yyue richessis, nether yilde yuel. If ony man makith a vow to tho, and yeldith not, tho axen not this.

35 Tho delyueren not a man fro deth, nether rauyschen a sijk man fro a miytiere.

36 Tho restoren not a blynd man to siyt; tho schulen not delyuere a man fro nede.

37 Tho schulen not haue merci on a widewe, nether tho schulen do good to fadirles children.

38 Her goddis of tre, and of stoon, and of gold, and of siluer, ben lijk stoonys of the mounteyn; forsothe thei that worschipen tho, schulen be schent.

39 Hou therfor is it to gesse, ether to seie,

40 that tho ben goddis? for whi yit whanne Caldeis onouren not tho. Which whanne thei heren that a doumb man mai not speke, offren hym to Bel, and axen of hym to speke;

41 as if thei that han no stiryng, moun feel. And thei, whanne thei schulen vndurstonde, schulen forsake tho idols; for tho goddis of hem han no wit.

42 Forsothe wymmen gird with roopis sitten in weies, and kyndelen boonys of olyues.

43 Sotheli whanne ony of tho wymmen is drawun awei of ony man passynge, and slepith with hym, sche dispisith her neiyboresse, that sche is not hadde worthi as hir silf, nether hir roop is brokun.

44 Forsothe alle thingis that ben don to tho, ben false. Hou therfor is it to gesse, ethir to seie, that tho ben goddis?

45 Forsothe the idols ben maad of smithis, and of goldsmithis. Tho schulen be noon other thing, no but that that prestis wolen, that tho be.

46 Also thilke goldsmithis that maken tho, ben not of myche tyme; therfor whether tho thingis that ben maad of them moun be goddis?

47 Sotheli thei leften false thingis, and schenschipe to men to comynge aftirward.

48 For whi whanne batels and yuels comen on hem, preestis thenken, where thei schulen hide hem silf with tho.

49 Hou therfor owen tho to be demyd, that tho ben goddis, which nether delyueren hem silf fro batel, nether delyueren hem silf fro yuelis?

50 For whi whanne tho ben of tree, and of stoon, and of gold, and of siluer, it schal be knowun aftirward of alle folkis, and kyngis, that tho thingis ben false, that ben maad open; for tho ben not goddis, but the werkis of hondis of men, and no werk of God is with tho.

51 Wherof therfor it is knowun, that tho ben not goddis, but the werkis of hondis of men, and no werk of God is in tho.

52 Tho reisen not a kyng to a cuntrei, nether schulen yyue reyn to men.

53 Also tho schulen not deme doom, nether tho schulen delyuere the cuntrei fro wrong.

54 For tho moun no thing, as litle crowis bitwixe the myddis of heuene and of erthe. For whanne fier fallith in to the hous of goddis of tree, and of gold, and of siluer, sotheli the prestis of tho schulen fle, and schulen be delyuered; but tho schulen be brent as beemys in the myddis.

55 Forsothe tho schulen not ayen stonde a kyng and batel. Hou therfor is it to gesse, or to resseyue, that tho ben goddis?

56 Goddis of tree, and of stoon, and of gold and of siluer, schulen not delyuere hem silf fro nyyt theues, nether fro dai theuys, and wickid men ben strongere than tho goddis.

57 Thei schulen take awei gold, and siluer, and cloth, bi which tho ben hilid, and thei schulen go awei; nether tho helpen hem silf.

58 Therfor it is betere to be a kyng schewynge his vertu, ether a profitable vessel in the hous, in which he schal haue glorie that weldith it, than false goddis; ether a dore in the hous, that kepith tho thingis that ben in it, is betere than false goddis.

59 Forsothe the sunne, and moone, and sterris, whan tho ben briyt, and sent out to profitis, obeien.

60 In lijk maner and leit, whanne it apperith, is cleer. Sotheli the same thing and wynd brethith in ech cuntrei.

61 And cloudis, to whiche, whanne it is comaundid of God to go thorouy al the world, perfourmen that, that is comaundid to tho.

62 Also fier 'that is sent fro aboue, to waste mounteyns and wodis, doith that, that is comaundid to it; but these idols ben not lijk to oon of tho thingis, nether bi fourmes, nether bi vertues.

63 Wherfor it is nether to gesse, nether to seie, that tho ben goddis, whanne tho moun not nether deme doom, nether do to men.

64 Therfor wite ye that tho ben not goddis, and drede ye not tho.

65 For tho schulen nether curse, nethir schulen blesse kyngis.

66 Also tho schewen not to hethene men signes in heuene, nether tho schulen schyne as the sunne, nether tho schulen yyue liyt as the moone.

67 Beestis that moun fle vndur a roof, and do profit to hem silf, ben betere than tho.

68 Therfor bi no maner it is open to you, that tho ben goddis.

69 For which thing drede ye not tho. For whi as 'a bugge, either a man of raggis, in a place where gourdis wexen, kepith no thing, so ben her goddis of tree, and of siluer, and of gold.

70 In the same maner and a whijt thorn in a gardyn kepith no thing, on which thorn ech brid sittith, in lijk maner and her goddis of tree, and of gold, and of siluer, ben lijk a deed man cast forth in derknessis.

71 Also of purpur and of marble, whiche thei holden aboue it; therfor ye schulen wite, that tho ben not goddis. Also tho ben etun at the laste, and it schal be in to schenschipe in the cuntrei.

72 Betere is a iust man, that hath no symylacris, for whi he schal be fer fro schenschipis.

BARUK

CAP 1

1 And these ben the wordis of the book, which Baruk, the sone of Nerie, sone of Maasie, sone of Sedechie, sone of Sedei, sone of Helchie, wroot in Babilonye;

2 in the fyuethe yeer, in the seuenthe dai of the monethe, in the tyme wherynne Caldeis token Jerusalem, and brenten it with fier.

3 And Baruk redde the wordis of this book to the eeris of Jeconye, sone of Joachym, kyng of Juda, and to the eeris of al the puple comynge to the book;

4 and to the eeris of the myyti sones of kyngis, and to the eeris of prestis, and to the eeris of the puple, fro the mooste 'til to the leeste of hem, of alle dwellynge in Babiloyne, and at the flood Sudi.

5 Whiche herden, and wepten, and fastiden, and preieden in the siyt of the Lord.

6 And thei gaderiden monei, bi that that ech mannus hond myyte;

7 and senten in to Jerusalem to Joachym, the prest, sone of Helchie, sone of Salen, and to the preestis, and to al the puple that weren foundun with hym in Jerusalem;

8 whanne he took the vessels of the temple of the Lord, that weren takun awei fro the temple, to ayen clepe in to the lond of Juda, in the tenthe dai of the monethe Siban; the siluerne vessels, which Sedechie, the kyng of Juda, the sone of Josie, 9 made, aftir that Nabugodonosor, kyng of Babiloyne, hadde take Jeconye, and princes, and alle myyti men, and the puple of the lond fro Jerusalem, and ledde hem boundun in to Babiloyne.

10 And thei seiden, Lo! we han sent to you richessis, of whiche bie ye brent sacrifices, and encense, and make ye sacrifice, and offre ye for synne at the auter of youre Lord God.

11 And preye ye for the lijf of Nabugodonosor, king of Babiloyne, and for the lijf of Balthasar, his sone, that the daies of hem ben on erthe as the daies of heuene;

12 that the Lord yyue vertu to vs, and liytne oure iyen, that we lyue vndur the schadewe of Nabugodonosor, kyng of Babiloyne, and vndur the schadewe of Balthasar, his sone; and that we serue hem bi many daies, and fynde grace in the siyt of hem.

13 And preye ye for 'vs silf to our Lord God, for we han synned to oure Lord God, and his strong veniaunce is not turned awei fro vs, 'til in to this dai.

14 And rede ye this book, which we senten to you, to be rehersid in the temple of the Lord, in a solempne dai, and in a couenable dai.

15 And ye schulen seie, Riytfulnesse is to oure Lord God, but schenschipe of oure face is to vs, as this dai is, to al Juda, and to dwelleris in Jerusalem,

16 to oure kyngis, and to oure princes, to oure preestis, and to oure profetis, and to oure fadris.

17 We synneden bifor oure Lord God, and bileuyden not, and tristiden not in hym.

18 And we weren not redi to be suget to hym, and we obeiden not to the vois of oure Lord God, that we yeden in hise comaundementis, whiche he yaf to vs;

19 fro the dai in which he ledde oure fadris out of the lond of Egipt, til in to this dai, we weren vnbileueful to oure Lord God; and we weren scaterid, and yeden awei, that we herden not the vois of hym.

20 And many yuels and cursyngis, whiche the Lord ordeynede to his seruaunt Moises, cleuyden to vs; which Lord ledde oure fadris out of the lond of Egipt, to yyue to vs a lond flowynge mylk and hony, as in this dai.

21 And we herden not the vois of oure Lord God, bi alle the wordis of prophetis, whiche he sente to vs, and to oure iugis;

22 and we yeden awei, ech man in to the wit of his yuel herte, to worche to alien goddis, and we diden yuels bifore the iyen of oure Lord God.

CAP 2

1 For which thing oure Lord God settide stidfastli his word, which he spak to vs, and to oure iugis, that demyden in Israel, and to oure kyngis, and to oure princes, and to al Israel and Juda;

2 that the Lord schulde brynge on vs grete yuels, that weren not don vndur heuene, as tho ben doon in Jerusalem; bi tho thingis that ben writun in the lawe of Moises,

3 that a man schulde ete the fleischis of his sone, and the fleischis of his douyter.

4 And he yaf hem in to the hond of alle kyngis, that ben in oure cumpas, in to schenschipe, and in to desolacioun in alle puplis, among whiche the Lord scateride vs.

5 And we ben maad bynethe, and not aboue; for we synneden to oure Lord God, in not obeiynge to the vois of hym.

6 Riytfulnesse is to oure Lord God, but schenschipe of face is to vs and to oure fadris, as this dai is.

7 For the Lord spak on vs alle these yuels, that camen on vs.

8 And we bisouyten not the face of oure Lord God, that we schulden turne ayen, ech of vs fro oure worste weies.

9 And the Lord wakide in yuels, and brouyte tho on vs; for the Lord is iust in alle hise werkis, whiche he comaundide to vs.

10 And we herden not the vois of hym, that we schulden go in the comaundementis of the Lord, whiche he yaf bifore oure face.

11 And now, Lord God of Israel, that leddist thi puple out of the lond of Egipt in a strong hond, and in myraclis, and in grete wondris, and in thi greet vertu, and in an hiy arm, and madist to thee a name, as this dai is;

12 we han synned, we han do vnfeithfuli, we han do wickidli, oure Lord God, in alle thi riytfulnessis.

13 Thi wrath be turned awey fro vs; for we ben left a fewe among hethene men, where thou scateridist vs.

14 Lord, here thou oure axyngis, and oure preyeris, and lede vs out for thee; and yyue thou to vs to fynde grace bifore the face of hem, that ledden vs awei;

15 that al erthe knowe, that thou art oure Lord God, and that thi name is clepid to help on Israel, and on the kyn of hym.

16 Lord, bihold thou fro thin hooli hous on vs, and bouwe doun thin eere, and here vs.

17 Opene thin iyen, and se; for not deed men that ben in helle, whos spirit is takun fro her entrails, schulen yyue onour and iustefiyng to the Lord;

18 but a soule which is sori on the greetnesse of yuel, and goith bowid, and sijk, and iyen failynge, and an hungri soule, yyueth glorie to thee, and riytfulnesse to the Lord.

19 For not bi the riytfulnesses of oure fadris we 'scheden merci bifore thi siyt, oure Lord God;

20 but for thou sentist thi wraththe and thi stronge veniaunce on vs, as thou spakest in the hondis of thi children profetis,

21 and seidist, Thus seith the Lord, Bowe ye youre schuldur, and youre necke, and do ye trauel to the kyng of Babiloyne; and ye schulen sitte in the lond, which Y yaf to youre fadris.

22 That if ye don not, nethir heren the vois of youre Lord God, to worche to the kyng of Babiloyne, Y schal make youre failyng fro the citees of Juda, and fro the yatis of Jerusalem;

23 and Y schal take awei fro you the vois of gladnesse, and the vois of ioye, and the vois of spouse, and the vois of spousesse; and al the lond schal be with out step of hem that dwellen therynne.

24 And thei herden not thi vois, that thei schulden worche to the kyng of Babiloyne; and thou hast set stidfastli thi wordis, whiche thou spakist in the hondis of thi children, prophetis; that the boonys of oure kyngis, and the boonys of oure fadris schulen be borun ouer fro her place.

25 And lo! tho ben cast forth in the heete of the sunne, and in the frost of niyt; and men ben deed in the worste sorewis, in hungur, and in swerd, and in sending out.

26 And thou hast set the temple in which thi name was clepid to help, as this dai schewith, for the wickidnesse of the hous of Israel, and of the hous of Juda.

27 And thou, oure Lord God, hast do in vs bi al thi goodnesse, and bi al that greet merciful doyng of thee,

28 as thou spakest in the hond of thi child Moises, in the dai in which thou comaundidist to hym to write thi lawe bifore the sones of Israel, and seidist,

29 If ye heren not my vois, this greet ournyng and myche schal be turned in to the leest among hethene men, whidur Y schal scatere hem.

30 For Y woot, that the puple schal not here me, for it is a puple of hard nol. And it schal turne to her herte in the lond of her caitiftee;

31 and thei schulen wite, that Y am the Lord God of hem. And Y schal yyue to hem an herte, and thei schulen vndurstonde, and eeris, and thei schulen here.

32 And thei schulen herie me in the lond of her caitiftee, and thei schulen be myndeful of my name.

33 Thei schulen turne awei hem silf fro her hard bak, and fro her wickidnessis; for thei schulen haue mynde of the wei of her fadris, that synneden ayens me.

34 And Y schal ayen clepe hem in to the lond, which Y swoor to yyue to the fadris of hem, to Abraham, Isaac, and Jacob; and thei schulen be lordis of it. And Y schal multiplie hem, and thei schulen not be maad lesse.

35 And Y schal ordeyne to hem an other testament euerlastynge, that Y be to hem in to God, and thei schulen be to me in to a puple. And Y schal no more moue my puple, the sones of Israel, fro the lond which Y yaf to hem.

1 And now, Lord almiyti, God of Israel, a soule in angwischis and a spirit anoied crieth to thee.

2 Lord, here thou, and haue merci, for thou art merciful God; and haue thou merci on vs, for we han synned bifor thee,
3 that sittist withouten ende, and we schulen not perische withouten ende.
4 Lord God almiyti, God of Israel, here thou now the preier of the deed men of Israel, and of the sones of hem, that synneden bifor thee, and herden not the vois of her Lord God, and yuels ben fastned to vs.
5 Nyle thou haue mynde on the wickidnesse of oure fadris, but haue thou mynde on thin hond and on thi name in this tyme;
6 for thou art oure Lord God, and, Lord, we schulen herie thee.
7 For whi for this thing thou hast youe thi drede in oure hertis, that we clepe thi name to help, and herie thee in oure caitiftee; for we schulen be conuertid fro the wickidnesse of oure fadris, that synneden ayens thee.
8 And lo! we ben in oure caitiftee to dai, whidur thou scateridist vs, in to schenschipe, and in to cursyng, and in to synne, bi al the wickidnesse of oure fadris, that yeden awei fro thee, thou oure Lord God.

CAP 3

9 Israel, here thou the comaundementis of lijf; perseyue thou with eeris, that thou kunne prudence.
10 Israel, what is it, that thou art in the lond of enemyes?
11 Thou wexidist eld in an alien lond, thou art defoulid with deed men, thou art arettid with hem, that goon doun in to helle?
12 Thou hast forsake the welle of wisdom;
13 for whi if thou haddist gon in the weies of God, sotheli thou haddist dwellid in pees on erthe.
14 Lerne thou, where is wisdom, where is prudence, where is vertu, where is vndurstondyng, that thou wite togidere, where is long duryng of lijf and lijf lode, where is liyt of iyen, and pees.
15 Who foond the place therof, and who entride in to the tresouris therof?
16 Where ben the princes of hethene men, and that ben lordis ouer the beestis, that ben on erthe?
17 Whiche pleien with the briddis of heuene;
18 whiche tresoren siluer and gold, in which men tristen, and noon ende is of the purchasyng of hem? Which maken siluer, and ben busi, and no fyndyng is of her werkis?
19 Thei ben distried, and yeden doun to hellis; and othere men riseden in the place of hem.
20 The yonge men of hem sien liyt, 'and dwelliden on erthe. But thei knewen not the weie of wisdom, nether vndurstoden the pathis therof;
21 nether the sones of hem resseyueden it. It was maad fer fro the face of hem;
22 it is not herd in the lond of Canaan, nether is seyn in Theman.
23 Also the sones of Agar, that souyten out prudence which is of erthe, the marchauntis of erthe, and of Theman, and the tale telleris, and sekeris out of prudence and of vndurstondyng. But thei knewen not the weie of wisdom, nether hadden mynde on the paththis therof.
24 O! Israel, the hous of God is ful greet, and the place of his possessioun is greet;
25 it is greet and hath noon ende, hiy and greet without mesure.

26 Namyd giauntis weren there; thei that weren of greet stature at the bigynnyng, and knewen batel.
27 The Lord chees not these, nether thei founden the weie of wisdom; therfor thei perischiden.
28 And for thei hadden not wisdom, thei perischiden for her vnwisdom.
29 Who stiede in to heuene, and took that wisdom, and brouyte it doun fro the cloudis?
30 Who passide ouer the see, and foond it, and brouyte it more than chosun gold?
31 Noon is, that mai knowe the weie therof, nethir that sekith the pathis therof;
32 but he that han alle thingis, knewe it, and foond it bi his prudence. Which made redi the erthe in euerlastynge tyme, and fillide it with twei footid beestis, and foure footid beestis.
33 Which sendith out liyt, and it goith, and clepide it; and it obeieth to hym in tremblyng.
34 Forsothe sterris yauen liyt in her kepyngis, and weren glad;
35 tho weren clepid, and tho seiden, We ben present; and tho schyneden to hym with mirthe, that made tho.
36 This is oure God, and noon other schal be gessid ayens hym.
37 This foond ech weie of wisdom, and yaf it to Jacob, his child, and to Israel, his derlyng.
38 Aftir these thingis he was seyn in londis, and lyuede with men.

CAP 4

1 This book of Goddis heestis, and the lawe which is withouten ende. Alle that holden it, schulen come to lijf. But thei that han forsake it, schulen come in to deth.
2 Jacob, be thou conuertid, and take thou it; go thou bi the weie at the briytnesse therof, ayens the liyt therof. Yyue thou not thi glorie to another, and thi dignyte to an alien folc. Israel, we ben blessid; for tho thingis that plesen God, ben open to vs.
5 The puple of God, Israel worthi to be had in mynde, be thou 'of betere coumfort.
6 Ye ben seeld to hethene men, not in to perdicioun; but for that that ye in ire terreden God to wrathfulnesse, ye ben bitakun to aduersaries.
7 For ye wraththiden thilke God euerlastynge, that made you; and ye offriden to fendis, and not to God.
8 For ye foryaten hym that nurschide you, and ye maden sori youre nurse, Jerusalem.
9 For it siy wrathfulnesse of God comynge to you, and it seide, Ye niy coostis of Sion, here; forsothe God hath brouyte greet morenyng to me.
10 For Y siy the caitiftee of my puple, of my sones and douytris, which he that is with out bigynnyng and ende brouyte on hem.
11 For Y nurschide hem with myrthe; but Y lefte hem with wepyng and morenyng.
12 No man haue ioye on me, a wedewe and desolat. Y am forsakun of manye for the synnes of my sones; for thei bowiden awei fro the lawe of God.
13 Forsothe thei knewen not 'the riytfulnessis of hym; nether thei yeden bi the weies of Goddis heestis, nether bi the pathis of his treuthe thei entriden with riytfulnesse.
14 The niy coostis of Sion come, and haue thei mynde on the caitifte of my sones and douytris, which he that is with out bigynnyng and ende brouyte on hem.

15 For he brouyte on hem a folk fro fer, an yuel folk, and of an other langage;

16 that reuerensiden not an eld man, nether hadden merci on children; and thei ledden awei the dereworthe sones of a widewe, and maden a womman aloone desolat of sones.

17 But what mai Y helpe you?

18 For he that brouyte on you yuels, shal delyuer you fro the hondis of youre enemyes.

19 Go ye, sones, go ye; for Y am forsakun aloone. Y haue vnclothid me of the stoole of pees; but Y haue clothid me with a sak of bisechyng, and Y schal crie to the hiyeste in my daies.

21 Sones, be ye of betere comfort; crie ye to the Lord, and he schal delyuere you fro the hond of princes, that ben youre enemyes.

22 For Y hopide youre helthe with outen ende, and ioye cam to me fro the hooli on merci, that schal come to you fro youre sauyour without bigynnyng and ende.

23 For Y sente you out with mourenyng and wepyng; but God schal brynge you ayen to me with ioye and myrthe with outen ende.

24 For as the neiyboressis of Sion sien youre caitifte maad of God, so thei schulen se and in swiftnesse youre helthe of God, which helthe schal come to you fro aboue with greet onour and euerlastynge schynyng.

25 Sones, suffre ye pacientli ire, that cam on you; for thin enemy pursuede thee, but thou schalt se soone the perdicioun of hym, and thou schalt stie on the neckes of hym.

26 My delicat men yeden scharp weies; for thei as a floc 'that is rauyschid weren led of enemyes.

27 Sones, be ye pacientere, and crie ye fer to the Lord; for whi youre mynde schal be of hym that ledith you.

28 For as youre wit was, that ye erriden fro God, ye schulen conuerte eft, and schulen seke hym tensithis so myche.

29 For he that brouyte in yuels to you, schal brynge eft euerlastynge myrthe to you with youre helthe.

30 Jerusalem, be thou of betere coumfort; for he that nemyde thee, excitith thee.

31 Thei that traueliden thee, schulen perische gilti; and thei that thankiden in thi fallyng, schulen be punyschid.

32 Citees to which thi sones serueden, 'schulen be punyschid, and that citee that took thi sones, schal be punyschid.

33 For as Babiloyne made ioie in thi hurlyng doun, and was glad in thi fal, so it schal be maad sori in his desolacioun.

34 And the ful out ioye of the multitude therof schal be kit awei, and the ioie therof schal be in to mourenyng.

35 For whi fier schal come on it fro hym that is without bigynnyng and ende, in ful long daies; and it schal be enhabitid of fendis, in to the multitude of tyme.

36 Jerusalem, biholde aboute to the eest, and se thou myrthe comynge of God to thee.

37 For lo! thi sones comen, which thou leftist scatered; thei comen gaderid fro the eest 'til to the west in the word of the hooli, and maken ioie to the onour of God.

CAP 5

1 Jerusalem, vnclothe thee of the stoole of thi mourenyng, and trauelyng; and clothe thou thee in the fairnesse, and onour of it, which is of God to thee in euerlastynge glorie.

2 God of ryytfulnesse schal cumpasse thee with a double cloth, and schal sette on thin heed a mytre of euerlastynge onour.

3 For God schal schewe his briytnesse in thee, which is vndur heuene.

4 For thi name schal be namyd of God to thee with outen ende, The pees of riytfulnesse, and the onour of pitee.

5 Jerusalem, rise vp, and stonde in an hiy place, and biholde aboute to the eest; and se thi sones gaderid togidere fro the sunne risynge til to the west in the word of the hooli, that maken ioie in the mynde of God.

6 For thei yeden out fro thee, and weren led of enemyes on feet; but the Lord schal brynge to thee hem borun in to honour, as the sones of rewme.

7 For God hath ordeyned to make low ech hiy hil, and euerlastynge rochis of stoon, and gret valeis, to fille the uneuenesse of erthe; that Israel go diligentli in to the onour of God.

8 Forsothe wodis and ech tree of swetnesse schadewiden Israel, bi the comaundement of God.

9 For God schal brynge Israel with mirthe in the liyt of his maieste, with merci and riytfulnesse, which is of hym.

EZECHIEL

CAP 1

1 And it was don, in the thrittithe yeer, in the fourthe monethe, in the fyuethe dai of the moneth, whanne Y was in the myddis of caitifs, bisidis the flood Chobar, heuenes weren openyd, and Y siy the reuelaciouns of God.

2 In the fyueth dai of the monethe; thilke is the fyuethe yeer of passing ouer of Joachym, kyng of Juda;

3 the word of the Lord was maad to Ezechiel, preest, the sone of Busi, in the lond of Caldeis, bisidis the flood Chobar; and the hond of the Lord was maad there on hym.

4 And Y siy, and lo! a whirlewynd cam fro the north, and a greet cloude, and fier wlappynge in, and briytnesse in the cumpas therof; and as the licnesse of electre fro the myddis therof, that is, fro the myddis of the fier.

5 And of myddis therof was a licnesse of foure beestis. And this was the biholdyng of tho, the licnesse of a man in tho.

6 And foure faces weren to oon, and foure wyngis weren to oon.

7 And the feet of tho weren streiyt feet, and the soole of the foote of tho was as the soole of a foot of a calf, and sparclis, as the biholdynge of buylynge bras.

8 And the hondis of a man weren vndur the wyngis of tho, in foure partis. And tho hadden faces and wyngis bi foure partis;

9 and the wyngis of tho weren ioyned togidir of oon to another. Tho turneden not ayen, whanne tho yeden, but eche yede bifore his face.

10 Forsothe the licnesse 'of the face of tho was the face of a man and the face of a lioun at the riythalf of tho foure. Forsothe the face of an oxe was at the left half of tho foure; and the face of an egle was aboue tho foure.

11 And the faces of tho and the wengis of tho weren stretchid forth aboue. Twei wyngis of eche weren ioyned togidere, and tweyne hiliden the bodies of tho.

12 And ech of tho yede bifore his face. Where the fersnesse of the wynd was, thidur tho yeden, and turneden not ayen, whanne tho yeden.

13 And the licnesse of the beestis, and the biholdyng of tho, was as of brennynge coolis of fier, and as the biholdyng of laumpis. This was the siyt rennynge aboute in the myddis of beestis, the schynyng of fier, and leit goynge out of the fier.

14 And the beestis yeden, and turneden ayen at the licnesse of leit schynynge.

15 And whanne Y bihelde the beestis, o wheel, hauuynge foure faces, apperide on the erthe, bisidis the beestis.

16 And the biholdyng of the wheelis and the werk of tho was as the siyt of the see; and o licnesse was of tho foure; and the biholdyng and the werkis of tho, as if a wheel be in the myddis of a wheel.

17 Tho goynge yeden bi foure partis of tho, and turneden not ayen, whanne tho yeden.

18 Also stature, and hiynesse, and orible biholdyng was to the wheelis; and al the bodi was ful of iyen in the cumpas of tho foure.

19 And whanne the beestis yeden, the wheelis also yeden togidere bisidis tho. And whanne the beestis weren reisid fro the erthe, the wheelis also weren reisid togidere.

20 Whidur euere the spirit yede, whanne the spirit yede thedur, also the wheelis suynge it weren reisid togidere; for whi the spirit of lijf was in the wheelis.

21 Tho yeden with the beestis goynge, and tho stoden with the beestis stondynge. And with the beestis reisid fro erthe, also the wheelis suynge tho beestis weren reisid togidere; for the spirit of lijf was in the wheelis.

22 And the licnesse of the firmament was aboue the heed of the beestis, and as the biholdyng of orible cristal, and stretchid abrood on the heed of tho beestis aboue.

23 Forsothe vndur the firmament the wyngis of tho beestis weren streiyt, of oon to anothir; ech beeste hilide his bodi with twei wyngis, and an other was hilid in lijk maner.

24 And Y herde the sown of wyngis, as the sown of many watris, as the sown of hiy God. Whanne tho yeden, ther was as a sown of multitude, as the sown of oostis of batel; and whanne tho stoden, the wyngis of tho weren late doun.

25 For whi whanne a vois was maad on the firmament, that was on the heed of tho, tho stoden, and leten doun her wyngis.

26 And on the firmament, that was aboue the heed of tho, was as the biholdyng of a saphire stoon, the licnesse of a trone; and on the licnesse of the trone was a licnesse, as the biholdyng of a man aboue.

27 And Y siy as a licnesse of electre, as the biholding of fier with ynne, bi the cumpas therof; fro the lendis of hym and aboue, and fro the lendis of him til to bynethe, Y siy as the licnesse of fier schynynge in cumpas,

28 as the biholdynge of the reynbowe, whanne it is in the cloude in the dai of reyn. This was the biholdyng of schynyng bi cumpas.

CAP 2

1 This was a siyt of the licnesse of the glorie of the Lord. And Y siy, and felle doun on my face; and Y herde the vois of a spekere. And he seide to me, Thou, sone of man, stonde on thi feet, and Y schal speke with thee.

2 And the spirit entride in to me, after that he spak to me, and settide me on my feet. And Y herde oon spekynge to me,

3 and seiynge, Sone of man, Y sende thee to the sones of Israel, to folkis apostatas, 'ether goynge a bak fro feith, that yeden awei fro me; the fadris of hem braken my couenaunt til to this dai.

4 And the sones ben of hard face, and of vnchastisable herte, to whiche Y sende thee. And thou schalt seie to hem, The Lord God seith these thingis;

5 if perauenture nameli thei heren, and if perauenture thei resten, for it is an hous terrynge to wraththe. And thei schulen wite, that a profete is in the myddis of hem.

6 Therfore thou, sone of man, drede not hem, nether drede thou the wordis of hem; for vnbileueful men and distrieris ben with thee, and thou dwellist with scorpiouns. Drede thou not the wordis of hem, and drede thou not the faces of hem, for it is an hous terrynge to wraththe.

7 Therfor thou schalt speke my wordis to hem, if perauenture thei heren, and resten, for thei ben terreris to wraththe.

8 But thou, sone of man, here what euer thingis Y schal speke to thee; and nyle thou be a terrere to wraththe, as the hows of Israel is a terrere to wraththe. Opene thi mouth, and ete what euer thingis Y yyue to thee.

9 And Y siy, and lo! an hond was sent to me, in which a book was foldid togidere. And he spredde abrood it bifor me, that was writun with ynne and with outforth. And lamentaciouns, and song, and wo, weren writun ther ynne.

CAP 3

1 And he seide to me, Sone of man, ete thou what euer thing thou fyndist, ete thou this volym; and go thou, and speke to the sones of Israel.

2 And Y openyde my mouth, and he fedde me with that volym.

3 And he seide to me, Sone of man, thi wombe schal ete, and thin entrails schulen be fillid with this volym, which Y yyue to thee. And Y eet it, and it was maad as swete hony in my mouth.

4 And he seide to me, Sone of man, go thou to the hous of Israel, and thou schalt speke my wordis to hem.

5 For thou schalt not be sent to a puple of hiy word, and of vnknowun langage; thou schalt be sent to the hous of Israel,

6 nether to many puplis of hiy word, and of vnknowun langage, of whiche thou maist not here the wordis. And if thou were sent to hem, thei schulden here thee.

7 But the hous of Israel nylen here thee, for thei nylen here me. For al the hous of Israel is of vnschamefast forheed, and of hard herte.

8 Lo! Y yaf thi face strongere than the faces of hem, and thi forheed hardere than the forheedis of hem.

9 Y yaf thi face as an adamaunt, and as a flynt; drede thou not hem, nether drede thou of the face of hem, for it is an hous terrynge to wraththe.

10 And he seide to me, Sone of man, take in thin herte, and here with thin eeris alle these my wordis, whiche Y speke to thee.

11 And go thou, and entre to the passyng ouer, to the sones of thi puple. And thou schalt speke to hem, and thou schalt seie to hem, The Lord God seith these thingis, if perauenture thei heren, and resten.

12 And the spirit took me, and Y herde after me the vois of a greet mouyng. The blessid glorie of the Lord was herd fro his place;

13 and Y herde the vois of wyngis of the beestis smytynge oon an othir, and the vois of wheelis suynge the beestis, and the vois of greet stiryng.

14 Also the spirit reiside me, and took me. And Y yede forth bittir in the indignacioun of my spirit; for the hond of the Lord was with me, and coumfortide me.

15 And Y cam to the passyng ouer, to the heep of newe fruytis, to hem that dwelliden bisidis the flood Chobar. And Y sat where thei saten, and Y dwellide there seuene daies, weilynge, in the myddis of hem.

16 Forsothe whanne seuene daies weren passid, the word of the Lord was maad to me, and seide, Sone of man,

17 Y yaf thee 'a spiere to the hous of Israel. And thou schalt here of my mouth a word, and thou schalt telle to hem of me.
18 If whanne Y seie to the wickid man, Thou schalt die bi deth, thou tellist not to hym, and spekist not to hym, that he be turned fro his wickid weie, and lyue; thilke wickid man schal die in his wickidnesse, but Y schal seke his blood of thin hond.
19 Forsothe if thou tellist to the wickid man, and he is not conuertid fro his wickidnesse, and fro his wickid weie; sotheli he schal die in his wickidnesse, but thou hast delyuerid thi soule.
20 But also if a iust man is turned fro his riytfulnesse, and doith wickidnesse, Y schal sette an hirtyng bifor hym; he schal die, for thou teldist not to hym; he schal die in his synne, and hise riytfulnessis, whiche he dide, schulen not be in mynde, but Y schal seke his blood of thin hond.
21 Forsothe if thou tellist to a iust man, that a iust man do not synne, and he doith not synne, he lyuynge schal lyue, for thou teldist to hym, and thou hast delyuered thi soule.
22 And the hond of the Lord was maad on me, and he seide to me, Rise thou, and go out in to the feeld, and there Y schal speke with thee.
23 And Y roos, and yede out in to the feeld. And lo! the glorie of the Lord stood there, as the glorie which Y siy bisidis the flood Chobar; and Y felle doun on my face.
24 And the spirit entride in to me, and settide me on my feet. And he spak to me, and seide to me, Entre thou, and be thou closid in the myddis of thin hous.
25 And thou, sone of man, lo! boondis ben youun on thee, and thei schulen bynde thee with tho, and thou schalt not go out in the myddis of hem.
26 And Y schal make thi tunge to cleue to the roof of thi mouth, and thou schalt be doumbe, and thou schalt not be as a man rebuykinge; for it is an hous terrynge to wraththe.
27 But whanne Y schal speke to thee, Y schal opene thi mouth, and thou schalt seie to hem, The Lord God seith these thingis, He that herith, here, and he that restith, reste; for it is an hous terrynge to wraththe.

CAP 4

1 And thou, sone of man, take to thee a tijl stoon; and thou schalt sette it bifore thee, and thou schalt discriue ther ynne the citee of Jerusalem.
2 And thou schalt ordeyne bisegyng ayenus that Jerusalem; and thou schalt bilde strengthis, and thou schalt bere togidere erthe, and thou shalt yyue oostis of batel ayens it, and thou schalt sette engynes in cumpas.
3 And take thou to thee an irone friynge panne; and thou schalt sette it in to an irone wal bitwixe thee and bitwixe the cite; and thou schalt sette stidfastli thi face to it, and it schal be in to bisegyng, and thou schalt cumpasse it; it is a signe to the hous of Israel.
4 And thou schalt slepe on thi left side, and thou schalt putte the wickidnessis of the hous of Israel on that side, in the noumbre of daies in which thou shalt slepe on that side, and thou schalt take the wickidnesse of hem.
5 Forsothe Y yaf to thee the yeeris of the wickidnesse of hem bi noumbre of daies, thre hundrid and nynti daies; and thou schalt bere the wickidnesse of the hous of Israel.
6 And whanne thou hast fillid these thingis, thou schalt slepe the secounde tyme on thi riytside. And thou schalt take the wickidnesse of the hous of Juda bi fourti daies; Y yaf to thee a dai for a yeer, a dai sotheli for a yeer.

7 And thou schalt turne thi face to the biseging of Jerusalem; and thin arm schal be stretchid forth, and thou schalt profesie ayens it.
8 Lo! Y haue cumpassid thee with boondis, and thou schalt not turne thee fro thi side in 'to other side, tille thou fille the daies of thi bisegyng.
9 And take thou to thee wheete, and barli, and beenys, and tillis, and mylie, and vetchis; and thou schalt putte tho in to o vesselle. And thou schalt make to thee looues for the noumbre of daies, bi whiche thou schalt slepe on thi side; bi three hundrid and nynti daies thou schalt ete it.
10 Forsothe thi mete, which thou schalt ete, schal be in weiyte twenti staters in a dai; fro tyme til to tyme thou schalt ete it.
11 And thou schalt drynke watir in mesure, the sixte part of hyn; fro tyme til to tyme thou schalt drynke it.
12 And thou schalt ete it as barli breed bakun vndur the aischis; and with 'a toord that goith out of a man thou schalt hile, it bifore the iyen of hem.
13 The Lord seith these thingis, So the sones of Israel schulen ete her breed defoulid among hethene men, to whiche Y schal caste hem out.
14 And Y seide, A! A! A! Lord God, lo! my soule is not defoulid, and fro my yong childhed til to now Y eet not a thing deed bi it silf, and to-rent of beestis; and al vnclene fleisch entride not in to my mouth.
15 And he seide to me, Lo! Y haue youe to thee the dung of oxis for mennus toordis; and thou schalt make thi breed with it.
16 And he seide to me, Sone of man, lo! Y schal al to-breke the staf of breed in Jerusalem, and thei schulen ete her breed in weiyte and in bisynesse, and thei schulen drynke water in mesure and in angwisch;
17 that whanne breed and watir failen, eche man falle doun to his brother, and thei faile in her wickidnessis.

CAP 5

1 And thou, sone of man, take to thee a scharp swerd, schauynge heeris; and thou schalt take it, and schalt leede it bi thin heed, and bi thi berd. And thou schalt take to thee a balaunce of weiyte, and thou schalt departe tho.
2 Thou schalt brenne the thridde part with fier in the myddis of the citee, bi the fillyng of daies of bisegyng. And thou schalt take the thridde part, and schalt kitte bi swerd in the cumpas therof. But thou schalt scatere 'the tother thridde part in to the wynd; and Y schal make nakid a swerd aftir hem.
3 And thou schalt take therof a litil noumbre, and thou schalt bynde tho in the hiynesse of thi mentil.
4 And eft thou schalt take of hem, and thou schalt caste forth hem in to the myddis of the fier. And thou schalt brenne hem in fier; and fier schal go out of that in to al the hous of Israel.
5 The Lord God seith these thingis, This is Jerusalem; Y haue sette it in the myddis of hethene men, and londis in the cumpas therof.
6 And it dispiside my domes, that it was more wickid than hethene men; and it dispiside my comaundementis more than londis that ben in the cumpas therof. For thei han cast awei my domes, and thei yeden not in my comaundementis.
7 Therfor the Lord God seith these thingis, For ye 'han passid hethene men that ben in youre cumpas, and ye yeden not in my comaundementis, and ye diden not my domes, and ye wrouyten not bi the domes of hethene men that ben in youre cumpas;

8 therfor the Lord God seith these thingis, Lo! Y to thee, and Y my silf schal make domes in the myddis of thee, bifor the iyen of hethene men; and Y schal do thingis in thee,

9 whiche Y dide not, and to whiche Y schal no more make lijk thingis, for alle thin abhomynaciouns.

10 Therfor fadris schulen ete sones in the myddis of thee, and sones schulen ete her fadris; and Y schal make domes in thee, and Y schal wyndewe alle thin remenauntis in to ech wynd.

11 Therfor Y lyue, seith the Lord God, no but for that that thou defoulidist myn hooli thing in alle thin offenciouns, and in alle thin abhomynaciouns; and Y schal breke, and myn iye schal not spare, and Y schal not do merci.

12 The thridde part of thee schal die bi pestilence, and schal be wastid bi hungur in the middis of thee; and the thridde part of thee schal falle doun bi swerd in thi cumpas; forsothe Y schal scatere thi thridde part in to ech wynd, and Y schal drawe out a swerd after hem.

13 And Y schal fille my stronge veniaunce, and Y schal make myn indignacioun to reste in hem, and Y schal be coumfortid. And thei schulen wite, that Y the Lord spak in my feruent loue, whanne Y schal fille al myn indignacioun in hem.

14 And Y schal yyue thee in to desert, in to schenschipe to hethene men that ben in thi cumpas, in the siyt of ech that passith forth.

15 And thou schalt be schenschipe 'and blasfemye, ensaumple and wondryng, among hethene men that ben in thi cumpas, whanne Y schal make domes in thee, in strong veniaunce, and indignacioun, and in blamyngis of ire.

16 Y the Lord haue spoke, whanne Y schal sende in to hem the worste arowis of hungur, that schulen bere deth; and whiche Y schal sende, that Y leese you. And Y schal gadere hungur on you, and Y schal al to-breke in you the sadnesse of breed.

17 And Y schal sende in to you hungur, and worste beestis, til to the deth; and pestilence and blood schulen passe bi thee, and Y schal bringe in swerd on thee; Y the Lord spak.

CAP 6

1 And the word of the Lord was maad to me,

2 and he seide, Thou, sone of man, sette thi face to the hillis of Israel; and thou schalt profesie to tho hillis, and schalt seie,

3 Hillis of Israel, here ye the word of the Lord God. The Lord God seith these thingis to mounteyns, and litil hillis, to roochis of stoon, and to valeis, Lo! Y schal bringe in on you a swerd, and Y schal leese youre hiye thingis.

4 And Y schal distrie youre auteris, and youre symylacris schulen be brokun; and Y schal caste doun youre slayn men bifore youre idols.

5 dnA Y schal yyue the deed bodies of the sones of Israel bifor the face of youre symylacris, and Y schal scatere youre boonys

6 aboute youre auteris, in alle youre dwellingis. Citees schulen be forsakun, and hiy thingis schulen be distried, and schulen be scaterid; and youre auteris schulen perische, and schulen be brokun. And youre idols schulen ceesse, and youre templis of idols schulen be al to-brokun, and youre werkis schulen be doen awei.

7 And a slayn man schal falle doun in the myddis of you; and ye schulen wite, that Y am the Lord.

8 And Y schal leeue in you hem that fledden swerd among hethene men, whanne Y schal scatere you in to londis.

9 And youre delyuered men schulen haue mynde on me among hethene men, to whiche thei ben led prisoneris; for Y

haue al to-broke her herte doynge fornycacioun, and goynge awei fro me, and her iyen doynge fornicacioun aftir her idols. And thei schulen displese hem silf on the yuels, whiche thei diden in alle her abhomynaciouns.

10 And thei schulen wite, that Y the Lord spak not in veyn, that Y schulde do this yuel to hem.

11 The Lord God seith these thingis, Smyte thin hond, and hurtle thi foot, and seie, Alas! to alle abhomynaciouns of the yuelis of the hous of Israel; for thei schulen falle doun bi swerd, hungur, and pestilence. He that is fer, shal die bi pestilence.

12 Forsothe he that is niy, shal falle bi swerd. And he that is laft and bisegid, shal die bi hungur. And Y schal fille myn indignacioun in hem.

13 And ye schulen wite, that Y am the Lord, whanne youre slayn men schulen be in the myddis of youre idols, in the cumpas of youre auteris, in eche hiy litil hil, and in alle the hiynessis of mounteyns, and vndur ech tree ful of wode, and vndur ech ook ful of boowis, that is, a place where thei brenten encense swete smellynge to alle her idols.

14 And Y schal stretche forth myn hond on hem, and Y schal make her lond desolat and destitute, fro desert Deblata, in alle the dwellyngis of hem; and thei schulen wite, that Y am the Lord.

CAP 7

1 And the word of the Lord was maad to me,

2 'and he seide, And thou, sone of man, the Lord God of the lond of Israel seith these thingis, The ende cometh, the ende cometh, on foure coostis of the lond.

3 Now an ende is on thee, and Y shal sende in my strong veniaunce on thee, and Y schal deme thee bi thi weies, and Y schal sette alle thin abhomynaciouns ayens thee.

4 And myn iye shal not spare on thee, and Y schal not do mercy. But Y shal sette thi weies on thee, and thin abhomynaciouns schulen be in the myddis of thee; and ye schulen wite, that Y am the Lord.

5 The Lord God seith these thingis, O turment, lo!

6 turment cometh; the ende cometh, the ende cometh; it schal wake fulli ayens thee; lo! it cometh.

7 Sorewe cometh on thee, that dwellist in the lond; the tyme cometh, the dai of sleyng is niy, and not of glorie of hillis.

8 Now anoon Y schal schede out myn ire on thee, and Y schal fille my strong veniaunce in thee; and Y schal deme thee bi thi weies, and Y schal putte to thee alle thi grete trespassis.

9 And myn iye schal not spare, nether Y schal do merci; but Y schal putte on thee thi weies, and thin abhomynaciouns schulen be in the myddis of thee; and ye schulen wite, that Y am the Lord smytynge.

10 Lo! the dai, lo! it cometh; sorewe is gon out. A yerde flouride,

11 pride buriownede, wickidnesse roos in the yerde of vnpitee; not of hem, and not of the puple, nether of the sown of hem, and no reste shal be in hem.

12 The tyme cometh, the dai neiyede; he that bieth, be not glad, and he that sillith, mourne not; for whi ire is on al the puple therof.

13 For he that sillith, schal not turne ayen to that that he seelde, and yit the lijf of hem is in lyueris; for whi the reuelacioun to al the multitude therof shal not go ayen, and a man schal not be coumfortid in the wickidnesse of his lijf.

14 Synge ye with a trumpe, alle men be maad redi, and noon is that schal go to batel; for whi my wraththe is on al the puple therof.

15 Swerd is with out forth, pestilence and hungur with ynne; he that is in the feeld, schal die bi swerd; and thei that ben in the citee, schulen be deuourid bi pestilence and hungur.

16 And thei schulen be sauyd that fleen of hem; and thei schulen be as culueris of grete valeis in hillis, alle quakynge, ech man in his wickidnesse.

17 Alle hondis schulen be aclumsid, and alle knees schulen flowe with watris.

18 And thei schulen girde hem with heiris, and inward drede schal hile hem; and schenschipe schal be in ech face, and ballidnesse schal be in alle the heedis of hem.

19 The siluer of hem schal be cast out, and the gold of hem schal be in to a dunghil; the siluer of hem and the gold of hem schal not mowe delyuere hem in the dai of the strong veniaunce of the Lord. Thei schulen not fille her soule, and the wombis of hem schulen not be fillid; for it is maad the sclaundre of hir wickidnesse.

20 And thei setteden the ournement of her brochis in to pride; and thei maden of it the ymagis of her abhomynaciouns and simylacris. For this thing Y yaf it to hem, in to vnclennesse.

21 And Y schal yyue it in to the hondis of aliens, to rauysche, and to the vnpitouse men of erthe, in to prey, and thei schulen defoule it.

22 And Y schal turne awei my face fro hem, and thei schulen defoule my priuyte; and harlotis schulen entre in to it, and schulen defoule it.

23 Make thou a closyng to gidere; for the lond is ful of doom of bloodis, and the citee is ful of wickidnesse.

24 And Y schal brynge the worste of hethene men, and thei schulen haue in possessioun the housis of hem; and Y schal make the pride of miyti men to ceesse, and enemyes schulen haue in possessioun the seyntuaries of hem.

25 In anguysch comynge aboue thei schulen seke pees, and it schal not be.

26 Disturblyng schal come on disturblyng, and heryng on heryng; and thei schulen seke of the profete a reuelacioun, and lawe shal perische fro the preest, and counsel fro eldre men.

27 The kyng schal mourne, and the prince schal be clothid in weilyng, and the hondis of the puple of the lond schulen be disturblid; bi the weie of hem Y schal do to hem, and bi the domes of hem Y schal deme hem; and thei schulen wite, that Y am the Lord.

CAP 8

1 And it was doon in the sixte yeer, in the sixte monethe, in the fyuethe dai of the monethe, Y sat in myn hous, and the elde men of Juda saten bifore me; and the hond of the Lord God felle there on me.

2 And Y siy, and lo! a licnesse as the biholdyng of fier; fro the biholding of hise leendis and bynethe was fier, and fro hise leendis and aboue was as the biholdyng of schynyng, as the siyt of electre.

3 And the licnesse of an hond was sent out, and took me bi the heer of myn heed; and the spirit reiside me bitwixe heuene and erthe, and brouyte me in to Jerusalem, in the siyt of God, bisidis the ynnere dore that bihelde to the north, where the idol of enuye was set, to stire indignacioun.

4 And lo! the glorie of God of Israel was there, bi siyt which Y siy in the feeld.

5 And he seide to me, Thou, sone of man, reise thin iyen to the weie of the north; and Y reiside myn iyen to the weie of the north, and lo! fro the north of the yate of the auter the idol of enuye was in that entryng.

6 And he seide to me, Sone of man, gessist thou whether thou seest what thing these men doon, the grete abhomynaciouns whiche the hous of Israel doith here, that Y go fer awei fro my seyntuarie? and yit thou schalt turne, and schalt se grettere abhomynaciouns.

7 And he ledde me with ynne to the dore of the halle; and Y siy, and lo! oon hoole in the wal.

8 And he seide to me, Sone of man, digge thou the wal; and whanne Y hadde diggid the wal, o dore apperide.

9 And he seide to me, Entre thou, and se the worste abhomynaciouns, whiche these men doon here.

10 And Y entride, and siy; and lo! ech licnesse of 'crepynge beestis, and abhomynacioun of beestis, and alle idols of the hous of Israel, weren peyntid in the wal al aboute in cumpas.

11 And seuenti men of the eldere of the hous of Israel stoden; and Jeconye, the sone of Saphan, stood in the myddis of hem, stondynge bifore the peyntyngis; and ech man hadde a censere in his hond, and the smoke of a cloude of encense stiede.

12 And he seide to me, Certis, sone of man, thou seest what thingis the eldere men of the hous of Israel doen in derknessis, ech man in the hid place of his bed; for thei seiyn, The Lord seeth not vs, the Lord hath forsake the lond.

13 And the Lord seide to me, Yit thou schalt turne, and schalt se gretter abhomynaciouns, whiche these men doon.

14 And he ledde me with ynne, bi the dore of the yate of the hous of the Lord, which dore bihelde to the north; and lo! wymmen saten there, biweilynge Adonydes.

15 And the Lord seide to me, Certis, sone of man, thou hast seyn; yit thou schalt turne, and schalt se gretere abhomynaciouns than these.

16 And he ledde me with ynne, in to the ynnere halle of the hous of the Lord; and lo! in the dore of the temple of the Lord, bitwixe the porche and the auter, weren as fyue and twenti men hauynge the backis ayens the temple of the Lord, and her faces to the eest; and thei worschipiden at the risyng of the sunne.

17 And the Lord seide to me, Certis, sone of man, thou hast seyn; whether this is a liyt thing to the hous of Juda, that thei schulden do these abhomynaciouns, whiche thei diden here? For thei filliden the lond with wickidnesse, and turneden to terre me to wraththe; and lo! thei applien a braunche to her nose thirlis.

18 Therfor and Y schal do in strong veniaunce; myn iye schal not spare, nether Y schal do merci; and whanne thei schulen crie to myn eris with greet vois, Y schal not here hem.

CAP 9

1 And he criede in myn eeris with greet vois, and seide, The visityngis of the citee han neiyed, and ech man hath in his hond an instrument of sleyng.

2 And lo! sixe men camen fro the weie of the hiyere yate, that biholdith to the north, and the instrument of deth of ech man was in his hond; also o man in the myddis of hem was clothid with lynnun clothis, and a pennere of a writere at hise reynes; and thei entriden, and stoden bisidis the brasun auter.

3 And the glorie of the Lord of Israel was takun vp fro cherub, which glorie was on it, to the threisfold of the hous; and the Lord clepide the man that was clothid with lynun clothis, and hadde a pennere of a writere in hise leendis.

4 And the Lord seide to hym, Passe thou bi the myddis of the citee, in the myddis of Jerusalem, and marke thou Thau on the forhedis of men weilynge and sorewynge on alle abhomynaciouns that ben doon in the myddis therof.

5 And he seide to hem in myn heryng, Go ye thorouy the citee, and sue ye hym, and smytte ye; youre iye spare not, nether do ye merci.

6 Sle ye til to deth, an eld man, a yong man, and a virgyn, a litil child, and wymmen; but sle ye not ony man, on whom ye seen Thau; and bigynne ye at my seyntuarie. Therfore thei bigunnen at the eldere men, that weren bifore the face of the hous.

7 And he seide to hem, Defoule ye the hous, and fille ye the hallis with slayn men; go ye out. And thei yeden out, and killiden hem that weren in the citee.

8 And lo! whanne the sleyng was fillid, Y was left. And Y felle doun on my face, and Y criede, and seide, Alas! alas! alas! Lord God, therfor whether thou schalt leese alle remenauntis of Israel, and schalt schede out thi stronge veniaunce on Jerusalem?

9 And he seide to me, The wickidnesse of the hous of Israel and of Juda is ful greet, and the lond is fillid of bloodis, and the citee is fillid with turnyng awei; for thei seiden, The Lord hath forsake the lond, and the Lord seeth not.

10 Therfor and myn iye schal not spare, nether Y schal do merci; Y schal yelde the weie of hem on the heed of hem.

11 And lo! the man that was clothid in lynun clothis, that hadde a pennere in his bak, answeride a word, and seide, Y haue do, as thou comaundidist to me.

CAP 10

1 And Y siy, and lo! in the firmament that was on the heed of cherubyns, as a saphir stoon, and as the fourme of licnesse of a kyngis seete apperide theron.

2 And he seide to the man that was clothid in lynnun clothis, and spak, Entre thou in the myddis of wheelis, that ben vndur cherubyns, and fille thin hond with coolis of fier, that ben bitwixe cherubyns, and schede thou out on the citee.

3 And he entride in my siyt; forsothe cherubyns stoden at the riyt side of the hous, whanne the man entride, and a clowde fillide the ynnere halle.

4 And the glorie of the Lord was reisid fro aboue cherubyns to the threisfold of the hous; and the hous was fillid with a cloude, and the halle was fillid with schynyng of the glorie of the Lord.

5 And the sown of wyngis of cherubyns was herd til to the outermere halle, as the vois of almyyti God spekynge.

6 And whanne he hadde comaundid to the man that was clothid in lynnun clothis, and hadde seid, Take thou fier fro the myddis of the wheelis, that ben bitwixe cherubyns, he entride, and stood bisidis the wheel.

7 And cherub stretchide forth his hond fro the myddis of cherubyns, to the fier that was bitwixe cherubyns; and took, and yaf in to the hondis of hym that was clothid in lynnun clothis; and he took, and yede out.

8 And the licnesse of the hond of a man apperide in cherubyns, vndur the wyngis of tho.

9 And Y siy, and lo! foure wheelis weren bisidis cherubyns; o wheel bisidis o cherub, and another wheel bisidis another cherub; forsothe the licnesse of wheelis was as the siyt of the stoon crisolitis.

10 And the biholdyng of tho was o licnesse of foure, as if a wheel be in the myddis of a wheel.

11 And whanne tho yeden, tho yeden in to foure partis; tho turneden not ayen goynge, but to the place to which that that was the firste wheel bowide to go, also othere suyden, and turneden not ayen.

12 And al the bodi of tho wheelis, and the neckis, and hondis, and wyngis of the beestis, and the cerclis, weren ful of iyen, in the cumpas of foure wheelis.

13 And he clepide tho wheelis volible, ether able to go al aboute, in myn heryng.

14 Forsothe o beeste hadde foure faces; o face was the face of cherub, and the secounde face the face of a man, and in the thridde was the face of a lioun, and in the fourthe was the face of an egle;

15 and the cherubyns weren reisid. Thilke is the beeste, which Y hadde seyn bisidis the flood Chobar.

16 And whanne cherubyns yeden, also the wheelis bisidis tho yeden to gidere; whanne cherubyns reisiden her wyngis, that tho schulden be enhaunsid fro the erthe, the wheelis abididen not stille, but also tho weren bisidis cherubyns.

17 The wheelis stooden with tho cherubyns stondynge, and weren reisid with the cherubyns reisid; for the spirit of lijf was in tho wheelis.

18 And the glorie of the Lord yede out fro the threisfold of the temple, and stood on the cherubyns.

19 And cherubyns reisiden her wyngis, and weren enhaunsid fro the erthe bifore me; and whanne tho yeden out, also the wheelis sueden; and it stood in the entryng of the eest yate of the hous of the Lord, and the glorie of God of Israel was on tho.

20 Thilke is the beeste, which Y siy vndur God of Israel, bisidis the flood Chobar. And Y vndurstood that foure cherubyns weren;

21 foure faces weren to oon, and foure wyngys weren to oon; and the licnesse of the hond of a man was vndur the wyngis of tho.

22 And the licnesse of the cheris of tho weren thilke cheeris whiche Y hadde seyn bisidis the flood Chobar; and the biholdyng of tho, and the fersnesse of ech, was to entre bifor his face.

CAP 11

1 And the spirit reiside me, and ledde me with ynne to the eest yate of the hous of the Lord, that biholdith the risyng of the sunne. And lo! in the entryng of the yate weren fyue and twenti men; and Y siy in the myddis of hem Jeconye, the sone of Assur, and Pheltie, the sone of Banaie, princes of the puple.

2 And he seide to me, Thou, sone of man, these ben the men that thenken wickidnesse, and treten the worste counsel in this citee,

3 and seien, Whether housis weren not bildid a while ago? this is the cawdrun, forsothe we ben fleischis.

4 Therfor profesie thou of hem, profesie thou, sone of man.

5 And the Spirit of the Lord felle in to me, and seide to me, Speke thou, The Lord seith these thingis, Ye hous of Israel spaken thus, and Y knewe the thouytis of youre herte;

6 ye killiden ful many men in this citee, and ye filliden the weies therof with slayn men.

7 Therfor the Lord seith these thingis, Youre slayn men, whiche ye puttiden in the myddis therof, these ben fleischis, and this is the cawdrun; and Y schal lede you out of the myddis therof.

8 Ye dredden swerd, and Y schal brynge in swerd on you, seith the Lord God.

9 And Y schal caste you out of the myddis therof, and Y schal yyue you in to the hond of enemyes, and Y schal make domes in you.

10 Bi swerd ye schulen falle doun, Y schal deme you in the endis of Israel; and ye schulen wite, that Y am the Lord.

11 This schal not be to you in to a cawdrun, and ye schulen not be in to fleischis in the myddis therof; Y schal deme you in the endis of Israel,

12 and ye schulen wite, that Y am the Lord. For ye yeden not in myn heestis, and ye dyden not my domes, but ye wrouyten bi the domes of hethene men, that ben in youre cumpas.

13 And it was doon, whanne Y profesiede, Pheltie, the sone of Banaie, was deed; and Y felle doun on my face, and Y criede with greet vois, and seide, Alas! alas! alas! Lord God, thou makist endyng of the remenauntis of Israel.

14 And the word of the Lord was maad to me,

15 and he seide, Sone of man, thi britheren, thi kynes men, and al the hous of Israel, and alle men, to whiche the dwell-eris of Jerusalem seiden, Go ye awei fer fro the Lord, the lond is youun to vs in to possessioun.

16 Therfor the Lord God seith these thingis, For Y made hem fer among hethene men, and for Y scateride hem in londis, Y schal be to hem in to a litil halewyng, in the londis to whiche thei camen.

17 Therfor speke thou, The Lord God seith these thingis, Y schal gadere you fro puplis, and Y schal gadere you togidere fro londis, in whiche ye ben scatered; and Y schal yyue the erthe of Israel to you.

18 And thei schulen entre thidur, and schulen do awei alle offenciouns, and alle abhomynaciouns therof in that dai.

19 And Y schal yyue to hem oon herte, and Y schal yyue a newe spirit in the entrails of hem; and Y schal take awei a stony herte fro the fleisch of hem, and Y schal yyue to hem an herte of fleisch;

20 that thei go in my comaundementis, and kepe my domes, and do tho; and that thei be in to a puple to me, and Y be in to God to hem.

21 But of whiche the herte goith after her offendyngis and abhomynaciouns, Y schal sette the weie of hem in her heed, seith the Lord God.

22 And the cherubyns reisiden her wyngis, and the wheelis yeden with tho, and the glorie of God of Israel was on tho.

23 And the glorie of the Lord stiede fro the myddis of the citee, and stood on the hil, which is at the eest of the citee.

24 And the spirit reiside me, and brouyte me in to Caldee, to the passyng ouer, in visioun bi the spirit of God; and the visioun which Y hadde seyn, was takun awei fro me.

25 And Y spak to the passyng ouer alle the wordis of the Lord, whiche he hadde schewid to me.

CAP 12

1 And the word of the Lord was maad to me,

2 and he seide, Sone of man, thou dwellist in the myddis of an hous terrynge to wraththe, which han iyen to se, and seen not, and eeris to here, and heren not; for it is an hous terrynge to wraththe.

3 Therfor thou, sone of man, make to thee vessels of passing ouer, and thou schalt passe ouer bi dai bifor hem; forsothe thou schalt passe ouer fro thi place to another place, in the siyt of hem, if perauenture thei biholden, for it is an hous ter-rynge to wraththe.

4 And thou schalt bere withoutforth thi vessels, as the vessels of a man passynge ouer bi dai, in the siyt of hem; sotheli thou schalt go out in the euentid bifore hem, as a man passynge forth goith out.

5 Bifore the iyen of hem digge the wal to thee, and thou 6 schalt go out thorouy it in the siyt of hem. Thou schalt be borun on schuldris, thou schalt be borun out in derknesse; thou schalt hile thi face, and thou schalt not se the erthe, for Y haue youe thee a signe

7 of thing to comynge to the hous of Israel. Therfor Y dide as the Lord comaundide to me; Y brouyte forth my vessels, as the vessels of a man passynge ouer bi dai, and in the euentid Y diggide a wal to me with hond; Y yede out in derknesse, and Y was borun on schuldris,

8 in the siyt of hem. And the word of the Lord was maad eerli to me,

9 and he seide, Sone of man, whether the hous of Israel, the hous terrynge to wraththe, seiden not to thee, What doist thou?

10 Seie thou to hem, The Lord God seith these thingis, This birthun is on the duyk, which is in Jerusalem, and on al the hous of Israel, which is in the myddis of hem.

11 Seie thou, Y am youre signe of thing to comynge; as Y dide, so it schal be don to hem; thei schulen go in to passynge ouer, and in to caitifte.

12 And the duyk which is in the myddis of hem, schal be borun out on schuldris, and he schal go out in derknesse; thei schulen digge the wal, and lede hym out; his face schal be hilid, that he se not with iye the erthe.

13 And Y schal stretche forth my net on hym, and he schal be takun in my net; and Y schal lede hym in to Babiloyne, in to the lond of Caldeis, and he schal not se that lond, and he schal die there.

14 And Y schal scatere in to ech wynd alle men that ben aboute hym, his help, and hise cumpenyes; and Y schal draw out the swerd aftir hem.

15 And thei schulen wite, that Y am the Lord, whanne Y schal scatere hem among hethene men, and schal sowe hem abrood in londis.

16 And Y schal leue of hem a fewe men fro swerd, and hun-gur, and pestilence, that thei telle out alle the grete trespassis of hem among hethene men, to which thei schulen entre; and thei schulen wite, that Y am the Lord.

17 And the word of the Lord was maad to me,

18 and he seide, Thou, sone of man, ete thi breed in distur-blyng, but also drynke thi water in haaste and mourening.

19 And thou schalt seie to the puple of the lond, The Lord God seith these thingis to hem that dwellen in Jerusalem, in the lond of Israel, Thei schulen ete her breed in angwisch, and thei schulen drynke her watir in desolacioun; that the lond be desolat of his multitude, for the wickidnesse of alle men that dwellen ther ynne.

20 And citees that ben now enhabitid, shulen be desolat, and the lond schal be forsakun; and ye schulen wite, that Y am the Lord.

21 And the word of the Lord was maad to me,

22 and he seide, Sone of man, what is this prouerbe to you, of men seiynge in the lond of Israel, Daies schulen be differrid in to long tyme, and ech visioun shal perische?

23 Therfor seie thou to hem, The Lord God seith these thingis, Y schal make this prouerbe to ceesse, and it schal no more be seid comynli in Israel; and speke thou to hem, that the daies han neiyid, and ech word of profesie.

24 For whi ech visioun schal no more be voide, nether bifor tellyng of thing to comynge schal be douteful in the myddis of the sones of Israel;

25 for Y the Lord schal speke what euer word Y schal speke, and it schal be don; it schal no more be delaied, but in youre daies, ye hous terrynge to wraththe, Y schal speke a word, and Y schal do that word, seith the Lord God.

26 And the word of the Lord was maad to me, and he seide, Thou,

27 sone of man, lo! the hous of Israel, of hem that seien, The visioun which this man seeth, is in to manye daies, and this man profesieth in to longe tymes.

28 Therfor seie thou to hem, The Lord God seith these thingis, Ech word of me schal no more be deferrid; the word which Y schal speke, schal be fillid, seith the Lord God.

CAP 13

1 And the word of the Lord was maad to me,

2 and he seide, Sone of man, profesie thou to the profetis of Israel that profesien; and thou schalt seie to hem that profesien of her herte,

3 Here ye the word of the Lord. The Lord God seith these thingis, Wo to the vnwise profetis, that suen her spirit, and seen no thing;

4 Israel, thi profetis weren as foxis in desert.

5 Ye stieden not euene ayens, nether ayensettiden a wal for the hous of Israel, that ye shulden stonde in batel in the dai of the Lord.

6 Thei seen veyn thingis, and deuynen a leesyng, and seien, The Lord seith, whanne the Lord sente not hem; and thei contynueden to conferme the word.

7 Whether ye seen not a veyn visioun, and spaken fals diuynyng, and seiden, The Lord seith, whanne Y spak not?

8 Therfor the Lord God seith these thingis, For ye spaken veyn thingis, and sien a leesyng, therfor lo! Y to you, seith the Lord God.

9 And myn hond schal be on the profetis that seen veyn thingis, and dyuynen a leesyng; thei schulen not be in the councel of my puple, and thei schulen not be writun in the scripture of the hous of Israel, nether thei schulen entre in to the lond of Israel; and ye schulen wite, that Y am the Lord God.

10 For thei disseyueden my puple, and seiden, Pees, pees, and no pees is; and it bildide a wal, but thei pargitiden it with fen with out chaffis.

11 Seie thou to hem that pargiten with out temperure, that it schal falle doun; for a strong reyn schal be flowynge, and I shal yyue ful grete stoones fallinge fro aboue, and Y schal yyue a wynd of tempest that distrieth.

12 For lo! the wal felle doun. Whether it schal not be seid to you, Where is the pargetyng, which ye pargetiden?

13 Therfor the Lord God seith these thingis, And Y schal make the spirit of tempestis to breke out in myn indignacioun, and strong reyn flowynge in my strong veniaunce schal be, and greet stoonys in wraththe in to wastyng.

14 And Y schal distrie the wal, which ye pargetiden with out temperure, and Y schal make it euene with the erthe; and the foundement therof schal be schewid, and it schal falle doun, and it schal be wastid in the myddis therof; and ye schulen wite, that Y am the Lord.

15 And Y schal fille myn indignacioun in the wal, and in hem that pargeten it with out temperure; and Y schal seie to you, The wal is not, and thei ben not,

16 that pargeten it, the profetis of Israel, that profesien to Jerusalem, and seen to it the visioun of pees, and pees is not, seith the Lord God.

17 And thou, sone of man, sette thi face ayens the douytris of thi puple, that profesien of her herte; and profesie thou on hem,

18 and seie thou, The Lord God seith these thingis, Wo to hem that sowen togidere cuschens vndur ech cubit of hond, and maken pilewis vndur the heed of ech age, to take soulis; and whanne thei disseyueden the soulis of my puple, thei quykenyden the soulis of hem.

19 And thei defouliden me to my puple, for an handful of barli, and for a gobet of breed, that thei schulden sle soulis that dien not, and quykene soulis that lyuen not; and thei lieden to my puple, bileuynge to leesyngis.

20 For this thing the Lord God seith these thingis, Lo! Y to youre cuschens, bi whiche ye disseyuen soulis fliynge; and Y schal al to-breke tho fro youre armes, and Y schal delyuere soulis which ye disseyuen, soulis to fle.

21 And Y schal al to-breke youre pilewis, and Y schal delyuere my puple fro youre hond; and thei schulen no more be in youre hondis, to be robbid; and ye schulen wite, that Y am the Lord.

22 For that that ye maden falsli the herte of a iust man to morene, whom Y made not sori; and ye coumfortiden the hondis of a wickid man, that he schulde not turne ayen fro his yuel weie, and lyue.

23 Therfor ye schulen not se veyn thingis, and ye schulen no more dyuyne false dyuynyngis; and Y schal delyuere my puple fro youre hond, and ye schulen wite, that Y am the Lord.

CAP 14

1 And men of the eldris of Israel camen to me, and saten bifor me.

2 And the word of the Lord was maad to me, and he seide, Sone of man,

3 these men han set her vnclennesses in her hertis, and han set stidfastli the sclaundre of her wickidnesse ayens her face. Whether Y 'that am axid, schal answere to hem?

4 For this thing speke thou to hem, and thou schalt seie to hem, These thingis seith the Lord God, A man, a man of the hous of Israel, that settith hise vnclennessis in his herte, and settith stidfastli the sclaundre of his wickidnesse ayens his face, and cometh to the profete, and axith me bi hym, Y the Lord schal answere to hym in the multitude of hise vnclennessis;

5 that the hous of Israel be takun in her herte, bi which thei yeden awei fro me in alle her idols.

6 Therfor seie thou to the hous of Israel, The Lord God seith these thingis, Be ye conuertid, and go ye awei fro youre idols, and turne awei youre faces fro alle youre filthis.

7 For whi a man, a man of the hous of Israel, and of conuersis, who euer is a comelyng in Israel, if he is alienyd fro me, and settith hise idols in his herte, and settith stidfastli the sclaundir of his wickidnesse ayens his face, and he cometh to the profete, to axe me bi hym, Y the Lord schal answere hym bi my silf.

8 And Y schal sette my face on that man, and Y schal make hym in to ensaumple, and in to a prouerbe, and Y schal leese hym fro the myddis of my puple; and ye schulen wite, that Y am the Lord.

9 And whanne a profete errith, and spekith a word, Y the Lord schal disseyue that profete; and Y schal stretche forth myn hond on hym, and Y schal do hym awei fro the myddis of my puple Israel.

10 And thei schulen bere her wickidnesse; bi the wickidnesse of the axere, so the wickidnesse of the profete schal be;

11 that the hous of Israel erre no more fro me, nether be defoulid in alle her trespassyngis; but that it be in to a puple to me, and Y be in to a God to hem, seith the Lord of oostis.

12 And the word of the Lord was maad to me, and he seide,

13 Sone of man, whanne the lond synneth ayens me, that it trespassynge do trespas, Y schal stretche forth myn hond on it, and Y schal al to-breke the yerde of breed therof; and Y schal sende hungur in to it, and Y schal sle of it man and beeste.

14 And if these thre men Noe, Danyel, and Job, ben in the myddis therof, thei bi her riytfulnesse schulen delyuere her soulis, seith the Lord of oostis.

15 That if also Y brynge in worste beestis on the lond, that Y distrie it, and if it is with out weie, for that no passer is for the beestis,

16 and these thre men, that 'ben bifore seid, ben therynne, Y lyue, seith the Lord God, for thei schulen nethir delyuere sones, nether douytris, but thei aloone schulen be deliuered; forsothe the lond schal be maad desolat.

17 Ethir if Y brynge in swerd on that lond, and Y seie to the swerd, Passe thou thorouy the lond, and Y sle of it man and beeste,

18 and these thre men ben in the myddis therof, Y lyue, seith the Lord God, that thei schulen not delyuere sones nether douytris, but thei aloone schulen be delyuered.

19 Forsothe if Y brynge in also pestilence on that lond, and Y schede out myn indignacioun on it in blood, that Y do awei fro it man and beeste,

20 and Noe, and Danyel, and Joob, ben in the myddis therof, Y lyue, seith the Lord God, for thei schulen not delyuere a sone and a douyter, but thei bi her riytfulnesse schulen dely-uere her soulis.

21 For the Lord God seith these thingis, That thouy Y sende in my foure worste domes, swerd, and hungur, and yuele beestis, and pestilence, in to Jerusalem, that Y sle of it man and beeste,

22 netheles saluacioun of hem that leden out sones and douy-tris, schal be left ther ynne. Lo! thei schulen go out to you, and ye schulen se the weie of hem, and the fyndyngis of hem; and ye schulen be coumfortid on the yuel, which Y brouyte in on Jerusalem, in alle thingis whiche Y bar in on it.

23 And thei schulen coumforte you, whanne ye schulen se the weie of hem and the fyndyngis of hem; and ye schulen knowe, that not in veyn Y dide alle thingis, what euer thingis Y dide there ynne, seith the Lord almyyti.

CAP 15

1 And the word of the Lord was maad to me,

2 and he seide, Sone of man, what schal be don to the tre of a vyne, of alle the trees of woodis, that ben among the trees of woodis?

3 Whether tymbre schal be takun therof, that werk be maad? ether shal a stake be maad therof, that ony vessel hange ther onne?

4 Lo! it is youun in to mete; fier wastide euer eithir part therof, and the myddis therof is dryuun in to deed sparcle; whether it schal be profitable to werk?

5 Yhe, whanne it was hool, it was not couenable to werk; hou myche more whanne fier hath deuourid, and hath brent it, no thing of werk schal be maad therof?

6 Therfor the Lord God seith thes thingis, As the tre of a vyne is among the trees of woodis, which Y yaf to fier to deuoure, so Y yaf the dwelleris of Jerusalem,

7 and Y schal sette my face ayens hem. Thei schulen go out of the fier, and fier schal waaste hem; and ye schulen wite, that Y am the Lord, whanne Y schal sette my face ayens hem,

8 and schal yyue the lond with out weie and desolat, for thei weren trespassours, seith the Lord God.

CAP 16

1 And the word of the Lord was maad to me,

2 and he seide, Sone of man, make thou knowun to Jerusalem her abhomynaciouns; and thou schalt seie,

3 The Lord God seith these thingis. A! thou Jerusalem, thi rote and thi generacioun is of the lond of Canaan; thi fadir is Amorrei, and thi moder is Cetei.

4 And whanne thou were borun, thi nawle was not kit awei in the dai of thi birthe, and thou were not waischun in watir in to helthe, nethir saltid with salt, nether wlappid in clothis.

5 An iye sparide not on thee, that it hauynge merci on thee, dide to thee oon of these thingis; but thou were cast forth on the face of erthe, in the castynge out of thi soule, in the dai in which thou were borun.

6 Forsothe Y passide bi thee, and Y siy thee defoulid in thi blood; and Y seide to thee, whanne thou were in thi blood, Lyue thou; sotheli Y seide to thee in thi blood, Lyue thou.

7 Y yaf thee multiplied as the seed of a feeld, and thou were multiplied, and maad greet; and thou entridist, and camest fulli to wymmens ournyng; thi tetis wexiden greet, and thin heer wexide; and thou were nakid, and ful of schenschipe.

8 And Y passide bi thee, and Y siy thee, and lo! thi tyme, the tyme of louyeris; and Y spredde abrood my clothing on thee, and Y hilide thi schenschipe. And Y swoor to thee, and Y made a couenaunt with thee, seith the Lord God, and thou were maad a wijf to me.

9 And Y waischide thee in water, and Y clenside awei thi blood fro thee, and Y anoyntide thee with oile.

10 And Y clothide thee with clothis of dyuerse colours, and Y schodde thee in iacynct, and Y girde thee with biys;

11 and Y clothide thee with sutil thingis, and Y ournede thee with ournement.

12 And Y yaf bies in thin hondis, and a wrethe aboute thi necke; and Y yaf a ryng on thi mouth, and cerclis to thin eeris, and a coroun of fairnesse in thin heed.

13 And thou were ourned with gold and siluer, and thou were clothid with biys and ray cloth with rounde ymagis, and many colours. Thou etist cleene flour of wheete, and hony, and oile, and thou were maad fair ful greetli; and thou encreessidist in to a rewme,

14 and thi name yede out in to hethene men for thi fairnesse; for thou were perfit in my fairnesse which Y hadde sett on thee, seith the Lord God.

15 And thou haddist trist in thi fairnesse, and didist fornica-cioun in thi name; and thou settidist forth thi fornicacioun to ech that passide forth, that thou schuldist be maad his.

16 And thou tokist of my clothis, and madist to thee hiy thingis set aboute on ech side; and thou didist fornycacioun on tho, as it was not don, nether schal be don.

17 And thou tokist the vessels of thi fairnesse, of my gold and of my siluer, which Y yaf to thee; and thou madist to thee ymagis of men, and didist fornycacioun in tho.

18 And thou tokist thi clothis of many colours, and thou were clothid in tho; and thou settidist myn oile and myn encence in the siyt of tho.

19 And thou settidist my breed, which Y yaf to thee, flour of wheete, and oile, and hony, bi whiche Y nurschide thee, in the siyt of tho, in to odour of swetnesse; and it was don, seith the Lord God.

20 And thou tokist thi sones and thi douytris, whiche thou gendridist to me, and offridist to tho, for to be deuourid. Whether thi fornicacioun is litil?

21 Thou offridist my sones, and yauest hem, and halewidist to tho.

22 And aftir alle thin abhomynaciouns and fornicaciouns, thou bithouytist not on the daies of thi yong wexynge age, whanne thou were nakid, and ful of schenschipe, and were defoulid in thi blood.

23 And after al thi malice, wo, wo bifelle to thee, seith the Lord God.

24 And thou bildidist to thee a bordel hous, and madist to thee a place of hordom in alle stretis.

25 At ech heed of the weie thou bildidist a signe of thin hordom, and madist thi fairnesse abhomynable; and thou departidist thi feet to ech man passynge forth, and multepliedist thi fornicaciouns.

26 And thou didist fornicacioun with the sones of Egipt, thi neiyboris of grete fleischis, and thou multepliedist thi fornicacioun, to terre me to wraththe.

27 Lo! Y schal stretch forth myn hond on thee, and Y schal take awei thi iustifiyng; and Y schal yyue thee in to the soulis of hem that haten thee, of the douytris of Palestyns, that ben aschamed in thi weie ful of greet trespas.

28 And thou didist fornicacioun with the sones of Assiriens, for thou were not fillid yit; and after that thou didist fornicacioun, nether so thou were fillid.

29 And thou multipliedist thi fornycacioun in the lond of Canaan with Caldeis, and nether so thou were fillid.

30 In what thing schal Y clense thin herte, seith the Lord God, whanne thou doist alle these werkis of a womman an hoore, and gredi axere?

31 For thou madist thi bordel hous in 'the heed of ech weie, and thou madist thin hiy place in ech street; and thou were not maad as an hoore ful of anoiyng,

32 encreessynge prijs, but as a womman auowtresse, that bryngith in aliens on hir hosebonde.

33 Hiris ben youun to alle hooris, but thou hast youe hire to alle thi louyeris; and thou yauest to hem, that thei schulden entre to thee on ech side, to do fornycacioun with thee.

34 And it was don in thee ayens the custom of wymmen in thi fornycaciouns, and fornicacioun schal not be after thee; for in that that thou yauest hiris, and tokist not hiris, the contrarie was don in thee.

35 Therfor, thou hoore, here the word of the Lord.

36 The Lord God seith these thingis, For thi riches is sched out, and thi schenschipe is schewid in thi fornicaciouns on thi louyeris, and on the idols of thin abhomynaciouns, in the blood of thi sones, whiche thou yauest to hem; lo!

37 Y schal gadere to gidere alle thi louyeris, with whiche thou were meddlid, and alle men whiche thou louedist, with alle men whiche thou hatidist; and Y schal gadere hem on thee on ech side, and Y schal make nakid thi schenschipe bifore hem, and thei schulen se al thi filthe.

38 And Y schal deme thee bi the domes of auoutressis, and schedinge out blood;

39 And Y schal yyue thee in to the blood of strong veniaunce, and of feruour. And Y schal yyue thee in to the hondis of hem, and thei schulen destrie thi bordel hous, and thei schulen destrie the place of thin hordom; and thei schulen make thee nakid of thi clothis, and thei schulen take awei the vessels of thi fairnesse, and thei schulen forsake thee nakid, and ful of schenschipe.

40 And thei schulen bringe on thee a multitude, and thei schulen stoon thee with stoonys, and thei schulen sle thee with her swerdis.

41 And thei schulen brenne thin housis with fier, and thei schulen make domes in thee, bifor the iyen of ful many wymmen; and thou schalt ceese to do fornicacioun, and thou schalt no more yyue hiris.

42 And myn indignacioun schal reste in thee, and my feruent loue schal be takun awei fro thee; and Y schal reste, and Y schal no more be wrooth,

43 for thou haddist not mynde on the daies of thi yong wexynge age, and thou terridist me to ire in alle these thingis. Wherfor and Y yaf thi weies in thin heed, seith the Lord God, and Y dide not aftir thi grete trespassis, in alle these thin abhomynaciouns.

44 Lo! ech man that seith a prouerbe comynli, schal take it in thee,

45 and schal seie, As the modir, so and the douytir of hir. Thou art the douyter of thi modir, that castide awey hir hosebonde and hir sones; and thou art the sister of thi sistris, that castiden a wei her hosebondis and her sones. Thi modir is Cetei, and thi fadir is Ammorrei;

46 and thi gretter sister is Samarie, sche and hir douytris, that dwellen at thi left side; but thi sistir lesse than thou, that dwellith at thi riyt side, is Sodom, and hir douytris.

47 But thou yedist not in the weies of hem, nethir thou didist aftir the grete trespassis of hem; hast thou do almest a litil lesse cursidere dedis than thei, in alle thi weies?

48 Y lyue, seith the Lord God, for Sodom, thi sister, did not, sche and hir douytris, as thou didist, and thi douytris.

49 Lo! this was the wickidnesse of Sodom, thi sister, pride, fulnesse of breed, and habundaunce, and idilnesse of hir, and of hir douytris; and thei puttiden not hond to a nedi man and pore.

50 And thei weren enhaunsid, and diden other abhominaciouns bifore me; and Y took hem awei, as thou hast seyn.

51 And Samarie synnede not the half of thi synnes, but thou hast ouercome hem in thi grete trespassis; and thou hast iustified thi sistris in alle thin abhomynaciouns, whiche thou wrouytist.

52 Therfor and thou bere thi schenschipe, that hast ouercome thi sistris with thi synnes, and didist more cursidli than thei; for thei ben iustified of thee. Therfor and be thou schent, and bere thi schenschipe, which hast iustified thi sistris.

53 And Y schal conuerte and restore hem by the conuersioun of Sodom with hir douytris, and bi the conuersioun of Samarie and of hir douytris; and Y schal conuerte thi turnyng ayen in the myddis of hem,

54 that thou bere thi schenschipe, and be aschamed in alle thingis whiche thou didist, coumfortynge hem.

55 And thi sister Sodom and hir doytris schulen turne ayen to her eldnesse; and Samarie and hir douytris shulen turne ayen

to her eeldnesse; and thou and thi douytris turne ayen to youre eldnesse.

56 Forsothe Sodom, thi sister, was not herd in thi mouth, in the dai of thi pride,

57 bifore that thi malice was schewid, as in this tyme, in to schenschipe of the douytris of Sirie, and of alle douytris in thi cumpas, of the douytris of Palestyn that ben aboute thee bi cumpas.

58 Thou hast bore thi greet trespas, and thi schenschipe, seith the Lord God.

59 For the Lord God seith these thingis, And Y schal do to thee as thou dispisidist the ooth, that thou schuldist make voide the couenaunt;

60 and Y schal haue mynde on my couenaunt with thee in the daies of thi yongthe, and Y schal reise to thee a couenaunt euerlastynge.

61 And thou schalt haue mynde on thi weies, and schalt be aschamed, whanne thou schalt resseyue thi sistris grettere than thou, with thi lesse sistris; and Y schal yyue hem in to douytris to thee, but not of thi couenaunt.

62 And Y schal reise my couenaunt with thee, and thou schalt wite, that Y am the Lord, that thou haue mynde, and be aschamed;

63 and that it be no more to thee to opene the mouth for thi schame, whanne Y schal be plesid to thee in alle thingis whiche thou didist, seith the Lord God.

CAP 17

1 And the word of the Lord was maad to me,

2 and he seide, Sone of man, sette forth a derk speche, and telle thou a parable to the hous of Israel;

3 and thou schalt seie, The Lord God seith these thingis. A greet egle of grete wyngis, with long stretchyng out of membris, ful of fetheris and of dyuersite, cam to the Liban, and took awei the merowe of the cedre.

4 He pullide awei the hiynesse of boowis therof, and bar it ouer in to the lond of Chanaan, and settide it in the citee of marchauntis.

5 And he took of the seed of the lond, and settide it in the lond for seed, that it schulde make stidfast roote on many watris; he settide it in the hiyere part.

6 And whanne it hadde growe, it encreeside in to a largere vyner, in lowe stature; for the boowis therof bihelden to that egle, and the rootis therof weren vndur that egle; therof it was maad a vyner, and it made fruyt in to siouns, and sente out boowis.

7 And another greet egle was maad, with grete wyngis, and many fetheris; and lo! this vyner as sendynge hise rootis to that egle, stretchide forth his siouns to that egle, that he schulde moiste it of the cornfloris of his seed.

8 Which is plauntid in a good lond on many watris, that it make boowis, and bere fruyt, that it be in to a greet vyner.

9 Seie thou, Ezechiel, The Lord God seith these thingis, Therfor whether he schal haue prosperite? Whether Nabugodonosor schal not pulle awei the rootis of hym, and schal streyne the fruytis of hym? And he schal make drie alle the siouns of buriowning therof, and it schal be drie; and not in greet arm, nether in myche puple, that he schulde drawe it out bi the rootis.

10 Lo! it is plauntid, therfor whether it schal haue prosperite? Whether not whanne brennynge wynd schal touche it, it schal be maad drye, and schal wexe drie in the cornfloris of his seed?

11 And the word of the Lord was maad to me, and he seide, Seie thou to the hous terrynge to wraththe,

12 Witen ye not what these thingis signefien? Seie thou, Lo! the king of Babiloyne cometh in to Jerusalem; and he schal take the kyng and the princis therof, and he schal leede hem to hym silf in to Babiloyne.

13 And he schal take of the seed of the rewme, and schal smyte with it a boond of pees, and he schal take of it an ooth; but also he schal take awei the stronge men of the lond,

14 that it be a meke rewme, and be not reisid, but that it kepe the couenaunt of hym, and holde it.

15 Which yede awei fro hym, and sente messangeris in to Egipt, that it schulde yyue to hym horsis and miche puple. Whether he that dide these thingis, schal haue prosperite, ether schal gete helthe? and whether he that brekith couenaunt, schal ascape?

16 Y lyue, seith the Lord God, for in the place of the king that made hym kyng, whos ooth he made voide, and brak the couenaunt, which he hadde with hym, in the myddis of Babiloyne he schal die.

17 And not in greet oost, nether in myche puple Farao schal make batel ayens hym, in the castyng of erthe, and in bildyng of palis, that he sle many persones.

18 For he dispiside the ooth, that he schulde breke the boond of pees, and lo! he yaf his hond; and whanne he hath do alle these thingis, he schal not ascape.

19 Therfor the Lord God seith these thingis, Y lyue, for Y schal sette on his heed the ooth which he dispiside, and the boond of pees which he brak.

20 And Y schal spredde abrood my net on hym, and he schal be takun in my net, and Y schal brynge hym in to Babiloyne; and there Y schal deme hym in the trespassyng, bi which he dispiside me.

21 And alle hise flieris a wei with al his cumpenye schulen falle doun bi swerd, forsothe the remenauntis schulen be schaterid in to ech wynd; and ye schulen wite, that Y the Lord spak.

22 The Lord God seith these thingis, And Y schal take of the merowe of an hiy cedre, and Y schal sette a tendir thing of the cop of hise braunchis; Y schal streyne, and Y schal plaunte on an hiy hil, and apperynge fer.

23 In the hiy hil of Israel Y schal plaunte it; and it schal breke out in to buriownyng, and it schal make fruyt, and it schal be in to a greet cedre, and alle briddis schulen dwelle vndur it; ech volatil schal make nest vndur the schadewe of hise boowis.

24 And alle trees of the cuntrei schulen wite, that Y am the Lord; Y made low the hiy tre, and Y enhaunside the low tre, and Y made drie the greene tree, and Y made the drie tree to brynge forth boowis; Y the Lord haue spoke, and Y haue do.

CAP 18

1 And the word of the Lord was maad to me,

2 and he seide, What is it, that ye turnen a parable among you in to this prouerbe, in the lond of Israel, and seien, Fadris eeten a bittir grape, and the teeth of sones ben an egge, ether astonyed?

3 Y lyue, seith the Lord God, this parable schal no more be in to a prouerbe to you in Israel.

4 Lo! alle soulis ben myne; as the soule of the fadir, so and the soule of the sone is myn. Thilke soule that doith synne, schal die.

5 And if a man is iust, and doith doom and riytfulnesse,

6 etith not in hillis, and reisith not hise iyen to the idols of the hous of Israel; and defoulith not the wijf of his neiybore, and neiyeth not to a womman defoulid with vncleene blood;

7 and makith not a man sori, yeldith the wed to the dettour, rauyschith no thing bi violence, yyueth his breed to the hungri, and hilith a nakid man with a cloth;

8 leeneth not to vsure, and takith not more; turneth awei his hond fro wickidnesse, and makith trewe dom bitwixe man and man;

9 and goith in my comaundementis, and kepith my domes, that he do treuthe; this is a iust man, he schal lyue in lijf, seith the Lord God.

10 That if he gendrith a sone, a theef, shedinge out blood,

11 and doith oon of thes thingis, and sotheli not doing alle these thingis, but etinge in hillis, and defoulynge the wijf of his neiybore,

12 makynge soreuful a nedy man and pore, rauyschynge raueyns, not yeldinge a wed, reisynge hise iyen to idols, doynge abhomynacioun; yiuynge to vsure, and takynge more;

13 whether he schal lyue? he schal not lyue; whanne he hath do alle these abhomynable thingis, he schal die bi deth, his blood schal be in hym.

14 That if he gendrith a sone, which seeth alle the synnes of his fadir, whiche he dide, and dredith, and doith noon lijk tho;

15 etith not on hillis, and reisith not hise iyen to the idols of the hous of Israel; and defoulith not the wijf of his neiybore,

16 and makith not sori a man, witholdith not a wed, and rauyschith not raueyn, yyueth his breed to the hungri, and hilith the nakid with a cloth;

17 turneth a wei his hond fro the wrong of a pore man, takith not vsure and ouerhabundaunce, 'that is, no thing more than he lente, and doith my domes, and goith in my comaundementis; this sone schal not die in the wickidnesse of his fadir, but he schal lyue in lijf.

18 For his fadir made fals caleng, and dide violence to his brother, and wrouyte yuel in the myddis of his puple, lo! he is deed in his wickidnesse.

19 And ye seien, Whi berith not the sone the wickidnesse of the fadir? That is to seie, for the sone wrouyte doom and riytfulnesse, he kepte alle my comaundementis, and dide tho, he schal lyue in lijf.

20 Thilke soule that doith synne, schal die; the sone schal not bere the wickidnesse of the fadir, and the fadir schal not bere the wickednesse of the sone; the riytfulnesse of a iust man schal be on hym, and the wickidnesse of a wickid man schal be on hym.

21 Forsothe if a wickid man doith penaunce of alle hise synnes whiche he wrouyte, and kepith alle myn heestis, and doith dom and riytfulnesse, he schal lyue bi lijf, and schal not die.

22 Y schal not haue mynde of alle his wickidnessis whiche he wrouyte; he schal lyue in his riytfulnesse which he wrouyte.

23 Whether the deth of the wickid man is of my wille, seith the Lord God, and not that he be conuertid fro his weies, and lyue?

24 Forsothe if a iust man turneth awey hym silf fro his riytfulnesse, and doith wickidnesse bi alle hise abhomynaciouns, which a wickid man is wont to worche, whether he schal lyue? Alle hise riytfulnessis whiche he dide, schulen not be had in mynde; in his trespassyng bi which he trespasside, and in his synne which he synnede, he schal die in tho.

25 And ye seiden, The weie of the Lord is not euene. Therfor, the hous of Israel, here ye, whether my weie is not euene, and not more youre weies ben schrewid?

26 For whanne a riytful man turneth awei hym silf fro his riytfulnesse, and doith wickidnesse, he schal die in it, he schal die in the vnriytwisnesse which he wrouyte.

27 And whanne a wickid man turneth awei him silf fro his wickidnesse which he wrouyte, and doith dom and riytfulnesse, he schal quykene his soule.

28 For he biholdinge and turnynge awei hym silf fro alle hise wickidnessis which he wrouyte, schal lyue in lijf, and schal not die.

29 And the sones of Israel seien, The weie of the Lord is not euene. Whether my weies ben not euene, ye hous of Israel, and not more youre weies ben schrewid?

30 Therfor, thou hous of Israel, Y schal deme ech man bi hise weies, seith the Lord God. Turne ye togidere, and do ye penaunce for alle youre wickidnessis, and wickidnesse schal not be to you in to falling.

31 Caste awei fro you alle youre trespassingis, bi whiche ye trespassiden, and make ye a newe herte and a newe spirit to you, and whi schulen ye die, the hous of Israel?

32 For Y nyle the deeth of hym that dieth, seith the Lord God; turne ye ayen, and lyue ye.

CAP 19

1 And thou, sone of man, take weiling on the princes of Israel;

2 and thou schalt seie, Whi thi modir, a lionesse, lai among liouns? In the myddis of litle liouns sche nurschide hir whelpis,

3 and ledde out oon of hir litle liouns; he was maad a lioun, and he lernyde to take prei, and to ete men.

4 And hethene men herden of hym, and token hym not withouten her woundis; and thei brouyten hym in chaynes in to the lond of Egipt.

5 Which modir whanne sche hadde seyn, that sche was sijk, and the abiding of hym perischide, took oon of her litle liouns, and made hym a lioun.

6 Which yede among liouns, and was maad a lioun;

7 and lernede to take prey, and to deuoure men. He lernyde to make widewis, and to brynge the citees of men in to desert; and the lond and the fulnesse therof was maad desolat, of the vois of his roryng.

8 And hethene men camen togidere ayens hym on ech side fro prouynces, and spredden on hym her net; he was takun in the woundis of tho hethene men.

9 And thei senten hym in to a caue in chaines, and brouyten hym to the kyng of Babiloyne; and thei senten hym in to prisoun, that his vois were no more herd on the hillis of Israel.

10 Thi modir as a vyner in thi blood was plauntid on watre; the fruitis therof and the boowis therof encreessiden of many watris.

11 And sadde yerdis weren maad to it in to septris of lordis, and the stature therof was enhaunsid among boowis; and it siy his hiynesse in the multitude of hise siouns.

12 And it was drawun out in wraththe, and was cast forth in to erthe; and a brennynge wynd dryede the fruyt therof, and the yerdis of strengthe therof welewiden, and weren maad drie, and fier eet it.

13 And now it is plauntid ouer in desert, in a lond with out weie, and thristi.

14 And fier yede out of the yerde of the braunchis therof, that eet the fruyt therof. And a stronge yerde, the ceptre of lordis, was not in it. It is weilyng, and it schal be in to weilyng.

CAP 20

1 And it was doon in the seuenthe yeer, in the fyuethe monethe, in the tenthe dai of the monethe, men of the eldris of Israel camen to axe the Lord; and thei saten bifor me.

2 And the word of the Lord was maad to me,

3 and he seide, Sone of man, speke thou to the eldere men of Israel; and thou schalt seie to hem, The Lord God seith these thingis, Whether ye camen to axe me? Y lyue, for Y schal not answere to you, seith the Lord God. Sone of man,

4 if thou demest hem, if thou demest, schewe thou to hem the abhomynaciouns of her fadris.

5 And thou schalt seie to hem, The Lord God seith these thingis, In the dai in which Y chees Israel, and reiside myn hond for the generacioun of the hous of Jacob, and Y apperide to hem in the lond of Egipt, and Y reiside myn hond for hem, and Y seide, Y am youre Lord God,

6 in that dai Y reiside myn hond for hem, that Y schulde leede hem out of the lond of Egipt, in to the lond which Y hadde purueiede to hem, the lond flowynge with mylk and hony, which is noble among alle londis.

7 And Y seide to hem, Ech man caste awei the offenciouns of hise iyen, and nyle ye be defoulid in the idols of Egipt; Y am youre Lord God.

8 And thei terriden me to wraththe, and nolden here me; ech man castide not awei the abhomynaciouns of hise iyen, nether thei forsoken the idols of Egipt.

9 And Y seide, that Y wold schede out myn indignacioun on hem, and fille my wraththe in hem, in the myddis of the lond of Egipt. And Y dide for my name, that it schulde not be defoulid bifore hethene men, in the myddis of whiche thei weren, and among whiche Y apperide to hem, that Y schulde lede hem out of the lond of Egipt.

10 Therfor Y castide hem out of the lond of Egipt, and Y ledde hem out in to desert;

11 and Y yaf to hem my comaundementis, and Y schewide to hem my doomes, which a man schal do, and lyue in tho.

12 Ferthermore and Y yaf to hem my sabatis, that it schulde be a sygne bitwixe me and hem, and that thei schulden wite, that Y am the Lord halewynge hem.

13 And the hous of Israel terriden me to wraththe in desert; thei yeden not in my comaundementis, and thei castiden awei my domes, whiche a man that doith, schal lyue in tho; and thei defouliden greetli my sabatis. Therfor Y seide, that Y wolde schede out my strong veniaunce on hem in desert, and waste hem;

14 and Y dide for my name, lest it were defoulid bifor hethene men, fro whiche Y castide hem out in the siyt of tho.

15 Therfor Y reiside myn hond on hem in the desert, that Y brouyte not hem in to the lond which Y yaf to hem, the lond flowynge with mylk and hony, the beste of alle londis.

16 For thei castiden awei my domes, and yeden not in my comaundementis, and thei defouliden my sabatis; for the herte of hem yede after idols.

17 And myn iye sparide on hem, that Y killide not hem, nether Y wastide hem in the desert.

18 Forsothe Y seide to the sones of hem in wildirnesse, Nyle ye go in the comaundementis of youre fadris, nether kepe ye the domes of hem, nethir be ye defoulid in the idols of hem.

19 Y am youre Lord God, go ye in my comaundementis, and kepe ye my domes, and do ye tho.

20 And halowe ye my sabatis, that it be a signe bitwixe me and you, and that it be knowun, that Y am youre Lord God.

21 And the sones terriden me to wraththe, and yeden not in my comaundementis, and kepten not my domes, that thei diden tho, whiche whanne a man hath do, he schal lyue in tho, and thei defouliden my sabatis. And Y manaasside to hem, that Y wolde schede out my stronge veniaunce on hem, and fille my wraththe in hem in the desert.

22 But Y turnede awei myn hond, and Y dide this for my name, that it were not defoulid bifore hethene men, fro whiche Y castide hem out bifore the iyen of tho.

23 Eft Y reiside myn hond ayens hem in wildirnesse, that Y schulde scatere hem in to naciouns, and wyndewe hem in to londis;

24 for that that thei hadden not do my domes, and hadden repreuyd my comaundementis, and hadden defoulid my sabatis, and her iyen hadden be after the idols of her fadris.

25 Therfor and Y yaf to hem comaundementis not good, and domes in whiche thei schulen not lyue.

26 And Y defoulide hem in her yiftis, whanne thei offriden to me for her trespassis al thing that openeth the wombe; and thei schulen wite, that Y am the Lord.

27 Wherfor speke thou, sone of man, to the hous of Israel, and thou schalt seie to hem, The Lord God seith these thingis, Yit and in this youre fadris blasfemyden me, whanne thei dispisynge hadden forsake me,

28 and Y hadde brouyte hem in to the lond on which Y reiside myn hond, that Y schulde yiue to hem, thei siyen ech hiy litil hil, and ech tree ful of boowis, and thei offriden there her sacrifices, and thei yauen there her offryngis, in to terring to wraththe; and thei settiden there the odour of her swetnesse, and thei offriden her moiste sacrifices.

29 And Y seide to hem, What is the hiy thing, to whiche ye entren? And the name therof is clepid Hiy Thing til to this dai.

30 Therfor seie thou to the hous of Israel, The Lord God seith these thingis, Certis ye ben defoulid in the weie of youre fadris, and ye don fornycacioun aftir the offendingis of hem,

31 and in the offryng of youre yiftis, whanne ye leden ouer youre sones bi fier, ye ben defoulid in alle youre idols til to dai, and schal Y answere to you, the hous of Israel? Y lyue, seith the Lord God, for Y schal not answere to you;

32 nether the thouyte of youre soul schal be don, that seien, We schulen be as hethene men, and as naciouns of erthe, that we worschipe trees and stoonys.

33 Y lyue, seith the Lord God, for in strong hond, and in arm stretchid forth, and in strong veniaunce sched out, I schal regne on you.

34 And Y schal lede out you fro puplis, and Y schal gadere you fro londis, in whiche ye ben scaterid; in strong hond, and in arm stretchid forth, and in strong veniaunce sched out Y schal regne on you.

35 And Y schal bringe you in to desert of puplis, and Y schal be demed there with you face to face.

36 As Y stryuede in doom ayens youre fadris in the desert of the lond of Egipt, so Y schal deme you, seith the Lord;

37 and Y schal make you suget to my septre, and Y schal bringe in you in the boondis of pees.

38 And Y schal chese of you trespassouris, and wickid men; and Y schal leede hem out of the lond of her dwelling, and

thei schulen not entre in to the lond of Israel; and ye schulen wite, that Y am the Lord.

39 And ye, the hous of Israel, the Lord God seith these thingis, Go ye ech man aftir youre idols, and serue ye tho. That and if ye heren not me in this, and defoulen more myn hooli name in youre yiftis,

40 and in youre idols, in myn hooli hil, in the hiy hil of Israel, seith the Lord God, ye schulen be punyschid greuousliere. There al the hous of Israel schal serue me, sotheli alle men in the lond, in which thei schulen plese me; and there Y schal seke youre firste fruytis, and the bigynnyng of youre tithis in alle youre halewyngis.

41 Y schal resseiue you in to odour of swetnesse, whanne Y schal leede you out of puplis, and schal gadere you fro londis, in whiche ye weren scaterid; and Y schal be halewid in you bifor the iyen of naciouns.

42 And ye schulen wite, that Y am the Lord, whanne Y schal bringe you in to the lond of Israel, in to the lond for which Y reiside myn hond, that Y schulde yyue it to youre fadris.

43 And ye schulen haue mynde there on youre weies, and on alle youre grete trespassis, bi whiche ye ben defoulid in tho; and ye schulen displese you in youre siyt, in alle youre malices whiche ye diden.

44 And ye schulen wite, that Y am the Lord, whanne Y schal do wel to you for my name; not bi youre yuel weies, nether bi youre worste trespassis, ye hous of Israel, seith the Lord God.

45 And the word of the Lord was maad to me,

46 and he seide, Thou, sone of man, sette thi face ayens the weie of the south, and droppe thou to the south, and profesie thou to the forest of the myddai feeld.

47 And thou schalt seie to the myddai forest, Here thou the word of the Lord. The Lord God seith these thingis, Lo! Y schal kyndle a fier in thee, and Y schal brenne in thee ech green tre, and ech drie tre; the flawme of brennyng schal not be quenchid, and ech face schal be brent ther ynne, fro the south til to the north.

48 And ech man schal se, that Y the Lord haue kyndlid it, and it schal not be quenchid.

49 And Y seide, A! A! A! Lord God, thei seien of me, Whethir this man spekith not bi parablis?

CAP 21

1 And the word of the Lord was maad to me,

2 and he seide, Thou, sone of man, sette thi face to Jerusalem, and droppe thou to the seyntuaries, and profesie thou ayens the erthe of Israel.

3 And thou schalt seie to the lond of Israel, The Lord God seith these thingis, Lo! Y to thee, and Y schal caste my swerd out of his schethe, and Y schal sle in thee a iust man and a wickid man.

4 Forsothe for that that Y haue slayn in thee a iust man and a wickid man, therfor my swerd schal go out of his schethe to ech man, fro the south til to the north;

5 that ech man wite, that Y the Lord haue drawe out my swerd fro his schethe, that schal not be clepid ayen.

6 And thou, sone of man, weile in sorewe of leendis, and in bitternessis thou schalt weile bifore hem.

7 And whanne thei schulen seie to thee, Whi weilist thou? thou schalt seie, For hering, for it cometh; and ech herte shal faile, and alle hondis schulen be aclumsid, and ech spirit schal be sike, and watris schulen flete doun bi alle knees; lo! it cometh, and it shal be don, seith the Lord God.

8 And the word of the Lord was maad to me,

9 and he seide, Sone of man, profesie thou; and thou schalt seie, The Lord God seith these thingis, Speke thou, The swerd, the swerd is maad scharp, and is maad briyt;

10 it is maad scharp to sle sacrifices; it is maad briyt, that it schyne. Thou that mouest the ceptre of my sone, hast kit doun ech tree.

11 And Y yaf it to be forbischid, that it be holdun with hond; this swerd is maad scharp, and this is maad briyt, that it be in the hond of the sleere.

12 Sone of man, crie thou, and yelle, for this swerd is maad in my puple, this in alle the duykis of Israel; thei that fledden ben youun to swerd with my puple. Therfor smite thou on thin hipe, for it is preuyd;

13 and this whanne it hath distried the ceptre, and it schal not be, seith the Lord God.

14 Therfor, sone of man, profesie thou, and smyte thou hond to hond, and the swerd be doublid, and the swerd of sleeris be treblid; this is the swerd of greet sleyng, that schal make hem astonyed,

15 and to faile in herte, and multiplieth fallingis. In alle the yatis of hem Y yaf disturbling of a swerd, scharp and maad briyt to schyne, gird to sleynge.

16 Be thou maad scharp, go thou to the riyt side, ether to the left side, whidur euer the desir of thi face is.

17 Certis and Y schal smyte with hond to hond, and Y schal fille myn indignacioun; Y the Lord spak.

18 And the word of the Lord was maad to me,

19 and he seide, And thou, sone of man, sette to thee twei weies, that the swerd of the king of Babiloyne come; bothe schulen go out of o lond, and bi the hond he schal take coniecting; he schal coniecte in the heed of the weie of the citee,

20 settinge a weye, that the swerd come to Rabath of the sones of Amon, and to Juda in to Jerusalem moost strong.

21 For the king of Babiloyne stood in the meeting of twey weies, in the heed of twei weies, and souyte dyuynyng, and medlide arowis; he axide idols, and took councel at entrails.

22 Dyuynyng was maad to his riyt side on Jerusalem, that he sette engyns, that he opene mouth in sleyng, that he reise vois in yelling, that he sette engyns ayens the yatis, that he bere togidere erthe, that he bilde strengthinges.

23 And he shal be as counceling in veyn goddis answer bifor the iyen of hem, and seruynge the reste of sabatis; but he schal haue mynde on wickidnesse, to take.

24 Therfor the Lord God seith these thingis, For that that ye hadden mynde on youre wickidnesse, and schewiden youre trespassyngis, and youre synnes apperiden in alle youre thouytis, forsothe for that that ye hadden mynde, ye schulen be takun bi hond.

25 But thou, cursid wickid duyk of Israel, whos dai bifor determyned is comun in the tyme of wickidnesse,

26 the Lord God seith these thingis, Do awei the mitre, take awei the coroun; whether it is not this that reiside the meke man, and made low the hiy man?

27 Wickidnesse, wickidnesse, wickidnesse Y schal putte it; and this schal not be doon til he come, whos the doom is, and Y schal bitake to hym.

28 And thou, sone of man, profesie, and seie, The Lord God seith these thingis to the sones of Amon, and to the schenschipe of hem; and thou schalt seie, A! thou swerd, A! thou swerd, drawun out to sle, maad briyte, that thou sle and schyne,

29 whanne veyn thingis weren seien to thee, and leesingis weren dyuynyd, that thou schuldist be youun on the neckis of wickid men woundid, the dai of whiche bifore determyned schal come in the tyme of wickidnesse, turne thou ayen in to thi schethe,

30 in to the place in which thou were maad. Y schal deme thee in the lond of thi birthe,

31 and Y schal schede out myn indignacioun on thee; in the fier of my strong veniaunce Y schal blowe in thee, and Y schal yyue thee in to the hondis of vnwise men, and makinge deth.

32 Thou schalt be mete to fier, thi blood schal be in the middis of erthe; thou schalt be youun to foryetyng, for Y the Lord spak.

CAP 22

1 And the word of the Lord was maad to me,

2 and he seide, And thou, sone of man, whether thou demest not the citee of bloodis?

3 And thou schalt schewe to it alle hise abhomynaciouns, and thou schalt seie, The Lord God seith these thingis, This is a citee schedinge out blood in the myddis of it silf, that the tyme therof come; and which made idols ayens it silf, that it shulde be defoulid.

4 In thi blood which is shed out of thee, thou trespassidist, and thou art defoulid in thin idols whiche thou madist; and thou madist thi daies to neiye, and thou brouytist the time of thi yeeris. Therfor Y yaf thee schenschipe to hethene men, and scornyng to alle londis that ben niy thee,

5 and that ben fer fro thee; thou foul citee, noble, greet in perisching, thei schulen haue victorie of thee.

6 Lo! princes of Israel, alle in her arm, weren in thee, to schede out blood.

7 Thei punyschiden with wrongis fadir and modir in thee, thei calengiden falsli a comelyng in the myddis of thee, thei maden sori a fadirles child and a widewe at thee.

8 Ye dispisiden my seyntuaries, and ye defouliden my sabatis.

9 Men bacbiteris weren in thee, to schede out blood, and eten on hillis in thee; thei wrouyten greet trespas in the myddis of thee.

10 Thei vnhiliden the schamefulere thingis of the fadir in thee, thei maden low in thee the vnclenesse of a womman in vnclene blood.

11 And ech man wrouyte abhomynacioun ayens the wijf of his neiybore, and the fadir of the hosebonde defoulide his sones wijf vnleuefuli; a brother opprosside in thee his sister, the douytir of his fadir.

12 Thei token yiftis at thee, to schede out blood; thou tokist vsure and ouerabundaunce, and thou calengidist greedili thi neiyboris, and thou hast foryete me, seith the Lord God.

13 Lo! Y haue smyte togidere myn hondis on thin aueryce, which thou didist, and on the blood which is sched out in the myddis of thee.

14 Whether thin herte schal susteyne, ether thin hondis schulen haue power in the daies whiche Y schal make to thee? For Y the Lord spak, and Y schal do.

15 And Y schal scatere thee in to naciouns, and Y schal wyndewe thee in to londis; and Y schal make thin vnclennesse to faile fro thee,

16 and Y schal welde thee in the siyt of hethene men; and thou schalt wite, that Y am the Lord.

17 And the word of the Lord was maad to me, and he seide,

18 Thou, sone of man, the hous of Israel is turned to me in to dros, ether filthe of irun; alle these ben bras, and tyn, and irun, and leed, in the myddis of furneis, thei ben maad the dros of siluer.

19 Therfor the Lord God seith these thingis, For that alle ye ben turned in to dros, lo! Y schal gadere you togidere in the myddis of Jerusalem,

20 bi gadering togidere of siluer, and of latoun, and of irun, and of tyn, and of leed, in the myddis of furneis; and Y schal kindle ther ynne a fier, to welle togidere; so Y schal gadere you togidere in my strong veniaunce, and in my wraththe, and Y schal reste. And Y schal welle you togidere,

21 and Y schal gadere you togidere, and Y schal sette you a fier in the fier of my strong veniaunce, and ye schulen be wellid togidere in the myddis therof.

22 As siluer is wellid togidere in the myddis of a furneis, so ye schulen be in the myddis therof; and ye schulen wite, that Y am the Lord, whanne Y haue sched out myn indignacioun on you.

23 And the word of the Lord was maad to me,

24 and he seide, Sone of man, seie thou to it, Thou art a lond vncleene, and not bireyned in the dai of strong veniaunce.

25 Sweringe togidere, ether conspiringe of profetis is in the myddis therof; as a lioun roringe and takinge prei, thei deuouriden men, thei token richessis and prijs; thei multiplieden widewis therof in the myddis therof.

26 Preestis therof dispisiden my lawe, and defouliden my seyntuaries; thei hadden not difference bitwixe hooli thing and vnhooli, thei vndurstoden not bitwixe defoulid thing and cleene thing; and thei turneden awei her iyen fro my sabatis, and Y was defoulid in the myddis of hem.

27 The princes therof in the myddis therof weren as wolues rauyschinge prey, to schede out blood, and to leese men, and in suynge lucris gredili.

28 Forsothe the profetis therof pargetiden hem with out temperure, and seyen veyn thingis, and dyuyneden leesingis to hem, and seiden, The Lord God seith these thingis, whanne the Lord spak not.

29 The puples of the lond calengiden fals caleng, and rauyschiden bi violence; thei turmentiden a nedi man and pore, and oppressiden a comeling bi fals caleng, with out doom.

30 And Y souyte of hem a man, that schulde sette an hegge bitwixe, and stonde set ayens me for the lond, that Y schulde not distrie it, and Y foond not.

31 And Y schedde out on hem myn indignacioun, and Y wastide hem in the fier of my wraththe; Y yeldide the weie of hem on the heed of hem, seith the Lord God.

CAP 23

1 And the word of the Lord was maad to me,

2 and he seide, Thou, sone of man, twei wymmen weren the douytris of o modir, and diden fornycacioun in Egipt;

3 in her yonge wexynge age thei diden fornicacioun; there the brestis of hem weren maad low, and the tetis of the tyme of mariage of hem weren brokun.

4 Forsothe the names of hem ben, Oolla, the more sistir, and Ooliba the lesse sistir of hir. And Y hadde hem, and thei childiden sones and douytris; certis the names of hem ben Samarie Oolla, and Jerusalem Ooliba.

5 Therfor Oolla dide fornicacioun on me, and was wood on hir louyeris, on Assiriens neiyinge,

6 clothid with iacinct, princes, and magistratis, yonge men of coueytise, alle kniytis, and stieris of horsis.

7 And sche yaf hir fornicaciouns on hem, on alle the chosun sones of Assiriens; and in alle on whiche sche was wood, sche was defoulid in the vnclennessis of hem.

8 Ferthermore and sche lefte not hir fornicaciouns, whiche sche hadde in Egipt; for whi and thei slepten with hir in the yongthe of hir, and thei braken the tetis of the tyme of mariage of hir, and thei scheden out her fornicacioun on hir.

9 Therfor Y yaf hir in to the hondis of hir louyeris, in to the hondis of the sones of Assur, on whos letcherie sche was wood.

10 Thei diskyueriden the schenschipe of hir; thei token awei the sones and the douytris of hir, and killiden hir with swerd; and the wymmen weren maad famouse, that is, sclaundrid, and thei diden domes in hir.

11 And whanne hir sistir Ooliba hadde seyn this, sche was wood in letcherie more than that sistre, and yaf vnschamefastli hir fornicacioun on the fornicacioun of hir sistre,

12 to the sones of Assiriens, to duykis and magistratis comynge to hir, that weren clothid with dyuerse cloth, to knyytis that weren borun on horsis, and to yonge men with noble schap, to alle men.

13 And Y siy that o weie of both sistris was defoulid,

14 and sche encreeside hir fornycaciouns. And whanne sche hadde seyn men peyntid in the wal, the ymagis of Caldeis expressid with colouris,

15 and gird on the reynes with kniytis girdlis, and cappis peyntid in the heedis of hem, the foormes of alle duykis, the licnesse of the sones of Babiloyne, and of the lond of Caldeis, in which thei weren borun;

16 sche was wood on hem bi coueitise of hir iyen, and sche sente messangeris to hem in to Caldee.

17 And whanne the sones of Babiloyne weren comun to hir, to the bed of tetis, thei defouliden hir in her letcheries of virgyns; and sche was defoulid of hem, and the soule of hir was fillid of hem.

18 Also sche made nakid hir fornicaciouns, and diskyuered hir schenschipe; and my soule yede awei fro hir, as my soule hadde go awei fro hir sistir.

19 For sche multiplied hir fornicaciouns, and hadde mynde on the daies of hir yongthe, in whiche sche dide fornicacioun in the lond of Egipt.

20 And sche was wood in letcherie on the liggyng bi of hem, whos fleischis ben as the fleischis of assis, and as the membris of horsis ben the membris of hem.

21 And thou visitidist the grete trespas of thi yongthe, whanne thi brestis weren maad low in Egipt, and the tetis of the tyme of thi mariage weren brokun.

22 Therfor, thou Ooliba, the Lord God seith these thingis, Lo! Y schal reise alle thi louyeris ayens thee, of whiche thi soule was fillid, and Y schal gadere hem ayens thee in cumpas;

23 the sones of Babiloyne, and alle Caldeis, noble and miyti men, and princes, alle the sones of Assiriens, and yonge men of noble foorme, duykis, and magistratis, alle princes of princes, and named stieris of horsis.

24 And thei araied with chare and wheel schulen come on thee, the multitude of puplis schulen be armed with haburioun, and scheeld, and basynet, ayens thee on ech side; and Y schal yyue doom bifor hem, and thei schulen deme thee bi her domes.

25 And Y schal sette my feruour in thee, which thei schulen vse with thee in woodnesse; thei schulen kitte awei thi nose and thin eeris, and thei schulen sle with swerd tho thingis that weren left; thei schulen take thi sones and thi douytris, and thi laste thing schal be deuourid bi fier.

26 And thei schulen make thee nakid of thi clothis, and thei schulen take awei the vessels of thi glorie.

27 And Y schal make thi greet trespasse to reste fro thee, and thi fornicacioun fro the lond of Egipt; and thou schalt not reise thin iyen to hem, and thou schalt no more haue mynde on Egipt.

28 For the Lord God seith these thingis, Lo! Y schal yyue thee in to the hondis of hem whiche thou hatist, 'in to the hondis of hem of whiche thi soule was fillid,

29 and thei schulen do with thee in hatrede. And thei schulen take awei alle thi trauels, and thei schulen leeue thee nakid, and ful of schenschipe; and the schenschipe of thi fornicaciouns schal be schewid. Thi greet

30 trespas and thi fornycaciouns han do these thingis to thee; for thou didist fornicacioun aftir hethene men, among whiche thou were defoulid in the idols of hem.

31 Thou yedist in the weie of thi sister, and Y schal yyue the cuppe of hir in thin hond.

32 The Lord God seith these thingis, Thou schalt drinke the cuppe of thi sistir, the depthe, and the broodnesse; thou that art most able to take, schalt be in to scornyng, and in to mouwyng.

33 Thou schalt be fillid with drunkenesse and sorewe, with the cuppe of mourenyng and of heuynesse, with the cuppe of thi sister Samarie.

34 And thou schalt drynke it, and thou schalt drinke of til to the drastis, and thou schalt deuoure the relifs therof, and thou schalt to-reende thi brestis, for Y the Lord spak, seith the Lord God.

35 Therfor the Lord God seith these thingis, For thou hast foryete me, and hast cast forth me bihynde thi bodi, bere thou also thi greet trespas and thi fornicaciouns.

36 And the Lord God seide to me, and spak, Sone of man, whether thou demest Ooliba and Oolla, and tellist to hem the grete trespassis of hem?

37 For thei diden auowtrie, and blood was in the hondis of hem, and thei diden fornicacioun with her idols; ferthermore and thei offriden to tho the sones whiche thei gendriden to me, for to be deuourid.

38 But also thei diden this to me, thei defouleden my seyntuarie in that dai, and maden vnhooli my sabatis.

39 And whanne thei sacrifisiden her sones to her idols, and entriden in to my seyntuarie in that dai, that thei schulden defoule it, thei diden also these thingis in the myddis of myn hous.

40 Thei senten to men comyng fro fer, to whiche thei hadden sent messangeris. Therfor lo! thei camen, to whiche thou waischidist thee, and anoyntidist thin iyen with oynement of wymmen, and thou were ourned with wymmens atier.

41 Thou satist in a ful fair bed, and a boord was ourned bifor thee; thou settidist myn encense and myn oynement on it.

42 And a vois of multitude makynge ful out ioye was ther ynne; and in men that weren brouyt of the multitude of men, and camen fro desert, thei settiden bies in the hondis of hem, and faire corouns on the heedis of hem.

43 And Y seide to hir, that was defoulid in auoutries, Now also this schal do fornycacioun in hir fornicacioun.

44 And thei entriden to hir; as to a womman, an hoore, so thei entriden to Oolla and to Ooliba, cursid wymmen.

45 Therfor these men ben iust, these schulen deme thilke wymmen bi the doom of auoutressis, and bi the doom of hem

that scheden out blood; for thei ben auoutressis, and blood is in the hondis of hem, and thei diden fornicacioun with her idols.

46 For the Lord God seith these thingis, Bringe thou multitudis to hem, and yyue thou hem in to noise, and in to raueyn;

47 and be thei stoonyd with the stoonys of puplis, and be thei stikid togidere with the swerdis of hem. Thei schulen sle the sones and the douytris of hem, and thei schulen brenne with fier the housis of hem.

48 And Y schal do awei greet trespas fro the lond; and alle wymmen schulen lerne, that thei do not aftir the greet trespas of hem.

49 And thei schulen yyue youre grete trespas on you; and ye schulen bere the synnes of youre idols, and ye schulen wite, that Y am the Lord God.

CAP 24

1 And the word of the Lord was maad to me, in the nynthe yeer, and in the tenthe monethe, in the tenthe dai of the monethe,

2 and he seide, Thou, sone of man, write to thee the name of this dai, in which the king of Babiloyne is confermed ayens Jerusalem to dai.

3 And thou schalt seie bi a prouerbe a parable to the hous, terrere to wraththe, and thou schalt speke to hem, The Lord God seith these thingis, Sette thou a brasun pot, sette thou sotheli, and putte thou watir in to it. Take thou a beeste ful fat;

4 gadere thou togidere the gobetis therof in it, ech good part, and the hipe, and the schuldre, chosun thingis and ful of boonys.

5 Also dresse thou heepis of boonys vndur it; and the sething therof buylide out, and the boonys therof weren sodun in the myddis therof.

6 Therfor the Lord God seith these thingis, Wo to the citee of bloodis, to the pot whos rust is ther ynne, and the rust therof yede not out of it; caste thou out it bi partis, and bi hise partis; lot felle not on it.

7 For whi the blood therof is in the myddis therof; he schede it out on a ful cleer stoon, he schedde not it out on erthe,

8 that it mai be hilid with dust, that Y schulde bringe in myn indignacioun, and 'a venge bi veniaunce; Y yaf the blood therof on a ful cleer stoon, that it schulde not be hilid.

9 Therfor the Lord God seith these thingis, Wo to the citee of bloodis, whos brennyng Y schal make greet;

10 gadere thou togidire boonys, whiche Y schal kyndle with fier; fleischis schulen be wastid, and al the settyng togidere schal be sodun, and boonys schulen faile.

11 Also sette thou it voide on coolis, that the metal therof wexe hoot, and be meltid, and that the filthe therof be wellid togidere in the myddis therof, and the rust therof be wastid.

12 It was swat bi myche trauel, and the ouer greet rust therof yede not out therof, nether bi fier.

13 Thin vnclennesse is abhomynable, for Y wolde clense thee, and thou art not clensid fro thi filthis; but nether thou schalt be clensid bifore, til Y make myn indignacioun to reste in thee.

14 Y the Lord spak; it schal come, and Y schal make, Y schal not passe, nethir Y schal spare, nether Y schal be plesid; bi thi weies and bi thi fyndyngis Y schal deme thee, seith the Lord.

15 And the word of the Lord was maad to me,

16 and he seide, Thou, sone of man, lo! Y take awei fro thee the desirable thing of thin iyen in veniaunce, and thou schalt not weile, nether wepe, nether thi teeris schulen flete doun.

17 Weile thou beynge stille, thou schalt not make mourenyng of deed men; thi coroun be boundun aboute thin heed, and thi schoon schulen be in the feet, nether thou schalt hile the mouth with a cloth, nether thou schalt ete the metis of mourneris.

18 Therfor Y spak to the puple in the morewtid, and my wijf was deed in the euentid; and Y dide in the morewtid, as he hadde comaundid to me.

19 And the puple seide to me, Whi schewist thou not to vs what these thingis signefien, whiche thou doist?

20 And Y seide to hem, The word of the Lord was maad to me,

21 and he seide, Speke thou to the hous of Israel, The Lord God seith these thingis, Lo! Y schal defoule my seyntuarie, the pride of youre empire, and the desirable thing of youre iyen, and on which youre soule dredith; and youre sones and youre douytris, whiche ye leften, schulen falle bi swerd.

22 And ye schulen do, as Y dide; ye schulen not hile mouthis with cloth, and ye schulen not ete the mete of weileris.

23 Ye schulen haue corouns in youre heedis, and schoon in the feet; ye schulen not weile, nether ye schulen wepe, but ye schulen faile in wretchidnessis, for youre wickidnessis; and ech man schal weile to his brother.

24 And Ezechiel schal be to you in to a signe of thing to comynge; bi alle thingis whiche he dide, ye schulen do, whanne this thing schal come; and ye schulen wite, that Y am the Lord God.

25 And thou, sone of man, lo! in the dai in which Y schal take awei fro hem the strengthe of hem, and the ioie of dignyte, and the desire of her iyen, on whiche the soulis of hem resten, caste awei the sones and douytris of hem;

26 in that dai whanne a man fleynge schal come to thee, to telle to thee;

27 in that dai sotheli thou schalt opene thi mouth with hym that fledde; and thou schalt speke, and schalt no more be stille; and thou schalt be to hem in to a signe of thing to comynge, and ye schulen witen, that Y am the Lord.

CAP 25

1 And the word of the Lord was maad to me,

2 and he seide, Thou, sone of man, sette thi face ayens the sones of Amon, and thou schalt profesie of hem.

3 And thou schalt seie to the sones of Amon, Here ye the word of the Lord God; the Lord God seith these thingis, For that that ye seiden, Wel! wel! on my seyntuarie, for it is defoulid, and on the lond of Israel, for it is maad desolat, and on the hous of Juda, for thei ben led in to to caitifte; lo!

4 therfor Y schal yyue thee the sones of the eest in to eritage, and thei schulen sette her foldis in thee, and thei shulen sette her tentis in thee; thei schulen ete thi fruytis, and thei schulen drynke thi mylk.

5 And Y schal yyue Rabath in to a dwellyng place of camels, and the sones of Amon in to a bed of beestis; and ye schulen wite, that Y am the Lord.

6 For the Lord God seith these thingis, For that that thou flappidist with hond, and smytidist with the foot, and ioyedist of al desijr on the lond of Israel;

7 therfor lo! Y schal stretche forth myn hond on thee, and Y schal yyue thee in to rauyschyng of hethene men, and Y schal sle thee fro puplis, and Y schal leese thee, and al to-breke thee fro londis; and ye schulen wite, that Y am the Lord.

8 The Lord God seith these thingis, For that that Moab and Seir seiden, Lo! the hous of Juda is as alle folkis; therfor lo!

9 Y schal opene the schuldre of Moab of citees, sotheli of citees therof and of the endis therof, the noble citees of the lond, Bethiesmoth, and Beelmoth,

10 and Cariathaym, to the sones of the eest, with the sones of Amon. And Y schal yyue it in to eritage, that mynde of the sones of Amon be no more among hethene men,

11 and in Moab Y schal make domes; and thei schulen wite, that Y am the Lord.

12 The Lord God seith these thingis, For that that Ydumee dide veniaunce, that it avengide it silf of the sones of Juda, and synnede doynge trespas, and axide greetli veniaunce of hem;

13 therfor the Lord God seith these thingis, Y schal stretche forth myn hond on Idumee, and Y schal take awei fro it man and beeste, and Y schal make it desert of the south; and thei that ben in Dedan schulen falle bi swerd.

14 And Y schal yyue my veniaunce on Idumee, bi the hond of my puple Israel; and thei schulen do in Edom bi my wraththe, and bi my strong veniaunce; and thei schulen knowe my veniaunce, seith the Lord God.

15 The Lord God seith these thingis, For that that Palestyns diden veniaunce, and auengiden hem silf, with al wille sleynge, and fillynge elde enemytees;

16 therfor the Lord God seith these thingis, Lo! Y schal stretche forth myn hond on Palestyns, and Y schal sle sleeris, and Y schal leese the remenauntis of the se coost;

17 and Y schal make grete veniaunces in hem, and Y schal repreue in strong veniaunce; and thei schulen wite, that Y am the Lord, whanne Y schal yyue my veniaunce on hem.

CAP 26

1 And it was doon in the enleuenthe yeer, in the firste dai of the monethe, the word of the Lord was maad to me, and he seide,

2 Thou, sone of man, for that that Tire seide of Jerusalem, Wel! the yatis of puplis ben brokun, it is turned to me; Y schal be fillid, it is forsakun;

3 therfor the Lord God seith these thingis, Lo! Tire, Y on thee; and Y schal make many folkis to stie to thee, as the see flowynge stieth.

4 And thei schulen distrie the wallis of Tire, and thei schulen distrie the touris therof; and Y schal rase the dust therof fro it, and Y schal yyue it in to a 'moost clere stoon.

5 Driyng of nettis schal be in the myddis of the see, for Y spak, seith the Lord God. And Tire schal be in to rauysching to hethene men.

6 And the douytris therof that ben in the feeld, schulen be slayn bi swerd; and thei schulen wite, that Y am the Lord.

7 For whi the Lord God seith these thingis, Lo! Y schal brynge to Tire Nabugodonosor, the king of Babiloyne, fro the north, the kyng of kyngis, with horsis, and charis, and knyytis, and with a cumpeny, and greet puple.

8 He schal sle bi swerd thi douytris that ben in the feeld, and he schal cumpasse thee with strengthingis, and he schal bere togidere erthe in cumpas. And he schal reise a scheeld ayens thee,

9 and he schal tempre engynes lijc vineres, and engines 'that ben clepid wetheris ayens thi wallis; and he schal distrie thi touris bi his armure.

10 Bi flowynge of his horsis, the dust of tho schal hile thee; thi wallis schulen be mouyd of the soun of knyytis, and of wheelis, and of charis; whanne he schal entre bi the yatis, as bi entryngis of a citee distried,

11 with the clees of hise horsis he schal defoule alle thi stretis. He shal sle bi swerd thi puple, and thi noble ymagis schulen falle doun in to erthe.

12 Thei schulen waste thi richessis, thei schulen rauysche thi marchaundies; and thei schulen distrie thi wallis, and thei schulen distrie thin housis ful clere, and thi stoonys, and thi trees, and thei schulen putte thi dust in the myddis of watris.

13 And Y schal make to reste the multitude of thi syngeris, and the sown of thin harpis schal no more be herd;

14 and Y schal yyue thee in to a moost cleer stoon. Thou schalt be driyng of nettis, and thou schalt no more be bildid, for Y the Lord spak, seith the Lord God.

15 The Lord God seith these thingis of Tire, Whether ilis schulen not be moued of the sown of thi fal, and of weiling of thi slayn men, whanne thei ben slayn in the myddis of thee?

16 And alle the princis of the see schulen go doun of her seetis, and thei schulen do awei her mentils, ether spuylis of slayn enemyes, and thei schulen caste awei her dyuerse clothis, and schulen be clothid with wondring. Thei schulen sitte in the erthe, and thei schulen be astonyed, and thei schulen wondre of thi sodeyn fal.

17 And thei schulen take weilyng on thee, and schule seie to thee, Hou perischidist thou, noble citee, that dwellist in the see, that were strong in the see with thi dwelleris, whiche dwelleris alle men dredden?

18 Now schippis schulen wondre in the dai of thi drede, and ilis in the see schulen be disturblid, for noon goith out of thee.

19 For the Lord God seith these thingis, Whanne Y schal yyue thee a citee desolat, as the citees that ben not enhabitid, and Y schal bringe on thee the depthe of watris, and many watris schulen hile thee.

20 And Y schal drawe thee doun with hem that goon doun in to a lake, to the puple euerlastynge; and Y schal sette thee in the laste lond, as elde wildirnessis, with hem that ben led doun in to a lake, that thou be not enhabited. Certis whanne Y schal yyue glorye in the lond of lyueris,

21 Y schal dryue thee in to nouyt, and thou schalt not be; and thou schalt be souyt, and thou schalt no more be foundun with outen ende, seith the Lord God.

CAP 27

1 And the word of the Lord was maad to me,

2 and he seide, Therfor thou, sone of man, take weilyng on Tire.

3 And thou schalt seie to Tire, that dwellith in the entryng of the see, to the marchaundie of puplis to many ilis, The Lord God seith these thingis, O! Tire, thou seidist, Y am of perfit fairnesse,

4 and Y am set in the herte of the see. Thei that ben in thi coostis that bildiden thee, filliden thi fairnesse;

5 thei bildiden thee with fir trees of Sanyr, with alle werkis of boordis of the see; thei token a cedre of the Liban, to make a mast to thee.

6 Thei hewiden ookis of Bala in to thin ooris, thei maden to thee thi seetis of roweris of yuer of Ynde, and cabans of the ilis of Italie.

7 Dyuerse biys, 'ether whijt silk, of Egipt, was wouun to thee in to a veil, that it schulde be set in the mast; iacynct and purpur of the ilis of Elisa weren maad thin hiling.

8 The dwelleris of Sidon and Aradians weren thi roweris; Tire, thi wise men weren maad thi gouernouris.

9 The elde men of Biblos, and the prudent men therof, hadden schipmen to the seruyse of thi dyuerse araye of houshold; alle

the schippis of the see, and the schip men of tho, weren in the puple of thi marchaundie.

10 Perseis, and Lidians, and Libians weren in thin oost; thi men werriours hangiden in thee a scheeld and helm, for thin ournyng.

11 Sones Aradians with thin oost weren on thi wallis in thi cumpas; but also Pigmeis, that weren in thi touris, hangiden her arowe casis in thi wallis bi cumpas; thei filliden thi fairnesse.

12 Cartagynensis, thi marchauntis, of the multitude of alle richessis filliden thi feiris, with siluer, and irun, with tyn, and leed.

13 Greece, and Tubal, and Mosoch, thei weren thi marchauntis, and brouyten boonde men and brasun vessels to thi puple.

14 Fro the hous of Thogorma thei brouyten horsis, and horse men, and mulis, to thi chepyng.

15 The sones of Dedan weren thi marchauntis; many ilis the marchaundie of thin hond, chaungiden teeth of yuer, and of hebennus, in thi prijs.

16 Sirie was thi marchaunt, for the multitude of thi werkis thei settiden forth in thi marcat gemme, and purpur, and clothis wouun dyuersli at the maner of scheeldis, and bijs, and seelk, and cochod, ether auer de peis.

17 Juda and the lond of Israel weren thi marchauntis in the beste wheete, and settiden forth in thi feiris bawme, and hony, and oile, and resyn.

18 Damassen was thi marchaunt, in the multitude of thi werkis, in the multitude of dyuerse richessis, in fat wyn, in wollis of best colour.

19 Dan, and Greece, and Mosel, settiden forth in thi fairis irun maad suteli, gumme of myrre, and calamus, that is, a spice swete smellynge, in thi marchaundie.

20 Dedan weren thi marchauntis, in tapitis to sitte.

21 Arabie and alle the princes of Cedar, thei weren the marchauntis of thin hond; with lambren, and wetheris, and kidis thi marchauntis camen to thee.

22 The silleris of Saba and of Rema, thei weren thi marchauntis, with alle the beste swete smellynge spices, and preciouse stoon, and gold, which thei settiden forth in thi marcat.

23 Aran, and Chenne, and Eden, weren thi marchauntis; Sabba, and Assur, and Chelmath, weren thi silleris.

24 Thei weren thi marchaundis in many maneres, in fardels of iacinct and of clothis of many colours, and of preciouse richessis, that weren wlappid and boundun with coordis.

25 Also schippis of the see hadden cedris in her marchaundies; thi princes weren in thi marchaundie; and thou were fillid, and were glorified greetli in the herte of the see.

26 Thi rowers brouyten thee in many watris, the south wynd al to-brak thee; in the herte of the see weren thi richessis,

27 and thi tresours, and thi many fold instrument. Thi schip men, and thi gouernouris that helden thi purtenaunce of houshold, and weren souereyns of thi puple, and thi men werriours that weren in thee, with al thi multitude which is in the myddis of thee, schulen falle doun in the herte of the see, in the dai of thi fallyng.

28 Schippis schulen be disturblid of the sown of the cry of thi gouernours;

29 and alle men that helden oore, schulen go doun of her shippis. Shipmen and alle gouernouris of the see shulen stonde in the lond;

30 and schulen yelle on thee with greet vois. And thei shulen cry bitterli, and thei schulen caste poudur on her heedis, and schulen be spreynt with aische.

31 And thei schulen shaue ballidnesse on thee, and schulen be gird with hairis, and thei schulen biwepe thee in bitternesse of soule, with most bittir wepyng.

32 And thei schulen take on thee a song of mourenyng, and thei schulen biweile thee, Who is as Tire, that was doumb in the myddis of the see?

33 And thou, Tire, fillidist many puplis in the goyng out of thi marchaundies of the see; in the multitude of thi richessis, and of thi puplis, thou madist riche the kingis of erthe.

34 Now thou art al to-brokun of the see, in the depthis of watris. Thi richessis and al thi multitude that was in the myddis of thee fellen doun;

35 alle the dwelleris of ilis and the kyngis of tho weren astonyed on thee. Alle thei weren smytun with tempest, and chaungiden cheris;

36 the marchauntis of puplis hissiden on thee. Thou art brouyt to nouyt, and thou schalt not be til 'in to with outen ende.

CAP 28

1 And the word of the Lord was maad to me,

2 and he seide, Sone of man, seie thou to the prince of Tire, The Lord God seith these thingis, For thin herte was reisid, and thou seidist, Y am God, and Y sat in the chaier of God, in the herte of the see, sithen thou art man and not God, and thou yauest thin herte as the herte of God; lo!

3 thou art wisere than Danyel, ech priuetee is not hid fro thee;

4 in thi wisdom and prudence thou madist to thee strengthe, and thou gatist to thee gold and siluer in thi tresouris;

5 in the multitude of thi wisdom, and in thi marchaundie thou multipliedist to thee strengthe, and thin herte was reisid in thi strengthe;

6 therfor the Lord God seith these thingis, For thin herte was reisid as the herte of God, therfor lo!

7 Y schal brynge on thee aliens, the strongeste of hethene. And thei schulen make nakid her swerdis on the fairnesse of thi wisdom, and thei schulen defoule thi fairnesse.

8 Thei schulen sle, and drawe doun thee; and thou schalt die bi the deth of vncircumcidid men, in the herte of the see.

9 Whether thou schalt seie, and speke, Y am God, bifore hem that sleen thee; sithen thou art a man, and not God?

10 In the hond of hem that sleen thee, bi deth of vncircumcidid men, thou schalt die in the hond of aliens; for Y the Lord spak, seith the Lord God.

11 And the word of the Lord was maad to me, and he seide, Thou, sone of man, reise thou weilyng on the kyng of Tire;

12 and thou schalt seie to hym, The Lord God seith these thingis, Thou a preente of licnesse, ful of wisdom, perfit in fairnesse,

13 were in delicis of paradijs of God. Ech preciouse stoon was thin hilyng, sardius, topacius, and iaspis, crisolitus, and onix, and birille, safire, and carbuncle, and smaragde; also gold was the werk of thi fairnesse, and thin hoolis weren maad redi, in the dai in which thou were maad.

14 Thou were cherub holdun forth, and hilynge; and Y settide thee in the hooli hil of God. In the myddis of stoonus set a fier thou yedist,

15 perfit in thi weies fro the dai of thi makyng, til wickidnesse was foundun in thee.

16 In the multitude of thi marchaundie thin ynnere thingis weren fillid of wickidnesse, and thou didist synne; and Y castide thee out of the hil of God, and, thou cherub hilynge fer, Y loste thee fro the myddis of stoonys set a fier.

17 And thin herte was reisid in thi fairnesse, thou lostist thi wisdom in thi fairnesse. Y castide thee doun in to erthe, Y yaf thee bifore the face of kingis, that thei schulden se thee.
18 In the multitude of thi wickidnessis, and in wickidnesse of thi marchaundie thou defoulidist thin halewyng; therfor Y schal brynge forth fier of the myddis of thee, that schal ete thee; and Y schal yyue thee in to aische on erthe, in the siyt of alle men seynge thee.
19 Alle men that schulen se thee among hethene men, schulen be astonyed on thee; thou art maad nouyt, and thou schalt not be with outen ende.
20 And the word of the Lord was maad to me,
21 and he seide, Thou, sone of man, sette thi face ayens Sidon, and thou schalt profesie of it;
22 and schalt seie, The Lord God seith these thingis, Lo! Y to thee, Sidon, and Y schal be glorified in the myddis of thee; and thei schulen wite, that Y am the Lord, whanne Y schal do domes in it, and Y schal be halewid ther ynne.
23 And Y schal sende pestilence in to it, and blood in the stretis therof, and slayn men bi swerd schulen falle doun in the myddis therof bi cumpas; and thei schulen wite, that Y am the Lord God.
24 And there schal no more be an hirtyng of bitternesse to the hous of Israel, and a thorn bryngynge in sorewe on ech side bi the cumpas of hem that ben aduersaries to hem; and thei schulen wite, that Y am the Lord God.
25 The Lord God seith these thingis, Whanne Y schal gadere togidere the hous of Israel fro puplis, among whiche thei ben scaterid, Y schal be halewid in hem bifor hethene men. And thei schulen dwelle in her lond, which Y yaf to my seruaunt Jacob.
26 And thei schulen dwelle sikir ther ynne, and thei schulen bilde housis, and thei schulen plaunte vynes, and thei schulen dwelle tristili, whanne Y schal make domes in alle men that ben aduersaries to hem bi cumpas; and thei schulen wite, that Y am the Lord God of hem.

CAP 29

1 In the tenthe yeer, in the tweluethe monethe, in the firste dai of the monethe, the word of the Lord was maad to me, and he seide,
2 Thou, sone of man, sette thi face ayens Farao, king of Egipt; and thou schalt profesie of hym, and of al Egipt.
3 Speke thou, and thou schalt seie, The Lord God seith these thingis, Lo! Y to thee, thou Farao, kyng of Egipt, thou grete dragoun, that liggist in the myddis of thi floodis, and seist, The flood is myn, and Y made mysilf.
4 And Y schal sette a bridil in thi chekis, and Y schal glue the fischis of thi floodis to thi scalis; and Y schal drawe thee out of the myddis of thi floodis, and alle thi fischis schulen cleue to thi scalis.
5 And Y schal caste thee forth in to desert, and alle the fischis of thi flood; on the face of erthe thou schalt falle doun, thou schalt not be gaderid, nethir schalt be gaderid togidere; to the beestis of erthe, and to the volatilis of the eir Y yaf thee to be deuourid.
6 And alle the dwelleris of Egipt schulen knowe, that Y am the Lord. For that that thou were a staf of rehed to the hous of Israel, whanne thei token thee with hond,
7 and thou were brokun, and to-rentist ech schuldre of hem, and whanne thei restiden on thee, thou were maad lesse, and thou hast discoumfortid alle the reynes of hem;

8 therfor the Lord God seith these thingis, Lo! Y schal bringe a swerd on thee, and Y schal sle of thee man and beeste;
9 and the lond of Egipt schal be in to desert, and in to wildirnesse, and thei schulen wite, that Y am the Lord. For that that thou seidist, The flood is myn, and Y made it, therfor lo!
10 Y to thee, and to thi floodis. And Y schal yyue 'in to wildirnesses the lond of Egipt distried bi swerd, fro the tour of Sienes til to the termes of Ethiopie.
11 The foot of man schal not passe bi it, nether the foot of beeste schal go in it, and it schal not be enhabitid in fourti yeer.
12 And Y schal yyue the lond of Egipt forsakun, in the myddis of londis forsakun, and the citees therof in the myddis of a citee distried, and tho schulen be desolat bi fourti yeer. And Y schal scatere Egipcians in to naciouns, and Y schal wyndewe hem in to londis.
13 For the Lord God seith these thingis, After the ende of fourti yeer Y schal gadere togidere Egipt fro puplis, among whiche thei weren scaterid;
14 and Y schal bringe ayen the caitifte of Egipte. And Y schal sette hem in the lond of Phatures, in the lond of her birthe; and thei schulen be there in to a meke rewme,
15 and among othere rewmes it schal be most low, and it schal no more be reisid ouer naciouns. And Y schal make hem lesse, that thei regne not on hethene men;
16 and thei schulen no more be to the hous of Israel in trist, techinge wickidnesse, that thei fle, and sue hem; and thei schulen knowe, that Y am the Lord God.
17 And it was don in the seuene and twentithe yeer, in the firste monethe, in the firste dai of the monethe, the word of the Lord was maad to me,
18 and he seide, Thou, sone of man, Nabugodonosor, kyng of Babiloyne, made his oost to serue bi greet seruyce ayens Tire; ech heed was maad ballid, and ech schuldir was maad bare of heer, and meede was not yoldun of Tire to hym, nether to his oost, for the seruyce bi which he seruede to me ayens it.
19 Therfor the Lord God seith these thingis, Lo! Y schal yyue Nabugodonosor, kyng of Babiloyne, in the lond of Egipt, and he schal take the multitude therof; and he schal take in preye the clothis therof, and he schal rauysche the spuylis therof, and meede schal be to his oost,
20 and to the werk for which he seruyde to me ayens it; and Y yaf the lond of Egipt to hym, for that that he trauelide to me, seith the Lord God.
21 In that dai an horn of the hous of Israel schal come forth, and Y schal yyue to thee an open mouth in the myddis of hem; and thei schulen wite, that Y am the Lord.

CAP 30

1 And the word of the Lord was maad to me,
2 and he seide, Sone of man, profesie thou, and seie, The Lord God seith these thingis, Yelle ye, Wo!
3 wo! to the dai, for the dai is niy; and the dai of the Lord neiyith, the dai of a cloude. The tyme of hethene men schal be;
4 and a swerd schal come in to Egipt, and drede schal be in Ethiopie, whanne woundid men schulen falle doun in Egipt, and the multitude therof schal be takun awei, and the foundementis therof schulen be distried.
5 Ethiopie, and Libie, and Lidiens, and al the residue comyn puple, and Chub, and the sones of the lond of boond of pees schulen falle doun bi swerd with hem.

6 The Lord God seith these thingis, And thei that vndursetten Egipt schulen falle doun, and the pride of the lordschipe therof schal be destried; fro the tour of Sienes thei schulen falle bi swerd ther ynne, seith the Lord of oostis.

7 And thei schulen be distried in the myddis of londis maad desolat, and the citees therof schulen be in the myddis of citees forsakun.

8 And thei schulen wite, that Y am the Lord God, whanne Y schal yyue fier in Egipt, and alle the helperis therof schulen be al to-brokun.

9 In that dai messangeris schulen go out fro my face in schippis with thre ordris of ooris, to al to-breke the trist of Ethiopie; and drede schal be in hem in the dai of Egipt, for with out doute it schal come.

10 The Lord God seith these thingis, And I schal make to ceesse the multitude of Egipt in the hond of Nabugodonosor, king of Babiloyne.

11 He and his puple with hym, the strongeste men of hethene men, schulen be brouyt, to leese the lond; and thei schulen drawe out her swerdis on Egipt, and thei schulen fille the lond with slayn men.

12 And Y schal make drie the botmes of floodis, and Y schal yyue the lond in the hond of the worste men; and I schal distrie the lond, and the fulnesse therof in the hond of aliens; Y the Lord spak.

13 The Lord God seith these thingis, And Y schal leese simylacris, and Y schal make idols to ceesse fro Memphis, and a duyk of the lond of Egipt schal no more be. And Y schal yyue drede in the lond of Egipt,

14 and Y schal leese the lond of Phatures. And Y schal yyue fier in Tafnys, and Y schal make my domes in Alisaundre.

15 And Y schal schede out myn indignacioun on Pelusyum, the strengthe of Egipt; and Y schal sle the multitude of Alisaundre,

16 and Y schal yyue fier in Egipt. Pelusyum, as a womman trauelynge of child, schal haue sorewe, and Alisaundre schal be destried, and in Memphis schulen be ech daies angwischis.

17 The yonge men of Heliopoleos and of Bubasti schulen falle doun bi swerd, and tho citees schulen be led caitifs.

18 And in Thafnys the dai schal wexe blak, whanne Y schal al to-breke there the ceptris of Egipt, and the pride of the power therof schal faile there ynne. A cloude schal hile it; forsothe the douytris therof schulen be led in to caitifte, and Y schal make domes in Egipt;

19 and thei schulen wite, that Y am the Lord.

20 And it was doon in the enleuenthe yeer, in the firste monethe, in the seuenthe dai of the moneth, the word of the Lord was maad to me,

21 and he seide, Thou sone of man, Y haue broke the arm of Farao, kyng of Egipt; and lo! it is not wlappid, that helthe schulde be restorid therto, that it schulde be boundun with clothis, and woundun with lynnun clothis, and that he myyte holde swerd, whanne he hadde resseyued strengthe.

22 Therfor the Lord God seith these thingis, Lo! Y to Farao, king of Egipt; and Y schal make lesse his strong arm but brokun, and Y schal caste doun the swerd fro his hond.

23 And Y schal scatere Egipt among hethene men, and Y schal wyndewe hem in londis.

24 And Y schal coumforte the armes of the kyng of Babiloyne, and Y schal yyue my swerd in the hond of hym; and Y schal breke the armes of Farao, and men slayn bifore his face schulen weile bi weilyngis.

25 And Y schal coumforte the armes of the kyng of Babiloyne, and the armes of Farao schulen falle doun. And thei schulen wite, that Y am the Lord, whanne Y schal yyue my swerd in the hond of the kyng of Babiloyne; and he schal stretche forth it on the lond of Egipt.

26 And Y schal scatere Egipt in to naciouns, and Y schal wyndewe hem in to londis; and thei schulen wite, that Y am the Lord.

CAP 31

1 And it was don in the enleuenthe yeer, in the thridde moneth, in the firste dai of the monethe, the word of the Lord was maad to me,

2 and he seide, Thou, sone of man, seie to Farao, kyng of Egipt, and to his puple, To whom art thou maad lijk in thi greetnesse?

3 Lo! Assur as a cedre in Liban, fair in braunchis, and ful of boowis, and hiy bi hiynesse; and his heiyte was reisid among thicke bowis.

4 Watris nurschiden hym, the depthe of watris enhaunside him; hise floodis fletiden out in the cumpas of hise rootis, and he sente out hise strondis to alle the trees of the cuntrei.

5 Therfor his hiynesse was enhaunsid ouer alle trees of the cuntrei, and hise trees weren multiplied, and hise braunchis weren reisid, for many watris.

6 And whanne he hadde stretchid forth his schadewe, alle the volatils of the eir maden nestis in hise braunchis; and alle the beestis of forestis gendriden vndur hise boowis, and the cumpeny of ful many folkis dwellide vndur the schadewynge place of hym.

7 And he was ful fair in his greetnesse, and in alargyng of hise trees; for the roote of hym was bisidis many watris.

8 Cedris in the paradijs of God weren not hiyere than he; fir trees atteyneden not euenli to the hiynesse of hym, and plane trees weren not euene with the boowis of hym. Ech tree of paradijs of God was not maad lic hym and his fairnesse.

9 For Y made hym fair, and with many and thicke boowis; and alle the trees of lust, that weren in the paradijs of God, hadden enuye to hym.

10 Therfor the Lord God seith these thingis, For that that he was reisid in hiynesse, and he yaf his hyynesse greene and thicke, and his herte was reisid in his hiynesse;

11 now Y haue youe hym in to the hondis of the strongeste man of hethene men. And he doynge schal do to that Assur; aftir the vnfeithfulnesse of hym Y castide hym out.

12 And aliens, and the moost cruel men of naciouns, schulen kitte hym doun, and schulen caste hym forth on hillis. And hise braunchis schulen falle doun in alle grete valeis, and hise trees schulen be brokun in alle roochis of stoon of erthe. And alle the puplis of erthe schulen go awei fro his schadewing place, and schulen forsake hym.

13 Alle volatils of the eir dwelliden in the fallyng of hym, and alle beestis of the cuntrei weren in the braunchis of hym.

14 Wherfor alle the trees of watris schulen not be reisid in hir hiynesse, nether schulen sette hir hiynesse among places ful of woode, and ful of boowis, and alle trees that ben moistid of watris schulen not stonde in the hiynesse of tho. For alle thei ben youun in to deth, to the ferthest lond in the myddis of the sones of men, to hem that goon doun in to the lake.

15 The Lord God seith these thingis, In the dai whanne he yede doun to hellis, Y brouyte yn mourenyng; Y hilide hym with depthe of watris, and I forbede his flodis, and Y

refreynede many watris. The Liban was sori on him, and alle the trees of the feeld

16 weren shakun of the soun of his falling. I mouide togidere hethene men, whanne Y ledde hym doun to helle, with hem that yeden doun in to the lake. And alle trees of likyng, noble trees, and ful cleere in the Liban, alle that weren moistid with watris, weren coumfortid in the loweste lond.

17 For whi also thei schulen go doun with hym to helle, to slayn men with swerd; and the arm of ech man schal sitte vndur the schadewyng place of hym, in the myddis of naciouns.

18 To whom art thou licned, thou noble and hiy among the trees of likyng? Lo! thou art led doun with the trees of likyng to the fertheste lond. In the myddis of vncircumcidid men thou schalt slepe, with hem that ben slayn bi swerd. Thilke is Farao, and al the multitude of hym, seith the Lord God.

CAP 32

1 And it was don in the tweluethe yeer, in the tweluethe monethe, in the firste dai of the monethe, the word of the Lord was maad to me,

2 and he seide, Thou, sone of man, take weilyng on Farao, kyng of Egipt, and thou schalt seie to hym, Thou were maad lijk to a lioun of hethene men, and to a dragoun whiche is in the see. And thou wyndewist with horn in thi floodis, and thou disturblidist watris with thi feet, and defoulidist the floodis of tho.

3 Therfor the Lord God seith these thingis, Y schal spredde abrood my net on thee in the multitude of many puples, and Y schal drawe thee out in my net;

4 and Y schal caste forth thee in to erthe. On the face of the feeld Y schal caste thee awei, and Y schal make alle the volatils of heuene to dwelle on thee, and Y schal fille of thee the beestis of al erthe.

5 And Y schal yyue thi fleischis on hillis, and Y schal fille thi litle hillis with thi root;

6 and Y schal moiste the erthe with the stynk of thi blood on mounteyns, and valeis schulen be fillid of thee.

7 And whanne thou schalt be quenchid, Y schal hile heuenes, and Y schal make blak the sterris therof; Y schal kyuere the sunne with a clowde, and the moone schal not yyue hir liyt.

8 Y schal make alle the liyt yyueris of heuene to mourne on thee, and Y schal yyue derknessis on thi lond, seith the Lord God; whanne thi woundid men schulen falle doun in the myddis of erthe, seith the Lord God.

9 And Y schal terre to wraththe the herte of many puplis, whanne Y schal bringe in thi sorewe among folkis, on londis whiche thou knowist not.

10 And Y schal make many puplis to wondre on thee, and the kyngis of hem schulen drede with ful greet hidousnesse on thee, for alle thi wickidnessis whiche thou wrouytist, whanne my swerd schal bigynne to flee on the faces of hem. And alle men schulen be astonyed sudenli, for her lijf, in the dai of her fallyng.

11 For the Lord God seith these thingis, The swerd of the king of Babiloyne schal come to thee;

12 in swerdis of stronge men Y schal caste doun thi multitude, alle these folkis ben not able to be ouercomun. And thei schulen waste the pride of Egipt, and the multitude therof schal be distried.

13 And Y schal leese alle the beestis therof, that weren on ful many watris; and the foot of a man schal no more troble tho watris, nether the clee of beestis schal troble tho.

14 Thanne Y schal yelde the watris of hem clenneste, and Y schal brynge the floodis of hem as oile, seith the Lord God,

15 whanne Y schal yyue desolat the lond of Egipt. Forsothe the lond schal be forsakun of his fulnesse, whanne Y schal smyte alle the dwellers therof; and thei schulen wite, that Y am the Lord.

16 It is a weiling, and the douytris of hethene men schulen biweile hym; thei schulen biweile hym on Egipt, and thei schulen biweile hym on the multitude therof, seith the Lord God.

17 And it was don in the tweluethe yeer, in the fiftenthe dai of the monethe, the word of the Lord was maad to me,

18 and he seide, Sone of man, synge thou a song of weilyng on the multitude of Egipt, and drawe thou doun it the same, and the douytris of stronge hethene men to the laste lond, with hem that yeden doun in to the lake.

19 In as myche as thou art fairere, go doun, and slepe with vncircumcidid men.

20 In the myddis of slayn men thei schulen falle doun bi swerd; a swerd is youun, and thei drowen it to, and alle the puplis therof.

21 The myytieste of stronge men schulen speke to hym, fro the myddis of helle, whiche with her helperis yeden doun, and slepten vncircumcidid, and slayn bi swerd.

22 There is Assur, and al his multitude; the sepulcris of hem ben in the cumpas of hym, alle slayn men, and that fellen doun bi swerd,

23 whose sepulcris ben youun in the laste thingis of the lake. And the multitude of hym is maad bi the cumpas of his sepulcre, alle slayn men, and fallynge doun bi swerd, whiche yauen sum tyme her ferdfulnesse in the lond of lyuynge men.

24 There is Helam, and al the multitude therof bi the cumpas of his sepulcre; alle these weren slayn, and fallynge doun bi swerd, that yeden doun vncircumcidid to the laste lond; whiche settiden her drede in the lond of lyuynge men, and baren her schenschipe with hem that goon doun in to the lake.

25 In the myddis of slayn men thei puttiden his bed in alle the puplis of hym; his sepulcre is in the cumpas of hym. Alle these weren vncircumcidid and slayn bi swerd, for thei yauen drede in the lond of lyuynge men, and baren her schenschipe with hem that gon doun in to the lake; thei ben set in the myddis of slayn men.

26 There ben Mosoch and Tubal, and al the multitude therof; the sepulcris therof ben in the cumpasse therof. Alle these men vncircumcidid weren slayn, and fallynge doun bi swerd, for thei yauen her drede in the lond of lyuynge men.

27 And thei schulen not slepe with stronge men, and fallynge doun, and vncircumcidid, that yeden doun in to helle with her armuris, and puttiden her swerdis vndur her heedis. And the wickidnessis of hem weren in the boonys of hem, for thei weren maad the drede of stronge men in the lond of lyuynge men.

28 And thou therfor schalt be al to-foulid in the myddis of vncircumcidid men, and schalt slepe with hem that ben slayn bi swerd.

29 There is Idumee, and the kingis therof, and alle duykis therof, that ben youun with her oost, with men slayn bi swerd, and which slepten with vncircumcidid men, and with hem that yeden doun in to the lake.

30 There ben alle princes of the north, and alle hunteris, that weren led forth with slayn men, that ben dredinge and schent in her strengthe, which slepten vncircumcidid with men slayn

bi swerd, and baren her schenschipe with hem that yeden doun in to the lake.

31 Farao siy hem, and was coumfortid on al his multitude that was slayn bi swerd. And Farao and al his oost, seith the Lord God, baren her schenschipe with hem that yeden doun in to the lake;

32 for he yaf his drede in the lond of lyuynge men. And Farao and al his multitude slepte in the myddis of vncircumcidid men, with men slayn bi swerd, seith the Lord God.

CAP 33

1 And the word of the Lord was maad to me,

2 and he seide, Thou, sone of man, speke to the sones of thi puple, and thou schalt seie to hem, A lond whanne Y bringe in a swerd on it, and the puple of the lond takith o man of hise laste men, and makith hym aspiere on hym,

3 and he seeth a swerd comynge on the lond, and sowneth with a clarioun, and tellith to the puple,

4 forsothe a man that herith, who euer he is, the sowne of the clarioun, and kepith not him silf, and the swerd cometh, and takith hym awei, the blood of hym schal be on the heed of hym.

5 He herde the sown of the clarioun, and kepte not hym silf, his blood schal be in hym; forsothe if he kepith hym silf, he schal saue his lijf.

6 That if the aspiere seeth a swerd comynge, and sowneth not with a clarioun, and the puple kepith not hym silf, and the swerd cometh, and takith awei a man of hem, sotheli he is takun in his wickidnesse; but Y schal seke the blood of hym of the hond of the aspiere.

7 And, thou, sone of man, Y yaf thee aspiere to the hous of Israel; therfor thou schalt here of my mouth a word, and schalt telle to hem of me.

8 If whanne Y seie to the wickid man, Thou, wickid man, schalt die bi deth, thou spekist not, that the wickid man kepe hym silf fro his weie, thilke wickid man schal die in his wickidnesse, but Y schal seke his blood of thin hond.

9 Forsothe if whanne thou tellist to the wickid man, that he be conuertid fro his weies, he is not conuertid fro his weie, he schal die in his wickidnesse; certis thou hast delyuered thi soule.

10 Therfore thou, sone of man, seie to the hous of Israel, Thus ye spaken, seiynge, Oure wickidnessis and oure synnes ben on vs, and we failen in tho; hou therfor moun we lyue? seie thou to hem,

11 Y lyue, seith the Lord God, Y nyle the deth of the wickid man, but that the wickid man be conuertid fro his weie, and lyue; be ye conuertid fro youre worste weies, and whi schulen ye die, the hous of Israel?

12 Therfor thou, sone of man, seie to the sones of thi puple, The riytfulnesse of a riytful man schal not delyuere hym, in whateuer dai he doith synne; and the wickidnesse of a wickid man schal not anoye him, in what euere dai he is conuertid fro his wickidnesse; and a iust man schal not mowe lyue in his riytfulnesse, in what euer dai he doith synne.

13 Also if Y seie to a iust man, that he schal lyue bi lijf, and he tristith in his riytfulnesse, and doith wickidnesse, alle his riytfulnessis schulen be youun to foryetyng, and in his wickidnesse which he wrouyte, in that he schal die.

14 Forsothe if Y seie to the wickid man, Thou schalt die bi deth, and he doith penaunce for his synne, and doith dom and riytfulnesse,

15 and if thilke wickid man restorith a wed, and yeldith raueyn, and goith in comaundementis of lijf, and doith not ony vniust thing, he schal lyue bi lijf, and schal not die.

16 Alle hise synnes which he synnede, schulen not be arettid to hym; he dide doom and riytfulnesse, he schal lyue bi lijf.

17 And the sones of thi puple seiden, The weie of the Lord is not euene weiyte; and the weie of hem is vniust.

18 For whanne a iust man goith awei fro his riytfulnesse, and doith wickidnessis, he schal die in tho;

19 and whanne a wickid man goith awei fro his wickidnesse, and doith dom and riytfulnes, he schal lyue in tho.

20 And ye seien, The weie of the Lord is not riytful. Y schal deme ech man bi hise weies of you, the hous of Israel.

21 And it was doon in the tweluethe yeer, in the tenthe monethe, in the fyuethe dai of the monethe of our passyng ouer, he that fledde fro Jerusalem cam to me, and seide, The citee is distried.

22 Forsothe the hond of the Lord was maad to me in the euentid, bifore that he cam that fledde, and he openyde my mouth, til he cam to me eerli; and whanne my mouth was openyd, Y was no more stille.

23 And the word of the Lord was maad to me, and he seide,

24 Thou, sone of man, thei that dwellen in 'thingis in poynt to falle doun on the erthe of Israel, seien, spekynge, Abraham was oon, and bi eritage he hadde the lond in possessioun; forsothe we ben manye, the lond is youun to vs in to possessioun.

25 Therfor thou schalt seie to hem, The Lord God seith these thingis, Whether ye that eten in blood, and reisen youre iyen to youre vnclennessis, and scheden blood, schulen haue in possessioun the lond bi eritage?

26 Ye stoden in youre swerdis, ye diden youre abhomynaciouns, and ech man defoulide the wijf of his neiybore; and schulen ye welde the lond bi eritage?

27 Thou schalt seie these thingis to hem, Thus seith the Lord God, Y lyue, for thei that dwellen in 'thingis redi to falle doun, schulen falle doun bi swerd, and he that is in the feld, schal be youun to beestis to be deuourid; but thei that ben in stronge holdis and in dennes, schulen die bi pestilence.

28 And Y schal yyue the lond in to wildirnesse, and in to desert, and the pryde and strengthe therof schal faile; and the hillis of Israel schulen be maad desolat, for noon is that schal passe bi tho.

29 And thei schulen wite, that Y am the Lord, whanne Y schal yyue her lond desolat and desert, for alle her abhomynaciouns whiche thei wrouyten.

30 And thou, sone of man, the sones of thi puple that speken of thee bisidis wallis, and in the doris of housis, and seien, oon to an other, a man to his neiybore, and speken, Come ye, and here we, what is the word goynge out fro the Lord;

31 and thei comen to thee, as if my puple entrith, and my puple sitten bifore thee, and thei heren thi wordis, and doon not tho; for thei turnen tho in to the song of her mouth, and her herte sueth her auerice;

32 and it is to hem as a song of musik, which is songun bi soft and swete sown; and thei heren thi wordis, and thei doon not tho;

33 and whanne that that is bifore seide cometh, for lo! it cometh, thanne thei schulen wite, that 'profetis weren among hem.

CAP 34

1 And the word of the Lord was maad to me,

2 and he seide, Sone of man, profesie thou of the schepherdis of Israel, profesie thou; and thou schalt seie to the schepherdis, The Lord God seith these thingis, Wo to the schepherdis of Israel, that fedden hym silf; whether flockis ben not fed of schepherdis?

3 Ye eeten mylk, and weren hilid with wollis, and ye killiden that that was fat; but ye fedden not my floc.

4 Ye maden not sad that that was vnstidfast, and ye maden not hool that that was sijk; ye bounden not that that was brokun, and ye brouyten not ayen that that was cast awei, and ye souyten not that that perischide; but ye comaundiden to hem with sturnenesse, and with power.

5 And my scheep weren scaterid, for no sheepherde was; and thei weren maad in to deuouryng of alle beestis of the feeld, and thei weren scaterid.

6 My flockis erriden in alle mounteyns, and in ech hiy hil, and my flockis weren scaterid on al the face of erthe, and noon was that souyte.

7 Therfor, scheepherdis, here ye the word of the Lord;

8 Y lyue, seith the Lord God, for whi for that that my flockis ben maad in to raueyn, and my scheep in to deuouryng of alle beestis of the feeld, for that that no scheepherde was, for the scheepherdis souyten not my floc, but the scheepherdis fedden hem silf, and fedden not my flockis; therfor,

9 scheepherdis, here ye the word of the Lord,

10 The Lord God seith these thingis, Lo! Y my silf am ouer scheepherdis; Y schal seke my floc of the hond of hem, and Y schal make hem to ceesse, that thei fede no more my flok, and that the scheepherdis feede no more hem silf. And Y schal delyuere my floc fro the mouth of hem, and it schal no more be in to mete to hem.

11 For the Lord God seith these thingis, Lo! Y my silf schal seke my scheep, and Y schal visite hem.

12 As a scheepherde visitith his floc, in the dai whanne he is in the myddis of hise scheep 'that ben scaterid, so Y schal visite my scheep; and Y schal delyuere hem fro alle places in whiche thei weren scaterid, in the dai of cloude, and of derknesse.

13 And Y schal leede hem out of puplis, and Y schal gadere hem fro londis, and Y schal brynge hem in to her lond, and Y schal feede hem in the hillis of Israel, in ryueris, and in alle seetis of erthe.

14 Y schal feede hem in moost plenteouse pasturis, and the lesewis of hem schulen be in the hiy hillis of Israel; there thei schulen reste in greene eerbis, and in fatte lesewis thei schulen be fed on the hillis of Israel.

15 Y schal fede my scheep, and Y schal make hem to ligge, seith the Lord God.

16 I schal seke that that perischide, and Y schal brynge ayen that that was cast awei; and Y schal bynde that that was brokun, and Y schal make sad that that was sijk; and Y schal kepe that that was fat and strong; and Y schal feede hem in doom;

17 forsothe ye ben my flockis. The Lord God seith these thingis, Lo! Y deme bitwixe beeste and beeste, and a wethir and a buc of geet.

18 Whether it was not enowy to you to deuoure good pasturis? Ferthermore and ye defouliden with youre feet the remenauntis of youre lesewis, and whanne ye drunken clereste watir, ye disturbliden the residue with youre feet.

19 And my scheep weren fed with tho thingis that weren defoulid with youre feet; and thei drunken these thingis, that youre feet hadden troblid.

20 Therfor the Lord God seith these thingis to you, Lo! Y my silf deme bitwixe a fat beeste and a leene beeste.

21 For that that ye hurliden with sidis, and schuldris, and wyndewiden with youre hornes alle sike beestis, til tho weren scaterid withoutforth, I schal saue my floc,

22 and it schal no more be in to raueyn. And Y schal deme bitwixe beeste and beeste;

23 and Y schal reise on tho o sheepherde, my seruaunt Dauid, that schal fede tho; he schal fede tho, and he schal be 'in to a sheepherde to hem.

24 Forsothe Y the Lord schal be in to God to hem, and my seruaunt Dauid schal be prince in the myddis of hem; Y the Lord spak.

25 And Y schal make with hem a couenaunt of pees, and Y schal make worste beestis to ceesse fro erthe; and thei that dwellen in desert, schulen slepe sikur in forestis.

26 And Y schal sette hem blessyng in the cumpas of my litle hil, and Y schal lede doun reyn in his tyme. And reynes of blessyng schulen be,

27 and the tre of the feeld schal yyue his fruyt, and the erthe schal yyue his seed. And thei schulen be in her lond with out drede; and thei schulen wite, that Y am the Lord, whanne Y schal al to-breke the chaynes of her yok, and schal delyuere hem fro the hond of hem that comaunden to hem.

28 And thei schulen no more be in to raueyn in to hethene men, nether the beestis of erthe schulen deuoure hem, but thei schulen dwelle tristili with outen ony drede.

29 And Y schal reise to hem a iust buriownyng named; and thei schulen no more be maad lesse for hunger in erthe, and thei schulen no more bere the schenschipis of hethene men.

30 And thei schulen wite, that Y am her Lord God with hem, and thei ben my puple, the hous of Israel, seith the Lord God.

31 Forsothe ye my flockis ben men, the flockis of my lesewe; and Y am youre Lord God, seith the Lord God.

CAP 35

1 And the word of the Lord was maad to me,

2 and he seide, Thou, sone of man, sette thi face ayens the hil of Seir; and thou schalt profesie to it, and thou schalt seie to it,

3 The Lord God seith these thingis, Thou hil of Seir, lo! Y to thee; Y schal stretche forth myn hond on thee, and Y schal yyue thee desolat and forsakun.

4 Y schal distrie thi citees, and thou schalt be forsakun; and thou schalt wite, that Y am the Lord.

5 For thou were an enemye euerlastynge, and closidist togidere the sonis of Israel in to the hondis of swerd, in the tyme of her turment, in the tyme of the laste wickidnesse;

6 therfor Y lyue, seith the Lord God, for Y schal yyue thee to blood, and blood schal pursue thee; and sithen thou hatidist blood, blood schal pursue thee.

7 And Y schal yyue the hil of Seir desolat and forsakun, and Y schal take awei fro it a goere and a comere ayen;

8 and Y schal fille the hillis therof with the careyns of her slayn men. Men slayn by swerd schulen falle doun in thi litle hillis, and in thi valeys, and in thi strondis.

9 Y schal yyue thee in to euerlastynge wildirnessis, and thi citees schulen not be enhabitid; and ye schulen wite, that Y am the Lord God.

10 For thou seidist, Twei folkis and twei londis schulen be myne, and Y schal welde tho bi eritage, whanne the Lord was there;

11 therfor Y lyue, seith the Lord God, for Y schal do bi thi wraththe, and bi thin enuye, which thou didist, hatinge hem, and Y schal be made knowun bi hem, whanne Y schal deme thee;

12 and thou schalt wite, that Y am the Lord. Y herde alle thi schenschipis, whiche thou spakist of the hillis of Israel, and seidist, The hillis of Israel ben forsakun, and ben youun to vs, for to deuoure.

13 And ye han rise on me with youre mouth, and ye han deprauyd ayens me; Y herde youre wordis.

14 The Lord God seith these thingis, While al the lond is glad, Y schal turne thee in to wildernesse.

15 As thou haddist ioie on the eritage of the hous of Israel, for it was distried, so Y schal do to thee; the hil of Seir schal be distried, and al Ydumee; and thei schulen wite, that Y am the Lord.

CAP 36

1 Forsothe thou, sone of man, profesie on the hillis of Israel; and thou schalt seie, Hillis of Israel, here ye the word of the Lord.

2 The Lord God seith these thingis, For that that the enemy seide of you, Wel! euerlastyng hiynessis ben youun to vs in to eritage;

3 therefore profesie thou, and seie, The Lord God seith these thingis, For that that ye ben maad desolat, and defoulid bi cumpas, and ben maad in to eritage to othere folkis, and ye stieden on the lippe of tunge, and on the schenschipe of puple;

4 therfor, hillis of Israel, here ye the word of the Lord God. The Lord God seith these thingis to the mounteyns, and litle hillis, to strondis, and to valeis, and to peecis of wallis left, and to citees forsakun, that ben maad bare of puplis, and ben scorned of othere folkis bi cumpas;

5 therfore the Lord God seith these thingis, For in the fier of my feruour Y spak of othere folkis, and of al Idumee, that yauen my lond in to eritage to hem silf with ioie 'and al herte, and of entent, and castiden out it, to distrie it; therfor profesie thou on the erthe of Israel,

6 and thou schalt seie to mounteyns, and litle hillis, to the hiynesse of hillis, and to valeis, The Lord God seith these thingis, For that that ye ben desolat, lo! Y spak in my feruour and in my strong veniaunce. For that that ye suffriden schenschipe of hethene men;

7 therfor the Lord God seith these thingis, Lo! Y reiside myn hond ayens hethene men, that ben in youre cumpas, that thei bere her schenschipe.

8 Forsothe, ye hillis of Israel, brynge forth youre braunchis, and bringe ye fruit to my puple Israel; for it is niy that it come.

9 For lo! Y to you, and Y schal turne to you, and ye schulen be erid, and schulen take seed.

10 And in you I schal multiplie men, and al the hous of Israel; and citees schulen be enhabitid, and ruynouse thingis schulen be reparelid.

11 And Y schal fille you with men and beestis, and thei schulen be multiplied, and schulen encreesse; and Y schal make you to dwelle as at the bigynnyng, and Y schal rewarde with more goodis than ye hadden at the bigynnyng; and ye schulen wite, that Y am the Lord.

12 And Y schal brynge men on you, my puple Israel, and bi eritage thei schulen welde thee, and thou schalt be to hem in

to eritage; and thou schalt no more leie to, that thou be with out hem.

13 The Lord God seith these thingis, For that that thei seien of you, Thou art a deuouresse of men, and stranglist thi folk;

14 therfor thou schalt no more ete men, and thou schalt no more sle thi folk, seith the Lord God.

15 And Y schal no more make herd in thee the schenschipe of hethene men, and thou schalt no more bere the schenschipe of puplis, and thou schalt no more leese thi folk, seith the Lord God.

16 And the word of the Lord was maad to me, and he seide, Thou,

17 sone of man, the hous of Israel dwelliden in her lond, and thei defouliden it in her weies, and in her studies; bi the vnclennesse of a womman in rotun blood the weie of hem is maad bifor me.

18 And Y schedde out myn indignacioun on hem, for blood which thei schedden on the lond, and in her idols thei defouliden it.

19 And Y scateride hem among hethene men, and thei weren wyndewid to londis; Y demede hem bi the weies and fyndyngis of hem.

20 And thei entriden to hethene men, to whiche thei entriden, and defouliden myn hooli name, whanne it was seid of hem, This is the puple of the Lord, and thei yeden out of the lond of hym.

21 And Y sparide myn hooli name, which the hous of Israel hadde defoulid among hethene men, to whiche thei entriden.

22 Therfor thou schalt seie to the hous of Israel, The Lord God seith these thingis, O! ye hous of Israel, not for you Y schal do, but for myn hooli name, which ye defouliden among hethene men, to whiche ye entriden.

23 And Y schal halewe my greet name, which is defoulid among hethene men, whiche ye defouliden in the myddis of hem; that hethene men wite, that Y am the Lord, seith the Lord of oostis, whanne Y schal be halewid in you before hem.

24 For Y schal take awei you fro hethene men, and Y schal gadere you fro alle londis, and Y schal brynge you in to youre lond.

25 And Y schal schede out clene watir on you, and ye schulen be clensid fro alle youre filthis; and Y schal clense you fro alle youre idols.

26 And Y schal yyue to you a newe herte, and Y schal sette a newe spirit in the myddis of you; and Y schal do awei an herte of stoon fro youre fleisch, and Y schal yyue to you an herte of fleisch,

27 and Y schal sette my spirit in the myddis of you. And Y schal make that ye go in my comaundementis, and kepe and worche my domes.

28 And ye schulen dwelle in the lond, whiche Y yaf to youre fadris; and ye schulen be in to a puple to me, and Y schal be in to a God to you.

29 And Y schal saue you fro alle youre filthis; and Y schal clepe wheete, and Y schal multiplie it, and Y schal not put hungur on you.

30 And Y schal multiplie the fruyt of tree, and the seedis of the feeld, that ye bere no more the schenschipe of hungur among hethene men.

31 And ye schulen haue mynde on youre worste weies, and on studies not goode; and youre wickidnessis, and youre grete trespassis schulen displese you.

32 Not for you Y schal do, seith the Lord God, be it knowun to you; O! the hous of Israel, be ye schent, and be ye aschamed on youre weies.

33 The Lord God seith these thingis, In the dai in which Y schal clense you fro alle youre wickidnessis, and Y schal make citees to be enhabitid, and Y schal reparele ruynouse thingis,

34 and the desert lond schal be tilid, that was sum tyme desolat, bifor the iyen of ech weiegoere,

35 thei schulen seie, Thilke lond vntilid is maad as a gardyn of likyng, and citees forsakun and destitute and vndur myned saten maad strong; and hethene men,

36 whiche euer ben left in youre cumpas, schulen wite, that Y the Lord haue bildid distried thingis, and Y haue plauntid vntilid thingis; Y the Lord spak, and Y dide.

37 The Lord God seith these thingis, Yit in this thing the hous of Israel schulen fynde me, that Y do to hem; Y schal multiplie hem as the floc of men, as an hooli floc,

38 as the floc of Jerusalem in the solempnytees therof, so the citees that ben forsakun, schulen be fulle of the flockis of men; and thei schulen wite, that Y am the Lord.

CAP 37

1 The hond of the Lord was maad on me, and ledde me out in the spirit of the Lord; and he lefte me in the myddis of a feeld that was ful of boonys;

2 and he ledde me aboute bi tho in cumpas. Forsothe tho weren ful manye on the face of the feeld, and drie greetli.

3 And he seide to me, Gessist thou, sone of man, whether these boonys schulen lyue? And Y seide, Lord God, thou wost.

4 And he seide to me, Profesie thou of these boonys; and thou schalt seie to tho, Ye drie boonys, here the word of the Lord.

5 The Lord God seith these thingis to these boonys, Lo! Y schal sende in to you a spirit, and ye schulen lyue.

6 And Y schal yyue synewis on you, and Y schal make fleischis to wexe on you, and Y schal stretche forth aboue a skyn in you, and Y schal yyue a spirit to you, and ye schulen lyue; and ye schulen wite, that Y am the Lord.

7 And Y profesiede, as he comaundide to me; forsothe a sown was maad, while Y profesiede, and lo! a stiryng togidere, and boonys camen to boonys, ech to his ioynture.

8 And Y siy and lo! synewis and fleischis 'wexeden vpon tho, and skyn was stretchid forth aboue in hem, and tho hadden no spirit.

9 And he seide to me, Profesie thou to the spirit, profesie thou, sone of man; and thou schalt seie to the spirit, The Lord God seith these thingis, Come, thou spirit, fro foure wyndis, and blowe thou on these slayn men, and lyue thei ayen.

10 And Y profesiede, as he comaundide to me; and the spirit entride in to tho boonys, and thei lyueden, and stoden on her feet, a ful greet oost.

11 And the Lord seide to me, Thou sone of man, alle these boonys is the hous of Israel; thei seien, Oure boonys drieden, and oure hope perischide, and we ben kit awei.

12 Therfor profesie thou, and thou schalt seie to hem, The Lord God seith these thingis, Lo! Y schal opene youre graues, and Y schal lede you out of youre sepulcris, my puple, and Y schal lede you in to youre lond Israel.

13 And ye schulen wite, that Y am the Lord, whanne Y schal opene youre sepulcris, and schal lede you out of youre biriels, my puple;

14 and Y schal yyue my spirit in you, and ye schulen lyue. And Y schal make you for to reste on youre lond; and ye schulen wite, that Y the Lord spak, and dide, seith the Lord God.

15 And the word of the Lord was maad to me,

16 and he seide, And thou, sone of man, take to thee o tree, and write thou on it, To Juda, and to the sones of Israel, and to hise felowis. And take thou an other tree, and write on it, Joseph, the tree of Effraym, and of al the hous of Israel, and of hise felowis.

17 And ioyne thou tho trees oon to the tother in to o tree to thee; and tho schulen be in to onement in thin hond.

18 Sotheli whanne the sones of thi puple that speken, schulen seie to thee, Whether thou schewist not to vs, what thou wolt to thee in these thingis?

19 thou schalt speke to hem, The Lord God seith these thingis, Lo! Y schal take the tree of Joseph, which is in the hond of Effraym, and the lynagis of Israel, that ben ioyned to hym, and Y schal yyue hem togidere with the tree of Juda; and Y schal make hem in to o tree, and thei schulen be oon in the hond of hym.

20 Sotheli the trees, on whiche thou hast write, schulen be in thin hond bifore the iyen of hem.

21 And thou schalt seie to hem, The Lord God seith these thingis, Lo! Y schal take the sones of Israel fro the myddis of naciouns, to whiche thei yeden forth; and Y schal gadere hem togidere on ech side. And Y schal brynge hem to her lond,

22 and Y schal make hem o folc in the lond, in the hillis of Israel, and o kyng schal be comaundynge to alle: and thei schulen no more be twei folkis, and thei schulen no more be departid in to twey rewmes.

23 And thei schulen no more be defoulid in her idols, and her abhomynaciouns, and in alle her wickidnessis. And Y schal make hem saaf fro alle her seetis, in which thei synneden, and Y schal clense hem; and thei schulen be a puple to me, and Y schal be God to hem.

24 And my seruaunt Dauid schal be kyng on hem, and o scheepherde schal be of alle hem; thei schulen go in my domes, and thei schulen kepe my comaundementis, and schulen do tho.

25 And thei schulen dwelle on the lond, which Y yaf to my seruaunt Jacob, in which youre fadris dwelliden; and thei schulen dwelle on that lond, thei, and the sones of hem, and the sones of her sones, til in to with outen ende; and Dauid, my seruaunt, schal be the prince of hem with outen ende.

26 And Y schal smyte to hem a boond of pees; it schal be a couenaunt euerlastynge to hem, and Y schal founde hem, and Y schal multiplie, and Y schal yyue myn halewing in the myddis of hem with outen ende.

27 And my tabernacle schal be among hem, and Y schal be God to hem, and thei schulen be a puple to me.

28 And hethene men schulen wite, that Y am the Lord, halewere of Israel, whanne myn halewyng schal be in the myddis of hem with outen ende.

CAP 38

1 And the word of the Lord was maad to me,

2 and he seide, Thou, sone of man, Sette thi face ayens Gog, and ayens the lond of Magog, the prince of the heed of Mosoch and of Tubal; and profesie thou of hym.

3 And thou schalt seie to hym, The Lord God seith these thingis, A! Gog, lo! Y to thee, prince of the heed of Mosoch and of Tubal;

4 and Y schal lede thee aboute, and Y schal sette a bridil in thi chekis, and Y schal leede out thee, and al thin oost, horsis, and horsmen, alle clothid with haburiouns, a greet multitude of men, takynge spere, and scheeld, and swerd.

5 Perseis, Ethiopiens, and Libiens with hem, alle ben araied with scheeldis and helmes.

6 Gomer, and alle the cumpenyes of hym, the hous of Togorma, the sidis of the north, and al the strengthe therof, and many puplis ben with thee.

7 Make redi, and araye thee, and al thi multitude which is gaderid to thee, and be thou in to comaundement to hem.

8 Aftir many daies thou schalt be visitid, in the laste of yeeris thou schalt come to the lond, that turnede ayen fro swerd, and was gaderid of many puplis, to the hillis of Israel that weren desert ful ofte; this was led out of puplis, and alle men dwell-ide tristili ther ynne.

9 Forsothe thou schalt stie, and schalt come as a tempest, and as a cloude, for to hile the lond, thou, and alle thi cumpanyes, and many puplis with thee.

10 The Lord God seith these thingis, In that dai wordis schulen stie on thin herte, and thou schalt thenke the worste thouyt;

11 and schalt seie, Y schal stie to the lond with out wal, and Y schal come to hem that resten and dwellen sikirli; alle these dwellen with out wal, barris and yatis ben not to hem;

12 that thou rauysche spuylis, and asaile prei; that thou brynge in thin hond on hem that weren forsakun, and after-ward restorid, and on the puple which is gaderid of hethene men, that bigan to welde, and to be enhabitere of the nawle of erthe.

13 Saba, and Dedan, and the marchauntis of Tharsis, and alle the liouns therof schulen seie to thee, Whether thou comest to take spuylis? Lo! to rauysche prey thou hast gaderid thi multi-tude, that thou take awei gold and siluer, and do awei purte-naunce of houshold and catel, and that thou rauysche preyes with out noumbre.

14 Therfor profesie thou, sone of man; and thou schalt seie to Gog, The Lord God seith these thingis, Whether not in that dai, whanne my puple Israel schal dwelle tristili, thou schalt wite;

15 and schalt come fro thi place, fro the sidis of the north, thou, and many puplis with thee, alle stieris of horsis, a greet cumpany, and an huge oost;

16 and thou as a cloude schalt stie on my puple Israel, that thou hile the erthe? Thou schalt be in the laste daies, and Y schal brynge thee on my lond, that my folkis wite, whanne Y schal be halewid in thee, thou Gog, bifor the iyen of them.

17 The Lord God seith these thingis, Therfor thou art he of whom Y spak in elde daies, in the hond of my seruauntis, pro-fetis of Israel, that profesieden in the daies of tho tymes, that Y schulde bringe thee on hem.

18 And it schal be, in that dai, in the dai of the comyng of Gog on the lond of Israel, seith the Lord God, myn indigna-cioun schal stie in my strong veniaunce, and in my feruour;

19 Y spak in the fier of my wraththe.

20 For in that dai schal be grete mouyng on the lond of Israel; and fischis of the see, and beestis of erthe, and briddis of the eir, and ech crepynge beeste which is mouyd on erthe, and alle men that ben on the face of erthe, schulen be mouyd fro my face; and hillis schulen be vndurturned, and heggis schulen falle doun, and ech wal schal falle doun in to erthe.

21 And Y schal clepe togidere a swerd ayens hym in alle myn hillis, seith the Lord God; the swerd of ech man schal be dressid ayens his brother.

22 And thanne Y schal deme hym bi pestilence, and blood, and greet reyn, and bi greet stoonys; Y schal reyn fier and brymstoon on hym, and on his oost, and on many puplis that ben with hym.

23 And Y schal be magnefied, and Y shal be halewid, and Y shal be knowun bifore the iyen of many folkis; and thei schulen wite, that Y am the Lord.

1 But profesie thou, sone of man, ayens Gog; and thou schalt seie, The Lord God seith these thingis, Lo! Y on thee, thou Gog, prince of the heed of Mosoch and of Tubal.

2 And Y schal lede thee aboute, and Y schal disseyue thee, and Y schal make thee to stie fro the sidis of the north, and Y schal brynge thee on the hillis of Israel.

3 And Y schal smyte thi bouwe in thi left hond, and Y schal caste doun thin arowis fro thi riyt hond.

4 Thou schalt falle doun on the hillis of Israel, thou, and alle thi cumpenyes, and puplis that ben with thee; Y yaf thee for to be deuourid to wielde beestis, to briddis, and to ech volatil, and to the beestis of erthe.

5 Thou schalt falle doun on the face of the feeld; for Y the Lord haue spoke, seith the Lord God.

6 And Y schal sende fier in Magog, and in hem that dwellen tristili in ilis; and thei schulen wite, that Y am the Lord God of Israel.

7 And Y schal make myn hooli name knowun in the myddis of my puple Israel, and Y schal no more defoule myn hooli name; and hethene men schulen wite, that Y am the Lord God, the hooli of Israel.

8 Lo! it cometh, and it is don, seith the Lord God.

9 This is the day of which Y spak. And dwelleris schulen go out of the citees of Israel, and thei schulen set a fier, and schulen brenne armuris, scheeld and spere, bouwe and arowis, and stauys of hond, and schaftis with out irun; and thei schulen brenne tho in fier bi seuene yeer.

10 And thei schulen not bere trees of cuntries, nether schulen kitte doun of forestis, for thei schulen brenne armuris bi fier; and thei schulen take preies of hem, to whiche thei weren preies, and thei schulen rauysche her wasteris, seith the Lord God.

11 And it schal be in that dai, Y schal yyue to Gog a named place, a sepulcre in Israel, the valei of weigoeris at the eest of the see, that schal make hem that passen forth for to wondre; and thei schulen birie there Gog, and al the multitude of hym, and it schal be clepid the valei of the multitude of Gog.

12 And the hous of Israel schulen birie hem, that thei clense the lond in seuene monethis.

13 Forsothe al the puple of the lond schal byrie hym, and it schal be a named dai to hem, in which Y am glorified, seith the Lord God.

14 And thei schulen ordeyne bisili men cumpassynge the lond, that schulen birie and seke hem that weren left on the face of the lond, that thei clense it. Forsothe aftir seuene monethis thei schulen bigynne to seke,

15 and thei schulen cumpas goynge aboute the lond; and whanne thei schulen se the boon of a man, thei schulen sette a 'notable signe bisidis it, til the birieris of careyns birie it in the valei of the multitude of Gog.

16 Sotheli the name of the cite is Amona; and thei schulen clense the lond.

17 Forsothe, thou, sone of man, the Lord God seith these thingis, Seie thou to ech brid, and to alle foulis, and to alle beestis of the feeld, Come ye to gidere, and haste ye, renne ye togidere on ech side to my sacrifice, which Y sle to you, a greet sacrifice on the hillis of Israel, that ye ete fleischis and drynke blood.

18 Ye schulen ete the fleischis of stronge men, and ye schulen drynke the blood of prynces of erthe, of wetheris, of lambren, and of buckis of geet, and of bolis, and of beestis maad fat, and of alle fat thingis.

19 And ye schulen ete the ynnere fatnesse in to fulnesse, and ye schulen drynke the blood in to drunkenesse, of the sacrifice which Y schal sle to you.

20 And ye schulen be fillid on my boord, of hors, and of strong horse man, and of alle men werriours, seith the Lord God.

21 And Y schal sette my glorie among hethene men, and alle hethene men schulen se my doom, which Y haue do, and myn hond, which Y haue set on hem.

22 And the hous of Israel schulen wite, that Y am her Lord God, fro that dai and afterward.

23 And hethen men schulen wite, that the hous of Israel is takun in her wickidnesse, for that that thei forsoken me; and Y hidde my face fro hem, and Y bitook hem into the hondis of enemyes, and alle thei fellen doun bi swerd.

24 Bi the unclennes and greet trespasse of hem Y dide to hem, and Y hidde my face fro hem.

25 Therfor the Lord God seith these thingis, Now Y schal leede ayen the caitiftee of Jacob, and Y schal haue merci on al the hous of Israel; and Y schal take feruoure for myn hooli name.

26 And thei schulen bere here schenschipe, and al the trespassing bi which thei trespassiden ayens me, whanne thei dwelliden in her lond tristili, and dredden no man;

27 and whanne Y schal bringe hem ayen fro puplis, and schal gadere fro the londis of her enemyes, and schal be halewid in hem, bifor the iyen of ful many folkis.

28 And thei schulen wite, that Y am the Lord God of hem, for that Y translatide hem in to naciouns, and haue gaderid hem on her lond, and Y lefte not ony of hem there.

29 And Y schal no more hide my face fro hem, for Y haue schede out my spirit on al the hous of Israel, seith the Lord God.

CAP 40

1 In the fyue and twentithe yeer of oure passyng ouer, in the bigynnyng of the yeer, in the tenthe dai of the monethe, in the fourtenthe yeer after that the citee was smytun, in this same dai the hond of the Lord was maad on me, and he brouyte me thidur in the reuelaciouns of God.

2 And he brouyte me in to the lond of Israel, and he leet me doun on a ful hiy hil, on which was as the bildyng of a citee goynge to the south;

3 and he ledde me in thidur. And lo! a man, whos licnesse was as the licnesse of bras, and a coorde of flex was in his hond, and a reed of mesure in his hond; forsothe he stood in the yate.

4 And the same man spak to me, Thou sone of man, se with thin iyen, and here with thin eeris, and sette thin herte on alle thingis, whiche Y schal schewe to thee, for thou art brouyt hidur, that tho be schewid to thee; telle thou alle thingis whiche thou seest to the hous of Israel.

5 And lo! a wal withouteforth, in the cumpas of the hous on ech side; and in the hond of the man was a rehed of mesure of sixe cubitis and a spanne, that is, an handibreede; and he mat the breede of the bildyng with o rehed, and the hiynesse bi o rehed.

6 And he cam to the yate that bihelde the weie of the eest, and he stiede bi degrees of it; and he mat the lyntil of the yate bi o rehed the breede, that is, o lyntil bi o rehed in breede;

7 and he mat o chaumbre bi o rehed in lengthe, and bi o rehed in breed, and fyue cubitis bitwixe chaumbris;

8 and he mat the lyntil of the yate bisidis the porche of the yate with ynne, bi o rehed.

9 And he mat the porch of the yate of eiyte cubitis, and the frount therof bi twei cubitis; sotheli the porche of the yate was with ynne.

10 Certis the chaumbris of the yate at the weie of the eest weren thre on this side, and thre on that side; o mesure of thre, and o mesure of the frountis on euer ethir side.

11 And he mat the breede of the lyntel of the yate of ten cubitis, and the lengthe of the yate of threttene cubitis.

12 And he mat a margyn of a cubit bifor the chaumbris, and o cubit was the ende on ech side; forsothe the chaumbris weren of sixe cubitis on this side and on that side.

13 And he mat the yate fro the roof of the chaumbre til to the roof therof, the breede of fyue and twenti cubitis, a dore ayens a dore.

14 And he made frountes bi sixti cubitis, and at the frount an halle of the yate on ech side bi cumpas;

15 and bifor the face of the yate that stretchith forth til to the face of the porche of the ynner yate, he mat fifti cubitis.

16 And he mat wyndows naraw with out and large with ynne, in the chaumbris and frountis of tho, that weren with ynne the yate on ech side bi cumpas. Sotheli in lijk maner also wyndows weren in the porchis bi cumpas with ynne; and the peynture of palm trees was grauun bifor the frountis.

17 And he ledde me out to the outermere halle, and lo! tresories, and pawment arayed with stoon in the halle bi cumpas; thretti tresories in the cumpas of the pawment;

18 and the pawment was bynethe in the front of the yatis, bi the lengthe of the yatis.

19 And he mat the breede fro the face of the lowere yate til to the frount of the ynnere halle with outforth, an hundrid cubitis at the eest, and at the north.

20 And he mat bothe in lengthe and in breede the yate that bihelde the weie of the north, of the outermore halle.

21 And he mat the chaumbris therof, thre on this side, and thre on that side, and the frount therof, and the porche therof, bi the mesure of the formere yate; the lengthe therof of fifti cubitis, and the breede therof of fyue and twenti cubitis.

22 Sotheli the wyndows therof, and the porche, and the grauyngis, weren bi the mesure of the yate that bihelde to the eest; and the stiyng therof was of seuene degrees, and a porche was bifore it.

23 And the yate of the ynnere halle was ayens the yate of the north, and ayens the eest yate; and he mat fro the yate til to the yate an hundrid cubitis.

24 And he ledde me out to the weie of the south, and lo! the yate that bihelde to the south; and he mat the frount therof, and the porche therof, bi the formere mesuris;

25 and the wyndows therof, and the porchis in cumpas, as othere wyndows; the lengthe of fifti cubitis, and the breede of fyue and twenti cubitis.

26 And bi seuene degrees me stiede to it, and 'an halle was bifor the yatis therof; and palme trees weren grauun, oon in this side, and another in that side in the frount therof.

27 And the yate of the ynnere halle was in the weie of the south; and he mat fro the yate til to the yate in the weie of the south, an hundrid cubitis.

28 And he ledde me in to the ynnere halle, to the south yate; and he mat the yate bi the formere mesuris;

29 the chaumbre therof, and the frount therof, and the porche therof bi the same mesuris; and he mat the wyndows therof, and the porche therof in cumpas; fifti cubitis of lengthe, and fyue and twenti cubitis of breede.

30 And he mat the halle bi cumpas, the lengthe of fyue and twenti cubitis, and the breede therof of fyue cubitis.

31 And the porche therof was to the outermere halle, and the palm trees therof in the frount; and eiyte degrees weren, bi whiche me stiede thorouy it.

32 And he ledde me in to the ynnere halle, bi the eest weie; and he mat the yate by the formere mesures;

33 the chaumbre therof, and the frount therof, and the porchis therof, as aboue; and he mat the wyndows therof, and the porchis therof in cumpas; the lengthe of fifti cubitis, and the breede of fyue and twenti cubitis; and the porche therof,

34 that is, of the outermore halle; and palme trees grauun in the frount therof, on this side and on that side; and in eiyte degrees was the stiyng therof.

35 And he ledde me in to the yate that bihelde to the north; and he mat bi the formere mesuris;

36 the chaumbre therof, and the frount therof, and the porche therof, and the wyndows therof bi cumpas; the lengthe of fifti cubitis, and the breede of fyue and twenti cubitis.

37 The porche therof bihelde to the outermore halle; and the grauyng of palm trees was in the frount therof, on this side and on that side; and in eiyte degrees was the stiyng therof.

38 And bi alle tresories a dore was in the frountis of yatis; and there thei waischiden brent sacrifice.

39 And in the porche of the yate weren twei boordis on this side, and twei boordis on that side, that brent sacrifice be offrid on tho, 'bothe for synne and for trespasse.

40 And at the outermore side, which stieth to the dore of the yate that goith to the north, weren twei boordis; and at 'the tother side, bifor the porche of the yate, weren twei boordis.

41 Foure boordis on this side, and foure boordis on that side; bi the sidis of the yate weren eiyte boordis, on whiche thei offriden.

42 Forsothe foure boordis to brent sacrifice weren bildid of square stoonys, in the lengthe of o cubit and an half, and in the breed of o cubit and an half, and in the hiythe of o cubit; on whiche boordis thei schulen sette vessels, in whiche brent sacrifice and slayn sacrifice is offrid.

43 And the brenkis of tho boordis ben of oon handibreede, and ben bowid ayen with ynne bi cumpas; forsothe on the boordis weren fleischis of offryng.

44 And with out the ynnere yate weren tresories of chauntours, in the ynnere halle, that was in the side of the yate biholdynge to the north; and the faces of tho weren ayens the south weie; oon of the side of the eest yate, that bihelde to the weie of the north.

45 And he seide to me, This treserie, that biholdith the south weie, is of the prestis that waken in the kepyngis of the temple,

46 Sotheli the tresorye that biholdith to the weie of the north, schal be of the preestis that waken to the seruice of the auter;

these ben the sones of Sadoch, whiche of the sones of Leuy neiyen to the Lord, for to mynystre to hym.

47 And he mat the halle, the lengthe of an hundrid cubitis, and the breede of an hundrid cubitis, bi square, and the auter bifore the face of the temple.

48 And he ledde me in to the porche of the temple; and he mat the porche bi fyue cubitis on this side, and bi fyue cubitis on that side; and he mat the breede of the yate, of thre cubitis on this side, and of thre cubitis on that side.

49 But he mat the lengthe of the porche of twenti cubitis, and the breede of eleuene cubitis, and bi eiyte degrees me stiede to it; and pileris weren in the frountis, oon on this side, and 'another on that side.

CAP 41

1 And he ledde me in to the temple, and he mat the frountis, sixe cubitis of breede on this side, and sixe cubitis of breede on that side, the breede of the tabernacle.

2 And the breede of the yate was of ten cubitis; and he mat the sidis of the yate bi fyue cubitis on this side, and bi fyue cubitis on that side; and he mat the lengthe therof of fourti cubitis, and the breede of twenti cubitis.

3 And he entride with ynne, and he mat in the front of the yate twei cubitis; and he mat the yate of sixe cubitis, and the breede of the yate of seuene cubits.

4 And he mat the lengthe therof of twenti cubitis, and the breede of twenti cubitis, bifor the face of the temple.

5 And he seide to me, This is the hooli thing of hooli thingis. And he mat the wal of the hous of sixe cubitis, and the breede of the side of foure cubitis, on ech side bi cumpas of the hous.

6 Forsothe the sidis weren tweies thre and thretti, the side to the side; and tho weren stondynge an hiy, that entriden bi the wal of the hous, in the sidis bi cumpas, that tho helden togidere, and touchiden not the wal of the temple.

7 And a street was in round, and stiede vpward bi a vijs, and bar in to the soler of the temple bi cumpas; therfor the temple was braddere in the hiyere thingis; and so fro the lowere thingis me stiede to the hiyere thingis, and in to the myddis.

8 And Y siy in the hous an hiynesse bi cumpas, the sidis foundid at the mesure of a rehed in the space of sixe cubitis;

9 and the breede by the wal of the side with outforth, of fyue cubitis; and the ynnere hous was in the sidis of the hous.

10 And bitwixe treseries Y siy the breede of twenti cubitis in the cumpas of the hous on ech side;

11 and Y siy the dore of the side to preier; o dore to the weie of the north, and o dore to the weie of the south; and Y siy the breede of place to preier, of fyue cubitis in cumpas.

12 And the bildyng that was ioyned to the place departid, and turned to the weie biholdynge to the see, of the breede of seuenti cubitis; sotheli the wal of the bildyng of fyue cubitis of breede bi cumpas, and the lengthe therof of nynti cubitis.

13 And he mat the lengthe of the hous, of an hundrid cubitis; and that that was departid, the bildyng and the wallis therof, of lengthe of an hundrid cubitis.

14 Forsothe the breede of the street bifor the face of the hous, and of that that was departid ayens the eest, was of an hundrid cubitis.

15 And he mat the lengthe of the bildyng ayens the face of that, that was departid at the bak; he mat the boteraces on euer either side of an hundrid cubitis. And he mat the ynnere temple, and the porchis of the halle,

16 lyntels, and wyndows narowe withoutforth and broode with ynne; boteraces in cumpas bi thre partis, ayenst the lintel

of ech, and araied with tree bi cumpas al aboute; sotheli fro the erthe til to the wyndows, and the wyndows weren closid on the doris,

17 and til to the ynnere hous, and withoutforth bi al the wal in cumpas, with ynne and with outforth at mesure.

18 And cherubyns and palm trees weren maad craftili, and a palm tree bitwixe cherub and cherub; and cherub hadde twei faces,

19 the face of a man bisidis the palm tree on this side, and the face of a lioun expressid bisidis the palm tree on 'the tother side. Bi al the hous in cumpas, fro the erthe til to the hiyere part,

20 cherubyns and palm trees weren grauun in the wal of the temple.

21 A threisfold foure cornerid; and the face of the biholdyng of the seyntuarie was ayens the biholding of the auter of tree;

22 the heiythe therof was of thre cubitis, and the lengthe therof of twei cubitis; and the corneris therof, and the lengthe therof, and the wallis therof, weren of tree. And he spak to me, This is the boord bifor the Lord.

23 And twei doris weren in the temple, and in the seyntuarie.

24 And in the twei doris on euer either side weren twei litle doris, that weren foldun togidere in hem silf; for whi twei doris weren on euer either side of the doris.

25 And cherubyns and the grauyng of palm trees weren grauun in the doris of the temple, as also tho weren expressid in the wallis. Wherfor and grettere trees weren in the frount of the porche with outforth,

26 on whiche the wyndows narowe with out and large with ynne, and the licnesse of palm trees weren on this side and on that syde; in the litle vndursettyngis of the porche, bi the sidis of the hous, and bi the breede of the wallis.

CAP 42

1 And he ledde me out in to the outermere halle, bi the weie ledynge to the north; and he ledde me in to the treserie, that was ayens the bildyng departid, and ayens the hous goynge to the north;

2 in the face an hundrid cubitis of lengthe of the dore of the north, and fifti cubitis of breede,

3 ayens twenti cubitis of the ynnere halle, and ayens the pawment araied with stoon of the outermere halle, where a porche was ioyned to thre fold porche.

4 And bifor the tresories was a walkyng of ten cubitis of breede, biholdynge to the ynnere thingis of the weie of o cubit. And the doris of tho to the north,

5 where tresories weren lowere in the hiyere thingis; for tho baren vp the porchis that apperiden an hiy of tho fro the lowere thingis, and fro the myddil thingis of the bildyng.

6 For tho weren of thre stagis, and hadden not pileris, as weren the pilers of hallis; therfor tho stoden an hiy fro the lowere thingis, and fro the myddil thingis fro erthe, bi fifti cubitis.

7 And the outermore halle closynge the walkynge place was bi the treseries, that weren in the weie of the outermore halle, bifor the treseries; the lengthe therof was of fifti cubitis.

8 For the lengthe of the tresories of the outermore halle was of fifti cubitis, and the lengthe bifor the face of the temple was of an hundrid cubitis.

9 And vndur these tresories was an entring fro the eest, of men entringe in to tho, fro the outermere halle,

10 in the brede of the wal of the halle, that was ayens the eest weie in the face of the bilding departid. And treseries weren bifore the bilding,

11 and a weie was bifor the face of tho, bi the licnesse of treseries that weren in the weie of the north; bi the lengthe of tho, so was also the breede of tho. And al the entryng of tho, and the licnessis and doris of tho,

12 weren lijk the doris of treseries that weren in the weye biholdynge to the south; a dore was in the heed of the weye, which weie was bifor the porche departid to men entringe bi the eest weie.

13 And he seide to me, The treseries of the north, and the treseries of the south, that ben bifor the bildyng departid, these ben hooli treseries, in whiche the preestis ben clothid, that neiyen to the Lord in to the hooli of hooli thingis; there thei schulen putte the hooli of hooli thingis, and offryngis for synne, and for trespas; for it is an hooli place.

14 Sotheli whanne prestis han entrid, thei schulen go out of hooli thingis in to the outermore halle; and there thei schulen putte vp her clothis, in whiche thei mynystren, for tho ben hooli; and thei schulen be clothid in othere clothis, and so thei schulen go forth to the puple.

15 And whanne he hadde fillid the mesuris of the ynnere hous, he ledde me out bi the weie of the yate that biheelde to the eest weie; and he mat it on ech side bi cumpas.

16 Forsothe he mat ayens the eest wynd with the rehed of mesure bi cumpas fyue hundrid rehedis, in a rehed of mesure bi cumpas.

17 And he mat ayens the wynd of the north fiue hundred rehedis, in the rehed of mesure bi cumpas.

18 And at the south wynd he mat fyue hundrid rehedis, with a rehed of mesure bi cumpas.

19 And at the west wynd he mat fyue hundrid rehedis, with the rehed of mesure.

20 Bi foure wyndis he mat the wal therof on ech side bi cumpas, the lengthe of fyue hundrid, and the breede of fyue hundrid, departynge bitwixe the seyntuarie and the place of the comyn puple.

CAP 43

1 And he ledde me out to the yate, that bihelde to the eest weie.

2 And lo! the glorie of God of Israel entride bi the eest weie; and a vois was to it, as the vois of many watris, and the erthe schynede of the mageste of hym.

3 And Y siy a visioun, bi the licnesse whiche Y hadde seyn, whanne he cam to distrie the citee; and the licnesse was lijc the biholdyng whiche Y hadde seyn bisidis the flood Chobar.

4 And Y felle doun on my face, and the mageste of the Lord entride in to the temple, bi the weie of the yate that biheeld to the eest.

5 And the Spirit reiside me, and ledde me in to the ynnere halle; and lo! the hous was fillid of the glorie of the Lord.

6 And Y herde oon spekynge to me of the hous. And the man that stood bisidis me,

7 seide to me, Thou, son of man, this is the place of my seete, and the place of the steppis of my feet, where Y dwelle in the myddis of the sones of Israel withouten ende; and the hous of Israel schulen no more defoule myn hooli name, thei, and the kyngis of hem in her fornicaciouns, and in the fallyngis of her kyngis, and in hiy places.

8 Whiche maden her threisfold bisidis my threisfold, and her postis bisidis my postis, and a wal was bitwixe me and hem;

and thei defouliden myn hooli name in abhomynaciouns whiche thei diden; wherfor Y wastide hem in my wraththe.

9 Now therfor putte thei awei fer her fornicacioun, and the fallyng of her kyngis fro me; and Y schal dwelle euere in the myddis of hem.

10 But thou, sone of man, schewe the temple to the hous of Israel, and be thei schent of her wickidnessis; and mete thei the bilding,

11 and be thei aschamed of alle thingis whiche thei diden. Thou schalt schewe to hem, and thou schalt write bifore the iyen of hem the figure of the hous, and of the bildyng therof; the outgoyngis, and the entryngis, and al the discryuyng therof, and alle the comaundementis therof, and al the ordre therof, 'and alle the lawis therof; that thei kepe alle the discryuyngis therof, and comaundementis therof, and do tho.

12 This is the lawe of the hous, in the hiynesse of the hil; alle the coostis therof in cumpas is the hooli of hooli thingis; therfor this is the lawe of the hous.

13 Forsothe these ben the mesuris of the auter, in a verieste cubit, that hadde a cubit and a spanne; in the bosum therof was a cubit in lengthe, and a cubit in breede; and the ende therof til to the brenke, and o spanne in cumpas; also this was the diche of the auter.

14 And fro the bosum of the erthe til to the laste heiythe weren twei cubitis, and the breede of o cubit; and fro the lesse heiythe til to the grettere heiythe were foure cubitis, and the breede was of o cubit; forsothe thilke ariel, that is, the hiyere part of the auter, was of foure cubitis; and fro the auter 'til to aboue weren foure hornes.

16 And the auter of twelue cubitis in lengthe was foure cornerid with euene sidis, bi twelue cubitis of breede.

17 And the heiythe of fourtene cubitis of lengthe was bi fourtene cubitis of breede, in foure corneris therof. And a coroun of half a cubit was in the cumpas therof, and the bosum therof was of o cubit bi cumpas; forsothe the degrees therof weren turned to the eest.

18 And he seide to me, Thou, sone of man, the Lord God seith these thingis, These ben the customs of the auter, in what euer dai it is maad, that me offre on it brent sacrifice, and blood be sched out.

19 And thou schalt yyue to preestis and dekenes, that ben of the seed of Sadoch, that neiyen to me, seith the Lord God, that thei offre to me a calf of the drooue for synne.

20 And thou schalt take of the blood therof, and schalt putte on foure hornes therof, and on foure corneris of heiythe, and on the coroun in cumpas; and thou schalt clense it, and make clene.

21 And thou schalt take the calf which is offrid for synne, and thou schalt brenne it in a departid place of the hous, with out the seyntuarie.

22 And in the secounde dai thou schalt offre a buk of geet, which is with out wem, for synne; and thei schulen clense the auter, as thei clensiden in the calf.

23 And whanne thou hast fillid that clensyng, thou schalt offre a calf of the drooue, which calf is without wem, and a wether with out wem of the floc.

24 And thou schalt offre tho in the siyt of the Lord; and prestis schulen putte salt on tho, and schulen offre tho in to brent sacrifice to the Lord.

25 Bi seuene daies thou schalt make a buk of geet for synne, ech dai; and thei schulen offre a calf of the drooue, and a wether vnwemmed of scheep.

26 Bi seuene daies thei schulen clense the auter, and schulen make it cleene, and thei schulen fille the hond therof.

27 Forsothe whanne seuene daies ben fillid, in the eiythe dai and ferther prestis schulen make on the auter youre brent sacrifices, and tho thingis whiche thei offren for pees; and Y schal be plesid to you, seith the Lord God.

CAP 44

1 And he turnede me to the weie of the yate of the outermore seyntuarie, which yate byhelde to the eest, and was closid.

2 And the Lord seide to me, This yate schal be closid, and schal not be opened, and a man schal not passe thorou it; for the Lord God of Israel entride bi it, and it schal be closid to the prince.

3 The prince hym silf schal sitte ther ynne, that he ete breed bifor the Lord; he schal go yn bi the weie of the yate of the porche, and he schal go out bi the weie therof.

4 And he ledde me bi the weie of the north yate, in the siyt of the hous; and Y siy, and lo! the glorie of the Lord fillide the hous of the Lord; and Y felle doun on my face.

5 And the Lord seide to me, Thou, sone of man, sette thin herte, and se with thin iyen, and here with thin eeris alle thingis whiche Y speke to thee, of al the ceremonyes of the hous of the Lord, and of alle the lawis therof; and thou schalt sette thin herte in the weies of the temple, bi alle the goyngis out of the seyntuarie.

6 And thou schalt seie to the hous of Israel terrynge me to wraththe, The Lord God seith these thingis, Ye hous of Israel, alle youre grete trespassis suffice to you,

7 for ye bryngen in alien sones, vncircumcidid in herte, and vncircumcidid in fleisch, that thei be in my seyntuarie, and defoule myn hous. And ye offren my looues, ynnere fatnesse, and blood, and breken my couenaunt in alle youre grete trespassis.

8 And ye kepten not the comaundementis of my seyntuarie, and ye settiden keperis of my kepyngis in my seyntuarye to you silf.

9 The Lord God seith these thingis, Ech alien 'that is vncircumcidid in herte, and vncircumcidid in fleisch, schal not entre in to my seyntuarie; ech alien sone, which is in the myddis of the sones of Israel.

10 But also Leuytis, 'ether men of the lynage of Leuy, that yeden fer a wei fro me in the errour of the sones of Israel, and erriden fro me aftir her idols, and baren her wickidnesse,

11 thei schulen be kepers of housis in my seyntuarye, and porteris of yatis of the hous, and mynystris of the hous; thei schulen sle brent sacrifices, and sacrifices for victorie of the puple; and thei schulen stonde in the siyt of the prestis, for to mynystre to hem.

12 For that that thei mynystriden to tho in the siyt of her idols, and weren maad to the hous of Israel in to offendyng of wickidnesse; therfor Y reiside myn hond on them, seith the Lord God, and thei baren her wickidnesse.

13 And thei schulen not neiye to me, that thei vse preesthod to me, nether thei schulen neiye to al my seyntuarie bisidis hooly of hooli thingis, but thei schulen bere her schenschipe, and her grete trespassis whiche thei diden.

14 And Y schal make hem porteris of the hous, in al the seruyce therof, and in alle thingis that ben don ther ynne.

15 Forsothe preestis and dekenes, the sones of Sadoch, that kepten the cerymonyes of my seyntuarie, whanne the sones of Israel erriden fro me, thei schulen neiye to me, for to

mynystre to me; and thei schulen stonde in my siyt, that thei offre to me ynnere fatnesse and blood, seith the Lord God.

16 Thei schulen entre in to my seyntuarie, and thei schulen neiye to my boord, that thei mynystre to me, and kepe my ceremonyes.

17 And whanne thei schulen entre in to the yatis of the ynnere halle,

18 thei schulen be clothid with lynnun clothis, nether ony wollun thing schal 'be do on hem, whanne thei mynystren in the yatis of the ynnere halle, and with ynne; lynnun cappis, ether mytris, schulen be in the heedis of hem, and lynnun brechis schulen be in the leendis of hem, and thei schulen not be gird in swoot.

19 And whanne thei schulen go out at the outermere halle to the puple, thei schulen dispuyle hem of her clothis, in whiche thei mynystriden, and thei schulen leie tho vp in the treserie of seyntuarie; and thei schulen clothe hem silf in othere clothis, and thei schulen not halewe my puple in her clothis.

20 Forsothe thei schulen not schaue her heed, nether thei schulen nursche long heere, but thei clippynge schulen clippe her heedis.

21 And ech preest schal not drynke wyn, whanne he schal entre in to the ynnere halle.

22 And preestis schulen not take wyues a widewe, and a forsakun womman, but virgyns of the seed of the hous of Israel; but also thei schulen take a widewe, which is the widewe of a preest.

23 And thei schulen teche my puple, what is bitwixe hooli thing and defoulid; and thei schulen schewe to hem, what is bitwixe cleene thing and vncleene.

24 And whanne debate is, thei schulen stonde in my domes, and schulen deme my lawis; and thei schulen kepe my comaundementis in alle my solempnytees, and thei schulen halewe my sabatis.

25 And thei schulen not entre to a deed man, lest thei be defoulid, no but to fadir, and modir, and to sone, and douyter, and to brother, and sister that hadde not an hosebonde, in whiche thei schulen be defoulid.

26 And after that he is clensid, seuene daies schulen be noumbrid to hym.

27 And in the dai of his entryng in to the seyntuarie, to the ynnere halle, that he mynystre to me in the seyntuarie, he schal offre for his synne, seith the Lord God.

28 Forsothe noon eritage schal be to hem, Y am the eritage of hem; and ye schulen not yyue to hem possessioun in Israel, for Y am the possessioun of hem.

29 Thei schulen ete sacrifice, bothe for synne and for trespasse, and ech avow of Israel schal be hern.

30 And the firste thingis of alle firste gendrid thingis, and alle moiste sacrifices, of alle thingis that ben offrid, schulen be the prestis part; and ye schulen yyue the firste thingis of youre metis to the prest, that he leie vp blessyng to his hous.

31 Preestis schulen not ete ony thing deed bi it silf, and takun of a beeste, of foulis, and of scheep.

CAP 45

1 And whanne ye schulen bigynne to departe the lond bi partis, departe ye the firste thingis to the Lord, an halewid thing of the lond, fyue and twenti thousynde of rehedis in lengthe, and ten thousynde of rehedis in breede; it schal be halewid in al the coost therof by cumpas.

2 And it schal be halewid on ech part in fyue hundrid rehedis bi fyue hundrid, in foure sidis bi cumpas, and in fifti cubitis in to the subarbis therof bi cumpas.

3 And fro this mesure thou schalt mete the lengthe of fyue and twenti thousynde of rehedis, and the breede of ten thousynde; and the temple and the hooli of hooli thingis schal be in it.

4 An halewid thing of the lond schal be to prestis, the mynystris of seyntuarie, that neiyen to the seruyce of the Lord; and a place schal be to hem in to housis, and in to the seyntuarie of hoolynesse.

5 Sotheli fyue and twenti thousynde of lengthe schulen be, and ten thousynde of breede; but the dekenes that mynystren to the hous, thei schulen haue in possessioun twenti treseries.

6 And ye schulen yyue the possessioun of the citee, fyue thousynde rehedis of breede, and fyue and twenti thousynde of lengthe, bi the departyng of the seyntuarie, to al the hous of Israel.

7 And ye schulen yyue a porcioun to the prince on this side and on that side, bisidis the departyng of the seyntuarie, and bisidis the possessioun of the citee, ayens the face of departynge of seyntuarie, and ayens the face of possessioun of the citee; fro the side of the se til to the see, and fro the side of the eest 'til to the eest, schal be of the possessioun of the prince. Forsothe the lengthe bi ech of the partis, fro the west ende til to the eest ende of the lond,

8 schal be possessioun to hym in Israel; and the princes schulen no more robbe my puple, but thei schulen yyue the lond to the hous of Israel, bi the lynagis of hem.

9 The Lord God seith these thingis, O! princes of Israel, suffice it to you, leue ye wickidnesse 'and raueyns, and do ye doom and riytfulnesse; departe ye youre niy coostis fro my puple, seith the Lord God.

10 A iust balaunce, and a iust mesure clepid ephi, and a iust mesure clepid bathus, schulen be to you.

11 Ephi and bathus schulen be euene, and of o mesure, that bathus take the tenthe part of the mesure clepid corus, and that ephi take the tenthe part of the mesure corus; bi the mesure of corus schal be euene weiynge of tho.

12 Forsothe a sicle schal haue twenti halpens; certis twenti siclis, and fyue and twenti siclis, and fiftene siclis maken a besaunt.

13 And these ben the firste fruytis whiche ye schulen take awei; the sixte part of ephi of a corus of wheete, and the sixte part of ephi of a corus of barli.

14 Also the mesure of oile; a bathus of oile is the tenthe part of corus, and ten bathus maken o corus; for ten bathus fillen o corus.

15 And 'a ram of the floc of twei hundrid, of these whiche the men of Israel nurschen, in to sacrifice, and in to brent sacrifice, and in to pesible sacrifices, to clense for hem, seith the Lord God.

16 Al the puple of the lond schal be boundun in these firste fruytis to the prince of Israel.

17 And on the prince schulen be brent sacrifices, and sacrifice, and moiste sacrifices, in solempnytees, and in kalendis, ether bigynnyngis of monethis, and in sabatis, and in alle the solempnytees of the hous of Israel; he schal make sacrifice, for synne, and brent sacrifice, and pesible sacrifices, to clense for the hous of Israel.

18 The Lord God seith these thingis, In the firste moneth, in the firste dai of the monethe, thou schalt take a calf with out wem of the drooue, and thou schalt clense the seyntuarie.

19 And the preest schal take of the blood of the beeste, that schal be for synne; and he schal putte in the postis of the hous, and in foure corneris of the heiythe of the auter, and in the postis of the yate of the ynnere halle.

20 And thus thou schalt do in the seuenthe dai of the monethe, for ech that knew not, and was disseyued bi errour, and thou schalt clense for the hous.

21 In the firste monethe, in the fourtenthe dai of the monethe, the solempnytee of pask schal be to you; therf looues schulen be etun bi seuene daies.

22 And the prince schal make a calf for synne in that dai, for hym silf and for al the puple of the lond.

23 And in the solempnytee of seuene daies he schal make brent sacrifice to the Lord; he schal offre seuene caluys and seuene wetheris with out wem ech dai, bi seuene daies, and ech dai a buc of geet, for synne.

24 And he schal make the sacrifice of ephi by a calf, and of ephi by a wether, and of oile the mesure hyn, bi ech ephi.

25 In the seuenthe monethe, in the fiftenthe dai of the monethe, in the solempnytee, he schal make as tho ben biforseid, bi seuene daies, as wel for synne as for brent sacrifice, and in sacrifice, and in oile.

CAP 46

1 The Lord God seith these thingis, The yate of the ynnere halle, that biholdith to the eest, schal be closid bi sixe daies, in whiche werk is doon; for it schal be openid in the dai of sabat, but also it schal be openyd in the dai of kalendis.

2 And the prince schal entre bi the weie of the porche of the yate withoutforth, and he schal stonde in the threisfold of the yate; and preestis schulen make the brent sacrifice of hym, and the pesible sacrifices of hym; and he schal worschipe on the threisfold of the yate, and he schal go out; forsothe the yate schal not be closid til to the euentid.

3 And the puple of the lond schal worschipe at the dore of that yate, in sabatis, and in calendis, bifor the Lord.

4 Forsothe the prince schal offre this brent sacrifice to the Lord in the dai of sabat, sixe lambren with out wem, and a wether with out wem,

5 and the sacrifice of ephi bi a wether; but in the lambren he schal offre the sacrifice which his hond schal yiue, and of oile the mesure hyn, bi ech ephi.

6 But in the dai of calendis he schal offre a calf with out wem of the droue; and sixe lambren, and wetheris schulen be with out wem,

7 and ephi bi a calf. Also he schal make the sacrifice ephi bi a wether; but of lambren as his hond fyndith, and of oile the mesure hyn, bi ech ephi.

8 And whanne the prince schal entre, entre he bi the weie of the porche of the yate, and go he out bi the same weie.

9 And whanne the puple of the lond schal entre in the siyt of the Lord, in solempnytees, which puple entrith bi the yate of the north, for to worschipe, go it out bi the wei of the south yate. Certis the puple that entrith bi the weie of the south yate, go out bi the weie of the north yate. It schal not turne ayen bi the weie of the yate, bi which it entride, but euene ayens that weie it schal go out.

10 Forsothe the prince schal be in the myddis of hem; he schal entre with hem that entren, and he schal go out with hem that goen out.

11 And in feiris and in solempnytees, the sacrifice of ephi schal be bi a calf, and ephi bi a wether; in lambren schal be sacrifice as his hond fyndith, and of oile the mesure hyn, bi ech ephi.

12 Forsothe whanne the prince makith a wilful brent sacrifice, ether wilful pesible sacrifice to the Lord, the yate that biholdith to the eest, schal be openyd to hym; and he schal make his brent sacrifice, and hise pesible sacrifices, as it is wont to be doon in the dai of sabat; and he schal go out, and the yate schal be closid after that he yede out.

13 And he schal make brent sacrifice ech day to the Lord, a lomb with out wem of the same yeer; euere he schal make it in the morewtid,

14 and he schal make sacrifice on it ful eerli; eerli he schal make the sixte part of ephi, and of oile the thridde part of hyn, that it be meddlid with the floure of wheete; it is a lawful sacrifice, contynuel and euerlastinge, to the Lord.

15 He schal make a lomb, and sacrifice, and oile, ful eerli; he schal make eerli brent sacrifice euerlastynge.

16 The Lord God seith these thingis, If the prince yyueth an hous to ony of hise sones, the eritage of hym schal be of hise sones; thei schulen welde it bi eritage.

17 Forsothe if he yyueth a biquest of his eritage to oon of hise seruauntis, it schal be his 'til to the yeer of remyssioun, and it schal turne ayen to the prince; forsothe the eritage of hym schal be to hise sones.

18 And the prince schal not take bi violence of the eritage of the puple, and of the possessioun of hem; but of his owne possessioun he schal yyue eritage to hise sones, that my puple be not scaterid, ech man fro his possessioun.

19 And he ledde me in bi the entryng, that was on the side of the yate, in to the treseries of the seyntuarie to the preestis, whiche treseries bihelden to the north; and there was a place goynge to the west.

20 And he seide to me, This is the place where prestis schulen sethe, bothe for synne and for trespas; where thei schulen sethe sacrifice, that thei bere not out in to the outermere halle, and the puple be halewid.

21 And he ledde me out in to the outermere halle, and ledde me aboute bi the foure corneris of the halle; and lo! a litil halle was in the corner of the halle, alle litil hallis bi the corneris of the halle;

22 in foure corneris of the halle litle hallis weren disposid, of fourti cubitis bi lengthe, and of thretti bi breede;

23 foure weren of o mesure; and a wal bi cumpas yede aboute foure litle hallis; and kychenes weren maad vndur the porchis bi cumpas.

24 And he seide to me, This is the hous of kichenes, in which the mynystris of the hous of the Lord schulen sethe the sacrifices of the puple.

CAP 47

1 And he turnede me to the yate of the hous; and lo! watris yeden out vndur the threisfold of the hous to the eest; for the face of the hous bihelde to the eest; forsothe the watris camen doun in to the riyt side of the temple, to the south part of the auter.

2 And he ledde me out bi the weie of the north yate, and he turnede me to the weie with out the outermere yate, to the weie that biholdith to the eest; and lo! watris flowynge fro the riyt side,

3 whanne the man that hadde a coord in his hond, yede out to the eest. And he mat a thousynde cubitis, and ledde me ouer thorou the water til to the heelis.

4 And eft he mat a thousynde, and ledde me ouer thorouy the watir 'til to the knees.

5 And eft he mat a thousynde, and ledde me ouer thorouy the watir 'til to the reynes. And he mat a thousynde, the stronde which Y myyte not passe; for the depe watris of the stronde hadden wexe greet, that mai not be waad ouer.

6 And he seide to me, Certis, sone of man, thou hast seyn. And he seide to me; and he turnede me to the ryuere of the stronde.

7 And whanne Y hadde turned me, lo! in the ryuer of the stronde ful many trees on euer either side.

8 And he seide to me, These watris that goon out to the heepis of soond of the eest, and goen doun to pleyn places of desert, schulen entre in to the see, and schulen go out; and the watris schulen be heelid.

9 And ech lyuynge beeste that creepith, schal lyue, whidur euere the stronde schal come; and fischis many ynow schulen be, aftir that these watris comen thidur, and schulen be heelid, and schulen lyue; alle thingis to whiche the stronde schal come, schulen lyue.

10 And fisshers schulen stonde on tho watris; fro Engaddi 'til to Engallym schal be driyng of nettis; ful many kyndis of fischis therof schulen be, as the fischis of the greet see, of ful greet multitude;

11 but in brynkis therof and in maraisis watris shulen not be heelid, for tho 'schulen be youun in to places of makynge of salt.

12 And ech tree berynge fruit schal growe on the stronde, in the ryueris therof on ech side; a leef therof schal not falle doun, and the fruyt therof schal not faile; bi alle monethis it schal bere firste fruytis, for the watris therof schulen go out of the seyntuarie; and the fruytis therof schulen be in to mete, and the leeuys therof to medicyn.

13 The Lord God seith these thingis, This is the ende, in which ye schulen welde the lond, in the twelue lynagis of Israel; for Joseph hath double part.

14 Forsothe ye schulen welde it, ech man euenli as his brother; on which Y reiside myn hond, that Y schulde yyue to youre fadris; and this lond schal falle to you in to possessioun.

15 This is the ende of the lond at the north coost fro the grete see, the weie of Bethalon to men comynge to Sedala,

16 Emath, Beroth, Sabarym, which is in the myddis bitwixe Damask and niy coostis of Emath, the hous of Thichon, which is bisidis the endis of Auran.

17 And the ende schal be fro the see 'til to the porche of Ennon, the ende of Damask, and fro the north til to the north, the ende of Emath; forsothe this is the north coost.

18 Certis the eest coost fro the myddis of Auran, and fro the myddis of Damask, and fro the myddis of Galaad, and fro the myddis of the lond of Israel, is Jordan departynge at the eest see, also ye schulen mete the eest coost.

19 Forsothe the south coost of myddai is fro Thamar til to the watris of ayenseiyng of Cades; and the stronde til to the greet see, and the south coost at myddai.

20 And the coost of the see is the greet see, fro the niy coost bi streiyt, til thou come to Emath; this is the coost of the see.

21 And ye schulen departe this lond to you bi the lynagis of Israel;

22 and ye schulen sende it in to eritage to you, and to comelyngis that comen to you, that gendriden sones in the myddis of you; and thei schulen be to you as men borun in the lond among the sones of Israel; with you thei schulen departe possessioun, in the myddis of the lynages of Israel.

23 Forsothe in what euer lynage a comelyng is, there ye schulen yyue possessioun to hym, seith the Lord God.

CAP 48

1 And these ben the names of lynagis, fro the endis of the north, bisidis the weie Ethalon, to men goynge to Emath, the porche of Ennon, the terme of Damask, to the north bisidis Emath; and the eest coost schal be to it the see, o part schal be of Dan.

2 And fro the ende of Dan, fro the eest coost til to the coost of the see, o part schal be of Aser.

3 And on the ende of Azer, fro the eest coost til to the coost of the see, oon of Neptalym.

4 And on the terme of Neptalym, fro the eest coost til to the coost of the see, oon of Manasses.

5 And on the ende of Manasses, fro the eest coost til to the coost of the see, oon of Effraym.

6 And on the ende of Effraym, fro the eest coost til to the coost of the see, oon of Ruben.

7 And on the ende of Ruben, fro the eest coost til to the coost of the see, oon of Juda.

8 And on the ende of Juda, fro the eest coost til to the coost of the see, schulen be the firste fruytis, whiche ye schulen departe bi fyue and twenti thousynde reheedis of breede and of lengthe, as alle partis ben, fro the eest coost til to the coost of the see; and the seyntuarie schal be in the myddis therof.

9 The firste fruytis whiche ye schulen departe to the Lord, the lengthe schal be in fyue and twenty thousynde, and the breed in ten thousynde.

10 Forsothe these schulen be the firste fruytis of the seyntuarie of preestis; to the north fyue and twenti thousynde of lengthe, and to the see ten thousinde of breede; but to the eest ten thousynde of breede, and to the south fyue and twenti thousynde of lengthe; and the seyntuarie of the Lord schal be in the myddis therof.

11 The seyntuarie schal be to prestis of the sones of Sadoch, that kepten my cerymonyes, and erriden not, whanne the sones of Israel erriden, as also dekenes erriden.

12 And the firste fruytis schulen be to hem of the firste fruytis of the lond, the hooli of hooli thingis, bi the terme of dekenes.

13 But also to dekenes in lijk maner bi the coostis of preestis schulen be fyue and twenti thousynde of lengthe, and ten thousynde of breede; al the lengthe of fiue and twenti thousynde, and the breede of ten thousynde.

14 And thei schulen not sille therof, nether schulen chaunge; and the firste fruytis of the lond schulen not be translatid, for tho ben halewid to the Lord.

15 Sotheli the fyue thousynde, that ben left ouer in breede, bi fyue and twenti thousynde, schulen be the vnhooli thingis, ether comyn thingis, of the citee, in to dwellyng place, and in to subarbis; and the citee schal be in the myddis therof.

16 And these schulen be the mesuris therof; at the north coost, fyue hundrid and foure thousynde of rehedis, and at the south coost, fyue hundrid and foure thousynde, and at the eest coost, fyue hundrid and foure thousynde, and at the west coost, fyue hundrid and foure thousynde.

17 Forsothe the subarbis of the citee at the north schulen be twei hundrid and fifti, and at the southe twei hundrid and fifti, and at the eest twei hundrid and fifti, and at the see, that is, the west, twei hundrid and fifti.

18 But that that is residue in lengthe, bi the firste fruytis of the seyntuarie, ten thousynde in to the eest, and ten thousynde in to the west, schulen be as the firste fruitis of the seyntuarie; and the fruitis schulen be in to looues to hem that seruen the citee.

19 Forsothe thei that seruen the citee schulen worche, of alle the lynagis of Israel.

20 Alle the firste fruitis of fyue and twenti thousynde, bi fyue and twenti thousynde in square, schulen be departid in to the firste fruytis of seyntuarie, and in to possessioun of the citee.

21 Forsothe that that is residue, schal be the princes part, on ech side of the firste fruitis of seyntuarie, and of the possessioun of the citee, euene ayens fyue and twenti thousynde of the firste fruytis, til to the eest ende; but also to the see euene ayens fyue and twenti thousynde, til to the ende of the see, schal be in lijk maner in the partis of the prince; and the firste fruytis of the seyntuarye, and the seyntuarie of the temple schulen be in the myddis of it.

22 Forsothe fro the possessioun of dekenes, and fro the possessioun of the citee, which is in the myddis of partis of the prince, schal be in to the porcioun of Juda, and in to the porcioun of Beniamyn; and it schal perteyne to the prince.

23 And to other lynagis, fro the eest coost 'til to the west coost, oon to Beniamyn.

24 And ayens the porcioun of Beniamyn, fro the eest coost til to the west coost, oon to Symeon.

25 And on the terme of Symeon, fro the eest coost til to the west coost, oon to Isacar.

26 And on the terme of Isacar, fro the eest coost til to the west coost, oon to Zabulon.

27 And on the terme of Zabulon, fro the eest coost til to the coost of the see, oon to Gad.

28 And on the terme of Gad, to the coost of the south in to myddai; and the ende schal be fro Thamar til to the watris of ayenseying of Cades, and the eritage ayens the grete see.

29 This is the lond which ye schulen sende in to part to the lynagis of Israel, and these ben the partyngis of tho, seith the Lord God.

30 And these ben the goyngis out of the citee; fro the north coost thou schalt mete fyue hundrid and foure thousynde rehedis.

31 And yatis of the citee schulen be in alle the lynagis of Israel, thre yatis at the north; o yate of Ruben, o yate of Juda, o yate of Leuy.

32 And at the eest coost, fyue hundrid and foure thousynd rehedis, and thre yatis; o yate of Joseph, o yate of Beniamyn, o yate of Dan.

33 And at the south coost thou schalt mete fyue hundrid and foure thousynde rehedis, and thre yatis schulen be of tho; o yate of Symeon, o yate of Isacar, o yate of Zabulon.

34 And at the west coost, fyue hundrid and foure thousynde of rehedis, thre yatis of tho; o yate of Gad, o yate of Aser, o yate of Neptalym.

35 Bi cumpas eiytene miles; and the name schal be fro that dai, The Lord there. Amen.

DANIEL

CAP 1

1 In the thridde yeer of the rewme of Joachym, king of Juda, Nabugodonosor, the kyng of Babiloyne, cam to Jerusalem, and bisegide it.

2 And the Lord bitook in his hond Joachym, the kyng of Juda, and he took a part of the vessels of the hous of God; and he bar out tho in to the lond of Sennaar, in to the hous of his god, and he took the vessels in to the hous of tresour of his god.

3 And the kyng seide to Asphaneth, souereyn of his onest seruauntis and chast, that he schulde brynge yn of the sones of Israel, and of the kyngis seed, and the children of tirauntis, in whiche weren no wem,

4 faire in schap, and lerned in al wisdom, war in kunnyng, and tauyt in chastisyng, and that myyten stonde in the paleis of the kyng, that he schulde teche hem the lettris and langage of Caldeis.

5 And the king ordeynede to hem lijflode bi ech dai of hise meetis, and of the wyn wherof he drank; that thei nurschid bi thre yeer, schulden stonde aftirward bifor the siyt of the kyng.

6 Therfor Danyel, Ananye, Myzael, and Azarie, of the sones of Juda, weren among hem.

7 And the souereyn of onest seruauntis and chast puttide to hem names; to Danyel he puttide Balthasar; to Ananye, Sidrach; to Mysael, Misach; and to Azarie, Abdenago.

8 Forsothe Danyel purposide in his herte, that he schulde not be defoulid of the boord of the kyng, nether of the wyn of his drink; and he preiede the souereyn of onest seruauntis and chast, that he schulde not be defoulid.

9 Forsothe God yaf grace and merci to Daniel, in the siyt of the prince of onest seruauntis and chast.

10 And the prince of onest seruauntis and chast seide to Daniel, Y drede my lord the king, that ordeinede to you mete and drynk; and if he seeth youre faces lennere than othere yonge wexynge men, youre eueneeldis, ye schulen condempne myn heed to the kyng.

11 And Danyel seide to Malazar, whom the prince of onest seruauntis and chast hadde ordeynede on Danyel, Ananye, Mysael, and Asarie,

12 Y biseche, asaie thou vs thi seruauntis bi ten daies, and potagis be youun to vs to ete, and water to drynke; and biholde thou oure cheris,

13 and the cheris of children that eten the kyngis mete; and as thou seest, so do thou with thi seruauntis.

14 And whanne he herde siche a word, he asaiede hem bi ten daies.

15 Forsothe after ten daies the cheris of hem apperiden betere and fattere, than alle the children that eeten the kyngis mete.

16 Certis Malazar took the metis, and the wyn of the drynk of hem, and yaf to hem potagis.

17 Forsothe to these children God yaf kunnyng and lernyng in ech book, and in al wisdom; but to Daniel God yaf vndurstondyng of alle visiouns and dremys.

18 Therfor whanne the daies weren fillid, aftir whiche the kyng seide, that thei schulden be brouyt yn, the souereyn of onest seruauntis and chast brouyte in hem, in the siyt of Nabugodonosor.

19 And whanne the kyng hadde spoke to hem, siche weren not foundun of alle, as Daniel, Ananye, Misael, and Azarie; and thei stoden in the siyt of the king.

20 And ech word of wisdom and of vndurstondyng, which the king axide of hem, he foond in hem ten fold ouer alle false dyuynouris and astronomyens, that weren in al his rewme.

21 Forsothe Danyel was til to the firste yeer of king Cyrus.

CAP 2

1 In the secounde yeer of the rewme of Nabugodonosor, Nabugodonosor siy a dreem; and his spirit was aferd, and his dreem fledde awei fro hym.

2 Therfor the kyng comaundide, that the dyuynours, and astronomyens, and witchis, and Caldeis schulden be clepid togidere, that thei schulden telle to the kyng hise dremys; and whanne thei weren comun, thei stoden bifor the king.

3 And the king seide to hem, Y siy a dreem, and Y am schent in mynde, and Y knowe not what Y siy.

4 And Caldeis answeriden the kyng bi Sirik langage, Kyng, liue thou with outen ende; seie thi dreem to thi seruauntis, and we schulen schewe to thee the expownyng therof.

5 And the kyng answeride, and seide to Caldeis, The word is goen awei fro me; if ye schewen not to me the dreem, and expownyng therof, ye schulen perische, and youre housis schulen be forfetid.

6 Forsothe if ye tellen the dreem, and the expownyng therof, ye schulen take of me meedis and yiftis, and myche onour; therfor schewe ye to me the dreem, and the interpretyng therof.

7 Thei answeriden the secounde tyme, and seiden, The kyng seie the dreem to hise seruauntis, and we schulen schewe the interpretyng therof.

8 The kyng answeride, and seide, Certis Y woot, that ye ayenbien the tyme, and witen that the word is goen awei fro me.

9 Therfor if ye schewen not to me the dreem, o sentence is of you, for ye maken an interpretyng bothe fals and ful of disseit, that ye speke to me til the tyme passe; therfor seie ye the dreem to me, that Y wite, that ye speke also the veri interpretyng therof.

10 Therfor Caldeis answeriden bifor the kyng, and seiden, Kyng, no man is on erthe, that mai fille thi word; but nether ony greet man and myyti of kyngis axith siche a word of ony dyuynour, and astronomyen, and of a man of Caldee.

11 For the word which thou, kyng, axist, is greuouse, nether ony schal be foundun, that schal schewe it in the siyt of the king, outakun goddis, whos lyuyng is not with men.

12 And whanne this word was herd, the kyng comaundide, in woodnesse and in greet ire, that alle the wise men of Babiloyne schulden perische.

13 And bi the sentence goon out, the wise men weren slayn; and Danyel and hise felows weren souyt, that thei schulden perische.

14 Thanne Danyel axide of the lawe and sentence, of Ariok, prynce of chyualrie of the kyng, that was gon out to sle the wise men of Babiloyne.

15 And he axide hym, that hadde take power of the kyng, for what cause so cruel a sentence yede out fro the face of the kyng. Therfor whanne Ariok hadde schewid the thing to Danyel,

16 Danyel entride, and preyede the kyng, that he schulde yyue tyme to hym to schewe the soilyng to the kyng.

17 And he entride in to his hous, and schewide the nede to Ananye, and to Misael, and Asarie,

18 hise felowis, that thei schulden axe merci of the face of God of heuene on this sacrament; and that Danyel and hise felowis schulden not perische with othere wise men of Babiloyne.

19 Thanne the priuyte was schewid to Danyel bi a visioun in nyyt. And Danyel blesside God of heuene, and seide,

20 The name of the Lord be blessid fro the world, and til in to the world, for wisdom and strengthe ben hise;

21 and he chaungith tymes and ages, he translatith rewmes and ordeyneth; he yyueth wisdom to wise men, and kunnyng to hem that vndurstonden techyng, ether chastisyng;

22 he schewith deepe thingis and hid, and he knowith thingis set in derknessis, and liyt is with hym.

23 God of oure fadris, Y knowleche to thee, and Y herie thee, for thou hast youe wisdom and strengthe to me; and now thou hast schewid to me tho thingis, whiche we preieden thee, for thou hast openyd to vs the word of the kyng.

24 Aftir these thingis Danyel entride to Ariok, whom the kyng hadde ordeyned, that he schulde leese the wise men of Babiloyne, and thus he spak to hym, Leese thou not the wise men of Babiloyne; leede thou me in bifor the siyt of the kyng, and Y schal telle the soilyng to the kyng.

25 Thanne Ariok hastynge ledde in Danyel to the kyng, and seide to him, Y haue foundun a man of the sones of passyng ouer of Juda, that schal telle the soilyng to the kyng.

26 The kyng answeride, and seide to Danyel, to whom the name was Balthasar, Whethir gessist thou, that thou maist verili schewe to me the dreem which Y siy, and the interpretyng therof?

27 And Danyel answeride bifore the king, and seide, The priuytee which the kyng axith, wise men, and astronomyens, and dyuynours, and lokeris of auteris, moun not schewe to the kyng.

28 But God is in heuene, that schewith priuytees, which hath schewid to thee, thou king Nabugodonosor, what thingis schulen come in the laste tymes. Thi dreem and visiouns of thin heed, in thi bed, ben sich.

29 Thou, kyng, bigunnest to thenke in thi bed, what was to comynge aftir these thingis; and he that schewith priuetees, schewide to thee what thingis schulen come.

30 And this sacrament is schewid to me, not bi wisdom which is in me more than in alle lyuynge men, but that the interpretyng schulde be maad opyn to the kyng, and thou schuldist knowe the thouytis of thi soule.

31 Thou, kyng, siyest, and lo! as o greet ymage; thilke ymage was greet, and hiy in stature, and stood bifore thee, and the loking therof was ferdful.

32 The heed of this ymage was of best gold, but the brest and armes weren of siluer; certis the wombe and thies weren of bras,

33 but the leggis weren of irun; forsothe sum part of the feet was of irun, sum was of erthe.

34 Thou siyest thus, til a stoon was kit doun of the hil, with outen hondis, and smoot the ymage in the irun feet therof and erthene feet, and al to-brak tho.

35 Thanne the irun, tijl stoon, ether erthene vessel, bras, siluer, and gold, weren al to-brokun togidere, and dryuun as in to a deed sparcle of a large somer halle, that ben rauyschid of wynd, and no place is foundun to tho; forsothe the stoon, that smoot the ymage, was maad a greet hil, and fillide al erthe.

36 This is the dreem. Also, thou kyng, we schulen seie bifor thee the interpretyng therof.

37 Thou art kyng of kyngis, and God of heuene yaf to thee rewme, strengthe, and empire, and glorie;

38 and he yaf in thin hond alle thingis, in whiche the sones of men, and the beestis of the feeld, and the briddis of the eir dwellen, and ordeynede alle thingis vndur thi lordschip; therfor thou art the goldun heed.

39 And another rewme lesse than thou schal rise aftir thee; and the thridde rewme, an other of bras, that schal haue the empire of al erthe.

40 And the fourthe rewme schal be as irun, as irun makith lesse, and makith tame alle thingis, so it schal make lesse, and schal al to-breke alle these rewmes.

41 Forsothe that thou siest a part of the feet and fyngris of erthe of a pottere, and a part of irun, the rewme shal be departid; which netheles schal rise of the plauntyng of irun, 'bi that that thou siest irun meynd with a tijl stoon of clei,

42 and the toos of the feet in parti of irun, and in parti of erthe, in parti the rewme schal be sad, and in parti to-brokun.

43 Forsothe that thou siest irun meynd with a tiel stoon of clei, sotheli tho schulen be meynd togidere with mannus seed; but tho schulen not cleue to hem silf, as irun mai not be meddlid with tyel stoon.

44 Forsothe in the daies of tho rewmes, God of heuene shal reise a rewme, that schal not be distried with outen ende, and his rewme schal not be youun to another puple; it schal make lesse, and schal waste alle these rewmes, and it schal stonde with outen ende,

45 bi this that thou siest, that a stoon was kit doun of the hil with outen hondis, and maad lesse the tiel stoon, and irun, and bras, and siluer, and gold. Greet God hath schewid to the kyng, what thingis schulen come aftirward; and the dreem is trewe, and the interpretyng therof is feithful.

46 Thanne king Nabugodonosor felle doun on his face, and worschipide Danyel, and comaundide sacrifices and encense to be brouyt, that tho schulden be sacrifised to hym.

47 Therfor the kyng spak, and seide to Danyel, Verili youre God is God of goddis, and Lord of kyngis, that schewith mysteries, for thou miytist opene this sacrament.

48 Thanne the kyng reiside Danyel an hiy, and yaf many yiftis and grete to hym; and ordeynede hym prince and prefect, ether cheef iustise, ouer alle the prouynces of Babiloyne, and maister ouer alle the wise men of Babiloyne.

49 Forsothe Danyel axide of the kyng, and ordeynede Sidrac, Misaac, and Abdenago ouer alle the werkis of the prouynce of Babiloyne; but Danyel hym silf was in the yatis of the kyng.

CAP 3

1 Nabugodonosor, the kyng, made a goldun ymage, in the heiythe of sixti cubitis, and in the breede of sixe cubitis; and he settide it in the feeld of Duram, of the prouynce of Babiloyne.

2 Therfor Nabugodonosor sente to gadere togidere the wise men, magistratis, and iugis, and duykis, and tirauntis, and prefectis, and alle princes of cuntreis, that thei schulden come togidere to the halewyng of the ymage, which the kyng Nabugodonosor hadde reisid.

3 Thanne the wise men, magistratis, and iugis, and duykis, and tirauntis, and beste men, that weren set in poweris, and alle the princes of cuntreis, weren gaderid togidere, that thei schulden come togidere to the halewyng of the ymage, which the kyng Nabugodonosor hadde reisid. Forsothe thei stoden in the siyt of the ymage, which Nabugodonosor hadde set; and a bedele criede myytili,

4 It is seid to you, puplis, kynredis, and langagis;

5 in the our in which ye heren the soun of trumpe, and of pipe, and of harpe, of sambuke, of sawtre, and of symphonye, and of al kynde of musikis, falle ye doun, and worschipe the goldun ymage, which the kyng Nabugodonosor made.

6 Sotheli if ony man fallith not doun, and worschipith not, in the same our he schal be sent in to the furneis of fier brennynge.

7 Therfor aftir these thingis, anoon as alle puplis herden the sown of trumpe, of pipe, and of harpe, of sambuke, and of sawtre, of symphonye, and of al kynde of musikis, alle puplis, lynagis, and langagis fellen doun, and worschipiden the golden ymage, which the kyng Nabugodonosor hadde maad.

8 And anoon in that tyme men of Caldee neiyiden, and accusiden the Jewis,

9 and seiden to the kyng Nabugodonosor, Kyng, lyue thou with outen ende.

10 Thou, kyng, hast set a decree, that ech man that herith the sown of trumpe, of pipe, and of harpe, of sambuke, and of sawtree, and of symphonye, and of al kynde of musikis, bowe doun hym silf, and worschipe the goldun ymage; forsothe if ony man fallith not doun,

11 and worschipith not, be he sent in to the furneis of fier brennynge.

12 Therfor men Jewis ben, Sidrac, Mysaac, and Abdenago, whiche thou hast ordeynede on the werkis of the cuntrei of Babiloyne. Thou kyng, these men han dispisid thi decree; thei onouren not thi goddis, and thei worshipen not the goldun ymage, which thou reisidist.

13 Thanne Nabugodonosor comaundide, in woodnesse and in wraththe, that Sidrac, Mysaac, and Abdenago schulden be brouyt; whiche weren brouyt anoon in the siyt of the kyng.

14 And the kyng Nabugodonosor pronounside, and seide to hem, Whether verili Sidrac, Mysaac, and Abdenago, ye onouren not my goddis, and worschipen not the golden ymage, which Y made?

15 Now therfor be ye redi, in what euer our ye heren the sown of trumpe, of pipe, of harpe, of sambuke, of sawtree, and of symphonye, and of al kynde of musikis, bowe ye doun you, and worschipe the ymage which Y made; that if ye worschipen not, in the same our ye schulen be sent in to the furneis of fier brennynge; and who is God, that schal delyuere you fro myn hond?

16 Sidrac, Misaac, and Abdenago answeriden, and seiden to the king Nabugodonosor, It nedith not, that we answere of this thing to thee.

17 For whi oure God, whom we worschipen, mai rauysche vs fro the chymenei of fier brennynge, and mai delyuere fro thin hondis, thou kyng.

18 That if he nyle, be it knowun to thee, thou kyng, that we onouren not thi goddis, and we worschipen not the goldun ymage, which thou hast reisid.

19 Thanne Nabugodonosor was fillid of woodnesse, and the biholdyng of his face was chaungid on Sidrac, Misaac, and Abdenago. And he comaundide, that the furneis schulde be maad hattere seuenfold, than it was wont to be maad hoot.

20 And he comaundide to the strongeste men of his oost, that thei schulden bynde the feet of Sidrac, Mysaac, and Abdenago, and sende hem in to the furneis of fier brennynge.

21 And anoon tho men weren boundun, with brechis, and cappis, and schoon, and clothis, and weren sent in to the myddis of the furneis of fier brennynge;

22 for whi comaundement of the kyng constreinede. Forsothe the furneis was maad ful hoot; certis the flawme of the fier killid tho men, that hadden sent Sidrac, Misaac, and Abdenago in to the furneis.

23 Sotheli these thre men, Sidrac, Misaac, and Abdenago, fellen doun boundun in the mydis of the chymenei of fier brennynge.

24 And thei walkiden in the myddis of the flawme, and herieden God, and blessiden the Lord.

25 Forsothe Asarie stoode, and preiede thus; and he openyde his mouth in the myddis of the fier,

26 and seide, Lord God of oure fadris, thou art blessid, and worthi to be heried, and thi name is glorious in to worldis;

27 for thou art riytful in alle thingis whiche thou didist to vs, and alle thi werkis ben trewe; and thi weies ben riytful, and alle thi domes ben trewe.

28 For thou hast do trewe domes, bi alle thingis whiche thou brouytist yn on vs, and on Jerusalem, the hooli citee of oure fadris; for in trewthe and in doom thou brouytist yn alle these thingis for oure synnes.

29 For we synneden, and diden wickidli, goynge awei fro thee, and we trespassiden in alle thingis,

30 and we herden not, nether kepten thi comaundementis, nether we diden as thou comaundidist to vs, that it schulde be wele to vs.

31 Therfor thou didist bi veri doom alle thingis whiche thou brouytist yn on vs, and alle thingis whiche thou didist to vs;

32 and thou hast bitake vs in the hondis of enemyes, wickid men, and worst trespassouris, and to the vniust kyng, and worst ouer al erthe.

33 And now we moun not opene the mouth; we ben maad schame and schenschipe to thi seruauntis, and to hem that worschipen thee.

34 We bisechen, yyue thou not vs to enemyes with outen ende, for thi name, and distrie thou not thi testament,

35 and take thou not awei thi merci fro vs, for Abraham, thi derlyng, and Ysaac, thi seruaunt, and Israel, thin hooli;

36 to whiche thou spakist, biheetyng that thou schuldist multiplie her seed as the sterris of heuene, and as grauel which is in the brynke of the see.

37 For whi, Lord, we ben maad litle, more than alle folkis, and we ben lowe in al erthe to dai, for oure synnes.

38 And in this tyme is no prince, and duyk, and profete, nether brent sacrifice, nether sacrifice, nether offryng, nether encense, nether place of firste fruytis bifor thee,

39 that we moun fynde thi mercy; but be we resseyued in contrit soule, and in spirit of mekenesse.

40 As in brent sacrifice of rammes, and of bolis, and as in thousyndis of fatte lambren, so oure sacrifice be maad to dai in thi siyt, that it plese thee; for no schame is to hem that tristen in thee.

41 And now we suen thee in al the herte, and we dreden thee, and we seken thi face.

42 Schende thou not vs, but do with vs bi thi myldenesse, and bi the multitude of thi merci.

43 And delyuere thou vs in thy merueils, and yyue thou glorie to thi name, Lord;

44 and alle men ben schent, that schewen yuelis to thi seruauntis; be thei schent in all thi miyt, and the strengthe of hem be al to-brokun;

45 and thei schulen wite, that thou art the Lord God aloone, and glorious on the roundnesse of londis.

46 And the mynystris of the kyng, that hadden sent hem, ceessiden not to make hoot the furneis with syment, and herdis of flex, and pitche, and siouns of vynes.

47 And the flawme was sched out ouer the furneis bi nyne and fourti cubitis,

48 and brak out, and brente hem that it foond of Caldeis bisidis the furneis.

49 Forsothe the aungel of the Lord cam doun with Asarie and hise felowis, in to the furneis, and smoot out the flawme of the fier fro the furneis;

50 and made the myddis of the furneis as the wynd of deew blowynge; and outerli the fier touchide not hem, nether made sori, nether dide ony thing of disese.

51 Thanne these thre as of o mouth herieden and glorifieden God, and blessiden God in the furneis,

52 and seiden, Lord God of oure fadris, thou art blessid, and worthi to be preisid, and gloriouse, and aboue enhaunsid in to worldis; and blessid is the name of thi glorie, which name is hooli, and worthi to be heried, and aboue enhaunsid in alle worldis.

53 Thou art blessid in the hooli temple of thi glorie, and aboue preisable, and gloriouse in to worldis.

54 Thou art blessid in the trone of thi rewme, and aboue preisable, and aboue enhaunsid in to worldis.

55 Thou art blessid, that biholdist depthis of watris, and sittist on cherubyn, and art preisable, and aboue enhaunsid in to worldis.

56 Thou art blessid in the firmament of heuene, and preisable, and gloriouse in to worldis.

57 Alle werkis of the Lord, blesse ye the Lord, herie ye, and aboue enhaunse ye hym in to worldis.

58 Aungels of the Lord, blesse ye the Lord; herie ye, and aboue enhaunse ye hym in to worldis.

59 Heuenes, blesse ye the Lord; herie ye, and aboue enhaunse ye hym in to worldis.

60 Alle watris, that ben aboue heuenes, blesse ye the Lord; herie ye, and aboue enhaunse ye him into worldis.

61 Alle the vertues of the Lord, blesse ye the Lord; herie ye, and aboue enhaunse ye hym in to worldis.

62 Sunne and moone, blesse ye the Lord; herie ye, and aboue enhaunse ye hym in to worldis.

63 Sterris of heuene, blesse ye the Lord; herie ye, and aboue enhaunse ye hym in to worldis.

64 Reyn and deew, blesse ye the Lord; herie ye, and aboue enhaunse ye hym in to worldis.

65 Ech spirit of God, blesse ye the Lord; herie ye, and aboue enhaunse ye hym in to worldis.

66 Fier and heete, blesse ye the Lord; herie ye, and aboue enhaunse ye hym in to worldis.

67 Coold and somer, blesse ye the Lord; herie ye, and aboue enhaunse ye hym in to worldis.

68 Dewis and whijt forst, blesse ye the Lord; herie ye, and aboue enhaunse ye hym in to worldis.

69 Blac forst and coold, blesse ye the Lord; herie ye, and aboue enhaunse ye hym in to worldis.

70 Yces and snowis, blesse ye the Lord; herie ye, and aboue enhaunse ye hym in to worldis.

71 Niytis and daies, blesse ye the Lord; herie ye, and aboue enhaunse ye hym in to worldis.

72 Liyt and derknesse, blesse ye the Lord; herie ye, and aboue enhaunse ye hym in to worldis.

73 Leitis and cloudis, blesse ye the Lord; herie ye, and aboue enhaunse ye hym in to worldis.

74 The erthe blesse the Lord; herie it, and aboue enhaunse it hym in to worldis.

75 Mounteyns and litle hillis, blesse ye the Lord; herie ye, and aboue enhaunse ye hym in to worldis.

76 Alle buriownynge thingis in erthe, blesse ye the Lord; herie ye, and aboue enhaunse ye hym in to worldis.

77 Wellis, blesse ye the Lord; herie ye, and aboue enhaunse ye hym in to worldis.

78 Sees and floodis, blesse ye the Lord; herie ye, and aboue enhaunse ye hym in to worldis.

79 Whallis, and alle thingis that ben mouyd in watris, blesse ye the Lord; herie ye, and aboue enhaunse ye hym in to worldis.

80 Alle briddis of the eyr, blesse ye the Lord; herie ye, and aboue enhaunse ye hym in to worldis.

81 Alle wielde beestis and tame beestis, blesse ye the Lord; herie ye, and aboue enhaunse ye hym in to worldis.

82 Sones of men, blesse ye the Lord; herie ye, and aboue enhaunse ye hym in to worldis.

83 Israel blesse the Lord; herie it, and aboue enhaunse it hym in to worldis.

84 Prestis of the Lord, blesse ye the Lord; herie ye, and aboue enhaunse ye hym in to worldis.

85 Seruauntis of the Lord, blesse ye the Lord; herie ye, and aboue enhaunse ye hym in to worldis.

86 Spiritis and soulis of iust men, blesse ye the Lord; herie ye, and aboue enhaunse ye hym in to worldis.

87 Hooli men and meke of herte, blesse ye the Lord; herie ye, and aboue enhaunse ye hym in to worldis.

88 Ananye, Azarie, Mysael, blesse ye the Lord; herie ye, and aboue enhaunse ye hym in to worldis. Which Lord rauyschide vs fro helle, and 'made saaf fro the hond of deth, and delyueride fro the myddis of flawme brennynge, and rauyschide vs fro the myddis of fier.

89 Knowleche ye to the Lord, for he is good; for his merci is in to the world.

90 Alle religiouse men, blesse ye the Lord, God of goddis; herie ye, and knouleche ye to hym, for his merci is in to alle worldis.

91 Thanne kyng Nabugodonosor was astonyed, and roos hastily, and seide to hise beste men, Whether we senten not thre men feterid in to the myddis of the fier? Whiche answeriden the kyng, and seiden, Verili, kyng.

92 The kyng answeride, and seide, Lo! Y se foure men vnboundun, and goynge in the myddis of the fier, and no thing of corrupcioun is in hem; and the licnesse of the fourthe is lijk the sone of God.

93 Thanne the kyng Nabugodonosor neiyide to the dore of the furneis of fier brennynge, and seide, Sidrac, Mysaac, and Abdenago, the seruauntis of hiy God lyuynge, go ye out, and come ye. And anoon Sidrac, Mysaac, and Abdenago, yeden out of the myddis of the fier.

94 And the wise men, and magistratis, and iugis, and miyti men of the kyng, weren gaderid togidere, and bihelden tho men, for the fier hadde had no thing of power in the bodies of hem, and an heer of her heed was not brent; also the breechis of hem weren not chaungid, and the odour of fier hadde not passid bi hem.

95 And Nabugodonosor brac out, and seide, Blessid be the God of hem, that is, of Sidrac, Mysaac, and Abdenago, that sente his aungel, and delyueride hise seruauntis, that bileuyden in to hym, and chaungiden the word of the kyng, and yauen her bodies, that thei schulden not serue, and that thei schulden not worschipe ony god, outakun her God aloone.

96 Therfor this decree is set of me, that ech puple, and langagis, and lynagis, who euer spekith blasfemye ayen God of Sidrac, and of Mysaac, and of Abdenago, perische, and his hous be distried; for noon other is God, that mai saue so.

97 Thanne the kyng auaunside Sidrac, Mysaac, and Abdenago, in the prouynce of Babiloyne; and sente in to al the lond a pistle, conteynynge these wordis.

CAP 4

98 Nabugodonosor, the kyng, writith thus to alle puplis and langagis, that dwellen in al erthe, pees be multiplied to you.

99 Hiy God made at me myraclis and merueils;

100 therfor it pleside me to preche hise myraclis, for tho ben greet, and hise merueils, for tho ben stronge; and his rewme is an euerlastynge rewme, and his power is in generacioun and in to generacioun.

1 I, Nabugodonosor, was restful in myn hous, and flourynge in my paleis;

2 Y siy a dreem, that made me aferd; and my thouytis in my bed, and the siytis of myn heed disturbliden me.

3 And a decre was set forth bi me, that alle the wise men of Babiloyne schulden be brouyt in bifor my siyt, and that thei schulden schewe to me the soilyng of the dreem.

4 Than false dyuynours, astronomyens, Caldeis, and biholderis of auteris entriden; and Y telde the dreem in the siyt of hem, and thei schewiden not to me the soilyng therof, til the felowe in office,

5 Danyel, to whom the name was Balthasar, bi the name of my God, entride in my siyt, which Danyel hath the spirit of hooli goddis in hym silf; and Y spak the dreem bifor hym.

6 Balthasar, prince of dyuynouris, whom Y knowe, that thou hast in thee the spirit of hooli goddis, and ech sacrament, ether preuytee, is not vnpossible to thee, telle thou to me the visiouns of my dreemes, whiche Y siy, and the soilyng of tho.

7 This is the visioun of myn heed in my bed. Y siy, and lo! a tree was in the myddis of erthe, and the hiynesse therof was ful greet.

8 And the tree was greet and strong, and the heiythe therof touchide heuene, and the biholdynge therof was 'til to the endis of al erthe.

9 The leeuys therof weren ful faire, and the fruyt therof was ful myche, and the mete of alle was in it; beestis and wielde beestis dwelliden vndur it, and briddis of the eir lyuyden in the braunchis therof, and ech man ete of it.

10 Thus Y siy in the visioun of myn heed, on my bed. And lo! a wakere, and hooli man cam doun fro heuene,

11 and he criede strongli, and seide thus, Hewe ye doun the tree, and kitte ye doun the bowis therof, and schake ye awei the leeuys therof, and scatere ye abrood the fruytis therof; beestis fle awei, that be vndur it, and briddis fro the bowis therof.

12 Netheles suffre ye the seed of rootis therof in erthe, and be he boondun with a boond of irun and of bras, in erbis that ben with out forth, and in the deew of heuene be he died, and his part be with wielde beestis in the erbe of erthe.

13 His herte be chaungid fro mannus herte, and the herte of a wielde beeste be youun to hym, and seuene tymes be chaungid on hym.

14 In the sentence of wakeris it is demed, and it is the word and axyng of seyntis, til lyuynge men knowe, that hiy God is Lord in the rewme of men; and he schal yyue it to whom euere he wole, and he schal ordeyne on it the mekeste man.

15 Y, Nabugodonosor, the kyng, siy this dreem. Therfor thou, Balthasar, telle hastili the interpretyng, for alle the wise men

of my rewme moun not seie to me the soilyng; but thou maist, for the spirit of hooli goddis is in thee.

16 Thanne Danyel, to whom the name was Balthasar, began to thenke priueli with ynne hym silf, as in oon our, and hise thouytis disturbliden hym. Forsothe the kyng answeride, and seide, Balthasar, the dreem and the interpretyng therof disturble not thee. Balthasar answeride, and seide, My lord, the dreem be to hem that haten thee, and the interpretyng therof be to thin enemyes.

17 The tree which thou siyest hiy and strong, whos heiythe stretchith 'til to heuene, and the biholdyng therof in to ech lond,

18 and the faireste braunchis therof, and the fruyt therof ful myche, and the mete of alle in it, and beestis of the feeld dwellynge vndur it, and the briddis of the eir dwellynge in the boowis therof,

19 thou art, kyng, that art magnefied, and wexidist strong, and thi greetnesse encreesside, and cam 'til to heuene, and thi power in to the endis of al erthe.

20 Sotheli that the kyng siy a wakere and hooli come doun fro heuene, and seie, Hewe ye doun the tree, and distrie ye it, netheles leeue ye the seed of rootis therof in erthe, and be he boundun with irun and bras, in erbis with out forth, and be he bispreynt with the deew of heuene, and his mete be with wielde beestis, til seuene tymes be chaungid on hym;

21 this is the interpretyng of the sentence of the hiyeste, which sentence is comun on my lord, the kyng.

22 Thei schulen caste thee out fro men, and thi dwellyng schal be with beestys and wielde beestis, and thou schalt ete hey, as an oxe doith, but also thou schalt be bisched with the dew of heuene, also seuene tymes schulen be chaungid on thee, til thou knowe, that hiy God is Lord 'on the rewme of men, and yyueth it to whom euer he wole.

23 Forsothe that he comaundide, that the seed of rootis therof, that is, of the tree, schulde be left, thi rewme schal dwelle to thee, aftir that thou knowist that the power is of heuene.

24 Wherfor, kyng, my counsel plese thee, and ayenbie thi synnes with almesdedis, and ayenbie thi wickidnessis with mercies of pore men; in hap God schal foryyue thi trespassis.

25 Alle these thingis camen on Nabugodonosor, the kyng.

26 After the ende of twelue monethis he walkide in the halle of Babiloyne;

27 and the kyng answeride, and seide, Whether this is not Babiloyne, the greet citee, which Y bildide in to the hous of rewme, in the miyt of my strengthe, and in the glorie of my fairnesse?

28 Whanne the word was yit in the mouth of the kyng, a vois felle doun fro heuene, Nabugodonosor, kyng, it is seid to thee, Thi rewme is passid fro thee,

29 and thei schulen caste thee out fro men, and thi dwellyng schal be with beestis and wielde beestis; thou schalt ete hey, as an oxe doith, and seuene tymes schulen be chaungid on thee, til thou knowe, that hiy God is Lord in the rewme of men, and yyueth it to whom euere he wole.

30 In the same our the word was fillid on Nabugodonosor, and he was cast out fro men, and he eet hey, as an oxe doith, and his bodi was colouryd with the deew of heuene, til hise heeris wexiden at the licnesse of eglis, and hise nailis as the nailis of briddis.

31 Therfor after the ende of daies, Y, Nabugodonosor, reiside myn iyen to heuene, and my wit was yoldun to me; and Y blesside the hiyeste, and Y heriede, and glorifiede hym that lyueth with outen ende; for whi his power is euerlastynge

power, and his rewme is in generacioun and in to generacioun.

32 And alle the dwelleris of erthe ben arettid in to noyt at hym; for bi his wille he doith, bothe in the vertues of heuene, and in the dwelleris of erthe, and noon is, that ayenstondith his hond, and seith to hym, Whi didist thou so?

33 In that tyme my wit turnede ayen to me, and Y cam fulli to the onour and fairnesse of my rewme, and my figure turnede ayen to me; and my beste men and my magistratis souyten me, and Y was set in my rewme, and my greet doyng was encreessid grettir to me.

34 Now therfor Y Nabugodonosor herie, and magnefie, and glorifie the kyng of heuene; for alle hise werkis ben trewe, and alle his weies ben domes; and he may make meke hem that goon in pride.

CAP 5

1 Balthasar, the kyng, made a greet feeste to hise beste men a thousynde, and ech man drank aftir his age.

2 Forsothe the kyng thanne drunkun comaundide, that the goldun and siluerne vessels schulden be brouyt forth, whiche Nabugodonosor, his fadir, hadde borun out of the temple that was in Jerusalem, that the kyng, and hise beste men, hise wyues, and councubyns schulden drynke in tho vessels.

3 Thanne the goldun vessels and siluerne, whiche he hadde borun out of the temple that was in Jerusalem, weren brouyt forth; and the kyng, and hise beste men, and hise wyues, and concubyns, drunken in tho vessels.

4 Thei drunken wyn, and herieden her goddis of gold, and of siluer, of bras, and of irun, and of tree, and of stoon.

5 In the same our fyngris apperiden, as of the hond of a man, writynge ayens the candilstike, in the pleyn part of the wal of the kyngis halle; and the kyng bihelde the fyngris of the hond writynge.

6 Thanne the face of the kyng was chaungid, and hise thouytis disturbliden hym; and the ioyncturis of hise reynes weren loosid, and hise knees weren hurtlid to hem silf togidere.

7 Therfor the kyng criede strongli, that thei schulden brynge yn astronomyens, Caldeis, and dyuynouris bi lokyng of auteris. And the kyng spak, and seide to the wise men of Babiloyne, Who euer redith this scripture, and makith opyn the interpretyng therof to me, schal be clothid in purpur; and he schal haue a goldun bie in the necke, and he schal be the thridde in my rewme.

8 Thanne alle the wise men of the kyng entriden, and miyten not rede the scripture, nether schewe to the kyng the interpretyng therof.

9 Wherof kyng Balthasar was disturblid ynow, and his cheer was chaungid, but also hise beste men weren disturblid.

10 Forsothe the queen entride in to the hous of feeste, for the thing that hadde bifeld to the king, and beste men; and sche spak, and seide, Kyng, lyue thou withouten ende. Thi thouytis disturble not thee, and thi face be not chaungid.

11 A man is in thi rewme, that hath the spirit of hooli goddis in hym silf, and in the daies of thi fadir kunnyng and wisdom weren foundun in hym; for whi and Nabugodonosor, thi fadir, made him prince of astronomyens, of enchaunteris, of Caldeis, and of dyuynouris bi lokyng on auteris; sotheli thi fadir, thou kyng, dide this;

12 for more spirit, and more prudent, and vndurstondyng, and interpretyng of dremes, and schewyng of priuytees, and assoilyng of boundun thingis weren foundun in hym, that is, in Danyel, to whom the kyng puttide the name Balthasar.

Now therfor Daniel be clepid, and he schal telle the interpretyng. Therfor Daniel was brouyt in bifor the kyng. To whom
the forseid kyng seide,

13 Art thou Danyel, of the sones of caitifte of Juda, whom my
fader, the kyng, brouyte fro Judee?

14 Y haue herd of thee, that thou hast in thee the spirit of goddis, and more kunnyng, and vndurstondyng, and wisdom be
foundun in thee.

15 And now wise men, astronomyens, entriden in my siyt, to
rede this scripture, and to schewe to me the interpretyng
therof; and thei myyten not seie to me the vndurstondyng of
this word.

16 Certis Y haue herde of thee, that thou maist interprete derk
thingis, and vnbynde boundun thingis; therfor if thou maist
rede the scripture, and schewe to me the interpretyng therof,
thou schalt be clothid in purpur, and thou schalt haue a goldun bie aboute thi necke, and thou schalt be the thridde prince
in my rewme.

17 To whiche thingis Danyel answeride, and seide bifore the
kyng, Thi yiftis be to thee, and yyue thou to another man the
yiftis of thin hous; forsothe, kyng, Y schal rede the scripture
to thee, and Y schal schewe to thee the interpretyng therof.

18 O! thou kyng, hiyeste God yaf rewme, and greet worschipe, and glorie, and onour, to Nabugodonosor, thi fadir.

19 And for greet worschip which he hadde youe to thilke
Nabugodonosor, alle puplis, lynagis, and langagis, trembliden
and dredden hym; he killide whiche he wolde, and he smoot
whiche he wolde, and he enhaunside whiche he wolde, and
he made low which he wolde.

20 Forsothe whanne his herte was reisid, and his spirit was
maad obstynat in pride, he was put doun of the seete of his
rewme;

21 and his glorie was takun awei, and he was cast out fro the
sones of men; but also his herte was set with beestis, and his
dwellyng was with wielde assis; also he eet hei as an oxe
doith, and his bodi was colourid with the deew of heuene, til
he knewe, that the hiyeste hath power in the rewme of men,
and he schal reise on it whom euer he wole.

22 And thou, Balthasar, the sone of hym, mekidest not thin
herte, whanne thou knewist alle these thingis;

23 but thou were reisid ayens the Lord of heuene, and the vessels of his hous weren brouyt bifore thee, and thou, and thi
beste men, and thi wyues, and thi concubyns, drunken wyn in
tho vessels; and thou heriedist goddis of siluer, and of gold,
and of bras, and of irun, and of tree, and of stoon, that seen
not, nether heren, nether feelen; certis thou glorifiedist not
God, that hath thi blast, and alle thi weies in his hond.

24 Therfor the fyngur of the hond was sent of hym, which
hond wroot this thing that is writun.

25 Sotheli this is the scripture which is discryued, Mane,
Techel, Phares.

26 And this is the interpretyng of the word. Mane, God hath
noumbrid thi rewme, and hath fillid it;

27 Techel, thou art weied in a balaunce, and thou art foundun
hauynge lesse;

28 Phares, thi rewme is departid, and is youun to Medeis and
Perseis.

29 Thanne, for the kyng comaundide, Daniel was clothid in
purpur, and a goldun bie was youun aboute in his necke; and
it was prechid of hym, that he hadde power, and was the
thridde in the rewme.

30 In the same niyt Balthasar, the kyng of Caldeis, was slayn;

31 and Daryus of Medei was successour in to the rewme, and
he was two and sixti yeer eld.

CAP 6

1 It pleside Darius, and he ordeynede sixe score duykis ouer
the rewme, that thei schulden be in al his rewme.

2 And ouer hem he ordeynede thre princes, of whiche Danyel
was oon; that the duykis schulden yelde resoun to hem, and
that the kyng schulde not suffre ony disese.

3 Therfor Danyel ouercam alle the princes and duikis, for
more spirit of God was in hym.

4 Certis the kyng thouyte to ordeyne hym on al the rewme.
Wherfor princes and duikis souyten to fynde occasioun to
Danyel, of the side of the kyng; and thei miyten fynde no
cause and suspicioun, for he was feithful, and no blame and
suspicioun was foundun in hym.

5 Therfor tho men seiden, We schulen not fynde ony occasioun to this Danyel, no but in hap in the lawe of his God.

6 Thanne the princes and duykis maden fals suggestioun to
the kyng, and spaken thus to hym, Kyng Darius, lyue thou
with onten ende.

7 Alle the princes of thi rewme, and magistratis, and duykis,
senatours, and iugis, han maad a counsel, that a decree and
comaundement of the emperour go out, that ech man that
axith ony axyng of what euer god and man, til to thretti daies,
no but of thee, thou kyng, he be sent in to the lake of liouns.

8 Now therfor, kyng, conferme thou the sentence, and write
thou the decree, that this that is ordeyned of Medeis and Perseis be not chaungid, nethir be it leueful to ony man to breke.

9 Forsothe Darius, the kyng, settide forth, and confermyde
the decree.

10 And whanne Danyel hadde founde this thing, that is, the
lawe ordeyned, he entride in to his hous; and the while the
wyndows weren open in his soler ayens Jerusalem, in thre
tymes in the dai he bowide hise knees, and worschipide, and
knoulechide bifore his God, as he was wont to do bifore.

11 Therfor tho men enqueriden ful bisili, and founden
Danyel preiynge, and bisechynge his God.

12 And thei neiyiden and spaken to the kyng of the comaundement, Kyng, whether thou ordeynedist not, that ech man
that axide ony of goddis and of men, til to thretti daies, no but
thee, thou kyng, he schulde be sent in to the lake of liouns?
To whiche men the kyng answeride, and seide, The word is
soth, bi the decree of Medeis and Perseis, which it is not leueful to breke.

13 Thanne thei answeriden, and seiden bifore the kyng,
Danyel, of the sones of caitifte of Juda, reckide not of thi
lawe, and of the comaundement, which thou ordeynedist, but
thre tymes bi the dai he preieth in his bisechyng.

14 And whanne the kyng hadde herd this word, he was sori
ynow, and he settide the herte for Danyel, for to do delyuere
hym; and til to the goyng doun of the sunne he trauelide for to
do delyuere hym.

15 But tho men vndurstoden the kyng, and seiden to hym,
Wite thou, kyng, that it is the lawe of Medeis and of Perseis,
that it is not leueful that ony decree be chaungid,

16 which the kyng ordeyneth. Thanne the kyng comaundide,
and thei brouyten Danyel, and senten hym in to the lake of
liouns. And the kyng seide to Danyel, Thi God, whom thou
worschipist euere, he schal delyuere thee.

17 And o stoon was brouyt, and was put on the mouth of the
lake, which the kyng aselide with his ryng, and with the ryng
of hise beste men, lest ony thing were don ayens Danyel.

18 Thanne the kyng yede in to his hous, and slepte with out soper, and metis weren not brouyte bifore hym; ferthermore and sleep yede awei fro hym.

19 Thanne the kyng roos in the firste morewtid, and yede hastili to the lake of liouns;

20 And he neiyide to the lake, and criede on Danyel with wepynge vois, and spak to hym, Danyel, the seruaunt of God lyuynge, gessist thou, whether thi God, whom thou seruest euere, miyte delyuere thee fro liouns?

21 And Danyel answeride the kyng, and seide, King, lyue thou with outen ende.

22 My God sente his aungel, and closide togidere the mouthis of liouns, and tho noieden not me, for riytfulnesse is foundun in me bifore hym; but also, thou kyng, Y dide no trespas bifore thee.

23 Thanne the kyng made ioie greetli on hym, and comaundide Danyel to be led out of the lake. And Danyel was led out of the lake, and noon hirtyng was foundun in hym, for he bileuede to his God.

24 Forsothe the kyng comaundide, tho men, that accusiden Danyel, weren brouyt, and weren sent in to the lake of liouns, thei, and the sones of hem, and the wyues of hem; and thei camen not 'til to the pawment of the lake, til the liouns rauyschiden hem, and al to-braken alle the boonys of hem.

25 Thanne Darius, the kyng, wroot to alle puplis, lynagis, and langagis, dwellynge in al erthe, Pees be multiplied to you.

26 Therfor a decree is ordeyned of me, that in al myn empire and rewme men tremble, and drede the God of Danyel; for he is God lyuynge, and euerlastynge in to worldis, and his rewme schal not be distried, and his power is 'til in to with outen ende.

27 He is delyuerer and sauyour, makynge myraclis and merueils in heuene and in erthe, which delyuerede Danyel fro the lake of liouns.

28 Certis Danyel dwellide stabli 'til to the rewme of Darius, and 'til to the rewme of Sirus of Persey.

CAP 7

1 In the firste yeer of Balthasar, kyng of Babiloyne, Danyel siy a sweuene. Forsothe he wroot the visioun of his hed in his bed, and the dreem, and comprehendide in schort word; and he touchide schortli the sentence,

2 and seide, Y siy in my visioun in niyt, and lo! foure wyndis of heuene fouyten in the myddis of the greet see.

3 And foure grete beestis dyuerse bitwixe hem silf stieden fro the see.

4 The firste beeste was as a lionesse, and hadde wyngis of an egle. Y bihelde til the wyngis therof weren pullid awei, and it was takun awei fro erthe, and it stood as a man on the feet, and the herte therof was youun to it.

5 And lo! another beeste, lijk a bere in parti, stood, and thre ordris weren in the mouth therof, and thre princes in the teeth therof. And thus thei seiden to it, Rise thou, ete thou ful many fleischis.

6 Aftir these thingis Y bihelde, and lo! anothir beeste as a pard, and it hadde on it silf foure wyngis of a brid, and foure heedis weren in the beeste, and power was youun to it.

7 Aftir these thingis Y bihelde in the visioun of niyt, and lo! the fourthe beeste, ferdful, and wondirful, and ful strong. It hadde grete irun teeth, and it ete, and made lesse, and defoulide with hise feet othere thingis; forsothe it was vnlijk othere beestis, which Y hadde seyn bifore it, and it hadde ten hornes.

8 Y bihelde the hornes, and lo! an other litil horn cam forth of the myddis of tho, and thre of the firste hornes weren drawun out fro the face therof; and lo! iyen as iyen of a man weren in this horn, and a mouth spekynge grete thingis.

9 Y bihelde, til that trones weren set, and the elde of daies sat; his cloth was whijt as snow, and the heeris of his heed weren as cleene wolle, his trone was as flawmes of fier, hise wheelis weren fier kyndlid.

10 A flood of fier and rennynge faste yede out fro his face, a thousynde thousynde mynistriden to hym, and ten sithis a thousynde sithis an hundrid thousynde stoden niy hym; the dom sat, and bookis weren opened.

11 Y bihelde for the vois of grete wordis whiche thilke horn spak; and Y siy that the beeste was slayn, and his bodi was perischid, and was youun to be brent in fier.

12 And Y siy that the power of othere beestis was takun awei, and the tymes of lijf weren ordeyned to hem, til to tyme and tyme.

13 Therfor Y bihelde in the visyoun of niyt, and lo! as a sone of man cam with the cloudis of heuene; and he cam fulli til to the elde of daies, and in the siyt of hym thei offriden hym.

14 And he yaf to hym power, and onour, and rewme, and alle the puplis, lynagis, and langagis schulen serue hym; his power is euerlastynge power, that schal not be takun awei, and his rewme, that schal not be corrupt.

15 My spirit hadde orrour, ether hidousnesse; Y, Danyel, was aferd in these thingis, and the siytis of myn heed disturbliden me.

16 Y neiyede to oon of the stonderis niy, and Y axide of hym the treuthe of alle these thingis. And he seide to me the interpretyng of wordis, and he tauyte me.

17 These foure grete beestis ben foure rewmes, that schulen rise of erthe.

18 Forsothe hooli men schulen take the rewme of hiyeste God, and thei schulen holde the rewme, til in to the world, and 'til in to the world of worldis.

19 Aftir these thingis Y wolde lerne diligentli of the fourthe beeste, that was greetli vnlijk fro alle, and was ful ferdful, the teeth and nailis therof weren of irun; it eet, and made lesse, and defoulide with hise feet othere thingis.

20 And of ten hornes whiche it hadde in the heed, and of the tother horn, that cam forth, bifore which thre hornes fellen doun, and of that horn that hadde iyen, and a mouth spekynge grete thingis, and was grettere than othere;

21 I bihelde, and lo! thilke horn made batel ayens hooli men, and hadde maistrie of hem,

22 til the elde of daies cam, and hiy God yaf doom to hooli men; and lo! tyme cam, and hooli men goten rewme.

23 And he seide thus, The fourthe beeste schal be the fourthe rewme in erthe, that schal be more than alle rewmes, and it schal deuoure al erthe, and it schal defoule, and make lesse that erthe.

24 Forsothe ten hornes schulen be ten kyngis of that rewme; and another kyng schal rise after hem, and he schal be miytiere than the formere, and he schal make low thre kyngis.

25 And he schal speke wordis ayens the hiy God, and he schal defoule the seyntis of the hiyeste; and he schal gesse, that he mai chaunge tymes and lawis; and thei schulen be youun in to his hondis, til to tyme, and times, and the half of tyme.

26 And doom schal sitte, that the power be takun awei, and be al to-brokun, and perische til in to the ende.

27 Sotheli that the rewme, and power, and the greetnesse of rewme, which is vndur ech heuene, be youun to the puple of

the seintis of the hiyeste, whos rewme is euerlastynge rewme, and alle kingis schulen serue, and obeie to hym.

28 Hidur to is the ende of the word. Y, Danyel, was disturblid myche in my thouytis, and my face was chaungid in me; forsothe Y kepte the word in myn herte.

CAP 8

1 In the thridde yeer of the rewme of Balthasar, the king, a visioun apperide to me. Y, Danyel, after that thing that Y hadde seyn in the bigynnyng,

2 siy in my visioun, whanne Y was in the castel of Susis, which is in the cuntrei of Helam; sotheli Y siy in the visioun that Y was on the yate Vlay.

3 And Y reiside myn iyen, and Y siy; and lo! o ram stood bifor the mareis, and hadde hiy hornes, and oon hiyere than the tother, and vndurwexynge.

4 Aftirward Y siy the ram wyndewynge with hornes ayens the eest, and ayens the west, and ayens the north, and ayens the south; and alle beestis myyten not ayenstonde it, nether be delyuered fro the hondis of it. And it dide bi his wille, and was magnefied.

5 And Y vndurstood. Lo! forsothe a buk of geet cam fro the west on the face of al erthe, and touchide not the erthe; forsothe the buk of geet hadde a noble horn bitwixe hise iyen;

6 and he cam til to that horned ram, which Y hadde seyn stondynge bifore the yate, and he ran in the fersnesse of his strengthe to that ram.

7 And whanne he hadde neiyid niy the ram, he hurlide fersly on hym, and he smoot the ram, and al to-brak tweyne hornes of hym, and the ram miyte not ayenstonde hym. And whanne he hadde sent that ram in to erthe, he defoulide; and no man miyte delyuere the ram fro his hond.

8 Forsothe the buk of geet was maad ful greet; and whanne he hadde encreessid, the greet horn was brokun, and foure hornes risiden vndur it, bi foure wyndis of heuene.

9 Forsothe of oon of hem yede out o litil horn, and it was maad greet ayens the south, and ayens the eest, and ayens the strengthe.

10 And it was magnefied til to the strengthe of heuene, and it castide doun of the strengthe and of sterris, and defoulide tho.

11 And he was magnefied til to the prince of strengthe, and he took awei fro hym the contynuel sacrifice, and castide doun the place of his halewyng.

12 Forsothe strengthe was youun to hym ayens the contynuel sacrifice for synnes, and treuthe schal be cast doun in erthe; and he schal haue prosperite, and schal do.

13 And Y herde oon of hooli aungels spekynge; and oon hooli aungel seide to another, Y noot to whom spekinge, Hou long the visioun, and the contynuel sacrifice, and the synne of desolacioun, which is maad, and the seyntuarie, and the strengthe schal be defoulid?

14 And he seide to hym, Til to the euentid and morewtid, two thousynde daies and thre hundrid; and the seyntuarie schal be clensid.

15 Forsothe it was doon, whanne Y, Danyel, siy the visioun, and axide the vndurstondyng, lo! as the licnesse of a man stood in my siyt.

16 And Y herde the voys of a man bitwixe Vlai, and he criede, and seide, Gabriel, make thou Danyel to vndurstonde this visioun.

17 And he cam, and stood bisidis where Y stood; and whanne he was comun, Y dredde, and felle on my face. And

he seide to me, Thou, sone of man, vndurstonde, for the visioun schal be fillid in the tyme of ende.

18 And whanne he spak to me, Y slood doun 'plat to the erthe. And he touchide me, and settide me in my degree.

19 And he seide to me, Y schal schewe to thee what thingis schulen come in the laste of cursing, for the tyme hath his ende.

20 The ram, whom thou siyest haue hornes, is the kyng of Medeis and of Perseis.

21 Forsothe the buc of geet is the kyng of Grekis; and the greet horn that was bitwixe hise iyen, he is the firste kyng.

22 Forsothe that whanne that horn was brokun, foure hornes risiden for it, foure kyngis schulen rise of the folc of hym, but not in the strengthe of hym.

23 And after the rewme of hem, whanne 'wickidnessis han encreessid, a kyng schal rise vnschamefast in face, and vndurstondyng proposisiouns, ether resouns set forth; and his strengthe schal be maad stalworthe,

24 but not in hise strengthis. And more than it mai be bileuyd he schal waste alle thingis, and he schal haue prosperite, and schal do. And he schal sle stronge men, and the puple of seyntis,

25 bi his wille, and gile schal be dressid in his hond. And he schal magnefie his herte, and in abundaunce of alle thingis he schal sle ful many men. And he schal rise ayens the prince of princes, and withouten hond he schal be al to-brokun.

26 And the visioun, which is seid in the morewtid and euentid, is trewe. Therfor seele thou the visioun, for it schal be after many daies.

27 And Y, Danyel, was astonyed, and was sijk bi ful many daies; and whanne Y hadde rise, Y dide the werkis of the kyng; and Y was astonyed at the visioun, and 'noon was that interpretide.

CAP 9

1 In the firste yeer of Darius, the sone of Assuerus, of the seed of Medeis, that was emperour on the rewme of Caldeis,

2 in the firste yeer of his rewme, Y, Danyel, vndurstood in bookis the noumbre of yeeris, of which noumbre the word of the Lord was maad to Jeremye, the profete, that seuenti yeer of desolacioun of Jerusalem schulde be fillid.

3 And Y settide my face to my Lord God, to preie and to biseche in fastyngis, in sak, and aische.

4 And Y preiede my Lord God, and Y knoulechide, and seide, Y biseche, thou Lord God, greet and ferdful, kepynge couenaunt and mercy to hem that louen thee, and kepen thi comaundementis.

5 We han synned, we han do wickidnesse, we diden unfeithfuli, and yeden awei, and bowiden awei fro thi comaundementis and domes.

6 We obeieden not to thi seruauntis, profetis, that spaken in thi name to oure kyngis, to oure princes, and to oure fadris, and to al the puple of the lond.

7 Lord, riytfulnesse is to thee, forsothe schenschipe of face is to vs, as is to dai to a man of Juda, and to the dwelleris of Jerusalem, and to al Israel, to these men that ben niy, and to these men that ben afer in alle londis, to which thou castidist hem out for the wickidnessis of hem, in whiche, Lord, thei synneden ayens thee.

8 Schame of face is to vs, to oure kyngis, to oure princes, and to oure fadris, that synneden;

9 but merci and benygnytee is to thee, oure Lord God. For we yeden awei fro thee,

10 and herden not the vois of oure Lord God, that we schulden go in the lawe of hym, whiche he settide to vs bi hise seruauntis, profetis.

11 And al Israel braken thi lawe, and bowiden awei, that thei herden not thi vois; and cursyng, and wlatyng, which is writun in the book of Moises, the seruaunt of God, droppide on vs, for we synneden to hym.

12 And he ordeynede hise wordis, whiche he spak on vs, and on oure princes, that demyden vs, that thei schulden brynge in on vs greet yuel, what maner yuel was neuer vndur al heuene, bi that that is doon in Jerusalem,

13 as it is writun in the lawe of Moises. Al this yuel cam on vs, and, oure Lord God, we preieden not thi face, that we schulden turne ayen fro oure wickidnessis, and schulden thenke thi treuthe.

14 And the Lord wakide on malice, and brouyt it on vs; oure Lord God is iust in alle his werkis whiche he made, for we herden not his vois.

15 And now, Lord God, that leddist thi puple out of the lond of Egipt in strong hond, and madist to thee a name bi this dai, we han synnede,

16 we han do wickidnesse, Lord, ayens thi riytfulnesse. Y biseche, thi wraththe and thi stronge veniaunce be turned awey fro thi citee Jerusalem, and fro thi hooli hil; for whi for oure synnes, and for the wickidnessis of oure fadris, Jerusalem and thi puple ben in schenschipe, to alle men bi oure cumpas.

17 But now, oure God, here thou the preyer of thi seruaunt, and the bisechyngis of him, and schewe thi face on thi seyntuarie, which is forsakun.

18 My God, for thi silf boowe doun thin eere, and here; opene thin iyen, and se oure desolacioun, and the citee, on which thi name is clepid to help. For not in oure iustifiyngis we setten forth mekeli preiers bifor thi face, but in thi many merciful doyngis.

19 Lord, here thou; Lord, be thou plesid, perseyue thou, and do; my Lord God, tarie thou not, for thi silf, for thi name is clepid to help on the citee, and on thi puple.

20 And whanne Y spak yit, and preiede, and knoulechide my synnes, and the synnes of my puple Israel, that Y schulde sette forth mekeli my preieris in the siyt of my God, for the hooli hil of my God,

21 the while Y spak yit in my preyer, lo! the man Gabriel, whom Y hadde seyn in visioun at the bigynnyng, flei soone, and touchide me in the tyme of euentid sacrifice;

22 and he tauyt me, and he spak to me, and seide, Danyel, now Y yede out, that Y schulde teche thee, and thou schuldist vndurstonde.

23 Fro the bigynnyng of thi preieris a word yede out. Forsothe Y cam to schewe to thee, for thou art a man of desiris; therfor perseyue thou the word, and vndurstonde thou the visioun.

24 Seuenti woukis of yeeris ben abreggid on thi puple, and on thin hooli citee, that trespassyng be endid, and synne take an ende, and that wickidnesse be doon awei, and euerlastynge riytfulnesse be brouyt, and that the visioun, and prophesie be fillid, and the hooli of seyntis be anoyntid.

25 Therfor wite thou, and perseyue; fro the goyng out of the word, that Jerusalem be bildid eft, til to Crist, the duyk, schulen be seuene woukis of yeeris and two and sixti woukis of yeeris; and eft the street schal be bildid, and wallis, in the angwisch of tymes.

26 And after two and sixti woukis 'of yeeris Crist schal be slayn. And it schal not be his puple, that schal denye hym. And the puple with the duyk to comynge schal distrie the citee, and the seyntuarie; and the ende therof schal be distriyng, and after the ende of batel schal be ordeynede desolacioun.

27 Forsothe o wouk 'of yeeris schal conferme the couenaunt to many men, and the offryng and sacrifice schal faile in the myddis of the wouke of yeeris; and abhomynacioun of desolacioun schal be in the temple, and the desolacioun schal contynue til to the parformyng and ende.

CAP 10

1 In the thridde yeer of the rewme of Sirus, kyng of Perseis, a word was schewid to Danyel, Balthasar bi name; and a trewe word, and greet strengthe, and he vndurstood the word; for whi vndurstondyng is nedeful in visioun.

2 In tho daies Y, Danyel, mourenyde bi the daies of thre woukis;

3 Y eet not desirable breed, and fleisch, and wyn entride not into my mouth, but nethir Y was anoynted with oynement, til the daies of thre woukis weren fillid.

4 Forsothe in the foure and twentithe dai of the firste monethe, Y was bisidis the greet flood, which is Tigris.

5 And Y reiside myn iyen, and Y siy, and lo! o man was clothid with lynun clothis, and hise reynes weren gird with schynynge gold;

6 and his bodi was as crisolitus, and his face was as the licnesse of leit, and hise iyen weren as a brennynge laumpe, and hise armes and tho thingis that weren bynethe til to the feet weren as the licnesse of bras beynge whijt, and the vois of hise wordis was as the vois of multitude.

7 Forsothe Y, Danyel, aloone siy the visioun; certis the men that weren with me, sien not, but ful greet ferdfulnesse felle yn on hem, and thei fledden in to an hid place.

8 But Y was left aloone, and Y siy this greet visioun, and strengthe dwellide not in me; but also my licnesse was chaungid in me, and Y was stark, and Y hadde not in me ony thing of strengthis.

9 And Y herde the vois of hise wordis, and Y herde, and lay astonyed on my face, and my face cleuyde to the erthe.

10 And lo! an hond touchide me, and reiside me on my knees, and on the toes of my feet.

11 And he seide to me, Thou, Danyel, a man of desiris, vndurstonde the wordis whiche Y speke to thee, and stonde in thi degree; for now Y am sent to thee. And whanne he hadde seid this word to me, Y stood quakynge.

12 And he seide to me, Danyel, nyle thou drede, for fro the firste dai in which thou settidist thin herte to vndurstonde, that thou schuldist turmente thee in the siyt of thi God, thi wordis weren herd, and Y cam for thi wordis.

13 Forsothe the prince of the rewme of Perseis ayenstood me oon and twenti daies, and lo! Myyhel, oon of the firste princes, cam in to myn help, and Y dwellide stille there bisidis the kyng of Perseis.

14 Forsothe Y am comun to teche thee, what thingis schulen come to thi puple in the laste daies; for yit the visioun is delaied in to daies.

15 And whanne he spak to me bi siche wordis, Y castide doun my cheer to erthe, and was stille.

16 And lo! as the licnesse of sone of man touchide my lippis; and Y openyde my mouth, and spak, and seide to hym that

stood bifore me, My Lord, in thi siyt my ioynctis ben vnknit, and no thing of strengthis dwellide in me.

17 And hou schal the seruaunt of my Lord mow speke with my Lord? no thing of strengthis dwellide in me, but also my breeth is closyde bitwixe.

18 Therfor eft as the siyt of a man touchide me, and coumfortide me,

19 and seide, Man of desiris, nyle thou drede; pees be to thee, be thou coumfortid, and be thou strong. And whanne he spak with me, Y wexide strong and seide, My Lord, speke thou, for thou hast coumfortid me.

20 And he seide, Whether thou woost not, whi Y cam to thee? And now Y schal turne ayen, to fiyte ayens the prince of Perseis. For whanne Y yede out, the prince of Grekis apperide comynge.

21 Netheles Y schal telle to thee that, that is expressid in the scripture of treuthe; and noon is myn helpere in alle these thingis, no but Myyhel, youre prynce.

CAP 11

1 Forsothe fro the firste yeer of Darius of Medei Y stood, that he schulde be coumfortid, and maad strong.

2 And now Y schal telle to thee the treuthe. And lo! thre kyngis schulen stonde yit in Persis, and the fourthe schal be maad riche with ful many richessis ouer alle. And whanne he hath woxe strong bi hise richessis, he schal reise alle men ayens the rewme of Greece.

3 Forsothe a strong kyng schal rise, and shal be lord in greet power, and schal do that, that schal plese hym.

4 And whanne he schal stonde, his rewme schal be al tobrokun, and it schal be departid in to foure wyndis of heuene, but not in to hise eiris, nether bi the power of hym in which he was lord; for his rewme schal be to-rente, yhe, in to straungeris, outakun these.

5 And the kyng of the south schal be coumfortid; and of the princes of hym oon schal haue power aboue hym, and he schal be lord in power; for whi his lordschipe schal be myche.

6 And after the ende of yeeris 'thei schulen be knyt in pees; and the douyter of the kyng of the south schal come to the kyng of the north, to make frenschipe. And sche schal not gete strengthe of arm, nether the seed of hir schal stonde; and sche schal be bitakun, and the yonglyngis of hir that brouyten hir, and he that coumfortide hir in tymes.

7 And a plauntyng of the seed of the rootis of hir schal stonde; and he schal come with an oost, and schal entre in to the prouynce of the kyng of the north, and he schal mysuse hem, and he schal gete;

8 ferthir more he schal gete both the goddis of hem, and grauun ymagis. Also he schal lede into Egipt precious vessels of gold, and of siluer, takun in batel. He schal haue the maistrie ayens the kyng of the north;

9 And the kyng of the south schal entre in to the rewme, and schal turne ayen to his lond.

10 Forsothe the sones of hym schulen be stirid to wraththe, and thei schulen gadere togidere a multitude of ful many coostis. And he schal come hastynge and flowynge, and he schal turne ayen, and schal be stirid, and schal bigynne batel with his strengthe.

11 And the king of the south schal be stirid, and schal go out, and schal fiyte ayens the kyng of the north, and schal make redi a ful grete multitude; and the multitude schal be youun in his hond.

12 And he schal take the multitude, and his herte schal be enhaunsid; and he schal caste doun many thousyndis, but he schal not haue the maistrie.

13 For the kyng of the north schal turne, and schal make redi a multitude, myche more than bifore; and in the ende of tymes and of yeeris he schal come hastynge with a ful greet oost, and with ful many richessis.

14 And in tho tymes many men schulen rise togidere ayens the kyng of the south; and the sones of trespassouris of thi puple schulen be enhaunsid, that thei fille the visioun, and thei schulen falle doun.

15 And the kyng of the north schal come, and schal bere togidere erthe, he schal take strongeste citees; and the armes of the south schulen not susteyne. And the chosun men therof schulen rise togidere, to ayenstonde, and strengthe schal not be.

16 And he schal come on hym, and schal do bi his wille; and noon schal be, that schal stonde ayens his face. And he schal stonde in the noble lond, and it schal be wastid in his hond.

17 And he schal sette his face, that he come to holde al the rewme of him, and he schal do riytful thingis with hym. And he schal yyue to hym the douyter of wymmen, to distrie hym; and it schal not stonde, and it schal not be his.

18 And he schal turne his face to ilis, and he schal take many ilis. And he schal make ceesse the prince of his schenschipe, and his schenschipe schal turne in to hym.

19 And he schal turne his face to the lordschip of his loond, and he schal snapere, and falle doun, and he schal not be foundun.

20 And the vilest and vnworthi to the kyngis onour schal stonde in the place of hym, and in fewe daies he schal be al to-brokun, not in woodnesse, nether in batel.

21 And a dispisid man schal stonde in the place of hym, and the onour of a kyng schal not be youun to hym; and he schal come priueli, and he schal gete the rewme bi gile.

22 And the armes of the fiytere schulen be ouercomun of his face, and schulen be al to-brokun, ferthermore and the duyk of boond of pees.

23 And after frenschipe with hym, he schal do gile. And he schal stie, and he schal ouercome with litil puple;

24 and he schal entre in to grete and riche citees, and he schal do thingis which hise fadris and the fadris of hise fadris diden not. He schal distrie the raueyns, and prei, and richessis of hem, and ayens most stidfast thouytis he schal take counsel, and this 'vn to a tyme.

25 And the strengthe of hym, and the herte of hym schal be stirid ayens the kyng of the south with a greet oost. And the king of the south schal be stirid to batel with many helpis and ful stronge; and thei schulen not stonde, for thei schulen take counsels ayens hym.

26 And thei that eeten breed with hym schulen al to-breke hym; and his oost schal be oppressid, and ful many men of hise schulen be slayn, and falle doun.

27 And the herte of twei kyngis schal be, that thei do yuel, and at o boord thei schulen speke leesyng, and thei schulen not profite; for yit the ende schal be in to an other tyme.

28 And he schal turne ayen in to his lond with many richessis, and his herte schal be ayens the hooli testament, and he schal do, and schal turne ayen in to his lond.

29 In tyme ordeyned he schal turne ayen, and schal come to the south, and the laste schal not be lijk the formere.

30 And schippis with three ordris of ooris, and Romayns, schulen come on hym, and he schal be smytun. And he schal

turne ayen, and schal haue indignacioun ayens the testament of seyntuarie, and he schal do. And he schal turne ayen, and he schal thenke ayens hem that forsoken the testament of seyntuarie.

31 And armes of hym schulen stonde, and schulen defoule the seyntuarie, and schulen take awei the contynuel sacrifice, and schulen yyue abhomynacioun in to desolacioun.

32 And wickid men schulen feyne testament gilefuli; but the puple that knowith her God schal holde, and do.

33 And tauyt men in the puple schulen teche ful many men, and schulen falle in swerd, and in flawme, and in to caitifte, and in to raueyn of daies.

34 And whanne thei han feld doun, thei schulen be reisid bi a litil help; and ful many men schulen be applied to hym gilefuli.

35 And of lerud men schulen falle, that thei be wellid togidere, and be chosun, and be maad whijt til to a tyme determyned; for yit another tyme schal be.

36 And the kyng schal do bi his wille, and he schal be reisid, and magnefied ayens ech god, and ayens God of goddis he schal speke grete thingis; and he schal be dressid, til wrathfulnesse be fillid. For the determynynge is perfitli maad.

37 And he schal not arette the God of hise fadris, and he schal be in the coueitisis of wymmen, and he schal not charge ony of goddis, for he schal rise ayens alle thingis.

38 Forsothe he schal onoure god of Maosym in his place, and he schal worschipe god, whom hise fadris knewen not, with gold, and siluer, and preciouse stoon, and precious thingis.

39 And he schal do that he make strong Moosym, with the alien god which he knew. And he schal multiplie glorie, and schal yyue power to hem in many thingis, and schal departe the lond at his wille.

40 And in the tyme determyned the kyng of the south schal fiyte ayens hym, and the kyng of the north schal come as a tempest ayens hym, in charis, and with knyytis, and in greet nauei.

41 And he schal entre in to londis, and schal defoule hem; and he schal passe, and schal entre in to the gloriouse lond, and many schulen falle. Forsothe these londis aloone schulen be sauyd fro his hond, Edom, and Moab, and princes of the sones of Amon.

42 And he schal sende his hond in to londis, and the lond of Egipt schal not ascape.

43 And he schal be lord of tresouris of gold, and of siluer, and in alle preciouse thingis of Egipt; also he schal passe bi Libie and Ethiopie.

44 And fame fro the eest and fro the north schal disturble hym; and he schal come with a greet multitude, to al to-breke, and to sle ful many men.

45 And he schal sette his tabernacle in Apheduo, bitwixe the sees, on the noble hil and hooli; and he schal come til to the heiythe therof, and no man schal helpe hym.

CAP 12

1 Forsothe in that tyme Miyhel, the greet prince, schal rise, that stondith for the sones of thi puple. And tyme schal come, what maner tyme was not, fro that tyme fro which folkis bigunnen to be, 'vn to that tyme. And in that tyme thi puple schal be saüed, ech that is foundun writun in the book of life.

2 And many of hem that slepen in the dust of erthe, schulen awake fulli, summe in to euerlastynge lijf, and othere in to schenschipe, that thei se euere.

3 Forsothe thei that ben tauyt, schulen schyne as the schynyng of the firmament, and thei that techen many men to riytfulnesse, schulen schyne as sterris in to euerlastynge euerlastyngnessis.

4 But thou, Danyel, close the wordis, and aseele the book, til to the tyme ordeyned; ful many men schulen passe, and kunnyng schal be many fold.

5 And Y, Danyel, siy, and lo! as tweyne othere men stood; oon stood on this side, on the brenk of the flood, and another on that side, on the tother part of the flood.

6 And Y seide to the man, that was clothid in lynnun clothis, that stood on the watris of the flood, Hou long schal be the ende of these merueils?

7 And Y herde the man, that was clothid in lynnun clothis, that stood on the watris of the flood, whanne he hadde reisid his riythond and lefthond to heuene, and hadde sworun by hym that lyueth with outen ende, For in to a tyme, and tymes, and the half of tyme. And whanne the scateryng of the hoond of the hooli puple is fillid, alle these thingis schulen be fillid.

8 And Y herde, and vndurstood not; and Y seide, My lord, what schal be aftir these thingis?

9 And he seide, Go thou, Danyel, for the wordis ben closid and aseelid, til to the tyme determyned.

10 Many men schulen be chosun, and schulen be maad whijt, and schulen be preued as fier, and wickid men schulen do wickidli, nether alle wickid men schulen vndurstonde; certis tauyt men schulen vndurstonde.

11 And fro the tyme whanne contynuel sacrifice is takun awei, and abhomynacioun is set in to discoumfort, schulen be a thousynde daies two hundrid and nynti.

12 He is blessid, that abideth, and cometh fulli, til a thousynde daies thre hundrid and fyue and thritti.

13 But go thou, Danyel, to the tyme determyned; and thou schalt reste, and stonde in thi part, in the ende of daies.

CAP 13

1 A man was in Babiloyne, and his name was Joachim.

2 And he took a wijf, Susanne bi name, the douyter of Helchie, a womman ful fair, and dredynge the Lord.

3 Forsothe hir fadir and modir, whanne thei weren riytful, tauyten her douyter bi the lawe of Moises.

4 Sotheli Joachim was ful riche, and he hadde a gardyn niy his hous; and the Jewis camen to hym, for he was the moost worschipful of alle.

5 And tweyne elde men weren ordeyned iugis in that yeer, of whiche the Lord spak, that wickidnesse yede out of Babiloyne, of the eldere iugis that semeden to gouerne the puple.

6 These iugis vsiden oft the hous of Joachym; and alle men that hadden domes camen to hem.

7 Forsothe whanne the puple hadde turned ayen after myddai, Susanne entride, and walkide in the gardyn of hir hosebonde.

8 And the eldre men siyen hir entrynge ech dai, and walkynge; and thei brenten out in to 'the couetise of hir.

9 And thei turneden awei her wit, and bowiden doun her iyen, that thei siyen not heuene, nether bithouyten on iust domes.

10 Sotheli bothe weren woundid bi the loue of hir, and thei schewiden not her sorewe to hem silf togidere;

11 for thei weren aschamed to schewe to hem silf her coueitise, willynge to ligge fleischli bi hir.

12 And thei aspieden ech dai more bisili to se hir.

13 And oon seide to the tothir, Go we hoom, for the our of mete is. And thei yeden out, and departiden fro hem silf.

14 And whanne thei hadden turned ayen, thei camen in to o place; and thei axiden ech of othere the cause, and thei knoulechiden her coueitise. And thanne in comyn thei ordeyneden a tyme, whanne thei miyten fynde hir aloone.

15 Forsothe it was doon, whanne thei aspieden a couenable dai, sche entride sumtyme, as yistirdai and the thridde dai ago, with twei damysels aloone, and wolde be waischun in the gardyn; for whi heete was.

16 And no man was there, outakun tweyne elde men hid, biholdynge hir.

17 Therfor sche saide to the damysels, Bringe ye to me oile, and oynementis; and close ye the doris of the gardyn, that Y be waischun.

18 And thei diden as sche 'hadde comaundid; and thei closiden the doris of the gardyn, and yeden out bi a posterne, to bringe tho thingis that sche hadde comaundid. And thei wisten not, that the elde men weren hid with ynne.

19 Sotheli whanne the damysels weren gon out, tweyne elde men risiden, and runnen to hir, and seiden, Lo!

20 the doris of the gardyn ben closid, and no man seeth vs, and we ben in 'the coueitise of thee. Wherfor assente thou to vs, and be thou meddlid with vs.

21 That if thou wolt not, we schulen seie witnessyng ayens thee, that a yong man was with thee, and for this cause thou sentist out the damesels fro thee.

22 And Susanne inwardli sorewide, and seide, Angwischis ben to me on ech side; for if Y do this, deth is to me; forsothe if Y do not, Y schal not ascape youre hondis.

23 But it is betere for me to falle in to youre hondis without werk, than to do synne in the siyt of the Lord.

24 And Susanne criede 'an hiy with greet vois, but also the elde men crieden ayens hir.

25 Forsothe oon ran, and openede the door of the gardyn.

26 Sotheli whanne the seruauntis of the hous hadden herd the cry in the gardyn, thei fellen in bi the posterne, to se what it was.

27 But after that the elde men spaken, the seruauntis weren aschamed greetly, for neuer was siche a word seid of Susanne. And the morew dai was maad.

28 And whanne the puple was comyn to Joachym, hir hosebonde, also the twei prestis fulle of wickid thouyte camen ayens Susanne, for to sle hir.

29 And thei seiden bifor al the puple, Sende ye to Susanne, the douyter of Helchie, the wijf of Joachym. And anoon thei senten.

30 And sche cam with hir fadir, and modir, and children, and alle kynesmen.

31 Certis Susanne was ful delicat, and fair of schap.

32 And tho wickid men comaundiden, that sche schulde be vnhilid, for sche was kyuered; that nameli so thei schuldun be fillid of hir fairnesse.

33 Therfor hir kynesmen wepten, and alle that knewen hir.

34 Forsothe the twei prestis risiden togidere in the myddis of the puple, and settiden her hondis on the heed of hir.

35 And sche wepte, and bihelde to heuene, and hir herte hadde trist in the Lord.

36 And the prestis seiden, Whanne we walkiden aloone in the gardyn, this Susanne entride with twei damesels; and sche closide the dore of the gardyn, and lefte the damesels.

37 And a yong man, that was hid, cam to hir, and lai bi hir.

38 Certis whanne we weren in a corner of the gardyn, we sien the wickidnesse, and runnen to hem, and we sien hem meddlid togidere.

39 And sotheli we myyten not take hym, for he was strongere than we; and whanne he hadde opened the doris, he skippide out.

40 But whanne we hadde take this womman, we axiden, who was the yonge man; and sche nolde schewe to vs. Of this thing we ben witnessis.

41 The multitude bileuede to hem, as to the eldre men and iugis of the puple, and condempneden hir to deth.

42 Forsothe Susanne criede loud with greet vois, and seide, Lord God, without bigynnyng and ende, that art knowere of hid thingis, that knowist alle thingis bifore that tho ben don;

43 thou wost, that thei han bore fals witnessyng ayens me. And lo! Y dye, whanne Y haue not do ony of these thingis, whiche these men han maad maliciously ayens me.

44 Forsothe the Lord herde the vois of hir.

45 And whanne she was led to the deth, the Lord reiside the hooli spirit of a yonge child, whos name was Danyel.

46 And he criede loude with a greet vois, Y am cleene of the blood of this womman.

47 And al the puple turned ayen to hym, and seide, What is this word, which thou hast spoke?

48 And whanne he stood in the myddis of hem, he seide, So ye, fonned children of Israel, not demynge nether knowynge that that is trewe, condempneden the douyter of Israel.

49 Turne ye ayen to the dom, for thei spaken fals witnessyng ayens hir.

50 Therfor the puple turnede ayen with haaste. And the elde men seiden to hym, Come thou, and sitte in the myddis of vs, and schewe to vs; for God hath youe to thee the onour of eelde.

51 And Danyel seide to hem, Departe ye hem atwynny fer, and Y schal deme hem.

52 Therfor, whanne thei weren departid oon fro the tother, he clepide oon of hem, and seide to hym, Thou elde man of yuel daies, now thi synnes ben comun, whiche thou wrouytist bifore,

53 demynge vniust domes, oppressynge innocentis, and delyuerynge gilti men, whanne the Lord seith, Thou schalt not sle an innocent and iust man.

54 But now if thou siest hir, seie thou, vndur what tree thou siest hem spekynge togidere to hem silf? Which seide, Vndur an haw tree.

55 Forsothe Danyel seide, Riytli thou liest in thin heed; for lo! the angel of the Lord, bi a sentence takun of hym, schal kitte thee bi the myddil.

56 And whanne he was stirid awei, he comaundide the tother to come, and seide to hym, Thou seed of Canaan, and not of Juda, fairnesse hath disseyued thee, and coueitise hath misturned thin herte;

57 thus ye diden to the douytris of Israel, and thei dredden, and spaken to you, but the douyter of Juda suffride not youre wickidnesse.

58 Now therfor seie thou to me, vndur what tree thou siest hem spekynge togidere to hem silf?

59 Which seide, Vndur a blak thorn. Forsothe Danyel seide to hym, Riytli also thou liest in thin heed; for the aungel of the Lord dwellith, and hath a swerd, that he kitte thee bi the myddil, and sle you.

60 Therfor al the puple criede lowde with greet vois, and blessiden 'the Lord, that saueth hem that hopen in hym.

61 And thei risiden togidere ayens the twei preestis; for Danyel hadde conuyctid hem bi her mouth, that thei hadden

bore fals witnessyng; and thei diden to hem, as thei hadden do yuele ayens the neiyboresse,

62 that thei schulden do bi the lawe of Moises, and thei killiden hem. And giltles blood was sauyd in that dai.

63 Forsothe Helchie and his wijf herieden the Lord in that day, for Susanne, her douyter, with Joachym, hir hosebonde, and with alle hir kynesmen, for a foul thing was not foundun in hir.

64 Forsothe Danyel was maad greet in the siyt of the puple, fro that dai and afterward.

65 And kyng Astriages was put to his fadris, and Sirus of Perseis took his rewme.

1 Forsothe Danyel eet with the kyng, and was onourid aboue alle the frendis of hym.

CAP 14

2 Also an idol, Bel bi name, was at Babiloyne, and twelue mesuris of cleene flour, of whiche mesuris eche conteynede thre buyschels, and fourti scheep, and sixe mesuris of wyn, that ben clepid amfris, weren spendid in it ech day.

3 And the kyng worschipede that Beel, and yede ech dai to onoure hym; certis Danyel worschipide his God. And the kyng seide to hym, Whi worschipist thou not Beel?

4 Which answeride, and seide to him, For Y worschipe not idols maad bi hond, but God lyuynge, that made of nouyt heuene and erthe, and hath power of ech fleisch.

5 And the kyng seide to hym, Whether it semeth not to thee, that Bel is a lyuynge god? whether thou seest not, hou grete thingis he etith and drynkith ech dai?

6 And Daniel seide leiyinge, Kyng, erre thou not; for whi this Bel is of clei with ynne, and of bras withoutforth, and etith not ony tyme.

7 And the king was wroth, and clepide the preestis therof, and seide to hem, If ye seien not to me, who it is that etith these costis, ye schulen die.

8 Forsothe if ye schewen that Bel etith these thingis, Daniel schal die, for he blasfemede Bel. And Daniel seide to the king, Be it don bi thi word.

9 Forsothe the prestis of Bel weren seuenti, outakun wyues, and litle children, ether seruauntis, and sones. And the kyng cam with Daniel in to the temple of Bel.

10 And the preestis of Bel seiden, Lo! we schulen go out, and thou, kyng, sette meetis, and meddle wyn, and close thou the dore, and aseele it with thi ryng.

11 And whanne thou entrist eerli, if thou fyndist not alle thingis etun of Bel, we schulen die bi deth, ether Daniel schal die, that liede ayens vs.

12 Sotheli thei tristiden, for thei hadden maad a priuy entryng vndur the boord, and bi it thei entriden euere, and deuouriden tho thingis.

13 Forsothe it was don, aftir that thei yeden out, and the king settide metis bifor Bel, Daniel comaundide to hise children, and thei brouyten aischis, and he riddlide thorouy al the temple bifor the kyng. And thei yeden out, and closiden the dore, and aseeliden with the ryng of the kyng, and yeden forth.

14 But the preestis entriden in niyt, bi her custom, and the wyues, and children of hem, and eeten and drunken alle thingis.

15 Forsothe the kyng roos moost eerli, and Daniel with hym.

16 And the kyng seide, Daniel, whether the seelis ben saaf? And he answeride, King, tho ben saaf.

17 And anoon whanne thei hadden openyd the dore, the king biheelde the boord, and he criede an hiy with a greet vois, Bel, thou art greet, and no gile is at thee.

18 And Daniel leiyede, and he helde the kyng, that he entride not with ynne. And Daniel seide, Lo! the pawment, perseyue thou whos steppis these ben.

19 And the kyng seide, Y se steppis of men, and of wymmen, and of yonge children. And the kyng was wrooth.

20 Thanne the kyng took the preestis, and the wyues, and children of hem; and thei schewiden to hym litle priuy doris, bi whiche thei entriden, and wastiden tho thingis that weren on the boord.

21 Therfor the kyng killide hem, and bitook Bel in to the power of Daniel, which distriede thilke Bel, and his temple.

22 And a greet dragoun was in that place, and Babiloyns worschipiden it.

23 And the kyng seide to Daniel, Lo! now thou maist not seie, that this is not a quik god; therfor worschipe thou hym.

24 And Daniel seide to the kyng, Y worschipe my Lord God, for he is God lyuynge.

25 But thou, kyng, yyue power to me, and Y schal sle the dragoun, with out swerd and staf. And the kyng seide, Y yyue to thee.

26 Therfor Daniel took pitch, and talow, and heeris, and sethide togidere; and he made gobetis, and yaf in to the mouth of the dragun; and the dragun was al to-brokun. And Daniel seide, Lo! whom ye worschipiden.

27 And whanne Babiloynes hadden herd this thing, thei hadden indignacioun greetli; and thei weren gaderid ayens the king, and seiden, The king is maad a Jew; he distriede Bel, and killide the dragun, and slow the preestis.

28 And thei seiden, whanne thei weren comun to the kyng, Bitake thou to vs Daniel, that distriede Bel, and killide the dragun; ellis we schulen sle thee, and thin hous.

29 Therfor the kyng siy, that thei fellen in on hym greetli; and he was compellid bi nede, and he bitook Daniel to hem.

30 Whiche senten hym in to the lake of liouns, and he was there seuene daies.

31 Certis seuene liouns weren in the lake, and twei bodies and twei scheep weren youun to hem ech dai. And thanne tho weren not youun to hem, that thei schulden deuoure Daniel.

32 Forsothe Abacuk, the profete, was in Judee, and he hadde soden potage, and hadde set in looues in a litil panyere; and he yede in to the feeld, to bere to reperis.

33 And the aungel of the Lord seide to Abacuk, Bere thou the mete, which thou hast, in to Babiloyne, to Daniel, which is in the lake of liouns.

34 And Abacuk seide, Lord, Y siy not Babiloyne, and Y knew not the lake.

35 And the aungel of the Lord took hym bi his top, and bar hym bi the heer of his heed; and he 'settide thilke Abacuk in Babiloyne, on the lake, in the fersnesse of his spirit.

36 And Abacuk criede, and seide, Daniel, the seruaunt of God, take thou the mete, that God hath sent to thee.

37 And Daniel seide, Lord God, thou hast mynde on me, and hast not forsake hem that louen thee.

38 And Daniel roos, and eet; certis the aungel of the Lord restoride Abacuk anoon in his place.

39 Therfor the kyng cam in the seuenthe dai to biweile Danyel; and he cam to the lake, and lokide in, and lo! Daniel sittynge in the myddis of liouns.

40 The kyng criede an hiy with greet vois, and seide, Lord God of Daniel, thou art greet; and the kyng drow hym out of the lake.

41 Certis he sente in to the lake hem, that weren cause of his perdicioun, and thei weren deuourid in a moment bifor him.

42 Thanne the kyng seide, Thei that dwellen in al erthe, drede the God of Daniel, for he is God lyuynge in to worldis; he is delyuerere, and sauyour, doynge myraclis and meruels in heuene and in erthe, that delyuerede Daniel fro the lake of liouns.

OSEE

CAP 1

1 The word of the Lord that was maad to Osee, the sone of Bery, in the daies of Osie, Joathan, Achas, Ezechie, kingis of Juda, and in the daies of Jeroboam, sone of Joas, the kyng of Israel.

2 The bigynnyng of the spekyng to the Lord in Osee. And the Lord seide to Osee, Go thou, take to thee a wijf of fornycaciouns, and make to thee sones of fornycaciouns, for the lond doynge fornicacioun schal do fornicacioun fro the Lord.

3 And he yede, and took Gomer, the douyter of Debelaym; and sche conseyuede, and childide a sone to hym.

4 And the Lord seide to hym, Clepe thou the name of hym Jesrael; for yit a litil and Y schal visite the blood of Jesrael on the hous of Hieu, and Y schal make to reste the rewme of the hous of Israel.

5 And in that dai Y schal al to-breke the bowe of Israel in the valei of Jesrael.

6 And sche conseyuede yit, and childide a douyter. And the Lord seide to hym, Clepe thou the name of hir With out merci, for Y schal no more leye to, for to haue merci on the hous of Israel, but bi foryetyng Y schal foryete hem.

7 And Y schal haue merci on the hous of Juda, and Y schal saue hem in her Lord God; and Y schal not saue hem in bowe, and swerd, and batel, and in horsis, and in horse men, ether kniytis.

8 And he wenyde hir that was With out merci. And sche conseyuede, and childide a sone to hym.

9 And he seide, Clepe thou his name Not my puple, for ye schulen not be my puple, and Y schal not be youre God.

10 And the noumbre of the sones of Israel schal be as grauel of the see, which grauel is with out mesure, and it schal not be noumbrid; and it schal be in the place, where it schal be seid to hem, Ye ben not my puple; it schal be seid to hem, Ye ben the sones of God lyuynge.

11 And the sones of Juda and the sones of Israel schulen be gaderid togidere, and thei schulen sette oon heed to hem silf, and thei schulen stie fro erthe, for the dai of Jesrael is greet.

CAP 2

1 Sei ye to youre britheren, Thei ben my puple; and to youre sister that hath gete merci,

2 Deme ye youre modir, deme ye, for sche is not my wijf, and Y am not hir hosebonde. Do sche awey hir fornicaciouns fro hir face, and hir auowtries fro the myddis of hir brestis;

3 lest perauenture Y spuyle hir nakid, and sette hir nakid bi the dai of hir natyuyte. And Y schal sette hir as a wildirnesse, and Y schal ordeyne hir as a lond with out weie, and Y schal sle hir in thirst.

4 And Y schal not haue merci on the sones of hir, for thei ben sones of fornicaciouns;

5 for the modir of hem dide fornicacioun, sche is schent that conseyuede hem, for sche seide, Y schal go after my louyeris that yeuen looues to me, and my watris, and my wolle, and my flex, and myn oile, and my drynke.

6 For this thing lo! Y schal hegge thi weie with thornes, and Y schal hegge it with a wal, and sche schal not fynde hir pathis.

7 And sche schal sue hir louyeris, and schal not take hem, and sche schal seke hem, and schal not fynde; and sche schal seie, Y schal go, and turne ayen to my formere hosebonde, for it was wel to me thanne more than now.

8 And this Jerusalem wiste not, that Y yaf to hir wheete, wyn, and oile; and Y multiplied siluer and gold to hir, whiche thei maden to Baal.

9 Therfor Y schal turne, and take my wheete in his tyme, and my wiyn in his tyme; and Y schal delyuere my wolle, and my flex, bi which thei hiliden the schenschipe therof.

10 And now Y schal schewe the foli of hir bifore the iyen of hir louyeris, and a man schal not delyuere hir fro myn hond;

11 and Y schal make to ceesse al the ioye therof, the solempnyte therof, the neomenye therof, the sabat therof, and alle the feeste tymes therof.

12 And Y schal distrie the vyner therof, of whiche sche seide, These ben myn hiris, whiche my louyeris yauen to me; and Y schal sette it in to a forest, and a beeste of the feeld schal ete it.

13 And Y schal visite on it the daies of Baalym, in whiche it brente encense, and was ourned with hir eere ryng, and hir broche, and yede after hir louyeris, and foryat me, seith the Lord.

14 For this thing lo! Y schal yyue mylk to it, and Y schal brynge it in to wildirnesse, and Y schal speke to the herte therof.

15 And Y schal yyue to it vyn tilieris therof of the same place, and the valei of Achar, that is, of disturblyng, for to opene hope. And it schal synge there bi the daies of hir yongthe, and bi the daies of hir stiyng fro the lond of Egipt.

16 And it schal be in that dai, seith the Lord, sche schal clepe me Myn hosebonde, and sche schal no more clepe me Baalym;

17 and Y schal take awei the names of Baalym fro hir mouth, and sche schal no more haue mynde of the name of tho.

18 And Y schal smyte to hem a boond of pees in that dai with the beeste of the feeld, and with the brid of the eir, and with the crepynge beeste of erthe. And Y schal al to-breke bowe, and swerd, and batel fro erthe; and Y schal make hem to slepe tristili.

19 And Y schal spouse thee to me withouten ende; and Y schal spouse thee to me in riytfulnesse, and in dom, and in merci, and in merciful doyngis.

20 And Y schal spouse thee to me in feith; and thou schalt wite, that Y am the Lord.

21 And it schal be, in that dai Y schal here, seith the Lord, and Y schal here heuenes, and tho schulen here the erthe;

22 and the erthe schal here wheete, and wyn, and oile, and these schulen here Jesrael.

23 And Y schal sowe it to me in to a lond, and Y schal haue merci on it that was with out merci.

24 And Y schal seie to that, that is not my puple, Thou art my puple, and it schal seie, Thou art my God.

CAP 3

1 And the Lord seide to me, Yit go thou, and loue a womman loued of a frend, and a womman auoutresse, as the Lord loueth the sones of Israel; and thei biholden to alien goddis, and louen the draffis of grapis.

2 And Y dalf it to me bi fiftene pens, and bi a corus of barli, and bi half a corus of barli.

3 And Y seide to it, Bi many daies thou schalt abide me; thou schalt not do fornycacioun, and thou schalt not be with an hosebonde, but also Y schal abide thee.

4 For bi many daies the sones of Israel schulen sitte with out kyng, with out prince, and with out sacrifice, and with out auter, and with out prestis cloth, and with out terafyn, that is, ymagis.

5 And after these thingis the sones of Israel schulen turne ayen, and schulen seke her Lord God, and Dauid, her king; and thei schulen drede at the Lord, and at the good of him, in the laste of daies.

CAP 4

1 Sones of Israel, here ye the word of the Lord, for whi doom is to the Lord with the dwelleris of erthe; for whi trewthe is not, and merci is not, and kunnyng of the Lord is not in erthe.

2 Curs, and leesyng, and manquelling, and thefte, and auowtrie flowiden, and blood touchide blood.

3 For this thing the erthe schal mourne, and ech that dwellith in that lond, schal be sijk, in the beeste of the feeld, and in the brid of the eir; but also the fischis of the see schulen be gaderid togidere.

4 Netheles ech man deme not, and a man be not repreuyd; for thi puple is as thei that ayen seien the prest.

5 And thou schalt falle to dai, and the profete also schal falle with thee; in the niyt Y made thi modir to be stille.

6 My puple was stille, for it hadde not kunnyng; for thou hast putte awei kunnyng, Y schal putte thee awei, that thou vse not presthod to me; and for thou hast foryete the lawe of thi God, also Y schal foryete thi sones.

7 Bi the multitude of hem, so thei synneden ayens me. Y schal chaunge the glorie of hem in to schenschipe.

8 Thei schulen ete the synnes of my puple, and thei schulen reise the soulis of hem to the wickidnesse of hem.

9 And it schal be, as the puple so the prest; and Y schal visite on hym the weies of hym, and Y schal yelde to him the thouytis of hym.

10 And thei schulen ete, and thei schulen not be fillid; thei diden fornicacioun, and ceessiden not, for thei forsoken the Lord in not kepynge.

11 Fornycacioun, and wiyn, and drunkenesse doen awei the herte.

12 My puple axide in his tre, and the staf therof telde to it; for the spirit of fornicacioun disseyuede hem, and thei diden fornicacioun fro her God.

13 On the heedis of mounteyns thei maden sacrifice, and on the litil hillis thei brenten encense vndur an ook, and a popeler, and terebynte, for the schadewe therof was good. Therfor youre douytris schulen do fornicacioun, and youre wyues schulen be auoutressis.

14 Y schal not visite on youre douytris, whanne thei don fornicacioun, and on youre wyues, whanne thei doon auowtrie; for thei lyuyden with hooris, and maden sacrifice with men turned in to wymmens condiciouns. And the puple that vndirstondith not, schal be betun.

15 If thou, Israel, doist fornicacioun, nameli Juda trespasse not; and nyle ye entre in to Galgala, and stie ye not in to Bethauen, nether swere ye, The Lord lyueth.

16 For as a wielde cow Israel bowide awei; now the Lord schal fede hem as a lomb in broodnesse.

17 Effraym is the partener of idols, leeue thou him;

18 the feeste of hem is departid. Bi fornicacioun thei diden fornicacioun, the defenders therof louyden to brynge schenschipe.

19 The spirit boond hym in hise wyngis, and thei schulen be schent of her sacrifices.

CAP 5

1 Preestis, here ye this, and the hous of Israel, perseyue ye, and the hous of the kyng, herkne ye; for whi doom is to you, for ye ben maad a snare to lokyng afer, and as a net spred abrood on Thabor.

2 And ye bowiden doun sacrifices in to depthe; and Y am the lernere of alle hem.

3 Y knowe Effraym, and Israel is not hid fro me; for now Effraym dide fornicacioun, Israel is defoulid.

4 Thei schulen not yiue her thouytis, that thei turne ayen to her God; for the spirit of fornicacioun is in the myddis of hem, and thei knewen not the Lord.

5 And the boost of Israel schal answere in to the face therof, and Israel and Effraym schulen falle in her wickidnesse; also Judas schal falle with hem.

6 In her flockis, and in her droues thei schulen go to seke the Lord, and thei schulen not fynde; he is takun awei fro hem.

7 Thei trespassiden ayens the Lord, for thei gendriden alien sones; now the monethe schal deuoure hem with her partis.

8 Sowne ye with a clarioun in Gabaa, with a trumpe in Rama; yelle ye in Bethauen, after thi bak, Beniamyn.

9 Effraym schal be in to desolacioun, in the dai of amendyng, and in the lynagis of Israel Y schewide feith.

10 The princes of Juda ben maad as takynge terme; Y schal schede out on hem my wraththe as watir.

11 Effraym suffrith fals chalenge, and is brokun bi doom; for he bigan to go after filthis.

12 And Y am as a mouyte to Effraym, and as rot to the hous of Juda.

13 And Effraym siy his sikenesse, and Judas siy his boond. And Effraym yede to Assur, and sente to the kyng veniere. And he mai not saue you, nether he mai vnbynde the boond fro you.

14 For Y am as a lionesse to Effraym, and as a whelp of a lioun to the hous of Juda.

15 Y my silf schal take, and go, and take awei, and noon is that schal delyuere. I schal go, and turne ayen to my place, til ye failen, and seken my face.

CAP 6

1 In her tribulacioun thei schulen rise eerli to me. Come ye, and turne we ayen to the Lord;

2 for he took, and schal heele vs; he schal smyte, and schal make vs hool.

3 He schal quykene vs after twei daies, and in the thridde dai he schal reise vs, and we schulen lyue in his siyt. We schulen wite, and sue, that we knowe the Lord. His goyng out is maad redi at the morewtid, and he schal come as a reyn to vs, which is timeful and lateful to the erthe.

4 Effraym, what schal Y do to thee? Juda, what schal Y do to thee? Youre merci is as a cloude of the morewtid, and as deew passynge forth eerli.

5 For this thing Y hewide in profetis, Y killide hem in the wordis of my mouth;

6 and thi domes schulen go out as liyt. For Y wolde merci, and not sacrifice, and Y wolde the kunnyng of God, more than brent sacrificis.

7 But thei as Adam braken the couenaunt; there thei trespassiden ayens me.

8 Galaad the citee of hem that worchen idol, is supplauntid with blood; and

9 as the chekis of men 'that ben theues. Partener of prestis sleynge in the weie men goynge fro Sichem, for thei wrouyten greet trespasse.

10 In the hous of Israel Y siy an orible thing; there the fornicacious of Effraym.

11 Israel is defoulid; but also thou, Juda, sette heruest to thee, whanne Y schal turne the caitiftee of my puple.

CAP 7

1 Whanne Y wolde heele Israel, the wickidnesse of Effraym was schewid, and the malice of Samarie was schewid, for thei wrouyten a leesyng. And a niyt theef entride, and robbid; a dai theef was withoutforth.

2 And lest thei seien in her hertis, that Y haue mynde on al the malice of hem, now her fyndyngis han cumpassid hem, tho ben maad bifor my face.

3 In her malice thei gladiden the kyng, and in her leesyngys 'thei gladiden the princes.

4 Alle that doen auoutrie, ben as an ouene maad hoot of a bakere. The citee restide a litil fro the medlyng of sour douy, til al was maad sour 'of sour douy.

5 The dai of oure kyng; the princis bigunnen to be wood of wyn; he stretchide forth his hoond with scorneris.

6 For thei applieden her herte as an ouene, whanne he settide tresoun to hem. Al the niyt he slepte bakynge hem, in the morewtid he was maad hoot, as the fier of flawme.

7 Alle weren maad hoot as an ouene, and thei deuouriden her iugis. Alle the kyngis of hem fellen doun, and noon is among hem that crieth to me.

8 Effraym hym silf was medlid among puplis; Effraym was maad a loof bakun vndur aischis, which is not turned ayen.

9 Aliens eeten the strengthe of hym, and he knew not; but also hoor heeris weren sched out in hym, and he knew not.

10 And the pride of Israel schal be maad low in the face therof; thei turneden not ayen to her Lord God, and thei souyten not hym in alle these thingis.

11 And Effraym was maad as a culuer disseyued, not hauynge herte. Thei clepiden Egipt to help, thei yeden to Assiriens.

12 And whanne thei ben goen forth, Y schal sprede abrood on hem my net, Y schal drawe hem doun as a brid of the eir. Y schal beete hem, bi the heryng of the cumpany of hem.

13 Wo to hem, for thei yeden awei fro me; thei schulen be distried, for thei trespassiden ayens me. And Y ayenbouyte hem, and thei spaken leesyngis ayenus me.

14 And thei crieden not to me in her herte, but yelliden in her beddis. Thei chewiden code on wheete, and wyn, and thei yeden awei fro me.

15 And Y tauyte, and coumfortide the armes of hem, and thei thouyten malice ayens me.

16 Thei turneden ayen, that thei schulden be with out yok; thei ben maad as a gileful bowe. The princis of hem schulen falle doun bi swerd, for the woodnesse of her tunge; this is the scornyng of hem in the lond of Egipt.

CAP 8

1 A trumpe be in thi throte, as an egle on the hous of the Lord; for that that thei yeden ouer my boond of pees, and braken my lawe.

2 Thei clepiden me to helpe, A! my God, we Israel han knowe thee.

3 Israel hath cast awei good, the enemye schal pursue hym.

4 Thei regnyden, and not of me; thei weren princes, and Y knew not. Thei maden her gold and siluer idols to hem, that thei schulden perische.

5 A! Samarie, thi calf is cast awei; my strong veniaunce is wrooth ayens hem. Hou long moun thei not be clensid?

6 for also it is of Israel. A crafti man made it, and it is not god; for the calf of Samarie schal be in to webbis of ireyns.

7 For thei schulen sowe wynd, and thei schulen repe whirlewynd. A stalke stondynge is not in hem, the seed schal not make mele; that if also it makith mele, aliens schulen ete it.

8 Israel is deuouryd; now Israel is maad as an vnclene vessel among naciouns,

9 for thei stieden to Assur. Effraym is a wielde asse, solitarie to hym silf. Thei yauen yiftis to louyeris;

10 but also with meede thei hiriden naciouns. Now Y schal gadere hem togidere, and thei schulen reste a litil fro birthun of the kyng and of princes.

11 For Efraym multipliede auteris to do synne, auteris weren maad to hym in to trespas.

12 Y schal write to hem my many fold lawis, that ben arettid as alien lawis.

13 Thei schulen brynge sacrifices, thei shulen offre, and ete fleischis; and the Lord schal not resseyue tho. Now he schal haue mynde on the wickidnessis of hem, and he schal visite the synnes of hem; thei schulen turne in to Egipt.

14 And Israel foryat his makere, and bildide templis to idols, and Judas multipliede stronge citees; and Y schal sende fier in to the citees of hym, and it schal deuoure the housis of hym.

CAP 9

1 Israel, nyle thou be glad, nyle thou make ful out ioie as puplis; for thou hast do fornicacioun fro thi God. Thou louedist meede on alle the cornflooris of wheete.

2 The cornfloor and pressour schal not feede hem, and wyn schal lie to hem.

3 Thei schulen not dwelle in the lond of the Lord. Effraym turnede ayen in to Egipt, and eet defoulid thing among Assiriens.

4 Thei schulen not offre wyn to the Lord, and thei schulen not plese hym. The sacrificis of hem ben as breed of mourneris; alle that schulen ete it schulen be defoulid. For the breed of hem is to the lijf of hem; thei schulen not entre in to the hous of the Lord.

5 What schulen ye do in the solempne dai, in the dai of the feeste of the Lord?

6 For lo! thei ben goon out fro distriyng. Egipt schal gadere hem togidere, Memphis schal birie hem. A nettle schal enherite the desirable siluer of hem, a clote schal be in the tabernaclis of hem.

7 Daies of visitacioun ben comun, daies of yeldyng ben comun. Knowe ye, that Israel is a fool, a wood profete, a spir-

itual man, for the multitude of thi wickidnesse is also the multitude of woodnesse.

8 The biholdere of Effraym with my God is a profete; a snare of fallyng is maad now on alle the weies of hym, woodnesse is in the hous of his God.

9 Thei synneden deepli, as in the daies of Gabaa. The Lord schal haue mynde on the wickidnesse of hem, and schal visite the synnes of hem.

10 Y foond Israel as grapis in desert, Y siy the fadris of hem as the firste applis of a fige tree, in the cop therof; but thei entriden to Belfegor, and weren alienyd in confusioun, and thei weren maad abhomynable as tho thingis whiche thei louyden.

11 Effraym as a brid fley awei; the glorye of hem is of child-beryng, and of the wombe, and of conseyuyng.

12 That if thei nurschen her sones, Y schal make hem with out children among men. But also wo to hem, whanne Y schal go awei fro hem.

13 Y siy that Effraym was as Tire, foundid in fairnesse; and Effraym schal lede out hise sones to the sleere.

14 Lord, yyue thou to hem; what schalt thou yyue to hem? yyue thou to hem a wombe with out children, and drie tetis.

15 Alle the wickidnessis of hem ben in Galgal, for there Y hadde hem hateful; for the malice of her fyndyngis. Y schal caste hem out of myn hous; Y schal not leie to, that Y loue hem. Alle the princes of hem goen awei.

16 Effraym is smyten, the roote of hem is dried vp; thei schulen not make fruyt. That thouy thei gendren, Y schal sle the moost louyd thingis of her wombe.

17 My God schal caste hem awey, for thei herden not hym; and thei schulen be of vnstable dwellyng among naciouns.

CAP 10

1 Israel was a vyne ful of bowis, fruyt was maad euene to hym; bi the multitude of his fruyt he multipliede auteris, bi the plente of his lond he was plenteuouse.

2 In simylacris the herte of hem is departid, now thei schulen perische. He schal breke the simylacris of hem, he schal robbe the auteris of hem.

3 For thanne thei schulen seie, A kyng is not to vs, for we dreden not the Lord. And what schal a kyng do to vs?

4 Speke ye wordis of vnprofitable visioun, and ye schulen smyte boond of pees with leesyng; and doom as bittirnesse schal burioune on the forewis of the feeld.

5 The dwelleris of Samarie worschipiden the kien of Bethauen. For the puple therof mourenyde on that calf, and the keperis of the hous therof; thei maden ful out ioye on it in the glorie therof, for it passide fro that puple.

6 For also it was borun to Assur, a yifte to the king veniere. Confusioun schal take Effraym, and Israel schal be schent in his wille.

7 Samarie made his kyng to passe, as froth on the face of water. And the hiy thingis of idol, the synne of Israel, schulen be lost.

8 A cloote and a brere schal stie on the auters of hem. And thei schulen seie to mounteyns, Hile ye vs, and to litle hillis, Falle ye doun on vs.

9 Fro the daies of Gabaa Israel synnede; there thei stoden. Batel schal not take hem in Gabaa,

10 on the sones of wickidnesse. Bi my desir Y schal chastise hem; puplis schulen be gaderid togidere on hem, whanne thei schulen be chastisid for her twei wickidnessis.

11 Effraym is a cow calf, tauyt for to loue threischyng; and Y yede on the fairenesse of the necke therof. Y schal stie on Effraym. Judas schal ere, and Jacob schal breke forewis to hym silf.

12 Sowe ye to you riytfulnesse in treuthe, and repe ye in the mouthe of merci, and make ye newe to you a feld newli brouyte to tilthe. Forsothe tyme is to seke the Lord, whanne he cometh, that schal teche you riytfulnesse.

13 Ye han erid vnfeithfulnesse, ye han rope wickidnesse, ye han ete the corn of leesyng. For thou tristydist in thi weles, and in the multitude of thi stronge men.

14 Noise schal rise in thi puple, and alle thi stronge holdis schulen be distried; as Salmana was distried of the hous of hym, that took veniaunce on Baal; in the dai of batel, whanne the modir was hurlid doun on the sones.

15 So Bethel dide to you, for the face of malice of youre wickidnessis.

CAP 11

1 As the morewtid passith, the king of Israel schal passe forth. For Israel was a child, and Y louyde hym; and fro Egipt Y clepide my sone.

2 Thei clepiden hem, so thei yeden awei fro the face of hem. Thei offriden to Baalym, and maden sacrifice to symylacris.

3 And Y as a nursche of Effraym bare hem in myn armes, and thei wisten not, that Y kepte hem.

4 Y schal drawe hem in the ropis of Adam, in the boondis of charite. And Y schal be to hem as he that enhaunsith the yok on the chekis of hem; and Y bowide doun to hym, that he schulde ete.

5 He schal not turne ayen in to the lond of Egipt. And Assur, he schal be kyng of hym, for thei nolden turne.

6 A swerd bigan in the citees therof, and it schal waaste the chosun men therof, and schal eete the heedis of hem.

7 And my puple schal hange, at my comynge ayen. But a yok schal be put to hem togidere, that schal not be takun awei.

8 Hou schal Y yyue thee, Effraym? schal Y defende thee, Israel? hou schal Y yyue thee? As Adama Y schal sette thee; as Seboym. Myn herte is turned in me; my repentaunce is disturblid togidere.

9 Y schal not do the strong veniaunce of my wraththe. Y schal not turne, to leese Effraym; for Y am God, and not man. Y am hooli in the myddis of thee, and Y schal not entre in to a citee.

10 Thei schulen go after the Lord. He shal rore as a lioun, for he shal rore, and the sones of the see schulen drede.

11 And thei schulen fle awei as a brid fro Egipt, and as a culuer fro the lond of Assiriens. And Y schal sette hem in her housis, seith the Lord.

CAP 12

12 Effraym cumpasside me in denying, the hous of Israel in gile. But Judas a witnesse yede doun with God, and with feithful seyntis.

1 Effraym fedith wynd, and sueth heete. Al dai he multiplieth leesyng, and distriyng; and he made boond of pees with Assiriens, and bar oile in to Egipt.

2 Therfor the doom of the Lord is with Juda, and visityng is on Jacob; bi the weies of hym, and bi the fyndyngis of hym he schal yelde to hym.

3 In the wombe he supplauntide his brother, and in his strengthe he was dressid with the aungel.

4 And he was strong to the aungel, and was coumfortid; he wepte, and preiede hym; in Bethel he foond hym, and there he spak with vs.

5 And the Lord God of oostis, the Lord, is the memorial of hym.

6 And thou schalt turne to thi God. Kepe thou merci and doom, and hope thou euere in thi God.

7 Chanaan louyde fals caleng, a gileful balaunce in his hond.

8 And Effraym seide, Netheles Y am maad riche, Y haue founde an idol to me; alle my trauelis schulen not fynde to me the wickidnesse, whiche Y synnede.

9 And Y am thi Lord God fro the lond of Egipt; yit Y schal make thee to sitte in tabernaclis, as in the daies of feeste.

10 And Y spak bi profetis, and Y multiplied profesie, and Y was licned in the hond of profetis.

11 If Galaad worschipith an idol, therfor thei erren in veyn offryng to oxis in Galgal; for whi and the auteris of hem schulen be as heepis on the forewis of the feeld.

12 Jacob fledde in to the cuntrei of Sirie, and Israel seruyde for a wijf, and seruyde, ether kepte, for a wijf.

13 But bi a profete the Lord ledde Israel out of Egipt, and bi a profete he was kept.

14 Effraym terride me to wrathfulnesse in hise bitternessis, and the blood of hym schal come on hym; and his Lord schal restore to hym the schenschipe of him.

CAP 13

1 For Effraym spak, hidousnesse assailide Israel; and he trespasside in Baal, and was deed.

2 And now thei addiden to do synne, and maden to hem a yotun ymage of her siluer, as the licnesse of idols; al is the makyng of crafti men. To these thei seien, A! ye men, offre, and worschipe caluys.

3 Therfor thei schulen be as a morewtid cloude, and as the deew of morewtid, that passith forth, as dust rauyschide bi whirlewynd fro the corn floor, and as smoke of a chymenei.

4 Forsothe Y am thi Lord God, 'that ledde thee fro the loond of Egipt; and thou schalt not knowe God, outakun me, and no sauyour is, outakun me.

5 Y knewe thee in the desert, in the lond of wildirnesse.

6 Bi her lesewis thei weren fillid, and hadden abundaunce; thei reisiden her herte, and foryaten me.

7 And Y schal be as a lionesse to hem, as a parde in the weye of Assiriens.

8 Y as a femal bere, whanne the whelps ben rauyschid, schal mete hem; and schal al to-breke the ynnere thingis of the mawe of hem. And Y as a lioun schal waaste hem there; a beeste of the feeld schal al to-rende hem.

9 Israel, thi perdicioun is of thee; thin help is oneli of me.

10 Where is thi kyng? moost saue he thee now in alle thi citees; and where ben thi iugis, of whiche thou seidist, Yyue thou to me a kyng, and princes?

11 Y schal yyue to thee a kyng in my strong veniaunce, and Y schal take awei in myn indignacioun.

12 The wickidnesse of Effraym is boundun togidere; his synne is hid.

13 The sorewis of a womman trauelynge of child schulen come to hym; he is a sone not wijs. For now he schal not stonde in the defoulyng of sones.

14 Y schal delyuere hem fro the hoond of deeth, and Y schal ayenbie hem fro deth. Thou deth, Y schal be thi deth; thou helle, Y schal be thi mussel.

15 Coumfort is hid fro myn iyen, for he schal departe bitwixe britheren. The Lord schal brynge a brennynge wynd, stiynge fro desert; and it schal make drie the veynes therof, and it schal make desolat the welle therof; and he schal rauysche the tresour of ech desirable vessel.

CAP 14

1 Samarie perische, for it stiride his God to bittirnesse; perische it bi swerd. The litle children of hem be hurtlid doun, and the wymmen with child therof be koruun.

2 Israel, be thou conuertid to thi Lord God, for thou fellist doun in thi wickidnesse.

3 Take ye wordis with you, and be ye conuertid to the Lord; and seie ye to hym, Do thou awei al wickidnesse, and take thou good; and we schulen yelde the caluys of oure lippis.

4 Assur schal not saue vs, we schulen not stie on hors; and we schulen no more seie, Oure goddis ben the werkis of oure hondis; for thou schalt haue merci on that modirles child, which is in thee.

5 Y schal make hool the sorewis of hem; Y schal loue hem wilfuli, for my strong veniaunce is turned awei fro hem.

6 Y schal be as a dew, and Israel schal buriowne as a lilie. And the root therof schal breke out as of the Liban;

7 the braunchis therof schulen go. And the glorye therof schal be as an olyue tree, and the odour therof schal be as of the Liban.

8 Thei schulen be conuertid, and sitte in the schadewe of hym; thei schulen lyue bi wheete, and schulen buriowne as a vyne. The memorial therof schal be as the wyne of Liban.

9 Effraym, what schulen idols do more to me? Y schal here him, and Y schal dresse him as a greene fir tree. Thi fruit is foundun of me.

10 Who is wijs, and schal vndurstonde these thingis? who is vndurstondyng, and schal kunne these thingis? For the weies of the Lord ben riytful, and iust men schulen go in tho; but trespassours schulen falle in tho.

JOEL

CAP 1

1 The word of the Lord is this, that was maad to Joel, the sone of Phatuel.

2 Elde men, here ye this, and alle dwelleris of the lond, perseyue ye with eeris. If this thing was don in youre daies, ether in the daies of youre fadris.

3 Of this thing telle ye to your sones, and your sones telle to her sones, and the sones of hem telle to another generacioun.

4 A locuste eet the residue of a worte worm, and a bruke eet the residue of a locuste, and rust eet the residue of a bruke.

5 Drunken men, wake ye, and wepe; and yelle ye, alle that drynken wyn in swetnesse; for it perischide fro youre mouth.

6 For whi a folc strong and vnnoumbrable stiede on my lond. The teeth therof ben as the teeth of a lioun, and the cheek teeth therof ben as of a whelp of a lioun.

7 It settide my vyner in to desert, and took awei the riynde of my fige tre. It made nakid and spuylide that vyner, and castide forth; the braunchis therof ben maad white.

8 Weile thou, as a virgyn gird with a sak on the hosebonde of hir tyme of mariage.

9 Sacrifice and moist sacrifice perischide fro the hous of the Lord; and preestis, the mynystris of the Lord, moureneden.

10 The cuntrey is maad bare of puple. The erthe mourenyde; for whete is distried. Wyn is schent, and oile was sijk, ether failide.

11 The erthe tilieris ben schent, the vyn tilieris yelliden on wheete and barli; for the ripe corn of the feeld is perischid.

12 The vyner is schent; and the fige tre was sijk. The pomgarnate tre, and the palm tre, and the fir tre, and alle trees of the feeld drieden vp; for ioie is schent fro the sones of men.

13 Ye prestis, girde you, and weile; ye mynystris of the auter, yelle. Mynystris of my God, entre ye, ligge ye in sak; for whi sacrifice and moist sacrifice perischide fro the hous of youre God.

14 Halewe ye fastyng, clepe ye cumpeny, gadere ye togidere elde men, and alle dwelleris of the erthe in to the hous of youre God; and crie ye to the Lord, A!

15 A! A! to the dai; for the dai of the Lord is niy, and schal come as a tempest fro the myyti.

16 Whether foodis perischiden not bifore youre iyen; gladnesse and ful out ioie perischide fro the hous of youre God?

17 Beestis wexen rotun in her drit. Bernes ben distried, celeris ben distried, for wheete is schent.

18 Whi weilide a beeste? whi lowiden the flockis of oxun and kien? for no lesewe is to hem; but also the flockis of scheep perischiden.

19 Lord, Y schal crye to thee, for fier eet the faire thingis of desert, and flawme brente all the trees of the cuntrei.

20 But also beestis of the feeld, as a corn floor thirstynge reyn, bihelden to thee; for the wellis of watris ben dried vp, and fier deuouride the faire thingis of desert.

CAP 2

1 Synge ye with a trumpe in Sion, yelle ye in myn hooli hil. Alle the dwelleris of erthe be disturblid; for the dai of the Lord cometh,

2 for the dai of derknessis and of myist is niy, the dai of cloude and of whirlewynde. As the morewtid spred abrood on hillis, a myche puple and strong. Noon was lijk it fro the bigynnyng, and after it schal not be, til in to yeeris of generacioun and of generacioun.

3 Bifore the face therof schal be fier deuourynge, and after it schal be brennynge flawme; as a gardyn of liking the lond schal be bifor him, and wildirnesse of desert schal be after him, and noon is that schal ascape him.

4 The lokyng of hem schal be as the lokyng of horsis, and as horse men so thei schulen renne.

5 As the sown of cartis on the heedis of hillis thei schulen skippe; as the sowne of the flawme of fier deuourynge stobil, as a strong puple maad redi to batel.

6 Puplis schulen be turmentid of the face therof, alle facis schulen be dryuun in to a pot.

7 As stronge men thei schulen renne, as men werriours thei schulen stie on the wal. Men schulen go in her weies, and thei schulen not bowe awei fro her pathis.

8 Ech man schal not make streyt his brother, ech man schal go in his path; but also thei schulen falle doun bi wyndows, and schulen not be hirt.

9 Thei schulen entre in to the citee, thei schulen renne on the wal; thei schulen stie on housis, thei schulen entre as a niyt theef bi wyndows.

10 The erthe tremblide of his face, heuenys weren mouyd, the sunne and the moone weren maad derk, and sterris withdrowen her schynyng.

11 And the Lord yaf his vois bifor the face of his oost, for hise oostis ben ful manye; for tho ben stronge, and doen the word of hym. For the dai of the Lord is greet, and ful ferdful, and who schal suffre it?

12 Now therfor seith the Lord, Be ye conuertid to me in al youre herte, in fastyng, and wepyng, and weilyng;

13 and kerue ye youre hertis, and not youre clothis, and be ye conuertid to youre Lord God, for he is benygne, and merciful, pacient, and of myche merci, and abidynge, ether foryyuynge, on malice.

14 Who woot, if God be conuertid, and foryyue, and leeue blessyng aftir hym? sacrifice and moist sacrifice to oure Lord God.

15 Synge ye with a trumpe in Sion, halewe ye fastyng, clepe ye cumpany; gadere ye togidere the puple, halewe ye the chirche,

16 gadere ye togidere elde men, gadere ye togidere litle children, and soukynge the brestis; a spouse go out of his bed, and a spousesse of hir chaumbre.

17 Prestis, the mynystris of the Lord, schulen wepe bitwixe the porche and the auter, and schulen seie, Lord! spare thou, spare thi puple, and yyue thou not thin eritage in to schenschipe, that naciouns be lordis of hem. Whi seien thei among puplis, Where is the God of hem?

18 The Lord louyde gelousli his lond, and sparide his puple.

19 And the Lord answeride, and seide to his puple, Lo! Y schal sende to you wheete, and wyn, and oile, and ye schulen be fillid with tho; and Y schal no more yyue you schenschipe among hethene men.

20 And Y schal make hym that is at the north fer fro you; and Y schal cast hym out in to a lond with out weie, and desert; his face ayens the eest see, and the laste part therof at the last see; and the stynk therof schal stie, and the root therof schal stie, for he dide proudli.

21 Erthe, nyle thou drede, make thou ful out ioye, and be glad; for the Lord magnefiede that he schulde do.

22 Beestis of the cuntrei, nyle ye drede, for the faire thingis of desert buriowneden; for the tre brouyte his fruyt, the fige tre and vyner yauen her vertu.

23 And the sones of Sion, make ye ful out ioie, and be ye glad in youre Lord God, for he yaf to you a techere of riytfulnesse, and he schal make morewtid reyn and euentid reyn to come doun to you, as in the bigynnyng.

24 And cornflooris schulen be fillid of wheete, and pressours schulen flowe with wyn, and oile.

25 And Y schal yelde to you the yeris whiche the locuste, bruke, and rust, and wort worm, my greet strengthe, eet, which Y sente in to you.

26 And ye schulen ete etyng, and ye schulen be fillid; and ye schulen herie the name of youre Lord God, that made merueils with you; and my puple schal not be schent with outen ende.

27 And ye schulen wite, that Y am in the myddis of Israel; and Y am youre Lord God, and 'noon is more; and my puple schal not be schent with outen ende.

28 And it schal be, aftir these thingis Y schal schede out my spirit on ech man, and youre sones and youre douytris schulen profesie; youre elde men schulen dreme dremes, and youre yonge men schulen se visiouns.

29 But also Y schal schede out my spirit on my seruauntis, and handmaydis, in tho daies;

30 and Y schal yyue grete wondris in heuene, and in erthe, blood, and fier, and the heete of smoke.

31 The sunne schal be turned in to derknessis, and the moone in to blood, bifor that the greet dai and orrible of the Lord come.

32 And it schal be, ech that clepith to helpe the name of the Lord, schal be saaf; for whi saluacioun schal be in the hil of Sion and in Jerusalem, as the Lord seide, and in the residue men, whiche the Lord clepith.

CAP 3

1 For lo! in tho daies, and in that tyme, whanne Y schal turne the caitifte of Juda and of Jerusalem,

2 Y schal gadere alle folkis, and Y schal lede hem in to the valei of Josephat; and Y schal dispute there with hem on my puple, and myn eritage Israel, whiche thei scateriden among naciouns; and thei departiden my lond, and senten lot on my puple;

3 and thei settiden a knaue child in the bordel hous, and seelden a damesel for wyn, that thei schulden drynke.

4 But what to me and to you, thou Tire, and Sidon, and ech ende of Palestyns? Whethir ye schulen yelde vengyng to me? and if ye vengen you ayens me, soone swiftli Y schal yelde while to you on youre heed.

5 Ye token awey my siluer and gold, and ye brouyten my desirable thingis and faireste thingis in to youre templis of idols.

6 And ye selden the sones of Juda, and the sones of Jerusalem to the sones of Grekis, that ye schulden make hem fer fro her coostis.

7 Lo! Y schal reise hem fro the place in which ye seelden hem; and Y schal turne youre yeldyng in to youre heed.

8 And Y schal sille youre sones and youre douytris in the hondis of the sones of Juda, and thei schulen selle hem to Sabeis, a fer folc, for the Lord spak.

9 Crye ye this thing among hethene men, halewe ye batel, reise ye stronge men; alle men werriours, neiy, and stie.

10 Beete ye togydere youre plowis in to swerdis, and youre mattokkis in to speeris; a sijk man seie, that Y am strong.

11 Alle folkis, breke ye out, and come fro cumpas, and be ye gaderid togidere; there the Lord schal make thi stronge men to die.

12 Folkis rise togidere, and stie in to the valei of Josofat; for Y schal sitte there, to deme alle folkis in cumpas.

13 Sende ye sikelis, 'ether sithis, for ripe corn wexide; come ye, and go ye doun, for the pressour is ful; pressouris ben plenteuouse, for the malice of hem is multiplied.

14 Puplis, puplis in the valei of kittyng doun; for the dai of the Lord is nyy in the valei of kittyng doun.

15 The sunne and the moone ben maad derk, and sterris withdrowen her schynyng.

16 And the Lord schal rore fro Sion, and schal yyue his vois fro Jerusalem, and heuenes and erthe schulen be mouyd; and the Lord is the hope of his puple, and the strengthe of the sones of Israel.

17 And ye schulen wite, that Y am youre Lord God, dwellynge in Sion, in myn hooli hil; and Jerusalem schal be hooli, and aliens schulen no more passe bi it.

18 And it schal be, in that dai mounteyns schulen droppe swetnesse, and litle hillis schulen flowe with mylke, and watris schulen go bi alle the ryueris of Juda; and a welle schal go out of the hous of the Lord, and schal moiste the stronde of thornes.

19 Egipt schal be in to desolacioun, and Idume in to desert of perdicioun; for that that thei diden wickidli ayens the sones of Juda, and schedden out innocent blood in her lond.

20 And Judee schal be enhabited with outen ende, and Jerusalem in to generacioun and in to generacioun.

21 And Y schal clense the blood of hem, which Y hadde not clensid; and the Lord schal dwelle in Syon.

AMOS

CAP 1

1 The wordis of Amos ben these, that was in the schepherdis thingis of Thecue, whiche he siy on Israel, in the daies of Osie, king of Juda, and in the daies of Jeroboam, sone of Joas, kyng of Israel, bifor twei yeeris of the erthe mouynge.

2 And he seide, The Lord schal rore fro Sion, and schal yyue his vois fro Jerusalem; and the faire thingis of schepherdis mourenyden, and the cop of Carmele was maad drie.

3 The Lord seith these thingis, On thre grete trespassis of Damask, and on foure, I shal not conuerte it, for it threischide Galaad in irun waynes.

4 And Y schal sende fier in to the hous of Asael, and it schal deuoure the housis of Benadab.

5 And Y schal al to-breke the barre of Damask, and Y schal leese a dwellere fro the feeld of idol, and hym that holdith the ceptre fro the hous of lust and of letcherie; and the puple of Sirie schal be translatid to Sirenen, seith the Lord.

6 The Lord seith these thingis, On thre grete trespassis of Gasa, and on foure, Y schal not conuerte it, for it translatide perfit caitifte, to close that togidere in Idumee.

7 And Y schal sende fier in to the wal of Gasa, and it schal deuoure the housis therof.

8 And Y schal leese the dwelleris of Azotus, and hym that holdith the ceptre of Ascalon; and Y schal turne myn hond on Accaron, and the remenauntis of Filisteis schulen perische, seith the Lord God.

9 The Lord God seith these thingis, On thre grete trespassis of Tire, and on foure, Y schal not conuerte it, for thei closiden togidere perfit caitifte in Idumee, and hadde not mynde on the boond of pees of britheren.

10 And Y schal sende fier in to the wal of Tire, and it schal deuoure the housis therof.

11 The Lord seith these thingis, On thre grete trespassis of Edom, and on foure, Y schal not conuerte it, for it pursuede bi swerd his brother, and defoulide the merci of hym, and helde ferthere his woodnesse, and kepte his indignacioun 'til in to the ende.

12 Y schal sende fier in to Theman, and it schal deuoure the housis of Bosra.

13 The Lord seith these thingis, On thre grete trespassis of the sones of Amon, and on foure, Y schal not conuerte hym, for he karf the wymmen with childe of Galaad, for to alarge his terme.

14 And Y schal kyndle fier in the wal of Rabbe, and it schal deuoure the housis therof, in yellyng in the dai of batel, and in whirlwynd in the dai of mouyng togidere.

15 And Melchon schal go in to caitifte, he and hise princes togidere, seith the Lord.

CAP 2

1 The Lord God seith these thingis, On thre grete trespassis of Moab, and on foure, Y schal not conuerte it, for it brente the boonys of the kyng of Idumee til to aische.

2 And Y schal sende fier in to Moab, and it schal deuoure the housis of Carioth; and Moab schal die in sown, in the noise of a trumpe.

3 And Y schal leese a iuge of the myddis therof, and Y schal sle with it alle the princes therof, seith the Lord.

4 The Lord seith these thingis, On thre grete trespassis of Juda, and on foure, Y schal not conuerte hym, for he hath caste awei the lawe of the Lord, and kepte not the comaundementis of hym; for her idols, after whiche the fadris of hem yeden, disseyueden hem.

5 And Y schal sende fier in to Juda, and it schal deuoure the housis of Jerusalem.

6 The Lord seith these thingis, On thre grete trespassis of Israel, and on foure, Y schal not conuerte hym, for that that he seelde a iust man for siluer, and a pore man for schoon.

7 Whiche al to-foulen the heedis of pore men on the dust of erthe, and bowen awei the weie of meke men; and the sone and his fadir yeden to a damesele, that thei schulden defoule myn hooli name.

8 And thei eeten on clothis leid to wedde bisidis ech auter, and drunken the wyn of dampned men in the hous of her God.

9 Forsothe Y distriede Ammorrei fro the face of hem, whos hiynesse was the hiynesse of cedris, and he was strong as an ook; and Y al to-brak the fruyt of hym aboue, and the rootis of hym bynethe.

10 Y am, that made you to stie fro the lond of Egipt, and ledde you out in desert bi fourti yeer, that ye schulden welde the lond of Ammorrei.

11 And Y reiside of youre sones in to profetis, and Nayareis of youre yonge men. Whether it is not so, ye sones of Israel? seith the Lord.

12 And ye birliden wyn to Nayareis, and comaundiden to profetis, and seiden, Profecie ye not.

13 Lo! Y schal charke vndur you, as a wayn chargid with hei charkith.

14 And fliyt schal perische fro a swift man, and a strong man schal not holde his vertu, and a stalworthe man schal not saue his lijf;

15 and he that holdith a bowe schal not stonde, and a swift man schal not be sauyd by hise feet; and the stiere of an hors schal not saue his lijf,

16 and a stronge man of herte schal fle nakid among stronge men in that dai, seith the Lord.

CAP 3

1 Sones of Israel, here ye the word which the Lord spak on you, and on al the kynrede, which Y ledde out of the lond of Egipt,

2 and seide, Oneli Y knewe you of alle the kynredis of erthe; therfor Y schal visite on you alle youre wickidnessis.

3 Whether tweyne schulen go togidere, no but it acorde to hem?

4 Whether a lioun schal rore in a forest, no but he haue prey? Whether the whelp of a lioun schal yyue vois fro his denne, no but he take ony thing?

5 Whether a brid schal falle in to a snare of erthe, with outen a foulere? Whether a snare schal be takun awei fro erthe, bifor that it tak sum thing?

6 Whether a trumpe schal sowne in a citee, and the puple schal not drede? Whether yuel schal be in a citee, which yuel the Lord schal not make?

7 For the Lord God schal not make a word, no but he schewe his priuyte to hise seruauntis profetis.

8 A lioun schal rore, who schal not drede? the Lord God spak, who schal not profesie?

9 Make ye herd in the housis of Azotus, and in the housis of the lond of Egipt; and seie ye, Be ye gaderid togidere on the hillis of Samarye, and se ye many woodnessis in the myddis therof, and hem that suffren fals calenge in the priuy places therof.

10 And thei kouden not do riytful thing, seith the Lord, and tresouriden wickidnesse and raueyn in her housis.

11 Therfor the Lord God seith these thingis, The lond schal be troblid, and be cumpassid; and thi strengthe schal be drawun doun of thee, and thin housis schulen be rauyschid.

12 The Lord God seith these thingis, As if a schepherd rauyschith fro the mouth of a lioun tweyne hipis, ether the laste thing of the eere, so the children of Israel schulen be rauyschid, that dwellen in Samarie, in the cuntrei of bed, and in the bed of Damask.

13 Here ye, and witnesse ye in the hous of Jacob, seith the Lord God of oostis.

14 For in the dai, whanne Y schal bigynne to visite the trespassyngis of Israel on hym, Y schal visite also on the auteris of Bethel; and the hornes of the auter schulen be kit awei, and schulen falle doun in to erthe.

15 And Y schal smyte the wynter hous with the somer hous, and the housis of yuer schulen perische, and many housis schulen be distried, seith the Lord.

CAP 4

1 Ye fatte kien, that ben in the hil of Samarie, here this word; whiche maken fals caleng to nedi men, and breken pore men; which seien to youre lordis, Bringe ye, and we schulen drynke.

2 The Lord God swoor in his hooli, for lo! daies schulen come on you; and thei schulen reise you in schaftis, and youre remenauntis in buylynge pottis.

3 And ye schulen go out bi the openyngis, oon ayens another, and ye schulen be cast forth in to Armon, seith the Lord.

4 Come ye to Bethel, and do ye wickidli; to Galgala, and multiplie ye trespassyng; and offre ye eerli youre sacrifices, in thre daies youre tithis.

5 And sacrifice ye heriyng of breed maad sour, and clepe ye wilful offryngis, and telle ye; for ye, sones of Israel, wolden so, seith the Lord God.

6 Wherfor and Y yaf to you astonying of teeth in alle youre citees, and nedinesse of looues in alle youre places; and ye turneden not ayen to me, seith the Lord.

7 Also Y forbeed reyn fro you, whanne thre monethis weren yit 'to comyng, til to ripe corn; and Y reynede on o citee, and on another citee Y reynede not; o part was bireyned, and the part driede vp on which Y reynede not.

8 And tweyne and thre citees camen to o citee, to drynke watir, and tho weren not fillid; and ye camen not ayen to me, seith the Lord.

9 Y smoot you with brennynge wynd, and with rust, the multitude of youre orcherdis, and of youre vyneris; and a wort worm eet youre olyue places, and youre fige places; and ye camen not ayen to me, seith the Lord.

10 Y sente in to you deth in the weie of Egipt, Y smoot with swerd youre yonge men, 'til to the caitifte of youre horsis, and Y made the stynk of youre oostis to stie in to youre nose thirlis; and ye camen not ayen to me, seith the Lord.

11 Y distriede you, as God distriede Sodom and Gomorre, and ye ben maad as a brond rauyschid of brennyng; and ye turneden not ayen to me, seith the Lord.

12 Wherfor, thou Israel, Y schal do these thingis to thee; but aftir that Y schal do to thee these thingis, Israel, be maad redi in to ayen comyng of thi God.

13 For lo! he fourmeth hillis, and makith wynd, and tellith to man his speche; and he makith a 'morew myist, and goith on hiy thingis of erthe; the Lord God of oostis is the name of hym.

CAP 5

1 Here ye this word, for Y reise on you a weilyng.

2 The hous of Israel felle doun, he schal not put to, that it rise ayen; the virgyn of Israel is cast doun in to hir lond, noon is that schal reise hir.

3 For the Lord God seith these thingis, The citee of which a thousynde wenten out, an hundrid schulen be left ther ynne; and of which an hundrid wenten out, ten schulen be left ther ynne, in the hous of Israel.

4 For the Lord seith these thingis to the hous of Israel, Seke ye me, and ye schulen lyue;

5 and nyle ye seke Bethel, and nyle ye entre in to Galgala, and ye schulen not passe to Bersabee; for whi Galgal schal be led caitif, and Bethel schal be vnprofitable.

6 Seke ye the Lord, and lyue ye, lest perauenture the hous of Joseph be brent as fier; and it schal deuoure Bethel, and there schal not be, that schal quenche.

7 Whiche conuerten doom in to wermod, and forsaken riytwisnesse in the lond,

8 and forsaken hym that makith Arture and Orion, and hym that turneth derknessis in to the morewtid, and him that chaungith dai in to niyt; which clepith watris of the see, and heldith out hem on the face of erthe; the Lord is name of hym.

9 Which scorneth distriyng on the stronge, and bringith rob-byng on the myyti.

10 Thei hatiden a man repreuynge in the yate, and thei wlatiden a man spekynge perfitli.

11 Therfor for that that ye robbiden a pore man, and token fro hym the chosun prey, ye schulen bilde housis with square stoon, and ye schulen not dwelle in hem; ye schulen plaunte moost louyd vyneyerdis, and ye schulen not drynke the wyn of hem.

12 For Y knew youre grete trespassis many, and youre stronge synnes; enemyes of 'the riytwis man, takynge yifte, and berynge doun pore men in the yate.

13 Therfor a prudent man schal be stille in that time, for the time is yuel.

14 Seke ye good, and not yuel, that ye lyue, and the Lord God of oostis schal be with you, as ye seiden.

15 Hate ye yuel, and loue ye good, and ordeyne ye in the gate doom; if perauenture the Lord God of oostis haue merci on the remenauntis of Joseph.

16 Therfor the Lord God of oostis, hauynge lordschipe, seith these thingis, Weilyng schal be in alle stretis, and in alle thingis that ben withoutforth it schal be seid, Wo! wo! and thei schulen clepe an erthe tilier to mourenyng, and hem that kunnen weile, to weilyng.

17 And weilyng schal be in alle weies, for Y schal passe forth in the myddil of 'the see, seith the Lord.

18 Wo to hem that desiren the dai of the Lord; wher to desiren ye it to you? This dai of the Lord schal be derknessis, and not liyt.

19 As if a man renne fro the face of a lioun, and a bere renne to hym; and he entre in to the hous, and lene with his hond on the wal, and a serpent dwellynge in schadewe bite hym.

20 Whether the dai of the Lord schal not be derknessis, and not liyt; and myist, and not schynyng ther ynne?

21 Y hatide and castide awei youre feeste daies, and Y schal not take the odour of youre cumpenyes.

22 That if ye offren to me youre brent sacrifices, and yiftis, Y schal not resseyue, and Y schal not biholde avowis of youre fatte thingis.

23 Do thou awei fro me the noise of thi songis, and Y schal not here the songis of thin harpe.

24 And doom schal be schewid as watir, and riytfulnesse as a strong streem.

25 Whether ye, the hous of Israel, offriden to me sacrifices for enemyes to be ouercomun, and sacrifice in desert fourti yeeris?

26 And ye han bore tabernaclis to Moloch, youre god, and ymage of youre idols, the sterre of youre god, which ye maden to you.

27 And Y schal make you for to passe ouer Damask, seide the Lord; God of oostis is the name of him.

CAP 6

1 Wo to you, that ben ful of richessis in Sion, and tristen in the hil of Samarie, ye principal men, the heedis of puplis, that goen proudli in to the hous of Israel.

2 Go ye in to Calamye, and se ye, and go ye fro thennus in to Emath the greet; and go ye doun in to Geth of Palestyns, and to alle the beste rewmes of hem, if her terme be broddere than youre terme.

3 And ye ben departid in to yuel dai, and neiyen to the seete of wickidnesse;

4 and ye slepen in beddis of yuer, and doen letcherie in youre beddis; and ye eten a lomb of the flok, and calues of the myddil of droue;

5 and ye syngen at vois of sautree. As Dauid thei gessiden hem for to haue instrumentis of song, and drynken wyn in viols;

6 and with beste oynement thei weren anoynted; and in no thing thei hadden compassioun on the sorewe, ether defoulyng, of Joseph.

7 Wherfor now thei schulen passe in the heed of men passynge ouer, and the doyng of men doynge letcherie schal be don awei.

8 The Lord God swoor in his soule, seith the Lord God of oostis, Y wlate the pride of Jacob, and Y hate the housis of hym, and Y schal bitake the citee with hise dwelleris;

9 that if ten men ben left in oon hous, and thei schulen die.

10 And his neiybore schal take hym, and schal brenne hym, that he bere out boonys of the hous. And he schal seie to hym, that is in the priuy places of the hous,

11 Whether ther is yit anentis thee? And he schal answer, An ende is. And he schal seie to hym, Be thou stille, and thenke thou not on the name of the Lord.

12 For lo! the Lord schal comaunde, and schal smyte the grettere hous with fallyngis, and the lesse hous with brekyngis.

13 Whether horsis moun renne in stoonys, ether it mai be eerid with wielde oxun? For ye turneden doom in to bitternesse, and the fruyt of riytfulnesse in to wermod.

14 And ye ben glad in nouyt, and ye seien, Whether not in oure strengthe we token to vs hornes?

15 Lo! Y schal reise on you, the hous of Israel, seith the Lord God of oostis, a folc; and it schal al to-breke you fro entre of Emath 'til to the streem of desert.

CAP 7

1 The Lord God schewide these thingis to me; and lo! a makere of locust in bigynnyng of buriownynge thingis of euentid reyn, and lo! euentid reyn after the clippere of the kyng.

2 And it was don, whanne he hadde endid for to ete the erbe of erthe, Y seide, Lord God, Y biseche, be thou merciful; who schal reise Jacob, for he is litil?

3 The Lord hadde merci on this thing; It schal not be, seide the Lord God.

4 The Lord God schewide to me these thingis; and lo! the Lord God schal clepe doom to fier, and it schal deuoure myche depthe of watir, and it eet togidere a part.

5 And Y seide, Lord God, Y biseche, reste thou; who schal reise Jacob, for he is litil?

6 The Lord hadde merci on this thing; But and this thing schal not be, seide the Lord God.

7 The Lord God schewide to me these thingis; and lo! the Lord stondinge on a wal plastrid, and in the hond of hym was a trulle of a masoun.

8 And the Lord seide to me, What seest thou, Amos? And Y seide, A trulle of a masoun. And the Lord seide, Lo! I schal putte a trulle in the myddil of my puple Israel; Y schal no more putte to, for to ouerlede it;

9 and the hiy thingis of idol schulen be distried, and the halewyngis of Israel schulen be desolat; and Y schal rise on the hous of Jeroboam bi swerd.

10 And Amasie, prest of Bethel, sente to Jeroboam, kyng of Israel, and seide, Amos rebellide ayens thee, in the myddil of the hous of Israel; the lond mai not susteyne alle hise wordis.

11 For Amos seith these thingis, Jeroboam schal die bi swerd, and Israel caitif schal passe fro his lond.

12 And Amasie seide to Amos, Thou that seest, go; fle thou in to the lond of Juda, and ete thou there thi breed; and there thou schalt profesie.

13 And thou schalt no more put to, that thou profesie in Bethel, for it is the halewyng of the king, and is the hous of the rewme.

14 And Amos answeride, and seide to Amasie, Y am not a profete, and Y am not sone of profete; but an herde of neet Y am, drawyng vp sicomoris.

15 And the Lord took me, whanne Y suede the floc; and the Lord seide to me, Go, and profesie thou to my puple Israel.

16 And now here thou the word of the Lord. Thou seist, Thou schalt not profesie on Israel, and thou schal not droppe on the hous of idol.

17 For this thing the Lord seith these thingis, Thi wijf schal do fornicacioun in the citee, and thi sones and thi douytris schal falle bi swerd, and thi lond schal be motun with a litil coord; and thou schalt die in a pollutid lond, and Israel caitif schal passe fro his lond.

CAP 8

1 The Lord God schewide to me these thingis; and lo! an hook of applis.

2 And the Lord seide, What seist thou, Amos? And Y seide, An hook of applis. And the Lord seide to me, The ende is comun on my puple Israel; Y schal no more putte to, that Y passe bi hym.

3 And the herris, ether twistis, of the temple schulen greetli sowne in that dai, seith the Lord God. Many men schulen die, silence schal be cast forth in ech place.

4 Here ye this thing, whiche al to-breken a pore man, and maken nedi men of the lond for to faile;

5 and ye seien, Whanne schal heruest passe, and we schulen sille marchaundises? and the sabat, and we schulen opene wheete? that we make lesse the mesure, and encreesse the cicle, and 'vndur put gileful balauncis;

6 that we welde bi siluer nedi men and pore men for schoon, and we sille outcastyngis of wheete?

7 The Lord swoor ayens the pride of Jacob, Y schal not foryete til to the ende alle the werkis of hem.

8 Whether on this thing the erthe schal not be mouyd togidere, and eche dwellere therof schal mourene? And it schal stie vp as al the flood, and schal be cast out, and schal flete awei as the stronde of Egipt.

9 And it schal be, seith the Lord, in that dai the sunne schal go doun in myddai, and Y schal make the erthe for to be derk in the dai of liyt.

10 And Y schal conuerte youre feeste daies in to mourenyng, and alle youre songis in to weilyng; and Y schal brynge yn on ech bac of you a sak, and on ech heed of you ballidnesse; and Y schal put it as the mourenyng of oon bigetun sone, and the laste thingis therof as a bittir dai.

11 Lo! the daies comen, seith the Lord, and Y schal sende out hungur in to erthe; not hungur of breed, nether thirst of watir, but of herynge the word of God.

12 And thei schulen be mouyd to gidere fro the see til to the see, and fro the north til to the eest thei schulen cumpasse, sekynge the word of the Lord, and thei schulen not fynde.

13 In that dai faire maidens schulen faile, and yonge men in thirst, whiche sweren in trespas of Samarie,

14 and seien, Dan, thi god lyueth, and the weie of Bersabee lyueth; and thei schulen falle, and thei schulen no more rise ayen.

CAP 9

1 I siy the Lord stondynge on the auter, and he seide, Smyte thou the herre, and the ouer threshfoldis be mouyd togidere; for aueryce is in the heed of alle, and Y schal sle bi swerd the laste of hem; ther schal no fliyt be to hem, and he that schal fle of hem, schal not be sauyd.

2 If thei schulen go doun til to helle, fro thennus myn hond schal lede out hem; and if thei schulen 'stie til in to heuene, fro thennus Y schal drawe hem doun.

3 And if thei schulen be hid in the cop of Carmele, fro thennus Y sekynge schal do awei hem; and if thei schulen hide hem silf fro myn iyen in the depnesse of the see, there Y shal comaunde to a serpente, and it schal bite hem.

4 And if thei schulen go awei in to caitifte bifore her enemyes, there Y schal comaunde to swerd, and it schal sle hem. And Y schal putte myn iyen on hem in to yuel, and not in to good.

5 And the Lord God of oostis schal do these thingis, that touchith erthe, and it schal faile, and alle men dwellynge ther ynne schulen mourene; and it schal stie vp as ech stronde, and it schal flete awei as flood of Egipt.

6 He that bildith his stiyng vp in heuene, schal do these thingis, and foundide his birthun on erthe; which clepith watris of the see, and heldith out hem on the face of erthe; the Lord is name of hym.

7 Whether not as sones of Ethiopiens ye ben to me, the sones of Israel? seith the Lord God. Whether Y made not Israel for to stie vp fro the lond of Egipt, and Palestines fro Capodosie, and Siriens fro Cirenen?

8 Lo! the iyen of the Lord God ben on the rewme synnynge, and Y schal al to-breke it fro the face of erthe; netheles Y al to-brekynge schal not al to-breke the hous of Jacob, seith the Lord.

9 For lo! Y schal comaunde, and schal schake the hous of Israel in alle folkis, as wheete is in a riddil, and a litil stoon schal not falle on erthe.

10 Alle synneris of my puple schulen die bi swerd, whiche seien, Yuel schal not neiy, and schal not come on vs.

11 In that dai Y schal reise the tabernacle of Dauith, that felle doun, and Y schal ayen bilde openyngis of wallis therof, and Y schal restore the thingis that fellen doun; and Y schal ayen bilde it,

12 as in olde daies, that thei welde the remenauntis of Idume, and alle naciouns; for that my name is clepun to help on hem, seith the Lord doynge these thingis.

13 Lo! daies comen, seith the Lord, and the erere schal take the repere, and 'the stampere of grape schal take the man sowynge seed; and mounteyns schulen droppe swetnesse, and alle smale hillis schulen be tilid.

14 And Y schal conuerte the caitifte of my puple Israel, and thei schulen bilde forsakun citees, and schulen dwelle; and schulen plaunte vyneyerdis, and thei schulen drynke wyn of hem; and schulen make gardyns, and schulen ete fruitis of hem.

15 And Y schal plaunte hem on her lond, and Y schal no more drawe out hem of her lond, which Y yaf to hem, seith the Lord thi God.

ABDIAS

CAP 1

1 Visioun of Abdias. The Lord God seith these thingis to Edom. We herden an heryng of the Lord, and he sente a messanger to hethene men. Rise ye, and togidere rise we ayens hym in to batel.

2 Lo! Y yaf thee litil in hethene men, thou art ful myche 'worthi to be dispisid.

3 The pride of thin herte enhaunside thee, dwellynge in crasyngis of stoonys, areisynge thi seete. Whiche seist in thin herte, Who schal drawe me doun in to erthe?

4 Thouy thou schalt be reisid as an egle, and thouy thou schalt putte thi nest among sterris, fro thennus Y schal drawe thee doun, seith the Lord.

5 If niyt theuys hadden entrid to thee, if outlawis bi niyt, hou schuldist thou haue be stille? whether thei schulden not haue stole thingis ynow to hem? If gadereris of grapis hadden entrid to thee, whether thei schulden haue left nameli clustris to thee?

6 Hou souyten thei Esau, serchiden the hid thingis of him?

7 Til to the termes thei senten out thee; and alle men of thi couenaunt of pees scorneden thee, men of thi pees wexiden stronge ayens thee; thei that schulen ete with thee, schulen put aspies, ether tresouns, vndur thee; ther is no prudence in hym.

8 Whether not in that dai, seith the Lord, Y schal lese the wise men of Idumee, and prudence of the mount of Esau?

9 And thi stronge men schulen drede of myddai, that a man of the hil of Esau perische.

10 For sleyng and for wickidnesse ayens thi brother Jacob, confusioun schal hile thee, and thou schalt perische with outen ende.

11 In the dai whanne thou stodist ayens hym, whanne aliens token the oost of hym, and straungeris entriden the yatis of hym, and senten lot on Jerusalem, thou were also as oon of hem.

12 And thou schalt not dispise in the dai of thi brother, in the dai of his pilgrimage, and thou schalt not be glad on the sones of Juda, in the dai of perdicioun of hem; and thou schalt not magnefie thi mouth in the dai of angwisch,

13 nether schalt entre in to the yate of my puple, in the dai of fallyng of hem; and thou schalt not dispise in the yuels of hym, in the dai of his distriyng; and thou schalt not be sent out ayens his oost, in the day of his distriyng;

14 nether thou schalt stonde in the goynges out, that thou sle hem that fledden; and thou schalt not close togidere the residues, ether left men, of hym, in the day of tribulacioun,

15 for the dai of the Lord is niy on alle 'hethene men. As thou hast doon, it schal be doon to thee; he schal conuerte thi yeldyng in to thin heed.

16 For as ye drunken on myn hooli hil, alle hethene men schulen drynke bisili, and thei schulen drynke, and schulen soupe vp; and thei schulen be as if thei ben not.

17 And saluacioun schal be in the hil of Sion, and it schal be hooli; and the hous of Jacob schal welde hem whiche wel-diden hem.

18 And the hous of Jacob schal be fier, and the hous of Joseph schal be flawme, and the hous of Esau schal be stobil; and 'thei schulen be kyndlid in hem, and thei schulen deuoure hem; and relifs schulen not be of the hous of Esau, for the Lord spak.

19 And these that ben at the south, schulen enherite the hil of Esau; and thei that ben in the lowe feeldis, schulen enherite Filistiym; and thei schulen welde the cuntrei of Effraym, and cuntrei of Samarie; and Beniamyn schal welde Galaad.

20 And ouerpassyng of this oost of sones of Israel schal welde alle places of Cananeis, til to Sarepta; and the transmygracioun of Jerusalem, that is in Bosphoro, schal welde citees of the south.

21 And sauyours schulen stie in to the hil of Sion, for to deme the hil of Esau, and a rewme schal be to the Lord.

JONAS

CAP 1

1 And the word of the Lord was maad to Jonas,

2 sone of Amathi, and seide, Rise thou, and go in to Nynyue, the greet citee, and preche thou ther ynne, for the malice therof stieth vp bifore me.

3 And Jonas roos for to fle in to Tharsis, fro the face of the Lord. And he cam doun to Joppe, and foond a schip goynge in to Tharsis, and he yaf schip hire to hem; and he wente doun in to it, for to go with hem in to Tharsis, fro the face of the Lord.

4 Forsothe the Lord sente a greet wynd in the see, and a greet tempest was maad in the see, and the schip was in perel for to be al to-brokun.

5 And schip men dredden, and men crieden to her god; and senten vessels, that weren in the schip, in to the see, that it were maad liytere of hem. And Jonas wente doun in to the ynnere thingis of the schip, and slepte bi a greuouse sleep.

6 And the gouernour cam to him, and seide to hym, Whi art thou cast doun in sleep? rise thou, clepe thi God to help, if perauenture God ayenthenke of vs, and we perische not.

7 And a man seide to his felowe, Come ye, and caste we lottis, and wite we, whi this yuel is to vs. And thei kesten lottis, and lot felle on Jonas.

8 And thei seiden to hym, Schewe thou to vs, for cause of what thing this yuel is to vs; what is thi werk, which is thi lond, and whidur goist thou, ether of what puple art thou?

9 And he seide to hem, Y am an Ebrew, and Y drede the Lord God of heuene, that made the see and the drie lond.

10 And the men dredden with greet drede, and seiden to him, Whi didist thou this thing? for the men knewen that he flei fro the face of the Lord, for Jonas hadde schewide to hem.

11 And thei seiden to hym, What schulen we do to thee, and the see schal seesse fro vs? for the see wente, and wexe greet on hem.

12 And he seide to hem, Take ye me, and throwe in to the see, and the see schal ceesse fro you; for Y woot, that for me this greet tempest is on you.

13 And men rowiden, for to turne ayen to the drie lond, and thei miyten not, for the see wente, and wexe greet on hem.

14 And thei crieden to the Lord, and seiden, Lord, we bisechen, that we perische not in the lijf of this man, and that thou yyue not on vs innocent blood; for thou, Lord, didist as thou woldist.

15 And thei token Jonas, and threwen in to the see; and the see stood of his buylyng.

16 And the men dredden the Lord with greet drede, and offriden oostis to the Lord, and vowiden avowis.

CAP 2

1 And the Lord made redi a greet fisch, that he shulde swolowe Jonas; and Jonas was in the wombe of the fisch thre daies and thre niytis.

2 And Jonas preiede to the Lord his God fro the fischis wombe,

3 and seide, Y criede to God of my tribulacioun, and he herde me; fro the wombe of helle Y criede, and thou herdist my vois.

4 Thou castidist me doun in to depnesse, in the herte of the see, and the flood cumpasside me; alle thi swolowis and thi wawis passiden on me.

5 And Y seide, Y am cast awei fro siyt of thin iyen; netheles eftsoone Y schal see thin hooli temple.

6 Watris cumpassiden me 'til to my soule, depnesse enuyrownede me, the see hilide myn heed.

7 Y wente doun to the vtmeste places of hillis, the barris of erthe closiden me togidere, in to withouten ende; and thou, my Lord God, schalt reise vp my lijf fro corrupcioun.

8 Whanne my soule was angwisched in me, Y bithouyte on the Lord, that my preier come to thee, to thin hooli temple.

9 Thei that kepen vanytees, forsaken his merci idili.

10 But Y in vois of heriyng schal offre to thee; what euer thingis Y vowide, Y schal yelde to the Lord, for myn helthe.

11 And the Lord seide to the fisch, and it castide out Jonas 'in to the drie lond.

CAP 3

1 And the word of the Lord was maad the secounde tyme to Jonas, and seide, Rise thou,

2 and go in to Nynyue, the greet citee, and preche thou in it the prechyng which Y speke to thee.

3 And Jonas roos, and wente in to Nynyue, bi the word of the Lord. And Nynyue was a greet citee, of the iurnei of thre daies.

4 And Jonas bigan for to entre in to the citee, bi the iornei of o dai, and criede, and seide, Yit fourti daies, and Nynyue schal be 'turned vpsodoun.

5 And men of Nynyue bileueden to the Lord, and prechiden fastyng, and weren clothid with sackis, fro the more 'til to the lesse.

6 And the word cam til to the kyng of Nynyue; and he roos of his seete, and castide awei his clothing fro him, and was clothid with a sak, and sat in aische.

7 And he criede, and seide in Nynyue of the mouth of the kyng and of 'his princis, 'and seide, Men, and werk beestis, and oxun, and scheep taaste not ony thing, nether be fed, nether drynke watir.

8 And men be hilid with sackis, and werk beestis crie to the Lord in strengthe; 'and be a man conuertid fro his yuel weie, and fro wickidnesse that is in the hondis of hem.

9 Who woot, if God be conuertid, and foryyue, and be turned ayen fro woodnesse of his wraththe, and we schulen not perische?

10 And God sai the werkis of hem, that thei weren conuertid fro her yuel weie; and God hadde merci on the malice which he spac, that he schulde do to hem, and did not.

CAP 4

1 And Jonas was turmentid with greet turment, and was wrooth.

2 And he preiede the Lord, and seide, Lord, Y biseche, whether this is not my word, whanne Y was yit in my lond? For this thing Y purposide, for to fle in to Tharsis; for Y woot, that thou, God, art meke and merciful, pacient, and of merciful doyng, and foryyuynge on malice.

3 And now, Lord, Y preie, take my soule fro me; for deth is betere to me than lijf.

4 And the Lord seide, Gessist thou, whether thou art wel wrooth?

5 And Jonas wente out of the citee, and sat ayens the eest of the citee, and made to hym a schadewyng place there; and sat vndur it in schadewe, til he sai what bifelle to the citee.

6 And the Lord God made redy an yuy, and it stiede vp on the heed of Jonas, that schadewe were on his heed, and kyueride hym; for he hadde trauelid. And Jonas was glad on the yuy, with greet gladnesse.

7 And God made redi a worm, in stiyng up of grei dai on the morewe; and it smoot the yuy, and it driede up.

8 And whanne the sunne was risun, the Lord comaundide to the hoot wynd and brennyng; and the sunne smoot on the heed of Jonas, and he swalide. And he axide to his soule that he schulde die, and seide, It is betere to me for to die, than for to lyue.

9 And the Lord seide to Jonas, Gessist thou, whether thou art wel wrooth on the yuy? And he seide, Y am wel wrooth, til to the deth.

10 And the Lord seide, Thou art sori on the yuy, in which thou trauelidist not, nether madist that it wexide, which was growun vndur o nyyt, and perischide in o nyyt.

11 And schal Y not spare the grete citee Nynyue, in which ben more than sixe score thousynde of men, which witen not what is betwixe her riyt half and left, and many beestis?

MYCHEE

CAP 1

1 The word of the Lord, which was maad to 'Mychee of Morasti, in the daies of Joathan, Achas, Ezechie, kyngis of Juda; which word he sai on Samarie, and Jerusalem.

2 Here ye, alle puplis, and the erthe perseyue, and plentee therof, and be the Lord God to you in to a witnesse, the Lord fro his hooli temple.

3 For lo! the Lord schal go out of his place, and schal come doun, and schal trede on hiy thingis of erthe.

4 And mounteyns schulen be waastid vndur hym, and valeis schulen be kit, as wex fro the face of fier, as watirs that rennen in to a pit.

5 In the grete trespas of Jacob is al this thing, and in the synnes of the hous of Israel. Which is the greet trespas of Jacob? whether not Samarie? and whiche ben the hiy thingis of Juda? whether not Jerusalem?

6 And Y schal put Samarie as an heep of stoonys in the feeld, whanne a vynyerd is plauntid; and Y schal drawe awei the stoonys therof in to a valei, and Y schal schewe the foundementis therof.

7 And alle 'grauun ymagis therof schulen be betun togidere, and alle hiris therof schulen be brent in fier; and Y schal putte alle idols therof in to perdicioun; for of hiris of an hoore tho ben gaderid, and 'til to hire of an hoore tho schulen turne ayen.

8 On this thing Y schal weile and yelle, Y schal go spuylid and nakid; Y schal make weilyng of dragouns, and mournyng as of ostrigis.

9 For wounde therof is dispeirid; for it cam til to Juda, it touchide the yate of my puple, til to Jerusalem.

10 In Geth nyle ye telle, bi teeris wepe ye not; in the hous of dust with dust togidere sprynge you.

11 And ye a fair dwellyng passe, which is confoundid with yuel fame; it is not goon out, which dwellith in the goyng out; a niy hous schal take of you weilyng, which stood to it silf.

12 For it is maad sijk to good, which dwellith in bitternessis. For yuel cam doun fro the Lord in to the yate of Jerusalem, noise of foure horsid cart,

13 of drede to the puple dwellynge at Lachis. It is the bigynnyng of synne of the douyter of Sion, for the grete trespassis of Israel ben foundun in thee.

14 Therfor he schal yyue werriours on the eritage of Geth, on housis of leesyng in to deseit to kyngis of Israel.

15 Yit Y schal brynge an eir to thee, that dwellist in Maresa; the glorie of Israel schal come til to Odolla.

16 Be thou maad ballid, and be thou clippid on the sones of thi delices; alarge thi ballidnesse as an egle, for thei ben lad caitif fro thee.

CAP 2

1 Wo to you, that thenken vnprofitable thing, and worchen yuele in youre beddis; in the morewtid liyt thei don it, for the hond of hem is ayenus God.

2 Thei coueitiden feeldis, and tooken violentli; and rauyschiden housis, and falsli calengiden a man and his hous, a man and his eritage.

3 Therfor the Lord seith these thingis, Lo! Y thenke on this meynee yuel, fro which ye schulen not take awei youre neckis; and ye schulen not walke proude, for the worste tyme is.

4 In that dai a parable schal be takun on you, and a song schal be songun with swetnesse of men, seiynge, Bi robbyng we ben distried; a part of my puple is chaungid; hou schal he go awei fro me, whanne he turneth ayen that schal departe youre cuntreis?

5 For this thing 'noon schal be to thee sendynge a litil corde of sort in cumpeny of the Lord.

6 A! thou Israel, speke ye not spekyng; it schal not droppe on these men, confusioun schal not catche,

7 seith the hous of Jacob. Whether the Spirit of the Lord is abreggid, either siche ben the thouytis of hym? Whether my wordis ben not gode, with hym that goith riytli?

8 And ayenward my puple roos togidere in to an aduersarie; ye token awei the mantil aboue the coote, and ye turneden in to batel hem that wenten sympli.

9 Ye castiden the wymmen of my puple out of the hous of her delices; fro the litle children of hem ye token awei myn heriyng with outen ende.

10 Rise ye, and go, for here ye han not reste; for the vnclennesse therof it schal be corrupt with the worst rot.

11 Y wolde that Y were not a man hauynge spirit, and rathere Y spak a leesyng. Y schal droppe to thee in to wyn, and in to drunkenesse; and this puple schal be, on whom it is droppid.

12 With gaderyng Y schal gadere Jacob; Y schal lede togidere thee al in to oon, the relifs of Israel. Y schal put hym togidere, as a floc in folde; as scheep in the myddil of fooldis thei schulen make noise, of multitude of men.

13 For he schal stie schewynge weie bifore hem; thei schulen departe, and passe the yate, and schulen go out therbi; and the kyng of hem schal passe bifore hem, and the Lord in the heed of hem.

CAP 3

1 And Y seide, Ye princis of Jacob, and duykis of the hous of Israel, here. Whether it be not youre for to knowe doom, whiche haten good,

2 and louen yuele? Whiche violentli taken awei the skynnes of hem fro aboue hem, and the fleisch of hem fro aboue the bonys of hem.

3 Whiche eeten the fleisch of my puple, and hiliden the skyn of hem fro aboue; and broken togidere the boonys of hem, and kittiden togidere as in a cawdroun, and as fleisch in the myddil of a pot.

4 Thanne thei schulen crie to the Lord, and he schal not here hem; and he schal hide hise face fro hem in that tyme, as thei diden wickidli in her fyndingis.

5 The Lord God seith these thingis on the profetis that disseyuen my puple, and biten with her teeth, and prechen pees; and if ony man yyueth not in the mouth of hem ony thing, thei halewen batel on hym.

6 Therfor niyt schal be to you for visioun, or profesie, and derknessis to you for dyuynacioun; and sunne schal go doun on the profetis, and the dai schal be maad derk on hem.

7 And thei schulen be confoundid that seen visiouns, and dyuynours schulen be confoundid, and alle schulen hile her cheris, for it is not the answer of God.

8 Netheles Y am fillid with strengthe of Spirit of the Lord, and in doom and vertu, that Y schewe to Jacob his greet trespas, and to Israel his synne.

9 Here these thingis, ye princes of the hous of Jacob, and domesmen of the hous of Israel, whiche wlaten dom, and peruerten alle riyt thingis;

10 whiche bilden Sion in bloodis, and Jerusalem in wickidnesse.

11 Princes therof demyden for yiftis, and prestis therof tauyten for hire, and profetis therof dyuyneden for money; and on the Lord thei restiden, and seiden, Whether the Lord is not in the myddil of us? yuelis schulen not come on vs.

12 For this thing bi cause of you, Sion as a feeld schal be erid; and Jerusalem schal be as an heep of stoonys, and the hil of the temple schal be in to hiye thingis of woodis.

CAP 4

1 And in the laste of daies the hil of the hous of the Lord schal be maad redi in the cop of hillis, and hiy ouer smale hillis. And puplis schulen flete to him, and many puplis schulen haaste,

2 and shulen seie, Come ye, stie we til to the hil of the Lord, and to the hous of God of Jacob; and he schal teche vs of hise weies, and we schulen go in hise pathis. For lawe schal go out fro Syon, and the word of the Lord fro Jerusalem;

3 and he schal deme bitwixe many puplis, and schal chastise stronge folkis til in to fer. And thei schulen bete togidere her swerdis in to scharis, and her speris in to picoisis; a folc schal not take swerd ayens folc, and thei schulen no more lerne for to fiyte.

4 And a man schal sitte vndur his vyneyerd, and vndur his fige tree; and ther schal not be that schal make aferd, for the mouth of the Lord of oostis spak.

5 For alle puplis schulen go, ech man in the name of his Lord God; but we schulen walke in the name of oure Lord God in to the world, and ouer.

6 In that dai, seith the Lord, Y schal gadere the haltynge, and Y schal gadere hir that Y castide awei, and whom Y turmentide Y schal coumforte.

7 And Y schal putte the haltynge in to relifs, ether remenauntis, and hir that trauelide, in a strong folc. And the Lord schal regne on hem in the hil of Sion, fro this now and til in to with outen ende.

8 And thou, 'derk tour of the floc of the douyter of Sion, 'til to thee he schal come, and the first power schal come, the rewme of the douytir of Jerusalem.

9 Now whi art thou drawun togidere with mournyng? whether a kyng is not to thee, ether thi counselour perischide? for sorewe hath take thee, as a womman trauelinge of child.

10 Thou douyter of Sion, make sorewe, and haaste, as a womman trauelynge of child; for now thou schalt go out of the citee, and schalt dwelle in cuntree, and schalt come 'til to Babiloyne; there thou schalt be delyuered, there the Lord schal ayen bie thee, fro the hond of thin enemyes.

11 And now many folkis ben gaderid on thee, whiche seien, Be it stonyd, and oure iye biholde in to Sion.

12 Forsothe thei knewen not the thouytis of the Lord, and vndurstoden not the councel of hym, for he gaderide hem as the hei of feeld.

13 Rise thou, douyter of Sion, and threische, for Y schal putte thin horn of irun, and Y schal putte thi nailis brasun; and thou schalt make lesse, ether waste, many puplis, and schalt sle to the Lord the raueyns of hem, and the strengthe of hem to the Lord of al erthe.

1 Now thou, douyter of a theef, schalt be distried; thei puttiden on vs bisegyng, in a yerde thei schulen smyte the cheke of the iuge of Israel.

CAP 5

2 And thou, Bethleem Effrata, art litil in the thousyndis of Juda; he that is the lordli gouernour in Israel, schal go out of thee to me; and the goyng out of hym is fro bigynnyng, fro daies of euerlastyngnesse.

3 For this thing he shal yyue hem til to the tyme in which the trauelinge of child schal bere child, and the relifs of hise britheren schulen be conuertid to the sones of Israel.

4 And he schal stonde, and schal fede in the strengthe of the Lord, in the heiythe of the name of his Lord God; and thei schulen be conuertid, for now he schal be magnefied til to the endis of al erthe.

5 And this schal be pees, whanne Assirius schal come in to oure lond, and whanne he schal trede in oure housis; and we schulen reise on hym seuene scheepherdis, and eiyte primatis men, ether the firste in dignytee.

6 And thei schulen frete the lond of Assur bi swerd, and the lond of Nembroth bi speris of hym; and he schal delyuere vs fro Assur, whanne he schal come in to oure lond, and whanne he schal trede in oure coostis.

7 And relifs of Jacob schulen be in the myddil of many puplis, as dew of the Lord, and as dropis on erbe, whiche abidith not man, and schal not abide sones of men.

8 And relifs of Jacob schulen be in hethene men, in the myddil of many puplis, as a lioun in beestis of the woodis, and as a whelpe of a lioun rorynge in flockis of scheep; and whanne he passith, and defoulith, and takith, there is not that schal delyuere.

9 And thin hond schal be reisid on thin enemyes, and alle thin enemyes schulen perische.

10 And it schal be, in that dai, seith the Lord, Y schal take awei thin horsis fro the myddil of thee, and Y schal distrie thi foure horsid cartis.

11 And Y schal leese the citees of thi lond, and Y schal distrie alle thi strengthis; and Y schal do awei witchecraftis fro thin hond, and dyuynaciouns schulen not be in thee.

12 And Y schal make for to perische thi 'grauun ymagis, and Y schal breke togidere fro the myddil of thee thin ymagis, and thou schalt no more worschipe the werkis of thin hondis.

13 And Y schal drawe out of the middis of thee thi woodis, and Y schal al to-breke thi citees.

14 And Y schal make in woodnesse and indignacioun veniaunce in alle folkis, whiche herden not.

CAP 6

1 Here ye whiche thingis the Lord spekith. Rise thou, stryue thou bi doom ayens mounteyns, and litle hillis here thi vois.

2 Mounteyns, and the stronge foundementis of erthe, here the doom of the Lord; for the doom of the Lord with his puple, and he schal be demyd with Israel.

3 Mi puple, what haue Y don to thee, ether what was Y greuouse to thee? Answere thou to me.

4 For Y ledde thee out of the lond of Egipt, and of the hous of seruage Y delyuerede thee; and Y sente bifore thi face Moises, and Aaron, and Marye.

5 My puple, bithenke, Y preie, what Balaac, kyng of Moab, thouyte, and what Balaam, sone of Beor, of Sethym, answeride to hym til to Galgala, that thou schuldist knowe the riytwisnesse of the Lord.

6 What worthi thing schal Y offre to the Lord? schal Y bowe the knee to the hiye God? Whether Y schal offre to hym brent sacrifices, and calues of o yeer?

7 Whether God mai be paid in thousyndis of wetheris, ether in many thousyndis of fatte geet buckis? Whether Y schal yyue my firste bigetun for my greet trespas, the fruyt of my wombe for synne of my soule?

8 Y schal schewe to thee, thou man, what is good, and what the Lord axith of thee; forsothe for to do doom, and for to loue merci, and be bisi for to walke with thi God.

9 The vois of the Lord crieth to the citee, and heelthe schal be to alle men dredynge thi name. Ye lynagis, here; and who schal approue it?

10 Yit fier is in the hous of the vnpitouse man, the tresouris of wickidnesse, and a lesse mesure ful of wraththe.

11 Whether Y schal iustifie the wickid balaunce, and the gileful weiytis of litil sak,

12 in whiche riche men therof ben fillid with wickidnesse? And men dwellynge ther ynne spaken leesyng, and the tunge of hem was gileful in the mouth of hem.

13 And Y therfor bigan for to smyte thee, in perdicioun on thi synnes.

14 Thou schalt ete, and schalt not be fillid, and thi mekyng is in the middil of thee; and thou schalt take, and schalt not saue; and which thou schalt saue, Y schal yyue in to swerd.

15 Thou schalt sowe, and schal not repe; thou schalt trede the 'frut of oliue, and schalt not be anoyntid with oile; and must, and schalt not drynke wyn.

16 And thou keptist the heestis of Amry, and al the werk of the hous of Acab, and hast walkid in the lustis of hem, that Y schulde yyue thee in to perdicioun, and men dwellynge in it in to scornyng, and ye schulen bere the schenschipe of my puple.

CAP 7

1 Wo to me, for Y am maad as he that gaderith in heruest rasyns of grapis; there is no clustre for to ete; my soule desiride figis ripe bifore othere.

2 The hooli perischide fro erthe, and riytful is not in men; alle aspien, ether setten tresoun, in blood, a man huntith his brother to deth.

3 The yuel of her hondis thei seien good; the prince axith, and the domesman is in yeldyng; and a greet man spak the desir of his soule, and thei sturbliden togidere it.

4 He that is best in hem, is as a paluyre; and he that is riytful, is as a thorn of hegge. The dai of thi biholdyng, thi visityng cometh, now schal be distriyng of hem.

5 Nyle ye bileue to a frend, and nyle ye truste in a duyk; fro hir that slepith in thi bosum, kepe thou closyngis of thi mouth.

6 For the sone doith wrong to the fadir, and the douyter schal rise ayens hir modir, and the wijf of the sone ayens the modir of hir hosebonde; the enemyes of a man ben the homeli, ether houshold meynee, of hym.

7 Forsothe Y schal biholde to the Lord, Y schal abide God my sauyour; the Lord my God schal here me.

8 Thou, myn enemye, be not glad on me, for Y felle doun, Y schal rise; whanne Y sitte in derknessis, the Lord is my liyt.

9 Y schal bere wraththe of the Lord, for Y haue synned to hym, til he deme my cause, and make my doom; he schal lede out me in to liyt, Y schal se riytwisnesse of hym.

10 And myn enemye schal biholde me, and sche schal be hilid with confusioun, which seith to me, Where is thi Lord God? Myn iyen schulen se hir, now sche schal be in to defoulyng, as clei of stretis.

11 Dai schal come, that thi wallis be bildid; in that dai lawe schal be maad afer.

12 In that dai and Assur schal come til to thee, and 'til to stronge citees, and fro stronge citees til to flood; and to see fro see, and to hil fro hil.

13 And erthe schal be in to desolacioun for her dwelleris, and for fruyt of the thouytis of hem.

14 Fede thou thi puple in thi yerde, the floc of thin eritage, that dwellen aloone in wielde wode; in the myddil of Carmel thei schulen be fed of Basan and of Galaad,

15 bi elde daies, bi daies of thi goyng out of the lond of Egipt. Y schal schewe to hym wonderful thingis;

16 hethene men schulen se, and thei schulen be confoundid on al her strengthe; thei schulen putte hondis on her mouth, the eris of hem schulen be deef;

17 thei schulen licke dust as a serpent; as crepynge thingis of erthe thei schulen be disturblid of her housis; thei schulen not desire oure Lord God, and thei schulen drede thee.

18 God, who is lijk thee, that doist awei wickidnesse, and berist ouer the synne of relifs of thin eritage? He shal no more sende in his stronge veniaunce, for he is willynge merci; he schal turne ayen,

19 and haue merci on vs. He schal put doun oure wickidnessis, and schal caste fer in to depnesse of the see alle oure synnes.

20 Thou schalt yyue treuthe to Jacob, merci to Abraham, whiche thou sworist to oure fadris fro elde daies.

NAUM

CAP 1

1 The birthun of Nynyue; the book of visioun of Naum Helcesei.

2 The Lord is a punyschere, and the Lord is vengynge; the Lord is venginge, and hauynge strong veniaunce; the Lord is vengynge ayens hise aduersaries, and he is wraththing to hise enemyes.

3 The Lord is pacient, and greet in strengthe, and he clensynge schal not make innocent. The Lord cometh in tempest, and the weies of hym ben in whirlwynd, and cloudis ben the dust of hise feet;

4 he blameth the see, and drieth it, and bryngith alle flodis to desert. Basan is maad sijk, and Carmel, and the flour of Liban langwischide.

5 Mounteyns ben mouyd togidere of hym, and litil hillis ben desolat. And erthe tremblide togidere fro the face of him, and the roundenesse of erthe, and alle dwellynge ther ynne.

6 Who schal stonde bifore the face of his indignacioun? and who schal ayenstonde in the wraththe of his stronge veniaunce? His indignacioun is sched out as fier, and stoonys ben brokun of hym.

7 The Lord is good, and coumfortynge in the dai of tribulacioun, and knowynge hem that hopen in hym.

8 And in greet flood passynge forth, he schal make ende of his place; and derknessis schulen pursue hise enemyes.

9 What thenken ye ayens the Lord? He schal make ende; double tribulacioun schal not rise togidere.

10 For as thornes byclippen hem togidere, so the feeste of hem drynkynge togidere schal be wastyd, as stobul ful of drienesse.

11 Of thee schal go out a man thenkynge malice ayens the Lord, and trete trespassyng in soule.

12 The Lord seith these thingis, If thei schulen be parfit, and so manye, and thus thei shulen be clippid, and it schal passe bi. I turmentide thee, and Y schal no more turmente thee.

13 And now Y schal al to-breke the yerde of hym fro thi bak, and Y schal breke thi bondis.

14 And the Lord schal comaunde on thee, it schal no more be sowun of thi name. Of the hous of thi god Y schal sle; Y schal putte thi sepulcre a 'grauun ymage, and wellid togidere, for thou art vnworschipid.

15 Lo! on hillis the feet of the euangelisynge and tellynge pees. Juda, halewe thou thi feeste daies, and yelde thi vowis, for whi Belial schal no more put to, that he passe forth in thee; al Belial perischide.

CAP 2

1 He stiede up, that schal scatere bifore thee, that schal kepe bisechyng; biholde thou the weie, coumforte leendis, strengthe thou vertu greetli.

2 For as the Lord yeldide the pride of Jacob, so the pride of Israel; for distrieris scateriden hem, and distrieden the generaciouns of hem.

3 The scheld of stronge men of hym ben firi, men of the oost ben in rede clothis; raynes of fire of chare, in the dai of his makyng redi; and the leederis therof ben asleep.

4 In weies thei ben troblid togidere, cartis of foure horsis ben hurtlid togidere in stretis; the siyte of hem as laumpis, as leitis rennynge aboute.

5 He schal bithenke of his stronge men, thei schulen falle in her weies; and swiftli thei schulen stie on the wallis therof, and schadewyng place schal be maad redi.

6 Yatis of floodis ben openyd, and the temple is brokun doun to erthe.

7 And a knyyt is led awei caitif, and the handmaidis therof schulen be dryuun sorewynge as culueris, grutchynge in her hertis.

8 And Nynyue, as a cisterne of watris the watris therof; forsothe thei fledden; stonde ye, stonde ye, and there is not that schal turne ayen.

9 Rauysche ye siluer, rauysche ye gold; and there is noon ende of richessis, of alle desirable vessels.

10 It is distried, and kit, and to-rent, and herte failynge, and vnknyttinge of smale knees, and failynge in alle reynes; and the face of alle ben as blacnesse of a pot.

11 Where is the dwellyng of liouns, and lesewis of whelpis of liouns? To whiche citee the lioun yede, that the whelp of the lioun schulde entre thidur, and there is not that schal make aferd.

12 The lioun took ynow to hise whelpis, and slowy to his lionessis; and fillide her dennes with prei, and his couche with raueyn.

13 Lo! Y to thee, seith the Lord God of oostis; and Y schal brenne thi cartis of foure horsis til to the hiyeste, and swerd schal ete thi smale liouns; and Y schal distrie thi prei fro the lond, and the vois of thi messangeris schulen no more be herd.

CAP 3

1 Wo to the citee of bloodis, al of leesyng, ful of to-reendyng; raueyn shal not go awei fro thee.

2 Vois of scourge, and vois of bire of wheel, and of hors makynge noise, and of foure horsid carte brennynge, and of kniyt stiynge vp,

3 and of schynynge swerd, and glesenynge spere, and of slayn multitude, and of greuouse fallyng, nether ther is eende of careyns. And thei schulen falle togidere in her bodies,

4 for the multitude of fornicaciouns of the hoore fair and plesaunt, and hauynge witchecraftis; which seelde folkis in her fornicaciouns, and meynees in her enchauntementis, ether sorceries.

5 Lo! Y to thee, seith the Lord God of oostis; and Y schal schewe thi schameful thingis in thi face; and Y schal schewe to folkis thi nakidnesse, and to rewmes thin yuel fame.

6 And Y schal cast out on thee thin abhomynaciouns, and Y schal punysche thee with dispitis, and Y schal putte thee in to ensaumple.

7 And it schal be, ech man that schal se thee, schal skippe awei fro thee, and schal seie, Nynyue is distried. Who schal moue heed on thee? wherof schal Y seke to thee a coumfortour?

8 Whether thou art betere than Alisaundre of puplis, that dwellith in floodis? Watris ben in cumpas therof, whos richessis is the see, watris ben wallis therof.

9 Ethiope is strengthe therof, and Egipt, and there is noon ende; Affrik and Libie weren in help therof.

10 But and it in 'passyng ouer is led in to caitifte; the litle children therof ben hurtlid doun in the heed of alle weies. And on the noble men therof thei kesten lot, and alle grete men therof ben set togidere in gyues.

11 And thou therfor schalt be drunkun, and schalt be dispisid, and thou schalt seke helpe of enemye.

12 Al thi strengthis as a fige tree, with hise figis vnripe; if thei schulen be schakun, thei schulen falle in to the mouth of the etere.

13 Lo! thi puple ben wymmen in the myddil of thee; the yatis of thi lond schulen be schewid to openyng to thin enemyes; fier schal deuoure thin herris.

14 Drawe vp to thee water for asegyng, bilde thi strengthis; entre in fen, and trede, thou vndurgoynge holde a tiel stoon.

15 There fier schal ete thee, thou schalt perische bi swerd, it schal deuoure thee, as bruke doith; be thou gaderid togidere as a bruke, be thou multiplied as a locuste.

16 Thou madist thi marchaundises mo than ben sterris of heuene; a bruke is spred abrood, and flei awei.

17 Thi keperis ben as locustis, and thi litle children ben as locustis of locustis, whiche sitten togidere in heggis in the dai of coold; the sun is risun, and thei fledden awei, and the place of hem is not knowun, where thei weren.

18 Thi scheepherdis napten, thou kyng Assur, thi princes schulen be biried; thi puple ofte was hid in hillis, and ther is not that schal gadere.

19 Thi sorewe is not priuy, thi wounde is worst; alle men that herden thin heryng, pressiden togidere hond on thee, for on whom passide not thi malice euermore?

ABACUK

CAP 1

1 The birthun that Abacuk, the profete, sai.

2 Hou longe, Lord, schal Y crye, and thou schalt not here? Y suffrynge violence schal crie an hiy to thee, and thou schalt not saue?

3 Whi schewidist thou to me wickidnesse and trauel, for to se prey and vnriytwisnesse ayens me? Whi biholdist thou dispiseris, and art stille, the while an vnpitouse man defoulith a riytfulere than hym silf? And thou schalt make men as fischis of

the see, and as crepynge thingis not hauynge a ledere; and doom is maad, and ayenseiyng is more miyti.

4 For this thing lawe is 'to-brokun, and doom cometh not til to the ende; for the vnpitouse man hath miyt ayens the iust, therfor weiward doom schal go out.

5 Biholde ye in hethene men, and se ye, and wondre ye, and greetli drede ye; for a werk is doon in youre daies, which no man schal bileue, whanne it schal be teld.

6 For lo! Y schal reise Caldeis, a bittir folk and swift, goynge on the breede of erthe, that he welde tabernaclis not hise.

7 It is orible, and dredeful; the dom and birthun therof schal go out of it silf.

8 His horsis ben liytere than pardis, and swifter than euentyd woluys, and hise horse men schulen be scaterid abrood; for whi 'horse men schulen come fro fer, thei schulen fle as an egle hastynge to ete.

9 Alle men schulen come to preye, the faces of hem is as a brennynge wynd; and he schal gadere as grauel caitifte,

10 and he schal haue victorie of kyngis, and tirauntis schulen be of his scornyng. He schal leiye on al strengthe, and schal bere togidere heep of erthe, and schal take it.

11 Thanne the spirit schal be chaungid, and he schal passe forth, and falle doun; this is the strengthe of hym, of his god.

12 Whether 'thou, Lord, art not my God, myn hooli, and we schulen not die? Lord, in to doom thou hast set hym, and thou groundidist hym strong, that thou schuldist chastise.

13 Thin iyen ben clene, se thou not yuel, and thou schalt not mowe biholde to wickidnesse. Whi biholdist thou not on men doynge wickidli, and thou art stille, while the vnpitouse man deuourith a more iust man than hymsilf?

14 And thou schalt make men as fischis of the see, and as a crepynge thing not hauynge prince.

15 He schal lifte vp al in the hook; he drawide it in his greet net, and gaderide in to his net; on this thing he schal be glad, and make ioie with outforth.

16 Therfore he schal offere to his greet net, and schal make sacrifice to his net; for in hem his part is maad fat, and his mete is chosun.

17 Therfor for this thing he spredith abrood his greet net, and euere more he ceesith not for to sle folkis.

CAP 2

1 On my kepyng Y schal stonde, and schal pitche a grees on wardyng; and Y schal biholde, that Y se what thing schal be seid to me, and what Y schal answere to hym that repreuith me.

2 And the Lord answeride to me, and seide, Write thou the reuelacioun, and make it pleyn on tablis, that he renne, that schal rede it.

3 For yit the visioun is fer, and it schal appere in to ende, and schal not lie; if it schal make dwellyng, abide thou it, for it comynge schal come, and schal not tarie.

4 Lo! the soule of hym, that is vnbileueful, schal not be riytful in hym silf; forsothe the iust man schal lyue in his feith.

5 And as wyn disseyueth a man drynkynge, so schal the proude man be, and he schal not be maad feir; for as helle he alargide his soule, and he is as deth, and he is not fillid; and he schal gadere to hym alle folkis, and he shal kepe togidere to hym alle puplis.

6 Whether not alle these puplis schulen take a parable on hym, and the speking of derk sentencis of hym? And it schal be seid, Wo to hym that multiplieth thingis not his owne; hou longe, and he aggreggith ayens hym silf thicke clei?

7 Whether not sudeynli thei schulen rise to gidere, that schulen bite thee? And thei schulen be reisid to-teerynge thee, and thou schalt be in to raueyn to hem; and thin aspieris in yuel schulen wake.

8 For thou robbidist many folkis, alle schulen robbe thee, whiche schulen be left of puplis, for blood of man, and for wickidnesse of lond of the citee, and of alle men dwellynge in it.

9 Wo to hym that gaderith yuel coueitise to his hous, that his nest be in hiy, and gessith hym for to be delyuered of the hond of yuel.

10 Thou thouytist confusioun to thin hous; thou hast slayn many puplis, and thi soule synnede.

11 For a stoon of the wal schal crie, and a tree that is bitwixe ioynturis of bildyngis schal answere.

12 Wo to hym that bildith a citee in bloodis, and makith redi a citee in wickidnesse.

13 Whether not these thingis ben of the Lord of oostis? For puplis schulen trauele in myche fier, and folkis in veyn, and thei schulen faile.

14 For the erthe schal be fillid, that it knowe the glorie of the Lord, as watris hilynge the see.

15 Wo to hym that yyueth drynk to his frend, and sendith his galle, and makith drunkun, that he biholde his nakidnesse.

16 He is fillid with yuel fame for glorie; and thou drynke, and be aslept; the cuppe of the riythalf of the Lord schal cumpasse thee, and 'castynge vp of yuel fame on thi glorie.

17 For the wickidnesse of Liban schal kyuere thee, and distruccioun of beestis schal make hem aferd, of bloodis of man, and of wickidnesse of lond, and of the citee, and of alle men dwellynge ther ynne.

18 What profitith the 'grauun ymage, for his makere grauyde it, a wellid thing togidere and fals ymage? for the makere therof hopide in makyng, that he made doumbe symylacris.

19 Wo to hym that seith to a tre, Wake thou; Rise thou, to a stoon beynge stille; whether he schal mow teche? Lo! this is kyuerid with gold and siluer, and no spirit is in his entrails.

20 Forsothe the Lord is in his hooli temple, al erthe be stille fro his face.

CAP 3

1 The preier of Abacuk, the profete, for vnkunnynge men. Lord, Y herde thin heryng, and Y dredde;

2 Lord, it is thi werk, in the myddil of yeeris quykene thou it. In the middil of yeeris thou schalt make knowun; whanne thou schalt be wrooth, thou schalt haue mynde of mercy.

3 God schal come fro the south, and the hooli fro the mount of Faran. The glorie of hym kyueride heuenes, and the erthe is ful of his heryyng.

4 The schynyng of hym schal be as liyt; hornes in hondis of hym.

5 There the strengthe of hym was hid, deth schal go bifore his face; the deuel schal go out bifore hise feet.

6 He stood, and mat the erthe; he bihelde, and vnboond folkis, and hillis of the world weren al to-brokun; the litle hillis of the world weren bowid doun, of the weies of his euerlastyngnesse.

7 For wickidnesse Y saiy the tentis of Ethiope, the skynnes of the lond of Madian schulen be troblid.

8 Lord, whether in floodis thou art wrooth, ether in floodis is thi strong veniaunce, ether in the see is thin indignacioun? Which shalt stie on thin horsis; and thi foure horsid cartis is saluacioun.

9 Thou reisynge schalt reise thi bouwe, othis to lynagis whiche thou hast spoke; thou schalt departe the floodis of erthe.

10 Watris saien thee, and hillis sorewiden, the goter of watris passide; depnesse yaf his vois, hiynesse reiside hise hondis.

11 The sunne and moone stoden in her dwellyng place; in the liyt of thin arowis thei schulen go, in the schynyng of thi spere glisnynge.

12 In gnastyng thou schalt defoule erthe, and in strong veniaunce thou schalt astonye folkis.

13 Thou art gon out in to helthe of thi puple, in to helthe with thi crist; thou hast smyte the heed of the hous of the vnpitouse man, thou hast maad nakid the foundement til to the necke.

14 Thou cursidist the ceptris, ether powers, of hym, the heed of hise fiyteris, to men comynge as whirlewynde for to sca-tere me; the ioiyng withoutforth of hem, as of hym that deuourith a pore man in hidlis.

15 Thou madist a weie in the see to thin horsis, in clei of many watris.

16 Y herde, and my wombe is troblid togidere; my lippis trembliden togidere of the vois. Rot entre in my boonys, and sprenge vndur me; that Y reste ayen in the dai of tribulacioun, and Y schal stie vp to oure puple gird togidere.

17 For the fige tre schal not floure, and buriownyng schal not be in vynyerdis; the werk of olyue tre schal lie, and feeldis schulen not brynge mete; a scheep schal be kit awei fro the fold, and droue schal not be in cratchis.

18 Forsothe Y schal haue ioye in the Lord, and Y schal make ioie with outforth in God my Jhesu.

19 God the Lord is my strengthe, and he schal putte my feet as of hertis; and on myn hiye thingis, the ouercomere schal lede forth me, syngynge in salmes.

SOFONYE

CAP 1

1 The word of the Lord, that was maad to Sofonye, sone of Chusi, sone of Godolie, sone of Amasie, sone of Ezechie, in the daies of Josie, the sone of Amon, king of Juda.

2 Y gaderinge schal gadere alle thingis fro the face of erthe, seith the Lord;

3 Y gaderynge man and beeste, Y gaderynge volatils of heuene, and fischis of the see; and fallyngis of vnpitouse men schulen be, and Y schal leese men fro face of erthe, seith the Lord.

4 And Y schal stretche out myn hond on Juda, and on alle dwellers of Jerusalem; and Y schal lese fro this place the relifs of Baal, and the names of keperis of housis, with prestis;

5 and hem that worschipen on roouys the knyythod of heuene, and worschipen, and sweren in the Lord, and sweren in Melchon;

6 and whiche ben turned awei bihynde the bak of the Lord, and whiche 'souyten not the Lord, nether enserchiden hym.

7 Be ye stille fro the face of the Lord God, for niy is the dai of the Lord; for the Lord made redi a sacrifice, halewide hise clepid men.

8 And it schal be, in the dai of sacrifice of the Lord, Y schal visite on princes, and on sones of the kyng, and on alle that ben clothid with pilgrimys, ether straunge, clothing.

9 And Y schal visite on ech that proudli entrith on the threis-fold in that dai, whiche fillen the hous of her Lord God with wickidnesse and gile.

10 And ther schal be in that dai, seith the Lord, a vois of cry fro the yate of fischis, and yellynge fro the secounde yate, and greet defoulyng fro litle hillis.

11 Yelle ye, dwelleris of Pila; al the puple of Canaan was stille togidere, alle men wlappid in siluer perischiden.

12 And it schal be, in that tyme Y schal seke Jerusalem with lanternes, and Y schal visite on alle men piyt in her darstis, whiche seien in her hertis, The Lord schal not do wel, and he schal not do yuele.

13 And the strengthe of hem schal be in to rauyschyng, and the housis of hem in to desert; and thei schulen bilde housis, and schulen not enhabite; and thei schulen plaunte vyneyerdis, and thei schulen not drynke the wyn of hem.

14 Nyy is the greet dai of the Lord, niy and swift ful myche; the vois of the dai of the Lord is bittir, a strong man schal be in tribulacioun there.

15 'The ilke dai is a dai of wraththe, dai of tribulacioun and angwisch, dai of nedynesse and wretchidnesse, dai of derknessis and myist, dai of cloude and whirlewynd,

16 dai of trumpe and noise on strong citees and on hiye corneris.

17 And Y schal troble men, and thei schulen walke as blynde, for thei han synned ayens the Lord; and the blood of hem schal be sched out as erthe, and the bodies of hem schulen be as tordis.

18 But and the siluer of hem, and gold of hem, schal not mowe delyuere hem in the dai of wraththe of the Lord; in fier of his feruour al erthe schal be deuourid, for he schal make ende with haastyng to alle men enhabitynge the erthe.

CAP 2

1 Come ye togidere, be gaderid, ye folc not worthi to be loued,

2 bifore that comaundyng brynge forth as dust passyng dai; bifore that wraththe of strong veniaunce of the Lord come on you, bifor that the dai of his indignacioun come on you.

3 Alle myelde men of erthe, seke ye the Lord, whiche han wrouyt the doom of hym; seke ye the iust, seke ye the mylde, if ony maner ye be hid in the dai of strong veniaunce of the Lord.

4 For Gasa schal be distried, and Ascalon schal be in to desert; thei schulen caste out Azotus in myddai, and Accaron schal be drawun out bi the root.

5 Wo to you that dwellen in the litil part of the see, a folc of loste men. The word of the Lord on you, Canaan, the lond of Filisteis, and Y schal distrie thee, so that a dwellere be not;

6 and the litil part of the see schal be reste of scheepherdis, and foldis of scheep.

7 And it schal be a litil part of hym, that schal be left of the hous of Juda, there thei schulen be fed in the housis of Ascalon; at euentid thei schulen reste, for the Lord God of hem schal visite hem, and schal turne awei the caitifte of hem.

8 Y herde the schenschip of Moab, and blasfemyes of sones of Amon, whiche thei seiden schentfuli to my puple, and thei weren magnefied on the termes of hem.

9 Therfor Y lyue, seith the Lord of oostis, God of Israel, for Moab schal be as Sodom, and the sones of Amon as Gomorre; drynesse of thornes, and hepis of salt, and desert, til in to withouten ende. The relifs of my puple schulen rauysche hem, the residues of my folc schulen welde hem.

10 Sotheli this thing schal come to hem for her pride, for thei blasfemeden, and weren magnefied on the puple of the Lord of oostis.

11 The Lord schal be orible on hem, and he schal make feble alle goddis of erthe; and men of her place schulen worschipe hym, alle the ilis of hethene men.

12 But and ye, Ethiopiens, schulen be slayn bi my swerd.

13 And he schal stretche forth his hond on the north, and schal leese Assur; and he schal putte the feir citee Nynyue in to wildirnesse, and into with out weie, and as desert.

14 And flockis, and alle the beestis of folkis, schulen ligge in the myddil therof; and onacratalus, and irchun schulen dwelle in threshfoldis therof; vois of the syngynge in wyndow, and crow in the lyntil, for Y schal make thinne the strengthe therof.

15 This is the gloriouse citee dwellynge in trist, which seide in hir herte, Y am, and ther is noon other more withouten me. Hou is it maad vnto desert, a couche of beeste; ech man that schal passe bi it, schal hisse, and schal moue his hond.

CAP 3

1 Wo! thou citee, terrere to wraththe, and bouyt ayen a culuer.

2 It herde not the vois of the Lord, and resseyuede not techyng, ether chastisyng; it tristenyde not in the Lord, it neiyide not to her God.

3 Princes therof in myddil therof weren as liouns rorynge; iugis therof weren wolues, in the euentid thei leften not in to morewe.

4 Profetis therof weren woode, vnfeithful men; prestis therof defouliden hooli thing, thei diden vniustli ayens the lawe.

5 The Lord iust in the myddil therof, schal not do wickidnesse; erli, erli he schal yyue his dom in liyt, and it schal not be hid; forsothe the wickid puple knew not confusioun.

6 Y loste folkis, and the corneris of hem ben distried; Y made the weies of hem desert, while there is not that schal passe. The citees of hem ben desolat, for a man is not left, nether ony dwellere.

7 Y seide, Netheles thou schalt drede me, thou schalt resseyue techyng; and the dwellyng place therof schal not perische, for alle thingis in whiche Y visitide it; netheles ful eerli thei risynge han corrupt alle her thouytis.

8 Wherfor abide thou me, seith the Lord, in the dai of my rysyng ayen in to comynge. For my doom is, that Y gadere folkis, and Y schal gadere rewmes; and Y schal schede out on hem myn indignacioun, and al wraththe of my strong veniaunce; for in fier of my feruour al erthe schal be deuourid.

9 For thanne Y schal yelde to puplis a chosun lippe, that alle clepe inwardli in the name of the Lord, and serue to hym with o schuldre.

10 Ouer the floodis of Ethiopie, fro thens my bisecheris, the sones of my scaterid men, schulen brynge yifte to me.

11 In that day thou schalt not be confoundid on alle thi fyndyngis, in whiche thou trespassidist ayens me; for thanne Y schal take awei fro the myddil of thee grete spekeris of thi pride, and thou schalt no more put to, for to be enhaunsid in myn hooli hil.

12 And Y schal leeue in the myddil of thee a pore puple and nedi; and thei schulen hope in the name of the Lord.

13 The relifs of Israel schulen not do wickidnesse, nether schulen speke leesyng, and a gileful tunge schal not be foundun in the mouth of hem; for thei schulen be fed, and schulen reste, and ther schal not be that schal make aferd.

14 These thingis seith the Lord, Douyter of Sion, herie thou hertli, synge thou, Israel; be thou glad, and make thou ioie withoutforth in al thin herte, thou douyter of Jerusalem.

15 The Lord hath take a wei thi dom, hath turned a wey thin enemyes; the kyng of Israel the Lord is in myddil of thee, thou schalt no more drede yuel.

16 In that dai it schal be seid, Jerusalem, nyle thou drede; Sion, thin hondis be not clumsid.

17 Thi Lord God is strong in the myddil of thee, he schal saue; he schal make ioie on thee in gladnesse, he schal be stille in thi louyng, he schal make ioie withoutforth on thee in heriyng.

18 Y schal gadere the foolis, ether veyn men, that wenten awei fro the lawe, for thei weren of thee, that thou haue no more schenschipe on hem.

19 Lo! Y schal sle alle men that turmentiden thee in that tyme, and Y schal saue him that haltith, and Y schal gadere hir that was cast out; and Y schal putte hem in to heriyng, and in to name in ech lond of confusioun of hem, in that tyme in which Y schal brynge you,

20 and in the tyme in which Y schal gadre you. For Y schal yyue you in to name, and in to heriyng to alle puplis of erthe, whanne Y schal conuerte youre caitifte bifore youre iyen, seith the Lord.

AGGEY

CAP 1

1 In the secounde yeer of Darius, kyng of Persis, in the sixte monethe, in the firste dai of the monethe, the word of the Lord was maad in the hond of Aggey, profete, to Sorobabel, sone of Salatiel, duyk of Juda, and to Jhesu, the greet preest, sone of Josedech,

2 and seide, The Lord of oostis seith these thingis, and spekith, This puple seith, Yit cometh not the tyme of the hous of the Lord to be bildid.

3 And the word of the Lord was maad in the hond of Aggei,

4 profete, and seide, Whether it is tyme to you, that ye dwelle in housis couplid with tymbir, and this hous be forsakun?

5 And now the Lord of oostis seith these thingis, Putte ye youre hertis on youre weies.

6 Ye han sowe myche, and brouyte in litil; ye han etun, and ben not fillid; ye han drunke, and ye ben not ful of drynk; ye hiliden you, and ye ben not maad hoote; and he that gaderide hiris, sente tho in to a sak holid, ether brokun.

7 The Lord of oostis seith these thingis, Putte ye youre hertis on youre weies.

8 Stie ye vp in to the munteyn, bere ye trees, and bilde ye an hous; and it schal be acceptable to me, and Y schal be glorified, seith the Lord.

9 Ye bihelden to more, and lo! it is maad lesse; and ye brouyten in to the hous, and Y blew it out. For what cause, seith the Lord of oostis? for myn hous is desert, and ye hasten ech man in to his hous.

10 For this thing heuenes ben forbedun, that thei schulden not yyue dew on you; and the erthe is forbodun, that it schulde not yyue his buriownyng.

11 And Y clepide drynesse on erthe, and on mounteyns, and on wheete, and on wyn, and on oile, and what euer thingis the erthe bryngith forth; and on men, and on beestis, and on al labour of hondis.

12 And Sorobabel, the sone of Salatiel, and Jhesus, the greet preest, the sone of Josedech, and alle relifs of the puple, herden the vois of her God, and the wordis of Aggei, the profete, as the Lord God of hem sente him to hem; and al the puple dredde of the face of the Lord.

13 And Aggei, a messanger of the Lord, of the messangeris of the Lord, seide to the puple, and spak, Y am with you, seith the Lord.

14 And the Lord reiside the spirit of Sorobabel, the sone of Salatiel, duik of Juda, and the spirit of Jhesu, the greet preest, the sone of Josedech, and the spirit of the relifs of al puple; and thei entriden, and maden werk in the hous of the Lord of oostis, her God.

CAP 2

1 In the foure and twentithe dai of the monethe, in the sixte monethe, in the secunde yeer of kyng Darius.

2 In the seuenthe monethe, in the oon and twentith dai of the monethe, the word of the Lord was maad in the hond of Aggei, the profete, and seide,

3 Speke thou to Sorobabel, the sone of Salatiel, the duyk of Juda, and to Jhesu, the gret preest, the sone of Josedech, and to othere of the puple, and seie thou,

4 Who in you is left, that sai this hous in his firste glorie? and what seen ye this now? whether it is not thus, as if it be not bifore youre iyen?

5 And now, Sorobabel, be thou coumfortid, seith the Lord, and Jhesu, greet preest, sone of Josedech, be thou coumfortid, and al the puple of the lond, be thou coumfortid, seith the Lord of oostis; and do ye, for Y am with you, seith the Lord of oostis.

6 The word that Y couenauntide with you, whanne ye wenten out of the lond of Egipt, and my Spirit schal be in the myddil of you.

7 Nyle ye drede, for the Lord of oostis seith these thingis, Yit o litil thing is, and Y schal moue heuene, and erthe, and see, and drie lond;

8 and Y schal moue alle folkis, and the desirid to alle folkis schal come; and Y schal fille this hous with glorie, seith the Lord of oostis.

9 Myn is siluer, and myn is gold, seith the Lord of oostes.

10 The glorie of this laste hous schal be greet, more than the firste, seith the Lord of oostis. And in this place Y schal yyue pees, seith the Lord of oostis.

11 In the foure and twentithe dai of the nynthe monethe, in the secounde yeer of kyng Daryus, the word of the Lord was maad to Aggei, the profete, and seide, The Lord God of oostis seith these thingis,

12 Axe thou preestis the lawe, and seie thou,

13 If a man takith halewyd fleisch in the hem of his clothing, and touchith of the hiynesse therof breed, ether potage, ether wyn, ether oile, ether ony mete, whether it schal be halewid? Sotheli preestis answeriden, and seiden, Nai.

14 And Aggei seide, If a man defoulid in soule touchith of alle these thingis, whether it schal be defoulid? And prestis answeriden, and seiden, It schal be defoulid.

15 And Aggei answeride, and seide, So is this puple, and so is this folc bifor my face, seith the Lord, and so is al werk of her hondis; and alle thingis whiche thei offren there, schulen be defoulid.

16 And nowe putte ye youre hertis, fro this dai and aboue, bifor that a stoon on a stoon was put in temple of the Lord,

17 whanne ye wenten to an heep of twenti buischels, and there weren maad ten; ye entriden to the pressour, that ye schulden presse out fifti galouns, and there weren maad twenti.

18 Y smoot you with brennynge wynd; and with myldew, and hail, alle the werkis of youre hondis; and ther was noon in you that turnede ayen to me, seith the Lord.

19 Putte ye youre hertis fro this dai, and in to comynge, fro the foure and twentithe dai of the nynthe monethe, fro the dai in whiche foundementis of the temple of the Lord ben castun, putte ye on youre herte.

20 Whether now seed is in buriownyng? and yit vineyerd, and fige tre, and pomgarnade, and the tre of olyue flouride not.

21 Fro this dai Y schal blesse. And the word of the Lord was maad the secounde tyme to Aggei, in the foure and twentithe dai of the monethe,

22 and seide, Spek thou to Sorobabel, duik of Juda, and seie thou, Y shal moue heuene and erthe togidere, and Y schal distrie the seet of rewmes,

23 and Y schal al to-breke the strengthe of rewme of hethene men, and schal distrie a foure horsid carte, and the stiere therof; and horsis schulen go doun, and stieris of hem, a man bi swerd of his brother.

24 In that dai, seith the Lord of oostis, thou Sorobabel, sone of Salatiel, my seruaunt, Y schal take thee, seith the Lord; and Y schal putte thee as a signet, for Y chees thee, seith the Lord of oostis.

SACARIE

CAP 1

1 In the eiythe monethe, in the secounde yeer of Darius, the word of the Lord was maad to Sacarie, the sone of Barachie, the sone of Addo,

2 profete, and seide, The Lord is wrooth on youre fadris with wrathfulnesse.

3 And thou schalt seie to hem, The Lord of oostis seith these thingis. Be ye conuertid to me, seith the Lord of oostis, and Y schal be conuertid to you, seith the Lord of oostis.

4 Be ye not as youre fadris, to whiche the formere profetis crieden, seiynge, The Lord of oostis seith these thingis, Be ye conuertid fro youre yuel weies, and youre worste thouytis; and thei herden not, nether token tent to me, seith the Lord of oostis.

5 Where ben youre fadris and profetis? whether thei schulen lyue with outen ende?

6 Netheles my wordis and my lawful thingis, whiche Y comaundide to my seruauntis profetis, whether thei tauyten not youre fadris? And thei weren conuertid, and seiden, As the Lord of oostys thouyte for to do to vs bi oure weies, and bi oure fyndingis he dide to vs.

7 In the foure and twentithe dai of the enleuenthe monethe Sabath, in the secounde yeer of Darius, the word of the Lord was maad to Sacarie, sone of Barachie, sone of Addo,

8 profete, and seide, Y saiy bi niyt, and lo! a man stiynge on a reed hors; and he stood bitwixe places where mirtis wexen, that weren in the depthe, and aftir hym weren horsis reede, dyuerse, and white.

9 And Y seide, My lord, who ben these? And an aungel of the Lord seide to me, that spak in me, Y schal schewe to thee what these ben.

10 And the man that stood bitwix places where mirtis wexen, answeride, and seide, These it ben, whiche the Lord sente, that thei walke thorouy erthe.

11 And thei answeriden to the aungel of the Lord, that stood bitwixe places where mirtis wexen, and seiden, We han walkid thorouy erthe, and lo! al erthe is enhabitid, and restith.

12 And the aungel of the Lord answeride, and seide, Lord of oostis, hou long schalt thou not haue merci on Jerusalem, and citees of Juda, to whiche thou art wrooth? This now is the seuentithe yeer.

13 And the Lord answeride to the aungel, that spak in me, goode wordis, and wordis of coumfort.

14 And the aungel that spak in me, seide to me, Crie thou, seiynge, The Lord of oostis seith these thingis, Y louyde Jerusalem and Sion in greet feruour;

15 and in greet wraththe Y schal be wroth on riche folkis; for Y was wrooth a litil, forsothe thei helpiden in to yuel.

16 Therfor the Lord seith these thingis, Y schal turne ayen to Jerusalem in mercies. Myn hous schal be bildid in it, seith the Lord of oostis; and a plomet schal be streiyt out on Jerusalem.

17 Yit crie thou, seiynge, The Lord of oostis seith these thingis, Yit my citees schulen flete with goodis, and yit the Lord schal coumforte Sion, and yit he schal chese Jerusalem.

18 And Y reiside myn iyen, and Y saiy, and lo! foure hornes.

19 And Y seide to the aungel that spak in me, What ben these? And he seide to me, These ben hornes, that wynde-widen Juda, and Israel, and Jerusalem.

20 And the Lord schewide to me foure smythis.

21 And Y seide, What comen these for to do? Which spak, seiynge, These ben the hornes, that wyndewiden Juda bi alle men, and no man of hem reiside his heed; and these camen for to make hem aferd, that thei caste doun the hornes of heth-ene men, which reisiden horn on the lond of Juda, for to sca-tere it.

CAP 2

1 And Y reiside myn iyen, and siy, and lo! a man, and lo! in his hoond a litil coorde of meteris.

2 And Y seide, Whidir goist thou? And he seide to me, That Y mete Jerusalem, and Judee; hou myche is the breede therof, and hou myche is the lengthe therof.

3 And lo! the aungel that spak in me, wente out, and another aungel wente out in to the metyng of hym, and seide to hym,

4 Renne thou, speke to this child, and seie thou, Jerusalem shal be enhabitid with out wal, for the multitude of men and of beestis in the myddil therof.

5 And Y schal be to it, seith the Lord, a wal of fier in cumpas; and Y schal be in glorie in myddil therof.

6 A! A! A! fle ye fro the lond of the north, seith the Lord, for in foure wyndis of heuene Y scateride you, seith the Lord.

7 A! thou Sion, fle, that dwellist at the douyter of Babiloyne.

8 For the Lord of oostis seith these thingis, After glorie he sente me to hethene men, whiche robbiden you; for he that schal touche you, schal touche the apple of myn iye.

9 For lo! Y reise myn hond on hem, and thei schulen be preyes to these that seruyden hem; and ye schulen knowe, that the Lord of oostis sente me.

10 Douyter of Sion, herie thou, and be glad; for lo! Y come, and Y schal dwelle in myddil of thee, seith the Lord.

11 And many folkis schulen be applied to the Lord in that dai, and thei schulen be to me in to puple, and Y schal dwelle in myddil of thee; and thou schalt wite, that the Lord of oostis sente me to thee.

12 And the Lord schal welde Juda in to his part, in the loud halewid, and schal cheese yit Jerusalem.

13 Ech fleisch be stil fro the face of the Lord, for he roos of his hooli dwelling place.

CAP 3

1 And the Lord schewide to me the greet prest Jhesu, ston-dynge bifore the aungel of the Lord; and Sathan stood on his riythalf, that he schulde be aduersarie to hym.

2 And the Lord seide to Sathan, The Lord blame in thee, Sathan, and the Lord that chees Jerusalem, blame in thee. Whether this is not a deed broond rauyschid fro the fier?

3 And Jhesus was clothid with foule clothis, and stood bifor the face of the aungel.

4 Which answeride, and seide to hem that stoden bifor hym, and he seide, Do ye awei foule clothis fro him. And he seide to hym, Lo! Y haue don awei fro thee thi wickidnesse, and Y haue clothid thee with chaungynge clothis.

5 And he seide, Putte ye a clene mytre on his heed. And thei puttiden a cleene mytre on his heed, and clothide him with clothis. And the aungel of the Lord stood,

6 And the aungel of the Lord witnesside to Jhesu,

7 and seide, The Lord of oostis seith these thingis, If thou schalt go in my weies, and schalt kepe my kepynge, also and thou schalt deme myn hous, and schalt kepe my porchis; and Y schal yyue to thee goeris, of these that now here stonden niy.

8 Here thou, Jhesu, greet preest, thou and thi frendis that dwellen bifore thee, for thei ben men signefiynge thing to comyng. Lo! sotheli Y schal brynge my seruaunt spryngynge up, ether Crist borun.

9 For lo! the stoon which Y yaf bifor Jhesu, on o stoon ben seuene iyen; and lo! Y schal graue the grauyng therof, seith the Lord of oostis, and Y schal do a wei the wickidnesse of that lond in o dai.

10 In that dai, seith the Lord of oostis, a man schal clepe his frend vndur a vyn tre, and vndur a fige tre.

CAP 4

1 And the aungel turnede ayen, that spak in me, and reiside me, as a man that is reisid of his sleep.

2 And he seide to me, What seest thou? And Y seide, Y saiy, and lo! a candilstike al of gold, and the laumpe therof on the heed therof, and seuene lanternes therof on it, and seuene ves-sels for to holde oyle to the lanternes, that weren on the heed therof.

3 And twei olyues there onne, oon of the riythalf 'of the laumpe, and 'an other on the left half therof.

4 And Y answeride, and seide to the aungel that spak in me, and Y seide, What ben these thingis, my lord?

5 And the aungel that spak in me, answeride, and seide to me, Whether thou woist not what ben these thingis? And Y seide, No, my lord.

6 And he answeride, and seide to me, and spak, This is the word of the Lord, seiynge to Sorobabel, Not in oost, nether in strengthe, but in my spirit, seith the Lord of oostis.

7 Who art thou, greet hil, bifore Sorobabel in to pleyn? and he schal lede out the firste stoon, and schal make euene grace to grace therof.

8 And the word of the Lord was maad to me,

9 and seide, The hondis of Sorobabel foundiden this hous, and the hondis of hym schulen perfourme it; and ye schulen wite, that the Lord of oostis sente me to you.

10 Who forsothe dispiside litle daies? and thei schulen be glad, and schulen se a stoon of tyn in the hond of Sorobabel. These ben seuene iyen of the Lord, that rennen aboute in to al erthe.

11 And Y answeride, and seide to hym, What ben these tweyne olyues on the riythalf of the candilstike, and at the lift-half therof?

12 And Y answeryde the secounde tyme, and seide to hym, What ben the tweyne eeris, ether ripe fruyt, of olyues, that ben bisidis the twei bilis of gold, in whiche ben oile vesselis of gold?

13 And he seide to me, and spak, Whether thou woost not what ben these thingis?

14 And Y seide, No, my lord. And he seide, These ben twei sones of oile of schynyng, whiche stonden nyy to the lordli gouernour of al erthe.

CAP 5

1 And Y was conuertid, and reiside myn iyen, and siy, and lo! a book fleynge.

2 And he seide to me, What seest thou? And Y seide, Lo! Y se a book fleynge; the lengthe therof was of twenti cubitis, and the breede therof of ten cubitis.

3 And he seide to me, This is the curs, that goith on the face of al erthe; for ech theef schal be demed, as it is writun there; and ech man swerynge, schal be demyd of this also.

4 Y schal lede out it, seith the Lord of oostis, and it schal come to the hous of a theef, and to the hous of hym that swerith falsli in my name; and it schal dwelle in myddil of hys hous, and schal waaste hym, and hise trees, and hise stoonys.

5 And the aungel wente out, that spak in me, and seide to me, Reyse thin iyen, and se, what this thing is, that goith out.

6 And Y seide, What is it? And he seide, This is a pot goyng out. And he seide, This is the iye of hem in al erthe.

7 And lo! a talent of leed was borun; and lo! a womman sittynge in myddil of the pot.

8 And he seide, This is vnpite, ether vnfeithfulnesse. And he castide doun hir in myddil of the pot, and sente a gobet of leed in to the mouth therof.

9 And Y reiside myn iyen, and siy, and lo! twei wymmen goynge out, and a spirit in wyngis of hem; and thei hadden wyngis as wyngis of a kite, and reisiden the pot bitwixe heuene and erthe.

10 And Y seide to the aungel that spak in me, Whidur beren these the pot?

11 And he seide to me, That an hous be bildid therto in the lond of Sennaar, and be stablischid, and set there on his foundement.

CAP 6

1 And Y was conuertid, and reiside myn iyen, and siy, and lo! foure horsid cartis goynge out of the myddil of tweyne hillis, and the hillis weren hillis of bras.

2 In the firste foure horsid carte weren reed horsis, and in the secounde foure horsid carte weren blac horsis;

3 and in the thridde foure horsid carte weren white horsis, and in the fourthe foure horsid carte weren dyuerse horsis, and stronge.

4 And Y answeride, and seide to the aungel that spak in me, What ben these thingis, my lord?

5 And the aungel aunsweride, and seide to me, These ben foure wyndis of heuene, whiche goen out, that thei stonde bifor the lordschipere of al erthe.

6 In which weren blake horsis, wenten out in to the lond of the north; and the white wenten out aftir hem; and the dyuerse wenten out to the lond of the south.

7 Forsothe thei that weren strengeste wenten out, and souyten for to go, and renne aboute bi al erthe. And he seide, Go ye, and walke ye thorouy the erthe. And thei walkiden thorouy erthe.

8 And he clepide me, and spak to me, and seide, Lo! thei that goon out in to lond of north, maden my spirit for to reste in the lond of north.

9 And the word of the Lord was maad to me, and seide,

10 Take thou of the transmygracioun, ether caitiftee, of Oldai, and of Tobie, and of Idaye; and thou schalt come in that dai, and schalt entre in to the hous of Josie, sone of Sofonye, that camen fro Babiloyne.

11 And thou schalt take gold and siluer, and schalt make corouns, and putte on the heed of Jhesu, the greet preest, sone of Josedech;

12 and schalt speke to hym, and seie, The Lord of oostis seith these thingis, seiynge, Lo! a man, Comynge forth, ether Borun, is his name, and vndir him it schal sprynge. And he schal bilde a temple to the Lord,

13 and he schal make a temple to the Lord; and he schal bere glorie, and schal sitte, and schal be lord on his seete; and the preest schal be on his seete, and counsel of pees schal be bitwixe hem tweyne.

14 And corouns schulen be to Helem, and to Tobie, and to Idaie, and to Hen, sone of Sofonye, a memorial in the temple of the Lord.

15 And thei that ben fer, schulen come, and bilde in the temple of the Lord; and ye schulen wite, that the Lord of oostis sente me to you. Sotheli this thing schal be, if bi heryng ye schulen here the vois of youre Lord God.

CAP 7

1 And it is maad in the fourthe yeer of Darius, kyng, the word of the Lord was maad to Sacarie, in the fourthe dai of the nynthe monethe, that is Caslew.

2 And Sarasar, and Rogumelech, and men that weren with hem, senten to the hous of the Lord, for to preye the face of the Lord;

3 that thei schulden seie to prestis of the hous of the Lord of oostis, and to profetis, and speke, Whether it is to wepe to me in the fyuethe monethe, ether Y schal halowe me, as Y dide now many yeeris?

4 And the word of the Lord was maad to me,

5 and seide, Speke thou to al the puple of the lond, and to prestis, and seie thou, Whanne ye fastiden, and weiliden in the fyueth and seuenthe monethe, bi these seuenti yeeris, whether ye fastiden a fast to me?

6 And whanne ye eeten, and drunken, whether ye eten not to you, and drunken not to you silf?

7 Whether wordis of profetis ben not, whiche the Lord spak in the hond of the formere profetis, whanne yit Jerusalem was enhabited, and was ful of richessis, and it, and citees therof in cumpas therof, and at the south and in feeldi place was enhabited?

8 And the word of the Lord was maad to Sacarie, and seide, The Lord of oostis saith these thingis, and spekith,

9 Deme ye trewe dom, and do ye merci, and doyngis of merci, ech man with his brother.

10 And nyle ye falsli calenge a widewe, and fadirles, ether modirles, and comelyng, and pore man; and a man thenke not in his herte yuel to his brother.

11 And thei wolden not 'take heede, and thei turneden awei the schuldre, and yeden awei, and 'maden heuy her eeris, lest thei herden.

12 And thei puttiden her herte as adamaunt, lest thei herden the lawe, and wordis whiche the Lord of oostis sente in his Spirit, bi the hond of the formere profetis; and greet indignacioun was maad of the Lord of oostis.

13 And it is doon, as he spak; and as thei herden not, so thei schulen crie, and Y schal not here, seith the Lord of oostis.

14 And Y scateride hem bi alle rewmes, whiche thei knewen not, and the lond is desolat fro hem; for that there was not a man goynge and turnynge ayen, and thei han put desirable lond in to desert.

CAP 8

1 And the word of the Lord of oostis was maad to me,

2 and seide, The Lord of oostis seith these thingis, Y hatide Sion with greet feruour, and with greet indignacioun Y hatide it.

3 The Lord of oostis seith these thingis, Y am turned ayen to Sion, and Y schal dwelle in the myddil of Jerusalem; and Jerusalem schal be clepid a citee of treuthe, and hil of the Lord schal be clepid an hil halewid.

4 The Lord of oostis seith these thingis, Yit elde men and elde wymmen schulen dwelle in the stretis of Jerusalem, and the staf of man in his hond, for the multitude of yeeris.

5 And the stretis of the cite schulen be fillid with 'yonge children and maidens, pleiynge in the stretis 'of it.

6 The Lord of oostis seith these thingis, Though it schal be seyn hard bifor the iyen of relifs of this puple in tho daies, whether bifor myn iyen it schal be hard, seith the Lord of oostis?

7 The Lord of oostis seith these thingis, Lo! Y schal saue my puple fro the lond of the eest, and fro lond of goynge doun of the sunne;

8 and Y schal brynge hem, and thei schulen dwelle in the myddil of Jerusalem; and thei schulen be to me in to a puple, and Y schal be to hem in to God, and in treuthe, and in riytwisnesse.

9 The Lord of oostis seith these thingis, Be youre hondis coumfortid, whiche heren in these daies these wordis bi the mouth of profetis, in the dai in which the hous of the Lord of oostis is foundid, that the temple schulde be bildid.

10 Sotheli bifore tho daies hire of men was not, nether hire of werk beestis was, nether to man entrynge and goynge out was pees for tribulacioun; and Y lefte alle men, ech ayens his neiybore.

11 But now not after the formere daies Y schal do to relifs of this puple, seith the Lord of oostis,

12 but seed of pees schal be; vyneyerd schal yyue his fruyt, and erthe schal yyue his buriownyng, and heuenes schulen yyue her dew; and Y schal make the relifs of this puple for to welde alle these thingis.

13 And it schal be, as the hous of Juda and hous of Israel weren cursyng in hethene men, so Y schal saue you, and ye schulen be blessyng. Nyle ye drede, be youre hondis coumfortid;

14 for the Lord of oostis seith these thingis, As Y thouyte for to turmente you, whanne youre fadris hadden terrid me to wraththe,

15 seith the Lord, and Y hadde not merci, so Y conuertid thouyte in these daies for to do wel to the hous of Juda and Jerusalem; nyle ye drede.

16 Therfor these ben the wordis whiche ye schulen do; speke ye treuthe, ech man with his neiybore; deme ye treuthe and dom of pees in youre yatis;

17 and thenke ye not in youre hertis, ony man yuel ayens his frend, and loue ye not a fals ooth; for alle thes thingis it ben, whiche Y hate, seith the Lord.

18 And the word of the Lord of oostis was maad to me,

19 and seide, The Lord of oostis seith these thingis, Fastyng of the fourthe monethe, 'and fastyng of the fyuethe, and fastyng of the seuenthe, and fasting of the tenthe, schal be to the hous of Juda in to ioie and gladnes, and in to solempnitees ful cleer; loue ye oneli treuthe and pees.

20 The Lord of oostis seith these thingis, Puplis schulen come on ech side, and dwelle in many citees;

21 and the dwelleris schulen go, oon to an other, and seie, Go we, and biseche the face of the Lord, and seke we the Lord of oostis; also I shal go.

22 And many puplis schulen come, and strong folkis, for to seke the Lord of oostis in Jerusalem, and for to biseche the face of the Lord.

23 The Lord of oostis seith these thingis, In tho daies, in whiche ten men of alle langagis of hethene men schulen catche, and thei schulen catche the hemme of a man Jew, and seye, We schulen go with you; for we han herd, that God is with you.

CAP 9

1 The birthun of the word of the Lord, in the lond of Adrach, and of Damask, the reste therof; for 'of the Lord is the iye of man, and of alle lynagis of Israel.

2 And Emath in termes therof, and Tirus, and Sidon; for thei token to hem wisdom greetli.

3 And Tirus bildide his strengthing, and gaderide siluer as erthe, and gold as fen of stretis.

4 Lo! the Lord schal welde it, and schal smyte in the see the strengthe therof, and it schal be deuourid bi fier.

5 Ascalon schal see, and schal drede; and Gasa, 'and schal sorewe ful myche; and Accaron, for the hope therof is confoundid; and the kyng schal perische fro Gasa, and Ascalon schal not be enhabited;

6 and a departere schal sitte in Asotus, and Y schal distrie the pride of Filisteis.

7 And Y schal take awei the blood therof fro the mouth of him, and abhomynaciouns of hym fro the myddil of teeth of hym, and he also schal be left to our God; and he schal be as a duyk in Juda, and Accaron as Jebusei.

8 And Y schal cumpasse myn hous of these that holden kniythod to me, and goen, and turnen ayen; and 'an vniust axere schal no more passe on hem, for now Y siy with myn iyen.

9 Thou douyter of Sion, make ioie withoutforth ynow, synge, thou douyter of Jerusalem; lo! thi kyng schal come to thee, he iust, and sauyour; he pore, and stiynge on a sche asse, and on a fole, sone of a sche asse.

10 And Y schal leese foure horsid carte of Effraym, and an hors of Jerusalem, and the bouwe of batel schal be distried; and he schal speke pees to hethene men, and the power of him schal be fro see til to see, and fro floodis til to the endis of erthe.

11 And thou in blood of thi testament sentist out thi boundun men fro lake, in which is not water.

12 Ye boundun of hope, be conuertid to strengthing; and to dai Y schewynge schal yelde to thee double thingis,

13 for Y schal stretche forthe to me Juda as a bowe, Y fillide 'the lond of Effraym. And Y schal reise thi sones, thou Sion, on thi sones, thou lond of Grekis, and Y schal sette thee as the swerd of stronge men.

14 And the Lord God schal be seyn on hem, and the dart of him schal go out as leit.

15 And the Lord God schal synge in a trumpe, and schal go in whirlwynd of the south; the Lord of oostis schal defende hem, and thei schulen deuoure, and make suget with stoonys of a slynge; and thei drynkynge schulen be fillid as with wyn, and schulen be fillid as viols, and as hornes of the auter.

16 And the Lord God 'of hem schal saue hem in that dai, as a floc of his puple, for hooli stoonus schulen be reisid on the lond of hym.

17 For what is the good of hym, and what is the faire of hym, no but whete of chosun men, and wyn buriownynge virgyns?

CAP 10

1 Axe ye of the Lord reyn in late tyme, and the Lord schal make snowis, and reyn of myyt of cloude; and he schal yyue to hem, to ech bi hym silf, erbe in the feeld.

2 For symylacris spaken vnprofitable thing, and diuynours saien leesyng; and dremeris spaken veynli, ydily thei coumfortiden; therfor thei ben led awei as a floc, thei schulen be turmentid, for a scheepherd is not to hem.

3 On scheepherdis my strong veniaunce is wrooth, and on buckis of geet Y schal visite; for the Lord of oostis hath visitide his floc, the hous of Juda, and hath put hem as an hors of hys glorie in batel.

4 Of hym 'schal be a cornere, and of hym a litil pale, of hym a bowe of batel, and of hym ech vniust axere schal go out togidere.

5 And thei schulen be as stronge men, defoulynge clei of weies in batel, and thei schulen fiyte, for the Lord is with hem; and stieris of horsis schulen be confoundid.

6 And Y schal coumforte the hous of Juda, and Y schal saue the hous of Joseph; and Y schal conuerte hem, for Y schal haue merci on hem; and thei schulen be as thei weren, whanne Y hadde not cast awei hem; for Y schal be the Lord God of hem, and Y schal graciousli here hem.

7 And thei schulen be as the stronge of Effraym, and the herte of hem schal be glad, as of wyn; and sones of hem schulen se, and be glad, and the herte of hem schal make ioie withoutforth in the Lord.

8 Y schal hisse, 'ether softli speke, to hem, and Y schal gadere hem, for Y ayen bouyte hem, and Y schal multiplie hem, as thei weren multiplied bifore.

9 And Y schal sowe hem in puplis, and fro fer thei schulen bithenke of me; and thei schulen lyue with her sones, and schulen turne ayen.

10 And Y schal 'ayen lede hem fro the lond of Egipt, and Y schal gadere hem fro Assiriens; and Y schal brynge hem to the lond of Galaad and of Liban, and place schal not be foundun to hem.

11 And he schal passe in the wawe of the see, and schal smyte wawis in the see, and alle depnessis of flood schulen be confoundid; and the pride of Assur schal be mekid, and the ceptre of Egipt schal go awei.

12 Y schal coumforte hem in the Lord, and thei schulen walke in the name of hym, seith the Lord.

CAP 11

1 Thou Liban, opene thi yatis, and fier schal ete thi cedris.

2 Yelle, thou fir tre, for the cedre felle doun, for grete men ben distried; yelle, ye okis of Basan, for the stronge welde wode is kit doun.

3 Vois of yellyng of schepherdis, for the greet worschip of hem is distried; vois of roryng of liouns, for the pride of Jordan is wastid.

4 My Lord God seith these thingis, Fede thou beestis of slauyter,

5 whiche thei that weldiden slowen; and 'sorewiden not, and selden hem, and seiden, Blessid be the Lord, we ben maad riche. And schepherdis of hem spariden not hem,

6 and Y schal no more spare on 'men enhabitynge the erthe, seith the Lord. Lo! Y schal bitake men, ech in hond of his neiybour, and in hoond of his kyng, and thei schulen toreende togidere the lond; and Y schal not delyuere fro the hond of hem,

7 and Y schal fede the beeste of sleyng. For this thing, ye pore men of the floc, here. And Y took to me twei yerdis; oon Y clepide Fairnesse, and the tother Y clepide Litil Corde; and Y fedde the floc.

8 And Y kittide doun thre scheepherdis in o monethe, and my soule is drawun togidere in hem; for also the soule of hem variede in me.

9 And Y seide, Y schal not fede you; that that dieth, die; and that that is kit doun, be kit doun; and the residues deuoure, ech the fleisch of his neiybore.

10 And Y took my yerde, that was clepid Fairnesse, and Y kittide doun it, that Y schulde make void my couenaunt, that Y smoot with alle puplis.

11 And it 'is led forth voide in that dai; and the pore of floc that kepen to me, knewen thus, for it is the word of the Lord.

12 And Y seide to hem, If it is good in youre iyen, brynge ye my meede; and if nai, reste ye. And thei weieden my meede, thretti platis of siluer.

13 And the Lord seide to me, Caste awei it to a makere of ymagis, the fair prijs, bi which Y am preisid of hem. And Y took thritti platis of siluer, and Y castide forth hem in the hous of the Lord, to the makere of ymagis.

14 And Y kittide doun my secunde yerde, that was clepide Litil Corde, that Y schulde departe the brotherhed bitwixe Juda and Israel.

15 And the Lord seide to me, Yit take to thee vessels of a fonned scheepherde;

16 for lo! Y schal reise a scheepherde in erthe, which schal not visite forsakun thingis, schal not seke scatered thingis, and schal not heele 'the brokun togidere, and schal not nurische forth that that stondith. And he schal ete fleischis of the fat, and schal vnbynde the clees of hem.

17 A! the scheepherd, and ydol, forsakynge the floc; swerd on his arm, and on his riyt iye; the arm of hym schal be dried with drynesse, and his riyt iye wexynge derk schal be maad derk.

CAP 12

1 The birthun of the word of the Lord on Israel. And the Lord seide, stretchynge forth heuene, and founding erthe, and makynge the spirit of a man in hym, Lo!

2 Y schal putte Jerusalem a lyntel of glotonye to alle puplis in cumpas, but and Juda schal be in 'a segyng ayens Jerusalem.

3 And it schal be, in that dai Y schal putte Jerusalem a stoon of birthun to alle puplis; alle that schulen lifte it, schulen be to-drawun with kittyng doun, and alle rewmes of erthe schulen be gaderid ayens it.

4 In that dai, seith the Lord, Y schal smyte ech hors in drede, 'ether leesynge of mynde, and the stiere 'of hym in woodnesse; and on the hous of Juda Y schal opene myn iyen, and schal smyte with blyndnesse ech hors of puplis.

5 And duikis of Juda schulen seie in her hertis, Be the dwellers of Jerusalem coumfortid to me in the Lord of oostis, the God of hem.

6 In that dai Y schal putte the duykis of Juda as a chymnei of fier in trees, and as a broond of fier in hei; and thei schulen deuoure at the 'riythalf and lefthalf alle puplis in cumpas. And Jerusalem schal be enhabitid eftsoone in his place, 'in Jerusalem.

7 And the Lord schal saue the tabernaclis of Juda, as in bigynnyng, that the hous of Dauid 'glorie not greetli, and the glorie of men dwellynge in Jerusalem be not ayens Juda.

8 In that dai the Lord schal defende the dwelleris of Jerusalem; and he that schal offende of hem, schal be in that dai as Dauid, and the hous of Dauid schal be as of God, as the aungel of the Lord in the siyt of hym.

9 And it schal be, in that dai Y schal seke for to al to-breke alle folkis that comen ayens Jerusalem.

10 And Y schal helde out on the hous of Dauid, and on dwelleris of Jerusalem, the spirit of grace, and of preieris; and thei schulen biholde to me, whom thei 'fitchiden togidere. And thei schulen biweile hym with weilyng, as on 'the oon bigetun; and thei schulen sorewe on hym, as it is wont 'for to be sorewid in the deth of the firste bigetun.

11 In that dai greet weilyng schal be in Jerusalem, as the weilyng of Adremon in the feeld of Magedon.

12 And erthe schal weile; meynees and meynees bi hem silf; the meynees of the hous of Dauid bi hem silf, and the wymmen of hem bi hem silf;

13 meynees of the hous of Nathan bi hem silf, and the wymmen of hem bi hem silf; meynees of the hous of Leuy bi hem silf, and the wymmen of hem bi hem silf; meynees of Semei bi hem silf, and the wymmen of hem bi hem silf.

14 All othere meynees, meynees and meynees bi hem silf, and the wymmen of hem bi hem silf.

CAP 13

1 In that dai an open welle schal be to the hous of Dauid, and to men dwellynge at Jerusalem, in to waischyng a wey of a synful man, and of womman defoulid in vnclene blood.

2 And it schal be, in that dai, seith the Lord of oostis, Y schal distrie names of idols fro 'the lond, and thei schulen no more be 'thouyt on; and Y schal take awei fro erthe false profetis, and an vnclene spirit.

3 And it schal be, whanne ony man schal profesie ouer, his fadir and modir that gendriden hym, schulen seie to hym, Thou schalt not lyue, for thou hast spoke leesyng in the name of the Lord; and his fadir and his modir, gendreris of hym, schulen 'togidere fitche hym, whanne he hath profesied.

4 And it schal be, in that dai profetis schulen be confoundid, ech of his visioun, whanne he schal profesie; nether thei schulen be hilid with mentil of sak, that thei lie;

5 but 'thei schulen seie, Y am not a profete; Y am a man 'erthe tiliere, for Adam is myn ensaumple fro my yongthe.

6 And it schal be seid to hym, What ben these woundis in the myddil of thin hondis? And he schal seie, With these Y was woundid in the hous of hem that louyden me.

7 Swerd, be thou reisid on my scheepherde, and on a man cleuynge to me, seith the Lord of oostis; smyte thou the scheepherde, and scheep of the floc schulen be scaterid. And Y schal turne myn hond to the litle.

8 And twei partis schulen be in ech lond, seith the Lord, and thei schulen be scaterid, and schulen faile, and the thridde part schal be left in it.

9 And Y schal lede the thridde part bi fier, and Y schal brenne hem, as siluer is brent, and Y schal preue hem, as gold is preuyd. He schal clepe to help my name, and Y schal graciously here him; and Y schal seie, Thou art my puple, and he schal seie, Thou art my Lord God.

CAP 14

1 Lo! daies comen, seith the Lord, and thi spuylis schulen be departid in the myddil of thee.

2 And Y schal gadere alle folkis to Jerusalem, in to batel; and the citee schal be takun, and housis schulen be distried, and wymmen schulen be defoulid. And the myddil part of the citee schal go out in to caitiftee, and the 'tother part of the puple schal not be takun awei fro the citee.

3 And the Lord schal go out, and schal fiyte ayens tho folkis, as he fauyte in the dai of strijf.

4 And hise feet schulen stonde in that dai on the hil of olyues, that is ayens Jerusalem at the eest. And the hil of olyues schal be coruun of the myddil part therof to the eest and to the west, bi ful greet biforbrekyng; and the myddil of the hil schal be departid to the north, and the myddil therof to the south.

5 And ye schulen fle to the valei of myn hillis, for the valei of hillis schal be ioyned togidere til to the nexte. And ye schulen fle, as ye fledden fro the face of erthe mouyng in the daies of Osie, kyng of Juda; and my Lord God schal come, and alle seyntis with hym.

6 And it schal be, in that dai liyt schal not be, but coold and frost.

7 And 'ther schal be o dai, which is knowun to the Lord, not day, nether niyt, and in tyme of euentid liyt schal be.

8 And it schal be, in that dai quyke watris schulen go out of Jerusalem, the myddil of hem schal go out to the eest see, and the myddil of hem to the laste see; in somer and in wynter thei schulen be.

9 And the Lord schal be kyng on al erthe; in that dai there schal be o Lord, and his name schal be oon.

10 And al erthe schal turne ayen til to desert, fro the litil hil Remmon to the south of Jerusalem. And it schal be reisid, and schal dwelle in his place, fro the yate of Beniamyn til to place of the formere yate, and til to the yate of the corneris, and fro the tour of Ananyel til to the pressouris of the kyng.

11 And thei schulen dwelle there ynne, and cursidnesse schal no more be, but Jerusalem schal sitte sikir.

12 And this schal be the wounde, bi which the Lord schal smyte alle folkis, that fouyten ayens Jerusalem; the fleisch of ech man stondynge on hise feet schal faile, and hise iyen schulen faile togidere in her hoolis, and her tunge schal faile togidere in her mouth.

13 In that dai greet noise of the Lord schal be in hem, and a man schal catche the hond of his neiybore; and his hond schal be lockid togidere on hond of his neiybore.

14 But and Judas schal fiyte ayens Jerusalem; and richessis of alle folkis in cumpas schulen be gaderide togidere, gold, and siluer, and many clothis ynow.

15 And so fallyng schal be of hors, and mule, and camel, and asse, and of alle werk beestis, that weren in tho castels, as this fallyng.

16 And alle that schulen be residue of alle folkis, that camen ayens Jerusalem, schulen stie vp fro yeer in to yeer, that thei worschipe the kyng, Lord of oostis, and halewe the feeste of tabernaclis.

17 And it schal be, reyn schal not be on hem that schulen not stie vp of the meyneis of erthe to Jerusalem, 'that thei worschipe the king, Lord of oostis.

18 'That and if the meynee of Egipt schal not stie vp, and schal not come, nether on hem schal be reyn; but fallyng schal be, bi which the Lord schal smyte alle folkis, whiche stieden not, for to halewe the feeste of tabernaclis.

19 This schal be the synne of Egipt, and this the synne of alle folkis, that stieden not, for to halewe the feeste of tabernaclis.

20 In that dai, that that is on the bridil of hors schal be hooli to the Lord; and caudruns schulen be in the hous of the Lord, as cruetis bifor the auter.

21 And euery caudrun in Jerusalem and Juda schal be halewid to the Lord of oostis. And alle men schulen come offrynge, and schulen take of tho, and schulen sethe in tho; and a marchaunt schal no more be in the hous of the Lord of oostis in that day.

MALACHIE

CAP 1

1 The birthun of the word of the Lord to Israel, in the hond of Malachie, the profete.

2 Y louyde you, seith the Lord, and ye seiden, In what thing louydist thou vs? Whether Esau was not the brother of Jacob, seith the Lord, and Y louyde Jacob,

3 forsothe Y hatide Esau? And Y haue put Seir the hillis of hym in to wildirnesse, and his eritage in to dragouns of desert.

4 That if Idumee seith, We ben distried, but we schulen turne ayen, and bilde tho thingis that ben distried; the Lord of oostis seith these thingis, These schulen bilde, and Y schal distrie; and thei schulen be clepid termes of wickidnesse, and a puple to whom the Lord is wroth, til in to with outen ende.

5 And youre iyen schulen se, and ye schulen seie, The Lord be magnefied on the terme of Israel.

6 The sone onourith the fader, and the seruaunt schal drede his lord; therfor if Y am fadir, wher is myn onour? and if Y am lord, where is my drede? seith the Lord of oostis. A! ye prestis, to you that dispisen my name; and ye seiden, Wherynne han we dispisid thi name?

7 Ye offren on myn auter vncleene breed, and ye seien, Wherynne han we defoulid thee? In that thing that ye seien, The boord of the Lord is dispisid.

8 If ye offren a blynd beest to be sacrifisid, whether it is not yuel? And if ye offren a crokid and sike beeste, whether it is not yuel? Offre thou it to thi duyk, if it schal plese hym, ether if he schal resseyue thi face, seith the Lord of oostis.

9 And now biseche ye the cheer of the Lord, that he haue merci on you; for of youre hond this thing is doon, if in ony maner he resseiue youre faces, seith the Lord of oostis.

10 Who is 'in you that closith doris, and brenneth myn auter 'of his owne wille, ethir freli? Wille is not to me in you, seith the Lord of oostis; and Y schal not resseyue a yifte of youre hond.

11 For fro rysyng of the sunne til to goyng doun, my name is greet in hethene men; and in ech place a cleene offring is sacrifisid, and offrid to my name; for my name is greet in hethene men, seith the Lord of oostis.

12 And ye han defoulid it in that that ye seien, The boord of the Lord is defoulid, and that that is put aboue is 'worthi to be dispisid, with fier that deuourith it.

13 And ye seiden, Lo! of trauel; and ye han blowe it a wei, seith the Lord of oostis. And ye brouyten in of raueyns a crokid thlng and sijk, and brouyten in a yifte; whether Y schal resseyue it of youre hond? seith the Lord.

14 Cursid is the gileful, that hath in his floc a male beeste, and 'he makynge a vow offrith a feble to the Lord; for Y am a greet kyng, seith the Lord of oostis, and my name is dredeful 'in folkis.

CAP 2

1 And now, A! ye preestis, this maundement is to you.

2 If ye wolen here, and if ye 'wolen not putte on the herte, that ye yyue glorie to my name, seith the Lord of oostis, Y schal sende nedynesse in to you, and Y schal curse to youre blessyngis; and Y schal curse hem, for ye han not putte on the herte.

3 Lo! Y schal caste to you the arm, and Y schal scatere on youre cheere the drit of youre solempnytees, and it schal take you with it.

4 And ye schulen wite, that Y sente to you this maundement, that my couenaunt were with Leuy, seith the Lord of oostis.

5 My couenaunt was with hym of lijf and pees; and Y yaf to hym a drede, and he dredde me, and he dredde of face of my name.

6 The lawe of trewthe was in his mouth, and wickidnesse was not foundun in hise lippis; in pees and in equite he walkide with me, and he turnede awei many men fro wickidnesse.

7 For the lippis of a prest kepen science, and thei schulen ayen seke the lawe of 'the mouth of hym, for he is an aungel of the Lord of oostes.

8 But ye wenten awei fro the weie, and sclaundren ful many men in the lawe; ye maden voide the couenaunt of Leuy, seith the Lord of oostis.

9 For which thing and Y yaf you worthi to be dispisid, and bowen to alle puplis, as ye kepten not my weies, and token a face in the lawe.

10 Whether not o fadir is of alle you? whether o God made not of nouyt you? Whi therfor ech of you dispisith his brother, and defoulith the couenaunt of youre fadris?

11 Judas trespasside, and abhomynacioun is maad in Israel, and in Jerusalem; for Judas defoulide the halewyng of the Lord, which he louyde, and he hadde the douyter of an alien god.

12 The Lord schal distrie the man that dide this thing, the maister and disciple, fro the tabernacle of Jacob, and him that offrith a yifte to the Lord of oostis.

13 And eftsoone ye diden this thing; ye hiliden with teeris the auter of the Lord, with wepyng and mourenyng; so that Y biholde no more to sacrifice, nether resseyue ony thing plesaunt of youre hond.

14 And ye seiden, For what cause? For the Lord witnesside bitwixe thee and the wijf of thi 'puberte, that is, tyme of mariage, which thou dispisidist, and this is thi felowe, and wijf of thi couenaunt.

15 Whether oon made not, and residue of spirit is his? and what sekith oon, no but the seed of God? Therfore kepe ye youre spirit, and nyle thou dispise the wijf of thi yongthe;

16 whanne thou hatist hir, leue thou hir, seith the Lord God of Israel. Forsothe wickidnesse schal kyuere the closyng of hym,

seith the Lord of oostis; kepe ye youre spirit, and nyle ye dispise.

CAP 3

17 Ye maden the Lord for to trauele in youre wordis, and ye seiden, Wherynne maden we hym for to trauele? In that that ye seien, Ech man that doith yuel, is good in the siyt of the Lord, and siche plesen to hym; ether certis where is the God of doom?

1 Lo! Y sende myn aungel, and he schal make redi weie bifor my face; and anoon the lordshipere, whom ye seken, schal come to his hooli temple, and the aungel of testament, whom ye wolen. Lo! he cometh, seith the Lord of oostis;

2 and who schal mowe thenke the dai of his comyng? and who schal stonde for to se hym? For he schal be as fier wellynge togidere, and as erbe of fulleris;

3 and he schal sitte wellynge togidere and clensynge siluer, and he schal purge the sones of Leuy; and he schal purge hem as gold and as siluer, and thei schulen be offrynge to the Lord sacrifices in riytfulnesse.

4 And the sacrifice of Juda and of Jerusalem schal plese to the Lord, as the daies of the world, and as olde yeeris.

5 And Y schal come to you in doom, and Y schal be a swift witnesse to mysdoeris, 'ether enchaunteris of deuelis craft, and to auouteris, and forsworn men, and that falsli calengen the hire of the hirid man, and widewis, and fadirles, 'ether modirles, children, and oppressen a pilgrym, 'nether dredden me, seith the Lord of oostis.

6 Forsothe Y am the Lord, and am not chaungid; and ye sones of Jacob ben not wastid.

7 Forsothe fro daies of youre fadris ye wenten awei fro my lawful thingis, and kepten not; turne ye ayen to me, and Y schal ayen turne to you, seith the Lord of oostis. And ye seiden, In what thing schulen we turne ayen?

8 If a man schal turmente God, for ye 'togidere fitchen me. And ye seiden, In what thing 'togidere fitchen we thee? In tithis and in 'firste fruitis;

9 and ye ben cursid in nedynesse, and alle ye folc disseyuen me, and 'togidere fitchen.

10 Brynge ye yn ech tithe in to my berne, that mete be in myn hous, and preue ye me on this thing, seith the Lord, if Y schal not opene to you the goteris of heuene, and schal schede out to you blessyng, til to aboundaunce.

11 And Y schal blame for you that that deuourith, and he schal not distrie the fruit of youre lond; nether bareyn vyneyerd schal be in the feeld,

12 seith the Lord of oostis, and alle folkis schulen seie you blessid; for ye schulen be a desirable lond, seith the Lord of oostis.

13 Youre wordis wexiden strong on me, seith the Lord; and ye seiden, What han we spokun ayens thee?

14 And ye seiden, He is veyn, that serueth God; and what wynnyng for we kepten hise heestis, and for we wenten sorewful bifore the Lord of oostis?

15 Therfor now we seien proude men blessid; for thei ben bildid doynge vnpitee, and thei temptiden God, and ben maad saaf.

16 Thanne men dredynge God spaken, ech with his neiybore; and the Lord perseyuede, and herde, and a book of mynde is writun bifor hym 'men dredynge God, and thenkynge his name.

17 And thei schulen be to me, seith the Lord of oostis, in the dai in which Y schal make, in to a special tresour; and Y schal spare hem, as a man sparith his sone seruynge to hym.

18 And ye schulen be conuertid, and ye schulen se, what is bitwixe the iust man and vnpitouse, bitwixe 'the seruynge to the Lord and 'not seruynge to hym.

CAP 4

1 For lo! a dai schal come, brennynge as a chymenei; and alle proude men, and alle doynge vnpitee schulen be stobul; and the dai comynge schal enflaume hem, seith the Lord of oostis, which schal not leeue to hem rote and buriownyng.

2 And to you dredynge my name the sunne of riytwisnesse schal rise, and heelthe in pennys of hym; and ye schulen go out, and schulen skippe, as a calf of the droue.

3 And ye schulen to-trede vnpitouse men, whanne thei schulen be aische vndur the soole of youre feet, in the dai in which Y do, seith the Lord of oostis.

4 Bithenke ye on the lawe of my seruaunt Moises, which Y comaundide to hym in Oreb, to al Israel comaundementis and domes.

5 Lo! Y schal sende to you Elie, the profete, bifore that the greet dai and orible of the Lord come.

6 And he schal conuerte the herte of fadris to sones, and the herte of sones to fadris of hem, lest perauenture Y come, and smyte the erthe with curs.

1 MACHABEIS

CAP 1

1 And it was don, aftir that Alisaundre of Filip, king of Macedoyne, which regnede first in Grece, and yede out of the lond of Sethym, smoot Darius, king of Perseis and of Medeis,

2 he ordeynede many batels, and gat strengthis of alle; and he slow the kingis of erthe,

3 and passide forth til to endis of erthe, and took spuylis of multitude of folkis; and the erthe was stille in siyt of hym.

4 And he gaderide vertu, and oost ful strong, and the herte of hym was enhaunsid and lift vp.

5 And he gat the cuntreis of folkis, and tirauntis; and thei weren maad to hym in to tribut.

6 And after these thingis he felle in to bed, and knew that he schulde die.

7 And he clepide his noble children, that weren nurschid with hym fro yongthe, and departide to hem his kingdom, whanne he lyuede yit.

8 And Alisaundre regnede twelue yeer, and was deed.

9 And his children weldiden the rewme,

10 ech in his place, and alle puttiden to hem diademys aftir his deth, and the sones of hem after hem, many yeeris; and yuels weren multiplied in erthe.

11 And ther wente out of hem a roote of synne, Antiok the noble, the sone of Antiok kyng, that was at Rome in ostage, and regnede in the hundrid and seuene and thrittithe yeer of the rewme of Grekis.

12 In tho daies wickid sones 'of Israel wenten out, and counseiliden many, and seide, Go we, and ordeyne we testament with hethene men, that ben aboute vs; for sithen we departiden fro hem, many yuels foundun vs.

13 And the word was seyn good bifore the iyen of hem.

14 And summe of the puple senten, and wenten to the kyng; and he yaf power to hem for to do riytwisnesse of hethene men.

15 And thei bildiden a scole in Jerusalem, bi lawis of naciouns;

16 and maden to hem prepucies, and wenten awei fro the hooli testament, and weren ioyned to naciouns, and weren seeld for to do yuel.

17 And the rewme hadde prosperite in the siyt of Antiok, and he bigan for to regne in the lond of Egipt, that he schulde regne on twei rewmes.

18 And he entride in to Egipt with a greuouse multitude, in charis, and olifauntis, and horse men, 'ether kniytis, and plenteuouse multitude of schippis,

19 and he ordeynede batel ayens Tholome, kyng of Egipt; and Tolome dredde of his face, and flei; and many weren woundid, and fellen doun.

20 And he took the stronge citees in the lond of Egipt, and took the preies of the lond of Egipt.

21 And Antiok turnede, after that he smoot Egipt, in the hundrid and thre and fourtithe yeer, and stiede to Israel.

22 And he stiede to Jerusalem with a greuouse multitude,

23 and entride in to the halewyng with pride; and he took the goldun auter, and the candilstike of liyt, and alle vessels therof, and the boord of proposicioun, and vessels of fletynge sacrifices, and cruetis, and goldun morteris, and veil, and crownes, and goldun ournement that was in the face of the temple; and he brak alle.

24 And he took siluer and gold, and alle desirable vessels, and he took the priuy tresours, whiche he foond; and whanne he hadde takun vp alle thingis, he wente in to his lond.

25 And he made slauyter of men, and spak in greet pride.

26 And greet weilyng was maad in Israel, and in ech place of hem;

27 and princes sorewiden inwardli, and eldere men, and maidens, and yonge men weren maad sike, and fairnesse of wymmen was chaungid.

28 Ech hosebonde took weilyng, and thei that saten in hosebondis bed, morenyden.

29 And the lond was mouyd togidere on men dwellynge therynne, and al the hous of Jacob was clothid with confusioun.

30 And aftir twei yeeris of daies, the kyng sente a prince of tributis in to the citees of Juda, and he cam to Jerusalem with greet cumpanye.

31 And he spak to hem pesible wordis in gile, and thei bileuyden to hym.

32 And sudeynli he felle in on the citee, and smoot it with a greet wounde, and loste myche puple of Israel.

33 And he took preies of the citee, and brente it with fier, and distriede housis therof, and wallis therof in cumpas.

34 And thei ledden wymmen caitif, and children, and weldiden beestis.

35 And thei bildiden the citee of Dauid with greet wal and sad, and sadde touris; and it was maad to hem in to an hiy tour.

36 And thei puttiden there a folc of synneris, wickid men, and thei weren strong in it; and thei puttiden armeris, and metis, and gaderiden preies of Jerusalem;

37 and puttiden vp there, and weren maad in to a greet snare.

38 And this thing was maad to aspiyngis in yuel, 'ether tresouns, to halewyng, and in to an yuel deuel in Israel euere more.

39 And thei schedden out innocent blood, bi cumpas of the halewyng, and defouliden the halewyng.

40 And dwelleris of Jerusalem fledden for hem, and it was maad abitacioun of straungeris, and it was maad straunge to his seed, and sones therof forsoken it.

41 The halewyng therof was desolat as wildirnesse; feeste daies therof weren turned in to mourenyng, sabotis therof in to schenschip, onouris therof in to nouyt.

42 Bi the glorie therof the yuel fame therof was multiplied, and hyynesse therof was turned in to mournyng.

43 And kyng Antiok wroot to al his rewme, that al the puple schulde be oon. And thei forsoken ech man his lawe;

44 and alle folkis consentiden bi the word of kyng Antiok,

45 and many of Israel consentiden to him, and sacrifieden to idols, and defouliden sabot.

46 And king Antiok sente bokis bi the hondis of messangeris in to Jerusalem, and in to alle citees of Judee, that thei schulden sue lawis of folkis of erthe,

47 and schulden forbede brent sacrifices, and sacrifices, and plesyngis for to be don in the temple of God,

48 and that thei schulden forbede the sabot for to be halewid, and solempne daies,

49 and hooli thingis for to be defoulid, and the hooli puple of Israel;

50 And he comaundide auteris for to be bildid, and templis, and idols; and swynes fleisch for to be sacrifisid, and vncleene beestis;

51 and for to leeue her sones vncircumcidid, and the soulis of hem for to be defoulid in alle vnclennessis and abhomynaciouns, so that thei schulden foryete the lawe, and schulen chaunge alle the iustifiyngis of God.

52 And who euere dide not bi the word of kyng Antiok, schulden die.

53 Bi alle these wordis he wroot to al his rewme, and aboue settide princes to the puple, whiche schulden constreyne these thingis for to be don.

54 And thei comaundiden to citees of Juda for to make sacrifice.

55 And many of the puple weren gaderid to hem, whiche forsoken the lawe of the Lord, and diden yuels on erthe.

56 And thei dryueden out the puple of Israel fro priuy places, and in hid places of fleynge men.

57 In the fiftenthe dai of the monethe Casleu, in the hundrid and fyue and fourtithe yeer, king Antiok bildide abhominable idol of discoumfort on the auter of God; and bi alle citees of Judee in cumpas thei bildiden auters.

58 And bifore the yatis of housis and in stretis thei brenten encensis, and sacrifieden;

59 and brenten bi fier the bookis of the lawe of God, and keruyden hem.

60 And anentis whom euere the bookis of testament of the Lord weren foundun, and who euere kepte the lawe of the Lord, bi the maundement of the kyng thei slowen hym.

61 In her power thei diden these thingis to the puple of Israel, that was foundun in ech monethe in citees.

62 And in the fyue and twentithe dai of the monethe, thei sacrifieden on the auter, that was ayens the auter of God.

63 And wymmen, that circumcididen her sones, weren stranglid, bi comaundement of kyng Antiok;

64 and thei hangiden children bi the neckis, bi alle housis of hem, and strangliden hem that circumcididen hem.

65 And many of the puple of Israel determyneden anentis hem, that thei schulden not ete vnclene thingis, and chesiden more for to die, than for to be defoulid with vnclene metis.

66 And thei wolden not breke the hooli lawe of God, and thei weren slayn;

67 and ful greet wraththe was maad on the puple.

CAP 2

1 In tho daies Matatias, the sone of Joon, sone of Symeon, and he was prest of the sones of Joarym, roos fro Jerusalem, and sat in the hil Modyn.

2 And he hadde fyue sones; Joon, that was named Gaddis; and Symount, that was named Thasi;

3 and Judas, that was clepid Machabeus;

4 and Eleasarus, that was named Abaron;

5 and Jonathas, that was clepid Apphus.

6 These siyen the yuels that weren don in the puple of Juda and in Jerusalem.

7 And Matatias seide, Wo to me! wher to am Y borun, for to se the distriyng 'of my puple, and the defoulyng of the hooli citee, and for to sitte there, whanne it is youun in to the hondis of enemyes?

8 Hooli thingis ben maad in the hond of straungeris; the temple therof as a man vnnoble;

9 vessels of glorie therof ben led awei caitif. Elde men therof ben slayn in stretis, and yonge men therof fellen doun bi swerd of enemyes.

10 What folc enheritide not the kingdom therof, and weldide not preies therof?

11 Al ournyng therof is borun awei; sche that was fre, is maad handmaidun.

12 And lo! oure hooli thing, and oure fairnesse, and oure clerete, is desolat, and hethene men defouliden it.

13 What therfor is yit to vs for to lyue?

14 And Matatias and his sones to-renten her clothis, and hiliden hem with heiris, and weiliden greetli.

15 And thei that weren sent of kyng Antiok, camen thidur, for to constreyne hem that fledden togidere in to the cite of Modyn, for to offre and brenne encensis, and for to departe fro the lawe of God.

16 And many of the puple of Israel consentiden, and camen to hem; but Matatias and his sones stoden stidefastli.

17 And thei answeriden, that weren sent of Antiok, and seiden to Matatias, Thou art prince, and moost clere, and greet in this citee, and ourned with sones and britheren.

18 Therfor go thou the formere, and do the maundement of the kyng, as alle folkis han don, and men of Juda, and thei that leften in Jerusalem. And thou schalt be, and thi sones, among frendis of the king, and maad large in siluer and gold, and many yiftis.

19 And Matatias answeride, and seide with greet vois, Thouy alle folkis obeien to kyng Antiok, that thei go awei ech man fro seruice of the lawe of his fadris, and consenten to his maundementis,

20 Y, and my sones, and my britheren schulen obeie to the lawe of oure fadris.

21 God be helpful to vs; it is not profitable to vs for to forsake the lawe and riytwisnesses of God.

22 We schulen not here the wordis of kyng Antiok, nether schulen make sacrifice to idols, and breke the maundementis of oure lawe, that we go bi anothir weie.

23 And as he ceesside for to speke these wordis, sum Jew wente to, bifore the iyen of alle men, for to sacrifice to idols on the auter, in the citee Modyn, bi comaundement of the kyng.

24 And Matatias siy, and sorewide, and his reynes trembliden togidere, and his woodnesse was kyndlid bi doom of the lawe; and he skippide in, and slow hym on the auter.

25 But and he slow in that tyme the man whom king Antiok sente, which compellide for to offre, and he distriede the auter.

26 And he louyde feruentli the lawe, as Fynees dide to Sambri, sone of Salomy.

27 And Matatias criede with greet vois in the citee, and seide, Ech man that hath feruent loue of the lawe, ordeyne a testament, 'that is, a couenaunt, and go out after me.

28 And he flei, and hise sones, in to munteyns, and leften what euere thingis thei hadden in the citee.

29 Thanne many sekynge dom and riytwisnesse, wenten doun in to desert, that thei schulden sitte there,

30 thei, and the sones of hem, and wymmen of hem, and beestis of hem, for yuels weren hard on hem.

31 And it was teld to men of the kyng, and to the oost, that weren in Jerusalem, the citee of Dauid, that summen wenten awei, that distrieden maundement of the kyng, in to priuy places in desert; and many hadden go after hem.

32 And anoon thei wenten to hem, and ordeineden ayens hem batel, in the dai of sabatis;

33 and seiden to hem, Ayenstonde ye also now yit? go ye out, and do ye after the word of kyng Antiok, and ye schulen lyue.

34 And thei seiden, We schulen not go out, nether schulen do the word of the king, that we defoule the dai of sabatis.

35 And thei stiriden batel ayens hem.

36 And thei answeriden not to hem, nether threwen stoon to hem, nether stoppiden priuy places,

37 and seiden, Die we alle in oure simplenesse, and heuene and erthe schulen be witnessis on vs, that vniustli ye lesen vs.

38 And thei yauen to hem batel in sabatis, and thei weren deed, and wyues of hem, and sones of hem, and beestis of hem, til to a thousande persoones of men.

39 And Matatias knew, and his frendis; and thei hadden mournyng on hem greetli.

40 And a man seide to his neiybore, If we alle schulen do as oure britheren diden, and schulen not fiyte ayens hethene men, for oure lyues, and oure iustifiyngis, sunnere thei schulen distrie vs fro erthe.

41 And thei thouyten in that dai, and seiden, Ech man who euere cometh to vs in batel, in dai of sabotis, fiyte we ayens hym, and die we not alle, as oure britheren ben deed in priuy places.

42 Thanne the synagoge of Jewis, strong in myytis of Israel, was gaderid to hem. Euery wilful man in the lawe,

43 and alle that fledden fro yuels, weren addid to hem, and thei weren maad to hem to stidfastnesse.

44 And thei gaderiden an oost, and smytiden synneris in her wraththe, and wickid men in her indignacioun; and the tother fledden to naciouns, for to ascape.

45 And Matatias enuyrownede, and hise frendis, and distrieden auteris,

46 and circumcididen children vncircumcided, hou many euere thei founden in the coostis of Israel, 'in strengthe.

47 And thei pursueden the sones of pride, and the werk hadde prosperite in her hondis.

48 And thei gaten the lawe fro hondis of hethene men, and fro hondis of kyngis, and yauen not strengthe to the synnere.

49 And daies of Matatias of diynge neiyiden, and he seide to hise sones, Now pride is coumfortid, and chastisyng, and tyme of distruccioun, and the wraththe of indignacioun.

50 Now therfor, sones, be ye sueris, 'ether louyeris, of the lawe, and yyue ye youre lyues for the testament of fadris.

51 And bithenke ye on werkis of fadris, whiche thei diden in her generaciouns, and ye schulen resseyue greet glorie, and euerlastynge name.

52 Whether in temptacioun Abraham was not founden trewe, and it was arettid to hym to riytwisnes?

53 Joseph in time of his angwisch kepte comaundement, and was maad lord of Egipt.

54 Fynees, oure fadir, in feruentli louynge the feruent loue of God, took testament of euerlastynge preesthod.

55 Jhesus, 'ether Josue, while he fillide the word, was maad duyk in Israel.

56 Caleph, while he witnesside in the chirche, took eritage.

57 Dauid in his merci gat the sete of kyngdom, in to worldis.

58 Elie, while he feruentli louyde the feruent loue of the lawe, was resseyued in to heuene.

59 Ananyas, Azarias, Misael, bileuyden, and weren delyuered fro flawme.

60 Danyel in his symplenesse was delyuered fro the mouth of liouns.

61 And thus bithenke ye bi generacioun and generacioun, for alle that hopen in to hym ben not maad vnstidefast.

62 And drede ye not of the wordis of a man synnere, for the glorie of hym is tord and worm;

63 to dai he is enhaunsid, and to morewe he schal not be foundun, for he is turned in to his erthe, and his thouyt schal perische.

64 Therfor, ye sones, be coumfortid, and do ye manli in the lawe; for whanne ye schulen do tho thingis that ben bodun to you in the lawe of youre Lord God, in it ye schulen be gloriouse.

65 And lo! Symount, youre brother; Y woot, that he is a man of councel, here ye hym eueremore, and he schal be fadir to you.

66 And Judas Machabeus, stronge in miytis fro his yongthe, be to you a prince in knyythod, and he schal do batel of the puple.

67 And ye schulen brynge to you alle doeris of the lawe, and venge ye the veniaunce of youre puple.

68 Yelde ye yeldyng to hethene men, and take ye tent to the heeste of the lawe.

69 And he blesside hem, and was put to hise fadris.

70 And he was deed in the hundrid and 'sixe and fourti yeer, and was biried of hise sones in to sepulcre of hise fadris in Modyn; and al Israel weiliden hym with greet weilyng.

CAP 3

1 And Judas, that was clepid Machabeus, the sone of Matatias, roos for hym.

2 And alle hise britheren helpiden hym, and alle that ioyneden hem to his fadir, and thei fouyten the batel 'of Israel with gladnesse.

3 And he alargide glorie to his puple, and clothide hym with an haburiowne as a giaunt, and girde hym with hise armeris of batel in batels, and defendide castels with his swerd.

4 He was maad lijk a lioun in hise werkis, and as a whelp of lioun rorynge in his huntyng.

5 And he pursuede wickid men, and souyte hem; and he brente hem in flawmes, that disturbliden his puple.

6 And hise enemyes weren put abac for drede of hym, and alle worcheris of wickidnesse weren troblid to gidere; and heelthe was dressid in his hond.

7 And he wraththide many kyngis, and gladide Jacob in hise werkis, and in to world his mynde is in blessyng.

8 And he wente thorouy the citees of Juda, and loste vnpitouse men of hem, and turnede awei wraththe fro Israel.

9 And he was named til to the vtmest of erthe, and he gaderide men perischynge.

10 And Appollyne gaderide folkis, and fro Samarie myche vertu, and greet, for to fiyte ayens Israel.

11 And Judas knew, and wente out ayens hym, and smoot, and slow hym. And many woundid fellen doun, and the othere fledden; and he took preies of hem.

12 And Judas took awei the swerd of Appollyne, and was fiytynge therwith in alle daies.

13 And Seron, prince of the oost of Sirie, herde, that Judas gaderide a gaderyng, and the chirche of feithful men with hym.

14 And he seide, Y schal make to me a name, and Y schal be glorified in the rewme, and Y schal ouercome Judas, and hem that ben with hym, whiche dispisiden the kyngis word.

15 And he made redi hym; and the castels of vnpitouse men, stronge helperis, stieden vp with hym, for to do veniaunce on the sones of Israel.

16 And thei neiyiden 'til to Betheron; and Judas wente out ayens hem, with fewe men.

17 Forsothe as thei siyen the oost comynge to hem in metinge, thei seiden to Judas, Hou moun we fewe fiyten ayens so greet multitude, so strong; and we ben maad weri bi fastyng this dai?

18 And Judas seide, It is liyt, 'ether esy, that many be closid togidere in hond of fewe; and difference is not in siyt of God 'of heuene, for to delyuere in manye ether in fewe;

19 for not in multitude of oost is the victorie of batel, but of heuene is strengthe.

20 Thei comen to vs in rebel multitude, and pride, for to distrie vs, and oure wyues, and oure sones, and for to robbe vs.

21 Forsothe we schulen fiyte for oure lyues, and oure lawis;

22 and the Lord hym silf schal al to-breke hem bifore oure face; forsothe drede ye not hem.

23 Sotheli as he ceesside for to speke, he hurlide in 'in to hem sudenli; and Seron was al to-brokun, and his oost, in the siyt of hym.

24 And he pursuede hym in the goynge doun of Betheron, til in to the feeld; and eiyte hundrid men of hem fellen doun, the othere forsothe fledden in to the lond of Filistiym.

25 And the drede of Judas, and of his britheren, and the inward ferdnesse, felle on alle hethene men in cumpas of hem;

26 and the name of hym cam to the kyng, and alle folkis telden of the bateils of Judas.

27 Sotheli as king Antiok herde these wordis, he was wrooth in soule; and he sente, and gaderide the oost of al his rewme, ful stronge castels.

28 And he openyde his treserie, and yaf sowdis to the oost, in to a yeer, and comaundide hem, that thei schulden be redi to alle thingis.

29 And he sai, that money failide of hise tresouris, and tributis of the cuntrei weren litil, for dissencioun and veniaunce that he dide in the lond, for to do awei the lawful thingis that weren of the firste daies.

30 And he dredde, that he schulde not haue as onys and twies in to costis and yiftis, whiche he hadde youun bifore with large hond; and he was riche ouer kingis that weren bifore hym.

31 And he was astonyed in soule greetli, and thouyte for to go in to Persis, and for to take tributis of cuntreis, and for to gadre myche siluer.

32 And he lefte Lisias, a noble man of the kyngis kyn, on the kingis nedis, fro the flood Eufrates til to the flood of Egipt;

33 and that he schulde nursche Antiok, his sone, til he cam ayen.

34 And he bitook to hym the half of the oost, and olifauntis, and comaundide to hym of alle these thingis that he wolde, and of men enhabitynge Judee and Jerusalem;

35 and that he schulde sende to hem an oost, for to al to-breke, and to distrie vttirly the vertu of Israel, and relifs of Jerusalem, and for to do awey the mynde of hem fro place;

36 and for to ordeyne dwelleris sones aliens in alle the coostis of hem, and bi lot for to departe the lond of hem.

37 And the kyng took a part of the residue oost, and wente out of Antiochie, citee of his rewme, in the hundrid and seuene and fourti yeer; and passide ouer the flood Eufrates, and wente thorou the hiyere cuntreis.

38 And Lisias chees Tholome, the sone of Dorym, and Nycanore, and Gorgie, miyti men of the kyngis frendis.

39 And he sente with hem fourti thousynde of men, and seuene thousynde of hors men, 'ether knyytis, that thei schul-den come in to the lond of Juda, and distrie it, bi the word of the kyng.

40 And thei wenten forth, for to go with al her pouer; and thei camen, and londiden at Ammaum, in the feeldi lond.

41 And marchauntis of cuntreis herden the name of hem, and token siluer and gold ful miche, and children, and camen in to castels, for to take the sones of Israel in to seruauntis; and the oostes of Sirie and the londis of aliens weren addid to hem.

42 And Judas siy, and his britheren, that yuelis weren multi-plied, and the oost appliede, 'ether londide, at the coostis of hem; and thei knewen the wordis of the kyng, whiche he comaundide the puple for to do, in to perischyng and endyng.

43 And thei seiden, ech man to his neiybore, Reise we the castyng doun of oure puple, and fiyte we for oure puple, and oure hooli thingis.

44 And comyng togidere of oost was gaderid, for to be redi in to batel, and for to preie, and axe merci, and merciful doyn-gis.

45 And Jerusalem was not enhabitid, but was as desert; ther was not that entride and wente out, of children therof; and the hooli thing was defoulid, and sones of aliens weren in the hiy tour, ther was the dwellyng of hethene men; and the likyng was don awei fro Jacob, and pipe and harpe failide there.

46 And thei weren gaderid, and camen in to Masphat ayens Jerusalem; for place of preier was in Masphat, sunnere than in Jerusalem.

47 And thei fastiden in that dai, and clothiden hem with hairis, and puttiden aisch in her heed, and renten her clothis.

48 And thei spredden abrood bookis of lawe, of the whiche hethene men souyten licnesse of her symylacris;

49 and thei brouyten ournementis of prestis, and 'firste fruy-tis, and tithis; and thei reisiden Nazareis that hadden fillid daies.

50 And thei crieden with greet vois to heuene, and seiden, What schulen we do to these, and whidur schulen we lede hem?

51 And thin hooli thingis ben to-trodun, and defoulid, and thi prestis ben maad in to mourenyng,

52 and in to dispisyng. And lo! naciouns camen togidere ayens vs, for to distrie vs; thou wost what thingis thei thenken ayens vs.

53 Hou schulen we mow withstonde bifore the face of hem, no but thou, God, helpe vs?

54 And thei crieden in trumpis, with greet vois.

55 And aftir these thingis Judas ordeynede duykis of the puple, tribunes, and centuriouns, and pentacontrarkis, and decuriouns.

56 And he seide to these that bildiden housis, and wediden wyues, and plauntiden vyne yerdis, and to dredeful men, that thei schulden turne ayen, eche man in to his hous, bi the lawe.

57 And thei mouyden castels, and thei settiden togidere at the south of Ammaum.

58 And Judas seide, Be ye gird, and be ye miyti sones, and be ye redi 'in the morewnyng, and that ye fiyte ayens these naciouns, that camen togidere for to distrie vs, and oure hooli thingis.

59 For betere is, that we die in batel, than for to se yuels of oure folc and holi thingis.

60 Sotheli as wille schal be in heuene, so be it don.

CAP 4

1 And Gorgias took fyue thousynde of men, and a thousynde chosun horse men; and thei mouyden tentis bi niyt,

2 for to applie to the tentis of Jewis, and for to smyte hem sudenli; and sones that weren of the hiy tour, weren lederis to hem.

3 And Judas herde, and he roos, and miyti men, for to smyte the pouer of oostis of the kyng, that was in Ammaum;

4 for yit the oost was scaterid fro tentis.

5 And Gorgias cam in to the tentis of Judas bi niyt, and foond no man; and thei souyten hem in hillis, for he seide, These fleen fro vs.

6 And whanne dai was maad, Judas apperide in the feeld with thre thousyndis of men oneli, whiche hadden not hilyngis and swerdis.

7 And thei siyen the tentis of hethene men stronge, and men haburiowned, and the multitude of horse men in cumpas of hem, and these weren tauyt to batel.

8 And Judas seide to hise men, that weren with hym, Drede ye not the multitude of hem, and drede ye not inwardli the fersnesse of hem.

9 Bithenke ye hou oure fadris weren maad saaf in the Reed See, whanne Farao pursuede hem with mychel oost.

10 And now crie we to heuene, and the Lord schal haue mercy on vs, and schal be myndeful of the testament of oure fadris, and schal al to-breke this oost bifore oure face to dai.

11 And alle folkis schulen wite, that it is God, that schal ayen-bie, and delyuere Israel.

12 And aliens reisiden her iyen, and sien hem comynge of the contrarie part,

13 and wenten out of tentis in to batel. And thei that weren with Judas, songen in trumpe.

14 And thei wenten togidere, and hethene men weren al to-brokun, and fledden in to feeld;

15 forsothe the laste fellen doun bi swerd. And thei pursueden hem til to Gaseron, and til 'in to feeldis of Idumee, and Ayotus, and Jannye; and there fellen doun of hem til to thre thousyndis of men.

16 And Judas turnede ayen, and his oost suynge hym.

17 And he seide to the puple, Coueite ye not preies, for batel is ayens vs,

18 and Gorgias and his oost ben in the hil niy vs; but stonde ye now ayens oure enemyes, and ouercome hem, and after these thingis ye schulen take preyes sikirli.

19 And yit while Judas spak these thingis, lo! sum part apperide, biholdynge forth fro the hil.

20 And Gorgias siy, that hise helperis weren togidere turned in to fliyt, and tentis weren brent; for smoke that was seyn, declaride that that was don.

21 And whanne thei bihelden these thingis, thei dredden greetli, biholdynge togidere bothe Judas and the oost, redi to batel in the feeld.

22 And thei fledden alle in the feeld of aliens,

23 and Judas turnede ayen to preies of the tentis; and thei token myche gold, and siluer, and iacynct, and purpur of the see, and grete richessis.

24 And thei conuertiden, and songen an ympne, 'ether heriyng, and blessiden God in to heuene; for he is good, for the merci of hym is in to the world.

25 And greet helthe was maad in Israel in that dai.

26 Forsothe who euere of aliens ascapiden, camen, and telden to Lisias alle thingis that bifellen.

27 And whanne he herde these thingis, he was astonyed in soule, and failide; for not what maner thingis he wolde, siche bifellen in Israel, and what maner thingis the kyng comaundide.

28 And in the yeer suynge, Lisias 'gaderide of chosun men sixti thousyndis, and of horse men fyue thousynde, for to ouercome hem.

29 And thei camen in to Judee, and settiden tentis in Betheron; and Judas ran to hem with ten thousynde of men.

30 And thei sien strong oost, and he preiede, and seide, Blessid art thou, sauyour of Israel, that hast al to-brokun the feersnesse of the myyti Golias in the hond of thi seruaunt Dauid, and bitokist the castels of aliens in to the hondis of Jonathas, sone of Saul, and of his squyer.

31 Close thou togidere also this oost in the hond of thi puple Israel, and be thei confoundid in her oost, and horse men.

32 Yyue thou to hem inward drede, and make the hardynesse of her vertu to faile, and be thei mouyd togidere in her brekyng togidere.

33 Caste doun hem bi the swerd of men louynge thee, and alle that knowen thi name, togidere preyse thee in ympnys.

34 And thei ioyneden togidere batel, and fyue thousyndis of men fellen doun of the oost of Lisias.

35 Lisias forsothe siy the fliyt of hise men, and the hardynesse of Jewis; and that thei weren redi ether for to lyue, ether for to die strongli. And he wente to Antioche, and chees knyytis, that thei multiplied schulden come eftsoone in to Judee.

36 Forsothe Judas seide to hise britheren, Lo! oure enemyes ben al to-brokun; stie we now, for to clense hooli thingis, and 'make newe.

37 And al the oost was gaderid, and thei stieden in to the hil of Sion.

38 And thei siyen halewyng desert, and the auter vnhalewid, and the yatis brent, and in the porche tendur trees growun, as in wielde wode or munteyns, and litle cellis distried.

39 And thei renten her clothis, and weiliden with greet weilyng; and puttiden aische on her heed,

40 and fellen on the face of the erthe, and crieden in trumpis of signes, and crieden in to heuene.

41 Thanne Judas ordeynede men, for to fiyte ayens hem that weren in the hiy tour, as long as thei clensiden hooli thingis.

42 And he chees preestis with out wem, hauynge wille in the lawe of God;

43 and thei clensiden hooli thingis, and token awei stoonys of defoulyng in to an vnclene place.

44 And he thouyte on the auter of brent sacrifices, that was vnhalewid, what he schulde do therof.

45 And a good counsel felle in to him, for to distrie it, lest it were to hem in to schenschip, for hethene men defouliden it.

46 And thei distrieden it, and kepten stonys in the hil of the hous, in couenable place, til that a profete cam, and answeride of hem.

47 And thei token hoole stoonys, by the lawe, and bildiden a newe auter, lijk that that was bifore.

48 And thei bildiden hooli thingis, and the thingis that weren with ynne the hous with ynneforth; and thei halewiden the hous, and porchis.

49 And thei maden newe hooli vessels, and brouyten in a candilstike, and auter of encensis, and a boord in to the temple.

50 And puttide encense on the auter, and tenden lanternes, that weren on the candilstike, and yauen liyt in the temple.

51 And thei puttiden looues on the boord, and hangiden veiles, and endiden alle werkis that thei maden.

52 And bifore morewtid thei risiden, in the fyue and twentithe dai of the nynthe monethe, this is the monethe Casleu, of the hundrid and eiyte and fourtithe yeer.

53 And thei offriden sacrifice bi the lawe, on the newe auter of brent sacrifices, which thei maden bi tyme.

54 And bi the dai in which hethene men defouliden it, in that it was 'maad newe, in songis, and harpis, and cynaris, 'that ben instrumentis of musik, ether giternes, and cymbalis.

55 And al the puple felle on her face, and worschipiden, and blessiden in to heuene him that made prosperite to hem.

56 And thei maden halewyng of the auter in eiyte daies, and offriden brent sacrifices with gladnesse, and helful thing of heriyng.

57 And thei ourneden the face of the temple with goldun corouns, and smale scheeldis; and halewiden yatis, and litle housis, and puttiden to hem yatis.

58 And ful greet gladnesse was maad in the puple, and the schenschipe of hethene men was turned awei.

59 And Judas ordeynede, and hise britheren, and al the chirche of Israel, that the dai of halewyng of the auter be don in his tymes, fro yeer in to yeer, bi eiyte daies, fro the fyue and twentithe dai of the monethe Casleu, with gladnesse and ioye.

60 And thei bildiden in that tyme the hil of Sion, and bi cumpas hiy wallis, and sadde touris, lest ony tyme hethene men wolden come, and defoule it, as thei diden before.

61 And he sette there an oost, for to kepe it; and he wardide it, 'for to kepe Bethsura, that the puple schulde haue strengthing ayens the face of Ydume.

CAP 5

1 And it was don, as hethene men herden in cumpas, that the auter was bildid, and the seyntuarie as bifore, thei weren wroth greetli.

2 And thei thouyten for to do awei, 'ether distrie, the kyn of Jacob, that was among hem; and thei bigunnen for to sle of the puple, and pursue.

3 And Judas ouercam the sones of Esau in Ydume, and hem that weren in Arabathane, for thei saten aboute men of Israel; and he smoot hem with a greet wounde.

4 And he thouyte on the malice of sones of Bean, that weren in to gnare, and in to sclaundre to the puple of Israel, and aspieden it, 'ether settiden 'buyschementis to it, in the weie.

5 And thes weren closid togidere fro hym in the touris; and he appliede to hem, and curside hem, and brente with fier the touris of hem, with alle men that weren in hem.

6 And he passide to the sones of Amon, and foond strong hond, and plenteuouse puple, and Tymothe, duyk of hem.

7 And he smoot many batels with hem, and thei weren brokun in siyt of hym; and he smoot hem.

8 And he took the citee Jaser, and vilages therof; and he turnede ayen in to Judee.

9 And hethene men that weren in Galaad, weren gaderid ayens Israelitis, that weren in coostis of hem, for to do awei hem; and thei fledden in to the strengthing of Datheman.

10 And thei senten lettris to Judas, and hise britheren, and seiden, Hethene men ben gaderid ayens vs bi cumpas, that thei do awei vs;

11 and thei maken redi for to come, and ocupie the strengthing, in to which we fledden; and Tymothe is duyk of the oost of hem.

12 Now therfor come thou, and delyuere vs fro her hondis, for a multitude of vs felle doun;

13 and alle oure britheren that weren in places of Tubyn, euerywhere ben slayn; and thei ledden awei caitif the wyues of hem, and children, and token spuylis, and killiden there almeste a thousynde men.

14 And yit epistlis weren rad, and lo! othere messangeris camen fro Galile, with cootis to-rent,

15 and telden bi these wordis, and seiden, that men camen togidere ayens hem fro Tolomaida, and Tire, and Sidon, and al Galile is fillid with aliens, for to distrie vs.

16 Sotheli as Judas herde, and the puple, these wordis, a greet chirche cam togidere, for to thenke what thei schulden do to her britheren, that weren in tribulacioun, and weren ouer comun of hem.

17 And Judas seide to Symount, his brother, Chese to thee men, and go, and delyuere thi britheren in Galile; Y forsothe and my brother Jonathas schulen go in to Galatithym.

18 And he lefte Josafus, sone of Sacarie, and Azarie, duykis of the puple, with the residue oost in Judee to kepyng;

19 and comaundide to hem, and seide, Be ye souereyns to this puple, and nyle ye smyte batel ayens hethene men, til we turnen ayen.

20 And men weren youun to Simount thre thousyndis, for to go in to Galile; to Judas sotheli eiyte thousynde, in to Galatithym.

21 And Symount wente in to Galile, and ioynede many batels with hethene men. And hethene men weren al to-brokun fro his face, and

22 he pursuede hem til the yate of Tolomaida. And there fellen doun of hethene men almest thre thousynde of men;

23 and he took the spuylis of hem. And he took hem that weren in Galile, and in Arbathis, with wyues, and children, and alle thingis that weren to hem; and brouyte in to Judee with greet gladnesse.

24 And Judas Machabeis, and Jonathas, and hise britheren passiden Jordan, and wenten forth the weie of thre daies in to desert.

25 And Nabutheis camen ayens hem, and resseyueden hem pesibli, and telden to hem alle thingis that bifellen to her britheren in Galadithym;

26 and that manye of hem weren takun in Barasa, and Bosor, and in Alymys, and in Casphor, and Mathet, and Carnaym; alle these were strong citees and grete.

27 But and in othere citees of Galatithis thei ben holdun cauyt. And on the morewe thei ordeyneden for to moue oost to tho citees, and for to take, and do awei hem in o dai.

28 And Judas turnede, and his oost, the weie in to desert of Bosor sudenli; and ocupiede the citee, and slow ech male bi the scharpnesse of swerd, and took alle the spuylis of hem, and brente it with fier.

29 And thei risiden thennus in nyyt, and wenten 'til to the strengthing.

30 And it was maad in sprynging of dai, whanne thei reisiden her iyen, and lo! myche puple, of whom was no noumbre, berynge laddris and engynes, for to take the strengthing, and ouer come hem.

31 And Judas siy, that batel bigan, and crie of batel stiede in to heuene, as trumpe, and greet cry of citee.

32 And he seide to his oost, Fiyte ye to dai for youre britheren.

33 And he cam, and thre ordris after hem, and thei crieden with trumpis, and crieden in preier.

34 And oostis of Thymothe knewen, that it was Machabeus, and thei fledden fro his face. And thei han smytun hem with greet wounde; and there fellen doun of hem in that dai almost eiyte thousynde of men.

35 And Judas turnede awei in to Maspha; and ouercam and took it, and slow ech male therof, and took spuylis of it, and brente it with fier.

36 Fro thennus he wente, and took Casbon, and Mageth, and Bosor, and othere citees of Galathite.

37 Forsothe after these wordis Thymothe gaderide an other oost, and puttide tentis ayens Raphon, ouer the streem.

38 And Judas sente for to biholde the oost, and thei telden ayen to hym, and seide, That alle hethene men that ben in oure cumpas, ful myche oost, camen togidere to hym.

39 And thei hiriden Arabiens in to help to him, and thei han set tentis ouer the streem, and ben redi for to come to thee in to batel. And Judas wente ayens hem.

40 And Tymothe seide to princes of his oost, Whanne Judas neiyeth, and his oost, to the streem of water, if he passith formere to vs, we schulen not mowe abide hym, for he miyti schal mowe ayens vs.

41 Sotheli if he dredith for to passe, and settith tentis biyende the flood, passe we ouer to hem, and we schulen mowe ayens hym.

42 Forsothe as Judas neiyede to the streem of water, he ordeynede scribis, 'ether writeris of the puple, bisidis the streem, and comaundide to hem, and seide, Leeue ye noon of men, but come alle in to batel.

43 And he the formere passide ouer to hem, and al the puple after hym. And alle these hethene men weren brokun fro the face of hem, and thei castiden awei her armeris; and thei fledden to the temple, that was at Carnaym.

44 And Judas ocupiede 'the ilke citee, and brente the temple with fier, with alle that weren in it; and Carnaym was oppressid, and miyte not abide ayens the face of Judas.

45 And Judas gaderide alle Israelitis that weren in Galadithes, fro the leeste to the moste, and wyues of hem, and children, and ful greet oost, that thei schulden come in to the lond of Judee.

46 And thei camen til to Efron, and this greet citee put in the entre was ful strong; and ther was not for to bowe awei fro it, in riyt half or left, but the weie was thorou the myddil.

47 And thei that weren in the citee closiden in hem, and stoppiden the yatis with stoonys. And Judas sente to hem with pesible wordis, and seide,

48 Passe we bi youre lond, for to go in to oure lond, and no man schal anoie you, oneli on feet we schulen go.

49 And thei wolden not opene to hem. And Judas comaundide for to preche in tentis, 'ether oost, that ech man schulde applie, 'that is, asaile the citee, in what place he was.

50 And men of vertu applieden hem, and he fauyt ayens that citee al dai and al niyt, and the citee was bitakun in his hond.

51 And thei slowen ech 'knaue child bi the scharpnesse of swerd, and drow vp bi the rootis it, and took the spuylis therof, and passide bi al the citee on the slayn men.

52 And thei passiden ouer Jordan, in the greet feeld ayens the face of Bethsan.

53 And Judas was gaderynge the laste men, and monestide the puple bi al the weie, til thei camen in to the lond of Juda.

54 And thei stieden in to the hil of Sion with gladnesse and ioie, and offriden brent sacrifices, that no man of hem 'was deed, til thei turneden ayen in pees.

55 And in the daies in whiche Judas was, and Jonathas, in the lond of Galaad, and Symount, his brother, in Galilee, ayens the face of Tholomaida,

56 Josofus, sone of Zacarie, herde, and Azarias, prince of vertu, the thingis doon wel, and batels that weren maad.

57 And he seide, Make we also a name to vs, and go we for to fiyte ayens hethene men, that ben in oure cumpas.

58 And he comaundide to these that weren in his oost, and thei wenten forth to Jamnyan.

59 And Gorgias wente out of the citee, and hise men, ayens hem, in to fiyt.

60 And Josofus and Azarias weren dryuun 'til to the endis of Judee; and ther fellen doun in that dai of the puple of Israel, men to twei thousyndis. And a greet wounde was maad in the puple;

61 for thei herden not Judas and hise britheren, and gessiden hem to do strongli.

62 Forsothe thei weren not of the seed of tho men, bi whiche helthe was maad in Israel.

63 And men of Juda weren magnefied greetli in the siyt of al Israel, and of alle hethene men, where the name of hem was herd.

64 And thei camen togidere, criynge to hem 'prosperite, ether preisyngis.

65 And Judas wente out, and his britheren, and ouercamen the sones of Esau, in the lond that is at the south; and he smoot Chebron, and vilagis therof, and distriede 'the wardyngis therof, and wallis therof, and brente in fier touris therof in cumpas.

66 And he mouede tentis, for to go in to the lond of aliens; and wente thorou Samarie.

67 In that dai prestis fellen doun in batel, while thei wolden do strongli, while with out counsel thei wenten out in to batel.

68 And Judas bowide awei in to Asotus, in the lond of aliens, and distriede auteris of hem, and brenten in fier the spuylis of her goddis, and took preies of citees; and turnede ayen in to the lond of Juda.

CAP 6

1 And kyng Antiok walkide thorouy the hiyere cuntreis, and herde that a citee, Elymaides, was in Persis, the nobleste and plenteuouse in siluer and gold;

2 and a temple in it was ful riche, and there weren goldun veilis, and haburiowns, and scheldis, whiche Alisaundre of Filip, kyng of Macedo, lefte, that regnede the firste in Greece.

3 And he cam, and souyte for to take the citee, and robbe it; and miyte not, for the word was knowun to hem that weren in the citee.

4 And thei risiden vp in to batel, and he flei fro thennus, and wente awei with greet heuynesse, and turnede ayen to Babyloyne.

5 And ther cam, that telde to hym in Persis, that the oostis that weren in the lond 'of Juda weren dryuun,

6 and that Lisias wente with strong vertu in the beste men, and was dryuun fro the face of Jewis, and thei wexiden stronge in armeris, and strengthis, and many preies, whiche thei token of tentis, 'ether oostis, that thei slowen;

7 and that thei distrieden the abhomynacioun, which he bildide on the auter that was in Jerusalem, and thei cumpassiden with hiye wallis the halewyng, as bifore, but and Betsura, his citee.

8 And it was don, as the kyng herde these wordis, he dredde, and was mouyd greetli, and felle doun in to a bed, and felle in to a greet sikenesse for heuynesse, for it was not don as he thouyte.

9 And he was there many daies, for greet heuynesse was renulid in him, and he demide hym silf for to die.

10 And he clepide alle hise frendis, and seide to hem, Sleep passide awei fro myn iyen, and Y failide 'in herte, and felle doun for bisynesse;

11 and seide in myn herte, In to hou greet tribulacioun bicam Y, and in to what wawis of heuynesse in which Y am now, that was myrie, and 'bolnyde, ether delicat in my power?

12 Now forsothe Y bithenke on the yuels that Y dide to Jerusalem, fro whennus and Y took alle goldun spuylis, and siluerne, that weren ther ynne; and Y sente with out cause, that men dwellynge in Judee be don awei.

13 Therfor Y knew that these yuels founden me therfor, and lo! Y perische bi greet heuynesse in alien lond.

14 And he clepid Filip, oon of his frendis, and made him souereyn on al his rewme;

15 and yaf to hym diademe, and his stole, and ryng, for to lede Antiok, his sone, and nurische hym, and that he schulde regne.

16 And kyng Antiok diede there, in the hundrid and nyne and fourti yeer.

17 And Lisias knew, that the kyng was deed, and ordeynede Antiok, the sone of hym, for to regne, whom he nurschide yong; and clepide his name Eupator.

18 And thei that weren in the hiy tour, closiden togidere Israel in cumpas of hooli thingis, and souyten to hem yuels euer more, to strengthing of hethene men.

19 And Judas thouyte for to distrie hem, and clepide togidere al the puple, for to bisege hem.

20 And thei camen togidere, and bisegiden hem, in the hundrid and fiftithe yeer; and thei maden arblastis, 'ether trepeiettis, that is, an instrument for to caste schaftis, and stoonys, and engynes.

21 And summe of hem that weren bisegid, wenten out; and summe of vnfeithful men of Israel ioyneden hem silf to hem,

22 and wenten to the kyng, and seiden, Hou long doist thou not dom, and vengist not oure britheren?

23 And we demyden for to serue thi fadir, and for to walke in hise heestis, and obeische to hise comaundementis.

24 And the sones of oure puple alienyden hem fro vs for this thing; and whiche euere weren foundun of vs, weren slayn, and oure eritagis weren rauyschid awei.

25 And not oneli to vs thei stretchiden out the hond, but and in to alle oure coostis.

26 And lo! thei applieden to day to the hiy tour in Jerusalem, for to ocupie it, and thei strengthiden a strengthing in Beth-sura.

27 And if thou schalt not bifore come hem more swiftli, thei schulen do grettere thingis than thes, and thou schalt not mowe welde hem.

28 And the kyng was wroth, as he herde this thing, and clepide togidere alle hise frendis, and princes of his oost, and hem that weren ouer horsemen;

29 but also an hirid oost fro othere rewmes, and ilis, and see coostis camen to hym.

30 And the noumbre of his oost was an hundrid thousynde of foot men, and twenti thousynde of horse men, and two and thritti olifauntis tauyt to batel.

31 And thei camen bi Idumee, and thei applieden to Bethsura, and fouyten many daies; and thei maden engynes, and thei wenten out, and brenten hem in fier, and fouyten manli.

32 And Judas wente fro the hiy tour, and mouede tentis to Bethsacharan, ayens tentis of the kyng.

33 And the kyng roos bifore the liyt, and stiride the oost in to feersnesse, ayens the weie of Bethsacharan; and the oostis maden redi hem togidere in to batel, and songen in trumpis.

34 And to olifauntis thei schewiden blood of grape, and morus, 'or mulberie trees, for to whette hem in to batel.

35 And thei departiden the beestis bi legyouns; and to ech olifaunt a thousynde men stoden niy in haburiownes mailid togidere, and brasun helmes in her heedis, and fyue hundrid horse men chosun weren ordeyned to ech beeste.

36 These weren there bifore the tyme, where euere the beeste was; and whidur euere it wente, thei wente, and departiden not her fro.

37 But and sadde touris of tre weren on hem, defendinge bi alle the beestis, and on hem weren engynes, and on ech bi hem silf men of vertu two and thritti, whiche fouyten fro aboue, and with ynne was the maister of the beeste.

38 And he ordeinede the residue multitude of horse men on this half and that half, 'in to twei partis, for to moue togidere the oost with trumpis, and for to constreyne the men maad thicke in her legiouns.

39 And as the sunne schynede in to the goldun scheldis, and brasun, the hillis schyneden ayen of hem, and schyneden ayen, as laumpis of fier.

40 And a part of the kyngis oost was departid bi hiy hillis, and other bi lowe places; and thei wenten warli, and ordynatli.

41 And alle men dwellynge in the lond weren mouyd togidere of the vois of multitude of hem, and ingoyng of cumpeny, and hurtlyng togidere of armeris; for the oost was ful grete and strong.

42 And Judas and his oost neiyide in to batel; and there fellen doun of the kyngis oost sixe hundrid men.

43 And Eleasar, the sone of Saura, siy oon of the beestis haburiowned with haburiownes of the kyng, and it was hiy stondynge ouer othere beestis; and it was seyn to hym, that the kyng was on it.

44 And he yaf hym silf for to delyuere his puple, and for to gete to hym a name euerlastynge.

45 And he ran ther to hardili, in to the myddil of legioun, and killide on the riyt half and left; and thei fellen doun fro hym hidur and thidur.

46 And he wente vndur the feet of the olifaunt, and vndur puttide hym silf ther to, and slow it; and it felle doun in to erthe on hym, and he was deed there.

47 And thei siyen the vertu of the kyng, and fersnesse of his oost, and turneden awei hem silf fro hem.

48 Forsothe tentis of the kyng stieden vp ayens hem, in to Jerusalem; and tentis of the king applieden to Judee, and to the hil of Syon;

49 and he made pees with these that weren in Bethsura. And thei wenten out of the citee, for foodis weren not to hem closid togidere there, for the sabatis of erthe weren.

50 And the kyng took Bethsura, and ordeynede there kepyng, for to kepe it.

51 And he turnede the tentis to the place of halewyng many daies; and ordeynede there arblastis, and engynes, and dartis of fier, and turmentis for to caste stoonys and dartis, and scorpiens for to schete arows, and slyngis.

52 Forsothe and thei maden engynes ayens the engynes of hem, and fouyten many daies.

53 Forsothe metis weren not in the citee, for that it was the seuenthe yeer; and thei that leften of hethene men in Judee, hadden wastid the relifs of tho thingis that weren kept.

54 And fewe men leften in hooli thingis, for hungur hadde take hem; and thei weren scaterid, ech man in to his place.

55 And Lisias herde, that Filip, whom kyng Antiok ordeynede, whanne he lyuyde yit, that he schulde nursche Antiok, his sone, that he schulde regne,

56 turnede ayen fro Perse and Medei, and the oost that wente with hym. And that he sekith for to take the causis of the rewme,

57 Lisias hastide for to go, and seie to the kyng, and duykis of the oost, We failen ech dai, and litil mete is to vs, and the place which we bisegen, is strong, and it fallith to vs for to ordeyne of the rewme.

58 Therfor now yyue we riythondis to these men, and make we pees with hem, and with al the folc of hem;

59 and ordeyne we to hem, that thei go in lawful thingis as bifore; for whi for the lawful thingis of hem whiche we dispisiden, thei ben wrooth, and han don alle these thingis.

60 And the word plesid in the siyt of the kyng, and of princes; and he sente to hem for to make pees, and thei resseyueden it.

61 And the kyng swoor to hem, and princes; and thei wenten out of the strengthing.

62 And the kyng entride in to the mount Sion, and he siy the strengthing of the place; and he brak ful soone the ooth that he swoor, and comaundide for to distrie the wal in cumpas.

63 And he departide awei hastili, and turnede ayen to Antiochie, and foond Filip regnynge in the citee; and he fauyt ayens hym, and ocupiede the cyte bi strengthe.

CAP 7

1 In the hundrid yeer and oon and fifti Demetrie, sone of Sileuce, wente out fro the cite of Rome, and stiede with fewe men in to a citee niy the see, and regnede there.

2 And it was don, as he entride in to the hous of the rewme of his fadris, the oost cauyte Antiok, and Lisias, for to brynge hem to hym.

3 And the thing was knowun to hym, and he seide, Nyle ye schewe to me the face of hem.

4 And the oost slow hem. And Demetrie sat on the seete of his rewme;

5 and wickid men and vnfeithful of Israel camen to hym, and Alchymus, duyk of hem, that wolde be maad prest;

6 and accusiden the puple anentis the kyng, and seiden, Judas and hise britheren loste thi frendis, and dyuerseli loste vs fro oure lond.

7 Now therfor sende thou a man, to whom thou bileuest, that he go, and se al the distriyng that he hath don to vs, and to cuntreis of the kyng; and he punyschide alle frendis of hym, and helperis of hem.

8 And the kyng chees of his frendis Bachides, that was lord ouer the greet flood in the rewme, and trewe to the kyng, and sente hym,

9 for to see the distriyng that Judas dide; and he ordeynede vnfeithful Alchymus in to presthod, and bad hym do veniaunce on the sones of Israel.

10 And thei risiden, and camen with greet oost in to the lond of Juda; and thei senten messangeris, and spaken to Judas and his britheren, with pesible wordis in gile.

11 And thei yauen not tent to her wordis; for thei siyen, that thei camen with greet oost.

12 And the congregacioun of scribis camen togidere to Alchymus and Bachides, for to axe tho thingis that ben iust;

13 and the firste Assideis, that weren among the sones of Israel, and thei axiden of hem pees.

14 For thei seiden, A man, preist of the seed of Aaron, cometh, he schal not disseyue vs.

15 And he spak with hem pesible wordis, and swoor to hem, and seide, We schulen not brynge in to you yuels, nether to youre frendis.

16 And thei bileuyden to hym. And he cauyte of hem sixti men, and slow hem in o dai, bi the word that is writun,

17 Thei shedden out the fleischis of thi seyntis, and blood of hem in cumpas of Jerusalem, and there was not that biriede.

18 And drede and tremblyng felle in to al the puple, for thei seiden, Ther is not treuthe and dom in hem; for thei han brokun the ordynaunce, and the ooth that thei sworen.

19 And Bachides mouyde tentis fro Jerusalem, and appliede in to Bethseca; and sente, and cauyte many of hem that fledden fro hym; and he killide summe of the puple, and castide in to a greet pitte.

20 And he bitook the regioun to Alchymus, and left with hym help, in to helpyng of hym. And Bachides wente to the kyng, and Alchymus dide ynow,

21 for the princehod of his presthod.

22 And alle camen togidere to hym, whiche disturbliden her puple, and weldiden the lond of Juda; and diden greet veniaunce in Israel.

23 And Judas siy alle yuels, that Alchymus dide, and thei that weren with hym, to the sones of Israel, myche more than hethene men.

24 And he wente oute in to alle coostis of Judee in cumpas, and dide veniaunce on men forsakeris, and thei ceesiden for to go out ferthere in to the cuntrei.

25 Forsothe Alchimus siy, that Judas hadde victorie, and thei that weren with hym; and he knew that he mai not abide hem, and he wente ayen to the kyng, and accusiden hem in many synnes.

26 And the kyng sente Nicanor, oon of his noblere princes, that was hauntynge enemytees ayens Israel, and comaundide hym for to distrie the puple.

27 And Nycanor cam in to Jerusalem, with greet oost, and he sente to Judas and his britheren with gile, bi pesible wordis,

28 seiynge, Fiyte be not bitwixe me and you; Y schal come with fewe men, for to se youre faces with pees.

29 And he cam to Judas, and thei gretten hem togidere pesibli; and enemyes weren redi for to rauysche Judas.

30 And the word was knowun to Judas, that with gile he cam to hym; and he was aferd of hym, and he wolde no more se his face.

31 And Nicanor knew, that his councel was knowun, and he wente out ayens Judas in to fiyt, bisidis Cafarsalama.

32 And ther fellen doun of Nicanoris oost almest fyue thousynde men, and thei fledden in to the citee of Dauid.

33 And after these wordis Nicanor stiede in to the hil of Sion, and ther wenten out of prestis of the puple, for to grete hym in pees, and for to schewe to hym brent sacrifices, that weren offrid for the kyng.

34 And he scornyde and dispiside hem, and defoulide, and spak proudli,

35 and swoor with wraththe, seiynge, If Judas schal not be takun, and his oost, in to myn hondis, anoon whanne Y schal turne ayen in pees, Y schal brenne this hous. And he wente out with greet wraththe.

36 And prestis entriden, and stoden bifore the face of the auter and temple,

37 and wepynge seiden, Thou, Lord, hast chosun this hous, for to clepe to helpe thi name in it, that it schulde be an hous of preier and biseching to thi puple; do thou veniaunce in this man,

38 and his oost, and falle thei bi swerd; haue mynde on her blasfemyes, and yyue not to hem that thei abide.

39 And Nicanor wente out fro Jerusalem, and appliede tentis to Betheron; and the oost of Sirie cam to him.

40 And Judas appliede in Adarsa, with thre thousynde men.

41 And Judas preiede, and seide, Lord, an aungel wente out, and smoot an hundrid thousynde foure score and fyue thousyndis of hem, that weren sent fro the kyng Senacherib, for thei blasfemiden thee;

42 so al to-breke this oost in oure siyt to dai, and othere men wite, that he spak yuel on thin hooli thingis; and deme thou hym by the malice of hym.

43 And the oostis ioyneden batel in the thrittenthe dai of the monethe Adar; and tentis of Nicanor weren al to-brokun, and he felle doun the firste in batel.

44 Sothely as his oost siy, that Nicanor felle doun, thei castiden awei her armeris, and fledden.

45 And thei pursueden hem the weie of o dai, fro Adasor til me come in to Gasara; and thei sungen in trumpis after hem with signefiyngis.

46 And thei wenten out of alle castels of Judee in cumpas, and wyndewiden hem with hornes, and eftsoone weren conuertid to hem; and alle falliden bi swerd, and ther was not left of hem not oon.

47 And thei token the spuylis of hem to prey; and thei girdiden of the heed of Nicanor, and his riyt hond which he stretchide forth proudli, and thei brouyten, and hangiden ayens Jerusalem.

48 And the puple was glad greetli, and diden that dai in greet gladnesse;

49 and ordeyneden this dai for to be doon in alle yeeris, in the thritteneth day of the monethe Adar.

50 And the lond of Juda was stille a fewe dais.

CAP 8

1 And Judas herde the name of Romayns, that thei ben miyti in strengthis, and acorden to alle thingis that ben axid of hem; and who euere wente to hem, thei ordeineden with hem frendschipis; and that thei ben miyti in strengthis.

2 And thei herden batels of hem, and goode vertues, that thei diden in Galacie, for thei weldiden hem, and ledden vndur tribute;

3 and hou many thingis thei diden in the cuntre of Spayne, and that thei brouyten in to power metals of siluer and gold that ben there; and weldiden ech place with her councel and pacience, 'or wisdom, places that weren ful fer fro hem;

4 and thei al to-braken kyngis that camen on hem fro the vtmeste places of erthe, and thei smytiden hem with greet wounde; forsothe othere yyuen to hem tribute bi alle yeeris.

5 And thei al to-braken in batel Filip, and Persen, kyngis of Cethis, and othere that baren armeris ayens hem, and weldiden hem.

6 And thei weldiden Antiok, the greet king of Asie, that yaf batel to hem, and hadde an hundrid and twenti olifauntis, and multitude of horse men and charis, and ful greet oost al to brokun of hem;

7 and thei token hym quyk, and ordeyneden to hym, that he schulde yyue greet tribut, and thei that regnede after hym; and that he schulde yyue pleggis and ordynaunce, in the cuntre of Yndis;

8 and thei puttiden out men of Medei, and of Lidde, fro the beste cuntreis of hem, and thei yauen tho cuntreis takun of hem to kyng Eumeny;

9 and that thei that weren anentis Elada, wolden go, and take awei hem; and the word was knowun to these Romayns,

10 and thei senten to hem o duyk, and thei fouyten ayens hem; and many of hem fellen, and thei ledden her wyues caitifs, and sones, and robbiden hem; and weldiden the lond of hem, and distrieden the wallis of hem, and brouyten hem in to seruage, til in to this dai.

11 And thei distrieden othere rewmes and ilis, that sum tyme ayenstoden hem, and brouyten in to power.

12 Forsothe with her frendis, and that hadden reste in hem, thei kepten frenschip, and thei weldiden rewmes that weren next, and that weren fer; for who euere herden the name of hem, dredden hem.

13 For thei regnyden, to whiche thei wolden be in help for to regne; forsothe whiche thei wolden, thei disturbliden fro rewme; and thei weren greetli enhaunsid.

14 In alle these Romayns no man bar diademe, nether was clothid in purpur, for to be magnefied ther ynne.

15 And thei that maden to hem a court, and ech dai thei counseliden thre hundrid and twenti, doynge counsel euere more of multitude, that thei do what thingis ben worthi.

16 And thei bitaken to o man her maistrie, 'ether cheef gouernaunce, bi ech yeer, for to be lord of al her lond; and alle obeschen to oon, and enuye is not, 'nether wraththe among hem.

17 And Judas chees Eupolemus, the sone of Joon, sone of Jacob, and Jason, the sone of Eleasarus, and sente hem to Rome, for to ordeyne with hem frenschip and felouschip;

18 and that thei schulden take awei fro hem the yok of Grekis, for thei sien that thei oppressiden the rewme of Israel in to seruage.

19 And thei wenten to Rome, a ful greet weie, and thei entriden in to the court,

20 and seiden, Judas Machabeus, and hise britheren, and the puple of Jewis senten vs to you, for to ordeyne with you felouschip and pees, and for to write togidere vs youre felowis and freendis.

21 And the word pleside in the siyt of hem.

22 And this is the ayen writyng, which thei ayen writiden in brasun tablis, and senten in to Jerusalem, that it were there a memorial, 'ether a thing of mynde, of pees and felouschip.

23 Be it wel to Romayns, and to the folc of Jewis, in see and lond, with outen ende; and swerd and enemy be fer fro hem.

24 That if batel bifallith to Romayns bifore, ether to alle felowis of hem in al the lordschip 'of hem,

25 the folc of Jewis schal bere help, as time axith, with ful herte; and the Romayns schulen not yyue,

26 nether priuyli ministre to the Jewis fiytynge, wheete, armeris, monei, schippis, as it pleside to Romayns; and thei schulen kepe the maundementis of hem, and take no thing of hem.

27 Forsothe in lijk maner and if batel fallith bifore to the folc of Jewis, Romayns schulen helpe of herte, as tyme suffrith hem;

28 and to Romayns helpynge wheete schal not be youun, nether armeris, monei, nether schippis, as it pleside to Romayns; and thei schulen kepe the maundementis of hem with out gile.

29 Bi these wordis Romayns ordeyneden to the puple of Jewis,

30 That if after these wordis, these ether thei wolen put ony thing to, ether do awei, thei schulen do of her 'comyn assent; and what euere thingis thei schulen put to, ether do awei, thei schulen be stidfast.

31 But also of yuels whiche kyng Demetrie hath don ayens hem, we han writun to hym, and we seiden, Whi hast thou greuyd thi yok on oure frendis and felowis, the Jewis?

32 Therfor if eftsoone thei schulen come to vs ayens thee, we schulen do doom to hem, and schulen fiyte with thee bi lond and see.

CAP 9

1 In the mene tyme, where Demetrie herde that Nicanor felle, and his oost, in batel, he puttide to eftsoone for to sende Bachides and Alchymus in to Judee, and the riyt half schiltrun with hem.

2 And thei wenten the weie that ledith in to Galgala, and thei settiden tentis in Masoloth, that is in Arbellis; and thei ocupieden it, and slowen many persoones of men.

3 In the firste monethe of the hundrid and two and fifti yeer, thei applieden the oost to Jerusalem.

4 And twenti thousynde of men, and twei thousynde of horse men, han risun, and wenten in to Berea.

5 And Judas settide tentis in Laisa, and thre thousynde men chosun with hym.

6 And thei siyen the multitude of oost, that thei ben manye, and thei dredden greetli; and many withdrowen hem fro tentis, and there left not of hem no but eiyte hundrid men.

7 And Judas siy that his oost fleet awei, and batel constreynede hym, he was brokun togidere in herte, for he hadde not tyme to gadere hem, and he was discoumfortid.

8 And he seide to these that weren residue, Rise we, and go we to oure aduersaries, if we schulen mow fiyte ayens hem.

9 And thei turneden awei hym, and seiden, We schulen not moun, but delyuere we oure lyues, and turne ayen we to oure britheren, and thanne we schulen fiyte ayens hem; forsothe we ben fewe.

10 And Judas seide, Fer be it for to do this thing, that we fle fro hem; and if oure tyme hath neiyed, die we in vertu for oure britheren, and yyue we not cryme to oure glorie.

11 And the oost mouyde fro tentis, and thei stoden ayens hem. And horse men weren departid in to twei partis, and slyngeris and archeris wenten bifore the oost, and the firste men of batel alle miyti.

12 Forsothe Bachides was in the riyt schiltrun. And the legioun of twei partis cam nyy, and crieden with trumpis.

13 Forsothe and these that weren on the part of Judas, crieden also, and the erthe was mouyd togidere of the vois of oostis, and batel was ioyned fro the morewtid til to euentid.

14 And Judas siy, that the part of Bachides oost was saddere in the riyt half, and alle stidfast in herte camen togidere with hym.

15 And the riyt part was al to-brokun of hem; and he pursuede hem 'til to the hil of Asotus.

16 And thei that weren in the left scheltrun, siyen, that the riyt scheltrun was al to-brokun, and thei sueden at the bac aftir Judas, and hem that weren with hym.

17 And the batel was maad greuouse, and there fellen many woundid of these and of hem.

18 And Judas felle, and the othere fledden.

19 And Jonathas and Symount token her brother Judas, and birieden hym in sepulcre of his fadris, in the citee of Modyn.

20 And al Israel biwepten him with greet weilyng, and mourneden many daies,

21 and seiden, Hou felle the myyti, that made Israel saaf.

22 And othere wordis of batels of Judas, and of vertues that he dide, and of his greetnessis, ben not writun; for tho weren ful many.

23 And it was don, after the deth of Judas, alle wickid men in alle coostis of Israel risiden out, and alle that wrouyten wickidnesse camen forth.

24 In tho daies ful greet hungur was maad, and al the cuntrey of hem bitook hem silf to Bachides with hem.

25 And Bachides chees vnpitouse men, and ordeynede hem lordis of the cuntrei.

26 And thei axiden out, and souyten the frendis of Judas, and brouyten hem to Bachides; and he vengide on hem, and scornede.

27 And greet tribulacioun was maad in Israel, what maner was not fro the dai in which a profete was not seyn in Israel.

28 And alle the frendis of Judas weren gaderid, and seiden to Jonatas, Sithen thi brother Judas is deed,

29 ther is no man lijk hym, that schal go out ayens enemyes, Bachides and hem that ben enemyes of oure folc.

30 Therfor now we chesen thee to dai for to be prince and duyk to vs for hym, for to fiyte oure batel.

31 And Jonatas resseyuede in that tyme the prinshod, and roos in the place of Judas, his brother.

32 And Bachides knew, and souyte for to sle him.

33 And Jonatas knew, and Symount, his brother, and alle that weren with hym, and fledden in to desert of Thecue, and saten togidere at the water of the lake Asphar.

34 And Bachides knew, and in the dai of sabatis he cam, and al his oost, ouer Jordan.

35 And Jonathas sente his brother ledere of that puple, and preiede Nabutheis, his frendis, that he schulde bitake to hem his apparel, that was plenteuouse.

36 And sones of Jambri wenten out of Madaba, and cauyten Joon, and alle thingis that he hadde, and wenten awei, hauynge tho thingis.

37 After thes wordis it was teld ayen to Jonathas, and Symount, his brother, that the sones of Jambri maken grete weddyngis, and wedden a wijf of Madaba, the douyter of oon of the grete princis of Canaan, with greet pride and apparel.

38 And thei bithouyten on the blood of Joon, her brother, and stieden vp, and hidden hem silf vndur kyueryng of the hil.

39 And thei reisiden her iyen, and siyen, and lo! noise, and greet apparel; and a hosebonde cam forth, and hise frendis, and hise britheren, ayens hem, with tympans, and musikis, and many armeris.

40 And thei risiden to hem fro buyschementis, and slowen hem, and many woundid fellen doun, and the residues fledden in to hil, and thei token alle the spuylis of hem;

41 and weddyngis weren conuertid in to mourenyng, and vois of her musikis in to weilyng.

42 And thei vengiden the veniaunce of her brotheris blood, and turnyden ayen to the brynk of Jordan.

43 And Bachides herde, and cam in the dai of sabatis til to the vtmeste part of Jordan, in greet strengthe.

44 And Jonathas seide to hise, Rise we, and fiyte ayens oure enemyes; for it is not to dai as yistirdai and the thridde dai agoon.

45 For lo! batel is euene ayens; sotheli watir of Jordan is on this half and on that half, and ryuers, and mareis, and forestis, and ther is not place of turnyng awei.

46 Now therfor crie ye in to heuene, that ye be delyuerede fro hond of youre enemyes.

47 And batel was ioyned. And Jonathas strauyt out his hond, for to smyte Bachides, and he turnede awei fro him bihynde.

48 And Jonathas skipte doun, and thei that weren with hym, in to Jordan, and swommen ouer Jordan to hem.

49 And there fellen of Bachides part in that dai a thousande men, and thei turneden ayen in to Jerusalem;

50 and bildiden strong citees in Judee, the strengthe that was in Jerico, and in Ammaum, and in Betheron, and Bethel, and Thamathan, and Phara, and Copho, with hiye wallis, and yatis, and lockis.

51 And he settide kepyng in hem, that thei schulden haunte enemytees in Israel;

52 and he strengthide the citee Bethsura, and Gazaram, and the hiy tour, and puttide in hem helpis and apparel of metis.

53 And he took the sones of princes of the cuntrei in ostage, and puttide hem in the hiy tour in Jerusalem, in kepyng.

54 And in the hundrid yeer and thre and fifti, in the secounde monethe, Alchymus comaundide the wallis of the hooli ynnere hous for to be distried, and the werkis of profetis for to be distried, and he bigan for to distrie.

55 In that tyme Alchymus was smytun, and the werkis of hym weren lettid. And his mouth was closid, and he was dissoluyd, 'ether maad feble, bi palesie, nether he miyte speke more a word, and comaunde of his hous.

56 And Alchymus was deed in that tyme, with greet turment.

57 And Bachides siy, that Alchymus was deed, and he turnede ayen to the kyng, and the lond was stille twei yeeris.

58 And alle wickid men thouyten, seiynge, Lo! Jonathas, and thei that ben with hym, dwellen in silence, and tristen; now

therfor brynge we Bachides, and he schal take hem alle in o niyt.

59 And thei wenten forth, and yauen councel to hym.

60 And he roos, for to come with myche oost. And he sente epistlis priuyli to his felowis, that weren in Judee, that thei schulden catche Jonathas, and hem that weren with hym; but thei miyten not, for her councel was knowun to hem.

61 And Jonathas cauyte of men of the cuntre, that weren princis of knytyhod, fifti men, and slow hem.

62 And Jonathas and Symount wenten, and thei that weren with hym, in to Bethbesse, 'that is in desert, and bildiden the distried thingis therof, and maden it strong.

63 And Bachides knew, and gaderide al his multitude, and denounside to hem that weren of Judee.

64 And he cam, and settide tentis aboue Bethbesse, and fauyte ayens it many daies, and made engynes.

65 And Jonathas lefte Symount, his brother, in the citee, and wente oute in to cuntre, and cam with noumbre;

66 and smoot Odaren, and hise britheren, and sones of Faseron, in the tabernaclis of hem, and bigan for to smyte, and wexe in vertues.

67 Symount sotheli, and thei that weren with hym, wenten out of the citee, and brenten engynes.

68 And thei fouyten ayens Bachides, and he was al to-brokun of hem; and thei turmentiden hym gretli, for his councel and his assailyng was voide.

69 And he was wrooth ayens wickid men, that yauen councel to hym for to come in to her cuntre, and slow many of hem; forsothe he thouyte with othere for to go in to his cuntre.

70 And Jonathas knew, and sente legatis to hym, for to make pees with hym, and to yelde to him prisoneris.

71 And wilfuli he took, and dide bi his wordis, and swoor that he schulde not do to him ony yuel in alle daies of his lijf.

72 And he yeldide to him caitifte, which he took bi prey bifore of the lond of Juda. And he turnede, and wente in to his lond, and puttide no more for to come in to his coostis.

73 And swerd ceesside fro Israel. And Jonatas dwellide in Machynas, and there Jonathas bigan for to deme the puple, and he distriede the vnfeithful men of Israel.

CAP 10

1 And in the hundrid and sixtithe yeer Alisaundre, the sone of Antiok, stiede up, that is named noble, and ocupiede Tolomaide; and thei resseyueden hym, and he regnede there.

2 And kyng Demetrie herde, and gaderide an oost ful copiouse, and wente out ayens hym in to batel.

3 And Demetrie sente epistle to Jonathas with pesible wordis, for to magnefie hym.

4 For he seide, Bifore take we for to make pees with hym, bifore that he make with Alisaundre ayens vs;

5 for he schal haue mynde of alle yuels, that we han don 'ayens him, and ayens his brother, and ayens his folc.

6 And he yaf to hym power to gadere oost, and for to make armeris, and hym for to be his felowe. And he comaundide ostagis, 'ether pleggis, that weren in the hiy tour, for to be youun to hym.

7 And Jonathas cam in to Jerusalem, and radde epistlis, in heryng of al the puple, and of hem that weren in the hiy tour.

8 And thei dredden with greet drede, for thei herden, that the kyng yaf to hym power to gadere an oost.

9 And ostagis weren takun to Jonathas, and he yeldide hem to her fadris and modris.

10 And Jonathas dwelte in Jerusalem, and bigan for to bilde and renule the citee.

11 And he seide to men doynge werkis, that thei schulden make up the wallis, and the hil of Sion in cumpas, with square stonys to strengthing; and thei diden so.

12 And aliens fledden, that weren in the strengthis, whiche Bachides hadde bildid;

13 and ech man lefte his place, and wente in to his lond.

14 Oneli in Bethsura dwelten sum of hem, that forsoken the lawe and heestis of God; for whi this was to hem to refuyte.

15 And Alisaundre the kyng herde biheestis, that Demetrie bihiyte to Jonathas, and thei telden to hym the batels and vertues whiche he dide, and his britheren, and the trauelis whiche thei traueliden.

16 And he seide, Whether we schulen fynde ony such man? And now make we hym our frende and felowe.

17 And he wroot epistle, and sente bi these wordis,

18 seiynge, Kyng Alisaundre to Jonathas, brother, helthe.

19 We han herde of thee, that thou art a miyti man in strengthis, and art able that thou be oure frend.

20 And now we ordeynen thee to dai hiyest prest of thi folc, and that thou be clepid frend of the kyng. And he sente to hym purpur, and a goldun coroun, that thou feele with vs what thingis ben oure, and kepe frenschipis to vs.

21 And Jonathas clothide hym with hooly stoole, in the seuenthe monethe, in the hundrid and sixtithe yeer, in the solempne dai of Senofegie. And he gaderide an ooste, and made copiouse armeris.

22 And Demetrie herde these wordis, and was maad ful sorewful, and seide, What han we do this thing,

23 that Alisaundre bifor ocupiede vs, for to catche frenschip of Jewis to his strengthing?

24 And Y schal write to hym preiynge wordis, and dignitees, and yiftis, that he be with me in help.

25 And he wroot to hym by these wordis, Kyng Demetrie to the folc of Jewis, helthe.

26 For ye kepten to vs couenaunt, and dwelten in oure frenschip, and wenten not to oure enemyes, we herden, and ioieden.

27 And now laste ye yit for to kepe to vs feith;

28 and we schulen quyte to you good thingis, for these thingis that ye diden with vs, and we schulen foryyue to you many rentis, and we schulen yyue yiftis to you.

29 And now Y asoile you, and alle Jewis, of tributis, and Y foryyue to you the prices of salt, and foryyue corouns, and the thridde part of seed;

30 and Y leeue to you fro this dai and afterward the half part of fruyt of tre, that is of my porcioun, tha tit be not takun of the lond of Juda, and of thre citees that ben addid therto, of Samarie and Galile, fro this dai and in to al tyme.

31 And Jerusalem be hooli, and fre, with hise coostis; and tithis and tributis be of it.

32 Also Y foryiue the power of the hiy tour, that is in Jerusalem; and Y yyue it to the hiyest prest, that he ordeyne therynne men, whiche euere he schal chese, that schulen kepe it.

33 And ech persoone of Jewis, that is caitif of the lond of Juda, in al my rewme, Y delyuer fre wilfuli, that alle be soilid of her tributis, yhe, of her beestis.

34 And alle solempne daies, and sabatis, and neomenyes, and alle daies ordeyned, and thre daies bifor the solempne dai, and thre daies after the solempne dai, alle these be daies of

fraunchise, and of remissioun, to alle Jewis that ben in my rewme.

35 And no man schal haue power for to do ony thing, and moue causis ayens ony of hem in ony cause.

36 And that ther be writun of Jewis in the kingis oost, to thritti thousyndis of men; and plentees schulen be youun to hem, as it bihoueth to alle oostis of the kyng.

37 And of hem schulen be ordeyned, that be in the greet strengthis of the kyng;

38 of hem schulen be ordeyned ouer nedis of the rewme, that ben don of feith, and princes be of hem; and walke thei in her lawis, as the kyng comaundide in the lond of Juda. And thre citees, that ben addid to Judee of the cuntre of Samarie, be demyd with Judee; that thei be vndur oon, and obeie not to other power, no but to the hiyeste prest;

39 Tolomaida, and coostis therof, whiche Y haue youun a yifte to hooli men that ben in Jerusalem, to nedeful costis of seyntis.

40 And Y schal yyue in ech yeer fiftene thousynde of siclis of siluer, of the kyngis resouns, that perteynen to me;

41 and al that is residue, which thei that weren ouer nedis yeldiden not in formere yeeris, fro this tyme thei schulen yyue in to werkis of the hous.

42 And ouer this fyue thousynde siclis of siluer, whiche thei token of resoun of hooli thingis bi ech yeer; and these thingis schulen perteyne to prestis, that vsen mynysterie.

43 And who euere schulen fle to the temple that is in Jerusalem, and in alle coostis therof, and ben gilti to the king in ony cause, be releesid; and haue thei fre alle thingis, that ben to hem in my rewme.

44 And to bilde werkis of hooli thingis, costis schulen be youun of the kyngis rent,

45 and for to bilde out the wallis of Jerusalem; and for to make strong in cumpas, spensis schulen be youun of the kyngis rent, for to make out wallis in Judee.

46 As Jonathas and the puple herde these wordis, thei bileueden not to hem, nether resseyueden hem; for thei hadden mynde of the greet malice that he hadde don in Israel, and hadde troblid hem greetli.

47 And it pleside togidere to hem in to Alisaundre, for he was to hem prince of wordis of pees, and to hym thei baren help in alle daies.

48 And kyng Alisaundre gaderide a greet oost, and mouyde tentis ayens Demetrie.

49 And the kyngis ioyneden batel, and the oost of Demetrie fledde; and Alisaundre pursuede him, and lai on hem;

50 and the batel was ful strong, til the sunne wente doun, and Demetrie felle in that dai.

51 And Alisaundre sente to Tolome, king of Egipt, legatis bi these wordis,

52 and seide, For Y cam ayen in to my rewme, and sat in the seete of my fadris; and Y haue weldid princehod, and Y haue al to-brokun Demetrie, and haue weldid oure cuntrei;

53 and Y haue ioyned fiyt with hym, and he and his oostis ben al to-foulid of vs, and we saten in seete of his rewme.

54 And now ordeyne we togidere frenschip, and yyue thi douyter a wijf to me, and Y schal be thi douyter hosebonde; and Y schal yyue to thee yiftis, and to hir dignytee.

55 And 'Tolome, kyng, answeride, seiynge, Blessid is the dai in which thou turnedist ayen to the lond of thi fadris, and hast sotun in the seete of rewme of hem.

56 And now Y schal do to thee whiche thingis thou hast writun; but come thou ayens me to Tolomaida, that we se vs togidere, and Y biheete to thee, as thou seidist.

57 And Tolome wente out of Egipt, he, and Cleopatra, his douyter; and he cam to Tolomaida, in the hundrid and two and sixtithe yeer.

58 And Alisaundre, the king, came to hym; and he yaf to hym Cleopatra, his douytir, and made his weddingis at Tolomaida, as kyngis in greet glorie.

59 And kyng Alisaundre wroot to Jonathas, that he schulde come ayens hym.

60 And he wente with glorie to Tolomaida, and mette there twei kyngis, and yaue to hem myche siluer, and gold, and yiftis; and foond grace in the siyte of hem.

61 And men of Israel, ful of venym, camen togidere ayens hym, wickid men, axynge ayens hym, and the kyng took no tent to hem;

62 and comaundide Jonathas for to be maad nakid of his clothis, and hym for to be clothid in purpur; and thei diden so. And the king settide hym for to sitte with hym,

63 and seide to hise princis, Go ye out with hym in to the myddil of the citee, and preche ye, that no man axe ayens hym of ony cause, nether ony man be heuy to hym of ony resoun.

64 And it was don, as thei that axiden sien his glorie that was prechid, and hym kyuered with purpur, alle fledden.

65 And the kyng magnefiede hym, and wroot hym among the firste frendis, and puttide hym duyk, and felow of prinshod.

66 And Jonathas turnede ayen in to Jerusalem, with pees and gladnesse.

67 In the hundrid yeer and fyue and sixtithe, Demetrie, the sone of Demetrie, cam fro Crete in to the lond of his fadris.

68 And kyng Alisaundre herde, and was maad ful soreuful, and turnede ayen to Antiochie.

69 And Demetrie ordeynede Appolyne duyk, that was souereyn of Celesirie; and he gaderide his greet oost, and cam to Jamnam; and sente to Jonathas, hiyeste prest, and seide, Thou aloone ayenstondist vs;

70 Y am maad in to scorn and schenschip therfor, for thou hauntist power in hillis ayens vs.

71 Now therfor if thou tristist in thi vertues, come doun to vs in to the feeld; and there asemble we togidere, for with me is vertu of batels.

72 Axe thou, and lerne who Y am, and othere that ben in help to me, and whiche seien, that youre foot may not stonde ayens oure face, for thi fadris weren conuertid in to fliyt twies in to her lond.

73 And now hou schalt thou mow susteyne multitude of horse men, and so greet oost in the feeld, where is no stoon, ne rocke, nether place of fleynge?

74 Sotheli as Jonathas herde these wordis of Appollonye, he was mouyd in herte; and he chees ten thousynde of men, and wente out fro Jerusalem, and Symount, his brother, cam to hym in to help.

75 And thei applieden tentis in Joppe, and it schittide out hym fro the citee, for Joppe was the keping of Appolyne; and he fouyte ayens it.

76 And thei weren agast, that weren with ynne the citee, and openyden to hym; and Jonathas weldide Joppe.

77 And Appolyne herde, and mouyde thre thousynde of horse men, and myche oost;

78 and wente to Asotus, as makynge weie. And anoon he wente out in to the feeld, for that he hadde multitude of horse

men, and tristnyde in hem; and Jonathas suede hym in to Asotus, and thei ioyneden batel.

79 And Appoloyne lefte in tentis a thousynde horse men bihynde hem priueli.

80 And Jonathas knewe that buschementis weren bihynde hym, and thei enuirowneden his tentis, and castiden dartis in to the puple, fro morew til to euentid.

81 Forsothe the puple stood, as Jonathas comaundide, and the horsis of hem traueliden out.

82 And Symount ledde his oost, and ioyneden ayens the legioun; forsothe horse men weren maad weri, and weren al to-brokun of hym, and fledden.

83 And thei that weren scaterid in to the feeld, fledden in to Asotus; and entriden in to the hous of Dagon, her idol, that there thei schulden delyuere hem silf.

84 And Jonathas brente Asotus, and citees that weren in cumpas therof, and took spuylis of hem; and he brente in fier the temple of Dagon, and hem that fledden in to it.

85 And ther weren that fellen bi swerd with hem that weren brent, almeste eiyte thousynde of men.

86 And fro thennus Jonathas mouyde tentis, and appliede hem to Ascalon; and thei wenten out of the citee ayens hym in greet glorie.

87 And Jonathas turnede ayen in to Jerusalem with hise men, hauynge many spuylis.

88 And it was don, as king Alisaundre herde these wordis, he puttide to yit for to glorifie Jonathas.

89 And he sente to hym a goldun lace, 'ether nouche, as custom is for to be youun to cosyns of kingis; and he yaf to him Accoron, and alle coostis therof in to possessioun.

CAP 11

1 And the kyng of Egipt gaderide an oost, as grauel that is aboute the brynke of the see, and many schippis; and souyte for to welde the rewme of Alisaundre in gile, and adde it to his rewme.

2 And he wente out in to Sirie with pesible wordis, and thei openyden to hym citees, and camen to hym; for whi kyng Alisaundre comaundide for to go out ayens him, for he was fadir of the kyngis wijf.

3 Sotheli whanne Tolome entride in to a citee, he puttide kepyngis of kniytis in ech citee. And as he neiyede to Azotus, thei schewiden to hym the temple of Dagon brent in fier, and Azotus, and othere thingis therof distried, and bodies cast forth, and the biriels of hem that weren slayn in batel, whiche thei maden bisidis the weie.

5 And thei telden to the kyng, that Jonathas dide these thingis, for to make enuye to hym; and the kyng was stille.

6 And Jonathas cam to the kyng with glorie in to Joppen, and thei gretten hem togidere; and thei slepten there.

7 And Jonathas wente with the king til to the flood that is clepid Eleutherus, and turnede ayen in to Jerusalem.

8 Sotheli kyng Tolome weldide the lordschip of citees til to Seleuce, bi the eest coost, and thouyte ayens Alisaundre yuel counsels;

9 and sente legatis to Demetrie, and seide, Come thou, make we bitwixe vs couenaunt, and Y schal yyue to thee my douyter, whom Alisaundre hath, and thou schalt regne in rewme of thi fadir.

10 For it rewith me, that Y yaf to hym my douyter; for he souyte for to sle me.

11 And he dispiside him therfor, for he coueitide the rewme of hym.

12 And he took a wey his douyter, and yaf hir to Demetrie, and alienyde hym fro Alisaundre; and hise enemytees weren maad knowun.

13 And Tolome entride in to Antiochie, and puttide twei diademys to his heed, of Egipt and of Asie.

14 Forsothe Alisaundre, the kyng, was in Cilice in tho tymes, for thei rebelliden, that weren in tho places.

15 And Alisaundre herde, and cam to hym in to batel; and Tolome, kyng, brouyt forth oost, and cam to hym in strong hond, and droof hym.

16 And Alisaundre flei in to Arabie, for to be defendid there; sotheli kyng Tolome was enhaunsid.

17 And Gadiel of Arabie took awei Alisaundris heed, and sente to Tolome.

18 And kyng Tolome was deed in the thridde dai; and thei that weren in strengthis perischiden, of hem that weren with ynne the castels.

19 And Demetrie regnede in the hundrid yeer and seuene and sixtithe.

20 In tho daies Jonathas gaderide hem that weren in Judee, for to ouercome the hiy tour, that is in Jerusalem; and thei maden ayens it many engynes.

21 And summe wickid men, that hatiden her folc, wenten to the kyng Demetrie, and telden to hym, that Jonathas bisegide the hiy tour.

22 And as he herde, he was wroth, and anoon he cam to Tolomaida, and wroot to Jonathas, that he schulde not bisege the hiy tour, but schulde come to hym in haaste, to speke togidere.

23 Sotheli as Jonathas herde, he comaundide for to bisege; and he chees of the eldere men of Israel, and of prestis, and yaf hym to perel.

24 And he took gold, and siluer, and cloth, and many other presentis; and wente to the kyng, to Tolomaida, and foond grace in the siyt of hym.

25 And summe wickid men of his folc axiden ayens hym;

26 'and the kyng dide to him, as thei that weren bifore hym, diden to hym; and he enhaunside him in siyt of alle his frendis,

27 and ordeynede to hym prinsehod of presthod, and what euere othere preciouse thingis he hadde bifore; and made hym prince of hise frendis.

28 And Jonatas axide of the kyng, that he schulde make Judee fre, and thre prinshedis of thre places, and Samarie and niy coostis therof; and he bihiyte to hym thre hundrid talentis.

29 And the kyng consentide, and wroot to Jonatas epistles of alle these thingis, conteynynge this maner.

30 Kyng Demetrie to Jonathas, brother, heelthe, and to the folc of Jewis.

31 The ensaumple of epistle, which we han writun to Lascheny, oure fadir, of you, we senten to you, that ye schulden wite.

32 Kyng Demetrie to Lascheny, fadur, heelthe.

33 To the puple of Jewis, oure frendis, and kepynge whiche thingis ben iust anentis vs, we demyden for to do wel, for benygnyte of hem that thei han anentis vs.

34 Therfor we ordeynen to hem, alle the coostis of Judee, and thre citees of offryngis, Liddea, and Ramatha, and Faseron, that ben addid to Judee, and Samarie, and alle the niy coostis of hem, for to be departid to alle men doynge sacrifice in Jerusalem, for these thingis that the kyng took bifore of hem bi alle yeeris, and for fruytis of the erthe, and of applis.

35 And other thingis that perteyneden to vs, of tithis, and tributis, fro this tyme we foryyuen to hem; and the pleyn places of salt makyng, and the corouns that weren borun to vs, alle thingis we graunten to hem;

36 and no thing of these schal be voide, fro this and in to al tyme.

37 Now therfor bisie ye for to make ensaumple of these thingis, and be it youun to Jonathas, and be put in the holi mount, and in the solempne place.

38 And kyng Demetrie siy, that the lond was stille in his siyt, and that no thing ayenstood hym, and lefte al his oost, ech man in to his place, outakun the straunge oost, that he drow fro ilis of hethene men; and alle the oostis of his fadris weren enemyes to hym.

39 Forsothe oon Trifon was of the partis of Alisaundre bifore, and he siy that al the oost grutchide ayens Demetrie; and he wente to Machuel Arabian, that nurschide Antiok, the sone of Alisaundre.

40 And he maad greet instaunce to hym, that he schulde bitake him to hym, for to regne in stide of his fadir; and telde out to hym, hou grete thingis Demetrie hadde don, and the enemytees of his oostis ayens hym; and he dwelte there many daies.

41 And Jonathas sente to kyng Demetrie, that he schulde caste out hem, that weren in the hiy tour in Jerusalem, and whiche weren in strengthis, for thei inpugnyden Israel.

42 And Demetrie sente to Jonatas, and seide, Not oneli this Y schal do to thee, and thi folc, but Y schal make thee noble bi glorie, and thi folc, whanne it schal be couenable.

43 Now therfor riytli thou schalt do, if thou schalt sende men in to help to me, for al myn oost wente awei.

44 And Jonathas sente to hym thre thousynde of stronge men, to Antiochie; and thei camen to the kyng, and the kyng delitide in the comyng of hem.

45 And there camen togidere that weren of the citee sixe score thousynde of men, and wolden sle the kyng.

46 And the kyng fledde in to the halle. And thei that weren of the citee ocupieden the weies of the citee, and bigunnen for to fiyte.

47 And the kyng clepide Jewis in to help, and alle camen togidere to hym, and alle weren scaterid bi the citee;

48 and slowen in that dai an hundrid thousynde of men, and brenten the citee, and token many spuylis in that dai, and delyueriden the kyng.

49 And thei siyen, that weren of the citee, that Jewis hadden take the citee as thei wolden; and thei weren maad vnstidefast in her soule, and crieden to the king with preieris, and seiden,

50 Yyue to vs riythondis, and ceesse the Jewis for to fiyte ayens vs and the citee.

51 And thei castiden awei her armeris, and maden pees. And Jewis weren glorified in the siyt of the kyng, and in the siyt of alle men that weren in his rewme, and weren named in the rewme. And thei wenten ayen in to Jerusalem, hauynge many spuylis.

52 And kyng Demetrie sat in seete of his rewme, and the lond was stille in his siyt.

53 And he liede alle thingis, what euere he seide, and alienyde hym fro Jonathas, and yeldide not to hym bi beneficis, whiche he hadde youun to hym; and Demetrie trauelide hym greetli.

54 Aftir these thingis Trifon turnede ayen, and Antiok, a yong child, with hym; and regnede, and puttide on hym a diademe.

55 And alle oostis weren gaderid to him, whiche kyng Demetrie scateride; and thei fouyten ayens hym, and he flei, and turnyde backis.

56 And Trifon took beestis, and weldide Antiochie.

57 And Antiok the yonge wroot to Jonatas, and seide, Y ordeyne to thee the presthod, and Y ordeyne thee on foure citees, that thou be of the kyngis frendis.

58 And he sente to hym goldun vessels, in to mynysterie, and yaf to hym power to drynk in gold, and for to be in purpur, and for to haue a goldun lace, 'ether nouche.

59 And he ordeynede Symount, his brother, duyk fro the endis of Tirie til to the endis of Egipt.

60 And Jonathas wente out, and walkide ouer the flood bi citees; and al the oost of Sirie was gaderid to hym in to help. And he cam to Ascalon, and thei of the citee camen ayens hym worschipfuli.

61 And fro thennus he wente 'in to Gasa, and thei that weren at Gasa closiden hem togidere, and he bisegide it. And he brente what thingis weren in cumpas of the citee, and spuylide it bi prey.

62 And men of Gasa preyeden Jonatas, and he yaf to hem riyt hond, 'ether pees. And he took the sones of hem in ostage, and he sente hem in to Jerusalem, and walkide thorou the cuntre til to Damask.

63 And Jonathas herde, that the princes of Demetrie trespassiden in Cades, that is in Galilee, with myche oost, wilynge for to remoue him fro nede of the rewme; and he cam ayens hem.

64 Forsothe he lefte Symount, his brother, withynne the prouynce.

65 And Symount appliede to Bethsura, and fauyt ayens it many daies, and closide togidere hem.

66 And thei axiden of hym for to take riythondis, and he yaf to hem. And he castide out hem fro thennus, and took the citee, and puttide ther ynne strengthe.

67 And Jonathas and his tentis, 'ether oost, applieden to the water of Genasar, and bifor the liyt thei walkiden in the liyt of Asor.

68 And lo! the tentis, 'ether oostis, of aliens camen ayens in the feeld, and settiden to him aspies in the hillis. Sotheli he cam ayens of the contrarie part.

69 Sotheli the aspies risiden vp of her places, and ioyneden batel.

70 And alle that weren of Jonathas part fledden, and no man of hem was left, no but Matathias, sone of Absalomy, and Judas, sone of Calphi, prince of knyythod and oost.

71 And Jonathas torente hise clothingis, and puttide erthe in his heed, and preiede.

72 And Jonathas turnede ayen to hem in to batel, and togidere turnyde hem in to fliyt, and fouyten.

73 And thei of his part that fledden sayn, and thei turnyden ayen to hym, and pursueden with hym til to Cades, to her tentis, and fulli camen til thidur.

74 And ther felden doun in that dai of aliens thre thousynde of men, and Jonathas turnede ayen in to Jerusalem.

CAP 12

1 And Jonatas siy that the tyme helpith hym; and he chees men, and sente hem to Rome for to ordeyne and renule frendschip with hem.

2 And to Sparciates, and to other places, he sente epistlis bi the same forme.

3 And thei wenten to Rome, and entriden in to the court, and seiden, Jonathas, hiyeste prest, and the folc of Jewis, sente vs, for to renule frendschip and felouschip, bi the formere.

4 And thei yauen to hem epistlis to hem bi placis, that thei schulden lede forth hem in to the lond of Juda with pees.

5 And this is the ensaumple of pistlis, whiche Jonathas wroot to Sparciatis.

6 Jonathas, hiyeste preest, and the eldere men of the folc, and prestis, and othere puple of Jewis, to Sparciatis, britheren, helthe.

7 Now bifore epistlis weren sent to Onyas, hiyeste prest, fro Darius, that regnede anentis you; for ye ben oure britheren, as the rescrite conteyneth, that is vndur put.

8 And Onyas resseyuede the man, that was sent, with onour, and took epistlis, in whiche he was signefied of felouschip and frendschip.

9 Whanne we hadden no nede of these, and hadden in coumfort hooli bookis that ben in oure hondis,

10 we hadden leuere for to sende to you, for to renule britherhod and frenschip, lest perauenture we be maad aliens fro you; forwhi many tymes passiden, sithen ye senten to vs.

11 We therfor in al tyme with out ceessyng, in to solempne daies, and othere, in whiche it bihoueth, ben myndeful of you in sacrifices that we offren, and in obseruaunces, as leueful is, and bisemeth, for to haue hadde mynde of britheren.

12 Therfore we ben glad of youre glorie.

13 Forsothe many tribulaciouns and many batels enuyrownden vs; and kyngis, that ben in oure cumpas, 'fouyten ayens vs.

14 Therfore we wolden not be greuouse to you, nether to othere felowis, and oure frendis, in these batels.

15 For we hadden help of heuene, and ben delyuered, and oure enemyes ben maad lowe.

16 Therfor we han chosun Newmenyus, the sone of Antiok, and Antipatre, sone of Jasoun, and senten to Romayns, for to renule with hem both frendschip and formere felouschipe.

17 Therfor we comaundiden to hem, that thei come also to you, and grete you, and yelde to you oure pistlis of renulyng of oure britherhod.

18 And nowe ye schulen do wel, answerynge to vs to these thingis.

19 And this is the ayenwrityng of epistlis, that Onyas, the kyng of Sparciatis, sente.

20 Onyas to Jonathas, greet preest, heelthe.

21 It is foundyn in writyng of Sparciatis, and of Jewis, that thei ben britheren, and that thei ben of the kyn of Abraham.

22 And now sithen we knowen these thingis, ye don wel, writynge to vs of youre pees.

23 But and we han ayen writun to you. Oure beestis and oure possessiouns ben youre, and youre oure. Therfor we comaundiden, for to telle these thingis to you.

24 And Jonathas herde, that the princes of Demetrie wenten out with myche oost, ouer that bifore, for to fiyte ayens hym.

25 And he wente out fro Jerusalem, and ran ayens hem in the cuntre of Amathitha; for he yaf not space to hem, for to entre in to his cuntree.

26 And he sente aspies in the tentis of hem, and thei turneden ayen, and telden, that thei ordeyneden for to come ouer thidur in niyt.

27 Whanne the sunne hadde go doun, Jonathas badde his men wake, and be redi in armeris to batel al nyyt. And he settide keperis bi cumpas of tentis;

28 and aduersaries herden, that Jonathas was redi with hise men in batel, and thei dredden, and inwardli weren agast in her herte, and tendiden fieris in her tentis.

29 Forsothe Jonathas, and thei that weren with hym, knewen not til to the morewe; for thei siyen liytis brennynge.

30 And Jonathas suyde hem, and cauyte not hem; for thei passiden the flood Eleutherus.

31 And Jonathas turnede to Arabas, that weren clepid Sabadeis; and smoot hem, and took spuylis of hem; and ioynede,

32 and cam in to Damask, and walkide bi al that cuntre.

33 Forsothe Symount wente out, and cam til to Ascalon, and to the nexte strengthis; and he bowide doun in to Joppe, and ocupiede it.

34 For he herde, that thei wolden yyue help to partis of Demetrie; and he puttide there keperis, for to kepe it.

35 And Jonathas turnede ayen, and clepide togidere the eldere men of the puple, and thouyte with hem for to bilde strengthis in Judee,

36 and for to bilde wallis in Jerusalem, and for to reise a greet hiythe, bytwixe the myddil of the hiy tour and the citee, for to departe it fro the citee, that it were aloone, and nether thei bie, nether sille.

37 And thei camen togidere, for to bilde the citee. And the wal felle doun togidere, that was on the streem, fro the risyng of the sunne; and he reparalide it, that is clepid Cafeteta.

38 And Symount bildide Adiada in Sephela, and strengthide it, and puttide on yatis and lockis.

39 And whanne Trifon thouyte for to regne at Asie, and take a diademe, and stretche out hond in to Antiok kyng,

40 he dredde, lest perauenture Jonathas schulde not suffre hym, but fiyte ayens hym; and he souyte for to catche hym, and sle.

41 And he roos vp, and wente in to Bethsan. And Jonathas wente out ayens hym, with fourti thousynde of chosun men in to batel, and cam to Bethsan.

42 And Trifon siy, that Jonathas cam with myche oost, for to stretche out hondis in to hym.

43 And he dredde, and resseyuede hym with onour, and comendide hym to alle his frendis; and yaf to hym yiftis, and comaundide to his oostis, for to obeie to hym as to hym silf.

44 And he seide to Jonathas, Wherto hast thou trauelid al the puple, whanne batel is not to vs?

45 And now sende ayen hem in to her housis. But chese thou to thee a fewe men, that ben with thee, and come thou with me to Tolomayda, and Y schal yyue it to thee, and other strengthis, and oost, and alle souereyns of offices; and Y schal turne, and Y schal go awei. For whi therfor Y cam.

46 And he bileuyde to hym, and dide as he seide, and lefte the oost; and thei wente awei in to the lond of Juda.

47 Forsothe he withhelde with hym thre thousynde of men, of whiche he sente ayen in to Galilee two thousynde; sotheli a thousynde cam with hym.

48 Forsothe as Jonathas entride in to Tolomaida, men of Tolomaida schittiden the yatis, and cauyten hym; and slowen bi swerd alle that entriden with hym.

49 And Trifon sente oost, and horse men in to Galilee, and in to the greet feeld, for to leese alle the felowis of Jonathas.

50 And whanne thei knewen that Jonathas was takun, and perischide, and alle that weren with hym, thei monestiden hem silf, and wenten out redi in to batel.

51 And thei siyen that pursueden, that thing was to hem for the lijf, and turneden ayen.

52 Forsothe thei camen alle with pees in to the lond of Juda. And thei biweiliden Jonathas greetli, and alle that weren with hym, and Israel mourenyde with greet mourenyng.

53 And alle hethene men that weren in the cumpas of hem, souyte for to al to-breken hem;

54 for thei seiden, Thei han no prince and helpere; now therfor ouercome we hem, and take we awei fro men the mynde of hem.

CAP 13

1 And as Symount herde, that Trifon gaderide a greet oost, for to come in to the lond of Juda,

2 and for to distrie it, and siy that the puple was in tremblyng and drede, he stiy vp to Jerusalem, and gaderide the puple;

3 and monestide, and seide, Ye witen, hou grete thingis Y, and my britheren, and the hous of my fadir, han do, for lawis, and for hooli thingis, batels, and what maner angwischis we saien.

4 For loue of these thingis alle my britheren perischiden for Israel, and Y aloone am left.

5 And now bifalle it not to me, for to spare my lijf in al the tyme of tribulacioun; for Y am not betere than my britheren.

6 Therfor Y schal venge my folc, and hooli thingis, and oure children, and wyues; for alle hethene men ben gaderid, for to distrie vs, bi cause of enemyte.

7 And the spirit of the puple was kyndlid togidere, as it herde these wordis.

8 And thei answeriden with greet vois, seiynge, Thou art oure duyk in stide of Judas, and Jonathas, thi brother; fiyte thou oure batel,

9 and alle thingis what euere thou schalt seie to vs, we schulen do.

10 And he gaderide alle men fiyteris, and hastide for to ende alle wallis of Jerusalem, and strengthide it in cumpas.

11 And he sente Jonathas, the sone of Absolomy, and with hym a newe oost, in to Joppe. And whanne he hadde put out these men that weren in it, he dwelte there.

12 And Trifon mouyde fro Tolomaida with myche oost, for to come in to the lond of Juda, and Jonathas with hym in kepyng.

13 Forsothe Symount appliede in Addus, ayens the face of the feeld.

14 And as Trifon knew, that Symount roos in the stide of his brother Jonathas, and that he was to ioynynge batel with hym, he sente to hym legatis,

15 and seide, For siluer, that thi brother Jonatas ouyte in acountis of the kyng, we withhelden hym.

16 And nowe sende thou an hundrid talentis of siluer, and hise twei sones pleggis, that he not dismyttid fle fro vs, and we schulen ayensende hym.

17 And Symount knew, that with gile he spak with hym. Netheles he comaundide the siluer for to be youun, and children, leste he schulde take grete enemytee at the puple of Israel, seiynge, For he sente not to hym siluer and children,

18 therfor he perischide.

19 And he sente the children, and an hundrid talentis. And he liede, and dismyttide not Jonathas.

20 And after these thingis Trifon cam with ynne the cuntre, for to distrie it. And thei cumpassiden bi the weie that ledith to Ador; and Symount and his oost walkiden in to ech place, whidur euere thei wenten.

21 Sotheli thei that weren in the hiy tour, senten legatis to Trifon, for to haste to come bi desert, and sende to hem foodis.

22 And Trifon made redi al the multitude of horse men, for to come in that nyyt. Sotheli ther was ful myche snow, and he cam not in to Galadithym.

23 And whanne he neiyede to Baschama, he slow Jonathas and hise sones there.

24 And Trifon turnede, and wente in to his lond.

25 And Symount sente, and took the boonus of Jonathas, his brother, and biride tho in Modyn, the citee of hise fadris.

26 And al Israel biweiliden hym with greet weilyng, and thei bymourenyde hym many daies.

27 And Symount bildide on the sepulcre of his fadir and hise britheren an hiy bildyng in siyt, with stoon polischid bihynde and bifore.

28 And he ordeynede seuene smale bildyngis, brood bynethe and scharp aboue, oon ayens oon, to fadir, and modir, and foure britheren.

29 And to these he puttide aboute grete pilers, and on the pileris armeris, to euerlastynge mynde; and bisidis armeris schippis grauun, whiche schulden be seyn of men seilynge in the see.

30 This is the sepulcre that Symount maad in Modyn, til in to this day.

31 Forsothe whanne Trifon made weie with Antiok, the yonge kyng, in gile he slow hym, and regnyde in his stide;

32 and puttide on hym the diademe of Asie, and made greet veniaunce in the lond.

33 And Symount bildide strengthis of Judee, and wardide hem with hiy touris, and grete wallis, and yatis, and lockis; and puttide foodis in strengthingis.

34 And Symount chees men, and sente to kyng Demetrie, that he schulde make remyssioun to the cuntree, for alle dedis of Trifon weren don bi rauyschyng.

35 And kyng Demetrie answeride to hym to these wordis, and wroot suche epistle.

36 Kyng Demetrie to Symount, hiyeste prest, and frend of kyngis, and to the eldere men, and folc of Jewis, heelthe.

37 We resseyueden the goldun coroun, and baheu, which ye senten, and ben redi for to make with you greet pees, and for to write to prepostis of the kyng, for to releesse to you what thingis we foryauen;

38 for what euere thingis we ordeynen to you, ben stable. The strengthis that ye bildiden, be to you; and we forgyuen ignorances and synnes,

39 til in to this dai, and the coroun that ye ouyten; and if ony other thing was tributarie in Jerusalem, now be it not tributarie.

40 And if ony of you ben able for to be writun togidere among oure men, be thei writun togidere, and pees be bitwixe vs.

41 In the hundrid yeer and seuentithe, the yok of hethene men was takun awei fro Israel.

42 And the puple began for to write in tablis, and comyn doyngis, in the firste yeer vndur Symount, hiyeste prest, greet duyk, and prince of Jewis.

43 In tho daies Symount appliede to Gasan, and enuyrownyde it with tentis, and made engines, and appliede to the citee, and smoot o tour, and took it.

44 And thei that braken out, weren with ynne the engyne in the cite, and greet stiryng was maad in the cite.

45 And thei stieden vp, that weren in the cite, with her wyues, and sones, on the wal, with her cootis kit, and crieden with greet vois axynge of Symount that riythondis be youun to hem,

46 and seiden, Yelde thou not to vs bi oure malices, but bi thi mercies, and we schulen serue to thee.

47 And Symount was bowid, and fauyt not ayens hem; netheles he castide hem out of the citee, and clenside fulli the housis in whiche weren symylacris, and thanne he entride in to it with ympnes, and blesside the Lord.

48 And whanne alle vnclennesse was caste out therof, he settide therynne men, that schulden do the lawe; and he strengthide it, and made an abitacioun to him.

49 Forsothe thei that weren in the hiy tour of Jerusalem, weren forbodun for to go out and go yn, in to the cuntre, and bie, and sille; and thei hungriden greetli, and many of hem perischiden for hungur.

50 And thei crieden to Symount, for to take riyt hondis, and he yaf to hem; and he castide out hem fro thennus, and clenside the hiy tour fro defoulingis.

51 And thei entriden in to it in thre and twentithe dai of the secounde monethe, in the hundrid and oon and seuenty yeer, with heriyng, and braunchis of palmes, and instrumentis of musik, 'ether giternys, and cymbalis, and harpis, and ympnys, and songis, for the greet enemye of Israel was al to-brokun.

52 And he ordeynede, that in alle yeeris these daies schulden be don with gladnesse.

53 And he strengthide the hil of the temple, that was bisidis the hiy tour, and dwelte there, he, and thei that weren with hym.

54 And Symount siy Joon, his sone, that he was a man of batel, and he puttide hym duyk of alle vertues, and he dwelte in Gasaris.

CAP 14

1 In the hundrid and two and seuenti yeer kyng Demetrie gaderide his oost, and wente to Medei, for to drawe togidere helpis to hym, for to ouercome Trifon.

2 And as Arsases, kyng of Persis and Medei, herde that Demetrie entride in to his niy coostis, he sente oon of hise princes, for to take hym quyk, and that he schulde brynge hym to hym silf.

3 And he wente, and smoot tentis, 'ether oost, of Demetrie, and took hym, and ledde hym to Arsaces, and he puttide hym in to kepyng.

4 And the lond of Juda was pesible in alle daies of Symount, and he souyte goode thingis of his folc; and his power and his glorie pleside to hem in alle daies.

5 And with al his glorie he took Joppe in to hauene, and made entre in to ilis of the see;

6 and alargide the coostis of his puple, and weldide the cuntre.

7 And he gaderide myche caitifte, and was lord in Gasara, and Bethsura, and the hiy tour; and dide awei vnclennessis of it, and ther was not that ayenstood hym.

8 And ech man tilide his owne lond with pees, and the lond of Juda yaf hise fruitis, and trees of feeldis her fruitis.

9 Eldere men saten alle in stretis, and tretiden of goodis of the lond; and yonge men clothiden hem in glorie, and in stoolis of batel.

10 And to the citees he yaf foodis, and ordeynede tho, that tho weren vessels of strengthing, til that the name of his glorie was named til to the laste of erthe.

11 He made pees on the lond, and Israel was glad with greet gladnesse;

12 and ech man sat vndur his vyne, and vndur his fige tree, nether ther was that feeride hem.

13 The fiytynge man ayens hem failide on erthe; kyngis weren al to-brokun in tho daies.

14 And he confermyde alle meke men of his puple, and he souyte out the lawe, and dide awei al yuel and wickidnesse;

15 and he glorifiede hooli thingis, and multipliede vessels of hooli thingis.

16 And it was herd at Rome, that Jonathas was deed, and til in to Sparciatis, and thei weren ful soreuful.

17 Forsothe as thei herden, that Symount, his brother, was maad hiyeste preest in his stide, and he weldide the cuntre, and citees in it,

18 thei writiden to hym in brasun tablis, for to renule frenschip, and felouschip, that thei maden with Judas and Jonathas, his britheren;

19 and thei weren rad in the siyt of the chirche in Jerusalem. And this is ensaumple of pistlis, that Sparciatis senten.

20 The prince and citees of Sparciatis to Symount, greet prest, and to the eldere men, and prestis, and to othere puple of Jewis, britheren, heelthe.

21 Legatis that weren sente to oure puple, telden to vs of youre glorie, and onour, and gladnesse, and we ioieden in the entree of hem.

22 And we han write what thingis weren seid of hem in councels of puple, thus. Numenyus, the sone of Antiok, and Antipater, the sone of Jason, legatis of Jewis, camen to vs, and renulide with vs the formere frendschip.

23 And it pleside to the puple, for to resseyue the men gloriousli, and to putte ensaumple of her wordis in departid bookis of the puple, that it be to mynde to the puple of Sparciatis; forsothe we han write ensaumple of these thingis to Symount, the greet preest.

24 Forsothe aftir these thingis Symount sente Numenyus to Rome, hauynge a greet goldun scheeld, in weiyte of a thousynde besauntis, for to ordeyne felouschip with hem. Sotheli whanne the puple of Rome herde these wordis,

25 thei seiden, What doyng of thankyngis schulen we yelde to Symount, and his sones?

26 For he restoride his britheren, and ouercam the enemyes of Israel fro hem. And thei ordeyneden to hym liberte, and writiden in brasun tablis, and Jewis puttiden in titlis, in the mount of Sion.

27 And this is ensaumple of writyng. In the eiytenthe dai of the monethe Ebul, in the hundrid and two and seuenti yeer, the thridde yeer vndur Symount, greet preest, in Asaramael,

28 in the greet comyng togidere of prestis, of the puple, and princis, and folc, and 'eldere men of the cuntre, these thingis weren maad knowun; for many tymes batels weren don in youre cuntre.

29 Forsothe Symount, the sone of Matatias, of the sones of Jarib, and his britheren, yauen hem silf to perel, and ayenstoden aduersaries of her folc, that her hooli thingis and lawe schulde stonde; and bi greet glorye thei glorifieden her folc.

30 And Jonathas gaderide his folc, and was maad to hem a greet preest, and is put to his puple.

31 And the enemyes of hem wolden defoule holi thingis, and distrie the cuntre of hem, and stretche forth hond in to hooli thingis 'of hem.

32 Thanne Symount ayenstood, and fauyt for his puple, and yaf many richessis, and armyd men of vertu of his folc, and yaf to hem sowdis;

33 and strengthide the citees of Juda, and Bethsura, that was in the endis of Judee, where bifor weren armeris of enemyes, and he puttide there help, men of Jewis.

34 And he strengthide Joppe, that was at the see, and Gasara, that was in coostis of Asotus, in which enemyes dwelten bifore; and he settide there Jewis, and what euere thingis weren able to amendyng of hem, he puttede in hem.

35 And the puple siy the doyng of Symount, and glorie that he thouyte 'for to do to his folc, and thei maden hym her duyk, and prince of preestis, for that he hadde don alle these thingis, and riytwisnesse, and feith that he kepte to his folc; and he souyte out in al maner for to raise hys puple.

36 And in hise daies it hadde prosperite in his hondis, that hethene men weren takun awei fro the cuntre of hem, whiche weren in the citee of Dauid in Jerusalem, in the hiy tour; fro which thei camen out, and defouliden alle thingis that weren in cumpas of hooli thingis, and yauen greet wounde to chastite.

37 And he settide ther ynne men Jewis, to defendyng of the cuntre and citee, and reiside the wallis in Jerusalem.

38 And kyng Demetrie ordeynede to hym the hiyeste presthod;

39 bi this he made him his frend, and glorifiede hym in greet glorie.

40 For he herde, that Jewis weren clepid of Romayns frendis, and felowis, and britheren, and that thei resseyueden legatis of Symount gloriousli;

41 and that Jewis, and prestis of hem, consentiden, him for to be her duyk, and hiyeste preest with outen ende, til ther rise a feithful profete;

42 and that he be duyk on hem, and cure were to him for hooli thingis; and that he schulde ordeyne gouernouris on the werkis of hem, and on the cuntre, and on armeris, and on strengthis;

43 and cure be to hym of hooli thingis; and that he be herd of men, and alle writyngis in the cuntre be writun togidere vndur name of hym; and that he be keuered with purpur and gold;

44 and that it be not leueful to ony of the puple, and to prestis, for to make ony thing of these voide, and ayenseie to these thingis that ben seid of hym, ether for to clepe togidere couent in the cuntre with outen hym; and for to be clothid in purpur, and for to vse a goldun lace, 'ether noche.

45 Sotheli he that schal do with out this, ether schal make voide ony of these, schal be gilti.

46 And it pleside togidere to al the puple, for to ordeyne Symount, and do bi these wordis.

47 And Symount resseyuede, and it pleside hym, that he schulde vse hiyeste preesthod, and be duyk and prince of the folc of Jewis, and prestis, and be souereyn of alle men.

48 And thei ordeyneden for to put this writyng in brasun tablis, and put hem in the wal aboute the cumpassyng of hooli thingis, in solempne place;

49 forsothe for to putte ensaumple of these in the tresorie, that Symount haue and hise sones.

CAP 15

1 And kyng Antiok, the sone of Demetrie, sente epistlis fro ilis of the see to Symount, prest, and prince of folc of Jewis, and to al the folc;

2 and tho weren conteynynge this maner. Kyng Antiok to Symount, greet prest, and to the folc of Jewis, helthe.

3 For summen berynge pestilence weldiden the rewme of oure fadris, forsothe Y wole calenge the rewme, and restore it, as it was bifore; Y made a chosun multitude of oost, and Y made schippis of werre.

4 Forsothe Y wole go forth bi cuntrees, that Y do veniaunce on hem that distrieden oure cuntre, and that maden many citees desolat in my rewme.

5 Now therfor Y ordeyne to thee alle offryngis, that kyngis bifore me foryauen to thee, and 'what euere other yiftis thei foryauen to thee;

6 and Y suffre thee for to make prynte of thin owne monei, in thi regioun;

7 Sotheli Y suffre Jerusalem for to be hooli and fre, and alle armeris that ben maad, and strengthis, that thou hast maad out, and that thou holdist, dwelle to thee;

8 and al dette of the kyng, and tho that ben to comynge of kingis thingis, fro this and in to al tyme ben foryouun to thee.

9 Sotheli whanne we schulen welde oure rewme, we schulen glorifie thee, and thi folc, and temple, with greet glorie, so that youre glorie be schewid in al erthe.

10 In the hundrid yeer and foure and seuentithe yeer Antiok wente out in to the lond of his fadris, and alle oostis camen togidere to hym, so that fewe weren left with Trifon.

11 And king Antiok pursuede hym, and Trifon cam in to Doram, and fledde bi the see coost;

12 for he wiste, that yuels weren gaderid on hym, and the oost forsook hym.

13 And Antiok appliede on Doram, with sixe score thousynde of fiytynge men, and eiyte thousynde of horse men;

14 and he cumpasside the citee, and schippis camen fro the see; and thei traueliden the citee bi lond and see, and suffriden no man for to entre, ether go out.

15 Forsothe Numenyus cam, and thei that weren with hym, fro Rome, and hadden epistlis writun to kingis and cuntreis, in whiche these thingis weren conteyned.

16 Lucius, 'cheef gouernour of Romayns, to kyng Tolome, heelthe.

17 Messangeris of Jewis camen to vs, oure frendis, renulinge the formere frendschip and felouschip, sent of Symoun, prince of prestis, and puple of Jewis.

18 Sotheli thei brouyten also a goldun scheeld of a thousynde besauntis.

19 Therfor it pleside to vs for to write to kyngis and cuntreis, that thei do not yuels to hem, nether impugne hem, and her citees, and her cuntreis, and thei bere not help to men fiytynge ayens hem.

20 Forsothe it is seyn to vs, for to resseyue of hem the scheeld.

21 Therfor if ony men of pestilence schulen fle fro the cuntre of hem to you, bitake ye hem to Symount, prince of prestis, that he do veniaunce on hem bi his lawe.

22 These same thingis ben writun to kyng Demetrie, and Attalus, and Arabas,

23 and Arsaces, and in to alle cuntreis, and Sampsame, and Spartanyes, and Delo, and Mydo, and Sydone, and Carie, and Sanyum, and Pamfiliam, and Lisiam, and Alacarnasum, and Rodum, and Phaselida, and Choo, and Sidon, and Arodo, and Gortynam, and Gnydum, and Cipre, and Cirenen.

24 Forsothe thei han writun ensaumple of these to Symount, prince of prestis, and to the puple of Jewis.

25 Forsothe Antiok, the kyng, appliede tentis in Doram the secounde tyme, mouynge to it 'euere more hondis, and makynge engynes; and he closide togidere Trifon, lest he wente out.

26 And Symount sente to hym twei thousynde of chosun men, in to help, and siluer, and gold, and plenteuouse vessels;

27 and he wolde not take tho. But he brak alle thingis that he couenauntide with hym bifore, and alienyde him silf fro hym.
28 And he sente to hym Athenobius, oon of his frendis, for to trete with hym, and seide, Ye holden Joppe, and Gasaram, and the hiy tour that is in Jerusalem, citees of my rewme;
29 ye han wastid the coostis of hem, and han do greet distriyng in the lond, and with out coostis of Judee ye ben lordis bi many places in my rewme.
30 Now therfor yyue ye the citees, which ye ocupieden, and tributis of places, of whiche ye ben lordis, out of endis of Judee.
31 Ether ellis yyue ye for hem fyue hundrid talentis of siluer, and of distriyng that ye han distried, and of tributis of citees, othere fyue hundrid talentis; ether ellis we schulen come, and ouercome you.
32 And Athenobius, frend of the kyng, cam in to Jerusalem, and siy the glorie of Symount, and clerenesse, in gold, and siluer, and plenteuouse apparel, and was astonyed; and telde to him the wordis of the kyng.
33 And Symount answeride, and seide to hym, Nether we token alien lond, nether withholden other mennus thingis, but eritage of oure fadris, that was weldid some time vniustly of oure enemies.
34 Sotheli we han tyme, and calengen the eritage of oure fadris.
35 For whi of Joppe and Gasara that thou axist, thei diden greet veniaunce in oure puple, and cuntree; of these we yyuen an hundrid talentis.
36 And Athenobius answeride not a word. Sotheli he turnede ayen with wraththe to the kyng, and telde ayen to hym these wordis, and the glorie of Symount, and alle thingis that he siy. And the king was wroth with greet wraththe.
37 Forsothe Trifon flei bi schip 'in to Ortosaida.
38 And the kyng ordeynede Cendebeus, duyk of the see coost, and yaf to him oost of foot men and horse men;
39 and comaundide him for to moue tentis ayens the face of Judee; and comaundide hym for to bilde Cedron, and stoppe the yatis of the cite, and ouercome the puple; forsothe the kyng pursuede Trifon.
40 And Cendebius cam to Jamnyam, and bigan for to terre the puple to wraththe, and for to defoule Judee, and make the puple caitif, and sle, and bilde Cedron.
41 And he settide there horse men and oost, that thei schulden gon out, and schulden walke bi weie of Judee, as the kyng ordeynede to hym.

CAP 16

1 And Joon stiede fro Gasara, and telde to Symount, his fader, what thingis Cendebius dide in the puple of hem.
2 And Symount clepide his tweyne eldere sones, Judas and Joon, and seide to hem, Y, and my britheren, and the hous of my fadir, han ouercomun the enemyes of Israel, fro yongthe til in to this dai; and it hadde prosperite in oure hondis, for to delyuere Israel sum times.
3 Forsothe now Y haue eldid, but be ye in my stide, and of my brother, and go ye out, and fiyte for oure folc; forsothe helpe of heuene be with you.
4 And he chees of the cuntrei twenti thousynde of fiytinge men, and horse men; and thei wenten out to Cendebeus, and slepten in Modyn.
5 And thei risiden eerli, and wenten in to the feeld, and lo! a copiouse oost cam in to metyng of hem, of foot men and horse men; and a rennynge flood was bitwixe the myddis of hem.
6 And he and his puple mouede the scheltruns ayens the face of hem, and he siy the puple tremblynge to passe ouer the streeme of water, and he passide ouer the firste; and men siyen hym, and passiden aftir hym.
7 And he departide the puple and horse men in the myddil of foot men; forsothe the multitude of horse men of aduersaries was ful plenteuouse.
8 And thei crieden an hiy with hooli trumpis; and Cendebeus was turned in to fliyt, and his oost, and many of hem fellen woundid; sotheli the residues fledden in to strengthe.
9 Thanne Judas, the brother of Joon, was woundid; forsothe Joon pursuede hem, til Cendebeus cam to Cedrona, which he bildide.
10 And thei fledden til to touris, that weren in the feeldis of Azotus, and he brente hem with fier; and ther fellen of hem two thousynde of men, and he turnede ayen in to Judee in pees.
11 And Tolome, the sone of Abobi, was ordeyned duyk in the feld of Jerico, and hadde myche siluer and gold;
12 for he weddid the douyter of the hiyeste preest.
13 And the herte of hym was reisid, and he wolde welde the cuntre; and he thouyte gile ayens Symount and his sones, for to do awei hem.
14 Forsothe Symount walkide bi citees that weren in the cuntre of Judee, and bar bisynesse of hem, and cam doun in to Jerico, he, and Matatias, his sone, and Judas, in the hundrid yeer and seuene and seuentithe, in the enleuenthe monethe; this is the monethe Sabath.
15 And the sone of Abobi resseyuede him in to a litil strengthe, that is clepid Doth, with gile, which he bildide; and made to hem a greet feeste, and hidde men ther.
16 And whanne Symount was ful of drynk, and hise sones, Tolome roos with his, and token her armeris, and entriden in to the feeste, and slowen hym, and hise twei sones, and summe children of hym.
17 And he dide a greet disseit in Israel, and yeldide yuels for goodis.
18 And Tolome wroot these thingis, and sente to the kyng, for to sende to hym an oost in to help, and he schulde bitake to hym the cuntre and citees of hem, and tributis.
19 And he sente othere in to Gasara, for to do awei Joon; and to the tribunes he sente epistlis, that thei schulden come to hym, and he schulde yyue to hem siluer, and gold, and yiftis.
20 And he sente other men, for to ocupie Jerusalem, and the mount of the temple.
21 And sum man ran bifore, and told to Joon in Gasara, for that his fadir perischide, and his britheren, and that he sente that thou also be slayn.
22 Forsothe as he herde, he wondride greetli; and he cauyte the men that camen for to leese hym, and he slow hem; for he knew, that thei souyten for to leese hym.
23 And othere thingis of Joons wordis, and of his batels, and good vertues, in whiche he dide strongli, and of bildyng of wallis, whiche he fulli made, and of thingis don of him, lo!
24 these ben writun in book of daies of his presthod, sithen he was maad prince of prestis aftir his fadir.

2 MACHABEIS

CAP 1

1 To britheren Jewis, that ben scaterid thorouy Egipt, britheren, that ben in Jerusalem, Jewis, and that ben in the cuntre of Judee, seien heelthe and good pees.

2 God do wel to you, and haue mynde of his testament, that he spak to Abraham, Isaac, and Jacob, that ben of the noumbre of his trewe seruauntis;

3 and yyue he herte to you alle, that ye worschipe hym, and do the wille of hym with greet herte and wilful soule.

4 Opene he youre herte in his lawe, and in hise heestis, and make he pees;

5 here he graciousli youre preieris, and be reounceld to you, nether forsake you in yuel tyme.

6 And now we ben here preiynge for you.

7 While Demetrie regneth in the hundrid yeer and sixtithe and nynthe, we Jewis han writun to you in tribulacioun and fersnesse, that cam aboue to vs in these yeeris, and sithen Jason wente out of the hooli lond and rewme.

8 Thei brenten the yate, and schedden out innocent blood; and we preieden to the Lord, and we ben graciousli herd, and we han offrid sacrifice, and clene flour, and han tendid lanternes, and han put forth looues.

9 And now make ye solempne the daies of Cenefegye, 'ether clensyng of the temple, of the monethe Caslew.

10 In the hundrid yeer and eiyte and eiytithe, the puple that is in Jerusalem and in Judee, and the elde men, and Judas, to Aristoble, maister of Tolome, kyng, that is of the kyn anoyntid prestis, and to hem that ben in Egipt, Jewis, helthe of soule, and helthe of bodi.

11 We delyuered of God fro grete perelis, don thankyngis to hym hugely, as we that han fouyten ayens sich a kyng.

12 For he made for to buyle out of Persis hem that fouyten ayens vs and the hooli citee.

13 For whi whanne the duyk hym silf was in Persis, and with hym a greet oost, he felle in the temple of Nauee, and was disseyued bi councel of the prest of Nauee.

14 Forsothe Antiok cam to the place as to dwellynge with hym, and his frendis, and for to take many richessis bi name of dower.

15 And whanne prestis of Nauee hadden put forth tho, and he with fewe entride with ynne the cumpas of the temple, thei closiden the temple, whanne Antiok hadde entrid.

16 And whanne the pryuy entre of the temple was openyd, thei threwen stoonys, and smytiden the duik, and hem that weren with hym, and thei departiden lememeel; and whanne the heedis weren gird of, thei castiden out forth.

17 Bi alle thingis blessid be God, that bitook vnpitouse men.

18 Therfor we to makynge clensyng of the temple, in the fyue and twentithe dai of the monethe Caslew, ledden nedeful for to signefie to you, that and ye do also the dai of Scenofegie, and the dai of fier, that was youun, whanne Neemye offride sacrifices, after that the temple and auter weren bildid.

19 For whi whanne oure fadris weren led in to Persis, prestis that thanne weren worschiperis of God, hidden priueli fier takun of the auter, in a valei, where was a deep pit and drie; and there ynne thei kepten it, so that the place was vnknowun to alle men.

20 Forsothe whanne many yeeris hadden passid, and it pleside to God that Neemye was sent fro the kyng of Persis, he sente the sones sones of tho prestis that hidden, for to seke fier; and as thei telden to vs, thei founden not fier, but fat water.

21 And he comaundide hem 'for to drawe, and brynge to hym. And Neemye, preest, comaundide the sacrifices, that weren put on, for to be spreynt with the water, tho and the trees, and tho thingis that weren put aboue.

22 And as this was don, and the tyme cam, in which the sunne schon ayen, that bifore was in cloude, a greet fier was kyndlid, so that alle men wondriden.

23 Forsothe alle prestis maden preier, while the sacrifice was endid; and Jonathas bigan, and othere forsothe answeriden.

24 And the preier of Neemye was hauynge this maner. Lord God, maker of nouyt of alle thingis, dredeful and strong, iust and merciful, which aloone art good kyng,

25 aloone yyuynge, aloone iust, and almyyti, and with out bigynnyng and ende, which delyuerist Israel fro al yuel, which madist fadris chosun, and halewidist hem;

26 take thou sacrifice for al thi puple Israel, and kepe thi part, and halewe.

27 Gadere oure scateryng, delyuere hem that seruen to hethene men, and biholde thou dispisid men, and maad abhomynable, that hethene men wite, that thou art oure God.

28 Turmente thou men oppressynge vs, and doynge dispit in pride.

29 Ordeyne thi puple in thin hooli place, as Moises seide.

30 Forsothe prestis sungen ympnes, til the sacrifice was endid.

31 Forsothe whanne the sacrifice was endid, Neemye comaundide the more stoonys for to be bisched of the residue watir;

32 and as this thing was don, flawme was kyndlid of hem, but it was wastid of the liyt, that ayen schynede of the auter.

33 Forsothe after that the thing was knowun, it was teld to the kyng of Persis, that in the place in which the prestis that weren translatid, hadden hid fier, water apperide, of which Neemye and thei that weren with hym clensiden sacrifices.

34 Forsothe the kyng bihelde and diligentli examynede the thing, and made a temple to hym, for to preue that thing that was don.

35 And whanne he hadde preued, he yaf many goodis to prestis, and othere yiftis; and he took with his hoond, and he yaf to hem.

36 Forsothe Neemye clepte this place Nepthar, that is interpretid, 'ether expowned, clensyng; forsothe anentis many it is clepid Nephi.

CAP 2

1 Forsothe it is foundun in writyngis of Jeremye, the profete, that he comaundide hem that passiden ouer, for to take fier, as it is signefied, and as he bad to men 'passynge ouer.

2 And he yaf to hem the lawe, leste thei foryaten the heestis of the Lord; and that thei schulden not erre in soulis, seynge goldun and siluerne symylacris, and ournementis of hem.

3 And he seide othere siche thingis, and monestide, that thei schulden not remoue the lawe fro her herte.

4 Sotheli it was in that writyng, hou the profete bad, bi Goddis answere maad to hym, that the tabernacle and 'the arke folowe with hym, til he wente out in to the hil in which Moises ascendide, and siy the eritage of God.

5 And Jeremye cam, and foond ther a place of denne, and brouyte in thidur the tabernacle, and 'the arke, and auter of encense, and stoppide the dore.

6 And summen camen togidere that folewiden, for to marke the place to hem, and miyten not fynde.

7 Forsothe as Jeremye knew, he blamede hem, and seide, that the place schal be vnknowun, til God gadere the congregacioun of puple, and be maad helpful.

8 And thanne the Lord schal schewe these thinges, and the maieste of the Lord schal appere; and a cloude schal be, as and to Moises it was schewid, and as whanne Salomon axide, that the place schulde be halewid to greet God, this cloude schewide;

9 and as hauynge wisdom he offryde sacrifice of halewyng, and of performyng of the temple.

10 As and Moises preiede to the Lord, and fier cam doun fro heuene, and wastide the brent sacrifice; as and Salomon preiede, and fier cam doun fro heuene, and wastide the brent sacrifice.

11 And Moises seide, For that it is not clensid, that was for synne, and it was wastid.

12 Also and Salomon in eiyte daies made solempne the halewyng.

13 Forsothe and these same thingis weren put yn in discripciouns, and exposiciouns of Neemye; and as he makide a litle bible, and gaderide bookis of cuntrees, and bookis of profetis, and of Dauid, and epistlis of kyngis, and of yiftis.

14 Also sotheli and Judas gaderide alle tho thingis which he lernyde bi batel, that bifelle to vs, and thei ben anentis vs.

15 Therfor if ye disiren these, send ye whiche schulen bere to you.

16 Therfor we to doynge purifiyng, han write to you; therfor ye schulen do wel, if ye schulen do these daies.

17 Forsothe it is God that delyueride his puple, and yeldide his eritage to alle, and rewme, and presthod,

18 and halewyng, as he bihiyte in the lawe, we hopen that soone he schal haue merci on vs, and schal gadere fro vndur heuene in to the hooli place; for he delyuerede vs fro grete perelis,

19 and purgide the place.

20 Sotheli of Judas Machabeus, and hise britheren, and of purifiyng of the greet temple, and of halewyng of the auter;

21 but and of the batels, that perteynen to Antiok noble, and his son Eupator;

22 and of liytnyngis that weren maad fro heuene, to hem that strongli diden for Jewis, so that, whanne thei weren fewe, thei auengiden al the cuntre, and dryuun an hethene multitude,

23 and rekyueriden the most famouse temple in al the world; and delyueriden the citee, that and lawis that weren don a wei weren restorid; for the Lord was maad helpful to hem, with al pesiblete.

24 And also we asaieden for to abregge in o book, thingis comprehendid of Jason of Cirenen in fyue bookis.

25 Forsothe we bihelden the multitude and hardnesse of bookis, to men willynge for to bigynne the tellyngis of stories, for multitude of thingis;

26 and sotheli we hadden bisinesse, that it were likyng of soule to men willynge for to rede;

26 forsothe to studiouse men, that thei miyten liytliere bitake to mynde; forsothe that to alle men redynge profit be youun.

27 And sotheli we token to vs silf that resseyueden this werk, bi cause of abreggyng, not esi trauel, but sotheli a werk ful of wakynges and swoot.

28 As these that maken redi a feeste, and seken for to plese to the wille of othere men, for grace of many men, we suffren wilfuli trauel;

29 forsothe we graunten the treuthe of alle autoris, but we vs silf studien to schortnesse, bi the fourme youun.

30 Forsothe as it is to the cheef carpenter of 'a newe hous, to be bisie of al the bildyng; to him sotheli that bisieth for to peynte, tho thingis ben to be souyt out, that ben couenable to ournyng; so it is to be gessid also in vs.

31 Forsothe for to gadere vndurstondyng, and ordeyne a word, and ful bisili for to enquere alle partis of the storie, ech bi hem silf, acordith to an autour;

32 forsothe for to sue schortnesse of seiyng, and for to eschewe out suyngis of thingis, is to be grauntid to the breggere.

33 Therfor fro hennus forth we schulen bigynne the tellyng; be it ynow for to haue seid so myche of 'bifor spekyng; for it is foli for to flete out, ether be long, bifore the stori, but in that stori for to be maad schort.

CAP 3

1 Therfor whanne the hooli citee was enhabited in al pees, lawis also yit weren best kept, for the feithfulnesse of Onyas, bischop, and for soulis hatynge yuele thingis,

2 it was maad, that bothe thei kyngis and prynces ledden the place worthi hiyeste onour, and liytiden the temple with gretteste yiftis;

3 so that Seleucus, kyng of Asie, yaf of his rentis alle spensis perteynynge to the seruices of sacrifices.

4 Forsothe Symount, of the lynage of Beniamyn, that was ordeyned souereyn of the temple, whanne the prince of prestis ayenstood hym, stroof for to caste sum wickid thing in the citee.

5 But whanne he miyte not ouercome Onyas, he cam to Appollonye, sone of Tharsee, that in that tyme was duyk of Celescirie and Fenyce;

6 and telde to hym, that the treserie in Jerusalem was ful with richessis vnnoumbrable; and that comyn richessis ben grete, whiche perteynen not to the resoun of sacrifices; forsothe that it was possible, that alle thingis falle vndur power of the kyng.

7 And whanne Appolonye hadde telde to the kyng of richessis that weren borun in, he sente Heliodore clepid, that was on his nedis, with maundementis for to bere out the forseid monei.

8 And anoon Heliodore took the weie, sotheli bi forme as if he were to passynge bi Celessirie and Fenyce citees, but in trewe thing to parformynge the kyngis purpos.

9 But whanne he cam to Jerusalem, and was resseyued benygneli of the hiyeste prest in the citee, he telde of doom youun of the richessis, and openyde for cause of what thing he cam; forsothe he axide, if verili these thingis weren so.

10 Thanne the hiyeste prest schewide, that these thingis weren kept to the lijflodis of widewis, and of fadirles ether modirles children;

11 that summe sotheli weren of Ircan Tobie, a man ful noble in these thingis, that vnpitouse Symount hadde teld; forsothe that alle talentis of siluer weren foure hundrid, and of gold two hundrid;

12 for that it was impossible on al maner, that thei be disseyued, that bitoken her thingis to be kept to the place and temple, that bi al the world was onourid for his worschipyng, and holynesse.

13 And he seide, for these thingis that he hadde in maundementis of the kyng, that in al kynde tho schulden be borun to the kyng.

14 Forsothe in the dai ordeyned Heliodore entride, to ordeyne of these thingis; forsothe there was not a litil tremblyng thorouy al the citee.

15 Forsothe prestis castiden hem silf bifore the auter, with prestis stoolis, and clepiden to help fro heuene hym that yaf lawe of thingis put in kepyng, that he schulde kepe tho thingis saf to hem that hadden put tho in kepyng.

16 Now forsothe he that siy the cheer of the hiyeste prest, was woundid in soule; for the face and colour was chaungid, and declaride the inward sorewe of soule.

17 For sum soreufulnesse was sched aboute to the man, and hidousnesse of bodi, bi whiche the sorewe of herte was maad knowun to men biholdynge.

18 Also othere men 'weren gaderid togidere flocmeel, and camen out of housis, bisechynge with opyn bisechyng, for that that the place was to comynge in to dispit.

19 And wymmen weren gird on the brest with heiris, and flo-widen togidere bi stretis; but and virgyns, that weren closid togidere, runnen to Onyas; othere forsothe to the wallis, summe sotheli bihelden bi wyndowis.

20 Forsothe alle helden forth hondis in to heuene, and bisouyten;

21 for ther was a wretchid abidyng of multitude meynt, and of the hiyeste prest ordeyned in strijf.

22 And these sotheli clepiden almiyti God to help, that thingis takun in kepyng schulden be kept in al holynesse, to hem that hadden put tho in kepyng.

23 Forsothe Heliodore performyde that thing, that he hadde demyd, and he was present with his knyytis in the same place aboute the treserie.

24 But the spirit of almyyti God made greet euydence of his schewyng, so that alle that weren hardi for to obeie to hym, fellen doun bi vertu of God, and weren conuertid in to feble-nesse, and inward drede.

25 For an hors apperide to hem, and hadde a dredeful sittere, ourned with beste hilyngis; and he with fersnesse ruyschide the formere feet to Heliodore; forsothe he that sat on hym, semyde for to haue goldun armeris.

26 Also twei othere yonge men apperiden, faire in vertu, beste in glorie, and faire in clothing, that stoden aboute hym, and on ech side scourgiden hym with out ceessyng, and beeten with many woundis.

27 Sodenli forsothe Heliodore felle doun to erthe, and thei rauyschiden hym sched aboute with myche derknesse, and castiden out hym, putte in a pakke sadil, 'ether hors litir.

28 And he that entride with many renneris and knyytis in to the forseid tresorie, was borun, whanne no man helpide hym, for the opyn vertu of God was knowun;

29 and forsothe bi Goddis vertu he lay doumb, and priued of al hope and heelthe.

30 Forsothe these Jewis blessiden the Lord, for he magny-fiede his place; and the temple, that a litil bifore was ful of drede and noyse, is fillid with ioye and gladnesse, for the Lord almyyti apperide.

31 Thanne forsothe summe of Eliodoris frendis preieden anoon Onyas, for to clepe to help the Hiyeste, and for to yyue lijf to hym, that was set in the laste spirit.

32 Sotheli the hiyeste prest bihelde, lest perauenture the kyng wolde suppose ony malice fulli don aboute Jewis aboute Heliodore, and offride for helthe of the man an heelful sacri-fice.

33 And whanne the hiyeste prest preiede, the same yonglyn-gis, clothid in the same clothis, stooden niy Heliodore, and

seiden, Do thou thankyngis to Onyas, the prest; for whi for hym the Lord hath youun lijf to thee;

34 thou sotheli, that art scourgid of God, telle to alle men the grete doyngis and power of God. And whanne these thingis weren seid, thei apperiden not.

35 Heliodore sotheli, whanne a sacrifice was offrid to God, and grete avowis weren bihiyt to hym, that grauntide hym for to lyue, and dide thankyngis to Onyas; and whanne his oost was resseyued, he wente ayen to the kyng.

36 Sotheli he witnesside to alle men the werkis of greet God, whiche he siy vndur hise iyen.

37 Forsothe whanne the kyng axide Heliodore, who was able for to be sent yit onys to Jerusalem,

38 he seide, If thou hast ony enemye, ether traitour of thi rewme, sende thidur, and thou schalt resseyue hym betun, if netheles he schal scape; for sum vertu of God is verili in the place.

39 For whi he that hath dwellyng in heuenys, is visitere and helpere of that place; and he smytith and lesith hem, that comen to mysdo. Therfor of Heliodore, and kepyng of the tre-serie, thus the thing hath it silf.

CAP 4

1 Simount forsothe biforseid, accusere of 'cuntree, and of richessis, spak yuel of Onyas, as if he had stirid Heliodore to these thingis, and he hadde be stirere of yuels;

2 and he durst seie the puruyour of the citee, and defendere of his folc, and louyere of the lawe of God, traitour of the rewme.

3 But whanne enemytees camen forth in so myche, that also bi summe famyliar frendis of Symount mansleyngis weren don,

4 Onyas bihelde the perel of strijf, and that Appolonye was wood, as duyk of Celessirie and Fenyce, for to encreesse the malice of Symount. And Onyas yaf him silf to the kyng;

5 not as accusere of citeseyns, but biholdyng anentis him silf the comyn profit of al the multitude.

6 For he siy, that it was impossible that pees were youun to thingis with out the kyngis puruyaunce, and that Symount myyte not ceesse of his foli.

7 But after the passyng out of Seleucus lijf, whanne Antiok, that was clepid noble, hadde takun rewme, Jasoun, the brother of Onyas, coueitide the hiyeste presthod; and Jason yede to the kyng,

8 and bihiyte to hym thre hundrid talentis and sixti of siluer, and of othere rentes fourescore talentis;

9 ouer these thingis he bihiyte also othere talentis an hundrid and fifti, if it were grauntid to his power, for to ordeyne a scole, and gaderyng, 'ether bordel hous, of yonge men to hym; and for to write hem that weren in Jerusalem 'men of Antiochus.

10 And whanne the kyng hadde grauntid this, and he weldide the prynshod, anoon he bigan for to translate to hethene cus-tom men of his lynage.

11 And whanne these thingis weren don awei, whiche bi cause of humanyte, 'ether curtesie, weren ordeyned of kyngis to Jewis bi Joon, the fadir of Eupolemy, which was ordeyned in lawful message of frenschip and felouschip anentis Romayns, he distriede lawis of citeseyns, and made schrewid ordenaunces;

12 for he was hardi for to ordeyne a scole of hethenesse vndur that hiy tour, and for to put alle the beste of faire yonge men in bordel housis.

13 Forsothe this was not bigynnyng, but sum encreessyng and profit of hethene and alien lijf, for the vnleueful and vnherd greet trespas of vnpitouse, and not prest Jason;

14 so that prestis not now weren youun aboute offices of the auter, but thei dispisiden the temple, and leften sacrifices, and thei hastiden for to be maad felowis of wrastling, and of vniust yyuyng of hym, and in ocupaciouns of a disch, 'ether pleiyng with a ledun disch.

15 And sotheli thei hadden onouris of fadris at nouyt, and demyden Greke glories beste.

16 For cause of which perelouse contension hadde hem, and thei folewiden her ordynaunces; and bi alle thingis thei coueitiden hem for to be lijk hem, whiche thei hadden enemyes and distrieris.

17 Forsothe for to do vnfeithfuli ayens Goddis lawes it bifallith not with out peyne, but the tyme suynge schal declare these thingis.

18 Sotheli whanne iustus, doon onys in fyue yeer, was maad solempli in Tire, and the kyng was present,

19 Jason ful of grete trespassis sente fro Jerusalem men synneris, berynge thre hundrid double dragmes of siluer in to sacrifice of Erculis; whiche these men that baren out axiden, that tho weren not youun in sacrifices, for it nedide not, but that tho schulen be ordeyned in to othere spensis.

20 But sotheli these weren offrid of him that sente in to the sacrifice of Ercules; sotheli for men present tho ben youun in to makyng of grete schippis.

21 Forsothe Appolonye, sone of Nestei, was sent in to Egipt for primatis, 'ether princes, of Tolome Philometor, the kyng; whanne Antiok knew him maad alyen fro nedis of the rewme, he counselide for his owne profitis, and yede fro thennus, and cam to Joppe, and fro thennus to Jerusalem.

22 And he was resseyued of Jason and the citee worschipfuli, with liytis of brondis, and preisyngis, and wente yn, and fro thennus he turnede the oost in to Fenyce.

23 And aftir the tyme of thre yeer Jason sente Menelaus, the brother of Symount aboue seid, berynge richessis to the kyng, and of necessarie causis to berynge answeris.

24 And he was comendid to the kyng, and, whanne he hadde magnefiede the face of his power, he turnyde in to hym silf the hiyeste presthod, and settide aboue Jason thre hundrid talentis of siluer.

25 And bi maundementis takun of the kyng, he cam, sotheli hauynge no thing worthi to presthod; but he bar the soule of a cruel tiraunt, and wraththe of wielde beeste.

26 And sotheli thilke Jason, that took his owne brother caitif, was disseyued, and outlawid, and put out in to the cuntree of Amanythen.

27 But Menelaus forsothe weldide the prinshod, but of richessis bihiyt to the kyng he dide no thing, whanne Sostratus, that was souereyn of the hiy tour, made 'maisterful axyng,

28 for whi reisyng of tributis perteynede to hym; for whiche cause bothe weren clepid to the kyng.

29 And Menelaus was remoued fro presthod, and Lysimacus, his brother, was successour; sotheli Sostratus was maad souereyn of men of Cipre.

30 And whanne these thingis weren don, it bifelle Tarsensis and Mallotis for to moue debate, for that thei weren youun in yifte to the concubyn of Antiok, kyng.

31 Therefor the kyng hastili cam, for to swage hem, and lefte oon of his eerlis suffectus Andronyk 'in dignyte, 'ether lutenaunt.

32 Forsothe Menelaus demyde that he hadde taken couenable tyme, and stal summe goldun vessels of the temple, and yaf to Andronik, and he selde to Tire othere, and bi niy citees.

33 And whanne Onyas hadde knowun this thing most certeynli, he repreuyde hym, and helde him silf in a sikir place at Antiochie, bisidis Daphnen.

34 Wherfor Menelaus yede to Andronik, and preiede that he wolde sle Onyas. And whanne he cam to Onyas, and hadde youe riythondis with an ooth, thouy he was suspect to him, he counselide hym for to go forth of asile, and anoon he slow hym, and dredde not riytwisnes.

35 For which cause not oneli Jewis, but and othere naciouns, weren wrothe, and baren heuyli of the vniust deth of so greet a man.

36 But Jewis at Antiochie, and Grekis, togidere playneden of the vniust deth of Onyas, and wenten to the king, that turnede ayen fro places of Cilicie.

37 Therfor the kyng Antiok was sori in soule for Onyas, and was bowid to merci, and schedde teeris, and bithouyte on the sobrenesse and myldenesse of the deed man.

38 And his herte was kyndlid, and he comaundide that Andronyk, vnclothid of purpur, be led aboute bi al the citee, and that in that place in which he hadde don vnpitee ayens Onyas, the cursid man be priuyd of lijf; for the Lord yaf to hym euene worthi peyne.

39 Forsothe whanne manye sacrilegijs weren don of Lisymacus, bi counsel of Menelaus, in the temple, and the fame was pupplischid, multitude was gaderid ayens Lisymacus; for myche gold was thanne borun out.

40 Forsothe whanne the cumpenyes risiden, and soulis weren fillid with wraththe, Lisymacus bigan for to vse almest thre thousynd armyd wickid hondis, bi sum tyraunt ledere, elde in age and also in woodnesse.

41 But as thei vndurstoden the enforsyng of Lysimacus, othere token stoonys, othere stronge stafis, summe sotheli castiden aische in to Lysimacus.

42 And many sotheli weren woundid, summe forsothe weren cast doun, alle forsothe weren togidere turnyd in to fliyt; also thei slowen hym sacrilegere, ether 'theef of hooli thingis, bisidis the treserie.

43 Therfor of these thingis dom bigan for to be mouyd ayens Menelaus.

44 And whanne the kyng cam to Tire, thre men weren sent of the eldere men, and brouyten the cause to him.

45 And whanne Menelaus was ouercomun, he bihiyte for to yyue many richessis to Tolome, for to counsele the kyng.

46 Therfor Tolome wente to the king, set in sum porche, as for cause of refreityng, ether coolding, and ledde awei fro sentence;

47 and assoilide fro crymes Menelaus, gilti treuli of al the malice. Forsothe he dampnede bi deth these wretchis, whiche schulden be demed innocentis, yhe, if thei hadden led cause anentis Scitis.

48 Therfor soone thei yauen vniust peyne to hem, that pursueden cause for the citee, and puple, and hooli vessels.

49 Wherfor and men of Tire weren wrothe, and weren most liberal ayens the biriynge of hem.

50 Forsothe for coueitise of hem that weren in power, Menelaus dwelte in power, wexynge in malice, and to disseitis of citeseyns.

CAP 5

1 In the same tyme Antiok made redi the secounde goyng in to Egipt.

2 Forsothe it bifelle, that bi ech citee of men of Jerusalem, weren seyn bi fourti daies horse men rennynge aboute the eir, hauynge goldun stoolis, and schaftis, as cumpenyes of knyytis armyd;

3 and coursis of horsis wiseli set bi ordris, and asailyngis for to be maad niy, and mouyngis of scheldis, and multitude of helmyd men, with streyned swerdis, and castyngis of dartis, and schynyng of goldun armeris, and of al kynde of haburiouns.

4 Wherfor alle men preieden, that the monstris, 'ether wondris, tokene of thingis to comynge, be conuertid in to good.

5 But whanne fals tithing wente out, as if Antiok hadde goon out of lijf, Jason sudenli assaylide the citee, with men takun not lesse than a thousynde; and whanne citeseyns fledden to the wal togidere, and at the laste the citee was takun, Menelaus fledde to the hiy tour.

6 Forsothe Jason sparide not in sleynge his citeseyns, nether he thouyte prosperite ayens cosyns; and he demyde it for to be moost yuel, that he schulde take victories of enemyes, and not of citeseyns.

7 And sotheli he weldide not prinshod, but took confusioun ende of his disseitis; and he flei eft, and wente in to Ammanythen.

8 And at the last in to vndoyng of him, he was closid togidere of Areta, tiraunt of Arabeis, and fley fro citee in to citee, and was odious to alle men, as apostata, 'ether forsakere of lawis, and abhomynable, as enemye of cuntre and citeseyns, and was cast out in to Egipt.

9 And he that hadde put out many of her cuntre, perischide in pilgrimage, and yede to Lacedomonas, as for cosynage to haue there refut.

10 And he that castide awei many vnbiried, is cast out bothe vnweilid and vnbiried, and nether vsith straunge sepulture, nether takith part of fadris sepulcre.

11 And whanne these thingis weren don so, the kyng supposide, that Jewis schulden forsake felouschip; and for this he yede out of Egipt with woode soulis, and took the citee sotheli with armeris.

12 Forsothe he comaundide to the knyytis, for to sle, nether spare to men rennynge ayens, and to stie vp bi housis, and strangle.

13 Therfor ther weren maad sleyngis of yonge and eldere, distriyngis of wymmen and children, and dethis of maidens and litle children.

14 Forsothe in alle thre daies foure score thousynde weren slayn, fourti thousynde boundun, forsothe not lesse seld; but nether these thingis sufficen.

15 Also he was hardi for to entre in to the temple holiere than al the lond, bi Menelaus ledere, that was traitour of lawis and cuntre.

16 And he touchide vnworthily, and defoulide, takynge in cursid hondis the hooli vessels, that weren put of othere kyngis and citees, to ournyng and glorie of the place.

17 Antiok was so alienyd fro mynde, and bihelde not, that, for synnes of men enhabitynge, the Lord was wroth a litil to the citee; for which thing also dispisyng bifelle aboute the place.

18 Ellis if it had not bifeld hem for to be wlappid in many synnes, as Eliodore, that was sent fro kyng Seleucus for to robbe the treserie, also this anoon comynge schulde be betun, and forsothe put a bak fro hardynesse.

19 But the Lord chees not the folc for the place, but place for the folk.

20 And therfor also thilke place was maad parcener of yuelis of the puple; aftirward forsothe it schal be maad felowe also of goodis, and it, that is forsakun in wraththe of almyyti God, eftsoone in recounselyng of the greet Lord schal be enhaunsid with greet glorie.

21 Therfor Antiok, whanne he hadde takun awei a thousynde and eiyte hundrid talentis of the temple, swiftli turnede ayen to Antiochie, and demyde hym for pride to lede the lond for to seile, the see forsothe for to make iournei, for pride of soule.

22 Forsothe he lefte also souereyns, to turmente the folc, in Jerusalem sotheli Filip, of the kyn of Frigeus, cruelere than hym silf in maneris, of whom he was ordeyned;

23 forsothe in Garisym, Andronik and Menelaus, whiche more greuousli than othere laien on citeseyns.

24 And whanne he was set ayens Jewis, he sente an odious prince, Appollonye, with an oost two and twenti thousyndis, and comaundide to hym for to sle al of perfit age, for to sille wymmen and yonge children.

25 Whiche whanne he cam to Jerusalem, feynede pees, and restide til to the holi dai of sabat. And thanne while Jewis helden halidai, he comaundide his men for to take armeris,

26 and stranglide alle that camen forth togidere to the biholdyng; and he ran aboute the citee with armed men, and slowe a greet multitude.

27 Forsothe Judas Machabeus, that was the tenthe, wente in to desert place, and there ledde lijf with his men, among wielde beestis in hillis; and dwelten etynge mete of hey, lest thei weren parceneres of defoulyng.

CAP 6

1 But not aftir myche tyme the king sente an elde man of Antiochie, which schulde constreyne Jewis, that thei schulden translate hem silf fro lawis of fadris and of God;

2 also he schulde defoule the temple, 'that was in Jerusalem, and schulde clepe it of Jouis Olympij, and in Garisym, as thei weren, that enhabitiden the place, of Jouis hospital.

3 Forsothe the fallyng in of yuels was worste and greuouse to alle;

4 for whi the temple was ful of letcherie and glotenye of hethene men, and of men doynge letcherie with horis, aud wymmen baren in hem silf to halewid housis, at her owne wille, berynge with ynne tho thingis whiche it was not leueful.

5 Also the auter was ful of vnleueful thingis, whiche weren forbodun bi lawis.

6 Sotheli nether sabatis weren kept, nether solempne daies of fadris weren kept, nether sympli, 'ether opynli, ony man knoulechide hym a Jew.

7 Forsothe thei weren led with bittir nede in the dai of the kyngis birthe to sacrifices. And whanne hooli thingis of Liber, 'that is, Bacus, 'ether a false god, which hethene men clepiden god of wyn, weren maad solempli, thei weren crownyd with yuy, and weren constreyned for to go aboute with Liber.

8 Sotheli the doom wente out in to the nexte citees of hethene men, bi Tolomeis procurynge, that in lijk maner also thei schulden do ayens Jewis, that thei schulden do sacrifice;

9 sotheli that thei schulden sle hem, that wolden not passe to ordynaunces of hethene men. Therfor it was to se wretchidnesse.

10 For whi twei wymmen weren accusid, that thei hadden circumcidid her children; and whanne thei hadden ledde hem aboute opynli bi the citee, with infauntis hangid at brestis, thei castiden doun bi the wallis.

11 Forsothe othere men yeden togidere to the nexte dennes, and halewiden pryueli the dai of sabat, whanne thei weren schewid to Filip, thei weren brent in flawmes, for thei dredden for religioun and obseruaunce, for to bere help to hem silf with hond.

12 Therfore Y biseche hem, that schulen rede this book, that thei 'drede not for aduersitees; but arette thei tho thingis that bifellen to be not to perischyng, but to amendyng of oure kyn.

13 For whi for to not suffre bi myche tyme synneris for to do of sentence, but anoon for to yyue veniaunces, is the schewing of greet benefice.

14 For whi, not as in othere naciouns, the Lord abidith pacientli, that whanne the dai of dom schal come, he punysche hem in plente of synnes,

15 so and in vs he ordeyneth, that whanne oure synnes ben turned aboute in to ende, so at the laste he venge on vs.

16 For which thing sotheli he neuer remoueth his merci fro vs; but he chastisith his puple, and forsakith not in aduersitees.

17 But these thingis ben seid of vs in fewe wordis to the monestyng of men redynge; now forsothe it is to come to the tellyng.

18 Therfor Eleasarus, oon of the formere of scribis, a man wexun in age, and 'fair in cheer, was compellid, 'yanynge with open mouth, for to ete swynes fleisch.

19 And he 'biclippide, ether chees, more glorious deth, than hateful lijf, and wilfuli wente bifore to turment.

20 Forsothe he bihelde hou it bihofte for to go, and suffride pacientli, and ordeynede for to not do vnleueful thingis for the loue of lijf.

21 Sotheli these that stoden nyy, weren mouyd to gidere bi wickid merci, for eld frenschip of the man, and thei token hym priueli, and preiede that fleischis schulden be brouyt, whiche it was leueful to hym for to ete, that he were feyned to haue etun, as the kyng comaundide, of the fleischis of sacrifice;

22 that bi this dede he schulde be delyuered fro deth; and for eld frenschip of the man, thei dide this curtesie in hym.

23 And he bigan for to thenke the worthi excellence of age, and of his elde, and 'fre borun horenesse of noblei, and of best lyuyng fro child; and bi the ordynaunces of holi lawe, and maad of God, he answeride soone, seiynge, that he wolde be sent bifore in to helle.

24 For he seide, It is not worthi to oure age for to feyne, that many yonge men deme, that Eleasarus of foure score yeer and ten, hath passid to the lijf of aliens,

25 and that thei ben disseyued for my feynyng, and for litil tyme of corruptible lijf, and that bi this Y gete spotte and cursidnesse to myn eelde.

26 For whi thouy in present tyme Y be delyuered fro turmentis of men, but nether quyk nether deed Y schal ascape the hond of Almyyti.

27 Wherfor in passynge the lijf strongli, sotheli Y schal appere worthi of age;

28 forsothe Y schal leue stronge ensaumple to yonge men, if Y vse perfitli onest deth with redi wille, and strongli for the worthieste and holieste lawis. Whanne these thingis weren seid, anoon he was drawun to turment.

29 Forsothe these that ledden hym, and a litil bifore weren myldere, weren turned in to wraththe, for the wordis seid of hym, whiche thei demyden brouyt forth bi pride of herte.

30 But whanne he schulde be slayn with woundis, he sorewide inwardli, and seide, Lord, that hast hooli kunnyng, openli thou woost, that whanne Y myyte be delyuered fro deth, Y suffre hard sorewis of bodi; forsothe bi soule wilfuli Y suffre these thingis for thi drede.

31 And sotheli this man on this maner departide fro lijf; not oneli leuynge the mynde of his deth to yonge men, but and to al the folc, to ensaumple of vertu and strengthe.

CAP 7

1 Forsothe it bifelle, that seuene britheren takun togidere with the modir, weren constreyned of the kyng for to taaste ayens the lawe swynes fleischis; and weren turmentid with scourgyngis, and turment maad of bole lether.

2 Forsothe oon of hem, that was the first, seide thus, What sekist thou? and what wolt thou lerne of vs? we ben redi for to die, more than to breke the fadris lawes of God.

3 Therfor the kyng was wroth, and comaundide 'pannes of bras, and brasun pottis for to be maad ful hoot. And whan tho anoon werin maad ful hoot,

4 he comaundide the tunge for to be kit of fro hym that spak bifore; and whanne the skynne of the heed was drawun awei, he bad bothe the hiyeste partis of hondis and of feet 'of hym for to be kit of, the while othere britheren and the modir 'of hym bihelden.

5 And whanne he was maad thanne vnprofitable bi alle thingis, he comaundide fier for to be brouyt to him, and yit 'al quik brethinge for to be brent in the brasun panne; in which whanne he was longe turmentid, the othere togidere with the modir, 'coumfortiden hem togidere for to die strongli,

6 seiynge, The Lord God schal biholde treuthe, and schal 'yyue solace in vs, as Moises declaride 'in bifore witnessyng of song, and among his seruauntis he schal yife coumforte.

7 Therfor whanne thilke firste was deed in this maner, thei ledden forth the nexte for to be scornyd; and whanne the skyn of his heed was drawun of, with the heeris, thei axiden, if he wolde ete, bifore that he were punyschid in al the bodi, bi alle membris bi hem silf.

8 And he answeride bi the vois of fadris, and seide, Y schal not do it. For which 'cause this also, in a place faste bi, resseyuede lijk turmentis of the firste.

9 And whanne he was ordeyned in the laste spirit, he seide thus, Sotheli thou most wickid lesist vs in this lijf, but the kyng of the world schal reise 'vs that ben deede for his lawis, in ayenrisinge of euerlastinge lijf.

10 After this the thridde was scorned; and whanne he was bede, he 'profride soone forth the tunge, and stidfastli helde forth the hondis,

11 and 'seide, Of God of heuene Y welde these lymes, but for the lawis of God now Y dispise these same; for Y hope, that Y schal resseyue tho of him.

12 So that the kyng, and thei that weren with hym, wondriden on the wisdom of the yonge man, that he ledde the turmentis as nouyt.

13 And whanne this was thus deed, thei traueliden the fourthe, and turmentiden in lijk maner.

14 And whanne he was thanne at the deth, he seide thus, 'Wel the rather it is ned, that men youun to deth of men, abide hope of God, that schulen be reisid ayen 'eft of him; for ayen risyng to lijf schal not be to thee.

15 And whanne thei hadden brouyt the fyuethe, thei traueliden hym. And he bihelde in to hym,

16 and seide, Thou hast power among men, 'and thouy thou be corruptible, thou doist what thou wolt; but nyl thou gesse, that oure kyn is forsakun of God.

17 But abide thou pacientli, and thou schalt se the greet power of hym, hou he schal turmente thee, and thi seed.

18 After thei ledden also the sixte; and this bigan for to die, and seide thus, Nyle thou erre idili; for we suffren these thingis for vs silf, synnynge ayens oure God, and thingis worthi of wondryng ben maad in vs;

19 but deme thou not, that it schal be with out peyne to thee, that thou hast temptid for to fiyte ayens God.

20 Forsothe the 'merueylous moder of hem, and worthi the mynde of goode men, which bihelde seuene sones perischynge vndur the tyme of o day, 'and suffride aboue manere with good wille, for the hope that sche hadde in to God;

21 sche monestide ech of hem bi vois of fadris, 'that is, acordynge to the techyng of hooli fadris, and was strongli fillid with wisdom, and settide mannus witte to wommanys thouyt,

22 and seide to hem, Sones, Y woot not hou ye apperiden in my wombe; for nether Y haue youun to you spirit, and soule, and lijf, and Y my silf ioynede not togidere the membris of ech;

23 but the makere of nouyt of the world, that fourmyde natiuyte of man, and foond bigynnyng of alle, schal yelde eft to you spirit, and lijf, with merci, as now ye dispisen you silf for the lawis of hym.

24 Forsothe Antiok demyde hym for to be dispisid, and also bi dispisable vois of a repreuere, and whanne yit the yongere was 'on lyue, not oneli he monestide bi wordis, but and with an ooth he affirmyde, to make hym riche and blissful, and to haue frend, translatid fro lawis of fadris, and to yyue 'to hym nedeful thingis.

25 But whanne the yonge man was not bowid to these thingis, the kyng clepide the modir, and softli counselide hir, that sche schulde be maad to the yonge man in to helth.

26 Forsothe whanne he monestide hir bi many wordis, sche bihiyte hir for to counsele hir sone.

27 Therfor sche bowide down to hym, and scornyde the cruel tiraunt, and seide in cuntrei vois, Sone, haue merci on me, that bar thee in wombe nyne monethis, and yaf mylk bi thre yeer, and nurschide, and fulli brouyte in to this age.

28 Y axe, child, that thou biholde to heuene and erthe, and alle thingis that ben in hem, and vnderstonde, that God made hem of nouyt, and the kynde of men.

29 So it schal be don, that thou drede not this turmentour, but be thou maad worthi to thi britheren, and resseyue deth, that in that merci doyng Y resseyue thee with thi britheren.

30 Whanne sche seide yit these thingis, the yong man seide, Whom abiden ye? Y obeie not to biddyng of the kyng, but to comaundement of the lawe, that was youun to vs bi Moises.

31 Forsothe thou, that art maad fyndere of al malice ayens Ebrewis, schalt not ascape the hond of God.

32 For we suffren these thingis for oure synnes;

33 thouy oure Lord be a litil wroth to vs for blamyng and chastisyng, but eft he schal be recounselid to hise seruauntis.

34 Forsothe thou cursid, and most flagiciouse, ether fulleste of yuel doyngis, and stiryngis, of alle men, nyle thou veynli be enhaunsid, that art enflaumyd bi veyn hope ayens his seruauntis;

35 for thou hast not scapid yit the dom of almyyti God, and biholdynge alle thingis.

36 'For whi my britheren suffriden now a litil sorewe, and ben maad vndur testament of euerlastynge lijf; thou sotheli bi dom of God schalt paie iust peynes of pride.

37 Sotheli 'Y as my britheren, bitake my soule and bodi for lawis of fadris; and Y clepe God to help, that more ripeli he be maad helpful to oure folc, and that thou knouleche with turmentis 'and betyngis, that he is God aloone.

38 Forsothe the wraththe of Almyyti schal faile in me and in my britheren, which is iustli brouyte in on al oure kyn.

39 Thanne the kyng was kyndlid with wrath, and was fers ayens hym more crueli aboue alle; and bar vnworthili, 'ether heuyli, hym silf scorned.

40 Therfor and this was clene, and diede, tristynge bi alle thingis in the Lord.

41 Forsothe at the laste also the modir was wastid, after the sones.

42 Therfor of sacrifices, and ouer greet crueltees, is ynowy seid.

CAP 8

1 Forsothe Judas Machabeus, and thei that weren with hym, entriden priueli in to castels; and clepiden togidere cosyns, and frendis, and token hem that dwelten in Judee, ether in kepyng of the lawe of Jewis, and ledden out men to sixe thousyndis.

2 And thei clepiden the Lord to help, for to biholde on the puple, that was defoulid of alle men; for to haue merci on the temple, that was defoulid of vnpitouse men;

3 and for to haue merci on distriyng of the citee, that was anoon to be maad pleyn togidere; and for to here the vois of blood criynge to hym,

4 and for to haue mynde on the wikidiste dethis of litle children innocentis, and of blasfemyes youun to his name; and for to haue indignacioun on these thingis.

5 And Machabeus, with the multitude gaderid, was maad vnsuffrable to hethene men; for the wraththe of the Lord was conuertid in to merci.

6 And he aboue cam to castels and citees, vnwarned, and brente hem; and ocupiede couenable places, and yaf not fewe sleyngis of enemyes.

7 Sotheli in niytis he was most borun to seche out rennyngis; and fame of his vertu was sched out euery where.

8 Forsothe Filip siy, that the man bi litil and litil cam to encrees, and that ful ofte thingis bifalliden to hym 'in prosperite; and he wroot to Tolome, duyk of Celessirie and of Fenice, that he schulde bere help to the kyngis nedis.

9 And he swiftli sente Nycanor of Patrode, of the formere frendis, and yaf 'to hym not lesse than twenti thousyndis of armed folkis meynt togidere, for to do awei al the kyn of Jewis; and ordeynede to hym Gorgie, a knyytli man, and most expert in thingis of batel.

10 Forsothe Nycanor bihiyte stidfastly to the kyng, that he schulde fille the tribut that was to be youun to Romayns, two thousyndis of talentis, of the caitifte of Jewis.

11 And anoon he sente to citees of the see coost, and clepide togidere to euenbiyng of prisoneris, ether of boonde men, of Jewis; and bihiyte, that he schal sille nynti boonde men for a talent, not biholdynge to the veniaunce that schulde sue hym of Almiyti.

12 Forsothe whanne Judas foond, he schewide to these Jewis that weren with hym, the comyng of Nycanor.

13 Of which summe inwardli dredden, and bileuyden not to the riytwisnesse of God, and weren turned in to fliyt;

14 othere sotheli, if ony leften of hem, camen, and togidere bisouyten the Lord, for to delyuere hem fro wyckid Nycanor, which hadde seld hem bifore that he cam niy;

15 and thouy not for hem, for the testament that was to the fadris of hem, and for clepyng to help of his hooli name and greet on hem.

16 Forsothe Machabeus clepide togidere seuene thousyndis that weren with hym, and preiede, that thei schulden not be recounselid to enemyes, nether schulden drede the multitude of enemyes wickidli comynge ayens hem, but strongli schulden fiyte;

17 hauynge bifore the iyen the dispit that was don in the hooli place vniustli of hem, and also the wrong of the citee, had in scornyng; yit also the ordenaunces of elde men distried.

18 For whi he seide, Thei sotheli tristen in armeris togidere and hardynesse; forsothe we tristen in the Lord almyyti, that may do awei with o lokyng bothe hem that comen ayens vs, and al the world.

19 Forsothe he monestide hem also of helpis of God, that weren don ayens fadris; and that vndur Senacherib an hundrid thousynde foure score thousynde and fyue thousindes perischiden;

20 and of the batel that was to hem ayens Galatas, in Babiloyne; 'whether if it come to the thing, 'ethir treuthe, whanne alle felowis Macedoyns doutiden, thei sixe thousandis aloone slowen an hundrid thousynde and twenti thousyndis, for help youun to hem fro heuene; and for these thingis thei hadden ful many benefices.

21 Bi thes wordis thei weren maad stidfast, and redi for to die for lawis and cuntre.

22 Therfor he ordeynede his britheren lederis to ech ordre, Symount, and Josofus, and Jonathas, 'and made suget to ech a thousynde and fyue hundrid.

23 Also to this thing, whanne the hooli book was red to hem of Esra, and a tokene was youun of Goddis help, he was duyk in the firste scheltrun, and ioynede batel with Nycanor.

24 And for the Almyyty was maad helpere to hem, thei slowen ouer nyne thousynde of men; forsothe thei constreyneden the more part of Nycanoris oost, maad feble bi woundis, for to fle.

25 Forsothe whanne the richessis of hem that camen to the biyng of hem weren takun vp, on ech side thei pursueden hem;

26 but thei turneden ayen closid togidere bi an our; for whi it was bifor sabat, for which cause thei lastiden not pursuynge.

27 Forsothe thei gaderiden the armeris of hem, and spuylis, and diden sabat, and blessiden the Lord, that delyuerede hem in this dai, droppynge in to hem bigynnyng of merci.

28 Forsothe after the sabat thei departiden spuylis to the feble folkis, and fadirles, and modirles, and widewis; and thei with hern hadden the residues.

29 Whanne these thingis weren thus don, and comynli of alle men bysechyng was maad, thei axiden the merciful Lord, for to be recounselid in to the ende to hise seruauntis.

30 And of these that weren with Tymothe and Bachides, stryuynge ayens hem silf, thei slowen ouer twenti thousyndis, and thei weldiden hiye strengthis; and thei departiden mo preies, and maden euene porcioun to feble folc, fadirles, and modirles, and widewis, but and to eldere men.

31 And whanne thei hadden gaderid the armeris of hem, diligentli thei 'puttiden togidere alle thingis in couenable places; forsothe thei baren to Jerusalem the residue spuylis.

32 And thei slowen Filarces, that was with Tymothe, a man ful of grete trespassis, that hadde turmentide Jewis in many thingis.

33 And whanne feestis of victorie weren don in Jerusalem, thei brenten hem that hadden brent hooli yatis, that is to seie, Calastenes, whanne he hadde flowun in to an hous; for whi worthi meede was yoldun to hem for her vnpitousnessis.

34 Forsothe the wickidist Nycanor, that brouyte a thousynde marchauntis to the sillyng of Jewis,

35 was mekid bi help of the Lord, of hem which he gesside noon; and whanne he hadde put awei the cloth of glorie, he fledde aloon bi priuy places, and cam to Antiochie, and hadde hiyeste wretchidnesse of the deth of his oost.

36 And he that bihiyte hym for to restore tribute to Romayns, of the caitifte of men of Jerusalem, prechide now that Jewis hadde o defendere God, and for hym thei weren vnable for to be woundid, for thei sueden lawis ordeyned of hym.

CAP 9

1 In the same tyme Antiok turnede ayen vnonestli fro Perses.

2 For he hadde entrid into that citee, that is seid Persibolis, and he temptide for to robbe the temple, and oppresse the citee; but for multitude ran togidere to armeris, thei weren turned in to fliyt; and so it bifelle, that Antiok after fliyt viliche turnede ayen.

3 And whanne he cam aboute Ebathana, he knew what thingis weren don ayens Nycanor and Tymothe.

4 Forsothe he was enhaunsid in wraththe, and demede that he myyte turne in to Jewis the wrong of hem, that hadden dryuun hym. And therfor he bad the chare for to be led in haste, doynge iourney with out ceessyng; for whi heuenli doom constreynede hym, for that he spak so proudli, that he schal come to Jerusalem, and to make it a gaderyng of sepulcre of Jewis.

5 But the Lord God of Israel, that biholdith alle thingis, smoot hym with a wounde incurable and inuisible; for as he endide this same word, an hard sorewe of entrails took hym, and bittere turmentis of inward thingis.

6 And sotheli iustli ynowy, for he that hadde turmentid the entrails of othere men, with many and newe turmentis, thouy he in no maner ceesside of his malice.

7 Forsothe ouer this he was fillid with pride, and brethide fier in soule ayens Jewis, and comaundynge the nede for to be hastid, it bifelle, that he goynge in fersnesse fallide doun of the chare, and that the membris weren trauelid with the greuouse hurtlyng togidere of bodi.

8 And he that semyde to hym silf for to comaunde also to wawis of the see, and ouer mannus maner was fillid with pride, and for to weie in balaunce the hiythis of hillis, was maad low to erthe, and was borun in a beere, and witnesside in him silf the opyn vertu of God;

9 so that wormes buyliden out of the bodi of the vnpitouse man, and the quyke fleischis of hym fletiden out in sorewis. Also with the sauour 'of hym, and stynkynge, the oost 'of hym was greuyd;

10 and no man myyte bere hym, for vnsuffryng of stynk, that a litil bifore demyde hym for to touche the sterris of heuene.

11 Therfor herbi he was led doun fro greuouse pride, and bigan for to come to knowyng of hym silf, and was warned bi Goddis veniaunce, for bi alle momentis his sorewis token encreessis.

12 And whanne he myyte not thanne suffre his stynk, thus he seide, It is iust for to be suget to God, and that a deedli man feele not euene thingis to God.

13 Forsothe the cursid man preiede the Lord of these thingis, of whom he schulde 'not gete merci.

14 And now he desirith to yelde fre the citee, to which he cam hastynge, for to drawe doun it to erthe, and for to make a sepulcre of thingis borun togidere.

15 And now he bihetith to make the Jewis euene to men of Athenys, whiche Jewis he seide that he schulde not haue worthi, yhe, of sepulture, but to bitake to foulis and wielde beestis, for to be 'to-drawun, and for to distrie with litle children;

16 also to ourne with beste yiftis the hooli temple, which he robbide bifore, and to multiplie hooli vessels, and to yyuynge of his rentis costis perteynynge to sacrifices;

17 ouer these thingis and that he schal be maad a Jewe, and to walke bi ech place of the lond, and to preche 'the power of God.

18 But, for sorewis ceesiden not, the iust doom of God hadde aboue come on hym, he disperide, and wroot to Jewis, bi maner of bisechyng, 'a pistle, conteynynge thes thingis.

19 To the beste citeseyns, Jewis, moost heelthe, and welfare, and to be riche, 'ether in prosperite, the kyng and prince Antiok.

20 If ye faren wel, and youre sones, and alle thingis ben to you of sentence, we don moost thankyngis.

21 And Y am ordeyned in sikenesse, and sotheli Y am myndeful benygneli of you, and Y turnede ayen fro places of Persis, and am cauyt with greuouse infirmyte, and Y ledde nedeful for to haue cure for comyn profit; and Y dispeire not of my silf,

22 but Y haue myche hope to ascape sikenesse.

23 For Y biholde that also my fadir, in what tymes he ledde oost in hiyere places, schewide, who after hym schulde resseyue prinshod; if that ony contrarie thing bifelle,

24 or hard thing were teld, these that weren in cuntreis, schulden wite to whom the summe, 'ether charge, of thingis was left, and schulden not be troblid.

25 To these thingis Y bihelde of next, that alle the myyti men and neiyboris aspien tymes, and abiden comynge, and Y haue ordeyned my sone Antiok kyng, whom Y, rennynge ayen ofte in to hiye rewmes, comendide to many of you, and Y wroot to hym what thingis ben suget.

26 Therfor Y preie you, and axe, that ye ben myndeful of benefices opynli and priueli, and that ech of you kepe feith to me, and to my sone.

27 For Y triste, that he schal do myldely, and manli, and sue my purpos, and be tretable to you.

28 Therfor the manquellere and blasfemere was smytun worst, and as he hadde tretid othere, he diede in pilgrimage in mounteyns, in wretchidful deth.

29 Forsothe Filip, his euene soukere, translatide, 'ether bar ouer, the bodi; which dredde the sone of Antiok, and wente to Tolome Filomethore, in to Egipt.

CAP 10

1 Forsothe Machabeus, and thei that weren with hym, for the Lord defendide hem, resseyuede sotheli the temple, and citee.

2 Forsothe he distriede the auteris, that aliens maden bi stretis, and also templis of waisshyng.

3 And whanne the temple was purgid, thei maden an other auter, and of stoonys firid, 'ether flyntis, bi fier conseyued,

thei offriden sacrifices after two yeer, and puttiden encense, and lanternes, and looues of proposicioun.

4 And whanne these thingis weren don, thei weren cast doun to erthe, and preieden the Lord, that thei schulden no more falle in siche yuelis; but thouy in ony tyme thei hadden synned, that thei schulden be chastised of hym more esili, and schulden not be bitakun to barbaries, and blasfeme men.

5 Forsothe in what dai the temple was defoulid of aliens, it bifelle that in the same dai clensyng was maad, in the fyue and twentithe dai of the monethe, that was Casleu.

6 And with gladnesse in eiyte daies thei diden bi maner of tabernaclis, bithenkynge that bifore a litil of tyme thei hadden don the solempne dai of tabernaclis in hillis and in dennys, bi custom of beestis.

7 For which thing thei baren byfore roddis, and grene braunchis, and palmes, to hym that yaf prosperite for to clense his place.

8 And thei demyden with comyn heest, and with doom, to alle the folc of Jewis, for to do these feeste daies in alle yeeris.

9 And the endyng of lijf of Antiok, that was clepid noble, hadde it thus.

10 Now forsothe we schulen telle of Eupator, sone of vnpitouse Antiok, what thingis weren don, and bregge, 'ether schortli telle, the yuelis that weren don in batels.

11 For whanne this Eupator hadde resseyued the rewme, he ordeynede on nedis of the rewme a man Lisias, prince of knyythod, of Fenece and Sirie.

12 For whi Tolome, that was seid Macer, ordeynede for to holde iust thing ayens Jewis, and most for wickidnesse that was don ayens hem, and pesibli for to do with hem.

13 But for this thing he was accusid of frendis anentis Eupator, whanne he herde ofte, Thou traitour, for that he hadde forsakun Cipre, bitakun to hym of Filometor, and hadde translatid to Antiok noble, also he hadde go awei fro hym, with venym he endide the lijf.

14 Forsothe Gorgias, whanne he was duyk of places, with comelyngis takun, ouercam ofte Jewis in batel.

15 Forsothe Jewis that helden couenable strengthis, resseyueden men dryuun fro Jerusalem, and saieden for to fiyte.

16 These forsothe that weren with Machabeus, preieden the Lord bi preieris, that he schulde be helpere to hem, and thei maden asawt in to strengthis of Idumeis.

17 And thei weren bisi bi myche strengthe, and weldiden places, and slowen men rennynge ayen, and strangliden alle togidere, not lesse than fyue and twenti thousandes.

18 Forsothe whanne summe fledden togidere in to twei touris ful stronge, hauynge alle apparel to ayen fiyte,

19 Machabeus lefte Symount, and Josofus, and eft Sachee, and hem that weren with hem, many ynow, to the ouercomyng of hem; and he was conuertid to tho batels that constreyneden more.

20 Sotheli these that weren with Symount, weren led bi coueitise, and weren counselid bi monei, of summe that weren in the touris; and whanne thei hadden take seuenti thousynde double dragmes, thei leeten summe fle out.

21 Forsothe whanne that thing that was don, was teld to Machabeus, he gaderide the princes of puple, and he accuside, that thei hadden seld britheren for monei, for thei delyueriden aduersaries of hem.

22 Therfor he slow these maad traitouris, and anoon ocupiede the tweye touris.

23 Forsothe in doynge alle thingis 'in prosperite in armeris and hondis, he slow in the twei strengthis more than twenti thousyndis.

24 And Tymothe, that bifore was ouercomun of Jewis, clepide togidere an oost of straunge multitude, and gaderide the multitude of horse men of Asie, and cam with armeris, as to take Judee.

25 Forsothe Machabeus, and thei that weren with hym, whanne he neiyede, bisouyten God, and bispreynten the heed with erthe, and bifor girdiden the leendis with heiris,

26 and kneliden doun at the brynke of the auter, that he schulde be helpful to hem, forsothe that to enemyes of hem he were enemye, and were aduersarie to aduersaries, as the lawe seith.

27 And so after preier, whanne thei hadden take armeris, thei yeden forth fer fro the citee, and thei weren maad nexte to enemyes, and saten.

28 Forsothe in the firste risyng of the sunne, bothe ioyneden batel; these sotheli hadden the Lord bihetere of victorie and prosperite; for thei hadden hardynesse the duyk of batel.

29 But whanne greet fiyte was, fyue faire men, on horsis with goldun bridels, apperiden to aduersaries fro heuene, and yauen ledyng to Jewis;

30 of whiche tweyne hadden Machabeus in the myddil, and set aboute with her armeris, and kepten hym sownd. Forsothe thei castiden dartis and leitis ayens aduersaries; of which thing and thei weren schent with blyndenesse, and weren fillid with perturbacioun, and fellen doun.

31 Forsothe ther weren slayn of foote men twenti thousynde and fyue hundrid, and horse men sixe hundrid.

32 Sotheli Tymothe fledde in to the strong hold of Gasara, of which strong hold Cereas was souereyn.

33 Forsothe Machabeus, and thei that weren with hym, weren glad, and bisegiden the strong hold bi foure daies.

34 And thei that weren with ynne, tristiden in the sikirnesse of the place, and cursiden aboue maner, and castiden cursid wordis.

35 But whanne the fyuethe dai schynede, twenti yonge men of these that weren with Machabeus, weren kyndlid in soulis for blasfemye, and wenten manli to the wal, and thei yeden with fers wille, and stieden vp;

36 but and othere also stieden, and assailiden for to brenne touris and yatis, and togidere brenne the curseris quyke.

37 Forsothe by contynuel twei daies thei wastiden the strong hold, and slowen Tymothe, hidynge hym silf, foundun in sum place; and thei slowen his brother Cereas, and Appolloffanes.

38 Whanne these thingis weren don, thei blessiden the Lord in ympnes and confessiouns, whiche dide grete thingis in Israel, and yaf to hem victorie.

CAP 11

1 But a litil tyme after, Lisias, the procuratour of the kyng, and kynesman, and souereyn of offices, bar greuousli of these thingis that bifellen,

2 and gederide foure score thousyndis, and al the multitude of horse men, and cam ayens Jewis, and demyde hym silf to make the citee takun a dwellyng to hethene men,

3 forsothe to haue the temple in to wynnyng of monei, as othere templis of hethene men, and presthod 'set to sale bi ech yeer;

4 and bithouyte not on the power of God, but in mynde he was maad with out bridil, and tristide in multitude of foot

men, and in thousyndis of horse men, and in foure score olifauntis.

5 Sothely he yede in to Judee, and cam niy to Bethsura, that was in streit place, fro Jerusalem in space of fyue furlongis, and fauyt ayens that strengthe.

6 Sotheli whanne Machabeus, and thei that weren with hym, knewen that strengthis weren impugned, with wepyng and teeris thei preieden the Lord, and al the cumpenye togidere, for to sende a good aungel to the helthe of Israel.

7 And Machabeus hym silf took firste armeris, and monestide othere for to take togidere perel with hym, and bere help to her britheren.

8 And whanne thei wenten forth togidere with redi wille fro Jerusalem, an hors man apperide goynge bifore hem in whijt cloth, in goldun armeris, and florischynge a schaft.

9 Thanne alle togidere blessiden the merciful Lord, and woxen strong in soulis; and weren redi for to perse not oneli men, but and moost feerse beestis, and irun wallis.

10 Therfor thei wenten redi, hauynge an helpere of heuene, and the Lord hauynge merci on hem.

11 Sotheli bi custom of liouns, in feersnesse thei hurliden in to enemyes, and castiden doun of hem enleuene thousyndis of foot men, and a thousynde and sixe hundrid of horse men.

12 Sotheli thei turneden alle in to fliyt; forsothe many of hem woundid, ascapiden nakid, but and Lisias hym silf fouli fleynge ascapide.

13 And for he was not witles, he arettide with hym silf the makyng lesse don ayens hym, and vndurstood that Ebrews ben vnouercomun, and tristen to help of almyyti God;

14 and he sente to hem, and bihiyte hym to consente to alle thingis that ben iust, and to compelle the kyng for to be maad frend.

15 Forsothe Machabeus grauntide to preieris of Lisias, and counselide to profit in alle thingis; and what euere thingis Machabeus wroot of Jewis to Lisias, the kyng grauntide tho thingis.

16 For whi epistlis weren writun to Jewis fro Lisias, conteynynge this maner. Lisias to the puple of Jewis, heelthe.

17 Joon and Abesalon, that ben sent fro you, bitoken writtis, and axiden, that Y schulde fille tho thingis that weren signefied bi hem.

18 Therfor what euere thingis miyten be brouyt forth to the kyng, Y expownede, and whiche the thing suffride, he grauntide.

19 Therfor if in nedis ye kepen feith, also fro hennys forth Y schal enforse for to be cause of goode thingis to you.

20 Of othere thingis sotheli Y comaundide bi alle wordis, both to these and to hem that ben sent of me, for to speke togidere with you.

21 Fare ye wel. In the hundrid yeer and eiyte and fourtithe, in the foure and twentith dai of the monethe Dioscorus.

22 Forsothe 'the pistle of the kyng conteynede thes thingis. Kyng Antiok to Lisias, brother, heelthe.

23 For oure fadir is translatid among goddis, we wolen that thei that ben in oure rewme do with out noise, and yyue diligence to her thingis;

24 we han herd that Jewis assentiden not to the fadir, for to be translatid to the custom of Grekis, bot wolen holde her ordynaunce, and that therfor thei axen of vs, that her lawful thingis be grauntid to hem.

25 Therfor we wolen that also this folc be quyet, and han ordeyned and demed, that the temple be restorid to hem, that thei schulden do bi the custom of her grettere men.

26 Therfor thou schalt do wel, if thou schalt sende to hem, and schalt yyue riythond; that, whanne oure wille is knowun, thei be in good coumfort, and serue to her owne profitis.

27 Sotheli to the Jewis the kyngis pistle was sich. Kyng Antiok to the 'eldre men of Jewis, and to othere Jewis, heelthe.

28 If ye faren wel, so it is as we wolen, but and we silf faren wel.

29 Menelaus cam to vs, and seide, that ye wolen go doun to youre, that ben anentis vs.

30 Therfor to these that gon togidere, we yyuen riythondis of sikirnesse til to the thrittith dai of the monethe Xandici,

31 that Jewis vse her metis, and lawis, as and bifore; and no man of hem in ony maner suffre disese of these thingis, that ben don bi ignoraunce.

32 Sotheli we senten also Menelaus, that schal speke to you.

33 Fare ye wel. In the hundrid yeer and eiyte and fourtithe, the fifteenthe dai of the monethe Xandici,

34 also Romayns senten 'a pistle, hauynge it thus. Quintus Menneus and Titus Manylius, legatis of Romayns, to the puple of Jewis, heelthe.

35 Of these thingis that Lisias, cosyn of the kyng, hath grauntid to you, and also we grauntiden.

36 Forsothe of whiche thingis he demyde to be teld ayen to the kyng, anoon sende ye summan; and speke ye among you diligentiliere, that we deme as it acordith to you.

37 For we gon to Antiochie, and therfor haste ye for to ayen write, that and we wite of what wille ye ben.

38 Fare ye wel.

CAP 12

In the hundrid yeer and foure and fourtithe yeer, in the fiftenthe dai of the monethe Xandici,

1 whanne these couenauntis weren maad, Lisias wente to the king; forsothe Jewis yauen werk to erthe tilyng.

2 But these that dwelten, Tymothe, and Appollonye, the sone of Gennei, but and Jerom, and Demophon proud, and Nycanore, prince of Cipre, suffriden not hem for to do in silence and reste.

3 Forsothe men of Joppe han do sich a felonye; thei preyeden Jewis with whiche thei dwelten, for to stie vp, with wyues, and sones, in to smale botis, whiche thei hadden maad redi, as if noon enemytees laien priueli among hem.

4 Therfor bi the comyn dom of the citee, and for thei acordiden, and for cause of pees hadden no thing suspect, whanne thei camen in to the depthe, thei drenchiden two hundrid, not lesse.

5 And as Judas knew this cruelte don ayens men of his folc, he comaundide to men that weren with hym; and he clepide 'to help the iust domesman God, and he cam ayens the sleeris of britheren,

6 and bi nyyt he brente the hauene, he brente the bootis, forsothe he slow bi swerd hem that fledden fro fier.

7 And whanne he hadde don these thingis, he wente awei, as eft to turnynge ayen, and vttirli to distriynge alle men of Joppe.

8 But whanne he knew, that also thei that weren at Jamnye wolden do in lijk maner to Jewis dwellynge with hem,

9 also to Jamnytes he aboue cam bi nyyt, and brente the hauene, with schippis; so that the liyt apperide to Jerusalem fro two hundrid furlongis and fourty.

10 Whanne thei hadden go thanne fro thennus bi nyne furlongis, and maden iournei to Tymothe, men of Arabie, fyue thousynde men, and horse men fyue hundrid, ioyneden batel with hym.

11 And whanne strong fiyt was maad, and bi help of God it bifelle esili, 'ether bi prosperite, the residue of men of Arabie, 'that weren ouercomun, axiden of Judas the riythondis for to be youun to hem; bihetynge hem silf to yyue lesewis, and to profitynge in othir thingis.

12 Forsothe Judas demyde verili hem profitable in many thingis, and bihiyte pees; and whanne thei hadden take riythondis, thei departiden to her tabernaclis.

13 Forsothe he assailide also sum citee sad bi briggis, and aboute set with wallis, which was enhabitid of cumpenyes of hethene men meynd, bothe men and wymmen, to which the name was Casphym.

14 Forsothe these that weren with ynne, tristiden to the stablenesse of wallis, and in apparel of foodis, and diden slacliere, 'to-terrynge Judas with cursis, and blasfemynge, and speking whiche thingis it is not leueful.

15 Sotheli Machabeus clepide to help the greet prince of the world, which with out wetheris, 'that ben engynes lijk wetheris, and with out engynes, in the tymes of Jhesu, 'ether Josue, castide doun Jericho; and hurtlide feersli to the wallis,

16 and took the cytee bi wille of the Lord, and dide vnnoumbrable sleyngis; so that the pool of stondynge watir of twei furlongis of brede, semyde to flowe with blood of slayn men.

17 Fro thennus thei wenten seuene hundrid and fifti furlongis, and camen in to Characha, to tho Jewis that ben clepid Tubianei.

18 And sotheli thei cauyten not Tymothe in tho places; and whanne no iourney was fulli don, Tymothe turnede ayen while most sad strengthe was left in 'a certayn place.

19 Forsothe Dositheus and Sosipater, that weren duykis with Machabeus, slowen ten thousend men left of Tymothe in the strengthe.

20 And Machabeus ordeynede aboute hym sixe thousynde, and ordeynede bi 'cohortis, ether cumpenyes of knyytis, and wente forth ayens Tymothe, hauynge with hym an hundrid thousynde and twenti thousynde of foot men, and of horse men twei thousynde and fyue hundrid.

21 Forsothe whanne the comyng of Judas was knowun, Tymothe bifore sente wymmen, and sones, and othere apparel in to a strengthe that is seid Carmon; for it was 'vnable to be ouercomun, and hard in goynge to, for streytnesses of places.

22 And whanne the firste cumpanye of Judas apperide, drede was maad to enemyes bi presence of God, that biholdith alle thingis; and thei weren turned in to flight, oon after anothir, so that thei weren cast doun more of her owne, and weren feblid with strokis of her swerdis.

23 Judas sotheli contynuede greetli, punyschynge vnhooli men, and castide doun of hem thretti thousynde of men.

24 Tymothe sotheli hym silf felle in to the partis of Dositheus and Sosipater; and he axide bi many preieris, that he were dismittid quyk; for he hadde fadris, and modris, and britheren, of many of Jewis, whiche it schulde bifalle for to be disseyued bi his deth.

25 And whanne he hadde youun feith, that he schulde restore hem bi couenaunt, thei dismittiden hym vnhirt, for heelthe of britheren.

26 Forsothe Judas turnede ayen fro Carmon, after that he hadde slayn fyue and twenti thousyndis.

27 Aftir the fliyt and deth of these, he mouyde the oost of Effron, strong citee, in which the multitude of dyuerse folkis dwelte; and stronge yonge men, stondynge togidere for wal-

lis, strongli fouyten ayen; forsothe in this weren many engynes, and apparels of dartis.

28 But whanne thei hadden clepid to help the Almiyti, that bi his power al to-brekith myytis of enemyes, thei token the citee, and castiden doun of hem that weren with ynne fyue and twenti thousynde.

29 Fro thens thei wenten to the citee of Scitis, which was fer fro Jerusalem sixe hundrid furlongis.

30 Forsothe for these Jewis that weren anentis Scitopolistis witnessiden, that thei weren had 'of hem benygneli, yhe, in tymes of aduersite, and that thei diden myldeli with hem,

31 thei diden thankyngis to hem; and also stiriden fro hennys forth for to be benygne ayens her kyn, and came to Jerusalem, whanne the solempne dai of wokis neiyide.

32 And aftir Pentecost, thei wenten ayens Gorgias, souereyn of Idumee.

33 Sotheli he wente out with thre thousynde foot men, and foure hundrid horse men;

34 and whanne thei weren asemblid, it bifelle that a fewe Jewis fellen doun.

35 Forsothe Dositheus, an horseman of Bachenoris, a strong man, helde Gorgias; and whanne he wolde take hym quyk, an horse man of Traces felle on hym, and kittide of his schuldre, and so Gorgias flei in to Maresam.

36 And whanne thei that weren with Hesdrym fouyten lengere, and thei weren maad wery, Judas inwardli clepide the Lord for to be maad helpere, and duyk of batel; and he bigan with cuntrei vois,

37 and with ympnes reiside cry, and made the knyytis of Gorgias to fle.

38 Forsothe Judas with the oost gaderid, cam in to the citee Odolla; and whanne the seuenthe dai cam aboue, thei weren clensid bi custom, and diden sabat in the same place.

39 And in the dai suynge Judas cam with hise, for to take awei the bodies of men cast doun, and for to putte with fadris, and modris, in sepulcris of fadris.

40 Forsothe thei foundun vndur cootis of slayn men, of the yiftis of idols that weren at Jamnyam, fro whiche the lawe forbedith Jewis; therfor it was maad knowun to alle men, that thei 'fellen doun for this cause.

41 And therfor alle blessiden the iust dom of the Lord, which made priuy thingis knowun.

42 And so thei conuertiden to preieris, and preieden, that 'the ilke trespas that was don, were bitakun to foryetyng. And sotheli the strengeste Judas monestide the puple, for to kepe hem with out synne, seynge vndur iyen, what thingis weren don for synnes of hem that weren cast doun.

43 And whanne 'spekyng togidere was maad, he sente twelue thousynde dragmes of siluer to Jerusalem, to be offrid a sacrifice for synnes of deed men, and bithouyte wel and religiousli of ayenrisyng;

44 for if he hopide not, that thei that fellen schulden rise ayen, it was seyn superflu and veyn for to preye for deed men;

45 and for he bihelde, that thei that token slepyng, 'ether deth, with pitee, hadden best grace kept.

46 Therfor hooli and heelful thenkyng is, for to preie for deed men, that thei be releesid of synnes.

CAP 13

1 In the hundrid and nyne and fourtithe yeer Judas knew, that Antiok Eupator cam with multitude ayens Judee;

2 and with hym cam Lisias, procuratour and souereyn of offices, hauynge with hym an hundrid and ten thousynde of foot men, and of horse men fyue thousynde, and olifauntis two and twenti, charis with sithis thre hundrid.

3 Forsothe and Menelaus ioynede hym to hem, and with greet desseit bisouyte Antiok, not for heelthe of the cuntre, but hopynge that he schulde be ordeyned in to prinshod.

4 But the kyng of kyngis reiside the willis of Antiok ayens the synnere; and whanne Lisyas schewide that he was cause of alle yuels, he comaundide, as custom is to hem, hym takun for to be slayn in the same place.

5 Sotheli in the same place was a tour of fifti cubitis, hauynge on ech side a gaderyng of aische; this was biholdynge in to a diche.

6 Fro thennus he comaundide the sacrilegere, 'ether cursid man, for to be caste doun in to aische, whanne alle men puttiden forth hym to the deth.

7 And bi siche lawe it bifelle the brekere of lawe for to die, nether Menelaus for to be youun to erthe.

8 And forsothe iustli ynowy; for whi for he dide many trespassis ayens the auter of God, whos fier and aische was hooli, he was dampned in the deth of aische.

9 But the kyng with out bridil in mynde, cam to schewe hym worse to Jewis, than his fadir.

10 And whanne these thingis weren knowun, Judas comaundide the puple, that bi nyyt and dai thei schulden clepe to help the Lord; that as euere more, also now he schulde helpe hem;

11 whiche sotheli dredden for to be priuyd of lawe, and cuntree, and hooli temple; and that he suffride not the puple, that a while gon hadde a litil quykid ayen, for to be suget eftsoone to blasfeme naciouns.

12 Therfor whanne alle men diden togidere that thing, and axiden merci of the Lord with wepyng, in fastyngis bi alle thre daies, and kneliden, Judas monestide hem for to make hem redi.

13 Forsothe he with eldre men thouyte for to go out, bifore that the kyng mouede oost to Judee, and gat the citee, and to bitake the ende of the thing to the dom of the Lord.

14 Therfor he yaf power of alle thingis to God, makere of nouyt of the world, and monestide hise for to fiyte strongli, and stonde til to the deth, for lawis, temple, citee, cuntre, and citeseyns; and he ordeynede the oost aboute Modyn.

15 And whanne a tokene was youun to hise of victorie of God, he chees the strengeste yonge men, and bi niyt he asailide the kyngis halle in tentis, and he slow fourtene thousynde men, and the moste of olifauntis, with these that weren put aboue.

16 And thei filliden the tentis of enemyes with hiyeste drede and disturblyng, and whanne these thingis weren don 'in prosperite, thei wenten awei.

17 Forsothe this was don in the dai liytynge, for the proteccioun of the Lord helpide hym.

18 But whanne the kyng hadde takun taast of hardynesse 'of Jewis bi craft, he asaiede hardynessis of places; and mouede the tentis to Bethsura,

19 that was a strong hold of Jewis; but he was dryuun hurtlide and menusid.

20 Forsothe to these that weren with ynne, Judas sente nedeful thingis.

21 Forsothe Rodochus, sum of the oost of Jewis, telde out priuetees to enemyes; which was souyt, and takun, and prisoned.

22 Eftsoone the kyng hadde word to hem that weren in Bethsura, and yaf the riythond, and resseyuede, and wente awei. He ioynede batel with Judas, and Judas was ouercomun.

23 Forsothe as he knew that Filip hadde rebellid at Antiochie, which was left on nedis, he was astonyed in mynde, and bisouyte Jewis, and was suget to hem, and swoor of alle thingis, of whiche it was seyn iust; and he was recounselid, and offride sacrifice, and worschipide the temple, and puttide yiftis.

24 He biclippide, 'ether kisside, Machabeus, and made hym prince and duyk fro Tolomaida til to Garreyns.

25 Sotheli as he cam to Tolomaida, men of Tolomaida baren greuousli acordyng of frendschip, and hadde indignacioun, leste perauenture thei wolden breke pees.

26 Thanne Lisias stiede vp in to the dom place, and expownede resoun, and ceeside the puple, and turnyde ayen to Antiochie; and in this maner the kingis goynge out and turnynge ayen wenten forth.

CAP 14

1 But aftir tyme of thre yeer Judas knew, and thei that weren with hym, that Demetrie Seleucus stiede to couenable places, with strong multitude, and schippis, bi the hauene of Tripolis,

2 and hath holdun cuntreis ayens Antiok, and his duyk Lisias.

3 Forsothe oon Alchimus, that was hiyeste prest, but wilfuli was defoulid in tymes of myngyng togidere, bihelde that in no maner heelthe was to hym, nether neiyyng to the auter,

4 and he cam to kyng Demetrie, in the hundrid and fiftithe yeer, and offride hym a goldun coroun, and palme, ouer these thingis and offride vessels, that weren seyn for to be of the temple; and sotheli in that day he was stille.

5 Forsothe he gat a couenable tyme of his woodnesse, and he was clepid of Demetrie to counsel, and was axid with what thingis and counsels Jewis enforsiden, and he answeride,

6 Thei that ben seid Assideis of Jewis, of whiche Judas Machabeus is souereyn, nurschen batels, and mouen discenciouns, nether suffren the rewme for to be quyet.

7 For whi and Y am defraudid of glorie of fadir and modir, sotheli Y seie, of hiyest presthod, and Y cam hidur,

8 first sotheli kepyng feith to the kyngis profitis, the secounde tyme sotheli counselynge also the citeseyns, for whi bi schrewidnesse of hem al oure kyn is trauelid greetli.

9 But Y preie, thou kyng, whanne alle these thingis ben knowun, biholde to the cuntre and kyn, by thi manlynesse schewid to alle men.

10 For whi as long as Judas lyueth, it is impossible that pees be to nedis.

11 Forsothe whanne siche thingis weren seid of hym, and othere frendis, hauynge hem enemyly, enflawmeden Demetrie ayens Judas.

12 Whiche anoon sente Nycanor, souereyn of olifauntis, a duyk in to Judee,

13 with comaundementis youun for to take thilke Judas quyk, for to scatere sotheli hem that weren with hym, and for to ordeyne Alchymus hiyeste prest of the moste holy temple.

14 Thanne hethene men that fledden Judas fro Judee, flokmel ioyneden hem to Nycanor, and gessiden the wretchidnessis and dethis of Jewis prosperitees of her thingis.

15 Therfor whanne comyng of Nycanor was herd, and comyng togidere of naciouns, Jewis bispreynt with erthe preieden hym, that ordeynede his puple in to with outen ende for to kepe, and which defendith his part with open signes.

16 Forsothe for the duyk comaundide, anoon thei mouyden fro thennus, and camen togidere to castel Dessau.

17 Symount forsothe, brother of Judas, ioynede batel with Nycanor, but he was al to-brokun with sudeyn comyng of aduersaries.

18 Netheles Nycanor herde the vertu of Judas felowis, and greetnesse of hardynesse, which thei hadden for stryues of the cuntree, and dredde for to make dom bi blood.

19 Wherfor he bifore sente Possidonye, and Theodote, and Mathie, for to yyue riythondis, and take.

20 And whanne longe counsel was don of these thingis, and the duyk hym silf hadde teld to the multitude, o sentence was of alle, for to graunte to frenschipis.

21 Therfor thei ordeyneden a dai, in which thei schulden do priueli bitwixe hem silf; 'smale setis weren brouyt forth, and set to ech.

22 Forsothe Judas comaundide armed men for to be in couenable places, lest perauenture ony thing of yuel schulde rise sudenli of enemyes; and thei maden a couenable speche togidere.

23 Forsothe Nycanor dwelte in Jerusalem, and no thing dide yuel; and he lefte flockis of cumpenyes, that weren gaderid.

24 Forsothe he hadde Judas euere more dereworthe of herte, and was bowid to the man;

25 and preiede hym for to wedde a wijf, and gendre sones; and he made weddyngis, and dide quyetli, and thei lyueden comynli, 'ether togidere.

26 Alchimus forsothe siy the charite of hem togidere, and acordyngis, and cam to Demetrie, and seide, that Nycanor assentith to alyen thingis, and hath ordeynede Judas, traitour of the rewme, successour to hym.

27 Therfor the kyng was maad scharp, and terrid to wraththe with siche worste accusyngis, and wroot to Nycanor, and seide, that sotheli he bar greuously of acordyng of frendschipe, and netheles comaundide for to sende Machabeus boundun to Antiochie.

28 And whanne these thingis weren knowun, Nycanor was astonyed, and greuousli bar, if he made voide tho thingis that weren acordid, and he was no thing harmed of the man;

29 but for he myyte not ayen stonde the kyng, he kepte couenablete, in which he schulde perfourme the maundement.

30 And Machabeus siy, that Nycanor dide with hym most sterneli, and yaf fersliere customable comyng togidere, and he vndurstode that this sternesse was not of goode, and with a fewe of hise gaderid, he hidde hym fro Nycanor.

31 And as he knew this thing, that he was strongli bifore comun, 'ether aspied, of the man, he cam to the mooste and holieste temple, and he comaundide to the prestis offrynge customable sacrifices, that the man be takun to hym.

32 And whanne thei seiden with ooth, that thei wisten not, where he was that was souyt, he stretchide forth the hond to the temple,

33 and swoor, If ye schulen not bitake to me Judas boundun, Y schal drawe doun this temple of God in to pleynesse, and digge out the auter, and Y schal halewe this temple to Liber, ether Bachus, the fadir.

34 And whanne he hadde seid these thingis, he wente awei. Forsothe the prestis helden forth hondis in to heuene, and clepiden hym to help that euere is forfiytere of the folc of hem, and seiden these thingis,

35 Thou, Lord of 'alle creaturis, that of no thing hast nede, woldist that the temple of thin habitacioun be maad in vs.

36 And now, thou Lord, hooli of alle hooli, kepe with outen ende this hous vndefoulid, that a litil agon was clensid.

37 Forsothe Rasias, oon of the eldre men of Jerusalem, was accusid to Nycanor; and Rasias was a man, louyere of the citee, and wel herynge, that for affeccioun was clepid fadir of Jewis.

38 This man many tymes helde purpos of contynence in Judee, and was apayed for to bitake bodi and soule for perseueraunce, 'ether lastyng.

39 Forsothe Nycanor wolde schewe the hatrede, that he hadde ayens Jewis, and sente fyue hundrid knyytis, for to take him.

40 For he gesside, if he hadde disseyued hym, that he shulde bringe in most deth to Jewis.

41 Forsothe whanne cumpenyes coueitiden for to falle in to his hous, and for to breke the yate, and for to moue to fier, whanne now he was takun, he asailide hym silf with swerd;

42 chesynge for to die nobli, rather than for to be maad suget to synneris, and ayens his birthis for to be led with vnworthi wrongis.

43 But whanne bi hastyng he hadde youun wounde with vncerteyne strook, and cumpenyes bitwixe doris brasten in, he ran ayen hardli to the wal, and castide doun hym silf manli in to the cumpenyes.

44 And whanne thei yauen swiftli place to his fal, he cam bi the myddil of the nol,

45 and yit while he brethide, he was kyndlid in herte, and roos. And whanne his blood with greet flowyng flowide doun, and with most greuouse woundis he was woundid, bi rennyng he passide the cumpeny; and stood on an heey stoon,

46 and now was maad with out blood, and biclippide his entrailis with both hondis, and castide forth on the cumpenyes, and clepide to helpe the lordschipere of lijf and spirit, that he schulde yelde eftsoone these thingis to hym; and thus he was deed fro lijf.

CAP 15

1 Forsothe as Nycanor foond that Judas was in the place of Samarie, he thouyte for to ioyne batel in the dai of sabat with al fersnesse.

2 Forsothe whanne Jewis, that sueden hym bi nede, seiden, Do thou not so fersli and hethenli, but yyue thou onour to the dai of halewyng, and worschipe thou hym, that biholdith alle thingis.

3 And he vnblesside, axide, If ther is a myyti in heuene, that comaundide the dai of sabatis for to be don?

4 And whanne thei answeriden, Ther is a quyk Lord, and he is myyti in heuene, that comaundide the seuenthe dai for to be don.

5 And he seide, And Y am myyti on erthe, which comaunde armeris for to be takun, and nedis of the kyng for to be fillid. Netheles he gat not, for to perfourme counsel.

6 And sotheli Nycanor was enhaunsid with souereyn pride, and thouyte for to ordeyne a comyn victorie of Judas.

7 Forsothe Judas Machabeus tristide euere more with al hope, that help schulde come to hym of the Lord,

8 and he monestide hise, that thei schulden not inwardli drede at the comyng to of naciouns, but schulden haue in mynde the helpis don to hem of heuene, and now schulden hope that the victorie schulde come to hem of Almiyti.

9 And he spak to hem of the lawe, and profetis, and monestide, 'ether warnyde, of batels which thei diden bifore, and ordeynede hem rediere.

10 And so whanne the soulis of hem weren reisid, he schewide to gidere the falsnesse of hethene men, and brekyng of othis.

11 Forsothe he armede ech of hem, not bi strengthing of scheld and schaft, but with beste wordis and monestyngis, and expownede a sweuene worthi of bileue, bi which he gladide alle.

12 Sotheli the visioun was sich. Judas siy Onyas, that was hiyeste prest, a good man and benygne, schamefast in siyt, and mylde in maneres, and fair in speche, and which was exercisid in vertues fro a child, holdynge forth the hondis for to preie for al the puple of Jewis.

13 After this thing that also anothir man apperide, wondurful in age and glorie, and in hauynge of greet fairnesse aboute hym.

14 Forsothe he siy Onyas answerynge for to haue seid, This is the louyere of britheren, and of the puple of Israel; this is he, that myche preieth for the puple, and al the hooli citee, Jeremye, 'the profet of God.

15 Forsothe he siy that Jeremye hath streyt forth the riythond, and hath youun a goldun swerd to Judas, and seide,

16 Take thou the hooli swerd, a yift of God, in which thou schalt caste doun the aduersaries of my puple Israel.

17 Therfor thei weren monestid with ful good wordis of Judas, of whiche fersnesse miyte be enhaunsid, and soules of yonge men be coumfortid, and thei ordeyneden for to fiyte, and turmente togidere strongli, that vertu schulde deme of nedis, 'ether causis, for that the hooli citee and temple weren in perel.

18 For whi for wyues, and sones, and also for britheren, and cosyns, was lesse bisynesse, but the moste and firste drede was holynesse of the temple.

19 But not leste bisynesse hadde hem that weren in citee, for these that schulden asaile, 'ether fiyte togidere.

20 And whanne now alle men hopiden dom to be, and enemyes come, and the oost was ordeined, beestis and horse men put togidere in couenable place,

21 Machabeus bihelde the comyng of multitude, and dyuerse apparel of armeris, and fersnesse of beestis, and he stretchide out the hondis to heuene, and clepide to help the Lord doynge greet wondris, which not bi power of armeris, but as it plesith to hym, yyueth victorie to worthi men.

22 Forsothe he seide, clepynge to help in this maner, Thou Lord, that sentist thin aungel vndur Ezechie, kyng of Juda, and hast slayn of the tentis, 'ether oostis, of Sennacherib, an hundrid thousynde foure score and fyue thousynde; and now,

23 lordschipere of heuenes, sende thou thi good aungel bifore vs, in drede and tremblynge of greetnesse of thin arm, that thei drede,

24 that comen with blasfemye ayens thin hooli puple. And sotheli thus he perfitli preiede.

25 Forsothe Nycanor, and thei that weren with hym, moueden to with trumpis and songis.

26 Judas forsothe, and thei that weren with hym, clepiden God to help bi preieris, and wenten togidere.

27 Sotheli thei fiytynge with hond, but preiynge God in hertis, castiden doun fyue and thretti thousynde, not lesse, and delitiden greetli bi presence of God.

28 And whanne thei hadden ceessid, and with ioye turneden ayen, thei knewen that Nycanor hadde falle, with his armeris.

29 Therfor whanne cry was maad, and perturbacioun styride, bi cuntre vois thei blessiden the Lord almyyti.

30 Forsothe Judas, that bi alle thingis in bodi and soule was redi for to die for citeseyns, bad, that the heed of Nycanor, and hond with the schuldre gird of, schulde be brouyt forth to Jerusalem.

31 Whidur whanne he fulli cam, whanne men of his lynage weren clepid togidere, and prestis to the auter, he clepide also hem that weren in the hiy tour.

32 And whanne the heed of Nycanor was schewid, and the cursid hond, which he holdynge forth ayens the hooli hous of almyyti God greetli gloriede,

33 also he comaundide the tunge of vnpitouse Nycanor kit of, for to be youun to briddis gobet mel; forsothe he comaundide the hond of the wood man for to be hangid vp ayens the temple.

34 Therfor alle blessiden the Lord of heuene, and seiden, Blessid be the Lord, that kepte his place vndefoulid.

35 Forsothe he hangide vp Nycanoris heed in the hiyeste tour, that it were knowun, and an opyn signe of the help of God.

36 Therfor alle men by comyn counsel demyden in no maner for to passe this dai with out solempnytee,

37 but for to haue solempnyte in the threttenthe dai of the moneth Adar, that is seid, bi vois of Sirie, the firste dai of Mardocheus.

38 Therfor whanne these thingis weren don ayens Nicanor, and of tho tymes whanne the citee was weldid of Ebrews, also Y in these thingis schal make an ende of word.

39 And sotheli if wel and as it acordith to the stori, this thing and Y wolc; if ellis lesse worthili, it is to foryyue to me.

40 Sotheli as for to drynke euere more wyn, ether euere more watir, it is contrarie, but for to vse chaungeable, 'ether 'now oon, now another, is delitable; so to men redynge, if the word be euer more souyt to ech part, it schal not be plesynge; therfor here it schal be endid.

MATHEU

CAP 1

1 The book of the generacioun of Jhesu Crist, the sone of Dauid, the sone of Abraham.

2 Abraham bigat Isaac. Isaac bigat Jacob. Jacob bigat Judas and hise britheren.

3 Judas bigat Fares and Zaram, of Tamar. Fares bigat Esrom.

4 Esrom bigat Aram. Aram bigat Amynadab. Amynadab bigat Naason. Naason bigat Salmon.

5 Salmon bigat Booz, of Raab. Booz bigat Obeth, of Ruth. Obeth bigat Jesse. Jesse bigat Dauid the king.

6 Dauid the king bigat Salamon, of hir that was Vries wijf.

7 Salomon bigat Roboam. Roboam bigat Abias.

8 Abias bigat Asa. Asa bigat Josaphath. Josaphath bigat Joram. Joram bigat

9 Osias. Osias bigat Joathan. Joathan bigat Achaz. Achaz bigat Ezechie.

10 Ezechie bigat Manasses. Manasses bigat Amon.

11 Amon bigat Josias. Josias bigat Jeconyas and his britheren, in to the transmygracioun of Babiloyne.

12 And aftir the transmygracioun of Babiloyne, Jeconyas bigat Salatiel. Salatiel bigat Zorobabel.

13 Zorobabel bigat Abyut. Abyut bigat Eliachym. Eliachym bigat Asor.

14 Asor bigat Sadoc. Sadoc bigat Achym.

15 Achym bigat Elyut. Elyut bigat Eleasar. Eleasar bigat Mathan.

16 Mathan bigat Jacob. Jacob bigat Joseph, the hosebonde of Marye, of whom Jhesus was borun, that is clepid Christ.

17 And so alle generaciouns fro Abraham to Dauid ben fourtene generacions, and fro Dauid to the transmygracioun of Babiloyne ben fourtene generaciouns, and fro the transmygracioun of Babiloyne to Crist ben fourtene generaciouns.

18 But the generacioun of Crist was thus. Whanne Marie, the modir of Jhesu, was spousid to Joseph, bifore thei camen togidere, she was foundun hauynge of the Hooli Goost in the wombe.

19 And Joseph, hir hosebonde, for he was riytful, and wolde not puplische hir, he wolde priueli haue left hir.

20 But while he thouyte thes thingis, lo! the aungel of the Lord apperide 'in sleep to hym, and seide, Joseph, the sone of Dauid, nyle thou drede to take Marie, thi wijf; for that thing that is borun in hir is of the Hooli Goost.

21 And she shal bere a sone, and thou shalt clepe his name Jhesus; for he schal make his puple saaf fro her synnes.

22 For al this thing was don, that it schulde be fulfillid, that was seid of the Lord bi a prophete, seiynge, Lo!

23 a virgyn shal haue in wombe, and she schal bere a sone, and thei schulen clepe his name Emanuel, that is to seie, God with vs.

24 And Joseph roos fro sleepe, and dide as the aungel of the Lord comaundide hym, and took Marie, his wijf;

25 and he knew her not, til she hadde borun her firste bigete sone, and clepide his name Jhesus.

CAP 2

1 Therfor whanne Jhesus was borun in Bethleem of Juda, in the daies of king Eroude, lo! astromyenes camen fro the eest to Jerusalem,

2 and seiden, Where is he, that is borun king of Jewis? for we han seyn his sterre in the eest, and we comen to worschipe him.

3 But king Eroude herde, and was trublid, and al Jerusalem with hym.

4 And he gaderide to gidre alle the prynces of prestis, and scribis of the puple, and enqueride of hem, where Crist shulde be borun.

5 And thei seiden to hym, In Bethleem of Juda; for so it is writun bi a profete,

6 And thou, Bethleem, the lond of Juda, art not the leest among the pryncis of Juda; for of thee a duyk schal go out, that schal gouerne my puple of Israel.

7 Thanne Eroude clepide pryueli the astromyens, and lernyde bisili of hem the tyme of the sterre that apperide to hem.

8 And he sente hem in to Bethleem, and seide, Go ye, and axe ye bisili of the child, and whanne yee han foundun, telle ye it to me, that Y also come, and worschipe hym.

9 And whanne thei hadden herd the kyng, thei wenten forth. And lo! the sterre, that thei siyen in the eest, wente bifore hem, til it cam, and stood aboue, where the child was.

10 And thei siyen the sterre, and ioyeden with a ful greet ioye.

11 And thei entriden in to the hous, and founden the child with Marie, his modir; and thei felden doun, and worschipiden him. And whanne thei hadden openyd her tresouris, thei offryden to hym yiftis, gold, encense, and myrre.

12 And whanne thei hadden take an aunswere in sleep, that thei schulden not turne ayen to Eroude, thei turneden ayen bi anothir weie in to her cuntrey.

13 And whanne thei weren goon, lo! the aungel of the Lord apperide to Joseph in sleep, and seide, Rise vp, and take the child and his modir, and fle in to Egipt, and be thou there, til that I seie to thee; for it is to come, that Eroude seke the child, to destrie hym.

14 And Joseph roos, and took the child and his modir bi nyyt, and wente in to Egipt,

15 and he was there to the deeth of Eroude; that it schulde be fulfillid, that was seid of the Lord bi the profete, seiynge, Fro Egipt Y haue clepid my sone.

16 Thanne Eroude seynge that he was disseyued of the astromyens, was ful wrooth; and he sente, and slowe alle the children, that weren in Bethleem, and in alle the coostis therof, fro two yeer age and with inne, aftir the tyme that he had enquerid of the astromyens.

17 Thanne 'it was fulfillid, that was seid bi Jeremye, the profete,

18 seiynge, A vois was herd an hiy, wepynge and moche weilyng, Rachel biwepynge hir sones, and she wolde not be coumfortid, for thei ben noyt.

19 But whanne Eroude was deed, loo! the aungel of the Lord apperide to Joseph in sleep in Egipt,

20 and seide, Ryse vp, and take the child and his modir, and go in to the lond of Israel; for thei that souyten the lijf of the chijld ben deed.

21 Joseph roos, and took the child and his modir, and cam in to the loond of Israel.

22 And he herde that Archilaus regnede in Judee for Eroude, his fadir, and dredde to go thidir. And he was warned in sleep, and wente in to the parties of Galilee;

23 and cam, and dwelte in a citee, that ys clepid Nazareth, that it shulde be fulfillid, that was seid bi profetis, For he shal be clepid a Nazarey.

CAP 3

1 In tho daies Joon Baptist cam, and prechide in the desert of Judee,

2 and seide, Do ye penaunce, for the kyngdom of heuenes shal neiye.

3 For this is he, of whom it is seid bi Ysaie, the prophete, seyinge, A vois of a crier in desert, Make ye redi the weies of the Lord; make ye riyt the pathis of hym.

4 And this Joon hadde clothing of camels heeris, and a girdil of skynne aboute hise leendis; and his mete was honysoukis, and hony of the wode.

5 Thanne Jerusalem wente out to hym, and al Judee, and al the cuntre aboute Jordan;

6 and thei weren waischun of hym in Jordan, 'and knowlechiden her synnes.

7 But he siy manye of the Farysees and of Saduceis comynge to his baptym, and seide to hem, Generaciouns of eddris, who shewide to you to fle fro the wraththe that is to come?

8 Therfor do ye worthi fruyte of penaunce,

9 and nyle ye seie with ynne you, We han Abraham to fadir; for Y seie to you, that God is myyti to reise vp of these stoones the sones of Abraham.

10 And now the ax is put to the roote of the tree; therfore euery tree that makith not good fruyt, shal be kit doun, and shal be cast in to the fier.

11 Y waische you in water, in to penaunce; but he that shal come after me is strongere than Y, whos schoon Y am not worthi to bere; he shal baptise you in the Hooli Goost and fier.

12 Whos wynewing cloth is in his hoond, and he shal fulli clense his corn flore, and shal gadere his whete in to his berne; but the chaffe he shal brenne with fier that mai not be quenchid.

13 Thanne Jhesus cam fro Galilee in to Jordan to Joon, to be baptised of hym.

14 And Joon forbede him, and seide, Y owe to be baptisid of thee, and thou comest to me?

15 But Jhesus answeride, and seide to hym, Suffre nowe, for thus it fallith to vs to fulfille al riytfulnesse.

16 Thanne Joon suffride hym. And whanne Jhesus was baptisid, anoon he wente up fro the watir; and lo! heuenes weren openyd to hym, and he saie the Spirit of God comynge doun as a dowue, and comynge on hym; and loo!

17 a vois fro heuenes, seiynge, This is my louyd sone, in which Y haue plesid to me.

CAP 4

1 Thanne Jhesus was led of a spirit in to desert, to be temptid of the feend.

2 And whanne he hadde fastid fourti daies and fourti nyytis, aftirward he hungride.

3 And the tempter cam nyy, and seide to hym, If thou art Goddis sone, seie that thes stoones be maad looues.

4 Which answeride, and seide to hym, It is writun, Not oonli in breed luyeth man, but in ech word that cometh of Goddis mouth.

5 Thanne the feend took hym in to the hooli citee, and settide hym on the pynacle of the temple,

6 and seide to hym, If thou art Goddis sone, sende thee adoun; for it is writun, That to hise aungels he comaundide of thee, and thei schulen take thee in hondis, lest perauenture thou hirte thi foot at a stoon.

7 Eftsoone Jhesus seide to hym, It is writun, Thou shalt not tempte thi Lord God.

8 Eftsoone the feend took hym in to a ful hiy hil, and schewide to hym alle the rewmes of the world, and the ioye of hem;

9 and seide to hym, Alle these 'Y schal yyue to thee, if thou falle doun and worschipe me.

10 Thanne Jhesus seide to hym, Goo, Sathanas; for it is writun, Thou schalt worschipe thi Lord God, and to hym aloone thou shalt serue.

11 Thanne the feend lafte hym; and lo! aungels camen nyy, and serueden to hym.

12 But whanne Jhesus hadde herd that Joon was takun, he wente in to Galilee.

13 And he lefte the citee of Nazareth, and cam, and dwelte in the citee of Cafarnaum, biside the see, in the coostis of Zabulon and Neptalym,

14 that it shulde be fulfillid, that was seid by Ysaie, the profete, seiynge,

15 The lond of Sabulon and the lond of Neptalym, the weie of the see ouer Jordan, of Galilee of hethen men,

16 the puple that walkide in derknessis saye greet liyt, and while men satten in the cuntre of shadewe of deth, liyt aroos to hem.

17 Fro that tyme Jhesus bigan to preche, and seie, Do ye penaunce, for the kyngdom of heuenes schal come niy.

18 And Jhesus walkide bisidis the see of Galilee, and saye twei britheren, Symount, that is clepid Petre, and Andrewe, his brothir, castynge nettis in to the see; for thei weren fischeris.

19 And he seide to hem, Come ye aftir me, and Y shal make you to be maad fisscheris of men.

20 And anoon thei leften the nettis, and sueden hym.

21 And he yede forth fro that place, and saie tweyne othere britheren, James of Zebede, and Joon, his brother, in a schip with Zebede, her fadir, amendynge her nettis, and he clepide hem.

22 And anoon thei leften the nettis and the fadir, and sueden hym.

23 And Jhesus yede aboute al Galilee, techynge in the synagogis of hem, and prechynge the gospel of the kyngdom, and heelynge euery languor and eche sekenesse among the puple.

24 And his fame wente in to al Sirie; and thei brouyten to hym alle that weren at male ese, and that weren take with dyuerse languores and turmentis, and hem that hadden feendis, and lunatike men, and men in palesy, and he heelide hem.

25 And ther sueden hym myche puple of Galile, and of Decapoli, and of Jerusalem, and of Judee, and of biyende Jordan.

CAP 5

1 And Jhesus, seynge the puple, wente vp in to an hil; and whanne he was set, hise disciplis camen to hym.

2 And he openyde his mouth, and tauyte hem, and seide,

3 Blessed ben pore men in spirit, for the kyngdom of heuenes is herne.

4 Blessid ben mylde men, for thei schulen welde the erthe.

5 Blessid ben thei that mornen, for thei schulen be coumfortid.

6 Blessid ben thei that hungren and thristen riytwisnesse, for thei schulen be fulfillid.

7 Blessid ben merciful men, for thei schulen gete merci.

8 Blessid ben thei that ben of clene herte, for thei schulen se God.

9 Blessid ben pesible men, for thei schulen be clepid Goddis children.

10 Blessid ben thei that suffren persecusioun for riytfulnesse, for the kingdam of heuenes is herne.

11 'Ye schulen be blessid, whanne men schulen curse you, and schulen pursue you, and shulen seie al yuel ayens you liynge, for me.

12 Ioie ye, and be ye glad, for youre meede is plenteuouse in heuenes; for so thei han pursued 'also profetis that weren bifor you.

13 Ye ben salt of the erthe; that if the salt vanysche awey, whereynne schal it be saltid? To no thing it is worth ouere, no but that it be cast out, and be defoulid of men.

14 Ye ben liyt of the world; a citee set on an hil may not be hid;

15 ne me teendith not a lanterne, and puttith it vndur a busschel, but on a candilstike, that it yyue liyt to alle that ben in the hous.

16 So schyne youre liyt befor men, that thei se youre goode werkis, and glorifie youre fadir that is in heuenes.

17 Nil ye deme, that Y cam to vndo the lawe, or the profetis; Y cam not to vndo the lawe, but to fulfille.

18 Forsothe Y seie to you, til heuene and erthe passe, o lettir or o titel shal not passe fro the lawe, til alle thingis be doon.

19 Therfor he that brekith oon of these leeste maundementis, and techith thus men, schal be clepid the leste in the rewme of heuenes; 'but he that doith, and techith, schal be clepid greet in the kyngdom of heuenes.

20 And Y seie to you, that but your riytfulnesse be more plenteuouse than of scribis and of Farisees, ye schulen not entre into the kyngdom of heuenes.

21 Ye han herd that it was seid to elde men, Thou schalt not slee; and he that sleeth, schal be gilti to doom.

22 But Y seie to you, that ech man that is wrooth to his brothir, schal be gilti to doom; and he that seith to his brother, Fy! schal be gilti to the counseil; but he that seith, Fool, schal be gilti to the fier of helle.

23 Therfor if thou offrist thi yifte 'at the auter, and ther thou bithenkist, that thi brothir hath sum what ayens thee,

24 leeue there thi yifte bifor the auter, and go first to be recounselid to thi brothir, and thanne thou schalt come, and schalt offre thi yifte.

25 Be thou consentynge to thin aduersarie soone, while thou art in the weie with hym, lest perauenture thin aduersarie take thee to the domesman, and the domesman take thee to the mynystre, and thou be sent in to prisoun.

26 Treuli Y seie to thee, thou schalt not go out fro thennus, til thou yelde the last ferthing.

27 Ye han herd that it was seid to elde men, Thou schalt 'do no letcherie.

28 But Y seie to you, that euery man that seeth a womman for to coueite hir, hath now do letcherie bi hir in his herte.

29 That if thi riyt iye sclaundre thee, pulle hym out, and caste fro thee; for it spedith to thee, that oon of thi membris perische, than that al thi bodi go in to helle.

30 And if thi riyt hond sclaundre thee, kitte hym aweye, and caste fro thee; for it spedith to thee that oon of thi membris perische, than that al thi bodi go in to helle.

31 And it hath be seyd, Who euere leeueth his wijf, yyue he to hir a libel of forsakyng.

32 But Y seie to you, that euery man that leeueth his wijf, outtakun cause of fornycacioun, makith hir to do letcherie, and he that weddith the forsakun wijf, doith auowtrye.

33 Eftsoone ye han herd, that it was seid to elde men, Thou schalt not forswere, but thou schalt yelde thin othis to the Lord.

34 But Y seie to you, that ye swere not 'for ony thing; nethir bi heuene, for it is the trone of God;

35 nether bi the erthe, for it is the stole of his feet; nether bi Jerusalem, for it is the citee of a greet kyng; nether thou schalt not swere bi thin heed,

36 for thou maist not make oon heere white, ne blacke;

37 but be youre word, Yhe, yhe; Nay, nay; and that that is more than these, is of yuel.

38 Ye han herd that it hath be seid, Iye for iye, and tothe for tothe.

39 But Y seie to you, that ye ayenstonde not an yuel man; but if ony smyte thee in the riyt cheke, schewe to him also the tothir;

40 and to hym that wole stryue with thee in doom, and take awey thi coote, leeue thou 'to him also thi mantil;

41 and who euer constreyneth thee a thousynde pacis, go thou with hym othir tweyne.

42 Yyue thou to hym that axith of thee, and turne not awey fro hym that wole borewe of thee.

43 Ye han herd that it was seid, Thou schalt loue thi neiybore, and hate thin enemye.

44 But Y seie to you, loue ye youre enemyes, do ye wel to hem that hatiden you, and preye ye for hem that pursuen, and sclaundren you;

45 that ye be the sones of your fadir that is in heuenes, that makith his sunne to rise vpon goode 'and yuele men, and reyneth on iust men and vniuste.

46 For if ye louen hem that louen you, what mede schulen ye han? whether pupplicans doon not this?

47 And if ye greten youre britheren oonli, what schulen ye do more? ne doon not hethene men this?

48 Therfore be ye parfit, as youre heuenli fadir is parfit.

CAP 6

1 Takith hede, that ye do not youre riytwisnesse bifor men, to be seyn of hem, ellis ye schulen haue no meede at youre fadir that is in heuenes.

2 Therfore whanne thou doist almes, nyle thou trumpe tofore thee, as ypocritis doon in synagogis and stretis, that thei be worschipid of men; sotheli Y seie to you, they han resseyued her meede.

3 But whanne thou doist almes, knowe not thi left hond what thi riyt hond doith, that thin almes be in hidils,

4 and thi fadir that seeth in hiddils, schal quyte thee.

5 And whanne ye preyen, ye schulen not be as ipocritis, that louen to preye stondynge in synagogis and corneris of stretis, to be seyn of men; treuli Y seie to you, thei han resseyued her meede.

6 But whanne thou schalt preye, entre in to thi couche, and whanne the dore is schet, preye thi fadir in hidils, and thi fadir that seeth in hidils, schal yelde to thee.

7 But in preiyng nyle yee speke myche, as hethene men doon, for thei gessen that thei ben herd in her myche speche.

8 Therfor nyle ye be maad lich to hem, for your fadir woot what is nede to you, bifore that ye axen hym.

9 And thus ye schulen preye, Oure fadir that art in heuenes, halewid be thi name;

10 thi kyngdoom come to; be thi wille don 'in erthe as in heuene;

11 yyue to vs this dai oure 'breed ouer othir substaunce;

12 and foryyue to vs oure dettis, as we foryyuen to oure dettouris; and lede vs not in to temptacioun,

13 but delyuere vs fro yuel.

14 Amen. For if ye foryyuen to men her synnes, youre heuenli fadir schal foryyue to you youre trespassis.

15 Sotheli if ye foryyuen not to men, nether youre fadir schal foryyue to you youre synnes.

16 But whanne ye fasten, nyle ye be maad as ypocritis sorewful, for thei defacen hem silf, to seme fastyng to men; treuli Y seie to you, they han resseyued her meede.

17 But whanne thou fastist, anoynte thin heed, and waische thi face,

18 that thou be not seen fastynge to men, but to thi fadir that is in hidlis, and thi fadir that seeth in priuey, shal yelde to thee.

19 Nile ye tresoure to you tresouris in erthe, where ruste and mouyte destrieth, and where theues deluen out and stelen;

20 but gadere to you tresouris in heuene, where nether ruste ne mouyte distrieth, and where theues deluen not out, ne stelen.

21 For where thi tresoure is, there also thin herte is.

22 The lanterne of thi bodi is thin iye; if thin iye be symple, al thi bodi shal be liytful;

23 but if thin iye be weiward, al thi bodi shal be derk. If thanne the liyt that is in thee be derknessis, how grete schulen thilk derknessis be?

24 No man may serue tweyn lordis, for ethir he schal hate 'the toon, and loue the tother; ethir he shal susteyne 'the toon, and dispise the tothir. Ye moun not serue God and richessis.

25 Therfor I seie to you, that ye be not bisi to youre lijf, what ye schulen ete; nether to youre bodi, with what ye schulen be clothid. Whether lijf is not more than meete, and the bodie more than cloth?

26 Biholde ye the foulis of the eire, for thei sowen not, nethir repen, nethir gaderen in to bernes; and youre fadir of heuene fedith hem. Whether ye ben not more worthi than thei?

27 But who of you thenkynge mai putte to his stature o cubit?

28 And of clothing what ben ye bisye? Biholde ye the lilies of the feeld, how thei wexen. Thei trauelen not, nether spynnen;

29 and Y seie to you, Salomon in al his glorie was not keuered as oon of these.

30 And if God clothith thus the hei of the feeld, that to day is, and to morewe is cast in to an ouen, hou myche more you of litel feith?

31 Therfor nyle ye be bisi, seiynge, What schulen we ete? or, What schulen we drinke? or, With what thing schulen we be keuered?

32 For hethene men seken alle these thingis; and youre fadir woot, that ye han nede to alle these thingis.

33 Therfor seke ye first the kyngdom of God, and his riytfulnesse, and alle these thingis shulen be cast to you.

34 Therfor nyle ye be bisy in to the morew, for the morew shal be bisi to 'hym silf; for it suffisith to the dai his owen malice.

CAP 7

1 Nile ye deme, 'that ye be not demed; for in what doom ye demen,

2 ye schulen be demed, and in what mesure ye meten, it schal be meten ayen to you.

3 But what seest thou a litil mote in the iye of thi brother, and seest not a beem in thin owne iye?

4 Or hou seist thou to thi brothir, Brothir, suffre I schal do out a mote fro thin iye, and lo! a beem is in thin owne iye?

5 Ipocrite, 'do thou out first the beem of thin iye, and thanne thou schalt se to do out the mote of the iye of thi brothir.

6 Nile ye yyue hooli thing to houndis, nethir caste ye youre margaritis bifore swyne, lest perauenture thei defoulen hem with her feet, and the houndis be turned, and al to-tere you.

7 Axe ye, and it schal be youun to you; seke ye, and ye schulen fynde; knocke ye, and it schal be openyd to you.

8 For ech that axith, takith; and he that sekith, fyndith; and it schal be openyd to hym, that knockith.

9 What man of you is, that if his sone axe hym breed, whethir he wole take hym a stoon?

10 Or if he axe fische, whether he wole take hym an edder?

11 Therfor if ye, whanne ye ben yuele men, kunnen yyue good yiftis to youre sones, hou myche more youre fadir that is in heuenes schal yyue good thingis to men that axen hym?

12 Therfor alle thingis, what euere thingis ye wolen that men do to you, do ye to hem, for this is the lawe and the prophetis.

13 Entre ye bi the streyt yate; for the yate that ledith to perdicioun is large, and the weie is broode, and there ben many that entren bi it.

14 Hou streit is the yate, and narwy the weye, that ledith to lijf, and ther ben fewe that fynden it.

15 Be ye war of fals prophetis, that comen to you in clothingis of scheep, but withynneforth thei ben as wolues of raueyn;

16 of her fruytis ye schulen knowe hem. Whether men gaderen grapis of thornes, or figus of breris?

17 So euery good tre makith good fruytis; but an yuel tre makith yuel fruytis.

18 A good tre may not make yuel fruytis, nethir an yuel tre make good fruytis.

19 Euery tre that makith not good fruyt, schal be kyt doun, and schal be cast in to the fier.

20 Therfor of her fruytis ye schulen knowe hem.

21 Not ech man that seith to me, Lord, Lord, schal entre in to the kyngdom of heuenes; but he that doith the wille of my fadir that is in heuenes, he schal entre in to the kyngdoom of heuenes.

22 Many schulen seie to me in that dai, Lord, Lord, whether we han not prophesied in thi name, and han caste out feendis in thi name, and han doon many vertues in thi name?

23 And thanne Y schal knouleche to hem, That Y knewe you neuere; departe awei fro me, ye that worchen wickidnesse.

24 Therfor ech man that herith these my wordis, and doith hem, schal be maad lijk to a wise man, that hath bildid his hous on a stoon.

25 And reyn felde doun, and flodis camen, and wyndis blewen, and russchiden 'in to that hous; and it felde not doun, for it was foundun on a stoon.

26 And euery man that herith these my wordis, and doith hem not, is lijk to a fool, that hath bildid his hous on grauel.

27 And reyn cam doun, and floodis camen, and wyndis blewen, and thei hurliden ayen that hous; and it felde doun, and the fallyng doun therof was greet.

28 And it was doon, whanne Jhesus hadde endid these wordis, the puple wondride on his techyng;

29 for he tauyte hem, as he that hadde power, and not as the scribis 'of hem, and the Farisees.

CAP 8

1 But whanne Jhesus was come doun fro the hil, mych puple suede hym.

2 And loo! a leprouse man cam, and worschipide hym, and seide, Lord, if thou wolt, thou maist make me clene.

3 And Jhesus helde forth the hoond, and touchide hym, and seide, Y wole, be thou maad cleene. And anoon the lepre of him was clensid.

4 And Jhesus seide to hym, Se, seie thou to no man; but go, shewe thee to the prestis, and offre the yift that Moyses comaundide, in witnessyng to hem.

5 And whanne he hadde entrid in to Cafarnaum, 'the centurien neiyede to him, and preiede him,

6 and seide, Lord, my childe lijth in the hous sijk on the palesie, and is yuel turmentid.

7 And Jhesus seide to him, Y schal come, and schal heele him.

8 And the centurien answeride, and seide to hym, Lord, Y am not worthi, that thou entre vndur my roof; but oonli seie thou bi word, and my childe shal be heelid.

9 For whi Y am a man ordeyned vndur power, and haue knyytis vndir me; and Y seie to this, Go, and he goith; and to another, Come, and he cometh; and to my seruaunt, Do this, and he doith it.

10 And Jhesus herde these thingis, and wondride, and seide to men 'that sueden him, Treuli Y seie to you, Y foond not so greet feith in Israel.

11 And Y seie to you, that many schulen come fro the eest and the west, and schulen reste with Abraham and Ysaac and Jacob in the kyngdom of heuenes;

12 but the sones of the rewme schulen be cast out in to vtmer derknessis; there schal be wepyng, and grynting of teeth.

13 And Jhesus seide to the centurioun, Go, and as thou hast bileuyd, be it doon to thee. And the child was heelid fro that hour.

14 And whanne Jhesus was comun in to the hous of Symount Petre, he say his wyues modir liggynge, and shakun with feueris.

15 And he touchide hir hoond, and the feuer lefte hir; and she roos, and seruede hem.

16 And whanne it was euen, thei brouyten to hym manye that hadden deuelis, and he castide out spiritis bi word, and heelide alle that weren yuel at ese;

17 that it were fulfillid, that was seid by Ysaie, the profete, seiynge, He took oure infirmytees, and bar oure siknessis.

18 And Jhesus say myche puple aboute him, and bade hise disciplis go ouer the watir.

19 And a scribe neiyede, and seide to hym, Maistir, Y shal sue thee, whidir euer thou schalt go.

20 And Jhesus seide to hym, Foxis han dennes, and briddis of heuene han nestis, but mannus sone hath not where 'he schal reste his heed.

21 Anothir of his disciplis seide to him, Lord, suffre me to go first, and birie my fader.

22 But Jhesus seide to hym, Sue thou me, and lete deed men birie her deede men.

23 And whanne he was goon vp in to a litil schip, his disciplis sueden hym.

24 And loo! a greet stiring was maad in the see, so that the schip was hilid with wawes; but he slepte.

25 And hise disciplis camen to hym, and reysiden hym, and seiden, Lord, saue vs; we perischen.

26 And Jhesus seide to hem, What ben ye of litil feith agaste? Thanne he roos, and comaundide to the wyndis and the see, and a greet pesibilnesse was maad.

27 And men wondriden, and seiden, What maner man is he this, for the wyndis and the see obeischen to him?

28 And whanne Jhesus was comun ouer the watir in to the cuntre of men of Gerasa, twey men metten hym, that hadden deuelis, and camen out of graues, ful woode, so that noo man myyte go bi that weie.

29 And lo! thei crieden, and seiden, What to vs and to thee, Jhesu, the sone of God? 'art thou comun hidir bifore the tyme to turmente vs?

30 And not fer fro hem was a flocke of many swyne lesewynge.

31 And the deuelis preyeden hym, and seiden, If thou castist out vs fro hennes, sende vs in to the droue of swyne.

32 And he seide to hem, Go ye. And thei yeden out, and wenten in to the swyne; and loo! in a greet bire al the droue wente heedlyng in to the see, and thei weren deed in the watris.

33 And the hirdis fledden awey, and camen in to the citee, and telden alle these thingis, and of hem that hadden the feendis.

34 And lo! al the citee wente out ayens Jhesu; and whanne thei hadden seyn hym, thei preieden, that he wolde passe fro her coostis.

CAP 9

1 And Jhesus wente vp in to a boot, and passide ouer the watir, and cam in to his citee.

2 And lo! thei brouyten to hym a man sike in palesie, liggynge in a bed. And Jhesus saw the feith of hem, and seide to

the man sike in palesye, Sone, haue thou trist; thi synnes ben foryouun to thee.

3 And lo! summe of the scribis seiden withynne hem silf, This blasfemeth.

4 And whanne Jhesus hadde seyn her thouytis, he seide, Wherto thenken ye yuele thingis in youre hertis?

5 What is liytere to seye, Thi synnes ben foryouun to thee, ethir 'to seie, Rise thou, and walke?

6 But that ye wite that mannus sone hath power to foryyue synnes in erthe, thanne he seide to the sijk man in palesie, Rise vp; take thi bed, and go in to thin hous.

7 And he roos, and wente in to his hous.

8 And the puple seynge dredde, and glorifiede God, that yaf suche power to men.

9 And whanne Jhesus passide fro thennus, he say a man, Matheu bi name, sittynge in a tolbothe. And he seide to hym, Sue thou me.

10 And he roos, and folewide hym. And it was don, the while he sat 'at the mete in the hous, lo! many pupplicans and synful men camen, and saten 'at the mete with Jhesu and hise disciplis.

11 And Farisees sien, and seiden to hise disciplis, Whi etith youre maister with pupplicans and synful men?

12 And Jhesus herde, and seide, A leche is not nedeful to men that faren wel, but to men that ben yuel at ese.

13 But go ye, and lerne what it is, Y wole merci, and not sacrifice; for I cam, not to clepe riytful men, but synful men.

14 Thanne the disciplis of Joon camen to hym, and seiden, Whi we and Farisees fasten ofte, but thi disciplis fasten not?

15 And Jhesus seide to hem, Whether the sones of the spouse moun morne, as long as the spouse is with hem? But daies schulen come, whanne the spouse schal be takun a wei fro hem, and thanne thei schulen faste.

16 And no man putteth a clout of buystous clothe in to an elde clothing; for it doith awey the fulnesse of the cloth, and a wers breking is maad.

17 Nethir men putten newe wyne in to elde botelis, ellis the botels ben to-broke, and distried, and the wyn sched out. But men putten newe wyne in to newe botels, and bothe ben kept.

18 Whiles that Jhesus spak thes thingis to hem, lo! a prince cam, and worschipide hym, and seide, Lord, my douyter is now deed; but come thou, and putte thin hond on hir, and she schal lyue.

19 And Jhesus roos, and 'hise disciplis, and sueden hym.

20 And lo! a womman, that hadde the blodi flux twelue yere, neiyede bihynde, and touchide the hem of his cloth.

21 For sche seide with ynne hir self, Yif Y touche oonli the cloth of hym, Y schal be saaf.

22 And Jhesus turnede, and say hir, and seide, Douytir, haue thou trist; thi feith hath maad thee saaf. And the womman was hool fro that our.

23 And whanne Jhesus cam in to the hous of the prince, and say mynstrallis, and the puple makynge noise,

24 he seide, Go ye a wei, for the damysel is not deed, but slepith. And thei scornyden hym.

25 And whanne the folc was put out, he wente in, and helde hir hond; and the damysel roos.

26 And this fame wente out in to al that loond.

27 And whanne Jhesus passide fro thennus, twei blynde men criynge sueden hym, and seiden, Thou sone of Dauid, haue merci on vs.

28 And whanne he cam in to the hous, the blynde men camen to hym; and Jhesus seide to hem, What wolen ye, that I do to you? And thei seiden, Lord, that oure iyen be opened. And Jhesus seide, Bileuen ye, that Y mai do this thing to you? Thei seien to him, Yhe, Lord.

29 Thanne he touchide her iyen, and seide, Aftir youre feith be it doon to you.

30 And the iyen of hem were opened. And Jhesus thretenede hem, and seide, Se ye, that no man wite.

31 But thei yeden out, and diffameden hym thorou al that lond.

32 And whanne thei weren gon out, loo! thei brouyten to hym a doumbe man, hauynge a deuel.

33 And whanne the deuel was cast out, the doumb man spak. And the puple wondride, and seide, It hath not be say thus in Israel.

34 But the Farisees seiden, In the prince of deuelis he castith out deuelis.

35 And Jhesus wente 'aboute alle the 'citees and castels, techinge in the synagogis of hem, and prechynge the gospel of the kyngdom, and helynge euery langour and euery sijknesse.

36 And he siy the puple, and hadde reuthe on hem; for thei weren trauelid, and liggynge as scheep not hauynge a scheepherde.

37 Thanne he seide to hise disciplis, Sotheli there is myche ripe corn, but fewe werk men.

38 Therfor preye ye the lord of the ripe corn, that he sende werke men in to his ripe corn.

CAP 10

1 And whanne his twelue disciplis weren clepid togidere, he yaf to hem powere of vnclene spiritis, to caste hem out of men, and to heele eueri langour, and sijknesse.

2 And these ben the names of the twelue apostlis; the firste, Symount, that is clepid Petre, and Andrew, his brothir; James of Zebede, and Joon, his brothir; Filip, and Bartholomeu;

3 Thomas, and Matheu, pupplican; and James Alfey, and Tadee;

4 Symount Chananee, and Judas Scarioth, that bitrayede Crist.

5 Jhesus sente these twelue, and comaundide hem, and seide, Go ye not 'in to the weie of hethene men, and entre ye not in to the citees of Samaritans;

6 but rather go ye to the scheep of the hous of Israel, that han perischid.

7 And go ye, and preche ye, and seie, that the kyngdam of heuenes shal neiye;

8 heele ye sike men, reise ye deede men, clense ye mesels, caste ye out deuelis; freeli ye han takun, freli yyue ye.

9 Nyle ye welde gold, nether siluer, ne money in youre girdlis, not a scrippe in the weie,

10 nether twei cootis, nethir shoon, nether a yerde; for a werkman is worthi his mete.

11 In to what euere citee or castel ye schulen entre, axe ye who therynne is worthi, and there dwelle ye, til ye go out.

12 And whanne ye goon in to an hous, 'grete ye it, and seyn, Pees to this hous.

13 And if thilk hous be worthi, youre pees schal come on it; but if that hous be not worthi, youre pees schal turne ayen to you.

14 And who euere resseyueth not you, nethir herith youre wordis, go ye fro that hous or citee, and sprenge of the dust of youre feet.

15 Treuly Y seie to you, it shal be more suffrable to the loond of men of Sodom and of Gommor in the dai of iugement, than to thilke citee.

16 Lo! Y sende you as scheep in the myddil of wolues; therfor be ye sliy as serpentis, and symple as dowues.

17 But be ye war of men, for thei schulen take you in counseilis, and thei schulen bete you in her synagogis;

18 and to meyris, or presidentis, and to kyngis, ye schulen be lad for me, in witnessyng to hem, and to the hethen men.

19 But whanne thei take you, nyle ye thenke, hou or what thing ye schulen speke, for it shal be youun 'to you in that our, what ye schulen speke;

20 for it ben not ye that speken, but the spirit of youre fadir, that spekith in you.

21 'And the brother shal take the brother in to deeth, and the fader the sone, and sones schulen rise ayens fadir and modir, and schulen turmente hem bi deeth.

22 And ye schulen be in hate to alle men for my name; but he that shall dwelle stille in to the ende, shal be saaf.

23 And whanne thei pursuen you in this citee, fle ye in to anothir. Treuli Y seie to you, ye schulen not ende the citees of Israel, to for that mannus sone come.

24 The disciple is not aboue the maistir, ne the seruaunt aboue hys lord;

25 it is ynowy to the disciple, that he be as his maistir, and to the seruaunt as his lord. If thei han clepid the hosebonde man Belsabub, hou myche more his houshold meyne?

26 Therfor drede ye not hem; for no thing is hid, that schal not be shewid; and no thing is priuey, that schal not be wist.

27 That thing that Y seie to you in derknessis, seie ye in the liyt; and preche ye on housis, that thing that ye heeren in the ere.

28 And nyle ye drede hem that sleen the bodi; for thei moun not sle the soule; but rather drede ye hym, that mai lese bothe soule and bodi in to helle.

29 Whether twei sparewis ben not seeld for an halpeny? and oon of hem shal not falle on the erthe with outen youre fadir.

30 'And alle the heeris of youre heed ben noumbrid. Therfor nyle ye drede; ye ben betere than many sparewis.

31 Therfor euery man that schal knouleche me bifore men, Y schal knouleche hym bifor my fadir that is in heuenes.

33 But he that shal denye me bifor men, and I shal denye him bifor my fadir that is in heuenes.

34 Nile ye deme, that Y cam to sende pees in to erthe; Y cam not to sende pees, but swerd.

35 For Y cam to departe a man ayens his fadir, and the douytir ayens hir modir, and the sones wijf ayens the housbondis modir;

36 and the enemyes of a man ben 'thei, that ben homeli with him.

37 He that loueth fadir or modir more than me, is not worthi to me. And he that loueth sone or douyter ouer me, is not worthi to me.

38 And he that takith not his croos, and sueth me, is not worthi to me.

39 He that fyndith his lijf, shal lose it; and he that lesith his lijf for me, shal fynde it.

40 He that resseyueth you, resseyueth me; and he that resseyueth me, resseyueth hym that sente me.

41 He that resseyueth a prophete in the name of a prophete, shal take the mede of a prophete. And he that resseyueth a iust man in the name of a iust man, schal take the mede of a iust man.

42 And who euer yyueth drynke to oon of these leeste a cuppe of coolde watir oonli in the name of a disciple, treuli Y seie to you, he shal not leese his mede.

CAP 11

1 And it was doon, whanne Jhesus hadde endid, he comaundide to hise twelue disciplis, and passide fro thennus to teche and preche in the citees of hem.

2 But whanne Joon in boondis hadde herd the werkis of Crist, he sente tweyne of hise disciplis,

3 and seide to him, 'Art thou he that schal come, or we abiden another?

4 And Jhesus answeride, and seide 'to hem, Go ye, and telle ayen to Joon tho thingis that ye han herd and seyn.

5 Blynde men seen, crokid men goon, meselis ben maad clene, deefe men heren, deed men rysen ayen, pore men ben takun to 'prechyng of the gospel.

6 And he is blessid, that shal not be sclaundrid in me.

7 And whanne thei weren goon awei, Jhesus bigan to seie of Joon to the puple, What thing wenten ye out in to desert to se? a reed wawed with the wynd?

8 Or what thing wenten ye out to see? a man clothid with softe clothis? Lo! thei that ben clothid with softe clothis ben in the housis of kyngis.

9 But what thing wenten ye out to se? a prophete? Yhe, Y seie to you, and more than a prophete.

10 For this is he, of whom it is writun, Lo! Y sende myn aungel bifor thi face, that shal make redi thi weye bifor thee.

11 Treuli Y seie to you, ther roos noon more than Joon Baptist among the children of wymmen; but he that is lesse in the kyngdom of heuenes, is more than he.

12 And fro the daies of Joon Baptist til now the kyngdom of heuenes suffrith violence, and violent men rauyschen it.

13 For alle prophetis and the lawe 'til to Joon prophecieden; and if ye wolen resseyue,

14 he is Elie that is to come.

15 He that hath eris of heryng, here he.

16 But to whom schal Y gesse this generacioun lijk? It is lijk to children sittynge in chepyng, that crien to her peeris,

17 and seien, We han songun to you, and ye han not daunsid; we han morned to you, and ye han not weilid.

18 For Joon cam nether etynge ne drynkynge, and thei seien, He hath a deuel.

19 The sone of man cam etynge and drynkynge, and thei seien, Lo! a man a glotoun, and a drinkere of wijne, and a freend of pupplicans and of synful men. And wisdom is iustified of her sones.

20 Thanne Jhesus bigan to seye repreef to citees, in whiche ful manye vertues of him weren doon, for thei diden not penaunce.

21 Wo to thee! Corosaym, woo to thee! Bethsaida; for if the vertues that ben doon in you hadden be doon in Tyre and Sidon, sumtyme thei hadden don penaunce in heyre and aische.

22 Netheles Y seie to you, it schal be lesse peyne to Tire and Sidon in the dai of doom, than to you.

23 And thou, Cafarnaum, whethir thou schalt be arerid vp in to heuene? Thou schalt go doun in to helle. For if the vertues that ben don in thee, hadden be don in Sodom, perauenture thei schulden haue dwellid 'in to this dai.

24 Netheles Y seie to you, that to the lond of Sodom it schal be 'lesse peyne in the dai of doom, than to thee.

25 In thilke tyme Jhesus answeride, and seide, Y knowleche to thee, fadir, lord of heuene and of erthe, for thou hast hid these thingis fro wijse men, and redi, and hast schewid hem to litle children;

26 so, fadir, for so it was plesynge tofore thee.

27 Alle thingis ben youune to me of my fadir; and no man knewe the sone, but the fadir, nethir ony man knewe the fadir, but the sone, and to whom the sone wolde schewe.

28 Alle ye that traueilen, and ben chargid, come to me, and Y schal fulfille you.

29 Take ye my yok on you, and lerne ye of me, for Y am mylde and meke in herte; and ye schulen fynde reste to youre soulis.

30 'For my yok is softe, and my charge liyt.

CAP 12

1 In that tyme Jhesus wente bi cornes in the sabot day; and hise disciplis hungriden, and bigunnen to plucke the eris of corn, and to ete.

2 And Fariseis, seynge, seiden to hym, Lo! thi disciplis don that thing that is not leueful to hem to do in sabatis.

3 And he seide to hem, Whether ye han not red, what Dauid dide, whanne he hungride, and thei that weren with hym?

4 hou he entride in to the hous of God, and eet looues of proposicioun, whiche looues it was not leueful to hym to ete, nether to hem that weren with hym, but to prestis aloone?

5 Or whether ye han not red in the lawe, that in sabotis prestis in the temple defoulen the sabotis, and thei ben with oute blame?

6 And Y seie to you, that here is a gretter than the temple.

7 And if ye wisten, what it is, Y wole merci, and not sacrifice, ye schulden neuer haue condempned innocentis.

8 For mannus Sone is lord, yhe, of the sabat.

9 And whanne he passide fro thennus, he cam in to the synagoge of hem.

10 And lo! a man that hadde a drye hoond. And thei axiden hym, and seiden, Whether it be leueful to hele in the sabot? that thei schulden acuse hym.

11 And he seide to hem, What man of you schal be, that hath o scheep, and if it falle in to a diche in the sabotis, whether he schal not holde, and lifte it vp?

12 How myche more is a man better than a scheep? Therfor it is leueful to do good in the sabatis.

13 Thanne he seide to the man, Stretche forth thin hoond. And he strauyte forth; and it was restorid to heelthe as the tothir.

14 And the Farisees wenten out, and maden a counsel ayens hym, hou thei schulden distrie hym.

15 And Jhesus knewe it, and wente awei fro thennus; and many sueden hym, and he helide hem alle.

16 And he comaundide to hem, that thei schulden not make hym knowun;

17 that that thing were fulfillid, that was seid by Isaie, the prophete, seiynge, Lo!

18 my child, whom Y haue chosun, my derling, in whom it hath wel plesid to my soule; Y schal put my spirit on him, and he schal telle dom to hethen men.

19 He schal not stryue, ne crye, nethir ony man schal here his voice in stretis.

20 A brisid rehed he schal not breke, and he schal not quenche smokynge flax, til he caste out doom to victorie;

21 and hethene men schulen hope in his name.

22 Thanne a man blynde and doumbe, that hadde a feend, was brouyt to hym; and he helide hym, so that he spak, and say.

23 And al the puple wondride, and seide, Whether this be the sone of Dauid?

24 But the Farisees herden, and seiden, He this casteth not out feendis, but in Belsabub, prince of feendis.

25 And Jhesus, witynge her thouytis, seide to hem, Eche kingdom departid ayens it silf, schal be desolatid, and eche cite, or hous, departid ayens it self, schal not stonde.

26 And if Satanas castith out Satanas, he is departid ayens him silf; therfor hou schal his kingdom stonde?

27 And if Y in Belsabub caste out deuelis, in 'whom youre sones casten out? Therfor thei schulen be youre domes men.

28 But if Y in the Spirit of God caste out feendis, thanne the kyngdom of God is comen in to you.

29 Ethir hou may ony man entre in to the hous of a stronge man, and take awey hise vesselis, but 'he first bynde the stronge man, and thanne he schal spuyle his hous?

30 He that is not with me, is ayens me; and he that gaderith not togidere with me, scaterith abrood.

31 Therfor I seie to you, al synne and blasfemye schal be foryouun to men, but 'the spirit of blasfemye schal not be foryouun.

32 And who euere seith a word ayens mannus sone, it schal be foryouun to him; but who that seieth a word ayens the Hooli Goost, it schal not be foryouun to hym, nether in this world, ne in 'the tothir.

33 Ethir make ye the tree good, and his fruyt good; ether make ye the tree yuel and his fruyt yuel; for a tree is knowun of the fruyt.

34 Ye generacioun of eddris, hou moun ye speke goode thingis, whanne ye ben yuele? For the mouth spekith of plente of the herte.

35 A good man bryngith forth good thingis of good tresoure, and an yuel man bringith forth yuel thingis of yuel tresoure.

36 And Y seie to you, that of euery idel word, that men speken, thei schulen yelde resoun therof in the dai of doom;

37 for of thi wordis thou schalt be iustified, and of thi wordis thou shalt be dampned.

38 Thanne summe of the scribis and Farisees answeriden to hym, and seiden, Mayster, we wolen se a tokne of thee.

39 Which answeride, and seide to hem, An yuel kynrede and a spouse brekere sekith a tokene, and a tokene schal not be youun to it, but the tokene of Jonas, the prophete.

40 For as Jonas was in the wombe of a whal thre daies and thre nyytis, so mannus sone schal be in the herte of the erthe thre daies and thre nyytis.

41 Men of Nynyue schulen rise in doom with this generacioun, and schulen condempne it; for thei diden penaunce in the prechyng of Jonas, and lo! here a gretter than Jonas.

42 The queene of the south schal rise in doom with this generacioun, and schal condempne it; for she cam fro the eendis of the erthe to here the wisdom of Salomon, and lo! here a gretter than Salomon.

43 Whanne an vnclene spirit goith out fro a man, he goith bi drie places, 'and sekith rest, and fyndith not.

44 Thanne he seith, Y schal turne ayen in to myn hous, fro whannys Y wente out. And he cometh, and fyndith it voide, and clensid with besyms, and maad faire.

45 Thanne he goith, and takith with him seuene othere spiritis worse than hym silf; and thei entren, and dwellen there. And the laste thingis of that man ben maad worse than the formere. So it schal be to this worste generacioun.

46 Yit whil he spak to the puple, lo! his modir and his bretheren stoden withouteforth, sekynge to speke to hym.

47 And a man seide to hym, Lo! thi modir and thi britheren stonden withouteforth, sekynge thee.

48 He answeride to the man, that spak to hym, and seide, Who is my modir? and who ben my britheren?

49 And he helde forth his hoond in to hise disciplis, and seide, Lo! my modir and my bretheren;

50 for who euer doith the wille of my fadir that is in heuenes, he is my brothir, and sistir, and modir.

CAP 13

1 In that dai Jhesus yede out of the hous, and sat bisidis the see.

2 And myche puple was gaderid to hym, so that he wente up in to a boot, and sat; and al the puple stood on the brenke.

3 And he spac to hem many thingis in parablis, and seide, Lo! he that sowith, yede out to sowe his seed.

4 And while he sowith, summe seedis felden bisidis the weie, and briddis of the eir camen, and eeten hem.

5 But othere seedis felden in to stony places, where thei hadden not myche erthe; and anoon thei sprongen vp, for thei hadden not depnesse of erthe.

6 But whanne the sonne was risun, thei swaliden, and for thei hadden not roote, thei drieden vp.

7 And other seedis felden among thornes; and thornes woxen vp, and strangeleden hem.

8 But othere seedis felden in to good lond, and yauen fruyt; summe an hundrid foold, an othir sixti foold, an othir thritti foold.

9 He that hath eris of heryng, here he.

10 And the disciplis camen nyy, and seiden to him, Whi spekist thou in parablis to hem?

11 And he answeride, and seide to hem, 'For to you it is youun to knowe the priuytees of the kyngdom of heuenes; but it is not youun to hem.

12 For it shal be youun to hym that hath, and he shal haue plente; but if a man hath not, also that thing that he hath shal be takun awei fro hym.

13 Therfor Y speke to hem in parablis, for thei seynge seen not, and thei herynge heren not, nether vndurstonden;

14 that the prophesie of Ysaie 'seiynge be fulfillid 'in hem, With heryng ye schulen here, and ye shulen not vndurstonde; and ye seynge schulen se, and ye shulen not se;

15 for the herte of this puple is greetli fattid, and thei herden heuyli with eeris, and thei han closed her iyen, lest sumtime thei seen with iyen, and with eeris heeren, and vndirstonden in herte, and thei be conuertid, and Y heele hem.

16 But youre iyen that seen ben blesside, and youre eeris that heren.

17 Forsothe Y seie to you, that manye profetis and iust men coueitiden to se tho thingis that ye seen, and thei sayn not, and to heere tho thingis that ye heren, and thei herden not.

18 Therfor here ye the parable of the sowere.

19 Ech that herith the word of the rewme, and vndirstondith not, the yuel spirit cometh, and rauyschith that that is sowun in his herte; this it is, that is sowun bisidis the weie.

20 But this that is sowun on the stony loond, this it is, that herith the word of God, and anoon with ioye takith it.

21 And he hath not roote in hym silf, but is temporal. For whanne tribulacioun and persecucioun is maad for the word, anoon he is sclaundrid.

22 But he that is sowun in thornes, is this that heerith the word, and the bisynesse of this world, and the fallace of ritchessis strangulith the word, and it is maad with outen fruyt.

23 But he that is sowun in to good loond, is this that herith the word, and vnderstondeth, and bryngith forth fruyt. And summe makith an hundrid fold, treuli anothir sixti fold, and another thritti fold.

24 Anothir parable Jhesus puttide forth to hem, and seide, The kyngdom of heuenes is maad lijk to a man, that sewe good seed in his feld.

25 And whanne men slepten, his enemy cam, and sewe aboue taris in the myddil of whete, and wente awei.

26 But whanne the erbe was growed, and made fruyt, thanne the taris apperiden.

27 And the seruauntis of the hosebonde man camen, and seiden to hym, Lord, whether hast thou not sowun good seed in thi feeld? where of thanne hath it taris?

28 And he seide to hem, An enemy hath do this thing. And the seruauntis seiden to him, 'Wolt thou that we goon, and gaderen hem?

29 And he seide, Nay, lest perauenture ye in gaderynge taris drawen vp with hem the whete bi the roote.

30 Suffre ye hem bothe to wexe in to repyng tyme; and in the tyme of ripe corne Y shal seie to the reperis, First gadere ye to gidere the taris, and bynde hem to gidere in knytchis to be brent, but gadere ye whete in to my berne.

31 Another parable Jhesus puttide forth to hem, and seide, The kyngdom of heuenes is lijk to a corn of seneuey, which a man took, and sewe in his feeld.

32 Which is the leeste of alle seedis, but whanne it hath woxen, it is the moste of alle wortis, and is maad a tre; so that briddis of the eir comen, and dwellen in the bowis therof.

33 Another parable Jhesus spac to hem, The kyngdom of heuenes is lijk to sour douy, which a womman took, and hidde in thre mesuris of mele, til it were alle sowrid.

34 Jhesus spac alle thes thingis in parablis to the puple, and he spac not to hem with out parablis, that it schulde be fulfillid,

35 that is seid bi the prophete, seiynge, Y shal opene my mouth in parablis; Y shal telle out hid thingis fro the makyng of the world.

36 Thanne he lefte the puple, and cam in to an hous; and hise disciplis camen to him, and seiden, Expowne to vs the parable of taris of the feeld.

37 Which answeride, and seide, He that sowith good seed is mannus sone;

38 the feeld is the world; but the good seed, these ben sones of the kyngdom, but taris, these ben yuele children;

39 the enemye that sowith hem is the feend; and the ripe corn is the endyng of the world, the reperis ben aungels.

40 Therfor as taris ben gaderid togidere, and ben brent in fier, so it shal be in the endyng of the world.

41 Mannus sone shal sende hise aungels, and thei schulen gadere fro his rewme alle sclaundris, and hem that doon wickidnesse;

42 and thei schulen sende hem in to the chymney of fier, there shal be weping and betyng to gidere of teeth.

43 Thanne iuste men schulen schyne as the sunne, in the rewme of her fadir. He that hath eeris of heryng, here he.

44 The kyngdom of heuenes is lijk to tresour hid in a feld, which a man that fyndith, hidith; and for ioye of it he goith, and sillith alle thingis that he hath, and bieth thilk feeld.

45 Eftsoone the kyngdom of heuenes is lijk to a marchaunt, that sechith good margaritis;

46 but whanne he hath foundun o precious margarite, he wente, and selde alle thingis that he hadde, and bouyte it.

47 Eft the kyngdom of heuenes is lijk to a nette cast into the see, and that gaderith to gidere of al kynde of fisschis;

48 which whanne it was ful, thei drowen vp, and seten bi the brenke, and chesen the goode in to her vessels, but the yuel thei kesten out.

49 So it schal be in the endyng of the world. Aungels schulen go out, and schulen departe yuel men fro the myddil of iuste men.

50 And thei shulen sende hem in to the chymnei of fier; ther shal be weping and gryntyng of teeth.

51 Han ye vndirstonde alle these thingis? Thei seien to hym, Yhe.

52 He seith to hem, Therfor euery wise man of lawe in the kyngdom of heuenes, is lijk to an hosebonde man, that bryngith forth of his tresoure newe thingis and elde.

53 And it was doon, whanne Jhesus hadde endid these parablis, he passide fro thennus.

54 And he cam in to his cuntrei, and tauyte hem in her synagogis, so that thei wondriden, and seiden, Fro whennus this wisdam and vertues camen to this?

55 Whether 'is not this the sone of a carpentere? Whether his modir be not seid Marie? and hise britheren, James, and Joseph, and Symount, and Judas? and hise sistris,

56 whether thei alle ben not among us? Fro whennus thanne 'alle thes thingis camen to this?

57 And so thei weren sclaundrid in hym. But Jhesus seide to hem, A profete is not with oute worschip, but in his owen cuntre, and in his owen hous.

58 And he dide not there manye vertues, for the vnbileue of hem.

CAP 14

1 In that tyme Eroude tetrarke, prynce of the fourthe part, herde the fame of Jhesu;

2 and seide to hise children, This is Joon Baptist, he is rysun fro deeth, and therfor vertues worchen in hym.

3 For Heroude hadde holde Joon, and bounde hym, and puttide hym 'in to prisoun for Herodias, the wijf of his brothir.

4 For Joon seide to him, It is not leueful to thee to haue hir.

5 And he willynge to sle hym, dredde the puple; for thei hadden hym as a prophete.

6 But in the dai of Heroudis birthe, the douytir of Herodias daunside in the myddil, and pleside Heroude.

7 Wherfor with an ooth he bihiyte to yyue to hir, what euere thing she hadde axid of hym.

8 And she bifor warned of hir modir, seide, Yif thou to me here the heed of Joon Baptist in a disch.

9 And the kyng was sorewful, but for the ooth, and for hem that saten to gidere at the mete, he comaundide to be youun.

10 And he sente, and bihedide Joon in the prisoun.

11 And his heed was brouyt in a dische, and it was youun to the damysel, and she bar it to hir modir.

12 And hise disciplis camen, and token his bodi, and birieden it; and thei camen, and tolden to Jhesu.

13 And whanne Jhesus hadde herd this thing, he wente fro thennus in a boot, in to desert place bisides. And whanne the puple hadde herd, thei folewiden hym on her feet fro citees.

14 And Jhesus yede out, and sai a greet puple, and hadde reuthe on hem, and heelide the sike men of hem.

15 But whanne the euentid was com, hise disciplis camen to him, and seiden, The place is desert, and the tyme is now passid; lat the puple go in to townes, to bye hem mete.

16 Jhesus seide to hem, Thei han not nede to go; yyue ye hem sumwhat to ete.

17 Thei answeriden, We han not heere, but fyue looues and twei fischis.

18 And he seide to hem, Brynge ye hem hidur to me.

19 And whanne he hadde comaundid the puple to sitte to meete on the heye, he took fyue looues and twei fischis, and he bihelde in to heuene, and blesside, and brak, and yaf to hise disciplis; and the disciplis yauen to the puple.

20 And alle eten, and weren fulfillid. And thei tooken the relifs of brokun gobetis, twelue cofynes ful.

21 And the noumbre of men that eten was fyue thousynde of men, outakun wymmen and lytle children.

22 And anoon Jhesus compellide the disciplis to go vp in to a boot, and go bifor hym ouer the see, while he lefte the puple.

23 And whanne the puple was left, he stiede aloone in to an hil for to preie. But whanne the euenyng was come, he was there aloone.

24 And the boot in the myddel of the see was schoggid with wawis, for the wynd was contrarie to hem.

25 But in the fourthe wakyng of the niyt, he cam to hem walkynge aboue the see.

26 And thei, seynge hym walking on the see, weren disturblid, and seiden, That it is a fantum; and for drede thei crieden.

27 And anoon Jhesus spac to hem, and seide, Haue ye trust, Y am; nyle ye drede.

28 And Petre answeride, and seide, Lord, if thou art, comaunde me to come to thee on the watris.

29 And he seide, Come thou. And Petre yede doun fro the boot, and walkide on the watris to come to Jhesu.

30 But he siy the wynd strong, and was aferde; and whanne he bigan to drenche, he criede, and seide, Lord, make me saaf.

31 And anoon Jhesus helde forth his hoond, and took Petre, and seide to hym, Thou of litil feith, whi hast thou doutid?

32 And whanne he hadde stied in to the boot, the wynd ceessid.

33 And thei, that weren in the boot, camen, and worschipiden hym, and seiden, Verili, thou art Goddis sone.

34 And whanne thei hadden passid ouer the see, thei camen in to the loond of Genesar.

35 And whanne men of that place hadden knowe hym, thei senten in to al that cuntre; and thei brouyten to hym alle that hadden siknesse.

36 And thei preieden hym, that thei schulden touche the hemme of his clothing; and who euere touchiden weren maad saaf.

CAP 15

1 Thanne the scribis and the Farisees camen to hym fro Jerusalem, and seiden,

2 Whi breken thi disciplis the tradiciouns of eldere men? for thei waisschen not her hondis, whanne thei eten breed.

3 He answeride, and seide to hem, Whi breken ye the maundement of God for youre tradicioun?

4 For God seide, Honoure thi fadir and thi modir, and he that cursith fadir or modir, die bi deeth.

5 But ye seien, Who euer seith to fadir or modir, What euere yifte is of me, it schal profite to thee;

6 and he hath not worschipid his fadir or his modir; and ye han maad the maundement of God voide for youre tradicioun.

7 Ypocritis, Isaie, the prophete, prophesiede wel of you,

8 and seide, This puple honourith me with lippis, but her herte is fer fro me;

9 and thei worschipen me 'with outen cause, techynge the doctrines and maundementis of men.

10 And whanne the puple weren clepid to gidere to hym, he seide to hem, Here ye, and 'vndurstonde ye.

11 That thing that entrith in to the mouth, defoulith not a man; but that thing that cometh out of the mouth, defoulith a man.

12 Thanne hise disciplis camen, and seiden to hym, Thou knowist, that, if this word be herd, the Farisees ben sclaundrid?

13 And he answeride, and seide, Eueri plauntyng, that my fadir of heuene hath not plauntid, shal be drawun vp by the roote.

14 Suffre ye hem; thei ben blynde, and leederis of blynde men. And if a blynd man lede a blynd man, bothe fallen doun in to the diche.

15 Petre answeride, and seide to hym, Expowne to vs this parable.

16 And he seide, Yit 'ye ben also with oute vndurstondyng?

17 Vndurstonden ye not, that al thing that entrith in to the mouth, goith in to the wombe, and is sent out in to the goyng awei?

18 But tho thingis that comen forth fro the mouth, goon out of the herte, and tho thingis defoulen a man.

19 For of the herte goon out yuele thouytis, mansleyngis, auowtries, fornycaciouns, theftis, fals witnessyngis, blasfemyes.

20 Thes thingis it ben that defoulen a man; but to ete with hondis not waischun, defoulith not a man.

21 And Jhesus yede out fro thennus, and wente in to the coostis of Tire and Sidon.

22 And lo! a womman of Canane yede out of tho coostis, and criede, and seide to him, Lord, the sone of Dauid, haue merci on me; my douyter is yuel traueilid of a feend.

23 And he answeride not to hir a word. And hise disciplis camen, and preieden hym, and seiden, Leue thou hir, for she crieth aftir vs.

24 He answeride, and seide, Y am not sent, but to the scheep of the hous of Israel that perischiden.

25 And she cam, and worschipide hym, and seide, Lord, helpe me.

26 Which answeride, and seide, It is not good to take the breed of children, and caste to houndis.

27 And she seide, Yhis, Lord; for whelpis eten of the crummes, that fallen doun fro the bord of her lordis.

28 Thanne Jhesus answeride, and seide to hir, A! womman, thi feith is greet; be it doon to thee, as thou wolt. And hir douytir was helid fro that hour.

29 And whanne Jhesus hadde passed fro thennus, he cam bisidis the see of Galilee. And he yede vp in to an hil, and sat there.

30 And myche puple cam to hym, and hadden with hem doumbe men and crokid, feble and blynde, and many other; and thei castiden doun hem at hise feet. And he helide hem,

31 so that the puple wondriden seynge doumbe men spekynge, and crokid goynge, blynde men seynge; and thei magnyfieden God of Israel.

32 And Jhesus, whanne hise disciplis weren clepid to gidere, seide to hem, Y haue reuthe of the puple, for thei han abiden now thre daies with me, and han no thing to ete; and Y wole not leeue hem fastynge, lest thei failen in the weie.

33 And the disciplis seien to him, Wherof thanne so many looues among vs in desert, to fulfille so greet a puple?

34 And Jhesus seide to hem, Hou many looues han ye? And thei seiden, Seuene, and a fewe smale fisshis.

35 And he comaundide to the puple, to sitte to mete on the erthe.

36 And he took seuene looues and fyue fischis, and dide thankyngis, and brak, and yaf to hise disciplis; and the disciplis yauen to the puple.

37 And alle eten, and weren fulfillid, and thei token that that was left of relifes, seuene lepis fulle.

38 And thei that eten weren foure thousynde of men, with outen litle children and wymmen.

39 And whanne he hadde left the puple, he wente vp in to a boot, and cam in to the coostis of Magedan.

CAP 16

1 And the Farisees and the Saducees camen to hym temptynge, and preieden hym to schewe hem a tokene fro heuene.

2 And he answeride, and seide to hem, Whanne the euentid is comun, ye seien, It schal be clere, for heuene is rodi;

3 and the morewtid, To dai tempest, for heuene schyneth heueli.

4 Thanne ye kunne deme the face of heuene, but ye moun not wite the tokenes of tymes. An yuel generacioun and auoutresse sekith a tokene; and a tokene schal not be youun to it, but the tokene of Jonas, the profete. And whanne he hadde left hem, he wente forth.

5 And whanne his disciplis camen ouer the see, thei foryaten to take looues.

6 And he seide to hem, Biholde ye, and be war of the soure dowy of Farisees and Saducees.

7 And thei thouyten among hem, and seiden, For we han not take looues.

8 But Jhesus witynge seide to hem, What thenken ye among you of litel feith, for ye han not looues?

9 Yit 'vndurstonden not ye, nether han mynde of fyue looues in to fyue thousynde of men, and hou many cofyns ye token?

10 nether of seuene looues in to foure thousynde of men, and hou many lepis ye token?

11 Whi vndurstonden ye not, for Y seide not to you of breed, Be ye war of the sourdowy of Farisees and of Saducees?

12 Thanne thei vndurstooden, that he seide not to be war of sourdowy of looues, but of the techyng of Farisees and Saducees.

13 And Jhesus cam in to the parties of Cesarie of Filip, and axide hise disciplis, and seide, Whom seien men to be mannus sone?

14 And thei seiden, Summe Joon Baptist; othere Elie; and othere Jeremye, or oon of the prophetis.

15 Jhesus seide to hem, But whom seien ye me to be?

16 Symount Petre answeride, and seide, Thou art Crist, the sone of God lyuynge.

17 Jhesus answeride, and seide to him, Blessid art thou, Symount Bariona; for fleisch and blood schewide not to thee, but my fadir that is in heuenes.

18 And Y seie to thee, that thou art Petre, and on this stoon Y schal bilde my chirche, and the yatis of helle schulen not haue miyt ayens it.

19 And to thee Y schal yyue the keies of the kingdom of heuenes; and what euer thou shalt bynde on erthe, schal be

boundun also in heuenes; and what euer thou schalt vnbynde on erthe, schal be vnbounden also in heuenes.

20 Thanne he comaundide to hise disciplis, that thei schulden seie to no man, that he was Crist.

21 Fro that tyme Jhesus bigan to schewe to hise disciplis, that it bihofte hym go to Jerusalem, and suffre many thingis, of the eldere men, and of scribis, and princis of prestis; and be slayn, and the thridde dai to rise ayen.

22 And Petre took hym, and bigan to blame him, and seide, Fer be it fro thee, Lord; this thing schal not be to thee.

23 And he turnede, and seide to Petre, Sathanas, go after me; thou art a sclaundre to me; for thou sauerist not tho thingis that ben of God, but tho thingis that ben of men.

24 Thanne Jhesus seide to his disciplis, If ony man wole come after me, denye he hym silf, and take his cros, and sue me; for he that wole make his lijf saaf,

25 shal leese it; and he that schal leese his lijf for me, schal fynde it.

26 For what profitith it to a man, if he wynne al the world, and suffre peiryng of his soule? or what chaunging schal a man yyue for his soule?

27 For mannes sone schal come in glorie of his fader, with his aungels, and thanne he schal yelde to ech man after his werkis.

28 Treuli Y seie to you, 'ther ben summe of hem that stonden here, whiche schulen not taste deth, til thei seen mannus sone comynge in his kyngdom.

CAP 17

1 And after sixe daies Jhesus took Petre, and James, and Joon, his brother, and ledde hem aside in to an hiy hil,

2 and was turned in to an othir licnesse bifor hem. And his face schone as the sunne; and hise clothis weren maad white as snowe.

3 And lo! Moises and Elie apperiden to hem, and spaken with hym.

4 And Petre answeride, and seide to Jhesu, Lord, it is good vs to be here. If thou wolt, make we here thre tabernaclis; to thee oon, to Moises oon, and oon to Elye. Yit the while he spak, lo!

5 a briyt cloude ouerschadewide hem; and lo! a voice out of the cloude, that seide, This is my dereworth sone, in whom Y haue wel pleside to me; here ye hym.

6 And the disciplis herden, and felden doun on her faces, and dredden greetli.

7 And Jhesus cam, and touchide hem, and seide to hem, Rise vp, and nyle ye drede.

8 And thei liften vp her iyen, and saien no man, but Jhesu aloone.

9 And as thei camen doun of the hille, Jhesus comaundide to hem, and seide, Seie ye to no man the visioun, til mannus sone rise ayen fro deeth.

10 And his disciplis axiden hym, and seiden, What thanne seien the scribis, that it bihoueth that Elie come first?

11 He answeride, and seide to hem, Elie schal come, and he schal restore alle thingis.

12 And Y seie to you, that Elie is nowe comun, and thei knewen hym not, but thei diden in him what euer thingis thei wolden; and so mannus sone schal suffre of hem.

13 Thanne the disciplis vndurstoden, that he seide to hem of Joon Baptist.

14 And whanne he cam to the puple, a man cam to hym, and felde doun on hise knees bifor hym, and seide, Lord, haue merci on my sone; for he is lunatike, and suffrith yuele, for ofte tymes he fallith in to the fier, and ofte tymes in to water.

15 And Y brouyte hym to thi disciplis, and thei myyten not heele hym.

16 Jhesus answeride, and seide, A! thou generacion vnbileueful and weiward; hou long schal Y be with you? hou long schal Y suffre you? Brynge ye hym hider to me.

17 And Jhesus blamede hym, and the deuel wente out fro hym; and the child was heelid fro that our.

18 Thanne the disciplis camen to Jhesu priueli, and seiden to hym, Whi myyten not we caste hym out?

19 Jhesus seith to hem, For youre vnbileue. Treuli Y seie to you, if ye han feith, as a corn of seneueye, ye schulen seie to this hil, Passe thou hennus, and it schal passe; and no thing schal be vnpossible to you;

20 but this kynde is not caste out, but bi preiyng and fastyng.

21 And whilis thei weren abidynge togidere in Galilee, Jhesus seide to hem, Mannus sone schal be bitraied in to the hondis of men;

22 and thei schulen sle hym, and the thridde day he schal rise ayen to lijf.

23 And thei weren ful sori. And whanne thei camen to Cafarnaum, thei that token tribute, camen to Petre, and seiden to hym, Youre maister payeth not tribute?

24 And he seide, Yhis. And whanne he was comen in to the hous, Jhesus cam bifor hym, and seide, Symount, what semeth to thee? Kyngis of erthe, of whom taken thei tribute? of her sones, ether of aliens?

25 And he seide, Of aliens. Jhesus seide to hym, Thanne sones ben fre.

26 But that we sclaundre hem not, go to the see, and caste an hook, and take thilke fisch that first cometh vp; and, whanne his mouth is opened, thou schalt fynde a stater, and yyue for thee and for me.

CAP 18

1 In that our the disciplis camen to Jhesu, and seiden, Who, gessist thou, is gretter in the kyngdom of heuenes?

2 And Jhesus clepide a litil child, and putte hym in the myddil of hem;

3 and seide, Y seie treuthe to you, but ye be turned, and maad as litle children, ye schulen not entre in to the kyngdom of heuenes.

4 Therfor who euer mekith hym as this litil child, he is gretter in the kyngdom of heuenes.

5 And he that resseyueth o siche litil child in my name, resseyueth me.

6 But who so sclaundrith oon of these smale, that bileuen in me, it spedith to hym that a mylnstoon 'of assis be hangid in his necke, and he be drenchid in the depnesse of the see.

7 Woo to the world, for sclaundris; for it is nede that sclaundris come; netheles wo to thilke man bi whom a sclaundre cometh.

8 And if thin hoond or thi foot sclaundreth thee, kitte it of, and caste awei fro thee. It is betere to thee to entre to lijf feble, ethir crokid, than hauynge tweyne hoondis or twey feet to be sent in to euerlastynge fier.

9 And if thin iye sclaundre thee, pulle it out, and caste awei fro thee. It is betere to thee with oon iye to entre in to lijf, thanne hauynge tweyn iyen to be sent in to the fier of helle.

10 Se ye, that ye dispise not oon of these litle. For Y seie to you, that the aungels of hem in heuenes seen euermore the face of my fadir that is in heuenes.

11 For mannus sone cam to saue that thing that perischide.

12 What semeth to you? If ther weren to sum man an hundrid scheep, and oon of hem hath errid, whethir he schal not leeue nynti and nyne in desert, and schal go to seche that that erride?

13 And if it falle that he fynde it, treuli Y seie to you, that he schal haue ioye theron more than on nynti and nyne that erriden not.

14 So it is not the wille bifor youre fadir that is in heuenes, that oon of these litle perische.

15 But if thi brother synneth ayens thee, go thou, and repreue hym, bitwixe thee and hym aloone; if he herith thee, thou hast wonnun thi brother.

16 And if he herith thee not, take with thee oon or tweyne, that euery word stonde in the mouth of tweyne or thre witnessis.

17 And if he herith not hem, seie thou to the chirche. But if he herith not the chirche, be he as an hethen and a pupplican to thee.

18 Y seie to you treuli, what euer thingis ye bynden on erthe, tho schulen be boundun also in heuene; and what euer thingis ye vnbynden on erthe, tho schulen be vnboundun also in heuene.

19 Eftsoone Y seie to you, that if tweyne of you consenten on the erthe, of euery thing what euer thei axen, it schal be don to hem of my fadir that is in heuenes.

20 For where tweyne or thre ben gaderid in my name, there Y am in the myddil of hem.

21 Thanne Petre cam to hym, and seide, Lord, how ofte schal my brother synne ayens me, and Y schal foryyue hym?

22 Whether til seuen tymes? Jhesus seith to hym, Y seie not to thee, til seuene sithis; but til seuenti sithis seuene sithis.

23 Therfor the kyngdom of heuenes is licned to a kyng, that wolde rekyn with hise seruauntis.

24 And whanne he bigan to rekene, oon that ouyte ten thousynde talentis, was brouyt to hym.

25 And whanne he hadde not wherof to yelde, his lord comaundide hym to be seld, and his wijf, and children, and alle thingis that he hadde, and to be paied.

26 But thilke seruaunt felde doun, and preiede hym, and seide, Haue pacience in me, and Y schal yelde to thee alle thingis.

27 And the lord hadde merci on that seruaunt, and suffride hym to go, and foryaf to hym the dette.

28 But thilke seruaunt yede out, and foonde oon of his euen seruauntis, that ouyte hym an hundrid pens; and he helde hym, and stranglide hym, and seide, Yelde that that thou owest.

29 And his euen seruaunt felle doun, and preyede hym, and seide, Haue pacience in me, and Y schal quyte alle thingis to thee.

30 But he wolde not; but wente out, and putte hym in to prisoun, til he paiede al the dette.

31 And hise euen seruauntis, seynge the thingis that weren don, soreweden greetli. And thei camen, and telden to her lord alle the thingis that weren don.

32 Thanne his lord clepide hym, and seide to hym, Wickid seruaunt, Y foryaf to thee al the dette, for thou preiedist me.

33 Therfor whether it bihouede not also thee to haue merci on thin euen seruaunt, as Y hadde merci on thee?

34 And his lord was wroth, and took hym to turmentouris, til he paiede al the dette.

35 So my fadir of heuene schal do to you, if ye foryyuen not euery man to his brother, of youre hertes.

CAP 19

1 And it was don, whanne Jhesus hadde endid these wordis, he passide fro Galilee, and cam in to the coostis of Judee ouer Jordan.

2 And myche puple suede him, and he heelide hem there.

3 And Farisees camen to him, temptynge him, and seiden, Whether it be leueful to a man to leeue his wijf, for ony cause?

4 Which answeride, and seide to hem, Han ye not red, for he that made men at the bigynnyng, made hem male and female?

5 And he seide, For this thing a man schal leeue fadir and modir, and he schal draw to his wijf; and thei schulen be tweyne in o fleisch.

6 And so thei ben not now tweyne, but o fleisch. Therfor a man departe not that thing that God hath ioyned.

7 Thei seien to hym, What thanne comaundide Moises, to yyue a libel of forsakyng, and to leeue of?

8 And he seide to hem, For Moises, for the hardnesse of youre herte, suffride you leeue youre wyues; but fro the bigynnyng it was not so.

9 And Y seie to you, that who euer leeueth his wijf, but for fornycacioun, and weddith another, doith letcherie; and he that weddith the forsakun wijf, doith letcherie.

10 His disciplis seien to him, If the cause of a man with a wijf is so, it spedith not to be weddid.

11 And he seide to hem, Not alle men taken this word; but to whiche it is youun.

12 For ther ben geldingis, whiche ben thus born of the modris wombe; and ther ben geldyngis, that ben maad of men; and there ben geldyngis, that han geldid hem silf, for the kyngdom of heuenes. He that may take, 'take he.

13 Thanne litle children weren brouyte to hym, that he schulde putte hondis to hem, and preie.

14 And the disciplis blamyden hem. But Jhesus seide to hem, Suffre ye that litle children come to me, and nyle ye forbede hem; for of siche is the kyngdom of heuenes.

15 And whanne he hadde put to hem hondis, he wente fro thennus.

16 And lo! oon cam, and seide to hym, Good maister, what good schal Y do, that Y haue euerlastynge lijf?

17 Which seith to hym, What axist thou me of good thing? There is o good God. But if thou wolt entre to lijf, kepe the comaundementis.

18 He seith to hym, Whiche? And Jhesus seide, Thou schalt not do mansleying, thou schalt not do auowtrie, thou schalt not do thefte, thou schalt not seie fals witnessying;

19 worschipe thi fadir and thi modir, and, thou schalt loue thi neiybore as thi silf.

20 The yonge man seith to hym, Y haue kept alle these thingis fro my youthe, what yit failith to me?

21 Jhesus seith to hym, If thou wolt be perfite, go, and sille alle thingis that thou hast, and yyue to pore men, and thou schalt haue tresoure in heuene; and come, and sue me.

22 And whanne the yong man hadde herd these wordis, he wente awei sorewful, for he hadde many possessiouns.

23 And Jhesus seide to hise disciplis, Y seie to you treuthe, for a riche man of hard schal entre in to the kyngdom of heuenes.

24 And eftsoone Y seie to you, it is liyter a camel to passe thorou a needlis iye, thanne a riche man to entre in to the kyngdom of heuens.

25 Whanne these thingis weren herd, the disciplis wondriden greetli, and seiden, Who thanne may be saaf?

26 Jhesus bihelde, and seide to hem, Anentis men this thing is impossible; but anentis God alle thingis ben possible.

27 Thanne Petre answeride, and seide to hym, Lo! we han forsake alle thingis, and we han suede thee; what thanne schal be to vs?

28 Jhesus seide to hem, Truli I seie to you, that ye that han forsake alle thingis, and han sued me, in the regeneracioun whanne mannus sone schal sitte in the sete of his maieste, ye schulen sitte on twelue setis, demynge the twelue kynredis of Israel.

29 And euery man that forsakith hous, britheren or sistren, fadir or modir, wijf ethir children, or feeldis, for my name, he schal take an hundrid foold, and schal welde euerlastynge lijf.

30 But manye schulen be, the firste the laste, and the laste the firste.

CAP 20

1 The kyngdom of heuenes is lijc to an housbonde man, that wente out first bi the morewe, to hire werk men in to his vyneyerd.

2 And whanne the couenaunt was maad with werk men, of a peny for the dai, he sente hem in to his vyneyerd.

3 And he yede out aboute the thridde our, and say othere stondynge idel in the chepyng.

4 And he seide to hem, Go ye also in to myn vynyerd, and that that schal be riytful, Y schal yyue to you.

5 And thei wenten forth. Eftsoones he wente out aboute the sixte our, and the nynthe, and dide in lijk maner.

6 But aboute the elleuenthe our he wente out, and foond other stondynge; and he seide to hem, What stonden ye idel here al dai?

7 Thei seien to him, For no man hath hirid vs. He seith to hem, Go ye also in to my vyneyerd.

8 And whanne euenyng was comun, the lord of the vyneyerd seith to his procuratoure, Clepe the werk men, and yelde to hem her hire, and bigynne thou at the laste til to the firste.

9 And so whanne thei weren comun, that camen aboute the elleuenthe our, also thei token eueryche of hem a peny.

10 But the firste camen, and demeden, that thei schulden take more, but thei token ech oon bi hem silf a peny;

11 and in the takyng grutchiden ayens the hosebonde man, and seiden,

12 These laste wrouyten oon our, and thou hast maad hem euen to vs, that han born the charge of the dai, and heete?

13 And he answeride to oon of hem, and seide, Freend, Y do thee noon wrong; whether thou hast not acordid with me for a peny?

14 Take thou that that is thin, and go; for Y wole yyue to this laste man, as to thee.

15 Whether it is not leueful to me to do that that Y wole? Whether thin iye is wickid, for Y am good?

16 So the laste schulen be the firste, and the firste the laste; 'for many ben clepid, but fewe ben chosun.

17 And Jhesus wente vp to Jerusalem, and took hise twelue disciplis in priuetee, and seide to hem, Lo!

18 we goon vp to Jerusalem, and mannus sone schal be bitakun to princis of prestis, and scribis; and thei schulen condempne him to deeth.

19 And thei schulen bitake hym to hethene men, for to be scorned, and scourgid, and crucified; and the thridde day he schal rise ayen to lijf.

20 Thanne the modir of the sones of Zebedee cam to hym with hir sones, onourynge, and axynge sum thing of hym.

21 And he seide to hir, What wolt thou? She seith to hym, Seie that thes tweyne my sones sitte, oon at thi riythalf, and oon at thi lefthalf, in thi kyngdom.

22 Jhesus answeride, and seide, Ye witen not what ye axen. Moun ye drynke the cuppe which Y schal drynke? Thei seien to hym, We moun.

23 He seith to hem, Ye schulen drinke my cuppe; but to sitte at my riythalf or lefthalf, it is not myn to yyue to you; but to whiche it is maad redi of my fadir.

24 And the ten herynge, hadden indignacioun of the twei britheren.

25 But Jhesus clepide hem to hym, and seide, Ye witen, that princis of hethene men ben lordis of hem, and thei that ben gretter, vsen power on hem.

26 It schal not be so among you; but who euer wole be maad gretter among you, be he youre mynystre; and who euer among you wole be the firste, he schal be youre seruaunt.

28 As mannus sone cam not to be seruyd, but to serue, and to yyue his lijf redempcioun for manye.

29 And whanne thei yeden out of Jerico, miche puple suede him.

30 And lo! twei blynde men saten bisydis the weie, and herden that Jhesus passide; and thei crieden, and seiden, Lord, the sone of Dauid, haue merci on vs.

31 And the puple blamede hem, that thei schulden be stille; and thei crieden the more, and seiden, Lord, the sone of Dauid, haue merci on vs.

32 And Jhesus stood, and clepide hem, and seide, What wolen ye, that Y do to you?

33 Thei seien to him, Lord, that oure iyen be opened.

34 And Jhesus hadde merci on hem, and touchide her iyen; and anoon thei sayen, and sueden him.

CAP 21

1 And whanne Jhesus cam nyy to Jerusalem, and cam to Bethfage, at the mount of Olyuete, thanne sente he his twei disciplis, and seide to hem,

2 Go ye in to the castel that is ayens you, and anoon ye schulen fynde an asse tied, and a colt with hir; vntien ye, and brynge to me.

3 And if ony man seie to you ony thing, seie ye, that the Lord hath nede to hem; and anoon he schal leeue hem.

4 Al this was doon, that that thing schulde be fulfillid, that was seid bi the prophete, seiynge, Seie ye to the douyter of Syon, Lo!

5 thi kyng cometh to thee, meke, sittynge on an asse, and a fole of an asse vnder yok.

6 And the disciplis yeden, and diden as Jhesus comaundide hem.

7 And thei brouyten an asse, and the fole, and leiden her clothis on hem, and maden hym sitte aboue.

8 And ful myche puple strewiden her clothis in the weie; othere kittiden braunchis of trees, and strewiden in the weie.

9 And the puple that wente bifore, and that sueden, crieden, and seiden, Osanna to the sone of Dauid; blessid is he that cometh in the name of the Lord; Osanna in hiy thingis.

10 And whanne he was entrid in to Jerusalem, al the citee was stirid, and seide, Who is this?

11 But the puple seide, This is Jhesus, the prophete, of Nazareth of Galilee.

12 And Jhesus entride in to the temple of God, and castide out of the temple alle that bouyten and solden; and he turnede vpsedoun the bordis of chaungeris, and the chayeris of men that solden culueris.

13 And he seith to hem, It is writun, Myn hous schal be clepid an hous of preier; but ye han maad it a denne of theues.

14 And blynde and crokid camen to hym in the temple, and he heelide hem.

15 But the princis of prestis and scribis, seynge the merueilouse thingis that he dide, and children criynge in the temple, and seiynge, Osanna to the sone of Dauid, hadden indignacioun,

16 and seiden to hym, Herist thou what these seien? And Jhesus seide to hem, Yhe; whether ye han neuer redde, That of the mouth of yonge children, and of soukynge childryn, thou hast maad perfit heriyng?

17 And whanne he hadde left hem, he wente forth out of the citee, in to Bethanye; and there he dwelte, and tauyte hem of the kyngdom of God.

18 But on the morowe, he, turnynge ayen in to the citee, hungride.

19 And he saye a fige tree bisidis the weie, and cam to it, and foond no thing ther ynne but leeues oneli. And he seide to it, Neuer fruyt come forth of thee, in to with outen eende, And anoon the fige tre was dried vp.

20 And disciplis 'sawen, and wondriden, seiynge, Hou anoon it driede.

21 And Jhesus answeride, and seide to hem, Treuli Y seie to you, if ye haue feith, and douten not, not oonli ye schulen do of the fige tree, but also if ye seyn to this hil, Take, and caste thee in to the see, it schal be don so.

22 And alle thingis what euere ye bileuynge schulen axe in preyer, ye schulen take.

23 And whanne he cam in to the temple, the princis of prestis and elder men of the puple camen to hym that tauyte, and seiden, In what power doist thou these thingis? and who yaf thee this power?

24 Jhesus answeride, and seide to hem, And Y schal axe you o word, the which if ye tellen me, Y schal seie to you, in what power Y do these thingis.

25 Of whennys was the baptym of Joon; of heuene, or of men? And thei thouyten with ynne hem silf,

26 seiynge, If we seien of heuene, he schal seie to vs, Whi thanne bileuen ye not to hym? If we seien of men, we dreden the puple, for alle hadden Joon as a prophete.

27 And thei answeriden to Jhesu, and seiden, We witen not. And he seide to hem, Nether Y seie to you, in what power Y do these thingis.

28 But what semeth to you? A man hadde twey sones; and he cam to the firste, and seide, Sone, go worche this dai in my vyneyerd.

29 And he answeride, and seide, Y nyle; but afterward he forthouyte, and wente forth.

30 But he cam to 'the tother, and seide on lijk maner. And he answeride, and seide, Lord, Y go; and he wente not.

31 Who of the tweyne dide the fadris wille? Thei seien to hym, The firste. Jhesus seith to hem, Treuli Y seie to you, for pupplicans and hooris schulen go bifor you 'in to the kyngdom of God.

32 For Joon cam to you in the weie of riytwisnesse, and ye bileueden not to him; but pupplicans and hooris bileueden to hym. But ye sayn, and hadden no forthenkyng aftir, that ye bileueden to hym.

33 Here ye another parable. There was an hosebonde man, that plauntide a vynyerd, and heggide it aboute, and dalfe a presour ther ynne, and bildide a tour, and hiride it to erthe tilieris, and wente fer in pilgrimage.

34 But whanne the tyme of fruytis neiyede, he sente his seruauntis to the erthe tilieris, to take fruytis of it.

35 And the erthetilieris token his seruauntis, and beeten 'the toon, thei slowen another, and thei stonyden another.

36 Eftsoone he sente othere seruauntis, mo than the firste, and in lijk maner thei diden to hem.

37 And at the laste he sente his sone to hem, and seide, Thei schulen drede my sone.

38 But the erthe tilieris, seynge the sone, seiden with ynne hem silf, This is the eire; come ye, sle we hym, and we schulen haue his eritage.

39 And thei token, and castiden hym out of the vynyerd, and slowen hym.

40 Therfor whanne the lord of the vyneyerd schal come, what schal he do to thilke erthe tilieris?

41 Thei seien to hym, He schal leese yuele the yuele men, and he schal sette to hire his vyneyerd to othere erthetilieris, whyche schulen yelde to hym fruyt in her tymes.

42 Jhesus seith to hem, Redden ye neuer in scripturis, The stoon which bilderis repreueden, this is maad in to the heed of the corner? Of the Lord this thing is don, and it is merueilous bifor oure iyen.

43 Therfor Y seie to you, that the kyngdom of God schal be takun fro you, and shal be youun to a folc doynge fruytis of it.

44 And he that schal falle on this stoon, schal be brokun; but on whom it schal falle, it schal al tobrise hym.

45 And whanne the princes of prestis and Farisees hadden herd hise parablis, thei knewen that he seide of hem.

46 And thei souyten to holde hym, but thei dredden the puple, for thei hadden hym as a prophete.

CAP 22

1 And Jhesus answeride, and spak eftsoone in parablis to hem,

2 and seide, The kyngdom of heuenes is maad lijk to a kyng that made weddyngis to his sone.

3 And he sente hise seruauntis for to clepe men that weren bode to the weddyngis, and thei wolden not come.

4 Eftsoone he sente othere seruauntis, and seide, Seie ye to the men that ben bode to the feeste, Lo! Y haue maad redi my meete, my bolis and my volatilis ben slayn, and alle thingis ben redy; come ye to the weddyngis.

5 But thei dispisiden, and wenten forth, oon in to his toun, anothir to his marchaundise. But othere helden his seruauntis, and turmentiden hem, and slowen.

7 But the kyng, whanne he hadde herd, was wroth; and he sente hise oostis, and he distruyede tho manquelleris, and brente her citee.

8 Thanne he seide to hise seruauntis, The weddyngis ben redi, but thei that weren clepid to the feeste, weren not worthi.

9 Therfor go ye to the endis of weies, and whom euere ye fynden, clepe ye to the weddyngis.

10 And hise seruauntis yeden out in to weies, and gadriden togider alle that thei founden, good and yuele; and the bridale was fulfillid with men sittynge at the mete.

11 And the kyng entride, to se men sittynge at the mete; and he siye there a man not clothid with bride cloth.

12 And he seide to hym, Freend, hou entridist thou hidir with out bride clothis? And he was doumbe.

13 Thanne the kyng bad hise mynystris, Bynde hym bothe hondis and feet, and sende ye him in to vtmer derknessis; there schal be wepyng and grentyng of teeth.

14 For many ben clepid, but fewe ben chosun.

15 Thanne Farisees yeden awei, and token a counsel to take Jhesu in word.

16 And thei senden to hym her disciplis, with Erodians, and seien, Maister, we witen, that thou art sothefast, and thou techist in treuthe the weie of God, and thou chargist not of ony man, for thou biholdist not the persoone of men.

17 Therfor seie to vs, what it seemeth to thee. Is it leueful that tribute be youun to the emperoure, ether nay?

18 And whanne Jhesus hadde knowe the wickidnesse of hem, he seide, Ypocritis, what tempten ye me?

19 Schewe ye to me the prynte of the money. And thei brouyten to hym a peny.

20 And Jhesus seide to hem, Whos is this ymage, and the writyng aboue?

21 Thei seien to hym, The emperouris. Thanne he seide to hem, Therfor yelde ye to the emperoure tho thingis that ben the emperouris, and to God tho thingis that ben of God.

22 And thei herden, and wondriden; and thei leften hym, and wenten awey.

23 In that dai Saduceis, that seien there is no risyng ayen to lijf, camen to hym, and axiden him,

24 and seiden, Mayster, Moises seide, if ony man is deed, not hauynge a sone, that his brother wedde his wijf, and reise seed to his brothir.

25 And seuen britheren weren at vs; and the firste weddide a wijf, and is deed. And he hadde no seed, and lefte his wijf to his brother;

26 also the secounde, and the thridde, til to the seuenthe.

27 But the laste of alle, the woman is deed.

28 Also in the risyng ayen to lijf, whos wijf of the seuene schal sche be? for alle hadden hir.

29 Jhesus answeride, and seide to hem, Ye erren, 'and ye knowen not scripturis, ne the vertu of God.

30 For in the rysyng ayen to lijf, nether thei schulen wedde, nethir schulen be weddid; but thei ben as the aungels of God in heuene.

31 And of the risyng ayen of deed men, 'han ye not red, that is seid of the Lord, that seith to you,

32 Y am God of Abraham, and God of Ysaac, and God of Jacob? he is not God of deede men, but of lyuynge men.

33 And the puple herynge, wondriden in his techynge.

34 And Fariseis herden that he hadde put silence to Saduceis, and camen togidere.

35 And oon of hem, a techere of the lawe, axide Jhesu, and temptide him,

36 Maistir, which is a greet maundement in the lawe?

37 Jhesus seide to him, Thou schalt loue thi Lord God, of al thin herte, and in al thi soule, and in al thi mynde.

38 This is the firste and the moste maundement.

39 And the secounde is lijk to this; Thou schalt loue thi neiyebore as thi silf.

40 In these twey maundementis hangith al the lawe and the profetis.

41 And whanne the Farisees weren gederid togidere, Jhesus axide hem,

42 and seide, What semeth to you of Crist, whos sone is he? Thei seien to hym, Of Dauid.

43 He seith to hem, Hou thanne Dauid in spirit clepith hym Lord,

44 and seith, The Lord seide to my Lord, Sitte on my riythalf, til Y putte thin enemyes a stool of thi feet?

45 Thanne if Dauid clepith hym Lord, hou is he his sone?

46 And no man miyte answere a word to hym, nethir ony man was hardi fro that day, to axe hym more.

CAP 23

1 Thanne Jhesus spac to the puple, and to hise disciplis,

2 and seide, On the chayere of Moises, scribis and Farisees han sete.

3 Therfor kepe ye, and do ye alle thingis, what euer thingis thei seien to you. But nyle ye do aftir her werkis; for thei seien, and don not.

4 And thei bynden greuouse chargis, and that moun not be borun, and putten on schuldris of men; but with her fyngur thei wolen not moue hem.

5 Therfor thei don alle her werkis 'that thei be seen of men; for thei drawen abrood her filateries, and magnifien hemmes.

6 And thei louen the first sittyng placis in soperis, and the first chaieris in synagogis;

7 and salutaciouns in chepyng, and to be clepid of men maystir.

8 But nyle ye be clepid maister; for oon is youre maystir, and alle ye ben britheren.

9 And nyle ye clepe to you a fadir on erthe, for oon is your fadir, that is in heuenes.

10 Nether be ye clepid maistris, for oon is youre maister, Crist.

11 He that is grettest among you, schal be youre mynystre.

12 For he that hieth himself, schal be mekid; and he that mekith hym silf, schal be enhaunsid.

13 But wo to you, scribis and Farisees, ipocritis, that closen the kyngdom of heuenes bifore men; and ye entren not, nether suffren men entrynge to entre.

14 Wo to you, scribis and Farisees, ipocritis, that eten the housis of widowis, and preien bi longe preier; for this thing ye schulen take more doom.

15 Wo to you, scribis and Farisees, ypocritis, that goon aboute the see and the loond, to make o prosilite; and whanne he is maad, ye maken hym a sone of helle, double more than ye ben.

16 Wo to you, blynde lederis, that seien, Who euer swerith bi the temple of God, it is 'no thing; but he that swerith in the gold of the temple, is dettoure.

17 Ye foolis and blynde, for what is grettere, the gold, or the temple that halewith the gold?

18 And who euer swerith in the auter, it is no thing; but he that swerith in the yifte that is on the auter, owith.

19 Blynde men, for what is more, the yifte, or the auter that halewith the yifte?

20 Therfor he that swerith in the auter, swerith in it, and in alle thingis that ben ther on.

21 And he that swerith in the temple, swerith in it, and in hym that dwellith in the temple.

22 And he that swerith in heuene, swerith in the trone of God, and in hym that sittith ther on.

23 Wo to you, scribis and Farisees, ypocritis, that tithen mynte, anete, and cummyn, and han left tho thingis that ben of more charge of the lawe, doom, and merci, and feith. And it bihofte to do these thingis, and not to leeue tho.

24 Blynde lederis, clensinge a gnatte, but swolewynge a camel.

25 Woo to you, scribis and Farisees, ypocritis, that clensen the cuppe and the plater with outforth; but with ynne ye ben ful of raueyne and vnclennesse.

26 Thou blynde Farisee, clense the cuppe and the plater with ynneforth, that that that is with outforth be maad clene.

27 Wo to you, scribis and Farisees, ipocritis, that ben lijk to sepulcris whitid, whiche with outforth semen faire to men; but with ynne thei ben fulle of boonus of deed men, and of al filthe.

28 So ye with outforth semen iust to men; but with ynne ye ben ful of ypocrisy and wickidnesse.

29 Wo to you, scribis and Farisees, ipocritis, that bilden sepulcris of profetis, and maken faire the birielis of iust men,

30 and seien, If we hadden be in the daies of oure fadris, we schulden not haue be her felowis in the blood of prophetis.

31 And so ye ben in witnessyng to you silf, that ye ben the sones of hem that slowen the prophetis.

32 And fulfille ye the mesure of youre fadris.

33 Ye eddris, and eddris briddis, hou schulen ye fle fro the doom of helle?

34 Therfor lo! Y sende to you profetis, and wise men, and scribis; and of hem ye schulen sle and crucifie, and of hem ye schulen scourge in youre sinagogis, and schulen pursue fro cite in to citee;

35 that al the iust blood come on you, that was sched on the erthe, fro the blood of iust Abel to the blood of Zacarie, the sone of Barachie, whom ye slowen bitwixe the temple and the auter.

36 Treuli Y seie to you, alle these thingis schulen come on this generacioun.

37 Jerusalem, Jerusalem, that sleest prophetis, and stoonest hem that ben sent to thee, hou ofte wolde Y gadere togidere thi children, as an henne gaderith togidir her chikenes vndir hir wengis, and thou woldist not.

38 Lo! youre hous schal be left to you desert.

39 And Y seie to you, ye schulen not se me fro hennus forth, til ye seien, Blessid is he, that cometh in the name of the Lord.

CAP 24

1 And Jhesus wente out of the temple; and his disciplis camen to hym, to schewe hym the bildyngis of the temple.

2 But he answeride, and seide to hem, Seen ye alle these thingis? Treuli Y seie to you, a stoon schal not be left here on a stoon, that ne it schal be destried.

3 And whanne he satte on the hille of Olyuete, hise disciplis camen to hym priueli, and seiden, Seie vs, whanne these thingis schulen be, and what token of thi comyng, and of the ending of the world.

4 And Jhesus answeride, and seide to hem, Loke ye, that no man disseyue you.

5 For many schulen come in my name, and schulen seie, Y am Crist; and thei schulen disseyue manye.

6 For ye schulen here batels, and opyniouns of batels; se ye that ye be not disturblid; for it byhoueth these thingis to be don, but not yit is the ende.

7 Folk schal rise togidere ayens folc, and rewme ayens rewme, and pestilences, and hungris, and the erthemouyngis schulen be bi placis;

8 and alle these ben bigynnyngis of sorewes.

9 Thanne men schulen bitake you in to tribulacion, and schulen sle you, and ye schulen be in hate to alle folk for my name.

10 And thanne many schulen be sclaundrid, and bitraye ech other, and thei schulen hate ech other.

11 And many false prophetis schulen rise, and disseyue manye.

12 And for wickidnesse schal 'be plenteuouse, the charite of manye schal wexe coold;

13 but he that schal dwelle stable in to the ende, schal be saaf.

14 And this gospel of the kyngdom schal be prechid in al the world, in witnessyng to al folc;

15 and thanne the ende schal come. Therfor whanne ye se the abhomynacioun of discomfort, that is seid of Danyel, the prophete, stondynge in the hooli place; he that redith, vndirstonde he;

16 thanne thei that ben in Judee, fle to the mounteyns; and he that is in the hous roof,

17 come not doun to take ony thing of his hous; and he that is in the feeld,

18 turne not ayen to take his coote.

19 But wo to hem that ben with child, and nurischen in tho daies.

20 Preye ye, that youre fleyng be not maad in wynter, or in the saboth.

21 For thanne schal be greet tribulacioun, what maner 'was not fro the bigynnyng of the world to now, nether schal be maad.

22 And but tho daies hadden be abreggide, ech flesch schulde not be maad saaf; but tho daies schulen be maad schort, for the chosun men.

23 Thanne if ony man seie to you, Lo! here is Crist, or there, nyle ye bileue.

24 For false Cristis and false prophetis schulen rise, and thei schulen yyue grete tokenes and wondrys; so that also the chosun be led in to erroure, if it may be done.

25 Lo! Y haue bifor seid to you.

26 Therfor if thei seie to you, Lo! he is in desert, nyle ye go out; lo! in priuey placis, nyle ye trowe.

27 For as leit goith out fro the eest, and apperith in to the weste, so schal be also the coming of mannus sone.

28 Where euer the bodi schal be, also the eglis schulen be gaderid thidur.

29 And anoon after the tribulacioun of tho daies, the sunne schal be maad derk, and the moone schal not yyue hir liyt, and the sterris schulen falle fro heuene, and the vertues of heuenes schulen be moued.

30 And thanne the tokene of mannus sone schal appere in heuene, and thanne alle kynredis of the erthe schulen weile; and thei schulen see mannus sone comynge in the cloudis of heuene, with miche vertu and maieste.

31 And he schal sende hise aungels with a trumpe, and a greet vois; and thei schulen gedere hise chosun fro foure wyndis, fro the hiyest thingis of heuenes to the endis of hem.

32 And lerne ye the parable of a fige tre. Whanne his braunche is now tendir, and the leeues ben sprongun, ye witen that somer is nyy;

33 'so and ye whanne ye seen alle these thingis, wite ye that it is nyy, in the yatis.

34 Treuli Y seie to you, for this generacioun schal not passe, til alle thingis be don;

35 heuene and erthe schulen passe, but my wordis schulen not passe.

36 But of thilke dai and our no man wote, nethir aungels of heuenes, but the fadir aloone.

37 But as it was in the daies of Noe, so schal be the comyng of mannus sone.

38 For as in the daies bifore the greet flood, thei weren etynge and drynkynge, weddynge and takynge to weddyng, to that dai, that Noe entride in to the schippe;

39 and thei knewen not, til the greet flood cam, and took alle men, so schal be the comyng of mannus sone.

40 Thanne tweyne schulen be in o feeld, oon schal be takun, and another left;

41 twey wymmen schulen be gryndynge in o queerne, oon schal be takun, and 'the tother left; tweyn in a bedde, 'the toon schal be takun, and the tother left.

42 Therfor wake ye, for ye witen not in what our the Lord schal come.

43 But wite ye this, that if the hosebonde man wiste in what our the thefe were to come, certis he wolde wake, and suffre not his hous to be vndurmyned.

44 And therfor be ye redi, for in what our ye gessen not, mannus sone schal come.

45 Who gessist thou is a trewe seruaunt and prudent, whom his lord ordeyned on his meynee, to yyue hem mete in tyme?

46 Blessed is that seruaunt, whom 'his lord, whanne he schal come, schal fynde so doynge.

47 Treuli Y seye to you, for on alle his goodis he schal ordeyne hym.

48 But if thilke yuel seruaunt seie in his herte, My lord tarieth to come,

49 and bigynneth to smyte hise euen seruauntis, and ete, and drynke with drunken men;

50 the lord of that seruaunt schal come in the dai which he hopith not, and in the our that he knowith not,

50 and schal departe hym, and putte his part with ypocritis; there schal be wepyng, and gryntyng of teeth.

CAP 25

1 Thanne the kyngdoom of heuenes schal be lijk to ten virgyns, whiche token her laumpis, and wenten out ayens the hosebonde and the wijf;

2 and fyue of hem weren foolis, and fyue prudent.

3 But the fyue foolis token her laumpis, and token not oile with hem;

4 but the prudent token oile in her vessels with the laumpis.

5 And whilis the hosebonde tariede, alle thei nappiden and slepten.

6 But at mydnyyt a cryy was maad, Lo! the spouse cometh, go ye oute to mete with him.

7 Thanne alle tho virgyns risen vp, and araieden her laumpis.

8 And the foolis seiden to the wise, Yyue ye to vs of youre oile, for oure laumpis ben quenchid.

9 The prudent answeriden, and seiden, Lest perauenture it suffice not to vs and to you, go ye rather to men that sellen, and bie to you.

10 And while thei wenten for to bie, the spouse cam; and tho that weren redi, entreden with him to the weddyngis; and the yate was schit.

11 And at the last the othere virgyns camen, and seiden, Lord, lord, opene to vs.

12 And he answeride, and seide, Treuli Y seie to you, Y knowe you not.

13 Therfor wake ye, for ye witen not the dai ne the our.

14 For as a man that goith in pilgrimage, clepide hise seruauntis, and bitook to hem hise goodis;

15 and to oon he yaf fyue talentis, and to another tweyne, and to another oon, to ech after his owne vertu; and wente forth anoon.

16 And he that hadde fyue besauntis, wente forth, and wrouyte in hem, and wan othere fyue.

17 Also and he that hadde takun tweyne, wan othere tweyne.

18 But he that hadde takun oon, yede forth, and dalf in to the erthe, and hidde the money of his lord.

19 But after long tyme, the lord of tho seruauntis cam, and rekenede with hem.

20 And he that hadde takun fyue besauntis, cam, and brouyte othere fyue, and seide, Lord, thou bytokist to me fyue besauntis, loo! Y haue getun aboue fyue othere.

21 His lord seide to hym, Wel be thou, good seruaunt and feithful; for on fewe thingis thou hast be trewe, Y schal ordeyne thee on manye thingis; entre thou in to the ioye of thi lord.

22 And he that hadde takun twey talentis, cam, and seide, Lord, thou bitokist to me twey besauntis; loo!

23 Y haue wonnen ouer othir tweyne. His lord seide to him, Wel be thou, good seruaunt and trewe; for on fewe thingis thou hast be trewe, Y schal ordeyne thee on many thingis; entre thou in to the ioie of thi lord.

24 But he that hadde takun o besaunt, cam, and seide, Lord, Y woot that thou art an hard man; thou repist where thou hast not sowe, and thou gederist togidere where thou hast not spred abrood;

25 and Y dredynge wente, and hidde thi besaunt in the erthe; lo! thou hast that that is thin.

26 His lord answeride, and seide to hym, Yuel seruaunt and slowe, wistist thou that Y repe where Y sewe not, and gadir to gidere where Y spredde not abrood?

27 Therfor it bihofte thee to bitake my money to chaungeris, that whanne Y cam, Y schulde resseyue that that is myn with vsuris.

28 Therfor take awei fro hym the besaunt, and yyue ye to hym that hath ten besauntis.

29 For to euery man that hath me schal yyue, and he schal encreese; but fro hym that hath not, also that that hym semeth to haue, schal be taken awey fro him.

30 And caste ye out the vnprofitable seruaunt in to vtmer derknessis; ther schal be wepyng, and gryntyng of teeth.

31 Whanne mannus sone schal come in his maieste, and alle hise aungels with hym, thanne he schal sitte on the sege of his maieste;

32 and alle folkis schulen be gaderid bifor hym,

33 and he schal departe hem atwynne, as a scheeperde departith scheep from kidis; and he schal sette the scheep on his riythalf, and the kidis on the lefthalf.

34 Thanne the kyng schal seie to hem, that schulen be on his riythalf, Come ye, the blessid of my fadir, take ye in possessioun the kyngdoom maad redi to you fro the makyng of the world.

35 For Y hungride, and ye yauen me to ete; Y thristide, and ye yauen me to drynke; Y was herboreles, and ye herboriden me;

36 nakid, and ye hiliden me; sijk, and ye visitiden me; Y was in prisoun, and ye camen to me.

37 Thanne iust men schulen answere to hym, and seie, Lord, whanne siyen we thee hungry, and we fedden thee; thristi, and we yauen to thee drynk?

38 and whanne sayn we thee herborles, and we herboreden thee; or nakid, and we hiliden thee?

39 or whanne sayn we thee sijk, or in prisoun, and we camen to thee?

40 And the kyng answerynge schal seie to hem, Treuli Y seie to you, as longe as ye diden to oon of these my leeste britheren, ye diden to me.

41 Thanne the kyng schal seie also to hem, that schulen be on his lefthalf, Departe fro me, ye cursid, in to euerlastynge fijr, that is maad redi to the deuel and hise aungels.

42 For Y hungride, and ye yauen not me to ete; Y thristide, and ye yauen not me to drynke;

43 Y was herborles, and ye herberden not me; nakid, and ye keuerden not me; sijk, and in prisoun, and ye visitiden not me.

44 Thanne and thei schulen answere to hym, and schulen seie, Lord, whanne sayn we thee hungrynge, or thristynge, or herboreles, or nakid, or sijk, or in prisoun, and we serueden not to thee?

45 Thanne he schal answere to hem, and seie, Treuli Y seie to you, 'hou longe ye diden not to oon of these leeste, nether ye diden to me.

46 And these schulen goo in to euerlastynge turment; but the iust men schulen go in to euerlastynge lijf.

CAP 26

1 And it was doon, whanne Jhesus hadde endid alle these wordis, he seide to hise disciplis,

2 Ye witen, that aftir twei daies pask schal be maad, and mannus sone schal be bitakun to be crucified.

3 Than the princes of prestis and the elder men of the puple were gaderid in to the halle of the prince of prestis, that was seid Cayfas,

4 and maden a counsel to holde Jhesu with gile, and sle him;

5 but thei seiden, Not in the haliday, lest perauenture noyse were maad in the puple.

6 And whanne Jhesus was in Betanye, in the hous of Symount leprous,

7 a womman that hadde a box of alabastre of precious oynement, cam to hym, and schedde out on the heed of hym restynge.

8 And disciplis seynge hadden dedeyn, and seiden, Wherto this loss? for it myyte be seld for myche,

9 and be youun to pore men.

10 But Jhesus knewe, and seide to hem, What ben ye heuy to this womman? for sche hath wrouyt in me a good werk.

11 For ye schulen euere haue pore men with you, but ye schulen not algatis haue me.

12 This womman sendynge this oynement in to my bodi, dide to birie me.

13 Treuli Y seie to you, where euer this gospel schal be prechid in al the world, it schal be seid, that sche dide this, in mynde of hym.

14 Thanne oon of the twelue, that was clepid Judas Scarioth, wente forth to the princis of prestis,

15 and seide to hem, What wolen ye yyue to me, and Y schal bitake hym to you? And thei ordeyneden to hym thretti pans of siluer.

16 And fro that tyme he souyte oportunyte, to bitraye hym.

17 And in the firste dai of therf looues the disciplis camen to Jhesu, and seiden, Where wolt thou we make redi to thee, to ete paske?

18 Jhesus seide, Go ye into the citee to 'sum man, and seie to hym, The maistir seith, My tyme is nyy; at thee Y make paske with my disciplis.

19 And the disciplis diden, as Jhesus comaundide to hem; and thei maden the paske redi.

20 And whanne euentid was come, he sat to mete with hise twelue disciplis.

21 And he seide to hem, as thei eten, Treuli Y seie to you, that oon of you schal bitraye me.

22 And thei ful sori bigunnen ech bi hym silf to seie, Lord, whether 'Y am?

23 And he answeride, and seide, He that puttith with me his hoond in the plater, schal bitraye me.

24 Forsothe mannus sone goith, as it is writun of hym; but wo to that man, bi whom mannus sone schal be bitrayed; it were good to hym, if that man hadde not be borun.

25 But Judas that bitraiede hym, answeride, seiynge, Maister, whether 'Y am? Jhesus seide to hym, Thou hast seid.

26 And while thei soupeden, Jhesus took breed, and blesside, and brak, and yaf to hise disciplis, and seide, Take ye, and ete; this is my body.

27 And he took the cuppe, and dide thankyngis, and yaf to hem,

28 and seide, Drynke ye alle herof; this is my blood of the newe testament, which schal be sched for many, in to remissioun of synnes.

29 And Y seie to you, Y schal not drynke fro this tyme, of this fruyt of the vyne, in to that dai whanne Y schal drynke it newe with you, in the kyngdom of my fadir.

30 And whanne the ympne was seid, thei wenten out in to the mount of Olyuete.

31 Thanne Jhesus seide to hem, Alle ye schulen suffre sclaundre in me, in this niyt; for it is writun, Y schal smyte the scheeperde, and the scheep of the flok schulen be scaterid.

32 But aftir that Y schal rise ayen, Y schal go bifore you in to Galilee.

33 Petre answeride, and seide to hym, Thouy alle schulen be sclaundrid in thee, Y schal neuer be sclaundrid.

34 Jhesus seide to him, Treuli Y seie to thee, for in this nyyt bifor the cok crowe, thries thou schalt denye me.

35 Peter seide to him, Yhe, thouy it bihoue that Y die with thee, Y schal not denye thee. Also alle the disciplis seiden.

36 Thanne Jhesus cam with hem in to a toun, that is seid Jessamanye. And he seide to his disciplis, Sitte ye here, the while Y go thider, and preye.

37 And whanne he hadde take Peter, and twei sones of Zebedee, he bigan to be heuy and sori.

38 Thanne he seide to hem, My soule is soreuful to the deeth; abide ye here, and wake ye with me.

39 And he yede forth a litil, and felde doun on his face, preiynge, and seiynge, My fader, if it is possible, passe this cuppe fro me; netheles not as Y wole, but as thou wolt.

40 And he cam to his disciplis, and foond hem slepynge. And he seide to Petir, So, whethir ye myyten not oon our wake with me?

41 Wake ye, and preye ye, that ye entre not in to temptacioun; for the spirit is redi, but the fleisch is sijk.

42 Eft the secounde tyme he wente, and preyede, seiynge, My fadir, if this cuppe may not passe, but Y drynke hym, thi wille be doon.

43 And eftsoone he cam, and foond hem slepynge; for her iyen weren heuyed.

44 And he lefte hem, and wente eftsoone, and preiede the thridde tyme, and seide the same word.

45 Thanne he cam to his disciplis, and seide to hem, Slepe ye now, and reste ye; loo! the our hath neiyed, and mannus sone schal be takun in to the hondis of synneris;

46 rise ye, go we; loo! he that schal take me, is nyy.

47 Yit the while he spak, lo! Judas, oon of the twelue, cam, and with hym a greet cumpeny, with swerdis and battis, sent fro the princis of prestis, and fro the eldre men of the puple.

48 And he that bitraiede hym, yaf to hem a tokene, and seide, Whom euer Y schal kisse, he it is; holde ye hym.

49 And anoon he cam to Jhesu, and seid, Haile, maister;

50 and he kisside hym. And Jhesus seide to hym, Freend, wherto art thou comun? Thanne thei camen niy, and leiden hoondis on Jhesu, and helden hym.

51 And lo! oon of hem that weren with Jhesu, streiyte out his hoond, and drouy out his swerd; and he smoot the seruaunt of the prince of prestis, and kitte of his ere.

52 Thanne Jhesus seide to hym, Turne thi swerd in to his place; for alle that taken swerd, schulen perische bi swerd.

53 Whether gessist thou, that Y may not preie my fadir, and he schal yyue to me now mo than twelue legiouns of aungels?

54 Hou thanne schulen the scriptures be fulfilled? for so it bihoueth to be doon.

55 In that our Jhesus seide to the puple, As to a theef ye han gon out, with swerdis and battis, to take me; dai bi dai Y sat among you, and tauyt in the temple, and ye helden me not.

56 But al this thing was don, that the scripturis of profetis schulden be fulfillid. Thanne alle the disciplis fledden, and leften hym.

57 And thei helden Jhesu, and ledden hym to Cayfas, the prince of prestis, where the scribis and the Farisees, and the eldre men of the puple weren comun togidere.

58 But Petir swede him afer, in to the halle of the prince of prestis; and he wente in, and sat with the seruauntis, to se the ende.

59 And the prince of prestis, and al the counsel souyten fals witnessing ayens Jhesu, that thei schulden take hym to deeth;

60 and thei founden not, whanne manye false witnessis weren comun. But at the laste, twei false witnessis camen,

61 and seiden, 'This seide, Y may distruye the temple of God, and after the thridde dai bilde it ayen.

62 And the prince of prestis roos, and seide to hym, Answerist thou no thing to tho thingis, that these witnessen ayens thee?

63 But Jhesus was stille. And the prince of prestis seide to hym, Y coniure thee bi lyuynge God, that thou seie to vs, if thou art Crist, the sone of God.

64 Jhesus seide to him, Thou hast seid; netheles Y seie to you, 'fro hennus forth ye schulen se mannus sone sittinge at the riythalf of the vertu of God, and comynge in the cloudis of heuene.

65 Thanne the prince of prestis to-rente his clothis, and seide, He hath blasfemed; what yit han we nede to witnessis? lo! now ye han herd blasfemye; what semeth to you?

66 And thei answeriden, and seiden, He is gilti of deeth.

67 Thanne thei speten 'in to his face, and smyten hym with buffatis; and othere yauen strokis with the pawme of her hondis in his face,

68 and seide, Thou Crist, arede to vs, who is he that smoot thee?

69 And Petir sat with outen in the halle; and a damysel cam to hym, and seide, Thou were with Jhesu of Galilee.

70 And he denyede bifor alle men, and seide, Y woot not what thou seist.

71 And whanne he yede out at the yate, another damysel say hym, and seide to hem that weren there, And this was with Jhesu of Nazareth.

72 And eftsoone he denyede with an ooth, For I knewe not the man.

73 And a litil aftir, thei that stooden camen, and seiden to Petir, Treuli thou art of hem; for thi speche makith thee knowun.

74 Thanne he bigan to warie and to swere, that he knewe not the man. And anoon the cok crewe.

75 And Petir bithouyte on the word of Jhesu, that he hadde seid, Bifore the cok crowe, thries thou schalt denye me. And he yede out, and wepte bitterli.

CAP 27

1 But whanne the morowtid was comun, alle the princis of prestis, and the eldre men of the puple token counsel ayens Jhesu, that thei schulden take hym to the deeth.

2 And thei ledden him boundun, and bitoken to Pilat of Pounce, iustice.

3 Thanne Judas that bitraiede hym, say that he was dampned, he repentide, and brouyte ayen the thretti pans to the princis of prestis, and to the elder men of the puple,

4 and seide, Y haue synned, bitraiynge riytful blood. And thei seiden, What to vs? bise thee.

5 And whanne he hadde cast forth the siluer in the temple, he passide forth, and yede, and hongide hym silf with a snare.

6 And the princis of prestis token the siluer, and seide, It is not leueful to putte it in to the treserie, for it is the prijs of blood.

7 And whanne thei hadden take counsel, thei bouyten with it a feeld of a potter, in to biryyng of pilgrymys.

8 Herfor thilke feeld is clepid Acheldemac, that is, a feeld of blood, in to this dai.

9 Thanne that was fulfillid, that was seid bi the prophete Jeremye, seiynge, And thei han takun thretti pans, the prijs of a man preysid, whom thei preiseden of the children of Israel;

10 and thei yauen hem in to a feeld of a potter, as the Lord hath ordenyd to me.

11 And Jhesus stood bifor the domesman; and the iustice axide him, and seide, Art thou king of Jewis?

12 Jhesus seith to hym, Thou seist. And whanne he was accusid of the princis of prestis, and of the eldere men of the puple, he answeride no thing.

13 Thanne Pilat seith to him, Herist thou not, hou many witnessyngis thei seien ayens thee?

14 And he answeride not 'to hym ony word, so that the iustice wondride greetli.

15 But for a solempne dai the iustice was wont to delyuere to the puple oon boundun, whom thei wolden.

16 And he hadde tho a famous man boundun, that was seid Barrabas.

17 Therfor Pilate seide to hem, whanne thei weren to gidere, Whom wolen ye, that Y delyuere to you? whether Barabas, or Jhesu, that is seid Crist?

18 For he wiste, that bi enuye thei bitraieden hym.

19 And while he sat for domesman, his wijf sente to hym, and seide, No thing to thee and to that iust man; for Y haue suffrid this dai many thingis for hym, bi a visioun.

20 Forsothe the prince of prestis, and the eldere men coun-seiliden the puple, that thei schulden axe Barabas, but thei schulden distrye Jhesu.

21 But the iustice answeride, and seide to hem, Whom of the tweyn wolen ye, that be delyuerit to you? And thei seiden, Barabas.

22 Pilat seith to hem, What thanne schal Y do of Jhesu, that is seid Crist?

23 Alle seien, 'Be he crucified. The iustice seith to hem, What yuel hath he doon? And thei crieden more, and seiden, Be he crucified.

24 And Pilat seynge that he profitide no thing, but that the more noyse was maad, took watir, and waischide hise hondis bifor the puple, and seide, Y am giltles of the blood of this riytful man; bise you.

25 And al the puple answeride, and seide, His blood be on vs, and on oure children.

26 Thanne he deliuerede to hem Barabas, but he took to hem Jhesu scourgid, to be crucified.

27 Thanne knyytis of the iustice token Jhesu in the moot halle, and gadriden to hym al the cumpeny 'of knyytis.

28 And thei vnclothiden hym, and diden aboute hym a reed mantil;

29 and thei foldiden a coroun of thornes, and putten on his heed, and a rehed in his riyt hoond; and thei kneliden bifore hym, and scornyden hym, and seiden, Heil, kyng of Jewis.

30 And thei speten on hym, and tooken a rehed, and smoot his heed.

31 And aftir that thei hadden scorned him, thei vnclothiden hym of the mantil, and thei clothiden hym with hise clothis, and ledden hym to 'crucifien hym.

32 And as thei yeden out, thei founden a man of Cirenen comynge fro the toun, Symont bi name; thei constreyneden hym to take his cross.

33 And thei camen in to a place that is clepid Golgatha, that is, the place of Caluarie.

34 And thei yauen hym to drynke wyne meynd with galle; and whanne he hadde tastid, he wolde not drynke.

35 And aftir that thei hadden crucified hym, thei departiden his clothis, and kesten lotte, to fulfille that is seid bi the prophete, seiynge, Thei partiden to hem my clothis, and on my clooth thei kesten lott.

36 And thei seten, and kepten him;

37 and setten aboue his heed his cause writun, This is Jhesu of Nazareth, kyng of Jewis.

38 Thanne twey theues weren crucified with hym, oon on the riythalf, and oon on the lefthalf.

39 And men that passiden forth blasfemeden hym,

40 mouynge her heedis, and seiynge, Vath to thee, that distri-est the temple of God, and in the thridde dai bildist it ayen; saue thou thi silf; if thou art the sone of God, come doun of the cross.

41 Also and princis of prestis scornynge, with scribis and elder men,

42 seiden, He made othere men saaf, he may not make hym silf saaf; if he is kyng of Israel, come he now doun fro the crosse, and we bileuen to hym;

43 he tristide in God; delyuer he hym now, if he wole; for he seide, That Y am Goddis sone.

44 And the theues, that weren crucified with hym, vpbrei-diden hym of the same thing.

45 But fro the sixte our derknessis weren maad on al the erthe, to the nynthe our.

46 And aboute the nynthe our Jhesus criede with a greet vois, and seide, Heli, Heli, lamazabatany, that is, My God, my God, whi hast thou forsake me?

47 And summen that stoden there, and herynge, seiden, This clepith Helye.

48 And anoon oon of hem rennynge, took and fillide a spounge with vynegre, and puttide on a rehed, and yaf to hym to drynke.

49 But othir seiden, Suffre thou; se we whether Helie come to deliuer hym.

50 Forsothe Jhesus eftsoone criede with a greet voyce, and yaf vp the goost.

51 And lo! the veil of the temple was to-rent in twey parties, fro the hiest to the lowest. And the erthe schoke, and stoonus weren cloue; and birielis weren openyd,

52 and many bodies of seyntis that hadden slepte, rysen vp.

53 And thei yeden out of her birielis, and aftir his resurrec-cioun thei camen in to the holi citee, and apperiden to many.

54 And the centurien and thei that weren with hym kepinge Jhesu, whanne thei saien the erthe schakynge, and tho thingis that weren doon, thei dredden greetli,

55 and seiden, Verili this was Goddis sone. And ther weren there many wymmen afer, that sueden Jhesu fro Galilee, and mynystriden to hym.

56 Among whiche was Marie Magdalene, and Marie, the modir of James, and of Joseph, and the modir of Zebedees sones.

57 But whanne the euenyng was come, ther cam a riche man of Armathi, Joseph bi name, and he was a disciple of Jhesu.

58 He wente to Pilat, and axide the bodi of Jhesu.

59 Thanne Pilat comaundide the bodie to be youun. And whanne the bodi was takun, Joseph lappide it in a clene sen-del,

60 and leide it in his newe biriel, that he hadde hewun in a stoon; and he walewide a greet stoon to the dore of the biriel, and wente awei.

61 But Marie Maudelene and anothir Marie weren there, sit-tynge ayens the sepulcre.

62 And on 'the tother dai, that is aftir pask euen, the princis of prestis and the Farisees camen togidere to Pilat,

63 and seiden, Sir, we han mynde, that thilke giloure seide yit lyuynge, Aftir thre daies Y schal rise ayen to lijf.

64 Therfor comaunde thou, that the sepulcre be kept in to the thridde dai; lest hise disciplis comen, and stelen hym, and seie to the puple, He hath rise fro deeth; and the laste errour schal be worse than the formere.

65 Pilat seide to hem, Ye han the kepyng; go ye, kepe ye as ye kunnen.

66 And thei yeden forth, and kepten the sepulcre, markynge the stoon, with keperis.

CAP 28

1 But in the euentid of the sabat, that bigynneth to schyne in the firste dai of the woke, Marie Mawdelene cam, and another Marie, to se the sepulcre.

2 And lo! ther was maad a greet ertheschakyng; for the aungel of the Lord cam doun fro heuene, and neiyede, and turnede awei the stoon, and sat theron.

3 And his lokyng was as leit, and hise clothis as snowe;

4 and for drede of hym the keperis weren afeerd, and thei weren maad as deede men.

5 But the aungel answeride, and seide to the wymmen, Nyle ye drede, for Y woot that ye seken Jhesu, that was crucified;

6 he is not here, for he is risun, as he seide; come ye, and se ye the place, where the Lord was leid.

7 And go ye soone, and seie ye to his disciplis, that he is risun. And lo! he schal go bifore you in to Galilee; there ye schulen se hym.

8 Lo! Y haue biforseid to you. And thei wenten out soone fro the biriels, with drede and greet ioye, rennynge to telle to hise disciplis.

9 And lo! Jhesus mette hem, and seide, Heile ye. And thei neiyeden, and heelden his feet, and worschipiden him.

10 Thanne Jhesus seide to hem, Nyle ye drede; go ye, 'telle ye to my britheren, that thei go in to Galile; there thei schulen se me.

11 And whanne thei weren goon, lo! summe of the keperis camen in to the citee, and telden to the princis of prestis alle thingis that weren doon.

12 And whanne thei weren gaderid togidere with the elder men, and hadden take her counseil, thei yauen to the kniytis miche monei, and seiden, Seie ye,

13 that hise disciplis camen bi nyyt, and han stolen hym, while ye slepten.

14 And if this be herd of the iustice, we schulen counseile hym, and make you sikir.

15 And whanne the monei was takun, thei diden, as thei weren tauyt. And this word is pupplischid among the Jewis, til in to this day.

16 And the enleuen disciplis wenten in to Galilee, in to an hille, where Jhesus hadde ordeyned to hem.

17 And thei sayn hym, and worschipiden; but summe of hem doutiden.

18 And Jhesus cam nyy, and spak to hem, and seide, Al power in heuene and in erthe is youun to me.

19 Therfor go ye, and teche alle folkis, baptisynge hem in the name of the Fadir, and of the Sone, and of the Hooli Goost;

20 techynge hem to kepe alle thingis, what euer thingis Y haue comaundid to you; and lo! Y am with you in alle daies, in to the ende of the world.

MARK

CAP 1

1 The bigynnyng of the gospel of Jhesu Crist, the sone of God.

2 As it is writun in Ysaie, the prophete, Lo! Y sende myn aungel bifor thi face, that schal make thi weie redi bifor thee.

3 The vois of a crier in desert, Make ye redi the weie of the Lord, make ye hise paththis riyt.

4 Joon was in desert baptisynge, and prechynge the baptym of penaunce, in to remissioun of synnes.

5 And al the cuntre of Judee wente out to hym, and alle men of Jerusalem; and thei weren baptisid of hym in the flom Jordan, 'and knoulechiden her synnes.

6 And Joon was clothid with heeris of camels, and a girdil of skyn was about hise leendis; and he ete hony soukis, and wilde hony, and prechide,

7 and seide, A stronger than Y schal come aftir me, and Y am not worthi to knele doun, and vnlace his schoone.

8 Y haue baptisid you in watir; but he schal baptise you in the Hooli Goost.

9 And it was don in tho daies, Jhesus cam fro Nazareth of Galilee, and was baptisid of Joon in Jordan.

10 And anoon he wente up of the watir, and saye heuenes opened, and the Hooli Goost comynge doun as a culuer, and dwellynge in hym.

11 And a vois was maad fro heuenes, Thou art my loued sone, in thee Y am plesid.

12 And anoon the Spirit puttide hym forth in to deseert.

13 And he was in deseert fourti daies and fourti nyytis, and was temptid of Sathanas, and he was with beestis, and aungels mynystriden to hym.

14 But aftir that Joon was takun, Jhesus cam in to Galilee, and prechide the gospel of the kyngdoom of God,

15 and seide, That the tyme is fulfillid, and the kyngdoom of God schal come nyy; do ye penaunce, and bileue ye to the gospel.

16 And as he passide bisidis the see of Galilee, he say Symount, and Andrew, his brother, castynge her nettis in to the see; for thei weren fisscheris.

17 And Jhesus seide to hem, Come ye aftir me; Y schal make you to be maad fisscheris of men.

18 And anoon thei leften the nettis, and sueden hym.

19 And he yede forth fro thennus a litil, and siy James of Zebedee, and Joon, his brother, in a boot makynge nettis.

20 And anoon he clepide hem; and thei leften Zebedee, her fadir, in the boot with hiryd seruauntis, and thei suweden hym.

21 And thei entriden in to Capharnaum, and anoon in the sabatys he yede in to a synagoge, and tauyte hem.

22 And thei wondriden on his teching; for he tauyte hem, as he that hadde power, and not as scribis.

23 And in the synagoge of hem was a man in an vnclene spirit, and he criede out,

24 and seide, What to vs and to thee, thou Jhesu of Nazareth? hast thou come to distrie vs? Y woot that thou art the hooli of God.

25 And Jhesus thretenede hym, and seide, Wex doumbe, and go out of the man.

26 And the vnclene spirit debreidynge hym, and criynge with greet vois, wente out fro hym.

27 And alle men wondriden, so that thei souyten with ynne hem silf, and seiden, What thing is this? what newe doctrine is this? for in power he comaundith to vnclene spiritis, and thei obeyen to hym.

28 And the fame of hym wente forth anoon in to al the cuntree of Galilee.

29 And anoon thei yeden out of the synagoge, and camen into the hous of Symount and of Andrewe, with James and Joon.

30 And the modir of Symountis wijf lay sijk in fyueris; and anoon thei seien to hym of hyr.

31 And he cam nyy, and areride hir, and whanne he hadde take hir hoond, anoon the feuer lefte hir, and sche seruede hem.

32 But whanne the euentid was come, and the sonne was gon doun, thei brouyten to hym alle that weren of male ese, and hem that hadden fendis.

33 And al the citee was gaderid at the yate.

34 And he heelide many, that hadden dyuerse sijknessis, and he castide out many feendis, and he suffride hem not to speke, for thei knewen hym.

35 And he roos ful eerli, and yede out, and wente in to a desert place, and preiede there.

36 And Symount suede hym, and thei that weren with hym.

37 And whanne thei hadden founde hym, thei seiden to hym, That alle men seken thee.

38 And he seide to hem, Go we in to the next townes and cit-ees, that Y preche also there, for her to Y cam.

39 And he prechide in the synagogis of hem, and in al Gali-lee, and castide out feendis.

40 And a leprouse man cam to hym, and bisouyte, 'and kne-lide, and seide, If thou wolt, thou maist clense me.

41 And Jhesus hadde mercy on hym, and streiyte out his hoond, and towchyde hym, and seide to hym, I wole, be thou maad cleene.

42 And whanne he hadde seide this, anoon the lepre partyde awey fro hym, and he was clensyd.

43 And Jhesus thretenede hym, and anoon Jhesus putte hym out,

44 and seyde to hym, Se thou, seye to no man; but go, schewe thee to the pryncys of prestys, and offre for thi clensynge in to wytnessyng to hem, tho thingis that Moyses bad.

45 And he yede out, and bigan to preche, and publische the word, so that now he myyte not go opynli in to the citee, but be withoutforth in desert placis; and thei camen to hym on alle sidis.

CAP 2

1 And eft he entride in to Cafarnaum, aftir eiyte daies.

2 And it was herd, that he was in an hous, and many camen to gidir, so that thei miyten not be in the hous, ne at the yate. And he spak to hem the word.

3 And there camen to hym men that brouyten a man sijk in palesie, which was borun of foure.

4 And whanne thei myyten not brynge hym to Jhesu for the puple, thei vnhileden the roof where he was, and openede it, and thei leten doun the bed in which the sijk man in palesie laye.

5 And whanne Jhesus hadde seyn the feith of hem, he seide to the sijk man in palesie, Sone, thi synnes ben foryouun to thee.

6 But there weren summe of the scribis sittynge, and then-kynge in her hertis,

7 What spekith he thus? He blasfemeth; who may foryyue synnes, but God aloone?

8 And whanne Jhesus hadde knowe this bi the Hooli Goost, that thei thouyten so with ynne hem silf, he seith to hem, What thenken ye these thingis in youre hertis?

9 What is liyter to seie to the sijk man in palesie, Synnes ben foryouun to thee, or to seie, Ryse, take thi bed, and walke?

10 But that ye wite that mannus sone hath power in erthe to foryyue synnes, he seide to the sijk man in palesie, Y seie to thee,

11 ryse vp, take thi bed, and go in to thin hous.

12 And anoon he roos vp, and whanne he hadde take the bed, he wente bifor alle men, so that alle men wondriden, and onoureden God, and seiden, For we seien neuer so.

13 And he wente out eftsoone to the see, and al the puple cam to hym; and he tauyte hem.

14 And whanne he passide, he saiy Leuy 'of Alfei sittynge at the tolbothe, and he seide to hym, Sue me. And he roos, and suede hym.

15 And it was doon, whanne he sat at the mete in his hous, many pupplicans and synful men saten togidere at the mete with Jhesu and hise disciplis; for there weren many that fole-widen hym.

16 And scribis and Farisees seynge, that he eet with puppli-cans and synful men, seiden to hise disciplis, Whi etith and drynkith youre maystir with pupplicans and synneris?

17 Whanne this was herd, Jhesus seide to hem, Hoole men han no nede to a leche, but thei that ben yuel at eese; for Y cam not to clepe iust men, but synneris.

18 And the disciplis of Joon and the Farisees weren fastynge; and thei camen, and seien to hym, Whi fasten the disciplis of Joon, and the Farisees fasten, but thi disciplis fasten not?

19 And Jhesus seide to hem, Whether the sones of sposailis moun faste, as longe as the spouse is with hem? As long tyme as thei haue the spouse with hem, thei moun not faste.

20 But daies schulen come, whanne the spouse schal be takun awei fro hem, and thanne thei schulen faste in tho daies.

21 No man sewith a patche of newe clooth to an elde clooth, ellis he takith awei the newe patche fro the elde, and a more brekyng is maad.

22 And no man puttith newe wyn in to elde botelis, ellis the wyn schal breste the botels, and the wyn schal be sched out, and the botels schulen perische. But newe wyn schal be put into newe botels.

23 And it was doon eftsoones, whanne the Lord walkid in the sabotis bi the cornes, and hise disciplis bigunnen to passe forth, and plucke eeris of the corn.

24 And the Farisees seiden to hym, Lo! what thi disciplis doon in sabotis, that is not leeueful.

25 And he seide to hem, Radden ye neuer what Dauid dide, whanne he hadde nede, and he hungride, and thei that weren with hym?

26 Hou he wente in to the hous of God, vndur Abiathar, prince of prestis, and eete looues of proposicioun, which it was not leeueful to ete, but to preestis aloone, and he yaf to hem that weren with hym.

27 And he seide to hem, The sabat is maad for man, and not a man for the sabat; and so mannus sone is lord also of the sabat.

CAP 3

1 And he entride eftsoone in to the synagoge, and there was a man hauynge a drye hoond.

2 And thei aspieden hym, if he helide in the sabatis, to accuse him.

3 And he seide to the man that hadde a drie hoond, Rise in to the myddil.

4 And he seith to hem, Is it leeueful to do wel in the sabatis, ether yuel? to make a soul saaf, ether to leese? And thei weren stille.

5 And he biheeld hem aboute with wraththe, and hadde sorewe on the blyndnesse of her herte, and seith to the man, Hold forth thin hoond. And he helde forth, and his hoond was restorid to hym.

6 Sotheli Farisees yeden out anoon, and maden a counsel with Erodians ayens hym, hou thei schulden lese hym.

7 But Jhesus with hise disciplis wente to the see; and myche puple fro Galilee and Judee suede hym,

8 and fro Jerusalem, and fro Ydume, and fro biyondis Jordan, and thei that weren aboute Tire and Sidon, a greet multitude, heringe the thingis that he dide, and cam to hym.

9 And Jhesus seide to hise disciplis, that the boot schulde serue hym, for the puple, lest thei thristen hym;

10 for he heelide many, so that thei felden fast to hym, to tou-che hym. And hou many euer hadde syknessis, and vnclene spiritis,

11 whanne thei seyen hym, felden doun to hym, and crieden, seiynge, Thou art the sone of God.

12 And greetli he manasside hem, that thei schulden not make hym knowun.

13 And he wente in to an hille, and clepide to hym whom he wolde; and thei camen to hym.

14 And he made, that there weren twelue with hym, to sende hem to preche.

15 And he yaf to hem pouwer to heele sijknessis, and to caste out feendis.

16 And to Symount he yaf a name Petre, and he clepide James of Zebede and Joon,

17 the brother of James, and he yaf to hem names Boenarges, that is, sones of thundryng.

18 And he clepide Andrew and Filip, and Bartholomew and Matheu, and Thomas and James Alfey, and Thadee,

19 and Symount Cananee, and Judas Scarioth, that bitraiede hym.

20 And thei camen to an hous, and the puple cam togidere eftsoone, so that thei miyten not ete breed.

21 And whanne his kynnysmen hadden herd, thei wenten out 'to holde him; for thei seiden, that he is turned in to woodnesse.

22 And the scribis that camen doun fro Jerusalem, seiden, That he hath Belsabub, and that in the prince of deuelis he castith out fendis.

23 And he clepide hem togidir, and he seide to hem in parablis, Hou may Sathanas caste out Sathanas?

24 And if a rewme be departid ayens it silf, thilke rewme may not stonde.

25 And if an hous be disparpoilid on it silf, thilke hous may not stonde.

26 And if Sathanas hath risun ayens hym silf, he is departid, and he schal not mowe stonde, but hath an ende.

27 No man may go in to a stronge mannus hous, and take awey hise vessels, but he bynde first the stronge man, and thanne he schal spoile his hous.

28 Treuli Y seie to you, that alle synnes and blasfemyes, bi whiche thei han blasfemed, schulen be foryouun to the sones of men.

29 But he that blasfemeth ayens the Hooli Goost, hath not remissioun in to with outen ende, but he schal be gilty of euerlastynge trespas.

30 For thei seiden, He hath an vnclene spirit.

31 And his modir and britheren camen, and thei stoden withoutforth, and senten to hym, and clepiden hym.

32 And the puple sat aboute hym; and thei seien to hym, Lo! thi modir and thi britheren with outforth seken thee.

33 And he answeride to hem, and seide, Who is my modir and my britheren?

34 And he bihelde thilke that saten aboute hym, and seide, Lo! my modir and my britheren.

35 For who that doith the wille of God, he is my brothir, and my sistir, and modir.

CAP 4

1 And eft Jhesus bigan to teche at the see; and myche puple was gaderid to hym, so that he wente in to a boot, and sat in the see, and al the puple was aboute the see on the loond.

2 And he tauyte hem in parablis many thingis. And he seide to hem in his techyng,

3 Here ye. Lo! a man sowynge goith out to sowe.

4 And the while he sowith, summe seed felde aboute the weie, and briddis of heuene camen, and eeten it.

5 Othere felde doun on stony places, where it had not myche erthe; and anoon it spronge vp, for it had not depnesse of erthe.

6 And whanne the sunne roos vp, it welewide for heete, and it driede vp, for it hadde no roote.

7 And othere felde doun in to thornes, and thornes sprongen vp, and strangliden it, and it yaf not fruyt.

8 And other felde doun in to good loond, and yaf fruyt, springynge vp, and wexynge; and oon brouyte thretti foold, and oon sixti fold, and oon an hundrid fold.

9 And he seide, He that hath eeris of heryng, here he.

10 And whanne he was bi hym silf, tho twelue that weren with hym axiden hym to expowne the parable.

11 And he seide to hem, To you it is youun to knowe the priuete of the kyngdom of God. But to hem that ben with outforth, alle thingis be maad in parablis, that thei seynge se,

12 and se not, and thei herynge here and vnderstonde not; lest sum tyme thei be conuertid, and synnes be foryouun to hem.

13 And he seide to hem, Knowe not ye this parable? and hou ye schulen knowe alle parablis?

14 He that sowith, sowith a word.

15 But these it ben that ben aboute the weie, where the word is sowun; and whanne thei han herd, anoon cometh Satanas, and takith awei the word that is sowun in her hertis.

16 And in lijk maner ben these that ben sowun on stony placis, whiche whanne thei han herd the word, anoon thei taken it with ioye;

17 and thei han not roote in hem silf, but thei ben lastynge a litil tyme; aftirward whanne tribulacioun risith, and persecucioun for the word, anoon thei ben sclaundrid.

18 And ther ben othir that ben sowun in thornes; these it ben that heren the word,

19 and disese of the world, and disseit of ritchessis, and othir charge of coueytise entrith, and stranglith the word, and it is maad with out fruyt.

20 And these it ben that ben sowun on good lond, whiche heren the word, and taken, and maken fruyt, oon thritti fold, oon sixti fold, and oon an hundrid fold.

21 And he seide to hem, Wher a lanterne cometh, that it be put vndur a buschel, or vndur a bed? nay, but that it be put on a candilstike?

22 Ther is no thing hid, that schal not be maad opyn; nethir ony thing is pryuey, that schal not come in to opyn.

23 If ony man haue eeris of heryng, here he.

24 And he seide to hem, Se ye what ye heren. In what mesure ye meten, it schal be metun to you ayen, and be cast to you.

25 For it schal be youun to hym that hath, and it schal be takun awei fro him that hath not, also that that he hath.

26 And he seide, So the kingdom of God is, as if a man caste seede in to the erthe,

27 and he sleepe, and it rise up niyt and dai, and brynge forth seede, and wexe faste, while he woot not.

28 For the erthe makith fruyt, first the gras, aftirward the ere, and aftir ful fruyt in the ere.

29 And whanne of it silf it hath brouyt forth fruyt, anoon he sendith a sikil, for repyng tyme is come.

30 And he seide, To what thing schulen we likne the kyngdom of God? or to what parable schulen we comparisoun it?

31 As a corne of seneuei, which whanne it is sowun in the erthe, is lesse than alle seedis that ben in the erthe;

32 and whanne it is sprongun up, it waxith in to a tre, and is maad gretter than alle erbis; and it makith grete braunchis, so

that briddis of heuene moun dwelle vndur the schadewe
therof.

33 And in many suche parablis he spak to hem the word, as
thei myyten here;

34 and he spak not to hem with out parable. But he
expownede to hise disciplis alle thingis bi hemsilf.

35 And he seide to hem in that dai, whanne euenyng was
come, Passe we ayenward.

36 And thei leften the puple, and token hym, so that he was in
a boot; and othere bootys weren with hym.

37 And a greet storm of wynde was maad, and keste wawis in
to the boot, so that the boot was ful.

38 And he was in the hyndir part of the boot, and slepte on a
pilewe. And thei reisen hym, and seien to hym, Maistir,
perteyneth it not to thee, that we perischen?

39 And he roos vp, and manasside the wynde, and seide to the
see, Be stille, wexe doumbe. And the wynde ceesside, and
greet pesiblenesse was maad.

40 And he seide to hem, What dreden ye? 'Ye han no feith
yit? And thei dredden with greet drede, and seien 'ech to
other, Who, gessist thou, is this? for the wynde and the see
obeschen to hym.

CAP 5

1 And thei camen ouer the see in to the cuntree of Gerasenes.

2 And aftir that he was goon out of the boot, anoon a man in
an vncleene spirit ran out of birielis to hym.

3 Which man hadde an hous in biriels, and nether with cheynes now myyte ony man bynde hym.

4 For ofte tymes he was boundun in stockis and chaynes, and
he hadde broke the chaynes, and hadde broke the stockis to
smale gobetis, and no man myyte make hym tame.

5 And euermore, nyyt and dai, in birielis and in hillis, he was
criynge and betynge hym silf with stoonus.

6 And he siy Jhesus afer, and ran, and worschipide hym.

7 And he criede with greet voice, and seide, What to me and
to thee, thou Jhesu, the sone of the hiyest God? Y coniure
thee bi God, that thou turmente me not.

8 And Jhesus seide to hym, Thou vnclene spirit, go out fro the
man.

9 And Jhesus axide hym, What is thi name? And he seith to
hym, A legioun is my name; for we ben many.

10 And he preiede Jhesu myche, that he schulde not putte
hym out of the cuntrei.

11 And there was there aboute the hille a greet flok of swyn
lesewynge.

12 And the spiritis preieden Jhesu, and seiden, Sende vs into
the swyn, that we entre in to hem.

13 And anoon Jhesus grauntide to hem. And the vnclene spiritis yeden out, and entriden in to the swyn, and with a greet
birre the flocke was cast doun in to the see, a twei thousynde,
and thei weren dreynt in the see.

14 And thei that kepten hem, fledden, and tolden in to the
citee, and in to the feeldis; and thei wenten out, to se what
was don.

15 And thei camen to Jhesu, and sayn hym that hadde be
trauelid of the feend, syttynge clothid, and of hool mynde;
and thei dredden.

16 And thei that saien, hou it was don to hym that hadde a
feend, and of the swyne, telden to hem.

17 And thei bigunnen to preie hym, that he schulde go a wei
fro her coostis.

18 And whanne he yede up in to a boot, he that was trauelid
of the deuel, bigan to preie hym, that he schulde be with hym.

19 But Jhesus resseyuede hym not, but seide to hym, Go thou
in to thin hous to thine, and telle to hem, hou grete thingis the
Lord hath don to thee, and hadde merci of thee.

20 And he wente forth, and bigan to preche in Decapoli, hou
grete thingis Jhesus hadde don to hym; and alle men wondriden.

21 And whanne Jhesus hadde gon vp in to the boot eftsoone
ouer the see, myche puple cam togidere to him, and was
aboute the see.

22 And oon of the princis of synagogis, bi name Jayrus, cam,
and siy hym, and felde doun at hise feet,

23 and preyede hym myche, and seide, My douyter is nyy
deed; come thou, putte thin hoond on her, that sche be saaf,
and lyue.

24 And he wente forth with hym, and myche puple suede
hym, and thruste hym.

25 And a womman hadde ben in the blodi fluxe twelue yeer,

26 and hadde resseyued many thingis of ful many lechis, and
hadde spendid al hir good, and was nothing amendid, but was
rather the wors, whanne sche hadde herd of Jhesu,

27 sche cam among the puple bihynde, and touchide his cloth.

28 For sche seide, That if Y touche yhe his cloth, Y schal be
saaf.

29 And anoon the welle of hir blood was dried vp, and sche
felide in bodi that sche was heelid of the siknesse.

30 And anoon Jhesus knewe in hym silf the vertu that was
goon out of hym, and turnede to the puple, and seide, Who
touchide my clothis?

31 And hise disciplis seiden to hym, Thou seest the puple
thristynge thee, and seist, Who touchide me?

32 And Jhesus lokide aboute to se hir that hadde don this
thing.

33 And the womman dredde, and quakide, witynge that it was
doon in hir, and cam, and felde doun bifor hym, and seide to
hym al the treuthe.

34 And Jhesus seide to hyr, Douytir, thi feith hath maad thee
saaf; go in pees, and he thou hool of thi sijknesse.

35 Yit while he spak, messangeris camen to the prince of the
synagoge, and seien, Thi douytir is deed; what traueilist thou
the maistir ferther?

36 But whanne the word was herd that was seid, Jhesus seide
to the prince of the synagoge, Nyle thou drede, oonli bileue
thou.

37 And he took no man to sue hym, but Petir, and James, and
Joon, the brother of James.

38 And thei camen in to the hous of the prince of the synagoge. And he saie noyse, and men wepynge and weilynge
myche.

39 And he yede ynne, and seide to hem, What ben ye troublid, and wepen? The damesel is not deed, but slepith.

40 And thei scorneden hym. But whanne alle weren put out,
he takith the fadir and the modir of the damesel, and hem that
weren with hym, and thei entren, where the damysel laye.

41 And he helde the hoond of the damesel, and seide to hir,
Tabita, cumy, that is to seie, Damysel, Y seie to thee, arise.

42 And anoon the damysel roos, and walkide; and sche was
of twelue yeer. And thei weren abaischid with a greet stony-
ing. And he comaundide to hem greetli, that no man schulde
wite it.

43 And he comaundide to yyue hir mete.

CAP 6

1 And he yede out fro thennus, and wente in to his owne cuntre; and hise disciplis folewiden him.

2 And whanne the sabat was come, Jhesus bigan to teche in a
synagoge. And many herden, and wondriden in his techyng,
and seiden, Of whennus to this alle these thingis? and what is
the wisdom that is youun to hym, and siche vertues whiche
ben maad bi hise hondis?

3 Whether this is not a carpenter, the sone of Marie, the
brother of James and of Joseph and of Judas and of Symount?
whether hise sistris ben not here with vs? And thei weren
sclaundrid in hym.

4 And Jhesus seide to hem, That a profete is not without
onoure, but in his owne cuntrey, and among his kynne, and in
his hous.

5 And he myyte not do there ony vertu, saue that he helide a
fewe sijk men, leiynge on hem hise hoondis.

6 And he wondride for the vnbileue of hem. And he wente
aboute casteles on ech side, and tauyte.

7 And he clepide togidere twelue, and bigan to sende hem bi
two togidere; and yaf to hem power of vnclene spiritis,

8 and comaundide hem, that thei schulde not take ony thing in
the weie, but a yerde oneli, not a scrippe, ne breed, nether
money in the girdil,

9 but schod with sandalies, and that thei schulden not be
clothid with twei cootis.

10 And he seide to hem, Whidur euer ye entren in to an hous,
dwelle ye there, til ye goon out fro thennus.

11 And who euer resseyueth you not, ne herith you, go ye out
fro thennus, and schake awei the powdir fro youre feet, in to
witnessyng to hem.

12 And thei yeden forth, and prechiden, that men schulden do
penaunce.

13 And thei castiden out many feendis, and anoyntiden with
oyle many sijk men, and thei weren heelid.

14 And kyng Eroude herde, for his name was maad opyn, and
seide, That Joon Baptist hath risen ayen fro deeth, and therfor
vertues worchen in hym.

15 Othir seiden, That it is Helie; but othir seiden, That it is a
profete, as oon of profetis.

16 And whanne this thing was herd, Eroude seide, This Joon,
whom Y haue biheedide, is risun ayen fro deeth.

17 For thilke Eroude sente, and helde Joon, and boond hym in
to prisoun, for Erodias, the wijf of Filip, his brothir; for he
hadde weddid hir.

18 For Joon seide to Eroude, It is not leueful to thee, to haue
the wijf of thi brothir.

19 And Erodias leide aspies to hym, and wolde sle hym, and
myyte not.

20 And Eroude dredde Joon, and knewe hym a iust man and
hooli, and kepte hym. And Eroude herde hym, and he dide
many thingis, and gladli herde hym.

21 And whanne a couenable dai was fallun, Eroude in his
birthdai made a soper to the princis, and tribunes, and to the
grettest of Galilee.

22 And whanne the douyter of thilke Erodias was comun
ynne, and daunside, and pleside to Eroude, and also to men
that saten at the mete, the kyng seide to the damysel, Axe
thou of me what thou wolt, and Y schal yyue to thee.

23 And he swore to hir, That what euer thou axe, Y schal
yyue to thee, thouy it be half my kyngdom.

24 And whanne sche hadde goon out, sche seide to hir modir,
What schal Y axe? And sche seide, The heed of Joon Baptist.

25 And whanne sche was comun ynne anoon with haast to the
kyng, sche axide, and seide, Y wole that anoon thou yyue to
me in a dische the heed of Joon Baptist.

26 And the kyng was sori for the ooth, and for men that saten
togidere at the meete he wolde not make hir sori;

27 but sente a manqueller and comaundide, that Joones heed
were brouyt in a dissche. And he bihedide hym in the prisoun,

28 and brouyte his heed in a disch, and yaf it to the damysel,
and the damysel yaf to hir modir.

29 And whanne this thing was herd, hise disciplis camen, and
token his bodi, and leiden it in a biriel.

30 And the apostlis camen togidere to Jhesu, and telden to
hym alle thingis, that thei hadden don, and tauyt.

31 And he seide to hem, Come ye bi you silf in to a desert
place; and reste ye a litil. For there were many that camen,
and wenten ayen, and thei hadden not space to ete.

32 And thei yeden in to a boot, and wenten in to a desert place
bi hem silf.

33 And thei sayn hem go awei, and many knewen, and thei
wenten afoote fro alle citees, and runnen thidur, and camen
bifor hem.

34 And Jhesus yede out, and saiy myche puple, and hadde
reuth on hem, for thei weren as scheep not hauynge a
scheepherd. And he bigan to teche hem many thingis.

35 And whanne it was forth daies, hise disciplis camen, and
seiden, This is a desert place, and the tyme is now passid;

36 lete hem go in to the nexte townes and villagis, to bie hem
meete to ete.

37 And he answeride, and seide to hem, Yyue ye to hem to
ete. And thei seiden to hym, Go we, and bie we looues with
two hundrid pens, and we schulen yyue to hem to ete.

38 And he seith to hem, Hou many looues han ye? Go ye, and
se. And whanne thei hadden knowe, thei seien, Fyue, and two
fischis.

39 And he comaundide to hem, that thei schulden make alle
men sitte to mete bi cumpanyes, on greene heye.

40 And thei saten doun bi parties, bi hundridis, and bi fifties.

41 And whanne he hadde take the fyue looues, and twei fischis, he biheelde in to heuene, and blesside, and brak looues,
and yaf to hise disciplis, that thei schulden sette bifor hem.
And he departide twei fischis to alle;

42 and alle eeten, and weren fulfillid.

43 And thei token the relifs of brokun metis, twelue cofyns
ful, and of the fischis.

44 And thei that eeten, weren fyue thousynde of men.

45 And anoon he maad hise disciplis to go up in to a boot, to
passe bifor hym ouer the se to Bethsaida, the while he lefte
the puple.

46 And whanne he hadde left hem, he wente in to an hille, to
preye.

47 And whanne it was euen, the boot was in the myddil of the
see, and he aloone in the loond;

48 and he say hem trauelynge in rowyng; for the wynde was
contrarie to hem. And aboute the fourthe wakynge of the
nyyt, he wandride on the see, and cam to hem, and wolde
passe hem.

49 And as thei sayn hym wandrynge on the see, thei gessiden
that it weren a fantum, and crieden out;

50 for alle sayn hym, and thei weren afraied. And anoon he
spak with hem, and seide to hem, Triste ye, Y am; nyle ye
drede.

51 And he cam vp to hem in to the boot, and the wynde ceesside. And thei wondriden more 'with ynne hem silf;

52 for thei vndurstoden not of the looues; for her herte was blyndid.

53 And whanne thei weren passid ouer the see, thei camen in to the lond of Genasareth, and settiden to loond.

54 And whanne thei weren gon out of the boot, anoon thei knewen hym.

55 And thei ranne thorou al that cuntre, and bigunnen to brynge sijk men in beddis on eche side, where thei herden that he was.

56 And whidur euer 'he entride in to villagis, ethir in to townes, or in to citees, thei setten sijk men in stretis, and preiden hym, that thei schulden touche namely the hemme of his cloth; and hou many that touchiden hym, weren maad saaf.

CAP 7

1 And the Farisees and summe of the scribis camen fro Jerusalem togidir to hym.

2 And whanne thei hadden seen summe of hise disciplis ete breed with vnwaisschen hoondis, thei blameden.

3 The Farisees and alle the Jewis eten not, but thei waisschen ofte her hoondis, holdynge the tradiciouns of eldere men.

4 And whanne thei turnen ayen fro chepyng, thei eten not, but thei ben waisschen; and many other thingis ben, 'that ben taken 'to hem to kepe, wasschyngis of cuppis, and of watir vessels, and of vessels of bras, and of beddis.

5 And Farisees and scribis axiden hym, and seiden, Whi gon not thi disciplis aftir the tradicioun of eldere men, but with vnwasschen hondis thei eten breed?

6 And he answeride, and seide to hem, Ysaie prophesiede wel of you, ypocritis, as it is writun, This puple worschipith me with lippis, but her herte is fer fro me;

7 and in veyn thei worschipen me, techinge the doctrines and the heestis of men.

8 For ye leeuen the maundement of God, and holden the tradiciouns of men, wasschyngis of watir vessels, and of cuppis; and many othir thingis lijk to these ye doon.

9 And he seide to hem, Wel ye han maad the maundement of God voide, 'to kepe youre tradicioun.

10 For Moyses seide, Worschipe thi fadir and thi modir; and he that cursith fadir or modir, die he by deeth.

11 But ye seien, If a man seie to fadir or modir, Corban, that is, What euer yifte is of me, it schal profite to thee;

12 and ouer ye suffren not hym do ony thing to fadir or modir,

13 and ye breken the word of God bi youre tradicioun, that ye han youun; and ye don many suche thingis.

14 And he eftsoone clepide the puple, and seide to hem, Ye alle here me, and vndurstonde.

15 No thing that is withouten a man, that entrith in to hym, may defoule him; but tho thingis that comen forth of a man, tho it ben that defoulen a man.

16 If ony man haue eeris of hering, here he.

17 And whanne he was entrid in to an hous, fro the puple, hise disciplis axiden hym the parable.

18 And he seide to hem, Ye ben vnwise also. Vndurstonde ye not, that al thing without forth that entreth in to a man, may not defoule hym?

19 for it hath not entrid in to his herte, but in to the wombe, and bynethe it goith out, purgynge alle metis.

20 But he seide, The thingis that gon out of a man, tho defoulen a man.

21 For fro with ynne, of the herte of men comen forth yuel thouytis, auowtries,

22 fornycaciouns, mansleyingis, theftis, auaricis, wickidnessis, gile, vnchastite, yuel iye, blasfemyes, pride, foli.

23 Alle these yuels comen forth fro with ynne, and defoulen a man.

24 And Jhesus roos vp fro thennus, and wente in to the coostis of Tyre and of Sidon. And he yede in to an hous, and wolde that no man wiste; and he myyte not be hid.

25 For a womman, anoon as sche herd of hym, whos douytir hadde an vnclene spirit, entride, and fel doun at hise feet.

26 And the womman was hethen, of the generacioun of Sirofenyce. And sche preiede hym, that he wolde caste out a deuel fro hir douyter.

27 And he seide to hir, Suffre thou, that the children be fulfillid first; for it is not good to take the breed of children, and yyue to houndis.

28 And sche answeride, and seide to him, Yis, Lord; for litil whelpis eten vndur the bord, of the crummes of children.

29 And Jhesus seide to hir, Go thou, for this word the feend wente out of thi douytir.

30 And whanne sche was gon in to hir hous home, sche foonde the damysel ligynge on the bed, and the deuel gon out fro hir.

31 And eftsoones Jhesus yede out fro the coostis of Tire, and cam thorou Sidon to the see of Galilee, bitwixe the myddil of the coostis of Decapoleos.

32 And thei bryngen to hym a man deef and doumbe, and preieden hym to leye his hoond on hym.

33 And he took hym asidis fro the puple, and puttide hise fyngris in to hise eris; and he spetide, and touchide his tonge.

34 And he bihelde in to heuene, and sorewide with ynne, and seide, Effeta, that is, Be thou openyd.

35 And anoon hise eris weren openyd, and the boond of his tunge was vnboundun, and he spak riytli.

36 And he comaundide to hem, that thei schulden seie to no man; but hou myche he comaundide to hem, so myche more thei prechiden,

37 and bi so myche more thei wondriden, and seiden, He dide wel alle thingis, and he made deef men to here, and doumbe men to speke.

CAP 8

1 In tho daies eft, whanne myche puple was with Jhesu, and hadden not what thei schulden ete, whanne hise disciplis weren clepid togidir,

2 he seide to hem, I haue reuth on the puple, for lo! now the thridde dai thei abiden me, and han not what to ete;

3 and if Y leeue hem fastynge in to her hous, thei schulen faile in the weie; for summe of hem camen fro fer.

4 And hise disciplis answerden to hym, Wherof schal a man mowe fille hem with looues here in wildirnesse?

5 And he axide hem, Hou many looues han ye?

6 Whiche seiden, Seuene. And he comaundide the puple to sitte doun on the erthe. And he took the seuene looues, and dide thankyngis, and brak, and yaf to hise disciplis, that thei schulden sette forth. And thei settiden forth to the puple.

7 And thei hadden a few smale fischis; and he blesside hem, and comaundide, that thei weren sette forth.

8 And thei eten, and weren fulfillid; and thei token vp that that lefte of relifs, seuene lepis.

9 And thei that eeten, weren as foure thousynde of men; and he lefte hem.

10 And anoon he wente vp in to a boot, with hise disciplis, and cam in to the coostis of Dalmamytha.

11 And the Farisees wenten out, and bigunnen to dispuyte with hym, and axiden a tokne of hym fro heuene, and temptiden hym.

12 And he sorewynge 'with ynne in spirit, seide, What sekith this generacioun a tokne? Treuli Y seie to you, a tokene schal not be youun to this generacioun.

13 And he lefte hem, and wente vp eftsoone in to a boot, and wente ouer the see.

14 And thei foryaten to take breed, and thei hadden not with hem but o loof in the boot.

15 And he comaundide hem, and seide, Se ye, and 'be war of the sowre dowy of Farisees, and of the sowrdowy of Eroude.

16 And thei thouyten, and seiden oon to anothir, For we han not looues.

17 And whanne this thing was knowun, Jhesus seide to hem, What thenken ye, for ye han not looues? Yit ye knowun not, ne vndurstonden; yit ye han youre herte blyndid.

18 Ye hauynge iyen, seen not, and ye hauynge eeris, heren not; nethir ye han mynde,

19 whanne Y brak fyue looues among fyue thousynde, and hou many cofynes ful of brokun meete 'ye tokun vp? Thei seien to hym, Twelue.

20 Whanne also seuene looues among foure thousynde of men, hou many lepis of brokun mete tokun ye vp?

21 And thei seien to hym, Seuene. And he seide to hem, Hou vndurstonden ye not yit?

22 And thei camen to Bethsaida, and thei bryngen to hym a blynde man, and thei preieden hym, that he schulde touche hym.

23 And whanne he hadde take the blynde mannus hoond, he ledde hym out of the street, and spete in to hise iyen, and sette hise hoondis on hym; and he axide hym, if he saye ony thing.

24 And he bihelde, and seide, Y se men as trees walkynge.

25 Aftirward eftsoones he sette hise hondis on hise iyen, and he bigan to see, and he was restorid, so that he saiy cleerli alle thingis.

26 And he sente hym in to his hous, and seide, Go in to thin hous; and if thou goist in to the streete, seie to no man.

27 And Jhesus entride and hise disciplis in to the castels of Cesarye of Philip. And in the weie he axide hise disciplis, and seide to hem, Whom seien men that Y am?

28 Whiche answeriden to hym, and seiden, Summen seien, Joon Baptist; other seien, Heli; and other seien, as oon of the prophetis.

29 Thanne he seith to hem, But whom seien ye that Y am? Petre answeride, and seide to hym, Thou art Crist.

30 And he chargide hem, that thei schulden not seie of hym to ony man.

31 And he bigan to teche hem, that it bihoueth mannus sone to suffre many thingis, and to be repreued of the elder men, and of the hiyest prestis, and the scribis, and to be slayn, and aftir thre dayes, to rise ayen.

32 And he spak pleynli the word. And Peter took hym, and bigan to blame hym, and seide, Lord, be thou merciful to thee, for this schal not be.

33 And he turnede, and saiy hise disciplis, and manasside Petir, and seide, Go after me, Satanas; for thou sauerist not tho thingis that ben of God, but tho thingis that ben of men.

34 And whanne the puple was clepid togidere, with hise disciplis, he seide to hem, If ony man wole come after me, denye he hym silf, and take his cros, and sue he me.

35 For he that wole make saaf his lijf, schal leese it; and he that leesith his lijf for me, and for the gospel, schal make it saaf.

36 For what profitith it to a man, if he wynne al the world, and do peiryng to his soule?

37 or what chaunging schal a man yyue for his soule?

38 But who that knoulechith me and my wordis in this generacioun avowtresse and synful, also mannus sone schal knouleche him, whanne he schal come in the glorie of his fadir, with his aungels.

39 And he seide to hem, Treuli Y seie to you, that there ben summen stondynge here, whiche schulen not taste deth, til thei seen the rewme of God comynge in vertu.

CAP 9

1 And aftir sixe daies Jhesus took Petre, and James, and Joon, and ledde hem bi hem silf aloone in to an hiy hille; and he was transfigurid bifor hem.

2 And hise clothis weren maad ful schynynge and white as snow, whiche maner white clothis a fuller may not make on erthe.

3 And Helie with Moises apperide to hem, and thei spaken with Jhesu.

4 And Petre answeride, and seide to Jhesu, Maister, it is good vs to be here; and make we here thre tabernaclis, oon to thee, oon to Moyses, and oon to Helie.

5 For he wiste not what he schulde seie; for thei weren agaste bi drede.

6 And ther was maad a cloude overschadewynge hem; and a vois cam of the cloude, and seide, This is my moost derworth sone, here ye hym.

7 And anoon thei bihelden aboute, and sayn no more ony man, but Jhesu oonli with hem.

8 And whanne thei camen doun fro the hille, he comaundide hem, that thei schulden not telle to ony man tho thingis that thei hadden seen, but whanne mannus sone hath risun ayen fro deeth.

9 And thei helden the word at hem silf, sekynge what this schulde be, whanne he hadde risun ayen fro deth.

10 And thei axiden hym, and seiden, What thanne seien Farisees and scribis, for it bihoueth 'Helie to come first.

11 And he answeride, and seide to hem, Whanne Helie cometh, he schal first restore alle thingis; and as it is writun of mannus sone, that he suffre many thingis, and be dispisid.

12 And Y seie to you, that Helie is comun, and thei diden to hym what euer thingis thei wolden, as it is writun of hym.

13 And he comynge to hise disciplis, saiy a greet cumpany aboute hem, and scribis disputynge with hem.

14 And anoon al the puple seynge Jhesu, was astonyed, and thei dredden; and thei rennynge gretten hym.

15 And he axide hem, What disputen ye among you?

16 And oon of the cumpany answerde, and seide, Mayster, Y haue brouyt to thee my sone, that hath a doumbe spirit; and where euer he takith hym,

17 he hurtlith hym doun, and he fometh, and betith togidir with teeth, and wexith drye. And Y seide to thi disciplis, that thei schulden caste hym out, and thei myyten not.

18 And he answeride to hem, and seide, A! thou generacioun out of bileue, hou longe schal Y be among you, hou longe schal Y suffre you? Brynge ye hym to me.

19 And thei brouyten hym. And whanne he had seyn him, anoon the spirit troublide him; and was throw doun to grounde, and walewide, and fomede.

20 And he axide his fadir, Hou longe 'is it, sith this 'hath falle to hym? And he seide, Fro childhode;

21 and ofte he hath put hym in to fier, and in to watir, to leese hym; but if thou maiste ony thing, helpe vs, and haue merci on vs.

22 And Jhesus seide to hym, If thou maiste bileue, alle thingis ben possible to man that bileueth.

23 And anoon the fadir of the child criede with teeris, and seide, Lord, Y bileue; Lord, helpe thou myn vnbileue.

24 And whanne Jhesus hadde seyn the puple rennynge togidere, he manasside the vnclene spirit, and seide to hym, Thou deef and doumbe spirit, Y comaunde thee, go out fro hym, and entre no more in to hym.

25 And he criynge, and myche to breidynge him, wente out fro hym; and he was maad as deed, so that many seiden, that he was deed.

26 And Jhesus helde his hoond, and lifte hym vp; and he roos.

27 And whanne he hadde entrid in to an hous, hise disciplis axiden hym priueli, Whi myyten not we caste hym out?

28 And he seide to hem, This kynde in no thing may go out, but in preier and fastyng.

29 And thei yeden fro thennus, and wente forth in to Galile; and thei wolden not, that ony man wiste.

30 And he tauyte hise disciplis, and seide to hem, For mannus sone schal be bitrayed in to the hondis of men, and thei schulen sle hym, and he slayn schal ryse ayen on the thridde day.

31 And thei knewen not the word, and dredden to axe hym.

32 And thei camen to Cafarnaum. And whanne thei weren in the hous, he axide hem, What tretiden ye in the weie?

33 And thei weren stille; for thei disputiden among hem in the weie, who of hem schulde be grettest.

34 And he sat, and clepide the twelue, and seide to hem, If ony man wole be the firste among you, he schal be the laste of alle, and the mynyster of alle.

35 And he took a child, and sette hym in the myddil of hem; and whanne he hadde biclippid hym, he seide to hem,

36 Who euer resseyueth oon of such children in my name, he resseyueth me; and who euer resseyueth me, he resseyueth not me aloone, but hym that sente me.

37 Joon answeride to hym, and seide, Maister, we sayn oon castynge out feendis in thi name, which sueth not vs, and we han forbodun hym.

38 And Jhesus seide, Nyle ye forbede him; for ther is no man that doith vertu in my name, and may soone speke yuel of me.

39 He that is not ayens vs, is for vs.

40 And who euer yyueth you a cuppe of coold water to drynke in my name, for ye ben of Crist, treuli Y seie to you, he schal not leese his mede.

41 And who euer schal sclaundre oon of these litle that bileuen in me, it were betere to hym that a mylne stoon 'of assis were don aboute his necke, and he were cast in to the see.

42 And if thin hoond sclaundre thee, kitte it awey; it is betere to thee to entre feble in to lijf, than haue two hondis, and go in to helle, in to fier that neuer schal be quenchid,

43 where the worm of hem dieth not, and the fier is not quenchid.

44 And if thi foote sclaundre thee, kitte it of; it is betere to thee to entre crokid in to euerlastynge lijf, than haue twei feet, and be sent in to helle of fier, that neuer schal be quenchid,

45 where the worme of hem dieth not, and the fier is not quenchid.

46 That if thin iye sclaundre thee, cast it out; it is betere to thee to entre gogil iyed in to the reume of God, than haue twey iyen, and be sent in to helle of fier, where the worme of hem dieth not,

47 and the fier is not quenchid.

48 And euery man schal be saltid with fier, and euery slayn sacrifice schal be maad sauery with salt.

49 Salt is good; if salt be vnsauery, in what thing schulen ye make it sauery? Haue ye salt among you, and haue ye pees among you.

CAP 10

1 And Jhesus roos vp fro thennus, and cam in to the coostis of Judee ouer Jordan; and eftsoones the puple cam togidere to hym, and as he was wont, eftsoone he tauyte hem.

2 And the Farisees camen, and axiden hym, Whether it be leueful to a man to leeue his wijf? and thei temptiden hym.

3 And he answeride, and seide to hem, What comaundide Moises to you?

4 And thei seiden, Moises suffride to write a libel of forsaking, and to forsake.

5 'To whiche Jhesus answeride, and seide, For the hardnesse of youre herte Moises wroot to you this comaundement.

6 But fro the bigynnyng of creature God made hem male and female;

7 and seide, For this thing a man schal leeue his fadir and modir,

8 and schal drawe to hys wijf, and thei schulen be tweyne in o flesch. And so now thei ben not tweyne, but o flesch.

9 Therfor that thing that God ioynede togidere, no man departe.

10 And eftsoone in the hous hise disciplis axiden hym of the same thing.

11 And he seide to hem, Who euer leeuith his wijf, and weddith another, he doith auowtri on hir.

12 And if the wijf leeue hir housebonde, and be weddid to another man, sche doith letcherie.

13 And thei brouyten to hym litle children, that he schulde touche hem; and the disciplis threteneden the men, that brouyten hem.

14 And whanne Jhesus hadde seyn hem, he baar heuy, and seide to hem, Suffre ye litle children to come to me, and forbede ye hem not, for of suche is the kyngdom of God.

15 Treuli Y seie to you, who euer resseyueth not the kyngdom of God as a litil child, he schal not entre in to it.

16 And he biclippide hem, and leide hise hondis on hem, and blisside hem.

17 And whanne Jhesus was gon out in the weie, a man ranne bifore, and knelide bifor hym, and preiede hym, and seide, Good maister, what schal Y do, that Y resseyue euerlastynge lijf?

18 And Jhesus seide to hym, What seist thou, that Y am good? Ther is no man good, but God hym silf.

19 Thou knowist the comaundementis, do thou noon auowtrie, 'sle not, stele not, seie not fals witnessyng, do no fraude, worschipe thi fadir and thi modir.

20 And he answeride, and seide to hym, Maister, Y haue kept alle these thingis fro my yongthe.

21 And Jhesus bihelde hym, and louede hym, and seide to hym, O thing faileth to thee; go thou, and sille alle thingis that thou hast, and yyue to pore men, and thou schalt haue tresoure in heuene; and come, sue thou me.

22 And he was ful sori in the word, and wente awei mornyng, for he hadde many possessiouns.

23 And Jhesus bihelde aboute, and seide to hise disciplis, Hou hard thei that han ritchessis schulen entre in to the kyngdom of God.

24 And the disciplis weren astonyed in hise wordis. And Jhesus eftsoone answeride, and seide 'to hem, Ye litle children, hou hard it is for men that tristen in ritchessis to entre in to the kyngdom of God.

25 It is liyter a camele to passe thorou a nedlis iye, than a riche man to entre in to the kyngdom of God.

26 And thei wondriden more, and seiden among hem silf, And who may be sauyd?

27 And Jhesus bihelde hem, and seide, Anentis men it is impossible, but not anentis God; for alle thingis ben possible anentis God.

28 And Petir bigan to seie to hym, Lo! we han left alle thingis, and han sued thee.

29 Jhesus answeride, and seide, Treuli Y seie to you, ther is no man that leeueth hous, or britheren, or sistris, or fadir, or modir, or children, or feeldis for me and for the gospel,

30 which schal not take an hundrid fold so myche now in this tyme, housis, and britheren, and sistris, and modris, and children, and feeldis, with persecuciouns, and in the world to comynge euerlastynge lijf.

31 But many schulen be, the firste the last, and the last the firste.

32 And thei weren in the weie goynge vp to Jerusalem; and Jhesus wente bifor hem, and thei wondriden, and foleweden, and dredden. And eftsoone Jhesus took the twelue, and bigan to seie to hem, what thingis weren to come to hym.

33 For lo! we stien to Jerusalem, and mannus sone schal be bitraied to the princis of prestis, and to scribis, and to the eldre men; and thei schulen dampne hym bi deth, and thei schulen take hym to hethene men. And thei schulen scorne hym,

34 and bispete hym, and bete him; and thei schulen sle hym, and in the thridde dai he schal rise ayen.

35 And James and Joon, Zebedees sones, camen to hym, and seiden, Maister, we wolen, that what euer we axen, thou do to vs.

36 And he seide to hem, What wolen ye that Y do to you?

37 And thei seiden, Graunte to vs, that we sitten 'the toon at thi riythalf, and the tother at thi left half, in thi glorie.

38 And Jhesus seide to hem, Ye witen not what ye axen; moun ye drynke the cuppe, which Y schal drynke, or be waischun with the baptym, in which Y am baptisid?

39 And thei seiden to hym, We moun. And Jhesus seide to hem, Ye schulen drynke the cuppe that Y drynke, and ye schulen be waschun with the baptym, in which Y am baptisid;

40 but to sitte at my riythalf or lefthalf is not myn to yyue to you, but to whiche it is maad redi.

41 And the ten herden, and bigunnen to haue indignacioun of James and Joon.

42 But Jhesus clepide hem, and seide to hem, Ye witen, that thei that semen to haue prynshode of folkis, ben lordis of hem, and the princes of hem han power of hem.

43 But it is not so among you, but who euer wole be maad gretter, schal be youre mynyster;

44 and who euer wole be the firste among you, schal be seruaunt of alle.

45 For whi mannus sone cam not, that it schulde be mynystrid to hym, but that he schulde mynystre, and yyue his lijf ayenbiyng for manye.

46 And thei camen to Jerico; and whanne he yede forth fro Jerico, and hise disciplis, and a ful myche puple, Barthymeus, a blynde man, the sone of Thimei, sat bisidis the weie, and beggide.

47 And whanne he herde, that it is Jhesus of Nazareth, he bigan to crie, and seie, Jhesu, the sone of Dauid, haue merci on me.

48 And manye thretneden hym, that he schulde be stille; and he criede myche the more, Jhesu, the sone of Dauid, haue merci on me.

49 And Jhesus stood, and comaundide hym to be clepid; and thei clepen the blynde man, and seien to hym, Be thou of betere herte, rise vp, he clepith thee.

50 And he castide awei his cloth, and skippide, and cam to hym.

51 And Jhesus answeride, and seide to hym, What wolt thou, that Y schal do to thee? The blynde man seide to hym, Maister, that Y se.

52 Jhesus seide to hym, Go thou, thi feith hath maad thee saaf. And anoon he saye, and suede hym in the weie.

CAP 11

1 And whanne Jhesus cam nyy to Jerusalem and to Betanye, to the mount of Olyues, he sendith tweyne of hise disciplis, and seith to hem,

2 Go ye in to the castel that is ayens you; and anoon as ye entren there ye schulen fynde a colt tied, on which no man hath sete yit; vntie ye, and brynge hym.

3 And if ony man seye ony thing to you, What doen ye? seie ye, that he is nedeful to the Lord, and anoon he schal leeue hym hidir.

4 And thei yeden forth, and founden a colt tied bifor the yate with out forth, in the metyng of twei weies; and thei vntieden hym.

5 And summe of hem that stoden there seiden to hem, What doen ye, vntiynge the colt?

6 And thei seiden to hem, as Jhesus comaundide hem; and thei leften it to hem.

7 And thei brouyten the colt to Jhesu, and thei leiden on hym her clothis, and Jhesus sat on hym.

8 And many strewiden her clothis in the weie, othere men kittiden braunchis fro trees, and strewiden in the weie.

9 And thei that wenten bifor, and that sueden, crieden, and seiden, Osanna,

10 blissid is he that cometh in the name of the Lord; blessid be the kyngdom of oure fadir Dauid that is come; Osanna in hiyest thingis.

11 And he entride in to Jerusalem, in to the temple; and whanne he 'hadde seyn al thing aboute, whanne it was eue, he wente out in to Betanye, with the twelue.

12 And anothir daye, whanne he wente out of Betanye, he hungride.

13 And whanne he hadde seyn a fige tree afer hauynge leeues, he cam, if happili he schulde fynde ony thing theron; and whanne he cam to it, he foonde no thing, out takun leeues; for it was not tyme of figis.

14 And Jhesus answeride and seide to it, Now neuer ete ony man fruyt of thee more. And hise disciplis herden;

15 and thei camen to Jerusalem. And whanne he was entrid in to the temple, he bigan to caste out silleris and biggeris in the

temple; and he turnede vpsodoun the bordis of chaungeris, and the chayeris of men that selden culueris;

16 and he suffride not, that ony man schulde bere a vessel thorou the temple.

17 And he tauyte hem, and seide, Whether it is not writun, That myn hous schal be clepid the hous of preyng to alle folkis? but ye han maad it a denne of theues.

18 And whanne this thing was herd, the princis of prestis and scribis souyten hou thei schulden leese hym; for thei dredden hym, for al the puple wondride on his techyng.

19 And whanne euenyng was come, he wente out of the citee.

20 And as thei passiden forth eerli, thei sayn the fige tree maad drye fro the rootis.

21 And Petir bithouyte hym, and seide to hym, Maister, lo! the fige tree, whom thou cursidist, is dried vp.

22 And Jhesus answeride and seide to hem, Haue ye the feith of God;

23 treuli Y seie to you, that who euer seith to this hil, Be thou takun, and cast in to the see; and doute not in his herte, but bileueth, that what euer he seie, schal be don, it schal be don to hym.

24 Therfor Y seie to you, alle thingis what euer thingis ye preynge schulen axe, bileue ye that ye schulen take, and thei schulen come to you.

25 And whanne ye schulen stonde to preye, foryyue ye, if ye han ony thing ayens ony man, that youre fadir that is in heuenes, foryyue to you youre synnes.

26 And if ye foryyuen not, nether youre fadir that is in heuenes, schal foryyue to you youre synnes.

27 And eftsoone thei camen to Jerusalem. And whanne he walkide in the temple, the hiyeste prestis, and scribis, and the elder men camen to hym,

28 and seyn to hym, In what power doist thou these thingis? or who yaf to thee this power, that thou do these thingis?

29 Jhesus answeride and seide to hem, And Y schal axe you o word, and answere ye to me, and Y schal seie to you in what power Y do these thingis.

30 Whether was the baptym of Joon of heuene, or of men? answere ye to me.

31 And thei thouyten with ynne hem silf, seiynge, If we seien of heuene, he schal seie to vs, Whi thanne bileuen ye not to him;

32 if we seien of men, we dreden the puple; for alle men hadden Joon, that he was verili a prophete.

33 And thei answeryden, and seien to Jhesu, We witen neuer. And Jhesu answerde, and seide to hem, Nether Y seie to you, in what power Y do these thingis.

CAP 12

1 And Jhesus bigan to speke to hem in parablis. A man plauntide a vynyerd, and sette an hegge aboute it, and dalf a lake, and bildide a toure, and hiryde it to tilieris, and wente forth in pilgrimage.

2 And he sente to the erthe tilieris in tyme a seruaunt, to resseyue of the erthe tilieris of the fruyt of the vynyerd.

3 And thei token hym, and beeten, and leften hym voide.

4 And eftsoone he sente to hem anothir seruaunt, and thei woundiden hym in the heed, and turmentiden hym.

5 And eftsoone he sente another, and thei slowen hym, and othir mo, betynge summe, and sleynge othere.

6 But yit he hadde a moost derworth sone, and he sente hym last to hem, and seide, Perauenture thei schulen drede my sone.

7 But the erthetilieris seiden togidere, This is the eire; come ye, sle we hym, and the eritage schal be ourun.

8 And thei tokun hym, and killiden, and castiden out without the vynyerd.

9 Thanne what schal the lord of the vynyerd do? He schal come, and lese the tilieris, and yyue the vynyerd to othere.

10 Whether ye han not red this scripture, The stoon which the bilderis han disspisid, this is maad in to the heed of the corner?

11 This thing is doon of the Lord, and is wondirful in oure iyen.

12 And thei souyten to holde hym, and thei dredden the puple; for thei knewen that to hem he seide this parable; and thei leften hym,

13 and thei wenten awei. And thei senten to hym summe of the Farisees and Erodians, to take hym in word.

14 Whiche camen, and seien to hym, Maistir, we witen that thou art sothfast, and reckist not of ony man; for nethir thou biholdist in to the face of man, but thou techist the weie of God in treuthe. Is it leeueful that tribute be youun to the emperoure, or we schulen not yyue?

15 Which witynge her pryuei falsnesse, seide to hem, What tempten ye me? brynge ye to me a peny, that Y se.

16 And thei brouyten to hym. And he seide to hem, Whos is this ymage, and the writyng? Thei seien to him, The emperouris.

17 And Jhesus answeride and seide to hem, Thanne yelde ye to the emperour tho thingis that ben of the emperours; and to God tho thingis that ben of God.

18 And thei wondriden of hym. And Saduces, that seien that ther is no ressurreccioun, camen to hym, and axeden hym,

19 and seiden, Maister, Moyses wroot to vs, that if the brother of a man were deed, and lefte his wijf, and haue no sones, his brother take his wijf, and reise vp seed to his brother.

20 Thanne seuene britheren ther weren; and the firste took a wijf, and diede, and lefte no seed.

21 And the secounde took hir, and he diede, and nether this lefte seed.

22 And the thridde also. And in lijk manere the seuene token hir, and leften not seed. And the womman the laste of alle ‘is deed.

23 Thanne in the resurreccioun, whanne thei schulen rise ayen, whos wijf of these schal sche be? for seuene hadden hir to wijf.

24 And Jhesus answeride, and seide to hem, Whether ye erren not therfor, that ye knowe not scripturis, nethir the vertu of God?

25 For whanne thei schulen rise ayen fro deeth, nether thei schulen wedde, nethir schulen be weddid, but thei schulen be as aungels of God in heuenes.

26 And of deed men, that thei risen ayen, han ye not red in the book of Moises, on the buysch, hou God spak to hym, and seide, Y am God of Abraham, and God of Isaac, and God of Jacob?

27 He is not God of deed men, but of lyuynge men; therfor ye erren myche.

28 And oon of the scribis, that hadde herde hem dispuytynge togidir, cam nyy, and saiy that Jhesus had wel answeride hem, and axide hym, which was the firste maundement of alle.

29 And Jhesus answeride to him, that the firste maundement of alle is, Here thou, Israel, thi Lord God is o God;

30 and thou schalt loue thi Lord God of al thin herte, and of al thi soule, and of al thi mynde, and of al thi myyt.

31 This is the firste maundement. And the secounde is lijk to this, Thou schalt loue thi neiybore as thi silf. Ther is noon other maundement gretter than these.

32 And the scribe seide to hym, Maister, in treuthe thou hast wel seid; for o God is, and ther is noon other, outakun hym;

33 that he be loued of al the herte, and of al the mynde, and of al the vndurstondynge, and of al the soule, and of al strengthe, and to loue the neiybore as hym silf, is gretter than alle brent offryngis and sacrifices.

34 And Jhesus seynge that he hadde answerid wiseli, seide to hym, Thou art not fer fro the kyngdom of God.

35 And thanne no man durste axe hym no more ony thing. And Jhesus answeride and seide, techynge in the temple, Hou seien scribis, that Crist is the sone of Dauid?

36 For Dauid hym silf seide in the Hooli Goost, the Lord seide to my lord, Sitte on my riythalf, til Y putte thin enemyes the stool of thi feet.

37 Thanne Dauid hym silf clepith him lord, hou thanne is he his sone? And myche puple gladli herde hym.

38 And he seide to hem in his techyng, Be ye war of scribis, that wolen wandre in stolis,

39 and be salutid in chepyng, and sitte in synagogis in the firste chaieris, and the firste sittyng placis in soperis;

40 whiche deuouren the housis of widewis vndur colour of long preier; thei schulen take the longer doom.

41 And Jhesus sittynge ayens the tresorie, bihelde hou the puple castide monei in to the tresorie; and many riche men castiden many thingis.

42 But whanne a pore widewe was comun, sche keste two mynutis, that is, a ferthing.

43 And he clepide togidere hise disciplis, and seide to hem, Treuli Y seie to you, that this pore widewe keste more thanne alle, that kesten in to the tresorie.

44 For alle kesten of that thing that thei hadden plente of; but this of her pouert keste alle thingis that sche hadde, al hir lyuelode.

CAP 13

1 And whanne he wente out of the temple, oon of hise disciplis seide to hym, Maister, biholde, what maner stoonys, and what maner bildyngis.

2 And Jhesu answeride, and seide to hym, Seest thou alle these grete bildingis? ther schal not be left a stoon on a stoon, which schal not be distried.

3 And whanne he sat in the mount of Olyues ayens the temple, Petir and James and Joon and Andrew axiden hym bi hem silf,

4 Seie thou to vs, whanne these thingis schulen be don, and what tokene schal be, whanne alle these thingis schulen bigynne to be endid.

5 And Jhesus answeride, and bigan to seie to hem, Loke ye, that no man disseyue you;

6 for manye schulen come in my name, seiynge, That Y am; and thei schulen disseyue manye.

7 And whanne ye here batels and opynyouns of batels, drede ye not; for it bihoueth these thingis to be doon, but not yit anoon is the ende.

8 For folk schal rise on folk, and rewme on rewme, and erthe mouyngis and hungur schulen be bi placis; these thingis schulen be bigynnyngis of sorewis.

9 But se ye you silf, for thei schulen take you in counsels, and ye schulen be betun in synagogis; and ye schulen stonde bifor kyngis and domesmen for me, in witnessyng to hem.

10 And it bihoueth, that the gospel be first prechid among al folk.

11 And whanne thei taken you, and leden you forth, nyle ye bifore thenke what ye schulen speke, but speke ye that thing that schal be youun to you in that our; for ye ben not the spekeris, but the Hooli Goost.

12 For a brother schal bitake the brother in to deth, and the fadir the sone, and sones schulen rise togider ayens fadris and modris, and punysche hem bi deeth.

13 And ye schulen be in hate to alle men for my name; but he that lastith in to the ende, schal be saaf.

14 But whanne ye schulen se the abhomynacioun of discoumfort, stondynge where it owith not; he that redith, vndurstonde; thanne thei that be in Judee, fle 'in to hillis.

15 And he that is aboue the roof, come not doun in to the hous, nethir entre he, to take ony thing of his hous;

16 and he that schal be in the feeld, turne not ayen bihynde to take his cloth.

17 But wo to hem that ben with child, and norischen in tho daies.

18 Therfor preye ye, that thei be not don in wyntir.

19 But thilke daies of tribulacioun schulen be suche, whiche maner weren not fro the bigynnyng of creature, which God hath maad, til now, nethir schulen be.

20 And but the Lord hadde abredgide tho daies, al fleische hadde not be saaf; but for the chosun whiche he chees, the Lord hath maad schort the daies.

21 And thanne if ony man seie to you, Lo! here is Crist, lo! there, bileue ye not.

22 For false Cristis and false prophetis schulen rise, and schulen yyue tokenes and wondris, to disseyue, if it may be don, yhe, hem that be chosun.

23 Therfor take ye kepe; lo! Y haue bifor seid to you alle thingis.

24 But in tho daies, aftir that tribulacioun, the sunne schal be maad derk, and the moon schal not yyue hir liyt,

25 and the sterris of heuene schulen falle doun, and the vertues that ben in heuenes, schulen be moued.

26 And thanne thei schulen se mannus sone comynge in cloudis of heuene, with greet vertu and glorie.

27 And thanne he schal sende hise aungelis, and schal geder hise chosun fro the foure wyndis, fro the hiyest thing of erthe til to the hiyest thing of heuene.

28 But of the fige tree lerne ye the parable. Whanne now his braunche is tendre, and leeues ben sprongun out, ye knowen that somer is nyy.

29 So whanne ye seen these thingis be don, wite ye, that it is nyy in the doris.

30 Treuli Y seie to you, that this generacioun schal not passe awei, til alle these thingis be don.

31 Heuene and erthe schulen passe, but my wordis schulen not passe.

32 But of that dai or our no man woot, nether aungels in heuene, nether the sone, but the fadir.

33 Se ye, wake ye, and preie ye; for ye witen not, whanne the tyme is.

34 For as a man that is gon fer in pilgrimage, lefte his hous, and yaf to his seruauntis power of euery work, and comaundide to the porter, that he wake.

35 Therfor wake ye, for ye witen not, whanne the lord of the hous cometh, in the euentide, or at mydnyyt, or at cockis crowyng, or in the mornyng;

36 leste whanne he cometh sodenli, he fynde you slepynge.

37 Forsothe that that Y seie to you, Y seie to alle, Wake ye.

CAP 14

1 Pask and the feest of therf looues was after twei daies. And the hiyest preestis and scribis souyten, hou thei schulden holde hym with gile, and sle.

2 But thei seiden, Not in the feeste dai, lest perauenture a noyse were maad among the puple.

3 And whanne he was at Betanye, in the hous of Symount leprous, and restide, a womman cam, that hadde a boxe of alabastre of precious oynement spikenard; and whanne the boxe of alabastre was brokun, sche helde it on his heed.

4 But there weren summe that beren it heuyli with ynne hem silf, and seiden, Wher to is this losse of oynement maad?

5 For this oynement myyte haue be seld more than for thre hundrid pens, and be youun to pore men. And thei groyneden ayens hir.

6 But Jhesus seide, Suffre ye hir; what be ye heuy to hir? sche hath wrouyt a good werk in me.

7 For euermore ye schulen haue pore men with you, and whanne ye wolen, ye moun do wel to hem; but ye schulen not euer more haue me.

8 Sche dide that that sche hadde; sche cam bifore to anoynte my bodi in to biriyng.

9 Treuli Y seie to you, where euer this gospel be prechid in al the world, and that that 'this womman hath don, schal be told in to mynde of hym.

10 And Judas Scarioth, oon of the twelue, wente to the hiyest prestis, to bitraye hym to hem.

11 And thei herden, and ioyeden, and bihiyten to yyue hym money. And he souyt hou he schulde bitraye hym couenabli.

12 And the firste dai of therf looues, whanne thei offriden pask, the disciplis seyn to hym, Whidir 'wilt thou that we go, and make redi to thee, that thou ete the pask?

13 And he sendith tweyn of hise disciplis, and seith to hem, Go ye in to the citee, and a man berynge a galoun of watir schal meete you; sue ye hym.

14 And whidur euer he entrith, seie ye to the lord of the hous, That the maister seith, Where is myn etynge place, where Y schal ete pask with my disciplis?

15 And he schal schewe to you a grete soupyng place arayed, and there make ye redi to vs.

16 And hise disciplis wenten forth, and camen in to the citee, and founden as he hadde seid to hem; and thei maden redy the pask.

17 And whanne the euentid was come, he cam with the twelue.

18 And whanne thei saten 'at the mete, and eeten, Jhesus seide, Treuli Y seie to you, that oon of you that etith with me, schal bitray me.

19 And thei bigunnen to be sori, and to seie to hym, ech bi hem silf, Whether Y?

20 Which seide to hem, Oon of twelue that puttith the hoond with me in the platere.

21 And sotheli mannus sone goith, as it is writun of hym; but wo to that man, by whom mannus sone schal be bitrayed. It were good to hym, yf thilke man hadde not be borun.

22 And while thei eeten, Jhesus took breed, and blessid, and brak, and yaf to hem, and seide, Take ye; this is my bodi.

23 And whanne he hadde take the cuppe, he dide thankyngis, and yaf to hem, and alle dronken therof.

24 And he seide to hem, This is my blood of the newe testament, which schal be sched for many.

25 Treuli Y seye to you, for now Y schal not drynke of this fruyt of vyne, in to that dai whane Y schal drynke it newe in the rewme of God.

26 And whanne the ympne was seid, thei wenten out in to the hil of Olyues.

27 And Jhesus seide to hem, Alle ye schulen be sclaundrid in me in this nyyt; for it is writun, Y schal smyte the scheepherde, and the scheep of the flok schulen be disparplid.

28 But aftir that Y schal rise ayen, Y schal go bifor you in to Galilee.

29 And Petir seide to hym, Thouy alle schulen be sclaundrid, but not Y.

30 And Jhesus seide to hym, Treuli Y seie to thee, that to dai bifore that the cok in this niyt crowe twies, thou schalt thries denye me.

31 But he seide more, Thouy it bihoueth, that Y die togider with thee, Y schal not forsake thee. And in lijk maner alle seiden.

32 And thei camen in to a place, whos name is Gethsamany. And he seide to hise disciplis, Sitte ye here, while Y preye.

33 And he took Petir and James and Joon with hym, and bigan to drede, and to be anoyed.

34 And he seide to hem, My soule is soreweful to the deeth; abide ye here, and wake ye with me.

35 And whanne he was gon forth a litil, he felde doun on the erthe, and preiede, that if it myyte be, that the our schulde passe fro hym.

36 And he seide, Abba, fadir, alle thingis ben possible to thee, bere ouer fro me this cuppe; but not that Y wole, but that thou wolt, be don.

37 And he cam, and foond hem slepynge. And he seide to Petir, Symount, slepist thou? myytist thou not wake with me oon our?

38 Wake ye, and 'preie ye, that ye entre not in to temptacioun; for the spirit is redi, but the fleische is sijk.

39 And eftsoone he yede, and preiede, and seide the same word;

40 and turnede ayen eftsoone, and foond hem slepynge; for her iyen weren heuyed. And thei knewen not, what thei schulden answere to hym.

41 And he cam the thridde tyme, and seide to hem, Slepe ye now, and reste ye; it suffisith. The hour is comun; lo! mannus sone schal be bitraied in to the hondis of synful men.

42 Rise ye, go we; lo! he that schal bitraye me is nyy.

43 And yit while he spak, Judas Scarioth, oon of the twelue, cam, and with him miche puple with swerdis and staues, sent fro the hiyest prestis, and the scribis, and fro the eldre men.

44 And his traytour hadde youun to hem a tokene, and seide, Whom euer Y kisse, he it is; holde ye hym, and lede ye warli.

45 And whanne he cam, anoon he came to hym, and seide, Maistir; and he kisside hym.

46 And thei leiden hondis on hym, and helden hym.

47 But oon of the men that stoden aboute, drowy out a swerd, and smoot the seruaunt of the hiyest preest, and kittide of his eere.

48 And Jhesus answeride, and seide to hem, As to a theef ye han gon out with swerdis and staues, to take me?

49 Dai bi dai Y was among you, and tauyte in the temple, and ye helden not me; but that the scripturis be fulfillid.

50 Thanne alle hise disciplis forsoken hym, and fledden.

51 But a yong man, clothid with lynnun cloth on the bare, suede hym; and thei helden hym.

52 And he lefte the lynnyn clothing, and fleiy nakid awei fro hem.

53 And thei ledden Jhesu to the hiyeste preest. And alle the prestis and scribis and eldere men camen togidir.

54 But Petir suede hym afer in to the halle of the hiyest preest. And he sat with the mynystris, and warmede hym at the fier.

55 And the hiyest prestis, and al the counsel, souyten witnessyng ayens Jhesu to take hym to the deeth; but thei founden not.

56 For manye seiden fals witnessyng ayens hym, and the witnessyngis weren not couenable.

57 And summe risen vp, and baren fals witnessyng ayens hym,

58 and seiden, For we 'han herd hym seiynge, Y schal vndo this temple maad with hondis, and aftir the thridde dai Y schal bilde another not maad with hondis.

59 And the witnessyng 'of hem was not couenable.

60 And the hiyest prest roos vp in to the myddil, and axide Jhesu, and seide, Answerist thou no thing to tho thingis that ben put ayens thee of these?

61 But he was stille, and answeride no thing. Eftsoone the hiyest prest axide hym, and seide to hym, Art thou Crist, the sone of the blessid God?

62 And Jhesus seide to hym, Y am; and ye schulen se mannus sone sittynge on the riythalf of the vertu of God, and comynge in the cloudis of heuene.

63 And the hiyest preest torente hise clothis, and seide, What yit dissiren we witnessis?

64 Ye han herd blasfemye. What semeth to you? And thei alle condempneden hym to be gilti of deeth.

65 And summe bigunnen to bispete hym, 'and to hile his face, and to smite hym with buffetis, and seie to hym, Areede thou. And the mynystris beeten hym with strokis.

66 And whanne Petir was in the halle bynethen, oon of the damesels of the hiyest prest cam.

67 And whanne sche hadde seyn Petir warmynge hym, sche bihelde hym, and seide, And thou were with Jhesu of Nazareth.

68 And he denyede, and seide, Nethir Y woot, nethir Y knowe, what thou seist. And he wente without forth bifor the halle; and anoon the cok crewe.

69 And eftsoone whanne another damesel hadde seyn hym, sche bigan to seye to men that stoden aboute, That this is of hem.

70 And he eftsoone denyede. And aftir a litil, eftsoone thei that stoden nyy, seiden to Petir, Verili thou art of hem, for thou art of Galilee also.

71 But he bigan to curse and to swere, For Y knowe not this man, whom ye seien.

72 And anoon eftsoones the cok crew. And Petir bithouyte on the word that Jhesus hadde seide to hym, Bifor the cok crowe twies, thries thou schalt denye me. And he bigan to wepe.

CAP 15

1 And anoon in the morewtid the hiyeste prestis maden a counsel with the elder men, and the scribis, and with al the counsel, and bounden Jhesu and ledden, and bitoken hym to Pilat.

2 And Pilat axide hym, Art thou kynge of Jewis? And Jhesus answeride, and seide to hym, Thou seist.

3 And the hieste prestis accusiden hym in many thingis.

4 But Pilat eftsoone axide hym, and seide, Answerist thou no thing? Seest thou in hou many thingis thei accusen thee?

5 But Jhesus answeride no more, so that Pilat wondride.

6 But bi the feeste dai he was wont to leeue to hem oon of men boundun, whom euer thei axiden.

7 And 'oon ther was that was seid Barabas, that was boundun with men of dissencioun, that hadden don manslauytir in seducioun.

8 And whanne the puple was gon vp, he bigan to preie, as he euer more dide to hem.

9 And Pilat answeride 'to hem, and seide, Wolen ye Y leeue to you the kyng of Jewis?

10 For he wiste, that the hiyeste prestis hadden takun hym bi enuye.

11 But the bischopis stireden the puple, that he schulde rather leeue to hem Barabas.

12 And eftsoone Pilat answerde, and seide to hem, What thanne wolen ye that Y schal do to the kyng of Jewis?

13 And thei eftsoone crieden, Crucifie hym.

14 But Pilat seide to hem, What yuel hath he don? And thei crieden the more, Crucifie hym.

15 And Pilat, willynge to make aseeth to the puple, lefte to hem Barabas, and bitok to hem Jhesu, betun with scourgis, to be crucified.

16 And knyytis ledden hym with ynneforth, in to the porche of the mote halle. And thei clepiden togidir al the cumpany of knyytis,

17 and clothiden hym with purpur. And thei writhen a coroun of thornes, and puttiden on hym.

18 And thei bigunnen to grete hym, and seiden, Heile, thou kyng of Jewis.

19 And thei smyten his heed with a reed, and bispatten hym; and thei kneliden, and worschipiden hym.

20 And aftir that thei hadden scorned him, thei vnclothiden hym of purpur, and clothiden hym with hise clothis, and ledden out hym, to crucifie hym.

21 And thei compelliden a man that passide the weie, that cam fro the toun, Symount of Syrenen, the fader of Alisaundir and of Rufe, to bere his cross.

22 And thei ledden hym in to a place Golgatha, that is to seie, the place of Caluari.

23 And thei yauen to hym to drynke wyn meddlid with mirre, and he took not.

24 And thei crucifieden him, and departiden hise clothis, and kesten lot on tho, who schulde take what.

25 And it was the thridde our, and thei crucifieden hym.

26 And the titil of his cause was writun, Kyng of Jewis.

27 And thei crucifien with hym twei theues, oon 'at the riythalf and oon at his lefthalf.

28 And the scripture was fulfillid that seith, And he is ordeyned with wickid men.

29 And as thei passiden forth, thei blasfemyden hym, mouynge her heedis, and seiynge, Vath! thou that distriest the temple of God, and in 'thre daies bildist it ayen;

30 come adoun fro the crosse, and make thi silf saaf.

31 Also the hiyeste prestis scorneden hym ech to othir with the scribis, and seiden, He made othir men saaf, he may not saue hym silf.

32 Crist, kyng of Israel, come doun now fro the cross, that we seen, and bileuen. And thei that weren crucified with hym, dispiseden hym.

33 And whanne the sixte hour was come, derknessis weren made on al the erthe til in to the nynthe our.

34 And in the nynthe our Jhesus criede with a greet vois, and seide, Heloy, Heloy, lamasabatany, that is to seie, My God, my God, whi hast thou forsakun me?

35 And summe of men that stoden aboute herden, and seiden, Lo! he clepith Helye.

36 And oon ranne, and fillide a spounge with vynegre, and puttide aboute to a reede, and yaf to hym drynke, and seide, Suffre ye, se we, if Helie come to do hym doun.

37 And Jhesus yaf out a greet cry, and diede.

38 And the veil of the temple was rent atwo fro the hiyeste to bynethe.

39 But the centurien that stood forn ayens siy, that he so criynge hadde diede, and seide, Verili, this man was Goddis sone.

40 And ther weren also wymmen biholdynge fro afer, among whiche was Marie Maudeleyn, and Marie, the modir of James the lesse, and of Joseph, and of Salome.

41 And whanne Jhesus was in Galilee, thei folewiden hym, and mynystriden to hym, and many othere wymmen, that camen vp togidir with him to Jerusalem.

42 And whanne euentid was come, for it was the euentid which is bifor the sabat,

43 Joseph of Armathie, the noble decurioun, cam, and he abood the rewme of God; and booldli he entride to Pilat, and axide the bodi of Jhesu.

44 But Pilat wondride, if he were now deed.

45 And whanne the centurion was clepid, he axide hym, if he were deed; and whanne he knewe of the centurion, he grauntide the bodi of Jhesu to Joseph.

46 And Joseph bouyte lynnen cloth, and took hym doun, and wlappide in the lynnen cloth, and leide hym in a sepulcre that was hewun of a stoon, and walewide a stoon to the dore of the sepulcre.

47 And Marie Maudeleyne and Marie of Joseph bihelden, where he was leid.

CAP 16

1 And whanne the sabat was passid, Marie Maudeleyne, and Marie of James, and Salomee bouyten swete smellynge oynementis, to come and to anoynte Jhesu.

2 And ful eerli in oon of the woke daies, thei camen to the sepulcre, whanne the sunne was risun.

3 And thei seiden togidere, Who schal meue awey to vs the stoon fro the dore of the sepulcre?

4 And thei bihelden, and seien the stoon walewid awei, for it was ful greet.

5 And thei yeden in to the sepulcre, and sayn a yonglyng, hilide with a white stole, sittynge 'at the riythalf; and thei weren afeerd.

6 Which seith to hem, Nyle ye drede; ye seken Jhesu of Nazareth crucified; he is risun, he is not here; lo! the place where thei leiden hym.

7 But go ye, and seie ye to hise disciplis, and to Petir, that he schal go bifor you in to Galilee; there ye schulen se hym, as he seide to you.

8 And thei yeden out, and fledden fro the sepulcre; for drede and quakyng had assailed hem, and to no man thei seiden ony thing, for thei dredden.

9 And Jhesus roos eerli the firste dai of the woke, and apperid firste to Marie Maudeleyne, fro whom he had caste out seuene deuelis.

10 And sche yede, and tolde to hem that hadden ben with hym, whiche weren weilynge and wepynge.

11 And thei herynge that he lyuyde, and was seyn of hir, bileueden not.

12 But after these thingis whanne tweyne of hem wandriden, he was schewid in anothir liknesse to hem goynge in to a toun.

13 And thei yeden, and telden to the othir, and nether thei bileueden to hem.

14 But 'at the laste, whanne the enleuene disciplis saten at the mete, Jhesus apperide to hem, and repreuede the vnbileue of hem, and the hardnesse of herte, for thei bileueden not to hem, that hadden seyn that he was risun fro deeth.

15 And he seide to hem, Go ye in to al the world, and preche the gospel to eche creature.

16 Who that bileueth, and is baptisid, schal be saaf; but he that bileueth not, schal be dampned.

17 And these tokenes schulen sue hem, that bileuen. In my name thei schulen caste out feendis; thei schulen speke with newe tungis;

18 thei schulen do awei serpentis; and if thei drynke ony venym, it schal not noye hem. Thei schulen sette her hondis on sijk men, and thei schulen wexe hoole.

19 And the Lord Jhesu, aftir he hadde spokun to hem, was takun vp in to heuene, and he sittith on the riythalf of God.

20 And thei yeden forth, and prechiden euery where, for the Lord wrouyte with hem, and confermyde the word with signes folewynge.

LUKE

CAP 1

1 Forsothe for manye men enforceden to ordeyne the tellyng of thingis, whiche ben fillid in vs,

2 as thei that seyn atte the bigynnyng, and weren ministris of the word,

3 bitaken, it is seen also to me, hauynge alle thingis diligentli bi ordre, to write to thee,

4 thou best Theofile, that thou knowe the treuthe of tho wordis, of whiche thou art lerned.

5 In the daies of Eroude, kyng of Judee, ther was a prest, Sakarie bi name, of the sorte of Abia, and his wijf was of the douytris of Aaron, and hir name was Elizabeth.

6 And bothe weren iust bifor God, goynge in alle the maundementis and iustifiyngis of the Lord, withouten pleynt.

7 And thei hadden no child, for Elizabeth was bareyn, and bothe weren of grete age in her daies.

8 And it bifel, that whanne Zacarie schulde do the office of preesthod, in the ordre of his cours tofor God,

9 aftir the custome of the preesthod, he wente forth bi lot, and entride in to the temple, to encense.

10 And al the multitude of the puple was with outforth, and preiede in the our of encensyng.

11 And an aungel of the Lord apperide to hym, and stood on the riythalf of the auter of encense.

12 And Zacarie seynge was afraied, and drede fel vpon hym.

13 And the aungel seide to hym, Zacarie, drede thou not; for thi preyer is herd, and Elizabeth, thi wijf, schal bere to thee a sone, and his name schal be clepid Joon.

14 And ioye and gladyng schal be to thee; and many schulen 'haue ioye in his natyuyte.

15 For he schal be greet bifor the Lord, and he schal not drynke wyn and sidir, and he schal be fulfillid with the Hooli Goost yit of his modir wombe.

16 And he schal conuerte many of the children of Israel to her Lord God;

17 and he schal go bifor hym in the spirit and the vertu of Helie; and he schal turne the hertis of the fadris in to the sones, and men out of bileue to the prudence of iust men, to make redi a perfit puple to the Lord.

18 And Zacarie seide to the aungel, Wherof schal Y wite this? for Y am eld, and my wijf hath gon fer in to hir daies.

19 And the aungel answeride, and seide to hym, For Y am Gabriel, that stonde niy bifor God; and Y am sent to thee to speke, and to euangelize to thee these thingis.

20 And lo! thou schalt be doumbe, and thou schalt not mow speke til in to the dai, in which these thingis schulen be don; for thou hast not bileued to my wordis, whiche schulen be fulfillid in her tyme.

21 And the puple was abidynge Zacarie, and thei wondriden, that he tariede in the temple.

22 And he yede out, and myyte not speke to hem, and thei knewen that he hadde seyn a visioun in the temple. And he bikenyde to hem, and he dwellide stille doumbe.

23 And it was don, whanne the daies of his office weren fulfillid, he wente in to his hous.

24 And aftir these daies Elizabeth, his wijf, conseyuede, and hidde hir fyue monethis, and seide,

25 For so the Lord dide to me in the daies, in whiche he bihelde, to take awei my repreef among men.

26 But in the sixte moneth the aungel Gabriel was sent fro God in to a citee of Galilee, whos name was Nazareth,

27 to a maidyn, weddid to a man, whos name was Joseph, of the hous of Dauid; and the name of the maidun was Marie.

28 And the aungel entride to hir, and seide, Heil, ful of grace; the Lord be with thee; blessid be thou among wymmen.

29 And whanne sche hadde herd, sche was troublid in his word, and thouyte what maner salutacioun this was.

30 And the aungel seide to hir, Ne drede thou not, Marie, for thou hast foundun grace anentis God.

31 Lo! thou schalt conceyue in wombe, and schalt bere a sone, and thou schalt clepe his name Jhesus.

32 This schal be greet, and he schal be clepid the sone of the Hiyeste; and the Lord God schal yeue to hym the seete of Dauid, his fadir, and he schal regne in the hous of Jacob with outen ende,

33 and of his rewme schal be noon ende.

34 And Marie seide to the aungel, On what maner schal this thing be doon, for Y knowe not man?

35 And the aungel answeride, and seide to hir, The Hooly Goost schal come fro aboue in to thee, and the vertu of the Hiyeste schal ouerschadewe thee; and therfor that hooli thing that schal be borun of thee, schal be clepid the sone of God.

36 And lo! Elizabeth, thi cosyn, and sche also hath conceyued a sone in hir eelde, and this moneth is the sixte to hir that is clepid bareyn;

37 for euery word schal not be inpossible anentis God.

38 And Marie seide, Lo! the handmaydyn of the Lord; be it don to me aftir thi word. And the aungel departide fro hir.

39 And Marie roos vp in tho daies, and wente with haaste in to the mounteyns, in to a citee of Judee.

40 And sche entride in to the hous of Zacarie, and grette Elizabeth.

41 And it was don, as Elizabeth herde the salutacioun of Marie, the yong child in hir wombe gladide. And Elizabeth was fulfillid with the Hooli Goost,

42 and criede with a greet vois, and seide, Blessid be thou among wymmen, and blessid be the fruyt of thi wombe.

43 And whereof is this thing to me, that the modir of my Lord come to me?

44 For lo! as the voice of thi salutacioun was maad in myn eeris, the yong child gladide in ioye in my wombe.

45 And blessid be thou, that hast bileued, for thilke thingis that ben seid of the Lord to thee, schulen be parfitli don.

46 And Marie seide, Mi soule magnyfieth the Lord,

47 and my spirit hath gladid in God, myn helthe.

48 For he hath biholdun the mekenesse of his handmaidun.

49 For lo! of this alle generaciouns schulen seie that Y am blessid. For he that is myyti hath don to me grete thingis, and his name is hooli.

50 And his mercy is fro kynrede in to kynredes, to men that dreden hym.

51 He made myyt in his arme, he scaterede proude men with the thouyte of his herte.

52 He sette doun myyti men fro sete, and enhaunside meke men.

53 He hath fulfillid hungri men with goodis, and he hath left riche men voide.

54 He, hauynge mynde of his mercy, took Israel, his child;

55 as he hath spokun to oure fadris, to Abraham and to his seed, in to worldis.

56 And Marie dwellide with hir, as it were thre monethis, and turnede ayen in to hir hous.

57 But the tyme of beryng child was fulfillid to Elizabeth, and sche bare a sone.

58 And the neiyboris and cosyns of hir herden, that the Lord hadde magnyfied his mercy with hir; and thei thankiden hym.

59 And it was don in the eiyte dai, thei camen to circumcide the child; and thei clepiden hym Zacarie, bi the name of his fadir.

60 And his moder answeride, and seide, Nay, but he schal be clepid Joon.

61 And thei seiden to hir, For no man is in thi kynrede, that is clepid this name.

62 And thei bikeneden to his fadir, what he wolde that he were clepid.

63 And he axynge a poyntil, wroot, seiynge, Joon is his name. 64 And alle men wondriden. And anoon his mouth was openyd, and his tunge, and he spak, and blesside God.

65 And drede was maad on alle her neiyboris, and alle these wordis weren pupplischid on alle the mounteyns of Judee.

66 And alle men that herden puttiden in her herte, and seiden, What maner child schal this be? For the hoond of the Lord was with hym.

67 And Zacarie, his fadir, was fulfillid with the Hooli Goost, and prophesiede,

68 and seide, Blessid be the Lord God of Israel, for he hath visitid, and maad redempcioun of his puple.

69 And he hath rerid to vs an horn of heelthe in the hous of Dauid, his child.

70 As he spak bi the mouth of hise hooli prophetis, that weren fro the world.

71 Helthe fro oure enemyes, and fro the hoond of alle men that hatiden vs.

72 To do merci with oure fadris, and to haue mynde of his hooli testament.

73 The greet ooth that he swoor to Abraham, oure fadir, to yyue hym silf to vs.

74 That we with out drede delyuered fro the hoond of oure enemyes,

75 serue to hym, in hoolynesse and riytwisnesse bifor hym in alle oure daies.

76 And thou, child, schalt be clepid the prophete of the Hiyest; for thou schalt go bifor the face of the Lord, to make redi hise weies.

77 To yyue scyence of helthe to his puple, in to remyssioun of her synnes;

78 bi the inwardnesse of the merci of oure God, in the whiche he spryngynge vp fro an hiy hath visitid vs.

79 To yyue liyt to hem that sitten in derknessis and in schadewe of deeth; to dresse oure feet in to the weie of pees.

80 And the child wexide, and was coumfortid in spirit, and was in desert placis 'til to the dai of his schewing to Israel.

CAP 2

1 And it was don in tho daies, a maundement wente out fro the emperour August, that al the world schulde be discryued.

2 This firste discryuyng was maad of Cyryn, iustice of Sirie.

3 And alle men wenten to make professioun, ech in to his owne citee.

4 And Joseph wente vp fro Galilee, fro the citee Nazareth, in to Judee, in to a citee of Dauid, that is clepid Bethleem, for that he was of the hous and of the meyne of Dauid,

5 that he schulde knouleche with Marie, his wijf, that was weddid to hym, and was greet with child.

6 And it was don, while thei weren there, the daies weren fulfillid, that sche schulde bere child.

7 And sche bare hir first borun sone, and wlappide hym in clothis, and leide hym in a cratche, for ther was no place to hym in no chaumbir.

8 And scheepherdis weren in the same cuntre, wakynge and kepynge the watchis of the nyyt on her flok.

9 And lo! the aungel of the Lord stood bisidis hem, and the cleernesse of God schinede aboute hem; and thei dredden with greet drede.

10 And the aungel seide to hem, Nyle ye drede; for lo! Y preche to you a greet ioye, that schal be to al puple.

11 For a sauyoure is borun to dai to you, that is Crist the Lord, in the citee of Dauid.

12 And this is a tokene to you; ye schulen fynde a yong child wlappid in clothis, and leid in a cratche.

13 And sudenli ther was maad with the aungel a multitude of heuenli knyythod, heriynge God,

14 and seiynge, Glorie be in the hiyeste thingis to God, and in erthe pees be to men of good wille.

15 And it was don, as the 'aungelis passiden awei fro hem in to heuene, the scheephirdis spaken togider, and seiden, Go we ouer to Bethleem, and se we this word that is maad, which the Lord hath 'maad, and schewide to vs.

16 And thei hiyynge camen, and founden Marie and Joseph, and the yong child leid in a cratche.

17 And thei seynge, knewen of the word that was seid to hem of this child.

18 And alle men that herden wondriden, and of these thingis that weren seid to hem of the scheephirdis.

19 But Marie kepte alle these wordis, berynge togider in hir herte.

20 And the scheepherdis turneden ayen, glorifyinge and heriynge God in alle thingis that thei hadden herd and seyn, as it was seid to hem.

21 And aftir that the eiyte daies weren endid, that the child schulde be circumcided, his name was clepid Jhesus, which was clepid of the aungel, bifor that he was conceyued in the wombe.

22 And aftir that the daies of the purgacioun of Marie weren fulfillid, aftir Moyses lawe, thei token hym into Jerusalem, to offre hym to the Lord, as it is writun in the lawe of the Lord,

23 For euery male kynde openynge the wombe, schal be clepid holi to the Lord; and that thei schulen yyue an offryng,

24 aftir that it is seid in the lawe of the Lord, A peire of turturis, or twei culuer briddis.

25 And lo! a man was in Jerusalem, whos name was Symeon; and this man was iust and vertuous, and aboode the coumfort of Israel; and the Hooli Goost was in hym.

26 And he hadde takun an answere of the Hooli Goost, that he schulde not se deeth, but he sawy first the Crist of the Lord.

27 And he cam in spirit into the temple. And whanne his fadir and modir ledden the child Jhesu to do aftir the custom of the lawe for hym,

28 he took hym in to hise armes, and he blesside God,

29 and seide, Lord, now thou leuyst thi seruaunt aftir thi word in pees;

30 for myn iyen han seyn thin helthe,

31 which thou hast maad redi bifor the face of alle puplis;

32 liyt to the schewyng of hethene men, and glorie of thi puple Israel.

33 And his fadir and his modir weren wondrynge on these thingis, that weren seid of hym.

34 And Symeon blesside hem, and seide to Marie, his modir, Lo! this is set in to the fallyng doun and in to the risyng ayen of many men in Israel, and in to a tokene, to whom it schal be ayenseid.

35 And a swerd schal passe thorou thin owne soule, that the thouytis ben schewid of many hertis.

36 And Anna was a prophetesse, the douytir of Fanuel, of the lynage of Aser. And sche hadde goon forth in many daies, and hadde lyued with hir hosebonde seuene yeer fro hir maydynhode.

37 And this was a widewe to foure scoor yeer and foure; and sche departide not fro the temple, but seruyde to God nyyt and dai in fastyngis and preieris.

38 And this cam vpon hem in thilk our, and knoulechide to the Lord, and spak of hym to alle that abiden the redempcioun of Israel.

39 And as thei hadden ful don alle thingis, aftir the lawe of the Lord, thei turneden ayen in to Galilee, in to her citee Nazareth.

40 And the child wexe, and was coumfortid, ful of wisdom; and the grace of God was in hym.

41 And his fadir and modir wenten ech yeer in to Jerusalem, in the solempne dai of pask.

42 And whanne Jhesus was twelue yeer oold, thei wenten vp to Jerusalem, aftir the custom of the feeste dai.

43 And whanne the daies weren don, thei turneden ayen; and the child abood in Jerusalem, and his fadir and modir knewen it not.

44 For thei gessynge that he hadde be in the felowschip, camen a daies iourney, and souyten hym among hise cosyns and hise knouleche.

45 And whanne thei founden hym not, thei turneden ayen in to Jerusalem, and souyten hym.

46 And it bifelle, that aftir the thridde dai thei founden hym in the temple, sittynge in the myddil of the doctours, herynge hem and axynge hem.

47 And alle men that herden hym, wondriden on the prudence and the answeris of hym.

48 And thei seyn, and wondriden. And his modir seide to hym, Sone, what hast thou do to vs thus? Lo! thi fadir and Y sorewynge han souyte thee.

49 And he seide to hem, What is it that ye souyten me? wisten ye not that in tho thingis that ben of my fadir, it behoueth me to be?

50 And thei vndurstoden not the word, which he spak to hem.

51 And he cam doun with hem, and cam to Nazareth, and was suget to hem. And his moder kepte togidir alle these wordis, and bare hem in hir herte.

52 And Jhesus profitide in wisdom, age, and grace, anentis God and men.

CAP 3

1 In the fiftenthe yeer of the empire of Tiberie, the emperoure, whanne Pilat of Pounce gouernede Judee, and Eroude was prince of Galilee, and Filip, his brothir, was prince of Iturye, and of the cuntre of Tracon, and Lisanye was prince of Abilyn,

2 vndir the princis of prestis Annas and Caifas, the word of the Lord was maad on Joon, the sone of Zacarie, in desert.

3 And he cam in to al the cuntre of Jordan, and prechide baptym of penaunce in to remyssioun of synnes.

4 As it is wrytun in the book of the wordis of Isaye, the prophete, The voice of a crier in desert, Make ye redi the weie of the Lord, make ye hise pathis riyt.

5 Ech valey schal be fulfillid, and euery hil and litil hil schal be maad lowe; and schrewid thingis schulen ben in to dressid thingis, and scharp thingis in to pleyn weies;

6 and euery fleisch schal se the heelthe of God.

7 Therfor he seid to the puple, which wente out to be baptisid of hym, Kyndlyngis of eddris, who schewide to you to fle fro the wraththe to comynge?

8 Therfor do ye worthi fruytis of penaunce, and bigynne ye not to seie, We han a fadir Abraham; for Y seie to you, that God is myyti to reise of these stoonys the sones of Abraham.

9 And now an axe is sett to the roote of the tree; and therfor euery tre that makith no good fruyt, schal be kit doun, and schal be cast in to the fier.

10 And the puple axide hym, and seiden, What thanne schulen we do?

11 He answeride, and seide to hem, He that hath twei cootis, yyue to hym that hath noon; and he that hath metis, do in lijk maner.

12 And pupplicans camen to be baptisid; and thei seiden to hym, Maister, what schulen we do?

13 And he seide to hem, Do ye no thing more, than that that is ordeyned to you.

14 And knyytis axiden hym, and seiden, What schulen also we do? And he seide to hem, Smyte ye wrongfuli no man, nethir make ye fals chalenge, and be ye apayed with youre sowdis.

15 Whanne al the puple gesside, and alle men thouyten in her hertis of Joon, lest perauenture he were Crist,

16 Joon answeride, and seide to alle men, Y baptize you in watir; but a stronger than Y schal come aftir me, of whom Y am not worthi to vnbynde the lace of his schoon; he schal baptize you in the Hooli Goost and fier.

17 Whos 'wynewyng tool in his hond, and he schal purge his floor of corn, and schal gadere the whete in to his berne; but the chaffis he schal brenne with fier vnquenchable.

18 And many othere thingis also he spak, and prechide to the puple. But Eroude tetrark, whanne he was blamed of Joon for Erodias,

19 the wijf of his brother, and for alle the yuelis that Eroude dide,

20 encreside this ouer alle, and schitte Joon in prisoun.

21 And it was don, whanne al the puple was baptised, and whanne Jhesu was baptised, and preiede, heuene was openyd.

22 And the Hooli Goost cam doun in bodili licnesse, as a dowue on hym; and a vois was maad fro heuene, Thou art my derworth sone, in thee it hath plesid to me.

23 And Jhesu hym silf was bigynninge as of thritti yeer, that he was gessid the sone of Joseph, which was of Heli,

24 which was of Mathath, which was of Leuy, which was of Melchi, that was of Jamne,

25 that was of Joseph, that was of Matatie, that was of Amos, that was of Naum, that was of Hely, that was of Nagge,

26 that was of Mathath, that was of Matatie, that was of Semei, that was of Joseph, that was of Juda, that was of Johanna,

27 that was of Resa, that was of Zorobabel, that was of Salatiel,

28 that was of Neri, that was of Melchi, that was of Addi, that was of Cosan, that was of Elmadan, that was of Her,

29 that was of Jhesu, that was of Eleasar, that was of Jorum, that was of Matath,

30 that was of Leuy, that was of Symeon, that was of Juda, that was of Joseph, that was of Jona, that was of Eliachym,

31 that was of Melca, that was of Menna, that of Mathatha, that was of Nathan,

32 that was of Dauid, that was of Jesse, that was of Obeth, that was of Boz, that was of Salmon, that was of Nason,

33 that was of Amynadab, that was of Aram, that was of Esrom, that was of Fares,

34 that was of Judas, that was of Jacob, that was of Isaac, that was of Abraham, that was of Tare, that was of Nachor,

35 that was of Seruth, that was of Ragau, that was of Faleth, that was of Heber,

36 that was of Sale, that was of Chaynan, that was of Arfaxath, that was of Sem, that was of Noe, that was of Lameth,

37 that was of Matussale, that was of Enok, that was of Jareth, that was of Malaliel, that was of Cainan, that was of Enos,

38 that was of Seth, that was of Adam, that was of God.

CAP 4

1 And Jhesus ful of the Hooli Goost turnede ayen fro Jordan, and was led bi the spirit into desert fourti daies,

2 and was temptid of the deuel, and eet nothing in tho daies; and whanne tho daies weren endid, he hungride.

3 And the deuel seide to him, If thou art Goddis sone, seie to this stoon, that it be maad breed.

4 And Jhesus answeride to hym, It is writun, That a man lyueth not in breed aloone, but in euery word of God.

5 And the deuel ladde hym in to an hiy hil, and schewide to hym alle the rewmes of the world in a moment of tyme;

6 and seide to hym, Y schal yyue to thee al this power, and the glorie of hem, for to me thei ben youun, and to whom Y wole, Y yyue hem;

7 therfor if thou falle doun, and worschipe bifore me, alle thingis schulen be thine.

8 And Jhesus answeride, and seide to hym, It is writun, Thou schalt worschipe thi Lord God, and to hym aloone thou schalt serue.

9 And he ledde hym in to Jerusalem, and sette hym on the pynacle of the temple, and seide to hym, If thou art Goddis sone, sende thi silf fro hennes doun;

10 for it is writun, For he hath comaundide to hise aungels of thee, that thei kepe thee in alle thi weies,

11 and that thei schulen take thee in hondis, lest perauenture thou hirte thi foote at a stoon.

12 And Jhesus answeride, and seide to him, It is seid, Thou schalt not tempte thi Lord God.

13 And whanne euery temptacioun was endid, the feend wente a wei fro hym for a tyme.

14 And Jhesus turnede ayen in the vertu of the spirit in to Galilee, and the fame wente forth of hym thorou al the cuntre.

15 And he tauyte in the synagogis of hem, and was magnyfied of alle men.

16 And he cam to Nazareth, where he was norisschid, and entride aftir his custom in the sabat dai in to a synagoge, and roos to reed.

17 And the book of Ysaye, the prophete, was takun to hym; and as he turnede the book, he foond a place, where it was wrytun,

18 The Spirit of the Lord on me, for which thing he anoyntide me; he sente me to preche to pore men, to hele contrite men in herte,

19 and to preche remyssioun to prisoneris, and siyt to blynde men, and to delyuere brokun men in to remissioun; to preche the yeer of the Lord plesaunt, and the dai of yeldyng ayen.

20 And whanne he hadde closid the book, he yaf ayen to the mynystre, and sat; and the iyen of alle men in the synagoge were biholdynge in to hym.

21 And he bigan to seie to hem, For in this dai this scripture is fulfillid in youre eeris.

22 And alle men yauen witnessyng to hym, and wondriden in the wordis of grace, that camen forth of his mouth. And thei seiden, Whether this is not the sone of Joseph?

23 And he seide to hem, Sotheli ye schulen seie to me this liknesse, Leeche, heele thi silf. The Farisees seiden to Jhesu, Hou grete thingis han we herd don in Cafarnaum, do thou also here in thi cuntre.

24 And he seide, Treuli Y seie to you, that no profete is resseyued in his owne cuntre.

25 In treuthe Y seie to you, that many widowis weren in the daies of Elie, the prophete, in Israel, whanne heuene was closid thre yeer and sixe monethis, whanne greet hungur was maad in al the erthe;

26 and to noon of hem was Elye sent, but in to Sarepta of Sydon, to a widowe.

27 And many meseles weren in Israel, vndur Helisee, the prophete, and noon of hem was clensid, but Naaman of Sirye.

28 And alle in the synagoge herynge these thingis, weren fillid with wraththe.

29 And thei risen vp, and drouen hym out with out the citee, and ledden hym to the cop of the hil on which her citee was bildid, to caste hym doun.

30 But Jhesus passide, and wente thorou the myddil of hem; and cam doun in to Cafarnaum,

31 a citee of Galilee, and there he tauyte hem in sabotis.

32 And thei weren astonyed in his techyng, for his word was in power.

33 And in her synagoge was a man hauynge an vnclene feend, and he criede with greet vois,

34 and seide, Suffre, what to vs and to thee, Jhesu of Nazareth? art thou comun to leese vs? Y knowe, that thou art the hooli of God.

35 And Jhesus blamede hym, and seide, Wexe doumbe, and go out fro hym. And whanne the feend hadde cast hym forth in to the myddil, he wente a wei fro hym, and he noyede hym no thing.

36 And drede was maad in alle men, and thei spaken togider, and seiden, What is this word, for in power and vertu he comaundith to vnclene spiritis, and thei gon out?

37 And the fame was pupplischid of him in to ech place of the cuntre.

38 And Jhesus roos vp fro the synagoge, and entride in to the hous of Symount; and the modir of Symountis wijf was holdun with grete fyueris, and thei preieden hym for hir.

39 And Jhesus stood ouer hir, and comaundide to the feuer, and it lefte hir; and anoon sche roos vp, and seruede hem.

40 And whanne the sunne wente doun, alle that hadden sijke men with dyuerse langours, ledden hem to hym; and he sette his hoondis on ech bi 'hem silf, and heelide hem.

41 And feendis wenten out fro manye, and crieden, and seiden, For thou art the sone of God. And he blamede, and suffride hem not to speke, for thei wisten hym, that he was Crist.

42 And whanne the dai was come, he yede out, and wente in to a desert place; and the puple souyten hym, and thei camen to hym, and thei helden hym, that he schulde not go a wei fro hem.

43 To whiche he seide, For also to othere citees it bihoueth me to preche the kyngdom of God, for therfor Y am sent.

44 And he prechide in the synagogis of Galilee.

CAP 5

1 And it was don, whanne the puple cam fast to Jhesu, to here the word of God, he stood bisidis the pool of Genasereth,

2 and saiy two bootis stondynge bisidis the pool; and the fischeris weren go doun, and waischiden her nettis.

3 And he wente vp in to a boot, that was Symoundis, and preiede hym to lede it a litil fro the loond; and he seet, and tauyte the puple out of the boot.

4 And as he ceesside to speke, he seide to Symount, Lede thou in to the depthe, and slake youre nettis to take fisch.

5 And Symount answeride, and seide to hym, Comaundoure, we traueliden al the nyyt, and token no thing, but in thi word Y schal leye out the net.

6 And whanne thei hadden do this thing, thei closiden togidir a greet multitude of fischis; and her net was brokun.

7 And thei bikenyden to felawis, that weren in anothir boot, that thei schulden come, and helpe hem. And thei camen, and filliden bothe the bootis, so that thei weren almost drenchid.

8 And whanne Symount Petir saiy this thing, he felde doun to the knees of Jhesu, and seide, Lord, go fro me, for Y am a synful man.

9 For he was on ech side astonyed, and alle that weren with hym, in the takyng of fischis whiche thei token.

10 Sotheli in lijk maner James and Joon, the sones of Zebedee, that weren felowis of Symount Petre. And Jhesus seide to Symount, Nyle thou drede; now fro this tyme thou schalt take men.

11 And whanne the bootis weren led vp to the loond, thei leften alle thingis, and thei sueden hym.

12 And it was don, whanne he was in oon of the citees, lo! a man ful of lepre; and seynge Jhesu felle doun on his face, and preyede hym, and seide, Lord, if thou wolt, thou maist make me clene.

13 And Jhesus held forth his hoond, and touchide hym, and seide, Y wole, be thou maad cleene. And anoon the lepre passide awei fro hym.

14 And Jhesus comaundide to hym, that he schulde seie to no man; But go, schewe thou thee to a preest, and offre for thi clensyng, as Moises bad, in to witnessyng to hem.

15 And the word walkide aboute the more of hym; and myche puple camen togidere, to here, and to be heelid of her siknessis.

16 And he wente in to desert, and preiede.

17 And it was don in oon of the daies, he sat, and tauyte; and there weren Farisees sittynge, and doctouris of the lawe, that camen of eche castel of Galilee, and of Judee, and of Jerusalem; and the vertu of the Lord was to heele sike men.

18 And lo! men beren in a bed a man that was sijk in the palsye, and thei souyten to bere hym in, and sette bifor hym.

19 And thei founden not in what partie thei schulden bere hym in, for the puple, 'and thei wenten on the roof, and bi the sclattis thei leeten hym doun with the bed, in to the myddil, bifor Jhesus.

20 And whanne Jhesu saiy the feith of hem, he seide, Man, thi synnes ben foryouun to thee.

21 And the scribis and Farisees bigunnen to thenke, seiynge, Who is this, that spekith blasfemyes? who may foryyue synnes, but God aloone?

22 And as Jhesus knewe the thouytis of hem, he answeride, and seide to hem, What thenken ye yuele thingis in youre hertes?

23 What is liyter to seie, Synnes ben foryouun to thee, or to seie, Rise vp, and walke?

24 But that ye wite, that mannus sone hath power in erthe to foryyue synnes, he seide to the sijk man in palesie, Y seie to thee, ryse vp, take thi bed, and go in to thin hous.

25 And anoon he roos vp bifor hem, and took the bed in which he lay, and wente in to his hous, and magnyfiede God.

26 And greet wondur took alle, and thei magnyfieden God; and thei weren fulfillid with greet drede, and seiden, For we han seyn merueilouse thingis to dai.

27 And after these thingis Jhesus wente out, and saiy a pupplican, Leuy bi name, sittynge at the tolbothe. And he seide to hym, Sue thou me;

28 And whanne he hadde left alle thingis, he roos vp, and suede hym.

29 And Leuy made to hym a greet feeste in his hous; and ther was a greet cumpanye of pupplicans, and of othere that weren with hem, sittynge at the mete.

30 And Farisees and the scribis of hem grutchiden, and seiden to hise disciplis, Whi eten ye and drynken with pupplicans and synful men?

31 And Jhesus answeride, and seide to hem, Thei that ben hoole han no nede to a leche, but thei that ben sijke;

32 for Y cam not to clepe iuste men, but synful men to penaunce.

33 And thei seiden to hym, Whi the disciplis of Joon fasten ofte, and maken preieris, also and of Farisees, but thine eten and drynken?

34 To whiche he seide, Whether ye moun make the sones of the spouse to faste, while the spouse is with hem?

35 But daies schulen come, whanne the spouse schal be takun a wei fro hem, and thanne thei schulen faste in tho daies.

36 And he seide to hem also a liknesse; For no man takith a pece fro a newe cloth, and puttith it in to an oold clothing; ellis bothe he brekith the newe, and the pece of the newe acordith not to the elde.

37 And no man puttith newe wyne in to oolde botels; ellis the newe wyn schal breke the botels, and the wyn schal be sched out, and the botels schulen perische.

38 But newe wyne owith to be put in to newe botels, and bothe ben kept.

39 And no man drynkynge the elde, wole anoon the newe; for he seith, The olde is the betere.

CAP 6

1 And it was don in the secounde firste sabat, whanne he passid bi cornes, hise disciplis pluckiden eeris of corn; and thei frotynge with her hondis, eeten.

2 And summe of the Farisees seiden to hem, What doon ye that, that is not leeueful in the sabotis?

3 And Jhesus answeride, and seide to hem, Han ye not redde, what Dauith dide, whanne he hungride, and thei that weren with hym;

4 hou he entride in to the hous of God, and took looues of proposicioun, and eet, and yaf to hem that weren with hem; whiche looues it was not leeueful to eete, but oonli to prestis.

5 And he seide to hem, For mannus sone is lord, yhe, of the sabat.

6 And it was don in another sabat, that he entride in to a synagoge, and tauyte. And a man was there, and his riyt hoond was drie.

7 And the scribis and Farisees aspieden hym, if he wolde heele hym in the sabat, that thei schulden fynde cause, whereof thei schulden accuse hym.

8 And he wiste the thouytis of hem, and he seide to the man that hadde a drie hoond, Rise vp, and stonde in to the myddil. And he roos, and stood.

9 And Jhesus seide to hem, Y axe you, if it is leueful to do wel in the sabat, or yuel? to make a soule saaf, or to leese?

10 And whanne he hadde biholde alle men aboute, he seide to the man, Hold forth thin hoond. And he held forth, and his hond was restorid to helthe.

11 And thei weren fulfillid with vnwisdom, and spaken togidir, what thei schulden do of Jhesu.

12 And it was don in tho daies, he wente out in to an hil to preye; and he was al nyyt dwellynge in the preier of God.

13 And whanne the day was come, he clepide hise disciplis, and chees twelue of hem, whiche he clepide also apostlis;

14 Symount, whom he clepide Petir, and Andrew, his brothir, James and Joon,

15 Filip and Bartholomew, Matheu and Thomas, James Alphei, and Symount, that is clepid Zelotes,

16 Judas of James, and Judas Scarioth, that was traytoure.

17 And Jhesus cam doun fro the hil with hem, and stood in a feeldi place; and the cumpeny of hise disciplis, and a greet multitude of puple, of al Judee, and Jerusalem, and of the see coostis, and of Tyre and Sidon,

18 that camen to here hym, and to be heelid of her siknessis; and thei that weren trauelid of vncleene spiritis, weren heelid.

19 And al puple souyte to touche hym, for vertu wente out of hym, and heelide alle.

20 And whanne hise iyen weren cast vp in to hise disciplis, he seide, Blessid be ye, 'pore men, for the kyngdom of God is youre.

21 Blessid be ye, that now hungren, for ye schulen be fulfillid. Blessid be ye, that now wepen, for ye schulen leiye.

22 Ye schulen be blessid, whanne men schulen hate you, and departe you awei, and putte schenschip to you, and cast out youre name as yuel, for mannus sone.

23 Joye ye in that dai, and be ye glad; for lo! youre meede is myche in heuene; for aftir these thingis the fadris of hem diden to prophetis.

24 Netheles wo to you, riche men, that han youre coumfort.

25 Wo to you that ben fulfillid, for ye schulen hungre. Wo to you that now leiyen, for ye schulen morne, and wepe.

26 Wo to you, whanne alle men schulen blesse you; aftir these thingis the fadris of hem diden to profetis.

27 But Y seie to you that heren, loue ye youre enemyes, do ye wel to hem that hatiden you;

28 blesse ye men that cursen you, preye ye for men that defamen you.

29 And to him that smytith thee on o cheeke, schewe also the tothir; and fro hym that takith awei fro thee a cloth, nyle thou forbede the coote.

30 And yyue to eche that axith thee, and if a man takith awei tho thingis that ben thine, axe thou not ayen.

31 And as ye wolen that men do to you, do ye also to hem in lijk maner.

32 And if ye louen hem that louen you, what thanke is to you? for synful men louen men that louen hem.

33 And if ye don wel to hem that don wel to you, what grace is to you? synful men don this thing.

34 And if ye leenen to hem of whiche ye hopen to take ayen, what thanke is to you? for synful men leenen to synful men, to take ayen as myche.

35 Netheles loue ye youre enemyes, and do ye wel, and leene ye, hopinge no thing therof, and youre mede schal be myche, and ye schulen be the sones of the Heyest, for he is benygne on vnkynde men and yuele men.

36 Therfor be ye merciful, as youre fadir is merciful.

37 Nyle ye deme, and ye schulen not be demed. Nyle ye condempne, and ye schulen not be condempned; foryyue ye, and it schal be foryouun to you.

38 Yyue ye, and it schal be youun to you. Thei schulen yyue in to youre bosum a good mesure, and wel fillid, and schakun togidir, and ouerflowynge; for bi the same mesure, bi whiche ye meeten, it schal be metun 'ayen to you.

39 And he seide to hem a liknesse, Whether the blynde may leede the blynde? ne fallen thei not bothe 'in to the diche?

40 A disciple is not aboue the maistir; but eche schal be perfite, if he be as his maister.

41 And what seest thou in thi brotheris iye a moot, but thou biholdist not a beem, that is in thin owne iye?

42 Or hou maist thou seie to thi brother, Brothir, suffre, Y schal caste out the moot of thin iye, and thou biholdist not a beem in thin owne iye? Ipocrite, first take out the beem of thin iye, and thanne thou schalt se to take the moot of thi brotheris iye.

43 It is not a good tree, that makith yuel fruytis, nether an yuel tree, that makith good fruytis;

44 for euery tre is knowun of his fruyt. And men gaderen not figus of thornes, nethir men gaderen a grape of a buysche of breris.

45 A good man of the good tresoure of his herte bryngith forth good thingis, and an yuel man of the yuel tresoure bryngith forth yuel thingis; for of the plente of the herte the mouth spekith.

46 And what clepen ye me, Lord, Lord, and doon not tho thingis that Y seie.

47 Eche that cometh to me, and herith my wordis, and doith hem, Y schal schewe to you, to whom he is lijk.

48 He is lijk to a man that bildith an hous, that diggide deepe, and sette the foundement on a stoon. And whanne greet flood was maad, the flood was hurtlid to that hous, and it miyte not moue it, for it was foundid on a sad stoon.

49 But he that herith, and doith not, is lijk to a man bildynge his hous on erthe with outen foundement; in to which the flood was hurlid, and anoon it felle doun; and the fallyng doun of that hous was maad greet.

CAP 7

1 And whanne he hadde fulfillid alle hise wordis in to the eeris of the puple, he entride in to Cafarnaum.

2 But a seruaunt of a centurien, that was precious to hym, was sijk, and drawynge to the deeth.

3 And whanne he hadde herd of Jhesu, he sente to hym the eldere men of Jewis, and preiede hym, that he wolde come, and heele his seruaunt.

4 And whanne thei camen to Jhesu, thei preieden hym bisili, and seiden to hym, For he is worthi, that thou graunte to hym this thing;

5 for he loueth oure folk, and he bildide to vs a synagoge.

6 And Jhesus wente with hem. And whanne he was not fer fro the hous, the centurien sente to hym freendis, and seide, Lord, nyle thou be trauelid, for Y am not worthi, that thou entre vnder my roof;

7 for which thing and Y demede not my silf worthi, that Y come to thee; but seie thou bi word, and my child schal be helid.

8 For Y am a man ordeyned vndur power, and haue knyytis vndur me; and Y seie to this, Go, and he goith, and to anothir, Come, and he cometh, and to my seruaunt, Do this thing, and he doith.

9 And whanne this thing was herd, Jhesus wondride; and seide to the puple suynge hym, Treuli Y seie to you, nether in Israel Y foond so greet feith.

10 And thei that weren sent, turneden ayen home, and founden the seruaunt hool, which was sijk.

11 And it was don aftirward, Jhesus wente in to a citee, that is clepid Naym, and hise disciplis; and ful greet puple wente with hym.

12 And whanne he cam nyy to the yate of the citee, lo! the sone of a womman that hadde no mo children, was borun out deed; and this was a widowe; and myche puple of the citee with hir.

13 And whanne the Lord Jhesu hadde seyn hir, he hadde reuthe on hir, and seide to hir, Nyle thou wepe.

14 And he cam nyy, and touchide the beere; and thei that baren stoden. And he seide, Yonge man, Y seie to thee, rise vp.

15 And he that was deed sat vp ayen, and bigan to speke; and he yaf hym to his modir.

16 And drede took alle men, and thei magnyfieden God, and seiden, For a grete profete is rysun among vs, and, For God hath visitid his puple.

17 And this word wente out of hym in to al Judee, and in to al the cuntre aboute.

18 And Joones disciplis toolden hym of alle these thingis.

19 And Joon clepide tweyn of hise disciplis, and sente hem to Jhesu, and seide, Art thou he that is to come, or abiden we anothir?

20 And whanne the men cam to hym, thei seiden, Joon Baptist sente vs to thee, and seide, Art thou he that is to come, or we abiden anothir?

21 And in that our he heelide many men of her sijknessis, and woundis, and yuel spiritis; and he yaf siyt to many blynde men.

22 And Jhesus answerde, and seide to hem, Go ye ayen, and telle ye to Joon tho thingis that ye han herd and seyn; blynde men seyn, crokid men goen, mesels ben maad cleene, deef men heren, deed men risen ayen, pore men ben takun to pre-chyng of the gospel.

23 And he that schal not be sclaundrid in me, is blessid.

24 And whanne the messangeris of Joon weren go forth, he bigan to seie of Joon to the puple,

25 What wenten ye out in to desert to se? a reed waggid with the wynd?

26 But what wenten ye out to se? a man clothid with softe clothis? Lo! thei that ben in precious cloth and in delicis, ben in kyngis housis. But what wenten ye out to se? a profete? Yhe, Y seie to you, and more than a profete.

27 This is he, of whom it is writun, Lo! Y sende myn aungel bifor thi face, which schal make 'thi weie redi bifor thee.

28 Certis Y seie to you, there is no man more prophete among children of wymmen, than is Joon; but he that is lesse in the kyngdom of heuenes, is more than he.

29 And al the puple herynge, and pupplicans, that hadden be baptisid with baptym of Joon, iustifieden God;

30 but the Farisees and the wise men of the lawe, that weren not baptisid of hym, dispisiden the counsel of God ayens hem silf.

31 And the Lord seide, Therfor to whom schal Y seie 'men of this generacioun lijk, and to whom ben thei lijk?

32 Thei ben lijk to children sittynge in chepyng, and spe-kynge togider, and seiynge, We han sungun to you with pipis, and ye han not daunsid; we han maad mornyng, and ye han not wept.

33 For Joon Baptist cam, nethir etynge breed, ne drynkynge wyne, and ye seyen, He hath a feend.

34 Mannus sone cam etynge and drynkynge, and ye seien, Lo! a man a deuourer, and drynkynge wyne, a frend of pup-plicans and of synful men.

35 And wisdom is iustified of her sones.

36 But oon of the Farisees preiede Jhesu, that he schulde ete with hym. And he entride in to the hous of the Farise, and sat at the mete.

37 And lo! a synful womman, that was in the citee, as sche knewe, that Jhesu sat at the mete in the hous of the Farisee, sche brouyte an alabaustre box of oynement;

38 and sche stood bihynde bysidis hise feet, and bigan to moiste hise feet with teeris, and wipide with the heeris of hir heed, and kiste hise feet, and anoyntide with oynement.

39 And the Farise seynge, that hadde clepide hym, seide within hym silf, seiynge, If this were a prophete, he schulde wite, who and what maner womman it were that touchith hym, for sche is a synful womman.

40 And Jhesus answeride, and seide to hym, Symount, Y haue sumthing to seie to thee. And he seide, Maistir, seie thou.

41 And he answeride, Twei dettouris weren to o lener; and oon auyt fyue hundrid pans, and 'the other fifti; but whanne thei hadden not wherof 'thei schulden yeelde, he foryaf to bothe. Who thanne loueth hym more?

43 Symount answeride, and seide, Y gesse, that he to whom he foryaf more. And he answeride to hym, Thou hast demyd riytli.

44 And he turnede to the womman, and seide to Symount, Seest thou this womman? I entride into thin hous, thou yaf no watir to my feet; but this hath moistid my feet with teeris, and wipide with hir heeris.

45 Thou hast not youun to me a cosse; but this, sithen sche entride, ceesside not to kisse my feet.

46 Thou anoyntidist not myn heed with oile; but this anoyn-tide my feet with oynement.

47 For the which thing Y seie to thee, many synnes ben fory-ouun to hir, for sche hath loued myche; and to whom is lesse foryouun, he loueth lesse.

48 And Jhesus seide to hir, Thi synnes ben foryouun to thee.

49 And thei that saten to gider at the mete, bigunnen to seie with ynne hem silf, Who is this that foryyueth synnes.

50 But he seide to the womman, Thi feith hath maad thee saaf; go thou in pees.

CAP 8

1 And it was don aftirward, and Jhesus made iourney bi citees and castels, prechynge and euangelisynge the rewme of God, and twelue with hym;

2 and sum wymmen that weren heelid of wickid spiritis and sijknessis, Marie, that is clepid Maudeleyn, of whom seuene deuelis wenten out,

3 and Joone, the wijf of Chuse, the procuratoure of Eroude, and Susanne, and many othir, that mynystriden to hym of her ritchesse.

4 And whanne myche puple was come togidir, and men hiyeden to hym fro the citees, he seide bi a symylitude,

5 He that sowith, yede out to sowe his seed. And while he sowith, sum fel bisidis the weie, and was defoulid, and brid-dis of the eir eten it.

6 And othir fel on a stoon, and it sprunge vp, and driede, for it hadde not moysture.

7 And othir fel among thornes, and the thornes sprongen vp togider, and strangliden it.

8 And othir fel in to good erthe, and it sprungun made an hun-drid foold fruyt. He seide these thingis, and criede, He that hath eeris of heryng, here he.

9 But hise disciplis axiden him, what this parable was.

10 And he seide to hem, To you it is grauntid to knowe the pryuete of the kyngdom of God; but to othir men in parablis, that thei seynge se not, and thei herynge vndurstonde not.

11 And this is the parable.

12 The seed is Goddis word; and thei that ben bisidis the weie, ben these that heren; and aftirward the feend cometh, and takith awei the word fro her herte, lest thei bileuynge be maad saaf.

13 But thei that fel on a stoon, ben these that whanne thei han herd, resseyuen the word with ioye. And these han not rootis;

for at a tyme thei bileuen, and in tyme of temptacioun thei goen awei.

14 But that that fel among thornes, ben these that herden, and of bisynessis, and ritchessis, and lustis of lijf thei gon forth, and ben stranglid, and bryngen forth no fruyt.

15 But that that fel in to good erthe, ben these that, in a good herte, and best heren the word, and holdun, and brengen forth fruyt in pacience.

16 No man lityneth a lanterne, and hilith it with a vessel, or puttith it vndur a bed, but on a candilstike, that men that entren seen liyt.

17 For ther is no priuei thing, which schal not be openyd, nether hid thing, which schal not be knowun, and come in to open.

18 Therfor se ye, hou ye heren; for it schal be youun to hym that hath, and who euer hath not, also that that he weneth that he haue, schal be takun awei fro hym.

19 And his modir and britheren camen to hym; and thei myyten not come to hym for the puple.

20 And it was teeld to hym, Thi modir and thi britheren stonden with outforth, willynge to se thee.

21 And he answeride, and seide to hem, My modir and my britheren ben these, that heren the word of God, and doon it.

22 And it was don in oon of daies, he wente vp in to a boot, and hise disciplis. And he seide to hem, Passe we ouer the see. And thei wenten vp.

23 And while thei rowiden, he slepte. And a tempest of wynde cam doun in to the watir, and thei weren dryuun hidur and thidur with wawis, and weren in perel.

24 And thei camen nyy, and reisiden hym, and seiden, Comaundoure, we perischen. And he roos, and blamyde the wynde, and the tempest of the watir; and it ceesside, and pesibilte was maad.

25 And he seide to hem, Where is youre feith? Which dredynge wondriden, and seiden togidir, Who, gessist thou, is this? for he comaundith to wyndis and to the see, and thei obeien to hym.

26 And thei rowiden to the cuntree of Gerasenus, that is ayens Galilee.

27 And whanne he wente out to the loond, a man ran to hym, that hadde a deuel long tyme, and he was not clothid with cloth, nether dwellide in hous, but in sepulcris.

28 This, whanne he saiy Jhesu, fel doun bifor hym, and he criynge with a greet vois seide, What to me and to thee, Jhesu, the sone of the hiyest God? Y biseche thee, that thou turmente 'not me.

29 For he comaundide the vncleene spirit, that he schulde go out fro the man. For he took hym ofte tymes, and he was boundun with cheynes, and kept in stockis, and, whanne the boondis weren brokun, he was lad of deuelis in to desert.

30 And Jhesus axide hym, and seide, What name is to thee? And he seide, A legioun; for many deuelis weren entrid in to hym.

31 And thei preyden hym, that he schulde not comaunde hem, that thei schulden go in to helle.

32 And there was a flok of many swyne lesewynge in an hil, and thei preieden hym, that he schulde suffre hem to entre in to hem. And he suffride hem.

33 And so the deuelis wenten out fro the man, and entriden in to the swyne; and with a birre the flok wente heedlyng in to the pool, and was drenchid.

34 And whanne the hirdis sayn this thing don, thei flowen, and tolden in to the cite, and in to the townes.

35 And thei yeden out to se that thing that was don. And thei camen to Jhesu, and thei founden the man sittynge clothid, fro whom the deuelis wenten out, and in hool mynde at hise feet; and thei dredden.

36 And thei that sayn tolden to hem, hou he was maad hool of the legioun.

37 And al the multitude of the cuntre of Gerasenus preiede hym, that he schulde go fro hem, for thei werun holdun with greet drede. He wente vp in to a boot, and turnede ayen.

38 And the man of whom the deuelis weren gon out, preide hym, that he schulde be with hym. Jhesus lefte hym,

39 and seide, Go ayen in to thin hous, and telle hou grete thingis God hath don to thee. And he wente thorow al the cite, and prechide, hou grete thingis Jhesus hadde don to hym.

40 And it was don, whanne Jhesus was gon ayen, the puple resseyuede hym; for alle weren abidynge hym.

41 And lo! a man, to whom the name was Jayrus, and he was prynce of a synagoge; and he fel doun at the feet of Jhesu, and preiede hym, that he schulde entre in to his hous,

42 for he hadde but o douyter 'almost of twelue yeer eelde, and sche was deed. And it bifel, the while he wente, he was thrungun of the puple.

43 And a womman that hadde a flux of blood twelue yeer, and hadde spendid al hir catel in leechis, and sche miyte not be curid of ony,

44 and sche cam nyy bihynde, and touchide the hem of his cloth, and anoon the fluxe of hir blood ceesside.

45 And Jhesus seide, Who is that touchide me? And whanne alle men denyeden, Petre seide, and thei that weren with hym, Comaundour, the puple thristen, and disesen thee, and thou seist, Who touchide me?

46 And Jhesus seide, Summan hath touchid me, for that vertu yede out of me.

47 And the womman seynge, that it was not hid fro hym, cam tremblynge, and fel doun at hise feet, and for what cause sche hadde touchid hym sche schewide bifor al the puple, and hou anoon sche was helid.

48 And he seide to hir, Douytir, thi feith hath maad thee saaf; go thou in pees.

49 And yit while he spak, a man cam fro the prince of the synagoge, and seide to hym, Thi douytir is deed, nyle thou trauel the maister.

50 And whanne this word was herd, Jhesus answeride to the fadir of the damysel, Nyle thou drede, but bileue thou oonli, and sche schal be saaf.

51 And whanne he cam to the hous, he suffride no man to entre with hym, but Petir and Joon and James, and the fadir and the modir of the damysel.

52 And alle wepten, and biweileden hir. And he seide, Nyle ye wepe, for the damysel is not deed, but slepith.

53 And thei scorneden hym, and wisten that sche was deed.

54 But he helde hir hoond, and criede, and seide, Damysel, rise vp.

55 And hir spirit turnede ayen, and sche roos anoon. And he comaundide to yyue to hir to ete.

56 And hir fadir and modir wondriden greetli; and he comaundide hem, that thei schulden not seie to ony that thing that was don.

CAP 9

1 And whanne the twelue apostlis weren clepid togidir, Jhesus yaf to hem vertu and power on alle deuelis, and that thei schulden heele sijknessis.

2 And he sente hem for to preche the kyngdom of God, and to heele sijk men.

3 And he seide to hem, No thing take ye in the weie, nether yerde, ne scrippe, nether breed, ne money, and nether haue ye two cootis.

4 And in to what hous that ye entren, dwelle ye there, and go ye not out fro thennus.

5 And who euer resseyuen not you, go ye out of that citee, and schake ye of the poudir of youre feet in to witnessyng on hem.

6 And thei yeden forth, and wenten aboute bi castels, prechynge and helynge euery where.

7 And Eroude tetrak herde alle thingis that weren don of hym, and he doutide,

8 for that it was seide of sum men, that Joon was risen fro deth; and of summen, that Elie hadde apperid; but of othere, that oon of the elde prophetis was risun.

9 And Eroude seide, Y haue biheedid Joon; and who is this, of whom Y here siche thingis? And he souyte to se hym.

10 And the apostlis turneden ayen, and tolden to hym alle thingis that thei hadden don. And he took hem, and wente bisidis in to a desert place, that is Bethsada.

11 And whanne the puple knewen this, thei folewiden hym. And he resseyuede hem, and spak to hem of the kyngdom of God; and he heelide hem that hadden neede of cure.

12 And the dai bigan to bowe doun, and the twelue camen, and seiden to hym, Leeue the puple, that thei go, and turne in to castels and townes, that ben aboute, that thei fynde mete, for we ben here in a desert place.

13 And he seide to hem, Yue ye to hem to ete. And thei seiden, Ther ben not to vs mo than fyue looues and twei fischis, but perauenture that we go, and bie meetis to al this puple.

14 And the men weren almost fyue thousynde. And he seide to hise disciplis, Make ye hem sitte to mete bi cumpanyes, a fifti to gidir.

15 And thei diden so, and thei maden alle men sitte to mete.

16 And whanne he hadde take the fyue looues and twei fischis, he biheeld in to heuene, and blesside hem, and brak, and delide to hise disciplis, that thei schulden sette forth bifor the cumpanyes.

17 And alle men eeten, and weren fulfillid; and that that lefte to hem of brokun metis was takun vp, twelue cofyns.

18 And it was don, whanne he was aloone preiynge, hise disciplis weren with hym, and he axide hem, and seide, Whom seien the puple that Y am?

19 And thei answeriden, and seiden, Joon Baptist, othir seien Elie, and othir seien, o profete of the formere is risun.

20 And he seide to hem, But who seien ye that Y am? Symount Petir answeride, and seide, The Crist of God.

21 And he blamynge hem comaundide that thei schulden seie to no man,

22 and seide these thingis, For it bihoueth mannus sone to suffre many thingis, and to be repreued of the elder men, and of the princis of prestis, and of scribis, and to be slayn, and the thridde dai to rise ayen.

23 And he seide to alle, If ony wole come aftir me, denye he hym silf, and take he his cross euery dai, and sue he me.

24 For he that wole make his lijf saaf schal leese it; and he that leesith his lijf for me, schal make it saaf.

25 And what profitith it to a man, if he wynne al the world, and leese hymsilf, and do peiryng of him silf.

26 For who so schameth me and my wordis, mannus sone schal schame hym, whanne he cometh in his maieste, and of the fadris, and of the hooli aungels.

27 And Y seie to you, verily ther ben summe stondynge here, whiche schulen not taste deeth, til thei seen the rewme of God.

28 And it was don aftir these wordis almest eiyte daies, and he took Petre and James and Joon, and he stiede in to an hil, to preye.

29 And while he preiede, the licnesse of his cheer was chaungid, and his clothing was whit schynynge.

30 And lo! two men spaken with hym,

31 and Moises and Helie weren seen in maieste; and thei sayn his goyng out, which he schulde fulfille in Jerusalem.

32 And Petre, and thei that weren with hym, weren heuy of sleep, and thei wakynge saien his majeste, and the twey men that stoden with hym.

33 And it was don, whanne thei departiden fro hym, Petir seide to Jhesu, Comaundour, it is good that we be here, and make we here thre tabernaclis, oon to thee, and oon to Moises, and oon to Elie. And he wiste not what he schulde seie.

34 But while he spak these thingis, a cloude was maad, and ouerschadewide hem; and thei dredden, whanne thei entriden in to the cloude.

35 And a vois was maad out of the cloude, and seide, This is my derworth sone, here ye hym.

36 And while the vois was maad, Jhesu was foundun aloone. And thei weren stille, and to no man seiden in tho daies ouyt of tho thingis, that thei hadden seyn.

37 But it was doon in the dai suynge, whanne thei camen doun of the hil, myche puple mette hem.

38 And lo! a man of the cumpany criede, and seide, Maister, Y biseche thee, biholde my sone, for Y haue no mo; and lo!

39 a spirit takith hym, and sudenli he crieth, and hurtlith doun, and to-drawith hym with fome, and vnneth he goith awei al to-drawynge hym.

40 And Y preiede thi disciplis, that thei schulden caste hym out, and thei myyten not.

41 And Jhesus answerde and seide to hem, A! vnfeithful generacioun and weiward, hou long schal Y be at you, and suffre you? brynge hidur thi sone.

42 And whanne he cam nyy, the deuel hurtlide hym doun, and to-braidide hym. And Jhesus blamyde 'the vnclene spirit, and heelide the child, and yeldide him to his fadir.

43 And alle men wondriden greetli in the gretnesse of God. And whanne alle men wondriden in alle thingis that he dide, he seide to hise disciplis,

44 Putte ye these wordis in youre hertis, for it is to come, that mannus sone be bitrayed in to the hondis of men.

45 And thei knewen not this word, and it was hid bifor hem, that thei feeliden it not; and thei dredden to axe hym of this word.

46 But a thouyt entride in to hem, who of hem schulde be grettest.

47 And Jhesu, seynge the thouytis of the herte of hem, took a child, and settide hym bisidis hym;

48 and seide to hem, Who euer resseyueth this child in my name, resseyueth me; and who euer resseyueth me, resseiueth him that sente me; for he that is leest among you alle, is the grettest.

49 And Joon answeride and seide, Comaundoure, we sayn a man castynge out feendis in thi name, and we han forbedun hym, for he sueth not thee with vs.

50 And Jhesus seide to hym, Nyle ye forbede, for he that is not ayens vs, is for vs.

51 And it was don, whanne the daies of his takyng vp weren fulfillid, he settide faste his face, to go to Jerusalem,

52 and sente messangeris bifor his siyt. And thei yeden, and entriden in to a citee of Samaritans, to make redi to hym.

53 And thei resseyueden not hym, for the face 'was of hym goynge in to Jerusalem.

54 And whanne James and Joon, hise disciplis, seyn, thei seiden, Lord, wolt thou that we seien, that fier come doun fro heuene, and waste hem?

55 And he turnede, and blamyde hem, and seide, Ye witen not, whos spiritis ye ben;

56 for mannus sone cam not to leese mennus soulis, but to saue. And thei wenten in to another castel.

57 And it was don, whanne thei walkeden in the weie, a man seide to hym, Y schal sue thee, whidur euer thou go.

58 And Jhesus seide to hym, Foxis han dennes, and briddis of the eir han nestis, but mannus sone hath not where he reste his heed.

59 And he seide to another, Sue thou me. And he seide, Lord, suffre me first to go, and birie my fadir.

60 And Jhesus seide to hym, Suffre that deede men birie hir deede men; but go thou, and telle the kyngdom of God.

61 And another seide, Lord, Y schal sue thee, but first suffre me to leeue 'alle thingis that ben at hoom.

62 And Jhesus seide to hym, No man that puttith his hoond to the plouy, and biholdynge bacward, is able to the rewme of God.

CAP 10

1 And aftir these thingis the Lord Jhesu ordeynede also othir seuenti and tweyn, and sente hem bi tweyn and tweyn bifor his face in to euery citee and place, whidir he was to come.

2 And he seide to hem, There is myche ripe corn, and fewe werke men; therfor preie ye the lord of the ripe corn, that he sende werke men in to his ripe corn.

3 Go ye, lo! Y sende you as lambren among wolues.

4 Therfor nyle ye bere a sachel, nethir scrippe, nethir schoon, and greete ye no man bi the weie.

5 In to what hous that ye entren, first seie ye, Pees to this hous.

6 And if a sone of pees be there, youre pees schal reste on hym; but if noon, it schal turne ayen to you.

7 And dwelle ye in the same hous, etynge and drynkynge tho thingis that ben at hem; for a werk man is worthi his hire. Nyle ye passe from hous in to hous.

8 And in to what euer citee ye entren, and thei resseyuen you, ete ye tho thingis that ben set to you;

9 and heele ye the sijke men that ben in that citee. And seie ye to hem, The kyngdom of God schal neiye in to you.

10 In to what citee ye entren, and thei resseyuen you not, go ye out in to the streetis of it,

11 and seie ye, We wipen of ayens you the poudir that cleued to vs of youre citee; netheles wite ye this thing, that the rewme of God schal come nyy.

12 Y seie to you, that to Sodom it schal be esiere than to that citee in that dai.

13 Wo to thee, Corosayn; wo to thee, Bethsaida; for if in Tyre and Sidon the vertues hadden be don, whiche han be don in you, sum tyme thei wolden haue sete in heyre and asches, and haue don penaunce.

14 Netheles to Tire and Sidon it schal be esiere in the doom than to you.

15 And thou, Cafarnaum, art enhaunsid 'til to heuene; thou schalt be drenchid 'til in to helle.

16 He that herith you, herith me; and he that dispisith you, dispisith me; and he that dispisith me, dispisith hym that sente me.

17 And the two and seuenti disciplis turneden ayen with ioye, and seiden, Lord, also deuelis ben suget to vs in thi name.

18 And he seide to hem, Y saiy Sathnas fallynge doun fro heuene, as leit.

19 And lo! Y haue youun to you power to trede on serpentis, and on scorpyouns, and on al the vertu of the enemy, and nothing schal anoye you.

20 Netheles nyle ye ioye on this thing, that spiritis ben suget to you; but ioye ye, that youre names ben writun in heuenes.

21 In thilk our he gladide in the Hooli Goost, and seide, Y knouleche to thee, fadir, Lord of heuene and of erthe, for thou hast hid these thingis fro wise men and prudent, and hast schewid hem to smale children. Yhe, fadir, for so it pleside bifor thee.

22 Alle thingis ben youun to me of my fadir, and no man woot, who is the sone, but the fadir; and who is the fadir, but the sone, and to whom the sone wole schewe.

23 And he turnede to hise disciplis, and seide, Blessid ben the iyen, that seen tho thingis that ye seen.

24 For Y seie to you, that many prophetis and kyngis wolden haue seie tho thingis, that ye seen, and thei sayn not; and here tho thingis, that ye heren, and thei herden not.

25 And lo! a wise man of the lawe ros vp, temptynge hym, and seiynge, Maister, what thing schal Y do to haue euerlastynge lijf?

26 And he seide to hym, What is writun in the lawe? hou redist thou?

27 He answeride, and seide, Thou schalt loue thi Lord God of al thin herte, and of al thi soule, and of alle thi strengthis, and of al thi mynde; and thi neiybore as thi silf.

28 And Jhesus seide to hym, Thou hast answerid riytli; do this thing, and thou schalt lyue.

29 But he willynge to iustifie hym silf, seide to Jhesu, And who is my neiybore?

30 And Jhesu biheld, and seide, A man cam doun fro Jerusalem in to Jerico, and fel among theues, and thei robbiden hym, and woundiden hym, and wente awei, and leften the man half alyue.

31 And it bifel, that a prest cam doun the same weie, and passide forth, whanne he hadde seyn hym.

32 Also a dekene, whanne he was bisidis the place, and saiy him, passide forth.

33 But a Samaritan, goynge the weie, cam bisidis hym; and he siy hym, and hadde reuthe on hym;

34 and cam to hym, and boond togidir hise woundis, and helde in oyle and wynne; and leide hym on his beest, and ledde in to an ostrie, and dide the cure of hym.

35 And another dai he brouyte forth twey pans, and yaf to the ostiler, and seide, Haue the cure of hym; and what euer thou schalt yyue ouer, Y schal yelde to thee, whanne Y come ayen.

36 Who of these thre, semeth to thee, was neiybore to hym, that fel among theues?

37 And he seide, He that dide merci in to hym. And Jhesus seide to hym, Go thou, and do thou on lijk maner.

38 And it was don, while thei wenten, he entride in to a castel; and a womman, Martha bi name, resseyuede hym in to hir hous.

39 And to this was a sistir, Marie bi name, which also sat bisidis the feet of the Lord, and herde his word.

40 But Martha bisiede aboute the ofte seruyce. And sche stood, and seide, Lord, takist thou no kepe, that my sistir hath left me aloone to serue? therfor seie thou to hir, that sche helpe me.

41 And the Lord answerde, and seide to hir, Martha, Martha, thou art bysi, and art troublid aboute ful many thingis;

42 but o thing is necessarie.

43 Marie hath chosun the best part, which schal not be takun awei fro hir.

CAP 11

1 And it was don, whanne he was preiynge in a place, as he ceesside, oon of hise disciplis seide to hym, Lord, teche vs to preye, as Joon tauyte hise disciplis.

2 And he seide to hem, Whanne ye preien, seie ye, Fadir, halewid be thi name. Thi kyngdom come to.

3 Yyue 'to vs to dai oure ech daies breed.

4 And foryyue to vs oure synnes, as we foryyuen to ech man that owith to vs. And lede vs not in to temptacioun.

5 And he seide to hem, Who of you schal haue a freend, and schal go to hym at mydnyyt, and schal seie to hym, Freend, leene to me thre looues;

6 for my freend cometh to me fro the weie, and Y haue not what Y schal sette bifor hym.

7 And he with ynforth answere and seie, Nyle thou be heuy to me; the dore is now schit, and my children ben with me in bed; Y may not rise, and yyue to thee.

8 And if he schal dwelle stil knockynge, Y seie to you, thouy he schal not rise, and yyue to him, for that that he is his freend, netheles for his contynuel axyng he schal ryse, and yyue to hym, as many as he hath nede to.

9 And Y seie to you, axe ye, and it schal be youun to you; seke ye, and ye schulen fynde; knocke ye, and it schal be openyd to you.

10 For ech that axith, takith, and he that sekith, fyndith; and to a man that knockith, it schal be openyd.

11 Therfor who of you axith his fadir breed, whether he schal yyue hym a stoon? or if he axith fisch, whether he schal yyue hym a serpent for the fisch?

12 or if he axe an eye, whether he schal a reche hym a scorpioun?

13 Therfor if ye, whanne ye ben yuel, kunnen yyue good yiftis to youre children, hou myche more youre fadir of heuene schal yyue a good spirit to men that axith him.

14 And Jhesus was castynge out a feend, and he was doumbe. And whanne he hadde cast out the feend, the doumbe man spak; and the puple wondride.

15 And sum of hem seiden, In Belsabub, prince of deuelis, he castith out deuelis.

16 And othir temptinge axiden of hym a tokene fro heuene.

17 And as he saiy the thouytis of hem, he seide to hem, Euery rewme departid ayens it silf, schal be desolat, and an hous schal falle on an hous.

18 And if Sathanas be departid ayens hym silf, hou schal his rewme stonde? For ye seien, that Y caste out feendis in Belsabub.

19 And if Y in Belsabub caste out fendis, in whom casten out youre sones? Therfor thei schulen be youre domesmen.

20 But if Y caste out fendis in the fyngir of God, thanne the rewme of God is comun among you.

21 Whanne a strong armed man kepith his hous, alle thingis that he weldith ben in pees.

22 But if a stronger than he come vpon hym, and ouercome hym, he schal take awei al his armere, in which he tristide, and schal dele abrood his robries.

23 He that is not with me, is ayens me; and he that gederith not togidir with me, scaterith abrood.

24 Whanne an vnclene spirit goith out of a man, he wandrith bi drie placis, and sekith reste; and he fyndynge not, seith, Y schal turne ayen in to myn hous, fro whannes Y cam out.

25 And whanne he cometh, he fyndith it clansid with besyms, and fayre arayed.

26 Thanne he goith, and takith with hym seuene othere spirits worse than hym silf, and thei entren, and dwellen there. And the laste thingis of that man ben maad worse than the formere.

27 And it was don, whanne he hadde seid these thingis, a womman of the cumpanye reride hir vois, and seide to hym, Blessid be the wombe that bare thee, and blessid be the tetis that thou hast soken.

28 And he seide, But yhe blessid be thei, that heren the word of God, and kepen it.

29 And whanne the puple runnen togidere, he bigan to seie, This generacioun is a weiward generacioun; it sekith a token, and a tokene schal not be youun to it, but the tokene of Jonas, the profete.

30 For as Jonas was a tokene to men of Nynyue, so mannus sone schal be to this generacioun.

31 The queen of the south schal rise in doom with men of this generacioun, and schal condempne hem; for sche cam fro the endis of the erthe, for to here the wisdom of Salomon, and lo! here is a gretter than Salomon.

32 Men of Nynyue schulen rise in doom with this generacioun, and schulen condempne it; for thei diden penaunce in the prechyng of Jonas, and lo! here is a gretter than Jonas.

33 No man tendith a lanterne, and puttith in hidils, nether vndur a buyschel, but on a candilstike, that thei that goen in, se liyt.

34 The lanterne of thi bodi is thin iye; if thin iye be symple, al thi bodi schal be liyti; but if it be weyward, al thi bodi schal be derkful.

35 Therfor se thou, lest the liyt that is in thee, be derknessis.

36 Therfor if al thi bodi be briyt, and haue no part of derknessis, it schal be al briyt, and as a lanterne of briytnesse it schal yyue liyt to thee.

37 And whanne he spak, a Farisee preiede him, that he schulde ete with hym. And he entride, and sat to the meete.

38 And the Farisee bigan to seie, gessynge with ynne hym silf, whi he was not waschen bifor mete.

39 And the Lord seide to hym, Now ye Farisees clensen that that is with outenforth of the cuppe and the plater; but that thing that is with ynne of you, is ful of raueyn and wickidnesse.

40 Foolis, whether he that made that that is withoutenforth, made not also that that is with ynne?

41 Netheles that that is ouer plus, yyue ye almes, and lo! alle thingis ben cleene to you.

42 But wo to you, Farisees, that tithen mynte, and rue, and ech eerbe, and leeuen doom and the charite of God. For it bihofte to do these thingis, and not leeue tho.

43 Wo to you, Farisees, that louen the firste chaieris in synagogis, and salutaciouns in chepyng.

44 Wo to you, that ben as sepulcris, that ben not seyn, and
men walkynge aboue witen not.

45 But oon of the wise men of the lawe answeride, and seide
to hym, Maystir, thou seiynge these thingis, also to vs doist
dispit.

46 And he seide, Also wo to you, wise men of lawe, for ye
chargen men with birthuns which thei moun not bere, and ye
you silf with youre o fyngur touchen not the heuynessis.

47 Wo to you, that bilden toumbis of profetis; and youre
fadris slowen hem.

48 Treuli ye witnessen, that ye consenten to the werkis of
youre fadris; for thei slowen hem, but ye bilden her sepulcris.

49 Therfor the wisdom of God seide, Y schal sende to hem
profetis and apostlis, and of hem thei schulen sle and pursue,

50 that the blood of alle prophetis, that was sched fro the
making of the world, be souyt of this generacioun;

51 fro the blood of the iust Abel to the blood of Zacharie, that
was slayn bitwixe the auter and the hous. So Y seie to you, it
schal be souyt of this generacioun.

52 Wo to you, wise men of the lawe, for ye han takun awei
the keye of kunnyng; and ye yow silf entriden not, and ye han
forbeden hem that entriden.

53 And whanne he seide these thingis to hem, the Farisees
and wise men of lawe bigunnen greuousli to ayenstonde, and
stoppe his mouth of many thingis,

54 aspiynge hym, and sekynge to take sum thing of his
mouth, to accuse hym.

CAP 12

1 And whanne myche puple stood aboute, so that thei treden
ech on othir, he bigan to seie to hise disciplis, Be ye war of
the sourdouy of the Farisees, that is ypocrisie.

2 For no thing is hilid, that schal not be schewid; nether hid,
that schal not be wist.

3 For whi tho thingis that ye han seid in derknessis, schulen
be seid in liyt; and that that ye han spokun in eere in the
couchis, schal be prechid in roofes.

4 And Y seie to you, my freendis, be ye not a ferd of hem that
sleen the bodie, and aftir these thingis han no more what thei
schulen do.

5 But Y schal schewe to you, whom ye schulen drede; drede
ye hym, that aftir he hath slayn, he hath power to sende in to
helle. And so Y seie to you, drede ye hym.

6 Whether fyue sparowis ben not seld for twei halpens; and
oon of hem is not in foryetyng bifor God?

7 But also alle the heeris of youre heed ben noumbrid. Therfor nyle ye drede; ye ben of more prijs than many sparowis.

8 Treuli Y seie to you, ech man that knoulechith me bifor
men, mannus sone schal knouleche hym bifor the aungels of
God.

9 But he that denyeth me bifor men, schal be denyed bifor the
aungels of God.

10 And ech that seith a word ayens mannus sone, it schal be
foryouun to hym; but it schal not be foryouun to hym, that
blasfemeth ayens the Hooli Goost.

11 And whanne thei leden you in to synagogis, and to magistratis, and potestatis, nyle ye 'be bisie, hou or what ye schulen
answere, or what ye schulen seie.

12 For the Hooli Goost schal teche you in that our, what it
bihoueth you to seie.

13 And oon of the puple seide to hym, Maystir, seie to my
brothir, that he departe with me the eritage.

14 And he seyde to hym, Man, who ordeynede me a domesman, or a departere, on you?

15 And he seide to hem, Se ye, and be ye war of al coueytice;
for the lijf of a man is not in the abundaunce of tho thingis,
whiche he weldith.

16 And he tolde to hem a liknesse, and seide, The feeld of a
riche man brouyte forth plenteuouse fruytis.

17 And he thouyte with ynne hym silf, and seide, What schal
Y do, for Y haue not whidur Y schal gadere my fruytis?

18 And he seith, This thing Y schal do; Y schal throwe doun
my bernes, and Y schal make gretter, and thidir Y schal gadir
alle thingis that growen to me, and my goodis.

19 And Y schal seie to my soule, Soule, thou hast many goodis kept in to ful many yeeris; rest thou, ete, drynke, and
make feeste.

20 And God seide to hym, Fool, in this nyyt thei schulen take
thi lijf fro thee. And whos schulen tho thingis be, that thou
hast arayed?

21 So is he that tresourith to hym silf, and is not riche in God.

22 And he seide to hise disciplis, Therfor Y seie to you, nyle
ye be bisy to youre lijf, what ye schulen ete, nether to youre
bodi, with what ye schulen be clothid.

23 The lijf is more than mete, and the body more than clothing.

24 Biholde ye crowis, for thei sowen not, nethir repen, to
whiche is no celer, ne berne, and God fedith hem. Hou myche
more ye ben of more prijs than thei.

25 And who of you bithenkynge may put to o cubit to his stature?

26 Therfor if ye moun not that that is leest, what ben ye bisie
of othere thingis?

27 Biholde ye the lilies of the feeld, hou thei wexen; thei
trauelen not, nethir spynnen. And Y seie to you, that nethir
Salomon in al his glorie was clothid as oon of these.

28 And if God clothith thus the hey, that to dai is in the feeld,
and to morewe is cast in to an ouen; hou myche more you of
litil feith.

29 And nyle ye seke, what ye schulen ete, or what ye schulen
drynke; and nyle ye be reisid an hiy.

30 For folkis of the world seken alle these thingis; 'and your
fadir woot, that ye neden alle these thingis.

31 Netheles seke ye first the kyngdom of God, and alle these
thingis schulen be caste to you.

32 Nile ye, litil flok, drede, for it pleside to youre fadir to
yyue you a kyngdom.

33 Selle ye tho thingis that ye han in possessioun, and yyue
ye almes. And make to you sachels that wexen not oolde, tresoure that failith not in heuenes, whidir a theef neiyith not,
nether mouyt destruyeth.

34 For where is thi tresoure, there thin herte schal be.

35 Be youre leendis gird aboue, and lanternes brennynge in
youre hoondis;

36 and be ye lijk to men that abiden her lord, whanne he schal
turne ayen fro the weddyngis, that whanne he schal come, and
knocke, anoon thei openen to hym.

37 Blessid be tho seruauntis, that whanne the lord schal come,
he schal fynde wakynge. Treuli Y seie to you, that he schal
girde hym silf, and make hem sitte to mete, and he schal go,
and serue hem.

38 And if he come in the secounde wakynge, and if he come in the thridde wakynge, and fynde so, tho seruauntis ben blessid.

39 And wite ye this thing, for if an hosebonde man wiste, in what our the theef wolde come, sotheli he schulde wake, and not suffre his hous to be myned.

40 And be ye redi, for in what our ye gessen not, mannus sone schal come.

41 And Petre seide to hym, Lord, seist thou this parable to vs, or to alle?

42 And the Lord seide, Who, gessist thou, is a trewe dispend-ere, and a prudent, whom the lord hath ordeyned on his meyne, to yyue hem in tyme mesure of whete?

43 Blessid is that seruaunt, that the lord whanne he cometh, schal fynde so doynge.

44 Verili Y seie to you, that on alle thingis that he weldith, he schal ordeyne hym.

45 That if that seruaunt seie in his herte, My lord tarieth to come; and bigynne to smyte children, and handmaydenes, and ete, and drynke, and be fulfillid ouer mesure,

46 the lord of that seruaunt schal come, in the dai that he hop-ith not, and the our that he woot not; and schal departe hym, and putte his part with vnfeithful men.

47 But thilke seruaunt that knew the wille of his lord, and made not hym redi, and dide not aftir his wille, schal be betun with many betyngis.

48 But he that knew not, and dide worthi thingis of strokis, schal be betun with fewe. For to eche man to whom myche is youun, myche schal be axid of hym; and thei schulen axe more of hym, to whom thei bitoken myche.

49 Y cam to sende fier 'in to the erthe, and what wole Y, but that it be kyndlid?

50 And Y haue to be baptisid with a baptysm, and hou am Y constreyned, til that it be perfitli don?

51 Wene ye, that Y cam to yyue pees in to erthe? Nay, Y say to you, but departyng.

52 For fro this tyme ther schulen be fyue departid in oon hous; thre schulen be departid ayens tweyne, and tweyne schulen be departid ayens thre;

53 the fadir ayens the sone, and the sone ayens the fadir; the modir ayens the douytir, and the douytir ayens the modir; the hosebondis modir ayens the sones wijf, and and the sones wijf ayens hir hosebondis modir.

54 And he seide also to the puple, Whanne ye seen a cloude risynge fro the sunne goynge doun, anoon ye seien, Reyn cometh; and so it is don.

55 And whanne ye seen the south blowynge, ye seien, That heete schal be; and it is don.

56 Ypocritis, ye kunnen preue the face of heuene and of erthe, but hou preuen ye not this tyme.

57 But what and of you silf ye demen not that that is iust?

58 But whanne thou goist with thin aduersarie in the weie to the prince, do bisynesse to be delyuerid fro hym; lest per-auenture he take thee to the domesman, and the domesman bitake thee to the maistirful axer, and the maistirful axer sende thee in to prisoun.

59 Y seie to thee, thou schalt not go fro thennus, til thou yelde the laste ferthing.

CAP 13

1 And sum men weren present in that tyme, that telden to hym of the Galileis, whos blood Pilat myngide with the sacri-ficis of hem.

2 And he answeride, and seide to hem, Wenen ye, that these men of Galile weren synneris more than alle Galilees, for thei suffriden siche thingis?

3 Y seie to you, nay; alle ye schulen perische in lijk manere, but ye han penaunce.

4 And as tho eiytetene, on which the toure in Siloa fel doun, and slowe hem, gessen ye, for thei weren dettouris more than alle men that dwellen in Jerusalem?

5 Y seie to you, nai; but also 'ye alle schulen perische, if ye doon not penaunce.

6 And he seide this liknesse, A man hadde a fige tre plauntid in his vynyerd, and he cam sekynge fruyt in it, and foond noon.

7 And he seide to the tilier of the vynyerd, Lo! thre yeeris ben, sithen Y come sekynge fruyt in this fige tre, and Y fynde noon; therfor kitte it doun, whereto ocupieth it the erthe?

8 And he answerynge seide to hym, Lord, suffre it also this yeer, the while Y delue aboute it, and Y schal donge it;

9 if it schal make fruyt, if nay, in tyme comynge thou schalt kitte it doun.

10 And he was techinge in her synagoge in the sabatis.

11 And lo! a womman, that hadde a spirit of sijknesse eiytene yeeris, and was crokid, and 'nethir ony maner myyte loke vpward.

12 Whom whanne Jhesus hadde seyn, he clepide to hym, and seide to hir, Womman, thou art delyuerid of thi sijknesse.

13 And he settide on hir his hoondis, and anoon sche stood upriyt, and glorifiede God.

14 And the prince of the synagoge answerde, hauynge dedeyn for Jhesus hadde heelid in the sabat; and he seide to the puple, Ther ben sixe dayes, in whiche it bihoueth to worche; therfor come ye in these, and 'be ye heelid, and not in the daie of sabat.

15 But the Lord answeride to hym, and seide, Ypocrite, whether ech of you vntieth not in the sabat his oxe, or asse, fro the cratche, and ledith to watir?

16 Bihofte it not this douytir of Abraham, whom Satanas hath boundun, lo! eiytetene yeeris, to be vnboundun of this boond in the dai of the sabat?

17 And whanne he seide these thingis, alle hise aduersaries weren aschamed, and al the puple ioiede in alle thingis, that weren gloriousli don of hym.

18 Therfor he seide, To what thing is the kyngdom of God lijk? and to what thing schal Y gesse it to be lijk?

19 It is lijk to a corn of seneuey, which a man took, and cast in to his yerd; and it wax, and was maad in to a greet tree, and foulis of the eire restiden in the braunchis therof.

20 And eft soone he seide, To what thing schal Y gesse the kyngdom of God lijk?

21 It is lijk to sourdouy, that a womman took, and hidde it 'in to thre mesuris of mele, til al were sourid.

22 And he wente bi citees and castels, techynge and makynge a iourney in to Jerusalem.

23 And a man seide to hym, Lord, if there ben fewe, that ben saued? And he seide to hem,

24 Stryue ye to entre bi the streite yate; for Y seie to you, many seken to entre, and thei schulen not mowe.

25 For whanne the hosebonde man is entrid, and the dore is closid, ye schulen bigynne to stonde with out forth, and knocke at the dore, and seie, Lord, opyn to vs. And he schal answere, and seie to you, Y knowe you not, of whennus ye ben.

26 Thanne ye schulen bigynne to seye, We han etun bifor thee and drunkun, and in oure streetis thou hast tauyt.

27 And he schal seie to you, Y know you not, of whennus ye ben; go awei fro me, alle ye worcheris of wickidnesse.

28 There schal be wepyng and gruntyng of teeth, whanne ye schulen se Abraham, and Isaac, and Jacob, and alle the prophetis in the kyngdom of God; and you to be put out.

29 And thei schulen come fro the eest and west, and fro the north and south, and schulen sitte 'at the mete in the rewme of God.

30 And lo! thei that weren the firste, ben the laste; and thei that weren the laste, ben the firste.

31 In that day sum of the Farisees camen nyy, and seiden to hym, Go out, and go fro hennus, for Eroude wole sle thee.

32 And he seide to hem, Go ye, and seie to that foxe, Lo! Y caste out feendis, and Y make perfitli heelthis, to dai and to morew, and the thridde dai Y am endid.

33 Netheles it bihoueth me to dai, and to morewe, and the dai that sueth, to walke; for it fallith not a profete to perische out of Jerusalem.

34 Jerusalem, Jerusalem, that sleest profetis, and stonest hem that ben sent to thee, hou ofte wolde Y gadre togider thi sones, as a brid gaderith his nest vndur fethris, and thou woldist not.

35 Lo! youre hous schal be left to you desert. And Y seie to you, that ye schulen not se me, til it come, whanne ye schulen seie, Blessid is he, that cometh in the name of the Lord.

CAP 14

1 And it was don, whanne he hadde entrid in to the hous of a prince of Farisees, in the sabat, to ete breed, thei aspieden hym.

2 And lo! a man sijk in the dropesie was bifor hym.

3 And Jhesus answerynge spak to the wise men of lawe, and to the Farisees, and seide, Whethir it is leeueful to heele in the sabat?

4 And thei helden pees. And Jhesus took, and heelide hym, and let hym go.

5 And he answeride to hem, and seide, Whos asse or oxe of you schal falle in to a pit, and 'he schal not anoon drawe hym out in the dai of the sabat?

6 And thei myyten not answere to hym to these thingis.

7 He seide also a parable to men bodun to a feeste, and biheld hou thei chesen the first sittyng placis, and seide to hem,

8 Whanne thou art bodun to bridalis, sitte not 'at the mete in the firste place; lest perauenture a worthier than thou be bodun of hym,

9 and lest he come that clepide thee and hym, and seie to thee, Yyue place to this, and thanne thou schalt bigynne with schame to holde the lowest place.

10 But whanne thou art bedun to a feste, go, and sitte doun in the laste place, that whanne he cometh, that bad thee to the feeste, he seie to thee, Freend, come hiyer. Thanne worschip schal be to thee, bifor men that sitten at the mete.

11 For ech that enhaunsith hym, schal be lowid; and he that meketh hym, schal be hiyed.

12 And he seide to hym, that hadde bodun hym to the feeste, Whanne thou makist a mete, or a soper, nyle thou clepe thi freendis, nether thi britheren, nethir cosyns, nethir neiyboris, ne riche men; lest perauenture thei bidde thee ayen to the feeste, and it be yolde ayen to thee.

13 But whanne thou makist a feeste, clepe pore men,

14 feble, crokid, and blynde, and thou schalt be blessid; for thei han not wherof to yelde thee, for it schal be yoldun to thee in the risyng ayen of iust men.

15 And whanne oon of hem that saten togider at the mete hadde herd these thingis, he seide to hym, Blessid is he, that schal ete breed in the rewme of God.

16 And he seide to hym, A man made a greet soper, and clepide many.

17 And he sent his seruaunt in the our of soper, to seie to men that weren bodun to the feeste, that thei schulden come, for now alle thingis ben redi.

18 And alle bigunnen togidir to excusen hem. The firste seide, Y haue bouyt a toun, and Y haue nede to go out, and se it; Y preye thee, haue me excusid.

19 And the tother seide, Y haue bouyt fyue yockis of oxun, and Y go to preue hem; Y preye thee, haue me excusid.

20 And an othir seide, Y haue weddid a wijf; and therfor Y may not come.

21 And the seruaunt turnede ayen, and tolde these thingis to his lord. Thanne the hosebonde man was wrooth, and seide to his seruaunt, Go out swithe in to the grete stretis and smal stretis of the citee, and brynge ynne hidir pore men, and feble, blynde, and crokid.

22 And the seruaunt seide, Lord, it is don, as thou hast comaundid, and yit there is a void place.

23 And the lord seide to the seruaunt, Go out in to weies and heggis, and constreine men to entre, that myn hous be fulfillid.

24 For Y seie to you, that noon of tho men that ben clepid, schal taaste my soper.

25 And myche puple wenten with hym; and he turnede, and seide to hem,

26 If ony man cometh to me, and hatith not his fadir, and modir, and wijf, and sones, and britheren, and sistris, and yit his owne lijf, he may not be my disciple.

27 And he that berith not his cross, and cometh aftir me, may not be my disciple.

28 For who of you willynge to bilde a toure, whether he 'first sitte not, and countith the spensis that ben nedeful, if he haue to perfourme?

29 Lest aftir that he hath set the foundement, and mowe not perfourme, alle that seen, bigynnen to scorne hym, and seie, For this man bigan to bilde,

30 and myyte not make an ende.

31 Or what kyng that wole go to do a bataile ayens anothir kyng, whether he sittith not first, and bithenkith, if he may with ten thousynde go ayens hym that cometh ayens hym with twenti thousynde?

32 Ellis yit while he is afer, he sendynge a messanger, preieth tho thingis that ben of pees.

33 So therfor ech of you, that forsakith not alle thingis that he hath, may not be my disciple.

34 Salt is good; but if salt vanysche, in what thing schal it be sauerid?

35 Nethir in erthe, nethir in donghille it is profitable, but it schal be cast out. He that hath eeris of herynge, here he.

CAP 15

1 And pupplicans and synful men weren neiyynge to him, to here hym.

2 And the Farisees and scribis grutchiden, seiynge, For this resseyueth synful men, and etith with hem.

3 And he spak to hem this parable,

4 and seide, What man of you that hath an hundrith scheep, and if he hath lost oon of hem, whethir he leeueth not nynti and nyne in desert, and goith to it that perischide, til he fynde it?

5 And whanne he hath foundun it, he ioieth, and leyith it on hise schuldris; and he cometh hoom,

6 and clepith togidir hise freendis and neiyboris, and seith to hem, Be ye glad with me, for Y haue founde my scheep, that hadde perischid.

7 And Y seie to you, so ioye schal be in heuene on o synful man doynge penaunce, more than on nynti and nyne iuste, that han no nede to penaunce.

8 Or what womman hauynge ten besauntis, and if sche hath lost oo besaunt, whether sche teendith not a lanterne, and turneth vpsodoun the hows, and sekith diligentli, til that sche fynde it?

9 And whanne sche hath foundun, sche clepith togidir freendis and neiyboris, and seith, Be ye glad with me, for Y haue founde the besaunt, that Y hadde lost.

10 So Y seie to you, ioye schal be bifor aungels of God on o synful man doynge penaunce.

11 And he seide, A man hadde twei sones;

12 and the yonger of hem seide to the fadir, Fadir, yyue me the porcioun of catel, that fallith to me. And he departide to hem the catel.

13 And not aftir many daies, whanne alle thingis weren gederid togider, the yonger sone wente forth in pilgrymage in to a fer cuntre; and there he wastide hise goodis in lyuynge lecherously.

14 And aftir that he hadde endid alle thingis, a strong hungre was maad in that cuntre, and he bigan to haue nede.

15 And he wente, and drouy hym to oon of the citeseyns of that cuntre. And he sente hym in to his toun, to fede swyn.

16 And he coueitide to fille his wombe of the coddis that the hoggis eeten, and no man yaf hym.

17 And he turnede ayen to hym silf, and seide, Hou many hirid men in my fadir hous han plente of looues; and Y perische here thorouy hungir.

18 Y schal rise vp, and go to my fadir, and Y schal seie to hym, Fadir, Y haue synned in to heuene, and bifor thee;

19 and now Y am not worthi to be clepid thi sone, make me as oon of thin hirid men.

20 And he roos vp, and cam to his fadir. And whanne he was yit afer, his fadir saiy hym, and was stirrid bi mercy. And he ran, and fel on his necke, and kisside hym.

21 And the sone seide to hym, Fadir, Y haue synned in to heuene, and bifor thee; and now Y am not worthi to be clepid thi sone.

22 And the fadir seide to hise seruauntis, Swithe brynge ye forth the firste stoole, and clothe ye hym, and yyue ye a ryng in his hoond,

23 and schoon on hise feet; and brynge ye a fat calf, and sle ye, and ete we, and make we feeste.

24 For this my sone was deed, and hath lyued ayen; he perischid, and is foundun. And alle men bigunnen to ete.

25 But his eldere sone was in the feeld; and whanne he cam, and neiyede to the hous, he herde a symfonye and a croude.

26 And he clepide oon of the seruauntis, and axide, what these thingis weren.

27 And he seide to hym, Thi brother is comun, and thi fadir slewe a fat calf, for he resseyuede hym saaf.

28 And he was wrooth, and wolde not come in. Therfor his fadir wente out, and bigan to preye hym.

29 And he answerde to his fadir, and seide, Lo! so many yeeris Y serue thee, and Y neuer brak thi comaundement; and thou neuer yaf to me a kidde, that Y with my freendis schulde haue ete.

30 But aftir that this thi sone, that hath deuourid his substaunce with horis, cam, thou hast slayn to hym a fat calf.

31 And he seide to hym, Sone, thou art euer more with me, and alle my thingis ben thine.

32 But it bihofte for to make feeste, and to haue ioye; for this thi brother was deed, and lyuede ayen; he perischide, and is foundun.

CAP 16

1 He seide also to hise disciplis, Ther was a riche man, that hadde a baili; and this was defamed to him, as he hadde wastid his goodis.

2 And he clepide hym, and seide to hym, What here Y this thing of thee? yelde reckynyng of thi baili, for thou miyte not now be baili.

3 And the baili seide with ynne him silf, What schal Y do, for my lord takith awei fro me the baili? delfe mai Y not, I schame to begge.

4 Y woot what Y schal do, that whanne Y am remeued fro the baili, thei resseyue me in to her hous.

5 Therfor whanne alle the dettours of his lord weren clepid togider, he seide to the firste, Hou myche owist thou to my lord?

6 And he seide, An hundrid barelis of oyle. And he seide to hym, Take thi caucioun, and sitte soone, and write fifti.

7 Aftirward he seide to another, And hou myche owist thou? Which answerde, An hundrid coris of whete. And he seide to hym, Take thi lettris, and write foure scoore.

8 And the lord preiside the baili of wickydnesse, for he hadde do prudentli; for the sones of this world ben more prudent in her generacioun than the sones of liyt.

9 And Y seie to you, make ye to you freendis of the ritchesse of wickidnesse, that whanne ye schulen fayle, thei resseyue you in to euerlastynge tabernaclis.

10 He that is trewe in the leeste thing, is trewe also in the more; and he that is wickid in a litil thing, is wickid also in the more.

11 Therfor if ye weren not trewe in the wickid thing of ritchesse, who schal bitake to you that that is verry?

12 And if ye weren not trewe in othere mennus thing, who schal yyue to you that that is youre?

13 No seruaunt may serue to twei lordis; for ether he schal hate 'the toon, and loue the tothir; ethir he schal drawe to 'the toon, and schal dispise the tothir. Ye moun not serue to God and to ritchesse.

14 But the Farisees, that weren coueytous, herden alle these thingis, and thei scorneden hym.

15 And he seide to hem, Ye it ben, that iustifien you bifor men; but God hath knowun youre hertis, for that that is hiy to men, is abhomynacioun bifor God.

16 The lawe and prophetis til to Joon; fro that tyme the rewme of God is euangelisid, and ech man doith violence in to it.

17 Forsothe it is liyter heuene and erthe to passe, than that o titil falle fro the lawe.

18 Euery man that forsakith his wijf, and weddith an other, doith letcherie; and he that weddith the wijf forsakun of the hosebonde, doith auowtrie.

19 There was a riche man, and was clothid in purpur, and whit silk, and eete euery dai schynyngli.

20 And there was a begger, Lazarus bi name, that lai at his yate ful of bilis,

21 and coueitide to be fulfillid of the crummes, that fellen doun fro the riche mannus boord, and no man yaf to hym; but houndis camen, and lickiden hise bilis.

22 And it was don, that the begger diede, and was borun of aungels in to Abrahams bosum.

23 And the riche man was deed also, and was biried in helle. And he reiside hise iyen, whanne he was in turmentis, and say Abraham afer, and Lazarus in his bosum.

24 And he criede, and seide, Fadir Abraham, haue merci on me, and sende Lazarus, that he dippe the ende of his fyngur in watir, to kele my tunge; for Y am turmentid in this flawme.

25 And Abraham seide to hym, Sone, haue mynde, for thou hast resseyued good thingis in thi lijf, and Lazarus also yuel thingis; but he is now coumfortid, and thou art turmentid.

26 And in alle these thingis a greet derk place is stablischid betwixe vs and you; that thei that wolen fro hennus passe to you, moun not, nethir fro thennus passe ouer hidur.

27 And he seide, Thanne Y preie thee, fadir, that thou sende hym in to the hous of my fadir.

28 For Y haue fyue britheren, that he witnesse to hem, lest also thei come in to this place of turmentis.

29 And Abraham seide to him, Thei han Moyses and the prophetis; here thei hem.

30 And he seide, Nay, fadir Abraham, but if ony of deed men go to hem, thei schulen do penaunce.

31 And he seide to hym, If thei heren not Moises and prophetis, nethir if ony of deed men rise ayen, thei schulen bileue to hym.

CAP 17

1 And Jhesu seide to hise disciplis, It is impossible that sclaundris come not; but wo to that man, bi whom thei comen.

2 It is more profitable to him, if a mylne stoon be put aboute his necke, and he be cast in to the see, than that he sclaundre oon of these litle.

3 Take ye hede you silf; if thi brothir hath synned ayens thee, blame hym; and if he do penaunce, foryyue hym.

4 And if seuene sithis in the dai he do synne ayens thee, and seuene sithis in the dai he be conuertid to thee, and seie, It forthenkith me, foryyue thou hym.

5 And the apostlis seiden to the Lord, Encrese to vs feith.

6 And the Lord seide, If ye han feith as the corn of seneuei, ye schulen seie to this more tre, Be thou drawun vp bi the rote, and be ouerplauntid in to the see, and it schal obeie to you.

7 But who of you hath a seruaunt erynge, or lesewynge oxis, which seith to hym, whanne he turneth ayen fro the feeld, Anoon go, and sitte to mete;

8 and seith not to hym, Make redi, that Y soupe, and girde thee, and serue me, while Y ete and drynke, and aftir this thou schalt ete and drynke;

9 whether he hath grace to that seruaunt, for he dide that that he comaundide hym?

10 Nay, Y gesse. So ye, whanne ye han don alle thingis that ben comaundid to you, seie ye, We ben vnprofitable seruauntis, we han do that that we ouyten to do.

11 And it was do, the while Jhesus wente in to Jerusalem, he passide thorou the myddis of Samarie, and Galilee.

12 And whanne he entride in to a castel, ten leprouse men camen ayens hym, whiche stoden afer,

13 and reiseden her voys, and seiden, Jhesu, comaundoure, haue merci on vs.

14 And as he say hem, he seide, Go ye, 'schewe ye you to the prestis. And it was don, the while thei wenten, thei weren clensid.

15 And oon of hem, as he saiy that he was clensid, wente ayen, magnifiynge God with grete vois.

16 And he fel doun on the face bifore hise feet, and dide thankyngis; and this was a Samaritan.

17 And Jhesus answerde, and seide, Whether ten ben not clensid, and where ben the nyne?

18 There is noon foundun, that turnede ayen, and yaf glorie to God, but this alien.

19 And he seide to hym, Rise vp, go thou; for thi feith hath maad thee saaf.

20 And he was axid of Farisees, whanne the rewme of God cometh. And he answerde to hem, and seide, The rewme of God cometh not with aspiyng,

21 nether thei schulen seie, Lo! here, or lo there; for lo! the rewme of God is with ynne you.

22 And he seide to hise disciplis, Daies schulen come, whanne ye schulen desire to se o dai of mannus sone, and ye schulen not se.

23 And thei schulen seie to you, Lo! here, and lo there. Nyle ye go, nether sue ye;

24 for as leyt schynynge from vndur heuene schyneth in to tho thingis that ben vndur heuene, so schal mannus sone be in his dai.

25 But first it bihoueth hym to suffre many thingis, and to be repreued of this generacioun.

26 And as it was doon in the daies of Noe, so it schal be in the daies of mannys sone.

27 Thei eeten and drunkun, weddiden wyues, and weren youun to weddyngis, til in to the dai in the whych Noe entride in to the schip; and the greet flood cam, and loste alle.

28 Also as it was don in the daies of Loth, thei eeten and drunkun, bouyten and seelden, plauntiden and bildiden; but the dai that Loth wente out of Sodome,

29 the Lord reynede fier and brymstoon fro heuene, and loste alle.

30 Lijk this thing it schal be, in what dai mannys sone schal be schewid.

31 In that our he that is in the roof, and his vessels in the hous, come he not doun to take hem awei; and he that schal be in the feeld, also turne not ayen bihynde.

32 Be ye myndeful of the wijf of Loth.

33 Who euer seketh to make his lijf saaf, schal leese it; and who euer leesith it, schal quykene it.

34 But Y seie to you, in that nyyt twei schulen be in o bed, oon schal be takun, and the tothir forsakun;

35 twei wymmen schulen be gryndynge togidir, 'the toon schal be takun, and 'the tother forsakun; twei in a feeld, 'the toon schal be takun, and 'the tother left.

36 Thei answeren, and seien to hym, Where, Lord?

37 Which seide to hym, Where euer the bodi schal be, thidur schulen be gaderid togidere also the eglis.

CAP 18

1 And he seide to hem also a parable, that it bihoueth to preye euer more, and not faile;

2 and seide, There was a iuge in a citee, that dredde not God, nether schamede of men.

3 And a widowe was in that citee, and sche cam to hym, and seide, Venge me of myn aduersarie;

4 and he wolde not longe tyme. But aftir these thingis he seide with ynne hym silf, Thouy Y drede not God, and schame not of man,

5 netheles for this widewe is heuy to me, Y schal venge hir; lest at the laste sche comynge condempne me.

6 And the Lord seide, Here ye, what the domesman of wickidnesse seith;

7 and whether God schal not do veniaunce of hise chosun, criynge to hym dai and nyyt, and schal haue pacience in hem?

8 Sotheli Y seie to you, for soone he schal do veniaunce of hem. Netheles gessist thou, that mannus sone comynge schal fynde feith in erthe?

9 And he seide also to sum men, that tristiden in hem silf, as thei weren riytful, and dispiseden othere, this parable,

10 seiynge, Twei men wenten vp in to the temple to preye; the toon a Farisee, and the tother a pupplican.

11 And the Farisee stood, and preiede bi hym silf these thingis, and seide, God, Y do thankyngis to thee, for Y am not as other men, raueinouris, vniust, auoutreris, as also this pupplican;

12 Y faste twies in the woke, Y yyue tithis of alle thingis that Y haue in possessioun.

13 And the pupplican stood afer, and wolde nether reise hise iyen to heuene, but smoot his brest, and seide, God be merciful to me, synnere.

14 Treuli Y seie to you, this yede doun in to his hous, and was iustified fro the other. For ech that enhaunsith hym, schal be maad low, and he that mekith hym, schal be enhaunsid.

15 And thei brouyten to hym yonge children, that he schulde touche hem; and whanne the disciplis saien this thing, thei blameden hem.

16 But Jhesus clepide togider hem, and seide, Suffre ye children to come to me, and nyle ye forbede hem, for of siche is the kyngdom of heuenes.

17 Treuli Y seie to you, who euer schal not take the kyngdom of God as a child, he schal not entre in to it.

18 And a prince axide hym, and seide, Goode maister, in what thing doynge schal Y weilde euerlastynge lijf?

19 And Jhesus seide to hym, What seist thou me good? No man is good, but God aloone.

20 Thou knowist the comaundementis, Thou schalt not sle, Thou schalt not do letcherie, Thou schalt not do theft, Thou schalt not seie fals witnessyng, Worschipe thi fadir and thi modir.

21 Which seide, Y haue kept alle these thingis fro my yongthe.

22 And whanne this thing was herd, Jhesus seide to hym, Yit o thing failith 'to thee; sille thou alle thingis that thou hast, and yyue to pore men, and thou schalt haue tresour in heuene; and come, and sue thou me.

23 Whanne these thingis weren herd, he was soreful, for he was ful ryche.

24 And Jhesus seynge hym maad sorie, seide, How hard thei that han money schulen entre in to the kyngdom of God;

25 for it is liyter a camel to passe thorou a nedlis iye, than a riche man to entre in to the kyngdom of God.

26 And thei that herden these thingis seiden, Who may be maad saaf?

27 And he seide to hem, Tho thingis that ben impossible anentis men, ben possible anentis God.

28 But Petir seide, Lo! we han left alle thingis, and han sued thee.

29 And he seide to hym, Treuli Y seie to you, there is no man that schal forsake hous, or fadir, modir, or britheren, or wijf, or children, or feeldis, for the rewme of God,

30 and schal not resseyue many mo thingis in this tyme, and in the world to comynge euerlastynge lijf.

31 And Jhesus took hise twelue disciplis, and seide to hem, Lo! we gon vp to Jerusalem, and alle thingis schulen be endid, that ben writun bi the prophetis of mannus sone.

32 For he schal be bitraied to hethen men, and he schal be scorned, and scourgid, and bispat;

33 and aftir that thei han scourgid, thei schulen sle hym, and the thridde dai he schal rise ayen.

34 And thei vndurstoden no thing of these; and this word was hid fro hem, and thei vndurstoden not tho thingis that weren seid.

35 But it was don, whanne Jhesus cam nyy to Jerico, a blynde man sat bisidis the weie, and beggide.

36 And whanne he herde the puple passynge, he axide, what this was.

37 And thei seiden to hym, that Jhesus of Nazareth passide.

38 And he criede, and seide, Jhesu, the sone of Dauyd, haue mercy on me.

39 And thei that wenten bifor blamyden hym, that he schulde be stille; but he criede myche the more, Thou sone of Dauid, haue mercy on me.

40 And Jhesus stood, and comaundide hym to be brouyt forth to hym. And whanne he cam nyy, he axide hym,

41 and seide, What wolt thou that Y schal do to thee? And he seide, Lord, that Y se.

42 And Jhesus seide to hym, Biholde; thi feith hath maad thee saaf.

43 And anoon he say, and suede hym, and magnyfiede God. And al the puple, as it say, yaf heriyng to God.

CAP 19

1 And Jhesus 'goynge yn, walkide thorou Jericho.

2 And lo! a man, Sache bi name, and this was a prince of pupplicans, and he was riche.

3 And he souyte to se Jhesu, who he was, and he myyte not, for the puple, for he was litil in stature.

4 And he ran bifore, and stiyede in to a sicomoure tree, to se hym; for he was to passe fro thennus.

5 And Jhesus biheld vp, whanne he cam to the place, and saiy hym, and seide to hym, Sache, haste thee, and come doun, for to dai Y mot dwelle in thin hous.

6 And he hiyynge cam doun, and ioiynge resseyuede hym.

7 And whanne alle men sayn, thei grutchiden seiynge, For he hadde turned to a synful man.

8 But Sache stood, and seide to the Lord, Lo! Lord, Y yyue the half of my good to pore men; and if Y haue ony thing defraudid ony man, Y yelde foure so myche.

9 Jhesus seith to hym, For to dai heelthe is maad to this hous, for that he is Abrahams sone;

10 for mannus sone cam to seke, and make saaf that thing that perischide.

11 Whanne thei herden these thingis, he addide, and seide a parable, for that he was nyy Jerusalem, 'and for thei gessiden, that anoon the kyngdom of God schulde be schewid.

12 Therfor he seide, A worthi man wente in to a fer cuntre, to take to hym a kyngdom, and to turne ayen.

13 And whanne hise ten seruauntis weren clepid, he yaf to hem ten besauntis; and seide to hem, Chaffare ye, til Y come.

14 But hise citeseyns hatiden hym, and senten a messanger aftir hym, and seiden, We wolen not, that he regne on vs.

15 And it was don, that he turnede ayen, whan he hadde take the kyngdom; and he comaundide hise seruauntis to be clepid, to whiche he hadde yyue monei, to wite, hou myche ech hadde wonne bi chaffaryng.

16 And the firste cam, and seide, Lord, thi besaunt hath wonne ten besauntis.

17 He seide to hym, Wel be, thou good seruaunt; for in litil thing thou hast be trewe, thou schalt be hauynge power on ten citees.

18 And the tother cam, and seide, Lord, thi besaunt hath maad fyue besauntis.

19 And to this he seide, And be thou on fyue citees.

20 And the thridde cam, and seide, Lord, lo! thi besaunt, that Y hadde, put vp in a sudarie.

21 For Y dredde thee, for thou art 'a sterne man; thou takist awey that that thou settidist not, and thou repist that that thou hast not sowun.

22 He seith to hym, Wickid seruaunt, of thi mouth Y deme thee. Wistist thou, that Y am 'a sterne man, takynge awei that thing that Y settide not, and repyng ethat thing that Y sewe not?

23 and whi hast thou not youun my money to the bord, and Y comynge schulde haue axid it with vsuris?

24 And he seide to men stondynge nyy, Take ye awei fro hym the besaunt, and yyue ye to hym that hath ten beyauntis:

25 And thei seiden to hym, Lord, he hath ten besauntis.

26 And Y seie to you, to ech man that hath, it schal be youun, and he schal encreese; but fro him that hath not, also that thing that he hath, schal be takun of hym.

27 Netheles brynge ye hidur tho myn enemyes, that wolden not that Y regnede on hem, and sle ye bifor me.

28 And whanne these thingis weren seid, he wente bifore, and yede vp to Jerusalem.

29 And it was don, whanne Jhesus cam nyy to Bethfage and Betanye, at the mount, that is clepid of Olyuete, he sente hise twei disciplis, and seide,

30 Go ye in to the castel, that is ayens you; in to which as ye entren, ye schulen fynde a colt of an asse tied, on which neuer man sat; vntye ye hym, and brynge ye to me.

31 And if ony man axe you, whi ye vntien, thus ye schulen seie to hym, For the Lord desirith his werk.

32 And thei that weren sent, wenten forth, and fonden as he seide to hem, a colt stondynge.

33 And whanne thei vntieden the colt, the lordis of hym seiden to hem, What vntien ye the colt?

34 And thei seiden, For the Lord hath nede to hym.

35 And thei ledden hym to Jhesu; and thei castynge her clothis on the colt, setten Jhesu on hym.

36 And whanne he wente, thei strowiden her clothis in the weie.

37 And whanne he cam nyy to the comyng doun of the mount of Olyuete, al the puple that cam doun bygunnen to ioye, and to herie God with greet vois on alle the vertues, that thei hadden sayn,

38 and seiden, Blessid be the king, that cometh in the name of the Lord; pees in heuene, and glorie in hiye thingis.

39 And sum of the Farisees of the puple seiden to hym, Maister, blame thi disciplis.

40 And he seide to hem, Y seie to you, for if these ben stille, stoonus schulen crye.

41 And whanne he neiyede, 'he seiy the citee,

42 and wepte on it, and seide, For if thou haddist knowun, thou schuldist wepe also; for in this dai the thingis ben in pees to thee, but now thei ben hid fro thin iyen.

43 But daies schulen come in thee, and thin enemyes schulen enuyroun thee with a pale, and thei schulen go aboute thee, and make thee streit on alle sidis,

44 and caste thee doun to the erthe, and thi sones that ben in thee; and thei schulen not leeue in thee a stoon on a stoon, for thou hast not knowun the tyme of thi visitacioun.

45 And he entride in to the temple, and bigan to caste out men sellynge ther inne and biynge,

46 and seide to hem, It is writun, That myn hous is an hous of preyer, but ye han maad it a den of theues.

47 And he was techynge euerydai in the temple. And the princis of prestis, and the scribis, and the princis of the puple souyten to lese hym;

48 and thei founden not, what thei schulden do to hym, for al the puple was ocupied, and herde hym.

CAP 20

1 And it was don in oon of the daies, whanne he tauyte the puple in the temple, and prechide the gospel, the princis of preestis and scribis camen togidere with the elder men;

2 and thei seiden to hym, Seie to vs, in what power thou doist these thingis, or who is he that yaf to thee this power?

3 And Jhesus answeride, and seide to hem, And Y schal axe you o word; answere ye to me.

4 Was the baptym of Joon of heuene, or of men?

5 And thei thouyten with ynne hem silf, seiynge, For if we seien, Of heuene, he schal seie, Whi thanne bileuen ye not to hym?

6 and if we seien, Of men, al the puple schal stoone vs; for thei ben certeyn, that Joon is a prophete.

7 And thei answeriden, that thei knewen not, of whennus it was.

8 And Jhesus seide to hem, Nether Y seie to you, in what power Y do these thingis.

9 And he bigan to seie to the puple this parable. A man plauntide a vynyerd, and hiride it to tilieris; and he was in pilgrimage longe tyme.

10 And in the tyme of gaderynge of grapis, he sente a seruaunt to the tilieris, that thei schulden yyue to hym of the fruyt of the vynyerd; whiche beten hym, and leten hym go voide.

11 And he thouyte yit to sende another seruaunt; and thei beten this, and turmentiden hym sore, and leten hym go.

12 And he thouyte yit to sende the thridde, and hym also thei woundiden, and castiden out.

13 And the lord of the vyneyerd seide, What schal Y do? Y schal sende my dereworthe sone; perauenture, whanne thei seen hym, thei schulen drede.

14 And whanne the tilieris sayn hym, thei thouyten with ynne hem silf, and seiden, This is the eire, sle we hym, that the eritage be oure.

15 And thei castiden hym out of the vyneyerd, and killiden hym. What schal thanne the lord of the vyneyerd do to hem?

16 He schal come, and distruye these tilieris, and yyue the vyneyerd to othere. And whanne this thing was herd, thei seiden to hym, God forbede.

17 But he bihelde hem, and seide, What thanne is this that is writun, The stoon which men bildynge repreueden, this is maad in to the heed of the corner?

18 Ech that schal falle on that stoon, schal be to-brisid, but on whom it schal falle, it schal al to-breke him.

19 And the princis of prestis, and scribis, souyten to leye on hym hoondis in that our, and thei dredden the puple; for thei knewen that to hem he seide this liknesse.

20 And thei aspieden, and senten aspieris, that feyneden hem iust, that thei schulden take hym in word, and bitaak hym to the 'power of the prince, and to the power of the iustice.

21 And thei axiden hym, and seiden, Maister, we witen, that riytli thou seist and techist; and thou takist not the persoone of man, but thou techist in treuthe the weie of God.

22 Is it leueful to vs to yyue tribute to the emperoure, or nay?

23 And he biheld the disseit of hem, and seide to hem, What tempten ye me?

24 Shewe ye to me a peny; whos ymage and superscripcioun hath it? Thei answerden, and seiden to hym, The emperouris.

25 And he seide to hem, Yelde ye therfor to the emperoure tho thingis that ben the emperours, and tho thingis that ben of God, to God.

26 And thei myyten not repreue his word bifor the puple; and thei wondriden in his answere, and heelden pees.

27 Summe of the Saduceis, that denyeden the ayenrisyng fro deeth to lijf, camen, and axiden hym,

28 and seiden, Maister, Moises wroot to vs, if the brother of ony man haue a wijf, and be deed, and he was with outen eiris, that his brothir take his wijf, and reise seed to his brother.

29 And so there weren seuene britheren. The firste took a wijf, and is deed with outen eiris;

30 and the brothir suynge took hir, and he is deed with outen sone;

31 and the thridde took hir; also and alle seuene, and leften not seed, but ben deed;

32 and the laste of alle the womman is deed.

33 Therfor in the 'risyng ayen, whos wijf of hem schal sche be? for seuene hadden hir to wijf.

34 And Jhesus seide to hem, Sones of this world wedden, and ben youun to weddyngis;

35 but thei that schulen be had worthi of that world, and of the 'risyng ayen fro deeth, nethir ben wedded,

36 nethir wedden wyues, nethir schulen mowe die more; for thei ben euen with aungels, and ben the sones of God, sithen thei ben the sones of 'risyng ayen fro deeth.

37 And that deed men risen ayen, also Moises schewide bisidis the busch, as he seith, The Lord God of Abraham, and God of Ysaac, and God of Jacob.

38 And God is not of deed men, but of lyuynge men; for alle men lyuen to hym.

39 And summe of scribis answeringe, seiden, Maistir, thou hast wel seid.

40 And thei dursten no more axe hym ony thing.

41 But he seide to hem, How seien men, Crist to be the sone of Dauid,

42 and Dauid hym silf seith in the book of Salmes, The Lord seide to my lord, Sitte thou on my riythalf,

43 til that Y putte thin enemyes a stool of thi feet?

44 Therfor Dauid clepith hym lord, and hou is he his sone?

45 And in heryng of al the puple, he seide to hise disciplis,

46 Be ye war of scribis, that wolen wandre in stolis, and louen salutaciouns in chepyng, and the firste chaieris in synagogis, and the firste sittynge placis in feestis;

47 that deuouren the housis of widewis, and feynen long preiyng; these schulen take the more dampnacioun.

CAP 21

1 And he biheeld, and saye tho riche men, that casten her yiftis in to the treserie;

2 but he saye also a litil pore widewe castynge twei ferthingis.

3 And he seide, Treuli Y seie to you, that this pore widewe keste more than alle men.

4 For whi alle these of thing that was plenteuouse to hem casten in to the yiftis of God; but this widewe of that thing that failide to hir, caste al hir liflode, that sche hadde.

5 And whanne sum men seiden of the temple, that it was apparailid with gode stoonus and yiftis,

6 he seide, These thingis that ye seen, daies schulen come, in whiche a stoon schal not be left on a stoon, which schal not be destried.

7 And thei axiden hym, and seiden, Comaundour, whanne schulen these thingis be? and what tokne schal be, whanne thei schulen bigynne to be don?

8 And he seide, Se ye, that ye be not disseyued; for many schulen come in my name, seiynge, For Y am, and the tyme schal neiye; therfor nyle ye go aftir hem.

9 And whanne ye schulen here batailis and stryues with ynne, nyle ye be aferd; it bihoueth first these thingis to be don, but not yit anoon is an ende.

10 Thanne he seide to hem, Folk schal rise ayens folk, and rewme ayens rewme;

11 grete mouyngis of erthe schulen be bi placis, and pestilencis, and hungris, and dredis fro heuene, and grete tokenes schulen be.

12 But bifore alle these thingis thei schulen sette her hoondis on you, and schulen pursue, bitakynge in to synagogis and kepyngis, drawynge to kyngis and to iusticis, for my name;

13 but it schal falle to you in to witnessyng.

14 Therfor putte ye in youre hertis, not to thenke bifore, hou ye schulen answere; for Y schal yyue to you mouth and wisdom,

15 to whiche alle youre aduersaries schulen not mowe ayenstonde, and ayenseie.

16 And ye schulen be takun of fadir, and modir, and britheren, and cosyns, and freendis, and bi deeth thei schulen turmente of you;

17 and ye schulen be in haate to alle men for my name.

18 And an heere of youre heed schal not perische;

19 in youre pacience ye schulen welde youre soulis.

20 But whanne ye schulen se Jerusalem ben enuyround with an oost, thanne wite ye, that the desolacioun of it schal neiye;

21 Thanne thei that ben in Judee, fle to the mountans; and thei that ben in the mydil of it, gon awei; and thei that ben in the cuntreis, entre not in to it.

22 For these ben daies of veniaunce, that alle thingis that ben writun, be fulfillid.

23 And wo to hem, that ben with child, and norischen in tho daies; for a greet diseese schal be on the erthe, and wraththe to this puple.

24 And thei schulen falle bi the scharpnesse of swerd, and thei schulen be led prisoneris in to alle folkis; and Jerusalem schal be defoulid of hethene men, til the tymes of naciouns be fulfillid.

25 And tokenes schulen be in the sunne, and the mone, and in the sterris; and in the erthe ouerleiyng of folkis, for confusioun of sown of the see and of floodis;

26 for men schulen wexe drye for drede and abidyng that schulen come to al the world; for vertues of heuenes schulen be mouyd.

27 And thanne thei schulen se mannys sone comynge in a cloude, with greet power and maieste.

28 And whanne these thingis bigynnen to be maad, biholde ye, and reise ye youre heedis, for youre redempcioun neiyeth.

29 And he seide to hem a liknesse, Se ye the fige tre, and alle trees,

30 whanne thei bryngen forth now of hem silf fruyt, ye witen that somer is nyy;

31 so ye, whanne ye seen these thingis to be don, wite ye, that the kyngdom of God is nyy.

32 Treuli Y seie to you, that this generacioun schal not passe, til alle thingis be don.

33 Heuene and erthe schulen passe, but my wordis schulen not passe.

34 But take ye heede to you silf, lest perauenture youre hertis be greuyd with glotony, and drunkenesse, and bisynessis of this lijf, and thilke dai come sodein on you; for as a snare it schal come on alle men,

35 that sitten on the face of al erthe.

36 Therfor wake ye, preiynge in ech tyme, that ye be hadde worthi to fle alle these thingis that ben to come, and to stonde bifor mannus sone.

37 And in daies he was techynge in the temple, but in nyytis he yede out, and dwellide in the mount, that is clepid of Oly-uet.

38 And al the puple roos eerli, to come to hym in the temple, and to here hym.

CAP 22

1 And the halidai of therf looues, that is seid pask, neiyede.

2 And the princis of preestis and the scribis souyten, hou thei schulden sle Jhesu, but thei dredden the puple.

3 And Sathanas entride in to Judas, that was clepid Scarioth, oon of the twelue.

4 And he wente, and spak with the princis of preestis, and with the magistratis, hou he schulde bitray hym to hem.

5 And thei ioyeden, and maden couenaunt to yyue hym money.

6 And he bihiyte, and he souyte oportunyte, to bitraye hym, with outen puple.

7 But the daies of therf looues camen, in whiche it was neede, that the sacrifice of pask were slayn.

8 And he sente Petre and Joon, and seide, Go ye, and make ye redi to vs the pask, that we ete.

9 And thei seiden, Where wolt thou, that we make redi?

10 And he seide to hem, Lo! whanne ye schulen entre in to the citee, a man berynge a vessel of watir schal meete you; sue ye hym in to the hous, in to which he entrith.

11 And ye schulen seie to the hosebonde man of the hous, The maister seith to thee, Where is a chaumbre, where Y schal ete the pask with my disciplis?

12 And he schal schewe to you a greet soupyng place strewid, and there make ye redi.

13 And thei yeden, and founden as he seide to hem, and thei maden redi the pask.

14 And whanne the our was come, he sat to the mete, and the twelue apostlis with hym.

15 And he seide to hem, With desier Y haue desirid to ete with you this pask, bifor that Y suffre;

16 for Y seie to you, that fro this tyme Y schal not ete it, til it be fulfillid in the rewme of God.

17 And whanne he hadde take the cuppe, he dide gracis, and seide, Take ye, and departe ye among you;

18 for Y seie to you, that Y schal not drynke of the kynde of this vyne, til the rewme of God come.

19 And whanne he hadde take breed, he dide thankyngis, and brak, and yaf to hem, and seide, This is my bodi, that schal be youun for you; do ye this thing in mynde of me.

20 He took also the cuppe, aftir that he hadde soupid, and seide, This cuppe is the newe testament in my blood, that schal be sched for you.

21 Netheles lo! the hoond of hym that bitraieth me, is with me at the table.

22 And mannus sone goith, 'aftir that it is determyned; netheles wo to that man, bi whom he schal be bitraied.

23 And thei bigunnen to seke among hem, who it was of hem, that was to do this thing.

24 And strijf was maad among hem, which of hem schulde be seyn to be grettest.

25 But he seide to hem, Kyngis of hethen men ben lordis of hem, and thei that han power on hem ben clepid good doeris, but ye not so;

26 but he that is grettest among you, be maad as yongere, and he that is bifor goere, as a seruaunt.

27 For who is gretter, he that sittith at the mete, or he that mynystrith? whether not he that sittith at the mete? And Y am in the myddil of you, as he that mynystrith.

28 And ye ben, that han dwellid with me in my temptaciouns; and Y dispose to you,

29 as my fadir hath disposid to me,

30 a rewme, that ye ete and drynke on my boord in my rewme, and sitte on trones, and deme the twelue kynredis of Israel.

31 And the Lord seide to Symount, Symount, lo, Satanas hath axid you, that he schulde ridile as whete; but Y haue preyede for thee,

32 that thi feith faile not; and thou sum tyme conuertid, conferme thi britheren.

33 Which seide to hym, Lord, Y am redi to go in to prisoun and in to deeth with thee.

34 And he seide, Y seie to thee, Petir, the cok schal not crowe to dai, til thou thries forsake that thou knowist me.

35 And he seide to hem, Whanne Y sente you with outen sachel, and scrippe, and schone, whether ony thing failide to you?

36 And thei seiden, No thing. Therfor he seide to hem, But now he that hath a sachel, take also and a scrippe; and he that hath noon, selle his coote, and bigge a swerd.

37 For Y seie to you, that yit it bihoueth that thing that is writun to be fulfillid in me, And he is arettid with wickid men; for tho thingis that ben of me han ende.

38 And thei seiden, Lord, lo! twei swerdis here. And he seide to hem, It is ynowy.

39 And he yede out, and wente aftir the custom in to the hille of Olyues; and the disciplis sueden hym.

40 And whanne he cam to the place, he seide to hem, Preye ye, lest ye entren in to temptacioun.

41 And he was taken awei fro hem, so myche as is a stonys cast; and he knelide,

42 and preyede, and seide, Fadir, if thou wolt, do awei this cuppe fro me; netheles not my wille be don, but thin.

43 And an aungel apperide to hym fro heuene, and coumfortide hym. And he was maad in agonye, and preyede the lenger;

44 and his swot was maad as dropis of blood rennynge doun in to the erthe.

45 And whanne he was rysun fro preier, and was comun to hise disciplis, he foond hem slepynge for heuynesse.

46 And he seide to hem, What slepen ye? Rise ye, and preye ye, that ye entre not in to temptacioun.

47 Yit while he spak, lo! a company, and he that was clepid Judas, oon of the twelue, wente bifor hem; and he cam to Jhesu, to kisse hym.

48 And Jhesus seide to hym, Judas, 'with a coss 'thou bytrayest 'mannys sone.

49 And thei that weren aboute hym, and sayn that that was to come, seiden to hym, Lord, whether we smyten with swerd?

50 And oon of hem smoot the seruaunt of the prince of preestis, and kittide of his riyt eere.

51 But Jhesus answerde, and seide, Suffre ye til hidir. And whanne he hadde touchid his eere, he heelide hym.

52 And Jhesus seide to hem, that camen to hym, the princis of preestis, and maiestratis of the temple, and eldre men, As to a theef ye han gon out with swerdis and staues?

53 Whanne Y was ech dai with you in the temple, ye streiyten not out hondis in to me; but this is youre our, and the power of derknessis.

54 And thei token him, and ledden to the hous of the prince of prestis; and Petir suede hym afer.

55 And whanne a fier was kyndelid in the myddil of the greet hous, and thei saten aboute, Petir was in the myddil of hem.

56 Whom whanne a damysel hadde seyn sittynge 'at the liyt, and hadde biholdun hym, sche seide, And this was with hym.

57 And he denyede hym, and seide, Womman, Y knowe hym not.

58 And aftir a litil another man siy hym, and seide, And thou art of hem. But Petir seide, A! man, Y am not.

59 And whanne a space was maad as of on our, another affermyd, and seide, Treuli this was with hym; for also he is of Galilee.

60 And Petir seide, Man, Y noot what thou seist. And anoon yit while he spak, the cok crewe.

61 And the Lord turnede ayen, and bihelde Petre; and Petre hadde mynde on the word of Jhesu, as he hadde seid, For bifor that the cok crowe, thries thou schalt denye me.

62 And Petre yede out, and wepte bittirli.

63 And the men that helden hym scorneden hym, and smyten hym.

64 And thei blynfelden hym, and smyten his face, and axiden hym, and seiden, Arede, thou Crist, to vs, who is he that smoot thee?

65 Also thei blasfemynge seiden ayens hym many other thingis.

66 And as the day was come, the eldre men of the puple, and the princis of prestis, and the scribis camen togidir, and ledden hym in to her councel,

67 and seiden, If thou art Crist, seie to vs.

68 And he seide to hem, If Y seie to you, ye schulen not bileue to me; and if Y axe, ye schulen not answere to me, nethir ye schulen delyuere me.

69 But aftir this tyme mannys sone schal be sittynge on the riyt half of the vertu of God.

70 Therfor alle seiden, Thanne art thou the sone of God? And he seide, Ye seien that Y am.

71 And thei seiden, What yit desiren we witnessyng? for we vs silf han herd of his mouth.

CAP 23

1 And al the multitude of hem arysen, and ledden hym to Pilat.

2 And thei bigunnen to accuse hym, and seiden, We han foundun this turnynge vpsodoun oure folk, and forbedynge tributis to be youun to the emperour, and seiynge that hym silf is Crist and kyng.

3 And Pilat axide hym, and seide, Art thou kyng of Jewis? And he answeride, and seide, Thou seist.

4 And Pilat seide to the princis of prestis, and to the puple, Y fynde no thing of cause in this man.

5 And thei woxen stronger, and seiden, He moueth the puple, techynge thorou al Judee, bigynnynge fro Galile til hidir.

6 And Pilat herynge Galile axide, if he were a man of Galile.

7 And whanne he knewe that he was of the powere of Eroude, he sente hym to Eroude; which was at Jerusalem in tho daies.

8 And whanne Eroude siy Jhesu, he ioyede ful myche; for long tyme he coueitide to se hym, for he herde many thingis of hym, and hopide to see sum tokene 'to be don of hym.

9 And he axide hym in many wordis; and he answeride no thing to hym.

10 And the princis of preestis and the scribis stoden, stidfastli accusynge hym.

11 But Eroude with his oost dispiside hym, and scornede hym, and clothide with a white cloth, and sente hym ayen to Pilat.

12 And Eroude and Pilat weren maad freendis fro that dai; for bifor thei weren enemyes togidre.

13 And Pilat clepide togider the princis of prestis and the maiestratis of the puple, and seide to hem,

14 Ye han brouyt to me this man, as turnynge awey the puple, and lo! Y axynge bifor you fynde no cause in this man of these thingis, in whiche ye accusen hym;

15 nether Eroude, for he hath sent hym ayen to vs, and lo! no thing worthi of deth is don to hym.

16 And therfor Y schal amende hym, and delyuere hym.

17 But he moste nede delyuer to hem oon bi the feest dai.

18 And al the puple criede togidir, and seide, Do 'awei hym, and delyuer to vs Barabas;

19 which was sent 'in to prisoun for disturblyng maad in the cite, and for mansleynge.

20 And eftsoone Pilat spak to hem, and wolde delyuer Jhesu.

21 And thei vndurcrieden, and seiden, Crucifie, crucifie hym.

22 And the thridde tyme he seide to hem, For what yuel hath this don? Y fynde no cause of deeth in hym; therfor Y schal chastise hym, and Y schal delyuer.

23 And thei contynueden with greet voicis axynge, that he schulde be crucified; and the voicis of hem woxen stronge.

24 And Pilat demyde her axyng to be don.

25 And he delyueride to hem hym, that for mansleyng and sedicioun was sent in to prisoun, whom thei axiden; but he bitook Jhesu to her wille.

26 And whanne thei ledden hym, thei token a man, Symon of Syrenen, comynge fro the toun, and thei leiden on hym the cross to bere aftir Jhesu.

27 And there suede hym myche puple, and wymmen that weiliden, and bymorneden hym.

28 And Jhesus turnede to hem, and seide, Douytris of Jerusalem, nyle ye wepe on me, but wepe ye on youre silf and on youre sones.

29 For lo! daies schulen come, in whiche it schal be seid, Blessid be bareyn wymmen, and wombis that han not borun children, and the tetis that han not youun souke.

30 Thanne thei schulen bigynne to seie to mounteyns, Falle ye doun on vs, and to smale hillis, Keuere ye vs.

31 For if in a greene tre thei don these thingis, what schal be don in a drie?

32 Also othere twei wickid men weren led with hym, to be slayn.

33 And 'aftir that thei camen in to a place, that is clepid of Caluerie, there thei crucifieden hym, and the theues, oon on the riyt half, and 'the tother on the left half.

34 But Jhesus seide, Fadir, foryyue hem, for thei witen not what thei doon.

35 And thei departiden his clothis, and kesten lottis. And the puple stood abidynge; and the princis scorneden hym with hem, and seiden, Othere men he maad saaf; make he hym silf saaf, if this be Crist, the chosun of God.

36 And the knyytis neiyeden, and scorneden hym, and profreden vynegre to hym,

37 and seiden, If thou art king of Jewis, make thee saaf.

38 And the superscripcioun was writun ouer hym with Greke lettris, and of Latyn, and of Ebreu, This is the kyng of Jewis.

39 And oon of these theues that hangiden, blasfemyde hym, and seide, If thou art Crist, make thi silf saaf and vs.

40 But 'the tothir answerynge, blamyde hym, and seide, Nether thou dredist God, that art in the same dampnacioun?

41 And treuli we iustli, for we han resseiued worthi thingis to werkis; but this dide no thing of yuel.

42 And he seide to Jhesu, Lord, haue mynde of me, whanne thou comest 'in to thi kyngdom.

43 And Jhesus seide to hym, Treuli Y seie to thee, this dai thou schalt be with me in paradise.

44 And it was almest the sixte our, and derknessis weren maad in al the erthe 'in to the nynthe our.

45 And the sun was maad derk, and the veile of the temple was to-rent atwo.

46 And Jhesus criynge with a greet vois, seide, Fadir, in to thin hoondis Y bitake my spirit. And he seiynge these thingis, yaf vp the goost.

47 And the centurien seynge that thing that was don, glorifiede God, and seide, Verili this man was iust.

48 And al the puple of hem that weren there togidir at this spectacle, and sayn tho thingis that weren don, smyten her brestis, and turneden ayen.

49 But alle his knowun stoden afer, and wymmen that sueden hym fro Galile, seynge these thingis.

50 And lo! a man, Joseph bi name, of Aramathie, a cite of Judee, that was a decurien, a good man and a iust,

51 this man concentide not to the counseil and to the dedis of hem; and he abood the kyngdom of God.

52 This Joseph cam to Pilat, and axide the bodi of Jhesu,

53 and took it doun, and wlappide it in a cleene lynen cloth, and leide hym in a graue hewun, in which not yit ony man hadde be leid.

54 And the dai was the euen of the halidai, and the sabat bigan to schyne.

55 And the wymmen suynge, that camen with hym fro Galile, sayn the graue, and hou his bodi was leid.

56 And thei turneden ayen, and maden redi swete smellynge spicis, and oynementis; but in the sabat thei restiden, aftir the comaundement.

CAP 24

1 But in o dai of the woke ful eerli thei camen to the graue, and brouyten swete smellynge spices, that thei hadden arayed.

2 And thei founden the stoon turned awei fro the graue.

3 And thei yeden in, and founden not the bodi of the Lord Jhesu.

4 And it was don, the while thei weren astonyed in thouyt of this thing, lo! twei men stoden bisidis hem in schynynge cloth.

5 And whanne thei dredden, and boweden her semblaunt in to the erthe, thei seiden to hem, What seken ye hym that lyueth with deed men?

6 He is not here, but is risun. Haue ye mynde, hou he spak to you, whanne he was yit in Galile,

7 and seide, For it bihoueth mannys sone to be bitakun in to the hondis of synful men, and to be crucified, and the thridde dai to rise ayen.

8 And thei bithouyten on hise wordis.

9 And thei yeden ayen fro the graue, and telden alle these thingis to the enleuene, and to alle othir.

10 And ther was Marie Mawdeleyn, and Joone, and Marie of James, and other wymmen that weren with hem, that seiden to apostlis these thingis.

11 And these wordis weren seyn bifor hem as madnesse, and thei bileueden not to hem.

12 But Petir roos vp, and ran to the graue; and he bowide doun, and say the lynen clothis liynge aloone. And he wente bi him silf, wondrynge on that that was don.

13 And lo! tweyne of hem wenten in that dai in to a castel, that was fro Jerusalem the space of sixti furlongis, bi name Emaws.

14 And thei spaken togidir of alle these thingis that haddun bifallun.

15 And it was don, the while thei talkiden, and souyten bi hem silf, Jhesus hym silf neiyede, and wente with hem.

16 But her iyen weren holdun, that thei knewen him not.

17 And he seide to hem, What ben these wordis, that ye speken togidir wandrynge, and ye ben sorewful?

18 And oon, whos name was Cleofas, answerde, and seide, Thou thi silf art a pilgrym in Jerusalem, and hast thou not knowun, what thingis ben don in it in these daies?

19 To whom he seide, What thingis? And thei seiden to hym, Of Jhesu of Nazareth, that was a man prophete, myyti in werk and word bifor God and al the puple;

20 and hou the heiyest preestis of oure princis bitoken hym in to dampnacioun of deeth, and crucifieden hym.

21 But we hopiden, that he schulde haue ayenbouyt Israel. And now on alle these thingis the thridde dai is to dai, that these thingis weren don.

22 But also summe wymmen of ouris maden vs afered, whiche bifor dai weren at the graue; and whanne his bodi was not foundun,

23 thei camen, and seiden, that thei syen also a siyt of aungels, whiche seien, that he lyueth.

24 And summe of oure wenten to the graue, and thei founden so as the wymmen seiden, but thei founden not hym.

25 And he seide to hem, A! foolis, and slowe of herte to bileue in alle thingis that the prophetis han spokun.

26 Whethir it bihofte not Crist to suffre these thingis, and so to entre in to his glorie?

27 And he bigan at Moises and at alle the prophetis, and declaride to hem in alle scripturis, that weren of hym.

28 And thei camen nyy the castel, whidur thei wenten. And he made countenaunce that he wolde go ferthere.

29 And thei constreyneden hym, and seiden, Dwelle with vs, for it drawith to nyyt, and the dai is now bowid doun.

30 And he entride with hem. And it was don, while he sat at the mete with hem, he took breed, and blesside, and brak, and took to hem.

31 And the iyen of hem weren openyd, and thei knewen hym; and he vanyschide fro her iyen.

32 And thei seiden togidir, Whether oure herte was not bren-nynge in vs, while he spak in the weie, and openyde to vs scripturis?

33 And thei risen vp in the same our, and wenten ayen in to Jerusalem, and founden the enleuene gaderid togidir, and hem that weren with hem,

34 seiynge, That the Lord is risun verrili, and apperide to Symount.

35 And thei tolden what thingis weren don in the weie, and hou thei knewen hym in brekyng of breed.

36 And the while thei spaken these thingis, Jhesus stood in the myddil of hem, and seide to hem, Pees to you; Y am, nyle ye drede.

37 But thei weren affraied and agast, and gessiden hem to se a spirit.

38 And he seide to hem, What ben ye troblid, and thouytis comen vp in to youre hertis?

39 Se ye my hoondis and my feet, for Y my silf am. Fele ye, and se ye; for a spirit hath not fleisch and boonys, as ye seen that Y haue.

40 And whanne he hadde seid this thing, he schewide hoondis and feet to hem.

41 And yit while thei bileueden not, and wondriden for ioye, he seide, Han ye here ony thing that schal be etun?

42 And thei proferden hym a part of a fisch rostid, and an hony combe.

43 And whanne he hadde etun bifore hem, he took that that lefte, and yaf to hem;

44 and seide 'to hem, These ben the wordis that Y spak to you, whanne Y was yit with you; for it is nede that alle thingis ben fulfillid, that ben writun in the lawe of Moises, and in prophetis, and in salmes, of me.

45 Thanne he openyde to hem wit, that thei schulden vnder-stonde scripturis.

46 And he seide to hem, For thus it is writun, and thus it bihofte Crist to suffre, and ryse ayen fro deeth in the thridde dai;

47 and penaunce and remyssioun of synnes to be prechid in his name 'in to alle folkis, bigynnynge at Jerusalem.

48 And ye ben witnessis of these thingis.

49 And Y schal sende the biheest of my fadir in to you; but sitte ye in the citee, til that ye be clothid with vertu from an hiy.

50 And he ledde hem forth in to Betanye, and whanne his hondis weren lift vp, he blesside hem.

51 And it was don, the while he blesside hem, he departide fro hem, and was borun in to heuene.

52 And thei worschipiden, and wenten ayen in to Jerusalem with greet ioye,

53 and weren euermore in the temple, heriynge and blessynge God.

JOHN

CAP 1

1 In the bigynnyng was the word, and the word was at God, and God was the word.

2 This was in the bigynnyng at God.

3 Alle thingis weren maad bi hym, and withouten hym was maad no thing, that thing that was maad.

4 In hym was lijf, and the lijf was the liyt of men; and the liyt schyneth in derknessis,

5 and derknessis comprehendiden not it.

6 A man was sent fro God, to whom the name was Joon.

7 This man cam in to witnessyng, that he schulde bere wit-nessing of the liyt, that alle men schulden bileue bi hym.

8 He was not the liyt, but that he schulde bere witnessing of the liyt.

9 There was a very liyt, which liytneth ech man that cometh in to this world.

10 He was in the world, and the world was maad bi hym, and the world knew hym not.

11 He cam in to his owne thingis, and hise resseyueden hym not.

12 But hou many euer resseyueden hym, he yaf to hem power to be maad the sones of God, to hem that bileueden in his name; the whiche not of bloodis,

13 nether of the wille of fleische, nether of the wille of man, but ben borun of God.

14 And the word was maad man, and dwellyde among vs, and we han seyn the glorie of hym, as the glorie of the 'oon bige-tun sone of the fadir, ful of grace and of treuthe.

15 Joon berith witnessyng of hym, and crieth, and seith, This is, whom Y seide, He that schal come aftir me, is maad bifore me, for he was tofor me;

16 and of the plente of hym we alle han takun, and grace for grace.

17 For the lawe was youun bi Moises; but grace and treuthe 'is maad bi Jhesu Crist.

18 No man sai euer God, no but the 'oon bigetun sone, that is in the bosum of the fadir, he hath teld out.

19 And this is the witnessyng of Joon, whanne Jewis senten fro Jerusalem prestis and dekenes to hym, that thei schulden axe hym, Who art thou?

20 He knoulechide, and denyede not, and he knoulechide, For Y am not Crist.

21 And thei axiden hym, What thanne? Art thou Elie? And he seide, Y am not. Art thou a profete? And he answeride, Nay.

22 Therfor thei seiden to hym, Who art thou? that we yyue an answere to these that senten vs. What seist thou of thi silf?

23 He seide, Y am a vois of a crier in deseert, Dresse ye the weie of the Lord, as Ysaie, the prophete, seide.

24 And thei that weren sent, weren of the Fariseis.

25 And thei axiden hym, and seiden to hym, What thanne baptisist thou, if thou art not Crist, nether Elie, nether a pro-fete?

26 Joon answeride to hem, and seide, Y baptise in watir, but in the myddil of you hath stonde oon, that ye knowen not;

27 he it is, that schal come aftir me, that was maad bifor me, of whom Y am not worthi to louse the thwong of his schoo.

28 These thingis weren don in Bethanye biyende Jordan, where Joon was baptisyng.

29 Anothir day Joon say Jhesu comynge to hym, and he seide, Lo! the lomb of God; lo! he that doith awei the synnes of the world.

30 This is he, that Y seide of, Aftir me is comun a man, which was maad bifor me; for he was rather than Y.

31 And Y knew hym not, but that he be schewid in Israel, therfor Y cam baptisynge in watir.

32 And Joon bar witnessyng, and seide, That Y saiy the spirit comynge doun as a culuer fro heuene, and dwellide on hym.

33 And Y knew hym not; but he that sente me to baptise in watir, seide to me, On whom thou seest the Spirit comynge doun, and dwellynge on hym, this is he, that baptisith in the Hooli Goost.

34 And Y say, and bar witnessyng, that this is the sone of God.

35 Anothir dai Joon stood, and tweyne of hise disciplis;

36 and he biheeld Jhesu walkinge, and seith, Lo! the lomb of God.

37 And twei disciplis herden hym spekynge,

38 and foleweden Jhesu. And Jhesu turnede, and say hem suynge hym, and seith to hem, What seken ye? And thei seiden to hym, Rabi, that is to seie, Maistir, where dwellist thou?

39 And he seith to hem, Come ye, and se. And thei camen, and sayn where he dwellide; and dwelten with hym that dai. And it was as the tenthe our.

40 And Andrewe, the brother of Symount Petir, was oon of the tweyne, that herden of Joon, and hadden sued hym.

41 This foond first his brother Symount, and he seide to him, We han foundun Messias, that is to seie, Crist; and he ledde him to Jhesu.

42 And Jhesus bihelde hym, and seide, Thou art Symount, the sone of Johanna; thou schalt be clepid Cefas, that is to seie, Petre.

43 And on the morewe he wolde go out in to Galilee, and he foond Filip; and he seith to hym, Sue thou me.

44 Filip was of Bethsaida, the citee of Andrew and of Petre.

45 Filip foond Nathanael, and seide to hym, We han foundun Jhesu, the sone of Joseph, of Nazareth, whom Moyses wroot in the lawe and profetis.

46 And Nathanael seide to hym, Of Nazareth may sum good thing be?

47 Filip seide to hym, Come, and se. Jhesus siy Nathanael comynge to hym, and seide to hym, Lo! verili a man of Israel, in whom is no gile.

48 Nathanael seide to hym, Wherof hast thou knowun me? Jhesus 'answerde, and seide to hym, Bifor that Filip clepide thee, whanne thou were vndur the fige tree, Y saiy thee. Nathanael answerde to hym,

49 'and seide, Rabi, thou art the sone of God, thou art kyng of Israel.

50 Jhesus answerde, and seide to hym, For Y seide to thee, Y sawy thee vndur the fige tre, thou bileuest; thou schalt se more than these thingis.

51 And he seide to hem, Treuli, treuli, Y seie to you, ye schulen se heuene opened, and the aungels of God stiynge vp and comynge doun on mannys sone.

CAP 2

1 And the thridde dai weddyngis weren maad in the Cane of Galilee; and the modir of Jhesu was there.

2 And Jhesus was clepid, and hise disciplis, to the weddyngis.

3 And whanne wijn failide, the modir of Jhesu seide to hym, Thei han not wijn.

4 And Jhesus seith to hir, What to me and to thee, womman? myn our cam not yit.

5 His modir seith to the mynystris, What euere thing he seie to you, do ye.

6 And there weren set 'sixe stonun cannes, aftir the clensyng of the Jewis, holdynge ech tweyne ether thre metretis.

7 And Jhesus seith to hem, Fille ye the pottis with watir. And thei filliden hem, vp to the mouth.

8 And Jhesus seide to hem, Drawe ye now, and bere ye to the architriclyn. And thei baren.

9 And whanne the architriclyn hadde tastid the watir maad wiyn, and wiste not wherof it was, but the mynystris wisten that drowen the watir, the architriclyn clepith the spouse,

10 and seith to hym, Ech man settith first good wiyn, and whanne men ben fulfillid, thanne that that is worse; but thou hast kept the good wiyn 'in to this tyme.

11 Jhesus dide this the bigynnyng of signes in the Cane of Galilee, and schewide his glorie; and hise disciplis bileueden in hym.

12 Aftir these thingis he cam doun to Cafarnaum, and his modir, and hise britheren, and hise disciplis; and thei dwelliden 'there not many daies.

13 And the pask of Jewis was nyy, and Jhesus wente vp to Jerusalem.

14 And he foond in the temple men sillynge oxun, and scheep, and culueris, and chaungeris sittynge.

15 And whanne he hadde maad as it were a scourge of smale cordis, he droof out alle of the temple, and oxun, and scheep; and he schedde the money of chaungeris, and turnede vpsedoun the boordis.

16 And he seide to hem that selden culueris, Take awei fro hennus these thingis, and nyle ye make the hous of my fadir an hous of marchaundise.

17 And hise disciplis hadden mynde, for it was writun, The feruent loue of thin hous hath etun me.

18 Therfor the Jewis answeriden, and seiden to hym, What token schewist thou to vs, that thou doist these thingis?

19 Jhesus answerde, and seide to hem, Vndo ye this temple, and in thre daies Y schal reise it.

20 Therfor the Jewis seiden to hym, In fourti and sixe yeer this temple was bildid, and schalt thou in thre daies reise it?

21 But he seide of the temple of his bodi.

22 Therfor whanne he was risun fro deeth, hise disciplis hadden mynde, that he seide these thingis of his bodi; and thei bileueden to the scripture, and to the word that Jhesus seide.

23 And whanne Jhesus was at Jerusalem in pask, in the feeste dai, many bileueden in his name, seynge his signes that he dide.

24 But Jhesus trowide not hym silf to hem, for he knewe alle men;

25 and for it was not nede to hym, that ony man schulde bere witnessyng, for he wiste, what was in man.

CAP 3

1 And there was a man of the Farisees, Nychodeme bi name, a prince of the Jewis.

2 And he cam to Jhesu bi niyt, and seide to hym, Rabi, we witen, that thou art comun fro God maister; for no man may do these signes, that thou doist, but God be with hym.

3 Jhesus answerde, and seide to hym, Treuli, treuli, Y seie to thee, but a man be borun ayen, he may not se the kyngdom of God.

4 Nychodeme seide to hym, Hou may a man be borun, whanne he is eeld? whether he may entre ayen in to his modris wombe, and be borun ayen?

5 Jhesus answeride, Treuli, treuli, Y seie to thee, but a man be borun ayen of watir, and of the Hooli Goost, he may not entre in to the kyngdom of God.

6 'That that is borun of the fleisch, is fleisch; and 'that that is borun of spirit, is spirit.

7 Wondre thou not, for Y seide to thee, It bihoueth you to be borun ayen.

8 The spirit brethith where he wole, and thou herist his vois, but thou wost not, fro whennus he cometh, ne whidir he goith; so is ech man that is borun of the spirit.

9 Nychodeme answeride, and seide to hym, Hou moun these thingis be don?

10 Jhesus answeride, and seide to hym, Thou art a maister in Israel, and knowist not these thingis?

11 Treuli, treuli, Y seie to thee, for we speken that that we witen, and we witnessen that that we han seyn, and ye taken not oure witnessyng.

12 If Y haue seid to you ertheli thingis, and ye bileuen not, hou if Y seie to you heueneli thingis, schulen ye bileue?

13 And no man stieth in to heuene, but he that cam doun fro heuene, mannys sone that is in heuene.

14 And as Moises areride a serpent in desert, so it bihoueth mannys sone to be reisid,

15 that ech man that bileueth in hym, perische not, but haue euerlastynge lijf.

16 For God louede so the world, that he yaf his 'oon bigetun sone, that ech man that bileueth in him perische not, but haue euerlastynge lijf.

17 For God sente not his sone in to the world, that he iuge the world, but that the world be saued bi him.

18 He that bileueth in hym, is not demed; but he that bileueth not, is now demed, for he bileueth not in the name of the 'oon bigetun sone of God.

19 And this is the dom, for liyt cam in to the world, and men loueden more derknessis than liyt; for her werkes weren yuele.

20 For ech man that doith yuele, hatith the liyt; and he cometh not to the liyt, that hise werkis be not repreued.

21 But he that doith treuthe, cometh to the liyt, that hise werkis be schewid, that thei ben don in God.

22 Aftir these thingis Jhesus cam, and hise disciplis, in to the loond of Judee, and there he dwellide with hem, and baptiside.

23 And Joon was baptisinge in Ennon, bisidis Salym, for many watris weren there; and thei camen, and weren baptisid.

24 And Joon was not yit sent in to prisoun.

25 Therfor a questioun was maad of Jonys disciplis with the Jewis, of the purificacioun.

26 And thei camen to Joon, and seiden 'to hym, Maister, he that was with thee biyonde Jordan, to whom thou hast borun witnessyng, lo! he baptisith, and alle men comen to hym.

27 Joon answerde, and seide, A man may not take ony thing, but it be youun to hym fro heuene.

28 Ye you silf beren witnessyng to me, that Y seide, Y am not Crist, but that Y am sent bifore hym.

29 He that hath a wijf, is the hosebonde; but the freend of the spouse that stondith, and herith hym, ioieth with ioye, for the vois of the spouse. Therfor in this thing my ioye is fulfillid.

30 It bihoueth hym to wexe, but me to be maad lesse.

31 He that cam from aboue, is aboue alle; he that is of the erthe, spekith of the erthe; he that cometh from heuene, is aboue alle.

32 And he witnessith that thing that he hath seie, and herde, and no man takith his witnessing.

33 But he that takith his witnessyng, hath confermyd that God is sothefast.

34 But he whom God hath sent, spekith the wordis of God; for not to mesure God yyueth the spirit.

35 The fadir loueth the sone, and he hath youun alle thingis in his hoond.

36 He that bileueth in the sone, hath euerlastynge lijf; but he that is vnbileueful to the sone, schal not se euerlastynge lijf, but the wraththe of God dwellith on hym.

CAP 4

1 Therfor as Jhesu knew, that the Farisees herden, that Jhesu makith and baptisith mo disciplis than Joon,

2 thouy Jhesus baptiside not, but hise disciplis, he lefte Judee,

3 and wente ayen in to Galilee.

4 And it bihofte hym to passe bi Samarie.

5 Therfor Jhesus cam in to a citee of Samarie, that is seid Sicar, bisidis the place, that Jacob yaf to Joseph, his sone.

6 And the welle of Jacob was there; and Jhesus was weri of the iourney, and sat thus vpon the welle. And the our was, as it were the sixte.

7 And a womman cam fro Samarie, to drawe watir. And Jhesus seith to hir, Yyue me drynk.

8 And hise disciplis weren gon in to the citee, to bie mete.

9 Therfor thilke womman of Samarie seith to him, Hou thou, 'whanne thou art a Jewe, axist of me drynk, that am a womman of Samarie? for Jewis vsiden not to dele with Samaritans.

10 Jhesus answerde, and seide to hir, If thou wistist the yifte of God, and who 'he is, that seith to thee, Yyue me drynk, thou perauenture woldist haue axid of hym, and he schulde haue youun to thee quyk watir.

11 The womman seith to him, Sire, thou hast not where ynne to drawe, and the pit is deep; wherof thanne hast thou quik watir?

12 Whethir thou art grettere than oure fadir Jacob, that yaf to vs the pit? and he drank therof, and hise sones, and hise beestis.

13 Jhesus answerde, and seide to hir, Eche man that drynkith of this watir, schal thirste efte soone; but he that drynkith of the watir that Y schal yyue hym, schal not thirste with outen ende; but the watir that Y schal yyue hym,

14 schal be maad in hym a welle 'of watir, spryngynge vp in to euerlastynge lijf.

15 The womman seith to hym, Sire, yyue me this watir, that Y thirste not, nether come hidur to drawe.

16 Jhesus seith to hir, Go, clepe thin hosebonde, and come hidir.

17 The womman answerde, and seide, Y haue noon hosebonde. Jhesus seith to hir, Thou seidist wel, That Y haue noon hosebonde;

18 for thou hast hadde fyue hosebondis, and he that thou hast, is not thin hosebonde. This thing thou seidist sotheli.

19 The womman seith to hym, Lord, Y se, that thou art a prophete.

20 Oure fadris worschipiden in this hil, and ye seien, that at Jerusalem is a place, where it bihoueth to worschipe.

21 Jhesus seith to hir, Womman, bileue thou to me, for the our schal come, whanne nether in this hil, nethir in Jerusalem, ye schulen worschipe the fadir.

22 Ye worschipen that ye knowen not; we worschipen that that we knowen; for helthe is of the Jewis.

23 But the tyme is comun, and now it is, whanne trewe worschiperis schulen worschipe the fadir in spirit and treuthe; for also the fadir sekith suche, that worschipen hym.

24 God is a spirit, and it bihoueth hem that worschipen hym, to worschipe in spirit and treuthe.

25 The womman seith to hym, Y woot that Messias is comun, that is seid Crist; therfor whanne he cometh, he schal telle vs alle thingis.

26 Jhesus seith to hir, Y am he, that spekith with thee.

27 And anoon hise disciplis camen, and wondriden, that he spak with the womman; netheles no man seide to hym, What sekist thou, or, What spekist thou with hir?

28 Therfor the womman lefte hir watir pot, and wente in to the citee, and seide to tho men,

29 Come ye, and se ye a man, that seide to me alle thingis that Y haue don; whether he be Crist?

30 And thei wenten out of the citee, and camen to hym.

31 In the mene while hise disciplis preieden hym, and seiden, Maistir, ete.

32 But he seide to hem, Y haue mete to ete, that ye knowen not.

33 Therfor disciplis seiden togidir, Whether ony man hath brouyt him mete to ete?

34 Jhesus seith to hem, My mete is, that Y do the wille of hym that sente me, that Y perfourme the werk of hym.

35 Whether ye seien not, that yit foure monethis ben, and rype corn cometh? Lo! Y seie to you, lifte vp youre iyen, and se ye the feeldis, for now thei ben white to repe.

36 And he that repith takith hire, and gaderith fruyt in to euerlastynge lijf; that bothe he that sowith, and he that repith, haue ioye togidere.

37 In this thing is the word trewe, for anothir is that sowith, and anothir that repith.

38 Y sente you to repe, that that ye 'haue not trauelid; 'othere men han trauelid, and ye han entrid 'in to her trauels.

39 And of that citee many Samaritans bileueden in hym, for the word of the womman, that bare witnessyng, That he seide to me alle thingis that Y haue don.

40 Therfor whanne Samaritans camen to hym, thei preieden hym to dwelle there; and he dwelte there twey daies.

41 And many mo bileueden for his word,

42 and seiden to the womman, That now not for thi speche we bileuen; for we han herd, and we witen, that this is verili the sauyour of the world.

43 And aftir twei daies he wente out fro thennus, and wente in to Galilee.

44 And he bar witnessyng, that a profete in his owne cuntre hath noon onour.

45 Therfor whanne he cam in to Galilee, men of Galilee resseyueden hym, whanne thei hadden seyn alle thingis that he hadde don in Jerusalem in the feeste dai; for also thei hadden comun to the feeste dai.

46 Therfor he cam eftsoone in to the Cane of Galile, where he made the watir wiyn. And 'a litil kyng was, whos sone was sijk at Cafarnaum.

47 Whanne this hadde herd, that Jhesu schulde come fro Judee in to Galilee, he wente to hym, and preiede hym, that he schulde come doun, and heele his sone; for he bigan to die.

48 Therfor Jhesus seide to him, But ye se tokenes and grete wondris, ye bileuen not.

49 The litil kyng seith to hym, Lord, come doun, bifor that my sone die.

50 Jhesus seith to hym, Go, thi sone lyueth. The man bileuede to the word, that Jhesus seide to hym, and he wente.

51 And now whanne he cam doun, the seruauntis camen ayens hym, and telden to hym, and seiden, That his sone lyuede.

52 And he axide of hem the our, in which he was amendid. And thei seiden to hym, For yistirdai in the seuenthe our the feuer lefte him.

53 Therfor the fadir knewe, that thilke our it was, in which Jhesus seide to hym, Thi sone lyueth; and he bileuede, and al his hous.

54 Jhesus dide eft this secounde tokene, whanne he cam fro Judee in to Galilee.

CAP 5

1 Aftir these thingis ther was a feeste dai of Jewis, and Jhesus wente vp to Jerusalem.

2 And in Jerusalem is a waissynge place, that in Ebrew is named Bethsaida, and hath fyue porchis.

3 In these lay a greet multitude of sike men, blynde, crokid, and drie, abidynge the mouyng of the watir.

4 For the aungel 'of the Lord cam doun certeyne tymes in to the watir, and the watir was moued; and he that first cam doun in to the sisterne, aftir the mouynge of the watir, was maad hool of what euer sijknesse he was holdun.

5 And a man was there, hauynge eiyte and thritti yeer in his sikenesse.

6 And whanne Jhesus hadde seyn hym liggynge, and hadde knowun, that he hadde myche tyme, he seith to hym, Wolt thou be maad hool?

7 The sijk man answerde to hym, Lord, Y haue no man, that whanne the watir is moued, to putte me 'in to the cisterne; for the while Y come, anothir goith doun bifor me.

8 Jhesus seith to hym, Rise vp, take thi bed, and go.

9 And anoon the man was maad hool, and took vp his bed, and wente forth. And it was sabat in that dai.

10 Therfor the Jewis seiden to him that was maad hool, It is sabat, it is not leueful to thee, to take awei thi bed.

11 He answeride to hem, He that made me hool, seide to me, Take thi bed, and go.

12 Therfor thei axiden him, What man 'is that, that seide to thee, Take vp thi bed, and go?

13 But he that was maad hool, wiste not who it was. And Jhesus bowide awei fro the puple, that was set in the place.

14 Aftirward Jhesus foond hym in the temple, and seide to hym, Lo! thou art maad hool; now nyle thou do synne, lest any worse thing bifalle to thee.

15 Thilke man wente, and telde to the Jewis, that it was Jhesu that made hym hool.

16 Therfor the Jewis pursueden Jhesu, for he dide this thing in the sabat.

17 And Jhesus answeride to hem, My fadir worchith til now, and Y worche.

18 Therfor the Jewis souyten more to sle hym, for not oneli he brak the sabat, but he seide that God was his fadir, and made hym euene to God.

19 Therfor Jhesus answerde, and seide to hem, Treuli, treuli, Y seye to you, the sone may not of hym silf do ony thing, but that thing that he seeth the fadir doynge; for what euere thingis he doith, the sone doith in lijk maner tho thingis.

20 For the fadir loueth the sone, and schewith to hym alle thingis that he doith; and he schal schewe to hym grettere werkis than these, that ye wondren.

21 For as the fadir reisith deed men, and quykeneth, so the sone quykeneth whom he wole.

22 For nethir the fadir iugith ony man, but hath youun ech doom to the sone,

23 that alle men onoure the sone, as thei onouren the fadir. He that onourith not the sone, onourith not the fadir that sente hym.

24 Treuli, treuli, Y seie to you, that he that herith my word, and bileueth to hym that sente me, hath euerlastynge lijf, and he cometh not in to doom, but passith fro deeth in to lijf.

25 Treuli, treuli Y seie to you, for the our cometh, and now it is, whanne deed men schulen here the vois of 'Goddis sone, and thei that heren, schulen lyue.

26 For as the fadir hath lijf in hym silf, so he yaf to the sone, to haue lijf in him silf;

27 and he yaf to hym power to make doom, for he is mannys sone.

28 Nyle ye wondre this, for the our cometh, in which alle men that ben in birielis, schulen here the voice of Goddis sone.

29 And thei that han do goode thingis, schulen go in to ayen-risyng of lijf; but thei that han done yuele thingis, in to ayen-risyng of doom.

30 Y may no thing do of my silf, but as Y here, Y deme, and my doom is iust, for Y seke not my wille, but the wille of the fadir that sente me.

31 If Y bere witnessing of my silf, my witnessyng is not trewe;

32 another is that berith witnessyng of me, and Y woot that his witnessyng is trewe, that he berith of me.

33 Ye senten to Joon, and he bar witnessyng to treuthe.

34 But Y take not witnessyng of man; but Y seie these thingis, that ye be saaf.

35 He was a lanterne brennynge and schynynge; but ye wolden glade at an our in his liyt.

36 But Y haue more witnessyng than Joon, for the werkis that my fadir yaf to me to perfourme hem, thilke werkis that Y do beren witnessyng of me, that the fadir sente me.

37 And the fadir that sente me, he bar witnessyng of me. Nether ye herden euere his vois, nether ye seien his licnesse.

38 And ye han not his word dwellynge in you; for ye byleuen not to hym, whom he sente.

39 Seke ye scripturis, in which ye gessen to haue euer-lastynge lijf; and tho it ben, that beren witnessyng of me.

40 And ye wolen not come to me, that ye haue lijf.

41 Y take not clerenesse of men;

42 but Y haue knowun you, that ye han not the loue of God in you.

43 Y cam in the name of my fadir, and ye token not me. If another come in his owne name, ye schulen resseyue hym.

44 Hou moun ye bileue, that resseyuen glorie ech of othere, and ye seken not the glorie 'that is of God aloone?

45 Nyle ye gesse, that Y am to accuse you anentis the fadir; it is Moises that accusith you, in whom ye hopen.

46 For if ye bileueden to Moises, perauenture ye schulden bileue also to me; for he wroot of me.

47 But if ye bileuen not to hise lettris, hou schulen ye bileue to my wordis?

CAP 6

1 Aftir these thingis Jhesus wente ouere the see of Galilee, that is Tiberias.

2 And a greet multitude suede hym; for thei sayn the tokenes, that he dide on hem that weren sijke.

3 Therfor Jhesus wente in to an hil, and sat there with hise disciplis.

4 And the paske was ful niy, a feeste dai of the Jewis.

5 Therfor whanne Jhesus hadde lift vp hise iyen, and hadde seyn, that a greet multitude cam to hym, he seith to Filip, Wherof schulen we bie looues, that these men ete?

6 But he seide this thing, temptynge hym; for he wiste what he was to do.

7 Filip answerde to hym, The looues of tweyn hundrid pans sufficen not to hem, that ech man take a litil what.

8 Oon of hise disciplis, Andrew, the brothir of Symount Petre,

9 seith to him, A child is here, that hath fyue barli looues and twei fischis; but what ben these among so manye?

10 Therfor Jhesus seith, Make ye hem sitte to the mete. And there was myche hey in the place. And so men saten to the mete, as 'fyue thousynde in noumbre.

11 And Jhesus took fyue looues, and whanne he hadde do thankyngis, he departide to men that saten to the mete, and also of the fischis, as myche as thei wolden.

12 And whanne thei weren fillid, he seide to hise disciplis, Gadir ye the relifs that ben left, that thei perischen not.

13 And so thei gadriden, and filliden twelue cofyns of relif of the fyue barli looues and twei fischis, that lefte to hem that hadden etun.

14 Therfor tho men, whanne thei hadden seyn the signe that he hadde don, seiden, For this is verili the profete, that is to come in to the world.

15 And whanne Jhesus hadde knowun, that thei weren to come to take hym, and make hym kyng, he fleiy 'aloone eft in to an hille.

16 And whanne euentid was comun, his disciplis wenten doun to the see.

17 And thei wenten vp in to a boot, and thei camen ouer the see in to Cafarnaum. And derknessis weren maad thanne, and Jhesus was not come to hem.

18 And for a greet wynde blew, the see roos vp.

19 Therfor whanne thei hadden rowid as fyue and twenti fur-longis or thretti, thei seen Jhesus walkynge on the see, and to be neiy the boot; and thei dredden.

20 And he seide to hem, Y am; nyle ye drede.

21 Therfor thei wolden take hym in to the boot, and anoon the boot was at the loond, to which thei wenten.

22 On 'the tother dai the puple, that stood ouer the see, say, that ther was noon other boot there but oon, and that Jhesu entride not with hise disciplis in to the boot, but hise disciplis aloone wenten.

23 But othere bootis camen fro Tiberias bisidis the place, where thei hadden eetun breed, and diden thankyngis to God.

24 Therfor whanne the puple hadde seyn, that Jhesu was not there, nether hise disciplis, thei wenten vp in to bootis, and camen to Cafarnaum, sekynge Jhesu.

25 And whanne thei hadden foundun hym ouer the see, thei seiden to hym, Rabi, hou come thou hidur?

26 Jhesus answerde to hem, and seide, Treuli, treuli, Y seie to you, ye seken me, not for ye sayn the myraclis, but for ye eten of looues, and weren fillid.

27 Worche ye not mete that perischith, but that dwellith in to euerlastynge lijf, which mete mannys sone schal yyue to you; for God the fadir hath markid hym.

28 Therfor thei seiden to hym, What schulen we do, that we worche the werkis of God?

29 Jhesus answerde, and seide to hem, This is the werk of God, that ye bileue to hym, whom he sente.

30 Therfor thei seiden to hym, What tokene thanne doist thou, that we seen, and bileue to thee? what worchist thou?

31 Oure fadris eeten manna in desert, as it is writun, He yaf to hem breed fro heuene to ete.

32 Therfor Jhesus seith to hem, Treuli, treuli, Y seie to you, Moyses yaf you not breed fro heuene, but my fadir yyueth you veri breed fro heuene;

33 for it is very breed that cometh doun fro heuene, and yyueth lijf to the world.

34 Therfor thei seiden to hym, Lord, euere yyue vs this breed.

35 And Jhesus seide to hem, Y am breed of lijf; he that cometh to me, schal not hungur; he that bileueth in me, schal neuere thirste.

36 But Y seid to you, that ye han seyn me, and ye bileueden not.

37 Al thing, that the fadir yyueth to me, schal come to me; and Y schal not caste hym out, that cometh to me.

38 For Y cam doun fro heuene, not that Y do my wille, but the wille of hym that sente me.

39 And this is the wille of the fadir that sente me, that al thing that the fadir yaf me, Y leese not of it, but ayen reise it in the laste dai.

40 And this is the wille of my fadir that sente me, that ech man that seeth the sone, and bileueth in hym, haue euerlastynge lijf; and Y schal ayen reyse hym in the laste dai.

41 Therfor Jewis grutchiden of hym, for he hadde seid, Y am breed that cam doun fro heuene.

42 And thei seiden, Whether this is not Jhesus, the sone of Joseph, whos fadir and modir we han knowun. Hou thanne seith this, That Y cam doun fro heuene?

43 Therfor Jhesus answerde, and seide to hem, Nyle ye grutche togidere.

44 No man may come to me, but if the fadir that sente me, drawe hym; and Y schal ayen reise hym in the laste dai. It is writun in prophetis,

45 And alle men schulen be able for to be tauyt 'of God. Ech man that herde of the fadir, and hath lerned, cometh to me.

46 Not for ony man hath sey the fadir, but this that is of God, hath sey the fadir.

47 Sotheli, sotheli, Y seie to you, he that bileueth in me, hath euerlastynge lijf.

48 Y am breed of lijf.

49 Youre fadris eeten manna in desert, and ben deed.

50 This is breed comynge doun fro heuene, that if ony man ete therof, he die not.

51 Y am lyuynge breed, that cam doun fro heuene.

52 If ony man ete of this breed, he schal lyue withouten ende. And the breed that Y schal yyue, is my fleisch for the lijf of the world.

53 Therfor the Jewis chidden togidere, and seiden, Hou may this yyue to vs his fleisch to ete?

54 Therfor Jhesus seith to hem, Treuli, treuli, Y seie to you, but ye eten the fleisch of mannus sone, and drenken his blood, ye schulen not haue lijf in you.

55 He that etith my fleisch, and drynkith my blood, hath euerlastynge lijf, and Y schal ayen reise hym in the laste dai.

56 For my fleisch is veri mete, and my blood is very drynk.

57 He that etith my fleisch, and drynkith my blood, dwellith in me, and Y in hym.

58 As my fadir lyuynge sente me, and Y lyue for the fadir, and he that etith me, he schal lyue for me.

59 This is breed, that cam doun fro heuene. Not as youre fadris eten manna, and ben deed; he that etith this breed, schal lyue withouten ende.

60 He seide these thingis in the synagoge, techynge in Cafarnaum.

61 Therfor many of hise disciplis herynge, seiden, This word is hard, who may here it?

62 But Jhesus witynge at hym silf, that hise disciplis grutchiden of this thing, seide to hem, This thing sclaundrith you?

63 Therfor if ye seen mannus sone stiynge, where he was bifor?

64 It is the spirit that quykeneth, the fleisch profitith no thing; the wordis that Y haue spokun to you, ben spirit and lijf.

65 But ther ben summe of you that bileuen not. For Jhesus wiste fro the bigynnynge, which weren bileuynge, and who was to bitraye hym.

66 And he seide, Therfor Y seide to you, that no man may come to me, but it were youun to hym of my fadir.

67 Fro this tyme many of hise disciplis wenten abak, and wenten not now with hym.

68 Therfor Jhesus seide to the twelue, Whether ye wolen also go awei?

69 And Symount Petre answeride to hym, Lord, to whom schulen we gon? Thou hast wordis of euerlastynge lijf;

70 and we bileuen, and han knowun, that thou art Crist, the sone of God.

71 Therfor Jhesus answerde to hem, Whether Y chees not you twelue, and oon of you is a feend?

72 And he seide this of Judas of Symount Scarioth, for this was to bitraye hym, whanne he was oon of the twelue.

CAP 7

1 Aftir these thingis Jhesus walkide in to Galilee, for he wolde not walke in to Judee, for the Jewis souyten to sle hym.

2 And ther was neiy a feeste dai of the Jewis, Senofegia.

3 And hise britheren seiden to hym, Passe fro hennus, and go in to Judee, that also thi disciplis seen thi werkis that thou doist;

4 for no man doith ony thing in hiddlis, and hym silf sekith to be opyn. If thou doist these thingis, schewe thi silf to the world.

5 For nether hise britheren bileueden in hym.

6 Therfor Jhesus seith to hem, My tyme cam not yit, but youre tyme is euermore redi.

7 The world may not hate you, sothely it hatith me; for Y bere witnessyng therof, that the werkis of it ben yuele.

8 Go ye vp to this feeste dai, but Y schal not go vp to this feeste dai, for my tyme is not yit fulfillid.

9 Whanne he hadde seid these thingis, he dwelte in Galilee.

10 And aftir that hise britheren weren gon vp, thanne he yede vp to the feeste dai, not opynli, but as in priuyte.

11 Therfor the Jewis souyten hym in the feeste dai, and seiden, Where is he?

12 And myche grutchyng was of hym among the puple. For summe seiden, That he is good; and othere seiden, Nai, but he disceyueth the puple;

13 netheles no man spak opynli of hym, for drede of the Jewis.

14 But whanne the myddil feeste dai cam, Jhesus wente vp in to the temple, and tauyte.

15 And the Jewis wondriden, and seiden, Hou can this man lettris, sithen he hath not lerned?

16 Jhesus answerde to hem, and seide, My doctryne is not myn, but his that sente me.

17 If ony man wole do his wille, he schal knowe of the techyng, whethir it be of God, or Y speke of my silf.

18 He that spekith of hym silf, sekith his owne glorie; but he that sekith the glorie of hym that sente hym, is sothfast, and vnriytwisnesse is not in hym.

19 Whether Moises yaf not to you a lawe, and noon of you doith the lawe?

20 What seken ye to sle me? And the puple answerde, and seide, Thou hast a deuel; who sekith to sle thee?

21 Jhesus answerde, and seide to hem, Y haue don o werk, and alle ye wondren.

22 Therfor Moises yaf to you circumcisioun; not for it is of Moyses, but of the fadris; and in the sabat ye circumciden a man.

23 If a man take circumcicioun in the sabat, that the lawe of Moises be not brokun, han ye indignacioun to me, for Y made al a man hool in the sabat?

24 Nile ye deme aftir the face, but deme ye a riytful doom.

25 Therfor summe of Jerusalem seiden, Whethir this is not he, whom the Jewis seken to sle?

26 and lo! he spekith opynli, and thei seien no thing to hym. Whether the princes knewen verili, that this is Crist?

27 But we knowun this man, of whennus he is; but whanne Crist schal come, no man woot of whennus he is.

28 Therfor Jhesus criede in the temple 'techynge, and seide, Ye knowen me, and 'ye knowen of whennus Y am; and Y cam not of my silf, but he is trewe that sente me, whom ye knowen not.

29 Y knowe hym, and if Y seie that Y knowe hym not, Y schal be lijk to you, a liere; but Y knowe hym, for of hym Y am, and he sente me.

30 Therfor thei souyten to take hym, and no man sette on hym hoondis, for his our cam not yit.

31 And many of the puple bileueden in hym, and seiden, Whanne Crist schal come, whether he schal do mo tokenes, than tho that this doith?

32 Farisees herden the puple musinge of hym these thingis; and the princis and Farisees senten mynystris, to take hym.

33 Therfor Jhesus seide to hem, Yit a litil tyme Y am with you, and Y go to the fadir, that sente me.

34 Ye schulen seke me, and ye schulen not fynde; and where Y am, ye may not come.

35 Therfor the Jewis seiden to hem silf, Whidur schal this gon, for we schulen not fynde hym? whether he wole go in to the scateryng of hethene men, and wole teche the hethene?

36 What is this word, which he seide, Ye schulen seke me, and ye schulen not fynde; and where Y am, ye moun not come?

37 But in the laste dai of the greet feeste, Jhesus stood, and criede, and seide, If ony man thirstith, come he to me, and drynke.

38 He that bileueth in me, as the scripture seith, Floodis of quyk watir schulen flowe fro his wombe.

39 But he seide this thing of the Spirit, whom men that bileueden in hym schulden take; for the Spirit was not yit youun, for Jhesus was not yit glorified.

40 Therfor of that cumpanye, whanne thei hadden herd these wordis of hym, thei seiden, This is verili a prophete.

41 Othere seiden, This is Crist. 'But summe seiden, Whether Crist cometh fro Galilee?

42 Whether the scripture seith not, that of the seed of Dauid, and of the castel of Bethleem, where Dauid was, Crist cometh?

43 Therfor discencioun was maad among the puple for hym.

44 For summe of hem wolden haue take hym, but no man sette hondis on hym.

45 Therfor the mynystris camen to bischopis and Farisees, and thei seiden to hem, Whi brouyten ye not hym?

46 The mynystris answeriden, Neuere man spak so, as this man spekith.

47 Therfor the Farisees answeriden to hem, Whether ye ben disseyued also?

48 whether ony of the pryncis or of the Farisees bileueden in hym?

49 But this puple, that knowith not the lawe, ben cursid.

50 Nychodeme seith to hem, he that cam to hym bi nyyt, that was oon of hem, Whethir oure lawe demith a man,

51 but it haue first herde of hym, and knowe what he doith?

52 Thei answeriden, and seiden to hym, Whether thou art a man of Galilee also? Seke thou scripturis, and se thou, that a prophete risith not of Galilee.

53 And thei turneden ayen, ech in to his hous.

CAP 8

1 But Jhesus wente in to the mount of Olyuete.

2 And eerli eft he cam in to the temple; and al the puple cam to hym; and he sat, and tauyte hem.

3 And scribis and Fariseis bryngen a womman takun in auoutrye, and thei settiden hir in the myddil,

4 and seiden to hym, Maystir, this womman is now takun in auoutrie.

5 And in the lawe Moises comaundide vs to stoone suche; therfor what seist thou?

6 And thei seiden this thing temptynge hym, that thei myyten accuse hym. And Jhesus bowide hym silf doun, and wroot with his fyngur in the erthe.

7 And whanne thei abiden axynge hym, he reiside hym silf, and seide to hem, He of you that is without synne, first caste a stoon in to hir.

8 And eft he bowide hym silf, and wroot in the erthe.

9 And thei herynge these thingis, wenten awei oon aftir anothir, and thei bigunnen fro the eldre men; and Jhesus dwelte aloone, and the womman stondynge in the myddil.

10 And Jhesus reiside hym silf, and seide to hir, Womman, where ben thei that accusiden thee? no man hath dampned thee.

11 Sche seide, No man, Lord. Jhesus seide 'to hir, Nethir Y schal dampne thee; go thou, and now aftirward nyle thou synne more.

12 Therfor eft Jhesus spak to hem, and seide, Y am the liyt of the world; he that sueth me, walkith not in derknessis, but schal haue the liyt of lijf.

13 Therfor the Fariseis seiden, Thou berist witnessyng of thi silf; thi witnessyng is not trewe.

14 Jhesus answerde, and seide to hem, And if Y bere witnessyng of my silf, my witnessyng is trewe; for Y woot fro whennus Y cam, and whidur Y go.

15 But ye witen not fro whennus Y cam, ne whidur Y go. For ye demen aftir the fleisch, but Y deme no man;

16 and if Y deme, my doom is trewe, for Y am not aloone, but Y and the fadir that sente me.

17 And in youre lawe it is writun, that the witnessyng of twei men is trewe.

18 Y am, that bere witnessyng of my silf, and the fadir that sente me, berith witnessyng of me.

19 Therfor thei seiden to hym, Where is thi fadir? Jhesus answeride, Nether ye knowen me, nethir ye knowen my fadir; if ye knewen me, perauenture ye schulden knowe also my fadir.

20 Jhesus spak these wordis in the tresorie, techynge in the temple; and no man took hym, for his our cam not yit.

21 Therfor eft Jhesus seide to hem, Lo! Y go, and ye schulen seke me, and ye schulen die in youre synne; whidur Y go, ye moun not come.

22 Therfor the Jewis seiden, Whether he schal sle hym silf, for he seith, Whidur Y go, ye moun not come?

23 And he seide to hem, Ye ben of bynethe, Y am of aboue; ye ben of this world, Y am not of this world.

24 Therfor Y seide to you, that ye schulen die in youre synnes; for if ye bileuen not that Y am, ye schulen die in youre synne.

25 Therfor thei seiden to hym, Who art thou? Jhesus seide to hem, The bigynnyng, which also speke to you.

26 Y haue many thingis to speke, and deme of you, but he that sente me is sothefast; and Y speke in the world these thingis, that Y herde of hym.

27 And thei knewen not, that he clepide his fadir God.

28 Therfor Jhesus seith to hem, Whanne ye han areisid mannus sone, thanne ye schulen knowe, that Y am, and of my silf Y do no thing; but as my fadir tauyte me, Y speke these thingis.

29 And he that sente me is with me, and lefte me not aloone; for Y do euermore tho thingis, that ben plesynge to hym.

30 Whanne he spak these thingis, manye bileueden in hym.

31 Therfor Jhesus seide to the Jewis, that bileueden in hym, If ye dwellen in my word, verili ye schulen be my disciplis;

32 and ye schulen knowe the treuthe, and the treuthe schal make you fre.

33 Therfor the Jewis answeriden to hym, We ben the seed of Abraham, and we serueden neuere to man; hou seist thou, That ye schulen be fre?

34 Jhesus answeride to hem, Treuli, treuli, Y seie to you, ech man that doith synne, is seruaunt of synne.

35 And the seruaunt dwellith not in the hows with outen ende, but the sone dwellith with outen ende.

36 Therfor if the sone make you fre, verili ye schulen be fre.

37 Y woot that ye ben Abrahams sones, but ye seken to sle me, for my word takith not in you.

38 Y speke tho thingis, that Y say at my fadir; and ye doen tho thingis, that ye sayn at youre fadir.

39 Thei answerden, and seiden to hym, Abraham is oure fadir. Jhesus seith to hem, If ye ben the sones of Abraham, do ye the werkis of Abraham.

40 But now ye seken to sle 'me, a man that haue spoken to you treuthe, that Y herde of God; Abraham dide not this thing.

41 Ye doen the werkis of youre fadir. Therfor thei seiden to hym, We ben not borun of fornycacioun; we han o fadir, God.

42 But Jhesus seith to hem, If God were youre fadir, sotheli ye schulden loue me; for Y passide forth of God, and cam; for nether Y cam of my silf, but he sente me.

43 Whi knowen ye not my speche? for ye moun not here my word.

44 Ye ben of the fadir, the deuel, and ye wolen do the desyris of youre fadir. He was a mansleere fro the bigynnyng, and he stood not in treuthe; for treuthe is not in hym. Whanne he spekith lesyng, he spekith of his owne; for he is a liere, and fadir of it.

45 But for Y seie treuthe, ye bileuen not to me.

46 Who of you schal repreue me of synne? if Y sey treuthe, whi bileuen ye not to me?

47 He that is of God, herith the wordis of God; therfor ye heren not, for ye ben not of God.

48 Therfor the Jewis answeriden, and seiden, Whether we seien not wel, that thou art a Samaritan, and hast a deuel?

49 Jhesus answerde, and seide, Y haue not a deuel, but Y onoure my fadir, and ye han vnhonourid me.

50 For Y seke not my glorye; there is he, that sekith, and demeth.

51 Treuli, treuli, Y seie to you, if ony man kepe my word, he schal not taste deth with outen ende.

52 Therfor the Jewis seiden, Now we han knowun, that thou hast a deuel. Abraham is deed, and the prophetis, and thou seist, If ony man kepe my word, he schal not taste deth withouten ende.

53 Whether thou art grettere than oure fader Abraham, that is deed, and the prophetis ben deed; whom makist thou thi silf?

54 Jhesus answeride, If Y glorifie my silf, my glorie is nouyt; my fadir, is that glorifieth me, whom ye seien, that he is youre God.

55 And ye han not knowun hym, but Y haue knowun hym; and if Y seie that Y knowe hym not, Y schal be a liere lich to you; but Y knowe hym, and Y kepe his word.

56 Abraham, youre fadir, gladide to se my dai; and he saiy, and ioyede.

57 Thanne the Jewis seiden to hym, Thou hast not yit fifti yeer, and hast thou seien Abraham?

58 Therfor Jhesus seide to hem, Treuli, treuli, Y seie to you, bifor that Abraham schulde be, Y am.

59 Therfor thei token stonys, to caste to hym; but Jhesus hidde hym, and wente out of the temple.

CAP 9

1 And Jhesus passynge, seiy a man blynd fro the birthe.

2 And hise disciplis axiden hym, Maistir, what synnede this man, or hise eldris, that he schulde be borun blynd?

3 Jhesus answeride, Nether this man synnede, nether hise eldris; but that the werkis of God be schewid in hym.

4 It bihoueth me to worche the werkis of hym that sente me, as longe as the dai is; the nyyt schal come, whanne no man may worche.

5 As longe as Y am in the world, Y am the liyt of the world.

6 Whanne he hadde seid these thingis, he spette in to the erthe, and made cley of the spotil, and anoyntide the cley on hise iyen,

7 and seide to hym, Go, and be thou waisschun in the watir of Siloe, that is to seie, Sent. Thanne he wente, and waisschide, and cam seynge.

8 And so neiyboris, and thei that hadden seyn him bifor, for he was a beggere, seiden, Whether this is not he, that sat, and beggide?

9 Othere men seiden, That this it is; othere men seyden, Nai, but he is lijc hym.

10 But he seide, That Y am. Therfor thei seiden to hym, Hou ben thin iyen openyd?

11 He answerde, Thilke man, that is seid Jhesus, made clei, and anoyntide myn iyen, and seide to me, Go thou to the watre of Siloe, and wassche; and Y wente, and wasschide, and say.

12 And thei seiden to hym, Where is he? He seide, Y woot not.

13 Thei leden hym that was blynd to the Farisees.

14 And it was sabat, whanne Jhesus made cley, and openyde hise iyen.

15 Eft the Farisees axiden hym, hou he hadde seyn. And he seide to hem, He leide to me cley on the iyen; and Y wasschide, and Y se.

16 Therfor summe of the Fariseis seiden, This man is not of God, that kepith not the sabat. Othere men seiden, Hou may a synful man do these signes. And strijf was among hem.

17 Therfor thei seien eftsoone to the blynd man, What seist thou of hym, that openyde thin iyen? And he seide, That he is a prophete.

18 Therfor Jewis bileueden not of hym, that he was blynd, and hadde seyn, til thei clepiden his fadir and modir, that hadde seyn.

19 And thei axiden hem, and seiden, Is this youre sone, which ye seien was borun blynd? hou thanne seeth he now?

20 His fadir and modir answeriden to hem, and seiden, We witen, that this is oure sone, and that he was borun blynd;

21 but hou he seeth now, we witen neuer, or who openyde hise iyen, we witen nere; axe ye hym, he hath age, speke he of hym silf.

22 His fader and modir seiden these thingis, for thei dredden the Jewis; for thanne the Jewis hadden conspirid, that if ony man knoulechide hym Crist, he schulde be don out of the synagoge.

23 Therfor his fadir and modir seiden, That he hath age, axe ye hym.

24 Therfor eftsoone thei clepiden the man, that was blynd, and seiden to hym, Yyue thou glorie to God; we witen, that this man is a synnere.

25 Thanne he seide, If he is a synnere, Y woot neuer; o thing Y woot, that whanne Y was blynd, now Y se.

26 Therfor thei seiden to hym, What dide he to thee? hou openyde he thin iyen?

27 He answerde to hem, Y seide to you now, and ye herden; what wolen ye eftsoone here? whether ye wolen be maad hise discyplis?

28 Therfor thei cursiden hym, and seiden, Be thou his disciple; we ben disciplis of Moises.

29 We witen, that God spak to Moises; but we knowen not this, of whennus he is.

30 Thilke man answeride, and seide to hem, For in this is a wondurful thing, that ye witen not, of whennus he is, and he hath openyd myn iyen.

31 And we witen, that God herith not synful men, but if ony 'man is worschypere of God, and doith his wille, he herith hym.

32 Fro the world it is not herd, that ony man openyde the iyen of a blynd borun man; but this were of God,

33 he myyt not do ony thing.

34 Thei answeriden, and seiden to hym, Thou art al borun in synnes, and techist thou vs? And thei putten hym out.

35 Jhesus herd, that thei hadden putte hym out; and whanne he hadde founde hym, he seide to hym, Bileuest thou in the sone of God?

36 He answerde, and seide, Lord, who is he, that Y bileue in hym?

37 And Jhesus seide to hym, And thou hast seyn him, and he it is, that spekith with thee.

38 And he seide, Lord, Y byleue. And he felle doun, and worschipide hym.

39 Therfore Jhesus seide to hym, Y cam in to this world, 'in to doom, that thei that seen not, see, and thei that seen, be maad blynde.

40 And summe of the Faryseis herden, that weren with hym, and thei seiden to hym, Whether we ben blynde?

41 Jhesus seide to hem, If ye weren blynde, ye schulden not haue synne; but now ye seien, That we seen, youre synne dwellith stille.

CAP 10

1 Treuli, treuli, Y seie to you, he that cometh not in by the dore in to the foold of scheep, but stieth bi another weie, is a nyyt theef and a dai theef.

2 But he that entrith bi the dore, is the scheepherde of the scheep.

3 To this the porter openeth, and the scheep heren his vois, and he clepith his owne scheep bi name, and ledith hem out.

4 And whanne he hath don out his owne scheep, he goith bifor hem, and the scheep suen hym; for thei knowun his vois.

5 But thei suen not an alien, but fleen from hym; for thei han not knowun the vois of aliens.

6 Jhesus seide to hem this prouerbe; but thei knewen not what he spak to hem.

7 Therfor Jhesus seide to hem eftsoone, Treuli, treuli, Y seie to you, that Y am the dore of the scheep.

8 As many as han come, weren nyyt theues and day theues, but the scheep herden not hem.

9 Y am the dore. If ony man schal entre bi me, he schal be sauyd; and he schal go ynne, and schal go out, and he schal fynde lesewis.

10 A nyyt theef cometh not, but that he stele, sle, and leese; and Y cam, that thei han lijf, and haue more plenteousli.

11 I am a good scheepherde; a good scheepherde yyueth his lijf for hise scheep.

12 But an hirid hyne, and that is not the scheepherde, whos ben not the scheep his owne, seeth a wolf comynge, and he leeueth the scheep, and fleeth; and the wolf rauyschith, and disparplith the scheep.

13 And the hirid hyne fleeth, for he is an hirid hyne, and it parteyneth not to hym of the scheep.

14 Y am a good scheepherde, and Y knowe my scheep, and my scheep knowen me.

15 As the fadir hath knowun me, Y knowe the fadir; and Y putte my lijf for my scheep.

16 Y haue othere scheep, that ben not of this foolde, and it bihoueth me to brynge hem togidir, and thei schulen here my vois; and it schal be maad o foolde and o scheepherde.

17 Therfor the fadir loueth me, for Y putte my lijf, that eftsoone Y take it.

18 No man takith it fro me, but Y putte it of my silf. Y haue power to putte it, and Y haue power to take it ayen. This maundement Y haue takun of my fadir.

19 Eft dissencioun was maad among the Jewis for these wordis.

20 And many of hem seiden, He hath a deuel, and maddith; what heren ye hym?

21 Othere men seiden, These wordis ben not of a man that hath a feend. Whether the deuel may opene the iyen of blynde men?

22 But the feestis of halewyng of the temple weren maad in Jerusalem, and it was wyntir.

23 And Jhesus walkide in the temple, in the porche of Salomon.

24 Therfor the Jewis camen aboute hym, and seiden to hym, Hou long takist thou awei oure soule? if thou art Crist, seie thou to vs opynli.

25 Jhesus answerde to hem, Y speke to you, and ye bileuen not; the werkis that Y do in the name of my fadir, beren witnessyng of me.

26 But ye bileuen not, for ye ben not of my scheep.

27 My scheep heren my vois, and Y knowe hem, and thei suen me.

28 And Y yyue to hem euerelastynge lijf, and thei schulen not perische with outen ende, and noon schal rauysche hem fro myn hoond.

29 That thing that my fadir yaf to me, is more than alle thingis; and no man may rauysche fro my fadris hoond.

30 Y and the fadir ben oon.

31 The Jewis token vp stoonys, to stoone hym.

32 Jhesus answerde to hem, Y haue schewide to you many good werkis of my fadir, for which werk of hem stonen ye me?

33 The Jewis answerden to hym, We stoonen thee not of good werk, but of blasfemye, and for thou, sithen thou art a man, makist thi silf God.

34 Jhesus answerde to hem, Whether it is not writun in youre lawe, That Y seide, Ye ben goddis?

35 Yf he seide that thei weren goddis, to whiche the word of God was maad, and scripture may not be vndon,

36 thilke that the fadir hath halewid, and hath sent in to the world, ye seien, That 'thou blasfemest, for Y seide, Y am Goddis sone?

37 Yf Y do not the werkis of my fadir, nyle ye bileue to me;

38 but if Y do, thouy ye wolen not bileue to me, bileue ye to the werkis; that ye knowe and bileue, that the fadir is in me, and Y in the fadir.

39 Therfor thei souyten to take hym, and he wente out of her hondis.

40 And he wente eftsoone ouer Jordan, in to that place where Joon was firste baptisynge, and he dwelte there.

41 And manye camen to hym, and seiden, For Joon dide no myracle;

42 and alle thingis what euer Joon seide of this, weren sothe. And many bileueden in hym.

CAP 11

1 And ther was a sijk man, Lazarus of Bethanye, of the castel of Marie and Martha, hise sistris.

2 And it was Marye, which anoyntide the Lord with oynement, and wipte hise feet with hir heeris, whos brother Lazarus was sijk.

3 Therfor hise sistris senten to hym, and seide, Lord, lo! he whom thou louest, is sijk.

4 And Jhesus herde, and seide to hem, This syknesse is not to the deth, but for the glorie of God, that mannus sone be glorified bi hym.

5 And Jhesus louyde Martha, and hir sistir Marie, and Lazarus.

6 Therfor whanne Jhesus herde, that he was sijk, thanne he dwellide in the same place twei daies.

7 And after these thingis he seide to hise disciplis, Go we eft in to Judee.

8 The disciplis seien to hym, Maister, now the Jewis souyten for to stoone thee, and eft goist thou thidir?

9 Jhesus answerde, Whether ther ben not twelue ouris of the dai? If ony man wandre in the dai, he hirtith not, for he seeth the liyt of this world.

10 But if he wandre in the niyt, he stomblith, for liyt is not in him.

11 He seith these thingis, and aftir these thingis he seith to hem, Lazarus, oure freend, slepith, but Y go to reise hym fro sleep.

12 Therfor hise disciplis seiden, Lord, if he slepith, he schal be saaf.

13 But Jhesus hadde seid of his deth; but thei gessiden, that he seide of slepyng of sleep.

14 Thanne therfor Jhesus seide to hem opynli, Lazarus is deed;

15 and Y haue ioye for you, that ye bileue, for Y was not there; but go we to hym.

16 Therfor Thomas, that is seid Didymus, seide to euen disciplis, Go we also, that we dien with hym.

17 And so Jhesus cam, and foond hym hauynge thanne foure daies in the graue.

18 And Bethany was bisidis Jerusalem, as it were fiftene furlongis.

19 And many of the Jewis camen to Mary and Martha, to coumforte hem of her brothir.

20 Therfor as Martha herde, that Jhesu cam, sche ran to hym; but Mary sat at home.

21 Therfor Martha seide to Jhesu, Lord, if thou haddist be here, my brother hadde not be deed.

22 But now Y woot, that what euere thingis thou schalt axe of God, God schal yyue to thee.

23 Jhesus seith to hir, Thi brother schal rise ayen.

24 Martha seith to hym, Y woot, that he schal rise ayen in the ayen risyng in the laste dai.

25 Jhesus seith to hir, Y am ayen risyng and lijf; he that bileueth in me, yhe, thouy he be deed,

26 he schal lyue; and ech that lyueth, and bileueth in me, schal not die with outen ende. Bileuest thou this thing?

27 Sche seith to hym, Yhe, Lord, Y haue bileued, that thou art Crist, the sone of the lyuynge God, that hast come in to this world.

28 And whanne sche hadde seid this thing, sche wente, and clepide Marie, hir sistir, in silence, and seide, The maister cometh, and clepith thee.

29 Sche, as sche herd, aroos anoon, and cam to hym.

30 And Jhesus cam not yit 'in to the castel, but he was yit in that place, where Martha hadde comun ayens hym.

31 Therfor the Jewis that weren with hir in the hous, and coumfortiden hir, whanne thei sayn Marie, that sche roos swithe, and wente out, thei sueden hir, and seiden, For sche goith to the graue, to wepe there.

32 But whanne Marie was comun where Jhesus was, sche seynge hym felde doun to his feet, and seide to hym, Lord, if thou haddist be here, my brother hadde not be deed.

33 And therfor whanne Jhesu saiy hir wepyng, and the Jewis wepynge that weren with hir, he 'made noise in spirit, and troblide hym silf,

34 and seide, Where han ye leid hym? Thei seien to hym, Lord, come, and se.

35 And Jhesus wepte. Therfor the Jewis seiden,

36 Lo! hou he louede hym.

37 And summe of hem seiden, Whethir this man that openyde the iyen of the borun blynde man, myyte not make that this schulde not die?

38 Therfor Jhesus eft makynge noise in hym silf, cam to the graue. And there was a denne, and a stoon was leid theronne.

39 And Jhesus seith, Take ye awey the stoon. Martha, the sistir of hym that was deed, seith to hym, Lord, he stynkith now, for he hath leye foure daies.

40 Jhesus seith to hir, Haue Y not seid to thee, that if thou bileuest, thou schalt se the glorie of God?

41 Therfor thei token awei the stoon. And Jhesus lifte vp hise iyen, and seide, Fadir, Y do thankyngis to thee, for thou hast herd me; and Y wiste,

42 that thou euermore herist me, but for the puple that stondith aboute, Y seide, that thei bileue, that thou hast sent me.

43 Whanne he hadde seid these thingis, he criede with a greet vois, Lazarus, come thou forth.

44 And anoon he that was deed, cam out, boundun the hondis and feet with boondis, and his face boundun with a sudarie. And Jhesus seith to hem, Vnbynde ye hym, and suffre ye hym to go forth.

45 Therfor many of the Jewis that camen to Marie and Martha, and seyn what thingis Jhesus dide, bileueden in hym.

46 But summe of hem wente to the Farisees, and seiden to hem, what thingis Jhesus 'hadde don.

47 Therfor the bischopis and the Farisees gadriden a counsel ayens Jhesu, and seiden, What do we? for this man doith many myraclis.

48 If we leeue hym thus, alle men schulen bileue in hym; and Romayns schulen come, and schulen take our place and oure folk.

49 But oon of hem, Cayfas bi name, whanne he was bischop of that yeer, seide to hem,

50 Ye witen nothing, ne thenken, that it spedith to you, that o man die for the puple, and that al the folc perische not.

51 But he seide not this thing of hym silf, but whanne he was bischop of that yeer, he prophesiede, that Jhesu was to die for the folc,

52 and not oneli for the folc, but that he schulde gadere in to oon the sones of God that weren scaterid.

53 Therfor fro that day thei souyten for to sle hym.

54 Therfor Jhesus walkide not thanne opynli among the Jewis; but he wente in to a cuntre bisidis desert, in to a citee, that is seid Effren, and there he dwellide with hise disciplis.

55 And the pask of the Jewis was niy, and many of the cuntrey wenten vp to Jerusalem bifor the pask, to halewe hem silf.

56 Therfor thei souyten Jhesu, and spaken togidere, stondynge in the temple, What gessen ye, for he cometh not to the feeste day? For the bischopis and Farisees hadden youun a maundement, that if ony man knowe where he is, that he schewe, that thei take hym.

CAP 12

1 Therfor Jhesus bifor sixe daies of pask cam to Bethanye, where Lazarus hadde be deed, whom Jhesus reiside.

2 And thei maden to hym a soopere there, and Martha mynystride to hym; and Lazarus was oon of men that saten at the mete with hym.

3 Therfor Marie took a pound of oynement of trewe narde precious, and anoyntide the feet of Jhesu, and wipte hise feet with hir heeris; and the hous was fulfillid of the sauour of the oynement.

4 Therfor Judas Scarioth, oon of hise disciplis, that was to bitraye hym,

5 seide, Whi is not this oynement seeld for thre hundrid pens, and is youun to nedi men?

6 But he seide this thing, not for it perteynede to hym of nedi men, but for he was a theef, and he hadde the pursis, and bar' tho thingis that weren sent.

7 Therfor Jhesus seide, Suffre ye hir, that in to the day of my biriyng sche kepe that;

8 for ye schulen euermore haue pore men with you, but ye schulen not euermore haue me.

9 Therfore myche puple of Jewis knew, that Jhesus was there; and thei camen, not oonli for Jhesu, but to se Lazarus, whom he hadde reisid fro deth.

10 But the princis of prestis thouyten to sle Lazarus,

11 for manye of the Jewis wenten awei for him, and bileueden in Jhesu.

12 But on the morew a myche puple, that cam togidere to the feeste dai, whanne thei hadden herd, that Jhesus cam to Jerusalem,

13 token braunchis of palmes, and camen forth ayens hym, and crieden, Osanna, blessid is the kyng of Israel, that cometh in the name of the Lord.

14 And Jhesus foond a yonge asse, and sat on hym,

15 as it is writun, The douytir of Syon, nyle thou drede; lo! thi kyng cometh, sittynge on 'an asse fole.

16 Hise disciplis knewen not first these thingis, but whanne Jhesus was glorified, thanne thei hadden mynde, for these thingis weren writun of hym, and these thingis thei diden to hym.

17 Therfor the puple bar witnessyng, that was with hym, whanne he clepide Lazarus fro the graue, and reiside hym fro deth.

18 And therfor the puple cam, and mette with hym, for thei herden that he hadde don this signe.

19 Therfor the Farisees seiden to hem silf, Ye seen, that we profiten no thing; lo! al the world wente aftir hym.

20 And there weren summe hethene men, of hem that hadden come vp to worschipe in the feeste dai.

21 And these camen to Filip, that was of Bethsaida of Galilee, and preieden hym, and seiden, Sire, we wolen se Jhesu.

22 Filip cometh, and seith to Andrew; eft Andrew and Filip seiden to Jhesu.

23 And Jhesus answerde 'to hem, and seide, The our cometh, that mannus sone be clarified.

24 Treuli, treuli, Y seie to you, but a corn of whete falle in to the erthe, and be deed, it dwellith aloone;

25 but if it be deed, it bryngith myche fruyt. He that loueth his lijf, schal leese it; and he that hatith his lijf in this world, kepith it in to euerlastynge lijf.

26 If ony man serue me, sue he me; and where Y am, there my mynystre schal be. If ony man serue me, my fadir schal worschipe hym.

27 Now my soule is troublid, and what schal Y seie? Fadir, saue me fro this our; but therfor Y cam in to this our;

28 fadir, clarifie thi name. And a vois cam fro heuene, and seide, And Y haue clarified, and eft Y schal clarifie.

29 Therfor the puple that stood, and herde, seide, that 'thundur was maad; othere men seide, an aungel spak to hym.

30 Jhesus answerde, and seide, This vois cam not for me, but for you.

31 Now is the doom of the world, now the prince of this world schal be cast out.

32 And if Y schal be enhaunsid fro the erthe, Y schal drawe alle thingis to my silf.

33 And he seide this thing, signifiynge bi what deth he 'was to die.

34 And the puple answeride to hym, We han herd of the lawe, that Crist dwellith with outen ende; and hou seist thou, It bihoueth mannys sone to be arerid?

35 Who is this mannus sone? And thanne Jhesus seith to hem, Yit a litil liyt is in you; walke ye, the while ye han liyt, that derknessis catche you not; he that wandrith in derknessis, woot nere whidur he goith.

36 While ye han liyt, bileue ye in liyt, that ye be the children of liyt. Jhesus spak these thingis, and wente, and hidde hym fro hem.

37 And whanne he hadde don so many myraclis bifor hem, thei bileueden not 'in to hym;

38 that the word of Ysaie, the prophete, schulde be fulfillid, which he seide, Lord, who bileuede to oure heryng, and to whom is the arm of the Lord schewid?

39 Therfor thei myyten not bileue, for eft Ysaye seide,

40 He hath blyndid her iyen, and he hath maad hard the herte of hem, that thei se not with iyen, and vndurstonde with herte; and that thei be conuertid, and Y heele hem.

41 Ysaye seide these thingis, whanne he say the glorie of hym, and spak of hym.

42 Netheles 'of the pryncis manye bileueden in hym, but for the Farisees thei knowlechiden not, that thei schulden not be put out of the synagoge;

43 for thei loueden the glorie of men, more than the glorie of God.

44 And Jhesus criede, and seide, He that bileueth in me, bileueth not in me, but in hym that sente me.

45 He that seeth me, seeth hym that sente me.

46 Y liyt cam in to the world, that ech that bileueth in me, dwelle not in derknessis.

47 And if ony man herith my words, and kepith hem, Y deme hym not; for Y cam not, that Y deme the world, but that Y make the world saaf.

48 He that dispisith me, and takith not my wordis, hath hym that schal iuge hym; thilke word that Y haue spokun, schal deme hym in the last dai.

49 For Y haue not spokun of my silf, but thilke fadir that sente me, yaf to me a maundement, what Y schal seie, and what Y schal speke.

50 And Y woot, that his maundement is euerlastynge lijf; therfor tho thingis that Y speke, as the fadir seide to me, so Y speke.

CAP 13

1 Bifor the 'feeste dai of pask Jhesus witynge, that his our is comun, that he passe fro this world to the fadir, whanne he hadde loued hise that weren in the world, in to the ende he louede hem.

2 And whanne the souper was maad, whanne the deuel hadde put than in to the herte, that Judas of Symount Scarioth schulde bitraye hym,

3 he witynge that the fadir yaf alle thingis to hym in to hise hoondis, and that he wente out fro God,

4 and goith to God, he risith fro the souper, and doith of hise clothis; and whanne he hadde takun a lynun cloth, he girde hym.

5 And aftirward he putte watir in to a basyn, and biganne to waische the disciplis feet, and to wipe with the lynnen cloth, with which he was gird.

6 And so he cam to Symount Petre, and Petre seith to hym, Lord, waischist thou my feet?

7 Jhesus answerde, and seide to hym, What Y do, thou wost not now; but thou schalt wite aftirward.

8 Petre seith to hym, Thou schalt neuere waische my feet. Jhesus answeride to hym, If Y schal not waische thee, thou schalt not haue part with me.

9 Symount Petre seith to hym, Lord, not oneli my feet, but bothe the hoondis and the heed.

10 Jhesus seide to hym, He that is waischun, hath no nede but that he waische the feet, but he is al clene; and ye ben clene, but not alle.

11 For he wiste, who 'was he that schulde bitraye hym; therfor he seide, Ye ben not alle clene.

12 And so aftir that he hadde waischun 'the feet of hem, he took hise clothis; and whanne he was set to mete ayen, eft he seide to hem, Ye witen what Y haue don to you.

13 Ye clepen me maistir and lord, and ye seien wel; for Y am.

14 Therfor if Y, lord and maistir, haue waischun youre feet, and ye schulen waische oon anothers feet;

15 for Y haue youun 'ensaumple to you, 'that as I haue do to you, so do ye.

16 Treuli, treuli, Y seie to you, the seruaunt is not grettere than his lord, nether an apostle is grettere than he that sente hym.

17 If ye witen these thingis, ye schulen be blessid, if ye doen hem.

18 Y seie not of 'alle you, Y woot whiche Y haue chosun; but that the scripture be fulfillid, He that etith my breed, schal reise his heele ayens me.

19 Treuly, Y seie to you bifor it be don, that whanne it is don, ye bileue that Y am.

20 Treuli, treuli, Y seie to you, he that takith whom euere Y schal sende, resseyueth me; and he that resseyueth me, resseyueth hym that sente me.

21 Whanne Jhesus hadde seid these thingis, he was troblid in spirit, and witnesside, and seide, Treuli, treuli, Y seie to you, that oon of you schal bitraye me.

22 Therfor the disciplis lokiden togidere, doutynge of whom he seide.

23 And so oon of hise disciplis was restynge in the bosum of Jhesu, whom Jhesu louede.

24 Therfor Symount Petre bikeneth to hym, 'and seith to hym, Who is it, of whom he seith?

25 And so whanne he hadde restid ayen on the brest of Jhesu, he seith to hym, Lord, who is it?

26 Jhesus answerde, He it is, to whom Y schal areche a sop of breed. And whanne he hadde wet breed, he yaf to Judas of Symount Scarioth.

27 And aftir the mussel, thanne Sathanas entride in to hym. And Jhesus seith to hym, That thing that thou doist, do thou swithe.

28 And noon of hem that saten at the mete wiste, wherto he seide to hym.

29 For summe gessiden, for Judas hadde pursis, that Jhesus hadde seid to hym, Bie thou tho thingis, that ben nedeful to vs to the feeste dai, or that he schulde yyue sum thing to nedi men.

30 Therfor whanne he hadde takun the mussel, he wente out anoon; and it was nyyt.

31 And whanne he was gon out, Jhesus seide, Now mannus sone is clarified, and God is clarified in hym.

32 If God is clarified in hym, God schal clarifie hym in hym silf, and anoon he schal clarifie hym.

33 Litle sones, yit a litil Y am with you; ye schulen seke me, and, as Y seide to the Jewis, Whidur Y go, ye moun not come; and to you Y seie now.

34 Y yyue to you a newe maundement, that ye loue togidir, as Y louede you, 'and that ye loue togidir.

35 In this thing alle men schulen knowe, that ye ben my disciplis, if ye han loue togidere.

36 Symount Petre seith to hym, Lord, whidur goist thou? Jhesus answeride, Whidur Y go, thou mayst not sue me now, but thou schalt sue afterward.

37 Petre seith to hym, Whi may Y not sue thee now? Y schal putte my lijf for thee.

38 Jhesus answeride, Thou schalt putte thi lijf for me? Treuli, treuli, Y seie to thee, the cok schal not crowe, til thou schalt denye me thries. And he seith to hise disciplis.

CAP 14

1 Be not youre herte afraied, ne drede it; ye bileuen in God, and bileue ye in me.

2 In the hous of my fadir ben many dwellyngis; if ony thing lesse, Y hadde seid to you, for Y go to make redi to you a place.

3 And if Y go, and make redi to you a place, eftsoones Y come, and Y schal take you to my silf, that where Y am, ye be.

4 And whidur Y go, ye witen, and ye witen the weie.

5 Thomas seith to hym, Lord, we witen not whidur thou goist, and hou moun we wite the weie?

6 Jhesus seith to hym, Y am weie, treuthe, and lijf; no man cometh to the fadir, but bi me.

7 If ye hadden knowe me, sotheli ye hadden knowe also my fadir; and aftirward ye schulen knowe hym, and ye han seyn hym.

8 Filip seith to hym, Lord, schewe to vs the fadir, and it suffisith to vs.

9 Jhesus seith to hym, So long tyme Y am with you, and 'han ye not knowun me? Filip, he that seeth me, seeth also the fadir. Hou seist thou, schewe to vs the fadir?

10 Bileuest thou not, that Y am in the fadir, and the fadir is in me? The wordis that Y speke to you, Y speke not of my silf; but the fadir hym silf dwellynge in me, doith the werkis.

11 Bileue ye not, that Y am in the fadir, and the fadir is in me?

12 Ellis bileue ye for thilke werkis. Treuli, treuli, Y seie to you, if a man bileueth in me, also he schal do the werkis that Y do; and he schal do grettere werkis than these, for Y go to the fadir.

13 And what euere thing ye axen the fadir in my name, Y schal do this thing, that the fadir be glorified in the sone.

14 If ye axen ony thing in my name, Y schal do it.

15 If ye louen me, kepe ye my comaundementis.

16 And Y schal preye the fadir, and he schal yyue to you another coumfortour,

17 the spirit of treuthe, to dwelle with you with outen ende; which spirit the world may not take, for it seeth hym not, nether knowith hym. But ye schulen knowe hym, for he schal dwelle with you, and he schal be in you.

18 Y schal not leeue you fadirles, Y schal come to you.

19 Yit a litil, and the world seeth not now me; but ye schulen se me, for Y lyue, and ye schulen lyue.

20 In that dai ye schulen knowe, that Y am in my fadir, and ye in me, and Y in you.

21 He that hath my comaundementis, and kepith hem, he it is that loueth me; and he that loueth me, schal be loued of my fadir, and Y schal loue hym, and Y schal schewe to hym my silf.

22 Judas seith to hym, not he of Scarioth, Lord, what is don, that thou schalt schewe thi silf to vs, and not to the world?

23 Jhesus answerde, and seide 'to hym, If ony man loueth me, he schal kepe my word; and my fadir schal loue hym, and we schulen come to hym, and we schulen dwelle with hym.

24 He that loueth me not, kepith not my wordis; and the word which ye han herd, is not myn, but the fadris, that sente me.

25 These thingis Y haue spokun to you, dwellynge among you; but thilke Hooli Goost,

26 the coumfortour, whom the fadir schal sende in my name, he schal teche you alle thingis, 'and schal schewe to you alle thingis, what euere thingis Y schal seie to you.

27 Pees Y leeue to you, my pees Y yyue to you; not as the world yyueth, Y yiue to you; be not youre herte affrayed, ne drede it.

28 Ye han herd, that Y seide to you, Y go, and come to you. If ye loueden me, forsothe ye schulden haue ioye, for Y go to the fadir, for the fadir is grettere than Y.

29 And now Y haue seid to you, bifor that it be don, that whanne it is don, ye bileuen.

30 Now Y schal not speke many thingis with you; for the prince of this world cometh, and hath not in me ony thing.

31 But that the world knowe, that Y loue the fadir; and as the fadir yaf a comaundement to me, so Y do. 'Rise ye, go we hennus.

CAP 15

1 Y am a very vyne, and my fadir is an erthe tilier.

2 Ech braunch in me that berith not fruyt, he schal take awey it; and ech that berith fruyt, he schal purge it, that it bere the more fruyt.

3 Now ye ben clene, for the word that Y haue spokun to you.

4 Dwelle ye in me, and Y in you; as a braunche may not make fruyt of it silf, but it dwelle in the vyne, so nether ye, but ye dwelle in me.

5 Y am a vyne, ye the braunchis. Who that dwellith in me, and Y in hym, this berith myche fruyt, for with outen me ye moun no thing do.

6 If ony man dwellith not in me, he schal be caste out as a braunche, and schal wexe drie; and thei schulen gadere hym, and thei schulen caste hym in to the fier, and he brenneth.

7 If ye dwellen in me, and my wordis dwelle in you, what euer thing ye wolen, ye schulen axe, and it schal be don to you.

8 In this thing my fadir is clarified, that ye brynge forth ful myche fruyt, and that ye be maad my disciplis.

9 As my fadir louede me, Y haue loued you; dwelle ye in my loue.

10 If ye kepen my comaundementis, ye schulen dwelle in my loue; as Y haue kept the comaundementis of my fadir, and Y dwelle in his loue.

11 These thingis Y spak to you, that my ioye be in you, and youre ioye be fulfillid.

12 This is my comaundement, that ye loue togidere, as Y louede you.

13 No man hath more loue than this, that a man putte his lijf for hise freendis.

14 Ye ben my freendis if ye doen tho thingis, that Y comaunde to you.

15 Now Y schal not clepe you seruauntis, for the seruaunt woot not, what his lord schal do; but Y haue clepid you freendis, for alle thingis what euere Y herde of my fadir, Y haue maad knowun to you.

16 Ye han not chosun me, but Y chees you; and Y haue put you, that ye go, and brynge forth fruyt, and youre fruyt dwelle; that what euere thing ye axen the fadir in my name, he yyue to you.

17 These thingis Y comaunde to you, that ye loue togidere.

18 If the world hatith you, wite ye, that it hadde me in hate rather than you.

19 If ye hadden be of the world, the world schulde loue that thing that was his; but for ye ben not of the world, but Y chees you fro the world, therfor the world hatith you.

20 Haue ye mynde of my word, which Y seide to you, The seruaunt is not grettere than his lord. If thei han pursued me, thei schulen pursue you also; if thei han kept my word, thei schulen kepe youre also.

21 But thei schulen do to you alle these thingis for my name, for thei knowen not hym that sente me.

22 If Y hadde not comun, and hadde not spokun to hem, thei schulden not haue synne; but now thei haue noon excusacioun of her synne.

23 He that hatith me, hatith also my fadir.

24 If Y hadde not doon werkis in hem, whiche noon other man dide, thei schulden not haue synne; but now both thei han seyn, and hatid me and my fadir.

25 But that the word be fulfillid, that is writun in her lawe, For thei hadden me in hate with outen cause.

26 But whanne the coumfortour schal come, which Y schal sende to you fro the fadir, a spirit of treuthe, which cometh of the fadir, he schal bere witnessyng of me; and ye schulen bere witnessyng, for ye ben with me fro the bigynnyng.

CAP 16

1 These thingis Y haue spokun to you, that ye be not sclaundrid.

2 Thei schulen make you with outen the synagogis, but the our cometh, that ech man that sleeth you, deme that he doith seruyce to God.

3 And thei schulen do to you these thingis, for thei han not knowun the fadir, nether me.

4 But these thingis Y spak to you, that whanne the our 'of hem schal come, ye haue mynde, that Y seide to you.

5 Y seide not to you these thingis fro the bigynnyng, for Y was with you. And now Y go to hym that sente me, and no man of you axith me, Whidur 'thou goist?

6 but for Y haue spokun to you these thingis, heuynesse hath fulfillid youre herte.

7 But Y seie to you treuthe, it spedith to you, that Y go; for if Y go not forth, the coumfortour schal not come to you; but if Y go forth, Y schal sende hym to you.

8 And whanne he cometh, he schal repreue the world of synne, and of riytwisnesse, and of doom.

9 Of synne, for thei han not bileued in me;

10 and of riytwisnesse, for Y go to the fadir, and now ye schulen not se me;

11 but of doom, for the prince of this world is now demed.

12 Yit Y haue many thingis for to seie to you, but ye moun not bere hem now.

13 But whanne thilke spirit of treuthe cometh, he schal teche you al trewthe; for he schal not speke of hym silf, but what euer thinges he schal here, he schal speke; and he schal telle to you tho thingis that ben to come.

14 He schal clarifie me, for of myne he schal take, and schal telle to you.

15 Alle thingis 'whiche euer the fadir hath, ben myne; therfor Y seide to you, for of myne he schal take, and schal telle to you.

16 A litil, and thanne ye schulen not se me; and eftsoone a litil, and ye schulen se me, for Y go to the fadir.

17 Therfor summe of hise disciplis seiden togidere, What is this thing that he seith to vs, A litil, and ye schulen not se me; and eftsoone a litil, and ye schulen se me, for Y go to the fadir?

18 Therfor thei seiden, What is this that he seith to vs, A litil? we witen not what he spekith.

19 And Jhesus knew, that thei wolden axe hym, and he seide to hem, Of this thing ye seken among you, for Y seide, A litil, and ye schulen not se me; and eftsoone a litil, and ye schulen se me.

20 Treuli, treuli, Y seie to you, that ye schulen mourne and wepe, but the world schal haue ioye; and ye schulen be soreuful, but youre sorewe schal turne in to ioye.

21 A womman whanne sche berith child, hath heuynesse, for hir tyme is comun; but whanne sche hath borun a sone, now sche thenkith not on the peyne, for ioye, for a man is borun in to the world.

22 And therfor ye han now sorew, but eftsoone Y schal se you, and youre herte schal haue ioie, and no man schal take fro you youre ioie.

23 And in that day ye schulen not axe me ony thing; treuli, treuli, 'Y seie to you, if ye axen the fadir ony thing in my name, he schal yyue to you.

24 'Til now ye axiden no thing in my name; 'axe ye, 'and ye schulen take, that youre ioie be ful.

25 Y haue spokun to you these thingis in prouerbis; the our cometh, whanne now Y schal not speke to you in prouerbis, but opynli of my fadir Y schal telle to you.

26 In that dai ye schulen axe in my name; and Y seie not to you, that Y schal preye the fadir of you;

27 for the fadir hym silf loueth you, for ye han loued me, and han bileued, that Y wente out fro God.

28 Y wente out fro the fadir, and Y cam in to the world; eftsoone Y leeue the world, and Y go to the fadir.

29 Hise disciplis seiden to hym, Lo! now thou spekist opynli, and thou seist no prouerbe.

30 Now we witen, that thou wost alle thingis; and it is not nede to thee, that ony man axe thee. In this thing we bileuen, that thou wentist out fro God.

31 Jhesus answeride to hem, Now ye bileuen.

32 Lo! the our cometh, and now it cometh, that ye be dispar-plid, ech in to hise owne thingis, and that ye leeue me aloone; and Y am not aloone, for the fadir is with me.

33 These thingis Y haue spokun to you, that ye haue pees in me; in the world ye schulen haue disese, but trust ye, Y haue ouercomun the world.

CAP 17

1 These thingis Jhesus spak, and whanne he hadde cast vp hise iyen in to heuene, he seide, Fadir, the our cometh, clarifie thi sone, that thi sone clarifie thee.

2 As thou hast youun to hym power on ech fleisch, that al thing that thou hast youun to hym, he yyue to hem euer-lastynge lijf.

3 And this is euerlastynge lijf, that thei knowe thee very God aloone, and whom thou hast sent, Jhesu Crist.

4 Y haue clarified thee on the erthe, Y haue endid the werk, that thou hast youun to me to do.

5 And now, fadir, clarifie thou me at thi silf, with the clere-nesse that Y hadde at thee, bifor the world was maad.

6 Y haue schewid thi name to tho men, whiche thou hast youun to me of the world; thei weren thine, and thou hast youun hem to me, and thei han kept thi word.

7 And now thei han knowun, that alle thingis that thou hast youun to me, ben of thee.

8 For the wordis that thou hast youun to me, Y yaf to hem; and thei han takun, and han knowun verili, that Y wente out fro thee; and thei bileueden, that thou sentist me.

9 Y preie for hem, Y preye not for the world, but for hem that thou hast youun to me, for thei ben thine.

10 And alle my thingis ben thine, and thi thingis ben myne; and Y am clarified in hem.

11 And now Y am not in the world, and these ben in the world, and Y come to thee. Hooli fadir, kepe hem in thi name, whiche thou yauest to me, that thei ben oon, as we ben.

12 While Y was with hem, Y kepte hem in thi name; thilke that thou yauest to me, Y kepte, and noon of hem perischide, but the sone of perdicioun, that the scripture be fulfillid.

13 But now Y come to thee, and Y speke these thingis in the world, that thei haue my ioie fulfillid in hem silf.

14 Y yaf to hem thi word, and the world hadde hem in hate; for thei ben not of the world, as Y am not of the world.

15 Y preye not, that thou take hem awei fro the world, but that thou kepe hem fro yuel.

16 They ben not of the world, as Y am not of the world.

17 Halewe thou hem in treuth; thi word is treuthe.

18 As thou sentist me in to the world, also Y sente hem 'in to the world.

19 And Y halewe my silf for hem, that also thei ben halewid in treuthe.

20 And Y preye not oneli for hem, but also for hem that schulden bileue in to me bi the word of hem;

21 that all ben oon, as thou, fadir, in me, and Y in thee, that also thei in vs be oon; that the world bileue, that thou hast sent me.

22 And Y haue youun to hem the clerenesse, that thou hast youun to me, that thei ben oon,

23 as we ben oon; Y in hem, and thou in me, that thei be endid in to oon; and that the world knowe, that thou sentist me, and hast loued hem, as thou hast loued also me.

24 Fadir, thei whiche thou yauest to me, Y wole that where Y am, that thei be with me, that thei see my clerenesse, that thou hast youun to me; for thou louedist me bifor the makyng of the world.

25 Fadir, riytfuli the world knew thee not, but Y knew thee, and these knewen, that thou sentist me.

26 And Y haue maad thi name knowun to hem, and schal make knowun; that the loue bi which thou 'hast loued me, be in hem, and Y in hem.

CAP 18

1 Whanne Jhesus hadde seid these thingis, he wente out with hise disciplis ouer the strond of Cedron, where was a yerd, in to which he entride, and hise disciplis.

2 And Judas, that bitrayede hym, knew the place, for ofte Jhesus cam thidur with hise disciplis.

3 Therfor whanne Judas hadde takun a cumpany of knyytis, and mynystris of the bischopis and of the Fariseis, he cam thidur with lanternys, and brondis, and armeris.

4 And so Jhesus witynge alle thingis that weren to come on hym, wente forth, and seide to hem, Whom seken ye?

5 Thei answeriden to hym, Jhesu of Nazareth. Jhesus seith to hem, Y am. And Judas that bitraiede hym, stood with hem.

6 And whanne he seide to hem, Y am, thei wenten abak, and fellen doun on the erthe.

7 And eft he axide hem, Whom seken ye? And thei seiden, Jhesu of Nazareth.

8 He answeride to hem, Y seide to you, that Y am; therfor if ye seken me, suffre ye these to go awei.

9 That the word which he seide schulde be fulfillid, For Y loste not ony of hem, whiche thou 'hast youun to me.

10 Therfor Symount Petre hadde a swerd, and drow it out, and smoot the seruaunt of the bischop, and kittide of his riyt eer. And the name of the seruaunt was Malcus.

11 Therfor Jhesus seide to Petre, Putte thou thi swerd in to thi schethe; wolt thou not, that Y drynke the cuppe, that my fadir yaf to me?

12 Therfor the cumpenye of knyytis, and the tribune, and the mynystris of the Jewis, token Jhesu, and bounden hym,

13 and ledden hym first to Annas; for he was fadir of Caifas wijf, that was bischop of that yeer.

14 And it was Caifas, that yaf counsel to the Jewis, that it spedith, that o man die for the puple.

15 But Symount Petre suede Jhesu, and another disciple; and thilke disciple was knowun to the bischop. And he entride with Jhesu, in to the halle of the bischop;

16 but Petre stood at the dore with outforth. Therfor 'the tother disciple, that was knowun to the bischop, wente out, and seide to the womman that kepte the dore, and brouyte in Petre.

17 And the damysel, kepere of the dore, seide to Petre, Whether thou art also of this mannys disciplis? He seide, Y am not.

18 And the seruantis and mynystris stooden at the coolis, for it was coold, and thei warmyden hem; and Petre was with hem, stondynge and warmynge hym.

19 And the bischop axide Jhesu of hise disciplis, and of his techyng.

20 Jhesus answerde to hym, Y haue spokun opynli to the world; Y tauyte euermore in the synagoge, and in the temple,

whider alle the Jewis camen togidere, and in hiddlis Y spak no thing.

21 What axist thou me? axe hem that herden, what Y haue spokun to hem; lo! thei witen, what thingis Y haue seid.

22 Whanne he hadde seid these thingis, oon of the mynystris stondynge niy, yaf a buffat to Jhesu, and seide, Answerist thou so to the bischop?

23 Jhesus answeride to hym, If Y haue spokun yuel, bere thou witnessyng of yuel; but if Y seide wel, whi smytist thou me?

24 And Annas sente hym boundun to Caifas, the bischop.

25 And Symount Petre stood, and warmyde him; and thei seiden to hym, Whether also thou art his disciple? He denyede, and seide, Y am not.

26 Oon of the bischops seruantis, cosyn of hym, whos eere Petre kitte of, seide, Say Y thee not in the yerd with hym?

27 And Petre eftsoone denyede, and anoon the cok crew.

28 Thanne thei ledden Jhesu to Cayfas, in to the moot halle; and it was eerli, and thei entriden not in to the moot halle, that thei schulden not be defoulid, but that thei schulden ete pask.

29 Therfor Pilat wente out with outforth to hem, and seide, What accusyng brynge ye ayens this man?

30 Thei answeriden, and seiden to hym, If this were not a mysdoere, we hadden not bitakun hym to thee.

31 Thanne Pilat seith to hem, Take ye hym, and deme ye him, after youre lawe. And the Jewis seiden to hym, It is not leueful to vs to sle ony man;

32 that the word of Jhesu schulde be fulfillid, whiche he seide, signifiynge bi what deth he schulde die.

33 Therfor eftsoone Pilat entride in to the moot halle, and clepide Jhesu, and seide to hym, Art thou kyng of Jewis?

34 Jhesus answerde, and seide to hym, Seist thou this thing of thi silf, ether othere han seid to thee of me?

35 Pilat answeride, Whether Y am a Jewe? Thi folc and bischops bitoken thee to me; what hast thou don?

36 Jhesus answeride, My kingdom is not of this world; if my kingdom were of this world, my mynystris schulden stryue, that Y schulde not be takun to the Jewis; but now my kingdom is not here.

37 And so Pilat seide to hym, Thanne 'thou art a king. Jhesus answeride, Thou seist, that Y am a king. To this thing Y am borun, and to this Y 'am comun in to the world, to bere witnessing to treuthe. Eche that is of treuthe, herith my vois.

38 Pilat seith to hym, What is treuthe? And whanne he hadde seid this thing, eft he wente out to the Jewis, and seide to hem, Y fynde no cause in hym.

39 But it is a custom to you, that Y delyuere oon to you in pask; therfor wole ye that Y delyuere to you the kyng of Jewis?

40 Alle crieden eftsoone, and seiden, Not this, but Baraban. And Barabas was a theef.

CAP 19

1 Therfor Pilat took thanne Jhesu, and scourgide.

2 And kniytis writhen a coroun of thornes, and setten on his heed, and diden aboute hym a cloth of purpur,

3 and camen to him, and seiden, Heil, kyng of Jewis. And thei yauen to him buffatis.

4 Eftsoone Pilat wente out, and seide to hem, Lo! Y brynge hym out to you, that ye knowe, that Y fynde no cause in him.

5 And so Jhesus wente out, berynge a coroun of thornes, and a cloth of purpur. And he seith to hem, Lo! the man.

6 But whanne the bischopis and mynystris hadden seyn hym, thei crieden, and seiden, Crucifie, crucifie hym. Pilat seith to

hem, Take ye hym, and crucifie ye, for Y fynde no cause in hym.

7 The Jewis answeriden to hym. We han a lawe, and bi the lawe he owith to die, for he made hym Goddis sone.

8 Therfor whanne Pilat hadde herd this word, he dredde the more.

9 And he wente in to the moot halle eftsoone, and seide to Jhesu, Of whennus art thou? But Jhesus yaf noon answere to him.

10 Pilat seith to him, Spekist thou not to me? Woost thou not, that Y haue power to crucifie thee, and Y haue power to delyuere thee?

11 Jhesus answeride, Thou schuldist not 'haue ony power ayens me, but it were youun to thee from aboue; therfor he that bitook me to thee, hath the more synne.

12 Fro that tyme Pilat souyte to delyuere hym; but the Jewis crieden, and seiden, If thou delyuerist this man, thou art not the emperouris freend; for ech man that makith hym silf king, ayen seith the emperoure.

13 And Pilat, whanne he hadde herd these wordis, ledde Jhesu forth, and sat for domesman in a place, that is seid Licostratos, but in Ebrew Golgatha.

14 And it was pask eue, as it were the sixte our. And he seith to the Jewis, Lo! youre king.

15 But thei crieden, and seiden, Take awei, take awei; crucifie him. Pilat seith to hem, Schal I crucifie youre king? The bischops answeriden, We han no king but the emperour.

16 And thanne Pilat bitook him to hem, that he schulde be crucified. And thei token Jhesu, and ledden him out.

17 And he bar to hym silf a cros, and wente out in to that place, that is seid of Caluarie, in Ebreu Golgatha;

18 where thei crucifieden him, and othere tweyne with him, oon on this side and oon on that side, and Jhesus in the myddil.

19 And Pilat wroot a title, and sette on the cros; and it was writun, Jhesu of Nazareth, king of Jewis.

20 Therfor manye of the Jewis redden this title, for the place where Jhesus was crucified, was niy the citee, and it was writun in Ebreu, Greek, and Latyn.

21 Therfor the bischops of the Jewis seiden to Pilat, Nyle thou write kyng of Jewis, but for he seide, Y am king of Jewis.

22 Pilat answeride, That that Y haue writun, Y haue writun.

23 Therfor the knyytis whanne thei hadden crucified hym, token hise clothis, and maden foure partis, to ech knyyt a part, and a coot. And the coot was without seem, and wouun al aboute.

24 Therfor thei seiden togidere, Kitte we not it, but caste we lot, whos it is; that the scripture be fulfillid, seiynge, Thei partiden my clothis to hem, and on my cloth thei casten lot. And the kniytis diden these thingis.

25 But bisidis the cros of Jhesu stoden his modir, and the sistir of his modir, Marie Cleofe, and Marie Maudeleyne.

26 Therfor whanne Jhesu hadde seyn his modir, and the disciple stondynge, whom he louyde, he seith to hise modir, Womman, lo thi sone.

27 Aftyrward he seith to the disciple, Lo! thi modir. And fro that our the disciple took hir in to his modir.

28 Aftirward Jhesus witynge, that now alle thingis ben endid, that the scripture were fulfillid, he seith, Y thirste.

29 And a vessel was set ful of vynegre. And thei 'leiden in isope aboute the spounge ful of vynegre, and putten to his mouth.

30 Therfor whanne Jhesus hadde 'takun the vynegre, he seid, It is endid. And 'whanne his heed was bowid doun, 'he yaf vp the goost.

31 Therfor for it was the pask eue, that the bodies schulden not abide on the cros in the sabat, for that was a greet sabat dai, the Jewis preiden Pilat, that the hipis of hem schulden be brokun, and thei takun awei.

32 Therfor knyytis camen, and thei braken the thies of the firste, and of the tothere, that was crucified with hym.

33 But whanne thei weren comun to Jhesu, as thei sayn him deed thanne, thei braken not hise thies;

34 but oon of the knyytis openyde his side with a spere, and anoon blood and watir wenten out.

35 And he that saiy, bare witnessyng, and his witnessing is trewe; and he woot that he seith trewe thingis, that ye bileue.

36 And these thingis weren don, that the scripture schulde be fulfillid, Ye schulen not breke a boon of hym.

37 And eftsoone another scripture seith, Thei schulen se in whom thei piyten thorow.

38 But after these thingis Joseph of Armathi preyede Pilat, that he schulde take awei the bodi of Jhesu, for that he was a disciple of Jhesu, but priui for drede of the Jewis. And Pilat suffride. And so he cam, and took awei the bodi of Jhesu.

39 And Nychodeme cam also, that hadde come to hym first bi nyyt, and brouyte a meddlynge of myrre and aloes, as it were an hundrid pound.

40 And thei token the bodi of Jhesu, and boundun it in lynun clothis with swete smellynge oynementis, as it is custom to Jewis for to birie.

41 And in the place where he was crucified, was a yerd, and in the yerd a newe graue, in which yit no man was leid.

42 Therfor there thei putten Jhesu, for the vigilie of Jewis feeste, for the sepulcre was niy.

CAP 20

1 And in o dai of the wouke Marie Maudeleyn cam eerli to the graue, whanne it was yit derk. And sche say the stoon moued awei fro the graue.

2 Therfor sche ran, and cam to Symount Petre, and to another disciple, whom Jhesus louede, and seith to hem, Thei han takun the Lord fro the graue, and we witen not, where thei han leid hym.

3 Therfor Petre wente out, and thilke other disciple, and thei camen to the graue.

4 And thei tweyne runnen togidre, and thilke othere disciple ran bifor Petre, and cam first to the graue.

5 And whanne he stoupide, he sai the schetis liynge, netheles he entride not.

6 Therfor Symount Petre cam suynge hym, and he entride in to the graue, and he say the schetis leid,

7 and the sudarie that was on his heed, not leid with the schetis, but bi it silf wlappid in to a place.

8 Therfor thanne thilke disciple that cam first to the graue, entride, and sai, and bileuede.

9 For thei knewen not yit the scripture, that it behofte him to rise ayen fro deth.

10 Therfor the disciplis wenten eftsoone to hem silf.

11 But Marie stood at the graue with outforth wepynge. And the while sche wepte, sche bowide hir, and bihelde forth in to the graue.

12 And sche sai twei aungels sittinge in white, oon at the heed and oon at the feet, where the bodi of Jhesu was leid.

13 And thei seien to hir, Womman, what wepist thou? Sche seide to hem, For thei han take awei my lord, and Y woot not, where thei han leid him.

14 Whanne sche hadde seid these thingis, sche turnede bacward, and sai Jhesu stondinge, and wiste not that it was Jhesu.

15 Jhesus seith to hir, Womman, what wepist thou? whom sekist thou? She gessynge that he was a gardynere, seith to him, Sire, if thou hast takun him vp, seie to me, where thou hast leid him, and Y schal take hym awei.

16 Jhesus seith to hir, Marie. Sche 'turnede, and seith to hym, Rabony, that is to seie, Maister.

17 Jhesus seith to hir, Nyle thou touche me, for Y haue not yit stied to my fadir; but go to my britheren, and seie to hem, Y stie to my fadir and to youre fadir, to my God and to youre God.

18 Marie Maudeleyne cam, tellinge to the disciplis, That Y sai the Lord, and these thingis he seide to me.

19 Therfor whanne it was eue in that dai, oon of the sabatis, and the yatis weren schit, where the disciplis weren gaderid, for drede of the Jewis, Jhesus cam, and stood in the myddil of the disciplis, and he seith to hem, Pees to you.

20 And whanne he hadde seid this, he schewide to hem hondis and side; therfor the disciplis ioieden, for the Lord was seyn.

21 And he seith to hem eft, Pees to you; as the fadir sente me, Y sende you.

22 Whanne he had seid this, he blewe on hem, and seide, Take ye the Hooli Goost;

23 whos synnes ye foryyuen, tho ben foryouun to hem; and whos ye withholden, tho ben withholdun.

24 But Thomas, oon of the twelue, that is seid Didimus, was not with hem, whanne Jhesus cam.

25 Therfor the othere disciplis seiden, We han seyn the Lord. And he seide to hem, But Y se in hise hondis the fitchinge of the nailis, and putte my fyngur in to the places of the nailis, and putte myn hond in to his side, Y schal not bileue.

26 And after eiyte daies eftsoone thise disciplis weren with ynne, and Thomas with hem. Jhesus cam, while the yatis weren schit, and stood in the myddil, and seide, Pees to you.

27 Afterward he seith to Thomas, Putte in here thi fyngur, and se myn hondis, and putte hidur thin hond, and putte in to my side, and nyle thou be vnbileueful, but feithful.

28 Thomas answeride, and seide to him, My Lord and my God.

29 Jhesus seith to him, Thomas, for thou hast seyn me, thou bileuedist; blessid ben thei, that seyn not, and han bileued.

30 And Jhesus dide many othere signes in the siyt of hise disciplis, whiche ben not writun in this book.

31 But these ben writun, that ye bileue, that Jhesus 'is Crist, the sone of God, and that ye bileuynge haue lijf in his name.

CAP 21

1 Afterward Jhesus eftsoone schewide hym to hise disciplis, at the see of Tiberias.

2 And he schewide him thus. There weren togidere Symount Petre, and Thomas, that is seid Didimus, and Nathanael, that was of the Cane of Galilee, and the sones of Zebedee, and tweyne othere of hise disciplis.

3 Symount Petre seith to hem, Y go to fische. Thei seyn to hym, And we comen with thee. And 'thei wenten out, 'and wenten in to a boot. And in that niyt thei token no thing.

4 But whanne the morewe was comun, Jhesus stood in the brenke; netheles the disciplis knewen not, that it was Jhesus.

5 Therfor Jhesus seith to hem, Children, whethir ye han ony souping thing? Thei answeriden to hym, Nay. He seide to hem,

6 Putte ye the nett in to the riyt half of the rowing, and ye schulen fynde. And thei puttiden the nett; and thanne thei miyten not drawe it for multitude of fischis.

7 Therfor thilke disciple, whom Jhesus louede, seide to Petre, It is the Lord. Symount Petre, whanne he hadde herd that it is the Lord, girte hym with a coote, for he was nakid, and wente in to the see.

8 But the othere disciplis camen bi boot, for thei weren not fer fro the lond, but as a two hundrid cubitis, drawinge the nett of fischis.

9 And as thei camen doun in to the lond, thei sayn coolis liynge, and a fisch leid on, and breed.

10 Jhesus seith to hem, Bringe ye of the fyschis, whiche ye han takun now.

11 Symount Petre wente vp, and drowy the nett in to the lond, ful of grete fischis, an hundrid fifti and thre; and whanne thei weren so manye, the nett was not brokun.

12 Jhesus seith to hem, Come ye, ete ye. And no man of hem that saten at the mete, durste axe hym, Who art thou, witinge that it is the Lord.

13 And Jhesus cam, and took breed, an yaf to hem, and fisch also.

14 Now this thridde tyme Jhesus was schewid to hise disciplis, whanne he hadde risun ayen fro deth.

15 And whanne thei hadde etun, Jhesus seith to Simount Petre, Symount of Joon, louest thou me more than these? He seith to him, Yhe, Lord, thou woost that Y loue thee. Jhesus seith to hym, Fede thou my lambren.

16 Eft he seith to hym, Symount of Joon, louest thou me? He seith to him, Yhe, Lord, thou woost that Y loue thee. He seith to him, Fede thou my lambren.

17 He seith to him the thridde tyme, Simount of Joon, louest thou me? Petre was heuy, for he seith to hym the thridde tyme, Louest thou me, and he seith to him, Lord, thou knowist alle thingis; thou woost that Y loue thee. Jhesus seith to hym, Fede my scheep.

18 Treuli, treuli, Y seie to thee, whanne thou were yongere, thou girdidist thee, and wandridist where thou woldist; but whanne thou schalt waxe eldere, thou schalt holde forth thin hondis, and another schal girde thee, and schal lede thee whidur thou wolt not.

19 He seide this thing, signifynge bi what deth he schulde glorifie God. And whanne he hadde seid these thingis, he seith to hym, Sue thou me.

20 Petre turnede, and say thilke disciple suynge, whom Jhesus louede, which also restid in the soper on his brest, and he seide to hym, Lord, who is it, that schal bitraie thee?

21 Therfor whanne Petre hadde seyn this, he seith to Jhesu, Lord, but what this?

22 Jhesus seith to him, So I wole that he dwelle til that Y come, what to thee? sue thou me.

23 Therfor this word wente out among the britheren, that thilke disciple dieth not. And Jhesus seide not to hym, that he dieth not, but, So Y wole that he dwelle til Y come, what to thee?

24 This is thilke disciple, that berith witnessyng of these thingis, and wroot hem; and we witen, that his witnessyng is trewe.

25 And ther ben also manye othere thingis that Jhesus dide, whiche if thei ben writun bi ech bi hym silf, Y deme that the world hym silf schal not take tho bookis, that ben to be writun.

DEDIS OF APOSTLIS

CAP 1

1 Theofle, first 'Y made a sermoun of alle thingis, that Jhesu bigan to do and to teche,

2 in to the daie of his ascencioun, in which he comaundide bi the Hooli Goost to hise apostlis, whiche he hadde chosun;

3 to whiche he schewide hym silf 'alyue aftir his passioun, by many argumentis, apperinge to hem fourti daies, and spekinge of the rewme of God.

4 And he ete with hem, and comaundide, that thei schulden not departe fro Jerusalem, but abide the biheest of the fadir, which ye herden, he seide, bi my mouth;

5 for Joon baptiside in watir, but ye schulen be baptisid in the Hooli Goost, aftir these fewe daies.

6 Therfor thei that weren come to gidere, axiden hym, and seiden, Lord, whether in this time thou schalt restore the kingdom of Israel?

7 And he seide to hem, It is not youre to knowe the tymes ether momentis, whiche the fadir hath put in his power;

8 but ye schulen take the vertu of the Hooli Goost comynge fro aboue in to you, and ye schulen be my witnessis in Jerusalem, and in al Judee, and Samarie, and to the vtmeste of the erthe.

9 And whanne he had seid these thingis, in her siyt he was lift vp, and a cloude resseyuede him fro her iyen.

10 And whanne thei biheelden hym goynge in to heuene, lo! 'twei men stoden bisidis hem in white clothing, and seiden,

11 Men of Galile, what stonden ye biholdinge in to heuene? This Jhesu, which is takun vp 'fro you in to heuene, schal come, as ye seyn hym goynge in to heuene.

12 Thanne thei turneden ayen to Jerusalem, fro the hille that is clepid 'the hille of Olyuete, which is bisidis Jerusalem an halidaies iourney.

13 And whanne thei weren entrid in to the hous, where thei dwelliden, thei wenten vp in to the soler, Petir and Joon, James and Andreu, Philip and Thomas, Bartholomew and Matheu, James of Alphei, and Symount Zelotes, and Judas of James.

14 Alle these weren lastingli contynuynge with o wille in preier, with wymmen, and Marie, the moder of Jhesu, and with hise britheren.

15 In tho daies Petre roos vp in the myddil of the britheren, and seide; and ther was a company of men togidere, almest an hundrid and twenti;

16 Britheren, it bihoueth that the scripture be fillid, whiche the Hooly Goost bifore seide bi the mouth of Dauith, of Judas that was ledere of hem that token Jhesu;

17 and was noumbrid among vs, and gat a part of this seruyce.

18 And this Judas hadde a feeld of the hire of wickidnesse, and he was hangid, and 'to-brast the myddil, and alle hise entrailes weren sched abrood.

19 And it was maad knowun to alle men that dwelten in Jerusalem, so that the ilke feeld was clepid Acheldemak in the langage of hem, that is, the feeld of blood.

20 And it is writun in the book of Salmes, The abitacioun of hem be maad desert, and be ther noon that dwelle in it, and an other take his bishopriche.

21 Therfor it bihoueth of these men, that ben gaderid togidere with vs in al the tyme, in which the Lord Jhesu entride, and wente out among vs,

22 and bigan fro the baptym of Joon til in to the dai in which he was takun vp fro vs, that oon of these be maad a witnesse of his resurreccioun with vs.

23 And thei ordeyneden tweyn, Joseph, that was clepid Barsabas, that was named Just, and Mathie.

24 And thei preieden, and seiden, Thou, Lord, that knowist the hertis of alle men, schewe whom thou hast chosun of these tweyne,

25 that oon take the place of this seruyce and apostlehed, of which Judas trespasside, that he schulde go in to his place.

26 And thei yauen lottis to hem, and the lot felde on Mathie; and he was noumbrid with enleuen apostlis.

CAP 2

1 And whanne the daies of Pentecost weren fillid, alle the disciplis weren togidre in the same place.

2 And sodeynli ther was maad a sown fro heuene, as of a greet wynde comynge, and it fillide al the hous where thei saten.

3 And diuerse tungis as fier apperiden to hem, and it sat on ech of hem.

4 And alle weren fillid with the Hooli Goost, and thei bigunnen to speke diuerse langagis, as the Hooli Goost yaf to hem for to speke.

5 And ther weren in Jerusalem dwellinge Jewis, religiouse men, of ech nacioun that is vndur heuene.

6 And whanne this vois was maad, the multitude cam togidere, and thei weren astonyed in thouyt, for ech man herde hem spekinge in his langage.

7 And alle weren astonyed, and wondriden, and seiden togidere, Whether not alle these that speken ben men of Galyle,

8 and hou herden we ech man his langage in which we ben borun?

9 Parthi, and Medi, and Elamyte, and thei that dwellen at Mesopotami, Judee, and Capodosie, and Ponte,

10 and Asie, Frigie, and Pamfilie, Egipt, and the parties of Libie, that is aboue Sirenen, and 'comelingis Romayns, and Jewis,

11 and proselitis, men of Crete, and of Arabie, we han herd hem spekynge in oure langagis the grete thingis of God.

12 And alle weren astonyed, and wondriden, 'and seiden togidere, What wole this thing be?

13 And othere scorneden, and seiden, For these men ben ful of must.

14 But Petre stood with the enleuene, and reiside vp his vois, and spak to hem, Ye Jewis, and alle that dwellen at Jerusalem, be this knowun to you, and with eris perseyue ye my wordis.

15 For not as ye wenen, these ben dronkun, whanne it is the thridde our of the dai;

16 but this it is, that was seid bi the prophete Johel,

17 And it schal be in the laste daies, the Lord seith, Y schal helde out my spirit on ech fleisch; and youre sones and youre douytris schulen prophesie, and youre yonge men schulen se visiouns, and youre eldris schulen dreme sweuenes.

18 And on my seruauntis and myn handmaidens in tho daies Y schal schede out of my spirit, and thei schulen prophecie.

19 And Y schal yyue grete wondris in heuene aboue, and signes in erthe bynethe, blood, and fier, and heete of smoke.

20 The sunne schal be turned in to derknessis, and the moone in to blood, bifor that the greet and the opyn dai of the Lord come.

21 And it schal be, ech man which euere schal clepe to help the name of the Lord, schal be saaf.

22 Ye men of Israel, here ye these wordis. Jhesu of Nazareth, a man preued of God bifor you bi vertues, and wondris, and tokenes, which God dide bi hym in the myddil of you,

23 as ye witen, ye turmentiden, and killiden hym bi the hoondis of wyckid men, bi counseil determyned and bitakun bi the forknouwyng of God.

24 Whom God reiside, whanne sorewis of helle weren vnboundun, bi that that it was impossible that he were holdun of it.

25 For Dauid seith of hym, Y saiy afer the Lord bifore me euermore, for he is on my riythalf, that Y be not mouyd.

26 For this thing myn herte ioiede, and my tunge made ful out ioye, and more ouere my fleisch schal reste in hope.

27 For thou schalt not leeue my soule in helle, nethir thou schalt yiue thin hooli to se corrupcioun.

28 Thou hast maad knowun to me the weies of lijf, thou schalt fille me in myrthe with thi face.

29 Britheren, be it leueful boldli to seie to you of the patriark Dauid, for he is deed and biried, and his sepulcre is among vs in to this dai.

30 Therfore whanne he was a prophete, and wiste, that with a greet ooth God hadde sworn to hym, that of the fruyt of his leende schulde oon sitte on his seete,

31 he seynge afer spak of the resurreccioun of Crist, for nether he was left in helle, nether his fleisch saiy corrupcioun.

32 God reiside this Jhesu, to whom we alle ben witnessis.

33 Therfor he was enhaunsid bi the riythoond of God, and thorouy the biheest of the Hooli Goost that he took of the fadir, he schedde out this spirit, that ye seen and heren.

34 For Dauid stiede not in to heuene; but he seith, The Lord seide to my Lord,

35 Sitte thou on my riyt half, til Y putte thin enemyes a stool of thi feet.

36 Therfor moost certeynli wite al the hous of Israel, that God made hym bothe Lord and Crist, this Jhesu, whom ye crucefieden.

37 Whanne thei herden these thingis, thei weren compunct in herte; and thei seiden to Petre and othere apostlis, Britheren, what schulen we do?

38 And Petre seide to hem, Do ye penaunce, and eche of you be baptisid in the name of Jhesu Crist, in to remissioun of youre synnes; and ye schulen take the yifte of the Hooli Goost.

39 For the biheest is to you, and to youre sones, and to alle that ben fer, which euer oure Lord God hath clepid.

40 Also with othere wordis ful many he witnesside to hem, and monestide hem, and seide, Be ye sauyd fro this schrewid generacioun.

41 Thanne thei that resseyueden his word weren baptisid, and in that dai soulis weren encreesid, aboute thre thousinde;

42 and weren lastynge stabli in the teching of the apostlis, and in comynyng of the breking of breed, in preieris.

43 And drede was maad to ech man. And many wondris and signes weren don bi the apostlis in Jerusalem, and greet drede was in alle.

44 And alle that bileueden weren togidre, and hadden alle thingis comyn.

45 Thei selden possessiouns and catel, and departiden tho thingis to alle men, as it was nede to ech.

46 And ech dai thei dwelliden stabli with o wille in the temple, and braken breed aboute housis, and token mete with ful out ioye and symplenesse of herte,

47 and herieden togidere God, and hadden grace to al the folk. And the Lord encreside hem that weren maad saaf, ech dai in to the same thing.

CAP 3

1 And Petre and Joon wenten vp in to the temple, at the nynthe our of preiyng.

2 And a man that was lame fro the wombe of his modir, was borun, and was leid ech dai at the yate of the temple, that is seid feir, to axe almes of men that entriden in to the temple.

3 This, whanne he say Petre and Joon bigynnynge to entre in to the temple, preyede that he schulde take almes.

4 And Petre with Joon bihelde on hym, and seide, Biholde thou in to vs.

5 And he biheelde in to hem, and hopide, that he schulde take sumwhat of hem.

6 But Petre seide, Y haue nether siluer ne gold; but that that Y haue, Y yiue to thee. In the name of Jhesu Crist of Nazareth, rise thou vp, and go.

7 And he took hym bi the riythoond, and heuede hym vp; and anoon hise leggis and hise feet weren sowdid togidere;

8 and he lippide, and stood, and wandride. And he entride with hem in to the temple, and wandride, and lippide, and heriede God.

9 And al the puple sai hym walkinge, and heriynge God.

10 And thei knewen hym, that he it was that sat at almes at the feire yate of the temple. And thei weren fillid with wondryng, and stoniynge, in that thing that byfelde to hym.

11 But whanne thei sien Petre and Joon, al the puple ran to hem at the porche that was clepid of Salomon, and wondriden greetli.

12 And Petre siy, and answeride to the puple, Men of Israel, what wondren ye in this thing? ether what biholden ye vs, as by oure vertue ethir power we maden this man for to walke?

13 God of Abraham, and God of Ysaac, and God of Jacob, God of oure fadris, hath glorified his sone Jhesu, whom ye bitraieden, and denyeden bifor the face of Pilat, whanne he demede hym to be delyuered.

14 But ye denyeden the hooli and the riytful, and axiden a mansleer to be youun to you.

15 And ye slowen the maker of lijf, whom God reiside fro deth, of whom we ben witnessis.

16 And in the feith of his name he hath confermyd this man, whom ye seen and knowen; the name of hym, and the feith that is bi him, yaf to this man ful heelthe in the siyt of alle you.

17 And now, britheren, Y woot that bi vnwityng ye diden, as also youre princis.

18 But God that bifor telde bi the mouth of alle profetis, that his Crist schulde suffre, hath fillid so.

19 Therfor be ye repentaunt, and be ye conuertid, that youre synnes be don awei,

20 that whanne the tymes of refresching schulen come from the siyt of the Lord, and he schal sende thilke Jhesu Crist,

21 that is now prechid to you. Whom it bihoueth heuene to resseyue, in to the tymes of restitucioun of alle thingis, which the Lord spak bi the mouth of hise hooli prophetis fro the world.

22 For Moises seide, For the Lord youre God schal reise to you a profete, of youre britheren; as me, ye schulen here hym bi alle thingis, what euer he schal speke to you.

23 And it schal be, that euery man that schal not here the ilke profete, schal be distried fro the puple.

24 And alle prophetis fro Samuel and aftirward, that spaken, telden these daies.

25 But ye ben the sones of prophetis, and of the testament, that God ordeynede to oure fadris, and seide to Abraham, In thi seed alle the meynes of erthe schulen be blessid.

26 God reiside his sone first to you, and sente hym blessynge you, that ech man conuerte hym from his wickidnesse.

CAP 4

1 And while thei spaken to the puple, the preestis and magistratis of the temple, and the Saduceis camen vpon hem, and soreweden,

2 that thei tauyten the puple, and telden in Jhesu the ayenrisyng fro deth.

3 And thei leiden hondis on hem, and puttiden hem in to warde in to the morewe; for it was thanne euentid.

4 But manye of hem that hadden herd the word, bileueden; and the noumbre of men was maad fyue thousyndis.

5 And amorewe it was don, that the princis of hem, and eldre men and scribis weren gadirid in Jerusalem;

6 and Annas, prince of preestis, and Caifas, and Joon, and Alisaundre, and hou manye euere weren of the kynde of preestis.

7 And thei settiden hem in the myddil, and axiden, In what vertue, ether in what name, han ye don this thing?

8 Thanne Petre was fillid with the Hooli Goost, and seide to hem, Ye pryncis of the puple, and ye eldre men, here ye.

9 If we to dai be demyd in the good dede of a sijk man, in whom this man is maad saaf,

10 be it knowun to you alle, and to al the puple of Israel, that in the name of Jhesu Crist of Nazareth, whom ye crucifieden, whom God reiside fro deth, in this this man stondith hool bifor you.

11 This is the stoon, which was repreued of you bildinge, which is maad in to the heed of the corner;

12 and heelthe is not in ony othir. For nether other name vndur heuene is youun to men, in which it bihoueth vs to be maad saaf.

13 And thei siyen the stidfastnesse of Petre and of Joon, for it was foundun that thei weren men vnlettrid, and lewid men, and thei wondriden, and knewen hem that thei weren with Jhesu.

14 And thei siyen the man that was helid, stondinge with hem, and thei myyten no thing ayenseie.

15 But thei comaundiden hem to go forth with out the counsel. And thei spaken togidere,

16 and seiden, What schulen we do to these men? for the signe is maad knowun bi hem to alle men, that dwellen at Jerusalem; it is opyn, and we moun not denye.

17 But that it be no more pupplischid in to the puple, manasse we to hem, that thei speke no more in this name to ony men.

18 And thei clepiden hem, and denounsiden to hem, that on no maner thei schulden speke, nether teche, in the name of Jhesu.

19 But Petre and Joon answeriden, and seiden to hem, If it be riytful in the siyt of God to here you rather than God, deme ye.

20 For we moten nedis speke tho thingis, that we han sayn and herd.

21 And thei manassiden, and leften hem, and foundun not hou thei schulden punische hem, for the puple; for alle men clarifieden that thing that was don in that that was bifalle.

22 For the man was more than of fourty yeer, in which this signe of heelthe was maad.

23 And whanne thei weren delyuerid, thei camen to her felowis, and telden to hem, hou grete thingis the princis of preestis and the eldre men hadden seid to hem.

24 And whanne thei herden, with oon herte thei reiseden vois to the Lord, and seiden, Lord, thou that madist heuene and erthe, see, and alle thingis that ben in hem, which seidist bi the Hooli Goost,

25 bi the mouth of oure fadir Dauid, thi child, Whi hethen men gnastiden with teeth togidre, and the puplis thouyten veyn thingis?

26 Kyngis of the erthe stoden nyy, and princis camen togidre 'in to oon, ayens the Lord, and ayens his Crist.

27 For verili Eroude and Pounce Pilat, with hethene men, and puplis of Israel, camen togidre in this citee ayens thin hooli child Jhesu,

28 whom thou anoyntidist, to do the thingis, that thin hoond and thi counsel demyden to be don.

29 And now, Lord, biholde in to the thretnyngis of hem, and graunte to thi seruauntis to speke thi word with al trist,

30 in that thing that thou holde forth thin hond, that heelthis and signes and wondris be maad bi the name of thin hooli sone Jhesu.

31 And whanne thei hadden preyed, the place was moued, in which thei weren gaderid; and alle weren fillid with the Hooli Goost, and spaken the word of God with trist.

32 And of al the multitude of men bileuynge was oon herte and oon wille; nether ony man seide ony thingis of tho thingis that he weldide to be his owne, but alle thingis weren comyn to hem.

33 And with greet vertu the apostlis yeldiden witnessyng of the ayenrysyng of Jhesu Crist oure Lord, and greet grace was in alle hem.

34 For nether ony nedi man was among hem, for how manye euere weren possessouris of feeldis, ether of housis, thei seelden, and brouyten the pricis of tho thingis that thei seelden,

35 and leiden bifor the feet of the apostlis. And it was departid to ech, as it was nede to ech.

36 Forsothe Joseph, that was named Barsabas of apostlis, that is to seie, the sone of coumfort, of the lynage of Leuy,

37 a man of Cipre, whanne he hadde a feeld, seelde it, and brouyte the prijs, and leide it bifor the feet of apostlis.

CAP 5

1 But a man, Anany bi name, with Safira, his wijf,

2 seelde a feeld, and defraudide of the prijs of the feeld; and his wijf was witinge. And he brouyte a part, and leide bifor the feet of the apostlis.

3 And Petre seide to hym, Anany, whi hath Sathanas temptid thin herte, that thou lye to the Hooli Goost, and to defraude of the prijs of the feeld?

4 Whethir it vnseld was not thin; and whanne it was seld, it was in thi power? Whi hast thou put this thing in thin herte? Thou hast not lied to men, but to God.

5 Anany herde these wordis, and felde doun, and was deed. And greet drede was maad on alle that herden.

6 And yonge men risen, and mouyden hym awei, and baren hym out, and birieden.

7 And ther was maad as a space of thre ouris, and his wijf knewe not that thing that was don, and entride.

8 And Petre answerde to hir, Womman, seie to me, whether ye seelden the feeld for so mych? And sche seide, Yhe, for so mych.

9 And Petre seide to hyr, What bifelde to you, to tempte the spirit of the Lord? Lo! the feet of hem that han birieden thin hosebonde ben at the dore, and thei schulen bere thee out.

10 Anoon sche felde doun at hise feet, and diede. And the yonge men entriden, and founden hir deed, and thei baren hir out, and birieden to hir hosebonde.

11 And greet drede was maad in al the chirche, and in to alle that herden these thingis.

12 And bi the hoondis of the apostlis signes and many wondris weren maad in the puple. And alle weren of oon acord in the porche of Salomon.

13 But no man of othere durste ioyne hymsilf with hem, but the puple magnyfiede hem.

14 And the multitude of men and of wymmen bileuynge in the Lord was more encreessid,

15 so that thei brouyten out sike men in to stretis, and leiden in litle beddis and couchis, that whanne Petre cam, nameli the schadew of hym schulde schadewe ech of hem, and thei schulden be delyuerid fro her syknessis.

16 And the multitude of citees niy to Jerusalem ran, bryngynge sijk men, and that weren trauelid of vnclene spiritis, whiche alle weren heelid.

17 But the prince of preestis roos vp, and alle that weren with hym, that is the eresye of Saduceis, and weren fillid with enuye;

18 and leiden hondis on the apostlis, and puttiden hem in the comyn warde.

19 But the aungel of the Lord openyde bi nyyt the yatis of the prisoun, and ledde hem out, and seide, Go ye,

20 and stonde ye, and speke in the temple to the puple alle the wordis of this lijf.

21 Whom whanne thei hadden herd, thei entriden eerli in to the temple, and tauyten. And the prince of preestis cam, and thei that weren with him, and clepiden togidre the counsel, and alle the eldre men of the children of Israel; and senten to the prisoun, that thei schulden be brouyt forth.

22 And whanne the mynystris camen, founden hem not, and for the prisoun was openyd, thei turneden ayen,

23 and teelden, and seiden, We founden the prisoun schit with al diligence, and the keperis stondynge at the yatis; but we opneden, and founden no man ther ynne.

24 And as the maiestratis of the temple, and the princis of preestis herden these wordis, thei doutiden of hem, what was don.

25 But a man cam, and teelde to hem, For lo! tho men whiche ye han put in to prisoun, ben in the temple, and stonden, and techen the puple.

26 Thanne the magistrat wente with the mynystris, and brouyte hem with out violence; for thei dredden the puple, lest thei schulden be stonyd.

27 And whanne thei hadden brouyt hem, thei settiden hem in the counsel; and the princes of prestis axiden hem,

28 and seiden, In comaundement we comaundiden you, that ye schulden not teche in this name, and lo! ye han fillid Jerusalem with youre teching, and ye wolen bringe on vs the blood of this man.

29 And Petre answeride, and the apostlis, and seiden, It bihoueth to obeie to God, more than to men.

30 God of oure fadris reiside Jhesu, whom ye slowen, hangynge in a tre.

31 God enhaunside with his riythond this prince and sauyour, that penaunce were yyue to Israel, and remyssioun of synnes.

32 And we ben witnessis of these wordis, and the Hooli Goost, whom God yaf to alle obeischinge to him.

33 Whanne thei herden these thingis, thei weren turmentid, and thouyten to sle hem.

34 But a man roos in the counsel, a Farise, Gamaliel bi name, a doctour of the lawe, a worschipful man to al the puple, and comaundide the men to be put without forth for a while.

35 And he seide to hem, Ye men of Israel, take tent to you silf on these men, what ye schulen do.

36 For bifore these daies Teodas, that seide hym silf to be sum man, to whom a noumbre of men consentiden, aboute foure hundrid; which was slayn, and alle that bileueden to hym, weren disparplit, and brouyt to nouyt.

37 Aftir this, Judas of Galilee was in the daies of professioun, and turnyde awei the puple aftir hym; and alle hou manye euere consentiden to hym, weren scatered, and he perischide.

38 And now therfor Y seie to you, departe ye fro these men, and suffre ye hem; for if this counsel ether werk is of men, it schal be vndon;

39 but if it is of God, ye moun not vndo hem, lest perauenture ye be foundun to repugne God.

40 And thei consentiden to him; and thei clepiden togidere the apostlis, and denounsiden to hem, that weren betun, that thei schulden no more speke in the name of Jhesu, and thei leten hem go.

41 And thei wenten ioiynge fro the siyt of the counsel, that thei weren had worthi to suffre dispisyng for the name of Jhesu. But ech dai thei ceessiden not in the temple, and aboute housis, to teche and to preche Jhesu Crist.

CAP 6

1 But in tho daies, whanne the noumbre of disciplis encreesside, the Grekis grutchiden ayens the Ebrews, for that her widewis weren dispisid in euery daies mynystryng.

2 And the twelue clepiden togidere the multitude of disciplis, and seiden, It is not ryytful, that we leeuen the word of God, and mynystren to boordis.

3 Therfor, britheren, biholde ye men of you of good fame, ful of the Hooli Goost and of wisdom, whiche we schulen ordeyne on this werk;

4 for we schulen be bisi to preier, and preche the word of God.

5 And the word pleside bifor al the multitude; and thei chesiden Styuen, a man ful of feith and of the Hooli Goost, and Filip, and Procore, and Nycanor, and Tymon, and Parmanam, and Nycol, a comelyng, a man of Antioche.

6 Thei ordeyneden these bifor the siyt of apostlis, and thei preyeden, and leiden hoondis on hem.

7 And the word of the Lord wexide, and the noumbre of the disciplis in Jerusalem was myche multiplied; also myche cumpany of preestis obeiede to the feith.

8 And Steuen, ful of grace and of strengthe, made wondris and grete signes in the puple.

9 But summe rysen of the synagoge, that was clepid of Libertyns, and Cirenensis, and of men of Alisaundre, and of hem that weren of Cilice and of Asie, and disputiden with Steuene.

10 And thei miyten not withstonde the wisdom and the spirit, that spak.

11 Thanne thei priueli senten men, that schulden seie, that thei herden hym seiynge wordis of blasfemye ayens Moises and God.

12 And so thei moueden togidere the puple, and the eldre men, and the scribis; and thei rannen togidre, and token hym, and brouyten in to the counsel.

13 And thei ordeyneden false witnessis, that seiden, This man ceessith not to speke wordis ayens the hooli place, and the lawe.

14 For we herden hym seiynge, That this Jhesus of Nazareth schal destrye this place, and schal chaunge the tradiciouns, whiche Moyses bitook to us.

15 And alle men that seten in the counsel bihelden hym, and sayn his face as the face of an aungel.

CAP 7

1 And the prynce of prestis seide to Steuene, Whethir these thingis han hem so?

2 Which seide, Britheren and fadris, here ye. God of glorie apperide to oure fadir Abraham, whanne he was in Mesopotamie, bifor that he dwelte in Carram, and seide to hym,

3 Go out of thi loond, and of thi kynrede, and come in to the loond, which Y schal schewe to thee.

4 Thanne he wente out of the loond of Caldeis, and dwelte in Carram. And fro thens aftir that his fader was deed, he translatide him in to this loond, in which ye dwellen now.

5 And he yaf not to hym eritage in it, nethir a paas of a foot, but he bihiyte to yyue hym it in to possessioun, and to his seed aftir hym, whanne he hadde not a sone.

6 And God spak to hym, That his seed schal be comling in an alien lond, and thei schulen make hem suget to seruage, and schulen yuel trete hem, foure hundrid yeris and thritti;

7 and Y schal iuge the folk, to which thei schulen serue, seith the Lord. And after these thingis thei schulen go out, and thei schulen serue to me in this place.

8 And he yaf to hym the testament of circumcisioun; and so he gendride Ysaac, and circumcidide hym in the eiyt dai. And Isaac gendride Jacob, and Jacob gendride the twelue patriarkis.

9 And the patriarkis hadden enuye to Joseph, and selden hym in to Egipt.

10 And God was with hym, and delyuerede hym of alle hise tribulaciouns, and yaf to hym grace and wisdom in the siyt of Farao, king of Egipt. And he ordeynede hym souereyn on Egipt, and on al his hous.

11 And hungur cam in to al Egipt, and Canaan, and greet tribulacioun; and oure fadris founden not mete.

12 But whanne Jacob hadde herd, that whete was in Egipt, he sente oure fadris first.

13 And in the secounde tyme Joseph was knowun of hise britheren, and his kyn was maad knowun to Farao.

14 And Joseph sente, and clepide Jacob, his fadir, and al his kynrede, seuenti and fyue men.

15 And Jacob cam doun in to Egipt, and was deed, he and oure fadris;

16 and thei weren translatid in to Sichen, and weren leid in the sepulcre, that Abraham bouyte bi prijs of siluer of the sones of Emor, the sone of Sichen.

17 And whanne the tyme of biheeste cam niy, which God hadde knoulechid to Abraham, the puple waxede, and multipliede in Egipt,

18 til another kyng roos in Egipt, which knewe not Joseph.

19 This bigilide oure kyn, and turmentide oure fadris, that thei schulden putte awey her yonge children, for thei schulden not lyue.

20 In the same tyme Moyses was borun, and he was louyd of God; and he was norischid thre monethis in the hous of his fadir.

21 And whanne he was put out in the flood, the douyter of Farao took hym vp, and nurischide hym in to hir sone.

22 And Moises was lerned in al the wisdom of Egipcians, and he was myyti in his wordis and werkis.

23 But whanne the tyme of fourti yeer was fillid to hym, it roos vp 'in to his herte, that he schulde visite hise britheren, the sones of Israel.

24 And whanne he say a man suffringe wronge, he vengide hym, and dide veniaunce for hym that suffride the wronge, and he killide the Egipcian.

25 For he gesside that his britheren schulden vndurstonde, that God schulde yyue to hem helthe bi the hoond of hym; but thei vndurstoden not.

26 For in the dai suynge he apperide to hem chidinge, and he acordide hem in pees, and seide, Men, ye ben britheren; whi noyen ye ech othere?

27 But he that dide the wronge to his neiybore, puttide hym awey, and seide, Who ordeynede thee prince and domesman on vs?

28 Whethir thou wolt sle me, as yistirdai thou killidist the Egipcian?

29 And in this word Moises flei, and was maad a comeling in the loond of Madian, where he bigat twei sones.

30 And whanne he hadde fillid fourti yeer, an aungel apperide to hym in fier of flawme of a buysch, in desert of the mount of Syna.

31 And Moises siy, and wondride on the siyt. And whanne he neiyede to biholde, the vois of the Lord was maad to hym,

32 and seide, Y am God of youre fadris, God of Abraham, God of Ysaac, God of Jacob. Moises was maad tremblynge, and durste not biholde.

33 But God seide to hym, Do of the schoon of thi feet, for the place in which thou stondist is hooli erthe.

34 Y seynge say the turmentyng of my puple that is in Egipt, and Y herde the mornyng of hem, and Y cam doun to delyuere hem. And now come thou, and Y schal sende thee in to Egipt.

35 This Moises whom thei denyeden, seiynge, Who ordeynede thee prince and domesman on vs? God sente this prince and ayenbiere, with the hoond of the aungel, that apperide to hym in the busch.

36 This Moises ledde hem out, and dide wondris and signes in the loond of Egipt, and in the reed see, and in desert fourti yeeris.

37 This is Moises, that seide to the sones of Israel, God schal reise to you a profete of youre bretheren, as me ye schulen here him.

38 This it is, that was in the chirche in wildirnesse, with the aungel that spak to hym in the mount of Syna, and with oure fadris; which took words of lijf to yyue to vs.

39 To whom oure fadris wolden not obeie, but puttiden hym awei, and weren turned awei in hertis in to Egipt,

40 seiynge to Aaron, Make thou to vs goddis, that schulen go bifore vs; for to this Moyses that ledde vs out of the lond of Egipt, we witen not what is don to hym.

41 And thei maden a calf in tho daies, and offriden a sacrifice to the mawmet; and thei weren glad in the werkis of her hondis.

42 And God turnede, and bitook hem to serue to the knyythod of heuene, as it is writun in the book of profetis, Whether ye, hous of Israel, offriden to me slayn sacrificis, ether sacrificis, fourti yeris in desert?

43 And ye han take the tabernacle of Moloc, and the sterre of youre god Renfam, figuris that ye han maad to worschipe hem; and Y schal translate you in to Babiloyn.

44 The tabernacle of witnessing was with oure fadris in desert, as God disposide to hem, and spak to Moyses, that he schulde make it aftir the fourme that he say.

45 Which also oure fadris token with Jhesu, and brouyten in to the possessioun of hethene men, whiche God puttide awey fro the face of oure fadris, til in to the daies of Dauid,

46 that fonde grace anentis God, and axide that he schulde fynde a tabernacle to God of Jacob.

47 But Salomon bildide the hous 'to hym.

48 But the hiy God dwellith not in thingis maad bi hoond,

49 as he seith bi the profete, Heuene is a seete to me, and the erthe is the stool of my feet; what hous schulen ye bilde to me, seith the Lord, ether what place is of my restyng?

50 Whether myn hoond made not alle these thingis?

51 With hard nol, and vncircumcidid hertis and eris ye withstoden eueremore the Hooli Goost; and as youre fadris, so ye.

52 Whom of the profetis han not youre fadris pursued, and han slayn hem that bifor telden of the comyng of the riytful man, whos traitouris and mansleeris ye weren now?

53 Whiche token the lawe in ordynaunce of aungels, and han not kept it.

54 And thei herden these thingis, and weren dyuersli turmentid in her hertis, and grenneden with teeth on hym.

55 But whanne Steuene was ful of the Hooli Goost, he bihelde in to heuene, and say the glorie of God, and Jhesu stondinge on the riythalf of the vertu of God. And he seide, Lo! Y se heuenes openyd, and mannus sone stondynge on the riythalf of the vertu of God.

56 And thei crieden with a greet vois, and stoppiden her eris, and maden with o wille an assauyt in to hym.

57 And thei brouyten hym out of the citee, and stonyden. And the witnessis diden of her clothis, bisidis the feet of a yong man, that was clepid Saule.

58 And thei stonyden Steuene, that clepide God to help, seiynge, Lord Jhesu, resseyue my spirit.

59 And he knelide, and criede with a greet vois, and seide, Lord, sette not to hem this synne. And whanne he hadde seid this thing, he diede.

CAP 8

1 But Saul was consentynge to his deth. And greet persecucioun was maad that dai in the chirche, that was in Jerusalem. And alle men weren scatered bi the cuntrees of Judee and Samarie, outakun the apostlis.

2 But good men birieden Steuene, and maden greet mornyng on hym.

3 But Saul greetli distruyede the chirche, and entryde bi housis, and drowe men and wymmen, and bitook hem in to prisoun.

4 And thei that weren scaterid, passiden forth, prechynge the word of God.

5 And Filip cam doun in to a citee of Samarie, and prechide to hem Crist.

6 And the puple yaf tent to thes thingis that weren seid of Filip, with o wille herynge and seynge the signes that he dide.

7 For manye of hem that hadden vnclene spiritis, crieden with a greet vois, and wenten out.

8 And manye sijk in the palsi, and crokid, weren heelid.

9 Therfor greet ioye was maad in that citee. But there was a man in that citee, whos name was Symount, a witche, that hadde disseyued the folc of Samarie, seiynge, that him silf was sum greet man.

10 Whom alle herkeneden, fro the leest to the moost, and seiden, This is the vertu of God, which is clepid greet.

11 And thei leueden hym, for long tyme he hadde maddid hem with his witche craftis.

12 But whanne thei hadden bileued to Filip, 'that prechide of the kingdom of God, men and wymmen weren baptisid in the name of Jhesu Crist.

13 And thanne also Symount him silf bileued; and whanne he was baptisid, he drouy to Filip; and he sai also that signes and grete vertues weren don, he was astonyed, and wondride.

14 But whanne the apostlis that weren at Jerusalem, hadden herd that Samarie hadde resseyued the word of God, thei senten to hem Petre and Joon.

15 And whanne thei camen, thei preieden for hem, that thei schulden resseyue the Hooli Goost;

16 for he cam not yit in to ony of hem, but thei weren baptisid oonli in the name of the Lord Jhesu.

17 Thanne thei leiden hoondis on hem, and thei resseyueden the Hooli Goost.

18 And whanne Symount hadde seyn, that the Hooly Goost was youun bi leiyng on of the hoondis of the apostlis, and he proferide to hem money, and seide,

19 Yyue ye also to me this power, that whom euere Y schal leye on myn hoondis, that he resseyue the Hooli Goost.

20 But Petir seide to hym, Thi money be with thee into perdicioun, for thou gessidist the yifte of God schulde be had for monei.

21 Ther is no part, ne sort to thee, in this word, for thin herte is not riytful bifor God.

22 Therfor do thou penaunce for this wickidnesse of thee, and preie God, if perauenture this thouyt of thin herte be foryouun to thee.

23 For Y se that thou art in the gall of bitternesse and in the boond of wickidnesse.

24 And Symount answeride, and seide, Preie ye for me to the Lord, that no thing of these thingis that ye han seid, com on me.

25 And thei witnessiden, and spaken the word of the Lord, and yeden ayen to Jerusalem, and prechiden to many cuntrees of Samaritans.

26 And an aungel of the Lord spak to Filip, and seide, Ryse thou, and go ayens the south, to the weie that goith doun fro Jerusalem in to Gasa; this is desert.

27 And he roos, and wente forth. And lo! a man of Ethiopie, a myyti man seruaunt, a yelding of Candace, the queen of Ethi-

opiens, which was on alle her richessis, cam to worschipe in Jerusalem.

28 And he turnede ayen, sittinge on his chare, and redinge Isaie, the profete.

29 And the spirit seide to Filip, Neiye thou, and ioyne thee to this chare.

30 And Filip 'ran to, and herde hym redynge Ysaie, the prophete. And he seide, Gessist thou, whether thou vndirstondist, what thingis thou redist?

31 And he seide, How may Y, if no man schewe to me? And he preiede Filip, that he schulde come vp, and sitte with hym.

32 And the place of the scripture that he redde, was this, As a scheep he was led to sleyng, and as a lomb bifor a man that scherith him is doumb with out vois, so he openyde not his mouth.

33 In mekenesse his dom was takun vp; who schal telle out the generacioun of hym? For his lijf schal be takun awei fro the erthe.

34 And the gelding answeride to Filip, and seide, Y biseche thee, of 'what profete seith he this thing? of him silf, ethir of ony othere?

35 And Filip openyde his mouth, and bigan at this scripture, and prechide to him Jhesu.

36 And the while thei wenten bi the weie, thei camen to a water. And the gelding seide, Lo! watir; who forbedith me to be baptisid?

37 And Filip seide, If thou bileuest of al the herte, it is leueful. And he answeride, and seide, Y bileue that Jhesu Crist is the sone of God.

38 And he comaundide the chare to stonde stille. And thei wenten doun bothe into the watir, Filip and the gelding, and Filip baptiside hym.

39 And whanne thei weren come vp of the watir, the spirit of the Lord rauyschide Filip, and the gelding say hym no more.

40 And Filip was foundun in Azotus; and he passide forth, and prechide to alle citees, til he cam to Cesarie.

CAP 9

1 But Saul, yit a blower of manassis and of betingis ayens the disciplis of the Lord,

2 cam to the prince of preestis, and axide of hym lettris in to Damask, to the synagogis; that if he fond ony men and wymmen of this lijf, he schulde lede hem boundun to Jerusalem.

3 And whanne he made his iourney, it bifelde, that he cam nyy to Damask. And sudenli a liyt from heuene schoon aboute hym;

4 and he fallide to the erthe, and herde a vois seiynge to hym, Saul, Saul, what pursuest thou me?

5 And he seide, Who art thou, Lord? And he seide, Y am Jhesu of Nazareth, whom thou pursuest. It is hard to thee, to kike ayens the pricke.

6 And he tremblide, and wondride, and seide, Lord, what wolt thou that Y do?

7 And the Lord seide to hym, Rise vp, and entre in to the citee, and it schal be seide to thee, what it bihoueth thee to do. And tho men that wenten with hym, stoden astonyed; for thei herden a vois, but thei sien no man.

8 And Saul roos fro the earth; and whanne hise iyen weren opened, he say no thing. And thei drowen hym bi the hondis, and ledden hym in to Damask.

9 And he was thre daies not seynge; 'and he eete not, nether drank.

10 And a disciple, Ananye bi name, was at Damask. And the Lord seide to hym in 'a visioun, Ananye. And he seide, Lo!
11 Y, Lord. And the Lord seide to hym, Rise thou, and go in to a streete that is clepid Rectus; and seke, in the hous of Judas, Saul bi name of Tharse. For lo! he preieth; and he say a man,
12 Ananye bi name, entringe and leiynge on hym hoondis, that he resseyue siyt.
13 And Ananye answerde, Lord, Y haue herd of many of this man, how greete yuelis he dide to thi seyntis in Jerusalem;
14 and this hath power of the princis of preestis, to bynde alle men that clepen thi name to helpe.
15 And the Lord seide to hym, Go thou, for this is to me a vessel of chesing, that he bere my name bifore hethene men, and kingis, and tofore the sones of Israel.
16 For Y schal schewe to hym, how grete thingis it bihoueth hym to suffre for my name.
17 And Ananye wente, and entride in to the hous; and leide on hym his hondis, and seide, Saul brothir, the Lord Jhesu sente me, that apperide to thee in the weie, in which thou camest, that thou se, and be fulfillid with the Hooli Goost.
18 And anoon as the scalis felden fro hise iyen, he resseyuede siyt. And he roos, and was baptisid.
19 And whanne he hadde takun mete, he was coumfortid. And he was bi sum daies with the disciplis, that weren at Damask.
20 And anoon he entride in to the synagogis, and prechide the Lord Jhesu, for this is the sone of God.
21 And alle men that herden hym, wondriden, and seiden, Whether this is not he that impugnede in Jerusalem hem that clepiden to help this name? and hidir he cam for this thing, that he schulde leede hem boundun to the princis of preestis?
22 But Saul myche more wexede strong, and confoundide the Jewis that dwelliden at Damask, and affermyde that this is Crist.
23 And whanne manye daies weren fillid, Jewis maden a counsel, that thei schulden sle hym.
24 And the aspies of hem weren maad knowun to Saul. And thei kepten the yatis dai and niyt, that thei schulden sle him.
25 But hise disciplis token hym bi nyyt, and delyuereden hym, and leeten him doun in a leep bi the wal.
26 And whanne he cam in to Jerusalem, he assaiede to ioyne hym to the disciplis; and alle dredden hym, and leueden not that he was a disciple.
27 But Barnabas took, and ledde hym to the apostlis, and telde to hem, how in the weie he hadde seyn the Lord, and that he spak to hym, and hou in Damask he dide tristili in the name of Jhesu.
28 And he was with hem, and entride, and yede out in Jerusalem, and dide tristili in the name of Jhesu.
29 And he spak with hethene men, and disputide with Grekis. And thei souyten to sle hym.
30 Which thing whanne the britheren hadden knowe, thei ledden hym bi nyyt to Cesarie, and leten hym go to Tarsis.
31 And the chirche bi al Judee, and Galilee, and Samarie, hadde pees, and was edefied, and walkide in the drede of the Lord, and was fillid with coumfort of the Hooli Goost.
32 And it bifelde, that Petre, the while he passide aboute alle, cam to the hooli men that dwelliden at Lidde.
33 And he foond a man, Eneas bi name, that fro eiyte yeer he hadde leie 'in bed; and he was sijk in palsy.
34 And Petre seide to hym, Eneas, the Lord Jhesu Crist heele thee; rise thou, and araye thee. And anoon he roos.

35 And alle men that dwelten at Lidde, and at Sarone, saien hym, whiche weren conuertid to the Lord.
36 And in Joppe was a disciplesse, whos name was Tabita, that is to seie, Dorcas. This was ful of good werkis and almesdedis, that sche dide.
37 And it bifelde in tho daies, that sche was sijk, and diede. And whanne thei hadden waischun hir, thei leiden hir in a soler.
38 And for Lidda was nyy Joppe, the disciplis herden that Petre was thereynne, and senten twei men to hym, and preieden, That thou tarie not to come to vs.
39 And Petre roos vp, and cam with hem. And whanne he was comun, thei ledden hym in to the soler. And alle widewis stoden aboute hym, wepynge, and schewynge cootis and clothis, which Dorcas made to hem.
40 And whanne alle men weren put with out forth, Petre knelide, and preiede. And he turnede to the bodi, and seide, Tabita, rise thou. And sche openyde hir iyen, and whanne sche siy Petre, sche sat vp ayen.
41 And he took hir bi the hond, and reiside hir. And whanne he hadde clepid the hooli men and widewis, he assignede hir alyue.
42 And it was maad knowun bi al Joppe; and many bileueden in the Lord.
43 And it was maad, that many daies he dwellide in Joppe, at oon Symount, a curiour.

CAP 10

1 A man was in Cesarie, Cornelie bi name, a centurien of the cumpanye of knyytis, that is seid of Italie;
2 a religious man, and dredinge the Lord, with al his meyne; doynge many almessis to the puple, and preynge the Lord euere more.
3 This say in a visioun opinli, as in the nynthe oure of the dai, an aungel of God entringe in to hym, and seiynge to hym, Cornelie.
4 And he bihelde hym, and was a dred, and seide, Who art thou, Lord? And he seide to hym, Thi preieris and thin almesdedis han stied vp in to mynde, in the siyt of the Lord.
5 And now sende thou men in to Joppe, and clepe oon Symount, that is named Petre.
6 This is herborid at a man Symount, curiour, whos hous is bisidis the see. This schal seie to thee, what it bihoueth thee to do.
7 And whanne the aungel that spak to hym, was gon awei, he clepide twei men of his hous, and a knyyt that dredde the Lord, whiche weren at his bidding.
8 And whanne he hadde told hem alle these thingis, he sente hem in to Joppe.
9 And on the dai suynge, while thei maden iournei, and neiyeden to the citee, Petre wente vp in to the hiest place of the hous to preie, aboute the sixte our.
10 And whanne he was hungrid, he wolde haue ete. But while thei maden redi, a rauysching of spirit felde on hym;
11 and he say heuene openyd, and a vessel comynge doun, as a greet scheet with foure corneris, to be lette doun fro heuene in to erthe,
12 in which weren alle foure footid beestis, and crepinge of the erthe, and volatilis of heuene.
13 And a vois was maad to hym, Rise thou, Petre, and sle, and ete.
14 And Petre seide, Lord, forbede, for Y neuer ete ony comun thing and vnclene.

15 And eft the secounde tyme the vois was maad to him, That thing that God hath clensid, seye thou not vnclene.

16 And this thing was don bi thries; and anoon the vessel was resseyued ayen.

17 And while that Petre doutide with ynne hym silf, what the visioun was that he say, lo! the men, that weren sent fro Corneli, souyten the hous of Symount, and stoden at the yate.

18 And whanne thei hadden clepid, thei axiden if Symount, that is named Petre, hadde there herbore.

19 And while Petre thouyte on the visioun, the spirit seide to hym, Lo! thre men seken thee.

20 Therfor ryse thou, and go doun, and go with hem, and doute thou no thing, for Y sente hem.

21 And Petre cam doun to the men, and seide, Lo! Y am, whom ye seken; what is the cause, for which ye ben come?

22 And thei seiden, Cornelie, the centurien, a iust man, and dredinge God, and hath good witnessyng of alle the folc of Jewis, took aunswere of an hooli aungel, to clepe thee in to his hous, and to here wordis of thee.

23 Therfor he ledde hem inne, and resseyuede in herbore; and that nyyt thei dwelliden with hym. And in the dai suynge he roos, and wente forth with hem; and sum of the britheren folewiden hym fro Joppe, that thei be witnessis to Petre.

24 And the other dai he entride in to Cesarie. And Cornelie abood hem, with hise cousyns, and necessarie freendis, that weren clepid togidere.

25 And it was don, whanne Petre was come ynne, Corneli cam metynge hym, and felle doun at hise feet, and worschipide him.

26 But Petre reiside hym, and seide, Aryse thou, also Y my silf am a man, as thou.

27 And he spak with hym, and wente in, and foonde many that weren come togidere.

28 And he seide to hem, Ye witen, how abhomynable it is to a Jewe, to be ioyned ether to come to an alien; but God schewide to me, that no man seye a man comyn, ethir vnclene.

29 For which thing Y cam, whanne Y was clepid, with out douting. Therfor Y axe you, for what cause han ye clepid me?

30 And Cornelie seide, To dai foure daies in to this our, Y was preiynge and fastynge in the nynthe our in myn hous. And lo! a man stood bifore me in a whijt cloth, and seide,

31 Cornelie, thi preier is herd, and thin almesdedis ben in mynde in the siyt of God.

32 Therfor sende thou in to Joppe, and clepe Symount, that is named Petre; this is herborid in the hous of Symount coriour, bisidis the see. This, whanne he schal come, schal speke to thee.

33 Therfor anoon Y sente to thee, and thou didist wel in comynge to vs. 'Now therfor we alle ben present in thi siyt, to here the wordis, what euer ben comaundid to thee of the Lord.

34 And Petre openyde his mouth, and seide, In trewthe Y haue foundun, that God is no acceptor of persoones;

35 but in eche folk he that dredith God, and worchith riytwisnesse, is accept to hym.

36 God sente a word to the children of Israel, schewinge pees bi Jhesu Crist; this is Lord of alle thingis.

37 Ye witen the word that is maad thorou al Judee, and bigan at Galile, aftir the baptym that Joon prechide, Jhesu of Nazareth;

38 hou God anoyntide hym with the Hooli Goost, and vertu; which passide forth in doynge wel, and heelynge alle men oppressid of the deuel, for God was with hym.

39 And we ben witnessis of alle thingis, whiche he dide in the cuntrei of Jewis, and of Jerusalem; whom thei slowen, hangynge in a tre.

40 And God reiside this in the thridde dai, and yaf hym to be maad knowun,

41 not to al puple, but to witnessis bifor ordeyned of God; to vs that eeten and drunken with hym, after that he roos ayen fro deth.

42 And he comaundide to vs to preche to the puple, and to witnesse, that he it is, that is ordeyned of God domesman of the quyk and of deede.

43 To this alle prophetis beren witnessing, that alle men that bileuen in hym, schulen resseyue remyssioun of synnes bi his name.

44 And yit while that Petre spak these wordis, the Hooli Goost felde on alle that herden the word.

45 And the feithful men of circumcisioun, that camen with Petre, wondriden, that also in to naciouns the grace of the Hooli Goost is sched out.

46 For thei herden hem spekynge in langagis, and magnyfiynge God.

47 Thanne Petre answeride, Whether ony man may forbede watir, that these ben not baptisid, that han also resseyued the Hooli Goost as we?

48 And he comaundide hem to be baptisid in the name of the Lord Jhesu Crist. Thanne thei preieden hym, that he schulde dwelle with hem sum daies.

CAP 11

1 And the apostlis, and the britheren that weren in Judee, herden that also hethene men resseyueden the word of God, and thei glorifieden God.

2 But whanne Petre cam to Jerusalem, thei that weren of circumcisioun, disputiden ayens hym,

3 and seiden, Whi entridist thou to men that han prepucie, and hast eete with hem?

4 And Petre bigan, and expownede to hem bi ordre,

5 and seide, Y was in the citee of Joppe, and preiede, and Y sai in rauysching of my mynde a visioun, that a vessel cam doun, as a greet scheete with foure coordis, and was sent doun fro heuene; and it cam to me.

6 In to which Y lokinge biheld, and sai foure footid beestis of the erthe, and beestis, and crepynge beestis, and volatils of heuene.

7 And Y herde also a vois that seide to me, Petre, rise thou, and sle, and eete.

8 But Y seide, Nay, Lord; for comyn thing ether vnclene entride neuer in to my mouth.

9 And the vois answeride the secounde tyme fro heuene, That thing that God hath clensid, seie thou not vnclene.

10 And this was don bi thries, and alle thingis weren resseyued ayen in to heuene.

11 And lo! thre men anoon stooden in the hous, in which Y was; and thei weren sent fro Cesarie to me.

12 And the spirit seide to me, that Y schulde go with hem, and doute no thing. Yhe, and these sixe britheren camen with me, and we entriden in to the hous of the man.

13 And he telde to vs, how he say an aungel in his hous, stondinge and seiynge to hym, Sende thou in to Joppe, and clepe Symount, that is named Petre, which schal speke to thee wordis,

14 in whiche thou schalt be saaf, and al thin hous.

15 And whanne Y hadde bigunnun to speke, the Hooli Goost felle on hem, as in to vs in the bigynnyng.

16 And Y bithouyte on the word of the Lord, as he seide, For Joon baptiside in watir, but ye schulen be baptisid in the Hooli Goost.

17 Therfor if God yaf to hem the same grace, as to vs that bileueden in the Lord Jhesu Crist, who was Y, that myyte for-beede the Lord, that he yyue not the Hooli Goost to hem that bileueden in the name of Jhesu Crist?

18 Whanne these thingis weren herd, thei helden pees, and glorifieden God, and seiden, Therfor also to hethene men God hath youun penaunce to lijf.

19 And thei that weren scaterid of the tribulacioun that was maad vndir Steuene, walkiden forth to Fenyce, and to Cipre, and to Antioche, and spaken the word to no man, but to Jewis aloone.

20 But sum of hem weren men of Cipre, and of Cirenen; whiche whanne thei hadden entride in to Antioche, thei spa-ken to the Grekis, and prechiden the Lord Jhesu.

21 And the hond of the Lord was with hem, and myche noumbre of men bileuynge was conuertid to the Lord.

22 And the word cam to the eris of the chirche, that was at Jerusalem, on these thingis; and thei senten Barnabas to Anti-oche.

23 And whanne he was come, and siy the grace of the Lord, he ioyede, and monestide alle men to dwelle in the Lord in purpos of herte;

24 for he was a good man, and ful of the Hooli Goost, and of feith. And myche puple was encresid to the Lord.

25 And he wente forth to Tharsis, to seke Saul; and whanne he hadde foundun hym, he ledde to Antioche.

26 And al a yeer thei lyueden ther in the chirche, and tauyten myche puple, so that the disciplis weren namyd first at Anti-oche cristen men.

27 And in these daies profetis camen ouer fro Jerusalem to Antioche.

28 And oon of hem roos vp, Agabus bi name, and signefiede bi the spirit a greet hungur to comynge in al the world, which hungur was maad vndur Claudius.

29 And alle the disciplis purposiden, after that ech hadde, for to sende in to mynysterie to britheren that dwelliden in Judee.

30 Which thing also thei diden, and sente it to the eldre men, bi the hoondis of Barnabas and Saul.

CAP 12

1 And in the same tyme Eroude the king sente power, to tur-mente sum men of the chirche.

2 And he slowe bi swerd James, the brothir of Joon.

3 And he siy that it pleside to Jewis, and keste to take also Petre; and the daies of therf looues weren.

4 And whanne he hadde cauyte Petre, he sente hym in to pris-oun; and bitook to foure quaternyouns of knyytis, to kepe hym, and wolde aftir pask bringe hym forth to the puple.

5 And Petre was kept in prisoun; but preier was maad of the chirche with out ceessing to God for hym.

6 But whanne Eroude schulde bringe hym forth, in that nyyt Petre was slepinge bitwixe twei knyytis, and was boundun with twei cheynes; and the keperis bifor the dore kepten the prisoun.

7 And lo! an aungel of the Lord stoode nyy, and liyt schoon in the prisoun hous. And whanne he hadde smyte the side of Petre, he reiside hym, and seide, Rise thou swiftli. And anoon the cheynes felden doun fro hise hoondis.

8 And the aungel seide to hym, Girde thee, and do on thin hoosis. And he dide so. And he seide to hym, Do aboute thee thi clothis, and sue me.

9 And he yede out, and suede hym; and he wiste not that it was soth, that was don bi the aungel; for he gesside hym silf to haue sey a visioun.

10 And thei passiden the first and the secounde warde, and camen to the iren yate that ledith to the citee, which anoon was opened to hem. And thei yeden out, and camen in to o street, and anoon the aungel passide awei fro hym.

11 And Petre turnede ayen to hym silf, and seide, Now Y woot verili, that the Lord sente his aungel, 'and delyueride me fro the hoond of Eroude, and fro al the abiding of the puple of Jewis.

12 And he bihelde, and cam to the hous of Marie, modir of Joon, that is named Marcus, where many weren gaderid togi-dre, and preiynge.

13 And whanne he knockid at the dore of the yate, a damysel, Rode bi name, cam forth to se.

14 And whanne sche knewe the vois of Petre, for ioye sche openyde not the yate, but ran in, and telde, that Petre stood at the yate.

15 And thei seiden 'to hir, Thou maddist. But sche affermyde, that it was so. And thei seiden, It is his aungel.

16 But Petre abood stille, and knockide. And whanne thei hadden opened the dore, thei sayen hym, and wondriden.

17 And he bekenyde to hem with his hoond to be stille, and telde hou the Lord hadde led hym out of the prisoun. And he seide, Telle ye to James and to the britheren these thingis. And he yede out, and wente in to an othere place.

18 And whanne the dai was come, ther was not lytil troubling among the knyytis, what was don of Petre.

19 And whanne Eroude hadde souyt hym, and foonde not, aftir that he hadde made enqueryng of the keperis, he comaundide hem to be brouyt to hym. And he cam doun fro Judee in to Cesarie, and dwellide there.

20 And he was wroth to men of Tyre and of Sidon. And thei of oon acord camen to hym, whanne thei hadden counseilid with Bastus, that was the kingis chaumbirleyn, thei axiden pees, for as myche that her cuntrees weren vitailid of hym.

21 And in a dai that was ordeyned, Eroude was clothid with kyngis clothing, and sat for domesman, and spak to hem.

22 And the puple criede, The voicis of God, and not of man.

23 And anoon an aungel of the Lord smoot hym, for he hadde not youun onour to God; and he was wastid of wormes, and diede.

24 And the word of the Lord waxide, and was multiplied.

25 And Barnabas and Saul turneden ayen fro Jerusalem, whanne the mynystrie was fillid, and token Joon, that was named Marcus.

CAP 13

1 And profetis and doctouris weren in the chirche that was at Antioche, in which Barnabas, and Symount, that was clepid Blac, and Lucius Cironense, and Manaen, that was the soukynge fere of Eroude tetrarke, and Saul weren.

2 And whanne thei mynystriden to the Lord, and fastiden, the Hooli Goost seide to hem, Departe ye to me Saul and Barna-bas, in to the werk to which Y haue takun hem.

3 Thanne thei fastiden, and preieden, and leiden hondis on hem, and leten hem go.

4 But thei weren sent of the Hooli Goost, and wenten forth to Seleucia, and fro thennus thei wenten bi boot to Cipre.

5 And whanne thei camen to Salamyne, thei prechiden the word of God in the synagogis of Jewis; and thei hadden also Joon in mynystrie.

6 And whanne thei hadden walkid bi al the ile to Pafum, thei founden a man, a witche, a false profete, a Jewe, to whom the name was Bariesu,

7 that was with the proconsul Sergius Paule, a prudent man. This clepide Barnabas and Poul, and desiride to here the word of God.

8 But Elymas witche withstoode hem; for his name is expowned so; and he souyte to turne awei the proconsul fro bileue.

9 But Saul, which is seid also Paul, was fillid with the Hooli Goost, and bihelde in to hym, and seide, A!

10 thou ful of al gile, and al falsnesse, thou sone of the deuel, thou enemye of al riytwisnesse, thou leeuest not to turne vpsodoun the riytful weies of the Lord.

11 And now lo! the hoond of the Lord is on thee, and thou schalt be blynde, and not seynge the sunne in to a tyme. And anoon myste and derknesse felden doun on hym; and he yede aboute, and souyte hym that schulde yyue hoond to hym.

12 Thanne the proconsul, whanne he hadde seyn the dede, bileuede, wondringe on the techyng of the Lord.

13 And whanne fro Pafum Poul hadde go bi a boot, and thei that weren with hym, thei camen to Pergen of Pamfilie; but Joon departide fro hem, and turnede ayen to Jerusalem.

14 And thei yeden to Pergen, and camen to Antioche of Persidie; and thei entriden in to the synagoge in the dai of sabatis, and saten.

15 And after the redyng of the lawe and of the prophetis, the princis of the synagoge senten to hem, and seiden, Britheren, if ony word of exortacioun to the puple is in you, seie ye.

16 And Poul roos, and with hoond baad silence, and seide, Men of Israel, and ye that dreden God, here ye.

17 God of the puple of Israel chees oure fadris, and enhaunside the puple, whanne thei weren comelingis in the loond of Egipt, and in an hiy arme he ledde hem out of it;

18 and bi the tyme of fourti yeeris he suffride her maneres in desert.

19 And he destriede seuene folkis in the loond of Canaan, and bi sort departide to hem her lond,

20 as aftir foure hundrid and fifti yeeris. And aftir these thingis he yaf domesmen, to Samuel, the profete.

21 And fro that tyme thei axiden a kyng, and God yaf to hem Saul, the sone of Cis, a man of the lynage of Beniamyn, bi fourti yeeris.

22 And whanne he was don awei, he reiside to hem Dauid king, to whom he bar witnessing, and seide, Y haue foundun Dauid, the sone of Jesse, a man aftir myn herte, which schal do alle my willis.

23 Of whos seed bi the biheest God hath led out to Israel a sauyoure Jhesu,

24 whanne Joon prechide bifor the face of his comyng the baptym of penaunce to al the puple of Israel.

25 But whanne Joon fillide his cours, he seide, Y am not he, whom ye demen me to be; but lo! he cometh aftir me, and Y am not worthi to doon of the schoon of hise feet.

26 Britheren, and sones of the kynde of Abraham, and whiche that in you dreden God, to you the word of helthe is sent.

27 For thei that dwelliden at Jerusalem, and princis of it, that knewen not this Jhesu, and the voicis of prophetis, that by euery sabat ben red, demyden, and filliden;

28 and thei founden in hym no cause of deth, and axiden of Pilat, that thei schulden sle hym.

29 And whanne thei hadden endid alle thingis that weren writun of hym, thei token hym doun of the tre, and leiden hym in a graue.

30 And God reiside hym fro deth in the thridde dai; which was seyn bi mony daies to

31 hem that wenten vp togidere with hym fro Galilee in to Jerusalem, which ben til now his witnessis to the puple.

32 And we schewen to you the biheest that was maad to oure fadris;

33 for God hath fulfillid this to her sones, and ayenreisid Jhesu; as in the secounde salm it is writun, Thou art my sone, to dai Y bigat thee.

34 And he ayenreiside hym fro deth, that he schulde not turne ayen in to corrupcioun, seide thus, For Y schal yyue to you the hooli trewe thingis of Dauid.

35 And therfor and on an othere stide he seith, Thou schalt not yyue thin hooli to se corrupcioun.

36 But Dauid in his generacioun, whanne he hadde mynstrid to the wille of God, diede, and was leid with hise fadris, and say corrupcioun;

37 but he whom God reiside fro deth, say not corrupcioun.

38 Therfor, britheren, be it knowun to you, that bi hym remyssioun of synnes is teld to you, fro alle synnes, of whiche ye myyten not be iustified in the lawe of Moises.

39 In this ech man that bileueth, is iustified.

40 Therfor se ye, that it come not to you, that is biforeseid in the profetis,

41 Ye dispiseris, se ye, and wondre ye, and be ye scaterid abrood; for Y worche a werk in youre daies, a werk that ye schulen not bileue, if ony man schal telle it to you.

42 And whanne thei yeden out, thei preieden, that in the sabat suynge thei schulden speke to hem these wordis.

43 And whanne the synagoge was left, manye of Jewis and of comelingis worschypynge God supeden Poul and Barnabas; that spaken, and counseliden hem, that thei schulden dwelle in the grace of God.

44 And in the sabat suynge almest al the citee cam togidir, to here the word of God.

45 And Jewis sien the puple, and weren fillid with enuye, and ayenseiden these thingis that weren seyd of Poul, and blasfemyden.

46 Thanne Poul and Barnabas stidfastli seiden, To you it bihofte first to speke the word of God; but for ye putten it awei, and han demyd you vnworthi to euerlastinge lijf, lo! we turnen to hethen men.

47 For so the Lord comaundide vs, Y haue set thee in to liyt to hethen men, that thou be in to helthe to the vtmest of erthe.

48 And hethen men herden, 'and ioieden, and glorifieden the word of the Lord; and bileueden, as manye as weren bifore ordeyned to euerlastinge lijf.

49 And the word of the Lord was sowun bi al the cuntre.

50 But the Jewis stiriden religiouse wymmen, and onest, and the worthiest men of the citee, and stireden persecucioun ayens Poul and Barnabas, and dryuen hem out of her cuntreis.

51 And thei schoken awei in to hem the duste of her feet, and camen to Yconye.

52 And the disciplis weren fillid with ioye and the Hooli Goost.

CAP 14

1 But it bifelde at Yconye, that thei entriden togidir in to the synagoge of Jewis, and spaken, so that ful greet multitude of Jewis and Grekis bileueden.

2 But the Jewis that weren vnbileueful, reiseden persecucioun, and stiriden to wraththe the soulis of hethene men ayens the britheren; but the Lord yaf soone pees.

3 Therfor thei dwelliden myche tyme, and diden tristili in the Lord, berynge witnessyng to the word of his grace, yyuynge signes and wondris to be maad bi the hondis of hem.

4 But the multitude of the citee was departid, and sum weren with the Jewis, and sum with the apostlis.

5 But whanne ther was maad 'an asaute of the hethene men and the Jewis, with her princis, to turmenten and to stonen hem,

6 thei vndurstoden, and fledden togidere to the citees of Licaonye, and Listris, and Derben, and into al the cuntre aboute. And thei prechiden there the gospel, and al the multitude was moued togider in the teching of hem. Poul and Barnabas dwelten at Listris.

7 And a man at Listris was sijk in the feet, and hadde sete crokid fro his modris wombe, which neuer hadde goen.

8 This herde Poul spekinge; and Poul biheld hym, and siy that he hadde feith, that he schulde be maad saaf,

9 and seide with a greet vois, Rise thou 'vp riyt on thi feet. And he lippide, and walkide.

10 And the puple, whanne thei hadde seyn that that Poul dide, reriden her vois in Licaon tunge, and seiden, Goddis maad lijk to men ben comun doun to vs.

11 And thei clepiden Barnabas Jubiter, and Poul Mercurie, for he was ledere of the word.

12 And the preest of Jubiter that was bifor the citee, brouyte boolis and crownes bifor the yatis, with puplis, and wolde haue maad sacrifice.

13 And whanne the apostlis Barnabas and Poul herden this, thei to-renten her cootis; and thei skipten out among the puple,

14 and crieden, and seiden, Men, what don ye this thing? and we ben deedli men lijk you, and schewen to you, that ye be conuertid fro these veyn thingis to the lyuynge God, that maad heuene, and erthe, and the see, and alle thingis that ben in hem;

15 which in generaciouns passid suffride alle folkis to gon in to her owne weies.

16 And yit he lefte not hym silf with out witnessing in wel doyng, for he yaf reyns fro heuene, and times beringe fruyt, and fulfillide youre hertis with meete and gladnesse.

17 And thei seiynge these thingis, vnnethis swagiden the puple, that thei offriden not to men.

18 But sum Jewis camen ouer fro Antioche and Iconye, and counseilden the puple, and stonyden Poul, and drowen out of the citee, and gessiden that he was deed.

19 But whanne disciplis weren comun aboute him, he roos, and wente in to the citee; and in the dai suynge he wente forth with Barnabas in to Derben.

20 And whanne thei hadden prechid to the ilk citee, and tauyte manye, thei turneden ayen to Listris, and Iconye, and to Antioche; confermynge the soulis of disciplis,

21 and monestinge, that thei schulden dwelle in feith, and seiden, That bi many tribulaciouns it bihoueth vs to entre in to the kingdom of heuenes.

22 And whanne thei hadden ordeined prestis to hem bi alle citees, and hadden preied with fastyngis, thei bitoken hem to the Lord, in whom thei bileueden.

23 And thei passiden Persidie, and camen to Pamfilie;

24 and thei spaken the word 'of the Lord in Pergen, and camen doun in to Italie.

25 And fro thennys thei wenten bi boot to Antiochie, fro whennus thei weren takun to the grace of God, in to the werk that thei filliden.

26 And whanne thei weren comun, and hadden gaderid the chirche, thei telden hou grete thingis God dide with hem, and that he hadde openyde to hethene men the dore of feith.

27 And thei dwelliden not a litil tyme with the disciplis.

CAP 15

1 And summe camen doun fro Judee, and tauyten britheren, That but ye ben circumcidid after the lawe of Moises, ye moun not be maad saaf.

2 Therfor whanne ther was maad not a litil discencioun to Poul and Barnabas ayens hem, thei ordeyneden, that Poul and Barnabas, and summe othere of hem, schulden go vp to the apostlis and preestis in Jerusalem, on this questioun.

3 And so thei weren led forth of the chirche, and passiden bi Fenyce and Samarie; and thei telden the conuersacioun of hethene men, and thei maden greet ioie to alle the britheren.

4 And whanne thei camen to Jerusalem, thei weren resseyued of the chirche and of the apostlis, and of the eldre men, and telden, hou grete thingis God dide with hem.

5 But summe of the erise of Fariseis, that bileueden, risen vp, and seiden, That it bihoueth hem to be circumsidid, and to comaunde to kepe also the lawe of Moises.

6 And the apostlis and eldre men camen togidre, to se of 'this word.

7 And whanne there was maad a greet sekyng herof, Petre roos, and seide to hem, Britheren, ye witen, that of elde daies in you God chees bi my mouth hethene, to here the word of the gospel, and to bileue;

8 and God, that knewe hertis, bar witnessing, and yaf to hem the Hooli Goost, as also to vs;

9 and no thing diuerside bitwixe vs and hem, 'and clenside the hertis of hem bi feith.

10 Now thanne what tempten ye God, to putte a yok on the necke of the disciplis, which nether we, nether oure fadris miyten bere?

11 But bi the grace of oure Lord Jhesu Crist we bileuen to be saued, as also thei.

12 And al the multitude helde pees, and herden Barnaban and Poul, tellinge hou grete signes and wondris God dide bi hem in hethene men.

13 And aftir that thei helden pees, James answeride, and seide, Britheren, here ye me.

14 Symount telde, hou God visitide, first to take of hethene men a puple to his name.

15 And the wordis of prophetis acorden to him,

16 as it is writun, Aftir this Y schal turne ayen, and bilde the tabernacle of Dauid, that felle doun; and Y schal bilde ayen the cast doun thingis of it, and Y schal reise it;

17 that other men seke the Lord, and alle folkis on which my name is clepid to helpe; the Lord doynge this thing, seith.

18 Fro the world, the werk of the Lord is knowun to the Lord.

19 For which thing Y deme hem that of hethene men ben conuertid to God,

20 to be not disesid, but to write to hem, that thei absteyne hem fro defoulingis of maumetis, and fro fornicacioun, and stranglid thingis, and blood.

21 For Moyses of elde tymes hath in alle citees hem that prechen him in synagogis, where bi ech sabat he is red.

22 Thanne it pleside to the apostlis, and to the eldre men, with al the chirche, to chees men of hem, and sende to Antioche, with Poul and Barnabas, Judas, that was named Barsabas, and Silas, the firste men among britheren;

23 and wroten bi the hondis of hem, Apostlis and eldre britheren to hem that ben at Antioche, and Sirie, and Silice, britheren of hethen men, greting.

24 For we herden that summe wenten out fro vs, and trobliden you with wordis, and turneden vpsodoun youre soulis, to whiche men we comaundiden not,

25 it pleside to vs gaderid in to oon, to chese men, and sende to you, with oure most dereworthe Barnabas and Poul,

26 men that yauen her lyues for the name of oure Lord Jhesu Crist.

27 Therfor we senten Judas and Silas, and thei schulen telle the same thingis to you bi wordis.

28 For it is seyn to the Hooly Goost and to vs, to putte to you no thing more of charge, than these nedeful thingis,

29 that ye absteyne you fro the offrid thingis of maumetis, and blood stranglid, and fornicacioun. Fro whiche ye kepinge you, schulen do wel. Fare ye wel.

30 Therfor thei weren let go, and camen doun to Antioche; and whanne the multitude was gaderid, thei token the epistle;

31 which whanne thei hadden red, thei ioyden on the coumfort.

32 And Judas and Silas and thei, for thei weren prophetis, coumfortiden britheren, and confermyden with ful many wordis.

33 But aftir that thei hadden be there a lytil while, thei weren let go of britheren with pees, to hem that hadden sent hem.

34 But it was seyn to Silas, to dwelle there; and Judas wente aloone to Jerusalem.

35 And Poul and Barnabas dwelten at Antioche, techinge and prechinge the word of the Lord, with othere manye.

36 But after summe daies, Poul seide to Barnabas, Turne we ayen, and visite britheren bi alle citees, in whiche we han prechid the word of the Lord, hou thei han hem.

37 And Barnabas wolde take with hym Joon, that was named Marcus.

38 But Poul preiede him, that he that departide fro hem fro Pamfilie, and wente not with hem in to the werk, schulde not be resseyued.

39 And dissencioun was maad, so that thei departiden a twynny. And Barnabas took Mark, and cam bi boot to Cipre.

40 And Poul chees Silas, and wente forth fro the britheren, and was bitakun to the grace of God.

41 And he wente bi Sirie and Silice, and confermyde the chirche, comaundinge to kepe the heestis of apostlis and eldre men.

CAP 16

1 And he cam in to Derben and Listram. And lo! a disciple was there, bi name Timothe, the sone of a Jewesse cristen, and of the fadir hethen.

2 And britheren that weren in Listris and Iconye, yeldiden good witnessing to hym.

3 And Poul wolde that this man schulde go forth with him, and he took, and circumsidide hym, for Jewis that weren in the places. For alle wisten, that his fadir was hethen.

4 Whanne thei passiden bi citees, thei bitoken to hem to kepe the techingis, that weren demyd of apostlis and eldre men, that weren at Jerusalem.

5 And the chirches weren conformed in feith, and encreseden in noumbre eche dai.

6 And thei passiden Frigie, and the cuntre of Galathi, and weren forbedun of the Hooli Goost to speke the word of God in Asie.

7 And whanne thei camen in to Mysie, thei assaieden to go in to Bithynye, and the spirit of Jhesu suffride not hem.

8 But whanne thei hadden passid bi Mysie, thei camen doun to Troade;

9 and a visioun 'bi nyyt was schewid to Poul. But a man of Macedonye that stoode, preiede hym, and seide, Go thou in to Macedonye, and helpe vs.

10 And as he hadde sei the visioun, anoon we souyten to go forth in to Macedonye, and weren maad certeyn, that God hadde clepid vs to preche to hem.

11 And we yeden bi schip fro Troade, and camen to Samatrachia with streiyt cours; and the dai suynge to Neapolis;

12 and fro thennus to Filippis, that is the firste part of Macedonye, the citee colonye. And we weren in this citee summe daies, and spaken togidere.

13 And in the dai of sabotis we wenten forth with out the yate bisidis the flood, where preier semyde to be; and we saten, and spaken to wymmen that camen togidere.

14 And a womman, Lidda bi name, a purpuresse of the cite of Tiatirens, worschipinge God, herde; whos herte the Lord openyde to yyue tente to these thingis, that weren seid of Poul.

15 And whanne sche was baptisid and hir hous, sche preyede, and seide, If ye han demyd that Y am feithful to the Lord, entre ye in to myn hous, and dwelle.

16 And sche constreynede vs. And it was don, whanne we yeden to preier, that a damysel that hadde a spirit of diuynacioun, mette vs, which yaf greet wynnyng to her lordis in dyuynynge.

17 This suede Poul and vs, and criede, and seide, These men ben seruauntis of the hiy God, that tellen to you the weie of helthe.

18 And this sche dide in many daies. And Poul sorewide, and turnede, and seide to the spirit, Y comaunde thee in the name of Jhesu Crist, that thou go out of hir.

19 And he wente out in the same our. And the lordis of hir siyen, that the hope of her wynnyng wente awei, and thei token Poul and Silas, and ledden in to the 'dom place, to the princis.

20 And thei brouyten hem to the magistratis, and seiden, These men disturblen oure citee,

21 for thei ben Jewis, and schewen a custom, which it is not leueful to vs to resseyue, nether do, sithen we ben Romayns.

22 And the puple 'and magistratis runnen ayens hem, and when thei hadden to-rente the cootis of hem, thei comaundiden hem to be betun with yerdis.

23 And whanne thei hadden youun to hem many woundis, thei senten hem into prisoun, and comaundiden to the kepere, that he schulde kepe hem diligentli.

24 And whanne he hadde take siche a precept, he putte hem into the ynnere prisoun, and streynede the feet of hem in a tre.

25 And at mydniyt Poul and Silas worschipide, and heriden God; and thei that weren in kepyng herden hem.

26 And sudenli a greet erthe mouyng was maad, so that the foundementis of the prisoun weren moued. And anoon alle the doris weren openyd, and the boondis of alle weren lousid.

27 And the kepere of the prisoun was awakid, and siy the yatis 'of the prisoun openyd, and with a swerd drawun out he wolde haue slawe hym silf, and gesside that the men that weren boundun, hadden fled.

28 But Poul criede with a greet vois, and seide, Do thou noon harm to thi silf, for alle we ben here.

29 And he axide liyt, and entride, and tremblide, and felle doun to Poul and to Silas at her feet.

30 And he brouyte hem with out forth, and seide, Lordis, what bihoueth me to do, that Y be maad saaf?

31 And thei seiden, Bileue thou in the Lord Jhesu, and thou schalt be saaf, and thin hous.

32 And thei spaken to hym the word of the Lord, with alle that weren in his hous.

33 And he took hem in the ilke our of the niyt, and waschide her woundis. And he was baptisid, and al his hous anoon.

34 And whanne he hadde led hem in to his hous, he settide to hem a boord. And he was glad with al his hous, and bileuede to God.

35 And whanne dai was come, the magistratis senten catchepollis, and seiden, Delyuere thou tho men.

36 And the kepere of the prisoun telde these wordis to Poul, That the magistratis han sent, that ye be delyuered; now therfor go ye out, and go ye in pees.

37 And Poul seide to hem, Thei senten vs men of Rome in to prisoun, that weren betun openli and vndampned, and now priueli thei bringen vs out; not so, but come thei hem silf, and delyuere vs out.

38 And the catchepollis telden these wordis to the magistratis; and thei dredden, for thei herden that thei weren Romayns.

39 And thei camen, and bisechiden hem, and thei brouyten hem out, and preieden, that thei schulden go out of the citee.

40 And thei yeden out of the prisoun, and entriden to Lidie. And whanne thei siyen britheren, thei coumfortiden hem, and yeden forth.

CAP 17

1 And whanne thei hadden passid bi Amfipolis and Appollonye, thei camen to Thessolonyk, where was a synagoge of Jewis.

2 And bi custom Poul entride to hem, and bi thre sabatis he declaride to hem of scripturis,

3 and openyde, and schewide that it bihofte Crist to suffre, and rise ayen fro deth, and that this is Jhesus Crist, whom Y telle to you.

4 And summe of hem bileueden, and weren ioyned to Poul and to Silas; and a greet multitude of hethene men worschipide God, and noble wymmen not a fewe.

5 But the Jewis hadden enuye, and token of the comyn puple summe yuele men, and whanne thei hadden maad a cumpenye, thei moueden the citee. And thei camen to Jasouns hous, and souyten hem to brynge forth among the puple.

6 And whanne thei founden hem not, thei drowen Jasoun and summe britheren to the princis of the citee, and crieden, That these it ben, that mouen the world, and hidir thei camen,

7 whiche Jason resseyuede. And these alle don ayens the maundementis of the emperour, and seien, that Jhesu is anothir king.

8 And thei moueden the puple, and the princis of the citee, herynge these thingis.

9 And whanne satisfaccioun was takun of Jason, and of othere, thei leten Poul and Silas go.

10 And anoon bi niyt britheren leten Silas go in to Beroan. And whanne thei camen thidur, thei entriden in to the synagoge of the Jewis.

11 But these weren the worthier of hem that ben at Thessolonik, whiche resseyueden the word with al desire, eche dai sekinge scripturis, if these thingis hadden hem so.

12 And manye of hem bileueden and of hethen wymmen onest and men not a fewe.

13 But whanne the Jewis in Tessalonyk hadden knowe, that also at Bero the word of God was prechid of Poul, thei camen thidir, mouynge and disturblynge the multitude.

14 And tho anoon britheren delyuerden Poul, that he schulde go to the see; but Sylas and Tymothe dwelten there.

15 And thei that ledden forth Poul, ledden hym to Atenes. And whanne thei hadden take maundement of him to Silas and to Tymothe, that ful hiyyngli thei schulden come to hym, thei wenten forth.

16 And while Poul abood hem at Atenys, his spirit was moued in him, for he saiy the citee youun to ydolatrie.

17 Therfor he disputide in the synagoge with the Jewis, and with men that worschipiden God, and in the dom place, by alle daies to hem that herden.

18 And summe Epeicureis, and Stoisens, and filosofris disputiden with hym. And summe seiden, What wole this sowere of wordis seie? And othere seiden, He semeth to be a tellere of newe fendis; for he telde to hem Jhesu, and the ayenrisyng.

19 And thei token, and ledden hym to Ariopage, and seide, Moun we wite, what is this newe doctryne, that is seid of thee?

20 For thou bringist ynne summe newe thingis to oure eeris; therfor we wolen wite, what these thingis wolen be.

21 For alle men of Athenys and comlingis herborid yauen tent to noon other thing, but ether to seie, ethir to here, sum newe thing.

22 And Poul stood in the myddil of Ariopage, and seide, Men of Athenys, bi alle thingis Y se you as veyn worschipers.

23 For Y passide, and siy youre maumetis, and foond an auter, in which was writun, To the vnknowun God. Therfor which thing ye vnknowynge worschipen, this thing Y schew to you.

24 God that made the world and alle thingis that ben in it, this, for he is Lord of heuene and of erthe, dwellith not in templis maad with hoond,

25 nethir is worschipid bi mannus hoondis, nether hath nede of ony thing, for he yyueth lijf to alle men, and brethinge, and alle thingis;

26 and made of oon al the kinde of men to enhabite on al the face of the erthe, determynynge tymes ordeyned, and termes of the dwellynge of hem,

27 to seke God, if perauenture thei felen hym, ether fynden, thouy he be not fer fro eche of you.

28 For in hym we lyuen, and mouen, and ben. As also summe of youre poetis seiden, And we ben also the kynde of hym.

29 Therfor sithen we ben the kynde of God, we schulen not deme, that godli thing is lijk gold, and siluer, ethir stoon, ethir to grauyng of craft and thouyt of man.

30 For God dispisith the tymes of this vnkunnyng, and now schewith to men, that alle euery where doon penaunce; for that he hath ordeyned a dai,

31 in which he schal deme the world in equite, in a man in which he ordeynede, and yaf feith to alle men, and reiside hym fro deth.

32 And whanne thei hadden herd the ayenrysing of deed men, summe scorneden, and summe seiden, We schulen here thee eft of this thing.

33 So Poul wente out of the myddil of hem.

34 But summen drowen to hym, and bileueden. Among whiche Dynyse Aropagite was, and a womman, bi name Damaris, and othere men with hem.

CAP 18

1 Aftir these thingis Poul yede out of Atenes, and cam to Corinthie.

2 And he fonde a man, a Jewe, Aquila bi name, of Ponte bi kynde, that late cam from Ytalie, and Priscille, his wijf, for that Claudius comaundide alle Jewis to departe fro Rome; and he cam to hem.

3 And for he was of the same craft, he dwellide with hem, and wrouyte; and thei weren of roopmakeris craft.

4 And he disputide in the synagoge bi ech sabat, puttynge among the name of the Lord Jhesu; and he counselide Jewis and Grekis.

5 And whanne Silas and Tymothe camen fro Macedonye, Poul yaf bisynesse to the word, and witnesside to the Jewis, that Jhesu is Crist.

6 But whanne thei ayenseiden and blasfemyden, he schoke awei hise clothis, and seide to hem, Youre blood be on youre heed; Y schal be clene from hennus forth, and schal go to hethene men.

7 And he passide fro thennus, and entride in to the hous of a iust man, Tite bi name, that worschipide God, whos hous was ioyned to the synagoge.

8 And Crispe, prince of the synagoge, bileuede to the Lord, with al his hous. And many of the Corinthies herden, and bileueden, and weren cristened.

9 And the Lord seide bi nyyt to Poul bi a visioun, Nyle thou drede, but speke, and be not stille;

10 for Y am with thee, and no man schal be put to thee to noye thee, for myche puple is to me in this citee.

11 And he dwellide there a yeer and sixe monethis, techinge among hem the word of God.

12 But whanne Gallion was proconsul of Acaye, Jewis risen vp with oo wille ayens Poul, and ledden hym to the doom,

13 and seiden, Ayens the lawe this counselith men to worschipe God.

14 And whanne Poul bigan to opene his mouth, Gallion seide to the Jewis, If there were ony wickid thing, ether yuel trespas, ye Jewis, riytli Y schulde suffre you;

15 but if questiouns ben of the word, and of names of youre lawe, bisee you silf; Y wole not be domesman of these thingis.

16 And he droof hem fro the doom place.

17 And alle token Sostenes, prince of the synagoge, and smoten him bifor the doom place; and no thing of these was to charge to Gallion.

18 And whanne Poul hadde abidun many daies, he seide fare wel to britheren, and bi boot cam to Syrie. And Priscille and Aquila camen with hym, whiche hadden clippid his heed in Tencris; for he had a vow.

19 And he cam to Effesie, and there he lefte hem; and he yede in to the synagoge, and disputide with Jewis.

20 And whanne thei preieden, that he schulde dwelle more time,

21 he consentide not, but he made 'fare wel, and seide, Eft Y schal turne ayen to you, if God wole; and he wente forth fro Effesi.

22 And he cam doun to Cesarie, and he yede vp, and grette the chirche, and cam doun to Antiochie.

23 And whanne he hadde dwellide there sumwhat of time, he wente forth, walkinge bi rewe thorou the cuntrei of Galathie, and Frigie, and confermyde alle the disciplis.

24 But a Jewe, Apollo bi name, a man of Alisaundre of kinde, a man eloquent, cam to Effesie; and he was myyti in scripturis.

25 This man was tauyt the weie of the Lord, and was feruent in spirit, and spak, and tauyte diligentli tho thingis that weren of Jhesu, and knew oonli the baptym of Joon.

26 And this man bigan to do tristili in the synagoge. Whom whanne Priscille and Aquila herden, thei token hym, and more diligentli expowneden to hym the weie of the Lord.

27 And whanne he wolde go to Acaie, britheren excitiden, and wroten to the disciplis, that thei schulden resseyue hym; which whanne he cam, yaf myche to hem that bileueden.

28 For he greetli ouercam Jewis, and schewide opynli bi scripturis, that Jhesu is Crist.

CAP 19

1 And it bifelle, whanne Apollo was at Corinthi, that Poul whanne he hadde go the hiyer coostis, he cam to Efesie, and foond summe of disciplis.

2 And he seide to hem, Whethir ye that bileuen han resseyued the Hooli Goost? And thei seiden to hym, But nether 'han we herd, if the Hooli Goost is.

3 And he seide, Therfor in what thing ben ye baptisid? And thei seiden, In the baptym of Joon.

4 And Poul seide, Joon baptiside the puple in baptym of penaunce, and tauyte, that thei schulden bileue in hym that was to comynge 'after hym, that is, in Jhesu.

5 Whanne thei herden these thingis, thei weren baptisid in the name of the Lord Jhesu.

6 And whanne Poul hadde leid on hem his hoondis, the Hooli Goost cam in hem, and thei spaken with langagis, and profecieden.

7 And alle weren almest twelue men.

8 And he yede in to the synagoge, and spak with trist thre monethis, disputinge and tretinge of the kingdom of God.

9 But whanne summe weren hardid, and bileueden not, and cursiden the weie of the Lord bifor the multitude, he yede awei fro hem, and departide the disciplis, and disputide in the scole of a myyti man eche dai.

10 This was doon bi twei yeeris, so that alle that dwelliden in Asie herden the word of the Lord, Jewis and hethene men.

11 And God dide vertues not smale bi the hoond of Poul,

12 so that on sijk men the sudaries weren borun fro his bodye, and sijknessis departiden fro hem, and wickid spiritis wenten out.

13 But also summe of the Jewis exorsisists yeden aboute, and assaieden to clepe the name of the Lord Jhesu Crist on hem that hadden yuele spiritis, and seiden, Y coniure you bi Jhesu, whom Poul prechith.

14 And ther weren seuene sones of a Jewe, Steuen, a prince of preestis, that diden this thing.

15 But the yuel spirit answeride, and seide to hem, Y knowe Jhesu, and Y knowe Poul; but who ben ye?

16 And the man in which was the worste deuel, lippide on hem, and hadde victorie of bothe, and was stronge ayens hem, that thei nakid and woundid fledden awei fro that hous.

17 And this thing was maad knowun to alle the Jewis and to hethene men, that dwelliden at Effesie; and drede felle doun on hem alle, and thei magnyfieden the name of the Lord Jhesu.

18 And many men bileueden, and camen, knowlechinge and tellynge her dedis.

19 And manye of them that sueden curiouse thingis, brouyten togidere bookis, and brenneden hem bifor alle men; and whanne the prices of tho weren acountid, thei founden monei of fifti thousynd pens;

20 so strongli the word of God wexide, and was confermyd.

21 And whanne these thingis weren fillid, Poul purposide in spirit, aftir that Macedony was passid and Acaie, to go to Jerusalem, and seide, For aftir that Y schal be there, it bihoueth me 'to se also Rome.

22 And he sente in to Macedonye twey men, that mynystriden to hym, Tymothe, and Eraste, and he dwellide for a tyme in Asie.

23 And a greet troubling was maad in that dai, of the weie of the Lord.

24 For a man, Demetrie bi name, a worcher in siluer, makide siluer housis to Diane, and yaf to crafti men myche wynnyng;

25 which he clepide togidere 'hem that weren suche maner werkmen, and seide, Men, ye witen that of this craft wynnyng is to vs;

26 and ye seen and heren, that this Poul counseilith and turneth awei myche puple, not oonli of Effesie, but almest of al Asie, and seith, that thei ben not goddis, that ben maad with hoondis.

27 And not oonli this part schal be in perel to vs, to come in to repreef, but also the temple of the greet Dian schal be acountid in to nouyt; yhe, and the maieste of hir schal bigynne to be destried, whom al Asie and the world worschipith.

28 Whanne these thingis weren herd, thei weren fillid with ire, and crieden, and seiden, Greet is the Dian of Effesians.

29 And the citee was fillid with confusioun, and thei maden an asaut with oon wille in to the teaatre, and tooken Gayus and Aristark, men of Macedonye, felawis of Poul.

30 And whanne Poul would haue entrid in to the peple, the disciplis suffriden not.

31 And also summe of the princis of Asie, that weren hise freendis, senten to him. and preieden, that he schulde not yyue hym silf in to the teatre.

32 And othere men crieden othir thing; for the chirche was confusid, and many wisten not for what cause thei weren come togidere.

33 But of the puple thei drowen awei oon Alisaundre, while Jewis puttiden hym forth. And Alisaundre axide with his hoond silence, and wolde yelde a resoun to the puple.

34 And as thei knewen that he was a Jew, o vois of alle men was maad, criynge as bi tweyn ouris, Greet Dian of Effesians.

35 And whanne the scribe hadde ceessid the puple, he seide, Men of Effesie, what man is he, that knowith not, that the citee of Effesians is the worschipere of greet Dian, and of the child of Jubiter?

36 Therfor whanne it may not be ayenseid to these thingis, it behoueth you to be ceessid, and to do no thing folili;

37 for ye han brouyt these men, nethir sacrilegeris, nethir blasfemynge youre goddesse.

38 That if Demetrie, and the werk men that ben with hym, han cause ayens ony man, there ben courtis, and domes, and iugis; accusen thei eche other.

39 If ye seken ouyt of ony othir thing, it may be assoylid in the lawful chirche.

40 For whi we ben in perel to be repreuyd of this daies dissencioun, sithen no man is gilti, of whom we moun yelde resoun of this rennyng togidre. And whanne he hadde seid this thing, he lete the puple go.

CAP 20

1 And aftir the noise ceesside, Poul clepide the disciplis, and monestide hem, and seide fare wel; and he wente forth, to go in to Macedonye.

2 And whanne he hadde walkid bi tho coostis, and hadde monestid hem bi many wordis, he cam to Greece.

3 Where whanne he hadde be thre monethis, the Jewis leiden aspies for hym, that was to saile in to Sirie; and he hadde counsel to turne ayen bi Macedonye.

4 And Sosipater of Pirri Boroense folowide hym; of Thessolonycenses, Astirak, and Secoundus, and Gayus Derbeus, and Tymothe; and Asians, Titicus and Trofimus.

5 These for thei wenten bifore, aboden vs at Troade.

6 For we schippiden aftir the daies of therf looues fro Filippis, and cam to hem at Troade in fyue daies, where we dwelten seuene daies.

7 And in the first dai of the woke, whanne we camen to breke breed, Poul dispitide with hem, and schulde go forth in the morew;

8 and he drow along the sermoun til in to mydnyyt. And many laumpes weren in the soler, where we weren gaderyd togidir.

9 And a yong man, Euticus bi name, sat on the wyndowe, whanne he was fallun in to an heuy sleep, while Poul disputide long, al slepynge he felle doun fro the thridde stage; and he was takun vp, and was brouyt deed.

10 To whom whanne Poul cam doun, he lay on hym, and biclippide, and seide, Nyle ye be troblid; for his soule is in hym.

11 And he wente vp, and brak breed, and eete, and spak ynowy vnto the dai; and so he wente forth.

12 And thei brouyten the childe alyue, and thei weren coumfortid greetli.

13 And we wenten vp in to a schip, and schippiden in to Asson, to take Poul fro thennus; for so he hadde disposid to make iourney bi loond.

14 And whanne he foond vs in Asson, we token hym, and camen to Mitilene.

15 And fro thennus we schippiden in the dai suynge, and we camen ayens Chyum, and another dai we haueenyden at Samum, and in the dai suynge we camen to Mylete.

16 And Poul purposide to schip ouer to Efesi, lest ony tariyng were maad to hym in Asie; for he hiyede, if it were possible to hym, that he schulde be in the dai of Pentecost at Jerusalem.

17 Fro Mylete he sente to Effesi, and clepide the grettest men of birthe of the chirche.

18 And whanne thei camen to hym, and weren togidir, he seide to hem, Ye witen fro the firste dai, in which Y cam in to Asie, hou with you bi eche tyme Y was,

19 seruynge to the Lord with al mekenesse, and mildnesse, and teeris, and temptaciouns, that felden to me of aspiyngis of Jewis;

20 hou Y withdrowe not of profitable thingis to you, that Y telde not to you, and tauyte you opynli, and bi housis;

21 and Y witnesside to Jewis and to hethene men penaunce in to God, and feith in to oure Lord Jhesu Crist.

22 And now lo! Y am boundun in spirit, and go in to Jerusalem; and Y knowe not what thingis schulen come to me in it,

23 but that the Hooli Goost 'bi alle citees witnessith to me, and seith, that boondis and tribulaciouns at Jerusalem abiden me.

24 But Y drede no thing of these, nether Y make my lijf preciousere than my silf, so that Y end my cours, and the mynysterie of the word, which Y resseyuede of the Lord Jhesu, to witnesse the gospel of the grace of God.

25 And 'now lo! Y woot, that ye schulen no more se my face, alle ye bi whiche Y passide, prechynge the kingdom of God.

26 Wherfor Y witnesse to you this day, that Y am cleen of the blood of alle men.

27 For Y fley not awey, that Y telde not to you al the counsel of God.

28 Take ye tente to you, and to al the flocke, in which the Hooli Goost hath set you bischops, to reule the chirche of God, which he purchaside with his blood.

29 Y woot, that aftir my departyng, rauyschinge wolues schulen entre in to you, 'and spare not the flok;

30 and men spekinge schrewid thingis schulen rise of you silf, that thei leden awei disciplis aftir hem.

31 For which thing wake ye, holdinge in mynde that bi thre yeer nyyt and dai Y ceesside not with teeris monestinge ech of you.

32 And now Y bitake you to God and to the word of his grace, that is myyti to edifie and yyue eritage in alle that ben maad hooli.

33 And of no man Y coueitide siluer, and gold, ether cloth, as you silf witen;

34 for to tho thingis that weren nedeful to me, and to these that ben with me, these hoondis mynystriden.

35 Alle these thingis Y schewide to you, for so it bihoueth men trauelinge to resseyue sike men, and to haue mynde of the 'word of the Lord Jhesu; for he seide, It is more blesful to yyue, than to resseyue.

36 And whanne he hadde seid these thingis, he knelide, and he preiede with alle hem.

37 And greet weping of alle men was maad; and thei felden on the necke of Poul, and kissiden hym,

38 and sorewiden moost in the word that he seide, for thei schulen no more se his face. And thei ledden hym to the schip.

CAP 21

1 And whanne it was don, that we schulden seile, and weren passid awei fro hem, with streiyt cours we camen to Choum, and the day suynge to Rodis, and fro thennus to Patiram, and fro thennus to Myram.

2 And whanne we founden a schip passinge ouer to Fenyce, we wenten vp in to it, and sailden forth.

3 And whanne we apperiden to Cipre, we leften it at the left half, and seiliden in to Sirie, and camen to Tire. For there the schip schulde be vnchargid.

4 And whanne we foundun disciplis, we dwelliden there seuene daies; whiche seiden bi spirit to Poul, that he schulde not go vp to Jerusalem.

5 And whanne the daies weren fillid, we yeden forth, and alle men with wyues and children ledden forth vs with outen the citee; and we kneliden in the see brenke, and we preieden.

6 And whanne we hadden maad fare wel togidre, we wenten vp into the schip; and thei turneden ayen in to her owne places.

7 And whanne the schip sailinge was fillid fro Tire, we camen doun to Tolamayda, and whanne we hadden gret wel the britheren, we dwelliden o dai at hem.

8 And another dai we yeden forth, and camen to Cesarie. And we entriden in to the hous of Filip euangelist, that was oon of the seuene, and dwelliden at hym.

9 And to hym weren foure douytris, virgyns, that profecieden.

10 And whanne we dwelliden there bi summe daies, a profete, Agabus bi name, cam ouer fro Judee.

11 This whanne he cam to vs, took the girdil of Poul, and boond togidere hise feet and hoondis, and seide, The Hooli Goost seith these thingis, Thus Jewis schulen bynde in Jerusalem the man, whos is this girdil; and thei schulen bytake into hethene mennys hoondis.

12 Which thing whanne we herden, we preieden, and thei that weren of that place, that he schulde not go vp to Jerusalem.

13 Thanne Poul answeride, and seide, What doen ye, wepinge and turmentinge myn herte? For Y am redi, not oonli to be boundun, but also to die in Jerusalem for the name of the Lord Jhesu.

14 And whanne we myyten not counseile hym, we weren stille, and seiden, The wille of the Lord be don.

15 And aftir these daies we weren maad redi, and wenten vp to Jerusalem.

16 And summe of the disciplis camen with vs fro Cesarie, and ledden with hem a man, Jason of Cipre, an elde disciple, at whom we schulden be herborid.

17 And whanne we camen to Jerusalem, britheren resseyueden vs wilfulli.

18 And in the dai suynge Poul entride with vs to James, and alle the eldre men weren gaderid.

19 Whiche whanne he hadde gret, he telde bi alle thingis, what God hadde doon in hethene men, bi the mynysterie of hym.

20 And whanne thei herden, thei magnyfiden God, and seiden to hym, Brothir, thou seest how many thousyndis ben in Jewis, that han bileued to God, and alle ben loueris of the lawe.

21 And thei herden of thee, that thou techist departing fro Moises of thilk Jewis that ben bi hethene men, that seien, that thei owen not circumcide her sones, nether owen to entre by custom.

22 Therfor what is? It bihoueth that the multitude come togidre; for thei schulen here, that thou art come.

23 Therfor do thou this thing, that we seien to thee. Ther ben to vs foure men, that han a vow on hem.

24 Take thou these men, and halowe thee with hem; honge on hem, that thei schaue her heedis; and that alle men wite, that the thingis that thei herden of thee ben false, but that thou walkist, and thi silf kepist the lawe.

25 But of these that bileueden of hethene men, we writen, demynge that thei absteyne hem fro thing offrid to idols, and fro blood, and also fro stranglid thing, and fro fornicacioun.

26 Thanne Poul took the men, and in the dai suynge he was purified with hem, and entride in to the temple, and schewide the filling of daies of purifying, til the offring was offrid for ech of hem.

27 And whanne seuene daies weren endid, the Jewis that weren of Asie, whanne thei saien him in the temple, stiriden al the puple, and leyden hondis on hym,

28 and crieden, Men of Israel, helpe ye vs. This is the man, that ayens the puple and the lawe and this place techith euery where alle men, more ouer and hath led hethene men in to the temple, and hath defoulid this hooli place.

29 For thei seyen Trofimus of Effesi in the citee with hym, whom thei gessiden that Poul hadde brouyt in to the temple.

30 And al the citee was moued, and a rennyng togider of the puple was maad. And thei token Poul, and drowen him out of the temple; and anoon the yatis weren closid.

31 And whanne thei souyten to sle hym, it was teld to the tribune of the cumpany of knyytis, that al Jerusalem is confoundid.

32 Which anoon took knyytis, and centuriens, and ran to hem. And whanne thei hadden seen the tribune, and the knyytis, thei ceessiden to smyte Poul.

33 Thanne the tribune cam, and cauyte hym, and comaundide, that he were boundun with twei cheynes; and axide, who he was, and what he hadde don.

34 But othere crieden other thing among the puple. And whanne he miyte 'knowe no certeyn thing for the noise, he comaundide hym to be led in to the castels.

35 And whanne Poul cam to the grees, it bifel that he was borun of kniytis, for strengthe of the puple.

36 For the multitude of the puple suede hym, and criede, Take hym awei.

37 And whanne Poul bigan to be led in to the castels, he seide to the tribune, Whether it is leueful 'to me, to speke ony thing to thee?

38 And he seide, Kanst thou Greek? Whether thou art not the Egipcian, which bifor these daies mouedist a noise, and leddist out in to desert foure thousynde of men, mensleeris?

39 And Poul seide to hym, For Y am a Jew, of Tharse of Cilicie, a citeseyn, which citee is not vnknowun. And Y preye thee, suffre me to speke to the puple.

40 And whanne he suffride, Poul stood in the grees, and bikenede with the hoond to the puple. And whanne a greet silence was maad, he spak in Ebrew tunge, and seide,

CAP 22

1 Britheren and fadris, here ye what resoun Y yelde now to you.

2 And whanne sum herden that in Ebrew tunge he spak to hem, thei yauen the more silence.

3 And he seide, Y am a man a Jew, borun at Tharse of Cilicie, nurischid and in this citee bisidis the feet of Gamaliel, tauyt bi the treuthe of fadris lawe, a louyere of the lawe, as also ye alle ben to dai.

4 And Y pursuede this weie til to the deth, byndynge and bitakinge 'in to holdis men and wymmen,

5 as the prince of prestis yeldith witnessyng to me, and alle the grettest in birth. Of whom also Y took pistlis to britheren, and wente to Damask, to bring fro thennys men boundun in to Jerusalem, that thei schulden be peyned.

6 And it was don, while Y yede, and neiyede to Damask, at myddai sudeynli fro heuene a greet plente of liyt schoon aboute me.

7 And Y felde doun to the erthe, and herde a voice fro heuene, seiynge to me, Saul, Saul, what pursuest thou me? It is hard to thee to kike ayens the pricke.

8 And Y answeride, Who art thou, Lord? And he seide to me, Y am Jhesu of Nazareth, whom thou pursuest.

9 And thei that weren with me sien but the liyt, but thei herden not the vois of hym, that spak with me.

10 And Y seide, Lord, what schal Y do? And the Lord seide to me, Rise thou, and go to Damask; and there it schal be seid to thee, of alle thingis which it bihoueth thee to do.

11 And whanne Y saye not, for the clerete of that liyt, Y was led bi the hond of felowis, and Y cam to Damask.

12 And a man, Ananye, that bi the lawe hadde wytnessyng of alle Jewis dwellinge in Damask,

13 cam to me, and stood niy, and seide to me, Saul, brother, biholde. And Y in the same our biheelde in to hym.

14 And he seide, God of oure fadris hath bifor ordeyned thee, that thou schuldist knowe the wille of him, and schuldist se the riytful man, and here the vois of his mouth.

15 For thou schalt be his witnesse to alle men, of tho thingis that thou hast seyn and herd.

16 And now, what dwellist thou? Rise vp, and be baptisid, and waische awei thi synnes, bi the name of hym clepid to help.

17 And it was don to me, as Y turnede ayen in to Jerusalem, and preyede in the temple, that Y was maad in rauysching of soule,

18 and Y siy him seiynge to me, Hiye thou, and go out faste of Jerusalem, for thei schulen not resseyue thi witnessing of me.

19 And Y seide, Lord, thei witen, that Y was closing togidir 'in to prisoun, and betinge bi synagogis hem that bileueden 'in to thee.

20 And whanne the blood of Steuene, thi witnesse, was sched out, Y stood niy, and consentide, and kept the clothis of men that slowen hym.

21 And he seide to me, Go thou, for Y schal sende thee fer to naciouns.

22 And thei herden him til this word; and thei reiseden her vois, and seiden, Take awei fro the erthe siche a maner man; for it is not leueful, that he lyue.

23 And whanne thei crieden, and kesten awei her clothis, and threwen dust in to the eir,

24 the tribune comaundide hym to be led in to castels, and to be betun with scourgis, and to be turmentid, that he wiste, for what cause thei crieden so to him.

25 And whanne thei hadden boundun hym with cordis, Poul seide to a centurien stondinge niy to hym, Whether it is leueful to you, to scourge a Romayn, and vndampned?

26 And whanne this thing was herd, the centurien wente to the tribune, and telde to hym, and seide, What art thou to doynge? for this man is a citeseyn of Rome.

27 And the tribune cam niy, and seide to hym, Seie thou to me, whether thou art a Romayn?

28 And he seide, Yhe. And the tribune answeride, Y with myche summe gat this fredom. And Poul seide, And Y was borun a citeseyn of Rome.

29 Therfor anoon thei that schulden haue turmentid hym, departiden awei fro hym. And the tribune dredde, aftir that he wiste, that he was a citeseyn of Rome, and for he hadde boundun hym.

30 But in the dai suynge he wolde wite more diligentli, for what cause he were accusid of the Jewis, and vnbounde hym, and comaundide prestis and al the counsel to come togidir. And he brouyte forth Poul, and sette hym among hem.

CAP 23

1 And Poul bihelde in to the counsel, and seide, Britheren, Y with al good conscience haue lyued bifore God, 'til in to this dai.

2 And Anany, prince of prestis, comaundide to men that stoden nyy hym, that thei schulden smyte his mouth.

3 Thanne Poul seide to hym, Thou whitid wal, God smyte thee; thou sittist, and demest me bi the lawe, and ayens the law thou comaundist me to be smytun.

4 And thei that stoden niy, seiden, Cursist thou the hiyest prest of God?

5 And Poul seide, Britheren, Y wiste not, that he is prince of preestis; for it is writun, Thou schalt not curse the prince of thi puple.

6 But Poul wiste, that o parti was of Saduceis, and the othere of Fariseis; and he criede in the counsel, Britheren, Y am a Farisee, the sone of Farisees; Y am demyd of the hope and of the ayen rising of deed men.

7 And whanne he hadde seid this thing, dissencioun was maad bitwixe the Fariseis and the Saduceis, and the multitude was departid.

8 For Saduceis seien, that no 'rysing ayen of deed men is, nether aungel, nether spirit; but Fariseis knowlechen euer eithir.

9 And a greet cry was maad. And summe of Farisees rosen vp, and fouyten, seiynge, We fynden no thing of yuel in this man; what if a spirit, ether an aungel spak to hym?

10 And whanne greet discencioun was maad, the tribune dredde, lest Poul schulde be to-drawun of hem; and he comaundide knyytis to go doun, and to take hym fro the myddil of hem, and to lede hym in to castels.

11 And in the niyt suynge the Lord stood niy to hym, and seide, Be thou stidfast; for as thou hast witnessid of me in Jerusalem, so it bihoueth thee to witnesse also at Rome.

12 And whanne the dai was come, summe of the Jewis gaderiden hem, and maden 'avow, and seiden, that thei schulden nether eete, ne drinke, til thei slowen Poul.

13 And there weren mo than fourti men, that maden this sweryng togider.

14 And thei wenten to the princis of prestis, and eldre men, and seiden, With deuocioun we han a vowid, that we schulen not taste ony thing, til we sleen Poul.

15 Now therfor make ye knowun to the tribune, with the counsel, that he bringe hym forth to you, as if ye schulden knowe sum thing more certeynli of hym; and we ben redi to sle hym, bifor that he come.

16 And whanne the sone of Poulis sister hadde herd the aspies, he cam, and entride in to the castels, and telde to Poul.

17 And Poul clepide to hym oon of the centuriens, and seide, Lede this yonge man to the tribune, for he hath sum thing to schewe to hym.

18 And he took hym, and ledde to the tribune, and seide, Poul, that is boundun, preide me to lede to thee this yonge man, that hath sum thing to speke to thee.

19 And the tribune took his hoond, and wente with hym asidis half, and axide hym, What thing is it, that thou hast to schewe to me?

20 And he seide, The Jewis ben acordid to preye thee, that to morewe thou brynge forth Poul in to the counsel, as if thei schulden enquere sum thing more certeynli of hym.

21 But bileue thou not to hem; for mo than fourti men of hem aspien hym, which han a vowid, that thei schulen not eete nether drynke, til thei sleen hym; and now thei ben redi, abidinge thi biheest.

22 Therfor the tribune lefte the yonge man, and comaundide, that he schulde speke to no man, that he hadde maad these thingis knowun to hym.

23 And he clepide togidre twei centuriens, and he seide to hem, Make ye redi twei hundrid knyytis, that thei go to Cesarie, and horse men seuenti, and spere men twey hundrid, fro the thridde our of the nyyt.

24 And make ye redy an hors, for Poul to ride on, to lede hym saaf to Felix, the presydent.

25 For the tribune dredde, lest the Jewis wolden take hym bi the weie, and sle hym, and aftirward he miyte be chalengid, as he hadde take money.

26 And wroot hym 'a pistle, conteynynge these thingis. Claudius Lisias to the beste Felix, president, heelthe.

27 This man that was take of the Jewis, and bigan to be slayn, Y cam vpon hem with myn oost, and delyuerede hym fro hem, whanne Y knewe that he was a Romayn.

28 And Y wolde wite the cause, which thei puttiden ayens hym; and Y ledde hym to the counsel of hem.

29 And Y foond, that he was accusid of questiouns of her lawe, but he hadde no cryme worthi the deth, ethir boondis.

30 And whanne it was teeld me of the aspies, that thei arayden for hym, Y sente hym to thee, and Y warnede also the accuseris, that thei seie at thee. Fare wel.

31 And so the knyytis, as thei weren comaundid, token Poul, and ledde hym bi nyyt into Antipatriden.

32 And in the dai suynge, whanne the horsmen weren left, that schulden go with hym, thei turneden ayen to the castels.

33 And whanne thei camen to Cesarie, thei token the pistle to the president, and thei setten also Poul byfore him.

34 And whanne he hadde red, and axide, of what prouynce he was, and knewe that he was of Cilicie,

35 Y schal here thee, he seide, whanne thin accuseris comen. And he comaundide hym to be kept in the moot halle of Eroude.

CAP 24

1 And aftir fyue daies, Ananye, prince of preestis, cam doun with summe eldere men, and Terculle, a feir speker, which wenten to the precident ayens Poul.

2 And whanne Poul was somened, Terculle bigan to accuse hym, and seide, Whanne in myche pees we doon bi thee, and many thingis ben amendid bi thi wisdom, euere more and euery where,

3 thou best Felix, we han resseyued with al doyng of thankingis.

4 But lest Y tarie thee lengere, Y preie thee, schortly here vs for thi mekenesse.

5 We han foundun this wickid man stirynge dissencioun to alle Jewis in al the world, and auctour of dissencioun of the secte of Nazarenus; and he also enforside to defoule the temple;

6 whom also we token, and wolden deme, after oure lawe.

7 But Lisias, the trybune, cam with greet strengthe aboue, and delyuerede hym fro oure hoondis;

8 and comaundide hise accuseris to come to thee, of whom thou demynge, maist knowe of alle these thingis, of whiche we accusen hym.

9 And Jewis putten to, and seiden, that these thingis hadden hem so.

10 And Poul answeride, whanne the president grauntide hym to seie, Of mony yeeris Y knowe thee, that thou art domesman 'to this folk, and Y schal do ynowy for me with good resoun.

11 For thou maist knowe, for to me ben not more than twelue daies, sithen Y cam vp to worschipe in Jerusalem;

12 and nether in the temple thei founden me disputinge with ony man, nether makynge concours of puple, nether in synagogis, nether in citee;

13 nether thei moun preue to thee, of the whiche thingis thei now accusen me.

14 But Y knowleche to thee this thing, that aftir the secte which thei seien eresie, so Y serue to God the fadir, 'and Y bileue to alle thingis that ben writun in the lawe and profetis; and Y haue hope in God,

15 whiche also thei hem silf abiden, the ayenrisyng 'to comynge of iust men and wickid.

16 In this thing Y studie with outen hirtyng, to haue concience to God, and to men euermore.

17 But after many yeeris, Y cam to do almes dedis to my folc, and offryngis, and auowis;

18 in whiche thei founden me purified in the temple, not with company, nether with noise. And thei cauyten me, and thei crieden, and seiden, Take awei oure enemye.

19 And summe Jewis of Asie, whiche it behofte to be now present at thee, and accuse, if thei hadden ony thing ayens me,

20 ether these hem silf seie, if thei founden in me ony thing of wickidnesse, sithen Y stonde 'in the counsel,

21 but oneli of this vois, by which Y criede stondynge among hem, For of the ayenrisyng of deed men Y am demyd this dai of you.

22 Sothely Felix delayede hem, and knewe moost certeynli of the weie, and seide, Whanne Lisias, the tribune, schal come doun, Y schal here you.

23 And he comaundide to a centurien to kepe hym, and that he hadde reste, nethir to forbede ony man to mynystre of his owne thingis to him.

24 And after summe dayes Felix cam, with Drussille his wijf, that was a Jewesse, and clepide Poul, and herde of him the feith that is in Crist Jhesu.

25 And while he disputide of riytwisnesse, and chastite, and of dom to comynge, Felix was maad tremblinge, and answerde, That perteneth now, go; but in tyme couenable Y schal clepe thee.

26 Also he hopide, that money schulde be youun to hym of Poul; for which thing eft he clepide hym, and spak with hym.

27 And whanne twei yeeris weren fillid, Felix took a successoure, Porcius Festus; and Felix wolde yyue grace to Jewis, and lefte Poul boundun.

CAP 25

1 Therfor whanne Festus cam in to the prouynce, aftir the thridde dai he wente vp to Jerusalem fro Cesarie.

2 And the princis of prestis, and the worthieste of the Jewis wenten to hym ayens Poul, and preieden hym,

3 and axiden grace ayens hym, that he schulde comaunde hym to be led to Jerusalem; and thei settiden aspies to sle hym in the weie.

4 But Festus answerde, that Poul schulde be kept in Cesarie; sotheli that he hym silf schulde procede more auisili. Therfor he seide, Thei that in you ben myyti,

5 come doun togidere; and if ony crime is in the man, accuse thei hym.

6 And he dwellede among hem no more than eiyte ether ten daies, and cam doun to Cesarie; and the tother dai he sat for domesman, and comaundide Poul to be brouyt.

7 And whanne he was brouyt forth, Jewis stoden aboute hym, whiche camen doun fro Jerusalem, puttynge ayens hym many and greuouse causis, whiche thei miyten not preue.

8 For Poul yeldide resoun in alle thingis, That nether ayens the lawe of Jewis, nether ayens the temple, nether ayens the emperoure, Y synnede ony thing.

9 But Festus wolde do grace to the Jewis, and answeride to Poul, and seide, Wolt thou gon vp to Jerusalem, and there be demyd of these thingis bifore me?

10 And Poul seide, At the domplace of the emperour Y stonde, where it bihoueth me to be demed. Y haue not noied the Jewis, as thou knowist wel.

11 For if Y haue noyed, ether don ony thing worthi deth, Y forsake not to die; but if no thing of tho is, that thei accusen me, no man may yyue me to hem. Y appele to the emperour.

12 Thanne Festus spak with the counsel, and answerde, To the emperoure thou hast appelid, to the emperoure thou schalt go.

13 And whanne summe daies weren passid, Agrippa kyng, and Beronyce camen doun to Cesarie, to welcome Festus.

14 And whanne thei dwelliden there many daies, Festus schewide to the king of Poul, and seide, A man is left boundun of Felix,

15 of which, whanne Y was at Jerusalem, princis of preestis and the eldre men of Jewis camen to me, and axiden dampnacioun ayens hym.

16 To whiche Y answeride, That it is not custom to Romayns, to dampne ony man, bifore that he that is accusid haue hise accuseris present, and take place of defending, to putte awei the crymes, that ben putte ayens hym.

17 Therfor whanne thei camen togidere hidir, withouten ony delaye, in the dai suynge Y sat for domesman, and comaundide the man to be brouyt.

18 And whanne hise accuseris stoden, thei seiden no cause, of whiche thingis Y hadde suspicioun of yuel.

19 But thei hadden ayens hym summe questiouns of her veyn worschiping, and of oon Jhesu deed, whom Poul affermyde to lyue.

20 And Y doutide of siche maner questioun, and seide, Whether he wolde go to Jerusalem, and ther be demyd of these thingis?

21 But for Poul appelide, that he schulde be kept to the knowing of the emperoure, Y comaundide him to be kept, til Y sende hym to the emperoure.

22 And Agrippa seide to Festus, Y my silf wolde here the man. And he seide, To morew thou schalt here hym.

23 And on the tother day, whanne Agrippa and Beronyce camen with greet desire, and entriden in to the auditorie, with tribunes and the principal men of the citee, whanne Festus bad, Poul was brouyt.

24 And Festus seide, King Agrippa, and alle men that ben with vs, ye seen this man, of which al the multitude of Jewis preyede me at Jerusalem, and axide, and criede, that he schulde lyue no lenger.

25 But Y foond, that he hadde don no thing worthi of deth; and Y deme to sende hym to the emperoure, for he appelide this thing.

26 Of which man Y haue not certeyne, what thing Y schal write to the lord. For which thing Y brouyte hym to you, and moost to thee, thou king Agrippa, that whanne axing is maad, Y haue what Y schal write.

27 For it is seyn to me with out resoun, to sende a boundun man, and not to signifie the cause of hym.

CAP 26

1 And Agrippa seide to Poul, It is suffrid to thee, to speke for thi silf. Thanne Poul helde forth the hoond, and bigan to yelde resoun.

2 Of alle thingis, in whiche Y am accusid of the Jewis, thou king Agrippa, Y gesse me blessid at thee, whanne Y schal defende me this dai;

3 moost for thou knowist alle thingis that ben among Jewis, customes and questiouns. For which thing, Y biseche, here me pacientli.

4 For alle Jewis that bifor knewen me fro the bigynnyng, knewen my lijf fro yongthe; that fro the bigynnyng was in my folc in Jerusalem,

5 if thei wolen bere witnessing, that bi the moost certeyn sect of oure religioun, Y lyuede a Farisee.

6 And now for the hope of repromyssioun, that is maad to oure fadris of God, Y stonde suget in dom;

7 in which hope oure twelue lynagis seruynge niyt and dai hopen to come; of which hope, sir king, Y am accusid of the Jewis.

8 What vnbileueful thing is demed at you, if God reisith deed men?

9 And sotheli Y gesside, that Y ouyte do many contrarie thingis ayens the name of Jhesu Nazarene.

10 Which thing also Y dide in Jerusalem, and Y encloside manye of the seyntis in prisoun, whanne Y hadde take powere of the princis of preestis. And whanne thei weren slayn, Y brouyte the sentence.

11 And bi alle synagogis ofte Y punyschide hem, and constreynede to blasfeme; and more Y wex wood ayens hem, and pursuede in to alien citees.

12 In whiche, the while Y wente to Damask, with power and suffring of princis of preestis,

13 at myddai, in the weie Y say, sir king, that fro heuene liyt schynede aboute me, passing the schynyng of the sunne, and aboute hem that weren togidir with me.

14 And whanne we alle hadden falle doun in to the erthe, Y herde a vois seiynge to me in Ebrew tunge, Saul, Saul, what pursuest thou me? it is hard to thee, to kicke ayens the pricke.

15 And Y seide, Who art thou, Lord? And the Lord seide, Y am Jhesus, whom thou pursuest.

16 But rise vp, and stoond on thi feet. For whi to this thing Y apperide to thee, that Y ordeyne thee mynystre and witnesse of tho thingis that thou hast seyn, and of tho in whiche Y schal schewe to thee.

17 And Y schal delyuere thee fro puplis and folkis, to whiche now Y sende thee,

18 to opene the iyen of hem, that thei ben conuertid fro derknesse to liyt, and fro power of Sathnas to God, that thei take remyssioun of synnes, and part among seyntis, bi feith that is in me.

19 Wherfor, sir kyng Agrippa, Y was not vnbileueful to the heuenli visioun;

20 but Y tolde to hem that been at Damask first, and at Jerusalem, and bi al the cuntre of Judee, and to hethene men, that

thei schulden do penaunce, and be conuertid to God, and do worthi werkis of penaunce.

21 For this cause Jewis token me, whanne Y was in the temple, to sle me.

22 But Y was holpun bi the helpe of God in to this dai, and stonde, witnessinge to lesse and to more. And Y seye no thing ellis than whiche thingis the prophetis and Moises spaken that schulen come,

23 if Crist is to suffre, if he is the firste of the ayenrising of deed men, that schal schewe liyt to the puple and to hethene men.

24 Whanne he spak these thingis, and yeldide resoun, Festus seide with greet vois, Poul, thou maddist; many lettris turnen thee to woodnesse.

25 And Poul seide, Y madde not, thou beste Festus, but Y speke out the wordis of treuthe and of sobernesse.

26 For also the king, to whom Y speke stidfastli, woot of these thingis; for Y deme, that no thing of these is hid fro hym; for nether in a cornere was ouyt of these thingis don.

27 Bileuest thou, king Agrippa, 'to prophetis? Y woot that thou bileuest.

28 And Agrippa seide to Poul, In litil thing thou counseilist me to be maad a cristen man.

29 And Poul seide, Y desire anentis God, bothe in litil and in greet, not oneli thee, but alle these that heren to dai, to be maad sich as Y am, outakun these boondis.

30 And the kyng roos vp, and the president, and Beronyce, and thei that saten niy to hem.

31 And whanne thei wenten awei, thei spaken togider, and seiden, That this man hath not don ony thing worthi deth, nether boondis.

32 And Agrippa seide to Festus, This man miyt be delyuerid, if he hadde not appelid to the emperour.

CAP 27

1 But as it was demed hym to schippe into Ytalie, thei bitoken Poul with othere kepers to a centurien, bi name Julius, of the cumpeny of knyytis of the emperoure.

2 And we wenten vp in to the schip of Adrymetis, and bigunnen to seile, and weren borun aboute the placis of Asie, while Aristark of Macedonye, Tessalonycence, dwellide stille with vs.

3 And in the dai suynge, we camen to Sydon; and Julius tretyde curteisli Poul, and suffride to go to frendis, and do his nedis.

4 And whanne we remouede fro thennus, we vndurseiliden to Cipre, for that wyndis weren contrarie.

5 And we seiliden in the see of Silicie and Pamfilie, and camen to Listris, that is Licie.

6 And there the centurien foond a schip of Alisaundre, seilinge in to Ytalie, and puttide vs ouer in to it.

7 And whanne in many daies we seilden slowli, and vnnethe camen ayens Guydum, for the winde lettide vs, we seiliden to Crete, bisidis Salomona.

8 And vnnethe we seilden bisidis, and camen into a place, that is clepid of good hauen, to whom the cite Tessala was niy.

9 And whanne miche time was passid, and whanne seiling thanne was not sikir, for that fasting was passid, Poul coumfortide hem,

10 and seide to hem, Men, Y se that seiling bigynneth to be with wrong and myche harm, not oonli of charge and of the schip, but also of oure lyues.

11 But the centurien bileuede more to the gouernour, and to the lord of the schip, thanne to these thingis that weren seid of Poul.

12 And whanne the hauene was not able to dwelle in wynter, ful many ordeyneden counsel to seile fro thennus, if on ony maner thei miyten come to Fenyce, to dwelle in wynter at the hauene of Crete, which biholdith to Affrik, and to Corum.

13 And whanne the south blew, thei gessiden hem to holde purpos; and whanne thei hadden removed fro Asson, thei seiliden to Crete.

14 And not aftir miche, the wynde Tifonyk, that is clepid north eest, was ayens it.

15 And whanne the schip was rauyschid, and myyte not enforse ayens the wynde, whanne the schip was youun to the blowynges of the wynde, we weren borun with cours into an ile,

16 that is clepid Canda; and vnethe we miyten gete a litil boot.

17 And whanne this was takun vp, thei vsiden helpis, girdinge togidere the schippe; and dredden, lest thei schulden falle into sondi placis. And whanne the vessel was vndur set, so thei weren borun.

18 And for we weren throwun with strong tempest, in the dai suynge thei maden casting out.

19 And the thridde dai with her hoondis thei castiden awei the instrumentis of the schip.

20 And whanne the sunne nether the sterris weren seie bi many daies, and tempest not a litil neiyede, now al the hope of oure helthe was don awei.

21 And whanne myche fasting hadde be, thanne Poul stood in the myddil of hem, and seide, A! men, it bihofte, whanne ye herden me, not to haue take awei the schip fro Crete, and gete this wronge and casting out.

22 And now Y counsel you to be of good coumfort, for los of no persoone of you schal be, outakun of the schip.

23 For an aungel of God, whos Y am, and to whom Y serue, stood niy to me in this niyt, and seide, Poul, drede thou not;

24 it bihoueth thee to stonde bifore the emperour. And lo! God hath youun to thee alle that ben in the schip with thee.

25 For which thing, ye men, be ye of good coumfort; for Y bileue to my God, that so it schal be, as it is seid to me.

26 And it bihoueth vs to come into sum yle.

27 But aftirward that in the fourtenthe dai the niyt cam on vs seilinge in the stony see, aboute mydniyt the schipmen supposiden sum cuntre to appere to hem.

28 And thei kesten doun a plommet, and founden twenti pasis of depnesse. And aftir a litil thei weren departid fro thennus, and foundun fiftene pasis.

29 And thei dredden, lest we schulden haue fallun in to scharp placis; and fro the last parti of the schip thei senten foure ankeris, and desiriden that the dai hadde be come.

30 And whanne the schipmen souyten to fle fro the schip, whanne thei hadden sent a litil boot in to the see, vndur colour as thei schulden bigynne to stretche forth the ankeris fro the formere part of the schip,

31 Poul seide to the centurien and to the knyytis, But these dwellen in the schip, ye moun not be maad saaf.

32 Thanne knyytis kittiden awei the cordis of the litil boot, and suffriden it to falle awei.

33 And whanne the dai was come, Poul preiede alle men to take mete, and seide, The fourtenthe dai this dai ye 'abiden, and dwellen fastinge, and taken no thing.

34 Wherfor Y preie you to take mete, for youre helthe; for of noon of you the heer of the heed schal perische.

35 And whanne he hadde seid these thingis, Poul took breed, and dide thankyngis to God in the siyt of alle men; and whanne he hadde brokun, he bigan to eete.

36 And alle weren maad of betere coumfort, and thei token mete.

37 And we weren alle men in the schip, two hundrid seuenti and sexe.

38 And thei weren fillid with mete, and dischargiden the schip, and castiden whete in to the see.

39 And whanne the dai was comun, thei knewen no lond; and thei bihelden an hauene that hadde a watir bank, in to which thei thouyten, if thei miyten, to bringe vp the schip.

40 And whanne thei hadden take vp the ankeris, thei bitoken hem to the see, and slakiden togidir the ioyntours of gouernails. And with a litil seil lift vp, bi blowyng of the wynde thei wenten to the bank.

41 And whanne we felden into a place of grauel gon al aboute with the see, thei hurtliden the schip. And whanne the formere part was fitchid, it dwellide vnmouable, and the last part was brokun of strengthe of the see.

42 And counsel of the kniytis was, to sle men that weren in warde, lest ony schulde ascape, whanne he hadde swymmed out.

43 But the centurien wolde kepe Poul, and forbede it to be don. And he comaundide hem that miyte swymme, to go in to the see, and scape, and go out to the loond.

44 And thei baren summe othere on boordis, summe on tho thingis that weren of the schip. And so it was don, that alle men ascapiden to the lond.

CAP 28

1 And whanne we hadden ascapid, thanne we knewen that the ile was clepid Militene. And the hethene men diden to vs not litil curtesie.

2 And whanne a fier was kyndelid, thei refreschiden vs alle, for the reyn that cam, and the coold.

3 But whanne Poul hadde gederid 'a quantite of kittingis of vines, and leide on the fier, an edder sche cam forth fro the heete, and took hym bi the hoond.

4 And whanne the hethene men of the ile siyen the beest hangynge in his hoond, thei seiden togidir, For this man is a manquellere; and whanne he scapide fro the see, Goddis veniaunce suffrith hym not to lyue in erthe.

5 But he schoke awei the beest in to the fier, and hadde noon harm.

6 And thei gessiden that he schulde be turned 'in to swellyng, and falle doun sudenli, and die. But whanne thei abiden longe, and sien that no thing of yuel was don in him, thei turneden hem togider, and seiden, that he was God.

7 And in tho placis weren maners of the prince of the ile, Pupplius bi name, which resseyuede vs bi thre daies benygnli, and foond vs.

8 And it bifel, that the fader of Pupplius lai trauelid with fyueris and blodi flux. To whom Poul entride, and whanne he hadde preied, and leid his hondis on hym, he helide hym.

9 And whanne this thing was don, alle that in the ile hadden sijknesses, camen, and weren heelid.

10 Which also onouriden vs in many worschipis, and puttiden what thingis weren necessarie to vs, whanne we schippiden.

11 And after thre monethis we schippiden in a schip of Ali-saundre, that hadde wyntrid in the ile, to which was an excellent singne of Castours.

12 And whanne we camen to Siracusan, we dwelliden there thre daies.

13 Fro thennus we seiliden aboute, and camen to Regyum; and aftir oo dai, while the south blew, in the secounde dai we camen to Puteolos.

14 Where whanne we founden britheren, we weren preied to dwelle there anentis hem seuene daies. And so we camen to Rome.

15 And fro thennus whanne britheren hadden herd, thei camen to vs to the cheping of Appius, and to the Thre tauernes.

16 And whanne Poul hadde seyn hem, he dide thankyngis to God, and took trist. And whanne 'we camen to Rome, it was suffrid to Poul to dwelle bi hym silf, with a kniyt kepinge him.

17 And after the thridde dai, he clepide togidir the worthieste of the Jewis. And whanne thei camen, he seide to hem, Britheren, Y dide no thing ayens the puple ether custom of fadris, and Y was boundun at Jerusalem, and was bitakun in to the hondis of Romayns.

18 And whanne thei hadden axid of me, wolden haue dely-uerid me, for that no cause of deth was in me.

19 But for Jewis ayenseiden, Y was constreyned to appele to the emperour; not as hauynge ony thing to accuse my puple.

20 Therfor for this cause Y preiede to se you, and speke to you; for for the hope of Israel Y am gird aboute with this chayne.

21 And thei seiden to hym, Nether we han resseyued lettris of thee fro Judee, nether ony of britheren comynge schewide, ether spak ony yuel thing of thee.

22 But we preyen to here of thee, what thingis thou felist; for of this sect it is knowun to vs, that euerywhere me ayenseith it.

23 And whanne thei hadden ordeined a dai to hym, many men camen to hym in to the in. To whiche he expownede, wit-nessinge the kyngdom 'of God, and counseilide hem of Jhesu, of the lawe of Moyses, and profetis, for the morewe til to euentid.

24 And summe bileueden to these thingis that weren seid of Poul, summe bileueden not.

25 And whanne thei weren not consentinge togidir, thei departiden. And Poul seide o word, For the Hooli Goost spak wel bi Ysaye, the profete, to oure fadris,

26 and seide, Go thou to this puple, and seie to hem, With eere ye schulen here, and ye schulen not vndirstonde; and ye seynge schulen se, and ye schulen not biholde.

27 For the herte of this puple is greetli fattid, and with eeris thei herden heuyli, and thei closiden togider her iyen, lest per-auenture thei se with iyen, and with eeris here, and bi herte vndurstonde, and be conuertid, and Y hele hem.

28 Therfor be it knowun to you, that this helthe of God is sent to hethen men, and thei schulen here.

29 And whanne he hadde seid these thingis, Jewis wenten out fro hym, and hadden myche questioun, ethir musyng, among hem silf.

30 And he dwellide ful twei yeer in his hirid place; and he resseyuede alle that entryden to hym,

31 and prechide the kingdom of God, and tauyte tho thingis that ben of the Lord Jhesu Crist, with al trist, with out forbe-dyng. Amen.

ROMAYNES

CAP 1

1 Poul, the seruaunt of Jhesu Crist, clepid an apostle, departid in to the gospel of God;

2 which he hadde bihote tofore bi his profetis in holi scrip-turis of his sone,

3 which is maad to hym of the seed of Dauid bi the flesch,

4 and he was bifor ordeyned the sone of God in vertu, bi the spirit of halewyng of the ayenrisyng of deed men, of Jhesu Crist oure Lord,

5 bi whom we han resseyued grace and the office of apostle, to obeie to the feith in alle folkis for his name,

6 among whiche ye ben also clepid of Jhesu Crist,

7 to alle that ben at Rome, derlyngis of God, and clepid hooli, grace to you, and pees of God oure fadir, and of the Lord Jhesu Crist.

8 First Y do thankyngis to my God, bi Jhesu Crist, for alle you, for youre feith is schewid in al the world.

9 For God is a witnesse to me, to whom Y serue in my spirit, in the gospel of his sone,

10 that with outen ceessyng Y make mynde of you euere in my preieris, and biseche, if in ony maner sum tyme Y haue a spedi weie in the wille of God to come to you.

11 For Y desire to se you, to parten sumwhat of spiritual grace,

12 that ye be confermyd, that is, to be coumfortid togidere in you, bi feith that is bothe youre and myn togidere.

13 And, britheren, Y nyle, that ye vnknowun, that ofte Y pur-poside to come to you, and Y am lett to this tyme, that Y haue sum fruyt in you, as in othere folkis.

14 To Grekis and to barberyns, to wise men and to vnwise men,

15 Y am dettour, so that that is in me is redi to preche the gos-pel also to you that ben at Rome.

16 For Y schame not the gospel, for it is the vertu of God in to heelthe to ech man that bileueth, to the Jew first, and to the Greke.

17 For the riytwisnesse of God is schewid in it, of feith in to feith,

18 as it is writun, For a iust man lyueth of feith. For the wraththe of God is schewid fro heuene on al vnpite and wick-idnesse of tho men, that withholden the treuthe of God in vnriytwisnes.

19 For that thing of God that is knowun, is schewid to hem, for God hath schewid to hem.

20 For the vnuysible thingis of hym, that ben vndurstondun, ben biholdun of the creature of the world, bi tho thingis that ben maad, yhe, and the euerlastynge vertu of hym and the godhed, so that thei mowe not be excusid.

21 For whanne thei hadden knowe God, thei glorifieden hym not as God, nether diden thankyngis; but thei vanyschiden in her thouyts, and the vnwise herte of hem was derkid.

22 For thei 'seiynge that hem silf weren wise, thei weren maad foolis.

23 And thei chaungiden the glorie of 'God vncorruptible in to the licnesse of an ymage of a deedli man, and of briddis, and of foure footid beestis, and of serpentis.

24 For which thing God bitook hem in to the desiris of her herte, in to vnclennesse, that thei punysche with wrongis her bodies in hem silf.

25 The whiche chaungiden the treuthe of God in to leesyng, and herieden and serueden a creature rathere than to the creatoure, that is blessid in to worldis of worldis.

26 Amen. Therfor God bitook hem in to passiouns of schenschipe. For the wymmen of hem chaungiden the kyndli vss in to that vss that is ayens kynde.

27 Also the men forsoken the kyndli vss of womman, and brenneden in her desiris togidere, and men in to men wrouyten filthehed, and resseyueden in to hem silf the meede that bihofte of her errour.

28 And as thei preueden that thei hadden not God in knowyng, God bitook hem in to a repreuable wit, that thei do tho thingis that ben not couenable; that thei ben fulfillid with al wickidnesse,

29 malice, fornycacioun, coueitise, weiwardnesse, ful of enuye, mansleyngis, strijf, gile, yuel wille, preuy bacbiteris, detractouris,

30 hateful to God, debateris, proude, and hiy ouer mesure, fynderis of yuele thingis, not obeschynge to fadir and modir,

31 vnwise, vnmanerli, withouten loue, withouten boond of pees, with outen merci.

32 The whiche whanne thei hadden knowe the riytwisnesse of God, vndirstoden not, that thei that don siche thingis ben worthi the deth, not oneli thei that don tho thingis, but also thei that consenten to the doeris.

CAP 2

1 Wherfor thou art vnexcusable, ech man that demest, for in what thing thou demest anothir man, thou condempnest thi silf; for thou doist the same thingis whiche thou demest.

2 And we witen, that the doom of God is aftir treuthe ayens hem, that don siche thingis.

3 But gessist thou, man, that demest hem that doen siche thingis, and thou doist tho thingis, that thou schalt ascape the doom of God?

4 Whether 'dispisist thou the richessis of his goodnesse, and the pacience, and the long abidyng? Knowist thou not, that the benygnyte of God ledith thee to forthenkyng?

5 But aftir thin hardnesse and vnrepentaunt herte, thou tresorist to thee wraththe in the dai of wraththe and of schewyng of the riytful doom of God,

6 that schal yelde to ech man aftir his werkis;

7 sotheli to hem that ben bi pacience of good werk, glorie, and onour, and vncorrupcioun, to hem that seken euerlastynge lijf;

8 but to hem that ben of strijf, and that assenten not to treuthe, but bileuen to wickidnesse, wraththe and indignacioun, tribulacioun and angwisch,

9 in to ech soule of man that worchith yuel, to the Jew first, and to the Greke;

10 but glorie, and honour, and pees, to ech man that worchith good thing, to the Jew first, and to the Greke.

11 For accepcioun of persones is not anentis God.

12 For who euere han synned without the lawe, schulen perische withouten the lawe; and who euere han synned in the lawe, thei schulen be demyd bi the lawe.

13 For the hereris of lawe ben not iust anentis God, but the doeris of the lawe schulen be maad iust.

14 For whanne hethene men that han not lawe, don kyndli tho thingis that ben of the lawe, thei not hauynge suche manere lawe, ben lawe to hem silf,

15 that schewen the werk of the lawe writun in her hertis. For the conscience of hem yeldith to hem a witnessyng bytwixe hem silf of thouytis that ben accusynge or defendynge,

16 in the dai whanne God schal deme the priuy thingis of men aftir my gospel, bi Jhesu Crist.

17 But if thou art named a Jew, and restist in the lawe, and hast glorie in God,

18 and hast knowe his wille, and thou lerud bi lawe preuest the more profitable thingis,

19 and tristist thi silf to be a ledere of blynde men, the liyt of hem that ben in derknessis,

20 a techere of vnwise men, a maistir of yonge children, that hast the foorme of kunnyng and of treuthe in the lawe;

21 what thanne techist thou another, and techist not thi silf? Thou that prechist that me schal not stele, stelist?

22 Thou that techist that me schal 'do no letcherie, doist letcherie? Thou that wlatist maumetis, doist sacrilegie?

23 Thou that hast glorie in the lawe, vnworschipist God bi brekyng of the lawe?

24 For the name of God is blasfemed bi you among hethene men, as is writun.

25 For circumcisioun profitith, if thou kepe the lawe; but if thou be a trespassour ayens the lawe, thi circumsicioun is maad prepucie.

26 Therfor if prepucie kepe the riytwisnessis of the lawe, whethir his prepucie schal not be arettid in to circumcisioun?

27 And the prepucie of kynde that fulfillith the lawe, schal deme thee, that bi lettre and circumcisioun art trespassour ayens the lawe.

28 For he that is in opene is not a Jew, nether it is circumcisioun that is openli in the fleisch;

29 but he that is a Jew in hid, and the circumcisioun of herte, in spirit, not bi the lettre, whos preisyng is not of men, but of God.

CAP 3

1 What thanne is more to a Jew, or what profit of circumcisioun?

2 Myche bi al wise; first, for the spekyngis of God 'weren bitakun to hem.

3 And what if summe of hem bileueden not? Whethir the vnbileue of hem hath auoidid the feith of God?

4 God forbede. For God is sothefast, but ech man a liere; as it is writun, That thou be iustified in thi wordis, and ouercome, whanne thou art demed.

5 But if oure wickidnesse comende the riytwisnesse of God, what shulen we seie? Whether God is wickid, that bryngith in wraththe?

6 Aftir man Y seie. God forbede. Ellis hou schal God deme this world?

7 For if the treuthe of God hath aboundid in my lessyng, in to the glorie of hym, what yit am Y demed as a synner?

8 And not as we ben blasfemed, and as summen seien that we seien, Do we yuele thingis, that gode thingis come. Whos dampnacioun is iust.

9 What thanne? Passen we hem? Nay; for we han schewid bi skile, that alle bothe Jewis and Grekis ben vndur synne,

10 as it is writun, For ther is no man iust;

11 ther is no man vndurstondynge, nethir sekynge God.

12 Alle bowiden a wey, togidere thei ben maad vnprofitable; ther is noon that doith good thing, there is noon 'til to oon.

13 The throte of hem is an opyn sepulcre; with her tungis thei diden gilefuli; the venym of snakis is vndur her lippis.

14 The mouth of whiche is ful of cursyng and bitternesse;

15 the feet of hem ben swifte to schede blood.

16 Sorewe and cursidnesse ben in the weies of hem, and thei knewen not the weie of pees;

17

18 the drede of God is not bifor her iyen.

19 And we witen, that what euere thingis the lawe spekith, it spekith to hem that ben in the lawe, that ech mouth be stoppid, and ech world be maad suget to God.

20 For of the werkis of the lawe ech fleisch schal not be iustified bifor hym; for bi the lawe ther is knowyng of synne.

21 But now with outen the lawe the riytwisnesse of God is schewid, that is witnessid of the lawe and the profetis.

22 And the riytwisnesse of God is bi the feith of Jhesu Crist in to alle men and on alle men that bileuen in hym; for ther is no departyng.

23 For alle men synneden, and han nede to the glorie of God;

24 and ben iustified freli bi his grace, bi the ayenbiyng that is in 'Crist Jhesu.

25 Whom God ordeynede foryyuer, bi feith in his blood, to the schewyng of his riytwisnesse, for remyssioun of biforgoynge synnes,

26 in the beryng up of God, to the schewyng of his riytwisnesse in this tyme, that he be iust, and iustifyynge hym that is of the feith of Jhesu Crist.

27 Where thanne is thi gloriyng? It is excludid. Bi what lawe? Of dedis doyng? Nay, but by the lawe of feith.

28 For we demen a man to be iustified bi the feith, with outen werkis of the lawe.

29 Whethir of Jewis is God oneli? Whether he is not also of hethene men? Yhis, and of hethene men.

30 For 'oon God is, that iustefieth circumcisioun bi feith, and prepucie bi feith.

31 Distruye we therfor the lawe bi the feith? God forbede; but we stablischen the lawe.

CAP 4

1 What thanne schulen we seie, that Abraham oure fadir aftir the flesch foond?

2 For if Abraham is iustified of werkis of the lawe, he hath glorie, but not anentis God.

3 For what seith the scripture? Abraham bileued to God, and it was arettid to him to riytwisnesse.

4 And to hym that worchith mede is not arettid bi grace, but bi dette.

5 Sotheli to hym that worchith not, but bileueth in to hym that iustefieth a wickid man, his feith is arettid to riytwisnesse, aftir the purpos of Goddis grace.

6 As Dauid seith the blessidnesse of a man, whom God acceptith, he yyueth to hym riytwisnesse with outen werkis of the lawe,

7 Blessid ben thei, whos wickidnessis ben foryouun, and whos synnes ben hid.

8 Blessid is that man, to whom God arettide not synne.

9 Thanne whether dwellith this blisfulnesse oneli in circumcisioun, or also in prepucie? For we seien, that the feith was arettid to Abraham to riytwisnesse.

10 Hou thanne was it arettid? in circumcisioun, or in prepucie? Not in circumcisioun, but in prepucie.

11 And he took a signe of circumcisioun, a tokenyng of riytwisnesse of the feith which is in prepucie, that he be fadir of alle men bileuynge bi prepucie, that it be arettid also to hem to riytwisnesse;

12 and that he be fadir of circumcisioun, not onely to hem that ben of circumcisioun, but also to hem that suen the steppis of the feith, which feith is in prepucie of oure fader Abraham.

13 For not bi the lawe is biheest to Abraham, or to his seed, that he schulde be eir of the world, but bi the riytwisnesse of feith.

14 For if thei that ben of the lawe, ben eiris, feith is distried, biheest is don awey.

15 For the lawe worchith wraththe; for where is no lawe, there is no trespas, nethir is trespassyng.

16 Therfor riytfulnesse is of the feith, that bi grace biheeste be stable to ech seed, not to that seed oneli that is of the lawe, but to that that is of the feith of Abraham, which is fadir of vs alle.

17 As it is writun, For Y haue set thee fadir of many folkis, bifor God to whom thou hast bileued. Which God quykeneth deed men, and clepith tho thingis that ben not, as tho that ben.

18 Which Abraham ayens hope bileuede in to hope, that he schulde be maad fader of many folkis, as it was seid to hym, Thus schal thi seed be, as the sterris of heuene, and as the grauel that is in the brenke of the see.

19 And he was not maad vnstidfast in the bileue, nether he biheelde his bodi thanne nyy deed, whanne he was almost of an hundrid yeer, ne the wombe of Sare nyy deed.

20 Also in the biheeste of God he doutide not with vntrist; but he was coumfortid in bileue,

21 yyuynge glorie to God, witynge moost fulli that what euere thingis God hath bihiyt, he is myyti also to do.

22 Therfor it was arettid to hym to riytwisnesse.

23 And it is not writun oneli for him, that it was arettid to hym to riytwisnesse,

24 but also for vs, to whiche it schal be arettid, that bileuen in him that reiside oure Lord Jhesu Crist fro deeth.

25 Which was bitakun for oure synnes, and roos ayen for oure iustefiyng.

CAP 5

1 Therfor we, iustified of feith, haue we pees at God bi oure Lord Jhesu Crist.

2 Bi whom we han niy goyng to, bi feith in to this grace, in which we stonden, and han glorie in the hope of the glorie of Goddis children.

3 And not this oneli, but also we glorien in tribulaciouns, witynge that tribulacioun worchith pacience,

4 and pacience preuyng, and preuyng hope.

5 And hope confoundith not, for the charite of God is spred abrood in oure hertis bi the Hooli Goost, that is youun to vs.

6 And while that we weren sijk aftir the tyme, what diede Crist for wickid men?

7 For vnnethis dieth ony man for the iust man; and yit for a good man perauenture summan dar die.

8 But God comendith his charite in vs; for if whanne we weren yit synneris,

9 aftir the tyme Crist was deed for vs, thanne myche more now we iustified in his blood, schulen be saaf fro wraththe bi him.

10 For if whanne we weren enemyes, we ben recounselid to God bi the deth of his sone, myche more we recounselid schulen be saaf in the lijf of hym.

11 And not oneli this, but also we glorien in God, bi oure Lord Jhesu Crist, bi whom we han resseyued now recounseling.

12 Therfor as bi o man synne entride in to this world, and bi synne deth, and so deth passide forth in to alle men, in which man alle men synneden.

13 For 'til to the lawe synne was in the world; but synne was not rettid, whanne lawe was not.

14 But deth regnyde from Adam 'til to Moises, also in to hem that synneden not in licnesse of the trespassyng of Adam, the which is licnesse of Crist to comynge.

15 But not as gilt, so the yifte; for if thorouy the gilt of oon manye ben deed, myche more the grace of God and the yifte in the grace of o man Jhesu Crist hath aboundid in to many men.

16 And not as bi o synne, so bi the yifte; for the doom of oon in to condempnacioun, but grace of many giltis in to iustificacioun.

17 For if in the gilt of oon deth regnede thorouy oon, myche more men that takyn plente of grace, and of yyuyng, and of riytwisnesse, schulen regne in lijf bi oon Jhesu Crist.

18 Therfor as bi the gilt of oon in to alle men in to condempnacioun, so bi the riytwisnesse of oon in to alle men in to iustifiyng of lijf.

19 For as bi inobedience of o man manye ben maad synneris, so bi the obedience of oon manye schulen be iust.

20 And the lawe entride, that gilt schulde be plenteuouse; but where gilt was plenteuouse,

21 grace was more plenteuouse. That as synne regnede in to deth, so grace regne bi riytwisnesse in to euerlastynge lijf, bi 'Crist Jhesu oure Lord.

CAP 6

1 Therfor what schulen we seie? Schulen we dwelle in synne, that grace be plenteuouse?

2 God forbede. For hou schulen we that ben deed to synne, lyue yit ther ynne?

3 Whether, britheren, ye knowen not, that whiche euere we ben baptisid in Crist Jhesu, we ben baptisid in his deth?

4 For we ben togidere biried with hym bi baptym 'in to deth; that as Crist aroos fro deth bi the glorie of the fadir, so walke we in a newnesse of lijf.

5 For if we plauntid togidere ben maad to the licnesse of his deth, also we schulen be of the licnesse of his risyng ayen;

6 witynge this thing, that oure olde man is crucified togidere, that the bodi of synne be distruyed, that we serue no more to synne.

7 For he that is deed, is iustefied fro synne.

8 And if we ben deed with Crist, we bileuen that also we schulen lyue togidere with hym;

9 witinge for Crist, rysynge ayen fro deth, now dieth not, deeth schal no more haue lordschip on hym.

10 For that he was deed to synne, he was deed onys; but that he lyueth, he liueth to God.

11 So ye deme you silf to be deed to synne, but lyuynge to God in 'Jhesu Crist oure Lord.

12 Therfor regne not synne in youre deedli bodi, that ye obeische to hise coueityngis.

13 Nether yyue ye youre membris armuris of wickidnesse to synne, but yyue ye you silf to God, as thei that lyuen of deed men, and youre membris armuris of riytwisnesse to God.

14 For synne schal not haue lordschipe on you; for ye ben not vndur the lawe, but vndur grace.

15 What therfor? Schulen we do synne, for we ben not vndur the lawe, but vndur grace?

16 God forbede. Witen ye not, that to whom ye yyuen you seruauntis to obeie to, ye ben seruauntis of that thing, to which ye han obeschid, ether of synne to deth, ether of obedience to riytwisnesse?

17 But Y thanke God, that ye weren seruauntis of synne; but ye han obeischid of herte in to that fourme of techyng, in which ye ben bitakun.

18 And ye delyuered fro synne, ben maad seruauntis of riytwisnesse.

19 Y seie that thing that is of man, for the vnstidefastnesse of youre fleisch. But as ye han youun youre membris to serue to vnclennesse, and to wickidnesse 'in to wickidnesse, so now yyue ye youre membris to serue to riytwisnesse in to hoolynesse.

20 For whanne ye weren seruauntis of synne, ye weren fre of riytfulnesse.

21 Therfor what fruyt hadden ye thanne in tho thingis, in whiche ye schamen now? For the ende of hem is deth.

22 But now ye delyuered fro synne, and maad seruauntis to God, han your fruyt in to holinesse, and the ende euerlastinge lijf. For the wagis of synne is deth; the grace of God is euerlastynge lijf in Crist Jhesu our Lord.

CAP 7

1 Britheren, whethir ye knowun not; for Y speke to men 'that knowen the lawe; for the lawe hath lordschip in a man, as long tyme as it lyueth?

2 For that womman that is vndur an hosebonde, is boundun to the lawe, while the hosebonde lyeth; but if hir hosebonde is deed, sche is delyuered fro the lawe of the hosebonde.

3 Therfor sche schal be clepid auoutresse, if sche be with another man, while the hosebonde lyeth; but if hir hosebonde is deed, sche is delyuered fro the lawe of the hosebonde, that sche be not auoutresse, if sche be with another man.

4 And so, my britheren, ye ben maad deed to the lawe bi the bodi of Crist, that ye ben of another, that roos ayen fro deth, that ye bere fruyt to God.

5 For whanne we weren in fleisch, passiouns of synnes, that weren bi the lawe, wrouyten in oure membris, to bere fruyt to deth.

6 But now we ben vnboundun fro the lawe of deth, in which we weren holdun, so that we seruen in newnesse of spirit, and not in eldnesse of lettre.

7 What therfor schulen we seie? The lawe is synne? God forbede. But Y knew not synne, but bi lawe; for Y wiste not that coueitynge was synne, but for the lawe seide, Thou schalt not coueyte.

8 And thoruy occasioun takun, synne bi the maundement hath wrouyt in me al coueytise; for withouten the lawe, synne was deed.

9 And Y lyuede withouten the lawe sumtyme; but whanne the comaundement was comun, synne lyuede ayen.

10 But Y was deed, and this comaundement that was to lijf, was foundun to me, to be to deth.

11 For synne, thorouy occasioun takun bi the comaundement, disceyuede me, and bi that it slow me.

12 Therfor the lawe is hooli, and the comaundement is hooli, and iust, and good.

13 Is thanne that thing that is good, maad deth to me? God forbede. But synne, that it seme synne, thorouy good thing wrouyte deth to me, that me synne ouer maner thorouy the comaundement.

14 And we witen, that the lawe is spiritual; but Y am fleischli, seld vndur synne.

15 For Y vndurstonde not that that Y worche; for Y do not the good thing that Y wole, but Y do thilke yuel thing that Y hate.

16 And if Y do that thing that Y wole not, Y consente to the lawe, that it is good.

17 But now Y worche not it now, but the synne that dwellith in me.

18 But and Y woot, that in me, that is, in my fleisch, dwellith no good; for wille lieth to me, but Y fynde not to performe good thing.

19 For Y do not thilke good thing that Y wole, but Y do thilke yuel thing that Y wole not.

20 And if Y do that yuel thing that Y wole not, Y worche not it, but the synne that dwellith in me.

21 Therfor Y fynde the lawe to me willynge to do good thing, for yuel thing lieth to me.

22 For Y delite togidere to the lawe of God, aftir the ynnere man. But Y se another lawe in my membris,

23 ayenfiytynge the lawe of my soule, and makynge me caitif in the lawe of synne, that is in my membris.

24 Y am an vnceli man; who schal delyuer me fro the bodi of this synne?

25 The grace of God, bi Jhesu Crist oure Lord. Therfor Y my silf bi the soule serue to the lawe of God; but bi fleisch to the lawe of synne.

CAP 8

1 Therfor now no thing of dampnacioun is to hem that ben in Crist Jhesu, whiche wandren not after the flesch.

2 For the lawe of the spirit of lijf in Crist Jhesu hath delyuerid me fro the lawe of synne, and of deth.

3 For that that was vnpossible to the lawe, in what thing it was sijk bi flesch, God sente his sone in to the licknesse of fleisch of synne, and of synne dampnede synne in fleisch;

4 that the iustefiyng of the lawe were fulfillid in vs, that goen not aftir the fleisch, but aftir the spirit.

5 For thei that ben aftir the fleisch, saueren tho thingis that ben of the fleisch; but thei that ben after the spirit, feelen tho thingis that ben of the spirit. For the prudence of fleisch is deth;

6 but the prudence of spirit is lijf and pees.

7 For the wisdom of the fleisch is enemye to God; for it is not suget to the lawe of God, for nether it may.

8 And thei that ben in fleisch, moun not plese to God.

9 But ye ben not in fleisch, but in spirit; if netheles the spirit of God dwellith in you. But if ony hath not the spirit of Crist, this is not his.

10 For if Crist is in you, the bodi is deed for synne, but the spirit lyueth for iustefiyng.

11 And if the spirit of hym that reiside Jhesu Crist fro deth dwellith in you, he that reiside Jhesu Crist fro deth, shal quykene also youre deedli bodies, for the spirit of hym that dwellith in you.

12 Therfor, britheren, we ben dettouris, not to the flesch, that we lyuen aftir the flesch.

13 For if ye lyuen aftir the fleisch, ye schulen die; but if ye bi the spirit sleen the dedis of the fleisch, ye schulen lyue.

14 For who euere ben led bi the spirit of God, these ben the sones of God.

15 For ye han not take eftsoone the spirit of seruage in drede, but ye han taken the spirit of adopcioun of sones, in which we crien, Abba, fadir.

16 And the ilke spirit yeldith witnessyng to oure spirit, that we ben the sones of God;

17 if sones, and eiris, 'and eiris of God, and eiris togidere with Crist; if netheles we suffren togidere, that also we ben glorified togidere.

18 And Y deme, that the passiouns of this tyme ben not worthi to the glorie to comynge, that schal be schewid in vs.

19 For the abidyng of creature abidith the schewyng of the sones of God.

20 But the creature is suget to vanyte, not willynge, but for hym that made it suget in hope;

21 for the ilke creature schal be delyuered fro seruage of corrupcioun in to liberte of the glorie of the sones of God.

22 And we witen, that ech creature sorewith, and trauelith with peyne til yit.

23 And not oneli it, but also we vs silf, that han the first fruytis of the spirit, and we vs silf sorewen with ynne vs for the adopcioun of Goddis sonys, abidynge the ayenbiyng of oure bodi.

24 But bi hope we ben maad saaf. For hope that is seyn, is not hope; for who hopith that thing, that he seeth?

25 And if we hopen that thing that we seen not, we abiden bi pacience.

26 And also the spirit helpith oure infirmyte; for what we schulen preie, as it bihoueth, we witen not, but the ilke spirit axith for vs with sorewyngis, that moun not be teld out.

27 For he that sekith the hertis, woot what the spirit desirith, for bi God he axith for hooli men.

28 And we witen, that to men 'that louen God, alle thingis worchen togidere in to good, to hem that aftir purpos ben clepid seyntis.

29 For thilke that he knewe bifor, he bifor ordenede bi grace to be maad lijk to the ymage of his sone, that he be the first bigetun among many britheren.

30 And thilke that he bifore ordeynede to blis, hem he clepide; and whiche he clepide, hem he iustifiede; and whiche he iustifiede, and hem he glorifiede.

31 What thanne schulen we seie to these thingis? If God for vs, who is ayens vs?

32 The which also sparide not his owne sone, but 'for vs alle bitook hym, hou also yaf he not to vs alle thingis with hym?

33 Who schal accuse ayens the chosun men of God? It is God that iustifieth,

34 who is it that condempneth? It is Jhesus Crist that was deed, yhe, the which roos ayen, the which is on the riyt half of God, and the which preieth for vs.

35 Who thanne schal departe vs fro the charite of Crist? tribulacioun, or anguysch, or hungur, or nakidnesse, or persecucioun, or perel, or swerd?

36 As it is writun, For we ben slayn al dai for thee; we ben gessid as scheep of slauytir.

37 But in alle these thingis we ouercomen, for hym that louyde vs.

38 But Y am certeyn, that nethir deeth, nether lijf, nether aungels, nethir principatus, nether vertues, nether present thingis, nether thingis to comynge, nether strengthe,

39 nether heiyth, nether depnesse, nether noon othir creature may departe vs fro the charite of God, that is in 'Crist Jhesu oure Lord.

CAP 9

1 I seie treuthe in Crist Jhesu, Y lye not, for my conscience berith witnessyng to me in the Hooli Goost,

2 for greet heuynesse is to me, and contynuel sorewe to my herte.

3 For Y my silf desiride to be departid fro Crist for my britheren, that ben my cosyns aftir the fleisch, that ben men of Israel;

4 whos is adopcioun of sones, and glorie, and testament, and yyuyng of the lawe, and seruyce, and biheestis;

5 whos ben the fadris, and of which is Crist after the fleisch, that is God aboue alle thingis, blessid in to worldis.

6 Amen. But not that the word of God hath falle doun. For not alle that ben of Israel, these ben Israelitis.

7 Nethir thei that ben seed of Abraham, 'alle ben sonys; but in Ysaac the seed schal be clepid to thee;

8 that is to seie, not thei that ben sones of the fleisch, ben sones of God, but thei that ben sones of biheeste ben demed in the seed.

9 For whi this is the word of biheest, Aftir this tyme Y schal come, and a sone schal be to Sare.

10 And not oneli sche, but also Rebecca hadde twey sones of o liggyng bi of Ysaac, oure fadir.

11 And whanne thei weren not yit borun, nether hadden don ony thing of good ether of yuel, that the purpos of God schulde dwelle bi eleccioun,

12 not of werkis, but of God clepynge, it was seid to hym,

13 that the more schulde serue the lesse, as it is writun, Y louede Jacob, but Y hatide Esau.

14 What therfor schulen we seie? Whether wickidnesse be anentis God?

15 God forbede. For he seith to Moyses, Y schal haue merci on whom Y haue merci; and Y schal yyue merci on whom Y schal haue merci.

16 Therfor it is not nether of man willynge, nethir rennynge, but of God hauynge mercy.

17 And the scripture seith to Farao, For to this thing Y haue stirid thee, that Y schewe in thee my vertu, and that my name be teld in al erthe.

18 Therfor of whom God wole, he hath merci; and whom he wole, he endurith.

19 Thanne seist thou to me, What is souyt yit? for who withstondith his wille?

20 O! man, who art thou, that answerist to God? Whether a maad thing seith to hym that made it, What hast thou maad me so?

21 Whether a potter of cley hath not power to make of the same gobet o vessel in to honour, an othere in to dispit?

22 That if God willynge to schewe his wraththe, and to make his power knowun, hath suffrid in greet pacience vessels of wraththe able in to deth,

23 to schewe the riytchessis of his glorie in to vessels of merci, whiche he made redi in to glorie.

24 Whiche also he clepide not oneli of Jewis, but also of hethene men, as he seith in Osee.

25 Y schal clepe not my puple my puple, and not my loued my louyd, and not getynge mercy getynge merci;

26 and it schal be in the place, where it is seid to hem, Not ye my puple, there thei schulen be clepid the sones of 'God lyuynge.

27 But Isaye crieth for Israel, If the noumbre of Israel schal be as grauel of the see, the relifs schulen be maad saaf.

28 Forsothe a word makynge an ende, and abreggynge in equyte, for the Lord schal make a word breggid on al the erthe.

29 And as Ysaye bifor seide, But God of oostis hadde left to vs seed, we hadden be maad as Sodom, and we hadden be lijk as Gommor.

30 Therfor what schulen we seie? That hethene men that sueden not riytwisnesse, han gete riytwisnesse, yhe, the riytwisnesse that is of feith.

31 But Israel suynge the lawe of riytwisnesse, cam not parfitli in to the lawe of riytwisnesse.

32 Whi? For not of feith, but as of werkys. And thei spurneden ayens the stoon of offencioun,

33 as it is writun, Lo! Y putte a stoon of offensioun in Syon, and a stoon of sclaundre; and ech that schal bileue 'in it, schal not be confoundid.

CAP 10

1 Britheren, the wille of myn herte and mi biseching is maad to God for hem in to helthe.

2 But Y bere witnessyng to hem, that thei han loue of God, but not aftir kunnyng.

3 For thei vnknowynge Goddis riytwisnesse, and sekynge to make stidefast her owne riytfulnesse, ben not suget to the riytwisnesse of God.

4 For the ende of the lawe is Crist, to riytwisnesse to ech man that bileueth.

5 For Moises wroot, For the man that schal do riytwisnesse that is of the lawe, schal lyue in it.

6 But the riytwisnesse that is of bileue, seith thus, Seie thou not in thin herte, Who schal stie in to heuene? that is to seie, to lede doun Crist;

7 or who schal go doun in to helle? that is, to ayenclepe Crist fro deth.

8 But what seith the scripture? The word is nyy in thi mouth, and in thin herte; this is the word of bileue, which we prechen.

9 That if thou knoulechist in thi mouth the Lord Jhesu Crist, and bileuest in thin herte, that God reiside hym fro deth, thou schalt be saaf.

10 For bi herte me bileueth to riytwisnesse, but bi mouth knowleching is maad to helthe.

11 For whi the scripture seith, Ech that bileueth in hym, schal not be confoundid.

12 And ther is no distinccioun of Jew and of Greke; for the same Lord of alle is riche in alle, that inwardli clepen hym.

13 For ech man 'who euere schal inwardli clepe the name of the Lord, schal be saaf.

14 Hou thanne schulen thei inwardli clepe hym, in to whom thei han not bileued? or hou schulen thei bileue to hym, whom thei han not herd? Hou schulen thei here, with outen a prechour?

15 and hou schulen thei preche, but thei be sent? As it is writun, Hou faire ben the feet of hem that prechen pees, of hem that prechen good thingis.

16 But not alle men obeien to the gospel. For Ysaie seith, Lord, who bileuede to oure heryng?

17 Therfor feith is of heryng, but heryng bi the word of Crist.

18 But Y seie, Whether thei herden not? Yhis, sothely the word of hem wente out in to al the erthe, and her wordis in to the endis of the world.

19 But Y seie, Whether Israel knewe not? First Moyses seith, Y schal lede you to enuye, that ye ben no folc; that ye ben an vnwise folc, Y schal sende you in to wraththe.

20 And Ysaie is bold, and seith, Y am foundun of men that seken me not; opynli Y apperide to hem, that axiden not me.

21 But to Israel he seith, Al dai Y streiyte out myn hondis to a puple that bileuede not, but ayen seide me.

CAP 11

1 Therfor Y seie, Whether God hath put awei his puple? God forbede. For Y am an Israelite, of the seed of Abraham, of the lynage of Beniamyn.

2 God hath not put awei his puple, which he bifor knew. Whether ye witen not, what the scripture seith in Elie? Hou he preieth God ayens Israel,

3 Lord, thei han slayn thi prophetis, thei han vndurdoluun thin auteris, and Y am lefte aloone, and thei seken my lijf.

4 But what seith Goddis answere to hym? Y haue left to me seuene thousyndes of men, that han not bowid her knees bifore Baal.

5 So therfor also in this tyme, the relifs ben maad saaf, bi the chesyng of the grace of God.

6 And if it be bi the grace of God, it is not now of werkis; ellis grace is not now grace.

7 What thanne? Israel hath not getun this that he souyte, but eleccioun hath getun; and the othere ben blyndid.

8 As it is writun, God yaf to hem a spirit of compunccioun, iyen that thei se not, and eeris, that thei here not, in to this dai.

9 And Dauith seith, Be the boord of hem maad in to a gryn bifor hem, and in to catchyng, and in to sclaundre, and in to yeldyng to hem.

10 Be the iyen of hem maad derk, that thei se not; and bowe thou doun algatis the bak of hem.

11 Therfor Y seie, Whether thei offendiden so, that thei schulden falle doun? God forbede. But bi the gilt of hem helthe is maad to hethene men, that thei sue hem.

12 That if the gilt of hem ben richessis of the world, and the makyng lesse of hem ben richessis of hethene men, hou myche more the plente of hem?

13 But Y seie to you, hethene men, for as longe as Y am apostle of hethene men, Y schal onoure my mynysterie,

14 if in ony maner Y stire my fleisch for to folowe, and that Y make summe of hem saaf.

15 For if the loss of hem is the recouncelyng of the world, what is the takyng vp, but lijf of deede men?

16 For if a litil part of that that is tastid be hooli, the hool gobet is hooli; and if the roote is hooli, also the braunchis.

17 What if ony of the braunchis ben brokun, whanne thou were a wielde olyue tre, art graffid among hem, and art maad felowe of the roote, and of the fatnesse of the olyue tre,

18 nyle thou haue glorie ayens the braunchis. For if thou gloriest, thou berist not the roote, but the roote thee.

19 Therfor thou seist, The braunchis ben brokun, that Y be graffid in.

20 Wel, for vnbileue the braunchis ben brokun; but thou stondist bi feith. Nyle thou sauere hiye thing,

21 but drede thou, for if God sparide not the kyndli braunchis, lest perauenture he spare not thee.

22 Therfor se the goodnesse, and the fersnesse of God; yhe, the feersnesse in to hem that felden doun, but the goodnesse of God in to thee, if thou dwellist in goodnesse, ellis also thou schalt be kit doun.

23 Yhe, and thei schulen be set yn, if thei dwellen not in vnbileue. For God is myyti, to sette hem in eftsoone.

24 For if thou art kit doun of the kyndeli wielde olyue tre, and ayens kynd art set in to a good olyue tre, hou myche more thei that ben bi kynde, schulen be set in her olyue tree?

25 But, britheren, Y wole not that ye vnknowen this mysterie, that ye be not wise to you silf; for blyndenesse hath feld a parti in Israel, til that the plente of hethene men entride,

26 and so al Israel schulde be maad saaf. As it is writun, He schal come of Syon, that schal delyuere, and turne awei the wickidnesse of Jacob.

27 And this testament to hem of me, whanne Y schal do awei her synnes.

28 Aftir the gospel thei ben enemyes for you, but thei ben moost dereworthe bi the eleccioun for the fadris.

29 And the yiftis and the cleping of God ben with outen forthenkyng.

30 And as sum tyme also ye bileueden not to God, but now ye han gete mercy for the vnbileue of hem;

31 so and these now bileueden not in to youre merci, that also thei geten merci.

32 For God closide alle thingis togidere in vnbileue, that he haue mercy on alle.

33 O! the heiynesse of the ritchessis of the wisdom and of the kunnyng of God; hou incomprehensible ben hise domes, and hise weies ben vnserchable.

34 For whi who knew the wit of the Lord, or who was his counselour? or who formere yaf to hym,

35 and it schal be quyt to hym?

36 For of hym, and bi hym, and in hym ben alle thingis. To hym be glorie in to worldis. Amen.

CAP 12

1 Therfore, britheren, Y biseche you bi the mercy of God, that ye yyue youre bodies a lyuynge sacrifice, hooli, plesynge to God, and youre seruyse resonable.

2 And nyle ye be confourmyd to this world, but be ye reformed in newnesse of youre wit, that ye preue which is the wille of God, good, and wel plesynge, and parfit.

3 For Y seie, bi the grace that is youun to me, to alle that ben among you, that ye sauere no more than it bihoueth to sauere, but for to sauere to sobrenesse; and to ech man, as God hath departid the mesure of feith.

4 For as in o bodi we han many membris, but alle the membris han not the same dede;

5 so we many ben o bodi in Crist, and eche ben membris oon of anothir.

6 Therfor we that han yiftis dyuersynge, aftir the grace that is youun to vs,

7 ethir prophecie, aftir the resoun of feith; ethir seruise, in mynystryng; ether he that techith, in techyng;

8 he that stirith softli, in monestyng; he that yyueth, in symplenesse; he that is souereyn, in bisynesse; he that hath merci, in gladnesse.

9 Loue with outen feynyng, hatynge yuel, drawynge to good;

10 louynge togidere the charite of britherhod. Eche come bifore to worschipen othere;

11 not slow in bisynesse, feruent in spirit, seruynge to the Lord,

12 ioiynge in hope, pacient in tribulacioun, bisy in preier,

13 yyuynge good to the nedis of seyntis, kepynge hospitalite.

14 Blesse ye men that pursuen you; blesse ye, and nyle ye curse;

15 for to ioye with men that ioyen, for to wepe with men that wepen.

16 Fele ye the same thing togidere; not sauerynge heiy thingis, but consentynge to meke thingis. Nile ye be prudent anentis you silf;

17 to no man yeldynge yuel for yuel, but purueye ye good thingis, not oneli bifor God, but also bifor alle men.

18 If it may be don, that that is of you, haue ye pees with alle men.

19 Ye moost dere britheren, not defendynge you silf, but yyue ye place to wraththe; for it is writun, The Lord seith, To me veniaunce, and Y schal yelde.

20 But if thin enemy hungrith, fede thou hym; if he thirstith, yyue thou drynke to hym; for thou doynge this thing schalt gidere togidere colis on his heed.

21 Nyle thou be ouercomun of yuel, but ouercome thou yuel bi good.

CAP 13

1 Euery soule be suget to heiyere powers. For ther is no power but of God, and tho thingis that ben of God, ben ordeyned.

2 Therfor he that ayenstondith power, ayenstondith the ordynaunce of God; and thei that ayenstonden, geten to hem silf dampnacioun.

3 For princes ben not to the drede of good work, but of yuel. But wilt thou, that thou drede not power? Do thou good thing, and thou schalt haue preisyng of it;

4 for he is the mynystre of God to thee in to good. But if thou doist yuel, drede thou; for not with outen cause he berith the swerd, for he is the mynystre of God, vengere in to wraththe to hym that doith yuel.

5 And therfor bi nede be ye suget, not oneli for wraththe, but also for conscience.

6 For therfor ye yyuen tributis, thei ben the mynystris of God, and seruen for this same thing.

7 Therfor yelde ye to alle men dettis, to whom tribut, tribut, to whom tol, tol, to whom drede, drede, to whom onour, onour.

8 To no man owe ye ony thing, but that ye loue togidere. For he that loueth his neiybore, hath fulfillid the lawe.

9 For, Thou schalt do no letcherie, Thou schalt not sle, Thou schalt not stele, Thou schalt not seie fals witnessyng, Thou schalt not coueyte the thing of thi neiybore, and if ther be ony othere maundement, it is instorid in this word, Thou schalt loue thi neiybore as thi silf.

10 The loue of neiybore worchith not yuel; therfor loue is the fulfillyng of the lawe.

11 And we knowen this tyme, that the our is now, that we rise fro sleep; for now oure heelthe is neer, than whanne we bile-ueden.

12 The nyyt wente bifore, but the dai hath neiyed. Therfor caste we awei the werkis of derknessis, and be we clothid in the armeris of liyt.

13 As in dai wandre we onestli, not in superflu feestis and drunkenessis, not in beddis and vnchastitees, not in strijf and in enuye;

14 but be ye clothid in the Lord Jhesu Crist, and do ye not the bisynesse of fleisch in desiris.

CAP 14

1 But take ye a sijk man in bileue, not in demyngis of thouy-tis.

2 For another man leueth, that he mai ete alle thingis; but he that is sijk, ete wortis.

3 He that etith, dispise not hym that etith not; and he that etith not, deme not hym that etith. For God hath take him to hym.

4 Who art thou, that demest anothris seruaunt? To his lord he stondith, or fallith fro hym. But he schal stonde; for the Lord is myyti to make hym parfit.

5 For whi oon demeth a day bitwixe a dai, another demeth ech dai.

6 Ech man encrees in his wit. He that vnderstondith the dai, vnderstondith to the Lord. And he that etith, etith to the Lord, for he doith thankyngis to God. And he that etith not, etith not to the Lord, and doith thankyngis to God.

7 For no man of vs lyueth to hymsilf, and no man dieth to hymself.

8 For whether we lyuen, we lyuen to the Lord; and whethir we dien, we dien to the Lord. Therfor whethir we lyuen or dien, we ben of the Lord.

9 For whi for this thing Crist was deed, and roos ayen, that he be Lord bothe of quyke and of deed men.

10 But what demest thou thi brothir? or whi dispisist thou thi brothir? for alle we schulen stonde bifore the trone of Crist.

11 For it is writun, Y lyue, seith the Lord, for to me ech kne schal be bowid, and ech tunge schal knouleche to God.

12 Therfor ech of vs schal yelde resoun to God for hym silf.

13 Therfor 'no more deme we ech other; but more deme ye this thing, that ye putte not hirtyng, or sclaundre, to a brothir.

14 I woot and triste in the Lord Jhesu, that no thing is vnclene bi hym, no but to him that demeth ony thing to be vnclene, to him it is vnclene.

15 And if thi brother be maad sori in conscience for mete, now thou walkist not aftir charite. Nyle thou thorouy thi mete lese hym, for whom Crist diede.

16 Therfor be not oure good thing blasfemed.

17 For whi the rewme of God is not mete and drynk, but riytwisnesse and pees and ioye in the Hooli Goost.

18 And he that in this thing serueth Crist, plesith God, and is proued to men.

19 Therfor sue we tho thingis that ben of pees, and kepe we togidere 'tho thingis that ben of edificacioun.

20 Nyle thou for mete distrie the werk of God. For alle thingis ben clene, but it is yuel to the man that etith bi offendyng.

21 It is good to not ete fleisch, and to not drynke wyn, nethir in what thing thi brother offendith, or is sclaundrid, or is maad sijk.

22 Thou hast feith anentis thi silf, haue thou bifore God. Blessid is he that demeth not hym silf in that thing that he preueth.

23 For he that demeth, is dampned, if he etith; for it is not of feith. And al thing that is not of feith, is synne.

CAP 15

1 But we saddere men owen to susteyne the feblenesses of sijke men, and not plese to vs silf.

2 Eche of vs plese to his neiybore in good, to edificacioun.

3 For Crist pleside not to hym silf, as it is writun, The repreues of men dispisynge thee, felden on me.

4 For what euere thingis ben writun, tho ben writun to oure techynge, that bi pacience and coumfort of scripturis we haue hope.

5 But God of pacience and of solace yyue to you to vndurstonde the same thing, ech in to othere aftir Jhesu Crist,

6 that ye of o wille with o mouth worschipe God and the fadir of oure Lord Jhesu Crist.

7 For which thing take ye togidere, as also Crist took you in to the onour of God.

8 For Y seie, that Jhesu Crist was a mynystre of circumcisioun for the treuthe of God, to conferme the biheestis of fadris.

9 And hethene men owen to onoure God for merci; as it is writun, Therfor, Lord, Y schal knowleche to thee among hethene men, and Y schal synge to thi name.

10 And eft he seith, Ye hethene men, be ye glad with his puple.

11 And eft, Alle hethene men, herie ye the Lord; and alle puplis, magnefie ye hym.

12 And eft Isaie seith, Ther schal be a roote of Jesse, that schal rise vp to gouerne hethene men, and hethene men schulen hope in hym.

13 And God of hope fulfille you in al ioye and pees in bileuynge, that ye encrees in hope and vertu of the Hooli Goost.

14 And, britheren, Y my silf am certeyn of you, that also ye ben ful of loue, and ye ben fillid with al kunnyng, so that ye moun moneste ech other.

15 And, britheren, more boldli Y wroot to you a parti, as bryngynge you in to mynde, for the grace that is youun to me of God,

16 that Y be the mynystre of Crist Jhesu among hethene men. And Y halewe the gospel of God, that the offryng of hethene men be acceptid, and halewid in the Hooli Goost.

17 Therfor Y haue glorie in Crist Jhesu to God.

18 For Y dar not speke ony thing of tho thingis, whiche Crist doith not bi me, in to obedience of hethene men, in word and dedis,

19 in vertu of tokenes and grete wondris, in vertu of the Hooli Goost, so that fro Jerusalem bi cumpas to the Illirik see Y haue fillid the gospel of Crist.

20 And so Y haue prechid this gospel, not where Crist was named, lest Y bilde vpon anotheres ground, but as it is writun,

21 For to whom it is not teld of him, thei schulen se, and thei that herden not, schulen vndurstonde.

22 For which thing Y was lettid ful myche to come to you, and Y am lettid to this tyme.

23 And now Y haue not ferthere place in these cuntrees, but Y haue desire to come to you, of many yeris that ben passid.

24 Whanne Y bygynne to passe in to Spayne, Y hope that in my goyng Y schal se you, and of you Y schal be led thidur, if Y vse you first in parti.

25 Therfor now Y schal passe forth to Jerusalem, to mynystre to seyntis.

26 For Macedonye and Acaie han assaied to make sum yifte to pore men of seyntis, that ben in Jerusalem.

27 For it pleside to hem, and thei ben dettouris of hem; for hethene men ben maad parteneris of her goostli thingis, thei owen also in fleischli thingis to mynystre to hem.

28 Therfor whanne Y haue endid this thing, and haue asigned to hem this fruyt, Y schal passe bi you in to Spayne.

29 And Y woot, that Y comynge to you, schal come 'in to the abundaunce of the blessing of Crist.

30 Therfor, britheren, Y biseche you bi oure Lord Jhesu Crist, and bi charite of the Hooli Goost, that ye helpe me in youre preyeris to the Lord,

31 that Y be delyuerid fro the vnfeithful men, that ben in Judee, and that the offryng of my seruyce be acceptid in Jerusalem to seyntis;

32 that Y come to you in ioye, bi the wille of God, and that Y be refreischid with you. And God of pees be with you alle. Amen.

CAP 16

1 And Y comende to you Feben, oure sister, which is in the seruyce of the chirche that is at Teucris,

2 that ye resseyue hir in the Lord worthili to seyntis, and 'that ye helpe hir in what euere cause sche schal nede of you. For sche helpide many men, and my silf.

3 Grete ye Prisca and Aquyla, myn helperis in Crist Jhesu,

4 which vndurputtiden her neckis for my lijf; to whiche not Y aloone do thankyngis, but also alle the chirchis of hethene men.

5 And grete ye wel her meyneal chirche. Grete wel Efenete, louyd to me, that is the firste of Asie in Crist Jhesu.

6 Grete wel Marie, the whiche hath trauelid myche in vs.

7 Grete wel Andronyk and Julian, my cosyns, and myn euen prisouneris, which ben noble among the apostlis, and whiche weren bifor me in Crist.

8 Grete wel Ampliate, most dereworth to me in the Lord.

9 Grete wel Vrban, oure helpere in Crist Jhesus, and Stacchen, my derlyng.

10 Grete wel Appellem, the noble in Crist.

11 Grete wel hem that ben of Aristoblis hous. Grete wel Erodion, my cosyn. Grete wel hem that ben of Narciscies hous, that ben in the Lord.

12 Grete wel Trifenam and Trifosam, whiche wymmen trauelen in the Lord. Grete wel Persida, most dereworthe womman, that hath trauelid myche in the Lord.

13 Grete wel Rufus, chosun in the Lord, and his modir, and myn.

14 Grete wel Ansicrete, Flegoncia, Hermen, Patroban, Herman, and britheren that ben with hem.

15 Grete wel Filologus, and Julian, and Nereum, and his sistir, and Olympiades, and alle the seyntis that ben with hem.

16 Grete ye wel togidere in hooli coss. Alle the chirches of Crist greten you wel.

17 But, britheren, Y preye you, that ye aspie hem that maken discenciouns and hirtyngis, bisidis the doctryne that ye han lerned, and bowe ye awei fro hem.

18 For suche men seruen not to the Lord Crist, but to her wombe, and bi swete wordis and blessyngis disseyuen the hertis of innocent men.

19 But youre obedience is pupplischid in to euery place, therfor Y haue ioye in you. But Y wole that ye be wise in good thing, and symple in yuel.

20 And God of pees tredde Sathanas vndur youre feet swiftli. The grace of oure Lord Jhesu Crist be with you.

21 Tymothe, myn helpere, gretith you wel, and also Lucius, and Jason, and Sosipater, my cosyns.

22 Y Tercius grete you wel, that wroot this epistle, in the Lord.

23 Gayus, myn oost, gretith you wel, and al the chirche. Erastus, tresorere of the city, gretith you wel, and Quartus brother.

24 The grace of oure Lord Jhesu Crist be with you alle.

25 Amen. And onour and glorie be to hym, that is myyti to conferme you bi my gospel, and prechyng of Jhesu Crist, bi the reuelacioun of mysterie holdun stylle in tymes euerlastinge;

26 which mysterie is now maad opyn bi scripturis of prophetis, bi the comaundement of God with outen bigynnyng and endyng, to the obedience of feith in alle hethene men, the mysterie

27 knowun bi Jhesu Crist to God aloone wiss, to whom be onour and glorie in to worldis of worldis. Amen.

1 CORINTHIS

CAP 1

1 Poul, clepid apostle of Jhesu Crist, bi the wille of God, and Sostenes, brothir, to the chirche of God that is at Corynthe,

2 to hem that ben halewid in Crist Jhesu, and clepid seyntis, with alle that inwardli clepen the name of oure Lord Jhesu Crist, in ech place of hem and of oure,

3 grace to you and pees of God, oure fadir, and of the Lord Jhesu Crist.

4 Y do thankyngis to my God eueremore for you, in the grace of God that is youun to you in Crist Jhesu.

5 For in alle thingis ye ben maad riche in hym, in ech word, and in ech kunnyng,

6 as the witnessyng of Crist is confermyd in you;

7 so that no thing faile to you in ony grace, that abiden the schewyng of oure Lord Jhesu Crist;

8 which also schal conferme you in to the ende with outen cryme, in the dai of the comyng of oure Lord Jhesu Crist.

9 'A trewe God, bi whom ye ben clepid in to the felouschipe of his sone Jhesu Crist oure Lord.

10 But, britheren, Y biseche you, bi the name of oure Lord Jhesu Crist, that ye alle seie the same thing, and that dissenci- ouns be not among you; but be ye perfit in the same wit, and in the same kunnyng.

11 For, my britheren, it is teld to me of hem that ben at Cloes, that stryues ben among you.

12 And Y seie that, that ech of you seith, For Y am of Poul, and Y am of Apollo, and Y am of Cefas, but Y am of Crist.

13 Whether Crist is departid? whether Poul was crucified for you, ether ye ben baptisid in the name of Poul?

14 Y do thankyngis to my God, that Y baptiside noon of you, but Crispus and Gayus;

15 lest ony man seie, that ye ben baptisid in my name.

16 And Y baptiside also the hous of Stephan, but Y woot not, that Y baptiside ony other.

17 For Crist sente me not to baptise, but to preche the gospel; not in wisdom of word, that the cros of Crist be not voidid awei.

18 For the word of the cros is foli to hem that perischen; but to hem that ben maad saaf, that is to seie, to vs, it is the vertu of God.

19 For it is writun, Y schal distruye the wisdom of wise men, and Y schal reproue the prudence of prudent men.

20 Where is the wise man? where is the wise lawiere? where is the purchasour of this world? Whether God hath not maad the wisdom of this world fonned?

21 For the world in wisdom of God knewe not God bi wis- dom, it pleside to God, bi foli of prechyng, 'to maken hem saaf that bileueden.

22 For Jewis seken signes, and Grekis seken wisdom;

23 but we prechen Crist crucified, to Jewis sclaundre, and to hethene men foli;

24 but to tho Jewis and Grekis that ben clepid, we prechen Crist the vertu of God and the wisdom of God.

25 For that that is foli thing of God, is wiser than men; and that that is the feble thing of God, is strengere than men.

26 But, britheren, se ye youre clepyng; for not many wise men aftir the fleisch, not many myyti, not many noble.

27 But God chees tho thingis that ben fonned of the world, to confounde wise men;

28 and God chees the feble thingis of the world, to confounde the stronge thingis; and God chees the vnnoble thingis 'and

dispisable thingis of the world, and tho thingis that ben not, to distruye tho thingis that ben;

29 that ech man haue not glorie in his siyt.

30 But of hym ye ben in Crist Jhesu, which is maad of God to vs wisdom, and riytwisnesse, and holynesse, and ayenbiyng; that,

31 as it is wrytun, He that glorieth, haue glorie in the Lord.

CAP 2

1 And Y, britheren, whanne Y cam to you, cam not in the heiynesse of word, ethir of wisdom, tellynge to you the wit- nessyng of Crist.

2 For Y demede not me to kunne ony thing among you, but Crist Jhesu, and hym crucified.

3 And Y in sikenesse, and drede, and myche trembling, was among you;

4 and my word and my preching was not in suteli sturyng wordis of mannus wisdom, but in schewyng of spirit and of vertu;

5 that youre feith be not in the wisdom of men, but in the vertu of God.

6 For we speken wisdom among perfit men, but not wisdom of this world, nether of princes of this world, that ben distried;

7 but we speken the wisdom of God in mysterie, 'which wis- dom is hid; which wisdom God bifor ordeynede bifor worldis in to oure glorie,

8 which noon of the princes of this world knew; for if thei hadden knowe, thei schulden neuere haue crucified the Lord of glorie.

9 But as it is writun, That iye say not, ne eere herde, nether it stiede in to herte of man, what thingis God arayede to hem that louen hym;

10 but God schewide to vs bi his spirit. For whi the spirit ser- chith alle thingis, yhe, the depe thingis of God.

11 And who of men woot, what thingis ben of man, but the spirit of man that is in hym? So what thingis ben of God, no man knowith, but the spirit of God.

12 And we han not resseiued the spirit of this world, but the spirit that is of God, that we wite what thingis ben youun to vs of God.

13 Whiche thingis we speken also, not in wise wordis of man- nus wisdom, but in the doctryn of the spirit, and maken a lik- nesse of spiritual thingis to goostli men.

14 For a beestli man perseyueth not tho thingis that ben of the spirit of God; for it is foli to hym, and he may not vndurst- onde, for it is examyned goostli.

15 But a spiritual man demeth alle thingis, and he is demed of no man.

16 As it is writun, And who knew the wit of the Lord, or who tauyte hym? And we han the wit of Crist.

CAP 3

1 And Y, britheren, myyte not speke to you as to spiritual men, but as to fleischli men;

2 as to litle children in Crist, Y yaf to you mylk drynke, not mete; for ye myyten not yit, nether ye moun now, for yit ye ben fleischli.

3 For while strijf is among you, whether ye ben not fleischli, and ye gon aftir man?

4 For whanne summe seith, Y am of Poul, another, But Y am of Apollo, whethir ye ben not men? What therfor is Apollo, and what Poul?

5 Thei ben mynystris of hym, to whom ye han bileuyd; and to ech man as God hath youun.

6 Y plauntide, Apollo moystide, but God yaf encreessyng.

7 Therfor nether he that plauntith is ony thing, nethir he that moistith, but God that yiueth encreessyng.

8 And he that plauntith, and he that moistith, ben oon; and ech schal take his owne mede, aftir his trauel.

9 For we ben the helperis of God; ye ben the erthetiliyng of God, ye ben the bildyng of God.

10 Aftir the grace 'of God that is youun to me, as a wise maistir carpenter Y settide the foundement; and another bildith aboue. But ech man se, hou he bildith aboue.

11 For no man may sette another foundement, outtakun that that is sett, which is Crist Jhesus.

12 For if ony bildith ouer this foundement, gold, siluer, preciouse stoonys, stickis, hey, or stobil, euery mannus werk schal be open;

13 for the dai of the Lord schal declare, for it schal be schewid in fier; the fier schal preue the werk of ech man, what maner werk it is.

14 If the werk of ony man dwelle stille, which he bildide aboue, he schal resseyue mede.

15 If ony mannus werk brenne, he schal suffre harm; but he schal be saaf, so netheles as bi fier.

16 Witen ye not, that ye ben the temple of God, and the spirit of God dwellith in you?

17 And if ony defoulith the temple of God, God schal leese hym; for the temple of God is hooli, which ye ben.

18 No man disseyue hym silf. If ony man among you is seyn to be wiys in this world, be he maad a fool, that he be wijs.

19 For the wisdom of this world is foli anentis God; for it is writun, Y schal catche wise men in her fel wisdom;

20 and eft, The Lord knowith the thouytis of wise men, for tho ben veyn.

21 Therfor no man haue glorie in men.

22 For alle thingis ben youre, ethir Poul, ether Apollo, ether Cefas, ether the world, ether lijf, ether deth, ether thingis present, ethir thingis to comynge; for alle thingis ben youre,

23 and ye ben of Crist, and Crist is of God.

CAP 4

1 So a man gesse vs, as mynystris of Crist, and dispenderis of the mynysteries of God.

2 Now it is souyt here among the dispenderis, that a man be foundun trewe.

3 And to me it is for the leest thing, that Y be demyd of you, or of mannus dai; but nether Y deme my silf.

4 For Y am no thing ouer trowynge to my silf, but not in this thing Y am iustified; for he that demeth me, is the Lord.

5 Therfor nyle ye deme bifore the tyme, til that the Lord come, which schal liytne the hyd thingis of derknessis, and schal schewe the counseils of hertis; and thanne preisyng schal be to ech man of God.

6 And, britheren, Y haue transfigurid these thingis in to me and in to Apollo, for you; that in vs ye lerne, lest ouer that it is writun, oon ayens another be blowun with pride for another.

7 Who demeth thee? And what hast thou, that thou hast not resseyued? And if thou hast resseyued, what gloriest thou, as thou haddist not resseyued?

8 Nowe ye ben fyllid, now ye ben maad riche; ye regnen with outen vs; and Y wolde that ye regnen, that also we regnen with you.

9 And Y gesse, that God schewide vs the laste apostlis, as thilke that ben sent to the deth; for we ben maad a spectacle to the world, and to aungels, and to men.

10 We foolis for Crist, but ye prudent in Crist; we sike, but ye stronge; ye noble, but we vnnoble.

11 Til in to this our we hungren, and thirsten, and ben nakid, and ben smytun with buffatis,

12 and we ben vnstable, and we trauelen worchynge with oure hondis; we ben cursid, and we blessen; we suffren persecucioun, and we abiden longe; we ben blasfemyd, and we bisechen;

13 as clensyngis of this world we ben maad the 'out castyng of alle thingis 'til yit.

14 Y write not these thingis, that Y confounde you, but Y warne as my moste dereworthe sones.

15 For whi if ye han ten thousynde of vndur maistris in Crist, but not many fadris; for in Crist Jhesu Y haue gendrid you bi the gospel.

16 Therfor, britheren, Y preye you, be ye foleweris of me, as Y of Crist.

17 Therfor Y sente to you Tymothe, which is my most dereworthe sone, and feithful in the Lord, which schal teche you my weies, that ben in Crist Jhesu; as Y teche euery where in ech chirche.

18 As thouy Y schulde not come to you, so summe ben blowun with pride;

19 but Y schal come to you soone, if God wole; and Y schal knowe not the word of hem that ben blowun with pride, but the vertu.

20 For the rewme of God is not in word, but in vertu.

21 What wole ye? Schal Y come to you in a yerde, or in charite, and in spirit of myldenesse?

CAP 5

1 In al maner fornycacioun is herd among you, and siche fornycacioun, which is not among hethene men, so that summan haue the wijf of his fadir.

2 And ye ben bolnyd with pride, and not more hadden weilyng, that he that dide this werk, be takun awei fro the myddil of you.

3 And Y absent in bodi, but present in spirit, now haue demyd as present hym that hath thus wrouyt, whanne

4 ye ben gaderid togidere in the name of oure Lord Jhesu Crist, and my spirit, with the vertu of the Lord Jhesu,

5 to take siche a man to Sathanas, in to the perischyng of fleisch, that the spirit be saaf in the dai of oure Lord Jhesu Crist.

6 Youre gloriyng is not good. Witen ye not, that a litil sourdow apeyrith al the gobet?

7 Clense ye out the old sourdow, that ye be new sprengyng togidere, as ye ben therf. For Crist offrid is oure pask.

8 Therfor ete we, not in eld sourdowy, nether in sourdowy of malice and weywardnesse, but in therf thingis of clernesse and of treuthe.

9 I wroot to you in a pistle, that ye be not medlid with letchours,

10 not with letchours of this world, ne coueitous men, ne raueynours, ne with men seruynge to mawmetis, ellis ye schulden haue go out of this world.

11 But now Y wroot to you, that ye be not meynd. But if he that is named a brother among you, and is a letchour, or coueitouse, or seruynge to ydols, or cursere, or ful of drunkenesse, or raueynour, to take no mete with siche.

12 For what is it to me to deme of hem that ben with oute forth? Whether ye demen not of thingis that ben with ynne forth?

13 For God schal deme hem that ben withouten forth. Do ye awei yuel fro you silf.

CAP 6

1 Dar any of you that hath a cause ayens another, be demed at wickid men, and not at hooli men?

2 Whether ye witen not, that seyntis schulen deme of this world? And if the world schal be demed bi you, be ye vnworthi to deme of the leste thingis?

3 Witen ye not, that we schulen deme aungels? hou myche more worldli thingis?

4 Therfor if ye han worldli domes, ordeyne ye tho contemptible men, that ben in the chirche, to deme.

5 Y seie to make you aschamed. So ther is not ony wise man, that may deme bitwixe a brothir and his brothir;

6 but a brothir with brothir stryueth in dom, and that among vnfeithful men.

7 And now trespas is algatis in you, for ye han domes among you. Whi rather take ye no wrong? whi rather suffre ye not disseit?

8 But and ye doen wrong, and doen fraude, and that to britheren.

9 Whether ye witen not, that wickid men schulen not welde the kyngdom of God? Nyle ye erre; nethir letchours, nether men that seruen mawmetis, nether auouteris,

10 nether letchouris ayen kynde, nether thei that doon letcheri with men, nether theues, nether auerouse men, nethir 'ful of drunkenesse, nether curseris, nether rauenours, schulen welde the kyngdom of God.

11 And ye weren sum tyme these thingis; but ye ben waischun, but ye ben halewid, but ye ben iustefied in the name of oure Lord Jhesu Crist, and in the spirit of oure God.

12 Alle thingis ben leeueful to me, but not alle thingis ben spedeful. Alle thingis ben leeueful to me, but Y schal not be brouyt doun vndur ony mannus power.

13 Mete to the wombe, and the wombe to metis; and God schal distruye bothe this and that. And the bodi not to fornycacioun, but to the Lord, and the Lord to the bodi.

14 For God reiside the Lord, and schal reise vs bi his vertu.

15 Witen ye not, that youre bodies ben membris of Crist? Schal Y thanne take the membris of Crist, and schal Y make the membris of an hoore? God forbede.

16 Whether ye witen not, that he that cleueth to an hoore, is maad o bodi? For he seith, Ther schulen be tweyne in o fleisch.

17 And he that cleueth to the Lord, is o spirit.

18 Fle ye fornycacioun; al synne what euere synne a man doith, is with out the bodi; but he that doith fornycacioun, synneth ayens his bodi.

19 Whether ye witen not, that youre membris ben the temple of the Hooli Goost, that is in you, whom ye han of God, and ye ben not youre owne?

20 For ye ben bouyt with greet prijs. Glorifie ye, and bere ye God in youre bodi.

CAP 7

1 But of thilke thingis that ye han write to me, it is good to a man to touche not a womman.

2 But for fornycacioun eche man haue his owne wijf, and ech womman haue hir owne hosebonde.

3 The hosebonde yelde dette to the wijf, and also the wijf to the hosebonde.

4 The womman hath not power of hir bodi, but the hosebonde; and the hosebonde hath not power of his bodi, but the womman.

5 Nyle ye defraude eche to othere, but perauenture of consent to a tyme, that ye yyue tent to preier; and eft turne ye ayen to the same thing, lest Sathanas tempte you for youre vncontynence.

6 But Y seie this thing as yyuyng leeue, not bi comaundement.

7 For Y wole, that alle men be as my silf. But eche man hath his propre yifte of God; oon thus, and another thus.

8 But Y seie to hem, that ben not weddid, and to widewis, it is good to hem, if thei dwellen so as Y.

9 That if thei conteynen not hem silf, be thei weddid; for it is betere to be weddid, than to be brent.

10 But to hem that ben ioyned in matrymonye, Y comaunde, not Y, but the Lord, that the wijf departe not fro the hosebonde;

11 and that if sche departith, that sche dwelle vnweddid, or be recounselid to hir hosebonde; and the hosebonde forsake not the wijf.

12 But to othere Y seie, not the Lord. If ony brother hath an vnfeithful wijf, and sche consenteth to dwelle with hym, leeue he hir not.

13 And if ony womman hath an vnfeithful hosebonde, and this consentith to dwelle with hir, leeue sche not the hosebonde.

14 For the vnfeithful hosebonde is halewid bi the feithful womman, and the vnfeithful womman is halewid bi the feithful hosebonde. Ellis youre children weren vncleene, but now thei ben hooli.

15 That if the vnfeithful departith, departe he. For whi the brother or sistir is not suget to seruage in siche; for God hath clepid vs in pees.

16 And wherof wost thou, womman, if thou schalt make the man saaf; or wherof wost thou, man, if thou schalt make the womman saaf?

17 But as the Lord hath departid to ech, and as God hath clepid ech man, so go he, as Y teche in alle chirchis.

18 A man circumcidid is clepid, brynge he not to the prepucie. A man is clepid in prepucie, be he not circumcidid.

19 Circumcisioun is nouyt, and prepucie is nouyt, but the kepyng of the maundementis of God.

20 Ech man in what clepyng he is clepid, in that dwelle he.

21 Thou seruaunt art clepid, be it no charge to thee; but if thou maist be fre, 'the rather vse thou.

22 He that is a seruaunt, and is clepid in the Lord, is a freman of the Lord. Also he that is a freman, and is clepid, is the seruaunt of Crist.

23 With prijs ye ben bouyt; nyle ye be maad seruauntis of men.

24 Therfor ech man in what thing he is clepid a brothir, dwelle he in this anentis God.

25 But of virgyns Y haue no comaundement of God; but Y yyue counseil, as he that hath mercy of the Lord, that Y be trewe.

26 Therfor Y gesse, that this thing is good for the present nede; for it is good to a man to be so.

27 Thou art boundun to a wijf, nyle thou seke vnbyndyng; thou art vnboundun fro a wijf, nyle thou seke a wijf.

28 But if thou hast takun a wijf, thou hast not synned; and if a maidun is weddid, sche synnede not; nethelesse siche schulen haue tribulacioun of fleisch.

29 But Y spare you. Therfor, britheren, Y seie this thing, The tyme is schort. Another is this, that thei that han wyues, be as thouy thei hadden noon;

30 and thei that wepen, as thei wepten not; and thei that ioien, as thei ioieden not; and thei that bien, as thei hadden not;

31 and thei that vsen this world, as thei that vsen not. For whi the figure of this world passith.

32 But Y wole, that ye be without bisynesse, for he that is without wijf, is bisi what thingis ben of the Lord, hou he schal plese God.

33 But he that is with a wijf, is bysy what thingis ben of the world, hou he schal plese the wijf, and he is departid.

34 And a womman vnweddid and maidun thenkith what thingis ben of the Lord, that sche be hooli in bodi and spirit. But sche that is weddid, thenkith what thingis ben of the world, hou sche schal plese the hosebonde.

35 And Y seie these thingis to youre profit, not that Y caste to you a snare, but to that that is onest, and that yyueth esynesse, with outen lettyng to make preieris to the Lord.

36 And if ony man gessith hym silf to be seyn foule on his virgyn, that sche is ful woxun, and so it bihoueth to be doon, do sche that that sche wole; sche synneth not, if sche be weddid.

37 For he that ordeynede stabli in his herte, not hauynge nede, but hauynge power of his wille, and hath demed in his herte this thing, to kepe his virgyn, doith wel.

38 Therfore he that ioyneth his virgyn in matrymonye, doith wel; and he that ioyneth not, doith betere.

39 The womman is boundun to the lawe, as longe tyme as hir hosebonde lyueth; and if hir hosebonde is deed, sche is delyuered fro the lawe of the hosebonde, be sche weddid to whom sche wole, oneli in the Lord.

40 But sche schal be more blessid, if sche dwellith thus, aftir my counsel; and Y wene, that Y haue the Spirit of God.

CAP 8

1 But of these thingis that ben sacrified to ydols, we witen, for alle we han kunnyng. But kunnyng blowith, charite edefieth.

2 But if ony man gessith, that he kan ony thing, he hath not yit knowe hou it bihoueth hym to kunne.

3 And if ony man loueth God, this is knowun of hym.

4 But of metis that ben offrid to idols, we witen, that an idol is no thing in the world, and that ther is no God but oon.

5 For thouy ther ben summe that ben seid goddis, ethir in heuene, ether in erthe, as ther ben many goddis, and many lordis;

6 netheles to vs is o God, the fadir, of whom ben alle thingis, and we in hym; and o Lord Jhesu Crist, bi whom ben alle thingis, and we bi hym.

7 But not in alle men is kunnyng. For summen with conscience of ydol til now eten as thing offrid to idolis; and her conscience is defoulid, for it is sijk.

8 Mete comendith vs not to God; for nether we schulen faile, if we eten not, nether if we eten, we schulen haue plente.

9 But se ye, lest perauenture this your leeue be maad hurtyng to sijke men.

10 For if ony man schal se hym, that hath kunnyng, etynge in a place where idols ben worschipid, whethir his conscience, sithen it is sijke, schal not be edified to ete thingis offrid to idols?

11 And the sijk brothir, for whom Crist diede, schal perische in thi kunnyng.

12 For thus ye synnyng ayens britheren, and smytynge her sijk conscience synnen ayens Crist.

13 Wherfor if mete sclaundrith my brother, Y schal neuere ete fleisch, lest Y sclaundre my brothir.

CAP 9

1 Whether Y am not fre? Am Y not apostle? Whether Y saiy not 'Crist Jhesu, 'oure Lord? Whether ye ben not my werk in the Lord?

2 And thouy to othere Y am not apostle, but netheles to you Y am; for ye ben the litle signe of myn apostlehed in the Lord.

3 My defense to hem that axen me, that is.

4 Whether we han not power to ete and drynke?

5 Whether we han not power to lede aboute a womman a sistir, as also othere apostlis, and britheren of the Lord, and Cefas?

6 Or Y aloone and Barnabas han not power to worche these thingis?

7 Who traueilith ony tyme with hise owne wagis? Who plauntith a vynyerd, and etith not of his fruyt? Who kepith a flok, and etith not of the mylk of the flok?

8 Whether aftir man Y sey these thingis? whether also the lawe seith not these thingis?

9 For it is writun in the lawe of Moises, Thou schalt not bynde the mouth of the ox threischynge. Whethir of oxun is charge to God?

10 Whether for vs he seith these thingis? For whi tho ben writun for vs; for he that erith, owith to ere in hope, and he that threischith, in hope to take fruytis.

11 If we sowen spiritual thingis to you, is it grete, if we repen youre fleischli thingis?

12 If othere ben parteneris of youre power, whi not rathere we? But we vsen not this power, but we suffren alle thingis, that we yyuen no lettyng to the euangelie of Crist.

13 Witen ye not, that thei that worchen in the temple, eten tho thingis that ben of the temple, and thei that seruen to the auter, ben partyneris of the auter?

14 So the Lord ordeynede to hem that tellen the gospel, to lyue of the gospel.

15 But Y vside noon of these thingis; sotheli Y wroot not these thingis, that tho be don so in me; for it is good 'to me rather to die, than that ony man 'auoyde my glorie.

16 For if Y preche the gospel, glorie is not to me, for nedelich Y mot don it; for wo to me, if Y preche not the gospel.

17 But if Y do this thing wilfuli, Y haue mede; but if ayens my wille, dispending is bitakun to me.

18 What thanne is my mede? That Y prechynge the gospel, putte the gospel with outen otheris cost, that Y vse not my power in the gospel.

19 Forwhi whanne Y was fre of alle men, Y made me seruaunt of alle men, to wynne the mo men.

20 And to Jewis Y am maad as a Jew, to wynne the Jewis; to hem that ben vndur the lawe,

21 as Y were vndur the lawe, whanne Y was not vndur the lawe, to wynne hem that weren vndur the lawe; to hem that weren with out lawe, as Y were with out lawe, whanne Y was not with out the lawe of God, but Y was in the lawe of Crist, to wynne hem that weren with out lawe.

22 Y am maad sijk to sike men, to wynne sike men; to alle men Y am maad alle thingis, to make alle men saaf.

23 But Y do alle thingis for the gospel, that Y be maad partener of it.

24 Witen ye not, that thei that rennen in a furlong, alle rennen, but oon takith the prijs? So renne ye, that ye catche.

25 Ech man that stryueth in fiyt, absteyneth hym fro alle thingis; and thei, that thei take a corruptible coroun, but we an vncorrupt.

26 Therfor Y renne so, not as 'in to vncerteyn thing; thus Y fiyte, not as betynge the eir;

27 but Y chastise my bodi, and bryng it in to seruage; lest perauenture whanne Y preche to othere, Y my silf be maad repreuable.

CAP 10

1 Britheren, Y nyle, that ye vnknowe, that alle oure fadris weren vndur cloude, and alle passiden the see;

2 and alle weren baptisid in Moises, in the cloude and in the see;

3 and alle eeten the same spiritual mete,

4 and alle drunken the same spiritual drynke; thei drunken of the spiritual stoon folewynge hem; and the stoon was Crist.

5 But not in ful manye of hem it was wel pleasaunt to God; for whi thei weren cast doun in desert.

6 But these thingis ben don in figure of vs, that we be not coueyteris of yuele thingis, as thei coueitiden.

7 Nether be ye maad idolatreris, as summe of hem; as it is writun, The puple sat to ete and drynke, and thei risen vp to pleie.

8 Nether do we fornycacioun, as summe of hem diden fornicacioun, and thre and twenti thousyndis weren deed in o dai.

9 Nethir tempte we Crist, as summe of hem temptiden, and perischiden of serpentis.

10 Nether grutche ye, as summe of hem grutchiden, and thei perischiden of a distrier.

11 And alle these thingis felliden to hem in figure; but thei ben writun to oure amendyng, in to whiche the endis of the worldis ben comun.

12 Therfor he that gessith hym, 'that he stondith, se he, that he falle not.

13 Temptacioun take 'not you, but mannus temptacioun; for God is trewe, which schal not suffre you to be temptid aboue that that ye moun; but he schal make with temptacioun also purueyaunce, that ye moun suffre.

14 Wherfor, ye most dereworthe to me, fle ye fro worschiping of maumetis.

15 As to prudent men Y speke, deme ye you silf that thing that Y seie.

16 Whether the cuppe of blessyng which we blessen, is not the comynyng of Cristis blood? and whether the breed which we breken, is not the takyng of the bodi of the Lord?

17 For we manye ben o breed and o bodi, alle we that taken part of o breed and of o cuppe.

18 Se ye Israel aftir the fleisch, whethir thei that eeten sacrifices, ben not partyneris of the auter?

19 What therfor seie Y, that a thing that is offrid to idols is ony thing, or that the idol is ony thing?

20 But tho thingis that hethene men offren, thei offren to deuelis, and not to God. But Y nyle, that ye ben maad felowis of feendis; for ye moun not drynke the cuppe of the Lord, and the cuppe of fendis;

21 ye moun not be parteneris of the boord of the Lord, and of the bord of feendis.

22 Whether we han enuye to the Lord? whether we ben strengere then he? Alle thingis ben leeueful to me, but not alle thingis ben spedeful.

23 Alle thingis ben leeueful to me, but not alle thingis edifien.

24 No man seke that thing that is his owne, but that thing that is of an othere.

25 Al thing that is seld in the bocherie, ete ye, axynge no thing for conscience.

26 The erthe and the plente of it is, the Lordis.

27 If ony of hethene men clepith you to soper, and ye wole go, al thing that is set to you, ete ye, axynge no thing for conscience.

28 But if ony man seith, This thing is offrid to idols, nyle ye ete, for hym that schewide, and for conscience; and Y seie not,

29 thi conscience, but of an othere. But wherto is my fredom demed of an othere mannus conscience?

30 Therfor if Y take part with grace, what am Y blasfemed, for that that Y do thankyngis?

31 Therfor whether ye eten, or drynken, or don ony other thing, do ye alle thingis 'in to the glorie of God.

32 Be ye with outen sclaundre to Jewis, and to hethene men, and to the chirche of God;

33 as Y bi alle thingis plese to alle men, not sekynge that that is profitable to me, but that that is profitable to manye men, that thei be maad saaf.

CAP 11

1 Be ye my foleweris, as Y am of Crist.

2 And, britheren, Y preise you, that bi alle thingis ye ben myndeful of me; and as Y bitook to you my comaundementis, ye holden.

3 But Y wole that ye wite, that Crist is heed of ech man; but the heed of the womman is the man; and the heed of Crist is God.

4 Ech man preiynge, or profeciynge, whanne his heed is hilid, defoulith his heed.

5 But ech womman preiynge, or profeciynge, whanne hir heed is not hilid, defoulith hir heed; for it is oon, as if sche were pollid.

6 And if a womman be not keuered, be sche pollid; and if it is foul thing to a womman to be pollid, or to be maad ballid, hile sche hir heed.

7 But a man schal not hile his heed, for he is the ymage and the glorie of God; but a womman is the glorie of man.

8 For a man is not of the womman, but the womman of the man.

9 And the man is not maad for the womman, but the womman for the man.

10 Therfor the womman schal haue an hilyng on hir heed, also for aungelis.

11 Netheles nether the man is with outen womman, nether the womman is with oute man, in the Lord.

12 Forwhi as the womman is of man, so the man is bi the womman; but alle thingis ben of God.

13 Deme ye you silf; bisemeth it a womman not hilid on the heed to preye God?

14 Nether the kynde it silf techith vs, for if a man nursche longe heer, it is schenschipe to hym;

15 but if a womman nurische longe heer, it is glorie to hir, for heeris ben youun to hir for keueryng.

16 But if ony man is seyn to be ful of strijf, we han noon siche custom, nethir the chirche of God.

17 But this thing Y comaunde, not preisynge, that ye comen togidere not in to the betere, but in to the worse.

18 First for whanne ye comen togidere in to the chirche, Y here that discenciouns ben, and in parti Y bileue.

19 For it bihoueth eresies to be, that thei that ben prouyd, ben opynli knowun in you.

20 Therfor whanne ye comen togidere in to oon, now it is not to ete the Lordis soper;

21 for whi ech man bifor takith his soper to ete, and oon is hungry, and another is drunkun.

22 Whether ye han not housis to ete and drynke, or ye dispisen the chirche of God, and confounden hem that han noon? What schal Y seie to you? Y preise you, but here yn Y preise you not.

23 For Y haue takun of the Lord that thing, which Y haue bitakun to you. For the Lord Jhesu, in what niyt he was bitraied,

24 took breed, and dide thankyngis, and brak, and seide, Take ye, and ete ye; this is my bodi, which schal be bitraied for you; do ye this thing in to my mynde.

25 Also the cuppe, aftir that he hadde soupid, and seide, This cuppe is the newe testament in my blood; do ye this thing, as ofte as ye schulen drynke, in to my mynde.

26 For as ofte as ye schulen ete this breed, and schulen drynke the cuppe, ye schulen telle the deth of the Lord, til that he come.

27 Therfor who euere etith the breed, or drynkith the cuppe of the Lord vnworthili, he schal be gilti of the bodi and of the blood of the Lord.

28 But preue a man hym silf, and so ete he of 'the ilke breed, and drynke of the cuppe.

29 For he that etith and drinkith vnworthili, etith and drinkith doom to hym, not wiseli demyng the bodi of the Lord.

30 Therfor among you many ben sijke and feble, and manye slepen.

31 And if we demyden wiseli vs silf, we schulden not be demyd;

32 but while we ben demyd of the Lord, we ben chastisid, that we be not dampned with this world.

33 Therfor, my britheren, whanne ye comen togidere to ete, abide ye togidere.

34 If ony man hungrith, ete he at home, that ye come not togidere in to doom. And Y schal dispose othere thingis, whanne Y come.

CAP 12

1 But of spiritual thingis, britheren, Y nyle that ye vnknowun.

2 For ye witen, that whanne ye weren hethene men, hou ye weren led goynge to doumbe maumetis.

3 Therfor Y make knowun to you, that no man spekynge in the spirit of God, seith departyng fro Jhesu; and no man may seie the Lord Jhesu, but in the Hooli Goost.

4 And dyuerse graces ther ben, but it is al oon Spirit;

5 and dyuerse seruyces ther ben, but it is al oon Lord; and dyuerse worchingis ther ben,

6 but 'al is oon God, that worchith alle thingis in alle thingis.

7 And to ech man the schewyng of spirit is youun to profit. The word of wisdom is youun to oon bi spirit;

8 to another the word of kunnyng, bi the same spirit;

9 feith to another, in the same spirit; to anothere, grace of hel-this, in o spirit;

10 to another, the worchyng of vertues; to another, profecie; to another, very knowyng of spiritis; to another, kyndis of langagis; to another, expownyng of wordis.

11 And oon and the same spirit worchith alle these thingis, departynge to ech bi hem silf as he wole.

12 For as ther is o body, and hath many membris, and alle the membris of the bodi whanne tho ben manye, ben o bodi, so also Crist.

13 For in o spirit alle we ben baptisid 'in to o bodi, ether Jewis, ether hethene, ether seruauntis, ether free; and alle we ben fillid with drink in o spirit.

14 For the bodi is not o membre, but manye.

15 If the foot seith, For Y am not the hoond, Y am not of the bodi; not therfor it is not of the bodi.

16 And if the ere seith, For Y am not the iye, Y am not of the bodi; not therfor it is not of the bodi.

17 If al the bodi is the iye, where is heryng? and if al the bodi is heryng, where is smellyng?

18 But now God hath set membris, and ech of hem in the bodi, as he wolde.

19 That if alle weren o membre, where were the bodi?

20 But now ther ben many membris, but o bodi.

21 And the iye may not seie to the hond, Y haue no nede to thi werkis; or eft the heed to the feet, Ye ben not necessarie to me.

22 But myche more tho that ben seyn to be the lowere membris of the bodi, ben more nedeful;

23 and thilke that we gessen to be the vnworthier membris of the bodi, we yyuen more honour 'to hem; and tho membris that ben vnonest, han more oneste.

24 For oure oneste membris han nede of noon; but God tempride the bodi, yyuynge more worschip to it, to whom it failide,

25 that debate be not in the bodi, but that the membris be bisi in to the same thing ech for othere.

26 And if o membre suffrith ony thing, alle membris suffren therwith; ethir if o membre ioieth, alle membris ioien togidere.

27 And ye ben the bodi of Crist, and membris of membre.

28 But God sette sum men in the chirche, fyrst apostlis, the secunde tyme prophetis, the thridde techeris, aftirward vertues, aftirward graces of heelyngis, helpyngis, gouernails, kyndis of langagis, interpretaciouns of wordis.

29 Whether alle apostlis? whethir alle prophetis? whether alle techeris? whether alle vertues?

30 whether alle men han grace of heelyngis? whether alle speken with langagis? whether alle expownen?

31 But sue ye the betere goostli yiftis. And yit Y schewe to you a more exellent weye.

CAP 13

1 If Y speke with tungis of men and of aungels, and Y haue not charite, Y am maad as bras sownynge, or a cymbal tynkynge.

2 And if Y haue prophecie, and knowe alle mysteries, and al kunnynge, and if Y haue al feith, so that Y meue hillis fro her place, and Y haue not charite, Y am nouyt.

3 And if Y departe alle my goodis in to the metis of pore men, and yf Y bitake my bodi, so that Y brenne, and if Y haue not charite, it profitith to me no thing.

4 Charite is pacient, it is benygne; charite enuyeth not, it doith not wickidli, it is not blowun,

5 it is not coueytouse, it sekith not tho thingis that ben hise owne, it is not stirid to wraththe, it thenkith not yuel,

6 it ioyeth not on wickidnesse, but it ioieth togidere to treuthe;

7 it suffrith alle thingis, it bileueth alle thingis, it hopith alle thingis, it susteyneth alle thingis.

8 Charite fallith neuere doun, whether prophecies schulen be voidid, ethir langagis schulen ceesse, ethir science schal be distried.

9 For a parti we knowun, and a parti we prophecien;

10 but whanne that schal come that is parfit, that thing that is of parti schal be auoidid.

11 Whanne Y was a litil child, Y spak as a litil child, Y vndurstood as a litil child, Y thouyte as a litil child; but whanne Y was maad a man, Y auoidide tho thingis that weren of a litil child.

12 And we seen now bi a myrour in derknesse, but thanne face to face; now Y knowe of parti, but thanne Y schal knowe, as Y am knowun.

13 And now dwellen feith, hope, and charite, these thre; but the most of these is charite.

CAP 14

1 Sue ye charite, loue ye spiritual thingis, but more that ye prophecien.

2 And he that spekith in tunge, spekith not to men, but to God; for no man herith. But the spirit spekith mysteries.

3 For he that prophecieth, spekith to men to edificacioun, and monestyng, and coumfortyng.

4 He that spekith in tunge, edifieth hym silf; but he that prophecieth, edifieth the chirche of God.

5 And Y wole, that alle ye speke in tungis, but more that ye prophecie. For he that prophecieth, is more than he that spekith in langagis; but perauenture he expoune, that the chirche take edificacioun.

6 But now, britheren, if Y come to you, and speke in langagis, what schal Y profite to you, but if Y speke to you ethir in reuelacioun, ethir in science, ethir in prophecie, ether in techyng?

7 For tho thingis that ben withouten soule, and yyueth voices, ethir pipe, ether harpe, but tho yyuen distinccioun of sownyngis, hou schal it be knowun that is sungun, ether that that is trumpid?

8 For if a trumpe yyue an vncerteyn soune, who schal make hym silf redi to batel?

9 So but ye yyuen an opyn word bi tunge, hou schal that that is seid be knowun? For ye schulen be spekynge in veyn.

10 There ben many kyndis of langagis in this world, and no thing is with outen vois.

11 But if Y knowe not the vertu of a vois, Y schal be to hym, to whom Y schal speke, a barbarik; and he that spekith to me, schal be a barbarik.

12 So ye, for ye ben loueris of spiritis, seke ye that ye be plenteuouse to edificacioun of the chirche.

13 And therfor he that spekith in langage, preie, that he expowne.

14 For if Y preye in tunge, my spirit preieth; myn vndurstondyng is with outen fruyt.

15 What thanne? Y schal preye in spirit, Y schal preye in mynde; Y schal seie salm, in spirit, Y schal seie salm also in mynde.

16 For if thou blessist in spirit, who fillith the place of an ydiot, hou schal he seie Amen on thi blessyng, for he woot not, what thou seist?

17 For thou doist wel thankyngis, but an othir man is not edefied.

18 Y thanke my God, for Y speke in the langage of alle you;

19 but in the chirche Y wole speke fyue wordis in my wit, that also Y teche othere men, than ten thousynde of wordis in tunge.

20 Britheren, nyle ye be maad children in wittis, but in malice be ye children; but in wittis be ye parfit.

21 For in the lawe it is writun, That in othere tungis and othere lippis Y schal speke to this puple, and nether so thei schulen here me, seith the Lord.

22 Therfor langagis ben in to tokene, not to feithful men, but to men out of the feith; but prophecies ben not to men out of the feith, but to feithful men.

23 Therfor if alle the chirche come togidere in to oon, and alle men speken in tungis, if idiotis, ether men out of the feith, entren, whether thei schulen not seie, What ben ye woode?

24 But if alle men prophecien, if ony vnfeithful man or idiot entre, he is conuyct of alle, he is wiseli demyd of alle.

25 For the hid thingis of his herte ben knowun, and so he schal falle doun on the face, and schal worschipe God, and schewe verili that God is in you.

26 What thanne, britheren? Whanne ye comen togidere, ech of you hath a salm, he hath techyng, he hath apocalips, he hath tunge, he hath expownyng; alle thingis be thei don to edificacioun.

27 Whether a man spekith in tunge, bi twei men, ethir thre at the moste, and bi partis, that oon interprete.

28 But if there be not an interpretour, be he stille in the chirche, and speke he to hym silf and to God.

29 Prophetis tweine or thre seie, and othere wiseli deme.

30 But if ony thing be schewid to a sittere, the formere be stille.

31 For ye moun 'prophecie alle, ech bi hym silf, that alle men lerne, and alle moneste.

32 And the spiritis of prophetis ben suget to prophetis;

33 for whi God is not of discencioun, but of pees; as in alle chirchis of hooli men 'Y teche.

34 Wymmen in chirchis be stille; for it is not suffrid to hem to speke, but to be suget, as the lawe seith.

35 But if thei wolen ony thing lerne, 'at home axe thei her hosebondis; for it is foule thing to a womman to speke in chirche.

36 Whether 'of you the word of God cam forth, or to you aloone it cam?

37 If ony man is seyn to be a prophete, or spiritual, knowe he tho thingis that Y write to you, for tho ben the comaundementis of the Lord.

38 And if ony man vnknowith, he schal be vnknowun.

39 'Therfor, britheren, loue ye to prophecie, and nyle ye forbede to speke in tungis.

40 But be alle thingis don onestli, and bi due ordre in you.

CAP 15

1 'Sotheli, britheren, Y make the gospel knowun to you, which Y haue prechid to you, the which also ye han takun, in which ye stonden,

2 also bi which ye schulen be sauyd; 'bi which resoun Y haue prechid to you, if ye holden, 'if ye han not bileuyd ideli.

3 For Y bitook to you at the bigynnyng that thing which also Y haue resseyued; that Crist was deed for oure synnes, bi the scripturis;

4 and that he was biried, and that he roos ayen in the thridde dai, after scripturis;

5 and that he was seyn to Cephas, and aftir these thingis to enleuene;

6 aftirward he was seyn to mo than fyue hundrid britheren togidere, of whiche manye lyuen yit, but summe ben deed; aftirward he was seyn to James,

7 and aftirward to alle the apostlis.

8 And last of alle he was seyn also to me, as to a deed borun child.

9 For Y am the leste of apostlis, that am not worthi to be clepid apostle, for Y pursuede the chirche of God.

10 But bi the grace of God Y am that thing that Y am; and his grace was not voide in me. For Y trauelide more plenteuously than alle thei; but not Y, but the grace of God with me.

11 But whether Y, or thei, so we han prechid, and so ye han bileuyd.

12 And if Crist is prechid, that he roos ayen fro deeth, hou seien summen among you, that the ayenrisyng of deed men is not?

13 And if the ayenrisyng of deed men is not, nethir Crist roos ayen fro deeth.

14 And if Crist roos not, oure preching is veyn, oure feith is veyn.

15 And we ben foundun false witnessis of God, for we han seid witnessyng ayens God, that he reiside Crist, whom he reiside not, if deed men risen not ayen.

16 Forwhi if deed men risen not ayen, nether Crist roos ayen;

17 and if Crist roos not ayen, oure feith is veyn; and yit ye ben in youre synnes.

18 And thanne thei that han diede in Crist, han perischid.

19 If in this life oneli we ben hoping in Crist, we ben more wretchis than alle men.

20 But now Crist roos ayen fro deth, the firste fruit of deed men;

21 for deeth was bi a man, and bi a man is ayenrisyng fro deth.

22 And as in Adam alle men dien, so in Crist alle men schulen be quykenyd.

23 But ech man in his ordre; the firste fruit, Crist, afterward thei that ben of Crist, that bileueden in the comyng of Crist;

24 aftirward an ende, whanne he schal bitake the kyngdom to God and to the fadir, whanne he schal auoide al princehod, and power, and vertu.

25 But it bihoueth hym to regne, til he putte alle hise enemyes vndur hise feet.

26 And at the laste, deth the enemye schal be distried; for he hath maad suget alle thingis vndur hise feet.

27 And whanne he seith, alle thingis ben suget to hym, with outen doubt outakun hym that sugetide alle thingis to hym.

28 And whanne alle thingis ben suget to hym, thanne the sone hym silf schal be suget to hym, that made 'alle thingis suget to hym, that God be alle thingis in alle thingis.

29 Ellis what schulen thei do, that ben baptisid for deed men, if in no wise deed men risen ayen? wherto ben thei baptisid for hem?

30 And wherto ben we in perel euery our?

31 Ech dai Y die for youre glorie, britheren, which glorie Y haue in Crist Jhesu oure Lord.

32 If aftir man Y haue fouyten to beestis at Efesi, what profitith it to me, if deed men risen not ayen? Ete we, and drynke we, for we schulen die to morewe.

33 Nyle ye be disseyued; for yuel spechis distrien good thewis.

34 Awake ye, iuste men, and nyle ye do synne; for summen han ignoraunce of God, but to reuerence Y speke to you.

35 But summan seith, Hou schulen deed men rise ayen, or in what maner bodi schulen thei come?

36 Vnwise man, that thing that thou sowist, is not quykened, but it die first;

37 and that thing that thou sowist, 'thou sowist not the bodi that is to come, but a nakid corn, as of whete, or of summe othere seedis;

38 and God yyueth to it a bodi, as he wole, and to ech of seedis a propir bodi.

39 Not ech fleisch is the same fleisch, but oon is of men, another is of beestis, another is of briddis, an othere of fischis.

40 And 'heuenli bodies ben, and 'ertheli bodies ben; but oon glorie is of heuenely bodies, and anothir is of ertheli.

41 An othere clerenesse is of the sunne, anothere clerenesse is of the moone, and anothere clerenesse is of sterris; and a sterre dyuersith fro a sterre in clerenesse.

42 And so the ayenrisyng of deed men. It is sowun in corrupcioun, it schal rise in vncorrupcioun;

43 it is sowun in vnnoblei, it schal rise in glorie; it is sowun in infirmyte, it schal rise in vertu;

44 it is sowun a beestly bodi, it schal rise a spiritual bodi. If ther is a beestli bodi, ther is also a spiritual bodi;

45 as it is writun, The firste man Adam was maad in to a soule lyuynge, the laste Adam in to a spirit quykenynge.

46 But the firste is not that that is spiritual, but that that is beestlich, aftirward that that is spiritual.

47 The firste man of erthe is ertheli; the secounde man of heuene is heuenelich.

48 Such as the ertheli man is, such ben the ertheli men; and such as the heueneli man is, suche ben also the heueneli men.

49 Therfor as we han bore the ymage of the ertheli man, bere we also the ymage of the heuenli.

50 Britheren, Y seie this thing, that fleisch and bloud moun not welde the kyngdom of God, nethir corrupcioun schal welde vncorrupcioun.

51 Lo! Y seie to you priuyte of hooli thingis. And alle we schulen rise ayen, but not alle we schulen be chaungid;

52 in a moment, in the twynklyng of an iye, in the laste trumpe; for the trumpe schal sowne, and deed men schulen rise ayen, with oute corrupcioun, and we schulen be chaungid.

53 For it byhoueth this corruptible thing to clothe vncorrupcioun, and this deedli thing to putte awei vndeedlinesse.

54 But whanne this deedli thing schal clothe vndeedlynesse, thanne schal the word be doon, that is writun, Deth is sopun vp in victorie.

55 Deth, where is thi victorie? Deth, where is thi pricke?

56 But the pricke of deth is synne; and the vertu of synne is the lawe.

57 But do we thankyngis to God, that yaf to vs victorie bi oure Lord Jhesu Crist.

58 Therfore, my dereworthe britheren, be ye stidefast, and vnmouable, beynge plenteuouse in werk of the Lord, euere more witynge that youre trauel is not idel in the Lord.

CAP 16

1 But of the gaderyngis of money that ben maad in to seyntis, as Y ordeynede in the chirchis of Galathie, so also do ye o dai of the wouke.

2 Ech of you kepe at hym silf, kepynge that that plesith to him, that whanne Y come, the gaderyngis ben not maad.

3 And whanne Y schal be present, whiche men ye preuen, Y schal sende hem bi epistlis to bere youre grace in to Jerusalem.

4 That if it be worthi that also Y go, thei schulen go with me.

5 But Y schal come to you, whanne Y schal passe bi Macedonye; for whi Y schal passe bi Macedonye.

6 But perauenture Y schal dwelle at you, or also dwelle the wynter, that and ye lede me whidir euere Y schal go.

7 And Y wole not now se you in my passyng, for Y hope to dwelle with you awhile, if the Lord schal suffre.

8 But Y schal dwelle at Efesi, 'til to Witsuntide.

9 For a grete dore and an opyn is openyd to me, and many aduersaries.

10 And if Thimothe come, se ye that he be with out drede with you, for he worcheth the werk of the Lord, as Y.

11 Therfor no man dispise hym; but lede ye hym forth in pees, that he come to me; for Y abide hym with britheren.

12 But, britheren, Y make knowun to you of Apollo, that Y preiede him myche, that he schulde come to you, with britheren. But it was not his wille to come now; but he schal come, whanne he schal haue leiser.

13 Walke ye, and stonde ye in the feith; do ye manli, and be ye coumfortid in the Lord,

14 and be alle youre thingis don in charite.

15 And, britheren, Y biseche you, ye knowen the hous of Stephan, and of Fortunati, and Acaicy, for thei ben the firste fruytis of Acaie, and in to mynystrie of seyntis thei han ordeyned hem silf;

16 that also ye be sugetis to suche, and to ech worchynge togidere and trauelynge.

17 For Y haue ioie in the presence of Stephan, and of Fortunate, and Acaici;

18 for thei filliden that thing that failide to you; for thei han refreischid bothe my spirit and youre. Therfor knowe ye hem, that ben suche maner men.

19 Alle the chirchis of Asie greten you wel. Aquila and Prisca, with her homeli chirche, greten you myche in the Lord, at the whiche also Y am herborid.

20 Alle bretheren greten you wel. Grete ye wel togidere in hooli cos.

21 My gretyng bi Poulis hoond.

22 If ony man loueth not oure Lord Jhesu Crist, be he cursid, Maranatha.

23 The grace of oure Lord Jhesu Crist be with you.

24 My charite be with you alle in Crist Jhesu oure Lord. Amen.

2 CORINTHIS

CAP 1

1 Poul, apostle of Jhesu Crist, bi the wille of God, and Tymothe, brothir, to the chirche of God that is at Corinthi, with alle seyntis that ben in al Acaie, grace to you,

2 and pees of God oure fadir and of the Lord Jhesu Crist.

3 Blessid be God and the fadir of oure Lord Jhesu Crist, fadir of mercies, and God of al coumfort,

4 which coumfortith vs in al oure tribulacioun, that also we moun coumforte hem, that ben in al diseese, bi the monestyng bi which also we ben monestid of God.

5 For as the passiouns of Crist ben plenteuouse in vs, so also bi Crist oure coumfort is plenteuouse.

6 And whether we ben in tribulacioun, for youre tribulacioun and heelthe, ethir we ben coumfortid, for youre coumfort, ethir we ben monestid, for youre monestyng and heelthe. Which worchith in you the suffring of the same passiouns, whiche 'we also suffren,

7 that oure hope be sad for you; witynge for as ye ben felowis of passiouns, so ye schulen ben also of coumfort.

8 For, britheren, we wolen that ye wite of oure tribulacioun, that was don in Asie; for ouer maner we weren greued ouer myyt, so that it anoiede vs, yhe, to lyue.

9 But we in vs silf hadden answere of deth, that we truste not in vs, but in God that reisith deed men.

10 Which delyuerede vs, and delyuerith fro so grete perelis, in to whom we hopen, also yit he schal delyuere,

11 while also ye helpen in preier for vs; that of the persones of many faces of that yyuyng that is in vs, thankyngis ben don for vs bi many men to God.

12 For oure glorie is this, the witnessyng of oure conscience, that in symplenesse and clennesse of God, and not in fleischli wisdom, but in the grace of God, we lyueden in this world, but more plenteuousli to you.

13 And we writen not othere thingis to you, than tho that ye han red and knowe, and Y hope that in to the ende ye schulen knowe,

14 as also ye han knowe vs a parti; for we ben youre glorie, as also ye ben oure in the dai of oure Lord Jhesu Crist.

15 And in this tristyng Y wolde first come to you, that ye schulden haue the secounde grace,

16 and passe bi you in to Macedonye, and eft fro Macedonye come to you, and of you be led in to Judee.

17 But whanne Y wolde this thing, whether Y vside vnstidfastnesse, ether tho thingis that Y thenke, Y thenke aftir the fleisch, that at me be, it is and it is not?

18 But God is trewe, for oure word that was at you is and is not, is not ther ynne, but is is in it.

19 For whi Jhesus Crist, the sone of God, which is prechid among you bi vs, bi me, and Syluan, and Tymothe, ther was not in hym is and is not, but is was in hym.

20 For whi hou many euer ben biheestis of God, in thilke is, 'that is, ben fillid. And therfor and bi hym we seien amen to God, to oure glorie.

21 Sotheli it is God that confermeth vs with you in Crist, and the which God anoyntide vs,

22 and which markide vs, and yaf ernes of the spirit in oure hertis.

23 For Y clepide God to witnesse ayens my soule, that Y sparynge you cam not ouer to Corynthe; not that we ben lordis of youre feith, but we ben helperis of youre ioye; for thorouy bileue ye stonden.

CAP 2

1 And Y ordeynede this ilke thing at me, that Y schulde not come eftsoone in heuynes to you.

2 For if Y make you sori, who is he that gladith me, but he that is soreuful of me?

3 And this same thing Y wroot to you, that whanne Y come, Y haue not sorewe on sorewe, of the whiche it behofte me to haue ioie. And Y triste in you alle, that my ioye is of alle you.

4 For of myche tribulacioun and angwisch of herte Y wroot to you by many teeris, not that ye be sori, but that ye wite what charite Y haue more plenteuously in you.

5 For if ony man hath maad me soreuful, he hath not maad me sorewful but a parti, that Y charge not you alle.

6 This blamyng that ys maad of manye, suffisith to hym, that is sich oon;

7 so that ayenward ye rathir foryyuen and coumfort, lest per- auenture he that is suche a maner man, be sopun vp bi more grete heuynesse.

8 For which thing Y biseche you, that ye conferme charite in to hym.

9 For whi therfor Y wroot this, that Y knowe youre preuyng, whether in alle thingis ye ben obedient.

10 For to whom ye han foryyuen ony thing, also Y haue foryyue. For Y that that Y foryaf, yif Y foryaf ony thing, haue youun for you in the persone of Crist,

11 that we be not disseyued of Sathanas; for we knowen hise thouytis.

12 But whanne Y was comun to Troade for the gospel of Crist, and a dore was opened to me in the Lord,

13 Y hadde not rest to my spirit, for Y foond not my brother Tite, but Y seide to hem farewel, and Y passide in to Mace- donye.

14 And Y do thankyngis to God, that euere more makith vs to haue victorie in Crist Jhesu, and schewith bi vs the odour of his knowing in ech place;

15 for we ben the good odour of Crist to God, among these that ben maad saaf, and among these that perischen.

16 To othere sotheli odour of deth in to deth, but to othere we ben odour of lijf in to lijf. And to these thingis who is so able?

17 For we ben not as many, that don auoutrie bi the word of God, but we speken of clennesse, as of God, bifor God in Crist.

CAP 3

1 Bigynnen we therfor eftsoone to preise vs silf? or whether we neden, as summen, pistlis of preisinge to you, or of you?

2 Ye ben oure pistle, writun in oure hertis, which is knowun and red of alle men,

3 and maad opyn, for ye ben the pistle of Crist mynystrid of vs, and writun, not with enke, but bi the spirit of the lyuynge God; not in stony tablis, but in fleischli tablis of herte.

4 For we han such trist bi Crist to God;

5 not that we ben sufficient to thenke ony thing of vs, as of vs, but oure sufficience is of God.

6 Which also made vs able mynystris of the newe testament, not bi lettre, but bi spirit; for the lettre sleeth, but the spirit quykeneth.

7 And if the mynystracioun of deth write bi lettris in stoonys was in glorie, so that the children of Israel myyten not biholde in to the face of Moises, for the glorie of his cheer, which is auoidid,

8 hou schal not the mynystracioun of the spirit be more in glorie?

9 For if the mynystracioun of dampnacioun was in glorie, myche more the mynysterie of riytwisnesse is plenteuouse in glorie.

10 For nether that that was cleer was glorified in this part for the excellent glorie; and if that that is auoidid,

11 was bi glorie, myche more that that dwellith stille is in glo- rie.

12 Therfor we that han suche hope, vsen myche trist;

13 and not as Moises leide a veil on his face, that the children of Israel schulden not biholde in to his face, which veil is auoidid.

14 But the wittis of hem ben astonyed; for in to this dai the same veil in reding of the olde testament dwellith not sche- wid, for it is auoidid in Crist, but in to this dai,

15 whanne Moises is red, the veil is put on her hertis.

16 But whanne Israel schal be conuertid to God, the veil schal be don awei.

17 And the spirit is the Lord; and where the spirit of the Lord is, there is fredom.

18 And alle we that with open face seen the glorie of the Lord, ben transformed in to the same ymage, fro clerenesse in to clerenesse, as of the spirit of the Lord.

CAP 4

1 Therfor we that han this admynystracioun, aftir this that we han getun merci,

2 faile we not, but do we awei the preue thingis of schame, not walkinge in sutil gile, nether doynge auoutrye bi the word of God, but in schewynge of the treuthe comendynge vs silf to ech conscience of men bifor God.

3 For if also oure gospel is kyuerid, in these that perischen it is kyuerid;

4 in which God hath blent the soulis of vnfeithful men of this world, that the liytnyng of the gospel of the glorie of Crist, which is the ymage of God, schyne not.

5 But we prechen not vs silf, but oure Lord Jhesu Crist; and vs youre seruauntis bi Jhesu.

6 For God, that seide liyt to schyne of derknessis, he hath youe liyt in oure hertis, to the liytnyng of the science of the clerenesse of God, in the face of Jhesu Crist.

7 And we han this tresour in britil vessels, that the worthi- nesse be of Goddis vertu, and not of vs.

8 In alle thingis we suffren tribulacioun, but we ben not ang- wischid, or annoyed; we ben maad pore, but 'we lacken noth- ing; we suffren persecucioun,

9 but we ben not forsakun; we ben maad lowe, but we ben not confoundid; we ben cast doun, but we perischen not.

10 And euere more we beren aboute the sleyng of Jhesu in oure bodi, that also the lijf of Jhesu be schewid in oure bod- ies.

11 For euere more we that lyuen, ben takun in to deth for Jhesu, that the lijf of Jhesu be schewid in oure deedli fleisch.

12 Therfor deth worchith in vs, but lijf worchith in you.

13 And we han the same spirit of feith, as it is writun, Y haue bileuyd, Y haue spoke; and we bileuen, wherfor also we spe- ken;

14 witynge that he that reiside Jhesu, schal reise also vs with Jhesu, and schal ordeyne with you.

15 And alle thingis for you, that a plenteuouse grace bi many thankyngis be plenteuouse in to the glorie of God.

16 For which thing we failen not, for thouy oure vtter man be corruptid; netheles the ynner man is renewid fro dai to dai.

17 But that liyt thing of oure tribulacioun that lastith now, but as it were by a moment, worchith in vs ouer mesure an euer- lastynge birthin in to the heiynesse of glorie;

18 while that we biholden not tho thingis that ben seyn, but tho that ben not seyn. For tho thingis that ben seyn, ben but durynge for a schort tyme; but tho thingis that ben not seyn, ben euerlastynge.

CAP 5

1 And we witen, that if oure ertheli hous of this dwellynge be dissoluyd, that we han a bildyng of God, an hous not maad bi hondis, euerlastynge in heuenes.

2 For whi in this thing we mornen, coueitynge to be clothid aboue with oure dwellyng, which is of heuene; if netheles we ben foundun clothid,

3 and not nakid.

4 For whi and we that ben in this tabernacle, sorewen with ynne, and ben heuyed, for that we wolen not be spuylid, but be clothid aboue; that the ilke thing that is deedli, be sopun vp of lijf.

5 But who is it that makith vs in to this same thing? God, that yaf to vs the ernes of the spirit.

6 Therfor we ben hardi algatis, and witen that the while we ben in this bodi, we goen in pilgrymage fro the Lord;

7 for we walken bi feith, and not bi cleer siyt.

8 But we ben hardi, and han good wille, more to be in pilgrymage fro the bodi, and to be present to God.

9 And therfor we stryuen, whether absent, whether present, to plese hym.

10 For it bihoueth vs alle to be schewid bifor the trone of Crist, that euery man telle the propre thingis of the bodi, as he hath don, ethir good, ether yuel.

11 Therfor we witynge the drede of the Lord, councelen men, for to God we ben opyn; and Y hope, that we ben opyn also in youre consciencis.

12 We comenden not vs silf eftsoone to you, but we yyuen to you occasioun to haue glorie for vs, that ye haue to hem that glorien in the face, and not in the herte.

13 For ethir we bi mynde passen to God, ether we ben sobre to you.

14 For the charite of Crist dryueth vs; gessynge this thing, that if oon died for alle, thanne alle weren deed.

15 And Crist diede for alle, that thei that lyuen, lyue not now to hem silf, but to hym that diede for hem, and roos ayen.

16 Therfor we fro this tyme knowen no man aftir the fleische; thouy we knowun Crist aftir the fleisch, but nowe we knowun not.

17 Therfor if ony newe creature is in Crist, the elde thingis ben passid.

18 And lo! alle thingis ben of God, which recounselide vs to hym bi Crist, and yaf to vs the seruyce of recounselyng.

19 And God was in Crist, recounselynge to hym the world, not rettynge to hem her giltes, and puttide in vs the word of recounselyng.

20 Therfor we vsen message for Crist, as if God monestith bi vs; we bisechen for Crist, be ye recounselid to God.

21 God the fadir made hym synne for vs, which knewe not synne, that we schulden be maad riytwisnesse of God in hym.

CAP 6

1 But we helpynge monesten, that ye resseyuen not the grace of God in veyn.

2 For he seith, In tyme wel plesinge Y haue herd thee, and in the dai of heelthe Y haue helpid thee. Lo! now a tyme acceptable, lo! now a dai of heelthe.

3 Y yue we to no man ony offencioun, that oure seruyce be not repreued;

4 but in alle thingis yyue we vs silf as the mynystris of God, in myche pacience, in tribulaciouns,

5 in nedis, in angwischis, in betyngis, in prisours, in dissensiouns with ynne, in trauels, in wakyngis, in fastyngis,

6 in chastite, in kunnyng, in long abiding, in swetnesse, in the Hooli Goost,

7 in charite not feined, in the word of treuthe, in the vertu of God; bi armeris of riytwisnesse on the riythalf and on the lefthalf;

8 bi glorie and vnnoblei; bi yuel fame and good fame; as disseyueris, and trewe men; as thei that ben vnknowun, and knowun;

9 as men diynge, and lo! we lyuen; as chastisid, and not maad deed;

10 as sorewful, euere more ioiynge; as hauynge nede, but makynge many men riche; as no thing hauynge, and weldynge alle thingis.

11 A! ye Corynthies, oure mouth is open to you, oure herte is alargid;

12 ye ben not angwischid in vs, but ye ben anguischid in youre inwardnessis.

13 And Y seie as to sones, ye that han the same reward, be ye alargid.

14 Nyle ye bere the yok with vnfeithful men. For what parting of riytwisnes with wickidnesse? or what felouschipe of liyt to derknessis?

15 and what acording of Crist to Belial? or what part of a feithful with the vnfeithful?

16 and what consent to the temple of God with mawmetis? And ye ben the temple of the lyuynge God, as the Lord seith, For Y schal dwelle in hem, and Y schal walke among hem; and Y schal be God of hem, and thei schulen be a puple to me.

17 For which thing go ye out of the myddil of hem, and be ye departid, seith the Lord, and touche ye not vnclene thing;

18 and Y schal resseyue you, and schal be to you in to a fadir, and ye schulen be to me in to sones and douytris, seith the Lord almyyti.

CAP 7

1 Therfor, most dereworthe britheren, we that han these biheestis, clense we vs fro al filthe of the fleische and of the spirit, doynge holynesse in the drede of God.

2 Take ye vs; we han hirt no man, we han apeirid no man, we han bigilid no man.

3 Y seie not to youre condempnyng; for Y seide bifor, that ye ben in youre hertis, to die togidere and to lyue togidere.

4 Myche trist is to me anentis you, myche gloriyng is to me for you. Y am fillid with coumfort, Y am plenteuouse in ioie in al oure tribulacioun.

5 For whanne we weren comun to Macedonye, oure fleisch hadde no reste, but we suffriden al tribulacioun; with outforth fiytingis, and dredis with ynne.

6 But God that coumfortith meke men, coumfortide vs in the comyng of Tite.

7 And not oneli in the comyng of him, but also in the coumfort bi which he was coumfortid in you, tellinge to vs youre desire, youre weping, youre loue for me, so that Y ioiede more.

8 For thouy Y made you sorie in a pistle, it rewith me not; thouy it rewide, seynge that thouy thilke pistle made you sori at an our, now Y haue ioie;

9 not for ye weren maad soreuful, but for ye weren maad soreuful to penaunce. For whi ye ben maad sori aftir God, that in no thing ye suffre peirement of vs.

10 For the sorewe that is aftir God, worchith penaunce in to stidfast heelthe; but sorewe of the world worchith deth.

11 For lo! this same thing, that ye ben soreuful aftir God, hou myche bisynesse it worchith in you; but defendyng, but indignacioun, but drede, but desire, but loue, but veniaunce. In alle thingis ye han youun you silf to be vndefoulid in the cause.

12 Therfor thouy Y wroot to you, Y wroot not for hym that dide the iniurie, nether for hym that suffride, but to schewe oure bisinesse, which we han for you bifor God.

13 Therfor we ben coumfortid, but in youre coumfort more plenteuousli we ioyeden more on the ioie of Tite, for his spirit is fulfillid of alle you.

14 And if Y gloriede ony thing anentis hym of you, Y am not confoundid; but as we han spoke to you alle thingis, so also oure glorie that was at Tite, is maad treuthe.

15 And the inwardnesse of hym be more plenteuousli in you, which hath in mynde the obedience of you alle, hou with drede and trembling ye resseyueden hym.

16 Y haue ioye, that in alle thingis Y triste in you.

CAP 8

1 But, britheren, we maken knowun to you the grace of God, that is youun in the chirchis of Macedonye,

2 that in myche asaiyng of tribulacioun, the plente of the ioye of hem was, and the hiyeste pouert of hem was plenteuouse 'in to the richessis of the symplenesse of hem.

3 For Y bere witnessyng to hem, aftir miyt and aboue miyt thei weren wilful,

4 with myche monestyng bisechynge vs the grace and the comynyng of mynystring, that is maad to hooli men.

5 And not as we hopiden, but thei yauen hem silf first to the Lord, aftirward to vs bi the wille of God.

6 So that we preyeden Tite, that as he bigan, so also he performe in you this grace.

7 But as ye abounden in alle thingis, in feith, and word, and kunnyng, and al bisynesse, more ouer and in youre charite in to vs, that and in this grace ye abounden.

8 Y seie not as comaundinge, but bi the bisynesse of othere men appreuynge also the good wit of youre charite.

9 And ye witen the grace of oure Lord Jhesu Crist, for he was maad nedi for you, whanne he was riche, that ye schulden be maad riche bi his nedynesse.

10 And Y yyue counsel in this thing; for this is profitable to you, that not oneli han bigunne to do, but also ye bigunnen to haue wille fro the formere yere.

11 But now parfourme ye in deed, that as the discrecioun of wille is redi, so be it also of parformyng of that that ye han.

12 For if the wille be redi, it is acceptid aftir that that it hath, not aftir that that it hath not.

13 And not that it be remyssioun to othere men, and to you tribulacioun;

14 but of euenesse in the present tyme youre aboundance fulfille the myseese of hem, that also the aboundaunce of hem be a fulfillynge of youre myseise, that euenesse be maad; as it is writun,

15 He that gaderide myche, was not encresid, and he that gaderide litil, hadde not lesse.

16 And Y do thankyngis to God, that yaf the same bisynesse for you in the herte of Tite,

17 for he resseyuede exortacioun; but whanne he was bisier, bi his wille he wente forth to you.

18 And we senten with hym a brother, whose preisyng is in the gospel bi alle chirchis.

19 And not oneli, but also he is ordeyned of chirchis the felowe of oure pilgrimage in to this grace, that is mynystrid of vs to the glorie of the Lord, and to oure ordeyned wille;

20 eschewynge this thing, that no man blame vs in this plente, that is mynystrid of vs to the glorye of the Lord.

21 For we purueyen good thingis, not onely bifor God, but also bifor alle men.

22 For we senten with hem also oure brothir, whom we han preued in many thingis ofte, that he was bisi, but nowe myche bisier, for myche trist in you,

23 ethir for Tite, that is my felowe and helpere in you, ethir for oure britheren, apostlis of the chirches of the glorie of Crist.

24 Therfor schewe ye in to hem in the face of chirchis, that schewynge that is of youre charite and of oure glorie for you.

CAP 9

1 For of the mynystrie that is maad to hooli men, it is to me of plente to write to you.

2 For Y knowe youre wille, for the which Y haue glorie of you anentis Macedonyes, for also Acaie is redi fro a yeer passid, and youre loue hath stirid ful manye.

3 And we han sent britheren, that this thing that we glorien of you, be not auoidid in this parti, that as Y seide, ye be redi.

4 Lest whanne Macedonyes comen with me, and fynden you vnredi, we be schamed, that we seien you not, in this substaunce.

5 Therfor Y gesside necessarie to preie britheren, that thei come bifore to you, and make redi this bihiyt blessyng to be redi, so as blessing, and not as aueryce.

6 For Y seie this thing, he that sowith scarseli, schal also repe scarseli; and he that sowith in blessyngis, schal 'repe also of blessyngis.

7 Ech man as he castide in his herte, not of heuynesse, or of nede; for God loueth a glad yyuere.

8 And God is miyti to make al grace abounde in you, that ye in alle thingis euere more han al sufficience, and abounde in to al good werk;

9 as it is writun, He delide abrood, he yaf to pore men, his riytwisnesse dwellith withouten ende.

10 And he that mynystrith seed to the sowere, schal yyue also breed to ete, and he schal multiplie youre seed, and make myche the encreessingis of fruytis of youre riytwisnesse;

11 that in alle thingis ye maad riche waxen plenteuouse in to al symplenesse, which worchith bi vs doing of thankingis to God.

12 For the mynystrie of this office not oneli fillith tho thingis that failen to holi men, but also multiplieth many thankyngis to God,

13 bi the preuyng of this mynystrie, which glorifien God in the obedience of youre knouleching in the gospel of Crist, and in symplenesse of comynycacioun in to hem and in to alle,

14 and in the biseching of hem for you, that desiren you for the excellent grace of God in you.

15 Y do thankyngis to God of the yifte of hym, that may not be teld.

CAP 10

1 And Y my silf Poul biseche you, bi the myldenesse and softnesse of Crist, which in the face am meke among you, and Y absent triste in you.

2 For Y preie you, that lest Y present be not bold bi the trist, in which Y am gessid to be bold in to summe, that demen vs, as if we wandren aftir the fleisch.

3 For we walkynge in fleisch, fiyten not aftir the fleisch.

4 For the armuris of oure knyythod ben not fleischli, but myyti bi God to the distruccioun of strengthis. And we distrien counsels,

5 and alle hiynesse that hiyeth it silf ayens the science of God, and dryuen 'in to caitifte al vndirstonding in to the seruyce of Crist.

6 And we han redi to venge al vnobedience, whanne youre obedience schal be fillid.

7 Se ye the thingis that ben after the face. If ony man trustith to him silf, that he is of Crist, thenke he this thing eft anentis hym silf,

8 for as he is Cristis, so also we. For if Y schal glorie ony thing more of oure power, which the Lord yaf to vs in to edifiyng, and not in to youre distruccioun, Y schal not be schamed.

9 But that Y be not gessid as to fere you bi epistlis,

10 for thei seien, That epistlis ben greuouse and stronge, but the presence of the bodi is feble, and the word worthi to be dispisid.

11 He that is suche oon, thenke this, for suche as we absent ben in word bi pistlis, suche we ben present in dede.

12 For we doren not putte vs among, or comparisoune vs to summen, that comenden hem silf; but we mesuren vs in vs silf, and comparisounen vs silf to vs.

13 For we schulen not haue glorie ouer mesure, but bi the mesure of the reule which God mesuride to vs, the mesure that stretchith to you.

14 For we ouerstretchen not forth vs, as not stretchinge to you. For to you we camen in the gospel of Crist,

15 not gloriynge ouer mesure in othere mennus trauelis. For we 'han hope of youre feith that wexith in you to be magnefied bi oure reule in abundaunce,

16 also to preche in to tho thingis that ben biyendis you, not to haue glorie in othere mennus reule, in these thingis that ben maad redi.

17 He that glorieth, haue glorie in the Lord.

18 For not he that comendith hym silf is preuyd, but whom God comendith.

CAP 11

1 I wolde that ye wolden suffre a litil thing of myn vnwisdom, but also supporte ye me.

2 For Y loue you bi the loue of God; for Y haue spousid you to oon hosebonde, to yelde a chast virgyn to Crist.

3 But Y drede, lest as the serpent disseyuede Eue with his sutil fraude, so youre wittis ben corrupt, and fallen doun fro the symplenesse that is in Crist.

4 For if he that cometh, prechith anothir Crist, whom we precheden not, or if ye taken another spirit, whom ye token not, or another gospel, which ye resseyueden not, riytli ye schulden suffre.

5 For Y wene that Y haue don no thing lesse than the grete apostlis.

6 For thouy Y be vnlerud in word, but not in kunnyng. For in alle thingis Y am open to you.

7 Or whether Y haue don synne, mekynge my silf, that ye be enhaunsid, for freli Y prechide to you the gospel of God?

8 Y made nakid othere chirchis, and Y took sowde to youre seruyce.

9 And whanne Y was among you, and hadde nede, Y was chargeouse to no man; for britheren that camen fro Macedonye, fulfilliden that that failide to me. And in alle thingis Y haue kept, and schal kepe me with outen charge to you.

10 The treuthe of Crist is in me; for this glorie schal not be brokun in me in the cuntreis of Acaie.

11 Whi? for Y loue not you?

12 God woot. For that that Y do, and that Y schal do, is that Y kitte awei the occasioun of hem that wolen occasioun, that in the thing, in which thei glorien, thei be foundun as we.

13 For siche false apostlis ben trecherouse werk men, and transfiguren hem in to apostlis of Crist.

14 And no wondur, for Sathanas hym silf transfigurith hym in to an aungel of light.

15 Therfor it is not greet, if hise mynystris ben transfigurid as the mynystris of riytwisnesse, whos ende schal be aftir her werkis.

16 Eft Y seie, lest ony man gesse me to be vnwise; ellis take ye me as vnwise, that also Y haue glorie a litil what.

17 That that Y speke, Y speke not aftir God, but as in vnwisdom, in this substaunce of glorie.

18 For many men glorien aftir the fleisch, and Y schal glorie.

19 For ye suffren gladli vnwise men, whanne ye silf ben wise.

20 For ye susteynen, if ony man dryueth you in to seruage, if ony man deuourith, if ony man takith, if ony man is enhaunsid, if ony man smytith you on the face.

21 Bi vnnoblei Y seie, as if we weren sike in this parti. In what thing ony man dar, in vnwisdom Y seie, and Y dar.

22 Thei ben Ebrewis, and Y; thei ben Israelitis, and Y; thei ben the seed of Abraham, and Y;

23 thei ben the mynystris of Crist, and Y. As lesse wise Y seie, Y more; in ful many trauelis, in prisouns more plenteuousli, in woundis aboue maner, in deethis ofte tymes.

24 Y resseyuede of the Jewis fyue sithis fourti strokis oon lesse;

25 thries Y was betun with yerdis, onys Y was stonyd, thries Y was at shipbreche, a nyyt and a dai Y was in the depnesse of the see;

26 in weies ofte, in perelis of floodis, in perelis of theues, in perelis of kyn, in perelis of hethene men, in perelis in citee, in perelis in desert, in perelis in the see, in perelis among false britheren, in trauel and nedynesse,

27 in many wakyngis, in hungur, in thirst, in many fastyngis, in coold and nakidnesse.

28 Withouten tho thingis that ben withoutforth, myn ech daies trauelyng is the bisynesse of alle chirchis.

29 Who is sijk, and Y am not sijk? who is sclaundrid, and Y am not brent?

30 If it bihoueth to glorie, Y schal glorie in tho thingis that ben of myn infirmyte.

31 God and the fadir of oure Lord Jhesu Crist, that is blessid in to worldis, woot that Y lie not.

32 The preuost of Damask, of the kyng of the folk Arethe, kepte the citee of Damascenes to take me;

33 and bi a wyndow in a leep Y was latun doun bi the wal, and so Y ascapide hise hondis.

CAP 12

1 If it bihoueth to haue glorie, it spedith not; but Y schal come to the visiouns and to the reuelaciouns of the Lord.

2 I woot a man in Crist that bifore fouretene yeer; whether in bodi, whether out of the bodi, Y woot not, God woot; that siche a man was rauyschid 'til to the thridde heuene.

3 And Y woot sich a man; whether in bodi, or out of bodi, Y noot, God woot;

4 that he was rauyschid in to paradis, and herde preuy wordis, whiche it is not leueful to a man to speke.

5 For such maner thingis Y schal glorie; but for me no thing, no but in myn infirmytees.

6 For if Y schal wilne to glorie, Y schal not be vnwijs, for Y schal seie treuthe; but Y spare, lest ony man gesse me ouer that thing that he seeth in me, or herith ony thing of me.

7 And lest the greetnesse of reuelaciouns enhaunse me in pride, the pricke of my fleisch, an aungel of Sathanas, is youun to me, that he buffate me.

8 For whiche thing thries Y preiede the Lord, that it schulde go awei fro me.

9 And he seide to me, My grace suffisith to thee; for vertu is parfitli maad in infirmyte. Therfor gladli Y schal glorie in myn infirmytees, that the vertu of Crist dwelle in me.

10 For which thing Y am plesid in myn infirmytees, in dispisyngis, in nedis, in persecuciouns, in anguyschis, for Crist; for whanne Y am sijk, thanne Y am miyti.

11 Y am maad vnwitti, ye constreyneden me. For Y ouyte to be comendid of you; for Y dide no thing lesse than thei that ben apostlis 'aboue maner.

12 Thouy Y am nouyt, netheles the signes of myn apostilhed ben maad on you, in al pacience, and signes, and grete wondris, and vertues.

13 And what is it, that ye hadden lesse than othere chirchis, but that Y my silf greuyde you not? Foryyue ye to me this wrong.

14 Lo! this thridde tyme Y am redi to come to you, and Y schal not be greuous to you; for Y seke not tho thingis that ben youre, but you. For nether sones owen to tresoure to fadir and modir, but the fadir and modir to the sones.

15 For Y schal yyue moost wilfuli, and Y my silf schal be youun aboue for youre soulis; thouy Y more loue you, and be lesse louyd.

16 But be it; Y greuyde not you, but whanne Y was sutil, Y took you with gile.

17 Whether Y disseyuede you bi ony of hem, which Y sente to you?

18 Y preiede Tite, and Y sente with hym a brother. Whether Tite begilide you? whether we yeden not in the same spirit? whether not in the same steppis?

19 Sum tyme ye wenen, that we schulen excuse vs anentis you. Bifor God in Crist we speken; and, moost dere britheren, alle thingis for youre edifiyng.

20 But Y drede, lest whanne Y come, Y schal fynde you not suche as Y wole, and Y schal be foundun of you suche as ye wolen not; lest perauenture stryuyngis, enuyes, sturdynessis, dissenciouns and detraccions, preuy spechis of discord, bolnyngis bi pride, debatis ben among you;

21 and lest eftsoone whanne Y come, God make me low anentis you, and Y biweile many of hem, that bifor synneden, and diden not penaunce on the vnclennesse, and fornicacioun, and vnchastite, that thei han don.

CAP 13

1 Lo! this thridde tyme Y come to you, and in the mouth of tweyne or of thre witnessis euery word schal stonde.

2 Y seide bifor, and seie bifor, as present twies, and now absent, to hem that bifor han synned, and to alle othere; for if Y come eftsoone, Y schal not spare.

3 Whether ye seken the preef of that Crist, that spekith in me, which is not feble in you?

4 For thouy he was crucified of infirmyte, but he lyueth of the vertu of God. For also we ben sijk in hym, but we schulen lyue with him of the vertu of God in vs.

5 Asaie you silf, if ye ben in the feith; ye you silf preue. Whether ye knowen not you silf, for Crist Jhesu is in you? but in happe ye ben repreuable.

6 But Y hope, that ye knowen, that we ben not repreuable.

7 And we preien the Lord, that ye do no thing of yuel; not that we seme preued, but that ye do that that is good, and that we ben as repreuable.

8 For we moun no thing ayens treuthe, but for the treuthe.

9 For we ioyen, whanne we ben sijk, but ye ben myyti; and we preien this thing, youre perfeccioun.

10 Therfor Y absent write these thingis, that Y present do not hardere, bi the powere, which the Lord yaf to me in to edificacioun, and not in to youre distruccioun.

11 Britheren, 'hennus forward ioye ye, be ye perfit, excite ye; vndurstonde ye the same thing; haue ye pees, and God of pees and of loue schal be with you.

12 Grete ye wel togidere in hooli cos. Alle hooli men greten you wel.

13 The grace of oure Lord Jhesu Crist, and the charite of God, and the comynyng of the Hooli Gost, be with 'you alle. Amen.

GALATHIES

CAP 1

1 Poul the apostle, not of men, ne bi man, but bi Jhesu Crist, and God the fadir,

2 that reiside hym fro deth, and alle the britheren that ben with me, to the chirchis of Galathie,

3 grace to you and pees of God the fadir, and of the Lord Jhesu Crist,

4 that yaf hym silf for oure synnes, to delyuere vs fro the present wickid world, bi the wille of God and of oure fadir,

5 to whom is worschip and glorie in to worldis of worldis. Amen.

6 I wondur, that so soone ye be thus moued fro hym that clepid you in to the grace of Crist, in to another euangelie; which is not anothir,

7 but that ther ben summe that troublen you, and wolen mysturne the euangelie of Crist.

8 But thouy we, or an aungel of heuene, prechide to you, bisidis that that we han prechid to you, be he acursid.

9 As Y haue seid bifore, and now eftsoones Y seie, if ony preche to you bisidis that that ye han vndurfongun, be he cursid.

10 For now whether counsele Y men, or God? or whether Y seche to plese men? If Y pleside yit men, Y were not Cristis seruaunt.

11 For, britheren, Y make knowun to you the euangelie, that was prechid of me, for it is not bi man;

12 ne Y took it of man, ne lernyde, but bi reuelacioun of Jhesu Crist.

13 For ye han herd my conuersacioun sumtyme in the Jurie, and that Y pursuede passyngli the chirche of God, and fauyt ayen it.

14 And Y profitide in the Jurie aboue many of myn eueneldis in my kynrede, and was more aboundauntli a folewere of my fadris tradiciouns.

15 But whanne it pleside hym, that departide me fro my modir wombe,

16 and clepide bi his grace, to schewe his sone in me, that Y schulde preche hym among the hethene, anoon Y drowy me not to fleisch and blood; ne Y cam to Jerusalem to the apostlis,

17 that weren tofor me, but Y wente in to Arabie, and eftsoones Y turnede ayen in to Damask.

18 And sith thre yeer aftir Y cam to Jerusalem, to se Petre, and Y dwellide with hym fiftene daies;

19 but Y sawy noon othere of the apostlis, but James, oure Lordis brother.

20 And these thingis which Y write to you, lo! tofor God Y lie not.

21 Afterward Y cam in to the coostis of Syrie and Cilicie.

22 But Y was vnknowun bi face to the chirchis of Judee, that weren in Crist; and thei hadden oonli an heryng,

23 that he that pursuede vs sum tyme, prechide now the feith, ayens which he fauyte sum tyme;

24 and in me thei glorifieden God.

CAP 2

1 And sith fourtene yeer aftir, eftsones Y wente vp to Jerusalem with Barnabas, and took with me Tite.

2 Y wente vp bi reuelacioun, and spak with hem the euangelie, which Y preche among the hethene; and bi hem silf to these that semeden to be sumwhat, lest Y runne, or hadde runne in veyne.

3 And nother Tite, that hadde be with me, while he was hethene, was compellid to be circumsidid;

4 but for false britheren that weren brouyt ynne, whiche hadden entrid to aspie oure fredom, which we han in Jhesu Crist, to bring vs in to seruage.

5 But we yyue no place to subieccioun, that the treuthe of the gospel schulde dwelle with you.

6 But of these that semeden to be sumwhat; whiche thei weren sum tyme, it perteyneth not to me, for God takith not the persoone of man; for thei that semeden to be sumwhat, yauen me no thing.

7 But ayenward, whanne thei hadden seyn, that the euangelie of prepucie was youun to me, as the euangelie of circumcisioun was youun to Petre;

8 for he that wrouyte to Petre in apostlehed of circumcisioun, wrouyte also to me among the hethene;

9 and whanne thei hadden knowe the grace of God, that was youun to me, James, and Petre, and Joon, whiche weren seyn to be the pileris, thei yauen riythond of felowschip to me and to Barnabas, that we among the hethene, and thei in to circumcisioun;

10 oneli that we hadde mynde of pore men 'of Crist, the which thing Y was ful bisi to doon.

11 But whanne Petre was comun to Antioche, Y ayenstood hym in the face, for he was worthi to be vndirnommen.

12 For bifor that ther camen summen fro James, he eete with the hethene men; but whanne thei weren comun, he withdrowy, and departide hym, dredinge hem that weren of circumcisioun.

13 And the othere Jewis assentiden to his feynyng, so that Barnabas was drawun of hem in to that feynyng.

14 But whanne Y sawy, that thei walkiden not riytli to the treuthe of the gospel, Y seide to Petre bifor alle men, If thou, that art a Jew, lyuest hethenlich, and not Jewelich, hou constreynest thou hethene men to bicome Jewis?

15 We Jewis of kynde, and not synful men of the hethene,

16 knowen that a man is not iustified of the werkis of lawe, but bi the feith of Jhesu Crist; and we bileuen in Jhesu Crist, that we ben iustified of the feith of Crist, and not of the werkis of lawe. Wherfor of the werkis of lawe ech fleisch schal not be iustified.

17 And if we sechen to be iustified in Crist, we oure silf ben foundun synful men, whether Crist be mynystre of synne?

18 God forbede. And if Y bylde ayen thingis that Y haue distruyed, Y make my silf a trespassour.

19 For bi the lawe Y am deed to the lawe, and Y am fitchid to the crosse, that Y lyue to God with Crist.

20 And now lyue not Y, but Crist lyueth in me. But that Y lyue now in fleisch, Y lyue in the feith of Goddis sone, that louede me, and yaf hym silf for me.

21 Y caste not awey the grace of God; for if riytwisnesse be thoruy lawe, thanne Crist diede with out cause.

CAP 3

1 Vnwitti Galathies, tofor whos iyen Jhesu Crist is exilid, and is crucified in you, who hath disseyued you, that ye obeyen not to treuthe?

2 This oneli Y wilne to lerne of you, whether ye han vndurfonge the spirit of werkis of the lawe, or of heryng of bileue?

3 So ye ben foolis, that whanne ye han bigunne in spirit, ye ben endid in fleisch.

4 So grete thingis ye han suffrid without cause, if it be withoute cause.

5 He that yyueth to you spirit, and worchith vertues in you, whether of werkis of the lawe, or of hering of bileue?

6 As it is writun, Abraham bileuede to God, and it was rettid to hym to riytfulnesse.

7 And therfor knowe ye, that these that ben of bileue, ben the sones of Abraham.

8 And the scripture seynge afer, that God iustifieth the hethene, of bileue told tofor to Abraham, That in thee alle the hethene schulen be blessid.

9 And therfor these that ben of bileue, schulen be blessid with feithful Abraham.

10 For alle that ben of the werkis of the lawe, ben vndur curse; for it is writun, Ech man is cursid, that abidith not in alle thingis that ben writun in the book of the lawe, to do tho thingis.

11 And that no man is iustified in the lawe bifor God, it is opyn, for a riytful man lyueth of bileue.

12 But the lawe is not of bileue, but he that doith tho thingis of the lawe, schal lyue in hem.

13 But Crist ayenbouyte us fro the curse of the lawe, and was maad acursid for vs; for it is writun, Ech man is cursid that hangith in the tre;

14 that among the hethene the blessyng of Abraham were maad in 'Crist Jhesu, that we vndurfonge the biheeste of spirit thoruy bileue.

15 Britheren, Y seie aftir man, no man dispisith the testament of a man that is confermed, or ordeyneth aboue.

16 The biheestis weren seid to Abraham and to his seed; he seith not, In seedis, as in many, but as in oon, And to thi seed, that is, Crist.

17 But Y seie, this testament is confermed of God; the lawe that was maad after foure hundrid and thritti yeer, makith not the testament veyn to auoide awei the biheest.

18 For if eritage were of the lawe, it were not now of biheeste. But God grauntide to Abraham thoruy biheest.

19 What thanne the lawe? It was sett for trespassing, to the seed come, to whom he hadde maad his biheest. Whiche lawe was ordeyned bi aungels, in the hoond of a mediatour. But a mediatour is not of oon. But God is oon.

21 Is thanne the lawe ayens the biheestis of God? God forbede. For if the lawe were youun, that myyte quikene, verili were riytfulnesse of lawe.

22 But scripture hath concludid alle thingis vndir synne, that the biheeste of the feith of Jhesu Crist were yyuen to hem that bileuen.

23 And tofor that bileue cam, thei weren kept vndur the lawe, enclosid in to that bileue that was to be schewid.

24 And so the lawe was oure vndirsmaister in Crist, that we ben iustified of bileue.

25 But aftir that bileue cam, we ben not now vndur the vndurmaistir.

26 For alle ye ben the children of God thoruy the bileue of Jhesu Crist.

27 For alle ye that ben baptisid, ben clothid with Crist.

28 Ther is no Jewe, ne Greke, ne bond man, ne fre man, ne male, ne female; for alle ye ben oon in 'Jhesu Crist.

29 And if ye ben oon in 'Jhesu Crist, thanne ye ben the seed of Abraham, and eiris bi biheest.

CAP 4

1 But Y seie, as long tyme as the eir is a litil child, he dyuersith no thing fro a seruaunt, whanne he is lord of alle thingis;

2 but he is vndur keperis and tutoris, in to the tyme determyned of the fadir.

3 So we, whanne we weren litle children, we serueden vndur the elementis of the world.

4 But aftir that the fulfilling of tyme cam, God sente his sone,

5 maad of a womman, maad vndur the lawe, that he schulde ayenbie hem that weren vndur the lawe, that we schulden vnderfonge the adopcioun of sones.

6 And for ye ben Goddis sones, God sente his spirit in to youre hertis, criynge, Abba, fadir.

7 And so ther is not now a seruaunt, but a sone; and if he is a sone, he is an eir bi God.

8 But thanne ye vnknowynge God, serueden to hem that in kynde weren not goddis.

9 But now whanne ye han knowe God, and ben knowun of God, hou ben ye turned eftsoone to the febil and nedi elementis, to the whiche ye wolen eft serue?

10 Ye taken kepe to daies, and monethis, and tymes, and yeris.

11 But Y drede you, lest without cause Y haue trauelid among you.

12 Be ye as Y, for Y am as ye. Britheren, Y biseche you, ye han hurt me no thing.

13 But ye knowen, that bi infirmyte of fleisch Y haue prechid to you now bifore;

14 and ye dispiseden not, nether forsoken youre temptacioun in my fleisch, but ye resseyueden me as an aungel of God, as 'Crist Jhesu.

15 Where thanne is youre blessyng? For Y bere you witnesse, that if it myyte haue be don. ye wolden haue put out youre iyen, and haue yyuen hem to me.

16 Am Y thanne maad an enemye to you, seiynge to you the sothe?

17 Thei louen not you wel, but thei wolen exclude you, that ye suen hem.

18 But sue ye the good euermore in good, and not oneli whanne Y am present with you.

19 My smale children, whiche Y bere eftsoones, til that Crist be fourmed in you,

20 and Y wolde now be at you, and chaunge my vois, for Y am confoundid among you.

21 Seie to me, ye that wolen be vndir the lawe, 'han ye not red the lawe?

22 For it is writun, that Abraham hadde two sones, oon of a seruaunt, and oon of a fre womman.

23 But he that was of the seruaunt, was borun after the flesh; but he that was of the fre womman, by a biheeste.

24 The whiche thingis ben seid bi an othir vndirstonding. For these ben two testamentis; oon in the hille of Synai, gendringe in to seruage, which is Agar.

25 For Syna is an hille that is in Arabie, which hille is ioyned to it that is now Jerusalem, and seruith with hir children.

26 But that Jerusalem that is aboue, is fre, whiche is oure modir.

27 For it is writun, Be glad, thou bareyn, that berist not; breke out and crye, that bringist forth no children; for many sones ben of hir that is left of hir hosebonde, more than of hir that hath an hosebonde.

28 For, britheren, we ben sones of biheeste aftir Isaac;

29 but now as this that was borun after the fleisch pursuede him that was aftir the spirit, so now.

30 But what seith the scripture? Caste out the seruaunt and hir sone, for the sone of the seruaunt schal not be eir with the sone of the fre wijf.

31 And so, britheren, we ben not sones of the seruaunt, but of the fre wijf, bi which fredom Crist hath maad vs fre.

CAP 5

1 Stonde ye therfor, and nyl ye eftsoones be holdun in the yok of seruage.

2 Lo! Y Poul seie to you, that if ye ben circumcidid, Crist schal no thing profite to you.

3 And Y witnesse eftsoones to ech man that circumcidith hym silf, that he is dettour of al the lawe to be don.

4 And ye ben voidid awei fro Crist, and ye that be iustified in the lawe, ye han fallen awei fro grace.

5 For we thoruy the spirit of bileue abiden the hope of riytfulnesse.

6 For in Jhesu Crist nether circumcisioun is ony thing worth, nether prepucie, but the bileue that worchith bi charite.

7 Ye runnen wel; who lettide you that ye obeyede not to treuthe?

8 Consente ye to no man; for this counsel ys not of hym that hath clepid you.

9 A litil souredowy apeirith al the gobet.

10 I trust on you in oure Lord, that ye schulden vndurstonde noon other thing. And who that disturblith you, schal bere dom, who euere he be.

11 And, britheren, if Y preche yit circumcisioun, what suffre Y yit persecucioun? thanne the sclaundre of the crosse is auoidid.

12 Y wolde that thei weren cut awei, that disturblen you.

13 For, britheren, ye ben clepid in to fredom; oneli yyue ye not fredom in to occasioun of fleisch, but bi charite of spirit serue ye togidere.

14 For euery lawe is fulfillid in o word, Thou schalt loue thi neiybore as thi silf.

15 And if ye bite, and ete ech othere, se ye, lest ye be wastid ech fro othere.

16 And Y seie you in Crist, walke ye in spirit, and ye schulen not performe the desiris of the fleisch.

17 For the fleisch coueitith ayens the spirit, and the spirit ayen the fleisch; for these ben aduersaries togidere, that ye don not alle thingis that ye wolen.

18 That if ye be led bi spirit, ye ben not vnder the lawe.

19 And werkis of the fleisch ben opyn, whiche ben fornicacioun, vnclennes, vnchastite, letcherie, seruice of false goddis,

20 witchecraftis, enmytees, striuyngis, indignaciouns, wrathis, chidingis, discenciouns, sectis, enuyes,

21 manslauytris, dronkennessis, vnmesurable etyngis, and thingis lijk to these, whiche Y seie to you, as Y haue told to you 'to fore, for thei that doon suche thingis, schulen not haue the kyngdom of God.

22 But the fruyt of the spirit is charite, ioye, pees, pacience, long abidyng,

23 benygnyte, goodnesse, myldenesse, feith, temperaunce, contynence, chastite; ayen suche thingis is no lawe.

24 And they that ben of Crist, han crucified her fleisch with vices and coueytyngis.

25 If we lyuen bi spirit, walke we bi spirit; be we not made coueytouse of veyn glorie, stirynge ech othere to wraththe, or hauynge enuye ech to othere.

CAP 6

1 Britheren, if a man be occupied in ony gilt, ye that ben spiritual, enforme ye such oon in spirit of softnesse, biholdinge thi silf, lest that thou be temptid.

2 Ech bere othere chargis, and so ye schulen fulfille the lawe of Crist.

3 For who that trowith that he be ouyt, whanne he is nouyt, he bigilith him silf.

4 But ech man preue his owne werk, and so he schal haue glorie in him silf, and not in an othere.

5 For ech man schal bere his owne charge.

6 He that is tauyt bi word, comune he with him that techith hym, in 'alle goodis.

7 Nyle ye erre, God is not scorned;

8 for tho thingis that a man sowith, tho thingis he schal repe. For he that sowith in his fleisch, of the fleisch he schal repe corrupcioun; but he that sowith in the spirit, of the spirit he schal repe euerelastynge lijf.

9 And doynge good faile we not; for in his tyme we schal repe, not failinge.

10 Therfor while we han tyme, worche we good to alle men; but most to hem that ben homliche of the feith.

11 Se ye, what maner lettris Y haue write to you with myn owne hoond.

12 For who euere wole plese in the fleisch, 'this constreyneth you to be circumcidid, oonli that thei suffren not the persecucioun of Cristis crosse.

13 For nether thei that ben circumcidid kepen the lawe; but thei wolen that ye be circumcidid, that thei haue glorie in youre fleisch.

14 But fer be it fro me to haue glorie, no but in the crosse of oure Lord Jhesu Crist, bi whom the world is crucified to me, and Y to the world.

15 For in Jhesu Crist nether circumcisioun is ony thing worth, ne prepucie, but a newe creature.

16 And who euere suwen this reule, pees on hem, and merci, and on Israel of God.

17 And heraftir no man be heuy to me; for Y bere in my bodi the tokenes of oure Lord Jhesu Crist.

18 The grace of oure Lord Jhesu Crist be with youre spirit, britheren. Amen.

EFFESIES

CAP 1

1 Poul, the apostle of Jhesu Crist, bi the wille of God, to alle seyntis that ben at Effesie, and to the feithful men in Jhesu Crist,

2 grace be to you and pees of God, oure fader, and oure Lord Jhesu Crist.

3 Blessid be God and the fadir of oure Lord Jhesu Crist, that hath blessid vs in al spiritual blessing in heuenli thingis in Crist,

4 as he hath chosun vs in hym silf bifor the makyng of the world, that we weren hooli, and with out wem in his siyt, in charite.

5 Which hath bifor ordeyned vs in to adopcioun of sones bi Jhesu Crist in to hym, bi the purpos of his wille,

6 in to the heriyng of the glorie of his grace;

7 in which he hath glorified vs in his dereworthe sone. In whom we han redempcioun bi his blood, foryyuenesse of synnes, aftir the ritchessis of his grace,

8 that aboundide greetli in vs in al wisdom and prudence,

9 to make knowun to vs the sacrament of his wille, bi the good plesaunce of hym; the which sacrament he purposide in

10 hym in the dispensacioun of plente of tymes to enstore alle thingis in Crist, whiche ben in heuenes, and whiche ben in erthe, in hym.

11 In whom we ben clepid bi sort, bifor ordeyned bi the purpos of hym that worchith alle thingis bi the counsel of his wille;

12 that we be in to the heriyng of his glorie, we that han hopid bifor in Crist.

13 In whom also ye weren clepid, whanne ye herden the word of treuthe, the gospel of youre heelthe, in whom ye bileuynge ben merkid with the Hooli Goost of biheest, which is the ernes of oure eritage,

14 in to the redempcioun of purchasyng, in to heriyng of his glorie.

15 Therfor and Y herynge youre feith, that is in Crist Jhesu, and the loue in to alle seyntis,

16 ceesse not to do thankyngis for you, makynge mynde of you in my preieris;

17 that God of oure Lord Jhesu Crist, the fadir of glorie, yyue to you the spirit of wisdom and of reuelacioun, in to the knowyng of hym;

18 and the iyen of youre herte liytned, that ye wite, which is the hope of his clepyng, and whiche ben the richessis of the glorie of his eritage in seyntis;

19 and whych is the excellent greetnesse of his vertu in to vs that han bileuyd, bi the worchyng of the myyt of his vertu,

20 which he wrouyte in Crist, reisynge hym fro deth, and settynge him on his riyt half in heuenli thingis,

21 aboue ech principat, and potestat, and vertu, and domynacioun, and aboue ech name that is named, not oneli in this world, but also in the world to comynge;

22 and made alle thingis suget vndur hise feet, and yaf hym to be heed ouer al the chirche,

23 that is the bodi of hym, and the plente of hym, which is alle thingis in alle thingis fulfillid.

CAP 2

1 And whanne ye weren deed in youre giltis and synnes,
2 in which ye wandriden sum tyme aftir the cours of this world, aftir the prince of the power of this eir, of the spirit that worchith now in to the sones of vnbileue;
3 in which also we 'alle lyueden sum tyme in the desiris of oure fleisch, doynge the willis of the fleisch and of thouytis, and we weren bi kynde the sones of wraththe, as othere men;
4 but God, that is riche in merci, for his ful myche charite in which he louyde vs,
5 yhe, whanne we weren deed in synnes, quikenede vs togidere in Crist, bi whos grace ye ben sauyd, and ayen rei-side togidere,
6 and made togidere to sitte in heuenli thingis in Crist Jhesu;
7 that he schulde schewe in the worldis aboue comynge the plenteuouse ritchessis of his grace in goodnesse on vs in Crist Jhesu.
8 For bi grace ye ben sauyd bi feith, and this not of you; for it is the yifte of God,
9 not of werkis, that no man haue glorie.
10 For we ben the makyng of hym, maad of nouyt in Crist Jhesu, in good werkis, whiche God hath ordeyned, that we go in tho werkis.
11 For which thing be ye myndeful, that sumtyme ye weren hethene in fleisch, which weren seid prepucie, fro that that is seid circumcisioun maad bi hond in fleisch;
12 and ye weren in that time with out Crist, alienyd fro the lyuyng of Israel, and gestis of testamentis, not hauynge hope of biheest, and with outen God in this world.
13 But now in Crist Jhesu ye that weren sum tyme fer, ben maad nyy in the blood of Crist.
14 For he is oure pees, that made bothe oon, and vnbyndynge the myddil wal of a wal with out morter, enmytees in his fleisch;
15 and auoidide the lawe of maundementis bi domes, that he make twei in hym silf in to a newe man,
16 makynge pees, to recounsele bothe in o bodi to God bi the cros, sleynge the enemytees in hym silf.
17 And he comynge prechide pees to you that weren fer, and pees to hem that weren niy;
18 for bi hym we bothe han niy comyng in o spirit to the fadir.
19 Therfor now ye ben not gestis and straungeris, but ye ben citeseyns of seyntis, and houshold meine of God;
20 aboue bildid on the foundement of apostlis and of profetis, vpon that hiyeste corner stoon, Crist Jhesu;
21 in whom ech bildyng maad waxith in to an hooli temple in the Lord;
22 In whom also 'be ye bildid togidere in to the habitacle of God, in the Hooli Goost.

CAP 3

1 For the grace of this thing I Poul, the boundun of Crist Jhesu, for you hethene men,
2 if netheles ye han herd the dispensacioun of Goddis grace, that is youun to me in you.
3 For bi reuelacioun the sacrament is maad knowun to me, as Y aboue wroot in schort thing,
4 as ye moun rede, and vndurstonde my prudence in the mys-terie of Crist.

5 Which was not knowun to othere generaciouns to the sones of men, as it is now schewid to his hooli apostlis and prophe-tis in the spirit,
6 that hethene men ben euen eiris, and of oo bodi, and parten-eris togidere of his biheest in Crist Jhesu bi the euangelie;
7 whos mynystre Y am maad, bi the yifte of Goddis grace, which is youun to me bi the worchyng of his vertu.
8 To me, leeste of alle seyntis, this grace is youun to preche among hethene men the vnserchable richessis of Crist, and to liytne alle men,
9 which is the dispensacioun of sacrament hid fro worldis in God, that made alle thingis of nouyt;
10 that the myche fold wisdom of God be knowun to princis and potestatis in heuenli thingis bi the chirche,
11 bi the bifore ordinaunce of worldis, which he made in Crist Jhesu oure Lord.
12 In whom we han trist and nyy comyng, in tristenyng bi the feith of hym.
13 For which thing Y axe, that ye faile not in my tribula-ciouns for you, which is youre glorie.
14 For grace of this thing Y bowe my knees to the fadir of oure Lord Jhesu Crist,
15 of whom ech fadirhod in heuenes and in erthe is named,
16 that he yyue to you, aftir the richessis of his glorie, vertu to be strengthid bi his spirit in the ynnere man,
17 that Crist dwelle bi feith in youre hertis; that ye rootid and groundid in charite,
18 moun comprehende with alle seyntis, which is the breede, and the lengthe, and the hiynesse, and the depnesse;
19 also to wite the charite of Crist more excellent than sci-ence, that ye be fillid in al the plentee of God.
20 And to hym that is myyti to do alle thingis more plenteu-ousli than we axen or vndurstondun, bi the vertu that wor-chith in vs,
21 to hym be glorie in the chirche, and in Crist Jhesu, in to alle the generaciouns of the world of worldis. Amen.

CAP 4

1 Therfor Y boundun for the Lord biseche you, that ye walke worthili in the clepyng,
2 in which ye ben clepid, with al mekenesse and myldenesse, with pacience supportinge ech other in charite,
3 bisi to kepe vnyte of spirit in the boond of pees.
4 O bodi and o spirit, as ye ben clepid in oon hope of youre cleping;
5 o Lord,
6 o feith, o baptym, o God and fadir of alle, which is aboue alle men, and bi alle thingis, and in vs alle.
7 But to ech of vs grace is youun bi the mesure of the yyuyng of Crist;
8 for which thing he seith, He stiynge an hiy, ledde caitifte caitif, he yaf yiftis to men.
9 But what is it, that he stiede vp, no but that also he cam doun first in to the lowere partis of the erthe?
10 He it is that cam doun, and that stiede on alle heuenes, that he schulde fille alle thingis.
11 And he yaf summe apostlis, summe prophetis, othere euangelistis, othere scheepherdis and techeris,
12 to the ful endyng of seyntis, in to the werk of mynystrie, in to edificacioun of Cristis bodi,
13 til we rennen alle, in to vnyte of feith and of knowyng of Goddis sone, in to a parfit man, aftir the mesure of age of the plente of Crist;

14 that we be not now litle children, mouynge as wawis, and be not borun aboute with ech wynd of teching, in the weiwardnesse of men, in sutil wit, to the disseyuyng of errour.
15 But do we treuthe in charite, and wexe in him by alle thingis, that is Crist oure heed;
16 of whom alle the bodi set togidere, and boundun togidere bi ech ioynture of vnder seruyng, bi worching in to the mesure of ech membre, makith encreesyng of the bodi, in to edificacioun of it silf in charite.
17 Therfor Y seie and witnesse this thing in the Lord, that ye walke not now, as hethene men walken, in the vanyte of her wit;
18 that han vndurstondyng derkned with derknessis, and ben alienyd fro the lijf of God, bi ignoraunce that is in hem, for the blyndenesse of her herte.
19 Which dispeirynge bitoken hem silf to vnchastite, in to the worchyng of al vnclennesse in coueitise.
20 But ye han not so lerud Crist, if netheles ye herden hym,
21 and ben tauyt in hym, as is treuthe in Jhesu.
22 Do ye awey bi the elde lyuyng the elde man, that is corrupt bi the desiris of errour;
23 and be ye renewlid in the spirit of youre soule;
24 and clothe ye the newe man, which is maad aftir God in riytwisnesse and hoolynesse of treuthe.
25 For which thing 'ye putte awei leesyng, and speke ye treuthe ech man with his neiybore, for we ben membris ech to othere.
26 Be ye wrooth, and nyle ye do synne; the sunne falle not doun on youre wraththe.
27 Nyle ye yyue stide to the deuel.
28 He that stal, now stele he not; but more trauele he in worchinge with hise hondis that that is good, that he haue whereof he schal yyue to nedi.
29 Ech yuel word go not of youre mouth; but if ony is good to the edificacioun of feith, that it yyue grace to men that heren.
30 And nyle ye make the Hooli Goost of God sori, in which ye ben markid in the dai of redempcioun.
31 Al bitternesse, and wraththe, and indignacioun, and cry, and blasfemye be takun awey fro you, with al malice;
32 and be ye togidere benygne, merciful, foryyuynge togidere, as also God foryaf to you in Crist.

CAP 5

1 Therfor be ye foloweris of God, as moost dereworthe sones;
2 and walke ye in loue, as Crist louyde vs, and yaf hym silf for vs an offryng and a sacrifice to God, in to the odour of swetnesse.
3 And fornycacioun, and al vnclennesse, or aueryce, be not named among you, as it bicometh holi men;
4 ethir filthe, or foli speche, or harlatrye, that perteyneth not to profit, but more doyng of thankyngis.
5 For wite ye this, and vndurstonde, that ech letchour, or vnclene man, or coueytouse, that serueth to mawmetis, hath not eritage in the kingdom of Crist and of God.
6 No man disseyue you bi veyn wordis; for whi for these thingis the wraththe of God cam on the sones of vnbileue.
7 Therfor nyle ye be maad parteneris of hem.
8 For ye weren sum tyme derknessis, but now 'ye ben liyt in the Lord. Walke ye as the sones of liyt.
9 For the fruyt of liyt is in al goodnesse, and riytwisnesse, and treuthe.
10 And preue ye what 'thing is wel plesynge to God.

11 And nyle ye comyne to vnfruytouse werkis of derknessis; but more repreue ye.
12 For what thingis ben don of hem in priuy, it is foule, yhe, to speke.
13 And alle thingis that ben repreuyd of the liyt, ben opynli schewid; for al thing that is schewid, is liyt.
14 For which thing he seith, Rise thou that slepist, and rise vp fro deth, and Crist schal liytne thee.
15 Therfor, britheren, se ye, hou warli ye schulen go;
16 not as vnwise men, but as wise men, ayenbiynge tyme, for the daies ben yuele.
17 Therfor nyle ye be maad vnwise, but vndurstondynge which is the wille of God.
18 And nyle ye be drunkun of wyn, in which is letcherie, but be ye fillid with the Hooli Goost; and speke ye to you silf in salmes,
19 and ymnes, and spiritual songis, syngynge and seiynge salm in youre hertis to the Lord;
20 euermore doynge thankingis for alle thingis in the name of oure Lord Jhesu Crist to God and to the fadir.
21 Be ye suget togidere in the drede of Crist.
22 Wymmen, be thei suget to her hosebondis,
23 as to the Lord, for the man is heed of the wymman, as Crist is heed of the chirche; he is sauyour of his bodi.
24 But as the chirche is suget to Crist, so wymmen to her hosebondis in alle thingis.
25 Men, loue ye youre wyues, as Crist louyde the chirche, and yaf hym silf for it, to make it holi;
26 and clenside it with the waisching of watir, in the word of lijf,
27 to yyue the chirche gloriouse to hym silf, that it hadde no wem, ne ryueling, or ony siche thing, but that it be hooli and vndefoulid.
28 So and men 'schulen loue her wyues, as her owne bodies. He that loueth his wijf, loueth hym silf;
29 for no man hatide euere his owne fleisch, but nurischith and fostrith it, as Crist doith the chirche.
30 And we ben membris of his bodi, of his fleisch, and of his boonys.
31 For this thing a man schal forsake his fadir and modir, and he schal drawe to his wijf; and thei schulen be tweyne in o fleisch.
32 This sacrament is greet; yhe, Y seie in Crist, and in the chirche.
33 Netheles ye alle, ech man loue his wijf as hym silf; and the wijf drede hir hosebonde.

CAP 6

1 Sones, obeische ye to youre fadir and modir, in the Lord; for this thing is riytful.
2 Onoure thou thi fadir and thi modir, that is the firste maundement in biheest;
3 that it be wel to thee, and that thou be long lyuynge on the erthe.
4 And, fadris, nyle ye terre youre sones to wraththe; but nurische ye hem in the teching and chastising of the Lord.
5 Seruauntis, obeische ye to fleischli lordis with drede and trembling, in simplenesse of youre herte, as to Crist;
6 not seruynge at the iye, as plesinge to men, but as seruauntis of Crist; doynge the wille of God bi discrecioun,
7 with good wille seruynge as to the Lord, and not as to men;

8 witinge that ech man, what euere good thing he schal do, he schal resseyue this of the Lord, whether seruaunt, whether fre man.

9 And, ye lordis, do the same thingis to hem, foryyuynge manaasis; witinge that bothe her Lord and youre is in heuenes, and the taking of persones is not anentis God.

10 Her aftirward, britheren, be ye coumfortid in the Lord, and in the miyt of his vertu.

11 Clothe you with the armere of God, that ye moun stonde ayens aspiynges of the deuel.

12 For whi stryuyng is not to vs ayens fleisch and blood, but ayens princis and potestatis, ayens gouernours of the world of these derknessis, ayens spiritual thingis of wickidnesse, in heuenli thingis.

13 Therfor take ye the armere of God, that ye moun ayenstonde in the yuel dai; and in alle thingis stonde perfit.

14 Therfor stonde ye, and be gird aboute youre leendis in sothefastnesse, and clothid with the haburioun of riytwisnesse,

15 and youre feet schood in making redi of the gospel of pees.

16 In alle thingis take ye the scheld of feith, in which ye moun quenche alle the firy dartis of 'the worste.

17 And take ye the helm of helthe, and the swerd of the Goost, that is, the word of God.

18 Bi al preier and bisechyng preie ye al tyme in spirit, and in hym wakinge in al bisynesse, and bisechyng for alle hooli men, and for me;

19 that word be youun to me in openyng of my mouth, with trist to make knowun the mysterie of the gospel,

20 for which Y am set in message in a chayne; so that in it Y be hardi to speke, as it bihoueth me.

21 And ye wite, what thingis ben aboute me, what Y do, Titicus, my moost dere brother, and trewe mynystre in the Lord, schal make alle thingis knowun to you;

22 whom Y sente to you for this same thing, that ye knowe what thingis ben aboute vs, and that he coumforte youre hertis.

23 Pees to britheren, and charite, with feith of God oure fadir, and of the Lord Jhesu Crist.

24 Grace with alle men that louen oure Lord Jhesu Crist in vncorrupcioun. Amen, 'that is, So be it.

FILIPENSIS

CAP 1

1 Poul and Tymothe, seruauntis of Jhesu Crist, to alle the hooli men in Crist Jhesu, that ben at Filippis, with bischopis and dekenes,

2 grace and pees to you of God oure fadir, and of the Lord Jhesu Crist.

3 I do thankyngis to my God

4 in al mynde of you euere more in alle my preyeris for alle you with ioye, and

5 make a bisechyng on youre comynyng in the gospel of Crist, fro the firste day til nowe;

6 tristenynge this ilke thing, that he that bigan in you a good werk, schal perfourme it til in to the dai of Jhesu Crist.

7 As it is iust to me to feele this thing for alle you, for that Y haue you in herte, and in my boondis, and in defending and confermyng of the gospel, that alle ye be felowis of my ioye.

8 For God is a witnesse to me, hou Y coueyte alle you in the bowelis of Jhesu Crist.

9 And this thing Y preie, that youre charite be plenteuouse more and more in kunnyng, and in al wit;

10 that ye preue the betere thingis, that ye be clene and without offence in the dai of Crist;

11 fillid with the fruyt of riytwysnesse bi Jhesu Crist, in to the glory and the heriyng of God.

12 For, britheren, Y wole that ye wite, that the thingis that ben aboute me han comun more to the profit of the gospel,

13 so that my boondis weren maad knowun in Crist, in ech moot halle, and in alle other placis;

14 that mo of britheren tristinge in the Lord more plenteuously for my boondis, dursten without drede speke the word of God.

15 But summe for enuye and strijf, summe for good wille, prechen Crist;

16 and summe of charite, witinge that Y am put in the defense of the gospel.

17 But summe of strijf schewen Crist not cleneli, gessynge hem to reise tribulacioun to my boondis.

18 But what? the while on al maner, ethir bi occasioun, ethir bi treuthe, Crist is schewid; and in this thing Y haue ioye, but also Y schal haue ioye.

19 And Y woot, that this thing schal come to me in to heelthe bi youre preyer, and the vndurmynystring of the spirit of 'Jhesu Crist, bi myn abidyng and hope.

20 For in no thing Y schal be schamed, but in al trist as euere more and now, Crist schal be magnefied in my bodi, ether bi lijf, ether bi deth.

21 For me to lyue is Crist, and to die is wynnyng.

22 That if to lyue in fleisch, is fruyt of werk to me, lo! what Y schal chese, Y knowe not.

23 But Y am constreyned of twei thingis, Y haue desire to be dissolued, and to be with Crist, it is myche more betere; but to dwelle in fleisch,

24 is nedeful for you.

25 And Y tristinge this thing, woot that Y schal dwelle, and perfitli dwelle to alle you, to youre profit and ioye of feith,

26 that youre thanking abounde in Crist Jhesu in me, bi my comyng eftsoone to you.

27 Oneli lyue ye worthili to the gospel of Crist, that whether whanne Y come and se you, ethir absent Y here of you, that ye stonden in o spirit of o wille, trauelinge togidere to the feith of the gospel.

28 And in no thing be ye aferd of aduersaries, which is to hem cause of perdicioun,

29 but to you cause of heelthe. And this thing is of God. For it is youun to you for Crist, that not oneli ye bileuen in hym, but also that ye suffren for hym;

30 hauynge the same strijf, which ye saien in me, and now ye han herd of me.

CAP 2

1 Therfor if ony coumfort is in Crist, if ony solace of charite, if ony felouschipe of spirit, if ony inwardnesse of merci doyng,

2 fille ye my ioye, that ye vndurstonde the same thing, and haue the same charite, of o wille, and feelen the same thing;

3 no thing bi strijf, nether by veyn glorie, but in mekenesse, demynge eche othere to be heiyer than hym silf;

4 not biholdinge ech bi hym silf what thingis ben his owne, but tho thingis that ben of othere men.

5 And fele ye this thing in you, which also in Crist Jhesu;

6 that whanne he was in the forme of God, demyde not raueyn, that hym silf were euene to God;

7 but he lowide hym silf, takinge the forme of a seruaunt, and
was maad in to the licknesse of men, and in abite was foundun as a man.

8 He mekide hym silf, and was maad obedient to the deth,
yhe, to the deth of the cross.

9 For which thing God enhaunside hym, and yaf to hym a
name that is aboue al name;

10 that in the name of Jhesu ech kne be bowid, of heuenli
thingis, of ertheli thingis, and of hellis;

11 and ech tunge knouleche, that the Lord Jhesu Crist is in the
glorie of God the fadir.

12 Therfor, my most dereworthe britheren, as euere more ye
han obeischid, not in my presence onely, but myche more
now in myn absence, worche ye with drede and trembling
youre heelthe.

13 For it is God that worchith in you, bothe to wilne, and to
performe, for good wille.

14 And do ye alle thingis with out grutchingis and doutyngis;

15 that ye be with out playnt, and symple as the sones of God,
with out repreef, in the myddil of a schrewid nacioun and a
weiward; among whiche ye schynen as yyueris of liyt in the
world.

16 And holde ye togidere the word of lijf to my glorie in the
day of Crist; for Y haue not runnen in veyn, nether Y haue
trauelid in veyn.

17 But thouy Y be offrid or slayn on the sacrifice and seruyce
of youre feith, Y haue ioye, and Y thanke you alle.

18 And the same thing haue ye ioye, and thanke ye me.

19 And Y hope in the Lord Jhesu, that Y schal sende
Tymothe soone to you, that Y be of good coumfort, whanne
tho thingis ben knowun that ben aboute you.

20 For Y haue no man so of o wille, that is bisi for you with
clene affeccioun.

21 For alle men seken tho thingis that ben her owne, not tho
that ben of Crist Jhesu.

22 But knowe ye the asaie of hym, for as a sone to the fadir he
hath seruyd with me in the gospel.

23 Therfor Y hope that Y schal sende hym to you, anoon as Y
se what thingis ben aboute me.

24 And Y triste in the Lord, that also my silf schal come to
you soone.

25 And Y gesside it nedeful to sende to you Epafrodite, my
brother and euene worchere, and myn euene knyyt, but youre
apostle, and the mynystre of my nede.

26 For he desiride you alle, and he was sorewful, therfor that
ye herden that he was sijk.

27 For he was sijk to the deth, but God hadde merci on him;
and not oneli on hym, but also on me, lest Y hadde heuynesse
on heuynesse.

28 Therfor more hastili Y sente hym, that whanne ye han
seyn hym, ye haue ioye eft, and Y be withouten heuynesse.

29 Therfor resseyue ye hym with al ioye in the Lord, and
haue ye suche with al onour.

30 For the werk of Crist he wente to deth, yyuynge his lijf,
that he schulde fulfille that that failide of you anentis my
seruyce.

CAP 3

1 Hennus forward, my britheren, haue ye ioye in the Lord. To
write to you the same thingis, to me it is not slow, and to you
it is necessarie.

2 Se ye houndis, se ye yuele werk men, se ye dyuysioun.

3 For we ben circumcisioun, which bi spirit seruen to God,
and glorien in Crist Jhesu, and han not trist in the fleisch,

4 thouy Y haue trust, yhe, in the fleisch. If ony othere man is
seyn to triste in the fleisch,

5 Y more, that was circumcidid in the eiytthe dai, of the kyn
of Israel, of the lynage of Beniamyn, an Ebrew of Ebrewis, bi
the lawe a Farisee,

6 bi loue pursuynge the chirche of God, bi riytwisnesse that is
in the lawe lyuynge with out playnt.

7 But whiche thingis weren to me wynnyngis, Y haue demed
these apeyryngis for Crist.

8 Netheles Y gesse alle thingis to be peirement for the cleer
science of Jhesu Crist my Lord. For whom Y made alle
thingis peyrement, and Y deme as drit,

9 that Y wynne Crist, and that Y be foundun in hym, not
hauynge my riytwisnesse that is of the lawe, but that that is of
the feith of Crist Jhesu, that is of God the riytwisnesse in
feith,

10 to knowe hym, and the vertu of his risyng ayen, and the
felouschipe of his passioun, and be maad lijk to his deeth,

11 if on ony maner Y come to the resurreccioun that is fro
deth.

12 Not that now Y haue takun, or now am parfit; but Y sue, if
in ony maner Y comprehende, in which thing also Y am comprehendid of Crist Jhesu.

13 Bretheren, Y deme me not that Y haue comprehendid; but
o thing, Y foryete tho thingis that ben bihyndis, and stretche
forth my silf to tho thingis that ben bifore,

14 and pursue to the ordeyned mede of the hiy clepyng of
God in Crist Jhesu.

15 Therfor who euere we ben perfit, feele we this thing. And
if ye vndurstonden in othere manere ony thing, this thing God
schal schewe to you.

16 Netheles to what thing we han comun, that we vndurstonden the same thing, and that we perfitli dwelle in the same
reule.

17 Britheren, be ye my foleweris, and weyte ye hem that
walken so, as ye han oure fourme.

18 For many walken, whiche Y haue seid ofte to you, but now
Y wepinge seie, the enemyes of Cristis cros,

19 who ende is deth, whos god is the wombe, and the glorie
in confusioun of hem, that saueren ertheli thingis.

20 But oure lyuyng is in heuenes; fro whennus also we abiden
the sauyour oure Lord Jhesu Crist,

21 which schal reforme the bodi of oure mekenesse, that is
maad lijk to the bodi of his clerenesse, bi the worching bi
which he mai 'also make alle thingis suget to hym.

CAP 4

1 Therfor, my britheren most dereworthe and most desirid,
my ioye and my coroun, so stonde ye in the Lord, most dere
britheren.

2 Y preye Eucodiam, and biseche Synticem, to vndurstonde
the same thing in the Lord.

3 Also Y preye and thee, german felow, helpe thou the ilke
wymmen that traueliden with me in the gospel, with Clement
and othere myn helperis, whos names ben in the book of lijf.

4 Ioye ye in the Lord euere more; eft Y seie, ioye ye.

5 Be youre pacyence knowun to alle men; the Lord is niy.

6 Be ye nothing bisi, but in al preyer and biseching, with
doyng of thankyngis, be youre axyngis knowun at God.

7 And the pees of God, that passith al wit, kepe youre hertis and vndurstondingis in Crist Jhesu.

8 Fro hennus forth, britheren, what euere thingis ben sothe, what euere thingis chast, what euere thingis iust, what euere thingis hooli, what euere thingis able to be louyd, what euere thingis of good fame, if ony vertu, if ony preising of discipline, thenke ye these thingis,

9 that also ye han lerud, and take, and heed, and seyn in me. Do ye these thingis, and God of pees schal be with you.

10 But Y ioyede greetli in the Lord, that sum tyme aftirward ye floureden ayen to feele for me, as also ye feeliden. But ye weren ocupied, Y seie not as for nede,

11 for Y haue lerud to be sufficient in whiche thingis Y am.

12 And Y can also be lowid, Y can also haue plentee. Euery where and in alle thingis Y am tauyt to be fillid, and to hungur, and to abounde, and to suffre myseiste.

13 Y may alle thingis in hym that coumfortith me.

14 Netheles ye han doon wel, comynynge to my tribulacioun.

15 For and ye, Filipensis, witen, that in the bigynnyng of the gospel, whanne Y wente forth fro Macedonye, no chirche comynede with me in resoun of thing youun and takun, but ye aloone.

16 Whiche senten to Tessalonyk onys and twies also in to vss to me.

17 Not for Y seke yifte, but Y requyre fruyt aboundinge in youre resoun.

18 For Y haue alle thingis, and abounde; Y am fillid with tho thingis takun of Epafrodite, whiche ye senten in to the odour of swetnesse, a couenable sacrifice, plesynge to God.

19 And my God fil alle youre desire, by hise richessis in glorie in Crist Jhesu.

20 But to God and oure fadir be glorie in to worldis of worldis.

21 Amen. Grete ye wel euery hooli man in Crist Jhesu.

22 Tho britheren that ben with me, greten you wel. Alle hooli men greten you wel, moost sotheli thei that ben of the emperouris hous.

23 The grace of oure Lord Jhesu Crist be with youre spirit. Amen.

COLOSENCIS

CAP 1

1 Poul, apostle of 'Crist Jhesu, bi the wille of God,

2 and Tymothe, brother, to hem that ben at Colose, hooli and feithful britheren in Crist Jhesu,

3 grace and pees to you of God oure fadir and of the Lord Jhesu Crist. We don thankyngis to God, and to the fader of oure Lord Jhesu Crist, euermore preiynge for you, herynge youre feith in Crist Jhesu,

4 and the loue that ye han to alle hooli men,

5 for the hope that is kept to you in heuenes. Which ye herden in the word of treuthe of the gospel,

6 that cam to you, as also it is in al the world, and makith fruyt, and wexith, as in you, fro that dai in which ye herden and knewen the grace of God in treuthe.

7 As ye lerneden of Epafras, oure felawe most dereworthe, which is a trewe mynystre of Jhesu Crist for you;

8 which also schewide to vs youre louyng in spirit.

9 Therfor we fro the dai in which we herden, ceessen not to preye for you, and to axe, that ye be fillid with the knowing of his wille in al wisdom and goostli vndurstondyng;

10 that ye walke worthili to God plesynge bi alle thingis, and make fruyt in al good werk, and wexe in the science of God,

11 and ben coumfortid in al vertu bi the miyt of his clerenesse, in al pacience and long abiding with ioye,

12 that ye do thankyngis to God and to the fadir, which made you worthi in to the part of eritage of hooli men in liyt.

13 Which delyueride vs fro the power of derknessis, and translatide in to the kyngdom of the sone of his louyng,

14 in whom we han ayenbiyng and remyssioun of synnes.

15 Which is the ymage of God vnuysible, the first bigetun of ech creature.

16 For in hym alle thingis ben maad, in heuenes and in erthe, visible and vnuysible, ether trones, ether dominaciouns, ether princehodes, ethir poweris, alle thingis ben maad of nouyt bi hym, and in hym,

17 and he is bifor alle, and alle thingis ben in hym.

18 And he is heed of the bodi of the chirche; which is the bigynnyng and the firste bigetun of deede men, that he holde the firste dignyte in alle thingis.

19 For in hym it pleside al plente to inhabite,

20 and bi hym alle thingis to be recounselid in to hym, and made pees bi the blood of his cros, tho thingis that ben in erthis, ether that ben in heuenes.

21 And whanne ye weren sumtyme aliened, and enemyes bi wit in yuele werkis,

22 now he hath recounselid you in the bodi of his fleisch bi deth, to haue you hooli, and vnwemmyd, and with out repreef bifor hym.

23 If netheles ye dwellen in the feith, foundid, and stable, and vnmouable fro the hope of the gospel that ye han herd, which is prechid in al creature that is vndur heuene. Of which Y Poul am maad mynystre,

24 and now Y haue ioye in passioun for you, and Y fille tho thingis that failen of the passiouns of Crist in my fleisch, for his bodi, that is the chirche.

25 Of which Y Poul am maad mynystre bi the dispensacioun of God, that is youun to me in you,

26 that Y fille the word of God, the priuyte, that was hid fro worldis and generaciouns. But now it is schewid to his seyntis,

27 to whiche God wold make knowun the richessis of the glorie of this sacrament in hethene men, which is Crist in you, the hope of glorie.

28 Whom we schewen, repreuynge ech man, and techinge 'ech man in al wisdom, that we offre ech man perfit in Crist Jhesu.

29 In which thing also Y trauele in stryuynge bi the worching of hym, that he worchith in me in vertu.

CAP 2

1 But Y wole that ye wite, what bisynesse Y haue for you, and for hem that ben at Laodice, and whiche euere saien not my face in fleisch,

2 that her hertis ben coumfortid, and thei ben tauyt in charite, in to alle the richessis of the plente of the vndurstondyng, in to the knowyng of mysterie of God, the fadir of Jhesu Crist,

3 in whom alle the tresouris of wisdom and of science ben hid.

4 For this thing Y seie, that no man disseyue you in heiythe of wordis.

5 For thouy Y be absent in bodi, bi spirit Y am with you, ioiynge and seynge youre ordre and the sadnesse of youre bileue that is in Crist.

6 Therfor as ye han takun Jhesu Crist oure Lord,

7 walke ye in hym, and be ye rootid and bieldid aboue in hym, and confermyd in the bileue, as ye han lerud, aboundinge in hym in doynge of thankyngis.

8 Se ye that no man disseyue you bi filosofie and veyn fallace, aftir the tradicioun of men, aftir the elementis of the world, and not aftir Crist.

9 For in hym dwellith bodilich al the fulnesse of the Godhed.

10 And ye ben fillid in hym, that is heed of al principat and power.

11 In whom also ye ben circumcidid in circumcisioun not maad with hoond, in dispoyling of the bodi of fleisch, but in circumcisioun of Crist;

12 and ye ben biried togidere with hym in baptim, in whom also ye han rise ayen bi feith of the worching of God, that reiside hym fro deth.

13 And whanne ye weren deed in giltis, and in the prepucie of youre fleisch, he quikenyde togidere you with hym;

14 foryyuynge to you alle giltis, doynge awei that writing of decre that was ayens vs, that was contrarie to vs; and he took awei that fro the myddil, pitchinge it on the cros;

15 and he spuylide principatis and poweris, and ledde out tristili, opynli ouercomynge hem in hym silf.

16 Therfor no man iuge you in mete, or in drink, or in part of feeste dai, or of neomenye,

17 or of sabatis, whiche ben schadewe of thingis to comynge; for the bodi is of Crist.

18 No man disseyue you, willynge to teche in mekenesse, and religioun of aungelis, tho thingis whiche he hath not seyn, walkinge veynli, bolnyd with wit of his fleisch,

19 and not holdynge the heed, of which al the bodi, bi boondis and ioynyngis togidere vndur mynystrid and maad, wexith in to encreessing of God.

20 For if ye ben deed with Crist fro the elementis of this world, what yit as men lyuynge to the world demen ye?

21 That ye touche not, nether taaste,

22 nether trete with hoondis tho thingis, whiche alle ben in to deth bi the ilke vss, aftir the comaundementis and the techingis of men;

23 whiche han a resoun of wisdom in veyn religioun and mekenesse, and not to spare the bodi, not in ony onour to the fulfillyng of the fleisch.

CAP 3

1 Therfor if ye han risun togidere with Crist, seke ye tho thingis that ben aboue, where Crist is sittynge in the riythalf of God.

2 Sauere ye tho thingis, that ben aboue, not tho that ben on the erthe.

3 For ye ben deed, and youre lijf is hid with Crist in God.

4 For whanne Crist schal appere, youre lijf, thanne also ye schulen appere with hym in glorie.

5 Therfor sle ye youre membris, whiche ben on the erthe, fornycacioun, vnclennesse, letcherie, yuel coueitise, and aueryse, which is seruyse of mawmetis;

6 for whiche thingis the wraththe of God cam on the sones of vnbileue;

7 in whiche also ye walkiden sum tyme, whanne ye lyueden in hem.

8 But now putte ye awei alle thingis, wraththe, indignacioun, malice, blasfemye and foule word of youre mouth.

9 Nyle ye lie togidere; spuyle ye you fro the elde man with his dedes, and clothe ye the newe man,

10 that is maad newe ayen in to the knowing of God, aftir the ymage of hym that made hym;

11 where is not male and female, hethene man and Jew, circumcisioun and prepucie, barbarus and Scita, bonde man and fre man, but alle thingis and in alle thingis Crist.

12 Therfor ye, as the chosun of God, hooli and louyd, clothe you with the entrailis of merci, benygnite, and mekenesse, temperaunce, pacience;

13 and support ye echon other, and foryyue to you silf, if ony man ayens ony hath a querele; as the Lord foryaf to you, so also ye.

14 And vpon alle these thingis haue ye charite, that is the boond of perfeccioun.

15 And the pees of Crist enioye in youre hertis, in which ye ben clepid in o bodi, and be ye kynde.

16 The word of Crist dwelle in you plenteuousli, in al wisdom; and teche and moneste you silf in salmes, and ympnes, and spiritual songis, in grace synginge in youre hertis to the Lord.

17 Al thing, what euere thing ye don, in word or in dede, alle thingis in the name of oure Lord Jhesu Crist, doynge thankyngis to God and to the fadir bi hym.

18 Wymmen, be ye sugetis to youre hosebondis, as it bihoueth in the Lord.

19 Men, loue ye youre wyues, and nyle ye be bittere to hem.

20 Sones, obeie ye to youre fadir and modir bi alle thingis; for this is wel plesinge in the Lord.

21 Fadris, nyle ye terre youre sones to indignacioun, that thei be not maad feble hertid.

22 Seruauntis, obeie ye bi alle thingis to fleischli lordis, not seruynge at iye, as plesynge to men, but in symplenesse of herte, dredinge the Lord.

23 What euer ye doen, worche ye of wille, as to the Lord and not to men;

24 witinge that of the Lord ye schulen take yelding of eritage. Serue ye to the Lord Crist.

25 For he that doith iniurie, schal resseyue that that he dide yuele; and acceptacioun of persoones is not anentis God.

CAP 4

1 Lordis, yyue ye to seruauntis that that is iust and euene, witinge that also ye han a Lord in heuene.

2 Be ye bisi in preier, and wake in it, in doynge of thankyngis;

3 and preie ech for othere, and for vs, that God opene to vs the dore of word, to speke the misterie of Crist;

4 for which also Y am boundun, that Y schewe it, so as it bihoueth me to speke.

5 Walke ye in wisdom to hem that ben with outen forth, ayenbiynge tyme.

6 Youre word be sauered in salt eueremore in grace; that ye wite, hou it bihoueth you to answere to ech man.

7 Titicus, most dere brother, and feithful mynyster, and my felowe in the Lord, schal make alle thingis knowun to you, that ben aboute me.

8 Whom Y sente to you to this same thing, that he knowe what thingis ben aboute you, and coumforte youre hertis, with Onesyme,

9 most dere and feithful brother, which is of you; whiche schulen make alle thingis that ben doon here, knowun to you.

10 Aristark, prisoner with me, gretith you wel, and Mark, the cosyn of Barnabas, of whom ye han take maundementis; if he come to you, resseyue ye hym;

11 and Jhesus, that is seid Just; whiche ben of circumcisioun; thei aloone ben myn helperis in the kingdom of God, that weren to me in solace.

12 Epafras, that is of you, the seruaunt of Jhesu Crist, gretith you wel; euere bisi for you in preyeris, that ye stonde perfit and ful in al the wille of God.

13 And Y bere witnessyng to hym, that he hath myche trauel for you, and for hem that ben at Loadice, and that ben at Ierapolim.

14 Luk, the leche most dere, and Demas, greten you wel.

15 Grete ye wel the britheren that ben at Loadice, and the womman Nynfam, and the chirche that is in hir hous.

16 And whanne this pistle is red among you, do ye, that it be red in the chirche of Loadicensis; and rede ye that pistle that is of Loadicensis.

17 And seie ye to Archippus, Se the mynysterie, that thou hast takun in the Lord, that thou fille it.

18 My salutacioun, bi the hoond of Poul. Be ye myndeful of my boondis. The grace of the Lord Jhesu Crist be with you. Amen.

1 THESSALONYCENSIS

CAP 1

1 Poul, and Siluan, and Tymothe, to the chirche of Tessalonicensis, in God the fadir,

2 and in the Lord Jhesu Crist, grace and pees to you. We doon thankyngis to God euere more for alle you, and we maken mynde of you in oure preyeris withouten ceessyng;

3 hauynge mynde of the werk of youre feith, and trauel, and charite, and abydyng of the hope of oure Lord Jhesu Crist, bifor God and oure fadir.

4 Ye louyde britheren of God, we witinge youre chesing;

5 for oure gospel was not at you in word oneli, but also in vertu, and in the Hooli Goost, and in myche plente; as ye witen, whiche we weren among you for you;

6 and ye ben maad foleweris of vs, and of the Lord, resseyuynge the word in myche tribulacioun, with ioye of the Hooli Goost;

7 so that ye ben maad ensaumple to alle men that bileuen, in Macedonye and in Acaie.

8 For of you the word of the Lord is pupplischid, not oneli in Macedonye and Acaie, but youre feith that is to God, in ech place is gon forth; so that it is not nede to vs to speke ony thing.

9 For thei schewen of you, what maner entre we hadden to you, and hou ye ben conuertid to God fro maumettis, to serue to the lyuynge God and veri; and to abide his sone fro heuenes,

10 whom he reiside fro deth, the Lord Jhesu, that delyuerede us fro wraththe to comynge.

CAP 2

1 For, britheren, ye witen oure entre to you, for it was not veyn;

2 but first we suffriden, and weren punyschid with wrongis, as ye witen in Filippis, and hadden trust in oure Lord, to speke to you the gospel of God in myche bisynesse.

3 And oure exortacioun is not of errour, nether of vnclennesse, nether in gile,

4 but as we ben preued of God, that the gospel of God schulde be takun to vs, so we speken; not as plesynge to men, but to God that preueth oure hertis.

5 For nether we weren ony tyme in word of glosing, as ye witen, nether in occasioun of auerise; God is witnesse; nether sekinge glorie of men,

6 nether of you,

7 nether of othere, whanne we, as Cristis apostlis, miyten haue be in charge to you. But we weren maad litle in the myddil of you, as if a nursche fostre hir sones;

8 so we desiringe you with greet loue, wolden haue bitake to you, not oneli the gospel of God, but also oure lyues, for ye ben maad most dereworthe to vs.

9 For, britheren, ye ben myndeful of oure trauel and werynesse; we worchiden nyyt and day, that we schulden not greue ony of you, and prechiden to you the euangelie of God.

10 God and ye ben witnessis, hou holili, and iustli, and with outen pleynt, we weren to you that bileueden.

11 As ye witen, hou we preyeden you, and coumfortiden ech of you, as the fadir hise sones,

12 and we han witnessid, that ye schulden go worthili to God, that clepide you in to his kingdom and glorie.

13 Therfor we doon thankingis to God with outen ceessyng. For whanne ye hadden take of vs the word 'of the heryng of God, ye token it not as the word of men, but as 'it is verili, the word of God, that worchith in you that han bileued.

14 For, britheren, ye ben maad foleweris of the chirchis of God, that ben in Jude, in Crist Jhesu, for ye han suffrid the same thingis of youre euene lynagis, as thei of the Jewis.

15 Whiche slowen bothe the Lord Jhesu and the profetis, and pursueden vs, and thei plesen not to God, and thei ben aduersaries to alle men;

16 forbedinge vs to speke to hethene men, that thei be maad saaf, that thei fille her synnes euere more; for the wraththe of God cam on hem in to the ende.

17 And, britheren, we desolat fro you for a tyme, bi mouth and in biholding, but not in herte, han hiyed more plenteuousli to se youre face with greet desir.

18 For we wolden come to you, yhe, Y Poul, onys and eftsoone, but Sathanas lettide vs.

19 For whi what is oure hope, or ioye, or coroun of glorie? Whether ye ben not bifore oure Lord Jhesu Crist in his comyng?

20 For ye ben oure glorie and ioye.

CAP 3

1 For which thing we suffriden no lengere, and it pleside to vs to dwelle aloone at Atenys;

2 and we senten Tymothe, oure brother, and mynystre of God in the euangelie of Crist, to you to be confermyd, and to be tauyt for youre feith,

3 that no man be mouyd in these tribulaciouns. For ye silf witen, that in this this thing we ben set.

4 For whanne we weren at you, we biforseiden to you, that we schulden suffre tribulaciouns; as it is don, and ye witen.

5 Therfor Y Poul, no lenger abidinge, sente to knowe youre feith, lest perauenture he that temptith tempte you, and youre trauel be maad veyn.

6 But now, whanne Tymothe schal come to vs fro you, and telle to vs youre feith and charite, and that ye han good mynde of vs, euere desyringe to se vs, as we also you;

7 therfor, britheren, we ben coumfortid in you, in al oure nede and tribulacioun, bi youre feith.

8 For now we lyuen, if ye stonden in the Lord.

9 For what doyng of thankingis moun we yelde to God for you, in al ioye, in which we ioyen for you bifor oure Lord?

10 nyyt and dai more plenteuousli preiynge, that we se youre face, and fulfille tho thingis that failen to youre feith.

11 But God hym silf and oure fadir, and the Lord Jhesu Crist, dresse oure weye to you.

12 And the Lord multiplie you, and make youre charite to be plenteuouse of ech to othere, and in to alle men, as also we in you;

13 that youre hertis ben confermyd with outen pleynt in holynesse, bifor God and oure fadir, in the comyng of oure Lord Jhesu Crist with alle hise seyntis. Amen.

CAP 4

1 Therfor, britheren, fro hennus forward we preien you, and bisechen in the Lord Jhesu, that as ye han resseyued of vs, hou it bihoueth you to go and to plese God, so walke ye, that ye abounde the more.

2 For ye witen what comaundementis Y haue youun to you bi the Lord Jhesu.

3 For this is the wille of God, youre holynesse, that ye absteyne you fro fornycacioun.

4 That ech of you kunne welde his vessel in holynesse, and onour;

5 not in passioun of lust, as hethene men that knowen not God.

6 And that no man ouergo, nethir disseyue his brothir in chaffaring. For the Lord is venger of alle these thingis, as we biforseiden to you, and han witnessid.

7 For God clepide not vs in to vnclennesse, but in to holynesse.

8 Therfor he that dispisith these thingis, dispisith not man, but God, that also yaf his holi spirit in vs.

9 But of the charite of britherhed we hadden no nede to write to you; ye silf han lerud of God, that ye loue togidere;

10 for ye don that in to alle britheren in al Macedonye. And, britheren, we preyen you, that ye abounde more; and taken kepe, that ye be quyet;

11 and that ye do youre nede, and 'ye worche with youre hoondis, as we han comaundid to you; and that ye wandre onestli to hem that ben with outforth, and that of no mannus ye desir ony thing.

12 For, britheren, we wolen not, that ye vnknowe of men that dien, that ye be not soreuful, as othere that han not hope.

13 For if we bileuen, that Jhesu was deed, and roos ayen, so God schal lede with hym hem that ben deed bi Jhesu.

14 And we seien this thing to you in the word of the Lord, that we that lyuen, that ben left in the comyng of the Lord, schulen not come bifor hem that ben deed.

15 For the Lord hym silf schal come doun fro heuene, in the comaundement, and in the vois of an archaungel, and in the trumpe of God; and the deed men that ben in Crist, schulen rise ayen first.

16 Afterward we that lyuen, that ben left, schulen be rauyschid togidere with hem in cloudis, metinge Crist 'in to the eir; and so euere more we schulen be with the Lord.

17 Therfor be ye coumfortid togidere in these wordis.

CAP 5

1 But, britheren, of tymes and momentis ye neden not that Y write to you.

2 For ye silf witen diligentli, that the dai of the Lord schal come, as a theef in the niyt.

3 For whanne thei schulen seie pees is, and sikirnesse, thanne sudeyn deth schal come on hem, as sorewe to a womman that is with child, and thei schulen not scape.

4 But, britheren, ye ben not in derknessis, that the ilke dai as a theef catche you.

5 For alle ye ben the sones of liyt, and sones of dai; we ben not of niyt, nether of derknessis.

6 Therfor slepe we not as othere; but wake we, and be we sobre.

7 For thei that slepen, slepen in the niyt, and thei that ben drunkun, ben drunkun in the niyt.

8 But we that ben of the dai, ben sobre, clothid in the haburioun of feith and of charite, and in the helme of hope of heelthe.

9 For God puttide not vs in to wraththe, but in to the purchasing of heelthe bi oure Lord Jhesu Crist, that was deed for vs;

10 that whether we waken, whether we slepen, we lyue togidere with him.

11 For which thing comforte ye togidere, and edefie ye ech other, as ye doon.

12 And, britheren, we preien you, that ye knowen hem that trauelen among you, and ben souereyns to you in the Lord, and techen you,

13 that ye han hem more aboundantli in charyte; and for the werk of hem, haue ye pees with hem.

14 And, britheren, we preien you, repreue ye vnpesible men. Coumforte ye men of litil herte, resseyue ye sijke men, be ye pacient to alle men.

15 Se ye, that no man yelde yuel for yuel to ony man; but euere more sue ye that that is good, ech to othere and to alle men.

16 Euere more ioye ye; without ceessing preye ye;

17 in alle thingis do ye thankyngis.

18 For this is the wille of God in Crist Jhesu, in alle you.

19 Nyle ye quenche the spirit;

20 nyle ye dispise prophecies.

21 But preue ye alle thingis, and holde ye that thing that is good.

22 Absteyne you fro al yuel spice.

23 And God hym silf of pees make you hooli bi alle thingis, that youre spirit be kept hool, and soule, and bodi, without pleynt, in the comyng of oure Lord Jhesu Crist.

24 God is trewe, that clepide you, which also schal do.

25 Britheren, preye ye for vs.

26 Grete ye wel alle britheren in hooli cos.

27 Y coniure you bi the Lord, that this pistle be red to alle hooli britheren.

28 The grace of oure Lord Jhesu Crist be with you. Amen.

2 THESSALONYCENSIS

CAP 1

1 Poul, and Siluan, and Tymothe, to the chirche of Tessalonicensis, in God oure fadir,

2 and in the Lord Jhesu Crist, grace to you and pees of God, oure fadir, and of the Lord Jhesu Crist.

3 We owen to do thankyngis eueremore to God for you, britheren, so as it is worthi, for youre feith ouer wexith, and the charite of ech of you to othere aboundith.

4 So that we silf glorien in you in the chirchis of God, for youre pacience and feith in alle youre persecuciouns and tribulaciouns.

5 Whiche ye susteynen in to the ensaumple of the iust dom of God, that ye be had worthi in the kingdom of God, for which ye suffren.

6 If netheles it is iust tofor God to quite tribulacioun to hem that troblen you,

7 and to you that ben troblid, rest with vs in the schewing of the Lord Jhesu fro heuene, with aungelis of his vertu,

8 in the flawme of fier, that schal yyue veniaunce to hem that knowen not God, and that obeien not to the euangelie of oure Lord Jhesu Crist.

9 Whiche schulen suffre euere lastinge peynes, in perischinge fro the face of the Lord, and fro the glorie of his vertu,

10 whanne he schal come to be glorified in hise seyntis, and to be maad wondurful in alle men that bileueden, for oure witnessing is bileuyd on you, in that dai.

11 In which thing also we preien euere more for you, that oure God make you worthi to his cleping, and fille al the wille of his goodnesse, and the werk of feith in vertu;

12 that the name of oure Lord Jhesu Crist be clarified in you, and ye in hym, bi the grace of oure Lord Jhesu Crist.

CAP 2

1 But, britheren, we preien you bi the comyng of oure Lord Jhesu Crist, and of oure congregacioun in to the same comyng,

2 that ye be not mouyd soone fro youre witt, nether be aferd, nether bi spirit, nether bi word, nether bi epistle as sent bi vs, as if the dai of the Lord be nyy.

3 No man disseyue you in ony manere. For but dissencioun come first, and the man of synne be schewid, the sonne of perdicioun,

4 that is aduersarie, and is enhaunsid ouer 'al thing that is seid God, or that is worschipid, so that he sitte in the temple of God, and schewe hym silf as if he were God.

5 Whether ye holden not, that yit whanne Y was at you, Y seide these thingis to you?

6 And now what withholdith, ye witen, that he be schewid in his tyme.

7 For the priuete of wickidnesse worchith now; oneli that he that holdith now, holde, til he be do awei.

8 And thanne thilke wickid man schal be schewid, whom the Lord Jhesu schal sle with the spirit of his mouth, and schal distrie with liytnyng of his comyng;

9 hym, whos comyng is bi the worching of Sathanas, in al vertu, and signes,

10 and grete wondris, false, and in al disseit of wickidnesse, to hem that perischen. For that thei resseyueden not the charite of treuthe, that thei schulden be maad saaf. And therfor God schal sende to hem a worching of errour, that thei bileue to leesing,

11 that alle be demed, whiche bileueden not to treuthe, but consentiden to wickidnesse.

12 But, britheren louyd of God, we owen to do thankyngis euermore to God for you, that God chees vs the firste fruytis in to heelthe, in halewing of spirit and in feith of treuthe;

13 in which also he clepide you bi oure gospel, in to geting of the glorie of oure Lord Jhesu Crist.

14 Therfor, britheren, stonde ye, and holde ye the tradiciouns, that ye han lerud, ethir bi word, ethir bi oure pistle.

15 And oure Lord Jhesu Crist him silf, and God oure fadir, which louyde vs, and yaf euerlastinge coumfort and good hope in grace, stire youre hertis,

16 and conferme in al good werk and word.

CAP 3

1 Britheren, fro hennus forward preye ye for vs, that the word of God renne, and be clarified, as it is anentis you;

2 and that we be delyuered fro noyous and yuele men; for feith is not of alle men.

3 But the Lord is trewe, that schal conferme you, and schal kepe fro yuel.

4 And, britheren, we trusten of you in the Lord, for what euere thingis we comaunden to you, bothe ye don and schulen do.

5 And the Lord dresse youre hertis, in the charite of God, and in the pacience of Crist.

6 But, britheren, we denouncen to you in the name of oure Lord Jhesu Crist, that ye withdrawe you from ech brother that wandrith out of ordre, and not aftir the techyng, that thei resseyueden of vs.

7 For 'ye silf witen, hou it bihoueth to sue vs. For we weren not vnpesible among you,

8 nethir with outen oure owne trauel we eeten breed of ony man, but in trauel and werynesse worchiden niyt and dai, that we greuyden noon of you.

9 Not as we hadden not power, but that we schulden yyue vs silf ensaumple to you to sue vs.

10 For also whanne we weren among you, we denounsiden this thing to you, that if ony man wole not worche, nethir ete he.

11 For we han herd that summe among you goon in reste, and no thing worchen, but don curiousli.

12 But we denouncen to hem that ben suche men, and bisechen in the Lord Jhesu Crist, that thei worchen with silence, and ete her owne breed.

13 But nyle ye, britheren, faile wel doynge.

14 That if ony man obeie not to oure word bi epistle, marke ye him, and comyne ye not with hym, that he be schamed;

15 and nyle ye gesse hym as an enemye, but repreue ye hym as a brother. And God hym silf of pees yyue to you euerlastinge pees in al place.

16 The Lord be with 'you alle.

17 My salutacioun bi the hoond of Poul; which signe in ech epistle Y write thus.

18 The grace of oure Lord Jhesu Crist be with 'alle you. Amen.

1 TYMOTHE

CAP 1

1 Poul, apostle 'of Jhesu Crist, bi the comaundement of God oure sauyour, and of Jhesu Crist oure hope,

2 to Tymothe, bilouyd sone in the feith, grace and merci and pees, of God the fadir, and of Jhesu Crist, oure Lord.

3 As Y preyede thee, that thou schuldist dwelle at Effesi, whanne Y wente into Macedonye, that thou schuldist denounce to summe men, that thei schulden not teche othere weie,

4 nether yyue tent to fablis and genologies that ben vncerteyn, whiche yyuen questiouns, more than edificacioun of God, that is in the feith.

5 For the ende of comaundement is charite of clene herte, and good conscience, and of feith not feyned.

6 Fro whiche thingis sum men han errid, and ben turned in to veyn speche;

7 and willith to be techeris of the lawe, and vndurstonden not what thingis thei speken, nether of what thingis thei affermen.

8 And we witen that the lawe is good, if ony man vse it lawefulli;

9 and witinge this thing, that the lawe is not set to a iust man, but to vniust men and not suget, to wickid men and to synneris, to cursid men and defoulid, to sleeris of fadir, and sleeris of modir, to 'men sleeris and lechouris,

10 to hem that don letcherie with men, lesingmongeris and forsworun, and if ony othere thing is contrarie to the hoolsum teching,

11 that is aftir the euangelie of the glorie of blessid God, which is bitakun to me.

12 Y do thankingis to hym, that coumfortide me in Crist Jhesu oure Lord, for he gesside me feithful, and putte me in mynystrie,

13 that first was a blasfeme, and a pursuere, and ful of wrongis. But Y haue getun the merci of God, for Y vnknowinge dide in vnbileue.

14 But the grace of oure Lord ouer aboundide, with feith and loue that is in Crist Jhesu.

15 A trewe word and worthi al resseyuyng, for Crist Jhesu cam in to this world to make synful men saaf, of whiche Y am the firste.

16 But therfor Y haue getun merci, that Crist Jhesu schulde schewe in me first al pacience, to the enfourmyng of hem that schulen bileue to hym in to euerlastinge lijf.

17 And to the king of worldis, vndeedli and vnvysible God aloone, be onour and glorie in to worldis of worldis. Amen.

18 I bitake this comaundement to thee, thou sone Timothe, after the prophecies that han be hertofore in thee, that thou traueile in hem a good trauel,

19 hauynge feith and good conscience, which summen casten awei, and perischiden aboute the feith.

20 Of whiche is Ymeneus and Alisaundre, which Y bitook to Sathanas, that thei lerne 'to not blasfeme.

CAP 2

1 Therfor Y biseche first of alle thingis, that bisechingis, preieris, axyngis, doyngis of thankyngis, ben maad for alle men,

2 for kingis and alle that ben set in hiynesse, that we leden a quyet and a pesible lijf, in al pite and chastite.

3 For this thing is good and acceptid bifor God,

4 oure sauyour, that wole that alle men ben maad saaf, and that thei come to the knowyng of treuthe.

5 For o God and a mediatour is of God and of men, a man Crist Jhesus,

6 that yaf him silf redempcioun for alle men. Whos witnessing is confermyd in his tymes;

7 in which Y am set a prechour and an apostle. For Y seye treuthe, and Y lie not, that am a techere of hethene men in feith and in treuthe.

8 Therfor Y wole, that men preye in al place, liftinge vp clene hondis with outen wraththe and strijf.

9 Also wymmen in couenable abite, with schamefastnesse and sobrenesse araiynge hem silf, not in writhun heeris, ethir in gold, ethir peerlis, ethir preciouse cloth; but that that bicometh wymmen,

10 biheetinge pite bi good werkis.

11 A womman lerne in silence, with al subieccioun.

12 But Y suffre not a womman to teche, nether to haue lordschip on the hosebonde, but to be in silence.

13 For Adam was first formed, aftirward Eue;

14 and Adam was not disseyued, but the womman was disseyued, in breking of the lawe.

15 But sche schal be sauyd bi generacioun of children, if sche dwellith perfitli in feith, and loue, and hoolynesse, with sobrenesse.

CAP 3

1 A feithful word. If ony man desirith a bishopriche, he desirith a good werk.

2 Therfor it bihoueth a byschop to be with out repreef, the hosebonde of o wijf, sobre, prudent, chast, vertewous, holdinge hospitalite, a techere;

3 not youun myche to wyn, not a smytere, but temperat, not ful of chiding, not coueitouse, wel reulinge his hous,

4 and haue sones suget with al chastite;

5 for if ony man kan not gouerne his house, hou schal he haue diligence of the chirche of God? not new conuertid to the feith,

6 lest he be borun vp in to pride, and falle in to doom of the deuel.

7 For it bihoueth hym to haue also good witnessing of hem that ben with outforth, that he falle not in to repreef, and in to the snare of the deuel.

8 Also it bihoueth dekenes to be chast, not double tungid, not youun myche to wyn, not suynge foul wynnyng;

9 that han the mysterie of feith in clene conscience.

10 But be thei preued first, and mynystre so, hauynge no cryme.

11 Also it bihoueth wymmen to be chast, not bacbitinge, sobre, feithful in alle thingis.

12 Dekenes be hosebondis of o wijf; whiche gouerne wel her sones and her housis.

13 For thei that mynystren wel, schulen gete a good degre to hem silf, and myche triste in the feith, that is in Crist Jhesu.

14 Sone Timothe, Y write to thee these thingis, hopinge that Y schal come soone to thee;

15 but if Y tarie, that thou wite, hou it bihoueth thee to lyue in the hous of God, that is the chirche of lyuynge God, a pilere and sadnesse of treuthe.

16 And opynli it is a greet sacrament of pitee, that thing that was schewid in fleisch, it is iustified in spirit, it apperid to aungels, it is prechid to hethene men, it is bileuyd in the world, it is takun vp in glorie.

CAP 4

1 But the spirit seith opynli, that in the laste tymes summen schulen departe fro the feith, yyuynge tent to spiritis of errour, and to techingis of deuelis; that speken leesing in ipocrisie,

2 and haue her conscience corrupt,

3 forbedinge to be weddid, to absteyne fro metis, whiche God made to take with doyng of thankingis, to feithful men, and hem that han knowe the treuthe.

4 For ech creature of God is good, and no thing is to be cast awei, which is takun with doyng of thankyngis;

5 for it is halewid bi the word of God, and bi preyer.

6 Thou puttynge forth these thingis to britheren, schalt be a good mynystre of Crist Jhesu; nurschid with wordis of feith and of good doctryne, which thou hast gete.

7 But eschewe thou vncouenable fablis, and elde wymmenus fablis; haunte thi silf to pitee.

8 For bodili exercitacion is profitable to litle thing; but pitee is profitable to alle thingis, that hath a biheest of lijf that now is, and that is to come.

9 A trewe word, and worthi al acceptacioun.

10 And in this thing we trauelen, and ben cursid, for we hopen in lyuyng God, that is sauyour of alle men, moost of feithful men.

11 Comaunde thou this thing, and teche.

12 No man dispise thi yongthe, but be thou ensaumple of feithful men in word, in lyuyng, in charite, in feith, in chastite.

13 Tyl Y come, take tent to redyng, to exortacioun and teching.

14 Nyle thou litil charge the grace which is in thee, that is youun to thee bi profecie, with putting on of the hondis of preesthod.

15 Thenke thou these thingis, in these be thou, that thi profiting be schewid to alle men.

16 Take tent to thi silf and to doctryn; be bisi in hem. For thou doynge these thingis, schalt 'make bothe thi silf saaf, and hem that heren thee.

1 Blame thou not an eldere man, but biseche as a fadir, yonge men as britheren; elde wymmen as modris,

2 yonge wymmen as sistris, in al chastite.

CAP 5

3 Honoure thou widewis, that ben very widewis.

4 But if ony widewe hath children of sones, lerne sche first to gouerne her hous, and quyte to fadir and modir; for this thing is acceptid bifor God.

5 And sche that is a widewe verili, and desolate, hope in to God, and be bisy in bisechingis and preieris niyt and dai.

6 For sche that is lyuynge in delicis, is deed.

7 And comaunde thou this thing, that thei be withouten repreef.

8 For if ony man hath not cure of his owne, and most of hise household men, he hath denyed the feith, and is worse than an vnfeithful man.

9 A widewe be chosun not lesse than sixti yeer, that was wijf of oon hosebonde,

10 and hath witnessing in good werkis, if sche nurschede children, if sche resseyuede pore men to herbore, if sche hath waischun the feet of hooli men, if sche mynystride to men that suffriden tribulacioun, if sche folewide al good werk.

11 But eschewe thou yongere widewis; for whanne thei han do letcherie, thei wolen be weddid in Crist,

12 hauynge dampnacioun, for thei han maad voide the firste feith.

13 Also thei idil lernen to go aboute housis, not oneli ydel, but ful of wordis and curiouse, spekynge thingis that bihoueth not.

14 Therfor Y wole, that yongere widewis be weddid, and bringe forth children, and ben hosewyues, to yyue noon occasioun to the aduersarie, bi cause of cursid thing.

15 For now summe ben turned abak aftir Sathanas.

16 If ony feithful man hath widewis, mynystre he to hem, that the chirche be not greuyd, that it suffice to hem that ben very widewis.

17 The prestis that ben wel gouernoures, be thei had worthi to double onour; moost thei that trauelen in word and teching.

18 For scripture seith, Thou schalt not bridil the mouth of the oxe threischinge, and, A werk man is worthi his hire.

19 Nyle thou resseyue accusyng ayens a preest, but vndur tweyne or thre witnessis.

20 But reproue thou men that synnen bifor alle men, that also othere haue drede.

21 Y preie bifor God, and Jhesu Crist, and hise chosun aungelis, that thou kepe these thingis with oute preiudice, and do no thing in bowynge 'in to the othere side.

22 Put thou hondis to no man, nether anoon comyne thou with othere mennus synnes. Kepe thi silf chast.

23 Nyle thou yit drinke watir, but vse a litil wyn, for thi stomac, and 'for thin ofte fallynge infirmytees.

24 Sum mennus synnes ben opyn, bifor goynge to dom; but of summen thei comen aftir.

25 And also goode dedis ben opyn, and tho that han hem in othere maner, moun not be hid.

CAP 6

1 What euere seruauntis ben vndur yok, deme thei her lordis worthi al onour, lest the name of the Lord and the doctryn be blasfemyd.

2 And thei that han feithful lordis, dispise hem not, for thei ben britheren; but more serue thei, for thei ben feithful and louyd, whiche ben parceneris of benefice. Teche thou these thingis, and moneste thou these thingis.

3 If ony man techith othere wise, and acordith not to the hoolsum wordis of oure Lord Jhesu Crist, and to that teching that is bi pitee,

4 he is proud, and kan no thing, but langwischith aboute questiouns and stryuyng of wordis, of the whiche ben brouyt forth enuyes, stryues, blasfemyes, yuele suspiciouns, fiytingis of men,

5 that ben corrupt in soule, and that ben pryued fro treuthe, that demen wynnyng to be pitee.

6 But a greet wynnyng is pitee, with sufficience.

7 For we brouyten in no thing in to this world, and no doute, that we moun not bere 'awey ony thing.

8 But we hauynge foodis, and with what thingus we schulen be hilid, be we paied with these thingis.

9 For thei that wolen be maad riche, fallen in to temptacioun, and 'in to snare of the deuel, and in to many vnprofitable desiris and noyous, whiche drenchen men in to deth and perdicioun.

10 For the rote of alle yuelis is coueytise, which summen coueitinge erriden fro the feith, and bisettiden hem with many sorewis.

11 But, thou, man of God, fle these thingis; but sue thou riytwisnesse, pite, feith, charite, pacience, myldenesse.

12 Stryue thou a good strijf of feith, catche euerlastinge lijf, in to which thou art clepid, and hast knoulechid a good knouleching bifor many witnessis.

13 I comaunde to thee bifor God, that quikeneth alle thingis, and bifor Crist Jhesu, that yeldide a witnessing vnder Pilat of Pounce, a good confessioun,

14 that thou kepe the comaundement with out wem, with out repreef, in to the comyng of oure Lord Jhesu Crist;

15 whom the blessid and aloone miyti king of kyngis and Lord of lordis schal schewe in his tymes.

16 Which aloone hath vndeedlynesse, and dwellith in liyt, to which no man may come; whom no man say, nether may se; to whom glorie, and honour, and empire be with out ende.

17 Amen. Comaunde thou to the riche men of this world, that thei vndurstonde not hiyli, nether that thei hope in vncerteynte of richessis, but in the lyuynge God, that yyueth to vs alle thingis plenteuously to vse;

18 to do wel, to be maad riche in good werkis, liytli to yyue,

19 to comyne, to tresoure to hem silf a good foundement in to tyme to comynge, that thei catche euerlastinge lijf.

20 Thou Tymothe, kepe the thing bitakun to thee, eschewynge cursid noueltees of voicis, and opynyouns of fals name of kunnyng;

21 which summen bihetinge, aboute the feith fellen doun. The grace of God be with thee. Amen.

2 TYMOTHE

CAP 1

1 Poul, apostle of Jhesu Crist, bi the wille of God, bi the biheest of lijf that is in Crist Jhesu,

2 to Tymothe, his moost dereworthe sone, grace, merci, and pees of God the fadir, and of Jhesu Crist, oure Lord.

3 I do thankyngis to my God, to whom Y serue fro my progenytouris in clene conscience, that with outen ceessyng Y haue mynde of thee in my preyeris,

4 niyt and dai, desirynge to se thee; hauynge mynde of thi teeris, that Y be fillid with ioye.

5 And Y bithenke of that feith, that is in thee not feyned, which also dwellide firste in thin aunte Loide, and in thi modir Eunyce. And Y am certeyn, that also in thee.

6 For which cause Y moneste thee, that thou reise ayen the grace of God, that is in thee bi the settyng on of myn hondis.

7 For whi God yaf not to vs the spirit of drede, but of vertu, and of loue, and of sobrenesse.

8 Therfor nyl thou schame the witnessyng of oure Lord Jhesu Crist, nether me, his prisoner; but trauele thou togidere in the gospel bi the vertu of God;

9 that delyueride vs, and clepide with his hooli clepyng, not after oure werkis, but bi his purpos and grace, that is youun in Crist Jhesu bifore worldli tymes;

10 but now it is opyn bi the liytnyng of oure sauyour Jhesu Crist, which destriede deth, and liytnede lijf and vncorrupcioun bi the gospel.

11 In which Y am set a prechour and apostle, and maistir of hethene men.

12 For which cause also Y suffre these thingis; but Y am not confoundid. For Y woot to whom Y haue bileuyd, and Y am certeyne that he is miyti for to kepe that is take to my keping in to that dai.

13 Haue thou the fourme of hoolsum wordis, whiche thou herdist of me in feith and loue in Crist Jhesu.

14 Kepe thou the good takun to thi kepyng bi the Hooli Goost, that dwellith in vs.

15 Thou wost this, that alle that ben in Asie ben turnyd awey fro me, of whiche is Figelus and Ermogenes.

16 The Lord yyue merci to the hous of Onesyforus, for ofte he refreischide me, and schamyde not my chayne.

17 But whanne he cam to Rome, he souyte me bisili, and foond.

18 The Lord yyue to hym to fynde merci of God in that dai. And hou grete thingis he mynystride to me at Effesi, thou knowist betere.

CAP 2

1 Therfor thou, my sone, be coumfortid in grace that is in Crist Jhesu.

2 And what thingis thou hast herd of me bi many witnessis, bitake thou these to feithful men, whiche schulen 'be also able to teche othere men.

3 Trauele thou as a good knyyt of Crist Jhesu.

4 No man holdinge knyythod to God, wlappith hym silf with worldli nedis, that he plese to hym, to whom he hath preuyd hym silf.

5 For he that fiytith in a batel, schal not be corowned, but he fiyte lawfuli.

6 It bihoueth an erthetiliere to resseyue first of the fruytis.

7 Vndurstonde thou what thingis Y seie. For the Lord schal yyue to thee vndurstonding in alle thingis.

8 Be thou myndeful that the Lord Jhesu Crist of the seed of Dauid hath rise ayen fro deth,

9 aftir my gospel, in which Y trauele 'til to boondis, as worching yuele, but the word of God is not boundun.

10 Therfor Y suffre alle thingis for the chosun, that also thei gete the heelthe, that is in Crist Jhesu, with heuenli glorie.

11 A trewe word, that if we ben deed togidere, also we schulen liue togidere;

12 if we suffren, we schulen regne togidere; if we denyen, he schal denye vs;

13 if we bileuen not, he dwellith feithful, he mai not denye hym silf.

14 Teche thou these thingis, witnessinge bifore God. Nyle thou stryue in wordis; for to no thing it is profitable, but to the suberting of men that heren.

15 Bisili kepe to yyue thi silf a preued preisable werkman to God, with oute schame, riytli tretinge the word of treuthe.

16 But eschewe thou vnhooli and veyn spechis, for whi tho profiten myche to vnfeithfulnesse,

17 and the word of hem crepith as a canker. Of whiche Filete is, and Ymeneus,

18 whiche felden doun fro the treuthe, seiynge that the rising ayen is now doon, and thei subuertiden the feith of summen.

19 But the sad foundement of God stondith, hauynge this marke, The Lord knowith whiche ben hise, and, Ech man that nameth the name of the Lord, departith fro wickidnesse.

20 But in a greet hous ben not oneli vessels of gold and of siluer, but also of tree and of erthe; and so summen ben in to onour, and summe in to dispit.

21 Therfor if ony man clensith hym silf fro these, he schal be a vessel halewid in to onour, and profitable to the Lord, redi to al good werk.

22 And fle thou desiris of yongthe, but sue thou riytwisnesse, feith, charite, pees, with hem that inwardli clepen the Lord of a clene herte.

23 And eschewe thou foltische questiouns, and without kunnyng, wytynge that tho gendren chidyngis.

24 But it bihoueth the seruaunt of the Lord to chide not; but to be mylde to alle men, able to teche,

25 paciente, with temperaunce repreuynge hem that ayenstonden the treuthe, that sum tyme God yyue to hem forthenkyng, that thei knowen the treuthe,

26 and that thei rise ayen fro the snares of the deuel, of whom thei ben holdun prisoneris at his wille.

CAP 3

1 But wite thou this thing, that in the laste daies perelouse tymes schulen neiye, and men schulen be louynge hem silf,

2 coueitouse, hiy of bering, proude, blasfemeris, not obedient to fadir and modir, vnkynde,

3 cursid, with outen affeccioun, with out pees, false blameris, vncontynent, vnmylde,

4 with out benygnyte, traitouris, ouerthwert, bollun with proude thouytis, blynde, loueris of lustis more than of God,

5 hauynge the licknesse of pitee, but denyynge the vertu of it. And eschewe thou these men.

6 Of these thei ben that persen housis, and leden wymmen caitifs chargid with synnes, whiche ben led with dyuerse desiris, euere more lernynge,

7 and neuere perfitli comynge to the science of treuthe.

8 And as Jannes and Mambres ayenstoden Moises, so these ayenstonden treuthe, men corrupt in vndirstonding, repreuyd aboute the feith.

9 But ferthere thei schulen not profite, for the vnwisdom of hem schal be knowun to alle men, as hern was.

10 But thou hast getun my teching, ordinaunce, purposing, feith, long abiding, loue,

11 pacience, persecuciouns, passiouns, whiche weren maad to me at Antioche, at Ycony, at Listris, what maner persecucyouns Y suffride, and the Lord hath delyuered me of alle.

12 And alle men that wolen lyue feithfuli in Crist Jhesu, schulen suffre persecucioun.

13 But yuele men and disseyueris schulen encreese in to worse, errynge, and sendinge in to errour.

14 But dwelle thou in these thingis that thou hast lerud, and that ben bitakun to thee, witinge of whom thou hast lerud;

15 for thou hast knowun hooli lettris fro thi youthe, whiche moun lerne thee to heelthe, bi feith that is in Crist Jhesu.

16 For al scripture inspirid of God is profitable to teche, to repreue, to chastice, to lerne in riytwisnes, that the man of God be parfit, lerud to al good werk.

CAP 4

1 I witnesse bifore God and Crist Jhesu, that schal deme the quike and the deed, and bi the comyng of hym, and the kyngdom of hym,

2 preche the word, be thou bisi couenabli with outen rest, repreue thou, biseche thou, blame thou in al pacience and doctryn.

3 For tyme schal be, whanne men schulen not suffre hoolsum teching, but at her desiris thei schulen gadere 'togidere to hem silf maistris yitchinge to the eeris.

4 And treuli thei schulen turne awei the heryng fro treuthe, but to fablis thei schulen turne.

5 But wake thou, in alle thingis traueile thou, do the werk of an euangelist, fulfille thi seruyce, be thou sobre.

6 For Y am sacrifisid now, and the tyme of my departyng is nyy.

7 Y haue stryuun a good strijf, Y haue endid the cours, Y haue kept the feith.

8 In 'the tothir tyme a coroun of riytwisnesse is kept to me, which the Lord, a iust domesman, schal yelde to me in that dai; and not oneli to me, but also to these that louen his comyng.

9 Hyye thou to come to me soone. For Demas, louynge this world, hath forsakun me, and wente to Tessalonyk,

10 Crescens in to Galathi, Tite in to Dalmacie;

11 Luk aloone is with me. Take thou Mark, and brynge with thee; for he is profitable to me in to seruyce.

12 Forsothe Y sente Titicus to Effesi.

13 The cloth which Y lefte at Troade at Carpe, whanne thou comest, bringe with thee, and the bookis, but moost parchemyne.

14 Alisaundre, the tresorer, schewide to me myche yuele; 'the Lord schal yelde to hym aftir his werkis.

15 Whom also thou eschewe; for he ayenstood ful greetli oure wordis.

16 In my firste defence no man helpide me, but alle forsoken me; be it not arettid to hem.

17 But the Lord helpide me, and coumfortide me, that the preching be fillid bi me, and that alle folkis here, that Y am delyueride fro the mouth of the lioun.

18 And the Lord delyueride me fro al yuel werk, and schal make me saaf in to his heuenly kingdom, to whom be glorie in to worldis of worldis.

19 Amen. Grete wel Prisca, and Aquila, and the hous of Oneseforus.

20 Erastus lefte at Corynthi, and Y lefte Trofymus sijk at Mylete.

21 Hiye thou to come bifore wyntir. Eubolus, and Prudent, and Lynus, and Claudia, and alle britheren, greten thee wel.

22 Oure Lord Jhesu Crist be with thi spirit. The grace of God be with you. Amen.

TITE

CAP 1

1 Poul, the seruaunt of God, and apostle of Jhesu Crist, bi the feith of the chosun of God, and bi the knowing of the treuthe,

2 whiche is aftir pitee, in to the hope of euerlastinge lijf, which lijf God that lieth not, bihiyte bifore tymes of the world;

3 but he hath schewid in hise tymes his word in preching, that is bitakun to me bi the comaundement of 'God oure sauyour,

4 to Tite, most dereworthe sone bi the comyn feith, grace and pees of God the fadir, and of Crist Jhesu, oure sauyour.

5 For cause of this thing Y lefte thee at Crete, that thou amende tho thingis that failen, and ordeyne preestis bi citees, as also Y disposide to thee.

6 If ony man is withoute cryme, an hosebonde of o wijf, and hath feithful sones, not in accusacioun of letcherie, or not suget.

7 For it bihoueth a bischop to be without cryme, a dispendour of God, not proud, not wrathful, not drunkelew, not smytere, not coueytouse of foul wynnyng;

8 but holdinge hospitalite, benygne, prudent, sobre, iust,

9 hooli, contynent, takinge that trewe word, that is aftir doctryn; that he be miyti to amoneste in hoolsum techyng, and to repreue hem that ayenseien.

10 For ther ben many vnobedient, and veyn spekeris, and disseyueris, moost thei that ben of circumcisyoun,

11 whiche it bihoueth to be repreued; whiche subuerten alle housis, techinge whiche thingis it bihoueth not, for the loue of foul wynnyng.

12 And oon of hem, her propre profete, seide, Men of Crete ben euere more lyeris, yuele beestis, of slowe wombe.

13 This witnessyng is trewe. For what cause blame hem sore, that thei be hool in feith,

14 not yyuynge tent to fablis of Jewis, and to maundementis of men, that turnen awei hem fro treuthe.

15 And alle thingis ben clene to clene men; but to vnclene men and to vnfeithful no thing is clene, for the soule and conscience of hem ben maad vnclene.

16 Thei knoulechen that thei knowen God, but bi dedis thei denyen; whanne thei ben abhominable, and vnbileueful, and repreuable to al good werk.

CAP 2

1 But speke thou tho thingis that bisemen hoolsum teching;

2 that elde men be sobre, chast, prudent, hool in feith, in loue, and pacience;

3 also olde wymmen in hooli abite, not sclaundereris, not seruynge myche to wyn, wel techynge, that thei teche prudence.

4 Moneste thou yonge wymmen, that thei loue here hosebondis, that thei loue her children;

5 and that thei be prudent, chast, sobre, hauynge cure of the hous, benygne, suget to her hosebondis, that the word of God be not blasfemyd.

6 Also moneste thou yonge men, that thei be sobre.

7 In alle thingis yyue thi silf ensaumple of good werkis, in teching, in hoolnesse, in sadnesse.

8 An hoolsum word, and vnrepreuable; that he that is of the contrarie side, be aschamed, hauynge noon yuel thing to seie of you.

9 Moneste thou seruauntis to be suget to her lordis; in alle thingis plesinge, not ayenseiynge, not defraudynge,

10 but in alle thingis schewinge good feith, that thei onoure in alle thingis the doctryn of 'God, oure sauyour.

11 For the grace of 'God, oure sauyour,

12 hath apperid to alle men, and tauyte vs, that we forsake wickidnesse, and worldli desyris, lyue sobreli, and iustli, 'and piteuousli in this world,

13 abidinge the blessid hope and the comyng of the glorie of the greet God, and of oure sauyour Jhesu Crist;

14 that yaf hym silf for vs, to ayenbie vs fro al wickidnesse, and make clene to hym silf a puple acceptable, and suere of good werkis.

15 Speke thou these thingis, and moneste thou, and repreue thou with al comaundement; no man dispise thee.

CAP 3

1 Amoneste hem to be sugetis to prynces, and to poweris; to obeische to that that is seid, and to be redi to al good werk;

2 to blasfeme no man, to be not ful of chiding, but temperat, schewynge al myldenesse to alle men.

3 For we weren sum tyme vnwise, vnbileueful, errynge, and seruynge to desiris, and to dyuerse lustis, doynge in malice and enuye, worthi to be hatid, hatinge ech othere.

4 But whanne the benygnyte and the manhed of oure sauyour God aperide,

5 not of werkis of riytwisnesse that we diden, but bi his merci he made vs saaf, bi waischyng of ayen bigetyng, and ayen newyng of the Hooli Goost,

6 whom he schedde into vs plenteuousli bi Jhesu Crist,

7 oure saueour, that we iustified bi his grace, ben eiris by hope of euerlastinge lijf.

8 A trewe word is, and of these thingis Y wole that thou conferme othere, that thei that bileuen to God, be bisy to be aboue othere in good werkis. These thingis ben good, and profitable to men.

9 And eschewe thou foltische questiouns, and genologies, and stryues, and fiytyngis of the lawe; for tho ben vnprofitable and veyn.

10 Eschewe thou a man eretik, aftir oon and the secound correccioun;

11 witinge that he that is siche a maner man is subuertid, and trespassith, and is dampned bi his owne dom.

12 Whanne Y sende to thee Arteman, or Titicus, hiy thou to 'come to me to Nycopolis; for Y haue purposid to dwelle in wyntir there.

13 Bisili byfor sende Zenam, a wise man of lawe, and Apollo, that no thing faile to hem.

14 Thei that ben of ouris, lerne to be gouernouris in good werkis, to necessarie vsis, that thei be not with out fruyt.

15 Alle men that ben with me greeten thee wel. Grete thou wel hem, that louen vs in feith. The grace of God be with you alle. Amen.

FILEMON

CAP 1

1 Poul, the boundun of Crist Jhesu, and Timothe, brother, to Filemon, bilouyd, and oure helpere, and to Appia,

2 most dere sister, and to Archip, oure euene kniyt, and to the chirche that is in thin hous,

3 grace be to you, and pees of God oure fader, and of the Lord Jhesu Crist.

4 I do thankingis to my God, euere more makinge mynde of thee in my preieris,

5 heringe thi charite and feith, that thou hast in the Lord Jhesu, and to alle hooli men,

6 that the comynyng of thi feith be maad opyn, in knowing of al good thing in Crist Jhesu.

7 And Y hadde greet ioye and coumfort in thi charite, for the entrailis of hooli men restiden bi thee, brother.

8 For which thing Y hauynge myche trist in Crist Jhesu, to comaunde to thee that that perteyneth to profit;

9 but Y biseche more for charite, sithen thou art siche as the elde Poul, and now the boundun of Jhesu Crist.

10 Y biseche thee for my sone Onesyme, whom Y in boondis bigat,

11 which sumtyme was vnprofitable to thee, but now profitable bothe to thee and to me; whom Y sente ayen to thee.

12 And resseyue thou hym as myn entrailis;

13 whom Y wolde withholde with me, that he schulde serue for thee to me in boondis of the gospel;

14 but with out thi counseil Y wolde not do ony thing, that thi good schulde not be as of nede, but wilful.

15 For perauenture therfor he departide fro thee for a tyme, that thou schuldist resseyue hym with outen ende;

16 now not as a seruaunt, but for a seruaunt a most dere brother, most to me; and how myche more to thee, bothe in fleisch and in the Lord?

17 Therfor if thou hast me a felowe, resseyue hym as me; for if he hath ony thing anoied thee,

18 ethir owith, arette thou this thing to me.

19 Y Poul wroot with myn hoond, Y schal yelde; that Y seie not to thee, that also thou owist to me thi silf.

20 So, brothir, Y schal vse thee in the Lord; fille thou myn entrails in Crist.

21 Y tristnynge of thin obedience wroot to thee, witynge that thou schalt do ouer that that Y seie.

22 Also make thou redi to me an hous to dwelle in; for Y hope that bi youre preyeris Y schal be youun to you.

23 Epafras, prisoner with me in Crist Jhesu,

24 greetith thee wel, and Mark, Aristark, Demas, Lucas, myn helperis.

25 The grace of oure Lord Jhesu Crist be with youre spirit. Amen.

EBREWS

CAP 1

1 God, that spak sum tyme bi prophetis in many maneres to oure fadris, at the

2 laste in these daies he hath spoke to vs bi the sone; whom he hath ordeyned eir of alle thingis, and bi whom he made the worldis.

3 Which whanne also he is the briytnesse of glorie, and figure of his substaunce, and berith alle thingis bi word of his vertu, he makith purgacioun of synnes, and syttith on the riythalf of the maieste in heuenes;

4 and so myche is maad betere than aungels, bi hou myche he hath eneritid a more dyuerse name bifor hem.

5 For to whiche of the aungels seide God ony tyme, Thou art my sone, Y haue gendrid thee to dai? And eftsoone, Y schal be to hym in to a fadir, and he schal be to me in to a sone?

6 And whanne eftsoone he bryngith in the firste bigetun sone in to the world, he seith, And alle the aungels of God worschipe hym.

7 But he seith to aungels, He that makith hise aungels spiritis, and hise mynystris flawme of fier.

8 But to the sone he seith, God, thi trone is in to the world of world; a yerde of equite is the yerde of thi rewme;

9 thou hast louyd riytwisnesse, and hatidist wickidnesse; therfor the God, thi God, anoyntide thee with oile of ioye, more than thi felowis.

10 And, Thou, Lord, in the bigynnyng foundidist the erthe, and heuenes ben werkis of thin hondis; thei schulen perische,

11 but thou schalt perfitli dwelle; and alle schulen wexe elde as a cloth, and thou schalt chaunge hem as a cloth,

12 and thei schulen be chaungid. But thou art the same thi silf, and thi yeeris schulen not faile.

13 But to whiche of the aungels seide God at ony tyme, Sitte thou on my riythalf, till Y putte thin enemyes a stool of thi feet?

14 Whether thei alle ben not seruynge spiritis, sente to seruen for hem that taken the eritage of heelthe?

CAP 2

1 Therfor more plenteuousli it bihoueth vs to kepe tho thingis, that we han herd, lest perauenture we fleten awei.

2 For if the ilke word that was seid bi aungels, was maad sad, and ech brekyng of the lawe and vnobedience took iust retribucioun of meede,

3 hou schulen we ascape, if we despisen so greet an heelthe? Which, whanne it hadde takun bigynnyng to be told out by the Lord, of hem that herden is confermyd in to vs.

4 For God witnesside to gidere bi myraclis, and wondris, and grete merueilis, and dyuerse vertues, and departyngis of the Hooli Goost, bi his wille.

5 But not to aungels God sugetide the world that is to comynge, of which we speken.

6 But sum man witnesside in a place, and seide, What thing is man, that thou art myndeful of hym, or mannus sone, for thou visitist hym?

7 Thou hast maad hym a litil lesse than aungels; thou hast corowned hym with glorie and onour; and thou hast ordeyned him on the werkis of thin hondis.

8 Thou hast maad alle thingis suget vndur hise feet. And in that that he sugetide alle thingis to hym, he lefte no thing vnsuget to him. But now we seen not yit alle thingis suget to hym;

9 but we seen hym that was maad a litil lesse than aungels, Jhesu, for the passioun of deth crowned with glorie and onour, that he thorouy grace of God schulde taste deth for alle men.

10 For it bisemede hym, for whom alle thingis, and bi whom 'alle thingis weren maad, which hadde brouyt many sones into glorie, and was auctour of the heelthe of hem, that he hadde an ende bi passioun.

11 For he that halewith, and thei that ben halewid, ben alle of oon; for which cause he is not schamed to clepe hem britheren,

12 seiynge, Y schal telle thi name to my britheren; in the myddil of the chirche Y schal herie thee.

13 And eftsoone, Y schal be tristnynge in to hym; and eftsoone, Lo! Y and my children, whiche God yaf to me.

14 Therfor for children comyneden to fleisch and blood, and he also took part of the same, that bi deth he schulde destrie hym that hadde lordschipe of deth, that is to seie, the deuel,

15 and that he schulde delyuere hem that bi drede of deth, 'bi al lijf weren boundun to seruage.

16 And he took neuere aungelis, but he took the seed of Abraham.

17 Wherfor he ouyte to be likned to britheren bi alle thingis, that he schulde be maad merciful and a feithful bischop to God, that he schulde be merciful to the trespassis of the puple.

18 For in that thing in which he suffride, and was temptid, he is miyti to helpe also hem that ben temptid.

CAP 3

1 Therfor, hooli britheren, and parceneris of heuenli cleping, biholde ye the apostle and the bischop of oure confessioun, Jhesu,

2 which is trewe to hym that made hym, as also Moises in al the hous of hym.

3 But this byschop is had worthi of more glorie than Moises, bi as myche as he hath more honour of the hous, that made the hous.

4 For ech hous is maad of sum man; he that made alle thingis of nouyt is God.

5 And Moises was trewe in al his hous, as a seruaunt, in to witnessyng of tho thingis that weren to be seid;

6 but Crist as a sone in his hous. Which hous we ben, if we holden sad trist and glorie of hope in to the ende.

7 Wherfor as the Hooli Goost seith, To dai, if ye han herd his vois, nyle ye hardne youre hertis,

8 as in wraththing, lijk the dai of temptacioun in desert;

9 where youre fadris temptiden me, and preueden, and siyen my werkis fourti yeeris.

10 Wherfor Y was wrooth to this generacioun, and Y seide, Euere more thei erren in herte, for thei knewen not my weies;

11 to whiche Y swore in my wraththe, thei schulen not entre in to my reste.

12 Britheren, se ye, lest perauenture in ony of you be an yuel herte of vnbileue, to departe fro the lyuynge God.

13 But moneste you silf bi alle daies, the while to dai is named, that noon of you be hardned bi fallas of synne.

14 For we ben maad parceneris of Crist, if netheles we holden the bigynnyng of his substaunce sad in to the ende.

15 While it is seid, to dai, if ye han herd the vois of hym, nyle ye hardne youre hertis, as in that wraththing.

16 For summen heringe wraththiden, but not alle thei that wenten out of Egipt bi Moises.

17 But to whiche was he wraththid fourti yeeris? Whether not to hem that synneden, whos careyns weren cast doun in desert?

18 And to whiche swoor he, that thei schulden not entre in to the reste of hym, not but to hem that weren vnbileueful?

19 And we seen, that thei myyten not entre in to the reste of hym for vnbileue.

CAP 4

1 Therfor drede we, lest perauenture while the biheest of entryng in to his reste is left, that ony of vs be gessid to be awei.

2 For it is told also to vs, as to hem. And the word that was herd profitide not to hem, not meynd to feith of tho thingis that thei herden.

3 For we that han bileued, schulen entre in to reste, as he seide, As Y swoor in my wraththe, thei schulen not entre in to my reste. And whanne the werkis weren maad perfit at the ordynaunce of the world,

4 he seide thus in a place of the seuenthe dai, And God restide in the seuenthe dai from alle hise werkis.

5 And in this place eftsoone, Thei schulen not entre in to my reste.

6 Therfor for it sueth, that summen schulen entre in to it, and thei to whiche it was teld to bifor, entriden not for her vnbileue.

7 Eftsoone he termyneth sum dai, and seith in Dauith, To dai, aftir so myche tyme of tyme, as it is biforseid, To dai if ye han herd his vois, nyle ye hardne youre hertis.

8 For if Jhesus hadde youun reste to hem, he schulde neuere speke of othere aftir this dai.

9 Therfor the sabat is left to the puple of God.

10 For he that is entrid in to his reste, restide of hise werkis, as also God of hise.

11 Therfor haste we to entre in to that reste, that no man falle in to the same ensaumple of vnbileue. For the word of God is quyk,

12 and spedi in worching, and more able to perse than any tweyne eggid swerd, and stretchith forth to the departynge of the soule and of the spirit, and of the ioynturis and merewis, and demere of thouytis, and of intentis and hertis.

13 And no creature is vnuisible in the siyt of God. For alle thingis ben nakid and opyn to hise iyen, to whom a word to vs.

14 Therfor we that han a greet bischop, that perside heuenes, Jhesu, the sone of God, holde we the knoulechyng of oure hope.

15 For we han not a bischop, that may not haue compassioun on oure infirmytees, but was temptid bi alle thingis bi lyc-nesse, with oute synne.

16 Therfor go we with trist to the trone of his grace, that we gete merci, and fynde grace in couenable help.

CAP 5

1 For ech bischop takun of men, is ordeyned for men in these thingis 'that ben to God, that he offre yiftis and sacrifices for synnes.

2 Which may togidere sorewe with hem, that beth vnkun-nynge and erren; for also he is enuyrounned with infirmytee.

3 And therfor he owith, as for the puple, so also for hym silf, to offre for synnes.

4 Nethir ony man taketh to hym onour, but he that is clepid of God, as Aaron was.

5 So Crist clarifiede not hym silf, that he were bischop, but he that spak to hym, Thou art my sone, to dai Y gendride thee.

6 As 'in anothere place he seith, Thou art a prest with outen ende, aftir the ordre of Melchisedech.

7 Which in the daies of his fleisch offride, with greet cry and teeris, preieris and bisechingis to hym that myyte make hym saaf fro deth, and was herd for his reuerence.

8 And whanne he was Goddis sone, he lernyde obedience of these thingis that he suffride;

9 and he brouyt to the ende is maad cause of euerlastinge heelthe to alle that obeischen to hym, and is clepid of God a bischop,

10 bi the ordre of Melchisedech.

11 Of whom ther is to vs a greet word for to seie, and able to be expowned, for ye ben maad feble to here.

12 For whanne ye ouyten to be maistris for tyme, eftsoone ye neden that ye be tauyt, whiche ben the lettris of the bigyn-nyng of Goddis wordis. And ye ben maad thilke, to whiche is nede of mylk, and not sad mete.

13 For ech that is parcenere of mylk, is with out part of the word of riytwisnesse, for he is a litil child.

14 But of perfit men is sad mete, of hem that for custom han wittis exercisid to discrecioun of good and of yuel.

CAP 6

1 Therfor we bringinge in a word of the bigynnyng of Crist, be we borun to the perfeccioun of hym, not eftsoone leggynge the foundement of penaunce fro deed werkis, and of the feith to God, and of teching of baptimys,

2 and of leiynge on of hondis, and of risyng ayen of deed men, and of the euerlastinge doom.

3 And this thing we schulen do, if God schal suffre.

4 But it is impossible, that thei that ben onys liytned, and 'han tastid also an heuenly yifte, and ben maad parceneris of the Hooli Goost,

5 and netheles han tastid the good word of God, and the ver-tues of the world to comynge, and ben slidun fer awei,

6 that thei be renewid eftsoone to penaunce. Whiche eftsones crucifien to hem silf the sone of God, and han to scorn.

7 For the erthe that drinkith reyn ofte comynge on it, and bringith forth couenable erbe to hem of whiche it is tilid, takith blessing of God.

8 But that that is bringinge forth thornes and breris, is repreuable, and next to curs, whos endyng schal be in to bren-nyng.

9 But, ye moost dereworthe, we tristen of you betere thingis, and neer to helthe, thouy we speken so.

10 For God is not vniust, that he foryete youre werk and loue, whiche ye han schewid in his name; for ye han mynystrid to seyntis, 'and mynistren.

11 And we coueiten that ech of you schewe the same bisy-nesse to the fillyng of hope in to the ende;

12 that ye be not maad slowe, but also sueris of hem, whiche bi feith and pacience schulen enherite the biheestis.

13 For God bihetinge to Abraham, for he hadde noon grettere, bi whom he schulde swere, swoor bi hym silf,

14 and seide, Y blessinge schal blesse thee, and Y multi-pliynge schal multiplie thee;

15 and so he long abidinge hadde the biheeste.

16 For men sweren bi a grettere than hem silf, and the ende of al her ple is an ooth to confirmacioun.

17 In which thing God willynge to schewe plenteuouslier to the eiris of his biheest the sadnesse of his counsel,

18 puttide bitwixe an ooth, that bi twey thingis vnmeuable, bi whiche it is impossible that God lie, we han a strengeste

solace, 'we that fleen togidere to holde the hope that is put forth to vs.

19 Which hope as an ankir we han sikir to the soule, and sad, and goynge in to the ynnere thingis of hiding;

20 where the bifore goere, Jhesus, that is maad bischop with outen ende bi the ordre of Melchisedech, entride for vs.

CAP 7

1 And this Melchisedech, king of Salem, and preest of the hiyeste God, which mette with Abraham, as he turnede ayen fro the sleyng of kyngis, and blesside hym;

2 to whom also Abraham departide tithis of alle thingis; first he is seid king of riytwisnesse, and aftirward kyng of Salem, that is to seie, king of pees,

3 with out fadir, with out modir, with out genologie, nether hauynge bigynnyng of daies, nether ende of lijf; and he is lickened to the sone of God, and dwellith preest with outen ende.

4 But biholde ye how greet is this, to whom Abraham the patriark yaf tithis of the beste thingis.

5 For men of the sones of Leuy takinge presthod han maundement to take tithis of the puple, bi the lawe, that is to seie, of her britheren, thouy also thei wenten out of the leendis of Abraham.

6 But he whos generacioun is not noumbrid in hem, took tithis of Abraham; and he blesside this Abraham, which hadde repromyssiouns.

7 With outen ony ayenseiyng, that that is lesse, is blessid of the betere.

8 And heere deedli men taken tithis; but there he berith witnessyng, that he lyueth.

9 And that it be seid so, bi Abraham also Leuy, that took tithis, was tithid; and yit he was in his fadris leendis,

10 whanne Melchisedech mette with hym.

11 Therfor if perfeccioun was bi the preesthood of Leuy, for vndur hym the puple took the lawe, what yit was it nedeful, another preest to rise, bi the ordre of Melchisedech, and not to be seid bi the ordre of Aaron?

12 For whi whanne the preesthod is translatid, it is nede that also translacioun of the lawe be maad.

13 But he in whom these thingis ben seid, is of another lynage, of which no man was preest to the auter.

14 For it is opyn, that oure Lord is borun of Juda, in which lynage Moises spak no thing of preestis.

15 And more yit it is knowun, if bi the ordre of Melchisedech another preest is risun vp;

16 which is not maad bi the lawe of fleischli maundement, but bi vertu of lijf that may not be vndon.

17 For he witnessith, That thou art a preest with outen ende, bi the ordre of Melchisedech;

18 that repreuyng of the maundement bifor goynge is maad, for the vnsadnesse and vnprofit of it.

19 For whi the lawe brouyt no thing to perfeccioun, but there is a bringing in of a betere hope, bi which we neiyen to God.

20 And hou greet it is, not with out sweryng; but the othere ben maad preestis with outen an ooth;

21 but this preest with an ooth, bi hym that seide 'to hym, The Lord swoor, and it schal not rewe hym, Thou art a preest with outen ende, bi the ordre of Melchisedech;

22 in so myche Jhesus is maad biheetere of the betere testament.

23 And the othere weren maad manye preestis, 'therfor for thei weren forbedun bi deth to dwelle stille;

24 but this, for he dwellith with outen ende, hath an euerlastynge preesthod.

25 Wherfor also he may saue with outen ende, comynge nyy bi hym silf to God, and euermore lyueth to preye for vs.

26 For it bisemyde that sich a man were a bischop to vs, hooli, innocent, vndefoulid, clene, departid fro synful men, and maad hiyere than heuenes;

27 which hath not nede ech dai, as prestis, first for hise owne giltis to offre sacrifices, and aftirward for the puple; for he dide this thing in offringe hym silf onys.

28 And the lawe ordeynede men prestis hauynge sijknesse; but the word of swering, which is after the lawe, ordeynede the sone perfit with outen ende.

CAP 8

1 But a capitle on tho thingis that ben seid. We han siche a bischop, that sat in the riythalf of the seete of greetnesse in heuenes,

2 the mynystre of seyntis, and of the veri tabernacle, that God made, and not man.

3 For ech bischop is ordeyned to offre yiftis and sacrificis; wherfor it is nede, that also this bischop haue sum thing that he schal offre.

4 Therfor if he were on erthe, he were no preest, whanne ther weren that schulden offre yiftis bi the lawe,

5 whiche seruen to the saumpler and schadewe of heueneli thingis. As it was answerid to Moises, whanne he schulde ende the tabernacle, Se, he seide, make thou alle thingis bi the saumpler, that is schewid to thee in the mount.

6 But now he hath getun a betere mynysterie, bi so myche as he is a mediatour of a betere testament, which is confermyd with betere biheestis.

7 For if the ilke firste hadde lackid blame, the place of the secounde schulde not haue be souyt.

8 For he repreuynge hem seith, Lo! daies comen, seith the Lord, and Y schal make perfit a newe testament on the hous of Israel, and on the hous of Juda;

9 not lijk the testament that Y made to her fadris, 'in the dai in which Y cauyte her hond, that Y schulde lede hem out of the loond of Egipt; for thei dwelliden not perfitli in my testament, and Y haue dispisid hem, seith the Lord.

10 But this is the testament, which Y schal dispose to the hous of Israel aftir tho daies, seith the Lord, in yyuynge my lawis in to the soulis of hem, and in to the hertis of hem I schal aboue write hem; and Y schal be to hem in to a God, and they schulen be to me in to a puple.

11 And ech man schal not teche his neiyebore, and ech man his brother, seiynge, Knowe thou the Lord; for alle men schulen knowe me, fro the lesse to the more of hem.

12 For Y schal be merciful to the wickidnesse of hem, and now Y schal not bithenke on the synnes of hem.

13 But in seiynge a newe, the formere wexide eeld; and that that is of many daies, and wexith eeld, is nyy the deeth.

CAP 9

1 And the former testament hadde iustefiyngis of worschip, and hooli thing duringe for a tyme.

2 For the tabernacle was maad first, in which weren candilstikis, and boord, and setting forth of looues, which is seid hooli.

3 And after the veil, the secounde tabernacle, that is seid sancta sanctorum, that is, hooli of hooli thingis;

4 hauynge a goldun cenrer, and the arke of the testament, keuered aboute on ech side with gold, in which was a pot of gold hauynge manna, and the yerde of Aaron that florischide, and the tablis of the testament;

5 on whiche thingis weren cherubyns of glorie, ouerschadewinge the propiciatorie; of whiche thingis it is not now to seie bi alle.

6 But whanne these weren maad thus togidere, preestis entriden eueremore in the formere tabernacle, doynge the offices of sacrifices; but in the secounde tabernacle,

7 the bischop entride onys in the yeer, not without blood, which he offride for his ignoraunce and the puplis.

8 For the Hooli Goost signefiede this thing, that not yit the weie of seyntis was openyd, while the formere tabernacle hadde staat.

9 Which parable is of this present tyme, bi which also yiftis and sacrifices ben offrid, whiche moun not make a man seruynge perfit bi conscience, oneli in metis,

10 and drynkis, and dyuerse waischingis, and riytwisnessis of fleisch, that weren sett to the tyme of correccioun.

11 But Crist beynge a bischop of goodis to comynge, entride bi a largere and perfitere tabernacle, not maad bi hoond, that is to seye,

12 not of this makyng, nether bi blood of goot buckis, or of calues, but bi his owne blood, entride onys in to the hooli thingis, that weren foundun bi an euerlastinge redempcioun.

13 For if the blood of gootbuckis, and of boolis, and the aische of a cow calf spreynd, halewith vnclene men to the clensing of fleisch,

14 hou myche more the blood of Crist, which bi the Hooli Goost offride hym silf vnwemmyd to God, schal clense oure conscience fro deed werkis, to serue God that lyueth?

15 And therfor he is a mediatour of the newe testament, that bi deth fallinge bitwixe, in to redempcioun of tho trespassyngis that weren vndur the formere testament, thei that ben clepid take the biheest of euerlastinge eritage.

16 For where a testament is, it is nede, that the deth of the testament makere come bitwixe.

17 For a testament is confermed in deed men; ellis it is not worthe, while he lyueth, that made the testament.

18 Wherfor nether the firste testament was halewid without blood.

19 For whanne ech maundement of the lawe was red of Moises to al the puple, he took the blood of calues, and of buckis of geet, with watir, and reed wolle, and ysope, and bispreynde bothe thilke book and al the puple,

20 and seide, This is the blood of the testament, that God comaundide to you.

21 Also he spreynde with blood the tabernacle, and alle the vessels of the seruyce in lijk maner.

22 And almest alle thingis ben clensid in blood bi the lawe; and without scheding of blood remyssioun of synnes is not maad.

23 Therfor it is nede, that the saumpleris of heuenli thingis be clensid with these thingis; but thilke heuenli thingis with betere sacrificis than these.

24 For Jhesus entride not in to hooli thingis maad bi hoondis, that ben saumpleris of very thingis, but in to heuene it silf, that he appere now to the cheer of God for vs; nether that he offre him silf ofte,

25 as the bischop entride in to hooli thingis bi alle yeeris in alien blood,

26 ellis it bihofte hym to suffre ofte fro the bigynnyng of the world; but now onys in the ending of worldis, to distruccioun of synne bi his sacrifice he apperide.

27 And as it is ordeynede to men,

28 onys to die, but aftir this is the dom, so Crist was offrid onys, to auoyde the synnes of many men; the secounde tyme he schal appere with outen synne to men that abiden him in to heelthe.

CAP 10

1 For the lawe hauinge a schadewe of good thingis 'that ben to come, not the ilke image of thingis, mai neuer make men neiyinge perfit bi the ilke same sacrifices, which thei offren without ceessing bi alle yeeris;

2 ellis thei schulden haue ceessid to be offrid, for as myche as the worschiperis clensid onys, hadden not ferthermore conscience of synne.

3 But in hem mynde of synnes is maad bi alle yeris.

4 For it is impossible that synnes be doon awei bi blood of boolis, and of buckis of geet.

5 Therfor he entrynge in to the world, seith, Thou woldist not sacrifice and offryng; but thou hast schapun a bodi to me;

6 brent sacrificis also for synne plesiden not to thee.

7 Thanne Y seide, Lo! Y come; in the bigynnyng of the book it is writun of me, that Y do thi wille, God.

8 He seiynge bifor, That thou woldist not sacrificis, and offringis, and brent sacrifices for synne, ne tho thingis ben plesaunt to thee, whiche ben offrid bi the lawe,

9 thanne Y seide, Lo! Y come, that Y do thi wille, God. He doith awei the firste, that he make stidfast the secounde.

10 In which wille we ben halewid bi the offring of the bodi of Crist Jhesu onys.

11 And ech prest is redi mynystrynge ech dai, and ofte tymes offringe the same sacrifices, whiche moun neuere do awei synnes.

12 But this man offringe o sacrifice for synnes, for euere more sittith in the riythalf of God the fadir;

13 fro thennus forth abidinge, til hise enemyes ben put a stool of hise feet.

14 For bi oon offring he made perfit for euere halewid men.

15 And the Hooli Goost witnessith to vs; for aftir that he seide, This is the testament,

16 which Y schal witnesse to hem after tho daies, the Lord seith, in yyuynge my lawes in the hertis of hem, and in the soulis of hem Y schal aboue write hem;

17 and now Y schal no more thenke on the synnes and the wickidnessis of hem.

18 And where remyssioun of these is, now is ther noon offring for synne.

19 Therfor, britheren, hauynge trist in to the entring of hooli thingis in the blood of Crist,

20 which halewide to vs a newe weie, and lyuynge bi the hiling, that is to seie,

21 his fleisch, and we hauynge the greet preest on the hous of God,

22 neiye we with very herte in the plente of feith; and be oure hertis spreined fro an yuel conscience, and oure bodies waischun with clene watir,

23 and holde we the confessioun of oure hope, bowinge to no side; for he is trewe that hath made the biheeste.

24 And biholde we togidere in the stiring of charite and of good werkis; not forsakinge oure gadering togidere,

25 as it is of custom to sum men, but coumfortinge, and bi so myche the more, bi hou myche ye seen the dai neiyynge.

26 Forwhi now a sacrifice for synnes is not left to vs, that synnen wilfuli, aftir that we han take the knowyng of treuthe.

27 Forwhi sum abiding of the dom is dreedful, and the suyng of fier, which schal waste aduersaries.

28 Who that brekith Moises lawe, dieth withouten ony merci, bi tweine or thre witnessis;

29 hou myche more gessen ye, that he disserueth worse turmentis, which defouleth the sone of God, and holdith the blood of the testament pollut, in which he is halewid, and doith dispit to the spirit of grace?

30 For we knowen him that seide, To me veniaunce, and Y schal yelde. And eft, For the Lord schal deme his puple.

31 It is ferdful to falle in to the hondis of God lyuynge.

32 And haue ye mynde on the formere daies, in which ye weren liytned, and suffriden greet strijf of passiouns.

33 And in the 'tothir ye weren maad a spectacle bi schenschipis and tribulaciouns; in an othir ye weren maad felowis of men lyuynge so.

34 For also to boundun men ye hadden compassioun, and ye resseyueden with ioye the robbyng of youre goodis, knowinge that ye han a betere and a dwellinge substaunce.

35 Therfor nyle ye leese youre trist, which hath greet rewarding.

36 For pacience is nedeful to you, that ye do the wille of God, and bringe ayen the biheest.

37 For yit a litil, and he that is to comynge schal come, and he schal not tarie.

38 For my iust man lyueth of feith; that if he withdrawith hym silf, he schal not plese to my soule.

39 But we ben not the sones of withdrawing awei in to perdicioun, but of feith in to getynge of soule.

CAP 11

1 But feith is the substaunce of thingis that ben to be hopid, and an argument of thingis not apperynge.

2 And in this feith elde men han gete witnessyng.

3 Bi feith we vndurstonden that the worldis weren maad bi Goddis word, that visible thingis weren maad of vnuysible thingis.

4 Bi feith Abel offride a myche more sacrifice than Caym to God, bi which he gat witnessyng to be iust, for God bar witnessyng to hise yiftis; and bi that feith he deed spekith yit.

5 Bi feith Ennok was translatid, that he schulde not se deth; and he was not foundun, for the Lord translatide him. For bifore translacioun he hadde witnessing that he pleside God.

6 And it is impossible to plese God without feith. For it bihoueth that a man comynge to God, bileue that he is, and that he is rewardere to men that seken hym.

7 Bi feith Noe dredde, thorouy answere takun of these thingis that yit weren not seyn, and schapide a schip in to the helthe of his hous; bi which he dampnede the world, and is ordeyned eir of riytwisnesse, which is bi feith.

8 By feith he that is clepid Abraham, obeiede to go out in to a place, whiche he schulde take in to eritage; and he wente out, not witinge whidur he schulde go.

9 Bi feith he dwelte in the loond of biheest, as in an alien loond, dwellynge in litle housis with Ysaac and Jacob, euene heiris of the same biheest.

10 For he abood a citee hauynge foundementis, whos crafti man and maker is God.

11 Bi feith also the ilke Sara bareyn, took vertu in consceyuyng of seed, yhe, ayen the tyme of age; for sche bileuede hym trewe, that hadde bihiyte.

12 For which thing of oon, and yit nyy deed, ther ben borun as sterris of heuene in multitude, and as grauel that is at the see side out of noumbre.

13 Bi feith alle these ben deed, whanne the biheestis weren not takun, but thei bihelden hem afer, and gretynge hem wel, and knoulechide that thei weren pilgryms, and herboryd men on the erthe.

14 And thei that sayn these thingis, signifien that thei sechen a cuntre.

15 'If thei hadden hadde mynde of the ilke, of which thei wenten out, thei hadden tyme of turnyng ayen;

16 but now thei desiren a betere, that is to seie, heuenli. Therfor God is not confoundid to be clepid the God of hem; for he made redi to hem a citee.

17 Bi feith Abraham offride Ysaac, whanne he was temptid; and he offride the oon bigetun, whych had takun the biheestis;

18 to whom it was seid, For in Ysaac the seed schal be clepid to thee.

19 For he demyde, that God is myyti to reise hym, yhe, fro deth; wherfor he took hym also in to a parable.

20 Bi feith also of thingis to comynge, Ysaac blesside Jacob and Esau.

21 Bi feith Jacob diynge blesside alle the sones of Joseph, and onouride the hiynesse of his yerde.

22 Bi feith Joseph dyynge hadde mynde of the passyng forth of the children of Israel, and comaundide of hise boonys.

23 Bi feith Moyses borun, was hid thre monethis of his fadir and modir, for that thei seiyen the yonge child fair; and thei dredden not the maundement of the king.

24 Bi feith Moises was maad greet, and denyede that he was the sone of Faraos douytir,

25 and chees more to be turmentid with the puple of God, than to haue myrthe of temporal synne;

26 demynge the repreef of Crist more richessis than the tresours of Egipcians; for he bihelde in to the rewarding.

27 Bi feith he forsook Egipt, and dredde not the hardynesse of the king; for he abood, as seinge hym that was vnuysible.

28 Bi feith he halewide pask, and the scheding out of blood, that he that distriede the firste thingis of Egipcians, schulde not touche hem.

29 Bi feith thei passiden the reed see, as bi drye lond, which thing Egipcians asaiynge weren deuourid.

30 Bi feith the wallis of Jerico felden doun, bi cumpassyng of seuene daies.

31 Bi feith Raab hoor resseyuede the aspieris with pees, and perischide not with vnbileueful men.

32 And what yit schal Y seie? For tyme schal faile to me tellynge of Gedeon, Barak, Sampson, Jepte, Dauid, and Samuel, and of othere prophetis;

33 whiche bi feith ouercamen rewmes, wrouyten riytwisnesse, gaten repromyssiouns; thei stoppiden the mouthis of liouns,

34 thei quenchiden the feersnesse of fier, thei dryueden awei the egge of swerd, thei coueriden of sijknesse, thei weren maad strong in batel, thei turneden the oostis of aliens.

35 Wymmen resseyueden her deed children fro deth to lijf; but othere weren holdun forth, not takinge redempcioun, that thei schulden fynde a betere ayenrising.

36 And othere asaieden scornyngis and betingis, more ouer and boondis and prisouns.

37 Thei weren stoned, thei weren sawid, thei weren temptid, thei weren deed in sleyng of swerd. Thei wenten aboute in broc skynnes, and in skynnes of geet, nedi, angwischid, turmentid;

38 to whiche the world was not worthi. Thei erriden in wildernessis, in mounteynes and dennes, and caues of the erthe.

39 And alle these, preued bi witnessing of feith, token not repromyssioun;

40 for God purueiede sum betere thing for vs, that thei schulden not be maad perfit with outen vs.

CAP 12

1 Therfor we that han so greet a cloude of witnessis put to, do we awei al charge, and synne stondinge aboute vs, and bi pacience renne we to the batel purposid to vs,

2 biholdinge in to the makere of feith, and the perfit endere, Jhesu; which whanne ioye was purposid to hym, he suffride the cros, and dispiside confusioun, and sittith on the riythalf of the seet of God.

3 And bithenke ye on hym that suffride siche 'ayen seiynge of synful men ayens hym silf, that ye be not maad wery, failinge in youre soulis.

4 For ye ayenstoden not yit 'til to blood, fiytyng ayens synne.

5 And ye han foryet the coumfort that spekith to you as to sones, and seith, My sone, nyle thou dispise the teching of the Lord, nether be thou maad weri, the while thou art chastisid of hym.

6 For the Lord chastisith hym that he loueth; he betith euery sone that he resseyueth.

7 Abide ye stille in chastising; God proferith hym to you as to sones. For what sone is it, whom the fadir chastisith not?

8 That if ye 'ben out of chastising, whos parteneris ben ye alle maad, thanne ye ben auowtreris, and not sones.

9 And aftirward we hadden fadris of oure fleisch, techeris, and we with reuerence dredden hem. Whethir not myche more we schulen obeische to the fadir of spiritis, and we schulen lyue?

10 And thei in tyme of fewe dayes tauyten vs bi her wille; but this fadir techith to that thing that is profitable, in resseyuynge the halewing of hym.

11 And ech chastisyng in present tyme semeth to be not of ioye, but of sorewe; but aftirward it schal yelde fruyt of riytwisnesse moost pesible to men exercisid bi it.

12 For whiche thing reise ye slowe hondis,

13 and knees vnboundun, and make ye riytful steppis to youre feet; that no man haltinge erre, but more be heelid.

14 Sue ye pees with alle men, and holynesse, with out which no man schal se God.

15 Biholde ye, that no man faile to the grace of God, that no roote of bittirnesse buriownynge vpward lette, and manye ben defoulid bi it;

16 that no man be letchour, ether vnhooli, as Esau, which for o mete seelde hise firste thingis.

17 For wite ye, that afterward he coueitinge to enherite blessing, was repreued. For he foond not place of penaunce, thouy he souyte it with teeris.

18 But ye han not come to the fier able to be touchid, and able to come to, and to the whirlewynd, and myst, and tempest, and soun of trumpe, and vois of wordis;

19 which thei that herden, excusiden hem, that the word schulde not be maad to hem.

20 For thei beren not that that was seid, And if a beeste touchide the hil, it was stonyd.

21 And so dredeful it was that was seyn, that Moises seide, Y am a ferd, and ful of trembling.

22 But ye han come nyy to the hil Sion, and to the cite of God lyuynge, the heuenli Jerusalem, and to the multitude of many thousynde aungels,

23 and to the chirche of the firste men, whiche ben writun in heuenes, and to God, domesman of alle, and to the spirit of iust perfit men,

24 and to Jhesu, mediatour of the newe testament, and to the sprenging of blood, 'betere spekinge than Abel.

25 Se ye, that ye forsake not the spekere; for if thei that forsaken him that spak on the erthe, aschapide not, myche more we that turnen awei fro him that spekith to vs fro heuenes.

26 Whos vois than mouyde the erthe, but now he ayen bihetith, and seith, Yit onys and Y schal moue not oneli erthe, but also heuene.

27 And that he seith, Yit onys, he declarith the translacioun of mouable thingis, as of maad thingis, that tho thingis dwelle, that ben vnmouable.

28 Therfor we resseyuynge the kingdom vnmouable, haue we grace, bi which serue we plesynge to God with drede and reuerence.

29 For oure God is fier that wastith.

CAP 13

1 The charite of britherhod dwelle in you, and nyle ye foryete hospitalite;

2 for bi this summen plesiden to aungels, that weren resseyued to herborewe.

3 Thenke ye on boundun men, as ye weren togidere boundun, and of trauelinge men, as ye silf dwellinge in the body.

4 'Wedding is in alle thingis onourable, and bed vnwemmed; for God schal deme fornicatouris and auouteris.

5 Be youre maneres withoute coueitise, apaied with present thingis; for he seide, Y schal not leeue thee,

6 nether forsake, so that we seie tristily, The Lord is an helpere to me; Y schal not drede, what a man schal do to me.

7 Haue ye mynde of youre souereyns, that han spokun to you the word of God; of whiche 'biholde ye the goyng out of lyuynge, and sue ye the feith of hem,

8 Jhesu Crist, yistirdai, and to dai, he is also into worldis.

9 Nyle ye be led awei with dyuerse 'techingis, and straunge. For it is best to stable the herte with grace, not with metis, whiche profitiden not to men wandringe in hem.

10 We han an auter, of which thei that seruen to the tabernacle, han not power to ete.

11 For of whiche beestis the blood is borun in for synne in to hooli thingis bi the bischop, the bodies of hem ben brent with out the castels.

12 For which thing Jhesu, that he schulde halewe the puple bi his blood, suffride with out the gate.

13 Therfor go we out to hym with out the castels, berynge his repreef.

14 For we han not here a citee dwellynge, but we seken a citee to comynge.

15 Therfor bi hym offre we a sacrifice of heriyng euere more to God, that is to seye, the fruyt of lippis knoulechinge to his name.

16 And nyle ye foryete wel doynge, and comynyng; for bi siche sacrifices God is disserued.

17 Obeie ye to youre souereyns, and be ye suget to hem; for thei perfitli waken, as to yeldinge resoun for youre soulis, that thei do this thing with ioie, and not sorewinge; for this thing spedith not to you.

18 Preie ye for vs, and we tristen that we han good conscience in alle thingis, willynge to lyue wel.

19 More ouer Y biseche you to do, that Y be restorid the sunnere to you.

20 And God of pees, that ladde out fro deth the greet scheepherd of scheep, in the blood of euerlastinge testament, oure Lord Jhesu Crist,

21 schape you in al good thing, that ye do the wille of hym; and he do in you that thing that schal plese bifor hym, bi Jhesu Crist, to whom be glorie in to worldis of worldis. Amen.

22 And, britheren, Y preie you, that ye suffre a word of solace; for bi ful fewe thingis Y haue writun to you.

23 Knowe ye oure brother Tymothe, that is sent forth, with whom if he schal come more hastili, Y schal se you.

24 Grete ye wel alle youre souereyns, and alle hooli men. The britheren of Italie greten you wel.

25 The grace of God be with you alle. Amen.

JAMES

CAP 1

1 James, the seruaunt of God, and of oure Lord Jhesu Crist, to the twelue kinredis, that ben in scatering abrood, helthe.

2 My britheren, deme ye al ioye, whanne ye fallen in to diuerse temptaciouns, witynge,

3 that the preuyng of youre feith worchith pacience;

4 and pacience hath a perfit werk, that ye be perfit and hole, and faile in no thing.

5 And if ony of you nedith wisdom, axe he of God, which yyueth to alle men largeli, and vpbreidith not; and it schal be youun to hym.

6 But axe he in feith, and doute no thing; for he that doutith, is lijk to a wawe of the see, which is moued and borun a boute of wynde.

7 Therfor gesse not the ilke man, that he schal take ony thing of the Lord.

8 A man dowble in soule is vnstable in alle hise weies.

9 And a meke brother haue glorie in his enhaunsyng,

10 and a riche man in his lownesse; for as the flour of gras he schal passe.

11 The sunne roos vp with heete, and driede the gras, and the flour of it felde doun, and the fairnesse of his chere perischide; and so a riche man welewith in hise weies.

12 Blessid is the man, that suffrith temptacioun; for whanne he schal be preued, he schal resseyue the coroun of lijf, which God biheyte to men that louen hym.

13 No man whanne he is temptid, seie, that he is temptid of God; for whi God is not a temptere of yuele thingis, for he temptith no man.

14 But ech man is temptid, drawun and stirid of his owne coueiting.

15 Aftirward coueityng, whanne it hath conseyued, bringith forth synne; but synne, whanne it is fillid, gendrith deth.

16 Therfor, my most dereworthe britheren, nyle ye erre.

17 Ech good yifte, and ech perfit yifte is from aboue, and cometh doun fro the fadir of liytis, anentis whom is noon other chaungyng, ne ouerschadewyng of reward.

18 For wilfulli he bigat vs bi the word of treuthe, that we be a bigynnyng of his creature.

19 Wite ye, my britheren moost loued, be ech man swift to here, but slow to speke, and slow to wraththe;

20 for the wraththe of man worchith not the riytwisnesse of God.

21 For which thing caste ye awei al vnclennesse, and plentee of malice, and in myldenesse resseyue ye the word that is plauntid, that may saue youre soulis.

22 But be ye doeris of the word, and not hereris oneli, disseiuynge you silf.

23 For if ony man is an herere of the word, and not a doere, this schal be licned to a man that biholdith the cheer of his birthe in a mirour;

24 for he bihelde hym silf, and wente awei, and anoon he foryat which he was.

25 But he that biholdith in the lawe of perfit fredom, and dwellith in it, and is not maad a foryetful herere, but a doere of werk, this schal be blessid in his dede.

26 And if ony man gessith hym silf to be religiouse, and refreyneth not his tunge, but disseyueth his herte, the religioun of him is veyn.

27 A clene religioun, and an vnwemmed anentis God and the fadir, is this, to visite fadirles and modirles children, and widewis in her tribulacioun, and to kepe hym silf vndefoulid fro this world.

CAP 2

1 Mi britheren, nyle ye haue the feith of oure Lord Jhesu Crist of glorie, in accepcioun of persoones.

2 For if a man 'that hath a goldun ring, and in a feire clothing, cometh in youre cumpany, and a pore man entrith in a foul clothing,

3 and if ye biholden in to hym that is clothid with clere clothing, and if ye seie to hym, Sitte thou here wel; but to the pore man ye seien, Stonde thou there, ethir sitte vndur the stool of my feet; whether ye demen not anentis you silf,

4 and ben maad domesmen of wickid thouytis?

5 Heere ye, my moost dereworthe britheren, whethir God chees not pore men in this world, riche in feith, and eiris of the kyngdom, that God bihiyte to men that louen him?

6 But ye han dispisid the pore man. Whether riche men oppressen not you bi power, and thei drawen you to domes?

7 Whether thei blasfemen not the good name, that is clepid to help on you?

8 Netheles if ye performen the kingis lawe, bi scripturis, Thou schalt loue thi neiybour as thi silf, ye don wel.

9 But if ye taken persones, ye worchen synne, and ben repreued of the lawe, as trespasseris.

10 And who euere kepith al the lawe, but offendith in oon, he is maad gilti of alle.

11 For he that seide, Thou schalt do no letcherie, seide also, Thou schalt not sle; that if thou doist not letcherie, but thou sleest, thou art maad trespassour of the lawe.

12 Thus speke ye, and thus do ye, as bigynnynge to be demyd bi the lawe of fredom.

13 For whi dom with out merci is to hym, that doith no mercy; but merci aboue reisith dom.

14 Mi britheren, what schal it profite, if ony man seie that he hath feith, but he hath not the werkis? whether feith schal mowe saue hym?

15 And if a brother ethir sister be nakid, and han nede of ech daies lyuelode,

16 and if ony of you seie to hem, Go ye in pees, be ye maad hoot, and be ye fillid; but if ye yyuen not to hem tho thingis that ben necessarie to bodi, what schal it profite?

17 So also feith, if it hath not werkis, is deed in it silf.

18 But summan schal seie, Thou hast feith, and Y haue werkis; schewe thou to me thi feith with out werkis, and Y schal schewe to thee my feith of werkis.

19 Thou bileuest, that o God is; thou doist wel; and deuelis bileuen, and tremblen.

20 But wolt thou wite, thou veyn man, that feith with out werkis is idul?

21 Whether Abraham, oure fadir, was not iustified of werkis, offringe Ysaac, his sone, on the auter?

22 Therfor thou seest, that feith wrouyte with hise werkis, and his feith was fillid of werkis.

23 And the scripture was fillid, seiynge, Abraham bileuede to God, and it was arettid to hym to riytwisnesse, and he was clepid the freend of God.

24 Ye seen that a man is iustified of werkis, and not of feith oneli.

25 In lijk maner, and whether also Raab, the hoore, was not iustified of werkis, and resseyuede the messangeris, and sente hem out bi anothir weie?

26 For as the bodi with out spirit is deed, so also feith with out werkis is deed.

CAP 3

1 Mi britheren, nyle ye be maad many maistris, witynge that ye taken the more doom.

2 For alle we offenden in many thingis. If ony man offendith not in word, this is a perfit man; for also he may lede aboute al the bodi with a bridil.

3 For if we putten bridlis 'in to horsis mouthis, for to consente to vs, and we leden aboute al the bodi of hem.

4 And lo! schippis, whanne thei ben grete, and ben dryuun of stronge wyndis, yit thei ben borun about of a litil gouernaile, where the meuyng of the gouernour wole.

5 So also the tunge is but a litil membre, and reisith grete thingis. Lo! hou litil fier brenneth a ful greet wode.

6 And oure tunge is fier, the vniuersite of wickidnesse. The tunge is ordeyned in oure membris, which defoulith al the bodi; and it is enflawmed of helle, and enflawmeth the wheel of oure birthe.

7 And al the kynde of beestis, and of foulis, and of serpentis, and of othere is chastisid, and tho ben maad tame of mannus kinde; but no man mai chastise the tunge,

8 for it is an vnpesible yuel, and ful of deedli venym.

9 In it we blessen God, the fadir, and in it we cursen men, that ben maad to the licnesse of God.

10 Of the same mouth passith forth blessing and cursing. My britheren, it bihoueth not that these thingis be don so.

11 Whether a welle of the same hoole bringith forth swete and salt watir?

12 My britheren, whether a fige tre may make grapis, ethir a vyne figus? So nethir salt watir mai make swete watir.

13 Who is wijs, and tauyt among you? schewe he of good lyuyng his worching, in myldenesse of his wisdom.

14 That if ye han bitter enuye, and stryuyngis ben in youre hertis, nyle ye haue glorye, and be lyeris ayens the treuthe.

15 For this wisdom is not fro aboue comynge doun, but ertheli, and beestli, and feendli.

16 For where is enuye and strijf, there is vnstidfastnesse and al schrewid werk.

17 But wisdom that is from aboue, first it is chast, aftirward pesible, mylde, able to be counseilid, consentinge to goode thingis, ful of merci and of goode fruytis, demynge with out feynyng.

18 And the fruyt of riytwisnesse is sowun in pees, to men that maken pees.

CAP 4

1 Wherof ben batelis and cheestis among you? Whether not of youre coueitisis, that fiyten in youre membris?

2 Ye coueiten, and ye han not; ye sleen, and ye han enuye, and ye moun not gete. Ye chiden, and maken batel; and ye han not, for ye axen not.

3 Ye axen, and ye resseyuen not; for that ye axen yuele, as ye schewen opynli in youre coueitisis.

4 Auowtreris, witen not ye, that the frenschip of this world is enemye to God? Therfor who euere wole be frend of this world, is maad the enemye of God.

5 Whether ye gessen, that the scripture seith veynli, The spirit that dwellith in you, coueitith to enuye?

6 But he yyueth the more grace; for which thing he seith, God withstondith proude men, but to meke men he yyueth grace.

7 Therfor be ye suget to God; but withstonde ye the deuel, and he schal fle fro you.

8 Neiye ye to God, and he schal neiye to you. Ye synneris, clense ye hondis, and ye double in soule, purge ye the hertis.

9 Be ye wretchis, and weile ye; youre leiyyng be turned in to weping, and ioye in to sorewe of herte.

10 Be ye mekid in the siyt of the Lord, and he schal enhaunse you.

11 My britheren, nyle ye bacbite ech othere. He that bacbitith his brothir, ethir that demeth his brothir, bacbitith the lawe, and demeth the lawe. And if thou demest the lawe, thou art not a doere of the lawe, but a domesman.

12 But oon is makere of the lawe, and iuge, that may lese, and delyuere.

13 And who art thou, that demest thi neiybore? Lo! now ye, that seien, To dai ethir to morewe we schulen go in to thilke citee, and there we schulen dwelle a yeer, and we schulen make marchaundise, and we schulen make wynning;

14 whiche witen not, what is to you in the morewe.

15 For what is youre lijf? A smoke apperinge at a litil, and aftirward it schal be wastid. Therfor that ye seie, If the Lord wole, and if we liuen, we schulen do this thing, ether that thing.

16 And now ye maken ful out ioye in youre pridis; euery siche ioye is wickyd.

17 Therfor it is synne to hym, that kan do good, and doith not.

CAP 5

1 Do now, ye riche men, wepe ye, yellinge in youre wretchid-nessis that schulen come to you.

2 Youre richessis ben rotun, and youre clothis ben etun of mouytis.

3 Youre gold and siluer hath rustid, and the rust of hem schal be to you in to witnessyng, and schal ete youre fleischis, as fier. Ye han tresourid to you wraththe in the last daies.

4 Lo! the hire of youre werke men, that repiden youre feeldis, which is fraudid of you, crieth; and the cry of hem hath entrid in to the eeris of the Lord of oostis.

5 Ye han ete on the erthe, and in youre letcheries ye han nur-schid youre hertis. In the dai of sleyng ye brouyten,

6 and slowen the iust man, and he ayenstood not you.

7 Therfor, britheren, be ye pacient, til to the comyng of the Lord. Lo! an erthetilier abidith preciouse fruyt of the erthe, paciently suffrynge, til he resseyue 'tymeful and lateful fruyt.

8 And be ye pacient, and conferme ye youre hertis, for the comyng of the Lord schal neiye.

9 Britheren, nyle ye be sorewful ech to other, that ye be not demed. Lo! the iuge stondith niy bifor the yate.

10 Britheren, take ye ensaumple of yuel goyng out, and of long abidyng, and trauel, and of pacience, the prophetis, that speken to you in the name of the Lord.

11 Lo! we blessen hem that suffriden. Ye herden the 'suffring, ethir pacience, of Joob, and ye sayn the ende of the Lord, for the Lord is merciful, and doynge merci.

12 Bifor alle thingis, my britheren, nyle ye swere, nether bi heuene, nether bi erthe, nethir bi what euere other ooth. But be youre word Yhe, yhe, Nay, nay, that ye fallen not vndir doom.

13 And if ony of you is sorewful, preye he with pacient soule, and seie he a salm.

14 If ony of you is sijk, lede he in preestis of the chirche, and preie thei for hym, and anoynte with oile in the name of the Lord;

15 and the preier of feith schal saue the sijk man, and the Lord schal make hym liyt; and if he be in synnes, thei schulen be foryouun to hym.

16 Therfor knouleche ye ech to othere youre synnes, and preye ye ech for othere, that ye be sauyd. For the contynuel preyer of a iust man is myche worth.

17 Elye was a deedli man lijk vs, and in preier he preiede, that it schulde not reyne on the erthe, and it reynede not thre yeeris and sixe monethis.

18 And eftsoone he preiede, and heuene yaf reyn, and the erthe yaf his fruyt.

19 And, britheren, if ony of you errith fro trewthe, and ony conuertith hym,

20 he owith to wite, that he that makith a synner to be turned fro the errour of his weye, schal saue the soule of hym fro deth, and keuereth the multitude of synnes.

1 PETRE

CAP 1

1 Petre, apostle of Jhesu Crist, to the chosun men, to the comelingis of scateryng abrood, of Ponte, of Galathie, of Capadosie,

2 of Asye, and of Bitynye, bi the 'bifor knowyng of God, the fadir, in halewyng of spirit, bi obedience, and springyng of the blood of Jhesu Crist, grace and pees be multiplied to you.

3 Blessid be God, and the fadir of oure Lord Jhesu Crist, which bi his greet merci bigat vs ayen in to lyuynge hope, bi the ayen risyng of Jhesu Crist fro deth,

4 in to eritage vncorruptible, and vndefoulid, and that schal not fade, that is kept in heuenes for you,

5 that in the vertu of God ben kept bi the feith in to heelthe, and is redi to be schewid in the last tyme.

6 In which ye schulen make ioye, thouy it bihoueth now a litil to be sori in dyuerse temptaciouns;

7 that the preuyng of youre feith be myche more preciouse than gold, that is preuyd bi fier; and be foundun in to heriyng, and glorie, and onour, in the reuelacioun of Jhesu Crist.

8 Whom whanne ye han not seyn, ye louen; in to whom also now ye not seynge, bileuen; but ye that bileuen schulen haue ioye, and gladnesse that may not be told out,

9 and ye schulen be glorified, and haue the ende of youre feith, the helthe of youre soulis.

10 Of which helthe profetis souyten, and enserchiden, that profecieden of the grace to comyng in you,

11 and souyten which euer what maner tyme the spirit of Crist signyfiede in hem, and bifor telde tho passiouns, that ben in Crist, and the latere glories.

12 To which it was schewid, for not to hem silf, but to you thei mynystriden tho thingis, that now ben teld to you bi hem that prechiden to you bi the Hooli Goost sent fro heuene, in to whom aungelis desiren to biholde.

13 For which thing be ye gird the leendis of youre soule, sobre, perfit, and hope ye in to the ilke grace that is profrid to you bi the schewyng of Jhesu Crist,

14 as sones of obedience, not made lijk to the formere desiris of youre vnkunnyngnesse,

15 but lijk him that hath 'clepid you hooli; that also 'ye silf be hooli in 'al lyuyng;

16 for it is writun, Ye schulen be hooli, for Y am hooli.

17 And if ye inwardli clepe him fadir, which demeth withouten accepcioun of persoones bi the werk of ech man, lyue ye in drede in the time of youre pilgrimage; witynge that not bi corruptible gold,

18 ethir siluer, ye ben bouyt ayen of youre veyn liuynge of fadris tradicioun,

19 but bi the precious blood as of the lomb vndefoulid and vnspottid,

20 Crist Jhesu, that was knowun bifor the makyng of the world, but he is schewid in the laste tymes,

21 for you that bi hym ben feithful in God; that reiside hym fro deth, and yaf to hym euerlastynge glorie, that youre feith and hope were in God.

22 And make ye chast youre soulis in obedience of charite, in loue of britherhod; of simple herte loue ye togidre more bisili.

23 And be ye borun ayen, not of corruptible seed, 'but vncorruptible, bi the word of lyuynge God, and dwellynge in to with outen ende.

24 For ech fleisch is hey, and al the glorie of it is as flour of hey; the hei driede vp, and his flour felde doun;

25 but the word of the Lord dwellith with outen ende. And this is the word, that is prechid to you.

CAP 2

1 Therfor putte ye awei al malice, and al gile, and feynyngis, and enuyes, and alle bacbityngis;

2 as now borun yonge children, resonable, with out gile, coueite ye mylk, that in it ye wexe in to helthe; if netheles ye han tastid,

3 that the Lord is swete.

4 And neiye ye to hym, that is a lyuyng stoon, and repreuyd of men, but chosun of God, and onourid;

5 and ye silf as quyk stoonys be ye aboue bildid in to spiritual housis, and an hooli preesthod, to offre spiritual sacrifices, acceptable to God bi Jhesu Crist.

6 For which thing the scripture seith, Lo! Y schal sette in Syon the hiyeste corner stoon, chosun and preciouse; and he that schal belieue in hym, schal not be confoundid.

7 Therfor onour to you that bileuen; but to men that bileuen not, the stoon whom the bilderis repreuyden, this is maad in to the heed of the corner; and the stoon of hirtyng,

8 and stoon of sclaundre, to hem that offenden to the word, nethir bileuen it, in which thei ben set.

9 But ye ben a chosun kyn, a kyngli preesthod, hooli folc, a puple of purchasing, that ye telle the vertues of hym, that clepide you fro derknessis in to his wondirful liyt.

10 Which sum tyme were not a puple of God, but now ye ben the puple of God; which hadden not merci, but now ye han merci.

11 Moost dere, Y biseche you, as comelyngis and pilgrymys, to absteine you fro fleischli desiris, that fiyten ayens the soule;

12 and haue ye youre conuersacioun good among hethene men, that in that thing that thei bacbite of you, as of mysdoeris, thei biholden you of good werkis, and glorifie God in the dai of visitacioun.

13 Be ye suget to ech creature, for God; ethir to the kyng, as to hym that is hiyer in state,

14 ethir to duykis, as to thilke that ben sent of hym to the veniaunce of mysdoers, and to the preisyng of good men.

15 For so is the wille of God, that ye do wel, and make the vnkunnyngnesse of vnprudent men to be doumb.

16 As fre men, and not as hauynge fredom the keuering of malice, but as the seruauntis of God.

17 Onoure ye alle men, loue ye brithirhod, drede ye God, onoure ye the king.

18 Seruauntis, be ye sugetis in al drede to lordis, not oneli to good and to mylde, but also to tyrauntis.

19 For this is grace, if for conscience of God ony man suffrith heuynessis, and suffrith vniustli.

20 For what grace is it, if ye synnen, and ben buffatid, and suffren? But if ye don wel, and suffren pacientli, this is grace anentis God.

21 For to this thing ye ben clepid. For also Crist suffride for vs, and lefte ensaumple to you, that ye folewe the steppis of hym.

22 Which dide not synne, nethir gile was foundun in his mouth.

23 And whanne he was cursid, he curside not; whanne he suffride, he manasside not; but he bitook hym silf to hym, that demyde hym vniustli.

24 And he hym silf bar oure synnes in his bodi on a tre, that we be deed to synnes, and lyue to riytwisnesse, bi whos wan wounde ye ben heelid.

25 For ye weren as scheep errynge, but ye ben now turned to the schipherde, and bischop of youre soulis.

CAP 3

1 Also wymmen be thei suget to her hosebondis; that if ony man bileue not to the word, bi the conuersacioun of wymmen thei be wonnun with out word.

2 And biholde ye in drede youre hooli conuersacioun.

3 Of whiche 'ther be not with outforth curious ournyng of heer, ether doyng aboute of gold, ethir ournyng of clothing;

4 but thilke that is the hid man of herte, in vncorrupcioun, and of mylde spirit, which is riche in the siyt of God.

5 For so sumtyme hooli wymmen hopinge in God ourneden hem silf, and weren suget to her owne hosebondis.

6 As Sara obeied to Abraham, and clepide hym lord; of whom ye ben douytris wel doynge, and not dredynge ony perturbacioun.

7 Also men dwelle togidre, and bi kunnyng yyue ye onoure to the wommanus freeltee, as to the more feble, and as to euen eiris of grace and of lijf, that youre preieris be not lettid.

8 And in feith alle of oon wille in preier be ye eche suffringe with othere, loueris of britherhod, merciful, mylde, meke;

9 not yeldinge yuel for yuel, nether cursing for cursing, but ayenward blessinge; for in this thing ye ben clepid, that ye welde blessinge bi eritage.

10 For he that wole loue lijf, and se goode daies, constreyne his tunge from yuel, and hise lippis, that thei speke not gile.

11 And bowe he from yuel, and do good; seke he pees, and perfitli sue it.

12 For the iyen of the Lord ben on iust men, and hise eris on the preieris of hem; but the cheer of the Lord is on men that don yuels.

13 And who is it that schal anoye you, if ye ben sueris and louyeris of goodnesse?

14 But also if ye suffren ony thing for riytwisnesse, ye ben blessid; but drede ye not the drede of hem, that ye be not disturblid.

15 But halewe ye the Lord Crist in youre hertis, and euermore be ye redi to satisfaccioun to ech man axynge you resoun of that feith and hope that is in you,

16 but with myldenesse and drede, hauynge good conscience; that in that thing that thei bacbiten of you, thei ben confoundid, whiche chalengen falsly youre good conuersacioun in Crist.

17 For it is betere that ye do wel, and suffre, if the wille of God wole, than doynge yuele.

18 For also Crist onys diede for oure synnes, he iust for vniust, that he schulde offre to God vs, maad deed in fleisch, but maad quik in spirit.

19 For which thing he cam in spirit, and also to hem that weren closid togidre in prisoun prechide;

20 whiche weren sum tyme vnbileueful, whanne thei abididen the pacience of God in the daies of Noe, whanne the schip was maad, in which a few, that is to seie, eiyte soulis weren maad saaf bi water.

21 And so baptym of lijk forme makith vs saaf; not the puttyng awei of the filthis of fleisch, but the axyng of a good conscience in God, bi the ayenrysyng of oure Lord Jhesu Crist, that is in the riyt half of God,

22 and swolewith deth, that we schulden be made eiris of euerlastinge lijf. He yede in to heuene, and aungelis, and powers, and vertues, ben maad sugetis to hym.

CAP 4

1 Therfor for Crist suffride in fleisch, be ye also armed bi the same thenkynge; for he that suffride in fleisch ceesside fro synnes,

2 that that is left now in fleisch lyue not now to the desiris of men, but to the wille of God.

3 For the time that is passid is ynow to the wille of hethene men to be endid, whiche walkiden in letcheries, and lustis, in myche drinking of wyn, in vnmesurable etyngis, and drynkyngis, and vnleueful worschiping of mawmetis.

4 In whiche now thei ben astonyed, in which thing thei wondren, for ye rennen not togidere 'in to the same confusioun of letcherie, and blasfemen.

5 And thei schulen yyue resoun to hym, that is redi to deme the quyke and the deed.

6 For whi for this thing it is prechid also to deed men, that thei be demed bi men in fleisch, and that thei lyue bi God in spirit.

7 For the ende of alle thingis schal neiye. Therfor be ye prudent, and wake ye in preyeris;

8 bifore alle thingis haue ye charite ech to other in you silf algatis lastynge; for charite couerith the multitude of synnes.

9 Holde ye hospitalite togidere with out grutching;

10 ech man as he hath resseyued grace, mynystringe it in to ech othere, as good dispenderis of the manyfold grace of God.

11 If ony man spekith, speke he as the wordis of God; if ony man mynystrith, as of the vertu which God mynystrith; that God be onourid in alle thingis bi Jhesu Crist oure Lord, to whom is glorie and lordschip in to worldis 'of worldis.

12 Amen. Moost dere brytheren, nyle ye go in pilgrymage in feruour, that is maad to you to temptacioun, as if ony newe thing bifalle to you;

13 but comyne ye with the passiouns of Crist, and haue ye ioye, that also ye be glad, and haue ioye in the reuelacioun of his glorie.

14 If ye ben dispisid for the name of Crist, ye schulen be blessid; for that that is of the onour, and of the glorie, and of the vertu of God, and the spirit that is his, schal reste on you.

15 But no man of you suffre as a mansleere, ethir a theef, ether cursere, ethir a disirere of othere mennus goodis;

16 but if as a cristen man, schame he not, but glorifie he God in this name.

17 For tyme is, that doom bigynne at Goddis hous; and if it bigynne first at vs, what ende schal be of hem, that bileuen not to the gospel?

18 And if a iust man vnnethe schal be sauid, where schulen the vnfeithful man and the synnere appere? Therfor and thei that suffren bi the wille of God, bitaken her soulis in good dedis to the feithful makere of nouyt.

CAP 5

1 Therfor Y, an euene eldre man, and a witnesse of Cristis passiouns, which also am a comynere of that glorie, that schal be schewid in tyme to comynge; byseche ye the eldre men,

2 that ben among you, fede ye the flok of God, that is among you, and puruey ye, not as constreyned, but wilfulli, bi God; not for loue of foule wynnyng,

3 but wilfulli, nether as hauynge lordschip in the clergie, but that ye ben maad ensaumple of the floc, of wille.

4 And whanne the prince of scheepherdis schal appere, ye schulen resseyue the coroun of glorie, that may neuere fade.

5 Also, ye yonge men, be ye suget to eldre men, and alle schewe ye togidere mekenesse; for the Lord withstondith proude men, but he yyueth grace to meke men.

6 Therfor be ye mekid vndir the myyti hoond of God, that he reise you in the tyme of visitacioun,

7 and caste ye al youre bisynesse in to hym, for to hym is cure of you.

8 Be ye sobre, and wake ye, for youre aduersarie, the deuel, as a rorynge lioun goith aboute, sechinge whom he schal deuoure.

9 Whom ayenstonde ye, stronge in the feith, witynge that the same passioun is maad to thilke brithirhode of you, that is in the world.

10 And God of al grace, that clepide you in to his euerlastinge glorie, you suffrynge a litil, he schal performe, and schal conferme, and schal make sad.

11 To hym be glorie and lordschip, in to worldis of worldis. Amen.

12 Bi Siluan, feithful brother to you as Y deme, Y wroot schortli; bisechinge, and witnessinge that this is the very grace of God, in which ye stonden.

13 The chirche that is gaderid in Babiloyne, and Marcus, my sone, gretith you wel.

14 Grete ye wel togidere in hooli cos. Grace be to you alle that ben in Crist. Amen.

2 PETRE

CAP 1

1 Simount Petre, seruaunt and apostle of 'Jhesu Crist, to hem that han take with vs the euene feith, in the riytwisnesse of oure God and sauyour Jhesu Crist,

2 grace and pees be fillid to you, bi the knowing of oure Lord Jhesu Crist.

3 Hou alle thingis of his godlich vertu, that ben to lijf and pitee, ben youun to vs, bi the knowyng of hym, that clepide vs for his owne glorie and vertu.

4 Bi whom he yaf to vs moost preciouse biheestis; that bi these thingis ye schulen be maad felows of Goddis kynde, and fle the corrupcioun of that coueytise, that is in the world.

5 And bringe ye in alle bisynesse, and mynystre ye in youre feith vertu, and 'in vertu kunnyng;

6 in kunnyng abstinence, in abstynence pacience, in pacience pitee;

7 in pitee, love of britherhod, and in loue of britherhod charite.

8 For if these ben with you, and ouercomen, thei schulen not make you voide, nethir with out fruyt, in the knowyng of oure Lord Jhesu Crist.

9 But to whom these ben not redi, he is blynd, and gropith with his hoond, and foryetith the purgyng of his elde trespassis.

10 Wherfor, britheren, be ye more bisi, that by goode werkis ye make youre clepyng and chesyng certeyn;

11 for ye doynge these thingis schulen not do synne ony tyme. For thus the entryng in to euerlastynge kyngdom of oure Lord and sauyour Jhesu Crist, schal be mynystrid to you plenteuuousli.

12 For which thing Y schal bigynne to moneste you euere more of these thingis; and Y wole that ye be kunnynge, and confermyd in this present treuthe.

13 Forsothe Y deme iustli, as long as Y am in this tabernacle, to reise you in monesting; and Y am certeyn,

14 that the putting awei of my tabernacle is swift, bi this that oure Lord Jhesu Crist hath schewid to me.

15 But Y schal yyue bisynesse, and ofte after my deth ye haue mynde of these thingis.

16 For we not suynge vnwise talis, han maad knowun to you the vertu and the biforknowyng of oure Lord Jhesu Crist; but we weren maad biholderis of his greetnesse.

17 For he took of God the fadir onour and glorie, bi siche maner vois slidun doun to hym fro the greet glorie, This is my loued sone, in whom Y haue plesid to me; here ye hym.

18 And we herden this vois brouyt from heuene, whanne we weren with hym in the hooli hil.

19 And we han a saddere word of prophecie, to which ye yyuynge tent don wel, as to a lanterne that yyueth liyt in a derk place, til the dai bigynne to yyue liyt, and the dai sterre sprenge in youre hertis.

20 And firste vndurstonde ye this thing, that ech prophesie of scripture is not maad bi propre interpretacioun;

21 for prophesie was not brouyt ony tyme bi mannus wille, but the hooli men of God inspirid with the Hooli Goost spaken.

CAP 2

1 But also false prophetis weren in the puple, as in you schulen be maistris lieris, that schulen bringe in sectis of perdicioun; and thei denyen thilke Lord that bouyte hem, and bringen on hem silf hasti perdicioun.

2 And many schulen sue her letcheries, bi whiche the weie of treuthe schal be blasfemyd;

3 and thei schulen make marchaundie of you in coueytise bi feyned wordis. To whiche doom now a while ago ceessith not, and the perdicioun of hem nappith not.

4 For if God sparide not aungels synnynge, but bitook hem to be turmentid, and to be drawun doun with boondis of helle in to helle, to be kept in to dom;

5 and sparide not the firste world, but kept Noe, the eiythe man, the biforgoere of riytwisnesse, and brouyte in the greet flood to the world of vnfeithful men;

6 and he droof in to poudre the citees of men of Sodom and of men of Gommor, and dampnede bi turnyng vpsedoun, and putte hem the ensaumple of hem that weren to doynge yuele;

7 and delyuerid the iust Loth, oppressid of the wrong, and of the letcherouse conuersacioun of cursid men;

8 for in siyt and hering he was iust, and dwellide amongst hem that fro dai in to dai turmentiden with wickid werkis a iust soule.

9 For the Lord kan delyuere piteuouse men fro temptacioun, and kepe wickid men 'in to the dai of dom to be turmentid;

10 but more hem that walken aftir the fleisch, in coueytinge of vnclennesse, and dispisen lordschiping, and ben boold, plesynge hem silf, and dreden not to bringe in sectis, blasfemynge; where aungels,

11 whanne thei ben more in strengthe and vertu, beren not 'that was the execrable doom ayens hem.

12 But these ben as vnresonable beestis, kyndli in to takyng, and in to deth, blasfemynge in these thingis that thei knowen not, and schulen perische in her corrupcioun,

13 and resseyue the hire of vnriytwisnesse. And thei gessen delicis of defouling and of wemme, to be likyngis of dai, flowynge in her feestis with delicis, doynge letcherie with you,

14 and han iyen ful of auowtrie, and vnceessynge trespas, disseyuynge vnstidfast soulis, and han the herte excercisid to coueitise; the sones of cursyng,

15 that forsaken the riyt weie, and erriden, suynge the weie of Balaam of Bosor, which louyde the hire of wickidnesse.

16 But he hadde repreuyng of his woodnesse; a doumb beest vndur yok, that spak with vois of man, that forbede the vnwisdom of the profete.

17 These ben wellis with out watir, and mystis dryuun with 'whirlinge wyndys, to whiche the thicke mijst of derknessis is reseruyd.

18 And thei speken in pryde of vanyte, and disseyuen in desiris of fleisch of letcherie hem, that scapen a litil.

19 Whiche lyuen in errour, and biheten fredom to hem, whanne thei ben seruauntis of corrupcioun. For of whom ony man is ouercomun, of hym also he is seruaunt.

20 For if men forsaken the vnclennessis of the world, bi the knowyng of oure Lord and sauyour Jhesu Crist, and eftsone ben wlappid in these, and ben ouercomun, the lattere thingis ben maad to hem worse than the formere.

21 For it was betere to hem to not knowe the weie of riytwisnesse, than to turne ayen aftir the knowyng, fro that hooli maundement that was bitakun to hem.

22 For thilke very prouerb bifelde to hem, The hound turnede ayen to his castyng, and a sowe is waischun in walwyng in fenne.

CAP 3

1 Lo! ye moost dereworth britheren, Y write to you this secounde epistle, in which Y stire youre clere soule bi monesting togidere,

2 that ye be myndeful of tho wordis, that Y biforseide of the hooli prophetis, and of the maundementis of the hooli apostlis of the Lord and sauyour.

3 First wite ye this thing, that in the laste daies disseyueris schulen come in disseit, goynge aftir her owne coueityngis,

4 seiynge, Where is the biheest, or the comyng of hym? for sithen the fadris dieden, alle thingis lasten fro the bigynnyng of creature.

5 But it is hid fro hem willynge this thing, that heuenes were bifore, and the erthe of water was stondynge bi watir, of Goddis word;

6 bi which that ilke world clensid, thanne bi watir perischide.

7 But the heuenes that now ben, and the erthe, ben kept bi the same word, and ben reseruyd to fier in to the dai of doom and perdicioun of wickid men.

8 But, ye moost dere, this o thing be not hid to you, that o dai anentis God is as a thousynde yeeris, and a thousynde yeeris ben as o dai.

9 The Lord tarieth not his biheest, as summe gessen, but he doith pacientli for you, and wole not that ony men perische, but that alle turne ayen to penaunce.

10 For the dai of the Lord schal come as a theef, in which heuenes with greet bire schulen passe, and elementis schulen be dissoluyd bi heete, and the erthe, and alle the werkis that ben in it, schulen be brent.

11 Therfor whanne alle these thingis schulen be dissolued, what manner men bihoueth it you to be in hooli lyuyngis and pitees,

12 abidinge and hiyynge in to the comyng of the dai of oure Lord Jhesu Crist, bi whom heuenes brennynge schulen be dissoluyd, and elementis schulen faile bi brennyng of fier.

13 Also we abiden bi hise biheestis newe heuenes and newe erthe, in which riytwisnesse dwellith.

14 For which thing, ye moost dere, abidynge these thingis, be ye bisye to be foundun to hym in pees vnspottid and vndefoulid.

15 And deme ye long abiding of oure Lord Jhesu Crist youre heelthe, as also oure moost dere brother Poul wroot to you, bi wisdom youun to hym.

16 As and in alle epistlis he spekith 'in hem of these thingis; in which ben summe hard thingis to vndurstonde, whiche vnwise and vnstable men deprauen, as also thei don othere scripturis, to her owne perdicioun.

17 Therfor ye, britheren, bifor witynge kepe you silf, lest ye be disseyued bi errour of vnwise men, and falle awei fro youre owne sadnesse.

18 But wexe ye in the grace and the knowyng of oure Lord Jhesu Crist and oure Sauyour; to hym be glorie now and in to the dai of euerlastyngnesse. Amen.

1 JOON

CAP 1

1 That thing that was fro the bigynnyng, which we herden, which we sayn with oure iyen, which we bihelden, and oure hondis touchiden, of the word of lijf; and the lijf is schewid.
2 And we sayn, and we witnessen, and tellen to you the euerlastynge lijf, that was anentis the fadir, and apperide to vs.
3 Therfor 'we tellen to you that thing, that we seyn, and herden, that also ye haue felowschipe with vs, and oure felowschip be with the fadir, and with his sone Jhesu Crist.
4 And we writen this thing to you, that ye haue ioye, and that youre ioye be ful.
5 And this is the tellyng, that we herden of hym, and tellen to you, that God is liyt, and ther ben no derknessis in him.
6 If we seien, that we han felawschip with hym, and we wandren in derknessis, we lien, and don not treuthe.
7 But if we walken in liyt, as also he is in liyt, we han felawschip togidere; and the blood of Jhesu Crist, his sone, clensith vs fro al synne.
8 If we seien, that we han no synne, we disseyuen vs silf, and treuthe is not in vs.
9 If we knowlechen oure synnes, he is feithful and iust, that he foryyue to vs oure synnes, and clense vs from al wickidnesse.
10 And if we seien, we han not synned, we maken hym a liere, and his word is not in vs.

CAP 2

1 Mi litle sones, Y write to you these thingis, that ye synnen not. But if ony man synneth, we han an aduocat anentis the fadir,
2 Jhesu Crist, and he is the foryyuenes for oure synnes; and not oneli for oure synnes, but also for the synnes of al the world.
3 And in this thing we witen, that we knowen hym, if we kepen hise comaundementis.
4 He that seith that he knowith God, and kepith not hise comaundementis, is a liere, and trewthe is not in hym.
5 But the charite of God is perfit verili in hym, that kepith his word. In this thing we witen, that we ben in hym, if we ben perfit in hym.
6 He that seith, that he dwellith in hym, he owith for to walke, as he walkide.
7 Moost dere britheren, Y write to you, not a newe maundement, but the elde maundement, that ye hadden fro the bigynnyng. The elde maundement is the word, that ye herden.
8 Eftsoone Y write to you a newe maundement, that is trewe bothe in hym and in you; for derknessis ben passid, and veri liyt schyneth now.
9 He that seith, that he is in liyt, and hatith his brother, is in derknesse yit.
10 He that loueth his brothir, dwellith in liyt, and sclaundre is not in hym.
11 But he that hatith his brother, is in derknessis, and wandrith in derknessis, and woot not whidir he goith; for derknessis han blindid hise iyen.
12 Litle sones, Y write to you, that youre synnes ben foryouun to you for his name.
13 Fadris, Y write to you, for ye han knowun hym, that is fro the bigynnyng. Yonge men, Y write to you, for ye han ouercomun the wickid.
14 Y write to you, yonge children, for ye han knowe the fadir. Y write to you, britheren, for ye han knowen hym, that is fro the bigynnyng. Y write to you, yonge men, for ye ben

stronge, and the word of God dwellith in you, and ye han ouercomun the wickid.
15 Nyle ye loue the world, ne tho thingis that ben in the world. If ony man loueth the world, the charite of the fadir is not in hym.
16 For al thing that is in the world, is coueitise of fleisch, and coueitise of iyen, and pride of lijf, which is not of the fadir, but it is of the world.
17 And the world schal passe, and the coueitise of it; but he that doith the wille of God, dwellith with outen ende.
18 My litle sones, the laste our is; and as ye han herd, that antecrist cometh, now many antecristis ben maad; wherfor we witen, that it is the laste our.
19 Thei wenten forth fro vs, but thei weren not of vs; for if thei hadden be of vs, thei hadden dwelte with vs; but that thei be knowun, that thei ben not of vs.
20 But ye han anointyng of the Hooli Goost, and knowen alle thingis.
21 Y wroot not to you, as to men that knowen not treuthe, but as to men that knowen it, and for ech leesing is not of treuthe.
22 Who is a liere, but this that denyeth that Jhesu is not Crist? This is antecrist, that denyeth the fadir, and the sone.
23 So ech that denyeth the sone, hath not the fadir; but he that knowlechith the sone, hath also the fadir.
24 That thing that ye herden at the bigynnyng, dwelle it in you; for if that thing dwellith in you, which ye herden at the bigynnyng, ye schulen dwelle in the sone and in the fadir.
25 And this is the biheeste, that he bihiyte to vs euerlastinge lijf.
26 Y wroot these thingis to you, of hem that disseyuen you,
27 and that the anoyntyng which ye resseyueden of hym, dwelle in you. And ye han not nede, that ony man teche you, but as his anoyntyng techith you of alle thingis, and it is trewe, and it is not leesyng; and as he tauyte you, dwelle ye in hym.
28 And now, ye litle sones, dwelle ye in hym, that whanne he schal appere, we haue a trist, and be not confoundid of hym in his comyng.
29 If ye witen that he is iust, wite ye that also ech that doith riytwisnesse, is borun of hym.

CAP 3

1 Se ye what maner charite the fadir yaf to vs, that we be named the sones of God, and ben hise sones. For this thing the world knewe not vs, for it knew not hym.
2 Moost dere britheren, now we ben the sones of God, and yit it apperide not, what we schulen be. We witen, that whanne he schal appere, we schulen be lijk hym, for we schulen se hym as he is.
3 And ech man that hath this hope in hym, makith hym silf hooli, as he is hooli.
4 Ech man that doith synne, doith also wickidnesse, and synne is wickidnesse.
5 And ye witen, that he apperide to do awei synnes, and synne is not in hym.
6 Ech man that dwellith in hym, synneth not; and ech that synneth, seeth not hym, nether knew hym.
7 Litle sones, no man disseyue you; he that doith riytwysnesse, is iust, as also he is iust.
8 He that doith synne, is of the deuel; for the deuel synneth fro the bigynnyng. In this thing the sone of God apperide, that he vndo the werkis of the deuel.

9 Ech man that is borun of God, doith not synne; for the seed of God dwellith in hym, and he may not do synne, for he is borun of God.

10 In this thing the sones of God ben knowun, and the sones of the feend. Ech man that is not iust, is not of God, and he that loueth not his brothir.

11 For this is the tellyng, that ye herden at the bigynnyng, that ye loue ech othere;

12 not as Caym, that was of the yuele, and slouy his brother. And for what thing slouy he him? for hise werkis weren yuele, and hise brotheris iust.

13 Britheren, nyle ye wondre, if the world hatith you.

14 We witen, that we ben translatid fro deeth to lijf, for we louen britheren. He that loueth not, dwellith in deth.

15 Ech man that hatith his brother, is a man sleere; and ye witen, that ech mansleere hath not euerlastinge lijf dwellinge in hym.

16 In this thing we han knowe the charite of God, for he puttide his lijf for vs, and we owen to putte oure lyues for oure britheren.

17 He that hath the catel of this world, and seeth that his brothir hath nede, and closith his entrailis fro hym, hou dwellith the charite of God in hym?

18 Mi litle sones, loue we not in word, nethir in tunge, but in werk and treuthe.

19 In this thing we knowen, that we ben of treuthe, and in his siyt we monesten oure hertis.

20 For if oure herte repreueth vs, God is more than oure hert, and knowith alle thingis.

21 Moost dere britheren, if oure herte repreueth not vs, we han trust to God;

22 and what euer we schulen axe, we schulen resseyue of hym, for we kepen hise comaundementis, and we don tho thingis that ben plesaunt bifor hym.

23 And this is the comaundement of God, that we bileue in the name of his sone Jhesu Crist, and that we loue ech othere, as he yaf heeste to vs.

24 And he that kepith hise comaundementis, dwellith in hym, and he in hym. And in this thing we witen, that he dwellith in vs, bi the spirit, whom he yaf to vs.

CAP 4

1 Moost dere britheren, nyle ye bileue to ech spirit, but preue ye spiritis, if thei ben of God; for many false prophetis wenten out in to the world.

2 In this thing the spirit of God is knowun; ech spirit that knowlechith that Jhesu Crist hath come in fleisch, is of God;

3 and ech spirit that fordoith Jhesu, is not of God. And this is antecrist, of whom ye herden, that he cometh; and riyt now he is in the world.

4 Ye, litle sones, ben of God, and ye han ouercome hym; for he that is in you is more, than he that is in the world.

5 Thei ben of the world, therfor thei speken of the world, and the world herith hem.

6 We ben of God; he that knowith God, herith vs; he that is not of God, herith not vs. In this thing we knowen the spirit of treuthe, and the spirit of errour.

7 Moost dere britheren, loue we togidere, for charite is of God; and ech that loueth his brother, is borun of God, and knowith God.

8 He that loueth not, knowith not God; for God is charite.

9 In this thing the charite of God apperide in vs, for God sente hise oon bigetun sone in to the world, that we lyue bi hym.

10 In this thing is charite, not as we hadden loued God, but for he firste louede vs, and sente hise sone foryyuenesse for oure synnes.

11 Ye moost dere britheren, if God louede vs, we owen to loue ech other.

12 No man say euer God; if we louen togidre, God dwellith in vs, and the charite of hym is perfit in vs.

13 In this thing we knowen, that we dwellen in hym, and he in vs; for of his spirit he yaf to vs.

14 And we sayen, and witnessen, that the fadir sente his sone sauyour of the world.

15 Who euer knowlechith, that Jhesu is the sone of God, God dwellith in him, and he in God.

16 And we han knowun, and bileuen to the charite, that God hath in vs. God is charite, and he that dwellith in charite, dwellith in God, and God in hym.

17 In this thing is the perfit charite of God with vs, that we haue trist in the dai of dom; for as he is, also we ben in this world.

18 Drede is not in charite, but perfit charite puttith out drede; for drede hath peyne. But he that dredith, is not perfit in charite.

19 Therfor loue we God, for he louede vs bifore.

20 If ony man seith, that 'Y loue God, and hatith his brother, he is a liere. For he that loueth not his brothir, which he seeth, hou mai he loue God, whom he seeth not?

21 And we han this comaundement of God, that he that loueth God, loue also his brothir.

CAP 5

1 Ech man that bileueth that Jhesus is Crist, is borun of God; and ech man that loueth hym that gendride, loueth hym that is borun of hym.

2 In this thing we knowen, that we louen the children of God, whanne we louen God, and don his maundementis.

3 For this is the charite of God, that we kepe hise maundementis; and his maundementis ben not heuy.

4 For al thing that is borun of God, ouercometh the world; and this is the victorie that ouercometh the world, oure feith.

5 And who is he that ouercometh the world, but he that bileueth that Jhesus is the sone of God?

6 This is Jhesus Crist, that cam bi watir and blood; not in water oonli, but in watir and blood. And the spirit is he that witnessith, that Crist is treuthe.

7 For thre ben, that yyuen witnessing in heuene, the Fadir, the Sone, and the Hooli Goost; and these thre ben oon.

8 'And thre ben, that yyuen witnessing in erthe, the spirit, water, and blood; and these thre ben oon.

9 If we resseyuen the witnessing of men, the witnessing of God is more; for this is the witnessing of God, that is more, for he witnesside of his sone.

10 He that bileueth in the sone of God, hath the witnessing of God in hym. He that bileueth not to the sone, makith hym a liere; for he bileueth not in the witnessing, that God witnesside of his sone.

11 And this is the witnessyng, for God yaf to you euerlastinge lijf, and this lijf is in his sone.

12 He that hath the sone of God, hath also lijf; he that hath not the sone of God, hath not lijf.

13 I write to you these thingis, that ye wite, that ye han euerlastynge lijf, which bileuen in the name of Goddis sone.

14 And this is the trist which we han to God, that what euer thing we axen aftir his wille, he schal here vs.

15 And we witen, that he herith vs, what euer thing we axen; we witen, that we han the axyngis, which we axen of hym.

16 He that woot that his brother synneth a synne not to deth, axe he, and lijf schal be youun to hym that synneth not to deth. Ther is a synne to deth; 'not for it Y seie, that ony man preie.

17 Ech wickidnesse is synne, and ther is synne to deth.

18 We witen, that ech man that is borun of God, synneth not; but the generacioun of God kepith hym, and the wickid touchith hym not.

19 We witen, that we ben of God, and al the world is set in yuel.

20 And we witen, that the sone of God cam in fleisch, and yaf to vs wit, that we know veri God, and be in the veri sone of hym.

21 This is veri God, and euerlastynge lijf. My litle sones, kepe ye you fro maumetis.

2 JOON

CAP 1

1 The eldere man, to the chosun ladi, and to her children, whiche Y loue in treuthe; and not Y aloone, but also alle men that knowen treuthe;

2 for the treuthe that dwellith in you, and with you schal be with outen ende.

3 Grace be with you, merci, and pees of God the fadir, and of Jhesu Crist, the sone of the fadir, in treuthe and charite.

4 I ioiede ful myche, for Y foond of thi sones goynge in treuthe, as we resseyueden maundement of the fadir.

5 And now Y preye thee, ladi, not as writinge a newe maundement to thee, but that that we hadden fro the bigynnyng, that we loue ech other.

6 And this is charite, that we walke after his maundementis. For this is the comaundement, that as ye herden at the bigynnyng, walke ye in hym.

7 For many disseyueris wenten out in to the world, which knoulechen not that Jhesu Crist hath come in fleisch; this is a disseyuere and antecrist.

8 Se ye you silf, lest ye lesen the thingis that ye han wrouyt, that ye resseyue ful mede;

9 witynge that ech man that goith bifore, and dwellith not in the teching of Crist, hath not God. He that dwellith in the teching, hath bothe the sone and the fadir.

10 If ony man cometh to you, and bryngith not this teching, nyle ye resseyue hym in to hous, nether seie ye to hym, Heil.

11 For he that seith to hym, Heil, comyneth with hise yuel werkis. Lo! Y biforseide to you, that ye be not confoundid in the dai of oure Lord Jhesu Crist.

12 Y haue mo thingis to write to you, and Y wolde not bi parchemyn and enke; for Y hope that Y schal come to you, and speke mouth to mouth, that your ioye be ful.

13 The sones of thi chosun sistir greten thee wel. The grace of God be with thee. Amen.

3 JOON

CAP 1

1 The eldere man to Gayus, most dere brother, whom Y loue in treuthe.

2 Most dere brothir, of alle thingis Y make preyer, that thou entre, and fare welefuly, as thi soule doith welefuli.

3 Y ioyede greetli, for britheren camen, and baren witnessing to thi treuthe, 'as thou walkist in treuthe.

4 Y haue not more grace of these thingis, than that Y here that my sones walke in treuthe.

5 Most dere brother, thou doist feithfuli, what euer thou worchist in britheren, and that in to pilgrymys,

6 which yeldiden witnessing to thi charite, in the siyt of the chirche; which thou leddist forth, and doist wel worthili to God.

7 For thei wenten forth for his name, and token no thing of hethene men.

8 Therfor we owen to resseyue siche, that we be euen worcheris of treuthe.

9 I hadde write perauenture to the chirche, but this Diotrepes, that loueth to bere primacie in hem, resseyueth not vs.

10 For this thing, if Y schal come, Y schal moneste hise werkis, whiche he doith, chidinge ayens vs with yuel wordis. And as if these thingis suffisen not to hym, nether he resseyueth britheren, and forbedith hem that resseyuen, and puttith out of the chirche.

11 Moost dere brothir, nyle thou sue yuel thing, but that that is good thing. He that doith wel, is of God; he that doith yuel, seeth not God.

12 Witnessing is yoldun to Demetrie of alle men, and of treuthe it silf; but also we beren witnessing, and thou knowist, that oure witnessing is trewe.

13 Y hadde many thingis to wryte to thee, but Y wolde not write to thee bi enke and penne.

14 For Y hope soone to se thee, and we schulen speke mouth to mouth. Pees be to thee. Frendis greten thee wel. Greete thou wel frendis bi name.

JUDAS

CAP 1

1 Judas, the seruaunt of Jhesu Crist, and brother of James, to these that ben louyd, that ben in God the fadir, and to hem that ben clepid and kept of Jhesu Crist,

2 mercy, and pees, and charite be fillid to you.

3 Moost dere britheren, Y doynge al bisynesse to write to you of youre comyn helthe, hadde nede to write to you, and preye to striue strongli for the feith that is onys takun to seyntis.

4 For summe vnfeithful men priueli entriden, that sum tyme weren bifore writun in to this dom, and ouerturnen the grace of oure God in to letcherie, and denyen hym that is oneli a Lord, oure Lord Jhesu Crist.

5 But Y wole moneste you onys, that witen alle thingis, that Jhesus sauyde his puple fro the lond of Egipt, and the secunde tyme loste hem that bileueden not.

6 And he reseruede vndur derknesse aungels, that kepten not her prinshod, but forsoken her hous, in to the dom of the greet God, in to euerlastynge bondis.

7 As Sodom, and Gomorre, and the nyy coostid citees, that in lijk maner diden fornycacioun, and yeden awei aftir othir fleisch, and ben maad ensaumple, suffrynge peyne of euerelastinge fier.

8 In lijk maner also these that defoulen the fleisch, and dispisen lordschip, and blasfemen mageste.

9 Whanne Myyhel, arkaungel, disputide with the deuel, and stroof of Moises bodi, he was not hardi to brynge in dom of blasfemye, but seide, The Lord comaunde to thee.

10 But these men blasfemen, what euer thingis thei knowen not. For what euer thingis thei knowen kyndli as doumbe beestis, in these thei ben corupt.

11 Wo to hem that wenten the weie of Caym, and that ben sched out bi errour of Balaam for mede, and perischiden in the ayenseiyng of Chore.

12 These ben in her metis, feestynge togidere to filthe, with out drede fedinge hemsilf. These ben cloudis with out watir, that ben borun aboute of the wyndis; heruest trees with out fruyt, twies deed, drawun vp bi the roote;

13 wawis of the woode see, fomynge out her confusiouns; errynge sterris, to whiche the tempest of derknessis is kept with outen ende.

14 But Enoch, the seuenthe fro Adam, profeciede of these, and seide, Lo! the Lord cometh with hise hooli thousandis,

15 to do dom ayens alle men, and to repreue alle vnfeithful men of alle the werkis of the wickidnesse of hem, bi whiche thei diden wickidli, and of alle the harde wordis, that wyckid synneris han spoke ayens God.

16 These ben grutcheris ful of pleyntis, wandrynge aftir her desiris; and the mouth of hem spekith pride, worschipinge persoones, bi cause of wynnyng.

17 And ye, moost dere britheren, be myndeful of the wordis, whiche ben bifor seid of apostlis of oure Lord Jhesu Crist; whiche seiden to you,

18 that in the laste tymes ther schulen come gilours, wandringe aftir her owne desiris, not in pitee.

19 These ben, whiche departen hemsilf, beestli men, not hauynge spirit.

20 But ye, moost dere britheren, aboue bilde you silf on youre moost hooli feith, and preye ye in the Hooli Goost,

21 and kepe you silf in the loue of God, and abide ye the merci of oure Lord Jhesu Crist in to lijf euerlastynge.

22 And repreue ye these men that ben demed,

23 but saue ye hem, and take ye hem fro the fier. And do ye merci to othere men, in the drede of God, and hate ye also thilke defoulid coote, which is fleischli.

24 But to him that is miyti to kepe you with out synne, and to ordeyne bifore the siyt of his glorie you vnwemmed in ful out ioye, in the comynge of oure Lord Jhesu Crist, to God aloone oure sauyour,

25 bi Jhesu Crist oure Lord, be glorie, and magnefiyng, empire, and power, bifore alle worldis, 'and now and in to alle worldis of worldis. Amen.

APOCALIPS

CAP 1

1 Apocalips of Jhesu Crist, which God yaf to hym to make open to hise seruauntis, whiche thingis it bihoueth to be maad soone. And he signyfiede, sending bi his aungel to his seruaunt Joon,

2 whiche bar witnessing to the word of God, and witnessing of Jhesu Crist, in these thingis, what euer thingis he say.

3 Blessid is he that redith, and he that herith the wordis of this prophecie, and kepith tho thingis that ben writun in it; for the tyme is niy.

4 Joon to seuene chirchis, that ben in Asie, grace and pees to you, of him that is, and that was, and that is to comynge; and of the seuene spiritis, that ben in the siyt of his trone; and of Jhesu Crist,

5 that is a feithful witnesse, the firste bigetun of deed men, and prince of kingis of the erthe; which louyde vs, and waischide vs fro oure synnes in his blood,

6 and made vs a kyngdom, and preestis to God and to his fader; to hym be glorie and empire in to worldis of worldis.

7 Amen. Lo! he cometh with clowdis, and ech iye schal se hym, and thei that prickiden hym; and alle the kynredis of the erthe schulen beweile hem silf on hym.

8 Yhe, Amen! Y am alpha and oo, the bigynnyng and the ende, seith the Lord God, that is, and that was, and that is to comynge, almyyti.

9 I, Joon, youre brothir, and partener in tribulacioun, and kingdom, and pacience in Crist Jhesu, was in an ile, that is clepid Pathmos, for the word of God, and for the witnessyng of Jhesu.

10 Y was in spirit in the Lordis dai, and Y herde bihynde me a greet vois, as of a trumpe,

11 seiynge to me, Write thou in a book that thing that thou seest, and sende to the seuene chirchis that ben in Asie; to Ephesus, to Smyrma, and to Pergamus, and to Tiatira, and to Sardis, and to Filadelfia, and to Loadicia.

12 And Y turnede, that Y schulde se the vois that spak with me; and Y turnede, and Y say seuene candelstikis of gold,

13 and in the myddil of the seuene goldun candelstikis oon lijk to the sone of man, clothid with a long garnement, and gird at the tetis with a goldun girdil.

14 And the heed of hym and his heeris weren whijt, as whijt wolle, and as snow; and the iyen of hym as flawme of fier,

15 and hise feet lijk to latoun, as in a brennynge chymney; and the vois of hym as the vois of many watris.

16 And he hadde in his riyt hoond seuene sterris, and a swerd scharp on euer ethir side wente out of his mouth; and his face as the sunne schyneth in his virtu.

17 And whanne Y hadde seyn hym, Y felde doun at hise feet, as deed. And he puttide his riyt hond on me, and seide, Nyle thou drede; Y am the firste and the laste; and Y am alyue, and Y was deed;

18 and lo! Y am lyuynge in to worldis of worldis, and Y haue the keyes of deth and of helle.

19 Therfor write thou whiche thingis thou hast seyn, and whiche ben, and whiche it bihoueth to be don aftir these thingis.

20 The sacrament of the seuene sterris, which thou seiyest in my riyt hond, and the seuene goldun candelstikis; the seuene sterris ben aungels of the seuene chirchis, and the seuene candelstikis ben seuene chirchis.

CAP 2

1 And to the aungel of the chirche of Efesus write thou, These thingis seith he, that holdith the seuene sterris in his riyt hond, which walkith in the middil of the seuene goldun candilstikis.

2 Y woot thi werkis, and trauel, and thi pacience, and that thou maist not suffre yuele men; and thou hast asaied hem that seien that thei ben apostlis, and ben not, and thou hast foundun hem lieris;

3 and thou hast pacience, and thou hast suffrid for my name, and failidist not.

4 But Y haue ayens thee a fewe thingis, that thou hast left thi firste charite.

5 Therfor be thou myndeful fro whennus thou hast falle, and do penaunce, and do the firste werkis; ether ellis, Y come soone to thee, and Y schal moue thi candilstike fro his place, but 'thou do penaunce.

6 But thou hast this good thing, that thou hatidist the dedis of Nycholaitis, the whiche also Y hate.

7 He that hath eeris, here he, what the spirit seith to the chirchis. To hym that ouercometh Y schal yyue to ete of the tre of lijf, that is in the paradis of my God.

8 And to the aungel of the chirche of Smyrma write thou, These thingis seith the firste and the laste, that was deed, and lyueth.

9 Y woot thi tribulacioun, and thi pouert, but thou art riche; and thou art blasfemyd of hem, that seien, that thei ben Jewis, and ben not, but ben the synagoge of Sathanas.

10 Drede thou no thing of these thingis, whiche thou schalt suffre. Lo! the deuel schal sende summe of you in to prisoun, that ye be temptid; and ye schulen haue tribulacioun ten daies. Be thou feithful to the deth, and Y schal yyue to thee a coroun of lijf.

11 He that hath eeris, here he, what the spirit seith to the chirchis. He that ouercometh, schal not be hirt of the secounde deth.

12 And to the aungel of the chirche of Pergamus write thou, These thingis seith he, that hath the swerd scharp on ech side.

13 Y woot where thou dwellist, where the seete of Sathanas is; and thou holdist my name, and denyedist not my feith. And in tho daies was Antifas, my feithful witnesse, that was slayn at you, where Sathanas dwellith.

14 But Y haue ayens thee a fewe thingis; for thou hast 'there men holdinge the teching of Balaam, which tauyte Balaac for to sende sclaundre bifor the sones of Israel, to ete of sacrificis of ydols, and to do fornicacioun;

15 so also thou hast men holdinge the teching of Nycholaitis.

16 Also do thou penaunce; 'yif ony thing lesse, Y schal come soone to thee, and Y schal fiyte with hem with the swerd of my mouth.

17 He that hath eeris, here he, what the spirit seith to the chirches. To him that ouercometh Y schal yyue aungel mete hid; and Y schal yyue to hym a whiit stoon, and in the stoon a newe name writun, which no man knowith, but he that takith.

18 And to the aungel of the chirche of Tiatira write thou, These thingis seith the sone of God, that hath iyen as flawme of fier, and hise feet lijk latoun.

19 Y knowe thi werkis, and feith, and charite, and thi seruyce, and thi pacience, and thi laste werkis mo than the formere.

20 But Y haue ayens thee a fewe thingis; for thou suffrist the womman Jesabel, which seith that sche is a prophetesse, to teche and disseyue my seruauntis, to do letcherie, and to ete of thingis offrid to idols.

21 And Y yaf to hir time, that sche schulde do penaunce, and sche wolde not do penaunce of hir fornycacioun.

22 And lo! Y sende hir in to a bed, and thei that doen letcherie with hir schulen be in moost tribulacioun, but thei don penaunce of hir werkis.

23 And Y schal slee hir sones in to deth, and alle chirchis schulen wite, that Y am serchinge reynes and hertis; and Y schal yyue to ech man of you after hise werkis.

24 And Y seie to you, and to othere that ben at Tiatire, who euer han not this teching, and that knewen not the hiynesse of Sathanas, hou thei seien, Y schal not sende on you another charge; netheles holde ye that that ye han,

25 til Y come.

26 And to hym that schal ouercome, and that schal kepe til in to the ende my werkis, Y schal yyue power on folkis,

27 and he schal gouerne hem in an yrun yerde; and thei schulen be brokun to gidre,

28 as a vessel of a pottere, as also Y resseyuede of my fadir; and Y schal yyue to hym a morewe sterre.

29 He that hath eeris, here he, what the spirit seith to the chirchis.

CAP 3

1 And to the aungel of the chirche of Sardis write thou, These thingis seith he, that hath the seuene spiritis of God, and the seuene sterris. Y woot thi werkis, for thou hast a name, that thou lyuest, and thou art deed.

2 Be thou wakynge, and conferme thou othere thingis, that weren to diynge; for Y fynde not thi werkis fulle bifore my God.

3 Therfor haue thou in mynde, hou thou resseyuedist, and herdist; and kepe, and do penaunce. Therfor if thou wake not, Y schal come as a nyyt theef to thee, and thou schalt not wite in what our Y schal come to thee.

4 But thou hast a fewe names in Sardis, whiche han not defoulid her clothis; and thei schulen walke with me in whijt clothis, for thei ben worthi.

5 He that ouercometh, schal be clothid thus with whijt clothis; and Y schal not do awei his name fro the book of lijf, and Y schal knoueleche his name bifore my fadir, and bifore hise aungels.

6 He that hath eeris, here he, what the spirit seith to the chirchis.

7 And to the aungel of the chirche of Filadelfie write thou, These thingis seith the hooli and trewe, that hath the keie of Dauid; which openeth, and no man closith, he closith, and no man openith.

8 I woot thi werkis, and lo! Y yaf bifore thee a dore opened, which no man may close; for thou hast a litil vertu, and hast kept my word, and denyest not my name.

9 Lo! Y schal yyue to thee of the synagoge of Sathanas, whiche seien that thei ben Jewis, and ben not, but lyen. Lo! Y schal make hem, that thei come, and worschipe byfor thi feet; and thei schulen wite,

10 that Y louyde thee, for thou keptist the word of my pacience. And Y schal kepe thee fro the our of temptacioun, that is to comynge in to al the world, to tempte men that dwellen in erthe.

11 Lo! Y come soone; holde thou that that thou hast, that no man take thi coroun.

12 And hym that schal ouercome, Y schal make a pilere in the temple of my God, and he schal no more go out; and Y schal write on hym the name of my God, and the name of the citee of my God, of the newe Jerusalem, that cometh doun fro heuene of my God, and my newe name.

13 He that hath eeris, here he, what the spirit seith to the chirchis.

14 And to the aungel of the chirche of Laodice write thou, These thingis seith Amen, the feithful witnesse and trewe, which is bigynnyng of Goddis creature.

15 I woot thi werkis, for nether thou art cold, nether thou art hoot; Y wolde that thou were could, ethir hoot;

16 but for thou art lew, and nether cold, nether hoot, Y schal bigynne to caste thee out of my mouth.

17 For thou seist, That Y am riche, and ful of goodis, and Y haue nede of no thing; and thou wost not, that thou art a wretche, and wretcheful, 'and pore, and blynde, and nakid.

18 Y counsele thee to bie of me brent gold, and preued, that thou be maad riche, and be clothid with whijt clothis, that the confusioun of thi nakidnesse be not seen; and anoynte thin iyen with a collerie, that thou se.

19 Y repreue, and chastise whom Y loue; therfor sue thou goode men, and do penaunce.

20 Lo! Y stonde at the dore, and knocke; if ony man herith my voys, and openith the yate to me, Y shal entre to hym, and soupe with hym, and he with me.

21 And Y schal yyue to hym that schal ouercome, to sitte with me in my trone, as also Y ouercam, and sat with my fadir in his trone.

22 He that hath eeris, here he, what the spirit seith to the chirchis.

CAP 4

1 Aftir these thingis Y say, and lo! a dore was openyd in heuene. And the firste vois that Y herde, was as of a trumpe spekinge with me, and seide, Stye thou vp hidur, and Y shal schewe to thee whiche thingis it bihoueth to be don soone aftir these thingus.

2 Anoon Y was in spirit, and lo! a seete was sett in heuene, and vpon the seete oon sittynge.

3 And he that sat, was lijk the siyt of a stoon iaspis, and to sardyn; and a reynbowe was in cumpas of the seete, lijk the siyt of smaragdyn.

4 And in the cumpas of the seete weren foure and twenti smale seetis; and aboue the troones foure and twenti eldre men sittinge, hilid aboute with whijt clothis, and in the heedis of hem goldun corouns.

5 And leitis, and voices, and thundringis camen out of the trone; and seuene laumpis brennynge bifore the trone, whiche ben the seuene spiritis of God.

6 And bifor the seete as a see of glas, lijk a crystal, and in the myddil of the seete, and in the cumpas of the seete, foure beestis ful of iyen bifore and bihynde.

7 And the firste beeste lijk a lyoun; and the secounde beeste lijk a calf; and the thridde beeste hauynge a face as of a man; and the fourthe beeste lijk an egle fleynge.

8 And the foure beestis hadden euery of hem sixe wyngis; and al aboute and with ynne thei weren ful of iyen; and thei hadden not reste dai and nyyt, seiynge, Hooli, hooli, hooli, the Lord God almyyti, that was, and that is, and that is to comynge.

9 And whanne tho foure beestis yauen glorie, and honour, and blessing to hym that sat on the trone, that lyueth in to worldis of worldis,

10 the foure and twenti eldre men fellen doun bifor hym that sat on the trone, and worschipiden hym that lyueth in to worldis of worldis. And thei casten her corouns bifor the trone,

11 and seiden, Thou, Lord 'oure God, art worthi to take glorie, and onour, and vertu; for thou madist of nouyt alle thingis, and for thi wille tho weren, and ben maad of nouyt.

CAP 5

1 And Y say in the riythond of the sittere on the trone, a book writun with ynne and with out, and seelid with seuene seelis.

2 And Y say a strong aungel, prechynge with a greet vois, Who is worthi to opene the book, and to vndon the seelis of it?

3 And noon in heuene, nether in erthe, nether vnder erthe, myyte opene the book, nether biholde it.

4 And Y wepte myche, for noon was founde worthi to opene the book, nethir to se it.

5 And oon of the eldre men seide to me, Wepe thou not; lo! a lioun of the lynage of Juda, the roote of Dauid, hath ouercomun to opene the book, and to vndon the seuene seelis of it.

6 And Y say, and lo! in the myddil of the trone, and of the foure beestis, and in the myddil of the eldre men, a lombe

stondynge as slayn, that hadde seuene hornes, and seuene iyen, whiche ben seuene spiritis of God, sent in to al the erthe.

7 And he cam, and took of the riythond of the sittere in the trone the book.

8 And whanne he hadde opened the book, the foure beestis and the foure and twenti eldre men fellen doun bifore the lomb; and hadden ech of hem harpis, and goldun violis ful of odours, whiche ben the preyeris of seyntis.

9 And thei sungun a newe song, and seiden, Lord oure God, thou art worthi to take the book, and to opene the seelis of it; for thou were slayn, and ayenbouytist vs to God in thi blood, of ech lynage, 'and tunge, and puple, and nacioun;

10 and madist vs a kyngdom, and prestis to oure God; and we schulen regne on erthe.

11 And Y say, and herde the vois of many aungels al aboute the trone, and of the beestis, and of the eldre men. And the noumbre of hem was thousyndis of thousyndis, seiynge with a greet vois,

12 The lomb that was slayn, is worthi to take vertu, and godhed, and wisdom, and strengthe, and onour, and glorie, and blessing.

13 And ech creature that is in heuene, and that is on erthe, and vndur erthe, and the see, and whiche thingis ben in it, Y herde alle seiynge, To hym that sat in the trone, and to the lomb, blessyng, and onour, and glorie, and power, in to worldis of worldis.

14 And the foure beestis seiden, Amen. And the foure and twenti eldre men fellen doun on her faces, and worschipiden hym that lyueth in to worldis of worldis.

CAP 6

1 And Y sai, that the lomb hadde openyd oon of the seuene seelis. And Y herde oon of the foure beestis seiynge, as a vois of thundur, Come, and se.

2 And Y sai, and lo! a white hors; and he that sat on hym hadde a bouwe, and a coroun was youun to hym. And he wente out ouercomynge, that he schulde ouercome.

3 And whanne he hadde openyd the secounde seel, I herde the secounde beest seiynge, Come 'thou, and se.

4 And another reed hors wente out; and it was youun to hym that sat on hym, that he schulde take pees fro the erthe, and that thei sle to gidere hem silf; and a greet swerd was youun to hym.

5 And whanne he hadde openyd the thridde seel, Y herde the thridde beest seiynge, Come thou, and se. And lo! a blak hors; and he that sat on hym hadde a balaunce in his hond.

6 And Y herde 'as a vois in the myddil of the foure beestis, seiynge, A bilibre of wheete for a peny, and thre bilibris of barli for a peny; and hirte thou not wyn, ne oile.

7 And whanne he hadde openyd the fourthe seel, Y herde a vois of the 'foure beestis, seiynge, Come thou, and se.

8 And lo! a pale hors; and the name was Deth to hym that sat on hym, and helle suede hym. And power was youun to hym on foure partis of the erthe, for to sle with swerd, and with hungur, and with deth, and with beestis of the erthe.

9 And whanne he hadde opened the fyuethe seel, Y say vndur the auter the soulis of men slayn for the word of God, and for the witnessing that thei hadden.

10 And thei crieden with a geet vois, and seiden, Hou long thou, Lord, that art hooli and trewe, demest not, and vengest not oure blood of these that dwellen in the erthe?

11 And white stoolis, for ech soule a stoole, weren youun to hem; and it was seide to hem, that thei schulden reste yit a litil

tyme, til the noumbre of her felowis and of her britheren ben fulfillid, that ben to be slayn, as also thei.

12 And Y say, whanne he hadde openyd the sixte seel, and lo! a greet erthe mouyng was maad; and the sunne was maad blak, as a sak of heire, and al the moone was maad as blood.

13 And the sterris of heuene felden doun on the erthe, as a fige tre sendith his vnripe figis, whanne it is mouyd of a greet wynd.

14 And heuene wente awei, as a book wlappid in; and alle munteyns and ilis weren mouyd fro her placis.

15 And kingis of the erthe, and princis, and tribunes, and riche, and stronge, and ech bonde man, and freman, hidden hem in dennys and stoonys of hillis.

16 And thei seien to hillis and to stoonys, Falle ye on vs, and hide ye vs fro the face of hym that sittith on the trone, and fro the wrath of the lomb;

17 for the greet dai of her wraththe cometh, and who schal mowe stonde?

CAP 7

1 Aftir these thingis Y sai foure aungels stondinge on the foure corneris of the erthe, holdinge foure wyndis of the erthe, that thei blewen not on the erthe, nether on the see, nether on ony tre.

2 And Y sawy anothir aungel stiynge fro the risynge of the sunne, that hadde a signe of the lyuynge God. And he criede with a greet vois to the foure aungels, to whiche it was youun to noye the erthe, and the see,

3 and seide, Nyle ye noye the erthe, and see, nether trees, til we marken the seruauntis of oure God in the forhedis of hem.

4 And I herde the noumbre of men that weren markid, an hundrid thousynde and foure and fourti thousynde markid, of euery lynage of the sones of Israel;

5 of the lynage of Juda, twelue thousynde markid; of the lynage of Ruben, twelue thousynde markid; of the lynage of Gad, twelue thousynde markid;

6 of the lynage of Aser, twelue thousynde markid; of the lynage of Neptalym, twelue thousynde markid; of the lynage of Manasse, twelue thousynde markid;

7 of the lynage of Symeon, twelue thousynde markid; of the lynage of Leuy, twelue thousynde markid; of the lynage of Isachar, twelue thousynde markid;

8 of the lynage of Zabulon, twelue thousynde markid; of the lynage of Joseph, twelue thousynde markid; of the lynage of Beniamyn, twelue thousynde markid.

9 Aftir these thingis Y sai a greet puple, whom no man myyte noumbre, of alle folkis, and lynagis, and puplis, and langagis, stondinge bifore the trone, in the siyt of the lomb; and thei weren clothid with white stoolis, and palmes weren in the hondis of hem.

10 And thei crieden with greet vois, and seiden, Heelthe to oure God, that sittith on the troone, and to the lombe.

11 And alle aungels 'stoden al aboute the trone, and the eldre men, and the foure beestis. And thei fellen doun in the siyt of the trone, on her faces, and worschipiden God, and seiden, Amen!

12 blessyng, and clerenesse, and wisdom, and doynge of thankingis, and honour, and vertu, and strengthe to oure God, in to worldis of worldis.

13 Amen. And oon of the senyours answerde, and seide to me, Who ben these, that ben clothid with white stoolis? and fro whennus came thei?

14 And Y seide to hym, My lord, thou woost. And he seide to me, These ben thei, that camen fro greet tribulacioun, and waischiden her stoolis, and maden hem white in the blood of the lomb.

15 Therfor thei ben bifor the trone of God, and seruen to hym dai and niyt, in his temple. And he that sittith in the trone, dwellith on hem.

16 Thei schulen no more hungur, nether thirste, nether sunne schal falle on hem, ne ony heete.

17 For the lomb, that is in the myddil of the trone, schal gouerne hem, and schal lede forth hem to the wellis of watris of lijf; and God schal wipe awei ech teer fro the iyen of hem.

CAP 8

1 And whanne he hadde openyd the seuenthe seel, a silence was maad in heuene, as half an our.

2 And Y say seuene aungels stondinge in the siyt of God, and seuene trumpis weren youun to hem.

3 And another aungel cam, and stood bifor the auter, and hadde a goldun censer; and many encencis weren youun to hym, that he schulde yyue of the preiers of alle seyntis on the goldun auter, that is bifor the trone of God.

4 And the smoke of encencis of the preiers of the hooli men stiede vp fro the aungels hoond bifor God.

5 And the aungel took the censere, and fillide it of the fier of the auter, and castide in to the erthe. And thundris, and voices, and leityngis weren maad, and a greet erthe mouyng.

6 And the seuene aungels, that hadden seuene trumpis, maden hem redi, that thei schulden trumpe.

7 And the firste aungel trumpide; and hail was maad, and fier meynd togidere in blood; and it was sent in to the erthe. And the thridde part of the erthe was brent, and the thridde part of trees was brent, and al the green gras was brent.

8 And the secunde aungel trumpide; and as a greet hil brennynge with fier was cast in to the see;

9 and the thridde part of the see was maad blood, and the thridde part of creature was deed, that hadde lyues in the see, and the thridde part of schippis perischide.

10 And the thridde aungel trumpide; and a greet sterre brennynge as a litil brond, felle fro heuene; and it felle in to the thridde part of floodis, and in to the wellis of watris.

11 And the name of the sterre is seid Wormod. And the thridde part of watris was maad in to wormod; and many men weren deed of the watris, for tho weren maad bittere.

12 And the fourthe aungel trumpide; and the thridde part of the sunne was smytun, and the thridde part of the moone, and the thridde part of sterris, so that the thridde part of hem was derkid, and the thridde part of the dai schynede not, and also of the nyyt.

13 And Y say, and herde the vois of an egle fleynge bi the myddil of heuene, and seiynge with a greet vois, Wo! wo! wo! to men that dwellen in erthe, of the othir voices of thre aungels, that schulen trumpe aftir.

CAP 9

1 And the fyuethe aungel trumpide; and Y say, that a sterre hadde falle doun fro heuene in to erthe; and the keye of the pit of depnesse was youun to it.

2 And it openede the pit of depnesse, and a smoke of the pit stiede vp, as the smoke of a greet furneis; and the sunne was derkid, and the eir, of the smoke of the pit.

3 And locustis wenten out of the smoke of the pit in to erthe; and power was youun to hem, as scorpiouns of the erthe han power.

4 And it was comaundid to hem, that thei schulden not hirte the gras of erthe, nether ony grene thing, nether ony tre, but oneli men, that han not the signe of God in her forhedis.

5 And it was youun to hem, that thei schulden not sle hem, but that thei schulden 'be turmentid fyue monethis; and the turmentyng of hem, as the turmentyng of a scorpioun, whanne he smytith a man.

6 And in tho daies men schulen seke deth, and thei schulen not fynde it; and thei schulen desire to die, and deth schal fle fro hem.

7 And the licnesse of locustis ben lijk horsis maad redi 'in to batel; and on the heedis of hem as corouns lijk gold, and the facis of hem as the faces of men.

8 And thei hadden heeris, as heeris of wymmen; and the teeth of hem weren as teeth of liouns.

9 And thei hadden haburiouns, as yren haburiouns, and the vois of her wengis as the vois of charis of many horsis ren-nynge 'in to batel.

10 And thei hadden tailis lijk scorpiouns, and prickis weren in the tailis of hem; and the myyt of hem was to noye men fyue monethis.

11 And thei hadden on hem a kyng, the aungel of depnesse, to whom the name bi Ebrew is Laabadon, but bi Greek Appol-lion, and bi Latyn 'he hath a name 'Extermynans, that is, a distriere.

12 O wo is passid, and lo! yit comen twei woes.

13 Aftir these thingis also the sixte aungel trumpide; and Y herde a vois fro foure corneris of the goldun auter, that is bifore the iyen of God,

14 and seide to the sixte aungel that hadde a trumpe, Vnbynde thou foure aungels, that ben boundun in the greet flood Eufrates.

15 And the foure aungels weren vnboundun, whiche weren redi in to our, and dai, and monethe, and yeer, to sle the thridde part of men.

16 And the noumbre of the oost of horse men was twenti thousynde sithis ten thousynde. Y herde the noumbre of hem.

17 And so Y say horsis in visioun; and thei that saten on hem hadden firy haburiouns, and of iacynt, and of brymstoon. And the heedis of the horsis weren as heedis of liouns; and fier, and smoke, and brymston, cometh forth of the mouth of hem.

18 Of these thre plagis the thridde part of men was slayn, of the fier, and of the smoke, and of the brymston, that camen out of the mouth of hem.

19 For the power of the horsis is in the mouth of hem, and in the tailis of hem; for the tailis of hem ben lyk to serpentis, hauynge heedis, and in hem thei noyen.

20 And the tothir men, that weren not slayn in these plagis, nether dyden penaunce of the werkis of her hondis, that thei worschipeden not deuelis, and simylacris of gold, and of siluer, and of bras, and of stoon, and of tre, whiche nethir mown se, nether heere, nether wandre;

21 and diden not penaunce of her mansleyngis, nether of her witchecraftis, nethir of her fornicacioun, nethir of her theftis, weren slayn.

CAP 10

1 And Y say another stronge aungel comynge doun fro heuene, clothid with a cloude, and the reynbowe on his heed; and the face of him was as the sunne, and the feet of hym as a piler of fier.

2 And he hadde in his hoond a litil book openyd; and he sette his riyt foot on the see, and the left foot on the erthe.

3 And he criede with a greet vois, as a lioun whanne he roreth; and whanne he hadde cried, the seuene thundris spa-ken her voicis.

4 And whanne the seuene thundris hadden spoken her voicis, Y was to writynge. And Y herde a vois fro heuene, seiynge, Marke thou what thingis the seuene thundris spaken, and nyle thou write hem.

5 And the aungel whom Y say stondinge aboue the see, and aboue the erthe, lifte vp his hond to heuene,

6 and swoor bi hym that lyueth in to worldis of worldis, that maad of nouyt heuene, and tho thingis whiche ben in it, and the erthe, and tho thingis that ben in it, and the see, and tho thingis that ben in it, that time schal no more be.

7 But in the daies of the vois of the seuenethe aungel, whanne he schal bigynne to trumpe, the mysterie of God schal be endid, as he prechide bi hise seruauntis prophetis.

8 And Y herde a vois fro heuene eftsoone spekynge with me, and seiynge, Go thou, and take the book, that is openyd, fro the hoond of the aungel, that stondith aboue the see, and on the lond.

9 And Y wente to the aungel, and seide to hym, that he schulde yyue me the book. And he seide to me, Take the book, and deuoure it; and it schal make thi wombe to be bittir, but in thi mouth it schal be swete as hony.

10 And Y took the book of the aungels hond, and deuouride it, and it was in my mouth as swete hony; and whanne Y hadde deuourid it, my wombe was bittere. And he seide to me, It bihoueth thee eftsoone to prophesie to hethene men, and to puplis, and langagis, and to many kingis.

CAP 11

1 And a reed lijk a yerde was youun to me, and it was seid to me, Rise thou, and meete the temple of God, and the auter, and men that worschipen in it.

2 But caste thou out the foryerd, that is with out the temple, and mete not it; for it is youun to hethene men, and thei schulen defoule the hooli citee bi fourti monethis and tweyne.

3 And Y schal yyue 'to my twey witnessis, and thei schulen prophesie a thousynde daies two hundrid and sixti, and schulen be clothid with sackis.

4 These ben tweyne olyues, and twei candilstikis, and thei stonden in the siyt of the Lord of the erthe.

5 And if ony man wole anoye hem, fier schal go out of the mouth of hem, and schal deuoure her enemyes. And if ony wole hirte hem, thus it bihoueth hym to be slayn.

6 These han power to close heuene, that it reyne not in the daies of her prophesie; and thei han power on watris, to turne hem in to blood; and to smyte the erthe with euery plage, and as ofte as thei wolen.

7 And whanne thei schulen ende her witnessing, the beeste that stieth vp fro depnesse, schal make batel ayens hem, and schal ouercome hem, and schal sle hem.

8 And the bodies of hem schulen ligge in the stretis of the greet citee, that is clepid goostli Sodom, and Egipt, where the Lord of hem was crucified.

9 And summe of lynagis, and of puplis, and of langagis, and of hethene men, schulen se the bodies of hem bi thre daies and an half; and thei schulen not suffre the bodies of hem to be put in biriels.

10 And men enhabitynge the erthe schulen haue ioye on hem; and thei schulen make myrie, and schulen sende yiftis togidere, for these twei prophetis turmentiden hem that dwellen on the erthe.

11 And aftir thre daies and an half, the spirit of lijf of God entride in to hem; and thei stoden on her feet, and greet dreed felle on hem that sayn hem.

12 And thei herden a greet vois fro heuene, seiynge to hem, Come vp hidir. And thei stieden in to heuene in a cloude, and the enemyes of hem sayn hem.

13 And in that our a greet erthe mouyng was maad, and the tenthe part of the citee felle doun; and the names of men seuene thousynde weren slayn in the erthe mouyng; and the tother weren sent in to drede, and yauen glorie to God of heuene.

14 The secounde wo is gon, and lo! the thridde wo schal come soone.

15 And the seuenthe aungel trumpide, and grete voicis weren maad in heuene, and seiden, The rewme of this world is maad 'oure Lordis, and of Crist, his sone; and he schal regne in to worldis of worldis.

16 Amen. And the foure and twenti eldre men, that saten in her seetis in the siyt of the Lord, fellen on her faces, and worschipiden God,

17 and seiden, We don thankyngis to thee, Lord God almyyti, which art, and which were, and which art to comynge; which hast takun thi greet vertu, and hast regned.

18 And folkis ben wrooth, and thi wraththe cam, and tyme of dede men to be demyd, and to yelde mede to thi seruauntis, and prophetis, and halewis, and dredynge thi name, to smale and to grete, and to distrie hem that corrumpiden the erthe.

CAP 12

19 And the temple of God in heuene was openyd, and the arke of his testament was seyn in his temple; and leityngis weren maad, and voices, and thondris, and 'erthe mouyng, and greet hail.

1 And a greet signe apperide in heuene; a womman clothid with the sunne, and the moone vndur hir feet, and in the heed of hir a coroun of twelue sterris.

2 And sche hadde in wombe, and sche crieth, trauelynge of child, and is turmentid, that sche bere child.

3 And another signe was seyn in heuene; and lo! a greet reede dragoun, that hadde seuene heedis, and ten hornes, and in the heedis of hym seuene diademes.

4 And the tail of hym drow the thridde part of sterris of heuene, and sente hem in to the erthe. And the dragoun stood bifore the womman, that was to berynge child, that whanne sche hadde borun child, he schulde deuoure hir sone.

5 And sche bar a knaue child, that was to reulinge alle folkis in an yrun yerde; and hir sone was rauyschid to God, and to his trone.

6 And the womman flei in to wildirnesse, where sche hath a place maad redi of God, that he fede hir there a thousynde daies two hundrid and sixti.

7 And a greet batel was maad in heuene, and Myyhel and hise aungels fouyten with the dragoun. And the dragoun fauyt, and hise aungels;

8 and thei hadden not myyt, nether the place of hem was foundun more in heuene.

9 And thilke dragoun was cast doun, the greet elde serpent, that is clepid the Deuel, and Sathanas, that disseyueth al the world; he was cast doun in to the erthe, and hise aungels weren sent with hym.

10 And Y herde a greet vois in heuene, seiynge, Now is maad helthe, and vertu, and kyngdom of oure God, and the power of his Crist; for the accuser of oure britheren is cast doun, which accuside hem bifor the siyte of oure God dai and nyyt.

11 And thei ouercamen hym for the blood of the lomb, and for the word of his witnessing; and thei louyden not her lyues til to deth.

12 Therfor, ye heuenes, be ye glad, and ye that dwellen in hem. Wo to the erthe, and to the see; for the fend is come doun to you, and hath greet wraththe, witynge that he hath litil tyme.

13 And after that the dragoun sai, that he was cast doun to the erthe, he pursuede the womman, that bare the knaue child.

14 And twei wengis of a greet egle weren youun to the womman, that sche schulde flee in to deseert, in to hir place, where sche is fed by tyme, and tymes, and half a tyme, fro the face of the serpent.

15 And the serpent sente out of his mouth aftir the womman watir as a flood, that he schulde make hir to be drawun of the flood.

16 And the erthe helpide the womman, and the erthe openyde his mouth, and soop up the flood, that the dragoun sente of his mouth.

17 And the dragoun was wrooth ayens the womman, and he wente to make batel with othere of hir seed, that kepen the maundementis of God, and han the witnessing of Jhesu Crist.

18 And he stood on the grauel of the see.

CAP 13

1 And Y sai a beeste stiynge vp of the see, hauynge seuene heedis, and ten hornes; and on hise hornes ten diademes, and on hise heedis the names of blasfemye.

2 And the beeste, whom Y sai, was lijk a pard, and hise feet as the feet of a beere, and his mouth as the mouth of a lioun; and the dragoun yaf his vertu and greet power to hym.

3 And Y sai oon of hise heedis, as slayn in to deth; and the wounde of his deth was curid. And al erthe wondride after the beeste.

4 And thei worschipiden the dragoun, that yaf power to the beeste; and thei worschipeden the beeste, and seiden, Who is lijk the beeste, and who schal mowe fiyte with it?

5 And a mouth spekynge grete thingis, and blasfemyes, was youun 'to it; and power was youun to it, to do two and fourti monethis.

6 And it openyde his mouth in to blasfemyes to God, to blasfeme his name, and his tabernacle, and hem that dwellen in heuene.

7 And it was youun to hym to make batel with seyntis, and to ouercome hem; and power was youun to hym in to ech lynage, and puple, and langage, and folk.

8 And alle men worschipiden it, that dwellen in erthe, whos names ben not writun in the book of lijf of the lomb, that was slayn fro the bigynnyng of the world.

9 If ony man hath eeris, here he.

10 He that ledith in to caitifte, schal go in to caitifte; he that sleeth with swerd, it bihoueth hym to be slayn with swerd. This is the pacience and the feith of seyntis.

11 And Y sai another beeste stiynge vp fro the erthe, and it hadde two hornes, lijk the lomb; and it spak as the dragoun,

12 and dide al the power of the formere beeste, in his siyt. And it made the erthe, and men dwellinge in it, to worschipe the firste beeste, whos wounde of deth was curid.

13 And it dide grete signes, that also it made fier to come doun fro heuene in to the erthe, in the siyt of alle men.

14 And it disseyueth men, that dwellen in erthe, for signes whiche ben youun 'to it to do in the siyt of the beeste; seiynge to men dwellinge in erthe, that thei make an ymage of the beeste, that hath the wounde of swerd, and lyuede.

15 And it was youun to hym, that he schulde yyue spirit to the ymage of the beeste, and that the ymage of the beeste speke. And he schal make, that who euere honouren not the ymage of the beeste, be slayn.

16 And he schal make alle, smale and grete, and riche and pore, and fre men and bonde men, to haue a carecter in her riythoond, ethir in her forheedis; that no man may bie,

17 ethir sille, but thei han the caracter, ether the name of the beeste, ethir the noumbre of his name.

18 Here is wisdom; he that hath vndurstonding, acounte the noumbre of the beeste; for it is the noumbre of man, and his noumbre is sixe hundrid sixti and sixe.

CAP 14

1 And Y sai, and lo! lomb stood on the mount of Sion, and with hym an hundrid thousynde and foure and fourti thousynde, hauynge his name, and the name of his fadir writun in her forhedis.

2 And Y herde a vois fro heuene, as the vois of many watris, and as the vois of a greet thundur; and the vois which is herd, was as of many harperis harpinge in her harpis.

3 And thei sungun as a newe song bifor the seete of God, and bifore the foure beestis, and senyouris. And no man miyte seie the song, but thei an hundrid thousynde and foure and fourti thousynde, that ben bouyt fro the erthe.

4 These it ben, that ben not defoulid with wymmen; for thei ben virgyns. These suen the lomb, whidir euer he schal go; these ben bouyt of alle men, the firste fruytis to God, and to the lomb;

5 and in the mouth of hem lesyng is not foundun; for thei ben with out wem bifor the trone of God.

6 And Y say another aungel, fliynge bi the myddil of heuene, hauynge an euerlastinge gospel, that he schulde preche to men sittynge on erthe, and on ech folk, and lynage, and langage, and puple;

7 and seide with a greet vois, Drede ye the Lord, and yyue ye to hym onour, for the our of his dom cometh; and worschipe ye hym, that made heuene and erthe, the see, and alle thingis that ben in hem, and the wellis of watris.

8 And anothir aungel suede, seiynge, Thilke greet Babiloyne fel doun, fel doun, which yaf drinke to alle folkis of the wyn of wraththe of her fornycacioun.

9 And the thridde aungel suede hem, and seide with a greet vois, If ony man worschipe the beeste, and the ymage of it, and takith the carecter in his forheed, ethir in his hoond,

10 this schal drynke of the wyn of Goddis wraththe, that is meynd with clere wyn in the cuppe of his wraththe, and schal be turmentid with fier and brymston, in the siyt of hooli aungels, and bifore the siyt of the lomb.

11 And the smoke of her turmentis schal stie vp in to the worldis of worldis; nether thei han reste dai and niyt, whiche worschipiden the beeste and his ymage, and yf ony man take the carect of his name.

12 Here is the pacience of seyntis, whiche kepen the maunde-mentis of God, and the feith of Jhesu.

13 And Y herde a vois fro heuene, seiynge to me, Write thou, Blessid ben deed men, that dien in the Lord; fro hennus forth now the spirit seith, that thei reste of her traueilis; for the werkis of hem suen hem.

14 And Y say, and lo! a white cloude, and aboue the cloude a sittere, lijk the sone of man, hauynge in his heed a goldun coroun, and in his hond a scharp sikil.

15 And another aungel wente out of the temple, and criede with greet vois to hym that sat on the cloude, Sende thi sikil, and repe, for the our cometh, that it be ropun; for the corn of the erthe is ripe.

16 And he that sat on the cloude, sente his sikil in to the erthe, and rap the erthe.

17 And another aungel wente out of the temple, that is in heuene, and he also hadde a scharp sikile.

18 And another aungel wente out fro the auter, that hadde power on fier and water; and he criede with a greet vois to hym that hadde the scharp sikil, and seide, Sende thi scharp sikil, and kitte awei the clustris of the vynyerd of the erthe, for the grapis of it ben ripe.

19 And the aungel sente his sikil in to the erthe, and gaderide grapis of the vynyerd of the erthe, and sente into the greet lake of Goddis wraththe.

20 And the lake was troddun without the citee, and the blood wente out of the lake til to the 'bridels of horsis, bi furlongis a thousynd and six hundrid.

CAP 15

1 And Y say another signe in heuene, greet and wondurful; seuene aungels hauynge 'seuene the laste veniauncis, for the wraththe of God is endid in hem.

2 And Y say as a glasun see meynd with fier, and hem that ouercamen the beeste, and his ymage, and the noumbre of his name, stondynge aboue the glasun see, hauynge the harpis of God;

3 and syngynge the song of Moises, the seruaunt of God, and the song of the lomb, and seiden, Grete and wondurful ben thi werkis, Lord God almyyti; thi weies ben iust and trewe, Lord, kyng of worldis.

4 Lord, who schal not drede thee, and magnyfie thi name? for thou aloone art merciful; for alle folkis schulen come, and worschipe in thi siyt, for thi domes ben open.

5 And aftir these thingis Y say, and lo! the temple of the tabernacle of witnessyng was opened in heuene;

6 and seuene aungels hauynge seuene plagis, wenten out of the temple, and weren clothid with a stoon clene and white, and weren bifor gird with goldun girdlis about the brestis.

7 And oon of the foure beestis yaf to the seuene aungels seuene goldun viols, ful of the wraththe of God, that lyueth in to worldis of worldis.

8 And the temple was fillid with smooke of the majestee of God, and of the vertu of hym; and no man myyte entre in to the temple, til the seuene plagis of seuene angels weren endid.

CAP 16

1 And Y herde a greet vois fro heuene, seiynge to the seuene aungels, Go ye, and schede out the seuene viols of Goddis wraththe in to erthe.

2 And the firste aungel wente, and schedde out his viol in to the erthe; and a wounde fers and werst was maad on alle that

hadden the carect of the beeste, and on hem that worschipiden the beeste, and his ymage.

3 And the secounde aungel schedde out his viol in to the see, and the blood was maad, as of a deed thing; and ech man lyuynge was deed in the see.

4 And the thridde aungel schedde out his viol on the floodis, and on the wellis of watris, and seide,

5 Just art thou, Lord, that art, and that were hooli, that demest these thingis;

6 for thei schedden out the blood of halewis and prophetis, and thou hast youun to hem blood to drinke; for thei ben worthi.

7 And I herde anothir seiynge, Yhe! Lord God almiyti, trewe and iust ben thi domes.

8 And the fourthe aungel schedde out his viol in to the sunne, and it was youun to hym to turmente men with heete and fier.

9 And men swaliden with greet heete, and blasfemyden the name of God hauynge power on these plagis, nether thei diden penaunce, that thei schulden yyue glorie to hym.

10 And the fifte aungel schedde out his viol on the seete of the beeste, and his kyngdom was maad derk; and thei eten togidere her tungis for sorewe,

11 and thei blasfemyden God of heuene, for sorewis of her woundis; and thei diden not penaunce of her werkis.

12 And the sixte aungel schedde out his viol in 'that ilke greet flood Eufratis, and driede the watir of it, that weie were maad redi to kingis fro the sunne rysyng.

13 And Y say thre vnclene spiritis bi the manner of froggis go out of the mouth of the dragoun, and of the mouth of the beeste, and of the mouth of the fals prophete.

14 For thei ben spiritis of deuels, makynge signes, and thei gon forth to kingis of al erthe, to gadere hem in to batel, to the greet dai of almiyti God.

15 Lo! Y come, as a niyt theefe. Blessid is he that wakith, and kepith hise clothis, that he wandre not nakid, and that thei se not the filthhed of hym.

16 And he schal gadre hem in to a place, that is clepid in Ebreu Hermagedon.

17 And the seuenthe aungel schedde out his viol in to the eyr, and a greet vois wente out of heuene fro the trone, and seide, It is don.

18 And leityngis weren maad, and voices, and thundris; and a greet erthe mouyng was maad, which manere neuere was, sithen men weren on erthe, siche 'erthe mouyng so greet.

19 And the greet citee was maad in to thre parties, and the citees of hethene men felden doun; and greet Babiloyne cam in to mynde byfor God, to yyue to it the cuppe of wyn of the indignacyoun of his wraththe.

20 And ech ile flei awei, and hillis ben not foundun.

21 And greet hail as a talent cam doun fro heuene in to men; and men blasfemyden God, for the plage of hail, for it was maad ful greet.

CAP 17

1 And oon of the seuene aungels cam, that hadde seuene viols, and spak with me, and seide, Come thou, Y schal schewe to thee the dampnacioun of the greet hoore, that sittith on many watris, with which kyngis of erthe diden fornicacioun;

2 and thei that dwellen in the erthe ben maad drunkun of the wyn of her letcherie.

3 And he took me in to desert in spirit. And Y say a womman sittynge on a reed beeste, ful of names of blasfemye, hauynge seuene heedis, and ten hornes.

4 And the womman was enuyround with purpur, and reed, and ouergild with gold, and preciouse stoon, and peerls, hauynge a goldun cuppe in hir hoond, ful of abhomynaciouns and vnclennesse of her fornycacioun.

5 And a name writun in the forheed of hir, Mysterie, Babiloyn the greet, modir of fornycaciouns, and of abhomynaciouns of erthe.

6 And Y say a womman drunkun of the blood of seyntis, and of the blood of martris of Jhesu. And whanne Y say hir, Y wondride with greet wondryng.

7 And the aungel seide to me, Whi wondrist thou? I schal seie to thee the sacrament yf the womman, and of the beeste that berith hir, that hath seuene heedis and ten hornes.

8 The beeste which thou seist, was, and is not; and sche schal stie fro depnesse, and sche schal go 'in to perisching. And men dwellinge in erthe schulen wondre, whos names ben not writun in the book of lijf fro the makinge of the world, seynge the beeste, that was, and is not.

9 And this is the witt, who that hath wisdom. The seuene heedis ben seuene hillis, on whiche the womman sittith, and kyngis seuene ben.

10 Fyue han feld doun, oon is, and anothir cometh not yit. And whanne he schal come, it bihoueth hym to dwelle a schort tyme.

11 And the beeste that was, and is not, and sche is the eiytthe, and is of the seuene, and schal go in to perischyng.

12 And the ten hornes whiche thou hast seyn, ben ten kyngis, that yit han not take kyngdom; but thei schulen take power as kingis, oon our after the beeste.

13 These han a counsel, and schulen bitake her vertu and power to the beeste.

14 These schulen fiyte with the lomb, and the lomb schal ouercome hem; for he is Lord of lordis, and kyng of kyngis; and thei that ben with hym, ben clepid, chosun, and feithful.

15 And he seide to me, The watris whiche thou hast seyn, where the hoore sittith, ben puplis, and folkis, and langagis.

16 And the ten hornes that thou hast seyn in the beeste, these schulen make hir desolat and nakid, and schulen ete the fleischis of hir, and schulen brenne togidere hir with fier.

17 For God yaf in to the hertis of hem, that thei do that that is pleasaunt to hym, that thei yyue her kyngdom to the beeste, til the wordis of God ben endid.

18 And the womman whom thou hast seyn, is the greet citee, that hath kingdom on kyngis of the erthe.

CAP 18

1 And aftir these thingis Y siy another aungel comynge doun fro heuene, hauynge greet power; and the erthe was liytned of his glorie.

2 'And he criede with strong vois, 'and seide, Greet Babiloyn felde doun, felde doun, and is maad the habitacioun of deuelis, and the keping of ech vnclene spirit, and 'the keping of ech vnclene foul, and hateful.

3 For alle folkis drunkun of the wraththe of fornycacioun of hir, and kingis of the erthe, and marchauntis of the erthe, diden fornycacioun with hir; and thei ben maad riche of the vertu of delices of hir.

4 And Y herde another vois of heuene, seiynge, My puple, go ye out of it, and be ye not parceneris of the trespassis of it, and ye schulen not resseyue of the woundis of it.

5 For the synnes of it camen 'til to heuene, and the Lord hadde mynde of the wickidnesse of it.

6 Yelde ye to it, as sche yeldide to you; and double ye double thingis, aftir her werkis; in the drynke that she meddlid to you, mynge ye double to hir.

7 As myche as sche glorifiede hir silf, and was in delicis, so myche turment yyue to hir, and weilyng; for in hir herte sche seith, Y sitte a queen, and Y am not a widewe, and Y schal not se weiling.

8 And therfor in o day hir woundis schulen come, deth, and mornyng, and hungur; and sche schal be brent in fier, for God is strong, that schal deme hir.

9 And the kingis of the erthe schulen biwepe, and biweile hem silf on hir, whiche diden fornicacioun with hir, and lyueden in delicis, whanne thei schulen se the smoke of the brennyng of it;

10 stondynge fer, for drede of the turmentis of it, and seiynge, Wo! wo! wo! thilke greet citee Babiloyn, and thilke stronge citee; for in oon our thi dom cometh.

11 And marchauntis of the erthe schulen wepe on it, and morne, for no man schal bie more the marchaundise of hem;

12 the marchaundies of gold, and of siluer, and of preciouse stoon, and of peerl, and of bies, and of purpur, and of silk, and coctyn, and ech tre tymus, and alle vessels of yuer, and alle vessels of preciouse stoon, and of bras, and of yrun, and of marbil,

13 and canel, and amonye, and of swete smellinge thingis, and oynementis, and encense, and of wyn, and of oyle, and of flour, and of whete, and of werk beestis, and of scheep, and of horsis, and of cartis, and of seruauntis, and other lyues of men.

14 And thin applis of the desire of thi lijf wenten awei fro thee, and alle fatte thingis, and ful clere perischiden fro thee.

15 And marchaundis of these thingis schulen no more fynde tho thingis. Thei that ben maad riche of it, schulen stonde fer, for drede of turmentis of it, wepynge, and mornynge, and seiynge, Wo!

16 wo! thilke greet citee, that was clothid with bijs, and purpur, and reed scarlet, and was ouergild with gold, and preciouse stoon, and margaritis,

17 for in oon our so many richessis ben destitute. And ech gouernour, and alle that saylen bi schip in to place, and maryneris, and that worchen in the see, stoden fer,

18 and crieden, seynge the place of the brennyng of it, seiynge, What is lijk this greet citee?

19 And thei casten poudre on her heedis, and crieden, wepynge, and mornynge, and seiynge, Wo! wo! thilke greet citee, in which alle that han schippis in the see ben maad riche of pricis of it; for in oon our it is desolat.

20 Heuene, and hooli apostlis, and prophetis, make ye ful out ioye on it, for God hath demed youre dom of it.

21 And o stronge aungel took vp a stoon, as a greet mylne stoon, and keste in to the see, and seide, In this bire thilke greet citee Babiloyn schal be sent, and now it schal no more be foundun.

22 And the vois of harpis, and of men of musik, and syngynge with pipe and trumpe, schal no more be herd in it. And ech crafti man, and ech craft, schal no more be foundun in it. And the vois of mylne stoon schal no more be herde in thee,

23 and the liyt of lanterne schal no more schyne to thee, and the vois of the hosebonde and of the wijf schal no more yit be herd in thee; for thi marchauntis weren princis of the erthe. For in thi witchecraftis alle folkis erriden.

24 And the blood of prophetis and seyntis is foundun in it, and of alle men that ben slayn in erthe.

CAP 19

1 Aftir these thingis Y herde as a greet vois of many trumpis in heuene, seiynge, Alleluya; heriynge, and glorie, and vertu is to oure God;

2 for trewe and iust ben the domes of hym, whiche demede of the greet hoore, that defoulide the erthe in her letcherye, and vengide the blood of hise seruauntis, of the hondis of hir.

3 And eft thei seiden, Alleluya. And the smoke of it stieth vp, in to worldis of worldis.

4 And the foure and twenti senyouris and foure beestis felden doun, and worschipiden God sittynge on the trone, and seiden, Amen, Alleluya.

5 And a vois wente out of the trone, and seide, Alle the seruauntis of oure God, seie ye heriyngus to oure God, and ye that dreden God, smale and grete.

6 And Y herde a vois of a grete trumpe, as the vois of many watris, and as the vois of grete thundris, seiynge, Alleluya; for oure Lord God almyyti hath regned.

7 Ioye we, and make we myrthe, and yyue glorie to hym; for the weddingis of the lomb camen, and the wijf of hym made redy hir silf.

8 And it is youun to hir, that sche kyuere hir with white bissyn schynynge; for whi bissyn is iustifiyngis of seyntis.

9 And he seide to me, Write thou, Blessid ben thei that ben clepid to the soper of weddyngis of the lomb. And he seide to me, These wordis of God ben trewe.

10 And Y felde doun bifore hise feet, to worschipe hym. And he seide to me, Se thou, that thou do not; Y am a seruaunt with thee, and of thi britheren, hauynge the witnessyng of Jhesu; worschipe thou God. For the witnessing of Jhesu is spirit of profesie.

11 And Y say heuene openyd, and lo! a whit hors, and he that sat on hym was clepid Feithful and sothefast; and with riytwisnesse he demeth, and fiytith.

12 And 'the iyen of hym weren as flawme of fier, and in his heed many diademys; and he hadde a name writun, which no man knew, but he.

13 And he was clothid in a cloth spreynt with blood; and the name of hym was clepid The sone of God.

14 And the oostis that ben in heuene, sueden hym on white horsis, clothid with bissyn, white and clene.

15 And a swerd scharp on ech side cam forth of his mouth, that with it he smyte folkis; and he shal reule hem with an yren yerde. And he tredith the pressour of wyn of stronge veniaunce of the wraththe of almyyti God.

16 And he hath writun in his cloth, and in the hemme, Kyng of kyngis and Lord of lordis.

17 And Y say an aungel, stondynge in the sunne; and he criede with greet vois, and seide to alle briddis that flowen bi the myddil of heuene, Come ye, and be ye gaderid to the greet soper of God,

18 that ye ete the fleisch of kingis, and fleisch of tribunes, and fleisch of stronge men, and fleisch of horsis, and of tho that sitten on hem, and the fleisch of alle fre men and bonde men, and of smale and of grete.

19 And Y sai the beeste, and the kyngis of the erthe, and the oostis of hem gaderid, to make batel with hym, that sat on the hors, and with his oost.

20 And the beeste was cauyt, and with hir the false prophete, that made signes bifor hir; in whiche he disseyuede hem that

token the carect of the beeste, and that worschipiden the ymage of it. These tweyne weren sent quyke in to the pool of fier, brennynge with brymstoon.

21 And the othere weren slayn of swerd of hym that sat on the hors, that cometh forth of the mouth of hym; and alle briddis weren fillid with the fleisch of hem.

CAP 20

1 And Y say an aungel comynge doun fro heuene, hauynge the keie of depnesse, and a greet chayne in his hoond.

2 And he cauyte the dragoun, the elde serpent, that is the deuel and Sathanas; and he boonde hym bi a thousynde yeeris.

3 And he sente hym 'in to depnesse, and closide on hym, that he disseyue no more the folkis, til a thousynde yeeris be fillid. Aftir these thingis it bihoueth hym to be vnboundun a litil tyme.

4 And Y say seetis, and thei saten on hem, and doom was youun to hem. And the soulis of men biheedid for the witnessyng of Jhesu, and for the word of God, and hem that worschipiden not the beeste, nether the ymage of it, nethir token the carect of it in her forheedis, nethir in her hoondis. And thei lyueden, and regneden with Crist a thousynde yeeris.

5 Othere of deed men lyueden not, til a thousynde yeeris ben endid. This is the first ayen risynge.

6 Blessid and hooli is he, that hath part in the firste ayenrysyng. In these men the secunde deth hath not power; but thei schulen be prestis of God, and of Crist, and thei schulen regne with hym a thousynde yeeris.

7 And whanne a thousynde yeeris schulen be endid, Sathanas schal be vnboundun of his prisoun; and he schal go out, and schal disseyue folkis, that ben on foure corners of the erthe, Gog and Magog. And he schal gadere hem in to batel, whos noumbre is as the grauel of the see.

8 And thei stieden vp on the broodnesse of erthe, and enuyrounede the castels of seyntis, and the louyd citee.

9 And fier cam doun 'of God fro heuene, and deuourede hem. And the deuel, that disseyuede hem, was sent in to the pool of fier and of brymston,

10 where bothe the beeste and fals prophetis schulen be turmentid dai and niyt, in to worldis of worldis.

11 Amen. And Y say a greet white trone, and oon sittynge on it, fro whos siyt erthe fled and heuene; and the place is not foundun 'of hem.

12 And Y sai deed men, grete and smale, stondynge in the siyt of the trone; and bookis weren opened, and deed men weren demed of these thingis that weren writun in the bookis, aftir the werkis of hem.

13 And the see yaf his deed men, that weren in it; and deth and helle yauen her deed men, that weren in hem. And it was demed of ech, aftir the werkis of hem.

14 And helle and deth weren sent in to a poole of fier. 'This is the secunde deth.

15 And he that was not foundun writun in the book of lijf, was sent in to the pool of fier.

CAP 21

1 And Y sai newe heuene and newe erthe; for the firste heuene and the firste erthe wenten awei, and the see is not now.

2 And Y Joon say the hooli citee Jerusalem, newe, comynge doun fro heuene, maad redi of God, as a wijf ourned to hir hosebonde.

3 And Y herde a greet vois fro the trone, seiynge, Lo! the tabernacle of God is with men, and he schal dwelle with hem; and thei schulen be his puple, and he God with hem schal be her God.

4 And God schal wipe awei ech teer fro the iyen of hem; and deth schal no more be, nether mornyng, nether criyng, nether sorewe schal be ouer; whiche 'firste thingis wenten awei.

5 And he seide, that sat in the trone, Lo! Y make alle thingis newe. And he seide to me, Write thou, for these wordis ben moost feithful and trewe.

6 And he seide to me, It is don; I am alpha and oo, the bigynnyng and ende. Y schal yyue freli of the welle of quic watir to hym that thirsteth.

7 He that schal ouercome, schal welde these things; and Y schal be God to hym, and he schal be sone to me.

8 But to ferdful men, and vnbileueful, and cursid, and manquelleris, and fornycatouris, and to witchis, and worschiperis of idols, and to alle lieris, the part of hem shal be in the pool brennynge with fier and brymstoon, that is the secounde deth.

9 And oon cam of the seuene aungels, hauynge violis fulle of 'seuene the laste veniauncis. And he spak with me, and seide, Come thou, and Y schal schewe to thee the spousesse, the wijf of the lomb.

10 And he took me vp in spirit in to a greet hille and hiy; and he schewide to me the hooli citee Jerusalem, comynge doun fro heuene of God,

11 hauynge the clerete of God; and the liyt of it lijk a preciouse stoon, as the stoon iaspis, as cristal.

12 And it hadde a walle greet and hiy, hauynge twelue yatis, and in the yatis of it twelue aungels, and names writun in, that ben the names of twelue lynagis of the sones of Israel; fro the east thre yatis,

13 and fro the north thre yatis, and fro the south thre yatis, and fro the west thre yatis.

14 And the wal of the citee hadde twelue foundementis, and in hem the twelue names of twelue apostlis, and of the lomb.

15 And he that spak with me, hadde a goldun mesure of a rehed, that he schulde mete the citee, and the yatis of it, and the wal.

16 And the citee was set in square; and the lengthe of it is so miche, 'as miche as is the breede. And he mat the citee with the rehed, bi furlongis twelue thousyndis. And the heiythe, and the lengthe and breede of it, ben euene.

17 And he mat the wallis of it, of an hundrid and 'foure and fourti cubitis, bi mesure of man, that is, of an aungel.

18 And the bildyng of the wal therof was of the stoon iaspis. And the citee it silf was clene gold, lijk clene glas.

19 And the foundementis of the wal of the citee weren ourned with al precious stoon. The firste foundement, iaspis; the secounde, safiris; the thridde, calcedonyus; the fourthe, smaragdus;

20 the fyuethe, sardony; the sixte, sardius; the seuenthe, crisolitus; the eiytthe, berillus; the nynthe, topacius; the tenthe, crisopassus; the eleuenthe, iacinctus; the tweluethe, ametistus.

21 And twelue yatis ben twelue margaritis, bi ech; 'and ech yate was of ech margarete. And the stretis of the citee weren clene gold, as of glas ful schynynge.

22 And Y say no temple in it, for the Lord God almyyti and the lomb, is temple of it.

23 And the citee hath no nede of sunne, nethir moone, that thei schyne in it; for the clerete of God schal liytne it; and the lomb is the lanterne of it.

24 And folkis schulen walke in liyt of it; and the kyngis of the erthe schulen brynge her glorie and onour in to it.

25 And the yatis of it schulen not be closid bi dai; and niyt schal not be there.

26 And thei schulen brynge the glorie and onour of folkis in to it.

27 Nether ony man defoulid, and doynge abhominacioun and leesyng, schal entre in to it; but thei that ben writun in the book of lijf and of the lomb.

CAP 22

1 And he schewide to me a flood of quic watir, schinynge as cristal, comynge forth of the seete of God, and of the lomb,

2 in the myddil of the street of it. And on ech side of the flood, the tree of lijf, bryngynge forth twelue fruytis, yeldinge his fruit bi ech monethe; and the leeues of the tree ben to heelthe of folkis.

3 And ech cursid thing schal no more be; but the seetis of God and of the lomb schulen be in it. And the seruauntis of hym schulen serue to hym.

4 And thei schulen see his face, and his name in her forheedis.

5 And niyt schal no more be, and thei schulen not haue nede to the liyt of lanterne, nethir to liyt of sunne; for the Lord God schal lyytne hem, and thei schulen regne in to worldis of worldis.

6 And he seide to me, These wordis ben moost feithful and trewe. And the Lord God of spiritis of prophetis sente his aungel, to schewe his seruauntis, what thingis it bihoueth to be don soone.

7 'And lo! Y come swiftli. Blessid is he, that kepith the wordis of prophesie of this book.

8 And Y am Joon, that herde and say these thingis. And aftirward that Y hadde 'herd and seyn, Y felde doun, to worschipe bifor the feet of the aungel, that schewide to me these thingis.

9 And he seide to me, Se thou, that thou do not; for Y am seruaunt 'with thee, and of thi britheren, prophetis, and of hem that kepen the wordis of prophesie of this book; worschipe thou God.

10 And he seide to me, 'Signe, ether seele, thou not the wordis of prophesie of this book; for the tyme is niy.

11 He that noyeth, noye he yit; and he that is in filthis, wexe foul yit; and a iust man, be iustified yit, and the hooli, be halewid yit.

12 Lo! Y come soone, and my mede with me, to yelde to ech man aftir hise werkis.

13 Y am alpha and oo, the firste and the laste, bigynnyng and ende.

14 Blessid be thei, that waischen her stoolis, that the power of hem be in the tree of lijf, and entre bi the yatis in to the citee.

15 For with outen forth houndis, and witchis, and unchast men, and manquelleris, and seruynge to idols, and ech that loueth and makith leesyng.

16 I Jhesus sente myn aungel, to witnesse to you these thingis in chirchis. Y am the roote and kyn of Dauid, and the schynynge morewe sterre.

17 And the spirit and the spousesse seien, Come thou. And he that herith, seie, Come thou; and he that thirstith, come; and he that wole, take he freli the watir of lijf.

18 And I witnesse to ech man herynge the wordis of prophesie of this book, if ony man schal putte to these thingis, God schal putte on hym the veniauncis writun in this book.

19 And if ony man do awei of the wordis of the book of this prophesie, God schal take awei the part of hym fro the book of lijf, and fro the hooli citee, and fro these thingis that ben writun in this book.

20 He seith, that berith witnessyng of these thingis, Yhe, amen. I come soone. Amen. Come thou, Lord Jhesu.

21 The grace of oure Lord Jhesu Crist be with you alle. Amen.

LAODICENSIS

CAP 1

1 Poul, apostle, not of men, ne by man, but bi Jhesu Crist, 'to the britheren that ben at Laodice,

2 grace to you, and pees of God the fadir, and of the Lord Jhesu Crist.

3 I do thankyngis to my God bi al my preier, that ye be dwelling and lastyng in him, abiding the biheest in the day of doom.

4 For neithir the veyn spekyng of summe vnwise men hath lettide you, the whiche wolden turne you fro the treuthe of the gospel, that is prechid of me.

5 And now hem that ben of me, to the profiyt of truthe of the gospel, God schal make disseruyng, and doyng benygnyte of werkis, and helthe of euerlasting lijf.

6 And now my boondis ben open, which Y suffre in Crist Jhesu, in whiche Y glade and ioie.

7 And that is to me to euerlastyng helthe, that this same thing be doon by youre preiers, and mynystryng of the Holi Goost, either bi lijf, either bi deeth.

8 Forsothe to me it is lijf to lyue in Crist, and to die ioie.

9 And his mercy schal do in you the same thing, that ye moun haue the same loue, and that ye be of oo will.

10 Therfore, ye weel biloued britheren, holde ye, and do ye in the dreede of God, as ye han herde the presence of me; and lijf schal be to you withouten eende.

11 Sotheli it is God that worchith in you.

12 And, my weel biloued britheren, do ye without eny withdrawyng what euer thingis ye don.

13 Joie ye in Crist, and eschewe ye men defoulid in lucre, 'either foul wynnyng.

14 Be alle youre askyngis open anentis God, and be ye stidefast in the witt of Crist.

15 And do ye tho thingis that ben hool,

16 and trewe, 'and chaast, and iust, and able to be loued; and kepe ye in herte tho thingis that ye haue herd and take;

17 and pees schal be to you.

18 Alle holi men greten you weel.

19 The grace of oure Lord Jhesu Crist be with youre spirit.

20 And do ye that pistil of Colocensis to be red to you.

Made in the USA
Las Vegas, NV
09 June 2021

24414412R00453